I0816427

Dedicated in gratitude to

the memories of

***Yael and Micha Taubman** z"l*

whose lives were bound in love with and dedication
to Torah, Am Yisrael and Eretz Yisrael

The Steinsaltz Ketuvim

The Steinsaltz Ketuvim

Translation and Commentary

Commentary by

Rabbi Adin Even-Israel Steinsaltz

Koren Publishers Jerusalem

The Steinsaltz Ketuvim

Commentary by
Rabbi Adin Even-Israel Steinsaltz
First Hebrew/English edition 2019

Koren Publishers Jerusalem Ltd.
POB 4044, Jerusalem 91040, ISRAEL
POB 8531, New Milford, CT 06776, USA

www.korenpub.com

Steinsaltz Center is the parent organization
of institutions established by Rabbi Adin Even-Israel Steinsaltz
POB 45187, Jerusalem 91450 ISRAEL
Telephone: +972 2 646 0900, Fax +972 2 624 9454
www.steinsaltz-center.org

ISBN 978-965-7760-25-3

Supported by the Matanel Foundation

Second printing
Printed in PRC

Steinsaltz Center

Executive Director, Steinsaltz Center

Rabbi Meni Even-Israel

Executive Editors

Rabbi Joshua Schreier
Rabbi Dr. Joshua Amaru

Editors

Rabbi Ayal Geffon, Senior Content Editor
Rabbi Yaakov Blinder, Senior Editor
Rabbi Yehoshua Duker, Senior Editor
Rabbi Avi Grossman, Senior Editor
Rabbi Yedidya Naveh, Senior Editor
Rabbi Michael Siev, Senior Editor
Rabbi Aryeh Sklar, Content Curator
Rabbi Alan Haber
Yisrael Kalker
Elisha Loewenstern
Rabbi Eli Ozarowski
Avi Steinhart
Rabbi David Strauss

Hebrew Edition Editors

Sara Friedland Ben Arza
Rabbi Yossi Ben Arza
Rabbi Meir Klein
Rabbi Daniel Eliav

Technical Staff

Tani Bednarsh
Adena Frazer
Shaltiel Shmidman

Editor in Chief

Rabbi Jason Rappoport

Copy Editors

Caryn Meltz, Manager
Aliza Israel, Consultant
Debbie Ismailoff, Senior Copy Editor
Ita Olesker, Senior Copy Editor
Chava Boylan
Suri Brand
Ilana Brown
Carolyn Budow Ben-David
Rachelle Emanuel
Charmaine Gruber
Deborah Meghnagi Bailey
Deena Nataf
Dvora Rhein
Elisheva Ruffer
Ilana Sobel

Maps Editors

Ilana Sobel, Map Curator
Rabbi Dr. Joshua Amaru, Senior Map Editor
Rabbi Alan Haber
Rabbi Aryeh Sklar

Language Experts

Dr. Stéphanie E. Binder, Greek & Latin
Rabbi Yaakov Hoffman, Arabic
Shira Shmidman, Aramaic

Design & Typesetting

Avishai Magence, Production Manager
Eliyahu Misgav, Art Director
Estie Dishon, Design & Typesetting
Bentzi Binder, Design

PSALMS

For Dawne
who is Dina

from her sisters
Lesley, Margot and Serena

Thursday

Dedicated in loving memory of our mother,
grandmother, and great-grandmother,
Edith Kaufthal, Esther bat Mordechai HaKohen,
who said Psalms every day for her family's well-being
and had enormous faith in their redemptive power.

Linda and Ilan Kaufthal
Abby and Joshua Kaufthal
Lori and David Kaufthal
Laura and Daniel Kaufthal
Judy and Uri Kaufthal
Dina and Jonathan Kaufthal
Keren and Jeremy Kaufthal
Alison and Joshua Kaufthal

Joseph Leo
Sydney Rose
Jack Ezra
Fred
Ella Julia
Leo Howard
Maximilian Julius
Bill Abraham
Jenna Lily
Evan Leo
Jacob Asher
Noah Cory
Maya Eden

Friday

We are honored to dedicate this section of Rabbi Steinsaltz's
work in honor of our children Judd, Lauren, and Emma.
May their connection to our faith be ever strong.

David & Leslie Fastenberg

Shabbat

Dedicated to Rav Adin Steinsaltz
הרב עדין אבן-ישראל שטיינזלץ שליט״א
with profound respect
for his monumental contribution to the Jewish people

Lewis and Gaya Aranoff Bernstein

Sunday

Dedicated in honor of my beautiful wife, Tatiana,
whose wisdom, humor, warmth,
and love makes our family.

Michael G. Reiff

Monday

In memory of Efraim ben Hilik, Gnesya bat Aaron,
Genya Golda bat Emmanuel, Yosefa bat Boris
and Mark ben Alexander
and in honor of our children
David and Chana Michal Shifra and their children
Sara Nessa, Odelia, Shylie Efrat, and Brielle

Boris and Anna Gulko

Tuesday

In memory of my grandparents Devora and Isaac Glassman
and their journey; my mother, Florence Glassman Carr,
whose kindness, courage, humor, and resilience
supported all around her; and the inspiring lives of
my brothers Robert and Jay.

Daniel B. Carr

Wednesday

Dedicated in honor of
Rose and Lawrence Shaykin
Marilyn and Jack Shechtman
May their memory always be for a blessing
With love from their children

Leonard and Maura Shaykin

PROVERBS

Dedicated in Memory of my beloved wife,

Susan

My life partner, my best friend, my love, my business partner, my soul mate, my eternal soul mate.

May her memory be for a Blessing.

Melvin Fastow

This volume
pays tribute to the memory of

Mr. Sami Rohr ז״ל

ר׳ **שמואל** ב״ר **יהושע אליהו** ז״ל

who served his Maker with joy,
and whose far-reaching vision, warm open hand, love of Torah,
and love for every Jew were catalysts for revival and growth of
vibrant Jewish life in the former Soviet Union
and in countless communities the world over,

and to the memory of his beloved wife

Mrs. Charlotte Rohr *(née Kastner)* ע״ה

שרה בת ר׳ **יקותיאל יהודה** ע״ה

who survived the flames of the Shoah to become
the elegant and gracious matriarch,
first in Colombia and later in the United States,
of three generations of a family
nurtured by her love and unstinting devotion.
She found grace in the eyes of all those whose lives she touched.

Together they merited to see all their children
build lives enriched by faithful commitment
to the spreading of Torah and *Ahavat Yisrael*.

Dedicated with love by

The Rohr Family

New York, USA

THE SONG OF SONGS

Dedicated in honor of
my beautiful wife,

Tatiana

whose wisdom, humor, warmth,

and love makes our family.

Michael G. Reiff

פיה פתחה בחכמה ותורת חסד על לשונה.... קמו בניה ויאשרוה בעלה ויהללה. (משלי לא:כו–כח)

She opens her mouth with wisdom, and the Torah of kindness is on her tongue....
Her children arise and laud her; her husband, and he praises her. (Proverbs 31:26–28)

ישלם יהוה פעלך ותהי משכרתך שלמה מעם יהוה אלהי ישראל אשר ברת לחסות תחת כנפיו. (רות ב:יב)

May the Lord reward your conduct, and may your payment be complete from the Lord,
God of Israel, under whose wings you came to find refuge. (Ruth 2:12)

In loving memory of our wife, mother and grandmother,

Geneviève* רות *Werthenschlag

on the 30th anniversary of her passing.

She epitomized the Woman of Valor and
strengthened and comforted many
with her kindness and faith.

We, her family,
continue to sing her praise
and while we long for her every day,
we carry her example of *reut, tzedakah,*
ḥesed, and *ahavat yisrael* in our minds and deeds.

May her *neshama* have an *aliya*.

LAMENTATIONS

"Where are you?"

This question goes unanswered in Lamentations.

Rabbi Steinsaltz,

your work challenges us to take up this question.
You have unlocked our texts so that we may seek the answer.
We are honored to join you in your sacred and restorative mission:
"Let My People Know"

Thank you for inspiring and educating us.

ECCLESIASTES

We dedicate this commentary
on the book of Kohelet
to our parents and grandparents
who believed in Jewish destiny
even in the darkest hours
of Soviet oppression.

Polina and Michael Liberman

דור לדור ישבח מעשיך

In honor of our grandchildren

Rena Ayelet, Tova Aliza, Ora Adina

Andrew Jeremy, Benjamin Zachary, Jonathan Meir

Aliza Ruth, Sophia Bella, Ayala Tamima, Samuel Issachar

Ella Orianna, Lily Claire, Ruby Jacqueline

Dedicated by

Monique and Mordecai Katz

DANIEL

We dedicate this work

in memory of our father

Howard Altman

in honor of our parents

Judy Altman
Linda and Ilan Kaufthal

and with gratitude for our children

Leo Howard and Maximilian Julius

Laura and Daniel Kaufthal

Table of Contents

Introduction to The Steinsaltz Ketuvim

Scholars and lay readers alike are aware that writing a new commentary on the Bible requires assistance and blessings from Above, as well as substantial effort from below. Two fundamental challenges stand before one who seeks to write a commentary on the Bible: First, the aspiration to relate to the loftiest and holiest text and to explain it faithfully risks hubris. Second, a huge number of commentaries on the Bible have been composed over the course of the past three thousand years by the greatest people in our history. Who has the audacity to attempt to join this holy assembly or even grasp its coattails?

Sanction for undertaking this daunting task can be found in Rashi's statement to his grandson Rashbam, himself the author of an important commentary on the Torah. Rashbam reports Rashi to have said that if he had had the strength, he would have written another commentary in accordance with the "plain meanings that are renewed every day" (Rashbam, Genesis 37:2).

In every generation and on each passing day, fresh light can be shed on the verses of the Bible and new perspectives can be found. Not only are new answers offered to old questions, but in every era additional questions are raised by students of the Bible, due to both the diversity of the personalities, and the differing interests and perspectives, of each era. Throughout the ages, the great commentaries have discussed a wide range of different issues. To this day, thank God, there are many scholars and students of the Bible raising unique questions and challenges that require attention, analysis, and investigation. All these illuminate the eternal words of the Torah through a range of viewpoints and give rise to "plain meanings that are renewed every day."

This commentary seeks to offer the reader the plain meaning of the text, the *peshat*. Ostensibly, this is the simplest level of interpretation, but the elucidation of the plain meaning is actually the most difficult type of interpretation. Other kinds of interpretation, based on allusion [*remez*], midrashic hermeneutics [*derash*], or esoteric, mystical traditions [*sod*], are free to forge links between the text and the sources from which they draw and are not constrained by the language and concepts of the Bible. In contrast, discovering the plain meaning of the text requires the interpreter to adhere closely to the literal meaning of the words while paying attention to syntax and context.

Although this commentary includes references to many other commentaries, it is not an anthology. It was not intended to provide a comprehensive array of interpretations from across the generations. The aim of the references is to show that a suggested interpretation is based on earlier sources or discusses a similar question. Moreover, this work does not aspire to be revolutionary or novel. Rather, it aims to present what might be called a "transparent" commentary, one whose explanations should go almost unnoticed and serve only to give the reader and student the sense that there is no barrier between him or her and the text. The aim is to let the Torah speak for itself, to allow the prophets to prophesy and the wise men to impart their wisdom. In order to enable the "voice" of the verses to be heard, the annotations are brief, serving as a thin, barely perceptible screen rather than a heavy, concealing coat of armor.

At Mount Sinai, the entire Jewish people heard "a great voice" (Deuteronomy 5:18), which the Sages interpret to mean a voice that has never ceased (*Targum Onkelos*; *Sanhedrin* 17a). It is my hope that this project will help people hear the voice of the Torah even in our busy, noisy world.

Rabbi Adin Even-Israel Steinsaltz

Introduction by the Hebrew Editors

The purpose of this commentary is to assist the contemporary reader by bridging the gaps in language, outlook, and culture between us and the world of the Bible. As far as possible, it seeks to clarify ambiguities, elucidate problematic passages, and remove obstacles to understanding while dealing with both explicit and implicit difficulties.

The commentary consists of several parts, which complement but are independent of one another. The literal translation of the verses appears in boldface. Woven into the biblical text in non-bold typeface are brief explanatory comments and elaborations. Below the text are notes that offer more elaborate discussion of topics that appear in the verses as well as insights into the general context and scientific and historical realia that surround the biblical text.

The biblical text is divided into units based on subject matter, which do not always accord with the standard division into chapters. Each unit is prefaced by a heading and a short introduction. This structure should not be viewed as a definitive partition of the biblical text but as a suggestion, part of the commentary, for the reader's convenience and orientation.

The commentary seeks to concisely clarify the language and context at the most basic level so as not to encumber the reader. Consequently, it is not committed to a particular exegetical method and does not systematically defer to any particular commentator. In cases where there are differing explanations of a passage, alternative explanations may be cited. In cases where the halakhic tradition expounds a verse in a manner not consistent with the plain meaning, this will be noted and explained briefly in the annotations themselves or by means of a reference, allowing the plain meaning of the text to be preserved while not disregarding the interpretation of the Oral Law.

It must be stated that even when written without qualification, the interpretations offered are not meant to be seen as authoritative. They are no more than suggestions, occasionally novel ones, which are compatible with the simple meaning of the text and which speak to the average reader. There are no systematic exegetical considerations behind the decision to adopt any particular interpretation.

Much thought and labor have been invested to ensure that the design of this work is as aesthetically pleasing and convenient for the user as possible. This design is the fruit of an ongoing collaboration between the team at the Institute for Talmudic Publications and Koren Publishers. Our thanks to Rabbi Meir Hanegbi, whose wisdom, conviviality, and efficiency contributed greatly to the success of the project. Rabbi Hanokh Ben Arza, may his memory be for a blessing, was the father of the two editors in chief of the Hebrew edition; his spirit and respect for the written word inspired them in their work.

The Editors

Introduction by the Translators

ON THE TRANSLATION OF THE KETUVIM

The English translation of *The Steinsaltz Ketuvim* includes a completely new translation of the Bible based on Rabbi Adin Even-Israel Steinsaltz's Hebrew commentary. Translation is necessarily an act of interpretation. In general, we have done our best, at Rabbi Steinsaltz's behest, to stay as close as possible to the original Hebrew verses so that the English reader will encounter the complexities of the text directly. In the course of translating, we have consulted other English translations, as well as relying heavily upon Onkelos' Aramaic translation and the classic medieval Jewish commentaries of the Torah: Rav Se'adya Gaon, Rashi, Ibn Ezra, Ramban, and Rashbam. Our goal throughout has been to produce a translation that is true to the original Hebrew text and commentary, yet at the same time is readable and accessible to a broad range of readers, from those who are familiar with Hebrew and seek to deepen their understanding of the Torah to those who will gain access to the text only by reading it in English. The commentary and notes are written in modern American English. In the spirit of the Hebrew edition, we have tried to preserve the lofty register of the biblical text while providing a commentary that is relevant and inspiring to our own generation. We hope that the Author of the Torah has aided us in achieving this goal.

THE LAYOUT OF THIS EDITION

On the left-hand side of each set of facing pages is the Hebrew text of the Bible with the traditional cantillation marks, meticulously edited over decades by the team at Koren Publishers, Jerusalem. On the facing page, the Steinsaltz translation of the Bible appears in boldface with the commentary interspersed between the words of the text in non-bold typeface. This enables the reader to easily follow either the direct translation alone or the translation augmented by the elucidated text.

The notes at the foot of the page are divided into two categories. Discussion notes provide background material, internal biblical parallels, alternative explanations, and a wealth of midrashic and philosophical ideas from Jewish commentaries over the generations. Background notes provide linguistic, historical, archaeological, and scientific information that is relevant to places, nations, flora and fauna, and other realia mentioned in the verses. Integrated into both the commentary and the notes are pictures, maps, and other graphics to aid the reader in grasping the biblical text.

References and sources for the commentary appear as endnotes, while the references and sources for the notes are interspersed throughout the notes themselves in parentheses. These references and sources, compiled by the Hebrew editors, include citations of other verses in the Bible, commentary elsewhere in the Bible, insights of the rabbinic Sages in the Talmud and *midrashim*, interpretations of the classical biblical commentaries, and citations of philosophical works and responsa by the early authorities [*rishonim*].

The translation of the verses of *Ketuvim* was undertaken by Rabbi Joshua Schreier and reviewed meticulously by Rabbi Dr. Joshua Amaru. The verses from Daniel were reviewed by Rabbi Ayal Geffon. Special thanks to Gaya Aranoff Bernstein and to Laurie E. Fialkoff for contributing their insights and knowledge to Psalms, which greatly enhanced the readability of the text. Many talented editors and translators participated in the translation of the commentary and notes as listed in the credits. We thank Matthew Miller, Avishai Magence, and the devoted and gifted team at Koren Publishers. We are grateful to Rabbi Meni Even-Israel, Executive Director of the Steinsaltz Center, whose wisdom and guidance have made this publication possible. We also thank Rabbi Dr. Natan Slifkin of the Biblical Museum of Natural History in Beit Shemesh for his help in identifying some animals and providing suitable images.

TRANSLITERATION

In general, we have tried to keep transliteration to a minimum and have relied upon it only for proper nouns and in places where a point of commentary relates to a Hebrew term. In the case of proper nouns, we have sought a middle ground between a rigorous adherence to Hebrew phonology and the use of anglicized versions of names taken from earlier translations of the Bible. For familiar names of both places and people, where encountering a transliteration would be jarring to many readers, we have used the well-known anglicized versions, such as Canaan, Egypt, Abraham, and Moses. Otherwise, proper nouns are transliterated according to the rules listed below. These transliterations offer the English reader an experience that is closer to that of the Hebrew reader.

Of course, determining which names count as familiar and which are not is not an exact science; the policy has been to use the anglicized names of familiar figures such as the names of prophets and books of the Bible, and some other well-known characters and place-names. The transliteration scheme generally follows modern Israeli Hebrew pronunciation, but note the following points:

- For proper nouns, no special characters are used to designate sounds that do not exist in English. For example, the name אֲחִיעֶזֶר will not be rendered Aḥiezer (with a diacritic for the letter *ḥet* that is used for the transliteration of Hebrew terms that are not proper nouns) but rather Ahiezer. Consequently, the letter ח is rendered as *h* (like the letter ה).
- The letter *h*, representing the Hebrew letter ה, has been omitted at the end of a word unless its omission could lead to mispronunciation. For example, שלה is written Shela, while נינוה is written Nineveh.
- The soft letter כ is rendered as *kh*.
- No distinction has been made between a letter containing a *dagesh ḥazak* (elsewhere represented by a double consonant) and one without. For example, it is Hukat as opposed to Hukkat.
- Apostrophes indicating glottal stops are employed only where a name could be mispronounced without them. For example, it is Se'ir as opposed to Seir.
- We have maintained a more technical transliteration scheme for citations, including the diacritic *ḥ* and consonant doubling for cases of a *dagesh*. For example, in the citation *Tanḥuma, Korah* 5, *Tanḥuma* retains the diacritic *ḥ*, whereas *Korah* does not.

On behalf of the team of inspired and dedicated translators, editors, and copy editors with whom it has been a great privilege to work, I express my hope that the decisions we have made have produced a translation that is faithful to the Hebrew, readable, accessible, and useful to the reader.

Jason Rappoport
Editor in Chief

Cantillation Marks (*Trop*)

שמות הטעמים וסימניהם

אשכנזים: מֵרְכָ֥א טִפְּחָ֖א מֻנַּ֣ח אֶתְנַחְתָּ֑א מֵרְכָ֥א טִפְּחָ֖א סוֹף־פָּסֽוּק

מַהְפַּ֤ךְ פַּשְׁטָ֨א מֻנַּ֣ח זָקֵף־קָטֹ֔ן זָקֵף־גָּד֕וֹל מֻנַּ֣ח ׀ מֻנַּ֣ח רְבִ֗יעַ

קַדְמָ֨א דַּרְגָּ֧א תְּבִ֛יר מֻנַּ֣ח זַרְקָ֮א מֻנַּ֣ח סֶגּ֒וֹל תְּ֠לִישָׁא־גְדוֹלָה

תְּלִישָׁא־קְטַנָּה֩ קַדְמָ֨א וְאַזְלָ֨א אַזְלָא־גֵּ֜רֵשׁ גֵּרְשַׁ֞יִם פָּזֵ֡ר

יְ֚תִיב שַׁלְשֶׁ֓לֶת גַּלְגַּ֪ל קַרְנֵי־פָ֟רָה מֵרְכָא־כְּפוּלָ֦ה

לְ֣גַרְמֵ֣הּ ׀ סוֹף־פָּסֽוּק׃

ספרדים: זַרְקָ֮א מַקַּף־שׁוֹפָר־הוֹלֵ֣ךְ סְגוֹלְתָּ֒א פָּזֵר־גָּד֡וֹל

תְּ֠לִשָׁא תְּלִשָׁ֩א אַזְלָא־גֵּ֜רִישׁ פָּסֵק ׀ רְבִ֗יעַ שְׁנֵי־גֵרְשַׁ֞יִן

דַּרְגָּ֧א תְּבִ֛יר מַאֲרִ֥יךְ טַרְחָ֖א אַתְנָ֑ח שׁוֹפָר־מְהֻפָּ֤ךְ

קַדְמָ֨א תְּרֵי־קַדְמִ֨ין זָקֵף־קָטֹ֔ן זָקֵף־גָּד֕וֹל שַׁלְשֶׁ֓לֶת

גַּלְגַּ֪ל קַרְנֵי־פָ֟רָה תְּרֵי־טַעֲמֵ֨י יְ֚תִיב סוֹף־פָּסֽוּק׃

Psalms

Psalms

INTRODUCTION TO PSALMS

The book of Psalms is unique among the books of the Bible. Taken as a whole, the Bible depicts the relationship between God and mankind, and more particularly between God and the people of Israel. In most books of the Bible, the relationship is primarily portrayed as proceeding from the top down, from God to man. By contrast, Psalms is the only book of the Bible where the relationship flows in the opposite direction, from man to God, in other words, where an individual turns to God and communicates with Him. Psalms is traditionally divided into five books, containing a total of 150 chapters. Some suggest that these are meant to correspond to the five books of the Torah. This parallelism also serves to illustrate that the relationship between God and man runs in both directions. Thus, despite their wide variation in subject matter and tone, the individual chapters comprising Psalms are all narrated from a human perspective, with all the limitations and complexity this entails.

The Hebrew title of the book, *Tehillim*, means "praises," and there is much in the way of praise in its chapters. Yet Psalms is much more than a compendium of ways to praise God. In fact, one can find in it almost any thought or feeling a person might wish to express to God. It includes a wide variety of poetic forms, with personal poetry alongside epic poems, as well as philosophical musings and introspection on matters pertaining to the nation of Israel and to mankind. But what pervades all of the psalms, whether clearly expressed or implicit, is the voice of the individual psalmist.

Just as the topics of the psalms vary, so does the persona of the psalmist. The psalmist is seen as alternately dejected and elated; there are psalms of defeat and surrender alongside powerful, exultant victory songs. Moreover, some of the psalms express disquiet, originating in a crisis of faith or a grievance, whereas others bespeak peace and tranquility. To use a musical metaphor, some psalms are staccato, others legato; some largo, others presto. In similar fashion, the psalmist can be compared to a harp, each of whose many strings has its own unique sound while simultaneously working in harmony.

Psalms deals with a number of recurring themes. Many of its chapters contain prayers and supplications that seem to correspond to actual events in the life of King David. But despite their various allusions to historical events, the psalms are not autobiographical. While many of them are attributed to David, neither his private nor his public persona is readily discernible. What emerges from most of the psalms is not the voice of a specific historical figure but rather that of Everyman.

As the bounds of the personal are transcended, the psalms enter the realm of the universal. For instance, while King David was surrounded for most of his life by followers, friends, and admirers, what is most striking in the psalms of supplication attributed to David is the loneliness they convey. Only rarely do we get a sense of David as part of a larger "us." The image is that of a man who feels alone even in the midst of a crowd. This quality, somewhat paradoxically, makes Psalms not only a collection of songs that can be sung aloud in a chorus of voices, but also an expression of many people's most private life experiences, whether joyous or distressing. As the verse says: "The heart alone knows its own bitterness, and no stranger can share in its joy" (Proverbs 14:10). People first feel their own pain and happiness, and only after that can they identify with the feelings and experiences of others.

The logic behind the psalms' arrangement remains unclear. There are no obvious differences between the five books, or sections, of Psalms. And while here and there a group of psalms appears to have certain structural or thematic similarities, these are the exceptions to the rule. It appears likely that the disarray is intentional, reflecting the perspective of a work that above all expresses human emotions. For emotions, like existence itself, have no fixed order; there are no predetermined conditions governing a person's feeling happy, sorrowful, introspective, or grateful. Psalms mirrors life in all its vicissitudes and inconsistencies, demonstrating that despite our most strenuous efforts, life can never be fully organized or controlled.

The chapters of Psalms differ from one another in structure and style as well as content and length. Psalms contains the shortest chapter in the Bible (two verses) and almost immediately following it, the longest chapter (176 verses). Some of the psalms have the rhythm and tone of epic poetry. Some are simple entreaties, and others are an outpouring of feeling emanating from the depths of the soul. There are many tearful prayers in Psalms, and often no explanation is provided for the psalmist's distress other than that something is wrong. Some psalms are distinctly meditative and deal with a well-defined topic. Others are songs of a historical nature. Also quite a few psalms offer straightforward, moral instruction.

Despite all the differences between them, the psalms share one outstanding characteristic: truth. There is no smoothing of rough edges, no attempt to ignore or gloss over difficult issues in order to create a sense of harmony. Indeed, many of the psalms have a kind of built-in dissonance that results from the psalmist's refusal to relinquish a point of truth even at the expense of disrupting the overall melody. Undoubtedly, this aspect of Psalms is partially why it continues to speak to so many people in all corners of the world. While Psalms very much belongs to a specific place (the Land of Israel) and a specific period (the biblical era), it nonetheless transcends all boundaries of space and time.

Like Job and Ecclesiastes, Psalms has a special, unique set of cantillations. The cantillation signs serve to punctuate the verses as well as to indicate specific musical notes. In Psalms, the musical component of the cantillations has been entirely lost. We know that certain psalms were sung in the Temple during the era of the Second Temple and possibly even before that. But beyond this we lack any reliable tradition pertaining to the melodies that were sung.

Until the period of the Sages, Psalms consisted of 147 chapters. Most of these texts have a heading and a clear internal structure. A later, non-Jewish division of Psalms produced the current 150 chapters, a few of which appear to be incomplete or not self-contained. Most of the psalms are attributed to David, as indicated in the psalms themselves, using descriptions such as: "the prayers of David son of Yishai" (Psalms 72:20). Nevertheless, according to the Sages in *Bava Batra* 14b–15a, various psalms were authored by ten others, among them Adam and Moses.

Apart from its literary value, Psalms enjoys an exceptional status in the biblical canon. No book of the Bible has evoked more tears or more words of gratitude and joy. Over the course of Jewish history, Psalms has been utilized more than any other book, not just by poets, but by all who seek to articulate the appropriate words and phrases with which to beseech, express gratitude to, pour out the sorrows of their soul to, or simply have a conversation with God. Whether it is a lonely widow weeping over her travails, a leader grappling with a military or political crisis, or an individual inspired to sing a song of thanksgiving, Psalms provides a mouthpiece for everyone. Indeed, if King David is termed "the sweet singer of Israel" (II Samuel 23:1), it is because he sang the song of an entire people.

Psalms

PSALM 1

PSALMS 1:1–6

A psalm that offers general observations about the joy experienced by an individual who conducts his life in the proper manner, and about the contrasting lives of those who are evil and sinful.

1 1 **Happy [*ashrei*][D] is the man who has not walked in the counsel of the wicked, has not stood in the path of sinners.** A person who shuns evil leads a fortunate, happy life. The phrase *atzat resha'im*, "counsel of the wicked," refers to bad advice given by wicked people. The happy man described here has not accepted or followed that advice. Since in other places the word *atzat* can be defined as "company" as well as "counsel," this verse can also be interpreted to mean that a good man does not associate with wicked people, refusing to be considered part of their society. **And has not sat in the company of scoffers.** In modern Hebrew, *letzim*, translated here as "scoffers," are clowns or jokers. But in Psalms, as in Proverbs and other sources, the word has a darker, more pejorative meaning. Scoffers are characterized by their frivolity and their breezy attitude toward that which is good. Even if they have no evil intent and do not actually behave in an evil manner, their mode of thinking and speaking opens the door to all manner of forbidden actions. The phrase "has not sat in the company of scoffers" emphasizes that even if one is not an active participant in such a group, and merely sits among them, he is exposing himself to wrongdoing.

BOOK ONE

Sunday

1st day of month

2 **But whose desire is the Torah of the Lord.**[D] The good and happy person desires God's Torah, which is a guidebook for a way of life. **He meditates on His Torah day and night.** The pronoun "His" can also be said to be referring to the person studying the Torah rather than to God. This phrase, then, emphasizes each specific individual's understanding of Torah, what he knows of it in his mind and heart. The term *yehgeh*, translated here as "meditates," can also mean "utters." When one chooses to spend all his time thinking and speaking of God's Torah, he distances himself from evil and clings to good, and for this he is rewarded as described in the following verse.

3 **He is like a tree planted by streams of water.** The tree described here lacks nothing, as even without rain it has sufficient water. It is a tree **which brings forth its fruit in season and whose leaf does not wither.** Trees that lack water often bear their fruit late, and their leaves shrivel and fall, but this tree is eternally fresh and thriving. This image is not merely one of blessing but also a concrete promise of ongoing fruitfulness in all its manifestations. The fruit of the righteous person's Torah, as well as that of his everyday labors, will ripen at the right time, bringing benefit both to himself and to others. He will not suffer from premature decline or withering, and **whatever he does will prosper.**

"Like a tree planted by streams of water"

4 By contrast, **not so the wicked, who** are not at all like well-rooted trees but instead **are like chaff that wind blows away.** Chaff is incapable of growth, and lacking a secure place of its own, is scattered by the wind in all directions. The wicked have a similar fate. They have no real place and no plan, but simply conform to shifting influences.

"Chaff that wind blows away"

5 **Therefore the wicked will not stand up in judgment.** When the time of judgment comes, the wicked will have no standing, **nor evildoers among the righteous.** Not only will evildoers not be acquitted, but they will not even be able to join the company of the righteous.

6 **For the Lord knows the way of the righteous.** Here, as elsewhere, *yode'a*, translated as "knows," specifically implies connectedness and love. God loves the righteous, and He therefore guides and assists them on their journey through life. **But** by contrast, **the way of the wicked will perish.** The way of the wicked results not only in the loss of eternal existence but also in an inability to withstand the vicissitudes of this life. Their path inevitably ends in ruin.

תהלים

א
ספר ראשון
יום ראשון
א לחודש

א א אַ֥שְֽׁרֵי־הָאִ֗ישׁ אֲשֶׁ֤ר ׀ לֹ֥א הָלַךְ֮ בַּעֲצַ֪ת רְשָׁ֫עִ֥ים וּבְדֶ֣רֶךְ חַ֭טָּאִים לֹ֥א עָמָ֑ד וּבְמוֹשַׁ֥ב
ב ג לֵ֝צִ֗ים לֹ֣א יָשָֽׁב׃ כִּ֤י אִ֥ם בְּתוֹרַ֥ת יהוה חֶ֫פְצ֥וֹ וּֽבְתוֹרָת֥וֹ יֶהְגֶּ֗ה יוֹמָ֥ם וָלָֽיְלָה׃ וְֽהָיָ֗ה
כְּעֵץ֮ שָׁת֪וּל עַֽל־פַּלְגֵ֫י מָ֥יִם אֲשֶׁ֤ר פִּרְי֨וֹ ׀ יִתֵּ֬ן בְּעִתּ֗וֹ וְעָלֵ֥הוּ לֹֽא־יִבּ֑וֹל וְכֹ֖ל אֲשֶׁר־
ד ה יַעֲשֶׂ֣ה יַצְלִֽיחַ׃ לֹא־כֵ֥ן הָרְשָׁעִ֑ים כִּ֥י אִם־כַּ֝מֹּ֗ץ אֲֽשֶׁר־תִּדְּפֶ֥נּוּ רֽוּחַ׃ עַל־כֵּ֤ן ׀ לֹא־יָקֻ֣מוּ
ו רְ֭שָׁעִים בַּמִּשְׁפָּ֑ט וְ֝חַטָּאִ֗ים בַּעֲדַ֥ת צַדִּיקִֽים׃ כִּֽי־יוֹדֵ֣עַ יהוה דֶּ֣רֶךְ צַדִּיקִ֑ים וְדֶ֖רֶךְ
רְשָׁעִ֣ים תֹּאבֵֽד׃

ב א ב לָ֭מָּה רָגְשׁ֣וּ גוֹיִ֑ם וּ֝לְאֻמִּ֗ים יֶהְגּוּ־רִֽיק׃ יִתְיַצְּב֨וּ ׀ מַלְכֵי־אֶ֗רֶץ וְרוֹזְנִ֥ים נֽוֹסְדוּ־יָ֑חַד
ג עַל־יהוה וְעַל־מְשִׁיחֽוֹ׃ נְֽ֭נַתְּקָה אֶת־מֽוֹסְרוֹתֵ֑ימוֹ וְנַשְׁלִ֖יכָה מִמֶּ֣נּוּ עֲבֹתֵֽימוֹ׃

PSALM 2

PSALMS 2:1–12

A psalm without a heading in honor of a king who is mentioned several times. The psalm's content and visionary language indicate that it is not describing a specific king but rather depicts a prophetic vision of the future redeemer, the Messiah.

2 1 **Why do nations rage** and stir up a great commotion, **and peoples meditate in vain?** Why do they deliberate and make declarations that ultimately are no more than empty threats?

2 **The kings of the earth have assembled, and rulers are gathered together against the Lord and against His anointed one,** the king. Those in power consult with one another, gathering together in order to plot against God and His anointed one, as described in the following verse.

3 **Let us snap off their chains,** a metaphor for the rule and control that Israel exerts over them, **and throw off their bonds.** The main objective of their rebellion against the king is to be free of God, as the king represents the nation's connection to God.

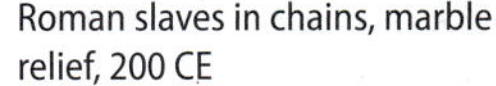

Roman slaves in chains, marble relief, 200 CE

"Let us snap off their chains"

DISCUSSION

1:1 | **Ashrei:** This word, translated here as "happy," serves as the opening word of several psalms. It indicates not only the subjective traits of happiness [*osher*] and satisfaction, but also objective uprightness and correctness [*yosher*].

1:2 | **Whose desire is the Torah of the Lord:** The psalmist here presents a definition of the righteous person: He is good in thought and in action, and even his inner will is directed toward God's Torah. When he has no other tasks to occupy him, neither sacred nor mundane, he directs his speech and thoughts to God's Torah.

4 **He whose seat is in heaven will laugh; the Lord will ridicule them.** All those rulers' plans will come to naught, for they are void of any true substance. What actually will come to pass is punishment from on high.

5 **Then He will talk to them in His anger; in His wrath He will frighten them** and say:

6 **Yet I have anointed My king on Zion, My holy mountain.** The continuation of the psalm is spoken by the king himself:

7 **I will tell of the decree.** I will set forth the basic premise of all my actions. **The Lord said to me: You are My son; today I begat you.** The king, chosen by God, can be likened to a man's beloved son. When he ascends to the throne, it is as if he is being reborn.

8 God has told me: **Make your request of Me, and I will make nations your inheritance; the ends of earth will be your portion.** You will reign over many nations; your sovereignty will extend to the ends of the earth.

Shattered potter's vessels

9 **You will smash them with an iron rod, shatter them like a potter's vessel.** You will destroy all your enemies as easily as one shatters a clay vessel.

10 **So now, kings, be wise; accept admonishment, judges of the earth.** Understand that God has placed the privilege of sovereignty in my hands, and consequently you are powerless against me. For this reason, one should follow the advice given in the next verse:

11 **Serve the Lord with reverence,** aware of the consequences that await you if you do not serve Him, **and rejoice with trembling.** Although you will be able to rejoice under the rule of the king, this joy must be tempered with a trembling awe, as a hidden threat will always be present: If you do not serve God, you will be punished in various ways.

12 **Kiss the son.** Most commentators define *bar* here as "son," which is the meaning of this word in Aramaic, referring to the king, as God said: "You are My son" (verse 7). The kiss is an expression of homage and affection. **Lest He be angry and you lose your way, even if His anger burns only slightly.** You cannot withstand God's fury; you cannot weather even His slightest anger. By contrast, **happy are all who rely on Him.** Those who put their faith in God will find the world beautiful and full of goodness.

PSALM 3

PSALMS 3:1–9

A psalm referring to an episode in which David is surrounded by enemies and considered by everyone to be in a hopeless situation. Nevertheless, he trusts in God to deliver him from his enemies and lead him to victory and peace.

3 1 **A psalm by David when he fled from Avshalom his son.** Although the heading makes reference to a specific episode, the psalm speaks generally of a situation of great distress. It is an entreaty to God, coupled with an expression of faith that He will rescue the psalmist from his dire straits.

2 **Lord, how numerous are my tormentors; many rise up against me.** Not only are they enemies, but they are rebels from within my own ranks.

3 In addition to these enemies and rebels, principally Avshalom's army, there are **many** others who **say of me: There is no salvation for him in God.** Although they were not actively involved in the insurgency, they nonetheless believed that David's reign had ended and that his predicament was hopeless. **Selah.**[D]

4 **But You, Lord, protect me. You are my glory,** or alternatively, You are the source of my glory, and **You lift my head.** You keep me from being completely cast off and humiliated.

5 **I cried aloud to the Lord and He answered me from His holy mount, Selah.** It is as if I can hear the voice of God speaking to me from the holy mount in Jerusalem.

6 **I lay down and slept,** often dejected and with no expectation that I would live to see the following day. But **I awoke** and did not succumb to eternal sleep, **because the Lord sustains me** and gave me strength to carry on.

7 And because God sustains me, **I shall have no fear of the myriads that surround me and oppose me.** I am not afraid of tens of thousands of people, all of whom are poised to attack me.

8 **Arise, Lord.** This is a call for God to reveal Himself in a recognizable way. **Save me, my God. For You have smitten my enemies on the cheek.** You have slapped the faces of all the enemies who surround me. This notion of a painful blow to the enemy's cheek resonates with the subsequent imagery: **You have broken the teeth of the wicked.**

9 In summation, David declares: **Salvation belongs to the Lord.** Even if salvation from God does not appear to be imminent, eventually it becomes apparent that **Your blessing is on Your people, Selah.**

ד ה יוֹשֵׁב בַּשָּׁמַיִם יִשְׂחָק אֲדֹנָי יִלְעַג־לָמוֹ׃ אָז יְדַבֵּר אֵלֵימוֹ בְאַפּוֹ וּבַחֲרוֹנוֹ יְבַהֲלֵמוֹ׃
ו ז וַאֲנִי נָסַכְתִּי מַלְכִּי עַל־צִיּוֹן הַר־קָדְשִׁי׃ אֲסַפְּרָה אֶל חֹק יְהוָה אָמַר אֵלַי בְּנִי־
ח אַתָּה אֲנִי הַיּוֹם יְלִדְתִּיךָ׃ שְׁאַל מִמֶּנִּי וְאֶתְּנָה גוֹיִם נַחֲלָתֶךָ וַאֲחֻזָּתְךָ אַפְסֵי־אָרֶץ׃
ט י תְּרֹעֵם בְּשֵׁבֶט בַּרְזֶל כִּכְלִי יוֹצֵר תְּנַפְּצֵם׃ וְעַתָּה מְלָכִים הַשְׂכִּילוּ הִוָּסְרוּ שֹׁפְטֵי
יא יב אָרֶץ׃ עִבְדוּ אֶת־יְהוָה בְּיִרְאָה וְגִילוּ בִּרְעָדָה׃ נַשְּׁקוּ־בַר פֶּן־יֶאֱנַף ׀ וְתֹאבְדוּ דֶרֶךְ
כִּי־יִבְעַר כִּמְעַט אַפּוֹ אַשְׁרֵי כָּל־חוֹסֵי בוֹ׃
ג א ב מִזְמוֹר לְדָוִד בְּבָרְחוֹ מִפְּנֵי ׀ אַבְשָׁלוֹם בְּנוֹ׃ יְהוָה מָה־רַבּוּ צָרָי רַבִּים קָמִים עָלָי׃
ג ד רַבִּים אֹמְרִים לְנַפְשִׁי אֵין יְשׁוּעָתָה לּוֹ בֵאלֹהִים סֶלָה׃ וְאַתָּה יְהוָה מָגֵן בַּעֲדִי
ה ו כְּבוֹדִי וּמֵרִים רֹאשִׁי׃ קוֹלִי אֶל־יְהוָה אֶקְרָא וַיַּעֲנֵנִי מֵהַר קָדְשׁוֹ סֶלָה׃ אֲנִי שָׁכַבְתִּי
ז וָאִישָׁנָה הֱקִיצוֹתִי כִּי יְהוָה יִסְמְכֵנִי׃ לֹא־אִירָא מֵרִבְבוֹת עָם אֲשֶׁר סָבִיב שָׁתוּ
ח עָלָי׃ קוּמָה יְהוָה ׀ הוֹשִׁיעֵנִי אֱלֹהַי כִּי־הִכִּיתָ אֶת־כָּל־אֹיְבַי לֶחִי שִׁנֵּי רְשָׁעִים
ט שִׁבַּרְתָּ׃ לַיהוָה הַיְשׁוּעָה עַל־עַמְּךָ בִרְכָתֶךָ סֶּלָה׃
ד א ב לַמְנַצֵּחַ בִּנְגִינוֹת מִזְמוֹר לְדָוִד׃ בְּקָרְאִי עֲנֵנִי ׀ אֱלֹהֵי צִדְקִי בַּצָּר הִרְחַבְתָּ לִּי חָנֵּנִי

PSALM 4

PSALMS 4:1–9

A psalm of entreaty on the part of one who is being vilified and pursued groundlessly. The psalmist calls upon God, as He both saves the blameless and foils the schemes of the wicked.

4 1 **For the chief musician, on stringed instruments,**[D] **a psalm by David.** Like the preceding psalm, this is essentially a prayer, though it does not speak of a specific struggle or imminent danger but rather conveys a more generalized state of distress. It also includes expressions of encouragement for others.

2 **When I call, answer me, God of my righteousness. In my**

DISCUSSION

3:3 | **Selah:** The meaning of this word, found almost exclusively in the book of Psalms, where it occurs frequently, is not entirely clear. According to an ancient tradition it means "forever" or "for all time." Often this sense is compatible with the context of the word, but sometimes this meaning can be applied only with difficulty. Some commentators are of the opinion that Selah indicates reinforcement for the preceding statement, meaning approximately "And so it is" or "Indeed it is so." Others believe that it is a musical term, indicating that the voice was to be raised at this point. Still others maintain that it is an instruction to lengthen the preceding word in order to conform to the meter of the song. Lastly, there are those who state that it indicates the end of a section of a song.

4:1 | **For the chief musician, on stringed instruments [*neginot*]:** This heading indicates that the psalm is addressed to the person who conducts its musical recital, known as the *menatze'aḥ* or "chief musician." This is one of a number of instructive openings to individual psalms. Some mention the type of musical instruments to be used, whereas others refer to a specific ancient melody. Some say that the plural word *neginot* indicates that this psalm has several tunes or involves several instruments. Apparently even the word *mizmor*, translated here as "psalm," serves to identify a particular type of melody.

distress, I feel as though I am confined. The word *batzar*, translated here as "distress," literally means "in a narrow place." This implies a feeling of paralysis, as though to say: My very existence, whether physical or spiritual, is so pressured that I am unable even to move. **You have relieved me.** The word *hirḥavta*, "you have relieved," or literally, "you have widened," describes one's feeling when redemption follows profound distress; it is as if all the sources of pressure have receded into the background and one can again breathe and move freely. Now, God, **be gracious to me and hear my prayer.**

3 **Sons of man.** The psalmist now turns to *benei ish*, "sons of man," namely, the leaders among his adversaries. Throughout the Bible, the word *ish* usually indicates a person of seniority and status. **How long will you put my honor to shame?** To what extent will you continue to denigrate and embarrass me? How long will you **love emptiness?** David's humiliation and his enemies' fight against him are not a consequence of his own deficiencies or mistakes. They constitute an unfounded war brought about by people who are propagating empty distortions and disseminating lies. How long will you **seek deception?** They go out of their way to seek out lies and deceptions concerning me. **Selah.**

4 Rather than pursuing me for baseless, deceptive reasons, **know,** be aware, **that the Lord has set apart the devoted for Himself; the Lord hears when I call to Him.** God has a special relationship with those who are faithful to Him. David's devotion to God and desire to be close to Him were acknowledged by all, even during his lifetime. He repeatedly refers to the special way in which God sets apart those who seek Him.

5 **Tremble and do not sin.** In this psalm, the word *rigzu*, defined here as "tremble," connotes agitation, though elsewhere the word refers to anger. The psalmist bids his antagonists to shake off their evil ways. **Say in your heart, upon your bed.** He calls on people to bestir themselves, to change their mind-set, and to transform their outlook on life so that they will not be drawn toward habitual sin. It is as if the psalmist is saying: Consider these matters in private, at a time before bed, rather than in the company of other people. Whereas public discussion can lead to distorted thought and convoluted expression, private contemplation facilitates a clearer understanding of the truth. **And be still, Selah.** The psalmist further enjoins individuals to be still and remain silent. One should not offer opinions or be drawn into discussion about matters unrelated to himself or outside the realm of his understanding. In the specific case at hand, rather than focusing on David and his deficiencies, people would be better off examining their own behavior and turning toward God.

6 **Offer sacrifices of righteousness, and trust in the Lord.**

7 **Many are saying** in their prayers: **Who will show us any good?** They seek out a source of blessing and goodness. **Bring forth the light of Your countenance upon us, Lord.** They ask God to bring forth His light and shine His countenance upon them. Alternatively, the word *nesa*, can mean "reveal Yourself." The psalmist goes on to say: I myself do not sit and contemplate the wrongs of others. I truly attempt to cleave to God.

8 **You put gladness in my heart, more than when their grain and new wine abounded.** You, God, have brought joy to my heart, a joy greater than that felt by others in possession of abundant grain and wine. I am not jealous of them; my inner joy suffices, and even increases in the face of the great success of others.

9 **I lie down and sleep, at peace together.** Apparently this means that when everything all together is peaceful, I will be able to sleep undisturbed. **For** even if **You** are **alone, Lord,** in seeking peace for me while all others are against me, this is sufficient for me, for You will **allow me to dwell in safety.**

PSALM 5

PSALMS 5:1–13

A psalm of prayer directed against those wicked individuals who are unworthy of God's kindness. The psalmist prays for his own righteousness to become apparent and for him to be granted salvation, as well as those found worthy.

5 1 **For the chief musician, for neḥilot accompaniment, a psalm by David.** Although we do not know the exact meaning of *neḥilot*, it is reasonable to assume that it was a musical instrument used to accompany this psalm. Some commentators say that it made a buzzing sound like that of a swarm [*neḥil*] of bees. Others believe it refers to an ancient melody known as *El HaNeḥilot* to which the words of this psalm were sung. Like the preceding psalms, this takes the form of a prayer, though it does not specify the psalmist's troubles. Instead, the psalmist presents the various ways in which people go astray, reiterating for himself and for others the importance of desiring closeness with God and choosing the right path.

2 **Give ear to my words, Lord; consider my meditation.** Please listen, God, to prayers of the heart as well as to those uttered by one's lips.

3 **Listen to the voice of my cry, my King and my God, for to You I pray.** The emphasis is on "to You"; I pray only to You, not to others.

4 **In the morning,** each morning, day after day, **Lord, You hear my voice. In the morning,** each morning, **I direct my prayer to You and await Your response.** These are the words of someone who is wholeheartedly set on choosing the right path to follow, someone who knows that the choice of any other path would defy the will of God.

ג וְשֹׁמֵעַ תְּפִלָּתִי: בְּנֵי־אִישׁ עַד־מֶה כְבוֹדִי לִכְלִמָּה תֶּאֱהָבוּן רִיק תְּבַקְשׁוּ כָזָב
ד ה סֶלָה: וּדְעוּ כִּי־הִפְלָה יְהוָה חָסִיד לוֹ יְהוָה יִשְׁמַע בְּקָרְאִי אֵלָיו: רִגְזוּ וְאַל־תֶּחֱטָאוּ
ו אִמְרוּ בִלְבַבְכֶם עַל־מִשְׁכַּבְכֶם וְדֹמּוּ סֶלָה: זִבְחוּ זִבְחֵי־צֶדֶק וּבִטְחוּ אֶל־יְהוָה:
ז ח רַבִּים אֹמְרִים מִי־יַרְאֵנוּ טוֹב נְסָה־עָלֵינוּ אוֹר פָּנֶיךָ יְהוָה: נָתַתָּה שִׂמְחָה בְלִבִּי
ט מֵעֵת דְּגָנָם וְתִירוֹשָׁם רָבּוּ: בְּשָׁלוֹם יַחְדָּו אֶשְׁכְּבָה וְאִישָׁן כִּי־אַתָּה יְהוָה לְבָדָד
לָבֶטַח תּוֹשִׁיבֵנִי:
ה א ב ג לַמְנַצֵּחַ אֶל־הַנְּחִילוֹת מִזְמוֹר לְדָוִד: אֲמָרַי הַאֲזִינָה | יְהוָה בִּינָה הֲגִיגִי: הַקְשִׁיבָה |
ד לְקוֹל שַׁוְעִי מַלְכִּי וֵאלֹהָי כִּי־אֵלֶיךָ אֶתְפַּלָּל: יְהוָה בֹּקֶר תִּשְׁמַע קוֹלִי בֹּקֶר אֶעֱרָךְ־
ה ו לְךָ וַאֲצַפֶּה: כִּי | לֹא אֵל־חָפֵץ רֶשַׁע | אָתָּה לֹא יְגֻרְךָ רָע: לֹא־יִתְיַצְּבוּ הוֹלְלִים
ז לְנֶגֶד עֵינֶיךָ שָׂנֵאתָ כָּל־פֹּעֲלֵי אָוֶן: תְּאַבֵּד דֹּבְרֵי כָזָב אִישׁ־דָּמִים וּמִרְמָה יְתָעֵב |
ח ט יְהוָה: וַאֲנִי בְּרֹב חַסְדְּךָ אָבוֹא בֵיתֶךָ אֶשְׁתַּחֲוֶה אֶל־הֵיכַל־קָדְשְׁךָ בְּיִרְאָתֶךָ: יְהוָה |
י נְחֵנִי בְצִדְקָתֶךָ לְמַעַן שׁוֹרְרָי הושר לְפָנַי דַּרְכֶּךָ: כִּי אֵין בְּפִיהוּ נְכוֹנָה קִרְבָּם הַוּוֹת הַיְשַׁר
יא קֶבֶר־פָּתוּחַ גְּרוֹנָם לְשׁוֹנָם יַחֲלִיקוּן: הַאֲשִׁימֵם | אֱלֹהִים יִפְּלוּ מִמֹּעֲצוֹתֵיהֶם בְּרֹב

5 **For You are not a God who takes pleasure in wickedness.** God's will is opposed to evil. **No evil dwells with You.**

6 **The foolish,** those who act impulsively, lack direction, and go astray, **will not stand before Your eyes.** You do not want them near You, for **You hate all evildoers.**

7 **You destroy those who speak falsehood; the Lord abhors a man of bloodshed and deceit.**

8 **But as for me, through Your abundant kindness, I will enter Your House.** The psalmist knows fully that he is not perfect. What matters is that he is trying to choose the right path. The fact that he is allowed to enter God's House is an expression of God's kindness toward him. **I will bow to Your Holy Temple in reverence to You.**

9 **Lead me, Lord, in Your righteousness.** Place me on the right path, guide me in Your righteous ways, so that I will be able to choose the appropriate way to stand **against my foes.** When surrounded by enemies, a person does not always have the ability to know how to act. It is precisely then that he needs guidance in how to remain on the proper path. **Straighten Your path before me** so that I will be able to walk easily in the path of righteousness.

10 **There is no truth in what they say.** In contrast with the divine path mentioned in the previous verse, the path of the enemies is marked by deceit. **Their inner being is misfortune.** All that is found within them is the disaster and trouble that they plot for others. **Their throat is an open grave.** Their mouths are likened to open tombs: They exude an inner decay; moreover, they entice and seduce others to fall within. **They deceive with their tongue,** frequently making use of deceptive accusations rather than honest argumentation.

"Open grave"

11 **Condemn them, God.** Judge them as they deserve to be judged, and find them guilty. **Let them fall by their own devices.** Alternatively, let them fall away from their schemes and

conspiracies. **Cast them out for their many transgressions, for they have rebelled against You** and are consequently deserving of punishment. *Pesha,* translated here as "transgression," indicates a sin committed deliberately.

12 The psalmist concludes on a more positive note: **But let all who put their trust in You rejoice; let them sing for joy forever, and You will shelter them. Those who love Your name will exult in You.**

13 **For it is You who blesses the righteous man, Lord, surrounding him with favor,**[D] **like** a large **shield** [***tzina***] that covers the entire body like a suit of armor. This is how God loves and is close to the righteous.

Relief depicting Assyrian archers behind a shield, Central Palace, Nimrud, 728 BCE

PSALM 6

PSALMS 6:1–11

A psalm of entreaty by a man who is both ill and persecuted by his enemies, crying out to God in his suffering and asking that God have mercy on him and heed his supplications.

6 1 **For the chief musician on stringed instruments, on the eight-stringed harp,**[B] **a psalm by David.**

2 **Lord, rebuke me not in Your anger**[D] **nor chasten me in Your displeasure.** The word *tokhiḥeni* refers to both rebuke and physical punishment. The psalmist entreats God: Do not rebuke me by means of physical punishment; pain can sometimes be unbearable.

African lyre with eight strings

3 **Be gracious to me, Lord, for I am miserable; heal me, Lord, for my bones are frightened.** The psalmist bases his request not on his own good deeds but rather on his inability to bear the intensity of the pain. The phrase "my bones are frightened" is almost certainly a poetic expression depicting fear and pain that have penetrated to the core.

4 **For I am in great terror.** More than just experiencing pain, the psalmist also fears that he will never recover from his illness, that he will die. He asks of God: **And You, Lord, how long** will You leave me in this dire and hopeless situation? When will I be healed?

5 **Return, Lord.** Pain and suffering can be understood as signs that one has been abandoned by God. This is the reason the psalmist beseeches God to return to him. **Rescue my soul.** Rescue me from this state of oppression. **Save me for the sake of Your kindness.** The rationale behind this request, "for the sake of Your kindness," appears frequently in the book of Psalms.

6 **For in death, there is no memory of You; in the grave, who can give You thanks?** The psalmist argues that it is not in God's interest to kill him, as he is capable of acknowledging and thanking God only while he is alive.

7 **I am depleted by my groaning.** Excessive groaning from pain can further sap the strength of a sick person. Alternatively, his pain is so great that it is difficult even to groan. **Every night I cause my bed to swim.** Because of all his weeping at night, his bed has practically become a pool of water. **I melt my couch with my tears.** I weep so profusely that my tears seem to dissolve my bed.

8 The psalmist's illness is not just his own private matter; it also arouses and encourages his enemies. He suffers both from the pain of the illness and from the awareness that his enemies are rejoicing in his misery, hoping daily for his demise. **My eye is weakened by anger, pulled out because of all my foes.** When I think of my adversaries celebrating my misfortune, I feel as if my eyes are falling out of their sockets. My vision has been weakened and clouded by grief. The foes in this psalm are not necessarily mortal flesh and blood; such imagery is rather an expression of the emotional state of a person who is desperately ill. He may feel that many different forces of evil are gathering against him, rejoicing in his misfortune. But when he recovers, all these dark feelings disappear. The concluding verses indicate the psalmist's abrupt shift in mood:

9 **Leave me, all you evildoers, for the Lord has heard the voice of my weeping** and has healed me.

10 **The Lord has heard my plea; the Lord will accept my prayer.** Once He accepts my prayer, I am able to recover.

11 **My enemies will be greatly ashamed and frightened; they will retreat, immediately be put to shame.** And once I recover, my enemies will disappear; they will even feel ashamed that they had been lying in wait for me.

יב פִּשְׁעֵיהֶם הַדִּיחֵמוֹ כִּי מָרוּ בָךְ: וְיִשְׂמְחוּ כָל־חוֹסֵי בָךְ לְעוֹלָם יְרַנֵּנוּ וְתָסֵךְ עָלֵימוֹ

יג וְיַעְלְצוּ בְךָ אֹהֲבֵי שְׁמֶךָ: כִּי־אַתָּה תְּבָרֵךְ צַדִּיק יהוה כַּצִּנָּה רָצוֹן תַּעְטְרֶנּוּ:

ו א ב לַמְנַצֵּחַ בִּנְגִינוֹת עַל־הַשְּׁמִינִית מִזְמוֹר לְדָוִד: יהוה אַל־בְּאַפְּךָ תוֹכִיחֵנִי וְאַל־

ג ד בַּחֲמָתְךָ תְיַסְּרֵנִי: חָנֵּנִי יהוה כִּי אֻמְלַל אָנִי רְפָאֵנִי יהוה כִּי נִבְהֲלוּ עֲצָמָי: וְנַפְשִׁי

ה נִבְהֲלָה מְאֹד וְאַתְּ יהוה עַד־מָתָי: שׁוּבָה יהוה חַלְּצָה נַפְשִׁי הוֹשִׁיעֵנִי לְמַעַן

ו ז חַסְדֶּךָ: כִּי אֵין בַּמָּוֶת זִכְרֶךָ בִּשְׁאוֹל מִי יוֹדֶה־לָּךְ: יָגַעְתִּי ׀ בְּאַנְחָתִי אַשְׂחֶה בְכָל־

ח לַיְלָה מִטָּתִי בְּדִמְעָתִי עַרְשִׂי אַמְסֶה: עָשְׁשָׁה מִכַּעַס עֵינִי עָתְקָה בְּכָל־צוֹרְרָי:

ט סוּרוּ מִמֶּנִּי כָּל־פֹּעֲלֵי אָוֶן כִּי־שָׁמַע יהוה קוֹל בִּכְיִי: שָׁמַע יהוה תְּחִנָּתִי יהוה

יא תְּפִלָּתִי יִקָּח: יֵבֹשׁוּ ׀ וְיִבָּהֲלוּ מְאֹד כָּל־אֹיְבָי יָשֻׁבוּ יֵבֹשׁוּ רָגַע:

ז א ב שִׁגָּיוֹן לְדָוִד אֲשֶׁר־שָׁר לַיהוה עַל־דִּבְרֵי־כוּשׁ בֶּן־יְמִינִי: יהוה אֱלֹהַי בְּךָ חָסִיתִי

PSALM 7

PSALMS 7:1–18

A psalm that offers the prayer of an individual beset by enemies and falsely accused of wrongdoing, who asks God to acknowledge his righteousness and requite his foes.

7 1 **A meditation[D] by David. A song that he sang to the Lord concerning the words of Kush the Benjamite.** There is no definitive identification for Kush the Benjamite. Some of the Sages suggest that it was another name for King Saul, who was from the tribe of Benjamin. A simpler explanation is that Kush was an ordinary Benjamite who spoke ill of David, possibly accusing him of being responsible for a military setback or of not fighting valiantly enough as a soldier in Saul's army.

2 **Lord, I put my faith in You. Deliver me from all my pursuers and rescue me,**

BACKGROUND

6:1 | **The eight-stringed harp [*sheminit*]:** The psalms were accompanied by various stringed instruments that differed according to their number of strings. Ancient drawings and reliefs display instruments varying from three to fourteen strings. *Sheminit*, from *shemoneh*, meaning "eight," alludes to eight strings, or perhaps to the stringed instrument called *sammu* in Akkadian (see also 92:4). Other commentators claim that the phrase *al hasheminit*, literally, "on the eighth," is an instruction for this particular psalm to be sung to the last of the eight melodies typically played on the instrument.

DISCUSSION

5:13 | **Surrounding him with favor [*ratzon*]:** The noun *ratzon* can mean "desire," or "wish," but it also indicates the fulfillment of the desire, the granting of goodness and satisfaction. The righteous are engulfed in God's love and in His willingness to hear and gratify their desires.

6:2 | **Rebuke me not in Your anger:** This psalm expresses the prayer of a man who is ill with a serious malady and does not know if he will ever recover from it. It ends with words of thanks, apparently because the prayer has been answered and he has been healed. The psalm makes mention of foes and evildoers, but this is not necessarily to be understood as referring to physical enemies. Rather, it is an expression of a sick person's feeling that various evil powers have aligned against him and are glad to see him suffer. When he recovers, these dark shadows disappear.

7:1 | **Meditation [*shigayon*]:** The simple explanation of this word appears to be that it is the name of a type of song or the name of a particular melody (see Rashi and Ibn Ezra; Habakkuk 3:1). However, some relate it to the word "mistake" [*shegi'a*] or "inadvertent act" [*shegaga*], meaning that this is a psalm of remorse for a mistake that David had made. The root of the word, *shin-gimmel-heh*, is sometimes used in the sense of "to think" or "to contemplate."

3 **lest he,** my enemy, **tear me like a lion, rending me in pieces, while there is no one to be my savior.** The psalmist now addresses the complaint that had been directed against him:

4 **Lord, my God, if I have done this,** if I have committed the misdeeds of which my enemies accuse me, **if my hands have done any wrong,**

5 **if I have repaid my friend with evil,** referring to someone who had once paid him a kind act, as *sholmi*, "my friend," is linguistically similar to *shalem*, "to pay," **or despoiled my enemy without cause,**

6 **then let the enemy pursue me and overtake me; let my life be trampled on the ground and my soul to the dust, Selah.** The word *kavod*, which usually means "honor," can also connote "being" or "soul." Hence the translation here and elsewhere of *kevodi* as "my life," "my being," or "my soul." Nevertheless, despite the psalmist's statement about being overtaken by the enemy and trampled to the ground, he continues:

7 **Arise, Lord, in Your anger.** It is fitting for You as well to be angered by the evil being done to me. **Lift Yourself up** and display Your power **against the wrath of my enemies. Awaken for me the judgment You commanded** concerning me.

8 **A congregation of nations will surround You, and with it return on high.** This is an image of God surrounded by an honor guard or entourage of the nations, all of whom have come to thank Him and escort Him to heaven, His holy abode on high.

9 **The Lord will be the Judge of the peoples.** When this time arrives, when God reveals Himself in judgment, I can request of Him as well to **judge me, Lord, as befits my righteousness and as befits my innocence.**

10 At that time **let the evil of the wicked come to an end, but give strength to the righteous one.** God has no need to examine external testimony in order to execute justice, **for men's hearts and minds are probed by the God of righteousness.** *Kelayot*, translated here as "minds," literally means "kidneys," which are considered the seat of a person's thoughts.

11 **God, the Savior of the upright of heart, is my shield.**

12 **God is a righteous Judge.** Because God is just, He exonerates the righteous. **And** at the same time, **the Almighty** also **shows His wrath** against the evildoers **every day**

13 **if he,** the evildoer, **does not repent** of his threats and evil plans against the righteous, **if he** persists and **sharpens his sword and pulls back his bow in readiness.**

14 **But** his plans will fail anyway, and the final result will be his own destruction; in the end, **he prepares deadly weapons against himself.** The very weapons the wicked aim at the righteous will instead target and destroy the wicked themselves. **His arrows are used against those who pursue.** The arrows directed against the righteous will instead be used against their pursuers.

15 **Behold how he conceives evil, is pregnant with iniquity, and gives birth to deceit.**[D] Whatever the wicked person creates and produces, the plans are undertaken in *aven*, translated here as "evil" but also meaning "nothingness," and in *amal*, translated as "iniquity" but also connoting toiling in vain. The final result is nothing but an empty lie.

16 **He,** the evildoer, **has dug a hole deep in the earth and has fallen into the pit he made.** Ultimately, the evil person falls into the hole that he dug for others.

17 **His wrongdoing will return to punish him; his violent behavior will come down on his head.** His own sins and evil deeds bring him trouble, suffering, and punitive consequences. He suffers even without the external infliction of punishment; he is essentially punished by his own wrongful deeds.

18 In conclusion: **I praise the Lord for His righteousness; I sing to the name of the Lord Most High.**

PSALM 8

PSALMS 8:1–10

A psalm that begins as a hymn of praise to God but is also an introspective poem that muses about man's place in the world.

8 1 **For the chief musician on the gittit,**[B] probably a musical instrument named after Gat, the city in which it may have been invented or where it was commonly played; **a psalm by David.** The psalm begins and ends with a proclamation of praise:

2 **Lord, our Master, how mighty is Your name throughout the world! You set Your glory in the heavens.** This verse can be understood to be an observation that God's name is glorified in heaven. Others explain it to mean: It would be befitting for You to bestow Your glory exclusively on the heavens.

3 **Out of the mouths of small children and suckling babes You founded strength.**[D] Their unique prayers are directed **against Your foes,** in order **to stop the enemy and the avenger.** Sung with childish sincerity, these songs are a positive force in the war against God's enemies. They represent a fundamental, basic strength that cannot be extinguished by adversaries, and they are a buffer against the waves of hatred that recur in every generation.

4 **When I see Your heavens, the work of Your fingers, the moon and the stars You have made.** I am thrilled by the enormity of Your all-encompassing greatness. But

"Out of the mouths of small children and suckling babes You founded strength." Children and their teacher, Samarkand, 1909

ג ד הוֹשִׁיעֵנִי מִכָּל־רֹדְפַי וְהַצִּילֵנִי׃ פֶּן־יִטְרֹף כְּאַרְיֵה נַפְשִׁי פֹּרֵק וְאֵין מַצִּיל׃ יְהוָה
ה אֱלֹהַי אִם־עָשִׂיתִי זֹאת אִם־יֶשׁ־עָוֶל בְּכַפָּי׃ אִם־גָּמַלְתִּי שׁוֹלְמִי רָע וָאֲחַלְּצָה
ו צוֹרְרִי רֵיקָם׃ יִרַדֹּף אוֹיֵב ׀ נַפְשִׁי וְיַשֵּׂג וְיִרְמֹס לָאָרֶץ חַיָּי וּכְבוֹדִי ׀ לֶעָפָר יַשְׁכֵּן
ז ח סֶלָה׃ קוּמָה יְהוָה ׀ בְּאַפֶּךָ הִנָּשֵׂא בְּעַבְרוֹת צוֹרְרָי וְעוּרָה אֵלַי מִשְׁפָּט צִוִּיתָ׃ וַעֲדַת
ט לְאֻמִּים תְּסוֹבְבֶךָּ וְעָלֶיהָ לַמָּרוֹם שׁוּבָה׃ יְהוָה יָדִין עַמִּים שָׁפְטֵנִי יְהוָה כְּצִדְקִי
י וּכְתֻמִּי עָלָי׃ יִגְמָר־נָא רַע ׀ רְשָׁעִים וּתְכוֹנֵן צַדִּיק וּבֹחֵן לִבּוֹת וּכְלָיוֹת אֱלֹהִים
יא יב צַדִּיק׃ מָגִנִּי עַל־אֱלֹהִים מוֹשִׁיעַ יִשְׁרֵי־לֵב׃ אֱלֹהִים שׁוֹפֵט צַדִּיק וְאֵל זֹעֵם בְּכָל־
יג יד יוֹם׃ אִם־לֹא יָשׁוּב חַרְבּוֹ יִלְטוֹשׁ קַשְׁתּוֹ דָרַךְ וַיְכוֹנְנֶהָ׃ וְלוֹ הֵכִין כְּלֵי־מָוֶת חִצָּיו
טו טז לְדֹלְקִים יִפְעָל׃ הִנֵּה יְחַבֶּל־אָוֶן וְהָרָה עָמָל וְיָלַד שָׁקֶר׃ בּוֹר כָּרָה וַיַּחְפְּרֵהוּ וַיִּפֹּל
יז יח בְּשַׁחַת יִפְעָל׃ יָשׁוּב עֲמָלוֹ בְרֹאשׁוֹ וְעַל קָדְקֳדוֹ חֲמָסוֹ יֵרֵד׃ אוֹדֶה יְהוָה כְּצִדְקוֹ
וַאֲזַמְּרָה שֵׁם־יְהוָה עֶלְיוֹן׃

ח א ב לַמְנַצֵּחַ עַל־הַגִּתִּית מִזְמוֹר לְדָוִד׃ יְהוָה אֲדֹנֵינוּ מָה־אַדִּיר שִׁמְךָ בְּכָל־הָאָרֶץ
ג אֲשֶׁר־תְּנָה הוֹדְךָ עַל־הַשָּׁמָיִם׃ מִפִּי עוֹלְלִים ׀ וְיֹנְקִים יִסַּדְתָּ עֹז לְמַעַן צוֹרְרֶיךָ
ד לְהַשְׁבִּית אוֹיֵב וּמִתְנַקֵּם׃ כִּי־אֶרְאֶה שָׁמֶיךָ מַעֲשֵׂה אֶצְבְּעֹתֶיךָ יָרֵחַ וְכוֹכָבִים אֲשֶׁר

BACKGROUND

8:1 | **Gittit:** A *gittit* is probably similar to a lyre [*nevel*]. The ancient lyre was arched in shape; its lower part was thick, and the strings were stretched from there to the upper, thinner section. Thus it was similar in appearance to a wine flask, which also had a thick base and a long neck, and which is also called *nevel* in the Bible (I Samuel 10:3, Jeremiah 13:12 and elsewhere). A *gat* is a winepress, and the derivative term *gittit* may have been used, by extension, as a name for the flask from which wine was drunk, and by further extension, to the musical instrument that resembled it in shape or that was played as an accompaniment to the drinking of wine or the trampling of grapes at the winepress.

DISCUSSION

7:15 | **He conceives evil, is pregnant with iniquity, and gives birth to deceit:** The schemes of the wicked that ultimately turn into actions are compared to stages in the development of a person: conception, pregnancy, and birth. The evil person sows words of evil, which develop into frustration and end with falsehood and failure (see also notes on Isaiah 59:4; Rambam, *Guide of the Perplexed* 1:7).

8:3 | **Out of the mouths of small children and suckling babes, You founded strength:** Praises and prayers offered to God are uttered not only by the lips of select wise men or elders; there is a special kind of divine praise that issues from the mouths of small children. Their words of praise, uttered in complete innocence, constitute the greatest praise of God, because they are devoid of guile or pretense. Their prayers do not suffer from the artificiality that is often a hallmark of "professional" religious poetry.

"Your heavens, the work of Your fingers, the moon and the stars You have made"

the sight of Your miraculous creations also raises doubts and uncertainty in my mind:
5 **What is a mortal that You remember him, a man that You take him into account?** After seeing the sun, moon, and stars, after contemplating enormous and distant worlds, one might conclude that man is an inconsequential and pitiful creation, fundamentally unworthy of attention from God above. Yet somehow, despite man's insignificance, You, God, have chosen to bestow on him manifold gifts.
6 **For You have made him a little less than divine.**[D] You have created him "in the image of God."[1] Consequently, God's spirit resides within man. An alternative interpretation of "divine" in this verse is that it refers to God's angels. You have bestowed upon man unique powers, making him only slightly inferior to the divine angels and **crowning him with honor and glory.**
7 In addition to creating man to be essentially superior to other beings, as is written in the book of Genesis, **You have made him ruler over the works of Your hands,** giving him permission and power to rule over Your handiwork. **You placed all things at his feet.** You charged him with reigning over all that exists,
8 **all sheep and cattle.** Domestic animals have been given over to man, and he also has dominion over **all the** wild **animals of the field,**
9 and over **the birds of the air and the fish of the sea, whatever crosses the sea's deep waters.** Man should thank God for giving him power over all the creatures of the land, sea, and sky. This vast power should be humbling. One might wonder: Is man truly worthy of it? This question can be instructive, helping one to realize that although man is in charge, his power stems from God, who, in His kindness, relegated it to him. When man considers his own insignificance vis-à-vis the immensity of the power placed in his hands, he should acknowledge that it is all a God-given gift. Therefore, he should say again, as in the opening verse of the psalm:

"Birds of the air"

"Fish of the sea, whatever crosses the sea's deep waters"

10 **Lord, our Master, how mighty is Your name throughout the world!**

PSALM 9

PSALMS 9:1–21

A psalm of thanksgiving by one who has been rescued from his enemies and led to victory. The psalmist prays that God will continue to be at his side against others who wage war against him.

9 1 **For the chief musician, on the death of Laben,**[D] **a psalm by David.** Written mostly in first-person singular, this psalm is intended to be studied and taught. To facilitate memorization, this Hebrew text, like many others, is arranged in an alphabetical acrostic. The alphabet is not complete, however, and there are non-alphabetical verses inserted between consecutive letters.
2 **I will thank You, Lord, with all my heart. I will tell of all Your wonders.**

DISCUSSION

8:5–6 | **What is a mortal that You remember him …For You have made him a little less than divine:** The psalmist moderates his statement of man's immense capabilities, by a sense of humility. He asks whether man is in fact deserving of all the power that has been granted to him. There is a lesson here for everyone: One must be aware of his great potential, but at the same time be grateful to God for having supplied him with dominion over nature.

9:1 | **On the death of Laben:** Since this psalm is generally one of thanksgiving to God and does not appear to be a lament about the loss of a son, certainly not one of David's own children, most commentators agree that the word *laben*, literally translated as "for the son," does not have that meaning here. Some commentators argue that Laben could be the name of an enemy king or commander unknown to us from other sources. Others speculate that *al mut Laben*, translated here as "on the death of Laben," actually has nothing to do with death, but rather was the name of a well-known song, and that this psalm was meant to be sung to its melody (see Rashi; Ibn Ezra; Malbim).

ה ו כּוֹנַנְתָּה׃ מָה־אֱנוֹשׁ כִּי־תִזְכְּרֶנּוּ וּבֶן־אָדָם כִּי תִפְקְדֶנּוּ׃ וַתְּחַסְּרֵהוּ מְּעַט מֵאֱלֹהִים
ז ח וְכָבוֹד וְהָדָר תְּעַטְּרֵהוּ׃ תַּמְשִׁילֵהוּ בְּמַעֲשֵׂי יָדֶיךָ כֹּל שַׁתָּה תַחַת־רַגְלָיו׃ צֹנֶה
ט י וַאֲלָפִים כֻּלָּם וְגַם בַּהֲמוֹת שָׂדָי׃ צִפּוֹר שָׁמַיִם וּדְגֵי הַיָּם עֹבֵר אָרְחוֹת יַמִּים׃ יהוה
אֲדֹנֵינוּ מָה־אַדִּיר שִׁמְךָ בְּכָל־הָאָרֶץ׃
ט א ב לַמְנַצֵּחַ עַל־מוּת לַבֵּן מִזְמוֹר לְדָוִד׃ אוֹדֶה יהוה בְּכָל־לִבִּי אֲסַפְּרָה כָּל־נִפְלְאוֹתֶיךָ׃
ג ד אֶשְׂמְחָה וְאֶעֶלְצָה בָךְ אֲזַמְּרָה שִׁמְךָ עֶלְיוֹן׃ בְּשׁוּב־אוֹיְבַי אָחוֹר יִכָּשְׁלוּ וְיֹאבְדוּ
ה ו מִפָּנֶיךָ׃ כִּי־עָשִׂיתָ מִשְׁפָּטִי וְדִינִי יָשַׁבְתָּ לְכִסֵּא שׁוֹפֵט צֶדֶק׃ גָּעַרְתָּ גוֹיִם אִבַּדְתָּ
ז רָשָׁע שְׁמָם מָחִיתָ לְעוֹלָם וָעֶד׃ הָאוֹיֵב ׀ תַּמּוּ חֳרָבוֹת לָנֶצַח וְעָרִים נָתַשְׁתָּ אָבַד
ח ט זִכְרָם הֵמָּה׃ וַיהוה לְעוֹלָם יֵשֵׁב כּוֹנֵן לַמִּשְׁפָּט כִּסְאוֹ׃ וְהוּא יִשְׁפֹּט־תֵּבֵל בְּצֶדֶק
י יא יָדִין לְאֻמִּים בְּמֵישָׁרִים׃ וִיהִי יהוה מִשְׂגָּב לַדָּךְ מִשְׂגָּב לְעִתּוֹת בַּצָּרָה׃ וְיִבְטְחוּ
יב בְךָ יוֹדְעֵי שְׁמֶךָ כִּי לֹא־עָזַבְתָּ דֹרְשֶׁיךָ יהוה׃ זַמְּרוּ לַיהוה יֹשֵׁב צִיּוֹן הַגִּידוּ בָעַמִּים
יג יד עֲלִילוֹתָיו׃ כִּי־דֹרֵשׁ דָּמִים אוֹתָם זָכָר לֹא־שָׁכַח צַעֲקַת עניים׃ חָנְנֵנִי יהוה רְאֵה עֲנָוִים

3 **I will be glad and delight in You. I will sing for Your name, Most High.**

4 **When my enemies are turned back, they stumble and perish before You.**

5 This will occur, **for You have performed my judgment and my verdict.** When the time came for me to be judged by You, I knew that You would find my enemies guilty. **You sat on Your throne** of justice, **Judge of righteousness.**

6 **You rebuked the nations,** and since God's rebuke manifests itself in the physical world of man, the outcome is that these evil nations are struck down. **You obliterated the wicked** to such an extent that **You blotted out their name forever and ever.**

7 **The enemy is no more,** and all that is left of their territory lies **in eternal ruin. You have destroyed their cities.** The word *natashta* is translated here as "You have destroyed," similar to the word *natatzta*, "You have shattered." **The memory of them is lost.** Not only have the cities fallen in conquest, but their memory has been obliterated as well.

8 **But** in contrast to the aforementioned enemies whose end is described here, **the Lord will endure forever. He has prepared His throne for judgment,**

9 **and He will judge the world in righteousness. He will administer fair judgment to the nations.**

10 **The Lord is a fortress for the oppressed, a fortress in times of trouble.**

11 **And those who know Your name,** who believe in You and recognize You, and are thus close to You, **place their trust in You, for You, Lord, do not forsake those who seek You.**

12 **Sing to the Lord** a song of thanksgiving, **dweller in Zion; make His deeds known among the peoples.** Tell all the nations how He saved you from danger and from the attacks of your enemies.

13 **For He avenges blood.** The word *doresh*, translated here as "avenges," literally means "searches." God investigates, as it were, incidents of bloodshed, and **He remembers them,** the righteous who have been unjustly slain. **He does not forget the cries of the humble,** those who have conducted themselves with righteousness and humility.

14 **Be gracious to me, Lord; see my deprivation, inflicted by my enemies. You lift me up from the gates of death,**

15 **so I might speak Your praise** when I experience Your salvation, **at the gates of the daughter of Zion.** The gates of a city were the public spaces, akin to a central plaza. **I rejoice in Your salvation** and tell others about it.

16 In contrast to my joy, **the nations have sunk into the pit they made, their feet trapped in the nets they hid.** The evil nations will fall into the very pits they dug; their feet will be caught in the traps they set for others.

17 **The Lord is known through the judgments He executes** throughout the world. **The evildoer is snared in the work of his own hands. Reflect upon this, Selah.** The word *higgayon*, translated here as "reflect upon this," can mean: This topic deserves consideration; think about it and discuss it with others.

18 **The wicked will return to,** or go in the direction of, **the netherworld.** Alternatively, one might say that in a certain sense, evildoers are creatures emanating from the netherworld who are forced to return to their origin. The same may be said of **all nations who have no memory of God.**

19 **For the needy will not always be forgotten** and **the hopes of the poor forever lost.** Even if the needy appear to be abandoned, hope is not lost; God ultimately turns toward them.

20 **Arise, Lord.** Stir Yourself to action and reveal Yourself through justice. **Let man not be arrogant.** The wicked will not prevail once God's presence is revealed in the world; no one then will dare to be insolent. **Let the nations be judged in Your sight.**

21 **Place fear in them, Lord.** While this spelling of *mora*, with a *heh*, means "edict," some interpret the word in the sense of *mora* with an *alef*, meaning "fear." Thus, the verse can either mean issue an edict against them or instill fear in them. Either way, this is **so that nations know they are but mortal men, Selah.** The nations must acknowledge that they are far from invincible; being human, they are *enosh*, "mortal," and both their power and their very lives will inevitably come to an end. The use of the word is significant in this context, as it evokes the similarly spelled word *anush*, someone who is critically ill.

PSALM 10

A psalm of prayer that rails against the rule of the wicked.

PSALMS 10:1–18

10 *2nd day of month*

1 **Why do You stand far off, Lord,** as if You were not here among us? **Why do You hide Yourself in times of trouble?**

2 **The wicked in their pride fervently pursue the afflicted, who are caught in the schemes they plot.**

3 **For the wicked one sings praises about his heart's desire.** If an evil person decides for some reason to praise God, it is only about the attainment of his own desires. **And the evil man [*botze'a*] blesses and reviles the Lord.** When that evil person blesses God, his blessing is so insincere that it is actually an affront to Him. An alternative translation of *botze'a* is "one who breaks bread." The meaning of this phrase, then, would be that an immoral person who steals bread from another and now sits down to eat it is committing a sacrilege by uttering a blessing over the bread.

4 **The wicked one, with his proud countenance,** or, alternatively, in his great wrath, **does not seek** God. The greater his pride or wrath, the less likely he is to seek and find God. **God is not in his thoughts.** A wicked person does not take God into consideration when he plots to do evil.

5 **His ways always prosper; Your judgments are on high, out of his sight.** It seems, especially to the evil people themselves, that Your judgments "on high" cannot affect them, for they seem to remain successful no matter what they do. **As for his foes, he blows at them.** With great ease, as if with a puff of air, the evil people blow away their rivals.

6 **He said in his heart: I will not stumble.** In his heart, the evil person believes himself to be secure, noting: I persist, I am stable; nothing can topple me. **Throughout generations I will never be in adversity.** He believes he can continue to live and do as he pleases, without anything untoward ever happening to him.

7 **His mouth is full of curses and deceit and intrigue; beneath his tongue are mischief and wickedness.**

8 The following is the wicked person's mode of action: **He lies in wait in courtyards; in hidden places he kills the innocent. He fixes his eyes on the downtrodden.** He lies in ambush in unguarded places, on the prowl for his victims.

9 **He lurks in a hiding place like a lion in its lair.** He lies in wait like a lion in the brambles, stalking its prey. **He lurks to catch the poor man; he catches the poor man and draws him into his net.** He is deceptive, entrapping the vulnerable person and setting obstacles in his path.

"He lurks in a hiding place like a lion in its lair; he lurks to catch"

10 **He crushes him, forces him to a crouch, and the downtrodden are toppled by his might.** He uses his might to crush and oppress the unfortunate, bringing them down.

11 **He says to himself: The Almighty has forgotten** about our existence. **He has hidden His face; He will never see.** Since God remains mostly unrevealed in His world, the wicked think

טו עָנְיִי מִשֹּׂנְאָי מְרוֹמְמִי מִשַּׁעֲרֵי־מָוֶת׃ לְמַעַן אֲסַפְּרָה כָּל־תְּהִלָּתֶיךָ בְּשַׁעֲרֵי בַת־
טז צִיּוֹן אָגִילָה בִּישׁוּעָתֶךָ׃ טָבְעוּ גוֹיִם בְּשַׁחַת עָשׂוּ בְּרֶשֶׁת־זוּ טָמָנוּ נִלְכְּדָה רַגְלָם׃
יז יח נוֹדַע ׀ יהוה מִשְׁפָּט עָשָׂה בְּפֹעַל כַּפָּיו נוֹקֵשׁ רָשָׁע הִגָּיוֹן סֶלָה׃ יָשׁוּבוּ רְשָׁעִים
יט לִשְׁאוֹלָה כָּל־גּוֹיִם שְׁכֵחֵי אֱלֹהִים׃ כִּי לֹא לָנֶצַח יִשָּׁכַח אֶבְיוֹן תִּקְוַת ענוים תֹּאבַד עֲנִיִּים
כ כא לָעַד׃ קוּמָה יהוה אַל־יָעֹז אֱנוֹשׁ יִשָּׁפְטוּ גוֹיִם עַל־פָּנֶיךָ׃ שִׁיתָה יהוה ׀ מוֹרָה לָהֶם
יֵדְעוּ גוֹיִם אֱנוֹשׁ הֵמָּה סֶּלָה׃
י א ב לָמָה יהוה תַּעֲמֹד בְּרָחוֹק תַּעְלִים לְעִתּוֹת בַּצָּרָה׃ בְּגַאֲוַת רָשָׁע יִדְלַק עָנִי יִתָּפְשׂוּ ׀ ב לחודש
ג ד בִּמְזִמּוֹת זוּ חָשָׁבוּ׃ כִּי־הִלֵּל רָשָׁע עַל־תַּאֲוַת נַפְשׁוֹ וּבֹצֵעַ בֵּרֵךְ נִאֵץ ׀ יהוה׃ רָשָׁע
ה כְּגֹבַהּ אַפּוֹ בַּל־יִדְרֹשׁ אֵין אֱלֹהִים כָּל־מְזִמּוֹתָיו׃ יָחִילוּ דְרָכָו ׀ בְּכָל־עֵת מָרוֹם
ו מִשְׁפָּטֶיךָ מִנֶּגְדּוֹ כָּל־צוֹרְרָיו יָפִיחַ בָּהֶם׃ אָמַר בְּלִבּוֹ בַּל־אֶמּוֹט לְדֹר וָדֹר אֲשֶׁר
ז ח לֹא־בְרָע׃ אָלָה ׀ פִּיהוּ מָלֵא וּמִרְמוֹת וָתֹךְ תַּחַת לְשׁוֹנוֹ עָמָל וָאָוֶן׃ יֵשֵׁב ׀ בְּמַאְרַב
ט חֲצֵרִים בַּמִּסְתָּרִים יַהֲרֹג נָקִי עֵינָיו לְחֵלְכָה יִצְפֹּנוּ׃ יֶאֱרֹב בַּמִּסְתָּר ׀ כְּאַרְיֵה בְסֻכֹּה
י יֶאֱרֹב לַחֲטוֹף עָנִי יַחְטֹף עָנִי בְּמָשְׁכוֹ בְרִשְׁתּוֹ׃ ודכה יָשֹׁחַ וְנָפַל בַּעֲצוּמָיו חלכאים׃ יִדְכֶּה חֵל כָּאִים
יא יב אָמַר בְּלִבּוֹ שָׁכַח אֵל הִסְתִּיר פָּנָיו בַּל־רָאָה לָנֶצַח׃ קוּמָה יהוה אֵל נְשָׂא יָדֶךָ
יג יד אַל־תִּשְׁכַּח עניים׃ עַל־מֶה ׀ נִאֵץ רָשָׁע ׀ אֱלֹהִים אָמַר בְּלִבּוֹ לֹא תִּדְרֹשׁ׃ רָאִתָה עֲנָוִים
כִּי־אַתָּה ׀ עָמָל וָכַעַס ׀ תַּבִּיט לָתֵת בְּיָדֶךָ עָלֶיךָ יַעֲזֹב חֵלֶכָה יָתוֹם אַתָּה ׀ הָיִיתָ
טו טז עוֹזֵר׃ שְׁבֹר זְרוֹעַ רָשָׁע וָרָע תִּדְרוֹשׁ־רִשְׁעוֹ בַל־תִּמְצָא׃ יהוה מֶלֶךְ עוֹלָם וָעֶד

they can do as they please. They are convinced that God does not see them.

12 Here begins the psalmist's prayer: **Arise, Lord God, raise Your hand,** reveal Your strength. **Do not forget the humble.**

13 **Why has the wicked man mocked God, saying to himself** of God: **You will not seek?** The wicked man believes that God is oblivious, that He has no interest in mankind.

14 But the truth is that **You have seen it; You have beheld mischief and anger.** You do look and You do see all the sins and the fury of the world, **and You gave it the power to be.** You Yourself are the one who makes it possible for evil to flourish in the world. **The poor rely on You; You have always helped the orphan.** Yet now the world appears to be completely abandoned by You. Because of this, the psalmist beseeches God:

15 **Break the arm of the wicked one and evildoer; purge his wickedness until You can find none.** Eradicate evil to such an extent that if You look for it, You will not find it.

16 **The Lord is King forever and ever; nations have perished from His land.** God has banished the wicked and immoral nations from His land.

17 **Lord, You hear the desire of the humble,** which they express in their prayers. **You will strengthen their heart; You will incline Your ear** to their prayers,

18 **to vindicate the orphan and the oppressed,** so that **it,** evil, **will no longer destroy mortals,** particularly those who are weak and vulnerable, **from the earth.**

PSALM 11

PSALMS 11:1–7

A contemplative psalm on evil, in which the psalmist depicts the way wicked people attack the righteous openly and secretly, lying in ambush against them, not realizing that God watches over the world and punishes those who deserve it.

11 1 **For the chief musician, by David. In the Lord I take refuge. How can you say to me: Wander away, bird, to your mountain?** How can you speak to me so harshly, with words that seem to say: Take off, bird, fly to the hills, get away from here?

"Wander away, bird, to your mountain"

2 The world is full of menace: **For behold, the wicked bend the bow; they have fixed their arrow on the string to shoot, in darkness,** when they cannot be detected, **at the upright of heart,** whom they intend to kill.

3 **If the** moral and societal **foundations** of the world **are destroyed, what can the righteous man do?** When the moral foundations of society are in ruins, what good can possibly come of the individual deeds of a righteous person?

4 And yet, there are grounds for a different kind of contemplation, one imbued with faith and hope: **The Lord is in His Holy Temple.** He has not abandoned His earthly abode. **The Lord's throne is in heaven,** and He rules over the world. **His eyes behold** all that occurs on earth; **He puts His gaze on the sons of man.**

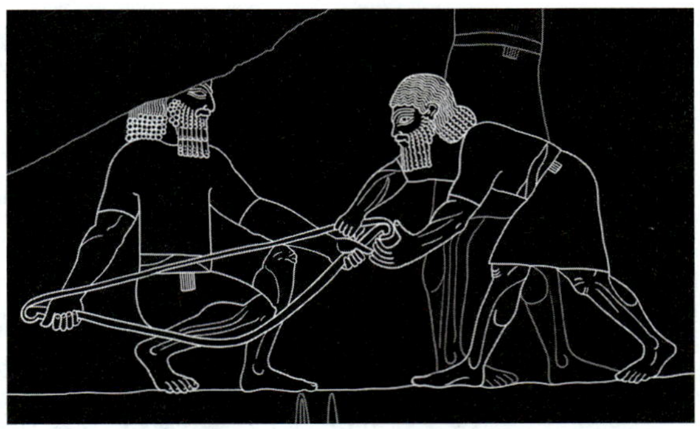

Assyrian soldiers drawing a bow and setting it for use, Assyrian relief, seventh century BCE

5 **The Lord attends to the righteous, but He hates the wicked and the lover of violence.**

6 **He will rain burning coal upon the wicked; fire and brimstone and windstorm will be their lot.**

7 **For the Lord is righteous and He** therefore **loves righteousness. Their faces,** the faces of the virtuous, **will behold the Upright One.**

PSALM 12

PSALMS 12:1–9

A plea against evildoers who seem to have the upper hand in the world, who speak of righteousness while fomenting evil. It is also a prayer to God to protect all those who follow the proper path.

12 1 **For the chief musician, on the eight-stringed harp** (see 6:1; 92:4), **a psalm by David.**

2 **Help, Lord, for the faithful man is no more, for trustworthiness has disappeared from among men.** There are no more righteous men; they are all gone, lost to mankind. Truth and loyalty have disappeared; only evil is left.

3 **People speak falsehood to one another.** Their words mean nothing, and their promises are worthless. **They speak with flattering lips and a double heart.** They are duplicitous; they do not reveal their true thoughts. They speak falsely, hiding their real intentions.

4 The psalmist pleads: **May the Lord cut off all flattering lips and the tongue that boasts.** Although flattery may be pleasing to those in power, to those who lack influence it is indicative of haughtiness and bravado.

5 And punish **those who say: With our tongue we will prevail; our lips are our own. Who is master over us?** Flatterers believe they can continue to deceive and threaten with impunity. What follows is a prayer and a message of good tidings:

6 God will not allow this situation to go on indefinitely. **Because of the robbery of the poor and the groans of the needy, the Lord says: Now I will arise** and reveal Myself to avenge these injustices. **I will bring deliverance; it,** this deliverance, **will be revealed to him,** the oppressed person, when he is rescued from the clutches of those who seek to harm him.

7 **The words of the Lord are pure words,** devoid of all pollutants. They are **like silver purified in the furnace of the earth.**

יז יח אַבְדוּ גוֹיִם מֵאַרְצוֹ׃ תַּאֲוַת עֲנָוִים שָׁמַעְתָּ יְהוָה תָּכִין לִבָּם תַּקְשִׁיב אָזְנֶךָ׃ לִשְׁפֹּט
יָתוֹם וָדָךְ בַּל־יוֹסִיף עוֹד לַעֲרֹץ אֱנוֹשׁ מִן־הָאָרֶץ׃

יא א ב לַמְנַצֵּחַ לְדָוִד בַּיהוָה ׀ חָסִיתִי אֵיךְ תֹּאמְרוּ לְנַפְשִׁי נודו הַרְכֶם צִפּוֹר׃ כִּי הִנֵּה נוּדִי
ג הָרְשָׁעִים יִדְרְכוּן קֶשֶׁת כּוֹנְנוּ חִצָּם עַל־יֶתֶר לִירוֹת בְּמוֹ־אֹפֶל לְיִשְׁרֵי־לֵב׃ כִּי
ד הַשָּׁתוֹת יֵהָרֵסוּן צַדִּיק מַה־פָּעָל׃ יְהוָה ׀ בְּהֵיכַל קָדְשׁוֹ יְהוָה בַּשָּׁמַיִם כִּסְאוֹ עֵינָיו
ה יֶחֱזוּ עַפְעַפָּיו יִבְחֲנוּ בְּנֵי אָדָם׃ יְהוָה צַדִּיק יִבְחָן וְרָשָׁע וְאֹהֵב חָמָס שָׂנְאָה נַפְשׁוֹ׃
ו ז יַמְטֵר עַל־רְשָׁעִים פַּחִים אֵשׁ וְגָפְרִית וְרוּחַ זִלְעָפוֹת מְנָת כּוֹסָם׃ כִּי־צַדִּיק יְהוָה ב
צְדָקוֹת אָהֵב יָשָׁר יֶחֱזוּ פָנֵימוֹ׃

יב א ב לַמְנַצֵּחַ עַל־הַשְּׁמִינִית מִזְמוֹר לְדָוִד׃ הוֹשִׁיעָה יְהוָה כִּי־גָמַר חָסִיד כִּי־פַסּוּ אֱמוּנִים
ג ד מִבְּנֵי אָדָם׃ שָׁוְא ׀ יְדַבְּרוּ אִישׁ אֶת־רֵעֵהוּ שְׂפַת חֲלָקוֹת בְּלֵב וָלֵב יְדַבֵּרוּ׃ יַכְרֵת
ה יְהוָה כָּל־שִׂפְתֵי חֲלָקוֹת לָשׁוֹן מְדַבֶּרֶת גְּדֹלוֹת׃ אֲשֶׁר אָמְרוּ ׀ לִלְשֹׁנֵנוּ נַגְבִּיר
ו שְׂפָתֵינוּ אִתָּנוּ מִי אָדוֹן לָנוּ׃ מִשֹּׁד עֲנִיִּים מֵאַנְקַת אֶבְיוֹנִים עַתָּה אָקוּם יֹאמַר
ז יְהוָה אָשִׁית בְּיֵשַׁע יָפִיחַ לוֹ׃ אִמֲרוֹת יְהוָה אֲמָרוֹת טְהֹרוֹת כֶּסֶף צָרוּף בַּעֲלִיל
ח ט לָאָרֶץ מְזֻקָּק שִׁבְעָתָיִם׃ אַתָּה־יְהוָה תִּשְׁמְרֵם תִּצְּרֶנּוּ ׀ מִן־הַדּוֹר זוּ לְעוֹלָם׃ סָבִיב
רְשָׁעִים יִתְהַלָּכוּן כְּרֻם זֻלּוּת לִבְנֵי אָדָם׃

יג א ב לַמְנַצֵּחַ מִזְמוֹר לְדָוִד׃ עַד־אָנָה יְהוָה תִּשְׁכָּחֵנִי נֶצַח עַד־אָנָה ׀ תַּסְתִּיר אֶת־פָּנֶיךָ

Alil, translated here as "furnace," can also mean "in plain view." The silver is **refined seven times,** so that it is completely free of impurities. That is to say, the words of God are utterly pure and perfect.

8 **You, Lord, will preserve them,** all the unfortunate and afflicted. **You will keep them secure from this generation,** which seems poised to endure **forever.**

9 God's protection is needed because **the wicked roam about, as lowliness [*kerum zulut*] is exalted among men.** Some translate *kerum zulut* as "leeches," which suck the blood of man. According to this reading, the wicked surround the downtrodden and exploit them, as if sucking their blood.

PSALM 13

PSALMS 13:1–6

A psalm of supplication. It seems to the psalmist that God has hidden His face from him and has delivered him into the hands of his enemies. He beseeches God to reveal His kindness and save him.

13 1 **For the chief musician, a psalm by David.**

2 **How long, Lord? Will You forget me forever? How long will You hide Your face from me?**

3 **How long must I devise plans** to escape the clutches of the
wicked? I seem to be unable to find the right way out. How long
must I **have sorrow in my heart** that overwhelms me **all day?**
My very existence is devoid of joy; all my thoughts are full of
gloom. **For how long will my enemies tower over me?**
4 **Look and answer me, Lord my God; bring light to my eyes**
to help me find the path to salvation, **lest I will sleep in** the
eternal sleep of **death,**
5 **lest my enemy say: I have overcome him,** and **lest my foes**
rejoice when I stumble.
6 **But** still **I trust in Your kindness,** my only solace. **My heart**
rejoices in anticipation of **Your salvation. I sing to the Lord,**
for He has dealt kindly with me.

PSALM 14

PSALMS 14:1–7

A psalm that contemplates the wicked of the world, who, lacking belief in God, are not afraid of Him, but rather go about their evil ways until the world is full of wrongdoing. The psalmist beseeches God for salvation in his time of trouble. The text closely resembles Psalm 53, with minor variations in language.

14 1 **For the chief musician, a psalm by David. The scoundrel,** a
mean, arrogant man, **says in his heart: There is no God.** He
does not acknowledge God's existence at all. Hence, **they have**
been corrupted, they have acted abominably; there is no
one who does good.
2 **The Lord looks down from heaven** into this world, **upon the**
sons of man, to see if there is anyone of understanding who
seeks God.
3 And He finds: **They have all gone sour, all of them together**
befouled. There is no one who does good, not even one.
4 **Have all the evildoers,** who deny God's existence and consequently have no qualms about their evil actions, **no knowledge?**
They, who devour my people as if eating bread, they who do
not call out to the Lord under any circumstances,
5 **there they are,** all the people of the generation, **in great fear,**
for God is only **with the righteous generation**. In a generation that is not righteous, no one feels that God's salvation is
imminent.
6 **You,** the wicked, **despise,** shame, **the counsel of the poor,**
discrediting their opinions, **for the Lord is their refuge,** and
they depend solely on Him. When God hides Himself and is
seemingly absent from this world, the wretched are bereft, with
no one to lean on. Following this dire description, the psalmist
concludes with a prayer:
7 **May the salvation of Israel emerge from Zion! When the**
Lord returns the captives of His people and settles them securely in their land, **Jacob will rejoice and Israel will exult.**

PSALM 15

PSALMS 15:1–5

A psalm that summarizes the positive personality traits of an individual. The Talmud[2] states that King David condensed all the commandments of the Torah into a mere eleven precepts. This psalm does not deal with observance of commandments but rather with personal virtues; the individual described here is not engaged in prayer or other religious rituals, yet he follows the path of the righteous in both demeanor and action.

15 1 **A psalm by David.**[D] **Lord, who may** claim the merit to **so-**
journ in Your tent? Who may dwell on Your holy mountain?
There is an element of poetic license to this question, since a tent is transported from place to place and those who dwell within it are sojourners, like guests who move on, whereas the Sanctuary on God's holy mountain is permanent and does not move. Some understand this opening question as follows: Who is truly worthy, and not simply permitted from the standpoint of Jewish law, to enter the grounds of the Holy Temple? It is likely, however, that the question is meant to be more general and abstract: Who is worthy of being close to God? The psalmist continues by specifying the characteristics that can make a person worthy of such intimacy.
2 It is **he who walks with integrity,** wholehearted in his honesty,
and does righteous works toward others, **and speaks the**
truth in his heart. He does not delude himself or deceive others; there is no contradiction between what he believes in his
heart and what he says with his mouth. His is a world of truth.

DISCUSSION

15:1 | **A psalm by David:** The eleven general precepts that are in the psalm describing "who may sojourn in Your tent" are regarded by the Talmud (*Makkot* 24a) as a synopsis of the Torah's 613 commandments. The psalm does not speak of the fulfillment of commandments per se, but primarily of human virtue. The person described here is unique not for his prayer, his divine service, or his level of knowledge, but for the refinement of his soul and the propriety of his actions.

ג מִמֶּנִּי׃ עַד־אָנָה אָשִׁית עֵצוֹת בְּנַפְשִׁי יָגוֹן בִּלְבָבִי יוֹמָם עַד־אָנָה ׀ יָרוּם אֹיְבִי עָלָי׃
ד ה הַבִּיטָה עֲנֵנִי יְהוָה אֱלֹהָי הָאִירָה עֵינַי פֶּן־אִישַׁן הַמָּוֶת׃ פֶּן־יֹאמַר אֹיְבִי יְכָלְתִּיו
ו צָרַי יָגִילוּ כִּי אֶמּוֹט׃ וַאֲנִי ׀ בְּחַסְדְּךָ בָטַחְתִּי יָגֵל לִבִּי בִּישׁוּעָתֶךָ אָשִׁירָה לַיהוָה
כִּי גָמַל עָלָי׃
יד א לַמְנַצֵּחַ לְדָוִד אָמַר נָבָל בְּלִבּוֹ אֵין אֱלֹהִים הִשְׁחִיתוּ הִתְעִיבוּ עֲלִילָה אֵין עֹשֵׂה־
ב טוֹב׃ יְהוָה מִשָּׁמַיִם הִשְׁקִיף עַל־בְּנֵי־אָדָם לִרְאוֹת הֲיֵשׁ מַשְׂכִּיל דֹּרֵשׁ אֶת־אֱלֹהִים׃
ג ד הַכֹּל סָר יַחְדָּו נֶאֱלָחוּ אֵין עֹשֵׂה־טוֹב אֵין גַּם־אֶחָד׃ הֲלֹא יָדְעוּ כָּל־פֹּעֲלֵי אָוֶן
ה אֹכְלֵי עַמִּי אָכְלוּ לֶחֶם יְהוָה לֹא קָרָאוּ׃ שָׁם ׀ פָּחֲדוּ פָחַד כִּי־אֱלֹהִים בְּדוֹר צַדִּיק׃
ו ז עֲצַת־עָנִי תָבִישׁוּ כִּי יְהוָה מַחְסֵהוּ׃ מִי יִתֵּן מִצִּיּוֹן יְשׁוּעַת יִשְׂרָאֵל בְּשׁוּב יְהוָה
שְׁבוּת עַמּוֹ יָגֵל יַעֲקֹב יִשְׂמַח יִשְׂרָאֵל׃
טו א ב מִזְמוֹר לְדָוִד יְהוָה מִי־יָגוּר בְּאָהֳלֶךָ מִי־יִשְׁכֹּן בְּהַר קָדְשֶׁךָ׃ הוֹלֵךְ תָּמִים וּפֹעֵל
ג צֶדֶק וְדֹבֵר אֱמֶת בִּלְבָבוֹ׃ לֹא־רָגַל ׀ עַל־לְשֹׁנוֹ לֹא־עָשָׂה לְרֵעֵהוּ רָעָה וְחֶרְפָּה
ד לֹא־נָשָׂא עַל־קְרֹבוֹ׃ נִבְזֶה ׀ בְּעֵינָיו נִמְאָס וְאֶת־יִרְאֵי יְהוָה יְכַבֵּד נִשְׁבַּע לְהָרַע
ה וְלֹא יָמִר׃ כַּסְפּוֹ ׀ לֹא־נָתַן בְּנֶשֶׁךְ וְשֹׁחַד עַל־נָקִי לֹא־לָקָח עֹשֵׂה־אֵלֶּה לֹא יִמּוֹט
לְעוֹלָם׃

3 **He who does not gossip with his tongue, nor does evil to his neighbor, nor tolerates disgrace for his friend.** He not only refrains from doing evil himself, but is also concerned about others. He tries to ensure that no disgrace will befall those who associate with him.

4 **In his own eyes he is despised and repugnant,** as he does not view himself as deserving of glory and honor, **but he honors those who fear the Lord.** Alternatively, the righteous man looks upon despicable people with repugnance, but honors those who fear God; he understands how to differentiate between the deserving and the undeserving. **He abides by his oaths, even if they cause him harm,** and he does not attempt to modify an oath or evade his responsibility.

5 **He does not lend with usury** or derive benefit from forbidden practices. **Nor,** if he is a judge or influential person, **does he take bribes against the innocent** to unjustly condemn them. **Whoever behaves in this manner,** consistent with all the ethical practices described above, **will never stumble**. It is he who is truly worthy of standing in God's Sanctuary.

PSALM 16

PSALMS 16:1–11

A psalm of thanksgiving to God for having guided the psalmist on a righteous path and for granting him the bliss of being close to Him.

16 1 **An instruction**[D] **by David. Almighty, protect me, for I take refuge in You.**
2 **You,** my soul, **said to the Lord: You are my Lord. I have no goodness but from You.** The literal meaning of this last phrase is "My goodness is not upon You," an obscure expression. It could mean the following: It is not incumbent upon You to bestow goodness on me. That is, I cannot consider myself virtuous and deserving of reward from You for having chosen to cling to You, for the goodness You have already bestowed upon me is boundless.
3 I join myself **with the holy of the earth,** righteous men, as opposed to the holy beings in heaven, the angels. **And the majestic ones, all my wishes are** to be counted **with them.** In contrast, the psalmist notes what he wishes to entirely avoid:
4 **They are engaged in many** mundane **matters, they who have dealings with strange things,** literally, "other things," meaning idols, which are often termed "other gods." **I will not pour their libations of blood or** even **carry their names on my lips.** The psalmist desires to thoroughly distance himself from anything related to idol worship.
5 Unlike them, **the Lord is my lot and my portion; You sustain my fate.**
6 With regard to his choice of acknowledging God, the psalmist says: **The lots [*ḥavalim*],** which can refer to portions of land, lottery slips, or the actual winnings of a lottery, **that have fallen to me are pleasant.** Since "You sustain my fate" (verse 5), I am assured that the portions that have fallen to me are the best. **My estate,** all that I have been fortunate to receive, **is lovely.**
7 **I bless the Lord who counsels me,** whose guidance has prevented me from choosing the wrong path. **Even on nights when my thoughts are anguished,** I am continually focused on finding the right path, and I regret the poor choices I have made in the past.
8 **I set the Lord before me always. He is on my right,** always coming to my assistance; **I will not stumble.**
9 **Because of this,** God's help, **my heart is glad. My being is joyous; my body rests securely.**
10 **For You will not abandon me to the netherworld; You will not allow Your devoted one to see the grave.**
11 **May You show me the path of life,** through which I may attain **abundance and joy in Your presence. Eternal pleasure is by Your right hand.** As you are my portion (verse 5), I forever merit the good and pleasure that result from being with you.

PSALM 17

PSALMS 17:1–15

A prayer to God to guard those who go in His path, saving them from their enemies and granting them joy and the merit of drawing close to Him.

17 1 **A prayer by David. Hear, Lord, what is just,** that which is sincere and true; **heed my cry. Give ear to my** earnest **prayer, which does not come from deceitful lips.**
2 **Let my judgment come forth from Your presence,** as I am confident that there will be a favorable outcome when God judges me. **Let Your eyes see what is right,** to see if there is any fault that lies within me.
3 **You have examined my heart, taken an account at night.** Your examination of me is applied not only to deeds, usually performed during the day, but also to the thoughts of the heart, which are just as active at night as by day. **You inspected me and found nothing.** The term *tzeraftani*, translated as "You inspected me," literally means "You refined me," as a silversmith refines silver by inspecting it and removing any impurities that he finds. But even at this level of scrutiny, You found nothing. **I pondered,** I examined my thoughts to ascertain that I had no unworthy musings, **and nothing passed my lips,** as I certainly did not utter anything unworthy aloud.
4 **In the doings of men,** in all my mundane actions and in everything that I do in this world, **I follow Your instruction. I have**

DISCUSSION

16:1 | **Instruction [*mikhtam*]:** A *mikhtam* is a kind of psalm that is characterized by its melody or by the method of its singing (see Abravanel, Exodus 15:1–2). It is also possible that this term indicates the special importance of the psalm's content, from the word *ketem*, meaning gold (see Ibn Ezra). According to the latter interpretation, this psalm is like a magnificent work of gold. Later in the book there appears a group of psalms, chapters 56–60, that are each called *mikhtam*; they reflect a personal and touching character of an individual who expresses his extreme closeness to God, which outweighs the existential difficulties facing him.

טז א ב מִכְתָּם לְדָוִד שָׁמְרֵנִי אֵל כִּי־חָסִיתִי בָךְ: אָמַרְתְּ לַיהוה אֲדֹנָי אָתָּה טוֹבָתִי בַּל־
ג ד עָלֶיךָ: לִקְדוֹשִׁים אֲשֶׁר־בָּאָרֶץ הֵמָּה וְאַדִּירֵי כָּל־חֶפְצִי־בָם: יִרְבּוּ עַצְּבוֹתָם אַחֵר
ה מָהָרוּ בַּל־אַסִּיךְ נִסְכֵּיהֶם מִדָּם וּבַל־אֶשָּׂא אֶת־שְׁמוֹתָם עַל־שְׂפָתָי: יהוה מְנָת־
ו חֶלְקִי וְכוֹסִי אַתָּה תּוֹמִיךְ גּוֹרָלִי: חֲבָלִים נָפְלוּ־לִי בַּנְּעִמִים אַף־נַחֲלָת שָׁפְרָה עָלָי:
ז ח אֲבָרֵךְ אֶת־יהוה אֲשֶׁר יְעָצָנִי אַף־לֵילוֹת יִסְּרוּנִי כִלְיוֹתָי: שִׁוִּיתִי יהוה לְנֶגְדִּי תָמִיד
ט י כִּי מִימִינִי בַּל־אֶמּוֹט: לָכֵן ׀ שָׂמַח לִבִּי וַיָּגֶל כְּבוֹדִי אַף־בְּשָׂרִי יִשְׁכֹּן לָבֶטַח: כִּי ׀
יא לֹא־תַעֲזֹב נַפְשִׁי לִשְׁאוֹל לֹא־תִתֵּן חסידיך לִרְאוֹת שָׁחַת: תּוֹדִיעֵנִי אֹרַח חַיִּים חֲסִידְךָ
שֹׂבַע שְׂמָחוֹת אֶת־פָּנֶיךָ נְעִמוֹת בִּימִינְךָ נֶצַח:
יז א תְּפִלָּה לְדָוִד שִׁמְעָה יהוה ׀ צֶדֶק הַקְשִׁיבָה רִנָּתִי הַאֲזִינָה תְפִלָּתִי בְּלֹא שִׂפְתֵי
ב ג מִרְמָה: מִלְּפָנֶיךָ מִשְׁפָּטִי יֵצֵא עֵינֶיךָ תֶּחֱזֶינָה מֵישָׁרִים: בָּחַנְתָּ לִבִּי ׀ פָּקַדְתָּ
ד לַּיְלָה צְרַפְתַּנִי בַל־תִּמְצָא זַמֹּתִי בַּל־יַעֲבָר־פִּי: לִפְעֻלּוֹת אָדָם בִּדְבַר שְׂפָתֶיךָ
ה ו אֲנִי שָׁמַרְתִּי אָרְחוֹת פָּרִיץ: תָּמֹךְ אֲשֻׁרַי בְּמַעְגְּלוֹתֶיךָ בַּל־נָמוֹטּוּ פְעָמָי: אֲנִי־
ז קְרָאתִיךָ כִי־תַעֲנֵנִי אֵל הַט־אָזְנְךָ לִי שְׁמַע אִמְרָתִי: הַפְלֵה חֲסָדֶיךָ מוֹשִׁיעַ
ח חוֹסִים מִמִּתְקוֹמְמִים בִּימִינֶךָ: שָׁמְרֵנִי כְּאִישׁוֹן בַּת־עָיִן בְּצֵל כְּנָפֶיךָ תַּסְתִּירֵנִי:
ט מִפְּנֵי רְשָׁעִים זוּ שַׁדּוּנִי אֹיְבַי בְּנֶפֶשׁ יַקִּיפוּ עָלָי: חֶלְבָּמוֹ סָּגְרוּ פִּימוֹ דִּבְּרוּ בְגֵאוּת:
יא יב אַשֻּׁרֵנוּ עַתָּה סבבוני עֵינֵיהֶם יָשִׁיתוּ לִנְטוֹת בָּאָרֶץ: דִּמְיֹנוֹ כְּאַרְיֵה יִכְסוֹף לִטְרֹף סְבָבוּנוּ

avoided the ways of trespassers, those whose evil respects no boundaries.

5 **Secure my steps on Your paths, so my feet will not stumble.**

6 **I call upon You** in the hope **that You** will **answer me, Almighty,** because I know You can help me. **Incline Your ear to me; hear my speech.**

7 **Reveal Your kindness, Redeemer of those who take refuge** in You, as You are protecting them **from the enemies who rise up** against You, whom I consider to be my own enemies as well, and You are **sheltering** them **in Your right hand.**

8 **Guard me like the pupil of an eye; hide me in the shadow of Your wings**

9 **from the wicked who rob me, my mortal enemies who encircle me.**

10 **They are encased in their fat.** In ancient times, obesity was a sign of wealth and power. **Their mouths speak with haughtiness.**

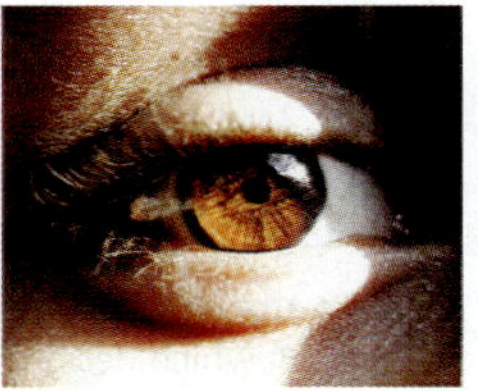

"Pupil of an eye"

11 **I see them now surrounding us. They cast their eyes, spreading them over the land.** The psalmist sees his enemies surrounding him, looking about in search of prey.

12 **He is akin to a lion yearning to tear at his prey, like a lion cub lurking in hidden lairs.**

13 The psalmist prays: **Arise, Lord, confront him and subdue him. Rescue me from the wicked with Your sword.** Reveal Yourself, God, and declare war on the enemy.

14 Furthermore, he asks for God's protection: To be **among those people** who are **under Your hand,** protected by You, **Lord, those people in the land whose portion,** thanks to Your assistance to them, **is life. Fill their bellies with Your hidden treasures; sate their sons, too, and let them leave what is left to their offspring.**

15 The psalmist concludes with a prayer and a request: **Truly, I shall see Your face; Your image will fill my waking vision.** Find me worthy of seeing Your presence revealed, as the prophets did, even while awake.

PSALM 18

A hymn of thanksgiving by David to God, replete with imagery of God's might.

PSALMS 18:1–51

18 1 **To the chief musician,**[D] **by David servant of the Lord, who spoke the words of this song to the Lord on the day the Lord saved him from the hands of all his enemies and from the hand of Saul.** This psalm also appears in II Samuel 22, with various minor linguistic differences. Psalm 18 is apparently a slightly revised version of the more ancient text found in Samuel, which contains archaic language and a number of expressions whose meanings remain unclear.

3rd day of month

2 **And he said: I love You, Lord, my strength.**[D] *Raḥamu* means "love" in Aramaic, though generally this root connotes "mercy" in Hebrew. This is also the meaning of the root in ancient Hebrew, and that is the sense of *erḥamkha* here, "I love You." David expresses his love for God, then continues with detailed words of praise:

3 **The Lord is my rock and my fortress, my Redeemer.** Several levels of protection are mentioned here. A rock is something one can lean on or climb onto in order to escape various troubles. A fortress is a protective physical structure. "My Redeemer" describes God as being actively involved in the rescue. **My Almighty, my mighty rock. I take refuge in Him, my shield, the horn of my salvation, my stronghold.** The verse describes God's continually increasing support.

4 **I call in praise to the Lord, and I am delivered from my enemies.**

5 **Cords of death were wrapped around me.** "Cords of death" [*ḥevlei mavet*] is a poetic phrase that has a double meaning. The simple meaning is that death is like a cord that ultimately binds and ropes in all men. But *ḥevlei* can also mean "pains," indicating physical suffering or connoting troubles and distress that envelop a person as though he were bound by cords. **Floods of wickedness terrified me.**

6 **Cords of the grave surrounded me; snares of death,** traps from which escape is all but impossible, **confronted me.**

7 **In my distress I called to the Lord, cried out to my God. From His dwelling place He heard my voice, and my cry reached His ears.**

8 The second part of this psalm depicts the glory and power of God's revelation. This section is not directly related to events in David's life. It is, rather, a general description of revelation, reminiscent of songs depicting the revelation at Mount Sinai and the like. **The earth shook and quaked. Foundations of mountains trembled, shaken because of His anger.**

9 **Smoke arose from His nostrils, a consuming fire from His mouth; burning coals emerged from Him.** These are descriptions of God's revelation in fire and smoke.

10 **He bent the heavens and came down.** It is not as if the Master of the Universe descends from the heavens, not even

DISCUSSION

18:1 | **To the chief musician:** The heading of Psalm 18, which designates its theme and content, tells us that it was not composed in David's youth, but in a period of his life when he was at the peak of his power, securely occupying his throne; thus he was able to summarize his life's achievements with optimism. Saul is mentioned specifically here because it was he who presented the greatest danger to David's life, and therefore the confrontation with him overshadowed all other events that took place subsequently.

18:2 | **I love You, Lord, my strength:** David is the quintessential image of a person who serves God. He acted throughout his life as an officiant in the House of God, the precursor to the Temple. That much can be deduced from the historical records of the book of Samuel, and even more clearly from the book of Psalms. His religious world was not merely a facet of his biography, but the focus of his entire life. He was a warrior and a politician, and had several wives, but his many mundane activities were secondary concerns for him. The essence of his life and his main occupation, from which he never deviated, was his love for God and his desire to serve Him (see further *Tanna deVei Eliyahu Rabba* 3).

יג וּכִכְפִיר יֹשֵׁב בְּמִסְתָּרִים׃ קוּמָה יהוה קַדְּמָה פָנָיו הַכְרִיעֵהוּ פַּלְּטָה נַפְשִׁי מֵרָשָׁע
יד חַרְבֶּךָ׃ מִמְתִים יָדְךָ ׀ יהוה מִמְתִים מֵחֶלֶד חֶלְקָם בַּחַיִּים וּצְפִינְךָ תְמַלֵּא בִטְנָם וּצְפוּנְךָ
טו יִשְׂבְּעוּ בָנִים וְהִנִּיחוּ יִתְרָם לְעוֹלְלֵיהֶם׃ אֲנִי בְּצֶדֶק אֶחֱזֶה פָנֶיךָ אֶשְׂבְּעָה בְהָקִיץ
תְּמוּנָתֶךָ׃
יח א לַמְנַצֵּחַ לְעֶבֶד יהוה לְדָוִד אֲשֶׁר דִּבֶּר ׀ לַיהוה אֶת־דִּבְרֵי הַשִּׁירָה הַזֹּאת בְּיוֹם ׀ ג לחודש
ב ג הִצִּיל־יהוה אוֹתוֹ מִכַּף כָּל־אֹיְבָיו וּמִיַּד שָׁאוּל׃ וַיֹּאמַר אֶרְחָמְךָ יהוה חִזְקִי׃ יהוה ׀
ד סַלְעִי וּמְצוּדָתִי וּמְפַלְטִי אֵלִי צוּרִי אֶחֱסֶה־בּוֹ מָגִנִּי וְקֶרֶן־יִשְׁעִי מִשְׂגַּבִּי׃ מְהֻלָּל
ה ו אֶקְרָא יהוה וּמִן־אֹיְבַי אִוָּשֵׁעַ׃ אֲפָפוּנִי חֶבְלֵי־מָוֶת וְנַחֲלֵי בְלִיַּעַל יְבַעֲתוּנִי׃ חֶבְלֵי
ז שְׁאוֹל סְבָבוּנִי קִדְּמוּנִי מוֹקְשֵׁי מָוֶת׃ בַּצַּר־לִי ׀ אֶקְרָא יהוה וְאֶל־אֱלֹהַי אֲשַׁוֵּעַ
ח יִשְׁמַע מֵהֵיכָלוֹ קוֹלִי וְשַׁוְעָתִי לְפָנָיו ׀ תָּבוֹא בְאָזְנָיו׃ וַתִּגְעַשׁ וַתִּרְעַשׁ ׀ הָאָרֶץ
ט וּמוֹסְדֵי הָרִים יִרְגָּזוּ וַיִּתְגָּעֲשׁוּ כִּי־חָרָה לוֹ׃ עָלָה עָשָׁן ׀ בְּאַפּוֹ וְאֵשׁ־מִפִּיו תֹּאכֵל
י יא גֶּחָלִים בָּעֲרוּ מִמֶּנּוּ׃ וַיֵּט שָׁמַיִם וַיֵּרַד וַעֲרָפֶל תַּחַת רַגְלָיו׃ וַיִּרְכַּב עַל־כְּרוּב וַיָּעֹף
יב וַיֵּדֶא עַל־כַּנְפֵי־רוּחַ׃ יָשֶׁת חֹשֶׁךְ ׀ סִתְרוֹ סְבִיבוֹתָיו סֻכָּתוֹ חֶשְׁכַת־מַיִם עָבֵי שְׁחָקִים׃
יג יד מִנֹּגַהּ נֶגְדּוֹ עָבָיו עָבְרוּ בָּרָד וְגַחֲלֵי־אֵשׁ׃ וַיַּרְעֵם בַּשָּׁמַיִם ׀ יהוה וְעֶלְיוֹן יִתֵּן קֹלוֹ
טו טז בָּרָד וְגַחֲלֵי־אֵשׁ׃ וַיִּשְׁלַח חִצָּיו וַיְפִיצֵם וּבְרָקִים רָב וַיְהֻמֵּם׃ וַיֵּרָאוּ ׀ אֲפִיקֵי מַיִם

metaphorically; rather, He lowers the heavens toward earth.[3] **A dense cloud is beneath His feet.**

11 **He mounted a cherub and flew.** Cherubs are symbolic of the divine chariot, as described in Ezekiel, as well as the Divine Presence, as in the Holy of Holies in the Temple.[4] **And He soared on wings of wind.**

12 **He engulfed His secret place in darkness, His sheltered surroundings, the darkness of waters.** This apparently refers to the darkness of black rainclouds, **clouds of the skies.**

13 Though engulfed in darkness, **from the radiance** that is **before Him,** behind all that concealment, **hail and coals of fire passed through His clouds.** Revelation is depicted here using imagery of hail and coals of fire breaking through the clouds of concealment.

14 **And the Lord thundered in the heavens, the voice of the Most High spewing forth hail and coals of fire.** The combination of ice and fire is an expression of divine power.

15 **He shot His arrows and dispersed them,** His enemies. **Many bolts of lightning confounded them.**

"Bolts of lightning"

16 In the midst of all this, **streams of water appeared.** The world was shaken up, causing sources of water to be displaced, as during the splitting of the Red Sea. **And the foundations of the world were laid bare.** The lower foundations of the world were exposed; unknown depths could be

seen. All this occurred as a consequence of God's wrath: **At Your rebuke, Lord, from the blast of the breath of Your nostrils.**

17 Until this point, the psalm describes God's power over the world. Yet His greatness also has a more intimate, personal aspect: **He sent** His hand, through various agents, **from above, and He took me** to lift me out of trouble. **He drew me out of surging waters.**

18 Or, in more concrete terms, without metaphor, **He rescued me from my mighty enemy, from those who hated me, when they were too strong for me.**

19 **They confronted me on the day of my calamity, but** at a time when enemies were poised and ready to attack, **the Lord was my support.**

20 **He brought me out into an open space.** He moved me from a place of distress to one of relief. **He rescued me because He delighted in me.**

21 There is a reason that God rescued me from adversity and attack: **God has rewarded me for my righteousness; for the purity of my hands He has requited me.**

22 **For I have kept the ways of the Lord and have not wickedly departed from my God.**

23 **For all His judgments were before me;** I was always aware of His laws, **and I did not dismiss His statutes.**

24 **I was blameless with Him and guarded myself from iniquity.**

25 **And the Lord requited me for my righteousness, for the purity of my hands in His eyes.** God, in His mercy, acknowledges my innocence. This attribute of mercy is the way of God, and He does not limit it to a particular person with whom He has a special relationship.

26 **With the pious You act mercifully; with a guileless man You behave without guile.**

27 **You are pure with the purehearted; with the crooked You are devious.** You behave forthrightly with the innocent, but You are cunning with those who take devious paths.

28 **For You rescue the poor, and,** on the other hand, You **abase those with haughty looks.**

29 Once again, the psalm takes on a personal tone: **For You light my lamp** to shine before me and lead the way, **Lord my God, illuminating my darkness.**

Lamp

30 **For with You,** with Your assistance, **I can shatter a troop. With my God,** with His help, **I can leap over walls.** This is an allusion to the cities captured by King David; it was as if he flew over their walls.

31 **The Almighty's way is blameless,** bestowing upon each individual the reward or punishment that exactly suits his deeds.

Battalion and its commander, Sumerian stone relief, 2450 BCE

The word of the Lord is purity. *Tzerufa*, translated as "purity," literally refers to the process of refinement of precious metals, purging them of impurities. **He is a shield for all who take refuge in Him.**

32 **For who is a god but the Lord? And who is a mighty rock except our God?**

33 The psalmist, relying on God, benefits from His protection: **The Almighty girds me with strength and shows me a straight path.**

34 **He makes my feet as swift as deer and sets me in high places.**

35 **He trains my hands for battle, and my arms are made** as unbreakable as **a bow of bronze.**

Deer running

36 **You have given me the shield of Your salvation,** Your protection, and the success it helps me achieve; **and Your right hand,** Your power and Your support, **assists me. Your humility,** Your willingness to descend to my aid, **makes me grow great.**

37 Metaphorically, **You lengthen my strides beneath me, and my feet do not stumble.** You have enabled me to advance rapidly, without falling.

38 Because of Your help in enabling me to stride broadly and swiftly, **I pursue my enemies and overtake them, and I will not turn back until they are utterly destroyed.**

39 **I crush them so they are unable to rise; they fall beneath my feet.**

40 **You girded me with strength for battle. You brought down beneath me those who rose against me.**

יז וַיִּגָּלוּ מוֹסְדוֹת תֵּבֵל מִגַּעֲרָתְךָ יְהוָה מִנִּשְׁמַת רוּחַ אַפֶּךָ: יִשְׁלַח מִמָּרוֹם יִקָּחֵנִי
יח יט יַמְשֵׁנִי מִמַּיִם רַבִּים: יַצִּילֵנִי מֵאֹיְבִי עָז וּמִשֹּׂנְאַי כִּי־אָמְצוּ מִמֶּנִּי: יְקַדְּמוּנִי בְיוֹם־
כ כא אֵידִי וַיְהִי־יְהוָה לְמִשְׁעָן לִי: וַיּוֹצִיאֵנִי לַמֶּרְחָב יְחַלְּצֵנִי כִּי חָפֵץ בִּי: יִגְמְלֵנִי יְהוָה
כב כג כְּצִדְקִי כְּבֹר יָדַי יָשִׁיב לִי: כִּי־שָׁמַרְתִּי דַּרְכֵי יְהוָה וְלֹא־רָשַׁעְתִּי מֵאֱלֹהָי: כִּי כָל־
כד מִשְׁפָּטָיו לְנֶגְדִּי וְחֻקֹּתָיו לֹא־אָסִיר מֶנִּי: וָאֱהִי תָמִים עִמּוֹ וָאֶשְׁתַּמֵּר מֵעֲוֺנִי:
כה כו וַיָּשֶׁב־יְהוָה לִי כְצִדְקִי כְּבֹר יָדַי לְנֶגֶד עֵינָיו: עִם־חָסִיד תִּתְחַסָּד עִם־גְּבַר תָּמִים
כז כח תִּתַּמָּם: עִם־נָבָר תִּתְבָּרָר וְעִם־עִקֵּשׁ תִּתְפַּתָּל: כִּי־אַתָּה עַם־עָנִי תוֹשִׁיעַ וְעֵינַיִם
כט ל רָמוֹת תַּשְׁפִּיל: כִּי־אַתָּה תָּאִיר נֵרִי יְהוָה אֱלֹהַי יַגִּיהַּ חָשְׁכִּי: כִּי־בְךָ אָרֻץ גְּדוּד
לא וּבֵאלֹהַי אֲדַלֶּג־שׁוּר: הָאֵל תָּמִים דַּרְכּוֹ אִמְרַת־יְהוָה צְרוּפָה מָגֵן הוּא לְכֹל ׀
לב לג הַחֹסִים בּוֹ: כִּי מִי אֱלוֹהַּ מִבַּלְעֲדֵי יְהוָה וּמִי צוּר זוּלָתִי אֱלֹהֵינוּ: הָאֵל הַמְאַזְּרֵנִי
לד לה חָיִל וַיִּתֵּן תָּמִים דַּרְכִּי: מְשַׁוֶּה רַגְלַי כָּאַיָּלוֹת וְעַל בָּמֹתַי יַעֲמִידֵנִי: מְלַמֵּד יָדַי
לו לַמִּלְחָמָה וְנִחֲתָה קֶשֶׁת־נְחוּשָׁה זְרוֹעֹתָי: וַתִּתֶּן־לִי מָגֵן יִשְׁעֶךָ וִימִינְךָ תִסְעָדֵנִי
לז לח וְעַנְוַתְךָ תַרְבֵּנִי: תַּרְחִיב צַעֲדִי תַחְתָּי וְלֹא מָעֲדוּ קַרְסֻלָּי: אֶרְדּוֹף אוֹיְבַי וְאַשִּׂיגֵם
לט מ וְלֹא־אָשׁוּב עַד־כַּלּוֹתָם: אֶמְחָצֵם וְלֹא־יֻכְלוּ קוּם יִפְּלוּ תַּחַת רַגְלָי: וַתְּאַזְּרֵנִי חַיִל
מא מב לַמִּלְחָמָה תַּכְרִיעַ קָמַי תַּחְתָּי: וְאֹיְבַי נָתַתָּה לִּי עֹרֶף וּמְשַׂנְאַי אַצְמִיתֵם: יְשַׁוְּעוּ
מג וְאֵין־מוֹשִׁיעַ עַל־יְהוָה וְלֹא עָנָם: וְאֶשְׁחָקֵם כְּעָפָר עַל־פְּנֵי־רוּחַ כְּטִיט חוּצוֹת
מד מה אֲרִיקֵם: תְּפַלְּטֵנִי מֵרִיבֵי עָם תְּשִׂימֵנִי לְרֹאשׁ גּוֹיִם עַם לֹא־יָדַעְתִּי יַעַבְדוּנִי: לְשֵׁמַע

41 **And you have made my enemies turn their backs to me** in flight; **I destroyed those who hated me.**

42 **They cried out for help, but there was no savior** for them; **they turned to the Lord, who did not answer them.**

43 **Then I beat them as fine as dust in the wind;** nothing at all was left of them. **I poured them out like mud in the streets.**

44 **You delivered me from the strife of** other **peoples; You placed me at the head of nations.** My success was so great that I ruled not only over nations neighboring the Land of Israel but also over faraway places, and **a people whom I have not known serve me.** The king's reputation of great power was such that even nations he did not know submitted to his sovereignty.

45 **As soon as they hear, they obey me; foreigners submit to me.** Foreigners who know me only by reputation are willing to submit to my commands. The word *yekhaḥashu*, translated here as "submit," literally means "to act with deceit." My enemies feign loyalty to me so they can benefit from my goodwill. The fact that his enemies feel obliged to conceal their adversarial status and lie and abase themselves before him is a clear manifestation of the ruler's power.

46 **Foreigners, exhausted, emerge** defeated **from their fortresses.**

47 The psalmist concludes: **The Lord lives; blessed is my mighty rock. Exalted be the God of my salvation,**

48 **the Almighty who executes vengeance for me and destroys nations beneath me.** Alternatively, the word *yadber*, translated here as "destroys," can mean "leads" or "brings": The Almighty brings nations under my rule.

49 He **rescues me from my enemies, lifts me above those who rise against me,** and **saves me from men of violence.**

50 **For this I give thanks to You among the nations, Lord, and sing praises to Your name.**

51 **He increases deliverance to His king.** God continually increases the support He gives to David, the king He chose. He **shows kindness to His anointed, to David and to his descendants,** to whom the kingship of Israel was promised **eternally.**

PSALM 19

PSALMS 19:1–15

A psalm about creation, Torah, and man, comprising three seemingly unconnected parts, which are revealed, ultimately, to be interrelated.

19 1 **To the chief musician, a psalm by David.**

2 **The heavens declare the glory of God,**[D] **and the sky tells the work of His hands.**

3 **Day to day gives utterance; night to night renders understanding.**[D]

4 **There is no talk, nor are there words; their voice is not heard.** This verse clarifies the words of the previous verse, "Day to day gives utterance." Obviously, the days do not actually talk; the fact of their existence makes them heard.

5 **Their influence encompasses the earth; their words reach to the end of the world.** Even though the declarations of the sky and of time have no voice and cannot actually be heard, they are transmitted to the ends of the earth. Their "words" are powerful enough to resound throughout the world. **In a tent within, He placed the sun.** The sky appears to serve as a dwelling place or tent for the sun, its most prominent object.

6 In describing his experience of observing the sun as it makes its way across the sky, the psalmist portrays the sunrise, **which** is **like a bridegroom leaving his bridal chamber;** the sun is blushing a little, but very happy. As it continues across the sky, it **rejoices like a warrior running his course,** not slackening its powerful run for a moment.

Sunrise. "Like a bridegroom leaving his bridal chamber"

7 **It rises from one end of the heavens, coursing the sky to the other edge; nothing escapes its heat.** The sun begins its run at one end of the sky, completes its arc, and concludes at the other end. All the while, as it shines and illuminates the earth, it evokes the full power of a warrior racing across the sky. No one can stop it.

8 The preceding verses describe the ways in which the skies, by their very existence, speak to someone who is able to hear them. The second part of this psalm is a hymn in praise of the Torah and its commandments. It is composed of six phrases, each of which describes a specific aspect of the Torah, followed by a quality inherently related to that aspect. A similar structure is found in Psalm 119. **The Torah of the Lord is perfect, restoring the soul,** bringing inner peace, a quality that is pure and unblemished. The reality of our world is replete with defects, dishonesty, cheating, and plotting; all result in spiritual exhaustion. The act of becoming absorbed in the Torah, which is whole and unblemished, soothes and restores the soul. **The testimony,** or Torah, **of the Lord can be trusted, making the simpleton,** one who lacks knowledge and understanding, **wise.** When the simpleton opens his mouth to explain something, his reasoning is usually distorted or inaccurate. However, when one states true, incontrovertible facts without elaboration, he speaks words of wisdom. This form of faithfulness can make even a simpleton wise.

9 **The precepts of the Lord,** namely, the commandments, **are upright, gladdening the heart.**[D] **The commandments of the Lord are clear, enlightening the eyes.** The commandments are described as "clear" in the sense of being pristine and pure. Although it is possible to see through something that is fogged or polluted by impurities, the eyes are strained in the process. By contrast, God's commandments, which are clear, spotless, and devoid of any impurities, brighten the eyes and clarify vision.

10 **Fear of the Lord is pure, and endures forever.** "Fear of the Lord" does not merely describe a relationship with God. In this context, it is also almost synonymous with the Torah, which is pure and eternal. The more complex something is, the more likely it is to change and eventually wear out. Complicated machinery is apt to malfunction when any of its interconnected parts is faulty. In contrast, something that is completely and intrinsically pure, even in the simplest physical sense, is more stable, as it contains no foreign matter, nothing liable to break down. This is also true of fear of God, which is pure in the most absolute sense; it endures forever because nothing can possibly

מה מו אֹזֶן יִשָּׁמְעוּ לִי בְּנֵי־נֵכָר יְכַחֲשׁוּ־לִי׃ בְּנֵי־נֵכָר יִבֹּלוּ וְיַחְרְגוּ מִמִּסְגְּרוֹתֵיהֶם׃ חַי־
מח יהוה וּבָרוּךְ צוּרִי וְיָרוּם אֱלוֹהֵי יִשְׁעִי׃ הָאֵל הַנּוֹתֵן נְקָמוֹת לִי וַיַּדְבֵּר עַמִּים תַּחְתָּי׃
מט נ מְפַלְּטִי מֵאֹיְבָי אַף מִן־קָמַי תְּרוֹמְמֵנִי מֵאִישׁ חָמָס תַּצִּילֵנִי׃ עַל־כֵּן ׀ אוֹדְךָ בַגּוֹיִם ׀
נא יהוה וּלְשִׁמְךָ אֲזַמֵּרָה׃ מַגְדִּל יְשׁוּעוֹת מַלְכּוֹ וְעֹשֶׂה חֶסֶד ׀ לִמְשִׁיחוֹ לְדָוִד וּלְזַרְעוֹ
עַד־עוֹלָם׃
יט א ב לַמְנַצֵּחַ מִזְמוֹר לְדָוִד׃ הַשָּׁמַיִם מְסַפְּרִים כְּבוֹד־אֵל וּמַעֲשֵׂה יָדָיו מַגִּיד הָרָקִיעַ׃
ג ד יוֹם לְיוֹם יַבִּיעַ אֹמֶר וְלַיְלָה לְּלַיְלָה יְחַוֶּה־דָּעַת׃ אֵין־אֹמֶר וְאֵין דְּבָרִים בְּלִי נִשְׁמָע
ה ו קוֹלָם׃ בְּכָל־הָאָרֶץ ׀ יָצָא קַוָּם וּבִקְצֵה תֵבֵל מִלֵּיהֶם לַשֶּׁמֶשׁ שָׂם־אֹהֶל בָּהֶם׃ וְהוּא
ז כְּחָתָן יֹצֵא מֵחֻפָּתוֹ יָשִׂישׂ כְּגִבּוֹר לָרוּץ אֹרַח׃ מִקְצֵה הַשָּׁמַיִם ׀ מוֹצָאוֹ וּתְקוּפָתוֹ
ח עַל־קְצוֹתָם וְאֵין נִסְתָּר מֵחַמָּתוֹ׃ תּוֹרַת יהוה תְּמִימָה מְשִׁיבַת נָפֶשׁ עֵדוּת יהוה
ט נֶאֱמָנָה מַחְכִּימַת פֶּתִי׃ פִּקּוּדֵי יהוה יְשָׁרִים מְשַׂמְּחֵי־לֵב מִצְוַת יהוה בָּרָה מְאִירַת
י עֵינָיִם׃ יִרְאַת יהוה ׀ טְהוֹרָה עוֹמֶדֶת לָעַד מִשְׁפְּטֵי־יהוה אֱמֶת צָדְקוּ יַחְדָּו׃

DISCUSSION

19:2 | **The heavens declare the glory of God:** This verse is not a depiction of God as Creator of the world, or a description of a miracle or the act of creation. It expresses a more introspective idea, that mere observation of the world makes a person aware of God's presence and engenders wonder at the world's existence. This is how "the sky tells the work of His hands"; its very presence speaks volumes. When a man looks at the sky, he is seeing God's glory revealed. The heavens, the planetary orbits, and the order of the universe are all evidence of God's handiwork. The psalmist is not searching for God's presence in the world; for him, the world is itself an expression of divine revelation.

19:3 | **Day to day gives utterance; night to night renders understanding:** Every day expresses God's glory; every night elicits new understanding. During the hours of daylight and heightened activity the so-called speech is more intense. Daylight hours are inherently active, and it is this activity that "speaks" of the glory of God. The night, on the other hand, is quieter, allowing for introspection. Its peace and tranquility also speak, as it were, but express a broader and possibly deeper understanding.

19:9 | **The precepts of the Lord are upright, gladdening the heart:** A connection between uprightness and joy is found in several other places, e.g., Psalms 97:11: "Light is sown for the righteous, and joy for the upright of heart." When one's heart is not "upright," there are twists and curves, which can bring about a situation in which, even in good times, and all the more so in less fortuitous circumstances, one finds himself incapable of experiencing joy. He is weighed down with doubts, suspicions, complications, and calculations. By contrast, the person with an upright heart is one who can see things clearly and accept goodness that comes his way with pure happiness. Moreover, the quality of uprightness itself brings one gladness. For this reason, God's commandments bring joy to the heart; they are devoid of fraudulence.

damage it. **The judgments of the Lord are true and altogether righteous.** This verse, as with those preceding it, presents a definition of truth. Something is "altogether" true when its separate parts are not contradictory when combined with one another; they remain true whether the components are seen individually or as a whole.

11 A more emotional description of the Torah follows: **They,** words of Torah and the commandments, **are more desirable than gold, than quantities of fine gold.** They are objects of desire, more precious than the finest gold. **And** they are **sweeter than honey and the juices of ripe fruit.** Moreover, while gold has no taste, words of Torah are sweet. These figurative definitions of Torah and the commandments serve as an appropriate transition to the third, most personal part of the psalm:

12 **Your servant,** I, the psalmist, **as well is mindful of them,** the commandments, **heeding them to the utmost.** The phrase *ekev rav*, translated here as "to the utmost," can also be understood to mean "crooked places." The psalmist avows that even in places where observance of the commandments is difficult he is conscientious in following God's precepts. Nevertheless, despite his vigilance, the psalmist acknowledges that there are obstacles to perfect observance:

13 **Who can discern his errors?** At times, an individual is apt to err unknowingly. Who can possibly be certain that his actions are faultless? **Acquit me of hidden faults.** The psalmist beseeches God: I need You to absolve me of misdeeds carried out unwittingly. Man cannot know what is hidden from him.[5]

14 There is an additional factor that can lead to an individual's downfall, namely, other people. **And keep Your servant far from sinners.** Protect me from the spiritually malevolent influence of evildoers. **Let them not have dominion over me,** for if they have me in their control they will be able to negatively impact my behavior. If You absolve me of mistakes I have made due to lack of knowledge or lack of understanding, and if You acquit me concerning matters I have done as a result of external factors beyond my control, **then I will be blameless and cleansed of great transgression.**

15 The psalm concludes with a prayer: **Let the words of my mouth and the meditation of my heart,** nonverbal sentiments, **be acceptable before You, Lord, my rock and my Redeemer.** In summary, this psalm expresses a parallel between the glory of God as it is perceived by contemplating the heavens, and His glory as revealed through Torah study. The third section of the psalm, then, is a specific, personal conclusion that derives from the general sentiments expressed in the first two sections.

PSALM 20

A psalm of intermingled prayer, supplication, and praise.

PSALMS 20:1–10

20 1 **To the chief musician, a psalm by David [*leDavid*].** This psalm appears to be a request on behalf of the king rather than a prayer by the king as a private individual. Therefore, some commentators interpret the word *leDavid* in this verse to mean "on behalf of David" and his reign.

2 **May the Lord answer you at a time of trouble; may the name of the God of Jacob fortify you.**

3 **May He send you help from the Sanctuary,** from His dwelling place on earth, **and support you from Zion,** the Temple Mount.

4 **May He remember** favorably **all your offerings** that you have brought to Him in the past, **and accept your burnt offering, Selah.** The word *yedashne*, translated here as "accept," is related to *deshen*, referring to fatness and choice quality. The psalmist prays: May your burnt offerings be accepted as the choicest of gifts.

5 **May He grant you your heart's desire and fulfill all your plans.**

6 **We will sing with joy at your salvation and raise banners in the name of our God,** in glorification of God's name; we will glorify His name as if waving it above us like a flag. **May the Lord fulfill all your wishes.**

7 **Now,** when victory comes, **I know that the Lord has rescued His anointed one,** the king of Israel; **He will answer him** and his prayers **from His holy heavens, with the mighty strength of His right hand,** which represents God's attributes of strength and beneficence. God provides the power to subdue the enemy, and He bestows the gift of redemption on the righteous.

8 **Some** of our adversaries **come** to wage war riding **on chariots,** the most formidable tool of war in ancient times, **and some on horses,** adding the elements of strength and swiftness to the attacking army, **but we invoke the name of the Lord our God.** We may not be armed with the most sophisticated weaponry, but we know that weapons do not determine the outcome of the battle; we derive our strength from God.

"Some come on chariots and some on horses." The battle of Kadesh, depicted on stone relief in the palace of Rameses II, Thebes

9 **They collapse and fall; we rise and take heart.**

10 **Deliver us, Lord. The King** of the universe **will answer us on the day we call.**

יא יב הַֽנֶּחֱמָדִים מִזָּהָב וּמִפַּז רָב וּמְתוּקִים מִדְּבַשׁ וְנֹפֶת צוּפִים: גַּם־עַבְדְּךָ נִזְהָר בָּהֶם
יג יד בְּשָׁמְרָם עֵקֶב רָב: שְׁגִיאוֹת מִי־יָבִין מִנִּסְתָּרוֹת נַקֵּנִי: גַּם מִזֵּדִים | חֲשֹׂךְ עַבְדֶּךָ
טו אַל־יִמְשְׁלוּ־בִי אָז אֵיתָם וְנִקֵּיתִי מִפֶּשַׁע רָב: יִהְיוּ לְרָצוֹן | אִמְרֵי־פִי וְהֶגְיוֹן לִבִּי
לְפָנֶיךָ יהוה צוּרִי וְגֹאֲלִי:
כ א ב לַמְנַצֵּחַ מִזְמוֹר לְדָוִד: יַעַנְךָ יהוה בְּיוֹם צָרָה יְשַׂגֶּבְךָ שֵׁם | אֱלֹהֵי יַעֲקֹב: יִשְׁלַח־
ג ד ה עֶזְרְךָ מִקֹּדֶשׁ וּמִצִּיּוֹן יִסְעָדֶךָּ: יִזְכֹּר כָּל־מִנְחֹתֶךָ וְעוֹלָתְךָ יְדַשְּׁנֶה סֶלָה: יִתֶּן־לְךָ
ו כִלְבָבֶךָ וְכָל־עֲצָתְךָ יְמַלֵּא: נְרַנְּנָה | בִּישׁוּעָתֶךָ וּבְשֵׁם־אֱלֹהֵינוּ נִדְגֹּל יְמַלֵּא יהוה
ז כָּל־מִשְׁאֲלוֹתֶיךָ: עַתָּה יָדַעְתִּי כִּי הוֹשִׁיעַ | יהוה מְשִׁיחוֹ יַעֲנֵהוּ מִשְּׁמֵי קָדְשׁוֹ
ח בִּגְבוּרוֹת יֵשַׁע יְמִינוֹ: אֵלֶּה בָרֶכֶב וְאֵלֶּה בַסּוּסִים וַאֲנַחְנוּ | בְּשֵׁם־יהוה אֱלֹהֵינוּ
ט י נַזְכִּיר: הֵמָּה כָּרְעוּ וְנָפָלוּ וַאֲנַחְנוּ קַּמְנוּ וַנִּתְעוֹדָד: יהוה הוֹשִׁיעָה הַמֶּלֶךְ יַעֲנֵנוּ ג
בְיוֹם־קָרְאֵנוּ:
כא א ב לַמְנַצֵּחַ מִזְמוֹר לְדָוִד: יהוה בְּעָזְּךָ יִשְׂמַח־מֶלֶךְ וּבִישׁוּעָתְךָ מַה־יגיל מְאֹד: תַּאֲוַת יָּגֶל
ג ד לִבּוֹ נָתַתָּה לּוֹ וַאֲרֶשֶׁת שְׂפָתָיו בַּל־מָנַעְתָּ סֶּלָה: כִּי־תְקַדְּמֶנּוּ בִּרְכוֹת טוֹב תָּשִׁית
ה ו לְרֹאשׁוֹ עֲטֶרֶת פָּז: חַיִּים | שָׁאַל מִמְּךָ נָתַתָּה לּוֹ אֹרֶךְ יָמִים עוֹלָם וָעֶד: גָּדוֹל
ז כְּבוֹדוֹ בִּישׁוּעָתֶךָ הוֹד וְהָדָר תְּשַׁוֶּה עָלָיו: כִּי־תְשִׁיתֵהוּ בְרָכוֹת לָעַד תְּחַדֵּהוּ

PSALM 21

PSALMS 21:1–14

A psalm in which the righteous king exalts and gives thanks to God; he trusts in God to overcome his enemies.

21 1 **To the chief musician, a psalm by David.**

2 **The king has joy in Your strength, Lord; how greatly he rejoices in Your salvation.**

3 **You gave him his heart's desire. You did not deny** his prayers, **the request of his lips, Selah.**

4 **You greet him with blessings of goodness,** literally, "You precede him with blessings"; even before he approaches You, You bestow Your blessings on him. **You set a crown of pure gold upon his head.**

5 **He asked You for life; You gave him** not only life for the moment but great longevity and **length of days.** May it be Your will that this continue **forevermore.**

6 **His honor is great in Your salvation.** The help You give him to win battles increases his honor and majesty. **You bestow splendor and glory upon him.**

7 **For You set** him as a recipient of **blessings** bestowed **upon him continually; You make him exceedingly joyous in Your presence.**

Golden crown

8 **For the king trusts in the Lord; in the kindness of the Most High he will not stumble.**
9 The psalmist proceeds to address the king: **Your hand will find,** reach, **all your enemies; your right hand will find those who hate you.**
10 **You will make them like a fiery oven at the time of your anger; the Lord will consume them with His wrath and let fire devour them.** When you direct your anger at your enemies, they will burn as if in a furnace. The fire of God's fury will consume them.
11 **You will destroy their offspring from the earth, and their descendants from among the sons of man.**
12 **Though they were inclined to evil against you, devising plots, they will not succeed.**
13 **For You make them turn back.** This phrase could also mean "You make them into targets," as **You aim Your bowstring at their faces.** You shoot them with arrows from Your bow.
14 In conclusion: **Be exalted, Lord, in Your strength.** Let the greatness of Your power be revealed to us, and then **we will sing and praise Your might.**

PSALM 22

PSALMS 22:1–32

A psalm that begins as a psalm of entreaty, a cry for help by someone who is isolated and surrounded by numerous enemies. It ends as a hymn of praise for the psalmist's salvation, which can be a source of hope for others.

22 1 **To the chief musician on ayelet hashaḥar,**[D] **a psalm by David.**
2 **My God, my God, why have You forsaken me?** This verse describes how the psalmist feels: Alone, pursued by adversaries, and abandoned by God. **So far from my deliverance are the words of my anguished cry.** In this context, "my deliverance" may refer to God. The psalmist feels that his cries are so distant from God that it seems as if they cannot reach Him.
3 **My God, I call You by day, but You do not answer; by night I have no solace.** I pray day and night, but my soul is not at peace.
4 **Yet You are holy, enthroned in the praises of Israel.** God is portrayed by the psalmist as sitting on a throne made of songs of praise sung to Him by generations of the people of Israel.
5 **In You our fathers placed their trust; they trusted, and You rescued them.** You delivered them from their sufferings.
6 **They cried out to You and escaped** from their precarious situations, **trusted in You and were not disappointed.**
7 **But I am a worm and not a man** in the eyes of my detractors, **an object of disgrace, scorned by the masses.**

Worm

8 **All who see me revile me, rejecting me with curled lip and wagging head.** Their insults are not even fully articulated; they consist of half-phrases accompanied by contemptuous snarls and head-shaking gesticulations, whether of contempt or pity.
9 **Let him turn toward the Lord; let Him rescue him; let Him save him, for He delights in him.** These are the words of the psalmist, voicing his inner feelings toward others.
10 **For You brought me forth from the womb; You made me secure at my mother's breast.**
11 **I have been cast upon You** to be dependent upon You **from the womb; from my mother's belly, You have been my God.** From earliest childhood, I have relied on You.
12 **Be not far from me, for trouble is near and there is no one** else **to help.**
13 **I am surrounded by** enemies that are like **many bulls,** large and dangerous animals, **encircled by the mighty bulls of Bashan,**[B] an unusually large kind of cattle.
14 **They open their mouths at me like a rapacious, roaring lion.**
15 **I am spilled out like water.** I feel depleted and vulnerable. **All my bones are disjointed. My heart is like wax, melting within me.** I have no inner strength to draw on.

Melting wax

16 **My vitality is parched like clay; my tongue cleaves to my palate. You have consigned me to the dust of death.** I feel barely alive; You have brought me to the brink of death.
17 **For dogs have surrounded me.**[B] The psalmist compares his enemies to hungry dogs. **A band of evildoers have encircled me, like a lion at my hands and feet.** I am surrounded by hordes of terrifying, evil foes. I am devastated and broken.
18 **I count all my bones,** because I feel that they are shattered. **They gaze and look at me.** My enemies are on the alert, waiting for my final downfall.
19 Even while I am still alive, **they divide my garments among them and cast lots for my clothing,** to decide who will get each garment.

ח ט בְּשִׂמְחָה אֶת־פָּנֶיךָ: כִּי־הַמֶּלֶךְ בֹּטֵחַ בַּיהוָה וּבְחֶסֶד עֶלְיוֹן בַּל־יִמּוֹט: תִּמְצָא יָדְךָ
י לְכָל־אֹיְבֶיךָ יְמִינְךָ תִּמְצָא שֹׂנְאֶיךָ: תְּשִׁיתֵמוֹ ׀ כְּתַנּוּר אֵשׁ לְעֵת פָּנֶיךָ יהוה בְּאַפּוֹ
יא יב יְבַלְּעֵם וְתֹאכְלֵם אֵשׁ: פִּרְיָמוֹ מֵאֶרֶץ תְּאַבֵּד וְזַרְעָם מִבְּנֵי אָדָם: כִּי־נָטוּ עָלֶיךָ
יג רָעָה חָשְׁבוּ מְזִמָּה בַּל־יוּכָלוּ: כִּי תְּשִׁיתֵמוֹ שֶׁכֶם בְּמֵיתָרֶיךָ תְּכוֹנֵן עַל־פְּנֵיהֶם:
יד רוּמָה יהוה בְעֻזֶּךָ נָשִׁירָה וּנְזַמְּרָה גְּבוּרָתֶךָ:
כב א ב לַמְנַצֵּחַ עַל־אַיֶּלֶת הַשַּׁחַר מִזְמוֹר לְדָוִד: אֵלִי אֵלִי לָמָה עֲזַבְתָּנִי רָחוֹק מִישׁוּעָתִי
ג ד דִּבְרֵי שַׁאֲגָתִי: אֱלֹהַי אֶקְרָא יוֹמָם וְלֹא תַעֲנֶה וְלַיְלָה וְלֹא־דוּמִיָּה לִי: וְאַתָּה קָדוֹשׁ
ה ו יוֹשֵׁב תְּהִלּוֹת יִשְׂרָאֵל: בְּךָ בָּטְחוּ אֲבֹתֵינוּ בָּטְחוּ וַתְּפַלְּטֵמוֹ: אֵלֶיךָ זָעֲקוּ וְנִמְלָטוּ
ז ח בְּךָ בָטְחוּ וְלֹא־בוֹשׁוּ: וְאָנֹכִי תוֹלַעַת וְלֹא־אִישׁ חֶרְפַּת אָדָם וּבְזוּי עָם: כָּל־רֹאַי
ט יַלְעִגוּ לִי יַפְטִירוּ בְשָׂפָה יָנִיעוּ רֹאשׁ: גֹּל אֶל־יהוה יְפַלְּטֵהוּ יַצִּילֵהוּ כִּי חָפֵץ בּוֹ:
י יא כִּי־אַתָּה גֹחִי מִבָּטֶן מַבְטִיחִי עַל־שְׁדֵי אִמִּי: עָלֶיךָ הָשְׁלַכְתִּי מֵרָחֶם מִבֶּטֶן אִמִּי
יב יג אֵלִי אָתָּה: אַל־תִּרְחַק מִמֶּנִּי כִּי־צָרָה קְרוֹבָה כִּי־אֵין עוֹזֵר: סְבָבוּנִי פָּרִים רַבִּים
יד טו אַבִּירֵי בָשָׁן כִּתְּרוּנִי: פָּצוּ עָלַי פִּיהֶם אַרְיֵה טֹרֵף וְשֹׁאֵג: כַּמַּיִם נִשְׁפַּכְתִּי וְהִתְפָּרְדוּ
טז כָּל־עַצְמוֹתָי הָיָה לִבִּי כַּדּוֹנָג נָמֵס בְּתוֹךְ מֵעָי: יָבֵשׁ כַּחֶרֶשׂ ׀ כֹּחִי וּלְשׁוֹנִי מֻדְבָּק
יז מַלְקוֹחָי וְלַעֲפַר־מָוֶת תִּשְׁפְּתֵנִי: כִּי סְבָבוּנִי כְּלָבִים עֲדַת מְרֵעִים הִקִּיפוּנִי כָּאֲרִי יָדַי
יח יט וְרַגְלָי: אֲסַפֵּר כָּל־עַצְמוֹתָי הֵמָּה יַבִּיטוּ יִרְאוּ־בִי: יְחַלְּקוּ בְגָדַי לָהֶם וְעַל־לְבוּשִׁי

BACKGROUND

22:13 | **The mighty bulls [*abirei*] of Bashan:** The Bashan area, fertile and rich with water, was known in ancient times as an area of fine pasture. The cattle and flocks that grew there were considered fat and of the highest quality (see, e.g., Deuteronomy 32:14; Ezekiel 39:18; Amos 4:1). *Abir* refers to a particularly strong and large animal. In this area, bones of *Bos primigenius* have been found; this species of wild cattle had giant horns, 3 m long, pointing forward, a height of 2 m at the shoulders, and weight approaching a metric ton (see verse 22).

22:17 | **Dogs have surrounded me:** Ownerless dogs gather together in bands in order to search for food. Bands of wild dogs sometimes attack other animals and even vulnerable humans. After they surround their victim they are likely to move in for the kill.

DISCUSSION

22:1 | **Ayelet hashaḥar:** This term, literally "deer of the dawn," is usually understood to refer to the beginning of dawn, or shortly before that, when the appearance of diverging "horns," rays, of light begin to appear, some time before the sun actually rises (see also *Aleh Yona*, pp. 23–30). It is possible that this psalm was composed to be recited at this particular time of day. In essence it is a psalm of lamentation and supplication, though it ends on a more positive note, just as the darkness of night ultimately yields to the sun's rays. Alternatively, *ayelet hashaḥar* is the name of the melody used for this psalm.

20 **But You, Lord, be not far off. My Strength, hasten to help me.**

21 **Rescue me from the sword, my soul from the grasp of the dog** that stands ready to attack me. The word *yeḥidati,* which means something singular and unique, is used here as a synonym for "my soul."

Vicious dog

22 **Save me from the lion's mouth, from the horns of the oryx;**[B] **answer me,** rescue me from these vicious animals.

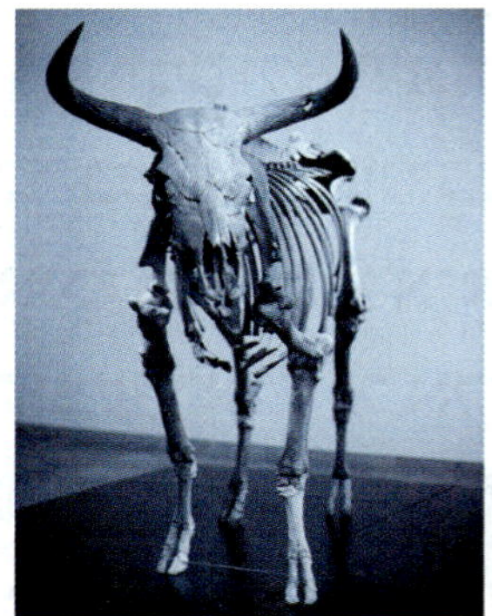
Horns of an oryx

23 The concluding verses of the psalm may have been composed at a later date, after the psalmist had been rescued from danger: **I will tell of Your name to my brothers; in the midst of the assembly I will praise You.** I will tell my kinsmen that You have rescued me from danger.

24 **You who fear the Lord, praise Him; may the progeny of Jacob honor Him, and may the progeny of Israel fear Him.**

25 **For** I, by my very survival, am testimony to the fact that **He did not despise or abhor the plea of the poor person, nor did He hide His face from him; when he cried to Him, He heard.**

26 **My praise will be of You in the great assembly.** I will praise You now in public, and **I will fulfill,** also in public, **my vows** that I made in my time of distress, **in the presence of those who fear Him.**

27 **The humble will eat and be satiated. Those who seek Him will praise the Lord; may your hearts be forever alive** due to your hope for God and His salvation.

28 **The ends of the earth will all remember and return to the Lord; all families of nations will bow down before You.**

29 **For kingship belongs to the Lord; He rules over nations.**

30 **The well-fed of the earth have all eaten and bowed down before Him; all who return to the dust,** that is, all men, **kneel before Him. Is there a soul to whom He has not given life?** Everyone alive is sustained by God. Every living, mortal soul, from privileged, prosperous people to those who are impoverished, should bow down before God in gratitude.

31 **Posterity will serve Him; coming generations will be told of the Lord.**

32 **They will come and declare His righteousness to a nation yet to be born,** to future generations, **for so He has done.** He has granted salvation to men in their times of distress.

PSALM 23

PSALMS 23:1–6

A psalm of devotion, in which the psalmist envisions himself as a lamb, wholly reliant on his devoted shepherd. The lamb trusts that the shepherd will lead him on a secure path and provide him with a dwelling in a good and happy place.

23 1 **A psalm by David. The Lord is my shepherd.**[D] Taking on the perspective of the lamb, the psalmist expresses gratitude to the shepherd for all he does. This metaphor is maintained throughout much of the psalm. Because God watches over me, **I lack nothing.**

4th day of month

2 **He has me lie down in green pastures.** Wherever I go, He provides me with resources that offer food and rest. **He leads me beside still,** gently flowing **waters,** streams that provide water in abundance without the danger that a strong current could pose to a lamb.

3 **He restores my soul.** The root of the Hebrew word *yeshovev,* translated here as "He restores," sometimes means "to grant rest," but its basic meaning is "to return." When one's soul is troubled or worried, it is not at peace, as though it is not in its natural place, but distanced and dislocated. When the soul returns to its true place, the result is inner peace. **He leads me in paths of righteousness.** *Maglei tzedek,* translated as "paths of righteousness," can also mean "correct paths," those fitting for the occasion. In the metaphor of the lamb and the shepherd, they represent paths suitable for a lamb to tread. In human terms, the phrase refers to one's course in life, a pathway that enables a person to remain righteous and that does not provide negative influences that contradict that goal. God cares for us **for His name's sake,** for His own sake, not necessarily because we are deserving of His protection. Whatever God's motivation, we, like the lamb, benefit from His tender care, as through it we attain serenity.

Flock of sheep

4 **Even when I walk through the valley of the shadow of death:** This phrase apparently refers to a vale that is accessed by a dangerous

כ כא יַפִּילוּ גוֹרָל׃ וְאַתָּה יְהוָה אַל־תִּרְחָק אֱיָלוּתִי לְעֶזְרָתִי חוּשָׁה׃ הַצִּילָה מֵחֶרֶב נַפְשִׁי
כב כג מִיַּד־כֶּלֶב יְחִידָתִי׃ הוֹשִׁיעֵנִי מִפִּי אַרְיֵה וּמִקַּרְנֵי רֵמִים עֲנִיתָנִי׃ אֲסַפְּרָה שִׁמְךָ
כד לְאֶחָי בְּתוֹךְ קָהָל אֲהַלְלֶךָּ׃ יִרְאֵי יְהוָה ׀ הַלְלוּהוּ כָּל־זֶרַע יַעֲקֹב כַּבְּדוּהוּ וְגוּרוּ
כה מִמֶּנּוּ כָּל־זֶרַע יִשְׂרָאֵל׃ כִּי לֹא־בָזָה וְלֹא שִׁקַּץ עֱנוּת עָנִי וְלֹא־הִסְתִּיר פָּנָיו מִמֶּנּוּ
כו כז וּבְשַׁוְּעוֹ אֵלָיו שָׁמֵעַ׃ מֵאִתְּךָ תְּהִלָּתִי בְּקָהָל רָב נְדָרַי אֲשַׁלֵּם נֶגֶד יְרֵאָיו׃ יֹאכְלוּ
כח עֲנָוִים ׀ וְיִשְׂבָּעוּ יְהַלְלוּ יְהוָה דֹּרְשָׁיו יְחִי לְבַבְכֶם לָעַד׃ יִזְכְּרוּ ׀ וְיָשֻׁבוּ אֶל־יְהוָה
כט כָּל־אַפְסֵי־אָרֶץ וְיִשְׁתַּחֲווּ לְפָנֶיךָ כָּל־מִשְׁפְּחוֹת גּוֹיִם׃ כִּי לַיהוָה הַמְּלוּכָה וּמֹשֵׁל
ל בַּגּוֹיִם׃ אָכְלוּ וַיִּשְׁתַּחֲווּ ׀ כָּל־דִּשְׁנֵי־אֶרֶץ לְפָנָיו יִכְרְעוּ כָּל־יוֹרְדֵי עָפָר וְנַפְשׁוֹ לֹא
לא לב חִיָּה׃ זֶרַע יַעַבְדֶנּוּ יְסֻפַּר לַאדֹנָי לַדּוֹר׃ יָבֹאוּ וְיַגִּידוּ צִדְקָתוֹ לְעַם נוֹלָד כִּי עָשָׂה׃
כג א ב מִזְמוֹר לְדָוִד יְהוָה רֹעִי לֹא אֶחְסָר׃ בִּנְאוֹת דֶּשֶׁא יַרְבִּיצֵנִי עַל־מֵי מְנֻחוֹת יְנַהֲלֵנִי׃ ד לחודש
ג ד נַפְשִׁי יְשׁוֹבֵב יַנְחֵנִי בְמַעְגְּלֵי־צֶדֶק לְמַעַן שְׁמוֹ׃ גַּם כִּי־אֵלֵךְ בְּגֵיא צַלְמָוֶת לֹא־
ה אִירָא רָע כִּי־אַתָּה עִמָּדִי שִׁבְטְךָ וּמִשְׁעַנְתֶּךָ הֵמָּה יְנַחֲמֻנִי׃ תַּעֲרֹךְ לְפָנַי ׀ שֻׁלְחָן

path, surrounded by pitfalls or perilous cliffs. Even when I traverse such a place, **I fear no evil.** I walk with confidence, **for You are with me. Your rod and Your staff,** instruments used by the shepherd to guide the flock, gently prodding those that stray back to the proper path, **they comfort me.**[D]

5 The images in this verse belong more to the human realm, but they too have a dual meaning: **You prepare a table before me in the presence of my enemies.** "Table" is used here in the broad sense of any place to eat. Even though enemies of all kinds may be lying in wait for me, I can sit and eat in peace,

BACKGROUND

22:22| **The horns of the oryx [*remim*]:** It is possible that *remim* are identical with the "mighty bulls" mentioned in verse 13, which have very large and dangerous horns. Herbivores with horns use them for self-defense from predators, but sometimes when they are aggravated or feel danger they use these horns to gore whatever is in their vicinity. Incidents of goring by cattle, which are common, are quite dangerous. With these depictions the psalmist illustrates his feelings of one who has become caught in a situation of immediate danger.

DISCUSSION

23:1| **The Lord is my shepherd:** This is a simple yet expressive song of thanksgiving, and for this reason it has become one of the most common psalms to be recited, both in the liturgy and in private prayer. Although the psalm contains references to specific events in David's life, its theme of thanksgiving is so general that anyone can identify with it. It is a song of thanksgiving from the point of view of a sheep that is grateful toward its shepherd for all the care that he bestows upon it. While the metaphoric meaning of the many expressions relating to the shepherd and his flock is self-evident, the psalm is not totally allegorical, and there are deviations from this central depiction.

23:4| **Your rod and Your staff, they comfort me:** From the perspective of the lamb, these implements are an integral part of the shepherd's image and are a source of comfort and security. The rod gives the shepherd the power to fend off enemies; the staff enables him to rescue the lamb from danger (see Zechariah 11:7). The top of the staff may be bent over so that the shepherd can grab hold of an errant sheep's neck and prod him back to the proper, safe path.

For humans, however, a rod often represents a means of punishment. This gives the phrase a second, deeper meaning: Both Your rod, Your instrument of punishment, and Your staff, literally, "Your support," are a source of comfort to me, because I know that whatever You do for me is ultimately in my best interest.

because You are with me, just as the lamb can graze, unafraid of predators, when the trusted shepherd is close. **You anoint my head with oil,** a practice that could impart comfort as well as impart cosmetic value to one's head. **My cup is full.** Literally, this expression means "my cup is one of saturation." That is, there is enough wine in the cup to enable me to drink my fill and adequately quench my thirst.

6 **May only goodness and kindness pursue me**[D] **all the days of my life, and I will dwell in the House of the Lord forever.** Relieved of fear of adversity, my happiness complete, I will be able to spend my time in the House of God, singing His praises without want or worry.

PSALM 24

A hymn depicting two different modes of entrance to the Holy Temple: That of man versus the majestic arrival of God.

PSALMS 24:1–10

24 1 **By David, a psalm. The earth is the Lord's, and all that it holds,** namely, **the world and all its inhabitants.**

2 **For He founded it upon the seas.** The terrain of the earth towers over the ocean below, as a building rises above its foundations. **And** He **established it upon the rivers.** The water flowing in the rivers has its origin in subterranean springs.

3 The focal point of the earth, its spiritual apex, is the Temple Mount, concerning which the psalmist asks: **Who may** be considered worthy to **ascend the mountain of the Lord? Who may stand in His holy place?** In this verse, and throughout the psalm, the "mountain of the Lord" refers both to the visible, physical Temple and to the concept of spiritual holiness on high, something that is beyond the physical world.

4 The psalmist answers the question posed in the preceding verse: **He who has clean hands and a pure heart,** one who is beyond reproach both in his deeds and in his thoughts; **he who has not raised up his soul for falsehood.**[D] He does not yearn for the attainment of false, corrupt goals. **Nor** has he **sworn deceitfully.** In its plain sense, "sworn deceitfully" refers to a person who is not engaged in actual evil deeds but allows himself to sin through false speech, even swearing a false oath. The phrase can also be translated more literally as "nor sworn for deceit." Not only is the virtuous man pure in deed and thought, as mentioned above, but he does not become involved in deceit practiced by others, through supporting them or obligating himself to ally with them through a covenantal oath.

5 **He,** the virtuous man described above, **will receive the blessing of the Lord, righteousness from the God of his deliverance.**

6 Of such people it may be said: **This is the generation of those who seek Him out,** who desire to follow His ways, **who seek Your countenance, the people of Jacob, Selah.**

7 Until this point, the psalm has described those worthy of entering and worshipping in the Holy Temple; among their characteristics are modesty and humility. The psalmist now depicts God's entrance to His Holy Temple, in grandeur and majesty. He addresses the gates of the Temple: **Lift up your heads, gates; be raised up, infinite portals,** as is befitting for the entrance of a visitor of great stature, **so the King of glory may enter.**

"Lift up your heads, gates." The Gate of Nikanor of the Temple courtyard, reproduction

8 **Who is the King of glory** that I refer to? Not a human warrior or a mortal of great renown, but rather **the Lord, strong and mighty; the Lord,** who enters His palace in the manner of a warrior **mighty in battle,** entering in triumphal procession.

9 The psalmist repeats his stirring call to the gates of entry to the Temple: **Lift up your heads, gates; raise yourselves up, infinite portals, so the King of glory may enter.**

10 **Who is He, this King of glory? The Lord of hosts,** the Ruler over all forces on earth and in the heavens, **He is the King of glory, Selah.**

ו נֶגֶד צֹרְרָי דִּשַּׁנְתָּ בַשֶּׁמֶן רֹאשִׁי כּוֹסִי רְוָיָה׃ אַךְ ׀ טוֹב וָחֶסֶד יִרְדְּפוּנִי כָּל־יְמֵי חַיָּי
וְשַׁבְתִּי בְּבֵית־יהוה לְאֹרֶךְ יָמִים׃
כד א ב לְדָוִד מִזְמוֹר לַיהוה הָאָרֶץ וּמְלוֹאָהּ תֵּבֵל וְיֹשְׁבֵי בָהּ׃ כִּי־הוּא עַל־יַמִּים יְסָדָהּ
ג ד וְעַל־נְהָרוֹת יְכוֹנְנֶהָ׃ מִי־יַעֲלֶה בְהַר־יהוה וּמִי־יָקוּם בִּמְקוֹם קָדְשׁוֹ׃ נְקִי כַפַּיִם
ה וּבַר־לֵבָב אֲשֶׁר לֹא־נָשָׂא לַשָּׁוְא נפשו וְלֹא נִשְׁבַּע לְמִרְמָה׃ יִשָּׂא בְרָכָה מֵאֵת יהוה נַפְשִׁי
ו ז וּצְדָקָה מֵאֱלֹהֵי יִשְׁעוֹ׃ זֶה דּוֹר דֹּרְשָׁו מְבַקְשֵׁי פָנֶיךָ יַעֲקֹב סֶלָה׃ שְׂאוּ שְׁעָרִים ׀
ח רָאשֵׁיכֶם וְהִנָּשְׂאוּ פִּתְחֵי עוֹלָם וְיָבוֹא מֶלֶךְ הַכָּבוֹד׃ מִי זֶה מֶלֶךְ הַכָּבוֹד יהוה
ט עִזּוּז וְגִבּוֹר יהוה גִּבּוֹר מִלְחָמָה׃ שְׂאוּ שְׁעָרִים ׀ רָאשֵׁיכֶם וּשְׂאוּ פִּתְחֵי עוֹלָם וְיָבֹא
י מֶלֶךְ הַכָּבוֹד׃ מִי הוּא זֶה מֶלֶךְ הַכָּבוֹד יהוה צְבָאוֹת הוּא מֶלֶךְ הַכָּבוֹד סֶלָה׃
כה א ב לְדָוִד אֵלֶיךָ יהוה נַפְשִׁי אֶשָּׂא׃ אֱלֹהַי בְּךָ בָטַחְתִּי אַל־אֵבוֹשָׁה אַל־יַעַלְצוּ אֹיְבַי
ג ד לִי׃ גַּם כָּל־קֹוֶיךָ לֹא יֵבֹשׁוּ יֵבֹשׁוּ הַבּוֹגְדִים רֵיקָם׃ דְּרָכֶיךָ יהוה הוֹדִיעֵנִי אֹרְחוֹתֶיךָ
ה לַמְּדֵנִי׃ הַדְרִיכֵנִי בַאֲמִתֶּךָ ׀ וְלַמְּדֵנִי כִּי־אַתָּה אֱלֹהֵי יִשְׁעִי אוֹתְךָ קִוִּיתִי כָּל־הַיּוֹם׃

PSALM 25

PSALMS 25:1–22

A prayer that does not address a specific topic but is rather the expression of one individual's desire to go in the path of God. Like other psalms offering moral instruction, its verses are arranged, for the most part, in alphabetical order. The final verse begins with the letter *peh*, which may signify the end of a chapter [*perek*] or paragraph [*piska*].

25 1 **A Psalm by David. To You, Lord, I lift up my soul,** elevating it to a higher level and bringing it closer to God.

2 **My God, in You do I trust,** and because I trust in You, **do not let me be shamed, nor let my enemies exult over me.**

3 **Indeed, all those who place their hope in You will not be ashamed,** for You will come to their aid; **ashamed will be those who deal treacherously without cause,** for no particular gain, but out of pure malice.

4 **Show me Your ways, Lord; teach me Your paths.**

5 **Lead me in Your truth and instruct me, for You are the God of my salvation; in You do I place my hope all day long.**

DISCUSSION

23:6 | **May only goodness and kindness pursue me:** While the literal meaning is that the psalmist wishes for his entire life to consist of experiences that are good and pleasant, the term "pursue me" would seem somewhat inappropriate in this context. It might be explained as follows: At times, a person does not recognize the path in life that will bring him happiness and therefore does not follow it. In such a case, he feels grateful when this path of goodness and kindness actively "pursues" him, as it were, and finds him despite his own lack of initiative.

24:4 | **He who has not raised up his soul [*nafshi*] for falsehood:** The word *nafshi*, translated here as "his soul," literally means "my soul," which is a difficult phrase in this context. Some interpret the entire psalm in a manner which accommodates this unusual expression. However, it may be that the psalmist, in a sudden emotional outburst, inserts his own soul into the discussion of the righteous man's virtues.

6 **Remember, Lord, Your mercy and kindness, for they are eternal.**

7 But **do not recall the sins of my youth or my transgressions,** committed out of impetuous, youthful desire. **Remember** for **me** my good deeds **with Your kindness, for the sake of Your goodness, Lord.**

8 **Good and upright is the Lord; therefore He instructs sinners in the** proper **way,** to help them find the path of righteousness and integrity.

9 **He guides the humble with justice, and He teaches the humble His way.**

10 **All the paths of the Lord are kindness and truth, for those who keep His covenant and His precepts.**

11 Act **for the sake of Your name, Lord, and pardon my iniquity, for it is great.**

12 **Who is the man,** how great is the man, **who fears the Lord, whom He instructs in the way that He chooses?**

13 **His soul will rest in good.** "Rest" here can refer both to ordinary sleep and to death; the righteous man's sleep, in both senses of the word, will be peaceful. **And his descendants will inherit the earth.**

14 **The secret of the Lord is** revealed **to those who fear Him. He will give them knowledge of His covenant** expressed in the words of the Torah.

15 **My eyes are ever toward the Lord, for He draws my feet out of the net.** He rescues me from traps and pitfalls that surround me even when I am unaware of them.

16 **Turn to me and be gracious to me, for I am lonely and afflicted** and in need of Your help.

17 **The troubles of my heart are widespread; free me from my distresses.**

18 **See my affliction and my toil, and forgive all my sins.**

19 **Regard my enemies, for they are many; they hate me with a hatred** born **of injustice,** a hatred that is driven by their desire to unjustly rob me of my possessions.

20 **Protect me and deliver me; do not let me be ashamed, for I take refuge in You.**

21 **Let** Your **integrity and uprightness preserve me, for I place my hope in You.**

22 In conclusion, a general request on behalf of the entire nation: **God, redeem Israel from all its troubles.**

PSALM 26

A psalm in which the psalmist prays for God's help, basing his request on his continual efforts to be as close to God as possible.

PSALMS 26:1–12

26 1 **By David. Judge me** for my thoughts and deeds, **Lord, for I have walked in innocence. I have trusted in the Lord, and** as I have chosen to follow a path of integrity and trust in God, I have faith that I **shall not falter.**

2 **Examine me, Lord, and try me,** and You will see that I truly am devoted to following Your way. **Purify my mind and my heart.**

3 **For Your kindness is before my eyes,** as I set my direction toward Your acts of kindness, **and I walk in** the path of **Your truth.**

4 **I do not sit with worthless men, nor do I go with those who** must **hide themselves** because of their nefarious activities.

5 **I abhor the assembly of evildoers and will not sit with the wicked.**

6 Rather, **I wash my hands in purity.** This may be understood both literally and figuratively. Literally, I wash my hands in preparation for prayer to You; figuratively, I keep my hands clean of evildoing. **And I circle Your altar, Lord,** in the manner of worshippers who come to pray at the Temple,

7 **proclaiming thankfulness** there, **and telling of all Your wonders.**

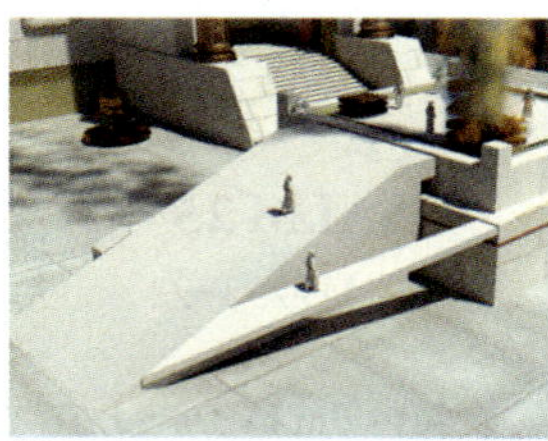

Altar in the Temple

8 The psalmist concludes: **Lord, I love the abode of Your House** and I frequent it, **the place where Your glory dwells.**

9 Therefore, I beseech You: **Do not gather in my soul with sinners** when You punish them; do not take **my life** along **with** those of **men of bloodshed,**

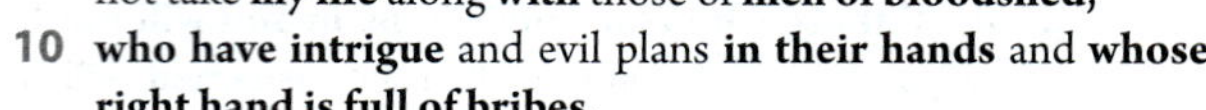

10 **who have intrigue** and evil plans **in their hands** and **whose right hand is full of bribes.**

11 **But I go in my innocence;** therefore, **redeem me and be gracious to me.**

12 **My foot stands on a straight path. In convocations** of the righteous **I will bless the Lord.**

ו ז זְכֹר־רַחֲמֶיךָ יְהוָה וַחֲסָדֶיךָ כִּי מֵעוֹלָם הֵמָּה׃ חַטֹּאות נְעוּרַי ׀ וּפְשָׁעַי אַל־תִּזְכֹּר
ח כְּחַסְדְּךָ זְכָר־לִי־אַתָּה לְמַעַן טוּבְךָ יְהוָה׃ טוֹב־וְיָשָׁר יְהוָה עַל־כֵּן יוֹרֶה חַטָּאִים
ט י בַּדָּרֶךְ׃ יַדְרֵךְ עֲנָוִים בַּמִּשְׁפָּט וִילַמֵּד עֲנָוִים דַּרְכּוֹ׃ כָּל־אָרְחוֹת יְהוָה חֶסֶד וֶאֱמֶת
יא יב לְנֹצְרֵי בְרִיתוֹ וְעֵדֹתָיו׃ לְמַעַן־שִׁמְךָ יְהוָה וְסָלַחְתָּ לַעֲוֹנִי כִּי רַב־הוּא׃ מִי־זֶה הָאִישׁ
יג יד יְרֵא יְהוָה יוֹרֶנּוּ בְּדֶרֶךְ יִבְחָר׃ נַפְשׁוֹ בְּטוֹב תָּלִין וְזַרְעוֹ יִירַשׁ אָרֶץ׃ סוֹד יְהוָה
טו לִירֵאָיו וּבְרִיתוֹ לְהוֹדִיעָם׃ עֵינַי תָּמִיד אֶל־יְהוָה כִּי הוּא־יוֹצִיא מֵרֶשֶׁת רַגְלָי׃
טז יז פְּנֵה־אֵלַי וְחָנֵּנִי כִּי־יָחִיד וְעָנִי אָנִי׃ צָרוֹת לְבָבִי הִרְחִיבוּ מִמְּצוּקוֹתַי הוֹצִיאֵנִי׃
יח יט רְאֵה עָנְיִי וַעֲמָלִי וְשָׂא לְכָל־חַטֹּאותָי׃ רְאֵה־אוֹיְבַי כִּי־רָבּוּ וְשִׂנְאַת חָמָס שְׂנֵאוּנִי׃
כ כא שָׁמְרָה נַפְשִׁי וְהַצִּילֵנִי אַל־אֵבוֹשׁ כִּי־חָסִיתִי בָךְ׃ תֹּם־וָיֹשֶׁר יִצְּרוּנִי כִּי קִוִּיתִיךָ׃
כב פְּדֵה אֱלֹהִים אֶת־יִשְׂרָאֵל מִכֹּל צָרוֹתָיו׃
כו א ב לְדָוִד ׀ שָׁפְטֵנִי יְהוָה כִּי־אֲנִי בְּתֻמִּי הָלַכְתִּי וּבַיהוָה בָּטַחְתִּי לֹא אֶמְעָד׃ בְּחָנֵנִי
ג יְהוָה וְנַסֵּנִי צרופה כִלְיוֹתַי וְלִבִּי׃ כִּי־חַסְדְּךָ לְנֶגֶד עֵינָי וְהִתְהַלַּכְתִּי בַּאֲמִתֶּךָ׃ צָרְפָה
ד ה לֹא־יָשַׁבְתִּי עִם־מְתֵי־שָׁוְא וְעִם נַעֲלָמִים לֹא אָבוֹא׃ שָׂנֵאתִי קְהַל מְרֵעִים וְעִם־
ו ז רְשָׁעִים לֹא אֵשֵׁב׃ אֶרְחַץ בְּנִקָּיוֹן כַּפָּי וַאֲסֹבְבָה אֶת־מִזְבַּחֲךָ יְהוָה׃ לַשְׁמִעַ בְּקוֹל
ח תּוֹדָה וּלְסַפֵּר כָּל־נִפְלְאוֹתֶיךָ׃ יְהוָה אָהַבְתִּי מְעוֹן בֵּיתֶךָ וּמְקוֹם מִשְׁכַּן כְּבוֹדֶךָ׃
ט י אַל־תֶּאֱסֹף עִם־חַטָּאִים נַפְשִׁי וְעִם־אַנְשֵׁי דָמִים חַיָּי׃ אֲשֶׁר־בִּידֵיהֶם זִמָּה וִימִינָם
יא יב מָלְאָה שֹּׁחַד׃ וַאֲנִי בְּתֻמִּי אֵלֵךְ פְּדֵנִי וְחָנֵּנִי׃ רַגְלִי עָמְדָה בְמִישׁוֹר בְּמַקְהֵלִים
אֲבָרֵךְ יְהוָה׃

PSALM 27

A psalm that combines gratitude for the past and supplication for the future, essentially a hymn of closeness to God.

PSALMS 27:1–14

27 1 **By David. The Lord is my light and my salvation.** Consequently, **whom shall I fear? The Lord is the stronghold of my life; of whom shall I be afraid?**

2 **When evildoers come upon me to devour my flesh, my foes and my adversaries, it is they who stumble and fall.**

3 **If an army besieges me, my heart will not fear. If war comes upon me, I will put my trust in this** realization that God is my light and salvation.

Roman legion, stone relief, Roman period

4 The psalmist is aware that God is his Protector and he is grateful for that. But his foremost desire and wish is in a different direction altogether. **One request have I made of the Lord; this is what I ask for: That I may dwell in the House of the Lord all the days of my life, to behold the goodness of the Lord and to visit His Temple.** This entreaty, especially when expressed by someone who, as neither priest nor Levite, has no tasks to perform in the daily Temple service, is not to be taken as a literal request to stay in the Temple to participate in its religious rituals. Rather, it is an ecstatic exclamation of devotion to God made by a person who enters His Temple and experiences the sheer joy of being close to God there.

5 **For in time of trouble He shelters me in His pavilion. He conceals me in the secret of His tent** to protect me from adversity. **He sets me high upon a mighty rock,** where no harm can come to me,

6 **so that now my head rises above my enemies around me. I will offer victory sacrifices [*zivḥei terua*] in His tent.** The unusual phrase *zivḥei terua* literally means "sacrifices with shofar blasts." It refers to thanksgiving sacrifices that are offered in the wake of a victory or triumph. **I will sing songs of praise to the Lord.**

7 Now, again, are words of prayer: **Hear, Lord, when I cry out** to You. **Be gracious to me and answer me.**

8 **For You,** on Your behalf, **my heart said: Seek Me.** When my heart says, "seek Me," it is quoting God, who is asking of me, and all others, to seek Him. To this divine call I can honestly respond: **Your presence, Lord, I do seek.**

9 **Do not hide Your face from me** by withholding Your assistance and abandoning me to the vicissitudes of life. **Do not turn Your servant away in anger,** even if Your wrath is justified. **You have been my succor** until this point; **do not abandon me or forsake me** now or in the future, **God of my salvation.**

10 **For my father and my mother may abandon me.** The bond between parent and child is one that endures almost unconditionally. For this reason, there is no greater sense of isolation than that felt by an abandoned child. **But the Lord will gather me up.** God's protection, however, covers everyone, even those who have been completely and utterly deserted. This verse is, therefore, a most powerful expression of trust in God and God alone.

11 **Teach me Your way,** the way of righteousness, **Lord, and lead me on a level path,** a correct and tranquil path in both the physical and the moral sense, **because of my foes,** in order for me to escape my foes.

12 **Do not deliver me to my foes, as is their desire, for they have risen against me as false witnesses,** making untrue accusations against me, **testifying unjustly.** An alternative interpretation is that *yafe'aḥ,* translated here as "testifying," may be related to *yifraḥ,* meaning to make something blossom or grow. The translation would then be "and they foment injustice."

13 If I survive unharmed, it is only because of my faith and prayers; I would have been vanquished **had I not believed that I would see the goodness of the Lord in the land of the living.** It was this faith that enabled me to continue fighting against my adversaries.

14 In conclusion, the psalmist offers words of encouragement to himself and to others: **Put your hope in the Lord; be strong and let your heart take courage, and** continue to **put your hope in the Lord** even if you do not see immediate results.

כז א ב לְדָוִד ׀ יְהוָה ׀ אוֹרִי וְיִשְׁעִי מִמִּי אִירָא יְהוָה מָעוֹז־חַיַּי מִמִּי אֶפְחָד׃ בִּקְרֹב עָלַי ׀
ג מְרֵעִים לֶאֱכֹל אֶת־בְּשָׂרִי צָרַי וְאֹיְבַי לִי הֵמָּה כָשְׁלוּ וְנָפָלוּ׃ אִם־תַּחֲנֶה עָלַי ׀ מַחֲנֶה
ד לֹא־יִירָא לִבִּי אִם־תָּקוּם עָלַי מִלְחָמָה בְּזֹאת אֲנִי בוֹטֵחַ׃ אַחַת ׀ שָׁאַלְתִּי מֵאֵת־
יְהוָה אוֹתָהּ אֲבַקֵּשׁ שִׁבְתִּי בְּבֵית־יְהוָה כָּל־יְמֵי חַיַּי לַחֲזוֹת בְּנֹעַם־יְהוָה וּלְבַקֵּר
ה ו בְּהֵיכָלוֹ׃ כִּי יִצְפְּנֵנִי ׀ בְּסֻכֹּה בְּיוֹם רָעָה יַסְתִּרֵנִי בְּסֵתֶר אָהֳלוֹ בְּצוּר יְרוֹמְמֵנִי׃ וְעַתָּה
יָרוּם רֹאשִׁי עַל אֹיְבַי סְבִיבוֹתַי וְאֶזְבְּחָה בְאָהֳלוֹ זִבְחֵי תְרוּעָה אָשִׁירָה וַאֲזַמְּרָה
ז ח לַיהוָה׃ שְׁמַע־יְהוָה קוֹלִי אֶקְרָא וְחָנֵּנִי וַעֲנֵנִי׃ לְךָ ׀ אָמַר לִבִּי בַּקְּשׁוּ פָנָי אֶת־פָּנֶיךָ
ט יְהוָה אֲבַקֵּשׁ׃ אַל־תַּסְתֵּר פָּנֶיךָ ׀ מִמֶּנִּי אַל תַּט־בְּאַף עַבְדֶּךָ עֶזְרָתִי הָיִיתָ אַל־
י יא תִּטְּשֵׁנִי וְאַל־תַּעַזְבֵנִי אֱלֹהֵי יִשְׁעִי׃ כִּי־אָבִי וְאִמִּי עֲזָבוּנִי וַיהוָה יַאַסְפֵנִי׃ הוֹרֵנִי
יב יְהוָה דַּרְכֶּךָ וּנְחֵנִי בְּאֹרַח מִישׁוֹר לְמַעַן שׁוֹרְרָי׃ אַל־תִּתְּנֵנִי בְּנֶפֶשׁ צָרָי כִּי קָמוּ־בִי
יג יד עֵדֵי־שֶׁקֶר וִיפֵחַ חָמָס׃ לוּלֵא הֶאֱמַנְתִּי לִרְאוֹת בְּטוּב־יְהוָה בְּאֶרֶץ חַיִּים׃ קַוֵּה
אֶל־יְהוָה חֲזַק וְיַאֲמֵץ לִבֶּךָ וְקַוֵּה אֶל־יְהוָה׃

כח א לְדָוִד אֵלֶיךָ יְהוָה ׀ אֶקְרָא צוּרִי אַל־תֶּחֱרַשׁ מִמֶּנִּי פֶּן־תֶּחֱשֶׁה מִמֶּנִּי וְנִמְשַׁלְתִּי
ב עִם־יוֹרְדֵי בוֹר׃ שְׁמַע קוֹל תַּחֲנוּנַי בְּשַׁוְּעִי אֵלֶיךָ בְּנָשְׂאִי יָדַי אֶל־דְּבִיר קָדְשֶׁךָ׃
ג אַל־תִּמְשְׁכֵנִי עִם־רְשָׁעִים וְעִם־פֹּעֲלֵי אָוֶן דֹּבְרֵי שָׁלוֹם עִם־רֵעֵיהֶם וְרָעָה בִּלְבָבָם׃
ד תֶּן־לָהֶם כְּפָעֳלָם וּכְרֹעַ מַעַלְלֵיהֶם כְּמַעֲשֵׂה יְדֵיהֶם תֵּן לָהֶם הָשֵׁב גְּמוּלָם לָהֶם׃

PSALM 28

A psalm that begins as a prayer for God's help and concludes with the psalmist's expression of gratitude for his salvation.

PSALMS 28:1–9

28 1 **By David. To You, Lord, I call. My rock,** my strength, **do not be deaf to me** by ignoring my plea, **for if You are silent I will be like those descending into the pit,** the grave. The psalmist's plea is for God's attentiveness, which is not only a source of strength but the very wellspring of his life.

2 **Hear the sound of my pleas when I cry to You for help, when I lift up my hands toward Your holy shrine.**

3 **Do not drag me away with the wicked,** do not include me in the ranks of wicked people, **and with evildoers,** those **who speak peaceably with their neighbors while malice is in their hearts.** Such people are even more dangerous than overt adversaries.

4 **Requite them according to their actions and wicked deeds; pay them back for what they have done; render to them what they deserve.** My prayer is only that they receive just punishment, no more.

5 **For they do not regard the works of the Lord, nor the deeds of His hands.** They do not understand that God is actively involved in His world; they would prefer not to think about the matter. In this way, they are able to continue engaging in wrongdoing. However, **He will tear them down and not build them up.** Intrigue and scheming will not save them from being destroyed.
6 **Blessed be the Lord, for He has heard the sound of my pleas.**
7 **The Lord is my strength and my shield; my heart trusts in Him, and I am helped** by Him. **My heart exults** in His salvation, **and with my song I give thanks to Him.** Alternatively, with my song I glorify Him.
8 **The Lord is their strength,** the strength of those who trust in Him; **He is a stronghold of salvation for His anointed one,** the king of Israel.
9 **Deliver Your people and bless Your possession,** a reference both to the people of Israel and the Land of Israel. **Shepherd them,** lead them as a shepherd leads his flock, **and raise them up forever.**

PSALM 29

PSALMS 29:1–11

A hymn about God's greatness and His revelation in the world, in which each different kind of revelation is termed "the voice of the Lord."

29 1 **A psalm by David. Give to the Lord, sons of the mighty.** Some commentators understand "sons of the mighty" to be angels; others say this represents the heavenly bodies. But the context of the verse implies that it is addressing human beings of great strength and stature; it is they who are best able to praise God in the most fitting manner. **Give to the Lord,** that is, praise Him, for His **glory and strength.**
2 **Give to the Lord the glory due His name; bow down to the Lord in holy splendor.**
3 From this point on, the psalmist elaborates on the various manifestations of God's revelation, which He terms "the voice of the Lord": **The voice of the Lord is on the waters; God of glory thunders; the Lord is** heard **upon surging waters.**
4 **The voice of the Lord is mighty,** and **the voice of the Lord is majestic.** He is also revealed in majestic beauty.
5 **The voice of the Lord** with its might **breaks cedars,** the strongest of trees; **the Lord splinters the cedars of Lebanon.** In essence, the revelation of God makes the entire world tremble.

Cedar forest in Lebanon

6 **He makes them,** the trees and all the creations in the world, jump from their place and **skip like calves;** the great mountains, such as the **Lebanon and** the **Siryon,**[B] skip **like young oryxes.**

"Siryon." Mount Hermon

7 **The voice of the Lord hews flames of fire.** It draws forth fire from the shattering mountains.
8 **The voice of the Lord makes the desert tremble** in awe. **The Lord makes the desert of Kadesh tremble.** This particular desert is mentioned to allude to the events that accompanied the revelation at Sinai, near Kadesh, as they are portrayed in several other psalms.[6]
9 **The voice of the Lord causes deer to calve.** The very same revelatory powers, the same voice that shakes the world, can also be a voice of gentleness, bringing fertility and fruitfulness to the world. **And** it also **strips the forests bare** by felling all their trees. **In His abode,** which is close to Him, as it were, the "voices of God" manifest themselves not in a display of power but rather in a tranquil manner, as **all proclaim His glory.**

Carmel forest, denuded after the fire of 2010

BACKGROUND

29:6| **Lebanon and Siryon:** The Lebanon is the name of a high mountain range opposite the Mediterranean in the northern part of the Land of Israel, today located in the country of Lebanon. To its east, across from the Beqaa Valley, is another mountain range, called the Anti-Lebanon Mountains, the southernmost peak of which is Mount Hermon, referred to here and elsewhere (Deuteronomy 3:9) by its Sidonite name, Siryon. These mountain ranges are like immense walls towering over the valley in between, which extends down to the Hula Valley and the Jordan River. They are also striking for their snow-capped peaks throughout most of the year.

ה ו כִּי לֹא יָבִינוּ אֶל־פְּעֻלֹּת יְהוָה וְאֶל־מַעֲשֵׂה יָדָיו יֶהֶרְסֵם וְלֹא יִבְנֵם׃ בָּרוּךְ יְהוָה
ז כִּי־שָׁמַע קוֹל תַּחֲנוּנָי׃ יְהוָה ׀ עֻזִּי וּמָגִנִּי בּוֹ בָטַח לִבִּי וְנֶעֱזָרְתִּי וַיַּעֲלֹז לִבִּי וּמִשִּׁירִי
ח ט אֲהוֹדֶנּוּ׃ יְהוָה עֹז־לָמוֹ וּמָעוֹז יְשׁוּעוֹת מְשִׁיחוֹ הוּא׃ הוֹשִׁיעָה ׀ אֶת־עַמֶּךָ וּבָרֵךְ
אֶת־נַחֲלָתֶךָ וּרְעֵם וְנַשְּׂאֵם עַד־הָעוֹלָם׃
כט א ב מִזְמוֹר לְדָוִד הָבוּ לַיהוָה בְּנֵי אֵלִים הָבוּ לַיהוָה כָּבוֹד וָעֹז׃ הָבוּ לַיהוָה כְּבוֹד שְׁמוֹ
ג הִשְׁתַּחֲווּ לַיהוָה בְּהַדְרַת־קֹדֶשׁ׃ קוֹל יְהוָה עַל־הַמָּיִם אֵל־הַכָּבוֹד הִרְעִים יְהוָה
ד ה עַל־מַיִם רַבִּים׃ קוֹל־יְהוָה בַּכֹּחַ קוֹל יְהוָה בֶּהָדָר׃ קוֹל יְהוָה שֹׁבֵר אֲרָזִים וַיְשַׁבֵּר
ו ז יְהוָה אֶת־אַרְזֵי הַלְּבָנוֹן׃ וַיַּרְקִידֵם כְּמוֹ־עֵגֶל לְבָנוֹן וְשִׂרְיוֹן כְּמוֹ בֶן־רְאֵמִים׃ קוֹל־
ח ט יְהוָה חֹצֵב לַהֲבוֹת אֵשׁ׃ קוֹל יְהוָה יָחִיל מִדְבָּר יָחִיל יְהוָה מִדְבַּר קָדֵשׁ׃ קוֹל
י יְהוָה ׀ יְחוֹלֵל אַיָּלוֹת וַיֶּחֱשֹׂף יְעָרוֹת וּבְהֵיכָלוֹ כֻּלּוֹ אֹמֵר כָּבוֹד׃ יְהוָה לַמַּבּוּל יָשָׁב
יא וַיֵּשֶׁב יְהוָה מֶלֶךְ לְעוֹלָם׃ יְהוָה עֹז לְעַמּוֹ יִתֵּן יְהוָה ׀ יְבָרֵךְ אֶת־עַמּוֹ בַשָּׁלוֹם׃ ד
ל א ב מִזְמוֹר שִׁיר־חֲנֻכַּת הַבַּיִת לְדָוִד׃ אֲרוֹמִמְךָ יְהוָה כִּי דִלִּיתָנִי וְלֹא־שִׂמַּחְתָּ אֹיְבַי לִי׃ יום שני
ג ד יְהוָה אֱלֹהָי שִׁוַּעְתִּי אֵלֶיךָ וַתִּרְפָּאֵנִי׃ יְהוָה הֶעֱלִיתָ מִן־שְׁאוֹל נַפְשִׁי חִיִּיתַנִי ה לחודש

10 **The Lord sat enthroned at the flood.** Some commentators say that *mabul*, "the flood," refers to the time when God sat in judgment and sentenced the earth to annihilation. It exemplifies how terrifying God's power can be. Others, however, believe that it is a name for God's throne of judgment. **The Lord sits as King forever,** as builder and creator upon earth, not as its destroyer.

11 **The Lord gives strength to His people,** so that they may be able to praise Him suitably; this requires strength, as the opening verse of the psalm stated. But at the same time, **the Lord will bless His people with peace.** He will grant a double blessing, combining physical strength and power with peace and tranquility.

PSALM 30

PSALMS 30:1–13

A psalm of thanks by one who, at a calm and peaceful period in his life, has suddenly been beset with great distress, a serious illness that has darkened his life. After turning to God in prayer, he regains his health and expresses his gratitude.

30 Monday *5th day of month*

1 **A psalm, a song for the dedication of the house, by David.** "The house" here is generally understood to be the Temple in Jerusalem. However, the text offers thanks for a completely different matter, namely, David's recovery from a grave illness or danger that suddenly befell him. It is possible, then, that he composed this hymn of praise to celebrate his recovery at the dedication of his private dwelling in Jerusalem.

2 **I extol You, Lord, for You lifted me up** out of the depths of despair, infirmity, and weakness, **and did not let my enemies rejoice over me,** gloating at my downfall.

3 **Lord my God, I cried out to You, and You healed me.**

4 **Lord, You lifted up my soul from the grave,** so close was I to death. **You kept me alive, kept me from going down to the pit,** another reference to the grave.

5 In his joy over his recovery, David calls upon others to join him in praising God: **Sing to the Lord, His devoted ones, and give thanks in remembrance of His holy name.**

6 **For His anger is but a moment.** An instant of God's anger can be devastating: Success, and life itself, can end in a heartbeat. But **in His desire, there is life.** If God wills it, a person can live a long, full life. **At night he goes to sleep weeping.** Night represents gloom and despair; it is also a time when sickness intensifies. **In the morning,** however, **there is** relief and optimism, and, in their wake, **joy.**

7 **I had said in my tranquility,** when all was going well for me: **I will never stumble.** I was certain things would remain that way.

8 **Lord, by Your will You put in place mighty mountains,** metaphorically, to obscure Your presence; **You hid Your face, and I was terrified.** When God "hides His face," that is, He withdraws His providence and protection, man is left vulnerable to all the forces of destruction wreaking havoc in the world.

9 In that dire hour, **to You, Lord, I called; I pleaded to my Lord** with the words of one who fears imminent death:

10 **What gain is** there **in** the shedding of **my blood, in my descending into the pit** of the grave, turning there to dust? **Can the dust thank You? Can it declare Your truth?**

11 The psalmist's plea continues: **Hear me, Lord, and be gracious to me; Lord, be my savior.**

12 When help from God does appear, David's prayer turns joyous: **You transformed my mourning** over my dismal fate **into** joyous **dancing; You loosened my sackcloth and girded me with joy.**

13 A person who has survived a near-fatal experience and has once again been given the gift of life knows well how to use this precious gift; it is **so that he may sing unceasing praises of glory to You. Lord my God, I will give thanks to You forever.**

PSALM 31

PSALMS 31:1–25

A psalm of entreaty and gratitude. Apparently written during a period of relative calm, it addresses the psalmist's past trials and fears alongside his present salvation.

31 1 **For the chief musician, a psalm by David.**

2 **In You, Lord, I place my trust,** and therefore I pray: **May I never be put to shame; rescue me in Your righteousness.**

3 **Incline Your ear to me,** to hear my prayer; **make haste to save me** from imminent danger. **Be my rock of refuge, a stronghold to deliver me.**

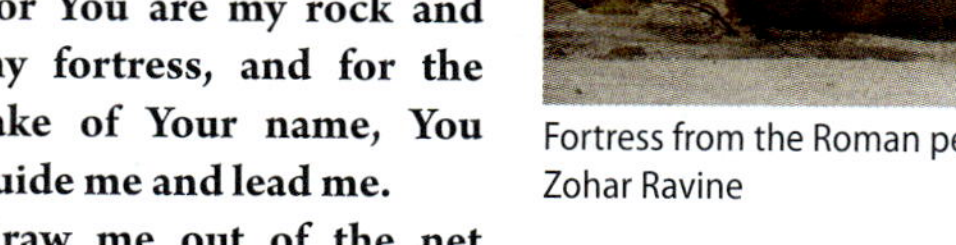

Fortress from the Roman period, Zohar Ravine

4 **For You are my rock and my fortress, and for the sake of Your name, You guide me and lead me.**

5 **Draw me out of the net they laid for me, for You are my stronghold.**

6 **Into Your hand I commit my spirit.** I entrust my life to You, depending on You to guard it. And indeed, **You have redeemed me, Lord, Almighty God of truth.**

7 **I hate those who rely on the vanities of falsehood,** namely, false gods. **As for me, I trust** only **in the Lord.**

8 **I rejoice and am happy in Your kindness, for You have seen my affliction. You have known my soul's distress,**

9 **and** because of this, **You did not deliver me into the hand of the enemy; You planted my feet in open space,** whereas I had previously been in a situation of confinement, as it were, unable to escape my desperate situation.

10 **Be gracious to me, Lord, for I am in distress; my eyes are weakened from vexation,**[B] as are **my soul and my belly.** It seems as if all the parts of my body are unable to function properly because of my distress.

11 **For my life has withered away in anguish and my years in sighing. In my iniquity, my strength has failed; my bones have decayed.**

12 **For all my foes I have become a disgrace,** an object of scorn, **and greatly so for my acquaintances.** I am scorned greatly by my acquaintances as well. **I am an object of dread to my well-wishers,** who fear for my well-being when they witness my deteriorating state. **Those who see me in the street flee from me.** My acquaintances see things in me that cause them to keep their distance. They avoid coming in contact with me because of my ill and miserable appearance.

BACKGROUND

31:10 | **My eyes are weakened from vexation:** It is known that mental stress can adversely affect one's vision, both by weakening the muscles that control the eye's focus and by altering the level of pressure inside the eyeball.

ה ו מיורדי־בור: זַמְּרוּ לַיהוָה חֲסִידָיו וְהוֹדוּ לְזֵכֶר קָדְשׁוֹ: כִּי רֶגַע ׀ בְּאַפּוֹ חַיִּים מִיָּרְדִי־
ז בִּרְצוֹנוֹ בָּעֶרֶב יָלִין בֶּכִי וְלַבֹּקֶר רִנָּה: וַאֲנִי אָמַרְתִּי בְשַׁלְוִי בַּל־אֶמּוֹט לְעוֹלָם:
ח ט יְהוָה בִּרְצוֹנְךָ הֶעֱמַדְתָּה לְהַרְרִי עֹז הִסְתַּרְתָּ פָנֶיךָ הָיִיתִי נִבְהָל: אֵלֶיךָ יְהוָה
י אֶקְרָא וְאֶל־אֲדֹנָי אֶתְחַנָּן: מַה־בֶּצַע בְּדָמִי בְּרִדְתִּי אֶל שָׁחַת הֲיוֹדְךָ עָפָר הֲיַגִּיד
יא יב אֲמִתֶּךָ: שְׁמַע־יְהוָה וְחָנֵּנִי יְהוָה הֱיֵה־עֹזֵר לִי: הָפַכְתָּ מִסְפְּדִי לְמָחוֹל לִי פִּתַּחְתָּ
יג שַׂקִּי וַתְּאַזְּרֵנִי שִׂמְחָה: לְמַעַן ׀ יְזַמֶּרְךָ כָבוֹד וְלֹא יִדֹּם יְהוָה אֱלֹהַי לְעוֹלָם אוֹדֶךָּ:
לא א ב לַמְנַצֵּחַ מִזְמוֹר לְדָוִד: בְּךָ־יְהוָה חָסִיתִי אַל־אֵבוֹשָׁה לְעוֹלָם בְּצִדְקָתְךָ פַלְּטֵנִי:
ג הַטֵּה אֵלַי ׀ אָזְנְךָ מְהֵרָה הַצִּילֵנִי הֱיֵה לִי ׀ לְצוּר־מָעוֹז לְבֵית מְצוּדוֹת לְהוֹשִׁיעֵנִי:
ד ה כִּי־סַלְעִי וּמְצוּדָתִי אָתָּה וּלְמַעַן שִׁמְךָ תַּנְחֵנִי וּתְנַהֲלֵנִי: תּוֹצִיאֵנִי מֵרֶשֶׁת זוּ טָמְנוּ
ו ז לִי כִּי־אַתָּה מָעוּזִּי: בְּיָדְךָ אַפְקִיד רוּחִי פָּדִיתָה אוֹתִי יְהוָה אֵל אֱמֶת: שָׂנֵאתִי
ח הַשֹּׁמְרִים הַבְלֵי־שָׁוְא וַאֲנִי אֶל־יְהוָה בָּטָחְתִּי: אָגִילָה וְאֶשְׂמְחָה בְּחַסְדֶּךָ אֲשֶׁר
ט רָאִיתָ אֶת־עָנְיִי יָדַעְתָּ בְּצָרוֹת נַפְשִׁי: וְלֹא הִסְגַּרְתַּנִי בְּיַד־אוֹיֵב הֶעֱמַדְתָּ בַמֶּרְחָב
י יא רַגְלָי: חָנֵּנִי יְהוָה כִּי צַר לִי עָשְׁשָׁה בְכַעַס עֵינִי נַפְשִׁי וּבִטְנִי: כִּי כָלוּ בְיָגוֹן חַיַּי וּשְׁנוֹתַי
יב בַּאֲנָחָה כָּשַׁל בַּעֲוֺנִי כֹחִי וַעֲצָמַי עָשֵׁשׁוּ: מִכָּל־צֹרְרַי הָיִיתִי חֶרְפָּה וְלִשְׁכֵנַי ׀ מְאֹד
יג יד וּפַחַד לִמְיֻדָּעָי רֹאַי בַּחוּץ נָדְדוּ מִמֶּנִּי: נִשְׁכַּחְתִּי כְּמֵת מִלֵּב הָיִיתִי כִּכְלִי אֹבֵד: כִּי
טו שָׁמַעְתִּי ׀ דִּבַּת רַבִּים מָגוֹר מִסָּבִיב בְּהִוָּסְדָם יַחַד עָלַי לָקַחַת נַפְשִׁי זָמָמוּ: וַאֲנִי ׀
טז עָלֶיךָ בָטַחְתִּי יְהוָה אָמַרְתִּי אֱלֹהַי אָתָּה: בְּיָדְךָ עִתֹּתָי הַצִּילֵנִי מִיַּד־אוֹיְבַי וּמֵרֹדְפָי:
יז יח הָאִירָה פָנֶיךָ עַל־עַבְדֶּךָ הוֹשִׁיעֵנִי בְחַסְדֶּךָ: יְהוָה אַל־אֵבוֹשָׁה כִּי קְרָאתִיךָ יֵבֹשׁוּ

13 **I am forgotten from men's hearts as a dead man,** whose memory fades away with time. **I am** forgotten **like a discarded tool.**

14 **For I have heard the slander of many. There is** nothing but **terror all around** me; **they have gathered together, scheming to take my life.**

15 **But as for me, I trust** only **in You, Lord. I say: You are my God.**

16 **My fate is in Your hand.** *Itotai,* literally "my times," denotes my life or my fate. **Save me from my enemies and from those who pursue me.**

17 **Shine Your countenance upon Your servant; deliver me in Your kindness.**

18 **Lord, let me not be shamed, for I have called upon You. Let** it be **the wicked** who will **be shamed; let them go silent to the grave.**

19 **Mute the lying lips that speak falsehood against the righteous with arrogance and contempt.**

20 The psalmist now turns from decrying the wicked to extolling the righteous and the salvation destined for them: **How great is the goodness You have in store for those who fear You.** They will be the beneficiaries of Your hidden gifts, which have not yet been bestowed upon man and **which You have created for those taking refuge in You, to be bestowed openly.**

21 **Conceal them in the secret place of Your presence; shelter them from man's intrigues in Your pavilion, away from the strife of** the slanderous **tongues** that are aimed against them.

22 **Blessed is the Lord, for He showed me wondrous kindness in a besieged city,** referring to either a literal or figurative siege.

23 **I had said in my anxious haste** while I was in distress: **I am cut off from Your view,** and You are no longer concerned about me. **But,** in fact, **You heard the voice of my pleas when I cried out to You.**

24 **Love the Lord, all His devoted ones,** for **the Lord is faithful** to reward those who trust in Him, **and He requites the arrogant with the bowstring,** punishing them with His arrows, as it were.

25 In conclusion, the psalmist proclaims: **Be strong and let your hearts take courage, all of you who put your hope in the Lord.** This verse can be seen not only as sound advice, but as a summation of the psalm. Evoking his own life experience as evidence, the psalmist concludes that God comes to the aid of those who rely on Him.

PSALM 32

A contemplative psalm that requests God's forgiveness and expresses hope for salvation.

PSALMS 32:1–11

32 1 **A contemplation, by David.** The word *maskil*, translated here as a "contemplation," apparently describes a type of psalm that is primarily introspective in nature, thoughts to be pondered rather than a psalm of prayer. Some commentators, however, suggest that *maskil* refers to the name of a particular melody. **Happy is he whose crime is forgiven, whose sin is pardoned.** The phrase *kesuy ḥata'a*, translated here as "whose sin is pardoned," literally means "who is covered up from sin"; it is as if he is protected from any connection with sin.

2 **Happy is the man in whom the Lord sees no iniquity and in whose spirit there is no deceit.** The psalmist admits: I do not always feel that I have attained the spiritual height of being without iniquity, but at least I honestly try to achieve repentance.

3 His sins have caused him physical suffering: **When I kept silent, my bones wasted away; so too when I roared** in prayer **throughout the day.** Whether I am silent or I cry out in prayer, my suffering does not abate.

4 **For day and night Your hand weighed upon me.** As I endured painful experiences and physical punishments, I felt as if a heavy hand was putting pressure on me. **My moisture,** my vitality, **has left me as if by summer heat, Selah.**

"My moisture has left me as if by summer heat." Parched land in the Negev

5 **I acknowledged my sin to You; I did not hide my iniquity. I said: I will confess my transgressions to the Lord. And You forgave the guilt of my sin, Selah.**

6 **Therefore, everyone who is devoted to You should pray at the time of searching,** in times of crisis or when he is at a crossroads in life, **so the torrent of mighty waters does not reach him,** so that he does not end up in a situation where he is drowning, as it were, in a torrent of surging water, hopelessly overwhelmed by troubles.

7 **You are my hiding place; protect me from enemies. Surround me with songs of deliverance** and gratitude, which will come in the wake of Your salvation, **Selah.**

8 In this next verse, the psalmist quotes what would be God's response to him: **I will instruct you and direct you in the path you should take. I will advise you,** as **My eye is upon you.**

9 This verse, shifting from singular to plural, is directed not just to the psalmist, but to all people: **Do not be like a horse or a mule,**[B] who, as mere animals, are **without understanding, whose wildness must be restrained with bit and bridle lest it approach you** and injure you.

Horse with a bridle

10 In summation: **There are many maladies for the wicked, but one trusting in the Lord is enveloped in kindness.**

11 **Rejoice in the Lord and be glad, you righteous ones; sing out with joy, all you whose hearts are upright.**

יט רְשָׁעִים יִדְּמוּ לִשְׁאוֹל׃ תֵּאָלַמְנָה שִׂפְתֵי שָׁקֶר הַדֹּבְרוֹת עַל־צַדִּיק עָתָק בְּגַאֲוָה
כ וָבוּז׃ מָה רַב טוּבְךָ אֲשֶׁר־צָפַנְתָּ לִּירֵאֶיךָ פָּעַלְתָּ לַחוֹסִים בָּךְ נֶגֶד בְּנֵי אָדָם׃
כא כב תַּסְתִּירֵם ׀ בְּסֵתֶר פָּנֶיךָ מֵרֻכְסֵי אִישׁ תִּצְפְּנֵם בְּסֻכָּה מֵרִיב לְשֹׁנוֹת׃ בָּרוּךְ יְהוָה
כג כִּי הִפְלִיא חַסְדּוֹ לִי בְּעִיר מָצוֹר׃ וַאֲנִי ׀ אָמַרְתִּי בְחָפְזִי נִגְרַזְתִּי מִנֶּגֶד עֵינֶיךָ אָכֵן
כד שָׁמַעְתָּ קוֹל תַּחֲנוּנַי בְּשַׁוְּעִי אֵלֶיךָ׃ אֶהֱבוּ אֶת־יְהוָה כָּל־חֲסִידָיו אֱמוּנִים נֹצֵר
כה יְהוָה וּמְשַׁלֵּם עַל־יֶתֶר עֹשֵׂה גַאֲוָה׃ חִזְקוּ וְיַאֲמֵץ לְבַבְכֶם כָּל־הַמְיַחֲלִים לַיהוָה׃
לב א ב לְדָוִד מַשְׂכִּיל אַשְׁרֵי נְשׂוּי־פֶּשַׁע כְּסוּי חֲטָאָה׃ אַשְׁרֵי־אָדָם לֹא יַחְשֹׁב יְהוָה לוֹ
ג ד עָוֺן וְאֵין בְּרוּחוֹ רְמִיָּה׃ כִּי־הֶחֱרַשְׁתִּי בָּלוּ עֲצָמָי בְּשַׁאֲגָתִי כָּל־הַיּוֹם׃ כִּי ׀ יוֹמָם
ה וָלַיְלָה תִּכְבַּד עָלַי יָדֶךָ נֶהְפַּךְ לְשַׁדִּי בְּחַרְבֹנֵי קַיִץ סֶלָה׃ חַטָּאתִי אוֹדִיעֲךָ וַעֲוֺנִי
לֹא־כִסִּיתִי אָמַרְתִּי אוֹדֶה עֲלֵי פְשָׁעַי לַיהוָה וְאַתָּה נָשָׂאתָ עֲוֺן חַטָּאתִי סֶלָה׃
ו עַל־זֹאת יִתְפַּלֵּל כָּל־חָסִיד ׀ אֵלֶיךָ לְעֵת מְצֹא רַק לְשֵׁטֶף מַיִם רַבִּים אֵלָיו לֹא
ז ח יַגִּיעוּ׃ אַתָּה ׀ סֵתֶר לִי מִצַּר תִּצְּרֵנִי רָנֵּי פַלֵּט תְּסוֹבְבֵנִי סֶלָה׃ אַשְׂכִּילְךָ ׀ וְאוֹרְךָ
ט בְּדֶרֶךְ־זוּ תֵלֵךְ אִיעֲצָה עָלֶיךָ עֵינִי׃ אַל־תִּהְיוּ ׀ כְּסוּס כְּפֶרֶד אֵין הָבִין בְּמֶתֶג־
י וָרֶסֶן עֶדְיוֹ לִבְלוֹם בַּל קְרֹב אֵלֶיךָ׃ רַבִּים מַכְאוֹבִים לָרָשָׁע וְהַבּוֹטֵחַ בַּיהוָה חֶסֶד
יא יְסוֹבְבֶנּוּ׃ שִׂמְחוּ בַיהוָה וְגִילוּ צַדִּיקִים וְהַרְנִינוּ כָּל־יִשְׁרֵי־לֵב׃

BACKGROUND

32:9 | **Like a horse or a mule:** Alongside the donkey, these animals were the main beasts used for transportation of people and goods in biblical times. In order to adapt them for pulling wagons or for riding, certain technical tools were necessary. Bridles and bits were placed on their heads and in their mouths for purposes of controlling their motion and speed. Horses and mules are mentioned specifically because they are usually used to pull wagons. Therefore, their response to bodily or oral signals on the part of the driver is somewhat diminished from that of a donkey, as the driver sitting on the wagon would be further removed from the animal's head.

PSALM 33

PSALMS 33:1–22

A psalm in praise of the greatness of God. Although it contains some instructive material, it focuses on God's beneficence on behalf of the world in general and humanity in particular.

33 1 **Rejoice in the Lord, righteous ones; it is comely for the upright to offer praise.**
2 **Give thanks to the Lord with the lyre; sing praises to Him
with a ten-stringed harp.**[B]
3 **Sing Him a new song.** It is
a greater tribute to God to
sing new songs and praises
than it is to repeat tributes
that have been sung before.
**Play beautifully with loud
sound.** The word *terua,*
translated as "loud sound,"
usually refers to music made
with a trumpet or horn.
4 And this is the song they
should sing: **For the word
of the Lord is upright,
all His deeds faithfully
wrought.** God's deeds are
characterized as "upright"
and "faithful," and these are
also attributes He seeks in
the world.

Krar, an African instrument similar to the biblical lyre

5 **He loves righteousness and justice; the Lord's kindness fills
the world.** The entire world is an expression of God's beneficence and generosity. From this we can learn that God values
these qualities in us as well.
6 **By the word of the Lord were the heavens made; by the
breath of His mouth, all their hosts.**
7 **He heaps together the waters of the sea, storing in vaults
the waters of the deep.** God has designated special places for
the concentrations of water found beneath the earth.
8 **Let the entire world be in awe of the Lord; let all earth's inhabitants fear Him** as they contemplate His immense power
in creation.
9 **For He spoke and it was done.** The world's creation was accomplished through God's mere utterance. **He commanded,
and it,** referring to everything created in the world, **took form.**
10 God's power manifests itself in creation in general, but particularly in His interaction with humanity: **The Lord overturns
the counsel of nations, annuls the schemes of peoples.**
11 In contrast to the futility of man's grand designs: **The Lord's
counsel endures forever; the plans of His heart** remain **for
all generations.**
12 But God not only created the world; He also chose a particular people to be His: **Happy is the nation whose God is the
Lord, the people whom He chose as His possession.**
13 **The Lord looks from heaven; He sees all mankind.**
14 **From His dwelling place** in the heavens, **He observes all the
inhabitants of the earth,**
15 **He who fashions all their hearts,** and **who** consequently **understands all their deeds.**
16 Since God observes and controls everything, it follows that all
outcomes are determined by Him: **The king is not saved by**
the fact that he has **a mighty army** at his disposal, and **the warrior** is **not rescued by** virtue of his **great strength.**
17 In ancient times, armies relied on horses and chariots both for
defense and for attack. But **a horse is false hope for victory**
if God does not will it, and **even in its great power, it cannot
offer escape.**
18 If not on horses and chariots, on what can one rely? **Truly, the
eye of the Lord is on those who fear Him, on those who
await His kindness**
19 **to deliver them from death** in battle, **to sustain them in
famine.**
20 **Our soul longs for the Lord; He is our help and our shield.**
21 **For our heart rejoices in Him, for we trust in His holy name**
that He will come to our aid.
22 The psalm ends with a request: **Let Your kindness, Lord, be
upon us, as we have put our hope in You.**

PSALM 34

PSALMS 34:1–23

A psalm relating to a specific incident in King David's life. Its verses are arranged alphabetically.

34 1 **By David, when he feigned madness**[D] **before Avimelekh,
who drove him away; and he left.** When David fled from
Saul, he found himself approaching the territory of Avimelekh
king of the Philistines. Fearing that the Philistines would murder him in revenge for the many battles he had waged against
them, David pretended to be mad, since madmen are generally
regarded as being harmless. The ruse succeeded; David was not
attacked, but rather was banished from Avimelekh's kingdom.[7]
There is no obvious connection between the content of this
psalm and the encounter with Avimelekh.
2 **I will bless the Lord at all times,** in times of glory and redemption as well as sorrow and trouble. **His praise will always**

לג א ב רַנְּנוּ צַדִּיקִים בַּיהוָה לַיְשָׁרִים נָאוָה תְהִלָּה: הוֹדוּ לַיהוָה בְּכִנּוֹר בְּנֵבֶל עָשׂוֹר
ג ד זַמְּרוּ־לוֹ: שִׁירוּ־לוֹ שִׁיר חָדָשׁ הֵיטִיבוּ נַגֵּן בִּתְרוּעָה: כִּי־יָשָׁר דְּבַר־יְהוָה וְכָל־
ה ו מַעֲשֵׂהוּ בֶּאֱמוּנָה: אֹהֵב צְדָקָה וּמִשְׁפָּט חֶסֶד יְהוָה מָלְאָה הָאָרֶץ: בִּדְבַר יְהוָה
ז שָׁמַיִם נַעֲשׂוּ וּבְרוּחַ פִּיו כָּל־צְבָאָם: כֹּנֵס כַּנֵּד מֵי הַיָּם נֹתֵן בְּאוֹצָרוֹת תְּהוֹמוֹת:
ח ט יִירְאוּ מֵיְהוָה כָּל־הָאָרֶץ מִמֶּנּוּ יָגוּרוּ כָּל־יֹשְׁבֵי תֵבֵל: כִּי הוּא אָמַר וַיֶּהִי הוּא־צִוָּה
י יא וַיַּעֲמֹד: יְהוָה הֵפִיר עֲצַת־גּוֹיִם הֵנִיא מַחְשְׁבוֹת עַמִּים: עֲצַת יְהוָה לְעוֹלָם תַּעֲמֹד
יב מַחְשְׁבוֹת לִבּוֹ לְדֹר וָדֹר: אַשְׁרֵי הַגּוֹי אֲשֶׁר־יְהוָה אֱלֹהָיו הָעָם | בָּחַר לְנַחֲלָה לוֹ:
יג יד מִשָּׁמַיִם הִבִּיט יְהוָה רָאָה אֶת־כָּל־בְּנֵי הָאָדָם: מִמְּכוֹן־שִׁבְתּוֹ הִשְׁגִּיחַ אֶל כָּל־יֹשְׁבֵי
טו טז הָאָרֶץ: הַיֹּצֵר יַחַד לִבָּם הַמֵּבִין אֶל־כָּל־מַעֲשֵׂיהֶם: אֵין־הַמֶּלֶךְ נוֹשָׁע בְּרָב־חָיִל
יז יח גִּבּוֹר לֹא־יִנָּצֵל בְּרָב־כֹּחַ: שֶׁקֶר הַסּוּס לִתְשׁוּעָה וּבְרֹב חֵילוֹ לֹא יְמַלֵּט: הִנֵּה עֵין
יט כ יְהוָה אֶל־יְרֵאָיו לַמְיַחֲלִים לְחַסְדּוֹ: לְהַצִּיל מִמָּוֶת נַפְשָׁם וּלְחַיּוֹתָם בָּרָעָב: נַפְשֵׁנוּ
כא חִכְּתָה לַיהוָה עֶזְרֵנוּ וּמָגִנֵּנוּ הוּא: כִּי־בוֹ יִשְׂמַח לִבֵּנוּ כִּי בְשֵׁם קָדְשׁוֹ בָטָחְנוּ:
כב יְהִי־חַסְדְּךָ יְהוָה עָלֵינוּ כַּאֲשֶׁר יִחַלְנוּ לָךְ:
לד א ב לְדָוִד בְּשַׁנּוֹתוֹ אֶת־טַעְמוֹ לִפְנֵי אֲבִימֶלֶךְ וַיְגָרְשֵׁהוּ וַיֵּלַךְ: אֲבָרְכָה אֶת־יְהוָה

BACKGROUND

33:2 | **With the lyre…with a ten-stringed harp:** The two main stringed instruments that were played before the ark in David's day, and later in the Temple, were the lyre and the harp. The lyre, a symmetrically shaped instrument, had horns fixed to the two sides of its wooden base, with the ends of the horns fastened to each other with a rod. From this upper rod strings were stretched onto the thick wooden base. Over time the horns were exchanged for wooden pieces, but the general shape of the instrument was preserved. The number of strings on the lyre varied from one instrument to another, ranging from three to ten.

The harp [*nevel*], by contrast, was nonsymmetrical, in the form of a bow or angled pieces of wood, with the strings stretched from one end of the bow or angle to the other. Its general shape was reminiscent of a long-necked wine flask, also called *nevel*, normally held in the hand. The ten-stringed harp had at least ten strings, as its name implies, but there were harps that had as many as fifteen. Such large harps were stationary (see Radak; Ibn Ezra).

DISCUSSION

34:1 | **By David, when he feigned madness:** The theme of this psalm is God's special providence and protection for the righteous; this may be the connection between the content of the psalm and the historical event mentioned in its heading (see Malbim). David may have written the psalm, which is didactic rather than emotive in tone, in order to demonstrate that he was indeed rational and in full control of his faculties. It is also possible that the alphabetical acrostic is employed as additional evidence that, despite his feigning madness, David was capable of clearly ordered thinking.

be in my mouth. External circumstances, be they good or bad, will not interfere with the psalmist's continual blessing of God.

3 **I will have glory in the Lord.** Here the psalmist explains how he is able to praise God at all times. If he dwells on his own problems, he is liable to feel anguish and doubt. But by thinking about God, he invariably comes to an awareness of God's greatness and glory, which are eternally present. **The humble will hear and rejoice.** The ability to praise God is unrelated to the state of man's glory; it is about the glory of God Himself. Even the humble, who regard themselves as unworthy, are able to rejoice and to sing God's praises.

4 Consequently, the psalmist calls on everyone to extol God: **Declare the greatness of the Lord with me; let us exalt His name together.**

5 **I sought the Lord and He answered me; He delivered me from all the things I dreaded.**

6 **Those who look to Him are illuminated, and their faces will never be ashamed.** The centrality of God's presence in their lives is a primary source of blessing and strength.

7 In addition, the psalmist affirms that God listens to them and comes to their aid: **A poor man cried out, and the Lord heard him and saved him from all his troubles.**

8 God's salvation is not always noticed by its beneficiary, but **the angel of the Lord encamps around those who fear Him, and rescues** and protects **them.**

9 **Taste and see that the Lord is good.** In order to come close to God, one needs to experience, or "taste," Him on some level so as to appreciate that "the Lord is good." **Happy is the man who takes refuge in Him.** Closeness to God, in and of itself, is the essence of good fortune, even when it is not rewarded by material gain.

10 Nonetheless, the psalmist offers assurance that closeness to God does bring tangible reward: **Fear the Lord, His holy ones,** those who dedicate themselves to serving Him. **For those who fear Him** are under His protection, and He sees to it that they **lack nothing.**

11 Even **young lions,** at the height of their physical power, **may** at times **suffer from want and hunger** for lack of prey. **But those who seek the Lord,** though they do not have the physical strength of lions, **will lack no good,** as God will see to it that their needs are met.

12 The psalmist continues with words of advice: **Come, children, listen to me; I will teach you to fear the Lord.** The following verses, addressed to students or young people, do not supply practical instruction for material success but are intended to define the proper behavior of God-fearing people.

13 **Who is the man who desires life, loving his days** of his life in order **to see good** during his lifetime?

14 Advice for such a person: **Guard your tongue from evil;** refrain from speaking derogatively, using coarse language, or shouting in anger even if you are justifiably upset, **and** guard **your lips from speaking** any words of **deceit.**

15 **Turn away from evil.** It is not always necessary to confront evil and fight against it; it is better to avoid contact with it from the outset. **And do good.** Actively pursuing good deeds is preferable to fighting off negative influences. In your dealings with other people, **seek peace,** for there is usually a way to resolve differences peacefully, **and pursue it.** Sometimes the peaceful approach is not the convenient one, and it is necessary to go out of one's way to actively pursue it.

16 The psalmist now speaks of promises made by God to the righteous: **The eyes of the Lord are on the righteous,** as He watches over them, never abandoning them, **and His ears are open to their cry.**

17 **The face of the Lord,** displaying His anger, **turns against evildoers.** He also attends to those who do evil; He does not allow their evil schemes to succeed, but turns **to excise their memory from the earth.**

18 **They,** the righteous, **cry out, and the Lord hears them, delivering them from all their troubles.**

19 God does not limit His attention to well-known righteous and God-fearing individuals; He also hearkens to the cries of the humblest and most downtrodden people: **The Lord is near to the** people whose suffering is so intense that they are **brokenhearted, and** He **saves those whose spirit is crushed.**

20 **Many evils may afflict a righteous man, but** ultimately **the Lord delivers him from them all.**

21 Even if the righteous man may fall, **He preserves all his bones** and ensures that **not one of them will be broken,** so extensive is God's protection of him.

22 **Evil causes the death of the wicked.** This is not necessarily referring to divine punishment; rather, evil by its very nature is essentially noxious and deadly. **And those who hate the righteous will be condemned** to failure and destroyed by their own actions.

DISCUSSION

35:3 | **Unsheathe [*veharek*] a spear:** This expression, which literally means "empty the spear" and which appears in the Torah as well (Exodus 15:9; Leviticus 26:33), is a picturesque term referring to a scabbard. This sheath of a spear or sword is left empty due to the frequent use of the weapon.

בְּכׇל־עֵת תָּמִיד תְּהִלָּתוֹ בְּפִי׃ בַּיהוה תִּתְהַלֵּל נַפְשִׁי יִשְׁמְעוּ עֲנָוִים וְיִשְׂמָחוּ׃ גַּדְּלוּ ג ד
לַיהוה אִתִּי וּנְרוֹמְמָה שְׁמוֹ יַחְדָּו׃ דָּרַשְׁתִּי אֶת־יהוה וְעָנָנִי וּמִכׇּל־מְגוּרוֹתַי הִצִּילָנִי׃ ה
הִבִּיטוּ אֵלָיו וְנָהָרוּ וּפְנֵיהֶם אַל־יֶחְפָּרוּ׃ זֶה עָנִי קָרָא וַיהוה שָׁמֵעַ וּמִכׇּל־צָרוֹתָיו ו ז
הוֹשִׁיעוֹ׃ חֹנֶה מַלְאַךְ־יהוה סָבִיב לִירֵאָיו וַיְחַלְּצֵם׃ טַעֲמוּ וּרְאוּ כִּי־טוֹב יהוה ח ט
אַשְׁרֵי הַגֶּבֶר יֶחֱסֶה־בּוֹ׃ יְראוּ אֶת־יהוה קְדֹשָׁיו כִּי־אֵין מַחְסוֹר לִירֵאָיו׃ כְּפִירִים י יא
רָשׁוּ וְרָעֵבוּ וְדֹרְשֵׁי יהוה לֹא־יַחְסְרוּ כׇל־טוֹב׃ לְכוּ־בָנִים שִׁמְעוּ־לִי יִרְאַת יהוה יב
אֲלַמֶּדְכֶם׃ מִי־הָאִישׁ הֶחָפֵץ חַיִּים אֹהֵב יָמִים לִרְאוֹת טוֹב׃ נְצֹר לְשׁוֹנְךָ מֵרָע יג יד
וּשְׂפָתֶיךָ מִדַּבֵּר מִרְמָה׃ סוּר מֵרָע וַעֲשֵׂה־טוֹב בַּקֵּשׁ שָׁלוֹם וְרׇדְפֵהוּ׃ עֵינֵי יהוה טו טז
אֶל־צַדִּיקִים וְאׇזְנָיו אֶל־שַׁוְעָתָם׃ פְּנֵי יהוה בְּעֹשֵׂי רָע לְהַכְרִית מֵאֶרֶץ זִכְרָם׃ יז
צָעֲקוּ וַיהוה שָׁמֵעַ וּמִכׇּל־צָרוֹתָם הִצִּילָם׃ קָרוֹב יהוה לְנִשְׁבְּרֵי־לֵב וְאֶת־דַּכְּאֵי־ יח יט
רוּחַ יוֹשִׁיעַ׃ רַבּוֹת רָעוֹת צַדִּיק וּמִכֻּלָּם יַצִּילֶנּוּ יהוה׃ שֹׁמֵר כׇּל־עַצְמוֹתָיו אַחַת כ כא
מֵהֵנָּה לֹא נִשְׁבָּרָה׃ תְּמוֹתֵת רָשָׁע רָעָה וְשֹׂנְאֵי צַדִּיק יֶאְשָׁמוּ׃ פּוֹדֶה יהוה נֶפֶשׁ כב כג
עֲבָדָיו וְלֹא יֶאְשְׁמוּ כׇּל־הַחֹסִים בּוֹ׃

ו לחודש לְדָוִד ׀ רִיבָה יהוה אֶת־יְרִיבַי לְחַם אֶת־לֹחֲמָי׃ הַחֲזֵק מָגֵן וְצִנָּה וְקוּמָה בְּעֶזְרָתִי׃ לה א ב
וְהָרֵק חֲנִית וּסְגֹר לִקְרַאת רֹדְפָי אֱמֹר לְנַפְשִׁי יְשֻׁעָתֵךְ אָנִי׃ יֵבֹשׁוּ וְיִכָּלְמוּ מְבַקְשֵׁי ג ד

23 This last verse, beginning with the letter *peh*, the significance of which is explained in the introduction to Psalm 25, is connected to the previous verse. In contrast to the fate of the evildoers, whom God abandons to the natural consequences of their sinful deeds, **the Lord redeems the souls of His servants,** sparing them from harm emanating from themselves or from others, **and none are condemned who take refuge in Him.**

PSALM 35

A psalm of prayer in which the psalmist beseeches God to actively protect and defend him against his many enemies.

PSALMS 35:1–28

35 *6th day of month*

1 **By David. Strive, Lord, against my rivals. Fight on my behalf.**
2 **Take hold of shield and armor and rise up to help me,**
3 **and unsheathe a spear**[D] **to block my pursuers; say to me: I am your salvation.**
4 **Let those who seek my life be ashamed and dishonored; may those devising evil against me be turned back and humiliated.**

5 **Let them be like chaff in the wind, with an angel of the Lord scattering them.**

6 **Let their way be dark and slippery,** two factors likely to cause one to lose his footing and fall, **with an angel of the Lord pursuing them.**

Chaff blowing away in the wind

7 **For without cause they have hidden ditches and nets against me** with which to trap me; **without cause they have dug pits for** the purpose of harming me or taking **my soul.**

8 **Let calamity come upon him,** upon my enemy, **unawares,** without him even understanding what it was that brought him down. **Let the net that he laid** for me **ensnare him** instead. **Let him plunge into that very calamity** that he had planned for me.

9 **As for me, I will rejoice in the Lord, happy in His salvation.**

10 **All my bones will say,** my entire body, as it were, will join with my mouth in praising God: **Lord, who is like You, who delivers the poor from those who are stronger, the poor and the needy from their despoiler?**

11 The psalmist describes some of the evil plans his enemies have employed against him: **Malicious,** false **witnesses arise** to accuse me, **asking me concerning things about which I know nothing** and imputing to me baseless claims.

12 What hurts most is that some of my accusers are people whom I used to help in their times of need. **They repay me evil for good, causing me grief.**

13 **Whereas I, when they were sick,** felt genuine sympathy for them; **my garb was sackcloth** as an expression of my distress over their troubles, and **I afflicted my soul in fasting. But my prayer returned to my breast.** They did not appreciate my commiseration and actions on their behalf; to them it was as though my prayers were being uttered for myself.

14 **As if with a beloved friend or brother I walked along** with them, sharing their burden, **bowed in gloom, as if grieving for** a deceased **mother.**

15 **But,** in marked contrast, **when I was limping** and hurting, **they rejoiced and gathered together** to gloat and to taunt me. **My attackers congregated without my knowing** what caused them to turn against me, **tearing at me,** at my clothing and my flesh, **without pause.**

16 **In their hypocrisy they made contemptuous gestures; they gnashed their teeth at me** in derision and enmity.

17 In the face of such hatred, the psalmist prays to God: **My Lord, how long will You look on** without coming to my aid? **Rescue me from their ravages** that they have schemed for me; **save my soul from** these enemies, who are ferocious like **young lions.**

18 After You heed my prayer and save me, **I will thank You in a great assembly,** and **I will praise You among a mighty throng.**

19 **Do not allow my false enemies,** enemies who had pretended to be my friends, **to gloat over me, or those who hate me without cause,** people with no reason to hate me, who therefore remained unsuspected by me, **to wink with their eyes** toward me in contempt.

20 **For they do not speak of peace** toward me; **they devise deceitful plans against those living serenely in the land,** who harbor no malice toward anyone.

21 And when they believe that they have witnessed my downfall, **they** mockingly **open their mouths wide against me, saying: Hurrah, hurrah! Our eyes have** finally **seen it,** his defeat.

22 **You have seen this, Lord; do not keep silent. Lord, do not be far from me.**

23 **Be bestirred and awaken to** do **justice for me; my God and my Lord,** come **to** aid me in **my struggle.**

24 **Vindicate me, Lord my God, as befits Your righteousness; do not let them rejoice over me.**

25 **Do not let them say in their heart: Hurrah for us,** for he has finally fallen! **Do not let them say: We have devoured** and destroyed **him.**

26 **May those who rejoice at my distress be altogether ashamed and humiliated; may those who glorify themselves about me,** about my misfortune, **be clothed in shame and dishonor.**

27 The psalmist ends on a positive note: **May those who desire my vindication sing out and rejoice, always saying: Great is the Lord who delights in the well-being of His servant** and has therefore granted him salvation.

28 **And** then **my tongue will utter Your righteousness,** and **Your praises all day long.**

DISCUSSION

36:1 | **By David servant of the Lord:** The unique phrasing of this introductory verse, "David servant of the Lord," is an expression of David's love and fear of God. Although the psalm addresses issues that are relevant to people in general, its personal expressions of devotion are based on the psalmist's life experience. Indeed, the expressions of closeness to God and love for Him in the psalm are striking.

ה נַפְשִׁי יִסֹּגוּ אָחוֹר וְיַחְפְּרוּ חֹשְׁבֵי רָעָתִי: יִהְיוּ כְּמֹץ לִפְנֵי־רוּחַ וּמַלְאַךְ יְהוָה דּוֹחֶה:
ו ז יְהִי־דַרְכָּם חֹשֶׁךְ וַחֲלַקְלַקֹּת וּמַלְאַךְ יְהוָה רֹדְפָם: כִּי־חִנָּם טָמְנוּ־לִי שַׁחַת רִשְׁתָּם
ח חִנָּם חָפְרוּ לְנַפְשִׁי: תְּבוֹאֵהוּ שׁוֹאָה לֹא־יֵדָע וְרִשְׁתּוֹ אֲשֶׁר־טָמַן תִּלְכְּדוֹ בְּשׁוֹאָה
ט י יִפָּל־בָּהּ: וְנַפְשִׁי תָּגִיל בַּיהוָה תָּשִׂישׂ בִּישׁוּעָתוֹ: כָּל עַצְמוֹתַי ׀ תֹּאמַרְנָה יְהוָה מִי
יא כָמוֹךָ מַצִּיל עָנִי מֵחָזָק מִמֶּנּוּ וְעָנִי וְאֶבְיוֹן מִגֹּזְלוֹ: יְקוּמוּן עֵדֵי חָמָס אֲשֶׁר לֹא־
יב יג יָדַעְתִּי יִשְׁאָלוּנִי: יְשַׁלְּמוּנִי רָעָה תַּחַת טוֹבָה שְׁכוֹל לְנַפְשִׁי: וַאֲנִי ׀ בַּחֲלוֹתָם לְבוּשִׁי
יד שָׂק עִנֵּיתִי בַצּוֹם נַפְשִׁי וּתְפִלָּתִי עַל־חֵיקִי תָשׁוּב: כְּרֵעַ־כְּאָח לִי הִתְהַלָּכְתִּי
טו כַּאֲבֶל־אֵם קֹדֵר שַׁחוֹתִי: וּבְצַלְעִי שָׂמְחוּ וְנֶאֱסָפוּ נֶאֶסְפוּ עָלַי נֵכִים וְלֹא יָדַעְתִּי
טז יז קָרְעוּ וְלֹא־דָמּוּ: בְּחַנְפֵי לַעֲגֵי מָעוֹג חָרֹק עָלַי שִׁנֵּימוֹ: אֲדֹנָי כַּמָּה תִּרְאֶה הָשִׁיבָה
יח יט נַפְשִׁי מִשֹּׁאֵיהֶם מִכְּפִירִים יְחִידָתִי: אוֹדְךָ בְּקָהָל רָב בְּעַם עָצוּם אֲהַלְלֶךָּ: אַל־
כ יִשְׂמְחוּ־לִי אֹיְבַי שֶׁקֶר שֹׂנְאַי חִנָּם יִקְרְצוּ־עָיִן: כִּי לֹא שָׁלוֹם יְדַבֵּרוּ וְעַל רִגְעֵי־אֶרֶץ
כא דִּבְרֵי מִרְמוֹת יַחֲשֹׁבוּן: וַיַּרְחִיבוּ עָלַי פִּיהֶם אָמְרוּ הֶאָח ׀ הֶאָח רָאֲתָה עֵינֵינוּ:
כב כג רָאִיתָה יְהוָה אַל־תֶּחֱרַשׁ אֲדֹנָי אַל־תִּרְחַק מִמֶּנִּי: הָעִירָה וְהָקִיצָה לְמִשְׁפָּטִי
כד כה אֱלֹהַי וַאדֹנָי לְרִיבִי: שָׁפְטֵנִי כְצִדְקְךָ יְהוָה אֱלֹהָי וְאַל־יִשְׂמְחוּ־לִי: אַל־יֹאמְרוּ
כו בְלִבָּם הֶאָח נַפְשֵׁנוּ אַל־יֹאמְרוּ בִּלַּעֲנוּהוּ: יֵבֹשׁוּ וְיַחְפְּרוּ ׀ יַחְדָּו שְׂמֵחֵי רָעָתִי
כז יִלְבְּשׁוּ־בֹשֶׁת וּכְלִמָּה הַמַּגְדִּילִים עָלָי: יָרֹנּוּ וְיִשְׂמְחוּ חֲפֵצֵי צִדְקִי וְיֹאמְרוּ תָמִיד
כח יִגְדַּל יְהוָה הֶחָפֵץ שְׁלוֹם עַבְדּוֹ: וּלְשׁוֹנִי תֶּהְגֶּה צִדְקֶךָ כָּל־הַיּוֹם תְּהִלָּתֶךָ: ה
לו א ב לַמְנַצֵּחַ ׀ לְעֶבֶד־יְהוָה לְדָוִד: נְאֻם־פֶּשַׁע לָרָשָׁע בְּקֶרֶב לִבִּי אֵין־פַּחַד אֱלֹהִים

PSALM 36

PSALMS 36:1–13

A psalm that contrasts the wicked person, who from lack of faith is drawn deeper and deeper into evil, with the righteous person, whose chief happiness is to cleave to God. The psalmist prays for the downfall of the wicked and the salvation of the righteous.

36 1 **For the chief musician, by David servant of the Lord.**[D]

2 **Sinfulness speaks to the wicked one.** This internal dialogue is known to me personally, because it sometimes takes place **in my** own **heart.** The central attribute of the wicked person is that **there is no fear of God before him,** even though he may acknowledge God's existence, and he therefore finds ways to rationalize his behavior and continue to sin.

3 **For in his eyes,** following his own misguided opinion, **he glides past Him.** The sinner thinks he can somehow evade God's attention **to** thereby **find,** or commit, **his iniquity,** and **to hate** others.
4 **The words of his mouth are wickedness and deceit; he has ceased to learn to do what is good.** He no longer tries to mend his ways, instead allowing his evil impulses free rein.
5 **He plots wickedness in his bed** as he goes to sleep, and when he arises, **he sets himself on a path of no good; he does not abhor evil.** This is a description of a person going through an internal spiritual crisis or breakdown. Even if he has not completely lost his faith in God, such faith no longer serves to block his negative thoughts or behavior. He is on a road spiraling downward.
6 But there is an alternative path, one that leads to enlightenment. Those who contemplate the matter should know that **Your kindness, Lord, extends to the heavens; Your faithfulness reaches the skies.**
7 **Your righteousness,** Your beneficence, **is** steadfast, **like mighty mountains,** and **Your judgments are** like **a fathomless deep. Lord, You save man and beast.** God's righteousness and faithfulness extend to everything He has created, man and beast alike.
8 Expressions of the psalmist's personal experience follow: **How precious is Your kindness, God; men take refuge in the shadow of Your garment.** Those who seek God's intimacy feel protected by Him, as if enveloped in His cloak.
9 **They are sated by the rich fare of Your House; You give them to drink from the stream of Your delights.** The experience of being close to God is comparable to having one's hunger satiated and his thirst slaked.
10 **For the source of life is with You,** and those who are close to You benefit from that life. **Through Your light we see light.** Closeness to God provides one with a sense of satisfaction and enlightenment.
11 **Extend Your kindness to those who know You,** those who love You and therefore strive to know You, **and** show **Your righteousness to the upright of heart,** those whose internal compass always points toward God, and who are therefore devoid of crookedness and deception.
12 The psalmist concludes with a request: **Let no arrogant foot come to me.** Do not let my actions be spoiled by arrogance, whether coming from others or from within myself. **Let no hand of the wicked drive me away** from You.
13 **There,** in the proximity of God, **the evildoers have fallen, cast down and unable to rise.**

PSALM 37

PSALMS 37:1–40

An instructive psalm, much of which is organized alphabetically. Its main theme is that the wicked, in all their varieties, are fated for destruction, despite any temporary success they may enjoy. In contrast, those who love and trust in God eventually flourish and endure.

37 1 **By David. Contend not with the wicked.** Do not compare your situation with that of evildoers. Do not compete with them nor emulate them, **nor be envious of evildoers.** A person who is not evil is harmed by putting himself in the same arena as the wicked; his image is damaged and his desires are corrupted.
2 In addition, while it may appear that the wicked always succeed, their success is fleeting: **They will soon be cut down like grass** that is cut while still green and used for animal feed, and they will **wither like the green herb.** They are like fields that turn a vibrant green after the rains begin, but, as experience shows, quickly dry out and turn brown.
3 **Trust in the Lord and do good; dwell in the land.** Avoid self-aggrandizement; instead, associate with the humbler people of the land **and cultivate faithfulness.** The literal meaning of the verb *re'eh*, translated here as "cultivate," is "to herd," "to graze," or "to feed oneself." A person who "grazes in faithfulness" is nourished and sustained by his faith in God. The phrase is thus a call to live modestly, subsisting on faithfulness, rather than seeking to attain material affluence.
4 **Take pleasure in the Lord** from being close to Him, **and** ultimately **He will grant you the desires of your heart.**
5 **Cast the path of your life onto the Lord.** *Gol*, translated here as "cast," literally means to roll something. The psalmist here encourages us to roll over, or transfer, the burdens of our daily life onto God, and to rely solely upon Him. **Trust in Him and He will act** in response, assisting you.
6 Even if others behave toward you with deceit, maintain your own goodness and innocence, and **He will bring your righteousness to light, your vindication bright as noon.**
7 **Be silent before the Lord and wait for Him; do not contend with one who prospers** through unjust means **or the man who is busy with intrigue.**
8 Maintain your righteousness not only in the realm of action but also in your emotions: **Leave off anger and forsake wrath,** both of which often cause a person to stray from the proper path. **Do not contend** and compete with the wicked, even if you do so **merely to make things go badly** for them, to avenge misdeeds they may have committed against you.
9 It is unnecessary for you to take revenge or punish those who have wronged you, **for evildoers will be cut off** even without your efforts, **while those who place their hope in the Lord will inherit the earth,** including the portions owned by those evildoers.

לנגד עיניו: כי־החליק אליו בעיניו למצא עונו לשנא: דברי־פיו און ומרמה ג ד
חדל להשכיל להיטיב: און | יחשב על־משכבו יתיצב על־דרך לא־טוב רע ה
לא ימאס: יהוה בהשמים חסדך אמונתך עד־שחקים: צדקתך | כהררי־אל ו ז
משפטיך תהום רבה אדם ובהמה תושיע | יהוה: מה־יקר חסדך אלהים ובני ח
אדם בצל כנפיך יחסיון: ירוין מדשן ביתך ונחל עדניך תשקם: כי־עמך מקור ט י
חיים באורך נראה־אור: משך חסדך לידעיך וצדקתך לישרי־לב: אל־תבואני יא יב
רגל גאוה ויד־רשעים אל־תנדני: שם נפלו פעלי און דחו ולא־יכלו קום: יג
לדוד | אל־תתחר במרעים אל־תקנא בעשי עולה: כי כחציר מהרה ימלו לז א ב
וכירק דשא יבולון: בטח ביהוה ועשה־טוב שכן־ארץ ורעה אמונה: והתענג ג ד
על־יהוה ויתן־לך משאלת לבך: גול על־יהוה דרכך ובטח עליו והוא יעשה: ה
והוציא כאור צדקך ומשפטך כצהרים: דום | ליהוה והתחולל לו אל־תתחר ו ז
במצליח דרכו באיש עשה מזמות: הרף מאף ועזב חמה אל־תתחר אך־ ח
להרע: כי־מרעים יכרתון וקוי יהוה המה יירשו־ארץ: ועוד מעט ואין רשע ט י
והתבוננת על־מקומו ואיננו: וענוים יירשו־ארץ והתענגו על־רב שלום: זמם יא יב
רשע לצדיק וחרק עליו שניו: אדני ישחק־לו כי־ראה כי־יבא יומו: חרב | יג יד
פתחו רשעים ודרכו קשתם להפיל עני ואביון לטבוח ישרי־דרך: חרבם תבוא טו
בלבם וקשתותם תשברנה: טוב־מעט לצדיק מהמון רשעים רבים: כי זרועות טז יז

10 **Soon the wicked man will be no more; you will gaze at his** former **place and he will be gone.** This can mean that he will no longer be alive, or that he will no longer be enjoying his former state of power and prosperity,

11 **while the humble,** as opposed to those sinners, will enjoy stability and **inherit the earth, delighting in abundant peace** and well-being.

12 **The wicked man plots against the righteous man,** menacingly **gnashing his teeth at him.**

13 But **the Lord laughs at him** and his evil schemes; **He sees his day** of downfall **coming.**

14 **The wicked draw their swords and stretch their bows** in order **to cast down the poor and the needy, to slaughter those who are upright in conduct.**

15 But ultimately **their swords will come into their own hearts, and their bows will be broken.**

16 **Better a little for the righteous man than abundance for many wicked people.** The goods and property possessed by the wicked are ephemeral,

17 **for the arms of the wicked will be broken, while the Lord supports the righteous.**

18 **The Lord knows** and loves **the days** and ways of life **of the blameless;** consequently, **their portion will last forever.**
19 **They are not put to shame** even **in difficult times; in days of famine they eat their fill.**
20 **But the wicked will perish, and the enemies of the Lord will be like the fat of rams,** consumed by others; **they will utterly vanish in smoke.**
21 **The wicked one borrows and does not repay.** It is typical of evil people to take whatever they can and not give to others even what they owe them. **The righteous one,** in contrast, **is gracious and gives** of his possessions to others, either as a loan or, if needed, as an outright gift.
22 **Those whom he,** the righteous man, **blesses inherit the earth; those whom he curses are cut off.**
23 **The Lord sets the footsteps of man; He desires his path,** the upright path of the righteous man.
24 **When he,** the righteous man, **stumbles, he will not fall down, because the Lord supports his hand.** The image here is of a father holding his child's hand; even if the child trips, he does not fall to the ground, since his father is supporting him.
25 **I was once a youth,** and **now I have grown old; and I have never seen a righteous man forsaken, nor his children seeking bread.** Even if a righteous person may not be counted among the prominent, wealthy people of his time, he and his children are never entirely forsaken. This is in contrast to the wicked, who ultimately experience utter ruin.
26 **All day long he is gracious and lending, and his children become a blessing.** The children of the righteous "become a blessing," not only in the sense of God rewarding them for their father's beneficence, but also, more practically, because people who benefited from their father's generosity will look after them.
27 **Turn from evil and do good, and** thereby **dwell securely forever,**
28 **for the Lord loves justice and does not forsake His pious ones. They are guarded forever, while the seed of the wicked is cut off.**
29 **The righteous will inherit the earth and dwell on it forever.**
30 The psalmist now describes the behavior of the righteous: **The mouth of the righteous utters wisdom, and his tongue speaks justice,** voicing proper and just statements.
31 **The teaching of his God is in his heart; his steps do not falter.**
32 To be sure, **the wicked man spies out the righteous man and seeks to kill him,**
33 **but the Lord will not leave him in his hand.** He will not abandon the righteous to the hands of the wicked **or let him be condemned when judged.**
34 **Put your hope in the Lord and follow His way, and** if you do, **He will** ultimately **raise you up** from your lowly position **to inherit the earth. When the wicked are cut off, you will see it.**
35 **I have seen a cruel and wicked man firmly rooted like a well-watered tree in its native soil.**
36 Yet, later I saw that despite his apparent sturdiness and robustness, **he passed away and was gone; I looked for him but he was no longer to be found.**
37 **Maintain** the path of **innocence, seek** the path of **integrity, for there is a** bright **future for the man of peace.**
38 **But transgressors,** in contrast, **will be altogether destroyed, the future of the wicked cut off.**
39 **The salvation of the righteous is from the Lord; He is their strength in times of trouble.**
40 **The Lord helps them and rescues them; He will rescue and deliver them from the wicked, because they took refuge in Him.**

PSALM 38

PSALMS 38:1–23

A psalm of supplication by one who suffers calamity and is wracked with physical pain and the anguish of being abandoned by formerly close friends. The psalmist acknowledges his transgressions and pleads to God for salvation, for apart from God, he has nothing.

38 1 **A psalm by David, to remind.** This psalm was apparently meant to remind God, as it were,[8] of how the psalmist suffered. It seems to have been written when the psalmist was gravely ill and in great physical pain. At the time, his enemies were convinced that his death was imminent, and they were hopeful that they would soon be able to celebrate his downfall.
2 The psalmist begins by pleading to God for relief from his pain: **Lord, do not rebuke me with Your fury and chastise me with Your burning anger.**
3 **Your arrows have pierced me,** a metaphorical description of God punishing him with pain and illness, and **Your hand has come down upon me** with a severe blow.
4 **There is nothing whole in my body,** no part of my body is well, **because of Your anger;** and there is **no tranquility in** any of **my bones, because of my sin.** This is not a complaint but a plea for mercy. The psalmist admits that he is suffering justly because of his sins, but he nevertheless prays for healing.

יח רְשָׁעִים תִּשָּׁבַרְנָה וְסוֹמֵךְ צַדִּיקִים יהוה׃ יוֹדֵעַ יהוה יְמֵי תְמִימִם וְנַחֲלָתָם לְעוֹלָם
יט כ תִּהְיֶה׃ לֹא־יֵבֹשׁוּ בְּעֵת רָעָה וּבִימֵי רְעָבוֹן יִשְׂבָּעוּ׃ כִּי רְשָׁעִים ׀ יֹאבֵדוּ וְאֹיְבֵי
כא כב יהוה כִּיקַר כָּרִים כָּלוּ בֶעָשָׁן כָּלוּ׃ לֹוֶה רָשָׁע וְלֹא יְשַׁלֵּם וְצַדִּיק חוֹנֵן וְנוֹתֵן׃ כִּי
כג מְבֹרָכָיו יִירְשׁוּ אָרֶץ וּמְקֻלָּלָיו יִכָּרֵתוּ׃ מֵיהוה מִצְעֲדֵי־גֶבֶר כּוֹנָנוּ וְדַרְכּוֹ יֶחְפָּץ׃
כד כה כִּי־יִפֹּל לֹא־יוּטָל כִּי־יהוה סוֹמֵךְ יָדוֹ׃ נַעַר ׀ הָיִיתִי גַּם־זָקַנְתִּי וְלֹא־רָאִיתִי צַדִּיק
כו כז נֶעֱזָב וְזַרְעוֹ מְבַקֶּשׁ־לָחֶם׃ כָּל־הַיּוֹם חוֹנֵן וּמַלְוֶה וְזַרְעוֹ לִבְרָכָה׃ סוּר מֵרָע וַעֲשֵׂה־
כח טוֹב וּשְׁכֹן לְעוֹלָם׃ כִּי יהוה ׀ אֹהֵב מִשְׁפָּט וְלֹא־יַעֲזֹב אֶת־חֲסִידָיו לְעוֹלָם נִשְׁמָרוּ
כט ל וְזֶרַע רְשָׁעִים נִכְרָת׃ צַדִּיקִים יִירְשׁוּ־אָרֶץ וְיִשְׁכְּנוּ לָעַד עָלֶיהָ׃ פִּי־צַדִּיק יֶהְגֶּה
לא לב חָכְמָה וּלְשׁוֹנוֹ תְּדַבֵּר מִשְׁפָּט׃ תּוֹרַת אֱלֹהָיו בְּלִבּוֹ לֹא תִמְעַד אֲשֻׁרָיו׃ צוֹפֶה
לג רָשָׁע לַצַּדִּיק וּמְבַקֵּשׁ לַהֲמִיתוֹ׃ יהוה לֹא־יַעַזְבֶנּוּ בְיָדוֹ וְלֹא יַרְשִׁיעֶנּוּ בְּהִשָּׁפְטוֹ׃
לד קַוֵּה אֶל־יהוה ׀ וּשְׁמֹר דַּרְכּוֹ וִירוֹמִמְךָ לָרֶשֶׁת אָרֶץ בְּהִכָּרֵת רְשָׁעִים תִּרְאֶה׃
לה לו רָאִיתִי רָשָׁע עָרִיץ וּמִתְעָרֶה כְּאֶזְרָח רַעֲנָן׃ וַיַּעֲבֹר וְהִנֵּה אֵינֶנּוּ וָאֲבַקְשֵׁהוּ וְלֹא
לז לח נִמְצָא׃ שְׁמָר־תָּם וּרְאֵה יָשָׁר כִּי־אַחֲרִית לְאִישׁ שָׁלוֹם׃ וּפֹשְׁעִים נִשְׁמְדוּ יַחְדָּו
לט מ אַחֲרִית רְשָׁעִים נִכְרָתָה׃ וּתְשׁוּעַת צַדִּיקִים מֵיהוה מָעוּזָּם בְּעֵת צָרָה׃ וַיַּעְזְרֵם
יהוה וַיְפַלְּטֵם יְפַלְּטֵם מֵרְשָׁעִים וְיוֹשִׁיעֵם כִּי־חָסוּ בוֹ׃

לח א ב ג מִזְמוֹר לְדָוִד לְהַזְכִּיר׃ יהוה אַל־בְּקֶצְפְּךָ תוֹכִיחֵנִי וּבַחֲמָתְךָ תְיַסְּרֵנִי׃ כִּי־חִצֶּיךָ
ד נִחֲתוּ בִי וַתִּנְחַת עָלַי יָדֶךָ׃ אֵין־מְתֹם בִּבְשָׂרִי מִפְּנֵי זַעְמֶךָ אֵין־שָׁלוֹם בַּעֲצָמַי
ה ו מִפְּנֵי חַטָּאתִי׃ כִּי עֲוֺנֹתַי עָבְרוּ רֹאשִׁי כְּמַשָּׂא כָבֵד יִכְבְּדוּ מִמֶּנִּי׃ הִבְאִישׁוּ נָמַקּוּ
ז ח חַבּוּרֹתָי מִפְּנֵי אִוַּלְתִּי׃ נַעֲוֵיתִי שַׁחֹתִי עַד־מְאֹד כָּל־הַיּוֹם קֹדֵר הִלָּכְתִּי׃ כִּי־כְסָלַי

5 **My iniquities** are so numerous, it is as if they have piled up and **have risen above my head; like an onerous burden, they are too heavy for me.**

6 **My wounds stink and fester because of my folly.** All this is punishment for my sins.

7 **I am greatly bent over and bowed; I walk about in gloom the entire day** because of my pain.

8 **My loins** can barely support me. I feel as if they **are filled with refuse; there is nothing whole** and healthy **in** all **my flesh.**

9 **I am depleted and utterly crushed; I roar from my heart's agitation.**
10 Yet the psalmist immediately realizes that there is no reason for him to cry out in pain: **My Lord, all my desires are** known **before You, and** even **my** muffled **sighs are not hidden from You.**
11 **My heart races,** my heartbeat is irregular, and **my strength fails me;** in my sickness and weakness it seems that **even the light of my eyes has left me.**
12 I suffer not only physically but also from lack of support: **My friends and companions stand aloof from my affliction, and those who are close to me keep their distance.** They do not come forward to help.
13 Moreover, **those who seek my life lay snares for me.** As they assume that my situation is hopeless, they feel free to plot against me. **Those who wish me ill speak of devastation** against me, **uttering deceit** about me **all day long.**
14 **And I,** out of weakness, **like one who is deaf, do not hear. I am like a mute who does not open his mouth.**
15 **Indeed, I am like a man who does not hear, a man with no power to rebuke** in response to their affronts.
16 My silence is not only a result of my weakness; it also stems from my faith, **for in You, Lord, I place my hope; Lord my God,** in my stead **You will answer** those who taunt me, since I am unable to do so.
17 **For I said: Lest they rejoice and become exalted over me when my leg falters.**
18 **For I am poised to stumble; my pain is always before me.**
19 **I will tell of my iniquity** and openly admit it; **I am anxious because of my sin.** For this reason, I do not complain that my punishment and suffering are unjustified.
20 **My enemies grow mighty; many are those who hate me without cause.**
21 **Those rendering evil for good,** who repay the good I did for them with hostility, **despise me because I pursue goodness.** The word *yistenuni* encompasses both hatred and accusation. It is not uncommon behavior for beneficiaries of aid to turn against their benefactors rather than show gratitude.
22 **Do not forsake me, Lord. My God, do not distance Yourself from me.**
23 **Make haste to help me, Lord, my salvation.**

PSALM 39

PSALMS 39:1–14

A psalm of prayer dealing with illness, pain, and the suffering inflicted by enemies. It also ponders the fate of humanity in a more general sense.

39 1 **For the chief musician, for Yedutun.** Yedutun was one of the
7th day Temple's chief musicians,[9] and David furnished this song to
of month him either to set it to music or to sing it. Some commentators are of the opinion that *yedutun* is the name of an existing melody to which this psalm was meant to be sung, or, alternatively, the name of a musical instrument. **A psalm by David.**
2 **I have said: I will guard my ways lest I sin with my tongue** by saying improper things. **I will muzzle my mouth while the wicked are in my presence.**
3 **I was mute and silent; I refrained even from speaking good,** lest I end up saying something inappropriate, **but my pain worsened.**
4 **My heart was hot within me while I was musing; the fire burned, and my tongue gave utterance,** not to complaints against God over my predicament but to meditations about matters of deeper significance:
5 **Lord, let me know my end and what will be the measure of my days.** The psalmist's request is primarily to be granted true awareness and appreciation of the transience of life, that we are here on earth only temporarily. He also expresses his desire to know when he will die, so that he can prepare for his death in a fitting manner. **Let me know when I will cease to be,** when all my suffering will come to an end; it is sometimes comforting to know this. In addition, the knowledge of one's mortality generates a different perspective on assessing one's life.
6 **Behold, You have given me days as handbreadths.** My life is so short, as though it could be quantified in handbreadths, a small unit of measurement. **My existence,** my world and everything in it, **is as nothing in Your sight. Indeed, everyone is like nothingness, every standing man, Selah.** Even when a person is alive and standing, he has no significance before You.
7 **Surely man walks about as a shadow,** living in a world of illusion and false images. **Indeed, he is in turmoil for naught, amassing riches and not knowing who will gather them** and benefit from them after his death. Life is short and of little meaning; all of man's endeavors lack real consequence.
8 Although the psalmist acknowledges that man is essentially insignificant, he still turns to God in prayer: **And now, Lord, on what do I rely? My hope resides** only **in You.** He does not expect help from anyone else.
9 I confess that I have sinned, but I beseech You to **deliver me from all my transgressions; do not disgrace me among the scoundrels.** Do not allow my enemies to overtake and shame me. Punishing me, besides being painful for me, would be a reward for them, and they are unworthy.

ט מָלְאוּ נִקְלֶה וְאֵין מְתֹם בִּבְשָׂרִי: נְפוּגוֹתִי וְנִדְכֵּיתִי עַד־מְאֹד שָׁאַגְתִּי מִנַּהֲמַת
י יא לִבִּי: אֲדֹנָי נֶגְדְּךָ כָל־תַּאֲוָתִי וְאַנְחָתִי מִמְּךָ לֹא־נִסְתָּרָה: לִבִּי סְחַרְחַר עֲזָבַנִי כֹחִי
יב וְאוֹר־עֵינַי גַּם־הֵם אֵין אִתִּי: אֹהֲבַי ׀ וְרֵעַי מִנֶּגֶד נִגְעִי יַעֲמֹדוּ וּקְרוֹבַי מֵרָחֹק עָמָדוּ:
יג יד וַיְנַקְשׁוּ ׀ מְבַקְשֵׁי נַפְשִׁי וְדֹרְשֵׁי רָעָתִי דִּבְּרוּ הַוּוֹת וּמִרְמוֹת כָּל־הַיּוֹם יֶהְגּוּ: וַאֲנִי
טו כְחֵרֵשׁ לֹא אֶשְׁמָע וּכְאִלֵּם לֹא יִפְתַּח־פִּיו: וָאֱהִי כְּאִישׁ אֲשֶׁר לֹא־שֹׁמֵעַ וְאֵין בְּפִיו
טז יז תּוֹכָחוֹת: כִּי־לְךָ יהוה הוֹחָלְתִּי אַתָּה תַעֲנֶה אֲדֹנָי אֱלֹהָי: כִּי־אָמַרְתִּי פֶּן־יִשְׂמְחוּ־
יח יט לִי בְּמוֹט רַגְלִי עָלַי הִגְדִּילוּ: כִּי־אֲנִי לְצֶלַע נָכוֹן וּמַכְאוֹבִי נֶגְדִּי תָמִיד: כִּי־עֲוֺנִי
כ כא אַגִּיד אֶדְאַג מֵחַטָּאתִי: וְאֹיְבַי חַיִּים עָצֵמוּ וְרַבּוּ שֹׂנְאַי שָׁקֶר: וּמְשַׁלְּמֵי רָעָה תַּחַת
כב טוֹבָה יִשְׂטְנוּנִי תַּחַת רדופי־טוֹב: אַל־תַּעַזְבֵנִי יהוה אֱלֹהַי אַל־תִּרְחַק מִמֶּנִּי: רֹדְפִי־
כג חוּשָׁה לְעֶזְרָתִי אֲדֹנָי תְּשׁוּעָתִי:

לט

א ב לַמְנַצֵּחַ לידיתון מִזְמוֹר לְדָוִד: אָמַרְתִּי אֶשְׁמְרָה דְרָכַי מֵחֲטוֹא בִלְשׁוֹנִי אֶשְׁמְרָה־ לִידוּתוּן
ג לְפִי מַחְסוֹם בְּעֹד רָשָׁע לְנֶגְדִּי: נֶאֱלַמְתִּי דוּמִיָּה הֶחֱשֵׁיתִי מִטּוֹב וּכְאֵבִי נֶעְכָּר: ז׳ לחודש
ד ה חַם־לִבִּי ׀ בְּקִרְבִּי בַּהֲגִיגִי תִבְעַר־אֵשׁ דִּבַּרְתִּי בִּלְשׁוֹנִי: הוֹדִיעֵנִי יהוה ׀ קִצִּי וּמִדַּת
ו יָמַי מַה־הִיא אֵדְעָה מֶה־חָדֵל אָנִי: הִנֵּה טְפָחוֹת ׀ נָתַתָּה יָמַי וְחֶלְדִּי כְאַיִן נֶגְדֶּךָ
ז אַךְ־כָּל־הֶבֶל כָּל־אָדָם נִצָּב סֶלָה: אַךְ־בְּצֶלֶם ׀ יִתְהַלֶּךְ־אִישׁ אַךְ־הֶבֶל יֶהֱמָיוּן
ח ט יִצְבֹּר וְלֹא־יֵדַע מִי־אֹסְפָם: וְעַתָּה מַה־קִּוִּיתִי אֲדֹנָי תּוֹחַלְתִּי לְךָ הִיא: מִכָּל־פְּשָׁעַי
י יא הַצִּילֵנִי חֶרְפַּת נָבָל אַל־תְּשִׂימֵנִי: נֶאֱלַמְתִּי לֹא אֶפְתַּח־פִּי כִּי אַתָּה עָשִׂיתָ: הָסֵר
יב מֵעָלַי נִגְעֶךָ מִתִּגְרַת יָדְךָ אֲנִי כָלִיתִי: בְּתוֹכָחוֹת עַל־עָוֺן ׀ יִסַּרְתָּ אִישׁ וַתֶּמֶס כָּעָשׁ
יג חֲמוּדוֹ אַךְ הֶבֶל כָּל־אָדָם סֶלָה: שִׁמְעָה תְפִלָּתִי ׀ יהוה וְשַׁוְעָתִי ׀ הַאֲזִינָה אֶל־

10 **I have become mute; I do not open my mouth** to argue or complain to You, **for,** regarding my suffering, I am aware that **it is Your doing.**

11 Nevertheless, I entreat God: **Remove Your plague from me; I am perishing from the blows of Your hand.**

12 **You chastise a man with punishments for his sin, consuming, like a moth, what is precious to him.** His possessions and his loved ones perish before him. **Surely man is mere nothingness, Selah.**

13 **Hear my prayer, Lord, and heed my cry; do not be silent at my tears. For I am a stranger with You, a sojourner, as were**

all my fathers. Precisely because I am such a fragile and transient being, perhaps I could be granted a respite from suffering. The reference to "all my fathers" indicates that the psalmist's plea does not pertain only to his own individual circumstances but is on behalf of all humanity. When compared with God's infinite existence, human life in this world is but an ephemeral interlude.

14 Therefore I pray: **Let me be, so I may have relief, before I depart and am no more.** If You do not give respite to a creature as short-lived and lowly as I am, my life will consist only of suffering and I will not have experienced what the world had in store for me.

PSALM 40

PSALMS 40:1–18

A psalm that contains an intermingling of praise and supplication and moves between past, present, and future. The concluding five verses of this psalm appear in almost identical form in Psalm 70.

40 1 **For the chief musician, a psalm by David.**
2 **I greatly hoped for the Lord, and He turned to me and heard my cry.**
3 **He brought me out of the pit of destruction, out of the swampy mud.** "Pit of destruction" apparently refers to a pit whose bottom is not firm but rather is full of slime and mud. This image is reinforced by the next phrase, "swampy mud," evoking a person who feels that he has nothing to lean on; the very ground beneath him does not support him, and he feels that he is liable at any moment to slip away and drown. But, continues the psalmist, God rescued me from this slippery peril, **and He set my feet upon a rock, making my footsteps firm.** Once he is rescued from the pit, the psalmist is grateful to God not only for his narrow escape from death but also for the opportunity to set himself on a new, more secure path.

Mud

4 **He placed a new song in my mouth, a song of praise for our God. Many will see** what happened to me, **and they will fear,** realizing just how far a man can slip and fall into peril. **And** they will also **trust in the Lord,** as they will understand that God can be relied upon to rescue man from such dire straits.
5 **Happy is the man who makes the Lord his trust, not turning** for help **to the proud,** who boast of their strengths and abilities, **and those who have strayed into falsehood,** whose promises are worthless.
6 **Many things, Lord my God, have You done; Your wondrous works and thoughts are for us.** Often it is only in retrospect that one can understand how certain situations that appeared to be incomprehensible or problematic actually worked out for the best. **No one compares to You** in comprehending all the hidden solutions to the problems and complications of life. **Though I declare and speak of Your miraculous deeds, they are too numerous to count.**
7 When one comes to give thanks to You, he realizes that **You do not desire sacrifice or meal offerings** as expressions of gratitude. Rather, **You have opened my ears** and given them the ability to hear and understand this: **You do not ask for burnt offerings or sin offerings.**
8 **So,** having contemplated all this, **I said: I have come with a written scroll of a book upon me.** I understand that I need to express my gratitude with words, both spoken and written.

Pupil reading from a "scroll of a book," 180–185 CE

9 **I delight in doing Your will, my God; Your teaching is in my belly.** It pervades my very core and informs everything I have to say.
10 **I proclaimed** the **righteousness** of Your deeds **in a great assembly,** so that everyone might hear of the mercies You showed me. **I will not restrain my lips, my Lord, as You know.**
11 **I did not conceal Your righteousness within my heart** by refraining to share knowledge of it with others; **I spoke of Your faithfulness and Your salvation. I did not hide Your kindness and Your truth from a great assembly.** In other words,

יד דִּמְעָתִי אַל־תֶּחֱרַשׁ כִּי גֵר אָנֹכִי עִמָּךְ תּוֹשָׁב כְּכָל־אֲבוֹתָי׃ הָשַׁע מִמֶּנִּי וְאַבְלִיגָה
בְּטֶרֶם אֵלֵךְ וְאֵינֶנִּי׃
מ א ב ג לַמְנַצֵּחַ לְדָוִד מִזְמוֹר׃ קַוֺּה קִוִּיתִי יהוה וַיֵּט אֵלַי וַיִּשְׁמַע שַׁוְעָתִי׃ וַיַּעֲלֵנִי ׀ מִבּוֹר
ד שָׁאוֹן מִטִּיט הַיָּוֵן וַיָּקֶם עַל־סֶלַע רַגְלַי כּוֹנֵן אֲשֻׁרָי׃ וַיִּתֵּן בְּפִי ׀ שִׁיר חָדָשׁ תְּהִלָּה
ה לֵאלֹהֵינוּ יִרְאוּ רַבִּים וְיִירָאוּ וְיִבְטְחוּ בַּיהוה׃ אַשְׁרֵי־הַגֶּבֶר אֲשֶׁר־שָׂם יהוה מִבְטַחוֹ
ו וְלֹא־פָנָה אֶל־רְהָבִים וְשָׂטֵי כָזָב׃ רַבּוֹת עָשִׂיתָ ׀ אַתָּה ׀ יהוה אֱלֹהַי נִפְלְאֹתֶיךָ
ז וּמַחְשְׁבֹתֶיךָ אֵלֵינוּ אֵין ׀ עֲרֹךְ אֵלֶיךָ אַגִּידָה וַאֲדַבֵּרָה עָצְמוּ מִסַּפֵּר׃ זֶבַח וּמִנְחָה ׀
ח לֹא־חָפַצְתָּ אָזְנַיִם כָּרִיתָ לִּי עוֹלָה וַחֲטָאָה לֹא שָׁאָלְתָּ׃ אָז אָמַרְתִּי הִנֵּה־בָאתִי
ט בִּמְגִלַּת־סֵפֶר כָּתוּב עָלָי׃ לַעֲשׂוֹת־רְצוֹנְךָ אֱלֹהַי חָפָצְתִּי וְתוֹרָתְךָ בְּתוֹךְ מֵעָי׃
י יא בִּשַּׂרְתִּי צֶדֶק ׀ בְּקָהָל רָב הִנֵּה שְׂפָתַי לֹא אֶכְלָא יהוה אַתָּה יָדָעְתָּ׃ צִדְקָתְךָ
לֹא־כִסִּיתִי ׀ בְּתוֹךְ לִבִּי אֱמוּנָתְךָ וּתְשׁוּעָתְךָ אָמָרְתִּי לֹא־כִחַדְתִּי חַסְדְּךָ וַאֲמִתְּךָ
יב לְקָהָל רָב׃ אַתָּה יהוה לֹא־תִכְלָא רַחֲמֶיךָ מִמֶּנִּי חַסְדְּךָ וַאֲמִתְּךָ תָּמִיד יִצְּרוּנִי׃
יג כִּי אָפְפוּ־עָלַי ׀ רָעוֹת עַד־אֵין מִסְפָּר הִשִּׂיגוּנִי עֲוֺנֹתַי וְלֹא־יָכֹלְתִּי לִרְאוֹת עָצְמוּ
יד טו מִשַּׂעֲרוֹת רֹאשִׁי וְלִבִּי עֲזָבָנִי׃ רְצֵה יהוה לְהַצִּילֵנִי יהוה לְעֶזְרָתִי חוּשָׁה׃ יֵבֹשׁוּ
טז וְיַחְפְּרוּ ׀ יַחַד מְבַקְשֵׁי נַפְשִׁי לִסְפּוֹתָהּ יִסֹּגוּ אָחוֹר וְיִכָּלְמוּ חֲפֵצֵי רָעָתִי׃ יָשֹׁמּוּ
יז עַל־עֵקֶב בָּשְׁתָּם הָאֹמְרִים לִי הֶאָח ׀ הֶאָח׃ יָשִׂישׂוּ וְיִשְׂמְחוּ ׀ בְּךָ כָּל־מְבַקְשֶׁיךָ

rather than offering sacrifices, it is psalms such as this, made public in their being transcribed and sung before "a great assembly," that properly express gratitude to God.

12 In turn, may it be that **You, Lord, will not withhold Your compassion from me; Your kindness and Your truth will always preserve me.**

13 The psalmist describes the dire situation he had faced before God's salvation: **For innumerable evils surrounded me.** But I realize that it is ultimately my fault, as **my iniquities, more numerous than the hairs on my head, overtook me. I was unable to see.** When my suffering afflicted me, it sapped my strength and my ability to see and understand that it was well deserved. **My heart,** my hope for deliverance, **failed me.**

14 At that time, I was only able to plead: **Please, Lord, deliver me; make haste to help me.**

15 **Let those who seek to destroy my life be utterly ashamed and humiliated. Let those who delight in my misfortune retreat in disgrace.**

16 **May those who say to me: Hurrah, hurrah! be confounded and turn on their heels in shame.** The word *yashomu* can mean both "may they be confounded" and "may they be destroyed."

17 Conversely, **let all who seek You be happy and rejoice in You; let those who love Your salvation always say: Great is the Lord.**

18 **As for me, poor and destitute,** having no importance on my own, **my Lord** nevertheless **takes me into account,** and because of that, **You are my help and my Savior. My God, do not tarry** with Your assistance to me.

PSALM 41

A psalm about illness and the suffering it causes.

PSALMS 41:1–14

41 1 **For the chief musician, a psalm by David.**
2 **Happy is one who attends to the helpless.** *Maskil*, translated here as "one who attends to," more literally means "one who shows understanding for." The psalmist speaks of a person who not only aids the sick but does so with sensitivity, in a way that maximizes benefit and minimizes embarrassment and shame. **The Lord will deliver him in times of trouble.**
3 **The Lord will preserve him and sustain him, and he will be made happy on earth. You will not give him over to the will** and evil desires **of his enemies.**
4 **The Lord will support him on his sickbed; You change his bedding during his illness.** God will see to it that he is cared for in his own illness. Changing the bed linens is just one example of how to aid a sick person.
5 **As for me, I said: Lord, be gracious to me; heal my soul, for I have sinned against You.** Although I have sinned against You and realize that I deserve to be punished for my sins, I still pray to You to grant me recovery.
6 **My enemies,** under the impression that I am mortally ill, **speak evil against me, saying: When will he die, and his name be lost?**
7 **And if someone comes to see me,** ostensibly for a thoughtful visit, **he speaks** his words of encouragement **falsely.** For in reality, **his heart gathers wickedness** that he does not speak out loud; only **when he goes outside, he speaks of it** to others.
8 **Together, all my enemies are whispering about me** and my dire situation, **considering the evil that has befallen me.**
9 This is what they are saying: **An incurable, evil** illness **has taken hold of him; now that he is bedridden, he will never rise again.**
10 **Even my ally, whom I trusted, he who partook of my bread** and was thereby graciously sustained by me, **has lifted his heel against me,** as if ready to trample me.
11 **But may You, Lord, be gracious to me and raise me up** from this sickbed, **so I might pay them back.**
12 **Then I will know You have favored me, for** then **my enemy will not** have occasion to **shout in triumph over me** any longer.
13 **And I, in my innocence, You have supported me; You have kept me upright before You always.**
14 This verse concludes the first of the five books of Psalms: **Blessed is the Lord, God of Israel, from eternity to eternity,** in all times, **amen and amen.**

PSALM 42

A psalm of prayer and yearning in which the psalmist describes himself in exile, hunted, despised, and alone. He knows that only God can deliver him from all his troubles.

PSALMS 42:1–12

42 1 **For the chief musician, a contemplation,**[10] **by the sons of**
BOOK TWO **Korah.** An alternative translation is "for the sons of Korah," meaning that the song was composed by someone else and given to them to sing.
2 **As a deer longs for brooks of water, so my soul longs for You, God.** The rare verb *ta'arog*, translated here as "longs," can also refer to the craving sound made by a deer. In either case the sense is the same.

Deer drinking water

3 **My soul thirsts for God, the living God Almighty. When will I come** to God's Temple **and appear before God's countenance?** The Torah refers to a visit to the House of God as "appearing before God's countenance."[11]
4 The psalmist describes his feelings when he is distant from God's Temple, or even in exile in a foreign land: **My tears have been my bread,** they are as common to me as my daily food, **day and night, when they,** my enemies, **say to me all day long: Where is your God?**
5 **These things I remember, and pour out my soul: When I used to go with a throng of people in a procession to the House of God, a celebrating multitude with voice of song and thanksgiving.**
6 The psalmist returns to speaking of his feelings while in exile. Addressing himself, he asks: **Why, my soul, are you stooped over,** downcast? **Why do you sigh for me? Have hope in God, for I will yet** be saved by Him and **thank Him for the salvation of His presence.**

יח יֹאמְרוּ תָמִיד יִגְדַּל יְהוָה אֹהֲבֵי תְּשׁוּעָתֶךָ: וַאֲנִי ׀ עָנִי וְאֶבְיוֹן אֲדֹנָי יַחֲשָׁב לִי עֶזְרָתִי
וּמְפַלְטִי אַתָּה אֱלֹהַי אַל־תְּאַחַר:
מא א ב ג לַמְנַצֵּחַ מִזְמוֹר לְדָוִד: אַשְׁרֵי מַשְׂכִּיל אֶל־דָּל בְּיוֹם רָעָה יְמַלְּטֵהוּ יְהוָה: יְהוָה ׀
ד יִשְׁמְרֵהוּ וִיחַיֵּהוּ יאשר בָּאָרֶץ וְאַל־תִּתְּנֵהוּ בְּנֶפֶשׁ אֹיְבָיו: יְהוָה יִסְעָדֶנּוּ עַל־עֶרֶשׂ וְאֻשַּׁר
ה דְּוָי כָּל־מִשְׁכָּבוֹ הָפַכְתָּ בְחָלְיוֹ: אֲנִי־אָמַרְתִּי יְהוָה חָנֵּנִי רְפָאָה נַפְשִׁי כִּי־חָטָאתִי
ו ז לָךְ: אוֹיְבַי יֹאמְרוּ רַע לִי מָתַי יָמוּת וְאָבַד שְׁמוֹ: וְאִם־בָּא לִרְאוֹת ׀ שָׁוְא יְדַבֵּר לִבּוֹ
ח יִקְבָּץ־אָוֶן לוֹ יֵצֵא לַחוּץ יְדַבֵּר: יַחַד עָלַי יִתְלַחֲשׁוּ כָּל־שֹׂנְאָי עָלַי ׀ יַחְשְׁבוּ רָעָה
ט י לִי: דְּבַר־בְּלִיַּעַל יָצוּק בּוֹ וַאֲשֶׁר שָׁכַב לֹא־יוֹסִיף לָקוּם: גַּם־אִישׁ שְׁלוֹמִי ׀ אֲשֶׁר־
יא בָּטַחְתִּי בוֹ אוֹכֵל לַחְמִי הִגְדִּיל עָלַי עָקֵב: וְאַתָּה יְהוָה חָנֵּנִי וַהֲקִימֵנִי וַאֲשַׁלְּמָה
יב יג לָהֶם: בְּזֹאת יָדַעְתִּי כִּי־חָפַצְתָּ בִּי כִּי לֹא־יָרִיעַ אֹיְבִי עָלָי: וַאֲנִי בְּתֻמִּי תָּמַכְתָּ בִּי
יד וַתַּצִּיבֵנִי לְפָנֶיךָ לְעוֹלָם: בָּרוּךְ יְהוָה ׀ אֱלֹהֵי יִשְׂרָאֵל מֵהָעוֹלָם וְעַד־הָעוֹלָם ׀ אָמֵן ׀ ו
וְאָמֵן:
מב א ב לַמְנַצֵּחַ מַשְׂכִּיל לִבְנֵי־קֹרַח: כְּאַיָּל תַּעֲרֹג עַל־אֲפִיקֵי־מָיִם כֵּן נַפְשִׁי תַעֲרֹג אֵלֶיךָ ספר שני
ג ד אֱלֹהִים: צָמְאָה נַפְשִׁי ׀ לֵאלֹהִים לְאֵל חָי מָתַי אָבוֹא וְאֵרָאֶה פְּנֵי אֱלֹהִים: הָיְתָה־
ה לִּי דִמְעָתִי לֶחֶם יוֹמָם וָלָיְלָה בֶּאֱמֹר אֵלַי כָּל־הַיּוֹם אַיֵּה אֱלֹהֶיךָ: אֵלֶּה אֶזְכְּרָה ׀
וְאֶשְׁפְּכָה עָלַי ׀ נַפְשִׁי כִּי אֶעֱבֹר ׀ בַּסָּךְ אֶדַּדֵּם עַד־בֵּית אֱלֹהִים בְּקוֹל־רִנָּה וְתוֹדָה
ו הָמוֹן חוֹגֵג: מַה־תִּשְׁתּוֹחֲחִי ׀ נַפְשִׁי וַתֶּהֱמִי עָלָי הוֹחִילִי לֵאלֹהִים כִּי־עוֹד אוֹדֶנּוּ

7 **My God, my soul is stooped over,** downcast; **thus I recall You from the lands of
Jordan and the Hermons,**[B] the territories
where the sources of the Jordan River are

"Lands of Jordan"

"And the Hermons"

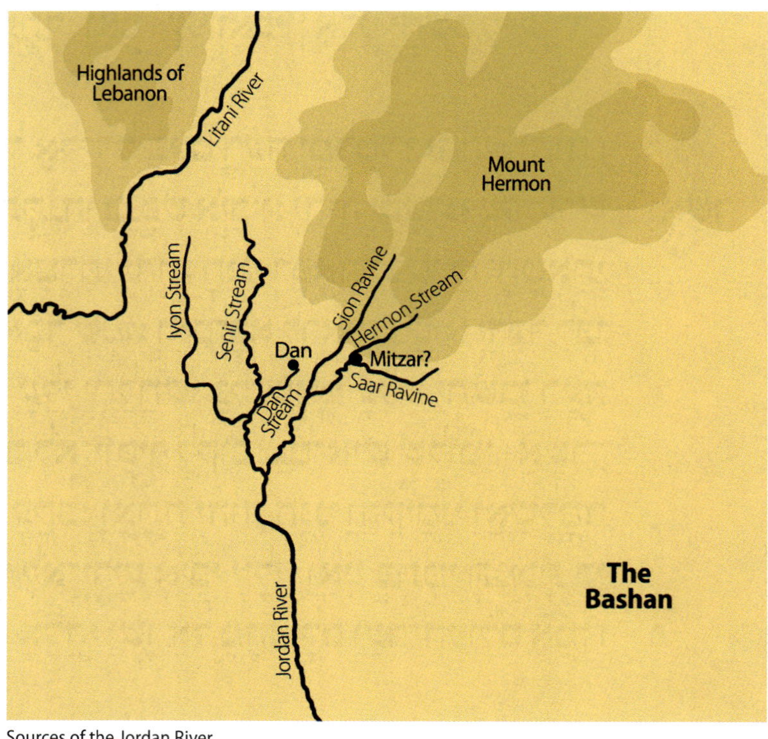

Sources of the Jordan River

located, near Mount Hermon, **from Mount Mitzar,**[B] apparently a mountain in that northern area.
8 **Deep calls to deep,** one body of abundant water calls to another, as it were, **in the sound of Your waterways.** For the
psalmist, the sound of cascading water is evocative of sadness.
All Your breakers and waves have passed over me, as if signifying my being overrun with torrents of troubles.
9 The psalmist expresses his devotion and hope: **The Lord commands His kindness** to me **by day,** so that **His song,** the song
of prayer that I sing to Him, **remains with me by night, a
prayer to the Almighty God of my life.**
10 In that prayer **I will say to God Almighty, my rock: Why have
You forgotten me? Why do I walk in gloom, oppressed by
the enemy?**
11 **I feel murder in my bones,** like actually being stabbed in my
bones, **as my foes ridicule me with their taunts, saying to me
all day long: Where is your God?** There is nothing more painful to me than this scornful question.
12 The psalmist again addresses his soul: **Why, my soul, are you
stooped over** and downcast? **Why do you sigh for me?** Rather,
have hope in God, for I will be saved by Him and **thank Him
again;** I will thank Him, **my salvation and my God,** before He
even redeems me, and again when He comes to my aid.

BACKGROUND

42:7 | **The lands of Jordan and the Hermons:** This describes the area of the headwaters of the Jordan: the Hermon, or Banias, Stream, flowing south from Mount Hermon; the Dan Stream; and the Senir, or Hatzbani, Stream. The area is characterized by an abundance of streams and high mountains.

Mount Mitzar: The mountain called Hermon actually comprises several peaks, which are called by various names. It is possible that Mount Mitzar, meaning "small," is the name of the lowest peak. Some believe that Mount Mitzar is situated south of Mount Hermon, in the area of the Saar Ravine in the northern Golan Heights, and the name may even be reflected in the village Zeura near the Saar Ravine.

ז יְשׁוּעוֹת פָּנָיו׃ אֱלֹהַי עָלַי נַפְשִׁי תִשְׁתּוֹחָח עַל־כֵּן אֶזְכָּרְךָ מֵאֶרֶץ יַרְדֵּן וְחֶרְמוֹנִים
ח מֵהַר מִצְעָר׃ תְּהוֹם־אֶל־תְּהוֹם קוֹרֵא לְקוֹל צִנּוֹרֶיךָ כָּל־מִשְׁבָּרֶיךָ וְגַלֶּיךָ עָלַי עָבָרוּ׃
ט י יוֹמָם ׀ יְצַוֶּה יהוה ׀ חַסְדּוֹ וּבַלַּיְלָה שִׁירֹה עִמִּי תְּפִלָּה לְאֵל חַיָּי׃ אוֹמְרָה ׀ לְאֵל
יא סַלְעִי לָמָה שְׁכַחְתָּנִי לָמָּה־קֹדֵר אֵלֵךְ בְּלַחַץ אוֹיֵב׃ בְּרֶצַח ׀ בְּעַצְמוֹתַי חֵרְפוּנִי
יב צוֹרְרָי בְּאָמְרָם אֵלַי כָּל־הַיּוֹם אַיֵּה אֱלֹהֶיךָ׃ מַה־תִּשְׁתּוֹחֲחִי ׀ נַפְשִׁי וּמַה־תֶּהֱמִי
עָלָי הוֹחִילִי לֵאלֹהִים כִּי־עוֹד אוֹדֶנּוּ יְשׁוּעֹת פָּנַי וֵאלֹהָי׃
מג א ב שָׁפְטֵנִי אֱלֹהִים ׀ וְרִיבָה רִיבִי מִגּוֹי לֹא־חָסִיד מֵאִישׁ־מִרְמָה וְעַוְלָה תְפַלְּטֵנִי׃ כִּי־
ג אַתָּה ׀ אֱלֹהֵי מָעוּזִּי לָמָה זְנַחְתָּנִי לָמָּה־קֹדֵר אֶתְהַלֵּךְ בְּלַחַץ אוֹיֵב׃ שְׁלַח־אוֹרְךָ
ד וַאֲמִתְּךָ הֵמָּה יַנְחוּנִי יְבִיאוּנִי אֶל־הַר־קָדְשְׁךָ וְאֶל־מִשְׁכְּנוֹתֶיךָ׃ וְאָבוֹאָה ׀ אֶל־
ה מִזְבַּח אֱלֹהִים אֶל־אֵל שִׂמְחַת גִּילִי וְאוֹדְךָ בְכִנּוֹר אֱלֹהִים אֱלֹהָי׃ מַה־תִּשְׁתּוֹחֲחִי ׀
נַפְשִׁי וּמַה־תֶּהֱמִי עָלָי הוֹחִילִי לֵאלֹהִים כִּי־עוֹד אוֹדֶנּוּ יְשׁוּעֹת פָּנַי וֵאלֹהָי׃

PSALM 43

PSALMS 43:1–5

Unquestionably a continuation of the preceding psalm. It is unclear why this psalm was made into a separate chapter.

43 1 **Vindicate me, God, and plead my cause against an unkind nation. Rescue me from a deceitful and unjust man.**

2 **For You are God of my stronghold. Why have You neglected me? Why must I walk about in gloom, oppressed by the enemy?**

3 **Send** me **Your light and Your truth; they will lead me. They will bring me** back **to Your holy mountain and Your dwelling place.**

4 **Then I will come to the altar of God, to the Almighty God of my abundant joy, and I will praise You on the lyre, God, my God.**

5 The psalmist concludes with the refrain from the previous psalm: **Why, my soul, are you stooped over** and downcast? **Why do you** only **sigh for me?** Instead, **have hope in God. For I will yet** be saved by Him and **thank Him,** as He is **my salvation and my God.**

PSALM 44

PSALMS 44:1–27

A psalm of prayer, entreaty, and complaint, whose subject is the difficulties faced by Israel as a result of being God's nation. The psalmist contrasts the glorious days of the nation's past with the harsh reality of its present situation.

44 8th day of month 1 **To the chief musician, a contemplation by the sons of Korah.** The contemplative aspect of this psalm deals with Israel's devotion to God as the cause of its present suffering. Thus, there is an element of complaint in the psalm, not with regard to the psalmist's personal woes but rather with regard to those of the nation. Containing both pleas and reminiscence, it has become ever more relevant with the passage of time.

2 **God, we have heard with our ears, our fathers have told us, of the deeds You did in their time, in days of old,** such as the conquest of the Land of Israel.

3 **You, with Your hand, drove out nations, and** You **planted them,** the people of Israel, in their stead; **You crushed peoples and sent them away.**

4 **For not by their own sword did they,** our ancestors, **inherit the land; their own arm did not deliver them.** Rather, **it was Your right hand and Your arm and the light of Your countenance** that accomplished this for them, **for You favored them.**

5 **You are my King, God; command** once again **victories for Jacob,** as You did in the past.

6 **Through You we gore our foes; through Your name we subdue those who rise against us.**

7 **For I do not put trust in my bow; nor will my sword save me.**

8 **For** it is **You** who **delivered us from our foes and shamed those who hate us.**

9 **In God we gloried all day long,** because of all our triumphs, and **we acknowledge Your name forever** as the One who enabled our successes, **Selah.**

10 **Yet** the present reality is completely different: Since then **You** have **neglected and disgraced us, and do not go forth** any longer **with our armies.** We no longer enjoy Your support.

11 **You have made us turn back** in retreat **from our foes; our enemies took spoils** of war from us **for themselves.**

12 **You made us like** helpless **sheep that are eaten, and** You **scattered us among the nations.**

13 **You sold Your people** to their enemies as captives **for a pittance; You did not set their value high.** We are enslaved and subjugated with very little cost to our oppressors.

14 **You made us a disgrace among our neighbors;** we have become objects of **scorn and mockery to those around us.**

15 **You made an example of us,** turning us into paradigms of degradation and disgrace, **among the nations;** we are **a cause for head shaking,** a gesture of pity and contempt, **among the peoples.**

16 **All day long my dishonor is before me, shame covering my face** because of the scorn and contempt heaped on me

17 **from the voices of revilers and blasphemers, among enemies and avengers.**

18 Words of prayer and complaint to God follow: **All this befell us, but we did not forget** our devotion to **You,** despite having been subjected to such humiliation and tragedy. **We did not deal falsely with Your covenant.** We still observe Your commandments.

19 **Our hearts did not turn back** from worshipping You, **though You caused our steps to stray from Your path,** from the path of Your assistance and salvation,

20 **when You crushed us in a place of** howling **jackals,** that is, in a situation comparable to a desolate wilderness, **covering us over in a place of the shadow of death,** in a dark and terrifying place.

21 **Had we** at times **forgotten the name of our God and stretched out our palms** in prayer **to a strange god,**

22 **would not God have discovered it, since He knows the secrets of the heart?** You therefore know the truth, that we have in fact remained loyal to You.

Jackal

23 **For we are killed all day long for You.** The enemies of God express their enmity toward Him by persecuting the people of Israel. **We are accounted as sheep for slaughter,** seen as easy prey.

24 **Arouse Yourself; why do You sleep, Lord?** Your disregard for our fate makes it appear as if You are asleep. **Awaken, do not neglect us forever.**

25 **Why do You conceal Your face and forget our affliction and oppression?**

26 **Our soul is stooped over into the dust.** We are dejected and of low spirits. It is as if **our belly cleaves to the earth,** so low have we sunk.

27 **Rise up, be our Savior; redeem us for the sake of Your kindness.**

מד א ב לַמְנַצֵּחַ לִבְנֵי־קֹרַח מַשְׂכִּיל׃ אֱלֹהִים ׀ בְּאׇזְנֵינוּ שָׁמַעְנוּ אֲבוֹתֵינוּ סִפְּרוּ־לָנוּ פֹּעַל־ ח לחודש
ג פָּעַלְתָּ בִימֵיהֶם בִּימֵי קֶדֶם׃ אַתָּה ׀ יָדְךָ גּוֹיִם הוֹרַשְׁתָּ וַתִּטָּעֵם תָּרַע לְאֻמִּים
ד וַתְּשַׁלְּחֵם׃ כִּי לֹא בְחַרְבָּם יָרְשׁוּ אָרֶץ וּזְרוֹעָם לֹא־הוֹשִׁיעָה לָּמוֹ כִּי־יְמִינְךָ וּזְרוֹעֲךָ
ה ו וְאוֹר פָּנֶיךָ כִּי רְצִיתָם׃ אַתָּה־הוּא מַלְכִּי אֱלֹהִים צַוֵּה יְשׁוּעוֹת יַעֲקֹב׃ בְּךָ צָרֵינוּ
ז ח נְנַגֵּחַ בְּשִׁמְךָ נָבוּס קָמֵינוּ׃ כִּי לֹא בְקַשְׁתִּי אֶבְטָח וְחַרְבִּי לֹא תוֹשִׁיעֵנִי׃ כִּי
ט הוֹשַׁעְתָּנוּ מִצָּרֵינוּ וּמְשַׂנְאֵינוּ הֱבִישׁוֹתָ׃ בֵּאלֹהִים הִלַּלְנוּ כׇל־הַיּוֹם וְשִׁמְךָ ׀ לְעוֹלָם
י יא נוֹדֶה סֶּלָה׃ אַף־זָנַחְתָּ וַתַּכְלִימֵנוּ וְלֹא־תֵצֵא בְּצִבְאוֹתֵינוּ׃ תְּשִׁיבֵנוּ אָחוֹר מִנִּי־צָר
יב יג וּמְשַׂנְאֵינוּ שָׁסוּ לָמוֹ׃ תִּתְּנֵנוּ כְּצֹאן מַאֲכָל וּבַגּוֹיִם זֵרִיתָנוּ׃ תִּמְכֹּר־עַמְּךָ בְלֹא־הוֹן
יד טו וְלֹא־רִבִּיתָ בִּמְחִירֵיהֶם׃ תְּשִׂימֵנוּ חֶרְפָּה לִשְׁכֵנֵינוּ לַעַג וָקֶלֶס לִסְבִיבוֹתֵינוּ׃ תְּשִׂימֵנוּ
טז מָשָׁל בַּגּוֹיִם מְנוֹד־רֹאשׁ בַּלְאֻמִּים׃ כׇּל־הַיּוֹם כְּלִמָּתִי נֶגְדִּי וּבֹשֶׁת פָּנַי כִּסָּתְנִי׃
יז יח מִקּוֹל מְחָרֵף וּמְגַדֵּף מִפְּנֵי אוֹיֵב וּמִתְנַקֵּם׃ כׇּל־זֹאת בָּאַתְנוּ וְלֹא שְׁכַחֲנוּךָ וְלֹא־
יט כ שִׁקַּרְנוּ בִּבְרִיתֶךָ׃ לֹא־נָסוֹג אָחוֹר לִבֵּנוּ וַתֵּט אֲשֻׁרֵינוּ מִנִּי אׇרְחֶךָ׃ כִּי דִכִּיתָנוּ
כא בִּמְקוֹם תַּנִּים וַתְּכַס עָלֵינוּ בְצַלְמָוֶת׃ אִם־שָׁכַחְנוּ שֵׁם אֱלֹהֵינוּ וַנִּפְרֹשׂ כַּפֵּינוּ לְאֵל
כב כג זָר׃ הֲלֹא אֱלֹהִים יַחֲקׇר־זֹאת כִּי־הוּא יֹדֵעַ תַּעֲלֻמוֹת לֵב׃ כִּי־עָלֶיךָ הֹרַגְנוּ כׇל־
כד הַיּוֹם נֶחְשַׁבְנוּ כְּצֹאן טִבְחָה׃ עוּרָה ׀ לָמָּה תִישַׁן ׀ אֲדֹנָי הָקִיצָה אַל־תִּזְנַח לָנֶצַח׃
כה כו לָמָּה־פָנֶיךָ תַסְתִּיר תִּשְׁכַּח עׇנְיֵנוּ וְלַחֲצֵנוּ׃ כִּי שָׁחָה לֶעָפָר נַפְשֵׁנוּ דָּבְקָה לָאָרֶץ
כז בִּטְנֵנוּ׃ קוּמָה עֶזְרָתָה לָּנוּ וּפְדֵנוּ לְמַעַן חַסְדֶּךָ׃

PSALM 45

PSALMS 45:1–18

A psalm in honor of the marriage of a warrior king. With a bit of poetic license the psalm can be applied to all bridegrooms, since a bridegroom on his wedding day is considered like a king.

45 1 **For the chief musician, on shoshanim.**[B] **A contemplation by the sons of Korah, a song of affection.** Unlike other psalms that have the word "contemplation" in their introductory verse, this psalm contains no incisive admonitions or discussions of lofty topics; rather, it contains advice and good wishes for the bride and groom. Some commentators suggest that the psalm was written in praise of King Solomon, or possibly the messianic king.

Judean coin bearing the imprint of a six-stringed harp

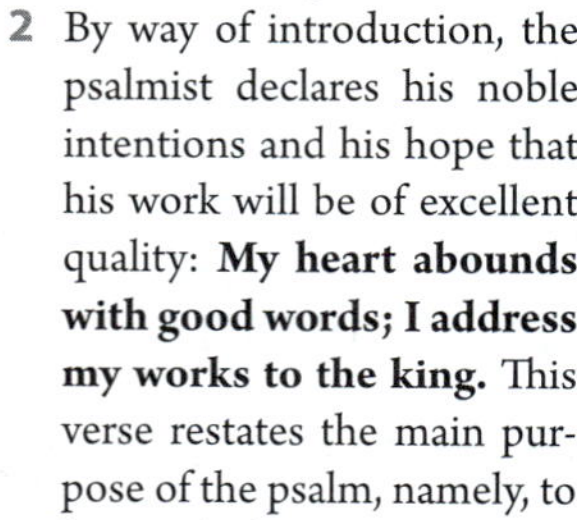

2 By way of introduction, the psalmist declares his noble intentions and his hope that his work will be of excellent quality: **My heart abounds with good words; I address my works to the king.** This verse restates the main purpose of the psalm, namely, to honor the king. **My tongue,** while reciting this song, **is** like **the pen of a swift transcriber.**

Assyrian scribes, wall painting, Til Barsip, Syria, eighth century BCE

3 **You are fairer than** all the other **sons of man; grace flows from your lips.** You express yourself gracefully, in a manner that is pleasant to hear. **Thus God has blessed you forever.**

4 As the king is also a warrior, the psalmist describes his military aspect: **Gird your sword upon your thigh, mighty one,** as this will be **for your majesty and glory.**

5 **Ride forth in your glory upon the word of truth.** The king's chariot, in a metaphorical sense, is the word of truth, **humility, and righteousness.** In addition to his role as warrior, the king serves as a judge. Here the military expressions acquire an additional metaphorical meaning: The glory and might of a king are manifest in his pursuit of truth in a manner that is both just and self-effacing. In similar fashion: **Let your right hand,** the symbol of both power and uprightness, **guide you along a wondrous path** that leads you to victory.

6 **Your arrows are sharp, piercing the hearts of the king's enemies; nations fall before you.**

7 **Your throne is** the throne **of God forever.** It is said of King Solomon that he "sat on the throne of the Lord."[12] **The staff of righteousness is the scepter of your kingship.**

8 **You love righteousness and abhor wickedness. Because of this, God your God has anointed you,** the king, **over your fellows with the oil of joy,** a reference to the oil used to anoint the king, as his rise to power, culminating in his coronation, is an occasion of great joy.

9 The psalmist describes the king as a bridegroom: **Myrrh,**[B] **aloes,**[B] **and cassia**[B] **were on all your garments as you went from ivory halls.** This was so ever **since they began to rejoice for you,** starting from when the wedding festivities began.

Myrrh

Aloes

Cassia

BACKGROUND

45:1 | **Shoshanim:** *Shoshanim* (see also 69:1, 80:1) is likely the name of a musical instrument that derived its name from the Akkadian word for lyre or from its six [*shesh*] strings. Similarly, the lily is called *shoshan* because of its six large, imposing petals. Alternatively, it may be the name of an ancient melody to which this psalm was to be sung.

45:9 | **Myrrh [*mor*]:** Myrrh was one of the most important spices of the ancient world, extracted from splitting the bark of various types of *Commiphora*, myrrh trees, which grow in Africa, southern Arabia, and eastern India. Myrrh even is mentioned in marriage contracts and other documents from the ancient East. Nevertheless, some disagree with the identification of *mor* as myrrh. In the Talmud (*Shabbat* 80b), *mor* is identified as *anpakinon*, a type of olive oil. According to the Rambam, *mor* is extracted from a gland of the musk deer.

Aloes [*ahalot*]: It is generally assumed that this item is identified with resin extracted from the core of the agarwood tree, *Aquilaria agallocha*, which grows in India and Indochina. It is considered one of the most expensive scents in the world.

Cassia: This is a type of cinnamon wood, from the tree *Cinnamomum cassia*. Pieces of its bark or powder extracted from it are used as a cooking spice and as scent.

45:10 | **Gold from Ofir:** This is a high-quality gold, mined in East Africa, southern Arabia, and India. Some suggest that the name Africa is derived from the place Ofir.

לַמְנַצֵּחַ עַל־שֹׁשַׁנִּים לִבְנֵי־קֹרַח מַשְׂכִּיל שִׁיר יְדִידֹת: רָחַשׁ לִבִּי ׀ דָּבָר טוֹב מה א ב
אֹמֵר אָנִי מַעֲשַׂי לְמֶלֶךְ לְשׁוֹנִי עֵט ׀ סוֹפֵר מָהִיר: יָפְיָפִיתָ מִבְּנֵי אָדָם הוּצַק חֵן ג
בְּשְׂפְתוֹתֶיךָ עַל־כֵּן בֵּרַכְךָ אֱלֹהִים לְעוֹלָם: חֲגוֹר־חַרְבְּךָ עַל־יָרֵךְ גִּבּוֹר הוֹדְךָ ד
וַהֲדָרֶךָ: וַהֲדָרְךָ ׀ צְלַח רְכַב עַל־דְּבַר־אֱמֶת וְעַנְוָה־צֶדֶק וְתוֹרְךָ נוֹרָאוֹת יְמִינֶךָ: ה
חִצֶּיךָ שְׁנוּנִים עַמִּים תַּחְתֶּיךָ יִפְּלוּ בְּלֵב אוֹיְבֵי הַמֶּלֶךְ: כִּסְאֲךָ אֱלֹהִים עוֹלָם וָעֶד ו ז
שֵׁבֶט מִישֹׁר שֵׁבֶט מַלְכוּתֶךָ: אָהַבְתָּ צֶּדֶק וַתִּשְׂנָא רֶשַׁע עַל־כֵּן ׀ מְשָׁחֲךָ אֱלֹהִים ח
אֱלֹהֶיךָ שֶׁמֶן שָׂשׂוֹן מֵחֲבֵרֶךָ: מֹר־וַאֲהָלוֹת קְצִיעוֹת כָּל־בִּגְדֹתֶיךָ מִן־הֵיכְלֵי שֵׁן ט
מִנִּי שִׂמְּחוּךָ: בְּנוֹת מְלָכִים בְּיִקְּרוֹתֶיךָ נִצְּבָה שֵׁגַל לִימִינְךָ בְּכֶתֶם אוֹפִיר: שִׁמְעִי־ י יא
בַת וּרְאִי וְהַטִּי אָזְנֵךְ וְשִׁכְחִי עַמֵּךְ וּבֵית אָבִיךְ: וְיִתְאָו הַמֶּלֶךְ יָפְיֵךְ כִּי־הוּא אֲדֹנַיִךְ יב
וְהִשְׁתַּחֲוִי־לוֹ: וּבַת־צֹר ׀ בְּמִנְחָה פָּנַיִךְ יְחַלּוּ עֲשִׁירֵי עָם: כָּל־כְּבוּדָּה בַת־מֶלֶךְ יג יד
פְּנִימָה מִמִּשְׁבְּצוֹת זָהָב לְבוּשָׁהּ: לִרְקָמוֹת תּוּבַל לַמֶּלֶךְ בְּתוּלוֹת אַחֲרֶיהָ רֵעוֹתֶיהָ טו
מוּבָאוֹת לָךְ: תּוּבַלְנָה בִּשְׂמָחֹת וָגִיל תְּבֹאֶינָה בְּהֵיכַל מֶלֶךְ: תַּחַת אֲבֹתֶיךָ יִהְיוּ טז יז
בָנֶיךָ תְּשִׁיתֵמוֹ לְשָׂרִים בְּכָל־הָאָרֶץ: אַזְכִּירָה שִׁמְךָ בְּכָל־דֹּר וָדֹר עַל־כֵּן עַמִּים יח
יְהוֹדֻךָ לְעוֹלָם וָעֶד:

10 **The daughters of kings are among those who honor you; at your right hand stands the consort,** the queen, **attired in gold from** faraway **Ofir,**[B] a land known for its fine gold.[13]

11 The psalmist now addresses the bride: **Listen, daughter, and take note** of all the splendor you will enjoy after your marriage; **incline your ear. Forget your people and your father's house** after you become the king's wife.

12 **The king will desire your beauty, as he is your master,** your king as well as your husband. **Bow to him.**

13 **The populace of Tyre will come with gifts** for the future queen, **seeking your favor, the wealthiest of the people.**

14 **All of the glory of the princess is within.** She does not appear in public; people honor her from a distance. **Her dress** is **interwoven with gold.**

15 **In embroidered clothing she is led to the king; her virgin companions follow her, escorting her to you,** the king.

16 **They,** the bride and her attendants, **are brought forth in gladness and rejoicing, entering the palace of the king.**

17 A blessing for the groom follows: **May your sons follow in the wake of your fathers.** May the dynasty remain unbroken, with your sons continuing to reign after you. **You will appoint them as ministers throughout the land.**

18 **I commemorate your name for all generations to come; thus nations will praise you forever.**

PSALM 46

PSALMS 46:1–12

A song of praise and thanksgiving to God in the wake of a victory. This triumph was preceded by a period of great distress, but following God's intervention a period of peace and tranquility ensues.

46 1 **For the chief musician, by the sons of Korah, a song on ala-**
mot. *Alamot,* literally, "young women," may have been the name
of a musical instrument played mostly by women. Alternatively,
it may have been the name of the melody used for this psalm.
2 **God is our refuge and our strength, our ever-present help**
in times of trouble.
3 **Therefore,** because God shelters us, **we will not fear during**
earth's upheaval, apparently a reference to an actual earthquake, or perhaps geopolitical turmoil, **when mountains**
tumble into the heart of the sea,
4 **though waters roar and foam** and **though mountains quake**
before His grandeur, as manifestations of God's great power,
Selah.
5 **There is a river whose streams gladden the city of God, the**
holy dwelling place of the Most High. As with the previous
description, the river and its streams can be understood not in
a literal sense, but as a metaphor for spiritual inspiration.
6 **God is in its midst,** in the midst of Jerusalem; therefore, **it will**
not topple. God will help it in the darkness that precedes the
dawn, **toward morning,** and not only during daylight hours.
7 **Nations raged, kingdoms tottered; He raised His voice and**
the earth melted.
8 **The Lord of hosts is with us.** "Lord of hosts" is one of the
names of God, depicting Him as ruler over all the powers of the
world. **The God of Jacob is our stronghold, Selah.**
9 **Come behold the works of the Lord,** His actions against the
enemies, carried out by the Lord **who made desolations,** total
devastation of them, **on the earth.**
10 **He makes wars,** the enemies' attacks against us, **cease**
throughout the earth; He breaks their **bows and severs** their
spears. He burns their **wagons,** used to transport soldiers or
supplies to the battlefront, **in fire.**
11 God now speaks to those enemies: **Desist** from your attempts
to wage war, **and know that I am God. I tower above nations,**
tower above the land.
12 The psalmist repeats, as a refrain: **The Lord of hosts is with us;**
the God of Jacob is our stronghold, Selah.

PSALM 47

PSALMS 47:1–10

A psalm devoted entirely to praising God's sovereignty over the universe. For this reason, it is associated with Rosh HaShana, the day of God's coronation; it is recited before the shofar is blown.

47 1 **For the chief musician, a psalm by the sons of Korah.**
2 **All people, clap your hands; shout to God with a joyous**
voice.
3 **For the Lord is most high and awesome, a great King over**
all the earth.
4 **He subdues peoples beneath us, nations under our feet.**
This verse and the next are references to the conquest of the
Land of Israel.
5 **He has chosen our portion,** the Land of Israel, **for us;** it is **the**
pride of Jacob, whom He loves, Selah.
6 **God ascends,** He is elevated and glorified, **with a clarion cry,**
which evokes majesty and glory; **the Lord** ascends **with the**
sound of a shofar.
7 **Sing praises to God, sing praises. Sing praises to our King,**
sing praises.
8 **For God is King of all the earth; sing thoughtful praises** in
His honor.
9 **God reigns over** all **the na-**
tions; God sits on His holy
throne.
10 **Ministers of the peoples**
have assembled, joining
with the people of the God
of Abraham. Nobles and
leaders of all nations gather
to join the people of Israel
in honoring God. Abraham
is mentioned here specifically because he was not only Israel's
forefather but also the propagator of monotheism in the
world.[14] **For the shields of the earth,** the power and ability to
safeguard the world, **belong to God;** in this, **He is greatly ele-**
vated. These words are a fitting conclusion to the psalm, which
is both a song of praise and a song of coronation for God as
King.

"With the sound of a shofar"

מו א ב לַמְנַצֵּחַ לִבְנֵי־קֹרַח עַל־עֲלָמוֹת שִׁיר׃ אֱלֹהִים לָנוּ מַחֲסֶה וָעֹז עֶזְרָה בְצָרוֹת נִמְצָא
ג ד מְאֹד׃ עַל־כֵּן לֹא־נִירָא בְּהָמִיר אָרֶץ וּבְמוֹט הָרִים בְּלֵב יַמִּים׃ יֶהֱמוּ יֶחְמְרוּ מֵימָיו
ה יִרְעֲשׁוּ־הָרִים בְּגַאֲוָתוֹ סֶלָה׃ נָהָר פְּלָגָיו יְשַׂמְּחוּ עִיר־אֱלֹהִים קְדֹשׁ מִשְׁכְּנֵי עֶלְיוֹן׃
ו ז אֱלֹהִים בְּקִרְבָּהּ בַּל־תִּמּוֹט יַעְזְרֶהָ אֱלֹהִים לִפְנוֹת בֹּקֶר׃ הָמוּ גוֹיִם מָטוּ מַמְלָכוֹת
ח ט נָתַן בְּקוֹלוֹ תָּמוּג אָרֶץ׃ יְהוָה צְבָאוֹת עִמָּנוּ מִשְׂגָּב לָנוּ אֱלֹהֵי יַעֲקֹב סֶלָה׃ לְכוּ־
י חֲזוּ מִפְעֲלוֹת יְהוָה אֲשֶׁר־שָׂם שַׁמּוֹת בָּאָרֶץ׃ מַשְׁבִּית מִלְחָמוֹת עַד־קְצֵה הָאָרֶץ
יא קֶשֶׁת יְשַׁבֵּר וְקִצֵּץ חֲנִית עֲגָלוֹת יִשְׂרֹף בָּאֵשׁ׃ הַרְפּוּ וּדְעוּ כִּי־אָנֹכִי אֱלֹהִים אָרוּם
יב בַּגּוֹיִם אָרוּם בָּאָרֶץ׃ יְהוָה צְבָאוֹת עִמָּנוּ מִשְׂגָּב לָנוּ אֱלֹהֵי יַעֲקֹב סֶלָה׃
מז א ב לַמְנַצֵּחַ לִבְנֵי־קֹרַח מִזְמוֹר׃ כָּל־הָעַמִּים תִּקְעוּ־כָף הָרִיעוּ לֵאלֹהִים בְּקוֹל רִנָּה׃
ג ד כִּי־יְהוָה עֶלְיוֹן נוֹרָא מֶלֶךְ גָּדוֹל עַל־כָּל־הָאָרֶץ׃ יַדְבֵּר עַמִּים תַּחְתֵּינוּ וּלְאֻמִּים
ה ו תַּחַת רַגְלֵינוּ׃ יִבְחַר־לָנוּ אֶת־נַחֲלָתֵנוּ אֶת גְּאוֹן יַעֲקֹב אֲשֶׁר־אָהֵב סֶלָה׃ עָלָה
ז אֱלֹהִים בִּתְרוּעָה יְהוָה בְּקוֹל שׁוֹפָר׃ זַמְּרוּ אֱלֹהִים זַמֵּרוּ זַמְּרוּ לְמַלְכֵּנוּ זַמֵּרוּ׃
ח ט כִּי מֶלֶךְ כָּל־הָאָרֶץ אֱלֹהִים זַמְּרוּ מַשְׂכִּיל׃ מָלַךְ אֱלֹהִים עַל־גּוֹיִם אֱלֹהִים יָשַׁב ׀
י עַל־כִּסֵּא קָדְשׁוֹ׃ נְדִיבֵי עַמִּים ׀ נֶאֱסָפוּ עַם אֱלֹהֵי אַבְרָהָם כִּי לֵאלֹהִים מָגִנֵּי־
אֶרֶץ מְאֹד נַעֲלָה׃
מח א ב ג שִׁיר מִזְמוֹר לִבְנֵי־קֹרַח׃ גָּדוֹל יְהוָה וּמְהֻלָּל מְאֹד בְּעִיר אֱלֹהֵינוּ הַר־קָדְשׁוֹ׃ יְפֵה נוֹף

PSALM 48

A psalm in praise and honor of Jerusalem in all its glory.

PSALMS 48:1–15

48 1 **A song, a psalm by the sons of Korah.**

2 **The Lord is great and exceedingly praised** when He appears **in the city of our God,** Jerusalem, and particularly when He appears **on His holy mountain,** the Temple Mount.

3 **Beautiful in its views, joy of all the world.** *Nof,* translated here as “views,” refers literally to the foliage of a tree. But the expression “beautiful foliage” is expanded to allude to the beauty of the entire city. The entire world sees Jerusalem as a paradigm of magnificence, whose pinnacle **is Mount Zion,** apparently a reference to the Temple Mount, as well as **the northern summit,** which contained palaces and, later, defense fortifications. It is **the city of the great king.** The “great king” may be a reference to King Solomon, whose palace was apparently situated in this northern part of the city.

4 **God, through its palaces,** referring to Jerusalem's largest and most exquisite structures, including public buildings and fortifications as well as homes of the wealthy and powerful, **is known as its stronghold.** For these structures are testimony to the city's greatness and strength.
5 **Behold, the kings convened** there, **passing** through the city **together.**
6 **They saw it** in all its splendor **and were amazed. They were terrified** by its strength; **they hastened** to leave the city, feeling overwhelmed and even threatened by its might.
7 **A fearful trembling seized them there, like the pangs of a woman giving birth,**
8 **or** like the terror of a seafarer who experiences **an east wind that breaks the ships of Tarshish.**[B] Although the east wind is rarely dangerous, it can acquire gale force during a severe storm, becoming powerful enough to destroy large ships. "Ships of Tarshish" were large, sturdy vessels built for long voyages, as Tarshish was a faraway port. Some say it was in Spain; others place its location in the eastern Mediterranean.
9 Those people who visit Jerusalem exclaim: **As we have heard** about Jerusalem in our home countries, **so we have seen** with our own eyes **in the city of the Lord of hosts, in the city of our God; may God establish it forever, Selah.**
10 Having witnessed the splendor of Jerusalem, **we envisage** a very different aspect of Godliness in Jerusalem, namely, **Your kindness, God,** which we do not see here, but is revealed **in the midst of Your Sanctuary.**
11 **As with Your name, God, so Your praise,** which people declare, is widespread and **reaches to the ends of the earth. Your right hand is filled with righteousness.** The image of God's "right hand" represents His power as well as His upright justice, an allusion to His faithfulness to His covenant.

Phoenician ship, stone engraving on a sarcophagus, Sidon, Lebanon, second century BCE

12 **Let Mount Zion be glad; let the daughters of Judah rejoice because of Your judgments.**
13 What follows is a call directed to those coming to Jerusalem: **Go about Zion,** the Temple Mount, which was surrounded by its own wall, **and encircle it; count** all **its towers,** the towers of the city as a whole.
14 **Pay attention to its ramparts** and **climb up to its palaces, so you may tell of it to the next generation.** Go from place to place so that you will be able to describe fully Jerusalem's greatness and glory.
15 Because Jerusalem is "the city of our God" and not merely the capital of a small country, the psalmist concludes with the following words: **For this is God, our God, forever and ever. He will guide us** forever, even **beyond death.**

PSALM 49

PSALMS 49:1–21

A psalm that focuses on death. It is recited nowadays in a house of mourning, and may have been composed for such a purpose.

49 1 **For the chief musician, a psalm by the sons of Korah.**
9th day of month 2 The psalm begins with a call for attention: **Hear this, all peoples; listen, all inhabitants of the world.** The word *ḥaled*, translated here as "the world," is usually defined more narrowly as land or soil. Given the similarities of sound, *ḥaled* also evokes a sense of termination or ending, as in the verb *ḥadal*, "to cease." In other words, it alludes to the ultimate return of all humanity to the dust of the earth.

BACKGROUND

48:8| **The ships of Tarshish:** Tarshish is the name of a port city or a geographical region that served as a maritime commercial center in the Mediterranean (see I Kings 10:22). Because of the similarity of names, it has been identified with Tarsus in southeastern Asia Minor, in today's Turkey, or with Tartessos in the southwest of the Iberian Peninsula. According to Ezekiel (27:12), Tarshish was a supply point for metals and other precious materials (see also Isaiah 2:15). It is possible that the term Tarshish was extended to refer to any place where similar activities took place, and to commercial ships that were used to transport merchandise great distances.

ד משוש כל־הארץ הר־ציון ירכתי צפון קרית מלך רב: אלהים בארמנותיה נודע
ה ו למשגב: כי־הנה המלכים נועדו עברו יחדו: המה ראו כן תמהו נבהלו נחפזו:
ז ח ט רעדה אחזתם שם חיל כיולדה: ברוח קדים תשבר אניות תרשיש: כאשר
שמענו | כן ראינו בעיר־יהוה צבאות בעיר אלהינו אלהים יכוננה עד־עולם
י יא סלה: דמינו אלהים חסדך בקרב היכלך: כשמך | אלהים כן תהלתך על־קצוי־
יב ארץ צדק מלאה ימינך: ישמח | הר־ציון תגלנה בנות יהודה למען משפטיך:
יג יד סבו ציון והקיפוה ספרו מגדליה: שיתו לבכם | לחילה פסגו ארמנותיה למען
טו תספרו לדור אחרון: כי זה | אלהים אלהינו עולם ועד הוא ינהגנו על־מות:
מט א ב ג למנצח לבני־קרח מזמור: שמעו־זאת כל־העמים האזינו כל־ישבי חלד: גם־ ט לחודש
ד בני אדם גם־בני־איש יחד עשיר ואביון: פי ידבר חכמות והגות לבי תבונות:
ה ו אשא למשל אזני אפתח בכנור חידתי: למה אירא בימי רע עון עקבי יסובני:
ז ח הבטחים על־חילם וברב עשרם יתהללו: אח לא־פדה יפדה איש לא־יתן
ט י לאלהים כפרו: ויקר פדיון נפשם וחדל לעולם: ויחי־עוד לנצח לא יראה

3 As noted in the previous verse, this psalm is directed to people in general, as its subject matter is universal, to **people and sons of man as well, rich and poor together.** *Benei adam*, translated here as "people," apparently refers to the common folk, whereas *benei ish*, "sons of man," refers to people of prominence, since *ish* is often used to indicate men of stature.

4 **My mouth will speak wisdom, understanding from my heart's meditation.** This verse indicates that the psalm is introspective in nature.

5 **I incline my ear for an allegory, opening with the lyre to state my sayings.** *Mashal*, translated here as "allegory," means a pithy or poetic utterance; in biblical Hebrew the word does not refer to a parable, a meaning it began to take on in the talmudic era. *Ḥidati*, translated here as "my sayings," refers to a kind of eloquent, clever statement, derived from the root *ḥad*, sharp. It does not necessarily denote a riddle or enigma, as it does elsewhere.

6 **Why should I fear in days of evil,** since all adversity eventually comes to an end, **though the iniquity of my feet surrounds me?** "Iniquity of my feet," literally, "iniquity of my heels," refers to sins committed as one walks along the path of life; alternatively, these are sins committed intentionally. I may be punished for my sins, but ultimately everything ceases.

7 The same may be said of **those who** are tranquil and comfortable in life, who **trust in their wealth and boast about their great riches.** In the end, death claims these people as well.

8 **A man can neither redeem his brother** from death **nor give God a ransom for him** to save him from that fate, nor can anyone else. When death calls, there is no escape.

9 **The redemption of their lives is too costly.** Even if it were possible to speak of a ransom from death, the price would be far too high, **and** it **can never be attained,** as it would exceed the value of everything in existence.

10 **Can one live forever, never seeing the grave?** Most people have illusions of immortality. They go about their daily lives, deluding themselves that they will live forever.

11 A man should realize that death is inevitable, **for he sees that** even the **wise men die. The foolish and the simpleminded** as well **all perish and leave** behind **their wealth to others.**

12 **Deep within them,** in their minds, **their houses will endure** in their possession **forever;** they imagine **their dwelling places will remain** theirs **for all generations. They name their lands after themselves,** expecting that their legacy will endure along with them.

13 **Yet man cannot abide** indefinitely **in his splendor.** In the end, all individuals are taken from this world. Worldly possessions, no matter how splendid, cannot save them from this fate. **He is like the beasts that perish,** dying just as animals do.

14 **This is their way of folly,** building their hopes and dreams on what they possess in this world, even though possessions are ephemeral and annulled by death. **So, too, those who follow,** subsequent generations, **speak the same desires** about indefinite continuation of life in this world, **Selah.**

15 **Like sheep, they are destined for the grave; death will shepherd them [*yirem*].** All of humanity is like a flock of sheep being led by a shepherd to inevitable death. Some commentators interpret *yirem* as "will consume them" rather than "will shepherd them." **The upright will rule over them** and take control of their property **in the morning,** in the future, after their death, while **their form,** their bodies, **will be consumed in the abode of the grave.**

16 In one of the few places in the Bible in which the continuing existence of the soul after death is mentioned, the psalmist now inserts a verse on a more positive note: **But God will redeem my soul from the grip of Sheol.** Usually *sheol* is translated as "the grave," a place one goes to after death. As such, elsewhere (55:16) this word is translated as "the netherworld." But sometimes, as here, it refers to a place of suffering and misery after death, a hell, where the souls of those who dedicated their lives exclusively to worldly matters go. The righteous, by contrast, will be redeemed from this fate by God. **He will take me in, Selah.** True redemption, real deliverance from Sheol, occurs when a soul reaches a level in which it is bound to God, a situation referred to in I Samuel 25:29 as the "bond of life with the Lord your God."

17 The psalmist turns to those people who choose to walk a righteous path but feel that the world does not value their choice: **Do not fear,** do not be concerned, **when a man becomes wealthy** and powerful, **increasing the honor of his house.** All this is ultimately of no consequence,

18 **for he will take nothing when he dies; his honor will not descend** to the grave **with him.** Wealth and honor have no meaning in the grave.

19 **Rather** than a person seeking out riches, **he should bring blessing upon himself during his life,** by doing good deeds that are seen as a blessing. Turning to such a person, the psalmist declares: Thereupon, **people will praise you** for your upright behavior, **and you** yourself **will benefit** from this. Righteous deeds are of benefit to the soul. People who are kind to others also help themselves thereby, and indeed, all that remains with one's soul in eternity is the good that it has done.

20 **Or** if not, **it,** man's soul, **will return to the generations of his fathers.** It will experience the same fate as the souls of his ancestors who did not follow this advice and **who forever will not behold the light.** All their material accomplishments will dim and fade after death.

21 The psalmist concludes with a summary of man's attitude toward his life: A **man** who is preoccupied with material life and basks **in his splendor does not understand** which things in life are truly meaningful and beneficial for his soul; **he is like the beasts that perish.** In life he is like an animal, devoid of understanding, and in death as well he is like a beast, in that there remains no memory of him and there is no hope for his soul.

PSALM 50

PSALMS 50:1–23

A psalm providing perspective about the offering of sacrifices in general. According to tradition, it was recited on one of the days of the Sukkot festival during the daily sacrifice.

50 1 **A psalm by Asaf. The Almighty God, the Lord, has spoken, addressing** all people of **the earth, from the rising of the sun to its setting,** from east to west.

2 **Out of Zion,** the Temple Mount, **the perfection of beauty, God shines forth.** The focal point of God's revelation is the Temple in Jerusalem.

3 **Our God arrives and is not silent;** His words will be heard. **Before Him a fire consumes** all, **and surrounding Him it is exceedingly stormy.** Divine revelation is accompanied by fire and stormy winds.[15]

4 **He summons the heavens above, and** He also calls upon **the earth,** in order **to judge His people.**

5 This is what He says to the earth: **Gather My devoted ones, those who establish a covenant with Me by sacrifice.**

6 In parallel: **The heavens declare His righteousness, for God Himself is Judge, Selah.**

7 God now directs His speech to His people in general, and more specifically to those who fear Him: **Hear, My people, and I will speak;** hear, **Israel,** and **I will bear witness to you.** Remember that **I am God, your God.** This is an allusion to the first of the Ten Precepts: "I am the Lord your God."[16]

יא הַשְׁחִת: כִּי יִרְאֶה ׀ חֲכָמִים יָמוּתוּ יַחַד כְּסִיל וָבַעַר יֹאבֵדוּ וְעָזְבוּ לַאֲחֵרִים חֵילָם:
יב יג קִרְבָּם בָּתֵּימוֹ ׀ לְעוֹלָם מִשְׁכְּנֹתָם לְדֹר וָדֹר קָרְאוּ בִשְׁמוֹתָם עֲלֵי אֲדָמוֹת: וְאָדָם
יד בִּיקָר בַּל־יָלִין נִמְשַׁל כַּבְּהֵמוֹת נִדְמוּ: זֶה דַרְכָּם כֵּסֶל לָמוֹ וְאַחֲרֵיהֶם ׀ בְּפִיהֶם
טו יִרְצוּ סֶלָה: כַּצֹּאן ׀ לִשְׁאוֹל שַׁתּוּ מָוֶת יִרְעֵם וַיִּרְדּוּ בָם יְשָׁרִים ׀ לַבֹּקֶר וְצִירָם וְצוּרָם
טז לְבַלּוֹת שְׁאוֹל מִזְּבֻל לוֹ: אַךְ־אֱלֹהִים יִפְדֶּה נַפְשִׁי מִיַּד שְׁאוֹל כִּי יִקָּחֵנִי סֶלָה:
יז יח אַל־תִּירָא כִּי־יַעֲשִׁר אִישׁ כִּי־יִרְבֶּה כְּבוֹד בֵּיתוֹ: כִּי לֹא בְמוֹתוֹ יִקַּח הַכֹּל לֹא־יֵרֵד
יט כ אַחֲרָיו כְּבוֹדוֹ: כִּי־נַפְשׁוֹ בְּחַיָּיו יְבָרֵךְ וְיוֹדֻךָ כִּי־תֵיטִיב לָךְ: תָּבוֹא עַד־דּוֹר אֲבוֹתָיו ז
כא עַד־נֵצַח לֹא יִרְאוּ־אוֹר: אָדָם בִּיקָר וְלֹא יָבִין נִמְשַׁל כַּבְּהֵמוֹת נִדְמוּ:
נ א מִזְמוֹר לְאָסָף אֵל ׀ אֱלֹהִים יְהוָה דִּבֶּר וַיִּקְרָא־אָרֶץ מִמִּזְרַח־שֶׁמֶשׁ עַד־מְבֹאוֹ:
ב ג מִצִּיּוֹן מִכְלַל־יֹפִי אֱלֹהִים הוֹפִיעַ: יָבֹא אֱלֹהֵינוּ וְאַל־יֶחֱרַשׁ אֵשׁ־לְפָנָיו תֹּאכֵל
ד ה וּסְבִיבָיו נִשְׂעֲרָה מְאֹד: יִקְרָא אֶל־הַשָּׁמַיִם מֵעָל וְאֶל־הָאָרֶץ לָדִין עַמּוֹ: אִסְפוּ־
ו לִי חֲסִידָי כֹּרְתֵי בְרִיתִי עֲלֵי־זָבַח: וַיַּגִּידוּ שָׁמַיִם צִדְקוֹ כִּי־אֱלֹהִים ׀ שֹׁפֵט הוּא
ז ח סֶלָה: שִׁמְעָה עַמִּי ׀ וַאֲדַבֵּרָה יִשְׂרָאֵל וְאָעִידָה בָּךְ אֱלֹהִים אֱלֹהֶיךָ אָנֹכִי: לֹא
ט עַל־זְבָחֶיךָ אוֹכִיחֶךָ וְעוֹלֹתֶיךָ לְנֶגְדִּי תָמִיד: לֹא־אֶקַּח מִבֵּיתְךָ פָר מִמִּכְלְאֹתֶיךָ
י יא עַתּוּדִים: כִּי־לִי כָל־חַיְתוֹ־יָעַר בְּהֵמוֹת בְּהַרְרֵי־אָלֶף: יָדַעְתִּי כָּל־עוֹף הָרִים וְזִיז
יב יג שָׂדַי עִמָּדִי: אִם־אֶרְעַב לֹא־אֹמַר לָךְ כִּי־לִי תֵבֵל וּמְלֹאָהּ: הַאוֹכַל בְּשַׂר אַבִּירִים

8 Although the Torah encourages animal sacrifices and gives extensive instructions concerning them, **I do not rebuke you for** not having offered **your sacrifices** to Me. **Nor are your burnt offerings always before Me.** They are not the focus of My attention. I do not need any of your sacrifices for My own sake. This point is clarified further in the following verses.

9 **I will not take** for Myself **a young bull from your house, or he-goats from your pens.**

10 I have no need of your animals, **for every beast of the forest is Mine, as are the cattle on thousands of hills.**

11 **I know every bird of the mountains; so too the large fowl of the field are with Me.** *Ziz*, translated here as "large fowl," is of uncertain meaning, but it appears to refer to a species of giant bird.[17]

12 Even **if** it were possible to imagine that **I were hungry, I would not tell you** and ask you to fulfill My need, **for the world and all it contains is Mine.**

"He-goat"

13 Of course, the scenario in the preceding verse is an absurdity, expressed ironically, for **do I eat the flesh of bulls or drink the blood of he-goats?** To believe that would be ludicrous.

14 It is clear, then, that God does not need the sacrifices we offer. Rather, they are a means by which we can express our relationship with God. **Offer God a thanksgiving sacrifice, and pay your** sacrificial **vows to the Most High** if you have pledged to bring a sacrifice in His honor.

15 And if you do fulfill your vows faithfully, you can always **call upon Me in times of trouble,** situations in which people are most inclined to make vows. **I will** accept your vow and **rescue you, and you will** subsequently **honor Me** by fulfilling the sacrificial vow.

16 All the foregoing relates to ordinary or specifically God-fearing individuals. **But to the wicked one God says: What right have you to speak of My statutes or to invoke My covenant** with Israel? Why do you profess to be a member of the holy nation of Israel and a party to their covenant with God?

17 **For** despite your claims, **you hate reproof, and you cast My words behind you,** following various paths of evil, as described in the following verses.

18 **When you see a thief, you run** to participate **with him** in his crime; **you join in with adulterers.**

19 **You let your mouth spew out evil, and** you **affix your tongue to deceit.**

20 **You sit and speak** even **against your brother** when in the company of others. **You slander your own mother's son.**

21 **You have done these** evil **things, and I kept silent,** not immediately responding to them. **Did you think I was like you, that I would** lower Myself to your level and come to **reprove you and set it,** your nefarious behavior, **before your eyes?**

22 God does not respond to evil in that way. But in the end, He does judge man: **Ponder this well, you who have forgotten God,** who believe that God has overlooked their sins entirely. Realize that the time of punishment will ultimately arrive, and repent, **lest I tear you to pieces, with no one to rescue you.**

23 The concluding verse is addressed to those who heed God's word: But **he who offers a thanksgiving sacrifice,** acting on his desire to show his gratitude to Me, **honors Me.** Such a sacrifice, made out of personal devotion, as opposed to an offering brought by one who thinks he is doing Me a favor, is a means of honoring Me. **And as for he who sets his path,** who consciously chooses to follow the paths of righteousness and propriety, **I will show him the salvation of God.**

PSALM 51

PSALMS 51:1–21

A psalm that is the classic text of confession and contrition, containing a plea for forgiveness and expressing hope for absolution.

51 1 **For the chief musician, a psalm by David,**

Tuesday 2 **when Natan the prophet came to him** to rebuke him **after he had been with Bathsheba.** Natan informed David that the consequences of his sin would be felt not only in his lifetime but also in the lives of his descendants. As recounted in the book of Samuel,[18] David acknowledged and deeply regretted his actions, and God accepted David's repentance, though he was not yet granted full atonement. This psalm offers David's perspective.

3 **Be gracious to me, God, as befits Your kindness; in the greatness of Your mercy, blot out my transgressions.** I offer no excuses; I plead only for compassion and mercy.

4 **Thoroughly wash [*kabbeseni*] my iniquity from me.** The word *kabbeseni* refers to an intense and thorough scrubbing to remove deeply ingrained dirt. **Purify me from my sin.**

5 **For I know my transgressions.** David is saying that he "knows" his transgressions, referring to sins committed deliberately, in the sense that he recognizes their severity. **My sin is always before me,** always on my mind; I am unable to forget what I have done.

6 **Against You alone I have sinned.** David does not mean to say that his sin did not affect other individuals, as clearly it harmed others: Bathsheba, Uriya, and other people who were involved. What David means is the following: My sin is so severe, so grave, that I cannot deal with it in any way other than by placing it before God to judge. In other words, his transgression was not only a crime and a violation of societal norms, but also a manifestation of a deeply ingrained flaw in his relationship with God. **I have done evil in Your eyes; so** I understand and accept that **You are just in your words and right in Your verdict,** whatever punishment it may involve.

7 At the same time, David offers an explanation that might mitigate his culpability. He notes that sin is not a onetime, exceptional occurrence in man's life but rather an intrinsic part

BACKGROUND

51:9 | **Hyssop:** Common hyssop, *Origanum syriacum*, is a perennial shrub used as an aromatic spice; it also possesses antiseptic and medicinal qualities and is an insect repellant. As it can grow in poor and dry soil, it serves as a symbol of hardiness, despite its humble size.

יד טו וְדַם עַתּוּדִים אֶשְׁתֶּה: זְבַח לֵאלֹהִים תּוֹדָה וְשַׁלֵּם לְעֶלְיוֹן נְדָרֶיךָ: וּקְרָאֵנִי בְּיוֹם
טז צָרָה אֲחַלֶּצְךָ וּתְכַבְּדֵנִי: וְלָרָשָׁע ׀ אָמַר אֱלֹהִים מַה־לְּךָ לְסַפֵּר חֻקָּי וַתִּשָּׂא בְרִיתִי
יז יח עֲלֵי־פִיךָ: וְאַתָּה שָׂנֵאתָ מוּסָר וַתַּשְׁלֵךְ דְּבָרַי אַחֲרֶיךָ: אִם־רָאִיתָ גַנָּב וַתִּרֶץ עִמּוֹ
יט כ וְעִם מְנָאֲפִים חֶלְקֶךָ: פִּיךָ שָׁלַחְתָּ בְרָעָה וּלְשׁוֹנְךָ תַּצְמִיד מִרְמָה: תֵּשֵׁב בְּאָחִיךָ
כא תְדַבֵּר בְּבֶן־אִמְּךָ תִּתֶּן־דֹּפִי: אֵלֶּה עָשִׂיתָ ׀ וְהֶחֱרַשְׁתִּי דִּמִּיתָ הֱיוֹת־אֶהְיֶה כָמוֹךָ
כב כג אוֹכִיחֲךָ וְאֶעֶרְכָה לְעֵינֶיךָ: בִּינוּ־נָא זֹאת שֹׁכְחֵי אֱלוֹהַּ פֶּן־אֶטְרֹף וְאֵין מַצִּיל: זֹבֵחַ
תּוֹדָה יְכַבְּדָנְנִי וְשָׂם דֶּרֶךְ אַרְאֶנּוּ בְּיֵשַׁע אֱלֹהִים:

נא א ב ג לַמְנַצֵּחַ מִזְמוֹר לְדָוִד: בְּבוֹא־אֵלָיו נָתָן הַנָּבִיא כַּאֲשֶׁר־בָּא אֶל־בַּת־שָׁבַע: חָנֵּנִי — יום שלישי
ד אֱלֹהִים כְּחַסְדֶּךָ כְּרֹב רַחֲמֶיךָ מְחֵה פְשָׁעָי: הרבה כַּבְּסֵנִי מֵעֲוֺנִי וּמֵחַטָּאתִי טַהֲרֵנִי: — הֶרֶב
ה ו כִּי־פְשָׁעַי אֲנִי אֵדָע וְחַטָּאתִי נֶגְדִּי תָמִיד: לְךָ לְבַדְּךָ ׀ חָטָאתִי וְהָרַע בְּעֵינֶיךָ
ז עָשִׂיתִי לְמַעַן תִּצְדַּק בְּדָבְרֶךָ תִּזְכֶּה בְשָׁפְטֶךָ: הֵן־בְּעָווֹן חוֹלָלְתִּי וּבְחֵטְא יֶחֱמַתְנִי
ח ט אִמִּי: הֵן־אֱמֶת חָפַצְתָּ בַטֻּחוֹת וּבְסָתֻם חָכְמָה תוֹדִיעֵנִי: תְּחַטְּאֵנִי בְאֵזוֹב וְאֶטְהָר
י יא תְּכַבְּסֵנִי וּמִשֶּׁלֶג אַלְבִּין: תַּשְׁמִיעֵנִי שָׂשׂוֹן וְשִׂמְחָה תָּגֵלְנָה עֲצָמוֹת דִּכִּיתָ: הַסְתֵּר

of his existence: **I was formed in iniquity; in sin my mother conceived me.** The very process of conception involves actions that are not necessarily driven by the purest impulses. Thus, from the beginning of man's existence, he is imbued with drives and passions, and this becomes part of human nature.

8 **You desire truth in the innermost parts.** The word *tuḥot*, translated here as "the innermost parts," literally means "the kidneys," regarded as the seat of counsel and decision. You desire that truth penetrate the innermost recesses of man's mind, and it is with this degree of sincerity that I confess my sin. **Show me wisdom,** the ability to understand the depth of my sin, **in the hidden place within** my soul, where my private thoughts reside.

9 David now beseeches God to purify him of his sin, alluding to methods described in the Torah to remove ritual impurity: **Purify me** as if **with hyssop,**[B] **and I will be clean.** Hyssop was used in the procedure of purification from the ritual impurity of leprosy,[19] as well as in the procedure of purification from the impurity contracted through contact with a corpse.[20] **Cleanse me [*tekhabbeseni*], so I will be whiter than snow.** As mentioned previously, *tekhabbeseni* refers to an intense cleansing. David is willing to accept the concomitant pain involved in this process.

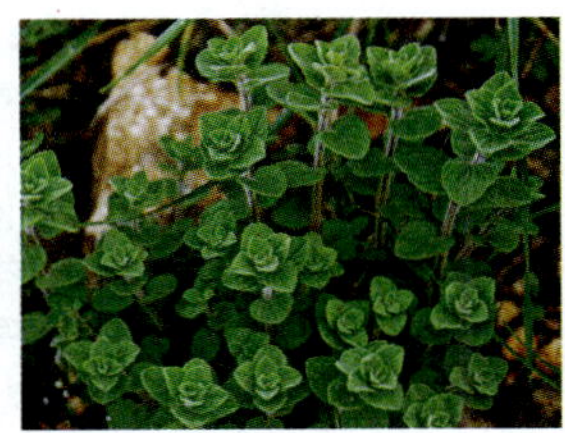
Hyssop

10 And when you purify me from my sin, this will **make me hear,** or experience, **joy and gladness** in the knowledge that my sin has been expiated. **Let the bones,** representing the essential, innermost part of me, **that You crushed rejoice.** The bones had been damaged by sins and guilt.

11 **Hide Your face from my sins** and do not keep them constantly in mind, **and blot out all my iniquities** in light of my repentance.

12 **Create in me a pure heart, God.** Replace my heart that has been damaged by my sins with a new heart. Grant me new understanding and feeling, **and renew a steadfast spirit within me.**

13 **Do not cast me away from Your presence** because of my sin, **and do not take** away **Your holy spirit from me.** Leave the holiness that is within me intact. David was not only a man of greatness; in many ways he was also a holy man.

14 **Restore the joy of Your salvation to me** by forgiving my sins. **Sustain me with a generous spirit** of divine grace.

15 Your acceptance of my repentance will be significant not only for me, but also for others who can learn from my experience, for **I will teach** about **Your ways** of forgiveness **to transgressors. Sinners will return to You** once they realize the potential of repentance.

16 **Save me from** the guilt of **bloodshed, God, the God of my salvation.** This is referring to David causing the death of Uriya, Bathsheba's husband. Save me from death for this sin, and then **my tongue will sing of Your righteousness** before others, who will learn from me the power of repentance.

17 **Lord, open my lips,** assist me in formulating these words, **so my mouth may declare Your praise.**

18 It is only the concepts discussed above that grant man atonement for his sins: the admission of wrongdoing, acceptance of punishment, and asking for forgiveness. Atonement cannot be achieved through sacrificial offerings alone, **for You do not desire me to offer a sacrifice; You are not pleased by a burnt offering.**

19 True **sacrifices to God are** not animal offerings, but **a broken,** contrite **spirit; You, God, will not reject a broken and crushed heart.**

20 Since David is the king of Israel as well as a private individual, he beseeches God to prevent his personal sins from harming the people of Israel as a whole: **Show Your favor to Zion; build the walls of Jerusalem.**

Wall of Jerusalem

21 **Then,** after atonement and forgiveness have been granted, **You will delight in righteous sacrifices,** sacrifices offered not for expiation but voluntary offerings that are expressive of our love, **in burnt offerings and whole burnt offerings. Then,** after true, heartfelt repentance, **young bulls will be offered on Your altar.**

PSALM 52

PSALMS 52:1–11

A prayer directed against liars and informers. While at times they appear to attain their devious goals, ultimately both the lie and the liar are discredited, while their innocent victim, with God's help, attains peace and tranquility.

52 1 **For the chief musician, a contemplation by David,**

2 composed **when Doeg the Edomite came and informed Saul, saying to him: David has come to the house of Ahimelekh.** As a result of what Doeg told Saul,[21] almost all the people of the house of Ahimelekh were killed for having harbored the fugitive David, despite their being innocent of any wrongdoing.

3 **Why do you boast of evil, you warrior?** Doeg was one of Saul's senior ministers and warriors. **The kindness of the Almighty,** which counteracts your evil deeds, **is all day long.**

4 **Your tongue contemplates wickedness. Like a honed razor, it works deceit.** A very sharp blade often "works deceit" by causing unintended scrapes.

5 **You love evil more than good, falsehood more than honest speech, Selah.**

6 **You love all slanderous words, a deceiving tongue.**

7 As punishment for this, **the Almighty will also shatter you forever; He will snatch you up, drag you from your tent, and uproot you from the land of the living, Selah.**

8 **And** when **the righteous will see** Doeg's downfall, they will have a twofold reaction: They will take note of the harshness of his punishment **and be awed, and** they **will laugh** and scoff **at him, saying:**

9 **Here is the man who did not make God his stronghold, relying** instead **on his great riches, fortifying himself in his wickedness.**

10 **But as for me,** one of the intended victims of Doeg's malevolent speech, **I am** thriving **like a verdant olive tree in the House of God; I trusted in the kindness of God forevermore** and emerged from the ordeal unscathed.

"Verdant olive tree"

11 **I will give thanks to You forever for what You have done, and I will place my hope in Your name, for it is good, in the presence of Your devoted ones.**

יב פָּנֶיךָ מֵחֲטָאָי וְכָל־עֲוֺנֹתַי מְחֵה׃ לֵב טָהוֹר בְּרָא־לִי אֱלֹהִים וְרוּחַ נָכוֹן חַדֵּשׁ
יג יד בְּקִרְבִּי׃ אַל־תַּשְׁלִיכֵנִי מִלְּפָנֶיךָ וְרוּחַ קָדְשְׁךָ אַל־תִּקַּח מִמֶּנִּי׃ הָשִׁיבָה לִּי שְׂשׂוֹן
טו יִשְׁעֶךָ וְרוּחַ נְדִיבָה תִסְמְכֵנִי׃ אֲלַמְּדָה פֹשְׁעִים דְּרָכֶיךָ וְחַטָּאִים אֵלֶיךָ יָשׁוּבוּ׃
טז יז הַצִּילֵנִי מִדָּמִים ׀ אֱלֹהִים אֱלֹהֵי תְּשׁוּעָתִי תְּרַנֵּן לְשׁוֹנִי צִדְקָתֶךָ׃ אֲדֹנָי שְׂפָתַי
יח יט תִּפְתָּח וּפִי יַגִּיד תְּהִלָּתֶךָ׃ כִּי ׀ לֹא־תַחְפֹּץ זֶבַח וְאֶתֵּנָה עוֹלָה לֹא תִרְצֶה׃ זִבְחֵי
כ אֱלֹהִים רוּחַ נִשְׁבָּרָה לֵב־נִשְׁבָּר וְנִדְכֶּה אֱלֹהִים לֹא תִבְזֶה׃ הֵיטִיבָה בִרְצוֹנְךָ אֶת־
כא צִיּוֹן תִּבְנֶה חוֹמוֹת יְרוּשָׁלָםִ׃ אָז תַּחְפֹּץ זִבְחֵי־צֶדֶק עוֹלָה וְכָלִיל אָז יַעֲלוּ עַל־
מִזְבַּחֲךָ פָרִים׃
נב א ב לַמְנַצֵּחַ מַשְׂכִּיל לְדָוִד׃ בְּבוֹא ׀ דּוֹאֵג הָאֲדֹמִי וַיַּגֵּד לְשָׁאוּל וַיֹּאמֶר לוֹ בָּא דָוִד
ג ד אֶל־בֵּית אֲחִימֶלֶךְ׃ מַה־תִּתְהַלֵּל בְּרָעָה הַגִּבּוֹר חֶסֶד אֵל כָּל־הַיּוֹם׃ הַוּוֹת תַּחְשֹׁב
ה לְשׁוֹנֶךָ כְּתַעַר מְלֻטָּשׁ עֹשֵׂה רְמִיָּה׃ אָהַבְתָּ רָּע מִטּוֹב שֶׁקֶר ׀ מִדַּבֵּר צֶדֶק סֶלָה׃
ו ז אָהַבְתָּ כָל־דִּבְרֵי־בָלַע לְשׁוֹן מִרְמָה׃ גַּם־אֵל יִתָּצְךָ לָנֶצַח יַחְתְּךָ וְיִסָּחֲךָ מֵאֹהֶל
ח ט וְשֵׁרֶשְׁךָ מֵאֶרֶץ חַיִּים סֶלָה׃ וְיִרְאוּ צַדִּיקִים וְיִירָאוּ וְעָלָיו יִשְׂחָקוּ׃ הִנֵּה הַגֶּבֶר
י לֹא יָשִׂים אֱלֹהִים מָעוּזּוֹ וַיִּבְטַח בְּרֹב עָשְׁרוֹ יָעֹז בְּהַוָּתוֹ׃ וַאֲנִי ׀ כְּזַיִת רַעֲנָן בְּבֵית
יא אֱלֹהִים בָּטַחְתִּי בְחֶסֶד־אֱלֹהִים עוֹלָם וָעֶד׃ אוֹדְךָ לְעוֹלָם כִּי עָשִׂיתָ וַאֲקַוֶּה שִׁמְךָ
כִּי־טוֹב נֶגֶד חֲסִידֶיךָ׃
נג א ב לַמְנַצֵּחַ עַל־מָחֲלַת מַשְׂכִּיל לְדָוִד׃ אָמַר נָבָל בְּלִבּוֹ אֵין אֱלֹהִים הִשְׁחִיתוּ וְהִתְעִיבוּ
ג עָוֶל אֵין עֹשֵׂה־טוֹב׃ אֱלֹהִים מִשָּׁמַיִם הִשְׁקִיף עַל־בְּנֵי־אָדָם לִרְאוֹת הֲיֵשׁ מַשְׂכִּיל

PSALM 53

PSALMS 53:1–7

A *maskil*, an introspective psalm about the deeds of the wicked. The psalmist sees the source of their evil in their lack of faith in divine providence and their misguided assumption that the world has been abandoned to those who are strong and lawless. Psalm 14 is a slightly different version of this psalm.

53 1 **For the chief musician, on the maḥalat, a contemplation by David.** It is unclear what *maḥalat* refers to. It was probably a type of musical instrument, or perhaps the name of a specific melody.

2 **The scoundrel says in his heart,** even if he does not declare it audibly: **There is no God.** His thoughts are evident from his behavior. **They have been corrupted and have acted abominably; there is no one who does good.** This belief partially underlies his abominable behavior.

3 **God looks down from heaven upon the sons of man to see if there is anyone of understanding who seeks God.**

4 The results of God's examination of mankind are discouraging. He finds that **it,** the entire generation, **has all gone sour** in the spiritual sense, **all of them together befouled; there is no one who does good, not even one.**

5 **Have the evildoers no knowledge, they, who devour my people as if eating bread, they who do not call out to God?** This verse depicts a world devoid of holiness. Evil people are present everywhere, attacking and harming those who are good.

6 **There they,** the few virtuous people, the victims of the evildoers, **were in great fear** of being swallowed up by the wicked. Turning to the righteous, the psalmist declares: **But,** in fact, **there was no** reason for you to **fear, for God has scattered the bones of those who** beset you and **encamped against you.** The psalmist addresses himself to the evildoers themselves: **You were put to shame!** And this is **because God despised them,** the evildoers.

7 The psalm closes with words of prayer: **May the salvation of Israel emerge from Zion! When God restores His captive people, Jacob will rejoice and Israel will exult.**

PSALM 54

PSALMS 54:1–9

A prayer against the wicked in which the psalmist expresses his faith that God will save him from his enemies and mete out just punishment for their misdeeds.

54 1 **For the chief musician on stringed instruments, a contemplation by David.**

2 It was composed **when the Zifites**[B] **came**[D] **and said to Saul: David is hiding among us,** whereupon Saul sent his men to capture him. Warned in advance, however, David managed to escape,[22] a turn of events for which he offers his thanks here.

3 **God, by Your name save me, and vindicate me by Your might.**

4 **God, hear my prayer; listen to the words of my mouth.**

5 **For strangers,** people who do not even know me and should have no reason to wish me ill, **have risen against me, and violent foes have sought my life.** They are acting unjustly toward me, demonstrating that **they have not set God before them, Selah.**

6 **Behold, God is my helper; the Lord is counted among those who support me.**

7 **He will repay evil to my foes.** Turning to God, David prays: **Destroy them by Your truth.**

8 **I will** then **bring a freewill sacrifice to You** for Your salvation; **I will give thanks to Your name, Lord, for it is good.**

9 **For He delivered me from all trouble, and my eyes have gazed upon** the downfall of **my enemies.**

PSALM 55

PSALMS 55:1–24

A psalm of prayer and supplication, relating to a time when the psalmist was beset by enemies, including traitors from among his own camp. According to some, the text alludes to the insurgency of Avshalom and the treachery of Ahitofel and others in supporting it.

55 *10th day of month* 1 **For the chief musician on stringed instruments, a contemplation by David.**

2 **Listen to my prayer, God; do not ignore my plea.** The psalmist's request that God heed his prayer is followed by a more modest request, that God not ignore him.

3 **Heed me and answer me as I lament with my speech,** as I speak of my pain and suffering, **and cry out**

4 **at the enemy's voice, at the oppression of the wicked, casting** their **evil upon me and hating me with wrath.**

5 **My heart is fearful within me; terrors of death descend upon me** because of all their threats.

6 **Fear and trembling enter me; I am enveloped in horror.**

7 **I said: Would that I had wings like a dove; I would fly away** to another place, anywhere else but here, **and come to rest.**

8 **I would wander far away to reside in the wilderness.** Although I might be isolated there, at least I would be safe. **Selah.**

9 **I would hasten to** seek out **a place of refuge, away from the stormy wind and tempest.**

10 The psalmist now shifts his attention to his foes, asking God for aid: **Confound them, Lord, confuse their tongue** and bring an end to their calumnies, **for I see injustice and strife in the city** when they are in control.

Dove spreading out its wings

11 **Day and night they encircle its walls** with injustice, **and there is iniquity and mischief within,**

12 **disasters within, intrigue and deceit not quitting its streets.**

13 The psalmist now turns to a particularly painful matter: **For it is not an enemy who taunts me, which I could bear.** It would

ד ה דֹּרֵשׁ אֶת־אֱלֹהִים׃ כֻּלּוֹ סָג יַחְדָּו נֶאֱלָחוּ אֵין עֹשֵׂה־טוֹב אֵין גַּם־אֶחָד׃ הֲלֹא יָדְעוּ

ו פֹּעֲלֵי אָוֶן אֹכְלֵי עַמִּי אָכְלוּ לֶחֶם אֱלֹהִים לֹא קָרָאוּ׃ שָׁם ׀ פָּחֲדוּ־פַחַד לֹא־הָיָה

ז פָחַד כִּי־אֱלֹהִים פִּזַּר עַצְמוֹת חֹנָךְ הֱבִשֹׁתָה כִּי־אֱלֹהִים מְאָסָם׃ מִי יִתֵּן מִצִּיּוֹן

יְשֻׁעוֹת יִשְׂרָאֵל בְּשׁוּב אֱלֹהִים שְׁבוּת עַמּוֹ יָגֵל יַעֲקֹב יִשְׂמַח יִשְׂרָאֵל׃

נד א ב לַמְנַצֵּחַ בִּנְגִינֹת מַשְׂכִּיל לְדָוִד׃ בְּבוֹא הַזִּיפִים וַיֹּאמְרוּ לְשָׁאוּל הֲלֹא דָוִד מִסְתַּתֵּר

ג ד עִמָּנוּ׃ אֱלֹהִים בְּשִׁמְךָ הוֹשִׁיעֵנִי וּבִגְבוּרָתְךָ תְדִינֵנִי׃ אֱלֹהִים שְׁמַע תְּפִלָּתִי הַאֲזִינָה

ה לְאִמְרֵי־פִי׃ כִּי זָרִים ׀ קָמוּ עָלַי וְעָרִיצִים בִּקְשׁוּ נַפְשִׁי לֹא שָׂמוּ אֱלֹהִים לְנֶגְדָּם

ו ז סֶלָה׃ הִנֵּה אֱלֹהִים עֹזֵר לִי אֲדֹנָי בְּסֹמְכֵי נַפְשִׁי׃ ישוב הָרַע לְשֹׁרְרָי בַּאֲמִתְּךָ — יָשִׁיב

ח ט הַצְמִיתֵם׃ בִּנְדָבָה אֶזְבְּחָה־לָּךְ אוֹדֶה שִּׁמְךָ יְהוָה כִּי־טוֹב׃ כִּי מִכָּל־צָרָה הִצִּילָנִי

וּבְאֹיְבַי רָאֲתָה עֵינִי׃

נה א ב לַמְנַצֵּחַ בִּנְגִינֹת מַשְׂכִּיל לְדָוִד׃ הַאֲזִינָה אֱלֹהִים תְּפִלָּתִי וְאַל־תִּתְעַלַּם מִתְּחִנָּתִי׃ — י לחודש

ג ד הַקְשִׁיבָה לִּי וַעֲנֵנִי אָרִיד בְּשִׂיחִי וְאָהִימָה׃ מִקּוֹל אוֹיֵב מִפְּנֵי עָקַת רָשָׁע כִּי־יָמִיטוּ

ה ו עָלַי אָוֶן וּבְאַף יִשְׂטְמוּנִי׃ לִבִּי יָחִיל בְּקִרְבִּי וְאֵימוֹת מָוֶת נָפְלוּ עָלָי׃ יִרְאָה וָרַעַד

ז ח יָבֹא בִי וַתְּכַסֵּנִי פַּלָּצוּת׃ וָאֹמַר מִי־יִתֶּן־לִּי אֵבֶר כַּיּוֹנָה אָעוּפָה וְאֶשְׁכֹּנָה׃ הִנֵּה

ט י אַרְחִיק נְדֹד אָלִין בַּמִּדְבָּר סֶלָה׃ אָחִישָׁה מִפְלָט לִי מֵרוּחַ סֹעָה מִסָּעַר׃ בַּלַּע

יא אֲדֹנָי פַּלַּג לְשׁוֹנָם כִּי־רָאִיתִי חָמָס וְרִיב בָּעִיר׃ יוֹמָם וָלַיְלָה יְסוֹבְבֻהָ עַל־חוֹמֹתֶיהָ

יב יג וְאָוֶן וְעָמָל בְּקִרְבָּהּ׃ הַוּוֹת בְּקִרְבָּהּ וְלֹא־יָמִישׁ מֵרְחֹבָהּ תֹּךְ וּמִרְמָה׃ כִּי לֹא־אוֹיֵב

DISCUSSION

54:1–2 | **A contemplation…when the Zifites came:** In this psalm the contemplation, or deep thought, can perhaps be seen from the relationship between the psalm's heading and its content. Although this psalm was written during a difficult time in David's life, he still expresses gratitude for a temporary reprieve from his troubles. It is a thought worthy of contemplation that in the midst of a series of deprivations and difficult situations the psalmist finds a moment to give thanks to God for his salvations, minor though they may be in comparison to his present misfortune.

BACKGROUND

54:2 | **Zif:** A city in the portion of the tribe of Judah (Joshua 15:55), identified with present-day Tel Zif. It is located approximately 7 km south of Hebron, near the modern-day town of Yatta. Remains of a city wall and other artifacts from the period of the Judean monarchy have been found in Tel Zif.

not be so bad if a known enemy would be scorning me. **Nor is it one of my foes who has grown threatening, from whom I could hide.**

14 David addresses his antagonist: **But rather it is you,** the one who is assailing me, **a man who was** always considered by me to be **my equal,** and moreover **my guide and companion.**

15 In our friendship **we shared confidences** with each other; **we walked** together **with great feeling in the House of God.** The pain is much greater, since my betrayal comes from one who had been a close friend.

16 David prays: **May He bring up death upon them; let them go down, still living, to the netherworld.** This may allude to the rebellion of Korah,[23] in which this was the fate of those who instigated an internal insurrection against Moses' leadership. **For evil is in their dwelling place,** that is, it is **inside them.**

17 **I call upon God; the Lord will save me.**

18 **Evening and morning and noon, I speak** in prayer **and cry aloud, and He hears my voice.**

19 At this point, there is a shift in the psalm's tone, evidently describing events that occurred at a later time: **He redeemed me unharmed from the battle waged against me, for there were many with me** supporting me, and for their sake God saved me from harm. It is also possible that this verse is describing occasions in the past in which David was rescued by God.

20 **The Almighty, He who abides from days of yore, will hear, and He will answer them,** those who have remained loyal to me, **Selah.** Referring now to the enemies: **They do not change;** as always, **they do not fear God.**

21 **He,** my antagonist, **raised his arms against his** erstwhile **comrades, violating his covenant** with them.

22 **His speech was smoother than cream, but** actually **war was in his heart. His words were softer than oil, yet they,** those words, **were** like **drawn swords** or, alternatively, like snares.

23 The psalmist offers general words of encouragement: **Cast your burden upon the Lord, and He will sustain you. He will never let the righteous slip.**

24 But as for his enemies: **You, God, will bring them down to the pit of destruction. Men of bloodshed and deceit will not live out** even **half their days, but I shall trust in You.**

PSALM 56

PSALMS 56:1–14

Another psalm of prayer and supplication that also contains expressions of faith and hope.

56 1 **For the chief musician, on yonat elem reḥokim.** The heading of this psalm is, in all likelihood, the name of a melody to be used for this particular text. **An instruction by David,** composed **when the Philistines seized him in Gat.**[B] David fled from Saul, seeking shelter with the Philistines in Gat,[24] where he was beset by further troubles.

2 **Be gracious to me, God, for men seek to devour me; fighters harass me all day long.**

3 **My foes seek to devour me all day long. But** despite the enemy's relentless pressure, there is reason for hope, as **many on high,** angels in heaven, **are fighting for me.**

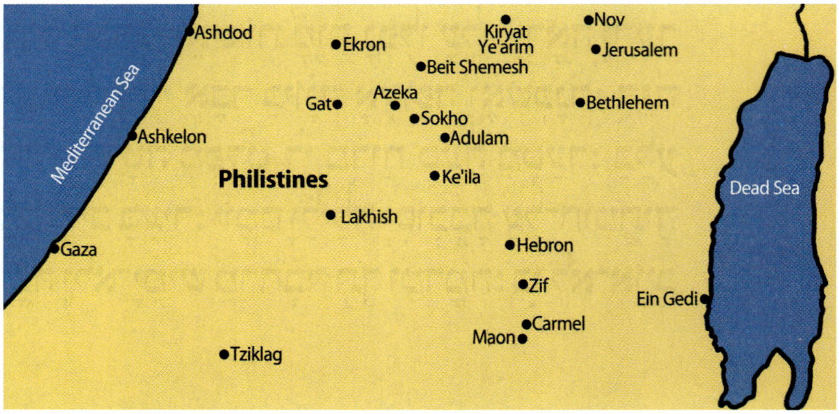

4 **On a day when I am afraid, I put my trust in You.**

Area of David's wanderings

5 **I praise the word of God. In God I trust; I shall not be afraid. What,** then, **can** a mortal man of **mere flesh do to me?**

BACKGROUND

56:1 | **Gat:** One of the five cities of the Philistines (mentioned in Joshua 13:3 and elsewhere), Gat has been identified with Tel Tzafit in the Judean lowlands. Two layers of ruins were discovered there: The earlier one is from the end of the ninth century BCE, consistent with the narrative in II Kings 12:18 concerning its destruction by Hazael king of Aram. The later layer testifies to the city's destruction at the hands of the Assyrians at the end of the eighth century BCE (II Kings 18).

יד יְחָרְפֵנִי וְאֶשָּׂא לֹא־מְשַׂנְאִי עָלַי הִגְדִּיל וְאֶסָּתֵר מִמֶּנּוּ: וְאַתָּה אֱנוֹשׁ כְּעֶרְכִּי אַלּוּפִי
טו טז וּמְיֻדָּעִי: אֲשֶׁר יַחְדָּו נַמְתִּיק סוֹד בְּבֵית אֱלֹהִים נְהַלֵּךְ בְּרָגֶשׁ: יְשִׁימוֹת | עָלֵימוֹ
יז יֵרְדוּ שְׁאוֹל חַיִּים כִּי־רָעוֹת בִּמְגוּרָם בְּקִרְבָּם: אֲנִי אֶל־אֱלֹהִים אֶקְרָא וַיהוה
יח יט יוֹשִׁיעֵנִי: עֶרֶב וָבֹקֶר וְצָהֳרַיִם אָשִׂיחָה וְאֶהֱמֶה וַיִּשְׁמַע קוֹלִי: פָּדָה בְשָׁלוֹם נַפְשִׁי
כ מִקְּרָב־לִי כִּי־בְרַבִּים הָיוּ עִמָּדִי: יִשְׁמַע | אֵל | וְיַעֲנֵם וְיֹשֵׁב קֶדֶם סֶלָה אֲשֶׁר אֵין
כא כב חֲלִיפוֹת לָמוֹ וְלֹא יָרְאוּ אֱלֹהִים: שָׁלַח יָדָיו בִּשְׁלֹמָיו חִלֵּל בְּרִיתוֹ: חָלְקוּ | מַחְמָאֹת
כג פִּיו וּקֲרָב־לִבּוֹ רַכּוּ דְבָרָיו מִשֶּׁמֶן וְהֵמָּה פְתִחוֹת: הַשְׁלֵךְ עַל־יהוה | יְהָבְךָ וְהוּא
כד יְכַלְכְּלֶךָ לֹא־יִתֵּן לְעוֹלָם מוֹט לַצַּדִּיק: וְאַתָּה אֱלֹהִים | תּוֹרִדֵם לִבְאֵר שַׁחַת אַנְשֵׁי
דָמִים וּמִרְמָה לֹא־יֶחֱצוּ יְמֵיהֶם וַאֲנִי אֶבְטַח־בָּךְ:
נו א ב לַמְנַצֵּחַ | עַל־יוֹנַת אֵלֶם רְחֹקִים לְדָוִד מִכְתָּם בֶּאֱחֹז אֹתוֹ פְלִשְׁתִּים בְּגַת: חָנֵּנִי
ג אֱלֹהִים כִּי־שְׁאָפַנִי אֱנוֹשׁ כָּל־הַיּוֹם לֹחֵם יִלְחָצֵנִי: שָׁאֲפוּ שׁוֹרְרַי כָּל־הַיּוֹם כִּי־רַבִּים
ד ה לֹחֲמִים לִי מָרוֹם: יוֹם אִירָא אֲנִי אֵלֶיךָ אֶבְטָח: בֵּאלֹהִים אֲהַלֵּל דְּבָרוֹ בֵּאלֹהִים
ו בָּטַחְתִּי לֹא אִירָא מַה־יַּעֲשֶׂה בָשָׂר לִי: כָּל־הַיּוֹם דְּבָרַי יְעַצֵּבוּ עָלַי כָּל־מַחְשְׁבֹתָם
ז ח לָרָע: יָגוּרוּ | יִצְפִּינוּ הֵמָּה עֲקֵבַי יִשְׁמֹרוּ כַּאֲשֶׁר קִוּוּ נַפְשִׁי: עַל־אָוֶן פַּלֶּט־לָמוֹ בְּאַף
ט עַמִּים | הוֹרֵד אֱלֹהִים: נֹדִי סָפַרְתָּה אָתָּה שִׂימָה דִמְעָתִי בְנֹאדֶךָ הֲלֹא בְּסִפְרָתֶךָ:
י יא אָז | יָשׁוּבוּ אוֹיְבַי אָחוֹר בְּיוֹם אֶקְרָא זֶה־יָדַעְתִּי כִּי־אֱלֹהִים לִי: בֵּאלֹהִים אֲהַלֵּל

יַשִּׁיא | מָוֶת

יִצְפֹּנוּ

6 **All day long they ponder my doings, their thoughts of evil directed against me.**

7 **They lie in wait in their dwelling places, they watch my footsteps in hopes of taking my life.**

8 **Cast them out for their iniquity; bring down nations, God, in anger.**

9 **You have taken** an **account of my** numerous places of **wandering. Put my tears in Your flask,** that is, take note of them and value them. There is a play on words here: The Hebrew word for both "wandering" and "flask" is *nod*. **Indeed, keep them in Your reckoning.**

10 **Then, on the day that I call** out to You in prayer, I trust that **my enemies will turn back** in retreat. But in any event, **this I know, that God is with me.**

11 **I praise the word of God; I praise the word of the Lord.** This verse invokes two of God's names, "God," referring to His attribute of justice, and "the Lord," alluding to His attribute of mercy. The psalmist declares his praise of God whatever the situation, whether He manifests Himself as stern Judge or merciful Protector.

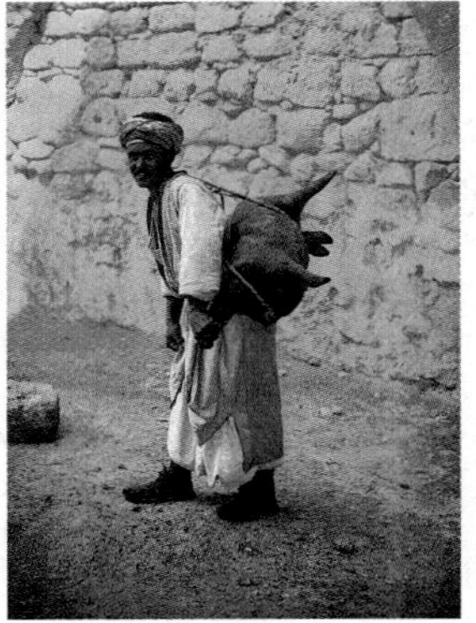

Man with skin flask

12 **In God I trust; I shall not be afraid. What can man do to me?**
13 **I will fulfill the vows I made to You; I will offer thanksgiving sacrifices to You.**
14 **For You have delivered me from death, indeed kept my feet from stumbling, so that I might walk before God in the light of the living.**

PSALM 57

PSALMS 57:1–12

A psalm in which, in a time of great distress, the psalmist turns to God. Although surrounded by enemies, he is confident that he will be rescued; indeed, he already thanks God for His assistance.

57 1 **For the chief musician, al tashḥet,** apparently a reference to
an ancient poem or melody on which this psalm is based. **An
instruction by David,** written **when he was in the cave fleeing from Saul,** an incident described in I Samuel 24.
2 **Be gracious to me, God, be gracious to me. For in You I take
refuge; in the shadow of Your wings I will shelter, until calamity passes.**
3 **I cry out to God Most High, to the Almighty who completes
for me.** The word *gomer*, translated here as "completes," is interpreted by some commentators as if it were written *gomel*,
meaning "who repays me for my good deeds." If *gomer* is understood literally, it seems that David is asking God to bring
his rescue to a successful conclusion. David's situation in the
meantime remains precarious; he has found no more than a
temporary shelter.
4 **May He send forth from heaven and deliver me, and put to
shame those who desire my destruction, Selah. May God
dispatch His kindness and His truth.**
5 **I lie amid** men who are as ferocious as **lions, anxious beasts,
among men whose teeth are spears and arrows, whose
tongues are a honed sword.**
The people surrounding me are even more dangerous than beasts, because they are armed. Moreover, their mouths, through their slander and disparagement, are as perilous as actual weapons.

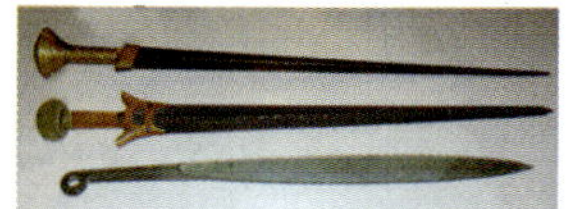
Mycenaean swords, reproductions

6 The psalmist turns to God
in prayer: **Rise above the
heavens, God; let Your
glory extend over all the
earth.**
7 **They prepared a net for
me to step onto, to bend
my spirit; they dug a pit
before me, but** ultimately
they themselves **fell into it,
Selah.**

Spearheads, Roman period

8 From here, the psalm concludes with words of praise and gratitude: **My heart is ready, God, my heart is ready. I will sing
and give praise.**
9 **Awaken, my soul! Awaken,** my **harp and lyre** with which I
sing God's praises; **I will wake the dawn.** Even before daybreak
I will begin to sing this psalm.
10 **I will give thanks to You, my Lord, among the peoples; I
will sing Your praise among the nations.**
11 **For Your kindness is great, reaching to the heavens, Your
truth,** in fulfillment of Your promise to protect me, **to the sky.**
12 The psalm ends by repeating verse 6 as a refrain: **Rise above
the heavens, God; let Your glory extend over all the earth.**

PSALM 58

PSALMS 58:1–12

A prayer against the wicked, who are full of evil thoughts. The psalmist beseeches God to destroy them.

58 1 **For the chief musician, al tashḥet.** This expression is explained above, in 57:1. **An instruction by David.**
2 The psalmist begins by addressing his enemies: **Do you violent
men really speak with righteousness? Do you judge men
honestly?**
3 No, **you plan wrongful deeds in your heart; with your hands
you mete out injustice in the land.**
4 **The wicked are corrupt from the womb; from birth, liars go
astray.**
5 **They have poison like the
venom of a serpent, like
a deaf cobra blocking its
ear,**[B]
6 **which does not hear** or react to **the voice of charmers,
skillful casters of spells.**[B]
Most snakes can be calmed
by charmers, but the "deaf

"Venom of a serpent." Venom dripping from the teeth of a rattlesnake

יב דָּבָר בַּיהוה אֲהַלֵּל דָּבָר: בֵּאלֹהִים בָּטַחְתִּי לֹא אִירָא מַה־יַּעֲשֶׂה אָדָם לִי:
יג יד עָלַי אֱלֹהִים נְדָרֶיךָ אֲשַׁלֵּם תּוֹדֹת לָךְ: כִּי הִצַּלְתָּ נַפְשִׁי מִמָּוֶת הֲלֹא רַגְלַי מִדֶּחִי
לְהִתְהַלֵּךְ לִפְנֵי אֱלֹהִים בְּאוֹר הַחַיִּים:
נז א ב לַמְנַצֵּחַ אַל־תַּשְׁחֵת לְדָוִד מִכְתָּם בְּבָרְחוֹ מִפְּנֵי־שָׁאוּל בַּמְּעָרָה: חָנֵּנִי אֱלֹהִים ׀
ג חָנֵּנִי כִּי בְךָ חָסָיָה נַפְשִׁי וּבְצֵל־כְּנָפֶיךָ אֶחְסֶה עַד יַעֲבֹר הַוּוֹת: אֶקְרָא לֵאלֹהִים
ד עֶלְיוֹן לָאֵל גֹּמֵר עָלָי: יִשְׁלַח מִשָּׁמַיִם ׀ וְיוֹשִׁיעֵנִי חֵרֵף שֹׁאֲפִי סֶלָה יִשְׁלַח אֱלֹהִים
ה חַסְדּוֹ וַאֲמִתּוֹ: נַפְשִׁי ׀ בְּתוֹךְ לְבָאִם אֶשְׁכְּבָה לֹהֲטִים בְּנֵי־אָדָם שִׁנֵּיהֶם חֲנִית
ו וְחִצִּים וּלְשׁוֹנָם חֶרֶב חַדָּה: רוּמָה עַל־הַשָּׁמַיִם אֱלֹהִים עַל כָּל־הָאָרֶץ כְּבוֹדֶךָ:
ז ח רֶשֶׁת ׀ הֵכִינוּ לִפְעָמַי כָּפַף נַפְשִׁי כָּרוּ לְפָנַי שִׁיחָה נָפְלוּ בְתוֹכָהּ סֶלָה: נָכוֹן לִבִּי
ט אֱלֹהִים נָכוֹן לִבִּי אָשִׁירָה וַאֲזַמֵּרָה: עוּרָה כְבוֹדִי עוּרָה הַנֵּבֶל וְכִנּוֹר אָעִירָה שָּׁחַר:
י יא אוֹדְךָ בָעַמִּים ׀ אֲדֹנָי אֲזַמֶּרְךָ בַּלְאֻמִּים: כִּי־גָדֹל עַד־שָׁמַיִם חַסְדֶּךָ וְעַד־שְׁחָקִים
יב אֲמִתֶּךָ: רוּמָה עַל־שָׁמַיִם אֱלֹהִים עַל כָּל־הָאָרֶץ כְּבוֹדֶךָ: ח
נח א ב לַמְנַצֵּחַ אַל־תַּשְׁחֵת לְדָוִד מִכְתָּם: הַאֻמְנָם אֵלֶם צֶדֶק תְּדַבֵּרוּן מֵישָׁרִים
ג ד תִּשְׁפְּטוּ בְּנֵי אָדָם: אַף־בְּלֵב עוֹלֹת תִּפְעָלוּן בָּאָרֶץ חֲמַס יְדֵיכֶם תְּפַלֵּסוּן: זֹרוּ
ה רְשָׁעִים מֵרָחֶם תָּעוּ מִבֶּטֶן דֹּבְרֵי כָזָב: חֲמַת־לָמוֹ כִּדְמוּת חֲמַת־נָחָשׁ כְּמוֹ־
ו פֶתֶן חֵרֵשׁ יַאְטֵם אָזְנוֹ: אֲשֶׁר לֹא־יִשְׁמַע לְקוֹל מְלַחֲשִׁים חוֹבֵר חֲבָרִים מְחֻכָּם:

BACKGROUND

58:5 | **Like a deaf cobra blocking its ear:** The black desert cobra, also known as *Walterinnesia*, is fairly common in Israel. All snakes have low-functioning ears. They have no outer ear, eardrum, or middle ear, and their inner ear serves primarily for maintaining the snake's balance. Therefore, their hearing is extremely weak and can detect only low frequencies of sound. It seems that snake charmers do not affect the snake through their music but through the movement of their bodies, which the snake imitates as part of its biting instinct.

58:6 | **Casters [*hover*] of spells:** This refers to a sorcerer or snake charmer, possibly akin to the Persian root *ayin-beit-reish*. In Akkadian, a priest is called *abaru*, and a hunter, perhaps specifically a snake hunter, is *baru*.

viper" is resistant to such pacification. The wicked are compared to such serpents, incapable of being swayed by words.

7 The psalmist continues with a prayer that is more like a curse: **God, break their teeth in their mouths; shatter the fangs of the young lions, Lord.**

8 **Let them melt away like the runoff of water,** dispersing in all different directions; **when he aims his arrows, let them be crushed** and broken before they hit their targets.

9 **Let them be like snails that melt away as they go along.**[B]

Fangs of a young lion

Like a stillborn of a woman, which has never seen the sun.

10 The psalmist now addresses the evildoers directly: **Before reaching** the age of **understanding, your shoots will become** hardened like **a bramble** bush; **and** then, when **you will be** solidified **like a** discrete **plant,** you will be **swept away by a whirlwind of wrath.**

Slug

11 In the end, **the righteous one will rejoice in seeing vengeance; he will wash his feet in the blood of the wicked.**

12 **And** then **man will say: Surely there is a reward for the righteous;** and even if this reward is not always immediately evident, we nevertheless realize that **surely there is a God who judges on earth.**

PSALM 59

PSALMS 59:1–18

A psalm in which David prays to be rescued from foes who are gathering to attack him for no justifiable reason. He expresses his faith that those foes will not only be defeated but will also acknowledge their wrongdoing. In addition, he prays that he will be able to offer his wholehearted thanks to God.

59 1 **For the chief musician, al tashḥet** (see 57:1). **An instruction by David, when Saul sent men to watch the house in order to kill him.** This psalm relates to a specific event in David's life, when Saul sent messengers to David's house with orders to kill him. David succeeded in escaping at the last moment.[25] In the verses that follow, he prays to be rescued from the continuing danger posed by those seeking his life.

2 **Rescue me from my enemies, my God; secure me from those rising against me.**

3 **Rescue me from evildoers; save me from men of bloodshed.**

4 **For they lie in wait against me; fierce men have gathered against me for no transgression or sin of mine, Lord.**

5 **They run** toward me **and prepare themselves** to do me harm, **through no fault of my own. Bestir Yourself for me, and see!**

6 **As for You, Lord, God of hosts, God of Israel, arouse Yourself** and reveal Yourself, **to make reckoning with all the nations.** The mention of "all the nations" might be a reference to the fact that Saul, for a variety of reasons, made use of foreign mercenaries in his effort to rid himself of David. **Do not pardon all the treacherous evildoers, Selah.**

7 David offers a description of those trying to capture him: They are nowhere to be found during the day, but **they return toward evening, barking like dogs and roaming the city.** Like wild dogs, they wander through the city primarily at night.

8 **Here they are, making** threatening **declarations with their mouths,** as if they had **swords in their lips.** They feel that they can speak and act as they please, **for** they say to themselves: **Who hears?** They do not believe that God hears them and will hold them to account.

9 **But You, Lord, laugh at them; You mock all the nations,** knowing that none of their schemes will be realized.

10 **His strength!** This is a call to God's power. **I will** hope and **wait for You, for God is my fortress.**

11 **My merciful God will come toward me;** He will grant me consideration and come to protect me. **God will let me look upon** the downfall of **my foes.**

BACKGROUND

58:9| **Snails that melt away as they go along:** The reference is to a type of snail without a shell, known as a slug. The description here particularly fits the species *Limax flavus*, the yellow slug, whose soft body is covered with a slimy substance and which is often found in or adjacent to homes. This creature leaves behind a trail of mucus as it goes, giving the impression of melting away.

ז ח אֱלֹהִים הֲרָס־שִׁנֵּימוֹ בְּפִימוֹ מַלְתְּעוֹת כְּפִירִים נְתֹץ ׀ יְהוָה׃ יִמָּאֲסוּ כְמוֹ־מַיִם
ט יִתְהַלְּכוּ־לָמוֹ יִדְרֹךְ חִצָּו כְּמוֹ יִתְמֹלָלוּ׃ כְּמוֹ שַׁבְּלוּל תֶּמֶס יַהֲלֹךְ נֵפֶל אֵשֶׁת בַּל־
י יא חָזוּ שָׁמֶשׁ׃ בְּטֶרֶם יָבִינוּ סִּירֹתֵיכֶם אָטָד כְּמוֹ־חַי כְּמוֹ־חָרוֹן יִשְׂעָרֶנּוּ׃ יִשְׂמַח
יב צַדִּיק כִּי־חָזָה נָקָם פְּעָמָיו יִרְחַץ בְּדַם הָרָשָׁע׃ וְיֹאמַר אָדָם אַךְ־פְּרִי לַצַּדִּיק אַךְ
יֵשׁ־אֱלֹהִים שֹׁפְטִים בָּאָרֶץ׃

נט א לַמְנַצֵּחַ אַל־תַּשְׁחֵת לְדָוִד מִכְתָּם בִּשְׁלֹחַ שָׁאוּל וַיִּשְׁמְרוּ אֶת־הַבַּיִת לַהֲמִיתוֹ׃
ב ג הַצִּילֵנִי מֵאֹיְבַי ׀ אֱלֹהָי מִמִּתְקוֹמְמַי תְּשַׂגְּבֵנִי׃ הַצִּילֵנִי מִפֹּעֲלֵי אָוֶן וּמֵאַנְשֵׁי דָמִים
ד הוֹשִׁיעֵנִי׃ כִּי הִנֵּה אָרְבוּ לְנַפְשִׁי יָגוּרוּ עָלַי עַזִּים לֹא־פִשְׁעִי וְלֹא־חַטָּאתִי יְהוָה׃
ה ו בְּלִי־עָוֹן יְרֻצוּן וְיִכּוֹנָנוּ עוּרָה לִקְרָאתִי וּרְאֵה׃ וְאַתָּה יְהוָה־אֱלֹהִים ׀ צְבָאוֹת
ז אֱלֹהֵי יִשְׂרָאֵל הָקִיצָה לִפְקֹד כָּל־הַגּוֹיִם אַל־תָּחֹן כָּל־בֹּגְדֵי אָוֶן סֶלָה׃ יָשׁוּבוּ
ח לָעֶרֶב יֶהֱמוּ כַכָּלֶב וִיסוֹבְבוּ עִיר׃ הִנֵּה ׀ יַבִּיעוּן בְּפִיהֶם חֲרָבוֹת בְּשִׂפְתוֹתֵיהֶם כִּי־מִי
ט י שֹׁמֵעַ׃ וְאַתָּה יְהוָה תִּשְׂחַק־לָמוֹ תִּלְעַג לְכָל־גּוֹיִם׃ עֻזּוֹ אֵלֶיךָ אֶשְׁמֹרָה כִּי־אֱלֹהִים
יא יב מִשְׂגַּבִּי׃ אֱלֹהֵי חסדו יְקַדְּמֵנִי אֱלֹהִים יַרְאֵנִי בְשֹׁרְרָי׃ אַל־תַּהַרְגֵם ׀ פֶּן־יִשְׁכְּחוּ חַסְדִּי
יג עַמִּי הֲנִיעֵמוֹ בְחֵילְךָ וְהוֹרִידֵמוֹ מָגִנֵּנוּ אֲדֹנָי׃ חַטַּאת־פִּימוֹ דְּבַר־שְׂפָתֵימוֹ וְיִלָּכְדוּ
יד בִגְאוֹנָם וּמֵאָלָה וּמִכַּחַשׁ יְסַפֵּרוּ׃ כַּלֵּה בְחֵמָה כַּלֵּה וְאֵינֵמוֹ וְיֵדְעוּ כִּי־אֱלֹהִים מֹשֵׁל
טו טז בְּיַעֲקֹב לְאַפְסֵי הָאָרֶץ סֶלָה׃ וְיָשֻׁבוּ לָעֶרֶב יֶהֱמוּ כַכָּלֶב וִיסוֹבְבוּ עִיר׃ הֵמָּה ינועון יְנִיעוּן

12 The psalmist prays to God to deal with his pursuers: **Do not** simply **slay them, lest my people forget.** If you kill them, their nefarious deeds will be forgotten along with them. I pray that in their punishment they will remain alive, so that the people will be reminded of their misdeeds. **Scatter them by Your power and bring them down, our shield, my Lord.**

13 **There is sin in their mouths** and in **the words of their lips. Let them be trapped** and then led to defeat **by their** own **pride, by the curses and lies that they utter.**

14 **Destroy** them **in wrath, destroy so they are no more, and they,** everyone in the world, **will know that God rules over Jacob to the ends of the earth, Selah.**

15 The psalmist reiterates and expands upon his previous description of his foes: **And they return toward evening, barking like dogs and roaming the city.**

16 **They,** the dogs, **wander about,** searching for food **to eat; if they are not sated, they stay to sleep.** So too, Saul's mercenaries prowl about in an unfamiliar city, searching for me everywhere.

17 The psalmist ends with words of praise to God: **But as for me,**
I will sing of Your strength, and **I will joyfully sing of Your**
kindness in the morning, for You were my fortress and a
refuge on the day of my distress.
18 **My Strength,** God! **To You I sing praises. For God is my for-**
tress, my merciful God.

PSALM 60

PSALMS 60:1–14

A song of praise and thanksgiving in the wake of a military victory. It opens with a description of previous difficult times of setback and defeat, and continues with an expression of gratitude for the ultimate triumph, conveying the message that everything is in the hands of God.

60 1 **For the chief musician,** on **shushan edut,** meaning literally,
11th day "lily of testimony." This psalm, like those immediately preced-
of month ing it, was apparently accompanied by an ancient melody. The
psalm was written in celebration of major victories in a war, and
though the war might not have reached its decisive conclusion,
there was already ample reason to give thanks. The psalm is
called **an instruction by David to teach** because in addition to
being a prayer, it also teaches of past events.
2 David wrote this psalm **when** his armies were engaged in active combat on several fronts: **He contended with Aram**[B]
Naharayim,at the northernmost border of David's kingdom,
and with Aram Tzova,[B] to the northwest; **and Yoav,** his general, **returned** from those wars **and smote twelve thousand**
Edomites in the Valley of Salt,[B] apparently adjacent to the
Dead Sea, or Salt Sea as it is known in Hebrew, to the south. In
effect, then, David and his armies were fighting two major wars
and won battles on both fronts. The psalm is thus a combination of praise, thanks, and remembrance.
3 **God,** it appeared to us that **You** had **abandoned us** and that
You had **sundered us. You were angry with us,** and we beseeched You to **restore us.**
4 **You** had **made the land quake; You shattered it,** and we
prayed: **Heal its broken pieces, for it has toppled.**
5 **You showed Your people harshness; You gave us poison**
wine to drink, so to speak. The years prior to the current victories were characterized by difficulties and defeats, with enemies
pressing on all sides.
6 Now, however, **You have given those who fear You a banner**
of victory **to wave** proudly, **because of Your truth,** Your faithfulness in keeping the ancient covenant that You made with our
forefathers. **Selah.**
7 **So that Your beloved ones,** the people of Israel, **be saved, de-**
liver us with Your right hand; answer me.
8 The psalmist now describes the victories: **God spoke** to me **in**
His holiness, assuring me of victory; **I** therefore **exulted. I di-**
vided Shekhem and measured out the valley of Sukot. Until
this point, these regions had been only partially under the rule
of Israel; other nations had occupied and fortified portions of
them. After David's victories they fell completely under Israelite
control, and he was now able to divide these areas among the
people.
9 Israel's victory in battle was made possible by the fact that the
people of Israel were now united behind a single leader: **Gilad**
is mine, and Manasseh, who dwelled in Gilad and the Bashan,
is also **mine, and Ephraim is my stronghold. Judah** is **my**
lawgiver, the one who decides and sets the laws. All of the
tribes, even those who had not been on friendly terms with one
another, were unified under David's rule.
10 **Moav**[B] **is my washbasin,** an expression of contempt; **I will fling**
my shoe at Edom,[B] an insulting gesture recognized throughout
the Middle East. **Philistia**[B] **will be crushed because of me.**
11 **Who leads me to besiege the city, who guides me to Edom?**
12 **Is it not You, God, who had** previously **abandoned us, You,**
God, who would not go forth with our armies?

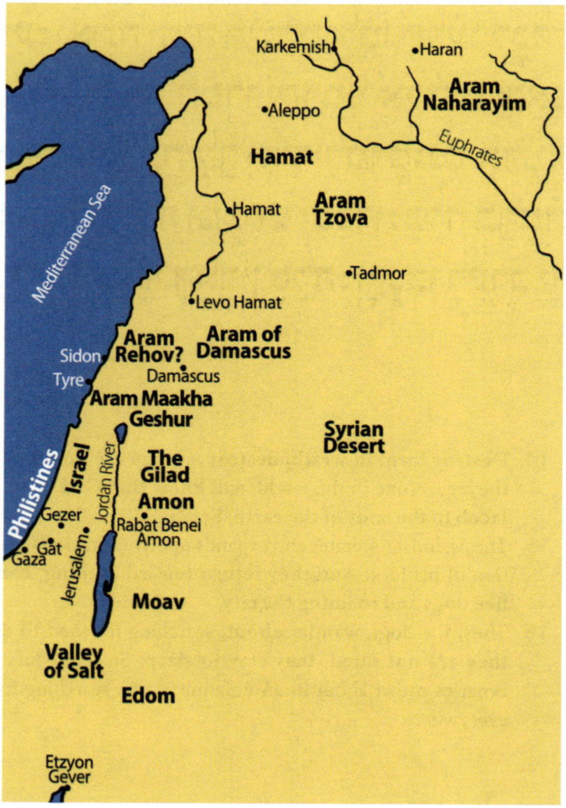

Nations surrounding David's kingdom

יז לֶאֱכֹל אִם־לֹא יִשְׂבְּעוּ וַיָּלִינוּ: וַאֲנִי ׀ אָשִׁיר עֻזֶּךָ וַאֲרַנֵּן לַבֹּקֶר חַסְדֶּךָ כִּי־הָיִיתָ
יח מִשְׂגָּב לִי וּמָנוֹס בְּיוֹם צַר־לִי: עֻזִּי אֵלֶיךָ אֲזַמֵּרָה כִּי־אֱלֹהִים מִשְׂגַּבִּי אֱלֹהֵי חַסְדִּי:
ס א ב לַמְנַצֵּחַ עַל־שׁוּשַׁן עֵדוּת מִכְתָּם לְדָוִד לְלַמֵּד: בְּהַצּוֹתוֹ ׀ אֶת אֲרַם נַהֲרַיִם וְאֶת־ יא לחודש
ג אֲרַם צוֹבָה וַיָּשָׁב יוֹאָב וַיַּךְ אֶת־אֱדוֹם בְּגֵיא־מֶלַח שְׁנֵים עָשָׂר אָלֶף: אֱלֹהִים
ד זְנַחְתָּנוּ פְרַצְתָּנוּ אָנַפְתָּ תְּשׁוֹבֵב לָנוּ: הִרְעַשְׁתָּה אֶרֶץ פְּצַמְתָּהּ רְפָה שְׁבָרֶיהָ
ה ו כִי־מָטָה: הִרְאִיתָ עַמְּךָ קָשָׁה הִשְׁקִיתָנוּ יַיִן תַּרְעֵלָה: נָתַתָּה לִּירֵאֶיךָ נֵּס לְהִתְנוֹסֵס
ז ח מִפְּנֵי קֹשֶׁט סֶלָה: לְמַעַן יֵחָלְצוּן יְדִידֶיךָ הוֹשִׁיעָה יְמִינְךָ ועננו: אֱלֹהִים ׀ דִּבֶּר וַעֲנֵנִי
ט בְּקָדְשׁוֹ אֶעְלֹזָה אֲחַלְּקָה שְׁכֶם וְעֵמֶק סֻכּוֹת אֲמַדֵּד: לִי גִלְעָד ׀ וְלִי מְנַשֶּׁה וְאֶפְרַיִם
י מָעוֹז רֹאשִׁי יְהוּדָה מְחֹקְקִי: מוֹאָב ׀ סִיר רַחְצִי עַל־אֱדוֹם אַשְׁלִיךְ נַעֲלִי עָלַי
יא יב פְּלֶשֶׁת הִתְרוֹעָעִי: מִי יֹבִלֵנִי עִיר מָצוֹר מִי נָחַנִי עַד־אֱדוֹם: הֲלֹא־אַתָּה אֱלֹהִים

BACKGROUND

60:2| **Aram:** This was a nation that dwelled between the Land of Israel and the Euphrates. It was split into several kingdoms: Aram of Damascus, Aram Tzova, Aram Beit Rehov, Aram Maakha, and Aram Naharayim. Its origins are Kir in eastern Babylonia (Amos 1:5).

Aram Tzova: Hadadezer king of Tzova expanded the borders of his country, Aram Tzova, up to the Euphrates River, but David's army, under the command of Yoav, succeeded in defeating Aram Tzova three times. At the time of the split-off of the Kingdom of Israel, Aram of Damascus conquered Aram Tzova, and the latter's final destruction took place under the Assyrian king Tiglat-Pileser III.

Valley of Salt: This valley stretches from the Dead Sea to the Red Sea, in the northern Arava. The ground of the Arava is salty, its aboveground water supply is limited, and some of its streams are saline. The northern Arava was a border area between Edom and Judah; it contains plains of poor, salt-laden soil, where halophytes, plants suited to salty soil, grow.

60:10| **Moav:** This was a kingdom east of the Dead Sea and south of the kingdom of Amon. The Moavites had shown animosity toward the Israelites even before the latter entered the land of Canaan, despite the familial relationship between the two nations (see Deuteronomy 23:4–5). David conquered Moav, but some of the Moavites, those in the southern region near Edom, maintained their independence. At a later time the Moavite king Mesha rebelled against the Israelite kings Ahav and Yehoram and reestablished his nation's independence.

Edom: This was a kingdom to the south of Judah, extending over both sides of the Arava, between the Dead Sea and the Red Sea. On the northeast it was bounded by Moav. Like the Moavites, the Edomites were hostile toward the Israelites even before the latter's conquest of the land of Canaan, despite their status as "brothers" of Israel (Numbers 20:14; Deuteronomy 23:8), having been descendants of Jacob's brother Esau. Although David conquered Edom and attached it to his kingdom, Israel later lost their control over Edom. Amatzya king of Judah defeated them at the Valley of Salt, but they rebelled against Judean control several times (see commentary on Genesis 27:40).

Philistia: This was a kingdom that stretched along the Mediterranean coast south of the lowlands of Judah. The Philistine people were a conglomeration of nations who came from the islands of the Mediterranean and left there for an unknown reason to infiltrate the Land of Israel some time at the end of the second millennium BCE. Their main settlement was in five cities: Gaza, Ashdod, Ashkelon, Ekron, and Gat. Another group of Philistines penetrated the northern parts of the Land of Israel, in the areas of the Yizre'el Valley and the Valley of Beit She'an. They were fierce enemies of Israel, and the latter were generally not able to conquer the Philistine areas during their conquest of the land. It was in their territory, in Gilboa, that King Saul was slain by them; David finally conquered them and attached their territory to his kingdom.

13 But now that You have once again come to our aid, **give us help against the foe, for deliverance by man** alone **is in vain.**

14 And if You come to our assistance, we will require no other form of salvation, for **with God we will triumph, and He will rout our foes.**

PSALM 61

PSALMS 61:1–9

A song of thanksgiving to God for providing aid and shelter at a time of distress. It is possible that it was written on the occasion of a great military victory.

61 1 **For the chief musician, upon neginat,** the name of a musical instrument or a type of melody, **by David.**
2 **Hear my singing, God; attend to my prayer,** in which I wish to praise You and to request an additional blessing from You.
3 **From the end of the earth I call to You when my heart is faint.** It is likely that the psalm was written when David was on a military campaign in a land far from the borders of Israel. **Guide me** to victory **against** an enemy so formidable that he is like **a rock that is** towering **high above me.**
4 **For You have been a refuge for me, a tower of strength against the enemy.**
5 **Let me dwell in Your tent forever; let me** always **take refuge in the shelter of Your wings, Selah.**
6 **For You, God, have heard my vows** that I undertook to fulfill if You would help me survive and win this war. **You granted the portion of those who fear Your name.** You rewarded them with what they deserve, namely, possession of the land that they retook from the enemy.
7 This is followed by David's additional request: **May you add years to the life of the king,** apparently a reference to himself, **so that his days extend over generations.**
8 **May he abide before the Lord forever. Make his portion kindness and truth;** bless the king with gifts of kindness and truth, **that they might preserve him.** In this translation, the word *man* is related to *mana*, "portion." The phrase can also be rendered: "Kindness and truth are what will preserve him."
9 **So I will sing praise to Your name forever, every day as I pay my vows,** expressing my gratitude to You for Your salvation.

PSALM 62

PSALMS 62:1–13

An introspective psalm that contrasts the lives of the wicked, whose apparent success is temporary, with those of individuals who embrace God and thus merit eternal life. It describes David's many enemies, as well as his hope to be rescued from them.

62 1 **For the chief musician, for Yedutun, a psalm by David.**
2 **For God alone does my soul wait silently** and anxiously, for **my salvation is from Him.**
3 **He alone is my rock and my salvation, my stronghold; I will not stumble** during times when adversity **greatly** besets me. An alternative understanding of *raba*, "greatly," in this phrase is: Even if I stumble a bit, I will not fall "greatly," all the way down to the ground.
4 The psalmist addresses his foes: **For how long will you terrorize a man?** This is the only time that the word *tehotetu*, translated as "terrorize," is used in the Bible. Its meaning is derived from the context of the verse. **You are murderers,** whether actual or potential killers, **all of you;** it is dangerous to be in your environs, **like** being near **a leaning wall or a tottering fence.**
5 **They scheme to bring down a man,** any man who has gained prominence, **from his lofty position.** And when they cannot attack him directly, **they** resort to slander and lies and **speak falsehood** against him. Or **they bless** him **with their mouths, but inwardly they curse, Selah.**
6 The psalmist repeats a variation of verse 2: **For God alone wait silently, my soul, for my hope is from Him.**
7 **He alone is my rock and my salvation, my stronghold; I will not stumble.**
8 **My** hope for **salvation and my** source of **glory are with God, rock of my strength; my refuge is in God.**
9 Speaking to members of the nation at large, the psalmist admonishes them: **Trust** only **in Him at all times, people,** for only on Him is it possible to rely fully. **Pour out your heart before Him** and tell Him of all your troubles, for only **God is a refuge for us, Selah.**
10 One should not put his trust in human beings, for **men are nothingness,** inconsequential and ephemeral; **men of rank are an illusion.** If one could weigh their worth, **they** would **rise together on the scales, lighter than nothingness.**
11 **Do not trust in** obtaining wealth through **fraud; do not delude yourselves by stealing.** Not only is it dishonest and sinful, but practically speaking, if you steal money, your wealth will prove to be elusive and short-lived. **If** you see in others that **wealth** built on deception and theft **increases, do not pay it heed,** for it will not last.
12 All these matters are decreed from on high; we are commanded by God to follow a path of proper behavior: **God has spoken once,** commanding us to follow in the path He has set for us,

יג זְנַחְתָּנוּ וְלֹא־תֵצֵא אֱלֹהִים בְּצִבְאוֹתֵינוּ׃ הָבָה־לָּנוּ עֶזְרָת מִצָּר וְשָׁוְא תְּשׁוּעַת
יד אָדָם׃ בֵּאלֹהִים נַעֲשֶׂה־חָיִל וְהוּא יָבוּס צָרֵינוּ׃
סא א ב ג לַמְנַצֵּחַ ׀ עַל־נְגִינַת לְדָוִד׃ שִׁמְעָה אֱלֹהִים רִנָּתִי הַקְשִׁיבָה תְּפִלָּתִי׃ מִקְצֵה
ד הָאָרֶץ ׀ אֵלֶיךָ אֶקְרָא בַּעֲטֹף לִבִּי בְּצוּר־יָרוּם מִמֶּנִּי תַנְחֵנִי׃ כִּי־הָיִיתָ מַחְסֶה
ה לִי מִגְדַּל־עֹז מִפְּנֵי אוֹיֵב׃ אָגוּרָה בְאׇהׇלְךָ עוֹלָמִים אֶחֱסֶה בְסֵתֶר כְּנָפֶיךָ סֶּלָה׃
ו ז כִּי־אַתָּה אֱלֹהִים שָׁמַעְתָּ לִנְדָרָי נָתַתָּ יְרֻשַּׁת יִרְאֵי שְׁמֶךָ׃ יָמִים עַל־יְמֵי־מֶלֶךְ
ח תּוֹסִיף שְׁנוֹתָיו כְּמוֹ־דֹר וָדֹר׃ יֵשֵׁב עוֹלָם לִפְנֵי אֱלֹהִים חֶסֶד וֶאֱמֶת מַן יִנְצְרֻהוּ׃
ט כֵּן אֲזַמְּרָה שִׁמְךָ לָעַד לְשַׁלְּמִי נְדָרַי יוֹם ׀ יוֹם׃
סב א ב לַמְנַצֵּחַ עַל־יְדוּתוּן מִזְמוֹר לְדָוִד׃ אַךְ אֶל־אֱלֹהִים דּוּמִיָּה נַפְשִׁי מִמֶּנּוּ יְשׁוּעָתִי׃
ג ד אַךְ־הוּא צוּרִי וִישׁוּעָתִי מִשְׂגַּבִּי לֹא־אֶמּוֹט רַבָּה׃ עַד־אָנָה ׀ תְּהוֹתְתוּ עַל־אִישׁ
ה תְּרָצְּחוּ כֻלְּכֶם כְּקִיר נָטוּי גָּדֵר הַדְּחוּיָה׃ אַךְ מִשְּׂאֵתוֹ ׀ יָעֲצוּ לְהַדִּיחַ יִרְצוּ כָזָב
ו בְּפִיו יְבָרֵכוּ וּבְקִרְבָּם יְקַלְלוּ־סֶלָה׃ אַךְ לֵאלֹהִים דּוֹמִּי נַפְשִׁי כִּי־מִמֶּנּוּ תִּקְוָתִי׃
ז ח אַךְ־הוּא צוּרִי וִישׁוּעָתִי מִשְׂגַּבִּי לֹא אֶמּוֹט׃ עַל־אֱלֹהִים יִשְׁעִי וּכְבוֹדִי צוּר־עֻזִּי
ט מַחְסִי בֵּאלֹהִים׃ בִּטְחוּ בוֹ בְכׇל־עֵת ׀ עָם שִׁפְכוּ־לְפָנָיו לְבַבְכֶם אֱלֹהִים מַחֲסֶה־
י לָּנוּ סֶלָה׃ אַךְ ׀ הֶבֶל בְּנֵי־אָדָם כָּזָב בְּנֵי אִישׁ בְּמֹאזְנַיִם לַעֲלוֹת הֵמָּה מֵהֶבֶל יָחַד׃
יא יב אַל־תִּבְטְחוּ בְעֹשֶׁק וּבְגָזֵל אַל־תֶּהְבָּלוּ חַיִל ׀ כִּי־יָנוּב אַל־תָּשִׁיתוּ לֵב׃ אַחַת ׀
יג דִּבֶּר אֱלֹהִים שְׁתַּיִם־זוּ שָׁמָעְתִּי כִּי עֹז לֵאלֹהִים׃ וּלְךָ־אֲדֹנָי חָסֶד כִּי־אַתָּה תְשַׁלֵּם
לְאִישׁ כְּמַעֲשֵׂהוּ׃

but **I have heard it twice.** This verse refers to the two aspects of God's commandments: to follow God's will, and to refrain from doing what opposes that will. The Torah, in essence, can be summed up in one phrase: "Turn from evil and do good" (34:15). **Might belongs to God,** and therefore we must be guided by His words.

13 Moreover, **kindness is Yours, my Lord, for You render** reward and punishment **to every man according to his deeds.**

PSALM 63

PSALMS 63:1–12

A psalm of devotion composed in the desert, a place of scarcity, thirst, and danger. The psalmist discovers that there is a yearning more powerful than thirst for water, namely, the yearning for closeness to God.

63 1 **A psalm by David, when he was in the Judean Desert.** This psalm depicts David's plight in the Judean Desert as he was fleeing from Saul, surrounded by enemies on all sides and suffering from constant deprivation. It is essentially a psalm of yearning for intimacy with God. The physical hardships of the desert intensify rather than diminish his desire for spirituality.
2 **God, You are my Almighty; I search for You. My soul thirsts for You; my flesh yearns for You, in a parched and thirsty land without water.** The psalmist's spiritual thirst for God is expressed against the backdrop of an arid desert in which man's physical needs are immediate and urgent. And yet, the psalmist's most intense thirst is not for water but for intimacy with God. It is precisely when his physical deprivation and isolation are most extreme that David realizes that his foremost longing in life is for spirituality.

"In a parched and thirsty land without water." The Judean Desert

3 **Indeed, in holiness I have seen You;** I imagine myself being enveloped in holiness, in a situation in which I am **beholding Your power and Your glory.** This is my dream and my desire.
4 **For Your kindness is better than life.** The realization that God's kindness is the source of all the goodness of the world means more to me than life itself. The mere recollection of Your kindness causes **my lips** to **praise You.**
5 **So I will bless You as long as I live.** My very life, the fact that I am alive, can be regarded as a means of blessing You. **I will lift up my hands** to pray **in Your name.**
6 **I am sated as with fat and rich fare.** My thoughts about You and the praises that I sing to You suffice to make me happy and fulfilled, providing gratification in the way that abundant good food satisfies a person. **My mouth offers praises with joyful lips,** not because of God's beneficence to me, but because I am filled with joy at sensing His presence.
7 **Even on my bed,** when it is time to relax and fall asleep, **I remember You. I meditate on You during the night watches.** A portion of the night, consisting of several hours, is called a "watch." People are sometimes roused from their sleep between one watch and the next, but they are not fully awake and immediately fall back asleep. I, however, says the psalmist, use these opportunities to meditate further upon You, which clearly indicates that You are central to all my thoughts. There is nothing more meaningful to me than awareness of God's presence; it occupies my heart and mind more than anything else.
8 **For You have been my help, and in the shadow of Your wings I sing for joy.** The psalmist here is thankful to God not only because He has kept him alive and relatively free, avoiding capture by Saul, but, more importantly, because of the feeling that he knows that God is always with him, providing him with protection.
9 **My soul clings to You;** it desires Your closeness, for **Your right hand has supported me.**
10 After describing his physical and spiritual state, the psalmist addresses the matter of his pursuers: **But they** who pursue me **seek my annihilation. May they descend into the depths of the earth.**
11 My enemies say that **they will shed his,** David's, **blood by the sword. May they become prey to the foxes** who prowl in the desert looking for dead animals and corpses.
12 **And may the king rejoice in God.** It is unclear whether the "king" refers to David himself, who had already been anointed by Samuel, or to Saul, whom David saw as still the legitimate king. David did not regard Saul as an enemy but rather as a man hounded by phantom terrors, driven to madness by his jealousy of David. David's hope was that if Saul could find happiness in God, he would no longer have cause to hate and pursue him. **And** may **everyone who swears by him,** one of the basic indicators of one's allegiance to the monarch, **be glorified, when the mouths of liars,** who have goaded Saul into jealousy of David, **are stopped.**

PSALM 64

PSALMS 64:1–11

A plea for protection by one who is pursued by enemies both visible and covert, all of whom use every means available in order to harm him.

64 1 **For the chief musician, a psalm by David.**
2 **Hear my voice, God, in my prayer; preserve my life from the terror of the enemy.**
3 **Hide me from the counsel of the wicked,** from their plans against me, **from the tumult of evildoers,**
4 **who whet their tongues like a sword, aiming their arrows,** a metaphor for their tongues, **with venomous words**
5 **to shoot furtively at the innocent. They shoot him suddenly,** with no warning, **and without fear,** since they perform their nefarious acts in secret.
6 **They bolster themselves with** engaging in **evil matters. They speak** among themselves **of laying hidden snares, saying: Who will see them?** Because they act furtively, they assume they will never be discovered.

סג א ב מִזְמ֥וֹר לְדָוִ֑ד בִּ֝הְיוֹת֗וֹ בְּמִדְבַּ֥ר יְהוּדָֽה׃ אֱלֹהִ֙ים ׀ אֵלִ֣י אַתָּה֮ אֲֽשַׁחֲ֫רֶ֥ךָּ צָמְאָ֬ה לְךָ֨ ׀

ג נַפְשִׁ֗י כָּמַ֣הּ לְךָ֣ בְשָׂרִ֑י בְּאֶֽרֶץ־צִיָּ֖ה וְעָיֵ֣ף בְּלִי־מָֽיִם׃ כֵּ֭ן בַּקֹּ֣דֶשׁ חֲזִיתִ֑ךָ לִרְא֥וֹת

ד ה עֻ֝זְּךָ֗ וּכְבוֹדֶֽךָ׃ כִּי־ט֣וֹב חַ֭סְדְּךָ מֵֽחַיִּ֗ים שְׂפָתַ֥י יְשַׁבְּחֽוּנְךָ׃ כֵּ֣ן אֲבָרֶכְךָ֣ בְחַיָּ֑י בְּ֝שִׁמְךָ֗

ו ז אֶשָּׂ֥א כַפָּֽי׃ כְּמ֤וֹ חֵ֣לֶב וָ֭דֶשֶׁן תִּשְׂבַּ֣ע נַפְשִׁ֑י וְשִׂפְתֵ֥י רְ֝נָנ֗וֹת יְהַלֶּל־פִּֽי׃ אִם־זְכַרְתִּ֥יךָ

ח ט עַל־יְצוּעָ֑י בְּ֝אַשְׁמֻר֗וֹת אֶהְגֶּה־בָּֽךְ׃ כִּֽי־הָיִ֣יתָ עֶזְרָ֣תָה לִּ֑י וּבְצֵ֖ל כְּנָפֶ֣יךָ אֲרַנֵּֽן׃ דָּבְקָ֣ה

י נַפְשִׁ֣י אַחֲרֶ֑יךָ בִּ֝֗י תָּמְכָ֥ה יְמִינֶֽךָ׃ וְהֵ֗מָּה לְ֭שׁוֹאָה יְבַקְשׁ֣וּ נַפְשִׁ֑י יָ֝בֹ֗אוּ בְּֽתַחְתִּיּ֥וֹת

יא יב הָאָֽרֶץ׃ יַגִּירֻ֥הוּ עַל־יְדֵי־חָ֑רֶב מְנָ֖ת שֻׁעָלִ֣ים יִהְיֽוּ׃ וְהַמֶּ֗לֶךְ יִשְׂמַ֥ח בֵּאלֹ֫הִ֥ים יִ֭תְהַלֵּל

כָּל־הַנִּשְׁבָּ֣ע בּ֑וֹ כִּ֥י יִ֝סָּכֵ֗ר פִּ֣י דֽוֹבְרֵי־שָֽׁקֶר׃

סד א ב ג לַמְנַצֵּ֗חַ מִזְמ֥וֹר לְדָוִֽד׃ שְׁמַע־אֱלֹהִ֣ים קוֹלִ֣י בְשִׂיחִ֑י מִפַּ֥חַד א֝וֹיֵ֗ב תִּצֹּ֥ר חַיָּֽי׃ תַּ֭סְתִּירֵנִי

ד מִסּ֣וֹד מְרֵעִ֑ים מֵ֝רִגְשַׁ֗ת פֹּ֣עֲלֵי אָֽוֶן׃ אֲשֶׁ֤ר שָׁנְנ֣וּ כַחֶ֣רֶב לְשׁוֹנָ֑ם דָּֽרְכ֥וּ חִ֝צָּ֗ם דָּבָ֥ר

ה ו מָֽר׃ לִירֹ֣ת בַּמִּסְתָּרִ֣ים תָּ֑ם פִּתְאֹ֥ם יֹ֝רֻ֗הוּ וְלֹ֣א יִירָֽאוּ׃ יְחַזְּקוּ־לָ֨מוֹ ׀ דָּ֘בָ֤ר רָ֗ע יְֽסַפְּר֗וּ

ז לִטְמ֣וֹן מוֹקְשִׁ֑ים אָ֝מְר֗וּ מִ֣י יִרְאֶה־לָּֽמוֹ׃ יַֽחְפְּֽשׂוּ־עוֹלֹ֗ת תַּ֭מְנוּ חֵ֣פֶשׂ מְחֻפָּ֑שׂ וְקֶ֥רֶב

ח ט אִ֝֗ישׁ וְלֵ֣ב עָמֹֽק׃ וַיֹּרֵ֗ם אֱלֹ֫הִ֥ים חֵ֥ץ פִּתְא֑וֹם הָ֝י֗וּ מַכּוֹתָֽם׃ וַיַּכְשִׁיל֣וּהוּ עָלֵ֣ימוֹ לְשׁוֹנָ֑ם

י יִ֝תְנֹֽדְד֗וּ כָּל־רֹ֥אֵה בָֽם׃ וַיִּֽירְא֗וּ כָּל־אָ֫דָ֥ם וַ֭יַּגִּידוּ פֹּ֣עַל אֱלֹהִ֑ים וּֽמַעֲשֵׂ֥הוּ הִשְׂכִּֽילוּ׃

יא יִשְׂמַ֬ח צַדִּ֣יק בַּ֭יהוָה וְחָ֣סָה ב֑וֹ וְ֝יִֽתְהַלְל֗וּ כָּל־יִשְׁרֵי־לֵֽב׃

סה א ב לַמְנַצֵּ֗חַ מִזְמ֥וֹר לְדָוִ֗ד שִֽׁיר׃ לְךָ֤ דֻֽמִיָּ֬ה תְהִלָּ֓ה אֱלֹהִ֣ים בְּצִיּ֑וֹן וּ֝לְךָ֗ יְשֻׁלַּם־נֶֽדֶר׃

7 They thoroughly seek out iniquities to commit, **to the very depths of a man's heart,** another reference to the clandestine nature of their plans and actions.

8 In this kind of situation, a person can only pray to God for help: **May God shoot them with an unexpected arrow, smiting them.**

9 Their own vicious **tongues will** backfire and **cause them,** instead of me, **to stumble.** May the tongues they used against me become the instrument of their own downfall. **All those who behold them** in defeat **will shudder** in revulsion and shock.

10 And all men who witness the downfall of the evildoers **will be in awe; they will declare it the work of God, understanding it as His doing.** When people see that the wicked are trapped and devastated by their own evil schemes, they will understand that the world is orchestrated by God's will.

11 The righteous will then **rejoice in the Lord and trust in Him, and all the upright in heart will be glorified.**

PSALM 65

PSALMS 65:1–14

A psalm of praise to God, who forgives sinners, embraces penitents, and fills the world with bounteous goodness and tranquility.

65 1 For the chief musician, a psalm by David, a song. This is a psalm of gratitude that depicts a time of spiritual tranquility and bounty.

2 For You, God of Zion, silence is praise, and a vow to You will be paid. While this verse can be interpreted in many ways, its central message is that all words in praise of God are insufficient. Words of praise can actually be shamefully inadequate, whereas silence includes all that can and cannot be verbalized. Instead of composing lengthy poems or songs in praise of God, we should praise Him with our deeds, by fulfilling the obligations we have undertaken to serve Him.

3 **You, who hear prayer, all flesh comes to You** to pray for their needs and to give thanks.

4 **Iniquities overwhelm me** and threaten to crush me with their weight, **but** despite the enormity of my sins, I have trust that **You forgive our transgressions.**

5 **Happy is the one You choose to bring near You, to dwell in Your Sanctuary. May we** be among their number, and **be sated by the bounty of Your House, the holiness of Your Temple.**

6 **Answer us justly with awesome deeds, God of our salvation and our shelter to the ends of the earth and the farthest sea.**

7 The following verses provide a fuller description of some of God's deeds: It is He **who sets mountains with His strength, girded with might.** God's divine might is expressed here by the image of a great mountain being set in place by Him, layer by layer, rock by rock.

8 God's power can also be portrayed in other ways. It is God **who stills the roaring of the seas, the roaring of their waves, and the tumult of nations.** God's power is depicted both with regard to the natural world and vis-à-vis the hubbub of human affairs.

9 Even **those who live at the ends of the earth are in awe of Your signs,** which are everywhere. Through those signs and miracles, **You make the place of dawn and dusk,** a poetic way of saying "east and west," **sing out.**

10 The psalmist also acknowledges His blessings: **You remember the earth and fulfill its desire, enriching it with abundance.** The earth's "desire" refers here, as in many other places, to water. **The streams of God are full of water.** Once the earth has been watered, it is ready to be cultivated: **You prepare their grain,** causing it to sprout and grow. **Indeed, You set it firmly in place,**[D] allowing it to continue its growth until it ripens.

11 **Saturate its furrows, satisfy its hollows, soften it with showers. Bless its vegetation.**

Furrows filled with rainwater

12 **You crown the year with Your bounty;** may these blessings continue all year round, "crowning" the year with plenty. **And** may **Your paths drip with rich abundance.** The word *ma'agalekha*, translated here as "Your paths," also refers to a recurring cycle of events.

13 **Oases in the desert overflow.** Ordinarily, oases are barely able to sustain themselves in their endless battle with the surrounding harshness of the desert. But You cause them, through an abundance of rain, to actually flow over to the surrounding arid terrain. **The hills gird themselves with joy.** The normally dry hills become covered with greenery and appear overjoyed by all the growth.

14 **The meadows are covered with flocks of sheep; the valleys,** the most fertile type of terrain, **are wrapped in grain. They shout for joy.** The word *yitro'a'u*, "shout for joy," has a second meaning as well: "They become friends." When there is widespread abundance, the earth and all that it produces appear to complement each other; they join together in harmony, **and they sing.**

"Meadows are covered with flocks of sheep"

PSALM 66

PSALMS 66:1–20

A psalm of praise to God for His revelation, both in general and in connection with specific historical events, beginning with the exodus from Egypt and the giving of the Torah at Mount Sinai, and continuing throughout the generations. The psalm concludes with a personal prayer by an individual who perceives divine providence in his own life.

66 1 **For the chief musician, a song, a psalm.** This psalm seems to
12th day of month allude to some kind of military victory, as it speaks of former obstacles and enemies who have now passed from existence. It is a hymn of gratitude to God, with its main theme expressed in the opening verse: **Shout out** with joy and thanks **to God, all the earth.**

2 **Sing the glory of His name; make His praise glorious.**

3 **Say to God: How awesome are Your works! Because of Your great power, Your enemies feign obedience to You.** God's enemies have been vanquished and subjugated; they are compelled to act with obedience, even if it is insincere.

DISCUSSION

65:7–10 | **Who sets [*mekhin*] mountains… You prepare [*takhin*] their grain; indeed [*khen*], You set it firmly in place [*tekhineha*]:** There is word play in the Hebrew. The root *kaf-vav-nun* appears several times in different senses: preparation, setting in place, setting firmly, and making straight. Furthermore, the use of setting firmly, *tekhineha*, is highly similar to the word "indeed," *khen*.

ג ד שֹׁמֵעַ תְּפִלָּה עָדֶיךָ כָּל־בָּשָׂר יָבֹאוּ׃ דִּבְרֵי עֲוֺנֹת גָּבְרוּ מֶנִּי פְּשָׁעֵינוּ אַתָּה תְכַפְּרֵם׃
ה ו אַשְׁרֵי ׀ תִּבְחַר וּתְקָרֵב יִשְׁכֹּן חֲצֵרֶיךָ נִשְׂבְּעָה בְּטוּב בֵּיתֶךָ קְדֹשׁ הֵיכָלֶךָ׃ נוֹרָאוֹת ׀
ז בְּצֶדֶק תַּעֲנֵנוּ אֱלֹהֵי יִשְׁעֵנוּ מִבְטָח כָּל־קַצְוֵי־אֶרֶץ וְיָם רְחֹקִים׃ מֵכִין הָרִים בְּכֹחוֹ
ח ט נֶאְזָר בִּגְבוּרָה׃ מַשְׁבִּיחַ ׀ שְׁאוֹן יַמִּים שְׁאוֹן גַּלֵּיהֶם וַהֲמוֹן לְאֻמִּים׃ וַיִּירְאוּ ׀ יֹשְׁבֵי
י קְצָוֺת מֵאוֹתֹתֶיךָ מוֹצָאֵי־בֹקֶר וָעֶרֶב תַּרְנִין׃ פָּקַדְתָּ הָאָרֶץ ׀ וַתְּשֹׁקְקֶהָ רַבַּת
יא תַּעְשְׁרֶנָּה פֶּלֶג אֱלֹהִים מָלֵא מָיִם תָּכִין דְּגָנָם כִּי־כֵן תְּכִינֶהָ׃ תְּלָמֶיהָ רַוֵּה נַחֵת
יב גְּדוּדֶהָ בִּרְבִיבִים תְּמֹגְגֶנָּה צִמְחָהּ תְּבָרֵךְ׃ עִטַּרְתָּ שְׁנַת טוֹבָתֶךָ וּמַעְגָּלֶיךָ יִרְעֲפוּן
יג יד דָּשֶׁן׃ יִרְעֲפוּ נְאוֹת מִדְבָּר וְגִיל גְּבָעוֹת תַּחְגֹּרְנָה׃ לָבְשׁוּ כָרִים ׀ הַצֹּאן וַעֲמָקִים
יַעַטְפוּ־בָר יִתְרוֹעֲעוּ אַף־יָשִׁירוּ׃

סו א ב לַמְנַצֵּחַ שִׁיר מִזְמוֹר הָרִיעוּ לֵאלֹהִים כָּל־הָאָרֶץ׃ זַמְּרוּ כְבוֹד־שְׁמוֹ שִׂימוּ כָבוֹד יב לחודש
ג ד תְּהִלָּתוֹ׃ אִמְרוּ לֵאלֹהִים מַה־נּוֹרָא מַעֲשֶׂיךָ בְּרֹב עֻזְּךָ יְכַחֲשׁוּ לְךָ אֹיְבֶיךָ׃ כָּל־
ה הָאָרֶץ ׀ יִשְׁתַּחֲווּ לְךָ וִיזַמְּרוּ־לָךְ יְזַמְּרוּ שִׁמְךָ סֶלָה׃ לְכוּ וּרְאוּ מִפְעֲלוֹת אֱלֹהִים
ו נוֹרָא עֲלִילָה עַל־בְּנֵי אָדָם׃ הָפַךְ יָם ׀ לְיַבָּשָׁה בַּנָּהָר יַעַבְרוּ בְרָגֶל שָׁם נִשְׂמְחָה־
ז בּוֹ׃ מֹשֵׁל בִּגְבוּרָתוֹ ׀ עוֹלָם עֵינָיו בַּגּוֹיִם תִּצְפֶּינָה הַסּוֹרְרִים ׀ אַל־ירימו לָמוֹ סֶלָה׃ יָרוּמוּ
ח ט בָּרְכוּ עַמִּים ׀ אֱלֹהֵינוּ וְהַשְׁמִיעוּ קוֹל תְּהִלָּתוֹ׃ הַשָּׂם נַפְשֵׁנוּ בַּחַיִּים וְלֹא־נָתַן
י יא לַמּוֹט רַגְלֵנוּ׃ כִּי־בְחַנְתָּנוּ אֱלֹהִים צְרַפְתָּנוּ כִּצְרָף־כָּסֶף׃ הֲבֵאתָנוּ בַמְּצוּדָה שַׂמְתָּ

4 **The entire earth will bow down to You and sing praises to You; they will sing praises to Your name, Selah.**

5 The psalmist now expresses specific praises of God: **Come and see the works of God, the awesome acts** that He has done **for the sons of man.**

6 **He turned the** Red **Sea into dry land** for the children of Israel; afterward **they passed through the** Jordan **River on foot. There we rejoiced in Him.**

7 **He rules the world with His might; His eyes keep watch on the nations,** ensuring that they are accorded their proper place. **The** people who are **rebellious** against God **will not be exalted,** for He will subdue them. **Selah.**

8 **Bless our God, you nations;** God's kindness toward Israel benefits all nations, and it is therefore fitting for all to praise Him. **Raise a voice in His praise,**

9 **to Him who keeps us alive and does not allow our feet to stumble.** This is the case even though, as described in the following verses, there have been many periods of struggle and testing.

10 **Though You have tested us, God; You refined us as silver is refined.** You have put us through many ordeals, similar to the harsh conditions of the refinement process.

11 **You brought us into the net** and **placed a tight belt around our loins.** These are all metaphors for situations of difficulty and distress.

12 **You let people ride over our heads;** that is, You have allowed us to be subjugated by others. **We went through fire and water,** both literally and figuratively. **But** in the end, **You drew us out** of these situations of pressure and anxiety **to** a situation of **relief.** The word *revaya*, translated here as "relief," literally refers to the slaking of thirst. Here it conveys the sense of relief felt by those who have been rescued and are now able to rest.
13 The psalmist continues on a personal note: **I will come to Your House with burnt offerings; I will pay You my vows,**
14 **those uttered by my lips and spoken by my mouth when I was in distress.** It is usually during difficult times that people make such vows.
15 **I will offer You burnt offerings of fattened animals with the smoking of rams,** that is, rams that are completely burned into smoke on the altar. **I will sacrifice bulls and he-goats, Selah.**
16 **Come and hear, all who fear God, and I will tell of what He has done for me.** I can personally attest to what God has done for me.
17 **I called to Him with my mouth, and He was extolled with my tongue.**
18 **Even if I sense wickedness in my heart, the Lord does not take notice.** Even if, like most people, I occasionally have wicked thoughts, God does not judge me harshly. He does not take my aberrant thoughts into consideration.
19 **Indeed, God listens, and** He **attends to the sound of my prayer.**
20 The psalmist concludes: **Blessed be God, who has not turned away my prayer nor withheld His kindness from me.**

PSALM 67

PSALMS 67:1–8

On the surface, this is a simple hymn of praise, consisting mainly of expressions of gratitude and a request for God's continued beneficence. A more insightful reading reveals a sophisticated structure to this brief psalm, and especially in kabbalistic literature it has been interpreted as containing veiled references to higher realms. Apart from its heading, the psalm has seven verses and a total of forty-nine words. The seven verses correspond to the seven branches of the Temple's candelabrum, and in some prayer books the psalm is even printed in the shape of such a candelabrum. On a deeper level, the psalm can be understood as a kind of roadmap marking the journey from the lowest world to the higher realms.

67 1 **For the chief musician, with instrumental music, a psalm, a song.** It appears that this psalm was intended to be sung in the Temple.
2 **May God be gracious to us and bless us; may He shine His countenance upon us, Selah.** This alludes to the priestly blessing, which contains similar wording.
3 Bless us **so that Your way is known on earth.** May God show us His guidance concerning which path to follow, and may He show everyone that He paves the way forward for those who love Him. May **Your salvation** be revealed **among all the nations.**

Psalm 67 written in the shape of the candelabrum, Denmark, eighteenth or nineteenth century CE

4 **Let the peoples praise You, God; let all the peoples praise You.** This psalm is directed not only to Israel but to all peoples of the world. It invites all nations to praise God for His kindness in general, and does not refer specifically to God's salvation of Israel.
5 **Let the nations be glad and sing for joy, for You judge all peoples fairly.** You provide a straight path for all nations to follow, one that is devoid of conflict or war, **and** you **guide the nations of the earth** to achieve appropriate goals. **Selah.**
6 **Let the peoples praise You, God; let all the peoples praise You.** This refrain emphasizes the psalm's universal relevance.
7 The following simple blessing is a further expression of the psalm's all-embracing theme: **The earth has yielded its crop** with sufficient produce to meet the needs of all. **May God, our God, bless us.** We beseech God to enrich the crops that grow naturally in the field with His divine blessing.
8 **May God bless us, and may** the people living in **all the ends of the earth fear Him.**

יב מוּעָקָה בְמָתְנֵינוּ׃ הִרְכַּבְתָּ אֱנוֹשׁ לְרֹאשֵׁנוּ בָּאנוּ־בָאֵשׁ וּבַמַּיִם וַתּוֹצִיאֵנוּ לָרְוָיָה׃
יג יד טו אָבוֹא בֵיתְךָ בְעוֹלוֹת אֲשַׁלֵּם לְךָ נְדָרָי׃ אֲשֶׁר־פָּצוּ שְׂפָתָי וְדִבֶּר־פִּי בַּצַּר־לִי׃ עֹלוֹת
טז מֵחִים אַעֲלֶה־לָּךְ עִם־קְטֹרֶת אֵילִים אֶעֱשֶׂה בָקָר עִם־עַתּוּדִים סֶלָה׃ לְכוּ־שִׁמְעוּ
יז וַאֲסַפְּרָה כָּל־יִרְאֵי אֱלֹהִים אֲשֶׁר עָשָׂה לְנַפְשִׁי׃ אֵלָיו פִּי־קָרָאתִי וְרוֹמַם תַּחַת
יח יט לְשׁוֹנִי׃ אָוֶן אִם־רָאִיתִי בְלִבִּי לֹא יִשְׁמַע ׀ אֲדֹנָי׃ אָכֵן שָׁמַע אֱלֹהִים הִקְשִׁיב בְּקוֹל
כ תְּפִלָּתִי׃ בָּרוּךְ אֱלֹהִים אֲשֶׁר לֹא־הֵסִיר תְּפִלָּתִי וְחַסְדּוֹ מֵאִתִּי׃
סז א ב לַמְנַצֵּחַ בִּנְגִינֹת מִזְמוֹר שִׁיר׃ אֱלֹהִים יְחָנֵּנוּ וִיבָרְכֵנוּ יָאֵר פָּנָיו אִתָּנוּ סֶלָה׃ לָדַעַת
ג ד ה בָּאָרֶץ דַּרְכֶּךָ בְּכָל־גּוֹיִם יְשׁוּעָתֶךָ׃ יוֹדוּךָ עַמִּים ׀ אֱלֹהִים יוֹדוּךָ עַמִּים כֻּלָּם׃ יִשְׂמְחוּ
ו וִירַנְּנוּ לְאֻמִּים כִּי־תִשְׁפֹּט עַמִּים מִישֹׁר וּלְאֻמִּים ׀ בָּאָרֶץ תַּנְחֵם סֶלָה׃ יוֹדוּךָ
ז עַמִּים ׀ אֱלֹהִים יוֹדוּךָ עַמִּים כֻּלָּם׃ אֶרֶץ נָתְנָה יְבוּלָהּ יְבָרְכֵנוּ אֱלֹהִים אֱלֹהֵינוּ׃
ח יְבָרְכֵנוּ אֱלֹהִים וְיִירְאוּ אוֹתוֹ כָּל־אַפְסֵי־אָרֶץ׃ ט
סח א ב לַמְנַצֵּחַ לְדָוִד מִזְמוֹר שִׁיר׃ יָקוּם אֱלֹהִים יָפוּצוּ אוֹיְבָיו וְיָנוּסוּ מְשַׂנְאָיו מִפָּנָיו׃
ג ד כְּהִנְדֹּף עָשָׁן תִּנְדֹּף כְּהִמֵּס דּוֹנַג מִפְּנֵי־אֵשׁ יֹאבְדוּ רְשָׁעִים מִפְּנֵי אֱלֹהִים׃ וְצַדִּיקִים
ה יִשְׂמְחוּ יַעַלְצוּ לִפְנֵי אֱלֹהִים וְיָשִׂישׂוּ בְשִׂמְחָה׃ שִׁירוּ ׀ לֵאלֹהִים זַמְּרוּ שְׁמוֹ סֹלּוּ
ו לָרֹכֵב בָּעֲרָבוֹת בְּיָהּ שְׁמוֹ וְעִלְזוּ לְפָנָיו׃ אֲבִי יְתוֹמִים וְדַיַּן אַלְמָנוֹת אֱלֹהִים

PSALM 68

PSALMS 68:1–36

An epic hymn in praise of the might of God, as manifested not only in military victories but also in the epitome of divine revelation that occurred at Mount Sinai. The text is noteworthy for its archaic and obscure Hebrew phrasing. It contains a number of words that are otherwise not found in the Bible, along with arcane verses and expressions that have been subject to a variety of interpretations.

68 1 **For the chief musician, a psalm by David, a song.** This is a psalm for times of war and other momentous historic events.

2 **May God arise and** may **His enemies scatter; may those who hate Him flee before Him.** This verse is an allusion to Numbers 10:35.

3 **Blow them away as smoke is wafted away** by a hand or fan, **as wax melts before fire; let the wicked perish before God,** so they disappear completely.

Smoke

4 **But let the righteous be happy. May they exult before God,** and **may they revel in happiness.** The apparently redundant phrase indicates that *sason*, which means "reveling," is the outward manifestation of *simḥa*, an internal feeling of "happiness."

5 **Sing to God; sing hymns to His name. Praise Him who rides in the highest heavens;** praise Him **with His name the Lord.** The Hebrew uses the name *Yah*, which is an abbreviated form of God's four-letter ineffable name, used occasionally in biblical songs of war and victory. **Be joyous before Him.**

6 God's greatness and revelation are manifested in various ways: **The Father of orphans, the Judge of widows, God is in His**

holy dwelling. God, in His majestic dwelling, watches over the meek.

7 This verse illustrates God's attention to every individual. **God settles the lonely in a home,** bringing isolated people together to marry and build a home. **He joyously leads forth prisoners.** The word *bakosharot,* translated here as "joyously," appears only here, and from the context it seems to indicate a deeply felt joy. **But the rebellious** are thrust aside to **dwell in a parched land.**

8 The exodus from Egypt and the giving of the Torah at Sinai are powerful examples of God's revelation: **God, when You went forth before Your people,** leading them out of Egypt, and **when You marched through the desolate land, Selah,**

9 **the earth quaked.** Physical manifestations of fear and awe in the presence of God included the trembling of Mount Sinai: **The heavens rained before God,** out of fear of Him. **This** quaking was what took place at Mount **Sinai,** which trembled **before God, the God of Israel.**[26]

10 Manifestations of divine revelation can also be calm and reassuring: **You scatter abundant rain** upon the earth, **God; You secure Your portion,** referring to the people and Land of Israel, **and** You also secure **the weary** people.

11 **Those You sustain have settled in it,** in the portion mentioned above, the Land of Israel. **In Your goodness, God, secure it for the needy,** for the needs of the people of Israel.

12 **My Lord gives the word, and the women herald the great armies.** When God gives the order, female choruses sing out in acclaim of the returning victorious armies.

13 And this is what they proclaim: **The kings of armies flee again and again,** abandoning their possessions as spoils of war, **while the women at home divide the spoils.** Even housewives, who may symbolically represent the people of Israel, who now live peacefully in their homes, go out to reap the spoils of war.

14 **Now you may lie within the sheepfolds.** This verse describes Israel in a time of tranquility, a time peaceful enough for a person to rest securely in a pasture where sheep graze. The following is a metaphorical depiction of the people of Israel: **Wings of the dove covered with silver, its pinions with green and gold.** Caught in the light of the sun, the dove's white feathers gleam like polished silver, and its wing tips sparkle with colors of green and gold.

Dove

15 **When the Almighty crushed the kings,** when powerful kings are brought down, God's glory is manifest. **Then it snowed in Tzalmon,** in the desert. The reversal of the existing political order is as stunning as snowfall in the desert.

16 **A mountain of God,** a mountain of vast proportions, **is Mount Bashan; a mountain of ridges**[B] **is Mount Bashan.**

17 **Why do you shudder, ridged mountains,** Bashan and others like it? Your shuddering is due to chagrin over the fact that **the mount that God desired for His abode** is Mount Sinai, mentioned in verse 9, or, according to others, Mount Moriah, the site of the Temple. Mount Moriah seems to be the more likely interpretation, given the conclusion of the verse: **There the Lord will surely dwell forever.**

18 The following verse returns to the revelation at Sinai: **The chariots of God,** though of course incorporeal, **are** compared in their might to a human camp of a **myriad,** comprising **thousands upon thousands of companies.** The word *shinan,* translated here as "companies," may also mean "angels" or "tents." **My Lord is among them, at Sinai, in holiness.**

19 The psalmist describes God as a victorious warrior: **You ascended on high; You took captives. You received tributes among men.** This may mean "tributes taken from men," or it may mean "tributes made up of men," that is, human captives. **Even the rebellious** ones, whom **You captured to dwell over** them, **Lord God.**

20 **Blessed be the Lord, who provides for us day by day, the Almighty of our deliverance, Selah.**

21 **The Almighty for us is the Almighty of deliverance,** who comes to our aid; as for those who refuse to submit to Him, **the Lord, my Lord, holds power over death** and will subject them to it.

22 **Indeed, God will shatter the heads of His enemies, hairy skulls of those walking in their guilt.**

23 At the same time, God seeks those of Israel who have lost their way, in order to bring them back: **The Lord said: I will bring them back from Bashan, I will bring them back from the**

BACKGROUND

68:16 | **Mount Bashan, a mountain of ridges:** The Bashan is a tall mountain range east of the Sea of Galilee, cut through by several ravines. In the eastern part of the Bashan there is an area of basalt rock punctuated by many clefts, called al-Laja, which is today part of Druze territory in Syria. There are several adjacent volcanic peaks in the area. The Bashan stands out from the neighboring geographic areas because of its many impressive cliffs, called here *gavnunim,* ridges.

ז בִּמְעוֹן קׇדְשׁוֹ: אֱלֹהִים ׀ מוֹשִׁיב יְחִידִים ׀ בַּיְתָה מוֹצִיא אֲסִירִים בַּכּוֹשָׁרוֹת אַךְ
ח ט סוֹרְרִים שָׁכְנוּ צְחִיחָה: אֱלֹהִים בְּצֵאתְךָ לִפְנֵי עַמֶּךָ בְּצַעְדְּךָ בִישִׁימוֹן סֶלָה: אֶרֶץ
רָעָשָׁה ׀ אַף־שָׁמַיִם נָטְפוּ מִפְּנֵי אֱלֹהִים זֶה סִינַי מִפְּנֵי אֱלֹהִים אֱלֹהֵי יִשְׂרָאֵל:
י יא גֶּשֶׁם נְדָבוֹת תָּנִיף אֱלֹהִים נַחֲלָתְךָ וְנִלְאָה אַתָּה כוֹנַנְתָּהּ: חַיָּתְךָ יָשְׁבוּ־בָהּ תָּכִין
יב יג בְּטוֹבָתְךָ לֶעָנִי אֱלֹהִים: אֲדֹנָי יִתֶּן־אֹמֶר הַמְבַשְּׂרוֹת צָבָא רָב: מַלְכֵי צְבָאוֹת יִדֹּדוּן
יד יִדֹּדוּן וּנְוַת־בַּיִת תְּחַלֵּק שָׁלָל: אִם־תִּשְׁכְּבוּן בֵּין שְׁפַתָּיִם כַּנְפֵי יוֹנָה נֶחְפָּה בַכֶּסֶף
טו טז וְאֶבְרוֹתֶיהָ בִּירַקְרַק חָרוּץ: בְּפָרֵשׂ שַׁדַּי מְלָכִים בָּהּ תַּשְׁלֵג בְּצַלְמוֹן: הַר־אֱלֹהִים
יז הַר־בָּשָׁן הַר גַּבְנֻנִּים הַר־בָּשָׁן: לָמָּה ׀ תְּרַצְּדוּן הָרִים גַּבְנֻנִּים הָהָר חָמַד אֱלֹהִים
יח לְשִׁבְתּוֹ אַף־יהוה יִשְׁכֹּן לָנֶצַח: רֶכֶב אֱלֹהִים רִבֹּתַיִם אַלְפֵי שִׁנְאָן אֲדֹנָי בָם סִינַי
יט בַּקֹּדֶשׁ: עָלִיתָ לַמָּרוֹם ׀ שָׁבִיתָ שֶּׁבִי לָקַחְתָּ מַתָּנוֹת בָּאָדָם וְאַף סוֹרְרִים לִשְׁכֹּן ׀
כ כא יָהּ אֱלֹהִים: בָּרוּךְ אֲדֹנָי יוֹם ׀ יוֹם יַעֲמׇס־לָנוּ הָאֵל יְשׁוּעָתֵנוּ סֶלָה: הָאֵל ׀ לָנוּ אֵל
כב לְמוֹשָׁעוֹת וְלֵיהוִה אֲדֹנָי לַמָּוֶת תּוֹצָאוֹת: אַךְ־אֱלֹהִים יִמְחַץ רֹאשׁ אֹיְבָיו קׇדְקֹד
כג כד שֵׂעָר מִתְהַלֵּךְ בַּאֲשָׁמָיו: אָמַר אֲדֹנָי מִבָּשָׁן אָשִׁיב אָשִׁיב מִמְּצֻלוֹת יָם: לְמַעַן ׀
כה תִּמְחַץ רַגְלְךָ בְּדָם לְשׁוֹן כְּלָבֶיךָ מֵאֹיְבִים מִנֵּהוּ: רָאוּ הֲלִיכוֹתֶיךָ אֱלֹהִים הֲלִיכוֹת
כו כז אֵלִי מַלְכִּי בַקֹּדֶשׁ: קִדְּמוּ שָׁרִים אַחַר נֹגְנִים בְּתוֹךְ עֲלָמוֹת תּוֹפֵפוֹת: בְּמַקְהֵלוֹת
כח בָּרְכוּ אֱלֹהִים אֲדֹנָי מִמְּקוֹר יִשְׂרָאֵל: שָׁם בִּנְיָמִן ׀ צָעִיר רֹדֵם שָׂרֵי יְהוּדָה רִגְמָתָם

depths of the sea. This last phrase may be an allusion to the splitting of the Red Sea.

24 The psalmist addresses the Israelites: God will bring you back **so that your foot might wade in** the **blood** of your enemies and **so your dogs' tongues might lick their portion** of the blood **of the enemy.**

25 What follows is a description of God's grandeur from the perspective of His people who honor Him in public ceremony: **They saw Your ways, God, the ways of my Almighty, my King in holiness.**

26 **First the singers, followed by musicians, amid the young women playing timbrels.** All of these people come out to greet the victorious King.

27 **Bless God among the great assemblies; the Lord, from the fount of Israel.**

28 **There,** at this musical tribute, **is** the tribe of **Benjamin,** who was **the youngest** of Jacob's sons, as well as the least populous tribe, **leading them; the chieftains of Judah in their throng, the chieftains of Zebulun, the chieftains of Naphtali.** In short, all the tribes of Israel, from one end to the other, were present.

29 The psalmist addresses Israel and its king: **Your God has decreed strength for you.** Then turning to God, he says: **Reveal Your strength, God, that You have employed on our behalf** in the past.

30 This strength that I speak of emanates **from Your Temple,** which is situated on Mount Moriah, **above Jerusalem. Kings** of all nations **bring gifts** and offerings **to You** there.

31 **Strike fear in the beasts among the reeds,** the wild animals lurking among the reeds near the water,[27] **and in the herd of cavalry horses going among the calves of the people.** The image is one of powerful war horses that cause the enemy to flee like calves caught in a stampede. The calves represent **those** vanquished people **who grovel** and seek to buy their safety from their invaders **for pieces of silver. He scatters the nations who desire battle.** The belligerent nations are dispersed by God; only those who have surrendered remain.

32 **Noblemen will arrive from Egypt; Kush,** in Africa, **will hasten to stretch out her hands** with gifts **to God.**

33 **Kingdoms of the earth, sing to God; sing praises to my Lord, Selah.**

34 Sing those praises **to Him who rides on the expanses of the highest, farthest heavens, who speaks with His voice, a mighty voice,** referring to the sound of thunder.

35 **Ascribe strength to God,** that is, praise Him for His strength, **whose majesty is over Israel.** God's power and greatness are made manifest through the people of Israel, **whose strength is in the heavens.**

36 **You are awesome,** feared, **God, from Your Sanctuary,** the source of God's revelation in the world. **The Almighty of Israel gives strength and power to the nation** of Israel. **Blessed be God.**

PSALM 69

PSALMS 69:1–37

A psalm of prayer and supplication. It is also the anguished cry of an individual caught in a vise of personal distress and attacks by an array of enemies. It ends on a hopeful note, which may reflect the psalmist's faith that God will come to his aid; alternatively, the ending may have been added at a later date, after the psalmist had been delivered from danger.

69 1 **For the chief musician, on shoshanim,[28] by David.**

13th day of month

2 The psalm begins with a plea from an individual who is in great peril: **Rescue me, God, for the waters have come up to my soul,** up to the point where they threaten my life.

3 **I am sinking in muddy depths without a foothold,** with no solid ground underneath to stop me from going under. **I am in deep water, and** I am unable to swim my way out of it because **a whirlpool is sweeping me away.**

Strong current in a river

Whirlpool

4 **I am weary from calling out** for help; **my throat is parched. My eyes are failing,** constantly looking out for the slightest sign of encouragement, **as I hope for my God.**

5 **More numerous than the hairs on my head are those who hate me without cause.** I am surrounded by enemies, many of whom have no justifiable reason to hate me. **Those who would destroy me, my deceitful enemies, have grown powerful.** The most evil among them have fabricated accusations against me for the sole purpose of bringing me down. Because of their false accusations, **I am made to give back** to them **what** in actuality **I never stole.**

6 The psalmist, as one who has dedicated himself completely to God, notes that although he is far from perfect, the hatred against him is not connected to his personal shortcomings: **God, You know my folly,** the sins that I have committed, which emanated from foolishness on my part; **my wrongs,** sins I have committed knowingly, **are** also **not hidden from You.** I am unable to hide these sins from You, and do not desire to do so.

7 **May those who place their hope in You not be dismayed because of me, my Lord, Lord of hosts.** I am regarded by others as a paradigm of a devoted servant of God. If I am allowed to perish, others will be discouraged from following my example. **May those who seek You not be shamed because of me, God of Israel.**

8 I have shown my complete dedication to You all my life, **for I have borne disgrace for Your sake, shame covering my face.** I have become an object of disdain and contempt because I am so closely bound with You. The path that I follow is not particularly popular, and it has set me apart from others.

9 The psalmist continues to describe the scorn to which he has been subjected: **I have been considered a stranger** even **by my brothers, an alien to my mother's sons.** Shunned even by my close family, I feel totally isolated.

10 **For zealotry for Your House has consumed me;** I have exhibited great passion and zeal for Your name and Your Temple. Therefore, **the insults of those who revile You fall on me.** Because I am so closely identified with You, those who revile You see me as an appropriate target of attack.

11 **I cry while fasting, and** thereby **become the object of abuse.**

כט שָׂרֵי זְבֻלוּן שָׂרֵי נַפְתָּלִי׃ צִוָּה אֱלֹהֶיךָ עֻזֶּךָ עוּזָּה אֱלֹהִים זוּ פָּעַלְתָּ לָּנוּ׃ מֵהֵיכָלֶךָ ל
לא עַל־יְרוּשָׁלָ͏ִם לְךָ יוֹבִילוּ מְלָכִים שָׁי׃ גְּעַר חַיַּת קָנֶה עֲדַת אַבִּירִים ׀ בְּעֶגְלֵי עַמִּים
לב מִתְרַפֵּס בְּרַצֵּי־כָסֶף בִּזַּר עַמִּים קְרָבוֹת יֶחְפָּצוּ׃ יֶאֱתָיוּ חַשְׁמַנִּים מִנִּי מִצְרָיִם כּוּשׁ
לג לד תָּרִיץ יָדָיו לֵאלֹהִים׃ מַמְלְכוֹת הָאָרֶץ שִׁירוּ לֵאלֹהִים זַמְּרוּ אֲדֹנָי סֶלָה׃ לָרֹכֵב
לה בִּשְׁמֵי שְׁמֵי־קֶדֶם הֵן יִתֵּן בְּקוֹלוֹ קוֹל עֹז׃ תְּנוּ עֹז לֵאלֹהִים עַל־יִשְׂרָאֵל גַּאֲוָתוֹ
לו וְעֻזּוֹ בַּשְּׁחָקִים׃ נוֹרָא אֱלֹהִים ׀ מִמִּקְדָּשֶׁיךָ אֵל יִשְׂרָאֵל הוּא נֹתֵן ׀ עֹז וְתַעֲצֻמוֹת
לָעָם בָּרוּךְ אֱלֹהִים׃

סט א ב ג לַמְנַצֵּחַ עַל־שׁוֹשַׁנִּים לְדָוִד׃ הוֹשִׁיעֵנִי אֱלֹהִים כִּי בָאוּ מַיִם עַד־נָפֶשׁ׃ טָבַעְתִּי ׀ יג לחודש
ד בִּיוֵן מְצוּלָה וְאֵין מָעֳמָד בָּאתִי בְמַעֲמַקֵּי־מַיִם וְשִׁבֹּלֶת שְׁטָפָתְנִי׃ יָגַעְתִּי בְקָרְאִי
ה נִחַר גְּרוֹנִי כָּלוּ עֵינַי מְיַחֵל לֵאלֹהָי׃ רַבּוּ ׀ מִשַּׂעֲרוֹת רֹאשִׁי שֹׂנְאַי חִנָּם עָצְמוּ
ו מַצְמִיתַי אֹיְבַי שֶׁקֶר אֲשֶׁר לֹא־גָזַלְתִּי אָז אָשִׁיב׃ אֱלֹהִים אַתָּה יָדַעְתָּ לְאִוַּלְתִּי
ז וְאַשְׁמוֹתַי מִמְּךָ לֹא־נִכְחָדוּ׃ אַל־יֵבֹשׁוּ בִי ׀ קֹוֶיךָ אֲדֹנָי יֱהֹוִה צְבָאוֹת אַל־יִכָּלְמוּ
ח ט בִי מְבַקְשֶׁיךָ אֱלֹהֵי יִשְׂרָאֵל׃ כִּי־עָלֶיךָ נָשָׂאתִי חֶרְפָּה כִּסְּתָה כְלִמָּה פָנָי׃ מוּזָר
י הָיִיתִי לְאֶחָי וְנָכְרִי לִבְנֵי אִמִּי׃ כִּי־קִנְאַת בֵּיתְךָ אֲכָלָתְנִי וְחֶרְפּוֹת חוֹרְפֶיךָ נָפְלוּ
יא יב עָלָי׃ וָאֶבְכֶּה בַצּוֹם נַפְשִׁי וַתְּהִי לַחֲרָפוֹת לִי׃ וָאֶתְּנָה לְבוּשִׁי שָׂק וָאֱהִי לָהֶם
יג יד לְמָשָׁל׃ יָשִׂיחוּ בִי יֹשְׁבֵי שָׁעַר וּנְגִינוֹת שׁוֹתֵי שֵׁכָר׃ וַאֲנִי תְפִלָּתִי־לְךָ ׀ יְהוָה עֵת
טו רָצוֹן אֱלֹהִים בְּרָב־חַסְדֶּךָ עֲנֵנִי בֶּאֱמֶת יִשְׁעֶךָ׃ הַצִּילֵנִי מִטִּיט וְאַל־אֶטְבָּעָה
טז אִנָּצְלָה מִשֹּׂנְאַי וּמִמַּעֲמַקֵּי־מָיִם׃ אַל־תִּשְׁטְפֵנִי ׀ שִׁבֹּלֶת מַיִם וְאַל־תִּבְלָעֵנִי

12 **And when I garb myself in sackcloth,** as a gesture of mourning or self-abnegation, **I am made an example** for derision.

13 **Those who sit at the gate,** the elders and prominent people of the city, **talk** derisively **about me; I am the subject of** mocking **songs by ale drinkers,** the common folk at the tavern.

14 **But as for me, let my prayer come to You, Lord, at a time of favor,** that this may be a time when You will be receptive to my prayers. **God, in the greatness of Your kindness, answer me with the truth of Your deliverance;** uphold faithfully that which You have promised, to come to my aid.

15 **Save me from the mire, lest I sink. May I be delivered from my foes and from the deep waters.** The psalmist returns to the imagery presented earlier, expressing his feeling of drowning.

16 **Do not let the whirlpool wash me away, nor the deep swallow**

Mouth of a well

me up, nor the well in which I am drowning **close its mouth over me,** preventing my escape.
17 **Answer me, Lord, for Your kindness is good. Turn to me** and save me **in the abundance of Your mercy.**
18 **Do not hide Your face,** or remove Your attention, **from Your servant, for I am in distress** and imminent danger, and I plead that You **make haste to answer me.**
19 **Draw near to me and redeem me; ransom me,** rescue me, **from my enemies,** who are in essence Your foes as well.
20 **You know of my humiliation, my shame, and my disgrace,** because **all** the actions of **my foes are before You.**
21 **Humiliation has broken my heart, and I have become desperately ill** from it. **I seek consolation, but there is none; I look for comforters** to treat me with compassion, **but** I **do not find any.**
22 Not only do they lack compassion, but they seek to harm me; **they put hemlock in my food, and for my thirst they give me vinegar to drink,** which only intensifies my thirst and increases my suffering.
23 In his misery, the psalmist curses his foes: **May their table become a trap.** May they be entrapped when they are sitting placidly at their table, and may **their** time of **tranquility** prove to be **a snare** for them.
24 **May their eyes grow dim so they cannot see; make their loins continuously unsteady** so they cannot stand.
25 **Pour out Your wrath on them; let the fierceness of Your anger overtake them** and punish them.
26 **May their fortress be desolate; may none dwell in their tents.**
27 The psalmist offers justification for his harsh words: **For they have pursued** me, **the one You have smitten.** God punished me for my personal sins and deficiencies, as God alone determines who suffers and who dies. **And** yet **they tell** with delight **of the pain of Your wounded;** my enemies take pleasure in speaking of my misery.
28 **Add** this **iniquity to their** other **iniquities;** when You judge them for their transgressions, **let them not be accorded Your righteousness,** which You normally extend to everyone.
29 When the time comes for You to record the fate of all, **may they be blotted out of the book of life. May they not be inscribed** for good **with the righteous;** record them instead among the wicked.
30 **As for me, afflicted and in pain, may Your salvation, God, strengthen me.**
31 And then **I will praise the name of God in song and magnify Him with thanksgiving,**
32 **and may it,** my meager tribute of song, **please the Lord more than** the sacrifice of **a** full-grown **bull with horns and hoofs.**
33 **The humble will see it,** Your salvation of me, **and be glad,** as I am an example to them of one who is fully devoted to God. **You who seek God** and witness His salvation of me, **let your hearts revive;** let this salvation provide you with hope and consolation.

Bull

34 **For the Lord hears the needy,** though they lack the means to vow sacrificial tributes to Him, **and** He **does not despise His prisoners,** who lack even freedom. He hears the prayers of the lowly people as well, and comes to their rescue.
35 **Let Him be praised by heaven and earth,** by **the seas and everything,** all the living creatures, **swarming within.**
36 And this is the praise all of them will declare to Him: **For God will save Zion and build** anew **the cities of Judah** that have been destroyed, **and people will settle there and possess it.**
37 **The descendants of His servants,** namely Israel, **will inherit it, and those who love His name,** as opposed to foreigners or enemies, **will dwell in it.**

PSALM 70
PSALMS 70:1–6

A short psalm of prayer, very similar in wording to the concluding verses of Psalm 40, in which David beseeches God to relieve him of his trials and tribulations.

70 1 **For the chief musician, by David, for remembrance.** This psalm was apparently written to remind God, as it were, of David's existence.
2 **God, hasten to deliver me.** The verb "hasten" is missing in the original Hebrew text, and is understood from the second half of the verse. **Lord, make haste to come to my aid.**
3 **Let those who seek my life be ashamed and humiliated. Let those who delight in my misfortune retreat in disgrace.**
4 **May those who say,** upon witnessing my misfortune: **Hurrah, hurrah! retreat on their heels in shame.**
5 **Let all who seek You be happy and rejoice in You; let those who love Your salvation always say: May God be magnified.**
6 In conclusion, the psalmist returns to his own personal situation: **As for me, poor and destitute, God, make haste,** for I am in urgent need of Your aid. **You are my help and my Savior; Lord, do not tarry;** save me from my misfortune.

יז מְצוּלָה וְאַל־תֶּאְטַר־עָלַי בְּאֵר פִּיהָ׃ עֲנֵנִי יהוה כִּי־טוֹב חַסְדֶּךָ כְּרֹב רַחֲמֶיךָ פְּנֵה
יח יט אֵלָי׃ וְאַל־תַּסְתֵּר פָּנֶיךָ מֵעַבְדֶּךָ כִּי־צַר־לִי מַהֵר עֲנֵנִי׃ קָרְבָה אֶל־נַפְשִׁי גְאָלָהּ
כ כא לְמַעַן אֹיְבַי פְּדֵנִי׃ אַתָּה יָדַעְתָּ חֶרְפָּתִי וּבָשְׁתִּי וּכְלִמָּתִי נֶגְדְּךָ כָּל־צוֹרְרָי׃ חֶרְפָּה ׀
כב שָׁבְרָה לִבִּי וָאָנוּשָׁה וָאֲקַוֶּה לָנוּד וָאַיִן וְלַמְנַחֲמִים וְלֹא מָצָאתִי׃ וַיִּתְּנוּ בְּבָרוּתִי
כג רֹאשׁ וְלִצְמָאִי יַשְׁקוּנִי חֹמֶץ׃ יְהִי־שֻׁלְחָנָם לִפְנֵיהֶם לְפָח וְלִשְׁלוֹמִים לְמוֹקֵשׁ׃
כד כה תֶּחְשַׁכְנָה עֵינֵיהֶם מֵרְאוֹת וּמָתְנֵיהֶם תָּמִיד הַמְעַד׃ שְׁפָךְ־עֲלֵיהֶם זַעְמֶךָ וַחֲרוֹן
כו כז אַפְּךָ יַשִּׂיגֵם׃ תְּהִי־טִירָתָם נְשַׁמָּה בְּאָהֳלֵיהֶם אַל־יְהִי יֹשֵׁב׃ כִּי־אַתָּה אֲשֶׁר־הִכִּיתָ
כח רָדָפוּ וְאֶל־מַכְאוֹב חֲלָלֶיךָ יְסַפֵּרוּ׃ תְּנָה־עָוֺן עַל־עֲוֺנָם וְאַל־יָבֹאוּ בְּצִדְקָתֶךָ׃
כט ל יִמָּחוּ מִסֵּפֶר חַיִּים וְעִם צַדִּיקִים אַל־יִכָּתֵבוּ׃ וַאֲנִי עָנִי וְכוֹאֵב יְשׁוּעָתְךָ אֱלֹהִים
לא לב תְּשַׂגְּבֵנִי׃ אֲהַלְלָה שֵׁם־אֱלֹהִים בְּשִׁיר וַאֲגַדְּלֶנּוּ בְתוֹדָה׃ וְתִיטַב לַיהוה מִשּׁוֹר
לג לד פָּר מַקְרִן מַפְרִיס׃ רָאוּ עֲנָוִים יִשְׂמָחוּ דֹּרְשֵׁי אֱלֹהִים וִיחִי לְבַבְכֶם׃ כִּי־שֹׁמֵעַ
לה אֶל־אֶבְיוֹנִים יהוה וְאֶת־אֲסִירָיו לֹא בָזָה׃ יְהַלְלוּהוּ שָׁמַיִם וָאָרֶץ יַמִּים וְכָל־רֹמֵשׂ
לו לז בָּם׃ כִּי אֱלֹהִים ׀ יוֹשִׁיעַ צִיּוֹן וְיִבְנֶה עָרֵי יְהוּדָה וְיָשְׁבוּ שָׁם וִירֵשׁוּהָ׃ וְזֶרַע עֲבָדָיו
יִנְחָלוּהָ וְאֹהֲבֵי שְׁמוֹ יִשְׁכְּנוּ־בָהּ׃

ע א ב ג לַמְנַצֵּחַ לְדָוִד לְהַזְכִּיר׃ אֱלֹהִים לְהַצִּילֵנִי יהוה לְעֶזְרָתִי חוּשָׁה׃ יֵבֹשׁוּ וְיַחְפְּרוּ
ד מְבַקְשֵׁי נַפְשִׁי יִסֹּגוּ אָחוֹר וְיִכָּלְמוּ חֲפֵצֵי רָעָתִי׃ יָשׁוּבוּ עַל־עֵקֶב בָּשְׁתָּם הָאֹמְרִים
ה הֶאָח ׀ הֶאָח׃ יָשִׂישׂוּ וְיִשְׂמְחוּ ׀ בְּךָ כָּל־מְבַקְשֶׁיךָ וְיֹאמְרוּ תָמִיד יִגְדַּל אֱלֹהִים
ו אֹהֲבֵי יְשׁוּעָתֶךָ׃ וַאֲנִי ׀ עָנִי וְאֶבְיוֹן אֱלֹהִים חוּשָׁה לִּי עֶזְרִי וּמְפַלְטִי אַתָּה יהוה
אַל־תְּאַחַר׃

PSALM 71

PSALMS 71:1–24

A psalm of request and thanksgiving. It begins with the psalmist beseeching God to rescue him from his enemies, and concludes with words of praise for his salvation.

71 1 **In You, Lord, I have taken refuge;**[B] therefore, **I shall never be ashamed.**
2 **Save me** from my enemies **and rescue me** from my troubles **in Your righteousness; incline Your ear to me and deliver me.**
3 **Be** like **a fortified dwelling for me, where I may enter at all times,** since **You have ordained my rescue, for You are my rock and my fortress.**
4 **My God, rescue me from the hand of the wicked, from the grasp of the wrongdoer and the violent man [*ḥometz*].** The word *ḥometz* is similar in meaning to *ḥomes*, "violent man" or "robber." It is also found in talmudic literature with a similar meaning.
5 **For You are my hope, my Lord God, my trust from the days of my youth.**
6 **I have relied on You from birth,** literally "from the belly," since emerging from the womb; **You brought me out of my mother's womb,** and I have been with You ever since. **I praise You always.**
7 **I have been an example for many.** David is aware that as king, his deeds and acts of courage are not private matters; people admire him as a symbol and role model. **And You are my mighty refuge.**
8 **Let my mouth be filled with praise for You;** enable me to praise You with a full mouth, with completion and perfection. May I be able to praise You **for Your glory all day long.**
9 The psalmist makes an additional request: **Do not cast me off in old age; do not forsake me when my strength fails.**
10 **For my enemies have spoken against me; those who keep watch over my soul,** those who await an opportunity to take my life, **have conspired together,**
11 **saying: God has forsaken him;** he no longer enjoys divine protection. Therefore, **pursue and seize him, for there is no one to rescue him.**
12 **God, do not be distant from me,** as my enemies would like; **my God, hasten to my aid.**
13 **May those who hate me be humiliated; may they perish. May those who seek my harm be wrapped in shame and disgrace.**
14 **But as for me, I will hope continually** for Your kindness and salvation, **and** when You do rescue me, **I will add to Your praises** that I have expressed in the past.
15 **My mouth will tell of Your righteousness, of Your salvation all day long, for they,** all Your acts of salvation toward me, **are beyond what I know to count.**
16 **If I come into** a position of **strength, my Lord God, I will invoke only Your righteousness,** for anything else that may have enabled me to achieve that power was only a tool in Your hands.
17 **God, You have taught me** everything that I know **from my youth, and until now I have told of Your wondrous deeds.**
18 **Also until I am old and gray,** as my strength diminishes, **God, do not forsake me, until I tell of Your strength to generations,** and until I tell **of Your might to all who come** into this world.
19 **For Your righteousness, God, reaches the heavens. For the great deeds you have done** for me, **God, who is comparable to You?**
20 **Though You brought upon me many severe troubles, You** always **come back and revive me; from the depths of the earth You come back and raise me up.**
21 **You** not only rescue me but even **increase my greatness; You turn** Your attention to me **to comfort me.**
22 **And I, I will give thanks to You with a harp; I will sing praises of Your truth, my God, on a lyre, Holy One of Israel.**
23 **My lips will sing out joyfully, along with my very soul that You redeemed** from peril.
24 **My tongue will also utter Your righteousness all day long, for those who sought to harm me have been confounded and brought to shame.** I can now express my gratitude, for You have indeed come to my rescue.

BACKGROUND

71:1 | **The chapter divisions of Psalms:** This psalm lacks a heading. Indeed, according to Mishael ben Uziel's *Kitab al-Ḥulaf* (The Book of Variations), chapters 70 and 71 of Psalms are in fact one single chapter. According to this division, there would be 149 chapters in the book rather than 150, and this count is supported by several ancient manuscripts and fragments from the Cairo Geniza. According to another opinion, mentioned in the Jerusalem Talmud (*Shabbat* 17:1) and *Masekhet Soferim* (16:11) there are 147 chapters in Psalms, and this view, too, is supported by manuscripts from the geniza.

עא א ב בְּךָ־יְהוָה חָסִיתִי אַל־אֵבוֹשָׁה לְעוֹלָם: בְּצִדְקָתְךָ תַּצִּילֵנִי וּתְפַלְּטֵנִי הַטֵּה־אֵלַי אָזְנְךָ

ג וְהוֹשִׁיעֵנִי: הֱיֵה לִי ׀ לְצוּר מָעוֹן לָבוֹא תָּמִיד צִוִּיתָ לְהוֹשִׁיעֵנִי כִּי־סַלְעִי וּמְצוּדָתִי

ד ה אָתָּה: אֱלֹהַי פַּלְּטֵנִי מִיַּד רָשָׁע מִכַּף מְעַוֵּל וְחוֹמֵץ: כִּי־אַתָּה תִקְוָתִי אֲדֹנָי יֱהֹוִה

ו מִבְטַחִי מִנְּעוּרָי: עָלֶיךָ ׀ נִסְמַכְתִּי מִבֶּטֶן מִמְּעֵי אִמִּי אַתָּה גוֹזִי בְּךָ תְהִלָּתִי תָמִיד:

ז ח כְּמוֹפֵת הָיִיתִי לְרַבִּים וְאַתָּה מַחֲסִי־עֹז: יִמָּלֵא פִי תְּהִלָּתֶךָ כָּל־הַיּוֹם תִּפְאַרְתֶּךָ:

ט י אַל־תַּשְׁלִיכֵנִי לְעֵת זִקְנָה כִּכְלוֹת כֹּחִי אַל־תַּעַזְבֵנִי: כִּי־אָמְרוּ אוֹיְבַי לִי וְשֹׁמְרֵי

יא יב נַפְשִׁי נוֹעֲצוּ יַחְדָּו: לֵאמֹר אֱלֹהִים עֲזָבוֹ רִדְפוּ וְתִפְשׂוּהוּ כִּי־אֵין מַצִּיל: אֱלֹהִים

יג אַל־תִּרְחַק מִמֶּנִּי אֱלֹהַי לְעֶזְרָתִי חישה: יֵבֹשׁוּ יִכְלוּ שֹׂטְנֵי נַפְשִׁי יַעֲטוּ חֶרְפָּה חוּשָׁה

יד טו וּכְלִמָּה מְבַקְשֵׁי רָעָתִי: וַאֲנִי תָּמִיד אֲיַחֵל וְהוֹסַפְתִּי עַל־כָּל־תְּהִלָּתֶךָ: פִּי ׀ יְסַפֵּר

טז צִדְקָתֶךָ כָּל־הַיּוֹם תְּשׁוּעָתֶךָ כִּי לֹא יָדַעְתִּי סְפֹרוֹת: אָבוֹא בִּגְבֻרוֹת אֲדֹנָי יֱהֹוִה

יז אַזְכִּיר צִדְקָתְךָ לְבַדֶּךָ: אֱלֹהִים לִמַּדְתַּנִי מִנְּעוּרָי וְעַד־הֵנָּה אַגִּיד נִפְלְאוֹתֶיךָ:

יח וְגַם עַד־זִקְנָה ׀ וְשֵׂיבָה אֱלֹהִים אַל־תַּעַזְבֵנִי עַד־אַגִּיד זְרוֹעֲךָ לְדוֹר לְכָל־יָבוֹא

יט גְּבוּרָתֶךָ: וְצִדְקָתְךָ אֱלֹהִים עַד־מָרוֹם אֲשֶׁר־עָשִׂיתָ גְדֹלוֹת אֱלֹהִים מִי כָמוֹךָ:

כ אֲשֶׁר הראיתנו ׀ צָרוֹת רַבּוֹת וְרָעוֹת תָּשׁוּב תחיינו וּמִתְּהֹמוֹת הָאָרֶץ תָּשׁוּב הִרְאִיתַנִי

כא כב תעלנו: תֶּרֶב ׀ גְּדֻלָּתִי וְתִסֹּב תְּנַחֲמֵנִי: גַּם־אֲנִי ׀ אוֹדְךָ בִכְלִי־נֶבֶל אֲמִתְּךָ אֱלֹהָי תְּחַיֵּנִי

כג אֲזַמְּרָה לְךָ בְכִנּוֹר קְדוֹשׁ יִשְׂרָאֵל: תְּרַנֵּנָּה שְׂפָתַי כִּי אֲזַמְּרָה־לָּךְ וְנַפְשִׁי אֲשֶׁר תַּעֲלֵנִי

כד פָּדִיתָ: גַּם־לְשׁוֹנִי כָּל־הַיּוֹם תֶּהְגֶּה צִדְקָתֶךָ כִּי־בֹשׁוּ כִי־חָפְרוּ מְבַקְשֵׁי רָעָתִי:

PSALM 72

PSALMS 72:1–20

A song and prayer regarding King Solomon. It also appears to contain words of prophecy concerning the future messiah, who will be a descendant of Solomon.

72 *14th day of month*

1 **For Solomon.** It appears likely that the psalm was written by David and dedicated to his son Solomon. **Endow the king,** apparently referring to David himself, **with Your justice, God;** enable me to carry out God's laws in the land. **And** endow **the king's son with Your righteousness;** may the king's son, his successor, be granted the ability to apply God's righteousness in the world.

2 **May he judge Your people with righteousness, and Your poor with justice.** *Tzedek*, "righteousness," is objective and absolute, and is administered toward the "people" at large. By contrast, *mishpat*, "justice," though not deviating from fairness, can take into account subjective factors such as financial hardship, and should be applied to the "poor."

3 When justice reigns supreme, there is tranquility in the land. **The mountains will bear peace for the people;** mountains often provide cover for enemies who may lurk there, but in his day, the mountains will shelter within them only peace, **and the hills** will bear **righteousness.**

4 **He will bring justice to the afflicted of the people,** as is his proper function. Beyond that, he will **save the destitute;** he will actively intervene to extend assistance to the most unfortunate, those whose needs go beyond fair justice. **And** he will **crush the oppressor** of the poor man. The king's judgments cannot always be soft and accommodating; at times he must take fierce action to battle oppression.

5 **They will fear You as long as the sun and moon endure.** In this idyllic land, the people will be consistently God-fearing, with the continuity and regularity of the sun and the moon, **throughout the generations.**

6 **It,** the king's righteous administration of justice, **will descend like rain on fleece.** The blessings of justice will never be wasted; they will be fully absorbed, like rain on the woolly fleece of lambs, and **like light showers that** gently **water the earth.**

7 **The righteous will flourish in his days,** as the king's virtuous rule will function as a shield to protect other righteous people with **abundant peace until the moon is no more,** that is, for all time.

8 In order for the tranquility of this kingdom, initiated by the righteous administration of justice, to be secure, it must also be accompanied by peace with the neighboring peoples: **He will** exert full **rule from sea to sea,** throughout the territory of the Land of Israel, which is surrounded by seas, and **from the river to the ends of the land.** In the Bible, "the river," when unspecified, refers to the Euphrates, which was actually a border of Solomon's territory.

9 **Seafarers** from distant lands who come to the Land of Israel **will kneel before him, and his enemies will** be brought so low that they will **lick the dust,** as it were.

10 The king's power and influence will extend far beyond the borders of the Land of Israel. **The kings of Tarshish,** a faraway city variously identified, located in Spain according to some, **and** the kings **of the islands will bring tribute** to the king. **The kings of Sheba and Seva,**[B] in farthest Arabia or Africa, **will offer gifts.**

11 **And all kings,** even from more distant lands than these, **will bow down before him; all nations will serve him** in one way or another.

12 This veneration of the king will take place both because of his military strength and also in appreciation of his wise and compassionate leadership, **for he will rescue,** both in his own realm and abroad, **the needy, who cry out** for assistance, **and the poor man with no one to help him.**

13 **He will have compassion on the poor and needy, and the lives of the needy he will save.**

14 **He will redeem them,** those powerless, vulnerable people, **from deceit and violence, and their blood,** their lives, **will be**

BACKGROUND

72:10| **Sheba and Seva:** The juxtaposition of these two nations suggests that they were related to each other. Seva is counted (Genesis 10:7) among the group of Kushite peoples who settled in eastern Africa, whereas Sheba is listed among the Shemites who lived in the southern Arabian peninsula, and later extended their rule to parts of eastern Africa, areas in present-day Eritrea and northern Ethiopia. It should be noted that in Isaiah (45:14) the Sevaites are identified as a tall, mercantile nation, and in fact the peoples of eastern Africa, like the Samburu south of Sudan and the Swahili, are quite tall. It is also possible that the name Seva was used to refer to all the nations of eastern Africa who were known as merchants (see commentary on Isaiah 43:3).

72:15| **The gold of Sheba:** The biblical record (II Chronicles 9:9), external Assyrian sources, and Greek and Roman historians all report that gold, precious stones, spices, and ivory were imported from Sheba in the Arabian peninsula. It is possible that the gold originated from the other side of the Red Sea, in the land of Punt in Africa, as this was the source of the gold imported by Egypt.

עב א ב לִשְׁלֹמֹה ׀ אֱלֹהִים מִשְׁפָּטֶיךָ לְמֶלֶךְ תֵּן וְצִדְקָתְךָ לְבֶן־מֶלֶךְ: יָדִין עַמְּךָ בְצֶדֶק יד לחודש
ג ד וַעֲנִיֶּיךָ בְמִשְׁפָּט: יִשְׂאוּ הָרִים שָׁלוֹם לָעָם וּגְבָעוֹת בִּצְדָקָה: יִשְׁפֹּט ׀ עֲנִיֵּי־עָם
ה ו יוֹשִׁיעַ לִבְנֵי אֶבְיוֹן וִידַכֵּא עוֹשֵׁק: יִירָאוּךָ עִם־שָׁמֶשׁ וְלִפְנֵי יָרֵחַ דּוֹר דּוֹרִים: יֵרֵד
ז כְּמָטָר עַל־גֵּז כִּרְבִיבִים זַרְזִיף אָרֶץ: יִפְרַח־בְּיָמָיו צַדִּיק וְרֹב שָׁלוֹם עַד־בְּלִי יָרֵחַ:
ח ט וְיֵרְדְּ מִיָּם עַד־יָם וּמִנָּהָר עַד־אַפְסֵי־אָרֶץ: לְפָנָיו יִכְרְעוּ צִיִּים וְאֹיְבָיו עָפָר יְלַחֵכוּ:
י יא מַלְכֵי תַרְשִׁישׁ וְאִיִּים מִנְחָה יָשִׁיבוּ מַלְכֵי שְׁבָא וּסְבָא אֶשְׁכָּר יַקְרִיבוּ: וְיִשְׁתַּחֲווּ־
יב יג לוֹ כָל־מְלָכִים כָּל־גּוֹיִם יַעַבְדוּהוּ: כִּי־יַצִּיל אֶבְיוֹן מְשַׁוֵּעַ וְעָנִי וְאֵין־עֹזֵר לוֹ: יָחֹס
יד עַל־דַּל וְאֶבְיוֹן וְנַפְשׁוֹת אֶבְיוֹנִים יוֹשִׁיעַ: מִתּוֹךְ וּמֵחָמָס יִגְאַל נַפְשָׁם וְיֵיקַר דָּמָם
טו טז בְּעֵינָיו: וִיחִי וְיִתֶּן־לוֹ מִזְּהַב שְׁבָא וְיִתְפַּלֵּל בַּעֲדוֹ תָמִיד כָּל־הַיּוֹם יְבָרֲכֶנְהוּ: יְהִי
פִסַּת־בַּר ׀ בָּאָרֶץ בְּרֹאשׁ הָרִים יִרְעַשׁ כַּלְּבָנוֹן פִּרְיוֹ וְיָצִיצוּ מֵעִיר כְּעֵשֶׂב הָאָרֶץ:
יז יח יְהִי שְׁמוֹ ׀ לְעוֹלָם לִפְנֵי־שֶׁמֶשׁ ינין שְׁמוֹ וְיִתְבָּרְכוּ בוֹ כָּל־גּוֹיִם יְאַשְּׁרוּהוּ: בָּרוּךְ ׀ יִנּוֹן
יט יְהוָה אֱלֹהִים אֱלֹהֵי יִשְׂרָאֵל עֹשֵׂה נִפְלָאוֹת לְבַדּוֹ: וּבָרוּךְ ׀ שֵׁם כְּבוֹדוֹ לְעוֹלָם
כ וְיִמָּלֵא כְבוֹדוֹ אֶת־כֹּל הָאָרֶץ אָמֵן ׀ וְאָמֵן: כָּלּוּ תְפִלּוֹת דָּוִד בֶּן־יִשָׁי: י

precious in his sight. This is unlike typical monarchs, who are indifferent to the suffering of the poor and downtrodden.

15 So will he live well, **and He will give him the gold of Sheba;**[B] God will grant him great wealth. **People will pray for him always; they will bless him all day long,** for he will be beloved by all.

16 In addition to the blessing of peace, **there will be abundance of grain in the land,** even **on the mountain tops,** where grain is not normally cultivated. **Its** trees will be so full of **fruit** that they **will rustle as** trees do in the great forest of **the Lebanon. There will be sprouting in the city like grass of the earth.** Useful vegetation will spring up like wild grass, in places that are not cultivated and sown.

17 This psalm sums up its prayer in the concluding verse: **May his name endure forever. May his name be praised as long as the sun shines,** that is, forever, **and may all people bless themselves by him;** may they consider him a paradigm of blessing. **May all the nations acclaim him,** or, more literally, may they declare: How fortunate he is! This verse marks the end of the content of the psalm. What follows are verses of conclusion to the second of the five sections that constitute the book of Psalms.

18 Blessed be the Lord God, the God of Israel, who alone works wonders.

19 And blessed be His glorious name forever; may the whole earth be filled with His glory, amen and amen. This concept is mirrored, in Aramaic, in the Kaddish prayer.

20 This verse concludes the second book of Psalms: **Here end the prayers of David son of Yishai.** Almost all the psalms up to this point were authored by David. Although some of the psalms that follow were also written by David, most are either unattributed or were authored by others.

PSALM 73

A psalm that raises troubling questions about the way the world operates, but also provides an answer to these questions.

PSALMS 73:1–28

73 BOOK THREE Wednesday

1 **A psalm** by **Asaf. Surely God is good to Israel, to those pure of heart,** although often this is not evident at all, as the psalmist goes on to describe.

2 **But as for me,** upon pondering this reality, **my feet came close to swerving, my steps nearly slipping away.** Several factors can lead to a person's stumbling from the right path, as the following verses point out.

3 **For I was jealous of the revelers; I saw the well-being of the wicked.** It seems as if the wicked are enjoying themselves since they experience success.

4 **For there are no chains** leading them **toward their death.** They do not seem to be fettered in chains as they are being led away to their deaths. **Indeed,** on the contrary, **they are** quite **healthy.**

5 **Theirs is no mortal toil.** They are not burdened with hard work like other people. **No plagues** or illnesses that are normally the lot **of man afflict them.**

6 **Therefore,** since their lives go so smoothly, **they carry pride as their necklace.** They display their pride as if it were an ornament, and **lawlessness envelops them like a mantle.**

7 **Their eyes bulge from fatness; the chambers of their hearts overflow.** They are so healthy and well fed that their eyes seem to be protruding, and their sense of well-being fills their hearts to the extent that it is clearly apparent in their external appearance.

8 **They are foul, speaking of wickedness and wrongdoing** toward others and toward God; **they speak out from their exalted place.** They have become foul, continually speaking ill both of others and of God. Encountering no hardships or obstacles in their lives, they allow themselves to say whatever they wish.

9 **They set their mouth against heaven; their tongue parades across the land,** spreading slander and calumny.

10 Among other evil things, they say: **Therefore, His people are in retreat, with only remnants of the waters of abundance.** The wicked believe that the righteous, and everyone else except themselves, receive only scraps of the bounty that they, the wicked, have accrued.

11 **And** since they feel free to speak against heaven (see verse 9), **they say: How does the Almighty know** what happens in the world, since He does not involve Himself with people's lives? **Is there knowledge in the Most High?** Their claim is that God neither knows nor cares about what happens in the world.

12 **Behold, they are wicked, at ease in their worldly attainments.**

13 In contrast to the ease and comfort of the wicked, the psalmist feels a sense of despair: **Indeed,** it seems that **it is all in vain that I have purified my heart and washed clean my hands** from wrongdoing,

14 **for** though I have followed the righteous path, **I have been stricken all day long and chastised** with suffering and hardship **every morning.**

15 **Had I said: I will speak of this,** were I to give a detailed account of the suffering the righteous are made to endure, **I would have betrayed generations of Your children,** as it would cause children of future generations to stray from the right path.

16 **When I sought to understand this,** why there seems to be so much injustice in the world, **it seemed futile in my eyes.** I have been at a loss when attempting to make sense of why the wicked prosper while the righteous suffer.

17 I did not comprehend this **until I entered the Temple of God,** where I was granted a greater level of understanding of God's manifestation in the world; **then I understood what would be their end.** I began to understand the true nature of the success of the wicked and the suffering of the righteous.

18 **Indeed, You set them on smooth paths.** God provides the wicked with a smooth path throughout their lives, and they are enticed to continue in their evil ways. But ultimately this path only leads them to disaster, as **You cast them down to destruction.**

19 Upon their downfall I see **how, in a moment, they are brought to desolation, swept away, annihilated by terror.**

20 **Like a dream after awakening,** when the sleeper realizes that all he has experienced is nothing but a dream, **Lord,** when You reveal Yourself **in the city, You make their image despised.** As stated often in the Bible, all the wicked's success and good fortune are temporary and ultimately lead to their undoing.

21 Concerning the fate of the righteous, the psalmist reflects: **When my heart is embittered, and in my mind I am filled with thoughts,** because I do not comprehend their destiny,

22 I remind myself that **I am a boor, unknowing** of God's mysterious ways; **I am like a beast before You.** I follow Him like an animal that is led by its master. Although this sort of blind obedience may seem to be lacking substance, it is in fact a tremendous privilege to be with God, as the psalmist goes on to acknowledge:

23 **Yet I am always with You; You grasp my right hand.** The fact that I choose to follow You means that You are leading me and providing me support.

עג א ב מִזְמוֹר לְאָסָף אַךְ טוֹב לְיִשְׂרָאֵל אֱלֹהִים לְבָרֵי לֵבָב: וַאֲנִי כִּמְעַט נטוי רַגְלָי כְּאַיִן ספר שלישי יום רביעי
ג ד שפכה אֲשֻׁרָי: כִּי־קִנֵּאתִי בַּהוֹלְלִים שְׁלוֹם רְשָׁעִים אֶרְאֶה: כִּי אֵין חַרְצֻבּוֹת נָטָיוּ
ה ו לְמוֹתָם וּבָרִיא אוּלָם: בַּעֲמַל אֱנוֹשׁ אֵינֵמוֹ וְעִם־אָדָם לֹא יְנֻגָּעוּ: לָכֵן עֲנָקַתְמוֹ שֻׁפְּכוּ
ז ח גַאֲוָה יַעֲטָף־שִׁית חָמָס לָמוֹ: יָצָא מֵחֵלֶב עֵינֵמוֹ עָבְרוּ מַשְׂכִּיּוֹת לֵבָב: יָמִיקוּ ׀
ט וִידַבְּרוּ בְרָע עֹשֶׁק מִמָּרוֹם יְדַבֵּרוּ: שַׁתּוּ בַשָּׁמַיִם פִּיהֶם וּלְשׁוֹנָם תִּהֲלַךְ בָּאָרֶץ:
י יא לָכֵן ׀ ישיב עַמּוֹ הֲלֹם וּמֵי מָלֵא יִמָּצוּ לָמוֹ: וְאָמְרוּ אֵיכָה יָדַע־אֵל וְיֵשׁ דֵּעָה יָשׁוּב
יב יג בְעֶלְיוֹן: הִנֵּה־אֵלֶּה רְשָׁעִים וְשַׁלְוֵי עוֹלָם הִשְׂגּוּ־חָיִל: אַךְ־רִיק זִכִּיתִי לְבָבִי וָאֶרְחַץ
יד טו בְּנִקָּיוֹן כַּפָּי: וָאֱהִי נָגוּעַ כָּל־הַיּוֹם וְתוֹכַחְתִּי לַבְּקָרִים: אִם־אָמַרְתִּי אֲסַפְּרָה כְמוֹ
טז יז הִנֵּה דוֹר בָּנֶיךָ בָגָדְתִּי: וָאֲחַשְּׁבָה לָדַעַת זֹאת עָמָל היא בְעֵינָי: עַד־אָבוֹא אֶל־ הוּא
יח מִקְדְּשֵׁי־אֵל אָבִינָה לְאַחֲרִיתָם: אַךְ בַּחֲלָקוֹת תָּשִׁית לָמוֹ הִפַּלְתָּם לְמַשּׁוּאוֹת:
יט כ אֵיךְ הָיוּ לְשַׁמָּה כְרָגַע סָפוּ תַמּוּ מִן־בַּלָּהוֹת: כַּחֲלוֹם מֵהָקִיץ אֲדֹנָי בָּעִיר ׀ צַלְמָם
כא כב תִּבְזֶה: כִּי יִתְחַמֵּץ לְבָבִי וְכִלְיוֹתַי אֶשְׁתּוֹנָן: וַאֲנִי־בַעַר וְלֹא אֵדָע בְּהֵמוֹת הָיִיתִי
כג כד עִמָּךְ: וַאֲנִי תָמִיד עִמָּךְ אָחַזְתָּ בְּיַד־יְמִינִי: בַּעֲצָתְךָ תַנְחֵנִי וְאַחַר כָּבוֹד תִּקָּחֵנִי:
כה כו מִי־לִי בַשָּׁמָיִם וְעִמְּךָ לֹא־חָפַצְתִּי בָאָרֶץ: כָּלָה שְׁאֵרִי וּלְבָבִי צוּר־לְבָבִי וְחֶלְקִי
כז כח אֱלֹהִים לְעוֹלָם: כִּי־הִנֵּה רְחֵקֶיךָ יֹאבֵדוּ הִצְמַתָּה כָּל־זוֹנֶה מִמֶּךָּ: וַאֲנִי ׀ קִרֲבַת
אֱלֹהִים לִי טוֹב שַׁתִּי ׀ בַּאדֹנָי יֱהֹוִה מַחְסִי לְסַפֵּר כָּל־מַלְאֲכוֹתֶיךָ:

24 **You guide me with Your counsel and lead me into honor.** In following God, I am close to Him, as He leads me to the right and worthy path. When a person is occupied with his yearning to draw close to God and to deepen his love of Him, external matters, including deprivation and the suffering of the righteous, lose their significance.

25 **Whom else do I have in heaven** whom I may trust? I recognize only You. I realize that despite all the worldly matters that may be attained **with You,** such as wealth, honor, and success, **I desire nothing on earth.** In light of my closeness to God, they are of no real importance to me.

26 **My flesh and my heart may fail, but** that is inconsequential, for **God is the strength of my heart and my portion forever.**

27 **Behold, those who are distant from You** ultimately **perish** from this world, and certainly from the World to Come; **You destroy all who stray from You.**

28 But **as for me, nearness to God is good; I put my trust in the Lord God so I may tell of all Your works.** This verse expresses the essence of the psalm, namely, the transition from an external perception of the world, in which evil people appear to be successful and on the ascendant, to the more introspective understanding that closeness to God is the greatest good.

PSALM 74

PSALMS 74:1–23

A psalm that depicts Israel at a time of crisis, when enemies prevail. The psalmist entreats God to once again display His miracles and bring about salvation as He has done before, both for the sake of His name as God of Israel and because of His covenant with them.

74 1 **A contemplation by Asaf.** The psalmist portrays a dire situation: **Why, God, have You abandoned us forever, Your anger smoldering against the sheep of Your fold?** To the psalmist, it appears as if God has abandoned His people in their time of distress.

2 **Remember Your congregation,** Israel, **which You acquired** for Yourself **of old, which You redeemed as the tribe of Your portion.** And remember **this Mount Zion** as well, **where You dwelled.**

3 **Lift Your footsteps** and bestir Yourself to action **toward the ongoing destruction** taking place on Mount Zion; see **all that the enemy has inflicted on the Sanctuary** itself.

4 **Your foes roared** with cries of victory **within Your meeting place,** where people once congregated in prayer and service to You, **setting their standards as signs;** their banners are now waving in our camp.

5 **It has become plainly known.** *Kemeivi lemala,* translated here as "plainly," literally means "as one lifts something up high" to show to all what he is holding. The enemy wantonly wreaks destruction **as an ax** cuts down many branches **in a thicket.**

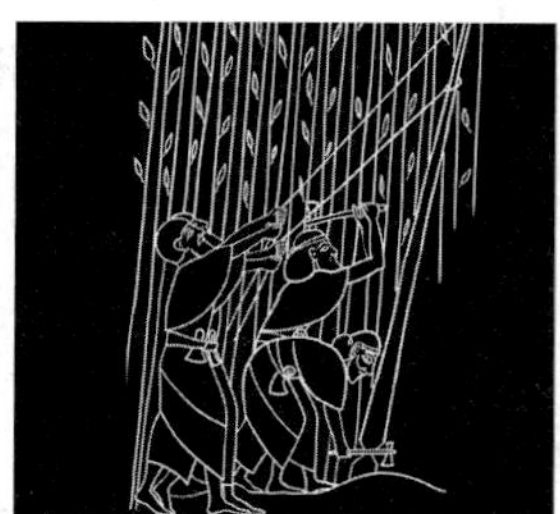

"As an ax in a thicket." Canaanite princes from Lebanon cutting down cedar trees for Pharaoh Seti I, illustration based on stone relief

6 **They smashed all its,** Jerusalem's, **entrances with axes and hatchets.**

7 **They burned Your Sanctuary; they defiled the dwelling place of Your name,** bringing **down** its glory **to the ground.**

8 **They said in their heart: Let us utterly destroy them. They burned all the meeting places of God in the land.** They destroyed not only Your Sanctuary but also other consecrated places. In later generations, such places would include synagogues and houses of study.

9 **We cannot see our signs.** We no longer experience the miracles that were wrought for us in the past. **There is no longer any prophet** to tell us when the destruction will finally come to an end, **nor is there any among us who knows for how long** this situation will continue.

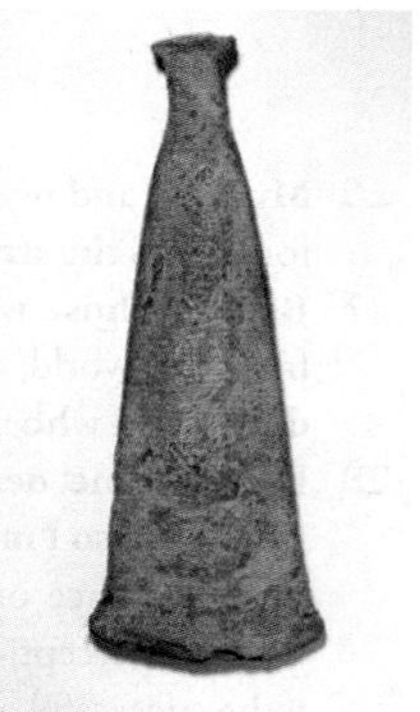

Hatchet blade, Egypt, Thirteenth Dynasty

10 Therefore, we ask: **How long, God, will the foe revile? Will the enemy eternally mock Your name?**

11 **Why do You withhold Your hand** from extending it in order to assist us? **Draw forth Your right hand from Your bosom.** We beseech You to draw forth not one but both of Your hands, as it were.

12 **For God is my King from times of old,** and in the past You have indeed come to our aid, **working deliverance in the midst of the land.**

13 **You shredded the sea with Your strength; You broke the heads of crocodiles on the waters.** *Tanninim,* translated here as "sea creatures," are giant creatures inhabiting the depths of the seas.[29]

14 **You crushed the heads of leviathan,** a giant sea creature; **You gave it as food to the nation, to the fleets,** feeding its flesh to people who never could have captured it on their own.

15 **You caused springs and streams to break forth** from the earth; **You dried up ever-flowing rivers.**

16 **The day is Yours, as Yours is the night,** for You rule at all times; **You founded** and created **light and the sun.**

17 **You laid down all the boundaries on earth.** You established the natural order of the world. **Summer and winter You created.**

18 And since Your power is so far-reaching, we beseech You: **Remember this: The enemy who reviled the Lord and the base people who scorned Your name.**

19 **Do not deliver Your dove,** the symbol of Israel, **to the wild beast,** their vicious enemy. **Do not eternally forget the lives of Your needy ones.**

20 **Look to the covenant** You forged with us and act to fulfill it, **for the earth is full of dark places and habitations of iniquity.**

21 **Let not the downtrodden one be turned back and shamed** because he has no one to protect him**; let the poor and needy praise Your name** after You have come to their aid.

22 **Arise, God, and strive on behalf of Your** own **cause** because, apart from harming us, the enemy is also desecrating Your name. **Recall the abuse of the scoundrels against You, all day long.**

23 **Do not forget the voice of Your foes, the endless tumult of those rising against You** through their scorn and desecration of Your name. For all these reasons, we beseech You to come to our salvation.

עד א ב מַשְׂכִּיל לְאָסָף לָמָה אֱלֹהִים זָנַחְתָּ לָנֶצַח יֶעְשַׁן אַפְּךָ בְּצֹאן מַרְעִיתֶךָ: זְכֹר
ג עֲדָתְךָ ׀ קָּנִיתָ קֶּדֶם גָּאַלְתָּ שֵׁבֶט נַחֲלָתֶךָ הַר־צִיּוֹן זֶה ׀ שָׁכַנְתָּ בּוֹ: הָרִימָה פְעָמֶיךָ
ד לְמַשֻּׁאוֹת נֶצַח כָּל־הֵרַע אוֹיֵב בַּקֹּדֶשׁ: שָׁאֲגוּ צֹרְרֶיךָ בְּקֶרֶב מוֹעֲדֶךָ שָׂמוּ אוֹתֹתָם
ה ו אֹתוֹת: יִוָּדַע כְּמֵבִיא לְמָעְלָה בִּסְבָךְ־עֵץ קַרְדֻּמּוֹת: וְעַתָּ פִּתּוּחֶיהָ יָּחַד בְּכַשִּׁיל
ז ח וְכֵילַפֹּת יַהֲלֹמוּן: שִׁלְחוּ בָאֵשׁ מִקְדָּשֶׁךָ לָאָרֶץ חִלְּלוּ מִשְׁכַּן־שְׁמֶךָ: אָמְרוּ בְלִבָּם
ט נִינָם יָחַד שָׂרְפוּ כָל־מוֹעֲדֵי־אֵל בָּאָרֶץ: אוֹתֹתֵינוּ לֹא־רָאִינוּ אֵין־עוֹד נָבִיא
י וְלֹא־אִתָּנוּ יֹדֵעַ עַד־מָה: עַד־מָתַי אֱלֹהִים יְחָרֶף צָר יְנָאֵץ אוֹיֵב שִׁמְךָ לָנֶצַח:
יא יב לָמָּה תָשִׁיב יָדְךָ וִימִינֶךָ מִקֶּרֶב חוקך כַלֵּה: וֵאלֹהִים מַלְכִּי מִקֶּדֶם פֹּעֵל יְשׁוּעוֹת חֵיקְךָ
יג יד בְּקֶרֶב הָאָרֶץ: אַתָּה פוֹרַרְתָּ בְעָזְּךָ יָם שִׁבַּרְתָּ רָאשֵׁי תַנִּינִים עַל־הַמָּיִם: אַתָּה
טו רִצַּצְתָּ רָאשֵׁי לִוְיָתָן תִּתְּנֶנּוּ מַאֲכָל לְעָם לְצִיִּים: אַתָּה בָקַעְתָּ מַעְיָן וָנָחַל אַתָּה
טז יז הוֹבַשְׁתָּ נַהֲרוֹת אֵיתָן: לְךָ יוֹם אַף־לְךָ לָיְלָה אַתָּה הֲכִינוֹתָ מָאוֹר וָשָׁמֶשׁ: אַתָּה
יח הִצַּבְתָּ כָּל־גְּבוּלוֹת אָרֶץ קַיִץ וָחֹרֶף אַתָּה יְצַרְתָּם: זְכָר־זֹאת אוֹיֵב חֵרֵף ׀ יְהוָה
יט וְעַם נָבָל נִאֲצוּ שְׁמֶךָ: אַל־תִּתֵּן לְחַיַּת נֶפֶשׁ תּוֹרֶךָ חַיַּת עֲנִיֶּיךָ אַל־תִּשְׁכַּח לָנֶצַח:
כ כא הַבֵּט לַבְּרִית כִּי מָלְאוּ מַחֲשַׁכֵּי־אֶרֶץ נְאוֹת חָמָס: אַל־יָשֹׁב דַּךְ נִכְלָם עָנִי וְאֶבְיוֹן
כב כג יְהַלְלוּ שְׁמֶךָ: קוּמָה אֱלֹהִים רִיבָה רִיבֶךָ זְכֹר חֶרְפָּתְךָ מִנִּי־נָבָל כָּל־הַיּוֹם: אַל־
תִּשְׁכַּח קוֹל צֹרְרֶיךָ שְׁאוֹן קָמֶיךָ עֹלֶה תָמִיד:
עה א ב לַמְנַצֵּחַ אַל־תַּשְׁחֵת מִזְמוֹר לְאָסָף שִׁיר: הוֹדִינוּ לְּךָ ׀ אֱלֹהִים הוֹדִינוּ וְקָרוֹב שְׁמֶךָ
ג ד סִפְּרוּ נִפְלְאוֹתֶיךָ: כִּי אֶקַּח מוֹעֵד אֲנִי מֵישָׁרִים אֶשְׁפֹּט: נְמֹגִים אֶרֶץ וְכָל־יֹשְׁבֶיהָ

PSALM 75

PSALMS 75:1–11

A psalm mainly expressing gratitude to God while also voicing the hope that God will continue to provide deliverance in times of trouble.

75 1 **For the chief musician, al tashḥet, a psalm by Asaf, a song.** The term *al tashḥet* is apparently a reference to an ancient poem or melody (see 57:1).

2 **We give thanks to You, God, we give thanks, and Your name is near** to us; it is constantly in our mouths. **They,** our forefathers and teachers, **have told** us **of Your wonders.**

3 Here God speaks, as it were: **When I set a time,** when the proper time arrives, **I will judge** the world **with equity.**

4 **The earth and all its inhabitants melt away; I set firm its**

pillars, Selah. Since I created the foundations of the earth, I can either shake them or keep them standing.
5 Now the psalmist speaks again: **I said to the revelers: Do not revel,** for your joy will not last forever. **And to the wicked** I said: **Do not raise a horn.** "Raising the horn" in biblical idiom refers to showing off one's strength or status.
6 **Do not raise your horn on high** in haughtiness and contempt, **speaking with insolent pride,** literally, "with a stiff neck," stretched out as a sign of pride and arrogance.
7 **For it is not from the east or the west** that victory and salvation come, **nor from the wilderness** of the south **or the mountains** of the north,
8 **but it is God who is the Judge; He humbles this one and raises that one.** In the end, it is only God who has the power to determine who will rise and who will fall.
9 **For a cup is in the hand of the Lord with foaming wine, filled with a mixture of spices, and He pours from it.** The cup of wine symbolizes God's administering of either deliverance, represented by the good-tasting wine, or vengeance. **But the** bitter **dregs,** which are not fit for drinking and which represent punishment, **are sucked,** their extract **drunk by all the wicked of the earth.**
10 **As for me, I will tell it,** God's praise, **forever; I will sing to the God of Jacob.**
11 The last verse is spoken by God: **All the horns of the wicked I will cut off, while the horns of the righteous shall be raised.**

PSALM 76

A psalm of praise about victory in war and the revelation of God.

PSALMS 76:1–13

76 1 **For the chief musician, on stringed instruments, a psalm by Asaf, a song.**
2 **God is known in Judah; His name is great in Israel.**
3 **His abode is in Shalem,** another name for Jerusalem, **His dwelling place in Zion.**
4 **There,** near Jerusalem, **He broke the sparks of the** enemy's **bow,** a poetic way of referring to arrows, and there He also broke the enemy's **shield and sword and war, Selah.**
5 **You,** God, **are radiant, mightier than mountains of prey,** tall and threatening mountains in which beasts of prey roam. All of these are subservient to God.
6 **The stout-hearted** men of the enemy's camp **ran rampant** and were inattentive to what was happening around them. Alternatively, **they fell into a stupor,** and this prevented them from recognizing the impending doom, **and warriors could not find their hands.** The enemies, taken by surprise, were helpless to respond.
7 **At Your rebuke, God of Jacob, it,** the enemy's camp, **fell into deep sleep, along with** the **chariot** driver **and horse.** In truth, even if they had remained awake, they would have been powerless against You.
8 **As for You, You are awesome; who can stand before You at the time of Your anger?**
9 **From heaven You pronounced judgment. The earth was frightened** at God's might, **and** then it **became calm,** after He destroyed the enemy,

Chariot and horse, Ur, 2500 BCE

10 **when God arose in judgment, to deliver all the humble of the earth, Selah.**
11 **For the wrathful man will praise You.** Violent aggressors will realize that they are powerless against You, and they will have no choice but to surrender and be grateful for their survival. **You stem the remnants of wrath.** You will rein in what remains of their wrath, allowing it expression only when You wish it.
12 The psalmist concludes by imploring everyone to give thanks to God for their salvation: **Make vows to the Lord your God** in thanksgiving for His salvation **and fulfill them; let all who are around Him bring gifts to the Awesome One.**
13 **He will cut off the spirit of rulers,** and all will admit that His might is great, **inspiring awe in kings of the earth.**

ה אָנֹכִי תִכַּנְתִּי עַמּוּדֶיהָ סֶּלָה׃ אָמַרְתִּי לַהוֹלְלִים אַל־תָּהֹלּוּ וְלָרְשָׁעִים אַל־תָּרִימוּ
ו ז קָרֶן׃ אַל־תָּרִימוּ לַמָּרוֹם קַרְנְכֶם תְּדַבְּרוּ בְצַוָּאר עָתָק׃ כִּי לֹא מִמּוֹצָא וּמִמַּעֲרָב
ח ט וְלֹא מִמִּדְבַּר הָרִים׃ כִּי־אֱלֹהִים שֹׁפֵט זֶה יַשְׁפִּיל וְזֶה יָרִים׃ כִּי כוֹס בְּיַד־יְהוָה וְיַיִן
י חָמַר | מָלֵא מֶסֶךְ וַיַּגֵּר מִזֶּה אַךְ־שְׁמָרֶיהָ יִמְצוּ יִשְׁתּוּ כֹּל רִשְׁעֵי־אָרֶץ׃ וַאֲנִי אַגִּיד
יא לְעֹלָם אֲזַמְּרָה לֵאלֹהֵי יַעֲקֹב׃ וְכָל־קַרְנֵי רְשָׁעִים אֲגַדֵּעַ תְּרוֹמַמְנָה קַרְנוֹת צַדִּיק׃
עו א ב לַמְנַצֵּחַ בִּנְגִינֹת מִזְמוֹר לְאָסָף שִׁיר׃ נוֹדָע בִּיהוּדָה אֱלֹהִים בְּיִשְׂרָאֵל גָּדוֹל שְׁמוֹ׃
ג ד וַיְהִי בְשָׁלֵם סֻכּוֹ וּמְעוֹנָתוֹ בְצִיּוֹן׃ שָׁמָּה שִׁבַּר רִשְׁפֵי־קָשֶׁת מָגֵן וְחֶרֶב וּמִלְחָמָה
ה ו סֶלָה׃ נָאוֹר אַתָּה אַדִּיר מֵהַרְרֵי־טָרֶף׃ אֶשְׁתּוֹלְלוּ | אַבִּירֵי לֵב נָמוּ שְׁנָתָם וְלֹא־
ז ח מָצְאוּ כָל־אַנְשֵׁי־חַיִל יְדֵיהֶם׃ מִגַּעֲרָתְךָ אֱלֹהֵי יַעֲקֹב נִרְדָּם וְרֶכֶב וָסוּס׃ אַתָּה | נוֹרָא
ט אַתָּה וּמִי־יַעֲמֹד לְפָנֶיךָ מֵאָז אַפֶּךָ׃ מִשָּׁמַיִם הִשְׁמַעְתָּ דִּין אֶרֶץ יָרְאָה וְשָׁקָטָה׃
י יא בְּקוּם־לַמִּשְׁפָּט אֱלֹהִים לְהוֹשִׁיעַ כָּל־עַנְוֵי־אֶרֶץ סֶלָה׃ כִּי־חֲמַת אָדָם תּוֹדֶךָּ
יב שְׁאֵרִית חֵמֹת תַּחְגֹּר׃ נִדְרוּ וְשַׁלְּמוּ לַיהוָה אֱלֹהֵיכֶם כָּל־סְבִיבָיו יֹבִילוּ שַׁי לַמּוֹרָא׃
יג יִבְצֹר רוּחַ נְגִידִים נוֹרָא לְמַלְכֵי־אָרֶץ׃
עז א ב לַמְנַצֵּחַ עַל־יְדִיתוּן לְאָסָף מִזְמוֹר׃ קוֹלִי אֶל־אֱלֹהִים וְאֶצְעָקָה קוֹלִי אֶל־אֱלֹהִים ידותון
ג וְהַאֲזִין אֵלָי׃ בְּיוֹם צָרָתִי אֲדֹנָי דָּרָשְׁתִּי יָדִי | לַיְלָה נִגְּרָה וְלֹא תָפוּג מֵאֲנָה הִנָּחֵם טו לחודש
ד ה נַפְשִׁי׃ אֶזְכְּרָה אֱלֹהִים וְאֶהֱמָיָה אָשִׂיחָה | וְתִתְעַטֵּף רוּחִי סֶלָה׃ אָחַזְתָּ שְׁמֻרוֹת

PSALM 77

PSALMS 77:1–21

A psalm that describes a time of suffering and calamity, in which the psalmist finds comfort in recalling God's previous deeds on behalf of His people.

77 *15th day of month* 1 **For the chief musician, for Yedutun, a psalm by Asaf.** As explained earlier,[30] the term *Yedutun* may be the name of a musical instrument, a type of psalm, the name of a poet, or a type of melody.

2 **I raise my voice to God and cry out; I raise my voice, and He listens to me.**

3 **On my day of trouble, I beseeched the Lord with my hand,** raising it up in prayer; **at night it,** my eye, **flowed** with tears **without cease** because of the magnitude of my overwhelming troubles**, and my soul refused to be comforted.**

4 **When I remember God, I moan; I cry out** because of my woes **until my spirit becomes faint, Selah.** The phrase *vetitatef ruḥi*, "my spirit becomes faint," literally, "my soul is wrapped up within me," is an expression of pain and distress. It also conveys the soul's becoming constricted, shrinking, almost as if enveloping itself in sorrow.

5 **You grasp my eyelids,** preventing me from sleeping;

moreover, I cannot pray or cry out to You at all times, for often **I am** too **agitated and cannot speak.**
6 In my present state of distress, **I ponder** the contrast of my current circumstances with **the days of old, the years of long ago.**
7 **I remember my song in the night,** when I used to thank God for His kindness; **I meditate with my heart, and my spirit searches.** Alongside these memories, my spirit has many questions that I continually turn over in my mind:
8 **Will the Lord abandon** us **forever? Will He never again find favor** with us?
9 **Has His kindness forever come to an end? Is His decision** to punish us **final for all generations?**
10 **Has God forgotten to be gracious** and forgive us? **Has He in anger closed off His mercy** and compassion? **Selah.**
11 **Then I said** to myself: **This is my prayer,** to reflect upon **the years of the Most High's right hand,** a very long span of time that includes periods of divine grace as well as times when God hid His presence. The psalmist prays to be able to perceive and understand this broader view of life.
12 The psalmist recalls those periods of divine grace: **I remember the deeds of the Lord, when I recall Your wonders of old.**
13 **I meditate on all of Your work, telling of Your glorious deeds** of the past.
14 **God, Your way is in holiness.** When You reveal Yourself, You are perceived as holy and exalted. **What god is as great as God?**
15 **You are the Almighty who works wonders; You proclaimed Your strength among the peoples.**
16 **With Your arm,** Your strength, **You redeemed Your people, the sons of Jacob and Joseph, Selah.**
17 The psalmist enumerates several instances of God's revelation: **The waters** of the Red Sea **saw you, God; the waters saw You and were frightened,** as it were, into receding and parting, **and the waters of the deep trembled.**
18 At that time, **the clouds poured out water; the skies gave voice as Your arrows,** bolts of lightning, **darted about.**
19 **Your thunder was all-encompassing; lightning lit up the world. The earth trembled and quaked.**
20 **Your way was through the** Red **Sea, Your path through the mighty waters,** clearing a trail through it for us to pass. **Your footprints left no trace.** When the splitting of the sea was over, the waters returned to their place, and there was no sign that the event had occurred.
21 Thereafter, **like a flock You led Your people** to the Land of Israel, **in the hands of Moses and Aaron.** When I consider this, I find that I still have hope, despite all my current troubles.

"Your way was through the sea, Your path through the mighty waters"

PSALM 78

PSALMS 78:1–72

An epic psalm covering the period from the exodus through the establishment of David's kingship, including descriptions of the ten plagues, the Israelites' journeys in the wilderness, and the conquest of the Land of Israel. The psalm focuses on God's continuous redemption of the people despite their many sins.

78 1 **A contemplation by Asaf.** As with other psalms containing the heading *maskil*, "contemplation," such as 32, 42, and 44, the focus of this psalm is contemplative and instructive rather than prayerful. It describes historical events with a poetic flair, and for this reason, some of the historical details and order of events differ from the way in which they appear in the Torah. First, however, the lengthy psalm begins with several statements of moral instruction: **Listen, my people, to my teaching. Incline your ears to the words of my mouth.**
2 **My mouth will open with a tale.** The word *mashal*, which in modern Hebrew pertains to a parable, refers here to a historical story told in poetic fashion. **I will recount stories from ancient times.** Here too the word *ḥidot* should not be understood in its modern sense of "riddles" or "challenging questions"; rather, it refers to artistically worded narratives (see also 49:5),
3 **those that we heard and knew** from tradition, **for our fathers told us.**
4 The psalmist continues by describing the tradition referred to in the previous verse: **We will not conceal it from their children, but will tell a later generation of the praises of the Lord and His might and the wonders He has done.**
5 **He set a precept in Jacob and imparted a teaching in Israel,** referring to the Torah in its entirety, among which are precepts commemorating certain historical events, **which He commanded our fathers to make known to their children,**
6 **so that the generation to come, children not yet born, may know** about these events that their fathers witnessed, and **they** in turn **will arise and tell their own children.**
7 Above and beyond historical interest, the lessons have a moral benefit: **So that they,** the new generations, will **place their trust in God, and not forget the Almighty's deeds, and keep His commandments,**
8 **and** they will **not be like** many of **their forefathers, a stubborn and rebellious generation that was not steadfast and whose spirit was not faithful to God,** as the psalmist now goes on to elaborate.
9 **The sons of Ephraim were archers equipped with bows, yet they turned back** and fled **on the day of battle.** It is not

ו ז עֵינָי נִפְעַמְתִּי וְלֹא אֲדַבֵּר: חִשַּׁבְתִּי יָמִים מִקֶּדֶם שְׁנוֹת עוֹלָמִים: אֶזְכְּרָה נְגִינָתִי
ח בַּלָּיְלָה עִם־לְבָבִי אָשִׂיחָה וַיְחַפֵּשׂ רוּחִי: הַלְעוֹלָמִים יִזְנַח | אֲדֹנָי וְלֹא־יֹסִיף לִרְצוֹת
ט י עוֹד: הֶאָפֵס לָנֶצַח חַסְדּוֹ גָּמַר אֹמֶר לְדֹר וָדֹר: הֲשָׁכַח חַנּוֹת אֵל אִם־קָפַץ בְּאַף
יא יב רַחֲמָיו סֶלָה: וָאֹמַר חַלּוֹתִי הִיא שְׁנוֹת יְמִין עֶלְיוֹן: אזכיר מַעַלְלֵי־יָהּ כִּי־אֶזְכְּרָה אֶזְכּוֹר
יג יד מִקֶּדֶם פִּלְאֶךָ: וְהָגִיתִי בְכָל־פָּעֳלֶךָ וּבַעֲלִילוֹתֶיךָ אָשִׂיחָה: אֱלֹהִים בַּקֹּדֶשׁ דַּרְכֶּךָ
טו טז מִי־אֵל גָּדוֹל כֵּאלֹהִים: אַתָּה הָאֵל עֹשֵׂה פֶלֶא הוֹדַעְתָּ בָעַמִּים עֻזֶּךָ: גָּאַלְתָּ
יז בִּזְרוֹעַ עַמֶּךָ בְּנֵי־יַעֲקֹב וְיוֹסֵף סֶלָה: רָאוּךָ מַּיִם | אֱלֹהִים רָאוּךָ מַּיִם יָחִילוּ אַף
יח יט יִרְגְּזוּ תְהֹמוֹת: זֹרְמוּ מַיִם | עָבוֹת קוֹל נָתְנוּ שְׁחָקִים אַף־חֲצָצֶיךָ יִתְהַלָּכוּ: קוֹל
כ רַעַמְךָ | בַּגַּלְגַּל הֵאִירוּ בְרָקִים תֵּבֵל רָגְזָה וַתִּרְעַשׁ הָאָרֶץ: בַּיָּם דַּרְכֶּךָ ושביליך וּשְׁבִילְךָ
כא בְּמַיִם רַבִּים וְעִקְּבוֹתֶיךָ לֹא נֹדָעוּ: נָחִיתָ כַצֹּאן עַמֶּךָ בְּיַד־מֹשֶׁה וְאַהֲרֹן:
עח א ב מַשְׂכִּיל לְאָסָף הַאֲזִינָה עַמִּי תּוֹרָתִי הַטּוּ אָזְנְכֶם לְאִמְרֵי־פִי: אֶפְתְּחָה בְמָשָׁל פִּי
ג ד אַבִּיעָה חִידוֹת מִנִּי־קֶדֶם: אֲשֶׁר שָׁמַעְנוּ וַנֵּדָעֵם וַאֲבוֹתֵינוּ סִפְּרוּ־לָנוּ: לֹא נְכַחֵד |
ה מִבְּנֵיהֶם לְדוֹר אַחֲרוֹן מְסַפְּרִים תְּהִלּוֹת יְהוָה וֶעֱזוּזוֹ וְנִפְלְאוֹתָיו אֲשֶׁר עָשָׂה: וַיָּקֶם
עֵדוּת | בְּיַעֲקֹב וְתוֹרָה שָׂם בְּיִשְׂרָאֵל אֲשֶׁר צִוָּה אֶת־אֲבוֹתֵינוּ לְהוֹדִיעָם לִבְנֵיהֶם:
ו ז לְמַעַן יֵדְעוּ | דּוֹר אַחֲרוֹן בָּנִים יִוָּלֵדוּ יָקֻמוּ וִיסַפְּרוּ לִבְנֵיהֶם: וְיָשִׂימוּ בֵאלֹהִים כִּסְלָם
ח וְלֹא יִשְׁכְּחוּ מַעַלְלֵי־אֵל וּמִצְוֹתָיו יִנְצֹרוּ: וְלֹא יִהְיוּ | כַּאֲבוֹתָם דּוֹר סוֹרֵר וּמֹרֶה דּוֹר
ט לֹא־הֵכִין לִבּוֹ וְלֹא־נֶאֶמְנָה אֶת־אֵל רוּחוֹ: בְּנֵי־אֶפְרַיִם נוֹשְׁקֵי רוֹמֵי־קָשֶׁת הָפְכוּ
י יא בְּיוֹם קְרָב: לֹא שָׁמְרוּ בְּרִית אֱלֹהִים וּבְתוֹרָתוֹ מֵאֲנוּ לָלֶכֶת: וַיִּשְׁכְּחוּ עֲלִילוֹתָיו
יב יג וְנִפְלְאוֹתָיו אֲשֶׁר הֶרְאָם: נֶגֶד אֲבוֹתָם עָשָׂה פֶלֶא בְּאֶרֶץ מִצְרַיִם שְׂדֵה־צֹעַן: בָּקַע

completely clear which historical event this verse is referring to. Some midrashim speak of an early attempt by the sons of Ephraim to leave Egypt before the time of the exodus.[31] The verse can also be understood as a reference to the kingdom of Ephraim, as the northern Kingdom of Israel is sometimes known, which abandoned the laws of the Torah.

10 **They did not keep the covenant of God, and they refused to walk in His law.**

11 **They forgot His deeds and the marvels He had shown them.**

12 **He had wrought wonders before their fathers in the land of Egypt, in the field of Tzo'an,** a poetic term for Egypt, as Tzo'an was a prominent Egyptian city that once served as its capital.

13 The psalmist enumerates the most noteworthy of the wonders wrought in Egypt: **He split the** Red **Sea and led them,** the children of Israel, **through** it; **He stood the waters** of the Red Sea **in a heap,** with walls of water forming on either side of the passing Israelites.

14 **Then He led them** through the wilderness **with a cloud by day, and throughout the night with the light of fire.**

15 **He split boulders in the desert and gave them drink,** with water gushing forth from the rocks as plentiful **as** water that springs **from the abundant depths.**

16 **And He brought forth streams from the rock, making the water come down like rivers** in the middle of the desert.

17 The psalm goes on to recount the Israelites' response to these miracles: **Yet they continued to sin against Him, to rebel against the Most High in the parched land.**

18 **In their hearts they tested the Almighty, asking for food for themselves,** as described in the Torah.[32]

19 **And they spoke against God,** putting Him to the test, **saying: Can the Almighty prepare a table in the wilderness?**

20 **Behold, He struck the rock so that waters gushed out and streams were flowing. Can He provide bread as well? Will He provide meat for His people?**[33]

21 **Thus the Lord was enraged when He heard this, and fire flared against Jacob, and wrath arose against Israel,**

22 **for they did not believe in God and did not trust in His deliverance.** The children of Israel were tested by these experiences in the wilderness, and they were found wanting.

23 Nevertheless, in response to their demands, **He commanded the skies above and opened the doors of heaven,**

24 **and He rained down manna for them to eat; grain from heaven,** again referring to the manna, **He gave them.**

25 **Men ate the bread of angels; He sent them provisions to satiation.**

26 Having supplied the people with abundant food in the form of manna, He addressed their desire for meat: **He stirred the east wind in the heavens; He drove the south wind with His might,**

27 **and He rained down meat upon them like dust, winged fowl like sand of the seas.** Both "meat" and "winged fowl" refer to the quail that God sent to the people to eat.[34]

28 **He let it fall in the midst of their camp, encircling their dwellings,**

29 **so they ate and were exceedingly sated; He brought them their desire** that they had requested.

30 The psalmist recounts what happened next, reviewing the events as recorded in the Torah:[35] **They had not yet taken leave of their desire. Their food was still in their mouths**

31 **when the anger of God rose against them. He slew the best among them; He struck down young warriors of Israel.**

32 **Nonetheless, they continued to sin and did not believe in His wonders.** Even after the episode of the quail and the plague that came in its wake, they continued to complain and to make various demands.

33 **He ended their days in futility, and their years in terror.** This is an allusion to the Israelites' punishment of wandering in the wilderness instead of being able to enter the Land of Israel.[36]

34 All of their years of wandering were characterized by a recurring pattern of behavior: **When He slew them, then they sought Him out; they returned and searched for the Almighty.**

35 **They remembered** in times of distress **that God was their rock, the Almighty Most High, their Redeemer.**

36 Their turning to God, however, was perfunctory rather than wholehearted: **But they beguiled Him with their mouth and lied to Him with their tongue.** They spoke as if they were faithful to Him, but in fact they were not.

37 **Their heart was not steadfast toward Him, nor were they faithful to His covenant.**

38 **Yet,** although God was aware of their insincerity, **He, being merciful, forgave iniquity and did not destroy** them for their sins. **He repeatedly restrained His anger and did not kindle all of His wrath.**

39 **He remembered that they were but flesh,** imperfect human beings, **a passing breeze that does not return.** God realizes that, given the frailties of human nature and the shortness of people's lives, one cannot make excessive demands on them.

40 **How often did they defy Him in the wilderness and distress Him in the desolate land!**

41 **They continually tested the Almighty; they marked the Holy One of Israel,** as if to make Him a target for additional provocations.

42 **They did not remember the strength of His hand on the day He redeemed them from their foes,**

43 **when He performed His signs in Egypt and His marvels in the field of Tzo'an.** The psalmist now turns to the story of the ten plagues and the exodus from Egypt:

44 **He turned their rivers to blood; their waters were unfit to drink.**

45 **He sent wild beasts among them, which devoured them, and frogs, which destroyed them,**

46 **and He gave their crops to grasshoppers, and the product of their labors to locusts.** The word *ḥasil,* translated here as "grasshoppers," is a synonym for locust. Alternatively, it may refer to a specific kind of locust.

Levant water frog

Desert locust

יד טו יָם וַיַּעֲבִירֵם וַיַּצֶּב־מַיִם כְּמוֹ־נֵד׃ וַיַּנְחֵם בֶּעָנָן יוֹמָם וְכָל־הַלַּיְלָה בְּאוֹר אֵשׁ׃ יְבַקַּע
טז צֻרִים בַּמִּדְבָּר וַיַּשְׁקְ כִּתְהֹמוֹת רַבָּה׃ וַיּוֹצִא נוֹזְלִים מִסָּלַע וַיּוֹרֶד כַּנְּהָרוֹת מָיִם׃
יז יח וַיּוֹסִיפוּ עוֹד לַחֲטֹא־לוֹ לַמְרוֹת עֶלְיוֹן בַּצִּיָּה׃ וַיְנַסּוּ־אֵל בִּלְבָבָם לִשְׁאָל־אֹכֶל
יט כ לְנַפְשָׁם׃ וַיְדַבְּרוּ בֵּאלֹהִים אָמְרוּ הֲיוּכַל אֵל לַעֲרֹךְ שֻׁלְחָן בַּמִּדְבָּר׃ הֵן הִכָּה־
כא צוּר ׀ וַיָּזוּבוּ מַיִם וּנְחָלִים יִשְׁטֹפוּ הֲגַם־לֶחֶם יוּכַל תֵּת אִם־יָכִין שְׁאֵר לְעַמּוֹ׃ לָכֵן ׀
כב שָׁמַע יהוה וַיִּתְעַבָּר וְאֵשׁ נִשְּׂקָה בְיַעֲקֹב וְגַם־אַף עָלָה בְיִשְׂרָאֵל׃ כִּי לֹא הֶאֱמִינוּ
כג כד בֵּאלֹהִים וְלֹא בָטְחוּ בִּישׁוּעָתוֹ׃ וַיְצַו שְׁחָקִים מִמָּעַל וְדַלְתֵי שָׁמַיִם פָּתָח׃ וַיַּמְטֵר
כה עֲלֵיהֶם מָן לֶאֱכֹל וּדְגַן־שָׁמַיִם נָתַן לָמוֹ׃ לֶחֶם אַבִּירִים אָכַל אִישׁ צֵידָה שָׁלַח
כו כז לָהֶם לָשֹׂבַע׃ יַסַּע קָדִים בַּשָּׁמָיִם וַיְנַהֵג בְּעֻזּוֹ תֵימָן׃ וַיַּמְטֵר עֲלֵיהֶם כֶּעָפָר שְׁאֵר
כח כט וּכְחוֹל יַמִּים עוֹף כָּנָף׃ וַיַּפֵּל בְּקֶרֶב מַחֲנֵהוּ סָבִיב לְמִשְׁכְּנֹתָיו׃ וַיֹּאכְלוּ וַיִּשְׂבְּעוּ
ל לא מְאֹד וְתַאֲוָתָם יָבִא לָהֶם׃ לֹא־זָרוּ מִתַּאֲוָתָם עוֹד אָכְלָם בְּפִיהֶם׃ וְאַף אֱלֹהִים ׀
לב עָלָה בָהֶם וַיַּהֲרֹג בְּמִשְׁמַנֵּיהֶם וּבַחוּרֵי יִשְׂרָאֵל הִכְרִיעַ׃ בְּכָל־זֹאת חָטְאוּ־עוֹד
לג לד וְלֹא הֶאֱמִינוּ בְּנִפְלְאוֹתָיו׃ וַיְכַל־בַּהֶבֶל יְמֵיהֶם וּשְׁנוֹתָם בַּבֶּהָלָה׃ אִם־הֲרָגָם
לה לו וּדְרָשׁוּהוּ וְשָׁבוּ וְשִׁחֲרוּ־אֵל׃ וַיִּזְכְּרוּ כִּי־אֱלֹהִים צוּרָם וְאֵל עֶלְיוֹן גֹּאֲלָם׃ וַיְפַתּוּהוּ
לז לח בְּפִיהֶם וּבִלְשׁוֹנָם יְכַזְּבוּ־לוֹ׃ וְלִבָּם לֹא־נָכוֹן עִמּוֹ וְלֹא נֶאֶמְנוּ בִּבְרִיתוֹ׃ וְהוּא יא
לט רַחוּם ׀ יְכַפֵּר עָוֺן וְלֹא־יַשְׁחִית וְהִרְבָּה לְהָשִׁיב אַפּוֹ וְלֹא־יָעִיר כָּל־חֲמָתוֹ׃ וַיִּזְכֹּר
מ כִּי־בָשָׂר הֵמָּה רוּחַ הוֹלֵךְ וְלֹא יָשׁוּב׃ כַּמָּה יַמְרוּהוּ בַמִּדְבָּר יַעֲצִיבוּהוּ בִּישִׁימוֹן׃
מא מב וַיָּשׁוּבוּ וַיְנַסּוּ אֵל וּקְדוֹשׁ יִשְׂרָאֵל הִתְווּ׃ לֹא־זָכְרוּ אֶת־יָדוֹ יוֹם אֲשֶׁר־פָּדָם מִנִּי־צָר׃
מג מד אֲשֶׁר־שָׂם בְּמִצְרַיִם אֹתוֹתָיו וּמוֹפְתָיו בִּשְׂדֵה־צֹעַן׃ וַיַּהֲפֹךְ לְדָם יְאֹרֵיהֶם וְנֹזְלֵיהֶם
מה מו בַּל־יִשְׁתָּיוּן׃ יְשַׁלַּח בָּהֶם עָרֹב וַיֹּאכְלֵם וּצְפַרְדֵּעַ וַתַּשְׁחִיתֵם׃ וַיִּתֵּן לֶחָסִיל יְבוּלָם

47 He destroyed their vines with hail and their sycamores with worms,

Sycamore tree

48 and He handed over their livestock to hail, their cattle to bolts of lightning.

49 He sent them His burning anger, fury, indignation, and trouble, a band of destroying angels. This verse refers to the pestilence that killed all the remaining livestock, which was delivered by angels of destruction.

50 He cleared a path, as it were, **for His anger** to reach Egypt; **He did not spare them from death; He delivered their animals to pestilence.**

51 He smote all the firstborn in Egypt, the first fruits of their vigor, another term for the firstborn, **in the tents of Ham,** referring to the Egyptians by the name of their forebear Ham.[37]

52 The aforementioned plagues led to the Israelites' exodus from Egypt: **Then He led forth His people like sheep,** which are led along a designated path by their caring shepherd, **and guided them in the wilderness like a flock.**

53 He guided them safely and they did not fear; the sea engulfed their enemies.

54 In the following verses, the psalmist turns from describing the events of the exodus to the conquest of the land: **He brought them to the boundary of His holiness,** the Land of Israel, **to the mountain owned by His right hand,** the mountain that is God's prized possession, Mount Zion, the choicest portion of the land.

55 He drove out the nations of Canaan **before them, dividing up their allotments of land** among the members of each of the twelve tribes. **He settled the tribes of Israel in their tents.**

56 Yet even after they were settled in the Land of Israel, the people continued to sin; **they tested and rebelled against God Most High, and they did not keep His precepts.**

57 They turned back from the path of propriety **and acted treacherously, as did their fathers** in the wilderness; **they became** unfaithful **like a crooked bow,** whose arrows fly off in all directions, far from the desired destination.

58 They provoked Him with their altars in high places dedicated to false gods, **and aroused His jealousy with their graven images.**

59 God heard of these depraved deeds **and grew angry; He utterly rejected Israel.**

60 He abandoned the Sanctuary at Shilo, which was apparently destroyed by the Philistines;[38] **He pitched a tent among men.** After the destruction of Shilo, God did not designate a specific alternative location as His dwelling place but instead dwelled among the people,

61 and He sent His strength into captivity, His glory into the hand of the foe. "His strength" and "His glory" refer to the powerful fortresses and cities that were overtaken by the enemy.

62 He delivered His people to the sword; He was filled with anger toward His portion, Israel.

63 Fire devoured His young men, and as a result of the men's deaths, **His virgins were not celebrated with wedding songs,** as they were left with no potential marriage partners.

64 His priests fell by the sword, and His widows could not weep for their husbands because they themselves were pursued and killed.

65 But after all the defeat and subjugation, there came a time for redemption: **Then the Lord awoke as if from sleep,** after seeming to be indifferent to Israel's suffering for so long, **like a warrior rising stridently from his wine,** after a refreshing reprieve from the battlefield.

66 He drove His foes into retreat, put them to everlasting shame.

67 And He rejected the tent of Joseph and did not choose the tribe of Ephraim. The tribe of Joseph and its branch Ephraim had been in power mostly during the period of the judges, and God now rejected their leadership.

68 Instead, **He chose the tribe of Judah, and Mount Zion** in Judah's territory, **which He loved** and selected as the site of His Temple,

69 and He built His holy place in the heights, establishing it, like the earth, for eternity.

70 And He chose David, His servant, from the tribe of Judah, **and took him from the sheepfolds,** where he had worked as a shepherd, to be king of Israel.

71 He brought him away from the suckling lambs to be a shepherd among Jacob, His people, and Israel, His portion. The verse notes the apt transition from shepherd of flocks to shepherd of Israel.

72 And He shepherded them with a pure heart and led them with skillful hands.

מז מח וִיגִיעָם לָאַרְבֶּה: יַהֲרֹג בַּבָּרָד גַּפְנָם וְשִׁקְמוֹתָם בַּחֲנָמַל: וַיַּסְגֵּר לַבָּרָד בְּעִירָם
מט וּמִקְנֵיהֶם לָרְשָׁפִים: יְשַׁלַּח־בָּם ׀ חֲרוֹן אַפּוֹ עֶבְרָה וָזַעַם וְצָרָה מִשְׁלַחַת מַלְאֲכֵי
נ נא רָעִים: יְפַלֵּס נָתִיב לְאַפּוֹ לֹא־חָשַׂךְ מִמָּוֶת נַפְשָׁם וְחַיָּתָם לַדֶּבֶר הִסְגִּיר: וַיַּךְ
נב כָּל־בְּכוֹר בְּמִצְרָיִם רֵאשִׁית אוֹנִים בְּאָהֳלֵי־חָם: וַיַּסַּע כַּצֹּאן עַמּוֹ וַיְנַהֲגֵם כַּעֵדֶר
נג נד בַּמִּדְבָּר: וַיַּנְחֵם לָבֶטַח וְלֹא פָחָדוּ וְאֶת־אוֹיְבֵיהֶם כִּסָּה הַיָּם: וַיְבִיאֵם אֶל־גְּבוּל
נה קָדְשׁוֹ הַר־זֶה קָנְתָה יְמִינוֹ: וַיְגָרֶשׁ מִפְּנֵיהֶם ׀ גּוֹיִם וַיַּפִּילֵם בְּחֶבֶל נַחֲלָה וַיַּשְׁכֵּן
נו בְּאָהֳלֵיהֶם שִׁבְטֵי יִשְׂרָאֵל: וַיְנַסּוּ וַיַּמְרוּ אֶת־אֱלֹהִים עֶלְיוֹן וְעֵדוֹתָיו לֹא שָׁמָרוּ:
נז נח וַיִּסֹּגוּ וַיִּבְגְּדוּ כַּאֲבוֹתָם נֶהְפְּכוּ כְּקֶשֶׁת רְמִיָּה: וַיַּכְעִיסוּהוּ בְּבָמוֹתָם וּבִפְסִילֵיהֶם
נט ס יַקְנִיאוּהוּ: שָׁמַע אֱלֹהִים וַיִּתְעַבָּר וַיִּמְאַס מְאֹד בְּיִשְׂרָאֵל: וַיִּטֹּשׁ מִשְׁכַּן שִׁלוֹ אֹהֶל
סא סב שִׁכֵּן בָּאָדָם: וַיִּתֵּן לַשְּׁבִי עֻזּוֹ וְתִפְאַרְתּוֹ בְיַד־צָר: וַיַּסְגֵּר לַחֶרֶב עַמּוֹ וּבְנַחֲלָתוֹ
סג סד הִתְעַבָּר: בַּחוּרָיו אָכְלָה־אֵשׁ וּבְתוּלֹתָיו לֹא הוּלָּלוּ: כֹּהֲנָיו בַּחֶרֶב נָפָלוּ וְאַלְמְנֹתָיו
סה סו לֹא תִבְכֶּינָה: וַיִּקַץ כְּיָשֵׁן ׀ אֲדֹנָי כְּגִבּוֹר מִתְרוֹנֵן מִיָּיִן: וַיַּךְ־צָרָיו אָחוֹר חֶרְפַּת עוֹלָם
סז סח נָתַן לָמוֹ: וַיִּמְאַס בְּאֹהֶל יוֹסֵף וּבְשֵׁבֶט אֶפְרַיִם לֹא בָחָר: וַיִּבְחַר אֶת־שֵׁבֶט יְהוּדָה
סט ע אֶת־הַר צִיּוֹן אֲשֶׁר אָהֵב: וַיִּבֶן כְּמוֹ־רָמִים מִקְדָּשׁוֹ כְּאֶרֶץ יְסָדָהּ לְעוֹלָם: וַיִּבְחַר
עא בְּדָוִד עַבְדּוֹ וַיִּקָּחֵהוּ מִמִּכְלְאֹת צֹאן: מֵאַחַר עָלוֹת הֱבִיאוֹ לִרְעוֹת בְּיַעֲקֹב עַמּוֹ
עב וּבְיִשְׂרָאֵל נַחֲלָתוֹ: וַיִּרְעֵם כְּתֹם לְבָבוֹ וּבִתְבוּנוֹת כַּפָּיו יַנְחֵם:
עט א מִזְמוֹר לְאָסָף אֱלֹהִים בָּאוּ גוֹיִם ׀ בְּנַחֲלָתֶךָ טִמְּאוּ אֶת־הֵיכַל קָדְשֶׁךָ שָׂמוּ אֶת־ טז לחודש
ב יְרוּשָׁלִַם לְעִיִּים: נָתְנוּ אֶת־נִבְלַת עֲבָדֶיךָ מַאֲכָל לְעוֹף הַשָּׁמָיִם בְּשַׂר חֲסִידֶיךָ

PSALM 79

A psalm of entreaty that describes the suffering and defeats of the Israelites and ends with a prayer for redemption.

PSALMS 79:1–13

79 1 *16th day of month* **A psalm by Asaf. God, the nations have invaded Your inherited land; they have defiled Your holy Temple. They have reduced Jerusalem to ruins.**

2 **They fed the corpses of Your servants to birds of the sky, the flesh of Your devoted ones to the beasts of the earth.** The people fell in the field, and as they lay there unburied, they were picked at by bird and beast.

3 **They spilled their blood like water around Jerusalem, and there was no one to bury them.**
4 **We have become a disgrace to our neighbors** as a result of our defeat and downfall, **an object of scorn and mockery to those around us.**
5 **How long, Lord? Will You be angry forever, Your jealousy burning like fire?** Even if we have sinned against You and incurred Your wrath, there has to be a limit to Your anger and to our suffering. This is all the more true if You compare our sins to those of our foes, as the following verse goes on to say:
6 If you are angry, **pour out Your wrath on the nations that do not acknowledge You** at all, rather than on us, **and on kingdoms that do not invoke Your name,** who are unquestionably more distant from You than we are,
7 **for they have devoured Jacob and made desolate his habitation.**
8 **Do not hold our former iniquities against us,** though we have indeed sinned. **Let Your mercy come to us quickly, for we are brought very low** and have been punished sufficiently.
9 **Help us, God of our salvation,** at least **for the glory of Your name,** even if we are undeserving; **deliver us and forgive us our sins for the sake of Your name.** We are associated with Your name, so our disgrace is a desecration of Your name.
10 **Why should the nations say: Where is their God?** If He is really their God, why doesn't He respond to our deeds against them? **Let us witness** it with our own eyes, and let it not happen in the distant future, **when there becomes known among the nations vengeance for the spilled blood of Your servants.**
11 **Let the captive's groaning come before You,** the cry of those held captive by the enemy. **By Your arm's great power, spare those doomed to die.**
12 **Pay back our neighbors to their bosom sevenfold for their abuse, for their reviling of You, Lord.**
13 **For we are Your people, the sheep of Your flock; we will give thanks to You forever, from generation to generation recounting Your praise.**

PSALM 80

PSALMS 80:1–20

A psalm that begins with recollections of Israel's past power and glory: first, when the nation left Egypt, and later, when God led the people to conquer and settle the Land of Israel. The psalmist goes on to describe the difficult times faced by the nation in his own time and finally ends with a prayer for God to renew His miracles and compassion.

80 1 **For the chief musician, for shoshanim, a testimony, a psalm by Asaf.** As noted earlier,[39] the term *shoshanim* refers to a particular melody or to a musical instrument. Perhaps this psalm is called a "testimony" because it contains elements of remembrance of past events, though it is also a prayer.
2 **Shepherd of Israel, listen. Appear to us, You who led Joseph like a flock, You who sit enthroned above the cherubs.** This verse entreats God to reveal Himself, as will be explained more fully in the following verses. The tribe of Joseph is accorded pride of place in this psalm, to the extent that the name Joseph, like Jacob or Israel, can be understood to represent the entire nation of Israel. God, in the Temple and elsewhere, is often depicted as riding on the cherubs.
3 **Rouse Your might before Ephraim, Benjamin, and Manasseh, and come to our rescue.** These three tribes, all descended from Rachel, are referred to as a single unit despite the fact that, from various historical perspectives, they did not maintain close ties.
4 **God, restore us.** The word *hashivenu*, literally "return us," in this instance means "turn toward us and save us" rather than being a request to bring us back from other lands. **Shine Your countenance on us and,** when You do so, **we will be delivered.**
5 **Lord, God of hosts, for how long will You fume against the prayer of Your people?** The expression "fume" is appropriate for depicting anger, as in Hebrew the common term for "wrath," *ḥaron af*, is literally "burning anger."
6 **You feed them the bread of tears.** They weep so much and so frequently in their sorrow that it is as if their very bread is soaked with tears. Indeed, **You give them** their **tears to drink in a threefold cup.** *Shalish*, translated here as a "threefold cup," is a type of measuring cup.
7 **You have made us a source of strife to our neighbors,** who fight with us constantly; and even when we are not the target of physical attack, **our enemies mock us.**
8 The psalmist repeats his entreaty: **God of hosts, restore us. Shine Your countenance on us and we will be delivered.**
9 What follows is a poetical-historical account of the nation of Israel, depicting them as a grapevine, an image found frequently in the words of the prophets: **You transported a vine,** representing the nation of Israel, **from Egypt** to the Land of Israel, a reference to the exodus. You **drove out the** Canaanite **nations and planted it,** Israel, there.
10 **You cleared space for it, and it took root and** spread out in all directions until it **filled the land.**
11 **The mountains were covered with its shade,** so tall and widespread was it; **its branches** were giant, **like cedars of the Almighty,** that is, cedars of vast proportions.
12 **It sent its boughs** westward **to the** Mediterranean **Sea, and its**

ג ד לְחַיְתוֹ־אָרֶץ׃ שָׁפְכוּ דָמָם ׀ כַּמַּיִם סְבִיבוֹת יְרוּשָׁלָ͏ִם וְאֵין קוֹבֵר׃ הָיִינוּ חֶרְפָּה

ה לִשְׁכֵנֵינוּ לַעַג וָקֶלֶס לִסְבִיבוֹתֵינוּ׃ עַד־מָה יהוה תֶּאֱנַף לָנֶצַח תִּבְעַר כְּמוֹ־אֵשׁ

ו קִנְאָתֶךָ׃ שְׁפֹךְ חֲמָתְךָ ׀ אֶל־הַגּוֹיִם אֲשֶׁר לֹא־יְדָעוּךָ וְעַל מַמְלָכוֹת אֲשֶׁר בְּשִׁמְךָ

ז ח לֹא קָרָאוּ׃ כִּי אָכַל אֶת־יַעֲקֹב וְאֶת־נָוֵהוּ הֵשַׁמּוּ׃ אַל־תִּזְכָּר־לָנוּ עֲוֺנֹת רִאשֹׁנִים

ט מַהֵר יְקַדְּמוּנוּ רַחֲמֶיךָ כִּי דַלּוֹנוּ מְאֹד׃ עָזְרֵנוּ ׀ אֱלֹהֵי יִשְׁעֵנוּ עַל־דְּבַר כְּבוֹד־שְׁמֶךָ

י וְהַצִּילֵנוּ וְכַפֵּר עַל־חַטֹּאתֵינוּ לְמַעַן שְׁמֶךָ׃ לָמָּה ׀ יֹאמְרוּ הַגּוֹיִם אַיֵּה אֱלֹהֵיהֶם

יא יִוָּדַע בגיים לְעֵינֵינוּ נִקְמַת דַּם־עֲבָדֶיךָ הַשָּׁפוּךְ׃ תָּבוֹא לְפָנֶיךָ אֶנְקַת אָסִיר כְּגֹדֶל בַּגּוֹיִם

יב זְרוֹעֲךָ הוֹתֵר בְּנֵי תְמוּתָה׃ וְהָשֵׁב לִשְׁכֵנֵינוּ שִׁבְעָתַיִם אֶל־חֵיקָם חֶרְפָּתָם אֲשֶׁר

יג חֵרְפוּךָ אֲדֹנָי׃ וַאֲנַחְנוּ עַמְּךָ ׀ וְצֹאן מַרְעִיתֶךָ נוֹדֶה לְּךָ לְעוֹלָם לְדוֹר וָדֹר נְסַפֵּר

תְּהִלָּתֶךָ׃

פ א ב לַמְנַצֵּחַ אֶל־שֹׁשַׁנִּים עֵדוּת לְאָסָף מִזְמוֹר׃ רֹעֵה יִשְׂרָאֵל ׀ הַאֲזִינָה נֹהֵג כַּצֹּאן יוֹסֵף

ג יֹשֵׁב הַכְּרוּבִים הוֹפִיעָה׃ לִפְנֵי אֶפְרַיִם ׀ וּבִנְיָמִן וּמְנַשֶּׁה עוֹרְרָה אֶת־גְּבוּרָתֶךָ וּלְכָה

ד ה לִישֻׁעָתָה לָּנוּ׃ אֱלֹהִים הֲשִׁיבֵנוּ וְהָאֵר פָּנֶיךָ וְנִוָּשֵׁעָה׃ יהוה אֱלֹהִים צְבָאוֹת עַד־

ו מָתַי עָשַׁנְתָּ בִּתְפִלַּת עַמֶּךָ׃ הֶאֱכַלְתָּם לֶחֶם דִּמְעָה וַתַּשְׁקֵמוֹ בִּדְמָעוֹת שָׁלִישׁ׃

ז ח תְּשִׂימֵנוּ מָדוֹן לִשְׁכֵנֵינוּ וְאֹיְבֵינוּ יִלְעֲגוּ־לָמוֹ׃ אֱלֹהִים צְבָאוֹת הֲשִׁיבֵנוּ וְהָאֵר פָּנֶיךָ

ט י וְנִוָּשֵׁעָה׃ גֶּפֶן מִמִּצְרַיִם תַּסִּיעַ תְּגָרֵשׁ גּוֹיִם וַתִּטָּעֶהָ׃ פִּנִּיתָ לְפָנֶיהָ וַתַּשְׁרֵשׁ שָׁרָשֶׁיהָ

יא יב וַתְּמַלֵּא־אָרֶץ׃ כָּסּוּ הָרִים צִלָּהּ וַעֲנָפֶיהָ אַרְזֵי־אֵל׃ תְּשַׁלַּח קְצִירֶהָ עַד־יָם וְאֶל־

shoots eastward **to the river,** a term that, when unspecified, generally refers to the Euphrates.

13 The preceding verses depicted the era of Israel's greatness. In the verses that follow, the psalmist describes the darker reality of his time: **Why have You breached its fences,** a vine's only protection from predators, **so that all who pass can pick its fruit?**

Wild boar

14 **The boar from the forest gnaws at it; the large fowl feed on it.**

15 The psalmist repeats his plea: **God of hosts, please return. Look from heaven and see, and take note of this vine,** and nurture it once again,

16 **and** take note of **the stock that Your right hand planted, and the son whom You embraced as Your own,** as the Torah states of the people of Israel, "You are children to the Lord."[40]

17 **It,** the vine, **is burned with fire and cut down; they,** Israel, **perish at the rebuke of Your countenance.**

Vine that appears dead in the winter

18 **Let Your hand sustain the man of Your right hand,** the one whom You hold in Your right hand, a symbol of honor and affection, **the son of man whom You embraced as Your own,**

19 **who never retreated from You. Revive us,** restore us to our past glory, **and we will call in Your name.**

20 The psalm ends with the plea of refrain: **Lord, God of hosts, restore us. Shine Your countenance on us and we will be delivered.**

PSALM 81

PSALMS 81:1–17

A psalm that makes reference to Rosh HaShana in the course of recounting miraculous events that led to the salvation of the Israelites, both collectively and as individuals. It teaches that such miracles can recur if Israel chooses to acknowledge the sovereignty of God and obey His laws.

81 1 **For the chief musician, on the gitit** (see 8:1), **a psalm by Asaf.**

2 **Sing for joy to God, our strength; shout with joy to the God of Jacob.**

3 **Take up the song. Sound the timbrel, a tuneful lyre with a harp.**

4 **Blow the shofar at the showing of the New Moon, at the appointed time of our holiday.** The word *ḥodesh*, related to *ḥadash*, new, refers to the New Moon. Here it refers to the specific New Moon of Rosh HaShana, a holiday marked by the blowing of the shofar.

5 **For it,** blowing the shofar on this day, **is a statute for Israel, a law of the God of Jacob.**

6 The psalmist now reminds us of times past, when God's kindness toward the Israelites in general, as well as toward specific individuals, was manifest: **He established it as a precept for Joseph when he went out** as ruler **over Egypt.** Speaking in Joseph's words, the psalmist says: **I learned a language I had not known** as a newcomer to Egypt.

7 Now the psalmist speaks in God's voice: **I removed a burden from his,** Joseph's, **shoulders,** as he had been imprisoned until I released him from prison, and thereby **freed his hands from** such menial chores as working with foodstuffs in **the** cooking **pot.**

8 God then speaks to Israel: **When you called in distress,** during your enslavement in Egypt, **I rescued you; I answered your secret call with thunder.** Though you prayed to Me silently, I rescued you with great commotion. This may also be an allusion to the giving of the Torah, which was accompanied by lightning and thunder. **I** also **tested you at the waters of Meriva,**[41] **Selah.** Although it was a test, the result was beneficial to you.

9 God now addresses the nation: **Listen, My people; I will warn you, Israel, if you listen to Me.**

10 Salvation from God is dependent on obedience to Him and to the laws of His Torah. Such obedience begins with the rejection of false gods: **Let there be no strange god among you; you shall not worship any foreign god.** This, along with the following verse, constitutes the first of the Ten Precepts; it is also the essence of the entire acceptance of God's rule.

11 **I am the Lord your God who brought you up from the land of Egypt.** If you follow these basic precepts, I will provide you with all your needs, as one might say to a child: **Open your mouth wide,** as if requesting food, **and I will fill it.**

12 **But My people did not listen to My voice; Israel did not heed Me** and keep My commandments.

13 **So I sent them in the way of their willful hearts.** I allowed them to follow their own will and **to walk in their own counsel,** and to suffer the consequences of their choices and their actions, without any assistance from Me.

יג יד נָהָר יוֹנְקוֹתֶיהָ: לָמָּה פָּרַצְתָּ גְדֵרֶיהָ וְאָרוּהָ כׇּל־עֹבְרֵי דָרֶךְ: יְכַרְסְמֶנָּה חֲזִיר מִיָּעַר
טו וְזִיז שָׂדַי יִרְעֶנָּה: אֱלֹהִים צְבָאוֹת שׁוּב נָא הַבֵּט מִשָּׁמַיִם וּרְאֵה וּפְקֹד גֶּפֶן זֹאת:
טז יז וְכַנָּה אֲשֶׁר־נָטְעָה יְמִינֶךָ וְעַל־בֵּן אִמַּצְתָּה לָּךְ: שְׂרֻפָה בָאֵשׁ כְּסוּחָה מִגַּעֲרַת
יח יט פָּנֶיךָ יֹאבֵדוּ: תְּהִי־יָדְךָ עַל־אִישׁ יְמִינֶךָ עַל־בֶּן־אָדָם אִמַּצְתָּ לָּךְ: וְלֹא־נָסוֹג מִמֶּךָּ
כ תְּחַיֵּנוּ וּבְשִׁמְךָ נִקְרָא: יְהוָה אֱלֹהִים צְבָאוֹת הֲשִׁיבֵנוּ הָאֵר פָּנֶיךָ וְנִוָּשֵׁעָה:
פא א ב ג לַמְנַצֵּחַ ׀ עַל־הַגִּתִּית לְאָסָף: הַרְנִינוּ לֵאלֹהִים עוּזֵּנוּ הָרִיעוּ לֵאלֹהֵי יַעֲקֹב: שְׂאוּ־
ד ה זִמְרָה וּתְנוּ־תֹף כִּנּוֹר נָעִים עִם־נָבֶל: תִּקְעוּ בַחֹדֶשׁ שׁוֹפָר בַּכֵּסֶה לְיוֹם חַגֵּנוּ: כִּי
ו חֹק לְיִשְׂרָאֵל הוּא מִשְׁפָּט לֵאלֹהֵי יַעֲקֹב: עֵדוּת ׀ בִּיהוֹסֵף שָׂמוֹ בְּצֵאתוֹ עַל־אֶרֶץ
ז מִצְרָיִם שְׂפַת לֹא־יָדַעְתִּי אֶשְׁמָע: הֲסִירוֹתִי מִסֵּבֶל שִׁכְמוֹ כַּפָּיו מִדּוּד תַּעֲבֹרְנָה:
ח ט בַּצָּרָה קָרָאתָ וָאֲחַלְּצֶךָּ אֶעֶנְךָ בְּסֵתֶר רַעַם אֶבְחָנְךָ עַל־מֵי מְרִיבָה סֶלָה: שְׁמַע
י עַמִּי וְאָעִידָה בָּךְ יִשְׂרָאֵל אִם־תִּשְׁמַע־לִי: לֹא־יִהְיֶה בְךָ אֵל זָר וְלֹא תִשְׁתַּחֲוֶה
יא לְאֵל נֵכָר: אָנֹכִי ׀ יְהוָה אֱלֹהֶיךָ הַמַּעַלְךָ מֵאֶרֶץ מִצְרָיִם הַרְחֶב־פִּיךָ וַאֲמַלְאֵהוּ:
יב יג וְלֹא־שָׁמַע עַמִּי לְקוֹלִי וְיִשְׂרָאֵל לֹא־אָבָה לִי: וָאֲשַׁלְּחֵהוּ בִּשְׁרִירוּת לִבָּם יֵלְכוּ
יד טו בְּמוֹעֲצוֹתֵיהֶם: לוּ עַמִּי שֹׁמֵעַ לִי יִשְׂרָאֵל בִּדְרָכַי יְהַלֵּכוּ: כִּמְעַט אוֹיְבֵיהֶם אַכְנִיעַ
טז יז וְעַל־צָרֵיהֶם אָשִׁיב יָדִי: מְשַׂנְאֵי יְהוָה יְכַחֲשׁוּ־לוֹ וִיהִי עִתָּם לְעוֹלָם: וַיַּאֲכִילֵהוּ
מֵחֵלֶב חִטָּה וּמִצּוּר דְּבַשׁ אַשְׂבִּיעֶךָ:

14 **If only My people would listen to Me,** if only **Israel would walk in My ways,** for if they did, the outcome would be a dramatic change for the better with regard to their fate.

15 **I would subdue their enemies in an instant; I would turn My hand against their foes.**

16 **Those who hate the Lord would feign obedience to Him,** as defeated enemies must do; **their time** of punishment **would last forever,**

17 **while,** after subduing and punishing Israel's enemies, **He would feed them,** the Israelites themselves, **the finest of wheat and sate them with honey drawn from the rock.**

PSALM 82

PSALMS 82:1–8

A psalm that both excoriates judges who do not perform their job in a manner befitting their office and offers guidelines for the proper meting out of justice.

82 1 **A psalm by Asaf. God stands,** that is, He is eternally present, **in the assembly of the Almighty,** a reference to a court that decides weighty matters, such as capital crimes. Such a court comprises twenty-three judges and is aptly called an assembly.[42] **In the midst of the judges He renders judgment.** The psalmist reminds these judges that whether they sense it or not, God Himself is present among them, keeping a watchful eye over all their decisions.

2 The judges are now admonished: **For how long will you judge wrongly and show favor to the wicked? Selah.** Your job is to be fair, to make sure that the powerless are defended properly, and yet you do the opposite: You show favoritism to the wicked at the expense of the weak.

3 The psalmist reminds the judges what their proper function should be: **Do justice to the lowly and the orphan; vindicate the poor and destitute,** even when they stand accused by powerful, wealthy people.

4 **Rescue the lowly and the needy; save them from the hands of the wicked.**

5 But **they,** the judges to whom the psalmist addresses his admonition, **neither know nor understand,** for they conduct themselves according to their own preconceptions. **They walk about in darkness,** unable to see the light of truth. Whether they act in secret or publicly, they are considered "walking in darkness" due to their unwillingness to see the truth, **while all the foundations of the earth collapse.** Their corrupt behavior threatens the very existence of society, which is founded upon the pillars of law and justice.

6 Initially **I had said: You are divine.** The word *elohim*, translated here as "divine," usually refers to God, but it can also be used to refer to angels and occasionally to judges (see verse 1). The psalmist here is admonishing the judges: Since you are called *elohim*, it is expected that you be faithful messengers of God, **like celestial beings,** angels, **all of you** executing His will among men.

7 The psalmist now understands that he has been mistaken and that judges are mortal, not divine: **Yet** now I see that I was mistaken, and I see that you are not angels; **as** mortal **men you will die; as any of the ministers you will fall.** You do not represent divine power but rather personal ambition, and consequently, like all ministers and powerful men, your grandeur will not endure.

8 The psalmist, disillusioned, closes with a plea to God: **Arise,** reveal Yourself, **God, and judge the earth** Yourself, Israelite and gentile alike, **for You possess all nations.**

PSALM 83

PSALMS 83:1–19

A psalm of supplication that appears to have been written at a time when all the nations surrounding Israel went on the attack. The text seems to place it in very ancient times, before the military victories of King David.

83 1 **A song, a psalm by Asaf.**

17th day of month 2 **God, do not be silent, do not hold Your peace. Almighty, do not be still.** I beg of You to act, to come to our aid.

3 **For behold, Your enemies are in an uproar; those who hate You have lifted their heads** in arrogance.

4 **They meet to lay devious plots against Your people, and conspire together against Your treasured ones.** *Tzefunekha,*

BACKGROUND

83:10| **The Kishon Stream:** This is the second largest drainage basin in the Land of Israel. It receives the runoff from the slopes of the Gilboa mountains, as well as the slopes of the lower Galilee and Mount Tavor, traverses the Yizre'el Valley, and flows into the sea at the southern end of Haifa Bay. The stream is known for its sudden floods when there is heavy rain in its basin area. These floods can sometimes turn large swaths of land into swamps that are difficult to cross.

83:11| **Ein Dor:** It is surmised that this city is located on the slopes of Givat HaMoreh, in the eastern Yizre'el Valley, which is mentioned as the site of Gideon's battle with the Midyanites (Judges 7:1). It is also there that the medium consulted by Saul lived (see I Samuel 28:7). Its identification with Khirbet Andur near the village Naghora, where archaeological artifacts from biblical times have been found, is consistent with the story of Saul's nighttime ride from Gilboa to Ein Dor and back. Its identification as the site of Sisera's defeat, which was in the Kishon Stream, is less satisfactory. It is possible that when stating, "They were destroyed at Ein Dor," the verse is referring only to Midyan's defeat at the hand of Gideon: The Midyanites encamped in the valley between Khirbet Andur and Mount Tavor, and from there fled eastward.

83:14| **Whirling sand [*galgal*]:** The meaning of this term, which literally means "wheel," is uncertain. It may be a type of rolling plant, or it may refer to another specific plant. According to Rashi's description of it here, it appears to be the European eryngo, a close relative to the Israeli *Eryngium creticum*. It may also be referring to the thorny plant *Gundelia tournefortii*, a kind of tumbleweed. Both of these straw-like plants roll in the wind, dispersing their seeds as they go.

פב א ב מִזְמוֹר לְאָסָף אֱלֹהִים נִצָּב בַּעֲדַת־אֵל בְּקֶרֶב אֱלֹהִים יִשְׁפֹּט: עַד־מָתַי תִּשְׁפְּטוּ־
ג ד עָוֶל וּפְנֵי רְשָׁעִים תִּשְׂאוּ־סֶלָה: שִׁפְטוּ־דַל וְיָתוֹם עָנִי וָרָשׁ הַצְדִּיקוּ: פַּלְּטוּ־דַל
ה וְאֶבְיוֹן מִיַּד רְשָׁעִים הַצִּילוּ: לֹא יָדְעוּ | וְלֹא יָבִינוּ בַּחֲשֵׁכָה יִתְהַלָּכוּ יִמּוֹטוּ כָּל־
ו ז מוֹסְדֵי אָרֶץ: אֲנִי־אָמַרְתִּי אֱלֹהִים אַתֶּם וּבְנֵי עֶלְיוֹן כֻּלְּכֶם: אָכֵן כְּאָדָם תְּמוּתוּן
ח וּכְאַחַד הַשָּׂרִים תִּפֹּלוּ: קוּמָה אֱלֹהִים שָׁפְטָה הָאָרֶץ כִּי־אַתָּה תִנְחַל בְּכָל־הַגּוֹיִם:
פג א ב ג שִׁיר מִזְמוֹר לְאָסָף: אֱלֹהִים אַל־דֳּמִי־לָךְ אַל־תֶּחֱרַשׁ וְאַל־תִּשְׁקֹט אֵל: כִּי־הִנֵּה יז לחודש
ד אוֹיְבֶיךָ יֶהֱמָיוּן וּמְשַׂנְאֶיךָ נָשְׂאוּ רֹאשׁ: עַל־עַמְּךָ יַעֲרִימוּ סוֹד וְיִתְיָעֲצוּ עַל־צְפוּנֶיךָ:
ה ו אָמְרוּ לְכוּ וְנַכְחִידֵם מִגּוֹי וְלֹא־יִזָּכֵר שֵׁם־יִשְׂרָאֵל עוֹד: כִּי נוֹעֲצוּ לֵב יַחְדָּו עָלֶיךָ
ז ח בְּרִית יִכְרֹתוּ: אָהֳלֵי אֱדוֹם וְיִשְׁמְעֵאלִים מוֹאָב וְהַגְרִים: גְּבָל וְעַמּוֹן וַעֲמָלֵק
ט פְּלֶשֶׁת עִם־יֹשְׁבֵי צוֹר: גַּם־אַשּׁוּר נִלְוָה עִמָּם הָיוּ זְרוֹעַ לִבְנֵי־לוֹט סֶלָה:
י יא עֲשֵׂה־לָהֶם כְּמִדְיָן כְּסִיסְרָא כְיָבִין בְּנַחַל קִישׁוֹן: נִשְׁמְדוּ בְעֵין־דֹּאר הָיוּ דֹּמֶן
יב יג לָאֲדָמָה: שִׁיתֵמוֹ נְדִיבֵמוֹ כְּעֹרֵב וְכִזְאֵב וּכְזֶבַח וּכְצַלְמֻנָּע כָּל־נְסִיכֵמוֹ: אֲשֶׁר
יד אָמְרוּ נִירְשָׁה לָּנוּ אֵת נְאוֹת אֱלֹהִים: אֱלֹהַי שִׁיתֵמוֹ כַגַּלְגַּל כְּקַשׁ לִפְנֵי־רוּחַ:

translated as "Your treasured ones," more literally means "Your hidden things," that which cannot be seen because they are spiritual in nature. They seek to destroy us both physically and spiritually.

5 Their plan is not merely to wage battle but to bring about our total annihilation: **They said: Come, let us wipe them out as a nation, so that the name of Israel is remembered no more.**

6 **For in unity they take counsel; against You they have made a pact.** War against Israel is ultimately a war waged against the God of Israel.

7 These enemies who seek our destruction are comprised of many parties: **the tents of Edom and the Ishmaelites, Moav and the Hagrites,** the descendants of Hagar,

8 **Geval,** a small kingdom to the north of Israel, **Amon, and Amalek, Philistia with the inhabitants of Tyre.**

9 **Assyria too has joined them,** despite its distance from the Land of Israel; **they give a hand to** the instigators of the conflict, **the sons of Lot,** the Moavites and Amonites, **Selah.**

10 The psalmist prays for God to rout these enemies: **Deal with them as** You did **with Midyan,**[43] **as with Sisera and Yavin**[44] **at the Kishon Stream.**[B]

11 **They,** Sisera and Yavin, **were destroyed at Ein Dor;**[B] in death **they became** as **dung for the ground.**

12 **Make their nobles like Orev and Ze'ev,** officers of Midyan slain by Gideon,[45] **all their princes like Zevah and Tzalmuna,** kings of Midyan who were also killed by Gideon,[46]

13 **who had said: Let us take the pleasant dwellings of God,** the Land of Israel, **for ourselves.**

14 **My God, make them like whirling sand,**[B] **like chaff** scattering **before the wind,**

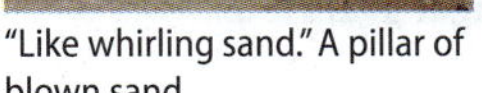

"Like whirling sand." A pillar of blown sand

Tumbleweed rolling in the wind

15 **like fire that consumes the forest, like flames that scorch mountains.**

16 **So may You pursue them with Your tempest, terrify them with Your storm.**

17 **Fill their faces with shame until** in desperation **they seek Your name** to save their lives, **Lord.**

18 **May they be ashamed and frightened forever; may they be humiliated and may they perish.**

19 **Then they will know that it is You alone whose name is the Lord.** It is only Your name and Your power that are eternal, and that it is You **who is Most High over all of the earth.**

PSALM 84

A psalm of prayer, expressing a yearning for intimacy with God and a desire to pray to Him at the Temple.

PSALMS 84:1–13

84 1 **For the chief musician, on the gitit, a psalm by the sons of Korah.**

2 **How pleasing are Your dwelling places, Lord of hosts.**

3 **My soul longs, indeed it yearns, for the courtyards of the Lord; my heart and my flesh sing with joy to the living Almighty.**

4 **Even the bird** that travels far and wide **has found a home,** and **the sparrow** too has **a nest for herself where she can put her young;** as for me, I wish my place of rest to be **at Your altars, Lord of hosts, my King and my God.**

Sparrow and her young

5 **Happy are those who dwell in Your House; they will continually praise You, Selah.**

6 **Happy are those whose strength is in You and whose hearts follow Your path.**

7 **When they pass through a valley of tears, they,** through their prayers and devotion to God, can **make it into a** flowing **spring.** Alternatively, the phrase *emek habakha*, translated here as "valley of tears," may also refer to a valley near Jerusalem where trees called *bakha* grew.[47] **Indeed, blessings cover** even **the guide** who leads the way into these places**.**

8 **They go from one success to another; they will be seen before God in Zion,** which is where their chosen path leads.

9 **Lord, God of hosts, hear my prayer. Listen, God of Jacob, Selah.**

10 **See** and assist **our shield,** the king who defends us, **God; look** with favor **upon the face of Your anointed one.**

11 **For one day in Your courtyard is better than a thousand** ordinary days; **I would rather stand at the threshold of the House of my God than dwell in tents of wickedness.**

12 **For the Lord God is a sun,** a source of light and strength, **and a shield** and protection; **the Lord gives grace and honor** to those who serve Him. **He withholds no good from those who walk uprightly.**

13 **Lord of hosts, happy is the man who trusts in You.**

PSALM 85

A psalm expressing gratitude to God, acknowledging that things have taken a turn for the better, though it also notes less auspicious times in the distant and more recent past.

PSALMS 85:1–14

85 1 **For the chief musician, a psalm by the sons of Korah.**

2 **Lord, You showed favor to Your land.** You turned Your attention toward the land with favor and love. **You returned Jacob** to it **from captivity.**

3 **You forgave the iniquity of Your people; You covered all of their sins, Selah.** That is, You have completely forgiven them (see 32:1), to the extent that their sins are no longer known. A person who truly repents is called *kesui ḥata'a*, someone whose sins have been completely "covered over."

4 **You gathered in,** that is, You have taken away, **all of Your fury; You turned away from Your fierce anger.**

5 The following are verses of entreaty: **Return to us, God of our salvation, and revoke Your anger against us.**

6 **Will You be enraged with us forever? Will You draw out Your wrath for generations?**

7 **Surely You will once again revive us, so Your people might rejoice in You.**

8 **Show us Your mercy, Lord, and grant us Your salvation.**

9 **I will hear what the Almighty Lord has to say** about my plea. The psalmist reveals God's response: **For He will speak peace to His people and to His devoted ones,** but on one condition: **If they do not return to folly,** sinful behavior, which is in essence a form of foolishness.

10 **Indeed, His salvation is near for those who fear Him,** and we will once again witness His revelation **so that glory may dwell in our land.**

11 **Kindness and truth have met;**[D] **justice and peace have**

טו טז כְּאֵשׁ תִּבְעַר־יָעַר וּכְלֶהָבָה תְּלַהֵט הָרִים׃ כֵּן תִּרְדְּפֵם בְּסַעֲרֶךָ וּבְסוּפָתְךָ תְבַהֲלֵם׃
יז יח מַלֵּא פְנֵיהֶם קָלוֹן וִיבַקְשׁוּ שִׁמְךָ יְהוָה׃ יֵבֹשׁוּ וְיִבָּהֲלוּ עֲדֵי־עַד וְיַחְפְּרוּ וְיֹאבֵדוּ׃
יט וְיֵדְעוּ כִּי־אַתָּה שִׁמְךָ יְהוָה לְבַדֶּךָ עֶלְיוֹן עַל־כָּל־הָאָרֶץ׃
פד א ב לַמְנַצֵּחַ עַל־הַגִּתִּית לִבְנֵי־קֹרַח מִזְמוֹר׃ מַה־יְּדִידוֹת מִשְׁכְּנוֹתֶיךָ יְהוָה צְבָאוֹת׃
ג ד נִכְסְפָה וְגַם־כָּלְתָה ׀ נַפְשִׁי לְחַצְרוֹת יְהוָה לִבִּי וּבְשָׂרִי יְרַנְּנוּ אֶל אֵל־חָי׃ גַּם־צִפּוֹר ׀
מָצְאָה בַיִת וּדְרוֹר ׀ קֵן ׀ לָהּ אֲשֶׁר־שָׁתָה אֶפְרֹחֶיהָ אֶת־מִזְבְּחוֹתֶיךָ יְהוָה צְבָאוֹת
ה ו מַלְכִּי וֵאלֹהָי׃ אַשְׁרֵי יוֹשְׁבֵי בֵיתֶךָ עוֹד יְהַלְלוּךָ סֶּלָה׃ אַשְׁרֵי אָדָם עוֹז־לוֹ בָךְ
ז מְסִלּוֹת בִּלְבָבָם׃ עֹבְרֵי ׀ בְּעֵמֶק הַבָּכָא מַעְיָן יְשִׁיתוּהוּ גַּם־בְּרָכוֹת יַעְטֶה מוֹרֶה׃
ח ט יֵלְכוּ מֵחַיִל אֶל־חָיִל יֵרָאֶה אֶל־אֱלֹהִים בְּצִיּוֹן׃ יְהוָה אֱלֹהִים צְבָאוֹת שִׁמְעָה
י יא תְפִלָּתִי הַאֲזִינָה אֱלֹהֵי יַעֲקֹב סֶלָה׃ מָגִנֵּנוּ רְאֵה אֱלֹהִים וְהַבֵּט פְּנֵי מְשִׁיחֶךָ׃ כִּי
יב טוֹב־יוֹם בַּחֲצֵרֶיךָ מֵאָלֶף בָּחַרְתִּי הִסְתּוֹפֵף בְּבֵית אֱלֹהַי מִדּוּר בְּאָהֳלֵי־רֶשַׁע׃ כִּי
שֶׁמֶשׁ ׀ וּמָגֵן יְהוָה אֱלֹהִים חֵן וְכָבוֹד יִתֵּן יְהוָה לֹא יִמְנַע־טוֹב לַהֹלְכִים בְּתָמִים׃
יג יְהוָה צְבָאוֹת אַשְׁרֵי אָדָם בֹּטֵחַ בָּךְ׃ יב
פה א ב ג לַמְנַצֵּחַ לִבְנֵי־קֹרַח מִזְמוֹר׃ רָצִיתָ יְהוָה אַרְצֶךָ שַׁבְתָּ שבות יַעֲקֹב׃ נָשָׂאתָ עֲוֺן שְׁבִית
ד ה עַמֶּךָ כִּסִּיתָ כָל־חַטָּאתָם סֶלָה׃ אָסַפְתָּ כָל־עֶבְרָתֶךָ הֱשִׁיבוֹתָ מֵחֲרוֹן אַפֶּךָ׃ שׁוּבֵנוּ
ו אֱלֹהֵי יִשְׁעֵנוּ וְהָפֵר כַּעַסְךָ עִמָּנוּ׃ הַלְעוֹלָם תֶּאֱנַף־בָּנוּ תִּמְשֹׁךְ אַפְּךָ לְדֹר וָדֹר׃
ז ח הֲלֹא־אַתָּה תָּשׁוּב תְּחַיֵּנוּ וְעַמְּךָ יִשְׂמְחוּ־בָךְ׃ הַרְאֵנוּ יְהוָה חַסְדֶּךָ וְיֶשְׁעֲךָ תִּתֶּן־
ט לָנוּ׃ אֶשְׁמְעָה מַה־יְדַבֵּר הָאֵל ׀ יְהוָה כִּי ׀ יְדַבֵּר שָׁלוֹם אֶל־עַמּוֹ וְאֶל־חֲסִידָיו
י יא וְאַל־יָשׁוּבוּ לְכִסְלָה׃ אַךְ קָרוֹב לִירֵאָיו יִשְׁעוֹ לִשְׁכֹּן כָּבוֹד בְּאַרְצֵנוּ׃ חֶסֶד־וֶאֱמֶת

DISCUSSION

85:11 | **Kindness and truth have met:** This describes the convergence of two attributes that are not always in harmony with each other, one often leading to the opposite course from that of the other. The same may be said for "justice and peace." Tensions arise from a clash of these attributes in the conflicted world known to us, put when the world reaches its perfected state of peace and serenity, they will all coexist in perfect harmony.

touched. All these qualities come together when God's revelation is realized.

12 At that time, **truth will spring up from the earth as righteousness looks down from heaven** and will be sensed by those on earth as well.

13 **Indeed, the Lord will bestow what is good** to everyone, **and our land will yield its produce.**

14 **Justice will go before Him as it sets its footsteps on the path.** Metaphorically speaking, justice will be witnessed and felt by all as if it is setting out on a path, and the glory of God follows.

PSALM 86

PSALMS 86:1–17

A psalm that essentially constitutes a cry to God for help. The psalmist is vulnerable and threatened from all sides. He prays to God not only to be saved but also to have the strength to remain on the right path.

86 1 **A prayer by David.** The psalmist begins with a general request: **Incline Your ear, Lord, answer me, for I am poor and needy** and worthy of Your compassion like any other unfortunate person.

2 Here the psalmist becomes more specific in his request: **Watch over me, for I am faithful;** I have chosen to follow a good and honest path. **You, who are my God, save your servant who trusts in You.**

3 **Have mercy on me, Lord, for I call to You all day long.**

4 **Gladden the soul of Your servant, for to You, Lord, I lift up my soul** in prayer, recognizing that You are my only source of strength and hope.

5 **For You, my Lord, are good and forgiving, abounding in kindness to all who call to You.**

6 **Listen, Lord, to my prayer; pay heed to the voice of my pleas.**

7 **In my time of trouble I call to You, for** I know that **You will answer me.**

8 **There is none like You among the gods, Lord, and nothing akin to Your deeds.**

9 Consequently, it is fitting that **all the nations You made will come and bow before You, Lord, and give honor to Your name.**

10 **For You are great and do wondrous deeds; You alone are God.**

11 The psalmist now presents his requests to God: **Teach me Your way, Lord, so I may walk in Your truth,** in the path that is proper and correct before You. **Dedicate my heart** so that it will be engaged in nothing else, but only **to fear Your name.**

12 **I give thanks to You, Lord my God, with all my heart, and I honor Your name forever.**

13 **For Your kindness to me is great; You rescued me from the depths of the netherworld.**

14 The psalmist now makes a specific, practical request of God: **God, wicked men have arisen against me; a band of violent foes has sought my life. They have not set You before them.** They do as they please, without taking Your will into consideration.

15 **But You, Lord, are Almighty, full of mercy and gracious, slow to anger and abundant in kindness and truth.**[48]

16 **Turn to me and be gracious to me. Give Your strength to Your servant; save the son of Your handmaid,** an expression indicating a slave born into slavery, who has never known personal independence nor had any other master.

17 **Show me a sign for good,** some indication, to myself and to others, that You indeed intend to come to my aid, **so that those who hate me may see it and be shamed, for** they will realize that **You, Lord, have helped and comforted me.**

PSALM 87

PSALMS 87:1–7

A psalm of praise with particular emphasis on Jerusalem.

87 1 **A song, a psalm by the sons of Korah; its foundation is in the holy mountains.** The main subject of this song is the mountains upon which Jerusalem rests, and specifically the Temple Mount.

2 **The Lord loves the gates of Zion more than all the dwelling places of Jacob,** because that is the city that He chose for Himself.

3 **Glorious things are spoken of you, city of God, Selah.**

4 Jerusalem, the city of God, is praiseworthy in comparison not only with other "dwelling places of Jacob" (verse 2) but also with all other places in the world. The psalmist offers a number of examples: **To those of my acquaintance, I mention Rahav,** literally "arrogance," another name for Egypt,[49] **and Babylon.** Egypt and Babylon were the two great empires of the time. **Behold Philistia and Tyre,** on the Mediterranean coast, **and Kush,** far to the south. In all these places there may

יב יג נִפְגָּשׁוּ צֶדֶק וְשָׁלוֹם נָשָׁקוּ: אֱמֶת מֵאֶרֶץ תִּצְמָח וְצֶדֶק מִשָּׁמַיִם נִשְׁקָף: גַּם־יהוה
יד יִתֵּן הַטּוֹב וְאַרְצֵנוּ תִּתֵּן יְבוּלָהּ: צֶדֶק לְפָנָיו יְהַלֵּךְ וְיָשֵׂם לְדֶרֶךְ פְּעָמָיו:
פו א ב תְּפִלָּה לְדָוִד הַטֵּה־יהוה אָזְנְךָ עֲנֵנִי כִּי־עָנִי וְאֶבְיוֹן אָנִי: שָׁמְרָה נַפְשִׁי כִּי־חָסִיד
ג אָנִי הוֹשַׁע עַבְדְּךָ אַתָּה אֱלֹהַי הַבּוֹטֵחַ אֵלֶיךָ: חָנֵּנִי אֲדֹנָי כִּי־אֵלֶיךָ אֶקְרָא כָּל־
ד ה הַיּוֹם: שַׂמֵּחַ נֶפֶשׁ עַבְדֶּךָ כִּי־אֵלֶיךָ אֲדֹנָי נַפְשִׁי אֶשָּׂא: כִּי־אַתָּה אֲדֹנָי טוֹב וְסַלָּח
ו ז וְרַב־חֶסֶד לְכָל־קֹרְאֶיךָ: הַאֲזִינָה יהוה תְּפִלָּתִי וְהַקְשִׁיבָה בְּקוֹל תַּחֲנוּנוֹתָי: בְּיוֹם
ח ט צָרָתִי אֶקְרָאֶךָּ כִּי תַעֲנֵנִי: אֵין־כָּמוֹךָ בָאֱלֹהִים ׀ אֲדֹנָי וְאֵין כְּמַעֲשֶׂיךָ: כָּל־גּוֹיִם ׀
י אֲשֶׁר עָשִׂיתָ יָבוֹאוּ ׀ וְיִשְׁתַּחֲווּ לְפָנֶיךָ אֲדֹנָי וִיכַבְּדוּ לִשְׁמֶךָ: כִּי־גָדוֹל אַתָּה וְעֹשֵׂה
יא נִפְלָאוֹת אַתָּה אֱלֹהִים לְבַדֶּךָ: הוֹרֵנִי יהוה ׀ דַּרְכֶּךָ אֲהַלֵּךְ בַּאֲמִתֶּךָ יַחֵד לְבָבִי
יב יג לְיִרְאָה שְׁמֶךָ: אוֹדְךָ ׀ אֲדֹנָי אֱלֹהַי בְּכָל־לְבָבִי וַאֲכַבְּדָה שִׁמְךָ לְעוֹלָם: כִּי־חַסְדְּךָ
יד גָּדוֹל עָלָי וְהִצַּלְתָּ נַפְשִׁי מִשְּׁאוֹל תַּחְתִּיָּה: אֱלֹהִים ׀ זֵדִים קָמוּ־עָלַי וַעֲדַת עָרִיצִים
טו בִּקְשׁוּ נַפְשִׁי וְלֹא שָׂמוּךָ לְנֶגְדָּם: וְאַתָּה אֲדֹנָי אֵל־רַחוּם וְחַנּוּן אֶרֶךְ אַפַּיִם וְרַב־
טז יז חֶסֶד וֶאֱמֶת: פְּנֵה אֵלַי וְחָנֵּנִי תְּנָה־עֻזְּךָ לְעַבְדֶּךָ וְהוֹשִׁיעָה לְבֶן־אֲמָתֶךָ: עֲשֵׂה־
עִמִּי אוֹת לְטוֹבָה וְיִרְאוּ שֹׂנְאַי וְיֵבֹשׁוּ כִּי־אַתָּה יהוה עֲזַרְתַּנִי וְנִחַמְתָּנִי:
פז א ב לִבְנֵי־קֹרַח מִזְמוֹר שִׁיר יְסוּדָתוֹ בְּהַרְרֵי־קֹדֶשׁ: אֹהֵב יהוה שַׁעֲרֵי צִיּוֹן מִכֹּל
ג ד מִשְׁכְּנוֹת יַעֲקֹב: נִכְבָּדוֹת מְדֻבָּר בָּךְ עִיר הָאֱלֹהִים סֶלָה: אַזְכִּיר ׀ רַהַב וּבָבֶל
ה לְיֹדְעָי הִנֵּה פְלֶשֶׁת וְצוֹר עִם־כּוּשׁ זֶה יֻלַּד־שָׁם: וּלְצִיּוֹן ׀ יֵאָמַר אִישׁ וְאִישׁ יֻלַּד־
ו ז בָּהּ וְהוּא יְכוֹנְנֶהָ עֶלְיוֹן: יהוה יִסְפֹּר בִּכְתוֹב עַמִּים זֶה יֻלַּד־שָׁם סֶלָה: וְשָׁרִים
כְּחֹלְלִים כָּל־מַעְיָנַי בָּךְ:

occasionally be found a native who brings pride to his country, and of whom it might be said: **This one was born there.**

5 **But of Zion it is said: This man and that man were born there. May the Most High establish it firmly.** *Ish*, translated as "man," often refers specifically to a person of prominence. It is not necessary to search in Zion for an occasional exceptional person; many great people are found there.

6 **When the Lord makes an account of the peoples,** there will still be one unique city, Jerusalem, concerning which it will be said of many prominent individuals: **This one was born there, Selah.**

7 **And singers and dancers alike** exclaim in honor of Jerusalem: **All my deepest desires are in you,** Jerusalem.

PSALM 88

PSALMS 88:1–19

A psalm of entreaty. The psalmist, suffering from a grave illness and shunned by those once close to him, prays to God to rescue him from his suffering and bring about his recovery. Unlike other psalms entreating God for relief, this psalm does not end on an optimistic note.

88 1 **A song, a psalm by the sons of Korah for the chief musician on maḥalat le'anot.** The word *le'anot* can mean "for response," and may indicate that this psalm is meant to be sung by two groups, the second responding to the first, with either a refrain or a complementary verse, which is common in songs of lamentation. **A contemplation by Heiman the Ezrahite.** This may be referring to the descendant of Korah by that name, a Levite who lived in the time of King David.[50] Alternatively, he may be identified as one of the descendants of Zerah, from the tribe of Judah.[51]

18th day of month

2 **Lord, God of my salvation, I cry out before You by day and by night.**

3 **Let my prayer come before You; incline Your ear to my plea.**

4 **For I am sated with evils.** I do not have the capacity to bear any further suffering. **My life is at the brink of the netherworld,** on the verge of death.

5 **I am reckoned** by some **as one who has** already died and **gone down to the pit,** buried in my grave; **I have become like a man with no** remaining **strength,**

6 **set free** from earthly concerns **among the dead, like those slain ones lying in the grave whom You no longer remember,** for You have no reason to be involved with those who are dead, **those cut off from Your hand,** or, alternatively, by Your hand.

7 **You put me in the lowest pit, in the dark places of the deep.** It is as if I am buried deep in the earth.

8 **Your wrath weighs upon me; You torment me with all Your breakers, Selah.** It feels as though all Your tidal waves, all the tribulations of the world, are directed against me.

9 **You have distanced me from my acquaintances; You have made me an object of loathing to them. I am shut in and cannot go out.**

10 **My eyes ache from misery. Lord, I call to You daily; I stretch out my hands to You** in prayer, yet my cries go unanswered.

11 Since I feel dead already, I cannot help but wonder: **Do You perform wonders for the dead? Do departed spirits rise and praise You?** Certainly not; they are beyond all hope. **Selah.**

12 **Is Your kindness recounted in the grave? Your faithfulness in the place of destruction?**

13 **Are Your wonders made known in the darkness? Your righteousness in the land of forgetfulness,** in the world of the dead?

14 **But I, Lord,** though I feel I am in just such a place, close to death, I **have cried out to You for help, and my prayer greets You** early **in the morning,** even before other people begin to pray.

15 And this is what I say in my prayer: **Lord, why do You neglect my soul, hide Your face from me?**

16 **From my youth I have been afflicted and near death.** Suffering is not new to me. **I bear Your terrors; my attention is turned to them,** for they surround me on all sides.

17 **Your furies have swept over me; Your horrors have silenced me** out of fear.

18 **They,** all my troubles and suffering, **surround me like water all day long.** I feel like a man who has fallen into a large body of water. **They encompass me altogether.**

19 There is no one to come to my aid, for **You have distanced** every **friend and comrade from me; those who know me are** as if **in darkness,** as I cannot see them anywhere.

PSALM 89

PSALMS 89:1–53

A psalm with two distinct parts: Praise for God for all His deeds from the beginning of Creation until the time of the reign of David, followed by entreaty and even protest against Him. Since it is essentially a psalm of prayer, the tone is not defiant.

89 1 **A contemplation by Eitan the Ezrahite.** Like other psalms with the heading *maskil,* this psalm seeks to present a specific idea, woven throughout the text, in a poetic and contemplative manner. The exact identity of Eitan the Ezrahite is unclear, as he is rarely mentioned in the Bible. Some commentators believe that the term "Ezrahite" indicates that he was Eitan son of Zerah,[52] from the tribe of Judah; others identify him with the Levite by that name who sang in the Temple in its early days.[53] According to one interpretation, Eitan is another name for the patriarch Abraham; if so, the events mentioned in the psalm represent his prophecy regarding incidents that would occur in the distant future, namely, the middle or end of the First Temple era.

2 **I will sing of the Lord's kindness forever. For all generations, my mouth will make known Your faithfulness.** *Emunatkha,* translated here as "Your faithfulness," may also mean "my faith in You," expressing the psalmist's unquestioning faith in God.

3 **For I said,** I have come to the conclusion, that **kindness is forever sustained; You set Your constancy in the heavens.** The word *emuna* is usually translated as "faith" and refers to the spiritual connection between man and God. However, here and

יח לחודש

פח א ב שִׁיר מִזְמוֹר לִבְנֵי קֹרַח לַמְנַצֵּחַ עַל־מָחֲלַת לְעַנּוֹת מַשְׂכִּיל לְהֵימָן הָאֶזְרָחִי׃ יְהוָה
ג אֱלֹהֵי יְשׁוּעָתִי יוֹם־צָעַקְתִּי בַלַּיְלָה נֶגְדֶּךָ׃ תָּבוֹא לְפָנֶיךָ תְּפִלָּתִי הַטֵּה אָזְנְךָ לְרִנָּתִי׃
ד ה כִּי־שָׂבְעָה בְרָעוֹת נַפְשִׁי וְחַיַּי לִשְׁאוֹל הִגִּיעוּ׃ נֶחְשַׁבְתִּי עִם־יוֹרְדֵי בוֹר הָיִיתִי
ו כְּגֶבֶר אֵין־אֱיָל׃ בַּמֵּתִים חָפְשִׁי כְּמוֹ חֲלָלִים ׀ שֹׁכְבֵי קֶבֶר אֲשֶׁר לֹא זְכַרְתָּם עוֹד
ז ח וְהֵמָּה מִיָּדְךָ נִגְזָרוּ׃ שַׁתַּנִי בְּבוֹר תַּחְתִּיּוֹת בְּמַחֲשַׁכִּים בִּמְצֹלוֹת׃ עָלַי סָמְכָה
ט חֲמָתֶךָ וְכָל־מִשְׁבָּרֶיךָ עִנִּיתָ סֶּלָה׃ הִרְחַקְתָּ מְיֻדָּעַי מִמֶּנִּי שַׁתַּנִי תוֹעֵבוֹת לָמוֹ כָּלֻא
י וְלֹא אֵצֵא׃ עֵינִי דָאֲבָה מִנִּי עֹנִי קְרָאתִיךָ יְהוָה בְּכָל־יוֹם שִׁטַּחְתִּי אֵלֶיךָ כַפָּי׃
יא יב הֲלַמֵּתִים תַּעֲשֶׂה־פֶּלֶא אִם־רְפָאִים יָקוּמוּ ׀ יוֹדוּךָ סֶּלָה׃ הַיְסֻפַּר בַּקֶּבֶר חַסְדֶּךָ
יג יד אֱמוּנָתְךָ בָּאֲבַדּוֹן׃ הֲיִוָּדַע בַּחֹשֶׁךְ פִּלְאֶךָ וְצִדְקָתְךָ בְּאֶרֶץ נְשִׁיָּה׃ וַאֲנִי ׀ אֵלֶיךָ
טו יְהוָה שִׁוַּעְתִּי וּבַבֹּקֶר תְּפִלָּתִי תְקַדְּמֶךָּ׃ לָמָה יְהוָה תִּזְנַח נַפְשִׁי תַּסְתִּיר פָּנֶיךָ
טז יז מִמֶּנִּי׃ עָנִי אֲנִי וְגֹוֵעַ מִנֹּעַר נָשָׂאתִי אֵמֶיךָ אָפוּנָה׃ עָלַי עָבְרוּ חֲרוֹנֶיךָ בִּעוּתֶיךָ
יח יט צִמְּתוּתֻנִי׃ סַבּוּנִי כַמַּיִם כָּל־הַיּוֹם הִקִּיפוּ עָלַי יָחַד׃ הִרְחַקְתָּ מִמֶּנִּי אֹהֵב וָרֵעַ
מְיֻדָּעַי מַחְשָׁךְ׃

פט א ב מַשְׂכִּיל לְאֵיתָן הָאֶזְרָחִי׃ חַסְדֵי יְהוָה עוֹלָם אָשִׁירָה לְדֹר וָדֹר ׀ אוֹדִיעַ אֱמוּנָתְךָ
ג ד בְּפִי׃ כִּי־אָמַרְתִּי עוֹלָם חֶסֶד יִבָּנֶה שָׁמַיִם ׀ תָּכִן אֱמוּנָתְךָ בָהֶם׃ כָּרַתִּי בְרִית
ה לִבְחִירִי נִשְׁבַּעְתִּי לְדָוִד עַבְדִּי׃ עַד־עוֹלָם אָכִין זַרְעֶךָ וּבָנִיתִי לְדֹר־וָדוֹר כִּסְאֲךָ
ו ז סֶלָה׃ וְיוֹדוּ שָׁמַיִם פִּלְאֲךָ יְהוָה אַף־אֱמוּנָתְךָ בִּקְהַל קְדֹשִׁים׃ כִּי מִי בַשַּׁחַק יַעֲרֹךְ

in several other verses of this psalm, the term conveys the notion of steadfastness and stability; hence, "Your constancy."

4 In the next two verses the speaker is God: **I established a covenant with My chosen one; I took an oath to David, My servant.** The psalmist here expresses his faith that God's constancy is also manifest in the everlasting covenant He made with the house of David, a covenant that is summarized in the next verse.

5 **I will establish your seed forever,** ensuring that your descendants will never cease to be, **and build up your throne for all** those **generations, Selah.**

6 The following are words of general praise of God: **The heavens praise Your wonders, Lord,** by exhibiting Your celestial marvels for all to see, **and Your constancy** is acknowledged **in the assembly of holy ones,** the angels.

7 **For who in the skies compares to the Lord? Who among sons of the mighty,** the divine angels, **is like the Lord?**

8 **The Almighty is revered in the great assembly of the holy ones,** the angels, **awesome to all who surround Him.**

9 **Lord, God of hosts,** a term depicting God's might among the hosts of the heavens, **who is like You, mighty Lord? Your constancy surrounds You.**

10 Just as God's rule extends through the heavens, so it is manifest in the world below: **You rule the swelling sea; when its waves rise,** even to great heights, **You still them.** At Your will, the waves become calm, even when they have risen to a point at which they seem to be unstoppable.

11 **You crushed Rahav like a corpse.** According to a number of commentaries, Rahav refers here to the leviathan, one of the great sea creatures mentioned in Genesis.[54] Based on this verse, they also say that the original male leviathan was killed by God in ancient times. **With the strength of Your arm, You scattered Your enemies.**

12 **Yours are the heavens, Yours too is the earth; You founded the world and all it contains.**

13 **You created the north and the south.** The great mountains **Tavor and Hermon sing with joy in Your name.** Tavor and Hermon are the two most prominent peaks in Israel, located at either end of the country's northern mountainous region.

Mount Tavor

14 **Your arm is powerful and Your hand is mighty; Your right hand, exalted.** Since the word *yadkha*, translated as "Your hand," is juxtaposed with *yeminekha*, "Your right hand," many commentators maintain that *yadkha* is referring to God's left hand, as it were.

15 **Righteousness and justice are at the base of Your throne; kindness and truth greet Your countenance.** Kindness and truth are personified in this verse, depicted as servants of God.

16 **Happy are the people,** Israel, **who know the clarion call,** who know how to praise God and sound the trumpet in His honor; **they walk, Lord, in the light of Your countenance.**

17 **They rejoice in Your name all day long; they are exalted through Your righteousness.** They rely on Your righteousness and are thereby exalted.

18 **For You are the glory of their strength; our horn,** our esteem and power, **is raised by Your favor.** When You favor us, we are exalted.

19 **For our protection is of the Lord; our king is of the Holy One of Israel,** for he rules in God's name.

20 Until this point, the psalm has focused on the greatness and glory of God in heaven and earth, and on His glory with regard to the Israelites in particular. The following section offers a more specific historical perspective: **You once spoke in a vision to Your devoted ones,** the prophets Samuel, Natan, and Gad, **saying: I aided the warrior; I raised the one chosen from the people.** The next verse identifies this warrior and chosen one whom God revealed to the prophets.

21 **I found David, My servant.** David was "found" in the sense that he had been an unknown figure, the youngest of Yishai's sons, living in a small town. **I anointed him with My holy oil,** a reference to Samuel's anointment of David as king of Israel,[55]

Anointment of David as king, fresco, synagogue in Dura-Europos, third century CE

22 **as the one whom My hand will establish; My arm will strengthen him.**

23 **The enemy will not rule over him; the wicked will not torment him,**

24 **and I will crush his foes before him and smite those who hate him.**

25 **My constancy and favor will be with him, and his horn,** his esteem and power, **will be raised in My name,** because he is protected by the power of God.

26 **I will set his hand upon the seas.** He will rule the coastline and the sea, and I will set **his right hand on the rivers.** This verse may be a reference to David's future victories, both to the east of the kingdom of Israel, at the Jordan River, and to its west, at the Mediterranean Sea.

27 **He will call to Me: You are my Father, my God, and the rock of my salvation.** He will remain connected and devoted to God.

28 **As for Me, I will make him My firstborn.** Not only will I consider him My son, but I will even regard him as the firstborn, being **supreme among kings of the earth.** King David will see God as his Father, and God in turn will treat David like a favored son.

29 **I will forever preserve My kindness to him; My covenant with him will be steadfast.**

ח לַיהוה יִדְמֶה לַיהוה בִּבְנֵי אֵלִים: אֵל נַעֲרָץ בְּסוֹד־קְדֹשִׁים רַבָּה וְנוֹרָא עַל־כָּל־

ט י סְבִיבָיו: יהוה ׀ אֱלֹהֵי צְבָאוֹת מִי־כָמוֹךָ חֲסִין ׀ יָהּ וֶאֱמוּנָתְךָ סְבִיבוֹתֶיךָ: אַתָּה

יא מוֹשֵׁל בְּגֵאוּת הַיָּם בְּשׂוֹא גַלָּיו אַתָּה תְשַׁבְּחֵם: אַתָּה דִכִּאתָ כֶחָלָל רָהַב בִּזְרוֹעַ

יב יג עֻזְּךָ פִּזַּרְתָּ אוֹיְבֶיךָ: לְךָ שָׁמַיִם אַף־לְךָ אָרֶץ תֵּבֵל וּמְלֹאָהּ אַתָּה יְסַדְתָּם: צָפוֹן

יד וְיָמִין אַתָּה בְרָאתָם תָּבוֹר וְחֶרְמוֹן בְּשִׁמְךָ יְרַנֵּנוּ: לְךָ זְרוֹעַ עִם־גְּבוּרָה תָּעֹז יָדְךָ

טו טז תָּרוּם יְמִינֶךָ: צֶדֶק וּמִשְׁפָּט מְכוֹן כִּסְאֶךָ חֶסֶד וֶאֱמֶת יְקַדְּמוּ פָנֶיךָ: אַשְׁרֵי הָעָם

יז יוֹדְעֵי תְרוּעָה יהוה בְּאוֹר־פָּנֶיךָ יְהַלֵּכוּן: בְּשִׁמְךָ יְגִילוּן כָּל־הַיּוֹם וּבְצִדְקָתְךָ יָרוּמוּ:

יח יט כִּי־תִפְאֶרֶת עֻזָּמוֹ אָתָּה וּבִרְצוֹנְךָ תרים קַרְנֵנוּ: כִּי לַיהוה מָגִנֵּנוּ וְלִקְדוֹשׁ יִשְׂרָאֵל תָּרוּם

כ מַלְכֵּנוּ: אָז דִּבַּרְתָּ בְחָזוֹן לַחֲסִידֶיךָ וַתֹּאמֶר שִׁוִּיתִי עֵזֶר עַל־גִּבּוֹר הֲרִימוֹתִי בָחוּר

כא כב מֵעָם: מָצָאתִי דָּוִד עַבְדִּי בְּשֶׁמֶן קָדְשִׁי מְשַׁחְתִּיו: אֲשֶׁר יָדִי תִּכּוֹן עִמּוֹ אַף־זְרוֹעִי

כג כד תְאַמְּצֶנּוּ: לֹא־יַשִּׁא אוֹיֵב בּוֹ וּבֶן־עַוְלָה לֹא יְעַנֶּנּוּ: וְכַתּוֹתִי מִפָּנָיו צָרָיו וּמְשַׂנְאָיו

כה כו אֶגּוֹף: וֶאֱמוּנָתִי וְחַסְדִּי עִמּוֹ וּבִשְׁמִי תָּרוּם קַרְנוֹ: וְשַׂמְתִּי בַיָּם יָדוֹ וּבַנְּהָרוֹת יְמִינוֹ:

כז כח הוּא יִקְרָאֵנִי אָבִי אָתָּה אֵלִי וְצוּר יְשׁוּעָתִי: אַף־אָנִי בְּכוֹר אֶתְּנֵהוּ עֶלְיוֹן לְמַלְכֵי־

כט ל אָרֶץ: לְעוֹלָם אשמור־לוֹ חַסְדִּי וּבְרִיתִי נֶאֱמֶנֶת לוֹ: וְשַׂמְתִּי לָעַד זַרְעוֹ וְכִסְאוֹ אֶשְׁמָר־

לא לב כִּימֵי שָׁמָיִם: אִם־יַעַזְבוּ בָנָיו תּוֹרָתִי וּבְמִשְׁפָּטַי לֹא יֵלֵכוּן: אִם־חֻקֹּתַי יְחַלֵּלוּ

לג לד וּמִצְוֹתַי לֹא יִשְׁמֹרוּ: וּפָקַדְתִּי בְשֵׁבֶט פִּשְׁעָם וּבִנְגָעִים עֲוֺנָם: וְחַסְדִּי לֹא־אָפִיר

לה לו מֵעִמּוֹ וְלֹא־אֲשַׁקֵּר בֶּאֱמוּנָתִי: לֹא־אֲחַלֵּל בְּרִיתִי וּמוֹצָא שְׂפָתַי לֹא אֲשַׁנֶּה: אַחַת

30 This everlasting kindness will be expressed in the fact that **I will eternally ensure his seed, and his throne will last as the days of the heavens,** forever. God's covenant is not only with David personally, but with his descendants forever.

31 However, this covenant has conditions that must be met: **If his sons forsake My teaching and do not walk according to My judgments,**

32 **if they violate My statutes and do not keep My commandments,**

33 **I shall punish their transgressions with a rod and their iniquity with plague.**

34 **But I will not remove My kindness from him or be false to My constancy.** Although David's descendants will not be immune from occasional sinful behavior, they will be punished as individuals. Their personal chastisement will not affect God's eternal covenant with the house of David at large.

35 **I will not violate My covenant, nor alter the utterance of My lips.**

36 **For I have sworn once** and for all **by My holiness; I will not be false to David.** I will never renege on My promise to him that his dynastic line will continue forever, as the next verse clarifies.

37 **His seed will endure forever, and his throne will be as** permanent as **the sun before Me,**
38 **eternal like the moon,** like the stars that are **a constant witness in the sky, Selah.**
39 Having reiterated the promises made by God to David and his descendants, the psalmist registers his complaint: **Yet You abandoned and repulsed** the house of David; **You became wrathful with Your anointed one,** referring to one or more of the kings who rose among David's descendants.
40 **You spurned the covenant of Your servant; You profaned his crown,** throwing it down, as it were, **on the ground.**
41 **You breached all his walls** that he built, **brought his fortresses to** rubble that is **a fright** to behold.
42 **All those passing on the way looted him,** the king himself as well as his people; **he was a disgrace to his neighbors,** who used his kingdom as a paradigm of disgrace and dishonor.
43 **You raised the right hand of his foes** by giving them strength and power; with this **You made all his enemies rejoice.**
44 **You even turned back the blade of his sword,** making it unreliable and useless; **You did not make him steadfast in battle,** and he was constantly defeated.
45 **You took away,** annulled his eminence, **from his** previous **brightness** and pureness, when he was impervious to harm. *Hishbata,* translated as "took away," more literally means "You annulled." You **cast his throne to the ground.**
46 **You shortened the days of his youth,** as he died at a young age, and **cloaked him with shame, Selah.** This description of the decline of the kingdom of the house of David expresses the psalmist's complaint and even protest against God for His seemingly broken promise regarding the eternal nature of the Davidic dynasty. It is followed by a concluding section of entreaty:
47 **How long, Lord? Will You hide Yourself forever?** The defeat and humiliation of Israel and of David's line are indications of God hiding His countenance from them. How long **will Your wrath burn like fire?**
48 **Remember what I am, what the world is.** *Ḥaled,* translated here as "world," is related to the word *ḥadal,* meaning "to come to an end." The psalmist calls to God to remember that the world is unstable and finite, and our lives in it are brief. **For what futile purpose did You create all the sons of man?**
49 Failure, shame, and hopelessness affect not only the king but the entire nation of Israel; we are all mortals. **Who is the man who can live and not see death; who can save his life from the netherworld? Selah.** In the face of each individual's inevitable death, it is still possible to carry on, as long as there remains a sense of hope and belief in a more certain future. In the present situation, however, the only certainty is death.
50 Therefore, the psalmist turns to God in prayer: **Where are Your former acts of kindness, Lord, those which You swore to David in Your constancy?**
51 **Remember, Lord, the humiliation of** us, **Your servants. My breast is burdened by all the many nations.** It is as if numerous nations were pressing on me, weighing me down, and I am unable to shake them off,
52 **for Your enemies revile the Lord.** In causing us pain and suffering, these nations are also desecrating God, whose name is linked with the nation of Israel and the house of David. **They revile the footsteps of Your anointed one.**
53 The psalm ends on a sad note of entreaty and complaint. There is, however, a final line that concludes the third book of Psalms. It is similar to the conclusion of the other books of Psalms, but it also relates specifically to the contents of this particular psalm: **Blessed be the Lord forever, amen and amen.**

PSALM 90

PSALMS 90:1–17

A psalm dealing with the human condition and with man's relationship with God. It includes elements of praise, complaint, and entreaty.

90 BOOK FOUR

Thursday *19th day of month*

1 **A prayer of Moses, man of God.**[D] The psalm begins with words of praise: **Lord, You have been a dwelling place for us from generation to generation;** we "dwell" within You forever in the sense that Your existence is the only thing that is essential and eternal, and all of creation exists only through You.[56]
2 **Before the birth of mountains, before You brought forth the earth and the world, forever and for eternity have You been the Almighty.**
3 The psalm now presents the crux of the problem: **You bring man down until he is crushed, and then You say: Return,** repent, **sons of man.**[D]
4 **Indeed, a thousand years in Your eyes are like yesterday gone by.** Time, as we know it, is irrelevant to God. For Him, a thousand years are like a day gone by; they leave no trace of palpable experience but only memory. **Like a watch of the night.** A portion of the night is known as a "watch." The years pass like a night watch, a period of time that goes unnoticed by mortals, who sleep through it.
5 **You make them,** man's days, **flow past, as if in sleep,** like a passing dream, not quite real. **In the morning,** when this sleep is finished, **they pass on like grass** that dries up and perishes,
6 **sprouting in the morning and then passing on, by evening broken and withered.** Such are the days of our lives compared

לז לח נִשְׁבַּעְתִּי בְקׇדְשִׁי אִם־לְדָוִד אֲכַזֵּב׃ זַרְעוֹ לְעוֹלָם יִהְיֶה וְכִסְאוֹ כַשֶּׁמֶשׁ נֶגְדִּי׃ כְּיָרֵחַ
לט יִכּוֹן עוֹלָם וְעֵד בַּשַּׁחַק נֶאֱמָן סֶלָה׃ וְאַתָּה זָנַחְתָּ וַתִּמְאָס הִתְעַבַּרְתָּ עִם־מְשִׁיחֶךָ׃
מ מא נֵאַרְתָּה בְּרִית עַבְדֶּךָ חִלַּלְתָּ לָאָרֶץ נִזְרוֹ׃ פָּרַצְתָּ כׇל־גְּדֵרֹתָיו שַׂמְתָּ מִבְצָרָיו
מב מג מְחִתָּה׃ שַׁסֻּהוּ כׇּל־עֹבְרֵי דָרֶךְ הָיָה חֶרְפָּה לִשְׁכֵנָיו׃ הֲרִימוֹתָ יְמִין צָרָיו הִשְׂמַחְתָּ
מד מה כׇּל־אוֹיְבָיו׃ אַף־תָּשִׁיב צוּר חַרְבּוֹ וְלֹא הֲקֵמֹתוֹ בַּמִּלְחָמָה׃ הִשְׁבַּתָּ מִטְּהָרוֹ וְכִסְאוֹ
מו מז לָאָרֶץ מִגַּרְתָּה׃ הִקְצַרְתָּ יְמֵי עֲלוּמָיו הֶעֱטִיתָ עָלָיו בּוּשָׁה סֶלָה׃ עַד־מָה יְהוָה
מח תִּסָּתֵר לָנֶצַח תִּבְעַר כְּמוֹ־אֵשׁ חֲמָתֶךָ׃ זְכׇר־אֲנִי מֶה־חָלֶד עַל־מַה־שָּׁוְא בָּרָאתָ
מט נ כׇל־בְּנֵי־אָדָם׃ מִי גֶבֶר יִחְיֶה וְלֹא יִרְאֶה־מָּוֶת יְמַלֵּט נַפְשׁוֹ מִיַּד־שְׁאוֹל סֶלָה׃ אַיֵּה ׀
נא חֲסָדֶיךָ הָרִאשֹׁנִים ׀ אֲדֹנָי נִשְׁבַּעְתָּ לְדָוִד בֶּאֱמוּנָתֶךָ׃ זְכֹר אֲדֹנָי חֶרְפַּת עֲבָדֶיךָ
נב שְׂאֵתִי בְחֵיקִי כׇּל־רַבִּים עַמִּים׃ אֲשֶׁר חֵרְפוּ אוֹיְבֶיךָ ׀ יְהוָה אֲשֶׁר חֵרְפוּ עִקְּבוֹת
נג מְשִׁיחֶךָ׃ בָּרוּךְ יְהוָה לְעוֹלָם אָמֵן ׀ וְאָמֵן׃

ספר רביעי
יום חמישי
יט לחודש

צ א ב תְּפִלָּה לְמֹשֶׁה אִישׁ־הָאֱלֹהִים אֲדֹנָי מָעוֹן אַתָּה הָיִיתָ לָּנוּ בְּדֹר וָדֹר׃ בְּטֶרֶם ׀
ג הָרִים יֻלָּדוּ וַתְּחוֹלֵל אֶרֶץ וְתֵבֵל וּמֵעוֹלָם עַד־עוֹלָם אַתָּה אֵל׃ תָּשֵׁב אֱנוֹשׁ עַד־
ד דַּכָּא וַתֹּאמֶר שׁוּבוּ בְנֵי־אָדָם׃ כִּי אֶלֶף שָׁנִים בְּעֵינֶיךָ כְּיוֹם אֶתְמוֹל כִּי יַעֲבֹר
ה ו וְאַשְׁמוּרָה בַלָּיְלָה׃ זְרַמְתָּם שֵׁנָה יִהְיוּ בַּבֹּקֶר כֶּחָצִיר יַחֲלֹף׃ בַּבֹּקֶר יָצִיץ וְחָלָף

DISCUSSION

90:1 | **A prayer of Moses, man of God:** This is the only chapter in Psalms attributed to a person who lived long before King David. Some Sages assert that the ten psalms that follow it were written by Moses as well. In any event, the topic and nature of the psalm remove it from the realm of prayers dealing with everyday affairs, and transfer it into a category that deals with sublime matters, fitting indeed for a prayer by Moses, the man of God. See also the Epistle of Comfort by Maimon, the father of Maimonides, which discusses primarily this psalm.

90:3 | **You bring man down until he is crushed, and then You say: Return, sons of man:** Moses reacts to the conditions of extreme difficulty, during which man is expected to return to God, and pleads: We, as human beings, are not always able to rise to the divine expectations of us. These words bring to mind other prayers mentioned in the Torah, in which Moses does not argue with divine justice per se, but presents the other side of the equation, the imperfection of human experience (see also *Sefer HaIkkarim* 4:37).

with divine eternity: an experience that is both ephemeral and inconsequential.
7 **We are consumed by Your wrath** even in the midst of our swiftly flowing days, **frightened by Your rage,** distressed and attempting to hide.
8 **You have placed our transgressions before You, our hidden things before the light of Your countenance.** Our clandestine acts are all plainly revealed before You; we cannot hide from You.
9 Being human, we sin, and we are punished, and **all of our days have passed by in Your fury; we have exhausted our years** fleetingly, **like an utterance,** which leaves no trace a moment after it is spoken.
10 **The days of our lives in it,** in this world, **are** a mere **seventy years, or if with might, eighty years;** and even **their pride,** referring to our greatest accomplishments, **is toil** in vain **and emptiness.** *Amal va'aven,* translated here as "toil and emptiness," can also mean "sin and wrongdoing." Our lives are **swiftly passing, and we fly away.** One of the reasons our achievements are insignificant is that our lives are exceedingly brief. We are so taken up with everyday, mundane matters that we invest neither the time nor the strength to consider what is truly important, namely, living in a proper manner and repenting any wrongdoing on our part.
11 **Who** among us **knows the** extent of the **power of Your wrath? As the fear of You, so is Your fury.** On the one hand, we are aware that sins bear consequences, even if we underestimate the severity of the punishment we might incur. On the other hand, we are rarely confronted with an opportunity to grasp reality and assess the significance of our lives.
12 **Teach us,** grant us the wisdom, **to count each of our days,** to realize that our lives are brief and that each day counts, **so we might** thereby **acquire a heart of wisdom.** If we attain this awareness of the passage of time, we might at least refrain from pursuing matters that are worthless or wrong; while they may be attractive in the short run, they have no lasting value and can lead us to incur punishment.
13 The last part of the psalm is an entreaty based less on man's goodness and more on his helplessness and mortality: **Return to us** and show us grace, **Lord; how long** will You remain distanced from us? **Have pity on Your servants.** This expression is used by Moses elsewhere as well;[57] it is an appeal to God to extend His mercy toward us even if we are not worthy of it.
14 **Sate us in the morning,** a reference to the early years of our lives, **with Your kindness, so we may sing and rejoice all our days.** Kindness shown to man in his youth is a source of joy throughout his life, as its memory always remains with him.
15 Alternatively, if You do not shower us with kindness at the beginning of our lives, **give us joy corresponding to the days You afflicted us, those years of evil that we saw,** so that at least the end of our lives will be good.
16 Once we have a measure of rest and tranquility, **Your deeds will be seen by Your servants;** we will be able to contemplate Your actions. This is also an implied request that God show us His mighty deeds. And let **Your majesty** be witnessed **by their children.**
17 The psalm ends with a general prayer for our lives: **May the graciousness of the Lord our God be upon us,** so that all of our difficult, tireless efforts in our endeavors, whose continuity and success we must not take for granted, will prove worthwhile in the long run, through Your **establishing the work of our hands for us** in our lifetime; **indeed, establishing the work of our hands.**

PSALM 91

PSALMS 91:1–16

A song of encouragement and consolation directed toward one who is under God's protection. The psalm alternates between voices: an individual praying and a chorus making general statements. The psalm concludes with God's words.

91 1 This verse is a kind of heading, clarifying that the psalm is directed at **he who dwells in the shelter of the Most High, who abides in the shadow of the Almighty,** seeking shelter from the troubles of this world, finding refuge in God, and dwelling under His protection.
2 The psalmist then opens with his prayer: **I will say of the Lord: He is my shelter and my fortress, my God in whom I trust,**
3 The chorus responds: It is indeed good to seek refuge in God, **for He will rescue you from the ensnaring trap, from devastating pestilence.**
4 Or, stated metaphorically: **He will cover You with His pinion; you will find refuge under His wings. His truth is** a source of protection from harm, like **a shield and armor.**
5 **You will not fear the terror of night.** At night one is more likely to fear being assaulted directly by an armed attacker. **Nor** will you fear **the arrow that flies by day.** Arrows are usually shot in the daytime, when their targets are in full sight.
6 **Nor** will you fear **the pestilence that stalks in darkness, nor the destruction that lays waste at noon.**

Shield, Greece, eighth century BCE

ז ח לָעֶרֶב יְמוֹלֵל וְיָבֵשׁ: כִּי־כָלִינוּ בְאַפֶּךָ וּבַחֲמָתְךָ נִבְהָלְנוּ: שַׁתָּ עֲוֺנֹתֵינוּ לְנֶגְדֶּךָ
ט י עֲלֻמֵנוּ לִמְאוֹר פָּנֶיךָ: כִּי כָל־יָמֵינוּ פָּנוּ בְעֶבְרָתֶךָ כִּלִּינוּ שָׁנֵינוּ כְמוֹ־הֶגֶה: יְמֵי־
שְׁנוֹתֵינוּ בָהֶם שִׁבְעִים שָׁנָה וְאִם בִּגְבוּרֹת ׀ שְׁמוֹנִים שָׁנָה וְרׇהְבָּם עָמָל וָאָוֶן כִּי־
יא יב גָז חִישׁ וַנָּעֻפָה: מִי־יוֹדֵעַ עֹז אַפֶּךָ וּכְיִרְאָתְךָ עֶבְרָתֶךָ: לִמְנוֹת יָמֵינוּ כֵּן הוֹדַע וְנָבִא
יג יד לְבַב חׇכְמָה: שׁוּבָה יְהוָה עַד־מָתָי וְהִנָּחֵם עַל־עֲבָדֶיךָ: שַׂבְּעֵנוּ בַבֹּקֶר חַסְדֶּךָ
טו טז וּנְרַנְּנָה וְנִשְׂמְחָה בְּכׇל־יָמֵינוּ: שַׂמְּחֵנוּ כִּימוֹת עִנִּיתָנוּ שְׁנוֹת רָאִינוּ רָעָה: יֵרָאֶה
יז אֶל־עֲבָדֶיךָ פׇעֳלֶךָ וַהֲדָרְךָ עַל־בְּנֵיהֶם: וִיהִי ׀ נֹעַם אֲדֹנָי אֱלֹהֵינוּ עָלֵינוּ וּמַעֲשֵׂה יג
יָדֵינוּ כּוֹנְנָה עָלֵינוּ וּמַעֲשֵׂה יָדֵינוּ כּוֹנְנֵהוּ:
צא א ב יֹשֵׁב בְּסֵתֶר עֶלְיוֹן בְּצֵל שַׁדַּי יִתְלוֹנָן: אֹמַר לַיהוָה מַחְסִי וּמְצוּדָתִי אֱלֹהַי אֶבְטַח־
ג ד בּוֹ: כִּי הוּא יַצִּילְךָ מִפַּח יָקוּשׁ מִדֶּבֶר הַוּוֹת: בְּאֶבְרָתוֹ ׀ יָסֶךְ לָךְ וְתַחַת־כְּנָפָיו
ה ו תֶּחְסֶה צִנָּה וְסֹחֵרָה אֲמִתּוֹ: לֹא־תִירָא מִפַּחַד לָיְלָה מֵחֵץ יָעוּף יוֹמָם: מִדֶּבֶר
ז בָּאֹפֶל יַהֲלֹךְ מִקֶּטֶב יָשׁוּד צׇהֳרָיִם: יִפֹּל מִצִּדְּךָ ׀ אֶלֶף וּרְבָבָה מִימִינֶךָ אֵלֶיךָ לֹא
ח ט יִגָּשׁ: רַק בְּעֵינֶיךָ תַבִּיט וְשִׁלֻּמַת רְשָׁעִים תִּרְאֶה: כִּי־אַתָּה יְהוָה מַחְסִי עֶלְיוֹן
י יא שַׂמְתָּ מְעוֹנֶךָ: לֹא־תְאֻנֶּה אֵלֶיךָ רָעָה וְנֶגַע לֹא־יִקְרַב בְּאׇהֳלֶךָ: כִּי מַלְאָכָיו יְצַוֶּה־
יב יג לָּךְ לִשְׁמׇרְךָ בְּכׇל־דְּרָכֶיךָ: עַל־כַּפַּיִם יִשָּׂאוּנְךָ פֶּן־תִּגֹּף בָּאֶבֶן רַגְלֶךָ: עַל־שַׁחַל
יד וָפֶתֶן תִּדְרֹךְ תִּרְמֹס כְּפִיר וְתַנִּין: כִּי בִי חָשַׁק וַאֲפַלְּטֵהוּ אֲשַׂגְּבֵהוּ כִּי־יָדַע שְׁמִי:

7 **A thousand may fall** victim to some calamity **at your side, and ten thousand at your right hand, but it will not reach you.**

8 **You will just look with your eyes and see the** just **punishment of the wicked,** that they receive.

9 The individual, who finds shelter in God, speaks again: **For You, Lord, are my shelter.** The chorus responds: It is fitting that you seek shelter in Him, for **you have made the Most High your dwelling place.**

10 As a result of your trust in Him, **no evil will befall you, and no plague will come near your tent,**

11 **for He will charge his angels on your behalf to guard you in all your ways.**

12 **They will carry you on their palms** of their hands, **lest your foot be struck by a stone.** As one lifts up a child and carries him when walking on perilous terrain, the angels will protect you from injury.

13 Because of this protection, **you will** be able to **tread** in complete safety, even **upon lions and cobras; you will** be able to **trample young lions and serpents.**

Black desert cobra

14 At this point, a third voice is heard, that of God: I grant this extraordinary protection to this individual **because he desired Me greatly.**

Therefore **I will rescue him; I will be his fortress, for he has known My name.**
15 **When he calls upon Me, I will answer him. I will be with him in times of trouble; I will deliver him and honor him.** Not only will I rescue him from distress, but I will also help him to achieve greatness and honor.
16 In addition, **I will sate him with length of days, and I will show him My salvation,** sparing him from both personal problems and general misfortunes.

PSALM 92

PSALMS 92:1–16

A psalm dedicated to the Sabbath day. At the same time, it is an all-encompassing meditation on matters of the world, reflecting, as if from on high, on good and evil, success and failure.

92 1 **A psalm, a song for the Sabbath day.** Although it was sung in the Temple every Sabbath, this psalm is not really about the Sabbath day as such, but rather what the Sages refer to as "the day that is entirely a Sabbath,"[58] that is, the Messianic Era, when a final reckoning will enable everything to be understood clearly in hindsight. In essence, the psalm is a reflection and overview of history, in which all negative events will be understood as ephemeral phenomena, and precursors of evil's ultimate downfall. The righteous, by contrast, will prove to have permanence, stability, and continuous prosperity.
2 **How good it is to give thanks to the Lord.** Gratitude is expressed for man's very ability to give thanks to God. We appreciate our ability **to sing praises to Your name, Most High,**
3 **to tell of Your kindness in the morning.** "In the morning" is a metaphor for a period when God's mercy is evident and revealed to us. **And** we express gratitude for **Your faithfulness in the nights.** The phrase "the nights" symbolizes dark times or periods of despondency, when it may appear as though God has withdrawn. At such times, it is faith in God that sustains a person.
4 We praise God **with a ten-stringed lute and with a harp, with meditative music on the lyre,** an instrument similar to a harp but with fewer strings (see commentary on 33:2). The word *higayon*, translated here as "meditative music," may refer to a certain type of melody or a specific style of playing the lyre.

Harp of eleven strings, perhaps the "ten-stringed lute." Illustration based on fresco, tomb of Rameses III, Egypt, 1156–1186 BCE

5 Here begins the actual content of the song: **For You, Lord, have made me happy by Your actions** in creating the world; **I will sing for joy at the work of Your hands,** all the creations found in the world.
6 **How great are Your works, Lord.** The quantity and quality of Your creations, which are manifest before us, give some indication of Your infinite greatness. **How profound** are **Your thoughts.** Aside from that which we can see ourselves, we realize the depth of Your thoughts, which are beyond our grasp.
7 And because of the depth of the divine thoughts, **a boor cannot know** their meaning and **a fool cannot understand this.**
8 They cannot understand, for instance, that **when the wicked sprout like grass,** everywhere, seemingly with no limitation, **and** when **evildoers flourish, it is only toward their eternal destruction.** In fact, the apparent success of the wicked is nothing more than a means leading to their total destruction. The metaphor is that of ridding a field of weeds: If one waters the ground, the weeds sprout and can be readily identified and eradicated, preparing the field for the sowing of crops.
9 **And You, Lord, are forever on high.** You see everything from above, and both the apparent rise of the wicked and their subsequent downfall are part of Your plan.
10 **For behold Your enemies, Lord, behold Your enemies perish** in the end; **all evildoers are scattered.**
11 As for me, the righteous one who serves You faithfully, **You raise my horn,** a metaphor for stature and power, **like** the tall, upright horns of **an oryx. I am anointed with fresh oil,** as I have achieved a position of greatness.
12 In my prosperity I have reached a position in which **my eye has seen** the downfall of **my foes. When the wicked rise against me, my ears will hear** of their defeat.
13 **The righteous man flourishes like a palm tree,** which soars to great heights and bears fruit even in the arid desert. **Like a** lofty **cedar in Lebanon he grows tall.**

Palm tree

Cedar in Lebanon

14 **Planted in the House of the Lord** and blessed by Him, **they blossom in the courts of our God.**
15 Even if they experience occasional hardship and adversity, **they will continue to yield fruit, even in old age.** While others wither and fade, **they will remain full and fresh.**

טו טז יִקְרָאֵנִי ׀ וְאֶעֱנֵהוּ עִמּוֹ־אָנֹכִי בְצָרָה אֲחַלְּצֵהוּ וַאֲכַבְּדֵהוּ׃ אֹרֶךְ יָמִים אַשְׂבִּיעֵהוּ
וְאַרְאֵהוּ בִּישׁוּעָתִי׃
צב א ב ג מִזְמוֹר שִׁיר לְיוֹם הַשַּׁבָּת׃ טוֹב לְהֹדוֹת לַיהוה וּלְזַמֵּר לְשִׁמְךָ עֶלְיוֹן׃ לְהַגִּיד בַּבֹּקֶר
ד ה חַסְדֶּךָ וֶאֱמוּנָתְךָ בַּלֵּילוֹת׃ עֲלֵי־עָשׂוֹר וַעֲלֵי־נָבֶל עֲלֵי הִגָּיוֹן בְּכִנּוֹר׃ כִּי שִׂמַּחְתַּנִי
ו יהוה בְּפָעֳלֶךָ בְּמַעֲשֵׂי יָדֶיךָ אֲרַנֵּן׃ מַה־גָּדְלוּ מַעֲשֶׂיךָ יהוה מְאֹד עָמְקוּ מַחְשְׁבֹתֶיךָ׃
ז ח אִישׁ־בַּעַר לֹא יֵדָע וּכְסִיל לֹא־יָבִין אֶת־זֹאת׃ בִּפְרֹחַ רְשָׁעִים ׀ כְּמוֹ עֵשֶׂב וַיָּצִיצוּ
ט י כׇּל־פֹּעֲלֵי אָוֶן לְהִשָּׁמְדָם עֲדֵי־עַד׃ וְאַתָּה מָרוֹם לְעֹלָם יהוה׃ כִּי הִנֵּה אֹיְבֶיךָ יהוה
יא כִּי־הִנֵּה אֹיְבֶיךָ יֹאבֵדוּ יִתְפָּרְדוּ כׇּל־פֹּעֲלֵי אָוֶן׃ וַתָּרֶם כִּרְאֵים קַרְנִי בַּלֹּתִי בְּשֶׁמֶן
יב יג רַעֲנָן׃ וַתַּבֵּט עֵינִי בְּשׁוּרָי בַּקָּמִים עָלַי מְרֵעִים תִּשְׁמַעְנָה אׇזְנָי׃ צַדִּיק כַּתָּמָר יִפְרָח
יד טו כְּאֶרֶז בַּלְּבָנוֹן יִשְׂגֶּה׃ שְׁתוּלִים בְּבֵית יהוה בְּחַצְרוֹת אֱלֹהֵינוּ יַפְרִיחוּ׃ עוֹד יְנוּבוּן
טז בְּשֵׂיבָה דְּשֵׁנִים וְרַעֲנַנִּים יִהְיוּ׃ לְהַגִּיד כִּי־יָשָׁר יהוה צוּרִי וְלֹא־עלתה בּוֹ׃ עוֹלָתָה
צג א ב יהוה מָלָךְ גֵּאוּת לָבֵשׁ לָבֵשׁ יהוה עֹז הִתְאַזָּר אַף־תִּכּוֹן תֵּבֵל בַּל־תִּמּוֹט׃ נָכוֹן
ג כִּסְאֲךָ מֵאָז מֵעוֹלָם אָתָּה׃ נָשְׂאוּ נְהָרוֹת ׀ יהוה נָשְׂאוּ נְהָרוֹת קוֹלָם יִשְׂאוּ נְהָרוֹת

16 This serves **to tell** all **that the Lord is upright** and His laws are just and true, even when His justice is concealed from human understanding. **He is my rock, and there is no wrongdoing in Him.** Even if the righteousness of God's justice is not evident to me, I must consider the future time, the End of Days, when it will become apparent that evil will have been eradicated from the world while goodness will remain permanent, vibrant, and fresh.

PSALM 93

PSALMS 93:1–5

A hymn about God's revelation in the world. In the wake of this revelation, all existence will be filled with song and all people will witness God's rule of the world and His presence within His Sanctuary.

93 **1** **The Lord reigns,** that is, when His reign is revealed to this world, **He is clothed in grandeur. The Lord is clothed** in glory **and has girded Himself with strength.** He is perceived as a king, cloaked in honor, girded in power. **The world is** then **firmly established, not to be shaken.** The world will be secure; wickedness, which is inherently unstable (see 92:8–10), will cease to exist.

2 **Your throne stands firm of old.** God's throne was already established in ancient times. **You are from eternity.**

3 When God's reign is revealed, the world sings in His honor: **The rivers raise, Lord; the rivers raise their voices. The rivers boost their towering waves,** singing and dancing, as it were, in honor of God.

4 **It is from the sound of many waters** that God's praises are heard, from **the mighty breakers of the sea,** singing their song. **The Lord is mighty on high.** God Himself is the mightiest of all.

5 This is the song they will "sing": **Your precepts,** or alternatively, "Your promises," **are completely true;** they have now been revealed and fulfilled. **Holiness adorns Your House; the Lord is for all length of days** and will abide in that House forever.

PSALM 94

PSALMS 94:1–23

A psalm of prayer about coping with the wicked. Although mainly descriptive and analytic, it also contains a personal prayer, as the psalmist is suffering from the evil around him and is in need of assistance and salvation.

94 1 **God of vengeance,**[D] **Lord, God of vengeance, appear.**

2 Because God's justice is not always manifest in the world and it can seem as if God hides Himself, withholding His power, the psalmist entreats Him: **Rise up, Judge of the earth;** reveal Yourself as the Ruler and Judge of the world. **Bring retribution to the arrogant.** The word *ge'im*, translated here and elsewhere in Psalms as "the arrogant," most often refers to wicked people who have no regard for others.

3 **How long for the wicked, Lord?** How long will You allow them to continue in their evil ways? **How long will the wicked exult?**

4 **They express themselves with arrogance; all the evildoers exalt themselves.** How long will all this persist?

5 In addition to engaging in self-aggrandizement, the wicked also cause suffering to others: **They crush Your people, Lord; they afflict** those who reside in **Your portion,** the Land of Israel. Alternatively, the words "Your portion" themselves refer to the people of Israel, who are at times called God's portion.

6 **They slay the widow and the proselyte, and they murder the orphan;** these all are the most vulnerable, with no personal protector.

7 When God chooses not to intervene, the wicked, unpunished, believe they can do as they please: **They say: The Lord does not see; the God of Jacob does not comprehend** what we are doing. Even if they believe that God exists, they assume that He takes no interest in people or in what they do. In their view, He has distanced Himself from the world to the extent that He is indifferent to its affairs.

8 The psalmist responds to this attitude: **Take heed, you boors among the people. Fools, when will you learn?**

9 **He who sets the ear in place, does He not hear? He who forms the eye, does He not see?**

10 **He who chastises nations, He who teaches man knowledge, shall He not rebuke?** Can it be that He who teaches all the nations will not instruct an individual human being? Is it possible that He who confers knowledge is incapable of understanding? On the contrary, when God chooses not to intervene, refraining from punishing the wicked or rewarding the good, He does so for reasons that are far beyond our comprehension, as the following verses detail.

11 **The Lord knows the thoughts of man, that they are vain,** transient, and insignificant. He knows that grandiose plans that the wicked make for themselves, trampling others in the process, ultimately come to naught.

12 The psalmist, turning his attention to those who suffer from the wicked, suggests an additional perspective: **Blessed is the man whom You chastise, Lord, whom You instruct with Your teaching.** Suffering serves as atonement for sin and a means of redirecting a person toward a better, loftier path. It is not an indication of God's indifference toward the one who is suffering, but rather, it is a form of instruction.

13 You arrange **to grant him respite in days of evil.** God's control in the world, which is not expressed through immediate reward and punishment, is not readily perceived by people. Still, He provides one receiving chastisement with a measure of relief that allows him to endure **until a pit is dug for the wicked** person, who will ultimately fall in and meet his destruction.

14 **Indeed,** even if it is not always evident, **the Lord will not abandon His people, nor will He forsake His portion.**

DISCUSSION

94:1 | **God of vengeance:** Vengeance is generally not considered positive; indeed, the Torah forbids it for man (Leviticus 19:18). It is fitting only for God, who alone can arrive at a truly just assessment and is devoid of human moral shortcomings. Divine vengeance is necessary both to prevent the wicked from doing evil in the future and to avenge the sinful acts they have already done. It is for this reason that elsewhere God is described as "zealous and vengeful" (Nahum 1:2); indeed, He testifies of Himself, "Vengeance and recompense are Mine" (Deuteronomy 32:35).

ד ה דָּכְיָם׃ מִקֹּלוֹת ׀ מַיִם רַבִּים אַדִּירִים מִשְׁבְּרֵי־יָם אַדִּיר בַּמָּרוֹם יְהוָה׃ עֵדֹתֶיךָ ׀
נֶאֶמְנוּ מְאֹד לְבֵיתְךָ נַאֲוָה־קֹדֶשׁ יְהוָה לְאֹרֶךְ יָמִים׃
צד א ב אֵל־נְקָמוֹת יְהוָה אֵל נְקָמוֹת הוֹפִיעַ׃ הִנָּשֵׂא שֹׁפֵט הָאָרֶץ הָשֵׁב גְּמוּל עַל־גֵּאִים׃
ג ד עַד־מָתַי רְשָׁעִים ׀ יְהוָה עַד־מָתַי רְשָׁעִים יַעֲלֹזוּ׃ יַבִּיעוּ יְדַבְּרוּ עָתָק יִתְאַמְּרוּ
ה ו כָּל־פֹּעֲלֵי אָוֶן׃ עַמְּךָ יְהוָה יְדַכְּאוּ וְנַחֲלָתְךָ יְעַנּוּ׃ אַלְמָנָה וְגֵר יַהֲרֹגוּ וִיתוֹמִים
ז ח יְרַצֵּחוּ׃ וַיֹּאמְרוּ לֹא יִרְאֶה־יָּהּ וְלֹא־יָבִין אֱלֹהֵי יַעֲקֹב׃ בִּינוּ בֹּעֲרִים בָּעָם וּכְסִילִים
ט י מָתַי תַּשְׂכִּילוּ׃ הֲנֹטַע אֹזֶן הֲלֹא יִשְׁמָע אִם־יֹצֵר עַיִן הֲלֹא יַבִּיט׃ הֲיֹסֵר גּוֹיִם הֲלֹא
יא יב יוֹכִיחַ הַמְלַמֵּד אָדָם דָּעַת׃ יְהוָה יֹדֵעַ מַחְשְׁבוֹת אָדָם כִּי־הֵמָּה הָבֶל׃ אַשְׁרֵי
יג הַגֶּבֶר אֲשֶׁר־תְּיַסְּרֶנּוּ יָּהּ וּמִתּוֹרָתְךָ תְלַמְּדֶנּוּ׃ לְהַשְׁקִיט לוֹ מִימֵי רָע עַד יִכָּרֶה
יד טו לָרָשָׁע שָׁחַת׃ כִּי ׀ לֹא־יִטֹּשׁ יְהוָה עַמּוֹ וְנַחֲלָתוֹ לֹא יַעֲזֹב׃ כִּי־עַד־צֶדֶק יָשׁוּב
טז מִשְׁפָּט וְאַחֲרָיו כָּל־יִשְׁרֵי־לֵב׃ מִי־יָקוּם לִי עִם־מְרֵעִים מִי־יִתְיַצֵּב לִי עִם־פֹּעֲלֵי
יז יח אָוֶן׃ לוּלֵי יְהוָה עֶזְרָתָה לִּי כִּמְעַט ׀ שָׁכְנָה דוּמָה נַפְשִׁי׃ אִם־אָמַרְתִּי מָטָה רַגְלִי
יט כ חַסְדְּךָ יְהוָה יִסְעָדֵנִי׃ בְּרֹב שַׂרְעַפַּי בְּקִרְבִּי תַּנְחוּמֶיךָ יְשַׁעַשְׁעוּ נַפְשִׁי׃ הַיְחָבְרְךָ
כא כב כִּסֵּא הַוּוֹת יֹצֵר עָמָל עֲלֵי־חֹק׃ יָגוֹדּוּ עַל־נֶפֶשׁ צַדִּיק וְדָם נָקִי יַרְשִׁיעוּ׃ וַיְהִי יְהוָה
כג לִי לְמִשְׂגָּב וֵאלֹהַי לְצוּר מַחְסִי׃ וַיָּשֶׁב עֲלֵיהֶם ׀ אֶת־אוֹנָם וּבְרָעָתָם יַצְמִיתֵם
יַצְמִיתֵם יְהוָה אֱלֹהֵינוּ׃

15 **Judgment will return with righteousness, and all the upright of heart will follow it.** After this judgment of the wicked, the hopes of the upright will be realized.

16 The psalmist muses: **Who will rise up for me,** to assist me to struggle **against the wicked? Who will take a stand for me against the evildoers?**

17 **Had the Lord not helped me, my soul would soon have dwelled in silence,** as I would have died and gone to the grave.

18 **When I say** to myself: **My foot is stumbling** and I am about to fall, **Your kindness, Lord,** comes to my aid and **supports me.**

19 **In the midst of my many troubled thoughts, Your consolations soothe me.** The realization that God assists me counteracts the thoughts of desperation and anguish that beset me.

20 **Can the seat of calamity,** the dominion of evil in the world, **be associated with You, that** seat **which creates evil that is** given a place of importance **above the law?**

21 **They,** those evildoers alluded to in the previous verse, **band themselves against the lives of the righteous and convict the blood of the innocent;** in condemning the innocent, they may even sentence them to death and thereby shed their blood.

22 **But the Lord is my stronghold; my God, the rock of my refuge.**

23 **He will requite them for their wickedness and destroy them in their own evil;** as noted in several places in the book of Proverbs, the evil done by sinners often serves as their own undoing, the means by which the wicked are punished and ultimately destroyed. **The Lord our God will destroy them.**

PSALM 95

A hymn in praise of God. It is also a call, based on Israel's history, to refrain from sin.

PSALMS 95:1–11

95 1 **Come, let us sing for joy to the Lord;** moreover, **let us make a joyful sound,** by raising our voices loudly in song or by playing musical instruments, **to the rock of our salvation.**

2 **Let us greet Him with** verbal declarations and sacrificial offerings of **thanksgiving. Let us cry out to Him joyfully, with song.**

3 **For the Lord is a great God, a great King, above all gods,** and therefore deserving of our praises and joyful singing,

4 **in whose hand are depths of the earth, and peaks of the mountains are His,**

5 **who owns the sea and made it, and whose hands formed the dry land.**

6 **Come, let us prostrate ourselves and bow down; let us kneel before the Lord our Maker.**

7 **For He is our God, and we are the people of His flock,** whom He leads and cares for, **and the sheep under His hand. Even today, would you only heed His voice;** to remain protected we must only obey and follow Him.

8 Using historical examples, the psalmist provides a reminder of the suffering that befalls those who do not follow God faithfully. In this verse and the following ones, God speaks to Israel: **Do not harden your hearts as you did at** the waters of **Meriva, or at Masa in the desert,** references to events described in the Torah.[59]

9 These were two representative incidents **when your fathers tested Me; they tried Me, and they also saw My work;** they saw that I fulfilled their requests and that I punished them for their unfaithfulness.

10 **For forty years I spurned that generation,** the generation of the exodus. **I said: They are a people who err in their hearts,** and **they do not know My ways.**

11 **Thus I swore in My wrath that they would not come to My resting place,** the Land of Israel. Alongside the benefit from seeking God's protection by following His commands, there is also a serious threat associated with rejecting God's authority: Just as those who trust in God are not treated neutrally but given all they need, those who deviate from His ways are not treated neutrally but are subjected to full severity of punishment.

PSALM 96

A hymn of praise for God. It is characterized as "a new song" because it is a novel formulation and expression of God's glory.

PSALMS 96:1–13

96 1 **Sing to the Lord a new song; sing to the Lord, all the earth.**

2 **Sing to the Lord, bless His name; proclaim the good tidings of His salvation day by day.**

3 **Tell of His glory among the nations** and **of His wonders among all the peoples.**

4 **For the Lord is great and** is **to be praised exceedingly; He is feared above all gods.**

5 **For all gods of the peoples are** merely useless, powerless **idols, but the Lord** possesses true power, as He **made the heavens.**

6 **Majesty and glory are** situated **before Him,** in the courtyard of his Temple, and **might and splendor are** found **in His Sanctuary.**

7 **Render to the Lord, you families of the peoples; render to the Lord honor and might.** Render honor by showing reverence to Him, and render might by clinging to Him with all your strength.

8 **Render to the Lord the glory due His name; bring an offering, and come into His courtyards,** to serve Him.

9 While there, **bow down to the Lord in** a mindset of **splendor of holiness,** that is, with the awe of awareness of His supreme holiness. **Tremble before Him, all the earth.**

10 **Say among the nations: The Lord reigns!** And when God's kingship is revealed, **the world is firmly established, not to be shaken;** it will no longer seem shaky and precarious, as it sometimes does now. **He will** then **minister fair judgment to the peoples.**

11 When God's glory becomes revealed, **the heavens will be happy, and the earth will rejoice. The sea and all its fullness will thunder.** The sea will thunder with its roaring waves, and all the creatures that fill it will join in the chorus of praise to God.

12 **The fields and everything within them will exult.** Even **all the trees of the forest** which, unlike cultivated fields, are not under man's dominion, **will then cry out for joy.**

13 All of these will sing out in joy **before the Lord when He comes** and reveals Himself in the world, **when He comes to judge the earth.** This revelation of God will take place when **He will judge the world with righteousness, and the peoples with His faithfulness.**

צה א ב ג לְכוּ נְרַנְּנָה לַיהוָה נָרִיעָה לְצוּר יִשְׁעֵנוּ׃ נְקַדְּמָה פָנָיו בְּתוֹדָה בִּזְמִרוֹת נָרִיעַ לוֹ׃ כִּי
ד אֵל גָּדוֹל יְהוָה וּמֶלֶךְ גָּדוֹל עַל־כָּל־אֱלֹהִים׃ אֲשֶׁר בְּיָדוֹ מֶחְקְרֵי־אָרֶץ וְתוֹעֲפוֹת
ה ו הָרִים לוֹ׃ אֲשֶׁר־לוֹ הַיָּם וְהוּא עָשָׂהוּ וְיַבֶּשֶׁת יָדָיו יָצָרוּ׃ בֹּאוּ נִשְׁתַּחֲוֶה וְנִכְרָעָה
ז נִבְרְכָה לִפְנֵי־יְהוָה עֹשֵׂנוּ׃ כִּי הוּא אֱלֹהֵינוּ וַאֲנַחְנוּ ׀ עַם מַרְעִיתוֹ וְצֹאן יָדוֹ הַיּוֹם
ח ט אִם־בְּקֹלוֹ תִשְׁמָעוּ׃ אַל־תַּקְשׁוּ לְבַבְכֶם כִּמְרִיבָה כְּיוֹם מַסָּה בַּמִּדְבָּר׃ אֲשֶׁר נִסּוּנִי
י אֲבוֹתֵיכֶם בְּחָנוּנִי גַּם־רָאוּ פָעֳלִי׃ אַרְבָּעִים שָׁנָה ׀ אָקוּט בְּדוֹר וָאֹמַר עַם תֹּעֵי
יא לֵבָב הֵם וְהֵם לֹא־יָדְעוּ דְרָכָי׃ אֲשֶׁר־נִשְׁבַּעְתִּי בְאַפִּי אִם־יְבֹאוּן אֶל־מְנוּחָתִי׃
צו א ב שִׁירוּ לַיהוָה שִׁיר חָדָשׁ שִׁירוּ לַיהוָה כָּל־הָאָרֶץ׃ שִׁירוּ לַיהוָה בָּרְכוּ שְׁמוֹ בַּשְּׂרוּ
ג ד מִיּוֹם־לְיוֹם יְשׁוּעָתוֹ׃ סַפְּרוּ בַגּוֹיִם כְּבוֹדוֹ בְּכָל־הָעַמִּים נִפְלְאוֹתָיו׃ כִּי גָדוֹל יְהוָה
ה וּמְהֻלָּל מְאֹד נוֹרָא הוּא עַל־כָּל־אֱלֹהִים׃ כִּי ׀ כָּל־אֱלֹהֵי הָעַמִּים אֱלִילִים וַיהוָה
ו ז שָׁמַיִם עָשָׂה׃ הוֹד־וְהָדָר לְפָנָיו עֹז וְתִפְאֶרֶת בְּמִקְדָּשׁוֹ׃ הָבוּ לַיהוָה מִשְׁפְּחוֹת
ח עַמִּים הָבוּ לַיהוָה כָּבוֹד וָעֹז׃ הָבוּ לַיהוָה כְּבוֹד שְׁמוֹ שְׂאוּ־מִנְחָה וּבֹאוּ לְחַצְרוֹתָיו׃
ט י הִשְׁתַּחֲווּ לַיהוָה בְּהַדְרַת־קֹדֶשׁ חִילוּ מִפָּנָיו כָּל־הָאָרֶץ׃ אִמְרוּ בַגּוֹיִם ׀ יְהוָה מָלָךְ
יא אַף־תִּכּוֹן תֵּבֵל בַּל־תִּמּוֹט יָדִין עַמִּים בְּמֵישָׁרִים׃ יִשְׂמְחוּ הַשָּׁמַיִם וְתָגֵל הָאָרֶץ
יב יג יִרְעַם הַיָּם וּמְלֹאוֹ׃ יַעֲלֹז שָׂדַי וְכָל־אֲשֶׁר־בּוֹ אָז יְרַנְּנוּ כָּל־עֲצֵי־יָעַר׃ לִפְנֵי יְהוָה ׀
כִּי בָא כִּי בָא לִשְׁפֹּט הָאָרֶץ יִשְׁפֹּט־תֵּבֵל בְּצֶדֶק וְעַמִּים בֶּאֱמוּנָתוֹ׃
צז א ב יְהוָה מָלָךְ תָּגֵל הָאָרֶץ יִשְׂמְחוּ אִיִּים רַבִּים׃ עָנָן וַעֲרָפֶל סְבִיבָיו צֶדֶק וּמִשְׁפָּט כ לחודש
ג ד מְכוֹן כִּסְאוֹ׃ אֵשׁ לְפָנָיו תֵּלֵךְ וּתְלַהֵט סָבִיב צָרָיו׃ הֵאִירוּ בְרָקָיו תֵּבֵל רָאֲתָה

PSALM 97

A hymn of praise that is essentially about God's revelation, but also concerns His sovereignty over the world.

PSALMS 97:1–12

97 1 **The Lord reigns,** and when He is revealed as sovereign, **the earth will rejoice. The many islands** all over the world **will be glad.**
20th day of month

2 The psalmist describes what this revelation will be like: **Cloud and fog surround Him** to conceal His glory as He sits upon His throne; **justice and judgment are the base of His throne.**

3 **Fire goes before Him,** an expression of His glory; but fire is also used as a tool for punishment, **and it burns around His foes.**

4 **His lightning illuminates the world; the earth sees, and trembles.**

5 **Mountains melt like wax** in fear **at the presence of the Lord, before the Master of all the earth.**
6 **The heavens declare His righteousness,** which will become apparent to all of creation, all the way up to the heavens; **all peoples behold His glory.**
7 At this time of revelation, **all those who worship images, who glorify idols, will be ashamed,** realizing the utter inanity of their belief. **All gods,** the heavenly powers and angels, **will bow down before Him.**

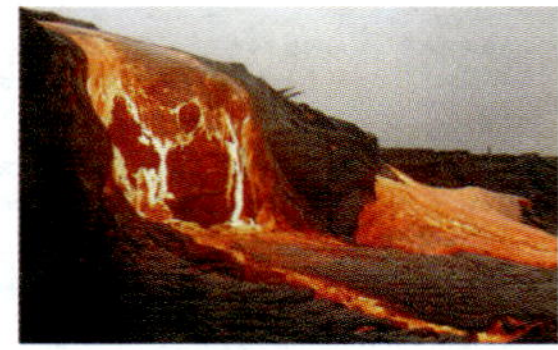
"Mountains melt like wax." Rivers of lava

8 **Zion will hear and be glad,** for it is the city of God; **and the daughters of Judah will rejoice because of Your judgments** that You will mete out upon this revelation, **Lord.**
9 **For You, Lord, are the Most High over all the earth; You are greatly exalted,** not only above us but **above all gods.**
10 The psalmist now turns to those who serve God: **You who love the Lord, hate evil.** It is not enough to cleave to God; you must also take a clear stand against evil. But you need not fear a backlash from the evildoers when you denounce them, for **He guards the lives of His devoted ones, saving them from the hand of the wicked.**
11 **Light is sown for the righteous, and joy for the upright of heart.** Light for the righteous, representing glory, exists, even though it is not always evident in the present. It is sown for them like seeds; eventually, their light will grow and be revealed to all.
12 **Rejoice in the Lord, you righteous ones, and give thanks at the mention of His holy name.**

PSALM 98

A psalm of general praise to God that describes how the world and its inhabitants sing and rejoice in His honor.

PSALMS 98:1–9

98 1 **A psalm. Sing to the Lord a new song, for He has done wonders; His right hand,** referring to His might, **and His holy arm have wrought salvation for Him.**
2 **The Lord has made known His salvation; before the eyes of the nations, He revealed His righteousness.**
3 One aspect of this revelation is connected specifically to the people of Israel: **He recalled His kindness and His faithfulness to the house of Israel,** and then **all the ends of the earth beheld the salvation of our God** that He wrought for Israel. Whenever God is revealed in all His power, Israel's greatness also becomes recognized.
4 But the psalmist calls to the people of all nations, not just Israel, to express joy in the divine revelation: **Shout with joy to the Lord, all the earth! Break forth,** or open your mouths wide, **and sing for joy; sing praises.**
5 **Sing to the Lord with lyre, with lyre and the melody of song.** The music begins softly, with stringed instruments.
6 It then increases in volume: **With trumpets and the sound of the shofar, make loud sound before the King, the Lord.**
7 And at this point, the forces of nature join in, accompanying the song, as it were: **Let the sea and all within it thunder, the world and all who dwell in it.**
8 **Rivers will clap hands.** The rivers join in the chorus of praise, though in a gentler manner than that of the thundering sea. The sound of the flowing rivers resembles that of clapping hands. **The mountains, in unison, will sing for joy.**
9 This great musical tribute is to take place **before the Lord, when He** reveals Himself and **comes to judge the earth.** At that time, **He will judge the world with righteousness and** judge **peoples with equity.**

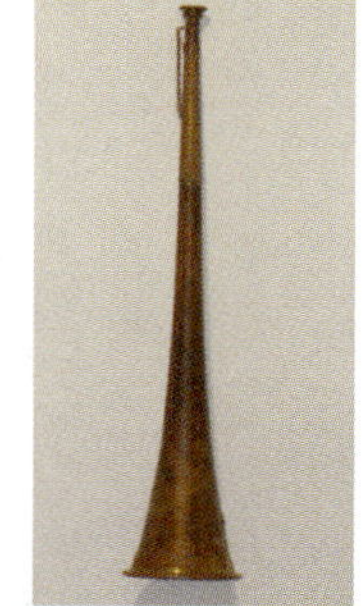
Trumpet

PSALM 99

A psalm that speaks of God's praise as it is revealed, in the course of history, through various historical figures.

PSALMS 99:1–9

99 1 **The Lord reigns,** and when God's sovereignty is revealed, **peoples tremble.** When **He is** sitting, **seated amidst** the **cherubs** that are atop the Holy Ark in the Temple and serve as God's throne on earth, as it were, **the earth shudders.**
2 **The Lord is great in Zion, and He is above all the peoples.**
3 **They acknowledge Your great and awesome name; it is holy.**
4 **The might of the King is that He loves justice.** God's strength manifests itself through His love of justice, not in arbitrary exercise of power. **You set it straight in place; You wrought judgment and justice in Jacob.** God's revelation on earth is based on law, order, and fairness, and thus the world is set "straight in place."
5 **Exalt the Lord our God and bow down at His footstool.** These verses portray God as if He is sitting on His throne, His feet resting on His "footstool," the Temple, thereby imparting sanctity to it. **He is holy.**

ה ו וַתָּחֵל הָאָרֶץ׃ הָרִים כַּדּוֹנַג נָמַסּוּ מִלִּפְנֵי יְהוָה מִלִּפְנֵי אֲדוֹן כָּל־הָאָרֶץ׃ הִגִּידוּ
ז הַשָּׁמַיִם צִדְקוֹ וְרָאוּ כָל־הָעַמִּים כְּבוֹדוֹ׃ יֵבֹשׁוּ ׀ כָּל־עֹבְדֵי פֶסֶל הַמִּתְהַלְלִים
ח בָּאֱלִילִים הִשְׁתַּחֲווּ־לוֹ כָּל־אֱלֹהִים׃ שָׁמְעָה וַתִּשְׂמַח ׀ צִיּוֹן וַתָּגֵלְנָה בְּנוֹת יְהוּדָה
ט לְמַעַן מִשְׁפָּטֶיךָ יְהוָה׃ כִּי־אַתָּה יְהוָה עֶלְיוֹן עַל־כָּל־הָאָרֶץ מְאֹד נַעֲלֵיתָ עַל־
י כָּל־אֱלֹהִים׃ אֹהֲבֵי יְהוָה שִׂנְאוּ רָע שֹׁמֵר נַפְשׁוֹת חֲסִידָיו מִיַּד רְשָׁעִים יַצִּילֵם׃
יא יב אוֹר זָרֻעַ לַצַּדִּיק וּלְיִשְׁרֵי־לֵב שִׂמְחָה׃ שִׂמְחוּ צַדִּיקִים בַּיהוָה וְהוֹדוּ לְזֵכֶר קָדְשׁוֹ׃
צח א מִזְמוֹר שִׁירוּ לַיהוָה ׀ שִׁיר חָדָשׁ כִּי־נִפְלָאוֹת עָשָׂה הוֹשִׁיעָה־לּוֹ יְמִינוֹ וּזְרוֹעַ
ב ג קָדְשׁוֹ׃ הוֹדִיעַ יְהוָה יְשׁוּעָתוֹ לְעֵינֵי הַגּוֹיִם גִּלָּה צִדְקָתוֹ׃ זָכַר חַסְדּוֹ ׀ וֶאֱמוּנָתוֹ
ד לְבֵית יִשְׂרָאֵל רָאוּ כָל־אַפְסֵי־אָרֶץ אֵת יְשׁוּעַת אֱלֹהֵינוּ׃ הָרִיעוּ לַיהוָה כָּל־הָאָרֶץ
ה ו פִּצְחוּ וְרַנְּנוּ וְזַמֵּרוּ׃ זַמְּרוּ לַיהוָה בְּכִנּוֹר בְּכִנּוֹר וְקוֹל זִמְרָה׃ בַּחֲצֹצְרוֹת וְקוֹל שׁוֹפָר
ז ח הָרִיעוּ לִפְנֵי ׀ הַמֶּלֶךְ יְהוָה׃ יִרְעַם הַיָּם וּמְלֹאוֹ תֵּבֵל וְיֹשְׁבֵי בָהּ׃ נְהָרוֹת יִמְחֲאוּ־כָף
ט יַחַד הָרִים יְרַנֵּנוּ׃ לִפְנֵי־יְהוָה כִּי בָא לִשְׁפֹּט הָאָרֶץ יִשְׁפֹּט־תֵּבֵל בְּצֶדֶק וְעַמִּים
בְּמֵישָׁרִים׃
צט א ב יְהוָה מָלָךְ יִרְגְּזוּ עַמִּים יֹשֵׁב כְּרוּבִים תָּנוּט הָאָרֶץ׃ יְהוָה בְּצִיּוֹן גָּדוֹל וְרָם הוּא
ג ד עַל־כָּל־הָעַמִּים׃ יוֹדוּ שִׁמְךָ גָּדוֹל וְנוֹרָא קָדוֹשׁ הוּא׃ וְעֹז מֶלֶךְ מִשְׁפָּט אָהֵב אַתָּה
ה כּוֹנַנְתָּ מֵישָׁרִים מִשְׁפָּט וּצְדָקָה בְּיַעֲקֹב ׀ אַתָּה עָשִׂיתָ׃ רוֹמְמוּ יְהוָה אֱלֹהֵינוּ
ו וְהִשְׁתַּחֲווּ לַהֲדֹם רַגְלָיו קָדוֹשׁ הוּא׃ מֹשֶׁה וְאַהֲרֹן ׀ בְּכֹהֲנָיו וּשְׁמוּאֵל בְּקֹרְאֵי
ז שְׁמוֹ קֹרְאִים אֶל־יְהוָה וְהוּא יַעֲנֵם׃ בְּעַמּוּד עָנָן יְדַבֵּר אֲלֵיהֶם שָׁמְרוּ עֵדֹתָיו וְחֹק

6 The psalmist proceeds to describe God's greatness as manifested in history: **Moses and Aaron were among His priests, and Samuel among those who called His name.** Beyond being a leader, Samuel was also responsible for the revival of Judaism in his generation. **They called to the Lord, and He answered them.**

7 **Through a pillar of cloud He spoke to them,** because **they kept His precepts and the statutes** of the Torah that **He gave them** as leaders.

8 **Lord our God, You answered them;** You answered their prayers. **You were a forgiving God to them, but You** also **took vengeance for their misdeeds.** This is proper, since God rules the world with justice.

9 **Exalt the Lord our God and bow down at His holy mountain,** the site of the Temple. **For the Lord our God is holy,** and it is fitting to show reverence to anything connected with Him.

PSALM 100

PSALMS 100:1–5

A psalm associated with the thanksgiving sacrifice; it may have been sung during the offering of that sacrifice. It is also a general expression of gratitude to God.

100 1 **A psalm of thanksgiving. Cry out joyously to the Lord, all the earth.**

2 **Serve the Lord with joy; come before Him,** to His Temple, **with song.**

3 **Know that the Lord is God. It is He who made us, and we belong to Him; we are His people and the sheep of His flock.**

4 **Enter His gates with thanksgiving;** bring thanksgiving offerings and, more generally, express gratitude to God. Enter **His courtyards with praise. Give thanks to Him; bless His name.**

5 **For the Lord is good, His kindness eternal. His faithfulness** toward those who are dedicated to His service **is for all generations.**

PSALM 101

PSALMS 101:1–8

A psalm about David that speaks of his deeds and intentions, both as a private individual and as king of Israel.

101 1 **A psalm of David. I sing kindness and justice; to You, Lord, I sing praises.**

2 **I ponder the path of integrity.** As I attempt to understand, to seek the right path and act with integrity, I ask of God: **When will You come** and reveal Yourself **to me?** David begins to describe his virtuous personal life: **I walk in the innocence of my heart in my house.**

3 **I set nothing contemptible before my eyes,** attempting to avoid even witnessing anything sinful. **I hate perversity; it does not cling to me.** I have nothing to do with it.

4 **A crooked heart stays far away from me. I** attempt to **know no evil.**

5 **One who secretly slanders his neighbor, I will cut him down.** Not only will I keep such a person out of favor, I will seek to destroy him. **I will not tolerate anyone with a proud demeanor or a lustful heart.**

6 **My eyes are** instead **on the faithful** and upright people **of the land,** insisting that only **they will dwell with me. He who walks in the path of integrity, it is** only **he who will serve me.**

7 **No deceiver or liar will dwell in my house; he will not stand firm before me.**

8 **Every morning I cut down all the wicked of the land, ridding the city of the Lord,** Jerusalem, **of all evildoers.**

PSALM 102

PSALMS 102:1–29

A psalm by an individual who is suffering greatly. His prayer to be rescued expresses his deep faith in God's omnipotence and compassion.

102 1 **The prayer of a poor man,** a weak and powerless man, **when he feels overwhelmed,** enveloped by distress and the sense of the world closing in on him. **And** he **pours out his woes before the Lord** in prayer to Him.

2 **Lord, hear my prayer; let my cry for help reach You.**

3 **Do not hide Your face from me at the time of my distress. Incline Your ear to** hear **me on the day that I call; answer me quickly.** My anguish and feeling of imminent destruction are so profound that I beg God for His immediate assistance.

4 **For my days are consumed** as if they are going up **in smoke,** destroyed without purpose; **and my bones, as in a pyre, are burnt hollow.**

5 **My heart is beaten down like** trampled **grass, and it withers, for** I am so overcome with pain and sorrow that I neglect to fulfill even my most basic needs; I even **forget to eat my bread.**

6 **From my groaning,** in my agony, I feel as though I am shriveling up, that **my bones cling to my flesh.**

7 **I am like a desert owl;**[B] **I have become like an owl of the ruins.**[B] Both of these nocturnal birds make sounds similar to crying or wailing.

Houbara bustard

"Owl of the ruins"

ח נֹתֵן־לָמוֹ: יהוה אֱלֹהֵינוּ אַתָּה עֲנִיתָם אֵל נֹשֵׂא הָיִיתָ לָהֶם וְנֹקֵם עַל־עֲלִילוֹתָם:
ט רוֹמְמוּ יהוה אֱלֹהֵינוּ וְהִשְׁתַּחֲווּ לְהַר קָדְשׁוֹ כִּי־קָדוֹשׁ יהוה אֱלֹהֵינוּ:
ק א ב מִזְמוֹר לְתוֹדָה הָרִיעוּ לַיהוה כָּל־הָאָרֶץ: עִבְדוּ אֶת־יהוה בְּשִׂמְחָה בֹּאוּ לְפָנָיו
ג בִּרְנָנָה: דְּעוּ כִּי־יהוה הוּא אֱלֹהִים הוּא עָשָׂנוּ וְלֹא אֲנַחְנוּ עַמּוֹ וְצֹאן מַרְעִיתוֹ: וְלוֹ
ד ה בֹּאוּ שְׁעָרָיו ׀ בְּתוֹדָה חֲצֵרֹתָיו בִּתְהִלָּה הוֹדוּ לוֹ בָּרְכוּ שְׁמוֹ: כִּי־טוֹב יהוה לְעוֹלָם
חַסְדּוֹ וְעַד־דֹּר וָדֹר אֱמוּנָתוֹ:
קא א ב לְדָוִד מִזְמוֹר חֶסֶד־וּמִשְׁפָּט אָשִׁירָה לְךָ יהוה אֲזַמֵּרָה: אַשְׂכִּילָה ׀ בְּדֶרֶךְ תָּמִים יד
ג מָתַי תָּבוֹא אֵלָי אֶתְהַלֵּךְ בְּתָם־לְבָבִי בְּקֶרֶב בֵּיתִי: לֹא־אָשִׁית ׀ לְנֶגֶד עֵינַי דְּבַר־
ד בְּלִיָּעַל עֲשֹׂה־סֵטִים שָׂנֵאתִי לֹא יִדְבַּק בִּי: לֵבָב עִקֵּשׁ יָסוּר מִמֶּנִּי רָע לֹא אֵדָע:
ה מלושני בַסֵּתֶר ׀ רֵעֵהוּ אוֹתוֹ אַצְמִית גְּבַהּ־עֵינַיִם וּרְחַב לֵבָב אֹתוֹ לֹא אוּכָל: מְלָשְׁנִי
ו ז עֵינַי ׀ בְּנֶאֶמְנֵי־אֶרֶץ לָשֶׁבֶת עִמָּדִי הֹלֵךְ בְּדֶרֶךְ תָּמִים הוּא יְשָׁרְתֵנִי: לֹא־יֵשֵׁב ׀
ח בְּקֶרֶב בֵּיתִי עֹשֵׂה רְמִיָּה דֹּבֵר שְׁקָרִים לֹא־יִכּוֹן לְנֶגֶד עֵינָי: לַבְּקָרִים אַצְמִית כָּל־
רִשְׁעֵי־אָרֶץ לְהַכְרִית מֵעִיר־יהוה כָּל־פֹּעֲלֵי אָוֶן:
קב א ב תְּפִלָּה לְעָנִי כִי־יַעֲטֹף וְלִפְנֵי יהוה יִשְׁפֹּךְ שִׂיחוֹ: יהוה שִׁמְעָה תְפִלָּתִי וְשַׁוְעָתִי
ג אֵלֶיךָ תָבוֹא: אַל־תַּסְתֵּר פָּנֶיךָ ׀ מִמֶּנִּי בְּיוֹם צַר לִי הַטֵּה־אֵלַי אָזְנֶךָ בְּיוֹם אֶקְרָא
ד ה מַהֵר עֲנֵנִי: כִּי־כָלוּ בְעָשָׁן יָמָי וְעַצְמוֹתַי כְּמוֹקֵד נִחָרוּ: הוּכָּה כָעֵשֶׂב וַיִּבַשׁ לִבִּי כִּי־
ו ז שָׁכַחְתִּי מֵאֲכֹל לַחְמִי: מִקּוֹל אַנְחָתִי דָּבְקָה עַצְמִי לִבְשָׂרִי: דָּמִיתִי לִקְאַת מִדְבָּר

BACKGROUND

102:7 | **Desert owl:** This is a predatory bird that lives in desolate, deserted areas. It is listed in the Torah as one of the birds that are forbidden to be eaten (Leviticus 11:18; Deuteronomy 14:17). Its name, *ke'a*, related to *ki*, vomit, indicates that it is a bird that spits out pellets, conglomerates of pieces of indigestible food, as is typical of night-time predators. Some identify the bird with *Strix butleri*, the Omani owl, or with the eagle owl, which is active in deserts. Others identify it as the houbara bustard, a large land bird with long legs and neck, whose height can reach 65 cm and whose wingspan is up to 150 cm.

Owl of the ruins: The Aramaic translations of this term, as well as that of the Septuagint, and most commentators and researchers, identify this bird as the one that is called in modern Hebrew *kos*, which is the Saharan little owl, *Athene noctue saharae*. This type of owl is a nighttime predator whose length can reach 22 cm, with a wingspan of 56 cm. The adult weighs up to 180 g. It is found mostly in open areas, often in ruins or rocky terrain. Like the desert owl, it produces a mournful sound.

8 **I am fixed in place,** unable to move from where I am, **and I am like a lonely bird on a rooftop,** with no one coming to my aid.
9 **My enemies taunt me all day long; my pursuers swear oaths by me,** using my name as a paradigm of wretchedness.
10 **I eat ashes as if bread.** Placing ashes on the head or dipping one's food in ashes is a sign of mourning. In my current state, the psalmist says, instead of just dipping my bread in ashes, the ashes have become my food, in place of bread, **and** all of **my drink is mixed with tears**
11 **because of Your wrath and Your fury,** which are the ultimate source of my suffering. **Indeed, You lifted me up and flung me away.** You lifted me up just as one picks up an object in order to cast it away.
12 **My days are like a cast shadow,** which has no tangible substance and constantly shifts in accordance with the moving of the sun. **And I wither away like grass** that is not watered.
13 Up to this point, the psalmist has described the pain and affliction of the poor man who is overwhelmed by hardship. Despite his suffering, he has faith and trust in God: **But You, Lord, abide forever,** without interruption or diminishment; **Your remembrance** is recalled **throughout the generations.**
14 And when it is Your will to show us grace, **You will arise** from Your place, as it were, **and have compassion for Zion, for it is time to be gracious to her, for the appointed time has come.**
15 Because we are devoted to You, we are determined to remain in Jerusalem, near Your Temple. **For Your servants desire her** very **stones and cherish her** very **dust,** loving even the inanimate and barren stones and dirt.
16 Therefore we pray: **May nations** also come to **fear the name of the Lord, and** may **all kings of the earth** learn to revere **Your glory,**
17 **when the Lord rebuilds Zion and is seen in His glory.**
18 **He has heeded the prayer of the juniper.**[B] The psalmist depicts one who is alone and without support as an *ar'ar*, a juniper, which is a desert shrub that can survive on very little water, but does not bear fruit. The word is related to *ariri*, meaning childless. **He did not despise their prayer.**
19 **Let this** divine salvation **be recorded for the generation to come, so that those yet to be born may praise the Lord.**
20 **For He gazed down from His holy height** to take note and to intervene in the events of this world; **from heaven the Lord looked upon the earth,**
21 **to hear the groaning of the captive, to unshackle those doomed to death,**
22 **so that the name of the Lord in Zion may be told, and His praise in Jerusalem,**
23 **when the peoples are gathered together** there in Jerusalem, **and kingdoms come** there **to serve the Lord.**
24 The psalmist believes that this redemption will come, and he prays that he may live to witness it. But in the meantime, his current state remains precarious: **Along the way,** along life's path as we await the future redemption, **He has weakened my strength,** and I feel as if **He has shortened my days.**
25 Therefore **I said** in prayer to Him: **My God, do not take me up in the midst of my days,** that is, do not bring an end to my life; **Your years last for all generations,** and You can grant me a long life.
26 **You laid the foundations of earth in times past,** at Creation; **the heavens are the work of Your hands.**
27 **Even they,** the works of Your hands, **will perish, but You will endure** forever. **All of them will wear out like a garment; You will change them like clothing, and they will be gone.** All the creations of the world will eventually wear out and be replaced.
28 **But You are He** who exists forever, **Your years never ending.**
29 Since You are eternal and omnipotent, You have the power to ensure that **the children of Your servants will dwell safely** and not be driven from their homes, **their descendants standing firmly before You** for all time.

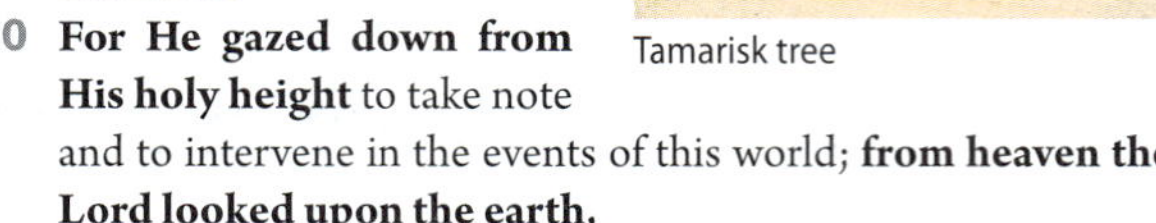
Tamarisk tree

BACKGROUND

102:18 | **Juniper:** Many possible identifications have been offered for this tree, called *ar'ar* in Hebrew: The tamarisk, *Tamarix*; tumbleweed, *Gundelia tournefortii*; and a short tree called *Edom arar* in modern Hebrew, *Juniperus phoenicea*. The last is a coniferous plant of the cypress family, which grows along the cliffs of Edom and the Arava. In dry areas its diminutive size makes it appear like a low bush, and it may even spread out along the ground itself.

103:5 | **Eagle [*nesher*]:** Many identify the *nesher*, or the Akkadian *nashru*, with the vulture, *Gyps fulvus*, a large bird characterized by its unique glide, its high nesting habits, and its swift swooping movements onto its prey, usually carrion (See Deuteronomy 28:49; Jeremiah 48:40; Obadiah 1:4; Micah 1:16; Habakkuk 1:8; Proverbs 23:5; Job 39:27–28). A similar bird was the imperial symbol of Egypt and Assyria. Its wingspan can reach 2.5 m, and it weighs approximately 10 kg. Its head and neck are without feathers, giving the impression that it has shed [*nashar*] them, which may be the source of its name. Some identify the *nesher* as the eagle, *Aquila chrysaetos*, which was used as an imperial symbol in the Roman period. Other researchers maintain that the *nesher* is a generic name for a number of large predatory birds.

ח ט הָיִיתִי כְּכוֹס חֳרָבוֹת: שָׁקַדְתִּי וָאֶהְיֶה כְּצִפּוֹר בּוֹדֵד עַל־גָּג: כָּל־הַיּוֹם חֵרְפוּנִי אוֹיְבָי
י יא מְהוֹלָלַי בִּי נִשְׁבָּעוּ: כִּי־אֵפֶר כַּלֶּחֶם אָכָלְתִּי וְשִׁקֻּוַי בִּבְכִי מָסָכְתִּי: מִפְּנֵי־זַעַמְךָ
יב יג וְקִצְפֶּךָ כִּי נְשָׂאתַנִי וַתַּשְׁלִיכֵנִי: יָמַי כְּצֵל נָטוּי וַאֲנִי כָּעֵשֶׂב אִיבָשׁ: וְאַתָּה יְהוָה
יד לְעוֹלָם תֵּשֵׁב וְזִכְרְךָ לְדֹר וָדֹר: אַתָּה תָקוּם תְּרַחֵם צִיּוֹן כִּי־עֵת לְחֶנְנָהּ כִּי־בָא
טו טז מוֹעֵד: כִּי־רָצוּ עֲבָדֶיךָ אֶת־אֲבָנֶיהָ וְאֶת־עֲפָרָהּ יְחֹנֵנוּ: וְיִירְאוּ גוֹיִם אֶת־שֵׁם יְהוָה
יז יח וְכָל־מַלְכֵי הָאָרֶץ אֶת־כְּבוֹדֶךָ: כִּי־בָנָה יְהוָה צִיּוֹן נִרְאָה בִּכְבוֹדוֹ: פָּנָה אֶל־תְּפִלַּת
יט הָעַרְעָר וְלֹא־בָזָה אֶת־תְּפִלָּתָם: תִּכָּתֶב זֹאת לְדוֹר אַחֲרוֹן וְעַם נִבְרָא יְהַלֶּל־
כ כא יָהּ: כִּי־הִשְׁקִיף מִמְּרוֹם קָדְשׁוֹ יְהוָה מִשָּׁמַיִם ׀ אֶל־אֶרֶץ הִבִּיט: לִשְׁמֹעַ אֶנְקַת
כב כג אָסִיר לְפַתֵּחַ בְּנֵי תְמוּתָה: לְסַפֵּר בְּצִיּוֹן שֵׁם יְהוָה וּתְהִלָּתוֹ בִּירוּשָׁלִָם: בְּהִקָּבֵץ
כד כה עַמִּים יַחְדָּו וּמַמְלָכוֹת לַעֲבֹד אֶת־יְהוָה: עִנָּה בַדֶּרֶךְ כחו קִצַּר יָמָי: אֹמַר אֵלִי כֹּחִי
כו אַל־תַּעֲלֵנִי בַּחֲצִי יָמָי בְּדוֹר דּוֹרִים שְׁנוֹתֶיךָ: לְפָנִים הָאָרֶץ יָסַדְתָּ וּמַעֲשֵׂה יָדֶיךָ
כז שָׁמָיִם: הֵמָּה ׀ יֹאבֵדוּ וְאַתָּה תַעֲמֹד וְכֻלָּם כַּבֶּגֶד יִבְלוּ כַּלְּבוּשׁ תַּחֲלִיפֵם וְיַחֲלֹפוּ:
כח כט וְאַתָּה־הוּא וּשְׁנוֹתֶיךָ לֹא יִתָּמּוּ: בְּנֵי־עֲבָדֶיךָ יִשְׁכּוֹנוּ וְזַרְעָם לְפָנֶיךָ יִכּוֹן:
קג א ב לְדָוִד ׀ בָּרְכִי נַפְשִׁי אֶת־יְהוָה וְכָל־קְרָבַי אֶת־שֵׁם קָדְשׁוֹ: בָּרְכִי נַפְשִׁי אֶת־יְהוָה
ג ד וְאַל־תִּשְׁכְּחִי כָּל־גְּמוּלָיו: הַסֹּלֵחַ לְכָל־עֲוֺנֵכִי הָרֹפֵא לְכָל־תַּחֲלֻאָיְכִי: הַגּוֹאֵל
ה מִשַּׁחַת חַיָּיְכִי הַמְעַטְּרֵכִי חֶסֶד וְרַחֲמִים: הַמַּשְׂבִּיעַ בַּטּוֹב עֶדְיֵךְ תִּתְחַדֵּשׁ כַּנֶּשֶׁר

PSALM 103

PSALMS 103:1–22

The first of two consecutive psalms beginning with the phrase "Bless the Lord, my soul." It deals mainly with the vicissitudes of human life, in both the physical and the spiritual realms. It also contains words of praise and supplication.

103 1 **By David. Bless the Lord, my soul, and all that is within me bless His holy name.**

2 **Bless the Lord, my soul, and do not forget all His acts of kindness.** In times of peace and abundance, people often forget God's past acts of beneficence; the psalmist warns against this.

3 **It is He who forgives all your iniquities, who heals all your diseases,** referring to both physical and spiritual ailments;

4 **who redeems your life from the pit** of the grave, from death; **who crowns you,** surrounds you, **with kindness and mercy;**

5 **who sates your spirit with good.** *Edyekh*, translated here as "your spirit," literally means an ornament, an item of beautification. Here it refers to the "beauty" of one's life, the spirit. Another interpretation of the word is "your body." **Your youth renewed like an eagle.**[B] Eagles live longer than other birds, and also retain their power and strength.

Vulture

6 The psalmist turns to another aspect of God's praises: **The Lord performs righteous deeds and metes out justice to all the oppressed.** Although people often undergo suffering, God ultimately delivers justice and rescues them from their enemies.

7 Proof for this can be brought not only from the experience of individuals, but also from history: **He made His ways known to Moses,** showing him repeatedly how He saved Israel from all the perils facing them, and proved **His deeds to the children of Israel.** The entire nation witnessed firsthand His miraculous deeds, from the exodus from Egypt onward.

8 **Merciful and gracious is the Lord, slow to anger and abounding in kindness.** This is an allusion to God's revelation to Moses by the cleft in the rock,[60] where He revealed His attributes of mercy, which include the words of this verse.

9 Even in times of trouble, we can take comfort in the fact that **He will not contend** with us **to eternity or forever keep His anger;** eventually He will forgive us and once again be our Protector.

10 **He has not dealt with us** as harshly **as** truly **befits our sins; He has not requited our iniquities in kind.**

11 **Rather, as high as the heavens above the earth, so is His kindness great for those who fear Him.**

12 **As far as east is from west, so has He distanced our transgressions from us,** in that He no longer remembers them or associates us with them.

13 **Just as a father has mercy on his children, so the Lord has mercy on those who fear Him.** God is merciful toward us, not necessarily because we are righteous, but because we are weak and are dependent on Him.

14 God is aware of how powerless we are and how much we need His kindness and mercy, **for He knows** how intense **our** evil **impulses** are, so likely to cause us to veer from the proper path. **He is mindful that we are but dust,** physical beings, children of the earth, and that because of this, He cannot expect perfection from us.

15 **As for man, his days are like grass,**[B] which dries up and withers. **He springs up** fleetingly **like a bud** of a wildflower **in the field,** which wilts shortly after it appears,

"His days are like grass"

"Bud in the field"

16 and **which, when a** hot east **wind passes over it, it** dries out and **ceases to be; its own place knows it no more,** as no trace of it remains.

17 **But** in contrast to man's fleeting, ephemeral existence, **the kindness of the Lord is forever to those who fear Him; His righteousness** extends even **for the children's progeny,**

18 **for those who keep His covenant and remember His precepts to observe them.**

19 **The Lord has established His throne in the heavens; His kingship rules over all** facets of creation.

20 The psalmist suggests words of praise that we humans, despite our limited power and brief life spans, can offer to God, by calling out to the angels: **Bless the Lord, His angels,** who are truly capable of praising Him properly, for they are **mighty in strength,** beings **who do His bidding** and whose entire reason for existence is the **heeding** of **His word.**

21 **Bless the Lord, all His hosts, His servants who do His will,** namely, all the creatures of the world, from the most exalted to the lowest.

22 **Bless the Lord, all of His works,** all of His creations, **in all places of His dominion,** throughout the entire universe. **Bless the Lord, my soul.** In reiterating the opening words of the psalm, "Bless the Lord, my soul," the psalmist emphasizes that this personal prayer is part of a universal chorus of praise.

BACKGROUND

103:15 | **Grass:** This term [*hatzir*] is applied to two different kinds of vegetation: the leek (see Numbers 11:5), and a grass-like covering of land unfit or inconvenient for cultivation. When the rains cease in summer and hot winds begin to blow, this latter vegetation dries out and remains withered throughout the summer. They are like the grassy spots that sprout on the roofs of stony structures and near drainpipes; as long as there is a water supply they thrive, but when that source disappears they dry out quickly.

ו ז נְעוּרָיְכִי׃ עֹשֵׂה צְדָקוֹת יְהוָה וּמִשְׁפָּטִים לְכָל־עֲשׁוּקִים׃ יוֹדִיעַ דְּרָכָיו לְמֹשֶׁה
ח ט לִבְנֵי יִשְׂרָאֵל עֲלִילוֹתָיו׃ רַחוּם וְחַנּוּן יְהוָה אֶרֶךְ אַפַּיִם וְרַב־חָסֶד׃ לֹא־לָנֶצַח יָרִיב
י יא וְלֹא לְעוֹלָם יִטּוֹר׃ לֹא כַחֲטָאֵינוּ עָשָׂה לָנוּ וְלֹא כַעֲוֺנֹתֵינוּ גָּמַל עָלֵינוּ׃ כִּי כִגְבֹהַּ
יב שָׁמַיִם עַל־הָאָרֶץ גָּבַר חַסְדּוֹ עַל־יְרֵאָיו׃ כִּרְחֹק מִזְרָח מִמַּעֲרָב הִרְחִיק מִמֶּנּוּ
יג יד אֶת־פְּשָׁעֵינוּ׃ כְּרַחֵם אָב עַל־בָּנִים רִחַם יְהוָה עַל־יְרֵאָיו׃ כִּי־הוּא יָדַע יִצְרֵנוּ
טו טז זָכוּר כִּי־עָפָר אֲנָחְנוּ׃ אֱנוֹשׁ כֶּחָצִיר יָמָיו כְּצִיץ הַשָּׂדֶה כֵּן יָצִיץ׃ כִּי רוּחַ עָבְרָה־
יז בּוֹ וְאֵינֶנּוּ וְלֹא־יַכִּירֶנּוּ עוֹד מְקוֹמוֹ׃ וְחֶסֶד יְהוָה ׀ מֵעוֹלָם וְעַד־עוֹלָם עַל־יְרֵאָיו
יח יט וְצִדְקָתוֹ לִבְנֵי בָנִים׃ לְשֹׁמְרֵי בְרִיתוֹ וּלְזֹכְרֵי פִקֻּדָיו לַעֲשׂוֹתָם׃ יְהוָה בַּשָּׁמַיִם הֵכִין
כ כִּסְאוֹ וּמַלְכוּתוֹ בַּכֹּל מָשָׁלָה׃ בָּרְכוּ יְהוָה מַלְאָכָיו גִּבֹּרֵי כֹחַ עֹשֵׂי דְבָרוֹ לִשְׁמֹעַ
כא כב בְּקוֹל דְּבָרוֹ׃ בָּרְכוּ יְהוָה כָּל־צְבָאָיו מְשָׁרְתָיו עֹשֵׂי רְצוֹנוֹ׃ בָּרְכוּ יְהוָה ׀ כָּל־מַעֲשָׂיו
בְּכָל־מְקֹמוֹת מֶמְשַׁלְתּוֹ בָּרְכִי נַפְשִׁי אֶת־יְהוָה׃
קד א ב בָּרְכִי נַפְשִׁי אֶת־יְהוָה יְהוָה אֱלֹהַי גָּדַלְתָּ מְּאֹד הוֹד וְהָדָר לָבָשְׁתָּ׃ עֹטֶה־אוֹר (כא לחודש)
ג כַּשַּׂלְמָה נוֹטֶה שָׁמַיִם כַּיְרִיעָה׃ הַמְקָרֶה בַמַּיִם עֲלִיּוֹתָיו הַשָּׂם־עָבִים רְכוּבוֹ
ד ה הַמְהַלֵּךְ עַל־כַּנְפֵי־רוּחַ׃ עֹשֶׂה מַלְאָכָיו רוּחוֹת מְשָׁרְתָיו אֵשׁ לֹהֵט׃ יָסַד־אֶרֶץ

PSALM 104

PSALMS 104:1–35

The second of two consecutive psalms beginning with the phrase "Bless the Lord, my soul." This is a hymn in praise of everything created by God, and it depicts the grand design of the world, of which man is but a small part.

104 *21st day of month*

1 **Bless the Lord, my soul.** This is more than an introductory phrase; it also evokes the spirit of this psalm, which is an outpouring of praise from an individual's point of view rather than a more dispassionate or seemingly objective outline of God's creation. The person praising God is central to this hymn of praise. **Lord my God, You are greatly exalted; You are clothed in splendor and glory.** The psalm begins with praise of God Himself before shifting to a broader, more detailed description of the world, depicted here as a kind of ornament or apparel for God.

2 **Enveloping** the world **with light as if with a cloak.** The expression *oteh or kasalma* is interpreted in other contexts as referring to God wrapping Himself, as it were, in a garment of light. Here, however, the explanation is that He envelops the world with light. **He spreads out the heavens like a tent cloth.**

3 **He covers His upper chambers with water.** As related in Genesis,[61] the heavens, called here the "upper chambers," are described as covered over with water. **He makes clouds His chariot; He moves on wings of wind.** God rides, as it were, upon the clouds and through the wind.

4 **He makes the winds His messengers** as they do His bidding, **the flaming fires His servants.**

5 **He established the earth on its foundations, never to be shaken.**

6 **He covered the depths,** the great subterranean stores of water, **as** one covers himself **with a garment;** He covered the depths with land. But at first, in the early stages of creation, **waters stood above** the entire earth, including **the mountains.**[62]

7 The waters covered the earth until God issued the command: "Let the water beneath the heavens be gathered to one place, and let the dry land appear."[63] Thereupon, **at Your rebuke they fled; at the sound of Your thunder they hastened away.** The next two verses provide further detail of this phenomenon.

8 **They rose to the mountains** and **descended in the valleys,** until they arrived at the sea, **to the place You established for them.**

9 After the waters converged into the seas, **You set a boundary,** the seashore, which **they could not cross, so they would not come back to cover the earth.**

10 Besides what is found in subterranean stores and in the sea, there is yet another source of water in the world: **He sends forth springs,** feeding streams that course **through the ravines; between the mountains they flow.**

11 Water is ubiquitous in nature, present in desolate as well as settled areas. But though it is an inanimate part of nature, it is closely linked to living creatures, for these waters sustain life: **They give drink to all beasts of the field; wild asses**[B] **quench their thirst** with them.

Asiatic wild asses

12 **Birds of the sky dwell alongside them,** as well as among the vegetation that grows near the streams, **giving voice among the branches.**

"Giving voice among the branches." Red-breasted robin singing

13 **He waters the mountains,** too high to obtain water from the springs, with rain that falls **from His upper chambers,** the heavens; **the earth is sated with the product of Your works,** the rain.

14 And through that rainfall, **He makes grass grow for the cattle, and vegetation for the labor of man,** for the beasts of burden with which he does his work, as well as ears of grain **for bringing forth bread from the earth** for man to eat.

15 **And** in addition to these, He brings forth from the ground grapes for **wine, which gladdens man's heart,** as well as olives, **making the face glisten from** their **oil,** by applying it to the skin as a moisturizer. **And bread, to sustain man's heart.** The three basic staples of life: bread, wine, and oil, all sprout from the earth, with the help of the rains.

16 **The trees of the Lord,** that is, trees of vast proportion, **sate themselves** from the rainwater and from the ground's nutrients; **the cedars of Lebanon** are a specific example of a very large tree **that He planted.**

"The stork has its home in the junipers"

17 In those trees is **where birds make their nests; the stork has its home in the junipers.**

18 **The high mountains are** habitats **for the ibex, the rocks a shelter for the hyrax.** Like the ibex, the rock hyrax, also known as the rock badger, lives in the mountains, and hide among the crags of the mountains for better protection from eagles.

"High mountains are for the ibex"

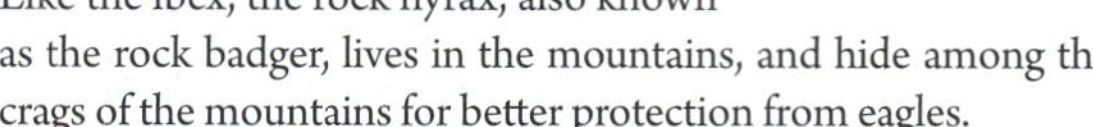

"Crags a shelter for the hyrax"

19 Having provided a geographical description of the world and all that grows in it, the psalmist shifts his attention to another aspect of the world, time: **He made the moon for appointed times,** by which dates of the month are established; **the sun knows its setting.** Whereas the movements of the moon are not completely regular, and its times of rising and setting change over the course of the month, the sun "knows" when to set, following a predictable pattern.

20 Shifts in time also affect the daily cycle of life: **You bring darkness and it becomes night, when all the beasts of the forest are astir,** as the animals of the forest, especially the predators, are active mostly at night.

21 **The young lions roar for prey, asking the Almighty for their food.** The roar of a lion sets its prey running in the direction that is most desirable for the lion; moreover, the prey is easier to spot and pursue when it runs. The psalmist poetically sees in the lion's roar not only a means to catch its prey, but also a kind of plea to God for food.

22 **When the sun rises they withdraw** and return to their lairs, **and crouch in their dens.**

23 At that point, when daylight arrives, **man goes out to his work and to his labor until evening.**

24 The psalmist exclaims his awe and wonder at God's works: **Lord, how manifold are Your deeds, in wisdom have**

ו עַל־מְכוֹנֶיהָ בַּל־תִּמּוֹט עוֹלָם וָעֶד׃ תְּהוֹם כַּלְּבוּשׁ כִּסִּיתוֹ עַל־הָרִים יַעַמְדוּ־מָיִם׃
ז ח מִן־גַּעֲרָתְךָ יְנוּסוּן מִן־קוֹל רַעַמְךָ יֵחָפֵזוּן׃ יַעֲלוּ הָרִים יֵרְדוּ בְקָעוֹת אֶל־מְקוֹם
ט י זֶה ׀ יָסַדְתָּ לָהֶם׃ גְּבוּל־שַׂמְתָּ בַּל־יַעֲבֹרוּן בַּל־יְשׁוּבוּן לְכַסּוֹת הָאָרֶץ׃ הַמְשַׁלֵּחַ
יא מַעְיָנִים בַּנְּחָלִים בֵּין הָרִים יְהַלֵּכוּן׃ יַשְׁקוּ כָּל־חַיְתוֹ שָׂדָי יִשְׁבְּרוּ פְרָאִים צְמָאָם׃
יב יג עֲלֵיהֶם עוֹף־הַשָּׁמַיִם יִשְׁכּוֹן מִבֵּין עֳפָאיִם יִתְּנוּ־קוֹל׃ מַשְׁקֶה הָרִים מֵעֲלִיּוֹתָיו
יד מִפְּרִי מַעֲשֶׂיךָ תִּשְׂבַּע הָאָרֶץ׃ מַצְמִיחַ חָצִיר ׀ לַבְּהֵמָה וְעֵשֶׂב לַעֲבֹדַת הָאָדָם
טו לְהוֹצִיא לֶחֶם מִן־הָאָרֶץ׃ וְיַיִן ׀ יְשַׂמַּח לְבַב־אֱנוֹשׁ לְהַצְהִיל פָּנִים מִשָּׁמֶן וְלֶחֶם
טז יז לְבַב־אֱנוֹשׁ יִסְעָד׃ יִשְׂבְּעוּ עֲצֵי יהוה אַרְזֵי לְבָנוֹן אֲשֶׁר נָטָע׃ אֲשֶׁר־שָׁם צִפֳּרִים
יח יְקַנֵּנוּ חֲסִידָה בְּרוֹשִׁים בֵּיתָהּ׃ הָרִים הַגְּבֹהִים לַיְּעֵלִים סְלָעִים מַחְסֶה לַשְׁפַנִּים׃
יט כ עָשָׂה יָרֵחַ לְמוֹעֲדִים שֶׁמֶשׁ יָדַע מְבוֹאוֹ׃ תָּשֶׁת־חֹשֶׁךְ וִיהִי לָיְלָה בּוֹ־תִרְמֹשׂ כָּל־
כא כב חַיְתוֹ־יָעַר׃ הַכְּפִירִים שֹׁאֲגִים לַטָּרֶף וּלְבַקֵּשׁ מֵאֵל אָכְלָם׃ תִּזְרַח הַשֶּׁמֶשׁ יֵאָסֵפוּן
כג כד וְאֶל־מְעוֹנֹתָם יִרְבָּצוּן׃ יֵצֵא אָדָם לְפָעֳלוֹ וְלַעֲבֹדָתוֹ עֲדֵי־עָרֶב׃ מָה־רַבּוּ מַעֲשֶׂיךָ ׀
כה יהוה כֻּלָּם בְּחָכְמָה עָשִׂיתָ מָלְאָה הָאָרֶץ קִנְיָנֶךָ׃ זֶה ׀ הַיָּם גָּדוֹל וּרְחַב יָדַיִם שָׁם־
כו רֶמֶשׂ וְאֵין מִסְפָּר חַיּוֹת קְטַנּוֹת עִם־גְּדֹלוֹת׃ שָׁם אֳנִיּוֹת יְהַלֵּכוּן לִוְיָתָן זֶה־יָצַרְתָּ

You made them all. Everything You created has its own unique niche and set of interactions with other creatures and with the environment as a whole. **The earth is full of Your possessions.**

25 Until this point, the psalmist has described the wonders of life on earth; here he proceeds to describe an area less visible to the human eye: **There is the sea, vast and broad; an innumerable swarm** of organisms **is in it, creatures both great and small.**

26 The sea is so vast that **there ships go,** traveling great distances; **and** it can house **the leviathan,** a giant sea creature, **which You created to frolic with,** as it were. Although it is massive beyond the dimensions of any other creature, even the leviathan is like a plaything in God's hands.

BACKGROUND

104:11 | **Wild asses:** The Asiatic wild ass, *Equus hemionus*, or in talmudic Hebrew *arod*, is the smallest of the undomesticated animals of the horse family. It is brownish gray with a dark mane, and it has a dark stripe that stretches along the spine from neck to tail. It is swift and difficult to catch and cannot be domesticated. This animal lives in the desert and used to be found throughout the Negev, the Judean Desert, in the deserts of northern Arabia, on the east bank of the Jordan, and in Syria up to the Euphrates, but it became extinct in those areas in the beginning of the last century. It was recently reintroduced to the area, and is found today near Mitzpe Ramon.

27 **They all,** all the creatures of the sea, land, and air mentioned earlier, **fix their hopes on You,** their true source of sustenance, **to give them their food at the proper time.**

28 **When You give it to them, they gather it.** At times, the food is available, but the creatures must search for it and gather what they can; at other times, **when You open Your hand** and release all Your bounty, **they are sated** amply **with good.**

29 On the other hand, there are also times **when You hide Your face,** withholding Your goodness from them. Since they are completely dependent on Your kindness, **they take fright,** distraught from the lack of sustenance. Moreover, eventually all life comes to an end; **when You take away their spirit, they die and return to their dust.**

30 Yet **when You send forth Your spirit, they are created.** Your creative spirit can also renew life, and **You renew the face of the land.**

31 Having completed his description of all the various creatures and their circumstances, the psalmist concludes: **May the glory of the Lord endure forever. May the Lord rejoice in His works.**

32 While God's glory is evident in the everyday functioning of the world, there are also occasions when God reveals His power in a more dramatic fashion: **He who looks at the earth, and it trembles** just from His stern gaze, like a servant who quakes at his master's scowl. **Who touches the mountains, and they smoke.** At a touch from God, as it were, volcanos spew fire and smoke.

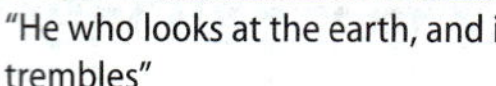

"He who looks at the earth, and it trembles"

"Who touches the mountains, and they smoke"

33 The psalmist now adds his personal note of praise: **I will sing to the Lord as long as I live; I will sing praise to my God as long as I am able.**

34 **May my utterance please Him,** may He accept it favorably. But in any event, **I rejoice in the Lord.**

35 After completing this description of the universe as a single, interconnected, harmonious entity comprised of countless varied parts and life forms, all of which are the work of God's hands, the psalmist cannot refrain from noting that there are those who spoil its beauty and perfection. It is for them that he prays at the end of this hymn: **May sinners be removed from the earth, and may the wicked be no more.** The psalmist concludes with the same words with which he opened the psalm: **Bless the Lord, my soul. Halleluya.** This word can be interpreted in two ways. It may be a composite of the two words *hallelu Ya*, meaning "praise the Lord." Alternatively, it may be understood as a single word, an expansion of the word *hallel*,[64] in which case it means "a great praise."

PSALM 105

PSALMS 105:1–45

A song expressing gratitude to God for His kindness throughout the generations. This psalm comprises an abbreviated account of the history of Israel until after the conquest of the land. Like Psalm 68, it is written in the form of an epic poem; it differs in that its tone is peaceful and serene rather than majestic or heroic.

105 1 The psalm begins with a celebratory declaration: **Give thanks to the Lord; proclaim His name.** This statement makes it clear from the outset that what follows is a song of thanksgiving to God for all He has done on our behalf. **Make His deeds known among the peoples.**

2 **Sing to Him, sing praises to Him. Speak of all His wonders,** referring not only to specific miraculous events, but to God's continual watching over us.

3 **Glory in His holy name,** and, through recalling the miracles He performed for us, **let the hearts of those who seek the Lord rejoice.**

4 **Search out the Lord and His strength; seek His presence always.**

5 **Remember the wonders He has done, His marvels, and the judgments of His mouth.** Remember not only God's miraculous deeds, but also His commandments.

DISCUSSION

105:8 | **For a thousand generations:** This expression does not refer to an exact number; rather it refers to a large amount in general. It is found in a similar sense in the Torah: "Who engages in kindness for the thousands" (Exodus 20:6), and "shall add to you one thousand times as you are" (Deuteronomy 1:11; see also Exodus 34:7; Deuteronomy 5:10).

כז כח לְשַׂחֶק־בּוֹ׃ כֻּלָּם אֵלֶיךָ יְשַׂבֵּרוּן לָתֵת אָכְלָם בְּעִתּוֹ׃ תִּתֵּן לָהֶם יִלְקֹטוּן תִּפְתַּח
כט יָדְךָ יִשְׂבְּעוּן טוֹב׃ תַּסְתִּיר פָּנֶיךָ יִבָּהֵלוּן תֹּסֵף רוּחָם יִגְוָעוּן וְאֶל־עֲפָרָם יְשׁוּבוּן׃
ל לא תְּשַׁלַּח רוּחֲךָ יִבָּרֵאוּן וּתְחַדֵּשׁ פְּנֵי אֲדָמָה׃ יְהִי כְבוֹד יְהוָה לְעוֹלָם יִשְׂמַח יְהוָה
לב לג בְּמַעֲשָׂיו׃ הַמַּבִּיט לָאָרֶץ וַתִּרְעָד יִגַּע בֶּהָרִים וְיֶעֱשָׁנוּ׃ אָשִׁירָה לַיהוָה בְּחַיָּי
לד לה אֲזַמְּרָה לֵאלֹהַי בְּעוֹדִי׃ יֶעֱרַב עָלָיו שִׂיחִי אָנֹכִי אֶשְׂמַח בַּיהוָה׃ יִתַּמּוּ חַטָּאִים ׀
מִן־הָאָרֶץ וּרְשָׁעִים ׀ עוֹד אֵינָם בָּרְכִי נַפְשִׁי אֶת־יְהוָה הַלְלוּ־יָהּ׃
קה א ב הוֹדוּ לַיהוָה קִרְאוּ בִּשְׁמוֹ הוֹדִיעוּ בָעַמִּים עֲלִילוֹתָיו׃ שִׁירוּ־לוֹ זַמְּרוּ־לוֹ שִׂיחוּ
ג ד בְּכָל־נִפְלְאוֹתָיו׃ הִתְהַלְלוּ בְּשֵׁם קָדְשׁוֹ יִשְׂמַח לֵב ׀ מְבַקְשֵׁי יְהוָה׃ דִּרְשׁוּ יְהוָה
ה ו וְעֻזּוֹ בַּקְּשׁוּ פָנָיו תָּמִיד׃ זִכְרוּ נִפְלְאוֹתָיו אֲשֶׁר־עָשָׂה מֹפְתָיו וּמִשְׁפְּטֵי־פִיו׃ זֶרַע
ז ח אַבְרָהָם עַבְדּוֹ בְּנֵי יַעֲקֹב בְּחִירָיו׃ הוּא יְהוָה אֱלֹהֵינוּ בְּכָל־הָאָרֶץ מִשְׁפָּטָיו׃ זָכַר
ט לְעוֹלָם בְּרִיתוֹ דָּבָר צִוָּה לְאֶלֶף דּוֹר׃ אֲשֶׁר כָּרַת אֶת־אַבְרָהָם וּשְׁבוּעָתוֹ לְיִשְׂחָק׃
י יא וַיַּעֲמִידֶהָ לְיַעֲקֹב לְחֹק לְיִשְׂרָאֵל בְּרִית עוֹלָם׃ לֵאמֹר לְךָ אֶתֵּן אֶת־אֶרֶץ־כְּנָעַן
יב יג חֶבֶל נַחֲלַתְכֶם׃ בִּהְיוֹתָם מְתֵי מִסְפָּר כִּמְעַט וְגָרִים בָּהּ׃ וַיִּתְהַלְּכוּ מִגּוֹי אֶל־
יד גּוֹי מִמַּמְלָכָה אֶל־עַם אַחֵר׃ לֹא־הִנִּיחַ אָדָם לְעָשְׁקָם וַיּוֹכַח עֲלֵיהֶם מְלָכִים׃

6 **Seed of Abraham, His servant; children of Jacob, His chosen ones,**

7 **He is the Lord our God; His judgments are throughout the land.** His words fill the world, which acts in accordance with His commands.

8 **He remembers His covenant** with the patriarchs **forever, the word that He ordained for a thousand generations.**[D]

9 This is the covenant **which He made with Abraham, and His oath to Isaac.** In this verse Isaac's Hebrew name is spelled *Yisḥak*, a variant of the usual spelling *Yitzḥak*; both words connote laughter, the basis for Isaac's name.[65]

10 **He set it,** this covenant, **for** Isaac's son **Jacob as a statute, for Israel as an everlasting covenant.** The name "Israel" here is synonymous with Jacob, but it also alludes more broadly to the nation of Israel, which descended from him.

11 **Saying: To you I will give the land of Canaan as your allotted portion.** In the covenant, God promised Abraham and, by extension, the nation of Israel, that the people would inherit the land of Canaan. The covenant addresses other issues as well, but since the purpose of this psalm is to express thanks to God for gifts bestowed upon Israel, only the promise of the land is mentioned here.

12 **It,** that covenant, **was** made **when they,** the nascent nation of Israel, **were a small number of people, just a few,** and, moreover, merely **sojourning within it,** not yet permanently settled in the land.

13 **They wandered from nation to nation.** All the patriarchs, Abraham, Isaac, and Jacob, were forced to wander away from the Land of Israel at one time or another, **from one kingdom to another people.** At times, their travels involved interaction with kings of other nations; in other instances, as when Jacob fled to Haran, they merely took up residence among "another people," the commoners.

14 Because of God's covenant with them, however, **He let no man oppress them** during all their travels, **and He** even **reproved**

kings on their account, as it is related in the Torah regarding Abraham and Isaac that God intervened to protect them.[66]
15 God told those kings: **Do not touch my anointed ones,** as the patriarchs, like anointed kings, merited special protection on God's part. **Do not harm My prophets.**[D]
16 Later, when Jacob was old, **He proclaimed a famine on the land; He broke every staff of bread,** every source of sustenance. The famine was so severe it affected even Egypt.
17 But to offset the devastating effects of that famine, **He had sent a man** to Egypt **before them,** namely, **Joseph,** to provide them with relief. Only in retrospect did it become evident that God had arranged for Joseph, **who had been sold as a slave,** to rise to power in Egypt to prepare for the arrival of the children of Israel.
18 When Joseph was enslaved, **they tortured his legs with chains** and **his body was placed in iron,**
19 and he remained in this situation **until the time** for his freedom, as predetermined by **His word, came to pass. The Lord's utterance purged him.** Joseph's suffering as a prisoner served to atone for his previous unworthy deeds.
20 And when that time ordained by God arrived, **He sent a king,** Pharaoh, **to release him** from his incarceration, **a ruler of a people who set him free.**
21 **He** then promoted Joseph and **made him master of his,** Pharaoh's, **house and ruler of all his possessions.**
22 Joseph was granted so much power that he was able **to imprison** even high-ranking **ministers at his will. He,** Joseph, **taught wisdom to his,** Pharaoh's, **elders.** Joseph advised Pharaoh how to avoid the ravages of the impending famine, and this wise counsel was given in the presence of all the elders and royal advisors of Egypt.
23 **Then Israel,** referring to Jacob, but also alluding to the nascent nation of Israel, **came to Egypt, and Jacob sojourned in the land of Ham.**[B]
24 **He,** God, **made His people** Israel **exceedingly fruitful, making them greater than their** Egyptian **foes.**
25 **Their hearts,** the hearts of the Egyptians, **changed** from their previous sympathy and respect for Israel. They began **to hate His people,** due to jealousy and suspicion, and **to harass His servants** with all the oppressive decrees described in the book of Exodus.
26 **He** then **sent Moses His servant, and Aaron, whom He had chosen** first as a prophet and subsequently to be the High Priest.
27 **They,** Moses and Aaron, **set before them,** before the Egyptians, **His signs, marvels in the land of Ham.**

The ten plagues of Egypt, Braginsky Leipnik Haggadah, 1739

28 Next comes a short description of the ten plagues, recounted here in a different order from that found in the book of Exodus: **He sent darkness and made it dark** in Egypt; **they,** Moses and Aaron, faithfully executed God's commands and **did not defy His word,** even though Moses initially voiced his misgivings about God's mode of action.[67]
29 **He turned their waters into blood and killed their fish.**
30 **Their land swarmed with frogs,** which found their way to every place in Egypt, **even in the chambers of their kings.**[68]
31 **He spoke, and wild beasts came; there were lice within all their borders.**
32 **He gave them hail for rain,** which was mixed with **flames of fire**[69] **in their land.**

BACKGROUND

105:23 | **In the land of Ham:** Egypt [*Mitzrayim*] is referred to as the land of Ham because Mitzrayim, the progenitor of the Egyptians, was one of Ham's descendants (Genesis 10:6). Of all of the nations descended from Ham, the Egyptian kingdom was by far the largest and most important.

DISCUSSION

105:15 | **Do not harm My prophets:** In Genesis (20:7), God refers to Abraham as a prophet in speaking to Avimelekh king of Gerar. The patriarchs are all called prophets here because God spoke to them. Their status was thus far higher than would be indicated by their material possessions or political capacities.

טו טז אַל־תִּגְּעוּ בִמְשִׁיחָי וְלִנְבִיאַי אַל־תָּרֵעוּ׃ וַיִּקְרָא רָעָב עַל־הָאָרֶץ כָּל־מַטֵּה־לֶחֶם
יז יח שָׁבָר׃ שָׁלַח לִפְנֵיהֶם אִישׁ לְעֶבֶד נִמְכַּר יוֹסֵף׃ עִנּוּ בַכֶּבֶל רַגְלָיו בַּרְזֶל בָּאָה נַפְשׁוֹ׃ (רַגְלוֹ)
יט כ עַד־עֵת בֹּא־דְבָרוֹ אִמְרַת יְהוָה צְרָפָתְהוּ׃ שָׁלַח מֶלֶךְ וַיַּתִּירֵהוּ מֹשֵׁל עַמִּים
כא כב וַיְפַתְּחֵהוּ׃ שָׂמוֹ אָדוֹן לְבֵיתוֹ וּמֹשֵׁל בְּכָל־קִנְיָנוֹ׃ לֶאְסֹר שָׂרָיו בְּנַפְשׁוֹ וּזְקֵנָיו יְחַכֵּם׃
כג כד וַיָּבֹא יִשְׂרָאֵל מִצְרָיִם וְיַעֲקֹב גָּר בְּאֶרֶץ־חָם׃ וַיֶּפֶר אֶת־עַמּוֹ מְאֹד וַיַּעֲצִמֵהוּ מִצָּרָיו׃
כה כו הָפַךְ לִבָּם לִשְׂנֹא עַמּוֹ לְהִתְנַכֵּל בַּעֲבָדָיו׃ שָׁלַח מֹשֶׁה עַבְדּוֹ אַהֲרֹן אֲשֶׁר בָּחַר־
כז כח בּוֹ׃ שָׂמוּ־בָם דִּבְרֵי אֹתוֹתָיו וּמֹפְתִים בְּאֶרֶץ חָם׃ שָׁלַח חֹשֶׁךְ וַיַּחְשִׁךְ וְלֹא־מָרוּ
כט ל אֶת־דבריו׃ הָפַךְ אֶת־מֵימֵיהֶם לְדָם וַיָּמֶת אֶת־דְּגָתָם׃ שָׁרַץ אַרְצָם צְפַרְדְּעִים (דְּבָרוֹ)
לא לב בְּחַדְרֵי מַלְכֵיהֶם׃ אָמַר וַיָּבֹא עָרֹב כִּנִּים בְּכָל־גְּבוּלָם׃ נָתַן גִּשְׁמֵיהֶם בָּרָד אֵשׁ
לג לד לֶהָבוֹת בְּאַרְצָם׃ וַיַּךְ גַּפְנָם וּתְאֵנָתָם וַיְשַׁבֵּר עֵץ גְּבוּלָם׃ אָמַר וַיָּבֹא אַרְבֶּה וְיֶלֶק
לה לו וְאֵין מִסְפָּר׃ וַיֹּאכַל כָּל־עֵשֶׂב בְּאַרְצָם וַיֹּאכַל פְּרִי אַדְמָתָם׃ וַיַּךְ כָּל־בְּכוֹר בְּאַרְצָם
לז לח רֵאשִׁית לְכָל־אוֹנָם׃ וַיּוֹצִיאֵם בְּכֶסֶף וְזָהָב וְאֵין בִּשְׁבָטָיו כּוֹשֵׁל׃ שָׂמַח מִצְרַיִם
לט מ בְּצֵאתָם כִּי־נָפַל פַּחְדָּם עֲלֵיהֶם׃ פָּרַשׂ עָנָן לְמָסָךְ וְאֵשׁ לְהָאִיר לָיְלָה׃ שָׁאַל וַיָּבֵא
מא מב שְׂלָו וְלֶחֶם שָׁמַיִם יַשְׂבִּיעֵם׃ פָּתַח צוּר וַיָּזוּבוּ מָיִם הָלְכוּ בַּצִּיּוֹת נָהָר׃ כִּי־זָכַר אֶת־

33 **It,** the destructive hail, **struck their vines and their fig trees, and it broke the trees** that grew within all **of their borders.** This was the most significant damage caused by the hail.

34 **He spoke, and locusts came, grasshoppers without number.**

35 **They ate all the vegetation in their land,** and **they ate the fruits of their soil.**

36 Then came the final plague: **He struck down every firstborn in their land, the first fruits of all their vigor,** a biblical expression synonymous with one's firstborn son.[70]

37 And following that final plague, **He brought them,** the Israelites, **out** of Egypt **with** the Egyptians' **silver and gold** taken as spoils; **none among His tribes faltered,** and no one was left behind.

38 As related in the Torah,[71] **Egypt rejoiced in their departure,** eager to be relieved of all the misfortunes that had befallen them, **for their dread,** dread of the Israelites, **had fallen upon them.**

39 The psalmist describes the people's wanderings in the desert after the exodus: **He spread out a cloud like a curtain** by day, with which to protect the people, **and fire to light up the night.**

40 **He,** Moses, **requested** meat from God on behalf of the people, **and He brought quail. He sated them with** manna, **the bread of heaven.**

41 **He opened a rock and water gushed forth** from it.[72] **They traveled through parched lands with a river** of fresh water alongside them.

42 God did all this for the Israelites, **for He remembered His holy word,** the covenant and oath he had made **to Abraham His servant.**

43 **And He brought out His people with joy, His chosen ones with joyous song,** and He led them through the wilderness until they arrived at the Land of Israel.

44 And there **He gave them the lands of nations,** the Canaanites and the surrounding peoples; **they inherited the fruit of the peoples' labor** during their conquest of the Land of Israel.

45 The gift of the land and all the bounty within it was given to Israel by God **so that they would keep His statutes and observe His teachings. Halleluya.**

PSALM 106

PSALMS 106:1–48

A psalm similar to the previous one, offering a poetic historical account of the people of Israel. Unlike Psalm 105, which is written in a tone of peace and serenity, the text here focuses largely on the sins committed by the people and the various ways in which they violated their covenant with God.

106 1 The psalm begins on a positive note with an expression of grati-
22nd day tude to God: **Halleluya. Give thanks to the Lord for He is**
of month **good, for His kindness is everlasting.** This verse is repeated several times throughout the book of Psalms and was apparently a set formulation of praise to God.

2 **Who can recount the mighty deeds of the Lord? Who can tell all His praises?**

3 **Happy are those who heed the law, who act with righteousness at all times.** In a sense, this is a reply to the question posed in the preceding verse. The person who constantly strives to act righteously is the one who deserves to "recount the mighty deeds" and tell all God's praises.

4 The next two verses constitute the only personal note in this psalm: **Remember me, Lord, when You favor Your people.** When the time comes for You to forgive and look favorably upon Your people, remember to count me among them. **Be mindful of me in Your salvation,**

5 **so I might see the prosperity of Your chosen ones, rejoice in the joy of Your nation** Israel, **and glory with Your portion,** referring both to the people and to the Land of Israel.

6 The confessional portion of the psalm begins here. It opens with a succinct acknowledgement of guilt before moving to a broader historical perspective: **We have sinned like our fathers; we have committed iniquity; we have behaved wickedly.**

7 **Our fathers in Egypt did not contemplate Your wonders** even as they occurred before their eyes; **they did not recall Your abundant acts of kindness. They rebelled by the sea, at the Red Sea,** complaining when Pharaoh pursued them to its shores.[73]

8 Nevertheless, **He rescued them** despite their rebelliousness, **for the sake of His name.** He saved them not for their own sake, as they were undeserving, but **to proclaim His might.**

9 **He rebuked the Red Sea and it dried up.** The water of the Red Sea withdrew as if shamed by God's rebuke, leaving dry land in its wake. **And He led them through the depths** on dry land, **as if** they were walking **through a desert.**

10 **He saved them from those who hated them,** referring to the pursuing Egyptians, and He **redeemed them from the hand of the enemy.**

11 **Water covered their foes.** Beyond preventing the Egyptians from pursuing the Israelites across the sea, the water of the Red Sea drowned them all, so that **not** even **one of them remained.**

12 **Then,** after the Israelites crossed the sea, **they believed in His words; they sang His praise,** referring to the Song at the Sea.[74]

13 But this reconciliation did not last long: **They quickly forgot His deeds; they did not await His counsel.** Whenever the children of Israel encountered any difficulty, they complained immediately, rather than trusting that God, who was leading them through the desert in a miraculous manner, would provide for their needs in due time.

14 Rather, **they craved with desire in the desert,** yearning for items that they lacked. Worse, **they tested the Almighty in the wilderness.** On some occasions, even when they lacked nothing they complained, solely to see if God could perform a certain deed, testing His omnipotence. This, too, was considered sinful on their part.

15 **He** ultimately **gave them their request,** sending them quail to eat, **but sent leanness into their souls,** for this quail led to the deaths of many people.[75]

16 In addition to testing God, **they became envious of Moses in the camp,** speaking ill of him, particularly during the uprising of Korah and his followers, **and** also speaking ill **of Aaron, the Lord's holy one,** questioning his right to the priesthood.[76]

17 **The earth opened and swallowed Datan, covering over the assembly of Aviram.** These two men were among the main instigators in Korah's rebellion.[77]

18 **A fire blazed in their assembly,** among those pretenders to the priesthood who had offered incense before the Tabernacle;[78] **flames consumed the wicked,** referring to the participants in this sin.

19 The psalmist now describes an even more grievous sin committed in the wilderness: **They made a calf in Horev,** another name for Mount Sinai, **bowing down to a molten image,**

מג מד דְּבַר קׇדְשׁוֹ אֶת־אַבְרָהָם עַבְדּוֹ: וַיּוֹצִא עַמּוֹ בְשָׂשׂוֹן בְּרִנָּה אֶת־בְּחִירָיו: וַיִּתֵּן לָהֶם
מה אַרְצוֹת גּוֹיִם וַעֲמַל לְאֻמִּים יִירָשׁוּ: בַּעֲבוּר ׀ יִשְׁמְרוּ חֻקָּיו וְתוֹרֹתָיו יִנְצֹרוּ הַלְלוּיָהּ: טו
קו א ב הַלְלוּיָהּ ׀ הוֹדוּ לַיהוה כִּי־טוֹב כִּי לְעוֹלָם חַסְדּוֹ: מִי יְמַלֵּל גְּבוּרוֹת יהוה יַשְׁמִיעַ כב לחודש
ג ד כׇּל־תְּהִלָּתוֹ: אַשְׁרֵי שֹׁמְרֵי מִשְׁפָּט עֹשֵׂה צְדָקָה בְכׇל־עֵת: זׇכְרֵנִי יהוה בִּרְצוֹן
ה עַמֶּךָ פׇּקְדֵנִי בִּישׁוּעָתֶךָ: לִרְאוֹת ׀ בְּטוֹבַת בְּחִירֶיךָ לִשְׂמֹחַ בְּשִׂמְחַת גּוֹיֶךָ לְהִתְהַלֵּל
ו ז עִם־נַחֲלָתֶךָ: חָטָאנוּ עִם־אֲבוֹתֵינוּ הֶעֱוִינוּ הִרְשָׁעְנוּ: אֲבוֹתֵינוּ בְמִצְרַיִם ׀ לֹא־
ח הִשְׂכִּילוּ נִפְלְאוֹתֶיךָ לֹא זָכְרוּ אֶת־רֹב חֲסָדֶיךָ וַיַּמְרוּ עַל־יָם בְּיַם־סוּף: וַיּוֹשִׁיעֵם
ט לְמַעַן שְׁמוֹ לְהוֹדִיעַ אֶת־גְּבוּרָתוֹ: וַיִּגְעַר בְּיַם־סוּף וַיֶּחֱרָב וַיּוֹלִיכֵם בַּתְּהֹמוֹת
י יא כַּמִּדְבָּר: וַיּוֹשִׁיעֵם מִיַּד שׂוֹנֵא וַיִּגְאָלֵם מִיַּד אוֹיֵב: וַיְכַסּוּ־מַיִם צָרֵיהֶם אֶחָד מֵהֶם
יב יג לֹא נוֹתָר: וַיַּאֲמִינוּ בִדְבָרָיו יָשִׁירוּ תְּהִלָּתוֹ: מִהֲרוּ שָׁכְחוּ מַעֲשָׂיו לֹא־חִכּוּ לַעֲצָתוֹ:
יד טו וַיִּתְאַוּוּ תַאֲוָה בַּמִּדְבָּר וַיְנַסּוּ־אֵל בִּישִׁימוֹן: וַיִּתֵּן לָהֶם שֶׁאֱלָתָם וַיְשַׁלַּח
טז יז רָזוֹן בְּנַפְשָׁם: וַיְקַנְאוּ לְמֹשֶׁה בַּמַּחֲנֶה לְאַהֲרֹן קְדוֹשׁ יהוה: תִּפְתַּח־אֶרֶץ וַתִּבְלַע
יח דָּתָן וַתְּכַס עַל־עֲדַת אֲבִירָם: וַתִּבְעַר־אֵשׁ בַּעֲדָתָם לֶהָבָה תְּלַהֵט רְשָׁעִים:
יט כ יַעֲשׂוּ־עֵגֶל בְּחֹרֵב וַיִּשְׁתַּחֲווּ לְמַסֵּכָה: וַיָּמִירוּ אֶת־כְּבוֹדָם בְּתַבְנִית שׁוֹר
כא כב אֹכֵל עֵשֶׂב: שָׁכְחוּ אֵל מוֹשִׁיעָם עֹשֶׂה גְדֹלוֹת בְּמִצְרָיִם: נִפְלָאוֹת בְּאֶרֶץ
כג חָם נוֹרָאוֹת עַל־יַם־סוּף: וַיֹּאמֶר לְהַשְׁמִידָם לוּלֵי מֹשֶׁה בְחִירוֹ עָמַד בַּפֶּרֶץ
כד לְפָנָיו לְהָשִׁיב חֲמָתוֹ מֵהַשְׁחִית: וַיִּמְאֲסוּ בְּאֶרֶץ חֶמְדָּה לֹא־הֶאֱמִינוּ לִדְבָרוֹ:

20 **and they exchanged their Glory,** the Almighty, **for the molded image of a grass-eating bull,** the Golden Calf.

21 **They forgot the Almighty, their Savior, who had done great things in Egypt,**

22 **wonders in the land of Ham,** and **awesome deeds by the Red Sea.**

Small bull idol found at worship site at heart of Israelite settlement in area of Samaria, twelfth century BCE

23 In the wake of the sin of the Golden Calf, **He said He would destroy them,** and would have done so **were it not for Moses, His chosen one, who stood before Him in the breach** and prayed **to turn back His wrath from destruction.**

24 The next grievous sin recounted here is that of the spies who were sent by Moses to scout the Land of Israel prior to the arrival of the children of Israel: Because of the frightening report brought back by the spies, **they despised the desirable Land** of Israel, and did not want to proceed to conquer it. **They did not have faith in His word,** His promise that they would be able to wage a successful conquest.

25 **They grumbled in their tents; they did not heed the voice of the Lord.**
26 **And He raised His hand** in a gesture of oath **concerning them, to cast them down,** to cause them to perish **in the desert,**
27 **to cast their seed among the nations and to scatter them among the lands.**[D]
28 The last of the grievous sins committed by the Israelites in the wilderness was the worship of the idols of the Moavites: **They clung to Baal Peor and ate sacrifices offered to the dead,** a disparaging term for idolatrous offerings.
29 **They provoked anger with their** other **deeds** that they committed on that occasion, **and a plague broke out among them.**
30 **Pinhas stood up to carry out judgment** by killing Zimri, one of the main perpetrators of sin in that incident,[79] **and** thereupon **the plague was stopped.**
31 **He was accorded merit for all generations to come, for eternity.** As a reward for his brave actions, Pinhas became the progenitor of a dynasty of priests who, aside from some brief interruptions, served as High Priests throughout the days of the Temple.
32 The psalmist mentions more sins committed by the Israelites. **They provoked** God **at the waters of Meriva, and Moses suffered on their account,** as it was he who was punished by being denied entry into the Promised Land.[80]
33 **For they,** the Israelites, **rebelled against him,** against Moses, accusing him of intentionally seeking to kill them, **and** because of their accusations, **he made an** unseemly **utterance with his lips.**[81] This verse seems to imply that Moses was punished not for his actions at Meriva but for what he said.
34 Later, after entering and possessing the Land of Israel, **they did not destroy the** Canaanite **peoples as the Lord told them to do,** to kill or expel all of them.
35 As a result of allowing the Canaanites to live among them, **they mingled with the nations, and** they **learned their practices**
36 **and served their idols, which became a snare for them.**
37 **They sacrificed their sons and their daughters to demons.** While this practice is not mentioned in other sources, an implicit reference is found in Leviticus 17:7.

38 **And they shed innocent blood, the blood of their sons and their daughters, whom they sacrificed to the idols of Canaan,** as part of the sacrificial rites to Molekh and other idols. **And the land became polluted with** that spilled **blood.**

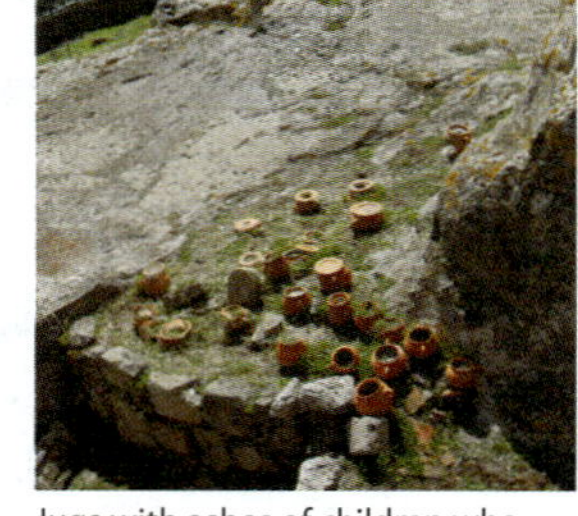
Jugs with ashes of children who were sacrificed at a child-sacrifice site, Sant'Antioco, Italy

39 **They were defiled by their practices; they went astray** from the service of God **with their deeds.** The description of these sins sums up the era of the judges.
40 Such abominations did not go unpunished: **The Lord's fury blazed against His people. He abhorred His portion,**
41 **and He delivered them into the hands of the nations,** who invaded the Land of Israel periodically. **Those who hated them ruled over them.**
42 **Their enemies oppressed them; they were subdued under their power,** as described in detail in the book of Judges.
43 **Many times did He rescue them** by the hand of the various judges and leaders who led them to victory. **But they were defiant in their counsel;** they took counsel among themselves and rebelled against God, **sinking low in their iniquity.**
44 **Yet He saw their distress when** time after time they cried out in prayer, and **He heard their cry.**
45 **He remembered His covenant for them and relented** from His intention to punish them severely, **because of His great kindness,**
46 **and He caused them to be pitied by all their captors.**[D]
47 The psalm closes with words of prayer: **Save us, Lord our God, and gather us in from among the nations,** where some of our nation are in exile, **so we might give thanks to Your holy name and glory in Your praise.**
48 The final verse of the psalm marks the conclusion of the fourth book of Psalms: **Blessed be the Lord, God of Israel, forever and ever. Let the entire nation say: Amen. Halleluya.**

DISCUSSION

106:27| **To cast their seed among the nations and to scatter them among the lands:** It seems that this verse is the source of the teaching of the Sages that due to the sin of the spies sent by Moses, which took place on the ninth of Av, many destructions and tragedies befell the Jewish people on that same date in future years. Many later calamities contained within them a portion of punishment for this sin as well (see *Sanhedrin* 104b; *Ta'anit* 29a, with emendations of Rav Yaakov Emden).

106:46| **By all their captors:** People from Israel were taken into captivity and were exiled over the course of many generations in biblical times. This may be learned from the verse (Obadiah 1:20): "The exile of this host of the children of Israel, who are among the Canaanites, up to Tzarefat, and the exile of Jerusalem that is in Sefarad" (see also Joel 4:6). This phenomenon occurred as far back as the beginning of the First Temple era.

כה כו וַיֵּרָגְנוּ בְאׇהֳלֵיהֶם לֹא שָׁמְעוּ בְּקוֹל יְהוָה׃ וַיִּשָּׂא יָדוֹ לָהֶם לְהַפִּיל אוֹתָם בַּמִּדְבָּר׃
כז כח וּלְהַפִּיל זַרְעָם בַּגּוֹיִם וּלְזָרוֹתָם בָּאֲרָצוֹת׃ וַיִּצָּמְדוּ לְבַעַל פְּעוֹר וַיֹּאכְלוּ זִבְחֵי מֵתִים׃
כט וַיַּכְעִיסוּ בְּמַעַלְלֵיהֶם וַתִּפְרׇץ־בָּם מַגֵּפָה׃ וַיַּעֲמֹד פִּינְחָס וַיְפַלֵּל וַתֵּעָצַר הַמַּגֵּפָה׃
ל לא לב וַתֵּחָשֶׁב לוֹ לִצְדָקָה לְדֹר וָדֹר עַד־עוֹלָם׃ וַיַּקְצִיפוּ עַל־מֵי מְרִיבָה וַיֵּרַע לְמֹשֶׁה
לג לד בַּעֲבוּרָם׃ כִּי־הִמְרוּ אֶת־רוּחוֹ וַיְבַטֵּא בִּשְׂפָתָיו׃ לֹא־הִשְׁמִידוּ אֶת־הָעַמִּים אֲשֶׁר
לה לו אָמַר יְהוָה לָהֶם׃ וַיִּתְעָרְבוּ בַגּוֹיִם וַיִּלְמְדוּ מַעֲשֵׂיהֶם׃ וַיַּעַבְדוּ אֶת־עֲצַבֵּיהֶם וַיִּהְיוּ
לז לח לָהֶם לְמוֹקֵשׁ׃ וַיִּזְבְּחוּ אֶת־בְּנֵיהֶם וְאֶת־בְּנוֹתֵיהֶם לַשֵּׁדִים׃ וַיִּשְׁפְּכוּ דָם נָקִי דַּם־
לט בְּנֵיהֶם וּבְנוֹתֵיהֶם אֲשֶׁר זִבְּחוּ לַעֲצַבֵּי כְנָעַן וַתֶּחֱנַף הָאָרֶץ בַּדָּמִים׃ וַיִּטְמְאוּ
מ מא בְמַעֲשֵׂיהֶם וַיִּזְנוּ בְּמַעַלְלֵיהֶם׃ וַיִּחַר־אַף יְהוָה בְּעַמּוֹ וַיְתָעֵב אֶת־נַחֲלָתוֹ׃ וַיִּתְּנֵם
מב מג בְּיַד־גּוֹיִם וַיִּמְשְׁלוּ בָהֶם שֹׂנְאֵיהֶם׃ וַיִּלְחָצוּם אוֹיְבֵיהֶם וַיִּכָּנְעוּ תַּחַת יָדָם׃ פְּעָמִים
מד רַבּוֹת יַצִּילֵם וְהֵמָּה יַמְרוּ בַעֲצָתָם וַיָּמֹכּוּ בַּעֲוֺנָם׃ וַיַּרְא בַּצַּר לָהֶם בְּשׇׁמְעוֹ אֶת־
מה מו רִנָּתָם׃ וַיִּזְכֹּר לָהֶם בְּרִיתוֹ וַיִּנָּחֵם כְּרֹב חֲסָדָו׃ וַיִּתֵּן אוֹתָם לְרַחֲמִים לִפְנֵי כׇּל־
מז שׁוֹבֵיהֶם׃ הוֹשִׁיעֵנוּ ׀ יְהוָה אֱלֹהֵינוּ וְקַבְּצֵנוּ מִן־הַגּוֹיִם לְהֹדוֹת לְשֵׁם קׇדְשֶׁךָ
מח לְהִשְׁתַּבֵּחַ בִּתְהִלָּתֶךָ׃ בָּרוּךְ יְהוָה ׀ אֱלֹהֵי יִשְׂרָאֵל מִן־הָעוֹלָם ׀ וְעַד הָעוֹלָם וְאָמַר
כׇּל־הָעָם אָמֵן הַלְלוּיָהּ׃

ספר חמישי

יום שישי

קז א ב הֹדוּ לַיהוָה כִּי־טוֹב כִּי לְעוֹלָם חַסְדּוֹ׃ יֹאמְרוּ גְּאוּלֵי יְהוָה אֲשֶׁר גְּאָלָם מִיַּד־צָר׃
ג ד וּמֵאֲרָצוֹת קִבְּצָם מִמִּזְרָח וּמִמַּעֲרָב מִצָּפוֹן וּמִיָּם׃ תָּעוּ בַמִּדְבָּר בִּישִׁימוֹן דֶּרֶךְ עִיר

PSALM 107

PSALMS 107:1–43

A psalm that depicts various perils that people may confront, their deliverance from these troubles, and their thanks to God for His salvation. It serves as a description of the basic forms of deliverance for which individuals were expected to bring a thanksgiving offering in Temple days and, in later generations, to recite the thanksgiving blessing known as *Birkat HaGomel*.

107
BOOK FIVE
Friday

1 The psalm opens with a verse of praise that appears in several other psalms as well: **Give thanks to the Lord, for He is good, for His kindness is forever.**

2 Those who have been redeemed from perilous situations should be especially grateful: **Let those the Lord redeemed say it, those He redeemed from the hand of the foe**

3 **and** whom He **gathered in from lands of the east, of the west, of the north, and from the sea.** The word *yam* often refers to the west, but because that direction has already been mentioned in this verse, it is translated here by its literal meaning of “sea.”

4 The psalmist now begins to describe the four groups of people who give thanks to God. The first: **They lost their way on a**

desolate path in the wilderness, not finding an inhabited place.
5 **Hungry and thirsty,** being lost in the wilderness, **their souls fainting within them,**
6 **they cried out to the Lord in their trouble,** while lost in the wilderness; **He rescued them from their distress,**
7 **and led them on a straight path toward an inhabited place,** from where they were able to find their way out of the wilderness.
8 **Let them give thanks to the Lord for His kindness and His wonders on behalf of man.**
9 **For He satisfied the thirsty soul and filled the hungry soul with goodness.**
10 The psalmist now refers to the second group of people: Prisoners, **dwellers in darkness and the shadow of death.** Jails were often dark, underground dungeons where prisoners were **fettered with affliction and iron,** both figuratively fettered by various forms of affliction and actually fettered with iron chains.
11 The prisoners described here are not necessarily people who were incarcerated unjustly: **For they had rebelled against the word of the Almighty, execrating the counsel of the Most High.**
12 **He subdued their hearts with toil,** with forced labor while in captivity; **they stumbled, and there was no one to help.**
13 **They cried out to the Lord in their trouble; He redeemed them from their distress.**
14 **He brought them out of darkness and the shadow of death, and He severed their chains.**
15 **Let them give thanks to the Lord for His kindness and His wonders on behalf of man.**
16 As in the first example, the psalmist concludes this second section with the exact reason why these people should express their gratitude: **For He shattered doors of bronze,** the mighty doors that sealed the prison, **and sundered iron bolts.**
17 The psalmist goes on to describe the third group of people who should give thanks: Those who have recovered from a serious illness. Here too their illness was often punishment for sins they committed: **Fools because of their path of sin were afflicted, and because of their transgressions.**
18 **Abhorring all food,** lacking an appetite because of their illness, they were in danger of dying; **they were at death's door.**
19 **They cried out to the Lord in their trouble; He delivered them from their distress.**
20 **He sent His word and healed them, and rescued them from the pit.** *Sheḥitotam*, translated here as "the pit," literally, "their pit," can also mean "their perversions." The term therefore refers both to the pit into which they figuratively fell, meaning their illness, as well as the sinful behavior that brought about their punishment.
21 **Let them give thanks to the Lord for His kindness and His wonders on behalf of man.**
22 **Let them offer thanksgiving sacrifices** after their recovery, **and tell of His deeds with joyful singing.**
23 The psalmist turns to the final group of people who should express their gratitude to God: **Those going to sea on ships, who do their work in the mighty waters,** such as sailors.

Phoenician ship carrying logs, Dur-Sharrukin, 713–716 BCE

24 **They saw the deeds of the Lord and His wonders in the deep,**
25 **how He spoke and produced a gale of wind, lifting its waves high.**
26 **They rose to the heavens** and **went down to the depths** as their ships were tossed by the waves. **Their souls dissolved in misery,** both from the discomfort of the rocking ship and from the terror of possibly sinking.
27 **They reeled and staggered** back and forth **like drunken men, all their skill come to naught.** When faced with the overwhelming power of a mighty storm at sea, the sailors' expertise is of no avail.
28 **They cried out to the Lord in their trouble, and He brought them out of their distress.**
29 **He turned the storm into silence, hushing its waves.**
30 **They,** the sea travelers, **rejoiced because they,** the storm's waves, **were quieted.** Now they would be able to resume their journey, and **He led them to their destination.**
31 **Let them give thanks to the Lord for His kindness and His wonders on behalf of man.**
32 **Let them exalt Him in the congregation of people, and praise Him in the company of** the **elders** of the community.
33 The psalmist now turns his attention from specific instances of peril and deliverance to the more general vicissitudes of life and God's mastery over nature. There are times when **He turns rivers into desert, turning springs of water into parched land,**

ה ו מוֹשָׁב לֹא מָצָאוּ׃ רְעֵבִים גַּם־צְמֵאִים נַפְשָׁם בָּהֶם תִּתְעַטָּף׃ וַיִּצְעֲקוּ אֶל־יהוה
ז בַּצַּר לָהֶם מִמְּצוּקוֹתֵיהֶם יַצִּילֵם׃ וַיַּדְרִיכֵם בְּדֶרֶךְ יְשָׁרָה לָלֶכֶת אֶל־עִיר מוֹשָׁב׃
ח ט יוֹדוּ לַיהוה חַסְדּוֹ וְנִפְלְאוֹתָיו לִבְנֵי אָדָם׃ כִּי־הִשְׂבִּיעַ נֶפֶשׁ שֹׁקֵקָה וְנֶפֶשׁ רְעֵבָה
י יא מִלֵּא־טוֹב׃ יֹשְׁבֵי חֹשֶׁךְ וְצַלְמָוֶת אֲסִירֵי עֳנִי וּבַרְזֶל׃ כִּי־הִמְרוּ אִמְרֵי־אֵל וַעֲצַת
יב יג עֶלְיוֹן נָאָצוּ׃ וַיַּכְנַע בֶּעָמָל לִבָּם כָּשְׁלוּ וְאֵין עֹזֵר׃ וַיִּזְעֲקוּ אֶל־יהוה בַּצַּר לָהֶם
יד טו מִמְּצֻקוֹתֵיהֶם יוֹשִׁיעֵם׃ יוֹצִיאֵם מֵחֹשֶׁךְ וְצַלְמָוֶת וּמוֹסְרוֹתֵיהֶם יְנַתֵּק׃ יוֹדוּ לַיהוה
טז יז חַסְדּוֹ וְנִפְלְאוֹתָיו לִבְנֵי אָדָם׃ כִּי־שִׁבַּר דַּלְתוֹת נְחֹשֶׁת וּבְרִיחֵי בַרְזֶל גִּדֵּעַ׃ אֱוִלִים
יח מִדֶּרֶךְ פִּשְׁעָם וּמֵעֲוֺנֹתֵיהֶם יִתְעַנּוּ׃ כׇּל־אֹכֶל תְּתַעֵב נַפְשָׁם וַיַּגִּיעוּ עַד־שַׁעֲרֵי מָוֶת׃
יט כ וַיִּזְעֲקוּ אֶל־יהוה בַּצַּר לָהֶם מִמְּצֻקוֹתֵיהֶם יוֹשִׁיעֵם׃ יִשְׁלַח דְּבָרוֹ וְיִרְפָּאֵם וִימַלֵּט
כא כב מִשְּׁחִיתוֹתָם׃ יוֹדוּ לַיהוה חַסְדּוֹ וְנִפְלְאוֹתָיו לִבְנֵי אָדָם׃ וְיִזְבְּחוּ זִבְחֵי תוֹדָה וִיסַפְּרוּ
כג מַעֲשָׂיו בְּרִנָּה׃ ׆ יוֹרְדֵי הַיָּם בָּאֳנִיּוֹת עֹשֵׂי מְלָאכָה בְּמַיִם
כד כה רַבִּים׃ ׆ הֵמָּה רָאוּ מַעֲשֵׂי יהוה וְנִפְלְאוֹתָיו בִּמְצוּלָה׃ ׆ וַיֹּאמֶר
כו וַיַּעֲמֵד רוּחַ סְעָרָה וַתְּרוֹמֵם גַּלָּיו׃ ׆ יַעֲלוּ שָׁמַיִם יֵרְדוּ תְהוֹמוֹת נַפְשָׁם בְּרָעָה
כז כח תִתְמוֹגָג׃ ׆ יָחוֹגּוּ וְיָנוּעוּ כַּשִּׁכּוֹר וְכׇל־חׇכְמָתָם תִּתְבַּלָּע׃ ׆ וַיִּצְעֲקוּ
כט אֶל־יהוה בַּצַּר לָהֶם וּמִמְּצוּקֹתֵיהֶם יוֹצִיאֵם׃ יָקֵם סְעָרָה לִדְמָמָה וַיֶּחֱשׁוּ גַּלֵּיהֶם׃
ל לא וַיִּשְׂמְחוּ כִי־יִשְׁתֹּקוּ וַיַּנְחֵם אֶל־מְחוֹז חֶפְצָם׃ יוֹדוּ לַיהוה חַסְדּוֹ וְנִפְלְאוֹתָיו לִבְנֵי
לב לג אָדָם׃ וִירוֹמְמוּהוּ בִּקְהַל־עָם וּבְמוֹשַׁב זְקֵנִים יְהַלְלוּהוּ׃ יָשֵׂם נְהָרוֹת לְמִדְבָּר
לד לה וּמֹצָאֵי מַיִם לְצִמָּאוֹן׃ אֶרֶץ פְּרִי לִמְלֵחָה מֵרָעַת יוֹשְׁבֵי בָהּ׃ יָשֵׂם מִדְבָּר לַאֲגַם־
לו לז מַיִם וְאֶרֶץ צִיָּה לְמֹצָאֵי מָיִם׃ וַיּוֹשֶׁב שָׁם רְעֵבִים וַיְכוֹנְנוּ עִיר מוֹשָׁב׃ וַיִּזְרְעוּ שָׂדוֹת

34 **a fruitful land into a salty wasteland.** As the underground water supply dries up, the remaining water becomes saline and unfit for drinking and irrigation. God does this as a punishment for the land, **because of the evil of those dwelling in it.**

35 However, droughts do not last forever, and opposite phenomena also occur: **He turns a desert into a lake of water and dry land into springs.**

36 **There,** in this newly fertile land, **He brings hungry people to dwell; they establish an inhabited city.**

37 There **they sow fields and plant vineyards, which bring forth fruits of produce.**

"And dry land into springs." Waterfall at Ein Gedi

38 **He blesses them and they multiply greatly; He does not let their cattle dwindle.**
39 **But** things can also change for the worse: **Then their numbers are diminished and they are brought down with distress, sorrow, and anguish.** Bad times cause loss and death, along with misery and sorrow for those who remain.
40 In another example of reversal of good fortune, **He pours contempt upon the wealthy,** taking away their wealth and impoverishing them, **and has them lose their way in a pathless wasteland,** a metaphor for their inability to extricate themselves from their difficult situation.
41 At the same time, **He gives shelter to the needy from affliction. He turns families** that had been weak and few in number **into** clans as numerous as **flocks** of sheep.
42 **The upright see this and are glad** over God's beneficence and mercy; **the mouth of iniquity,** of those who ordinarily speak only base and sinful words, **is stopped** and rendered inactive, as they too join in praising God.
43 In conclusion: **He who is wise will heed** and give heart to **these matters,** all these reversals of fortune in life, **and ponder the kindness of the Lord,** realizing that man's destiny is completely in God's hands.

PSALM 108

PSALMS 108:1–14

A psalm whose second half is a repetition, with minor changes, of the end of Psalm 60. Its different beginning, however, makes it a more straightforward song of praise. Unlike Psalm 60, which was written under specific historic circumstances (see 60:2), this psalm discusses more generally the contrast between the troubles of the past and the victories of the present.

108 1 **A song, a psalm by David.**
23rd day of month 2 **My heart is ready** to begin this song, **God; I will sing and give praise, and my soul as well.** Not only will I sing to You and praise You with my mouth, but my whole soul and being will join in.
3 The psalmist addresses his musical instruments: **Awaken, harp and lyre; I will wake the dawn.** Let us begin to play at the first glimmering of light.
4 **I will give thanks to You, Lord, among the peoples; I will sing Your praise among the nations.**
5 **For Your kindness is greater than the heavens; Your truth** in fulfilling Your covenant with us **reaches the skies.**
6 **Rise above the heavens, God,** revealing Your presence in the world; **let Your glory extend throughout the earth,**
7 **that Your beloved ones may be saved; deliver me with Your right hand and answer me.**
8 After an introductory section of supplication, the psalmist begins his song of praise: **God spoke in His holiness** to assure me of victory; **I exulted. I divided Shekhem and measured out the valley of Sukot.** Upon David's victories over the nations living in these regions, these places fell under Israelite control, and he was now able to divide them among the people (see commentary on 60:8).
9 The psalmist acknowledges those tribes of Israel who came to his aid: **Gilad,** a branch of Manasseh, **is mine,** the rest of **Manasseh is mine, and Ephraim is my stronghold, Judah my lawgiver.**
10 Now he mentions the enemies against whom he has fought: **Moav,** whom I have vanquished, I regard with contempt as if it **is** nothing more than **my washbasin; I will throw my shoe** in scorn **at Edom; against Philistia I will deliver a crushing defeat.**

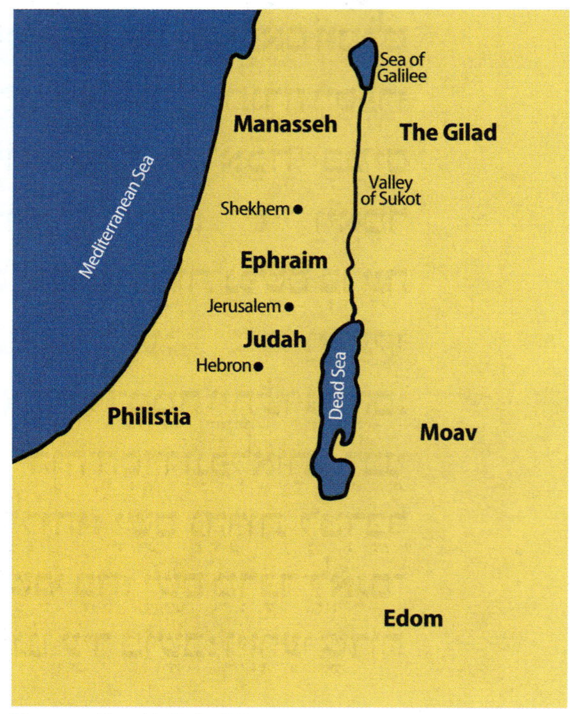

Places mentioned in Psalm 108

11 **Who leads me to a fortified city? Who guides me to Edom** to conquer it?
12 **Is it not You, God, who had abandoned us** in the past, **You, God, who would not go forth with our armies,** and that is why we were not victorious in the past? Now that You have come to our aid, however, we are triumphant.

לח וַיִּטְּעוּ כְרָמִים וַיַּעֲשׂוּ פְּרִי תְבוּאָה: וַיְבָרְכֵם וַיִּרְבּוּ מְאֹד וּבְהֶמְתָּם לֹא יַמְעִיט:
לט מ וַיִּמְעֲטוּ וַיָּשֹׁחוּ מֵעֹצֶר רָעָה וְיָגוֹן: ׆ שֹׁפֵךְ בּוּז עַל־נְדִיבִים וַיַּתְעֵם בְּתֹהוּ
מא מב לֹא־דָרֶךְ: וַיְשַׂגֵּב אֶבְיוֹן מֵעוֹנִי וַיָּשֶׂם כַּצֹּאן מִשְׁפָּחוֹת: יִרְאוּ יְשָׁרִים וְיִשְׂמָחוּ וְכָל־
מג עַוְלָה קָפְצָה פִּיהָ: מִי־חָכָם וְיִשְׁמָר־אֵלֶּה וְיִתְבּוֹנְנוּ חַסְדֵי יְהוָה:
קח א ב שִׁיר מִזְמוֹר לְדָוִד: נָכוֹן לִבִּי אֱלֹהִים אָשִׁירָה וַאֲזַמְּרָה אַף־כְּבוֹדִי: עוּרָה הַנֵּבֶל — כג לחודש
ג ד ה וְכִנּוֹר אָעִירָה שָּׁחַר: אוֹדְךָ בָעַמִּים ׀ יְהוָה וַאֲזַמֶּרְךָ בַּלְאֻמִּים: כִּי־גָדֹל מֵעַל־שָׁמַיִם
ו חַסְדֶּךָ וְעַד־שְׁחָקִים אֲמִתֶּךָ: רוּמָה עַל־שָׁמַיִם אֱלֹהִים וְעַל כָּל־הָאָרֶץ כְּבוֹדֶךָ:
ז ח לְמַעַן יֵחָלְצוּן יְדִידֶיךָ הוֹשִׁיעָה יְמִינְךָ ועננו: אֱלֹהִים ׀ דִּבֶּר בְּקָדְשׁוֹ אֶעְלֹזָה — וַעֲנֵנִי
ט אֲחַלְּקָה שְׁכֶם וְעֵמֶק סֻכּוֹת אֲמַדֵּד: לִי גִלְעָד ׀ לִי מְנַשֶּׁה וְאֶפְרַיִם מָעוֹז רֹאשִׁי
י יְהוּדָה מְחֹקְקִי: מוֹאָב ׀ סִיר רַחְצִי עַל־אֱדוֹם אַשְׁלִיךְ נַעֲלִי עֲלֵי־פְלֶשֶׁת אֶתְרוֹעָע:
יא יב מִי יֹבִלֵנִי עִיר מִבְצָר מִי נָחַנִי עַד־אֱדוֹם: הֲלֹא־אֱלֹהִים זְנַחְתָּנוּ וְלֹא־תֵצֵא אֱלֹהִים
יג יד בְּצִבְאֹתֵינוּ: הָבָה־לָּנוּ עֶזְרָת מִצָּר וְשָׁוְא תְּשׁוּעַת אָדָם: בֵּאלֹהִים נַעֲשֶׂה־חָיִל
וְהוּא יָבוּס צָרֵינוּ:
קט א ב לַמְנַצֵּחַ לְדָוִד מִזְמוֹר אֱלֹהֵי תְהִלָּתִי אַל־תֶּחֱרַשׁ: כִּי פִי רָשָׁע וּפִי־מִרְמָה עָלַי
ג ד פָּתָחוּ דִּבְּרוּ אִתִּי לְשׁוֹן שָׁקֶר: וְדִבְרֵי שִׂנְאָה סְבָבוּנִי וַיִּלָּחֲמוּנִי חִנָּם: תַּחַת־אַהֲבָתִי

13 **Give us aid against the foe, for deliverance by man is in vain.** Only God's assistance is of any avail.

14 The point is reiterated in the conclusion: **With God we will triumph, and He will rout our foes.**

PSALM 109

PSALMS 109:1–31

A psalm in which King David pleads for his life, which is endangered by his many enemies, and in which he recounts the enemies' harsh words against him.

109 1 **To the chief musician, a psalm by David. God of my praise, do not keep silent.** Although I am presently unable to respond to my enemies' taunts, may You not remain silent but punish them as they deserve.

2 **For the mouths of the wicked and the mouths of the deceitful have opened against me.** Some of the accusations against me are founded on deceit; others are simply malicious. **They speak of me with a lying tongue.**

3 **Hateful words surround me.** In the past, my enemies kept silent; it is only now, when I have fallen from power, that they are able to condemn me and fight against me. **They fought against me without cause.**

4 **In return for my love** toward them, **they accuse me; I am all prayer.** With this unusual expression, David defines himself not merely as someone who prays but as someone whose whole essence is prayer.

5 **They requited my good with evil, hatred in place of my love.** Assuming that the context of this psalm is Avshalom's rebellion, this verse refers both to a once-beloved son, who had been treated with great compassion by David, and to the king's former friends and deputies who joined the insurrection.

6 David now enumerates the curses cast upon him by his enemies. Addressing God, they said: **Appoint a wicked one,** that is, the forces of evil, administered by an avenging angel, **over him; have an adversary stand at his right.**

7 **When he is judged** before You, **may he be found guilty; may his prayer be regarded as sin,** unaccepted and dismissed with contempt.

8 **May his days be few,** may he die soon, and **may another take his position.**

9 **May his children be fatherless and his wife a widow.**

10 **May his** orphaned **children** have to **wander** from place to place **and beg** for their sustenance, **scrounging because of their ruin,** because nothing will be left of what their father had accrued.

11 **May creditors seize all that he has; may strangers plunder the fruit of his labor.**

12 **May there be no one to offer him kindness** during his lifetime, **no one to pity his orphans** after his death.

13 **May his legacy be cut off; may their names,** the names of David and his offspring, **be blotted out from the coming generations.**

14 With their names blotted out, the only preserved memories of them would be those of sin and iniquity: **May the iniquity of his fathers be remembered by the Lord; may his mother's sin not be erased.** This is not an allusion to any specific sins of David's parents, but to the many misdeeds that all human beings commit throughout their lifetimes.

15 **May these** sins **be before the Lord continually; may He cut off their memory from the earth.**

16 David's accusers now explain why they believe he deserves to be cursed in this manner: **For he did not remember to practice kindness. He drove to death the poor, the needy, and the brokenhearted.**

17 **He loved curses.** During his reign he disregarded the curses that his detractors might level at him, **and they will now come upon him.** He laughed off their curses, but now they would affect him. **He had no desire for blessings, and they will now be far from him.**

18 **May he be clothed in curses, as with a garment; may they enter his body like water** that is imbibed, **like oil** rubbed into the skin, seeping **into his bones.**

19 **May he wrap them as a garment around him,**[D] **like a belt he constantly fastens.**

20 Following this recitation of the curses hurled at him when he was downtrodden, pursued, and in a seemingly hopeless situation, curses that express pent-up hostility and possibly longstanding hatred, David goes on to say: **This is what those who hate me do, they who speak against me; it is from the Lord.**[D]

21 Having cited his enemies' deep hatred for him, David turns to God in prayer: **You, Lord my God, do to me for the sake of Your name; rescue me, for Your mercy is good.**

22 **For I am poor and needy, my heart hollow within me,** devoid of feeling, confidence, and strength.

23 **I walk along,** fading **like a lengthening shadow** as the sun is about to set, **tossed about like a locust** driven from place to place by the wind.

24 **My knees are weak from fasting, my flesh grown gaunt.**

25 **I have become a disgrace to them** in my weakness and desperation; **they see me and shake their heads** in disparagement and contempt.

26 David turns to God with a direct plea for assistance: **Help me, Lord my God; deliver me, as befits Your kindness.**

27 **They will know that** it is not my sins or lack of power that have brought about my vulnerable situation, but **it is Your hand, that You, Lord, have done it,** and consequently You can reverse the situation and restore me to my previously exalted position.

28 **They may curse, but You will bless. They rose against me, but they will be shamed, while Your servant will rejoice.**

29 **Those who hate me will be clothed in dishonor, wrapped in their shame like a cloak.** Once I return to power, my enemies will be left with nothing but shame for having conspired against me.

30 When that time comes, **with my mouth, I will give abundant thanks to the Lord; in the midst of multitudes I will glorify Him.**

31 **For He stands at the right hand of the needy, to deliver him from those who judge him.** Although attempts have been made to falsely charge him with all manner of evil, God will save him.

ה ו יִשְׂטְנוּנִי וַאֲנִי תְפִלָּה׃ וַיָּשִׂימוּ עָלַי רָעָה תַּחַת טוֹבָה וְשִׂנְאָה תַּחַת אַהֲבָתִי׃ הַפְקֵד
ז עָלָיו רָשָׁע וְשָׂטָן יַעֲמֹד עַל־יְמִינוֹ׃ בְּהִשָּׁפְטוֹ יֵצֵא רָשָׁע וּתְפִלָּתוֹ תִּהְיֶה לַחֲטָאָה׃
ח ט י יִהְיוּ־יָמָיו מְעַטִּים פְּקֻדָּתוֹ יִקַּח אַחֵר׃ יִהְיוּ־בָנָיו יְתוֹמִים וְאִשְׁתּוֹ אַלְמָנָה׃ וְנוֹעַ
יא יָנוּעוּ בָנָיו וְשִׁאֵלוּ וְדָרְשׁוּ מֵחָרְבוֹתֵיהֶם׃ יְנַקֵּשׁ נוֹשֶׁה לְכָל־אֲשֶׁר־לוֹ וְיָבֹזּוּ זָרִים
יב יג יְגִיעוֹ׃ אַל־יְהִי־לוֹ מֹשֵׁךְ חָסֶד וְאַל־יְהִי חוֹנֵן לִיתוֹמָיו׃ יְהִי־אַחֲרִיתוֹ לְהַכְרִית בְּדוֹר
יד טו אַחֵר יִמַּח שְׁמָם׃ יִזָּכֵר ׀ עֲוֺן אֲבֹתָיו אֶל־יְהֹוָה וְחַטַּאת אִמּוֹ אַל־תִּמָּח׃ יִהְיוּ נֶגֶד־
טז יְהֹוָה תָּמִיד וְיַכְרֵת מֵאֶרֶץ זִכְרָם׃ יַעַן אֲשֶׁר ׀ לֹא זָכַר עֲשׂוֹת חָסֶד וַיִּרְדֹּף אִישׁ־עָנִי
יז וְאֶבְיוֹן וְנִכְאֵה לֵבָב לְמוֹתֵת׃ וַיֶּאֱהַב קְלָלָה וַתְּבוֹאֵהוּ וְלֹא־חָפֵץ בִּבְרָכָה וַתִּרְחַק
יח יט מִמֶּנּוּ׃ וַיִּלְבַּשׁ קְלָלָה כְּמַדּוֹ וַתָּבֹא כַמַּיִם בְּקִרְבּוֹ וְכַשֶּׁמֶן בְּעַצְמוֹתָיו׃ תְּהִי־לוֹ
כ כְּבֶגֶד יַעְטֶה וּלְמֵזַח תָּמִיד יַחְגְּרֶהָ׃ זֹאת ׀ פְּעֻלַּת שֹׂטְנַי מֵאֵת יְהֹוָה וְהַדֹּבְרִים רָע
כא עַל־נַפְשִׁי׃ וְאַתָּה ׀ יֱהֹוִה אֲדֹנָי עֲשֵׂה־אִתִּי לְמַעַן שְׁמֶךָ כִּי־טוֹב חַסְדְּךָ הַצִּילֵנִי׃
כב כג כִּי־עָנִי וְאֶבְיוֹן אָנֹכִי וְלִבִּי חָלַל בְּקִרְבִּי׃ כְּצֵל כִּנְטוֹתוֹ נֶהֱלָכְתִּי נִנְעַרְתִּי כָּאַרְבֶּה׃
כד כה בִּרְכַּי כָּשְׁלוּ מִצּוֹם וּבְשָׂרִי כָּחַשׁ מִשָּׁמֶן׃ וַאֲנִי ׀ הָיִיתִי חֶרְפָּה לָהֶם יִרְאוּנִי יְנִיעוּן
כו כז רֹאשָׁם׃ עָזְרֵנִי יְהֹוָה אֱלֹהָי הוֹשִׁיעֵנִי כְחַסְדֶּךָ׃ וְיֵדְעוּ כִּי־יָדְךָ זֹּאת אַתָּה יְהֹוָה
כח כט עֲשִׂיתָהּ׃ יְקַלְלוּ־הֵמָּה וְאַתָּה תְבָרֵךְ קָמוּ ׀ וַיֵּבֹשׁוּ וְעַבְדְּךָ יִשְׂמָח׃ יִלְבְּשׁוּ שׂוֹטְנַי
ל לא כְּלִמָּה וְיַעֲטוּ כַמְעִיל בָּשְׁתָּם׃ אוֹדֶה יְהֹוָה מְאֹד בְּפִי וּבְתוֹךְ רַבִּים אֲהַלְלֶנּוּ׃ כִּי־
יַעֲמֹד לִימִין אֶבְיוֹן לְהוֹשִׁיעַ מִשֹּׁפְטֵי נַפְשׁוֹ׃

DISCUSSION

109:19 | **May he wrap them as a garment around him:** Many commentaries understand the maledictions of verses 6–19 as being uttered by David toward his enemies. According to this interpretation, David, under attack from all sides, abandons his usual composure and in his bitterness severely curses his enemies (see *Tzidkat HaTzaddik* 71). In our commentary, these harsh words are interpreted as imprecations hurled against David by his adversaries. Support for this approach can be found in the fact that the curses are directed against an individual, and David's many enemies are referred to in the plural at the beginning of the psalm. The general context, and even some of the specifics of this passage, are consistent with David's situation: Isolated, under siege, and accursed while fleeing from his own son Avshalom (II Samuel 13–18; see also I Kings 2:8).

109:20 | **This is what those who hate me do… It is from the Lord:** David, in his great faith, does not see in these curses merely expressions of the hostility of his enemies; he views them as manifestations of God's punishment for his past misdeeds. This is what he said in response to the imprecations of Shimi ben Gera as well: "He curses because the Lord said to him: Curse David. Who can say: Why did you do so?" (II Samuel 16:10).

PSALM 110

PSALMS 110:1–7

Apparently a coronation psalm, which may have been recited at David's formal coronation ceremony in Jerusalem. The introductory statement, *LeDavid mizmor*, usually translated as "A psalm by David," can also be rendered "A psalm for David," and that is evidently its meaning here.

110 1 **A psalm for David. The utterance of the Lord to my master,** the king: **Sit on My right**[D] **until I place your enemies as a stool for your feet.** God tells the king to sit, as it were, and wait while He fights his wars for him.

"Until I place your enemies as a stool for your feet." Tiglat Pileser placing his feet on the neck of the king of Gaza, illustration based on Assyrian stone relief, eighth century BCE

2 **The Lord will send your rod of strength from Zion;** with that rod, or royal scepter, you shall **rule among your enemies.**
3 **Your people will volunteer** to fight for you **on your day of battle in sacred glory,** with great reverence. **From the womb of the dawn,** since the day of your birth, you were destined for this glory; **yours is** and will remain **the dew,** the freshness and vigor, **of youth.**
4 In honor of the coronation, the psalmist declares: **The Lord has sworn, and He will not renounce it; you are chief forever by My decree.** The word *kohen* usually means priest, but the term can also refer to any leader or holder of a senior position of authority,[82] **like Malkitzedek.**[D]
5 **The Lord is at your right hand** to assist you; **He will crush kings** who fight against you **on the day of His wrath.**
6 **He will judge among the nations,** smiting all their warriors, **and make it full of corpses.** God will destroy your enemies in war, to the extent that the enemy camp will be full of corpses, **crushing** the **heads** of the enemies **over a broad land.** The imagery is of maimed warriors strewn across the battlefield.
7 As for the warrior in your camp, **he will drink** peacefully, with no opposition, **from the stream on the way. Thus will his head be raised** confidently when he moves on to the battlefield.

PSALM 111

PSALMS 111:1–10

A song of praise to God for His many acts of kindness. Both this psalm and the next one, which resemble each other in format, are instructional texts that are meant to be learned by heart. To facilitate memorization, the Hebrew verses are arranged in alphabetical order, with each verse containing two or three phrases that begin with consecutive Hebrew letters.

111 1 **Halleluya. I will thank the Lord with all my heart in the assembly and council of the upright.**
2 **Great are the works of the Lord, ready for all that is desired.** God's works are finely wrought and perfectly ready to be put into operation.
3 **Splendid and glorious is His work; His righteousness stands forever.**
4 **He has made His wonders a lasting memory.** God's wonders are not temporary phenomena but rather endure and leave a lasting memory. **The Lord is gracious and merciful.**
5 **He gives food to those who fear Him; He remembers forever His covenant** with those who cling to Him.
6 **He tells the power of His deeds to His people.** God informs His people what will transpire in the future, as all events that occur are ordained from above. But God does not merely tell

DISCUSSION

110:1 | **Sit on My right:** God places David on His right side, as it were, since in a sense the king who rules in Jerusalem sits upon the throne of God, the throne that He has prepared to be dedicated to Him so that his chosen one may sit on it, as it is stated concerning King Solomon (I Chronicles 29:23).

110:4 | **Malkitzedek:** He was the king of Shalem, which is Jerusalem, in the days of Abraham. In the Bible he is described as "a *kohen* of God the Most High" (Genesis 14:18; see also commentary on Joshua 10:1).

קי א לְדָוִד מִזְמוֹר נְאֻם יהוה ׀ לַאדֹנִי שֵׁב לִימִינִי עַד־אָשִׁית אֹיְבֶיךָ הֲדֹם לְרַגְלֶיךָ׃
ב ג מַטֵּה עֻזְּךָ יִשְׁלַח יהוה מִצִּיּוֹן רְדֵה בְּקֶרֶב אֹיְבֶיךָ׃ עַמְּךָ נְדָבֹת בְּיוֹם חֵילֶךָ בְּהַדְרֵי־
ד קֹדֶשׁ מֵרֶחֶם מִשְׁחָר לְךָ טַל יַלְדֻתֶיךָ׃ נִשְׁבַּע יהוה ׀ וְלֹא יִנָּחֵם אַתָּה־כֹהֵן לְעוֹלָם
ה ו עַל־דִּבְרָתִי מַלְכִּי־צֶדֶק׃ אֲדֹנָי עַל־יְמִינְךָ מָחַץ בְּיוֹם־אַפּוֹ מְלָכִים׃ יָדִין בַּגּוֹיִם
ז מָלֵא גְוִיּוֹת מָחַץ רֹאשׁ עַל־אֶרֶץ רַבָּה׃ מִנַּחַל בַּדֶּרֶךְ יִשְׁתֶּה עַל־כֵּן יָרִים רֹאשׁ׃
קיא א ב הַלְלוּיָהּ ׀ אוֹדֶה יהוה בְּכָל־לֵבָב בְּסוֹד יְשָׁרִים וְעֵדָה׃ גְּדֹלִים מַעֲשֵׂי יהוה דְּרוּשִׁים
ג ד לְכָל־חֶפְצֵיהֶם׃ הוֹד־וְהָדָר פָּעֳלוֹ וְצִדְקָתוֹ עֹמֶדֶת לָעַד׃ זֵכֶר עָשָׂה לְנִפְלְאֹתָיו
ה ו חַנּוּן וְרַחוּם יהוה׃ טֶרֶף נָתַן לִירֵאָיו יִזְכֹּר לְעוֹלָם בְּרִיתוֹ׃ כֹּחַ מַעֲשָׂיו הִגִּיד לְעַמּוֹ
ז ח לָתֵת לָהֶם נַחֲלַת גּוֹיִם׃ מַעֲשֵׂי יָדָיו אֱמֶת וּמִשְׁפָּט נֶאֱמָנִים כָּל־פִּקּוּדָיו׃ סְמוּכִים
ט לָעַד לְעוֹלָם עֲשׂוּיִם בֶּאֱמֶת וְיָשָׁר׃ פְּדוּת ׀ שָׁלַח לְעַמּוֹ צִוָּה־לְעוֹלָם בְּרִיתוֹ קָדוֹשׁ
י וְנוֹרָא שְׁמוֹ׃ רֵאשִׁית חָכְמָה ׀ יִרְאַת יהוה שֵׂכֶל טוֹב לְכָל־עֹשֵׂיהֶם תְּהִלָּתוֹ עֹמֶדֶת טז
לָעַד׃
קיב א ב הַלְלוּיָהּ ׀ אַשְׁרֵי־אִישׁ יָרֵא אֶת־יהוה בְּמִצְוֹתָיו חָפֵץ מְאֹד׃ גִּבּוֹר בָּאָרֶץ יִהְיֶה

them of promises; He also fulfills them, **giving them the portion of nations,** as He promised to the patriarchs.

7 **The works of His hands are truth and justice; steadfast are all His edicts.**

8 **They are set firmly for all eternity, fashioned in truth and uprightness.**

9 **He has sent redemption to His people, ordaining His covenant** with them **for all time. Holy and awesome is His name.**

10 In light of all that has been said, the psalmist summarizes: **Wisdom begins with fear of the Lord.** Fear of God should be the underlying principle of a person's conception of the world, the foundation upon which he constructs his worldview, for all **those who practice it will come to good sense. His praise stands forever.**

PSALM 112

PSALMS 112:1–10

A psalm in praise of the righteous. Like the preceding psalm, it is didactic and meant to be memorized, and it is similarly structured in alphabetical order.

112 1 **Halleluya. Happy is the man who fears the Lord and who greatly delights in His commandments.**

2 Such a person merits everything good this world has to offer: **His descendants will be mighty on earth.** Not only will he be successful himself, but he will also reap the blessing of having heroic and successful descendants. **He will be blessed with a generation of the upright,** with upright descendants.

3 **Wealth and riches are in his house.** But he does not hold on
to his wealth for himself; he shares it with others, **and his righteousness,** his benevolence, **stands forever.**
4 **Light dawns in darkness for the upright, for he is gracious
and compassionate and righteous.**
5 **It is good for a man to be gracious and to lend** to others without interest, **conducting his affairs with justice,** judiciously:
When appropriate, the money is given as charity, as in verse 3,
and when the situation warrants it, he lends it.
6 **For He will never stumble** in his lifetime, and even after his
death **the righteous man is remembered** favorably **forever.**
7 **He fears no evil tidings** because **his heart is steadfast, trusting in the Lord.**
8 **His heart is reliant** on God. **He will not fear** in the face of
threats or adversity **until** ultimately **he beholds the fall of his
foes.**
9 **He gives freely to the needy; his righteousness stands forever. His horn,** his good name or stature, **is raised high in
honor.**
10 In contrast to the righteous person, who prospers in all his
endeavors, **the wicked one sees and is angered.** The mere
existence of the righteous individual is vexing to the wicked
person. **He gnashes his teeth** in anger **and dissolves,** as it
were, in the realization that he has no recourse to harm the
righteous. **The desire of the wicked,** whether to cause harm
to the righteous or to attain any material success, **will come to
naught.**

PSALM 113

PSALMS 113:1–9

One of the most well-known chapters in Psalms as the opening psalm of the Hallel prayer recited on Jewish holidays, which consists of Psalms 113–118. It focuses on manifold and complementary aspects of God's greatness.

113 1 **Halleluya. Praise, you servants of the Lord.** These are not
24h day necessarily people of any particular status or position but sim-
of month ply those who regard themselves as serving God. **Praise the
name of the Lord.**
2 This is what you, the servants of God, should say: **Blessed
be the name of the Lord from now until eternity.** This is a
general statement of praise for God. This praise consists of two
distinct facets, as the psalmist goes on to elaborate.
3 The first facet is God's awesome greatness: **From the sun's rising place** in the east **to the place where it sets** in the west, **the
name of the Lord is praised.**
4 **Exalted above all nations is the Lord; above the heavens is
His glory.** God rules over the heavens, is above worldly existence, and is beyond the powers and forces of the world.
5 **Who is like the Lord our God, who sits on high,**[D]
6 **who looks down to see what is in heaven and earth?** Here we
come to the second facet of God's praise: His awareness of all
His creations on earth and His care for them. Because God is
"above the heavens" (verse 4) and "sits on high" (verse 5), even
when He observes what is in heaven He is looking down, as it
were. From His perspective, the heavens and everything within
them are no more exalted than the creatures of the earth; He
cares about everyone and everything to the same degree.
7 As a result of God's concern for all His creations, **He raises the
poor from the dust, lifts the needy from the refuse heap,**
8 **to set them among the rich and noble of His people.** The
poor receive divine care and are raised to a higher level, even in
this world.
9 **He sets the barren woman at home as a joyful mother of
children. Halleluya.**

PSALM 114

PSALMS 114:1–8

A song of praise concerning the exodus from Egypt. Rather than describing the events of the exodus historically, it depicts emotional responses to the revelation of God.

114 1 **When Israel went out of Egypt, the house of Jacob from a
foreign-speaking people,** "foreign," as the Egyptian language
was very different from Hebrew,
2 the tribe of **Judah became His holy one.** They became the lo-
cus of the manifestation of God's holiness. And **Israel** became

DISCUSSION

113:4–5 | **Above the heavens is His glory.... Who is like the Lord...who sits on high:** All the nations of the world who worship God acknowledge that His glory is in the heavens, because in their eyes He is the supreme spiritual power. However, the "servants of the Lord" (verse 1) realize that in fact He "sits on high," even beyond the heavens. He "looks down to see what is in heaven and earth" (verse 6), since He transcends both heaven and earth, which are His creations.

ג ד זַרְעוֹ דּוֹר יְשָׁרִים יְבֹרָךְ׃ הוֹן־וָעֹשֶׁר בְּבֵיתוֹ וְצִדְקָתוֹ עֹמֶדֶת לָעַד׃ זָרַח בַּחֹשֶׁךְ
ה אוֹר לַיְשָׁרִים חַנּוּן וְרַחוּם וְצַדִּיק׃ טוֹב־אִישׁ חוֹנֵן וּמַלְוֶה יְכַלְכֵּל דְּבָרָיו בְּמִשְׁפָּט׃
ו ז כִּי־לְעוֹלָם לֹא־יִמּוֹט לְזֵכֶר עוֹלָם יִהְיֶה צַדִּיק׃ מִשְּׁמוּעָה רָעָה לֹא יִירָא נָכוֹן לִבּוֹ
ח ט בָּטֻחַ בַּיהוָה׃ סָמוּךְ לִבּוֹ לֹא יִירָא עַד אֲשֶׁר־יִרְאֶה בְצָרָיו׃ פִּזַּר ׀ נָתַן לָאֶבְיוֹנִים
י צִדְקָתוֹ עֹמֶדֶת לָעַד קַרְנוֹ תָּרוּם בְּכָבוֹד׃ רָשָׁע יִרְאֶה ׀ וְכָעָס שִׁנָּיו יַחֲרֹק וְנָמָס
תַּאֲוַת רְשָׁעִים תֹּאבֵד׃
קיג א ב הַלְלוּיָהּ ׀ הַלְלוּ עַבְדֵי יְהוָה הַלְלוּ אֶת־שֵׁם יְהוָה׃ יְהִי שֵׁם יְהוָה מְבֹרָךְ מֵעַתָּה כד לחודש
ג ד וְעַד־עוֹלָם׃ מִמִּזְרַח־שֶׁמֶשׁ עַד־מְבוֹאוֹ מְהֻלָּל שֵׁם יְהוָה׃ רָם עַל־כָּל־גּוֹיִם ׀ יְהוָה
ה ו עַל הַשָּׁמַיִם כְּבוֹדוֹ׃ מִי כַּיהוָה אֱלֹהֵינוּ הַמַּגְבִּיהִי לָשָׁבֶת׃ הַמַּשְׁפִּילִי לִרְאוֹת
ז ח בַּשָּׁמַיִם וּבָאָרֶץ׃ מְקִימִי מֵעָפָר דָּל מֵאַשְׁפֹּת יָרִים אֶבְיוֹן׃ לְהוֹשִׁיבִי עִם־נְדִיבִים
ט עִם נְדִיבֵי עַמּוֹ׃ מוֹשִׁיבִי ׀ עֲקֶרֶת הַבַּיִת אֵם־הַבָּנִים שְׂמֵחָה הַלְלוּיָהּ׃
קיד א ב בְּצֵאת יִשְׂרָאֵל מִמִּצְרָיִם בֵּית יַעֲקֹב מֵעַם לֹעֵז׃ הָיְתָה יְהוּדָה לְקָדְשׁוֹ יִשְׂרָאֵל
ג ד מַמְשְׁלוֹתָיו׃ הַיָּם רָאָה וַיָּנֹס הַיַּרְדֵּן יִסֹּב לְאָחוֹר׃ הֶהָרִים רָקְדוּ כְאֵילִים גְּבָעוֹת
ה ו כִּבְנֵי־צֹאן׃ מַה־לְּךָ הַיָּם כִּי תָנוּס הַיַּרְדֵּן תִּסֹּב לְאָחוֹר׃ הֶהָרִים תִּרְקְדוּ כְאֵילִים

His dominion. They were the ones who accepted upon themselves God's sovereignty.

3 After that, the Almighty revealed Himself further to them: **The** Red **Sea saw and fled.** The verse describes the splitting of the Red Sea from the perspective of the water itself rather than the perspective of Israel's salvation. After witnessing the revelation of God's glory, the sea retreated in awe. And later, as the Israelites came to the Land of Israel, **the Jordan** River similarly **turned back** from its course to allow them to cross into the land.

4 **The mountains danced like rams, the hills like lambs.** The earth quaked, which made it appear as though the mountains and hills were dancing.

Ram

Lambs

5 The psalmist poetically turns to the inanimate objects involved and asks: **What is it, sea, that makes you flee? The Jordan, that you turn back?**

6 **The mountains, that you dance like rams? The hills, like lambs?**

7 They respond: We quake and flee **from before the Master, Creator of the earth, from before the God of Jacob,** who created everything and has the power to change the world as He desires.

8 Just as He can cause the sea to split and the mountains to quake, it is He **who turns the rock into a pool of water, flint into a fountain of water,** an allusion to the events described in Exodus 17 and Numbers 20.

PSALM 115

A psalm expressing thankfulness for the fact that Israel, as opposed to other nations, had the privilege of choosing God.

PSALMS 115:1–18

115 1 **Not for us, Lord, not for us** do we request salvation, **but for Your name give glory.** Here, and in a number of other places in Psalms, the psalmist expresses the idea that because we are so intimately connected and identified with God, His honor is diminished, as it were, whenever we are humiliated. Conversely, when we are rescued from trouble, this redounds to His honor. We ask of God: Give us honor not for our sake but for the sake of Your name, **for** the sake of **Your kindness** that you promised to show us, and **for** the sake of **Your truth,** Your faithfulness in upholding those promises.

2 The psalmist expands on this theme: **Why should the nations,** who can actually point to their gods, **say: Where now is their God,** who cannot be seen?

3 **But our God is in the heavens; whatever He desires, He does,** for all power is in His hands.

4 **Their idols,** by contrast, **are silver and gold, man's handiwork,** like inanimate, powerless manikins, as detailed in the following verses.

5 **Mouths they have, but cannot speak. Eyes they have, but cannot see.**

6 **Ears they have, but cannot hear. Noses they have, but cannot smell.**

7 **Their hands do not feel.** *Yemishun* can mean both "move" and "feel." These idols can neither move their hands nor feel anything with them. **Their feet do not walk. No utterance comes from their throat,** for they are incapable of speech.

8 The psalmist beseeches God: **May their makers,** those who crafted these idols, **become** silent and lifeless **like them; so too all who put their faith in them.**

9 The psalmist now addresses the nation in accordance with its different factions: **Israel, trust in the Lord** and do not put your faith in such worthless images; **He is their help and their shield.** The abrupt change from direct address to third person, in this verse and the succeeding ones, probably indicates that this ending was meant to be recited by a chorus as a kind of refrain.

10 **House of Aaron, trust in the Lord; He is their help and their shield.**

11 **You who fear the Lord,**[D] **trust in the Lord; He is their help and their shield.**

12 **May the Lord who remembers us** for good **give His blessing** to those who are deserving of it: **May He bless the house of Israel; may He bless the house of Aaron.**

13 **May He bless those who fear the Lord, the young with the old.**

14 **May the Lord increase your numbers, yours and your children's.**

15 **You are blessed by the Lord, the Maker of heaven and earth.**

16 The psalmist offers an explanation as to why he requests God's blessing: **The heavens are the heavens of the Lord,** and that is where He dwells, as it were, **while the earth He has given to the sons of man.** Our place is here on earth, not in the heavens, and we pray for the strength and ability to carry out our earthly, mundane tasks.

17 **The dead cannot praise the Lord.** Though they are also of the earth, they are no longer able to fulfill any kind of role or task, **nor can any who go down into silence** in the grave,

18 **but we will bless the Lord from now until eternity. Halleluya.**

DISCUSSION

115:11| **You who fear the Lord:** It is possible that this expression, which appears several times in Psalms, refers to a group of individuals who live a God-fearing way of life. It may also relate to a specific group of people, whose exact identity is unknown to us, who dedicated themselves to worshipping God, spending much of their time in the Temple engaged in prayer.

ז ח גְּבָעוֹת כִּבְנֵי־צֹאן׃ מִלִּפְנֵי אָדוֹן חוּלִי אָרֶץ מִלִּפְנֵי אֱלוֹהַּ יַעֲקֹב׃ הַהֹפְכִי הַצּוּר
אֲגַם־מָיִם חַלָּמִישׁ לְמַעְיְנוֹ־מָיִם׃
קטו א ב לֹא לָנוּ יְהוָה לֹא לָנוּ כִּי־לְשִׁמְךָ תֵּן כָּבוֹד עַל־חַסְדְּךָ עַל־אֲמִתֶּךָ׃ לָמָּה יֹאמְרוּ
ג ד הַגּוֹיִם אַיֵּה־נָא אֱלֹהֵיהֶם׃ וֵאלֹהֵינוּ בַשָּׁמָיִם כֹּל אֲשֶׁר־חָפֵץ עָשָׂה׃ עֲצַבֵּיהֶם כֶּסֶף
ה ו וְזָהָב מַעֲשֵׂה יְדֵי אָדָם׃ פֶּה־לָהֶם וְלֹא יְדַבֵּרוּ עֵינַיִם לָהֶם וְלֹא יִרְאוּ׃ אׇזְנַיִם לָהֶם
ז וְלֹא יִשְׁמָעוּ אַף לָהֶם וְלֹא יְרִיחוּן׃ יְדֵיהֶם ׀ וְלֹא יְמִישׁוּן רַגְלֵיהֶם וְלֹא יְהַלֵּכוּ לֹא־
ח ט יֶהְגּוּ בִּגְרוֹנָם׃ כְּמוֹהֶם יִהְיוּ עֹשֵׂיהֶם כֹּל אֲשֶׁר־בֹּטֵחַ בָּהֶם׃ יִשְׂרָאֵל בְּטַח בַּיהוָה
י יא עֶזְרָם וּמָגִנָּם הוּא׃ בֵּית אַהֲרֹן בִּטְחוּ בַיהוָה עֶזְרָם וּמָגִנָּם הוּא׃ יִרְאֵי יְהוָה בִּטְחוּ
יב בַיהוָה עֶזְרָם וּמָגִנָּם הוּא׃ יְהוָה זְכָרָנוּ יְבָרֵךְ יְבָרֵךְ אֶת־בֵּית יִשְׂרָאֵל יְבָרֵךְ אֶת־
יג יד בֵּית אַהֲרֹן׃ יְבָרֵךְ יִרְאֵי יְהוָה הַקְּטַנִּים עִם־הַגְּדֹלִים׃ יֹסֵף יְהוָה עֲלֵיכֶם עֲלֵיכֶם
טו טז וְעַל־בְּנֵיכֶם׃ בְּרוּכִים אַתֶּם לַיהוָה עֹשֵׂה שָׁמַיִם וָאָרֶץ׃ הַשָּׁמַיִם שָׁמַיִם לַיהוָה
יז יח וְהָאָרֶץ נָתַן לִבְנֵי־אָדָם׃ לֹא הַמֵּתִים יְהַלְלוּ־יָהּ וְלֹא כׇּל־יֹרְדֵי דוּמָה׃ וַאֲנַחְנוּ ׀
נְבָרֵךְ יָהּ מֵעַתָּה וְעַד־עוֹלָם הַלְלוּ־יָהּ׃
קטז א ב אָהַבְתִּי כִּי־יִשְׁמַע ׀ יְהוָה אֶת־קוֹלִי תַּחֲנוּנָי׃ כִּי־הִטָּה אׇזְנוֹ לִי וּבְיָמַי אֶקְרָא׃
ג ד אֲפָפוּנִי ׀ חֶבְלֵי־מָוֶת וּמְצָרֵי שְׁאוֹל מְצָאוּנִי צָרָה וְיָגוֹן אֶמְצָא׃ וּבְשֵׁם־יְהוָה
ה ו אֶקְרָא אָנָּה יְהוָה מַלְּטָה נַפְשִׁי׃ חַנּוּן יְהוָה וְצַדִּיק וֵאלֹהֵינוּ מְרַחֵם׃ שֹׁמֵר פְּתָאיִם

PSALM 116

A psalm of thanksgiving offered by one who has been rescued from great peril, such as serious illness.

PSALMS 116:1–19

116 1 **I am happy, for the Lord heard my voice, my pleas.** This opening verse summarizes the main theme of the psalm. The psalmist is joyful not only because he was rescued but also because God listened to his prayer.

2 **For He inclined His ear to me, and in all my days** of hardship and adversity **I call out to Him.**

3 **Cords of death were wrapped around me; agonies of the grave assailed me** when **I encountered distress and sorrow.**

4 In those situations, **I called in the name of the Lord: Please, Lord, save my life.**

5 **The Lord is gracious and righteous, and our God is merciful.**

6 **The Lord protects the simple.** The word *petayim*, translated here as "the simple," refers to people who are naïve and therefore likely to be enticed [*mitpateh*] into troublesome situations. Since they do not know how to protect themselves,

God protects them so they do not come to too much harm. **I was brought low, and He saved me.**
7 **Return, my soul, to restfulness, for the Lord has helped you.**
8 **For You rescued me from death, my eyes from tears, my feet from obstruction.**
9 Now that I have been saved from peril, **I walk before the Lord in the land of the living,** without concern for my survival.
10 **I believed** in You **as I spoke** my words of prayer before You, **when I was suffering greatly.**
11 **In my haste, I said: All men are false.** Suffering is a subjective experience that is often exacerbated by the sense of being alone and abandoned, and many people in distress jump to the mistaken conclusion that no one around them cares. In truth, even in the darkest hours, people have at least a few loyal friends who will not abandon them. But this may not be immediately apparent, and the seeming lack of support can lead to despondency.
12 The psalmist now turns to words of praise: **What shall I give to the Lord in return for all the good He rendered me?**
13 **I will lift a cup of salvation,** referring to a cup of wine that is raised in a public toast of thanksgiving, **and I will call in the name of the Lord** with words of thanks for Him.
14 Now that I have been delivered from danger, **I will fulfill my vows to the Lord,** which I undertook in my times of distress. When possible, I will fulfill them **in the presence of all His people,** in order to publicize God's kindness to me and to inspire others.
15 **Weighty in the eyes of the Lord is the death of His devoted ones.** God does not want to bring death to those who love Him.
16 With this in mind, the psalmist issues his plea: **I beseech You, Lord,** to come to my aid, **for I am Your servant, your servant the son of Your handmaid.** The phrase "I am Your servant, the son of Your handmaid" describes an individual born into a family of slaves who has never known any personal independence. But in contrast to the demeaning human institution of slavery, servitude to God is uplifting and liberating. In fact, the result has been that **You have loosened my bonds.** You have freed me from all my suffering and pain.
17 **I will offer a thanksgiving offering to You** for saving me from peril, **and I will call in the name of the Lord** with cries of thanksgiving.
18 **I will fulfill my** sacrificial **vows to the Lord in the presence of all His people.**
19 These vows, which include thanksgiving sacrifices, will be fulfilled in the main place of public gathering for the people of Israel, **in the courtyards of the House of the Lord, in your midst, Jerusalem. Halleluya.**

PSALM 117

PSALMS 117:1–2

The shortest psalm in the book of Psalms. Although it is counted as a separate chapter, it could easily be regarded as the conclusion of the preceding psalm or as the beginning of the one that follows.

117 1 **Praise the Lord, all nations; extol Him, all peoples.** All nations can see and extol the greatness of God, even when His miracles occur in other places or to other peoples.
2 **For His kindness toward us is overwhelming.** You, the nations of the world, can see the revelation of God's overwhelming kindness toward His people, His servants. **And the truth of the Lord is forever. Halleluya.**

PSALM 118

PSALMS 118:1–29

A song of thanksgiving, the concluding psalm of the Hallel prayer. In part, it describes how an individual person was rescued by God, but it is also a model for the nation as a whole, since the individual happens to be their king. It seems that this psalm too was written for a chorus, as many of its verses in praise of God are written in responsive form.

118 1 The psalm begins on a festive note, with a verse of thanksgiving for God's benevolence, which is found in a number of other chapters of Psalms as well: **Give thanks to the Lord, for He is good;** He has shown kindness toward us, **for His kindness is forever.**
2 **Let Israel now say: His kindness is forever.**
3 **Let the house of Aaron,** the priests who serve in the Temple, **now say: His kindness is forever.**
4 **Let those who fear the Lord now say: His kindness is forever.**
5 After the introductory declarations of praise, the main theme of the psalm, namely, thanksgiving to God for the deliverance He wrought, begins here. From the context (verse 10), it appears that the psalmist is referring to a rescue from a difficult military or political situation. **From the straits I called to the Lord.** When I began my prayer, I felt as though I were in a narrow, constricted space, as if the boundaries of my life were closing in on me. But then **the Lord answered me with a wide expanse.** He answered my prayers not with words but with action, placing me in a situation that alleviated my sense of distress and confinement.
6 **The Lord is with me; I shall not fear. What can man do to me** if God is with me?

ז ח יְהוָה דַּלּוֹתִי וְלִי יְהוֹשִׁיעַ: שׁוּבִי נַפְשִׁי לִמְנוּחָיְכִי כִּי־יְהוָה גָּמַל עָלָיְכִי: כִּי חִלַּצְתָּ
ט נַפְשִׁי מִמָּוֶת אֶת־עֵינִי מִן־דִּמְעָה אֶת־רַגְלִי מִדֶּחִי: אֶתְהַלֵּךְ לִפְנֵי יְהוָה בְּאַרְצוֹת
י יא הַחַיִּים: הֶאֱמַנְתִּי כִּי אֲדַבֵּר אֲנִי עָנִיתִי מְאֹד: אֲנִי אָמַרְתִּי בְחָפְזִי כָּל־הָאָדָם כֹּזֵב:
יב יג מָה־אָשִׁיב לַיהוָה כָּל־תַּגְמוּלוֹהִי עָלָי: כּוֹס־יְשׁוּעוֹת אֶשָּׂא וּבְשֵׁם יְהוָה אֶקְרָא:
יד טו נְדָרַי לַיהוָה אֲשַׁלֵּם נֶגְדָה־נָּא לְכָל־עַמּוֹ: יָקָר בְּעֵינֵי יְהוָה הַמָּוְתָה לַחֲסִידָיו:
טז יז אָנָּה יְהוָה כִּי־אֲנִי עַבְדֶּךָ אֲנִי־עַבְדְּךָ בֶּן־אֲמָתֶךָ פִּתַּחְתָּ לְמוֹסֵרָי: לְךָ־אֶזְבַּח זֶבַח
יח יט תּוֹדָה וּבְשֵׁם יְהוָה אֶקְרָא: נְדָרַי לַיהוָה אֲשַׁלֵּם נֶגְדָה־נָּא לְכָל־עַמּוֹ: בְּחַצְרוֹת ׀
בֵּית יְהוָה בְּתוֹכֵכִי יְרוּשָׁלָםִ הַלְלוּיָהּ:

קיז א ב הַלְלוּ אֶת־יְהוָה כָּל־גּוֹיִם שַׁבְּחוּהוּ כָּל־הָאֻמִּים: כִּי גָבַר עָלֵינוּ ׀ חַסְדּוֹ וֶאֱמֶת־
יְהוָה לְעוֹלָם הַלְלוּיָהּ:

קיח א ב הוֹדוּ לַיהוָה כִּי־טוֹב כִּי לְעוֹלָם חַסְדּוֹ: יֹאמַר־נָא יִשְׂרָאֵל כִּי לְעוֹלָם חַסְדּוֹ:
ג ד יֹאמְרוּ־נָא בֵית־אַהֲרֹן כִּי לְעוֹלָם חַסְדּוֹ: יֹאמְרוּ־נָא יִרְאֵי יְהוָה כִּי לְעוֹלָם חַסְדּוֹ:
ה ו מִן־הַמֵּצַר קָרָאתִי יָּהּ עָנָנִי בַמֶּרְחָב יָהּ: יְהוָה לִי לֹא אִירָא מַה־יַּעֲשֶׂה לִי אָדָם:
ז ח ט יְהוָה לִי בְּעֹזְרָי וַאֲנִי אֶרְאֶה בְשֹׂנְאָי: טוֹב לַחֲסוֹת בַּיהוָה מִבְּטֹחַ בָּאָדָם: טוֹב
י יא לַחֲסוֹת בַּיהוָה מִבְּטֹחַ בִּנְדִיבִים: כָּל־גּוֹיִם סְבָבוּנִי בְּשֵׁם יְהוָה כִּי אֲמִילַם: סַבּוּנִי
יב גַם־סְבָבוּנִי בְּשֵׁם יְהוָה כִּי אֲמִילַם: סַבּוּנִי כִדְבֹרִים דֹּעֲכוּ כְּאֵשׁ קוֹצִים בְּשֵׁם יְהוָה

7 **The Lord is with me, with those who help me; I will gaze upon** the downfall of **my enemies.**

8 **It is better to take refuge in the Lord than to trust in man,** both because of His superior power and, as is pointed out so frequently in Psalms, His unsurpassed trustworthiness.

9 **It is better to take refuge in the Lord than to trust in nobles.**

10 **All the nations surrounded me.** The psalmist depicts his desperation in the face of a military attack by his enemies, who were closing in from all sides. But, he declares: **It is in the name of the Lord** that I put my trust, and it is because of this **that I** am able to **cut them down.**

11 **They,** those enemies, **swarmed around me, indeed they surrounded me; it is in the name of the Lord that I cut them down.**

12 **They swarmed around me like bees** that attack one who approaches their hive, swarming around him, seeking to sting him and drive him away. **They flickered and faded like fire amid thorns.** The psalmist now depicts his enemies as a raging fire; but their conflagration is in fact nothing but a fire among thorns, which begins with a huge flame but very quickly dissipates. **It is in the name of the Lord that I cut them down.**

13 The psalmist now addresses his enemies: **You pushed me hard to make me fall, but the Lord helped me** to prevent this from happening.
14 **The Lord is my strength and song, and He has become my salvation.**[D] All my strength is derived from God, and therefore God is the object of all my songs of praise.
15 After God delivers me from my enemies, **a voice of song and deliverance is** heard **among the tents of the righteous,** who praise Him for His salvation, saying: **The right hand of the Lord brings success.** The "right hand" of God is a poetic symbol of power, as the right hand is generally the stronger one.
16 **The right hand of the Lord is exalted; the right hand of the Lord brings success.**
17 The psalmist now offers words of prayer: **May I not die but live, so I may tell the deeds of the Lord.** This is one of many verses in the Bible that reflect the idea that if a person survives mortal danger, it is incumbent on him to make his story known to others and acknowledge God's hand in his survival, thanking God publicly.
18 **The Lord chastised me severely** during those periods of peril and distress, **but He did not deliver me to death.**
19 Because of God's salvation in protecting me from death, I must recount His deeds and thank Him, and so I declare: **Open for me the gates of righteousness,** apparently a reference to the gates of the Temple, where the psalmist goes to offer his thanks in public. **I will enter through them; I will give thanks to the Lord.**
20 **This is the gate to the Lord; the vindicated,** those who were found by God to be deserving, and were granted victory by Him, **will enter through it** to praise God.
21 **I will give thanks to You, for You answered me** and my prayers; **You have been my salvation.**
22 **The stone that the builders rejected,** considering it of inferior quality or appearance, subsequently **became the cornerstone,** the most structurally essential and most visible part of the building. This metaphor is intended to express the idea that sometimes a person's perspective can change upon pondering past events. Things or people that may have at first seemed insignificant may turn out to be the key to one's deliverance.
23 Concerning such reversals of import and significance, it may be said: **This was from the Lord.** When seemingly decisive or critical events turn out to be inconsequential, or vice versa, it is God's doing. **It is wondrous,** remarkable and surprising, **in our eyes.**
24 **This** day of deliverance **is the day of the Lord's doing; we rejoice and exult in Him.**
25 The first part of this verse is a prayer offered during a time of distress: **Lord, save us, we beseech You!** It is followed by words that are said after the danger has passed: **Lord, grant us success, we beseech You!**
26 The preceding verse marks the end of the prayer of the person who, having been saved from peril, comes to the Temple to offer his thanks. At this point, the priests or others within the Temple offer their response: **Blessed be the one who comes in the name of the Lord; we bless you from the House of the Lord.**
27 Both parties continue: **The Lord is God; He has given us light** by delivering us from distress and darkness into bright salvation. **Bind the festival offering with cords,** in order to prevent it from running free and creating havoc, **and from there to the horns of the altar.**
28 The psalmist restates his gratitude to God: **You are my Almighty, and I will give thanks to You. My God, I will exalt You.**
29 The psalm ends with a repetition of the praise of the first verse: **Give thanks to the Lord, for He is good, for His kindness is forever.**

DISCUSSION

118:14 | **The Lord is my strength and song, and He has become my salvation:** These ancient words were first uttered by the Israelites in the Song at the Sea (Exodus 15:2). A very similar phrase appears in Isaiah (12:2). Several interpretations are offered for the first half of this verse: "Strength and song belong to the Lord"; "Song and praise for the strength of the Lord"; "Strength, expressed through the cutting off of His enemies, belongs to the Lord"; and "My strength and my song belong to the Lord."

יג יד כִּי אֲמִילַם׃ דַּחֹה דְחִיתַנִי לִנְפֹּל וַיהוה עֲזָרָנִי׃ עָזִּי וְזִמְרָת יָהּ וַיְהִי־לִי לִישׁוּעָה׃
טו טז קוֹל ׀ רִנָּה וִישׁוּעָה בְּאָהֳלֵי צַדִּיקִים יְמִין יהוה עֹשָׂה חָיִל׃ יְמִין יהוה רוֹמֵמָה יְמִין
יז יח יהוה עֹשָׂה חָיִל׃ לֹא־אָמוּת כִּי־אֶחְיֶה וַאֲסַפֵּר מַעֲשֵׂי יָהּ׃ יַסֹּר יִסְּרַנִּי יָּהּ וְלַמָּוֶת
יט כ לֹא נְתָנָנִי׃ פִּתְחוּ־לִי שַׁעֲרֵי־צֶדֶק אָבֹא־בָם אוֹדֶה יָהּ׃ זֶה־הַשַּׁעַר לַיהוה צַדִּיקִים
כא כב יָבֹאוּ בוֹ׃ אוֹדְךָ כִּי עֲנִיתָנִי וַתְּהִי־לִי לִישׁוּעָה׃ אֶבֶן מָאֲסוּ הַבּוֹנִים הָיְתָה לְרֹאשׁ
כג כד פִּנָּה׃ מֵאֵת יהוה הָיְתָה זֹּאת הִיא נִפְלָאת בְּעֵינֵינוּ׃ זֶה־הַיּוֹם עָשָׂה יהוה נָגִילָה
כה כו וְנִשְׂמְחָה בוֹ׃ אָנָּא יהוה הוֹשִׁיעָה נָּא אָנָּא יהוה הַצְלִיחָה נָּא׃ בָּרוּךְ הַבָּא בְּשֵׁם
כז יהוה בֵּרַכְנוּכֶם מִבֵּית יהוה׃ אֵל ׀ יהוה וַיָּאֶר לָנוּ אִסְרוּ־חַג בַּעֲבֹתִים עַד־קַרְנוֹת
כח כט הַמִּזְבֵּחַ׃ אֵלִי אַתָּה וְאוֹדֶךָּ אֱלֹהַי אֲרוֹמְמֶךָּ׃ הוֹדוּ לַיהוה כִּי־טוֹב כִּי לְעוֹלָם חַסְדּוֹ׃
קיט א ב אַשְׁרֵי תְמִימֵי־דָרֶךְ הַהֹלְכִים בְּתוֹרַת יהוה׃ אַשְׁרֵי נֹצְרֵי עֵדֹתָיו בְּכָל־לֵב יִדְרְשׁוּהוּ׃ כה לחודש
ג ד ה אַף לֹא־פָעֲלוּ עַוְלָה בִּדְרָכָיו הָלָכוּ׃ אַתָּה צִוִּיתָה פִקֻּדֶיךָ לִשְׁמֹר מְאֹד׃ אַחֲלַי
ו ז יִכֹּנוּ דְרָכָי לִשְׁמֹר חֻקֶּיךָ׃ אָז לֹא־אֵבוֹשׁ בְּהַבִּיטִי אֶל־כָּל־מִצְוֺתֶיךָ׃ אוֹדְךָ בְּיֹשֶׁר
ח לֵבָב בְּלָמְדִי מִשְׁפְּטֵי צִדְקֶךָ׃ אֶת־חֻקֶּיךָ אֶשְׁמֹר אַל־תַּעַזְבֵנִי עַד־מְאֹד׃

PSALM 119

PSALMS 119:1–176

A distinctly didactic psalm comprising short verses, often not linked to one another in terms of their content and arranged in alphabetical order, with eight verses allotted to each of the twenty-two letters of the Hebrew alphabet. Although each verse is an independent, disjointed unit, two features unify the psalm into a coherent whole. First, nearly all the verses are written in the first-person singular voice, reflecting an individual turning to the Almighty both to express his prayers and wishes and to recount His deeds. The second theme repeated throughout the psalm is that of praise for God's Torah and commandments. The unifying motif of the psalm is the psalmist's devotion to God and his moving ever closer to Him by perceiving His revelation in the Torah. A great deal has been written about the precision of phrasing and the recurring patterns in this psalm. Some commentators suggest that it is a collection of one-line sayings meant to be recited sequentially, one verse per day, meaning that two full cycles would be completed in a lunar year.

119 *25th day of month*

1 **Happy are those whose path is blameless,** those who follow the proper path, **who follow the teaching of the Lord.** Note that here and elsewhere in this psalm the word *Torah* is translated as "teaching."

2 **Happy are those who uphold His precepts and seek Him wholeheartedly** through observance of those commandments.

3 **They do not engage in wrongdoing, but rather walk in His ways** that He has set forth in His Torah.

4 The psalmist now speaks to God: **You commanded Your edicts to be diligently observed.**

5 **It is my wish that my ways be firmly set to observe Your statutes,**

6 **for then I would not be ashamed when looking upon all Your commandments,** for I will be able to honestly say that I have done my best to observe them.

7 **I give thanks to You with a sincere heart as I study Your righteous laws.** This verse can be understood in two ways: The very act of studying God's laws is a form of giving thanks. Alternatively, after having studied the laws, I give thanks to God for showing me, through the Torah, the true and proper path.

8 **I follow Your statutes.** I strive to observe Your commandments, and therefore I pray: **Do not utterly forsake me,** so that I can continue following this path.

9 **How can a young man bring merit to his path?** How can a young person choose the right path? **By observing what befits Your word,** by following everything You have commanded.

10 **I seek You with all my heart.** I desire to become close to You, and I pray to you: **Let me not stray from Your commandments.** Grant me the strength to continue observing Your commandments.

11 **I store Your saying in my heart, so as not to sin against You.** I keep Your teachings in my heart; this helps me to avoid sinning, or at least guards me from sinning out of ignorance.

12 A short prayer: **Blessed are You, Lord; teach me Your statutes.**

13 **With my lips I recount all the laws of Your mouth.** I speak words of Torah aloud and impart them to others as well.

14 **I rejoice in** following **the path of Your precepts as** a person would rejoice **over all riches,** over suddenly receiving a great fortune.

15 **I speak about Your edicts and** I also **look upon Your ways,** pondering their meaning.

16 **I delight in Your statutes.** Your commandments and Your Torah are not a burden for me. In fact, I actually delight in them, as I find them engaging and interesting. As a result, **I do not forget Your word** or your teachings.

17 **Grant kindness to** me, **Your servant, that I might live and keep Your word.**

18 **Uncover my eyes,** grant me understanding and insight, **so I might perceive the wonders of Your teaching.** To fully appreciate the greatness of the Torah, it is not sufficient merely to speak about it or to observe its commandments; therefore, the psalmist implores God for enlightenment.

19 **I am but a sojourner on earth.** I am here on earth for a limited time, like a traveler on the road, so **do not hide Your commandments from me.** Allow me to use the limited time that I have to learn Your commandments. This can be seen as a continuation of the previous verses, in which the psalmist prayed for life and enlightenment. Alternatively, the verse can be read as a plea for guidance: During my days on earth, I am like a stranger in a foreign land, requiring instruction in the laws and customs of the land, that is, the laws of Your Torah.

20 **My soul longingly partakes of Your laws at all times.** The word *garsa*, translated as "partakes," conjures up the image of someone eating a delicacy with great enthusiasm.

21 **You rebuke the accursed, insolent ones who stray from Your commandments.**

22 **Remove disgrace and abuse from me, for I have upheld Your precepts** and can therefore ask You to protect me from the shame and humiliation that is heaped upon me.

23 **Even when princes sit and talk about me,** engaging in a discussion that should interest me, Your servant, and elicit my participation, **Your servant** instead **reflects on Your statutes** and avoids joining the conversation.

24 **Also Your precepts are my delight.** Even my entertainment consists of studying Your Torah. Moreover, those precepts function as **my counselors,** in the sense that they provide me with guidance as to how to best conduct my life.

25 **My soul cleaves to the dust.** I am completely depressed and disheartened. In this difficult situation, all I can do is pray: **Revive me as Your word.** Grant me life just as there is life in the words of Your Torah.

26 **I told of my ways,** I recounted to You the various matters and troubles in my life, **and You answered me.** You responded to my prayers. Now that You have granted me relief, I have one primary request: **Teach me Your statutes.**

27 **Make me understand the way of Your edicts, and** then **I will** be able to **speak about Your wonders.**

28 **My soul is dripping with anguish.** The image here is of a soul crying incessantly, to the extent that it becomes wrung out and desiccated. Therefore, the psalmist pleads: **Sustain me, as befits Your word.**

29 **Remove the path of falsehood from me.** Allow me to learn only about the true path. This may also be seen as a request that God grant the wisdom to avoid living one's life in accordance with false beliefs. **Grant me** knowledge of **Your teaching.**

30 **I have chosen the path of faith; I have placed Your laws** before me.

31 Moreover, **I cleave to Your precepts; Lord, do not shame me.** Keep me from experiencing shame, since I am doing my utmost to follow Your laws.

32 **I run in the path of Your commandments, for You widen my heart.** If You grant me breadth of heart, that is, a good temperament and adequate ability, I will fulfill Your commandments with alacrity, as one might run down a path.

33 **Teach me, Lord, the way of Your statutes, and I will** then be able to **uphold it to the end.**

34 **Give me understanding, so I might** then **uphold Your teaching and follow it wholeheartedly.**

35 **Guide me in the path of Your commandments, for in it is my desire.** Although I freely desire and choose this path, I need guidance in following it.

36 **Incline my heart toward Your precepts,** so that they become my chief interest and delight, **and** do **not** direct it **toward** seeking **material gain.**

37 Similarly, **avert my eyes from seeing falsehood; through Your ways,** rather than through false ideas and visions, **give me life.**

38 **Fulfill the promise You made to Your servant, which is for those who fear You.** You have given Your word that those who serve and fear You are worthy of Your protection.

ט י בַּמֶּה יְזַכֶּה־נַּעַר אֶת־אָרְחוֹ לִשְׁמֹר כִּדְבָרֶךָ׃ בְּכָל־לִבִּי דְרַשְׁתִּיךָ אַל־תַּשְׁגֵּנִי
יא יב מִמִּצְוֺתֶיךָ׃ בְּלִבִּי צָפַנְתִּי אִמְרָתֶךָ לְמַעַן לֹא אֶחֱטָא־לָךְ׃ בָּרוּךְ אַתָּה יהוה לַמְּדֵנִי
יג יד חֻקֶּיךָ׃ בִּשְׂפָתַי סִפַּרְתִּי כֹּל מִשְׁפְּטֵי־פִיךָ׃ בְּדֶרֶךְ עֵדְוֺתֶיךָ שַׂשְׂתִּי כְּעַל כָּל־הוֹן׃
טו טז בְּפִקֻּדֶיךָ אָשִׂיחָה וְאַבִּיטָה אֹרְחֹתֶיךָ׃ בְּחֻקֹּתֶיךָ אֶשְׁתַּעֲשָׁע לֹא אֶשְׁכַּח דְּבָרֶךָ׃
יז יח גְּמֹל עַל־עַבְדְּךָ אֶחְיֶה וְאֶשְׁמְרָה דְבָרֶךָ׃ גַּל־עֵינַי וְאַבִּיטָה נִפְלָאוֹת מִתּוֹרָתֶךָ׃
יט כ גֵּר אָנֹכִי בָאָרֶץ אַל־תַּסְתֵּר מִמֶּנִּי מִצְוֺתֶיךָ׃ גָּרְסָה נַפְשִׁי לְתַאֲבָה אֶל־מִשְׁפָּטֶיךָ
כא כב בְכָל־עֵת׃ גָּעַרְתָּ זֵדִים אֲרוּרִים הַשֹּׁגִים מִמִּצְוֺתֶיךָ׃ גַּל מֵעָלַי חֶרְפָּה וָבוּז כִּי עֵדֹתֶיךָ
כג כד נָצָרְתִּי׃ גַּם יָשְׁבוּ שָׂרִים בִּי נִדְבָּרוּ עַבְדְּךָ יָשִׂיחַ בְּחֻקֶּיךָ׃ גַּם־עֵדֹתֶיךָ שַׁעֲשֻׁעָי
אַנְשֵׁי עֲצָתִי׃
כה כו כז דָּבְקָה לֶעָפָר נַפְשִׁי חַיֵּנִי כִּדְבָרֶךָ׃ דְּרָכַי סִפַּרְתִּי וַתַּעֲנֵנִי לַמְּדֵנִי חֻקֶּיךָ׃ דֶּרֶךְ־פִּקּוּדֶיךָ
כח כט הֲבִינֵנִי וְאָשִׂיחָה בְּנִפְלְאוֹתֶיךָ׃ דָּלְפָה נַפְשִׁי מִתּוּגָה קַיְּמֵנִי כִּדְבָרֶךָ׃ דֶּרֶךְ־שֶׁקֶר
ל לא הָסֵר מִמֶּנִּי וְתוֹרָתְךָ חָנֵּנִי׃ דֶּרֶךְ־אֱמוּנָה בָחָרְתִּי מִשְׁפָּטֶיךָ שִׁוִּיתִי׃ דָּבַקְתִּי בְעֵדְוֺתֶיךָ
לב יהוה אַל־תְּבִישֵׁנִי׃ דֶּרֶךְ־מִצְוֺתֶיךָ אָרוּץ כִּי תַרְחִיב לִבִּי׃
לג לד הוֹרֵנִי יהוה דֶּרֶךְ חֻקֶּיךָ וְאֶצְּרֶנָּה עֵקֶב׃ הֲבִינֵנִי וְאֶצְּרָה תוֹרָתֶךָ וְאֶשְׁמְרֶנָּה בְכָל־
לה לו לֵב׃ הַדְרִיכֵנִי בִּנְתִיב מִצְוֺתֶיךָ כִּי־בוֹ חָפָצְתִּי׃ הַט־לִבִּי אֶל־עֵדְוֺתֶיךָ וְאַל אֶל־בָּצַע׃
לז לח הַעֲבֵר עֵינַי מֵרְאוֹת שָׁוְא בִּדְרָכֶךָ חַיֵּנִי׃ הָקֵם לְעַבְדְּךָ אִמְרָתֶךָ אֲשֶׁר לְיִרְאָתֶךָ׃
לט מ הַעֲבֵר חֶרְפָּתִי אֲשֶׁר יָגֹרְתִּי כִּי מִשְׁפָּטֶיךָ טוֹבִים׃ הִנֵּה תָּאַבְתִּי לְפִקֻּדֶיךָ בְּצִדְקָתְךָ
חַיֵּנִי׃
מא מב וִיבֹאֻנִי חֲסָדֶךָ יהוה תְּשׁוּעָתְךָ כְּאִמְרָתֶךָ׃ וְאֶעֱנֶה חֹרְפִי דָבָר כִּי־בָטַחְתִּי בִּדְבָרֶךָ׃

39 **Remove my disgrace** that others have heaped upon me, **which I dread, for Your laws,** which I follow faithfully, **are good,** and it would be inappropriate to allow me to suffer such disgrace.

40 **How I long for Your edicts!** And for this reason, I pray to You: **In Your righteousness give me life.**

41 **Let Your kindness reach me, Lord, as well as Your deliverance, as befits Your promise.**

42 **And I will** have the strength and confidence to **answer** and stand firm against **those who revile me, for I trust in Your word,** which gives me the courage of conviction.

43 **Do not withhold the word of truth altogether from my mouth.** Do not hold back my ability to speak truth and avoid falsehood, **for I trust in Your laws** and therefore hope that You will help me in this matter. The word *yiḥalti*, translated here as "I trust," can be understood as both anticipation and hope.
44 **May I follow Your teaching always and forever.**
45 **Let me walk in a wide, expansive place,** free from the confinement of distress, **for I have sought Your edicts** and am therefore deserving of Your aid.
46 **I will recount Your precepts,** discussing the Torah and its commandments, **before kings,** perhaps referring even to foreign kings who have never heard of the Torah or its laws, **and not be ashamed** to do so, because I take such pride in Your Torah.
47 **I will delight in Your commandments, which I love.** Because I love the commandments, I enjoy occupying myself with them.
48 **I will lift my hands** in prayer **to** be able to delve more and more into **Your commandments, which I love, and I will reflect on Your statutes.**
49 **Remember the word to Your servant, with which You gave me hope.** This interpretation renders *yiḥaltani* as "You gave me hope." The word can also be translated as "You put Your trust in me," in which case the verse would read: I ask You to remember the promises You made to me because You put Your trust in me; that is, You found favor in me and brought me close to You.
50 **This is my comfort in my affliction.** My one consolation during times of distress is **that Your utterance revives me** and gives me relief.
51 **Evildoers mock me** and my way of life **greatly, but I do not veer from Your teaching.**
52 **I have always remembered Your laws, Lord, and I am** thereby **comforted.**
53 **Great distress has seized me because of the wicked who have forsaken Your teaching.** I cannot be indifferent to people who abandon Your Torah; their very existence weighs heavily on me and causes me pain.
54 **Your statutes were** as pleasant as **songs to me.** *Ḥukekha*, "Your statutes," usually refers to those commandments whose rationale is not known. Even these bring me great joy **in the house of my sojourning,** even when I am a sojourner in a strange place, not in a comfortable or tranquil setting.
55 **Lord, I remember Your name** even **in the night,** when I am alone, **and I follow Your teaching.**
56 **This,** an apparent reference to the comfort and success mentioned in the previous verses, **became mine, because I upheld Your precepts.**
57 **I have declared** my decision **that the Lord is my portion,** and therefore it is my desire **to follow Your words.**
58 **I plead for Your countenance with a whole heart; be gracious to me, as befits Your promise** to grant reward to those who follow Your ways.
59 I periodically **consider** and evaluate **my ways, and** when I find that improvement is needed, **I turn my feet toward Your precepts.**
60 **I hasten, I do not delay, in following Your commandments.**
61 **The pains of the wicked** that they inflicted upon me **contorted me, but** nevertheless, **I did not forget Your teaching.**
62 **At midnight,** a time when most people are asleep, **I rise to give thanks to You for Your righteous laws.**
63 **I am a friend to all who fear You.** I attempt to be close to such people, **to those who follow your edicts.**
64 **The earth is full of Your kindness, Lord,** and I pray: **Teach me Your statutes.** I wish not only to benefit from Your beneficence but also to understand Your ways.
65 **You dealt well with Your servant, Lord, as befits Your word,** Your promise to do good to the righteous.
66 **Teach me good discernment,** literally "a good taste," **and understanding.** Show me both the pleasure and the wisdom that are gained from Your Torah. **For I believe in Your commandments,** and therefore I beseech You to deepen my understanding so that I can delight even more in Your commandments.
67 **Before I discussed it,** before I immersed myself in the ways of the Torah, **I would go astray,** because I did not have sufficient knowledge to know what needed to be done; **but now** that I have studied the Torah, **I** faithfully **follow Your saying.**
68 **You are good and do good** for the entire world. **Teach me Your statutes.** My personal request is for Your goodness toward me to be reflected in Your teaching me Your laws.
69 **Evildoers pin falsehoods on me.** But **I** pay no heed to them and their slander, and **uphold Your edicts with a whole heart.**
70 **Their hearts are dulled, as if covered with fat,** without feeling or understanding. But **I delight in Your teaching** and have no interest in their illusory pleasures.
71 **It is good for me that I was afflicted** whenever I strayed from the proper path, for Your chastisement caused me to correct my conduct, **so I might learn Your statutes.**
72 **The teaching of Your mouth is better for me than thousands of gold and silver pieces.**
73 **Your hands made me and set me in place.** Now I request: **Give me understanding, so I might learn Your commandments.**
74 **May those** other people **who fear You see me and be glad, because I hope for Your word.** These God-fearing people are happy to see that I share their desire for the word of God.

מג מד וְאַל־תַּצֵּל מִפִּי דְבַר־אֱמֶת עַד־מְאֹד כִּי לְמִשְׁפָּטֶךָ יִחָלְתִּי׃ וְאֶשְׁמְרָה תוֹרָתְךָ
מה מו תָמִיד לְעוֹלָם וָעֶד׃ וְאֶתְהַלְּכָה בָרְחָבָה כִּי פִקֻּדֶיךָ דָרָשְׁתִּי׃ וַאֲדַבְּרָה בְעֵדֹתֶיךָ
מז מח נֶגֶד מְלָכִים וְלֹא אֵבוֹשׁ׃ וְאֶשְׁתַּעֲשַׁע בְּמִצְוֺתֶיךָ אֲשֶׁר אָהָבְתִּי׃ וְאֶשָּׂא־כַפַּי אֶל־
מִצְוֺתֶיךָ אֲשֶׁר אָהָבְתִּי וְאָשִׂיחָה בְחֻקֶּיךָ׃
מט נ נא זְכֹר־דָּבָר לְעַבְדֶּךָ עַל אֲשֶׁר יִחַלְתָּנִי׃ זֹאת נֶחָמָתִי בְעָנְיִי כִּי אִמְרָתְךָ חִיָּתְנִי׃ זֵדִים
נב הֱלִיצֻנִי עַד־מְאֹד מִתּוֹרָתְךָ לֹא נָטִיתִי׃ זָכַרְתִּי מִשְׁפָּטֶיךָ מֵעוֹלָם ׀ יְהוָה וָאֶתְנֶחָם׃
נג נד זַלְעָפָה אֲחָזַתְנִי מֵרְשָׁעִים עֹזְבֵי תּוֹרָתֶךָ׃ זְמִרוֹת הָיוּ־לִי חֻקֶּיךָ בְּבֵית מְגוּרָי׃
נה נו זָכַרְתִּי בַלַּיְלָה שִׁמְךָ יְהוָה וָאֶשְׁמְרָה תּוֹרָתֶךָ׃ זֹאת הָיְתָה־לִּי כִּי פִקֻּדֶיךָ נָצָרְתִּי׃
נז נח נט חֶלְקִי יְהוָה אָמַרְתִּי לִשְׁמֹר דְּבָרֶיךָ׃ חִלִּיתִי פָנֶיךָ בְכָל־לֵב חָנֵּנִי כְּאִמְרָתֶךָ׃ חִשַּׁבְתִּי
ס סא דְרָכָי וָאָשִׁיבָה רַגְלַי אֶל־עֵדֹתֶיךָ׃ חַשְׁתִּי וְלֹא הִתְמַהְמָהְתִּי לִשְׁמֹר מִצְוֺתֶיךָ׃ חֶבְלֵי
סב רְשָׁעִים עִוְּדֻנִי תּוֹרָתְךָ לֹא שָׁכָחְתִּי׃ חֲצוֹת־לַיְלָה אָקוּם לְהוֹדוֹת לָךְ עַל מִשְׁפְּטֵי
סג סד צִדְקֶךָ׃ חָבֵר אָנִי לְכָל־אֲשֶׁר יְרֵאוּךָ וּלְשֹׁמְרֵי פִּקּוּדֶיךָ׃ חַסְדְּךָ יְהוָה מָלְאָה הָאָרֶץ
חֻקֶּיךָ לַמְּדֵנִי׃
סה סו טוֹב עָשִׂיתָ עִם־עַבְדְּךָ יְהוָה כִּדְבָרֶךָ׃ טוּב טַעַם וָדַעַת לַמְּדֵנִי כִּי בְמִצְוֺתֶיךָ
סז סח הֶאֱמָנְתִּי׃ טֶרֶם אֶעֱנֶה אֲנִי שֹׁגֵג וְעַתָּה אִמְרָתְךָ שָׁמָרְתִּי׃ טוֹב־אַתָּה וּמֵטִיב לַמְּדֵנִי
סט ע חֻקֶּיךָ׃ טָפְלוּ עָלַי שֶׁקֶר זֵדִים אֲנִי בְּכָל־לֵב ׀ אֱצֹּר פִּקּוּדֶיךָ׃ טָפַשׁ כַּחֵלֶב לִבָּם אֲנִי
עא עב תּוֹרָתְךָ שִׁעֲשָׁעְתִּי׃ טוֹב־לִי כִי־עֻנֵּיתִי לְמַעַן אֶלְמַד חֻקֶּיךָ׃ טוֹב־לִי תוֹרַת־פִּיךָ יז
מֵאַלְפֵי זָהָב וָכָסֶף׃
עג עד יָדֶיךָ עָשׂוּנִי וַיְכוֹנְנוּנִי הֲבִינֵנִי וְאֶלְמְדָה מִצְוֺתֶיךָ׃ יְרֵאֶיךָ יִרְאוּנִי וְיִשְׂמָחוּ כִּי לִדְבָרְךָ

75 **I know, Lord, that Your rulings are just.** I acknowledge Your justice even when things do not go my way, **and that** when **You afflicted me,** You did so **in faithfulness,** with good reason.

76 **May Your kindness comfort me** in my times of distress, **as You promised Your servant** that You would come to his assistance.

77 **May Your mercy come to me, so I might live; Your teaching is my delight,** and I am therefore deserving of Your mercy.

78 **May the evildoers be shamed for contorting me with lies.** They defame me and my path of righteousness. But despite their falsehoods, **I will reflect on Your edicts.**

79 Even when I have sinned and caused the God-fearing people to shun me, **may those who fear You and who know Your precepts,** the people whom I respect and whose company I desire, **turn to me** and again draw near to me.

80 **May my heart be blameless in Your statutes,** may I conduct myself with complete integrity and virtue and not stray from the true path, **lest I be ashamed** of myself.

81 **My soul goes out in yearning for Your salvation; I await** the fulfillment of **Your word.**

82 **My eyes pine for** the fulfillment of **Your promise, saying: When will You comfort me?**

83 **Even when I am** in distress, **like a wineskin in steam,** which shrivels and shrinks, **I do not forget Your statutes.**

84 **How many are the days of Your servant?** The days of my life are numbered. Therefore, I ask: **When will You pass judgment on my pursuers?** This is not an expression of lack of faith in God but rather a request: Since my days are short, please allow me to see in my lifetime that my enemies receive the punishment they deserve.

85 **Evildoers dig pits,** traps, **that are meant for me; they do not act as befits Your teaching,** for they are careless about transgressing the Torah.

86 **All Your commandments are truth,** I believe in them faithfully, **yet they pursue me with lies,** the opposite of truth; **help me** to evade their pursuit.

87 **They nearly rid the earth of me,** yet despite my anguish, **I do not forsake Your edicts.**

88 **Give me life, as befits Your kindness, so I might** have the ability to **follow the precept of Your mouth.**

89 **Forever, Lord, does Your word stand in the heavens.**[D]

90 **Your faithfulness is for all generations; You established the earth, and it stands.** The earth, like the heavens mentioned in the previous verse, is upheld by God's word.

91 **They,** all the inhabitants of the world, **stand today for Your judgment, for all are Your servants,** subject to Your jurisdiction, even if they do not acknowledge it. From the context, it would appear that the word "today" refers to any and every day.

92 **Had Your teaching not been my delight,** expanding my heart, filling me with joy, and acting as a constant source of comfort, **I would have perished in my affliction.**

93 **I will never forget Your edicts,** not only out of dedication to them but for my very survival, **for through them You gave me life.**

94 **I am Yours; save me, for I have sought Your edicts.** The second half of the verse explains the first half: "I am Yours," in that I am always seeking out Your commandments.

95 **The wicked wish to destroy me,** and **I ponder Your precepts,** because they are a source of strength for me in the face of adversity. Moreover, "I ponder Your precepts" because they heighten my awareness of the fact that You oversee the world, and my enemies can do nothing to me against Your will.

96 **I see** that there is **an end to all** things, even **great** and complex **things, but Your commandments are exceedingly wide** and boundless; they have no end.

97 **How I love Your teaching! It is what I speak of all day.** I love
26th day of month the Torah to such an extent that it is the main subject of my conversation.

98 **Your commandments make me wiser than my enemies,** affording me protection from them, **for they are always mine.** I am constantly involved in their study and observance. The Torah is not only a spiritual guide but a fount of practical knowledge that enables me to triumph over my foes.

99 **I have gained discernment beyond that of all my teachers, for Your precepts are my conversation.** In addition to all the wisdom I received from my teachers, the fact that I constantly speak about the commandments has given me the ability to surpass them in knowledge.

100 **I gain insight from the elders, for I uphold Your edicts** and am thereby better able to hear and absorb the wisdom they impart.

101 **From all evil paths I bar my feet.** I fetter my feet, as it were, in order to prevent myself from going to inappropriate places, **so I might follow Your word.**

102 **I have not turned away from Your laws, for You Yourself have taught me** the proper, true path.

103 **How sweet is Your saying to my palate, more than honey to my mouth.**

104 **I gain insights from Your edicts; therefore, I hate every path of falsehood.** Your laws teach me not only how to conduct myself but also how to discern the true value of things.

עה עו יִחָלְתִּי: יָדַעְתִּי יְהוָה כִּי־צֶדֶק מִשְׁפָּטֶיךָ וֶאֱמוּנָה עִנִּיתָנִי: יְהִי־נָא חַסְדְּךָ לְנַחֲמֵנִי
עז עח כְּאִמְרָתְךָ לְעַבְדֶּךָ: יְבֹאוּנִי רַחֲמֶיךָ וְאֶחְיֶה כִּי־תוֹרָתְךָ שַׁעֲשֻׁעָי: יֵבֹשׁוּ זֵדִים כִּי־
עט פ שֶׁקֶר עִוְּתוּנִי אֲנִי אָשִׂיחַ בְּפִקּוּדֶיךָ: יָשׁוּבוּ לִי יְרֵאֶיךָ וידעו עֵדֹתֶיךָ: יְהִי־לִבִּי תָמִים וְיֹדְעֵי
בְּחֻקֶּיךָ לְמַעַן לֹא אֵבוֹשׁ:
פא פב כָּלְתָה לִתְשׁוּעָתְךָ נַפְשִׁי לִדְבָרְךָ יִחָלְתִּי: כָּלוּ עֵינַי לְאִמְרָתֶךָ לֵאמֹר מָתַי תְּנַחֲמֵנִי:
פג פד כִּי־הָיִיתִי כְּנֹאד בְּקִיטוֹר חֻקֶּיךָ לֹא שָׁכָחְתִּי: כַּמָּה יְמֵי־עַבְדֶּךָ מָתַי תַּעֲשֶׂה
פה פו בְרֹדְפַי מִשְׁפָּט: כָּרוּ־לִי זֵדִים שִׁיחוֹת אֲשֶׁר לֹא כְתוֹרָתֶךָ: כָּל־מִצְוֺתֶיךָ אֱמוּנָה
פז פח שֶׁקֶר רְדָפוּנִי עָזְרֵנִי: כִּמְעַט כִּלּוּנִי בָאָרֶץ וַאֲנִי לֹא־עָזַבְתִּי פִקֻּדֶיךָ: כְּחַסְדְּךָ חַיֵּנִי
וְאֶשְׁמְרָה עֵדוּת פִּיךָ:
פט צ לְעוֹלָם יְהוָה דְּבָרְךָ נִצָּב בַּשָּׁמָיִם: לְדֹר וָדֹר אֱמוּנָתֶךָ כּוֹנַנְתָּ אֶרֶץ וַתַּעֲמֹד:
צא צב לְמִשְׁפָּטֶיךָ עָמְדוּ הַיּוֹם כִּי הַכֹּל עֲבָדֶיךָ: לוּלֵי תוֹרָתְךָ שַׁעֲשֻׁעָי אָז אָבַדְתִּי בְעָנְיִי:
צג צד לְעוֹלָם לֹא־אֶשְׁכַּח פִּקּוּדֶיךָ כִּי־בָם חִיִּיתָנִי: לְךָ־אֲנִי הוֹשִׁיעֵנִי כִּי פִקּוּדֶיךָ דָרָשְׁתִּי:
צה צו לִי קִוּוּ רְשָׁעִים לְאַבְּדֵנִי עֵדֹתֶיךָ אֶתְבּוֹנָן: לְכָל־תִּכְלָה רָאִיתִי קֵץ רְחָבָה מִצְוָתְךָ
מְאֹד:
צז צח מָה־אָהַבְתִּי תוֹרָתֶךָ כָּל־הַיּוֹם הִיא שִׂיחָתִי: מֵאֹיְבַי תְּחַכְּמֵנִי מִצְוֺתֶךָ כִּי לְעוֹלָם כו לחודש
צט ק הִיא־לִי: מִכָּל־מְלַמְּדַי הִשְׂכַּלְתִּי כִּי עֵדְוֺתֶיךָ שִׂיחָה לִי: מִזְּקֵנִים אֶתְבּוֹנָן כִּי פִקּוּדֶיךָ
קא קב נָצָרְתִּי: מִכָּל־אֹרַח רָע כָּלִאתִי רַגְלָי לְמַעַן אֶשְׁמֹר דְּבָרֶךָ: מִמִּשְׁפָּטֶיךָ לֹא־סָרְתִּי
קג קד כִּי־אַתָּה הוֹרֵתָנִי: מַה־נִּמְלְצוּ לְחִכִּי אִמְרָתֶךָ מִדְּבַשׁ לְפִי: מִפִּקּוּדֶיךָ אֶתְבּוֹנָן
עַל־כֵּן שָׂנֵאתִי ׀ כָּל־אֹרַח שָׁקֶר:

DISCUSSION

119:89 | **Forever, Lord, does Your word stand in the heavens:** This verse has traditionally been interpreted to mean that the word of God, the utterance through which He created the world, remains until today and still upholds the heavens.

105 **A lamp to my feet is Your word,** because it guides me and shows me where to go, like a light in the dark, **and** it is **a light for my path.**
106 **I have sworn and will fulfill my oath, to follow Your righteous laws.**[D]
107 **I am exceedingly afflicted; give me life, Lord, as befits Your word.**
108 **Please, Lord, accept** favorably **the offerings of my mouth,** such as my words, my prayers, and my songs of praise, **and** continue to **teach me Your laws.**
109 **My life is always in my hand.** I am in such great and constant danger that it is as though I have to hold my life in my hand in order to protect it. **But** despite this, **I do not forget Your teaching.**
110 In a similar vein: **The wicked set a snare for me,** forcing me to alter my route to avoid them, **but** despite this, **I do not veer from Your edicts.**
111 **Your precepts are my possession forever,** my portion and inheritance in life, **for they are the joy of my heart,** not out of any special privilege but simply because I love them so deeply.
112 **I incline my heart to carry out Your statutes forever, to the end,** to the last detail.
113 **I hate what is twisted.** The word *se'afim* is related to *se'ifim*, the branches of a tree, which extend outward in haphazard directions. Here it refers to people or ideas that are "twisted," not upright and truthful. **But I love Your teaching.**
114 **You are my shelter and** my **shield; I hope** in anxious anticipation **for Your word.**
115 The psalmist prays, addressing himself to the sinners who torment him: **Depart from me, evildoers, so I might uphold the commandments of my God** without hindrance.
116 **Sustain me, as befits Your word, so I might live,** so I might survive the attacks of the evildoers. Alternatively, so I might live a good life. **Let me not be ashamed of my hope,** shame that would result from Your not granting me the ability to realize my aspirations.
117 **Support me and I will** thereby **be saved. And** then, when I can be relieved of the need to battle evil, **I will** be free to **always turn my attention to Your statutes.**
118 **You turn aside all those who stray from Your statutes, for their deception is a lie.** Evildoers attempt to justify their actions by means of deceptions and excuses. These justifications, however, are nothing but lies.
119 **Like dross, You destroy the wicked of the earth.** The wicked are likened to dross, waste that is separated from precious metal and discarded. **Therefore I love Your precepts,** so I should not be treated in the same fashion.
120 **My flesh prickles in fright,** or, alternatively, the hair of my body stands on end, **because of You, for I fear Your judgments.** Although this psalm is full of expressions of love and devotion, there are also many verses like this one that convey fear and awe of God.
121 **I have practiced justice and righteousness,** so **do not leave me to my oppressors.**
122 **Vouch for Your servant, for good.** Grant me protection. The word *arov*, translated here as "vouch for," literally refers to one who undertakes to be guarantor of a loan. **Keep evildoers from oppressing me.**
123 **My eyes pine for Your salvation,** Your assistance in times of trouble, **and** I also long for **Your righteous word,** by which You will grant me instruction for my future conduct.
124 **Deal with Your servant** beneficently, **as befits Your kindness.** Consider me with Your attribute of mercy; do not judge me harshly for my sins, **and teach me Your statutes.**
125 **I am Your servant; give me understanding, so I might know Your precepts.**
126 **It is time to act for the Lord, for they have violated Your teaching.** When a time arrives that the Torah has been widely abandoned, we are obligated to act with renewed effort and urgency to rectify the situation.
127 **Indeed, I love Your commandments more than gold, more than fine gold.**
128 **Indeed, I have dealt straightly with all Your edicts.** I try to stay on the straight path of Your commandments. **I hate every false path,** shunning everything that deviates from the straight path.
129 **Your precepts are wondrous; therefore my soul upholds them.**
130 **Your opening words enlighten.** From the very start, Your words bring enlightenment. **They bring understanding** even **to the simple.** Even those who are totally ignorant are granted a glimmer of understanding already at the very beginning of their study.
131 **I open my mouth wide and breathe in deep, longing for Your commandments.** I open my mouth as if to inhale whatever I can from the commandments, so great is my desire for them.
132 **Turn to me and treat me graciously, as befits those who love Your name.**
133 **Make my footsteps firm with Your saying** so that You **let no wrongdoing rule over me.**
134 **Redeem me from the oppression of man, so I might follow Your edicts,** for my enemies' constant oppression prevents me from devoting myself fully to following Your commandments.
135 **Shine Your face on Your servant,** show me Your favor, **and teach me Your statutes.**
136 **Streams of water flow from my eyes,** so much do I weep **for those who do not follow Your teaching.**

נֵר־לְרַגְלִי דְבָרֶךָ וְאוֹר לִנְתִיבָתִי: נִשְׁבַּעְתִּי וָאֲקַיֵּמָה לִשְׁמֹר מִשְׁפְּטֵי צִדְקֶךָ: נַעֲנֵיתִי קה קו קז
עַד־מְאֹד יהוה חַיֵּנִי כִדְבָרֶךָ: נִדְבוֹת פִּי רְצֵה־נָא יהוה וּמִשְׁפָּטֶיךָ לַמְּדֵנִי: נַפְשִׁי קח קט
בְכַפִּי תָמִיד וְתוֹרָתְךָ לֹא שָׁכָחְתִּי: נָתְנוּ רְשָׁעִים פַּח לִי וּמִפִּקּוּדֶיךָ לֹא תָעִיתִי: קי
נָחַלְתִּי עֵדְוֹתֶיךָ לְעוֹלָם כִּי־שְׂשׂוֹן לִבִּי הֵמָּה: נָטִיתִי לִבִּי לַעֲשׂוֹת חֻקֶּיךָ לְעוֹלָם קיא קיב
עֵקֶב:
סֵעֲפִים שָׂנֵאתִי וְתוֹרָתְךָ אָהָבְתִּי: סִתְרִי וּמָגִנִּי אָתָּה לִדְבָרְךָ יִחָלְתִּי: סוּרוּ מִמֶּנִּי קיג קיד קטו
מְרֵעִים וְאֶצְּרָה מִצְוֺת אֱלֹהָי: סָמְכֵנִי כְאִמְרָתְךָ וְאֶחְיֶה וְאַל־תְּבִישֵׁנִי מִשִּׂבְרִי: קטז
סְעָדֵנִי וְאִוָּשֵׁעָה וְאֶשְׁעָה בְחֻקֶּיךָ תָמִיד: סָלִיתָ כָּל־שׁוֹגִים מֵחֻקֶּיךָ כִּי־שֶׁקֶר קיז קיח
תַּרְמִיתָם: סִגִים הִשְׁבַּתָּ כָל־רִשְׁעֵי־אָרֶץ לָכֵן אָהַבְתִּי עֵדֹתֶיךָ: סָמַר מִפַּחְדְּךָ קיט קכ
בְשָׂרִי וּמִמִּשְׁפָּטֶיךָ יָרֵאתִי:
עָשִׂיתִי מִשְׁפָּט וָצֶדֶק בַּל־תַּנִּיחֵנִי לְעֹשְׁקָי: עֲרֹב עַבְדְּךָ לְטוֹב אַל־יַעַשְׁקֻנִי זֵדִים: קכא קכב
עֵינַי כָּלוּ לִישׁוּעָתֶךָ וּלְאִמְרַת צִדְקֶךָ: עֲשֵׂה עִם־עַבְדְּךָ כְחַסְדֶּךָ וְחֻקֶּיךָ לַמְּדֵנִי: קכג קכד
עַבְדְּךָ־אָנִי הֲבִינֵנִי וְאֵדְעָה עֵדֹתֶיךָ: עֵת לַעֲשׂוֹת לַיהוה הֵפֵרוּ תּוֹרָתֶךָ: עַל־כֵּן קכה קכו קכז
אָהַבְתִּי מִצְוֺתֶיךָ מִזָּהָב וּמִפָּז: עַל־כֵּן ׀ כָּל־פִּקּוּדֵי כֹל יִשָּׁרְתִּי כָּל־אֹרַח שֶׁקֶר קכח
שָׂנֵאתִי:
פְּלָאוֹת עֵדְוֹתֶיךָ עַל־כֵּן נְצָרָתַם נַפְשִׁי: פֵּתַח־דְּבָרֶיךָ יָאִיר מֵבִין פְּתָיִים: פִּי־פָעַרְתִּי קכט קל קלא
וָאֶשְׁאָפָה כִּי לְמִצְוֺתֶיךָ יָאָבְתִּי: פְּנֵה־אֵלַי וְחָנֵּנִי כְּמִשְׁפָּט לְאֹהֲבֵי שְׁמֶךָ: פְּעָמַי הָכֵן קלב קלג
בְּאִמְרָתֶךָ וְאַל־תַּשְׁלֶט־בִּי כָל־אָוֶן: פְּדֵנִי מֵעֹשֶׁק אָדָם וְאֶשְׁמְרָה פִּקּוּדֶיךָ: פָּנֶיךָ קלד קלה
הָאֵר בְּעַבְדֶּךָ וְלַמְּדֵנִי אֶת־חֻקֶּיךָ: פַּלְגֵי־מַיִם יָרְדוּ עֵינָי עַל לֹא־שָׁמְרוּ תוֹרָתֶךָ: קלו

DISCUSSION

119:106 | **I have sworn and will fulfill my oath, to follow Your righteous laws:** Although Jewish law generally discourages taking vows and oaths, an exception is made for vows pertaining to the observance of the Torah. Such a vow serves as a personal stimulus for an individual to fulfill his obligations (see *Nedarim* 8a).

137 **Righteous are You** at all times, **Lord, and upright are Your judgments,** even if we are not always able to understand how they are fair.
138 **With Your precepts, You greatly ordain righteousness and faith.** With Your commandments, You show us the path to righteousness and faith, for these two qualities are embedded in all the precepts of the Torah.
139 **My zealotry consumes me, for my foes have forgotten Your words.** I am consumed by anger against those who ignore Your words.
140 **Your saying is exceedingly pure, and Your servant loves it.**
141 **Young** and inexperienced **am I,** with limited knowledge, **and** I am therefore **disdained,** regarded as unworthy, both in my own eyes and in those of others. **Yet** despite this, **I do not forget Your edicts.**
142 **Your righteousness is eternal; Your teaching is truth.**
143 **Trouble and distress have found me** often during my life, but offsetting my suffering is the fact that **Your commandments are my delight.**
144 **Your precepts are forever righteous. Give me understanding, so I might live,** by understanding and cleaving to Your laws.
145 **I call out wholeheartedly** to You; **answer me, Lord,** and as a result of Your assistance, **I will** be better able to **uphold Your statutes.**
146 **I call out to You; save me, and I will follow Your precepts.**
147 **I rise before dawn and cry for help; for Your word I wait.**
148 **My eyes precede the** late **night watches.** I wake up while it is still nighttime **to reflect on Your word.**
149 **Hear my voice, as befits Your kindness; Lord, give me life when You judge me** mercifully.
150 **Pursuers of loathsomeness draw near** to their sinful ambitions. The word *zimma*, translated here as "loathsomeness," refers to wickedness in general and debauchery in particular. **They distance themselves from Your teaching.** They do not realize that the path they have chosen leads them farther and farther away from Your Torah.
151 **You are near** to me, **Lord, and all Your commandments are truth.**
152 **Your precepts, I know, are of old,** from the very beginning of time; **You established them for eternity,** and since they are eternal, I can always cleave to them.
153 **See my affliction and rescue me, for I have not forgotten Your teaching.**
154 **Plead my cause and redeem me; give me life, as befits Your promise.**
155 **Salvation is far from the wicked, for they do not seek Your statutes** and do not merit God's intervention on their behalf.
156 **Great are Your mercies, Lord; give me life when You judge me** in accordance with those mercies.
157 **Many are my pursuers and my foes,** and I am forced to take action to protect myself from my enemies, **yet I do not veer from Your precepts.**
158 **I see traitors and contend with them,** but not **for** my own sake; rather, it is because **they do not follow Your word.**
159 **See how I love Your edicts; Lord, give me life, as befits Your kindness.**
160 **Your word begins in truth; eternal are all Your righteous laws.** Introductory words of some written works are often of minor importance, but regarding Your Torah, everything You have said and ordained, from the very first word, is true and eternal.
161 **Princes,** those in powerful positions, **pursue me without cause, yet my heart fears** only **Your words,** not their threats.
162 **I rejoice at Your sayings, as one who finds great spoils.**
163 **I hate and abhor falsehood,** but **I love Your teaching.**
164 **Seven times a day do I praise You**[D] **for Your righteous laws.**
165 **Those who love Your teaching know great peace; for them there is no obstacle,** because this "great peace," granted by God, protects them.
166 **I await Your salvation, Lord, and I have fulfilled Your commandments,** even now, when Your salvation has not yet come.
167 **My soul follows your precepts, and I love them exceedingly.** I keep Your commandments not only out of a sense of obligation but because I have an emotional connection to them.
168 **I follow Your edicts and Your precepts.** Indeed, I am obliged to do so, and in fact I have no alternative, **for all my ways are before You,** and You are aware of everything I do.
169 **Let my song draw near You, Lord.** That is, accept my prayer favorably. **Give me understanding, as befits Your word.**
170 **Let my plea come before You; rescue me, as befits Your promise.**
171 **Let my lips utter praise, for You teach me Your statutes.** If You teach me Your laws, that will enable me both to speak about them and to offer words of praise for Your guidance.
172 **Let my tongue declare Your word** aloud, **for all Your commandments are just.**

צדיק אתה יהוה וישר משפטיך: צוית צדק עדתיך ואמונה מאד: צמתתני קלז קלח קלט
קנאתי כי־שכחו דבריך צרי: צרופה אמרתך מאד ועבדך אהבה: צעיר אנכי קמ קמא
ונבזה פקדיך לא שכחתי: צדקתך צדק לעולם ותורתך אמת: צר־ומצוק קמב קמג
מצאוני מצותיך שעשעי: צדק עדותיך לעולם הבינני ואחיה: קמד
קראתי בכל־לב ענני יהוה חקיך אצרה: קראתיך הושיעני ואשמרה עדתיך: קמה קמו
לדברך קדמתי בנשף ואשועה לדבריך יחלתי: קדמו עיני אשמרות לשיח באמרתך: קמז קמח
קולי שמעה כחסדך יהוה כמשפטך חיני: קרבו רדפי זמה מתורתך רחקו: קמט קנ
קרוב אתה יהוה וכל־מצותיך אמת: קדם ידעתי מעדתיך כי לעולם יסדתם: קנא קנב
ראה־עניי וחלצני כי־תורתך לא שכחתי: ריבה ריבי וגאלני לאמרתך חיני: קנג קנד
רחוק מרשעים ישועה כי־חקיך לא דרשו: רחמיך רבים ׀ יהוה כמשפטיך קנה קנו
חיני: רבים רדפי וצרי מעדותיך לא נטיתי: ראיתי בגדים ואתקוטטה אשר קנז קנח
אמרתך לא שמרו: ראה כי־פקודיך אהבתי יהוה כחסדך חיני: ראש־דברך קנט קס
אמת ולעולם כל־משפט צדקך:
ומדברך שרים רדפוני חנם ומדבריך פחד לבי: שש אנכי על־אמרתך כמוצא שלל קסא קסב
רב: שקר שנאתי ואתעבה תורתך אהבתי: שבע ביום הללתיך על משפטי קסג קסד
צדקך: שלום רב לאהבי תורתך ואין־למו מכשול: שברתי לישועתך יהוה קסה קסו
ומצותיך עשיתי: שמרה נפשי עדתיך ואהבם מאד: שמרתי פקודיך ועדתיך קסז קסח
כי כל־דרכי נגדך:
תקרב רנתי לפניך יהוה כדברך הבינני: תבוא תחנתי לפניך כאמרתך הצילני: קסט קע
תבענה שפתי תהלה כי תלמדני חקיך: תען לשוני אמרתך כי כל־מצותיך קעא קעב

DISCUSSION

119:164 | **Seven times a day do I praise You:** Seven is often a typological number in the Bible, indicating abundance. However, there are those who interpret this verse as an allusion to the daily prayers as they were established by the Sages, namely, the seven blessings they instituted to accompany the recitation of the morning and evening *Shema*, or to other series of blessings or prayers that number seven (see Jerusalem Talmud, *Berakhot* 1:5; see also *Tanḥuma*, *Bereshit*; *Roke'aḥ*, *Hilkhot Kaddish*; Malbim).

173 **Let Your hand be ready to help me, for I have chosen Your edicts.**
174 **I long for Your salvation, Lord, and Your teaching is my delight** at all times.
175 **May my soul live, so I might praise You; may Your laws come to my aid.**
176 **I have gone astray,** both physically and spiritually, **like a lost sheep. Seek Your servant,** as a shepherd searches for his lost sheep, **for** even when I am lost and cannot discern a straight path before me, **I do not forget Your commandments.**

The Songs of Ascents

PSALMS 120:1–134:3

Many explanations have been offered for the term "song of ascents," which introduces the next fifteen psalms. According to one interpretation, "ascents" refers to journeys to the Temple in Jerusalem for the three yearly pilgrimage festivals, and these fifteen songs were composed to be sung by the pilgrims on those occasions. Another opinion is that "ascents" refers to the fifteen stairs by which one ascended from the outer courtyard to the inner, sacred courtyard of the Temple area, upon which the Levites would stand with their instruments and sing these psalms. Yet others maintain that the term refers to a particular kind of musical style, like many similarly unfamiliar terms found in the introductory verses of other psalms.

PSALM 120

PSALMS 120:1–7

The first of the songs of ascents, a supplication for relief from the distress stemming from hostility on the part of internal and external enemies. The psalmist also expresses his gratitude to God for answering his prayers.

120 Shabbat *27th day of month*

1 **A song of ascents. I called out to the Lord in my distress, and He answered me.**
2 **Lord, save me from lying lips,** from the lies that people are spreading about me; save me **from a deceitful tongue.**
3 To this, the psalmist adds words of reproof: Lies, deceit, and slander offer nothing but twisted satisfaction to those who wish to harm others. **What gain will it give you, deceitful tongue? What will it avail?** While slander often spreads quickly and reaches a large number of people, causing great harm, it rarely benefits the slanderer.
4 Indeed, in some instances, the slanderer not only receives no benefit from his malicious speech, but is actually punished, whether directly or indirectly, and all he receives as a consequence of his malicious speech are the **sharp arrows of the warrior** that are aimed at him, and **burning coals of the broom bush,**[B] which burn for a considerable amount of time. Far from being rewarded, the slanderer will be punished with prolonged suffering.
5 The psalmist shifts to the suffering that is experienced by a person who is being maligned. Such a person feels akin to one facing hostile forces on all sides. **Woe is me, that I sojourn in Meshekh,**[B] a nation residing outside of the borders of the Land of Israel, **that I dwell among the tents of Kedar,**[B] the Ishmaelites. Both groups displayed longstanding hostility toward Israel and posed a continual threat of war.
6 **My soul has long dwelled,** that is, I find myself dwelling, **with those who hate peace.**
7 **I am all peace,** I desire peace; **yet when I speak** to them, **they are for war.**

BACKGROUND

120:4| **Broom bush:** This has been identified with *Retama raetam*, a perennial bush that is common in the Negev and in the coastal area, standing about 1.5–2 m tall, with rich and fragrant blossoms. Its green branches are long and slender, unlike those of other desert shrubs in those areas. Most of the year it is bare of leaves, but its dense, green branches provide shade nonetheless. Its shallower roots and its branches are used to produce coals that stay hot for an especially long time.

120:5| **Meshekh:** This nation is mentioned with Tuval in Ezekiel (27:13, 32:26, 38:2) as being under the common rule of Magog. A nation with a similar name, *Moshkhi*, appears in Assyrian sources, both in Asia Minor and in the Caucasus east of the Black Sea, in today's Abkhazia. For those who dwelled in the Land of Israel, their land constituted the northernmost outpost imaginable.

Kedar: Kedar was one of Ishmael's sons (Genesis 25:13) and was the name of a nomadic tribe or group of tribes that lived in the Syrian-Arabian desert and engaged in shepherding and trade (Isaiah 42:11, 60:7; Jeremiah 49:28). They are also mentioned in Assyrian and Babylonian documents of that period. While their central location was in Wadi al-Sirhan, parallel to the modern-day Jordanian-Saudi Arabian border, they often engaged in raids and attacks upon fertile areas. They could be distinguished by the dark black tents in which they lived. For those who dwelled in the Land of Israel, the Kedarites represented life far away from populated areas.

קעג קעד צֶדֶק׃ תְּהִי־יָדְךָ לְעׇזְרֵנִי כִּי פִקּוּדֶיךָ בָחָרְתִּי׃ תָּאַבְתִּי לִישׁוּעָתְךָ יְהֹוָה וְתוֹרָתְךָ
קעה קעו שַׁעֲשֻׁעָי׃ תְּחִי־נַפְשִׁי וּתְהַלְלֶךָּ וּמִשְׁפָּטֶךָ יַעְזְרֻנִי׃ תָּעִיתִי כְּשֶׂה אֹבֵד בַּקֵּשׁ עַבְדֶּךָ
כִּי מִצְוֺתֶיךָ לֹא שָׁכָחְתִּי׃

יום השבת
כז לחודש

כ א ב שִׁיר הַמַּעֲלוֹת אֶל־יְהֹוָה בַּצָּרָתָה לִּי קָרָאתִי וַיַּעֲנֵנִי׃ יְהֹוָה הַצִּילָה נַפְשִׁי מִשְּׂפַת־
ג ד שֶׁקֶר מִלָּשׁוֹן רְמִיָּה׃ מַה־יִּתֵּן לְךָ וּמַה־יֹּסִיף לָךְ לָשׁוֹן רְמִיָּה׃ חִצֵּי גִבּוֹר שְׁנוּנִים
ה ו עִם גַּחֲלֵי רְתָמִים׃ אוֹיָה־לִי כִּי־גַרְתִּי מֶשֶׁךְ שָׁכַנְתִּי עִם־אׇהֳלֵי קֵדָר׃ רַבַּת שָׁכְנָה־
ז לָּהּ נַפְשִׁי עִם שׂוֹנֵא שָׁלוֹם׃ אֲנִי־שָׁלוֹם וְכִי אֲדַבֵּר הֵמָּה לַמִּלְחָמָה׃

כא א ב שִׁיר לַמַּעֲלוֹת אֶשָּׂא עֵינַי אֶל־הֶהָרִים מֵאַיִן יָבֹא עֶזְרִי׃ עֶזְרִי מֵעִם יְהֹוָה עֹשֵׂה
ג ד שָׁמַיִם וָאָרֶץ׃ אַל־יִתֵּן לַמּוֹט רַגְלֶךָ אַל־יָנוּם שֹׁמְרֶךָ׃ הִנֵּה לֹא־יָנוּם וְלֹא יִישָׁן
ה ו שׁוֹמֵר יִשְׂרָאֵל׃ יְהֹוָה שֹׁמְרֶךָ יְהֹוָה צִלְּךָ עַל־יַד יְמִינֶךָ׃ יוֹמָם הַשֶּׁמֶשׁ לֹא־יַכֶּכָּה
ז ח וְיָרֵחַ בַּלָּיְלָה׃ יְהֹוָה יִשְׁמׇרְךָ מִכׇּל־רָע יִשְׁמֹר אֶת־נַפְשֶׁךָ׃ יְהֹוָה יִשְׁמׇר־צֵאתְךָ
וּבוֹאֶךָ מֵעַתָּה וְעַד־עוֹלָם׃

PSALM 121

PSALMS 121:1–8

A song of trust in God that is intended for all, even those who might seem to be utterly defenseless. It contains words of reassurance and encouragement rather than prayer.

121

1 **A song of ascents. I lift my eyes to the mountains; from where will my help come?** The opening verse depicts an individual, possibly under siege or belonging to an armed force facing imminent attack, who looks to the mountains, hoping to see signs of help on the way.

2 The psalmist answers his own question. There may in fact not be any help coming, in the form of soldiers, from the mountains. But that does not matter, for **my help is from the Lord, Maker of heaven and earth.** It is God who rules over the entire world, with all power in His hands.

3 The petitioner of the previous verses is now told: **He,** God, **will not let your foot give way. He who watches over you will not slumber.**

4 **Behold, the Guardian of Israel neither slumbers nor sleeps.** For the "Guardian of Israel," identified in the following verse as God, the concept of sleep does not apply.

5 **The Lord is your guardian.** As a guardian, God is so close to you that it is as if **the Lord is your shade,** your shadow, **by your right hand.** In this context, "right hand" conveys the notion of assistance and rescue.

6 God provides protection not only against human foes but also against perils of any other sort. **By day the sun will not strike you,** afflicting you with its heat. **Nor** will harm befall you when **the moon** shines, **at night.**

7 **The Lord will guard you from all evil; He will guard your life.**

8 **The Lord will guard your going and your coming.** God will watch over you wherever your travels take you, both to your destination and back, **from now until eternity.**

PSALM 122

PSALMS 122:1–9

A psalm of joy and praise to Jerusalem, sung by pilgrims making their ascent to the city during the three major festivals. The psalm describes the city in its glory at the time of the Temple, when all the tribes would assemble, and when the city served as the center of sovereignty of the Jewish nation.

122 1 **A song of ascents, of David.** "Of David" could indicate David's
authorship of this psalm, but it can also mean that it was written by someone else in his honor. **I rejoiced when they said
to me: Let us go to the House of the Lord.** The ascent to
Jerusalem is a joyous experience in its own right.
2 As the pilgrims approach the entrance to Jerusalem, they say:
Our feet are standing at your gates, Jerusalem.
3 From our vantage point at the city's gates, we can see how **the
built-up Jerusalem is like a city** that has been **joined together,** in a literal sense. The city was built on a cluster of adjacent
hills that, before the time of David, may have been separate
civic, and perhaps also military, units. It was David who unified
the city, though it was only during the reign of Solomon that
the wall encompassing it was built.
4 **There,** to Jerusalem, **the tribes went up, the tribes of the
Lord, a testimony for Israel,** who made the pilgrimage there
to give thanks to the name of the Lord.
5 The psalmist sings the praise of Jerusalem, which is not only the
Holy City but also the capital: **For there stood the thrones of
judgment,** as it was the seat of the supreme court of justice,
which convened near the Temple and the king's palace, and
it was there that were situated the **thrones of the house of
David.** David and his descendants who reigned after him acted
as both rulers and judges in all civil matters.
6 The psalmist offers his blessing to Jerusalem: **Pray for the
peace of Jerusalem; may those who love you be tranquil.**[D]
7 A further prayer for Jerusalem: **May peace be within your
walls,** *ḥeilekh* referring to a secondary, lower wall that surrounds parts of the main, fully fortified city wall. May there be
tranquility within your towers. *Armonot,* translated here as
"towers," usually refers to large palaces, but it can also connote
fortresses.
8 **For the sake of my brothers and companions I now say:
Peace be with you.** My prayer for Jerusalem is on behalf of all
those in the city, whether residents or visitors.
9 **For the sake of the House of the Lord our God,** itself located
here in Jerusalem, **I seek your good.**

PSALM 123

PSALMS 123:1–4

A song of entreaty and plea for assistance, written from the perspective of one who is downtrodden and held in contempt.

123 1 **A song of ascents. I lift my eyes to You.** I, so distant from
heaven, having reached the lowest point, raise my eyes in prayer
and supplication to You **who dwell in heaven.**
2 **Behold, as the eyes of servants to their master's hand,** and
even **as the eyes of a maid to the hand of her mistress,** for if
male servants are dependent and submissive, even more so are
maidservants, who are weaker, **so our eyes are to the Lord our
God until He is gracious to us.** A "master's hand" is the source
of giving and succor as well as punishment, and the slave has no
recourse other than his master's goodwill. Similarly, our position vis-à-vis God is that of utter dependency and submission,
and we thus wholeheartedly beseech His aid, in the knowledge
that only He can help us.
3 And this is our prayer: **Be gracious to us, Lord; be gracious
to us, for we are sated with scorn.** Beyond our other suffering,
we have been subjected to a full measure of degradation.
4 **We are sated with the mockery of the complacent, the
abuse of the arrogant.**[D]

DISCUSSION

122:6 | **Pray for the peace of Jerusalem; may those who love you be tranquil:** Besides the simple meaning of the verb "be tranquil" [*yishlayu*], there is an echo of another, similar-sounding word in the verse, "pray" [*sha'alu*]. "Those who love you," Jerusalem, are the ones who pray for your peace.

123:4 | **The abuse of the arrogant:** The translation "of the arrogant" accords with the word as it is written in the text, as one word, *ligeyonim*. However, it is pronounced as two separate words, *ligei yonim*. Some explain the pronounced version as follows: *Ligei* refers to arrogant people, and *yonim* refers to those who cause harassment and distress by means of contemptuous words or deeds.

קכב א ב שִׁיר הַמַּעֲלוֹת לְדָוִד שָׂמַחְתִּי בְּאֹמְרִים לִי בֵּית יְהוָה נֵלֵךְ׃ עֹמְדוֹת הָיוּ רַגְלֵינוּ
ג ד בִּשְׁעָרַיִךְ יְרוּשָׁלָם׃ יְרוּשָׁלַם הַבְּנוּיָה כְּעִיר שֶׁחֻבְּרָה־לָּהּ יַחְדָּו׃ שֶׁשָּׁם עָלוּ שְׁבָטִים
ה שִׁבְטֵי־יָהּ עֵדוּת לְיִשְׂרָאֵל לְהֹדוֹת לְשֵׁם יְהוָה׃ כִּי שָׁמָּה ׀ יָשְׁבוּ כִסְאוֹת לְמִשְׁפָּט
ו ז כִּסְאוֹת לְבֵית דָּוִד׃ שַׁאֲלוּ שְׁלוֹם יְרוּשָׁלָם יִשְׁלָיוּ אֹהֲבָיִךְ׃ יְהִי־שָׁלוֹם בְּחֵילֵךְ
ח ט שַׁלְוָה בְּאַרְמְנוֹתָיִךְ׃ לְמַעַן אַחַי וְרֵעָי אֲדַבְּרָה־נָּא שָׁלוֹם בָּךְ׃ לְמַעַן בֵּית־יְהוָה
אֱלֹהֵינוּ אֲבַקְשָׁה טוֹב לָךְ׃

קכג א ב שִׁיר הַמַּעֲלוֹת אֵלֶיךָ נָשָׂאתִי אֶת־עֵינַי הַיֹּשְׁבִי בַּשָּׁמָיִם׃ הִנֵּה כְעֵינֵי עֲבָדִים אֶל־יַד
אֲדוֹנֵיהֶם כְּעֵינֵי שִׁפְחָה אֶל־יַד גְּבִרְתָּהּ כֵּן עֵינֵינוּ אֶל־יְהוָה אֱלֹהֵינוּ עַד שֶׁיְּחָנֵּנוּ׃
ג ד חָנֵּנוּ יְהוָה חָנֵּנוּ כִּי־רַב שָׂבַעְנוּ בוּז׃ רַבַּת שָׂבְעָה־לָּהּ נַפְשֵׁנוּ הַלַּעַג הַשַּׁאֲנַנִּים
הַבּוּז לגאיונים׃ לִגְאֵי יוֹנִים

קכד א ב שִׁיר הַמַּעֲלוֹת לְדָוִד לוּלֵי יְהוָה שֶׁהָיָה לָנוּ יֹאמַר־נָא יִשְׂרָאֵל׃ לוּלֵי יְהוָה שֶׁהָיָה
ג ד לָנוּ בְּקוּם עָלֵינוּ אָדָם׃ אֲזַי חַיִּים בְּלָעוּנוּ בַּחֲרוֹת אַפָּם בָּנוּ׃ אֲזַי הַמַּיִם שְׁטָפוּנוּ
ה ו נַחְלָה עָבַר עַל־נַפְשֵׁנוּ׃ אֲזַי עָבַר עַל־נַפְשֵׁנוּ הַמַּיִם הַזֵּידוֹנִים׃ בָּרוּךְ יְהוָה שֶׁלֹּא

PSALM 124

A psalm of thanksgiving to God for rescuing His servants at a time when their situation appeared to be hopeless.

PSALMS 124:1–8

124 1 **A song of ascents, by David.** In a certain sense, this psalm of thanksgiving comes as a response to the previous psalm of supplication, as it mentions not only a prayer to God but also His resulting salvation. While it does not describe complete salvation, it does depict extrication from a dire predicament. **Let Israel now say: Had it not been for the Lord, who was with us.** This song of gratitude is written on the part of the entire nation, as indicated by the phrase "Let Israel now say."

2 **Had it not been for the Lord,** had God, **who was with us,** not supported our cause **when men rose against us,** to fight against us and disparage us,

3 **they would have swallowed us alive when their anger was kindled against us.**

4 **Then,** if God had not come to our aid, **the waters would have engulfed us.** We would have been washed away by the "waters" of hordes of many nations;[83] **the torrent would have swept over us.**

5 **Then the wicked waters would have swept over us.** Since the waters mentioned in these verses are a metaphor for an outpouring of malice and evil, the word "wicked" is appropriate here.

6 Now follows a more explicit expression of thanks to God: **Blessed be the Lord, who did not give us over as prey to**

their teeth. Although our enemies continually lie in wait, God does not allow them to trap us.

7 **We were like a bird escaping from a trapper's snare.** Occasionally a bird caught in a snare manages to break free of it. In our case as well, **the snare broke, and we escaped.**

8 This miraculous rescue occurred to us because **our help is in the name of the Lord, Maker of heaven and earth.**

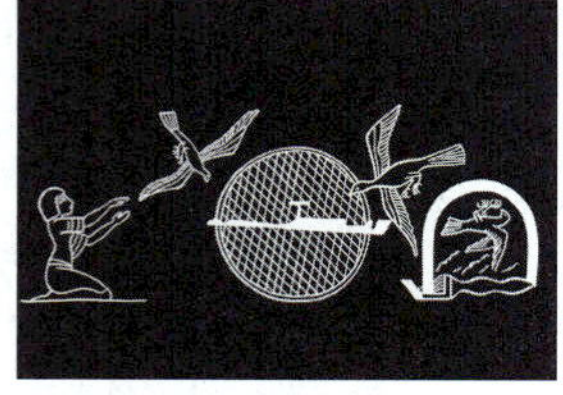
"Trapper's snare." Illustration based on depiction of bird trap, Egypt

PSALM 125

PSALMS 125:1–5

A song of prayer and thanksgiving, whose main theme is trust in God.

125 1 **A song of ascents. Those who trust in the Lord are like Mount Zion,**[B] **which will never topple and will forever endure.**

2 This comparison elicits another: **Jerusalem, mountains surround it.** Jerusalem is not situated on the highest hill in the area but rather is surrounded by a number of hills of the same approximate height, which can serve to fortify the city from every direction. **And the Lord surrounds His people.** Just as Jerusalem is surrounded and protected by mountains, so too God surrounds and protects His people from all evil, **from now until eternity.**

3 **Indeed, the rod of wickedness will not rest upon the lot of the righteous.** *Shevet*, translated here as "rod," also refers to the scepter of a king. God will not allow the righteous to fall under the rule of evil rulers, **lest the righteous set their hands to wrongdoing.** When evil men rule, even righteous people, in order to survive, have no choice but to be compliant to a greater or lesser extent, and then it is as if they themselves participate in wrongdoing.

4 **Be good, Lord, to those who are good, and to the upright of heart,** that is, all those who refrain from entering a world of evil and wrongdoing.

5 By contrast, **as for those who twist their crooked ways,** they believe they are permitted to act in devious ways in order to gain something or to extricate themselves from evil. Even though they are not completely wicked, they "twist their crooked ways," that is, they will not only follow crooked routes but will also make such paths even more twisted than they are. **May the Lord lead them away with the evildoers.** Because they are not honest and upright, God will carry them off with the outright evildoers. **Peace be to Israel.** But when people follow a path of righteousness and integrity, there will be peace upon Israel.

PSALM 126

PSALMS 126:1–6

A song of praise about the time of the final redemption, which, when it arrives, will make the previous experiences of suffering seem like a mere dream. The past will then be understood differently, revealed as a period of toil and preparation for the ultimate reward.

126 1 **A song of ascents. When the Lord brings about the return to Zion,** we will realize that all along **we were like dreamers.** The commentaries, from the time of the Talmud onward, interpret the phrase "we were like dreamers" as describing not the time of redemption, which will seem to be the fulfillment of a dream, but rather the time of exile, which is "dreamlike" in the sense that it is abnormal, even nightmarish. When we dream, we perceive the dream to be actual reality that is coherent and meaningful, despite its many distortions. Similarly, the time of exile incorporates distortions that seem normal, such as those regarding the relationship in exile between ruler and ruled, or between truth and lies. It is only with redemption, when we are restored to a true, non-distorted state of being, that we come to an awareness of how dreamlike our entire exilic existence actually was.

2 **Then our mouths will be filled with laughter, and our tongues with song.** The emphasis here is on "filled." While we certainly do laugh even when in exile, our laughter is always tempered by the knowledge that there are many problems in the world, and we are in a situation that constrains joy. Only with redemption will we be able to laugh wholeheartedly, without a trace of sadness. In addition, **then the nations will say: The Lord has done great things for them.** Even people from distant lands will speak about our redemption as a remarkable and unprecedented event.

3 And at that time, we too will be able to say that **the Lord has done great things for us.** He has done more for us than we deserve; His deliverance has exceeded our wildest expectations. Then we will be able to exclaim that **we are joyful** in the fullest sense.

"Riverbeds in the Negev." Flash flood above Ein Maarif, in a tributary of the Tzin Ravine

4 **Lord, bring about our return, like riverbeds in the**

ז נְתָנָנוּ טֶרֶף לְשִׁנֵּיהֶם: נַפְשֵׁנוּ כְּצִפּוֹר נִמְלְטָה מִפַּח יוֹקְשִׁים הַפַּח נִשְׁבָּר וַאֲנַחְנוּ
ח נִמְלָטְנוּ: עֶזְרֵנוּ בְּשֵׁם יהוה עֹשֵׂה שָׁמַיִם וָאָרֶץ:
קכה א ב שִׁיר הַמַּעֲלוֹת הַבֹּטְחִים בַּיהוה כְּהַר־צִיּוֹן לֹא־יִמּוֹט לְעוֹלָם יֵשֵׁב: יְרוּשָׁלַם הָרִים
ג סָבִיב לָהּ וַיהוה סָבִיב לְעַמּוֹ מֵעַתָּה וְעַד־עוֹלָם: כִּי לֹא יָנוּחַ שֵׁבֶט הָרֶשַׁע עַל
ד גּוֹרַל הַצַּדִּיקִים לְמַעַן לֹא־יִשְׁלְחוּ הַצַּדִּיקִים | בְּעַוְלָתָה יְדֵיהֶם: הֵיטִיבָה יהוה
ה לַטּוֹבִים וְלִישָׁרִים בְּלִבּוֹתָם: וְהַמַּטִּים עֲקַלְקַלּוֹתָם יוֹלִיכֵם יהוה אֶת־פֹּעֲלֵי הָאָוֶן
שָׁלוֹם עַל־יִשְׂרָאֵל:
קכו א ב שִׁיר הַמַּעֲלוֹת בְּשׁוּב יהוה אֶת־שִׁיבַת צִיּוֹן הָיִינוּ כְּחֹלְמִים: אָז יִמָּלֵא שְׂחוֹק
ג פִּינוּ וּלְשׁוֹנֵנוּ רִנָּה אָז יֹאמְרוּ בַגּוֹיִם הִגְדִּיל יהוה לַעֲשׂוֹת עִם־אֵלֶּה: הִגְדִּיל
ד יהוה לַעֲשׂוֹת עִמָּנוּ הָיִינוּ שְׂמֵחִים: שׁוּבָה יהוה אֶת־שבותנו כַּאֲפִיקִים בַּנֶּגֶב: שְׁבִיתֵנוּ
ה ו הַזֹּרְעִים בְּדִמְעָה בְּרִנָּה יִקְצֹרוּ: הָלוֹךְ יֵלֵךְ | וּבָכֹה נֹשֵׂא מֶשֶׁךְ־הַזָּרַע בֹּא־יָבֹא
בְרִנָּה נֹשֵׂא אֲלֻמֹּתָיו:

Negev.[B] This situation is likened to that of a farmer sowing his seeds:

5 **Those who sow,** toil **in tears.** Sowing seeds is hard work that requires tremendous effort, and it is invariably accompanied by anxiety: Will the seeds bear fruit? But when harvest time comes, **with joyous song they reap.**

6 The psalm concludes with a broader description of the toil of sowing and the joy of reaping: **He who weeps as he walks to and fro, bearing his sack of seed,** which the farmer scatters with a certain amount of trepidation, as the seeds could have been, and perhaps should have been, used for food rather than having them decompose in the ground. In the end, however, he **indeed returns in joyous song,** this time too, **bearing** a burden, but now he carries **his sheaves** of bounteous harvest in his arms.

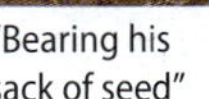

"Bearing his sack of seed"

"Bearing his sheaves"

BACKGROUND

125:1| **Mount Zion:** This is a name for Jerusalem as a whole, and for the Temple Mount in particular (Isaiah 4:5, 8:18, 29:8; Lamentations 5:18), elsewhere referred to as Mount Moriah (II Chronicles 3:1). The common contemporary application of the name Mount Zion to refer to a mountain to the west of David's city began in the Byzantine period, under the influence of Christian sources.

126:4| **Riverbeds in the Negev:** The riverbeds in the Negev, the Land of Israel's southern desert, are almost always dry. Since the desert soil does not absorb the water, the rainfall on the surface joins together to form massive flows on the mountain slopes that cascade through the dry riverbeds with great force; in a flash flood, the riverbeds are filled all at once with a torrent of water, the outcome of a distant rainfall. This description is not only a plea for the coming of the redemption, for which we continually wait, but also a prayer that it will come even if the existing reality makes it seem impossible. While redemption and exile are described here as two entirely different states of being, in truth they are linked. Exile, with all its concomitant suffering, serves as preparation for redemption; although in exile we have no respite, and the manifest reality is one of exile and exile only, still there is hope for redemption.

PSALM 127

PSALMS 127:1–5

A psalm of moral instruction attributed to Solomon, or perhaps written by King David for his son Solomon. Its main message is that man's actions, in and of themselves, can never guarantee success. It is only God's graciousness that helps us, even in the things that we ourselves do.

127 1 **A song of ascents, by Solomon,** or alternatively, for Solomon. **If the Lord does not build a house,** the house will collapse, and **those who build it labor in vain. If the Lord does not guard a city, in vain does the watchman keep vigil.** The city's defenses will be breached if God does not provide His protection.

2 God also determines success or failure in matters involving day-to-day sustenance. This verse describes those who believe that success is a matter of diligence: **It is futile, you early risers,** getting to work early, **and you who linger,** working long after everyone else is gone, **you who eat the bread of sorrow.** They are consumed with planning and worrying, too distracted even to enjoy their food. **For surely He grants sleep to His beloved.** Those whom God assists are granted a good night's sleep and still succeed in their everyday affairs, whereas those who are continually obsessed with thoughts and plans may find that those plans all come to naught.

3 This holds true for other things in life that are essentially gifts from God. **Truly, children are a portion of the Lord.** Children are God's greatest gift, the one most readily recognized as having been bestowed by God. **Reward is the fruit of one's womb.** They are the greatest reward, the most valuable assets one can obtain in this world.

4 **Like arrows in the hand of a warrior, so are the children of youth.** The children born to us in our youth are those who shape the future.

5 The arrow imagery is further developed in the concluding verse: **Happy is the man who fills his quiver with them.** A man with many children is like a well-armed warrior. **They will not be put to shame when they confront enemies at the gate.** Their physical numbers will enable them to withstand attack. Moreover, they will have the requisite wisdom to take part in public meetings held at the city gate, in which internal affairs and the best means of combating foes are discussed. The phrase *ki yedabberu*, translated here as "when they confront," can also mean "when they speak to."

Quiver on the back of an archer, stone relief, palace of Assurbanipal, Nineveh, seventh century BCE

PSALM 128

PSALMS 128:1–6

A hymn that depicts blessing in the form of tranquility, while offering praise for those who fear God.

128 1 **A song of ascents. Blessed are all who fear the Lord, who walk in His ways.**

2 Such people are not necessarily occupied with great, grandiose matters. Rather, **when You eat of the labor of your hands, you are happy.** Happiness is the lot of a simple, ordinary person who enjoys the fruits of his labor. **And it is good for you,** for honest physical labor provides spiritual tranquility as well as the basic necessities.

3 In this pastoral image, a large and flourishing vine is growing on the side of the house it is leaning against, and the whole family is nourished by it. **Your wife is like a fruitful vine by the side of your house.** The wife is likened to this nourishing vine. **Your children** are **like young olive trees surrounding your table.** The children are depicted as young olive shoots sitting serenely around their father's table. This latter image is true to nature: When left undisturbed, an olive tree often sprouts sprigs from its roots that encircle its trunk.

"A fruitful vine by the side of your house"

4 **Indeed, so shall a man who fears the Lord be blessed.** The blessing is that of a serene and happy domestic life.

5 **May the Lord bless you from Zion; may you see the prosperity of Jerusalem all the days of your life.** This is an additional blessing addressed to the God-fearing man mentioned in the previous verse.

"Young olive trees." Olive shoots at the side of the tree trunk

6 To this are added other blessings: **And may you see the children of your children.** This God-fearing man will also merit seeing the continuity of generations, not only children but also grandchildren. And finally, **peace to Israel,** a concluding blessing that encompasses everything.

קכז א שִׁיר הַמַּעֲלוֹת לִשְׁלֹמֹה אִם־יְהוָה ׀ לֹא־יִבְנֶה בַיִת שָׁוְא עָמְלוּ בוֹנָיו בּוֹ אִם־יְהוָה
ב לֹא־יִשְׁמָר־עִיר שָׁוְא ׀ שָׁקַד שׁוֹמֵר׃ שָׁוְא לָכֶם ׀ מַשְׁכִּימֵי קוּם מְאַחֲרֵי־שֶׁבֶת אֹכְלֵי
ג לֶחֶם הָעֲצָבִים כֵּן יִתֵּן לִידִידוֹ שֵׁנָא׃ הִנֵּה נַחֲלַת יְהוָה בָּנִים שָׂכָר פְּרִי הַבָּטֶן׃
ד ה כְּחִצִּים בְּיַד־גִּבּוֹר כֵּן בְּנֵי הַנְּעוּרִים׃ אַשְׁרֵי הַגֶּבֶר אֲשֶׁר מִלֵּא אֶת־אַשְׁפָּתוֹ מֵהֶם
לֹא־יֵבֹשׁוּ כִּי־יְדַבְּרוּ אֶת־אוֹיְבִים בַּשָּׁעַר׃
קכח א ב שִׁיר הַמַּעֲלוֹת אַשְׁרֵי כָּל־יְרֵא יְהוָה הַהֹלֵךְ בִּדְרָכָיו׃ יְגִיעַ כַּפֶּיךָ כִּי תֹאכֵל אַשְׁרֶיךָ
ג וְטוֹב לָךְ׃ אֶשְׁתְּךָ ׀ כְּגֶפֶן פֹּרִיָּה בְּיַרְכְּתֵי בֵיתֶךָ בָּנֶיךָ כִּשְׁתִלֵי זֵיתִים סָבִיב לְשֻׁלְחָנֶךָ׃
ד ה הִנֵּה כִי־כֵן יְבֹרַךְ גָּבֶר יְרֵא יְהוָה׃ יְבָרֶכְךָ יְהוָה מִצִּיּוֹן וּרְאֵה בְּטוּב יְרוּשָׁלָםִ כֹּל
ו יְמֵי חַיֶּיךָ׃ וּרְאֵה־בָנִים לְבָנֶיךָ שָׁלוֹם עַל־יִשְׂרָאֵל׃ יח
קכט א ב שִׁיר הַמַּעֲלוֹת רַבַּת צְרָרוּנִי מִנְּעוּרַי יֹאמַר־נָא יִשְׂרָאֵל׃ רַבַּת צְרָרוּנִי מִנְּעוּרָי גַּם
ג ד לֹא־יָכְלוּ לִי׃ עַל־גַּבִּי חָרְשׁוּ חֹרְשִׁים הֶאֱרִיכוּ למענותם׃ יְהוָה צַדִּיק קִצֵּץ עֲבוֹת לְמַעֲנִיתָם
ה ו רְשָׁעִים׃ יֵבֹשׁוּ וְיִסֹּגוּ אָחוֹר כֹּל שֹׂנְאֵי צִיּוֹן׃ יִהְיוּ כַּחֲצִיר גַּגּוֹת שֶׁקַּדְמַת שָׁלַף יָבֵשׁ׃
ז ח שֶׁלֹּא מִלֵּא כַפּוֹ קוֹצֵר וְחִצְנוֹ מְעַמֵּר׃ וְלֹא אָמְרוּ ׀ הָעֹבְרִים בִּרְכַּת־יְהוָה אֲלֵיכֶם
בֵּרַכְנוּ אֶתְכֶם בְּשֵׁם יְהוָה׃

PSALM 129

PSALMS 129:1–8

A psalm combining gratitude and rebuke: Gratitude to God for His salvation, and rebuke to those who plot against the righteous.

129 1 **A song of ascents. Let Israel now say: They have greatly beleaguered me, from the time of my youth.** The nation of Israel can truthfully claim that it has been surrounded by enemies from the very dawn of its history.

2 **They have greatly beleaguered me from the time of my youth, yet they did not prevail against me.** Even though I have been plagued relentlessly by foes, they have been unsuccessful in their attempts to destroy me.

3 **Across my back the plowers plowed,** as though they slashed at my flesh. **They extended their furrows,** creating a seemingly endless furrow.

4 But **the Lord is righteous; He cuts the cords of the wicked,** the thick cords by which they try to bind the righteous.

5 And eventually, **all those who hate Zion will be put to shame and made to retreat.**

6 The psalmist now presents a graphic image of what will eventually befall these enemies. Houses in those days had flat roofs, some of which were made of a mixture of mud and clay. Therefore, at times seeds of grain would take root, though these never got beyond the initial stage of sprouting, as there was not enough soil to sustain their growth. The psalmist expresses his wish that the enemies be like this roof grass: **They will be like grass on a roof, which withers before it flowers** or produces grain,

7 and **which does not fill the palm of the reaper, nor the bosom of the sheaf binder,** as there are no stalks to harvest.

8 **And those who pass by will not say: The blessing of the Lord be upon you; we bless you in the name of the Lord.** The custom was for passersby to offer a blessing to those engaged in harvesting. No such blessing is issued in this case, for there is nothing to harvest.

PSALM 130

PSALMS 130:1–8

A psalm of supplication and a plea for forgiveness that is recited on special days of prayer, including the Ten Days of Repentance between Rosh HaShana and Yom Kippur.

130 1 **A song of ascents. Out of the depths I call to You, Lord.** The word *mima'amakim*, "out of the depths," has a twofold meaning: I feel like someone thrust into a deep pit, and I am calling from the innermost depths of my heart.

2 And this is what I call out to Him: **Lord, hear my voice; let Your ears be attentive to the sound of my pleas.**

3 **If You hold fast, Lord, to iniquities,** if You remember and keep a record of all our sins, **my Lord, who can stand?** We cannot survive. Our sins are many, and without Your forgiveness, we will not be able to bear their accumulated weight.

4 **Yet forgiveness is with You, that You might be feared.** God's forgiveness instills in man a desire to remain in His good graces and to avoid future sin. By contrast, in a world without forgiveness, there would also be no fear of God. If man knew there was no remedy for him, he would, in his hopelessness, simply do as he pleased.

5 **I hope, Lord, my soul hopes; I long for His word.**

6 **My soul awaits the Lord,** I anticipate and await God, **more than watchers for the morning, watchers for the morning,** even more than those who awaken at dawn in anticipation of redemption and relief.

7 **Await the Lord, Israel, for kindness is with the Lord, and abundant redemption is with Him.** God has the power to redeem and save whomever and whatever He wants.

8 **And** consequently, **He will redeem Israel from all its iniquities.**

PSALM 131

PSALMS 131:1–3

A song of devotion to God, characterized not by ecstasy or passion but rather by the sense of inner peace that comes from adopting a loving self-abandonment for the sake of God.

131 1 **A song of ascents, by David.** In common with several other psalms among the Songs of Ascents, this one develops a single idea, or essentially a single image: **Lord, my heart is not haughty, nor my eyes lofty.** A haughty heart and lofty eyes are expressions not only of arrogance but also of desire for riches. **And I do not aspire to something too great or too wonderful for me.** I have no such aspirations. I remain where I am, and as I am.

2 **Instead I have composed and quieted my soul.** *Shivviti*, translated here as "composed," literally means "equal to." It describes the absence of any ambition, the sense of being completely at peace with the status quo. The soul is in a state of silence and quiet acceptance, **like a weaned child on its mother.** This central image of a weaned child held in its mother's bosom conveys both intimacy and great serenity. Unlike a nursing baby who cuddles in his mother's lap because he both wants and needs to nurse, the weaned child nestling in his mother's arms is seeking and receiving only one thing, an intimacy devoid of any material desire. **Like a weaned child is my soul.** By way of analogy, the psalmist's soul experiences a state of intimacy and devotion that is characterized by an all-encompassing inner peace and quiet.

"Like a weaned child on its mother." Judean mother and her children, Lakhish reliefs, 700–692 BCE

3 The psalmist concludes with what may be seen as overall advice to Israel: **Await the Lord, Israel, from now until eternity.** Try to achieve intimacy with God that is free of any request or desire, other than that of being close to Him.

קל א ב שִׁיר הַמַּעֲלוֹת מִמַּעֲמַקִּים קְרָאתִיךָ יהוה: אֲדֹנָי שִׁמְעָה בְקוֹלִי תִּהְיֶינָה אָזְנֶיךָ
ג ד קַשֻּׁבוֹת לְקוֹל תַּחֲנוּנָי: אִם־עֲוֺנוֹת תִּשְׁמָר־יָהּ אֲדֹנָי מִי יַעֲמֹד: כִּי־עִמְּךָ הַסְּלִיחָה
ה ו לְמַעַן תִּוָּרֵא: קִוִּיתִי יהוה קִוְּתָה נַפְשִׁי וְלִדְבָרוֹ הוֹחָלְתִּי: נַפְשִׁי לַאדֹנָי מִשֹּׁמְרִים
ז לַבֹּקֶר שֹׁמְרִים לַבֹּקֶר: יַחֵל יִשְׂרָאֵל אֶל־יהוה כִּי־עִם־יהוה הַחֶסֶד וְהַרְבֵּה עִמּוֹ
ח פְדוּת: וְהוּא יִפְדֶּה אֶת־יִשְׂרָאֵל מִכֹּל עֲוֺנוֹתָיו:

קלא א שִׁיר הַמַּעֲלוֹת לְדָוִד יהוה | לֹא־גָבַהּ לִבִּי וְלֹא־רָמוּ עֵינַי וְלֹא־הִלַּכְתִּי | בִּגְדֹלוֹת
ב וּבְנִפְלָאוֹת מִמֶּנִּי: אִם־לֹא שִׁוִּיתִי | וְדוֹמַמְתִּי נַפְשִׁי כְּגָמֻל עֲלֵי אִמּוֹ כַּגָּמֻל עָלַי
ג נַפְשִׁי: יַחֵל יִשְׂרָאֵל אֶל־יהוה מֵעַתָּה וְעַד־עוֹלָם:

קלב א ב שִׁיר הַמַּעֲלוֹת זְכוֹר־יהוה לְדָוִד אֵת כָּל־עֻנּוֹתוֹ: אֲשֶׁר נִשְׁבַּע לַיהוה נָדַר לַאֲבִיר
ג ד יַעֲקֹב: אִם־אָבֹא בְּאֹהֶל בֵּיתִי אִם־אֶעֱלֶה עַל־עֶרֶשׂ יְצוּעָי: אִם־אֶתֵּן שְׁנַת לְעֵינָי
ה ו לְעַפְעַפַּי תְּנוּמָה: עַד־אֶמְצָא מָקוֹם לַיהוה מִשְׁכָּנוֹת לַאֲבִיר יַעֲקֹב: הִנֵּה־שְׁמַעֲנוּהָ
ז ח בְאֶפְרָתָה מְצָאנוּהָ בִּשְׂדֵי־יָעַר: נָבוֹאָה לְמִשְׁכְּנוֹתָיו נִשְׁתַּחֲוֶה לַהֲדֹם רַגְלָיו: קוּמָה
ט י יהוה לִמְנוּחָתֶךָ אַתָּה וַאֲרוֹן עֻזֶּךָ: כֹּהֲנֶיךָ יִלְבְּשׁוּ־צֶדֶק וַחֲסִידֶיךָ יְרַנֵּנוּ: בַּעֲבוּר דָּוִד

PSALM 132

PSALMS 132:1–18

A song in honor of King David, describing his efforts to build the Temple in Jerusalem and the preparations he made for it. This psalm also contains God's promise to David and his descendants throughout the generations.

132 1 **A song of ascents. Remember, Lord, all of David's afflictions.** After this brief reminder of David's many trials and tribulations, the psalm goes on to praise him:

2 Remember **how he swore to the Lord and vowed to the Champion of Jacob,** an unusual expression referring to the Almighty.

3 This is the vow that David undertook: **I will not enter the roof of my house nor lie on my bed,**

4 **I will not give sleep to my eyes nor slumber to my eyelids,**

5 **until I find a place for the Lord, a dwelling place for the Champion of Jacob.** In David's time, the Ark of the Covenant had no permanent abode, but was transferred from place to place. David's great dream was to build the Temple, which would house the ark.

6 The people of Israel speak next: **Indeed, we heard it,** the good tidings that the Temple would be built, while David was still **in Efrat,** or Bethlehem. **We found it,** the actualization of this plan, **in the fields of the forest,** referring to the granary of Aravna the Yevusite, the site that David consecrated for the building of the Temple.[84]

7 The psalmist continues, full of passion: **Let us go to His dwelling place; let us bow down toward His footstool,** the Temple.

8 **Arise, Lord, to Your resting place.** This verse is similar to the words recited when the Ark of the Covenant was moved from one place to another in the wilderness.[85] **You and the ark of Your strength,** the symbol of the revelation of the Divine Presence.

9 In the Temple, the service of God will return to its rightful place: **Your priests will be clothed in righteousness; Your devoted ones will sing for joy.**

10 All this will come to pass **for the sake of David, Your servant,**

because of his great efforts to bring the ark to a permanent place and to build the Temple. For his sake, **do not turn away the face of Your anointed one.**

11 And David is indeed rewarded: **The Lord has sworn a true oath to David and will not recant** for all time: **From the fruit of your loins I will establish a throne for you.** God promised David that the monarchy would be passed on to his descendants for all generations to come.

12 But this promise carries a proviso: Only **if your sons follow My covenant and My precept, which I will teach them,** then **their sons too shall sit upon your throne forever.**

13 **For the Lord has chosen Zion; He desired it for His dwelling.**

14 Here the psalmist speaks in the name of God: **This is My resting place forever.** I have chosen Jerusalem as My eternal dwelling place. **Here I will settle, for I desired it.**

15 **I will bless its provisions abundantly; I will satisfy its needy ones with bread.**

16 **I will clothe its priests with salvation.** The priests will be clothed in the priestly garments, and God will ensure that they enjoy respect and stature in the Temple: **Its devoted ones will truly sing for joy.**

17 **There I will make the horn of David spring forth.** This image is a figurative way of describing greatness that is perceived by all. God promises to grant David extraordinary strength and power. **I have prepared a lamp for My anointed one.**[B] This verse teaches that it was customary to light a lantern in honor of kings and other important individuals.

18 **I will clothe his enemies in humiliation; on him a crown will glitter.** God will humiliate David's enemies while bringing glory to his monarchy.

PSALM 133

A psalm of praise about the glory of Jerusalem and the Temple during an era of tranquility.

PSALMS 133:1–3

133 1 **A song of ascents, by David. Indeed, how good and how pleasant it is for brothers to dwell together in unity.** How good it is when all of the people of Israel, and the people of Jerusalem in particular, are in the place where they belong, enjoying one another's company.

2 These people, sitting at ease and in good fellowship, behold the priests in their glory as they anoint their heads with fragrant oil; this is a description of both dignity and ease. **It is like fine oil** applied **on the head,** which subsequently drips and goes **running down the beard,** in this case **the beard of Aaron** as well as those of his descendants the priests, **coming down onto his robes.** The image of precious scented oil, glistening from the top of the head to the bottom of the beard, is a symbol of greatness and contentment. In the case of Aaron and his sons, their beards, and hence the scented oil, reached their priestly garments. This, too, is a depiction of abundance and tranquility.

3 The concluding verse makes use of contrasting images to depict a life of great wealth. It is **like the dew of Hermon,**[B] a place of great moisture, **descending upon the** more arid **mountains of Zion, for** it is **there** that **the Lord commanded the blessing of life, for eternity,** that is, life in all its fullness.

"Like the dew of Hermon descending upon the mountains of Zion." Hermon Stream

BACKGROUND

132:17 | **I have prepared a lamp for My anointed one:** The lighting of candles as a symbol of honor may be traced to the candelabrum of the Temple, which was lit solely for the honor of God (see *Bemidbar Rabba* 15). The Sabbath candles may also be explained as being lit in honor of the Sabbath, which is personified as a queen. Lighting candles in someone's honor is known in other cultures as well, such as Persian, Hellenistic, and Far Eastern societies, but in Western culture the phenomenon took on added significance because of its biblical overtones.

133:3 | **The dew of Hermon:** Dew is the condensation of moisture found in the air, which takes place in conditions of high humidity or low temperatures. On summer nights, when the temperature of the air is low enough to allow water condensation, dew forms on the surface of items that are cooler than the air, such as rocks and leaves. Mount Hermon lies in the path of southwestern winds that blow in from the Mediterranean, carrying a large amount of moisture. As the air rises, pushed up by the slope of the mountain, a mist is formed from the cold and the condensation of water in the air. As a result, rainfall often occurs when the water droplets of this mist merge together. Similarly, the condensed water forms dew before the droplets converge into raindrops. Mount Hermon is one of the most dew-laden areas of the Land of Israel because of its height, and its mist often leaves dew drops on the rocks and ground.

יא עַבְדֶּךָ אַל־תָּשֵׁב פְּנֵי מְשִׁיחֶךָ׃ נִשְׁבַּע־יְהוָה ׀ לְדָוִד אֱמֶת לֹא־יָשׁוּב מִמֶּנָּה מִפְּרִי
יב בִטְנְךָ אָשִׁית לְכִסֵּא־לָךְ׃ אִם־יִשְׁמְרוּ בָנֶיךָ ׀ בְּרִיתִי וְעֵדֹתִי זוֹ אֲלַמְּדֵם גַּם־בְּנֵיהֶם
יג יד עֲדֵי־עַד יֵשְׁבוּ לְכִסֵּא־לָךְ׃ כִּי־בָחַר יְהוָה בְּצִיּוֹן אִוָּהּ לְמוֹשָׁב לוֹ׃ זֹאת־מְנוּחָתִי
טו טז עֲדֵי־עַד פֹּה אֵשֵׁב כִּי אִוִּתִיהָ׃ צֵידָהּ בָּרֵךְ אֲבָרֵךְ אֶבְיוֹנֶיהָ אַשְׂבִּיעַ לָחֶם׃ וְכֹהֲנֶיהָ
יז אַלְבִּישׁ יֶשַׁע וַחֲסִידֶיהָ רַנֵּן יְרַנֵּנוּ׃ שָׁם אַצְמִיחַ קֶרֶן לְדָוִד עָרַכְתִּי נֵר לִמְשִׁיחִי׃
יח אוֹיְבָיו אַלְבִּישׁ בֹּשֶׁת וְעָלָיו יָצִיץ נִזְרוֹ׃
קלג א ב שִׁיר הַמַּעֲלוֹת לְדָוִד הִנֵּה מַה־טּוֹב וּמַה־נָּעִים שֶׁבֶת אַחִים גַּם־יָחַד׃ כַּשֶּׁמֶן הַטּוֹב ׀
ג עַל־הָרֹאשׁ יֹרֵד עַל־הַזָּקָן זְקַן־אַהֲרֹן שֶׁיֹּרֵד עַל־פִּי מִדּוֹתָיו׃ כְּטַל־חֶרְמוֹן שֶׁיֹּרֵד
עַל־הַרְרֵי צִיּוֹן כִּי שָׁם ׀ צִוָּה יְהוָה אֶת־הַבְּרָכָה חַיִּים עַד־הָעוֹלָם׃
קלד א שִׁיר הַמַּעֲלוֹת הִנֵּה ׀ בָּרְכוּ אֶת־יְהוָה כָּל־עַבְדֵי יְהוָה הָעֹמְדִים בְּבֵית־יְהוָה
ב ג בַּלֵּילוֹת׃ שְׂאוּ־יְדֵכֶם קֹדֶשׁ וּבָרְכוּ אֶת־יְהוָה׃ יְבָרֶכְךָ יְהוָה מִצִּיּוֹן עֹשֵׂה שָׁמַיִם
וָאָרֶץ׃
קלה א ב הַלְלוּיָהּ ׀ הַלְלוּ אֶת־שֵׁם יְהוָה הַלְלוּ עַבְדֵי יְהוָה׃ שֶׁעֹמְדִים בְּבֵית יְהוָה בְּחַצְרוֹת כח לחודש

PSALM 134

PSALMS 134:1–3

The last of the fifteen Songs of Ascents, another psalm of praise and glorification of the Temple.

134 1 **A song of ascents. Indeed, bless the Lord, all you servants of the Lord who stand** and serve **by night in the House of the Lord.** Since sacrifices were not brought at night, this verse may be referring to individuals who would come regularly to the Temple at night to stand before God in devotion or to pray.

2 **Lift up your hands toward the Sanctuary and bless the Lord.**

3 The concluding verse offers a blessing for all of Israel: **The Lord who made heaven and earth will bless you from Zion.**

PSALM 135

PSALMS 135:1–21

A psalm of Halleluya, meaning "praise of God." Its main theme is God's greatness in the world and how this is revealed through the history of the people of Israel.

135 1 **Halleluya. Praise the name of the Lord. Praise Him, servants of the Lord,**

28th day of month 2 **who stand in the House of the Lord, in the courts of the House of our God.** This verse could refer to the Levites who, as choristers in the Temple, sang these psalms. Or it could refer both to Levites and to other God-fearing people who join in their singing.

3 **Praise the Lord, for the Lord is good. Sing praises to His name, for He is pleasant.**
4 **For the Lord has chosen Jacob for Himself, Israel as His treasured possession,** His chosen people.
5 **For I know the Lord is great, and that our Master is above all gods.**
6 **Whatever the Lord desires to do, He does,** for He rules over all aspects of creation: **In the heavens and on the earth, in the seas and all the depths.**
7 **He makes clouds ascend from the ends of the earth; He makes lightning for the rain.**[B] Lightning and thunder often herald rain. **He brings out winds from His vaults.** In the imagery of this verse, the winds of the world are stored in a special repository and are taken out and released by God.
8 The psalmist turns from God's greatness in the world to His greatness in history: **He smote the firstborn of Egypt, from man to beast,** during the last and most severe of the ten plagues brought upon Egypt, as related in the book of Exodus.
9 The smiting of the firstborn marked the end and summation of the period when **He sent signs and wonders into the midst of Egypt, among Pharaoh and among all his servants.**
10 **He struck down many nations and slew mighty kings.** This verse refers to the wars waged by the children of Israel when they came to the Land of Israel.
11 The psalmist cites some illustrious examples of these "mighty kings": **Sihon king of the Emorites,**[B] **Og king of Bashan,**[B] **and all the kingdoms of Canaan.** A host of Canaanite kings were defeated over the course of several years of conquest. The two kings specifically mentioned here, Sihon and Og, controlled more extensive territories than did the other Canaanite kings.
12 **And He gave their lands as a portion, a portion to Israel, His people.**
13 The following verses offer words of praise and gratitude to God: **Lord, Your name is eternal; Your remembrance, Lord, for all generations.**[D]
14 **For the Lord will judge His people and will take pity on His servants.** When God juxtaposes the people of Israel, His servants, to other nations of the world, what is most apparent, and what stands in their favor, is their closeness to Him.
15 **The idols of the nations are silver and gold, the work of man's hands.** As the next verses demonstrate, these idols are devoid of life.
16 **Mouths they have but cannot speak. Eyes they have but cannot see.**
17 **Ears they have, yet they do not hear; nor is there any breath in their mouths.** They are nothing but lifeless dolls.
18 The psalmist's reaction to these facts combines mockery with imprecation: **May their makers become like them,** as lifeless as the idols themselves. **So too all who trust in them.**
19 In contrast to the other nations and their idols, **house of Israel, bless the Lord; house of Aaron,** the priests, **bless the Lord.**
20 **House of Levi, bless the Lord; you who fear the Lord,** probably referring to those who worship God and who, unlike the priests and Levites, have no specific or designated role in the Temple service, **bless the Lord.**
21 All say, in unison: **Blessed be the Lord from Zion, He who dwells in Jerusalem. Halleluya.**

BACKGROUND

135:7 | **He makes clouds ascend from the ends of the earth; He makes lightning for the rain:** The term *nesi'im*, translated here as "clouds," appears also in Jeremiah (10:13, 51:16), in connection with strong winds, lightning, and heavy rain. It appears that *nesi'im* are the large clouds called *Cumulonimbus*, which, owing to their great size, appear to stretch out to the end of the horizon. The force of gravity causes the water particles in the cloud to fall, colliding with each other in the process, thereby producing an electric charge which expresses itself as thunder and lightning.

135:11 | **Sihon king of the Emorites:** According to the description of Moses' conquest of the land, found in the books of Numbers and Joshua, Sihon's kingdom, the capital of which was Heshbon, spread over the eastern side of the Jordan River from the Sea of Galilee to the Arnon Stream. North of this was the territory of Og king of Bashan. Some scholars believe that the name Sihon is preserved in the place name Tel Shihan, located between Heshbon and Kir of Moav, south of the Arnon Stream.

Og king of Bashan: Bashan is the fertile area at the northern end of the east bank of the Jordan River, stretching from the Yarmuk River to Mount Hermon, and from the Jordan Valley in the east to the Druze mountains in the west. This area includes what is today called the Golan Heights. Moses and the children of Israel conquered the kingdom of Bashan before their entry into the Promised Land, the land of Canaan proper. Og is described as a giant, a remnant of the ancient Refaim people. Some scholars attribute to the Refaim culture the large megalithic structures such as Rujm al-Hiri in the Golan, which apparently had some astronomical significance. The name Og is found in Ugaritic as "Ben Ago," and in Aramaic as "Aga."

DISCUSSION

135:13 | **Lord, Your name is eternal [*le'olam*]; Your remembrance [*zikhrekha*], Lord, for all generations:** The psalmist here echoes the words of God to Moses as He appeared to him in the burning bush, at the beginning of his mission to free the children of Israel: "That is My name forever [*le'olam*] and that is My appellation [*zikhri*] for all generations" (Exodus 3:15).

ג ד בֵּית אֱלֹהֵינוּ: הַלְלוּיָהּ כִּי־טוֹב יְהוָה זַמְּרוּ לִשְׁמוֹ כִּי נָעִים: כִּי־יַעֲקֹב בָּחַר לוֹ יָהּ
ה ו יִשְׂרָאֵל לִסְגֻלָּתוֹ: כִּי אֲנִי יָדַעְתִּי כִּי־גָדוֹל יְהוָה וַאֲדֹנֵינוּ מִכָּל־אֱלֹהִים: כֹּל אֲשֶׁר־
ז חָפֵץ יְהוָה עָשָׂה בַּשָּׁמַיִם וּבָאָרֶץ בַּיַּמִּים וְכָל־תְּהֹמוֹת: מַעֲלֶה נְשִׂאִים מִקְצֵה
ח הָאָרֶץ בְּרָקִים לַמָּטָר עָשָׂה מֽוֹצֵא־רוּחַ מֵאוֹצְרוֹתָיו: שֶׁהִכָּה בְּכוֹרֵי מִצְרָיִם מֵאָדָם
ט י עַד־בְּהֵמָה: שָׁלַח ׀ אוֹתֹת וּמֹפְתִים בְּתוֹכֵכִי מִצְרָיִם בְּפַרְעֹה וּבְכָל־עֲבָדָיו: שֶׁהִכָּה
יא גּוֹיִם רַבִּים וְהָרַג מְלָכִים עֲצוּמִים: לְסִיחוֹן ׀ מֶלֶךְ הָאֱמֹרִי וּלְעוֹג מֶלֶךְ הַבָּשָׁן וּלְכֹל
יב יג מַמְלְכוֹת כְּנָעַן: וְנָתַן אַרְצָם נַחֲלָה נַחֲלָה לְיִשְׂרָאֵל עַמּוֹ: יְהוָה שִׁמְךָ לְעוֹלָם
יד טו יְהוָה זִכְרְךָ לְדֹר־וָדֹר: כִּי־יָדִין יְהוָה עַמּוֹ וְעַל־עֲבָדָיו יִתְנֶחָם: עֲצַבֵּי הַגּוֹיִם כֶּסֶף
טז יז וְזָהָב מַעֲשֵׂה יְדֵי אָדָם: פֶּה־לָהֶם וְלֹא יְדַבֵּרוּ עֵינַיִם לָהֶם וְלֹא יִרְאוּ: אָזְנַיִם לָהֶם
יח וְלֹא יַאֲזִינוּ אַף אֵין־יֶשׁ־רוּחַ בְּפִיהֶם: כְּמוֹהֶם יִהְיוּ עֹשֵׂיהֶם כֹּל אֲשֶׁר־בֹּטֵחַ בָּהֶם:
יט כ בֵּית יִשְׂרָאֵל בָּרְכוּ אֶת־יְהוָה בֵּית אַהֲרֹן בָּרְכוּ אֶת־יְהוָה: בֵּית הַלֵּוִי בָּרְכוּ אֶת־
כא יְהוָה יִרְאֵי יְהוָה בָּרְכוּ אֶת־יְהוָה: בָּרוּךְ יְהוָה ׀ מִצִּיּוֹן שֹׁכֵן יְרוּשָׁלָםִ הַלְלוּיָהּ:
קלו א ב הוֹדוּ לַיהוָה כִּי־טוֹב כִּי לְעוֹלָם חַסְדּוֹ: הוֹדוּ לֵאלֹהֵי הָאֱלֹהִים כִּי לְעוֹלָם חַסְדּוֹ:
ג ד הוֹדוּ לַאֲדֹנֵי הָאֲדֹנִים כִּי לְעוֹלָם חַסְדּוֹ: לְעֹשֵׂה נִפְלָאוֹת גְּדֹלוֹת לְבַדּוֹ כִּי לְעוֹלָם
ה ו חַסְדּוֹ: לְעֹשֵׂה הַשָּׁמַיִם בִּתְבוּנָה כִּי לְעוֹלָם חַסְדּוֹ: לְרֹקַע הָאָרֶץ עַל־הַמָּיִם כִּי

PSALM 136

PSALMS 136:1–26

Another psalm in praise of God, very similar to the preceding psalm in content and wording. The main difference between them is that this psalm is clearly meant to be recited responsively. Each of its verses begins with a specific praise of God, which is answered by the refrain: "For His kindness is forever."

136

1 The leader exclaims: **Give thanks to the Lord, for He is good!** And the chorus or congregation responds: **For His kindness is forever.** The pattern continues throughout the psalm.

2 **Give thanks to the God of heavenly powers, for His kindness is forever.**

3 **Give thanks to the Master of masters, for His kindness is forever.**

4 **To Him who alone does great wonders, for His kindness is forever.** Only God is capable of performing great miracles.

5 A description of some of these miracles follows: **To Him who made the heavens with wisdom, for His kindness is forever.**

6 **To Him who spreads out the earth above the waters, for His kindness is forever.** The earth is depicted here as covering all the subterranean waters of the world.

7 **He who made the great lights, for His kindness is forever:**
8 **The sun to rule by day, for His kindness is forever,**
9 and **the moon and stars to rule by night, for His kindness is forever.**

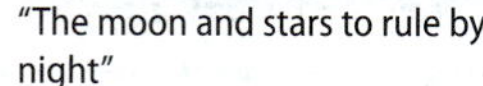
"The moon and stars to rule by night"

"The sun to rule by day"

10 As in the preceding psalm, the psalmist proceeds from a general
description of God's greatness in the world to examples of His
greatness as manifested in historical events: It is **He who smote**
Egypt through their firstborn, for His kindness is forever,
11 **and who brought Israel out from their midst,** from the midst
of the Egyptians, **for His kindness is forever,**
12 **with a strong hand and an outstretched arm, for His kindness is forever.**

13 It is **He who split the Red Sea asunder, for His kindness is**
forever. The splitting of the Red Sea was a three-part miracle;
this is the first part.
14 **And** He **led Israel through its midst,** the midst of the sea, the
second part of the miracle, **for His kindness is forever,**
15 **while He hurled Pharaoh and his army into the Red Sea,** the
third part of the miracle, **for His kindness is forever.**
16 It is **He who led His people through the wilderness, for His**
kindness is forever. Throughout their wanderings, God supplied the people with all their needs.
17 It is **He who smote great kings** in the course of the conquest of
the Canaanites, **for His kindness is forever,**
18 **and slew mighty kings, for His kindness is forever.**
19 Two of those kings are now mentioned: **Sihon king of the**
Emorites, for His kindness is forever,
20 **and Og king of Bashan, for His kindness is forever.**
21 **He gave their land as a portion, for His kindness is forever,**
22 **a portion to Israel His servant, for His kindness is forever.**
23 Here the psalmist offers two general examples of God's kindness that do not pertain to any specific historical event: It is
God **who in our lowliness remembered us** and rescued us at
times of decline and degradation, **for His kindness is forever,**
24 **and He freed us from our foes, for His kindness is forever.**
25 Finally, each and every day: **He gives food to all flesh.** God
sustains all the creatures of the world, **for His kindness is forever.**
26 The psalmist concludes on a joyous note: **Give thanks to the**
Almighty of heaven, for His kindness is forever.

PSALM 137

PSALMS 137:1–9

An elegy of people in exile who are in a state of utmost decline and humiliation. It contains reminiscences of the destruction of Jerusalem as well as a prayer that punishment be meted out to the enemy.

137 1 The speakers are the exiles who arrived in Babylon. They say:
By the rivers of Babylon, there we sat and also wept, when
we remembered Zion and our exile from there to a foreign land.
2 **On the willows in its midst,** in Babylon's midst, **we hung our**
lyres. The people lamenting were sitting by rivers, where willows often grow. Hanging the lyres on the willows was a way of saying that the exiles did not want to use them, because they were no longer willing, or able, to sing.
3 **For there our captors asked us for songs, and our tormentors, mirth.** The captors asked their captives to play for them, in some instances because of their curiosity to hear different types of melodies and, in other cases, as a way of tormenting them. They said: **Sing to us of the songs of Zion.** There were many kinds of songs sung in Jerusalem, but the term "Zion" refers specifically to the Temple Mount. The captors were thus asking the captives to sing the songs that had been sung in the Temple.

Judeans playing their lyres as they go into exile, Lakhish reliefs, 700–692 BCE

ז ח לְעוֹלָם חַסְדּוֹ: לְעֹשֵׂה אוֹרִים גְּדֹלִים כִּי לְעוֹלָם חַסְדּוֹ: אֶת־הַשֶּׁמֶשׁ לְמֶמְשֶׁלֶת
ט בַּיּוֹם כִּי לְעוֹלָם חַסְדּוֹ: אֶת־הַיָּרֵחַ וְכוֹכָבִים לְמֶמְשְׁלוֹת בַּלָּיְלָה כִּי לְעוֹלָם חַסְדּוֹ:
י יא לְמַכֵּה מִצְרַיִם בִּבְכוֹרֵיהֶם כִּי לְעוֹלָם חַסְדּוֹ: וַיּוֹצֵא יִשְׂרָאֵל מִתּוֹכָם כִּי לְעוֹלָם
יב יג חַסְדּוֹ: בְּיָד חֲזָקָה וּבִזְרוֹעַ נְטוּיָה כִּי לְעוֹלָם חַסְדּוֹ: לְגֹזֵר יַם־סוּף לִגְזָרִים כִּי לְעוֹלָם
יד טו חַסְדּוֹ: וְהֶעֱבִיר יִשְׂרָאֵל בְּתוֹכוֹ כִּי לְעוֹלָם חַסְדּוֹ: וְנִעֵר פַּרְעֹה וְחֵילוֹ בְיַם־סוּף כִּי
טז יז לְעוֹלָם חַסְדּוֹ: לְמוֹלִיךְ עַמּוֹ בַּמִּדְבָּר כִּי לְעוֹלָם חַסְדּוֹ: לְמַכֵּה מְלָכִים גְּדֹלִים כִּי
יח יט לְעוֹלָם חַסְדּוֹ: וַיַּהֲרֹג מְלָכִים אַדִּירִים כִּי לְעוֹלָם חַסְדּוֹ: לְסִיחוֹן מֶלֶךְ הָאֱמֹרִי כִּי
כ כא לְעוֹלָם חַסְדּוֹ: וּלְעוֹג מֶלֶךְ הַבָּשָׁן כִּי לְעוֹלָם חַסְדּוֹ: וְנָתַן אַרְצָם לְנַחֲלָה כִּי לְעוֹלָם
כב כג חַסְדּוֹ: נַחֲלָה לְיִשְׂרָאֵל עַבְדּוֹ כִּי לְעוֹלָם חַסְדּוֹ: שֶׁבְּשִׁפְלֵנוּ זָכַר לָנוּ כִּי לְעוֹלָם
כד כה חַסְדּוֹ: וַיִּפְרְקֵנוּ מִצָּרֵינוּ כִּי לְעוֹלָם חַסְדּוֹ: נֹתֵן לֶחֶם לְכָל־בָּשָׂר כִּי לְעוֹלָם חַסְדּוֹ:
כו הוֹדוּ לְאֵל הַשָּׁמָיִם כִּי לְעוֹלָם חַסְדּוֹ:
לז א ב עַל־נַהֲרוֹת | בָּבֶל שָׁם יָשַׁבְנוּ גַּם־בָּכִינוּ בְּזָכְרֵנוּ אֶת־צִיּוֹן: עַל־עֲרָבִים בְּתוֹכָהּ
ג תָּלִינוּ כִּנֹּרוֹתֵינוּ: כִּי שָׁם | שְׁאֵלוּנוּ שׁוֹבֵינוּ דִּבְרֵי־שִׁיר וְתוֹלָלֵינוּ שִׂמְחָה שִׁירוּ לָנוּ
ד ה מִשִּׁיר צִיּוֹן: אֵיךְ נָשִׁיר אֶת־שִׁיר־יְהוָה עַל אַדְמַת נֵכָר: אִם־אֶשְׁכָּחֵךְ יְרוּשָׁלָםִ
ו תִּשְׁכַּח יְמִינִי: תִּדְבַּק לְשׁוֹנִי | לְחִכִּי אִם־לֹא אֶזְכְּרֵכִי אִם־לֹא אַעֲלֶה אֶת־יְרוּשָׁלַםִ
ז עַל רֹאשׁ שִׂמְחָתִי: זְכֹר יְהוָה | לִבְנֵי אֱדוֹם אֵת יוֹם יְרוּשָׁלָםִ הָאֹמְרִים עָרוּ | עָרוּ

4 The captives respond: **How can we sing the song of the Lord,** the Temple, **on foreign soil?**

5 The exiles then speak about the memory of Jerusalem: **If I forget you, Jerusalem, let my right hand,** my stronger hand, **lose its power.**

6 **Let my tongue cleave to my palate,** so that I will be unable to speak, **if I do not recall you.** If I do not recall the memory of Jerusalem, **if I do not set Jerusalem above my foremost joy,** it would be best for me not to speak at all. Even at the height of personal joy I will never forget Jerusalem and the humiliation it suffered.

7 Besides remembering the destruction of Jerusalem, we will also never forget the war and our enemies. **Remember, Lord, the day of** the destruction and downfall of **Jerusalem, for the sons of Edom,** who joined forces with the other enemies of Israel and **who said: Tear it down, tear it down, to its**

very foundation.[B] They called not only for the conquest of Jerusalem, but also for its total destruction.

8 **Thieving daughter of Babylon, happy is he who pays you back for what you did to us,** and does to you what you have done to us.

9 **Happy is he who will seize and dash your infants against the rock.** The psalmist does not say that he, personally, would like to carry out vengeance, but rather wishes that someone else would do so.

PSALM 138

A psalm of thanksgiving for God's help to individuals and to the nation as a whole.

PSALMS 138:1–8

138 1 **By David. I praise You with all my heart; before divine beings, I sing praises to You.** This verse refers to "divine beings," or angels. The psalmist, as it were, is singing not only among men but also before angels, who cannot themselves give thanks to God in the same way as people.

2 **I bow down toward Your holy Sanctuary, and I acclaim Your name for Your kindness and Your truth.** "Truth" refers to God's faithful fulfillment of His promises to David. **For You have made Your word greater than Your entire name.** Your kindness and Your fulfillment of Your word exceed everything I previously knew about Your name.

3 **On the day that I called, You answered me; You gave my soul strength and made it exalted.** You emboldened my soul to such an extent that it reached an elevated, exalted state.

4 **All kings of the earth will give thanks to You, Lord, when they hear the words of Your mouth.** Those among the kings and rulers who have heard the word of God will thank Him.

5 **They will sing** praises **of the ways of the Lord, for great is the Lord's honor** throughout the world.

6 **Though the Lord is exalted,** though God is in the highest heavens, **He sees the lowly** and pays heed to the lowest of the low. **The haughty He knows from afar.** He is also cognizant of those who are arrogant, and can punish them accordingly.

7 **Though I walk in the midst of distress,** when I am surrounded by adversity on all sides, **You keep me alive. In spite of** the attempts of **my enemies** to harm me, they are unsuccessful; **You send forth Your hand; Your right hand saves me.**

8 **The Lord will complete [*yigmor*] this for me.** Some commentators understand the word *yigmor* in the sense of *gemul*, or recompense, so that the verse is saying: God will repay me for my good deeds. However, it can also be interpreted literally, in the sense of finishing or completing for me the things that I want to do. **Your kindness, Lord, is forever; do not forsake the works of Your hands,** but rather help them to accomplish their goals to completion.

PSALM 139

A psalm of introspection and devotion; in essence, it constitutes praise of God's closeness.

PSALMS 139:1–24

139 1 **For the chief musician, a psalm by David. Lord, You have searched me, and You know me.**

2 **You know when I sit and when I rise.** Every move I make is known to You. **You understand my thoughts from afar.** You know me inside and out.

3 **You discern my path and my resting place.** You know my actions both when I am traveling on a path and when I am resting in one place. **You are familiar with all my ways.**

4 **Even when there is no word on my tongue,** as nothing that I say is new to You, **truly, Lord, You know it all,** even words that I wish to say but have not yet uttered.

5 **From back and front, You shaped me.** From the outset, You have been as close to me as can possibly be, for You created and shaped me. Moreover, from the beginning, **You placed Your palm on me;** I have been under Your protection. In this sense of divine intimacy, God always knows and cares for people and, despite His unfathomable greatness, is always close at hand.

6 **This knowledge is too wonderful for me.** It is like a wonder, beyond my comprehension. **It is sublime; I cannot reach it.** I cannot fathom the fact that You are always with me and that no side of me is unexposed, unexamined, or unrevealed to You.

7 **Where can I go from Your spirit?** Even if I wanted to escape from You, to go away and vanish, there is no way I could. **And where can I flee from Your presence,** since You are everywhere, and in everything?

8 **If I ascend to heaven, You are there; if I lie down in the netherworld, You are there.**

9 **Were I to travel on the wings of dawn,** to the easternmost point, or **were I to dwell at the end of the sea,** to the west,

"The wings of dawn"

"The end of the sea"

ח עַד הַיְסוֹד בָּהּ: בַּת־בָּבֶל הַשְּׁדוּדָה אַשְׁרֵי שֶׁיְשַׁלֶּם־לָךְ אֶת־גְּמוּלֵךְ שֶׁגָּמַלְתְּ לָנוּ:
ט אַשְׁרֵי ׀ שֶׁיֹּאחֵז וְנִפֵּץ אֶת־עֹלָלַיִךְ אֶל־הַסָּלַע:
לח א ב לְדָוִד ׀ אוֹדְךָ בְכָל־לִבִּי נֶגֶד אֱלֹהִים אֲזַמְּרֶךָּ: אֶשְׁתַּחֲוֶה אֶל־הֵיכַל קָדְשְׁךָ וְאוֹדֶה
ג אֶת־שְׁמֶךָ עַל־חַסְדְּךָ וְעַל־אֲמִתֶּךָ כִּי־הִגְדַּלְתָּ עַל־כָּל־שִׁמְךָ אִמְרָתֶךָ: בְּיוֹם
ד קָרָאתִי וַתַּעֲנֵנִי תַּרְהִבֵנִי בְנַפְשִׁי עֹז: יוֹדוּךָ יהוה כָּל־מַלְכֵי־אָרֶץ כִּי שָׁמְעוּ אִמְרֵי־
ה ו פִיךָ: וְיָשִׁירוּ בְּדַרְכֵי יהוה כִּי־גָדוֹל כְּבוֹד יהוה: כִּי־רָם יהוה וְשָׁפָל יִרְאֶה וְגָבֹהַּ
ז מִמֶּרְחָק יְיֵדָע: אִם־אֵלֵךְ ׀ בְּקֶרֶב צָרָה תְּחַיֵּנִי עַל אַף אֹיְבַי תִּשְׁלַח יָדֶךָ וְתוֹשִׁיעֵנִי
ח יְמִינֶךָ: יהוה יִגְמֹר בַּעֲדִי יהוה חַסְדְּךָ לְעוֹלָם מַעֲשֵׂי יָדֶיךָ אַל־תֶּרֶף:
לט א ב לַמְנַצֵּחַ לְדָוִד מִזְמוֹר יהוה חֲקַרְתַּנִי וַתֵּדָע: אַתָּה יָדַעְתָּ שִׁבְתִּי וְקוּמִי בַּנְתָּה
ג ד לְרֵעִי מֵרָחוֹק: אָרְחִי וְרִבְעִי זֵרִיתָ וְכָל־דְּרָכַי הִסְכַּנְתָּה: כִּי אֵין מִלָּה בִּלְשׁוֹנִי
ה ו הֵן יהוה יָדַעְתָּ כֻלָּהּ: אָחוֹר וָקֶדֶם צַרְתָּנִי וַתָּשֶׁת עָלַי כַּפֶּכָה: פלאיה דַעַת פְּלִיאָה
ז ח מִמֶּנִּי נִשְׂגְּבָה לֹא־אוּכַל לָהּ: אָנָה אֵלֵךְ מֵרוּחֶךָ וְאָנָה מִפָּנֶיךָ אֶבְרָח: אִם־אֶסַּק
ט שָׁמַיִם שָׁם אָתָּה וְאַצִּיעָה שְּׁאוֹל הִנֶּךָּ: אֶשָּׂא כַנְפֵי־שָׁחַר אֶשְׁכְּנָה בְּאַחֲרִית יָם:

BACKGROUND

137:7 | **Tear it down, tear it down, to its very foundation:** During Nebuchadnezzar's conquest of Judah, which ended in the destruction of the Temple and the Babylonian exile, the flourishing kingdom of Edom, located south of the Dead Sea and in the Arava, was destroyed first. The Edomites wandered westward into the Negev. Already at the end of the period of the kings of Judah, fortifications were built to defend against the Edomites. At Tel Arad, where one such fortress stood, an ostracon was discovered that reads: "The Edomites are coming." The Edomites, who spread out into the southern part of the Kingdom of Judah, also participated in the killing of Judean refugees and exiles who had escaped the destruction of Jerusalem.

10 **even there Your hand would guide me.** No matter how far away I may go, You are there. **Your right hand would hold me fast.**
11 **Even if I say that darkness will conceal me, that night, for me, is light.** In this verse, the word "light" is used euphemistically to mean just the opposite, darkness. Alternatively: Even if I say that darkness conceals me, that would be incorrect, for the night is unable to hide me from You; it is as if the dark night is actually light.
12 **Even darkness does not darken for You.** No matter how dark the night becomes, it cannot hide me from You. **The night, as if day, gives forth light.** For You, darkness does not conceal; it is as if night is as bright as day. **Darkness and light are the same.** Although for us light and darkness are opposites, from God's perspective, there is no difference between them.
13 The psalmist goes on to express the sentiment that everything he has done is actually a result of God's creation of him. **For You formed my innermost parts.** From the very beginning, my being has been Your handiwork. Everything in my life stems from Your creation of me, even my innermost, hidden parts. **You sheltered me in my mother's womb.**
14 **I will give thanks to You, for I was made in a wondrous manner.** My complex, unique existence is the work of Your hands. **Wonderful are Your works.** Your deeds are miraculous both in their entirety and in their smallest details. **I know this well.**
15 **My essence was not hidden from You when I was wrought in a secret place,** in my mother's womb. There I was **knitted,** formed, in a place hidden from sight as though **in the depths of the earth.**
16 You recognized and shaped the template of my being, both physical and spiritual. **Your eyes saw my unformed parts.** You know me not only as I am now, fully formed and distinct, but also as nothing more than a shapeless mass. **In Your book, they are all recorded.** Every individual is counted and recorded before You. Moreover, God regards each and every day and its events not only in the general sense of a unit of time, but also as a unique entity: **Of the days that were created, each one is His.**
17 **How precious to me,** when I ponder my reality and my existence as an individual, **are thoughts of You, God.** I realize how important to me are my thoughts and ideas about You. **How vast is their beginning,** the essentials, the foundations of my thoughts, concerning God!
18 **When I count them,** my thoughts about You, Your being, and Your greatness, **they outnumber the sand,** as they are more numerous than grains of sand. **When I awake, I am still with You.** These thoughts are with me at all times, whether it is evident to others or not. Although I do not think about You when I sleep, as soon as I awake, I once again find myself close to You.
19 As in other psalms contemplating the unity and harmony of God vis-à-vis His world and creations, this psalm also addresses darker matters, namely, flaws and imperfections in the world. These flaws are not intrinsic to creation but rather are the outcome of human behavior. Only humans, who have been given free will, are capable of consciously doing evil; only they can create the blemishes and distortions that mar the world's harmony. The psalmist thus beseeches God: **If only You, God, would slay the wicked, and men of bloodshed would turn away from me,** the world would be a brighter place.
20 If only you would slay **Your enemies, who defy You for the sake of intrigue, exalting themselves in vain.** Whenever people aspire to greatness and scheme to promote themselves, their efforts are for naught. The phrase "exalting themselves in vain" refers not only to the outcome of their behavior but also to their very aspirations, which are devoid of any value or substance.
21 Although these enemies are not the psalmist's personal foes, he cannot remain on the sidelines in this war between good and evil. **For surely Your enemies, Lord, I hate, and I contend with those who rise against You.**
22 **I hate them with utter hatred; they have become my enemies.** I hate them not because they have at any time harmed me or caused me distress, but because I am obligated to take Your part in a war that is essentially directed against You. At the very least, I am obliged to state which side I support and which side I oppose.
23 **Search me, God,** concerning these and other matters, **and know my heart.** Know that my most profound intentions are directed solely toward You. **Test me and know my thoughts,**
24 **and see if there is any grievous way in me.** If You find that my heart's inclination has in any way led me astray, **lead me on the path to eternity;** guide me to the right path, that which leads to eternity.

PSALM 140

PSALMS 140:1–14

A psalm of supplication and entreaty, written by David at a time when he was pursued by King Saul's men while being slandered and falsely accused.

140 1 **For the chief musician, a psalm by David.**
29th day of month 2 **Rescue me, Lord, from evil people; protect me from unjust men,**
3 **those who devise wicked plans in their hearts, each day provoking wars.** It is as if they live their lives in continual warfare.

י יא גַּם־שָׁם יָדְךָ תַנְחֵנִי וְתֹאחֲזֵנִי יְמִינֶךָ: וָאֹמַר אַךְ־חֹשֶׁךְ יְשׁוּפֵנִי וְלַיְלָה אוֹר בַּעֲדֵנִי:
יב יג גַּם־חֹשֶׁךְ לֹא־יַחְשִׁיךְ מִמֶּךָ וְלַיְלָה כַּיּוֹם יָאִיר כַּחֲשֵׁיכָה כָּאוֹרָה: כִּי־אַתָּה קָנִיתָ
יד כִלְיֹתָי תְּסֻכֵּנִי בְּבֶטֶן אִמִּי: אוֹדְךָ עַל כִּי נוֹרָאוֹת נִפְלֵיתִי נִפְלָאִים מַעֲשֶׂיךָ וְנַפְשִׁי
טו יֹדַעַת מְאֹד: לֹא־נִכְחַד עָצְמִי מִמֶּךָּ אֲשֶׁר־עֻשֵּׂיתִי בַסֵּתֶר רֻקַּמְתִּי בְּתַחְתִּיּוֹת
טז יז אָרֶץ: גָּלְמִי ׀ רָאוּ עֵינֶיךָ וְעַל־סִפְרְךָ כֻּלָּם יִכָּתֵבוּ יָמִים יֻצָּרוּ ולא אֶחָד בָּהֶם: וְלִי וְלוֹ
יח מַה־יָּקְרוּ רֵעֶיךָ אֵל מֶה עָצְמוּ רָאשֵׁיהֶם: אֶסְפְּרֵם מֵחוֹל יִרְבּוּן הֱקִיצֹתִי וְעוֹדִי
יט כ עִמָּךְ: אִם־תִּקְטֹל אֱלוֹהַּ ׀ רָשָׁע וְאַנְשֵׁי דָמִים סוּרוּ מֶנִּי: אֲשֶׁר יֹמְרוּךָ לִמְזִמָּה נָשֻׂא
כא כב לַשָּׁוְא עָרֶיךָ: הֲלוֹא־מְשַׂנְאֶיךָ יהוה ׀ אֶשְׂנָא וּבִתְקוֹמְמֶיךָ אֶתְקוֹטָט: תַּכְלִית
כג כד שִׂנְאָה שְׂנֵאתִים לְאוֹיְבִים הָיוּ לִי: חָקְרֵנִי אֵל וְדַע לְבָבִי בְּחָנֵנִי וְדַע שַׂרְעַפָּי: וּרְאֵה
אִם־דֶּרֶךְ־עֹצֶב בִּי וּנְחֵנִי בְּדֶרֶךְ עוֹלָם:

קמ א ב ג לַמְנַצֵּחַ מִזְמוֹר לְדָוִד: חַלְּצֵנִי יהוה מֵאָדָם רָע מֵאִישׁ חֲמָסִים תִּנְצְרֵנִי: אֲשֶׁר חָשְׁבוּ כט לחודש
ד רָעוֹת בְּלֵב כָּל־יוֹם יָגוּרוּ מִלְחָמוֹת: שָׁנְנוּ לְשׁוֹנָם כְּמוֹ־נָחָשׁ חֲמַת עַכְשׁוּב תַּחַת
ה שְׂפָתֵימוֹ סֶלָה: שָׁמְרֵנִי יהוה ׀ מִידֵי רָשָׁע מֵאִישׁ חֲמָסִים תִּנְצְרֵנִי אֲשֶׁר חָשְׁבוּ
ו לִדְחוֹת פְּעָמָי: טָמְנוּ־גֵאִים ׀ פַּח לִי וַחֲבָלִים פָּרְשׂוּ רֶשֶׁת לְיַד־מַעְגָּל מֹקְשִׁים

4 **They sharpen their tongues like a serpent.** In the book of Psalms and elsewhere in the Bible, the serpent's tongue symbolizes slander. **The venom of spiders**[B] **is under their lips, Selah.**

5 **Guard me, Lord, from the hands of the wicked; protect me from unjust men who seek to trip my feet.**

6 Such men attempt to bring about my downfall, and for this purpose they use all manner of cunning tricks. **The arrogant laid a trap for me; they spread a net with cords by the wayside.**[B] Animals are often trapped in this fashion; their feet get entangled in netting that is put near places that they frequent. **And set snares for me, Selah.** The psalmist is referring to various traps that his enemies set for him.

BACKGROUND

140:4 | **The venom of spiders:** The identity of the *akhshuv*, translated here as "spider," is uncertain. It may be a poisonous snake, or a spider [*akavish*] with inversion of the word's letters, as Rashi seems to suggest, or another aggressive arthropod. The word *ḥamat*, which literally means "wrath," here refers to venom. This may be an allusion to the ferociousness of the spider as it swiftly wraps up its prey and paralyzes it. The word *akhshuv* in modern Hebrew refers to *Solifugae*, an arachnid that is similar to the spider but which does not spin a web. It is found mostly in dry and desert areas, with five species existing in Israel.

140:6 | **They spread a net with cords by the wayside:** The word *ma'agal*, literally "circle," often means "way" or "road" (see, e.g., Isaiah 26:7; Proverbs 4:26). It may also be the name of a kind of trap consisting of nets twisted together in a circle around the animal's lair, as *ma'agal* may refer to the center of a circle (see commentary on I Samuel 26:5). By means of noise, smoke, an animal used as bait, or other such methods, the animal is lured from its lair and trapped in the tightly knit net, which resembles a spider web.

7 At such times, the psalmist has no recourse other than prayer. **I said to the Lord: You are my God; listen, Lord, to the sound of my pleas.**

8 **Lord, my Lord, strength of my deliverance, You shielded my head on the day of battle.**

9 **Lord, do not grant the desires of the wicked. Do not bring their scheme to fruition.** Do not allow the wicked to succeed in carrying out their evil plans. **May they depart** from me, **Selah.**

10 **May the mischief of their lips cover the heads of those who surround me.** The essence of David's request is that the evildoers be brought down by their own evil.

11 **May burning coals fall on them; may they be cast into the fire, into deep pits,** another means of trapping animals, **never to rise.**

12 **May slanderers have no place in the land; may evil trap unjust men and thrust them into the depths.**

13 In contrast to the fate of the wicked, who are brought down by their own evil deeds, the righteous will eventually be aided and rescued. **I know the Lord will minister justice to the poor,** and mete out fair **judgment to the needy.**

14 And after the enemy has collapsed, **the righteous will surely give thanks to Your name; the upright will dwell** in peace **in Your presence.**

PSALM 141

PSALMS 141:1–10

Another psalm depicting an individual pursued by enemies, whose wickedness he decries. In addition, the psalmist prays to be spared from becoming like his foes; he wants no part of their modes of behavior.

141 1 **A psalm by David. Lord, I have called out to You; make haste to help me.** I am in need of immediate rescue. **Listen to my voice as I call out to You.**

2 **Let my prayer stand as an offering of incense before You.** Although my prayer consists only of words, let it be considered as pleasing before You as an incense offering. **The lifting of my hands, an evening offering.** Let my hands lifted in prayer be deemed a sacrificial offering.

3 And this is the prayer I offer up to You: **Place a sentinel, Lord, at my mouth,** so that I will not engage in evil speech as do my enemies. **Guard the door to my lips** and enable me to remain silent.

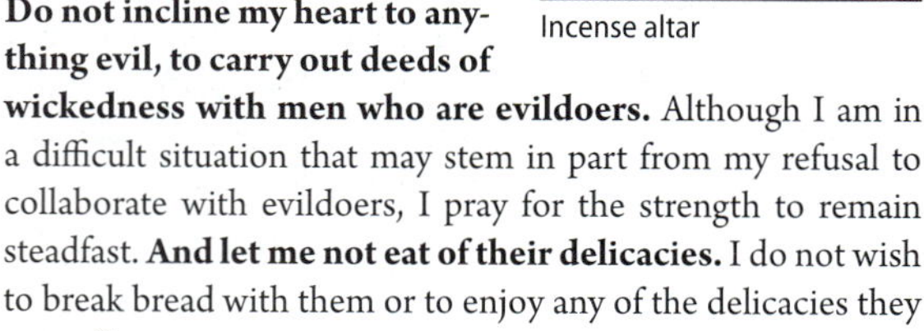

Incense altar

4 **Do not incline my heart to anything evil, to carry out deeds of wickedness with men who are evildoers.** Although I am in a difficult situation that may stem in part from my refusal to collaborate with evildoers, I pray for the strength to remain steadfast. **And let me not eat of their delicacies.** I do not wish to break bread with them or to enjoy any of the delicacies they may offer.

5 **May the Righteous One strike me, for it is a kindness.** Even if You hit me, You are righteous, and You do me a kindness, as it causes me to improve myself. **May He rebuke me; it is like fragrant oil.** Your rebuke is like fragrant oil anointing my head, and I pray: **Let it,** this oil, **not be removed from my head; my prayer is still against their evildoings.** As I continue on my way, I pray to be rescued from my enemies.

6 **Their judges will slip down from the rocks.** "Their judges" refers to their leaders. Ultimately, they will collapse, as if tumbling off a boulder, and **they will hear my words, for they are pleasing.** At that point, my enemies may be ready to understand that I am not at the root of the animosity between us. On the contrary, I am trying to conduct myself in the best possible way, for their sake as well as my own.

7 In the meantime, however, **as if** a woodcutter is **chopping and breaking the earth,** where in the course of chopping and splitting wood he makes holes in the ground underneath, I am receiving blows from all sides. Moreover, I feel as though **our**

"Guard me from the trap...snares...nets." Fish caught in a trap, illustration based on stone relief, tomb of Mereruka, Sixth Dynasty, Saqqara, Egypt, 2345–2333 BCE

ז ח שָׁתוּ־לִי סֶלָה: אָמַרְתִּי לַיהוה אֵלִי אָתָּה הַאֲזִינָה יהוה קוֹל תַּחֲנוּנָי: יֱהֹוִה
ט אֲדֹנָי עֹז יְשׁוּעָתִי סַכֹּתָה לְרֹאשִׁי בְּיוֹם נָשֶׁק: אַל־תִּתֵּן יהוה מַאֲוַיֵּי רָשָׁע זְמָמוֹ
י יא אַל־תָּפֵק יָרוּמוּ סֶלָה: רֹאשׁ מְסִבָּי עֲמַל שְׂפָתֵימוֹ יכסומו: ימיטו עֲלֵיהֶם גֶּחָלִים יְכַסֵּמוֹ
יב בָּאֵשׁ יַפִּלֵם בְּמַהֲמֹרוֹת בַּל־יָקוּמוּ: אִישׁ לָשׁוֹן בַּל־יִכּוֹן בָּאָרֶץ אִישׁ־חָמָס רָע יִמּוֹטוּ
יג יד יְצוּדֶנּוּ לְמַדְחֵפֹת: ידעת כִּי־יַעֲשֶׂה יהוה דִּין עָנִי מִשְׁפַּט אֶבְיֹנִים: אַךְ צַדִּיקִים יט
יוֹדוּ לִשְׁמֶךָ יֵשְׁבוּ יְשָׁרִים אֶת־פָּנֶיךָ:
מא א ב מִזְמוֹר לְדָוִד יהוה קְרָאתִיךָ חוּשָׁה לִּי הַאֲזִינָה קוֹלִי בְּקָרְאִי־לָךְ: תִּכּוֹן תְּפִלָּתִי
ג קְטֹרֶת לְפָנֶיךָ מַשְׂאַת כַּפַּי מִנְחַת־עָרֶב: שִׁיתָה יהוה שָׁמְרָה לְפִי נִצְּרָה עַל־דַּל
ד שְׂפָתָי: אַל־תַּט־לִבִּי ׀ לְדָבָר ׀ רָע לְהִתְעוֹלֵל עֲלִלוֹת ׀ בְּרֶשַׁע אֶת־אִישִׁים פֹּעֲלֵי־
ה אָוֶן וּבַל־אֶלְחַם בְּמַנְעַמֵּיהֶם: יֶהֶלְמֵנִי צַדִּיק ׀ חֶסֶד וְיוֹכִיחֵנִי שֶׁמֶן רֹאשׁ אַל־יָנִי
ו רֹאשִׁי כִּי־עוֹד וּתְפִלָּתִי בְּרָעוֹתֵיהֶם: נִשְׁמְטוּ בִידֵי־סֶלַע שֹׁפְטֵיהֶם וְשָׁמְעוּ אֲמָרַי
ז ח כִּי נָעֵמוּ: כְּמוֹ פֹלֵחַ וּבֹקֵעַ בָּאָרֶץ נִפְזְרוּ עֲצָמֵינוּ לְפִי שְׁאוֹל: כִּי אֵלֶיךָ ׀ יֱהֹוִה אֲדֹנָי
ט עֵינָי בְּכָה חָסִיתִי אַל־תְּעַר נַפְשִׁי: שָׁמְרֵנִי מִידֵי פַח יָקְשׁוּ לִי וּמֹקְשׁוֹת פֹּעֲלֵי אָוֶן:
י יִפְּלוּ בְמַכְמֹרָיו רְשָׁעִים יַחַד אָנֹכִי עַד־אֶעֱבוֹר:

bones are scattered at the mouth of the grave, as if we are being torn apart, leading to our death.

8 **Yet my eyes are toward You, Lord my God. In You I take refuge; do not discard me.**

9 **Guard me from the trap they laid for me, from the snares of evildoers.**

10 **Let the wicked fall together into their own nets.** May they all be snared by their own devices **until I escape,** so that I may emerge safely.

PSALM 142

A psalm of entreaty by one who is isolated. Surrounded by hatred and by enemies pursuing him, he prays to be rescued.

PSALMS 142:1–8

142 1 **A contemplation by David**[D] **when he was in the cave,** hiding
from Saul's henchmen;[86] it is also **a** song of **prayer.**
2 **My voice is to the Lord when I cry out; my voice is to the
Lord when I plead.**
3 **I pour out my woe before Him.** The word *siḥi*, translated here
as "my woe," connotes both prayer and sorrow. **Before Him, I
speak of my trouble.**
4 **When my spirit grows faint** (see 77:4), **You know my way.**
You know that the path I follow is not one of evil. Nonetheless,
on the road where I go, they have laid a trap for me.
5 **Look on the right,** as one's right side represents his strength,
and see. "The right" may also refer to the place where one's
friends stand by him. **I have no one who knows me,** and I am
completely alone; **there is nowhere to flee. No one seeks my
well-being.** No one is looking after me or seeking ways to help
me.
6 **I cried out to You, Lord, and said: You are my** only **refuge,
my portion in the land of the living,** my only source of help
in this world.
7 **Listen to my cry, for I am greatly weakened. Rescue me
from my pursuers, for they are too strong for me.** I have
become so weakened that I cannot hold my own against my
enemies.
8 **Release me from confinement, so I may give thanks to Your
name. The righteous, through me, will be glorified when
You deal kindly with me.**

PSALM 143

A song of prayer and entreaty at a time of distress caused mainly by outside enemies.

PSALMS 143:1–12

143 1 **A psalm by David. Lord, hear my prayer, listen to my pleas.
In Your faithfulness, in Your righteousness, answer me.**
David's plea for help and protection is grounded on God's
mercy. Despite his admitted imperfections, David emphasizes
that he has always striven to be close to God and to serve Him.
Thus, he entreats God to heed his prayer out of His mercy and
righteousness.
2 **Do not put Your servant to judgment.** I am not requesting
justice but rather mercy. And it is not only for myself that I say
this, **for no living thing can be justified before You.** Were I to
be judged, I would certainly be found guilty.
3 In the meantime, however, I am suffering. **Indeed, the enemy
has pursued me** and **crushed my life to the ground;** my foes
are crushing the life out of me. They **made me dwell in dark
places, like those forever dead.**
4 **My spirit grows faint** (see 77:4). **My heart is stunned within
me.**
5 **I remember days of old** when I was at ease, **when I meditated
on all Your doings and spoke of the work of Your hands.**
6 **I stretch out my hands to You** in prayer; **my soul** reaches out,
like a parched land, to You, Selah. I turn to you as desperately
as parched earth needs rain.
7 **Answer me quickly, Lord; my spirit fails.** I feel as though I
am suffocating. **Do not hide Your face from me, lest I be like
those who descend to the pit.** If You do not turn to me, I will
be like someone who is already dead.
8 **Let me hear Your kindness in the morning, for in You I have
trusted.** I have always been bound and connected to You, and
You are my main support. **Show me the way in which I should
walk, for I lift up my soul to You** now, as I have always done in
the past.
9 **Rescue me from my enemies, Lord, for in You I take cover.**
You are my shelter and my protective armor.
10 **Teach me to do Your will,** as perhaps I err inadvertently in my
ways, **for You are my God. Your spirit is good;** You can lead
me on the correct path. **Lead me to a level land.** Mountain
paths are tortuous and dangerous, whereas on a level path one
can move more freely and see both far and near.
11 **For the sake of Your name, Lord, save my life. In Your righteousness, free me from distress.**
12 **And in Your kindness** toward me, **destroy my enemies; lay
waste to all my foes, for I am Your servant,** and as one under
Your protection, I ask for Your help.

DISCUSSION

142:1 | **A contemplation by David:** The Sages comment: What is meant here by "a contemplation by David"? When Saul and David were together in the cave, David saw and realized that a man does not survive by his money, his wisdom, or his might. What is it that sustains man? His prayers. David contemplated this and knew that the best course of action for him at that time was to pray (*Midrash Tehillim*).

מב א ב מַשְׂכִּיל לְדָוִד בִּהְיוֹתוֹ בַמְּעָרָה תְפִלָּה: קוֹלִי אֶל־יְהוָה אֶזְעָק קוֹלִי אֶל־יְהוָה
ג ד אֶתְחַנָּן: אֶשְׁפֹּךְ לְפָנָיו שִׂיחִי צָרָתִי לְפָנָיו אַגִּיד: בְּהִתְעַטֵּף עָלַי ׀ רוּחִי וְאַתָּה
ה יָדַעְתָּ נְתִיבָתִי בְּאֹרַח־זוּ אֲהַלֵּךְ טָמְנוּ פַח לִי: הַבֵּיט יָמִין ׀ וּרְאֵה וְאֵין־לִי מַכִּיר
ו אָבַד מָנוֹס מִמֶּנִּי אֵין דּוֹרֵשׁ לְנַפְשִׁי: זָעַקְתִּי אֵלֶיךָ יְהוָה אָמַרְתִּי אַתָּה מַחְסִי
ז חֶלְקִי בְּאֶרֶץ הַחַיִּים: הַקְשִׁיבָה ׀ אֶל־רִנָּתִי כִּי־דַלּוֹתִי מְאֹד הַצִּילֵנִי מֵרֹדְפַי כִּי
ח אָמְצוּ מִמֶּנִּי: הוֹצִיאָה מִמַּסְגֵּר ׀ נַפְשִׁי לְהוֹדוֹת אֶת־שְׁמֶךָ בִּי יַכְתִּרוּ צַדִּיקִים כִּי
תִגְמֹל עָלָי:
מג א מִזְמוֹר לְדָוִד יְהוָה ׀ שְׁמַע תְּפִלָּתִי הַאֲזִינָה אֶל־תַּחֲנוּנַי בֶּאֱמֻנָתְךָ עֲנֵנִי בְּצִדְקָתֶךָ:
ב ג וְאַל־תָּבוֹא בְמִשְׁפָּט אֶת־עַבְדֶּךָ כִּי לֹא־יִצְדַּק לְפָנֶיךָ כָל־חָי: כִּי רָדַף אוֹיֵב ׀ נַפְשִׁי
ד דִּכָּא לָאָרֶץ חַיָּתִי הוֹשִׁיבַנִי בְמַחֲשַׁכִּים כְּמֵתֵי עוֹלָם: וַתִּתְעַטֵּף עָלַי רוּחִי בְּתוֹכִי
ה יִשְׁתּוֹמֵם לִבִּי: זָכַרְתִּי יָמִים ׀ מִקֶּדֶם הָגִיתִי בְכָל־פָּעֳלֶךָ בְּמַעֲשֵׂה יָדֶיךָ אֲשׂוֹחֵחַ:
ו ז פֵּרַשְׂתִּי יָדַי אֵלֶיךָ נַפְשִׁי ׀ כְּאֶרֶץ־עֲיֵפָה לְךָ סֶלָה: מַהֵר עֲנֵנִי ׀ יְהוָה כָּלְתָה רוּחִי
ח אַל־תַּסְתֵּר פָּנֶיךָ מִמֶּנִּי וְנִמְשַׁלְתִּי עִם־יֹרְדֵי בוֹר: הַשְׁמִיעֵנִי בַבֹּקֶר ׀ חַסְדֶּךָ כִּי־בְךָ
ט בָטָחְתִּי הוֹדִיעֵנִי דֶּרֶךְ־זוּ אֵלֵךְ כִּי־אֵלֶיךָ נָשָׂאתִי נַפְשִׁי: הַצִּילֵנִי מֵאֹיְבַי ׀ יְהוָה
י אֵלֶיךָ כִסִּתִי: לַמְּדֵנִי ׀ לַעֲשׂוֹת רְצוֹנֶךָ כִּי־אַתָּה אֱלוֹהָי רוּחֲךָ טוֹבָה תַּנְחֵנִי בְּאֶרֶץ
יא יב מִישׁוֹר: לְמַעַן־שִׁמְךָ יְהוָה תְּחַיֵּנִי בְּצִדְקָתְךָ ׀ תוֹצִיא מִצָּרָה נַפְשִׁי: וּבְחַסְדְּךָ
תַּצְמִית אֹיְבָי וְהַאֲבַדְתָּ כָּל־צֹרְרֵי נַפְשִׁי כִּי אֲנִי עַבְדֶּךָ:

PSALM 144

PSALMS 144:1–15

A psalm depicting a time of war, a prayer for God's help and an expression of gratitude for the victory that was wrought. It concludes with a description of ensuing peace and tranquility in the land, once there are no longer any enemies to threaten it.

144 1 **By David. Blessed is the Lord, my rock, who trains my hands for battle and my fingers for warfare,** enabling me to be victorious.

2 You are **my kindness,** the one who bestows kindness upon me, **and my fortress,** who protects me, **my stronghold and my rescuer, my shield in whom I shelter;** You are He **who subdues my people under me,** enabling me to be a king and leader of my people.

3 This is a song of gratitude, not glorification, as even the victorious king knows well that God's beneficence is responsible for his victory. This leads him to reflect: **Lord, what is man that You should know him?** Why should humans merit Your love and attention? **A mortal that You should consider him?** What is their worth, that You think about them and accord them status?

4 After all, **man is like vapor.** Human life is ephemeral, like a whiff of vapor or a blowing wind. **His days** are **like a passing shadow.** Man's life has even less substance than a fixed shadow; it is like a "passing shadow," such as that of a moving cloud or a bird. Therefore, the psalmist prays for God's continued beneficence instead of arguing that man has any special merit.

5 The psalmist prays for victory in the wars he is waging: **Lord, tilt Your heavens** to bring them closer to earth, so to speak, **and descend** so that You can intervene in what is happening. **Touch the mountains, and they will smolder.** When You merely touch the mountains, they begin to burn.

6 **Send forth lightning and scatter them,** my enemies; **let fly Your arrows and confound them.**

7 **Stretch out Your hand from above** to aid me; **deliver and rescue me from surging waters,** a metaphor that the psalmist proceeds to clarify: **From the hands of foreigners** who are waging war against me.

8 Those foreigners are dangerous not only as foes but also as allies, because their loyalty cannot be trusted: They are people **whose mouths speak deceit, whose right hand,** the hand generally extended in assistance or in the forging of a covenant, **is a right hand of lies.**

9 **God, I will sing a new song to You, on a harp of ten strings.** A ten-stringed harp is unusual; harps of that time generally had at most seven or eight strings. **I will sing praises to You,**

10 and this is my song of praise: You are He **who gives salvation to kings, who delivers David His servant from the sword of evil.** He saves me in times of battle and also from any form of evil.

11 The psalmist repeats his plea: **Deliver and rescue me from the hands of foreigners whose mouths speak deceit, whose right hand is a right hand of lies,**

12 **so that our sons will be like saplings tended in their youth.** After the descriptions of war, this verse and the ones that follow depict the nation during an era of tranquility and prosperity following their victory. The nation's sons are likened to saplings that grow without impediments. **Our daughters** will be **like shapely corner pillars, like the form of a palace [*heikhal*].** The daughters are described as decorated pillars in a palace. *Heikhal* is a word that can also refer to the Temple. This description evokes not only beauty but holiness and perfection.

13 **Our storehouses are full, supplying all manner of goods; our flocks are multiplying to thousands and tens of thousands in our marketplaces.**

14 **Our oxen are laden** with goods. **There is no breach** of a barrier **and no going forth.** This sentence refers both to the cattle, which remain safely confined, and to the people, who are tranquil and secure and do not go forth to battle. **There is no shrieking** out of anger, or fighting **in our streets.**

"Our oxen are laden." Oxen pulling a pile of straw

15 **Happy is the nation for whom this is so,** who is blessed by God with a good life of peace and prosperity; **happy is the nation whose God is the Lord.**

PSALM 145

PSALMS 145:1–21

A psalm that is essentially one of praise and thanks for God's eternal kindness; it contains no entreaties or requests. It is structured alphabetically, and while there is no continuous line of thought from one verse to the next, all the verses taken together form a portrait of God's beneficence in the world.

145 1 **A psalm of praise, by David.**[D] The heading, "a psalm of praise," is a fitting characterization of this psalm. Two main themes are presented in the verses that follow. The first pertains to the Holy One as a gracious God who sustains His world. The second describes God's majesty and might, which are referred to repeatedly, both explicitly and implicitly. Thus, **I extol You, my God, the King.** I give You honor, and in this way Your greatness in the world is magnified. The second half of the verse reiterates

30th day of month

מד א ב לְדָוִד ׀ בָּרוּךְ יְהוָה ׀ צוּרִי הַמְלַמֵּד יָדַי לַקְרָב אֶצְבְּעוֹתַי לַמִּלְחָמָה: חַסְדִּי וּמְצוּדָתִי
ג מִשְׂגַּבִּי וּמְפַלְטִי לִי מָגִנִּי וּבוֹ חָסִיתִי הָרוֹדֵד עַמִּי תַחְתָּי: יְהוָה מָה־אָדָם וַתֵּדָעֵהוּ
ד ה בֶּן־אֱנוֹשׁ וַתְּחַשְּׁבֵהוּ: אָדָם לַהֶבֶל דָּמָה יָמָיו כְּצֵל עוֹבֵר: יְהוָה הַט־שָׁמֶיךָ וְתֵרֵד
ו ז גַּע בֶּהָרִים וְיֶעֱשָׁנוּ: בְּרוֹק בָּרָק וּתְפִיצֵם שְׁלַח חִצֶּיךָ וּתְהֻמֵּם: שְׁלַח יָדֶיךָ מִמָּרוֹם
ח פְּצֵנִי וְהַצִּילֵנִי מִמַּיִם רַבִּים מִיַּד בְּנֵי נֵכָר: אֲשֶׁר פִּיהֶם דִּבֶּר־שָׁוְא וִימִינָם יְמִין
ט י שָׁקֶר: אֱלֹהִים שִׁיר חָדָשׁ אָשִׁירָה לָּךְ בְּנֵבֶל עָשׂוֹר אֲזַמְּרָה־לָּךְ: הַנּוֹתֵן תְּשׁוּעָה
יא לַמְּלָכִים הַפּוֹצֶה אֶת־דָּוִד עַבְדּוֹ מֵחֶרֶב רָעָה: פְּצֵנִי וְהַצִּילֵנִי מִיַּד בְּנֵי־נֵכָר אֲשֶׁר
יב פִּיהֶם דִּבֶּר־שָׁוְא וִימִינָם יְמִין שָׁקֶר: אֲשֶׁר בָּנֵינוּ ׀ כִּנְטִעִים מְגֻדָּלִים בִּנְעוּרֵיהֶם
יג בְּנוֹתֵינוּ כְזָוִיֹּת מְחֻטָּבוֹת תַּבְנִית הֵיכָל: מְזָוֵינוּ מְלֵאִים מְפִיקִים מִזַּן אֶל זַן צֹאונֵנוּ
יד מַאֲלִיפוֹת מְרֻבָּבוֹת בְּחוּצוֹתֵינוּ: אַלּוּפֵינוּ מְסֻבָּלִים אֵין פֶּרֶץ וְאֵין יוֹצֵאת וְאֵין
טו צְוָחָה בִּרְחֹבֹתֵינוּ: אַשְׁרֵי הָעָם שֶׁכָּכָה לּוֹ אַשְׁרֵי הָעָם שֶׁיְהוָה אֱלֹהָיו:
מה א ב תְּהִלָּה לְדָוִד אֲרוֹמִמְךָ אֱלוֹהַי הַמֶּלֶךְ וַאֲבָרְכָה שִׁמְךָ לְעוֹלָם וָעֶד: בְּכָל־יוֹם ל לחודש
ג אֲבָרְכֶךָּ וַאֲהַלְלָה שִׁמְךָ לְעוֹלָם וָעֶד: גָּדוֹל יְהוָה וּמְהֻלָּל מְאֹד וְלִגְדֻלָּתוֹ אֵין חֵקֶר:

and emphasizes this point: **And I bless Your name forever and ever.** "Forever" means that God is blessed at all times, continually; "and ever" indicates that He is blessed for eternity.

2 **Every day I bless You. And I praise Your name forever and ever.**[D]

3 **The Lord is great and highly extolled.** Nevertheless, the manifold forms of praise offered to God cannot convey the full extent of His greatness, **and His greatness is unfathomable,** beyond human comprehension.

DISCUSSION

145:1 | **A psalm of praise, by David:** This is arguably the best-known chapter in all of Psalms, because the Sages inserted it into the daily prayers to be recited three times a day (see *Berakhot* 4b). The psalm's second verse, "Every day I bless you" may be one reason why the chapter was chosen for daily recitation. In the liturgy, the verse 84:5 and the preceding verse, 144:15, are appended to the beginning of the psalm, and another verse (115:18) is added at the end, in order to complement ideas that pertain to those who come to pray in the synagogue.

For many generations, this psalm, together with the following five, which begin and end with "Halleluya" and are the closing chapters of the book, has customarily been recited daily in all Jewish communities during the morning service.

145:2 | **Every day I bless You. And I praise Your name forever and ever:** There is a tension or perhaps a complement between one's everyday obligation to bless God and the giving of praise that is eternal, "forever and ever." Indeed, all the verses of the chapter, with one significant exception, are divided into two sections, one of which is either a reprise of the other or a complement to it. It is also possible, over the course of the psalm, to discern the development of a single theme: The increasing intensity of God's praise. Whereas in the beginning, "Every day I bless You" mentions the psalmist's personal blessing, the continuation, "Your devoted ones bless You" (verse 10), and finally "all flesh blesses His holy name" (verse 21), reflects this heightened intensity.

4 **From generation to generation Your works are praised.** Every generation transmits its praises of God to the generation that follows; in this way, praise of God is continually being created, added to, and renewed. **And they tell of Your mighty acts.** Although this is a hymn of praise for God's kindness, His attribute of might, while not expounded here, is always in the background.
5 **I speak about the glorious honor of Your majesty;** I will say everything that can possibly be said to honor and glorify God, **and** I speak **of Your wondrous deeds.**
6 **They speak of the power of Your awesome acts.** God's attributes of power and awesomeness appear elsewhere in Psalms and throughout the Bible. **And I tell of Your greatness;** "greatness" refers to a softer, more merciful aspect of God's power.
7 **They,** those who worship You, **give voice to the recollection of Your great goodness, and of Your righteousness,** Your beneficence and generosity on their behalf and on behalf of the entire world, **they joyously sing.**
8 And this is their praise that they sing: **Gracious and merciful is the Lord, slow to anger, and great in kindness.**
9 **The Lord is good to all, and His mercy extends to all His creations.** A new idea is introduced here: God's beneficence is not limited to a specific category of creation. It is all-inclusive and therefore also balanced. It follows that if God is good "to all," He is good to celestial as well as earthly beings, merciful to predators as well as to their prey.
10 **All Your creations thank You, Lord.** Everything You have created is grateful to You. **And Your devoted ones,** those who are closest to You, **bless You.**
11 After mentioning giving thanks in general, more specific praise is articulated: **They speak of the honor of Your kingdom, and they tell of Your might.**
12 It is important to speak about these matters and **to make known to people His mighty acts and the honored splendor of His kingdom,** as when they are explained to others, it enables God's greatness to be acknowledged by all. It is the obligation of those who know this, and who can tell about it, to do so.
13 A partial list of praise follows: **Your kingship is an eternal kingship, and Your reign is in every generation.** God's sovereignty is eternal. There is a difference in nuance between the two terms used in this verse for ruling. *Malkhut*, "kingship," conveys a knowing and willing acceptance of God's sovereignty, whereas *memshala*, "reign," refers to God's controlling rule, which exists independent of man's awareness and acknowledgment. In accordance with the alphabetical structure of the psalm, the next verse should begin with the letter *nun*. However, this letter is skipped,[87] and the psalm continues with a verse beginning with the following letter, *samekh*:
14 **The Lord supports all those who fall.** The word *hanofelim*, translated here as "those who fall," refers to people who are unstable and thus liable to fall unless they are somehow supported. **And He straightens all who are bent over.**
15 **The eyes of all** mankind, and all of creation, **look to You in hope.** You are the focus of all hope. **And You** indeed **give them,** all the world's creatures, **their food in its proper time.**
16 **You open Your hand, and satisfy the desire of every living thing.** You see to it that the needs and desires of every living thing are met.
17 **Just is the Lord in all His ways.** As has been noted in many places, our comprehension is exceedingly limited, and because of this we sometimes perceive the ways in which the world works as being unjust. It is precisely for this reason that we are called upon to offer these words of praise. **And kind in all His deeds.** Beyond being just, God extends kindness that greatly exceeds the criteria of justice.
18 **The Lord is close to all who call Him, to all who call Him in truth.** When people turn to God in prayer, He is always near. Or, more precisely, He is always accessible to those who reach out to Him in a sincere manner, calling to Him "in truth." This explanation is indicated by the structure of the verse, the only one in this psalm that does not consist of two parallel clauses. As previously noted, in all the other verses, the second clause expands upon the first, whereas here the second clause, "to all who call Him in truth," serves to define and qualify the meaning of the first clause, namely, that those who do not call to God with sincerity do not achieve closeness to Him or are answered.
19 When the righteous call out to Him, as mentioned in the previous verse, **He grants the wishes of those who fear Him; and He hears their cry** when they call out to Him in time of need, **and** He **saves them.**
20 **The Lord watches over all who love Him, and He will destroy all the wicked.**
21 In conclusion: **My mouth speaks praise of the Lord.** With this psalm, I, the psalmist, express the glory of God. **And** in turn it is my hope that **all flesh,** that is, all people, and perhaps all beings in creation, **will bless His holy name forever and ever.**

ד ה דור לדור ישבח מעשיך וגבורתיך יגידו: הדר כבוד הודך ודברי נפלאתיך
ו ז אשיחה: ועזוז נוראתיך יאמרו וגדלותיך אספרנה: זכר רב־טובך יביעו וגדולתך
ח ט וצדקתך ירננו: חנון ורחום יהוה ארך אפים וגדל־חסד: טוב־יהוה לכל ורחמיו
י יא על־כל־מעשיו: יודוך יהוה כל־מעשיך וחסידיך יברכוכה: כבוד מלכותך
יב יאמרו וגבורתך ידברו: להודיע | לבני האדם גבורתיו וכבוד הדר מלכותו:
יג יד מלכותך מלכות כל־עלמים וממשלתך בכל־דור ודר: סומך יהוה לכל־הנפלים
טו וזוקף לכל־הכפופים: עיני־כל אליך ישברו ואתה נותן־להם את־אכלם בעתו:
טז יז פותח את־ידך ומשביע לכל־חי רצון: צדיק יהוה בכל־דרכיו וחסיד בכל־
יח יט מעשיו: קרוב יהוה לכל־קראיו לכל אשר יקראהו באמת: רצון־יראיו יעשה
כ ואת־שועתם ישמע ויושיעם: שומר יהוה את־כל־אהביו ואת כל־הרשעים
כא ישמיד: תהלת יהוה ידבר פי ויברך כל־בשר שם קדשו לעולם ועד:
מו א ב הללויה הללי נפשי את־יהוה: אהללה יהוה בחיי אזמרה לאלהי בעודי:
ג ד אל־תבטחו בנדיבים בבן־אדם | שאין לו תשועה: תצא רוחו ישב לאדמתו
ה ביום ההוא אבדו עשתנתיו: אשרי שאל יעקב בעזרו שברו על־יהוה אלהיו:
ו עשה | שמים וארץ את־הים ואת־כל־אשר־בם השמר אמת לעולם:

PSALM 146

A psalm glorifying God's kindness and beneficence, and avowing that He alone is the source of all good.

PSALMS 146:1–10

146 1 **Halleluya. Praise the Lord, my soul.**

2 **I will praise the Lord as long as I live; I will sing praises to my God as long as I am** alive.

3 **Do not trust in princes.** It is important to keep in mind that no one, no matter how rich, powerful, generous, or kind, is entirely in control of his fate. Individuals invariably depend on others, and many factors are beyond human control. Even if the person has the best intentions, he is not completely reliable, for one can never truly trust **in man, in whom there is no salvation.** Humans can never be a stable, permanent source of security.

4 For when a person dies, **his spirit departs** and **he returns to the earth; on that day, his plans cease to be.** His thoughts and plans for the future are buried with him. This holds true for everyone, even for those who, while still alive, are true to their word.

5 In contrast, **happy is he whose help is from the God of Jacob, whose hope is in the Lord his God,** who is both everlasting and omnipotent, as the following verse elaborates:

6 It is He **who made heaven, and earth,** and **the sea, and all that is in them, who guards truth forever.** God's truth, and His promises, are unassailable.

7 Moreover, God not only created the world, but continues to watch over it, **performing justice for the** ones who are **oppressed** and abused and who have no one else to rely upon, and also **giving bread to the hungry. The Lord releases the imprisoned.**

8 **The Lord opens the eyes of the blind; the Lord straightens those who are bent over. The Lord loves the righteous** and protects them even when they have no human protector.

9 **The Lord protects proselytes,** who have no family or tribe to lean on for support. **He heartens the orphan and the widow,** who are similarly helpless, **and** by contrast, He **twists the path of the wicked,** thwarting them in their ways.

10 In light of all the above, it is proper to praise God and pray: **May the Lord reign forever;** may **your God, Zion,** rule **for all generations. Halleluya.**

PSALM 147

PSALMS 147:1–20

A song of praise whose distinctive beauty lies in its continual movement from one theme to another, oscillating between the personal and the more general, the national and the cosmic, man's problems and the magnitude of the universe. It is akin to an orchestral piece in which a variety of instruments have been given solo parts.

147 1 **Halleluya, for it is good to sing to our God.** Praising God is good not only in a moral sense; it also brings happiness to the person praising Him, **for it is pleasant** to sing to Him. **Praise is lovely.**

2 In the following verses the psalmist begins with praise of God's greatness and emphasizes the way in which His power is manifest in the cosmos as a whole. God also provides assistance to all people and to other beings in distress. **The Lord is the builder of Jerusalem; He gathers in the dispersed of Israel.** God will bring back those who have fled or who have been exiled to different places.

3 **He heals the brokenhearted and binds their wounds.** The word *atzvotam*, translated here as "their wounds," more literally means "their sorrows." God "binds their wounds" spiritually as well as physically, providing solace for those in sorrow.

4 While God attends to even the smallest of matters, He is, at the same time, sovereign over all that exists: **He sets a number for the stars.** The stars belong to Him; they are all numbered by Him. **And** He **calls them all by name;** because they all belong to Him, He gives each one a name.

"He sets a number for the stars, and calls them all by name"

5 **Our Lord is great and abundant in strength; His understanding is beyond measure.**

6 Here the psalmist returns from discussing the cosmos to the world of man: **The Lord heartens the humble and casts the wicked to the ground.**

"The fledgling ravens when they call"

7 **Sing to the Lord with songs of thanksgiving; sing praises with the lyre to our God,** lauding His providence and greatness always and everywhere.

8 Our God is He **who covers the heavens with clouds, who provides the earth with rain,** and **who makes grass grow on the mountains.**

9 **He gives food to the beasts.** God cares for all His creatures, **and** attends even **to the fledgling ravens,** among the most pitiful and unsightly creatures, **when they call.**[D]

10 Such care is solely an expression of God's kindness; it is in no way indicative of a reciprocal relationship between God and His creatures: **It is not the might of horses that He desires; nor does He want the legs of a man,** the legs representing a person's main source of stability and strength.

11 **The Lord wants those who fear Him,** regardless of whether they are powerful or brave, **those who long for His kindness.**

12 The psalmist shifts focus: **Extol the Lord, Jerusalem; praise your God, Zion.** God has a special relationship with Jerusalem, His city, and with His Temple.

13 **For He has strengthened the bars of your gates.** With His divine protection, He bolsters, as it were, the bars of the city's gates against enemy forces trying to gain entrance. **He has blessed your sons within.**

BACKGROUND

147:9 | **To the fledgling ravens when they call:** When the adult ravens approach the nest, their famished offspring let out a shrieking sound, giving the impression of desperation, and as a result of their loud calls with their beaks wide open, they are at last supplied with food by their parents. This verse would seem to support the popular notion that ravens abandon their young (see *Eiruvin* 22a; *Ketubot* 49b; see also Job 38:41).

ז ח עֹשֶׂה מִשְׁפָּט ׀ לָעֲשׁוּקִים נֹתֵן לֶחֶם לָרְעֵבִים יהוה מַתִּיר אֲסוּרִים: יהוה ׀ פֹּקֵחַ
ט עִוְרִים יהוה זֹקֵף כְּפוּפִים יהוה אֹהֵב צַדִּיקִים: יהוה ׀ שֹׁמֵר אֶת־גֵּרִים יָתוֹם
י וְאַלְמָנָה יְעוֹדֵד וְדֶרֶךְ רְשָׁעִים יְעַוֵּת: יִמְלֹךְ יהוה ׀ לְעוֹלָם אֱלֹהַיִךְ צִיּוֹן לְדֹר וָדֹר
הַלְלוּיָהּ:
מז א ב הַלְלוּיָהּ ׀ כִּי־טוֹב זַמְּרָה אֱלֹהֵינוּ כִּי־נָעִים נָאוָה תְהִלָּה: בּוֹנֵה יְרוּשָׁלַםִ יהוה נִדְחֵי
ג ד יִשְׂרָאֵל יְכַנֵּס: הָרֹפֵא לִשְׁבוּרֵי לֵב וּמְחַבֵּשׁ לְעַצְּבוֹתָם: מוֹנֶה מִסְפָּר לַכּוֹכָבִים
ה ו לְכֻלָּם שֵׁמוֹת יִקְרָא: גָּדוֹל אֲדוֹנֵינוּ וְרַב־כֹּחַ לִתְבוּנָתוֹ אֵין מִסְפָּר: מְעוֹדֵד עֲנָוִים
ז יהוה מַשְׁפִּיל רְשָׁעִים עֲדֵי־אָרֶץ: עֱנוּ לַיהוה בְּתוֹדָה זַמְּרוּ לֵאלֹהֵינוּ בְכִנּוֹר:
ח ט הַמְכַסֶּה שָׁמַיִם ׀ בְּעָבִים הַמֵּכִין לָאָרֶץ מָטָר הַמַּצְמִיחַ הָרִים חָצִיר: נוֹתֵן לִבְהֵמָה
י לַחְמָהּ לִבְנֵי עֹרֵב אֲשֶׁר יִקְרָאוּ: לֹא בִגְבוּרַת הַסּוּס יֶחְפָּץ לֹא־בְשׁוֹקֵי הָאִישׁ
יא יב יִרְצֶה: רוֹצֶה יהוה אֶת־יְרֵאָיו אֶת־הַמְיַחֲלִים לְחַסְדּוֹ: שַׁבְּחִי יְרוּשָׁלַםִ אֶת־יהוה
יג יד הַלְלִי אֱלֹהַיִךְ צִיּוֹן: כִּי־חִזַּק בְּרִיחֵי שְׁעָרָיִךְ בֵּרַךְ בָּנַיִךְ בְּקִרְבֵּךְ: הַשָּׂם־גְּבוּלֵךְ
טו טז שָׁלוֹם חֵלֶב חִטִּים יַשְׂבִּיעֵךְ: הַשֹּׁלֵחַ אִמְרָתוֹ אָרֶץ עַד־מְהֵרָה יָרוּץ דְּבָרוֹ: הַנֹּתֵן
יז יח שֶׁלֶג כַּצָּמֶר כְּפוֹר כָּאֵפֶר יְפַזֵּר: מַשְׁלִיךְ קַרְחוֹ כְפִתִּים לִפְנֵי קָרָתוֹ מִי יַעֲמֹד: יִשְׁלַח
יט דְּבָרוֹ וְיַמְסֵם יַשֵּׁב רוּחוֹ יִזְּלוּ־מָיִם: מַגִּיד דְּבָרָו לְיַעֲקֹב חֻקָּיו וּמִשְׁפָּטָיו לְיִשְׂרָאֵל:
כ לֹא עָשָׂה כֵן ׀ לְכָל־גּוֹי וּמִשְׁפָּטִים בַּל־יְדָעוּם הַלְלוּיָהּ:

14 It is He **who sets your borders at peace,** referring both to the borders of the Land of Israel and to those of Jerusalem, and **sates you with the fat of wheat,** the most desired and nutritious part of the wheat kernel.

15 Here the psalmist returns to the world as a whole: It is God **who sends His commands to earth, His word swiftly running.** God's commandments have an immediate impact on earth.

16 **Who bestows snow** that is **like fleece** in its pure whiteness, and **scatters frost like ashes,** as a layer of frost on the ground is as fine and smooth as a layer of ash;

"Who bestows snow like fleece"

17 **flinging His ice,** in the form of hail and snow, **like crumbs. Who can withstand His cold?**

18 But then, in time **He sends His word and melts them.** At God's word, all the ice and snow melt. **He makes His wind blow.** His warm breeze, God's breath, as it were, melts them, **and they flow like water.**

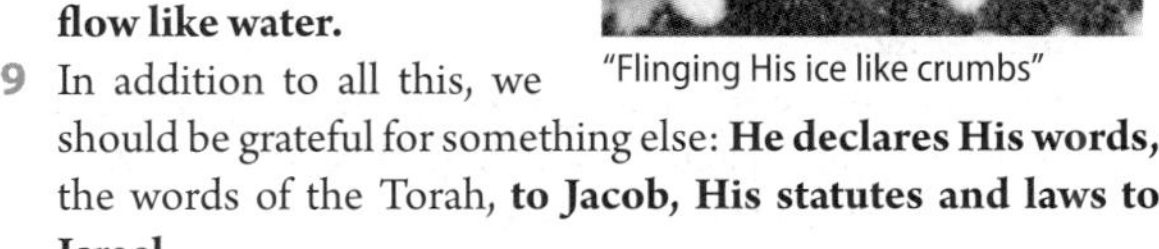
"Flinging His ice like crumbs"

19 In addition to all this, we should be grateful for something else: **He declares His words,** the words of the Torah, **to Jacob, His statutes and laws to Israel.**

20 **He did not do so with any other nation; they do not know the laws** of God. The Torah and its commandments are God's exclusive gift to the people of Israel. **Halleluya.**

PSALM 148

PSALMS 148:1–14

A hymn of praise calling on all of creation to sing God's praises. The first part of the psalm addresses heavenly bodies and creatures; the second is a similar appeal to earthly beings.

148 1 **Halleluya. Praise the Lord from the heavens; praise Him in
the heights.**
2 The psalmist specifies which heavenly bodies and creatures are
being called upon to praise God: **Praise Him, all His angels;
praise Him, all His hosts.** "His angels" are spiritual beings
created to fulfill specific missions for God, whether by way of
verbal pronouncement or by more direct intervention in the affairs of lower worlds. "His hosts" include celestial beings, such
as those described in chapter 1 of the book of Ezekiel.
3 **Praise Him, sun and moon.** These, too, are located on high,
though they are not in heaven in the same sense as the celestial
beings. **Praise Him, all stars giving light.**
4 **Praise Him, heavens on heavens, and the waters above the
heavens.** The heavens are perceived as multilayered, one layer
above the other; our Sages speak of seven heavens. The waters
that are "above the heavens" are the heavenly reservoirs of water
and rain from which bounty flows down to our world.
5 **Let them praise the name of the Lord.** They praise Him for
their very existence, as they have no material needs; they thank
Him **for** the fact that **He commanded and they were created.**
6 **He established them,** the heavens and all they contain, **forever, for all time; He gave a statute,** the laws of nature and
physics, **that will not be revoked.** From our perspective, all of
these phenomena are constant and eternal.
7 In the second part of the psalm, God's legions on earth are addressed: **Praise the Lord from the earth, sea creatures and
all depths.** "Depths" in this verse complements the "waters
above the heavens" in verse 4.
8 Joining in the praise of God are **fire and hail, snow and vapor,
storm wind that carries out
His word,**
9 **the mountains and all the
hills, fruit trees and** also **all
the cedars,** the non-fruit-
bearing trees, which also
participate in singing God's
praises,
10 **beasts and all cattle, creep-
ing things, and winged
fowl,**

"Hail, snow and vapor, storm wind that carries out His word"

11 **kings of the earth and all nations, princes and all judges on
earth,**
12 **young men and maidens,** and **old men with youths.** Not
only the great, but also the common folk, one and all, are called
upon to sing God's praises.
13 The psalmist concludes: **Let them** all **praise the name of the
Lord, for His name alone is exalted,** and **His glory** is **across
earth and heaven.** God's glory illuminates earth and the heavens, and therefore they must both praise Him.
14 **He raises a horn,** denoting uplifting with glory, **for His people, glory for all His devoted ones,** as those who are close
to God are uplifted by Him. He does this **for the children of
Israel, the people who are near to Him. Halleluya.**

PSALM 149

PSALMS 149:1–9

A psalm of praise that becomes ever more vigorous in tone, as if to reflect the psalmist's hope that the scenes he depicts will one day be realized.

149 1 **Halleluya. Sing to the Lord a new song;** sing **His praise in
the assembly of the devoted.** "A new song" usually refers to
one that offers new insight on a well-known topic. Part of this
psalm is addressed specifically to "the assembly of the devoted,"
those who regard themselves as being most loyal to God and
most profoundly connected to Him.
2 **Let Israel rejoice in its Maker; let the sons of Zion delight in
their King.**
3 **Let them praise His name with dance.** *Mahol*, translated here
as "dance," may also refer to a musical instrument. **With timbrel and lyre let them sing to Him.**
4 This is the main focus of gratitude: **For the Lord desires
His people; He glorifies the humble with salvation.** When
salvation arrives, all who have been oppressed and humbled
will be raised to positions of honor.
5 **Let the devoted ones exult in honor** when that salvation
occurs; **let them sing for joy** even when **in their beds,** after
retiring for the night.
6 The devoted ones do not merely benefit from God's salvation;
they are also expected to exert themselves in order to change
and improve the world.
Although the psalm
speaks of God's salvation,
man's efforts also facilitate
its arrival: **Exaltation of
the Almighty is in their
throats, and** at the same

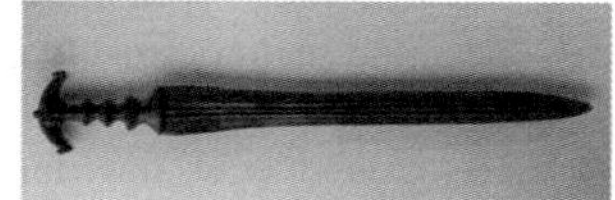
"Double-edged sword." Iran, 900–800 BCE

מח א ב הַלְלוּיָהּ ׀ הַלְלוּ אֶת־יהוה מִן־הַשָּׁמַיִם הַלְלוּהוּ בַּמְּרוֹמִים׃ הַלְלוּהוּ כָל־מַלְאָכָיו
ג ד הַלְלוּהוּ כָּל־צְבָאָו׃ הַלְלוּהוּ שֶׁמֶשׁ וְיָרֵחַ הַלְלוּהוּ כָּל־כּוֹכְבֵי אוֹר׃ הַלְלוּהוּ שְׁמֵי
ה הַשָּׁמָיִם וְהַמַּיִם אֲשֶׁר ׀ מֵעַל הַשָּׁמָיִם׃ יְהַלְלוּ אֶת־שֵׁם יהוה כִּי הוּא צִוָּה וְנִבְרָאוּ׃
ו ז וַיַּעֲמִידֵם לָעַד לְעוֹלָם חָק־נָתַן וְלֹא יַעֲבוֹר׃ הַלְלוּ אֶת־יהוה מִן־הָאָרֶץ תַּנִּינִים
ח ט וְכָל־תְּהֹמוֹת׃ אֵשׁ וּבָרָד שֶׁלֶג וְקִיטוֹר רוּחַ סְעָרָה עֹשָׂה דְבָרוֹ׃ הֶהָרִים וְכָל־
י יא גְּבָעוֹת עֵץ פְּרִי וְכָל־אֲרָזִים׃ הַחַיָּה וְכָל־בְּהֵמָה רֶמֶשׂ וְצִפּוֹר כָּנָף׃ מַלְכֵי־אֶרֶץ
יב וְכָל־לְאֻמִּים שָׂרִים וְכָל־שֹׁפְטֵי אָרֶץ׃ בַּחוּרִים וְגַם־בְּתוּלוֹת זְקֵנִים עִם־נְעָרִים׃
יג יד יְהַלְלוּ ׀ אֶת־שֵׁם יהוה כִּי־נִשְׂגָּב שְׁמוֹ לְבַדּוֹ הוֹדוֹ עַל־אֶרֶץ וְשָׁמָיִם׃ וַיָּרֶם קֶרֶן ׀
לְעַמּוֹ תְּהִלָּה לְכָל־חֲסִידָיו לִבְנֵי יִשְׂרָאֵל עַם קְרֹבוֹ הַלְלוּיָהּ׃

מט א ב הַלְלוּיָהּ ׀ שִׁירוּ לַיהוה שִׁיר חָדָשׁ תְּהִלָּתוֹ בִּקְהַל חֲסִידִים׃ יִשְׂמַח יִשְׂרָאֵל
ג ד בְּעֹשָׂיו בְּנֵי־צִיּוֹן יָגִילוּ בְמַלְכָּם׃ יְהַלְלוּ שְׁמוֹ בְמָחוֹל בְּתֹף וְכִנּוֹר יְזַמְּרוּ־לוֹ׃ כִּי־
ה רוֹצֶה יהוה בְּעַמּוֹ יְפָאֵר עֲנָוִים בִּישׁוּעָה׃ יַעְלְזוּ חֲסִידִים בְּכָבוֹד יְרַנְּנוּ עַל־
ו ז מִשְׁכְּבוֹתָם׃ רוֹמְמוֹת אֵל בִּגְרוֹנָם וְחֶרֶב פִּיפִיּוֹת בְּיָדָם׃ לַעֲשׂוֹת נְקָמָה בַּגּוֹיִם
ח ט תּוֹכֵחוֹת בַּלְאֻמִּים׃ לֶאְסֹר מַלְכֵיהֶם בְּזִקִּים וְנִכְבְּדֵיהֶם בְּכַבְלֵי בַרְזֶל׃ לַעֲשׂוֹת
בָּהֶם ׀ מִשְׁפָּט כָּתוּב הָדָר הוּא לְכָל־חֲסִידָיו הַלְלוּיָהּ׃

time **a double-edged sword** with which to wage war **is in their hand,**

7 **to wreak vengeance on the nations** and **rebuke among the peoples,**

8 **to bind their kings with fetters and their nobles with iron chains,** an act carried out in the wake of a final and total victory,

9 and **to execute judgment as it is written.** Judgment will be carried out "as it is written" in the book of justice, with each individual receiving his just punishment. Although the act of bringing enemies to justice does not fall within the category of singing songs of praises in holy places, being instead a matter of taking vigorous action in this world, **this is** nonetheless **glory for all His devoted ones. Halleluya.**

PSALM 150

A psalm that calls on everyone to praise God in all ways, both in terms of ideas and in a variety of sounds.

PSALMS 150:1–6

150 1 **Halleluya. Praise the Almighty in His holy place,** in His holy precincts here on earth, when His presence is revealed to us; and **praise Him in His heavenly stronghold,** when He is exalted in the worlds beyond.

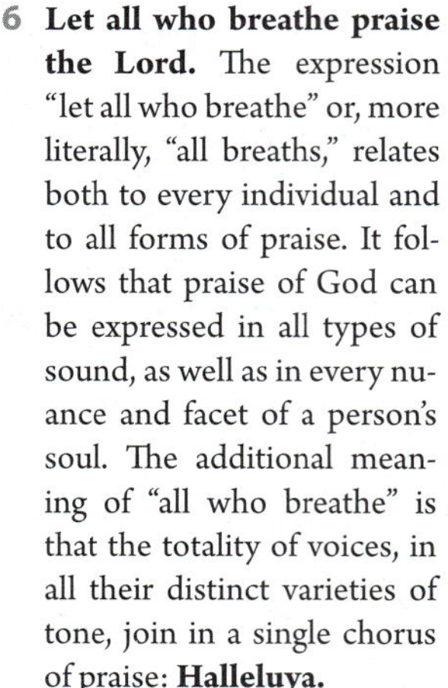

Flutes

2 **Praise Him for His mighty deeds,** and also **praise Him as befits His abundant might,** His power as expressed in splendor and kindness.

3 Such praise is carried out in various ways, each one expressing a different facet of tribute: **Praise Him with the blowing of the shofar,** which is expressive of glory and majesty. And **praise Him** as well **with harp and lyre,** such stringed instruments producing a more delicate, lyrical sound.

4 **Praise Him with timbrel and tambourine,** which produce sound through percussion. The word *maḥol* is often translated as "dance" (see 149:3), but here it refers to a musical instrument similar to a timbrel, or perhaps to a drum frame surrounded by bells. **Praise Him with stringed instruments and flute,** which, in contrast to the percussion instruments, produce gentler sounds.

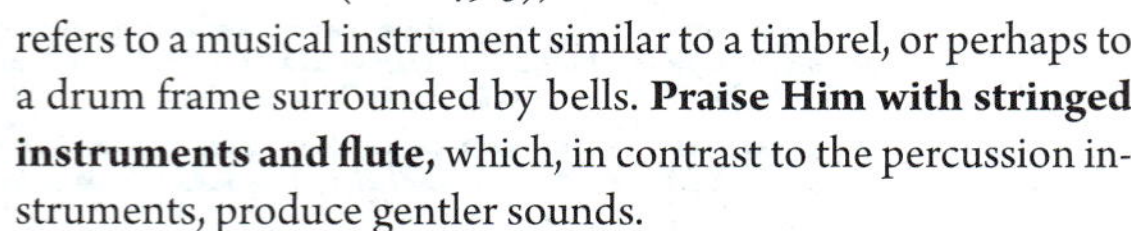

5 **Praise Him with the sound of cymbals;**[B] **praise Him with crashing cymbals.** Two types of cymbals are mentioned here. One was apparently a small cymbal that was used to accompany another instrument, whereas the "crashing cymbals" refer to a larger instrument that produced loud clanging sounds. Here, too, different aspects of song and praise are expressed by the combination of stronger and more delicate sounds.

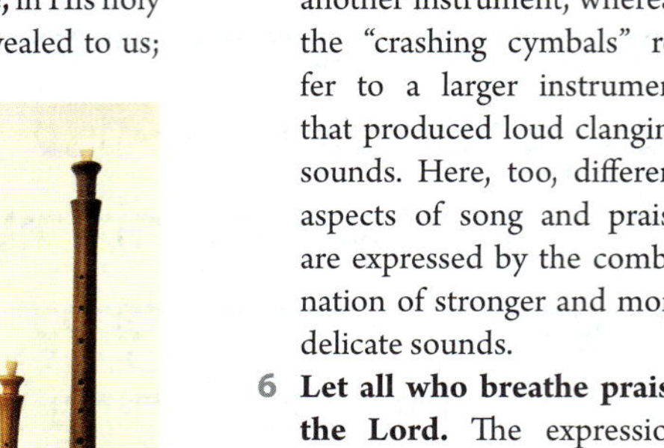

6 **Let all who breathe praise the Lord.** The expression "let all who breathe" or, more literally, "all breaths," relates both to every individual and to all forms of praise. It follows that praise of God can be expressed in all types of sound, as well as in every nuance and facet of a person's soul. The additional meaning of "all who breathe" is that the totality of voices, in all their distinct varieties of tone, join in a single chorus of praise: **Halleluya.**

"Sound of cymbals." Mosaic of street musician playing small cymbals, Villa of Cicero, first century BCE

"Crashing cymbals." Large cymbal, ancient Greece, fifth century BCE

BACKGROUND

150:5 | **Cymbals:** These are percussion instruments made of copper. Many cymbals, their diameter reaching 10 cm, have been found among the artifacts in the Land of Israel. They produce their sound by striking one against the other, striking a single cymbal with a rock or piece of metal, or by beating it with a drumstick. Alongside the name *tziltzelim* mentioned here and in II Samuel (6:5), it is also known as *metzaltayim* in Ezra and Chronicles. It is recounted of the cymbal used in the Temple that although it was only one of several instruments played there, its loud sound could be heard at great distances (see *Arakhin* 13b; *Tamid* 30b).

קנ א ב הַֽלְלוּיָ֨הּ ׀ הַֽלְלוּ־אֵ֥ל בְּקׇדְשׁ֑וֹ הַ֝לְל֗וּהוּ בִּרְקִ֥יעַ עֻזּֽוֹ׃ הַלְל֥וּהוּ בִגְבוּרֹתָ֑יו הַ֝לְל֗וּהוּ
ג ד כְּרֹ֣ב גֻּדְלֽוֹ׃ הַ֭לְלוּהוּ בְּתֵ֣קַע שׁוֹפָ֑ר הַ֝לְל֗וּהוּ בְּנֵ֣בֶל וְכִנּֽוֹר׃ הַ֭לְלוּהוּ בְתֹ֣ף וּמָח֑וֹל
ה ו הַ֝לְל֗וּהוּ בְּמִנִּ֥ים וְעֻגָֽב׃ הַלְל֥וּהוּ בְצִלְצְלֵי־שָׁ֑מַע הַ֝לְל֗וּהוּ בְּֽצִלְצְלֵ֥י תְרוּעָֽה׃ כֹּ֣ל
הַ֭נְּשָׁמָה תְּהַלֵּ֥ל יָ֗הּ הַֽלְלוּיָֽהּ׃

Proverbs

Proverbs

INTRODUCTION TO PROVERBS

The book of Proverbs, or *Mishlei*, is also called "the Book of Wisdom,"[1] as it contains words of wisdom authored by King Solomon, who was the wisest of all men.[2] The book is composed of proverbs, ideas expressed through brief, pithy phrases, and poetic images.[3] The book also contains allegories and metaphors, which is the meaning of the term *meshalim*, or, in the construct state, *mishlei*, according to contemporary usage (see, e.g., 1:17, 11:22).

Solomon's aphorisms that have been collected in this book include instructions and guidance for life. A significant part of the book is dedicated to young people just setting out on their path in life, who do not understand the complexity and challenges of the world. Solomon warns them against various temptations, such as crime and problematic women, teaches them which things have positive value and which should be avoided, and instructs them about the proper ways to live with regard to work, interpersonal relations, and other life situations. In addition to the teachings that address the young and inexperienced, there are also words of advice for adults, as well as educational guidance.

The wisdom discussed in this book is not metaphysical, supernal wisdom, and neither, according to its simple meaning, does it address the sublime aspects of serving God. Rather, it is practical wisdom that is primarily focused on worldly matters such as the value of work and industriousness, avoiding the provision of financial guarantees for other people, the dangers of flatterers and addiction to alcohol, and the importance of choosing proper friends and remaining loyal to them. Nearly all of these goals are expressed in the first chapter, which serves as a general introduction to the book and states its primary mission: To teach those who lack experience or do not have the ability to understand things deeply. Because the book of Proverbs gives rationales for its instruction to act in a certain manner, it is expected that everyone will accept these guidelines.

The book is composed primarily of short sayings, one or two verses each, which express pearls of wisdom, each of which forms an independent unit. At the same time, there are also many instances of images and themes that are spread out over the course of several verses. Although the majority of the sayings in the book are written in very clear language and draw on examples from everyday life, many verses demonstrate great ingenuity and sophistication and require much thought and effort in order to fully understand them.

One of the more conspicuous characteristics of the majority of the book of Proverbs is its lack of any apparent overall structure. Verses that deal with related topics are not necessarily consecutive; often they are scattered among the various chapters of the book. However, a few larger units can be discerned within the book, such as the proverbs that condemn drunkenness (23:28–34; 31:4–7), those that warn against being drawn after a strange woman (chap. 5, 6:32–7:27), those in praise of wisdom (chaps. 8–9), and the alphabetical song in praise of the woman of valor (30:10–31).

It seems that this collection of aphorisms, which Solomon either wrote himself[4] or which he formulated and others transcribed, was not committed to writing at one time or for a single purpose. In addition to the collections of Solomon's sayings (see 1:1, 10:1, 25:1), there are also quotations from other wise people.[5]

The Sages generally agreed that the content of this book was written when Solomon was middle-aged.[6] However, some of the collections of Solomon's wisdom contained therein were edited many generations later, even as late as the days of Hizkiya king of Judah (see 25:1).

Proverbs

The Book's Title and Statement of Purpose

PROVERBS 1:1–7

After a short preamble, which provides the book's name and author, its purpose is defined: To guide, advise, and present words of wisdom, mainly for those in special need of it. The introduction concludes with a basic proclamation about the first steps toward acquiring knowledge.

1 1 **The** following are **proverbs of Solomon son of David, king of Israel.**

2 To a great extent, this opening declaration stating the aim of the work applies to the entire book; it is to teach one **to know wisdom and admonition** and **to comprehend statements of understanding.** Not only does the book incorporate words of wisdom, it provides encouragement and instruction on how to seek out such important matters and how to try to understand them;

3 **to accept,** acquire and appreciate, **admonition of prudence,** lessons and practical conclusions for the performance of **righteousness** and **justice, and** how to follow the path of **fairness;**

4 and **to give cleverness,** practical wisdom, **to the naïve.** In other words, the book offers **knowledge and prudence to the** inexperienced **lad.**

5 Although the book of Proverbs is designed mainly for people who have no knowledge of the world,[7] it is also written to **let the wise one hear** these ideas **and gain a lesson,** as the book's sayings will be useful to him as well, **and** to **let the discerning one acquire strategies,**[D] insights into reality,[8]

6 **to understand proverbs and aphorisms, the words of the wise and their riddles.**

7 At the outset, the book issues a fundamental declaration: **The fear of the Lord is the beginning of** all **knowledge.**[D] From this basic starting point it is possible to construct various forms of knowledge, but **fools scorn wisdom and admonition** that include the fear of God.

A Warning against Temptations, and Exhortations to Accept Wisdom and Admonition

PROVERBS 1:8–2:22

8 **Hear,** listen and accept,[9] **my son,** referring to a student, typically one who is young, **the admonition,** rules of behavior and reproof, **of your father, and do not forsake the teaching of your mother.** You must hold firm to the education you receive in your parents' home, as it can be assumed that parents want their child to follow the right path.[10]

9 It is fitting for you to attend to these words of discipline and Torah and to observe them, **for they will be** like **a graceful adornment,** a fine, decorative, ribbon, **for your head and** like **necklaces for your neck.**[B]

Necklace, Egypt, 750–525 BCE

10 **My son, if sinners tempt you, do not accede.**

11 **If they,** uncouth street youths, **say** to you: **Come with us,** join our gang; **let us lie in wait for blood,** we can ambush and rob people,[11] **let us lurk for the innocent** passerby, **without cost,** without any risk or investment on our part, and thereby increase our profits;

"For they will be a graceful adornment for your head, and necklaces for your neck." Illustration based on wall fresco, Egypt, 3000 BCE

משלי

א ב מִשְׁלֵי שְׁלֹמֹה בֶן־דָּוִד מֶלֶךְ יִשְׂרָאֵל׃ לָדַעַת חָכְמָה וּמוּסָר לְהָבִין אִמְרֵי בִינָה׃ א
ג ד לָקַחַת מוּסַר הַשְׂכֵּל צֶדֶק וּמִשְׁפָּט וּמֵשָׁרִים׃ לָתֵת לִפְתָאיִם עָרְמָה לְנַעַר דַּעַת
ה ו וּמְזִמָּה׃ יִשְׁמַע חָכָם וְיוֹסֶף לֶקַח וְנָבוֹן תַּחְבֻּלוֹת יִקְנֶה׃ לְהָבִין מָשָׁל וּמְלִיצָה
ז דִּבְרֵי חֲכָמִים וְחִידֹתָם׃ יִרְאַת יהוה רֵאשִׁית דָּעַת חָכְמָה וּמוּסָר אֱוִילִים בָּזוּ׃
ח ט שְׁמַע בְּנִי מוּסַר אָבִיךָ וְאַל־תִּטֹּשׁ תּוֹרַת אִמֶּךָ׃ כִּי ׀ לִוְיַת חֵן הֵם לְרֹאשֶׁךָ וַעֲנָקִים
י יא לְגַרְגְּרֹתֶיךָ׃ בְּנִי אִם־יְפַתּוּךָ חַטָּאִים אַל־תֹּבֵא׃ אִם־יֹאמְרוּ לְכָה אִתָּנוּ נֶאֶרְבָה

DISCUSSION

1:4–5 | To give cleverness [*orma*] to the naïve [*petayim*]...and prudence [*mezima*] to the lad... and let the discerning one acquire strategies [*taḥbulot*]: The translations of these words provided here, in the context of the book of Proverbs, do not convey the same negative connotations they carry in contemporary Hebrew.

The *peti* is not a fool, but an innocent and naïve individual, such as a young person setting out on his path in life (see Rav Yosef Naḥmias). The book of Proverbs is designed to provide guidance to such people, instructing them how to live their lives. In this context, *orma* means shrewdness and practical wisdom, and *mezima* refers to thoughtfulness and ingenuity, as opposed to other contexts where it implies something negative (see Deuteronomy 19:19; Psalms 21:12; Job 21:27). Even *taḥbulot*, which elsewhere has a negative connotation meaning tricks or plots, simply means wise and sophisticated courses of action.

1:7 | The fear of the Lord is the beginning of knowledge: This idea is repeated multiple times in this book, as well as in other places (see, e.g., 9:10; Psalms 111:10; see also Mishna *Avot* 3:9). This is also similar to the opening words of Rambam's *Mishne Torah*: The foundation of all foundations, and the pillar of all wisdom, is the knowledge that there is a First Cause (*Sefer HaMadda*, *Hilkhot Yesodei HaTorah* 1:1). All wisdom is based on fundamental principles, and since the fear of God is the basis of everything, all other knowledge is built upon it.

BACKGROUND

1:9 | For they will be a graceful adornment [*liveyat*] for your head and necklaces [*anakim*] for your neck: Apparently, a *liveya* is an ornament that encircles the head, as a similar Akkadian word, *lawu*, means to encircle. An *anak* is an ornament for the neck comprised of a ring, or a chain with rings or beads. In several Semitic languages, *anak* means neck. In ancient Egypt, the head and neck were often decorated with a variety of beads, precious stones, and gold, which served to accentuate the significance of the head and heart.

12 **let us swallow them,** the innocent, **as the grave** ultimately **does to** all **the living, and the blameless will be like those cast down into a pit,** that is, the grave. We have the power to do all this without leaving a trace.

13 Through these actions, **we will find all precious wealth, we will fill our houses with spoils,**

14 so **cast your lot among us,** as not only will we allow you to participate in our exploits, but **there will be one purse for us all;** we will also divide our gains between us.

15 **My son, do not walk on a way,** any kind of way,[12] **with them; prevent your foot from their pathway.**

16 **For** ultimately **their feet** will **run to evil, and they** will **hasten to shed blood.** Even if they claim that they will easily succeed in grabbing spoils, and they will take only a few luxury items from the rich, and other such claims, in practice they run toward evil, and it will not be long before they even commit murder.[13]

17 **For the net is spread for nothing in the eyes of any winged creature.**[B] From a bird's perspective, the net is spread for no reason, and as they do not know it is a trap, they are liable to be caught in it. Likewise, those sinners who are enticed to gain their livelihood by taking money from others are in fact caught in a trap and are seeking to snare you unawares as well. This is a group of apparently clever, successful people, but in truth they do not understand what they are doing.

"For the net is spread for nothing in the eyes of any winged creature." Birds flying into a trap, Tacuinum Sanitatis, a medical text from the Middle Ages

18 These sinners think that they are waiting to ambush others, but it is not so simple, for in reality **they lie in wait for their own blood; they lurk,** set a trap, **for their own lives,** as they will eventually be caught and punished.[14]

19 **So are the ways of every pursuer of ill-gotten gain; it,** this path, **takes the life of its owners.** This is true not only in a moral, lofty sense, but even in this world, a life of theft and banditry is no life at all.[15]

20 A person outside the home is exposed to more than just enticement to sin. **Wisdom** also **sings out in the street; it projects its voice in the squares,** issuing an invitation to all. The verse personifies wisdom, comparing it to a peddler woman advertising her wares with a melodious cry in the streets and thoroughfares.

21 **It calls** out **at the head of throngs, at the entrances of the gates; in the city, it says its sayings:**

22 **How long, naïfs, will you love naïveté,** and how long will **scoffers covet scoffing for themselves, and fools,** until when will they **hate knowledge?** These categories represent three levels of recklessness: naïve people with little understanding, who are liable to believe anything; cynics who tend not to believe anything; and complete fools.[16]

23 Wisdom continues: **Return at my rebuke.** If you will only listen to it, then **behold, I will express my spirit to you,** I will provide you with guidance and direction, and thus **I will make known to you my words.** All you need to do is listen.

24 But **because I have called** you, **and you have refused; I have extended my hand** as a signal for you to come to me,[17] **and** yet **there is no one listening;**

25 **you neglect all my counsel and are unwilling to receive my rebuke,** because you do as you wish, you do not listen to my words of reproof at all, and nothing can compel you to change your ways,

26 since you will not even consider amending your behavior, **I too will laugh at your** coming **calamity; I will mock** you **with the coming of your fear.** When your bitter end arrives, you will feel as though I am standing to the side and scorning you for your foolishness,

27 **with the coming of your fear like a cataclysm, and your calamity appearing like a storm, with trouble and distress coming upon you,** and you stand helpless.

28 **Then they will call me, but I,** Wisdom, **will not answer; they will look for me, but they will not find me,**

29 **because they hated knowledge and did not choose fear of the Lord.**

30 **They were unreceptive to my counsel; they reviled** and entirely rejected **all my rebuke,**

31 **and** ultimately **they will eat of the fruit of their way;** they will

יב יג לְדָם נִצְפְּנָה לְנָקִי חִנָּם: נִבְלָעֵם כִּשְׁאוֹל חַיִּים וּתְמִימִים כְּיוֹרְדֵי בוֹר: כָּל־הוֹן
יד יָקָר נִמְצָא נְמַלֵּא בָתֵּינוּ שָׁלָל: גּוֹרָלְךָ תַּפִּיל בְּתוֹכֵנוּ כִּיס אֶחָד יִהְיֶה לְכֻלָּנוּ:
טו טז בְּנִי אַל־תֵּלֵךְ בְּדֶרֶךְ אִתָּם מְנַע רַגְלְךָ מִנְּתִיבָתָם: כִּי רַגְלֵיהֶם לָרַע יָרוּצוּ וִימַהֲרוּ
יז יח לִשְׁפָּךְ־דָּם: כִּי־חִנָּם מְזֹרָה הָרָשֶׁת בְּעֵינֵי כָּל־בַּעַל כָּנָף: וְהֵם לְדָמָם יֶאֱרֹבוּ יִצְפְּנוּ
יט לְנַפְשֹׁתָם: כֵּן אָרְחוֹת כָּל־בֹּצֵעַ בָּצַע אֶת־נֶפֶשׁ בְּעָלָיו יִקָּח:
כ כא חָכְמוֹת בַּחוּץ תָּרֹנָּה בָּרְחֹבוֹת תִּתֵּן קוֹלָהּ: בְּרֹאשׁ הֹמִיּוֹת תִּקְרָא בְּפִתְחֵי
כב שְׁעָרִים בָּעִיר אֲמָרֶיהָ תֹאמֵר: עַד־מָתַי ׀ פְּתָיִם תְּאֵהֲבוּ פֶתִי וְלֵצִים לָצוֹן חָמְדוּ
כג לָהֶם וּכְסִילִים יִשְׂנְאוּ־דָעַת: תָּשׁוּבוּ לְתוֹכַחְתִּי הִנֵּה אַבִּיעָה לָכֶם רוּחִי אוֹדִיעָה
כד כה דְבָרַי אֶתְכֶם: יַעַן קָרָאתִי וַתְּמָאֵנוּ נָטִיתִי יָדִי וְאֵין מַקְשִׁיב: וַתִּפְרְעוּ כָל־עֲצָתִי
כו כז וְתוֹכַחְתִּי לֹא אֲבִיתֶם: גַּם־אֲנִי בְּאֵידְכֶם אֶשְׂחָק אֶלְעַג בְּבֹא פַחְדְּכֶם: בְּבֹא
כח כשאוה ׀ פַּחְדְּכֶם וְאֵידְכֶם כְּסוּפָה יֶאֱתֶה בְּבֹא עֲלֵיכֶם צָרָה וְצוּקָה: אָז יִקְרָאֻנְנִי כְּשׁוֹאָה
כט וְלֹא אֶעֱנֶה יְשַׁחֲרֻנְנִי וְלֹא יִמְצָאֻנְנִי: תַּחַת כִּי־שָׂנְאוּ דָעַת וְיִרְאַת יְהוָה לֹא בָחָרוּ:
ל לא לֹא־אָבוּ לַעֲצָתִי נָאֲצוּ כָּל־תּוֹכַחְתִּי: וְיֹאכְלוּ מִפְּרִי דַרְכָּם וּמִמֹּעֲצֹתֵיהֶם יִשְׂבָּעוּ:

BACKGROUND

1:17 | **For the net is spread for nothing in the eyes of any winged creature:** To this day, birds are trapped in nets, especially during migratory seasons. The birds do not notice the nets, or are unaware of the danger they pose, and they become entangled in them, unable to break free. The majority of such traps are vertical, but there are also nets spread horizontally, slightly above the ground, sometimes with seeds inside them as bait.

bear the consequences of the corrupt path they chose, **and be sated with their** own evil **intrigues.**

32 Those consequences will be disastrous, **for the waywardness**[18] **of the naïve will kill them, and the complacency of fools,** who do not take into account that they will have to pay for their sins, **will** itself **destroy them.**

33 **But one who heeds me,** Wisdom, who seeks to straighten his path, **will reside securely and tranquilly, without fear of evil.**

2 1 The father-instructor continues with his words of encouragement to his son-disciple, urging him to acquire wisdom and accept reproof: **My son, if you will take my sayings** to heart **and reserve my commandments with you,**

2 **make your ear listen to wisdom and incline your heart to sagacity.**

3 **For if you** not only incline your ear to listen, but also **cry out for understanding,**[D] by praying and seeking it of your own initiative,[19] **and raise your voice for sagacity,** yearning for it fervently,

4 **if you seek it,** understanding, **like** those who love **silver** and can never have enough of it, **and search for it like** one searches **for hidden treasures,** in a comprehensive and attentive manner, with vigor, joy, and desire, despite the difficulties and disappointments such a search will entail,[20]

"Treasures." Trove of silver coins, found on Mount Carmel

5 **then you will understand fear of the Lord, and you will find knowledge of God.**

6 **For the Lord grants wisdom;**[D] **from His mouth,** an expression indicative of closeness and great affection,[21] **are knowledge and sagacity.**

7 **He,** God, **reserves resourcefulness,** insight and practical abilities, **for the upright; He is a shield for those who walk honestly,**

8 so that they will be able **to guard the paths of justice** and honesty; **He will protect the way of His virtuous ones.**

9 **Then you will understand righteousness, justice, and uprightness,** and you will know **every good track,** how to live a good way of life.

10 **For wisdom will come into your heart, and knowledge will please your soul.**[22]

11 Then **prudence,** thought, analysis, and flashes of inspiration, **will protect you,** and **sagacity will safeguard you,**

12 **saving you from the way of evil, from a man speaking duplicity,** persuasive lies,

13 from **those who forsake the paths of uprightness** in order **to walk in the ways of darkness,**

14 **who rejoice to do evil and exult in the duplicity,** distortion, **of evil.** Such individuals are happy when evil is regarded as good, and good evil, and when there is confusion between those different worlds.

15 They are people **whose ways are crooked and** who **are corrupt in their tracks,** their way of life.

16 Discretion and discernment will guard you also **to save you from a strange woman, from the foreign woman who smooths her sayings,** who speaks flattery. Apparently, at that time there were married women who would seek adventures for themselves when their husbands were away from home. A woman of this type would seek to tempt young, inexperienced boys and to entice them with her seductive words.

17 This is a woman **who forsakes the husband of her youth,** is unfaithful to her husband, **and** at the same time **has forgotten the covenant of her God.** The covenant of marriage is significant not only as a commitment between two people but also as part of one's relationship with God.[23]

18 **For her house sags**[24] **toward death, and her tracks are** leading **to the ghosts.** The ways of this woman lead directly to the netherworld.

19 **All who come to her will not return,** as they cannot extract themselves from her influence, **and they will not attain the paths of life.**

20 All this admonition is expressed **so that you may walk in the way of the good and keep the paths of the righteous.**

21 **For the upright will dwell** securely **in the land, and the honest,** the faithful and righteous, **will be left in it.** Only those who follow the upright path and observe the ways of God can merit living in a good land;

22 **and** by contrast, **the wicked will be eliminated from the land,** as their existence there is merely temporary, **and the treacherous will be uprooted**[25] **from it.**

לב לג כִּי מְשׁוּבַת פְּתָיִם תַּהַרְגֵם וְשַׁלְוַת כְּסִילִים תְּאַבְּדֵם: וְשֹׁמֵעַ לִי יִשְׁכָּן־בֶּטַח וְשַׁאֲנַן
מִפַּחַד רָעָה:

ב

א ב בְּנִי אִם־תִּקַּח אֲמָרָי וּמִצְוֺתַי תִּצְפֹּן אִתָּךְ: לְהַקְשִׁיב לַחָכְמָה אָזְנֶךָ תַּטֶּה לִבְּךָ
ג ד לַתְּבוּנָה: כִּי אִם לַבִּינָה תִקְרָא לַתְּבוּנָה תִּתֵּן קוֹלֶךָ: אִם־תְּבַקְשֶׁנָּה כַכָּסֶף
ה ו וְכַמַּטְמוֹנִים תַּחְפְּשֶׂנָּה: אָז תָּבִין יִרְאַת יהוה וְדַעַת אֱלֹהִים תִּמְצָא: כִּי־יהוה יִתֵּן
ז ח חָכְמָה מִפִּיו דַּעַת וּתְבוּנָה: וצפן לַיְשָׁרִים תּוּשִׁיָּה מָגֵן לְהֹלְכֵי תֹם: לִנְצֹר אָרְחוֹת יִצְפֹּן
ט י מִשְׁפָּט וְדֶרֶךְ חֲסִידָו יִשְׁמֹר: אָז תָּבִין צֶדֶק וּמִשְׁפָּט וּמֵישָׁרִים כָּל־מַעְגַּל־טוֹב: כִּי־
יא תָבוֹא חָכְמָה בְלִבֶּךָ וְדַעַת לְנַפְשְׁךָ יִנְעָם: מְזִמָּה תִּשְׁמֹר עָלֶיךָ תְּבוּנָה תִנְצְרֶכָּה:
יב יג לְהַצִּילְךָ מִדֶּרֶךְ רָע מֵאִישׁ מְדַבֵּר תַּהְפֻּכוֹת: הַעֹזְבִים אָרְחוֹת יֹשֶׁר לָלֶכֶת בְּדַרְכֵי־
יד טו חֹשֶׁךְ: הַשְּׂמֵחִים לַעֲשׂוֹת רָע יָגִילוּ בְּתַהְפֻּכוֹת רָע: אֲשֶׁר אָרְחֹתֵיהֶם עִקְּשִׁים
טז יז וּנְלוֹזִים בְּמַעְגְּלוֹתָם: לְהַצִּילְךָ מֵאִשָּׁה זָרָה מִנָּכְרִיָּה אֲמָרֶיהָ הֶחֱלִיקָה: הַעֹזֶבֶת
יח אַלּוּף נְעוּרֶיהָ וְאֶת־בְּרִית אֱלֹהֶיהָ שָׁכֵחָה: כִּי שָׁחָה אֶל־מָוֶת בֵּיתָהּ וְאֶל־רְפָאִים
יט כ מַעְגְּלֹתֶיהָ: כָּל־בָּאֶיהָ לֹא יְשׁוּבוּן וְלֹא־יַשִּׂיגוּ אָרְחוֹת חַיִּים: לְמַעַן תֵּלֵךְ בְּדֶרֶךְ
כא טוֹבִים וְאָרְחוֹת צַדִּיקִים תִּשְׁמֹר: כִּי־יְשָׁרִים יִשְׁכְּנוּ־אָרֶץ וּתְמִימִים יִוָּתְרוּ בָהּ:
כב וּרְשָׁעִים מֵאֶרֶץ יִכָּרֵתוּ וּבוֹגְדִים יִסְּחוּ מִמֶּנָּה:

DISCUSSION

2:3 | **For if [*im*] you cry out for understanding:** According to the Aramaic translation and the Sages, this verse is interpreted as if it said *em*, meaning "mother," instead of *im*, meaning "if," and indeed there are several extant manuscripts with this vocalization (see *Targum*; *Berakhot* 57a; *Bemidbar Rabba* 40:9). If so, the verse would read: Call understanding your mother. This reading of the verse implies that one should relate to understanding as to a mother. This association, and the similar comparison of wisdom to a sister (see 7:4; *Berakhot* 57a), carry great significance.

2:6 | **For the Lord grants wisdom:** In the book of Proverbs, wisdom is understood as more than mere knowledge and literacy. It is identified with the Torah itself, which teaches how to walk in the ways of God. Although the book of Proverbs includes practical advice, urging listeners to work studiously and to avoid laziness and drunkenness and the like, it also contains much deeper ideas that can elevate an individual to great spiritual heights, as will become clear later in the book.

Guidance to the Youth Regarding Torah, God, and One's Fellow Man

PROVERBS 3:1–35

Alongside statements about wisdom, understanding, and general good behavior, this section offers the disciple pieces of personal advice which touch on various matters, as well as pronouncements on the greatness of Torah in the broad sense.

3 1 The chapter begins with general statements on the adoption of wisdom and the observance of the commandments. The wise father-instructor tells his son-disciple: **My son, do not forget my teaching, and let your heart keep my commandments.**

2 **For they,** these teachings and commandments, **will add length of days, years of life, and peace,** tranquility and satisfaction, **to you.**

3 **Do not,** my son, **let kindness and truth forsake you. Bind them upon your neck,** like a necklace; **write them upon the tablet of your heart.** These are allegoric expressions of ideas that accompany a person wherever he turns, and which he remembers at all times.

4 **And you will** thereby **find grace and** be considered someone who has **high favor in the eyes of God and man.** You will be liked by all.

5 Next come a few short instructions on one's relationship with God: **Trust in the Lord** and turn to Him always **with all your heart,** so that He will guide you on your path and support you, **and do not lean on your own understanding.** Even when the path of God or His word do not appear correct to you, it is preferable to rely on Him rather than your own wisdom. In many areas one must trust in God.

6 **In all your ways** and deeds **be cognizant of Him,** remember God, draw close and connect to Him, **and** when He becomes the focus of all your deeds, **He will smooth your paths,** even if the paths themselves are uneven.[26]

7 The primary temptation for the youth to whom these words of admonition are addressed is not necessarily the performance of evil for its own sake. Rather, typically he will start to lower his standards of conduct due to the natural inclination to cut corners and choose the easiest course of conduct, even if not entirely permitted. Therefore, he is warned: **Do not be wise in your own eyes; fear the Lord and turn away from evil.**

8 Then **it,** the fear of God, **will be healing for your navel, and an elixir for your bones.** It will provide strength and vitality for your entire being, from root to branch.[27]

9 **Honor the Lord with your wealth,** your possessions, **and with the first fruits of all your produce.** The ways of honoring God include making monetary donations to the Sanctuary and to charitable causes, and separating *terumot* and tithes from one's produce, as well as contributing one's strengths, talents, and other resources in the service of God.[28]

10 **And** then, **your silos**[B] **will be filled with plenty,** you will enjoy a satisfying crop, **and your wineries will burst with wine.**

"And your silos will be filled with plenty." Illustration based on a nineteenth-century representation of ancient Egyptian silos

11 In general, words of Torah and good advice are enjoyable, or at least painless; however, punishment and reproof can cause pain and stress. Nonetheless, **the admonition of the Lord do not despise, my son, and do not loathe His rebuke,** whether delivered directly by God Himself or transmitted through the agency of people who serve as His messengers.

12 There is no need to see suffering as an evil, **for he whom the Lord loves He rebukes,** whereas He has no particular concern for those whom He does not love. Therefore, if God causes pain to you but not to others, know that He is occupying Himself with you and is interested in you. **And He reconciles** with His creations **like a father** reconciles **with a son** after striking him. The verse uses the image of an authoritative father, who is occasionally advised to use the rod. Although he does not want to hurt his son, he sometimes employs this disciplinary measure in order to educate him about proper conduct, which, in the long run, improves their relationship as well.

13 The text further praises the wisdom of the Torah: **Happy is the man who has found wisdom, and a man who comes upon,** who knows how to find, **sagacity.**

14 **For trading in it is better** and more profitable **than trading in silver, and its yield** is greater **than** that of **fine gold.**[B]

Block of fine gold

ג א ב בְּנִי תּוֹרָתִי אַל־תִּשְׁכָּח וּמִצְוֺתַי יִצֹּר לִבֶּךָ: כִּי אֹרֶךְ יָמִים וּשְׁנוֹת חַיִּים וְשָׁלוֹם
ג יוֹסִיפוּ לָךְ: חֶסֶד וֶאֱמֶת אַל־יַעַזְבֻךָ קָשְׁרֵם עַל־גַּרְגְּרוֹתֶיךָ כָּתְבֵם עַל־לוּחַ לִבֶּךָ:
ד וּמְצָא־חֵן וְשֵׂכֶל־טוֹב בְּעֵינֵי אֱלֹהִים וְאָדָם:
ה ו בְּטַח אֶל־יהוה בְּכָל־לִבֶּךָ וְאֶל־בִּינָתְךָ אַל־תִּשָּׁעֵן: בְּכָל־דְּרָכֶיךָ דָעֵהוּ וְהוּא יְיַשֵּׁר
ז ח אֹרְחֹתֶיךָ: אַל־תְּהִי חָכָם בְּעֵינֶיךָ יְרָא אֶת־יהוה וְסוּר מֵרָע: רִפְאוּת תְּהִי לְשָׁרֶּךָ
ט י וְשִׁקּוּי לְעַצְמוֹתֶיךָ: כַּבֵּד אֶת־יהוה מֵהוֹנֶךָ וּמֵרֵאשִׁית כָּל־תְּבוּאָתֶךָ: וְיִמָּלְאוּ
אֲסָמֶיךָ שָׂבָע וְתִירוֹשׁ יְקָבֶיךָ יִפְרֹצוּ:
יא יב מוּסַר יהוה בְּנִי אַל־תִּמְאָס וְאַל־תָּקֹץ בְּתוֹכַחְתּוֹ: כִּי אֶת אֲשֶׁר יֶאֱהַב יהוה יוֹכִיחַ
יג יד וּכְאָב אֶת־בֵּן יִרְצֶה: אַשְׁרֵי אָדָם מָצָא חָכְמָה וְאָדָם יָפִיק תְּבוּנָה: כִּי טוֹב סַחְרָהּ
טו מִסְּחַר־כָּסֶף וּמֵחָרוּץ תְּבוּאָתָהּ: יְקָרָה הִיא מפניים וְכָל־חֲפָצֶיךָ לֹא יִשְׁווּ־בָהּ: מִפְּנִינִים
טז יז אֹרֶךְ יָמִים בִּימִינָהּ בִּשְׂמֹאולָהּ עֹשֶׁר וְכָבוֹד: דְּרָכֶיהָ דַרְכֵי־נֹעַם וְכָל־נְתִיבוֹתֶיהָ
יח שָׁלוֹם: עֵץ־חַיִּים הִיא לַמַּחֲזִיקִים בָּהּ וְתֹמְכֶיהָ מְאֻשָּׁר:

15 **It,** wisdom, **is more precious than pearls,**[B] **and all the objects of your desire do not equal it.**

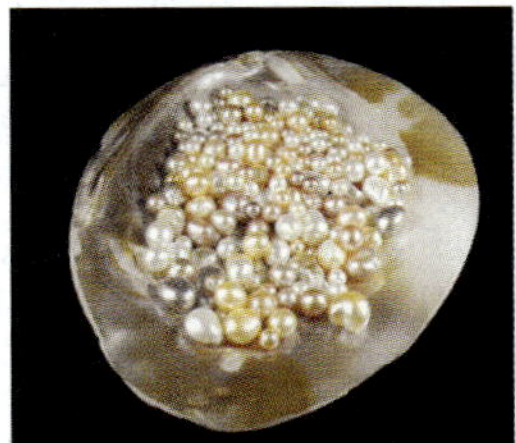

Pearls

Precious stones

16 The Torah provides a plethora of gifts: **Length of days is on its right; on its left is wealth and honor.** From the right, the stronger side, one receives long life, a gift that is beyond human effort; the left side of the Torah, which represents the aspect that is of lesser prominence, proffers material gifts, which are of lesser importance than long life.[29]

17 **Its ways are** ultimately **ways of pleasantness, and all its pathways are peace.** These are the Torah's foundational principles and its goals, according to which it operates.[30]

18 **It is a tree of life for those who hold on to it, and its supporters,** who observe its commandments in full,[31] **are happy,** strong, and successful.

BACKGROUND

3:10| **Silos:** Grain was kept in silos for future use, especially for a time of scarcity. Some of the silos of the time were walled pits, others were caverns hewn from rock, and yet others were constructed from bricks.

3:14| **Fine gold [*ḥarutz*]:** *Ḥarutz* is a term for gold similar to *harusu* in Akkadian. The Bible employs numerous terms for gold, depending on its quality and source. The term *ḥarutz* refers to superior-quality gold, which is called *zahav sagur* elsewhere in the Bible (e.g., I Kings 6:20, 7:49; II Chronicles 4:20, 22, 9:20). In Ugaritic and Canaanite-Phoenician, gold is called *ḥarutz*.

3:15| **Pearls [*peninim*]:** This word refers to round, precious stones; some say it refers to pearls, which are called *peninim* in modern Hebrew. A similar word means a spherical knob in Egyptian, while in Akkadian a similar term refers to a precious stone that comes from the sea, which perhaps corresponds to the *peninim* of modern Hebrew as well as to corals.

19 The Torah has been portrayed here as practical, relatable wisdom, which provides individuals with counsel on how to conduct themselves. It is for this reason that it is called "the admonition of your father" and "the teaching of your mother" (1:8), as it is clear that one who grows up in a good home receives advice and instruction of this kind from his parents. However, the Torah is also far more than that, as **the Lord founded the earth with,** by means of, **wisdom,** and **established the heavens with sagacity.**

20 **With His knowledge the depths were breached, and** with His wisdom **the skies deposit dew.** The Torah in its broad heavenly scope incorporates all of wisdom, understanding, and knowledge and is the instrument with which God created the world.[32]

21 **My son, may they,** the words of Torah, **not go astray from your eyes; safeguard resourcefulness and prudence.**

22 **They will be** sources of **life,** vitality and sustenance, **for your soul and grace for your neck.** They are useful for preserving life itself and also provide grace and beauty.

23 **Then,** when you observe the Torah, **you will walk on your way in security,** your path will be assured, **and your foot will not be struck.** You will not trip over stumbling blocks.

24 Not only when you are on the move, but also **when you lie down, you will not be afraid; you will lie down, and your sleep will be sweet** and peaceful.[33]

25 **Fear not from sudden terror, and from the cataclysm of the wicked when it comes** upon them, as you will not be affected,

26 **for the Lord will be your hope**[D] and haven, **and** He **will protect your foot from being trapped** in any obstacle.

27 The chapter moves on to providing advice on interpersonal relations: **Do not withhold good from its owner,** from someone to whom it is due, **when it is in your power to do so,** to do good. Even if you are not obligated to do something, if you can help others by taking action, do not refrain from doing so.[34]

28 **Do not say to your friend** who asks you for something: **Go** now **and return, and I will give** you that which you request when you come back **tomorrow, and** in fact **you have it with you** now. Sometimes one rebuffs his neighbor for no good reason, either due to simple unwillingness to help or out of laziness. One might even refuse repeatedly so that the neighbor will sense how hard it is for him to give the item, or so that the neighbor will be more pleased when he finally receives the object of his request. This is inappropriate behavior, and it is even more problematic when the requested item is money that is owed to the recipient.[35]

29 **Do not devise** a plan to do **harm against your friend who lives securely with you,** who feels comfortable with you and has no suspicions of you.[36] This verse can be explained as referring to someone who plans to dissolve a partnership without his partner's knowledge. The Sages interpret it in relation to a man who is living with a woman while in his heart he is planning to divorce her.[37]

30 **Do not quarrel with a man for nothing if he caused you no harm.** However, it can be inferred from this that if someone has indeed harmed you, you might have legitimate cause to quarrel with him.

31 **Do not envy a man of villainy,** a robber, **and do not choose any of his ways.** Do not envy him, despite the fact that such people sometimes become models of success.

32 **For the corrupt person is an abomination to the Lord, and His counsel is with the upright,** who are His confidants, as it were. Only one who acts correctly and has perfected his personality traits will merit receiving wisdom from God.[38]

33 Even if at present the righteous do not always receive goodness and blessing, eventually **the curse of the Lord is on the house of the wicked, and He blesses the abode of the righteous.**

34 Man's free choice has consequences: **If it is to scoffers** that one turns, **he** too **will scoff,** as God will not prevent him from being influenced by their ways. **But to** one who chooses to be among **the humble, He gives favor** and grace from above.[39]

35 **The wise will inherit honor, and fools appropriate disgrace.** Even fools earn publicity, but they become renowned for their disgrace and stupidity.[40]

DISCUSSION

3:26 | **For the Lord will be your hope [*kislecha*]:** The word *kesel* has different meanings, which may be connected to each other. In this context, it refers to the source of strength and security, the foundation upon which one is supported, like *kesalim*, which means hips (see Psalms 38:8; Malbim, Leviticus 3:5). An additional meaning of this root relates to the constellation Orion, known in Hebrew as Kesil (see Amos 5:8). Possibly it is called this due to its brightness and strength.

4:7 | **The beginning of wisdom: Acquire wisdom:** The hallmark of a genuine scholar is that he never stops studying. This explains the difference between the Jewish term *talmid hakham*, literally "student of a scholar," which refers to a wise person as someone who remains a student, and the Greek term *philosophus*, which means simply "lover of wisdom."

יט כ יהוה בחכמה יסד־ארץ כונן שמים בתבונה: בדעתו תהומות נבקעו ושחקים
כא כב ירעפו־טל: בני אל־ילזו מעיניך נצר תשיה ומזמה: ויהיו חיים לנפשך וחן
כג כד לגרגרתיך: אז תלך לבטח דרכך ורגלך לא תגוף: אם־תשכב לא־תפחד
כה כו ושכבת וערבה שנתך: אל־תירא מפחד פתאם ומשאת רשעים כי תבא: כי־
כז יהוה יהיה בכסלך ושמר רגלך מלכד: אל־תמנע־טוב מבעליו בהיות לאל
כח כט ידיך לעשות: אל־תאמר לרעיך | לך ושוב ומחר אתן ויש אתך: אל־תחרש ידך לרעך
ל על־רעך רעה והוא־יושב לבטח אתך: אל־תרוב עם־אדם חנם אם־לא גמלך תריב
לא לב רעה: אל־תקנא באיש חמס ואל־תבחר בכל־דרכיו: כי תועבת יהוה נלוז
לג לד ואת־ישרים סודו: מארת יהוה בבית רשע ונוה צדיקים יברך: אם־ללצים
לה הוא־יליץ ולעניים יתן־חן: כבוד חכמים ינחלו וכסילים מרים קלון: ולענוים
א ב שמעו בנים מוסר אב והקשיבו לדעת בינה: כי לקח טוב נתתי לכם תורתי
ג ד אל־תעזבו: כי־בן הייתי לאבי רך ויחיד לפני אמי: וירני ויאמר לי יתמך־דברי
ה לבך שמר מצותי וחיה: קנה חכמה קנה בינה אל־תשכח ואל־תט מאמרי־פי:
ו ז אל־תעזבה ותשמרך אהבה ותצרך: ראשית חכמה קנה חכמה ובכל־קנינך

Preserving Wisdom and the Upright Path

PROVERBS 4:1–27

The book continues with general words of praise for the acquisition of wisdom, alongside statements of encouragement to heed reproof and to stay on the straight path.

4 1 **Hear, children, a father's admonition, and listen to know understanding.**

2 **For a good lesson I have given you: My Torah, do not forsake it.**

3 **For I was a son to my father, the tender,** pampered,[41] **and only one before my mother.**

4 As his young, only son, my father gave me a gift; **he instructed me and said to me: Let your heart grasp my words: Observe my commandments and** thereby **live.** This is what will be useful to you in life.

5 **Acquire wisdom** as best you can; **acquire understanding** and reflection. After you have received instruction, **do not forget and do not deviate from the sayings of my mouth.**

6 **Do not forsake it,** wisdom, **and it will protect you; love it, and** then **it will safeguard you.**

7 **The beginning of wisdom: Acquire wisdom.**[D] The first step toward wisdom is the desire and passion to acquire more and more wisdom. **And of all your** potential **acquisitions,** the first one you should pursue is to **acquire understanding.** alternatively, if you have acquired wisdom first, then anything you achieve later will come with additional insight.[42]

8 **Prize it,** pay attention to, cultivate, and glorify wisdom,[43] **and** then **it will elevate you; it will honor you when you embrace it.**
9 **It will give your head an adornment of grace.** A wise person is accompanied by a certain grace, even if he is not physically attractive. **It will bestow upon you** [*temaggeneka*] **a crown of glory,** a splendid garland,[44] or, alternatively, it will give you a shield [*magen*].[45]
10 **Hear, my son, and accept my sayings, and they will add for you years of life.**
11 **I have instructed you** to walk **in a way of wisdom; I have directed you in tracks of uprightness,** or in the straight path.
12 If you follow this path, then **when you walk, your steps will not be restricted.** You will not have to shorten your steps, since one who walks along a straight, paved road can march with broad, confident steps. **And if you run, you will not stumble.**
13 **Hold fast to admonition, do not let go; safeguard it,** the way of wisdom you have learned, **as it is your life.**
14 **Do not enter the path of the wicked, and do not proceed on the way of evildoers,**[46] or, alternatively, do not encourage, or give sanction to, the path of evildoers. Do not think that theirs is the correct path.[47] This advice is not given to one who has an evil heart, but to one who is merely inexperienced. He feels that walking along the good, upright path is boring, and that the other roads, those that are not paved and signposted, are more attractive and offer greater freedom.
15 **Avoid**[48] **it,** the path of evildoers, or, alternatively, ruin it,[49] **do not pass on it; turn aside from it, and pass,** travel, **on** a different route.
16 **For they,** the wicked, **do not sleep.** They cannot fall asleep **if they do not do harm, and their sleep is robbed if they do not make** someone **stumble.** This path to which you are attracted is not neutral; those who follow it are compelled to harm people.
17 **For they eat the bread of wickedness,** food acquired through evil deeds, **and drink the wine of villainies,** robbery.
18 **But the path of the righteous is** bright and gleaming **like a dawning light, growing brighter until the day is established.** Even if you cannot see it at present, know that those who follow the path of righteousness are marching toward the sun, which illuminates with increasing brightness, until the light of the day reaches its zenith.

"Growing brighter until the day is established"

19 By contrast, **the way of the wicked is like the blackness; they do not know on what they stumble.**
20 **My son, listen to my words; incline your ear to my statements.**
21 **Let them,** these sayings, **not go astray from your eyes; keep them within your heart.**
22 **For they are** a source of **life for those who find them, and** they provide **healing for all one's flesh.**
23 The verse now offers additional advice, more basic and comprehensive: **Above all else, safeguard your heart, as from it are the sources of life.** One's heart is the source of his vitality, and therefore it must be guarded well. Deviation of the heart from the proper path is the root cause of the suffering a person brings upon himself.[50]
24 **Remove from yourself crookedness of mouth, and distance from yourself corruption of lips.** If one follows a crooked path, people will talk about him. Do not let yourself become the object of gossip and suspicion.[51]
25 **Your eyes should look straight ahead,** toward your upright path,[52] **and your eyelids** should **point directly opposite you.** Rather than looking to the sides and seeking a corner where you can hide, or a shortcut, watch the road ahead of you.[53]
26 **Smooth,** or straighten, find the right balance, for **the track of your feet,**[54] **and** thereby **all your ways will be established.**
27 **Do not turn aside** from the proper path **right or left;**[D] **remove your foot from evil.**

DISCUSSION

4:27| **Do not turn aside right or left:** At first glance, this advice does not seem particularly exciting or inspiring, as it does not encourage adventures or exhilarating experiences. Rather, it urges the listener to act prudently, to follow the correct course of action, and to exercise caution.

The approach reflected here is quite straightforward: There is a straight path, and there are crooked ones. A person who follows the true, good, straight path is rewarded with life, while those who walk down the crooked ones are headed toward destruction. In general, people know the correct way to live, but at times they consider it unappealing or are tempted to pursue other approaches. A young person, who does not fully understand where all the different paths lead, is in particular danger of being tempted into embarking on a small adventure. Therefore, he is warned: Although the straight path is not always appealing to you, it is the only correct and safe way.

קְנֵה בִינָה׃ סַלְסְלֶהָ וּתְרוֹמְמֶךָּ תְּכַבֵּדְךָ כִּי תְחַבְּקֶנָּה׃ תִּתֵּן לְרֹאשְׁךָ לִוְיַת־חֵן ח ט
עֲטֶרֶת תִּפְאֶרֶת תְּמַגְּנֶךָּ׃ שְׁמַע בְּנִי וְקַח אֲמָרָי וְיִרְבּוּ לְךָ שְׁנוֹת חַיִּים׃ בְּדֶרֶךְ י יא
חָכְמָה הֹרֵתִיךָ הִדְרַכְתִּיךָ בְּמַעְגְּלֵי־יֹשֶׁר׃ בְּלֶכְתְּךָ לֹא־יֵצַר צַעֲדֶךָ וְאִם־תָּרוּץ יב
לֹא תִכָּשֵׁל׃ הַחֲזֵק בַּמּוּסָר אַל־תֶּרֶף נִצְּרֶהָ כִּי־הִיא חַיֶּיךָ׃ בְּאֹרַח רְשָׁעִים אַל־ יג יד
תָּבֹא וְאַל־תְּאַשֵּׁר בְּדֶרֶךְ רָעִים׃ פְּרָעֵהוּ אַל־תַּעֲבָר־בּוֹ שְׂטֵה מֵעָלָיו וַעֲבוֹר׃ כִּי טו טז
יַכְשִׁילוּ לֹא יִשְׁנוּ אִם־לֹא יָרֵעוּ וְנִגְזְלָה שְׁנָתָם אִם־לֹא יכשולו׃ כִּי לָחֲמוּ לֶחֶם רֶשַׁע וְיֵין יז
חֲמָסִים יִשְׁתּוּ׃ וְאֹרַח צַדִּיקִים כְּאוֹר נֹגַהּ הוֹלֵךְ וָאוֹר עַד־נְכוֹן הַיּוֹם׃ דֶּרֶךְ רְשָׁעִים יח יט
כָּאֲפֵלָה לֹא יָדְעוּ בַּמֶּה יִכָּשֵׁלוּ׃ בְּנִי לִדְבָרַי הַקְשִׁיבָה לַאֲמָרַי כ
הַט־אָזְנֶךָ׃ אַל־יַלִּיזוּ מֵעֵינֶיךָ שָׁמְרֵם בְּתוֹךְ לְבָבֶךָ׃ כִּי־חַיִּים הֵם לְמֹצְאֵיהֶם וּלְכָל־ כא כב
בְּשָׂרוֹ מַרְפֵּא׃ מִכָּל־מִשְׁמָר נְצֹר לִבֶּךָ כִּי־מִמֶּנּוּ תּוֹצְאוֹת חַיִּים׃ הָסֵר מִמְּךָ עִקְּשׁוּת כג כד
פֶּה וּלְזוּת שְׂפָתַיִם הַרְחֵק מִמֶּךָּ׃ עֵינֶיךָ לְנֹכַח יַבִּיטוּ וְעַפְעַפֶּיךָ יַיְשִׁרוּ נֶגְדֶּךָ׃ פַּלֵּס כה כו
מַעְגַּל רַגְלֶךָ וְכָל־דְּרָכֶיךָ יִכֹּנוּ׃ אַל־תֵּט־יָמִין וּשְׂמֹאול הָסֵר רַגְלְךָ מֵרָע׃ כז
בְּנִי לְחָכְמָתִי הַקְשִׁיבָה לִתְבוּנָתִי הַט־אָזְנֶךָ׃ לִשְׁמֹר מְזִמּוֹת וְדַעַת שְׂפָתֶיךָ יִנְצֹרוּ׃ ה א ב

Keeping Away from the Strange Woman

PROVERBS 5:1–23

The main topic of this section is a warning to young men to steer clear of strange women. Not infrequently, a man turns from his wife to the arms of another woman whom he considers at the time to be beautiful, smart, and charming, although there is no objective justification for this. The text cautions such a man, who seeks a taste of forbidden fruit, to keep his distance from the seductive woman.

Throughout the generations, the "strange woman" described here has been interpreted as an allegory for ideologies that are in conflict with the Torah.[55] Like the strange woman, such an idea can be attractive and seductive and can become the basis for an entire heretical culture. Indeed, the coming verses can be understood on two levels, according to their simple meaning and as an allegory.

Rambam interprets the verse "golden apples in silver ornaments" (25:11) as a reference to precisely this sort of dual meaning, with a hidden message expressed through a parable. In such a situation, each of the two levels is independently significant; the simple reading of the passage can be understood on its own merits, while the deeper, allegorical meaning can be even more beautiful and sublime.[56]

5 1 **My son, listen to my wisdom,** which was acquired through life experience; **incline your ear to my sagacity,**

2 in order **to maintain prudence and have your lips conserve knowledge,** so that you will guard your speech and speak only intelligent statements.[57]

3 **For the lips of a strange woman,** who seeks to entrap you, **drip honey,** sweet, pleasant words of seduction, **and her palate is smoother than oil,**

Common wormwood

Double-edged sword

4 **but** although her initial comments are smooth, flattering, and sweet, **her end is bitter as wormwood,**[B] and in contrast to her smooth talk, it is **sharp as a double-edged sword.**

5 **Her feet go down to death.** She walks toward death,[58] or, alternatively, her end is death;[59] **to the grave her steps are directed.** If you submit to temptation and accompany her, she will take you there with her.

6 Be careful **lest you mark out a path of life** that you think is quick and easy but is actually dangerous. **Her tracks wander; you will not know.** Due to your limited life experience, you might think that the road to the strange woman's house and back again is fast and easy, but what appears to you as a short detour is really a dangerous path. The ways of this seemingly smooth reality are actually twisted and tangled.[60]

7 **Now, children, listen to me, and do not depart from the sayings of my mouth.**

8 **Distance your way from her,** this woman, **and do not go near the entrance of her house.** This refers to a married woman who seeks out young men, sometimes only for a short adventure and at other times for a deeper connection. The man who is seduced by her finds himself in all sorts of trouble.

9 Beware, **lest you give** away **your glory,** your splendor and possessions, **to others.** You might lend the woman money, bestow gifts upon her, or invest energy in her. Be careful, lest she take everything from you, **and** lest you give **your years to the cruel.** If she takes advantage of you, you might waste all your days in pursuit of her.

10 **Lest strangers** eat and **be sated with your strength,** all that you have, **and your toils,** the property for which you labored, **be in the house of a stranger.** Ultimately, you will find that behind this woman lies an entire network that is extorting money from you.

11 **You will moan at your end,** as you will grow angry and cry out in pain **with the demise of your flesh and your body,**[61] which is the eventual result of this process.

12 **You will say: How is it that I hated admonition and my heart spurned rebuke,**

13 **and I did not heed the voice of my instructors, and to my teachers I did not incline my ear?**

14 As a result of my actions, **I was on the verge of complete degradation in the midst of a congregation and assembly,** society and its judges.

15 **Drink water from your** own **cistern, and** draw **fluids from your** own **well.** If you seek intimacy, turn to your own wife, not to a different woman.[62]

16 Rather than going to other water sources, **may your** own **springs,** your blessings, **be dispersed abroad, and** let **streams of water** flow **in the** open **squares,** so that the earth will be saturated and sprout forth its bounty. Thus you will be a flowing source of blessings.

Cistern, Kina Ravine, assumed to be from the Nabatean period

Well, Tel Lakhish, second millennium BCE

17 **They,** the waters, **will be your own, and there will be nothing for strangers with you.** Preserve that which you have: Your home and your life.

18 **May your fount be blessed, and** may you **rejoice from the wife of your youth.**

Spring at Ein Bokek

19 Your wife is **a lovely doe and a graceful ibex,** so let **her breasts satisfy you at any time; in her love you will always be intoxicated,** so that you contemplate and think of her at all times.

Doe

Ibex

ג ד כִּי נֹפֶת תִּטֹּפְנָה שִׂפְתֵי זָרָה וְחָלָק מִשֶּׁמֶן חִכָּהּ: וְאַחֲרִיתָהּ מָרָה כַלַּעֲנָה חַדָּה
ה ו כְּחֶרֶב פִּיּוֹת: רַגְלֶיהָ יֹרְדוֹת מָוֶת שְׁאוֹל צְעָדֶיהָ יִתְמֹכוּ: אֹרַח חַיִּים פֶּן־תְּפַלֵּס
נָעוּ מַעְגְּלֹתֶיהָ לֹא תֵדָע:
ז ח וְעַתָּה בָנִים שִׁמְעוּ־לִי וְאַל־תָּסוּרוּ מֵאִמְרֵי־פִי: הַרְחֵק מֵעָלֶיהָ דַרְכֶּךָ וְאַל־תִּקְרַב
ט י אֶל־פֶּתַח בֵּיתָהּ: פֶּן־תִּתֵּן לַאֲחֵרִים הוֹדֶךָ וּשְׁנֹתֶיךָ לְאַכְזָרִי: פֶּן־יִשְׂבְּעוּ זָרִים כֹּחֶךָ
יא יב וַעֲצָבֶיךָ בְּבֵית נָכְרִי: וְנָהַמְתָּ בְאַחֲרִיתֶךָ בִּכְלוֹת בְּשָׂרְךָ וּשְׁאֵרֶךָ: וְאָמַרְתָּ אֵיךְ
יג שָׂנֵאתִי מוּסָר וְתוֹכַחַת נָאַץ לִבִּי: וְלֹא־שָׁמַעְתִּי בְּקוֹל מוֹרָי וְלִמְלַמְּדַי לֹא־הִטִּיתִי
יד טו אָזְנִי: כִּמְעַט הָיִיתִי בְכָל־רָע בְּתוֹךְ קָהָל וְעֵדָה: שְׁתֵה־מַיִם מִבּוֹרֶךָ וְנֹזְלִים מִתּוֹךְ
טז יז בְּאֵרֶךָ: יָפוּצוּ מַעְיְנֹתֶיךָ חוּצָה בָּרְחֹבוֹת פַּלְגֵי־מָיִם: יִהְיוּ־לְךָ לְבַדֶּךָ וְאֵין לְזָרִים ב
יח יט אִתָּךְ: יְהִי־מְקוֹרְךָ בָרוּךְ וּשְׂמַח מֵאֵשֶׁת נְעוּרֶךָ: אַיֶּלֶת אֲהָבִים וְיַעֲלַת־חֵן דַּדֶּיהָ
כ יְרַוֻּךָ בְכָל־עֵת בְּאַהֲבָתָהּ תִּשְׁגֶּה תָמִיד: וְלָמָּה תִשְׁגֶּה בְנִי בְזָרָה וּתְחַבֵּק חֵק
כא כב נָכְרִיָּה: כִּי נֹכַח ׀ עֵינֵי יְהוָה דַּרְכֵי־אִישׁ וְכָל־מַעְגְּלֹתָיו מְפַלֵּס: עֲווֹנֹתָיו יִלְכְּדֻנוֹ
כג אֶת־הָרָשָׁע וּבְחַבְלֵי חַטָּאתוֹ יִתָּמֵךְ: הוּא יָמוּת בְּאֵין מוּסָר וּבְרֹב אִוַּלְתּוֹ יִשְׁגֶּה:

20 You have a beautiful, loving wife, who provides you with all your physical and spiritual needs. **Why would you be intoxicated, my son, by a strange woman, and embrace the bosom of a stranger?**

21 **For the ways of man are before the eyes of the Lord;** God observes all man's actions, **and He smooths all his tracks,** his ways of life.

22 **His** own **iniquities will trap him, the wicked one, and he will be caught,** become entwined, **in the ropes of his** own **sin.** There is no need for external punishments, as man fashions his own traps.

23 **He will die for lack of admonishment, and in his abundant foolishness he will err.** The young person to whom these warnings are directed views himself as his own master. Wandering the streets of the city, he may encounter the strange woman either at her initiative or at his own. These verses explain to him that the other woman, to whom men are naturally attracted, is nothing but a beautiful illusion, who will ultimately lead him to physical and spiritual destruction. As explained above, on the symbolic level the temptress represents foreign ideologies. The message here is that you have the Torah that is yours; why do you turn to other systems of thought or religions? If you allow yourself to be seduced into following them, you will ultimately lose out, become trapped, and destroyed.

BACKGROUND

5:4| **Wormwood [*la'ana*]:** The term *la'ana* can refer to a specific bitter plant, or it can be used as a generic term for various bitter or poisonous plants. Since *la'ana* is frequently mentioned in the Bible alongside hemlock [*rosh*], most researchers identify it with wormwood, *Artemisia absinthium*, which is common in Israel. The plant's flowers are yellow, and it reaches a height and width of 1.5 m.

Further Advice for the Young

PROVERBS 6:1–19

More counsel to the youth against unfavorable dealings, general neglect, and dubious company.

6 1 **My son, if you became a guarantor for** the debt of **your friend** or acquaintance, **if you have shaken hands for a stranger,** you have thereby taken upon yourself a monetary liability. Serving as a guarantor is a serious obligation, which should be undertaken only with great caution. Sometimes inexperienced individuals agree to the request of someone with whom they have a tenuous connection to sign on a guarantee, without taking into account the possibility that they might have to pay the debt themselves. On such occasions, one rashly accepts the obligation without paying sufficient attention to the possible consequences.

2 In a case of this kind, **you have been snared by the sayings of your** own **mouth;** you are **trapped by the sayings of your mouth.**

3 **Do this, then, my son, and be delivered, as you have come into the hand,** under the control **of, your friend,** as you are obligated to him. **Go, ingratiate yourself,**[63] **and exalt your friend,** and explain to him that you are unable to fulfill this obligation you accepted upon yourself.[64]

4 **Do not grant sleep to your eyes or slumber to your eyelids** until you rid yourself of this source of trouble.

5 **Be delivered like a gazelle** escapes **from the hand** of a hunter **and like a bird** escapes **from the hand of a trap.** Try to extricate yourself from any guarantee as quickly as possible. You should accept a responsibility of this kind only for trustworthy people with whom you are very close; do not sign a guarantee on the basis of vague familiarity.

Hunting gazelles, relief from tomb of Ineni, Egypt, 1479–1425 BCE

6 The book now offers advice with regard to laziness: **Idler, go to the ant;**[B] **see its ways and become wise.** Sit near an ant colony and watch how these creatures work.

7 **Though it does not have a commander, officer, or governor,** as the industrious ant does all the work alone, without commanders or officers,

8 **it prepares its bread in the summer and amasses its food at the harvest** season, for later use. Learn from the ant how to perform work right away; do not hesitate and procrastinate.

Harvester ants at work

9 **How long will you lie down, idler? When will you arise from your sleep?**

10 If you say: I will have **a little sleep, a little slumber,** and then **a little** more **folding of arms to lie down** and relax while awake,

11 **your poverty will come like a** seasoned **marcher,** who is used to marching forward tirelessly, **and your lack** will surely arrive **like a shielded man,** an energetic soldier bearing a shield who advances confidently with none stopping him.[65] Alternatively, this refers to the bearer of the large shield who stays close to his officer to protect him. Poverty will certainly come to one who does not act but instead idly lets the time pass.

12 The chapter moves from the denigration of the lazy to criticism of another type of person: **A wicked person, a man of iniquity, goes about**[66] **with a crooked mouth;** he enjoys distorting matters and speaking evil of others.[67]

13 When this base person is unable to speak and yet wishes to slander someone, **he winks with his eyes, shuffles with his feet,** or **points with his fingers** to hint at something negative or to indicate that matters are not as they seem.

14 **Duplicity is in his heart; he devises evil at all times, inciting strife.**

15 **Therefore, his calamity will come suddenly; abruptly he will be broken, and there is no remedy.** This will be the end of a person with an evil tongue, who slanders and gossips even when he does not stand to gain anything from it.

16 **They are six** evil attributes **that the Lord hates, and seven that are an abomination to His soul.** The seventh is the worst of them all, and the greatest abomination.[68] This literary style employing increasing numbers recurs toward the end of the book (see 30:15, 18, 21, 29).[69]

17 These attributes are as follows: **haughty eyes, a lying tongue, and hands that shed innocent blood,**

18 **a heart devising iniquitous thoughts, feet hastening to run to evil,**

19 **he who utters lies as a false witness, and he who incites discord among brethren.** One who incites discord among friends and brethren employs all the other six evil attributes and causes great harm to others.[70] For this reason, it is the worst of them all.

ו א ב בְּנִי אִם־עָרַבְתָּ לְרֵעֶךָ תָּקַעְתָּ לַזָּר כַּפֶּיךָ: נוֹקַשְׁתָּ בְאִמְרֵי־פִיךָ נִלְכַּדְתָּ בְּאִמְרֵי־
ג פִיךָ: עֲשֵׂה זֹאת אֵפוֹא ׀ בְּנִי וְהִנָּצֵל כִּי בָאתָ בְכַף־רֵעֶךָ לֵךְ הִתְרַפֵּס וּרְהַב רֵעֶיךָ:
ד ה אַל־תִּתֵּן שֵׁנָה לְעֵינֶיךָ וּתְנוּמָה לְעַפְעַפֶּיךָ: הִנָּצֵל כִּצְבִי מִיָּד וּכְצִפּוֹר מִיַּד יָקוּשׁ:
ו ז לֵךְ־אֶל־נְמָלָה עָצֵל רְאֵה דְרָכֶיהָ וַחֲכָם: אֲשֶׁר אֵין־לָהּ קָצִין שֹׁטֵר וּמֹשֵׁל:
ח ט תָּכִין בַּקַּיִץ לַחְמָהּ אָגְרָה בַקָּצִיר מַאֲכָלָהּ: עַד־מָתַי עָצֵל ׀ תִּשְׁכָּב מָתַי תָּקוּם
י יא מִשְּׁנָתֶךָ: מְעַט שֵׁנוֹת מְעַט תְּנוּמוֹת מְעַט ׀ חִבֻּק יָדַיִם לִשְׁכָּב: וּבָא־כִמְהַלֵּךְ
רֵאשֶׁךָ וּמַחְסֹרְךָ כְּאִישׁ מָגֵן:
יב יג אָדָם בְּלִיַּעַל אִישׁ אָוֶן הוֹלֵךְ עִקְּשׁוּת פֶּה: קֹרֵץ בְּעֵינָו מֹלֵל בְּרַגְלָו מֹרֶה
יד טו בְּאֶצְבְּעֹתָיו: תַּהְפֻּכוֹת ׀ בְּלִבּוֹ חֹרֵשׁ רָע בְּכָל־עֵת מדנים יְשַׁלֵּחַ: עַל־כֵּן פִּתְאֹם מְדָיְנִים
יָבוֹא אֵידוֹ פֶּתַע יִשָּׁבֵר וְאֵין מַרְפֵּא:
טז יז שֶׁשׁ־הֵנָּה שָׂנֵא יְהוָה וְשֶׁבַע תועבות נַפְשׁוֹ: עֵינַיִם רָמוֹת לְשׁוֹן שָׁקֶר וְיָדַיִם תּוֹעֲבַת
יח יט שֹׁפְכוֹת דָּם־נָקִי: לֵב חֹרֵשׁ מַחְשְׁבוֹת אָוֶן רַגְלַיִם מְמַהֲרוֹת לָרוּץ לָרָעָה: יָפִיחַ
כ כְּזָבִים עֵד שָׁקֶר וּמְשַׁלֵּחַ מְדָנִים בֵּין אַחִים: נְצֹר בְּנִי מִצְוַת אָבִיךָ
כא כב וְאַל־תִּטֹּשׁ תּוֹרַת אִמֶּךָ: קָשְׁרֵם עַל־לִבְּךָ תָמִיד עָנְדֵם עַל־גַּרְגְּרֹתֶךָ: בְּהִתְהַלֶּכְךָ ׀

Repeated Warnings about the Seductions of a Married Woman

PROVERBS 6:20–7:27

The detailed description in this section depicts an immoral woman who seeks to entice young men, as well as the devastation and loss that result from her seduction. Although the main ideas of this passage have already been stated above, the advice is repeated for the benefit of the young person who considers himself an adult, as he is liable to pay a hefty price for his impetuousness.

20 **My son, keep the commandment of your father, and do not forsake the teaching of your mother.**

21 **Bind them upon your heart always; fasten them** as a remembrance **upon your neck.**

22 **It,** your parents' instruction, **will guide you when you walk,** and it will accompany you always: **When you lie down, it will protect you, and when you awaken,** both in the morning, and much later, at the resurrection of the dead, **it will be** the topic of **your conversation.**[71]

BACKGROUND

6:6 | **Ant [*nemala*]:** The descriptions here indicate that this is the creature nowadays called the harvester ant, *Messor*, which is common in Israel. There are some twenty species of this ant. The working collector ants are 4–11 mm in size, while soldier ants reach up to 15 mm. The collector ants are especially active in fields in the summer season, when they gather several kilograms of food and transport them to their nests.

23 **For the commandment is** like **a lamp** filled with oil that lights up the dark, and **the Torah is** not a lone candle, a mere physical object, but abstract, broad **light;**[72] **and rebukes of admonition is the way of life.**

24 These have the power **to protect you from an evil woman, from the smoothness of the tongue of the foreign woman.**

25 **Do not covet her beauty in your heart, and do not let her take you with her eyelids.** You desire her beauty, and she winks at you with her eyes, and thereby traps you.

26 **For on account of a licentious woman, one** who is ensnared by her charms will become impoverished to the point that he lacks basic necessities and **is brought to** beg for **a loaf of bread. And a married woman** who seeks relations with others **hunts** even for **a precious soul,** the pure, exceptional soul.[73]

27 **Can a man stoke fire,** sweep up burning coals **in his bosom,** between his garment and his body, **and his clothes not be burned?**

28 **If a man walks on hot coals, will his feet not be scalded?**

29 **So,** like one who holds fire and walks on coals, **is he who consorts with his friend's wife; all who touch her will not be absolved** from punishment even in this world, and certainly not in the next world.

30 **They,** people, **do not scorn a thief who steals to fill himself when he is hungry,**

31 **but** even so, **when he is found, he must pay sevenfold,** a hefty price for his theft, and **he must** even **give all the wealth of his house** for this purpose. Even a pauper who was so hungry and miserable that he resorted to theft, so that there is some sort of justification for his deeds, will nevertheless receive his punishment; how much more so is this true of one who engages in adultery, as he has no such defense.

32 **He who commits adultery with a woman lacks a heart;**[74] he has no wisdom. **He who would destroy his** own **soul does so.**

33 **He will find affliction and disgrace, and his disrepute** for the adulterous act **will not be erased.**

34 **For jealousy is the fury of man.** The anger of that woman's husband, which is based on jealousy, will be great. **And he will not have compassion on the day of vengeance.** The husband will avenge himself mercilessly.

35 **He,** the husband, **will not accept any ransom.** He will not be placated by any payment, unlike in the case of a thief. **He will be unwilling** to be appeased even **if you multiply bribes.** Adultery is an ugly, immoral, and unjustified deed, and furthermore, it is also dangerous.

7 1 Once again, **my son, keep my sayings, and store my commandments with you.**

2 **Observe my commandments and** thereby you will **live, and** preserve **my teaching,** just **as the apple of your eye,** the pupil, is guarded constantly and reflexively by the eyelids, which protect this most sensitive and vulnerable of organs.

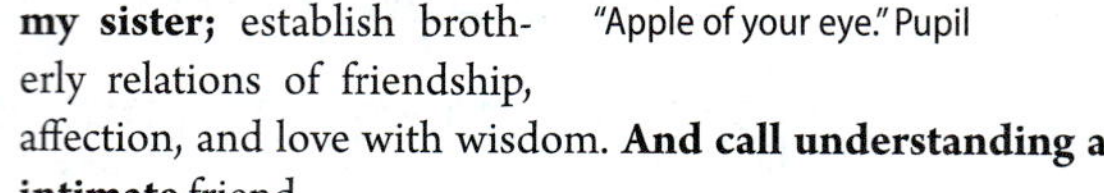

"Apple of your eye." Pupil

3 **Bind them,** my statements, **on your fingers,** just as one ties an ornament, seal, or sign as a reminder on his finger; **inscribe them on the tablet of your heart.**

4 **Say to wisdom: You are my sister;** establish brotherly relations of friendship, affection, and love with wisdom. **And call understanding an intimate** friend.

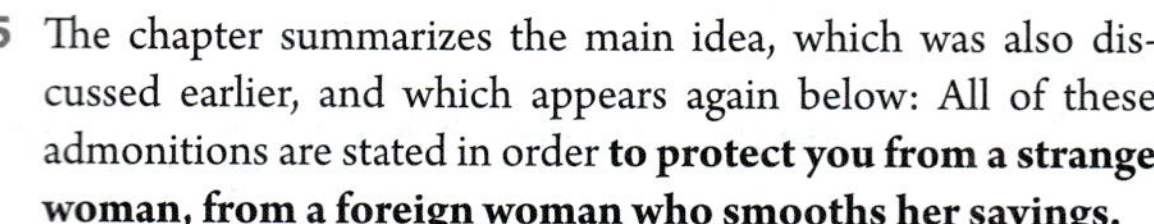

5 The chapter summarizes the main idea, which was also discussed earlier, and which appears again below: All of these admonitions are stated in order **to protect you from a strange woman, from a foreign woman who smooths her sayings.**

6 The youth's problem, on both the literal and the metaphorical levels, is vividly described by the father-instructor as he reflects upon the young man who is attracted by the seductive married woman, unaware of the harm he is doing to himself: **For from the window of my house, through my lattice,**[B] **I looked;**

Woman looking through a window, Arslan Tash, Syria, eighth century BCE

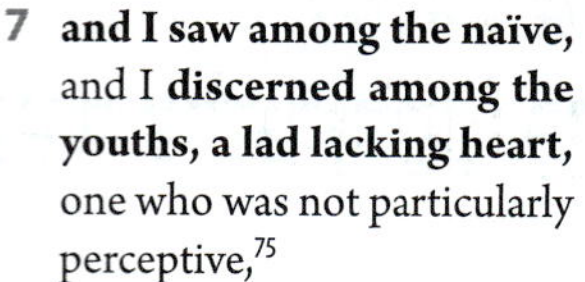

7 **and I saw among the naïve,** and I **discerned among the youths, a lad lacking heart,** one who was not particularly perceptive,[75]

8 **who passes in the street near her corner,** where the strange woman sits, **and on the way to her house he treads.**

9 This all happened **in the twilight, in the evening of the day, in the dead of night and blackness,**[76] at a time when a young man departs from his friends and goes on his way or returns home.

10 **And behold, a woman** appears and **is there to meet him with the attire** and manner[77] **of a harlot, and** she is **set of heart.** She harbors no doubts or pangs of conscience; she knows what she wants and is determined to entrap the young man.[78]

11 **She is turbulent and rebellious; her feet do not dwell in her house,** as she is constantly venturing outside.

12 **Sometimes** she is walking **in the street, sometimes in the** public **squares; she lurks at every corner,** seeking adventure everywhere.[79]

13 When she saw a victim approaching, **she seized him,** the naïve

כג תנחה אתך בשכבך תשמר עליך והקיצות היא תשיחך: כי נר מצוה ותורה
כד כה אור ודרך חיים תוכחות מוסר: לשמרך מאשת רע מחלקת לשון נכריה: אל-
כו תחמד יפיה בלבבך ואל-תקחך בעפעפיה: כי בעד-אשה זונה עד-ככר לחם
כז ואשת איש נפש יקרה תצוד: היחתה איש אש בחיקו ובגדיו לא תשרפנה:
כח כט אם-יהלך איש על-הגחלים ורגליו לא תכוינה: כן הבא אל-אשת רעהו לא
ל לא ינקה כל-הנגע בה: לא-יבוזו לגנב כי יגנוב למלא נפשו כי ירעב: ונמצא ישלם
לב שבעתים את-כל-הון ביתו יתן: נאף אשה חסר-לב משחית נפשו הוא יעשנה:
לג לד נגע-וקלון ימצא וחרפתו לא תמחה: כי-קנאה חמת-גבר ולא-יחמול ביום
לה ז א נקם: לא-ישא פני כל-כפר ולא-יאבה כי תרבה-שחד: בני
ב שמר אמרי ומצותי תצפן אתך: שמר מצותי וחיה ותורתי כאישון עיניך:
ג ד קשרם על-אצבעתיך כתבם על-לוח לבך: אמר לחכמה אחתי את ומדע
ה ו לבינה תקרא: לשמרך מאשה זרה מנכריה אמריה החליקה: כי בחלון ביתי
ז ח בעד אשנבי נשקפתי: וארא בפתאים אבינה בבנים נער חסר-לב: עבר בשוק
ט י אצל פנה ודרך ביתה יצעד: בנשף-בערב יום באישון לילה ואפלה: והנה
יא אשה לקראתו שית זונה ונצרת לב: המיה היא וסררת בביתה לא-ישכנו
יב יג רגליה: פעם | בחוץ פעם ברחבות ואצל כל-פנה תארב: והחזיקה בו ונשקה

BACKGROUND

7:6| **Lattice [*eshnav*]:** It is surmised that this term is derived from a similar Akkadian word that refers to an opening in a wall through which the wind can blow. This description suits the appearance of the word in connection to Sisera's mother (Judges 5:28). From ancient times, and even up to the present day, mainly in Islamic lands, windows in the house would often contain wooden, metal, or stone latticework, *mashrabiya* in Arabic. This feature enables one to look outside while remaining unobserved. A latticework window also keeps the house shaded while allowing for ventilation.

youth, **and kissed him; she was brazen and** shamelessly **said to him:**
14 **Peace offerings were incumbent upon me,** as I had vowed to bring them; **today I paid my vows.** By this statement she is hinting to him that her house is full of good food, and also that she hopes to receive an abundance of blessing.
15 **Therefore, I came out to meet you, to seek your face, and I have** indeed **found you.**
16 **I have adorned my bed with coverlets,** and the blankets are **fitted** and made **of fine** and elegant **Egyptian linen.**[80]
17 **I have perfumed my bed with myrrh,**[B] **aloes,**[B] **and cinnamon.**[B]

Myrrh

Indian aloe tree

Slenderleaf iceplant

Cinnamon

18 The verse cites the woman's offer, which is an audacious, simple, and unambiguous invitation: **Come, let us sate ourselves with love until the morning.** Spend the night with me; **let us delight ourselves in lovemaking.**

19 **For** if you are afraid of being discovered by my husband, **the man is not in his home; he has gone on a distant journey.**[81]
20 **He took the purse of silver with him** and has gone off on a business trip; only **at the appointed time he will come** back **to his home.** In the meantime, you and I will be undisturbed.

"Purse of silver." Pouch with coins

21 **She swayed him,** the youth, **with the abundance of her eloquence; with the smoothness of her lips,** her smooth talk, **she leads him astray.** She tells him how good things will be for him and that everything is ready, arranged, and safe.
22 **He follows her unconsciously,** unawares, seduced, **like an ox comes to the slaughter, or like a snake** that slithers confidently **to** administer **the admonishment of an** unsuspecting **fool** by biting him,[82]
23 **until an arrow splits his liver;** the young simpleton rushes **like the hastening of a bird to the snare, not knowing that it,** this deed, **is at the cost of his life.**
24 **Now, sons, heed me, and listen to the sayings of my mouth.**
25 Each and every one of you, **let your heart not turn aside to her,** this woman's, **ways; do not wander onto her paths,** the direction she proposes.

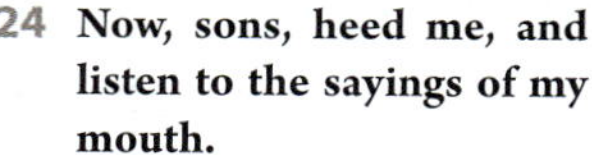

Snare for birds

DISCUSSION

7:26 | **For many slain has she felled:** Some temptations are not presented as good but simply emphasize the pleasure and enjoyment they offer, wrapped in assurances of security and serenity. People are convinced to perform morally base actions due to someone whispering in their ear: This is your opportunity to enjoy life, and it may not come again! Because of this, they destroy themselves.

For example, this is how people begin to take illicit drugs. Someone tells them all of the advantages of the drug and promises that no bad consequences will result from taking it. Many have succumbed to these temptations and condemned themselves to material and spiritual hell as a result.

Similarly, this is how young people get involved with crime. A naïve youngster is wandering about, and someone suggests that he assist a group of people in burglarizing a particular home, promising that there is money and jewelry in the home, and that within just a few minutes all of them can be safely outside, dividing up the spoils of their crime completely undetected. The temptations of evil acts can be complex, attractive, and well constructed, which is why they are effective. There is no hope other than to continually warn the youth to put his energies into obtaining wisdom and to give him practical advice.

יד טו לוֹ הֵעֵזָה פָנֶיהָ וַתֹּאמַר לוֹ: זִבְחֵי שְׁלָמִים עָלָי הַיּוֹם שִׁלַּמְתִּי נְדָרָי: עַל־כֵּן יָצָאתִי

טז לִקְרָאתֶךָ לְשַׁחֵר פָּנֶיךָ וָאֶמְצָאֶךָּ: מַרְבַדִּים רָבַדְתִּי עַרְשִׂי חֲטֻבוֹת אֵטוּן מִצְרָיִם:

יז יח נַפְתִּי מִשְׁכָּבִי מֹר אֲהָלִים וְקִנָּמוֹן: לְכָה נִרְוֶה דֹדִים עַד־הַבֹּקֶר נִתְעַלְּסָה בָּאֳהָבִים:

יט כ כִּי אֵין הָאִישׁ בְּבֵיתוֹ הָלַךְ בְּדֶרֶךְ מֵרָחוֹק: צְרוֹר־הַכֶּסֶף לָקַח בְּיָדוֹ לְיוֹם הַכֵּסֶא

כא כב יָבֹא בֵיתוֹ: הִטַּתּוּ בְּרֹב לִקְחָהּ בְּחֵלֶק שְׂפָתֶיהָ תַּדִּיחֶנּוּ: הוֹלֵךְ אַחֲרֶיהָ פִּתְאֹם

כג כְּשׁוֹר אֶל־טָבַח יָבֹא וּכְעֶכֶס אֶל־מוּסַר אֱוִיל: עַד יְפַלַּח חֵץ כְּבֵדוֹ כְּמַהֵר צִפּוֹר

אֶל־פָּח וְלֹא־יָדַע כִּי־בְנַפְשׁוֹ הוּא:

כד כה וְעַתָּה בָנִים שִׁמְעוּ־לִי וְהַקְשִׁיבוּ לְאִמְרֵי־פִי: אַל־יֵשְׂטְ אֶל־דְּרָכֶיהָ לִבֶּךָ אַל־תֵּתַע

כו כז בִּנְתִיבוֹתֶיהָ: כִּי־רַבִּים חֲלָלִים הִפִּילָה וַעֲצֻמִים כָּל־הֲרֻגֶיהָ: דַּרְכֵי שְׁאוֹל בֵּיתָהּ

26 Indeed, you are neither the first nor the last, **for many slain has she felled,**[D] **and considerable are all her killed.** She does not cease killing men through one method or another. She seduces them and then casts them aside.

27 **The paths to the grave are to her house, descending to the chambers of death.** The seductions of the impressive, well-dressed woman promising love are perhaps very powerful. However, they will ultimately lead to destruction, to pain and suffering, to heartache and pangs of conscience, and to losses, punishment, and vengeance. As mentioned above, just as this advice is helpful when it comes to avoiding a seductive adulteress, it is equally vital when it comes to harmful wisdom. Wisdom based on heresy is still wisdom. It is attractive and seductive, just like the wisdom of Torah. However, in reality it creates a counterculture, and "her feet go down to death" (5:5).

BACKGROUND

7:17 | **Myrrh [*mor*]:** One of the most important perfumes in the ancient world, myrrh is extracted by piercing the bark of thorny trees of the genus *Commiphora*, which grow in Africa, southern Arabia, and eastern India. Inscriptions and documents from the ancient East mention myrrh. The Talmud (*Shabbat* 80b) identifies *mor* with *anfiknon*, a type of olive oil. According to Rambam, *mor* is extracted from the glandular secretions of the male musk deer.

Aloes [*ahalim*]: Aloe is generally identified with the perfume that is extracted from the Indian aloe tree, *Aquilaria agallocha*, which grows in India and Indochina, and is considered one of the most expensive perfumes in the world. Some say it is the desert plant known nowadays as the slenderleaf iceplant, *Mesembryanthemum nodiflorum*. This fleshy plant, which grows low along the ground, contains a fragrant sap. It grows quickly and covers wide areas with a vivid green color.

Cinnamon [*kinnamon*]: Many commentaries identify this as the bark of the cinnamon tree, *Cinnamomum zeylanicum*, which is found in tropical regions and grows up to a height of 10 m. Others say that *kinnamon* is *Andropogon nardus*, a fragrant plant from the Graminae family, which comes from eastern Asia (Ramban).

Wisdom's Speech

PROVERBS 8:1–36

The previous sections offered mainly practical wisdom, including counsel to young people on how to conduct themselves and what to avoid, as well as a description of seductive wisdom using the imagery of a strange woman. This section depicts a different aspect of wisdom and consists mainly of a poetic soliloquy delivered by an anthropomorphized wisdom. This is a unique speech in the book of Proverbs and, indeed, in the Bible as a whole. Wisdom is described here from its greatest heights down to its lowest levels, from subjects that go beyond metaphysics and the upper worlds to everyday advice given to a young man venturing forth into the world.[83]

8 1 **Doesn't wisdom call out, and sagacity project its voice?**
2 **She stands atop the heights,** at the highest spots, visible to
all,[84] **along the way, at the crossroads;**
3 **she shouts near the gates, at the mouth of the city,** the central gathering place,[85] **at the approach to the entrances.**
4 This is her speech: **To you, men, I call, and my voice is** raised
to the sons of man.
5 **Naïfs,** who are uneducated and inexperienced, **understand**
cleverness, and fools, who do not possess wisdom, **be of an**
understanding heart, learn from me.
6 **Hear** my words, **for I will speak of matters of consequence.**[86]
Alternatively, this may be translated to mean: I will give clear
and concise instructions.[87] **And from the parting of my lips**
will be fairness, honest and just statements.
7 **For my palate will express truth, and wickedness is an**
abomination to my lips. Wisdom is judged by its truthfulness;
it cannot bear distortion and unfairness.[88]
8 **All the sayings of my mouth are** stated **in righteousness;**
there is nothing twisted or crooked in them.
9 **They are all correct to the one who understands.** One who
reflects on them will discover that all my sayings are correct,
and they are **right to those who find knowledge.** My statements are not always straightforward, and not all people can
fully understand them without assistance, but one who analyzes them will realize their truth.
10 Wisdom further glorifies herself: **Take my admonishment,**
and do **not** take **silver.** It is preferable to acquire the instruction I am offering than to accumulate money. **And knowledge**
should be taken **rather than choice gold.**[89]
11 **For wisdom is better,** more advantageous, valuable, and useful **than pearls, and all objects cannot equal it.**[D] No material
object is worth as much as wisdom.
12 It is clear that the wisdom referred to here is not merely good
instruction and advice. Evidently, this wisdom rises beyond the
realm of practical activity, as the text is alluding to the Torah
itself, which is the perfect wisdom of God, and to which nothing in the world can compare.[90] Therefore, wisdom adds: **I am**
wisdom; I dwell in cleverness, I do not deal only in abstract
statements; I also have the ability to act astutely in the world,
and will find, become familiar with, **knowledge of plans,**
thoughts, stratagems, and solutions.
13 **Fear of the Lord,** which is identified here with wisdom, **is**
hatred of evil; consequently, **pride, arrogance, the evil way,**
and the duplicitous mouth, I hate.
14 **Counsel and resourcefulness are mine;** those who are connected to me[91] can provide good advice, and they possess
sound wisdom. Wise men offer assistance, insight into various
situations, and they can resolve problems. Since **I am under-**
standing, might is mine.
15 Therefore, **through me kings reign, and princes legislate jus-**
tice, just laws.
16 **Through me rulers rule, and nobles** reign with my assistance,
all righteous judges. Wisdom prepares those who acquire her
for these roles, and guides them on their path.
17 **I love those who love me,** and therefore I reveal my secrets
to them,[92] **and those who seek me will find me.** On the one
hand, wisdom sells herself and declares to all: Acquire me; grab
hold of me. On the other hand, since all worthwhile matters are
contained within it, wisdom is extremely valuable and consequently one should actively seek it out.
18 **Riches and honor are** also found **with me, great wealth and**
righteousness.
19 **My fruit is better than gold and fine gold, and my yield** that
I provide is worth more **than choice silver.**
20 **I walk on the path of righteousness, in the midst of the**
pathways of justice. My benefits cannot be obtained through
deception and evil acts, but only by acting fairly and righteously.
21 My aim is **to bequeath** spiritual **substance [*yesh*],** which exists eternally,[93] **to those who love me, and I will** also **fill their**
treasuries. The term *yesh*, meaning something that exists, is an
unusual case where the Bible employs abstract terminology.
22 Up to this point, the passage has discussed earthly wisdom,
such as that of human leadership as well as how to relate to the
world. Now the focus turns to heavenly wisdom. The description of Torah portrayed in the following passage, in abstract
stages and in a very broad scope, is unparalleled anywhere
else in the Bible. **The Lord made me at the beginning of His**
way, the earliest of His undertakings of old. I am His first
undertaking, as wisdom is the first creation, and is necessary to
enable the rest of creation.[94] The Sages state that the Torah existed for two thousand years before the creation of the world.[95]
23 **I was crowned from ancient times, from the beginning,**
from before the earth. I was anointed as a princess or queen

ח א ב יֹרְד֗וֹת אֶל־חַדְרֵי־מָֽוֶת׃ הֲֽלֹא־חָכְמָ֥ה תִקְרָ֑א וּ֝תְבוּנָ֗ה תִּתֵּ֥ן קוֹלָֽהּ׃ בְּרֹאשׁ־מְרֹמִ֥ים

ג עֲלֵי־דָ֑רֶךְ בֵּ֖ית נְתִיב֣וֹת נִצָּֽבָה׃ לְיַד־שְׁעָרִ֥ים לְפִי־קָ֑רֶת מְב֖וֹא פְתָחִ֣ים תָּרֹֽנָּה׃

ד ה אֲלֵיכֶ֣ם אִישִׁ֣ים אֶקְרָ֑א וְ֝קוֹלִ֗י אֶל־בְּנֵ֥י אָדָֽם׃ הָבִ֣ינוּ פְתָאיִ֣ם עָרְמָ֑ה וּ֝כְסִילִ֗ים

ו ז הָבִ֥ינוּ לֵֽב׃ שִׁ֭מְעוּ כִּֽי־נְגִידִ֣ים אֲדַבֵּ֑ר וּמִפְתַּ֥ח שְׂ֝פָתַ֗י מֵישָׁרִֽים׃ כִּֽי־אֱ֭מֶת יֶהְגֶּ֣ה

ח ט חִכִּ֑י וְתוֹעֲבַ֖ת שְׂפָתַ֣י רֶֽשַׁע׃ בְּצֶ֥דֶק כָּל־אִמְרֵי־פִ֑י אֵ֥ין בָּ֝הֶ֗ם נִפְתָּ֥ל וְעִקֵּֽשׁ׃ כֻּלָּ֣ם

י נְ֭כֹחִים לַמֵּבִ֑ין וִ֝ישָׁרִ֗ים לְמֹ֣צְאֵי דָֽעַת׃ קְחֽוּ־מוּסָרִ֥י וְאַל־כָּ֑סֶף וְ֝דַ֗עַת מֵחָר֥וּץ

יא יב נִבְחָֽר׃ כִּֽי־טוֹבָ֣ה חָ֭כְמָה מִפְּנִינִ֑ים וְכָל־חֲ֝פָצִ֗ים לֹ֣א יִשְׁווּ־בָֽהּ׃ אֲֽנִי־חָ֭כְמָה שָׁכַ֣נְתִּי

יג עָרְמָ֑ה וְדַ֖עַת מְזִמּ֣וֹת אֶמְצָֽא׃ יִֽרְאַ֣ת יהוה֮ שְֽׂנֹ֫את רָ֥ע גֵּ֘אָ֤ה וְגָא֨וֹן ׀ וְדֶ֣רֶךְ רָ֭ע

יד טו וּפִ֥י תַהְפֻּכ֗וֹת שָׂנֵֽאתִי׃ לִֽי־עֵ֭צָה וְתוּשִׁיָּ֑ה אֲנִ֥י בִ֝ינָ֗ה לִ֣י גְבוּרָֽה׃ בִּ֭י מְלָכִ֣ים יִמְלֹ֑כוּ

טז יז וְ֝רֹזְנִ֗ים יְחֹקְק֥וּ צֶֽדֶק׃ בִּ֭י שָׂרִ֣ים יָשֹׂ֑רוּ וּ֝נְדִיבִ֗ים כָּל־שֹׁ֥פְטֵי צֶֽדֶק׃ אֲ֭נִי אֹהֲבַ֣יהָ אֵהָ֑ב אֹהֲבַ֣י

יח יט וּ֝מְשַׁחֲרַ֗י יִמְצָאֻֽנְנִי׃ עֹֽשֶׁר־וְכָב֥וֹד אִתִּ֑י ה֥וֹן עָ֝תֵ֗ק וּצְדָקָֽה׃ ט֣וֹב פִּ֭רְיִי מֵחָר֣וּץ וּמִפָּ֑ז

כ כא וּ֝תְבוּאָתִ֗י מִכֶּ֥סֶף נִבְחָֽר׃ בְּאֹֽרַח־צְדָקָ֥ה אֲהַלֵּ֑ךְ בְּ֝ת֗וֹךְ נְתִיב֥וֹת מִשְׁפָּֽט׃ לְהַנְחִ֖יל

אֹהֲבַ֥י ׀ יֵ֑שׁ וְאֹ֖צְרֹתֵיהֶ֣ם אֲמַלֵּֽא׃

כב כג יְֽהוָ֗ה קָ֭נָנִי רֵאשִׁ֣ית דַּרְכּ֑וֹ קֶ֖דֶם מִפְעָלָ֣יו מֵאָֽז׃ מֵ֭עוֹלָם נִסַּ֣כְתִּי מֵרֹ֗אשׁ מִקַּדְמֵי־

DISCUSSION

8:11 | **All objects cannot equal it:** The Sages interpret the phrase "all objects [*ḥafatzim*]," which can also be translated "all desirable things," as referring to the performance of a commandment. The verse is consequently stating that studying the wisdom of the Torah is of greater importance than the performance of the commandments written therein. Based on this, the Sages declare that performing a commandment that can be done by another or performed later is not sufficient justification to interrupt one's Torah study (see *Moed Katan* 9b).

before the world came into being. From a certain perspective, the Torah is the ruler of the world.[96]

24 **When there were no depths, I was generated;** I came into being **when there were no springs laden with water,** as they had not yet been created.

25 **Before the mountains were formed, before the hills** were created, **I was generated,**

26 **while He had not yet made lands and** their surrounding **environs,**[97] **or the beginning of the dust of the world;**

27 **when He prepared the heavens, there I was;**[D] I was with God **when He set a circle,** the circle of the world, **on the face of the depths,** when he established the boundaries of the deep underneath the land;[98]

28 **when He buttressed the skies above, when the springs of the depths** increased and **became mighty,**

29 **when He set His limit to the sea, and the waters would not violate His mandate,** or its edge, as no matter how stormy the sea, there is a boundary it does not cross; **when He fixed the foundations of the earth,** I already existed;

"When He set His limit to the sea"

30 **I was with Him, as a protégé;**[99] God nurtured and trained me, and **I was** like a child, **a delight day after day,** before the world came into being, when only God and I, His Torah, existed; I was **playing before Him at all times.** However, I did not just remain in heaven to play; I also descended to the world and continued to operate after Creation as well.

31 I was **playing in the world of His earth;** divine wisdom charts the earth, as the world is the playing field of the wisdom of God; **and my delights are with the sons of man.**[D]

32 The Torah continues to speak, but here the speech moves from Torah in the lofty, abstract form to its status in the practical world: **Now, sons, heed me, as happy are those who observe my ways.**

33 **Heed admonition and become wise; do not avoid it** or ignore my instructions.

34 **Happy is the man who heeds me,** who has the tenacity **to persist at my gates,** faithfully, **day after day,** in order **to protect** and observe **the doorposts of my entrances.** One who wants to learn wisdom should come to visit me every day.

35 **For he who finds me finds life, and** thereby **derives favor from the Lord.**

36 **But he who sins against me** does not harm others; rather, he **wrongs his** own **soul; all who hate me love death,** as death is the opposite of wisdom. The Torah not only enriches life, it is also the source and the fountain of life.

The Calls of Wisdom and Folly to the Simpleminded

PROVERBS 9:1–18

In this section, wisdom and folly are presented symbolically as two women who generously proffer their wares. Both of them address the simple folk, who must choose between them.

9 1 **Wisdom has built her house,** and in order to establish it firmly she **has hewed her seven pillars.** Seven is a symbolic number that represents sanctity.[100]

2 Inside her home, **she has prepared her meat, mixed her wine,** and **set her table.**[D] Everything is ready for a feast.

3 **She has sent out her young women; she will** have them **call** out her invitation from **upon,**[101] or from the edges of, **the heights,** the roofs or towers **of the city.** Wisdom's maidens openly publicize their mistress's feast:

4 **Whoever is a naïf,** without wisdom, **let him turn here; to he who lacks heart, she says to him:**

5 **Come, partake of my bread,** which I myself prepared, **and drink of the wine that I have mixed.** Come and receive from me basic, beneficial, and pleasing items that I have to offer.

6 **Forsake naïveté and live, and step on the way of understanding.**

7 This invitation is not addressed to sages, who will seek wisdom of their own accord, but it is also not for scoffers, who denigrate wisdom and mock ideas and people out of an exaggerated sense of self-confidence, whether as a joke or otherwise. For **he who admonishes a scoffer takes disgrace upon himself.** One who censures such a person will not receive honor, as the mocker is not interested in listening to him. **And** the same **is** true of **he who rebukes the wicked for his shortcomings,** as such people do not like reproof and they do not respond well to criticism. Alternatively, this last clause means: And his fate will be like someone who reproves a wicked man for his shortcomings.[102]

8 **Do not rebuke a scoffer, lest he hate you** for it; by contrast, **rebuke the wise,** alert him to his errors, **and he will love you;** he will be pleased and will thank you for helping him amend his ways.

9 **Give** a suggestion or an idea **to the wise person, and he will become wiser; inform the righteous person** of what he should do, **and he will add learning.** It is both possible and appropriate to offer words of wisdom to wise and righteous people, as they are interested in hearing them. Although wisdom directs her invitation to all, she takes into account that not

כד כה אָרֶץ׃ בְּאֵין־תְּהֹמוֹת חוֹלָלְתִּי בְּאֵין מַעְיָנוֹת נִכְבַּדֵּי־מָיִם׃ בְּטֶרֶם הָרִים הָטְבָּעוּ
כו כז לִפְנֵי גְבָעוֹת חוֹלָלְתִּי׃ עַד־לֹא עָשָׂה אֶרֶץ וְחוּצוֹת וְרֹאשׁ עַפְרוֹת תֵּבֵל׃ בַּהֲכִינוֹ
כח שָׁמַיִם שָׁם אָנִי בְּחוּקוֹ חוּג עַל־פְּנֵי תְהוֹם׃ בְּאַמְּצוֹ שְׁחָקִים מִמָּעַל בַּעֲזוֹז עִינוֹת
כט ל תְּהוֹם׃ בְּשׂוּמוֹ לַיָּם ׀ חֻקּוֹ וּמַיִם לֹא יַעַבְרוּ־פִיו בְּחוּקוֹ מוֹסְדֵי אָרֶץ׃ וָאֶהְיֶה אֶצְלוֹ
לא אָמוֹן וָאֶהְיֶה שַׁעֲשֻׁעִים יוֹם ׀ יוֹם מְשַׂחֶקֶת לְפָנָיו בְּכָל־עֵת׃ מְשַׂחֶקֶת בְּתֵבֵל
אַרְצוֹ וְשַׁעֲשֻׁעַי אֶת־בְּנֵי אָדָם׃
לב לג וְעַתָּה בָנִים שִׁמְעוּ־לִי וְאַשְׁרֵי דְּרָכַי יִשְׁמֹרוּ׃ שִׁמְעוּ מוּסָר וַחֲכָמוּ וְאַל־תִּפְרָעוּ׃
לד לה אַשְׁרֵי־אָדָם שֹׁמֵעַ לִי לִשְׁקֹד עַל־דַּלְתֹתַי יוֹם ׀ יוֹם לִשְׁמֹר מְזוּזֹת פְּתָחָי׃ כִּי מֹצְאִי
לו מצאי חַיִּים וַיָּפֶק רָצוֹן מֵיְהוָה׃ וְחֹטְאִי חֹמֵס נַפְשׁוֹ כָּל־מְשַׂנְאַי אָהֲבוּ מָוֶת׃ מָצָא
ט א ב חָכְמוֹת בָּנְתָה בֵיתָהּ חָצְבָה עַמּוּדֶיהָ שִׁבְעָה׃ טָבְחָה טִבְחָהּ מָסְכָה יֵינָהּ אַף
ג ד עָרְכָה שֻׁלְחָנָהּ׃ שָׁלְחָה נַעֲרֹתֶיהָ תִקְרָא עַל־גַּפֵּי מְרֹמֵי קָרֶת׃ מִי־פֶתִי יָסֻר הֵנָּה
ה ו חֲסַר־לֵב אָמְרָה לּוֹ׃ לְכוּ לַחֲמוּ בְלַחֲמִי וּשְׁתוּ בְּיַיִן מָסָכְתִּי׃ עִזְבוּ פְתָאיִם וִחְיוּ
ז ח וְאִשְׁרוּ בְּדֶרֶךְ בִּינָה׃ יֹסֵר ׀ לֵץ לֹקֵחַ לוֹ קָלוֹן וּמוֹכִיחַ לְרָשָׁע מוּמוֹ׃ אַל־תּוֹכַח לֵץ
ט פֶּן־יִשְׂנָאֶךָּ הוֹכַח לְחָכָם וְיֶאֱהָבֶךָּ׃ תֵּן לְחָכָם וְיֶחְכַּם־עוֹד הוֹדַע לְצַדִּיק וְיוֹסֶף לֶקַח׃

DISCUSSION

8:27 | **When He prepared the heavens, there I was:** The Midrash derives from these words that the Torah is the most supreme wisdom of God, into which He looked in order to create the world (see *Bereshit Rabba* 1:1).

8:30–31 | **A delight day after day...and my delights are with the sons of man:** At its highest level and in its essence, the Torah is not simply practical wisdom or advice about how to live a proper, moral life. In its original form, prior to the creation of the world, it was not designed to be a guidebook for life or to be used for any purpose. It was simply the delight of God, a level that is described in kabbalistic literature as the delight of the King in His Essence (see *Emek HaMelekh*). Even in its lower manifestation, the Torah is not necessarily perceived as a facilitator or a means to an end for humans, but rather as a delight or plaything. When people study Torah, they should enjoy it and delight in it, in accordance with the words of the daily blessing recited on the Torah: Please sweeten the words of Your Torah in our mouths (see Rabbeinu Yona, *Avot* 2:18). This reality is described as a kind of triangle: God plays, as it were, with the world as well as with the Torah; human beings may also take part in God's game.

9:2 | **Mixed her wine, set her table [*shulḥana*]:** The name of the important halakhic work written by Rabbi Yosef Karo known as the *Shulḥan Arukh* certainly alludes to the furnishing of the table of wisdom referred to in this verse.

everyone wants to hear what she has to say, and that her ideas will not be beneficial to all people.

10 **The beginning of wisdom is fear of the Lord, and knowledge of the holy,** of God, or angels and lofty beings,[103] **is understanding.** Alternatively, this means that the knowledge of holy people, the knowledge of their statements, and the adoption of their customs, is the basis of understanding.[104]

11 **For with me,** the wisdom of the Torah, **your days will be increased, and years of life will be added for you.** The wisdom of the Torah is the source of strength and life.

12 **If you became wise** and chose the side of wisdom, **you became wise for yourself;** you will be the first to reap the benefits. **And** likewise **if you** chose the other path and **scoffed, you will bear it,** the consequences, **alone.** With regard to both wisdom and scorn, the responsibility lies with you. Even if the choice does not affect your social status, it will make a difference in your life.

13 Up to this point, wisdom has been described as attempting to sell her wares, perhaps without great success. Although she can bestow all manner of good upon people, give them food and drink, teach them the plain and homiletic meaning of texts, and both exoteric and esoteric knowledge, this is a highly focused and defined form of wisdom. Wisdom's counsel is not an abstract, sophisticated, intellectual exercise; rather, it is based on the fear of God, and it includes reproof and ethics. Therefore, it is not the most popular type of advice, and indeed, wisdom's rival is no less available to all: **The woman of folly is clamorous;** she is talkative and loud, appearing on every stage and communicating through all types of media. However, she exists **in naïveté, and does not** actually **know anything.** Although her claims are vague, she nevertheless tries to tempt people into buying her merchandise.

14 **She sits at the entrance of her house, on a chair in the heights of the city.** Like wisdom, folly too seeks publicity in the open thoroughfares.

15 Her aim is **to call to the passersby who** seek to **straighten their paths.** Folly calls out in the same manner as wisdom:

16 **Whoever is a naïf, let him turn here; to he who lacks heart, she says** her statements **to him.** Just like wisdom, folly addresses young, inexperienced individuals who wish to broaden their horizons. She suggests they should learn from her own experiences, which differ greatly from those of wisdom. She declares:

17 **Stolen waters are sweet,** their taste seems sweet because they were stolen; **and clandestine bread,** obtained in secret, dishonest ways, **is pleasing.** Sin is attractive. Folly advises a person to stray a little from the correct path in order to add spice to his boring, aimless life.

18 Here the wise person notes: **And he,** the naïf, **does not know that the ghosts** of the dead, demonic forces **are** found **there; her,** folly's, **guests are** living **in the depths of the grave.** Like wisdom, folly has also prepared an elaborate feast for her guests. However, that, which appears to them to be a fine restaurant, is actually a deep cellar crawling with ghosts and shadows of the dead.

A Collection of Proverbs on Good and Bad Behavior

PROVERBS 10:1–22:16

The opening portion of the book, which dealt with wisdom, and incidentally with folly as well, is followed by a large collection of hundreds of short aphorisms, which are not necessarily related to each other and are not arranged in any logical order or pattern. These proverbs follow a standard structure; virtually all of them contain roughly eight words and consist of two hemistiches. In the first group, the hemistiches express an idea and its opposite, such as in the opening proverb: "A wise son brings joy to his father, but a foolish son is his mother's sorrow" (10:1). These are followed by a second group in which the two hemistiches are roughly synonymous, e.g., "He who is slow to anger is better than the mighty, and the ruler of his spirit than the capturer of a city" (16:32). Interestingly, some have counted the number of proverbs in this section and arrived at a total of 375, which is the numerical value of the Hebrew word for Solomon [*Shlomo*].[105]

Although Solomon's many aphorisms cover a range of topics, they consist primarily of practical instructions and advice for life: to follow the upright path; to avoid twisted routes, which will eventually lead to one's downfall; to complete one's work on time; and the like. Most of the proverbs, according to their plain meaning, do not rise to great philosophical heights or express exceptionally profound ideas. Rather, they offer the counsel and guidance of a wise man with regard to the actual state of affairs in the world. In general, these are instructions to follow the middle path: to conduct oneself with moderation and fairness, to act wisely, and to try to maintain a framework of life that incorporates righteousness and kindness. There are no exceptional demands here, in any direction. The clear message is that one must seek to do good as best he can, while avoiding evil, and then he will enjoy a good life.

Even if they are not necessarily exciting, these guidelines can bring blessings to the lives of those who memorize them and take them to heart. In the larger scheme, the wicked will indeed fail and the miserly will ultimately lose their possessions, despite the fact that people do not always have the patience to wait to see them receive their just deserts.

י יא תְּחִלַּת חָכְמָה יִרְאַת יְהוָה וְדַעַת קְדֹשִׁים בִּינָה׃ כִּי־בִי יִרְבּוּ יָמֶיךָ וְיוֹסִיפוּ לְּךָ שְׁנוֹת ג

יב יג חַיִּים׃ אִם־חָכַמְתָּ חָכַמְתָּ לָּךְ וְלַצְתָּ לְבַדְּךָ תִשָּׂא׃ אֵשֶׁת כְּסִילוּת הֹמִיָּה פְּתַיּוּת

יד טו וּבַל־יָדְעָה מָּה׃ וְיָשְׁבָה לְפֶתַח בֵּיתָהּ עַל־כִּסֵּא מְרֹמֵי קָרֶת׃ לִקְרֹא לְעֹבְרֵי־דָרֶךְ

טז יז הַמְיַשְּׁרִים אֹרְחוֹתָם׃ מִי־פֶתִי יָסֻר הֵנָּה וַחֲסַר־לֵב וְאָמְרָה לּוֹ׃ מַיִם־גְּנוּבִים יִמְתָּקוּ

יח וְלֶחֶם סְתָרִים יִנְעָם׃ וְלֹא־יָדַע כִּי־רְפָאִים שָׁם בְּעִמְקֵי שְׁאוֹל קְרֻאֶיהָ׃

י א ב מִשְׁלֵי שְׁלֹמֹה בֵּן חָכָם יְשַׂמַּח־אָב וּבֵן כְּסִיל תּוּגַת אִמּוֹ׃ לֹא־יוֹעִילוּ אוֹצְרוֹת

ג רֶשַׁע וּצְדָקָה תַּצִּיל מִמָּוֶת׃ לֹא־יַרְעִיב יְהוָה נֶפֶשׁ צַדִּיק וְהַוַּת רְשָׁעִים יֶהְדֹּף׃

ד ה רָאשׁ עֹשֶׂה כַף־רְמִיָּה וְיַד חָרוּצִים תַּעֲשִׁיר׃ אֹגֵר בַּקַּיִץ בֵּן מַשְׂכִּיל נִרְדָּם בַּקָּצִיר

Righteous and Wicked; Upright and Deceptive; Wise and Foolish

PROVERBS 10:1–32

10 1 **The proverbs of Solomon;** short, didactic sayings that express Solomon's wisdom about life and his advice: **A wise son brings joy to his father, but a foolish son is his mother's sorrow.** The wise son engages in productive activity, is active in society, and participates in public events, and his father rejoices in his accomplishments and success. By contrast, the foolish son presumably sits at home, doing nothing productive. Consequently, it is his mother, generally the parental figure in the house most of the time, who is brought to tears at his imprudent behavior.[106]

2 **Treasures of wickedness,** collected through evil means, **will not avail, but** in contrast, **righteousness delivers from death.** If there is money that is truly useful, it is not the funds one has accumulated for himself, but funds that he has distributed to charity.[107]

3 **The Lord will not starve the soul of the righteous,** as He fulfills his requests; **and He averts the devastation of the wicked,** the disaster that the wicked seek to bring upon the virtuous. Although the wicked may have more power and options available to them than the righteous, God does not allow their plots to come to fruition.[108] Alternatively, the latter phrase of this verse can be interpreted to mean that God brings devastation upon the wicked. This interpretation suits better the contrast between the two hemistiches of the verse.[109]

4 **A poor person is made by a negligent hand,** meaning that if one is lazy he will become poor; alternatively, this means that one who deals dishonestly will become poor;[110] **but the hand of the diligent enriches** its owner.

5 **He who stores during the summer,** the season of the ripening and harvesting of produce, **is a successful son.** He is

industrious and works not only to reap the crop but also to gather and store the produce. **And he who sleeps during the harvest,** when the staple foods are gathered in, **is a shameful son,** a disappointment. This unsuccessful son lets time pass until he is compelled to rush and grab what is left. He will suffer from the pangs of hunger when winter arrives.

"He who stores during the summer." Harvest transported for processing and storage, fresco, Tomb of Panehsi, Egypt, 1298–1235 BCE

6 **Blessings are** bestowed **upon the head of the righteous.** All bless the righteous man, who himself is constantly showering others with blessings;[111] **and villainy will cover the mouth of the wicked.** Wicked men are cursed by their own speech, as their wickedness envelops them and causes them harm.[112]

7 **The memory of the righteous,** when people recall righteous individuals, it **is for a blessing; and the name of the wicked will rot,**[D] as their names will not be remembered.[113]

8 **The wisehearted will accept commandments,** as the wise person prefers to perform good deeds rather than talk extensively; **and he who is of foolish lips,** who constantly prattles nonsense, **will be bewildered,** he will lose his way and get into trouble.[114]

9 **He who walks honestly will walk securely;** he does not stumble nor is he afraid, as he is not trying to hide anything;[115] **but** in contrast, **he who distorts his ways will suffer** pain,[116] or will be found out.[117]

10 **He who winks his eye,** to signal that he does not mean what he says, or to deprecate others, **causes sadness.** The winker thinks that most people do not notice his subtle hints, or that his insinuations are accepted in good spirits, but in fact he causes trouble and angers people. **And** likewise, **he who is of foolish lips,** who does not know how to guard his tongue, **will be bewildered,** as he will soon acquire the reputation of a fool.

11 **The mouth of the righteous is a source of life,** as it brings life to the world, **but the mouth of the wicked will cover** the world **with villainy,**[D] as his speech leads to violent robbery.[118]

12 **Hatred** in the heart **arouses strife,** and it causes a person to find reason to quarrel over even trivial matters. **And love covers all transgressions,** as the lover does not see the faults of the one he loves, or he perceives them in an entirely different light.

13 **In the lips of the discerning will be found wisdom,** as he knows how to talk and which matters are worthy of a response; **but a** whipping **rod is** found **for the back of one without heart.** One who is not wise and fails to grasp what he is told requires drastic measures to ensure comprehension.[119]

14 **Wise men store knowledge** in their hearts, without speaking much; **and the mouth of the fool is imminent ruin,**[D] as he causes his own destruction.

15 **The wealth of the rich is,** at least in his own mind, **his fortified city;**[120] by contrast, the cause of **the ruin of the impoverished is their poverty,** which causes their troubles. This verse is more of an observation than a piece of advice.

16 **The act of the righteous is for life;** the righteous brings life into the world, directly or indirectly; but **the yield of the wicked is for sin,** as he produces more transgressions or punishments.[121]

17 **Heeding admonition is a path for life,** the path which leads to life, health, success, and blessings; **but forsaking rebuke,** a refusal to listen to criticism, either due to foolishness or wickedness, **leads** one **astray** and brings troubles upon himself and others.

18 On the one hand, **the concealer of hatred** in his heart **has lying lips, and** on the other hand, **the spreader**[D] **of slander,** who says everything he thinks, **is a fool.**[122]

19 Similarly, **in** using **abundant words, transgression will be unceasing,** as excessive talk leads to sin,[123] **but he who restrains his lips** from speaking too much **is sensible.** Not only does he not sin, but this is generally a wiser practice as well.[124]

20 **The tongue of the righteous,** who speaks only fine, correct matters, **is choice silver,** acceptable to all, whereas **the heart of the wicked is negligible,** like a small, insignificant item.[125] Unlike the righteous, the wicked have nothing of substance to give to others.

21 **The lips of the righteous lead many,** as he instructs and sustains multitudes; **and fools,** who feature in Proverbs as the opposite of the righteous on numerous occasions (see, e.g., 1:7, 10:8, 10:14, 12:15, 14:3), **will die from lack of heart,** knowledge and correct thinking.[126]

22 **The blessing of the Lord, it will enrich, without adding toil [*etzev*] with it.** Alternatively, the word *etzev* refers to sorrow and suffering. Certain blessings are delivered as a gift from Heaven, unaccompanied by any suffering, or not requiring toil. By contrast, achievements that are not a blessing from God, and which are sometimes the result of drudgery or improper actions, will always increase one's sorrow.[127]

23 **The performance of lechery is like a game for a fool.** For such an individual, immorality and other evil schemes are easy and routine. **And wisdom is** likewise easy and pleasant[128] **for a man of sagacity.** The natural occupation of a discerning individual is wisdom.

ו ז בֵּן מֵבִישׁ: בְּרָכוֹת לְרֹאשׁ צַדִּיק וּפִי רְשָׁעִים יְכַסֶּה חָמָס: זֵכֶר צַדִּיק לִבְרָכָה וְשֵׁם
ח ט רְשָׁעִים יִרְקָב: חֲכַם־לֵב יִקַּח מִצְוֹת וֶאֱוִיל שְׂפָתַיִם יִלָּבֵט: הוֹלֵךְ בַּתֹּם יֵלֶךְ בֶּטַח
י יא וּמְעַקֵּשׁ דְּרָכָיו יִוָּדֵעַ: קֹרֵץ עַיִן יִתֵּן עַצָּבֶת וֶאֱוִיל שְׂפָתַיִם יִלָּבֵט: מְקוֹר חַיִּים פִּי
יב צַדִּיק וּפִי רְשָׁעִים יְכַסֶּה חָמָס: שִׂנְאָה תְּעֹרֵר מְדָנִים וְעַל כָּל־פְּשָׁעִים תְּכַסֶּה
יג יד אַהֲבָה: בְּשִׂפְתֵי נָבוֹן תִּמָּצֵא חָכְמָה וְשֵׁבֶט לְגֵו חֲסַר־לֵב: חֲכָמִים יִצְפְּנוּ־דָעַת
טו טז וּפִי־אֱוִיל מְחִתָּה קְרֹבָה: הוֹן עָשִׁיר קִרְיַת עֻזּוֹ מְחִתַּת דַּלִּים רֵישָׁם: פְּעֻלַּת
יז צַדִּיק לְחַיִּים תְּבוּאַת רָשָׁע לְחַטָּאת: אֹרַח לְחַיִּים שׁוֹמֵר מוּסָר וְעֹזֵב תּוֹכַחַת
יח יט מַתְעֶה: מְכַסֶּה שִׂנְאָה שִׂפְתֵי־שָׁקֶר וּמוֹצִא דִבָּה הוּא כְסִיל: בְּרֹב דְּבָרִים לֹא
כ יֶחְדַּל־פָּשַׁע וְחוֹשֵׂךְ שְׂפָתָיו מַשְׂכִּיל: כֶּסֶף נִבְחָר לְשׁוֹן צַדִּיק לֵב רְשָׁעִים כִּמְעָט:
כא כב שִׂפְתֵי צַדִּיק יִרְעוּ רַבִּים וֶאֱוִילִים בַּחֲסַר־לֵב יָמוּתוּ: בִּרְכַּת יְהוָה הִיא תַעֲשִׁיר
כג וְלֹא־יוֹסִף עֶצֶב עִמָּהּ: כִּשְׂחוֹק לִכְסִיל עֲשׂוֹת זִמָּה וְחָכְמָה לְאִישׁ תְּבוּנָה:

DISCUSSION

10:7 | The memory of the righteous is for a blessing, and the name of the wicked will rot: The Sages derived from here that when mentioning the name of a righteous individual who has passed away, one blesses him by saying: *Zekher tzaddik livrakha*, the memory of the righteous is for a blessing, which is often abbreviated as *zatzal*, an acronym composed of the first letters of these Hebrew words. This formulation is still used today. Similarly, there were times when it was customary to write *shin-reish-yod* following the name of the wicked, which is an acronym for the phrase: The name of the wicked will rot. Moreover, Jews throughout history have endeavored to use names of righteous, good people for their children, thereby eliminating the names of the wicked by not perpetuating them (see *Yoma* 38b; Rabbeinu Yona).

10:11 | The mouth of the wicked will cover with villainy: The second part of this verse in Hebrew is identical to the Hebrew in the second part of 10:6. In the context of the earlier verse, the wicked person's fate is contrasted with that of the righteous and the passage is therefore translated with villainy as the subject, as that which covers the mouth of the wicked. Here, the first part of the verse reveals that it is addressing the effect of righteousness or wickedness, and therefore the mouth of the wicked is the subject, covering the world with villainy.

10:14 | The mouth of the fool is imminent ruin: There are some fools who waste their time and the time of those listening to them with inane chatter, while other fools mislead people with incorrect information. This verse refers to one who speaks excessively and thereby publicizes that which should not be disclosed. The words of such fools always cause trouble.

10:18 | The concealer…the spreader: The advice given until this point is not particularly complex or surprising. It is based on the simple assumption that there is a correct and proper way in which a person should conduct himself; there are appropriate manners with which to speak and to act, and one who follows these methods can avoid evil and achieve positive results. However, this proverb reflects a more complex problem: Is it preferable for a person to speak or to be silent? Hatred sometimes results from a conflict that develops between one individual and another. One who decides not to speak about it at all ends up lying and concealing the hatred in his heart, while one who speaks about everything with everyone is considered a fool (see Rabbeinu Yona).

24 This verse again compares the fate of the wicked to the righteous: **The dread of the wicked, it will come upon him;** a wicked person will eventually receive that which he fears. **And He will grant the craving of the righteous.** The righteous will be granted all their desires by God. This principle does not always appear to be actualized in practice; sometimes one must wait to witness its fulfillment.[129]

25 **When the storm passes,** when destructive events occur in the world, **there are no wicked,** as the wicked are uprooted and vanish; **but the righteous** individual is not swept away, and what is more, he **is the foundation of the world.**

26 **Like vinegar,** which is painful **to the teeth, and like smoke,** which is hurtful **to the eyes, so is the idler to those who send him.**[D] When a lazy person is sent on a mission, he will not perform the task properly and certainly not punctually, thereby disappointing his senders.[130] The phrase: "Like vinegar to the teeth and like smoke to the eyes," is sometimes used by the Sages to refer to unpleasant experiences or to express that a different Sage's halakhic argument defies logic.[131]

27 The chapter continues with more aphorisms that deal with the reward of the righteous in contrast to those who stray from the proper path. Unlike other types of fear, which lead to detrimental anxieties,[132] **the fear of the Lord will add days, but the years of the wicked will be shortened.** This may be because the wicked are often involved in dangerous pursuits. On a deeper level, the reason is that all the days of a God-fearing individual are meaningful, whereas the wicked shorten their years by wasting most of them in the pursuit of unrealized lusts and greed.

28 **The expectation of the righteous is** a source of **joy,** as it will eventually be fulfilled; **but the hope of the wicked will perish.**

29 **The way of the Lord is a stronghold,** a haven, **to the honest, but** the very same path of the Lord brings **ruin to the performers of iniquity.** The Sages similarly state that the Torah is an "elixir of life" to those who are occupied with it with good intentions and who have fine character traits, but an "elixir of death" to others.[133]

30 **The righteous will never collapse, and the wicked will not dwell in the land** in tranquility for an extended period of time.

31 **The mouth of the righteous produces,** or expresses,[134] **wisdom, and the duplicitous tongue will be excised.** It does not deserve to survive and will not last.

32 **The lips of the righteous know conciliation.** The righteous, who speaks helpful and pleasing words, knows how to placate and satisfy people;[135] **and the mouth of the wicked is duplicity,** which brings no satisfaction to anyone.

Integrity, Money, and Blessings

PROVERBS 11:1–31

11 1 **Scales of deceit,** with which one can cheat, e.g., when one of its weights is inaccurate, **are an abomination to the Lord, and a true,** exact, **weight is His will.**

Scales for weighing by means of a stone, Ein Gedi, seventh to sixth century BCE

2 **With the arrival of spite [*zadon*], disgrace has arrived; and wisdom is with the humble,** who wish to listen more than voice their own opinions.[136] The word *zadon* includes bad intentions, haughtiness, and deception of the kind discussed in the previous verse.[137]

3 **The honesty of the upright,** their sincere and faithful conduct, **will guide them** on the proper path; **and the distortion of the treacherous** will not bring them the benefit they seek. Moreover, it **will** bring **plunder** and other disaster upon **them.**

4 **Wealth will not avail** the rich **on the day of ire,** when retribution arrives;[138] **but righteousness will deliver** a person **from death.**

5 **The righteousness of the honest will straighten his way, and the wicked will fall in his wickedness.**

DISCUSSION

10:26 | **So is the idler to those who send him:** The notion of one who is wise and reliable is mentioned a number of times in Proverbs. This verse declares that a messenger who does not bear these qualities will cause more harm than good during his mission (see 13:17, 25:13, 26:6). The imagery of vinegar and smoke used to describe the actions of a sluggard in relation to the one who sends him can allude to the fact that even if there is some benefit to his actions, they are accompanied by damage due to his lack of attentiveness. This is similar to vinegar, which is sometimes used for medicinal purposes, or a burning fire used for cooking and heating, which can cause significant damage if not properly supervised (see, e.g., Rabbeinu Baḥya, introduction to *Teruma*).

מְגוֹרַת רָשָׁע הִיא תְבוֹאֶנּוּ וְתַאֲוַת צַדִּיקִים יִתֵּן׃ כַּעֲבוֹר סוּפָה וְאֵין רָשָׁע וְצַדִּיק כד כה
יְסוֹד עוֹלָם׃ כַּחֹמֶץ לַשִּׁנַּיִם וְכֶעָשָׁן לָעֵינָיִם כֵּן הֶעָצֵל לְשֹׁלְחָיו׃ יִרְאַת יְהוָה תּוֹסִיף כו כז
יָמִים וּשְׁנוֹת רְשָׁעִים תִּקְצֹרְנָה׃ תּוֹחֶלֶת צַדִּיקִים שִׂמְחָה וְתִקְוַת רְשָׁעִים תֹּאבֵד׃ כח
מָעוֹז לַתֹּם דֶּרֶךְ יְהוָה וּמְחִתָּה לְפֹעֲלֵי אָוֶן׃ צַדִּיק לְעוֹלָם בַּל־יִמּוֹט וּרְשָׁעִים לֹא כט ל
יִשְׁכְּנוּ־אָרֶץ׃ פִּי־צַדִּיק יָנוּב חָכְמָה וּלְשׁוֹן תַּהְפֻּכוֹת תִּכָּרֵת׃ שִׂפְתֵי צַדִּיק יֵדְעוּן לא לב
רָצוֹן וּפִי רְשָׁעִים תַּהְפֻּכוֹת׃ מֹאזְנֵי מִרְמָה תּוֹעֲבַת יְהוָה וְאֶבֶן שְׁלֵמָה רְצוֹנוֹ׃ א
בָּא־זָדוֹן וַיָּבֹא קָלוֹן וְאֶת־צְנוּעִים חָכְמָה׃ תֻּמַּת יְשָׁרִים תַּנְחֵם וְסֶלֶף בֹּגְדִים ב ג
יְשָׁדֵּם ושדם׃ לֹא־יוֹעִיל הוֹן בְּיוֹם עֶבְרָה וּצְדָקָה תַּצִּיל מִמָּוֶת׃ צִדְקַת תָּמִים תְּיַשֵּׁר ד ה
דַּרְכּוֹ וּבְרִשְׁעָתוֹ יִפֹּל רָשָׁע׃ צִדְקַת יְשָׁרִים תַּצִּילֵם וּבְהַוַּת בֹּגְדִים יִלָּכֵדוּ׃ בְּמוֹת ו ז
אָדָם רָשָׁע תֹּאבַד תִּקְוָה וְתוֹחֶלֶת אוֹנִים אָבָדָה׃ צַדִּיק מִצָּרָה נֶחֱלָץ וַיָּבֹא רָשָׁע ח
תַּחְתָּיו׃ בְּפֶה חָנֵף יַשְׁחִת רֵעֵהוּ וּבְדַעַת צַדִּיקִים יֵחָלֵצוּ׃ בְּטוּב צַדִּיקִים תַּעֲלֹץ ט י
קִרְיָה וּבַאֲבֹד רְשָׁעִים רִנָּה׃ בְּבִרְכַּת יְשָׁרִים תָּרוּם קָרֶת וּבְפִי רְשָׁעִים תֵּהָרֵס׃ יא
בָּז־לְרֵעֵהוּ חֲסַר־לֵב וְאִישׁ תְּבוּנוֹת יַחֲרִישׁ׃ הוֹלֵךְ רָכִיל מְגַלֶּה־סּוֹד וְנֶאֱמַן־רוּחַ יב יג

6 **The righteousness of the upright will deliver them, and the treacherous will be trapped in devastation,** their crises, or their evil desires.[139]

7 **With the death of a wicked person hope is lost.** A wicked person does not leave behind him any anticipation of good from his works or promises. **And the expectation of the iniquitous,**[140] or violent individuals, **is lost.**[141] Other interpretations: As long as the wicked person is still alive he can amend his ways, but once he is dead all hope of his repentance is lost;[142] since a wicked individual is focused on himself and his hopes mainly concern his own bodily pleasures, upon his death they are lost together with him.[143]

8 **The righteous is extricated from trouble, and the wicked enters into his place.** There are cases where a righteous person escapes from a trap, and a wicked individual falls there in his place, despite all his stratagems to avoid punishment.

9 **With a flattering mouth he,** a wicked individual, **destroys his friend,** who believes his words of flattery; **but with** their **knowledge the righteous will be extricated** from this danger.[144]

10 **With the good of the righteous the city exults,** as the righteous are beloved by the residents of the city; **and with the perishing of the wicked there is singing,** as they cause harm to the residents of the city and therefore their demise brings joy.[145]

11 **With the blessing of the upright,** which they receive due to their conduct and speech, **a city is exalted; and by the mouth of the wicked,** who gossip, lie, curse, and insult,[146] **it,** the city, **is destroyed.**

12 **He who scorns his friend is lacking of heart, and a man of sagacity,** when he hears the insults of that foolish individual, **will be silent.** A sagacious individual knows when to hold back and not become involved in pointless disputes.[147]

13 **He who gossips reveals secrets.** Even if he does not mean to do so, his constant chatter and stories eventually cause him to reveal matters that should have remained hidden; **but he who**

is of faithful spirit conceals a matter. He keeps such details to himself and does not publicize them.

14 **Without strategies a people will fall,** as nations require wisdom, as well as cunning and good strategizing, in order to survive. **And salvation is** achieved **in,** through, **abundant counsel.**

15 **Harm will come when one is guarantor for a stranger.**[148] As stated earlier, it is inadvisable to serve as a guarantor for one whose character and means are unknown (see 6:1–5). Sometimes it might seem that a certain person is trustworthy and that he will certainly repay his debts, yet it is eventually discovered that he is unreliable. **And the hater of handshakes,** who refrains from obligating himself and issuing promises, **is secure.**[149]

16 **A woman of grace supports** people deserving of **honor,** including her husband. **And** by contrast, **the strong,** powerful men [***aritzim***], apparently the polar opposite of a "woman of grace," **support** those who have **wealth.** Unlike the honorable, who are supported by delicate, sensitive souls, the wealthy are supported by the powerful. It should be noted that in the Bible the word *aritz* does not necessarily have the negative connotation that later became associated with the term.[150]

17 **He who cares for himself is a man of kindness,** generous and sensitive, as he is aware of his own needs and takes them into consideration, and will also notice and care for the needs of others; **and he who abuses his** own **flesh,** by engaging in harsh ascetic practices,[151] **is** often **cruel** to others, alienated and inconsiderate.

18 **The wicked performs acts of falsity,** as his deeds do not rest on a stable foundation; **and the sower of righteousness has a true reward,** unlike others who sow seeds, who do not necessarily benefit from their investment.[152]

19 **Righteousness is the base of a life,**[153] or it is a proper attribute for life. The basis of life is righteousness. **And** by contrast, **one** who **pursues evil** leads himself **to his death.**

20 **The crooked of heart are an abomination to the Lord,** as God pushes away those who lack both internal and external integrity; **and His will is** fulfilled by **those of honest way.**

21 **Those of one hand to another [*yad leyad*] will not be absolved.** One who frequently shakes hands, signifying agreements or guarantees he makes to others, will not go unpunished. This does not mean that one should avoid all commitments; rather, he must take into account his ability to fulfill his obligations, and understand the seriousness of a handshake. **And the descendant of the righteous will escape** from this source of trouble. An alternative interpretation: One who performs good deeds in order to receive immediate [*miyad*] reward is not meritorious enough to escape punishment, whereas the righteous, who act with pure motivations, preserve their goodness for their descendants.[154]

22 **A beautiful woman without sense,** who lacks understanding, **is a ring of gold** hanging **in the snout of a pig,** with which the animal is always rummaging around in garbage. Not only does such a ring fail to adorn the pig, it is clearly out of place and gets filthy. Similarly, the beauty of a woman who does not possess intelligence or personality is a waste and a disappointment.

Ring in the snout of a pig

23 **The craving of the righteous,** who are generous, **is only** for **good; the hope of the wicked,** who are selfish, **is ire.** The hopes of the wicked are directed toward matters that unavoidably lead to anger and retribution.

24 **Some distribute** money to charity, or invest in business, **and gain more** profits as a result; **but** regarding **he who spares integrity,** who saves and is miserly, **it will be only for loss.** As stated above, one must be cautious, but miserliness can consume a person and lead to his downfall. In some instances, only one who is willing to spend money will be able to gain.

25 **A beneficent soul,** the generous person who provides for others and wishes them well, **will be fortified** and content; **and one who satisfies** others, **he too will be satisfied.** His life will be full and tranquil.

26 **The withholder of grain** from others will find that **the nation,** his fellow citizens, **will curse him.** Some commentaries interpret this verse in reference to one who causes the price of basic commodities to rise.[155] In times of famine or shortage, not only does this person refrain from donating some of his produce to others, he does not even sell it, as he keeps it for himself in order to raise prices. **But blessing will be on the head of the provider** of food, who does not preserve it all for himself.

27 **He who quests for** the **good** of others **will** always **seek conciliation,** as he looks for peaceful relations; additionally, he himself will be at peace with others. **And** as for **he who seeks evil, it will come to him.**[156]

28 **He who trusts his wealth will fall,** despite all this wealth; **but the righteous will sprout like a leaf,** which perhaps does not appear to be especially grand, and on occasion withers temporarily, but will always grow again.[157]

"The righteous will sprout like a leaf"

29 **The abuser of his house,** by being overly demanding, miserly, or apathetic, **will inherit wind,** emptiness or

יד טו מְכַסֶּה דָבָר׃ בְּאֵין תַּחְבֻּלוֹת יִפָּל־עָם וּתְשׁוּעָה בְּרֹב יוֹעֵץ׃ רַע־יֵרוֹעַ כִּי־עָרַב
טז יז זָר וְשֹׂנֵא תֹקְעִים בּוֹטֵחַ׃ אֵשֶׁת־חֵן תִּתְמֹךְ כָּבוֹד וְעָרִיצִים יִתְמְכוּ־עֹשֶׁר׃ גֹּמֵל
יח נַפְשׁוֹ אִישׁ חָסֶד וְעֹכֵר שְׁאֵרוֹ אַכְזָרִי׃ רָשָׁע עֹשֶׂה פְעֻלַּת־שָׁקֶר וְזֹרֵעַ צְדָקָה שֶׂכֶר
יט כ אֱמֶת׃ כֵּן־צְדָקָה לְחַיִּים וּמְרַדֵּף רָעָה לְמוֹתוֹ׃ תּוֹעֲבַת יהוה עִקְּשֵׁי־לֵב וּרְצוֹנוֹ
כא כב תְּמִימֵי דָרֶךְ׃ יָד לְיָד לֹא־יִנָּקֶה רָּע וְזֶרַע צַדִּיקִים נִמְלָט׃ נֶזֶם זָהָב בְּאַף חֲזִיר
כג כד אִשָּׁה יָפָה וְסָרַת טָעַם׃ תַּאֲוַת צַדִּיקִים אַךְ־טוֹב תִּקְוַת רְשָׁעִים עֶבְרָה׃ יֵשׁ מְפַזֵּר
כה וְנוֹסָף עוֹד וְחוֹשֵׂךְ מִיֹּשֶׁר אַךְ־לְמַחְסוֹר׃ נֶפֶשׁ־בְּרָכָה תְדֻשָּׁן וּמַרְוֶה גַּם־הוּא יוֹרֶא׃
כו כז מֹנֵעַ בָּר יִקְּבֻהוּ לְאוֹם וּבְרָכָה לְרֹאשׁ מַשְׁבִּיר׃ שֹׁחֵר טוֹב יְבַקֵּשׁ רָצוֹן וְדֹרֵשׁ רָעָה
כח כט תְבוֹאֶנּוּ׃ בּוֹטֵחַ בְּעָשְׁרוֹ הוּא יִפֹּל וְכֶעָלֶה צַדִּיקִים יִפְרָחוּ׃ עוֹכֵר בֵּיתוֹ יִנְחַל־רוּחַ
ל לא וְעֶבֶד אֱוִיל לַחֲכַם־לֵב׃ פְּרִי־צַדִּיק עֵץ חַיִּים וְלֹקֵחַ נְפָשׁוֹת חָכָם׃ הֵן צַדִּיק בָּאָרֶץ
יב א ב יְשֻׁלָּם אַף כִּי־רָשָׁע וְחוֹטֵא׃ אֹהֵב מוּסָר אֹהֵב דָּעַת וְשֹׂנֵא תוֹכַחַת בָּעַר׃ טוֹב
ג יָפִיק רָצוֹן מֵיהוה וְאִישׁ מְזִמּוֹת יַרְשִׁיעַ׃ לֹא־יִכּוֹן אָדָם בְּרֶשַׁע וְשֹׁרֶשׁ צַדִּיקִים

anger.[158] The assumption that such behavior will bring any kind of benefit is incorrect and foolish. **And the fool will** inevitably **become servant to the wisehearted.** It is therefore proper to cultivate wisdom and sensitivity, rather than run one's household with a stingy, short-tempered attitude.

30 **The fruit of the righteous is a tree of life, and he who gathers souls,** educating and taking care of them, **is wise.** The wise invest in what is truly important, which is people.[159]

31 **Behold, restitution will be made to the righteous on the earth,** meaning that even the righteous shall be punished for his occasional misdeeds; **all the more so the wicked and the sinner** will certainly be punished.

The Righteous, Good, Wise, and Industrious, and Their Antitheses

PROVERBS 12:1–15:32

12 1 **He who loves admonition loves knowledge.** Since he wants to increase his knowledge and understanding, he listens to criticism and amends his ways. **And he who hates rebuke is a boor.** Since he does not comprehend that criticism is an aid to self-improvement and the acquisition of knowledge, he remains as brutish as before.

2 **The good will elicit favor from the Lord,** as he will receive God's blessing and kindness; **but a man of** evil **schemes, He will condemn;** alternatively: A man of wicked devices will condemn the good man.

3 **A person will not be established by wickedness, but** conversely, **the root of the righteous will not collapse.** Even if they occasionally falter, their roots will grow again.[160]

4 **A woman of valor is** like **the crown** on the head **of her husband, but a shameful one is like rot in his bones.** Like many wise sayings, this is more a description of reality than a piece of practical advice, although the perceptive will take this observation to heart and act accordingly.

5 **Thoughts of the righteous are** always **of justice,** honesty, and righteousness, but **the strategies of the wicked are deceit.** The thoughts of the wicked invariably center on how to cheat and deceive others.

6 Sometimes wicked people seem to be speaking and acting properly. However, the **words** and preoccupations **of the wicked are** really **an ambush for blood,** as they are invariably considering how to take advantage of others.[161] **And the mouth of the upright will deliver them** from the wicked. Alternatively, the mouth of the upright will rescue others from the wicked.[162]

7 **Overturn the wicked and they are no more.** The wicked appear stable, but as soon as they lose power, nothing remains of them. **But the house of the righteous will stand,** even if it faces difficulties.[163]

8 **According to his sense a man will be praised.** A person's reputation is determined in accordance with his measure of intelligence. **But the bent of heart will incur contempt.** In the book of Proverbs and elsewhere in the Bible, the heart is the seat of understanding, not only emotion.[164]

9 **Better is the disgraceful,** one who is considered inferior from a social perspective, **with a servant,** but has someone to perform his labor for him, **than the self-important,** and important in the eyes of others, **who** in fact **is lacking bread.** One who is not too proud to work hard, just as a servant does, even if the labor is demeaning according to his social status, is better than one who refuses to lower himself by working, and maintains his high social status but eventually is lacking even his necessities.[165]

10 **The righteous knows the nature of his animal,** he knows and takes care of the urges and needs of his animals; **and the mercies of the wicked are cruel.** Even when a wicked person appears to show mercy to people or animals and spoils them, his actions are tainted with cruelty.[166] Sometimes wicked people can be seen playing with their pets, and yet they do so in a sadistic manner that causes pain.

11 **He who works his** own **land will have bread to satisfaction, and he who pursues emptiness,** wasteful, unsubstantial matters, **lacks a heart,** and of course will lack bread as well.

12 **The wicked** who, unlike the foolish and naïve, has malicious plans, **covets the trap of evil ones,** with which to ensnare others; **and the root of the righteous,** or one who descends from righteous individuals, **will** constantly **provide** goodness and blessings for others.[167]

13 **In the transgression of the lips is an evil snare.** Evil speech does not remain floating in the air; rather, people hear it and it causes distress and trouble. **But the righteous** individual, who takes care not to talk in such a manner, **emerges from** that **trouble.**

14 **From the fruit,** output, **of a man's mouth he will be sated with good;** one's good speech will come back to him and bring him positive consequences. **And the reward of a person's hands,** his labor, **will come back to him;** he will receive returns on his investments.

15 **The way of a fool is upright in his own eyes.** A fool has an exaggerated sense of self-confidence. Therefore, he is convinced that his path is the correct one, and refuses to heed advice. **And he who heeds counsel is wise.** A wise person will investigate and clarify, and he is willing to listen to others. Alternatively, the verse means that one who hearkens to counsel becomes wise.

16 **A fool's anger will be known that** very **day.**[168] Alternatively, this means that the fool's anger will become as clear as day to all.[169] When he becomes angry, his foolishness also becomes known, as the Sages state: In three matters a person's true character is ascertained: in his cup, meaning his behavior when he drinks; in his pocket, meaning his financial dealings with others; and in his anger.[170] **And a clever man,** who acts astutely, **conceals disgrace,** as he is master over his feelings and does not let them erupt.

17 The text continues with the theme of speech: **He who utters faithfully** and spreads truth is one who **will disclose righteousness.** A person who speaks with honesty and relates matters as they are, thereby enhances his credibility; **but a witness of falsehoods,** who distorts the truth, increases **deceit.**

DISCUSSION

12:19 | **Truth and falsehood:** The book of Proverbs speaks extensively about truth and falsehood. It is unclear whether speaking falsehood is considered an absolute transgression. It would appear that the Torah forbids lies that are damaging to others, or lies spoken with intention to profit dishonestly (see Leviticus 19:11; *Shevuot* 26a; Rambam, *Sefer Hafla'a*, *Hilkhot Shevuot* 1:8). In contrast, here falsehood is presented as intrinsically base and inappropriate both ethically and socially (see also *Mesillat Yesharim* 12).

12:25 | **Suppress it [*yashḥena*]:** This rare word has multiple interpretations. In addition to the simple meaning, i.e., a person will suppress his worry, some interpret it to mean: He will relate about it to others [*yesiḥena*, spelled with a *sin*]. Others interpret it to mean: He should remove it [*yesiḥena* with a *samekh*], meaning that it is preferable for him to remove this worry from his mind (see Rashi; *Yoma* 45a).

ד ה בַּל־יִמּוֹט׃ אֵשֶׁת־חַיִל עֲטֶרֶת בַּעְלָהּ וּכְרָקָב בְּעַצְמוֹתָיו מְבִישָׁה׃ מַחְשְׁבוֹת
ו צַדִּיקִים מִשְׁפָּט תַּחְבֻּלוֹת רְשָׁעִים מִרְמָה׃ דִּבְרֵי רְשָׁעִים אֱרָב־דָּם וּפִי יְשָׁרִים
ז ח יַצִּילֵם׃ הָפוֹךְ רְשָׁעִים וְאֵינָם וּבֵית צַדִּיקִים יַעֲמֹד׃ לְפִי־שִׂכְלוֹ יְהֻלַּל־אִישׁ וְנַעֲוֵה־
ט י לֵב יִהְיֶה לָבוּז׃ טוֹב נִקְלֶה וְעֶבֶד לוֹ מִמִּתְכַּבֵּד וַחֲסַר־לָחֶם׃ יוֹדֵעַ צַדִּיק נֶפֶשׁ
יא בְּהֶמְתּוֹ וְרַחֲמֵי רְשָׁעִים אַכְזָרִי׃ עֹבֵד אַדְמָתוֹ יִשְׂבַּע־לָחֶם וּמְרַדֵּף רֵיקִים חֲסַר־
יב יג לֵב׃ חָמַד רָשָׁע מְצוֹד רָעִים וְשֹׁרֶשׁ צַדִּיקִים יִתֵּן׃ בְּפֶשַׁע שְׂפָתַיִם מוֹקֵשׁ רָע וַיֵּצֵא
יד טו מִצָּרָה צַדִּיק׃ מִפְּרִי פִי־אִישׁ יִשְׂבַּע־טוֹב וּגְמוּל יְדֵי־אָדָם ישוב לוֹ׃ דֶּרֶךְ אֱוִיל יָשִׁיב
טז יז יָשָׁר בְּעֵינָיו וְשֹׁמֵעַ לְעֵצָה חָכָם׃ אֱוִיל בַּיּוֹם יִוָּדַע כַּעְסוֹ וְכֹסֶה קָלוֹן עָרוּם׃ יָפִיחַ
יח אֱמוּנָה יַגִּיד צֶדֶק וְעֵד שְׁקָרִים מִרְמָה׃ יֵשׁ בּוֹטֶה כְּמַדְקְרוֹת חָרֶב וּלְשׁוֹן חֲכָמִים
יט כ מַרְפֵּא׃ שְׂפַת־אֱמֶת תִּכּוֹן לָעַד וְעַד־אַרְגִּיעָה לְשׁוֹן שָׁקֶר׃ מִרְמָה בְּלֶב־חֹרְשֵׁי רָע
כא כב וּלְיֹעֲצֵי שָׁלוֹם שִׂמְחָה׃ לֹא־יְאֻנֶּה לַצַּדִּיק כָּל־אָוֶן וּרְשָׁעִים מָלְאוּ רָע׃ תּוֹעֲבַת
כג יְהוָה שִׂפְתֵי־שָׁקֶר וְעֹשֵׂי אֱמוּנָה רְצוֹנוֹ׃ אָדָם עָרוּם כֹּסֶה דָּעַת וְלֵב כְּסִילִים יִקְרָא
כד כה אִוֶּלֶת׃ יַד־חָרוּצִים תִּמְשׁוֹל וּרְמִיָּה תִּהְיֶה לָמַס׃ דְּאָגָה בְלֶב־אִישׁ יַשְׁחֶנָּה וְדָבָר

18 **There is one who expresses** matters in hurtful ways, **like stabbings of a sword, but the tongue of the wise is a cure.** Even when the wise issue deprecatory comments, their statements heal rather than harm.[171]

19 **The language of truth will be established forever, but a tongue of falsehood**[D] **is only for a moment.** Falsehood does not last. This is one of the differences between truth and lies, both from an analytical, philosophical perspective and in the practical realm: Those things which have a continued existence are true, but that which does not survive is false in its very essence.

20 **Deceit is in the heart of devisers of evil, but to the counselors of peace** there is **joy,** as they are not afraid of revealing their thoughts, and they enjoy the benefits accrued from their speech.

21 **No iniquity** and dishonesty[172] **will befall the righteous** individual. Since he has no deception in his heart and does not lust after such matters, he will not sin even accidentally; **but the wicked are filled with evil.**

22 **Lips of falsehood are an abomination to the Lord,** as God hates falsehood; **but they who deal faithfully are** fulfilling **His will.** He cherishes those who conduct themselves truthfully, and is close to them.[173]

23 **A clever person conceals knowledge** inside himself, **and the heart of fools proclaims folly;** the fool is unable to hide anything, and proclaims his imprudence to all.[174]

24 **The hand of the diligent,** of those who work in the proper manner, **will rule.** Their power will increase thanks to the superior quality of their labor;[175] **and** in contrast, those who act with **deceit will be subject to tribute.** The end state of the deceitful and lazy will be one of weakness and subjugation, and they will have to pay a tribute to others.[176] Alternatively, the verse means that the accomplishments of such individuals will dissipate,[177] as phony activity will not be productive.

25 When there is **worry in the heart of a man he should suppress it.**[D] He should not let his worries overpower him, but he should conquer them.[178] **And a good word,** or matter, **renders it,** the worry, into **joy.**

26 **The righteous has an advantage [*yater*] over his friend.** Alternatively, he receives an advantage from him. Some claim that *yater* is from the root *tav-vav-reish*: The righteous seeks out [*tar*] a good path for his friend.[179] **And the way of the wicked,** which they imagine will take them to a good place, **will** actually **lead them astray.**

27 **The deceitful will not scorch his prey** in the manner of hunters, who would break or slightly scorch the wings of the captured birds so that they would not escape. In other words, anything obtained by deception will not be preserved.[180] **But the wealth of a worthy man is choice gold,** or: One earns his wealth through his diligence and honesty;[181] alternatively: The wealth of a diligent man is dear to him. A cheater seeks to cut corners and find easy routes to his goals, but he will ultimately be left with nothing. By contrast, the industrious, who perform their work faithfully and follow the proper path, will preserve their money, and success will shine favorably upon them.

28 **In the path of righteousness is** an increase of **life,**[182] **and along its pathway there is no death.**

13 1 **A wise son is** one who learns **from a father's admonition;**[183] **and a scoffer,** a cynical person, who does not learn nor consider matters carefully, **did not hear castigation.**

2 **From the fruit of a man's mouth he will partake of goodness;** he is sustained by his good speech.[184] Some interpret this proverb as a continuation of the previous verse: The wise son is one who eats from the fruit of the mouth of his father who rebukes him. **And the soul of the treacherous** will partake of **villainy.**

3 **He who guards his mouth** from superfluous speech thereby **protects his life, and he who parts wide his lips** and relates everything without discrimination, **it is** a habit that will bring **ruin for him.**

4 **The idler's soul craves and has nothing,** he is left discontented; **and the soul of the diligent will luxuriate,** satisfied and comfortable.

5 **The righteous hates a false word, and the wicked disgusts,** by acting in a manner that repulses others, **and brings disrepute.**

6 **Righteousness safeguards he whose way is honest, and wickedness distorts,** negatively impacts, **the sinner.**[185]

7 **Some act affluent, but there is nothing** in his possession; and **some act poor and there is great wealth.**

8 **The ransom of a man's life is his wealth.** When necessary, one's wealth can serve as ransom for him, **and the poor does not hear castigation.** Reprimanding the poor person is often ineffective. On the one hand, he is not susceptible to threats that may concern one who is wealthy, as the poor man has nothing to lose. On the other hand, a poor person who has sinned cannot afford to pay restitution.

9 **The light of the righteous will rejoice;** it will shine. The term "rejoice" in this context is a poetic expression of affection for the light, similar to "the light is sweet."[186] **And** in contrast to the righteous, or perhaps in consequence of their righteousness,[187] **the lamp of the wicked will dim.** The soul of the righteous is referred to here as "light," whereas the soul of the wicked is dubbed a "lamp." This is because the wicked focus on material objects, and their light is feeble and temporary.[188]

10 One who acts by **spite alone,** or through crushing others without consideration for them, **will generate contention, and those who seek counsel** from others will find **wisdom,** as they will act in a reasonable, deliberate manner.

11 **Wealth will diminish from,** as a result of, **futility** failing to take action or acting recklessly; **and he who gathers** patiently **by hand,** little by little, **will increase** his property. Wealth does not necessarily come in large quantities at one time; occasionally, it is those who act properly and with restraint who gradually accumulate a fortune.

12 **Expectation deferred,** an extended but unfulfilled anticipation, **sickens the heart, and craving realized is a tree of life** for the recipient. When someone's wishes come true, he is revived. Alternatively, by connecting to the "tree of life," the source of goodness and wisdom, one's desire is fulfilled. With regard to this verse, the Talmud states: Anyone who prolongs his prayer and expects it to be answered, will ultimately come to heartache… And what is the remedy for one afflicted with that illness? He should engage in Torah study.[189]

13 **He who scorns something will be injured by it.** In all realms of life, one should be careful not to scorn anything. Eventually, he will encounter that very same object in a different context, and will be injured by it.[190] **And he who fears a commandment,** who not only refrains from mocking but treats God's commandments with respect and observes them, he **will be rewarded.**

14 **The Torah of the wise is a fount of life,** which helps him **to turn** away **from the snares of death.** The training and studies of the wise prevent them from falling into evil ways.

15 **Good sense grants favor.** One's insight is among the various features and reasons why one gains the appreciation of others. **But the way of the treacherous is hard,** tough and inflexible in its stance, as they are unwilling to learn from anyone else. Consequently, they do not find favor in people's eyes.

16 **Everyone clever will act with knowledge, and a fool will spread folly** through his actions. He surrounds himself with stupidity on all sides.

17 **A wicked agent,** who does not fulfill his mission properly,[191] **will fall into harm,** which he brings upon himself; **and a faithful emissary is** able to provide **a cure.** The question of whether

כו כז טוֹב יְשַׂמְּחֶנָּה׃ יָתֵר מֵרֵעֵהוּ צַדִּיק וְדֶרֶךְ רְשָׁעִים תַּתְעֵם׃ לֹא־יַחֲרֹךְ רְמִיָּה צֵידוֹ

כח וְהוֹן־אָדָם יָקָר חָרוּץ׃ בְּאֹרַח־צְדָקָה חַיִּים וְדֶרֶךְ נְתִיבָה אַל־מָוֶת׃

יג א ב בֵּן חָכָם מוּסַר אָב וְלֵץ לֹא־שָׁמַע גְּעָרָה׃ מִפְּרִי פִי־אִישׁ יֹאכַל טוֹב וְנֶפֶשׁ בֹּגְדִים

ג ד חָמָס׃ נֹצֵר פִּיו שֹׁמֵר נַפְשׁוֹ פֹּשֵׂק שְׂפָתָיו מְחִתָּה־לוֹ׃ מִתְאַוָּה וָאַיִן נַפְשׁוֹ עָצֵל

ה ו וְנֶפֶשׁ חָרֻצִים תְּדֻשָּׁן׃ דְּבַר־שֶׁקֶר יִשְׂנָא צַדִּיק וְרָשָׁע יַבְאִישׁ וְיַחְפִּיר׃ צְדָקָה

ז תִּצֹּר תָּם־דָּרֶךְ וְרִשְׁעָה תְּסַלֵּף חַטָּאת׃ יֵשׁ מִתְעַשֵּׁר וְאֵין כֹּל מִתְרוֹשֵׁשׁ וְהוֹן רָב׃

ח ט כֹּפֶר נֶפֶשׁ־אִישׁ עָשְׁרוֹ וְרָשׁ לֹא־שָׁמַע גְּעָרָה׃ אוֹר־צַדִּיקִים יִשְׂמָח וְנֵר רְשָׁעִים

י יא יִדְעָךְ׃ רַק־בְּזָדוֹן יִתֵּן מַצָּה וְאֶת־נוֹעָצִים חָכְמָה׃ הוֹן מֵהֶבֶל יִמְעָט וְקֹבֵץ עַל־יָד

יב יג יַרְבֶּה׃ תּוֹחֶלֶת מְמֻשָּׁכָה מַחֲלָה־לֵב וְעֵץ חַיִּים תַּאֲוָה בָאָה׃ בָּז לְדָבָר יֵחָבֶל לוֹ

יד טו וִירֵא מִצְוָה הוּא יְשֻׁלָּם׃ תּוֹרַת חָכָם מְקוֹר חַיִּים לָסוּר מִמֹּקְשֵׁי מָוֶת׃ שֵׂכֶל־טוֹב

טז יז יִתֶּן־חֵן וְדֶרֶךְ בֹּגְדִים אֵיתָן׃ כָּל־עָרוּם יַעֲשֶׂה בְדָעַת וּכְסִיל יִפְרֹשׂ אִוֶּלֶת׃ מַלְאָךְ

יח רָשָׁע יִפֹּל בְּרָע וְצִיר אֱמוּנִים מַרְפֵּא׃ רֵישׁ וְקָלוֹן פּוֹרֵעַ מוּסָר וְשׁוֹמֵר תּוֹכַחַת

יט כ יְכֻבָּד׃ תַּאֲוָה נִהְיָה תֶּעֱרַב לְנָפֶשׁ וְתוֹעֲבַת כְּסִילִים סוּר מֵרָע׃ הלוך אֶת־חֲכָמִים הוֹלֵךְ

כא כב וחכם וְרֹעֶה כְסִילִים יֵרוֹעַ׃ חַטָּאִים תְּרַדֵּף רָעָה וְאֶת־צַדִּיקִים יְשַׁלֶּם־טוֹב׃ טוֹב יֶחְכָּם

כג יַנְחִיל בְּנֵי־בָנִים וְצָפוּן לַצַּדִּיק חֵיל חוֹטֵא׃ רָב־אֹכֶל נִיר רָאשִׁים וְיֵשׁ נִסְפֶּה בְּלֹא

or not a messenger is faithful to those who sent him can be a matter of life or death.

18 **Poverty and disgrace is for one who avoids admonition,** a reckless individual who does not listen to criticism; **but** in contrast, **the keeper of rebuke will be honored.**

19 **Craving realized is pleasant for the soul,**[192] **and turning from evil is the abomination of fools.** Fools follow a path that does not enable their desires to be fulfilled at any point, and they thereby draw closer to evil. Indeed, the converse is the case: The fools consider it an abomination to turn away from something evil that they desire.

20 **He who** constantly **walks with the wise will become wise,** as he will grow wiser merely by keeping their company; **and he who shepherds**[193] or leads[194] **fools will be broken.**[195]

21 **Evil** itself **pursues** and harms **sinners, and the righteous will be rewarded with goodness.** Alternatively, goodness itself will reward the righteous.[196]

22 **The good will** merit to **bequeath** an inheritance **to** his **grandchildren; and the wealth of the sinner is stored,** reserved, **for the righteous,** while nothing will remain for the sinner himself.

23 **Much food is in the plowing of the poor.** A poor person, who has no option but to invest great effort in his undertakings, will eventually enjoy the fruits of his labor.[197] Alternatively, the yield from the poor man's plowing will be the sustenance of the wealthy. If so, the principle stated in the second part of the verse expands upon the first part rather than standing in contrast to it. **And some are swept away without justice.** Some people invest great effort but are unsuccessful and are lost.[198]

24 **He who spares his rod,** and thereby refrains from disciplining his son, in effect **hates his son,** as the child will not learn anything, which means that his father has caused him harm. **And he who loves him,** his son, **seeks for him admonition.** He takes care to chastise him, which includes the occasional use of the rod. A life of complete freedom, without any fear or discipline, is dangerous.

25 **The righteous eats to his own satisfaction;** he consumes only that which he requires, and if there is more than he needs he will leave some over.[199] **And the stomach of the wicked will lack.** The wicked is never satisfied, and is always craving for more; he feels a constant lack in his stomach.

14 1 **The wise among women**[200] **builds her house.** The home, in both the material and the spiritual sense, is to a large extent built by the woman; **and the foolish** woman **will destroy it with her hands,** even if she does not intend to do so.

2 **He who fears the Lord walks in his uprightness,** meaning that one who follows the straight, proper path fears God,[201] or that one who fears God will act honestly, **and he whose ways are crooked scorns Him.** Although people do not always keep this in mind, the actions of a crooked swindler do not only break the law and get him into trouble with the authorities, they also desecrate the name of God.[202]

3 **In the mouth of the fool is a staff of pride.** The fool imagines that he is wise and tries to express his supposed greatness in his speech. However, not only is his pride unfounded, his very self-exposure serves to belittle him. **And the lips of the wise will protect them** from imprudent comments.

4 **Without oxen there is no trough,** a vessel for storing produce; alternatively: The trough is clean and empty. Oxen provided the main source of labor in agriculture, including in plowing, reaping, and transportation. **And abundant yield is** gained **through the strength of the ox.** One cannot extract something from nothing. Great success requires serious investment in a workforce and other resources.

Plowing with oxen

5 **A trustworthy witness will not lie.** One can rely on such a witness. Not only will he not speak falsehoods, he also will not waste his words. **And a false witness utters** and spreads **lies.** One who is generally accustomed to speaking deceitfully is not reliable as a witness.[203]

6 **A scoffer seeks wisdom, and there is none.** Such lightheaded individuals are unwilling to make the requisite effort, and therefore wisdom will elude them. **But knowledge is easy** to acquire **for the discerning.**

7 **Go** far **away from a foolish man.** When you see a fool, cross over to the other side of the street, as you will gain nothing from meeting him. **And** keep your distance **from** those **whom you do not know to have knowledgeable lips,** as it is not worth your while to converse with those who do not speak intelligently.[204]

8 **The wisdom of the clever is understanding his own way,** discerning for himself the proper path to follow; **and deceit is the folly of fools.** Their foolishness causes them to stray from the path of honesty, and they are constantly making mistakes and causing others to err as well.[205]

9 **Guilt causes fools to talk.** Their conversation revolves around their sins, guilt, or the amends they must make.[206] Some explain the verse to mean that fools distort the concept of sin. **And** in contrast, there is **good will among the upright.** The conversation of the upright is motivated by good deeds, kindness, and blessings. Consequently, one who keeps the company of fools will find guilt in various forms, whereas among sincere and upstanding people feelings of good will, closeness, and love will be cultivated.

10 **The heart knows the bitterness of itself, and no stranger can share in its joy.** A person experiences his own pain and joy directly; no one else can experience these feelings with the same force.

11 **The house of the wicked will be destroyed, and the tent of the upright will flourish.** Honest individuals have good hope for the future.

12 **There is** sometimes **a** path that appears to be the **right way before a man, and** yet **its end is** like **the ways of death,** the paths that lead to desolation. Therefore, one must exercise caution and be constantly vigilant on his path, while hoping for divine assistance.[207]

13 **Even in laughter the heart aches.** If people are suffering from depression or are in a state of sorrow, their pain endures even while they laugh, **and** often **grief is the end of joy.** The sadness resurfaces again immediately after the joy has passed.

14 **A wayward heart will be sated from its ways.** A person whose heart turns from the proper path will be full of the bitterness with which he feeds himself. **And a good man will remove** himself **from him,** the individual with a wayward heart, and will not follow his path and stumble.

15 **The naïf,** who can be easily duped and does not examine matters thoroughly or reflect upon them, **believes everything** he hears to be factually correct; **and the clever** individual **will understand it correctly,** and in the appropriate manner.

כד כה מִשְׁפָּט׃ חוֹשֵׂךְ שִׁבְטוֹ שׂוֹנֵא בְנוֹ וְאֹהֲבוֹ שִׁחֲרוֹ מוּסָר׃ צַדִּיק אֹכֵל לְשֹׂבַע נַפְשׁוֹ
א ב וּבֶטֶן רְשָׁעִים תֶּחְסָר׃ חַכְמוֹת נָשִׁים בָּנְתָה בֵיתָהּ וְאִוֶּלֶת בְּיָדֶיהָ תֶהֶרְסֶנּוּ׃ הוֹלֵךְ
ג בְּיָשְׁרוֹ יְרֵא יְהוָה וּנְלוֹז דְּרָכָיו בּוֹזֵהוּ׃ בְּפִי־אֱוִיל חֹטֶר גַּאֲוָה וְשִׂפְתֵי חֲכָמִים ד
ד ה תִּשְׁמוּרֵם׃ בְּאֵין אֲלָפִים אֵבוּס בָּר וְרָב־תְּבוּאוֹת בְּכֹחַ שׁוֹר׃ עֵד אֱמוּנִים לֹא יְכַזֵּב
ו ז וְיָפִיחַ כְּזָבִים עֵד שָׁקֶר׃ בִּקֶּשׁ־לֵץ חָכְמָה וָאָיִן וְדַעַת לְנָבוֹן נָקָל׃ לֵךְ מִנֶּגֶד לְאִישׁ
ח כְּסִיל וּבַל־יָדַעְתָּ שִׂפְתֵי־דָעַת׃ חָכְמַת עָרוּם הָבִין דַּרְכּוֹ וְאִוֶּלֶת כְּסִילִים מִרְמָה׃
ט י אֱוִלִים יָלִיץ אָשָׁם וּבֵין יְשָׁרִים רָצוֹן׃ לֵב יוֹדֵעַ מָרַּת נַפְשׁוֹ וּבְשִׂמְחָתוֹ לֹא־יִתְעָרַב
יא יב זָר׃ בֵּית רְשָׁעִים יִשָּׁמֵד וְאֹהֶל יְשָׁרִים יַפְרִיחַ׃ יֵשׁ דֶּרֶךְ יָשָׁר לִפְנֵי־אִישׁ וְאַחֲרִיתָהּ
יג יד דַּרְכֵי־מָוֶת׃ גַּם־בִּשְׂחוֹק יִכְאַב־לֵב וְאַחֲרִיתָהּ שִׂמְחָה תוּגָה׃ מִדְּרָכָיו יִשְׂבַּע סוּג
טו טז לֵב וּמֵעָלָיו אִישׁ טוֹב׃ פֶּתִי יַאֲמִין לְכָל־דָּבָר וְעָרוּם יָבִין לַאֲשֻׁרוֹ׃ חָכָם יָרֵא וְסָר
יז מֵרָע וּכְסִיל מִתְעַבֵּר וּבוֹטֵחַ׃ קְצַר־אַפַּיִם יַעֲשֶׂה אִוֶּלֶת וְאִישׁ מְזִמּוֹת יִשָּׂנֵא׃
יח יט נָחֲלוּ פְתָאיִם אִוֶּלֶת וַעֲרוּמִים יַכְתִּרוּ דָעַת׃ שַׁחוּ רָעִים לִפְנֵי טוֹבִים וּרְשָׁעִים
כ כא עַל־שַׁעֲרֵי צַדִּיק׃ גַּם־לְרֵעֵהוּ יִשָּׂנֵא רָשׁ וְאֹהֲבֵי עָשִׁיר רַבִּים׃ בָּז־לְרֵעֵהוּ חוֹטֵא
כב כג וּמְחוֹנֵן עניים אַשְׁרָיו׃ הֲלוֹא־יִתְעוּ חֹרְשֵׁי רָע וְחֶסֶד וֶאֱמֶת חֹרְשֵׁי טוֹב׃ בְּכָל־עֶצֶב עֲנָוִים

16 **A wise man fears** and is cautious, **and** therefore he **turns from evil, but the** arrogant **fool becomes enraged and confident** in himself, his greatness, and his power.[208]

17 **The quick to anger will commit folly,** as he will err due to his lack of patience; **and** at the same time, **a man of schemes,** who overanalyzes and formulates numerous detailed plans, **will be hated** by people. One should follow the moderate path, not to always react instantly and rashly, but also to refrain from devising endless schemes.

18 **Naïfs,** who are incapable of discerning between diverse issues, will eventually **have inherited folly, and the clever,** who examine matters until they fully understand them, **will** ultimately **be crowned with knowledge.**[209] Alternatively, the latter phrase may be translated to mean: The clever glorify knowledge.

19 **The evil** will ultimately **bow before the good, and the wicked** will come and prostrate themselves **at the gates of the righteous** individual to seek his forgiveness.

20 The text now turns to topics that pertain to the nature of society: **The poor is hated even**[210] **by his friend.** A pauper is despised by all; even his friends are estranged from him. **But the lovers of the rich are many.**

21 **He who scorns his friend is** thereby **a sinner, and happy** and blessed **is he who is kind to the humble** and has mercy upon them.

22 **Truly, those who devise evil will** become confused, lose their way, and **wander; and those who devise good will have kindness and truth.**

23 **In all toil** [*etzev*] **there is advantage;** hard work brings positive results. Some explain: Even from sadness [*etzev*] some advantage can accrue.[211] **But lips' talk is only for detriment.** Nothing useful will come of mere speech.[212]

24 **The crown** upon the head **of the wise is their wealth,** as wealth is suitable for the wise; **and the folly of fools is** no more than **folly,** even if they are rich.[213]

25 **A true witness saves souls,** as his testimony ensures that the guilty will be condemned and the innocent vindicated; **and he who utters lies is** all **deceit.** By spreading his falsehoods, the liar will only disappoint.

26 **In the fear of the Lord is a stalwart stronghold;** this type of fear serves as a powerful stronghold that protects a person; **and for his children there will be shelter.** Even if his children do not attain their father's level, they will at least be able to take refuge in the fortress he constructed.

27 **The fear of the Lord is a fount of life,** and it helps a person **to turn from the snares of death.**

28 **In the multitude of people is the glory of a king,** in that he rules over them; **and in the lack of a nation,** when the number of the people dwindle, **is the ruin of a prince.**

29 **The** one who is **slow to anger is of great understanding,** as a perceptive person realizes it is proper to have patience; **and the impatient** person **exalts folly.**

30 **A healing heart is the life of the flesh.** A good and calm heart provides healthy life for one's entire body. **And envy is the rot of bones.** Envy does not build anything; it causes the body to disintegrate. When envy takes hold of a person, it erodes him and reduces his power.

31 **He who oppresses,** takes advantage of and shortchanges, **the poor** not only harms that pauper, he also **reviles his Maker,** he disparages God Himself; **and he who is gracious to the needy** and has mercy upon them thereby **honors Him,** who created the needy. The act of compassion toward the poor is itself a manner of honoring God. Since God Himself does not require gifts, whereas the destitute are in need of them, the way to honor God is by giving to the poor.

32 **In his evil the wicked is rejected,** and he fails to accomplish anything of value; **and the righteous finds refuge in his** own **death.** The righteous remains steadfast in his trust in God even as he dies.[214]

33 **In the heart of the discerning will** naturally **rest** a quiet, internal **wisdom, and within fools it will be made known.** The fool proclaims to all the little wisdom he does possess, or alternatively, the fact that he lacks wisdom entirely.[215] Some explain the verse to mean that the wisdom of the discerning individual reaches everywhere and becomes known even to fools, who come to realize the extent of their lack of wisdom.[216]

34 **Righteousness will exalt a nation,** as an entire nation can be raised up by the performance of righteousness; **and kindness of nations is sin.**[217] The kindness performed by various nations is actually sin, not true kindness, as nations often support each other not out of a desire to do good, but merely due to political considerations.[218]

35 **The king's favor is to a successful servant,** as he is gratified by such a servant and gives him his support; **and his anger will be to the shameful,** the negligent, substandard servant from whom he derives no benefit.

15 1 **A gentle** and courteous **response assuages** the **fury** of one who is angry. During a quarrel or a sensitive situation that is liable to deteriorate into a fight, a calm response can quell someone's growing rage. **And a tiresome word provokes wrath.** A harsh or insulting retort will only increase the tension. One should therefore accustom oneself to speaking in a gentle manner.

2 **The tongue of the wise improves knowledge, and the mouth of fools** habitually **expresses folly.** Even if a fool learns something, whatever comes out of his mouth will be foolish.

3 **The eyes of the Lord are in every place, gazing at the wicked and the good.** One must keep in mind that God is always watching both evil people and good people, and there is no escape from His sight.

4 Another aphorism on the topic of speech: **A** soft-spoken, **healing tongue,**[219] or alternatively, the healing of the spirit by means of the tongue,[220] **is a tree of life,** producing life, health, happiness, and welfare; **and distortion with it,** the tongue, **is an injury to the spirit,** a source of despondency, bitter disappointment, and pain.

5 More on the subject of the foolish and the wise, and the righteous and the wicked: **A fool scorns** and rejects **his father's admonishment, and he who heeds** the **rebuke** he receives **will become clever** and discerning.

6 **The house of the righteous is a great storehouse,** as anything the righteous individual stores in his house will last for a long time; **and in the produce of the wicked** there is **spoilage.**[221]

7 **The lips of the wise will disperse knowledge, but not so the heart of fools.** The fool does not distribute or acquire knowledge; indeed, he does not even pay any attention to it. Alternatively, this phrase means: The heart of the foolish is not right or properly directed.

8 **The offering of the wicked is an abomination to the Lord;** even when a wicked person brings a sacrifice, God despises it. **And the prayer of the upright,** even without any sacrifice, **is His gratification,** and God responds with blessing.

9 **The way of the wicked,** his general conduct, actions, and dealings, **is an abomination to the Lord, and He loves a pursuer of righteousness [*tzedaka*].** In the Bible, the term *tzedaka*, which later came to mean charity, includes not only giving to the poor and the pursuit of justice, but the observance of the Torah and the performance of good deeds as well.

כד יִהְיֶה מוֹתָר וּדְבַר־שְׂפָתַיִם אַךְ־לְמַחְסוֹר׃ עֲטֶרֶת חֲכָמִים עָשְׁרָם אִוֶּלֶת כְּסִילִים
כה כו אִוֶּלֶת׃ מַצִּיל נְפָשׁוֹת עֵד אֱמֶת וְיָפִחַ כְּזָבִים מִרְמָה׃ בְּיִרְאַת יְהוָה מִבְטַח־עֹז
כז כח וּלְבָנָיו יִהְיֶה מַחְסֶה׃ יִרְאַת יְהוָה מְקוֹר חַיִּים לָסוּר מִמֹּקְשֵׁי מָוֶת׃ בְּרָב־עָם
כט הַדְרַת־מֶלֶךְ וּבְאֶפֶס לְאֹם מְחִתַּת רָזוֹן׃ אֶרֶךְ אַפַּיִם רַב־תְּבוּנָה וּקְצַר־רוּחַ מֵרִים
ל לא אִוֶּלֶת׃ חַיֵּי בְשָׂרִים לֵב מַרְפֵּא וּרְקַב עֲצָמוֹת קִנְאָה׃ עֹשֵׁק דָּל חֵרֵף עֹשֵׂהוּ וּמְכַבְּדוֹ
לב לג חֹנֵן אֶבְיוֹן׃ בְּרָעָתוֹ יִדָּחֶה רָשָׁע וְחֹסֶה בְמוֹתוֹ צַדִּיק׃ בְּלֵב נָבוֹן תָּנוּחַ חָכְמָה
לד לה וּבְקֶרֶב כְּסִילִים תִּוָּדֵעַ׃ צְדָקָה תְרוֹמֵם־גּוֹי וְחֶסֶד לְאֻמִּים חַטָּאת׃ רְצוֹן־מֶלֶךְ
טו א לְעֶבֶד מַשְׂכִּיל וְעֶבְרָתוֹ תִּהְיֶה מֵבִישׁ׃ מַעֲנֶה־רַּךְ יָשִׁיב חֵמָה וּדְבַר־עֶצֶב יַעֲלֶה־
ב ג אָף׃ לְשׁוֹן חֲכָמִים תֵּיטִיב דָּעַת וּפִי כְסִילִים יַבִּיעַ אִוֶּלֶת׃ בְּכָל־מָקוֹם עֵינֵי יְהוָה
ד ה צֹפוֹת רָעִים וְטוֹבִים׃ מַרְפֵּא לָשׁוֹן עֵץ חַיִּים וְסֶלֶף בָּהּ שֶׁבֶר בְּרוּחַ׃ אֱוִיל יִנְאַץ
ו מוּסַר אָבִיו וְשֹׁמֵר תּוֹכַחַת יַעְרִם׃ בֵּית צַדִּיק חֹסֶן רָב וּבִתְבוּאַת רָשָׁע נֶעְכָּרֶת׃
ז ח שִׂפְתֵי חֲכָמִים יְזָרוּ דָעַת וְלֵב כְּסִילִים לֹא־כֵן׃ זֶבַח רְשָׁעִים תּוֹעֲבַת יְהוָה וּתְפִלַּת
ט י יְשָׁרִים רְצוֹנוֹ׃ תּוֹעֲבַת יְהוָה דֶּרֶךְ רָשָׁע וּמְרַדֵּף צְדָקָה יֶאֱהָב׃ מוּסָר רָע לְעֹזֵב
יא אֹרַח שׂוֹנֵא תוֹכַחַת יָמוּת׃ שְׁאוֹל וַאֲבַדּוֹן נֶגֶד יְהוָה אַף כִּי־לִבּוֹת בְּנֵי־אָדָם׃
יב יג לֹא־יֶאֱהַב לֵץ הוֹכֵחַ לוֹ אֶל־חֲכָמִים לֹא יֵלֵךְ׃ לֵב שָׂמֵחַ יֵיטִב פָּנִים וּבְעַצְּבַת־לֵב
יד טו רוּחַ נְכֵאָה׃ לֵב נָבוֹן יְבַקֶּשׁ־דָּעַת וּפְנֵי כְסִילִים יִרְעֶה אִוֶּלֶת׃ כָּל־יְמֵי עָנִי רָעִים וּפִי

10 There is **harsh admonition for he who forsakes the** proper **path. He who hates rebuke will die** in his wickedness; even suffering will not move him, because he refuses to accept any guidance or instruction.[222]

11 Even **the grave and oblivion,** which seemingly are bereft of substance and are of no interest or value, **are before the Lord;** all the **more so the hearts of the** living **sons of man,** within whom a lofty soul resides, are revealed before God.[223]

12 **A scoffer,** a flighty, arrogant person, **does not love his own rebuking;** therefore, **to the wise he will not go,** as he assumes they will tell him things he does not wish to hear.

13 **A joyous heart cheers the face, and with heartache is a spirit dejected;** at a time of misery, it is evident to outside observers that one's spirit is broken. Feelings of both happiness and sadness are reflected in a person's appearance.

14 **The discerning heart seeks knowledge, and the mouth of fools befriends folly.** The mouth of a foolish person constantly speaks nonsense.[224]

15 **All the days of the poor are wretched.** Even situations that are not particularly difficult can be very damaging to a poor person. If something is broken, he might not be able to have it fixed immediately; if he is ill, be might not have the funds to receive proper medical attention. Consequently, his problems only worsen. **But the goodhearted has a perpetual feast.** He is happy with his lot and can celebrate at all times.

16 Nevertheless, despite the difficulties the poor must face, **better is little,** a small amount of property, that is acquired **with fear of the Lord, than great treasure and with it, confusion,** or quarrels.[225]

17 This verse expresses a similar idea to the previous one: **A** simple and inexpensive **meal of greens and love there is better,** more pleasant, **than** the meat of **a fattened ox and** yet there is **hatred with it.**

18 **A furious man,** one who is constantly angry, **arouses strife, and he who is slow to anger quiets quarreling.**

19 **The way of the idler is like a hedge of thorns,**[B] which blocks the path and forces passersby to either turn away[226] or struggle through the thicket while they are pricked by the thorns. **But the path of the upright is paved;** it is comfortable for walking and contains no stumbling blocks.[227]

"A hedge of thorns." Branches with thorns, constituting a barrier

"The path of the upright is paved." Ancient Roman path, Syria

20 On wisdom and foolishness: **A wise son gladdens a father, and a foolish man,** through his deeds, **scorns his mother.** Even after he has matured, his foolishness still disgraces his mother.

21 **Folly is** a cause of **joy to he who is lacking of heart,** as such a person enjoys foolish matters; **and a man of sagacity will walk forthrightly,** since he involves himself with matters of reason. Alternatively, the verse means that joy is foolishness to one who lacks understanding, but is beneficial to a discerning person in straightening his path.[228]

22 **Plans are impeded without counsel.** Plans will not come to fruition if they are not formed through shared discussion and general consultations. **And with an abundance of advisors they,** the plans, **will endure.**

23 **There is joy for a man in the reply of his mouth;** when one answers correctly and accurately, it pleases him. **And how good is a word at its** proper **time.**

24 On morality, humility, and righteousness: **The path of life goes upward for the sensible;** the way of life of the discerning individual is directed upward, to sacred matters, **so that he may turn away from the grave beneath.** If a person does not want to fall all the way down to the netherworld below, he must attempt to advance and climb higher.[229]

25 **The Lord will uproot the house of the arrogant** and aggressive;[230] **and He will set** firmly **the border of the widow.** God will guard the territory of the weak widow from cruel, arrogant individuals.[231]

26 **Thoughts of** an **evil** person **are an abomination to the Lord, and sayings of pleasantness** and kindness[232] **are pure;** they are considered beautiful and desirable to God.

27 **A seeker of ill-gotten gain,** who lives for monetary gain, is one who **abuses,** destroys, **his** own **house.** The continuous attempt to earn more money by any means, both honest and dishonest, will eventually bring harm upon a person and his family. **And a hater of gifts will live.** Even if the gifts are not given in the form of bribes, they disrupt the proper order of things, and therefore it is appropriate to avoid accepting them as much as possible.[233]

28 **The heart of the righteous will** carefully **consider** his reply **in answering.**[234] Alternatively, he speaks about refreshing matters in a pleasant manner,[235] or talks with humility and modesty.[236] **And the mouth of the wicked will express evil,** as wicked people are always occupied with such matters.

29 **The Lord is far from the wicked, and He hears the prayer of the righteous.** The same idea is expressed somewhat differently in the book of Psalms: The Lord is close to all who call Him, to all who call Him in truth.[237]

30 **Brightness of the eyes,** a pleasant countenance, **gladdens the heart.** Alternative interpretations: Seeing a precious item brings joy to the heart; one who is able to perceive the good in the world will thereby cause his heart to rejoice. **And good news fortifies**[238] **bones.**[B]

31 **An ear that heeds life's rebuke,** words of rebuke that are meaningful for life, even if the person himself is not wise and

BACKGROUND

15:19| **Thorns [*ḥedek*]:** A prickly plant, or a general term for thorns used in fences and for closing off breaches in barriers (see, e.g., Micah 7:4; Mishna *Eiruvin* 10:8). Some contend that this is a species of nightshade, *Solaum incanum*, which grows in the lower Jordan Valley and which is also called *ḥedek* in Arabic (Imanuel Löw, *Die Flora der Juden*. Band III, Pedaliaceae-Zygophyllaceae. Vienna and Leipzig: R. Löwit, 1924 [German], 376).

15:30| **And good news fortifies [*tedashen*] bones:** The word *tedashen* literally means fatten. It was an accepted idea in ancient times that fat people were healthier than thin people, as they were more resistant to the effects of the frequent droughts and famines that plagued the ancient world. Consequently, the portly body was a sign of health and success. The verse is speaking of the soul's effect on the body: Good news that breathes hope into a person can even improve his physical health, expressed here through the concept of fortified bones. The converse is also true: Despair and despondency are represented by dry bones (see 17:22; Ezekiel 37:11).

ו כָּל־גְּבַהּ־לֵב יָד לְיָד לֹא יִנָּקֶה׃ בְּחֶסֶד וֶאֱמֶת יְכֻפַּר עָוֺן וּבְיִרְאַת יהוה סוּר מֵרָע׃
ז ח בִּרְצוֹת יהוה דַּרְכֵי־אִישׁ גַּם־אוֹיְבָיו יַשְׁלִם אִתּוֹ׃ טוֹב מְעַט בִּצְדָקָה מֵרֹב תְּבוּאוֹת
ט י בְּלֹא מִשְׁפָּט׃ לֵב אָדָם יְחַשֵּׁב דַּרְכּוֹ וַיהוה יָכִין צַעֲדוֹ׃ קֶסֶם ׀ עַל־שִׂפְתֵי־מֶלֶךְ
יא בְּמִשְׁפָּט לֹא יִמְעַל־פִּיו׃ פֶּלֶס ׀ וּמֹאזְנֵי מִשְׁפָּט לַיהוה מַעֲשֵׂהוּ כָּל־אַבְנֵי־כִיס׃
יב יג תּוֹעֲבַת מְלָכִים עֲשׂוֹת רֶשַׁע כִּי בִצְדָקָה יִכּוֹן כִּסֵּא׃ רְצוֹן מְלָכִים שִׂפְתֵי־צֶדֶק וְדֹבֵר
יד טו יְשָׁרִים יֶאֱהָב׃ חֲמַת־מֶלֶךְ מַלְאֲכֵי־מָוֶת וְאִישׁ חָכָם יְכַפְּרֶנָּה׃ בְּאוֹר־פְּנֵי־מֶלֶךְ חַיִּים
טז וּרְצוֹנוֹ כְּעָב מַלְקוֹשׁ׃ קְנֹה־חָכְמָה מַה־טּוֹב מֵחָרוּץ וּקְנוֹת בִּינָה נִבְחָר מִכָּסֶף׃
יז יח מְסִלַּת יְשָׁרִים סוּר מֵרָע שֹׁמֵר נַפְשׁוֹ נֹצֵר דַּרְכּוֹ׃ לִפְנֵי־שֶׁבֶר גָּאוֹן וְלִפְנֵי כִשָּׁלוֹן
יט כ גֹּבַהּ רוּחַ׃ טוֹב שְׁפַל־רוּחַ אֶת־עניים מֵחַלֵּק שָׁלָל אֶת־גֵּאִים׃ מַשְׂכִּיל עַל־דָּבָר עֲנָוִים
כא יִמְצָא־טוֹב וּבוֹטֵחַ בַּיהוה אַשְׁרָיו׃ לַחֲכַם־לֵב יִקָּרֵא נָבוֹן וּמֶתֶק שְׂפָתַיִם יֹסִיף
כב כג לֶקַח׃ מְקוֹר חַיִּים שֵׂכֶל בְּעָלָיו וּמוּסַר אֱוִלִים אִוֶּלֶת׃ לֵב חָכָם יַשְׂכִּיל פִּיהוּ וְעַל־
כד כה שְׂפָתָיו יֹסִיף לֶקַח׃ צוּף־דְּבַשׁ אִמְרֵי־נֹעַם מָתוֹק לַנֶּפֶשׁ וּמַרְפֵּא לָעָצֶם׃ יֵשׁ דֶּרֶךְ

Wisdom and Refined Character Traits

PROVERBS 16:16–32

16 **How much better is the acquisition of wisdom than** the acquisition of **fine gold! And the acquisition of understanding is choicer than silver.**

17 **The way of the upright,** the essence of their path, **is turning from evil; the protector of his soul safeguards his way.**

18 **Pride goes before** and causes **destruction, and** likewise **a haughty spirit** comes **before a fall.** Even if it appears that someone is safely following the proper path, pride and haughtiness can lead him to disaster in one form or another.[253]

19 **Better to be lowly of spirit** together **with the humble than to divide spoils with the proud.**

20 **He who contemplates a matter will find goodness** in it, in the form of wisdom, understanding, innovation, or truth, **and he who trusts in the Lord, happy is he.**[254]

21 **The wisehearted,** one who is endowed with the ability to learn and comprehend, **is called discerning, and** someone who is gifted with **sweetness of lips,** who knows how to express himself precisely and how to please an audience, **will increase learning** for himself and others.[255]

22 **Intelligence is a fount of life,** which produces fruit **for its possessor, and the admonition of fools is folly.** Anything stated by fools, including their rebukes and attempts to teach others proper conduct, is simply foolishness.[256]

23 **The heart of the wise will make his mouth accomplished.** The wise are unevenly blessed in their oratorical talents, but their statements always emanate from the wisdom of their hearts, which give them knowledge and is the key to the success of their speeches. **And** the inner wisdom of the heart of the wise person **increases the learning on his lips.**

24 **Pleasant sayings are date honey: Sweet to the soul and a cure for the bone.**[B]

Dates and date honey

25 Sometimes **there is a way**

that seems right before a man, but he later discovers that **its end is the ways of death,** as it can lead to his demise.[257]

26 **The toiling soul toils against him, for his mouth has compelled him.** Some explain the verse as follows: One who is suffering has only himself to blame, as the statements of his own mouth have led to this outcome. If a person issues statements that are better left unsaid, he will become embroiled in others' problems and will eventually have to work hard in order to extricate himself from them.[258] Others interpret this verse in a positive manner: The spirit that toils to advance in his studies will acquire knowledge to such an extent that the material he has learned will become part of him.

27 **A wicked man,** an uninhibited individual who accepts no responsibilities, **digs up evil.** Whenever he speaks or acts, he attempts to dig traps in which he can ensnare others. **And on his lips is like a searing fire.** His words are painful and harmful.[259]

28 **A fickle man incites strife.** His instability, as he continuously transfers his allegiance from one person to the next and constantly alters his opinion from one extreme to the other, leads to quarrels, even when he is not personally involved. **And a grumbler,** who constantly complains and is critical of everything, **alienates friends.**[260]

29 **A man of villainy seduces his friend and leads him on a way that is not good,** even when he appears to provide him with sound advice.

30 **He who shuts his eyes,** exerting himself **to consider duplicity,** and **hints with his lips,** acting with cunning and trickery, will not stop with mere thoughts and hints, as eventually he will be found **completing the evil** acts that he has contemplated.[261]

31 **Gray hair is a crown of glory** for the elderly; **it will be found in the way of righteousness,** one who follows a righteous path. A person who lives a worthy life will merit this mark of distinction. People will observe him, learn from his actions, and speak his praises.

32 **He who is slow to anger is better than the mighty, and the ruler of his spirit,** one who refrains from erupting in rage, is better **than the capturer of a city.** The conquest of a city is a single victory, whereas one who seeks to control his spirit engages in a never-ending struggle.

Social Interactions, Family, and Character Traits

PROVERBS 16:33–22:16

33 **The lot is cast in the bosom,** individuals cast lots in private to determine their destiny, **and** yet in actuality, one's fate is not in human hands; rather, **all of one's judgment is from the Lord.** A person's destiny and future are determined by God alone.

17 1 The aphorisms in this passage deal primarily with human relations, both within and outside the family structure. **Dry,** plain **bread,** without any condiments,[262] **and** a life of **tranquility with it, is better than a house full of feasts of strife,**[D] a home where fancy meals are served but whose residents are constantly quarreling hatefully with each other.

2 This proverb also deals with the difference between what is outwardly visible and true reality: **A successful servant,** who loyally fulfills his responsibilities, **will rule over a shameful son,** who fails to fulfill his responsibilities. The dependable servant will eventually elevate himself to a higher status than the son, as the servant is the reliable one. **And** moreover, the servant **will share an inheritance among brothers.**[D] He will ultimately receive a portion of the family inheritance, whether officially or otherwise.[263]

3 **A refining pot is** the utensil used **for** purifying **silver, and a crucible** is **for** melting **gold.** Through these implements one can determine the metal's level of purity. **And the Lord is the tester of hearts.** One's heart can be evaluated only by God. He alone assesses an individual's level of purity and discerns any

DISCUSSION

17:1 | **Dry bread and tranquility with it is better than a house full of feasts of strife:** It would seem obvious that it is preferable to live a peaceful life in poverty than to live in a wealthy home that is full of arguments and upheavals. However, there are people who imagine that they can enjoy the feasts while avoiding the fights. Although that is always possible, it is still important to stress that it is not necessarily poverty that stands in the way of a happy, tranquil life, nor material wealth that guarantees such a life. There are houses that contain an abundance of material goodness without any actual satisfaction.

17:2 | **Will share an inheritance among brothers:** It has happened on more than one occasion in wealthy families that a laborer who lacked status, or even a slave, overcame all the rightful heirs to take over the family inheritance. An example of this is the Hasmonean family, toward the end of the Second Temple period, when the highly effective and successful slaves from the house of Herod managed to seize control of the throne, even though they were hardly righteous individuals.

כו יְשַׁר לִפְנֵי־אִישׁ וְאַחֲרִיתָהּ דַּרְכֵי־מָוֶת: נֶפֶשׁ עָמֵל עָמְלָה לּוֹ כִּי־אָכַף עָלָיו פִּיהוּ:
כז כח אִישׁ בְּלִיַּעַל כֹּרֶה רָעָה וְעַל־שפתיו כְּאֵשׁ צָרָבֶת: אִישׁ תַּהְפֻּכוֹת יְשַׁלַּח מָדוֹן שְׂפָתוֹ
כט ל וְנִרְגָּן מַפְרִיד אַלּוּף: אִישׁ חָמָס יְפַתֶּה רֵעֵהוּ וְהוֹלִיכוֹ בְּדֶרֶךְ לֹא־טוֹב: עֹצֶה עֵינָיו
לא לַחְשֹׁב תַּהְפֻּכוֹת קֹרֵץ שְׂפָתָיו כִּלָּה רָעָה: עֲטֶרֶת תִּפְאֶרֶת שֵׂיבָה בְּדֶרֶךְ צְדָקָה
לב לג תִּמָּצֵא: טוֹב אֶרֶךְ אַפַּיִם מִגִּבּוֹר וּמֹשֵׁל בְּרוּחוֹ מִלֹּכֵד עִיר: בַּחֵיק יוּטַל אֶת־הַגּוֹרָל
ז א ב וּמֵיהוה כָּל־מִשְׁפָּטוֹ: טוֹב פַּת חֲרֵבָה וְשַׁלְוָה־בָהּ מִבַּיִת מָלֵא זִבְחֵי־רִיב: עֶבֶד־
ג מַשְׂכִּיל יִמְשֹׁל בְּבֵן מֵבִישׁ וּבְתוֹךְ אַחִים יַחֲלֹק נַחֲלָה: מַצְרֵף לַכֶּסֶף וְכוּר לַזָּהָב
ד ה וּבֹחֵן לִבּוֹת יהוה: מֵרַע מַקְשִׁיב עַל־שְׂפַת־אָוֶן שֶׁקֶר מֵזִין עַל־לְשׁוֹן הַוֹּת: לֹעֵג
ו לָרָשׁ חֵרֵף עֹשֵׂהוּ שָׂמֵחַ לְאֵיד לֹא יִנָּקֶה: עֲטֶרֶת זְקֵנִים בְּנֵי בָנִים וְתִפְאֶרֶת בָּנִים
ז ח אֲבוֹתָם: לֹא־נָאוָה לְנָבָל שְׂפַת־יֶתֶר אַף כִּי־לְנָדִיב שְׂפַת־שָׁקֶר: אֶבֶן־חֵן הַשֹּׁחַד

Refining metals in a crucible

admixture of impure elements. Not even the person himself is always aware of his character deficiencies.[264]

4 **Evil listens to speech of iniquity; falsehood is nourished by a tongue of ruin.** This is not necessarily referring to an evil person; rather, evil in the abstract gives heed to the language of wickedness and of sin.[265] Evil and falsehood will be found in an environment that is characterized by offensive discourse. They listen to these exchanges, so to speak, and enjoy them.

5 **He who mocks the poor** for any reason, whether for his disheveled clothing or his miserable way of life, not only acts inappropriately in human terms, but he also **reviles his,** the poor person's, **Maker.** Neither the rich nor the poor created themselves or arranged their lot in life; both wealth and poverty are apportioned by heavenly calculations.[266] **He who rejoices at** the **calamity** of others **will not be absolved.** Even if such an individual is not subject to human retribution, God will ensure that he receives his fitting punishment.

6 **The crown,** the adornment and mark of honor, **of elders is grandchildren,** as they provide their grandparents with joy and honor. The grandchildren draw confidence from their grandparents, and the grandparents see their grandchildren as their successors. **And** meanwhile, **the glory of children is their fathers.** Children glory in the good reputation of their parents and grandparents, while the elders take pride in their grandchildren and their accomplishments.[267]

7 **Excessive speech is unbecoming in a scoundrel,** or one who is stingy. It is preferable for a miser to remain silent than to speak arrogantly, as his statements will not increase his honor. **More so** is **false speech** unbecoming **to the noble,** an honorable person, the opposite of a scoundrel.[268] Sometimes generous individuals exaggerate the extent of their generosity and even relate stories of their acts of kindness that are entirely false.

8 This proverb describes reality rather than offering instructive advice: **A bribe is a precious stone in the eyes of its possessor; wherever he turns, he will succeed.** Just as a precious stone is beautiful and decorative, so too a bribe is valuable in the eyes of its giver. One who is prepared to smooth his path through bribes thinks he will automatically succeed wherever he turns. Gates will be opened before him, and the law will be removed from his path, as though he had an amulet, a kind of a free entry pass.[269]

9 **He who obscures transgression,** whether intentionally or because he simply fails to perceive that the sinner has done anything wrong, does so because he **seeks love.** In his love for something or someone, he is uninterested in discerning and exposing the flaws of the object or person.[270] **And** by contrast, **he who repeats the thing,** and continuously refers to a transgression or flaw, **alienates** and creates divisiveness between himself and **a friend,** or an important minister.[271]

10 **The affliction of castigation for he who understands is more than striking a fool a hundred** lashes. Not even one hundred lashes will have an impact upon the fool, whereas it is enough to rebuke a man of understanding once. Teachers are well aware that a student's level of sensitivity is an important factor in his education.

11 **The evil man seeks only defiance,** or angry and bitter statements, **and a cruel messenger will** ultimately **be sent against him.**[272]

12 **Let a man meet a bereaved bear,**[B] a frightening and dangerous beast, **but not a fool in his folly.** An encounter with a dangerous animal is preferable to meeting someone who behaves foolishly, as such a person is likely to be even more dangerous. The fool does not necessarily act with evil intentions, but nevertheless he can draw a person into intractable difficulties.

Syrian brown bear

13 **He who repays good with evil,** his punishment is that **evil will not move from his house.** Troubles will constantly pursue him.

14 **The beginning of strife is like the release of water.** A quarrel often begins with a minor matter, before quickly developing into a broader fight, like the opening of a small dam. The uncontrollable rushing waters soon expand the opening further, until they sweep everything away. Likewise, a dispute can easily escalate out of control, **and** therefore **before the quarrel erupts, leave.** Since there are two sides to every squabble, if one party backs off at the right time, the argument will dissipate.

"Release of water." Opening the gates of a dam

15 **He who exonerates the wicked and he who condemns the righteous, both of them are an abomination to the Lord,** as God despises any plainly false judgment.

16 **Why is there payment in the hand of a fool to purchase wisdom, but there is no heart?** How will it help a fool to pay to study if he is incapable of understanding? The Sages interpret this verse in reference to individuals who possess Torah knowledge but have no fear of Heaven.[273]

17 **The friend loves at all times.** A true friend loves a person regardless of his situation. One who is friendly toward another only when that person is successful is not a real friend. **And a brother is born for adversity.** In times of trouble, one realizes who truly acts as a brother, as worthless friends and acquaintances scatter and abruptly disappear.

18 **A man lacking heart,** common sense, **shakes hands,** making promises and accepting commitments, and serves as **guarantor of a guarantee before his friend.** Unless absolutely necessary, it is not recommended to serve as guarantor for another, to avoid becoming enmeshed in superfluous problems. This piece of advice recurs many times in the book of Proverbs (see 6:1, 11:15, 20:16, 22:26, 27:13).

19 **He who loves transgression loves strife.** One who enjoys quarreling in effect loves sin, as strife invariably leads to undesirable consequences.[274] **He who elevates his entrance,** choosing to be inaccessible, **seeks destruction.** Sometimes important people make it difficult for others to get close to them, but when they themselves encounter troubles, it becomes clear that they have lost their friends. Ultimately, people who are always quarreling, as well as those who endeavor to avoid any contact with others, will not receive help in their time of need.

20 **The crooked of heart,** one whose intellect is warped, **will not find goodness, and the duplicitous of tongue,** who speaks

BACKGROUND

17:12| **A bereaved bear:** The Syrian brown bear, *Ursus arctos syriacus*, was common in the thick forests that covered Israel up to the nineteenth century. The length of its body reaches 2 m and its height 1.85 m, and it can weigh up to 200 kg. The bear is used in the Bible as a symbol of danger, rage, and cruelty (I Samuel 17:34–35; II Kings 2:24; Hosea 13:8; Amos 5:19). The expression "a bereaved bear," which appears several times in the Bible, refers to a bear that has lost its offspring and in its pain will attack furiously.

ט בְּעֵינֵי בְעָלָיו אֶל־כָּל־אֲשֶׁר יִפְנֶה יַשְׂכִּיל: מְכַסֶּה־פֶּשַׁע מְבַקֵּשׁ אַהֲבָה וְשֹׁנֶה בְדָבָר
י יא מַפְרִיד אַלּוּף: תֵּחַת גְּעָרָה בְמֵבִין מֵהַכּוֹת כְּסִיל מֵאָה: אַךְ־מְרִי יְבַקֶּשׁ־רָע וּמַלְאָךְ
יב יג אַכְזָרִי יְשֻׁלַּח־בּוֹ: פָּגוֹשׁ דֹּב שַׁכּוּל בְּאִישׁ וְאַל־כְּסִיל בְּאִוַּלְתּוֹ: מֵשִׁיב רָעָה תַּחַת
יד טוֹבָה לֹא־תָמִישׁ רָעָה מִבֵּיתוֹ: פּוֹטֵר מַיִם רֵאשִׁית מָדוֹן וְלִפְנֵי הִתְגַּלַּע הָרִיב תָּמוּשׁ
טו טז נְטוֹשׁ: מַצְדִּיק רָשָׁע וּמַרְשִׁיעַ צַדִּיק תּוֹעֲבַת יהוה גַּם־שְׁנֵיהֶם: לָמָּה־זֶּה מְחִיר
יז יח בְּיַד־כְּסִיל לִקְנוֹת חָכְמָה וְלֶב־אָיִן: בְּכָל־עֵת אֹהֵב הָרֵעַ וְאָח לְצָרָה יִוָּלֵד: אָדָם
יט חֲסַר־לֵב תּוֹקֵעַ כָּף עֹרֵב עֲרֻבָּה לִפְנֵי רֵעֵהוּ: אֹהֵב פֶּשַׁע אֹהֵב מַצָּה מַגְבִּיהַּ פִּתְחוֹ
כ כא מְבַקֶּשׁ־שָׁבֶר: עִקֶּשׁ־לֵב לֹא יִמְצָא־טוֹב וְנֶהְפָּךְ בִּלְשׁוֹנוֹ יִפּוֹל בְּרָעָה: יֹלֵד כְּסִיל
כב לְתוּגָה לוֹ וְלֹא־יִשְׂמַח אֲבִי נָבָל: לֵב שָׂמֵחַ יֵיטִב גֵּהָה וְרוּחַ נְכֵאָה תְּיַבֶּשׁ־גָּרֶם:
כג שֹׁחַד מֵחֵק רָשָׁע יִקָּח לְהַטּוֹת אָרְחוֹת מִשְׁפָּט:
כד כה אֶת־פְּנֵי מֵבִין חָכְמָה וְעֵינֵי כְסִיל בִּקְצֵה־אָרֶץ: כַּעַס לְאָבִיו בֵּן כְּסִיל וּמֶמֶר
כו כז לְיוֹלַדְתּוֹ: גַּם עֲנוֹשׁ לַצַּדִּיק לֹא־טוֹב לְהַכּוֹת נְדִיבִים עֲלֵי־יֹשֶׁר: חוֹשֵׂךְ אֲמָרָיו

deceptively and inconsistently, **will fall into harm.** Sometimes it seems that it is easier to get ahead using falsehood and flattery, but an unreliable person will ultimately stumble.

21 The aphorist adds a disheartening comment: **The begetter of a fool, it is sorrow for him,** as his son will provide him with nothing but anguish, **and the father of a scoundrel will not rejoice.** The father of a miserly and wicked person can only sigh in despair.

22 **A joyous heart will improve healing,** accelerating one's recovery from illness, as joy itself improves one's health. **And** by contrast, **a depressed spirit** of sadness and gloom **dries bones.** Joy and sadness are not only abstract emotions; they physically affect the body's health and appearance.[275]

23 **A bribe from the bosom of the wicked is taken** by a judge or another official **to pervert the paths of justice.** A bribe is always donated by the wicked or by one whose claim does not deserve a favorable judgment.[276] Even in places where it is common to give a bribe and it is not thought of as a bribe but rather as an expression of friendship or a mark of gratitude, it is designed for the same purpose, to diverge from the path of honesty and justice.

24 **Wisdom is** found **in front of the understanding.** A person of insight will discover wisdom in his own vicinity. **And the eyes of a fool are** always focused **at the ends of the earth.** He goes off to search for wisdom in the far-flung corners of the world.[277]

25 This verse also deals with the damage caused by foolishness: **A foolish son is** a cause of **vexation to his father, and bitterness,** or rebellion, **to the one who bore him,** his mother.[278]

26 **Surely punishment is not good for the righteous,** it is not good when the righteous are punished,[279] **striking the noble despite their uprightness.** It is inadvisable for a king to punish the righteous, even if on occasion they do not heed his royal instructions. Alternatively, it is unfortunate that social arrangements sometimes require the noble and righteous to endure suffering without any protection. Another interpretation of the first part of the verse is that it is not good for the righteous to mete out punishment to others.[280]

27 **He who spares his sayings** thereby indicates that he **knows knowledge.** Those who know much do not speak a lot. In contrast, one who talks about every subject is not necessarily well informed, and it is likely that his knowledge is minimal. **And a man of sagacity is** gentle and **noble of spirit.** He treats his words as precious and does not speak at length.[281]

28 **Even a fool, being silent, is considered wise.**[D] When a fool refrains from prattling away to others, they will think that he is wise. **And he who seals his lips** is esteemed as **discerning.**

18 1 **The** individual who is unconcerned about breaking social norms and possibly becoming **isolated** from society **will seek** the **satisfaction of** every **craving; with all resourcefulness he will be exposed.** The insight or advice of a wise man will eventually expose that individual's true actions and intentions. Some interpret the first clause as follows: One who pursues his own desires will ultimately separate himself from his friends and his Creator, or, alternatively, the pursuit of desire is inherently self-centered.

2 More on fools and the wicked, and wise men and the righteous: When **a fool** speaks, he **does not desire sagacity, but only the revealing of his heart,** self-expression. The urge to verbalize one's thoughts and feelings does not necessarily lead to the disclosure of wise or beneficial ideas.

3 **With the coming of the wicked** to a specific place **comes also contempt** for those surrounding him; **and with disgrace** that the wicked bring, there is also **disrepute** to others.[282]

4 **The words of a** wise **man's mouth are deep waters,** while the man himself is like **a flowing stream, a fount of wisdom.** People who speak wisely keep revealing profound and refreshing ideas, which would not otherwise have been understood.[283]

"A flowing stream." Tzipori Stream

5 **Favoring the wicked** in judgment **is no good,** both because one is thereby vindicating the wicked and because one is **distorting the righteous in judgment.** When righteous and wicked individuals are engaged in a dispute, it is sometimes easier to help the wicked and thereby prevent disturbances. However, bias toward the wicked is wrong and will ultimately lead to punishment.

6 **The lips of a fool come with quarreling.** Even when a fool lacks evil intentions, his statements lead to quarrels, either due to his manner of speech or because of his foolishness. **And** likewise, **his mouth invites blows.** His comments lead to disputes and fights.[284]

7 **A fool's mouth is ruin for him, and his lips are a snare for his soul,** as time and again he finds himself trapped by his own statements.

8 The aphorist now analyzes various character traits: **The words of a grumbler,** or an instigator, **are like blows,** harmful to others. One who wishes to besmirch people is critical of everything and everyone. **And** although his comments appear to be unimportant and easily disregarded, in actual fact **they descend into the chambers of the belly** and do upset people. This is not always noticeable, as such a person is considered a negative influence whom people try to ignore, but nevertheless his insults can indeed strike deep into the heart.[285]

9 **Even he who is lax in his work is brother,** similar, **to a master of destruction.** One who shirks his responsibilities will at times cause as much damage as one who actively destroys. A destroyer breaks things, while one who slacks off causes them to be broken, and thus from the perceptive of the end result, the two are akin.

10 **The name of the Lord is** like **a tower of strength; by it the righteous will run** confidently, without stumbling blocks or delays, **and be exalted.** Righteous individuals will be protected and strengthened by the name of God, to whom they cleave.[286]

11 In contrast to the security of the righteous, **the wealth of the rich is his fortified city, and** it is **like a high wall** built **in his** decorated **chamber,** or his treasuries. The wealthy think that they are protected by the power of their money.[287]

12 **Before destruction a man's heart grows haughty, and before honor, humility.** Haughtiness generally comes before destruction, and conversely, humility is followed by honor. When someone acts with authentic humility, he is likely to receive honor, as true honor pursues one who is not interested in it and is not overjoyed to receive it.[288]

13 **He who responds before he hears** the second side, as he believes that he already knows what the other person will say, **it is folly for him and humiliation,** as perhaps he is mistaken about what his interlocutor intended to say.

14 **The spirit** of confidence and joy **of a man will sustain him,** his body, **in his illness,** and he will endure;[289] **but a depressed spirit, who can bear it?** Who can bear prolonged sadness, gloominess, and depression? Even if such moods do not lead to immediate crises, they make life too difficult to tolerate. One's

DISCUSSION

17:28 | **Even a fool, being silent, is considered wise:** As the Sages state: Silence is fitting for the wise, and even more so for fools (*Pesaḥim* 99b). For fools, silence is vital. One who discovers that he was not born wise can study, but as he cannot change his nature entirely, it is best for him to pay attention to the counsel of the wise and at least refrain from publicizing his stupidity. Often, however, a dullard errs in his self-estimation. It is sound advice to teach a student or son of limited intelligence to choose silence and listen to others instead of always voicing his uninformed opinion.

כח יוֹדֵעַ דָּעַת וקר־רוּחַ אִישׁ תְּבוּנָה׃ גַּם אֱוִיל מַחֲרִישׁ חָכָם יֵחָשֵׁב אֹטֵם שְׂפָתָיו יְקַר־
ח א ב נָבוֹן׃ לְתַאֲוָה יְבַקֵּשׁ נִפְרָד בְּכָל־תּוּשִׁיָּה יִתְגַּלָּע׃ לֹא־יַחְפֹּץ כְּסִיל בִּתְבוּנָה כִּי
ג ד אִם־בְּהִתְגַּלּוֹת לִבּוֹ׃ בְּבוֹא־רָשָׁע בָּא גַם־בּוּז וְעִם־קָלוֹן חֶרְפָּה׃ מַיִם עֲמֻקִּים
ה דִּבְרֵי פִי־אִישׁ נַחַל נֹבֵעַ מְקוֹר חָכְמָה׃ שְׂאֵת פְּנֵי־רָשָׁע לֹא־טוֹב לְהַטּוֹת צַדִּיק
ו ז בַּמִּשְׁפָּט׃ שִׂפְתֵי כְסִיל יָבֹאוּ בְרִיב וּפִיו לְמַהֲלֻמוֹת יִקְרָא׃ פִּי־כְסִיל מְחִתָּה־לוֹ
ח ט וּשְׂפָתָיו מוֹקֵשׁ נַפְשׁוֹ׃ דִּבְרֵי נִרְגָּן כְּמִתְלַהֲמִים וְהֵם יָרְדוּ חַדְרֵי־בָטֶן׃ גַּם מִתְרַפֶּה
י בִמְלַאכְתּוֹ אָח הוּא לְבַעַל מַשְׁחִית׃ מִגְדַּל־עֹז שֵׁם יְהוָה בּוֹ־יָרוּץ צַדִּיק וְנִשְׂגָּב׃ ה
יא יב הוֹן עָשִׁיר קִרְיַת עֻזּוֹ וּכְחוֹמָה נִשְׂגָּבָה בְּמַשְׂכִּיתוֹ׃ לִפְנֵי־שֶׁבֶר יִגְבַּהּ לֵב־אִישׁ וְלִפְנֵי
יג יד כָבוֹד עֲנָוָה׃ מֵשִׁיב דָּבָר בְּטֶרֶם יִשְׁמָע אִוֶּלֶת הִיא־לוֹ וּכְלִמָּה׃ רוּחַ־אִישׁ יְכַלְכֵּל
טו מַחֲלֵהוּ וְרוּחַ נְכֵאָה מִי יִשָּׂאֶנָּה׃ לֵב נָבוֹן יִקְנֶה־דָּעַת וְאֹזֶן חֲכָמִים תְּבַקֶּשׁ־דָּעַת׃
טז יז מַתָּן אָדָם יַרְחִיב לוֹ וְלִפְנֵי גְדֹלִים יַנְחֶנּוּ׃ צַדִּיק הָרִאשׁוֹן בְּרִיבוֹ יבא־רֵעֵהוּ וַחֲקָרוֹ׃ וּבָא־
יח יט מִדְיָנִים יַשְׁבִּית הַגּוֹרָל וּבֵין עֲצוּמִים יַפְרִיד׃ אָח נִפְשָׁע מִקִּרְיַת־עֹז ומדונים כִּבְרִיחַ וּמִדְיָנִים

mood can have a great effect on one's material reality, including his physical well-being, for better or worse.

15 **The discerning heart** is not satisfied only with what he already knows; rather, he **will** continuously **acquire** more **knowledge. And the ear of the wise** does not suffice with the wisdom he has acquired; rather, he persistently **seeks** to earn more **knowledge.**

16 **A man's giving** to others, in any form, **expands** and provides benefit for **him and will guide him before the great.** Society grants prominence to those who support its goals.

17 The aphorist now discusses disputes and adjudication: When two individuals appear for judgment, **the** one who presents his side **first seems righteous in his case, and then his counterpart comes and interrogates him.** Both with regard to a children's quarrel, or a dispute in court between adults, the one who presents his version of events first often sounds correct, until his statements are critiqued or refuted by the other side. However, even when the second party gets the chance to present his own case, it is sometimes difficult for him to change the picture that has already been etched into the judge's consciousness.[290]

18 **Casting lots may quiet contentions and** by contrast, the lot sometimes **may estrange disputants.** According to some commentaries, this means that casting a lot can either enable disputing parties to resolve their quarrel, or it may cause the two sides to decide that they are unable to live together.[291] However, most commentaries maintain that the second clause is also referring to a positive separation between the litigants, upon the resolution of their dispute.

19 **A treacherous brother is worse than a fortified city.** Alternatively, the power of a negligent brother, a traitor, can shatter even a strong city. **And** his **strife is** strong, **like the bars of a** large gate of **a palace** that is locked before the quarreling parties.[292] Some explain this clause as saying that their contentions are similar to a bar whose removal opens the castle gates to the enemy.

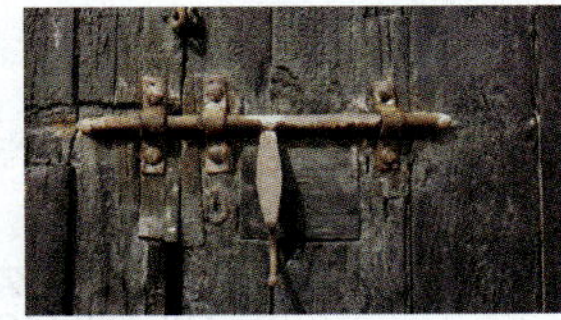
Bar to lock a gate

20 This aphorist cites two more statements involving speech and human interactions: **From the fruit of a man's mouth his belly will be satisfied,** he can profit from his positive speech, and **with the produce of his lips he will be satisfied.** He will bear the consequences of whatever emerges from his mouth. The tongue has tremendous power, for both good and evil.

21 **Death and life are in the power of the tongue, and those who love it,** the tongue, who guard it and use it appropriately,[293] **will eat its fruit.**

22 **He who has found a wife has found goodness and,** moreover, he **elicits favor from the Lord.** Some actions are considered pleasant by humans alone, but finding a wife is viewed pleasing both to the man and to God.[294]

23 **A poor person speaks** regularly with **supplications,** as he cannot offer anything substantial in return for favors, **and a rich one responds with impudence,** with regard to both issues that pertain to him and those matters that are not connected to him at all.[295]

24 **A friendly man is fragile.** One who makes many friends easily is likely to end up hurt. Having too many friends does not help a person, but rather consumes his time and energy. **But there is** a single **loved one who is closer than a brother.**[296]

19 1 **Better a poor man walking honestly than one of crooked lips who is a fool.** One who speaks in a perverse manner is essentially a fool.[297]

2 **Without knowledge, even the soul is no good.** One who lacks knowledge is bereft of a good soul as well, whereas someone who guides his conduct through wisdom has a worthy soul. Alternatively, actions performed without knowledge are not beneficial for the soul, or the verse is saying that it is not good to be unfamiliar with the nature of one's soul. **And he who hastens with his feet,** without knowing where and why he is running, in effect **sins,** as one should act only after careful consideration of all relevant factors.[298]

3 **The folly of man will distort his way, and** eventually when he stumbles, **his heart will rage against the Lord.** Sometimes people err or sin intentionally and thereby cause their own downfall, or they are simply unsuccessful, but instead of accepting the blame themselves, they cast aspersions upon God.[299]

4 **Wealth will add many friends,** as many people seek a close relationship with a wealthy individual, **but the impoverished is separated from his friend,** as he finds himself abandoned by all his acquaintances.

5 **A false witness will** ultimately **not be absolved, and** even **he who utters** and spreads **lies will not escape.**

6 It was stated above that many people seek to become friends with the wealthy (verse 4). This verse speaks of one who is not only wealthy but is also known to be generous: **Many will** endeavor to have a face-to-face meeting so that they can **court the presence of the generous one, and all are friendly to a man of gifts,** who is known to give gifts to others.

7 In contrast, **all the brethren of the poor** man, who actually requires assistance, **hate him; certainly his friends disengage from him. He pursues assurances that are for him.**[D] He seeks promises and assurances from others, and sometimes invents assurances that he has supposedly received. Alternatively, the latter clause means that people fabricate negative comments, which they attribute to the poor in order to justify keeping their distance from them. This interpretation is based on the word *lo* as it is written, *lamed-alef,* which means "no." There is a Masoretic note indicating that although the word should be written this way, it should be read as though it was written *lamed-vav,* in which case it means "him" and refers to the poor man, in accordance with the previously mentioned interpretations.

8 **He who acquires a heart,** wisdom, is someone who **loves himself** and pursues what is good for himself. **He who awaits** and desires **sagacity will** cause himself to **find good.**

9 **A false witness will not be absolved.** This was already stated above (verse 5), but the continuation here is even more severe: **And he who utters lies will** not only fail to escape punishment, as stated there, but he will actually **perish.**

10 **Pleasure is unbecoming for a fool.** A fool who lives a life of opulence feels like he is a supreme ruler, which is an

DISCUSSION

19:7 | **He pursues assurances that are for him:** It should be noted that the third clause in this verse is quite unusual for the book of Proverbs, whose verses generally contain only two parallel clauses. It is possible to read this last clause as connected to the following verse and to interpret it to mean: One who pursues words will acquire them but nothing else, but one who acquires a heart, meaning wisdom, loves himself.

BACKGROUND

19:12 | **Like a lion's roar:** A lion generally roars when it must defend its territory and that of its pride. Its powerful roar can be heard from a distance of up to 8 km.

Dew: Dew is the condensation of atmospheric moisture in the air, generated by humid conditions or low temperatures. It generally appears on cold surfaces, such as stones and leaves. Dew adds moisture and freshness to vegetation, and it is indirectly beneficial to the animals that later consume the produce.

אַרְמוֹן: מִפְּרִי פִי־אִישׁ תִּשְׂבַּע בִּטְנוֹ תְּבוּאַת שְׂפָתָיו יִשְׂבָּע: מָוֶת וְחַיִּים בְּיַד־ כ כא
לָשׁוֹן וְאֹהֲבֶיהָ יֹאכַל פִּרְיָהּ: מָצָא אִשָּׁה מָצָא טוֹב וַיָּפֶק רָצוֹן מֵיְהוָה: תַּחֲנוּנִים כב כג
יְדַבֶּר־רָשׁ וְעָשִׁיר יַעֲנֶה עַזּוֹת: אִישׁ רֵעִים לְהִתְרֹעֵעַ וְיֵשׁ אֹהֵב דָּבֵק מֵאָח: טוֹב כד יט א
רָשׁ הוֹלֵךְ בְּתֻמּוֹ מֵעִקֵּשׁ שְׂפָתָיו וְהוּא כְסִיל: גַּם בְּלֹא־דַעַת נֶפֶשׁ לֹא־טוֹב וְאָץ ב
בְּרַגְלַיִם חוֹטֵא: אִוֶּלֶת אָדָם תְּסַלֵּף דַּרְכּוֹ וְעַל־יְהוָה יִזְעַף לִבּוֹ: הוֹן יֹסִיף רֵעִים ג ד
רַבִּים וְדָל מֵרֵעֵהוּ יִפָּרֵד: עֵד שְׁקָרִים לֹא יִנָּקֶה וְיָפִיחַ כְּזָבִים לֹא יִמָּלֵט: רַבִּים ה ו
יְחַלּוּ פְנֵי־נָדִיב וְכָל־הָרֵעַ לְאִישׁ מַתָּן: כָּל אֲחֵי־רָשׁ ׀ שְׂנֵאֻהוּ אַף כִּי מְרֵעֵהוּ רָחֲקוּ ז
לוֹ־ מִמֶּנּוּ מְרַדֵּף אֲמָרִים לא־הֵמָּה: קֹנֶה־לֵּב אֹהֵב נַפְשׁוֹ שֹׁמֵר תְּבוּנָה לִמְצֹא־טוֹב: ח
עֵד שְׁקָרִים לֹא יִנָּקֶה וְיָפִיחַ כְּזָבִים יֹאבֵד: ט
לֹא־נָאוֶה לִכְסִיל תַּעֲנוּג אַף כִּי־לְעֶבֶד ׀ מְשֹׁל בְּשָׂרִים: שֵׂכֶל אָדָם הֶאֱרִיךְ אַפּוֹ י יא
וְתִפְאַרְתּוֹ עֲבֹר עַל־פָּשַׁע: נַהַם כַּכְּפִיר זַעַף מֶלֶךְ וּכְטַל עַל־עֵשֶׂב רְצוֹנוֹ: הַוֺּת יב יג
לְאָבִיו בֵּן כְּסִיל וְדֶלֶף טֹרֵד מִדְיְנֵי אִשָּׁה: בַּיִת וָהוֹן נַחֲלַת אָבוֹת וּמֵיְהוָה אִשָּׁה יד
מַשְׂכָּלֶת: עַצְלָה תַּפִּיל תַּרְדֵּמָה וְנֶפֶשׁ רְמִיָּה תִרְעָב: שֹׁמֵר מִצְוָה שֹׁמֵר נַפְשׁוֹ טו טז

undesirable state of affairs. It is **certainly** not appropriate or recommended **for a servant to** be elevated to a status where he will **rule over princes** and other dignitaries.[300]

11 **A man's sense slows his anger.** One's intellect teaches him to be slow to anger, control his temper, and refrain from erupting in rage. **And his glory is** in his **overlooking transgression.** It is unwise to be particular with others, to get involved in frequent quarrels, or regularly become angry.

12 **A king's wrath is like a** threatening **lion's roar,**[B] **and** by contrast, **his favor is like dew**[B] **on grass,** which causes it to sprout. Whereas the anger of a king is often dangerous, his favor can be most beneficial.[301]

"Dew on grass"

13 **A foolish son is a calamity to his father, and the contentions of a wife are an annoying drip.** Although spousal quarrels and a wife's criticisms and complaints may not be the worst calamity, they can still cause a husband to go out of his mind.

Drip

14 **House and wealth are** received by a person as **the inheritance of** his **fathers, but a capable** and wise **wife is** a gift **from the Lord,** and cannot be bequeathed by one's father. The husband must therefore recognize and appreciate that he has received his wife from God, and he should express his gratitude to Him.[302]

15 **Sloth casts a deep sleep.** One who is lazy will ultimately grow tired and fall asleep, **and the deceitful soul,** someone who spends his time scheming instead of working, **will hunger.**

16 **He who keeps a commandment** thereby **protects his soul, and he who scorns His ways** and follows the desires of his own heart **will die** for his sin.

17 **He who cares for the poor,** by giving him gifts, is considered as though he **lends to the Lord,** as he has thereby fulfilled God's responsibility, as it were. **And** therefore **He will pay his reward.**[303] God will repay the loan by giving him reward.

18 **Admonish your son, as there is hope.** Rebuking and disciplining one's son, even by striking him, can help improve his behavior,[304] **and** you should do so very cautiously, and **do not set yourself to causing his death.** You must refrain from overly severe punishments that might kill him or squelch his spirit.[305]

19 On the contrary, **a person of great wrath is subject to punishment.** Outbursts of anger do not resolve a problem but simply have negative consequences for the one who becomes angry. **Rather,** instead of becoming furious over what has been lost, **deliver,** save what may still be salvaged, **and add more** assistance for those who truly require it. Alternatively, if you save your enemy in his time of trouble, you will merit an increase of days and goodness.[306]

20 **Hear counsel and accept admonishment, so that you will become wise by your end.** Even if you fail to internalize the advice immediately, it will eventually make you wiser. Therefore, it is appropriate to view in a positive light those who critique or admonish you.[307]

21 **Many are the thoughts** and plans **in the heart of a man, but** ultimately **it is the counsel of the Lord that will stand.** Some explain that one should seek out and attempt to identify the counsel of God, which is actually present within one's heart among his many other thoughts.[308]

22 **A person's craving should be his kindness.** One should crave to perform acts of kindness, as one should desire to help others. Alternatively, the kindnesses one performs attract the admiration of others and cause them to desire his company.[309] **And better** to be **a poor man,** despite one's miserable fate, **than a man of deceit.**

23 **The fear of the Lord leads to life, and he will lodge in satisfaction; he will not be visited by evil.**[D]

24 **The idler inserts his hand into the dish [*tzalaḥat*]**[310] **and will not even return it to his mouth.** He is so lazy that he cannot even muster sufficient strength to bring his hand to his mouth. An indolent person begins a task but fails to complete it, even in order to provide for his own needs, and consequently he will remain hungry and needy. Other commentaries interpret *tzalaḥat* as a type of pocket.[311] If so, the verse means that one who is slothful effectively buries his hand in his pocket and therefore will not have any food to put in his mouth.

25 **Strike the scoffer,** who is arrogant and acts inappropriately, **and the naïf will become clever** and wise. The scoffer himself is always confident that he is in the right, and therefore he will learn nothing from being struck. However, the naïf, who does not understand much and therefore does not arouse enmity and so is not beaten like the scoffer, will learn something when he observes the scoffer being struck. **If you rebuke the discerning, he will achieve knowledge** and benefit from the rebuke and criticism he has received.

26 **He who robs,** or tramples upon, **his father will** also **drive away his mother** from the house, even if the son does nothing to her directly. Such is **a shameful, disreputable son.** A child must honor his parents even when they are not perfect and he has reason to answer back, as this preserves the stability of the home.

27 **Cease, my son, from hearing admonition in order to,** if you wish to, **deviate from sayings of knowledge.** If one fails to listen to good advice or hear rebuke, he will ultimately stray from a balanced path. Alternatively, there is no benefit to hearing instruction if one does not intend to act accordingly.

28 **A wicked witness will scoff at justice,** which he portrays as evil, **and the mouth of the wicked will swallow,** or conceal, **iniquity.**

29 **Punishments are prepared for scoffers,**[D] who live in a carefree, self-confident manner, **and blows** are prepared **for the back of fools.**

DISCUSSION

19:23 | **And he will lodge in satisfaction; he will not be visited by evil:** The second part of this verse can be interpreted as a separate idea, unrelated to the fear of God: Even one who cannot afford to buy things for himself is advised to go to bed satisfied, so that he will benefit from a comfortable night's sleep. The Sages state with regard to this verse: Evil tidings will not be delivered to whomever fills himself with Torah. Perhaps the Sages sought, through this interpretation, to link the two sections of the verse together (see *Berakhot* 14b, and Maharsha ad loc.).

19:29 | **Punishments are prepared for scoffers:** In the bustle of everyday life, many people are occupied solely with the present, but the wise reflect on matters from a distance, and therefore they can discern who will ultimately stumble and suffer. Similarly, people prefer to continue along their chosen paths, as they do not like to hear rebuke and criticism, and certainly no one enjoys punishments. However, one who considers life from a broad perspective will realize that reproof is beneficial and increases one's knowledge.

יז יח בּוֹזֵה דְרָכָיו יומת׃ מַלְוֵה יְהוָה חוֹנֵן דָּל וּגְמֻלוֹ יְשַׁלֶּם־לוֹ׃ יַסֵּר בִּנְךָ כִּי־יֵשׁ תִּקְוָה — יָמוּת
יט וְאֶל־הֲמִיתוֹ אַל־תִּשָּׂא נַפְשֶׁךָ׃ גרל־חֵמָה נֹשֵׂא עֹנֶשׁ כִּי אִם־תַּצִּיל וְעוֹד תּוֹסִף׃ — גְּדָל־
כ כא שְׁמַע עֵצָה וְקַבֵּל מוּסָר לְמַעַן תֶּחְכַּם בְּאַחֲרִיתֶךָ׃ רַבּוֹת מַחֲשָׁבוֹת בְּלֶב־אִישׁ
כב כג וַעֲצַת יְהוָה הִיא תָקוּם׃ תַּאֲוַת אָדָם חַסְדּוֹ וְטוֹב־רָשׁ מֵאִישׁ כָּזָב׃ יִרְאַת יְהוָה
כד לְחַיִּים וְשָׂבֵעַ יָלִין בַּל־יִפָּקֶד רָע׃ טָמַן עָצֵל יָדוֹ בַּצַּלָּחַת גַּם־אֶל־פִּיהוּ לֹא יְשִׁיבֶנָּה׃
כה כו לֵץ תַּכֶּה וּפֶתִי יַעְרִם וְהוֹכִיחַ לְנָבוֹן יָבִין דָּעַת׃ מְשַׁדֶּד־אָב יַבְרִיחַ אֵם בֵּן מֵבִישׁ
כז כח וּמַחְפִּיר׃ חֲדַל־בְּנִי לִשְׁמֹעַ מוּסָר לִשְׁגוֹת מֵאִמְרֵי־דָעַת׃ עֵד בְּלִיַּעַל יָלִיץ מִשְׁפָּט
כט כ א וּפִי רְשָׁעִים יְבַלַּע־אָוֶן׃ נָכוֹנוּ לַלֵּצִים שְׁפָטִים וּמַהֲלֻמוֹת לְגֵו כְּסִילִים׃ לֵץ הַיַּיִן
ב הֹמֶה שֵׁכָר וְכָל־שֹׁגֶה בּוֹ לֹא יֶחְכָּם׃ נַהַם כַּכְּפִיר אֵימַת מֶלֶךְ מִתְעַבְּרוֹ חוֹטֵא
ג ד נַפְשׁוֹ׃ כָּבוֹד לָאִישׁ שֶׁבֶת מֵרִיב וְכָל־אֱוִיל יִתְגַּלָּע׃ מֵחֹרֶף עָצֵל לֹא־יַחֲרֹשׁ ישאל — וְשָׁאַל
ה ו בַקָּצִיר וָאָיִן׃ מַיִם עֲמֻקִּים עֵצָה בְלֶב־אִישׁ וְאִישׁ תְּבוּנָה יִדְלֶנָּה׃ רָב־אָדָם יִקְרָא
ז אִישׁ חַסְדּוֹ וְאִישׁ אֱמוּנִים מִי יִמְצָא׃ מִתְהַלֵּךְ בְּתֻמּוֹ צַדִּיק אַשְׁרֵי בָנָיו אַחֲרָיו׃
ח ט מֶלֶךְ יוֹשֵׁב עַל־כִּסֵּא־דִין מְזָרֶה בְעֵינָיו כָּל־רָע׃ מִי־יֹאמַר זִכִּיתִי לִבִּי טָהַרְתִּי

20

1 **Wine is** like **a scoffer,** as it causes inconsistency, a lack of serious behavior, and a general lack of discipline.[312] **Strong drink is tumultuous** inside the body of the drinker, **and any** who is **misled,** tempted, **by it will not become wise.** The excessive consumption of alcohol will decrease one's knowledge; therefore, one should limit his intake.

2 **A king's wrath is a roar like the lion; he who provokes him,** the king, **forfeits his life.**

3 **Refraining from a quarrel is honor for a man.** One who refrains from quarrels thereby demonstrates his dignity. **And every fool will be exposed,** as fools are drawn into any argument.

4 **From the winter, the idler will not plow; he will ask** for produce **at harvest, and there is nothing.** One who has not toiled during the winter months cannot expect to receive any crop yield in the summer.

5 **Counsel in the heart of a man is** latent like **deep water;** therefore, it is sometimes insufficiently clear or known even to oneself. **And a man of sagacity,** who converses with that individual, **will draw it out** through questioning, listening, and reflection.

6 **One may call many a person his man of grace,** whether by relating that the person assisted him or that he is anticipating a favor from him, **but who can find a reliable man?** It is rare to find a truly dependable ally.[313] Alternatively, the verse may be translated to mean that many people present themselves as men of grace, but it is difficult to find someone who is fully reliable in his portrayal of his own deeds.[314]

7 **He who walks honestly,** and acts only with pure motives, **is a righteous man.**[315] **Happy are his children after him,** as they are directly influenced by him, and they also benefit from his fine reputation.[316]

8 When **a king** is **sitting on the throne of judgment,** he discerns and **scatters with his eyes all evil.**

9 Some individuals are relatively pure spiritually, others are less so, but **who can say: I have cleansed my heart, I am purified from sin?** No one is ever entirely free of transgression.

10 One who holds **differing weights,** one heavier than the other, **and differing measures,**[D] one of which is bigger than the other, in order to use one to measure merchandise that he is selling and the other to measure merchandise that he is buying, **both of them are an abomination to the Lord.**

11 **Even a lad is recognized through his deeds** and antics, which indicate **if his action is pure or upright.** It stands to reason that a child's current conduct is often a good indicator of his future behavior over the course of his life, as it is unlikely that his personality will change significantly.

12 **A hearing ear and a seeing eye, the Lord made them both,** and He certainly is aware of, and supervises, all that occurs.

13 **Do not love sleep, lest you become impoverished. Open your eyes,** be alert and active, and then **you will be sated with food.**

14 **Bad, bad, the buyer says.** When a person purchases goods, he speaks negatively about them in an attempt to lower the price. **And** after he has completed his purchase, **he goes off,** and **then he glories** in his acquisition: What a great item I have purchased at such a low price. This verse is not offering advice, but rather it is describing what has always been a common mode of behavior.

15 **There is gold, and an abundance of gems, but lips of knowledge are a** rare, **precious vessel,** more useful and valuable than gems.[317]

16 This verse reiterates a warning against serving as a guarantor for a stranger. It is not uncommon for people to say to a lender: **Take his,** the guarantor's, **garment for he was guarantor for a stranger.** Since he entered this risky situation of his own accord, there is no reason to have compassion upon him. Perhaps the guarantor thought that he was simply providing the borrower with his signature, but ultimately he will discover that he may well lose his very garment. **And** in a different context, one can sometimes hear the following statement: **Take it as collateral for a foreign woman.** A man was kind to a foreign woman and provided her with guarantees. After he has forgotten all about the encounter, he is forced to give up his garment due to his imprudent commitment.

17 **Bread of falsehood is sweet to a man.** Food obtained in a dishonest manner can seem especially tasty at the time, **but afterward his mouth will be filled with gravel.** Instead of delicious and nutritious bread, he will discover that he has the taste of gravel in his mouth.[318]

18 One's **thoughts** in all areas of life **will be** well **established** and preserved **through counsel** with others. In order to solidify one's plans, he should consult with others. **And with strategies,** not simply with brute force, one should **wage war.** One who employs sophisticated schemes can defeat even a more physically powerful enemy.

19 **He who goes about as a gossip reveals secrets.** Even if he did not initially intend to do so, various secrets will inevitably be revealed through his prattling. Therefore, **do not be involved with one who spreads wide his lips.** Do not maintain close ties with someone who is unable to control his speech, as he will relate matters that you prefer to be kept secret.

20 **He who curses his father or his mother, his lamp will** ultimately **be extinguished into black darkness.** Utter darkness, death, and evil will befall him.[319]

21 **An estate seized hastily at the start will not be blessed in its end.** For instance, when relatives divide an inheritance, sometimes the portions are not distributed in an organized fashion that clearly establishes legal ownership. In such cases, problems will not have been resolved, and they are likely to recur at a later stage.[320]

22 **Do not say,** when quarreling with someone: **I will repay evil;** I will treat the evildoer as he deserves. Rather, **wait for the Lord, and He will save you** and avenge the wrong on your behalf.[321]

23 **Differing,** falsified, **weights are an abomination to the Lord, and scales of deceit are no good.** It is possible that this is referring not only to using inconsistent weights, but also to using inconsistent standards in judging others, or to applying different standards to oneself and to others.[322]

24 **A man's steps are from,** directed by, **the Lord; and a person, what does he understand of his way?** What does he know about his own path? People act in accordance with their plans, and it might appear to them that everything is functioning smoothly, but the path they have chosen for themselves may not be beneficial, or may even be dangerous. It is therefore best for one to rely upon God and hope that He will lead him to the right place.[323]

DISCUSSION

20:10 | **Differing weights, and differing measures:** Using unreliable weights is a Torah prohibition, which appears in a similar form in Deuteronomy (25:13–16). The book of Proverbs does not repeat laws of the Torah that are clearly religious in nature, such as observing the Sabbath or keeping kosher. However, as part of its focus on social ills, it will occasionally reiterate commandments of the Torah related to interpersonal relations, which it will further develop or analyze (see Rabbeinu Baḥya, introduction to *Va'ethanan*).

BACKGROUND

20:26 | **And he turns a wheel upon them:** Trampling the enemy with the wheels of heavy chariots was a military strategy as well as a method of torture deployed in the ancient world. A model of a chariot, which contains wheels with special spokes designed specifically for this purpose, has been unearthed by archaeologists in Egypt.

י יא מְחַטָּאתִי׃ אֶבֶן וָאֶבֶן אֵיפָה וְאֵיפָה תּוֹעֲבַת יהוה גַּם־שְׁנֵיהֶם׃ גַּם בְּמַעֲלָלָיו
יב יִתְנַכֶּר־נָעַר אִם־זַךְ וְאִם־יָשָׁר פָּעֳלוֹ׃ אֹזֶן שֹׁמַעַת וְעַיִן רֹאָה יהוה עָשָׂה גַם־
יג יד שְׁנֵיהֶם׃ אַל־תֶּאֱהַב שֵׁנָה פֶּן־תִּוָּרֵשׁ פְּקַח עֵינֶיךָ שְׂבַע־לָחֶם׃ רַע רַע יֹאמַר הַקּוֹנֶה
טו טז וְאֹזֵל לוֹ אָז יִתְהַלָּל׃ יֵשׁ זָהָב וְרָב־פְּנִינִים וּכְלִי יְקָר שִׂפְתֵי־דָעַת׃ לְקַח־בִּגְדוֹ כִּי־
יז עָרַב זָר וּבְעַד נכרים חַבְלֵהוּ׃ עָרֵב לָאִישׁ לֶחֶם שָׁקֶר וְאַחַר יִמָּלֵא־פִיהוּ חָצָץ׃ נָכְרִיָּה
יח יט מַחֲשָׁבוֹת בְּעֵצָה תִכּוֹן וּבְתַחְבֻּלוֹת עֲשֵׂה מִלְחָמָה׃ גּוֹלֶה־סּוֹד הוֹלֵךְ רָכִיל וּלְפֹתֶה
כ כא שְׂפָתָיו לֹא תִתְעָרָב׃ מְקַלֵּל אָבִיו וְאִמּוֹ יִדְעַךְ נֵרוֹ באישון חֹשֶׁךְ׃ נַחֲלָה מבחלת בֶּאֱשׁוּן מְבֹהֶלֶת
כב בָּרִאשֹׁנָה וְאַחֲרִיתָהּ לֹא תְבֹרָךְ׃ אַל־תֹּאמַר אֲשַׁלְּמָה־רָע קַוֵּה לַיהוה וְיֹשַׁע
כג כד לָךְ׃ תּוֹעֲבַת יהוה אֶבֶן וָאָבֶן וּמֹאזְנֵי מִרְמָה לֹא־טוֹב׃ מֵיהוה מִצְעֲדֵי־גָבֶר וְאָדָם
כה כו מַה־יָּבִין דַּרְכּוֹ׃ מוֹקֵשׁ אָדָם יָלַע קֹדֶשׁ וְאַחַר נְדָרִים לְבַקֵּר׃ מְזָרֶה רְשָׁעִים מֶלֶךְ
כז כח חָכָם וַיָּשֶׁב עֲלֵיהֶם אוֹפָן׃ נֵר יהוה נִשְׁמַת אָדָם חֹפֵשׂ כָּל־חַדְרֵי־בָטֶן׃ חֶסֶד וֶאֱמֶת
כט יִצְּרוּ־מֶלֶךְ וְסָעַד בַּחֶסֶד כִּסְאוֹ׃ תִּפְאֶרֶת בַּחוּרִים כֹּחָם וַהֲדַר זְקֵנִים שֵׂיבָה׃

25 **It is a snare for a person to spout sanctity,** to carelessly make vows; **scrutiny must follow vows.** One who has made a vow must remember to investigate whether he has indeed fulfilled his vow. Although no one will come to ensure that the vow is carried out, it is nevertheless a commitment to God, and one who vows causes himself harm if he fails to keep his word. It is dangerous to be reckless or playful and use unnecessary language when dealing with holy matters.

26 **A wise king scatters the wicked** so that they are not concentrated together, **and he turns a wheel upon them.**[B] The wheel was used as a means of threshing and flattening agricultural products, and occasionally for trampling humans as well. The verse allows for both interpretations: It may refer to both a king who separates the good and evil in his kingdom, as one would separate chaff from wheat, and to one who oppresses the wicked as a punishment.[324]

27 **The spirit of man is the lamp of the Lord, who searches all the chambers of the belly.** God examines the inner life of a person by means of his own soul, which serves as a lamp. Thus, everything is revealed before Him, including matters that are concealed from the person himself.[325]

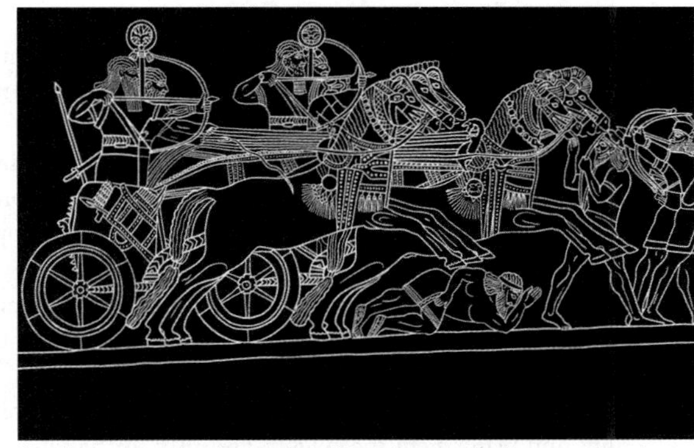

"And he turns a wheel upon them." Assyrian war chariot trampling the enemy, illustration based on stone relief, Nimrud, Iraq, ninth century BCE

28 **Kindness and truth will safeguard the king** when they are employed in his kingdom, **and his throne is supported with** the **kindness** and mercy he extends to others.[326]

29 **The glory of young men is their strength, and the splendor of elders,** who no longer possess abundant strength, **is** their **gray hair.**

30 **Injurious wounds purge evil.** Alternatively, they are the final repayment of evil. Open wounds are a result of one's evil deeds, but they also atone for those deeds. **And** likewise, **blows to the chambers of the belly** are also a means of both punishment and atonement. This refers to concealed wounds that are not immediately noticeable and that sometimes appear only a long time after the incident that caused them.

21 1 **A king's heart in the hand of the Lord is streams of water.** People may believe that a particular ruler is stable and reliable. However, just as canals or tributaries are carved and shaped by the owner of the field, the hearts of kings are entirely in the hand of God: **To wherever He wishes He turns it.**[327] This is the case even though the king himself is often unable to sense his change of direction.

"Streams of water; to wherever He wishes He turns it." Preparing a ditch for irrigating a field

2 **Every way of a man is right in his own eyes,** as he is confident that he is pursuing the proper path, **but** only **the Lord measures,** evaluates, **hearts.**

3 **Acting with righteousness and justice is preferential to the Lord than sacrifice.** This notion that justice is preferable to bringing offerings is expressed numerous times by the prophets.[328]

4 **Haughtiness and a proud heart,** full of great and pretentious desires, **are a furrow of the wicked, a** path comprised entirely of **sin.**[329]

5 **The thoughts of the diligent** individual, who evaluates his actions and plans them thoroughly, **are only for benefit.** They are nothing but advantageous and profitable, even though the execution of the task itself is thereby delayed.[330] **And all** the **hastiness** of those continuously rushing to make a profit **is only for detriment.**[331]

6 **Making treasures through a false tongue is fleeting vapor.** Those who act in that manner accomplish nothing substantial. On the contrary, **they are** in effect **seekers of death** and destruction.

7 **The wicked's pillaging will cause them to fear,**[332] **for they refuse to act with justice,** and all of their actions are wicked.

8 **Erratic is the way of man, and strange.** Many people act in inconsistent and unreasonable ways, both in their personal and public lives, yet are not even aware of this fact. **And the** individual is **pure** in his own eyes; **his conduct is upright.** Alternatively, the latter half of the verse is the inverse of the first half. The verse, then, is conveying that most people act in ways that are erratic and strange, and only the pure-hearted conduct themselves in an upright manner.

9 **Better** for one **to live on the** secluded **corner of a roof,** even if it is uncomfortable or lacks protection, **than** to reside **with a woman of strife in a comfortable house,** one that is spacious and has other people around. It is better to live in a secluded, quiet area than to live in a comfortable and social framework with a contentious woman.

10 **The soul of the wicked desires evil;** therefore **his friend will not find favor in his eyes.** He has no mercy or compassion upon his neighbor.[333]

11 **With the punishment of a scoffer, the naïf becomes wise.** Although a naïve person does not understand very much, he can learn from the experience of the scorner (see 19:25). **And with the education of the wise, he acquires knowledge** and insight. Consequently, there are three levels here: Scorners, who fail to learn at all; the naïve, who do not gain knowledge on their own, but when they reflect upon the punishment of others they can understand the difference between appropriate and inappropriate conduct; and the wise, who can recognize proper behavior on their own even without a living example.[334]

12 **The righteous advising the house of the wicked** only further **suborns the wicked,** leading him **to** greater **evil.** Some wicked individuals are merely encouraged to persist in their evil ways by the attempts of others to help or guide them.[335]

13 **He who seals his ears to the cry of the impoverished,** because he is preoccupied with other matters, **he too** will ultimately become destitute as well, or suffer some other calamity, and he **will call and not be answered.**[336]

14 An inappropriate **gift,** such as a bribe, given **in secret overcomes wrath, and a bribe** found **in the bosom** appeases **harsh fury.** Giving such gifts is wrong, but this is the reality.[337]

15 **Acting with justice is a joy to the righteous,** whether the just act is performed by the righteous person himself or someone else. In either case, when justice is achieved, the righteous are happy, **but** the same situation brings fear and **ruin to the performers of iniquity,** criminals.[338] Alternatively, this is referring specifically to wicked people who try to perform justice. Since they are unhappy when justice is achieved, their judgment will emerge twisted.[339]

א ל א חברות פצע תמריק ברע ומכות חדרי־בטן: פלגי־מים לב־מלך ביד־יהוה תמרוק
ב ג על־כל־אשר יחפץ יטנו: כל־דרך־איש ישר בעיניו ותכן לבות יהוה: עשה
ד צדקה ומשפט נבחר ליהוה מזבח: רום־עינים ורחב־לב נר רשעים חטאת:
ה ו מחשבות חרוץ אך־למותר וכל־אץ אך־למחסור: פעל אצרות בלשון שקר
ז ח הבל נדף מבקשי־מות: שד־רשעים יגורם כי מאנו לעשות משפט: הפכפך
ט דרך איש וזר וזך ישר פעלו: טוב לשבת על־פנת־גג מאשת מדונים ובית מדינים
י יא חבר: נפש רשע אותה־רע לא־יחן בעיניו רעהו: בענש־לץ יחכם־פתי ובהשכיל
יב יג לחכם יקח־דעת: משכיל צדיק לבית רשע מסלף רשעים לרע: אטם אזנו
יד מזעקת־דל גם־הוא יקרא ולא יענה: מתן בסתר יכפה־אף ושחד בחק חמה
טו טז עזה: שמחה לצדיק עשות משפט ומחתה לפעלי און: אדם תועה מדרך
יז השכל בקהל רפאים ינוח: איש מחסור אהב שמחה אהב יין־ושמן לא יעשיר:
יח יט כפר לצדיק רשע ותחת ישרים בוגד: טוב שבת בארץ־מדבר מאשת מדונים מדינים
כ כא וכעס: אוצר | נחמד ושמן בנוה חכם וכסיל אדם יבלענו: רדף צדקה וחסד
כב כג ימצא חיים צדקה וכבוד: עיר גברים עלה חכם וירד עז מבטחה: שמר פיו

16 **A person who wanders from the way of sense,** the proper path, **will** ultimately **rest in the congregation of ghosts.** He is fast approaching the dwelling of the dead.[340]

17 **He who loves rejoicing** and pursues excessive indulgence **is a man who lacks,** as he will never be satisfied.[341] Likewise, **he who loves** drinking **wine and** smearing **oil** upon himself, chasing a life of physical gratification, **will not become rich.**

18 **The wicked is ransom for the righteous.** The wicked will find himself ensnared in the troubles from which the righteous has just escaped, **and the treacherous will take the place of the upright** and be struck by calamity in their place.[342]

19 **Better to live in a wilderness land,** not merely on a corner of a roof, as stated above (verse 9), **than** to live **with a woman of strife and anger.** Life with such a woman is more unpleasant and harmful than remaining in complete isolation.

20 **Precious treasure and** scented **oil are** often found **in the abode of the wise, and the foolish person will swallow it,** as he destroys the entire supply.

21 **He who pursues righteousness and kindness will find** a reward of long **life** and health, as well as **righteousness,** or merit and blessing,[343] **and honor,** which he receives for the acts of kindness he has performed.[344]

22 **The wise goes up against the** well-protected **city of the mighty and removes the strength of its stronghold.**[345] It is therefore advisable to let a wise individual take command in such situations.[346]

23 **He who guards his mouth and his tongue guards himself from troubles.** Silence generally does not lead to serious negative consequences, but improper speech, even uttered on a single occasion, can cause major harm. Alternatively, the

expression "guards his mouth" is referring to guarding one's mouth from eating unhealthy foods.[347]

24 **A spiteful and arrogant man, scoffer is his name; he acts with spiteful ire.** Some people present themselves as somewhat flighty or lightheaded, but in fact they engage in highly calculated acts of evil. They may try to conceal their evil intentions and make it seem as though their actions are unintentional, but they are actually premeditated and thoroughly planned.[348]

25 **The craving of the idler will kill him, as his hands refuse to do anything.** When one's inaction causes his desires to be left unfulfilled, he is left empty and hungry. A great unfilled desire can cause harm and even death.

26 **All day he,** that lazy person, **is seized with craving,** and yet he is not prepared to expend effort in order to achieve his desires. **But** by contrast, **the righteous will give** him charity **and not stint,**[D] despite the fact that the recipient is responsible for his own troubles.[349]

27 **The sacrifice of the wicked is** always **an abomination; certainly, when he brings it in depravity,** with wicked thoughts. The wicked brings an offering in an attempt to extricate himself from a difficult situation. He supposes that he can obtain atonement for his sins without emending his ways, and he will thereby be saved from the hand of God, so to speak. However, God despises his offering.[350]

28 **A lying witness will perish, and a man who listens,** and is insightful and examines matters carefully,[351] **will forever speak,** as people will always be interested in hearing what he has to say.

29 **A wicked man is insolent,** impudent and defiant; **and the upright, he discerns his way** and walks with confidence.

30 **There is no wisdom, no sagacity, and no counsel** to act **against the Lord.** As much as one might try to outsmart God or scheme against Him in order to achieve his goals, the will of God will ultimately be fulfilled.[352]

31 **A horse is ready for the day of battle,**[B] **but** although the horse is an important weapon of war, **salvation is for the Lord.** Horses and weaponry do not win the war; success is in God's hands, and one should look to Him for salvation.[353]

"A horse is ready for the day of battle." Assyrian archer shooting while riding a horse, Nimrud, Iraq, eighth century BCE

22 1 **A name is preferable to great wealth.** One's good reputation is priceless; it can be preserved more easily than wealth, and it does not entail worry or weigh heavily on a person like material riches. **And** likewise, **good grace** should be preferred **to silver and gold.** The ability to understand the world and to conduct oneself with grace and tact is more valuable than silver and gold.[354]

2 **Rich and poor meet** in certain situations, despite the fact that they are on opposite ends of the social spectrum, as ultimately **the Lord is the Maker of them all.** God created both the rich and the poor, and therefore they share many common qualities that enable them to meet, interact, and even assist one another at times.[355] Some commentaries connect this verse to the

DISCUSSION

21:26 | **All day he is seized with craving, but the righteous will give and not stint:** This contrast between the righteous individual and the lazy one alludes to the proper manner of acquiring wisdom and following the path of truth. An idle person is unwilling to toil in order to achieve the wisdom he seeks, whereas the righteous person invests all his energy into his studies and avoids wasting his time (Rambam, *Guide of the Perplexed* 1:34).

22:4 | **In the wake [*ekev*] of humility are fear of the Lord:** In a homiletical vein, the Sages explain that fear of the Lord is like a lowly heel [*akev*] in relation to humility (see Jerusalem Talmud, *Shabbat* 1:3). This is because humility is a great and important attribute from which various forms of goodness and blessings flow, including fear of the Lord, riches, honor, and life.

BACKGROUND

21:31 | **A horse is ready for the day of battle:** War horses were the most proficient weapon used by ancient armies. They were trained to move in response to very slight motions of the rider, which freed both the rider's hands to hold weapons with which he could attack the enemy. These horses were swift and would gallop fearlessly toward the enemy or any other challenge. Man's improper reliance upon the power of horses as opposed to faith in God is mentioned several times in the Bible (see Psalms 20:8).

כד כה ולשונו שמר מצרות נפשו: זד יהיר לץ שמו עושה בעברת זדון: תאות עצל
כו תמיתנו כי־מאנו ידיו לעשות: כל־היום התאוה תאוה וצדיק יתן ולא יחשך:
כז כח זבח רשעים תועבה אף כי־בזמה יביאנו: עד־כזבים יאבד ואיש שומע לנצח
כט ל ידבר: העז איש רשע בפניו וישר הוא ׀ יכין דרכיו: אין חכמה ואין תבונה יָבִין
לא ב א ואין עצה לנגד יהוה: סוס מוכן ליום מלחמה וליהוה התשועה: נבחר שם דְּרָכוֹ
ב ג מעשר רב מכסף ומזהב חן טוב: עשיר ורש נפגשו עשה כלם יהוה: ערום ׀
ד ראה רעה ויסתר ופתיים עברו ונענשו: עקב ענוה יראת יהוה עשר וכבוד ונסתר
ה ו וחיים: צנים פחים בדרך עקש שומר נפשו ירחק מהם: חנך לנער על־פי דרכו
ז גם כי־יזקין לא־יסור ממנה: עשיר ברשים ימשול ועבד לוה לאיש מלוה:
ח ט זורע עולה יקצור־און ושבט עברתו יכלה: טוב־עין הוא יברך כי־נתן מלחמו יִקְצָר־
י יא לדל: גרש לץ ויצא מדון וישבת דין וקלון: אהב טהור־לב חן שפתיו רעהו טְהָר־

previous one: The rich and the poor can both achieve a good name and grace, as these qualities are independent of one's wealth.

3 **The clever one sees harm,** as he discerns when trouble is approaching **and hides** himself from it, **but naïfs pass** near it **and are punished.** They are harmed due to their lack of caution.[356]

4 **In the wake of humility are fear of the Lord,**[D] **wealth, honor, and life.**[357]

5 **Thorns and traps,**[358] or cold and heat,[359] **are in the way of the crooked,** a warped individual, whereas **the guardian of his soul will distance himself from them.** A cautious person will naturally protect himself from such dangers, but a crooked person is drawn to them and becomes entangled in them.

6 **Train the lad in accordance with his way,** in a manner appropriate for him, which allows him to easily comprehend and apply what he is taught. If you do so properly, and avoid pressuring the child to follow a direction unsuitable for him, **even when he grows old, he will not turn from it.** Success in education does not depend merely on fine theories. Only a method that suits the personality and character of a particular student will fully leave its mark on him. If one attempts to educate someone in a fashion that is not in keeping with his natural character, when he becomes an adult he will likely find for himself a more suitable path.[360]

7 **The wealthy will rule over the poor, and a borrower is servant to a man who lends.**

8 **He who sows injustice will reap iniquity.** One who harms others will ultimately suffer from evil himself, **and his ire's rod,** his strength, **will fail.** The devastating consequences of evil behavior will ricochet upon those who performed it.[361]

9 **A generous eye,** one who looks at others in a positive manner and endeavors to provide them with what they lack,[362] **will** himself **be blessed, for he gives of his bread to the impoverished.**

10 **Expel** from your house or company **the scoffer,** who is frivolous and refuses to take responsibility for his actions, **and** thereby **strife will depart, and contention and disgrace will cease.** The scorner does not always quarrel directly with those in his immediate surroundings, but nevertheless he complicates their lives by incessantly involving himself in arguments and crises. Once he has departed, quiet will reign.

11 **One who loves,** and **is pure of heart, has grace on his lips;**[363] **his friend is** like **a king.**

12 **The eyes of the Lord safeguard knowledge,** or knowledgeable and truthful people,[364] **and** as God watches everything, **He distorts the words of the treacherous.** God will negate the will and plans of those who betray His word.[365]
13 **The idler,** who prefers not to leave his house, **says: There is a lion** prowling **in the street; I will be murdered in the squares.** Lions are not commonly found in city streets, and it is unlikely that a passerby would be killed, but the idler invents all sorts of excuses to avoid activity.
14 **The mouth of deviance,** a bad, repulsive mouth, **is a deep pit; he who has infuriated the Lord will fall there,** into this mouth, which is essentially a trap.[366]
15 **Folly is bound in the heart of a lad,** as a youngster occasionally entertains an idea without realizing that it is foolish,[367] and **the rod of admonishment will distance it from him.** Beating the lad will remove his foolishness (see 19:18).
16 **He who exploits the impoverished to gain for himself,** or **he who gives to the wealthy, it is only for loss.** Neither one who oppresses the poor in order to increase his own wealth, nor one who gives to the rich to win their favor, will thereby benefit. There is nothing to be gained from this type of giving or taking, which only causes harm.[368]

Warnings and Instructions for a Student

PROVERBS 22:17–24:34

This section contains advice and warnings addressed directly to a student, who is also called "my son." This title might simply be a term of endearment, indicative of a close relationship with the student, or perhaps these particular instructions were originally formulated for the benefit of the speaker's own biological son. The opening verses of this section can be read as the conclusion of the preceding lengthy section of short proverbs. In any case, the style of these verses is similar to those of the beginning of the book.

17 **Incline your ear and hear the words of the wise, and set your heart to** the task of absorbing **my knowledge.**[D]
18 **For it is pleasant** for you **if you keep them in your belly,** if you internalize and remember these instructions,[369] and if **they shall be fixed together on your lips** as a clear and orderly doctrine.[370]
19 If you do so, you will merit **to place your trust in the Lord.** The aphorist stresses again: **I have informed you today, even for you.**[371]
20 **Didn't I write it for you,** and reiterate it at least **three times,**[372] **with** wise **counsel and knowledge,**[373]
21 in order **to** faithfully and precisely **inform you of the certainty of sayings of truth?** Alternatively, this means: I did so to inform you of sayings of truth whose precision and correctness is clearly recognized by all.[374] I did not inform you of this only for yourself, but also **to respond with sayings of truth to those who sent you,** your parents who have sent you off to study, or those who ask questions of you.[375]
22 The aphorist offers specific warnings and advice: **Do not rob the impoverished, as he is impoverished,** and has no one to help him,[376] **and do not oppress the poor at the gate,** in courts of justice,[377] or in your business dealings in the city, where the rich and poor often interact,[378]
23 **for the Lord will fight their,** the wretched people's, **battle and will deprive those who deprive them of life.**[379] Even when it is necessary to rebuke or punish one of these unfortunate people, such acts must be carried out with great mercy and respect.[380]
24 The verses now cite a series of instructions involving one's social environment: **Do not befriend he who is disposed to wrath, and do not approach the man of fury.** Do not associate with him.
25 The reason for the above advice, to keep away from someone who is prone to fits of rage, is not because he will inevitably turn his anger upon you, as you are his friend. Nevertheless, you should avoid his company **lest you become versed in his ways** and accustomed to acting accordingly, **and** as a result, you will **bring a snare upon your soul.** It is best to avoid being overly involved with those who serve as a negative role model.
26 **Do not be among those who shake hands,** make promises, **among the guarantors of loans.** Even if you are surrounded by people who make this type of commitment, either to boast about their ill-advised generosity or for some other reason, you

DISCUSSION

22:17| **Incline your ear and hear the words of the wise, and set your heart to my knowledge:** In contrast to the claims of many parents, educators, and rabbis, that only their opinions should be taken into account, this teacher advises his student to listen to other scholars as well. Nevertheless, he also tells him that his own instruction is worth attention, as he is his advisor, father, or rabbi. A disciple should listen carefully to his teacher or guide, while allowing others to add wisdom and explanations of their own. By taking all these to heart, the student can find his own path (see Ralbag).

יב יג מלך: עיני יהוה נצרו דעת ויסלף דברי בגד: אמר עצל ארי בחוץ בתוך רחבות
יד טו ארצח: שוחה עמקה פי זרות זעום יהוה יפול־שם: אולת קשורה בלב־נער יפל־
טז שבט מוסר ירחיקנה ממנו: עשק דל להרבות לו נתן לעשיר אך־למחסור:
יז יח הט אזנך ושמע דברי חכמים ולבך תשית לדעתי: כי־נעים כי־תשמרם בבטנך
יט כ יכנו יחדו על־שפתיך: להיות ביהוה מבטחך הודעתיך היום אף־אתה: הלא ו
כא כתבתי לך שלשום במעצות ודעת: להודיעך קשט אמרי אמת להשיב שלישים
כב אמרים אמת לשלחיך: אל־תגזל־דל כי דל־הוא ואל־תדכא עני
כג כד בשער: כי־יהוה יריב ריבם וקבע את־קבעיהם נפש: אל־תתרע את־בעל
כה אף ואת־איש חמות לא תבוא: פן־תאלף ארחתו ולקחת מוקש לנפשך:
כו כז אל־תהי בתקעי־כף בערבים משאות: אם־אין־לך לשלם למה יקח משכבך
כח כט מתחתיך: אל־תסג גבול עולם אשר עשו אבותיך: חזית איש ׀ מהיר במלאכתו
א לפני־מלכים יתיצב בל־יתיצב לפני חשכים: כי־תשב ללחום את־מושל בין
ב ג תבין את־אשר לפניך: ושמת שכין בלעך אם־בעל נפש אתה: אל־תתאו

should resist the social pressure to follow suit. Think carefully about your options and remember that you are under no obligation to commit yourself.[381]

27 **If** you agreed to serve as a guarantor, and it eventually turns out that **you do not have with what to pay, why should** you put yourself in a situation where **he,** the creditor, can **take** away your property, even **your bed from under you?**

28 **Do not move** back **the ancient boundary that your ancestors established** to demarcate property boundaries.

29 **Have you seen a man** who is **quick,** determined, and efficient **in his work?** If so, rest assured that he will go far. **He will** advance and eventually **stand before kings. He will not stand before dark ones,** lowly men; alternatively, he will not stand in hidden and dark places. Consequently, it is worthwhile to learn from him and emulate his actions.[382]

23 **1** The aphorist offers advice on how to act with members of the ruling class: **When you sit to break bread with a ruler,** you must **discern well that which is before you.** Regardless of the identity of this ruler, such a feast cannot be treated as a regular meal among friends.

2 Even if the ruler displayed great generosity by inviting you to feast with him, you must be careful. Therefore, **put a knife into your throat,** so that you do not speak too much at this meal, **if you are a** wise and **sensitive person,** as unnecessary disclosures can harm you. Some explain that the verse means to say: Put a knife into your throat so that you do not eat too much if you are someone with a large appetite.

3 **Do not crave his delicacies, as it is the bread of deceit.** The ruler certainly did not invite you to feast with him merely because he likes you; his generosity is designed to make you incur a debt that you will eventually be forced to pay.[383] This idea is reiterated many generations later by the Sages, who also advise against becoming too close to the governing authorities, as powerful people generally have only their own interests at heart and do not care about others.[384]

4 The aphorist speaks about wealth: **Do not weary yourself to become rich,** to acquire wealth beyond your needs; **cease your discerning,** your investigating ways of amassing more and more money.[385]

5 **If you cast your eyes on it,** even if you do manage to acquire wealth, as soon as you look upon the money **it is gone, as it will make wings for itself** and disappear quickly. **Like an eagle it will fly to the heavens,** leaving no trace of the hard work you invested in amassing your wealth.

"Like an eagle it will fly to the heavens"

6 This proverb deals with a stingy person: **Do not break bread on the bread of a miser, and do not crave his delicacies.**

7 **For as he deems in his mind, so he is.** His true attitude is internal and may not be revealed through his actions.[386] If you are his guest, he might perhaps invite you politely: **Eat and drink, he says to you; but** nevertheless, **his heart is not with you.** He has no interest in your partaking of his food.

8 **You ate your loaf** at his invitation, but it will make you uncomfortable and **you will vomit it,** so that it will be as though you had never eaten at all. **And you** will have **destroyed your pleasant words.** The pleasantries you heaped upon him and your genuine compliments will amount to nothing. You will derive no benefit from associating with someone who is not interested in you or your well-being.[387]

9 This advice is perhaps connected to the previous proverb:[388] **Do not speak in the ears of a fool, as he will** not benefit from your statements and will even **scorn the insight of your words.** Therefore, any discussion or attempt to criticize him will be useless.[389]

10 This verse also deals with money and the social arena, and it expands upon an ancient idea recorded in the earliest sources:[390] **Do not move the ancient boundary,** in order to enlarge your property by encroaching on land belonging to others, **and do not encroach** as a trespasser **on the fields of orphans.** Although it is tempting to take over a nearby field that is currently neglected because it belongs to orphans, you must refrain from doing so,

11 **for** even if the orphans have no relatives who can defend their interests, **their Redeemer** in heaven **is strong; He will conduct their quarrel with you,** and you will be held accountable for your actions.

12 This section deals with ethics and education. **Bring your heart to admonition,** listen carefully to rebuke, while retaining an open mind,[391] **and** open **your ears to** hear **sayings of knowledge.**

13 **Do not refrain from admonishing a lad** even by means of physical punishment, as necessary; **when you** occasionally **strike him** lightly **with the rod, he will not die** from such treatment.

14 On the contrary, **you should strike him with the rod and** thereby **deliver his soul from the grave.** A minor blow will cause only slight physical pain, but it will save his soul from destruction and eternal punishment. Unlike many of the previous exhortations, which are geared primarily toward young people, that they should listen, internalize, and obey, this warning is for adults who are concerned about their children's welfare. Such individuals must remember that being strict is not necessarily harmful.

15 **My son,** a figurative reference to a student in addition to its literal meaning, **if your heart is wise, my heart too**[392] **will rejoice.** If you grow ever wiser, I will not become jealous of you. On the contrary, I will rejoice and take pleasure in your success. The Sages similarly state: A person is jealous of everyone, except for his son and his student.[393]

16 **And my kidneys will delight,** I will be filled with genuine happiness, **when your lips are speaking fairness,** truthful and honest statements.

17 **Let your heart not envy sinners,** and take no notice of their deeds. **Rather, be** involved only[394] **in fear of the Lord all day.** Some explain the verse as follows: Do not direct your envy at a person who has acquired wealth illegally, and do not seek the status of a powerful individual. It is much better to envy one who fears God and to contemplate how to emulate his righteousness.[395]

18 **For indeed,**[396] **there is a future,** a purpose and a goal for all things, **and** therefore **your hope** for a successful outcome **will not be eliminated.** Accordingly, do not be jealous of sinners who enjoy temporary good fortune.[397]

19 **Hear you, my son, and** try to **become wise, and** then you will be able to **persist in the way of your heart,** the appropriate path.

20 **Do not be among the guzzlers of wine,** those who drink until they are intoxicated, or **among the gorgers of meat for themselves,** who consume large amounts of meat for pleasure. Gluttony is an abhorrent trait, especially when one eats not merely staple foods such as bread, water, and milk but gorges himself on luxuries such as meat and wine.

21 **For a guzzler and a gorger will become poor, and** the **slumber** of an inebriated, hedonistic, or lazy individual **will** impoverish and ultimately **clothe you in tatters.** Instead of drowning oneself in physical pleasures, one should work for his livelihood.[398]

הֲתָעִיף לְמַטְעַמּוֹתָיו וְהוּא לֶחֶם כְּזָבִים: אַל־תִּיגַע לְהַעֲשִׁיר מִבִּינָתְךָ חֲדָל: התעוף עֵינֶיךָ ד ה
יָעוּף בּוֹ וְאֵינֶנּוּ כִּי עָשֹׂה יַעֲשֶׂה־לּוֹ כְנָפַיִם כְּנֶשֶׁר ועוף הַשָּׁמָיִם: אַל־תִּלְחַם אֶת־לֶחֶם ו
רַע עָיִן וְאַל־תִּתְאָו לְמַטְעַמֹּתָיו: כִּי ׀ כְּמוֹ־שָׁעַר בְּנַפְשׁוֹ כֶּן־הוּא אֱכוֹל וּשְׁתֵה ז
יֹאמַר לָךְ וְלִבּוֹ בַּל־עִמָּךְ: פִּתְּךָ־אָכַלְתָּ תְקִיאֶנָּה וְשִׁחַתָּ דְּבָרֶיךָ הַנְּעִימִים: בְּאָזְנֵי ח ט
כְסִיל אַל־תְּדַבֵּר כִּי־יָבוּז לְשֵׂכֶל מִלֶּיךָ: אַל־תַּסֵּג גְּבוּל עוֹלָם וּבִשְׂדֵי יְתוֹמִים י
אַל־תָּבֹא: כִּי־גֹאֲלָם חָזָק הוּא־יָרִיב אֶת־רִיבָם אִתָּךְ: הָבִיאָה לַמּוּסָר לִבֶּךָ וְאָזְנֶךָ יא יב
לְאִמְרֵי־דָעַת: אַל־תִּמְנַע מִנַּעַר מוּסָר כִּי־תַכֶּנּוּ בַשֵּׁבֶט לֹא יָמוּת: אַתָּה בַּשֵּׁבֶט יג יד
תַּכֶּנּוּ וְנַפְשׁוֹ מִשְּׁאוֹל תַּצִּיל: בְּנִי אִם־חָכַם לִבֶּךָ יִשְׂמַח לִבִּי גַם־אָנִי: וְתַעְלֹזְנָה טו טז
כִלְיוֹתָי בְּדַבֵּר שְׂפָתֶיךָ מֵישָׁרִים: אַל־יְקַנֵּא לִבְּךָ בַּחַטָּאִים כִּי אִם־בְּיִרְאַת־יהוה יז
כָּל־הַיּוֹם: כִּי אִם־יֵשׁ אַחֲרִית וְתִקְוָתְךָ לֹא תִכָּרֵת: שְׁמַע־אַתָּה בְנִי וַחֲכָם וְאַשֵּׁר יח יט
בַּדֶּרֶךְ לִבֶּךָ: אַל־תְּהִי בְסֹבְאֵי־יָיִן בְּזֹלְלֵי בָשָׂר לָמוֹ: כִּי־סֹבֵא וְזוֹלֵל יִוָּרֵשׁ וּקְרָעִים כ כא
גִּיל | יָגִיל | תַּלְבִּישׁ נוּמָה: שְׁמַע לְאָבִיךָ זֶה יְלָדֶךָ וְאַל־תָּבוּז כִּי־זָקְנָה אִמֶּךָ: אֱמֶת קְנֵה כב כג
וְיוֹלֵד | יִשְׂמַח וְאַל־תִּמְכֹּר חָכְמָה וּמוּסָר וּבִינָה: גול יָגוּל אֲבִי צַדִּיק יולד חָכָם וישמח בּוֹ: כד
תִּצֹּרְנָה יִשְׂמַח־אָבִיךָ וְאִמֶּךָ וְתָגֵל יוֹלַדְתֶּךָ: תְּנָה־בְנִי לִבְּךָ לִי וְעֵינֶיךָ דְּרָכַי תרצנה: כִּי־ כה כו כז

22 **Heed your father,** as **it is he who begot you, and do not scorn when your mother has aged.** Such attitudes should be avoided, not only because they are disrespectful, but also because one can learn important lessons from one's parents.[399] Evidently, the familiar depiction of parents as old people who do not understand modern life and whose ideas are no longer relevant was prevalent in ancient times as well.

23 Invest the necessary effort and resources to **acquire truth,** even if that requires one to spend money purchasing books or traveling to a distant land to study.[400] **And** after you have acquired truth, **do not sell it,** do not attempt to earn a profit by selling truth for more than you spent acquiring it. Rather, the acquisition of truth itself, alongside **wisdom, good conduct, and understanding,** should be your reward. In addition, the Sages explain that even if you have spent money to learn Torah, you should still teach others free of charge.[401]

24 **The father of the righteous will revel with happiness, and the begetter of the wise will rejoice in him.** Therefore, you should make every effort to be among those who bring joy to their parents.

25 **Your father and your mother will rejoice, and she who bore you,** an appellation that includes the nurse who raised you,[402] **will be happy** when they see you behave properly.

26 **My son, give me your heart,** listen to my advice, **and your eyes will safeguard my ways,** so that you can avoid temptation.

27 Maintain control over your eyes and your desires, which try to

draw you after them,[403] **for a harlot is a deep pit,** a trap, **and a foreign woman is a narrow well,** from which it is very difficult to escape.[404] This refers not only to an actual harlot, but also to a woman of loose morals who acts promiscuously for pleasure alone.

"Deep pit." Pit used as a trap for animals

"Narrow well"

28 **She too will lie in ambush like a kidnapper,** who attacks suddenly. When a woman of this kind encounters a man, she initially appears charming and delightful, but she is actually a vicious predator waiting to ensnare him, **and** she will **increase the treacherous among men.** Such a woman is generally married, and her adultery leads to more faithlessness, strife, and troubles.

29 This warning is comprised of poetic refrains regarding one who drinks wine: **To whom,** who can be expected to cry out: **Woe? To whom: Alas? To whom strife? To whom talk** of complaints and bitterness? **To whom wounds** that he received **without cause? To whom redness of the eyes?**[405]

30 These phenomena are common **to those who linger,** who sit until late at night, **over wine.** Their eyes are red from all their drinking and lack of sleep, and they sometimes suffer injuries in unnecessary brawls. The same applies **to those who come to assess the** quality of the **mixture** of their drink. Instead of discussing matters of Torah and fear of God, they stay up late debating which alcoholic drink is best.[406]

31 **Do not see wine in its redness,** do not allow its attractive color to seduce you, **for he who directs his eye to the cup will walk inattentively.** When one gazes at wine and is tempted by its color, the goblet, or its fragrance and taste, he can overindulge and become addicted to alcohol. This will cause him to be inattentive to the pitfalls around him, as he will not notice where he has to turn or take a detour to avoid obstacles. Drunk people lack inhibitions, and their judgment is often impaired.[407]

32 Although wine is initially pleasant and enjoyable, **in its end it bites like a serpent and secretes like** a venomous **adder.** It can cause severe harm to those who get drunk.[408]

33 When you are drunk, **your eyes will see illusions.** An intoxicated individual can start to hallucinate. **And your heart will speak contradictions.** You will be illogical.[409]

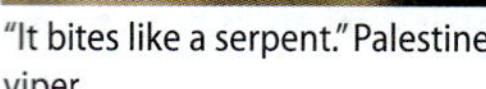

"It bites like a serpent." Palestine viper

"Secretes like an adder." Venom dripping from snake's mouth

34 **You will be like one lying in the midst of the sea,** among the waves rocking him back and forth, **or like one lying at the top of a mast** blowing in the winds. One who drinks too much is frequently dizzy.

"Lying in the midst of the sea." People drowning at sea, stone relief, palace of Ashurbanipal, Nineveh, seventh century BCE

"Top of a mast." Boat with two masts, stone relief, Carthage, Roman period

35 The drunkard declares: Indeed **they struck me, but I did not feel pain; they beat me, but I did not know.** Feeling as though the entire world is spinning, he nevertheless states: **When will I awaken? I will continue to seek it.** He only wants to drink more wine. This brief but vivid depiction of the stages through which a drunkard passes from start to finish are an attempt to dissuade a young man from drinking.

24 1 **Do not envy** the success of **men of evil, and do not crave to be among them,** or to associate with them.

2 No benefit will come from such a relationship, **for their heart contemplates robbery, and their lips speak** evil and **mischief.** They are no good for anything, and one should not rely on them.

3 By contrast, **with wisdom a house is built, and with sagacity it is established** and will endure;[410]

4 **with knowledge, chambers are filled with all precious and pleasant wealth.** Wisdom, understanding, and knowledge are creative, constructive, and reliable qualities.

5 Therefore, **a wise man has might,**[411] as he gains power and fortitude from his wisdom, **and a man of knowledge exerts** his **strength.** Strength is not merely a physical quality; it also depends on the character of the individual in question.

6 **For** it is not only with force but also **with strategies** that **you will wage war for yourself, and** at a time of conflict and in

כח שׁוּחָה עֲמֻקָּה זוֹנָה וּבְאֵר צָרָה נָכְרִיָּה: אַף־הִיא כְּחֶתֶף תֶּאֱרֹב וּבוֹגְדִים בְּאָדָם
כט תּוֹסִף: לְמִי אוֹי לְמִי אֲבוֹי לְמִי מדונים | לְמִי שִׂיחַ לְמִי פְּצָעִים חִנָּם לְמִי חַכְלִלוּת מִדְיָנִים
ל לא עֵינָיִם: לַמְאַחֲרִים עַל־הַיָּיִן לַבָּאִים לַחְקֹר מִמְסָךְ: אַל־תֵּרֶא יַיִן כִּי יִתְאַדָּם כִּי־
לב לג יִתֵּן בכיס עֵינוֹ יִתְהַלֵּךְ בְּמֵישָׁרִים: אַחֲרִיתוֹ כְּנָחָשׁ יִשָּׁךְ וּכְצִפְעֹנִי יַפְרִשׁ: עֵינֶיךָ בַּכּוֹס
לד יִרְאוּ זָרוֹת וְלִבְּךָ יְדַבֵּר תַּהְפֻּכוֹת: וְהָיִיתָ כְּשֹׁכֵב בְּלֶב־יָם וּכְשֹׁכֵב בְּרֹאשׁ חִבֵּל:
לה א הִכּוּנִי בַל־חָלִיתִי הֲלָמוּנִי בַּל־יָדָעְתִּי מָתַי אָקִיץ אוֹסִיף אֲבַקְשֶׁנּוּ עוֹד: אַל־תְּקַנֵּא
ב בְּאַנְשֵׁי רָעָה וְאַל־תִּתְאָו לִהְיוֹת אִתָּם: כִּי־שֹׁד יֶהְגֶּה לִבָּם וְעָמָל שִׂפְתֵיהֶם
ג ד תְּדַבֵּרְנָה: בְּחָכְמָה יִבָּנֶה בָּיִת וּבִתְבוּנָה יִתְכּוֹנָן: וּבְדַעַת חֲדָרִים יִמָּלְאוּ כָּל־הוֹן
ה ו יָקָר וְנָעִים: גֶּבֶר־חָכָם בַּעוֹז וְאִישׁ־דַּעַת מְאַמֶּץ־כֹּחַ: כִּי בְתַחְבֻּלוֹת תַּעֲשֶׂה־לְּךָ
ז מִלְחָמָה וּתְשׁוּעָה בְּרֹב יוֹעֵץ: רָאמוֹת לֶאֱוִיל חָכְמוֹת בַּשַּׁעַר לֹא יִפְתַּח־פִּיהוּ:
ח ט מְחַשֵּׁב לְהָרֵעַ לוֹ בַּעַל־מְזִמּוֹת יִקְרָאוּ: זִמַּת אִוֶּלֶת חַטָּאת וְתוֹעֲבַת לְאָדָם לֵץ:
י יא הִתְרַפִּיתָ בְּיוֹם צָרָה צַר כֹּחֶכָה: הַצֵּל לְקֻחִים לַמָּוֶת וּמָטִים לַהֶרֶג אִם־תַּחְשׂוֹךְ:
יב כִּי־תֹאמַר הֵן לֹא־יָדַעְנוּ זֶה הֲלֹא־תֹכֵן לִבּוֹת | הוּא־יָבִין וְנֹצֵר נַפְשְׁךָ הוּא יֵדָע

battle, **salvation is with** the wisdom and insight of **abundant counsel,** many advisors.[412]

7 **Wisdom is lofty to a fool,** like an unreachably high place.[413] Since the fool feels that wisdom is entirely beyond his reach, he does not even attempt to study or acquire it, and therefore **at the** city **gate,** where the important people congregate, **he will not open his mouth,** as he has nothing to add to their learned conversations.

8 **He who calculates to do harm** to others, **they will call him a schemer.** In general, one who plans to harm another does so surreptitiously. When his plot is eventually discovered, he earns a reputation as one who uses his wisdom for illegitimate personal gains.[414]

9 A mere **scheme of folly is sin,** even if it is not brought to fruition, **and abomination is for a scoffing person.** Revulsion is the appropriate reaction to individuals who scoff at important matters.

10 **If you falter on a day of trouble, your strength will be curbed.** It is more important to show strength at times of trouble than when everything is running smoothly.[415]

11 This proverb is perhaps an illustration of the previous verse:[416] You must **deliver,** save, **those** people who are being **taken to death.** You must take any action you can to save such individuals. **If only you would save those likely to be killed.**[417] Some explain this as a question: Will you, due to weakness, absolve yourself of responsibility and refrain from taking action on such a day of trouble?

12 You will not escape responsibility for failing to respond. Even **if you say: Behold, we did not know this,** we could not have known that those people were in danger or that we could have saved them, this will not save you. **Truly, the Assessor of hearts, He understands, and the Safeguard of your soul, He knows.** Even if such excuses convince others that you are absolved of responsibility, such claims will be ineffective before God. He knows exactly what you did and did not know, **and** God **repays each man in accordance with his actions.**

13 **Eat honey, my son, as it is good, and nectar is sweet on your palate;**
14 **so** too **is knowing wisdom.** Just as honey is pleasing to the palate, you will find wisdom similarly pleasing **for your soul; if you have found it, there will be a future** for you, **and your hope will not be lost.**[418]
15 The aphorist speaks directly to the wicked person: **Do not lie in wait, wicked one, by the abode of the righteous,** if you see that he is about to suffer financial collapse or is forced to abandon his home.[419] **Do not plunder,** or destroy, **his resting place.** You should know that a righteous individual differs greatly from you,
16 **as the righteous falls seven times,** for everyone experiences downfalls during their lifetime,[420] **and** yet he **rises** up again. **But the wicked** ones, like you, **will stumble into harm,** and will not rise up again. Consequently, if you attempt to harm the righteous, it is you who will ultimately be destroyed by your own plot.
17 The aphorist turns to the righteous: **With the fall of your enemy, rejoice not, and in his stumbling, let your heart not be glad.** Such a reaction is immoral; there are no legitimate justifications for happiness over someone's sad fate.[421]
18 Furthermore, such rejoicing can be counterproductive: Do not rejoice in your enemy's fall **lest the Lord see it, and it is evil in His eyes, and** as a result **He** will **turn His wrath from him.** God does not want people to rejoice over the failure and suffering of others. If He observes you enjoying your enemy's downfall, He might reduce his suffering. In that case, your happiness has indirectly saved your enemy from the full extent of the punishment he deserves.[422]
19 **Do not compete with evildoers.** Alternatively, do not mingle with them and attempt to emulate their ways,[423] and **do not envy the wicked.**
20 Such envy is entirely misguided, **for there will be no future for,** or no remnant of, **the evil one,** and **the lamp of the wicked will** ultimately **go out.**
21 **Fear the Lord, my son, and** also be wary of **the king; do not mix with those who are different,** people with foreign opinions and ways,[424]
22 **for their calamity will rise suddenly** and unexpectedly, **and who knows the tragedy of both of them,** those who have foreign ideas and those who mingle with them?[425] Alternatively, the latter phrase refers to those who disobey God and those who defy the king.[426] It is impossible to know when they will be punished and in what manner. This fundamental idea is a recurring theme throughout the book of Proverbs: If you are not absolutely certain of all the details of a situation, it is preferable not to get involved.
23 **These,** the following proverbs, **too are** designed **for the wise** people, many of whom are important individuals, including judges:[427] **Showing preference in judgment,** creating the impression or appearance of favoring one party, **is no good.** Not only is such conduct expressly prohibited by the Torah, it also causes goodness to be withheld from the individual and society.[428]
24 **He who says to the wicked: You are righteous,** all **peoples will curse him,** and **nations will be furious with him.**
25 Conversely, **for the rebukers it will be pleasant, and a blessing of goodness will come upon them,** as people will bless them. A judge who maintains his objectivity and refrains from unjustly favoring anyone is not necessarily a passive individual. On the contrary, the prohibition against showing favoritism includes an obligation to rebuke those who act improperly, even if they are legally in the right.[429]
26 Everyone's **lips will kiss he who responds with sensible,** clear, and just **words.** People admire such an individual. Some explain that one who gives a right answer is comparable to one who kisses the lips of his listeners.[430]
27 **Prepare your labor outside, and ready them** for future use **for you in the field;** and only **afterward you will build your house.**[D]
28 **Do not be a witness against your friend for nothing,** unnecessarily,[431] **nor** should you **spread wide your lips** to prattle. It is inappropriate to meddle in other people's affairs, or to waste time with meaningless chatter.
29 **Do not say: I will do to him as he did to me; I will repay the man according to his actions.** Do not take revenge.
30 The following passage is a rebuke to lazy people: **I have passed by an idle man's field and the vineyard of a person lacking heart,** meaning devoid of understanding,

Weeds in a vineyard

DISCUSSION

24:27 | Prepare your labor outside, and ready them for you in the field; afterward you will build your house: The Rambam (*Sefer HaMadda, Hilkhot Deot* 5:11) derives from here that one should first plant a vineyard as a source of livelihood, then build a house, and lastly take a wife. This is the appropriate order, and one who deviates from it is likely to encounter difficulties (see *Metzudat David*; Malbim; *Sota* 44a).

יג יד וְהֵשִׁיב לְאָדָם כְּפָעֳלוֹ׃ אֱכָל־בְּנִי דְבַשׁ כִּי־טוֹב וְנֹפֶת מָתוֹק עַל־חִכֶּךָ׃ כֵּן ׀ דְּעֶה
טו חָכְמָה לְנַפְשֶׁךָ אִם־מָצָאתָ וְיֵשׁ אַחֲרִית וְתִקְוָתְךָ לֹא תִכָּרֵת׃ אַל־תֶּאֱרֹב רָשָׁע
טז לִנְוֵה צַדִּיק אַל־תְּשַׁדֵּד רִבְצוֹ׃ כִּי שֶׁבַע ׀ יִפּוֹל צַדִּיק וָקָם וּרְשָׁעִים יִכָּשְׁלוּ בְרָעָה׃
יז יח בִּנְפֹל אויביך אַל־תִּשְׂמָח וּבִכָּשְׁלוֹ אַל־יָגֵל לִבֶּךָ׃ פֶּן־יִרְאֶה יְהוָה וְרַע בְּעֵינָיו (אוֹיִבְךָ)
וְהֵשִׁיב מֵעָלָיו אַפּוֹ׃
יט כ אַל־תִּתְחַר בַּמְּרֵעִים אַל־תְּקַנֵּא בָּרְשָׁעִים׃ כִּי ׀ לֹא־תִהְיֶה אַחֲרִית לָרָע נֵר רְשָׁעִים
כא כב יִדְעָךְ׃ יְרָא־אֶת־יְהוָה בְּנִי וָמֶלֶךְ עִם־שׁוֹנִים אַל־תִּתְעָרָב׃ כִּי־פִתְאֹם יָקוּם אֵידָם
וּפִיד שְׁנֵיהֶם מִי יוֹדֵעַ׃
כג כד גַּם־אֵלֶּה לַחֲכָמִים הַכֵּר־פָּנִים בְּמִשְׁפָּט בַּל־טוֹב׃ אֹמֵר ׀ לְרָשָׁע צַדִּיק אָתָּה
כה יִקְּבֻהוּ עַמִּים יִזְעָמוּהוּ לְאֻמִּים׃ וְלַמּוֹכִיחִים יִנְעָם וַעֲלֵיהֶם תָּבוֹא בִרְכַּת־טוֹב׃
כו כז שְׂפָתַיִם יִשָּׁק מֵשִׁיב דְּבָרִים נְכֹחִים׃ הָכֵן בַּחוּץ ׀ מְלַאכְתֶּךָ וְעַתְּדָהּ בַּשָּׂדֶה לָךְ
אַחַר וּבָנִיתָ בֵיתֶךָ׃
כח כט אַל־תְּהִי עֵד־חִנָּם בְּרֵעֶךָ וַהֲפִתִּיתָ בִּשְׂפָתֶיךָ׃ אַל־תֹּאמַר כַּאֲשֶׁר עָשָׂה־לִי כֵּן
אֶעֱשֶׂה־לּוֹ אָשִׁיב לָאִישׁ כְּפָעֳלוֹ׃
ל לא עַל־שְׂדֵה אִישׁ־עָצֵל עָבַרְתִּי וְעַל־כֶּרֶם אָדָם חֲסַר־לֵב׃ וְהִנֵּה עָלָה כֻלּוֹ ׀ קִמְּשֹׂנִים
לב כָּסּוּ פָנָיו חֲרֻלִּים וְגֶדֶר אֲבָנָיו נֶהֱרָסָה׃ וָאֶחֱזֶה אָנֹכִי אָשִׁית לִבִּי רָאִיתִי לָקַחְתִּי
לג לד מוּסָר׃ מְעַט שֵׁנוֹת מְעַט תְּנוּמוֹת מְעַט ׀ חִבֻּק יָדַיִם לִשְׁכָּב׃ וּבָא־מִתְהַלֵּךְ רֵישֶׁךָ
וּמַחְסֹרֶיךָ כְּאִישׁ מָגֵן׃

31 **and behold, it was all overgrown with nettles, its surface covered with** various prickly plants and **thorns, and its stone fence,** which had previously enclosed the area, was **destroyed.**

32 **I saw, and I set my heart; I saw, and received admonition** by contemplating his neglected property.

33 The aphorist summarizes the pattern of the lazy person's habits: **A little sleep, a little slumber, a little folding of the hands to lie down.** First he sleeps a little, then he slumbers, and even after he eventually wakes up, he simply folds his hands and continues to rest.[432]

34 **Your poverty will come walking about** confidently, **and your lack** will come with certainty, **like a military man.** You carry out your affairs slowly, without any sense of urgency. By contrast, the consequences of your indolence will arrive swiftly and with determination.

Proverbs Copied by King Hizkiya's Men

PROVERBS 25:1–29:27

The following sayings do not differ substantively from the previous collection of Solomon's proverbs, although here one can more easily discern divisions into topics and links between the verses. It is possible that unlike the large, central compendium of proverbs, which was widespread and famous, this collection remained hidden until the time of King Hizkiya.

25 1 **These too,** the upcoming aphorisms, **are proverbs of Solomon that the men of Hizkiya king of Judah copied.**[D]

Matters Concerning Kings

PROVERBS 25:2–7

The book of Proverbs was composed by a king. It is therefore fitting that although the image of the king it portrays is not always ideal, the king invariably appears as a powerful figure.

2 **Concealing a matter is the glory of God.** God created the world without explaining its ultimate meaning. The universe has many hidden secrets, and so does God's Torah. These mysteries reflect His glory.[433] **But** by contrast, **the glory of** human **kings is to investigate a matter.** Kings are constantly investigating matters, seeking to reveal their causes, and this is their glory. The mysteries of existence, and the human desire and capacity to reveal them, complement one another.[434]

3 **The heavens** are unreachable **for,** on account of, their great **height, and the earth** is similarly unfathomable **for** its great **depth, and** likewise, **the heart of kings is** also **inscrutable.**[D] It cannot be entirely understood. A king has the ultimate authority over, and responsibility for, everything that happens in his realm. Even if he is not a great or wise individual, he presides over a government that is necessarily complex. Since he must make the ultimate decisions in this difficult environment, he must try to take into account the countless needs, desires, claims, and opinions of all the various individuals and groups under his control, even though he cannot know all the details. Such calculations are potentially endless.[435]

4 **Remove the dross from silver,**[B] **and** only then **a** completed[436] **vessel will emerge for the smith.**

5 Likewise, **remove the wicked** person **from** serving as an officer **before the king, and** then **his throne will be established in righteousness.** Just as it is difficult to fashion a magnificent vessel from silver that is full of dross, so too a king who has wicked people among his advisors will be unable to establish a grand and stable kingdom.

6 **Do not glorify yourself,** do not adorn yourself and attempt to draw attention to yourself, **before a king, and do not stand in the place of the great,** where nobles are present.

7 Instead, it is advisable for you to remain in your place, **as it is better that it should be said to you: Come up here, than that you should be demeaned before a prince, whom your eyes have seen,** with whom you are familiar. Even if you do not attain the highest levels, as you perhaps had hoped, at least someone might notice you at some point and help you advance. This situation is preferable to the alternative: If you forcefully push yourself to the center of power, ultimately you are likely to be demoted when a superior candidate is found.[437]

Methods of Communication

PROVERBS 25:8–28

8 **Do not go forth hastily to quarrel.** Avoid arguments, **lest you not know what to do** and how to react **in the end, when your friend humiliates you.**[438]

9 On a related matter: If you wish to quarrel, then **fight your battle with your friend.** If a disagreement remains within a limited circle of friends or associates, one can argue more freely, without fear of being humiliated or that the dispute will spin out of control. Even if the parties are unable to arrive at a mutually acceptable solution, a quarrel of this kind will not lead to shame. **But** even then, **do not reveal the secret of another** person,

10 **lest the listener humiliate you,**[D] **and your slandering,** the negative reports that your opponent will use to besmirch your reputation, **will not be rescinded.** It will be publicized, and you will remain helpless to prevent it.

11 **A word spoken appropriately is like golden apples,** or small balls, wrapped **in** decorative **silver ornaments,**[BD] which frame the gold balls. At first glance one notices only the silver, but upon more careful

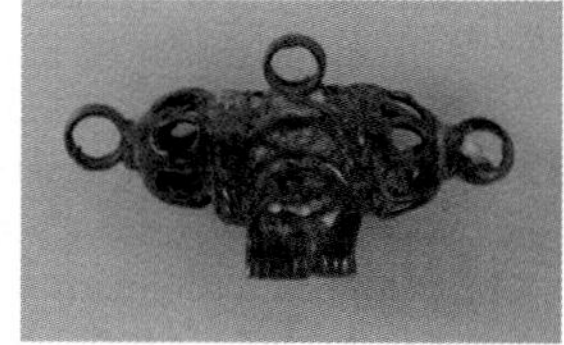

Silver ornament, Egypt, tenth to eighth century BCE

ה א ב גַּם־אֵלֶּה מִשְׁלֵי שְׁלֹמֹה אֲשֶׁר הֶעְתִּיקוּ אַנְשֵׁי ׀ חִזְקִיָּה מֶלֶךְ־יְהוּדָה׃ כְּבֹד אֱלֹהִים
ג הַסְתֵּר דָּבָר וּכְבֹד מְלָכִים חֲקֹר דָּבָר׃ שָׁמַיִם לָרוּם וָאָרֶץ לָעֹמֶק וְלֵב מְלָכִים
ד ה אֵין חֵקֶר׃ הָגוֹ סִיגִים מִכָּסֶף וַיֵּצֵא לַצֹּרֵף כֶּלִי׃ הָגוֹ רָשָׁע לִפְנֵי־מֶלֶךְ וְיִכּוֹן בַּצֶּדֶק
ו ז כִּסְאוֹ׃ אַל־תִּתְהַדַּר לִפְנֵי־מֶלֶךְ וּבִמְקוֹם גְּדֹלִים אַל־תַּעֲמֹד׃ כִּי טוֹב אֲמָר־לְךָ
ח עֲלֵה הֵנָּה מֵהַשְׁפִּילְךָ לִפְנֵי נָדִיב אֲשֶׁר רָאוּ עֵינֶיךָ׃ אַל־תֵּצֵא לָרִב מַהֵר פֶּן מַה־
ט תַּעֲשֶׂה בְּאַחֲרִיתָהּ בְּהַכְלִים אֹתְךָ רֵעֶךָ׃ רִיבְךָ רִיב אֶת־רֵעֶךָ וְסוֹד אַחֵר אַל־תְּגָל׃
י יא פֶּן־יְחַסֶּדְךָ שֹׁמֵעַ וְדִבָּתְךָ לֹא תָשׁוּב׃ תַּפּוּחֵי זָהָב בְּמַשְׂכִּיּוֹת כָּסֶף דָּבָר דָּבֻר עַל־

BACKGROUND

25:4 | **Dross from silver:** Silver is a noble metal, which means that it resists corrosion or oxidation through reactions with other elements, including oxygen. It is naturally found mixed with lead, sulfur, and other elements. Since ancient times, methods have been developed to purify silver by removing these materials, called dross. Most of these methods were only partially successful.

25:11 | **Golden apples in silver ornaments:** This is apparently referring to filigree, a type of jewelry metalwork comprised of silver threads arranged in various geometric patterns. The play of colors of the golden balls visible through the holes in the silver wrapping is considered exquisite and elegant. Interestingly, the combination of gold and silver also features in the procedures surrounding the paschal offering (see Mishna *Pesaḥim* 5:5).

DISCUSSION

25:1 | **That the men of Hizkiya king of Judah copied:** As a result of King Hizkiya's encouragement, love of Torah and its study thrived during his reign (see II Chronicles 30:22, 31:4). The Sages state that during that period everyone learned Torah, from the smallest to the greatest (see *Sanhedrin* 94b; *Sifrei*, *Va'ethanan* 32). Elsewhere the Bible recounts other great projects undertaken by Hizkiya, such as the fortifications he built and the wars he waged, perhaps in an attempt to restore the borders of Israel to their location during Solomon's days (see II Kings 18–19; II Chronicles 32). It is revealed here that another project that occupied his men was the literary work of collecting ancient manuscripts (see Rashi; Vilna Gaon).

25:3 | **The heavens for height, and the earth for depth, and the heart of kings is inscrutable:** This idea was reformulated by the Sages many generations later: Even if all the seas were ink, and the reeds that grow near swamps quills, and the heavens parchment, and all the people scribes, all of these are insufficient to write down the unquantifiable scope of governmental authority, that is, all the considerations with which a government must concern itself (*Shabbat* 11a).

25:10 | **Lest the listener humiliate you [*yeḥassedkha*]:** The root of *yeḥassedkha*, *ḥet-samekh-dalet*, bears two meanings. Its more widespread meaning is a positive one, indicating goodness, charity, grace, and pleasantness. However, it can also denote disgrace and shame. For example, in the book of Leviticus (20:17), one type of licentious act is called *ḥesed*. It is interesting to note that in Aramaic this root is more commonly used in its negative denotation of shame than in its positive meaning.

25:11 | **Golden apples in silver ornaments:** In the introduction to his *Guide of the Perplexed*, the Rambam uses this image in reference to the statements of the Sages, which invariably include multiple levels of meaning. One who comprehends their sayings on a simple level will at least receive settings of silver, whereas one who analyzes them in depth will merit golden apples. The Rambam adds that the proverbs of this book themselves contain hidden wisdom, beyond their plain meaning of advice for practical conduct that is advantageous to both the individual and society. Many commentaries follow this method in their interpretations of these chapters (see, e.g., Ralbag's commentary on Proverbs; Rabbeinu Baḥya, introduction to *Vayak'hel*).

inspection, one can discern the gold balls through the openings in the ornamental covering. Similarly, when a person speaks wisely, his statements contain nuances and deeper interpretations beneath the simple meaning of his words.[439]

12 This proverb employs a similar metaphor: **A wise rebuker in a heedful ear is a nose ring of gold and an** exquisite **adornment of fine gold.** When a wise person rebukes someone who is not particularly inclined to listen, his statement is generally not as effective as it could be. Similarly, if the one issuing the rebuke is not wise, his comments are sometimes unworthy of being heard. However, the combination of a wise person rebuking someone who is willing to listen is like a beautiful material that has been skillfully crafted into a beautiful shape.

"A nose ring of gold and an adornment of fine gold." Golden ornaments, Nimrud, Iraq

13 **An emissary loyal to his sender is** refreshing **like the cold of snow** when it falls **on a** hot summer **day** at the time **of** the wheat **harvest,**[B] as **he restores the soul of his master.** One can never be absolutely certain that his messenger will carry out a task correctly. Important objectives are frequently missed and opportunities lost because of an agent's failures. However, a faithful messenger who fulfills his mission dependably will refresh the soul of his sender.

14 **A man who glories in a false gift is clouds and wind but no rain.** The presence of clouds and wind create an expectation for rain, and if it does not fall, people experience great frustration. A similar disappointment results when one announces with great pride that he intends to make a generous contribution to some important cause but fails to fulfill his word.

"Clouds and wind but no rain"

15 **With forbearance,** patience and calm, **is** even **a** military **commander,** or a civilian of elevated stature, **enticed, and a soft tongue breaks a bone.** A tolerant approach and gentle speech can be highly effective when dealing with aristocrats or difficult officials.

16 **You found honey; eat enough for yourself,** for your actual needs, **lest you** overeat, because it is so sweet and you came across it unexpectedly, and you will **be** too **sated with it, and vomit it.**[D]

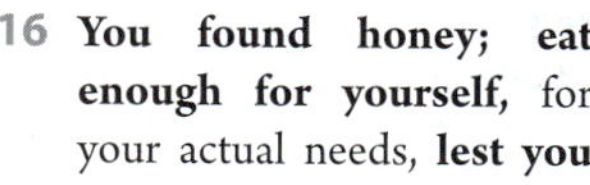

Honey

17 Likewise, **let your foot be scarce in your friend's house.** Refrain from visiting there too frequently.[440] Alternatively, make your foot precious [*yakar*] and important to him, by not spending too much time in his home.[441] Do not visit him too often, even if he is your friend. You must maintain a certain distance, **lest he be sated with you and hate you.**[D] Just as one must be careful to eat sweet honey in moderation, so too you should not overstay your welcome in your friend's house, as this might lead him to push you away.

18 **A man who bears false witness against his friend is a battering ram,**[B] **a sword, and a sharp arrow.** Such a witness shatters, pierces, and kills, and it is hard to thwart his destructive act.

"Sharp arrow." Arrowheads, City of David, Hasmonean period

"Battering ram." Illustration based on relief from Nimrud, ninth century BCE

19 **Trust in a traitor on a day of trouble is a loose tooth and an unsteady** or dislocated **foot.** One who tries to use them will be frustrated and feel greater pain than if the tooth or foot were simply missing. Those who rely on the assurances of an unfaithful person will similarly suffer; it is when their assistance is most necessary that their lack of trustworthiness becomes clear.[442]

20 **Removing**[443] **a garment on a cold day is vinegar** that one pours **on natron,** a detergent, **and as he who sings songs to a sorrowful heart.** In chemical terms, natron, or niter, is a base, and therefore when an acidic substance is poured on it, the two substances neutralize one another. The idea is that one who

יב אָפְנָיו: נֶזֶם זָהָב וַחֲלִי־כָתֶם מוֹכִיחַ חָכָם עַל־אֹזֶן שֹׁמָעַת:
יג כְּצִנַּת־שֶׁלֶג ׀ בְּיוֹם קָצִיר צִיר נֶאֱמָן לְשֹׁלְחָיו וְנֶפֶשׁ אֲדֹנָיו יָשִׁיב: ז
יד טו נְשִׂיאִים וְרוּחַ וְגֶשֶׁם אָיִן אִישׁ מִתְהַלֵּל בְּמַתַּת־שָׁקֶר: בְּאֹרֶךְ אַפַּיִם יְפֻתֶּה קָצִין
טז יז וְלָשׁוֹן רַכָּה תִּשְׁבָּר־גָּרֶם: דְּבַשׁ מָצָאתָ אֱכֹל דַּיֶּךָּ פֶּן־תִּשְׂבָּעֶנּוּ וַהֲקֵאתוֹ: הֹקַר
יח רַגְלְךָ מִבֵּית רֵעֶךָ פֶּן־יִשְׂבָּעֲךָ וּשְׂנֵאֶךָ: מֵפִיץ וְחֶרֶב וְחֵץ שָׁנוּן אִישׁ־עֹנֶה בְרֵעֵהוּ
יט כ עֵד שָׁקֶר: שֵׁן רֹעָה וְרֶגֶל מוּעָדֶת מִבְטָח בּוֹגֵד בְּיוֹם צָרָה: מַעֲדֶה־בֶּגֶד ׀ בְּיוֹם
כא קָרָה חֹמֶץ עַל־נָתֶר וְשָׁר בַּשִּׁרִים עַל לֶב־רָע: אִם־רָעֵב שֹׂנַאֲךָ הַאֲכִלֵהוּ לָחֶם
כב וְאִם־צָמֵא הַשְׁקֵהוּ מָיִם: כִּי גֶחָלִים אַתָּה חֹתֶה עַל־רֹאשׁוֹ וַיהוָה יְשַׁלֶּם־לָךְ:
כג כד רוּחַ צָפוֹן תְּחוֹלֵל גָּשֶׁם וּפָנִים נִזְעָמִים לְשׁוֹן סָתֶר: טוֹב שֶׁבֶת עַל־פִּנַּת־גָּג מֵאֵשֶׁת
מדונים וּבֵית חָבֶר: מִדְיָנִים

sings in an attempt to bring joy and pleasure to a mourner actually increases his pain, just as vinegar damages niter.

21 **If your enemy is hungry, feed him bread; and if thirsty, give him water to drink.** Although your natural inclination is to take revenge, you should resist such temptation and help him instead,

22 **as you are raking coals upon his head.** His knowledge that he has become dependent on his enemy, who is feeding him and has repaid his evil deeds with kindness, is humiliating for him. Furthermore, it is an inherently good deed, **and** therefore, **the Lord will reward you** for performing this kind act. By showing him kindness you will benefit twice; you will achieve the highest form of sweet and effective revenge, and you will also be rewarded.[444]

23 **A north wind generates rain,**[B] **and an angry face** generates **a stealthy tongue.** Just as the north wind generally brings rain clouds in the Land of Israel, so too, when someone has an angry face but is unable to express his thoughts publicly, he will eventually let out his rage by speaking in secret.

24 **Better to live** alone, like a bird **on** an exposed **corner of a roof,**

BACKGROUND

25:13| **Like the cold of snow on a day of harvest:** This unusual imagery was perhaps inspired by the snow that can be seen on Mount Hermon, or by tall mountains that remain snowcapped even during summer, a phenomenon that was known even in antiquity. There are also historical references to snow that was transported and sold in the markets of Tyre and even Egypt as a luxury item for cooling drinks (see Eusebius of Caesarea, *Das Onomastikon der Biblischen Ortsnamen*, E. Klostermann, ed., Hildesheim, Germany: Georg Olms Publishers, 1966 [Greek and Latin], 21). In addition, the Mishna discusses the use of snow to fill a ritual bath in situations where rainwater is unavailable (*Mikvaot* 7:1).

25:18| **Battering ram [*mefitz*]:** Battering rams were used in siege warfare to apply repeated blows to walls and fortifications, and thereby weaken and destroy them. This instrument, in various forms, was common throughout the ancient world.

25:23| **A north wind generates rain:** The majority of the rain in the Land of Israel comes from the west or northwest, due to low-pressure systems from the regions of Italy or Cyprus. Occasionally, powerful winds arrive directly from the north, the area of Russia, bringing rainstorms and even snow.

DISCUSSION

25:16| **Lest you be sated with it and vomit it:** It is possible that this consumption of honey symbolizes the analysis of complex, esoteric wisdom, which must also be performed with care and by observing boundaries (see Rambam, *Guide of the Perplexed* 1:32; Rabbeinu Baḥya, introduction to *Pekudei*).

25:17| **Let your foot be scarce in your friend's house, lest he be sated with you and hate you:** Some Sages apply this principle even to pilgrims to the Temple. It is unbecoming to visit God's Temple too often (see Rambam, *Guide of the Perplexed* 3:47, based on *Ḥagiga* 7a). This saying suits the overall spirit of the book of Proverbs, that actions are pleasing and suitable when they are performed in moderation.

with no shelter or room to move, **than** to live **with a woman of strife in a comfortable house,** which has enough space for social events.

25 **Cold water on a weary soul,** which revives it, **is** as **good news** that arrives unexpectedly **from a distant land.** Such news likewise renews and revives one's soul.

26 **A righteous man who** collapses and **grovels before the wicked is** like **a muddied** and polluted **spring and a ruined fount.** A righteous person is a source of blessing, and therefore he should feel protected and secure. His downfall before a wicked person is particularly painful, like the ruins of a formerly clear and refreshing spring.[445] Some commentaries interpret this analogy in a positive manner, that the righteous who fall before the wicked will ultimately rise again and be restored, just as a muddied spring eventually returns to its pristine state.[446]

27 **Eating much honey is no good, but assessing their honor is honorable.** Although investigating and evaluating matters brings glory, one should limit his analysis of goodness or wisdom, just as there is a limit to how much honey one should eat.[447] Alternatively, many commentaries interpret the verse as presenting two opposite ideas: Whereas the consumption of honey should be limited, one should publicize the glory of the righteous and the statements of the wise as much as possible.

28 **A man with no constraint to his spirit is a breached city without a** protective **wall.** People who speak without inhibitions harm both others and themselves.

The Fool and His Dealings

PROVERBS 26:1–12

26 1 **Like snow** that comes **in the summer and like rain** that falls **during the harvest,** bizarre occurrences that are not in accordance with the proper order of nature cause general discomfort, and are even harmful to crops, **so is honor not fitting for a fool.**[448]

2 **Like the bird wandering,** and **like the swallow**[B] **flying,** which eventually return to the nests they left,[449] **so the pointless curse,** a curse uttered without reason, **will come** only **upon him** [***lo***], the one who curses. It will not cause harm to another person. The translation follows the vocalization of the word *lo*, *lamed-vav*, as prescribed by the oral tradition. According to the Masoretic spelling of the word, *lamed-alef*, the end of the verse would mean: "So the pointless curse will not come about."

Swallow

Sparrows

3 **A whip** is designed **for** striking **the horse, a bit**[B] **for** leading **the donkey, and a rod for** hitting **the back,** or body, **of fools.** The rod is the most effective implement for the education of fools.[450]

4 **Do not answer a fool according to his folly,** in the same manner that he speaks, **lest you too** come to **resemble him.** When you argue with him, you will necessarily converse in his language and style.

"Whip for the horse." Illustration on amphora, Athens, 700 BCE

Bit in horse's mouth

5 Surprisingly, this aphorism is the reverse of the previous one: **Answer a fool**[D] **according to his folly, lest he become wise in his own eyes.** If you do not respond to him in a way that he can understand, he will imagine that he is clever and that

DISCUSSION

26:4–5 | **Do not answer a fool…Answer a fool:** The juxtaposition of these two verses prompts many of the commentaries to discuss their relationship. The Sages state that in general one should not answer a fool unless he inquires with regard to matters of Torah, in which case one should respond to him (*Shabbat* 30b). Although when speaking with him one necessarily begins to speak in his style, which lowers the level of the conversation, there are nevertheless some occasions when one must protest and inform the public that the fool is not correct. Therefore, in specific cases one must deliberate whether it is worthwhile to show everyone that the fool has received a response, even if his question consisted of pure foolishness (see Ralbag).

מַיִם קָרִים עַל־נֶפֶשׁ עֲיֵפָה וּשְׁמוּעָה טוֹבָה מֵאֶרֶץ מֶרְחָק׃ מַעְיָן נִרְפָּשׂ וּמָקוֹר כה כו
מִשְׁחָת צַדִּיק מָט לִפְנֵי־רָשָׁע׃ אָכֹל דְּבַשׁ הַרְבּוֹת לֹא־טוֹב וְחֵקֶר כְּבֹדָם כָּבוֹד׃ כז
עִיר פְּרוּצָה אֵין חוֹמָה אִישׁ אֲשֶׁר אֵין מַעְצָר לְרוּחוֹ׃ כַּשֶּׁלֶג ׀ בַּקַּיִץ וְכַמָּטָר כח א
בַּקָּצִיר כֵּן לֹא־נָאוֶה לִכְסִיל כָּבוֹד׃ כַּצִּפּוֹר לָנוּד כַּדְּרוֹר לָעוּף כֵּן קִלְלַת חִנָּם ב
לֹא תָבֹא׃ שׁוֹט לַסּוּס מֶתֶג לַחֲמוֹר וְשֵׁבֶט לְגֵו כְּסִילִים׃ אַל־תַּעַן כְּסִיל כְּאִוַּלְתּוֹ ג ד לוֹ
פֶּן־תִּשְׁוֶה־לּוֹ גַם־אָתָּה׃ עֲנֵה כְסִיל כְּאִוַּלְתּוֹ פֶּן־יִהְיֶה חָכָם בְּעֵינָיו׃ מְקַצֶּה רַגְלַיִם ה ו
חָמָס שֹׁתֶה שֹׁלֵחַ דְּבָרִים בְּיַד־כְּסִיל׃ דַּלְיוּ שֹׁקַיִם מִפִּסֵּחַ וּמָשָׁל בְּפִי כְסִילִים׃ ז
כִּצְרוֹר אֶבֶן בְּמַרְגֵּמָה כֵּן־נוֹתֵן לִכְסִיל כָּבוֹד׃ חוֹחַ עָלָה בְיַד־שִׁכּוֹר וּמָשָׁל בְּפִי ח ט

he has won the argument. It would seem from the contradictory nature of these aphorisms that no single solution is always effective in dealing with fools. On the one hand, one who responds to them becomes similar to them; on the other hand, if they are left to talk unchallenged, they will appear justified.

6 **He who sends things by the hand of a fool cuts off his feet and drinks rancor,** anger or injustice. Some explain that a mission through the agency of a fool is a self-negating act, comparable to one who sends a messenger while cutting off his feet and thereby incapacitating him. Furthermore, the sender himself is hurt as well, as the outcome will not be to his liking: The fool will not reach his destination at all, or at the very least, the mission will not be performed properly.

7 **As calves protrude from the lame, so is a proverb in the mouth of fools.** Since the calves of a lame person are improperly positioned, they appear to protrude and seem bent and twisted.[451] Likewise, even on the rare occasion when a fool attempts to utter a proverb, his statement comes out distorted and inaccurate.

8 **Like** one who places **a pebble in a sling,**[B] a device for throwing stones, **so is he who gives honor to a fool.** It will bring no benefit to anyone, as it is unknown what effect this honor will have and what damage it might cause.[452]

9 Like **a thorn that enters the hand of a drunkard, so is a proverb in the mouth of fools.** When a drunkard walks, he cannot properly discern objects that lie in his way, and therefore he is liable to grasp onto thorns. Likewise, when a fool relates a proverb or utters a wise statement, he chooses something unsuitable for the time and place. This distorts the wise statement he repeats and can even be somewhat dangerous.[453]

BACKGROUND

26:2| **Swallow** [***deror***]: The identity of this bird is uncertain. However, its qualities that are mentioned in the Bible and by the Sages, such as its proximity to human habitats (Psalms 84:4; *Shabbat* 106b), its small dimensions (*Tosefta, Shabbat* 8:19), and its ability to elude capture even in enclosed areas (*Shabbat* 106b), match the description of a number of birds: the turtledove, the swallow, and the sparrow. Various Bible translations, as well as some of the commentaries, identify the *deror* as any one of these species. Even *Metzudat Tzion*, who interprets it as the *atalef*, may be referring to the swallow, as the word *atalef*, which in modern Hebrew refers to a bat, was used to denote the swallow until the nineteenth century.

26:3| **Bit:** This is a thin, short, metal bar which is placed in the mouth of an animal and attached to the reins with rings, in order to lead and halt the animal. The pulling of a bridle by the rider through the reins is sharply felt by the animal in its mouth, and causes it to respond by stopping or turning.

26:8| **Sling** [***margema***]: The word *regima* means the act of throwing stones. Consequently, a *margema* is an implement used for this purpose, a sling. This is not referring to the catapult, a large device used for flinging stones a great distance, as that device postdates the biblical period. Some explain that a *margema* is a heap of stones, similar to the Arabic *rujm*. Accordingly, the verse would be alluding to the pagan rite of throwing a stone upon a pile of stones (*Ḥullin* 133a; see *Tosefta, Avoda Zara* 7:18).

10 **The great man may bring about anything and** yet **he hires a fool and hires the disobedient.** Although the master has many projects, they are not done properly because he hires a fool or the disobedient to do the job.[454]
11 **Like a dog returns to its vomit**[B] and attempts to eat it, **so a fool repeats his folly,** the nonsense he spews, over and over again. In biblical times, dogs frequently rummaged around and searched for food.[455]
12 **Have you seen a man** who is **wise in his own eyes? There is more hope for a fool than for him.** One's self-image as a wise person is dangerous, as it holds him back from improving. Consequently, even an actual fool has a greater chance to better himself than such an individual.

The Idler

PROVERBS 26:13–16

13 **The idler says: There is a lion on the way, a lion** is wandering **in the squares.** All the sluggard wants to do is stay at home, and he finds all kinds of excuses to refrain from venturing out into the street.
14 **The door turns** from side to side **on its hinges, and** similarly **the idler** is still turning **on his bed,** over and again, refusing to budge.[456]
15 **The idler inserts his hand into the dish; he is too weary to return it to his mouth.** He is so lazy that he cannot find the strength to finish a task he has begun, not even the basic act of eating, and he ultimately remains hungry.[457]
16 **The idler is wiser in his own eyes than seven who respond sensibly,** who speak words of substance and issue intelligent replies. A lazy person prefers to rest secure in his own wisdom, and he does not even care to consult the many sayings of the wise that are available to him.

Men of Strife and Hatred

PROVERBS 26:17–28

17 **A passerby who is angered over a quarrel not his is** like **one who grasps the ears of a dog.** One who interferes in a dispute that does not concern him is comparable to one who grabs hold of the ears of a dog for no reason, provoking the animal, that is likely to bite him.[458]
18 **Like the prankster who shoots firebrands, arrows, and death,** deadly arrows, all for fun,[459]
19 **so is a man who deceives** and harms **his friend** with his words, **and** then **says:** After all, **aren't I** only **joking?** I did not mean to hurt you; I was just playing.[460]
20 **In the absence of wood the fire will be extinguished, and without a grumbler,** one who instigates quarrels, **strife is silenced.** With his absence, arguments are also quelled and disappear.
21 Likewise, **like charcoal** used **to** produce **coals, and wood to** kindle **fire, so is** the behavior of **a contentious man to inciting a quarrel.**

"Like charcoal to coals and wood to fire"

22 **The words of a grumbler,** or one who is looking to pick a fight, **are like blows, and** ultimately **they descend into the chambers of the belly** and cause offense, even if the intention of the speaker was not to do so (see 18:8).
23 If one has **ardent lips,** which speak with passion and sometimes too sweetly, **but an evil heart,** one's words **are** like **silver dross coating earthenware.**[B] Insincere speech may sound

BACKGROUND

26:11| **Like a dog returns to its vomit:** Domesticated dogs have become accustomed to a different diet than the rest of the dog family. However, wild dogs sometimes find the enzymes they lack by eating their excrement and vomit, to which enzymes have been added by the digestive system. Sometimes their lack of enzymes is simply due to a shortage of food, especially in the case of wandering dogs that rummage in garbage.

26:23| **Silver dross [*sigim*] coating earthenware:** In ancient times people would often use metal dross, mainly silica and metal oxides, for glazing and externally sealing earthenware vessels, a process called *safsag* in Hitite and Ugaritic. A furnace was used for this process.

י כְּסִילִים: רַב מְחוֹלֵל־כֹּל וְשֹׂכֵר כְּסִיל וְשֹׂכֵר עֹבְרִים:
יא יב כְּכֶלֶב שָׁב עַל־קֵאוֹ כְּסִיל שׁוֹנֶה בְאִוַּלְתּוֹ: רָאִיתָ אִישׁ חָכָם בְּעֵינָיו תִּקְוָה לִכְסִיל
יג יד מִמֶּנּוּ: אָמַר עָצֵל שַׁחַל בַּדָּרֶךְ אֲרִי בֵּין הָרְחֹבוֹת: הַדֶּלֶת תִּסּוֹב עַל־צִירָהּ
טו טז וְעָצֵל עַל־מִטָּתוֹ: טָמַן עָצֵל יָדוֹ בַּצַּלָּחַת נִלְאָה לַהֲשִׁיבָהּ אֶל־פִּיו: חָכָם עָצֵל
יז בְּעֵינָיו מִשִּׁבְעָה מְשִׁיבֵי טָעַם: מַחֲזִיק בְּאָזְנֵי־כָלֶב עֹבֵר מִתְעַבֵּר עַל־רִיב לֹּא־לוֹ:
יח יט כְּמִתְלַהְלֵהַּ הַיֹּרֶה זִקִּים חִצִּים וָמָוֶת: כֵּן־אִישׁ רִמָּה אֶת־רֵעֵהוּ וְאָמַר הֲלֹא־מְשַׂחֵק
כ כא אָנִי: בְּאֶפֶס עֵצִים תִּכְבֶּה־אֵשׁ וּבְאֵין נִרְגָּן יִשְׁתֹּק מָדוֹן: פֶּחָם לְגֶחָלִים וְעֵצִים
לְאֵשׁ וְאִישׁ מדונים לְחַרְחַר־רִיב: מִדְיָנִים
כב כג דִּבְרֵי נִרְגָּן כְּמִתְלַהֲמִים וְהֵם יָרְדוּ חַדְרֵי־בָטֶן: כֶּסֶף סִיגִים מְצֻפֶּה עַל־חָרֶשׂ
כד כה שְׂפָתַיִם דֹּלְקִים וְלֶב־רָע: בִּשְׂפָתָו יִנָּכֵר שׂוֹנֵא וּבְקִרְבּוֹ יָשִׁית מִרְמָה: כִּי־יְחַנֵּן
כו קוֹלוֹ אַל־תַּאֲמֶן־בּוֹ כִּי שֶׁבַע תּוֹעֵבוֹת בְּלִבּוֹ: תִּכַּסֶּה שִׂנְאָה בְּמַשָּׁאוֹן תִּגָּלֶה
כז כח רָעָתוֹ בְקָהָל: כֹּרֶה־שַּׁחַת בָּהּ יִפֹּל וְגֹלֵל אֶבֶן אֵלָיו תָּשׁוּב: לְשׁוֹן־שֶׁקֶר יִשְׂנָא
ז א דַכָּיו וּפֶה חָלָק יַעֲשֶׂה מִדְחֶה: אַל־תִּתְהַלֵּל בְּיוֹם מָחָר כִּי לֹא־תֵדַע מַה־יֵּלֶד

sweet but is inherently worthless, just like impure silver covering cheap earthenware.

24 **An enemy dissembles with his lips,** as he disguises himself in order to appear to love the person he despises, **and** despite his friendly face, **within himself he places deceit.**

25 **When he ingratiates with his voice,** seeking to find favor or plead his case, **do not trust him, as there are seven,** many, **abominations,** repulsive matters, **in his heart.**

26 **Hatred will be concealed by desolation.** Eventually his hatred will be covered with destruction, and **his wickedness will be revealed before the congregation,** in public. Do not believe an evil person even if he is speaks kindly. When events develop naturally, he will ultimately harm his own cause and reveal the true feelings in his heart.[461]

27 For **he who digs a pit will** himself **fall into it, and** with regard to **he who rolls a stone** up the incline of a hill, the likely result is that **it will return onto him.** Ultimately, wickedness harms the perpetrator himself.

28 One who has **a lying tongue hates the pure,** anything that is pristine and clean. Alternatively, he hates the unfortunate people he exploits, or he hates those who reprove him. **And a slippery,** or smooth, **mouth will make mistakes.** One should therefore keep away from a lying tongue that instigates hatred and evil, and from flattering statements that only deceive and cause trouble.

Boastfulness, Anger, and Hatred

PROVERBS 27:1–6

27 1 **Do not glory in tomorrow;** do not glorify yourself in all the wonderful things you expect will happen to you in the future, **for you do not know what a day will bring about,** what will actually occur.

2 **Let a stranger praise you, and not your own mouth.** When it comes to compliments about you, it is better that they come from others rather than from yourself. Let **a foreigner** praise you, **and not your own lips.**
3 **Heavy is a stone and** likewise **weighty is the sand, but the anger of a fool is heavier than both of them.** There are many heavy, wearisome objects in the world, but the anger of a fool is more oppressive than all of them.
4 **Cruelty is** often the result of **fury and a torrent of wrath, but who can withstand jealousy?** Jealousy is harsher than anger, as it can completely engulf a person.
5 **Better open rebuke than concealed love.** Love that has no external expression is of minimal benefit. By contrast, an actual rebuke, which is unpleasant at first, might ultimately have a positive effect.[462]
6 **Faithful,** suitable and acceptable, **are the wounds of a friend, and the kisses of an enemy are onerous.**[463] Reproof and castigation delivered by someone who cares are for the good, whereas the apparently favorable approaches of an enemy are invariably unhelpful.[464]

The Senses, Wisdom, and Friendship

PROVERBS 27:7–22

7 **The sated soul will reject honey.** One who has eaten too much will lose his appetite entirely and reject even sweet, tasty foods; **and for the hungry soul everything bitter is sweet.** Even bitter foods are welcome to the palate of the hungry.
8 **Like a bird wandering from its nest** to seek food or to escape some disturbance will find no rest until it returns to its home, **so is a man who wanders from his place** to earn a livelihood or to flee from trouble. He too yearns to come back, and is not at ease and settled until he returns.

Wandering bird

9 Refreshing **oil and** fragrant **incense gladden the heart, and** this is similar to **the sweetness of one's friend** that comes **from profound counsel.**[D] There is a special sweetness and joy in receiving sincere advice from a good friend.
10 This proverb continues the theme of the previous one: **Do not forsake your friend or your father's friend;** remain faithful. **And do not go to your brother's house on the day of your calamity,** because he, unlike your friend, suffers together with you, and your presence will only make things harder for him. **A close friend is better,** more useful and effective, **than a distant brother.** If your brother remains distant and is uninterested in drawing close to you, he will not provide you with support.[465]
11 **Be wise, my son, and** thereby **my heart will be glad, and I will have an answer for him who reviles** and curses **me.** People sometimes curse a person for the failure of his student or son. A successful son or disciple protects the parent or educator from disparagement or humiliation.[466]
12 **The clever,** discerning **one sees** potential **harm** ahead **and** immediately **hides, but naïfs,** by contrast, **pass** right through the dangerous spot, **and are punished** for their recklessness, as they do not know how to exercise caution. This advice was mentioned above (22:3).

DISCUSSION

27:8–9 | **So is a man who wanders from his place...and the sweetness of one's friend from profound counsel:** It is possible that the juxtaposition of these verses indicates the unique attention one should give to a stranger or a guest from another locale (see Rabbeinu Baḥya, introduction to *Tetzaveh*).

BACKGROUND

27:17 | **Iron sharpens iron:** In the ancient world, iron was the hardest known material (see Daniel 2:40). Therefore, iron files were used for sharpening other iron implements.

27:18 | **The guardian of [*notzer*] a fig tree:** Some explain that *notzer* is derived from *netzer*, a stem. In other words, one who plants the stem of a fig tree shall eat its fruit (see Jeremiah 31:5). Planting the stems of fig trees was one of the oldest agricultural activities practiced in the ancient world. According to this interpretation, the verse is emphasizing the right of one who plants a fig tree to enjoy its fruit.

יוֹם׃ יְהַלֶּלְךָ זָר וְלֹא־פִיךָ נָכְרִי וְאַל־שְׂפָתֶיךָ׃ כֹּבֶד־אֶבֶן וְנֵטֶל הַחוֹל וְכַעַס אֱוִיל ב ג
כָּבֵד מִשְּׁנֵיהֶם׃ אַכְזְרִיּוּת חֵמָה וְשֶׁטֶף אָף וּמִי יַעֲמֹד לִפְנֵי קִנְאָה׃ טוֹבָה תּוֹכַחַת ד ה
מְגֻלָּה מֵאַהֲבָה מְסֻתָּרֶת׃ נֶאֱמָנִים פִּצְעֵי אוֹהֵב וְנַעְתָּרוֹת נְשִׁיקוֹת שׂוֹנֵא׃ נֶפֶשׁ ו ז
שְׂבֵעָה תָּבוּס נֹפֶת וְנֶפֶשׁ רְעֵבָה כָּל־מַר מָתוֹק׃ כְּצִפּוֹר נוֹדֶדֶת מִן־קִנָּהּ כֵּן־אִישׁ ח
וְרֵעַ נוֹדֵד מִמְּקוֹמוֹ׃ שֶׁמֶן וּקְטֹרֶת יְשַׂמַּח־לֵב וּמֶתֶק רֵעֵהוּ מֵעֲצַת־נָפֶשׁ׃ רֵעֲךָ ורעה ט י
אָבִיךָ אַל־תַּעֲזֹב וּבֵית אָחִיךָ אַל־תָּבוֹא בְּיוֹם אֵידֶךָ טוֹב שָׁכֵן קָרוֹב מֵאָח רָחוֹק׃
חֲכַם בְּנִי וְשַׂמַּח לִבִּי וְאָשִׁיבָה חֹרְפִי דָבָר׃ עָרוּם רָאָה רָעָה נִסְתָּר פְּתָאיִם עָבְרוּ יא יב
נֶעֱנָשׁוּ׃ קַח־בִּגְדוֹ כִּי־עָרַב זָר וּבְעַד נָכְרִיָּה חַבְלֵהוּ׃ מְבָרֵךְ רֵעֵהוּ ׀ בְּקוֹל גָּדוֹל יג יד
מִדְיָנִים בַּבֹּקֶר הַשְׁכֵּים קְלָלָה תֵּחָשֶׁב לוֹ׃ דֶּלֶף טוֹרֵד בְּיוֹם סַגְרִיר וְאֵשֶׁת מדונים נִשְׁתָּוָה׃ טו
צֹפְנֶיהָ צָפַן־רוּחַ וְשֶׁמֶן יְמִינוֹ יִקְרָא׃ בַּרְזֶל בְּבַרְזֶל יָחַד וְאִישׁ יַחַד פְּנֵי־רֵעֵהוּ׃ נֹצֵר טז יז יח

13 A lender is often told: **Take his garment,** the garment of so-and-so, **for he was** a **guarantor** on a loan **for a stranger** and needlessly acted against his own interests. **And take it as collateral for a foreign woman,** for whom he signed as a guarantor in order to help extricate her from trouble. It is better not to become involved in the debts of others, certainly not strangers who request a supposedly small favor. By becoming involved a person is liable to lose his possessions. This advice also appeared earlier (20:16; and see, e.g., 6:1, 17:18).[467]

14 **He who blesses his friend in a loud voice early in the morning,** when all can hear his blessing, in an overly eager manner or at an unseemly hour, **it will be considered a curse to him.** Not everyone likes to be blessed loudly. Furthermore, too many public blessings and praises can be harmful. If it is openly proclaimed that someone is generous, for example, too many people might come to his door seeking support and assistance. It is better to bless someone in private and in the appropriate circumstances.[468]

15 **A bothersome drip** inside one's home **on a cold rainy day and a contentious woman are alike,** equally unpleasant.[469]

16 In fact, a contentious woman is even worse than dripping water, as **he who hides her** flaws is like one who **hides wind,** an impossible task, **and** she is like **the oil** [*shemen*] **of his right hand** which **proclaims** or declares itself. Her presence cannot be concealed, like oil smeared on the right hand, which leaves its traces on everything.[470] Other interpretations: He will eventually hurt his right hand and will have to smear it with oil; trying to hide her is like attempting to hide oil in one's hand, a pointless effort; or he will have to call upon his fattened [*shemena*], strong, right hand in order to control a contentious woman.

17 **Iron sharpens** other **iron**[B] when the two items are rubbed against each other; **and** so too **a man sharpens in the presence of** [***penei***] **his friend.** When two friends sit together, they sharpen each other's minds.[471] Some translate: He makes the countenance of [*penei*] his friend joyful.

"Iron sharpens iron"

18 **The guardian of a fig tree,**[B] whose fruit ripens in stages over a lengthy period of time rather than in a single

Fig tree with fruits emerging

day, is the one who **will eat its fruit.** In order to take the fruit, it is necessary to remain next to the tree and guard the figs from damage when they fall as well as ensure that they are neither taken by others nor eaten by animals. **And** likewise, **the** diligent and devoted **protector of his master,** or teacher, **will be honored.** He will earn honor, which is the fruit of his labor.[472]

19 **As water reflects a face** back **to the face** that looks into it, **so does the heart of a person** reflect his feelings **to a person** who faces him. One who looks into water will see his own face, as in a mirror, and every distortion of his features, whether due to affection or anger, will appear there. Similarly, one's heart reflects back the feelings of another, as a person treats a friend in the manner in which he is treated by his friend.

20 **The grave and oblivion are not sated,** as more and more people enter into them, **and** likewise **the eyes of man are not sated;** they are always craving more. Endless greed is a kind of internal hell within a person.[473]

21 **The refining pot is** used **for** testing and purifying **silver, and the crucible,** which is even hotter than a refining pot,[474] is **for gold, and a man is** tested, and his quality can be ascertained, **according to his praise,** the compliments that people pay him.[475] Alternatively, the verse means that the more one is praised, the more exacting the scrutiny of his conduct; or: The nature of a person can be established by that which he himself praises.

22 **If you crush a fool among the groats in a mortar** and strike him **with a pestle,**[B] a small stone rod, that is, even if you chastise him, **his folly will not be removed from him.** He will remain foolish, and therefore there is no point in reprimanding him.

Mortar and pestle, Neolithic Age

The Owner of Flocks

PROVERBS 27:23–27

This section is addressed specifically to one who owns flocks, but it is basically an encouragement to all owners of small businesses and those with modest incomes to take care not to neglect them. A secure, stable investment can accumulate and ultimately serve the investor well.

23 **Know the faces of your flocks,** their nature and needs, **and pay attention to the herds,** despite the fact that they generally do not require close supervision;

24 **for prosperity,** material wealth and power, **is not forever, nor is a crown,** a precious item or exalted state, something that will necessarily remain **from generation to generation.** Not even a crown lasts forever, and therefore one should pay attention to minor, prosaic matters as well, such as taking care of one's flock, despite the dull nature of such occupations.[476]

25 The text explains why taking care of one's flock is a good investment: **Pasture is revealed, and grass is seen, and the vegetation of the mountains,** the flocks' pasture, **is gathered,** and it grows again each season so that the animals have a constant source of food.

26 The wool of the **lambs will be for your garments and he-goats** will serve **for the price of a field.** Male goats produce neither milk nor wool, but they can be sold in order to fund the acquisition of a field.[477]

Flock at pasture

27 **Goats' milk will suffice for your food, for the food of your household,** your entire family; **and** the milk will also provide **nourishment for your maids.**

People and Their Influence on Society

PROVERBS 28:1–29:27

The pearls of wisdom and moral maxims presented here deal with human behavior in general, without focusing on a specific area. Nevertheless, considerable space is devoted here to matters involving society and its rulers, government, and public organizations.

28 1 **The wicked flee without a pursuer.** Ultimately, the wicked will be afraid even when no one is chasing them; **but the righteous will** all **be** as **secure** in their dwelling places **as a young lion,** which does not fear other animals (see 30:30).

2 **Through the transgression of a land,** when the inhabitants of a country do not act properly, **its princes are many,** because a small government cannot restrain the people. Alternatively, the verse means that when numerous people hold governmental or quasi-governmental posts, thereby weakening the central government, it is a sign of widespread corruption in the land.[478] **But with an understanding and knowledgeable person, so he will endure.** His status will be established, and the matters that are under his jurisdiction will not be dispersed among all those officers.[479]

3 **A man who is poor and oppresses the impoverished is** like **a torrential rain that leaves no food.** One who tyrannizes the poor without even gaining anything is utterly evil. Persecuting others when one does not stand to benefit is comparable to

יט תְּאֵנָה יֹאכַל פִּרְיָהּ וְשֹׁמֵר אֲדֹנָיו יְכֻבָּד׃ כַּמַּיִם הַפָּנִים לַפָּנִים כֵּן לֵב הָאָדָם לָאָדָם׃
כ שְׁאוֹל וַאֲבַדֹּה לֹא תִשְׂבַּעְנָה וְעֵינֵי הָאָדָם לֹא תִשְׂבַּעְנָה׃
כא כב מַצְרֵף לַכֶּסֶף וְכוּר לַזָּהָב וְאִישׁ לְפִי מַהֲלָלוֹ׃ אִם־תִּכְתּוֹשׁ אֶת־הָאֱוִיל ׀ בַּמַּכְתֵּשׁ
בְּתוֹךְ הָרִיפוֹת בַּעֱלִי לֹא־תָסוּר מֵעָלָיו אִוַּלְתּוֹ׃
כג כד יָדֹעַ תֵּדַע פְּנֵי צֹאנֶךָ שִׁית לִבְּךָ לַעֲדָרִים׃ כִּי לֹא לְעוֹלָם חֹסֶן וְאִם־נֵזֶר לְדוֹר דוֹר׃ וָדוֹר
כה כו גָּלָה חָצִיר וְנִרְאָה־דֶשֶׁא וְנֶאֶסְפוּ עִשְּׂבוֹת הָרִים׃ כְּבָשִׂים לִלְבוּשֶׁךָ וּמְחִיר שָׂדֶה
ח כז א עַתּוּדִים׃ וְדֵי ׀ חֲלֵב עִזִּים לְלַחְמְךָ לְלֶחֶם בֵּיתֶךָ וְחַיִּים לְנַעֲרוֹתֶיךָ׃ נָסוּ וְאֵין־
ב רֹדֵף רָשָׁע וְצַדִּיקִים כִּכְפִיר יִבְטָח׃ בְּפֶשַׁע אֶרֶץ רַבִּים שָׂרֶיהָ וּבְאָדָם מֵבִין יֹדֵעַ
ג ד כֵּן יַאֲרִיךְ׃ גֶּבֶר רָשׁ וְעֹשֵׁק דַּלִּים מָטָר סֹחֵף וְאֵין לָחֶם׃ עֹזְבֵי תוֹרָה יְהַלְלוּ רָשָׁע
ה וְשֹׁמְרֵי תוֹרָה יִתְגָּרוּ בָם׃ אַנְשֵׁי־רָע לֹא־יָבִינוּ מִשְׁפָּט וּמְבַקְשֵׁי יהוה יָבִינוּ כֹל׃
ו ז טוֹב־רָשׁ הוֹלֵךְ בְּתֻמּוֹ מֵעִקֵּשׁ דְּרָכַיִם וְהוּא עָשִׁיר׃ נוֹצֵר תּוֹרָה בֵּן מֵבִין וְרֹעֶה
ח זוֹלְלִים יַכְלִים אָבִיו׃ מַרְבֶּה הוֹנוֹ בְּנֶשֶׁךְ ובתרבית לְחוֹנֵן דַּלִּים יִקְבְּצֶנּוּ׃ וְתַרְבִּית

torrential rain that is unpleasant and causes harm, without even providing the compensatory benefit of sprouting food crops.

4 **Those who forsake the Torah praise the wicked;** they rejoice in them and glorify in their success; **and keepers of the Torah will** refuse to accept the wicked and even **provoke** and struggle against **them.** Beyond the question of how people themselves behave, they are tested by their attitude toward others. Those who abandon the Torah and have no moral compass are likely to praise the wicked, whereas those who observe the Torah will express their objections to such people.

5 **Men of evil will not understand justice.** They are even incapable of understanding the principles of fairness and justice, as they block themselves off from such matters. **But seekers of the Lord will** truly **understand everything.** They are willing to listen, and wish to comprehend even opinions that do not accord with their state of mind.[480]

6 **Better a poor man walking honestly than one of crooked ways who is rich.** The unusual form of the plural "ways [*derakhayim*]," literally, "two ways," indicates that this is referring to one who has at least two paths open before him, and on each occasion he chooses a different one, whichever he feels is convenient at the time. Even if such a person is rich, he is worse off than a simple man who follows a single path in an upright and consistent manner.

7 **He who safeguards the Torah is an understanding son, and a companion of gluttons humiliates his father.**

8 **He who increases his wealth through accrual and interest,** which are both unethical and forbidden by Torah law, will

BACKGROUND

27:22| **A mortar with a pestle:** A mortar is a hard receptacle, while a pestle is a hard rod used for pounding. These are the oldest tools in the world for grinding food. In addition to their use in the preparation of food, such as the groats mentioned in the verse, mortars and pestles were employed for crushing medicines and spices. In the Temple, they were used for pounding the ingredients of the incense (see II Chronicles 24:14, and Rashi ad loc.; Jerusalem Talmud, *Yoma* 4:5). To this day, mortars and pestles serve as tools for crushing hard kernels, and are used mainly as household implements.

ultimately see that he **amasses it for the sake of he who cares for the poor,** one who follows the opposite path and gives his own money to the poor. This money earned through interest will eventually find its way to a philanthropist. The difference between accrual [*neshekh*] and interest [*tarbit*] is that accrual is collected through a loan that bites [*noshekh*], so to speak, as the borrower's debt grows exponentially with time, whereas in a case of interest, a fixed sum, albeit larger than the original loan, must be repaid by a specific date.[481]

9 **He who removes his ear from hearing Torah, even his prayer is an abomination.** Some people are uninterested in learning and obeying God's Torah, and yet they still have demands from God. Since they do not heed the instruction of God as expressed in His Torah, He too does not wish to hear their prayers.

10 **He who misleads the upright on a harmful way, he will fall into his own pit,** a pit he himself dug; **and the honest,** despite their naïveté, **will inherit goodness** and will avoid that pit.[482]

11 **A rich man is wise in his own eyes;** he considers himself clever, with an authoritative opinion on all matters; **and the impoverished one who understands will examine him.** He analyzes the rich man's statements carefully and discovers what he really knows and what he does not.

12 **With the exultation of the righteous the splendor is great.** A society in which the righteous are joyful is a glorious one, as it provides benefit to many, **and with the rise of the wicked** to rule, an honest **person will** have to **be sought** out and yet will not be found, as upright people hide themselves at such times.

13 **He who conceals his transgressions,** who refuses to admit his sins, his repentance is incomplete, and therefore he **will not succeed,** and people will not forgive him even when they are uncertain that he has wronged them; **and he who confesses** his sins **and** also **forsakes** them **will** ultimately **find mercy,** as people are likely to have compassion upon him and forgive him.[483]

14 **Happy is a person who is always afraid,** who is cautious, afraid of making mistakes, and prepares himself for all kinds of eventualities; **but he who inures his heart,** who is overly confident in himself and is never afraid, **will fall into** unanticipated **harm.**[484]

15 **A wicked governor** who lords **over an impoverished people is** like **a roaring lion and a growling bear.**[B] There is no escaping a ruler of this type, just as one cannot evade a vicious beast that seeks its prey.

16 **A ruler,** a powerful man of exalted status, **may lack sagacity and engage in much exploitation,** as he steals much in order to amass a fortune and is thereby likely to shorten his life.[485] Conversely, **haters of ill-gotten gain**[486] **will extend their days.**

17 **A man blamed for the blood of a person,** accused of murder and wanted by the authorities, **even if he flees to a pit, no one will support him.** He has lost everything, and all his good deeds will be of no avail.[487]

18 **He who walks honestly will be saved** from adversity, **and he who is crooked in his ways,** who attempts to employ different tricks and shortcuts each time, **will fall** all **at once.**

19 **He who works his land will be sated with bread** through his toil, **and he who pursues vanities** instead of working **will be sated with poverty.** He will be left with nothing.[488]

20 **A man of** good **faith will abound with blessings, and he who hastens to become rich** without caring whom he crushes on his way and what wrongdoings he performs in his quest **will not be absolved** of punishment, neither in this world nor in the World to Come.

21 **Showing partiality** by granting someone preferential treatment unjustly **is no good.** This is referring particularly to a judge, but it applies to others as well, if they are partial to someone who they know does not act properly. However, alongside the obligation to treat people in accordance with the requirements of law and justice rather than personal motives, one must take into account that some errors are more forgivable than others, **and a man will transgress for a portion of bread.** Sometimes people commit crimes due to hunger, and the sinner's situation at the time should be taken into consideration.

22 **A miserly man rushes after wealth,** as he is always chasing after more possessions, **and** he **does not know that** ultimately **lack will come upon him.** His incessant pursuit of money will eventually cause him losses rather than increase his wealth.

23 **He who rebukes a person will later** [*aḥarai*][489] **find more favor** with the recipient of the rebuke **than one with a slippery tongue.** Although people instinctively like those who flatter them, ultimately they stop believing them and relinquish their

BACKGROUND

28:15 | **And a growling [*shokek*] bear:** Bears looking for food produce a wide variety of noises, including a clicking sound with the tongue, similar to licking [*likuk*], and low pants that to the human ear sound like a longing cry [*hishtokekut*]. The term *shokek* here may refer to one of these sounds.

ט י מֵסִיר אָזְנוֹ מִשְּׁמֹעַ תּוֹרָה גַּם־תְּפִלָּתוֹ תּוֹעֵבָה: מַשְׁגֶּה יְשָׁרִים ׀ בְּדֶרֶךְ רָע בִּשְׁחוּתוֹ
יא הוּא־יִפּוֹל וּתְמִימִים יִנְחֲלוּ־טוֹב: חָכָם בְּעֵינָיו אִישׁ עָשִׁיר וְדַל מֵבִין יַחְקְרֶנּוּ:
יב יג בַּעֲלֹץ צַדִּיקִים רַבָּה תִפְאָרֶת וּבְקוּם רְשָׁעִים יְחֻפַּשׂ אָדָם: מְכַסֶּה פְשָׁעָיו לֹא
יד יַצְלִיחַ וּמוֹדֶה וְעֹזֵב יְרֻחָם: אַשְׁרֵי אָדָם מְפַחֵד תָּמִיד וּמַקְשֶׁה לִבּוֹ יִפּוֹל בְּרָעָה:
טו אֲרִי־נֹהֵם וְדֹב שׁוֹקֵק מוֹשֵׁל רָשָׁע עַל עַם־דָּל:
טז נָגִיד חֲסַר תְּבוּנוֹת וְרַב מַעֲשַׁקּוֹת שֹׂנאֵי בֶצַע יַאֲרִיךְ יָמִים: ח שֹׂנֵא
יז יח אָדָם עָשֻׁק בְּדַם־נָפֶשׁ עַד־בּוֹר יָנוּס אַל־יִתְמְכוּ־בוֹ: הוֹלֵךְ תָּמִים יִוָּשֵׁעַ וְנֶעְקַשׁ
יט כ דְּרָכַיִם יִפּוֹל בְּאֶחָת: עֹבֵד אַדְמָתוֹ יִשְׂבַּע־לָחֶם וּמְרַדֵּף רֵיקִים יִשְׂבַּע־רִישׁ: אִישׁ
כא אֱמוּנוֹת רַב־בְּרָכוֹת וְאָץ לְהַעֲשִׁיר לֹא יִנָּקֶה: הַכֵּר־פָּנִים לֹא־טוֹב וְעַל־פַּת־לֶחֶם
כב כג יִפְשַׁע־גָּבֶר: נִבֳהָל לַהוֹן אִישׁ רַע עָיִן וְלֹא־יֵדַע כִּי־חֶסֶר יְבֹאֶנּוּ: מוֹכִיחַ אָדָם אַחֲרַי
כד חֵן יִמְצָא מִמַּחֲלִיק לָשׁוֹן: גּוֹזֵל ׀ אָבִיו וְאִמּוֹ וְאֹמֵר אֵין־פָּשַׁע חָבֵר הוּא לְאִישׁ
כה כו מַשְׁחִית: רְחַב־נֶפֶשׁ יְגָרֶה מָדוֹן וּבֹטֵחַ עַל־יְהוָה יְדֻשָּׁן: בּוֹטֵחַ בְּלִבּוֹ הוּא כְסִיל
כז וְהוֹלֵךְ בְּחָכְמָה הוּא יִמָּלֵט: נוֹתֵן לָרָשׁ אֵין מַחְסוֹר וּמַעְלִים עֵינָיו רַב־מְאֵרוֹת:
כח כט א בְּקוּם רְשָׁעִים יִסָּתֵר אָדָם וּבְאָבְדָם יִרְבּוּ צַדִּיקִים: אִישׁ תּוֹכָחוֹת מַקְשֶׁה־עֹרֶף

support. Some interpret *aḥarai* as: After Me, a reference to one who rebukes a man, admonishing him to follow God.

24 **He who robs his father and his mother and says: There is no transgression,** as they are always making efforts on my behalf and giving me things, and anyway I will eventually inherit their property, **he is a companion to a man of destruction.** He too is a robber, as the property is currently not his, and he is therefore performing a prohibited act.

25 **A greedy,** lustful, **soul provokes strife,** both because people will not agree to his extravagant demands and because a dissatisfied individual is frequently angry and often involved in fights;[490] **and he who trusts** in **the Lord** and is satisfied with little **will luxuriate,** as he will merit both goodness and pleasure.

26 **One who trusts in his** own **heart,** imagining that he knows everything, **he is a fool; and one who walks with wisdom, he will escape** troubles, because he takes potential problems, obstacles, and misgivings into account and does not suffer from over-confidence.

27 **He who gives** charity **to the poor has no lack, but he who averts his eyes** from the suffering of others **will have many curses** fall upon him.

28 **With the rise of the wicked,** when they attain elevated status, an upright **person should hide** and try not to stand out; **and with their,** the wicked people's, **eradication, the righteous increase,** as they allow themselves to be seen, at which point it becomes apparent that there are more righteous people than one might have thought.

29 **1** **A man rebuked who stiffens his neck** and takes no notice **will suddenly be broken, and there is no remedy.** The apparent strength of stubborn men who remain apathetic to criticism for their wrongdoings is merely transitory and soon passes.

2 **With the rise of the righteous** to a position of power **the people rejoice, and with the rule of the wicked the people sigh** in pain and disappointment.
3 **A man who loves wisdom gladdens his father, and a companion of harlots** not only brings his father no joy but **will** also **lose a fortune.**
4 **A king will uphold the land with** the performance of **justice,** as his state is maintained by his fairness and the order he imposes, **but** if he is **a man of donations,** a man seeking donations, whether he demands money in order to give to others, or he is weak and requires the funds himself, he **will** thereby **destroy it,** the land. A king cannot establish his realm by distributing donations or by taking them for himself but by staying loyal to law and order.[491]
5 **A man who flatters his friend spreads a net for his feet.** Through his seemingly sweet, pleasant statements, he effectively traps and imprisons the other person.[492]
6 **In the transgression of an evil man there is a snare** for himself; **but the righteous,** who act with integrity, **will** eventually **sing and be joyous.** Some explain the end of the verse to mean that the righteous will rejoice in the removal of those who perform evil.[493]
7 **The righteous man knows the cause of the poor** and the helpless. Intimately aware of their misery, the righteous person is sensitive to the poor, and he tries to help them and protect their interests. By contrast, **the wicked one will not understand knowledge** at all, and certainly ignores the poor and even treads upon them, until he himself falls, as stated in the previous verse.
8 **Scoffing men will agitate a city,** as they create a destructive atmosphere and thereby harm not only themselves and those who listen to them but an entire city;[494] alternatively, this means that they bring pain and bitter disappointment upon a city. **And wise men will assuage** the **wrath** that hovers over a city.
9 **A wise man judged** in a case **with a foolish man may be wrathful or amused, but** either way **there is no satisfaction.** No good will come of this dispute, as the foolish individual will not react properly no matter what the wise man does. Therefore, quarreling with a fool is always completely pointless.[495]
10 **Bloody men,** criminals, **hate a virtuous person.** Even when an artless person has no quarrel with such individuals, his innocence bothers them, and his abstention from their way of life upsets them. **And the upright,** by contrast, are favorable toward the virtuous one and **seek him out,** to do good to him and learn from his ways.[496]
11 **The fool vents all his spirit.** One of the signs of a fool is that he says everything on his mind, whether it is wise or unintelligent, whether it is suitable for the occasion or inappropriate. Furthermore, he reveals all of his spirit, his desire and intentions.[497] **But the wise man will soothe it, keeping it back.** Even when he has an urge to say something, he knows when it is best not to talk.[498] Some explain: The wise man silences and pushes aside the words of the fool when the latter "vents all his spirit."
12 In the case of **a ruler who listens to falsehood,** it is not the failing of one person alone, but **all his servants are wicked.** When people see that the head of a system accepts lies, a whole group of criminals will gather around him. For this reason the Bible always places ultimate blame for the sins of a generation upon its kings and other leaders.
13 **The poor** man **and the deceitful man** sometimes **meet** in the course of a quarrel or a conversation. Generally, there is nothing to be gained from an encounter of this kind, as even if the trickster successfully deceives the poor man, his victim does not have anything to give him. However, on occasion, **the Lord enlightens the eyes of both of them,** in which case they might discover a new path they were not previously familiar with, and perhaps they will receive mutual benefit from the meeting.
14 **The king who judges the impoverished truthfully** and consistently, **his throne will be established forever.**
15 Both the **rod** of punishment **and** verbal **rebuke will grant wisdom,** as some people change their ways as soon as they hear rebuke, whereas others become wise only when they are struck with the rod. **And a dissolute,** wild and abandoned, **youth shames his mother,** who was unsuccessful at raising him properly.
16 Transgression does not thrive in a vacuum. Rather, **with the increase of the wicked** who perform such acts, **transgression** likewise **increases. But** because sin is not constructive and instead brings ruin and disaster, **the righteous**[D] **will** ultimately **see their fall,** the fall of the wicked and sinful.

DISCUSSION

29:16 | **The wicked...the righteous:** The wicked and righteous are often contrasted. The distinction between them is expressed in every realm, including their conduct, their speech, their friends and confidants, and those they choose to distance themselves from. The notion that emerges from the description here, and from the book of Proverbs in general, is that a person must take a stand and decide with which camp he wishes to associate himself. His choices will inevitably affect the details of his life in every area.

ב פֶּתַע יִשָּׁבֵר וְאֵין מַרְפֵּא׃ בִּרְבוֹת צַדִּיקִים יִשְׂמַח הָעָם וּבִמְשֹׁל רָשָׁע יֵאָנַח עָם׃
ג ד אִישׁ־אֹהֵב חָכְמָה יְשַׂמַּח אָבִיו וְרֹעֶה זוֹנוֹת יְאַבֶּד־הוֹן׃ מֶלֶךְ בְּמִשְׁפָּט יַעֲמִיד
ה אָרֶץ וְאִישׁ תְּרוּמוֹת יֶהֶרְסֶנָּה׃ גֶּבֶר מַחֲלִיק עַל־רֵעֵהוּ רֶשֶׁת פּוֹרֵשׂ עַל־פְּעָמָיו׃
ו ז בְּפֶשַׁע אִישׁ רָע מוֹקֵשׁ וְצַדִּיק יָרוּן וְשָׂמֵחַ׃ יֹדֵעַ צַדִּיק דִּין דַּלִּים רָשָׁע לֹא־יָבִין
ח ט דָּעַת׃ אַנְשֵׁי לָצוֹן יָפִיחוּ קִרְיָה וַחֲכָמִים יָשִׁיבוּ אָף׃ אִישׁ־חָכָם נִשְׁפָּט אֶת־אִישׁ
י אֱוִיל וְרָגַז וְשָׂחַק וְאֵין נָחַת׃ אַנְשֵׁי דָמִים יִשְׂנְאוּ־תָם וִישָׁרִים יְבַקְשׁוּ נַפְשׁוֹ׃
יא יב כָּל־רוּחוֹ יוֹצִיא כְסִיל וְחָכָם בְּאָחוֹר יְשַׁבְּחֶנָּה׃ מֹשֵׁל מַקְשִׁיב עַל־דְּבַר־שָׁקֶר
יג יד כָּל־מְשָׁרְתָיו רְשָׁעִים׃ רָשׁ וְאִישׁ תְּכָכִים נִפְגָּשׁוּ מֵאִיר־עֵינֵי שְׁנֵיהֶם יהוה׃ מֶלֶךְ
טו שׁוֹפֵט בֶּאֱמֶת דַּלִּים כִּסְאוֹ לָעַד יִכּוֹן׃ שֵׁבֶט וְתוֹכַחַת יִתֵּן חָכְמָה וְנַעַר מְשֻׁלָּח
טז יז מֵבִישׁ אִמּוֹ׃ בִּרְבוֹת רְשָׁעִים יִרְבֶּה־פָּשַׁע וְצַדִּיקִים בְּמַפַּלְתָּם יִרְאוּ׃ יַסֵּר בִּנְךָ
וִינִיחֶךָ וְיִתֵּן מַעֲדַנִּים לְנַפְשֶׁךָ׃
יח יט בְּאֵין חָזוֹן יִפָּרַע עָם וְשֹׁמֵר תּוֹרָה אַשְׁרֵהוּ׃ בִּדְבָרִים לֹא־יִוָּסֶר עָבֶד כִּי־יָבִין וְאֵין
כ כא מַעֲנֶה׃ חָזִיתָ אִישׁ אָץ בִּדְבָרָיו תִּקְוָה לִכְסִיל מִמֶּנּוּ׃ מְפַנֵּק מִנֹּעַר עַבְדּוֹ וְאַחֲרִיתוֹ
כב כג יִהְיֶה מָנוֹן׃ אִישׁ־אַף יְגָרֶה מָדוֹן וּבַעַל חֵמָה רַב־פָּשַׁע׃ גַּאֲוַת אָדָם תַּשְׁפִּילֶנּוּ

17 **Admonish your son** both verbally and by dispensing punishments, **and he will give you rest,** comfort and satisfaction; **and** what is more, he will **provide delights to your soul.** It is therefore important to concern yourself with educating and disciplining your children.

18 **Where there is no** broad **vision,** prophecy, ideal, or plan for the future, **the people become unruly,** wild and uninhibited; **and happy is he who keeps the Torah,** which provides him with vision and ideals.

19 **A servant will not be admonished** and trained **with words; though he understands** what he is told, **there is no response.** He does not respond or accept authority. A servant who is not particularly sharp or faithful will not act based upon internal motivation, nor is he willing to listen to reproof. Consequently, he should be addressed in a different manner.

20 **Have you seen a man hasty in his affairs,** who makes impulsive decisions? **From him there is hope** even **for a fool,** as such a person will certainly commit many errors (see 26:12), and even a fool will be able to take advantage of him.

21 **He who pampers his servant from youth, in the end he,** the servant, **will become master** [***manon***] of the house.[499] Some explain *manon* to refer to weakness and sluggishness. If one indulges his servant excessively he will become indolent.[500] If a servant is not interested in working, it is inadvisable to allow him to do as he wishes.

22 **A man of wrath provokes strife.** One who becomes angry with everything and everyone will over time amass many enemies for himself. **And a man of fury** ultimately also **abounds in transgression.**

23 **A man's pride will debase him.** One who grows excessively arrogant will eventually be lowered by that very haughtiness. Pride is not merely a repulsive character trait; it is an actual stumbling block in life. **And the lowly spirit will attain honor.**

24 **He who shares with a thief hates himself.** Apart from wretched individuals who steal bread to eat, thieves generally require a partner with whom to trade their stolen wares. Although the partner does not steal, he still harms himself, as **he will hear an oath** imposed by the government upon the public, compelling anyone who knows details of the crime to speak to the authorities, **but** he **will not tell.**[501] In addition to the fact that he has violated the prohibition against being an accomplice to a crime, this person will eventually suffer the same downfall as the thief.[502]

25 **A man's fear sets a snare** for himself, as he falls into the trap; **and he who trusts** in **the Lord** while remaining aware of potential dangers on his path **will be exalted,** established in a strong, protected place.

26 **Many seek a ruler's favor,** as they are under the assumption that he fixes the outcome of legal cases, **but** in fact **a man's judgment is from the Lord.** True judgment comes from God, while the ruler is merely a tool in His hand. Therefore, rather than flattering the ruler, one should approach the One who leads him.[503]

27 **A man of iniquity is an abomination to the righteous, and** the reverse is also true, as **the** individual who is **straight of path is an abomination to the wicked.** The wicked person loathes a man of integrity. The righteous not only performs good deeds, but also combats evil. Correspondingly, the wicked person is not satisfied with merely performing evil; he actively hates those that follow the upright path, as their very existence is a reproach to him.

Other Sayings of the Wise

PROVERBS 30:1–31:9

This last collection of aphorisms in the book of Proverbs differs from the previous ones in several respects. First, these proverbs are longer than the previous ones, as they comprise several verses. Second, the text does not attribute them to King Solomon but to other figures. It is possible that Solomon collected various aphorisms or copied the style of well-known composers of maxims.[504] In addition, the earlier proverbs of Solomon are mainly words of reproof and practical instructions about daily behavior, whereas this section consists primarily of descriptions of reality and facts of life through which, if one contemplates them, one can become wise. Some of the wise sayings in this chapter are linked through their analogous use of numbers.

30 1 **The words of Agur son of Yakeh,** an unknown personage.[505] The Sages maintain that this is one of the names of King Solomon himself. Solomon had many names: The Bible itself calls him both Solomon and Yedidya,[506] and it is accepted that the title Kohelet[507] refers to Solomon as well. Accordingly, the Sages expound the name Agur son of Yakeh as a description of one who collects [*oger*] words of wisdom and then spits them out [*mekiam*], or emits them for others to hear.[508] These words are **the oration [*massa*],** a kind of prophetic vision. Alternatively, *Massa* is part of Agur's name or title, reflecting the name of his hometown or ethnic group. **The utterance of the man to Itiel,** or alternatively, by Itiel. Whether Itiel is the one delivering the speech or Agur's intended audience, his identity is unknown.[509] However, his name can be interpreted literally, which appears to be the way it is used in the final phrase of the verse: **To Itiel and Ukal,** meaning God [*El*] is with me [*iti*], and therefore I am capable of [*ukhal*] succeeding.[510] This is an esoteric introduction to the oration that follows.

2 The address begins with a declaration whose context is also unknown: **For I am a boor among men,** I lack discernment in comparison to others, **and the understanding of man is not mine,** as I am merely a simple person.

3 **I have not learned wisdom, nor do I know the sacred knowledge.**

4 Nevertheless, I would like to understand a few points: **Who went up to heaven and** then **came down? Who gathered the wind in his fists? Who bound water in his garment?** This is a reference to the clouds, which are spread across the sky like garments. **Who established** and built up **all the ends of the earth? What is his name, and what is his son's name, if you know?** The answer to these questions is that there is no human being who could do such things. It is all the work of God, about whom it is impossible to know many details. All I know is that God is the omnipotent Master of the world.

DISCUSSION

30:7 | **Two I ask of You:** This is not the only example of a collection of sayings arranged based on numbers. Another well-known instance appears in chapter 6 of *Pirkei Avot*. In addition, some works of wisdom of gentile origin are also arranged according to this structure.

30:8 | **Do not give me poverty or wealth:** The Sages throughout the generations have expanded the meaning of these words, viewing them as an allusion to a request for the balanced usage of a person's various capabilities, such as the force of desire and the intellect (see, e.g., Ralbag; *Tzidkat HaTzaddik* 214, 258; *Mikhtav MeEliyahu* vol. 4, p. 39).

כד וְשְׁפַל־ר֗וּחַ יִתְמֹ֥ךְ כָּבֽוֹד׃ חוֹלֵ֣ק עִם־גַּ֭נָּב שׂוֹנֵ֣א נַפְשׁ֑וֹ אָלָ֥ה יִ֝שְׁמַ֗ע וְלֹ֣א יַגִּֽיד׃
כה כו חֶרְדַּ֣ת אָ֭דָם יִתֵּ֣ן מוֹקֵ֑שׁ וּבוֹטֵ֖חַ בַּיהוָ֣ה יְשֻׂגָּֽב׃ רַ֭בִּים מְבַקְשִׁ֣ים פְּנֵי־מוֹשֵׁ֑ל וּ֝מֵיְהוָ֗ה
כז מִשְׁפַּט־אִֽישׁ׃ תּוֹעֲבַ֣ת צַ֭דִּיקִים אִ֣ישׁ עָ֑וֶל וְתוֹעֲבַ֖ת רָשָׁ֣ע יְשַׁר־דָּֽרֶךְ׃
א ב דִּבְרֵ֤י ׀ אָג֣וּר בִּן־יָקֶ֗ה הַמַּ֫שָּׂ֥א נְאֻ֣ם הַ֭גֶּבֶר לְאִ֥יתִיאֵ֑ל לְאִ֖יתִיאֵ֣ל וְאֻכָֽל׃ כִּ֤י בַ֣עַר
ג ד אָ֭נֹכִי מֵאִ֑ישׁ וְלֹֽא־בִינַ֖ת אָדָ֣ם לִֽי׃ וְלֹֽא־לָמַ֥דְתִּי חָכְמָ֑ה וְדַ֖עַת קְדֹשִׁ֣ים אֵדָֽע׃ מִ֤י
עָלָֽה־שָׁמַ֨יִם ׀ וַיֵּרַ֡ד מִ֤י אָֽסַף־ר֨וּחַ ׀ בְּחָפְנָ֡יו מִ֤י צָֽרַר־מַ֨יִם ׀ בַּשִּׂמְלָ֗ה מִ֭י הֵקִ֣ים כָּל־
ה אַפְסֵי־אָ֑רֶץ מַה־שְּׁמ֥וֹ וּמַה־שֶּׁם־בְּ֝נ֗וֹ כִּ֣י תֵדָֽע׃ כָּל־אִמְרַ֣ת אֱל֣וֹהַּ צְרוּפָ֑ה מָגֵ֥ן ה֝֗וּא
ו ז לַחֹסִ֥ים בּֽוֹ׃ אַל־תּ֥וֹסְףְּ עַל־דְּבָרָ֑יו פֶּן־יוֹכִ֖יחַ בְּךָ֣ וְנִכְזָֽבְתָּ׃ שְׁ֭תַּיִם
ח שָׁאַ֣לְתִּי מֵאִתָּ֑ךְ אַל־תִּמְנַ֥ע מִ֝מֶּ֗נִּי בְּטֶ֣רֶם אָמֽוּת׃ שָׁ֤וְא ׀ וּֽדְבַר־כָּזָ֡ב הַרְחֵ֬ק מִמֶּ֗נִּי
ט רֵ֣אשׁ וָ֭עֹשֶׁר אַל־תִּֽתֶּן־לִ֑י הַ֝טְרִיפֵ֗נִי לֶ֣חֶם חֻקִּֽי׃ פֶּן־אֶשְׂבַּ֤ע ׀ וְכִחַ֗שְׁתִּי וְאָמַ֗רְתִּי
י מִ֣י יְהוָ֑ה וּפֶּן־אִוָּרֵ֥שׁ וְגָנַ֑בְתִּי וְ֝תָפַ֗שְׂתִּי שֵׁ֣ם אֱלֹהָֽי׃ אַל־תַּלְשֵׁ֣ן עֶ֭בֶד
יא יב אֶל־אֲדֹנָ֑ו פֶּן־יְקַלֶּלְךָ֥ וְאָשָֽׁמְתָּ׃ דּ֣וֹר אָבִ֣יו יְקַלֵּ֑ל וְאֶת־אִ֝מּ֗וֹ לֹ֣א יְבָרֵֽךְ׃ דּ֭וֹר טָה֣וֹר

5 **Every saying of God is refined; He is a shield to those who rely on Him,** whether or not they understand His ways. Therefore, they must listen to Him.

6 **Do not add to His words,** because you cannot comprehend all that occurs in the world, **lest He rebuke you** that your addition to His words is incorrect, **and you will be found to be false.** Alternatively, you will be disappointed, or you will become untrue to God, abandoning His word.[511]

7 Agur now addresses God: **Two** matters **I ask of You;**[D] **do not deny me before I die:** feed me my allotted bread.

8 First, **distance vanity and falsehood from me;** and second, **do not give me** either **poverty or wealth;**[D] rather, **feed me with my allotted bread,** the food I require.[512]

9 Agur explains why he wishes to avoid both excessive wealth and poverty: **Lest I become** too **sated** with money, **and renounce** God, **and say,** out of a sense that everything belongs to me and has been acquired as a result of my own strength: **Who is the Lord?** I do not know Him. **And,** by contrast, **lest I become poor and** be forced to **steal, and** when I am caught or accused of the crime, I **appropriate the name of my God** by swearing falsely in His name or by cursing in bitterness over my situation. It is dangerous both to be too wealthy and to be too poor, and therefore I request to receive only the food that I need, in a state of tranquility and comfort.

10 **Do not slander a servant to his master,** that he has not performed his service properly, **lest he,** the servant, **curse you** when he is punished as a result of your report, **and you will be guilty** of causing him harm, as you are not obliged to become involved with the relationship between a servant and his master. Your interference will backfire to your own detriment.[513] The reason for the placement of these words of reproof in the context of this passage is unclear.

11 The previous passages discussed the world at large as well as humanity as a whole. The next proverbs address specific generations of people, which are subject to the constraints of time. It is not clear which generation the speaker refers to, but the description here could be applied to many different periods. **It is a generation that will curse its father and will not bless its mother,**

12 **a generation pure in its own eyes, but it has not been cleansed from its own excrement.** The members of this generation have not grown up, and they are as soiled and fetid as infants in need of a clean diaper. This verse is perhaps referring to people who are preoccupied with external cleanliness while remaining impure inside;[514]

13 **a generation, how haughty are its eyes, and its eyelids are raised up.** They are haughty individuals who act as though they peer down on the world from above;

14 **a generation whose teeth are** like **swords, and its incisors** like slaughtering **knives,** as they seek **to devour the poor from the earth, and the indigent from among mankind.** This is a predatory, corrupt, and filthy generation.

15 This aphorism is the first of a series that follow the recurring pattern of three and four, which is familiar from elsewhere in the Bible, and is often indicative of abundance in general:[515] **The leech,**[B] a parasite that attaches itself to animals and sucks their blood, **has two daughters,** who say: **Give, give.** This is an image of a creature that eats and devours without limits. Some consider the leech a symbol for Gehenna.[516] **There are three** things **that,** like the leech, **will not be sated, four that do not say: Enough.**[517]

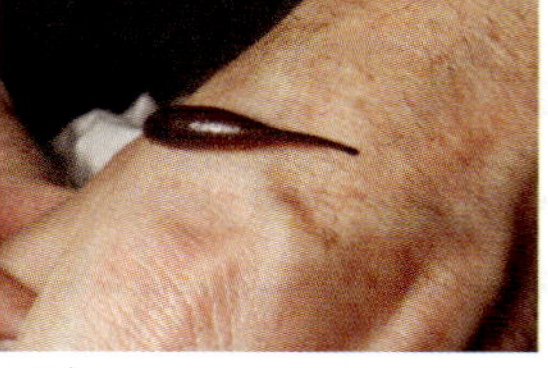
Leech

16 These are the things that are never satisfied: **The grave,** or Gehenna; **the barren womb,** or the desire for offspring, which come from the womb; **earth is not sated with water,** as the earth continually swallows any water that is poured onto it; **and fire does not say: Enough,** but continues to burn whatever it encounters. The two daughters of the leech that demand: Give, give, represent these two pairs of items that incessantly take, one pair from the material world, the earth and fire, and the other from human life, the grave and the womb.[518]

17 The verse adds: **An eye** of a son **that mocks a father** for his forgetfulness and general inactivity in his old age, **and scorns the wrinkles of his mother,** her old age and the marks it leaves on her physical appearance,[519] **the ravens of the ravine will gouge it,**[B] **and eaglets will eat it.** Ravens are neither large nor particularly strong birds. Consequently, when they find a carcass they pluck out its soft, external parts, including the eyes. Likewise, young eagles find it hard to penetrate the hide of carcasses, and therefore they eat its eyes. This will be the punishment of one who uses his eyes to harm others.

Raven

18 **They are three** things **that are beyond me,** which I do not understand, **and four that I do not know:** Generally, in proverbs of this type, the fourth item is the focal point of the saying.[520]

19 **The way of an eagle in the heavens,** how the heavy eagle manages to soar through the sky; **the way of a serpent on a rock,** the manner in which a serpent crawls and finds its way on a rock despite its lack of feet; **the way of a ship in the midst of the sea,** as it too charts a course without holding onto anything; **and** the fourth mystery is **the way of a man with a young woman,** the nature of their relationship and how it is formed. Much has been written on aeronautics, zoology, and seamanship, but even more has been composed about the male-female relationship; yet it still remains a mystery. Part of the wonder of these phenomena is that these creatures and objects leave no traces behind them.[521]

"Eagle in the heavens"

"Serpent on a rock"

"Ship in the midst of the sea"

20 So too **is the way of an adulterous woman: She eats, and wipes her mouth, and says: I did not do wrong.** This is a graphic way of saying that the relationship between a man and a woman also leaves no traces, and no one else can truly know what transpired between the pair.[522]

21 The text cites another aphorism which follows the same pattern: **Because of three** phenomena **the earth quakes, and because of four,** the fourth occurrence, **it cannot bear:**

22 **Because of a slave when he becomes king; and a scoundrel,** a wicked, miserly individual, **when he is sated with bread,** is successful and thrives;

23 **because of a hated,** adulterous **woman,**[523] **when it is she who is consorted with** by her husband, while another wife receives no attention; **and a maidservant when she supplants her mistress.** The humiliation and disgrace which inevitably result from the reign of a servant are even more accentuated when a handmaid, whose status is even lower than that of a male servant, inherits her mistress's position, and the mistress has no choice but to watch this unbearable sight submissively.[524] Such injustices shock the world, causing it to "quake," as it were.

24 **They are four** creatures **that are little upon earth, but** in practice **they are exceedingly wise,** and their unique talents enable them to thrive despite their diminutive size:

25 **The ants are a people,** a community, **not mighty** (see commentary on 6:8), **yet they prepare their food in the summer.** They are

"The ants are a people not mighty, yet they prepare their food in the summer"

יג יד בְּעֵינָיו וּמִצֹּאָתוֹ לֹא רֻחָץ: דּוֹר מָה־רָמוּ עֵינָיו וְעַפְעַפָּיו יִנָּשֵׂאוּ: דּוֹר ׀ חֲרָבוֹת שִׁנָּיו
וּמַאֲכָלוֹת מְתַלְּעֹתָיו לֶאֱכֹל עֲנִיִּים מֵאֶרֶץ וְאֶבְיוֹנִים מֵאָדָם:
טו לַעֲלוּקָה ׀ שְׁתֵּי בָנוֹת הַב ׀ הַב שָׁלוֹשׁ הֵנָּה לֹא תִשְׂבַּעְנָה אַרְבַּע לֹא־אָמְרוּ הוֹן:
טז יז שְׁאוֹל וְעֹצֶר רָחַם אֶרֶץ לֹא־שָׂבְעָה מַּיִם וְאֵשׁ לֹא־אָמְרָה הוֹן: עַיִן ׀ תִּלְעַג לְאָב
יח וְתָבוּז לִיקֲּהַת אֵם יִקְּרוּהָ עֹרְבֵי־נַחַל וְיֹאכְלוּהָ בְנֵי־נָשֶׁר: שְׁלֹשָׁה
יט הֵמָּה נִפְלְאוּ מִמֶּנִּי וְאַרְבַּע לֹא יְדַעְתִּים: דֶּרֶךְ הַנֶּשֶׁר ׀ בַּשָּׁמַיִם דֶּרֶךְ נָחָשׁ עֲלֵי צוּר
כ דֶּרֶךְ־אֳנִיָּה בְלֶב־יָם וְדֶרֶךְ גֶּבֶר בְּעַלְמָה: כֵּן ׀ דֶּרֶךְ אִשָּׁה מְנָאָפֶת אָכְלָה וּמָחֲתָה
פִיהָ וְאָמְרָה לֹא־פָעַלְתִּי אָוֶן:
כא כב תַּחַת שָׁלוֹשׁ רָגְזָה אֶרֶץ וְתַחַת אַרְבַּע לֹא־תוּכַל שְׂאֵת: תַּחַת עֶבֶד כִּי יִמְלוֹךְ
כג וְנָבָל כִּי יִשְׂבַּע־לָחֶם: תַּחַת שְׂנוּאָה כִּי תִבָּעֵל וְשִׁפְחָה כִּי־תִירַשׁ גְּבִרְתָּהּ:
כד כה אַרְבָּעָה הֵם קְטַנֵּי־אָרֶץ וְהֵמָּה חֲכָמִים מְחֻכָּמִים: הַנְּמָלִים עַם לֹא־עָז וַיָּכִינוּ

BACKGROUND

30:15 | **Leech [*aluka*]:** According to the majority of the commentaries, the *aluka* is a segmented worm-like animal from the subclass *Hirudinea*, which lives in or near water sources. It can grow from a single centimeter to 15 cm, and it can store in its body up to five times its weight in blood. When sucking blood, the creature releases anticoagulants and other agents that inhibit one's sensation of the wound. Due to these qualities, one of the hundreds of its species, the medical leech, *Hirudo medicinalis*, was used in various medical procedures such as bloodletting.

30:17 | **The ravens of the ravine will gouge it:** Ravens, *Corvidae*, are intelligent omnivores who remember their favorite and most easily available foods. They often eat carrion, though they are not strong enough to tear through the flesh by themselves. However, they are capable of plucking out the eyes of carcasses to reach the innards when there is no other opening to the body. Since the eye reflects light, it is visible at great distances from a dark body. For the same reason, ravens have a habit of collecting shiny objects, which they snatch even from open windows.

intelligent enough, as it were, to prepare their food for the winter during the summer.

26 **The hyraxes**[B] **are a people not powerful,** they are not strong, and **yet they place their house in the rock,** as unlike other creatures they are capable of living in crevices in cliffs, where they can find shelter.

"Hyraxes…place their house in the rock"

27 **There is no king for locusts,**[B] and **yet they all go out in ranks** to work together. When a swarm of locusts leaves its place, hundreds of thousands or even millions of them spread forth as one;

"There is no king for locusts, yet they all go out in ranks." Swarm of locusts attacking a field

28 **the gecko**[B] **grasps with hands,** taking hold of surfaces with its legs in order to climb walls and even walk along ceilings, **and** yet **it is** found everywhere, even **in the king's palaces.**

29 **There are three** creatures **that are accomplished marchers,** which walk well, **and four accomplished walkers,** as the fourth marches best of all:[525]

30 **A lion is the mightiest among animals, and it does not retreat before anything;** it marches securely without the need to watch its surroundings;[526]

31 **the greyhound,**[D] a kind of hunting dog, which is also impudent and walks arrogantly; **or the billy goat,** as it likewise walks with confidence; **and the** powerful

Gecko grasping onto a wall and climbing it

Saluki hunting dog, relief sunken in stone, tomb of Sarenput I, Egypt, Twelfth Dynasty

Billy goats

king, against whom no one rises.[527] This a derisive comparison: The king is listed together with three animals that are not actually important but simply march with confidence. Similarly, the king may have great pride, but he often barely moves from his place. On the one hand, the list of these proud walkers serves as a warning to others not to challenge them; on the other hand, it is a subtle but sharp mockery of the arrogant behavior of kings.

32 **If you were demeaned, it is due to arrogance;** if you have fallen and have been humiliated, it is because you initially sought to lift yourself up. You praised yourself with your words, but these ultimately brought shame upon you. **If you conspired [*zammota*], put hand to mouth,** be quiet. Alternatively, the verse means that if you block your mouth with your hand, like a muzzle [*zemam*] on an animal, no harm will befall you.

33 **For compression of milk produces butter, and compression of a nose produces blood, and compression of wrath produces quarreling.** The product of anger is a quarrel. One should remember that while beneficial products can be extracted from milk, a far less pleasant substance, blood, comes from the nose, and the least appealing product of all is that which comes from anger.

31 1 **The words of Lemuel the king,**[D] which are **the oration,** a speech that contains harsh reproof,[528] **with which his mother admonished him.**

BACKGROUND

30:26 | **Hyraxes:** This creature is also mentioned in Psalms (104:18) as an animal that lives in rocky areas. Its accepted identification is the rock hyrax, *Procavia capensis syriaca*, which can be found in the cliffs of Israel. The rock hyrax weighs 2–5 kg and is roughly 50 cm in length. It lives in crevices in cliffs that are difficult for other creatures to access, and this protects it from predators (see commentary on Leviticus 11:5).

30:27 | **Locusts:** This refers to *Schistocerca gregaria*, flying insects from East Africa, specifically Sudan. These grasshoppers are ordinarily solitary creatures, but under certain conditions they reproduce at tremendous rates and undergo physiological transformations of color and size, growing to as much as 7 cm in length. When this occurs, their behavior also changes, and they gather into swarms that can contain as many as ten billion creatures. Aided by the wind, swarms of these locusts can travel vast distances in search of food, from southern Sudan and Ethiopia to neighboring countries along the Red Sea and even Sinai and Israel. Along the way, these locusts can destroy the harvests of very large swaths of land, as they can eat daily an amount of food equal to their body weight.

30:28 | **Gecko [*semamit*]:** Although some claim that the *semamit* is a spider, it is more likely the Mediterranean house gecko, *Hemidactylus turcicus*, a semi-translucent, soft-skinned lizard. This creature climbs on walls and other vertical objects, and even on ceilings, while remaining close to small indentations on the surface. It can reach a maximum size of 14 cm. The gecko spends most of its time in small, hidden crevices in both small and large houses, where it finds its food, such as tiny bugs, butterflies, and moths.

כו כז בַּקַּיִץ לַחְמָם׃ שְׁפַנִּים עַם לֹא־עָצוּם וַיָּשִׂימוּ בַסֶּלַע בֵּיתָם׃ מֶלֶךְ אֵין לָאַרְבֶּה
כח וַיֵּצֵא חֹצֵץ כֻּלּוֹ׃ שְׂמָמִית בְּיָדַיִם תְּתַפֵּשׂ וְהִיא בְּהֵיכְלֵי מֶלֶךְ׃
כט ל שְׁלֹשָׁה הֵמָּה מֵיטִיבֵי צָעַד וְאַרְבָּעָה מֵיטִבֵי לָכֶת׃ לַיִשׁ גִּבּוֹר בַּבְּהֵמָה וְלֹא־יָשׁוּב
לא לב מִפְּנֵי־כֹל׃ זַרְזִיר מָתְנַיִם אוֹ־תָיִשׁ וּמֶלֶךְ אַלְקוּם עִמּוֹ׃ אִם־נָבַלְתָּ בְהִתְנַשֵּׂא וְאִם־
לג זַמּוֹתָ יָד לְפֶה׃ כִּי מִיץ חָלָב יוֹצִיא חֶמְאָה וּמִיץ־אַף יוֹצִיא דָם וּמִיץ אַפַּיִם יוֹצִיא
א ב רִיב׃ דִּבְרֵי לְמוּאֵל מֶלֶךְ מַשָּׂא אֲשֶׁר־יִסְּרַתּוּ אִמּוֹ׃ מַה־בְּרִי
ג וּמַה־בַּר־בִּטְנִי וּמֶה בַּר־נְדָרָי׃ אַל־תִּתֵּן לַנָּשִׁים חֵילֶךָ וּדְרָכֶיךָ לַמְחוֹת מְלָכִין׃
ד ה אַל לַמְלָכִים ׀ לְמוֹאֵל אַל לַמְלָכִים שְׁתוֹ־יָיִן וּלְרוֹזְנִים או שֵׁכָר׃ פֶּן־יִשְׁתֶּה וְיִשְׁכַּח אֵי

2 **What, my son, and what, son of my womb?** You have performed an action of little importance.[529] Alternatively: What is this worthless thing you have done, my son?[530] **And what, son of my vows?** You were born only thanks to the vows I uttered. Therefore, my speech is not only the reprimand of a mother to her son; rather, it is delivered in a particular context.[531]

3 **Do not give** all **your strength to** loving **women, or let your ways rub out advice.** Do not allow your personality and behavioral traits to negate sound counsel when it is given to you. One who gives his strength to women thereby negates himself and loses his value. Alternatively, this clause means: Do not give your ways to that which destroys the strength of kings.[532]

4 **It is not for kings, Lemuel, it is not for kings to drink wine** excessively and certainly not to get drunk, **or for princes** to say: **Where is strong drink?** It is unbecoming for them to occupy themselves with drinking. This idea that imbibing wine impairs the power and authority of the king appears elsewhere in the Bible as well.[533] Lemuel's mother warns him against giving in to passing temptations in the form of women and alcohol. Such conduct is especially dangerous for a king, who might thereby lose his strength and forfeit his capacity to perform his leadership role.[534]

5 **Lest he drink, and forget that which was legislated,** the written laws, **and** also **pervert the justice of all the children**

DISCUSSION

30:31 | **The greyhound [*zarzir motnayim*]:** The Peshiteta and the Septuagint translate *zarzir motnayim* as the chicken. Later commentaries translate this term as a hunting dog, or greyhound. From its juxtaposition with the he-goat and the king, it would seem that it is a quick animal that is intelligent and controlling of others. In fact, the commonality of all four members of this group is their ability to lead and to rule over others. There is usually one lion that leads a group of female and younger lions; the he-goat assists the shepherd in leading the flock; and with regard to greyhounds as well, there is generally a leader of the pack when they hunt or pull sleds. If this term is translated as a chicken, the analogy also fits, as sometimes a rooster leads and controls the actions of a group of other chickens.

31:1 | **The words of Lemuel the king:** It is possible there was in fact a king with this name, but the Sages interpreted the name Lemuel as a reference to King Solomon himself (see Rashi; Ibn Ezra; *Sanhedrin* 70b). Lemuel may be a nickname whose meaning is one who is associated with and goes to God (see Ralbag; *Metzudat David*; Rashi, verse 4), which is similar to the meaning of Solomon's second name, Yedidya (see II Samuel 12:25), one who is close with God.

If the following verses are indeed attributed to Solomon's mother, then they are not a product of Solomon's own wisdom, but ideas spoken to him. These words of rebuke address general topics that are appropriate to be discussed with every person individually, though it is not known that Solomon specifically drank wine and became inebriated on a frequent basis. Perhaps for this reason, the Sages stated that these words of rebuke were spoken in a particular context. It is related that on the day the construction of the Temple was completed, King Solomon married the daughter of Pharaoh. As a result, he did not arise at the proper time in the morning. Everyone was awaiting his arrival, and his lateness delayed the Temple service. After this incident, Solomon's mother rebuked him that it was because he was with his wife, or had drunk an excessive amount of wine, that he did not awaken (see Rashi; *Bemidbar Rabba* 10:4).

of the poor, the causes of all the unfortunate members of society.[535] When he is inebriated, the king will not be exact with the particulars, and even if he does not intend to perform an injustice, he will judge hastily and commit errors. In such situations, it is the people on the margins of society who will suffer the most.

6 There is no absolute objection here to drinking wine itself, as there are instances where wine is good and beneficial: **Give strong drink to the desolate,**[D] to the miserable individual who feels that he is wasting away, **and** giving **wine** is also suitable **to** cheer up **embittered souls.**

7 **Let him,** the desolate one or the bitter individual, **drink and forget his poverty** and his terrible situation, **and remember his toil** and frustration **no more.**

8 This verse provides further advice for a king, who also functions as a judge: **Open your mouth for the mute,** whether he is literally dumb, or simply unable to speak about the matter at hand, such as one at a trial who cannot express himself properly. A righteous judge is obligated to assist those who are incapable of pleading their cases, and act **for the judgment for all the fragile,** people who have no security and stability and whose claims are liable to be negated by the opposing party. Perhaps they came to the court inadequately prepared, while far more powerful, educated individuals of a higher status sit across from them, and therefore they are stifled. A king must pay careful attention to such a case, and try to redress the balance in favor of the weaker side.[536]

9 **Open your mouth, rule justly,**[D] **and judge the poor and indigent.** The righteous judge is obliged not only to decide between the competing parties but to examine the matter in detail, and clarify the claims as best he can. Consequently, a king is not permitted to enjoy physical pleasures like any other person, because he must be careful to retain his strength and clarity of mind at all times. Only in this way can he fulfill his task of leading his country and establishing righteous judgment.

A Woman of Valor

PROVERBS 31:10–31

Proverbs concludes with the following hymn about a woman of valor. Its structure is that of an alphabetical acrostic, a form that is found in other biblical books, such as Psalms and Lamentations, typically in chapters that bear a didactic message. But this form is unique for the book of Proverbs. The hymn illustrates the noble qualities of a woman of valor.

The book of Proverbs contains many references to women. It generally depicts the best ones as those who stay at home and engage in household matters. By contrast, here it celebrates an active woman who takes initiative. She is one who alongside complete management of her household also engages in business. She is the driving force both within the home and outside of it. Moreover, she is an independent personality whose character traits and spiritual and religious qualities shape the nature of the home, as she lovingly cares for all the members of her family. This passage does not describe merely a righteous woman or a woman who is adept at business. Rather, she has the ability to combine the home and family arena with the organizational and business arena, which merge together to compose her religious world. The combination of these elements transforms her into the unique woman depicted here.

10 **A woman of valor,** a strong woman who successfully performs great tasks, **who can find?** It is not easy to find such a woman, and **far beyond pearls is her value** (see commentary on 3:15). She is rarer and more valuable than precious stones.[537]

11 **Her husband's heart relies on her;** he relies upon all her deeds, **and he will not lack treasure.** He can leave the running of all their household affairs in her trustworthy hands without fear of loss.[538]

12 **She bestows** only **good and not evil upon him,**[D] **all the days of her life.**

13 She herself performs the household tasks properly: **She seeks** out **wool and flax** for spinning. In the Bible and the Mishna, spinning wool or flax was a task generally attributed to women.[539] **And her hands work willingly;**[540] alternatively, this means that she works with good, expert hands.

Spun wool

Flax straw, yarn, and rope

BACKGROUND

31:15 | She arises while still night and provides fare for her household: Baking bread in ancient times required the woman to rise while it was yet dark in order to grind flour, to knead and arrange the dough, and afterward to bake bread for the members of her household who had to leave for their work at daybreak.

ו ז מְחֻקָּק וִישַׁנֶּה דִּין כָּל־בְּנֵי־עֹנִי׃ תְּנוּ־שֵׁכָר לְאוֹבֵד וְיַיִן לְמָרֵי נָפֶשׁ׃ יִשְׁתֶּה וְיִשְׁכַּח
ח ט רִישׁוֹ וַעֲמָלוֹ לֹא יִזְכָּר־עוֹד׃ פְּתַח־פִּיךָ לְאִלֵּם אֶל־דִּין כָּל־בְּנֵי חֲלוֹף׃ פְּתַח־פִּיךָ
שְׁפָט־צֶדֶק וְדִין עָנִי וְאֶבְיוֹן׃
י יא אֵשֶׁת־חַיִל מִי יִמְצָא וְרָחֹק מִפְּנִינִים מִכְרָהּ׃ בָּטַח בָּהּ לֵב בַּעְלָהּ וְשָׁלָל לֹא
יב יג יֶחְסָר׃ גְּמָלַתְהוּ טוֹב וְלֹא־רָע כֹּל יְמֵי חַיֶּיהָ׃ דָּרְשָׁה צֶמֶר וּפִשְׁתִּים וַתַּעַשׂ בְּחֵפֶץ
יד טו כַּפֶּיהָ׃ הָיְתָה כָּאֳנִיּוֹת סוֹחֵר מִמֶּרְחָק תָּבִיא לַחְמָהּ׃ וַתָּקָם ׀ בְּעוֹד לַיְלָה וַתִּתֵּן

14 The woman of valor is not satisfied with sitting passively and fulfilling her basic duties. **She is like the merchant ships,** which sail great distances to procure goods, **bringing her food from afar.** She takes initiative, is creative, and travels to bring food to her home.

15 **She arises while still night and provides fare for her household.**[B] She takes care to prepare food for the members of her household ahead of time; **and** she provides **a** fixed **portion to her young women.** She gives every one of her maids sufficient provisions for their needs.

Woman grating cheese, Greece, 500–475 BCE

Phoenician merchant ships, illustration based on stone relief, palace of Sargon II, Dur-Sharrukin, Assyria, 722–705 BCE

DISCUSSION

31:6| **Give strong drink to the desolate:** If individuals who do not have any plans for the future or who are very fearful drink wine, they can forget their situation. For this reason, when the Sanhedrin judged capital cases, they would give the one on trial who was about to receive the death penalty wine to drink in order to reduce his level of suffering (see *Sanhedrin* 43a).

31:9| **Open your mouth, rule justly:** The king is not simply the leader of his country; he also has the responsibility to ensure that fair judgment is carried out. In this regard, it appears that the king possesses a unique level of authority of judgment that goes beyond that of ordinary courts. This role is somewhat comparable to that of the Supreme Court today, whose role is to ensure societal justice rather than simply reviewing earlier decisions.

From the few examples found in the Bible that illustrate this role, it would seem that people occasionally came directly to the king to beg for mercy. In these instances, there was no complaint of perversion of justice with regard to any specific law. Rather, a litigant who agreed that he was legally obligated to compensate the other party but did not have the wherewithal to do so would approach the king and plead for him to use his unique authority to help him. In other words, these were requests for a type of justice and fairness that went beyond the letter of the law. They were directed to the king, as he was the final arbiter of justice, who was not accountable to anyone other than God (see II Samuel 14:4–11, and commentary on verse 4; I Kings 20:39–40; II Kings 8:3–6).

31:12| **She bestows good and not evil upon him:** Within every society, some people may bestow good upon others while simultaneously causing evil in other ways. By contrast, despite all the activities the woman of valor is engaged in and her successes, she is not controlling or angry, and she does not denounce her husband or make life difficult for him. She does not limit the realm of her husband in any way in order to increase her reputation or her standing. She maintains this quality during her entire life, which means that it is not dependent upon her being young and active, or being older and wiser. Rather, she acts with honesty and strength all her life.

16 In addition to capably managing her household, **she considers** purchasing **a field, and purchases it; with the fruit of her hands,** the products of her labor, **she plants a vineyard.** She does not simply accumulate her profits, nor does she buy jewelry for herself with her earnings. Rather, the fruit of her labor produces enough money for her to procure land and plant a vineyard.

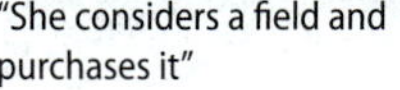

"She considers a field and purchases it"

Vineyard in the Golan Heights

17 **She girds her loins with might,** she acts quickly and decisively, **and strengthens her arms.** She does not sit idle, but acts constantly with vigor.[541]

18 **She perceives that her merchandise,** i.e., the products of her dealings as well as her actions in general, **is good; her lamp does not go out at night.** After awaking early to care for all the needs of her family, she continues to be active at night, as she always has work that can be done in her home.

19 **She extends her hands to the distaff, and her palms support the spindle,**[B] spinning implements. Her hands ensure that the spindle turns in the proper manner.

Woman spinning with distaff and spindle, illustration based on picture from Roman period

"As her entire household is clothed in scarlet wool." Woman weaving on a loom

20 Although she herself works, she does not hoard the money she earns to spend on her own pleasures; she is not materialistic. **She opens her palm to the poor and extends her hands to the indigent.** She provides sustenance to the poor as well.

21 Not only does the woman of valor run affairs of the present in the best possible way, she also thinks long term and plans for the future: **She does not fear snow,** the harshest winter days, **for her household, as her entire household is clothed in scarlet wool,**[B] which protects them from the cold and also looks beautiful.[542]

22 **She has made coverlets,** bedding or linings, **for herself; her clothing is** fine **linen and** expensive **purple wool.** Both beauty and wealth are on display in her home.[543]

23 But she is not concerned for her own dress alone: **Her husband is renowned** for his fine appearance[544] **at the** city **gates,** the main communal centers, **where he sits with the elders of the land,** its leaders and dignitaries.

24 **She makes a linen sheet and sells it;** even when she does not need linen garments she fashions them for sale; **and** she **gives a belt,** whose preparation is more complicated than simple bedding,[545] **to the merchant.**[B] Although her main occupation is within the home, and this includes the making of colorful clothing and bedding, she sells any surplus items to outsiders.

25 **Might and grandeur are her clothing;** she wears dignified clothes that are both durable and beautiful; **and she laughs** and rejoices **to the final day** of her life. Her garments are not merely for adornment in the present, as everything she makes withstands the test of time and does not get worn out.

26 Beyond her practical capabilities in running the household and her business initiatives for increasing the family income from other sources, she is also a wise, good-hearted woman: **She opens her mouth with** words of **wisdom, and the Torah of kindness is on her tongue.** She teaches religious ideas that incorporate love and generosity.

27 **She supervises the proceedings of her household,** as she takes care that the house, with all its people and servants, is properly managed, **and she does not eat the bread of idleness.** She does not simply sit back and enjoy the sight of her servants or family members doing all the work; rather, she prefers to be active herself.

28 Therefore, **her children arise and laud her** [***vayasheruha***]; alternatively, they note that she follows the upright [*yeshara*] path; **her husband** also rises up, **and he praises her**[546] with the following declaration:

29 **Many daughters,** many women, **have performed valiantly,** have been successful in one way or another, **but you have surpassed them all.** You have achieved perfection in all your qualities. You are creative, active, generous, strong, organized, and wise.

30 Her husband and children further state:[547] **Grace is falsehood,** as one's appearance can change and disappoint, **and beauty is futility,** since it eventually wastes away and is lost; but **a woman who fears the Lord,** when this quality becomes an inherent part of her personality, **she will be praised** forever. The verse is not rejecting grace and beauty entirely; rather, it is saying that these fine qualities when utilized by themselves can lead one astray, and are transient and unstable.[548]

31 **Give her from the fruit of her hands.** She does not require any external gifts, as she is content to receive the fruit of her labor and the wages of her toil. **And may her actions praise her at the gates.**[D] She is in no need of praise from afar or honorary titles granted by others. Her own works are her praise.

טז טֶרֶף לְבֵיתָהּ וְחֹק לְנַעֲרֹתֶיהָ׃ זָמְמָה שָׂדֶה וַתִּקָּחֵהוּ מִפְּרִי כַפֶּיהָ נָטַע כָּרֶם׃
יז יח חָגְרָה בְעוֹז מָתְנֶיהָ וַתְּאַמֵּץ זְרוֹעֹתֶיהָ׃ טָעֲמָה כִּי־טוֹב סַחְרָהּ לֹא־יִכְבֶּה בַלַּיְל
יט כ נֵרָהּ׃ יָדֶיהָ שִׁלְּחָה בַכִּישׁוֹר וְכַפֶּיהָ תָּמְכוּ פָלֶךְ׃ כַּפָּהּ פָּרְשָׂה לֶעָנִי וְיָדֶיהָ שִׁלְּחָה
כא כב לָאֶבְיוֹן׃ לֹא־תִירָא לְבֵיתָהּ מִשָּׁלֶג כִּי כָל־בֵּיתָהּ לָבֻשׁ שָׁנִים׃ מַרְבַדִּים עָשְׂתָה־
כג כד לָּהּ שֵׁשׁ וְאַרְגָּמָן לְבוּשָׁהּ׃ נוֹדָע בַּשְּׁעָרִים בַּעְלָהּ בְּשִׁבְתּוֹ עִם־זִקְנֵי־אָרֶץ׃ סָדִין
כה עָשְׂתָה וַתִּמְכֹּר וַחֲגוֹר נָתְנָה לַכְּנַעֲנִי׃ עֹז־וְהָדָר לְבוּשָׁהּ וַתִּשְׂחַק לְיוֹם אַחֲרוֹן׃
כו כז פִּיהָ פָּתְחָה בְחָכְמָה וְתוֹרַת־חֶסֶד עַל־לְשׁוֹנָהּ׃ צוֹפִיָּה הילכות בֵּיתָהּ וְלֶחֶם הֲלִיכוֹת
כח כט עַצְלוּת לֹא תֹאכֵל׃ קָמוּ בָנֶיהָ וַיְאַשְּׁרוּהָ בַּעְלָהּ וַיְהַלְלָהּ׃ רַבּוֹת בָּנוֹת עָשׂוּ חָיִל
ל וְאַתְּ עָלִית עַל־כֻּלָּנָה׃ שֶׁקֶר הַחֵן וְהֶבֶל הַיֹּפִי אִשָּׁה יִרְאַת־יהוה הִיא תִתְהַלָּל׃
לא תְּנוּ־לָהּ מִפְּרִי יָדֶיהָ וִיהַלְלוּהָ בַשְּׁעָרִים מַעֲשֶׂיהָ׃

BACKGROUND

31:19| **Distaff and spindle:** Spinning with a distaff and spindle was a woman's task in ancient times. A distaff is a rod around which the raw material, the wool or flax, is wrapped, and from which the thread is drawn, while a spindle is a short rod, to which an additional weight is sometimes tied, and around which one wraps the thread that was rolled and spun between the fingers of the hand.

31:21| **Scarlet wool [*shanim*]:** In Akkadian, the similar word *sannitu* means a colorful woven cloth. The Hebrew term *shani*, or *shanim*, refers to wool dyed a bright shade of red, almost orange, extracted from the blood of the *tola'at shani*, a type of insect.

31:24| **The merchant [*kena'ani*]:** In ancient times, most Israelites did not engage in commercial dealings, which was primarily the arena of the Canaanites. For this reason, the word used for merchant is *kena'ani*.

DISCUSSION

31:31| **And may her actions praise her at the gates:** As can be seen from this passage, the woman of valor is described as the ideal woman, one who also possesses many qualities of modern women. She is not merely submissive to her husband and closeted in her house. Rather, she is a creative, active individual, who leads others without attempting to control them or force her desires upon them. She engages in commerce and gives charity. In addition, she is responsible and trustworthy, with regard to both her business dealings and her simple, daily tasks. Her image is strikingly different from the other images of women described in the Bible. In addition, the description of her praises and positive qualities does not include her external appearance, which is often highlighted with regard to other women in the Bible. Rather, the woman of valor stands out as having a reputation of one whose every action brings only good and blessing. Therefore, a man should aspire to marry such a woman and search for one like her.

Job

Job

INTRODUCTION TO JOB

The long-suffering figure of Job is at the center of this book. In the wake of the terrible tragedies Job experiences, he engages in a dispute with God over his righteousness. God does not hurry to respond to him, but Job's friends, who arrive to comfort him in his despair, refute his claims. The majority of the book consists of speeches; some are delivered by Job himself, while some are addressed to Job by his friends.

Although the book starts and ends with prose, it is written mostly in a poetic style and includes some of the most beautiful descriptions of nature in the entire Bible. The speeches constituting the main part of the book are delivered in a flowery style that is not easily understood. Not only do they employ a lexicon of irregular and difficult words, but their content is also complex and weighty. This unusual book certainly provides an opening for people seeking to inveigh against God because of their troubles and to criticize His leadership of the world. However, it also provides a divine perspective on human questions. Reading the book causes one to consider whether posing these profound questions is in fact justified, and whether receiving responses to those questions is a real possibility.

Job

Job's Test

JOB 1:1–2:13

The book of Job is framed by a background story. The first section of this story occurs in two different arenas: on earth (verses 1–5) and in heaven (verses 6–12).

1 1 **There was a man in the land of Utz,**[B] in the region of Aram[1] or Edom,[2] **whose name was Job;**[D] **that man was virtuous and upright, God-fearing, and he shunned evil.** He excelled in all aspects of character and conduct.

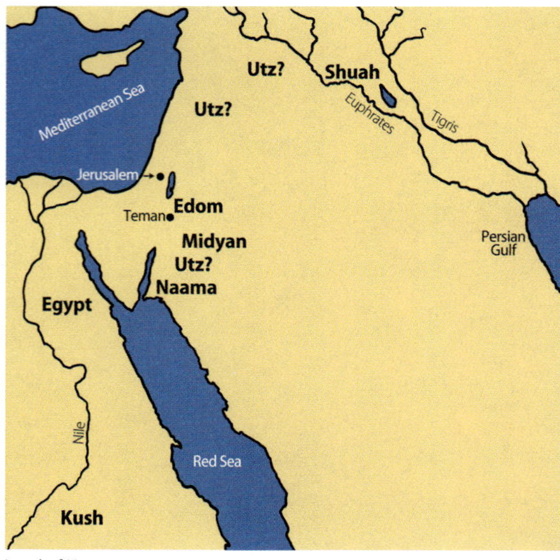

Land of Utz

2 **Seven sons and three daughters were born to him.**

3 **His livestock was seven thousand sheep, three thousand camels, five hundred pairs of oxen, five hundred female donkeys, as well as a great many servants.**[3] **This man was greater** in wealth and honor[4] **than all the people of the East.** With his large family and vast properties, Job was almost like a king.

4 **His sons would go and make a feast in the house of each** son **on his day.** Every day of the week, or occasionally,[5] a different son would invite the entire family for a feast in his house. **They would send and invite their three sisters,** who were presumably unmarried, **to eat and drink with them.** The family was close and lived a tranquil life, enjoying each other's company during extended family meals.

5 **It was when the cycle of the days of their feasting was completed that Job would send and sanctify them.** Job was careful to purify his children from various types of impurity. Perhaps they might have contracted impurities during their feasts.[6] Other commentaries explain that he invited them to join him. **And he,** Job, **would rise early in the morning and proffer up burnt offerings corresponding to the number of all of them,** all his children. **For Job would say: Perhaps my sons have sinned and blasphemed [*berekhu*] God in their hearts.** The word *berekhu* means "they blessed," but here, as elsewhere, it is used euphemistically so as to avoid any explicit association of blasphemy in connection with God.[7] Job was concerned that in their excessive levity or smugness, during the feasts, his children might have entertained negative thoughts about God, even if such notions were not expressed verbally. **So would Job,** this successful, wealthy, and God-fearing individual, **do always.**

6 **It was one day, and the children of the great,**[D] the angels, **came to stand before the Lord,** in a kind of heavenly meeting. **And the accuser too came among them,** as he is also an angel with a task, which is not necessarily evil, to fulfill. He is assigned the role of prosecutor, whose duty is to ensure that all cases are conducted in accordance with the letter of the law and to raise allegations if there are grounds to do so.[8]

7 **The Lord said to the accuser: From where have you come? The accuser answered the Lord and said: From wandering the earth, and from walking around it.** I have traveled throughout the world, observing, executing my duty. Satan does not remain in heaven, as his primary occupation involves this world. It is clear that God and Satan maintain friendly ties, so to speak.

8 **The Lord said to the accuser: Have you noticed My servant Job? For there is no one like him on the earth, a virtuous and upright man, revering God and shunning evil.** Look at him. Don't you agree that he is an impressive figure?

9 **Then the accuser answered the Lord and said: Is it for nothing that Job reveres God?** He has good reason for revering You.

10 **Haven't You sheltered him, his household, and everything around that is his?** You have spread over him a net of assistance, protection, and patronage.[9] **You blessed his handiwork,**

איוב

א אִישׁ הָיָה בְאֶרֶץ־עוּץ אִיּוֹב שְׁמוֹ וְהָיָה ׀ הָאִישׁ הַהוּא תָּם וְיָשָׁר וִירֵא אֱלֹהִים א
ב ג וְסָר מֵרָע: וַיִּוָּלְדוּ לוֹ שִׁבְעָה בָנִים וְשָׁלוֹשׁ בָּנוֹת: וַיְהִי מִקְנֵהוּ שִׁבְעַת אַלְפֵי־צֹאן
וּשְׁלֹשֶׁת אַלְפֵי גְמַלִּים וַחֲמֵשׁ מֵאוֹת צֶמֶד־בָּקָר וַחֲמֵשׁ מֵאוֹת אֲתוֹנוֹת וַעֲבֻדָּה
ד רַבָּה מְאֹד וַיְהִי הָאִישׁ הַהוּא גָּדוֹל מִכָּל־בְּנֵי־קֶדֶם: וְהָלְכוּ בָנָיו וְעָשׂוּ מִשְׁתֶּה
ה בֵּית אִישׁ יוֹמוֹ וְשָׁלְחוּ וְקָרְאוּ לִשְׁלֹשֶׁת אַחְיֹתֵיהֶם לֶאֱכֹל וְלִשְׁתּוֹת עִמָּהֶם: וַיְהִי
כִּי הִקִּיפוּ יְמֵי הַמִּשְׁתֶּה וַיִּשְׁלַח אִיּוֹב וַיְקַדְּשֵׁם וְהִשְׁכִּים בַּבֹּקֶר וְהֶעֱלָה עֹלוֹת
מִסְפַּר כֻּלָּם כִּי אָמַר אִיּוֹב אוּלַי חָטְאוּ בָנַי וּבֵרֲכוּ אֱלֹהִים בִּלְבָבָם כָּכָה יַעֲשֶׂה
ו אִיּוֹב כָּל־הַיָּמִים: וַיְהִי הַיּוֹם וַיָּבֹאוּ בְּנֵי הָאֱלֹהִים לְהִתְיַצֵּב עַל־
ז יהוה וַיָּבוֹא גַם־הַשָּׂטָן בְּתוֹכָם: וַיֹּאמֶר יהוה אֶל־הַשָּׂטָן מֵאַיִן תָּבֹא וַיַּעַן הַשָּׂטָן
ח אֶת־יהוה וַיֹּאמַר מִשּׁוּט בָּאָרֶץ וּמֵהִתְהַלֵּךְ בָּהּ: וַיֹּאמֶר יהוה אֶל־הַשָּׂטָן הֲשַׂמְתָּ
לִבְּךָ עַל־עַבְדִּי אִיּוֹב כִּי אֵין כָּמֹהוּ בָּאָרֶץ אִישׁ תָּם וְיָשָׁר יְרֵא אֱלֹהִים וְסָר מֵרָע:
ט וַיַּעַן הַשָּׂטָן אֶת־יהוה וַיֹּאמַר הַחִנָּם יָרֵא אִיּוֹב אֱלֹהִים: הֲלֹא־אַתָּ שַׂכְתָּ בַעֲדוֹ

BACKGROUND

1:1 | **Utz:** This is the name of an Aramean tribe or nation (see Genesis 10:23, 22:21) that apparently lived in the region of the people of the East (see verse 3; Genesis 29:1), in the eastern and northeastern areas of the Land of Israel. Josephus identifies Utz with the region of Bashan, which is near Aram. Others suggest that Utz was located near the Euphrates River. However, the listing of Utz together with the descendants of Se'ir and Edom (Genesis 36:28; Lamentations 4:21) indicates that it was close to Edom. This suggestion is supported by the mention in verse 15 of Sheba, which was also a southern kingdom.

DISCUSSION

1:1 | **Job:** The identity of Job is unknown, but the name of his birthplace and other details of his life indicate that he was not an Israelite. The period in which he lived is also uncertain. Some claim that he was a contemporary of the patriarch Abraham, while others maintain that he lived more than a thousand years later. According to one opinion, it can be inferred from the mystery that envelops the figure of Job that he "never existed and was never created; rather, he was a parable" (*Bava Batra* 15a). In other words, the plot of this book is fictional and is designed to evoke discussions about its important topics. However, elsewhere Job is mentioned alongside Noah and Daniel as one of the righteous men of the world (see Ezekiel 14:14).

It seems that this figure was etched into the collective memory of the Jewish people over the generations. Indeed, a story like Job's could have occurred in a variety of places and periods; his words have ramifications that go far beyond his own time and place, whenever and wherever that may have been.

1:6 | **The children of the great [*benei ha'elohim*]:** The expression *benei ha'elohim* appears only in Job (1:6, 2:1, 38:7) and Genesis (6:2, 4). An alternative translation of this term might be "children of God." In Job, the term refers to the members of the heavenly court, which also includes the accuser mentioned here. It is more difficult to claim that the *benei ha'elohim* referred to in Genesis are angels, since there they are said to marry human women.

and his livestock has spread out in the land. You help him, bless him, and grant him success. His world is calm and serene, and his every desire is fulfilled. He has never had to struggle in any way. This is why he acts in a wholehearted and upright manner.

11 **However, extend Your hand now, and touch,** harm, something of **all that he has. Won't he blaspheme You to Your face?** The verse employs the term *yevarkheka*, literally, bless You, as a euphemism for blaspheme You. Under those circumstances Job would undoubtedly change his ways.

12 **The Lord said to the accuser: Behold, everything that he has is in your hand.** You have permission to test Job to see whether, as you claim, he will abandon and even blaspheme Me in his suffering. **Only do not extend your hand against him.** Do not harm Job bodily. **The accuser emerged from the presence of the Lord** to act on the permission he had received to test Job.

13 **It was one day, and his,** Job's, **sons and his daughters were eating and drinking wine** in their usual manner **in the house of their firstborn brother,**

14 **and a messenger came to Job and said: The oxen were plowing** in the field, **and the female donkeys were grazing**[B] **alongside them,** as they cannot be used for plowing like the oxen,

15 **and Sheba**[B] **fell upon them and took them** away. People from the kingdom of Sheba attacked them and plundered all the animals;[10] **they smote** all of **the lads,** the servants working there, who were not necessarily youths, **by the sword and only I alone escaped to tell you.** I alone survived to relate what happened.

16 **This one,** the first messenger, **was still speaking** and relating his story, **and that one,** another messenger, **came and said: A fire of God,** a fire with no apparent cause, or alternatively, a massive fire,[11] **fell from the heavens, and it burned among the sheep and the lads** that were tending the sheep **and consumed them.** Everything was destroyed, **and only I alone escaped to tell you.**

17 **This one,** the second messenger, **was still speaking, and that one,** a third messenger, **came** with further bad news **and said: The Chaldeans,** Babylonians, **set three columns,** organized their army into three fronts, **and made a raid against the camels and took them; they smote the lads** that were with the camels **by the sword and only I alone escaped to tell you.** Each messenger related to Job an additional calamity that had befallen his possessions and men.

18 **This one was still speaking, and that one,** yet another messenger, **came and said: Your sons and your daughters were eating and drinking wine in the house of their firstborn brother,**

19 **and behold, a great wind came from across,** from the direction of, **the wilderness, and it,** the wind, **struck the four corners of the house, and it fell on the lads** who were inside, **and they died; and only I alone escaped to tell you.** Job is informed that not only are his possessions lost, but his family has perished as well.

20 **Job rose, and he rent his robe, sheared** the hair off **his head** as a sign of mourning, **and** he **fell to the ground and prostrated himself** before God.[12]

21 **He said: Naked I emerged from my mother's womb, and naked I will return there.** Now that I have lost all that I acquired over the course of my life, I will return to my starting point in this world. Just as I was born without any possessions or children, so too will I die without them. **The Lord gave** me the gifts of family, possessions, and power, **and the Lord has** now **taken** them away; **blessed be the name of the Lord** for all His deeds.

22 **With all this,** despite all these tragedies, **Job did not sin and did not ascribe misconduct to God.** He did not utter any complaints about what had occurred to him.[13] Although he was shattered by the many tragedies he endured, he nevertheless accepted his fate, and refused to question it or discuss it. Instead, he wished to bless God and continue to live.

2 1 **It was one day,** after Job had already lost his possessions and most of his family, **and the children of the great,** the angels, **came to stand before the Lord.** They regularly gathered to stand before Him, like in a military roll call. **And the accuser too came to stand before the Lord.**

2 **The Lord said to the accuser: From where have you come? The accuser answered the Lord and said: From wandering the earth, and from walking around it.**

BACKGROUND

1:14 | **The oxen were plowing, and the female donkeys were grazing:** Donkeys were generally used for carrying, not plowing. It is also possible that the verse stresses the distinction between the oxen plowing and the donkeys grazing to indicate that Job's men were careful to avoid any violation of the prohibition against plowing with diverse species, that is, plowing with oxen and donkeys together (Deuteronomy 22:10). This prohibition was not observed by the other peoples of the East.

1:15 | **Sheba:** Sheba is generally identified as a nation and kingdom that originated in the southwestern area of the Arabian Peninsula. Sheba was known for its manufacture of myrrh and frankincense. Based on the description below (6:19), and in other books of the Bible, Sheba was a source of commerce for gold, precious stones, and spices (see, e.g., I Kings 10:1; Ezekiel 27:22; Psalms 72:15), a claim supported by Assyrian documents and Roman historical records.

וּבְעַד־בֵּיתוֹ וּבְעַד כָּל־אֲשֶׁר־לוֹ מִסָּבִיב מַעֲשֵׂה יָדָיו בֵּרַכְתָּ וּמִקְנֵהוּ פָּרַץ בָּאָרֶץ׃
יא יב וְאוּלָם שְׁלַח־נָא יָדְךָ וְגַע בְּכָל־אֲשֶׁר־לוֹ אִם־לֹא עַל־פָּנֶיךָ יְבָרְכֶךָּ׃ וַיֹּאמֶר יהוה
אֶל־הַשָּׂטָן הִנֵּה כָל־אֲשֶׁר־לוֹ בְּיָדֶךָ רַק אֵלָיו אַל־תִּשְׁלַח יָדֶךָ וַיֵּצֵא הַשָּׂטָן מֵעִם
יג פְּנֵי יהוה׃ וַיְהִי הַיּוֹם וּבָנָיו וּבְנֹתָיו אֹכְלִים וְשֹׁתִים יַיִן בְּבֵית אֲחִיהֶם הַבְּכוֹר׃
יד וּמַלְאָךְ בָּא אֶל־אִיּוֹב וַיֹּאמַר הַבָּקָר הָיוּ חֹרְשׁוֹת וְהָאֲתֹנוֹת רֹעוֹת עַל־יְדֵיהֶם׃
טו וַתִּפֹּל שְׁבָא וַתִּקָּחֵם וְאֶת־הַנְּעָרִים הִכּוּ לְפִי־חָרֶב וָאִמָּלְטָה רַק־אֲנִי לְבַדִּי לְהַגִּיד
טז לָךְ׃ עוֹד ׀ זֶה מְדַבֵּר וְזֶה בָּא וַיֹּאמַר אֵשׁ אֱלֹהִים נָפְלָה מִן־הַשָּׁמַיִם וַתִּבְעַר בַּצֹּאן
יז וּבַנְּעָרִים וַתֹּאכְלֵם וָאִמָּלְטָה רַק־אֲנִי לְבַדִּי לְהַגִּיד לָךְ׃ עוֹד ׀ זֶה מְדַבֵּר וְזֶה בָּא
וַיֹּאמַר כַּשְׂדִּים שָׂמוּ ׀ שְׁלֹשָׁה רָאשִׁים וַיִּפְשְׁטוּ עַל־הַגְּמַלִּים וַיִּקָּחוּם וְאֶת־הַנְּעָרִים
יח הִכּוּ לְפִי־חָרֶב וָאִמָּלְטָה רַק־אֲנִי לְבַדִּי לְהַגִּיד לָךְ׃ עַד זֶה מְדַבֵּר וְזֶה בָּא וַיֹּאמַר
יט בָּנֶיךָ וּבְנוֹתֶיךָ אֹכְלִים וְשֹׁתִים יַיִן בְּבֵית אֲחִיהֶם הַבְּכוֹר׃ וְהִנֵּה רוּחַ גְּדוֹלָה בָּאָה ׀
מֵעֵבֶר הַמִּדְבָּר וַיִּגַּע בְּאַרְבַּע פִּנּוֹת הַבַּיִת וַיִּפֹּל עַל־הַנְּעָרִים וַיָּמוּתוּ וָאִמָּלְטָה רַק־
כ אֲנִי לְבַדִּי לְהַגִּיד לָךְ׃ וַיָּקָם אִיּוֹב וַיִּקְרַע אֶת־מְעִלוֹ וַיָּגָז אֶת־רֹאשׁוֹ וַיִּפֹּל אַרְצָה
כא וַיִּשְׁתָּחוּ׃ וַיֹּאמֶר עָרֹם יָצָתִי מִבֶּטֶן אִמִּי וְעָרֹם אָשׁוּב שָׁמָה יהוה נָתַן וַיהוה לָקָח
כב ב א יְהִי שֵׁם יהוה מְבֹרָךְ׃ בְּכָל־זֹאת לֹא־חָטָא אִיּוֹב וְלֹא־נָתַן תִּפְלָה לֵאלֹהִים׃ וַיְהִי
הַיּוֹם וַיָּבֹאוּ בְּנֵי הָאֱלֹהִים לְהִתְיַצֵּב עַל־יהוה וַיָּבוֹא גַם־הַשָּׂטָן בְּתֹכָם לְהִתְיַצֵּב
ב עַל־יהוה׃ וַיֹּאמֶר יהוה אֶל־הַשָּׂטָן אֵי מִזֶּה תָּבֹא וַיַּעַן הַשָּׂטָן אֶת־יהוה וַיֹּאמַר
ג מִשֻּׁט בָּאָרֶץ וּמֵהִתְהַלֵּךְ בָּהּ׃ וַיֹּאמֶר יהוה אֶל־הַשָּׂטָן הֲשַׂמְתָּ לִבְּךָ אֶל־עַבְדִּי
אִיּוֹב כִּי אֵין כָּמֹהוּ בָּאָרֶץ אִישׁ תָּם וְיָשָׁר יְרֵא אֱלֹהִים וְסָר מֵרָע וְעֹדֶנּוּ מַחֲזִיק
ד בְּתֻמָּתוֹ וַתְּסִיתֵנִי בוֹ לְבַלְּעוֹ חִנָּם׃ וַיַּעַן הַשָּׂטָן אֶת־יהוה וַיֹּאמַר עוֹר בְּעַד־עוֹר

3 **The Lord said to the accuser: Did you notice My servant Job?** Observe him, **for there is no one like him on the earth, a virtuous and upright man, revering God and shunning evil.** Despite all the calamities that have befallen him, **he still maintains his virtuousness, and you incited Me against him, to destroy him without cause,** as it has become evident that he did not deserve any of this. What do you say about him now?

4 **The accuser answered the Lord and said: Skin for skin.** A person is always prepared to sacrifice the skin of another

instead of his own. Alternatively, someone in danger will use the skin of his hands to protect the skin of his head or some other critical limb of the body.[14] **Everything that a man has he will give for his life.** If someone feels threatened, he will focus on defending himself. In his struggle to survive, he will agree to give up everything else in exchange for his life.[15] Up to this point, only Job's children and his possessions had been harmed; his body remained intact, and Satan argued that that is why he blessed God.

5 **However, extend Your hand now, and touch his bone and his flesh.** If his very body is harmed, **won't he blaspheme You to Your face?** Again this is a euphemism, as the word used in the text, *yevarkheka*, literally means that he will bless You.

6 **The Lord said to the accuser: Behold, he is in your hand.** You have permission to afflict him as much as you wish. **Only spare his life.** Ensure that he remains alive.

7 **The accuser emerged from the presence of the Lord, and he struck Job with a terrible rash**[B] **from the sole of his foot to the crown of his head.** Not only is the afflicted individual greatly tormented by such a disease, but it also forces him to maintain a distance from others, as it is contagious. Therefore, not only did Job suffer from the physical symptom of the disease, the itching all over his body, but he was also rendered miserable, lonely, and contemptible because of it.

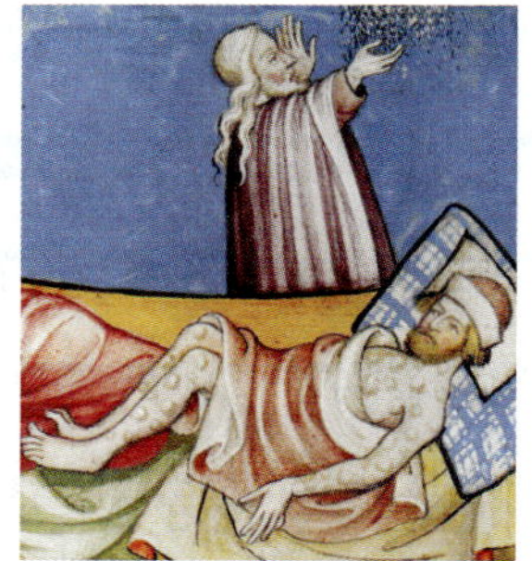
People stricken with terrible rashes, miniature from the Toggenburg Bible, fifteenth century

8 Therefore, **he took for himself a potsherd to scratch with it and sat in the ashes.** The itching caused by the boils and the resulting lesions were aggravated by the woolen garments customarily worn in the days of Job. Thin ash is a soft and gentle surface that is soothing for one whose skin is inflamed, and it would have eased the pain of the boils and the severe itching.[16]

9 **His wife said to him: Do you still maintain your wholeheartedness** and remain God-fearing after all this suffering? **Blaspheme God and die.** God will punish you with death for blaspheming Him, and then you will be free of pain and thus find peace. Job's wife argued that there is no way to evade suffering brought by God Himself other than by bringing about one's own death.[17]

10 **He said to her: You are speaking like one of the disgraceful women speak,** and yet you are a decent woman. **Shall we accept the good from God, and not accept the evil?** Do we stipulate that we will worship God only if He provides for us from His goodness? **With all this,** despite everything that had happened to him, **Job did not sin with his lips.** His life was not worth living, he was broken, tormented, and ill, but still he would not utter anything negative about God.

11 **Job's three friends heard of all this evil that had come upon him, and each came from his place, Elifaz the Temanite,**[B] from the city of Teman in Edom,[18] **and Bildad the Shuhite,**[B] **and Tzofar the Naamatite.**[B] **They met together to come to commiserate with him,** to share in his sorrow, **and to comfort him** to the best of their ability.

12 **They lifted their eyes from afar,** in his direction, **but they did not recognize him.** They saw that his surroundings were all in ruins, he had been struck with boils, and was presumably naked or at least partially unclothed, due to the pain of the boils. **They raised their voice and wept. Each rent his robe, and they threw dust on their heads heavenward,** which are various gestures of mourning over this troubling scene.

13 **They sat down with him on the ground seven days and seven nights, and no one spoke a word to him,**[D] **as they saw that the pain was very great.** They realized that in his great pain, anything they said would only cause additional suffering and distress. So they sat, waiting for him to make the first move, and participated in his sorrow as friends.

DISCUSSION

2:13 | **And no one spoke a word to him:** A *halakha* practiced to this day is derived from this verse. Comforters who come to the house of a mourner during the seven days of mourning may not start a conversation; rather, they must wait for the mourner himself to speak first (see *Moed Katan* 28b; *Shulḥan Arukh, Yoreh De'a* 376:1).

ה וְכֹל אֲשֶׁר לָאִישׁ יִתֵּן בְּעַד נַפְשׁוֹ׃ אוּלָם שְׁלַח־נָא יָדְךָ וְגַע אֶל־עַצְמוֹ וְאֶל־בְּשָׂרוֹ
ו אִם־לֹא אֶל־פָּנֶיךָ יְבָרְכֶךָּ׃ וַיֹּאמֶר יְהוָה אֶל־הַשָּׂטָן הִנּוֹ בְיָדֶךָ אַךְ אֶת־נַפְשׁוֹ שְׁמֹר׃
ז וַיֵּצֵא הַשָּׂטָן מֵאֵת פְּנֵי יְהוָה וַיַּךְ אֶת־אִיּוֹב בִּשְׁחִין רָע מִכַּף רַגְלוֹ עַד קָדְקֳדוֹ׃ וְעַד
ח ט וַיִּקַּח־לוֹ חֶרֶשׂ לְהִתְגָּרֵד בּוֹ וְהוּא יֹשֵׁב בְּתוֹךְ־הָאֵפֶר׃ וַתֹּאמֶר לוֹ אִשְׁתּוֹ עֹדְךָ
י מַחֲזִיק בְּתֻמָּתֶךָ בָּרֵךְ אֱלֹהִים וָמֻת׃ וַיֹּאמֶר אֵלֶיהָ כְּדַבֵּר אַחַת הַנְּבָלוֹת תְּדַבֵּרִי
גַּם אֶת־הַטּוֹב נְקַבֵּל מֵאֵת הָאֱלֹהִים וְאֶת־הָרָע לֹא נְקַבֵּל בְּכָל־זֹאת לֹא־חָטָא
אִיּוֹב בִּשְׂפָתָיו׃
יא וַיִּשְׁמְעוּ שְׁלֹשֶׁת ׀ רֵעֵי אִיּוֹב אֵת כָּל־הָרָעָה הַזֹּאת הַבָּאָה עָלָיו וַיָּבֹאוּ אִישׁ מִמְּקֹמוֹ
אֱלִיפַז הַתֵּימָנִי וּבִלְדַּד הַשּׁוּחִי וְצוֹפַר הַנַּעֲמָתִי וַיִּוָּעֲדוּ יַחְדָּו לָבוֹא לָנוּד־לוֹ וּלְנַחֲמוֹ׃
יב וַיִּשְׂאוּ אֶת־עֵינֵיהֶם מֵרָחוֹק וְלֹא הִכִּירֻהוּ וַיִּשְׂאוּ קוֹלָם וַיִּבְכּוּ וַיִּקְרְעוּ אִישׁ מְעִלוֹ
יג וַיִּזְרְקוּ עָפָר עַל־רָאשֵׁיהֶם הַשָּׁמָיְמָה׃ וַיֵּשְׁבוּ אִתּוֹ לָאָרֶץ שִׁבְעַת יָמִים וְשִׁבְעַת

BACKGROUND

2:7 | **Rash [*sheḥin*]:** The same word is used for the sixth plague in Egypt. In most Semitic languages, the root *shin-ḥet-nun* is associated with heat. Researchers have suggested several skin conditions that cause fever and painful itching that may be identified with this rash. One such condition is urticaria, or hives, whose symptoms include a sudden outbreak of red lesions on the skin that cause itching and which can be brought on by great stress. It might also be smallpox, which causes high fever and an outbreak of very distinct and ugly lesions. The descriptions of Job's dry and cracked skin, which appear later in the book, also match the symptoms of a severe case of dermatitis, eczema, or scabies. Whatever skin affliction this was, since he remained able to engage in extensive discussions with his friends and ultimately with God, Job does not appear to have suffered from a life-threatening disease.

2:11 | **The Temanite:** Teman was a city in southern Edom, as well as a name for the southern region of Edom. According to the identification of Eusebius in his *Onomasticon*, Teman was located in el-Yaval, in the high mountain range east of Petra. Accordingly, it is generally identified with Tawilan, approximately 5 km east of Petra (see the map at the beginning of this section).

The Shuhite: The area known as Shuah, or Suhum, was located along the banks of the middle Euphrates, in modern-day eastern Syria. Shuah was under the control of the kingdom of Mari, where it was referred to as Suhu. Later, Assyria and Babylonia strove for control of this area (see the map at the beginning of this section).

The Naamatite: Some identify Naama as being near the city of Tabuk in northwestern Arabia, close to the Gulf of Eilat. In ancient times, the kingdom of Midyan extended into this region (see the map at the beginning of this section).

Job's Response to His Condition

JOB 3:1–26

Job is broken and ruined. He has lost most of his possessions, his family, and his future. In addition, due to his skin affliction he no longer has the ability to lead a normal life, and people have distanced themselves from him. His close friends have come to visit but have not yet dared to speak, in light of the pain he is suffering.

In his miserable condition, Job begins to curse his life. He claims that the very beginnings of his life were cursed, and he fantasizes about not having been born into such a cruel world. If life is void of meaning and full of pain, he thinks, it is better to live in the world of the dead. Indeed, the grave is described here as an almost idyllic place where freedom and equality reign. But at this stage Job still does not complain directly to God, nor does he challenge the divine calculations.

3 1 **Thereafter,** after having sat in silence, **Job opened his mouth, and he cursed his day.** He expressed his pain over having lost everything and questioned the value of his life in this lowly state. However, he does not accuse God regarding what has occurred.

2 **Job exclaimed and said:**

3 Job curses his life: **Perish the day I was born, and** also **the night it was said: A man,** I, a boy who later became a man, **has been conceived.**[19]

4 **Let that day** on which I was born **be** one of **darkness; let God above not seek it,** but let it be forgotten, **and may light not shine on it.**

5 **May darkness and the shadow of death sully it;**[20] **may a cloud dwell upon** and darken **it; may it,** that day, **be terrorized as if by day-demons** or other evil forces that appear every day.[21]

6 **May that night** on which I was created **be taken** and swallowed **by blackness; let it not be counted among the days of the year; may it not enter the tally of months.** That night should be erased from the calendar so that it will not be included in the calculations of the days or months.[22]

7 **Behold, may that night be desolate,** may it remain alone;[23] **may no joy come in it.**

8 **They who curse the day,**[24] **who prepare for rousing the leviathan**[B] to swallow them up, or alternatively, those who know how to arouse even the awesome leviathan from its place, **may they scorn it,** that night that I was created.

9 **Let the stars of its twilight,** or, alternatively, the stars of that night, **be dark; it hopes for light, but there is none,** as light should never arrive to conclude that night; **let it not see the eyes of dawn.** The metaphorical eyes of that night should not merit to be opened by the morning.[25]

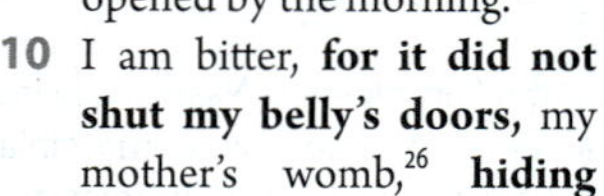

"The eyes of dawn"

10 I am bitter, **for it did not shut my belly's doors,** my mother's womb,[26] **hiding trouble from my eyes.** Had those doors closed, preventing my birth, everything would have been better, as then I would have been spared all this suffering.[27]

11 **Why didn't I die from the womb, and** at least **expire when I emerged from the belly?** It would have been better for me to have died immediately following my birth.[28]

12 And if I had to be born, **why did** the **knees** on which I was placed after my birth **wait for me? And for what were there breasts for me to suck?** For what purpose did I nurse at my mother's breasts?[29]

13 It would have been better had I not been born, or had I not received immediate care at birth, **for now, I would lie** in the grave **and be silent.**[30] **I would sleep,** and **then there would be rest for me.** I would rest peacefully, having joined the dead resting in the grave,

14 and there in the grave, I would have resided **with kings and counselors of the world, who build** cities, which were formerly **ruins, for themselves,**[B] where they could spread their reputation[31] before departing from the world,

15 **or with princes who have gold, who fill their houses with silver,** but ultimately die.

16 **Or why am I not like a buried stillborn, like infants who did not see light,** who died before they could see the world? Job is asking: Why couldn't mine have been a hidden, buried, untimely birth, like that of infants who never see the light of the world?[32]

17 It would have been preferable for me not to have lived at all, as **there,** in the grave, **distress has ceased** even **for the wicked,** as they are spared suffering, worries, and strife. There even the wicked don't scheme as they did in their lifetimes; **and there,** in the grave, **rest those whose strength is sapped.**[33]

18 **Together,** all **prisoners are tranquil;** they are no longer beaten, **not hearing the** raised, oppressive **voice of the taskmaster.**

19 **Small or great, he is there.** Whatever the status of the person when alive, in the grave, everyone is equal, **and the slave is free from his master.** Death frees everyone from social status and troubles and provides each person with freedom and rest.

20 That being the case, **why does He give** the **light** of the world **to the sufferer, and** what is the reason that **life** is granted **to embittered souls,** the pitiful

21 **who** suffer their entire lives, and **wait for death, but it is not? They dig for it** as though hunting for death in holes and crevices, **more than** one would search **for hidden treasures,**[34]

א לֵילוֹת וְאֵין־דֹּבֵר אֵלָיו דָּבָר כִּי רָאוּ כִּי־גָדַל הַכְּאֵב מְאֹד׃ אַחֲרֵי־כֵן פָּתַח אִיּוֹב
אֶת־פִּיהוּ וַיְקַלֵּל אֶת־יוֹמוֹ׃
ב ג ד וַיַּעַן אִיּוֹב וַיֹּאמַר׃ יֹאבַד יוֹם אִוָּלֶד בּוֹ וְהַלַּיְלָה אָמַר הֹרָה גָבֶר׃ הַיּוֹם הַהוּא יְהִי
ה חֹשֶׁךְ אַל־יִדְרְשֵׁהוּ אֱלוֹהַּ מִמָּעַל וְאַל־תּוֹפַע עָלָיו נְהָרָה׃ יִגְאָלֻהוּ חֹשֶׁךְ וְצַלְמָוֶת
ו תִּשְׁכָּן־עָלָיו עֲנָנָה יְבַעֲתֻהוּ כִּמְרִירֵי יוֹם׃ הַלַּיְלָה הַהוּא יִקָּחֵהוּ אֹפֶל אַל־יִחַדְּ
ז בִּימֵי שָׁנָה בְּמִסְפַּר יְרָחִים אַל־יָבֹא׃ הִנֵּה הַלַּיְלָה הַהוּא יְהִי גַלְמוּד אַל־תָּבֹא
ח ט רְנָנָה בוֹ׃ יִקְּבֻהוּ אֹרְרֵי־יוֹם הָעֲתִידִים עֹרֵר לִוְיָתָן׃ יֶחְשְׁכוּ כּוֹכְבֵי נִשְׁפּוֹ יְקַו־לְאוֹר
י וָאַיִן וְאַל־יִרְאֶה בְּעַפְעַפֵּי־שָׁחַר׃ כִּי לֹא סָגַר דַּלְתֵי בִטְנִי וַיַּסְתֵּר עָמָל מֵעֵינָי׃
יא יב לָמָּה לֹּא מֵרֶחֶם אָמוּת מִבֶּטֶן יָצָאתִי וְאֶגְוָע׃ מַדּוּעַ קִדְּמוּנִי בִרְכָּיִם וּמַה־שָּׁדַיִם
יג יד כִּי אִינָק׃ כִּי־עַתָּה שָׁכַבְתִּי וְאֶשְׁקוֹט יָשַׁנְתִּי אָז ׀ יָנוּחַ לִי׃ עִם־מְלָכִים וְיֹעֲצֵי
טו אָרֶץ הַבֹּנִים חֳרָבוֹת לָמוֹ׃ אוֹ עִם־שָׂרִים זָהָב לָהֶם הַמְמַלְאִים בָּתֵּיהֶם כָּסֶף׃
טז יז אוֹ כְנֵפֶל טָמוּן לֹא אֶהְיֶה כְּעֹלְלִים לֹא־רָאוּ אוֹר׃ שָׁם רְשָׁעִים חָדְלוּ רֹגֶז וְשָׁם
יח יט יָנוּחוּ יְגִיעֵי כֹחַ׃ יַחַד אֲסִירִים שַׁאֲנָנוּ לֹא שָׁמְעוּ קוֹל נֹגֵשׂ׃ קָטֹן וְגָדוֹל שָׁם הוּא
כ כא וְעֶבֶד חָפְשִׁי מֵאֲדֹנָיו׃ לָמָּה יִתֵּן לְעָמֵל אוֹר וְחַיִּים לְמָרֵי נָפֶשׁ׃ הַמְחַכִּים לַמָּוֶת

BACKGROUND

3:8 | **Leviathan:** This refers to an awe-inspiring primordial creature of which nothing definitive is known. It was not a whale, despite various translations of the Bible rendering it as such, furnishing the basis for the modern Hebrew term for whale as *livyatan*. Verses in the book of Job and elsewhere in the Bible link this creature to water and to the primordial deep that existed prior to the six days of Creation. It is likely that the leviathan is not an animal in the zoological sense at all but rather represents one of several primeval forces that cannot be readily classified (see below, chaps. 40–41; Isaiah 27:1; Psalms 74:14, 104:26).

3:14 | **Who build ruins for themselves:** In many archaeological excavations, in Israel and around the world, cities have been unearthed that were constructed upon the ruins of earlier cities at the initiative of new rulers. For example, Jericho was rebuilt in the days of Ahav after it had been destroyed by Joshua (Joshua 6:26; I Kings 16:34). The ruins of at least five different once-populated cities have been found there, one on top of the other (see commentary on Jeremiah 30:18).

22 **rejoicing with cries of exultation, glad when they find the grave.**
23 **It,** all of this, **is** stated **for** myself, **a man whose way is hidden,** whose world has darkened, **and against whom God has set a screen** so that he will no longer see His face.[35]
24 **For my groaning** in pain **will come before my food,** before I eat my food, **and my screams pour out like water.**[36]
25 **For that** very matter **which I feared has come upon me, and that which daunted me has come to me.**
26 **I was not serene, was not silent, and I did not rest, but turmoil came.**

Elifaz's First Speech

JOB 4:1–5:27

Job's friends, all God-fearing individuals, had initially sat alongside him in silence as a sign of support for their friend in distress. In their presence, Job eventually spoke, cursing the day of his birth and expressing disgust at his existence and his life of suffering. He did not mention possible reasons for these misfortunes. It is his friends, those faring better than he, who now drag him into a theological discussion on such topics. Each of them will deliver an impressive discourse in an attempt to rebuke Job, stated with a sense of superiority.

Elifaz, the first speaker, demands that Job remain true to his own method of dealing with suffering experienced by others (see 4:3–4). Although Job has done nothing more than mourn over his bitter fate, Elifaz senses in Job's words a latent desire to dispute with his Creator over the justice of the events. Therefore, he shares a prophetic experience of his own with Job. In a jolting nighttime vision, he was shown the massive chasm between man and God. His conclusion is that a human cannot possibly emerge victorious from judgment with God. Elifaz proceeds to rebuke those who fail to turn to God, and instructs Job to understand the following message from his misery: Suffering is sent from Above as part of divine communication with man. If Job successfully internalizes this message, Elifaz claims, he might merit a good end. He concludes his speech with words of encouragement.

4 1 **Elifaz the Temanite answered and said:**
2 What has happened to you? **If a matter tries [*hanissa*] you, will you be enervated?** Will you be weary and broken immediately after a test [*nisayon*], calamity, or other upheaval?[37] **Who can restrain his words?** It is impossible to remain silent after hearing your comments.[38]
3 **Behold, you have** previously **chastised many,** advising them how to act, **and** you **have strengthened feeble hands.** When you enjoyed an elevated social standing, unfortunates turned to you, and you invariably lifted their spirits.
4 **Your words have raised the weakened, and you have strengthened** the **unsteady knees** of those too infirm to stand.
5 **But now it,** suffering, **comes upon you and you are enervated? It touches you and you panic?** How is this possible?
6 **Shouldn't your reverence** of God **be your** source of **security [*kislatekha*]** and stability, **your hope and the virtuousness of your way?** You can rely on your past perfect behavior. *Kislatekha* is based on the word *kesalim*, the flanks, which are the strongest and most stable part of an animal.
7 **Please remember, who is the innocent who perished?** Was anyone who suffered ever entirely innocent? **And where are the upright who were destroyed?** You know that this is not the case.[39]
8 **According to what I have seen, they who plow,** plan, **iniquity and sow travail,** sin, **will reap them,**[D] will have to bear the results of their plots and deeds.
9 **They will** immediately **perish** merely **by the** angry **breath of God,**[40] **and from the blast of His wrath they will cease** and be destroyed.
10 Even the initial manifestation of divine rage affects the strongest creatures, as immediately in response **the roar of the lion**[B] **and the voice of the great cat** are heard, **and the teeth of the lion cubs are broken.**[41]

"The roar of the lion and the voice of the great cat"

11 **The lion [*layish*],** another name for a lion, perhaps referring to a lion at some particular stage of its life or to a specific species of lion,[42] in addition to the three names in the previous verse, **perishes for lack of prey,**[43] **and the** young **children of the lion,** which remain together while they are young for protection, **are scattered**[B] in a panic and are lost. When God roars, even those who consider themselves as strong as lions are broken and destroyed.
12 Elifaz is indicating that he was imbued with a heavenly spirit. Here he describes a prophetic vision he received that referred to the secrets behind events that occur in the world. As is the case for other gentile prophets, his prophetic experience occurred in the middle of the night.[44] **A matter was smuggled to me,** which I did not hear directly,[45] **and my ear received a trace,** a slight hint **of it.**
13 The source of my knowledge of heavenly matters is **in thoughts** that come **from** the dreamlike **visions of the night.** I heard these hints at a time **when slumber falls on men.**
14 **Fear summoned me, and trembling** at the revelation; **it made my many bones quake.**
15 A heavenly **spirit would pass before me; it would cause the hair of my flesh to bristle.**
16 I could tell that **it,** whatever it was, **would stop, but I would not recognize its appearance. It was a form before my eyes,**

כב כג וְאֵינֶנּוּ וַֽיַּחְפְּרֻהוּ מִמַּטְמוֹנִֽים׃ הַשְּׂמֵחִים אֱלֵי־גִיל יָשִׂישׂוּ כִּי יִמְצְאוּ־קָֽבֶר׃ לְגֶבֶר
כד אֲשֶׁר־דַּרְכּוֹ נִסְתָּרָה וַיָּסֶךְ אֱלוֹהַּ בַּעֲדֽוֹ׃ כִּֽי־לִפְנֵי לַחְמִי אַנְחָתִי תָבֹא וַֽיִּתְּכוּ כַמַּיִם
כה כו שַׁאֲגֹתָֽי׃ כִּי פַחַד פָּחַדְתִּי וַיֶּאֱתָיֵנִי וַאֲשֶׁר יָגֹרְתִּי יָבֹא לִֽי׃ לֹא שָׁלַוְתִּי ׀ וְלֹא שָׁקַטְתִּי
וְלֹא־נָחְתִּי וַיָּבֹא רֹֽגֶז׃

א ב ג וַיַּעַן אֱלִיפַז הַֽתֵּימָנִי וַיֹּאמַֽר׃ הֲנִסָּה דָבָר אֵלֶיךָ תִּלְאֶה וַעְצֹר בְּמִלִּין מִי יוּכָֽל׃ הִנֵּה
ד ה יִסַּרְתָּ רַבִּים וְיָדַיִם רָפוֹת תְּחַזֵּֽק׃ כּוֹשֵׁל יְקִימוּן מִלֶּיךָ וּבִרְכַּיִם כֹּרְעוֹת תְּאַמֵּֽץ׃ כִּי
ו עַתָּה ׀ תָּבוֹא אֵלֶיךָ וַתֵּלֶא תִּגַּע עָדֶיךָ וַתִּבָּהֵֽל׃ הֲלֹא יִרְאָתְךָ כִּסְלָתֶךָ תִּקְוָתְךָ
ז ח וְתֹם דְּרָכֶֽיךָ׃ זְכָר־נָא מִי הוּא נָקִי אָבָד וְאֵיפֹה יְשָׁרִים נִכְחָֽדוּ׃ כַּאֲשֶׁר רָאִיתִי
ט י חֹרְשֵׁי אָוֶן וְזֹרְעֵי עָמָל יִקְצְרֻֽהוּ׃ מִנִּשְׁמַת אֱלוֹהַּ יֹאבֵדוּ וּמֵרוּחַ אַפּוֹ יִכְלֽוּ׃ שַׁאֲגַת
יא אַרְיֵה וְקוֹל שָׁחַל וְשִׁנֵּי כְפִירִים נִתָּֽעוּ׃ לַיִשׁ אֹבֵד מִבְּלִי־טָרֶף וּבְנֵי לָבִיא יִתְפָּרָֽדוּ׃
יב יג וְאֵלַי דָּבָר יְגֻנָּב וַתִּקַּח אָזְנִי שֵׁמֶץ מֶֽנְהוּ׃ בִּשְׂעִפִּים מֵחֶזְיֹנוֹת לָיְלָה בִּנְפֹל תַּרְדֵּמָה
יד טו עַל־אֲנָשִֽׁים׃ פַּחַד קְרָאַנִי וּרְעָדָה וְרֹב עַצְמוֹתַי הִפְחִֽיד׃ וְרוּחַ עַל־פָּנַי יַחֲלֹף תְּסַמֵּר
טז שַׂעֲרַת בְּשָׂרִֽי׃ יַעֲמֹד ׀ וְלֹא־אַכִּיר מַרְאֵהוּ תְּמוּנָה לְנֶגֶד עֵינָי דְּמָמָה וָקוֹל אֶשְׁמָֽע׃

DISCUSSION

4:8 | **They who plow iniquity and sow travail will reap them:** In this verse, Elifaz employs images from the agricultural world. Plowing corresponds to plotting and forethought, which prepare the ground for the seed of the negative act, whose outcome is then reaped. "Iniquity" [*aven*] and "travail" [*amal*] are synonyms for sin, and both express the vanity and insubstantiality of such behavior. *Aven* is related to *ayin*, nothing, while *amal* can mean hard but useless toil (see Isaiah 59:4).

BACKGROUND

4:10 | **The roar of the lion:** A lion generally roars when it must defend its territory and its pride. Its powerful roar can be heard from a distance of up to 8 km.

4:11 | **The lion perishes for lack of prey, and the children of the lion are scattered:** Most lions live in groups known as prides, which are comprised of lionesses, their offspring, and one or more males. Lions obtain their food most successfully by working together as a group. When the pride becomes too large for its hunters to find enough food for all the members, some lions may be ejected. The lions' offspring remain faithful to the pride until they become adults, at approximately the age of two or three. The existence of solitary lions that are not part of a pride is generally indicative of a drought. It is a struggle for solitary lions to survive for extended periods.

but I did not know what it was. **I would hear silence and a voice.** There was silence, and yet a voice came from within the silence.[46]

17 The voice declared:[47] **Will a human be more just than God**[D] in a debate between them? **Will a man be purer than his Maker?**

18 **Behold, He does not trust** even **His servants,** the angels and heavenly hosts, **and to His angels He attributes misconduct,** as He considers them blemished[48] and does not rely on them.

19 **All the more so** is He aware of the weaknesses of **dwellers in houses of clay,**[B] the physical body,[49] **whose founding is in dust, who are made despondent** and destroyed **before,** by means of,[50] **a moth.**[B]

Moth

"Houses of clay." Egypt

20 **From morning to evening they,** people, **are broken.** What starts in the morning as a mere crack in their world can turn into a complete rupture by night.[51] **Forever unnoticed, they perish.** They are lost forever without anyone paying attention to them.

21 **Hasn't their remnant gone away from them?** Alternatively, when God brings tragedy upon people, aren't their remains scattered? They are ruined and eradicated, ultimately **dying without wisdom.** In his dispute with God, man, who is small and lowly in comparison, will never emerge triumphant.

5 1 If you wish to cry out, then **call now;** but **is there anyone answering you? To which of the holy ones,** the angels, **will you turn?** You can turn only to God in prayer.

2 **For anger kills the fool, and envy will put the naïf to death.** It is characteristic of the unwise to be swayed by strong emotions, and a dire fate awaits such individuals.[52] The fool Elifaz is describing is one who fails to turn to God. It is possible that this includes even Job himself.

3 **I have seen the fool taking root,** growing and developing,[53] **and I cursed his house with suddenness.** I cursed his home that a calamity should suddenly fall upon it and halt his development.

4 **His,** the foolish man's, **children are distanced from salvation** and will not be rescued, **and** they **are made despondent,** or oppressed, **at the gate,** the location of the city court,[54] **without a deliverer.**

5 **His,** the fool's, **harvest, the hungry eat and** starving individuals **put into baskets,** or, alternatively, his harvest is taken from him even if it is surrounded by a fence of thorns, **and the thirsty**[55] **imbibe their wealth.** They seek to swallow the portion belonging to the fool's children.[56]

6 Elifaz elaborates on the downfall of the foolish: **For iniquity does not emerge from the dust, and travail does not grow from the ground.** Nature does not sin,[57]

DISCUSSION

4:17 | **Will a human be more just than God:** Elifaz is not a prophet sent to deliver a concrete message from God to man. Although he appears to be the most erudite of Job's friends, he offers no explanation for Job's suffering. His conception of the relationship between man and his Creator is based on the fear and terror that fall upon a person when he receives a revelation. Later in the book it will become clear that the prophetic experience itself does not necessarily support a stance of the kind presented by Elifaz, as Job himself will merit a comforting prophecy.

BACKGROUND

4:19 | **Dwellers in houses of clay:** To this day, in the dry regions of the Middle East, houses are constructed with bricks of dried clay, as this is an easy, quick, and effective method of building. The bricks are composed of straw mixed with clay soil and are dried in the sun. However, the neglect of such a structure, strong rainstorms, or floods can cause parts of the building to erode and collapse. The prayer of the High Priest on Yom Kippur that the houses of the inhabitants of the Sharon region should not become their graves (Jerusalem Talmud, *Yoma* 5:2) was apparently referring to dangers of this kind.

Moth: In the larval stage, many species of moths feed on organic materials, and they are similar to the larvae found on corpses. The adult flying moth, *Aglossa cuprina*, also known as the grease moth, consumes the fat of living animals as well as grease produced by bacteria that feed on decaying matter. For this reason, grease moths are often found circling the air near corpses.

הַאֱנוֹשׁ מֵאֱלוֹהַּ יִצְדָּק אִם־מֵעֹשֵׂהוּ יִטְהַר־גָּבֶר׃ הֵן בַּעֲבָדָיו לֹא יַאֲמִין וּבְמַלְאָכָיו יז יח
יָשִׂים תָּהֳלָה׃ אַף ׀ שֹׁכְנֵי בָתֵּי־חֹמֶר אֲשֶׁר־בֶּעָפָר יְסוֹדָם יְדַכְּאוּם לִפְנֵי־עָשׁ׃ יט
מִבֹּקֶר לָעֶרֶב יֻכַּתּוּ מִבְּלִי מֵשִׂים לָנֶצַח יֹאבֵדוּ׃ הֲלֹא־נִסַּע יִתְרָם בָּם יָמוּתוּ וְלֹא כ כא
בְחָכְמָה׃ קְרָא־נָא הֲיֵשׁ עוֹנֶךָּ וְאֶל־מִי מִקְּדֹשִׁים תִּפְנֶה׃ כִּי־לֶאֱוִיל יַהֲרָג־כָּעַשׂ ה א ב
וּפֹתֶה תָּמִית קִנְאָה׃ אֲנִי־רָאִיתִי אֱוִיל מַשְׁרִישׁ וָאֶקּוֹב נָוֵהוּ פִתְאֹם׃ יִרְחֲקוּ בָנָיו ג ד
מִיֶּשַׁע וְיִדַּכְּאוּ בַשַּׁעַר וְאֵין מַצִּיל׃ אֲשֶׁר קְצִירוֹ ׀ רָעֵב יֹאכֵל וְאֶל־מִצִּנִּים יִקָּחֵהוּ ה
וְשָׁאַף צַמִּים חֵילָם׃ כִּי ׀ לֹא־יֵצֵא מֵעָפָר אָוֶן וּמֵאֲדָמָה לֹא־יִצְמַח עָמָל׃ כִּי־אָדָם ו ז
לְעָמָל יוּלָּד וּבְנֵי־רֶשֶׁף יַגְבִּיהוּ עוּף׃ אוּלָם אֲנִי אֶדְרֹשׁ אֶל־אֵל וְאֶל־אֱלֹהִים אָשִׂים ח
דִּבְרָתִי׃ עֹשֶׂה גְדֹלוֹת וְאֵין חֵקֶר נִפְלָאוֹת עַד־אֵין מִסְפָּר׃ הַנֹּתֵן מָטָר עַל־פְּנֵי־ ט י
אָרֶץ וְשֹׁלֵחַ מַיִם עַל־פְּנֵי חוּצוֹת׃ לָשׂוּם שְׁפָלִים לְמָרוֹם וְקֹדְרִים שָׂגְבוּ יֶשַׁע׃ יא
מֵפֵר מַחְשְׁבוֹת עֲרוּמִים וְלֹא־תַעֲשֶׂינָה יְדֵיהֶם תּוּשִׁיָּה׃ לֹכֵד חֲכָמִים בְּעָרְמָם יב יג
וַעֲצַת נִפְתָּלִים נִמְהָרָה׃ יוֹמָם יְפַגְּשׁוּ־חֹשֶׁךְ וְכַלַּיְלָה יְמַשְׁשׁוּ בַצָּהֳרָיִם׃ וַיֹּשַׁע יד טו
מֵחֶרֶב מִפִּיהֶם וּמִיַּד חָזָק אֶבְיוֹן׃ וַתְּהִי לַדַּל תִּקְוָה וְעֹלָתָה קָפְצָה פִּיהָ׃ הִנֵּה טז יז
אַשְׁרֵי אֱנוֹשׁ יוֹכִחֶנּוּ אֱלוֹהַּ וּמוּסַר שַׁדַּי אַל־תִּמְאָס׃ כִּי הוּא יַכְאִיב וְיֶחְבָּשׁ יִמְחַץ יח

7 **for man is born to travail** and sin, just **as sparks fly upward.** Just as sparks naturally fly upward, so too, it is natural for people to sin.[58]

8 **However,** unlike the foolish or simple person, **I would seek for God, and to God I will direct my words.**[59]

9 One can certainly rely upon God, as it is He **who performs great things, and there is no fathoming** them, **wonders without number.**

10 He is the One **who gives rain over the face of the earth, and sends** down **water over the surface of fields,**

11 **setting the lowly on high,** raising them to heaven, **and** He directs matters so that **the dejected,** the broken and downcast, **are exalted with salvation.**

12 At the same time, **He thwarts the thoughts of the crafty,** those who rely on their cunning, **and their hands do not act with resourcefulness.** They are unable to execute the plots they devise.[60]

13 **He,** God, **traps the wise with their craftiness,** He traps them in their own guile, **and the counsel of the wily is hasty,** impulsive and foolish.[61]

14 Their punishment will be that **during the day they encounter darkness, and at noon they grope** to find their way **like at night.**

15 But **He saves the indigent from the sword** of the wicked, He saves them **from their** devouring **mouth,**[62] **and** He rescues them **from the hand of the mighty.**

16 **There is hope for the impoverished, and iniquity will clench its mouth.** People's fortunes change; therefore, do not despair.

17 Do not reject suffering, as it is part of God's communication with man.[63] **Behold, happy is the man whom God rebukes; do not despise the chastisement of,** the suffering brought upon you by **the Almighty.**

18 **For He causes pain and He bandages** the injury that He

brought upon you; **He crushes and** subsequently **His hands heal.** He strikes, and then He cures.

19 **In six troubles He will deliver you, and in seven, no harm will touch you.** God will save you from every distress. Six and seven are generic numbers that signify large quantities.[64]

20 **In famine, He redeems you from death, and in war** He saves you **from the sword.**

21 **From the scourge of the tongue you will be hidden.** God will protect you[65] when people utter hurtful or damaging comments about you, **and you will not fear pillage when it comes.**

22 **At pillage and hunger you will laugh,** as they will not threaten you, **and from the beasts of the earth, do not fear,** as God will protect you from them.

"From the beasts of the earth." Leopard on a morning stroll, He'etekim Cliff, near Ein Gedi

23 **For your covenant will be with the rocks of the field [*avnei hasadeh*].** The rocks themselves will ensure that you do not stumble while you walk,[66] as all of nature will join forces with you. Alternatively, *avnei hasadeh* should be interpreted as *adnei hasadeh*, a mysterious creature that is half-human, half-beast.[67] **And the beasts of the field will make peace with you** and will do you no harm.[68]

"Rocks of the field." Samaria

24 **You will know that your tent is at peace,** as tranquility will reign there; **and visiting your abode,** when you arrive home from a journey, **you will not be lacking,** for everything will have remained intact.

25 **You shall know also that your descendants will be many,** you will have many children, **and your offspring** will increase **like the grass of the earth.**

26 **You will come to the grave at the right time [*kelaḥ*],** after a good and long life,[69] or alternatively, refreshed, with vigor, **like a grain pile** harvested **at its time,** after it dries in the field and is ready to move to the next stage in the production process.[70]

27 Elifaz concludes his speech: **Behold, we have investigated this; it is so,** this is the way of the world. Ultimately, the pure and upright person will not be lost, unlike fools. **Hear it,** Job, **and know for yourself.** Consider my comments in a personal context as well. Elifaz is implicitly saying to Job: If you accept that God has intentionally inflicted this suffering upon you, and you submit to it, you will experience salvation in your lifetime. God will restore to you all that you have lost, and you will enjoy a good end.

"Grain pile." Bundled grain sheaves

BACKGROUND

6:5 | **Onager:** The onager, *Equus hemionus*, is the smallest of the wild donkeys and lives in the wilderness. It is grayish brown, its mane is dark, and it has a broad dark stripe that extends along the back of its spine all the way to the tail. The onager is quick and hard to trap, and cannot be domesticated. This animal was commonly found in the Negev, the Judean Desert, the wilderness of the northern Arabian Peninsula, the region east of the Jordan River, Syria, and from there all the way to the Euphrates River. However, it became extinct in these areas in the early twentieth century. It has recently been returned to Israel and can be found today in the area of Mitzpe Ramon.

יט כ וְיָדָו תִּרְפֶּֽינָה׃ בְּשֵׁשׁ צָרוֹת יַצִּילֶךָּ וּבְשֶׁבַע ׀ לֹא־יִגַּע בְּךָ רָֽע׃ בְּרָעָב פָּדְךָ מִמָּוֶת
כא כב וּבְמִלְחָמָה מִידֵי חָֽרֶב׃ בְּשׁוֹט לָשׁוֹן תֵּחָבֵא וְלֹא־תִירָא מִשֹּׁד כִּי יָבֽוֹא׃ לְשֹׁד
כג וּלְכָפָן תִּשְׂחָק וּֽמֵחַיַּת הָאָרֶץ אַל־תִּירָֽא׃ כִּי עִם־אַבְנֵי הַשָּׂדֶה בְרִיתֶךָ וְחַיַּת הַשָּׂדֶה
כד כה הָשְׁלְמָה־לָֽךְ׃ וְֽיָדַעְתָּ כִּי־שָׁלוֹם אָהֳלֶךָ וּפָקַדְתָּ נָוְךָ וְלֹא תֶחֱטָֽא׃ וְֽיָדַעְתָּ כִּי־רַב
כו זַרְעֶךָ וְצֶאֱצָאֶיךָ כְּעֵשֶׂב הָאָֽרֶץ׃ תָּבוֹא בְכֶלַח אֱלֵי־קָבֶר כַּעֲלוֹת גָּדִישׁ בְּעִתּֽוֹ׃
ו כז א הִנֵּה־זֹאת חֲקַרְנוּהָ כֶּן־הִיא שְׁמָעֶנָּה וְאַתָּה דַע־לָֽךְ׃ וַיַּעַן אִיּוֹב ב
ב ג וַיֹּאמַֽר׃ לוּ שָׁקוֹל יִשָּׁקֵל כַּעְשִׂי וְהַיָּתִי בְּמֹאזְנַיִם יִשְׂאוּ־יָֽחַד׃ כִּי־עַתָּה מֵחוֹל יַמִּים וְהַוָּתִי
ד יִכְבָּד עַל־כֵּן דְּבָרַי לָֽעוּ׃ כִּי חִצֵּי שַׁדַּי עִמָּדִי אֲשֶׁר חֲמָתָם שֹׁתָה רוּחִי בִּעוּתֵי
ה ו אֱלוֹהַּ יַעַרְכֽוּנִי׃ הֲיִנְהַק־פֶּרֶא עֲלֵי־דֶשֶׁא אִם יִגְעֶה־שּׁוֹר עַל־בְּלִילֽוֹ׃ הֲיֵאָכֵל תָּפֵל

Job's First Response to Elifaz

JOB 6:1–7:21

In this book, Job and his friends generally do not directly respond to the specific theological points raised by the other. Rather, they exchange a series of speeches in which each individual in turn expresses his thoughts. Nevertheless, here Job is possibly responding to Elifaz's implicit request that he take hold of himself and refrain from arguing with God. Job retorts that it is hard to withhold complaints that emanate from a state of true distress. His comments also contain harsh criticism of his supposed friends, who have disappointed and betrayed him by their reactions to his turmoil.

In this monologue, Job expresses his personal pain against the background of the limitations of man's life in general. Man's life span is limited, he is like a laborer who merely seeks to obtain some compensation for his work and some respite from his labor, and his inevitable death is already known from the beginning. When severe suffering is added to such conditions, man grows weary with his lot in life and wishes to die. Nevertheless, although Job voices his desire to die, he does nothing to actualize this desire.

Job's comments indicate that he realizes that his suffering comes from God, but he cannot understand why he has been so afflicted. He cannot imagine that he, a mere mortal, presents any danger to the world. Job also wonders why God constantly focuses on humans, examining their actions and testing them. Job's speech starts and concludes with a series of scathing rhetorical questions.

6 1 **Job answered and said:**

2 **If only my anger** and pain **were weighed, and my calamity borne, together on a scale,**

3 **for now it,** the weight of my pain, **would weigh heavier than** all of **the sand of the seas** in the world, as my suffering is too great to be measured; **therefore, my words waver,** they are incoherent and improperly formulated.[71]

4 **For the arrows of the Almighty,** which He shot at me, **are** still **in me, whose poison my spirit drinks;**[72] **the terrors of God are arrayed** in battle **against me.**[73]

5 **Does the onager**[B] **bray** in dissatisfaction **over grass?** When it has ample food, this creature eats in silence. **Does the ox low over his mash?** My complaints do not emanate from a state of satisfaction and content. If all were well, I would not cry out in pain.

6 As for your response, Elifaz, it is insufficient to assuage my hunger and misery:[74] **Can the bland be eaten without salt?** It is

Onagers eating grass

Oxen eating

impossible to eat such food. **Is there flavor in mallow sap,**[B] a plant whose liquid is tasteless?[75]

Bull mallow

Common alkanet

Marsh mallow

Gibber saltbush

Asphaltic seablite

7 Job continues: Your comments are comparable to those tasteless foods. **My soul refuses to touch them; they are like the food of suffering for me.**
8 **If only my request would be accepted,** fulfilled, **and God would grant my hope,**
9 **and God would agree to crush me** entirely;[76] **freeing**[77] **His hand, and eliminating me.**[78] If He were to kill me, my suffering would end.
10 **May it,** this death, **yet be my consolation,**[79] **as I shake in terror,** due to my request to God to kill me **without compassion, that I did not ignore the sayings of the Holy One.**
11 **What is my strength that I should wait?** I no longer have enough energy to wait and hope. **What will be my end, that my soul should endure** more suffering? For what can I hope? I am broken financially, socially, mentally, and physically.
12 **Is my strength the strength of stones? Is my flesh** made of **bronze?**[80] I am merely human, and I am not as tough and durable as stones or brass.
13 **Is there no help for me?** Even those friends who supposedly arrived to comfort me do not support my statements.[81] **Has resourcefulness been denied me?**
14 Have assistance and sound wisdom abandoned me,[82] **for the sake of one who deprives [*lamas*] his neighbor of kindness,** one who withholds kindness from his friend and dissolves [*memoses*] it, so to speak,[83] **or one who forsakes reverence of the Almighty?**

"Betrayed like a ravine, like the channel through which streams pass." Temporary flooding of the Tzin Ravine, Negev

15 **My brethren,** upon whom I thought I could rely, **have betrayed** me **like a ravine** through which water flows irregularly, **like the channel through which streams** usually **pass** but is currently dry. The waters of such a seasonal stream disappoint those who rely upon them both in cold and hot conditions, as described in the following verses.
16 These are brooks **which are frozen,**[84] **because of ice, and upon which snow accumulates.**
17 However, **when scorched,** during a heat wave,[85] **they disappear** and are cut off; **in its,** the channel's,[86] **heat, they dwindle,** or disappear, **from their place,** leaving nothing behind.
18 **Their courses' ways are winding;**[87] **they go up into emptiness and are lost.**
19 **They looked to the caravans of Tema;**[B] **the convoys of Sheba, they hoped for them.** Those who were thirsty and were disappointed by the drying of the streams,[88] or the streams themselves,[89] looked for the caravans coming and going from Tema, a city in Arabia, and waited for the convoys going back and forth from Sheba (see 1:15), hoping to obtain water from them.

Convoy in the wilderness

BACKGROUND

6:6 | **Mallow sap [*ḥalamut*]:** This has been identified with several edible plants from the mallow family, which contain an abundance of mucilage: bull mallow, *Malva nicaeensis*; okra, also known as gumbo, Mulukhiyah, or Nalta jute, which have a mucilaginous texture and are tasteless in their natural form; common alkanet, *Anchusa undulata*, known in Syriac as *helmeta*; a salty plant called the saltbush, *Atriplex*; and the Asphaltic seablite, *Suaeda asphaltica*. Some identify the *ḥalamut* with the marsh mallow, *Althaea officinalis*, which is rich in mucilage (Rambam). Alternatively, *ḥalamut* is defined as the yolk of an egg.

6:19 | **Tema:** This is the name of one of the sons of Ishmael, whose descendants dwelled in the wilderness east of Canaan (Genesis 25:15). Tema is also a large oasis located in northern Arabia, approximately 400 km southeast of Eilat. This oasis is located at the crossroads where the route from southern Arabia to Babylonia and the road leading to the Mediterranean regions meet.

ז מִבְּלִי־מֶלַח אִם־יֶשׁ־טַעַם בְּרִיר חַלָּמוּת: מֵאֲנָה לִנְגּוֹעַ נַפְשִׁי הֵמָּה כִּדְוֵי לַחְמִי:
ח ט מִי־יִתֵּן תָּבוֹא שֶׁאֱלָתִי וְתִקְוָתִי יִתֵּן אֱלוֹהַּ: וְיֹאֵל אֱלוֹהַּ וִידַכְּאֵנִי יַתֵּר יָדוֹ וִיבַצְּעֵנִי:
י וּתְהִי־עוֹד ׀ נֶחָמָתִי וַאֲסַלְּדָה בְחִילָה לֹא יַחְמוֹל כִּי־לֹא כִחַדְתִּי אִמְרֵי קָדוֹשׁ:
יא יב מַה־כֹּחִי כִי־אֲיַחֵל וּמַה־קִּצִּי כִּי־אַאֲרִיךְ נַפְשִׁי: אִם־כֹּחַ אֲבָנִים כֹּחִי אִם־בְּשָׂרִי
יג יד נָחוּשׁ: הַאִם אֵין עֶזְרָתִי בִי וְתֻשִׁיָּה נִדְּחָה מִמֶּנִּי: לַמָּס מֵרֵעֵהוּ חָסֶד וְיִרְאַת שַׁדַּי
טו טז יַעֲזוֹב: אַחַי בָּגְדוּ כְמוֹ־נָחַל כַּאֲפִיק נְחָלִים יַעֲבֹרוּ: הַקֹּדְרִים מִנִּי־קָרַח עָלֵימוֹ
יז יח יִתְעַלֶּם־שָׁלֶג: בְּעֵת יְזֹרְבוּ נִצְמָתוּ בְּחֻמּוֹ נִדְעֲכוּ מִמְּקוֹמָם: יִלָּפְתוּ אָרְחוֹת דַּרְכָּם
יט כ יַעֲלוּ בַתֹּהוּ וְיֹאבֵדוּ: הִבִּיטוּ אָרְחוֹת תֵּמָא הֲלִיכֹת שְׁבָא קִוּוּ־לָמוֹ: בֹּשׁוּ כִּי־בָטָח
כא כב בָּאוּ עָדֶיהָ וַיֶּחְפָּרוּ: כִּי־עַתָּה הֱיִיתֶם לוֹ תִּרְאוּ חֲתַת וַתִּירָאוּ: הֲכִי־אָמַרְתִּי הָבוּ
כג כד לִי וּמִכֹּחֲכֶם שִׁחֲדוּ בַעֲדִי: וּמַלְּטוּנִי מִיַּד־צָר וּמִיַּד עָרִיצִים תִּפְדּוּנִי: הוֹרוּנִי וַאֲנִי
כה אַחֲרִישׁ וּמַה־שָּׁגִיתִי הָבִינוּ לִי: מַה־נִּמְרְצוּ אִמְרֵי־יֹשֶׁר וּמַה־יּוֹכִיחַ הוֹכֵחַ מִכֶּם:
כו כז הַלְהוֹכַח מִלִּים תַּחְשֹׁבוּ וּלְרוּחַ אִמְרֵי נֹאָשׁ: אַף־עַל־יָתוֹם תַּפִּילוּ וְתִכְרוּ עַל־

20 But **they were embarrassed** and disappointed **because they** had previously **trusted; they,** the ones searching for water, **came there,** to each of the caravans in which they had placed their hopes, **and were humiliated.** Their disappointment at failing to receive the water they thirsted for shamed them and lowered their spirits. This metaphor reflects Job's disappointment in his brothers, or in those who came to comfort him. He compares his anticipation for authentic comfort to one who thirsts for water. The person initially puts his hopes in seasonal streams, but they fail to provide water to quench his thirst. He subsequently seeks salvation from nomads living in the wilderness; however, they too do not provide him with the water he needs.

21 **For now you** are not devoted to me, but you **have become it** [***lo***]. You have become like that seasonal stream, which does not provide water when it is needed.[90] Alternatively, you act as though you cannot comfort me because you belong to Him, God.[91] Some commentaries read *lo* as *lamed-alef,* meaning no, instead of *lamed-vav,* meaning his or it. According to this version, Job is saying that he placed his hopes in them, and yet they were unable to deliver. The support he anticipated never materialized. **You see calamity,** or some sort of crisis, **and you are afraid.** You do not share my misery and you provide me with no assistance.

22 **Did I say: Give me, or** did I ask: **Pay a bribe,** or a ransom, **for me from your wealth,** your possessions?

23 **Or** did I expect you to **rescue me from the hand of an enemy, or** to **redeem me,** save me, **from the hand of the mighty?** I did not ask for anything from you. Why, then, have you renounced me?

24 If you wish to teach me, then indeed **teach me, and I will be silent; explain to me what I have done wrong.**

25 **How forceful**[92] **are sayings of uprightness?** But **what rebuke is there from you?** What reproach do you have for me?

26 **Do you consider** mere **words to be a rebuke?** Do you think that by merely stating words you are successfully offering a rebuke? In uttering empty words, **are** you not treating **the statements of the despairing,** my despair, as just **wind?**

27 **You would even fall upon an orphan,** who is defenseless. Job compares the lack of regard for his despair in response to his situation to harming an orphan. **And** you would **dig a pit for your friend,** into which he would stumble.

28 It is likely that at this point Job's friends turned their faces away
from him.[93] Therefore, Job calls out to them: **Now** therefore, if
you have complaints against me, **agree to look at me; to your
faces I will not lie.**[94]
29 Job perhaps sees his friends preparing to leave. Therefore, he
says to them:[95] **Come back, please; let there be no iniquity.**
Let me demonstrate that I have not sinned. **Stay** a while **longer,**[96] as **my justice is in it,** my claim.
30 **Is there iniquity on my tongue? Doesn't my palate,** my
mouth, my speech, **discern disasters,** the calamities that have
befallen me?

7 **1** **Truly, there is a** limited **term,** years of life, **for man on earth,
and his days are like the days of a hireling.** Just as a laborer is
hired to work for a fixed period but no longer, one's days in this
world are limited. When one has completed his service, he does
not remain a single moment longer in the world.
2 Man in this world is **like a servant who yearns for shade.** He
is not free to do as he wishes during his period of servitude,
but yearns to at least rest for a bit in the shade, **and** he is **like a
hireling who hopes for his wages.**[97]
3 Just as a servant's time is limited and is entirely dependent upon
his master, **so have months of futility,** empty of content, **been
bequeathed,** allocated, **to me, and nights of travail** and suffering **been appointed for me.**[98]
4 **When I lie down** at night, **I say: When will I arise? Measuring**
the length of **the night,** as in my suffering I await the end of the
night,[99] **I am filled with restlessness until dawn.**[100]
5 **My flesh is covered with worms; my skin is a clod of earth;**[B]
it is **cracked and has become repulsive.**[101]
6 Unlike the nights of suffering, which feel as though they continue without end, **my days,** the days of good, **were swifter than
a weaver's shuttle,**[102] as they left me quickly, **and they ended
with no hope.**
7 God, **remember that my life is** passing by as **wind.** I am not an
immortal creature, and I cannot bear this misery. **My eye will
not again see good,** as it once saw in the past.
8 After I die, **the eye of one who sees me,** or who wishes to see
me, **will not behold me; Your eyes are on me, and I am not.**

Weaver's shuttle, used to hold the yarn for the weft and quickly send back and forth while weaving

You could cause my death by setting your eyes on me without
causing me to suffer.[103]
9 Just as **a cloud dissipates and goes away, so one who descends to the grave will not come up.** Death is irreversible.
10 **He,** the deceased, **will not return to his house; his** dignified
place that he maintained in his lifetime **will no longer recognize him.** He will lose all connection to the place where he
lived, and no memory of him will be preserved.
11 Job continues to speak to God: You do not ease my suffering,
and therefore **I too will not restrain my mouth** from speaking
to You.[104] **I will speak in,** out of, **the anguish of my spirit; I
will converse in the bitterness of my soul.**
12 **Am I a sea** that threatens to drown everything within it, **or a
sea monster,** an ancient creature that You have retained under
Your direct control,[105] **that You place a watch over me?** I am
not a monster that seeks to rule over the entire inhabited world
and that must be stopped in its tracks.
13 **For I said** to myself that I hoped that **my bed will console me,**
that **my bedding will bear my discourse.** I will find respite
from my troubles and bitterness while sleeping, but I am unable to rest in tranquility,
14 **and You frighten me with dreams and terrify me from visions** of the night.
15 **My soul prefers strangling,**[D] **death, rather than** living this life
in **my bones,** my body.[106]
16 **I loathe it,** my present life, and as **I will not live forever, let me
be, as my days are futility.** Stop afflicting me and let me live a
life blessed with meaning and hope.

BACKGROUND

7:5 | **My flesh is covered with worms; my skin is a clod of earth:** As mentioned above (commentary on 2:7), the boils with which Job was afflicted were perhaps symptoms of eczema. In some forms of eczema, pustules break out on the skin that appear dark on top and can feel like worms crawling on the skin. In addition, the disease can produce dry patches of wrinkles that resemble a clod of earth or the bark of a tree.

DISCUSSION

7:15 | **My soul prefers strangling:** Although Job would prefer to die than continue living in his current state, he does not listen to his wife's advice to "blaspheme God and die" (2:9), nor does he perform any action that might hasten his demise.

כח כט רֵיעֲכֶם׃ וְעַתָּה הוֹאִילוּ פְנוּ־בִי וְעַל־פְּנֵיכֶם אִם־אֲכַזֵּב׃ שֻׁבוּ־נָא אַל־תְּהִי עַוְלָה

ל א וְשֻׁבִי עוֹד צִדְקִי־בָהּ׃ הֲיֵשׁ־בִּלְשׁוֹנִי עַוְלָה אִם־חִכִּי לֹא־יָבִין הַוּוֹת׃ הֲלֹא־צָבָא וְשׁוּבוּ

ב ג לֶאֱנוֹשׁ עֲלֵ־אָרֶץ וְכִימֵי שָׂכִיר יָמָיו׃ כְּעֶבֶד יִשְׁאַף־צֵל וּכְשָׂכִיר יְקַוֶּה פָעֳלוֹ׃ כֵּן

ד הָנְחַלְתִּי לִי יַרְחֵי־שָׁוְא וְלֵילוֹת עָמָל מִנּוּ־לִי׃ אִם־שָׁכַבְתִּי וְאָמַרְתִּי מָתַי אָקוּם

ה וּמִדַּד־עָרֶב וְשָׂבַעְתִּי נְדֻדִים עֲדֵי־נָשֶׁף׃ לָבַשׁ בְּשָׂרִי רִמָּה וגיש עָפָר עוֹרִי רָגַע וְגוּשׁ

ו ז וַיִּמָּאֵס׃ יָמַי קַלּוּ מִנִּי־אָרֶג וַיִּכְלוּ בְּאֶפֶס תִּקְוָה׃ זְכֹר כִּי־רוּחַ חַיָּי לֹא־תָשׁוּב עֵינִי

ח ט לִרְאוֹת טוֹב׃ לֹא־תְשׁוּרֵנִי עֵין רֹאִי עֵינֶיךָ בִּי וְאֵינֶנִּי׃ כָּלָה עָנָן וַיֵּלַךְ כֵּן יוֹרֵד שְׁאוֹל

י יא לֹא יַעֲלֶה׃ לֹא־יָשׁוּב עוֹד לְבֵיתוֹ וְלֹא־יַכִּירֶנּוּ עוֹד מְקוֹמוֹ׃ גַּם־אֲנִי לֹא אֶחֱשָׂךְ

יב פִּי אֲדַבְּרָה בְּצַר רוּחִי אָשִׂיחָה בְּמַר נַפְשִׁי׃ הֲיָם־אָנִי אִם־תַּנִּין כִּי־תָשִׂים עָלַי

יג יד מִשְׁמָר׃ כִּי־אָמַרְתִּי תְּנַחֲמֵנִי עַרְשִׂי יִשָּׂא בְשִׂיחִי מִשְׁכָּבִי׃ וְחִתַּתַּנִי בַחֲלֹמוֹת

טו טז וּמֵחֶזְיֹנוֹת תְּבַעֲתַנִּי׃ וַתִּבְחַר מַחֲנָק נַפְשִׁי מָוֶת מֵעַצְמוֹתָי׃ מָאַסְתִּי לֹא־לְעֹלָם

יז אֶחְיֶה חֲדַל מִמֶּנִּי כִּי־הֶבֶל יָמָי׃ מָה־אֱנוֹשׁ כִּי תְגַדְּלֶנּוּ וְכִי־תָשִׁית אֵלָיו לִבֶּךָ׃

יח יט וַתִּפְקְדֶנּוּ לִבְקָרִים לִרְגָעִים תִּבְחָנֶנּוּ׃ כַּמָּה לֹא־תִשְׁעֶה מִמֶּנִּי לֹא־תַרְפֵּנִי עַד־בִּלְעִי

כ רֻקִּי׃ חָטָאתִי מָה אֶפְעַל ׀ לָךְ נֹצֵר הָאָדָם לָמָה שַׂמְתַּנִי לְמִפְגָּע לָךְ וָאֶהְיֶה עָלַי

כא לְמַשָּׂא׃ וּמֶה ׀ לֹא־תִשָּׂא פִשְׁעִי וְתַעֲבִיר אֶת־עֲוֺנִי כִּי־עַתָּה לֶעָפָר אֶשְׁכָּב וְשִׁחַרְתַּנִי

17 **What is man,** and what is his significance, **that You make him great, and** that **You set Your heart toward him?**

18 **You remember him** to watch over him **each morning**[107] **and test him each moment.** Why are You constantly examining man's traits and deeds?[108]

19 For **how long will You not release me,**[109] **not let me be, even to swallow my spittle?** You do not leave me alone even for the short time necessary to swallow my saliva.[110]

20 Even if **I have sinned, what have I done to You, Guardian of man?** My sins do not affect You at all, as You are exalted above everything. **Why did You set me as Your target,** a target for You to strike, or, alternatively, why do You treat me as one who can strike You, as it were, **and** why do You treat me as though **I have become a burden to myself,** that is, to You?

21 **Why don't You bear my transgression and overlook my iniquity? For now,** in a short while, **I will lie** down buried **in the dust; You will seek me, but I will not be.** Please free me from this suffering. I want to live in whatever manner I wish. I will die when I die, but there is no need to add any further torment. Although here Job speaks of his sins, he does not consider them the primary source of his suffering. He admits that, being human, he might have erred, but he argues that the punishments he has received do not correspond to the sum total of all the transgressions he could have conceivably committed. He therefore cannot understand why all this has happened to him. Moreover, he complains about his misery. Whereas he previously merely described his difficulties and the extent of his suffering, he now requests simply to be left to die in peace.

Bildad's First Speech

JOB 8:1–22

Bildad the Shuhite, Job's second friend, also perceives in Job's laments a complaint directed at God. By means of an analogy from the plant world, he conveys to Job his basic faith that one who suffers is struck for a reason, and the eventual portion of every righteous individual is good. Bildad speaks in a more blunt manner than Elifaz the Temanite. He explicitly describes the children of Job as deserving of their fate and indirectly accuses Job himself of sin.

8 1 **Bildad the Shuhite answered and said:**

2 **Until when will you pronounce these, and** until when **will the sayings of your mouth be a great wind,** an attack, against God?[111]

3 **Would God pervert judgment? Does the Almighty pervert justice?** Bildad castigates Job for ideas that he did not express. Job merely articulated the pain he was feeling and wondered why God was striking him ceaselessly, as though the rest of the world required protection from his baleful influence. Nevertheless, like Elifaz, Bildad infers from Job's comments that he maintains a grievance against God's system of judgment in the world. Bildad therefore responds to his understanding of Job's beliefs.

4 **If your children sinned against Him, He sent them** to death **into the hand of,** due to, **their transgression.**[112]

5 It would be good **if you,** in contrast to them, **would seek God, and plead to the Almighty;**

6 **if you are** truly **pure and upright, right now He will rouse Himself** to bring goodness **for you,**[113] **and He will restore the abode of your righteousness,**[114] or He will recompense you properly for your righteous habitation.

7 **Your beginning may be small,** as you started lowly and poor, **but your end will soar very high.** Alternatively, the good you possessed initially will be considered minor in comparison to what you will ultimately receive.[115]

8 **For ask now of the first generation, and attend,** direct your attention, **to the investigation of their fathers,** the early generations,

9 **for we are** but **of yesterday,** we are very young, **and** therefore **do not know** everything, **for our days on earth are** as **a** passing **shadow.**

10 **Won't they,** your fathers,[116] **teach you, say to you, and from their heart, words will emerge,** to explain to you the proper order of nature?[117]

11 **Can a reed,**[B] a plant that sprouts near swamps and streams, **grow tall without a marsh? Can rushes,**[B] a generic term for shrubbery that grows alongside water,[118] or a type of willow, **rise without water?**

Reeds in a marsh

12 With no source of water, even though **it is still in its bud,** or fresh, and is **not** supposed to be **plucked** so quickly,[119] **and** yet nevertheless **it will wither before any other grass.**

13 **So are the paths of all forgetters of God.** They will wither quickly, because they abandoned their source of sustenance,[120] and **the hypocrite's hope will perish;**

14 **it is he whose support,** upon which he relies, **is gossamer,** a thin web,[121] or his confidence will be cut down and diminished,[122] **and whose trust is a spider's web.** He places his trust in flimsy webs.

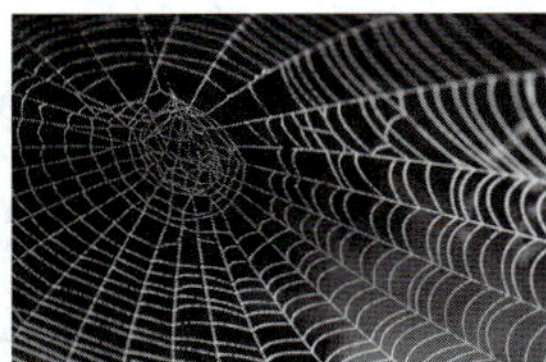

"Whose trust is a spider's web"

15 **He will lean on his house, but it will not stand; he will grasp it, but it will not endure.** One cannot rely upon such a house.

16 **It,** this plant, the wicked individual,[123] **is moist before the** rising of the **sun,** before retribution arrives,[124] or it is moist and flourishing when it is in the sunshine; **and its shoots**[125] **go forth over,** into, **his garden.** Some interpret this set of verses (16–19) as referring to a righteous individual who ultimately attains a good portion despite temporary suffering.[126]

17 However, if[127] **on a heap** of stones,[128] **its roots are entangled,** then **it looks for a place among the stones,** and the plant has nothing to take hold of and has no source of sustenance.

18 **If it is cleared away,** uprooted, **from its place, and** then its place[129] **will deny it** and say: **I did not see you.** I never knew you at all. Nothing will be left of you.[130]

19 **Behold, this is the gladness,** the supposed success, **of its way,** or, alternatively, the dissolving or rotting of his path. This plant is about to rot, **and** hopefully **from other earth they,** its roots, **will grow.** The roots of the plant will spring again elsewhere on earth, in a different form.

20 **Behold, God will not despise the blameless.** If you are indeed an upright individual, God will come to your aid. **And** He **will not support the evildoers,**[131]

21 since if you are righteous, He will assist you **until He fills your mouth with laughter and your lips with celebration.**

22 But **Your enemies will be clothed in shame, and the tent of the wicked shall be no more.**

א ב וְאֵינֶֽנִּי׃ וַיַּעַן בִּלְדַּד הַשּׁוּחִי וַיֹּאמַר׃ עַד־אָן תְּמַלֶּל־אֵלֶּה וְרוּחַ כַּבִּיר
ג ד אִמְרֵי־פִֽיךָ׃ הַאֵל יְעַוֵּת מִשְׁפָּט וְאִם־שַׁדַּי יְעַוֵּת־צֶֽדֶק׃ אִם־בָּנֶיךָ חָֽטְאוּ־לוֹ וַֽיְשַׁלְּחֵם
ה ו בְּיַד־פִּשְׁעָֽם׃ אִם־אַתָּה תְּשַׁחֵר אֶל־אֵל וְאֶל־שַׁדַּי תִּתְחַנָּֽן׃ אִם־זַךְ וְיָשָׁר אָתָּה
ז כִּֽי־עַתָּה יָעִיר עָלֶיךָ וְשִׁלַּם נְוַת צִדְקֶֽךָ׃ וְהָיָה רֵאשִׁיתְךָ מִצְעָר וְאַחֲרִיתְךָ יִשְׂגֶּה
ח ט מְאֹֽד׃ כִּֽי־שְׁאַל־נָא לְדֹר רִישׁוֹן וְכוֹנֵן לְחֵקֶר אֲבוֹתָֽם׃ כִּֽי־תְמוֹל אֲנַחְנוּ וְלֹא נֵדָע
י יא כִּי צֵל יָמֵינוּ עֲלֵי־אָֽרֶץ׃ הֲלֹא־הֵם יוֹרוּךָ יֹאמְרוּ לָךְ וּמִלִּבָּם יוֹצִאוּ מִלִּֽים׃ הֲיִגְאֶה־
יב גֹּמֶא בְּלֹא בִצָּה יִשְׂגֶּא־אָחוּ בְלִי־מָֽיִם׃ עֹדֶנּוּ בְאִבּוֹ לֹא יִקָּטֵף וְלִפְנֵי כָל־חָצִיר
יג יד יִיבָֽשׁ׃ כֵּן אָרְחוֹת כָּל־שֹׁכְחֵי אֵל וְתִקְוַת חָנֵף תֹּאבֵֽד׃ אֲשֶׁר־יָקוֹט כִּסְלוֹ וּבֵית
טו טז עַכָּבִישׁ מִבְטַחֽוֹ׃ יִשָּׁעֵן עַל־בֵּיתוֹ וְלֹא יַעֲמֹד יַחֲזִיק בּוֹ וְלֹא יָקֽוּם׃ רָטֹב הוּא
יז לִפְנֵי־שָׁמֶשׁ וְעַל־גַּנָּתוֹ יֹנַקְתּוֹ תֵצֵֽא׃ עַל־גַּל שָׁרָשָׁיו יְסֻבָּכוּ בֵּית אֲבָנִים יֶחֱזֶֽה׃
יח יט אִם־יְבַלְּעֶנּוּ מִמְּקֹמוֹ וְכִחֶשׁ בּוֹ לֹא רְאִיתִֽיךָ׃ הֶן־הוּא מְשׂוֹשׂ דַּרְכּוֹ וּמֵעָפָר אַחֵר
כ כא יִצְמָֽחוּ׃ הֶן־אֵל לֹא יִמְאַס־תָּם וְלֹא־יַחֲזִיק בְּיַד־מְרֵעִֽים׃ עַד־יְמַלֵּה שְׂחוֹק פִּיךָ
כב וּשְׂפָתֶיךָ תְרוּעָֽה׃ שֹׂנְאֶיךָ יִלְבְּשׁוּ־בֹשֶׁת וְאֹהֶל רְשָׁעִים אֵינֶֽנּוּ׃

BACKGROUND

8:11 | **Reed:** This refers to the papyrus sedge, *Cyperus papyrus*, a large reed that grows near rivers and reaches a height of 4–5 m. The well-known papyrus of ancient times, it has been used for mats, ropes, sandals, basket weaving, the construction of boats, and the manufacture of writing paper.

Rushes [*aḥu*]: In Egyptian, the term *acha* means green. Indeed, *aḥu* is the word used to refer to the location where the cows grazed in Pharaoh's dream (Genesis 41:2).

Job's First Response to Bildad

JOB 9:1–10:22

Job begins this speech by expressing the greatness of God, thereby highlighting the helplessness of one who wishes to contend with Him. Despite this reality, Job continues to protest his innocence against Bildad's claim that there is no suffering without sin and against accusations charging Job and his sons with responsibility for their own suffering.

In this speech, Job protests the injustice he perceives in God's actions. He acknowledges God's providence over each of His creatures from the moment of their formation and His absolute knowledge of everything that encompasses their entire existence. Therefore, he again wonders why God seems to be harassing him.

9 1 **Job answered and said:**
2 **Indeed, I know that it is so.** As you say, God is great, and one
cannot challenge Him. Therefore, **how can man justify himself with God?** I know that one who seeks to contend with
Him will not emerge victorious.
3 **If he desires to contend with Him, He would not answer
him** concerning even **one** claim out **of a thousand.**
4 As **He,** God, **is wise of heart and mighty of power, who has
castigated Him** with his speech[132] **and prospered** [*vayish-
lam*], or emerged whole [*shalem*] from this confrontation?[133]
5 It is **He who moves mountains and they do not know, who
overturns them in His wrath;**
6 **who shakes**[134] **the earth from its place, its pillars swaying;**
7 **who says to the sun** to halt, **and it** obeys and **does not shine,**[135]
and seals, or conceals, **the stars;**[136]
8 **who spreads the heavens alone and treads on the** high **crests
of the sea;**
9 **who made** the constellations **Ursa
Major, Orion, and** the **Pleiades,**[B]
and the chambers of the south, perhaps a reference to a specific southern
constellation;[137]

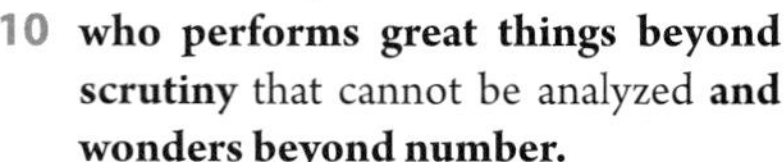

Orion

10 **who performs great things beyond
scrutiny** that cannot be analyzed **and
wonders beyond number.**

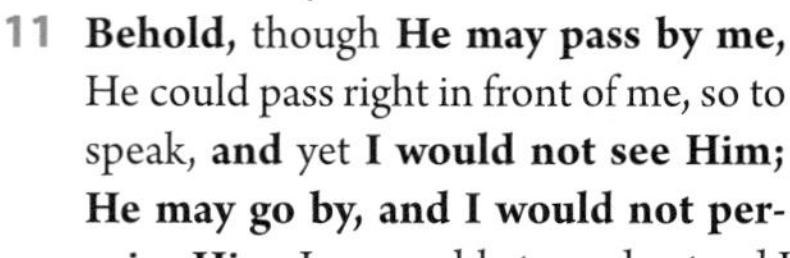

The Pleiades

11 **Behold,** though **He may pass by me,**
He could pass right in front of me, so to
speak, **and** yet **I would not see Him;
He may go by, and I would not per-
ceive Him.** I am unable to understand His ways.

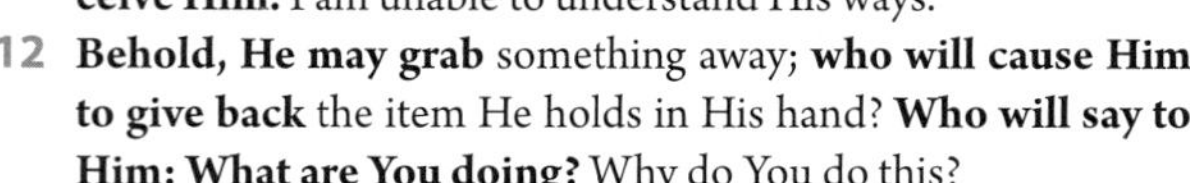

12 **Behold, He may grab** something away; **who will cause Him
to give back** the item He holds in His hand? **Who will say to
Him: What are You doing?** Why do You do this?
13 **God will not restrain His wrath; beneath Him the helpers
of Rahav,**[D] a creature or force that rises up against God's rule in
the world, **are bowed** and submit to Him.
14 Since that is so, **how then can I,** a mere mortal, **answer Him
and choose my words with Him?** I am certainly unable to
contend with God.[138]
15 **Even though I am justified, I could not answer.** I could
not press claims against Him.[139] Instead, **I would plead to my
Judge,** to God.
16 However, I am not optimistic about that strategy either, as even
if I called, and even if **He answered me, I would not believe
that He would listen to my voice** and heed my supplication.
17 **It is He who crushes me with a storm and increases my
wounds without cause.**
18 **He does not allow me to catch my breath,** to allow my spirit
to calm,[140] **for He sates me with** more and more **bitterness.**
19 I am helpless when pitted against God. **If it is a matter,** a contest, **of strength, the Mighty One is here, and if it is** a matter
for judgment that I must seek, **who will set an appointment
for me** for a judgment against God?
20 **Even if I am righteous, my** own **mouth will condemn me** out
of fear of denouncing God;[141] **I am blameless, but He will distort** matters **against me** and I will ultimately carry the blame.
21 Although I cannot prove it in a trial, nevertheless I know[142] that
I am blameless. Do I not know myself?[143] **I despise my life.**
22 I have a definitive conclusion from all of this: **One thing,
therefore, I say: The blameless and the wicked He destroys.**
I fail to perceive justice in the world, as the fate of the innocent
is identical to that of the sinner.
23 **If a lash** strikes and **causes death suddenly,** if retribution
descends to the earth, **He mocks at the undoing**[144] **of the
innocent.**
24 **The earth is given** over by God **into the hand,** the control, **of
the wicked one; he covers the faces of its,** the earth's, **judges**
to prevent them from seeing the truth. In such a corrupt situation, I must ask: **If not, then who is it?** If my statement that the

DISCUSSION

9:13 | **Rahav:** The Talmud interprets this term as the name of the angelic minister of the sea (*Bava Batra* 74b). It may also be a reference to Egypt (Rashi; see commentary on Isaiah 27:1, 30:7).

א ב ג וַיַּעַן אִיּוֹב וַיֹּאמַר: אָמְנָם יָדַעְתִּי כִי־כֵן וּמַה־יִּצְדַּק אֱנוֹשׁ עִם־אֵל: אִם־יַחְפֹּץ לָרִיב

ד עִמּוֹ לֹא־יַעֲנֶנּוּ אַחַת מִנִּי־אָלֶף: חֲכַם לֵבָב וְאַמִּיץ כֹּחַ מִי־הִקְשָׁה אֵלָיו וַיִּשְׁלָם:

ה ו הַמַּעְתִּיק הָרִים וְלֹא יָדָעוּ אֲשֶׁר הֲפָכָם בְּאַפּוֹ: הַמַּרְגִּיז אֶרֶץ מִמְּקוֹמָהּ וְעַמּוּדֶיהָ

ז ח יִתְפַלָּצוּן: הָאֹמֵר לַחֶרֶס וְלֹא יִזְרָח וּבְעַד כּוֹכָבִים יַחְתֹּם: נֹטֶה שָׁמַיִם לְבַדּוֹ וְדוֹרֵךְ

ט י עַל־בָּמֳתֵי יָם: עֹשֶׂה־עָשׁ כְּסִיל וְכִימָה וְחַדְרֵי תֵמָן: עֹשֶׂה גְדֹלוֹת עַד־אֵין חֵקֶר

יא יב וְנִפְלָאוֹת עַד־אֵין מִסְפָּר: הֵן יַעֲבֹר עָלַי וְלֹא אֶרְאֶה וְיַחֲלֹף וְלֹא־אָבִין לוֹ: הֵן יַחְתֹּף

יג מִי יְשִׁיבֶנּוּ מִי־יֹאמַר אֵלָיו מַה־תַּעֲשֶׂה: אֱלוֹהַּ לֹא־יָשִׁיב אַפּוֹ תַּחְתָּו שָׁחֲחוּ עֹזְרֵי

יד טו רָהַב: אַף כִּי־אָנֹכִי אֶעֱנֶנּוּ אֶבְחֲרָה דְבָרַי עִמּוֹ: אֲשֶׁר אִם־צָדַקְתִּי לֹא אֶעֱנֶה

טז יז לִמְשֹׁפְטִי אֶתְחַנָּן: אִם־קָרָאתִי וַיַּעֲנֵנִי לֹא־אַאֲמִין כִּי־יַאֲזִין קוֹלִי: אֲשֶׁר־בִּשְׂעָרָה

יח יט יְשׁוּפֵנִי וְהִרְבָּה פְצָעַי חִנָּם: לֹא־יִתְּנֵנִי הָשֵׁב רוּחִי כִּי יַשְׂבִּעַנִי מַמְּרֹרִים: אִם־לְכֹחַ

כ אַמִּיץ הִנֵּה וְאִם־לְמִשְׁפָּט מִי יוֹעִידֵנִי: אִם־אֶצְדָּק פִּי יַרְשִׁיעֵנִי תָּם־אָנִי וַיַּעְקְשֵׁנִי:

כא כב תָּם־אָנִי לֹא־אֵדַע נַפְשִׁי אֶמְאַס חַיָּי: אַחַת הִיא עַל־כֵּן אָמַרְתִּי תָּם וְרָשָׁע הוּא

כג כד מְכַלֶּה: אִם־שׁוֹט יָמִית פִּתְאֹם לְמַסַּת נְקִיִּם יִלְעָג: אֶרֶץ ׀ נִתְּנָה בְיַד־רָשָׁע פְּנֵי־

BACKGROUND

9:9 | **Ursa Major [Ash], Orion [Kesil], and Pleiades [Kima]:** Ancient scholars accumulated astronomical knowledge by extended tracking of the stars. Names, which often varied from one culture to another, were given to prominent asterisms (patterns of stars visible in the night sky) and to particularly bright stars.

Ash, also called Ayish (see 38:32), has been identified as Arcturus of the constellation Boötes, which is the brightest star in the northern celestial hemisphere. According to a different opinion, it is the nearby constellation Ursa Major, which points toward the North Star. Kesil is identified as the bright constellation Orion, while Kima is traditionally associated with a group of stars called Pleiades or Seven Sisters (see *Berakhot* 58b–59a; *Rosh HaShana* 11b–12a).

fates of both the righteous and the wicked are placed into the hands of the wicked is not correct, then who is responsible for the corruption and evil we experience?[145]

25 **My** good **days are** dissipating **swifter than a runner,** a speedy messenger; **they flee,** as though[146] **not seeing good.**

26 **They go by with** the speed of **reed**[147] **boats.**[B] Boats fashioned from reeds sail in the river quickly, **like the eagle that swoops over prey.**[B] An eagle can reach very high speeds when swooping over its prey.[148] Hence, the sailing of the reed ship and the swooping of the eagle are two metaphors describing how swiftly all of Job's good times faded away and were forgotten.

Reed boat

Griffon vulture swooping over its prey

27 **If I say: I will forget my pain,**[149] **I will abandon my claims,**[150] or rage,[151] **and be restrained,**

28 **fearing all my suffering** and wishing to push it away,[152] **I know that You will not acquit me,** but will continue to harm me.

29 Therefore, since **I will be condemned, why should I toil in futility?**

30 Even **if I bathed in snow water, and** even if I washed and **purified my hands with soap,**[B]

31 **then You would** remove me from the cleansing water and instead **immerse me in the pit,** the grave, and even **my** own **garments would abhor me** and be revolted by my body. I will never be able to purify myself in Your eyes.[153]

Soapwort

32 **For He is not a man like me that I could** dare to **answer Him** or **to come together in judgment,** in a trial between us.

33 **There is no arbiter between us.** In a judgment between us, there can be no one who could prove the justness of one side. There is no one **to place his hand upon the two of us,** to whose authority we would both submit.[154]

34 However, **let Him remove His scepter,** His rule, **from me, and let His dread not terrify me.**

35 **I would speak, and I would not fear Him; but it is not so, I am with myself.** In practice, no one can help me; I remain alone.

10 1 **My soul is sick of my life; I will allow myself complaint.** I will give free rein to my complaint. **I will speak in the bitterness of my soul.**

2 **I will say to God: Do not condemn** and punish **me; let me know why You contend with me.** I want to know of what crime I am accused.

3 **Is it good for You that You should exploit** me and treat me unjustly, **that You should despise Your handiwork?** You invested effort in me; why, then, do You loathe me **and** at the same time **appear** to aid **in the counsel of the wicked,** who continue to live in tranquility?[155]

4 **Do You have eyes of flesh; do You see as man sees?** You know what is hidden in the hearts of men, and You are aware of the deeds they perform in secret, as well as the larger picture of world events. If so, why do You exchange the fates of the innocent with that of the wicked?[156]

5 Man, with his limited vision, is sometimes swayed by foreign considerations and interests that stem from his concerns and worries as a mortal. The nature of man's plans and his urge to actualize them swiftly are motivated by his knowledge that his life will soon end. This is not true of God: **Are Your days like the days of a mortal? Are Your years like the days of a man,**

6 **that You seek my iniquity and search for my sin?** In comparison to Your eternal existence, none of these have any value. Why, then, do You plot against me by amassing proofs against me? Aren't You beyond all such considerations,[157]

7 **even though You know**[158] **that I would not sin,** that I cannot commit a crime against You, **and** that even if I did do so,[159] **there is no deliverer from Your hand?** If I did sin, I will not be saved.

8 Furthermore, **Your hands shaped me and fashioned me,** enveloped me **together on all sides,** and yet with those same hands that surround me, You have ruined Your creation, as **You destroy me** from all sides.

9 **Please, remember that You have fashioned me like** one kneads and shapes **clay, and** ultimately **to dust You will return me.** The description of the creation of the first man from the earth can be metaphorically applied to all people.[160]

10 **Truly, You have liquefied me like milk,** as the process of my formation in the womb involved the transformation of solids into liquids, **and curdled me like cheese.**[B] Likewise, certain liquids solidified during my creation, similar to the cheese-making process.[161]

"Curdled me like cheese." Blocks of cheese

11 **You clothed me with skin and flesh** when You created me, **and** You **covered me**[162] **with bones and sinews.**

12 Throughout, **You granted me life and grace, and Your command preserved my spirit.**

כה שֹׁפְטֶיהָ יְכַסֶּה אִם־לֹא אֵפוֹא מִי־הוּא: וְיָמַי קַלּוּ מִנִּי־רָץ בָּרְחוּ לֹא־רָאוּ טוֹבָה:
כו כז חָלְפוּ עִם־אֳנִיּוֹת אֵבֶה כְּנֶשֶׁר יָטוּשׂ עֲלֵי־אֹכֶל: אִם־אָמְרִי אֶשְׁכְּחָה שִׂיחִי אֶעֶזְבָה
כח כט פָנַי וְאַבְלִיגָה: יָגֹרְתִּי כָל־עַצְּבֹתָי יָדַעְתִּי כִּי־לֹא תְנַקֵּנִי: אָנֹכִי אֶרְשָׁע לָמָּה־זֶּה
ל לא הֶבֶל אִיגָע: אִם־הִתְרָחַצְתִּי בְמוֹ־שָׁלֶג וַהֲזִכּוֹתִי בְּבֹר כַּפָּי: אָז בַּשַּׁחַת תִּטְבְּלֵנִי בְּמֵי־
לב לג וְתִעֲבוּנִי שַׂלְמוֹתָי: כִּי־לֹא־אִישׁ כָּמֹנִי אֶעֱנֶנּוּ נָבוֹא יַחְדָּו בַּמִּשְׁפָּט: לֹא יֵשׁ־בֵּינֵינוּ
לד לה מוֹכִיחַ יָשֵׁת יָדוֹ עַל־שְׁנֵינוּ: יָסֵר מֵעָלַי שִׁבְטוֹ וְאֵמָתוֹ אַל־תְּבַעֲתַנִּי: אֲדַבְּרָה
א וְלֹא אִירָאֶנּוּ כִּי־לֹא־כֵן אָנֹכִי עִמָּדִי: נָקְטָה נַפְשִׁי בְּחַיָּי אֶעֶזְבָה עָלַי שִׂיחִי אֲדַבְּרָה
ב ג בְּמַר נַפְשִׁי: אֹמַר אֶל־אֱלוֹהַּ אַל־תַּרְשִׁיעֵנִי הוֹדִיעֵנִי עַל מַה־תְּרִיבֵנִי: הֲטוֹב
ד לְךָ ׀ כִּי־תַעֲשֹׁק כִּי־תִמְאַס יְגִיעַ כַּפֶּיךָ וְעַל־עֲצַת רְשָׁעִים הוֹפָעְתָּ: הַעֵינֵי בָשָׂר
ה ו לָךְ אִם־כִּרְאוֹת אֱנוֹשׁ תִּרְאֶה: הֲכִימֵי אֱנוֹשׁ יָמֶיךָ אִם־שְׁנוֹתֶיךָ כִּימֵי גָבֶר: כִּי־
ז תְבַקֵּשׁ לַעֲוֺנִי וּלְחַטָּאתִי תִדְרוֹשׁ: עַל־דַּעְתְּךָ כִּי־לֹא אֶרְשָׁע וְאֵין מִיָּדְךָ מַצִּיל:
ח ט יָדֶיךָ עִצְּבוּנִי וַיַּעֲשׂוּנִי יַחַד סָבִיב וַתְּבַלְּעֵנִי: זְכָר־נָא כִּי־כַחֹמֶר עֲשִׂיתָנִי וְאֶל־
י יא עָפָר תְּשִׁיבֵנִי: הֲלֹא כֶחָלָב תַּתִּיכֵנִי וְכַגְּבִנָּה תַּקְפִּיאֵנִי: עוֹר וּבָשָׂר תַּלְבִּישֵׁנִי
יב וּבַעֲצָמוֹת וְגִידִים תְּשֹׂכְכֵנִי: חַיִּים וָחֶסֶד עָשִׂיתָ עִמָּדִי וּפְקֻדָּתְךָ שָׁמְרָה רוּחִי:

BACKGROUND

9:26 | **Reed [*eveh*] boats:** Based on the context, these could be fast-moving ships or boats from a place called Eveh. It is also possible that the term *eveh* refers to the reeds or stalks that grow on the banks of streams, such as papyri, as in the verses "As the barley was just ripened [*aviv*]" (Exodus 9:31, and Rashi ad loc.) and "The budding [*ibei*] of the vale" (Song of Songs 6:11). There is a similar word in Akkadian. Boats made of tied bundles of reeds were common in the ancient East and remain in use to this day, since they are easy to construct and navigate. Furthermore, due to their light weight, they are very swift.

Like the eagle [*nesher*] that swoops over prey: Some identify the *nesher* as the eagle, *Aquila chrysaetos*, which was a very important Roman symbol. Others identify it as the griffon vulture, *Gyps fulvus*, a large bird that nests and soars at markedly high altitudes, more than 10 km above the ground. This enables the bird to identify its prey from afar and glide swiftly toward its food (see 39:27–28; Jeremiah 48:40; Obadiah 1:4; Micah 1:16; Habakkuk 1:8). Its wingspan stretches up to 2.5 m, and it weighs roughly 10 kg. Its head and neck are bare of feathers, appearing as though they have been shed [*nashar*]; perhaps this accounts for the bird's name. Other researchers maintain that *nesher* is a general term for several different birds of prey.

9:30 | **Purified my hands with soap [*bevor*]:** Some explain that this is a reference to a substance that is also called *borit* (Isaiah 1:25; Jeremiah 2:22). *Borit* is a cleanser produced by burning certain plants, such as soapwort, *Saponaria*, a plant from the carnation family, or by burning plants that thrive in saline environments, whose tissues are rich in potassium.

10:10 | **Truly, You have liquefied me like milk and curdled me like cheese:** During the development of a fetus, processes of liquefaction and solidification occur. The primary fetal cells first develop within a mucous, semi-liquid tissue within the uterine wall. Later, the fetus solidifies and grows limbs. However, it also eventually expels certain liquids that contribute to the amniotic fluid, inside of which the development of the fetus continues until birth. At birth, the amniotic fluid bursts from the womb.

13 Yet all **these matters You concealed in Your heart.** You are intimately familiar with every secret detail of my creation and my life. **I know that** all **this is with You.** A similar idea, in a different context and style, is found in Psalms 139.
14 **If I sin, You detain me.** You are aware of it and do not turn a blind eye to my transgression,[163] **and** You **do not cleanse me of my iniquity.**
15 **If I am wicked, woe is me, and** yet even **if I am righteous, I will not lift up my head; I am sated with shame and I see**[164] **my disgrace,** since in any case You will be dissatisfied with me.[165]
16 **It,** my poverty and disgrace, **will be lifted up,** will increase,[166] when **You will hunt me like** one hunts **a lion**[167] **and intensify Your blows upon me again.**[168]
17 **You will renew** gathering **Your witnesses against me, and Your anger with me will increase; it transforms, but it is constantly with me.** My afflictions are constantly changing form, but they each strike me at fixed times.[169] Alternatively, a mass of afflictions strike me.
18 **Why did You take me out from the womb?** It would have been better for me not to have been born. **I would have expired** quietly in the womb as a stillborn,[170] **and no eye would have seen me.**
19 **I would have been as one who had not been; I would have been** a stillborn, **carried** straight **from the womb to the grave.**

"You will hunt me like a lion." Lion hunt, relief, Nimrud, Iraq, seventh century BCE

This would have been preferable to all the suffering I experienced throughout my life.
20 **Aren't my days few? Cease and let me be,**[171] **and I will compose myself,** or rest,[172] **a little**
21 **before I go, not to return, to the land of darkness and the shadow of death,** to the provinces of death and the netherworld,
22 **a land of** thick and amplified **darkness, like blackness, the shadow of death**[B] **and disarray,** as Gehenna is characterized by a lack of structure or stability, **looking like blackness.** Even the light that shines in that place is dark.

Tzofar's First Speech

JOB 11:1–20

Tzofar emboldens himself, and perhaps Job's other interlocutors do so as well, to confront Job's eloquent presentation. Expressing his faith in divine justice, Tzofar, like his two predecessors, casts doubt on Job's righteousness. He argues that since the way in which God's justice descends to the world is hidden from human perception, Job should not pretend that he can accurately evaluate God's ways, wisdom, or actions. Nevertheless, he assures Job that if he prays and directs his heart and deeds to God, he will experience renewal, tranquility, and security.

11 1 **Tzofar the Naamatite answered and said:**
2 **Should** one who speaks **so many words not be answered?** Do you think that your verbosity is enough to end all discussion, so that the debate will of necessity end with your stated position? **And should an eloquent man,** a skilled rhetorician, **be vindicated** simply by virtue of his eloquence?
3 **Your fabrications have silenced men; you have mocked, and there is no one to reproach you.** No one rebukes you or stops you. Perhaps Tzofar is referring to others who are present at the scene apart from Elifaz and Bildad, who heard Job's discourse and were left speechless by his declarations.[173]
4 **You said: My discourse is pure, and I am clean in your eyes.** I am considered innocent by my audience.[174]
5 **However, if only God would speak and** instead of letting you go astray with such thoughts, **open His lips** to speak **against you.**
6 **He would tell you the secrets of wisdom,** the esoteric knowledge that is hidden from you, **as sagacity is double-sided** and has many things to reveal to you. **Know that God may overlook some of your iniquities for you.** Alternatively, God can forget your sins, that is, forgive you for them.[175] However, you must listen to Him and speak less.
7 **Can you discover the understanding of God,** His ultimate intentions? **Can you discover the purpose of the Almighty?** Do you think that you can examine and understand God?
8 In the **heights of heavens, what can you do?** What power do you have to change the heavenly spheres? God's wisdom is **deeper than the grave; what can you know** of it?
9 **Its measure is longer than the earth, and** its expanse is **broader than the sea.** You are trying to understand matters that are beyond your comprehension.
10 **If He causes** those who have sinned against Him **to pass on,** to be cut off or killed, **or** if He **confines,** imprisons, **or assembles**

יג יד וְאֵלֶּה צָפַנְתָּ בִלְבָבֶךָ יָדַעְתִּי כִּי־זֹאת עִמָּךְ׃ אִם־חָטָאתִי וּשְׁמַרְתָּנִי וּמֵעֲוֺנִי לֹא

טו תְנַקֵּנִי׃ אִם־רָשַׁעְתִּי אַלְלַי לִי וְצָדַקְתִּי לֹא־אֶשָּׂא רֹאשִׁי שְׂבַע קָלוֹן וּרְאֵה עָנְיִי׃

טז יז וְיִגְאֶה כַּשַּׁחַל תְּצוּדֵנִי וְתָשֹׁב תִּתְפַּלָּא בִי׃ תְּחַדֵּשׁ עֵדֶיךָ ׀ נֶגְדִּי וְתֶרֶב כַּעַשְׂךָ עִמָּדִי

יח יט חֲלִיפוֹת וְצָבָא עִמִּי׃ וְלָמָּה מֵרֶחֶם הֹצֵאתָנִי אֶגְוַע וְעַיִן לֹא־תִרְאֵנִי׃ כַּאֲשֶׁר לֹא־

כ הָיִיתִי אֶהְיֶה מִבֶּטֶן לַקֶּבֶר אוּבָל׃ הֲלֹא־מְעַט יָמַי יחדל ישית מִמֶּנִּי וְאַבְלִיגָה

וחדל וְשִׁית

כא כב מְּעָט׃ בְּטֶרֶם אֵלֵךְ וְלֹא אָשׁוּב אֶל־אֶרֶץ חֹשֶׁךְ וְצַלְמָוֶת׃ אֶרֶץ עֵיפָתָה ׀ כְּמוֹ אֹפֶל

א ב צַלְמָוֶת וְלֹא סְדָרִים וַתֹּפַע כְּמוֹ־אֹפֶל׃ וַיַּעַן צֹפַר הַנַּעֲמָתִי וַיֹּאמַר׃ הֲרֹב

ג דְּבָרִים לֹא יֵעָנֶה וְאִם־אִישׁ שְׂפָתַיִם יִצְדָּק׃ בַּדֶּיךָ מְתִים יַחֲרִישׁוּ וַתִּלְעַג וְאֵין

ד ה מַכְלִם׃ וַתֹּאמֶר זַךְ לִקְחִי וּבַר הָיִיתִי בְעֵינֶיךָ׃ וְאוּלָם מִי־יִתֵּן אֱלוֹהַּ דַּבֵּר וְיִפְתַּח

ו שְׂפָתָיו עִמָּךְ׃ וְיַגֶּד־לְךָ ׀ תַּעֲלֻמוֹת חָכְמָה כִּי־כִפְלַיִם לְתוּשִׁיָּה וְדַע ׀ כִּי־יַשֶּׁה לְךָ

ז ח אֱלוֹהַּ מֵעֲוֺנֶךָ׃ הַחֵקֶר אֱלוֹהַּ תִּמְצָא אִם עַד־תַּכְלִית שַׁדַּי תִּמְצָא׃ גָּבְהֵי שָׁמַיִם

ט י מַה־תִּפְעָל עֲמֻקָּה מִשְּׁאוֹל מַה־תֵּדָע׃ אֲרֻכָּה מֵאֶרֶץ מִדָּהּ וּרְחָבָה מִנִּי־יָם׃ אִם־

BACKGROUND

10:22 | **Land of darkness, like blackness, the shadow of death:** Job expresses the common belief that upon their deaths, most people enter the netherworld, where they exist as shadowy ghosts lacking any substance. Indeed, the Talmud depicts Gehenna as an extremely vast expanse (*Pesaḥim* 94a). However, in several places, the Bible indicates that not everyone who dies need descend to the netherworld (see I Samuel 2:6, 25:29; Hosea 13:14; Psalms 16:10–11, 49:16).

In many ancient cultures, it was customary to build elaborate mausoleums for kings and princes due to the belief that they would merit eternal life, while the fate of most other humans after death would not be substantially different from that of animals. By contrast, the assumption in Jewish tradition is different. The Mishna states: All of Israel has a portion in the World to Come (*Sanhedrin* 10:1). Unless a person has committed an unusually severe transgression, he will merit eternal life.

them, **who can restrain Him?** Who can prevent Him from doing so?[176]

11 **For He knows vain men.** He is familiar with sinners. **He sees iniquity without looking for it.** He does not need to pause to reflect on the details; He knows everything immediately.

12 **But a hollow man can take heart.** In contrast to God, man is an empty receptacle; therefore, his heart can be filled with understanding, as a **colt of an onager**[B] **can be born a man.** When a person is born, he is like the colt of a wild ass, and he must then grow and develop into a man.[177]

13 Therefore, **if you,** Job, **prepare your heart, and spread your hands to Him** in prayer,

14 **if there is iniquity in your hand, banish it** from you; **do not let injustice dwell in your tents,**

15 **for then you can raise your face without blemish.** You will not have to bow your head due to your blemish. **You will be steadfast and will not fear.**

16 **For** in this state, **you will forget your travail** and misery; **you will remember it like water that has passed.** You will have only vague memories of your pain, like the bare trace of passing waters.

17 **The world will rise up** and be built **brighter than** the light of **noon;**[178] it **will be illuminated; like the morning it will be.** Then the world will shine for you and be renewed as the morning.[179]

18 **You will be secure because there is hope; you will be entrenched** [***veḥafarta***] **and lie down in security.** You will be as secure as if you were surrounded by excavated moats [*ḥafira*] that protect you from your enemies.[180] Alternatively, you will have security in the World to Come when you arrive at your grave, which has already been dug [*ḥafur*].[181]

19 **You will lie down without threat, and many will court your favor.** They will come to your door to seek your advice.

20 Unlike those who are innocent of sin, **the eyes of the wicked will fail** in their expectation of being saved from their misfortune, **and escape will be lost for them; their hope will become** nothing but **despair.**

Job's First Response to Tzofar

JOB 12:1–14:22

After having heard all his friends speak at length of God's might, Job retorts that their statements offer nothing new, as even animals and inanimate objects are aware of God's abilities. However, this knowledge does not reassure him, since God's power can be channeled not only constructively but destructively as well. Job does not deny God's strength, but unlike his friends, whose reaction to this fact is to utter statements of flattery and falsehood that he considers a form of hypocritical obsequiousness, Job is determined to stand resolutely before God and sound his claims honestly.

After responding to his friends, Job addresses God directly. At the beginning of his direct address to God, he requests conditions that would allow him to speak freely and openly. He goes on to ask God how many and which sins might possibly justify his suffering and travails. Job further speaks of the brevity of man's life and the vanity and pointlessness of his existence. His travails lead him to wonder about what he deems as a personal vendetta against him and why a lofty and noble God would harass a lowly, limited, and hopeless creature like man.

12 1 **Job answered** sarcastically **and said:**

2 **Indeed, you are a people.** You are the majority, and this gives you confidence that you possess the truth[182] **and** that together **with you, wisdom will die.**[183]

3 However, **I too have a heart,**[184] **like you.** The heart is considered the seat of understanding.[185] **I am no less than you. Who does not have this?** Who does not comprehend these matters?[186] You are not saying anything new.

4 **I have become one mocked by his neighbor.** Alternatively, they considered me one who mocks others. I was once **one who had called to God and He answered him,** but my lot now **is** to be **a laughingstock of the completely righteous,** all of you.[187]

5 I have become **a calamity that brings contempt to complacent composure, ready for those whose foot slips.** A disaster[188] that undermines the confidence of one who is at ease and self-assured is prepared for those who have slipped.

6 By contrast, **the tents are tranquil for robbers.** They dwell serenely in their homes, **and there is security** in life **for the provokers of God.** Yet I know that this too is only **as the hand of God engenders.** Such unexpected and incomprehensible outcomes are also controlled by God.[189]

7 **But ask now the animals, and** even **they will teach you,**[190] as they all know that everything is in God's hands, **and** you may also ask **the birds of the heavens, and they will tell you,**

8 **or converse with the earth, and it will teach you, and the fish of the sea will** also **relate** this truth **to you.**

9 **Who does not know, among all these, that the hand of the Lord has done** all **this?**

10 He **in whose hand is the life of every living thing and the spirit of all flesh of man.**

11 **Doesn't** God control even **the ear,** which can **discern words, and the palate,** which can **taste food?**[191]

12 **Wisdom is with the aged, and with length of days, sagacity.** These too are gifts bestowed upon them by God.

13 **Wisdom and might are with Him; counsel and sagacity are His.**

14 **Behold, He demolishes, and** then **it will not be rebuilt; He shuts a man in, and** afterward, **it will not be opened.**

יא יַחֲלֹף וְיַסְגִּיר וְיַקְהִיל וּמִי יְשִׁיבֶנּוּ׃ כִּי־הוּא יָדַע מְתֵי־שָׁוְא וַיַּרְא־אָוֶן וְלֹא יִתְבּוֹנָן׃

יב יג וְאִישׁ נָבוּב יִלָּבֵב וְעַיִר פֶּרֶא אָדָם יִוָּלֵד׃ אִם־אַתָּה הֲכִינוֹתָ לִבֶּךָ וּפָרַשְׂתָּ אֵלָיו

יד טו כַּפֶּךָ׃ אִם־אָוֶן בְּיָדְךָ הַרְחִיקֵהוּ וְאַל־תַּשְׁכֵּן בְּאֹהָלֶיךָ עַוְלָה׃ כִּי־אָז ׀ תִּשָּׂא פָנֶיךָ

טז יז מִמּוּם וְהָיִיתָ מֻצָק וְלֹא תִירָא׃ כִּי־אַתָּה עָמָל תִּשְׁכָּח כְּמַיִם עָבְרוּ תִזְכֹּר׃ וּמִצָּהֳרַיִם

יח יָקוּם חָלֶד תָּעֻפָה כַּבֹּקֶר תִּהְיֶה׃ וּבָטַחְתָּ כִּי־יֵשׁ תִּקְוָה וְחָפַרְתָּ לָבֶטַח תִּשְׁכָּב׃

יט כ וְרָבַצְתָּ וְאֵין מַחֲרִיד וְחִלּוּ פָנֶיךָ רַבִּים׃ וְעֵינֵי רְשָׁעִים תִּכְלֶינָה וּמָנוֹס אָבַד מִנְהֶם ג

א ב וְתִקְוָתָם מַפַּח־נָפֶשׁ׃ וַיַּעַן אִיּוֹב וַיֹּאמַר׃ אָמְנָם כִּי אַתֶּם־עָם

ג וְעִמָּכֶם תָּמוּת חָכְמָה׃ גַּם־לִי לֵבָב ׀ כְּמוֹכֶם לֹא־נֹפֵל אָנֹכִי מִכֶּם וְאֶת־מִי־אֵין

ד ה כְּמוֹ־אֵלֶּה׃ שְׂחֹק לְרֵעֵהוּ ׀ אֶהְיֶה קֹרֵא לֶאֱלוֹהַּ וַיַּעֲנֵהוּ שְׂחוֹק צַדִּיק תָּמִים׃ לַפִּיד

ו בּוּז לְעַשְׁתּוּת שַׁאֲנָן נָכוֹן לְמוֹעֲדֵי רָגֶל׃ יִשְׁלָיוּ אֹהָלִים ׀ לְשֹׁדְדִים וּבַטֻּחוֹת לְמַרְגִּיזֵי

ז אֵל לַאֲשֶׁר הֵבִיא אֱלוֹהַּ בְּיָדוֹ׃ וְאוּלָם שְׁאַל־נָא בְהֵמוֹת וְתֹרֶךָּ וְעוֹף הַשָּׁמַיִם

ח ט וְיַגֶּד־לָךְ׃ אוֹ שִׂיחַ לָאָרֶץ וְתֹרֶךָּ וִיסַפְּרוּ לְךָ דְּגֵי הַיָּם׃ מִי לֹא־יָדַע בְּכָל־אֵלֶּה כִּי

י יא יַד־יְהוָה עָשְׂתָה זֹּאת׃ אֲשֶׁר בְּיָדוֹ נֶפֶשׁ כָּל־חָי וְרוּחַ כָּל־בְּשַׂר־אִישׁ׃ הֲלֹא־אֹזֶן

יב יג מִלִּין תִּבְחָן וְחֵךְ אֹכֶל יִטְעַם־לוֹ׃ בִּישִׁישִׁים חָכְמָה וְאֹרֶךְ יָמִים תְּבוּנָה׃ עִמּוֹ

יד חָכְמָה וּגְבוּרָה לוֹ עֵצָה וּתְבוּנָה׃ הֵן יַהֲרוֹס וְלֹא יִבָּנֶה יִסְגֹּר עַל־אִישׁ וְלֹא יִפָּתֵחַ׃

BACKGROUND

11:12| **Colt of an onager [*ayir pereh*]:** An *ayir* is a young ass or a male ass (see Genesis 32:15). Even young domesticated animals are known for their convulsive movements before they are trained, and here the verse is referring to a wild animal. It is well known that a wild male ass cannot be domesticated.

15 **Behold, He halts the water and it dries; He releases it** to flood, **and they,** the waters, **overturn the earth.**
16 **With Him are strength and resourcefulness; the misled,** the unintentional sinner, **and the misleading,** Satan,[192] **are** also **His.**
17 **He leads counselors,** those who are supposedly wise and independent of thought, **astray, and** He **renders judges fools,** or mad.[193]
18 On the one hand, **He removes the restraints,** the ruling power, **of kings,** as God removes their authority, **and** on the other hand, it is He who **binds a belt on their waists.** He is also the one who gives them the power to reign.[194]
19 **He leads priests astray and the mighty He corrupts** and misleads.[195]
20 **He removes speech from the** established, **reliable** men so that they forget how to speak or are struck dumb by events, **and** He **takes** away **the sense,** understanding, **of elders.**
21 **He pours contempt on the noble,** the wealthy and dignified, **and weakens the dam of the watercourses.** He releases the masses upon them like water currents breaking through dams.[196]
22 **He reveals depths from the darkness and brings the shadow of death to light.**
23 **He** sometimes **increases the** power of **nations, and** at other times **He eliminates them; He spreads traps for the nations,**[197] **but He** also **guides them.**[198]
24 **He removes the heart,** understanding, **of the leaders**[199] **of the people of the land and misleads them through trackless emptiness.**
25 **They grope in the dark without light, and He causes them to veer like a drunk.**

13 1 After Job has acknowledged that he is aware of God's might, he returns to the point he made at the beginning of the speech: **Behold, my eye has seen all** that you have described of the greatness of God and His unlimited power. **My ear has** also **heard and understood.**
2 **What you know** about God's greatness, **I too know; I am no less than you.**
3 **But** unlike you, whose awareness of God's might leads you to submission and silence toward Him, **I would** prefer to **speak to the Almighty, and to argue with God I desire,** even to contend with Him.
4 **But you are spreaders**[200] **of falsehood, physicians of folly, all of you.** Your statements provide no form of healing.
5 **Would that you were silent, and it,** your silence, **would be wisdom for you.**
6 **Hear now my argument, and listen to the contentions of my lips.**
7 Furthermore, **will you speak injustice,** falsely, **on behalf of**[201] **God, and for Him** will you **speak deceit?** You know that you do not speak the truth. You merely talk in this manner because you think that this is what one is supposed to say, either because it is written in the holy books or because it is your tradition. Your justification of God in our dispute is nothing more than hypocritical bias toward Him.
8 **Will you favor Him? Will you contend on behalf of God,** to justify and defend Him?
9 **Will it be good if He examines you?** Do you think it would be to your benefit if He were to examine you? In doing so, He would expose your hypocrisy and insincere flattery. **Will you fool Him as one fools a man?**
10 No, **He will rebuke** and punish **you if you secretly favor** Him.
11 **Won't dread of Him terrify you, and His fear fall upon you?**
12 **Your slogans,** the matters you keep mentioning and repeating, **are comparable to ashes,** as they will not last; **your bodies are** comparable to **bodies**[202] **of clay.** You are not solid creatures; rather, you are fashioned from pliable material that turns into any shape that is imprinted on it. You speak with self-assurance, but your statements are no more stable or resilient than your bodies are.
13 **Be silent to me, and I will speak, and let happen to me what may.**
14 **For what should I take my flesh in my teeth?** Why should I bite my skin in order to refrain from talking,[203] **and** why should I **place my life,** my breath,[204] **in my hand,** in order to hold my peace? Alternatively, this phrase may be understood as saying: I will put my life in my hand. That is, I am even willing to risk my life to say what is on my mind.[205]
15 **Though He kills me, I will yearn for Him.** Even then, my love for God and devotion to Him will not cease. **But** nevertheless, **I will** still **argue my ways.** There is no rebellion in my words.[206] I will lay out my claims **before Him** in the hope that He will accept them.
16 **Moreover, He is my salvation.** I, not you, will merit salvation, **as the hypocrite will not come before Him.** Therefore, God will not accept your flattery.
17 **Hear my word, and let my articulation be in your ears.**
18 **Behold now, I have arranged my case** before God; **I know that I will be vindicated.**
19 **Who is it who will contend with me? For then,** if I could find someone who could argue against me, **I would be silent and expire.** However, in reality, there is no one who can prevent me from staking my claim for justice.
20 Now Job addresses God directly. **But two** things **do not do to me,** and **then I will not hide from You.** I will reveal all that is in my heart if you do not do the following two things:[207]

טו טז הֵן יַעְצֹר בַּמַּיִם וְיִבָשׁוּ וִישַׁלְּחֵם וְיַהַפְכוּ־אָרֶץ׃ עִמּוֹ עֹז וְתוּשִׁיָּה לוֹ שֹׁגֵג וּמַשְׁגֶּה׃
יז יח מוֹלִיךְ יוֹעֲצִים שׁוֹלָל וְשֹׁפְטִים יְהוֹלֵל׃ מוּסַר מְלָכִים פִּתֵּחַ וַיֶּאְסֹר אֵזוֹר בְּמָתְנֵיהֶם׃
יט כ מוֹלִיךְ כֹּהֲנִים שׁוֹלָל וְאֵתָנִים יְסַלֵּף׃ מֵסִיר שָׂפָה לְנֶאֱמָנִים וְטַעַם זְקֵנִים יִקָּח׃
כא כב שׁוֹפֵךְ בּוּז עַל־נְדִיבִים וּמְזִיחַ אֲפִיקִים רִפָּה׃ מְגַלֶּה עֲמֻקוֹת מִנִּי־חֹשֶׁךְ וַיֹּצֵא לָאוֹר
כג כד צַלְמָוֶת׃ מַשְׂגִּיא לַגּוֹיִם וַיְאַבְּדֵם שֹׁטֵחַ לַגּוֹיִם וַיַּנְחֵם׃ מֵסִיר לֵב רָאשֵׁי עַם־הָאָרֶץ
כה א וַיַּתְעֵם בְּתֹהוּ לֹא־דָרֶךְ׃ יְמַשְׁשׁוּ־חֹשֶׁךְ וְלֹא־אוֹר וַיַּתְעֵם כַּשִּׁכּוֹר׃ הֶן־כֹּל רָאֲתָה
ב ג עֵינִי שָׁמְעָה אָזְנִי וַתָּבֶן לָהּ׃ כְּדַעְתְּכֶם יָדַעְתִּי גַם־אָנִי לֹא־נֹפֵל אָנֹכִי מִכֶּם׃ אוּלָם
ד אֲנִי אֶל־שַׁדַּי אֲדַבֵּר וְהוֹכֵחַ אֶל־אֵל אֶחְפָּץ׃ וְאוּלָם אַתֶּם טֹפְלֵי־שָׁקֶר רֹפְאֵי אֱלִל
ה ו כֻּלְּכֶם׃ מִי־יִתֵּן הַחֲרֵשׁ תַּחֲרִישׁוּן וּתְהִי לָכֶם לְחָכְמָה׃ שִׁמְעוּ־נָא תוֹכַחְתִּי וְרִבוֹת
ז ח שְׂפָתַי הַקְשִׁיבוּ׃ הַלְאֵל תְּדַבְּרוּ עַוְלָה וְלוֹ תְּדַבְּרוּ רְמִיָּה׃ הֲפָנָיו תִּשָּׂאוּן אִם־לָאֵל
ט י תְּרִיבוּן׃ הֲטוֹב כִּי־יַחְקֹר אֶתְכֶם אִם־כְּהָתֵל בֶּאֱנוֹשׁ תְּהָתֵלּוּ בוֹ׃ הוֹכֵחַ יוֹכִיחַ
יא אֶתְכֶם אִם־בַּסֵּתֶר פָּנִים תִּשָּׂאוּן׃ הֲלֹא שְׂאֵתוֹ תְּבַעֵת אֶתְכֶם וּפַחְדּוֹ יִפֹּל עֲלֵיכֶם׃
יב יג זִכְרֹנֵיכֶם מִשְׁלֵי־אֵפֶר לְגַבֵּי־חֹמֶר גַּבֵּיכֶם׃ הַחֲרִישׁוּ מִמֶּנִּי וַאֲדַבְּרָה־אָנִי וְיַעֲבֹר
יד טו עָלַי מָה׃ עַל־מָה ׀ אֶשָּׂא בְשָׂרִי בְשִׁנָּי וְנַפְשִׁי אָשִׂים בְּכַפִּי׃ הֵן יִקְטְלֵנִי לֹא אֲיַחֵל לוֹ
טז יז אַךְ־דְּרָכַי אֶל־פָּנָיו אוֹכִיחַ׃ גַּם־הוּא־לִי לִישׁוּעָה כִּי־לֹא לְפָנָיו חָנֵף יָבוֹא׃ שִׁמְעוּ
יח שָׁמוֹעַ מִלָּתִי וְאַחֲוָתִי בְּאָזְנֵיכֶם׃ הִנֵּה־נָא עָרַכְתִּי מִשְׁפָּט יָדַעְתִּי כִּי־אֲנִי אֶצְדָּק׃
יט כ מִי־הוּא יָרִיב עִמָּדִי כִּי־עַתָּה אַחֲרִישׁ וְאֶגְוָע׃ אַךְ־שְׁתַּיִם אַל־תַּעַשׂ עִמָּדִי אָז

21 First, **distance Your** heavy **hand** that strikes me with these blows[208] **from me, and** second, **may Your dread not terrify me.** Do not scare me. As long as I am reduced by the suffering I am experiencing and by my dread of You, I am unable to express the musings of my heart. I require a certain measure of freedom in order to speak my piece.

22 If these two conditions are fulfilled, then **call, and I will answer; or I will speak, and You answer me.** We will be able to engage in a conversation.

23 I am requesting that You clarify for me: **How many iniquities and sins do I have? Inform me of** the nature of **my transgression and my sin.**

24 **Why do You hide Your face and consider me as Your enemy?** I do not know how many and what kinds of sins might justify such an antagonistic attitude toward me.

25 **Will You break**[209] **a driven leaf,** which has already fallen from the tree, **and will You pursue dry straw,**

26 such **that You write noxious matters,** issue such bitter decrees,[210] **about me and bequeath me the iniquities of my youth,** those sins for which I have already atoned and made amends, or those transgressions I committed before I matured?[211]

27 **You place my feet in the stocks,** a type of wooden shackle used to hold the feet of prisoners,[212] **and You watch all my paths; You constrict the soles of my feet,** so that I cannot move or do anything.[213]

28 Why do You treat my body so harshly? As **he,** man in general, **decays like carrion** and wastes away **like a garment eaten by a moth,** full of holes, ruined, and rendered useless.

14 1 **Man is born of a woman, few of days and sated with vexation.** Man's life span is limited, while his troubles and suffering are too great.

2 **He emerges like a flower and withers;**[B] **he flees like an** insubstantial **shadow,** whose size and shape is constantly changing **and does not endure.** Man is ephemeral.

"He emerges like a flower and withers." The short-lived blossom of an almond tree

3 Is it not enough for You to reflect upon and watch over all the great creatures and plants in the world? Yet **even on this,** ephemeral man, **You opened Your eyes, and You would bring me,** a lowly mortal, **to judgment with You?**

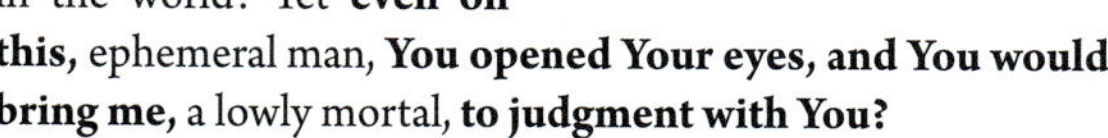

4 In this judgment, **who can generate the pure from the impure? Isn't it the One?** Only the One, God,[214] can justify man, even if he is impure and wicked, when He comes to judge him. Yet why should He punish such a puny creature?

Stocks

5 **If his days are determined,** circumscribed and limited,[215] and **the number of his months is** fixed and established **with You, and You have established his allotment** of time and options, **and it will not be surpassed,**

6 **let him be, and it will cease.** Let him rest from his pain[216] **until, like a hired laborer, he finishes** the work of **his day.** Let him conclude his life in peace.

7 **For the tree has hope:**[B] **If it is hewed, it may yet regenerate,** it can sprout again, **and its roots will not cease.** They will not disappear but will grow again.

8 **If its root grows old in the earth and its trunk** apparently **dies in the dirt,**

9 **it will blossom at the scent of water,** even if the tree is given only the smallest amount of water, **and produce branches**[217] **like a sapling.**[218]

"For the tree has hope: If it is hewed, it may yet regenerate, and its roots will not cease." Renewal of a tree after it has been cut down

10 **But** in contrast, **man dies and weakens; a human expires, and where is he?**

11 Just as **water has gone out of the sea, and** as **a river has dried and is parched,** irreversible processes,

12 so too, **a man lies down** dead **and will not rise until the heavens** wear out and **are no more;**[219] **they,** the dead, **will not** ever **awaken and will not** ever **be roused from their sleep.**

13 **If only You would hide me in the grave** and **would conceal me** there **until Your wrath subsides; You would** watch over me there and **set for me a portion,** a limit for my suffering, **and** then You **would** eventually **remember me** and bring me out of the grave.

כא כב מִפָּנֶיךָ לֹא אֶסָּתֵר׃ כַּפְּךָ מֵעָלַי הַרְחַק וְאֵמָתְךָ אַל־תְּבַעֲתַנִּי׃ וּקְרָא וְאָנֹכִי אֶעֱנֶה
כג כד אוֹ־אֲדַבֵּר וַהֲשִׁיבֵנִי׃ כַּמָּה לִי עֲוֺנוֹת וְחַטָּאוֹת פִּשְׁעִי וְחַטָּאתִי הֹדִיעֵנִי׃ לָמָּה־פָנֶיךָ
כה כו תַסְתִּיר וְתַחְשְׁבֵנִי לְאוֹיֵב לָךְ׃ הֶעָלֶה נִדָּף תַּעֲרוֹץ וְאֶת־קַשׁ יָבֵשׁ תִּרְדֹּף׃ כִּי־תִכְתֹּב
כז עָלַי מְרֹרוֹת וְתוֹרִישֵׁנִי עֲוֺנוֹת נְעוּרָי׃ וְתָשֵׂם בַּסַּד ׀ רַגְלַי וְתִשְׁמוֹר כָּל־אָרְחֹתָי
כח א עַל־שָׁרְשֵׁי רַגְלַי תִּתְחַקֶּה׃ וְהוּא כְּרָקָב יִבְלֶה כְּבֶגֶד אֲכָלוֹ עָשׁ׃ אָדָם יְלוּד אִשָּׁה
ב ג קְצַר יָמִים וּשְׂבַע־רֹגֶז׃ כְּצִיץ יָצָא וַיִּמָּל וַיִּבְרַח כַּצֵּל וְלֹא יַעֲמוֹד׃ אַף־עַל־זֶה
ד ה פָּקַחְתָּ עֵינֶךָ וְאֹתִי תָבִיא בְמִשְׁפָּט עִמָּךְ׃ מִי־יִתֵּן טָהוֹר מִטָּמֵא לֹא אֶחָד׃ אִם־
ו חֲרוּצִים ׀ יָמָיו מִסְפַּר־חֳדָשָׁיו אִתָּךְ חֻקָּו עָשִׂיתָ וְלֹא יַעֲבֹר׃ שְׁעֵה מֵעָלָיו וְיֶחְדָּל
ז עַד־יִרְצֶה כְּשָׂכִיר יוֹמוֹ׃ כִּי יֵשׁ לָעֵץ תִּקְוָה אִם־יִכָּרֵת וְעוֹד יַחֲלִיף וְיֹנַקְתּוֹ לֹא
ח ט תֶחְדָּל׃ אִם־יַזְקִין בָּאָרֶץ שָׁרְשׁוֹ וּבֶעָפָר יָמוּת גִּזְעוֹ׃ מֵרֵיחַ מַיִם יַפְרִחַ וְעָשָׂה
י יא קָצִיר כְּמוֹ־נָטַע׃ וְגֶבֶר יָמוּת וַיֶּחֱלָשׁ וַיִּגְוַע אָדָם וְאַיּוֹ׃ אָזְלוּ־מַיִם מִנִּי־יָם וְנָהָר
יב יֶחֱרַב וְיָבֵשׁ׃ וְאִישׁ שָׁכַב וְלֹא־יָקוּם עַד־בִּלְתִּי שָׁמַיִם לֹא יָקִיצוּ וְלֹא־יֵעֹרוּ מִשְּׁנָתָם׃
יג מִי יִתֵּן ׀ בִּשְׁאוֹל תַּצְפִּנֵנִי תַּסְתִּירֵנִי עַד־שׁוּב אַפֶּךָ תָּשִׁית לִי חֹק וְתִזְכְּרֵנִי׃

BACKGROUND

14:2 | **He emerges like a flower and withers:** Most fruit trees in the region of the Land of Israel blossom for a brief period, roughly one to three weeks. The shedding of masses of flowers is impressive, both in the carpet of flowers that fall to the ground and the sudden change in the appearance of the tree. This phenomenon is especially noticeable in the almond tree, which blossoms even before its leaves bud.

14:7 | **For the tree has hope:** Even after they have been chopped down, trees can return to life and be renewed through embryonic buds found in their various parts. Chopping the tree at a high point will lead to the growth of new branches and a fresh blossoming of its leaves. Chopping at a low point will cause the growth of new, straight trunks. Sometimes a tree is even deliberately cut down in order to stimulate the growth of such trunks (see *Bava Batra* 80b; *Tosefta*, *Menaḥot* 13:4). In certain species, chopping at an even lower point will cause a renewal of shoots that sprout directly from the roots in the soil. However, there are some trees that do not renew themselves, such as cedar and palm trees.

14 **If a man dies, will he live? All the days of my** apportioned
time of life, **I wait until my passing,** the time for my departure
from the world,[220] **comes.**
15 **Call, and I will answer You; yearn for Your handiwork.** Job
requests from God: Call to me and I will answer; desire the response of the work of Your hands.[221]
16 **For now,** please **count my steps.** Watch over me and ensure
that I do not fall. **Do not keep watch over my sin.** Alternatively,
do not remember my sin forever, or if I have sinned, punish me
for it immediately, without delay.[222]
17 Currently, **my transgression is sealed** up with You as **in a bundle, and You have added to my iniquity.** You pile more sins
upon me.[223]
18 **However,** just as the mightiest elements of nature do not last
forever, as **a falling mountain will crumble** into dust, **and
bedrock will be moved from its place** and does not remain
firm,
19 and as **stones are worn away by water,** since **its torrents wash
away the dust** or the aftergrowth **of the earth,** so too[224] **the
hope of man You destroy.**
20 **You overpower him,** man,
forever, and he is gone from
the world and dies;[225] **You alter his countenance** as he
ages **and send him away**
from the world.
21 **His sons attain** a position
of **honor, but he does not
know** this; **they suffer, but
he does not empathize with them.**
22 **But his flesh on him is painful, and his soul mourns over
him.**

"Stones are worn away by water"

Elifaz's Second Speech

JOB 15:1–35

At this point, one round of exchanges has concluded. Now Elifaz, the first to respond to Job, speaks again. His comments this time offer no substantial change to his first speech or any great novelty, but it appears that his tone here is harsher and more sarcastic.

In the first part of this speech, Elifaz issues a personal reproof to Job. He expresses his disappointment in his friend, whom he had thought wise and righteous. However, now he considers Job's statements as full of nonsense and evil. He accuses Job of pretentions unworthy of him. Elifaz then describes the wicked and the disasters that will ultimately befall them. He also warns Job that his contemptuous words against God identify him as one of them.

15 1 **Elifaz the Temanite answered and said:**
2 **Should the wise answer with windy knowledge,** vanity, **and
have the** dry **east wind fill his belly?** How can it be that you,
a man who is considered wise, actually have no true wisdom
inside you? Only empty words arise from your belly.
3 **You,** the wise man, **rebuke** and judge **with useless talk**[226] **and**
pointless **words with no effect in them.**
4 **Indeed,** with your comments **you nullify reverence** of God
and make belittling and flawed **speech**[227] **before God.**
5 **For your iniquity trains your mouth** what to say. Your words
do not emanate from the heart of the righteous man I knew;
rather, they are an expression of the sinner within you. **And**
this is so even though you do not openly utter prohibited or heretical statements; instead, **you choose clever language,** crafty
sayings that only allude to such wicked matters.[228]
6 **Your mouth condemns you, and not I.** What you yourself
have said is enough to condemn you. I do not need to add anything; **your** own **lips testify against you.**
7 You speak with confidence, as though there was never a person
like you. **Are you the first man** who was **born** in the world?
Were you made before the hills? Has no experience and
knowledge been accumulated in the world until now? There are
people from whom you can inquire and learn.[229] What is the
source of your supposedly certain knowledge?
8 **Do you listen in the council of God and extract wisdom for
yourself?**[230]
9 **What do you know that we do not know?** What **do you understand that is not with us,** in our consciousness?
10 **Both the graybeard and the aged are among us,** and some of
us are **greater in days**[231] **than your father.**
11 **Is it not enough for you, the consolations of God,** the good
that God has wrought for you until now?[232] Alternatively, are
the consolations in our statements about God too meager
for you?[233] Are you not satisfied with **the matter** that God
whispered[234] **to you,** which He revealed to you through your
friends?
12 **To what,** or to where, **does your heart take you, and what do
your eyes intimate?**
13 Only **when you turn your spirit toward God,** then **you can
express words** of truth **from your mouth.**
14 **What is man that he should be exonerated, and that one
born of a woman be justified?** Man can never be considered
entirely innocent and righteous.
15 **Behold,** even **in His holy ones,** the angels,[235] **He does not
trust,** as even their shortcomings are revealed to God; therefore, He does not fully trust them. **And** even **the heavens are
not pure in His eyes.**

יד טו אִם־יָמוּת גֶּבֶר הֲיִחְיֶה כָּל־יְמֵי צְבָאִי אֲיַחֵל עַד־בּוֹא חֲלִיפָתִי: תִּקְרָא וְאָנֹכִי אֶעֱנֶךָּ
טז יז לְמַעֲשֵׂה יָדֶיךָ תִכְסֹף: כִּי־עַתָּה צְעָדַי תִּסְפּוֹר לֹא־תִשְׁמֹר עַל־חַטָּאתִי: חָתֻם
יח בִּצְרוֹר פִּשְׁעִי וַתִּטְפֹּל עַל־עֲוֹנִי: וְאוּלָם הַר־נוֹפֵל יִבּוֹל וְצוּר יֶעְתַּק מִמְּקֹמוֹ:
יט כ אֲבָנִים ׀ שָׁחֲקוּ מַיִם תִּשְׁטֹף־סְפִיחֶיהָ עֲפַר־אָרֶץ וְתִקְוַת אֱנוֹשׁ הֶאֱבַדְתָּ: תִּתְקְפֵהוּ
כא לָנֶצַח וַיַּהֲלֹךְ מְשַׁנֶּה פָנָיו וַתְּשַׁלְּחֵהוּ: יִכְבְּדוּ בָנָיו וְלֹא יֵדָע וְיִצְעֲרוּ וְלֹא־יָבִין לָמוֹ:
כב טו א אַךְ־בְּשָׂרוֹ עָלָיו יִכְאָב וְנַפְשׁוֹ עָלָיו תֶּאֱבָל: וַיַּעַן אֱלִיפַז הַתֵּימָנִי וַיֹּאמַר:
ב ג הֶחָכָם יַעֲנֶה דַעַת־רוּחַ וִימַלֵּא קָדִים בִּטְנוֹ: הוֹכֵחַ בְּדָבָר לֹא יִסְכּוֹן וּמִלִּים לֹא־
ד ה יוֹעִיל בָּם: אַף־אַתָּה תָּפֵר יִרְאָה וְתִגְרַע שִׂיחָה לִפְנֵי־אֵל: כִּי יְאַלֵּף עֲוֹנְךָ פִיךָ
ו ז וְתִבְחַר לְשׁוֹן עֲרוּמִים: יַרְשִׁיעֲךָ פִיךָ וְלֹא־אָנִי וּשְׂפָתֶיךָ יַעֲנוּ־בָךְ: הֲרִאישׁוֹן אָדָם
ח ט תִּוָּלֵד וְלִפְנֵי גְבָעוֹת חוֹלָלְתָּ: הַבְסוֹד אֱלוֹהַ תִּשְׁמָע וְתִגְרַע אֵלֶיךָ חָכְמָה: מַה־
י יָּדַעְתָּ וְלֹא נֵדָע תָּבִין וְלֹא־עִמָּנוּ הוּא: גַּם־שָׂב גַּם־יָשִׁישׁ בָּנוּ כַּבִּיר מֵאָבִיךָ יָמִים:
יא יב הַמְעַט מִמְּךָ תַּנְחֻמוֹת אֵל וְדָבָר לָאַט עִמָּךְ: מַה־יִּקָּחֲךָ לִבֶּךָ וּמַה־יִּרְזְמוּן עֵינֶיךָ:
יג יד כִּי־תָשִׁיב אֶל־אֵל רוּחֶךָ וְהֹצֵאתָ מִפִּיךָ מִלִּין: מָה־אֱנוֹשׁ כִּי־יִזְכֶּה וְכִי־יִצְדַּק יְלוּד
טו טז אִשָּׁה: הֵן בִּקְדֹשָׁו לֹא יַאֲמִין וְשָׁמַיִם לֹא־זַכּוּ בְעֵינָיו: אַף כִּי־נִתְעָב וְנֶאֱלָח אִישׁ־
יז יח שֹׁתֶה כַמַּיִם עַוְלָה: אֲחַוְךָ שְׁמַע־לִי וְזֶה־חָזִיתִי וַאֲסַפֵּרָה: אֲשֶׁר־חֲכָמִים יַגִּידוּ
יט כ וְלֹא כִחֲדוּ מֵאֲבוֹתָם: לָהֶם לְבַדָּם נִתְּנָה הָאָרֶץ וְלֹא־עָבַר זָר בְּתוֹכָם: כָּל־יְמֵי
כא רָשָׁע הוּא מִתְחוֹלֵל וּמִסְפַּר שָׁנִים נִצְפְּנוּ לֶעָרִיץ: קוֹל־פְּחָדִים בְּאָזְנָיו בַּשָּׁלוֹם

16 If He does not place His faith in angels and heavenly beings, **all the more so** He will not rely on **one abominable and revolting, a man who drinks iniquity like water,** who pursues crime and amasses more and more sins.

17 **I will tell you;**[236] **hear me, this I have seen,** in a vision or in my thoughts, **and will relate.**

18 I will tell you **that which the wise** men **tell and which is** received[237] **from their fathers and** that which **they do not withhold,**

19 the righteous, upright fathers[238] **to whom alone the land,** the world, **was given, and no stranger has passed among them.** Even if there were others who inherited the world, they are considered of no importance at all.

20 This is what the wise men relate: **All the days of the wicked, he trembles** with fear;[239] **a number of years is set aside,** allotted, **for the powerful,** and until his imminent demise, he lives a life of terror.

21 **The sound of terrors is** always **in his ears;** even **in** peaceful years of **tranquility, the robber will come upon him.**[240]

22 **He does not believe that he will return from darkness, and**
despite the gloom, **he is visible to a sword,** as the one holding
the sword can perceive him.[241]
23 **He wanders for bread,** asking: **Where is it? He knows that**
the day of darkness is ready at hand for him. It awaits him.[242]
24 **Trouble,**[243] or enemies, **and distress terrorize** or startle **him;**
they attack him like a king destined for a siege.
25 **Because he,** the wicked, **extended his hand against God and**
would overcome the Almighty, since the wicked man is prepared to fight against God,
26 **he runs at Him,** or against Him **defiantly, with the thickness**
of his exposed shields.
27 Until now, the wicked has enjoyed a life of pleasure. **Because**
he has covered his face with his fat and he has made a flesh
fold [*pima*], the folds of fat that appear like a mouth [*peh*],[244]
over his loins,[245]
28 his sins are inevitably followed by punishment: **He shall dwell**
in desolate cities and **in houses in which one would not**
live, in structures **which are destined to become** demolished
heaps.
29 **He shall not become rich, and his wealth shall not endure,**
his wealth will not last;[246] **nothing of theirs will extend over**
the earth, or be left on earth to give to others.[247]
30 **He will not turn away from** his place of **darkness; the flame**
will dry his shoots, and they will pass away from the world[248]
by the breath of His mouth.
31 **Let him,** the wicked, **not trust in** lies and **futility that**
momentarily **misleads, for emptiness will be his compensa-**
tion. Falsehood begets nothing but more falsehood.[249]
32 **It will be concluded before his time.** He will die early, **and his**
treetop will not be green.
33 **He will shed his unripe grapes like a vine** whose clusters have
not yet formed, **and he will cast off his blossoms like an olive**
tree. The children, life, or deeds of the wicked will end before
they come to fruition, like the unripe grapes and flowers of an
olive tree that are shed and scattered before they develop into
edible fruits.

Unripe grapes

Olive blossoms and young olives

34 **For the company of the hypocrite** and cheater **will** ultimately **be** lonely and **desolate, and fire will** eventually **consume**
the tents of people who erected them with money obtained
through **bribery.**[250]
35 **They,** these wicked people, think of sin so much, it is as though
they **conceive** or become pregnant with **travail;** therefore,
they give birth to iniquity, and their belly prepares deceit.

Job's Second Response to Elifaz

JOB 16:1–17:16

Job opens his response to Elifaz's second speech by expressing his anger at his friends. He claims that their words have offered him no fresh insights, as he himself could have said everything that he heard from them. Job rejects their worthless consolations. He returns to his descriptions of his suffering and the feelings of anguish that accompany his travails for the very reason that he knows that they are nothing but God's wishes and intentions. Yet, although he is a broken man, he still cleaves to God. He pours out his heart and presents his questions to Him. The abandoned Job insults his friends, accusing them of having no wisdom, being full of flattery, and making statements that do nothing but torment him. This lamentation of Job's concludes with harsh depictions of his proximity to the grave.

16 1 **Job answered and said:**
2 **I have heard many** statements **like these.** You have not told
me anything new. **All of you are useless comforters,** toilers in
vain, worthless and false.[251]
3 **Is there an end to windy,** empty, **words? Or what is it that**
drives you, motivates or applies pressure upon each one of
you, **that you respond?**[252]
4 **I also** could and **would speak as you do, if your life were in**
place of my life, if you were in my place. **I would amass words**
against you, in the manner of preachers and eulogizers. I am
very familiar with the style of a sermon, and were it not for
my suffering I could moralize just as well as you do. **And** I too
would **shake my head at you,** as a mark of sorrow.
5 **I would** likewise **encourage you with my mouth,** just as until now you have offered me no practical assistance, **and the**
movement of my lips would relieve your grief,[253] or, alternatively, my grief.[254]
6 But why should I dwell on fantasies, for **if I speak, my pain**
will not be lessened, and if I refrain from talking and remain
silent, **what will go from me?** What part of my pain will be
removed?[255]
7 **But now it,** or all this talk, or this pain,[256] **has wearied me;**
You[257] **have devastated all my congregation,** or my family.[258]
8 **You have shriveled me**[259] through the want and suffering You
have inflicted upon me; the mark **it** has made on me **is a wit-**
ness. My gauntness stands to testify **against me; it testifies**
before me.

כב כג שודד יבואנו׃ לא־יאמין שוב מני־חשך וצפו הוא אלי־חרב׃ נדד הוא ללחם וצפוי
כד איה ידע | כי־נכון בידו יום־חשך׃ יבעתהו צר ומצוקה תתקפהו כמלך | עתיד
כה כו לכידור׃ כי־נטה אל־אל ידו ואל־שדי יתגבר׃ ירוץ אליו בצואר בעבי גבי
כז כח מגניו׃ כי־כסה פניו בחלבו ויעש פימה עלי־כסל׃ וישכון | ערים נכחדות בתים
כט לא־ישבו למו אשר התעתדו לגלים׃ לא־יעשר ולא־יקום חילו ולא־יטה
ל לא לארץ מנלם׃ לא־יסור | מני־חשך ינקתו תיבש שלהבת ויסור ברוח פיו׃ אל־
לב יאמן בשו נתעה כי־שוא תהיה תמורתו׃ בלא־יומו תמלא וכפתו לא רעננה׃
לג לד יחמס כגפן בסרו וישלך כזית נצתו׃ כי־עדת חנף גלמוד ואש אכלה אהלי־
לה טז א שחד׃ הרה עמל וילד און ובטנם תכין מרמה׃ ויען איוב ויאמר׃
ב ג שמעתי כאלה רבות מנחמי עמל כלכם׃ הקץ לדברי־רוח או מה־ימריצך כי
ד תענה׃ גם | אנכי כככם אדברה לו־יש נפשכם תחת נפשי אחבירה עליכם
ה ו במלים ואניעה עליכם במו ראשי׃ אאמצכם במו־פי וניד שפתי יחשך׃ אם־
ז אדברה לא־יחשך כאבי ואחדלה מה־מני יהלך׃ אך־עתה הלאני השמות
ח ט כל־עדתי׃ ותקמטני לעד היה ויקם בי כחשי בפני יענה׃ אפו טרף | וישטמני
י חרק עלי בשניו צרי | ילטוש עיניו לי׃ פערו עלי | בפיהם בחרפה הכו לחיי
יא יב יחד עלי יתמלאון׃ יסגירני אל אל עויל ועל־ידי רשעים ירטני׃ שלו הייתי |
יג ויפרפרני ואחז בערפי ויפצפצני ויקימני לו למטרה׃ יסבו עלי | רביו יפלח
יד כליותי ולא יחמל ישפך לארץ מררתי׃ יפרצני פרץ על־פני־פרץ ירץ עלי

9 **His wrath has mauled and He hates me; He has gnashed His teeth at me; my enemy sharpens**[260] **his eyes toward me** and plots how to increase my suffering.

10 **They have opened wide their mouth against me,** to shout at me; **they strike my cheek in disgrace,** scornfully, to humiliate me; **together they convene against me.**[261]

11 **God hands me over to the unjust,** those who perform evil acts,[262] **and by means of the wicked, He misdirects me.**[263]

12 **I was tranquil, and He agitated me,** or, alternatively, He crushed me;[264] **He seized my nape and shattered me;**[265] **He set me as His target** in order to shoot me.[266]

13 **His marksmen surround me; He pierces my kidneys** with their arrows, and He **does not show compassion; He spills my bile onto the ground.**[267]

14 **He** strikes and **breaks me, break after break,** one blow after another; **He runs at me** to hurt me **like a warrior** attacking in battle.[268]

15 **I sewed sackcloth over my skin**[269] as a sign of mourning for
myself, **and I have set in dust my renown.** I placed dust upon
my head.[270]
16 **My face is enflamed from weeping,**[271] **and the shadow of
death**[272] **is on my eyelids.**
17 All this has befallen me **for no villainy that is in my hands,** for
nothing; **my prayer** before You **has been pure.** If so, why am I
experiencing such terrible suffering?
18 **Earth, do not cover my blood.** I prefer it to remain exposed,
as a constant reminder of the injustice I have suffered. **And let
there be no resting place for my outcry,** so that it may continue to be heard by all, or by God.[273]
19 **Now too, behold, my witness is** located **in the heavens, and
my witness is on high.**
20 **My eloquent ones,** or, alternatively, those who distort my
claims, **my friends: My eye streams** as I weep **to God.**
21 **Can a man argue with God**[274] **as a person does with his
friend?** One can rightfully respond only to his friend, another
mortal.
22 **For but a few years pass** me, **and I will go on the path** of life
from which I will not return. One cannot return from this
path.

17 1 **My spirit is crushed,** or bruised from all the troubles that have
been visited upon me. **My days are dwindling,** my days fade
and are lost.[275] **Graves are mine.** They are all that is left to me of
my children.
2 **Truly,** or I swear, **mockers are with me,**[276] **and my eye goes to
sleep with the embitterment they cause** me.[277]
3 Job now turns to God with a request: **Promise now, guarantee
me with You.** Be my guarantor, for if You will not assure my
safety, **who is it who will shake hands with me?** No mortal
will obligate himself as my guarantor. The shaking of hands is a
symbolic act that expresses one's obligation to the other.[278]
4 **For You have concealed their heart from understanding,**
my friends do not comprehend at all,[279] **and therefore, You
will not exalt them.**
5 **The conniver will report friends,**[280] **and the eyes of his children will languish,** from peering in unrequited expectation.[281]
6 **He,** this treacherous friend, the pain, Elifaz,[282] or God,[283]
rendered me a byword[284] **of the people.** Indeed, over the
generations, Job has become known as the archetype of the suffering man. **I will be** the classic example of **he who is already
in hell** even before his death.[285]
7 **My eye has dimmed,** and my vision is blurred **from** my **anger,
and my limbs**[286] do not function and **are all** insubstantial,[287]
like a shadow.
8 **The upright are outraged** and rise up **at this; the pure are
aroused against the** mocking **hypocrite** to reprove him.[288]
9 **The righteous stays his course,** despite the retribution that
descends upon the earth, **and the clean-handed will add
strength.**
10 After these general comments, Job addresses his friends with a
direct attack: **Even if all of you return** and speak, **and come
now, I will not find a wise man among you.**
11 **My days have passed,** or are passing; **my thoughts**[289] **are
severed** due to all my pain and aggravation; **they are the inheritance of my heart.**[290]
12 **They,** my friends,[291] or my torments, **transform night into day,**
as they deprive me of sleep, **approaching light into darkness.**
The light that seems near is actually fading.[292]
13 **Truly, I hope that the grave will be my home; in the darkness,** the grave, **I will cushion my bedding.**
14 **I called to the pit** of the netherworld: **You are my father;** and
to the maggots I declared: You are **my mother and my sister,**
as I live with them. My mother and my sister eat my flesh.
15 **Where then is my hope, and my hope, who can see it?**
16 **It,** my hope, **descends the levels**[293] **of the grave, comes to rest
together** with me **on the dirt.**[294]

Bildad's Second Speech

JOB 18:1–21

After a short introduction in which he expresses his reservations over Job's long soliloquy and his critique of his friends, Bildad describes the bitter fate that awaits the wicked. He does not focus on any specific faults in Job's behavior and does not speak directly to him, but it is clear from the context that Bildad believes that one who suffers as much as Job must be a wicked person.

18 1 **Bildad the Shuhite answered and said:**
2 **When will you,** Job, **put an end to the words?** When will you
stop talking?[295] Whenever you appear to be ready to conclude
speaking, you begin a new topic.[296] First you should **contemplate, and afterward we will speak.** It should be noted that
Bildad speaks here to Job in the second person plural, a somewhat indirect form of address.
3 **Why have we been considered like a beast, obtuse in your
eyes?** Why do you consider us bereft of understanding and
insight?[297]
4 You are **one who mauls** and harms **himself in his wrath; will
the earth be forsaken for you and the rock removed from
its place?** Do you expect the natural laws of the world to be
overturned for your sake? Others interpret this as a reference
to God, who is referred to in the Bible as a rock.[298] If so, the
final phrase in the verse reads: Do you expect God to alter His
normal ways for you?
5 **Rather, the light of the wicked will dim,**[299] **and the spark**[300]
of his fire will not glow.

טו טז כְּגִבּוֹר׃ שַׂק תָּפַרְתִּי עֲלֵי גִלְדִּי וְעֹלַלְתִּי בֶעָפָר קַרְנִי׃ פָּנַי חמרמרה מִנִּי־בֶכִי וְעַל חֳמַרְמְרוּ

יז יח עַפְעַפַּי צַלְמָוֶת׃ עַל לֹא־חָמָס בְּכַפָּי וּתְפִלָּתִי זַכָּה׃ אֶרֶץ אַל־תְּכַסִּי דָמִי וְאַל־יְהִי

יט כ מָקוֹם לְזַעֲקָתִי׃ גַּם־עַתָּה הִנֵּה־בַשָּׁמַיִם עֵדִי וְשָׂהֲדִי בַּמְּרוֹמִים׃ מְלִיצַי רֵעָי אֶל־

כא כב אֱלוֹהַּ דָּלְפָה עֵינִי׃ וְיוֹכַח לְגֶבֶר עִם־אֱלוֹהַּ וּבֶן־אָדָם לְרֵעֵהוּ׃ כִּי־שְׁנוֹת מִסְפָּר

ז א ב יֶאֱתָיוּ וְאֹרַח לֹא־אָשׁוּב אֶהֱלֹךְ׃ רוּחִי חֻבָּלָה יָמַי נִזְעָכוּ קְבָרִים לִי׃ אִם־לֹא

ג הֲתֻלִים עִמָּדִי וּבְהַמְּרוֹתָם תָּלַן עֵינִי׃ שִׂימָה־נָּא עָרְבֵנִי עִמָּךְ מִי הוּא לְיָדִי יִתָּקֵעַ׃

ד ה כִּי־לִבָּם צָפַנְתָּ מִּשָּׂכֶל עַל־כֵּן לֹא תְרֹמֵם׃ לְחֵלֶק יַגִּיד רֵעִים וְעֵינֵי בָנָיו תִּכְלֶנָה׃

ו ז וְהִצִּגַנִי לִמְשֹׁל עַמִּים וְתֹפֶת לְפָנִים אֶהְיֶה׃ וַתֵּכַהּ מִכַּעַשׂ עֵינִי וִיצֻרַי כַּצֵּל כֻּלָּם׃

ח ט יָשֹׁמּוּ יְשָׁרִים עַל־זֹאת וְנָקִי עַל־חָנֵף יִתְעֹרָר׃ וְיֹאחֵז צַדִּיק דַּרְכּוֹ וּטֳהָר־יָדַיִם ד

י יא יֹסִיף אֹמֶץ׃ וְאוּלָם כֻּלָּם תָּשֻׁבוּ וּבֹאוּ נָא וְלֹא־אֶמְצָא בָכֶם חָכָם׃ יָמַי עָבְרוּ זִמֹּתַי

יב יג נִתְּקוּ מוֹרָשֵׁי לְבָבִי׃ לַיְלָה לְיוֹם יָשִׂימוּ אוֹר קָרוֹב מִפְּנֵי־חֹשֶׁךְ׃ אִם־אֲקַוֶּה שְׁאוֹל

יד טו בֵּיתִי בַּחֹשֶׁךְ רִפַּדְתִּי יְצוּעָי׃ לַשַּׁחַת קָרָאתִי אָבִי אָתָּה אִמִּי וַאֲחֹתִי לָרִמָּה׃ וְאַיֵּה

טז אֵפוֹ תִקְוָתִי וְתִקְוָתִי מִי יְשׁוּרֶנָּה׃ בַּדֵּי שְׁאֹל תֵּרַדְנָה אִם־יַחַד עַל־עָפָר

ז א ב נָחַת׃ וַיַּעַן בִּלְדַּד הַשֻּׁחִי וַיֹּאמַר׃ עַד־אָנָה ׀ תְּשִׂימוּן קִנְצֵי לְמִלִּין

ג ד תָּבִינוּ וְאַחַר נְדַבֵּר׃ מַדּוּעַ נֶחְשַׁבְנוּ כַבְּהֵמָה נִטְמִינוּ בְּעֵינֵיכֶם׃ טֹרֵף נַפְשׁוֹ בְּאַפּוֹ

ה הַלְמַעַנְךָ תֵּעָזַב אָרֶץ וְיֶעְתַּק־צוּר מִמְּקֹמוֹ׃ גַּם אוֹר רְשָׁעִים יִדְעָךְ וְלֹא־יִגַּהּ שְׁבִיב

ו ז אִשּׁוֹ׃ אוֹר חָשַׁךְ בְּאָהֳלוֹ וְנֵרוֹ עָלָיו יִדְעָךְ׃ יֵצְרוּ צַעֲדֵי אוֹנוֹ וְתַשְׁלִיכֵהוּ עֲצָתוֹ׃

ח ט כִּי־שֻׁלַּח בְּרֶשֶׁת בְּרַגְלָיו וְעַל־שְׂבָכָה יִתְהַלָּךְ׃ יֹאחֵז בְּעָקֵב פָּח יַחֲזֵק עָלָיו צַמִּים׃

6 **The light will have darkened in his tent, and his lamp will dim over him.**

7 **The strides of his strength will be shortened.** His steps shall become short, like those of a weak person, **and his** own **counsel will cast him down,** cause his downfall,[301]

8 **for he is caught in a net by his feet, and he walks on a snag,** a tangle of branches placed over a trap.[302]

9 **A snare will seize a heel;**[303] **its strings will tighten upon him.** The knots of the snare will tighten around him.[304]

"He is caught in a net by his feet." Deer caught in a net, Edfu, Egypt, 257–237 BCE

10 **His rope** to ensnare him **is hidden in the ground, and his trap** is prepared **on the path.**
11 **Terrors,** or demons,[305] **will frighten him on all sides and scatter his feet.** In his terror, his limbs will be scattered, so to speak, and rendered useless,[306] and he will fall.
12 **His progeny will be hungry,**[307] **and calamity is set by his side.**[308]
13 **It will consume the branches,** pieces, **of his skin; death's firstborn,** the angel of death, **will consume his branches,** will devour his children.[309]
14 **Its support will be severed from his tent.** That which provides stability for the tent, possibly the peg that holds it in place, will be removed.[310] This is possibly an allusion to his wife. **And** it **will march him to the king of terrors,** the king of demons.[311]
15 **She,** his wife, who has become a widow, **will dwell in his tent without him;**[312] **sulfur,**[B] which destroys everything, **will be scattered** and will rain **on his abode.**

Sulfur crystal

16 **Below, his roots will dry, and above, his harvest will wither.**
17 **His memory will perish from the earth, and there will be no name for him in the street.**[313]

"Below, his roots will dry, and above, his harvest will wither"

18 **He will be driven from light to darkness, and he will be banished from the world.**[314]
19 **He will have neither son**[315] **nor grandson among his people, and there will be no remnant in his dwellings.**
20 **The recent,** later generations, **are astonished at his day,** when they contemplate his fate, **and the ancient,** earlier generations, **are seized with agitation** [*sa'ar*], shaking in fear as though confronted with stormy [*se'ara*] winds.[316]
21 Bildad concludes his appraisal of the lot of the wicked: **But these are** the events that shall befall **the habitations of the wicked, and this is the place** of residence **of one who does not know God.**

Job's Second Response to Bildad

JOB 19:1–29

Job rebukes his friends, whose comments have upset him, and he again places the responsibility for his situation upon God. He expresses his claim that his misfortune is due to God through a series of images, some of which parallel expressions of grief employed in the book of Lamentations. In this speech, Job stresses his feelings of isolation and estrangement in his time of tragedy from those who were formerly closest to him. His friends, members of his household, and even his servants have all turned their backs on him. Not only has his social circle shrunk, but his wrecked body has atrophied as well.

Yet all this does not bring Job to a state of heresy or even total despair. He declares that through his tragedy he has direct knowledge of God and he even believes in the possibility that God will bring him salvation. It is for this very reason that he cannot bear to listen to those who chant to him theological platitudes.

19 1 **Job answered and said:**
2 **How long will you aggrieve**[317] **my soul and oppress me with words?**
3 **These ten times,** numerous occasions,[318] **you have humiliated** and insulted **me,** either explicitly or by intimation; **you are not ashamed to estrange yourselves from me.**[319]
4 **If indeed I erred, with me my error rests.** Any errors I may have committed have not harmed those around me or the world in general, and therefore I do not deserve such a severe punishment.[320]
5 **If indeed you will overload against me, and rebuke me with my disgrace,** if you continue to argue that I have sinned greatly,
6 because you consider me exceedingly wicked and you judge me by my misfortunes, you should **know then that** I am not guilty, but rather **God has sabotaged me, and He has surrounded me with His trap.**[321]
7 **Behold, I call: Villainy, but I am not answered; I plead, but there is no justice.**
8 **He has fenced my path and I cannot pass, and He places darkness on my paths,** so that I cannot continue.
9 **He has stripped me of my honor,** my former stature, **and removed the crown from my head.**
10 **He,** God, **smashes me all around, and I go.** I will soon die because I cannot bear any more pain. **He has transplanted my hope like an** uprooted **tree.**[322]
11 **He has enflamed His wrath against me, and He considers me as** one of **His adversaries.**
12 **His troops,** the tragedies that have befallen me,[323] **come** to attack me **together.** It is difficult for me to view the series of catastrophes that have befallen me with such frequency as anything other than a coordinated and deliberate attack. **They beat a path against me,** crushing me beneath them, **and** they **encamp around my tent.**
13 **He has distanced my brethren from me, and my acquaintances have become estranged from me,** or they act cruelly

טָמוּן בָּאָרֶץ חַבְלוֹ וּמַלְכֻּדְתּוֹ עֲלֵי נָתִיב׃ סָבִיב בִּעֲתֻהוּ בַלָּהוֹת וֶהֱפִיצֻהוּ לְרַגְלָיו׃ י יא
יְהִי־רָעֵב אֹנוֹ וְאֵיד נָכוֹן לְצַלְעוֹ׃ יֹאכַל בַּדֵּי עוֹרוֹ יֹאכַל בַּדָּיו בְּכוֹר מָוֶת׃ יִנָּתֵק יב יג יד
מֵאָהֳלוֹ מִבְטַחוֹ וְתַצְעִדֵהוּ לְמֶלֶךְ בַּלָּהוֹת׃ תִּשְׁכּוֹן בְּאָהֳלוֹ מִבְּלִי־לוֹ יְזֹרֶה עַל־ טו
נָוֵהוּ גָפְרִית׃ מִתַּחַת שָׁרָשָׁיו יִבָשׁוּ וּמִמַּעַל יִמַּל קְצִירוֹ׃ זִכְרוֹ־אָבַד מִנִּי־אָרֶץ טז יז
וְלֹא־שֵׁם לוֹ עַל־פְּנֵי־חוּץ׃ יֶהְדְּפֻהוּ מֵאוֹר אֶל־חֹשֶׁךְ וּמִתֵּבֵל יְנִדֻּהוּ׃ לֹא נִין לוֹ יח יט
וְלֹא־נֶכֶד בְּעַמּוֹ וְאֵין שָׂרִיד בִּמְגוּרָיו׃ עַל־יוֹמוֹ נָשַׁמּוּ אַחֲרֹנִים וְקַדְמֹנִים אָחֲזוּ כ
שָׂעַר׃ אַךְ־אֵלֶּה מִשְׁכְּנוֹת עַוָּל וְזֶה מְקוֹם לֹא־יָדַע־אֵל׃ וַיַּעַן אִיּוֹב כא א
וַיֹּאמַר׃ עַד־אָנָה תּוֹגְיוּן נַפְשִׁי וּתְדַכְּאוּנַנִי בְמִלִּים׃ זֶה עֶשֶׂר פְּעָמִים תַּכְלִימוּנִי ב ג
לֹא־תֵבֹשׁוּ תַּהְכְּרוּ־לִי׃ וְאַף־אָמְנָם שָׁגִיתִי אִתִּי תָּלִין מְשׁוּגָתִי׃ אִם־אָמְנָם עָלַי ד ה
תַּגְדִּילוּ וְתוֹכִיחוּ עָלַי חֶרְפָּתִי׃ דְּעוּ־אֵפוֹ כִּי־אֱלוֹהַּ עִוְּתָנִי וּמְצוּדוֹ עָלַי הִקִּיף׃ הֵן ו ז
אֶצְעַק חָמָס וְלֹא אֵעָנֶה אֲשַׁוַּע וְאֵין מִשְׁפָּט׃ אָרְחִי גָדַר וְלֹא אֶעֱבוֹר וְעַל־נְתִיבוֹתַי ח
חֹשֶׁךְ יָשִׂים׃ כְּבוֹדִי מֵעָלַי הִפְשִׁיט וַיָּסַר עֲטֶרֶת רֹאשִׁי׃ יִתְּצֵנִי סָבִיב וָאֵלַךְ ט י
וַיַּסַּע כָּעֵץ תִּקְוָתִי׃ וַיַּחַר עָלַי אַפּוֹ וַיַּחְשְׁבֵנִי לוֹ כְצָרָיו׃ יַחַד ׀ יָבֹאוּ גְדוּדָיו וַיָּסֹלּוּ יא יב
עָלַי דַּרְכָּם וַיַּחֲנוּ סָבִיב לְאָהֳלִי׃ אַחַי מֵעָלַי הִרְחִיק וְיֹדְעַי אַךְ־זָרוּ מִמֶּנִּי׃ יג

BACKGROUND

18:15 | **Sulfur:** Sulfur, or brimstone, is first mentioned as an inflammatory substance in the story of the destruction of Sodom and Gomorrah (Genesis 19:24). In ancient times, sulfur was used to kindle and fan the flames of a fire. It was also utilized for burning the waste products of fields and vineyards, and perhaps also to destroy fields and granaries in time of war. In Israel, naturally occurring sulfur can be found south of Gaza, near Be'eri, and in sedimentary rock deposits in the Jordan Valley.

toward me.[324] Not only am I destitute, but my skin disease keeps people at bay.

14 **My relatives have departed,** or disappeared, **and my acquaintances have forgotten me.**

15 **The residents of my house and my maidservants consider me a stranger; I have become a foreigner in their eyes.**

16 **I called for my servant, but he would not answer me,** as I no longer have any authority. He does not obey me and even ignores my calls, **though I plead with him with my own mouth.**

17 **My spirit,** my soul, **is estranged** even **from my wife, and my pleas, from the children of my belly.** My entreaties are foreign even to those I raised in my home as though they were my own children.[325]

18 **Even delinquents,** a mob of youths,[326] **have despised me; I arise and they speak against me** with derision.[327]

19 **All my** former **confidants abhor me and those I loved have turned against me**[328] and have become my enemies.

20 As for my body, **my bones stick to my skin and to my flesh;** I have become physically weak and shriveled.[329] I have lost everything I had, **and I escaped by the skin of my teeth.** After all the tragedies that have befallen me I am left with nothing, and even my skin is badly afflicted; only the skin around my teeth remains intact.[330]

21 **Pity me, pity me,** as **you are my friends; for** I have not done anything wrong, but **the hand of God has touched,** harmed, **me.**

22 **Why do you pursue me like God** oppresses me? You see that I am suffering, and yet you only add to my anguish **and are not sated with my flesh.** You continue to hound me in one way or another, and you are still not satisfied.[331]

23 **If only my words were indeed written; if only they were in a scroll and inscribed,**[D] engraved for all time,

24 **with an iron pen or with lead,** from which molds can be cast, **that they be etched in the rock forever.**[B] If only my words would be recorded and remembered eternally.

25 **But I,** although I protest the injustice that God has done to me, **I know that my Redeemer lives, and He will stand last on the dust.** After all else has ceased to exist, God alone will remain.[332]

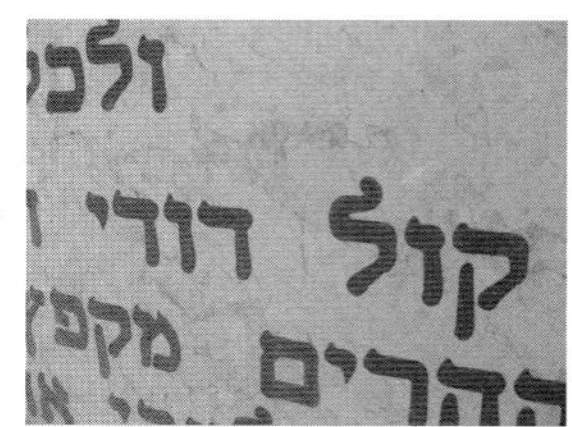

"With an iron pen or with lead, that they be etched in the rock forever." Inscription etched in rock and then filled with lead

26 **After my skin** has been destroyed, **this** bone **was struck** as well,[333] **and from my flesh,** directly, without any intermediary, **I will view God.**

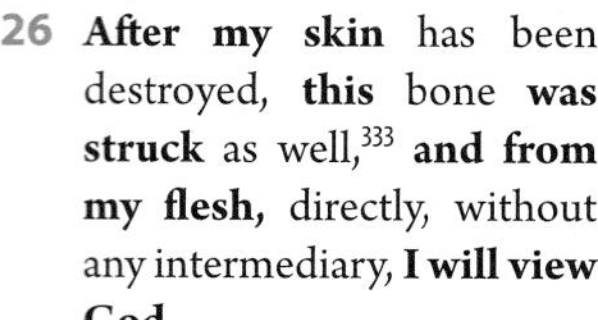

27 **What I view for myself,** seeing God through my pain, **my eyes will see, not** those of **a stranger.** You cannot stand in my shoes, cannot perceive what God is showing to me through my own suffering. Therefore your explanations of my experiences will inevitably fail. Only I can understand[334] how **my kidneys are lost within me,** that I have suffered internal injuries.

28 **If you say: For what is he persecuted, and isn't the root of the matter found in me?** Some read the verse as follows: If only you would say with compassion:[335] Why is he persecuted, and what is the root cause of sin within him? But it did not occur to you to think this way.[336]

29 **Beware of the sword,** which will eventually exact vengeance upon you. Since you are abandoning me due to theological assumptions rather than a genuine understanding of the situation, I know you will be punished. **For** divine **fury by the sword**[337] **will be for** severe **iniquity, so that you will know that there is judgment [*shadun*].**[338] *Shadun* can also be interpreted with the connotation of robbery, and therefore these words would read: So that you will eventually be robbed [*shod*]. Alternatively, based on the Aramaic word *shadi,* the verse says: So that you will be cast off. Possibly, Job is saying: You will be made to understand robbery and affliction so that in the future you will have compassion for the downtrodden.[339]

DISCUSSION

19:23 | **If only my words were indeed written; if only they were in a scroll and inscribed:** Job expresses his hope that his sufferings will lead to the writing of a book of lamentations and reflections. It is unlikely that he imagined that this wish would indeed come to pass.

BACKGROUND

19:24 | **With an iron pen or with lead, that they be etched in the rock forever:** In antiquity, inscriptions were chiseled into rock with hard iron pens. For important inscriptions, the carving might be widened and deepened and filled with lead, whose dark coloring would serve to emphasize the writing against the lighter-hued rock. Soft lead could easily be poured into horizontal inscriptions or hammered into vertical captions. This technique of filling chiseled indentations with lead is employed even nowadays for inscriptions on stone monuments or gravestones.

חדלו קרובי ומידעי שכחוני: גרי ביתי ואמהתי לזר תחשבני נכרי הייתי יד טו
בעיניהם: לעבדי קראתי ולא יענה במו־פי אתחנן־לו: רוחי זרה לאשתי וחנתי טז יז
לבני בטני: גם־עוילים מאסו בי אקומה וידברו־בי: תעבוני כל־מתי סודי יח יט
וזה־אהבתי נהפכו־בי: בעורי ובבשרי דבקה עצמי ואתמלטה בעור שני: כ
חנני חנני אתם רעי כי יד־אלוה נגעה בי: למה תרדפני כמו־אל ומבשרי לא כא כב
תשבעו: מי־יתן אפו ויכתבון מלי מי־יתן בספר ויחקו: בעט־ברזל ועפרת כג כד
לעד בצור יחצבון: ואני ידעתי גאלי חי ואחרון על־עפר יקום: ואחר עורי כה כו
נקפו־זאת ומבשרי אחזה אלוה: אשר אני | אחזה־לי ועיני ראו ולא־זר כלו כז
כליתי בחקי: כי תאמרו מה־נרדף־לו ושרש דבר נמצא־בי: גורו לכם | מפני־ כח כט
חרב כי־חמה עונות חרב למען תדעון שדין: ויען צופר הנעמתי שדון א כ
ויאמר: לכן שעפי ישיבוני ובעבור חושי בי: מוסר כלמתי אשמע ורוח מבינתי ב ג
יענני: הזאת ידעת מני־עד מני שים אדם עלי־ארץ: כי רננת רשעים מקרוב ד ה
ושמחת חנף עדי־רגע: אם־יעלה לשמים שיאו וראשו לעב יגיע: כגללו לנצח ו ז
יאבד ראיו יאמרו איו: כחלום יעוף ולא ימצאהו וידד כחזיון לילה: עין שזפתו ח ט

Tzofar's Second Speech

JOB 20:1–29

Like his two partners who spoke before him in this round of speeches, Tzofar also presents a lengthy soliloquy on the bitter fate that awaits the wicked. The wicked individual, who trusts in himself, soars briefly, but very quickly his possessions, strength, and body are diminished. Like his friends, Tzofar does not explicitly state that Job is wicked, but once again, the context does not leave much room for doubt; his scathing comments contain a severe accusation against Job.

20 1 **Tzofar the Naamatite answered and said:**

2 **Indeed,** after hearing your statements, **my thoughts respond** to the questions you have raised **for me,** because I have remained silent and attentive. **And because my feelings are in me,**

3 **I hear my humiliating chastisement** that you issued, **but the spirit of my understanding will answer for me,** and I will respond accordingly.

4 My spirit says to me the following: **Have you known this forever,** have you not always been aware of what I am about to say,[340] **from when man was placed upon the earth?**

5 You must know **that the rejoicing** and song **of the wicked is recent,** it has begun only recently,[341] **and the joy of the hypocrite is fleeting.** It is very brief.

6 **Though his crown,** the height of the wicked, **ascends to the heavens, and his head reaches to the clouds,**

7 **he will perish forever like his dung.** His great height is nothing more than a tower of dung, which will eventually crumble and be annihilated. **They who saw him will say: Where is he?** How did he disappear so completely?

8 **He will dissipate like a dream** fades, **and they will not find him; he will wander**[342] **like a vision of the night.** The greatness of the wicked fades away without leaving a trace, like a dream in the night.

9 **The eye that glimpsed him will not again, and he will no longer be looked upon by** the people of[343] **his place.**

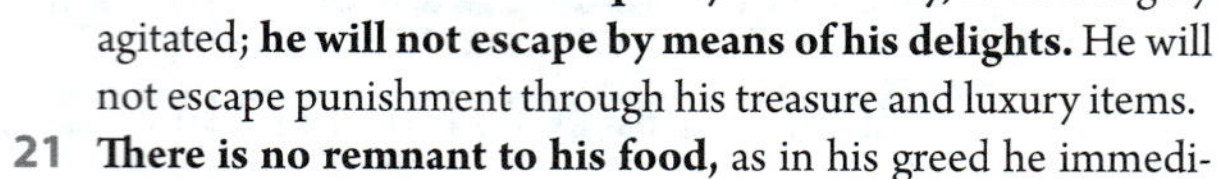

10 **His children shall** have to **appease the poor** whom he robbed,[344] **and his hands shall recompense his wickedness.** He will have to reverse the outcome of his wicked deeds.[345]
11 **His bones were** once **full** of the energy **of his youthfulness, but with him it will lie in the dust.** His youthful vigor will be buried with him. This may mean that he will die young.[346]
12 **Though evil,** which is like spoiled or poisonous food, **is sweet in his mouth, he conceals it under his tongue,** since if the wicked conceive a plot that cannot be executed immediately, they secretly hold on to it for a more convenient time.[347]
13 **He will have compassion for it,** his wicked plan, **and will not forsake it; he will withhold it within his palate.**
14 After he swallows **his food,** carries out his nefarious plans, it **will turn in his gut; it will be** like **cobras' venom**[B] **within him,** in his stomach.[348]

Black cobra

15 **He swallowed,** amassed, **wealth and will vomit it; God will dispossess him of his belly,** even though he has already digested it, as it were.
16 **He will suck the poison**[349] **of cobras,** those creatures will bite him; **the viper's**[B] **tongue will kill him.**

Saw-scaled viper

17 **He will not** merit to **see the brooks, the** abundance of the **rivers, the streams of honey and butter.**[B] This bounty is not meant for him.

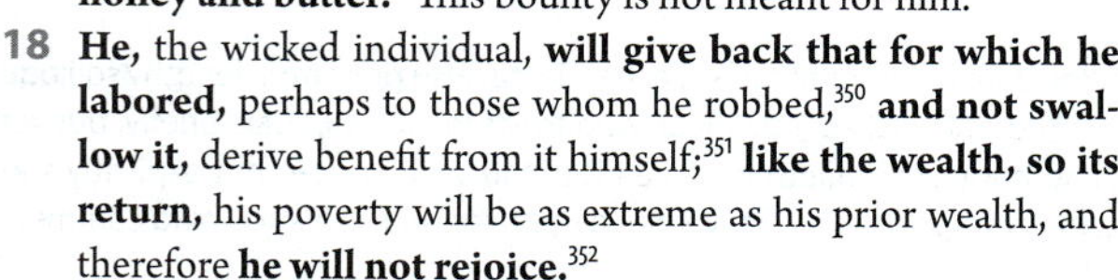

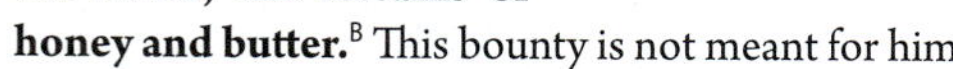

18 **He,** the wicked individual, **will give back that for which he labored,** perhaps to those whom he robbed,[350] **and not swallow it,** derive benefit from it himself;[351] **like the wealth, so its return,** his poverty will be as extreme as his prior wealth, and therefore **he will not rejoice.**[352]
19 **For he has broken, forsaken the impoverished; he robbed a house and would not build it.**
20 **For he does not know tranquility in his belly,** as he is highly agitated; **he will not escape by means of his delights.** He will not escape punishment through his treasure and luxury items.
21 **There is no remnant to his food,** as in his greed he immediately consumes everything;[353] **therefore, he will not sustain his prosperity.** He will not have the ability to preserve his bounty.[354]
22 **With the satisfaction of his needs,** when he has everything he needs, it is then that trouble will befall him and **he will be troubled; the hand of all travail will come upon him,** or a wicked and dangerous individual[355] will strike him and persecute him.
23 **When he is filling his belly, He,** God, **will send against him His enflamed wrath, and rain upon him with His fire** [***bilḥumo***]. This interpretation defines *bilḥumo* as being related to *ḥam*, implying the heat of anger.[356] Alternatively, *bilḥumo* can be related to the word for war [*milḥama*]: He will rain upon him in His war [*beloḥamo*] against him.
24 **He will flee from an iron weapon; the brass bow,** with arrowheads of brass, **will pass through him.** The arrows of this powerful bow will pierce the body of the wicked.[357]
25 **He,** his enemy, **drew,** his weapon,[358] **and it** struck the wicked and **emerged from his back; the blade through his gall bladder**[359] **will strike terror in him.**[360]
26 **All darkness is destined for his concealed acts,** due to his secret transgressions;[361] **a fire not fanned,** either a supernatural fire or a natural one that is not fanned to increase its flames, so that instead it will burn him more slowly and thereby increase his suffering,[362] **will consume him; it will harm the remnant in his tent.** He who is left in his tent will be broken and collapse.[363]
27 **The heavens will reveal his iniquity** before all, **and the earth will rise** up **against him,** as it will not want to receive him.
28 **The produce of his house will be exiled,**[364] and God's punishment will be **poured out on the day of His wrath.**[365]
29 **That is the fate of a wicked man from God, and the inheritance decreed upon him from God.**

Job's Second Response to Tzofar

JOB 21:1–34

Throughout this second series of speeches, the friends' recurring claim is that one who suffers must certainly be wicked. The last, Tzofar, particularly emphasized this point. It can be inferred from his presentation that in his opinion, Job's sufferings are an indication that he has sinned greatly. In his response, Job claims that even if a terrible fate does await the wicked, it generally does not transpire in the public eye. More than a few wicked people live out comfortable and happy lives. He also rejects the idea that the punishment of the wicked is meted out upon their children, arguing that if that were the case, the sinner and those around him would not be able to identify divine justice from which they could draw the appropriate conclusions.

21 **1** **Job answered and said:**
2 **Hear my word and may this be your consolation.** You will comfort me by listening to me.[366]
3 **Bear with me,** be patient, **and I will speak, and after my speaking,** Tzofar, **you may mock** what you have heard.
4 **Do I converse with a man? If so, why should I not be**

י וְלֹא תוֹסִיף וְלֹא־עוֹד תְּשׁוּרֶנּוּ מְקוֹמוֹ׃ בָּנָיו יְרַצּוּ דַלִּים וְיָדָיו תָּשֵׁבְנָה אוֹנוֹ׃
יא יב עַצְמוֹתָיו מָלְאוּ עֲלוּמָו וְעִמּוֹ עַל־עָפָר תִּשְׁכָּב׃ אִם־תַּמְתִּיק בְּפִיו רָעָה יַכְחִידֶנָּה
יג יד תַּחַת לְשׁוֹנוֹ׃ יַחְמֹל עָלֶיהָ וְלֹא יַעַזְבֶנָּה וְיִמְנָעֶנָּה בְּתוֹךְ חִכּוֹ׃ לַחְמוֹ בְּמֵעָיו נֶהְפָּךְ
טו טז מְרוֹרַת פְּתָנִים בְּקִרְבּוֹ׃ חַיִל בָּלַע וַיְקִאֶנּוּ מִבִּטְנוֹ יֹרִשֶׁנּוּ אֵל׃ רֹאשׁ־פְּתָנִים יִינָק
יז יח תַּהַרְגֵהוּ לְשׁוֹן אֶפְעֶה׃ אַל־יֵרֶא בִפְלַגּוֹת נַהֲרֵי נַחֲלֵי דְּבַשׁ וְחֶמְאָה׃ מֵשִׁיב יָגָע
יט וְלֹא יִבְלָע כְּחֵיל תְּמוּרָתוֹ וְלֹא יַעֲלֹס׃ כִּי־רִצַּץ עָזַב דַּלִּים בַּיִת גָּזַל וְלֹא יִבֶנֵהוּ׃
כ כא כִּי ׀ לֹא־יָדַע שָׁלֵו בְּבִטְנוֹ בַּחֲמוּדוֹ לֹא יְמַלֵּט׃ אֵין־שָׂרִיד לְאָכְלוֹ עַל־כֵּן לֹא־יָחִיל
כב כג טוּבוֹ׃ בִּמְלֹאות שִׂפְקוֹ יֵצֶר לוֹ כָּל־יַד עָמֵל תְּבֹאֶנּוּ׃ יְהִי ׀ לְמַלֵּא בִטְנוֹ יְשַׁלַּח־בּוֹ
כד חֲרוֹן אַפּוֹ וְיַמְטֵר עָלֵימוֹ בִּלְחוּמוֹ׃ יִבְרַח מִנֶּשֶׁק בַּרְזֶל תַּחְלְפֵהוּ קֶשֶׁת נְחוּשָׁה׃
כה כו שָׁלַף וַיֵּצֵא מִגֵּוָה וּבָרָק מִמְּרֹרָתוֹ יַהֲלֹךְ עָלָיו אֵמִים׃ כָּל־חֹשֶׁךְ טָמוּן לִצְפּוּנָיו
כז תְּאָכְלֵהוּ אֵשׁ לֹא־נֻפָּח יֵרַע שָׂרִיד בְּאָהֳלוֹ׃ יְגַלּוּ שָׁמַיִם עֲוֹנוֹ וְאֶרֶץ מִתְקוֹמָמָה
כח כט לוֹ׃ יִגֶל יְבוּל בֵּיתוֹ נִגָּרוֹת בְּיוֹם אַפּוֹ׃ זֶה ׀ חֵלֶק־אָדָם רָשָׁע מֵאֱלֹהִים וְנַחֲלַת אִמְרוֹ
א ב א מֵאֵל׃ וַיַּעַן אִיּוֹב וַיֹּאמַר׃ שִׁמְעוּ שָׁמוֹעַ מִלָּתִי וּתְהִי־זֹאת תַּנְחוּמֹתֵיכֶם׃
ג ד שָׂאוּנִי וְאָנֹכִי אֲדַבֵּר וְאַחַר דַּבְּרִי תַלְעִיג׃ הֶאָנֹכִי לְאָדָם שִׂיחִי וְאִם־מַדּוּעַ לֹא־

BACKGROUND

20:14| **Cobras' venom:** The bitter taste of a food is generally an indication that it has spoiled or is otherwise harmful. In many instances, toxic substances produced by animals also have a bitter taste. Accordingly, snake venom is called *merora*, which is related to the word *mar*, bitter, despite the fact that the venom generally does not come into contact with one's taste buds. Cobras, which are venomous snakes from the Elapidae family, are among the most venomous snakes in the world. One of them, the black desert cobra, *Walterinnesia aegyptia*, is fairly common in Israel, in the Jordan Valley and the Negev.

20:16| **Viper:** A Midrash (*Mekhilta*, *Beshalah* 1; *Tanḥuma*, *Beshalah* 18) calls this snake the *akhas*, which is similar to *Echis*, the scientific name for saw-scaled vipers, from the family of vipers. Although they are some of the smallest snakes in the venomous Viperidae family, they are aggressive and unpredictable. They produce warning sounds by moving their bodies in a circular motion and rubbing the scales at the sides of their bodies together.

20:17| **Honey and butter:** Butter, or curd, which is produced from whole milk, is considered a high-quality and conservable product of sheep, goats, and cattle. The honey mentioned here is the concentrated, conservable juice of figs and dates. From ancient to contemporary times, the combination of these products has symbolized high-quality food. The Land of Israel is praised many times in the Bible as a land flowing with milk and honey (see, e.g., Exodus 3:8; Deuteronomy 11:9).

losing patience? Since my grievance is directed to God, why
shouldn't I be impatient at His silence? I cannot hold back my
complaints.[367]
5 **Turn to me and be astonished, and place** your **hand over**
your **mouth.** Be silent.[368]
6 You will not be the only ones who are shocked by my speech.
When I myself **remember** my claims, **I am startled, and shud-**
dering seizes my flesh.
7 **Why do the wicked live,** and furthermore, they **grow old,**[369]
and **even become powerful,** growing ever stronger?
8 **Their offspring are well placed** and successful **before them,**
with them, and their descendants are before their eyes.
They see their descendants flourish.
9 **Their houses are peaceful without fear, and the rod of God**
is not upon them. They feel
no threat of divine
punishment.
10 **His bull breeds** with their
cow **and does not fail,** as its
seed is not expelled from the
womb;[370] **his cow calves and**
does not miscarry.
11 **They,** the wicked, **send out**
their youngsters freely,
without fear, **like a flock,**
and their children prance
like young goats and lambs.[371]
12 **They sing** with gladness **to**
the music of **the drum**[B] **and**
harp[B] **and rejoice at the**
sound of the pipe.

Cow calving, wooden statue, Egypt, Twelfth Dynasty

Young goats prancing

Woman playing drum, ceramic figurine, Shikmona, eighth century BCE

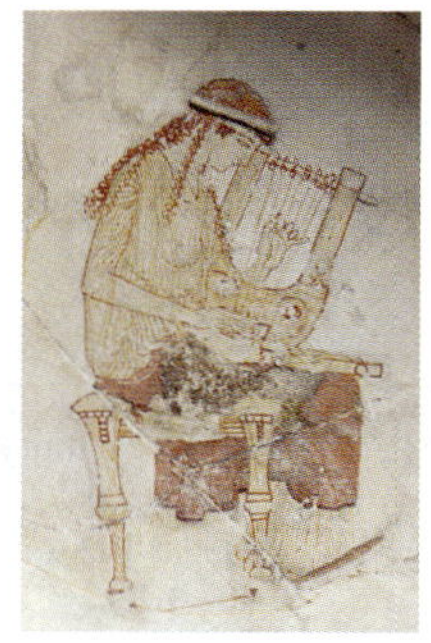
Playing a harp, illustration on a vessel, Greece, fifth century BCE

Pipe players, 14th century haggada

13 **They spend their days in prosperity, and** even when it is
time for them to die, **they descend to the grave in a moment,**
quickly and painlessly, without suffering or experiencing severe
illnesses.[372]
14 **They say to God: Turn away from us;** we are not interested in
You, and **we do not desire the knowledge of Your ways.**
15 **What is the Almighty that we should serve Him? What**
good will it do if we encounter Him, pray to Him?
16 **Behold,** in actual fact, **their prosperity is not in their hand,**
as it is God who has granted them their good life,[373] and therefore, **the fate of the wicked is obscure to me.** I cannot fathom
it.[374]
17 **How often is the lamp of the wicked extinguished, does**
their calamity come upon them, does He deal out their por-
tion in His wrath? It is a rare occurrence that the wicked receive
their due punishment.[375]
18 How often[376] **are they like**
straw blown **before the**
wind, and like chaff the
storm carried off?
19 If you claim that **God re-**
serves for his children
his wickedness, as He will
punish the children of the
wicked for their father's evil deeds,[377] in that case God's judgment is hidden from the wicked and his associates who are
aware of his sins. Rather, **let Him pay it to him,** the evildoer
himself, **and he will know.** It would be preferable for God to
punish the wicked one himself.[378]

Chaff blowing in the wind

20 **Let his** own **eyes see his destruction,**[379] **and let him drink**
from the fury of the Almighty. It would be better for the wicked one himself to experience God's wrath.[380]
21 **For what does he care for his household after him?** He does
not know what will happen to his descendants after his death.
If the punishment is meted out to his children after he is gone,
he himself will have been untouched by retribution and will not
have learned anything from it, as **the number of his months,**
his life span, **is defined,** determined in advance, and he has not
been harmed.[381]
22 Job offers another argument: **Will anyone teach knowledge**
to God? It is He who judges from the heights. Alternatively,
can anyone teach the knowledge of God's ways, seeing that He
judges in accordance with principles beyond understanding?[382]
How can you assume to explain God's lofty ways?
23 **This one,** one person, **dies**
in his full vigor, without his
body having been smitten,[383]
tranquil[384] **and serene,**
24 **his udders filled with**
milk, and the marrow of
his bones moistened.[385]

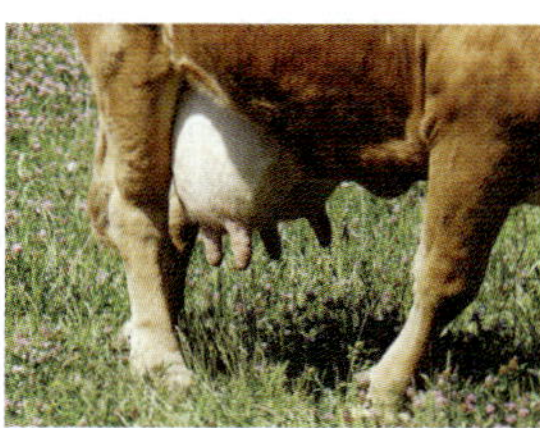
Udders of a cow

ה ו תִּקְצַר רוּחִי׃ פְּנוּ־אֵלַי וְהָשַׁמּוּ וְשִׂימוּ יָד עַל־פֶּה׃ וְאִם־זָכַרְתִּי וְנִבְהָלְתִּי וְאָחַז
ז ח בְּשָׂרִי פַּלָּצוּת׃ מַדּוּעַ רְשָׁעִים יִחְיוּ עָתְקוּ גַּם־גָּבְרוּ חָיִל׃ זַרְעָם נָכוֹן לִפְנֵיהֶם עִמָּם
ט י וְצֶאֱצָאֵיהֶם לְעֵינֵיהֶם׃ בָּתֵּיהֶם שָׁלוֹם מִפָּחַד וְלֹא שֵׁבֶט אֱלוֹהַּ עֲלֵיהֶם׃ שׁוֹרוֹ עִבַּר
יא וְלֹא יַגְעִל תְּפַלֵּט פָּרָתוֹ וְלֹא תְשַׁכֵּל׃ יְשַׁלְּחוּ כַצֹּאן עֲוִילֵיהֶם וְיַלְדֵיהֶם יְרַקֵּדוּן׃
יב יג יִשְׂאוּ כְּתֹף וְכִנּוֹר וְיִשְׂמְחוּ לְקוֹל עוּגָב׃ יבלו בַטּוֹב יְמֵיהֶם וּבְרֶגַע שְׁאוֹל יֵחָתּוּ׃ יְכַלּוּ
יד טו וַיֹּאמְרוּ לָאֵל סוּר מִמֶּנּוּ וְדַעַת דְּרָכֶיךָ לֹא חָפָצְנוּ׃ מַה־שַּׁדַּי כִּי־נַעַבְדֶנּוּ וּמַה־
טז יז נּוֹעִיל כִּי נִפְגַּע־בּוֹ׃ הֵן לֹא בְיָדָם טוּבָם עֲצַת רְשָׁעִים רָחֲקָה מֶנִּי׃ כַּמָּה ׀ נֵר־
יח רְשָׁעִים יִדְעָךְ וְיָבֹא עָלֵימוֹ אֵידָם חֲבָלִים יְחַלֵּק בְּאַפּוֹ׃ יִהְיוּ כְּתֶבֶן לִפְנֵי־רוּחַ
יט כ וּכְמֹץ גְּנָבַתּוּ סוּפָה׃ אֱלוֹהַּ יִצְפֹּן־לְבָנָיו אוֹנוֹ יְשַׁלֵּם אֵלָיו וְיֵדָע׃ יִרְאוּ עֵינָו כִּידוֹ
כא כב וּמֵחֲמַת שַׁדַּי יִשְׁתֶּה׃ כִּי מַה־חֶפְצוֹ בְּבֵיתוֹ אַחֲרָיו וּמִסְפַּר חֳדָשָׁיו חֻצָּצוּ׃ הַלְאֵל
כג כד יְלַמֶּד־דָּעַת וְהוּא רָמִים יִשְׁפּוֹט׃ זֶה יָמוּת בְּעֶצֶם תֻּמּוֹ כֻּלּוֹ שַׁלְאֲנַן וְשָׁלֵיו׃ עֲטִינָיו
כה כו מָלְאוּ חָלָב וּמֹחַ עַצְמוֹתָיו יְשֻׁקֶּה׃ וְזֶה יָמוּת בְּנֶפֶשׁ מָרָה וְלֹא־אָכַל בַּטּוֹבָה׃ יַחַד
כז עַל־עָפָר יִשְׁכָּבוּ וְרִמָּה תְּכַסֶּה עֲלֵיהֶם׃ הֵן יָדַעְתִּי מַחְשְׁבוֹתֵיכֶם וּמְזִמּוֹת עָלַי

Blessings rest both upon what emerges from his body and his insides.

25 **And that one,** another individual, **dies with an embittered soul and has never tasted goodness.** One might conclude that the first person was righteous, while the second was wicked.

26 However, there is no difference between their ultimate fates, as **together they lie in the dust, and maggots**[B] **cover them.** They are both buried in the ground, and their flesh is consumed by worms.

27 **Behold, I know your thoughts, and** I am aware of **the schemes that you devise against me,**

Maggots

BACKGROUND

21:12| **Drum:** A percussion instrument (see Exodus 15:20) that is used even nowadays to provide rhythm in songs and dance. This drum is fashioned from a circular wooden frame over which the skin of an animal or sometimes even that of a fish is stretched and glued or tied. Metal disks are often attached to the frame, and they jingle when the instrument is shaken. The drum is carried by hand, and the player taps on it with his fingers.

Harp: This was a symmetrical string instrument with a thick wooden base. Horns were attached at its two sides, a pole ran across the top from one horn to the other, and strings were stretched from the pole at the top to the base. Over time, the horns were replaced with wood, but the basic form of the harp has been preserved. The precise number of strings on the harp depends on the particular instrument, but ranges from three to ten.

21:26| **Maggots:** This refers to the larvae stage of development of various insects after they hatch. The larvae are sustained from rotting flesh, and therefore they grow in corpses.

28 **when you say: Where is the house of the wealthy?**[386] **And where is the tent of the dwelling of the wicked?** You wonder how the beautiful house of the wealthy Job, whom you consider wicked, has become a ruin.
29 **Haven't you asked** these questions of **the passersby? You do not recognize their signs.** You do not understand the signs they give in response.[387] You ignore the answers of those who understand events in the world at large.
30 **For evil is reserved for the day of calamity; they will be brought on for the day of ire.** His punishments accumulate and will be administered on the day of his calamity; his recompense will be brought forth on the day of wrath.[388]
31 **But who will tell his way to his face; when he acts, who will repay him?** Who is able to rebuke the wicked for his misdeeds and administer his punishment to him?[389]
32 Even in his death, **he,** the wicked, **will be brought to burial and he will be hastened to a mound [*gadish*].** He is buried quickly and ceremoniously in his dignified burial plot, which is raised high like a pile of grain [*gadish*].[390]
33 **The streamside earth,** where he is buried, **is sweet to him; following him** to death **are all men, and** likewise **before him, innumerable** men passed away.[391]
34 Since there is no evident causal relationship between a person's conduct and his fate, **how do you comfort me with futility? Of your answers, treachery remains.**

Elifaz's Third Speech

JOB 22:1–30

After Job has criticized his friends and their vain attempts to console him, Elifaz sharpens his message in the next round of speeches. He begins by rebuking Job for his audacious demand that God answer him. He continues by directly and bluntly accusing Job of committing severe transgressions. Finally, he concludes on an optimistic note, by reminding Job of the possibility of repentance. He declares that if Job chooses this path, he will be saved and will even be given the chance to have a positive impact on the welfare of others.

22 1 **Elifaz the Temanite answered and said:**
2 **Can a man be of use**[392] **to God? Rather, let the sensible man be of use to himself.** He who is wise is profitable only to himself.[393] Elifaz is saying to Job: God derives no benefit from speaking with you.
3 **Is it out of the Almighty's desire that you are righteous and is there profit** to Him **if you make your ways whole,** straighten your ways?
4 **Does He rebuke you from His fear of you, entering into judgment with you?** Is it from fear of you that He contends with you? God has no need to respond to your arguments.
5 After many insinuations, Elifaz finally levels a direct, blunt indictment: **Isn't your wickedness great, and there is no end to your iniquities?**
6 **For you take collateral**[394] **from your brother for naught,** undeservedly, by force, **and you strip** the last **garments of the naked** and leave them bare.[395]
7 **No water to the thirsty do you give to drink, and from the hungry you withhold bread.**
8 **A violent** and mighty **man, the earth is his;** you gave him land. **And a man of favor will live in it.** An important man of rank, or one whose debts you forgave in judgment, dwells in the land.[396] This indicates that Job served as a judge, and the fate of those who came before him for judgment was sealed by his word.[397]
9 **Widows,** who do not have the power to sue their oppressors, **you dispatched empty-handed,** leaving them destitute, **and the arms,** the strength, **of the orphans,** who also have no one to defend them, **you oppressed.**[398]
10 **Therefore, there are snares all around you, and sudden fear terrifies you,**
11 **or darkness, you cannot see, and a torrent of water covers you.** In your darkness, you cannot perceive the truth, as you are covered by an abundance of waters, your pain.[399]
12 Therefore, you err in thinking: **Isn't God** located **at the apex of heaven? See the height of the stars, how lofty they are.** The distance between God and myself is so great that He does not pay any attention to me at all.[400]
13 **You say: What does God know? Can He judge through the fog?** Is God aware of what is happening beyond the fog? Under the cover of haze and distance, I can do as I please.
14 You suppose that **clouds obscure for Him and** therefore **He does not see; in the circuit**[401] **of the heavens He makes His way.** Therefore, when He is on the side that is far from me, He cannot see me.
15 **Will you keep** and remember **the eternal path**[402] **upon which men of evil have trodden?**
16 These are wicked men **who were eliminated**[403] **before their time,** in their youth, **a river poured for their foundation.** Alternatively, these are wicked men whose foundation, even in their lifetime, was unstable and poured out like a stream, or melted away.[404]
17 These are wicked men **who say to God: Turn away from us** and do not interfere with our lives. **How will the Almighty act toward them?** They mistakenly think that God does not affect their lives at all.
18 **And** yet **He filled their houses with good.** Elifaz adds: **May the counsel of the wicked be distant from me.** I want no part of it.[405]

תַּחְמֹסוּ׃ כִּי תֹאמְרוּ אַיֵּה בֵית־נָדִיב וְאַיֵּה אֹהֶל ׀ מִשְׁכְּנוֹת רְשָׁעִים׃ הֲלֹא שְׁאֶלְתֶּם כח כט
עוֹבְרֵי דָרֶךְ וְאֹתֹתָם לֹא תְנַכֵּרוּ׃ כִּי לְיוֹם אֵיד יֵחָשֶׂךְ רָע לְיוֹם עֲבָרוֹת יוּבָלוּ׃ ל
מִי־יַגִּיד עַל־פָּנָיו דַּרְכּוֹ וְהוּא־עָשָׂה מִי יְשַׁלֶּם־לוֹ׃ וְהוּא לִקְבָרוֹת יוּבָל וְעַל־גָּדִישׁ לא לב
יִשְׁקוֹד׃ מָתְקוּ־לוֹ רִגְבֵי נָחַל וְאַחֲרָיו כָּל־אָדָם יִמְשׁוֹךְ וּלְפָנָיו אֵין מִסְפָּר׃ וְאֵיךְ לג לד
תְּנַחֲמוּנִי הָבֶל וּתְשׁוּבֹתֵיכֶם נִשְׁאַר־מָעַל׃ וַיַּעַן אֱלִיפַז הַתֵּמָנִי כב א
וַיֹּאמַר׃ הַלְאֵל יִסְכָּן־גָּבֶר כִּי־יִסְכֹּן עָלֵימוֹ מַשְׂכִּיל׃ הַחֵפֶץ לְשַׁדַּי כִּי תִצְדָּק וְאִם־ ב ג
בֶּצַע כִּי־תַתֵּם דְּרָכֶיךָ׃ הֲמִיִּרְאָתְךָ יֹכִיחֶךָ יָבוֹא עִמְּךָ בַּמִּשְׁפָּט׃ הֲלֹא רָעָתְךָ רַבָּה ד ה
וְאֵין־קֵץ לַעֲוֹנֹתֶיךָ׃ כִּי־תַחְבֹּל אַחֶיךָ חִנָּם וּבִגְדֵי עֲרוּמִּים תַּפְשִׁיט׃ לֹא־מַיִם עָיֵף ו ז
תַּשְׁקֶה וּמֵרָעֵב תִּמְנַע־לָחֶם׃ וְאִישׁ זְרוֹעַ לוֹ הָאָרֶץ וּנְשׂוּא פָנִים יֵשֶׁב בָּהּ׃ אַלְמָנוֹת ח ט
שִׁלַּחְתָּ רֵיקָם וּזְרֹעוֹת יְתֹמִים יְדֻכָּא׃ עַל־כֵּן סְבִיבוֹתֶיךָ פַחִים וִיבַהֶלְךָ פַּחַד פִּתְאֹם׃ י
אוֹ־חֹשֶׁךְ לֹא־תִרְאֶה וְשִׁפְעַת־מַיִם תְּכַסֶּךָּ׃ הֲלֹא־אֱלוֹהַּ גֹּבַהּ שָׁמָיִם וּרְאֵה רֹאשׁ יא יב
כּוֹכָבִים כִּי־רָמּוּ׃ וְאָמַרְתָּ מַה־יָּדַע אֵל הַבְעַד עֲרָפֶל יִשְׁפּוֹט׃ עָבִים סֵתֶר־לוֹ וְלֹא יג יד
יִרְאֶה וְחוּג שָׁמַיִם יִתְהַלָּךְ׃ הַאֹרַח עוֹלָם תִּשְׁמוֹר אֲשֶׁר דָּרְכוּ מְתֵי־אָוֶן׃ אֲשֶׁר־ טו טז
קֻמְּטוּ וְלֹא־עֵת נָהָר יוּצַק יְסוֹדָם׃ הָאֹמְרִים לָאֵל סוּר מִמֶּנּוּ וּמַה־יִּפְעַל שַׁדַּי יז
לָמוֹ׃ וְהוּא מִלֵּא בָתֵּיהֶם טוֹב וַעֲצַת רְשָׁעִים רָחֲקָה מֶנִּי׃ יִרְאוּ צַדִּיקִים וְיִשְׂמָחוּ יח יט
וְנָקִי יִלְעַג־לָמוֹ׃ אִם־לֹא נִכְחַד קִימָנוּ וְיִתְרָם אָכְלָה אֵשׁ׃ הַסְכֶּן־נָא עִמּוֹ וּשְׁלֹם כ כא
בָּהֶם תְּבוֹאַתְךָ טוֹבָה׃ קַח־נָא מִפִּיו תּוֹרָה וְשִׂים אֲמָרָיו בִּלְבָבֶךָ׃ אִם־תָּשׁוּב כב כג
עַד־שַׁדַּי תִּבָּנֶה תַּרְחִיק עַוְלָה מֵאָהֳלֶךָ׃ וְשִׁית־עַל־עָפָר בָּצֶר וּבְצוּר נְחָלִים כד

19 By contrast, **may the righteous see it,** the downfall of the wicked, **and rejoice, and the pure mock them,** those who imagine that they are not dependent upon God.

20 The righteous say as follows: **Surely, they who would rise against us [*kimanu*] have been annihilated.** Alternatively, surely our existence [*kiyumenu*], that is, our dwelling place, has not been destroyed.[406] Another interpretation: If we, the innocent, have not been eliminated, it is because God has sustained us [*kiyemanu*].[407] **And** by contrast, **those who are left of them,** the wicked, **fire has consumed.**

21 **Please, attune yourself to Him,** accustom yourself to following God's ways,[408] **and** then you will **be complete,** whole; **thereby,** through such behavior, **goodness will come upon you.**[409]

22 **Please receive Torah from His mouth, and place His sayings in your heart.**

23 **If you return to the Almighty,** then **you will be built up; you will distance injustice from your tents**

24 **and** then you will become so wealthy[410] that you **will set your treasure,** precious commodities,[411] perhaps a collection of

highly valuable minerals, **on the dust, and the** valuable **gold of Ofir**[B] **among the stones of ravines,** in an unprotected spot.[412]
25 **The Almighty will be with,** will protect, **your treasures.** Alternatively, the Almighty will fight your enemies.[413] **And** a **vast** [***to'afot***] amount of **silver will be yours.**[414] Alternatively, silver will fly [*ya'uf*] to you.[415]
26 **For then you will delight in the Almighty, and you will lift your face to God.**
27 **You will pray to Him, and He will hear you, and you will fulfill your vows** when He fulfills your wishes.
28 **You will decide something, and** God will ensure that **He will fulfill it for you, and light will shine upon your ways.** You will be successful in all your endeavors.
29 **With the downtrodden,** when you see people who are downtrodden,[416] **you will** promise them[417] and **say: There will be exaltation,**[418] **as** you know that **He saves the humble** person, the miserable.[419]
30 It will then be in your merit[420] that **He will rescue the impure, and he,** the sinner, **will escape by,** due to, **the cleanness of your hands.** Elifaz's speech is rather scathing, but he ends by reminding Job that he can still amend his ways. His main point is that if someone acts in a sinful manner, thinking that he can hide from God, he will be severely punished. However, if he repents and turns to God, he will receive goodness and blessing. He therefore tells Job: Everything depends upon your actions, and you should not blame God for your fate.

Job's Third Response to Elifaz

JOB 23:1–24:25

At the start of this response, Job addresses the opening of Elifaz's speech. He complains that God remains hidden and also asks God to conduct a trial directly with him. Job continues by disputing both aspects of Elifaz's claim about divine justice: First Job argues that he is suffering despite the fact that he is righteous, and then he asserts that there are wicked individuals who live comfortable lives.

23 1 **Job answered and said:**
2 **Today too,** after hearing your speech,[421] **my discourse is bitter;**[422] **the hand against me is heavier than my groaning.** My afflictions are heavier than my groaning.[423] I cannot adequately express the extent of my suffering.
3 **If only I could know** God **and find Him, I would come up to His seat,** the place where He resides.[424]
4 **I would organize my case before Him and fill my mouth with arguments** pertaining to my current condition. I am not afraid to enter a trial with God, but currently I cannot present my arguments before Him.
5 **I would know,** comprehend, **the words that He would answer me, and I would understand what He would say to me.**
6 **Would He quarrel with me in His great power,** in a power struggle whose outcome is a foregone conclusion? **No; rather, He would invigorate me.** He would grant me the strength to stand before Him in judgment.[425]
7 **There,** in the court of justice,[426] **I would argue with Him uprightly,** or directly, **and I would escape** from **my judgment forever.**
8 **Behold, I go forward,** or eastward,[427] **but He is not there,** I cannot find Him, **and** I go **backward,** or westward,[428] **but I do not perceive Him,** or His location;[429]
9 **to the left,** the north,[430] **when He acts, but I do not behold Him,** I cannot perceive His works:[431] **He hides**[432] **on the right,** the south,[433] **and I do not see Him.**
10 Whichever direction I turn I cannot reach Him. He hides,[434] **for He knows the way that was with me,** that the path I was on was good; **when He tries me,** even by inflicting great suffering upon me, **I will emerge** pure **like gold.**
11 **My foot held fast to His steps.**[435] I have followed God's path. **I kept His way, and I did not diverge** from it.
12 **From the commandment of His lips I would not move.** I have loyally observed His commandments.[436] **It was my practice to treasure the sayings of His mouth.** I have habitually guarded the words of His mouth.[437]
13 **He is of one mind,** or He follows His one path, His own path, **and who can respond to Him** and dispute with Him? **His soul desires and He does.** Anything that God wants He can make happen.
14 **For He will complete my portion,** the suffering He has decreed for me; **there are many like that,** the retributions that He desires, **with Him.**
15 **Therefore, I am panic-stricken at His presence; I consider, and I fear Him.**

BACKGROUND

22:24| **Ofir:** There are three main opinions with regard to the location of this place, which was renowned as a source of high-quality gold: East Africa, southern Arabia, or India. It has been suggested that the very name Africa is derived from the name Ofir.

24:5| **Onagers in the wilderness:** Onagers that live in the wilderness (see commentary on 6:5) never cease searching for their food, the sparse desert vegetation, especially during the hot desert summers.

אוֹפִֽיר׃ וְהָיָ֣ה שַׁדַּ֣י בְּצָרֶ֑יךָ וְכֶ֖סֶף תּוֹעָפ֣וֹת לָֽךְ׃ כִּי־אָ֖ז עַל־שַׁדַּ֣י תִּתְעַנָּ֑ג וְתִשָּׂ֖א כה כו
אֶל־אֱל֣וֹהַּ פָּנֶֽיךָ׃ תַּעְתִּ֣יר אֵ֭לָיו וְיִשְׁמָעֶ֑ךָּ וּנְדָרֶ֥יךָ תְשַׁלֵּֽם׃ וְֽתִגְזַר־א֭וֹמֶר וְיָ֣קָם לָ֑ךְ כז כח
וְעַל־דְּ֝רָכֶ֗יךָ נָ֣גַהּ אֽוֹר׃ כִּֽי־הִ֭שְׁפִּילוּ וַתֹּ֣אמֶר גֵּוָ֑ה וְשַׁ֖ח עֵינַ֣יִם יוֹשִֽׁעַ׃ יְֽמַלֵּ֥ט אִֽי־נָקִ֑י ה כט ל
וְ֝נִמְלַ֗ט בְּבֹ֣ר כַּפֶּֽיךָ׃ וַיַּ֥עַן אִיּ֗וֹב וַיֹּאמַֽר׃ גַּם־הַ֭יּוֹם מְרִ֣י שִׂחִ֑י יָ֝דִ֗י א ב
כָּבְדָ֥ה עַל־אַנְחָתִֽי׃ מִֽי־יִתֵּ֣ן יָ֭דַעְתִּי וְאֶמְצָאֵ֑הוּ אָ֝ב֗וֹא עַד־תְּכוּנָתֽוֹ׃ אֶעֶרְכָ֣ה לְפָנָ֣יו ג ד
מִשְׁפָּ֑ט וּ֝פִ֗י אֲמַלֵּ֥א תוֹכָחֽוֹת׃ אֵ֭דְעָה מִלִּ֣ים יַעֲנֵ֑נִי וְ֝אָבִ֗ינָה מַה־יֹּ֥אמַר לִֽי׃ הַבְּרָב־ ה ו
כֹּ֭חַ יָרִ֣יב עִמָּדִ֑י לֹ֥א אַךְ־ה֝֗וּא יָ֣שִׂם בִּֽי׃ שָׁ֗ם יָ֭שָׁר נוֹכָ֣ח עִמּ֑וֹ וַ֝אֲפַלְּטָ֗ה לָ֝נֶ֗צַח מִשֹּׁפְטִֽי׃ ז
הֵ֤ן קֶ֣דֶם אֶהֱלֹ֣ךְ וְאֵינֶ֑נּוּ וְ֝אָח֗וֹר וְֽלֹא־אָבִ֥ין לֽוֹ׃ שְׂמֹ֣אול בַּעֲשֹׂת֣וֹ וְלֹא־אָ֑חַז יַעְטֹ֥ף ח ט
יָ֝מִ֗ין וְלֹ֣א אֶרְאֶֽה׃ כִּֽי־יָ֭דַע דֶּ֣רֶךְ עִמָּדִ֑י בְּ֝חָנַ֗נִי כַּזָּהָ֥ב אֵצֵֽא׃ בַּ֭אֲשֻׁרוֹ אָחֲזָ֣ה רַגְלִ֑י י יא
דַּרְכּ֖וֹ שָׁמַ֣רְתִּי וְלֹא־אָֽט׃ מִצְוַ֣ת שְׂ֭פָתָיו וְלֹ֣א אָמִ֑ישׁ מֵ֝חֻקִּ֗י צָפַ֥נְתִּי אִמְרֵי־פִֽיו׃ יב
וְה֣וּא בְ֭אֶחָד וּמִ֣י יְשִׁיבֶ֑נּוּ וְנַפְשׁ֖וֹ אִוְּתָ֣ה וַיָּֽעַשׂ׃ כִּ֭י יַשְׁלִ֣ים חֻקִּ֑י וְכָהֵ֖נָּה רַבּ֣וֹת עִמּֽוֹ׃ יג יד
עַל־כֵּ֭ן מִפָּנָ֣יו אֶבָּהֵ֑ל אֶ֝תְבּוֹנֵ֗ן וְאֶפְחַ֥ד מִמֶּֽנּוּ׃ וְ֭אֵל הֵרַ֣ךְ לִבִּ֑י וְ֝שַׁדַּ֗י הִבְהִילָֽנִי׃ כִּי־לֹ֣א טו טז יז
נִ֭צְמַתִּי מִפְּנֵי־חֹ֑שֶׁךְ וּ֝מִפָּנַ֗י כִּסָּה־אֹֽפֶל׃ מַדּ֗וּעַ מִ֭שַּׁדַּי לֹא־נִצְפְּנ֣וּ עִתִּ֑ים א
וְ֝יֹדְעָ֗ו לֹא־חָ֥זוּ יָמָֽיו׃ גְּבֻל֥וֹת יַשִּׂ֑יגוּ עֵ֥דֶר גָּ֝זְל֗וּ וַיִּרְעֽוּ׃ חֲמ֣וֹר יְתוֹמִ֣ים יִנְהָ֑גוּ יַ֝חְבְּל֗וּ ב ג
שׁ֣וֹר אַלְמָנָֽה׃ יַטּ֣וּ אֶבְיֹנִ֣ים מִדָּ֑רֶךְ יַ֥חַד חֻ֝בְּא֗וּ ענוי־אָֽרֶץ׃ הֵ֤ן פְּרָאִ֨ים ׀ בַּמִּדְבָּ֗ר יָֽצְא֣וּ עֲנִיֵּי־ ד ה
בְּ֭פָעֳלָם מְשַׁחֲרֵ֣י לַטָּ֑רֶף עֲרָבָ֥ה ל֥וֹ לֶ֝֗חֶם לַנְּעָרִֽים׃ בַּ֭שָּׂדֶה בְּלִיל֣וֹ יקצירו וְכֶ֖רֶם יִקְצ֑וֹרוּ ו

16 **God has made my heart faint, and the Almighty has caused me to panic,**

17 **for I was not** utterly **annihilated**[438] **before the darkness** and suffering that befell me,[439] **nor**[440] **did blackness conceal** the horrors of retribution **from my face.** He kept me alive to experience all this pain.

24 1 **Why are times not concealed from the Almighty?** Why shouldn't one think that events are hidden from God? **Those who know Him cannot foresee His days.** After all, even those who know Him, who should be able to explain divine providence, are unable to do so.[441]

2 **They,** wicked individuals, **move boundaries** in order to expropriate land; **they steal a flock and shepherd it** in fields that do not belong to them, for their own benefit.[442]

3 **They drive the donkey of orphans,** which they appropriate for themselves; they **take as collateral the ox of a widow,** in violation of the Torah's command: "You shall not take a widow's garment as collateral."[443]

4 **They** impose their fear on the weak, and thereby **turn the indigent from the way; together, the poor of the land hide.**

5 **Behold, like onagers** that live **in the wilderness,**[B] **they go out to their tasks, seeking prey; the desert is his, food for the young.**[444] The wicked are compared to wild donkeys because they are violent and uninhibited.[445] They prefer to derive their sustenance in the unprotected wilderness, where they can rob passersby, rather than in civilized regions.[446]

6 **They,** the wild asses, that is, the wicked, **reap in the field at night** [*belilo*],[447] **and the wicked harvest the vineyard.** Some

claim that *belilo* is a contraction of *beli lo*, meaning not theirs, implying that they harvest the grain of others.[448]

7 **They have them pass the night naked without clothing, and there is no covering in the cold.** The wicked take from the poor everything they have, including their clothing,[449] leaving them lying naked, with no covering at all.

8 **They,** the poor, **are soaked by the streams of the mountains,** the waters that flow from the mountains, **and they embrace the rock for lack of shelter.** Since the poor lack basic shelter, they have no choice but to press themselves against rocks for some degree of protection.[450]

9 **They snatch an orphan from the breast** of his mother,[451] **and from upon the poor they take collateral,** by removing their very clothing from their bodies,

10 so that **they,** the poor, must **walk about naked, without clothing, and the hungry carry** to those oppressive wicked people **a sheaf** of grain.[452] These destitute individuals have to work for the evildoers, harvesting and transporting their crops while they themselves are starving.

11 **They,** the poor workers, **would make oil between their rows** of the olive groves belonging to these wicked men; **they have trodden** grapes in their **winepresses and are thirsty,** while the owners do not allow them to taste the beverages they themselves help to produce.[453]

Rows of olive trees

Treading grapes in a winepress, fresco on tomb wall, Egypt, fifteenth century BCE

12 **From a populated city they,** the poor and oppressed men,[454] or the residents of a conquered city, **groan, and the souls of the dead plead,** beseech for help; **but God does not treat it as indecency.** He does not see anything improper in their situation.[455]

13 **These** wicked men **were among the rebels against** God, **the** source of **light,** goodness, and truth;[456] **they did not recognize His ways, and they did not live by His paths.**

14 **The murderer would rise up in broad daylight, he would kill the poor and indigent,** as he does not accept the yoke of Heaven at all, **and at night he would be like a thief,** who surreptitiously carries out his nefarious acts.

15 **The eye of the adulterer,** who searches for a strange woman with whom he can sin, **awaits the night, saying: No eye will behold me, and he directs his glance clandestinely** toward her.[457]

16 **In the dark they burrow under** in order to break into **houses; during the day they conceal it; they know not light.** During the daylight hours, they cover up the area they dug in the previous night, so that no one will discover their evil plans. Alternatively, during the daytime they hide themselves so that no one will see them.[458]

17 **For them together, morning is the shadow of death, for they will be recognized; it is the terrors,** or the demons,[459] **of the shadow of death.** The morning is a frightful time for them, as they could be identified in the light of day.[460]

18 After describing the evil ways of the wicked, Job depicts the punishment they deserve:[461] **He will be light upon the surface of the water.** The wicked will not have any durable existence or honor; rather, it will be as though they are floating on the water. **Their portion in the land is cursed; no one will turn aside through the vineyards.** No one will turn to their vineyards, because they will be rendered impassable due to all the thorns that will sprout there.[462]

19 Just as **desolation as well as heat rob** and easily eradicate **snow water,** so does[463] **the grave** eliminate **those who** have **sinned.**

20 **The womb** of his mother **will forget him.**[464] The fate of the wicked will be like that of an aborted fetus. **He will be sweet for the maggots** in the ground;[465] **he will no longer be remembered, and** thus **injustice will be broken like a tree.**

21 **He consorts with the barren who will not give birth, and to the widow he will do no good.** The wicked individual will live with a barren woman, and after he dies he will leave her nothing for her livelihood.

22 However, despite their evil deeds, God supports the wicked: **He perpetuates the powerful in his strength.** God extends the lives of the mighty, wicked people.[466] **He,** each of them, **rises up, though he does not believe in life,** even if he reaches a point where he does not believe he will live.[467]

23 **He gives him security on which he relies,** God gives the wicked a crutch to support the wicked, **and His eyes are on their ways.** He watches and protects them.

ז ח רָשָׁע יְלַקֵּשׁוּ: עָרוֹם יָלִינוּ מִבְּלִי לְבוּשׁ וְאֵין כְּסוּת בַּקָּרָה: מִזֶּרֶם הָרִים יִרְטָבוּ
ט י וּמִבְּלִי מַחְסֶה חִבְּקוּ־צוּר: יִגְזְלוּ מִשֹּׁד יָתוֹם וְעַל־עָנִי יַחְבֹּלוּ: עָרוֹם הִלְּכוּ בְּלִי
יא יב לְבוּשׁ וּרְעֵבִים נָשְׂאוּ עֹמֶר: בֵּין־שׁוּרֹתָם יַצְהִירוּ יְקָבִים דָּרְכוּ וַיִּצְמָאוּ: מֵעִיר
יג מְתִים ׀ יִנְאָקוּ וְנֶפֶשׁ־חֲלָלִים תְּשַׁוֵּעַ וֶאֱלוֹהַּ לֹא־יָשִׂים תִּפְלָה: הֵמָּה ׀ הָיוּ בְּמֹרְדֵי
יד אוֹר לֹא־הִכִּירוּ דְרָכָיו וְלֹא יָשְׁבוּ בִּנְתִיבֹתָיו: לָאוֹר יָקוּם רוֹצֵחַ יִקְטָל־עָנִי וְאֶבְיוֹן
טו וּבַלַּיְלָה יְהִי כַגַּנָּב: וְעֵין נֹאֵף ׀ שָׁמְרָה נֶשֶׁף לֵאמֹר לֹא־תְשׁוּרֵנִי עָיִן וְסֵתֶר פָּנִים
טז יז יָשִׂים: חָתַר בַּחֹשֶׁךְ בָּתִּים יוֹמָם חִתְּמוּ־לָמוֹ לֹא־יָדְעוּ אוֹר: כִּי יַחְדָּו ׀ בֹּקֶר לָמוֹ
יח צַלְמָוֶת כִּי־יַכִּיר בַּלְהוֹת צַלְמָוֶת: קַל־הוּא ׀ עַל־פְּנֵי־מַיִם תְּקֻלַּל חֶלְקָתָם בָּאָרֶץ
יט כ לֹא־יִפְנֶה דֶּרֶךְ כְּרָמִים: צִיָּה גַם־חֹם יִגְזְלוּ מֵימֵי־שֶׁלֶג שְׁאוֹל חָטָאוּ: יִשְׁכָּחֵהוּ
כא רֶחֶם ׀ מְתָקוֹ רִמָּה עוֹד לֹא־יִזָּכֵר וַתִּשָּׁבֵר כָּעֵץ עַוְלָה: רֹעֶה עֲקָרָה לֹא תֵלֵד
כב כג וְאַלְמָנָה לֹא יְיֵטִיב: וּמָשַׁךְ אַבִּירִים בְּכֹחוֹ יָקוּם וְלֹא־יַאֲמִין בַּחַיִּין: יִתֶּן־לוֹ לָבֶטַח
כד וְיִשָּׁעֵן וְעֵינֵיהוּ עַל־דַּרְכֵיהֶם: רוֹמּוּ מְּעַט ׀ וְאֵינֶנּוּ וְהֻמְּכוּ כַּכֹּל יִקָּפְצוּן וּכְרֹאשׁ
ה כה א שִׁבֹּלֶת יִמָּלוּ: וְאִם־לֹא אֵפוֹ מִי יַכְזִיבֵנִי וְיָשֵׂם לְאַל מִלָּתִי: וַיַּעַן
ב ג בִּלְדַּד הַשֻּׁחִי וַיֹּאמַר: הַמְשֵׁל וָפַחַד עִמּוֹ עֹשֶׂה שָׁלוֹם בִּמְרוֹמָיו: הֲיֵשׁ מִסְפָּר
ד לִגְדוּדָיו וְעַל־מִי לֹא־יָקוּם אוֹרֵהוּ: וּמַה־יִּצְדַּק אֱנוֹשׁ עִם־אֵל וּמַה־יִּזְכֶּה יְלוּד

24 **If lifted for a while, they would be gone; lowered at all, they would be cut off and would wither like the top of the stalk.** Were the eyes of God to be lifted even briefly from the wicked, they would be gone; it is only God's special protection that sustains them.[468] If God's eyes were lowered from the wicked at all, they would be gathered in from their place and cut off,[469] and they would wither and be lost like the top of an ear of corn.[470]

25 **If it is indeed not so,** if my depiction of reality is incorrect, **who will** contradict me or **refute me and negate my word,** my comments?

Bildad's Third Speech

JOB 25:1–6

This short speech, like the earlier ones, is a critique of Job for his impudence in seeking to contest God's judgment.

25 1 **Bildad the Shuhite answered and said:**

2 **Dominion and fear are with Him.** God has supreme authority and power; therefore, He casts His awe upon all. **He** also **makes peace in His heights.**

3 **Is there a number to His troops?** The forces of God are unlimited. **On whom does His light not rise?**[471] No one can hide from Him.

4 **How, then, can man be vindicated** in his case **with God? Or how can one** who is **born of a woman be exonerated** in his

judgment with God? You cannot possibly emerge vindicated in your dispute with God.

5 **Behold,** in comparison with God's light, **even**[472] **the moon does not shine,**[473] **and the stars** and their light **are not pure in His eyes;**

6 **how much less so** pure and shining is **man, a maggot; the son of man,** who is **a worm.** A mere puny mortal, so much lower than those celestial bodies, should not open his mouth against God.

Job's Third Response to Bildad

JOB 26:1–14

Job refuses to acquiesce to Bildad's demand that he remain silent due to his insignificance in comparison with God's greatness. In this speech, Job reiterates to his friends that he recognizes God's greatness no less than they do. Furthermore, although he speaks of the wonders of creation, and of cosmic, powerful forces, he is aware that he can describe only a small part of the divine might. To a certain extent, Job continues from where Bildad left off; however, in contrast to Bildad's depiction of a harmonious world, Job chooses to portray creation and the greatness of the Creator in a stormy, raging, and mysterious fashion. It seems that this is Job's way of saying that there is no contradiction between his knowledge and awe of the astounding powers of God, and his right to argue his case before the Creator.

26 1 **Job answered and said:**

2 **How you have helped without power!** How can you claim to have helped, when you have no power? You have **saved with a powerless arm!** In what sense have you saved, when your arm is without strength?

3 **How you have counseled without wisdom;** you have sought to give counsel when you have no wisdom. **And** do you imagine that you **have shown much resourcefulness?**[474]

4 **To whom have you related** these **words?** For whom do you feel that your banal comments were considered a novelty?[475] **And whose spirit emerged from you?** What spirit rested upon you that enabled you to speak such lofty words of wisdom?[476] Job thus rejects Bildad's argument with sarcastic derision.

5 Job now provides his own description of God's greatness, power, and awe. **The dead**[477] **will tremble beneath the water and its dwellers,** in the netherworld.[478]

6 **The grave is bare,** exposed, **before Him, and destruction has no cover.** They are both clearly revealed before God.

7 **He spreads the north**[479] **over emptiness**[D] **and suspends the earth over nothingness.**[480] His creation is wondrous, and its essence is beyond all logic.

8 **He amasses water in His clouds, and the cloud does not burst due to it.** Despite the weight of the water they contain, the clouds do not burst open; rather, they let their water out in drops.

9 **He grasps the surface of His throne,** a metaphor for heaven,[481] **and spreads**[482] **His cloud over it,** His throne, the firmament in the sky.[483]

10 **He has circumscribed a boundary,** in the form of an encompassing line, **on the surface of the water.** God set a limit upon the sea so that its waters should not flood the land.[484] Alternatively, the boundary refers to the sky, which surrounds all the different bodies of waters in a great circle (22:14). This boundary reaches **until the far reaches of light and darkness,** the edges where light meets darkness, that is, the limits of reality.[485]

11 The world and all that it contains have no defense against Him: **The pillars of heaven sag,** are weakened, **and they are undermined by His castigation.**

12 **With His power, He has calmed the sea, and with His understanding, He crushed Rahav,** a kind of whale or sea monster which represents the forces of rebellion against God.[486]

13 **With His wind, the heavens are enhanced,** as God's spirit fixes the heavens;[487] **His hand has slain the bar serpent,**[D] Rahav, mentioned in the previous verse.[488] God creates mysterious, incomprehensible worlds, and He also strikes and destroys the forces of chaos.

14 **Behold, these** matters I spoke of here **are but the edges of His ways, and how** but **a trace** of His full greatness **is heard about Him.**[489] **Who can understand the** whole **thunder of His might** in all its power? No one can grasp the full might of God. Job accepts Bildad's claim about God's greatness and power, and goes even further, depicting those strengths of God that do not provide harmony on earth. Yet, while Bildad inferred from the reality of God's power that a human cannot emerge victorious in his contentions with the Divine, Job remains silent in that regard. It is clear from the context that his silence is a refusal to accept Bildad's conclusion. Job insists that his recognition of God's greatness does not mean that he must refrain from complaining. Perhaps Job is arguing that his friends, who have based their claims on wisdom, actually have limited access to true wisdom, which belongs to God alone. Nevertheless, it is also possible that in this speech, Job is less reactive to his friends. Rather, he is giving expression to his own confrontation with his current pitiful state. If so, then he is acknowledging the inability of human intelligence to find explanations for the unfathomable situation in which he finds himself.

ה ו אִשָּׁה: הֵן עַד־יָרֵחַ וְלֹא יַאֲהִיל וְכוֹכָבִים לֹא־זַכּוּ בְעֵינָיו: אַף כִּי־אֱנוֹשׁ רִמָּה
א ב וּבֶן־אָדָם תּוֹלֵעָה: וַיַּעַן אִיּוֹב וַיֹּאמַר: מֶה־עָזַרְתָּ לְלֹא־כֹחַ הוֹשַׁעְתָּ
ג ד זְרוֹעַ לֹא־עֹז: מַה־יָּעַצְתָּ לְלֹא חָכְמָה וְתֻשִׁיָּה לָרֹב הוֹדָעְתָּ: אֶת־מִי הִגַּדְתָּ מִלִּין
ה ו וְנִשְׁמַת־מִי יָצְאָה מִמֶּךָּ: הָרְפָאִים יְחוֹלָלוּ מִתַּחַת מַיִם וְשֹׁכְנֵיהֶם: עָרוֹם שְׁאוֹל
ז ח נֶגְדּוֹ וְאֵין כְּסוּת לָאֲבַדּוֹן: נֹטֶה צָפוֹן עַל־תֹּהוּ תֹּלֶה אֶרֶץ עַל־בְּלִימָה: צֹרֵר מַיִם
ט י בְּעָבָיו וְלֹא־נִבְקַע עָנָן תַּחְתָּם: מְאַחֵז פְּנֵי־כִסֵּה פַּרְשֵׁז עָלָיו עֲנָנוֹ: חֹק־חָג עַל־
יא פְּנֵי־מָיִם עַד־תַּכְלִית אוֹר עִם־חֹשֶׁךְ: עַמּוּדֵי שָׁמַיִם יְרוֹפָפוּ וְיִתְמְהוּ מִגַּעֲרָתוֹ:
יב יג בְּכֹחוֹ רָגַע הַיָּם ובתובנתו מָחַץ רָהַב: בְּרוּחוֹ שָׁמַיִם שִׁפְרָה חֹלֲלָה יָדוֹ נָחָשׁ וּבִתְבוּנָתוֹ
יד בָּרִחַ: הֶן־אֵלֶּה | קְצוֹת דְּרָכוֹ וּמַה־שֵּׁמֶץ דָּבָר נִשְׁמַע־בּוֹ וְרַעַם גְּבוּרֹתָו מִי

DISCUSSION

26:7 | **He spreads the north over emptiness:** In the Land of Israel and the surrounding areas, the north was often considered the most dark and mysterious area of the world, because the sun always appears on the southern side of the sky. This is the meaning of the statement of the Sages that the northern side of the world is not closed, so to speak (*Bava Batra* 25; *Pirkei deRabbi Eliezer* 3).

26:13 | **The bar serpent:** This mysterious creature is perhaps one of the *taninim*, the great serpents, mentioned in the Creation account (See Genesis 1:21, and Rashbam ad loc.; *Bava Batra* 74b). In Isaiah (27:1), the bar serpent is referred to as the leviathan bar serpent and mentioned along with the leviathan twisted serpent. In the prophetic and midrashic literature, these creatures fail to fit any zoological classification and instead represent primordial forces that exist somewhere in between the physical and metaphysical worlds. Although they are not necessarily evil, they prevent God from exercising His full dominion over the world (see *Targum*; Ezekiel 26:12–13, 40:25–32; *Sukka* 52a; *Kiddushin* 29b; *Bava Batra* 75a). Their description as creatures of the deep sea alludes to the mysteriousness in which they act. The prophet Isaiah foresees that at the end of days God will kill them, because they embody reality's persistent opposition to His dominion.

Job's First Speech

JOB 27:1–28:28

Since Tzofar did not reply to Job in this exchange, Job continues with two speeches that are called "orations," or "parables." The two orations, likely to have been two parts of a single speech, were possibly divided due to their length.[490] In the first oration, Job echoes his friends' comments on the bitter end of the wicked; the difference between Job's comments and those of his friends is that they have Job's fate in mind, whereas he alludes to the punishment that he believes awaits them. He then addresses the ability of people to investigate all materials and treasures of the world. He notes that wisdom, which is immeasurably more valuable than the riches of nature, is not in their hands. Rather, wisdom belongs to God, and man cannot truly comprehend it fully; he can only adjust himself to its guidelines by cleaving to God in fear and by turning away from evil.

27 1 **Job again took up his oration,** or parable, **and said:**

2 **As God lives,** I take an oath in the name of God, though **He has averted my justice, and the Almighty,** though He **has embittered my soul,**

3 **that as long as my soul is in me and the spirit of God is in my nostrils,** as long as I am alive,

4 **my lips will not speak injustice, and my tongue will not utter deceit.**

5 **Far be it from me to justify** the arguments **you** put forward, even though I confront a puzzle that I cannot solve; **until I expire, I will not set aside my virtuousness from myself.** I will not sin by agreeing with you, for if I confess to sins that I have not committed, I will have betrayed my integrity and impaired my ability to walk wholly with God.

6 **I have held on to my righteousness, and I will not relent; my heart has not shamed me,** I have not entertained any shameful thoughts,[491] **all my days.**

7 **Let my enemy be** considered **like the wicked, and they who oppose me like the unjust.** Job is speaking of the bitter end of the wicked. While his friends were alluding to him when they engaged in such talk, Job believes in his own righteousness, and refers to the harsh retribution that he believes awaits them.[492]

8 **For what is the hope of the hypocrite,** the wicked, **when he profits,** if he steals; after all, he will derive no benefit from his sin, **as God will disburden him of,** throw away,[493] **his life?**

9 **Will God hear his,** the wicked man's, **cry when trouble comes upon him?**

10 **Will he delight in the Almighty and call to God at all times?** Since the wicked man is not close to God, he will not merit His assistance.

11 **I will instruct you about the hand of God;** I can state that everything is entrusted into the hands of God; **I will not deny that it is with the Almighty.** God has power over all.

12 **Behold, all of you have seen it,** what goes on in the world; **why are you blathering this futility?** Why do you make such empty statements?

13 **This,** the punishment detailed below, **is the portion of a wicked person,** which is kept for him **with God and** it is **the lot that the mighty** ones **receive from the Almighty.**[494]

14 **If his children are many, it,** his progeny, **is for the sword, and his offspring will not have their fill of bread;** they will experience shortage and hunger.

15 **His survivors,** those who were not destroyed by the sword,[495] **will be buried by pestilence, and his widows will not cry,** as there will be no surviving widows, or because the widows will be too preoccupied with their own cares to mourn, or because their captors will not permit them to eulogize their late husbands.[496]

16 **If he,** the wicked, **amasses** much **silver, like dust,** which is accessible to all, **and assembles** a great deal of **garments, like** the plentiful **dirt** of the mountains,

17 **he will assemble** those garments, **but** it will be **the righteous** who **will don** them; **and of the silver** he amassed, **the innocent will partake,** receive.[497]

18 **He has built his house like** the thin cocoon of **a moth**[B] pupa. His house will be unstable and will not protect him, and it will be flimsy, **like a booth made by a watchman.**[B] Such booths were designed to last for only a brief period.

Booth near a vineyard

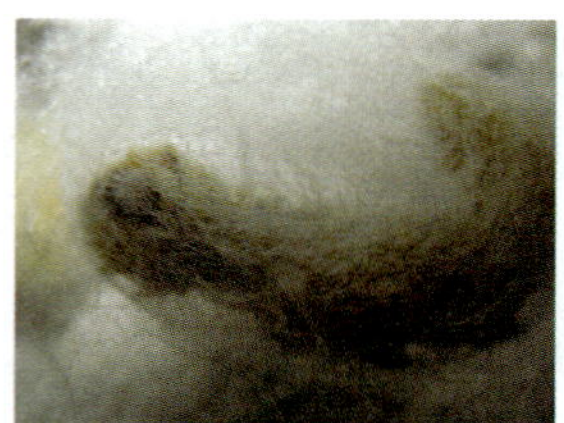
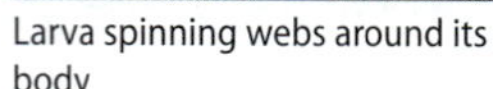
Larva spinning webs around its body

Moth breaking out of its cocoon

19 **He will lie down** due to illness when he is **rich, but he will not so die.** He will pass away without all his wealth,[498] for when **he has opened his eyes,** he is still alive, **and it is not.** His wealth is gone, as it has been plundered while he lay ill.

20 **Terrors,**[499] or demons and other harmful beings,[500] **will overtake him** and wash him away **like water; a storm abducts him at night.**

21 **The east wind will pick him up, and he will be gone; it,** the storm, **sweeps him from his place.**[501]

יתבונן: ויסף איוב שאת משלו ויאמר: חי־אל הסיר משפטי א ב
ושדי המר נפשי: כי־כל־עוד נשמתי בי ורוח אלוה באפי: אם־תדברנה שפתי ג ד
עולה ולשוני אם־יהגה רמיה: חלילה לי אם־אצדיק אתכם עד־אגוע לא־ ה
אסיר תמתי ממני: בצדקתי החזקתי ולא ארפה לא־יחרף לבבי מימי: יהי ו ז
כרשע איבי ומתקוממי כעול: כי מה־תקות חנף כי יבצע כי ישל אלוה נפשו: ח
הצעקתו ישמע ׀ אל כי־תבוא עליו צרה: אם־על־שדי יתענג יקרא אלוה ט י
בכל־עת: אורה אתכם ביד־אל אשר עם־שדי לא אכחד: הן אתם כלכם יא יב
חזיתם ולמה־זה הבל תהבלו: זה ׀ חלק־אדם רשע ׀ עם־אל ונחלת עריצים יג
משדי יקחו: אם־ירבו בניו למו־חרב וצאצאיו לא ישבעו־לחם: שרידיו במות יד טו
יקברו ואלמנתיו לא תבכינה: אם־יצבר כעפר כסף וכחמר יכין מלבוש: יכין טז יז
וצדיק ילבש וכסף נקי יחלק: בנה כעש ביתו וכסכה עשה נצר: עשיר ישכב יח יט
ולא יאסף עיניו פקח ואיננו: תשיגהו כמים בלהות לילה גנבתו סופה: ישאהו כ כא
קדים וילך וישערהו ממקמו: וישלך עליו ולא יחמל מידו ברוח יברח: ישפק כב כג

22 **He will cast upon him** His anger,[502] **and** will **have no compassion; it,** his wealth,[503] or he, the one who would previously help him,[504] **will flee from his hand.**

23 **He,** the wicked person, **will clap his hands over it** in a gesture of worry and sorrow, **and howl** and hiss in astonishment **over it,** his former helper or his lost wealth, **from his place.**

BACKGROUND

27:18| **He has built his house like a moth:** The larvae of many species of moth spin thin webs forming cocoons, in which they wrap themselves for their development as pupae. The cocoon serves as the larva's house during this stage. At the end of this developmental period, the adult moth easily tears open this cocoon and emerges from it. For more about the moth, see commentary on 4:19.

A booth made by a watchman: Booths are temporary structures made from branches, fieldstones, and foliage, which have been built since ancient times and are still used to this day. They were generally constructed for vineyard guards to use during the period in which grapes ripened; therefore, their use was seasonal and temporary. Occasionally, they were built to serve as shelters from the hot summer sun. In Israel, one can find square guard booths made of branches in the coastal regions and the plains, as well as round booths fashioned from fieldstones on hill slopes. The roofs of all such booths were constructed from leaves and plants, as is required for the booth known as the *sukka*, constructed for the festival of Sukkot.

28 1 Man can investigate the sources of precious materials, near and far: **For there is a source of silver,**[B] an area where silver is found or extracted, **and a place where gold is refined** from dross.

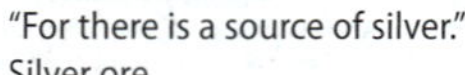
"For there is a source of silver." Silver ore

"And a place where gold is refined." Gold ore

2 **Iron is taken from the dust,**[B] **and copper is** similarly **smelted from rock.**[B] Pure copper is rare in nature. Rather, it is found in ore and then separated, refined, and melted.[505] Job is saying that practical human knowledge can reach far below the surface of the earth.

"Iron is taken from the dust." Red, iron-rich dust

"Copper is smelted from rock." Copper ore

3 **He,** man, **sets an end to darkness and investigates every end;** man's[506] search for knowledge encompasses even **the stone of thick darkness and the shadow of death,** which lie deep in the ground. Some commentaries explain that the subject of the verse is God.[507]
4 In order to expose hidden metals, **he,** man, **drives,** or digs, **a shaft** far **away from** inhabited areas, **habitation**[508] **which is forgotten by foot traffic,** where no one else travels, places **removed**[509] **from humanity,** abandoned by their former residents **who have moved on.**
5 There is the **earth, from which bread emerges.** What lies below it is concealed, but at times **its bowels are overturned as if by fire,** by an earthquake or a volcanic eruption.[510]
6 At such times, it is discovered that **its stones are a source of sapphires, and its dust has gold.**

"Its bowels are overturned as if by fire." Boiling lava in a volcanic crater

7 This is **a path** that is so far-flung and hidden that it is even **unknown by bird of prey,**[B] **and the eye of the buzzard**[B] **has not seen it,** despite the fact that it is a bird which can see from great distances;[511]

Bonelli's eagle

Eastern imperial eagle

European honey buzzard

8 **wild beasts**[512] **have not trodden it,** this path, **and the lion**[B] **did not find prey on it,** or tear its prey there.[513]
9 **He,** man, **extends his hand to the flinty rock,** or large boulder, and searches for metals and treasures of the ground; alternatively, the reference is to God, who undermines the supposedly unshakeable forces of nature;[514] **he overturns mountains from the root,**[D] from their foundations.

"Flinty rock"

10 **He breaks channels through the rocks, and his eye sees everything precious** that is hidden there. Here too, while some commentaries understand that this verse refers to God,[515] others explain that it refers to man.[516]
11 **He dams the depths of the rivers** with all the secrets hidden in them,[517] **and** thus **brings hidden** treasures swept away in the water[518] **to light** by uncovering them.
12 Natural treasures can be hidden deep inside the earth, far from civilization, or covered by water, and yet man can discover them following earthquakes or other dramatic events, as well

DISCUSSION

28:9 | **He extends his hand to the flinty rock; he overturns mountains from the root:** Some commentaries understand this description of transforming an inhabited area into a destroyed, desolate wasteland as an allusion to the destruction of Sodom and the cities of the plain (*Bereshit Rabba* 51:4).

א ב עלימו כפימו וישרק עליו ממקמו: כי יש לכסף מוצא ומקום לזהב יזקו: ברזל
ג מעפר יקח ואבן יצוק נחושה: קץ | שם לחשך ולכל-תכלית הוא חוקר אבן
ד ה אפל וצלמות: פרץ נחל | מעם-גר הנשכחים מני-רגל דלו מאנוש נעו: ארץ
ו ממנה יצא-לחם ותחתיה נהפך כמו-אש: מקום-ספיר אבניה ועפרת זהב לו:
ז ח נתיב לא-ידעו עיט ולא שזפתו עין איה: לא-הדריכוהו בני-שחץ לא-עדה
ט י עליו שחל: בחלמיש שלח ידו הפך משרש הרים: בצורות יארים בקע וכל-
יא יב יקר ראתה עינו: מבכי נהרות חבש ותעלמה יצא אור: והחכמה

BACKGROUND

28:1 | **For there is a source of silver:** No silver mines have been found in the region of Israel. Such mines are known only in the north and west, e.g., in Asia Minor and the Attica region of Greece (see Jeremiah 10:9). A small amount of silver can be extracted with difficulty during the process of refining gold.

28:2 | **Iron is taken from the dust:** Iron was extracted in a crucible in which iron ores were burned together with wood charcoal to purify them. After people smelted the ore, they would beat out the solid metal. In ancient times, iron ore was found in Asia Minor and in Ajloun, east of the Jordan. Minute quantities of iron from meteors that struck the earth have also been discovered. Extracting iron was hard work, evident from the fact that the land in which the Israelites were subjected to backbreaking labor, Egypt, is referred to as "the iron crucible" (e.g., Deuteronomy 4:20; Jeremiah 11:4).

Copper [*neḥoshet*] is smelted from rock: Copper, which bears a similar name in Phoenician, was the first metal that was extracted on a large scale by casting in crucibles. Most of the metal was brought from afar, from the mountains of Armenia, Asia Minor, and Cyprus, although modest amounts were also found in the Sinai Peninsula and in Timna in the Negev. Copper is a relatively soft metal.

28:7 | **Bird of prey [*ayit*]:** This is referring to a bird of prey from the Accipitridae family, specifically its subfamily Aegypiinae (see Genesis 15:11), including Bonelli's eagle and the eastern imperial eagle, which are found in Israel and the surrounding region. These birds fly high and have sharp vision.

Buzzard [*ayya*]: This bird has particularly sharp eyesight [*re'iya*] and can see from great distances. It is generally identified as the common buzzard, *Buteo buteo*, a nomadic bird of prey from the Accipitridae family, with a wingspan of about 120 cm and a weight of up to 900 g (Yehuda Felix, *The Animal World of the Bible*. Tel Aviv: Sinai, 1956 [Hebrew], 65). Alternatively, it is the European honey buzzard, *Pernis apivorus*, also a nomadic bird of prey from the Accipitridae family which is found in Israel. It is of medium size, with a body length of 53–58 cm, a wingspan of around 145 cm, and a weight of around 460–800 g.

28:8 | **Lion [*shaḥal*]:** There are six names for a lion in the Bible: *ari*, *kefir*, *lavi*, *layish*, *shaḥal*, and *shaḥatz* (see *Avot deRabbi Natan*, version I, 39). Some maintain that these many names correspond to different stages in the animal's appearance and development (Rashi; Radak). Others contend that the different terms refer to a variety of species of lion, which come from different lands of origin and which are distinguishable in their size and shape. It is also possible that the *shaḥal* and the *kefir* are snakes, or some other large animal (Naftali Herz Tur-Sinai, *Halashon Vehasefer* ["The Language and the Book"]: *Studies in Hebrew Language*, vol 1. Jerusalem: Bialik Institute 1959 [Hebrew], 380–382; see Psalms 91:13).

as through his own searches. **But** in contrast, when it comes to **wisdom, where will it be found? And where is the place of understanding?**

13 **Man does not know its value, and it is not found in the land of the living.**

14 **The deep says: It is not** located **in me; and the sea says: It is not with me.**

15 **One will not give gold in exchange for it.**[519] One cannot acquire wisdom by paying for it with gold, **and silver cannot be weighed as its price.**

16 **It cannot be assessed** or praised by comparison,[520] saying that it is **like gold** that comes from the land **of Ofir,**[521] or **like precious onyx or sapphire.**

Onyx

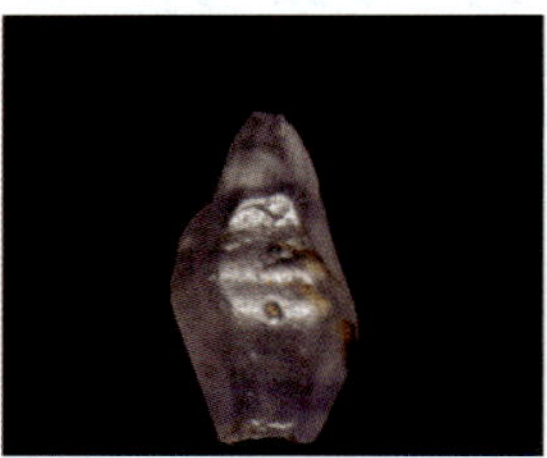
Sapphire crystal

17 **It cannot be valued like gold and glass [*zekhukhit*];**[B] its worth cannot be gauged by a comparison to these substances, **or its exchange be vessels of fine gold.**[522] *Zekhukhit* is perhaps a precious stone that is pure [*zaka*] or transparent; or possibly the *zekhukhit* of modern Hebrew, glass,[523] which was highly valuable in those days.

Glass vessel from the Cyclades, fourth century BCE

18 **Coral and crystal,** precious materials,[524] **will not be mentioned** in relation to wisdom; **the acquisition [*meshekh*] of wisdom is greater than pearls [*peninim*].** More effort is necessary to draw in [*limshokh*] and absorb wisdom than is used in acquiring pearls. *Peninim* might be a general term for round precious stones, or it might refer to pearls extracted from the shells of oysters. Pearls are *peninim* in modern Hebrew.[525]

Crystal

19 **It cannot be valued like the peridot of Kush,** a precious stone from Ethiopia; **it cannot be assessed like pure gold.**[526]

20 These wonderful natural treasures can be discovered through much toil and effort and then brought from distant lands. **But wisdom, from where will it come,** which as stated, is inestimably more valuable than such items? **And where is the place of understanding?**

Peridot

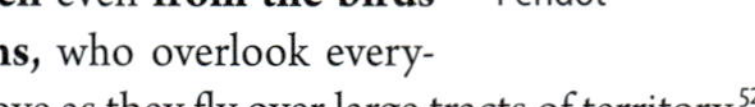

21 **It is vanished from the eyes of all living and hidden** even **from the birds of the heavens,** who overlook everything from above as they fly over large tracts of territory.[527]

22 **Destruction and death,** which exist on the margins of reality, **say: We have heard** only **a rumor with our ears,** but it is not in our midst.

23 **God** alone **understands its,** wisdom's, **way, and** only **He knows its place.**

24 **For He gazes to the ends of the earth, and that which is beneath all the heavens He sees;** nothing is hidden from His gaze.

25 He uses wisdom **to set the calibration of the wind,** as He measures the appropriate speed and strength of the wind in every place,[528] **and** to **allocate water by measure,**

26 **in setting an allotment,** an arrangement and plan, **for the rain, and** in making **a way for lightning and thunder.**[529]

27 **Then He,** who knows all these matters, **saw and quantified it,** wisdom; He was exacting in its size and details,[530] or: He formulated it in a book of instructions,[531] **prepared it, and also investigated it.**

28 **He,** God, **said to man:** Indeed, wisdom is with Me, and you cannot know it all, and **behold,** for your purposes, **the fear of the Lord, it is wisdom, and turning away,** refraining **from evil, is understanding** for you.

BACKGROUND

28:17 | **Glass [*zekhukhit*]:** Glass was fashioned everywhere in the Middle East, from Mesopotamia, through Phoenicia and Israel, all the way to Egypt. It was produced by melting silica sand together with plant ashes. Sometimes calcium carbonate or sodium carbonate would be added. Glass in ancient times was murky and opaque; the production of transparent glass was a difficult, expensive process. Indeed, the Talmud attests that the value of a white or transparent glass cup was four hundred *zuz* (*Berakhot* 31b), which was a year's income.

יג מֵאַיִן תִּמָּצֵא וְאֵי זֶה מְקוֹם בִּינָה׃ לֹא־יָדַע אֱנוֹשׁ עֶרְכָּהּ וְלֹא תִמָּצֵא בְּאֶרֶץ
יד טו הַחַיִּים׃ תְּהוֹם אָמַר לֹא בִי־הִיא וְיָם אָמַר אֵין עִמָּדִי׃ לֹא־יֻתַּן סְגוֹר תַּחְתֶּיהָ וְלֹא
טז יז יִשָּׁקֵל כֶּסֶף מְחִירָהּ׃ לֹא־תְסֻלֶּה בְּכֶתֶם אוֹפִיר בְּשֹׁהַם יָקָר וְסַפִּיר׃ לֹא־יַעַרְכֶנָּה
יח זָהָב וּזְכוֹכִית וּתְמוּרָתָהּ כְּלִי־פָז׃ רָאמוֹת וְגָבִישׁ לֹא יִזָּכֵר וּמֶשֶׁךְ חָכְמָה מִפְּנִינִים׃
יט כ לֹא־יַעַרְכֶנָּה פִּטְדַת־כּוּשׁ בְּכֶתֶם טָהוֹר לֹא תְסֻלֶּה׃ וְהַחָכְמָה
כא מֵאַיִן תָּבוֹא וְאֵי זֶה מְקוֹם בִּינָה׃ וְנֶעֶלְמָה מֵעֵינֵי כָל־חָי וּמֵעוֹף הַשָּׁמַיִם נִסְתָּרָה׃
כב כג אֲבַדּוֹן וָמָוֶת אָמְרוּ בְּאָזְנֵינוּ שָׁמַעְנוּ שִׁמְעָהּ׃ אֱלֹהִים הֵבִין דַּרְכָּהּ וְהוּא יָדַע אֶת־
כד כה מְקוֹמָהּ׃ כִּי־הוּא לִקְצוֹת־הָאָרֶץ יַבִּיט תַּחַת כָּל־הַשָּׁמַיִם יִרְאֶה׃ לַעֲשׂוֹת לָרוּחַ
כו כז מִשְׁקָל וּמַיִם תִּכֵּן בְּמִדָּה׃ בַּעֲשֹׂתוֹ לַמָּטָר חֹק וְדֶרֶךְ לַחֲזִיז קֹלוֹת׃ אָז רָאָהּ וַיְסַפְּרָהּ
כח הֱכִינָהּ וְגַם־חֲקָרָהּ׃ וַיֹּאמֶר ׀ לָאָדָם הֵן יִרְאַת אֲדֹנָי הִיא חָכְמָה וְסוּר מֵרָע
כט א ב בִּינָה׃ וַיֹּסֶף אִיּוֹב שְׂאֵת מְשָׁלוֹ וַיֹּאמַר׃ מִי־יִתְּנֵנִי כְיַרְחֵי־קֶדֶם כִּימֵי

Job's Second Speech

JOB 29:1–31:40

Following his speech about the greatness of God and His lofty wisdom in the first parable, Job then speaks of his own life in his second oration. He describes his existence prior to the disasters that befell him, the life of a secure, wealthy, esteemed individual, widely praised for his generous and sensitive conduct. He then moves on to his current pitiful state, in which he is scorned by even the lowliest members of society. Finally, in a series of rhetorical questions, he makes an oath that he has acted righteously and with integrity in various realms of life.

29 1 **Job again took up his oration and said:**
2 **If only I were as in the months of old;**[D] if only I could go back and live again **as** I did **in the days when God would protect me;**[532]

DISCUSSION

29:2 | **If only I were as in the months of old:** Although the phrase "as in the months of old" refers to one's entire past, some commentaries understand the phrase as meaning that Job was yearning specifically for the time when he was in his mother's womb. At that time, a person experiences total ecstasy, a feeling that does not return anytime during one's life. The following verse, "when His lamp would shine over my head, and by His light I would walk through darkness," is interpreted in a similar manner as well: A lit lamp is placed above the head of a fetus, and he can see from one end of the world to the other (see *Nidda* 30b).

3 **when His lamp would shine over my head,** when God protected me, **and by His light I**
would walk even **through**
darkness.
4 I wish I could return to my
previous existence, **as I was**
in the days of my youth,[D]
the period of my growth,
with the intimacy of God,[533]
His closeness, or special
providence, **over my tent;**

Lamp

5 **when the Almighty was still with me, and** at the time when
my lads, my servants and assistants, **surrounded me,** I was
protected and strong;
6 **when my feet**[534] **were bathed in butter,**[535] I enjoyed economic
bounty in those days, **and the rock poured for me rivers of**
oil. This rock perhaps represents Job's secure fortress, surrounded by rivers of oil, so to speak;
7 I was not merely secure and wealthy; I also enjoyed a lofty social status: **When I would go out to the gate of the city, and**
in the plaza, in the square, another place where the leaders sat,
I would prepare, establish, **my seat.**
8 In those days, **lads saw me and hid,** in awe of my greatness,
and even **elders rose and stood** in my honor.
9 **Princes ceased their words** in my presence, **and placed a**
hand to their mouths, as a signal for silence;
10 **the voice of rulers**[536] **was hushed, and their tongue cleaved**
in silence **to their palate.**
11 All these people gave me respect, **for the ear** of all **heard and**
affirmed me, my fine demeanor and speech, **and the eye** of everyone **saw and attested to me,** my good deeds,[537]
12 **that I would rescue the crying poor and the orphan with no**
one to help him.
13 Furthermore, since I helped those who had lost their way, or
property, **the blessing of the lost would come to me, and**
the heart of the widow I would gladden, as she had no other
means of support.
14 **I donned righteousness, and it clothed me.** I acted with
righteousness, and it suited my character; **like a robe,** to wrap
around myself,[538] **and a mitre was my justice.**
15 **Eyes, I was, to the blind, and feet to the lame was I.** I helped
all those who suffered from blemishes and all those who required assistance.
16 **I was father to the indigent and,** when hearing of **a quarrel**
about which I did not know, as it did not relate to my life directly, **I would investigate it.** I cannot bear a fight; therefore,
I got involved even in conflicts that did not concern me, and I
sought to reconcile the difficulties.
17 It was not enough for me to investigate these cases; I was also
an active participant in punishing the guilty: **I would break the**
jaws[B] **of the unjust** man, **and from his teeth,** which he used to
oppress and harm his neighbors, **I would cast out** and rescue
the **prey.**
18 **I would say: I will expire in my nest,** in my place of security, as
I do not require the kindnesses of others, and I can rest in peace
for the rest of my life in my home, **and I will multiply my days**
like sand.[D] My days will be as many as the multitude of grains
of sand.[539] In many places in the Bible, sand represents increase
and multiplicity.[540]
19 **My root will be open to water,** from which it will draw its sustenance. My existence will be as secure as a tree planted near
water, an image which appears elsewhere in the Bible.[541] **And**
dew will lie during the night **on my branch.**[542]
20 **My honor is renewed** and strengthened repeatedly[543] **in me,**
and my bow, my might,[544] **will** constantly **be rejuvenated in**
my hand.
21 **To me, they listened and looked forward** to hearing more;
they were silent for my counsel.[545]
22 **They would not deviate from following my word** and my
instructions,[546] **and my utterance would rain upon them.**

DISCUSSION

29:4 | **In the days of my youth [*horpi*]:** It is possible that this expression relates to a calendar structure in which the year begins in the winter [*horef*] because that is when one begins to plant the coming year's crops. Accordingly, the winter is compared to one's youth, and the end of one's life is symbolized by the summer, when everything is wilted (see Ralbag).

29:18 | **I will multiply my days like sand [*hol*]:** According to the midrash, the word *hol* refers to the supernatural bird known as the phoenix. This bird lives for an extremely long time, and when its time comes to die, it is capable of renewing itself instead (see Rashi; Malbim; *Sanhedrin* 108b; *Bereshit Rabba* 19:5).

BACKGROUND

29:17 | **The jaws [*metalot*]:** This term, which also appears as *malte'ot*, refers to the special teeth of predators that enable them to cut up their prey and break their bones. These extremely sharp teeth are located behind the canines, the long, protruding teeth used for catching prey. As indicated here, and in Psalms 58:7, when these teeth are smashed, the animal cannot catch its prey.

אלוה ישמרני: בהלו נרו עלי ראשי לאורו אלך חשך: כאשר הייתי בימי חרפי ג ד
בסוד אלוה עלי אהלי: בעוד שדי עמדי סביבותי נערי: ברחץ הליכי בחמה ה ו
וצור יצוק עמדי פלגי־שמן: בצאתי שער עלי־קרת ברחוב אכין מושבי: ראוני ז ח
נערים ונחבאו וישישים קמו עמדו: שרים עצרו במלים וכף ישימו לפיהם: ט
קול־נגידים נחבאו ולשונם לחכם דבקה: כי אזן שמעה ותאשרני ועין ראתה י יא
ותעידני: כי־אמלט עני משוע ויתום ולא־עזר לו: ברכת אבד עלי תבא ולב יב יג
ו אלמנה ארנן: צדק לבשתי וילבשני כמעיל וצניף משפטי: עינים הייתי לעור יד טו
ורגלים לפסח אני: אב אנכי לאביונים ורב לא־ידעתי אחקרהו: ואשברה טז יז
מתלעות עול ומשניו אשליך טרף: ואמר עם־קני אגוע וכחול ארבה ימים: יח
שרשי פתוח אלי־מים וטל ילין בקצירי: כבודי חדש עמדי וקשתי בידי תחליף: יט כ
לי־שמעו ויחלו וידמו למו עצתי: אחרי דברי לא ישנו ועלימו תטף מלתי: כא כב
ויחלו כמטר לי ופיהם פערו למלקוש: אשחק אלהם לא יאמינו ואור פני לא כג כד
יפילון: אבחר דרכם ואשב ראש ואשכון כמלך בגדוד כאשר אבלים ינחם: כה
ועתה ׀ שחקו עלי צעירים ממני לימים אשר־מאסתי אבותם לשית עם־כלבי א
צאני: גם־כח ידיהם למה לי עלימו אבד כלח: בחסר ובכפן גלמוד הערקים ב ג

My statements nurtured my listeners like drops of rainwater, or the dew that irrigates soil.[547]

23 **They looked forward to me as if** they were waiting **for rain, and** they **opened their mouth wide** to absorb my words as though they were thirsty **for** a few more drops of **spring rain.**

24 Due to my lofty status, **I would joke with them and they would not believe it.** Though joking is unbecoming of one so respected, it would still remain exalted in their eyes, **and the light of my face would not diminish.**[548]

25 **I chose their way; I sat at the head**[549] **and lived as a king among the troop, as one who consoles the mourners.**

30 1 **But now** even **those younger in days than I laugh at me,** and not merely youths, but **those whose fathers I rejected from placing with the dogs of my flock.** I would not have placed the fathers of these lads even among the dogs that guard my sheep.

Dog with flock

2 In order to further illustrate his own degraded status, Job depicts in detail the inferiority and contemptibility of those who scorn him: **The strength of their hands, too, why do I need it?** It cannot help me.[550] **Vigor,** power, freshness, and vitality,[551] **is lost to them.** Despite their youth, their strength is exhausted.

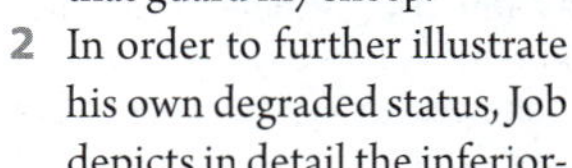

3 **They,** those who despise me, **are** themselves **in want, and in**

famine; they are lonely,[552] **fleeing** in their disgrace **to the wil-**
derness, a place of **gloom, destruction, and desolation,**[553]
4 **who pick saltwort,** a desert
shrub from which nomads
living in the wilderness
sustain themselves, **from**
bushes;[B] **and the root of the**
retama is their food.[B] They
eat the roots of the shrub,
or they use the roots of the
shrub to warm themselves.[554]

Mediterranean saltbush

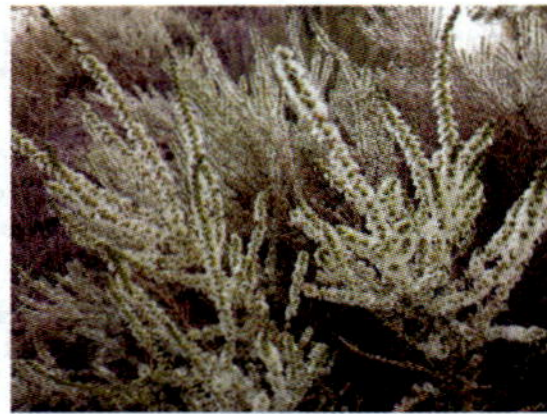
Mediterranean saltwort

White broom

5 **They,** those who despise me, **are driven out from inside** the
city;[555] **they,** the residents of
the city,[556] **raise a cry at**
them, declaring their shame,
like a thief.
6 Since they are expelled from
inhabited areas, **in channels**
of ravines they reside, in
holes in the dirt and rocks.
7 **Among the bushes they**

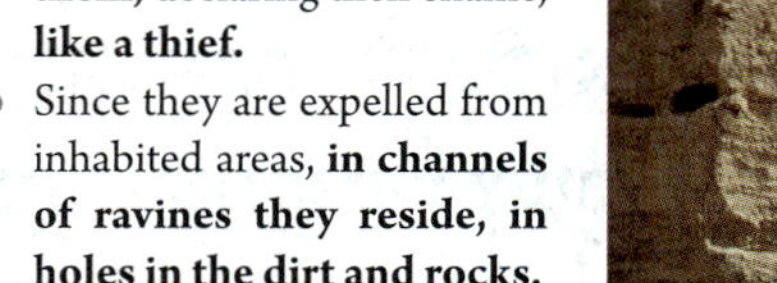

"In holes in the dirt and rocks." Caves in Ein Gedi

bray like wild asses;[557] **under the nettles,** or thorns, **they are**
gathered to sit together.[558]
8 **They are children of** wicked and despicable **scoundrels, also**
children of the nameless, even **lower than the earth.**
9 Job graphically depicts the despicable rabble that mocks him.
These are people who lack property, power, place and status
in society, and good reputation. In light of this description of
those who scorn him, Job's present position seems even low-
lier: **Now I have become their song,** they sing mocking songs
about me; **I am a byword to them;** I am the subject of their
ditties and gossip.
10 **They detest me, they distance themselves from me, and**
they do not even **spare spittle from my face.**
11 **For He,** God, or he, the man who mocks me,[559] **has opened my**
cord,[560] with which I girded my loins as an expression of my
strength,[561] my connections and the defenses that protect me,
and afflicted me, and they have cast aside restraint with re-
gard to me. Their behavior was restrained as long as I retained
my power and status. Now, these people allow themselves to
harm me.
12 **On my right,** instead of my respectable group of dignitaries,
young ruffians, mischievous youths,[562] **will rise up; they cast**
aside, push against, **my feet and press me onto their ways of**
calamity. They now seek to transfer to me the banishment and
troubles they have experienced.[563]
13 **They have smashed my path;**[564] through their actions, **they**
have exacerbated my situation, which is of **no help to them-**
selves. They derive no personal benefit from their actions,
which they perform purely for the sake of evil itself.[565]
14 **They come like a wide torrent,** like a broad wave they come to
wash over me; **they roll under foreboding clouds.**[566]

BACKGROUND

30:4 | Saltwort [*malu'aḥ*] from bushes: *Malu'aḥ*, which means salty, is a general term for a variety of plants which thrive in salty environments. Saltwort is the common name of several genera of plants that fit this category, such as the genus *Salsola*, meaning salty in Latin, or *Halogeton*, meaning neighbor of salt in Greek, both of the Amaranthaceae family. It is also possible to identify the "*malu'aḥ* from bushes" as the saltbush, or the name of the most prominent of them, the Mediterranean saltbush, also of the Amaranthaceae family. It is a perennial shrub whose height ranges from 50–200 cm. Its leaves are small, ovoid, hairy, and somewhat gray in color. It is found in wilderness areas in the Middle East, especially in areas of salty soil, river channels, and near the sea. The Talmud (*Kiddushin* 66a) relates that a certain *malu'aḥ* shrub was eaten by the builders of the Temple, who made do with little food in stressful conditions, and some identify this as referring to saltbush. To this day, Bedouins and village dwellers on the edge of the wilderness gather saltbush leaves and use them as food.

The root of the retama is their food: *Retama raetam*, white broom, is a white shrub from the Fabaceae family. It is a perennial, olive-green, desert plant which reaches a height of around 1.5–2 m. This shrub grows primarily in coastal areas, the Negev, and in the wilderness. Its branches are long and thin. Unlike other desert shrubs, for most of the year it does not grow leaves, and only the green and dense branches can be used for shade. It sprouts an abundance of fragrant flowers, while coals made from its aerial roots are of excellent quality and preserve heat for an extended period. Indeed, the plant is mentioned in Psalms 120:4 as kindling material. To this day, Bedouins in the Sinai desert prepare coals from its roots in order to bake their bread, among other purposes. There is an opinion that the "cake baked on coals" that Elijah ate when he fled to the wilderness of Sinai was baked on the coals of this shrub, under which he sat (I Kings 19:4–6).

צִיָּה אֶמֶשׁ שׁוֹאָה וּמְשֹׁאָה׃ ד הַקֹּטְפִים מַלּוּחַ עֲלֵי־שִׂיחַ וְשֹׁרֶשׁ רְתָמִים לַחְמָם׃
ה ו ז מִן־גֵּו יְגֹרָשׁוּ יָרִיעוּ עָלֵימוֹ כַּגַּנָּב׃ בַּעֲרוּץ נְחָלִים לִשְׁכֹּן חֹרֵי עָפָר וְכֵפִים׃ בֵּין־
ח שִׂיחִים יִנְהָקוּ תַּחַת חָרוּל יְסֻפָּחוּ׃ בְּנֵי־נָבָל גַּם־בְּנֵי בְלִי־שֵׁם נִכְּאוּ מִן־הָאָרֶץ׃
ט י וְעַתָּה נְגִינָתָם הָיִיתִי וָאֱהִי לָהֶם לְמִלָּה׃ תִּעֲבוּנִי רָחֲקוּ מֶנִּי וּמִפָּנַי לֹא־חָשְׂכוּ רֹק׃
יא יב כִּי־יתרו פִתַּח וַיְעַנֵּנִי וְרֶסֶן מִפָּנַי שִׁלֵּחוּ׃ עַל־יָמִין פִּרְחַח יָקוּמוּ רַגְלַי שִׁלֵּחוּ וַיָּסֹלּוּ יִתְרִי
יג יד עָלַי אָרְחוֹת אֵידָם׃ נָתְסוּ נְתִיבָתִי להיתי יֹעִילוּ לֹא עֹזֵר לָמוֹ׃ כְּפֶרֶץ רָחָב יֶאֱתָיוּ לְהַוָּתִי
טו תַּחַת שֹׁאָה הִתְגַּלְגָּלוּ׃ הָהְפַּךְ עָלַי בַּלָּהוֹת תִּרְדֹּף כָּרוּחַ נְדִבָתִי וּכְעָב עָבְרָה
טז יז יְשֻׁעָתִי׃ וְעַתָּה עָלַי תִּשְׁתַּפֵּךְ נַפְשִׁי יֹאחֲזוּנִי יְמֵי־עֹנִי׃ לַיְלָה עֲצָמַי נִקַּר מֵעָלָי
יח יט וְעֹרְקַי לֹא יִשְׁכָּבוּן׃ בְּרָב־כֹּחַ יִתְחַפֵּשׂ לְבוּשִׁי כְּפִי כֻתָּנְתִּי יַאַזְרֵנִי׃ הֹרָנִי לַחֹמֶר
כ כא וָאֶתְמַשֵּׁל כֶּעָפָר וָאֵפֶר׃ אֲשַׁוַּע אֵלֶיךָ וְלֹא תַעֲנֵנִי עָמַדְתִּי וַתִּתְבֹּנֶן בִּי׃ תֵּהָפֵךְ
כב לְאַכְזָר לִי בְּעֹצֶם יָדְךָ תִשְׂטְמֵנִי׃ תִּשָּׂאֵנִי אֶל־רוּחַ תַּרְכִּיבֵנִי וּתְמֹגְגֵנִי תשוה׃ תְּשִׁיָּה
כג כד כִּי־יָדַעְתִּי מָוֶת תְּשִׁיבֵנִי וּבֵית מוֹעֵד לְכָל־חָי׃ אַךְ לֹא־בְעִי יִשְׁלַח־יָד אִם־בְּפִידוֹ
כה כו לָהֶן שׁוּעַ׃ אִם־לֹא בָכִיתִי לִקְשֵׁה־יוֹם עָגְמָה נַפְשִׁי לָאֶבְיוֹן׃ כִּי טוֹב קִוִּיתִי וַיָּבֹא

15 **Terrors** and nightmares **overwhelm me; it,** terror, **pursues my virtue,** my generosity and fine attributes, **like the wind; and like a cloud, my salvation passes on.**

16 **Now, my soul pours out of me** in tears; **days of affliction have seized me.**[567]

17 **At night my bones are pierced** and painful, as though they are **overcoming me, and my sinews do not rest** from suffering. The pain, both external and internal, has penetrated deep within me.

18 **With great force it,** the pain, **imitates my garment.** The pain forcefully adheres to me, as though it were my clothing;[568] **like the collar of my tunic it,** the pain, **is wrapped around me.** It surrounds me in a kind of chokehold.[569]

19 **It,** the pain, **directed me to be** like **clay,**[570] or it has thrown me[571] to the dust,[572] **and I have become like dust and ashes.**

20 Job now turns to God: **I cry to You, but You do not answer me; I stand** before You in prayer, **and You look at me;** You see me, and yet You do not respond.

21 **You have become cruel with regard to me; with the might of Your hand You despise me.**

22 **You lift me to the wind, it will transport me and dissolve my resourcefulness,** my insight and understanding.

23 **For I know that you will reply to me with death and with the appointed house for all living.** All living beings, including myself, will eventually arrive at death's door.

24 **Yet no one will extend a hand to** rescue me from **a heap,** the grave;[573] **if ruin is upon him, does he have wealth?** At the time of a calamity, one's wealth will be of no assistance.[574]

25 Job concludes this lengthy speech with a series of oaths and declarations of his righteousness in various areas of life, despite which he has suffered from numerous disasters: **Truly,** I make an oath that in my period of greatness **I wept for the downtrodden; my soul grieved for the indigent** when I observed his sorry state.

26 **For I hoped for good,** by treating other people with compassion, **and** yet **evil came; I longed for light, and darkness came.** Now that I am in trouble, no one has taken pity on me.

27 **My innards burn** in pain **and do not quiet,** they are not calmed;[575] more **days of affliction await me.**[576]

28 **I walk in gloom, without** feeling the **sun.** Not only do I cry when I am alone, but **I rise in the assembly, and** yet I can do nothing but **cry out** for help.

29 In my cries, **I have become** like **a brother to jackals and a companion to eagle owls,**[B] which make similar cries.[577]

Jackal

Eagle owl

Little owl

30 **My skin is blackened**[578] **upon me, and my bones are dried,** parched,[579] **from** the **heat** of my illness.

31 **My harp is for mourning, and my pipe is for the voice of weepers.** My musical instruments, which were formerly used for rejoicing and the pleasures of life, now produce sounds of eulogy and lamentation.

31 1 Job again declares his decency and good character: **I established a covenant with my eyes,** I placed an obligation upon my eyes, **that I would not look upon a virgin.** Although I am not forbidden to a maiden, I refrained from such matters due to my desire to conduct myself with holiness.[580]

2 **What is the portion of God from above,** given to me for my righteousness,[581] **and** what is **the inheritance of the Almighty** that is apportioned to me **from on high?**

3 **Isn't it** right that God should bring[582] **calamity for the unjust, and alienation [*nekher*] for the performers of iniquity?** Let Him estrange Himself [*yitnaker*] from such people, not me.

4 After all, God knows everything about me: **Doesn't He see my ways and count all my steps?** Every little action of mine is revealed before Him.

5 He knows[583] **whether I have walked with futility,** or lies, **and** if **my foot has hastened to** perform **deceit,**

6 **let Him weigh me on a just scale, and God will know my virtue;** that I am innocent and that I deserved all the good that I received.

7 **Did my feet deviate from the** proper **way, and my heart follow my eyes,** was I attracted by items that were not mine; **and did anything,** a blemish or a forbidden or impure object,[584] **stick to my palms?**

8 If so, I would accept my punishment: **Let me sow, but another eat** the fruit of my labor; **and let my offspring be uprooted** and destroyed.

9 **Was my heart seduced by a** married **woman**[585] **and I lay in wait at my neighbor's entrance** for him to exit so that I could enter his house?[586]

10 If so, **let my wife grind for another,** be given over to another,[587] **and let others kneel over her,** have relations with her.

11 A person should not engage in adultery, **for that is lewdness, and it is a heinous iniquity.**

12 **For it is a fire that consumes until destruction, and it will uproot all my produce.**

13 **Did I despise justice for my slave and my maidservant**[D] and treat them unfairly **when they quarreled with me?**

14 **What then will I do when God rises** to demand justice for them in trial, **and when He reckons** my deeds; **what will I answer Him?**

15 **Didn't He make him,** my servant, **in the belly that made me?** He was created in the same manner as myself. **And** didn't He **form us** both **in one womb?** Since we are both people, how can I disparage him?

16 **Did I deprive the poor of their needs and cause the widow's eyes,** desperately looking for my help, **to yearn?** Did I disappoint her?[588]

17 **Did I eat my bread alone? Did an orphan not partake of it?**

18 **For from my youth, these** characteristics and moral qualities[589] **raised me up as a father, and from the belly of my mother I acted so,** by helping others.

19 **Did I see one** miserable wanderer **lost without garments, or** give **no clothing for the indigent** and remain indifferent?

20 **Truly, his loins blessed me;**[590] I take an oath that I covered him with garments, thereby warming him and causing his loins to bless me, **and from the fleece of my** shorn **sheep, he would be warmed.**

21 **If I raised up my hand against an orphan** to strike him **because I saw my support in the gate,** the court; if I took advantage of my preferable status and my connections with the judges to plot against helpless orphans,[591]

22 then **let my shoulder fall from its shoulder blade** and shatter, **and my forearm be broken from the upper arm,**[592] or from the shoulder.

23 **For calamity,** punishment, **from God is a fright to me, and I am unable to bear its weight;** I cannot act in such a manner due to my fear of the severity of His punishment.[593]

רַע וָאֲיַחֲלָה לְאוֹר וַיָּבֹא אֹפֶל׃ מֵעַי רֻתְּחוּ וְלֹא־דָמּוּ קִדְּמֻנִי יְמֵי־עֹנִי׃ קֹדֵר הִלַּכְתִּי כז כח
בְּלֹא חַמָּה קַמְתִּי בַקָּהָל אֲשַׁוֵּעַ׃ אָח הָיִיתִי לְתַנִּים וְרֵעַ לִבְנוֹת יַעֲנָה׃ עוֹרִי שָׁחַר כט ל
מֵעָלָי וְעַצְמִי־חָרָה מִנִּי־חֹרֶב׃ וַיְהִי לְאֵבֶל כִּנֹּרִי וְעֻגָבִי לְקוֹל בֹּכִים׃ בְּרִית כָּרַתִּי לא לא א
לְעֵינָי וּמָה אֶתְבּוֹנֵן עַל־בְּתוּלָה׃ וּמֶה ׀ חֵלֶק אֱלוֹהַּ מִמָּעַל וְנַחֲלַת שַׁדַּי מִמְּרֹמִים׃ ב
הֲלֹא־אֵיד לְעַוָּל וְנֵכֶר לְפֹעֲלֵי אָוֶן׃ הֲלֹא־הוּא יִרְאֶה דְרָכָי וְכָל־צְעָדַי יִסְפּוֹר׃ ג ד
אִם־הָלַכְתִּי עִם־שָׁוְא וַתַּחַשׁ עַל־מִרְמָה רַגְלִי׃ יִשְׁקְלֵנִי בְמֹאזְנֵי־צֶדֶק וְיֵדַע אֱלוֹהַּ ה ו
תֻּמָּתִי׃ אִם־תִּטֶּה אַשֻּׁרִי מִנִּי הַדָּרֶךְ וְאַחַר עֵינַי הָלַךְ לִבִּי וּבְכַפַּי דָּבַק מְאוּם׃ ז
אֶזְרְעָה וְאַחֵר יֹאכֵל וְצֶאֱצָאַי יְשֹׁרָשׁוּ׃ אִם־נִפְתָּה לִבִּי עַל־אִשָּׁה וְעַל־פֶּתַח רֵעִי ח ט
אָרָבְתִּי׃ תִּטְחַן לְאַחֵר אִשְׁתִּי וְעָלֶיהָ יִכְרְעוּן אֲחֵרִין׃ כִּי־הִוא זִמָּה וְהִיא עָוֹן י יא
הִיא וְהוּא
פְּלִילִים׃ כִּי אֵשׁ הִיא עַד־אֲבַדּוֹן תֹּאכֵל וּבְכָל־תְּבוּאָתִי תְשָׁרֵשׁ׃ אִם־אֶמְאַס יב יג
מִשְׁפַּט עַבְדִּי וַאֲמָתִי בְּרִבָם עִמָּדִי׃ וּמָה אֶעֱשֶׂה כִּי־יָקוּם אֵל וְכִי־יִפְקֹד מָה יד
אֲשִׁיבֶנּוּ׃ הֲלֹא־בַבֶּטֶן עֹשֵׂנִי עָשָׂהוּ וַיְכֻנֶנּוּ בָּרֶחֶם אֶחָד׃ אִם־אֶמְנַע מֵחֵפֶץ דַּלִּים טו טז
וְעֵינֵי אַלְמָנָה אֲכַלֶּה׃ וְאֹכַל פִּתִּי לְבַדִּי וְלֹא־אָכַל יָתוֹם מִמֶּנָּה׃ כִּי מִנְּעוּרַי גְּדֵלַנִי יז יח
כְאָב וּמִבֶּטֶן אִמִּי אַנְחֶנָּה׃ אִם־אֶרְאֶה אוֹבֵד מִבְּלִי לְבוּשׁ וְאֵין כְּסוּת לָאֶבְיוֹן׃ יט
אִם־לֹא בֵרְכוּנִי חֲלָצָו וּמִגֵּז כְּבָשַׂי יִתְחַמָּם׃ אִם־הֲנִיפוֹתִי עַל־יָתוֹם יָדִי כִּי־אֶרְאֶה כ כא
בַשַּׁעַר עֶזְרָתִי׃ כְּתֵפִי מִשִּׁכְמָה תִפּוֹל וְאֶזְרֹעִי מִקָּנָה תִשָּׁבֵר׃ כִּי־פַחַד אֵלַי אֵיד כב כג

BACKGROUND

30:29 | **Eagle owls [*benot ya'ana*]:** The context indicates that this is an animal that wails. The *bat ya'ana* is a non-kosher bird of prey (Leviticus 11:16) which is mentioned elsewhere in the Bible alongside desert animals and birds (Isaiah 34:13; Jeremiah 50:39; Micah 1:8). The root of the name is probably *vav-ayin-nun* or *yod-ayin-nun*, which means "hungry" in Syriac. Alternatively, it is from the root *ayin-nun-yod* or *ayin-nun-heh* due to its screech [*aniya*]. Since it is listed in the verse in Leviticus (11:16) together with nocturnal birds of prey from the owl family, some identify it as the pharaoh eagle owl, *Bubo ascalaphus*, which has a body length of approximately 40 cm and a weight of roughly 2 kg. This bird emits a howling sound. Others say it is the little owl, *Athene noctua*, a small, nocturnal bird that lives in desolate areas, among other locations. Yet others maintain, based on Onkelos and the *Targum*, that it is the ostrich, *Struthio camelus*, the largest extant species of birds that once roamed the deserts of Syria, Iraq, the Arabian Peninsula, and the Negev (Rav Se'adya Gaon; Malbim). The ostrich is the only bird in the Struthionidae family. Its wingspan is approximately 2 m, and it can reach around 2.5 m in height. The ostrich weighs around 150 kg. The ostrich is also the fastest animal with two legs, reaching speeds of up to 65 kph. However, this identification does not quite fit this verse, as ostriches do not have real vocal cords.

DISCUSSION

31:13 | **Did I despise justice for my slave and my maidservant:** In this verse, Job points to his innocence even with regard to matters that most individuals would not treat very seriously. He claims that he refrained from these negative actions because he knew that otherwise he would not emerge innocent and pure in the eyes of God. It should be noted that the notion that one should respect every person, including those beholden to him, because they too were created by the same Creator, was not widely accepted until a much later period in history.

24 **Did I place my dependence on gold;** have I trusted in **or** did I **say to** fine **gold:**[594] You are **my reliance?**
25 **Did I rejoice because my wealth,** or power, **was great, or because my hand had found abundance?**
26 **Did I see** the **light** of the sun[595] **when it shines, or the passing of the precious moon,**[596]
27 **and my heart was secretly enticed, and my mouth kissed my hand?** Did I send a kiss from afar to the sun, moon, stars, or constellations, in an idolatrous gesture?[597]
28 **It too,** such a deed, **would have been a heinous iniquity, for** although the action would usually not be seen by others, and even if it were, it would not be considered a serious offense, nevertheless **I would have denied God above,** I would have betrayed Him.
29 **Did I rejoice at the downfall of my enemy or was I bolstered** and felt strengthened **when evil found him?**
30 **I did not allow my palate to sin** with my speech, not even by **asking for his life with a curse,** by cursing my enemy that he should die.
31 **Didn't the men of my tent,** my guests, **say:** The meat that he has fed us is so tasty; **if only we will never be sated from his meat?** We wish that our stomachs were not full from his meat, so that we could eat more and more of it.[598]
32 When I was at the height of my power and influence, **the stranger did not stay the night outside,** but in my house; **my doors I opened for the guest.**
33 **Truly,** I take an oath that **I did not hide my transgressions as people do,**[599] **concealing my iniquity in my hiding place**[600]
34 **because I feared the great horde and the contempt of families breaking me, and I would be silent and not go out of the entrance.** I did not remain silent due to social pressures, and did not refrain from venturing out of my home on account of others. On the contrary, if any sins had weighed upon my conscience, I would have voiced them. I was not afraid of public opinion.
35 **If only there was someone to hear me** proclaim this declaration of innocence; that my life is clean of all sin, in thought, speech, and deed, and in every area of human activity; **behold my writing,** my written statement,[601] **let the Almighty answer me** and testify about me, **and let the scroll** of indictment **be written by my adversary**, so that the matter will be out in the open.
36 **Truly, wouldn't I carry it,** the book written against me, or the person who wrote it, **on my shoulder,** wouldn't I **tie it on me,** upon my head, **as a crown?** I would greatly respect it.[602]
37 **I would tell him the number of my steps;** I would reveal all the necessary details before the writer of this indictment;[603] **like** one approaches **a ruler**[604] **I would draw him near.**
38 Job concludes this speech with a parable from the world of agriculture. In this parable, he again accepts severe punishments upon himself, if he deserves them. However, he is convinced that he is clear of any blame. **If my land would cry out against me,** my corrupt deeds, **and its furrows would weep together,**
39 **if I have eaten its produce without silver,** by stealing it, **or** if I **deflated** and pained **the spirit of its owners,**[605]
40 I would curse myself: **Let thistles come out** of my field **instead of wheat, and instead of barley, stinkweed,**[B] bad or malodorous weeds. **The words of Job are concluded.**

Spotted golden thistle

Wheat field

Stinkweed

BACKGROUND

31:40 | **Stinkweed** [*ba'esha*]**:** This is a general name for weeds that sprout alongside wheat or other cultivated crops. They can have a deleterious effect on one's desired crop. The "sour grapes" [*be'ushim*] of Isaiah 5:2 can be explained in a similar manner.

DISCUSSION

32:2 | **Elihu son of Barakhel the Buzite, from the family of Ram:** While the names of the friends who spoke previously do not appear to be in Hebrew, the name and father's name of this speaker appear to be Hebrew in origin. In fact, the term "Buzi" is also used to refer to the father of the prophet Ezekiel (Ezekiel 1:3).

כד כה אֵ֣ל וּ֝מִשְּׂאֵת֗וֹ לֹ֣א אוּכָֽל׃ אִם־שַׂ֣מְתִּי זָהָ֣ב כִּסְלִ֑י וְ֝לַכֶּ֗תֶם אָמַ֥רְתִּי מִבְטַחִֽי׃ אִם־
כו אֶ֭שְׂמַח כִּי־רַ֣ב חֵילִ֑י וְכִֽי־כַ֝בִּ֗יר מָצְאָ֥ה יָדִֽי׃ אִם־אֶרְאֶ֣ה א֭וֹר כִּ֣י יָהֵ֑ל וְ֝יָרֵ֗חַ יָקָ֥ר
כז כח הֹלֵֽךְ׃ וַיִּ֣פְתְּ בַּסֵּ֣תֶר לִבִּ֑י וַתִּשַּׁ֖ק יָדִ֣י לְפִֽי׃ גַּם־ה֭וּא עָוֺ֣ן פְּלִילִ֑י כִּֽי־כִחַ֖שְׁתִּי לָאֵ֣ל
כט ל מִמָּֽעַל׃ אִם־אֶ֭שְׂמַח בְּפִ֣יד מְשַׂנְאִ֑י וְ֝הִתְעֹרַ֗רְתִּי כִּֽי־מְצָ֥אוֹ רָֽע׃ וְלֹא־נָתַ֣תִּי לַחֲטֹ֣א
לא חִכִּ֑י לִשְׁאֹ֖ל בְּאָלָ֣ה נַפְשֽׁוֹ׃ אִם־לֹ֣א אָ֭מְרוּ מְתֵ֣י אָהֳלִ֑י מִֽי־יִתֵּ֥ן מִ֝בְּשָׂר֗וֹ לֹ֣א נִשְׂבָּֽע׃
לב לג בַּ֭חוּץ לֹא־יָלִ֣ין גֵּ֑ר דְּ֝לָתַ֗י לָאֹ֥רַח אֶפְתָּֽח׃ אִם־כִּסִּ֣יתִי כְאָדָ֣ם פְּשָׁעָ֑י לִטְמ֖וֹן בְּחֻבִּ֣י
לד לה עֲוֺנִֽי׃ כִּ֤י אֶֽעֱר֨וֹץ ׀ הָ֘מ֤וֹן רַבָּ֗ה וּֽבוּז־מִשְׁפָּח֥וֹת יְחִתֵּ֑נִי וָ֝אֶדֹּ֗ם לֹא־אֵ֥צֵא פָֽתַח׃ מִ֤י
לו יִתֶּן־לִ֨י ׀ שֹׁ֘מֵ֤עַֽ לִ֗י הֶן־תָּ֭וִי שַׁדַּ֣י יַעֲנֵ֑נִי וְסֵ֥פֶר כָּ֝תַ֗ב אִ֣ישׁ רִיבִֽי׃ אִם־לֹ֣א עַל־שִׁ֭כְמִי
לז לח אֶשָּׂאֶ֑נּוּ אֶֽעֶנְדֶ֖נּוּ עֲטָר֣וֹת לִֽי׃ מִסְפַּ֣ר צְ֭עָדַי אַגִּידֶ֑נּוּ כְּמוֹ־נָ֝גִ֗יד אֲקָרְבֶֽנּוּ׃ אִם־עָ֭לַי
לט אַדְמָתִ֣י תִזְעָ֑ק וְ֝יַ֗חַד תְּלָמֶ֥יהָ יִבְכָּיֽוּן׃ אִם־כֹּ֭חָהּ אָכַ֣לְתִּי בְלִי־כָ֑סֶף וְנֶ֖פֶשׁ בְּעָלֶ֣יהָ
מ הִפָּֽחְתִּי׃ תַּ֤חַת חִטָּ֨ה ׀ יֵ֣צֵא ח֭וֹחַ וְתַֽחַת־שְׂעֹרָ֣ה בָאְשָׁ֑ה תַּ֝֗מּוּ דִּבְרֵ֥י אִיּֽוֹב׃
לב א וַֽיִּשְׁבְּת֡וּ שְׁלֹ֤שֶׁת הָאֲנָשִׁ֣ים הָ֭אֵלֶּה מֵעֲנ֣וֹת אֶת־אִיּ֑וֹב כִּ֤י ה֖וּא צַדִּ֣יק
ב בְּעֵינָֽיו׃ וַיִּ֤חַר אַ֨ף ׀ אֱלִיה֣וּא בֶן־בַּרַכְאֵ֮ל הַבּוּזִ֪י מִמִּשְׁפַּ֫חַ֥ת רָ֥ם

Elihu's Speech

JOB 32:1–37:24

It seems that the speeches and responses of Job and his friends were delivered in a public setting. After Job's previous response, a young man from the audience, Elihu, stands up and addresses Job and his friends. Like the three friends, Elihu's language is not always clear. However, unlike them, Elihu is apparently an Israelite, as indicated by his own name, his father's name, and his family name.

Elihu's speech is split into four separate responses to Job, which are presented consecutively. He starts by stressing God's superiority over everything. He infers from this fact that it is impossible for God to perform injustice. Since God is not beholden to anyone, nor does He require any assistance to act, there is no conceivable reason for Him to engage in corrupt deeds. Man's good behavior gives God nothing, nor does any negative conduct on the part of humans harm Him in any way. Although one cannot argue with God due to His lofty position, communication exists between Him and man, through visions and dreams as well as through the suffering that He brings. Rather than viewing suffering as a punishment that is indicative of wrongdoing, Elihu proposes that someone who is suffering should see his pain as a message, calling on him to respond to his afflictions and accept them with love.

Finally, through a lengthy description of rainfall, clouds, thunder, and lightning, Elihu vividly illustrates the greatness and wonder of God. Elihu's aim in portraying God's power to Job is to persuade him that his attempts to contend with God are futile. This detailed depiction of nature can also be viewed as a preparation for the next section, in which God Himself speaks directly to Job.

32 1 **These three men,** Elifaz, Bildad, and Tzofar, **ceased to answer Job because** they realized that he would not be persuaded by anything they said, as **he was righteous in his own eyes,** convinced of his own righteousness.

2 **The wrath of Elihu son of Barakhel the Buzite, from the family of Ram,**[D] **was enflamed. His wrath was enflamed against Job because he regarded himself as more just than God.**[606]

3 **Against his,** Job's, **three friends his wrath was enflamed**
because they did not find a response to Job's plight, **and**
therefore they **condemned Job.**
4 **Elihu had waited** until this point **for Job with his words.**
Elihu had not yet said anything, **as they,** Job and his three
friends, **were older in days than he.**
5 **Elihu saw that there was no response in the mouths of the**
three men, and his wrath was enflamed to the point that he
felt he had to interject.
6 **Elihu son of Barakhel the Buzite answered and said: I am**
young in days, and you are old; therefore, I was intimidat-
ed, and I feared expressing my opinion to you. I was afraid of
speaking in your presence.
7 **I said** to myself: **Age should speak, and the multitude of**
years should expound wisdom. I assumed that the longer a
person lives, the greater his wisdom would be.
8 **Indeed,** in truth, **it,** wisdom, **is a spirit in man, and the soul**
from the Almighty causes them, men, **to understand.** One
receives insight through the soul, which comes from God; it
does not depend on age.
9 **It is not the mature** ones **who become wise or the elderly**
who always **understand judgment.**
10 **Therefore, I say: Listen to me; I too will express my opinion.**
11 **Behold, I waited for,** anticipated, **your words; I listened**
to your insights until you had investigated with words,
until you had found the right words and completed all your
arguments.
12 **I look to you,** I am watching you, **and behold, there is no one**
among you arguing successfully **against Job,** properly **an-**
swering his statements.
13 **Lest you** insist and **say:** For our part, **we have found wisdom,**
and we understand the reason for Job's suffering, know that
only **God will vanquish him,** Job, **not man,** as no one can refute his claims.
14 True, **he,** Job, **did not direct his words to me,** and he was not
arguing with me. **And** still, even if he had, **with your state-**
ments, I would not answer him.
15 **They,** the friends, **are afraid, they do not answer anymore;**
words are removed from them.
16 **I waited until they,** the friends, **were not speaking, for them**
to cease and not answer anymore.
17 Since the friends were unable to win the argument, **I too will**
answer my part; I too will express my opinion.
18 **For I am full of words; the spirit in my belly,** full of tempestu-
ous thoughts and emotions, **is bothering me.**[607]
19 **Behold, my belly is** agitated, **like** an **unopened,** sealed vessel of fermenting **wine; like new wineskins, it will burst.**[608]
When wine ferments in a new container, the pressure inside the

"Like unopened wine." Closed pitchers, illustration based on a mural, Tomb of Nebamun, Egypt, fifteenth century BCE. Foam resulting from fermentation seeps from the top of the two jars on the left

vessel increases as the wine ferments until it eventually smashes
the vessel or bursts open the wineskin.
20 Therefore, **I will speak and be relieved; I will open my lips**
and answer. At long last, I will express myself.
21 **Please, let me not show favor to any man.** I will flatter no one,
and I will give titles to no person. I will not address them with
honorary names, or in an indirect, deferential manner.[609]
22 **For I do not know how to give titles.** It is not my way to address people according to the dictates of etiquette or to speak in
a cultured manner. Moreover, I do not value such efforts, as the
matters of which I wish to speak are too important and are also
rather urgent. **In a moment, my Maker would carry me away.**
In a flash, God could take my life.[610]
33 1 **However, Job, hear, please, my words, and listen to all my**
statements.
2 **Behold, now I have opened my mouth; my tongue has spo-**
ken on my palate.
3 **My sayings are from the uprightness of my heart; my lips**
speak clear knowledge. A clear opinion will issue forth from
my mouth.[611]
4 **The spirit of God has formed me, and the spirit of the**
Almighty has given me life. I am only human. However, I will
nevertheless present some arguments to you as one speaks to a
friend who is an equal.[612]
5 **If you can, answer me; formulate your claims,** arrange your
arguments, **before me** and **stand** to debate me. You said that
you cannot contend with God because you are overwhelmingly
in awe of Him (9:32–35). However, you can speak comfortably
with me.
6 **Behold, I am like you to God.** We are both equal before Him.
I too was formed from clay.[613]

ג בְּאִיּוֹב חָרָה אַפּוֹ עַל־צַדְּקוֹ נַפְשׁוֹ מֵאֱלֹהִים׃ וּבִשְׁלֹשֶׁת רֵעָיו חָרָה אַפּוֹ עַל אֲשֶׁר
ד לֹא־מָצְאוּ מַעֲנֶה וַיַּרְשִׁיעוּ אֶת־אִיּוֹב׃ וֶאֱלִיהוּ חִכָּה אֶת־אִיּוֹב בִּדְבָרִים כִּי זְקֵנִים־
ה הֵמָּה מִמֶּנּוּ לְיָמִים׃ וַיַּרְא אֱלִיהוּא כִּי אֵין מַעֲנֶה בְּפִי שְׁלֹשֶׁת הָאֲנָשִׁים וַיִּחַר
ו אַפּוֹ׃ וַיַּעַן ׀ אֱלִיהוּא בֶן־בַּרַכְאֵל הַבּוּזִי וַיֹּאמַר צָעִיר אֲנִי לְיָמִים
ז וְאַתֶּם יְשִׁישִׁים עַל־כֵּן זָחַלְתִּי וָאִירָא ׀ מֵחַוֺּת דֵּעִי אֶתְכֶם׃ אָמַרְתִּי יָמִים יְדַבֵּרוּ
ח ט וְרֹב שָׁנִים יֹדִיעוּ חָכְמָה׃ אָכֵן רוּחַ־הִיא בֶאֱנוֹשׁ וְנִשְׁמַת שַׁדַּי תְּבִינֵם׃ לֹא־רַבִּים
י יא יֶחְכָּמוּ וּזְקֵנִים יָבִינוּ מִשְׁפָּט׃ לָכֵן אָמַרְתִּי שִׁמְעָה־לִּי אֲחַוֶּה דֵעִי אַף־אָנִי׃ הֵן
יב הוֹחַלְתִּי ׀ לְדִבְרֵיכֶם אָזִין עַד־תְּבוּנֹתֵיכֶם עַד־תַּחְקְרוּן מִלִּין׃ וְעָדֵיכֶם אֶתְבּוֹנָן
יג וְהִנֵּה אֵין לְאִיּוֹב מוֹכִיחַ עוֹנֶה אֲמָרָיו מִכֶּם׃ פֶּן־תֹּאמְרוּ מָצָאנוּ חָכְמָה אֵל יִדְּפֶנּוּ
יד טו לֹא־אִישׁ׃ וְלֹא־עָרַךְ אֵלַי מִלִּין וּבְאִמְרֵיכֶם לֹא אֲשִׁיבֶנּוּ׃ חַתּוּ לֹא־עָנוּ עוֹד
טז יז הֶעְתִּיקוּ מֵהֶם מִלִּים׃ וְהוֹחַלְתִּי כִּי־לֹא יְדַבֵּרוּ כִּי עָמְדוּ לֹא־עָנוּ עוֹד׃ אַעֲנֶה אַף־
יח יט אֲנִי חֶלְקִי אֲחַוֶּה דֵעִי אַף־אָנִי׃ כִּי מָלֵתִי מִלִּים הֱצִיקַתְנִי רוּחַ בִּטְנִי׃ הִנֵּה בִטְנִי
כ כְּיַיִן לֹא־יִפָּתֵחַ כְּאֹבוֹת חֲדָשִׁים יִבָּקֵעַ׃ אֲדַבְּרָה וְיִרְוַח־לִי אֶפְתַּח שְׂפָתַי וְאֶעֱנֶה׃
כא כב אַל־נָא אֶשָּׂא פְנֵי־אִישׁ וְאֶל־אָדָם לֹא אֲכַנֶּה׃ כִּי לֹא יָדַעְתִּי אֲכַנֶּה כִּמְעַט יִשָּׂאֵנִי
א ב עֹשֵׂנִי׃ וְאוּלָם שְׁמַע־נָא אִיּוֹב מִלָּי וְכָל־דְּבָרַי הַאֲזִינָה׃ הִנֵּה־נָא פָּתַחְתִּי פִי דִּבְּרָה
ג ד לְשׁוֹנִי בְחִכִּי׃ יֹשֶׁר־לִבִּי אֲמָרָי וְדַעַת שְׂפָתַי בָּרוּר מִלֵּלוּ׃ רוּחַ־אֵל עָשָׂתְנִי וְנִשְׁמַת
ה ו שַׁדַּי תְּחַיֵּנִי׃ אִם־תּוּכַל הֲשִׁיבֵנִי עֶרְכָה לְפָנַי הִתְיַצָּבָה׃ הֵן־אֲנִי כְפִיךָ לָאֵל מֵחֹמֶר

7 **Behold, fear of me will not terrify you.** You have nothing to fear from me, **and my coercion will not weigh upon you.**[614]

8 **Indeed, what you have said in my ears, and the sound of the words I have heard.** I will summarize what you said:

9 **I am pure, without transgression, I am innocent, and there is no iniquity in me.**

10 **Behold, He finds pretexts** to spread libel **against me,** and although I am close to God and fear Him, **He considers me His enemy.**

11 **He puts my feet in stocks.** He binds me and restricts my movement.[615] **He watches all my paths.** He tracks me and thereby limits the paths I may take.

12 **Behold, in this,** your claim that God is seeking an excuse to harm you,[616] **you are not right. I answer you, as** the truth is that **God is greater than man.** He is far above man, and He would not act unjustly.

13 **Why do you contend against Him that He does not reply to any statements?** Why do you claim that He will certainly not answer any of your complaints? After all, sometimes people do receive a response from Heaven.[617]

14 **For God speaks** to people **once,**[618] or in one way,[619] **and** also **twice,** or in two ways, **to he who does not see.** He speaks twice to one who does not see what God wishes to show him,

15 **in a dream, in a night vision, when deep sleep falls upon men, in sleep upon a bed.**

16 **Then He uncovers the ears of men,** God reveals His word to them, **and** likewise **with their chastisement,** the reproof and moral instruction He delivers to them or, alternatively, the suffering He brings upon them to teach them a lesson, **He imprints,** engraves, His message upon them,[620]

17 in order **to turn a person away from an action** that is wrong, from his usual bad conduct,[621] **and** to **conceal the body [*geva*] from man,**[622] or, alternatively, his pride [*ga'ava*],[623] so that a person will not act according to the dictates of his bodily needs or pride.

18 God brings suffering upon a person or issues a verbal reproof to him, and thereby **He spares his soul from perdition,** from death and the netherworld, **and his life,**[624] or his soul,[625] **from perishing by the sword.**[626]

19 **He,** man, **is rebuked with pain on his bed, and it,** the pain, **is strong in his many bones.**[627] The suffering itself is God's punitive response to man.

20 **Disgusted is his life,** the sick man's soul[628] is nauseated, **by bread,**[629] **and his soul** is disgusted even **by desirable food.**

21 He becomes so weak that **his flesh is consumed from sight.** He is so thin that it is as though his flesh cannot be seen. **And his bones are crushed,**[630] even to the extent that they are virtually **invisible.**

22 He senses that **his soul approaches perdition and** that **his life** is given **to the killers,** angels of destruction.[631]

23 **If there is for him an angel, an advocate, one out of a thousand** angels who prosecute him,[632] **to relate a person's uprightness,**[633]

24 **He will be gracious to him,** God will have mercy upon him, **and He will say: Save him from descending to perdition,** from dying;[634] **I have found ransom,** an atonement for his sins.

25 Then **his flesh will be fresher,** moister and fatter,[635] **than in youth,** more than it was even when he was young;[636] **let him return to the days of his boyhood.**

26 When he recovers from his illness, **he will entreat God, and He will accept him; he will see His face with joyous acclamation.**[637] **And He will restore to man** the reward for **his righteousness.**

27 **He will gaze upon men,**[638] or he will march among men,[639] rectify his past deeds,[640] or surround himself with men,[641] **and say** his confession to them: **I sinned, I perverted what was straight, and it was not worth it for me.**[642]

28 **He,** God, **redeems his soul,** the soul of this man who returned to Him, **from passing into perdition,** from dying, **and his life will see the light.** No man's fate is predetermined. Sometimes God allows a person to recover his health, in which case he can return to the condition of his earlier years.

29 **Behold, all these God does, twice, thrice,** several times, **with a man,** by addressing him, either by means of rebuke in a dream or through suffering,

30 in order **to restore his soul from perdition, to be enlightened with the light of life.**

31 **Listen, Job, hear me; be silent, and I will speak.**

32 **If there are words** in your mouth in response, **answer me; speak, as** I do not want to accuse you of wrongdoing. On the contrary, **I wish to vindicate you.**

33 **If not,** if you do not have anything to say, **hear me; be silent, and I will teach you wisdom,** if you will allow me to do so.

34 1 **Elihu answered and said:**

2 **Hear my words, wise ones, and listen to me, knowledgeable ones.** Listen to my next speech.

3 **For the ear evaluates,** tests, the quality of **words, and** likewise **a palate tastes** and discerns the quality of **food.**[643]

4 **Let us so choose justice for ourselves.** We can examine the matters at hand objectively and understand them properly. **Let it become known between us what is good.** Although Elihu presents himself as a neutral party rather than taking one side or the other in the debate, it will become apparent that he does take a specific stance.

5 Elihu first summarizes the claim until this point. **For Job said: I am righteous, but God has taken fair judgment away from me,** as He has not judged me correctly.

6 **I will reject my judgment as false; my arrow is fatal,** it has caused a grave wound,[644] **though I am without transgression.**

ז ח קֹרַצְתִּי גַם־אָנִי׃ הִנֵּה אֵמָתִי לֹא תְבַעֲתֶךָּ וְאַכְפִּי עָלֶיךָ לֹא־יִכְבָּד׃ אַךְ אָמַרְתָּ
ט י בְאָזְנָי וְקוֹל מִלִּין אֶשְׁמָע׃ זַךְ אֲנִי בְּלִי פָשַׁע חַף אָנֹכִי וְלֹא עָוֺן לִי׃ הֵן תְּנוּאוֹת
יא יב עָלַי יִמְצָא יַחְשְׁבֵנִי לְאוֹיֵב לוֹ׃ יָשֵׂם בַּסַּד רַגְלָי יִשְׁמֹר כָּל־אָרְחֹתָי׃ הֶן־זֹאת לֹא־
יג צָדַקְתָּ אֶעֱנֶךָּ כִּי־יִרְבֶּה אֱלוֹהַּ מֵאֱנוֹשׁ׃ מַדּוּעַ אֵלָיו רִיבוֹתָ כִּי כָל־דְּבָרָיו לֹא־יַעֲנֶה׃
יד טו כִּי־בְאַחַת יְדַבֶּר־אֵל וּבִשְׁתַּיִם לֹא יְשׁוּרֶנָּה׃ בַּחֲלוֹם ׀ חֶזְיוֹן לַיְלָה בִּנְפֹל תַּרְדֵּמָה
טז יז עַל־אֲנָשִׁים בִּתְנוּמוֹת עֲלֵי מִשְׁכָּב׃ אָז יִגְלֶה אֹזֶן אֲנָשִׁים וּבְמֹסָרָם יַחְתֹּם׃ לְהָסִיר
יח אָדָם מַעֲשֶׂה וְגֵוָה מִגֶּבֶר יְכַסֶּה׃ יַחְשֹׂךְ נַפְשׁוֹ מִנִּי־שָׁחַת וְחַיָּתוֹ מֵעֲבֹר בַּשָּׁלַח׃
יט כ וְהוּכַח בְּמַכְאוֹב עַל־מִשְׁכָּבוֹ וריב עֲצָמָיו אֵתָן׃ וְזִהֲמַתּוּ חַיָּתוֹ לָחֶם וְנַפְשׁוֹ מַאֲכַל וְרוֹב
כא כב תַּאֲוָה׃ יִכֶל בְּשָׂרוֹ מֵרֹאִי ושפי עַצְמֹתָיו לֹא רֻאּוּ׃ וַתִּקְרַב לַשַּׁחַת נַפְשׁוֹ וְחַיָּתוֹ וְשֻׁפּוּ
כג כד לַמְמִתִים׃ אִם־יֵשׁ עָלָיו ׀ מַלְאָךְ מֵלִיץ אֶחָד מִנִּי־אָלֶף לְהַגִּיד לְאָדָם יָשְׁרוֹ׃ וַיְחֻנֶּנּוּ
כה וַיֹּאמֶר פְּדָעֵהוּ מֵרֶדֶת שָׁחַת מָצָאתִי כֹפֶר׃ רֻטֲפַשׁ בְּשָׂרוֹ מִנֹּעַר יָשׁוּב לִימֵי עֲלוּמָיו׃
כו כז יֶעְתַּר אֶל־אֱלוֹהַּ ׀ וַיִּרְצֵהוּ וַיַּרְא פָּנָיו בִּתְרוּעָה וַיָּשֶׁב לֶאֱנוֹשׁ צִדְקָתוֹ׃ יָשֹׁר ׀ עַל־
כח אֲנָשִׁים וַיֹּאמֶר חָטָאתִי וְיָשָׁר הֶעֱוֵיתִי וְלֹא־שָׁוָה לִי׃ פָּדָה נפשי מֵעֲבֹר בַּשָּׁחַת נַפְשׁוֹ
כט ל וחיתי בָּאוֹר תִּרְאֶה׃ הֶן־כָּל־אֵלֶּה יִפְעַל־אֵל פַּעֲמַיִם שָׁלוֹשׁ עִם־גָּבֶר׃ לְהָשִׁיב וְחַיָּתוֹ
לא נַפְשׁוֹ מִנִּי־שָׁחַת לֵאוֹר בְּאוֹר הַחַיִּים׃ הַקְשֵׁב אִיּוֹב שְׁמַע־לִי הַחֲרֵשׁ וְאָנֹכִי אֲדַבֵּר׃
לב לג אִם־יֵשׁ־מִלִּין הֲשִׁיבֵנִי דַּבֵּר כִּי־חָפַצְתִּי צַדְּקֶךָּ׃ אִם־אַיִן אַתָּה שְׁמַע־לִי הַחֲרֵשׁ ז
א ב וַאֲאַלֶּפְךָ חָכְמָה׃ וַיַּעַן אֱלִיהוּא וַיֹּאמַר׃ שִׁמְעוּ חֲכָמִים מִלָּי וְיֹדְעִים
ג ד הַאֲזִינוּ לִי׃ כִּי־אֹזֶן מִלִּין תִּבְחָן וְחֵךְ יִטְעַם לֶאֱכֹל׃ מִשְׁפָּט נִבְחֲרָה־לָּנוּ נֵדְעָה
ה ו בֵינֵינוּ מַה־טּוֹב׃ כִּי־אָמַר אִיּוֹב צָדַקְתִּי וְאֵל הֵסִיר מִשְׁפָּטִי׃ עַל־מִשְׁפָּטִי אֲכַזֵּב

7 **Who is a man like Job,** in turning from evil, and yet he is someone **who drinks scoffing,** whose mouth is full of mockery and
whose criticism of God flows out of his mouth **like water,**
8 **who keeps company with performers of injustice and walks
with men of wickedness?**
9 **For he said: It is of no use to man that he wishes to be with
God,** that he wishes to conduct himself in accord with God.[645]
Job's claim is that one derives no benefit from performing the
will of God and following Him wholeheartedly.[646]
10 **Therefore, men of heart [*levav*], hear me:** First, I must say
that **far be it from God to act with wickedness, and** second,
far be it **from the Almighty to do injustice.** God does not perform evil. In many places in the Bible, the heart [*lev*] is the seat
of understanding rather than emotion.[647]
11 **For He repays a person for his action, and according to the
conduct of a man He will provide for him.**
12 **For indeed,** truthfully,[648] **God will not be wicked, and the
Almighty will not distort justice.**
13 **Who commanded Him about the earth?** Who commanded
Him to create the world?[649] Since He does not answer to anyone, it is unreasonable to suggest that He requires a pretext
to harass you.[650] **And who set in place,** created,[651] **the entire
world?** Since He is the source of everything, He would not perform wicked acts.
14 **If He** only **directs His heart to him,** and wishes to do evil to
man, He would not have to accuse him falsely; **his spirit and his
soul He will** simply **gather to Him,** killing him immediately.[652]
15 **All flesh will perish together, and humanity will return to
dust.**
16 In his second speech, Elihu started by addressing everyone
present. Now Elihu turns to Job: **If there is understanding** in
you,[653] **hear this; heed the sound of my words.**
17 **Should one who hates justice** be the one to **govern** the
world?[654] **Will you condemn He who is greatly righteous?**
18 **Can it be said of a king,** as you do: **Lowlife,** that he is a lowly
person who cannot possibly rise from his current state? Or can
one declare **to nobles:** You are **wicked?**
19 For you know that **it is He who does not show favor** in judgment **to princes and does not prefer the wealthy,** those in
positions of power and those who are lofty in status, **over the
poor, as they are all His handiwork,** the princes, influential
people, and the destitute together.
20 For if He so wishes, **in a moment they will die, and at midnight,** on their beds in the dark, **the people** who honored the
powerful and trusted in their strength **will shudder,**[655] **and
they,** the powerful ones, **will pass on;**[656] **the mighty will be
removed without effort.**[657]
21 **For His eyes are on the ways of a man, and all his steps He
sees.**
22 **There is no darkness** for God, **and there is no shadow of
death where the performers of injustice can hide.** Evildoers
have nowhere to escape from Him.
23 **For on no man does He place overmuch** blame. He does
not accuse an individual of committing more sins than he has
performed,[658] giving cause to the person **to go** and complain
before God in judgment.[659]
24 **He shatters the powerful without number.** God has the power to crush the strongest of men[660] in great numbers (9:10), **and**
after their collapse, He **sets others in their place.**
25 **Therefore,** as everything is revealed before God, **He knows
their,** men's, **activities, and He turns it,** their lives' light, **into
night,**[661] **and they are crushed** and broken.[662]
26 **He strikes them** without delay[663] **in the place**[664] **of the wicked, in a place with onlookers,**[665]
27 **because they strayed from following Him, and they did not
appreciate** or learn from **any of His ways,**
28 **bringing the cry of the impoverished before Him.** The deviation of powerful individuals from the path of God caused the
poor to cry to Him,[666] **and He hears the cry of the poor.**
29 **He quiets,** brings calm, to certain people, **and** then **who can
do harm?** No one can harm them. When **He conceals His
face, who can see Him? To a nation,** or a king, **and to an individual alike.** This is the way that God acts toward a nation, or a
king,[667] as well as toward an individual.[668]
30 **He,** God, **prevents a hypocritical person from reigning,**[669]
and likewise He refrains **from setting hindrances for the people,** which would harm them.
31 **For to God one should say: I will bear it; I will not cause
harm.** It is proper for one to say to God: I have received my
punishment and will perform no more destructive acts.[670]
32 **That which I cannot view** of my own accord, **teach me;** and
then **if I have performed injustice, I will** accept upon myself
not to **continue.**
33 **Is it with you,** through consultation with you, Job, **that He will
repay** good or evil?[671] **For you rejected** the suffering that God
has brought upon you.[672] **Will it be you who chooses and not
I?** Do you imagine that you can choose the recompense that
you deserve rather than God? **What do you know that** motivates **you** to **speak?**
34 **Men of heart say to me, and a wise man hears** and agrees with
me:
35 **Job speaks unwisely** in his demand for judgment with God,
and his words are spoken **without intelligence.**
36 **My wish is that**[673] **Job** should **be tried until eternity,** through
all kinds of tests, **for answers regarding men of injustice,**[674]
or because he answers together with the wicked with whom he
keeps company.[675]

ז ח אנוש חצי בלי־פשע: מי־גבר כאיוב ישתה־לעג כמים: וארח לחברה עם־
ט פעלי און וללכת עם־אנשי־רשע: כי־אמר לא יסכן־גבר ברצתו עם־אלהים:
י יא לכן ׀ אנשי לבב שמעו לי חללה לאל מרשע ושדי מעול: כי פעל אדם ישלם־
יב לו וכארח איש ימצאנו: אף־אמנם אל לא־ירשיע ושדי לא־יעות משפט:
יג יד מי־פקד עליו ארצה ומי שם תבל כלה: אם־ישים אליו לבו רוחו ונשמתו אליו
טו טז יאסף: יגוע כל־בשר יחד ואדם על־עפר ישוב: ואם־בינה שמעה־זאת האזינה
יז יח לקול מלי: האף שונא משפט יחבוש ואם־צדיק כביר תרשיע: האמר למלך
יט בליעל רשע אל־נדיבים: אשר לא־נשא ׀ פני שרים ולא נכר־שוע לפני־דל
כ כי־מעשה ידיו כלם: רגע ׀ ימתו וחצות לילה יגעשו עם ויעברו ויסירו אביר
כא כב לא ביד: כי־עיניו על־דרכי־איש וכל־צעדיו יראה: אין־חשך ואין צלמות
כג להסתר שם פעלי און: כי לא על־איש ישים עוד להלך אל־אל במשפט:
כד כה ירע כבירים לא־חקר ויעמד אחרים תחתם: לכן יכיר מעבדיהם והפך לילה
כו כז וידכאו: תחת־רשעים ספקם במקום ראים: אשר על־כן סרו מאחריו וכל־
כח כט דרכיו לא השכילו: להביא עליו צעקת־דל וצעקת עניים ישמע: והוא ישקט ׀
ל ומי ירשע ויסתר פנים ומי ישורנו ועל־גוי ועל־אדם יחד: ממלך אדם חנף
לא לב ממקשי עם: כי־אל־אל האמר נשאתי לא אחבל: בלעדי אחזה אתה הרני
לג אם־עול פעלתי לא אסיף: המעמך ישלמנה ׀ כי־מאסת כי־אתה תבחר ולא־
לד לה אני ומה־ידעת דבר: אנשי לבב יאמרו לי וגבר חכם שמע לי: איוב לא־בדעת
לו ידבר ודבריו לא בהשכיל: אבי יבחן איוב עד־נצח על־תשבת באנשי־און:

37 **For** with his piercing statements, **he,** Job, **adds transgression**
to his sin, he strikes with his words,[676] or he speaks too much
among us,[677] **and** furthermore, not only does he talk in this
manner to us, but **he proliferates his** harsh **sayings against**
God.
35 1 **Elihu,** continuing his repudiation of Job and his assertions, **an-**
swered and said:
2 **Is this what you consider justice,** to enter into judgment with
God? Alternatively, do you think that you speak rightly? **You**
say: My righteousness is greater than God's![678]
3 **When you** think it proper to **ask: What use will it be for you,**
the righteous? What do you gain by following the upright path?
What advantage will it, my righteousness,[679] **be for me more**
than from my sinning? Whichever course of action I choose,
my fate will be the same.
4 **I will answer you** about this **with words, and** even **your**
friends with you.
5 **Look heavenward and see** what you can, **and see the skies;**
they are so much **loftier than you.** When you speak of God's
judgment, you must take into account that you are no more
than a small, ignorant creature standing before the great,
mighty God. Perhaps you require your claims of righteousness
and good deeds for your own personal needs, but you simply do not have the capacity to perceive the larger picture of
reality.[680]
6 **If you have sinned, how have you acted against Him?** How
do you harm Him? **If your transgressions proliferate, what**
will you have done to Him?
7 Likewise, **if you are righteous, what have you given Him, or**
what has He taken from your hand? Some mistakenly think
that if they have fulfilled God's commandments, then they have
helped Him in some way. However, the actions of such a puny
creature as you, whether for good or evil, have no discernible
effect on the infinite God.
8 **Your wickedness is for a man like you,** your evil acts can only
harm a man like yourself, **and your righteousness** can bring
benefit **for a person,** but all this has no meaning for God.
9 **From conflict the exploited cry out.** Due to fights and theft,[681]
the oppressed victims cry out. **They** beg and **plead due to the**
arm of many, because of the forceful acts of the many oppressors and robbers.
10 **But he didn't say,** or it is not right that one should say in accusation: **Where is God my Maker, who allows mishaps,**
who allows people to cut down others and cause damage,[682] **in**
the night, when no one is watching, as social crime is man's
responsibility,
11 **who teaches us**[683] **through the animals of the earth and**
makes us wiser from the birds of the heavens? God provides
us with instruction through the behavior of the beasts and
birds.[684]
12 **There they cry, but He does not respond, because of the**
pride of the evil. When one reflects upon the quarrels of animals, he sees that they cry, but no one answers, because of the
pride of the vicious beasts that attack them. One should learn
from packs of wolves, flocks of sheep, and hunted birds not
to involve God in disputes arising from the actions of other
people.
13 Although God does not always respond to the cries of living
creatures, **it is vanity,** in vain, to say **that God does not hear**
and that the Almighty will not see it, your distress.
14 **Although you say you do not see Him** or His righteous
judgment,[685] **the case is before Him, and you must wait** and
hope **for Him,**[686] as His righteous judgment will eventually be
revealed.
15 **Now, as you do not,** as you do not have hope and will not wait
for Him patiently,[687] you think that **He visited His wrath** upon
you and afflicted you unjustly in His rage **and did not know**
its great extent. It seems to you as though God is completely
unaware of your great cry.[688]
16 Elihu ends this section by referring to Job in the third person:
Job, in his failure to wait for God to reveal the righteousness of
His judgment, **futility issues from his mouth; he proliferates**
words without knowledge.
36 1 **Elihu continued and said:**
2 **Wait for me a bit** more, **and I** will **convey to you, as there are**
more words to say **on God's behalf,** in His name.[689]
3 **I will project my opinion afar, and I will ascribe righteous-**
ness to my Maker. I will make known His righteousness.
4 **Indeed, my words are not false.** I am not against you, Job, as
one of sound opinions is with you. I am speaking to you honestly, with full understanding of your feelings.
5 **Behold, God is mighty; He does not despise any** man, or,
alternatively, He will not ruin and destroy anyone for no reason.[690] For **He is great in strength of heart.** He can tolerate
much due to His might and wisdom.
6 Yet **He will not keep the wicked alive; He will give justice to**
the poor. In accordance with the demands of the law, He will
punish the wicked who harm the poor.
7 **He will not withdraw His eyes from the righteous,** watching over them carefully, **and** he places **kings upon the throne.**
He has seated them there
to reign **forever,**[691] **and they**
are exalted.
8 In contrast, **if there are**
those bound in shackles[692]
or trapped in the pangs of
affliction,[693]

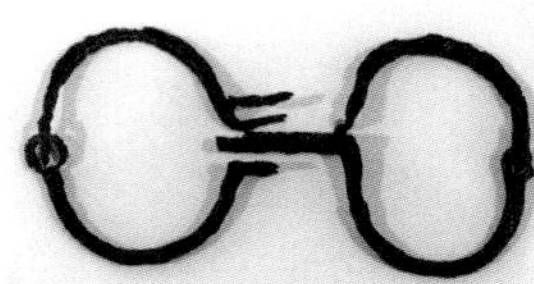
Iron shackles, Roman period

כִּי יֹסִיף עַל־חַטָּאתוֹ פֶשַׁע בֵּינֵינוּ יִסְפּוֹק וְיֶרֶב אֲמָרָיו לָאֵל׃ וַיַּעַן אֱלִיהוּ לז א ה
וַיֹּאמַר׃ הֲזֹאת חָשַׁבְתָּ לְמִשְׁפָּט אָמַרְתָּ צִדְקִי מֵאֵל׃ כִּי־תֹאמַר מַה־יִּסְכָּן־לָךְ ב ג
מָה־אֹעִיל מֵחַטָּאתִי׃ אֲנִי אֲשִׁיבְךָ מִלִּין וְאֶת־רֵעֶיךָ עִמָּךְ׃ הַבֵּט שָׁמַיִם וּרְאֵה ד ה
וְשׁוּר שְׁחָקִים גָּבְהוּ מִמֶּךָּ׃ אִם־חָטָאתָ מַה־תִּפְעָל־בּוֹ וְרַבּוּ פְשָׁעֶיךָ מַה־תַּעֲשֶׂה־ ו
לּוֹ׃ אִם־צָדַקְתָּ מַה־תִּתֶּן־לוֹ אוֹ מַה־מִיָּדְךָ יִקָּח׃ לְאִישׁ־כָּמוֹךָ רִשְׁעֶךָ וּלְבֶן־אָדָם ז ח
צִדְקָתֶךָ׃ מֵרֹב עֲשׁוּקִים יַזְעִיקוּ יְשַׁוְּעוּ מִזְּרוֹעַ רַבִּים׃ וְלֹא־אָמַר אַיֵּה אֱלוֹהַּ עֹשָׂי ט י
נֹתֵן זְמִרוֹת בַּלָּיְלָה׃ מַלְּפֵנוּ מִבַּהֲמוֹת אָרֶץ וּמֵעוֹף הַשָּׁמַיִם יְחַכְּמֵנוּ׃ שָׁם יִצְעֲקוּ יא יב
וְלֹא יַעֲנֶה מִפְּנֵי גְּאוֹן רָעִים׃ אַךְ־שָׁוְא לֹא־יִשְׁמַע ׀ אֵל וְשַׁדַּי לֹא יְשׁוּרֶנָּה׃ אַף יג יד
כִּי־תֹאמַר לֹא תְשׁוּרֶנּוּ דִּין לְפָנָיו וּתְחוֹלֵל לוֹ׃ וְעַתָּה כִּי־אַיִן פָּקַד אַפּוֹ וְלֹא־יָדַע טו
בַּפַּשׁ מְאֹד׃ וְאִיּוֹב הֶבֶל יִפְצֶה־פִּיהוּ בִּבְלִי־דַעַת מִלִּין יַכְבִּר׃ טז

וַיֹּסֶף אֱלִיהוּא וַיֹּאמַר׃ כַּתַּר־לִי זְעֵיר וַאֲחַוֶּךָּ כִּי־עוֹד לֶאֱלוֹהַּ מִלִּים׃ אֶשָּׂא דֵעִי א ב ג ו
לְמֵרָחוֹק וּלְפֹעֲלִי אֶתֵּן־צֶדֶק׃ כִּי־אָמְנָם לֹא־שֶׁקֶר מִלָּי תְּמִים דֵּעוֹת עִמָּךְ׃ הֶן־ ד ה
אֵל כַּבִּיר וְלֹא יִמְאָס כַּבִּיר כֹּחַ לֵב׃ לֹא־יְחַיֶּה רָשָׁע וּמִשְׁפַּט עֲנִיִּים יִתֵּן׃ לֹא־יִגְרַע ו ז
מִצַּדִּיק עֵינָיו וְאֶת־מְלָכִים לַכִּסֵּא וַיֹּשִׁיבֵם לָנֶצַח וַיִּגְבָּהוּ׃ וְאִם־אֲסוּרִים בַּזִּקִּים ח
יִלָּכְדוּן בְּחַבְלֵי־עֹנִי׃ וַיַּגֵּד לָהֶם פָּעֳלָם וּפִשְׁעֵיהֶם כִּי יִתְגַּבָּרוּ׃ וַיִּגֶל אָזְנָם לַמּוּסָר ט י
וַיֹּאמֶר כִּי־יְשֻׁבוּן מֵאָוֶן׃ אִם־יִשְׁמְעוּ וְיַעֲבֹדוּ יְכַלּוּ יְמֵיהֶם בַּטּוֹב וּשְׁנֵיהֶם בַּנְּעִימִים׃ יא
וְאִם־לֹא יִשְׁמְעוּ בְּשֶׁלַח יַעֲבֹרוּ וְיִגְוְעוּ בִּבְלִי־דָעַת׃ וְחַנְפֵי־לֵב יָשִׂימוּ אָף לֹא יב יג
יְשַׁוְּעוּ כִּי אֲסָרָם׃ תָּמֹת בַּנֹּעַר נַפְשָׁם וְחַיָּתָם בַּקְּדֵשִׁים׃ יְחַלֵּץ עָנִי בְעָנְיוֹ וְיִגֶל יד טו

9 know that **He has told them,** through the suffering He brings upon them,[694] **of their actions,** their evil deeds, **and their transgressions, that they are** steadily **increasing.**

10 In this manner,[695] **He has exposed their ear to** receive **chastisement and said** to them, through their suffering,[696] **that they should repent from iniquity.**

11 If they heed the word of God, which is revealed to them through their pain,[697] **and serve Him, they will end**[698] **their days in ease and their years in pleasantness.**

12 But if they do not heed, they will be dispatched by the sword and expire without knowledge.

13 But the hypocritical of heart, the wicked, **will arouse** God's **wrath; they do not cry out** to Him for help even **when He binds them** with their troubles.[699]

14 Their souls will die in youth, and their lives will be ended in a disrespectful manner, **among the male cult prostitutes.**[700]

15 Elihu returns to discussing people who perceive their suffering as a message from God: **He rescues the poor in His affliction,**

and He exposes their ear by oppression. They are able to hear the word of God, which is expressed through their suffering.[701]
16 After describing the people who listen to the word of God as expressed through their pain, as well as those who deny it, Elihu now addresses Job directly: My comments apply to you personally,[702] as it is through the very suffering that God has brought upon you that **He has even moved you** far **from a narrow opening, its bottom wide and insubstantial.** Gehenna is compared to an oven, which is typically wide below and narrow on top so that its heat and smoke accumulate inside.[703] **And** furthermore,[704] **the comfort of your table,** set there gently by God, **is full of fat.** Not only are you spared the punishment of Gehenna through your suffering, but it also earns you the reward of tranquility and great benefit.[705]
17 Even if[706] **the sentence of the wicked,** the judgment that the wicked deserve, **has filled you, yet** you should know that **the sentence and justice will assist you.** Such punishments will actually help you in the long term.[707]
18 This will be **when** you are **subject to** God's great **wrath.**[708] But beware **lest you be misled** from the upright path **by** the evil inclination[709] due to your **uncertainty** or a blow you received,[710] **and** take care that **great ransom,** your suffering, **does not divert you** from the truth. Alternatively, not even a large ransom of money can rescue you from God's wrath.
19 **Would your plea be formulated without distress?** Suffering awakens a person to turn to God. Would you articulate your prayers if you were not experiencing troubles?[711] **And** can you set forth your prayer without **any exertions of effort?**
20 **Do not long for** the speedy arrival of **the night,** death,[712] **to remove**[713] **peoples from their place,** for a time will come when you will have such power that you will even be able to remove, or cut off,[714] peoples from their place.
21 **Beware, do not turn to injustice, for it is that,** sin, **which you have chosen** and preferred until now, **over submission.**[715]
22 **Behold, God is exalted** and mighty **in His power; who is a teacher like Him?** Who can teach people like He does?[716]
23 **Who has commanded Him His way?** One cannot command God to do one thing or another. **Who has said** to Him: **You have performed injustice?** One cannot claim that God has acted improperly.
24 **Remember** His deeds because **when you exalt** Him, you will see the greatness of **His work,**[717] **of which men have sung,** composed songs.[718]
25 **All that men have seen in it,** anything they have seen of His presence, **man looks** at only **from afar.**[719] Man can only stand at a distance and receive a general impression of the ways of God.
26 **Behold, God is exalted, and we cannot know; the number of His years is beyond scrutiny.** He is not subject to the dimension of time; He is eternal.[720]
27 **For** we do not know when **He emits drops of water,** when He causes them to drip down,[721] **distilling,** filtering or condensing them, **into** drops of **rain from His vapor,**
28 **which the skies pour out, raining on many people.** Man cannot fully comprehend the greatness of God and His deeds; he cannot understand the secret of rainfall.
29 Not only is he unable to comprehend the falling of rain, but **does he understand the sails of a cloud,** the place to which the cloud floats,[722] **the sounds of His covering,** His thunder?[723]
30 **Behold, He spreads His light,** lightning, **over it,** the cloud, **and covers the roots,** or the edge,[724] **of the sea.**
31 **For with these,** lightning and rain,[725] **He judges peoples;** through them, **He** also **provides food in abundance.**
32 **He covers the light with His hands,** with His clouds,[726] **and commands it,** one cloud,[727] **to collide** into another cloud in order to produce rain.[728]

"He spreads His light over it." Lightning

33 **Its,** the thunder's, **noise**[729] **tells about Him,** God and His greatness, or about the rain. The thunder is like **the nose's breath that rises up** from God, so to speak.

37 1 **Even at this,** the thunder,[730] **my heart trembles, and** it beats so hard that it feels as though it **leaps from its place.**[731]
2 **Hear the fury of His voice** and **the sound that emerges from His mouth.**
3 **He appears,** or renders His effects noticeable, **under all the heavens, and His lightning** extends **to the ends of the earth.**[732]
4 **After it,** the lightning, **a sound** of thunder **roars,**[733] **thunders with the voice** of the expression **of His majesty, and He does not tarry after them.** He does not delay the sound of the thunder following the lightning[734] **as His voice is heard.**
5 **God thunders wondrously,** in a miraculous manner, **with His voice; He performs great things, and we do not know.** We are unaware of the great things that God performs all the time.
6 This verse specifies one of those great things: **For He says to the snow: Be** placed[735] **on the earth,** unlike the rain, which penetrates the earth. **And the rain He pours down; the downpour of the rain is His might,** as He causes the rain and snow to descend to the earth.
7 Furthermore, **it,** the mighty rain, **seals the hand of every person,** confines him within his home, to prevent him **from** leaving and **knowing his actions.**[D] The rain prevents him from supervising his business matters and workers.[736]
8 Because of the rain, even **the beast comes into a lair,** a place of hiding,[737] **and it rests in its dens.**

טז בְּלַחַץ אָזְנָם׃ וְאַף הֲסִיתְךָ ׀ מִפִּי־צָר רַחַב לֹא־מוּצָק תַּחְתֶּיהָ וְנַחַת שֻׁלְחָנְךָ מָלֵא

יז יח דָשֶׁן׃ וְדִין־רָשָׁע מָלֵאתָ דִּין וּמִשְׁפָּט יִתְמֹכוּ׃ כִּי־חֵמָה פֶּן־יְסִיתְךָ בְשָׂפֶק וְרָב־כֹּפֶר

יט כ אַל־יַטֶּךָּ׃ הֲיַעֲרֹךְ שׁוּעֲךָ לֹא בְצָר וְכֹל מַאֲמַצֵּי־כֹחַ׃ אַל־תִּשְׁאַף הַלָּיְלָה לַעֲלוֹת

כא כב עַמִּים תַּחְתָּם׃ הִשָּׁמֶר אַל־תֵּפֶן אֶל־אָוֶן כִּי עַל־זֶה בָּחַרְתָּ מֵעֹנִי׃ הֶן־אֵל יַשְׂגִּיב

כג כד בְּכֹחוֹ מִי כָמֹהוּ מוֹרֶה׃ מִי־פָקַד עָלָיו דַּרְכּוֹ וּמִי־אָמַר פָּעַלְתָּ עַוְלָה׃ זְכֹר כִּי־

כה כו תַשְׂגִּיא פָעֳלוֹ אֲשֶׁר שֹׁרְרוּ אֲנָשִׁים׃ כָּל־אָדָם חָזוּ־בוֹ אֱנוֹשׁ יַבִּיט מֵרָחוֹק׃ הֶן־אֵל

כז שַׂגִּיא וְלֹא נֵדָע מִסְפַּר שָׁנָיו וְלֹא־חֵקֶר׃ כִּי יְגָרַע נִטְפֵי־מָיִם יָזֹקּוּ מָטָר לְאֵדוֹ׃

כח כט אֲשֶׁר־יִזְּלוּ שְׁחָקִים יִרְעֲפוּ עֲלֵי ׀ אָדָם רָב׃ אַף אִם־יָבִין מִפְרְשֵׂי־עָב תְּשֻׁאוֹת

ל לא סֻכָּתוֹ׃ הֵן־פָּרַשׂ עָלָיו אוֹרוֹ וְשָׁרְשֵׁי הַיָּם כִּסָּה׃ כִּי־בָם יָדִין עַמִּים יִתֶּן־אֹכֶל

לב לג לְמַכְבִּיר׃ עַל־כַּפַּיִם כִּסָּה־אוֹר וַיְצַו עָלֶיהָ בְמַפְגִּיעַ׃ יַגִּיד עָלָיו רֵעוֹ מִקְנֶה אַף

לז א ב עַל־עוֹלֶה׃ אַף־לְזֹאת יֶחֱרַד לִבִּי וְיִתַּר מִמְּקוֹמוֹ׃ שִׁמְעוּ שָׁמוֹעַ בְּרֹגֶז קֹלוֹ וְהֶגֶה

ג ד מִפִּיו יֵצֵא׃ תַּחַת־כָּל־הַשָּׁמַיִם יִשְׁרֵהוּ וְאוֹרוֹ עַל־כַּנְפוֹת הָאָרֶץ׃ אַחֲרָיו ׀ יִשְׁאַג־

ה קוֹל יַרְעֵם בְּקוֹל גְּאוֹנוֹ וְלֹא יְעַקְּבֵם כִּי־יִשָּׁמַע קוֹלוֹ׃ יַרְעֵם אֵל בְּקוֹלוֹ נִפְלָאוֹת

ו עֹשֶׂה גְדֹלוֹת וְלֹא נֵדָע׃ כִּי לַשֶּׁלֶג ׀ יֹאמַר הֱוֵא אָרֶץ וְגֶשֶׁם מָטָר וְגֶשֶׁם מִטְרוֹת

ז ח עֻזּוֹ׃ בְּיַד־כָּל־אָדָם יַחְתּוֹם לָדַעַת כָּל־אַנְשֵׁי מַעֲשֵׂהוּ׃ וַתָּבוֹא חַיָּה בְמוֹ־אָרֶב

DISCUSSION

37:7 | **It seals [*yaḥtom*] the hand of every person from knowing his actions:** In addition to the simple understanding of the verse as referring to rain, the Sages interpreted it as referring to the soul. When a person's soul ascends to heaven after death, it signs [*ḥotem*] a document containing a list of sins that the person committed during his lifetime, affirming that it is correct. Some commentaries have even suggested that each night, while a person is sleeping, his soul ascends to heaven to write and ratify a document in which the day's events are recorded (*Shela*, glosses to *Ḥullin* 18, based on *Zohar*, *Hayei Sarah*).

9 At that time,[738] **from the chamber,** the place where it resides, **comes the storm, and frost** comes **from the** special **storehouses.**[739]
10 **From the breath**[740] **of God, He gives ice.** His breath forms ice, just as the world was created through the speech of His mouth.[741] **And the breadth,** abundance, **of the waters becomes solid.**[742]
11 **Even on a clear day, He loads the thick cloud.** Sometimes God brings the thick cloud even on a clear day,[743] and **the cloud scatters its light,** or rain.
12 **It,** the cloud, **turns and reverses by His strategies,** by God's unexpected instructions, **to perform them, all that He commands them,** e.g., sounding claps of thunder and dispatching bolts of lightning, as well as causing rain and snow to fall **upon the face of the world, on earth.**[744]
13 **Whether for the rod,** for punishment, **when it is for His land,**[745] **or for grace, He will provide it.** When a cloud comes over the earth, it may be to strike the land, or to bestow blessing upon it. The nature of a cloud's mission is determined by God.
14 **Listen to this, Job; stand and consider the wonders of God.**
15 **Do you know when God placed them,** clouds, **over them,** people,[746] **and** when **the lightning of His cloud appeared?**
16 **Do you know the layers of the cloud,** or the path cleared by a cloud, and can you comprehend **the wonders of He who is complete in knowledge?**
17 Do you understand **why** after rainfall and a storm **your garments are warm when the earth is calmed** and quiet **from the** hot **south** wind?[747]
18 **Would you**[748] **ascend with Him to the heavens, which**

Mirror, Egypt, 800–100 BCE

are as strong as a cast mirror?[B] Can you ascend with God to the heavens to make them as strong as a polished mirror? When the skies are entirely clear, they seem solid and dry, like a huge domed mirror over the face of the earth.[749]
19 If you can reach such heights, **inform us what we should say to Him.**[750] However, you know as well as we do that you cannot do so, **for we cannot arrange ourselves,** our speech, before God[751] or stand before Him, **due to** the **darkness** that envelops us[752] or that surrounds God and hides Him from our sight.[753]
20 However, it is not necessary to inform God of anything:[754] **Need it be related to Him that I speak?** Must I relate what I have to say to God in order for Him to hear my words?[755] **Can a man say** anything **so it would be concealed** from God?[756]
21 **Now they,** human beings, **do not see the light,** as it is covered by clouds; **it is bright in the heavens,** and yet it exists even though it is not revealed to them,[757] **and** then **a wind passes,** scatters the clouds, **and clears them.**
22 **From the north comes gold,** the light of God's splendor; **about God is awesome glory.** The golden splendor covers God with awesome majesty. Unlike the warm, quiet south, the north is the source of storms and rain, and yet it is the direction from which God will appear and reveal Himself to you.[758] Perhaps Elihu is telling Job here that it is through his very suffering and spiritual upheavals that God will be revealed to him.
23 **The Almighty, we cannot find him; He is exalted in power and judgment and abundant in righteousness. He will not afflict.** He would not bring arbitrary suffering upon His creatures.[759]
24 **Therefore, men revere Him,** as He is unparalleled in power and mighty in judgment; and yet **He does not regard all** who are **wise of heart.** God controls this wondrous, mysterious world, and He does not see fit to justify Himself to human understanding.[760]

BACKGROUND

37:18| **As strong as a cast mirror:** The mirror in ancient times was a thin, round plate of metal, usually bronze, that could be polished but could also withstand distortions and not become bent.

ט י וּבִמְעוֹנֹתֶ֥יהָ תִשְׁכֹּֽן׃ מִֽן־הַ֭חֶדֶר תָּב֣וֹא סוּפָ֑ה וּֽמִמְּזָרִ֥ים קָרָֽה׃ מִנִּשְׁמַת־אֵ֥ל יִתֶּן־
יא יב קָ֑רַח וְרֹ֖חַב מַ֣יִם בְּמוּצָֽק׃ אַף־בְּ֭רִי יַטְרִ֣יחַ עָ֑ב יָ֝פִ֗יץ עֲנַ֣ן אוֹרֽוֹ׃ וְה֤וּא מְסִבּ֨וֹת ׀
יג מִתְהַפֵּ֣ךְ בְּתַחְבּוּלֹתָ֣ו לְפָעֳלָ֑ם כֹּ֖ל אֲשֶׁ֥ר יְצַוֵּ֨ם ׀ עַל־פְּנֵ֖י תֵבֵ֣ל אָֽרְצָה׃ אִם־לְשֵׁ֥בֶט
יד אִם־לְאַרְצ֑וֹ אִם־לְ֝חֶ֗סֶד יַמְצִאֵֽהוּ׃ הַאֲזִ֣ינָה זֹּ֣את אִיּ֑וֹב עֲ֝מֹ֗ד וְהִתְבּוֹנֵ֤ן ׀ נִפְלְא֬וֹת
טו טז אֵֽל׃ הֲ֭תֵדַע בְּשׂוּם־אֱל֣וֹהַּ עֲלֵיהֶ֑ם וְ֝הוֹפִ֗יעַ א֣וֹר עֲנָנֽוֹ׃ הֲ֭תֵדַע עַל־מִפְלְשֵׂי־עָ֑ב
יז יח מִ֝פְלְא֗וֹת תְּמִ֣ים דֵּעִֽים׃ אֲשֶׁר־בְּגָדֶ֥יךָ חַמִּ֑ים בְּהַשְׁקִ֥ט אֶ֝֗רֶץ מִדָּרֽוֹם׃ תַּרְקִ֣יעַ עִ֭מּוֹ
יט לִשְׁחָקִ֑ים חֲ֝זָקִ֗ים כִּרְאִ֥י מוּצָֽק׃ ה֭וֹדִיעֵנוּ מַה־נֹּ֣אמַר ל֑וֹ לֹ֥א נַ֝עֲרֹ֗ךְ מִפְּנֵי־חֹֽשֶׁךְ׃
כ כא הַיְסֻפַּר־ל֭וֹ כִּ֣י אֲדַבֵּ֑ר אִם־אָ֥מַר אִ֝֗ישׁ כִּ֣י יְבֻלָּֽע׃ וְעַתָּ֤ה ׀ לֹ֥א רָא֡וּ א֗וֹר בָּהִ֣יר ה֭וּא
כב כג בַּשְּׁחָקִ֑ים וְר֥וּחַ עָ֝בְרָ֗ה וַֽתְּטַהֲרֵֽם׃ מִ֭צָּפוֹן זָהָ֣ב יֶאֱתֶ֑ה עַל־אֱ֝ל֗וֹהַּ נ֣וֹרָא הֽוֹד׃ שַׁדַּ֣י
כד לֹֽא־מְ֭צָאנֻהוּ שַׂגִּיא־כֹ֑חַ וּמִשְׁפָּ֥ט וְרֹב־צְ֝דָקָ֗ה לֹ֣א יְעַנֶּֽה׃ לָ֭כֵן יְרֵא֣וּהוּ אֲנָשִׁ֑ים לֹֽא־
לח א יִ֝רְאֶ֗ה כָּל־חַכְמֵי־לֵֽב׃ וַיַּֽעַן־יְהוָ֣ה אֶת־אִ֭יּוֹב מִנהסערה וַיֹּאמַֽר׃ מִן ׀ הַסְּעָרָ֗ה
ב ג מִ֤י זֶ֨ה ׀ מַחְשִׁ֖יךְ עֵצָ֥ה בְמִלִּ֗ין בְּֽלִי־דָֽעַת׃ אֱזָר־נָ֣א כְגֶ֣בֶר חֲלָצֶ֑יךָ וְ֝אֶשְׁאָלְךָ֗ וְהוֹדִיעֵֽנִי׃

God's First Response to Job

JOB 38:1–40:2

God's answer to Job essentially consists of a long series of rhetorical questions in which the Creator says to him: Since you do not have the power to create the detailed and complex reality that you see before you, you cannot supervise and manage the world, nor can you comprehend the mysteries in which it is enveloped. It is therefore best that you remain in your place, give Me the necessary awe and respect, and cease debating with Me.

In His response to Job, God does not give him new information about the way He conducts the world, nor does He explain anything about Job's suffering that he did not already know. Nevertheless, in God's answer, Job receives something of what he has been seeking. Job had demanded that he be allowed to stand before God and make his claims to Him. Now, after Elihu has described to him some of God's mighty deeds, Job merits a direct response from God. The content of Elihu's speech can thus be seen as preparation for God's answer from the tempest. In both cases, the unbridgeable chasm between God and man is emphasized. However, the description of the world in God's response is on a greater scale than Elihu's depiction. The depiction of the world in this section moves from the beginning of existence to God's routine management of the world: From the heavens, the heavenly bodies, and precipitation to the earth and its foundations, from His control over the spreading seas to His concern for feeding the diverse species of wild animals, thereby ensuring their continued existence.

Furthermore, the confrontation itself is an especially dramatic event. Despite the unfathomable gap between God and man, Job merits a revelation. The power of this response lies less in its content than in the actual encounter itself.

38 1 **The Lord answered Job from the tempest,** the wind that brought down the house of his firstborn and killed his sons,[761] **and said:**

2 **Who is this who,** instead of uttering enlightening words of wisdom, **darkens counsel with ignorant words?**[762]

3 **Gird now your loins like a man.** Stand and ready yourself, as **I will ask you, and you will inform Me,** attempt to respond to Me. God's speech consists of a series of rhetorical questions.

4 **Where were you when I founded the earth? Tell, if you have achieved understanding,** if you have any knowledge of the matter:
5 **Who set its dimensions, if you know, or who extended the measure,** a measuring implement, **over it?** You are not familiar with My plans for the world or the manner of its formation.
6 **Upon what were its bases** for the pillars upon which the world rests, so to speak, **sunk?** You do not know what the world stands on, **or who established its cornerstone,**[B] the foundation of the earth,[763]
7 **when the morning stars** first **sang together**[764] **and all the children of the great,** the angels,[765] **shouted** for joy?
8 After asking questions that demonstrate to Job that he is unfamiliar with the beginning of the world and the secret of its formation and existence, God then depicts the might of the sea, whose waves can be halted only by divine power. He starts by proclaiming that from creation, the sea has been held back so that it cannot break out beyond its boundaries: **Who dammed the sea with doors** so that it should not flood the earth **when it burst out and emerged from the womb,** at the time of the sea's birth,[766]
9 **when I placed a cloud as its garment,** when I dressed the sea with a cloud, **and fog** I placed **as its swaddling**? It appears as though the great sea reaches to the edges of heaven, with the clouds and fog wrapped around it like a garment.[767]
10 **I imposed My limitations upon it.** I stopped the sea's advance[768] by means of the boundary I erected for it,[769] **and I set a bar and doors** against the sea, preventing it from encroaching upon the land.
11 **I said** to the sea: **You shall come this far and not continue** any further, **and here the foam of your waves,** which seek to rise ever higher,[770] **will be set.**[771]
12 After depicting the sea, God speaks of the light:[772] **In all your days,**[773] **have you commanded** the appearance of **the morning, and** have you ever **apprised the dawn of its place**[774]
13 that it might spread from there **to seize the ends of the earth, and the wicked will be shaken from it?** When the light shines on the earth, the wicked, who act under the cover of darkness, cease their nefarious activities.[775]
14 Each morning, **it,** the land,[776] **changes like the** soft **clay of a seal,**[B] which can be shaped into various forms, as the sun affects it in different ways,[777] **and they,** people, **present themselves** upon it **like a** fresh **garment** every day.[778]
15 **Their light,** the light of the sun, **will be withheld from the wicked, and the upraised,** strong, and powerful **arm** of the haughty **will be broken.** This will occur in the future, when this light shines on the entire land.
16 **Have you entered into the depths**[779] **of the sea? Have you walked in the recesses of the deep?** Do you know what goes on in the depths?[780]

"Clay of a seal." Left: stone cylinder seal, Mesopotamia; right: relief in ceramic clay

17 **Have the gates of death been revealed to you? Have you seen the gates of the shadow of death?** Death is also part of existence. Have you deciphered its secrets?
18 **Have you gazed until the expanses of the earth? Tell, if you know all of it.** You do not know everything about the world.
19 **On which path does the light dwell, and darkness, what is its place**
20 **that you would take it,** both the light and the darkness, and bring each one **to its domain,** its proper place, **and that you would understand** which are **the paths of its home,** leading to those places?
21 Before continuing to lay out His questions before Job, which serve to emphasize the lowliness of man and his brief life span, God tells him mockingly: If **you know** all these matters, the reason must be **for you were born then,** when the world was created, **and the number of your days is many.** One who has lived less than the duration of the world cannot know all these things; they are known only to Me.
22 **Have you come to the storehouses of snow, and have you seen the storehouses of hail**
23 **that I have withheld for a time of trouble,** or, alternatively, for the time to punish the enemy, **for a day of battle and war?** When I wage war against the wicked, I will bring down upon them a flood of snow and hail.[781]
24 **What is the way that the light breaks through?** From where is it that **the east wind is scattered upon the earth?**
25 **Who cleaved a channel for the torrent,** a path through which the rain descends from the clouds so that it reaches particular areas,[782] **and** who cleared **a way for the flash of the thunder**[783]
26 **to rain** even **on a land with no man, a wilderness, no person in it,**
27 in order **to sate the desolation and wasteland,** the neglected places that no one cares to irrigate,[784] **and to cause the grass to sprout** there?
28 **Does the rain have a father? And who begot the drops of dew?** What is the source of precipitation?

ד ה אֵיפֹה הָיִיתָ בְּיָסְדִי־אָרֶץ הַגֵּד אִם־יָדַעְתָּ בִינָה׃ מִי־שָׂם מְמַדֶּיהָ כִּי תֵדָע אוֹ מִי־
ו ז נָטָה עָלֶיהָ קָּו׃ עַל־מָה אֲדָנֶיהָ הָטְבָּעוּ אוֹ מִי־יָרָה אֶבֶן פִּנָּתָהּ׃ בְּרָן־יַחַד כּוֹכְבֵי
ח ט בֹקֶר וַיָּרִיעוּ כָּל־בְּנֵי אֱלֹהִים׃ וַיָּסֶךְ בִּדְלָתַיִם יָם בְּגִיחוֹ מֵרֶחֶם יֵצֵא׃ בְּשׂוּמִי עָנָן
י יא לְבֻשׁוֹ וַעֲרָפֶל חֲתֻלָּתוֹ׃ וָאֶשְׁבֹּר עָלָיו חֻקִּי וָאָשִׂים בְּרִיחַ וּדְלָתָיִם׃ וָאֹמַר עַד־פֹּה
יב תָבוֹא וְלֹא תֹסִיף וּפֹא־יָשִׁית בִּגְאוֹן גַּלֶּיךָ׃ הֲמִיָּמֶיךָ צִוִּיתָ בֹּקֶר יִדַּעְתָּה שַׁחַר הַשַּׁחַר
יג יד מְקֹמוֹ׃ לֶאֱחֹז בְּכַנְפוֹת הָאָרֶץ וְיִנָּעֲרוּ רְשָׁעִים מִמֶּנָּה׃ תִּתְהַפֵּךְ כְּחֹמֶר חוֹתָם
טו טז וְיִתְיַצְּבוּ כְּמוֹ לְבוּשׁ׃ וְיִמָּנַע מֵרְשָׁעִים אוֹרָם וּזְרוֹעַ רָמָה תִּשָּׁבֵר׃ הֲבָאתָ עַד־
יז נִבְכֵי־יָם וּבְחֵקֶר תְּהוֹם הִתְהַלָּכְתָּ׃ הֲנִגְלוּ לְךָ שַׁעֲרֵי־מָוֶת וְשַׁעֲרֵי צַלְמָוֶת תִּרְאֶה׃
יח יט הִתְבֹּנַנְתָּ עַד־רַחֲבֵי־אָרֶץ הַגֵּד אִם־יָדַעְתָּ כֻלָּהּ׃ אֵי־זֶה הַדֶּרֶךְ יִשְׁכָּן־אוֹר וְחֹשֶׁךְ
כ כא אֵי־זֶה מְקֹמוֹ׃ כִּי תִקָּחֶנּוּ אֶל־גְּבוּלוֹ וְכִי תָבִין נְתִיבוֹת בֵּיתוֹ׃ יָדַעְתָּ כִּי־אָז תִּוָּלֵד
כב כג וּמִסְפַּר יָמֶיךָ רַבִּים׃ הֲבָאתָ אֶל־אֹצְרוֹת שָׁלֶג וְאוֹצְרוֹת בָּרָד תִּרְאֶה׃ אֲשֶׁר־
כד חָשַׂכְתִּי לְעֶת־צָר לְיוֹם קְרָב וּמִלְחָמָה׃ אֵי־זֶה הַדֶּרֶךְ יֵחָלֶק אוֹר יָפֵץ קָדִים
כה כו עֲלֵי־אָרֶץ׃ מִי־פִלַּג לַשֶּׁטֶף תְּעָלָה וְדֶרֶךְ לַחֲזִיז קֹלוֹת׃ לְהַמְטִיר עַל־אֶרֶץ לֹא־
כז כח אִישׁ מִדְבָּר לֹא־אָדָם בּוֹ׃ לְהַשְׂבִּיעַ שֹׁאָה וּמְשֹׁאָה וּלְהַצְמִיחַ מֹצָא דֶשֶׁא׃ הֲיֵשׁ־

BACKGROUND

38:6| **Cornerstone:** The construction of stone and brick houses generally started with the placement of a cornerstone in order to establish the exact location of the house, the directions of the walls that extended from the cornerstone, and even the right angles where the walls would meet. Since the placing of a cornerstone was viewed as a necessary stage in the proper construction of a durable and aesthetically pleasing edifice, it was considered of great importance.

38:14| **The clay of a seal:** The use of clay for a seal comes from Mesopotamia. From there, the practice spread in the form of cylinder seals throughout the ancient Near East, including Egypt. The manufacturers of such seals had to take into account the fact that the desired picture would be the reverse of how it appeared on the seal, in the form of indentations rather than protrusions.

29 **From whose belly did the ice emerge, and the frost of heav-
en, who gave birth to it?**
30 **Like stone, water hides itself** when it turns into blocks of
ice,[785] **and the face of the deep,** where large amounts of water
are gathered,[786] **congeals** into ice.[787]
31 God now speaks of the stars: **Will you tie the chains of the
Pleiades?** Can you confine and control the star clusters, such
as Pleiades? **Or** can you **untie the reins of Orion?** Orion is a
constellation of stars (see commentary on 9:9).
32 **Will you bring out the constellations in their season and
guide Ursa,** a bright star in the star cluster of Pleiades (see
commentary on 9:9), **with her sons,** smaller stars?[788]
33 **Do you know the rules of the heavens,** the laws of the heavenly bodies? **Will you establish its,** heaven's,[789] **dominion on
earth?**
34 **Will you raise your voice to the cloud** and instruct it where to
move, so **that a cascade of water,** rainwater, **will** immediately
cover you?
35 **Will you** have the power to **cast lightning and** then **it will go
and say to you,** in submission and readiness to fulfill your instructions: **Here we are?**
36 **Who set wisdom in ob-
scurity,** in concealed, secret
places,[790] or, alternatively, in
the kidneys or innards? **Or
who gave understanding to
the heart,**[791] or to the rooster,
so that it knows to crow at
regular times of the day?[792]

Rooster

37 **Who will relate about the
skies with wisdom, and
who can lay down the con-
tainers of the heavens,** the
clouds that are filled with
water, so that they rain down
on the world,[793]

"Who can lay down the containers of the heavens?"

38 **when the dust consolidates
into a mass and the clods
stick together** from the rainfall?[794]
39 God returns to His descriptions of life on earth: **Will you hunt
prey for the lion**[D] **or fill the need of young lions?** Can you
provide the needs of wild animals
40 **when they crouch**[795] **in their dens and wait in a lair for their
ambush** of their prey?
41 **Who prepares for the
unsightly crow,**[B] the most
despised of birds,[796] **its prey
when its young,** its wretched offspring, plead and **cry
to God, wandering without
food?**

Lion crouching in ambush, ready to leap on its prey

"Who prepares for the crow its prey?"

"When its young cry to God"

39 1 **Have you** ever **known the
time when ibexes give
birth? Will you mark,** do
you remember precisely, **the
calving of hinds?**
2 **Will you count the months
of their reaching term,** the
months of their pregnancy
until they give birth, **and
know the time when they give birth,** so that you can assist
them?

Ibex and its young

DISCUSSION

38:39| **Will you hunt prey for the lion:** The detailed description of the world presented here complements the description of nature and God's providence of the world that appears in Psalms 104, where a poetic style is also utilized. However, in Psalms 104, the human author expresses his amazement at the harmony of the world and blesses God for being allowed to perceive it. By contrast, here the Creator Himself attests to the complexity of the world. This complexity demonstrates to Job, who is ill, wounded, and lonely, his lowliness in comparison to God.

כט לַמָּטָר אָב אוֹ מִי־הוֹלִיד אֶגְלֵי־טָל: מִבֶּטֶן מִי יָצָא הַקָּרַח וּכְפֹר שָׁמַיִם מִי יְלָדוֹ:
ל לא כְּאֶבֶן מַיִם יִתְחַבָּאוּ וּפְנֵי תְהוֹם יִתְלַכָּדוּ: הַתְקַשֵּׁר מַעֲדַנּוֹת כִּימָה אוֹ־מֹשְׁכוֹת
לב לג כְּסִיל תְּפַתֵּחַ: הֲתֹצִיא מַזָּרוֹת בְּעִתּוֹ וְעַיִשׁ עַל־בָּנֶיהָ תַנְחֵם: הֲיָדַעְתָּ חֻקּוֹת שָׁמָיִם
לד לה אִם־תָּשִׂים מִשְׁטָרוֹ בָאָרֶץ: הֲתָרִים לָעָב קוֹלֶךָ וְשִׁפְעַת־מַיִם תְּכַסֶּךָּ: הַתְשַׁלַּח ח
לו בְּרָקִים וְיֵלֵכוּ וְיֹאמְרוּ לְךָ הִנֵּנוּ: מִי־שָׁת בַּטֻּחוֹת חָכְמָה אוֹ מִי־נָתַן לַשֶּׂכְוִי בִינָה:
לז לח מִי־יְסַפֵּר שְׁחָקִים בְּחָכְמָה וְנִבְלֵי שָׁמַיִם מִי יַשְׁכִּיב: בְּצֶקֶת עָפָר לַמּוּצָק וּרְגָבִים
לט מ יְדֻבָּקוּ: הֲתָצוּד לְלָבִיא טָרֶף וְחַיַּת כְּפִירִים תְּמַלֵּא: כִּי־יָשֹׁחוּ בַמְּעוֹנוֹת יֵשְׁבוּ
מא בַסֻּכָּה לְמוֹ־אָרֶב: מִי יָכִין לָעֹרֵב צֵידוֹ כִּי־יְלָדָו אֶל־אֵל יְשַׁוֵּעוּ יִתְעוּ לִבְלִי־אֹכֶל:
א ב הֲיָדַעְתָּ עֵת לֶדֶת יַעֲלֵי־סָלַע חֹלֵל אַיָּלוֹת תִּשְׁמֹר: תִּסְפֹּר יְרָחִים תְּמַלֶּאנָה וְיָדַעְתָּ
ג ד עֵת לִדְתָּנָה: תִּכְרַעְנָה יַלְדֵיהֶן תְּפַלַּחְנָה חֶבְלֵיהֶם תְּשַׁלַּחְנָה: יַחְלְמוּ בְנֵיהֶם יִרְבּוּ
ה ו בַבָּר יָצְאוּ וְלֹא־שָׁבוּ לָמוֹ: מִי־שִׁלַּח פֶּרֶא חָפְשִׁי וּמֹסְרוֹת עָרוֹד מִי פִתֵּחַ: אֲשֶׁר־

3 When **they crouch, their young emerge** from their sundered bodies,[797] **and they cast off their labor pains,** as their birth pangs elapse on their own.[798] Man can feed domestic animals and even help them give birth, whereas wild animals are nourished and procreate without any human knowledge or involvement at all.

4 **Their young,** those of wild goats and hinds, **grow strong; they grow** outside **in the wild; they emerge** on their own **and do not return to them,** their mothers.

5 **Who sent the onager** [*pereh*] (see commentary on 6:5) **free,** so that it cannot be tamed at all? **Who loosened the reins of the wild ass** [*arod*],[B]

Onager

African wild donkey

6 **for whom I rendered,** established, the **wilderness his home, and salt land,** desert regions, **his dwelling?**

BACKGROUND

38:41 | **Crow:** The hooded crow, *Corvus cornix*, is one of the most common birds in Israel. Its length is 44–51 cm, and it has a wingspan of 84–100 cm. Its body is gray, while its head, chest, wings, and feet are black. An omnivorous bird, it will often gather its food near human habitation. The cry of the offspring of crows to God is also mentioned in Psalms (147:9). The crow is listed among the non-kosher birds (Leviticus 11:15).

39:5 | **Wild ass [*arod*]:** This is the African wild donkey, *Equus africanus*, which is a different species of wild donkey than the onager, or *pereh*, mentioned in the first clause of the verse. The *arod* is gray in the winter and has lighter-colored legs, with dark, hairy rings. This animal is larger than the *pereh*; its shoulder height is 135 cm, and it is very fast. The males of this wild donkey aggressively guard their habitats, and territorial fights between them are violent and cruel. The *arod* is more similar to a domesticated donkey than the *pereh*.

7 Since this animal lives only in uninhabited areas, **he scoffs at
the tumult of the city,** the sounds of work that can be heard
there.[799] He **does not hear the shouts of the oppressor,** who
is tyrannizing others.
8 **He scouts the hills for his pasture,** he roams and explores the
mountains for his pasture,[800] **and seeks everything green,**
vegetation.
9 **Will the aurochs,**[B] large, strong wild animals, **be willing to
serve you? Will he stay the night near your trough** and feed
there? Many creatures in the world are not dependent upon
man and receive no assistance from him.
10 **Can you bind the aurochs with his rope to a furrow,** to have
him plow there? **Will he loosen,** turn over, **the soil of valleys
after you?**

Oxen plowing a furrow

11 **Will you trust him because his strength is great? Will you**
therefore **leave your toil** in your sown field **for him?**[801]
12 **Will you trust him that he will restore your seed and gather
from your threshing floor?** Perhaps you might try to train the
wild ox and harness it for your labor in light of its size and power. However, it is too strong for humans to control and use for
their needs.
13 The chapter now describes wonders involving birds: Did you
create[802] **the wing of the songbird [*renanim*],** which **beats
joyously? Are its pinions and plumage of a stork?** Did you
create the wing joints and feathers of the stork?[803] Some maintain that *renanim* refers to a songbird,[804] while others say that it
refers to a bird with colorful
wings, which glorifies itself
in its colors.[805]
14 **For it leaves its eggs on the
earth,**[B] as this bird does not
nest in trees or on rocks but
on the ground, **and warms
them on dust,**

Ostrich warming its eggs on dust

15 **and it forgets,** does not take into account, **that a foot** of any
creature **may** step on an egg and **crush it or a beast of the field**
may **trample it.**
16 **It,** that bird, **is harsh to its young,** as certain birds become
estranged from their offspring and abandon them, **as though
they are not from it; its toil** in hatching the eggs **is in vain,
without concern** that its fledglings might be taken from it,
17 **for God deprived it of wisdom,** or made it forget its wisdom,[806] **and did not allot understanding to it.**
18 **In time,** when it wishes to fly,[807] **it will soar on high and scoff
at the horse and its rider,** as they cannot harm it, since God
watches over this bird.[808]
19 **Do you give the horse
strength?**[B] **Do you clothe
its neck with a mane?**
20 **Do you cause it to rever-
berate like a locust?** Do you
enable the horse to emit a
noise like that which is produced by locusts when they
swarm upon fields?[809] **The
glory of its snorting is terror,** terrifying.[810]

Archer on a horse, stone relief, palace of Ashurbanipal, Nineveh, 645–635 BCE

21 When **it,** a war horse, gallops, it **gouges in the valley**[811] **and
rejoices with strength; it issues forth toward weapons.** This
animal is ready for battle.
22 **It scoffs at fear**[812] **and is not dismayed; it does not retreat
from a sword.**
23 **Upon it the quiver rattles,**[813] a noise produced by **the blade of**
the **spear and javelin** striking the arrows in the quiver.
24 **Noisily and speedily it swallows the land,** or gallops over
the land, **and** in its joy **does not forbear due to the sound of
the shofar** that it hears, calling the soldiers to war and warning
them about the approaching enemy. The animal lusts so greatly
for war that it can scarcely believe the battle has arrived.[814]
25 **With the sounding of the shofar,**[815] which signals the com-
mencement of battle, **it says: Hurrah.** The horse rejoices in
anticipation of war. **From afar it smells the war** and hears **the
thundering of the officers** of war[816] **and the shouting.** Unlike
the wild animals discussed in previous verses, war horses are
constantly in close contact with humans.
26 God returns to discussing birds: **Is
it by your understanding that the
hawk flies, stretches its wings to
the south?** Migrating hawks pass
through the Land of Israel on their
way south.[817] Is the hawk's knowledge that it must fly southward for
the winter derived from human
understanding?

Hawk

ז שַׂמְתִּי עֲרָבָה בֵיתוֹ וּמִשְׁכְּנוֹתָיו מְלֵחָה: יִשְׂחַק לַהֲמוֹן קִרְיָה תְּשֻׁאוֹת נוֹגֵשׂ לֹא
ח ט יִשְׁמָע: יְתוּר הָרִים מִרְעֵהוּ וְאַחַר כָּל־יָרוֹק יִדְרוֹשׁ: הֲיֹאבֶה רֵים עָבְדֶךָ אִם־יָלִין
י יא עַל־אֲבוּסֶךָ: הֲתִקְשָׁר־רֵים בְּתֶלֶם עֲבֹתוֹ אִם־יְשַׂדֵּד עֲמָקִים אַחֲרֶיךָ: הֲתִבְטַח־
יב בּוֹ כִּי־רַב כֹּחוֹ וְתַעֲזֹב אֵלָיו יְגִיעֶךָ: הֲתַאֲמִין בּוֹ כִּי־ישוב זַרְעֶךָ וְגָרְנְךָ יֶאֱסֹף: יָשִׁיב
יג יד כְּנַף־רְנָנִים נֶעֱלָסָה אִם־אֶבְרָה חֲסִידָה וְנֹצָה: כִּי־תַעֲזֹב לָאָרֶץ בֵּצֶיהָ וְעַל־עָפָר
טו טז תְּחַמֵּם: וַתִּשְׁכַּח כִּי־רֶגֶל תְּזוּרֶהָ וְחַיַּת הַשָּׂדֶה תְּדוּשֶׁהָ: הִקְשִׁיחַ בָּנֶיהָ לְּלֹא־לָהּ
יז יח לְרִיק יְגִיעָהּ בְּלִי־פָחַד: כִּי־הִשָּׁהּ אֱלוֹהַּ חָכְמָה וְלֹא־חָלַק לָהּ בַּבִּינָה: כָּעֵת בַּמָּרוֹם
יט תַּמְרִיא תִּשְׂחַק לַסּוּס וּלְרֹכְבוֹ: הֲתִתֵּן לַסּוּס גְּבוּרָה הֲתַלְבִּישׁ צַוָּארוֹ רַעְמָה:
כ כא הֲתַרְעִישֶׁנּוּ כָּאַרְבֶּה הוֹד נַחְרוֹ אֵימָה: יַחְפְּרוּ בָעֵמֶק וְיָשִׂישׂ בְּכֹחַ יֵצֵא לִקְרַאת־
כב כג נָשֶׁק: יִשְׂחַק לְפַחַד וְלֹא יֵחָת וְלֹא־יָשׁוּב מִפְּנֵי־חָרֶב: עָלָיו תִּרְנֶה אַשְׁפָּה לַהַב
כד כה חֲנִית וְכִידוֹן: בְּרַעַשׁ וְרֹגֶז יְגַמֶּא־אָרֶץ וְלֹא־יַאֲמִין כִּי־קוֹל שׁוֹפָר: בְּדֵי שֹׁפָר ׀
כו יֹאמַר הֶאָח וּמֵרָחוֹק יָרִיחַ מִלְחָמָה רַעַם שָׂרִים וּתְרוּעָה: הֲמִבִּינָתְךָ יַאֲבֶר־נֵץ

BACKGROUND

39:9| **The aurochs [*reim*]:** The *reim*, or *re'em*, refers to the aurochs, an extinct species of large wild cattle, *Bos primigenius*. Aurochs were common in Israel in biblical times, and remains of their skeletons have been found in the Golan Heights. They were far larger than modern-day cattle, reaching roughly 3 m in length, while the height of their shoulders was about 2 m, and they weighed up to a ton. Their huge horns, angled toward the front, were at least the height of an average person. This is not the *re'em* of modern Hebrew, which is the oryx, called *dishon* in the Bible.

39:14| **It leaves its eggs on the earth:** The descriptions in these verses suit the peacock, genus *Pavo*, or the common ostrich, *Struthio camelus*, with its unusual height (2–2.5 m) and variegated feathering, which can be black-white, brown-white, or striped brown-white. The feathers of both these birds have been used from ancient times for decorating elegant items of clothing, especially the crowns of nobles and kings. The verse mentions the habit of the females of these species to lay their eggs on the surface of the ground.

39:19| **Do you give the horse strength?:** In the ancient world, horses were not used for labor but for riding and war. It seems that in those times, a method of harnessing horses for plowing that did not concurrently cause pain to the animal had not yet been discovered (see commentary on Exodus 14:7). Horses were trained to fearlessly participate in attacks against an enemy during battle. In the height of battle, amid the chaos, commotion, and attempts to strike the opponents with swords and kill them, these animals needed to be obedient to their masters. Occasionally, they took a more active role in the battle as well; in addition to carrying their riders, they were also sometimes expected to kick the enemy or to bite them.

27 **Does the eagle ascend** to fly **at your directive and raise** on
high places **its nest?**[818]
28 **On a rock it dwells and**
stays the night, sleeps, **on**
the crag of the rock and the
stronghold.
29 **From there,** the mountain
heights, **it spies food;**[819] **its**
eyes look afar.[B]
30 The eagle itself eats some of
the carrion it finds, while it
brings a portion for its offspring in the nest: **Its young swallow**
blood,[820] as they too are nourished from carcasses; **where the**
slain are found, **there it is.**

Eagle's nest on a high crag

40 1 After it has been called to Job's attention that he is only one of
God's many creatures, and that despite his highly developed
consciousness he is incapable of running the world, he no
longer voices his complaints, but prefers to remain silent. **The**
Lord answered Job and said:
2 **Should one who quarrels with the Almighty be chastised?**
Is he likely to accept reproof? Alternatively, does one who contends with God act in a moral manner?[821] **Let one who rebukes**
God please **respond to it,** God's reproof. You are invited to try
to respond to Me.[822]

Job's First Response to God

JOB 40:3–5

Job's complaints are silenced in the face of the divine communication. At the conclusion of His address to Job, God invited Job to respond to His words, but Job has nothing to say.

3 **Job answered the Lord and said:**
4 **I am insignificant** in my own eyes; **what will I answer You?** I
have no response. **I place my hand to my mouth** as a mark of
silence.
5 **I have spoken once, but I will not respond; twice, but I will**
not continue. I have indeed spoken too much.

God's Second Response to Job

JOB 40:6–41:26

In this next series of rhetorical questions, God mocks the human pretention of mastery over the animal kingdom, that man can control the beasts of enormous dimensions that are found both in the sea and on land. Through detailed presentations of two giant creatures, God vividly reminds Job of his smallness and insignificance in the universe, especially when faced with his Creator. These descriptions are not designed to provide Job with information, nor are they a direct response to his claims. Rather, they are meant to evoke in him feelings of wonder, humility, and awe in the presence of divine greatness.

6 **The Lord answered Job from the tempest and said:**
7 **Gird now your loins like a man,** prepare yourself, for **I will**
ask you; I will show you other natural phenomena, **and you**
will inform Me, respond to Me.
8 **Will you even disavow My justice,** by claiming that My judgment is unfair? **Will you condemn Me** by claiming that I am
wicked **so that you may be vindicated?**
9 **Do you have an arm,** strength, **like God?** If you are wiser and
more righteous than I, perhaps you are also as strong as I.[823] **Can**
you thunder with a voice like Him?
10 **Adorn**[824] **yourself now with grandeur and eminence, and**
don glory and majesty like Me.[825]
11 **Scatter your irate wrath, and see every proud one, and**
abase him.
12 **See every proud one and subdue him, and crush**[826] **the wicked in their place.**
13 **Hide them in the dust together; cover their faces in**
concealment,[827]
14 **and I also will concede to you if your right hand can save**
you. If you can do with your strength that which I am able to
do, I will concede your righteousness.[828] God scorns
Job's efforts to confront Him, as though there is any comparison between him and his Creator. In effect, He is saying to Job:
If you run the world better than I do, then I will confess that you
are correct and I will praise you.
15 If you cannot control humans that are arrogant, go and seek
other creatures:[829] **Behold now** the **behemoth,**[D] the name of a
large animal,[830] **which I made with you,** which shares the world
with you;[831] **it eats hay like cattle.** This creature is herbivorous.
16 **Behold now, its strength is in its loins, and its potency is in**
the muscles of its belly.
17 **It shakes its tail** quickly,[832] **like a cedar.** Its massive tail looks
like a cedar tree swaying in
the wind.[833] **The veins of its**
testicles are knit together,
like the boughs of a tree.[834]
18 **Its bones are like chunks**[835]
of bronze; its bones are
like an iron bar.
19 **It is the first of the ways of**
God, the most important
of God's creatures,[836] or the

Cedar

כז כח יפרש כנפו לתימן: אם־על־פיך יגביה נשר וכי ירים קנו: סלע ישכן ויתלנן
כט ל על־שן־סלע ומצודה: משם חפר־אכל למרחוק עיניו יביטו: ואפרחו יעלעו־
א ב דם ובאשר חללים שם הוא: ויען יהוה את־איוב ויאמר: הרב עם־
ג ד שדי יסור מוכיח אלוה יעננה: ויען איוב את־יהוה ויאמר: הן קלתי
ה מה אשיבך ידי שמתי למו־פי: אחת דברתי ולא אענה ושתים ולא
ו ז אוסיף: ויען־יהוה את־איוב מנסערה ויאמר: אזר־נא כגבר חלציך
ח ט אשאלך והודיעני: האף תפר משפטי תרשיעני למען תצדק: ואם־זרוע כאל ׀
י יא לך ובקול כמהו תרעם: עדה־נא גאון וגבה והוד והדר תלבש: הפץ עברות
יב אפך וראה כל־גאה והשפילהו: ראה כל־גאה הכניעהו והדך רשעים תחתם:
יג יד טמנם בעפר יחד פניהם חבש בטמון: וגם־אני אודך כי־תושע לך ימינך:
טו טז הנה־נא בהמות אשר־עשיתי עמך חציר כבקר יאכל: הנה־נא כחו במתניו
יז יח ואונו בשרירי בטנו: יחפץ זנבו כמו־ארז גידי פחדו ישרגו: עצמיו אפיקי
יט כ נחשה גרמיו כמטיל ברזל: הוא ראשית דרכי־אל העשו יגש חרבו: כי־בול
כא הרים ישאו־לו וכל־חית השדה ישחקו־שם: תחת־צאלים ישכב בסתר קנה

מן | סערה

first animal created by God.[837] This animal is invulnerable to any attack from hunters or beasts of prey; only **its Maker may present His sword** to kill it.[838]

20 **For produce of mountains will be carried to it,** they will bring it food produced by the mountains, **and all the beasts of the field play there,** where it lies down. The behemoth does not prey upon nor harm any other animal.[839]

21 **It lies beneath the lotuses [*tze'elim*]**[B] **in the cover of reed and swamp.** Alternatively, *tze'elim* is a general name for trees that provide shade [*tzel*], or it refers to shadows [*tzelalim*].[840]

"Reed and swamp." Hula Lake nature reserve

BACKGROUND

39:29 | **Its eyes look afar:** The eagle builds its nests in rocky heights, where its eggs and offspring are protected from predators. It feeds partly on carcasses, which it can see from a distance due to its sharp vision (see commentary on 9:26).

40:21 | **The lotuses [*tze'elim*]:** Some say that this is the Christ's thorn jujube, *Ziziphus spina-christi*, which grows on the banks of the Jordan, alongside other plants that grow on riverbanks, such as willows and reeds. It is a prickly tree, roughly 5 m in height, and it provides sweet but poor-quality fruit. As a riverside plant, it is frequently used for browsing and as a hiding place by local animals, even the largest ones. Others maintain that *tze'elim* is the acacia tree, based on its similarity to the Arabic term.

DISCUSSION

40:15 | **Behemoth:** It is difficult to ascertain whether the reference is to an actual creature, perhaps a hippopotamus or an elephant. The Sages called the behemoth a wild ox, a massive animal that lives in the unknown reaches of the world about which travelers would relate fantastical and exaggerated stories (Ibn Ezra; *Bava Batra* 74b; *Bereshit Rabba* 7:4; *Bemidbar Rabba* 21:18; *Midrash Tanḥuma*, *Pinhas* 12).

22 **The lotuses cover it with their shade;**[841] **the willows of the brook surround it.**

23 **Behold,** this beast is so large that **it can swallow a river; it need not rush.** It has the strength to swallow a river, and it will not rush due to any fear, as it is not afraid of any other creature. **It is secure, even if it draws the Jordan into its mouth,** even if the behemoth were to attempt to suck in the river.[842]

24 **Before its eyes it takes it; it will pierce its nose with snags.** In its desire to swallow the entire Jordan, the behemoth will lower its face and appear to ingest it through its eyes, and thereby pierce its own nose on the rocks that can be found on the riverbed.[843]

25 From the behemoth, the most massive land animal, God moves on to a description of the leviathan, the largest creature in the sea: **Can you pull up a leviathan**[B] **with a hook or grip its tongue with a cord,** catch it using a rod inserted in its tongue?[844]

26 **Can you put a** bent **hook**[845] **into its nose or pierce its cheek with a barb**[B] in order to trap it?

Pointed stalk used for fishing, illustration based on fresco from Beni Hasan cemetery, Egypt, twenty-fourth century BCE

27 If you did try to catch the enormous leviathan, **will** you expect **it** to **make many supplications to you or will it speak softly to you,** entreating you not to carry out your plan?[846]

28 **Will it establish a covenant with you** in order to escape the threat you pose? **Will** it agree that **you** may **take it as an eternal slave?**

29 **Will you play with it like** one plays **with a bird, or will you bind it for your girls,** as a toy for your children?[847]

30 **Will enchanters,** or wise men and sorcerers,[848] or bands of merchants,[849] **make a banquet of it?**[850] **Will they divide it,** divide up its flesh, **among merchants?**[851]

31 **Can you fill its skin with darts,** or thorns, in order to capture the leviathan **or** pierce **its head with fish spears,** sharp implements for catching fish?[852]

32 If you have already tried to **lay your hand upon it** in an attempt to capture the huge creature, **remember war** and act **no more.** The memory of the struggle will prevent you from having any further desire to do so, as your provocation of the leviathan would certainly have been a traumatic experience for you.[853]

Spears for catching large fish

41 1 **Behold, hope for it,** for capturing the leviathan,[854] **is futile; isn't one cast down** in fright **even at the sight of it?**[855]

2 **No one is so fierce as to rouse it** from its rest;[856] **who is it who can stand before Me?** God invites anyone who imagines that he can defeat the leviathan to engage Him, so to speak.

3 **Who surpasses Me? I will pay.** If there is one who is more successful than Me in this confrontation, I will pay him the sum of this wager. I can pay him, as **everything beneath the heavens is Mine.**

4 If there were such a cruel and mighty individual, **I would not be silent about his exploits,** his mighty actions, **and about speaking of his feats, and the elegance of his shapeliness,** the grace of his limbs. Some explain this verse as a rhetorical question rather than a statement.

5 God returns to the description of the leviathan:[857] **Who can reveal that which is under the front of its garment,** what is hidden within its mantle of scales? **Who can approach its double bridle,** the spot between its jaws, where a bridle might be placed? No one would dare venture near there.

6 **Who can open the doors of its face,** its mouth?[858] **Around its teeth** there **is terror.** Its teeth threaten all those in its vicinity.

7 **Rows of scales,** the ridges of its scales, **are its pride,** so that its flesh is **closed** beneath them, as **with a tight seal.**

8 **One meets another,** the scales touch each other, so that **no space comes between them.**

9 **Each is stuck to the other; they are interlocked** into a single sheet of armor **and cannot be separated.**

10 **Its sneezes flash light.** When the leviathan sneezes, it appears as though it is emitting lightning, **and its eyes are like the eyes of dawn.** Its eyes glow like the reddening of the skies before sunrise.[859]

11 **Torches proceed from its mouth, and** even **sparks of fire escape** from it.[860]

כב כג וּבִצָּה׃ יְסֻכֻּהוּ צֶאֱלִים צִלֲלוֹ יְסֻבּוּהוּ עַרְבֵי־נָחַל׃ הֵן יַעֲשֹׁק נָהָר וְלֹא יַחְפּוֹז יִבְטַח ׀
כד כה כִּי־יָגִיחַ יַרְדֵּן אֶל־פִּיהוּ׃ בְּעֵינָיו יִקָּחֶנּוּ בְּמוֹקְשִׁים יִנְקָב־אָף׃ תִּמְשֹׁךְ לִוְיָתָן בְּחַכָּה
כו כז וּבְחֶבֶל תַּשְׁקִיעַ לְשֹׁנוֹ׃ הֲתָשִׂים אַגְמֹן בְּאַפּוֹ וּבְחוֹחַ תִּקֹּב לֶחֱיוֹ׃ הֲיַרְבֶּה אֵלֶיךָ
כח תַּחֲנוּנִים אִם־יְדַבֵּר אֵלֶיךָ רַכּוֹת׃ הֲיִכְרֹת בְּרִית עִמָּךְ תִּקָּחֶנּוּ לְעֶבֶד עוֹלָם׃
כט ל הַתְשַׂחֶק־בּוֹ כַּצִּפּוֹר וְתִקְשְׁרֶנּוּ לְנַעֲרוֹתֶיךָ׃ יִכְרוּ עָלָיו חַבָּרִים יֶחֱצוּהוּ בֵּין כְּנַעֲנִים׃
לא לב הַתְמַלֵּא בְשֻׂכּוֹת עוֹרוֹ וּבְצִלְצַל דָּגִים רֹאשׁוֹ׃ שִׂים־עָלָיו כַּפֶּךָ זְכֹר מִלְחָמָה אַל־
א א ב תּוֹסַף׃ הֵן־תֹּחַלְתּוֹ נִכְזָבָה הֲגַם אֶל־מַרְאָיו יֻטָל׃ לֹא־אַכְזָר כִּי יְעוּרֶנּוּ וּמִי הוּא
ג ד לְפָנַי יִתְיַצָּב׃ מִי הִקְדִּימַנִי וַאֲשַׁלֵּם תַּחַת כָּל־הַשָּׁמַיִם לִי־הוּא׃ לֹא־אַחֲרִישׁ בַּדָּיו לוֹ־
ה ו וּדְבַר־גְּבוּרוֹת וְחִין עֶרְכּוֹ׃ מִי־גִלָּה פְּנֵי לְבוּשׁוֹ בְּכֶפֶל רִסְנוֹ מִי יָבוֹא׃ דַּלְתֵי פָנָיו
ז ח מִי פִתֵּחַ סְבִיבוֹת שִׁנָּיו אֵימָה׃ גַּאֲוָה אֲפִיקֵי מָגִנִּים סָגוּר חוֹתָם צָר׃ אֶחָד בְּאֶחָד
ט י יִגַּשׁוּ וְרוּחַ לֹא־יָבֹא בֵינֵיהֶם׃ אִישׁ־בְּאָחִיהוּ יְדֻבָּקוּ יִתְלַכְּדוּ וְלֹא יִתְפָּרָדוּ׃ עֲטִישֹׁתָיו
יא תָּהֶל אוֹר וְעֵינָיו כְּעַפְעַפֵּי־שָׁחַר׃ מִפִּיו לַפִּידִים יַהֲלֹכוּ כִּידוֹדֵי אֵשׁ יִתְמַלָּטוּ׃

BACKGROUND

40:25 | **Leviathan:** It is unclear which creature is referred to by the term "leviathan." The crocodile possesses some, but not all, of the characteristics described here. For instance, its scales are extremely strong and have the ability to withstand the blow of weapons (41:19–21). The leviathan's other characteristics are consistent with the shark, which is certainly a terrifying predator. For example, the description of the creature's formidable teeth (41:6) is consistent with the numerous teeth of the crocodile as well as the lower teeth of the shark, which could easily crush a fisherman's raft. Moreover, the teeth of a crocodile are exposed even when its mouth is not open. Nevertheless, the overall description, which in its plain meaning includes emitting flames from its mouth (41:11, 13) as well as possessing a neck (41:14), is not consistent with the known characteristics of these animals or any other animal. Like the behemoth, it seems that this massive, mysterious creature is not an actual living being that is found in the world known to humans today.

40:26 | **Or pierce its cheek with a barb:** In ancient times they would use reed stalks when fishing to both kill the fish and carry it away. They would pierce the fish with the pointed stalk, which they would then thread through its body. The large thorns of thistles were used as rods, while metal rings were passed through the nostrils or cheeks of the animal in order to control it and lead it in the desired direction.

12 **Smoke emerges from its nostrils, like** steam that rises **from a boiling vat or** bubbling **cauldron.**[861]

Steam emerging from a boiling vat

13 **Its breath ignites** like **coals, and flame emerges from its mouth.**

14 Great **might rests in its neck, and** even **anguish,** worry and pain,[862] **rejoices**[863] **before it.** It has no concerns or sadness. Alternatively, since it devours and ruins everything, it sows terror upon its surroundings, and therefore only the attributes of worry and distress feel at ease before it.

15 **The layers of its flesh are joined, cast upon it, will not collapse.** Its body is solid, consolidated, and tightly compressed.

16 **Its heart is cast like a stone.** It does not get nervous or scared but rather is **cast like a lower millstone.** Unlike an upper millstone, a lower millstone does not revolve.[864]

Lower and upper millstones

17 **From its rearing up, the mighty fear.** The mighty are terrified of it,[865] and **breakers are damaged.** When faced with the leviathan, even the waves are left damaged.[866]

18 The leviathan is resistant to all weapons: **One who reaches it with a sword will not recover.** Alternatively, the one who attacks it with a sword will be unable to maintain a stance against it.[867] The sword will not succeed against this creature, **or** even if one attacks **with a spear,** a larger weapon,[868] **and armor,** he will have no chance against the leviathan.[869]

"With a spear and armor." Warrior wearing armor and holding a spear, based on an illustration from ancient Greece

19 If one attempts to harm the leviathan with iron weapons, **it considers iron to be like straw,** as the iron will slip off it as though the metal were as soft as straw, **and bronze** is treated by the leviathan, due to the creature's hard, strong scales, **like rotten wood.**

20 **The arrow does not cause it to flee; slingshots** flung at it **are transformed for it into straw.** They are nothing more than stubble to the leviathan.

Aiming arrows, Lakhish reliefs, Nineveh, 700–692 BCE

Carrying slingshots, Lakhish reliefs, Nineveh, 700–692 BCE

21 The attacks of **weapons**[870] **seem like straw** to it; **it scoffs at the sound of a javelin.** Implements of destruction have no effect on the leviathan.

22 **Jagged shards are** placed **under it,** in the place where it lies, and yet they do not bother the creature at all. If **it is cushioned**

יב יג מִנְּחִירָיו יֵצֵא עָשָׁן כְּדוּד נָפוּחַ וְאַגְמֹן׃ נַפְשׁוֹ גֶּחָלִים תְּלַהֵט וְלַהַב מִפִּיו יֵצֵא׃
יד טו בְּצַוָּארוֹ יָלִין עֹז וּלְפָנָיו תָּדוּץ דְּאָבָה׃ מַפְּלֵי בְשָׂרוֹ דָבֵקוּ יָצוּק עָלָיו בַּל־יִמּוֹט׃
טז יז לִבּוֹ יָצוּק כְּמוֹ־אָבֶן וְיָצוּק כְּפֶלַח תַּחְתִּית׃ מִשֵּׂתוֹ יָגוּרוּ אֵלִים מִשְּׁבָרִים יִתְחַטָּאוּ׃
יח יט מַשִּׂיגֵהוּ חֶרֶב בְּלִי תָקוּם חֲנִית מַסָּע וְשִׁרְיָה׃ יַחְשֹׁב לְתֶבֶן בַּרְזֶל לְעֵץ רִקָּבוֹן
כ כא נְחוּשָׁה׃ לֹא־יַבְרִיחֶנּוּ בֶן־קָשֶׁת לְקַשׁ נֶהְפְּכוּ־לוֹ אַבְנֵי־קָלַע׃ כְּקַשׁ נֶחְשְׁבוּ תוֹתָח
כב כג וְיִשְׂחַק לְרַעַשׁ כִּידוֹן׃ תַּחְתָּיו חַדּוּדֵי חָרֶשׂ יִרְפַּד חָרוּץ עֲלֵי־טִיט׃ יַרְתִּיחַ כַּסִּיר
כד כה מְצוּלָה יָם יָשִׂים כַּמֶּרְקָחָה׃ אַחֲרָיו יָאִיר נָתִיב יַחְשֹׁב תְּהוֹם לְשֵׂיבָה׃ אֵין־עַל־
כו עָפָר מָשְׁלוֹ הֶעָשׂוּ לִבְלִי־חָת׃ אֵת כָּל־גָּבֹהַּ יִרְאֶה הוּא מֶלֶךְ עַל־כָּל־בְּנֵי־
ב א ב שָׁחַץ׃ וַיַּעַן אִיּוֹב אֶת־יהוה וַיֹּאמַר׃ יָדַעְתָּ כִּי־כֹל תּוּכָל וְלֹא־יִבָּצֵר
ג מִמְּךָ מְזִמָּה׃ מִי זֶה ׀ מַעְלִים עֵצָה בְּלִי דָעַת לָכֵן הִגַּדְתִּי וְלֹא אָבִין נִפְלָאוֹת מִמֶּנִּי
ד ה וְלֹא אֵדָע׃ שְׁמַע־נָא וְאָנֹכִי אֲדַבֵּר אֶשְׁאָלְךָ וְהוֹדִיעֵנִי׃ לְשֵׁמַע־אֹזֶן שְׁמַעְתִּיךָ

on a spiked **threshing sledge,** it can rest upon it **as** though it were lying **on mud.**[871] It is resistant to all sharp objects.

23 **It causes the depths** of the sea **to boil like a pot, renders the sea like a concoction** of spices.[872] The movement of this mammoth creature stirs everything in its surroundings, creating turmoil in the water.

24 **Following it, a path is illuminated.** Its quick movement leaves behind a trace in the water, like after the passage of a boat.[873] **It causes the deep to seem white-haired** like an old man, as the creature leaves white foam in its wake.[874]

25 **On land there is nothing comparable,** there is no similar creature,[875] **that is made to be** entirely **fearless.**

26 **It sees all that is exalted; it is king over all the prideful,** large beasts.[876]

Spiked threshing implement

Job's Second Response to God

JOB 42:1–6

Job's short reply to God's second speech reveals the main message of the book. God did not address the questions Job repeatedly asked. However, he finds comfort in the very fact of God's closeness to him. The presence of God is the only answer there is. In the wake of Job's direct encounter with the great truth of God, questions of ultimate meaning and justice lose their force.[877]

42 1 **Job answered the Lord and said:**

2 **I know** now what I knew before as well, **that You are able to do anything and that no purpose,** thought,[878] **is precluded for You.**

3 All that is true, and yet my consciousness has undergone such a great transformation that I wonder: **Who is this who obscures counsel, is ignorant?** How was this knowledge concealed from me before?[879] **Consequently,** I apologize, as **I have stated** until now **but did not understand;** I spoke of **matters** that **were beyond me, and I did not know.**

4 In my lack of knowledge, I said to You: **Please, hear** what I have to say, **and I will speak; I will ask You and You will inform me,** respond to me.

5 In the past, **I had heard You with the hearing of the ear.** What I knew of You was from secondhand reports, **but now**

my eye has seen You. Due to the direct revelation of Your glory before my eyes, my entire worldview has changed;[880]
6 **therefore, I recant** everything I previously said[881] **and** feel **regret over** the statements I, **dust and ashes,** a lowly mortal, have uttered. Alternatively, the power of my encounter with You led me to reject things that I previously considered valuable in my life. By Your turning to me, I have found comfort for the pain I felt while sitting in dust and ashes in lament over my sufferings.[882]

The Friends' Repentance and the Restoration of Job

JOB 42:7–17

This section, which completes the narrative of the book of Job, provides a positive ending to the terrible events with which the book opened. After the discussions and responses that took up the bulk of the book, God revealed Himself to Job. Although Job's questions were not answered in this encounter, the revelation itself was enough to lead him to a new evaluation of life, and he sees no reason to continue arguing. Here, at the end of the book, divine judgment is fully expressed: God calls Job His servant, while He demands from Job's friends that they bring sacrifices for atonement and request Job's forgiveness.

7 **It was after the Lord had spoken these matters to Job, and the Lord said to Elifaz the Temanite: My wrath is enflamed against you and against your two friends, as you have not spoken rightly of Me,** or for My sake, **like My servant Job.** Job's statements, which were uttered out of pain and anguish, were justified. Job knew that there were limits he must not cross even when he was protesting. He adamantly rejected his wife's suggestion to blaspheme God (see 2:9). By contrast, his friends spoke improperly: In their efforts to justify God, they blamed Job for what had happened to him, and when they were faced with the real suffering of their friend, they reacted by turning to abstract philosophical and theological debates.[883]

Bull

Ram

8 **Now, take for yourselves seven bulls and seven rams, and go to My servant Job, and offer up a burnt offering for yourselves** to atone for your sins. **My servant Job will pray for you,** both because you sinned toward him and because he is a good, upright man, **for I will favor** only **him, so as not to treat you degradingly,** a great evil. Only his merit can protect you from the punishment you deserve,[884] **for you have not spoken rightly of Me, like My servant Job.**
9 **Elifaz the Temanite, Bildad the Shuhite, and Tzofar the Naamatite went, and they did as the Lord had spoken to them.** They offered sacrifices, sought Job's forgiveness, and he prayed for them, **and the Lord favored Job.**
10 **The Lord restored the loss of Job when he prayed for his friends.** Job did not bear a grudge against his friends, but prayed for them. **And the Lord added to Job double of all that he had before.**
11 **All his brothers, all his sisters, and all his previous acquaintances,** who had abandoned him in his hour of distress (19:13–19), **came and ate bread with him in his house; and they commiserated with him,** they shared in his sorrow, **and consoled him over all the harm that the Lord had brought upon him. Each gave him one kesita,**[B] a coin[885] or a small sheep,[886] **and each, one gold nose ring.**

Sheep

Gold nose rings

12 **The Lord blessed the latter period of Job more than** all he possessed at **his beginning, and he had fourteen thousand sheep, six thousand camels, one thousand yokes of oxen, and one thousand female donkeys.**
13 **He had twice seven sons,** or two sets of seven sons,[887] **and three daughters.** He had double the number of sons, while the number of his daughters remained the same. However, as his daughters were special, the chapter proceeds to list them by their names, which perhaps alludes to their beauty.[888]
14 **He called the name of the first Yemima,** as bright as the day [*yom*];[889] **the name of the second, Ketzia,** the name of a perfume; **and the name of the third, Keren Hapukh,** a cosmetic implement.
15 **There were not found women as beautiful as the daughters of Job in all the land, and their father gave them an inheritance among their brothers.** They were of distinguished lineage and beauty, and they were also wealthy.

ו וְעַתָּה עֵינִי רָאָתְךָ: עַל־כֵּן אֶמְאַס וְנִחַמְתִּי עַל־עָפָר וָאֵפֶר:
ז וַיְהִי אַחַר דִּבֶּר יְהוָה אֶת־הַדְּבָרִים הָאֵלֶּה אֶל־אִיּוֹב וַיֹּאמֶר יְהוָה אֶל־אֱלִיפַז
הַתֵּימָנִי חָרָה אַפִּי בְךָ וּבִשְׁנֵי רֵעֶיךָ כִּי לֹא דִבַּרְתֶּם אֵלַי נְכוֹנָה כְּעַבְדִּי אִיּוֹב:
ח וְעַתָּה קְחוּ־לָכֶם שִׁבְעָה־פָרִים וְשִׁבְעָה אֵילִים וּלְכוּ ׀ אֶל־עַבְדִּי אִיּוֹב וְהַעֲלִיתֶם
עוֹלָה בַּעַדְכֶם וְאִיּוֹב עַבְדִּי יִתְפַּלֵּל עֲלֵיכֶם כִּי אִם־פָּנָיו אֶשָּׂא לְבִלְתִּי עֲשׂוֹת עִמָּכֶם
ט נְבָלָה כִּי לֹא דִבַּרְתֶּם אֵלַי נְכוֹנָה כְּעַבְדִּי אִיּוֹב: וַיֵּלְכוּ אֱלִיפַז הַתֵּימָנִי וּבִלְדַּד
הַשּׁוּחִי צֹפַר הַנַּעֲמָתִי וַיַּעֲשׂוּ כַּאֲשֶׁר דִּבֶּר אֲלֵיהֶם יְהוָה וַיִּשָּׂא יְהוָה אֶת־פְּנֵי אִיּוֹב:
י וַיהוָה שָׁב אֶת־שבית אִיּוֹב בְּהִתְפַּלְלוֹ בְּעַד רֵעֵהוּ וַיֹּסֶף יְהוָה אֶת־כָּל־אֲשֶׁר שְׁבוּת
יא לְאִיּוֹב לְמִשְׁנֶה: וַיָּבֹאוּ אֵלָיו כָּל־אֶחָיו וְכָל־אַחְיֹתָיו וְכָל־יֹדְעָיו לְפָנִים וַיֹּאכְלוּ
עִמּוֹ לֶחֶם בְּבֵיתוֹ וַיָּנֻדוּ לוֹ וַיְנַחֲמוּ אֹתוֹ עַל כָּל־הָרָעָה אֲשֶׁר־הֵבִיא יְהוָה עָלָיו
יב וַיִּתְּנוּ־לוֹ אִישׁ קְשִׂיטָה אֶחָת וְאִישׁ נֶזֶם זָהָב אֶחָד: וַיהוָה בֵּרַךְ אֶת־אַחֲרִית אִיּוֹב
מֵרֵאשִׁתוֹ וַיְהִי־לוֹ אַרְבָּעָה עָשָׂר אֶלֶף צֹאן וְשֵׁשֶׁת אֲלָפִים גְּמַלִּים וְאֶלֶף־צֶמֶד
יג יד בָּקָר וְאֶלֶף אֲתוֹנוֹת: וַיְהִי־לוֹ שִׁבְעָנָה בָנִים וְשָׁלוֹשׁ בָּנוֹת: וַיִּקְרָא שֵׁם־הָאַחַת
טו יְמִימָה וְשֵׁם הַשֵּׁנִית קְצִיעָה וְשֵׁם הַשְּׁלִישִׁית קֶרֶן הַפּוּךְ: וְלֹא נִמְצָא נָשִׁים יָפוֹת
טז כִּבְנוֹת אִיּוֹב בְּכָל־הָאָרֶץ וַיִּתֵּן לָהֶם אֲבִיהֶם נַחֲלָה בְּתוֹךְ אֲחֵיהֶם: וַיְחִי אִיּוֹב
אַחֲרֵי־זֹאת מֵאָה וְאַרְבָּעִים שָׁנָה וַיִּרְא אֶת־בָּנָיו וְאֶת־בְּנֵי בָנָיו אַרְבָּעָה דֹּרוֹת:
יז וַיָּמָת אִיּוֹב זָקֵן וּשְׂבַע יָמִים:

16 **After this, Job lived for one hundred and forty years.** Whatever his age was when the catastrophes befell him, his former life was entirely ruined. The new life with which he was blessed was twice as long as man's standard seventy years.[890] **He saw his sons, and his sons' sons, four generations.**

17 **Job died, old and full of days.**

BACKGROUND

42:11 | **One kesita:** A similar word in Akkadian, *sikkultu*, means sheep or a valuable item. The *Targum* on this verse, as well as Onkelos and the Septuagint in Genesis (33:19) render the term *kesita* as sheep. This translation is supported by the mention of Job's sheep in the next verse. Others claim that the *kesita* is a unit of weight, perhaps of silver. Another possibility is that it came to refer to a type of coin, perhaps with an image of a sheep imprinted on it. Rabbi Akiva is cited in the Talmud as saying: When I went to Africa, they would call a *ma'a*, which is a type of coin, a *kesita* (*Rosh HaShana* 26a).

The Song of Songs

The Song of Songs

INTRODUCTION TO THE SONG OF SONGS

The Song of Songs is a collection of love poetry. Despite the literary unity of the book and its themes, it is hard to discern a coherent narrative running through it all. Between the obscure starting point of the book and its conclusion, which could point toward marriage, there are elusive circles of mutual courtship and pursuit. Nevertheless, there is an overall harmony to the poems, and despite the peaks and troughs in the relationship between the lovers who are the poems' focus, there is no open conflict between them. They occasionally become distanced from one another, but soon return and become close once again.

Other characters apart from the two lovers make brief appearances, but they do not participate in the main events, and are marginal figures, who sometimes serve to provide a different perspective on the relationship between the principal couple.

The encounters depicted here are more intimate than the accepted manners of courtship in the ancient Jewish world. It is certainly possible that the poems do not tell of real face-to-face meetings, but rather represent the lovers' tender fantasies. The dreamlike vagueness of the narrative throughout the book supports this suggestion.

The love between man and woman, which is the focus of the entire book, has been understood throughout the generations as an allegory for the relationship between the people of Israel as a whole and the Holy One.[1] The Song of Songs evokes a relationship of intense longing and intimacy using very specific imagery. This representation of the love between God and His people through metaphors of sexual love is far from unique in the Bible, and not at all foreign to Jewish tradition. In the Bible this characterization is especially prevalent in the Prophets. Some of the prophets evoke a marital relationship, both as the ideal of the covenant and as the model for the betrayal and jealousy felt by God when Israel sins.[2] This imagery is often highly physical and even erotic. Nevertheless, the tone of The Song of Songs differs from these metaphors.

Allegorical love poems that express religious devotion and a believer's feeling for his god were not unusual in the ancient Middle East. For example, ancient Sumerian poems have been discovered that are broadly similar in their themes to The Song of Songs, and some of them were expressly designed for use in ritual ceremonies of worship. This fact serves to undermine the oft-heard suggestion that the allegorical reading of The Song of Songs offered by the Sages is the anachronistic reaction of a prudish culture shocked by its explicitness. It is rather an instance of an ancient and well-established phenomenon.

Notwithstanding the similarities between The Song of Songs and similar poems from other cultures, The Song of Songs is neither generic nor universal. The images are well defined, detailed, and local. They refer to the Land of Israel, its scenery and ways of life, with especial attention paid to Jerusalem and its environs. Although there is a certain continuity in the setting of the characters and events described, the book does not provide a well-articulated representation of the characters and their relationship as one finds typically in ancient Greek literature. Every so often, the characters shift and display different aspects of themselves, and thus another feature of the poem is revealed, inviting more and more exegetical interpretations and further investigations into hidden levels of meaning. Each detail remains vital and sensuous, and yet at the same time symbolic and fundamental. Over the generations, The Song of Songs has become a timeless recounting of the love between the nation of Israel and God.

It has been the custom since the Middle Ages to recite The Song of Songs on the festival of Passover, which always occurs in the spring. This is the season of the events described in the book, and Passover also represents the springtime of Israel as a nation.[3]

Many communities also have the custom of reading The Song of Songs every week, just before the start of Shabbat.

The Song of Songs

Song of the Young Woman to Her Beloved

THE SONG OF SONGS 1:1

At the simplest level, The Song of Songs is the poetic expression of the passion of two young lovers. It has always been understood as referring also to other sorts of love relationships. Beyond the allegorical reading of the Sages, in which The Song of Songs depicts the love between the Jewish people and God, the entire book can be read as the portrayal of the love of an individual soul for its Creator. Each level of interpretation, that of the collective Jewish people's relationship with God and that of the individual's relationship with God, makes use of different symbols.

1 1 **The song of songs,**[D] the most special of poems, **which is Solomon's.**[D] Solomon king of Israel is said to have composed a great number of poems.[4]

The Opening Poem

THE SONG OF SONGS 1:2–4

The first poem expresses the intensity of new love, while hinting at other dimensions of the love relationship.

2 The poem opens without identifying its speaker, but its grammatical context, which addresses a male beloved, leaves no doubt that these are the words of a young woman: **May he kiss me with the kisses of his mouth, as your love**[B] **is better than wine.** Alternatively: The wetness of your mouth is better than wine.[5] The speaker's transition from employing third person pronouns to directly addressing her subject likely alludes to a process in which passionate fantasies feel more and more real, eventually giving the impression that the beloved is present even if he is not.

3 The woman continues to praise her beloved: **By the fragrance of your good oils,** even **your name is** pleasant **like poured oil** [***shemen turak***],[B] and **therefore, the young women love you.** The young woman speaks not only of love for her partner and a yearning for personal closeness to him, but also of her admiration for him, noting that he is loved by all.

4 **Draw me; after you we will run** together. The verse portrays a budding romance: The young man woos the young woman, and she takes hold of his hand and runs with him. However, they do not run aimlessly: **The king brought me to his** private **chambers.** At this point, another layer is added to the poem, as the woman discovers that her beloved is no ordinary man but the king himself. Although the beloved will sometimes be described as a shepherd, perhaps the king prefers to appear as a simple man rather than a ruler when courting his loved one. However, when they finally run together, the king takes her specifically to his palace chambers. Alternatively, in the eyes of the woman, her beloved shepherd is a king, and she feels like a queen whose groom, the king, is leading her to his home.[6] This motif does not seem typical of a love poem. It reveals another layer of meaning: The soul, which until now has wandered in the familiar outside world, finds itself inside the chamber of the beloved king. There **let us exult and rejoice in you. We will recount your love,** which is sweeter and **more** intoxicating **than wine. Rightly** [***meisharim***] **do they love you,** or upright individuals love you.

An Address to the Daughters of Jerusalem

THE SONG OF SONGS 1:5–6

In the following few verses, the woman speaks to other figures, real or metaphorical.

5 The woman declares: **I am black but lovely,**[BD] **daughters of Jerusalem.** The city of Jerusalem serves as the backdrop for the poem. I am black **like the tents of** the tribes of **Kedar.**[B] These tents were made from the wool of the local goats, which were typically black, **like the curtains of Solomon,**[B] which were most splendid, and perhaps also black. The woman's black and beautiful appearance is illustrated by a pair of contrasting images: coarse wool and royal drapes.

Tents in the wilderness

שיר השירים

א

א ב שִׁיר הַשִּׁירִים אֲשֶׁר לִשְׁלֹמֹה: יִשָּׁקֵנִי מִנְּשִׁיקוֹת פִּיהוּ כִּי־טוֹבִים דֹּדֶיךָ מִיָּיִן:
ג ד לְרֵיחַ שְׁמָנֶיךָ טוֹבִים שֶׁמֶן תּוּרַק שְׁמֶךָ עַל־כֵּן עֲלָמוֹת אֲהֵבוּךָ: מָשְׁכֵנִי אַחֲרֶיךָ
נָּרוּצָה הֱבִיאַנִי הַמֶּלֶךְ חֲדָרָיו נָגִילָה וְנִשְׂמְחָה בָּךְ נַזְכִּירָה דֹדֶיךָ מִיַּיִן מֵישָׁרִים
ה אֲהֵבוּךָ: שְׁחוֹרָה אֲנִי וְנָאוָה בְּנוֹת יְרוּשָׁלִָם כְּאָהֳלֵי קֵדָר כִּירִיעוֹת

BACKGROUND

1:2| **Your love [*dodekha*]:** This word has two meanings: First, it is the plural form of *dod*, "beloved," as in the verse "This is my beloved [*dodi*], and this is my companion" (5:16). Second, it denotes lovemaking, based on a similar Akkadian term, and this is the meaning of *dodekha* in this verse (see also verse 4, 4:10, 7:13; Proverbs 7:18).

1:3| **Poured oil [*shemen turak*]:** The word *turak* means poured or emptied. Alternatively, it is related to *tamruk*, cosmetics (see Vilna Gaon). According to this interpretation, *shemen turak* is perfumed oil. A similar term in Akkadian means a perfume or spice.

1:5| **I am black, but lovely [*nava*]:** In Akkadian, *nawru* means sparkling, shiny, and colorful. Indeed, a woman whose skin was darkened as a result of guarding vineyards (see verse 6) might stand out among her friends. It is worth noting the statement in the Mishna (*Nega'im* 2:1) concerning the typical complexion of the Jewish people in ancient times: "Rabbi Yishmael says: The children of Israel, may I be an atonement for them! They are like the box tree, neither black nor white, but in between." The color of the box tree, of the genus *Buxus*, is somewhere between ivory and light brown.

Kedar: In the Torah, Kedar is listed as Ishmael's second son (Genesis 25:13), and in the Prophets it refers to a nomadic tribe, or group of tribes, that raised cattle and camels and engaged in commerce (see Isaiah 42:11, 60:7; Jeremiah 49:28; Ezekiel 27:21). Assyrian records refer to the leaders of Kedar and their wanderings in the region of the Syrian-Arabian desert. Pliny the Elder lists them together with the Nabateans as migrants and settlers in Babylonia, present-day Jordan, and the Sinai Peninsula.

Like the tents of Kedar, like the curtains of Solomon: The root *kuf-dalet-reish* means dark or black. The tribes of Kedar were known by this name due to their dark clothing and tents. Against the background of the desert rocks and light sands, the dark tents of Kedar could be seen from a great distance. The comparison of a woman to Solomon's colorful woven curtains can be understood by noting that royal tents, as well as the Tent of Meeting in the wilderness, had two layers: an outer one of a uniform color, made of goats' wool, and an inner, multicolored one.

DISCUSSION

1:1| **The Song of songs:** The Sages teach: All the Writings, or in a different version, all the poems, are holy, but The Song of Songs is the holy of holies (Mishna *Yadayim* 3:5; see *Shir HaShirim Rabba* 1:11). From a grammatical perspective, the phrase "song of songs" can be considered an expression of emphasis, like "slave of slaves" (Genesis 9:25, and Ibn Ezra ad loc.). The title of the book also reflects its dual nature: The Song of Songs is simultaneously a single prose poem or story and a compilation of individual poems each relating its own partial narrative. Indeed, the transitions from one section to another are not always smooth and are likely to leave the reader seeking clarification.

Which is Solomon's: Solomon makes several appearances in The Song of Songs, not only as its author but also as a character, albeit with a somewhat obscure role. He is sometimes portrayed as a third party independent of the lovers, sometimes as a kind of custodian of the young woman, whom he presents to others. At other times, Solomon appears in the role of the beloved himself, although several other verses indicate that the beloved is not a king but a shepherd. According to the allegory, the figure of King Solomon in The Song of Songs represents God (see, e.g., *Shevuot* 38b). But even without resorting to the allegory, it is clear that the figure of Solomon is an amalgamation of a historical person and a symbol. This is one of the many fluid and enigmatic aspects of the book.

1:5| **I am black, but lovely:** This expression has been understood in an apologetic light: Although I am dark or tanned, and I do not perfectly match your image of ideal beauty, I am nevertheless beautiful. The perception of beauty expressed in the verse is typical of the ancient Middle East, where the inhabitants, particularly the poorer ones who worked outside, were usually of a dark complexion, while paler skin tones were associated with the elites and were considered more beautiful.

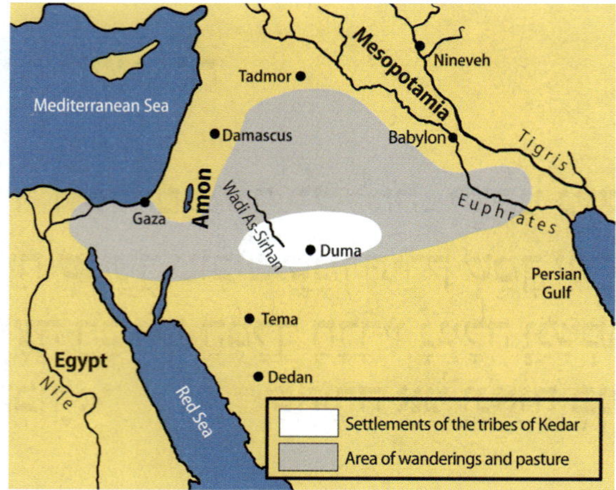

Wanderings of the tribes of Kedar

6 **Do not gaze at me** disrespectfully,[7] seeing **that I am dark, for**
this is not my natural color; rather, **the sun has tanned me.**[8]

The woman now addresses how a fair and modest daughter of Jerusalem faced such exposure to the sun: **The sons of my mother were incensed at me; they placed me as guard of the** family **vineyards,**[B] to chase away any animals that attempted to infiltrate. However, because of the task imposed upon me, **my own vineyard I did not guard.** I too have a vineyard of my own, but the members of my family who quarreled with me cared only for their vineyards, while mine was left abandoned. This verse can be understood as the personal struggle of a woman who wishes to extricate herself from the plight of her perceived external ugliness, and to reveal her hidden beauty. However, the verse can also be interpreted metaphorically as a declaration by the Jewish people: Admittedly we are not clean and pure as snow, but the blackness of our sins is not a natural blemish, nor was it caused by circumstances of our own choosing. As a nation, we have been forced to wander frequently. Because of the other nations, we were forced to fulfill various roles for the benefit of the world, to preserve their vineyards. Therefore, we were left without the time or opportunity to protect our own vineyard.

The Young Woman's Declaration and the Beloved's Response

THE SONG OF SONGS 1:7–2:7

The woman now turns to her beloved, who presumably was not present during her conversation with the daughters of Jerusalem. Perhaps this is not a real exchange, but an expression of a secret wish.

7 **Tell me,** you **whom my soul loves, where do you herd**[D] your
flock? **Where do you rest your flock at noon?**[B] **Why should**
I be as one bound to the
flocks of your colleagues? Alternatively: Why should I wrap myself up or veil myself for reasons of modesty, in following the flocks of other shepherds? If you tell me where to find you, I will not be forced to wander in the company of strangers.

Flock of sheep

8 For the first time, the lover's response is heard: **If you do not**
know where I am, you, **the fairest among women, go out in the footsteps of the sheep and herd your kids.** Apparently, in addition to being a keeper of vineyards, the woman is also a shepherdess. A young shepherdess would generally be given a small flock of kids, while the larger flocks were shepherded by men. The matriarch Rachel likely shepherded such a small flock.[9] You must seek me **by the tents of the shepherds.** The beloved is unable to give the young woman an address where she can find him. Rather, she must go out to seek him. Similarly, the final destination of the soul's great journey, like that of Israel's travels in the wilderness, lies beyond the horizon.

9 The lover briefly expresses his love for the woman, even more
emphatically than her expressions of affection for him: **To a mare in Pharaoh's chariots I have likened you, my love.** Horses are generally considered beautiful creatures. A horse harnessed to one of Pharaoh's chariots would be perfect and adorned with decorations.[10]

Horse pulling Pharaoh's chariot, fresco, Abu Simbel, southern Egypt, thirteenth century BCE

ו שְׁלֹמֹה: אַל־תִּרְאוּנִי שֶׁאֲנִי שְׁחַרְחֹרֶת שֶׁשֱּׁזָפַתְנִי הַשָּׁמֶשׁ בְּנֵי אִמִּי נִחֲרוּ־בִי שָׂמֻנִי
ז נֹטֵרָה אֶת־הַכְּרָמִים כַּרְמִי שֶׁלִּי לֹא נָטָרְתִּי: הַגִּידָה לִּי שֶׁאָהֲבָה נַפְשִׁי אֵיכָה
ח תִרְעֶה אֵיכָה תַּרְבִּיץ בַּצָּהֳרָיִם שַׁלָּמָה אֶהְיֶה כְּעֹטְיָה עַל עֶדְרֵי חֲבֵרֶיךָ: אִם־לֹא
תֵדְעִי לָךְ הַיָּפָה בַּנָּשִׁים צְאִי־לָךְ בְּעִקְבֵי הַצֹּאן וּרְעִי אֶת־גְּדִיֹּתַיִךְ עַל מִשְׁכְּנוֹת
ט י הָרֹעִים: לְסֻסָתִי בְּרִכְבֵי פַרְעֹה דִּמִּיתִיךְ רַעְיָתִי: נָאווּ לְחָיַיִךְ בַּתֹּרִים
יא יב צַוָּארֵךְ בַּחֲרוּזִים: תּוֹרֵי זָהָב נַעֲשֶׂה־לָּךְ עִם נְקֻדּוֹת הַכָּסֶף: עַד־שֶׁהַמֶּלֶךְ בִּמְסִבּוֹ

10 Like the horse in Pharaoh's chariot, **your cheeks are lovely** and decorated **with rings,** apparently large earrings that rest on the cheeks; **your neck** is decorated **with beads.**

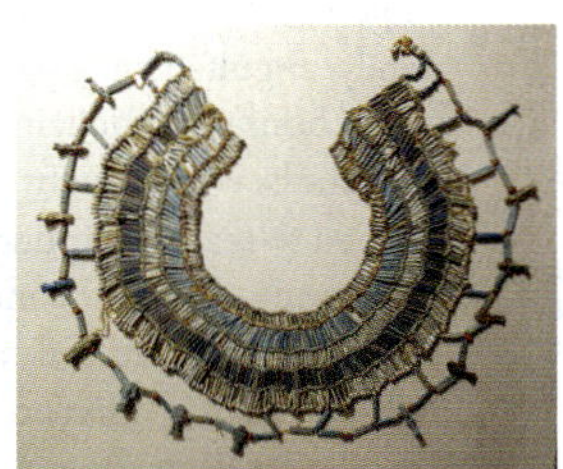

Necklace, Egypt, seventh century BCE

11 You are worthy of even grander jewelry: **We will make you golden rings with studs**[11] **of silver.**[B] Silver studs stand out prominently on a golden background, like white spots on dark fur. Allegorically, the chariots of Pharaoh recall Israel's exodus from Egypt, while the various ornaments are reminiscent of the great wealth taken from there by the children of Israel. This combination of gold and silver has been given many other interpretations, some of them mystical.

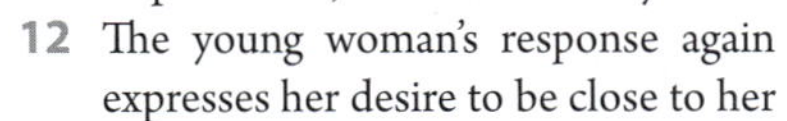

12 The young woman's response again expresses her desire to be close to her

Gold earring, Italy, fourth century BCE

BACKGROUND

1:6 | **Guard of the vineyards:** The main work in a vineyard, namely the harvesting and storage of grapes, and the production of wine and raisins from the fruit, is performed over the course of a three- to five-month period. During this time, the vineyard is vulnerable to animals and to thieves who might take grapes without permission. To protect against these threats, vineyard owners and their families would guard their vineyards. In many cases, round, tall structures suitable as lookouts were built to house the guards. These structures were typically constructed from stones gathered from a clearing, with a booth erected at the top of each of them.

1:7 | **Rest your flock at noon:** A day of shepherding is generally divided into three stages: In the morning hours, the sheep graze in the fields; during the noon hours, the flock rests in the shade and chews its cud; in the afternoon, the flock grazes again until close to sunset, before returning to its pen or shelter for the night.

1:11 | **We will make you golden rings with studs of silver:** It is possible that these silver studs are to be integrated between golden spherules, in order to enhance the visual effect. The combination of gold and silver is a motif in other sources as well (see Proverbs 25:11; Mishna *Pesaḥim* 5:5).

DISCUSSION

1:7 | **Where do you herd:** This question is left unanswered. The only response the woman receives is that she should continue looking. This constant searching is an attribute of the soul and can also be metaphorically ascribed to the heavenly bodies that are constantly orbiting. This idea is echoed by the question attributed to the angels, in which they ask repeatedly: Where is the place of His glory? (*Musaf* prayer for Shabbat and festivals; see *Ḥagiga* 13b; *Pirkei deRabbi Eliezer* 4). This question appears in a different form as a request by Moses: "If I have found favor now in Your eyes, inform me, please, of Your ways.... Show me, please, Your glory" (Exodus 33:13–18). As with the request of the young woman, Moses appeals to God: If You love me, then allow me to approach You and to know You.

beloved: **While the king was at his feast, my lavender**[B] **emitted its fragrance.** Among all the fragrances at the king's feast, the scent of my lavender is the most pronounced.[12]

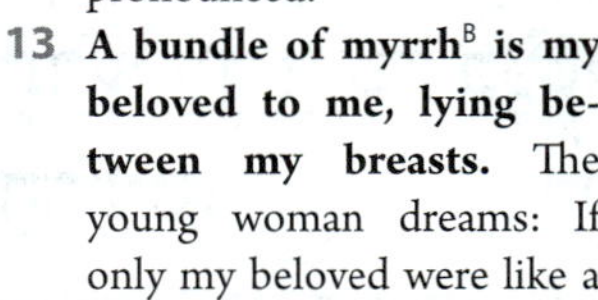

Lavender

13 **A bundle of myrrh**[B] **is my beloved to me, lying between my breasts.** The young woman dreams: If only my beloved were like a bundle of myrrh hanging from my neck and resting in my bosom.

Pendant with receptacle for fragrant herbs, Egypt, first century BCE

Trees from which myrrh is extracted

14 **A cluster of henna,**[B] a fragrant plant whose fruit grows in clusters, **my beloved is to me, in the vineyards of Ein Gedi,** where henna apparently grew. Perhaps the woman anticipates meeting her lover there.

Cluster from a henna tree

Date flowers

15 As the pace of the exchange between the beloved and his lover increases, the beloved speaks again: **Behold, you are fair, my love; behold, you are fair; your eyes are like doves.** Doves are a symbol of beauty and grace; the comparison of the woman's eyes to doves is also indicative of perfection and tranquility, which arouse the man's love.[13]

16 The young woman responds: **Behold, you are fair, my beloved,** your company is **pleasant too; indeed our bed is fresh.** She fantasizes of a shared home and bed.

17 **The beams of our houses are** made of **cedars,**[B] **and our rafters are junipers.**[B] Two aspects of the lovers' relationship are intertwined in this passage. Alongside passionate love, there is a motif of calm and the stability of home. When the woman calls to her lover, "Draw me; after you we will run" (verse 4), the intention is not to run and play aimlessly, as the same verse concludes: "The king brought me to his chambers." The blossoming love between them, which is expressed by the fresh bed of the previous verse, is followed by the dream of sharing a home. Their relationship must eventually be brought into a stable framework. The young man and woman, though completely engulfed in a passionate love, still set as their goal a shared home, symbolizing the nation of Israel in Egypt or in the wilderness who, caught up in their romance with God, still yearned to reach their homeland.

Greek juniper

2 1 The young woman continues: **I am** as beautiful as **a daffodil of the Sharon,**[B] **a lily of the valleys.**[B]

Sea daffodil

2 Her beloved confirms: Indeed, **like a lily among the thorns, so is my love among the girls.** You stand out among all the other girls, and you are different from them. Furthermore, just as one can enjoy the conspicuous beauty of a lily, but it is difficult to approach the flower due to the thorns, so too you are not easily accessible. This depiction alludes to the simultaneous intimacy and distance present in their relationship, which can be understood at all levels of interpretation.

Madonna lily

3 The young woman praises her beloved: **Like an apple tree,**[B] with its distinct aroma,[14] **among the** plain **trees of the forest, so is my beloved among the boys.** In addition to its scent, the apple tree possesses other advantages: **In its shade I delighted and I sat, and its fruit was sweet to my palate.**

Apple tree

יג יד נִרְדִּי נָתַן רֵיחוֹ: צְרוֹר הַמֹּר ׀ דּוֹדִי לִי בֵּין שָׁדַי יָלִין: אֶשְׁכֹּל הַכֹּפֶר ׀ דּוֹדִי לִי בְּכַרְמֵי
טו טז עֵין גֶּדִי: הִנָּךְ יָפָה רַעְיָתִי הִנָּךְ יָפָה עֵינַיִךְ יוֹנִים: הִנְּךָ יָפֶה דוֹדִי אַף
יז א נָעִים אַף־עַרְשֵׂנוּ רַעֲנָנָה: קֹרוֹת בָּתֵּינוּ אֲרָזִים רחיטנו בְּרוֹתִים: אֲנִי חֲבַצֶּלֶת רָהִיטֵנוּ
ב ג הַשָּׁרוֹן שׁוֹשַׁנַּת הָעֲמָקִים: כְּשׁוֹשַׁנָּה בֵּין הַחוֹחִים כֵּן רַעְיָתִי בֵּין הַבָּנוֹת: כְּתַפּוּחַ

BACKGROUND

1:12| **Lavender [*nerd*]:** Later in The Song of Songs (4:14), *nerd* appears in a list of fragrant plants. As to its identity, there are two main suggestions. The first identifies it as lavender, *Lavandula angustifolia*, that grows wild throughout the Middle East and is a common feature of modern Israel's landscape. Its flowers emit a familiar scent, and are arranged like stalks [*shibbolet*] on their twigs, leading the Sages to refer to it as *shibbolet nerd* (see *Karetot* 6a). In Ancient Greek, lavender is known as *nardus*.

The second suggested identification is spikenard, *Nardostachys jatamansi*, a plant that grows in the Himalayan mountains. The leaves and root of the spikenard are the source of a valuable fragrant oil whose aroma is similar to musk, and whose scent is agreeable to some more than others. According to this interpretation, the term *shibbolet nerd* refers to hairs that cover the underside of the spikenard's stalk.

The Aramaic translations of the Bible, as well as some researchers, suggest other identifications for *nerd*, such as turmeric, the rose, or *Moringa peregrine*, which is found in desert oases in Israel.

1:13| **Myrrh [*mor*]:** One of the most important spices in the ancient world, myrrh was extracted from the resin of trees of the genus *Commiphora*, native to Africa, southern Arabia, and eastern India. Myrrh is mentioned in inscriptions and manuscripts from the ancient Orient and was used in cosmetics until modern times. Alternatively, *mor* has been identified with *anpakinon*, oil extracted from unripe olives (*Shabbat* 80b), used as a depilatory. According to the Rambam, *mor* is extracted from the glands of musk deer (see Ramban, Exodus 30:23).

1:14| **Henna [*kofer*]:** Most researchers identify the *kofer* plant with the henna tree, *Lawsonia inermis*, which stands 1–6 m tall. Requiring a warm climate, it once grew on the terraces of the oasis of Ein Gedi. Its clusters of flowers are fragrant, and the natural henna dye is extracted from its roots. Other possible identifications of the *kofer* include date palm flowers, known as *kufra* in the Talmud; cloves and the camphor tree, neither of which grows in Israel; the cypress, and early ripening grapes, which could conceivably have been grown in Ein Gedi.

1:17| **Cedars:** The cedar, genus *Cedrus*, is a large and beautiful conifer tree. The tree, which can reach a height of 40 m, grows in elevated and cold regions, and is common in Lebanon. Due to its strength and flexibility, cedar wood was particularly useful in the construction of public structures and palaces.

According to Egyptian and Assyrian records from the first and second millennia BCE, the forests of Lebanon were a main source of building materials for large buildings and ships as well as ritual boats, furniture, and coffins. Cedars were imported from Lebanon for the construction of both the First Temple (I Kings 5:20) and the Second Temple (Ezra 3:7).

Junipers [*berotim*]: *Berotim*, or *beroshim*, usually appear in the Bible alongside cedars, and this tree also grows in the mountains of Lebanon (see II Kings 19:23; Ezekiel 27:5). The term *berotim* does not refer to the genus *Cupressus*, known in modern Hebrew as the *berosh*, but rather to the Greek juniper, *Juniperus excelsa*. This tree is common in Lebanon and reaches a height of 30 m.

2:1| **Daffodil [*ḥavatzelet*] of the Sharon:** The Sharon is the coastal plain of Israel immediately north of what is now the Tel Aviv area. An inscription on the sarcophagus of Eshmunazar II, a Phoenician king of Sidon, as well as ancient Egyptian sources, refer to the region by this name. On the beaches of this region one can find the sea daffodil, *Pancratium maritimum*, from the Amaryllidaceae family. Its attractive flowers are white and fragrant. The petals have a diameter of roughly 10 cm, and it grows to a height of 60 cm. The mature flower has a great deal of nectar and emits a strong, pleasant aroma. The *ḥavatzelet* of the Sharon has been previously identified as the Madonna lily, the narcissus, or even the saffron crocus, but none of these flowers is typically found in the Sharon.

Lily [*shoshana*] of the valleys: There are numerous opinions with regard to the identity of the *shoshana*. Based on a similar Akkadian term, the *shoshana* is the flower known as the Madonna lily, *Lilium candidum*. Alternatively, it is the water lily, or the blue lotus, *Nymphaea caerulea*. The identification of the *shoshana* as the Madonna lily fits the next verse, "a lily [*shoshana*] among the thorns," since thorn bushes are sometimes found near this plant. Nevertheless, it is not a wild plant that grows in the valleys. By contrast, the water lily flourishes in freshwater pools, or in marshes in lowlands or valleys. However, thorns do not grow around it.

Another possible identification of the *shoshana* is *Rosa phoenicia*, a prickly shrub with beautiful and fragrant white flowers that grows in Israel on the banks of valley streams, which fits both characterizations in the verses. It is also possible that the *shoshana* of the valleys and the *shoshana* among the thorns are different species. If so, then one may identify the *shoshana* of the valleys as the lotus, which grows in the valleys, and the *shoshana* among the thorns as the Madonna lily.

Yet another possibility is that *shoshana* is a general term for beautiful multi-petaled flowers. If so, the date palm could also be referred to as a *shoshana* of the valleys due to the terrain in which it grows, its resemblance to a flower with splendid petals, and the fact that just above the ground it is surrounded with prickly shoots. This identification is also supported by the proto-Ionic capital design found on columns in the area, which were called *timorot*, comparable to *tamar*, the date (see I Kings 7:19, and commentary ad loc.).

4 **He brought me to the wine house,** a kind of tavern where men would drink. It is not clear whether such a tavern would serve women as well. Consequently, it seems that this phrase is an expression of the young woman's wish that her lover would allow her to accompany him wherever he goes. It is also possible that this wine house was the equivalent of a modern-day café. Alternatively, this term refers to a vineyard. **And his gaze** [***diglo***] **upon me is love.** *Diglu* in Akkadian indicates seeing or gazing. Alternatively, our love is his banner [*degel*]; he takes pride in displaying to others the love that radiates from us.[15]

5 **Support me with raisin cakes,**[16] **cushion me with** a bed of **apples, for I am lovesick.** In her weakness, the woman requests to be surrounded by fruit so as to create an aromatic, pleasant environment.[17] It is possible that she mentions raisin cakes [*ashishot*] because of the reinforcement [*ishush*] that she requires. They were known by this name because they were considered to give strength to those who ate them. The raisin cakes and apples literarily parallel the wine house and the apple tree mentioned in the previous two verses.

6 **His left** arm **is under my head and his right embraces me.** In pining for her beloved, she imagines that she is lying close to him.

7 **I administer an oath to you, daughters of Jerusalem,** who are not active participants in the story but background characters surrounding the woman, **by the gazelles,**[B] **and by the deer of the field,**[B] **that you not awaken and not rouse love, until it desires** to awaken by itself. Do not stir the love from the outside; let it develop naturally. Since this oath involves matters of the heart, the woman invokes animals that symbolize beauty and love. This obscure language, which is repeated elsewhere in The Song of Songs (3:5, 8:4), indicates that the young woman is confident that her relationship with her beloved will ultimately blossom, and so she requests that her love be allowed to advance at the appropriate pace. Her fantasies of constant and public companionship, represented by the wine house, do not need to come to fruition immediately; on the contrary, she is worried that they might materialize prematurely. Still, she yearns for her beloved to reveal their mutual love before all at the appropriate time. Allegorically understood, the nation of Israel wishes for God to reveal Himself and display before all the nations His love and closeness to Israel.

It is noteworthy that one does not ordinarily take an oath by gazelles or deer. In choosing these images, the woman evokes different names of God. In Hebrew, the word "gazelles" [*tzeva'ot*] alludes to one of God's names: Lord of Hosts [*Adonai Tzeva'ot*], while the term "deer of the field" [*ayalot hasadeh*] resembles another: God Almighty [*El Shadai*].

Gazelles

Roe deer

Entreaties and Rejections

THE SONG OF SONGS 2:8–3:5

Alongside declarations of mutual love and desire, the poem emphasizes the fluctuations of the developing connection between the lovers. The need for patience with regard to matters of the heart is stressed as well.

8 **The sound of** the footsteps of **my beloved, behold he approaches, leaping on the mountains, bounding on the hills** toward me.

9 **My beloved is like a gazelle or a fawn,** skipping speedily over the hills, in all its splendor; **behold, he is** already **standing behind our wall.** I can hear him behind the wall, and I can sense his presence,[18] **watching from the windows, peering** at me **through the cracks.** Like the events of national redemption, an individual's relationship with God is neither linear nor orderly. The gazelle racing over the mountains is alternately visible and hidden, as is the woman's beloved as he stands behind the wall, only visible through a crack in the structure. The metaphor of the wall expresses varying stages of revelation and concealment.

10 Drawing near, **my beloved** turned to me and **spoke up, and he said to me: Get up, my love, my fair one, and go** by yourself. Alternatively, come with me. The time has arrived for you to venture forth on a journey and to progress to a higher plane.

11 **For, behold, the winter** [***setav***], the rainy season, **has passed; the rain is over and gone.** Although in modern Hebrew *setav* means autumn, in this verse it refers to winter, and this is also its meaning in Aramaic.[19] In fact, it is questionable whether the Land of Israel has an autumn season at all, since its two principal seasons are a hot, dry summer and a rainy winter.[20]

Almond blossom

12 **The blossoms have been seen in the land, the time of the nightingale**[B] **has arrived, and the** characteristic **sound of the turtledove**[B] **is**

בַּעֲצֵי הַיַּעַר כֵּן דּוֹדִי בֵּין הַבָּנִים בְּצִלּוֹ חִמַּדְתִּי וְיָשַׁבְתִּי וּפִרְיוֹ מָתוֹק לְחִכִּי׃ הֱבִיאַנִי ד
אֶל־בֵּית הַיָּיִן וְדִגְלוֹ עָלַי אַהֲבָה׃ סַמְּכוּנִי בָּאֲשִׁישׁוֹת רַפְּדוּנִי בַּתַּפּוּחִים כִּי־חוֹלַת ה
אַהֲבָה אָנִי׃ שְׂמֹאלוֹ תַּחַת לְרֹאשִׁי וִימִינוֹ תְּחַבְּקֵנִי׃ הִשְׁבַּעְתִּי אֶתְכֶם בְּנוֹת ו ז
יְרוּשָׁלִַם בִּצְבָאוֹת אוֹ בְּאַיְלוֹת הַשָּׂדֶה אִם־תָּעִירוּ ׀ וְאִם־תְּעוֹרְרוּ אֶת־הָאַהֲבָה
עַד שֶׁתֶּחְפָּץ׃ קוֹל דּוֹדִי הִנֵּה־זֶה בָּא מְדַלֵּג עַל־הֶהָרִים מְקַפֵּץ עַל־ ח
הַגְּבָעוֹת׃ דּוֹמֶה דוֹדִי לִצְבִי אוֹ לְעֹפֶר הָאַיָּלִים הִנֵּה־זֶה עוֹמֵד אַחַר כָּתְלֵנוּ מַשְׁגִּיחַ ט
מִן־הַחֲלֹּנוֹת מֵצִיץ מִן־הַחֲרַכִּים׃ עָנָה דוֹדִי וְאָמַר לִי קוּמִי לָךְ רַעְיָתִי יָפָתִי וּלְכִי־ י
לָךְ׃ כִּי־הִנֵּה הַסְּתָו עָבָר הַגֶּשֶׁם חָלַף הָלַךְ לוֹ׃ הַנִּצָּנִים נִרְאוּ בָאָרֶץ עֵת הַזָּמִיר יא יב

BACKGROUND

2:3| **Apple tree [*tapuaḥ*]:** The verse is almost certainly referring to one of the ancestors of the modern-day apple tree, *Malus domestica*, a species of deciduous fruit trees from the Rosaceae family. The wild apple, *Malus sieversii*, with its multicolored peel, grows in Kazakhstan. The yellow and fragrant European crab apple, *Malus sylvestris*, grows throughout Europe. The oriental apple, *Malus orientalis*, a hybrid produced from wild and crab apple strains, grows in Turkey. All naturally occurring apple trees grow in forests or on the outskirts of forests, and produce beautiful, fragrant, whitish-pink flowers. Some of them are also prickly. According to the *Targum*, the *tapuaḥ* is actually the *etrog* (see *Tosafot*, *Shabbat* 88a). The apple tree appears later in The Song of Songs as a shady, aromatic location suitable for a lovers' rendezvous (see 7:9, 8:5).

2:7| **Gazelles:** The mountain gazelle, *Gazella gazella*, is a swift, long-legged antelope of the family Bovidae. Gazelles generally live in groups and herds, and their activity can be best viewed at night, in the light of a full moon. They are gentle, cautious creatures and, like all antelope, are kosher, since they both chew the cud and have cloven hoofs. The coat of the gazelle is light brown in color, while its belly and rump are white, making its short, black tail conspicuous. Both males and females have straight horns that grow throughout their lifetime. As part of their mating ritual, the male chases the female for long distances until the latter accedes; hence the phrase "until it desires" (see also 3:5).

Deer of the field: These are generally identified as the roe deer, *Capreolus capreolus*, and a member of the family Cervidae. Like all deer, roe deer are kosher, since they chew the cud and have cloven hoofs. Originally indigenous to the Land of Israel, this breed of deer disappeared from the area in the early twentieth century. Attempts have been made in recent years to restore the breed to its natural habitat on Mount Carmel.

The roe deer grows to a length of 95–135 cm and a height of approximately 75 cm, weighing on average 15–30 kg. As opposed to gazelles, only the male roe deer have antlers, which regrow annually. During mating season, the males seek out the females, who attract them to their territories.

2:12| **Nightingale [*zamir*]:** This refers to the common nightingale, *Luscinia megarhynchos*, a brown bird with a reddish tail. The nightingale measures roughly 15 cm in length and passes through Israel on its migratory flight to Europe from Africa, mainly during the Hebrew month of Nisan, at the beginning of spring. Some remain in Israel throughout the summer. The nightingale is named, in both Hebrew and English, for its loud, sweet song [*zemer*], which is especially noticeable at night.

Turtledove [*tor*]: This is the European turtledove, *Streptopelia turtur*, a migratory bird from the Columbidae family that flocks to Israel from Africa during the spring. During their migration, some of these birds continue northward, while others remain until the autumn migratory season when they return south. The turtledove varies in color, ranging from gray to chestnut. It has bright patches on its neck, and its body is approximately 28 cm long. During mating season, the male turtledove emits a characteristic cooing sound, which is the origin of its name in Hebrew and Arabic, as well as in a number of European languages.

heard in our land. These migratory birds pass through Israel during the spring, and are therefore a sign of winter's end.

Common nightingale

Turtledove

13 **The fig tree formed its unripe figs.** Unripe figs begin to form in early spring. **And the** blossoming **vines** have formed their **budding,** and **emitted** their pleasant **fragrance.** These buds appear as clusters of small white flowers. **Get up, my love, my fair one, and go.** Spring is the best time for walking in nature.

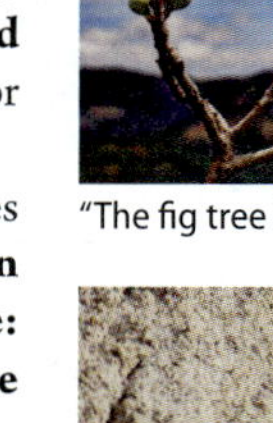
"The fig tree formed its unripe figs"

14 **My dove,** my love, who hides **in the clefts of the rock, in the covert of the terrace:** Come out, and **show me your appearance, let me hear your voice, for your voice is pleasant, and your appearance is lovely.** The time has come for you to reveal yourself. This can be understood as a call to the individual soul or the nation of Israel to take action, as the time of redemption has arrived. According to the Sages' allegorical reading, these verses allude to Israel's exodus from Egypt, which took place in the spring. According to the allegory of the individual soul's yearning for God, these verses describe how the periods of cold and darkness during which the soul was in hibernation are over, and have been replaced with light and life; it is therefore time to rise and venture forth.

Dove in the cleft of a rock

15 However, the path ahead is neither straight nor smooth: **Catch for us** the **foxes,** those **little foxes that ruin the vineyards,**[B] **as our vineyards are** already **in bud,** and the damage caused by the foxes can be significant. The little foxes symbolize the troubles of both the individual and the collective. Although they are not dangerous to humans, they can cause significant damage to vineyards as the grapes begin to grow. Likewise, even when the lovers' romance begins to blossom, other troubles lie ahead.

Jackal

Fox

16 Although there are obstacles to our coming together, this is not due to emotional distance: **My beloved is mine, and I am his, who herds among the lilies.** Although my beloved shepherds among the lilies, as I gather from his pleasant scent,[21] he always remembers me, and I him; so the love between us will last. Even when I must chase away the foxes that ruin the vineyard, and he is occupied with important matters in his own world, there can be no doubting our bond.

17 We cannot see each other **until the day is great,** until the sun shines fully, or until the wind blows,[22] **and the shadows flee.** In the meantime, **turn** around, **my beloved, and be like a gazelle or a young hart on the cleft mountains,** mountains that are scored by ravines and valleys. Alongside the yearning for closeness, the partners give each other space. This point is often lost between lovers. Not all times are ripe for intense passion, and it is sometimes preferable to allow one's beloved to tend to his or her own matters. Here the young woman is confident in the strength of their bond; she is certain that her beloved will return. Whether this verse refers to historical events in the process of national redemption or to the experiences of the individual's soul, there are times of passion, revelation, and intimacy, and there are also times of calm, concealment, and distance. In these moments of distance, the couple is not truly separated from one another. Rather, their connection is toned down, demanding less of each of them. Love requires moments of respite so that its intensity does not become overwhelming.

"Cleft mountain." Mount Arbel

3 1 While the woman's beloved runs over the hills, she remains at home, yearning for him: **On my bed during the nights I sought the one whom my soul loves.** In light of verse 4 below, it seems her sleeping chambers are not in her parents' house. **I sought him, but I did not find him.** He was not close by. One of the symbolic interpretations of this description is that the soul seeks God at times of loneliness and difficulty, only to find Him distant.

2 She takes action: **I will rise now, and go about the city, in the streets and in the squares. I will seek the one whom my soul loves;** perhaps he can be found in the city streets. However, again, **I sought him, but I did not find him.**

יג הִגִּיעַ וְקוֹל הַתּוֹר נִשְׁמַע בְּאַרְצֵנוּ: הַתְּאֵנָה חָנְטָה פַגֶּיהָ וְהַגְּפָנִים ׀ סְמָדַר נָתְנוּ
יד רֵיחַ קוּמִי לָכִי רַעְיָתִי יָפָתִי וּלְכִי־לָךְ: יוֹנָתִי בְּחַגְוֵי הַסֶּלַע בְּסֵתֶר לָךְ
הַמַּדְרֵגָה הַרְאִינִי אֶת־מַרְאַיִךְ הַשְׁמִיעִנִי אֶת־קוֹלֵךְ כִּי־קוֹלֵךְ עָרֵב וּמַרְאֵיךְ
טו נָאוֶה: אֶחֱזוּ־לָנוּ שׁוּעָלִים שֻׁעָלִים קְטַנִּים מְחַבְּלִים כְּרָמִים וּכְרָמֵינוּ
טז יז סְמָדַר: דּוֹדִי לִי וַאֲנִי לוֹ הָרֹעֶה בַּשּׁוֹשַׁנִּים: עַד שֶׁיָּפוּחַ הַיּוֹם וְנָסוּ הַצְּלָלִים סֹב
א דְּמֵה־לְךָ דוֹדִי לִצְבִי אוֹ לְעֹפֶר הָאַיָּלִים עַל־הָרֵי בָתֶר: עַל־
ב מִשְׁכָּבִי בַּלֵּילוֹת בִּקַּשְׁתִּי אֵת שֶׁאָהֲבָה נַפְשִׁי בִּקַּשְׁתִּיו וְלֹא מְצָאתִיו: אָקוּמָה
נָּא וַאֲסוֹבְבָה בָעִיר בַּשְּׁוָקִים וּבָרְחֹבוֹת אֲבַקְשָׁה אֵת שֶׁאָהֲבָה נַפְשִׁי בִּקַּשְׁתִּיו
ג וְלֹא מְצָאתִיו: מְצָאוּנִי הַשֹּׁמְרִים הַסֹּבְבִים בָּעִיר אֵת שֶׁאָהֲבָה נַפְשִׁי רְאִיתֶם:
ד כִּמְעַט שֶׁעָבַרְתִּי מֵהֶם עַד שֶׁמָּצָאתִי אֵת שֶׁאָהֲבָה נַפְשִׁי אֲחַזְתִּיו וְלֹא אַרְפֶּנּוּ
ה עַד־שֶׁהֲבֵיאתִיו אֶל־בֵּית אִמִּי וְאֶל־חֶדֶר הוֹרָתִי: הִשְׁבַּעְתִּי אֶתְכֶם בְּנוֹת יְרוּשָׁלִַם

3 **The watchmen who patrol the city found me,** and I asked them: **Have you seen the one whom my soul loves?** It appears that they too had not seen her beloved. The appearance of watchmen indicates that this takes place in an established city, probably Jerusalem, which contains not only marketplaces and streets but also a patrol.

4 Since the watchmen offer no help, she turns elsewhere. **I had almost passed them, when I found the one whom my soul loves.** After three desperate attempts to find her beloved, first at home, then in the streets, and finally after asking others, she finds him. **I grasped him and I would not release him until I brought him to my mother's house, and to the chamber of the one who conceived me.** Unlike in other parts of the text, where the house and bed represent erotic love (e.g., 1:4, 16), in this verse the home symbolizes emotional closeness and family. In terms of the soul's experience, the soul seeks the object of its love in order to return to the emotional relationships of its childhood. One's parents' house is the place of his initial development. Therefore, the relationship must be built there. Symbolically, returning to the mother's home represents the Jewish people returning to their national homeland from their exile among the gentile nations, and in a spiritual sense, returning to God. The people of Israel implore God: Let us return to our original state.

5 Once again, the woman issues her warning: **I administer an oath to you, daughters of Jerusalem, by the gazelles, or by the deer of the field, that you not awaken and not rouse love, until it desires** to awaken by itself. As mentioned above (2:7), love has a natural course of development, and it must be allowed to intensify on its own at the appropriate pace. Elsewhere, the poem contains expressions of great passion, but this verse speaks of a contrasting idea: Let love develop on its own terms; do not fan its flames prematurely.

BACKGROUND

2:15| **Little foxes [*shu'alim*] that ruin the vineyards:** The term *shu'al* likely refers to the red fox, *Vulpes vulpes*, which can be found in Israel and whose diet includes fruit. It can also refer to the golden jackal, *Canis aureus*. The jackal is often found near populated areas, where it takes advantage of the local agricultural supply for food in the spring and summer. In the ancient world, the hills of Jerusalem and Hebron were terraced mostly with vineyards. When these blossomed in the spring, and when the grapes ripened in the summer, jackals searching for food would be attracted to them (see commentary on 1:6; Judges 15:4).

The Young Woman's Appearance and Solomon's Splendor

THE SONG OF SONGS 3:6–11

This section opens with praise for the woman, envisioned coming out of the wilderness, perhaps to meet her groom. It then moves on to a description of the magnificent canopy and crown of King Solomon. There is no definitive explanation as to why King Solomon appears at this point. Perhaps the mysterious beloved is none other than Solomon himself, who until now has been anonymously walking through the streets of Jerusalem, courting a young woman unaware of his identity. Alternatively, King Solomon's appearance is meant only to provide background imagery for the story. In order to highlight the simplicity of the love between the Jerusalemite woman and her beloved and their modest lives, the poem portrays Solomon as reigning majestically over the city, surrounded by guards. According to the Sages, the name Solomon in The Song of Songs refers to the highest king, God Himself, who is constantly present in the backdrop of the narrative.

6 **Who is this coming up from the wilderness like columns of smoke,** which are visible in the desert from afar? This is not regular smoke, but **perfumed with myrrh and frankincense,**[B] fragrant spices, **and with all the powders of the merchant.** Merchants used to travel from place to place peddling cosmetics and jewelry to women.

Frankincense

"Like columns of smoke." Smoke from incense altar

7 At this point, the story turns in a new direction. King Solomon, who until now was mentioned only in the opening verse of the book, appears as a character in the story, as a king among his people: **Behold the bed of Solomon: There are sixty valiant men**[D] forming one or several perimeters **around it,**[B] **from the valiant of Israel.**

8 **All** these valiant men are **armed with a sword, trained in war; each man, a sword on his thigh, from fear in the nights.** There are fears that prey even on great rulers such as Solomon, and the guards therefore surround his bed. Although they primarily served as a guard of honor, these valiant men also protect Solomon from sudden attack in the night.

King in palanquin with canopy, illustration based on fresco, Ancient Egypt

9 **King Solomon made himself a** grand **canopy,** or perhaps a canopied bed, **from the wood of Lebanon.**

10 **He made its pillars of silver, its cushioning of gold,** and **its seat of** valuable **purple wool.**[B] Solomon's guards protect his canopy against strangers approaching from the outside, but **its interior is inlaid with love, from the daughters of Jerusalem** who came to King Solomon's bed. This could refer to Solomon's many wives and concubines (see 6:8).

11 **Emerge, daughters of Zion,** who represent the surrounding public, **and gaze at King Solomon,**[D] **at the crown with which his mother crowned him on the day of his wedding,**[D] **and on the day of the rejoicing of his heart.**[B]

Gold garland crown, Greece, 320–300 BCE

DISCUSSION

3:7 | **Sixty valiant men:** The number sixty has symbolic significance. It appears later in the book as the number of queens, also apparently of King Solomon (6:8; Rashbam). The Sages offer various allegorical explanations for this number. For example, the queens have been said to symbolize the sixty tractates of the Talmud (see *Shir HaShirim Rabba* 6:8), while the sixty valiant men have been interpreted as an allusion to the sixty letters in the priestly blessings (see *Shir HaShirim Rabba* 3:7).

בִּצְבָאוֹת אוֹ בְּאַיְלוֹת הַשָּׂדֶה אִם־תָּעִירוּ ׀ וְאִם־תְּעוֹרְרוּ אֶת־הָאַהֲבָה עַד

ו שֶׁתֶּחְפָּץ׃ מִי זֹאת עֹלָה מִן־הַמִּדְבָּר כְּתִימֲרוֹת עָשָׁן מְקֻטֶּרֶת

ז מֹר וּלְבוֹנָה מִכֹּל אַבְקַת רוֹכֵל׃ הִנֵּה מִטָּתוֹ שֶׁלִּשְׁלֹמֹה שִׁשִּׁים גִּבֹּרִים סָבִיב לָהּ

ח מִגִּבֹּרֵי יִשְׂרָאֵל׃ כֻּלָּם אֲחֻזֵי חֶרֶב מְלֻמְּדֵי מִלְחָמָה אִישׁ חַרְבּוֹ עַל־יְרֵכוֹ מִפַּחַד

ט י בַּלֵּילוֹת׃ אַפִּרְיוֹן עָשָׂה לוֹ הַמֶּלֶךְ שְׁלֹמֹה מֵעֲצֵי הַלְּבָנוֹן׃ עַמּוּדָיו

עָשָׂה כֶסֶף רְפִידָתוֹ זָהָב מֶרְכָּבוֹ אַרְגָּמָן תּוֹכוֹ רָצוּף אַהֲבָה מִבְּנוֹת יְרוּשָׁלָםִ׃

יא צְאֶינָה ׀ וּרְאֶינָה בְּנוֹת צִיּוֹן בַּמֶּלֶךְ שְׁלֹמֹה בָּעֲטָרָה שֶׁעִטְּרָה־לּוֹ אִמּוֹ בְּיוֹם חֲתֻנָּתוֹ

BACKGROUND

3:6| **Perfumed with myrrh and frankincense [*levona*]:** Frankincense is a fragrant, whitish-yellow resin derived from *Boswellia sacra* trees. Its name in Hebrew, *levona*, is probably due to its whitish [*lavan*] color. Frankincense grows in the southern part of the Arabian Peninsula, as well as in Somalia and Ethiopia. In King Solomon's time, it was probably grown in the Jordan Valley. Frankincense, which produces a fragrant smoke when burned, was used as part of the meal offerings in the Tabernacle in the wilderness, and in the Temple in Jerusalem (see Leviticus 2:1, and commentary ad loc.). With regard to myrrh, see commentary on 1:13.

3:7| **The bed of Solomon: There are sixty valiant men around it:** In ancient times the royal guard served both to guard a monarch or ruler in case of rebellion, and as a symbol of his importance. It seems that King David also had a special guard, comprising two groups of thirty soldiers each (see I Chronicles 11, and *Da'at Mikra* ad loc.). During the tranquil period of Solomon's reign, these "valiant men" served primarily as an honor guard. Even today, it is still customary for kings and rulers to maintain such an honor guard, such as the Household Division of the British monarch.

3:10| **Purple wool [*argaman*]:** *Argaman* is a general name for a reddish-purple dye produced from the spiny dye-murex, *Murex brandaris*, a snail that lives in the Mediterranean Sea. The liquid used for preparing this dye was extracted from a secretion of the snail found in minute quantities in its hypobranchial gland. Thus, many thousands of snails were required to dye a fabric. Ancient documents attest that wool dyed with this substance was forty times more expensive than wool dyed with other colors (see, e.g., Daniel 5:7). Consequently, *argaman* was used mainly for priests, kings, and ministers. Due to its importance and high price, its production was controlled, and at times, free trade of the dye was prohibited.

3:11| **At the crown with which his mother crowned him on the day of his wedding, and on the day of the rejoicing of his heart:** In ancient times, it was customary in many cultures to adorn the heads of bridegrooms and brides with crowns. The crowns of bridegrooms were generally made from expensive metals such as silver and gold, but there were also wreaths of flowers and reeds.

DISCUSSION

3:11| **King Solomon [*Shelomo*]:** If this is a reference to God, who is described as the One for whom peace [*shalom*] is His, then this entire portrayal relates to Him. The Sages explain that "the day of his wedding" refers to the giving of the Torah, and "the day of the rejoicing of his heart" refers to the building of the Temple. Solomon is of course the king who oversaw the construction of the Temple (Mishna *Ta'anit* 4:8; see I Kings 6). The canopy is reminiscent of the Holy of Holies, the innermost and most intimate chamber in the Sanctuary (see *Shir HaShirim Rabba*). This canopy is constructed from extremely valuable materials, and it is filled with the love of the daughters of Jerusalem, which represents the connection between man below and God above. According to this interpretation, these verses depict the appearance of the King in His glory over the course of history as a Savior, and as the One who holds the future in His hand.

At the crown with which his mother crowned him on the day of his wedding: The Talmud states that crowns were placed on the heads of the children of Israel in honor of the giving of the Torah (*Shabbat* 88a). It was customary to place a crown on the heads of bridegrooms on their wedding day, but this practice was suspended after the destruction of the Temple (see Mishna *Sota* 9:14). In certain places there developed a custom to place the crown of the Torah scroll on the head of the groom, and the authorities discuss the appropriateness of this custom. See *Shulḥan Arukh*, *Oraḥ Ḥayyim* 154:10, where the ruling is that this custom should not be practiced.

The First Song of the Beloved to the Young Woman

THE SONG OF SONGS 4:1–7

The beloved now uses imagery from various landscapes to praise the beauty of his love. However, toward the end of the passage he announces a temporary separation.

4 1 The beloved's praise for the young woman's beauty is not superficial; it first focuses on those parts of the body through which the personality finds expression: **Behold, you are fair, my love; behold, you are fair; your eyes are** graceful and calming as a pair of **doves;**[B] they peer out from **behind your braid,** which rests partly on your face. In the context of God's song to Israel, these dovelike eyes have been interpreted as an allusion to the willingness to accept a burden without complaint, and to go wherever one is sent. **Your hair is like a flock of goats that stream down from the highlands of Gilad,**[B] an area of pasture. The goats in this imagery are black, and more active than sheep, evoking the way a young woman's curly black locks flow down her head.

Pair of doves

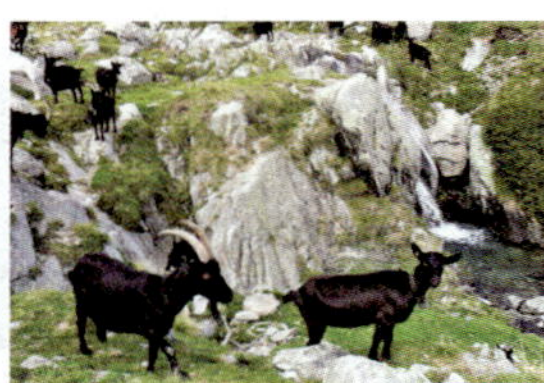
Flock of goats moving down a mountain

2 **Your teeth are like a flock of ordered ewes that have come up from being washed,** when they are extremely white and clean. As the ewes emerge simultaneously from the water, the entire herd is lined up like white teeth, **that are all paired, and there is none missing among them.**

3 **Your lips are like a scarlet**[B] **thread, and your speech is lovely.** Some people have beautiful mouths but as soon as they open them to speak, their charm fades. In your case, however, your speech complements your physical beauty. **Your temple [*rakkatekh*] is like a pomegranate slice** which is exposed **behind your braid.** The Sages expound *rakkatekh* based on the word *reik*, empty. Even the emptiest or most depraved member of Israel is like a pomegranate slice containing numerous seeds, which represent good deeds.

Pomegranate slices

4 **Your neck is like the tower of David,** long and upright, **built magnificently [*talpiyot*].** This tower of David is not the construction known by that name today, but another tall tower in ancient Jerusalem that no longer stands. Here, the beloved praises the posture of the bride, the nation of Israel. The Sages explain this verse as a reference to the Temple, which stood on the hill [*tel*] to which all mouths [*piyot*] turn in prayer. **One thousand bucklers are hung upon it, all the shields of the mighty.**[B] The mighty men in the fortress would hang their shields on the tower as a show of strength. This tower on which a thousand shields hung resembled the woman's upright neck decorated with many ornaments.

Pendant necklace in the shape of warriors' shields, Iran, first millennium BCE

5 **Your two breasts are like two fawns, twins of a gazelle.**[B] The birth of twins is not a particularly common phenomenon among gazelles or deer. When twin fawns stand together, their black noses stand out, **which** is especially striking when they **graze among the** white **lilies.**

Two fawns

6 In the meantime, **until the day is great,** or until the hot wind blows, that is, until noon, **and the shadows flee, I will go to the mountain of myrrh,** the mountain where myrrh grows, **and to the hill of frankincense,** where the air is fragrant and pleasant. The beloved, who grazes his flock among the lilies and wanders in the mountains, tells his love that he is leaving for a short while and will return home when the sun is at full strength.

7 The beloved concludes his poem with a verse that echoes its beginning: **All of you is fair, my love, and there is no blemish in you;** you are perfect. When one is in love, one sees no flaw in the object of one's love. Even if certain blemishes or problems appear, one considers them no more than temporary stains and passing shadows, and the overall picture remains perfect. This holds true even with regard to divine love.

וּבְיוֹם שִׂמְחַת לִבּוֹ׃ הִנָּךְ יָפָה רַעְיָתִי הִנָּךְ יָפָה עֵינַיִךְ יוֹנִים מִבַּעַד א
ב לְצַמָּתֵךְ שַׂעְרֵךְ כְּעֵדֶר הָעִזִּים שֶׁגָּלְשׁוּ מֵהַר גִּלְעָד׃ שִׁנַּיִךְ כְּעֵדֶר הַקְּצוּבוֹת שֶׁעָלוּ
ג מִן־הָרַחְצָה שֶׁכֻּלָּם מַתְאִימוֹת וְשַׁכֻּלָה אֵין בָּהֶם׃ כְּחוּט הַשָּׁנִי שִׂפְתוֹתַיִךְ וּמִדְבָּרֵיךְ
ד נָאוֶה כְּפֶלַח הָרִמּוֹן רַקָּתֵךְ מִבַּעַד לְצַמָּתֵךְ׃ כְּמִגְדַּל דָּוִיד צַוָּארֵךְ בָּנוּי לְתַלְפִּיּוֹת
ה אֶלֶף הַמָּגֵן תָּלוּי עָלָיו כֹּל שִׁלְטֵי הַגִּבּוֹרִים׃ שְׁנֵי שָׁדַיִךְ כִּשְׁנֵי עֳפָרִים תְּאוֹמֵי צְבִיָּה
ו הָרוֹעִים בַּשּׁוֹשַׁנִּים׃ עַד שֶׁיָּפוּחַ הַיּוֹם וְנָסוּ הַצְּלָלִים אֵלֶךְ לִי אֶל־הַר הַמּוֹר וְאֶל־
ז ח גִּבְעַת הַלְּבוֹנָה׃ כֻּלָּךְ יָפָה רַעְיָתִי וּמוּם אֵין בָּךְ׃ אִתִּי מִלְּבָנוֹן

The Beloved's Second Poem

THE SONG OF SONGS 4:8–11

In the second love poem, the beloved expresses deepening emotions. The young woman, who was previously called his love, is now referred to as his bride, and he addresses her with increasing frequency.

8 **With me from** Mount **Lebanon, my bride, with me from Lebanon, come.** Let us wander together in Lebanon and return. Perhaps the beloved is approaching from northern Israel. **Look from the peak of Amana,**[B] **from the peak of Senir and Hermon.** Senir is another name for Mount Hermon, perhaps a specific side of the mountain. Look out **from the dens of**

BACKGROUND

4:1| **Your eyes are doves:** The rock dove, *Columba livia*, which is common in Israel, nests in terraced fields, near human residences, or in rocky areas in the hills. Doves are monogamous birds; they change mates only after the death of their partner. The male and female are practically identical in appearance, predominantly gray with black stripes. The verse may be alluding to the color of the girl's eyes. The domestic pigeon is a domesticated subspecies of the rock dove, and it resembles the latter in both behavior and appearance. Domestic pigeons are also monogamous.

A flock of goats that stream down from the highlands of Gilad: The region known as Gilad extends from the Sea of Galilee to the Dead Sea on the eastern side of the Jordan River. It is a hilly region, rich in water sources and vegetation, and suitable for pasture (see Numbers 32:1). However, it is relatively unsuitable for farming. The woman's hair is compared to the sight of black goats streaming down a hill, black lines against the bright background of the highlands of Gilad.

4:3| **Scarlet [*shani*]:** A dye of bright red, produced from a scale insect known as a kermes. The dye is extracted from the creatures by drying them, crushing them, and then cooking them. Besides its use in dying expensive fabrics, this substance was used in the ritual for the purification of lepers (Leviticus 14:4, 49) and of people who had come in contact with a dead body (Numbers 19:6). In the description of the building of the Temple (II Chronicles 2:6, 13), the term *karmil* appears instead of *shani*, *karmil* being the Hebrew name for the kermes insect (Rav Se'adya Gaon; Rashi; Radak).

4:4| **All the shields of the mighty:** Early necklaces were made from long, colorful beads that were threaded in rows. These would rest upon the neck like shields hanging from a wall or tower.

4:5| **Twins of a gazelle:** There are two types of gazelle in Israel: the mountain gazelle, also known as the Levantine mountain gazelle, and the dorcas gazelle. It is possible that the verse is referring to another type of gazelle that lived in this region, the black-tailed gazelle, *Gazella subgutturosa*, which currently inhabits an area spanning from the Arabian Peninsula to central Asia, and was once very common in Jordan and Syria. Between the ages of three and eight, when a female black-tailed gazelle is at her most fertile, she can bear twins (Azarya Alon, ed., *Plants and Animals of the Land of Israel: An Illustrated Encyclopedia*. Ministry of Defense/Society for the Protection of Nature, 1983–1990 [Hebrew]).

4:8| **From the peak of Amana:** Since Amana is listed alongside Senir and Hermon, which are in the southern Anti-Lebanon Mountains, it appears that Amana is a peak in the same range, near the source of the Amana River, which is mentioned as one of the rivers of Damascus. This river is generally identified with the Barada River, which cuts through the city. In Sumerian documents, Amana is mentioned as Amanum, and until the Roman era there was a waystation of this name. Amana has been identified with Mount Zabadani, which is northwest of Damascus and reaches a height of 1800 m. Amana's forests and rocky cliffs are features of its impressive landscape. The Amana of this verse should not be confused with the Amanos Mountains in southeastern Turkey.

lions, from the mountains of leopards.[B] These forested areas were largely uncultivated expanses in which lions and leopards roamed. The wild regions of Lebanon, with their array of predators, serve as a contrasting background to the gentle bride, the Jewish people, or the soul.

Mount Hermon

Lebanon

9 **You have charmed me, my sister,**[D] my love, **my bride; you have charmed me with** my seeing even just **one of your eyes, with** even **one bead of your necklace.** Even the smallest glimpse of you moves me.
10 **How fair is your loving,** or the moistness of your mouth, **my sister, my bride. How much better is your loving than wine, and the fragrance of your oils,** even the simplest of them, is more delightful **than all spices.**
11 **Your lips drip nectar, my bride, honey and milk are under your tongue,** your taste is sweet and pleasant, **and the scent of your garments is like the scent of Lebanon,** a rainy, fertile, and forested region.

The Third Poem and the Bride's Invitation to Her Beloved

THE SONG OF SONGS 4:12–5:1

In his third poem, the beloved praises the bride's qualities of modesty and loyalty, and concludes with a wish. After the poem, the text briefly hints at unification between the lovers.

12 **A locked garden is my sister, my bride; a locked fountainhead,**[23] **a sealed spring.** Although your beauty is arresting, it is not in the public domain; it is designated for one man only.
13 **Your branches,**[24] your external appearance, your garments and coverings, **are** like the pleasant sight of **an orchard of pomegranates, with delicious fruit,** and they are scented like **hennas with lavenders,** perfumes (see 1:12, 14). You radiate beauty from every angle.
14 Your garments are scented like **lavender and saffron,**[B] **lemongrass and cinnamon,**[B] **with all trees of frankincense; myrrh and aloes,**[B] **with all the finest spices.**[25] Of the eleven spices blended into the incense used in the Temple, only four are specified by name in the Torah. Almost all of the rest are taken from this list.
15 The singer returns to the image of the bride as a spring in a locked garden: She is a source of life, **a garden spring, a well of spring water, and flowing streams from Lebanon.** The spring's source is in the distant and fertile mountain peaks.[26]

Sealed spring

"Orchard of pomegranates"

Saffron crocus

Cinnamon

Frankincense tree

Indian aloe tree

16 **Awake, north wind, and come, south wind; blow upon my garden,** my bride, and **its perfume will spread,** or: The sap of its perfumed trees will flow. Unlike many places in the Bible that mention the covenant between God and Israel and its ensuing obligations, this passage expresses the romantic aspect of the covenant. This poem of love and praise is reminiscent of Jeremiah's invocation of the nuptial love between God and Israel in the wilderness.[27] At the starting point in their shared journey, there was a sense of confidence and mutual commitment regarding the future, a faith that all would be well. The groom is moved by the perfect beauty and loyalty of the bride, and he waits for her lovely scent to spread across great distances.

כַּלָּ֔ה אִתִּ֖י מִלְּבָנ֣וֹן תָּב֑וֹאִי תָּשׁ֣וּרִי ׀ מֵרֹ֣אשׁ אֲמָנָ֗ה מֵרֹ֤אשׁ שְׂנִיר֙ וְחֶרְמ֔וֹן מִמְּעֹנ֣וֹת
ט אֲרָי֔וֹת מֵֽהַרְרֵ֖י נְמֵרִֽים׃ לִבַּבְתִּ֖נִי אֲחֹתִ֣י כַלָּ֑ה לִבַּבְתִּ֙נִי֙ באחד מֵעֵינַ֔יִךְ בְּאַחַ֥ד עֲנָ֖ק בְּאַחַ֥ת
י מִצַּוְּרֹנָֽיִךְ׃ מַה־יָּפ֥וּ דֹדַ֖יִךְ אֲחֹתִ֣י כַלָּ֑ה מַה־טֹּ֤בוּ דֹדַ֙יִךְ֙ מִיַּ֔יִן וְרֵ֥יחַ שְׁמָנַ֖יִךְ מִכָּל־
יא בְּשָׂמִֽים׃ נֹ֛פֶת תִּטֹּ֥פְנָה שִׂפְתוֹתַ֖יִךְ כַּלָּ֑ה דְּבַ֤שׁ וְחָלָב֙ תַּ֣חַת לְשׁוֹנֵ֔ךְ וְרֵ֥יחַ שַׂלְמֹתַ֖יִךְ
יב יג כְּרֵ֥יחַ לְבָנֽוֹן׃ גַּ֥ן ׀ נָע֖וּל אֲחֹתִ֣י כַלָּ֑ה גַּ֥ל נָע֖וּל מַעְיָ֥ן חָתֽוּם׃ שְׁלָחַ֙יִךְ֙
יד פַּרְדֵּ֣ס רִמּוֹנִ֔ים עִ֖ם פְּרִ֣י מְגָדִ֑ים כְּפָרִ֖ים עִם־נְרָדִֽים׃ נֵ֣רְדְּ ׀ וְכַרְכֹּ֗ם קָנֶה֙ וְקִנָּמ֔וֹן עִ֖ם
טו כָּל־עֲצֵ֣י לְבוֹנָ֑ה מֹ֚ר וַאֲהָל֔וֹת עִ֖ם כָּל־רָאשֵׁ֥י בְשָׂמִֽים׃ מַעְיַ֣ן גַּנִּ֔ים בְּאֵ֖ר מַ֣יִם חַיִּ֑ים
טז וְנֹזְלִ֖ים מִן־לְבָנֽוֹן׃ ע֤וּרִי צָפוֹן֙ וּב֣וֹאִי תֵימָ֔ן הָפִ֥יחִי גַנִּ֖י יִזְּל֣וּ בְשָׂמָ֑יו יָבֹ֤א דוֹדִי֙ לְגַנּ֔וֹ

BACKGROUND

From the mountains of leopards: This refers to the Arabian leopard, *Panthera pardus nimr*, one of the smallest leopards in the world. The Arabian leopard is a solitary predator, weighing 20–30 kg. It can be found in the mountains of the Judean Desert, and in the Negev in the region of Mitzpe Ramon.

4:14| **Saffron:** Since ancient times, saffron has been obtained from the *Crocus sativus* flower. It is used mainly as a seasoning and coloring agent in food and is still one of the world's most expensive spices.

Lemongrass and cinnamon [*kaneh vekinnamon*]: Some consider *kaneh vekinnamon* the name of a single spice (Septuagint). Perhaps this spice was cinnamon extracted from the inner bark of the tropical cinnamon tree, of the genus *Cinnamomum*, which grows in the Far East. This hypothesis is supported by the verse: "And the good cane [*kaneh*] from a distant land" (Jeremiah 6:20). The bark of this tree curls up when dried and looks like a stick, the literal meaning of the word *kaneh*. Others identify *kaneh* with a plant from the lemongrass genus, *Cymbopogon*, whose leaves contain aromatic oils. Yet another opinion identifies *kaneh* as *Acorus calamus*, also called sweet flag, a plant of the Acoraceae family with fragrant roots (Zohar Amar, *Flora of the Bible*. Jerusalem: Rubin Mass Ltd., 2012 [Hebrew], p. 181).

Aloes [*ahalot*]: *Ahal* is generally identified with one of the species of the tropical Indian aloe tree, genus *Aquilaria*, from whose bark a potent and expensive perfume is extracted.

DISCUSSION

4:9| **My sister:** This term for a lover has been in use from ancient times and can be found also in modern Hebrew poetry. Although the title is sometimes used in a literal sense, as when Abraham said of Sarah that she was his sister (Genesis 20:2), it can also be indicative of a relationship that is not familial. In various monarchies in the ancient Orient, the queen was sometimes called the king's sister, whether or not she was actually his sister, although on more than one occasion this was indeed the case.

After all this praise by the beloved, the bride responds with a brief, modest invitation: **Let my beloved come to his garden and eat his delicious fruits.** The garden is not locked to you; the fountain is open before you.

5 1 After the bride's invitation, the beloved describes the satisfaction he found in his perfect bride: **I came to my garden,** filled with all types of goodness, **my sister, my bride; I gathered my myrrh with my perfume; I ate my honeycomb with my honey; I drank my wine with my milk. Eat, friends; drink, and make love.** The image is of a romantic lovers' tryst.

Honeycomb

The Longing of the Young Woman

THE SONG OF SONGS 5:2–6:3

Now the woman relates her experiences. She opens with a story, perhaps only a dream,[28] of a missed opportunity in which she failed to meet her beloved because of her hesitation to open her door to him. Now, she is regretful and lonely, and she yearns for him.

2 **I am sleeping, but my heart is awake.** In this semiconscious state, something inside me alerted me: **The sound of my beloved is knocking.**[D] Despite my drowsiness, some part of me was alert, eagerly listening for him. I could hear him calling out to me: **Open for me, my sister, my love, my faultless dove,** my perfect beauty. There is a tone of familiarity and closeness in these expressions of affection by the male protagonist. He continues: Open for me, **for my head is filled with dew** from waiting outside at night; **my locks** are filled with the **drops of night,** dew. I am wet, it is uncomfortable outdoors, and I seek shelter.

Dew

3 The woman says to herself: **I have** already **taken off my tunic; how can I don it** now? **I have washed my feet** before bed; **how can I soil them** by walking on the floor to open the door? She does not answer her beloved's call.

4 **My beloved extended his hand through the hole**[D] in the door.[29] When he did so, my love welled up **and my core** [*me'ay*] **was moved for him,** my insides turned over from excitement. Although in modern Hebrew the term *me'ayim* refers specifically to the intestines, in the Bible it refers to the internal cavity of one's body, and by extension, to the heart and soul.[30]

5 Despite my hesitations, when I realized that my beloved was almost inside I could no longer restrain myself: **I arose to open for my beloved; my** perfumed **hands were dripping with** liquid **myrrh, and my fingers with myrrh passing onto the handles of the latch.** The scent of myrrh reached outside.

Bolt on a door

6 **I opened for my beloved; but** while I had hesitated, **my beloved had slipped away, was gone. My soul had departed with his speaking.** When he turned to me before, my heart stopped due to my profound love and longing. Now he was nowhere to be found. **I sought him, but I did not find him; I called him, but he did not answer me.** The verse possibly describes not an actual event, but a lover's troubled dream brought on by anxiety over a potential missed opportunity. Allegorically, this episode refers to real missed opportunities for redemption, on both a national and a personal level. Historically and personally, complacency and other obstacles to salvation prevent the long-sought union with God from taking place.

7 After searching for my beloved near the house to no avail, I went out into the streets. There **the sentries patrolling in the city found me,** and when they saw that I was wandering alone at night **they struck me, they wounded me;** apparently, they considered me a loiterer deserving of punishment. **The guards of the walls took my shawl from upon me.** The guards of the walls are not necessarily her enemies. Since they are charged with preserving the public order, they punish the woman for what they perceive as inappropriate behavior. Similarly, the individual's soul or the nation as a whole can react to a missed opportunity counterproductively. Plagued with visions of what might have been, it can attempt to seize the moment after it has passed, and in the process transgress boundaries. Such transgression always incurs punishment.

8 Here, it seems, the dream comes to an end. Now the woman addresses her friends: **I administer an oath to you, daughters of Jerusalem;** now, come to my aid: **If you find my beloved, what should you tell him?** Tell him **that I am lovesick.** Previously she bid the daughters of Jerusalem to promise that they would let the love awaken by itself (2:7, 3:5). Now, after the nocturnal episode, whether real or imagined, she no longer has the strength to hide her feelings or to keep up appearances. She entreats the daughters of Jerusalem to reveal her powerful love to her beloved.

ה א וְיֹאכַל פְּרִי מְגָדָיו׃ בָּאתִי לְגַנִּי אֲחֹתִי כַלָּה אָרִיתִי מוֹרִי עִם־בְּשָׂמִי אָכַלְתִּי יַעְרִי
ב עִם־דִּבְשִׁי שָׁתִיתִי יֵינִי עִם־חֲלָבִי אִכְלוּ רֵעִים שְׁתוּ וְשִׁכְרוּ דּוֹדִים׃ אֲנִי
יְשֵׁנָה וְלִבִּי עֵר קוֹל ׀ דּוֹדִי דוֹפֵק פִּתְחִי־לִי אֲחֹתִי רַעְיָתִי יוֹנָתִי תַמָּתִי שֶׁרֹּאשִׁי
ג נִמְלָא־טָל קְוֻצּוֹתַי רְסִיסֵי לָיְלָה׃ פָּשַׁטְתִּי אֶת־כֻּתָּנְתִּי אֵיכָכָה אֶלְבָּשֶׁנָּה רָחַצְתִּי
ד ה אֶת־רַגְלַי אֵיכָכָה אֲטַנְּפֵם׃ דּוֹדִי שָׁלַח יָדוֹ מִן־הַחֹר וּמֵעַי הָמוּ עָלָיו׃ קַמְתִּי אֲנִי
ו לִפְתֹּחַ לְדוֹדִי וְיָדַי נָטְפוּ־מוֹר וְאֶצְבְּעֹתַי מוֹר עֹבֵר עַל כַּפּוֹת הַמַּנְעוּל׃ פָּתַחְתִּי
אֲנִי לְדוֹדִי וְדוֹדִי חָמַק עָבָר נַפְשִׁי יָצְאָה בְדַבְּרוֹ בִּקַּשְׁתִּיהוּ וְלֹא מְצָאתִיהוּ
ז קְרָאתִיו וְלֹא עָנָנִי׃ מְצָאֻנִי הַשֹּׁמְרִים הַסֹּבְבִים בָּעִיר הִכּוּנִי פְצָעוּנִי נָשְׂאוּ אֶת־
ח רְדִידִי מֵעָלַי שֹׁמְרֵי הַחֹמוֹת׃ הִשְׁבַּעְתִּי אֶתְכֶם בְּנוֹת יְרוּשָׁלָם אִם־תִּמְצְאוּ אֶת־
ט דּוֹדִי מַה־תַּגִּידוּ לוֹ שֶׁחוֹלַת אַהֲבָה אָנִי׃ מַה־דּוֹדֵךְ מִדּוֹד הַיָּפָה בַּנָּשִׁים מַה־דּוֹדֵךְ
י יא מִדּוֹד שֶׁכָּכָה הִשְׁבַּעְתָּנוּ׃ דּוֹדִי צַח וְאָדוֹם דָּגוּל מֵרְבָבָה׃ רֹאשׁוֹ כֶּתֶם פָּז קְוֻצּוֹתָיו

9 The women ask her: **How is your beloved more than another beloved, O fairest of women?** Who is your beloved? How can we recognize him? **How is your beloved more** special **than another beloved, that you administer an oath to us so?** Notably, in The Song of Songs, the beloved is unknown. He appears intermittently and then vanishes, and no one can identify or locate him. In the background of the text hovers the question of how real the beloved actually is. For the time being, he has no formal relationship with the woman. They rarely meet, and at this stage of the story they are never seen together in public. Allegorically understood, the mysterious nature of the beloved represents the mysterious nature of God.

10 The young woman responds: The face of **my beloved is clear and ruddy,** his skin is clean and white, and his cheeks are red like a beautiful youth.[31] This mixture of red and white is consistent with the image of an apple to which the beloved was previously compared (2:3). My beloved is **more eminent** [***dagul***] **than ten thousand.** Like a flag [*degel*], my beloved stands out from the masses, unique.

11 **His head is** impressively shaped as a work of **the finest gold;**[32]

DISCUSSION

5:2 | **I am sleeping...My beloved is knocking:** On more than one occasion in history, the people of Israel were given a chance to redeem themselves, but they slumbered, failing to seize the moment. On the most fundamental level, and in the depths of the nation's heart, it is true that "I am my beloved's, and my beloved is mine" (6:3; see also 2:16), I desire redemption and a connection to God. But alas, I am lazy and slow to act. Throughout these love poems, with all their ups and downs, the lovers constantly desire one another, but external circumstances do not allow them to unite easily and they are frequently left alone with their longings. The beloved's knocking awakens her love, but she is too slow to act, and by the time she rises he has passed. In the wake of this vision, the woman is left with strengthened passion and will, but an opportunity has been missed.

5:4 | **My beloved extended his hand through the hole:** Locking a door from the inside was performed in biblical times by means of a vertical or horizontal bolt, which was wedged into the doorpost, the lintel, or the doorstep, thus preventing the door from being opened from the outside. The hole mentioned here probably served as means of grasping the door in order to open or close it when unlocked. Although in the ancient world there were locking mechanisms, which required the insertion of a key through a hole from the outside, such mechanisms have been found in the Land of Israel only from the Roman period.

his locks are curls, black as a raven. In ancient times, the hair color of Israelites was typically black.[33]

12 **His eyes are** perfect, radiating beauty and calm, **like doves beside streams of water.** This is a pastoral image of grace and tranquility. A dove drinks by sucking water[34] into its beak and directly into its throat, making no swallowing movement of its head. A pair of doves drinking thus appears to be in synchrony, as they change neither their stance nor their movements. His dark eyes are set against the backdrop of his light skin as if **they are bathed in milk, well set** like precious stones, neither protruding nor sunken.[35]

Dove beside water

13 **His cheeks are like a bed of fragrant plants, growths of spice mixtures.** An Israelite of the time would not be clean-shaven, and as the beloved is young, his beard is likely to be short, like small herbs growing in their beds. **His lips are** colored,[36] or velvety and fragrant[37] like **lilies;**[B] **dripping with flowing,** fragrant **myrrh.**

14 **His hands are** built as **rods of gold set with beryl [*tarshish*];**[B] **his belly is** like a solid **slab of ivory covered with sapphires.**[B]

15 **His calves are pillars of marble, set on bases of fine gold.** The beloved is compared to a work of art. **His appearance is like** the forested region of **Lebanon,** fertile and teeming with life, **choice like** the tall, impressive **cedars** that grow there.

16 **His palate is sweet and all of him is delightful. This is my beloved, and this is my companion, daughters of Jerusalem.** The bride lovingly depicts her beloved as the epitome of beauty. In her eyes, all of his features are wonderful and perfect. Her descriptions do not provide her listeners with practical details that might help them locate her beloved, but they illustrate her feelings for him. Many allegorical interpretations have been offered for these descriptions. The question: "How is your beloved more than another beloved"? (verse 9) has been posed to the nation of Israel for over two thousand years. The answer to this question is: You may not be able to see Him until He reveals Himself, but we can see that He is perfect, and we can do nothing other than seek Him everywhere.

Aquamarine

"Slab of ivory"

Peridot

Sapphire

6 1 The daughters of Jerusalem respond in unison: **Where did your beloved go, fairest of women? Where did your beloved turn? We will seek him with you.**

2 The woman responds: **My beloved descended to his garden, to the beds of fragrant plants.** She does not provide an exact location, but she knows that he is supposed to be in a place of beauty and fragrance, **to herd** his flock **in the gardens, and to gather lilies** for himself.

"Beds of fragrant plants"

3 She concludes: **I am my beloved's, and my beloved is mine.** It is he **who herds among the lilies.** Though he is not currently with me, this does not mean he is avoiding me. I am certain that our love is real. For now, however, my beloved has descended to his garden. Perhaps he will return to me with flowers.

The Beloved and His Love Grow Closer

THE SONG OF SONGS 6:4–7:14

The exchanges between the beloved and his love intensify in their passion with the rising intensity depicted by increasingly overt and bold imagery. The couple stand in wonder at their mutual love. Although it has not been fully consummated, they have full faith in its reality, despite temporary separations, sudden disappearances, and delays.

4 The beloved himself speaks, though the object of his love is likely not present. **You are fair, my love, like Tirtza,**[B] a small city in the portion of Manasseh, which at one point served as the capital of the Kingdom of Israel.[38] It is possible that its beauty played a role in its being chosen as the capital. You are **lovely like Jerusalem**[39] and you are **formidable like banners [*nidgalot*].** You stand out as a banner on display as it flutters

יב תַּלְתַּלִּים שְׁחֹרוֹת כָּעוֹרֵב׃ עֵינָיו כְּיוֹנִים עַל־אֲפִיקֵי מָיִם רֹחֲצוֹת בֶּחָלָב יֹשְׁבוֹת
יג עַל־מִלֵּאת׃ לְחָיָו כַּעֲרוּגַת הַבֹּשֶׂם מִגְדְּלוֹת מֶרְקָחִים שִׂפְתוֹתָיו שׁוֹשַׁנִּים נֹטְפוֹת
יד מוֹר עֹבֵר׃ יָדָיו גְּלִילֵי זָהָב מְמֻלָּאִים בַּתַּרְשִׁישׁ מֵעָיו עֶשֶׁת שֵׁן מְעֻלֶּפֶת סַפִּירִים׃
טו טז שׁוֹקָיו עַמּוּדֵי שֵׁשׁ מְיֻסָּדִים עַל־אַדְנֵי־פָז מַרְאֵהוּ כַּלְּבָנוֹן בָּחוּר כָּאֲרָזִים׃ חִכּוֹ
ו א מַמְתַקִּים וְכֻלּוֹ מַחֲמַדִּים זֶה דוֹדִי וְזֶה רֵעִי בְּנוֹת יְרוּשָׁלָםִ׃ אָנָה הָלַךְ דּוֹדֵךְ הַיָּפָה
ב בַּנָּשִׁים אָנָה פָּנָה דוֹדֵךְ וּנְבַקְשֶׁנּוּ עִמָּךְ׃ דּוֹדִי יָרַד לְגַנּוֹ לַעֲרֻגוֹת הַבֹּשֶׂם לִרְעוֹת
ג בַּגַּנִּים וְלִלְקֹט שׁוֹשַׁנִּים׃ אֲנִי לְדוֹדִי וְדוֹדִי לִי הָרֹעֶה בַּשּׁוֹשַׁנִּים׃
ד ה יָפָה אַתְּ רַעְיָתִי כְּתִרְצָה נָאוָה כִּירוּשָׁלָםִ אֲיֻמָּה כַּנִּדְגָּלוֹת׃ הָסֵבִּי עֵינַיִךְ מִנֶּגְדִּי
ו שֶׁהֵם הִרְהִיבֻנִי שַׂעְרֵךְ כְּעֵדֶר הָעִזִּים שֶׁגָּלְשׁוּ מִן־הַגִּלְעָד׃ שִׁנַּיִךְ כְּעֵדֶר הָרְחֵלִים
ז שֶׁעָלוּ מִן־הָרַחְצָה שֶׁכֻּלָּם מַתְאִימוֹת וְשַׁכֻּלָה אֵין בָּהֶם׃ כְּפֶלַח הָרִמּוֹן רַקָּתֵךְ

high above. Alternatively, *nidgalot* refers to arrays of decorated soldiers.[40]

5 **Avert your eyes from me, as they excite my arrogance,** or passion,[41] when they gaze upon me. **Your** black, curly **hair,** flowing down your back, **is like a flock of goats that has streamed down from the Gilad.**

Tirtza Ravine

6 **Your teeth are like a flock of ewes that have come up from being washed, that are all paired, and there is none missing among them.** Your teeth are perfect and beautiful.

7 **Your temple is like a pomegranate slice,** round and beautiful, **behind your braid,** or lock of hair, falling over your face and sides.

BACKGROUND

5:13 | **His lips are lilies [*shoshanim*]:** The identity of the *shoshana* is unclear (see commentary on 2:1). If this description refers to the color of his lips, then the *shoshana* must be red (see Alsheikh). If so, it likely refers to the rose and not the white Madonna lily. However, it is possible that the verse intends to describe the shape or feel of the beloved's lips, rather than their color, in which case the *shoshana* can still be identified as the Madonna lily.

5:14 | **Beryl [*tarshish*]:** *Tarshish* is one of the precious stones set into the breast piece of the High Priest (Exodus 28:20). Various opinions are offered in rabbinic literature and the Aramaic translations regarding the identity and color of *tarshish*. Nowadays, it is commonly accepted to identify *tarshish* with peridot or with the bluish-green variety of beryl known as aquamarine. Some have noted a similarity between the word *tarshish* and the Akkadian word for red, *rususu*.

Sapphire: A blue variety of the extremely hard mineral corundum, the sapphire is valued as a precious stone for jewelry. Corundum can also appear in other colors. The red variety is called ruby.

6:4 | **Tirtza:** Tirtza was an important city in the territory of the tribe of Manasseh, identified with Tel el-Far'a, approximately 10 km northeast of Shekhem. This city controlled the roads leading from Shekhem to the crossings of the Jordan River near Adam and to Beit She'an. Archaeological discoveries in the area reflect the biblical accounts of Tirtza. Nearby, there is a large spring, Ein el-Far'a.

The city was protected by ravines on three sides. The beautiful, green, and water-rich environment surrounding Tirtza, along with its strategic location, justified its choice as the capital city of the Kingdom of Israel. During a rebellion it was destroyed, and the more fortified city of Samaria was selected in its stead.

8 **They are sixty queens,** wives of King Solomon, **and eighty concubines, and** around him there are also **young women without number.** Perhaps this is a poem composed about or by King Solomon, presumably in his youth.[42]

9 Despite Solomon's many women, **unique is my faultless dove;** she stands above them all. **Unique to her mother,** there is no woman like her; she is **pure to the one who bore her. Girls see her and laud her, queens and concubines** see her **and praise her.**

10 The beloved continues to praise his bride: **Who is she who appears** in the distance, glowing **like** the **dawn, fair like the moon, pure** and shining **like the sun?** The initial light of dawn is very gentle; the light of the moon is not strong, but it is pleasant and clear; the sun that eventually shines forth is the brightest of all.[43] She is **formidable like banners.**

Dawn

11 Here the narrator could be either the beloved or his love, but it is probably the latter:[44] **I have gone down to the nut garden to look at the budding [*ibbei*] of the vale,**[45] the fresh fruits or plants of the valley. Perhaps the word *aviv*, spring, is derived from *ibbei*, as spring is the season of regrowth and vitality.[46] I have gone **to see whether the vine has blossomed and the pomegranates are in bloom.** This takes place in spring, when people generally venture down to gardens and streams to see the blossoming plants. Many commentaries explain this image of initial growth as representing the exodus from Egypt.

Unripe nuts

Unripe dates

"Pomegranates are in bloom"

12 I am utterly amazed by the experience, as if **I do not know my own soul** in this surreal state that resembles a dream. **It has set me,** I feel as though I have been set **on chariots of my noble [*nadiv*] people,** as if he has taken me upon his chariot among his soldiers. Some suggest that the phrase *ami nadiv*, my noble people, is an allusion to Aminadav father of Nahshon, the prince of Judah.

7 1 This part of the song evokes the dancing young women, calling to the most beautiful among them: **Return, return,** turn around, or rejoin our dancing, **the Shulamite.** This is probably not a person's name, but an appellation for a perfect [*mushlemet*], beautiful girl, the bride of the beloved. **Return, return, and we will gaze upon you.** And a response: **Why will you gaze at the Shulamite like a dance of two companies** of dancers? Why do you look at the Shulamite in this circle of dancers? Although the Shulamite appears together with all the other girls, she stands out. Allegorically understood, the Shulamite could be a metaphor for Israel among the nations or for the soul that shines out from the body.

2 The Shulamite's beauty is now described in detail, from her toes to her head: **How fair are your steps,**[47] or your feet,[48] **in sandals, daughter of a nobleman. Your rounded thighs are like ornaments, the handiwork of a master craftsman,**[B] perfect as a work of art.

Necklace of gold links, Egypt, Roman period

3 **Your navel is a moon-shaped goblet,** or bowl. **May it not lack mixed wine. Your belly is** round, smooth, and symmetrical, like **a pile of wheat** in a granary, **hedged with lilies.** This last expression is an image of carefully guarded beauty.[49]

Pile of threshed wheat

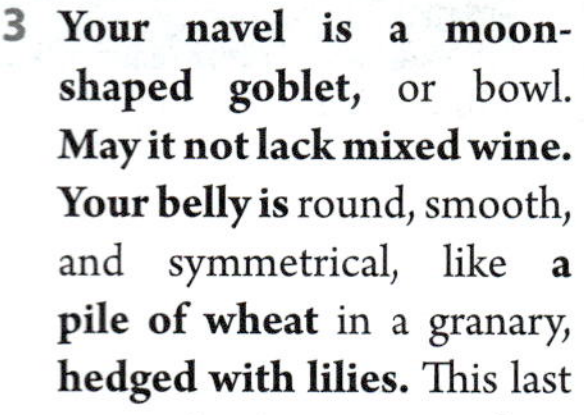

4 **Your two breasts are like two fawns, twins of a gazelle.** This simile relies on both the fawns' physical shape and their aesthetic beauty.

5 **Your neck is** upright, white, and beautiful, **like an ivory tower; your eyes are** like the **pools in Heshbon,**[B] **by the gate of Bat Rabim.** Heshbon was an ancient city located on the eastern side of the Jordan River that served as a political and commercial center even before Israel entered the land of Canaan. It is possible that Heshbon boasted two large pools near its city gates, perhaps in a public square where many people [*rabim*] would gather.[50] The imagery evokes large, deep, and tranquil eyes. **Your nose,**[D] or your forehead, **is like the tower of Lebanon overlooking Damascus** in the distance.[51]

ח מִבַּ֖עַד לְצַמָּתֵֽךְ׃ שִׁשִּׁ֥ים הֵ֙מָּה֙ מְּלָכ֔וֹת וּשְׁמֹנִ֖ים פִּֽילַגְשִׁ֑ים וַעֲלָמ֖וֹת אֵ֥ין מִסְפָּֽר׃
ט אַחַ֥ת הִיא֙ יוֹנָתִ֣י תַמָּתִ֔י אַחַ֥ת הִיא֙ לְאִמָּ֔הּ בָּרָ֥ה הִ֖יא לְיֽוֹלַדְתָּ֑הּ רָא֤וּהָ בָנוֹת֙
י וַֽיְאַשְּׁר֔וּהָ מְלָכ֥וֹת וּפִֽילַגְשִׁ֖ים וַֽיְהַלְלֽוּהָ׃ מִי־זֹ֥את הַנִּשְׁקָפָ֖ה כְּמוֹ־שָׁ֑חַר
יא יָפָ֣ה כַלְּבָנָ֗ה בָּרָה֙ כַּֽחַמָּ֔ה אֲיֻמָּ֖ה כַּנִּדְגָּלֽוֹת׃ אֶל־גִּנַּ֤ת אֱגוֹז֙ יָרַ֔דְתִּי לִרְא֖וֹת בְּאִבֵּ֣י
יב הַנָּ֑חַל לִרְאוֹת֙ הֲפָֽרְחָ֣ה הַגֶּ֔פֶן הֵנֵ֖צוּ הָרִמֹּנִֽים׃ לֹ֣א יָדַ֔עְתִּי נַפְשִׁ֣י שָׂמַ֔תְנִי מַרְכְּב֖וֹת
א עַמִּ֥י נָדִֽיב׃ שׁ֤וּבִי שׁ֙וּבִי֙ הַשּׁ֣וּלַמִּ֔ית שׁ֥וּבִי שׁ֖וּבִי וְנֶחֱזֶה־בָּ֑ךְ מַה־תֶּֽחֱזוּ֙ בַּשּׁ֣וּלַמִּ֔ית
ב כִּמְחֹלַ֖ת הַֽמַּחֲנָֽיִם׃ מַה־יָּפ֧וּ פְעָמַ֛יִךְ בַּנְּעָלִ֖ים בַּת־נָדִ֑יב חַמּוּקֵ֣י יְרֵכַ֔יִךְ כְּמ֣וֹ חֲלָאִ֔ים
ג מַעֲשֵׂ֖ה יְדֵ֥י אָמָּֽן׃ שָׁרְרֵךְ֙ אַגַּ֣ן הַסַּ֔הַר אַל־יֶחְסַ֖ר הַמָּ֑זֶג בִּטְנֵךְ֙ עֲרֵמַ֣ת חִטִּ֔ים סוּגָ֖ה
ד ה בַּשּׁוֹשַׁנִּֽים׃ שְׁנֵ֥י שָׁדַ֛יִךְ כִּשְׁנֵ֥י עֳפָרִ֖ים תָּאֳמֵ֥י צְבִיָּֽה׃ צַוָּארֵ֖ךְ כְּמִגְדַּ֣ל הַשֵּׁ֑ן עֵינַ֜יִךְ
בְּרֵכ֣וֹת בְּחֶשְׁבּ֗וֹן עַל־שַׁ֙עַר֙ בַּת־רַבִּ֔ים אַפֵּךְ֙ כְּמִגְדַּ֣ל הַלְּבָנ֔וֹן צוֹפֶ֖ה פְּנֵ֥י דַמָּֽשֶׂק׃

BACKGROUND

7:2 | **Your rounded thighs are like ornaments [*ḥala'im*], the handiwork of a master craftsman:** The word *ḥelya*, or *ḥali*, apparently refers to a round ornament. The *ḥali* is also mentioned alongside earrings in the book of Proverbs (25:2). Some associate this term with the word *ḥuliya*, a term used by the Sages to denote a link in a chain or bead (Rashi). Alternatively, *ḥali* may be related to a similar Akkadian word that means loins. If so, the beloved is praising the figure of his love as suitable for birthing children.

7:5 | **Heshbon:** Heshbon was an important city located on the border between the territories of Gad and Reuben (Joshua 13:17). It is generally identified with Tel Hesban, which is located on the ancient King's Highway, on the highlands above the Madaba Plains, about 20 km southwest of Rabat Amon, or present-day Amman. According to Josephus, control of Heshbon changed hands during various wars, and was under Jewish control during the Hasmonean period. It can be inferred from this verse that the people of Israel were familiar with this city (see also Ramban, Numbers 32:38). Although the surrounding region was fertile, the city was located on the edge of the desert. It was therefore necessary to channel the water that flowed through nearby ravines in the winter, and to store it in pools.

DISCUSSION

7:5 | **Your nose [*apekh*]:** Rashi notes that a large nose is not considered a sign of beauty, and he therefore maintains that the word *apekh* here refers to the forehead, since the face as a whole can be referred to as *apayim*. Others maintain that *apekh* indeed refers to her nose, as in verse 9 that follows, and explain that the comparison between the young woman's nose and the tower of Lebanon refers to its renowned beauty and straightness, not its size (see Ibn Ezra; Rav Yosef Kara; Rav Yeshaya of Trani).

6 **Your head is** elegantly set **upon you like the Carmel.** This could also be a reference to the woman's curly hair, since Mount Carmel has lush vegetation. **And the locks of your head are** carefully arranged **like** soft strands of **purple wool,** displayed in magnificent arrangements due to the wool's rarity and price.[52] **A king,** the beloved, is **bound in the tresses.**[BD]

Mount Carmel

"King bound in the tresses." Tasseled headdress, Troy, Bronze Age

7 The previous description of the bride, which was the most intimate so far, is now followed by expressions of the mutual adoration between the lovers: **How fair you are and how pleasant you are, love in its delights.** Love waxes and wanes, and includes, alongside dreams and aspirations, also heartache. However, love in its delights is consummated love, in which joy is fully realized.

8 The beloved's poem of intimacy: **This, your stature, is likened to a** tall, beautiful **date palm, and your breasts** are likened **to** round **clusters** of dates that hang at its sides.

9 The image of the date palm continues: **I said** to myself: **I will ascend the date palm, I will grasp its branches;**[53] **and please may your breasts be like clusters of the vine, and the fragrance of your nose** pleasant **like apples.**

Date palms

Date palm branches

"Clusters of the vine"

10 **Your palate,** the taste of your kisses, **is like fine wine that goes pleasantly with my lovemaking [*dodi*],** or that goes pleasantly into my mouth.[54] Another possible interpretation is that the word *dodi* here means "my beloved," a reference to the male lover. If so, this phrase is recited by the bride. However, since the first phrase, "Your palate is like fine wine," is addressed to the female lover, then this latter phrase must be an interjection as the young woman completes her beloved's sentence. The man continues: Your palate is like fine wine, **moving the lips of the sleeping** so that they speak.[55]

11 The woman responds: **I am my beloved's,** or I yearn for my beloved, **and his desire is toward me.**

12 **Come, my beloved, let us go out** alone **to the field; let us stay the night in the villages.** These are not necessarily actual plans. They may simply be fantasies that convey the depth of her emotion and passion.

13 **Let us arise early to the vineyards; let us see whether the vine has blossomed, the grape bud has sprouted.**[56] Let us see whether **the pomegranates have bloomed.**[B] This scene takes place during the spring, when the flowers of the pomegranate tree appear, undoubtedly a beautiful sight. **There,** in the tranquil and beautiful vineyard, **I will give my love to you.** These descriptions of springtime can also be understood as an allusion to the exodus from Egypt, as Passover is always in the spring. There is a special obligation to remember the exodus, which was itself the springtime blossoming of Israel into a nation, during the month in which all of nature blossoms and the promise of the future beckons.

"The grape bud has sprouted." Tiny grapes visible between stamens

14 After a while, **the mandrakes have emitted fragrance.**[B] Mandrakes do not emit their pleasant fragrance in the spring. Rather, they ripen approximately one and a half months later, at the time of the wheat harvest. Therefore, a considerable time must have passed since the invitation of the previous verse. **And at our entrance are** the scents of **all types of delicacies,** both **new,** which have sprouted recently, **and old.** All of this sweetness, new and old, **I have hidden them away for you, my beloved.** At this point, the courtship that has been developing throughout the entire story reaches its conclusion. The love between the beloved and his bride is depicted here at its apex, when the beloved describes his love as utterly beautiful and graceful, and she responds by noting that all of nature is ripe for the consummation of their love, and that she waits only for him.

Mandrakes

ו ז רֹאשֵׁךְ עָלַיִךְ כַּכַּרְמֶל וְדַלַּת רֹאשֵׁךְ כָּאַרְגָּמָן מֶלֶךְ אָסוּר בָּרְהָטִים׃ מַה־יָּפִית
ח וּמַה־נָּעַמְתְּ אַהֲבָה בַּתַּעֲנוּגִים׃ זֹאת קוֹמָתֵךְ דָּמְתָה לְתָמָר וְשָׁדַיִךְ לְאַשְׁכֹּלוֹת׃
ט אָמַרְתִּי אֶעֱלֶה בְתָמָר אֹחֲזָה בְּסַנְסִנָּיו וְיִהְיוּ־נָא שָׁדַיִךְ כְּאֶשְׁכְּלוֹת הַגֶּפֶן וְרֵיחַ
י יא אַפֵּךְ כַּתַּפּוּחִים׃ וְחִכֵּךְ כְּיֵין הַטּוֹב הוֹלֵךְ לְדוֹדִי לְמֵישָׁרִים דּוֹבֵב שִׂפְתֵי יְשֵׁנִים׃ אֲנִי
יב יג לְדוֹדִי וְעָלַי תְּשׁוּקָתוֹ׃ לְכָה דוֹדִי נֵצֵא הַשָּׂדֶה נָלִינָה בַּכְּפָרִים׃ נַשְׁכִּימָה לַכְּרָמִים
נִרְאֶה אִם־פָּרְחָה הַגֶּפֶן פִּתַּח הַסְּמָדַר הֵנֵצוּ הָרִמּוֹנִים שָׁם אֶתֵּן אֶת־דֹּדַי לָךְ׃
יד הַדּוּדָאִים נָתְנוּ־רֵיחַ וְעַל־פְּתָחֵינוּ כָּל־מְגָדִים חֲדָשִׁים גַּם־יְשָׁנִים דּוֹדִי צָפַנְתִּי
ח א לָךְ׃ מִי יִתֶּנְךָ כְּאָח לִי יוֹנֵק שְׁדֵי אִמִּי אֶמְצָאֲךָ בַחוּץ אֶשָּׁקְךָ גַּם לֹא־יָבוּזוּ לִי׃

Toward a Permanent Covenant

THE SONG OF SONGS 8:1–14

In this last section, though the poem remains the same poem and the love the same love, one can discern a new element. At the conclusion of The Song of Songs the reader finds premonitions of significant changes in the relationship between the beloved and his love. The previous descriptions of a vague, open-ended love gradually transition to a more functional, almost legal form. This section also includes certain insights on the nature of love, and the accompanying emotion of jealousy.

8 1 Until this point, the poem described a love bounded neither by space nor by time, with the lovers seemingly everywhere and nowhere at once. In the following verses, the woman expresses her desire to strengthen and stabilize her bond with her beloved: **If only you were like a brother to me, who sucked the breasts of my mother. I would find you outside; I would kiss you, yet they would not despise me.** Kissing a brother in public is not considered an undignified act. The young woman yearns to openly display her love for her beloved in such a natural manner.

BACKGROUND

7:6| **A king [*melekh*] bound in the tresses [*barehatim*]:** Some suggest that the word *melekh* in this context does not mean king at all but is derived from the Akkadian term *malu*, which means an uncombed lock of hair. A similar Greek word, *mallu*, refers to a curl of wool or hair. If this is correct, then the word *rehatim* should be understood as the beams of a loom, such that the entire phrase means: Her hair is naturally arranged like weaving on the beams of a loom.

7:13| **The vine has blossomed, the grape bud has sprouted, the pomegranates have bloomed:** After the start of the spring season, when the flowers of the field bloom, and the nightingale and turtledove have appeared (see 2:12), springtime reaches its peak, culminating in the blossoming of the vine and pomegranate. At this stage, one can observe the shedding of the joined, closed petals of the grape bud, as the stamen and pistils are released for pollination.

7:14| **The mandrakes have emitted fragrance:** The mandrake, *Mandragora autumnalis*, which grows in Israel, ripens during the wheat harvest. It possesses a bright orange color and emits a pungent fragrance. The mandrake grows throughout the winter surrounded by purple flowers in a rosette of leaves close to the ground. The fruit is edible; however, its leaves, roots, and seeds are poisonous. In folklore, the mandrake is considered to have medicinal properties, and to be a remedy for infertility.

DISCUSSION

7:6| **King bound in the tresses [*melekh asur barehatim*]:** Despite his power, wealth, and freedom, the king is captivated by her hair (see Ibn Ezra). Some explain that the tresses, *rehatim*, are not the bride's hair but the ribbons and fine chains decorating it, which were now tied around the king's head, according to the ancient custom for a bridegroom to tie his bride's hair decorations around his own head. It is also possible to translate the verse as follows: And the locks of your head are like purple wool of the king, bound in ribbons.

2 **I would lead you** unabashedly, I **would bring you to my mother's house, who teaches me;**[57] there **I would give you from the spiced wine to drink, from the juice of my pomegranate.**
3 Another fantasy: **His left** arm **is under my head, and his right embraces me** intimately.
4 Nevertheless, **I administer an oath to you, daughters of Jerusalem: For what do you awaken and for what do you rouse love, until it desires**[D] to awaken by itself? Let the love develop at its own pace.
5 This verse is spoken by a third party, depicting the relationship from a more stable, objective perspective: **Who is that coming up from the wilderness, leaning upon her beloved?**[58] Is it not the woman, who says to her beloved: **Under the apple tree** I met you and **I roused you** from your slumber; or, I roused your love for me. **There your mother conceived you; there she who bore you conceived.** The word *ḥibela*, translated here as "conceived," could also mean "suffered birth pangs." The shade of the apple tree is the beloved's place of origin, and it is there that he now encounters his love. Previously, the woman sought to bring her beloved into her mother's house; now, she arrives from an unknown wilderness, drawn to the place where her beloved was formed. Though she does not meet his parents, she makes reference to them. Understood allegorically, this verse refers to the soul's quest to rise above the mundane, and to find God in its own source and origin.

Apple tree

6 The woman asks of her beloved: **Set me as a seal upon your heart, as a seal upon your arm.**[B] Let me be like your seal, a personal item unique to you. This is another symbol of the increasing permanence of their bond. So powerful is the woman's devotion that she wishes to relinquish her independent existence altogether, preferring to attach herself to her beloved as a seal. There is, however, another side to this, **as love is as intense as death.** Alongside the delights of love, there is also a dark side. Just as death swallows everything and cannot be deferred, so too the feelings of love are so overpowering as to be inescapable. Furthermore, **jealousy is as cruel as the grave.** This refers to the demand for exclusive possession of the object of one's love. Such jealousy is a profound emotion that is difficult to bear. Understood allegorically, the jealousy that is built into love for God, who demands complete devotion, is very difficult for other peoples to comprehend. To the nation of Israel, the relationship with God is not only its most important bond, but the only thing in the world that matters. This feeling is as harsh, absolute, and uncompromising as the grave. **Its sparks,** the sparks of love, **are the sparks of fire,** which can burn and even destroy a person. Love is **a great conflagration.**
7 If love is true, **much water cannot extinguish** the fire of that **love, and rivers cannot wash it away;** even **if a man were to give all the wealth of his house for** the purchase of **love, he would be scorned.**[D] By means of gestures, gifts, and displays of emotion, one can acquire a certain level of friendship, but not love.
8 Now, relatives of the lovers begin to openly discuss their relationship. The brothers of the young woman speak first: **We have a little sister, and she has no breasts,** she is too young and insufficiently developed. Therefore, **what shall we do for our sister on the day that she will be spoken for** concerning marriage? Since she is not yet ready for marriage, what shall we do when the proposal arrives? How long can we delay it?
9 As long as the little sister was simply playing outside, singing and dancing, the brothers did not take much notice of her behavior. Now, however, they begin to appraise her character: **If she is a wall,** guarded and modest, **we will build upon her a silver parapet,**[B] we will decorate her with conspicuous jewelry. **And if she is a door,** which can be open and unguarded, **we will affix on her cedar panels** to protect her.[59]

Headdress with parapet on statuette, Rome, second century CE

10 The young woman responds: First, **I am a wall,** not a door, **and** second, **my breasts** are **like the towers.** I have breasts; you have merely failed to notice how much I have grown. **Then,** in this state, **I was in his eyes,** the eyes of the beloved, who is perhaps not immediately present, **as one who finds peace.** My beloved already knows that I have found my peace with my choice of him. You should have no misgivings

"I am a wall"

ב ג אֶנְהָגֲךָ אֲבִיאֲךָ אֶל־בֵּית אִמִּי תְּלַמְּדֵנִי אַשְׁקְךָ מִיַּיִן הָרֶקַח מֵעֲסִיס רִמֹּנִי׃ שְׂמֹאלוֹ
ד תַּחַת רֹאשִׁי וִימִינוֹ תְּחַבְּקֵנִי׃ הִשְׁבַּעְתִּי אֶתְכֶם בְּנוֹת יְרוּשָׁלִָם מַה־תָּעִירוּ ׀ וּמַה־
ה תְּעֹרְרוּ אֶת־הָאַהֲבָה עַד שֶׁתֶּחְפָּץ׃ מִי זֹאת עֹלָה מִן־הַמִּדְבָּר
מִתְרַפֶּקֶת עַל־דּוֹדָהּ תַּחַת הַתַּפּוּחַ עוֹרַרְתִּיךָ שָׁמָּה חִבְּלַתְךָ אִמֶּךָ שָׁמָּה חִבְּלָה
ו יְלָדַתְךָ׃ שִׂימֵנִי כַחוֹתָם עַל־לִבֶּךָ כַּחוֹתָם עַל־זְרוֹעֶךָ כִּי־עַזָּה כַמָּוֶת אַהֲבָה
ז קָשָׁה כִשְׁאוֹל קִנְאָה רְשָׁפֶיהָ רִשְׁפֵּי אֵשׁ שַׁלְהֶבֶתְיָה׃ מַיִם רַבִּים לֹא יוּכְלוּ לְכַבּוֹת
אֶת־הָאַהֲבָה וּנְהָרוֹת לֹא יִשְׁטְפוּהָ אִם־יִתֵּן אִישׁ אֶת־כָּל־הוֹן בֵּיתוֹ בָּאַהֲבָה בּוֹז
ח יָבוּזוּ לוֹ׃ אָחוֹת לָנוּ קְטַנָּה וְשָׁדַיִם אֵין לָהּ מַה־נַּעֲשֶׂה לַאֲחוֹתֵנוּ
ט בַּיּוֹם שֶׁיְּדֻבַּר־בָּהּ׃ אִם־חוֹמָה הִיא נִבְנֶה עָלֶיהָ טִירַת כָּסֶף וְאִם־דֶּלֶת הִיא נָצוּר
י עָלֶיהָ לוּחַ אָרֶז׃ אֲנִי חוֹמָה וְשָׁדַי כַּמִּגְדָּלוֹת אָז הָיִיתִי בְעֵינָיו כְּמוֹצְאֵת שָׁלוֹם׃

BACKGROUND

8:6 | **Set me as a seal upon your heart, as a seal upon your arm:** The seal was a valuable personal accessory, used mainly for signing and confirming contracts or statutes. It was used primarily by men, and was framed within a ring that was worn on one's finger, or hung around one's neck. The seal would be sunk and rolled in a soft substance, such as wax or clay, which would later harden, retaining the design that was imprinted on it.

8:9 | **Silver parapet [*tira*]:** In both the Bible and the Mishna, a *tira* refers to a low fence or parapet that surrounds a defined area (see Genesis 25:16; Ezekiel 46:23; Mishna *Kelim* 3:5). Later, the word *tira* came to mean a palace and fortress, as in modern Hebrew. It is possible that this silver *tira* is actually a crown-like ornament, like the "city of gold" mentioned in the Mishna (*Shabbat* 6:1; *Eduyyot* 2:7; *Kelim* 11:8).

DISCUSSION

8:4 | **For what do you rouse love, until it desires:** This phrase is repeated throughout the book. Even when the love is mutual and clear, it cannot be enhanced by artificial means, by external displays, or through the participation of gossiping strangers. To goad emotion from the outside can even disturb or delay the fruition of love. Furthermore, the request to not rouse love prematurely displays a confidence that the love is real and strong, and not to be anxious or fretted about. Therefore, the daughters of Jerusalem are told not to involve themselves in the situation, which is solely between the woman and her beloved.

8:7 | **If a man were to give all the wealth of his house for love, he would be scorned:** Sometimes it seems that anything can be bought, so long as one finds the right price. However, no matter how great one's fortune, love cannot be purchased. When it appears that a person has succeeded in buying love, in practice he has acquired no more than a person's body. Furthermore, love cannot be relinquished or sold.

about my relationship. I am ready physically, emotionally, and morally to be married.

11 An anonymous third party provides background for the continuation of the woman's speech: King **Solomon had a vineyard at Baal Hamon.**[B] **He gave the vineyard to the guards,** to take care of it. **Each would bring,** earn in exchange **for its fruit, a** sizable income of one **thousand** pieces **of silver.** The vineyard symbolizes a woman, specifically the female protagonist of the poem, and Solomon is her guardian, the closest thing to a paternal figure, who has appointed the brothers to look after their sister. These guards of the vineyard receive a handsome payment for fruits of the vineyard. Allegorically, the nation of Israel is the vineyard. When it fulfills its divine purpose, its profits are distributed among the nations, if they only know to appreciate the vineyard and show responsibility for it.

Vineyard

12 Now, the young woman, who considers herself mature, decides for herself the fate of her vineyard: **My vineyard is before me,** and I intend to give it to my beloved; I intend to marry him. As part of the arrangement, the profits from the vineyard will be distributed: **The thousand is for you, Solomon,** the custodian, **and two hundred** will be given **for those who guard its fruit.** Now, when the couple wishes to establish their bond in marriage, they erect boundaries. Allegorically speaking, the bride is the individual soul or the Jewish people that yearns and seeks to be married to God. In this context, the Sages expound that "the day of his wedding" (3:11) refers to the giving of the Torah, and "the day of the rejoicing of his heart" refers to the building of the Temple (see commentary on 3:11). Of course, there was love between God and Israel before these events, but their relationship was not cemented in a formal covenant. The giving of the Torah was the wedding of Israel to God, as it was at that moment that a binding relationship was established. Likewise, when God dwelled among the nation of Israel with the building of the Temple, it was as if the bride and groom had created a new, shared household. On every level of interpretation, the same questions are posed: Who is the bride? Is she worthy? Is she ready for marriage or must she wait a few more years? And on every level of interpretation, a permanent relationship consists of agreements and commitments, and carries with it a price. The great King Solomon clearly does not require more money. Still, in order to finalize the agreement, the bride must relinquish part of her inheritance and give her vineyard as a dowry.

13 Throughout this dialogue, the beloved was not present. Now, he addresses his bride-to-be: You, **the one who dwells in the gardens,** whose **companions listen to your voice,** as you proved when you spoke to the brothers: **Let me hear it.** I wish to meet you and listen to your sweet voice myself.

14 She responds: Indeed, the consummation of our relationship is nearer than ever, but its time has not yet arrived. In the meantime, **flee, my beloved, and be like a gazelle or a young deer on the mountains of spices.** You are assured of my love; I am yours. Now leap on the hills and enjoy their fragrance, for I know that you will return.

BACKGROUND

8:11 | **Baal Hamon:** No place of this name has been identified. Perhaps Baal Hamon is not the name of a place, but a phrase referring to the work by a contractor for the owner [*baal*] of a fortune [*hamon*] (see Ecclesiastes 5:9). Some suggest that this is Baal Hermon, located on the slopes of the Hermon (see Judges 3:3). This is a fertile and well-watered area, and it produces quality vines even today. According to the *Targum* and Rashi, Baal Hamon is Jerusalem, where masses [*hamon*] of people gathered, especially on Passover, the spring festival.

יא כֶּ֣רֶם הָיָ֤ה לִשְׁלֹמֹה֙ בְּבַ֣עַל הָמ֔וֹן נָתַ֥ן אֶת־הַכֶּ֖רֶם לַנֹּטְרִ֑ים אִ֛ישׁ יָבִ֥א בְּפִרְי֖וֹ אֶ֥לֶף
יב יג כָּֽסֶף׃ כַּרְמִ֥י שֶׁלִּ֖י לְפָנָ֑י הָאֶ֤לֶף לְךָ֙ שְׁלֹמֹ֔ה וּמָאתַ֖יִם לְנֹטְרִ֥ים אֶת־פִּרְיֽוֹ׃ הַיּוֹשֶׁ֣בֶת
יד בַּגַּנִּ֗ים חֲבֵרִ֛ים מַקְשִׁיבִ֥ים לְקוֹלֵ֖ךְ הַשְׁמִיעִֽנִי׃ בְּרַ֣ח ׀ דּוֹדִ֗י וּֽדְמֵה־לְךָ֤ לִצְבִי֙ א֛וֹ
לְעֹ֥פֶר הָֽאַיָּלִ֖ים עַ֥ל הָרֵ֥י בְשָׂמִֽים׃

Ruth

Ruth

INTRODUCTION TO RUTH

The story of the book of Ruth can be described as a kind of idyll. It unfolds in a quiet Judean community during the era of the judges, in Israel's early history. No earth-shattering miracles occur in this book, nor any events of historical import. While there is a certain amount of conflict in the story, a sense of calmness and harmony infuses the narrative. The book's main characters are memorable not for their fastidiously correct behavior, but for their personal decisions to conduct themselves with kindness and generosity toward one another.

The central focus of this book is the personal story of a daughter-in-law and her mother-in-law who are left to wander through the world destitute, before they eventually achieve security. Only the final verses, which relate how the eponymous heroine, Ruth, becomes the mother of the royal dynasty of Israel, transform the plot from a personal, human story to one of national significance. The conclusion also shows how God guides events in the world, as He nurtures a person on the margins of society, a female Moavite convert, until she becomes the ancestor of King David himself. One of David's psalms contains a verse that aptly describes the plot of this book: "The stone that the builders rejected became the cornerstone."[1]

Ruth

Elimelekh and His Family in Moav

RUTH 1:1–5

The story of Ruth begins with a famine in the Land of Israel, which causes Elimelekh's family to relocate from Bethlehem to Moav. This move is not as strange as it might first seem, as the Moavite nation shared common roots with the Jewish people. The founding ancestor of the nation Moav was a son of Lot, the nephew of Abraham our patriarch. Ancient inscriptions indicate that the Moavite language was very similar to Hebrew. Accordingly, Elimelekh's family remains within the same broad cultural context, despite the numerous differences between the nations. While residing in Moav, the exiled family is struck by a series of tragedies, and only Naomi survives.

1 1 **It was in the days when the judges judged;**[D] **there was a fam-**
ine in the land due to a drought. **And a** wealthy, prominent
man[2] **from Bethlehem,** which was in the territory **of Judah,**[B]
near Jerusalem, **went to reside** temporarily **in the fields of**
Moav, where conditions were better, **he, his wife, and his two**
sons. The verse specifies Bethlehem in Judah in order to distinguish this place from the town of Bethlehem located in the
Galilee.[3]

Bethlehem, illustration, 1894

2 **The name of the man was Elimelekh, the name of his wife**
was Naomi, and the names of his two sons were Mahlon and

Mountains of Moav, view from Eretz Yisrael to the east

Kilyon.[D] **They were Efratites from Bethlehem of Judah.** The
region near Bethlehem was named after their family of Efrat,[4]
who was a descendant of Hur.[5] **They came to the fields of**
Moav and were there for some time.

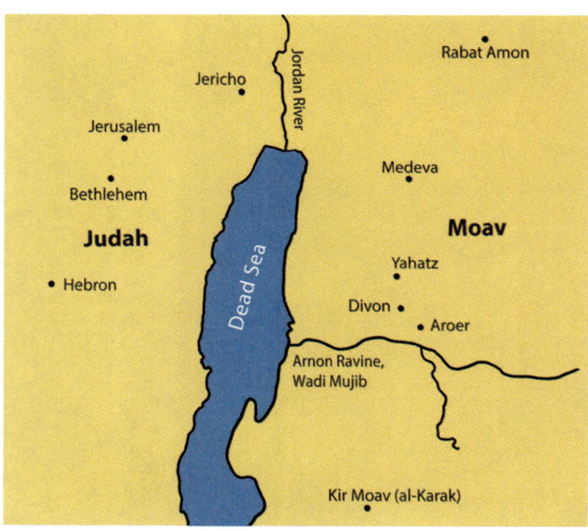

Bethlehem of Judah and the fields of Moav

3 **Elimelekh, Naomi's husband, died** while they were living
in Moav, **and she and her two sons remained** in the fields of
Moav.
4 **They,** Naomi's two sons, **married** local **Moavite women: The**
name of the one was Orpa, and the name of the second
Ruth;[D] **they lived there approximately ten years.**
5 **Also both of them, Mahlon and Kilyon, died** childless; **and**
the woman, Naomi, **remained of her two children and her**
husband.

רות

א וַיְהִי בִּימֵי שְׁפֹט הַשֹּׁפְטִים וַיְהִי רָעָב בָּאָרֶץ וַיֵּלֶךְ אִישׁ מִבֵּית לֶחֶם יְהוּדָה לָגוּר
ב בִּשְׂדֵי מוֹאָב הוּא וְאִשְׁתּוֹ וּשְׁנֵי בָנָיו: וְשֵׁם הָאִישׁ אֱלִימֶלֶךְ וְשֵׁם אִשְׁתּוֹ נָעֳמִי
וְשֵׁם שְׁנֵי־בָנָיו | מַחְלוֹן וְכִלְיוֹן אֶפְרָתִים מִבֵּית לֶחֶם יְהוּדָה וַיָּבֹאוּ שְׂדֵי־מוֹאָב
ג ד וַיִּהְיוּ־שָׁם: וַיָּמָת אֱלִימֶלֶךְ אִישׁ נָעֳמִי וַתִּשָּׁאֵר הִיא וּשְׁנֵי בָנֶיהָ: וַיִּשְׂאוּ לָהֶם
נָשִׁים מֹאֲבִיּוֹת שֵׁם הָאַחַת עָרְפָּה וְשֵׁם הַשֵּׁנִית רוּת וַיֵּשְׁבוּ שָׁם כְּעֶשֶׂר שָׁנִים:
ה ו וַיָּמֻתוּ גַם־שְׁנֵיהֶם מַחְלוֹן וְכִלְיוֹן וַתִּשָּׁאֵר הָאִשָּׁה מִשְּׁנֵי יְלָדֶיהָ וּמֵאִישָׁהּ: וַתָּקָם
הִיא וְכַלֹּתֶיהָ וַתָּשָׁב מִשְּׂדֵי מוֹאָב כִּי שָׁמְעָה בִּשְׂדֵה מוֹאָב כִּי־פָקַד יהוה אֶת־עַמּוֹ

The Return from Moav to Judah

RUTH 1:6–22

Naomi, the sole survivor of the family that had traveled to Moav, returns to the land of Judah in a miserable state. As Naomi is an impressive individual, her daughters-in-law seek to come with her to the Land of Israel, and it is clear from the text that there is an especially warm relationship between this mother-in-law and her daughters-in-law. After Naomi urges them to remain in their land, Ruth alone insists on accompanying her, and Ruth arrives with Naomi in Bethlehem of Judah.

6 **She and her daughters-in-law rose, and returned from the fields of Moav,** not only because Naomi had lost her husband and sons, but also **because she had heard in the fields of Moav that the Lord had remembered His people to give**

BACKGROUND

1:1 | **Bethlehem of Judah:** This has been identified with the hill that extends eastward from the center of the modern city of Bethlehem, approximately 9 km south of Jerusalem, and 1.5 km east of the ancient road along the central ridge of the highlands of the Land of Israel known as the Way of the Patriarchs. It is possible that the city was named for the fertile plains on its eastern side, where wheat and barley were grown. Bethlehem is also referred to as Efrat, according to the verse "Efrata, the father of Bethlehem" (I Chronicles 4:4).

DISCUSSION

1:1 | **In the days when the judges judged:** During this period, the setting for the book of Judges, tribes and families were the most important social units in Israel, although the people were still one nation. There were periodic skirmishes with enemies, but Israel did not engage in any major wars. The Torah and its commandments were generally observed in accordance with the tradition that the people had received. Nevertheless, the stories related in the Judges that span this lengthy period depict Israel as a people with a warped ethical sensibility, along with a corrupt religious and national consciousness.

1:2 | **Mahlon and Kilyon:** There is a possible allusion to the story of Elimelekh's family in I Chronicles (4:22), although the names that appear there differ from the ones mentioned here. If that verse indeed refers to the same story, Mahlon and Kilyon might not have been their real names, but pseudonyms given to them following their deaths at a young age. While the name Mahlon seems to connote sickness (*mahala*), it can also be interpreted in a positive sense, similar to Mahli (Exodus 6:19) and Ahlai (I Chronicles 2:31), which mean jewelry (see, e.g., Proverbs 25:12). It could also be related to sweetness, as indicated by the root in Arabic, from which the name for the modern sesame snack halva is derived. However, the name Kilyon, literally "annihilation" (see Isaiah 10:22), bears an unambiguously negative connotation (see Ibn Ezra; *Bava Batra* 91b; *Ruth Rabba* 2:5). Appropriately, as evident from the continuation of the narrative, Kilyon did not merit a lasting remembrance, whereas Mahlon's name was perpetuated and glorified by his widow, Ruth.

1:4 | **Orpa and Ruth:** The text does not reveal anything about the identity of these two women. According to Jewish tradition, Ruth descended from the royal line of Moav, while Orpa apparently came from an upper-class

▸ *family*

them bread. In the meantime, the famine had ended and normal life had resumed in the land of Judah.

7 **She departed from the place where she was, and her two daughters-in-law were with her,** as they were her only surviving family members; **they went on the way to return to the land of Judah.**

8 **Naomi said to her two daughters-in-law:** I am returning to my home and my people, but as for you, **go, each return to her mother's house** and family. She added with great affection: **May the Lord deal kindly with you** and assist you, **as you have dealt with the dead and with me.**

9 **May the Lord grant you that you find repose, each in the house of her husband.** I bless each of you that you should both remarry and live in peace with new husbands. Since nothing remains from our family relationship, there is no reason for you to accompany me. Naomi wished to treat these two women fairly, as they were apparently relatively young, having married a mere few years earlier. She therefore encouraged them to resume their lives elsewhere. **She,** Naomi, **kissed them** a farewell kiss; **and they,** possibly all three of them, **raised their voices and wept.** This shared weeping is indicative of the profound ties between them, despite the fact that the pair were not Naomi's biological daughters.

10 **They said to her: No, for we will return with you to your people** and live among your nation. We are one family, and we will continue to remain a family.

11 **Naomi said: Return, my daughters; why would you go with me?** There is no reason for you to do so. **Do I have more sons in my womb**[6] **who will be husbands for you?** Is there any chance that I will give birth to boys who might later marry you and produce offspring?[7]

12 Accordingly, **return, my daughters; go, as I am too old to** remarry and **have a** second **husband.** Even **if I were to** entertain an utterly unrealistic idea and **say: I have hope, then even if I had a husband tonight, and even if I were to bear sons,**

13 **would you wait for them,** these imaginary sons, **until they grow up? For them, would you constrain yourselves** and stop your lives, **to not have a husband? No, my daughters, for I am embittered on your account** that I am unable to assist you or provide you with anything, **for the hand of the Lord has been extended against me.** I am left wretched and hopeless. Apparently, any property or possessions the family had once owned had been lost over the years.

14 **They raised their voices and wept more; Orpa kissed her mother-in-law** farewell, as she had been convinced by Naomi's argument and decided to return home, **but Ruth clung to her** and would not consent to any separation.

15 **She,** Naomi, **said** to Ruth: **Behold, your sister-in-law returned to her people and to her god;**[D] **return after your sister-in-law.**

16 **Ruth said: Do not implore me to leave you,**[8] **to return from following you,** to abandon you. **For wherever you will go, I will go; and wherever you lodge, I will lodge;** moreover, **your people is my people, and your God my God.**[D] You said that Orpa should return to her nation and her gods, but Moav is no longer my nation, and the gods of Moav are no longer my gods. My ties to your family and way of life are not an accident, and I no longer feel any connection to the Moavite nation and its faith;

17 **wherever you die, I will die, and there I will be buried.** I will remain alongside you until death, and I will be buried together with you. I swear that **so may the Lord do to me, and so may He continue, for death will separate between me and you.** Note that Ruth takes an oath in the name of the God of Israel.

18 **She,** Naomi, **saw that she was resolute to go with her,** despite her best efforts to convince Ruth that she should return home, **and she ceased speaking with her** and urging her to return.

19 **The two of them walked until they arrived in Bethlehem.** Since Bethlehem was not far from Moav, they presumably walked for only a few days. **It was, upon their arriving in Bethlehem, that the whole city was in a tumult over them; the women said: Is that Naomi?** No one was familiar with Ruth, but everyone in the small city knew the distinguished Naomi. At this stage, however, she had not only aged physically, but her dress and her appearance had changed, as the vicissitudes of life had left their scars.[9]

20 **She said to them: Do not call me Naomi,** meaning pleasant [*no'am*], as I have not had any pleasantness in my life; rather, **call me Bitterness [*Mara*].**[10] This name is more appropriate, **as the Almighty has greatly embittered me** and brought much bitterness and suffering upon me.

DISCUSSION

family as well. The prominent status of these women is consistent with the supposition that Elimelekh and his family did not come to Moav as beggars, but rather as distinguished individuals, and that they traveled there in order to live in an honorable fashion (see Rashi, verse 2; *Targum*; *Ruth Rabba* 2; *Nazir* 23b).

1:15| **Returned to her people and to her god:** The marriage of Orpa and Ruth to men from Judah would likely have included their acceptance of the commandments of the Torah. Although it is unknown whether any sort of ceremony was performed to mark the occasion, foreign women who married into an Israelite household accepted upon themselves

▸ *the*

ז לָתֵת לָהֶם לָחֶם׃ וַתֵּצֵא מִן־הַמָּקוֹם אֲשֶׁר הָיְתָה־שָׁמָּה וּשְׁתֵּי כַלֹּתֶיהָ עִמָּהּ
ח וַתֵּלַכְנָה בַדֶּרֶךְ לָשׁוּב אֶל־אֶרֶץ יְהוּדָה׃ וַתֹּאמֶר נָעֳמִי לִשְׁתֵּי כַלֹּתֶיהָ לֵכְנָה שֹּׁבְנָה
אִשָּׁה לְבֵית אִמָּהּ יַעֲשֶׂה יְהוָה עִמָּכֶם חֶסֶד כַּאֲשֶׁר עֲשִׂיתֶם עִם־הַמֵּתִים וְעִמָּדִי׃ יַעַשׂ
ט יִתֵּן יְהוָה לָכֶם וּמְצֶאןָ מְנוּחָה אִשָּׁה בֵּית אִישָׁהּ וַתִּשַּׁק לָהֶן וַתִּשֶּׂאנָה קוֹלָן
י יא וַתִּבְכֶּינָה׃ וַתֹּאמַרְנָה־לָּהּ כִּי־אִתָּךְ נָשׁוּב לְעַמֵּךְ׃ וַתֹּאמֶר נָעֳמִי שֹׁבְנָה בְנֹתַי לָמָּה
יב תֵלַכְנָה עִמִּי הַעוֹד־לִי בָנִים בְּמֵעַי וְהָיוּ לָכֶם לַאֲנָשִׁים׃ שֹׁבְנָה בְנֹתַי לֵכְןָ כִּי זָקַנְתִּי
מִהְיוֹת לְאִישׁ כִּי אָמַרְתִּי יֶשׁ־לִי תִקְוָה גַּם הָיִיתִי הַלַּיְלָה לְאִישׁ וְגַם יָלַדְתִּי בָנִים׃
יג הֲלָהֵן ׀ תְּשַׂבֵּרְנָה עַד אֲשֶׁר יִגְדָּלוּ הֲלָהֵן תֵּעָגֵנָה לְבִלְתִּי הֱיוֹת לְאִישׁ אַל בְּנֹתַי
יד כִּי־מַר־לִי מְאֹד מִכֶּם כִּי־יָצְאָה בִי יַד־יְהוָה׃ וַתִּשֶּׂנָה קוֹלָן וַתִּבְכֶּינָה עוֹד וַתִּשַּׁק
טו עָרְפָּה לַחֲמוֹתָהּ וְרוּת דָּבְקָה בָּהּ׃ וַתֹּאמֶר הִנֵּה שָׁבָה יְבִמְתֵּךְ אֶל־עַמָּהּ וְאֶל־
טז אֱלֹהֶיהָ שׁוּבִי אַחֲרֵי יְבִמְתֵּךְ׃ וַתֹּאמֶר רוּת אַל־תִּפְגְּעִי־בִי לְעָזְבֵךְ לָשׁוּב מֵאַחֲרָיִךְ
יז כִּי אֶל־אֲשֶׁר תֵּלְכִי אֵלֵךְ וּבַאֲשֶׁר תָּלִינִי אָלִין עַמֵּךְ עַמִּי וֵאלֹהַיִךְ אֱלֹהָי׃ בַּאֲשֶׁר
תָּמוּתִי אָמוּת וְשָׁם אֶקָּבֵר כֹּה יַעֲשֶׂה יְהוָה לִי וְכֹה יֹסִיף כִּי הַמָּוֶת יַפְרִיד בֵּינִי
יח יט וּבֵינֵךְ׃ וַתֵּרֶא כִּי־מִתְאַמֶּצֶת הִיא לָלֶכֶת אִתָּהּ וַתֶּחְדַּל לְדַבֵּר אֵלֶיהָ׃ וַתֵּלַכְנָה
שְׁתֵּיהֶם עַד־בּוֹאָנָה בֵּית לָחֶם וַיְהִי כְּבוֹאָנָה בֵּית לֶחֶם וַתֵּהֹם כָּל־הָעִיר עֲלֵיהֶן
כ וַתֹּאמַרְנָה הֲזֹאת נָעֳמִי׃ וַתֹּאמֶר אֲלֵיהֶן אַל־תִּקְרֶאנָה לִי נָעֳמִי קְרֶאןָ לִי מָרָא

DISCUSSION

the service of God. Even though the process of conversion is ordinarily administered by the court, it is possible that a would-be convert who fulfills the Torah in its entirety may be considered Jewish even without explicit action by a court (see *Yevamot* 45b). With regard to Orpa, although she had joined the Israelite nation to a limited extent, when her connection was terminated against her will by the death of her husband, she returned home and once again resumed the status of a Moavite who worshipped the Moavite gods (see Alsheikh; *Ruth Rabba* 2:21; Rambam, *Hilkhot Issurei Bia* 13:15–17).

1:16| **Your people is my people, and your God my God:** The relationship between Ruth and Naomi began with Ruth's marriage to Mahlon, but over the years Ruth had fully adopted her new family's way of life. For this reason, she serves as a model convert for future generations. Her attachment to God, the Israelite people, and its ways of life has become a symbol of the experience of a true convert. He or she must feel that the conversion is not temporary, and that it does not depend on location or convenience. Rather, the change of status must be due to total identification with Israel. The transformation that Ruth underwent led her to deny any further connection to her homeland and her past. As far as she was concerned, she had been born anew as a daughter to Naomi. Although there was no longer any formal familial relationship between them, the two remained extremely close.

21 **I went**[11] **full,** with a husband, children, and possessions, **and the Lord returned me empty,** with nothing; **why would you call me Naomi, and the Lord has testified against me**[12] and rebuked me for my sins; alternatively, He has warned me **and the Almighty has harmed me?**

22 **Naomi returned, and Ruth the Moavite, her daughter-in-law, was with her, who returned from the fields of Moav; they came to Bethlehem at the beginning of the barley harvest,** the period after the festival of Passover, when barley is first reaped. Thus, it was relatively easy to find food during this time of the year.

Beginning of the barley harvest

Ruth's First Visit to the Field of Boaz

RUTH 2:1–23

Several gestures of kindness figure prominently in this section: Ruth, a foreigner, volunteers to go out and glean in the harvested fields for herself and her mother-in-law, while Boaz, the owner of the field where she finds herself, takes steps to ease Ruth's difficult task. Indeed, the overall context is one of kindness, as the residents of Bethlehem are presented as fulfilling the Torah's command to leave any fallen or forgotten stalks in the field for the needy.

2 1 **Naomi had an acquaintance**[13] **of her husband,** who was a **mighty man of valor,** prominent in stature, **from the family of Elimelekh, and his name was Boaz.**[D]

2 **Ruth the Moavite said to Naomi: Let me now go to the field, and glean among the stalks of grain,**[D] in accordance with the common practice of the poor, which Ruth had apparently noticed, **following anyone in whose eyes I find favor.** I will go to the field of someone in whose eyes I find favor and who will allow me to glean there.[14] Although the Torah requires the owner of a field to leave gleanings of his harvest for the destitute, in practice not every landowner welcomed the poor graciously. Some were concerned that the poor might distract the reapers from their work, while others suspected them of dishonesty, and there might even have been some individuals who did not wish to interact with or assist others at all. **She,** Naomi, **said to her: Go, my daughter.**

3 **She went, and came, and gleaned** the stalks that had fallen or had not been harvested **in the field after the reapers; it happened for her that it was the tract of land belonging to Boaz, who was from the family of Elimelekh,** without prior knowledge of the landowner's identity.

4 **Behold,** at that time **Boaz came from Bethlehem** to his field outside the city, presumably in order to supervise the harvest. **And** Boaz **said to the reapers** a greeting in the form of a blessing: **The Lord be with you** and assist you. **They said to him: The Lord bless you.**[D]

5 **Boaz said to his lad set over the reapers** to ensure that the harvest was performed properly: **Whose young woman is this?** With whom is she associated? Bethlehem was not a large city, and Boaz, one of the long-standing residents of the city, was surprised to see a young woman whom he did not recognize.

Harvest, illustration based on fresco, Egypt

Reapers

כא כִּי־הֵמַר שַׁדַּי לִי מְאֹד: אֲנִי מְלֵאָה הָלַכְתִּי וְרֵיקָם הֱשִׁיבַנִי יהוה לָמָּה תִקְרֶאנָה
כב לִי נָעֳמִי וַיהוה עָנָה בִי וְשַׁדַּי הֵרַע־לִי: וַתָּשָׁב נָעֳמִי וְרוּת הַמּוֹאֲבִיָּה כַלָּתָהּ עִמָּהּ
א הַשָּׁבָה מִשְּׂדֵי מוֹאָב וְהֵמָּה בָּאוּ בֵּית לֶחֶם בִּתְחִלַּת קְצִיר שְׂעֹרִים: וּלְנָעֳמִי מידע מוֹדַע
ב לְאִישָׁהּ אִישׁ גִּבּוֹר חַיִל מִמִּשְׁפַּחַת אֱלִימֶלֶךְ וּשְׁמוֹ בֹּעַז: וַתֹּאמֶר רוּת הַמּוֹאֲבִיָּה
אֶל־נָעֳמִי אֵלְכָה־נָּא הַשָּׂדֶה וַאֲלַקֳטָה בַשִּׁבֳּלִים אַחַר אֲשֶׁר אֶמְצָא־חֵן בְּעֵינָיו
ג וַתֹּאמֶר לָהּ לְכִי בִתִּי: וַתֵּלֶךְ וַתָּבוֹא וַתְּלַקֵּט בַּשָּׂדֶה אַחֲרֵי הַקֹּצְרִים וַיִּקֶר מִקְרֶהָ
ד חֶלְקַת הַשָּׂדֶה לְבֹעַז אֲשֶׁר מִמִּשְׁפַּחַת אֱלִימֶלֶךְ: וְהִנֵּה־בֹעַז בָּא מִבֵּית לֶחֶם
ה וַיֹּאמֶר לַקּוֹצְרִים יהוה עִמָּכֶם וַיֹּאמְרוּ לוֹ יְבָרֶכְךָ יהוה: וַיֹּאמֶר בֹּעַז לְנַעֲרוֹ הַנִּצָּב
ו עַל־הַקּוֹצְרִים לְמִי הַנַּעֲרָה הַזֹּאת: וַיַּעַן הַנַּעַר הַנִּצָּב עַל־הַקּוֹצְרִים וַיֹּאמַר נַעֲרָה
ז מוֹאֲבִיָּה הִיא הַשָּׁבָה עִם־נָעֳמִי מִשְּׂדֵי מוֹאָב: וַתֹּאמֶר אֲלַקֳטָה־נָּא וְאָסַפְתִּי
בָעֳמָרִים אַחֲרֵי הַקּוֹצְרִים וַתָּבוֹא וַתַּעֲמוֹד מֵאָז הַבֹּקֶר וְעַד־עַתָּה זֶה שִׁבְתָּהּ
ח הַבַּיִת מְעָט: וַיֹּאמֶר בֹּעַז אֶל־רוּת הֲלוֹא שָׁמַעַתְּ בִּתִּי אַל־תֵּלְכִי לִלְקֹט בְּשָׂדֶה

6 **The lad set over the reapers answered and said: She is a young Moavite woman who returned with Naomi from the fields of Moav.**

7 **She said,** asked of us:[15] **Please let me glean and gather among the sheaves, following the reapers. She came and has been standing** in the field **from the morning until now; she sat in the house only a bit.** She went to a nearby house to rest for a short time, before returning to the field.[16]

Sheaves in the field

8 **Boaz said to Ruth: Hear truly, my daughter; do not go to glean in a different field; also do not pass on from here** to another field, as my field is sufficiently large, **but** rather **attach**

DISCUSSION

2:1| **Boaz:** Little is related about Boaz in the book of Ruth itself, although his high social status is evident from the narrative, and his noble lineage appears at the conclusion of the book. Some Sages identify him with the judge Ivtzan of Bethlehem (see *Bava Batra* 91a; *Ruth Rabba* 3:6; Judges 12:8–10, and Radak ad loc.). Furthermore, the book later indicates that he was one of the judges of the city, perhaps even the most senior of them (see 4:1–2, and Ralbag ad loc.).

2:2| **And glean among the stalks of grain:** The Torah commands the owner of land to give gifts to the poor from his field: "When you reap the harvest of your land, you shall not finish reaping the corner of your field, and the gleanings of your harvest you shall not gather. Your vineyard you shall not harvest completely, and the fallen fruit of your vineyard you shall not gather; for the poor and for the stranger you shall leave them" (Leviticus 19:9–10; see also Leviticus 23:22). According to this commandment, the farmer and his workers must leave the stalks that fall during the time of harvest for the poor. Furthermore, the commandment of forgotten produce (Deuteronomy 24:19) requires a harvester who forgot grain or other crops in the field, whether harvested or not harvested, to leave them there for the needy, rather than returning and taking them for himself. Although there was no centrally organized government in the period of the judges to enforce the Torah, many of the commandments of the Torah were transmitted by tradition and observed. The book of Ruth teaches that at that time the poor did in fact benefit from these philanthropic commandments.

2:4| **The Lord be with you.... The Lord bless you:** Boaz likely did not create this formulation; rather, it was already an accepted greeting, as it appears elsewhere as well (see Judges 6:12; *Berakhot* 63a).

yourself to my young women. Keep close to my maidservants
and go with them.
9 **Let your eyes be on the field that they reap, and follow**
them, the other maidservants. **Haven't I commanded the lads**
not to touch you, and bother you, but rather treat you with
respect? Moreover, as you are outside in the heat, **when you**
become thirsty, go to the vessels that contain water for the
reapers, **and drink from that which the lads have drawn.** I
permit you to drink from their water, so that you can continue
to reap here in comfort.[17]
10 **She fell on her face and prostrated herself to the ground;**
she said to him: Why have I found favor in your eyes, that
you should acknowledge me and treat me in such a friendly
manner, **and I am a foreigner?** I am not from the house of
Israel, and I am a stranger to this area.
11 **Boaz answered and said to her:** Although I have not seen you
until now, **everything that you did for your mother-in-law**
after the death of your husband was told to me; you left
your father and your mother, and the land of your birth,
and you went to a people that you did not know previously.
12 **May the Lord reward your conduct, and may your payment**
be complete from the Lord, God of Israel, under whose
wings you came to find refuge. Boaz understood that Ruth
had not converted for merely social or financial reasons, and
that she did not come to the Land of Israel just in order to accompany her mother-in-law. Rather, she wished to be close to
God.
13 **She said: May I find favor in your eyes, my lord.** I am grateful
that I have found favor in your eyes;[18] **for you have comforted**
me, for you have spoken to the heart of your maidservant.
You have encouraged me and treated me in a special manner,
though I am not worthy **even** of a status **as one of your**
maidservants.[19]
14 **Boaz said to her** sometime later, **at mealtime,** when the reapers gathered to sit and eat: **Come over here, and eat from the bread** shared by the reapers, **and dip your piece in the vinegar**[B] that is used as a sauce for the bread. **She sat beside the reapers,** not mingling with them, **and he,** Boaz, **handed her** kernels of **roasted** fresh **grain.** Some of the starch inside of these kernels is converted to sugar when heated, and the slightly sweet roasted kernels were considered a delicacy. **And she ate and was satisfied, and left over.** Boaz had given her a sizable portion, which was more than enough to satisfy her.

To the left: fresh wheat kernels; to the right: dry wheat kernels

15 **She rose to glean, and Boaz commanded his lads, saying:**
She is permitted to glean in the field not only after you have removed the bound-together sheaves of harvested grain, but **let**
her glean among the sheaves as well, and do not shame her.
You must allow her to glean without voicing any objections;[20]
16 **also pull some for her from the bundles.** You are to forget, or intentionally remove,[21] some stalks from those that are tied together ready to be harvested with the sickle, **and leave them, and let her glean, and do not rebuke her.**

Bundle of grain

17 **She gleaned in the field until evening.** Since Ruth had been given a comfortable place to rest, perhaps in the shade near the reapers, and provided with food and drink, she did not need to return home in the middle of the day. **And she beat out that which she had gleaned,** in order to separate the kernels of grain from the stalks, **and it was approximately an ephah of barley,** a sizable dry measure equivalent to roughly 24 L.

Beating kernels with a stick

18 **She took it up,** the barley, **and came to the city, and her**
mother-in-law saw that which she had gleaned, a larger
quantity than Naomi had expected;[22] **she took out and gave**
to her that which she had left over from her fill. As stated,
Ruth did not eat all of what Boaz had given her. She brought her
mother-in-law roasted grain in addition to the barley.
19 **Her mother-in-law said to her: Where did you glean today**
and where did you work? Blessed be he who acknowledged
you, who assisted you, and who treated you with exceptional
generosity. **She told her mother-in-law** the identity of the man
with whom she worked, and said: The name of the man, the
owner of the field, **with whom I worked today is Boaz.**
20 **Naomi said to her daughter-in-law: Blessed be he to the**
Lord, who has not forsaken His kindness to the living and to
the dead. Boaz had maintained close ties with the family when
Naomi's husband and sons were still alive, and he was now honoring their memory by helping Naomi and Ruth.[23] **Naomi said**
to her: I am familiar with him not only as a resident of this city,

ט אַחַר וְגַם לֹא תַעֲבוּרִי מִזֶּה וְכֹה תִדְבָּקִין עִם־נַעֲרֹתָי׃ עֵינַיִךְ בַּשָּׂדֶה אֲשֶׁר־יִקְצֹרוּן
וְהָלַכְתְּ אַחֲרֵיהֶן הֲלוֹא צִוִּיתִי אֶת־הַנְּעָרִים לְבִלְתִּי נָגְעֵךְ וְצָמִת וְהָלַכְתְּ אֶל־
י הַכֵּלִים וְשָׁתִית מֵאֲשֶׁר יִשְׁאֲבוּן הַנְּעָרִים׃ וַתִּפֹּל עַל־פָּנֶיהָ וַתִּשְׁתַּחוּ אָרְצָה וַתֹּאמֶר
יא אֵלָיו מַדּוּעַ מָצָאתִי חֵן בְּעֵינֶיךָ לְהַכִּירֵנִי וְאָנֹכִי נָכְרִיָּה׃ וַיַּעַן בֹּעַז וַיֹּאמֶר לָהּ הֻגֵּד
הֻגַּד לִי כֹּל אֲשֶׁר־עָשִׂית אֶת־חֲמוֹתֵךְ אַחֲרֵי מוֹת אִישֵׁךְ וַתַּעַזְבִי אָבִיךְ וְאִמֵּךְ
יב וְאֶרֶץ מוֹלַדְתֵּךְ וַתֵּלְכִי אֶל־עַם אֲשֶׁר לֹא־יָדַעַתְּ תְּמוֹל שִׁלְשׁוֹם׃ יְשַׁלֵּם יְהוָה
פָּעֳלֵךְ וּתְהִי מַשְׂכֻּרְתֵּךְ שְׁלֵמָה מֵעִם יְהוָה אֱלֹהֵי יִשְׂרָאֵל אֲשֶׁר־בָּאת לַחֲסוֹת
יג תַּחַת־כְּנָפָיו׃ וַתֹּאמֶר אֶמְצָא־חֵן בְּעֵינֶיךָ אֲדֹנִי כִּי נִחַמְתָּנִי וְכִי דִבַּרְתָּ עַל־לֵב
יד שִׁפְחָתֶךָ וְאָנֹכִי לֹא אֶהְיֶה כְּאַחַת שִׁפְחֹתֶיךָ׃ וַיֹּאמֶר לָה בֹעַז לְעֵת הָאֹכֶל גֹּשִׁי
הֲלֹם וְאָכַלְתְּ מִן־הַלֶּחֶם וְטָבַלְתְּ פִּתֵּךְ בַּחֹמֶץ וַתֵּשֶׁב מִצַּד הַקֹּצְרִים וַיִּצְבָּט־לָהּ
טו קָלִי וַתֹּאכַל וַתִּשְׂבַּע וַתֹּתַר׃ וַתָּקָם לְלַקֵּט וַיְצַו בֹּעַז אֶת־נְעָרָיו לֵאמֹר גַּם בֵּין
טז הָעֳמָרִים תְּלַקֵּט וְלֹא תַכְלִימוּהָ׃ וְגַם שֹׁל־תָּשֹׁלּוּ לָהּ מִן־הַצְּבָתִים וַעֲזַבְתֶּם
יז וְלִקְּטָה וְלֹא תִגְעֲרוּ־בָהּ׃ וַתְּלַקֵּט בַּשָּׂדֶה עַד־הָעָרֶב וַתַּחְבֹּט אֵת אֲשֶׁר־לִקֵּטָה
יח וַיְהִי כְּאֵיפָה שְׂעֹרִים׃ וַתִּשָּׂא וַתָּבוֹא הָעִיר וַתֵּרֶא חֲמוֹתָהּ אֵת אֲשֶׁר־לִקֵּטָה
יט וַתּוֹצֵא וַתִּתֶּן־לָהּ אֵת אֲשֶׁר־הוֹתִרָה מִשָּׂבְעָהּ׃ וַתֹּאמֶר לָהּ חֲמוֹתָהּ אֵיפֹה לִקַּטְתְּ
הַיּוֹם וְאָנָה עָשִׂית יְהִי מַכִּירֵךְ בָּרוּךְ וַתַּגֵּד לַחֲמוֹתָהּ אֵת אֲשֶׁר־עָשְׂתָה עִמּוֹ
כ וַתֹּאמֶר שֵׁם הָאִישׁ אֲשֶׁר עָשִׂיתִי עִמּוֹ הַיּוֹם בֹּעַז׃ וַתֹּאמֶר נָעֳמִי לְכַלָּתָהּ בָּרוּךְ
הוּא לַיהוָה אֲשֶׁר לֹא־עָזַב חַסְדּוֹ אֶת־הַחַיִּים וְאֶת־הַמֵּתִים וַתֹּאמֶר לָהּ נָעֳמִי

but **the man is** also **related to us, he is among our redeemers [*go'aleinu*].** When someone becomes poor and is forced to sell his field, a relative may redeem the field from the buyer if he can afford to do so.[24] Although some Sages maintain that it is obligatory for such a relative to do so, the *halakha* is that it is optional.[25] This purchase is called the redemption [*ge'ula*] of the field, and every relative is considered a potential redeemer [*go'el*].

BACKGROUND

2:14| **In the vinegar:** In ancient times, vinegar was considered to have cooling features, and it would be used on hot days. This notion appears both in ancient scientific documents, such as Pliny's encyclopedia, *Natural History* (first century CE), and in statements of the Sages in reference to this verse: It is derived from here that vinegar is beneficial in hot weather (*Shabbat* 113b; *Pesikta Zutreta*, *Ruth* 2:14).

21 In keeping with Naomi's excitement and the praises she had bestowed upon Boaz, **Ruth the Moavite said** in the same vein: **Indeed, he said to me: You shall attach yourself to my lads** and continue gleaning with them, **until they complete my entire harvest.**

22 **Naomi said to Ruth, her daughter-in-law:** Since Boaz is treating you so well, **my daughter, it is better that you go out with his young women** and remain in his field, **that you not be accosted in another field.**

23 **She attached herself to Boaz's young women to glean until the end of barley harvest and wheat harvest.** The barley harvest begins in the spring and lasts for some seven weeks. It is followed by the wheat harvest, which generally starts at around the time of Shavuot, which is called the Festival of the First Fruits of the wheat harvest.[26] This harvest concludes approximately three months after the start of the barley harvest.[27] **And she lived with her mother-in-law.** During that entire period, Ruth would glean in the field and bring the grain home to her mother-in-law.

Wheat

Field at the end of the harvest

Barley

Ruth's Descent to the Threshing Floor

RUTH 3:1–18

In this section, Ruth meets Boaz under different circumstances and for a very different purpose. In contrast to her daily, public visits to his field during the harvest season, this encounter occurs at night when Ruth comes alone to the threshing floor. Whereas Ruth arrived in the field to glean in order to provide for herself and her mother-in-law, she now goes, at Naomi's initiative, to the threshing floor in order to find a permanent solution for their plight. Naomi's motive for this stems not only from her role as mother-in-law but also as Ruth's teacher and mentor, and from her sense of responsibility for Ruth's future.

3 1 **Naomi, her mother-in-law, said to her: My daughter, do I not seek repose for you, so that it may be well for you?** You are currently living in a temporary manner; I wish to find a more permanent arrangement for you. Naomi had expressed a similar wish while they were still in Moav (see 1:9).

2 **Now, isn't Boaz our acquaintance** and friend, **that you were with his young women? Behold, he is winnowing**[B] **the barley threshing floor**[B] **tonight.** Boaz was not married at that time; some maintain that he was a widower.[28] Naomi sought to arrange a match between him and Ruth.

Winnowing on a threshing floor

3 **Bathe, anoint yourself** with oil in order to enhance your appearance, **place your** most attractive **garment upon**[29] **you,**[D] **and descend to the threshing floor; do not make yourself known to the man.** Hide in the threshing floor so that Boaz will not discover you **until he finishes eating and drinking.**

4 **It shall be that when he lies down** to sleep on the threshing floor that night, in order to guard the grain, or perhaps because he wishes to resume work early in the morning, **you shall know the place where he lies, and you shall come and uncover his feet.** Even in the summer the evenings in the Judean hills are not particularly hot, and therefore Boaz's feet would be covered. **And lie down** near his feet. **He will tell you what you shall do.** Allow him to proceed in whatever manner he sees fit. Through this unusual act, which is direct and authentic, but at the same time discreet and non-binding, Ruth will issue an unconventional proposition: A request for Boaz's full protection, which means that in essence she is asking him to marry her.[30]

DISCUSSION

3:3 | **Place your garment upon you:** The Sages explain that this is referring to the fine garments that are worn on the Sabbath (*Ruth Rabba* 5:12).

כא קרוב לנו האיש מגאלנו הוא: ותאמר רות המואביה גם | כי־אמר אלי עם־
כב הנערים אשר־לי תדבקין עד אם־כלו את כל־הקציר אשר־לי: ותאמר נעמי
אל־רות כלתה טוב בתי כי תצאי עם־נערותיו ולא יפגעו־בך בשדה אחר:
כג ותדבק בנערות בעז ללקט עד־כלות קציר־השערים וקציר החטים ותשב
ג א את־חמותה: ותאמר לה נעמי חמותה בתי הלא אבקש־לך מנוח אשר ייטב־
ב לך: ועתה הלא בעז מדעתנו אשר היית את־נערותיו הנה־הוא זרה את־גרן
ג השערים הלילה: ורחצת | וסכת ושמת שמלתך עליך וירדתי הגרן אל־תודעי (שמלתיך, וירדת)
ד לאיש עד כלתו לאכל ולשתות: ויהי בשכבו וידעת את־המקום אשר ישכב־
ה שם ובאת וגלית מרגלתיו ושכבתי והוא יגיד לך את אשר תעשין: ותאמר (ושכבת)
ו אליה כל אשר־תאמרי אעשה: ותרד הגרן ותעש ככל אשר־צותה חמותה: (אלי)
ז ויאכל בעז וישת וייטב לבו ויבא לשכב בקצה הערמה ותבא בלט ותגל

5 **She,** Ruth, **said to her: Everything that you say to me, I will do.** Ruth could have hesitated to follow such a strange suggestion, which was not in keeping with conventional norms of decency and modesty. Nevertheless, she accepted her mother-in-law's plan without hesitation.

6 **She went down to the threshing floor, and acted in accordance with everything that her mother-in-law had commanded her.**

7 When the workday was concluded, **Boaz ate and drank** wine, **and his heart was merry, and he came to lie at the end of the pile of grain,** the mound of grain stalks, where there is grain on the ground that is comfortable to lie on and where he could also watch over the harvested grain. **She came surreptitiously, and she uncovered his feet, and she lay down** at his feet, per Naomi's instruction.

"At the end of the pile of grain"

BACKGROUND

3:2| **Winnowing:** After barley was gathered in the threshing floor, it was threshed in order to separate the kernels from the stalks, either by beating it with flails or by having an animal tread on it on a hard surface. The kernels were then winnowed in order to separate the grain from the husks by tossing it in the air with a shovel or a fork when there is a wind. The heavier grain fell back down while the husks, called chaff, blew away. Winnowing was usually performed in the late afternoon, evening, or early morning hours, when there is often a breeze in many parts of Israel.

The threshing floor: This was a public area that was exposed to the air and the wind, where the harvested grain was threshed and winnowed.

8 **It was midnight, and the man was startled and recoiled** in confusion,[31] as he had gone to sleep alone, and now he suddenly discerned the presence of another person;[32] **behold, a woman was lying at his feet.**

9 **He said** in complete surprise: **Who are you? She said: I am Ruth, your maidservant,** whom you know; **spread the corner of your garment,** your patronage, **over your maidservant,** and take me as your wife, **for you are a redeemer.** Owing to your familial ties to Naomi, you are also related to me, as I am her son's widow. Naomi had presumably explained to Ruth the significance of this type of redemption as practiced among the Israelites.

10 **He said: Blessed be you to the Lord, my daughter; your latter kindness,** when you chose to marry a relative of your deceased husband, **is greater than the former,**[D] when you left your land and accompanied your mother-in-law,[33] **in not going after the lads, whether poor or rich.** Had you sought to marry merely in order to reestablish your own life, you would have chosen a young man, closer in age to yourself. By selecting me, a man who is far older than you, because of my formal status as a redeemer, you have revealed the purity of your intentions.[34]

11 **Now, my daughter, do not fear, everything that you say I will do for you, for everyone** who is found **at the gate of my people,** the important men of the city,[35] **knows that you are a woman of valor [*eshet ḥayil*],** an unusual personality and an exceptional person. The term *eshet ḥayil* here parallels the phrase "mighty man of valor" [*gibbor ḥayil*] that appeared earlier in reference to Boaz (2:1). It also features as a general expression of praise in the book of Proverbs, which was written by King Solomon, a descendant of Ruth and Boaz.[36]

12 **Now it is true that I am a redeemer,** as I am part of the family; **however, there is a redeemer who is closer than I,** and the proper order must be maintained with regard to these matters.[37]

13 Therefore, **stay** here **tonight, and when it is morning, if he,** the redeemer who has a closer relationship to you, **redeems you,** then it is **good [*tov*], he will redeem,** as he has the right.[38] Alternatively, the word *tov* is the name of the redeemer.[39] According to this interpretation, the verse reads: And when it is morning, if Tov performs his role as redeemer, then let him do so. **But if he does not wish to redeem you, I will redeem you,**[D] as I will then be the next in line to redeem you. I swear **as the Lord lives; lie** down **until the morning** and rest; I will not touch you.[40]

14 **She lay at his feet until the morning, and rose before one could discern another. He,** Boaz, **said: Let it not be known that the woman came to the threshing floor.** Since he did not want her to be identified or her actions publicized, she departed before the light of day.[41]

15 **He,** Boaz, **said** to Ruth: **Hand me the** large **kerchief that is upon you, and hold it out; and she held it out. He measured six measures of barley,**[42] a sizable amount, **and placed it,** the full kerchief, **on her; and he** too **entered the city,** to take care of his business.

16 **She came to her mother-in-law,** when it was still quite early in the morning, and therefore she was unable to identify Ruth immediately.[43] **And she,** Naomi, **said: Who are you, my daughter? She told her everything that the man had done for her.**

17 **She,** Ruth, **said: These six measures of barley he gave me, as he said to me: Do not go empty**-handed **to your mother-in-law.** This is not a payment of any sort, but a gift to bring to your mother-in-law.[44]

18 **She said: Sit** and wait, **my daughter, until you know how the matter will develop; for the man will not rest until he completes the matter today.** I know that he is a determined man, and I am certain that he will not delay.

The Redemption of the Field and the Redemption of Ruth

RUTH 4:1–12

Boaz wants to marry Ruth, but he first has to deal with a formal limitation: According to the laws of inheritance and monetary rights, there is another individual who has a closer familial relationship to Elimelekh. Consequently, the right to redeem Naomi's field and to marry Ruth as a wife belongs to him. For this reason Ruth has not yet received a definite answer from Boaz with regard to her future. The response has to be given the next day in public, after a conversation with the other potential redeemer. The section concludes with the confirmation of the legal action, and with a blessing from the elders and the residents of the city to Boaz on the occasion of his marriage to Ruth.

4 1 Boaz did not postpone the matter of the redemption. **Boaz went up to the gate,**[B] the place of judgment, where the dignitaries of the city were present, **and sat there, and behold, the redeemer of whom Boaz had spoken was passing. He,** Boaz, **said: Turn aside** from wherever you are going and enter, **sit here, So-and-So. He turned aside and he sat.** The redeemer's name is not stated here, either because it is not known, or because he acted inappropriately by refusing the redemption.[45]

2 **He,** Boaz, **took ten men of the elders of the city, and said: Sit here** to serve as judges; **and they sat** down.

ח מַרְגְּלֹתָיו וַתִּשְׁכָּב׃ וַיְהִי בַּחֲצִי הַלַּיְלָה וַיֶּחֱרַד הָאִישׁ וַיִּלָּפֵת וְהִנֵּה אִשָּׁה שֹׁכֶבֶת
ט מַרְגְּלֹתָיו׃ וַיֹּאמֶר מִי־אָתְּ וַתֹּאמֶר אָנֹכִי רוּת אֲמָתֶךָ וּפָרַשְׂתָּ כְנָפֶךָ עַל־אֲמָתְךָ
י כִּי גֹאֵל אָתָּה׃ וַיֹּאמֶר בְּרוּכָה אַתְּ לַיהוָה בִּתִּי הֵיטַבְתְּ חַסְדֵּךְ הָאַחֲרוֹן מִן־הָרִאשׁוֹן
יא לְבִלְתִּי־לֶכֶת אַחֲרֵי הַבַּחוּרִים אִם־דַּל וְאִם־עָשִׁיר׃ וְעַתָּה בִּתִּי אַל־תִּירְאִי כֹּל
יב אֲשֶׁר־תֹּאמְרִי אֶעֱשֶׂה־לָּךְ כִּי יוֹדֵעַ כָּל־שַׁעַר עַמִּי כִּי אֵשֶׁת חַיִל אָתְּ׃ וְעַתָּה כִּי
יג אָמְנָם כִּי אם גֹאֵל אָנֹכִי וְגַם יֵשׁ גֹּאֵל קָרוֹב מִמֶּנִּי׃ לִינִי ׀ הַלַּיְלָה וְהָיָה בַבֹּקֶר
אִם־יִגְאָלֵךְ טוֹב יִגְאָל וְאִם־לֹא יַחְפֹּץ לְגָאֳלֵךְ וּגְאַלְתִּיךְ אָנֹכִי חַי־יְהוָה שִׁכְבִי
יד עַד־הַבֹּקֶר׃ וַתִּשְׁכַּב מַרְגְּלוֹתוֹ עַד־הַבֹּקֶר וַתָּקָם בטרום יַכִּיר אִישׁ אֶת־רֵעֵהוּ בְּטֶרֶם
טו וַיֹּאמֶר אַל־יִוָּדַע כִּי־בָאָה הָאִשָּׁה הַגֹּרֶן׃ וַיֹּאמֶר הָבִי הַמִּטְפַּחַת אֲשֶׁר־עָלַיִךְ
טז וְאֶחֳזִי־בָהּ וַתֹּאחֶז בָּהּ וַיָּמָד שֵׁשׁ־שְׂעֹרִים וַיָּשֶׁת עָלֶיהָ וַיָּבֹא הָעִיר׃ וַתָּבוֹא אֶל־
יז חֲמוֹתָהּ וַתֹּאמֶר מִי־אַתְּ בִּתִּי וַתַּגֶּד־לָהּ אֵת כָּל־אֲשֶׁר עָשָׂה־לָהּ הָאִישׁ׃ וַתֹּאמֶר
יח שֵׁשׁ־הַשְּׂעֹרִים הָאֵלֶּה נָתַן לִי כִּי אָמַר ° אַל־תָּבוֹאִי רֵיקָם אֶל־חֲמוֹתֵךְ׃ וַתֹּאמֶר אֵלַי
שְׁבִי בִתִּי עַד אֲשֶׁר תֵּדְעִין אֵיךְ יִפֹּל דָּבָר כִּי לֹא יִשְׁקֹט הָאִישׁ כִּי־אִם־כִּלָּה הַדָּבָר
א הַיּוֹם׃ וּבֹעַז עָלָה הַשַּׁעַר וַיֵּשֶׁב שָׁם וְהִנֵּה הַגֹּאֵל עֹבֵר אֲשֶׁר דִּבֶּר־בֹּעַז וַיֹּאמֶר
ב סוּרָה שְׁבָה־פֹּה פְּלֹנִי אַלְמֹנִי וַיָּסַר וַיֵּשֵׁב׃ וַיִּקַּח עֲשָׂרָה אֲנָשִׁים מִזִּקְנֵי הָעִיר וַיֹּאמֶר

DISCUSSION

3:10 | **Your latter kindness is greater than the former:** The biblical commandment of levirate marriage applies to the brother of a married man who died childless. The Torah commands that the living brother should marry the widow, so that the children who will be born to them will continue the name of the deceased (see Deuteronomy 25:5). This chapter is not referring to a standard levirate marriage, as neither Boaz nor the anonymous man discussed below (verse 12) were Ruth's brothers-in-law. Rather, it is speaking of an analogous type of redemption based on a more distant relationship.

3:13 | **But if he does not wish to redeem you, I will redeem you:** Some claim that Elimelekh, Boaz's father, and the redeemer, whose name might have been Tov, and who is also referred to below as *Ploni Almoni*, So-and-So (4:1), were all brothers (see 4:3; *Ruth Rabba* 6:3; *Bava Batra* 91a; *Midrash Tanḥuma, Behar* 3). However, this was not necessarily the case, as in any event this was not an ordinary levirate marriage. If the redeemer and Boaz were brothers, then the anonymous redeemer was the older brother. If they were not brothers, then he was a closer relative to Elimelekh than Boaz.

BACKGROUND

4:1 | **The gate:** The city gate was the center of communal life. Archaeological evidence and various passages from the Bible indicate that the actual structure of the gate, as well as the adjacent area, was used for legal trials (see Genesis 23:10; Deuteronomy 21:19, 22:24; Joshua 20:4; Amos 5:15). In addition, the gate was a place for the sacrificial rites of the shrines, sometimes called "high places," which were eventually prohibited (II Kings 23:8), as well as economic transactions, announcements, public rebukes (Jeremiah 17:19, 19:2; Amos 5:10), and special gatherings of the people (Nehemiah 8:1). In several ancient cities that have been subject to archaeological research, communal structures unearthed close to the gate might also have been part of this complex. Due to the centrality of the gate, the expression "the gate of the city" sometimes refers to the entire city (see, e.g., Exodus 20:10; Deuteronomy 15:7, 23:17; I Kings 8:37).

3 **He said to the redeemer:** Regarding **the tract of land that belonged to our brother, to Elimelekh, Naomi, who has returned from the fields of Moav, is selling,** that is, she has put up the land for sale.[46] Naomi and Ruth could not work the field alone, and the money from the sale would help sustain them financially.
4 **I said: I will inform you, saying: Acquire before those who are sitting here, and before the elders of my people.** If you have not heard about it, I hereby inform you that the field is for sale, and you may purchase it officially in a public manner before all those who sit here. **If you would redeem, redeem,** as you have the first right to do so. **But if you will not redeem, tell me, and I will know. For there is no one besides you to redeem, and I am after you.** According to the laws of redemption, there is no other potential redeemer in the family apart from myself. If you refuse to redeem it, I will purchase it instead. **He,** the man, **said: I will redeem** it, by purchasing it.
5 The anonymous redeemer agreed to purchase the field belonging to the family of his relatives, but he did not realize that whoever redeems the field must also marry the young surviving widow, and thereby preserve the family by having more children. This is not a biblical obligation, as according to Torah law the redemption of an inheritance of a relative is not automatically accompanied by the obligation to marry his widow. Nevertheless, the practice was that anyone who takes over the inheritance of a relative must also marry his wife, similar to levirate marriage.[47] **Boaz said: On the day of your acquisition of the field from the hand of Naomi, and from Ruth the Moavite,**[D] **you acquire the wife of the dead;** the practice of redemption includes marrying her in order **to perpetuate the name of the dead upon his inheritance.** By marrying the widow of the deceased childless husband and fathering children with her, the name of the deceased will be perpetuated.
6 **The redeemer said: I cannot redeem for myself, lest I ruin my inheritance,** harm my family; **you redeem my redemption** in my place, **as I cannot redeem** it. Apparently, he did not want to marry Ruth because she was a foreign woman, and worse, a Moavite.[48] Alternatively, he was wary of bringing a younger wife into his home as a rival to his current wife, a move that would cause marital strife.[49]
7 **This was the tradition in Israel,** in the ancient past, **concerning redemption** of fields **and concerning exchange** of goods, in order **to validate any matter: A man removed his shoe,**

Shoe used in *ḥalitza* ceremony abrogating levirate marriage, New York, twentieth century

and he gave it to another; that action of removing one's shoe **was the testament in Israel.** It was a symbolic expression of the completion of a transaction.[50]
8 **The redeemer said to Boaz: Acquire it for yourself;** I waive my right to the purchase; **and he removed his shoe,** to indicate that he was prepared to validate the arrangement.
9 **Boaz said to the elders and to all the people: You are witnesses this day that I have acquired everything that was Elimelekh's and everything that was Kilyon's and Mahlon's from the hand of Naomi.**
10 **And Ruth the Moavite, wife of Mahlon, I have acquired as my wife,** similar to the levirate marriage discussed in the Torah.[51] Here too my intention is **to perpetuate the name of the dead upon his inheritance,** both by buying his field as well as through the descendants of his widow, **and** thus **the name of the dead will not be eliminated from among his brethren and from the gate of his place.** Any children from the match will be named after the deceased, and in this manner his existence will be continued in this world in a certain sense.[52] **You are witnesses today.** Boaz thereby invited the elders and the people to validate the proceedings.
11 **All the people who were at the gate, and the elders, said: We are witnesses,** and we all affirm your statement. Since Boaz intended to marry Ruth, they also blessed him: **May the Lord grant that the woman who is coming into your house be like Rachel and like Leah, both of whom built the house of Israel. Prosper in Efrat, and proclaim a name in Bethlehem.** Some explain that the last phrase means that you should merit

DISCUSSION

4:5 | **The Moavite:** The Torah prohibits marriage with converts from Moav: "An Amonite or a Moavite shall not enter into the assembly of the Lord; even the tenth generation shall not enter into the assembly of the Lord forever, because they did not greet you with bread and with water on the way upon your exodus from Egypt, and because he hired against you Bilam son of Beor, from Petor, Aram Naharayim, to

▸ curse

ג שְׁבוּ־פֹה וַיֵּשֵׁבוּ׃ וַיֹּאמֶר לַגֹּאֵל חֶלְקַת הַשָּׂדֶה אֲשֶׁר לְאָחִינוּ לֶאֱלִימֶלֶךְ מָכְרָה
ד נָעֳמִי הַשָּׁבָה מִשְּׂדֵה מוֹאָב׃ וַאֲנִי אָמַרְתִּי אֶגְלֶה אָזְנְךָ לֵאמֹר קְנֵה נֶגֶד הַיֹּשְׁבִים
וְנֶגֶד זִקְנֵי עַמִּי אִם־תִּגְאַל גְּאָל וְאִם־לֹא יִגְאַל הַגִּידָה לִּי וְאֵדַע כִּי אֵין זוּלָתְךָ
ה לִגְאוֹל וְאָנֹכִי אַחֲרֶיךָ וַיֹּאמֶר אָנֹכִי אֶגְאָל׃ וַיֹּאמֶר בֹּעַז בְּיוֹם־קְנוֹתְךָ הַשָּׂדֶה מִיַּד
נָעֳמִי וּמֵאֵת רוּת הַמּוֹאֲבִיָּה אֵשֶׁת־הַמֵּת קניתי לְהָקִים שֵׁם־הַמֵּת עַל־נַחֲלָתוֹ׃ קָנִיתָ
ו וַיֹּאמֶר הַגֹּאֵל לֹא אוּכַל לגאול־לִי פֶּן־אַשְׁחִית אֶת־נַחֲלָתִי גְּאַל־לְךָ אַתָּה אֶת־ לִגְאָל־
ז גְּאֻלָּתִי כִּי לֹא־אוּכַל לִגְאֹל׃ וְזֹאת לְפָנִים בְּיִשְׂרָאֵל עַל־הַגְּאוּלָּה וְעַל־הַתְּמוּרָה
ח לְקַיֵּם כָּל־דָּבָר שָׁלַף אִישׁ נַעֲלוֹ וְנָתַן לְרֵעֵהוּ וְזֹאת הַתְּעוּדָה בְּיִשְׂרָאֵל׃ וַיֹּאמֶר
ט הַגֹּאֵל לְבֹעַז קְנֵה־לָךְ וַיִּשְׁלֹף נַעֲלוֹ׃ וַיֹּאמֶר בֹּעַז לַזְּקֵנִים וְכָל־הָעָם עֵדִים אַתֶּם
הַיּוֹם כִּי קָנִיתִי אֶת־כָּל־אֲשֶׁר לֶאֱלִימֶלֶךְ וְאֵת כָּל־אֲשֶׁר לְכִלְיוֹן וּמַחְלוֹן מִיַּד
י נָעֳמִי׃ וְגַם אֶת־רוּת הַמֹּאֲבִיָּה אֵשֶׁת מַחְלוֹן קָנִיתִי לִי לְאִשָּׁה לְהָקִים שֵׁם־הַמֵּת
עַל־נַחֲלָתוֹ וְלֹא־יִכָּרֵת שֵׁם־הַמֵּת מֵעִם אֶחָיו וּמִשַּׁעַר מְקוֹמוֹ עֵדִים אַתֶּם הַיּוֹם׃
יא וַיֹּאמְרוּ כָּל־הָעָם אֲשֶׁר־בַּשַּׁעַר וְהַזְּקֵנִים עֵדִים יִתֵּן יהוה אֶת־הָאִשָּׁה הַבָּאָה
אֶל־בֵּיתֶךָ כְּרָחֵל ׀ וּכְלֵאָה אֲשֶׁר בָּנוּ שְׁתֵּיהֶם אֶת־בֵּית יִשְׂרָאֵל וַעֲשֵׂה־חַיִל
יב בְּאֶפְרָתָה וּקְרָא־שֵׁם בְּבֵית לָחֶם׃ וִיהִי בֵיתְךָ כְּבֵית פֶּרֶץ אֲשֶׁר־יָלְדָה תָמָר

offspring from this marriage in Bethlehem,[53] which was near Efrata, or the very same place (see 1:2).

12 May your house be like the house of Peretz, your ancestor,[54] **whom Tamar bore to Judah,**[D] **from the descendants that the Lord will give you from this young woman.**

DISCUSSION

curse you" (Deuteronomy 23:4–5). The Oral Law teaches that this prohibition applies only to Moavite men, not women. This *halakha* was not well known at the time, and was not accepted in practice on a regular basis (see *Yevamot* 77a). The redeemer's refusal to marry Ruth may have been out of his misunderstanding of this law (see *Ruth Rabba* 7:10).

4:12| **Like the house of Peretz whom Tamar bore to Judah:** Although Peretz was not Judah's firstborn, the sons of Tamar continued the legacy of Judah, and the leaders of the tribe of Judah came from this lineage for many generations. The mention of Tamar and Judah in the people's blessing highlights the similarity between the match of Ruth and Boaz and that story. Just as the marriage of Boaz to Ruth did not involve a simple case of levirate marriage, Judah and Tamar's relationship was also not a standard levirate marriage, as Judah was the father, not the brother, of the deceased.

There are other dimensions to this comparison to Judah and Tamar. In both stories, pure God-fearing women are placed in difficult circumstances, and they must devise unusual plans of action that breach the standard norms in order to maintain their ties to the family of Judah. Ultimately, both Tamar and Ruth successfully build the future royal family of David (see Alsheikh; Malbim).

Ruth's Marriage and the Birth of Her Son

RUTH 4:13–17

The hopes that have been placed upon Ruth and Boaz and the blessings bestowed upon them indeed come to pass. Naomi is not abandoned either, as the son born to Ruth is considered a redeemer for her as well. His birth preserves the name of her deceased son, and in her old age she helps to raise the child and serves as a kind of mother and nurse for him.

13 **Boaz took Ruth, and she became his wife; and he consorted with her, and the Lord granted her pregnancy, and she bore**[D] **a son.**[D]

14 Following the birth of a son to Ruth, **the women said to Naomi: Blessed be the Lord, who did not leave you today without a redeemer.** He is considered the heir of your deceased son, as he preserves his memory and existence in this world, like the child born from a levirate marriage. In this manner, he redeems you, as though you had given birth to an additional son. **And let his name be called in Israel.** Now your family lineage will be continued.

15 Furthermore, **may he be for you a restorer of life** merely by virtue of his existence, **and one to sustain your old age.** When he grows up and you grow old, you can rely upon him to care for you. **For your daughter-in-law, who loves you, who is better for you than seven sons, bore him.**

16 **Naomi took the child, and she placed him in her bosom,** despite the lack of any direct blood relationship between her and the boy, **and was a nurse for him.** She felt an unusual affinity to this boy for two reasons: First, he carried her deceased son's legacy, and in a certain sense, his very existence. Second, he was the son of Ruth, who was like a daughter to her, and perhaps even closer than that, as Naomi considered Ruth her successor.[55]

17 In fact, Naomi was treated as the mother of the child by those in her immediate surroundings. **The women neighbors called him a name, saying: A son is born to Naomi.**[56] **They called his name Oved; he is the father of Yishai,** who was **the father of David.**

The Lineage of the House of David

RUTH 4:18–22

Since the previous passage concluded with the list of generations from Boaz to King David, the book ends with the broader family lineage, starting with Peretz, who was the son of Judah, the father of the tribe. The purpose of this family lineage is to trace the roots of King David, whose remarkable deeds and accomplishments justify all of the difficulties and suffering described in the book of Ruth.

18 **These are the generations of** the family of **Peretz: Peretz begot Hetzron;**

19 **and Hetzron begot Ram, and Ram begot Aminadav;**

20 **and Aminadav begot Nahshon,** the prince of the tribe of Judah at the time of the exodus from Egypt,[57] **and Nahshon begot Salmon;**

21 **and Salmon begot Boaz, and Boaz begot Oved;**

22 **and Oved begot Yishai, and Yishai begot David.**[D]

Supposed graves of Yishai and Ruth, Hebron

יג לִיהוּדָה מִן־הַזֶּרַע אֲשֶׁר יִתֵּן יהוה לְךָ מִן־הַנַּעֲרָה הַזֹּאת: וַיִּקַּח בֹּעַז אֶת־רוּת
יד וַתְּהִי־לוֹ לְאִשָּׁה וַיָּבֹא אֵלֶיהָ וַיִּתֵּן יהוה לָהּ הֵרָיוֹן וַתֵּלֶד בֵּן: וַתֹּאמַרְנָה הַנָּשִׁים
אֶל־נָעֳמִי בָּרוּךְ יהוה אֲשֶׁר לֹא הִשְׁבִּית לָךְ גֹּאֵל הַיּוֹם וְיִקָּרֵא שְׁמוֹ בְּיִשְׂרָאֵל:
טו וְהָיָה לָךְ לְמֵשִׁיב נֶפֶשׁ וּלְכַלְכֵּל אֶת־שֵׂיבָתֵךְ כִּי כַלָּתֵךְ אֲשֶׁר־אֲהֵבַתֶךְ יְלָדַתּוּ
טז אֲשֶׁר־הִיא טוֹבָה לָךְ מִשִּׁבְעָה בָּנִים: וַתִּקַּח נָעֳמִי אֶת־הַיֶּלֶד וַתְּשִׁתֵהוּ בְחֵיקָהּ
יז וַתְּהִי־לוֹ לְאֹמֶנֶת: וַתִּקְרֶאנָה לוֹ הַשְּׁכֵנוֹת שֵׁם לֵאמֹר יֻלַּד־בֵּן לְנָעֳמִי וַתִּקְרֶאנָה
שְׁמוֹ עוֹבֵד הוּא אֲבִי־יִשַׁי אֲבִי דָוִד:
יח יט וְאֵלֶּה תּוֹלְדוֹת פָּרֶץ פֶּרֶץ הוֹלִיד אֶת־חֶצְרוֹן: וְחֶצְרוֹן הוֹלִיד אֶת־רָם וְרָם הוֹלִיד
כ כא אֶת־עַמִּינָדָב: וְעַמִּינָדָב הוֹלִיד אֶת־נַחְשׁוֹן וְנַחְשׁוֹן הוֹלִיד אֶת־שַׂלְמָה: וְשַׂלְמוֹן
כב הוֹלִיד אֶת־בֹּעַז וּבֹעַז הוֹלִיד אֶת־עוֹבֵד: וְעֹבֵד הוֹלִיד אֶת־יִשָׁי וְיִשַׁי הוֹלִיד אֶת־
דָּוִד:

DISCUSSION

4:13 | **And the Lord granted her pregnancy, and she bore:** This conception occurred with divine assistance. After all, Ruth was previously married to a man younger than Boaz, yet did not bear him any children. According to the Sages, this event was especially miraculous, as they state that Boaz passed away on the night after Ruth became pregnant (see Alsheikh; Malbim; *Midrash Ruth Zuta* 4).

And she bore a son: The narrative involving Ruth concludes here. Nothing is stated about the remainder of her life. However, the Sages say that she lived to a very old age, and merited to see not only King David, her grandson, but also his son, King Solomon (*Bava Batra* 91b).

4:22 | **And Yishai begot David:** It is unclear whether this is a complete family lineage covering every generation, as many years separate the generation of Peretz from that of David. If this is in fact a full list, each of the individuals mentioned here must have lived to a very old age and fathered children very late in life (see Ibn Ezra; *Yalkut Shimoni*; *Bereshit Rabba* 96:4; Ramban, Genesis 46:15). It is more plausible that certain individuals of lesser importance were omitted from this list (see Ibn Ezra; *Yalkut Shimoni*; commentary on I Chronicles 2:51).

Lamentations

Lamentations

INTRODUCTION TO LAMENTATIONS

According to tradition, the book of Lamentations was authored by the prophet Jeremiah.[1] However, the Sages explain that in fact it was Barukh ben Neriya the scribe, Jeremiah's friend, who wrote the book, based on the words of Jeremiah.[2] This book does not contain a running narrative or description of events, but rather consists of lamentations over the downfall of Israel: the killings, famine, exile, and sufferings of the Jewish people.

These lamentations are usually understood as specifically addressing the destruction of the Temple, but this interpretation is not absolute. Although they are lamentations for the downfall of an entire kingdom and describe the departure of the nation into exile, they are actually missing an explicit and detailed description of the destruction of the Temple. It is therefore possible that a large portion of these lamentations were written prior to the destruction of the Temple. Support for this suggestion can be found in a verse elsewhere in the Bible that describes the aftermath of the death of King Yoshiya, decades before the destruction of Jerusalem: "And Jeremiah lamented Yoshiya, and all the male and female singers spoke of Yoshiya in their lamentations until this day, and they made them a statute over Israel, and behold, they are written in the lamentations."[3] This indicates that many years before the destruction of the Temple, a collection of lamentations was compiled in which those of Jeremiah over the death of Yoshiya appeared. It would seem, therefore, that the earlier compilation of lamentations is in fact the book of Lamentations. The downfall of Yoshiya is especially fitting as the subject of the third lamentation, which is unique with regard to its length and structure.[4]

The death of King Yoshiya signified the conclusion of an era. This was understood by those with foresight who lived at the time, despite the fact that, in practice, Yoshiya's three sons as well as his grandson reigned in Judah after his death. During the reigns of Yoshiya's successors, Jerusalem was conquered twice, once by the Egyptians, who exiled the king of Judah, and later by the Babylonians, who after an extended siege took another king captive. Repeated attempts to rebel against Babylonian rule did not succeed. It is therefore certainly possible that the military defeat at Megiddo in which Yoshiya was killed was already perceived as the beginning of the end of the kingdom of Judah.

The lamentations in this book do not describe an absolute destruction or the final end of the Jewish people. Rather, alongside mourning, themes of hope for consolation in the future are also present. Nevertheless, the catastrophic nature of the downfall is not in doubt, and the lamenter does not anticipate the kingdom's revival in the near future. Consolation is only for the distant future. It is therefore understandable that these lamentations were written down for future generations, and it is logical that their recitation has become a permanent custom among the Jewish people.

Most of the lamentations were written according to an alphabetical acrostic arrangement, with some minor departures. Only the final chapter does not use this acrostic method; even so, it consists of twenty-two verses, just like all the others. This highly stylized method of writing attests to the fact that the contents of the book were composed deliberately, rather than being a spontaneous emotional outpouring. Their form may also indicate an awareness that they would be read on a regular basis. Even one in the midst of mourning, who has difficulty finding the appropriate words to articulate his or her pain, will be able to find an appropriate expression of his emotions within this book.

Lamentations

Jerusalem

LAMENTATIONS 1:1–22

This lamentation depicts the miserable condition of Jerusalem in its destroyed state in comparison with its past eminence. The lamenter describes the loneliness, siege, famine, killing, robbery, captivity, and exile of the inhabitants of the city, as well as the degradation of the city itself. Three times the lamenter pauses in his harsh descriptions and cries out to God, that He should see what He has done. The lamenter is not complaining or accusing God; on the contrary, toward the end of the lamentation he justifies the divine sentence that was passed against Jerusalem due to the sins of its inhabitants. Still, in his cries to Heaven, he expresses his bewilderment at the harshness of the punishment. The lamentation ends with a plea for revenge against Judah's enemies.

1 1 **How does the** once **greatly crowded city** of Jerusalem now **sit alone? She has become** without support, **like a widow.**[D] **Great** and important **among the nations,**[5] **a princess,** ruler, and minister **among the states: She has become a vassal,** subservient to others! Jerusalem, which was the seat of a great and glorious kingdom, has completely lost its prestige.

2 **She,** the helpless widow, Jerusalem, **weeps at night,** as she is ashamed to weep in the daytime when people can see her, **and her tears are on her cheeks.** She attempts to hide her tears from the eyes of strangers. **Of all her lovers,** or political allies, **she has no one to comfort her. All her allies have betrayed her; they have become her enemies;** all the countries that had friendly relationships with her abandoned her after her downfall.

3 **Judah has been exiled in affliction and in great enslavement. She has settled among the nations, finding no rest,** because **all her pursuers,** her perpetual enemies, who had borne animosity toward her for generations, **have overtaken her.** They seized the opportunity to take revenge against her while she was pressed **within the straits,** narrow areas with no escape routes.[6]

Men and women going into exile on a wagon, Lakhish reliefs, Nineveh, 701 BCE

4 In normal times, the roads to Jerusalem were busy, particularly during the pilgrimage festivals when all of Israel would travel there. But now, **the ways**, the roads, **of Zion mourn,** they are desolate, **without pilgrims to the festival; all her gates are desolate; her priests sigh,** as the city is destroyed and the Temple is deserted.[7] **Her young women are melancholy, and she is embittered.**

5 **Her besiegers are ascendant, her enemies are tranquil, for the Lord has tormented her for her abundant transgressions; her infants are led into captivity before the besieger,** at the time of Yehoyakhin's exile to Babylonia.

6 **All her splendor has gone out of the daughter of Zion. Her** free and esteemed **princes are** hungry and lost, **like deer that have not found pasture.**[8] **They went powerless before the pursuer;** they were led into captivity by their new masters.

Hunting deer, relief at the Palace of Ashurbanipal, Nineveh, 645–635 BCE

7 **In the days of her affliction and her wretchedness,** her suffering,[9] **Jerusalem recalled all her delights that were from the days of old.** At the moment of her downfall, Jerusalem remembers the good days of yesteryear. **With the fall of her people into the hand of the besieger, with no one to help her, the besiegers saw her; they mocked her deficiencies.** Even those who did not actively participate in her destruction took pleasure in her downtrodden state.

איכה

א איכה ׀ ישבה בדד העיר רבתי עם היתה כאלמנה רבתי בגוים שרתי במדינות
ב היתה למס: בכו תבכה בלילה ודמעתה על לחיה אין־לה מנחם מכל־אהביה
ג כל־רעיה בגדו בה היו לה לאיבים: גלתה יהודה מעני ומרב עבדה היא ישבה
ד בגוים לא מצאה מנוח כל־רדפיה השיגוה בין המצרים: דרכי ציון אבלות
מבלי באי מועד כל־שעריה שוממין כהניה נאנחים בתולתיה נוגות והיא
ה מר־לה: היו צריה לראש איביה שלו כי־יהוה הוגה על־רב פשעיה עולליה
ו הלכו שבי לפני־צר: ויצא מן בת־ציון כל־הדרה היו שריה כאילים לא־מצאו מבת־
ז מרעה וילכו בלא־כח לפני רודף: זכרה ירושלם ימי עניה ומרודיה כל מחמדיה
אשר היו מימי קדם בנפל עמה ביד־צר ואין עוזר לה ראוה צרים שחקו על־
ח משבתה: חטא חטאה ירושלם על־כן לנידה היתה כל־מכבדיה הזילוה
ט כי־ראו ערותה גם־היא נאנחה ותשב אחור: טמאתה בשוליה לא זכרה

8 **A sin has Jerusalem sinned; therefore she has become a pariah.**[D] **All who honored her have demeaned her, because they saw her nakedness;** her shortcomings and agonies have been exposed to all.[10] **Even she** herself **sighs and has regressed.** She has become weak and therefore does not actively respond; instead, she sighs and resigns herself to her misery and desolation.

9 **Her impurity,** the blood of her menstruation, **is** perceptible **on the edges of her skirts,** the hems of her garment; in other words, her sins are obvious. **She had not considered** the fact

DISCUSSION

1:1| **She has become like a widow:** In its simple sense, the verse is declaring Jerusalem akin to a widow simply because she is devoid of protection and her status has become low. But there is also a sense that the city's "husband," God, has abandoned her. A similar expression is found in the last lamentation (5:3): "We have become orphans, fatherless; our mothers are like widows." This verse can be read literally, but it can also be seen as an allegory of the sense of orphanhood felt by the people of the city toward their Father in Heaven; the subjective feeling of Jerusalem, or the people of Israel, that they have been abandoned forever (Rashi; *Targum Yonatan*; *Eikha Rabba* 1:3; *Targum Yonatan* and *Pesikta Zutreta* on 5:3; see also Isaiah 54:4–5).

1:8| **She has become a pariah [*nidda*]:** The Hebrew word *nidda* denotes something kept at a distance or shunned. It is also used to refer to a menstruating woman. Presumably, this usage arose due to the observance of the laws of ritual purity in Temple times. In order to avoid becoming impure, pure individuals would often avoid menstruating women and others who were ritually impure (see, e.g., Jerusalem Talmud, *Shekalim* 8:1). The imagery used here and in the next verse is of Jerusalem as a shunned menstruating woman. According to the Talmud (*Ta'anit* 20a), this metaphor was chosen to provide a sense of hope for the future: "Just as a menstruating woman will become permitted, so too Jerusalem will be restored."

that this would be **her end.**[11] **She has declined extraordinarily,** far beyond expectations;[12] **there is no one to comfort her.** Consequently, the lamenter pleads: **See, Lord, my affliction, for the enemy has expanded** his power; he acts in Jerusalem as he pleases.

10 **The besieger spread his hand over all her delights,** i.e., he has taken them, **as she saw the nations entering her Sanctuary,** those nations **whom You had commanded that they should not enter Your assembly.** This is referring to the Amonites and the Moavites, whom the Torah denies even the possibility of conversion to Judaism.[13] The entry of such banned and inferior nations into the Temple is therefore doubly insulting.[14]

"The besieger spread his hand over all her delights." Romans carrying away the Temple vessels in their victory march, stone relief, Arch of Titus, Rome, 82 CE

11 **All her people are sighing, seeking bread** during the siege; **they have given** all **their delights,** their most valuable items, **for food to sustain**[15] **life.** Again the lamenter requests that God look at him, but now his request is in the name of Jerusalem: **See, Lord, and look, for I have become abject.**[16] Alternatively, the lamenter is saying that the reason people are starving for bread is that in the past the city was full of gluttony.[17]

12 Desolate Jerusalem now turns to the people who pass through it unheedingly, and expresses its wishes for them: **May it not befall you, all wayfarers.** Let troubles like mine never befall you.[18] **Behold and see: Is there any pain like my pain, which has been done to me,**[19] **with which the Lord has tormented me on the day of His enflamed wrath?**

13 **From on high He sent fire into my bones, and He crushed them,** flattened and destroyed them. **He spread a net for my feet,** and once I was caught in it, **He set me back. He rendered me desolate, suffering,** ill and in pain, or, distanced like a menstruating woman,[20] **all day.**

14 **The yoke of my transgressions is preserved**[21] **in His hand;** the transgressions are **becoming entangled, coming upon my neck** like a yoke, **sapping my strength. The Lord delivered me into the hands of those against whom I cannot stand.**

15 **The Lord trampled**[22] **all my mighty in my midst; He proclaimed a festival** of many enemies **against me** in order **to break my young men; the Lord has trodden the virgin daughter of Judah,** a moniker for the tribe of Judah or the residents of Jerusalem, **in a winepress.** We have all been trampled like grapes by the enemy, and our blood has been spilled like wine in a winepress.[23]

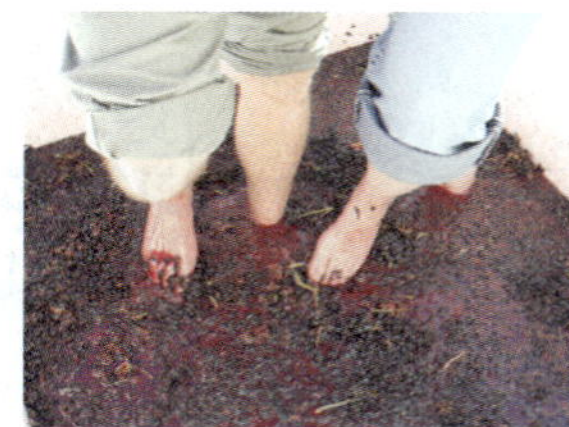

Treading in a winepress

16 **For these I weep; my eye, my eye sheds water,** tears, **for a comforter,** a king or other savior, **restorer of my soul, has grown distant from me. My children have become desolate,** with no guide or supporter, **because the enemy has prevailed.**

17 **Zion spread her hands** as a sign of surrender, defeat, and despair;[24] **there was no comforter for her. The Lord has commanded for Jacob that his besiegers surround him** from all sides.[25] **Jerusalem has become like a pariah among them,** even more distanced and disgraced.[26]

18 The lamentation is composed with the mindset of acceptance of God's sentence: **The Lord,** who has done all this to us, **is righteous;** His judgment is correct, **for I have defied,** transgressed, **His word. Hear now all you peoples,** what God has done to us, **and see my pain: My young women and young men have gone into captivity.**

19 **I called to my lovers,** those who had presented themselves as my friends and allies,[27] but **they deceived me.** Meanwhile, **my priests and my elders,** who are usually sustained by public funds (see 4:16), **perished in the city, while they sought food for themselves,** as the public did not have the means to support them during the siege; they tried **to restore their lives** and sustain themselves, but to no avail.

"My young women and young men have gone into captivity." Jews exiled from Lakhish, above left: men, above right: women; Lakhish reliefs, Nineveh, 701 BCE

י אַחֲרִיתָהּ וַתֵּרֶד פְּלָאִים אֵין מְנַחֵם לָהּ רְאֵה יהוה אֶת־עׇנְיִי כִּי הִגְדִּיל אוֹיֵב׃ יָדוֹ
פָּרַשׂ צָר עַל כׇּל־מַחֲמַדֶּיהָ כִּי־רָאֲתָה גוֹיִם בָּאוּ מִקְדָּשָׁהּ אֲשֶׁר צִוִּיתָה לֹא־יָבֹאוּ
יא בַקָּהָל לָךְ׃ כׇּל־עַמָּהּ נֶאֱנָחִים מְבַקְּשִׁים לֶחֶם נָתְנוּ מחמודיהֶם בְּאֹכֶל לְהָשִׁיב מַחֲמַדֵּיהֶם
יב נָפֶשׁ רְאֵה יהוה וְהַבִּיטָה כִּי הָיִיתִי זוֹלֵלָה׃ לוֹא אֲלֵיכֶם כׇּל־עֹבְרֵי דֶרֶךְ הַבִּיטוּ
וּרְאוּ אִם־יֵשׁ מַכְאוֹב כְּמַכְאֹבִי אֲשֶׁר עוֹלַל לִי אֲשֶׁר הוֹגָה יהוה בְּיוֹם חֲרוֹן אַפּוֹ׃
יג מִמָּרוֹם שָׁלַח־אֵשׁ בְּעַצְמֹתַי וַיִּרְדֶּנָּה פָּרַשׂ רֶשֶׁת לְרַגְלַי הֱשִׁיבַנִי אָחוֹר נְתָנַנִי
יד שֹׁמֵמָה כׇּל־הַיּוֹם דָּוָה׃ נִשְׂקַד עֹל פְּשָׁעַי בְּיָדוֹ יִשְׂתָּרְגוּ עָלוּ עַל־צַוָּארִי הִכְשִׁיל
טו כֹּחִי נְתָנַנִי אֲדֹנָי בִּידֵי לֹא־אוּכַל קוּם׃ סִלָּה כׇל־אַבִּירַי ׀ אֲדֹנָי בְּקִרְבִּי קָרָא עָלַי
טז מוֹעֵד לִשְׁבֹּר בַּחוּרָי גַּת דָּרַךְ אֲדֹנָי לִבְתוּלַת בַּת־יְהוּדָה׃ עַל־אֵלֶּה ׀ אֲנִי בוֹכִיָּה
עֵינִי ׀ עֵינִי יֹרְדָה מַּיִם כִּי־רָחַק מִמֶּנִּי מְנַחֵם מֵשִׁיב נַפְשִׁי הָיוּ בָנַי שׁוֹמֵמִים כִּי גָבַר
יז אוֹיֵב׃ פֵּרְשָׂה צִיּוֹן בְּיָדֶיהָ אֵין מְנַחֵם לָהּ צִוָּה יהוה לְיַעֲקֹב סְבִיבָיו צָרָיו הָיְתָה
יח יְרוּשָׁלַםִ לְנִדָּה בֵּינֵיהֶם׃ צַדִּיק הוּא יהוה כִּי פִיהוּ מָרִיתִי שִׁמְעוּ־נָא כׇל־עַמִּים הָעַמִּים
יט וּרְאוּ מַכְאֹבִי בְּתוּלֹתַי וּבַחוּרַי הָלְכוּ בַשֶּׁבִי׃ קָרָאתִי לַמְאַהֲבַי הֵמָּה רִמּוּנִי כֹּהֲנַי
כ וּזְקֵנַי בָּעִיר גָּוָעוּ כִּי־בִקְשׁוּ אֹכֶל לָמוֹ וְיָשִׁיבוּ אֶת־נַפְשָׁם׃ רְאֵה יהוה כִּי־צַר־לִי
מֵעַי חֳמַרְמָרוּ נֶהְפַּךְ לִבִּי בְּקִרְבִּי כִּי מָרוֹ מָרִיתִי מִחוּץ שִׁכְּלָה־חֶרֶב בַּבַּיִת כַּמָּוֶת׃
כא שָׁמְעוּ כִּי נֶאֱנָחָה אָנִי אֵין מְנַחֵם לִי כׇּל־אֹיְבַי שָׁמְעוּ רָעָתִי שָׂשׂוּ כִּי אַתָּה עָשִׂיתָ
כב הֵבֵאתָ יוֹם־קָרָאתָ וְיִהְיוּ כָמוֹנִי׃ תָּבֹא כׇל־רָעָתָם לְפָנֶיךָ וְעוֹלֵל לָמוֹ כַּאֲשֶׁר עוֹלַלְתָּ
לִי עַל כׇּל־פְּשָׁעָי כִּי־רַבּוֹת אַנְחֹתַי וְלִבִּי דַוָּי׃

20 The lamenter again turns to God, and this time he is apparently representing both himself and Jerusalem as one: **See, Lord, for I am in distress, my innards burn;**[28] my entire body hurts, including my innards. I feel as if **my heart is overturned within me, for I have rebelled,** transgressed the word of God. **Outside, the sword bereaves; in the house, it is like death.** Outside the house, people are being killed, but even inside the house, the terror of death is found.

21 **They heard that I sigh; there is no comforter for me; all my enemies heard of my misfortune, were glad** at my misfortune, **because You acted.** The lamenter now begs:[29] Please, **may You bring the day that You proclaimed, and** punish them so that **they will be like me,** with similar suffering to mine.

22 **Let all their wickedness,** of those who pretended to be my friends and allies, **come before You, and do to them as You did to me for all my transgressions, for my sighs are many and my heart is suffering,** suffering from pain.

God's Treatment of the Daughter of Zion

LAMENTATIONS 2:1–22

Whereas the previous lamentation emphasized the enemy whom God sent to torment Jerusalem for her sins, this one opens by stressing the lamenter's astonishment at God's affliction of "the daughter of Zion," "the daughter of Jerusalem," and "the daughter of Judah." The word "daughter" appears eleven times in this lamentation. Here, it is God who degrades Israel and its leaders and destroys their homes and fortresses. God appears as an enemy Himself, not only as He who sent the enemy.

The lamenter subsequently accuses the false prophets of Jerusalem of having prevented the inhabitants of Jerusalem from confronting their sins and changing their ways by soothing them with false prophecies. Now, there are no longer any prophecies, and the sounds of rejoicing of those who would come for the pilgrimage festivals no longer emanate from the city. Instead, the sounds that are heard in Jerusalem are those of babies crying for food and drink; the shouts and cries of its defeated inhabitants; expressions of astonishment and sorrow, as well as eulogies, by those who pass through the ruined city; and the voices of enemies rejoicing over Israel's misfortune.

2 1 **How the Lord has clouded** over **the daughter of Zion in His wrath. He cast the splendor of Israel from the heavens to the earth and did not remember His footstool,** a flowery metaphor for the Temple,[30] **on the day of His wrath.**

2 **The Lord has demolished and has had no compassion for all the** pleasant **habitations of Jacob; He destroyed, in His ire, the strongholds of the daughter of Judah. He brought them to the ground;**[31] **He profaned,** disgraced, and eliminated **a kingdom and its princes.**

"He destroyed, in His ire, the strongholds of the daughter of Judah." The siege of Lakhish and the stronghold under attack, illustration based on Lakhish reliefs, Nineveh,

3 **He severed in enflamed wrath all the grandeur of Israel.** In normal times, God protects His nation and does not allow the enemy to do as it wishes toward it; but now, **He retracted His right hand,** which prevents the enemy from harming Israel, **from being before the enemy,** allowing the enemy to act unrestrained,[32] **who burned Jacob like flaming fire, consuming all around.**

4 **He,** God himself, **drew His bow** against us **as an enemy.** Not only did God withhold His hand from restraining the enemy, but **His right hand stood** against us **as a besieger, and He killed all delights of the eye. In the tent of the daughter of Zion, He poured His fury like fire.**

Arrows stretched for firing, relief at the Palace of Ashurbanipal, Nineveh, 645–635 BCE

"He poured His fury like fire." Burnt room, City of David, Jerusalem, sixth century BCE

5 **The Lord was like an enemy; He demolished Israel, demolished all its palaces, destroyed its strongholds, and multiplied** sounds of **mourning and moaning in the daughter of Judah.**[33]

6 **He stripped His shrine,** His dwelling place,[34] picking all its fruits, **like a garden;**[35] **He destroyed His place of assembly,** or the place where He attended.[36] **The Lord caused festival and Sabbath to be forgotten in Zion.** The times have become so bitter and hard that the festivals, and even the Sabbaths, are no longer discernable. The routine of life has become poor, dull, and sad. **And He,** God, **scorned,** cursed and harmed, **king and priest** of Israel **in His furious wrath.**

7 **The Lord forsook His altar, cursed** and ceased to protect **His Temple. He gave into the hand of the enemy the walls of her palaces.** Since the whole city has been delivered to the control of foreigners, **they made** a loud **noise in the House of the Lord, like a day of festival.** The sounds of the massacre and battle in the Temple brought back memories of voices raised in song and thanks that would emanate from those celebrating the festivals in previous years.[37]

8 **The Lord resolved to destroy the wall of the daughter of Zion; He drew,** marked **a line** in preparation of His plan of action, and **did not withdraw His hand from demolishing,** but implemented His plan. **He caused rampart and wall to mourn, together they languish.**

9 **Her gates sank into the ground;** essentially, they have disappeared, because people have stopped using them and therefore they no longer serve any purpose. **He eradicated and broke her bars,** which would have been used to close the gates. **Her king and her princes are** exiled **among the nations** and cannot help. **There is no Torah; her prophets, too, could not find a vision from the Lord.** All is hidden and unknown. The leaders have gone into exile, and those who are left offer no comfort.

10 **The elders of the daughter of Zion sit on the ground, are silent.**[38] **They have placed dust on their heads, have girded themselves with sackcloth. The young women of Jerusalem have lowered their heads to the ground.** Both the young and the old mourn.

א אֵיכָה יָעִיב בְּאַפּוֹ | אֲדֹנָי אֶת־בַּת־צִיּוֹן הִשְׁלִיךְ מִשָּׁמַיִם אֶרֶץ תִּפְאֶרֶת יִשְׂרָאֵל
ב וְלֹא־זָכַר הֲדֹם־רַגְלָיו בְּיוֹם אַפּוֹ: בִּלַּע אֲדֹנָי לא חָמַל אֵת כָּל־נְאוֹת יַעֲקֹב הָרַס וְלֹא
ג בְּעֶבְרָתוֹ מִבְצְרֵי בַת־יְהוּדָה הִגִּיעַ לָאָרֶץ חִלֵּל מַמְלָכָה וְשָׂרֶיהָ: גָּדַע בָּחֳרִי־אַף
כֹּל קֶרֶן יִשְׂרָאֵל הֵשִׁיב אָחוֹר יְמִינוֹ מִפְּנֵי אוֹיֵב וַיִּבְעַר בְּיַעֲקֹב כְּאֵשׁ לֶהָבָה אָכְלָה
ד סָבִיב: דָּרַךְ קַשְׁתּוֹ כְּאוֹיֵב נִצָּב יְמִינוֹ כְּצָר וַיַּהֲרֹג כֹּל מַחֲמַדֵּי־עָיִן בְּאֹהֶל בַּת־צִיּוֹן
ה שָׁפַךְ כָּאֵשׁ חֲמָתוֹ: הָיָה אֲדֹנָי | כְּאוֹיֵב בִּלַּע יִשְׂרָאֵל בִּלַּע כָּל־אַרְמְנוֹתֶיהָ שִׁחֵת
ו מִבְצָרָיו וַיֶּרֶב בְּבַת־יְהוּדָה תַּאֲנִיָּה וַאֲנִיָּה: וַיַּחְמֹס כַּגַּן שֻׂכּוֹ שִׁחֵת מֹעֲדוֹ שִׁכַּח
ז יְהוָה | בְּצִיּוֹן מוֹעֵד וְשַׁבָּת וַיִּנְאַץ בְּזַעַם־אַפּוֹ מֶלֶךְ וְכֹהֵן: זָנַח אֲדֹנָי | מִזְבְּחוֹ נִאֵר
מִקְדָּשׁוֹ הִסְגִּיר בְּיַד־אוֹיֵב חוֹמֹת אַרְמְנוֹתֶיהָ קוֹל נָתְנוּ בְּבֵית־יְהוָה כְּיוֹם מוֹעֵד:
ח חָשַׁב יְהוָה | לְהַשְׁחִית חוֹמַת בַּת־צִיּוֹן נָטָה קָו לֹא־הֵשִׁיב יָדוֹ מִבַּלֵּעַ וַיַּאֲבֶל־חֵל
ט וְחוֹמָה יַחְדָּו אֻמְלָלוּ: טָבְעוּ בָאָרֶץ שְׁעָרֶיהָ אִבַּד וְשִׁבַּר בְּרִיחֶיהָ מַלְכָּהּ וְשָׂרֶיהָ
י בַגּוֹיִם אֵין תּוֹרָה גַּם־נְבִיאֶיהָ לֹא־מָצְאוּ חָזוֹן מֵיְהוָה: יֵשְׁבוּ לָאָרֶץ יִדְּמוּ זִקְנֵי בַת־
צִיּוֹן הֶעֱלוּ עָפָר עַל־רֹאשָׁם חָגְרוּ שַׂקִּים הוֹרִידוּ לָאָרֶץ רֹאשָׁן בְּתוּלֹת יְרוּשָׁלִָם:
יא כָּלוּ בַדְּמָעוֹת עֵינַי חֳמַרְמְרוּ מֵעַי נִשְׁפַּךְ לָאָרֶץ כְּבֵדִי עַל־שֶׁבֶר בַּת־עַמִּי בֵּעָטֵף
יב עוֹלֵל וְיוֹנֵק בִּרְחֹבוֹת קִרְיָה: לְאִמֹּתָם יֹאמְרוּ אַיֵּה דָּגָן וָיָיִן בְּהִתְעַטְּפָם כֶּחָלָל
יג בִּרְחֹבוֹת עִיר בְּהִשְׁתַּפֵּךְ נַפְשָׁם אֶל־חֵיק אִמֹּתָם: מָה־אעודך מָה אֲדַמֶּה־לָּךְ אֲעִידֵךְ
הַבַּת יְרוּשָׁלִַם מָה אַשְׁוֶה־לָּךְ וַאֲנַחֲמֵךְ בְּתוּלַת בַּת־צִיּוֹן כִּי־גָדוֹל כַּיָּם שִׁבְרֵךְ

11 The lamenter's distress at the sight of his eyes is so great that he feels as though it physically harms him: **My eyes fail from** the many **tears; my innards burn.**[39] I am overcome with a terrible stomachache; **my liver is poured on the earth over the disaster of the daughter of my people, as the infants and the suckling babes faint in the city squares.**

12 **To their mothers they,** the young children, **say: Where is grain and** if there is no bread, where is there **wine** to refresh our souls? **while fainting like the wounded,** as lifeless corpses **in the city squares, while their souls are poured into their mothers' bosoms.**

13 **What shall I attest to you?** What similar case can I cite in order to comfort you?[40] **To what shall I liken you,** what metaphors can I use in order to explain your situation, **daughter of Jerusalem? To what shall I equate you,** with what can I compare your suffering, **and** thereby **comfort you, virgin daughter of Zion? For your disaster is as vast as the sea; who can heal you?** No one can.

14 **Your prophets,** who were not true prophets of God, **envisioned** and delivered prophecies of **futility and foolishness for you,** as they had no substance, **and did not reveal your iniquity to bring about your rehabilitation,** to return you to your previous state. They betrayed their mission, which was to castigate you for your sins and inspire you to repent. Instead, **they** allowed you to deteriorate and **envisioned for you prophecies of futility and deviance,** or incitement, which incited you to abandon the correct path.[41] Instead of telling you the hard truth, which would have convinced you to change your ways and repent, your prophets affirmed your behavior, enabling you to continue your evil ways unimpeded.

15 **All wayfarers clapped their hands at you; they whistled and shook their heads,** expressions of grief, **at the daughter of Jerusalem.** At the sight of your ruin, they wonder: **Is this the city that was said to be perfect beauty, the joy of the entire earth?**

16 **All your enemies opened their mouths wide,** jeering **against you; they whistled and gnashed** their **teeth,** expressions of anger or animosity. **They said: We have demolished** her; **indeed, this is the day for which we hoped,** the day of Jerusalem's downfall; now **we found** it, **we saw** it.

17 **The Lord accomplished that which He devised;**[D] **He implemented His statement that He commanded from the days of old.** He had warned you in His Torah of defeat and destruction, starvation and war, and now His retribution for your sins has come to pass.[42] **He destroyed and had no compassion. He caused the enemy to rejoice over you, raised the horn of your antagonists.** He has empowered them in their own eyes.

18 **Their hearts,** the hearts of the city's inhabitants, **cried to the Lord. Wall of the daughter of Zion, let tears fall like a stream, day and night; do not give yourself respite; let the apple of your eye not cease.** Do not allow yourself to stop weeping.[43]

19 The lamenter now turns to Israel: **Arise, cry out** while eulogizing **at night,**[44] **at the beginning of the watches.** For watchmen, the night is divided into shifts, and the time at the beginning of each shift is opportune for prayer.[45] **Pour out your heart like water,** sob uncontrollably during these hours of the night **before the face of the Lord** over your situation. **Lift up your hands to Him** in prayer **for the life of your infants, who are faint with hunger at the head of every street.** Not only the adults are starving to death; even the young children have nothing to eat.

20 Like the previous lamentation, this one also concludes with a call to God to see how lowly Jerusalem has become, and once again the lamenter personally identifies with Jerusalem: **See, Lord, and behold to whom You have done this. Shall women eat their fruit, the infants of their nurturing?** Was it Your intention that the starvation should be so terrible as to cause this to happen? **Shall the priest and the prophet be slain in the Temple of the Lord,** which is supposed to be a place of refuge? Was that Your intent?

21 **Lad and elder lay on the ground in the streets; my young women and my young men fell by the sword. You killed on the day of Your wrath; You slaughtered, had no compassion.** You have harmed us mercilessly.

22 **You have called,** invited, **as on an appointed day, my fears** to come **from all around, and there was no survivor or remnant on the day of the Lord's wrath.** All the houses, gardens, books, public works, and **those** children **whom I nurtured and reared, my enemy annihilated;** I remain alone in the world.

The Man Who Views the Suffering of His Nation

LAMENTATIONS 3:1–66

The third lamentation is distinct from the others in structure, style, and content.

As opposed to the other lamentations, whose verses are long and composed of several parts, the verses here are short. Most of the other lamentations feature one verse beginning with each letter of the Hebrew alphabet, forming an alphabetic acrostic; here, while the alphabetic acrostic structure is maintained, there are three verses for each letter.

Stylistically, the broad use of first person singular is conspicuous. Although throughout the book of Lamentations there are verses where the prophet speaks of his own personal anguish and pain upon observing the destruction, nevertheless Jerusalem is generally referred to in the third person, sometimes assuming the persona of a woman. This lamentation, by contrast, is recited by a man who considers himself an example and a symbol for the entire nation, and therefore his personal experience is emphasized.

There are further differences between this lamentation and the others that relate to the content: Whereas in the other lamentations the prophet describes the historical context for his feelings, including references to starvation and murder, the physical destruction of Jerusalem, and the enemies inflicting this destruction and rejoicing in it, this lamentation does not present any such descriptions. Instead, it focuses on the lamenter's personal suffering; his wavering between hope and despair; and his fluctuation between surrender and acceptance of the situation on the one hand, and his pain, cries, and struggling on the other. There is no question of "how [*eikha*] this can have happened," as is found in the other lamentations, only a description of the current situation.

The lamentation ends with a prayer that God deliver appropriate retribution to the enemy for mocking and inflicting destruction on the Jewish people.

3 1 **I am the man who has seen** and suffered **affliction by the rod of His fury.**[46]

2 **He,** God, **conducted and led me in darkness and not in light.**

יד מִי יְרַפֵּא־לָךְ׃ נְבִיאַיִךְ חָזוּ לָךְ שָׁוְא וְתָפֵל וְלֹא־גִלּוּ עַל־עֲוֺנֵךְ לְהָשִׁיב שביתך שְׁבוּתֵךְ

טו וַיֶּחֱזוּ לָךְ מַשְׂאוֹת שָׁוְא וּמַדּוּחִים׃ סָפְקוּ עָלַיִךְ כַּפַּיִם כָּל־עֹבְרֵי דֶרֶךְ שָׁרְקוּ וַיָּנִעוּ

רֹאשָׁם עַל־בַּת יְרוּשָׁלָ͏ִם הֲזֹאת הָעִיר שֶׁיֹּאמְרוּ כְּלִילַת יֹפִי מָשׂוֹשׂ לְכָל־הָאָרֶץ׃

טז פָּצוּ עָלַיִךְ פִּיהֶם כָּל־אוֹיְבַיִךְ שָׁרְקוּ וַיַּחַרְקוּ־שֵׁן אָמְרוּ בִּלָּעְנוּ אַךְ זֶה הַיּוֹם שֶׁקִּוִּינֻהוּ

יז מָצָאנוּ רָאִינוּ׃ עָשָׂה יְהוָה אֲשֶׁר זָמָם בִּצַּע אֶמְרָתוֹ אֲשֶׁר צִוָּה מִימֵי־קֶדֶם הָרַס

יח וְלֹא חָמָל וַיְשַׂמַּח עָלַיִךְ אוֹיֵב הֵרִים קֶרֶן צָרָיִךְ׃ צָעַק לִבָּם אֶל־אֲדֹנָי חוֹמַת בַּת־

צִיּוֹן הוֹרִידִי כַנַּחַל דִּמְעָה יוֹמָם וָלַיְלָה אַל־תִּתְּנִי פוּגַת לָךְ אַל־תִּדֹּם בַּת־עֵינֵךְ׃

יט קוּמִי ׀ רֹנִּי בַלַּיִל לְרֹאשׁ אַשְׁמֻרוֹת שִׁפְכִי כַמַּיִם לִבֵּךְ נֹכַח פְּנֵי אֲדֹנָי שְׂאִי אֵלָיו

כ כַּפַּיִךְ עַל־נֶפֶשׁ עוֹלָלַיִךְ הָעֲטוּפִים בְּרָעָב בְּרֹאשׁ כָּל־חוּצוֹת׃ רְאֵה יְהוָה וְהַבִּיטָה

לְמִי עוֹלַלְתָּ כֹּה אִם־תֹּאכַלְנָה נָשִׁים פִּרְיָם עֹלֲלֵי טִפֻּחִים אִם־יֵהָרֵג בְּמִקְדַּשׁ אֲדֹנָי

כא כֹּהֵן וְנָבִיא׃ שָׁכְבוּ לָאָרֶץ חוּצוֹת נַעַר וְזָקֵן בְּתוּלֹתַי וּבַחוּרַי נָפְלוּ בֶחָרֶב הָרַגְתָּ

כב בְּיוֹם אַפֶּךָ טָבַחְתָּ לֹא חָמָלְתָּ׃ תִּקְרָא כְיוֹם מוֹעֵד מְגוּרַי מִסָּבִיב וְלֹא הָיָה בְּיוֹם

אַף־יְהוָה פָּלִיט וְשָׂרִיד אֲשֶׁר־טִפַּחְתִּי וְרִבִּיתִי אֹיְבִי כִלָּם׃

א ב אֲנִי הַגֶּבֶר רָאָה עֳנִי בְּשֵׁבֶט עֶבְרָתוֹ׃ אוֹתִי נָהַג וַיֹּלַךְ חֹשֶׁךְ וְלֹא־אוֹר׃

DISCUSSION

2:16–17 | **All your enemies opened their mouths…The Lord accomplished that which He devised:** Although this lamentation, like the other lamentations, is written in alphabetical order, verses 16 and 17 begin with *peh* and *ayin*, respectively, which is contrary to the common order. This change to the alphabetical order appears in the third and fourth lamentations as well (3:46–51; 4:16–17). There are various interpretive explanations for this phenomenon, but it is possible that in those days the order of the Hebrew alphabet was not entirely fixed (see also *Sanhedrin* 104b; *Eikha Rabba* 2:20).

3 **Indeed, against me He will again turn His hand all day.** God came back again and again to strike me relentlessly.
4 **He wore away my flesh and my skin, broke my bones.**
5 **He built against me** a wall of siege,[47] **and surrounded me with gall,**[B] a bitter and poisonous weed,[48] **and adversity.**

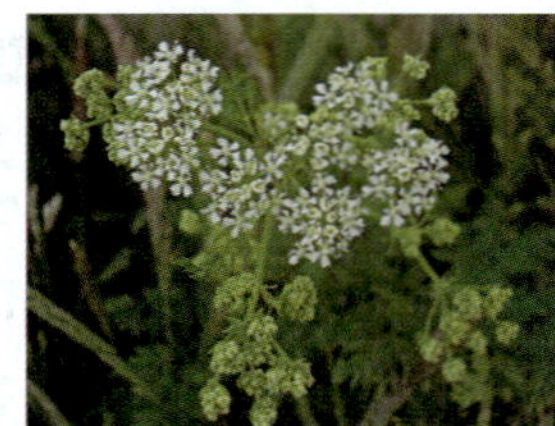
Gall, hemlock

6 **He settled me in darkness, like those long dead,** who dwell in eternal darkness.
7 **He fenced me in,** limited my movement, so **that I would not emerge;** He **made my fetters heavy,** so that they bind me down.[49]

Remains of fetters, Roman period

8 **Even as I cry and plead, He blocks my prayer,**[50] preventing it from reaching Him and being accepted.
9 **He fenced my ways with hewn stone,** stones for construction that block roads; He **distorted my paths.** Not only does He not redeem me from my troubles, but He gives me new ones.
10 **He,** God, **is like a bear in ambush to me, a lion in hiding.** Therefore, dangers appear in my life repeatedly.

Bear, detail from the Birds Mosaic, Caesarea, Byzantine period

11 **He has twisted my ways,**[51] or, He has covered my ways with thorns,[52] **and mauled me,** torn me to pieces,[53] **rendered me desolate** and alone.
12 **He drew His bow and set me as the target for the arrow.**
13 **He** then **pierced my kidneys with** His arrows, **the contents of His quiver.**
14 **I have become a laughingstock to all my people, their song**[D] **all day.** I have become an object of mockery and satirical songs. The lamenter here is referring to himself, or alternatively, he is speaking of the people, in first person, as their representative.
15 **He,** God, **filled me with bitterness, sated me with** a solution of **wormwood,**[B] a bitter or poisonous drink.
16 Since God has withheld food from me, **He has ground my teeth with gravel,** forcing me to eat it, and He has **covered me in ashes.**[54]
17 **My soul has forsaken peace;** my soul has abandoned its hope for peace. **I have forgotten** the possibility of **goodness** because I am engulfed in distress.

Wormwood

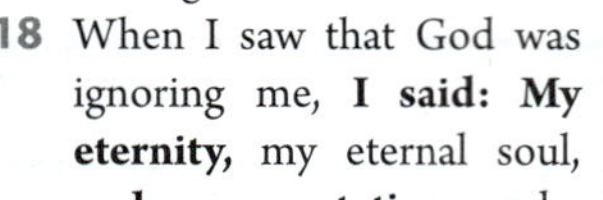

18 When I saw that God was ignoring me, **I said: My eternity,** my eternal soul, **and my expectation,** my hope, **have perished,** are lost, **from the Lord.**[55]
19 **Remember my affliction and my anguish,** my hardship, which is bitter like **wormwood and gall.**
20 In the future **You will remember, and** yet in the meantime, my soul **is bowed** down **within me** from the toil and suffering.[56]
21 Despite the pain and anguish that God has wrought upon me, almost leading me to despair, **this I will reply to my heart;** I constantly remind myself of the following principle, and **therefore I will await,** or I have hope.[57]
22 **It is** due to **the Lord's kindnesses that we have not ceased.** Thanks to the Lord's mercies we have not been utterly consumed; we still exist, despite all the troubles, **for His mercies have not ended.** This faith was expressed by the Jewish people in all of their exiles.[58]
23 **New every morning, great is the trust in You.**[D] Alternatively, every morning my faith in You strengthens anew.
24 **The Lord is my portion, says my soul,** choosing to be loyal to God.[59] **Therefore I will await Him.**
25 **The Lord is good to those who hope for Him, to the soul that seeks Him.**
26 **It is good** for a man **to await silently**[60] **the salvation of the Lord.**
27 The prophet further consoles himself: **It is good for a man that he bears a yoke in his youth.** Just as a young man can carry a heavy burden without getting injured, so too let him accept the challenge described in the next verse.
28 **Let him sit alone and be silent, because he took it upon himself;** he has accepted this life situation, despite its hardship.[61]
29 **Let him** subdue himself and **put his mouth in the dust,** so that he cannot speak;[62] **perhaps there is hope.**
30 Instead of striking back, **let him offer his cheek to one who strikes him; let him be filled with disgrace,** as he is smitten from every direction.
31 Nevertheless, there is still hope, **for the Lord will not forsake forever.**
32 **For,** even **if He torments,** ultimately **He will have compassion, according to His abundant kindness.**[63]
33 **For He does not afflict** people **willingly** for no reason, **and** He does not **torment the children of men** capriciously.[64]

ג ד ה אַךְ בִּי יָשֻׁב יַהֲפֹךְ יָדוֹ כָּל־הַיּוֹם: בִּלָּה בְשָׂרִי וְעוֹרִי שִׁבַּר עַצְמוֹתָי: בָּנָה עָלַי וַיַּקַּף
ו ז רֹאשׁ וּתְלָאָה: בְּמַחֲשַׁכִּים הוֹשִׁיבַנִי כְּמֵתֵי עוֹלָם: גָּדַר בַּעֲדִי וְלֹא אֵצֵא הִכְבִּיד
ח ט י נְחָשְׁתִּי: גַּם כִּי אֶזְעַק וַאֲשַׁוֵּעַ שָׂתַם תְּפִלָּתִי: גָּדַר דְּרָכַי בְּגָזִית נְתִיבֹתַי עִוָּה: דֹּב
יא יב אֹרֵב הוּא לִי אריה בְּמִסְתָּרִים: דְּרָכַי סוֹרֵר וַיְפַשְּׁחֵנִי שָׂמַנִי שֹׁמֵם: דָּרַךְ קַשְׁתּוֹ אֲרִי
יג יד וַיַּצִּיבֵנִי כַּמַּטָּרָא לַחֵץ: הֵבִיא בְּכִלְיוֹתָי בְּנֵי אַשְׁפָּתוֹ: הָיִיתִי שְּׂחֹק לְכָל־עַמִּי נְגִינָתָם
טו טז כָּל־הַיּוֹם: הִשְׂבִּיעַנִי בַמְּרוֹרִים הִרְוַנִי לַעֲנָה: וַיַּגְרֵס בֶּחָצָץ שִׁנָּי הִכְפִּישַׁנִי בָּאֵפֶר:
יז יח יט וַתִּזְנַח מִשָּׁלוֹם נַפְשִׁי נָשִׁיתִי טוֹבָה: וָאֹמַר אָבַד נִצְחִי וְתוֹחַלְתִּי מֵיהוָה: זְכָר־עָנְיִי
כ כא וּמְרוּדִי לַעֲנָה וָרֹאשׁ: זָכוֹר תִּזְכּוֹר ותשיח עָלַי נַפְשִׁי: זֹאת אָשִׁיב אֶל־לִבִּי עַל־ וְתָשׁוֹחַ
כב כג כֵּן אוֹחִיל: חַסְדֵי יהוה כִּי לֹא־תָמְנוּ כִּי לֹא־כָלוּ רַחֲמָיו: חֲדָשִׁים לַבְּקָרִים רַבָּה
כד כה אֱמוּנָתֶךָ: חֶלְקִי יהוה אָמְרָה נַפְשִׁי עַל־כֵּן אוֹחִיל לוֹ: טוֹב יהוה לְקֹוָו לְנֶפֶשׁ
כו כז תִּדְרְשֶׁנּוּ: טוֹב וְיָחִיל וְדוּמָם לִתְשׁוּעַת יהוה: טוֹב לַגֶּבֶר כִּי־יִשָּׂא עֹל בִּנְעוּרָיו:
כח כט ל יֵשֵׁב בָּדָד וְיִדֹּם כִּי נָטַל עָלָיו: יִתֵּן בֶּעָפָר פִּיהוּ אוּלַי יֵשׁ תִּקְוָה: יִתֵּן לְמַכֵּהוּ לֶחִי
לא לב לג יִשְׂבַּע בְּחֶרְפָּה: כִּי לֹא יִזְנַח לְעוֹלָם אֲדֹנָי: כִּי אִם־הוֹגָה וְרִחַם כְּרֹב חֲסָדָו: כִּי לֹא

BACKGROUND

3:5 | **Gall [*rosh*]:** *Rosh* is commonly identified as hemlock, *Conium maculatum*, an extremely poisonous plant that was used for the execution of criminals in ancient Greece. An herbaceous plant of the Apiaceae family that reaches a height of 1.5 m, hemlock has white flowers and its stalk is speckled with black spots; it grows wild, typically by the roadside or on the edges of cultivated fields. Others identify *rosh* as the opium poppy, *Papaver somniferum*. The fruit of the poppy resembles a head [*rosh*], and it is used to produce opium. Alternatively, *rosh* might be golden henbane, *Hyoscyamus aureus*, which also contains a strong poison.

3:15 | **Wormwood [*la'ana*]:** *La'ana* is commonly identified with wormwood, *Artemisia absinthium*, which is common in Israel. The plant's flowers are yellow, and it reaches a height and width of 1.5 m. Alternatively, *la'ana* is a generic term for various bitter or poisonous plants.

DISCUSSION

3:14 | **A laughingstock to all my people, their song:** This verse can be seen as a description of the suffering of the prophets due to the way they were perceived by the people, as demonstrated in the verse: "The prophet is a fool, the man of the spirit is mad" (Hosea 9:7). Unlike the metaphors used in the previous verses, this one relates to the actual reality of the prophet's life and his standing among his listeners. He was confined to a hopeless existence, where the people around him would shoot arrows of derision at him.

3:23 | **New every morning, great is the trust in You:** Jews recite the following passage, based on this verse, every morning upon waking up: I offer thanks before You, living and eternal King, for You have mercifully restored my soul within me; Your faithfulness is great.

34 He does not want[65] **to subdue under His feet all the prisoners of the earth.**

"To subdue under his feet." Tiglat Pileser subduing his enemy under his feet, Nimrud, Iraq, 747–727 BCE

35 And it is not His habit[66] **to distort the judgment of man before the face of the Most High.** God does not pervert justice,
36 **to subvert a man in his quarrel,** his cause, **the Lord has deemed it unfit.**[67]
37 **Who is this,** what enemy could there be, **who said** that he would harm Israel **and it occurred,** whose declaration was fulfilled, **if the Lord did not command** it? If Israel suffers harm, it is certainly a divine decree.[68]
38 **From the mouth of the Most High, evil and good do not emerge.** God leaves the world in the hands of man's free will.[69]
39 When all is said and done, **what shall a living man complain?** His complaints about his difficulties and troubles are unjustified, as **each man for his sins.**[D] His dire situation is merely the result of his own evil deeds.[70]
40 Therefore, **let us search and examine our ways, and return to the Lord.**
41 **Let us lift up our heart with our hands, to God in the heavens.** Let us rip out our heart and give it, as it were, to God.[71]
42 Despite the call for appeasement and hope, notwithstanding the theodicy and logical explanations, the cry toward God reemerges: Although **we have transgressed and defied,** and we were therefore deserving of punishment, nevertheless, we would have expected You to pardon us, not only the way a master pardons his slaves, but as a father forgives his children.[72] However, **You have not forgiven.**
43 **You are covered with wrath,** or: You distanced yourself and hid behind a wall of wrath,[73] **and have pursued us; You killed; You did not have compassion.**
44 **You have covered Yourself,** as if **with a cloud, so that no prayer can pass** through, as though the gates of heaven are closed to our prayers.[74] The prophet speaks here in the name of all the people of Israel.
45 **You render us**[75] **filth and refuse in the midst of the peoples.**
46 **All our enemies have opened their mouth** wide **against us,** and we cannot respond.
47 **Terror and a trap,** or obstacles,[76] **came upon us, desolation and disaster.**[77]
48 The prophet returns to speaking in first person singular: When faced with our shameful state among the nations, **streams of water pour down from my eye,** crying **for the disaster of the daughter of my people.**
49 **My eye will flow** with tears **and will not cease,**[78] **from lack of respite.** The tears do not cease because there is no respite from our troubles.[79]
50 I cry continuously, **until the Lord looks out and sees** our misery **from the heavens,** and redeems us soon. Expressions of hope, loyalty, and faith in future salvation again come to the fore.
51 **My eye distressed my soul,**[80] or contaminated my soul,[81] **more than all the daughters of my city.** Alternatively: Jeremiah is lamenting over the fact that he has seen all of his neighbors and relatives going into exile or getting killed, while his own sobbing eyes are the only ones left to cry for all the rest, like an incompletely formed cluster of grapes [*olelet*] left on the vine during the harvest.
52 **My enemies hunted me like a bird** is hunted, **without cause.**
53 **They bound my life in the pit.**[82] **And** furthermore, they **cast stones at me.**
54 The pit was full of water; **waters rose over my head. I said: I am doomed.** My end has come.
55 **I called** upon **Your name,** I prayed to You, **Lord, from the depths of the pit.**[D]

"My enemies hunted me like a bird." Hunting birds, relief, Tomb of Nebamun, Eighteenth Dynasty, Egypt

56 **You heard my voice,** which is itself a minor salvation; please, **let Your ear not disregard my cry, for my comfort.** The prophet begs God not to ignore his plea, so that his conditions may improve.[83]
57 I had hope when **You approached on the day that I called You. You said** to me: **Do not fear.**
58 In the end, **Lord, You have fought the battles of my soul; You redeemed my life.**
59 **Lord, You have seen my wrongs,** the injustice that was done to me;[84] please **adjudicate my case.**
60 **You have seen all their,** the enemies', **vengeance, all their** evil **thoughts against me.**

לד לה עָנָה מִלִּבּוֹ וַיַּגֶּה בְּנֵי־אִישׁ׃ לְדַכֵּא תַּחַת רַגְלָיו כֹּל אֲסִירֵי אָרֶץ׃ לְהַטּוֹת מִשְׁפַּט־
לו לז גָּבֶר נֶגֶד פְּנֵי עֶלְיוֹן׃ לְעַוֵּת אָדָם בְּרִיבוֹ אֲדֹנָי לֹא רָאָה׃ מִי זֶה אָמַר וַתֶּהִי אֲדֹנָי לֹא
לח לט צִוָּה׃ מִפִּי עֶלְיוֹן לֹא תֵצֵא הָרָעוֹת וְהַטּוֹב׃ מַה־יִּתְאוֹנֵן אָדָם חָי גֶּבֶר עַל־חֲטָאָו׃
מ מא נַחְפְּשָׂה דְרָכֵינוּ וְנַחְקֹרָה וְנָשׁוּבָה עַד־יְהוָה׃ נִשָּׂא לְבָבֵנוּ אֶל־כַּפָּיִם אֶל־אֵל
מב מג בַּשָּׁמָיִם׃ נַחְנוּ פָשַׁעְנוּ וּמָרִינוּ אַתָּה לֹא סָלָחְתָּ׃ סַכּוֹתָה בָאַף וַתִּרְדְּפֵנוּ הָרַגְתָּ לֹא
מד מה חָמָלְתָּ׃ סַכֹּתָה בֶעָנָן לָךְ מֵעֲבוֹר תְּפִלָּה׃ סְחִי וּמָאוֹס תְּשִׂימֵנוּ בְּקֶרֶב הָעַמִּים׃
מו מז מח פָּצוּ עָלֵינוּ פִּיהֶם כָּל־אֹיְבֵינוּ׃ פַּחַד וָפַחַת הָיָה לָנוּ הַשֵּׁאת וְהַשָּׁבֶר׃ פַּלְגֵי־מַיִם
מט נ תֵּרַד עֵינִי עַל־שֶׁבֶר בַּת־עַמִּי׃ עֵינִי נִגְּרָה וְלֹא תִדְמֶה מֵאֵין הֲפֻגוֹת׃ עַד־יַשְׁקִיף
נא נב וְיֵרֶא יְהוָה מִשָּׁמָיִם׃ עֵינִי עוֹלְלָה לְנַפְשִׁי מִכֹּל בְּנוֹת עִירִי׃ צוֹד צָדוּנִי כַּצִּפּוֹר אֹיְבַי
נג נד נה חִנָּם׃ צָמְתוּ בַבּוֹר חַיָּי וַיַּדּוּ־אֶבֶן בִּי׃ צָפוּ־מַיִם עַל־רֹאשִׁי אָמַרְתִּי נִגְזָרְתִּי׃ קָרָאתִי
נו שִׁמְךָ יְהוָה מִבּוֹר תַּחְתִּיּוֹת׃ קוֹלִי שָׁמָעְתָּ אַל־תַּעְלֵם אָזְנְךָ לְרַוְחָתִי לְשַׁוְעָתִי׃
נז נח קָרַבְתָּ בְּיוֹם אֶקְרָאֶךָּ אָמַרְתָּ אַל־תִּירָא׃ רַבְתָּ אֲדֹנָי רִיבֵי נַפְשִׁי גָּאַלְתָּ חַיָּי׃
נט ס רָאִיתָה יְהוָה עַוָּתָתִי שָׁפְטָה מִשְׁפָּטִי׃ רָאִיתָה כָּל־נִקְמָתָם כָּל־מַחְשְׁבֹתָם לִי׃
סא סב שָׁמַעְתָּ חֶרְפָּתָם יְהוָה כָּל־מַחְשְׁבֹתָם עָלָי׃ שִׂפְתֵי קָמַי וְהֶגְיוֹנָם עָלַי כָּל־הַיּוֹם׃

61 **You heard their taunt,**[85] **Lord, all their thoughts about me.** When Jeremiah's harsh prophecies for the future did not materialize, his listeners would ridicule him and throw stones at him. When the prophecies were eventually fulfilled, the same people took revenge against him, as though he were to blame for the events, even though his statements had been meant merely to warn them.

62 **The lips,** the words, **of those who rise against me, and their thoughts, are against me all day.** In all their statements and thoughts, I am considered the sole guilty party.[86]

DISCUSSION

3:39 | **What shall a living man complain? Each man for his sins:** King David said similarly: "Evil shall kill the wicked" (Psalms 34:22). Evil deeds are the cause of their author's misfortunes.

3:53–55 | **They bound my life in the pit…waters rose over my head…from the depths of the pit:** These are not merely metaphoric expressions of confinement and humiliation; according to the book of Jeremiah (38:6), this actually happened to Jeremiah: "They took Jeremiah and they cast him into the pit of Malkiyahu the king's son, which was in the court of internment, and they lowered Jeremiah with ropes. And in the pit there was no water but only mud, and Jeremiah was drowning in the mud."

63 **Look at their sitting and their rising,** look at what they do constantly; **I am** the subject of **their song,** the object of their mockery and ridicule.
64 **Pay them retribution, Lord,** punish them, **according to their handiwork.**
65 **May you give them hardness of heart,** troubles that seal up the heart;[87] may **Your curse** be **upon them.**[88]
66 **May you pursue them in wrath and destroy them from beneath the heavens of the Lord.**

The Destruction of the Precious Sons of Zion

LAMENTATIONS 4:1–22

Due to its sins, Jerusalem was filled with victims, those dead of starvation and those killed by the sword. This lamentation describes the deterioration of the people of Jerusalem, from their previous stature as a refined population, to the lowest level it is possible to reach, through siege and war. The residents of Jerusalem had placed their trust in foreign aid and had also hoped that their king would save them, but their hopes were dashed. The lamentation ends with words of comfort: Edom, which rejoices in the misfortune of Israel, will be destroyed too, and Jerusalem's disaster will end.

4 1 **How can** shiny **gold tarnish?**[89] How can the appearance of **the fine gold change?**[90] **The sacred stones are spilled at the head of every street.** How is all that was beautiful and precious disgraced and gone to waste?
2 **The precious sons of Zion, who were valued as gold,**[91] **how are they** now **considered** as worthless as **earthenware jugs, the handiwork of the hands of the potter?**
3 **Even jackals take out a breast,**[B] **nurse their pups.** Even these animals, some of whom are predatory, are merciful in certain situations; but **the daughter of my people has become cruel.** The mothers of Jerusalem are malnourished; their breasts have shriveled, and their survival instincts prevent them from supplying the needs of their children.[92] They are **like ostriches,**[B] who abandon their offspring[93] **in the wilderness.** This is what has befallen Israel. Jerusalem has become like a wilderness, a place where people do not care for each other.

Female jackal and her offspring

"Nurse their pups." Female whale and her offspring

"Ostriches in the wilderness"

4 **The tongue of the suckling babe sticks to its palate from thirst,** because there is no milk for the nursing infants; **infants request bread, and no one breaks it for them,** because of the siege upon Jerusalem.
5 **The eaters of delicacies are** now **desolate** and penniless **in the streets; those reared**[94] **in** expensive **scarlet** garments now **embrace heaps of refuse,** as they are left with nothing.
6 **The iniquity of the daughter of my people** must have **exceeded the sin of Sodom,** as her punishment was more severe than that of Sodom, **which was overthrown in a moment, and no** enemy **hands seized it,** whereas in Jerusalem the suffering is continuous.[95]
7 In past times, **its,** Jerusalem's, **nazirites used to be purer than snow, whiter than milk; their appearance**[96] **was ruddier than gems,**[B] **their form a sapphire.**

Sapphire

Gems

8 The people of Jerusalem were clean, pure, refined, and beautiful. In better times, they engaged only in matters of holiness. Now, however, **their countenance is blacker than coal; they are not recognized in the streets. Their skin is shriveled on their bones;**[97] **it has become dry as wood.**
9 **Those killed by sword** in battle **were better off than those killed by hunger, for** from their **ruptured** bodies,[98] **they,** the victims of hunger, **leak with,** emit various liquids from, **the produce of the field.**[99] Alternatively, "these" refers to the victims of the sword, who were stabbed through while sated.[100]
10 **The hands of merciful women cooked their children; they,** the children, **were food for them,** their mothers,[101] **in** the time of **the disaster of the daughter of my people.**

סג סד שִׁבְתָּם וְקִימָתָם הַבִּיטָה אֲנִי מַנְגִּינָתָם: תָּשִׁיב לָהֶם גְּמוּל יהוה כְּמַעֲשֵׂה יְדֵיהֶם:
סה סו תִּתֵּן לָהֶם מְגִנַּת־לֵב תַּאֲלָתְךָ לָהֶם: תִּרְדֹּף בְּאַף וְתַשְׁמִידֵם מִתַּחַת שְׁמֵי יהוה:
א אֵיכָה יוּעַם זָהָב יִשְׁנֶא הַכֶּתֶם הַטּוֹב תִּשְׁתַּפֵּכְנָה אַבְנֵי־קֹדֶשׁ בְּרֹאשׁ כָּל־חוּצוֹת:
ב בְּנֵי צִיּוֹן הַיְקָרִים הַמְסֻלָּאִים בַּפָּז אֵיכָה נֶחְשְׁבוּ לְנִבְלֵי־חֶרֶשׂ מַעֲשֵׂה יְדֵי יוֹצֵר:
ג ד גַּם־תנין חָלְצוּ שַׁד הֵינִיקוּ גּוּרֵיהֶן בַּת־עַמִּי לְאַכְזָר כי ענים בַּמִּדְבָּר: דָּבַק לְשׁוֹן
ה יוֹנֵק אֶל־חִכּוֹ בַּצָּמָא עוֹלָלִים שָׁאֲלוּ לֶחֶם פֹּרֵשׂ אֵין לָהֶם: הָאֹכְלִים לְמַעֲדַנִּים נָשַׁמּוּ
ו בַּחוּצוֹת הָאֱמֻנִים עֲלֵי תוֹלָע חִבְּקוּ אַשְׁפַּתּוֹת: וַיִּגְדַּל עֲוֹן בַּת־עַמִּי מֵחַטַּאת סְדֹם
ז הַהֲפוּכָה כְמוֹ־רָגַע וְלֹא־חָלוּ בָהּ יָדָיִם: זַכּוּ נְזִירֶיהָ מִשֶּׁלֶג צַחוּ מֵחָלָב אָדְמוּ עֶצֶם
ח מִפְּנִינִים סַפִּיר גִּזְרָתָם: חָשַׁךְ מִשְּׁחוֹר תָּאֳרָם לֹא נִכְּרוּ בַּחוּצוֹת צָפַד עוֹרָם עַל־
ט עַצְמָם יָבֵשׁ הָיָה כָעֵץ: טוֹבִים הָיוּ חַלְלֵי־חֶרֶב מֵחַלְלֵי רָעָב שֶׁהֵם יָזוּבוּ מְדֻקָּרִים
י מִתְּנוּבֹת שָׂדָי: יְדֵי נָשִׁים רַחֲמָנִיּוֹת בִּשְּׁלוּ יַלְדֵיהֶן הָיוּ לְבָרוֹת לָמוֹ בְּשֶׁבֶר בַּת־

תַּנִּים
כַּיְעֵנִים

BACKGROUND

4:3 | **Jackals [*tannim*] take out a breast:** According to the written text, the word is spelled *tannin*. This leads to the interpretation by some that the verse is referring to whales, which did exist in the Mediterranean Sea, though it is not their natural habitat. It may be suggested that the expression "take out a breast" supports this interpretation, as the nursing parts of the female whale are covered in pockets of skin and need to be drawn out for nursing. On the other hand, according to the traditional vocalization of the text, the word is *tannim*, the plural of *tan*, which is a jackal, an animal similar to a fox that feeds on various animals and carrion. The *tan* is mentioned in the Bible as a howling desert animal. This interpretation of the verse is supported by the comparison to the ostrich, another desert animal (see Isaiah 13:21–22, 34:13; 43:20). Alternatively, some identify the *tan* with the Pharaoh eagle-owl (*bubo ascalaphus*), a nocturnal bird of prey that dwells in ruins and crevices.

Like ostriches [*ye'enim*]: An ostrich does not have a nest; it leaves its eggs on the ground, without incubation. Perhaps for this reason it is described as cruel toward its offspring. A similar behavior is criticized in the book of Job (39:13–15): "The wing of the songbird beats joyously; are its pinions and its plumage of a stork? For it leaves its eggs on the earth and warms them on dust, and it forgets that a foot may crush it or a beast of the field trample it." There is an opinion that the term *ye'enim* refers not to a type of animal, but is the name of a tribe, based on one reading of Psalms 55:20 (*Tur Sinai*).

4:7 | **Gems [*peninim*]:** In biblical Hebrew and in the Aramaic translations of the Bible, *peninim* are specific kinds of round precious stones, or alternatively, a generic word for all precious stones. In Ibn Ezra's commentary on Song of Songs (5:14), he interprets *peninim* to mean sapphires. However, others maintain that the term refers to pearls, which are formed in seashells from organic matter and are generally white, silver, or black. In ancient Egyptian, a similar word denotes a spherical marble, and in Akkadian, there is a similar word that refers to a precious stone that comes from the sea and perhaps means pearl or coral.

11 **The Lord vented His fury, He poured out His enflamed wrath. He kindled a fire in Zion, and it consumed** even **its foundations.**

12 **The kings of the earth and all the inhabitants of the world did not believe that a besieger and enemy would enter the gates of Jerusalem,**[B] which was such a central, fortified, and secure city.

"The gates of Jerusalem." Damascus Gate, 1910

13 **It,** this entire catastrophe, **was due to the sins of her** false **prophets,**[102] and because **of the iniquities of her priests, who shed the blood of the righteous in her midst,** in order to achieve wealth and honor.

14 The entire city was filled with the blood of the dead. **They wandered blind in the streets.** Alternatively, blind men wander in the streets without a guide, **having been sullied with blood,** as they could not see where the corpses were, **so that one could not touch their** filthy **garments.**

15 It was necessary to warn those approaching: **Turn away, impure, they called to them; turn away, turn away, do not touch, because they were begrimed,** had become dirty, **as well as wandering. They said among the nations: They will not continue to reside here,** in our land, or in Jerusalem.[103]

16 **The attention of the Lord has divided them;** God has scattered them in His anger.[104] **He will not continue to look at them,** as **they did not respect priests and were not gracious to elders.** They did not help the needy.[105]

17 **Our eyes yet fail, seeking deliverance in vain;** our hopes for help have turned out to be in vain. **In our waiting, we awaited a** foreign **nation that** we hoped would come to our aid, but it **cannot save** us.[106]

18 **They,** the enemies, **hunted our steps,** even preventing us[107] **from walking in our squares; our end approaches, our days are filled, as our end has come.**

19 Even those who did not stay in the city could not find refuge because **our pursuers were swifter than the eagles**[B] **of the heavens,** and they captured us. **They chased us on the mountains; they ambushed us in the wilderness.**

20 **The breath of our nostrils, the anointed of the Lord,**[D] a reference to the king of Judah, who was anointed with a special oil, **was captured in their traps.** This is the king **of whom we said: In his shade we will live among the nations.**

21 The lamenter expresses bitter scorn toward the people of Edom, who, during this period, enjoyed calm and bliss: **Be glad and rejoice, daughter of Edom,**[D] **who resides in the land of Utz.**[B] But not for long, as **the cup** of vengeance and destruction **will pass to you too; you will get drunk** from drinking it, **and you will be overturned,** ruined.[108]

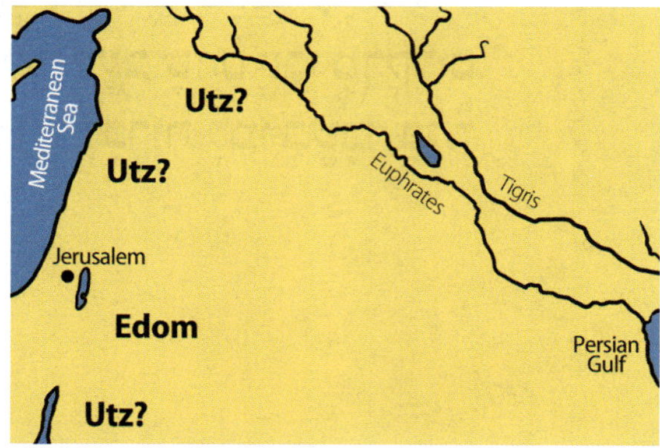

Possible locations for the land of Utz

22 **Your iniquity is completed, daughter of Zion; He,** God, **will not continue to exile you.** You have received the entire punishment that you deserved and have consequently paid for all your sins. On the other hand, **He reckons your iniquity, daughter of Edom; He will expose your sins.** He will yet settle His account with you for your sins.

DISCUSSION

4:20 | **The anointed of the Lord:** The Sages identified this king as Yoshiya, the last great king of Judah, upon whom Israel placed their final hope for defense. This hope ended in disappointment when Yoshiya was shot dead by the Egyptian army (II Chronicles 35:23; *Tosefta*, *Ta'anit* 2:10; see introduction to this lamentation).

4:21 | **Edom:** The people of Edom supported Judah's enemies and mocked the inhabitants of Jerusalem during their destruction (see Obadiah 1:12–14). The final word of this verse is the rare verb *titari*, used by the prophet to prophesy the destruction of Edom. It literally means "you shall make yourself naked"; its implied meaning is that Israel will be overturned, torn down, and ruined. It paraphrases Edom's joyous exclamation when they celebrated Israel's defeat, encouraging their total destruction (Psalms 137:7): "Tear it down [*aru*], tear it down [*aru*], until its very foundation."

יא יב עַמִּי: כִּלָּה יהוה אֶת־חֲמָתוֹ שָׁפַךְ חֲרוֹן אַפּוֹ וַיַּצֶּת־אֵשׁ בְּצִיּוֹן וַתֹּאכַל יְסוֹדֹתֶיהָ: לֹא
יג הֶאֱמִינוּ מַלְכֵי־אֶרֶץ וכל יֹשְׁבֵי תֵבֵל כִּי יָבֹא צַר וְאוֹיֵב בְּשַׁעֲרֵי יְרוּשָׁלִָם: מֵחַטֹּאת כֹּל
יד נְבִיאֶיהָ עֲוֺנֹת כֹּהֲנֶיהָ הַשֹּׁפְכִים בְּקִרְבָּהּ דַּם צַדִּיקִים: נָעוּ עִוְרִים בַּחוּצוֹת נְגֹאֲלוּ
טו בַּדָּם בְּלֹא יוּכְלוּ יִגְּעוּ בִּלְבֻשֵׁיהֶם: סוּרוּ טָמֵא קָרְאוּ לָמוֹ סוּרוּ סוּרוּ אַל־תִּגָּעוּ כִּי
טז נָצוּ גַּם־נָעוּ אָמְרוּ בַּגּוֹיִם לֹא יוֹסִפוּ לָגוּר: פְּנֵי יהוה חִלְּקָם לֹא יוֹסִיף לְהַבִּיטָם
יז פְּנֵי כֹהֲנִים לֹא נָשָׂאוּ זקנים לֹא חָנָנוּ: עודינה תִּכְלֶינָה עֵינֵינוּ אֶל־עֶזְרָתֵנוּ הָבֶל וּזְקֵנִים עוֹדֵינוּ
יח בְּצִפִּיָּתֵנוּ צִפִּינוּ אֶל־גּוֹי לֹא יוֹשִׁעַ: צָדוּ צְעָדֵינוּ מִלֶּכֶת בִּרְחֹבֹתֵינוּ קָרַב קִצֵּנוּ
יט מָלְאוּ יָמֵינוּ כִּי־בָא קִצֵּנוּ: קַלִּים הָיוּ רֹדְפֵינוּ מִנִּשְׁרֵי שָׁמָיִם עַל־הֶהָרִים דְּלָקֻנוּ
כ בַּמִּדְבָּר אָרְבוּ לָנוּ: רוּחַ אַפֵּינוּ מְשִׁיחַ יהוה נִלְכַּד בִּשְׁחִיתוֹתָם אֲשֶׁר אָמַרְנוּ בְּצִלּוֹ
כא נִחְיֶה בַגּוֹיִם: שִׂישִׂי וְשִׂמְחִי בַּת־אֱדוֹם יושבתי בְּאֶרֶץ עוּץ גַּם־עָלַיִךְ תַּעֲבָר־כּוֹס יוֹשֶׁבֶת
כב תִּשְׁכְּרִי וְתִתְעָרִי: תַּם־עֲוֺנֵךְ בַּת־צִיּוֹן לֹא יוֹסִיף לְהַגְלוֹתֵךְ פָּקַד עֲוֺנֵךְ בַּת־אֱדוֹם
גִּלָּה עַל־חַטֹּאתָיִךְ:

BACKGROUND

4:12 | **That a besieger and enemy would enter the gates of Jerusalem:** Nebuchadnezzar's conquest of Jerusalem and his subsequent coronation of Tzidkiya are described in a Babylonian chronicle that was discovered during excavations of the city of Babylon: "In the seventh year of the month of Kislev, the king of Akkad [Nebuchadnezzar] gathered his soldiers and went to the land of the Hitites [Syria and Israel], and encamped by the city of Judah; and in the month of Adar, on the second day [of the month], he seized the city and captured the king, appointed in it a king whom he trusted, and took a heavy tax from it, and came to Babylon."

4:19 | **Eagle [*nesher*]:** Some explain that this is the griffon vulture, *Gyps fulvus*, a large bird that nests and soars at markedly high altitudes, which enables it to glide swiftly toward its food (see Jeremiah 48:40; Obadiah 1:4; Micah 1:16; Habakkuk 1:8; Job 39:27–28). This bird was a royal symbol in both Egypt and Assyria. Its wingspan stretches to 2.5 m and it weighs roughly 10 kg. Its head and neck are bare of feathers, as though they were plucked [*nashar*]; perhaps this accounts for the name. Some identify the *nesher* with the golden eagle, *Aquila chrysaetos*, which was an important Roman symbol, while yet others maintain that *nesher* is a general term that refers to several different types of birds of prey.

4:21 | **The land of Utz:** Apparently, there were several lands called Utz. In Genesis there is a son of Aram named Utz (10:23). In addition, the land of Utz appears as one of the lands of the Children of the East in the book of Job (1:3). Therefore, some place it somewhere in or near modern-day Syria. Ancient historians, e.g., Josephus Flavius, identified it as being in an area of the Bashan, now known as the Golan Heights. In addition, there was a grandson of Se'ir named Utz (Genesis 36:28), and that source and the verse here indicate that there was also a land called Utz in the Edomite region further south, in what is now Jordan.

Humiliation, Orphanhood, and Eternal Hope

LAMENTATIONS 5:1–22

This lamentation is different from the others in that it is not an alphabetical acrostic. But it is similar to most of them in that it has twenty-two verses, and in addition, like the previous lamentations, the suffering and troubles of the people of Jerusalem are described. Toward the end, the lamenter focuses his anguish on the destruction of Mount Zion, the source of his heartache. However, he emphasizes that although God's dwelling place in the world has been destroyed, He still remains. This provides hope for the restoration of the relationship and the covenant between God and His people.

5 1 **Remember, Lord, what befell us,** our terrible troubles. Alternatively, this means: Remember our glorious past, and on the other hand, **look and see our** current **disgrace.**[109]

2 **Our inheritance has been transferred to strangers,** after they invaded and plundered it, **our houses** have been given **to foreigners.**

3 **We have become orphans, fatherless; our mothers are like widows.**[110]

4 When the water reservoirs were full, there was no need to pay for water;[111] but during the siege, **our water we drank for money.** In better days, there was no shortage of wood that could be collected easily; now, **our wood comes at a price.**

5 Up **to our necks we were pursued; we are exhausted, and we have no respite.**

6 **We extended a hand to Egypt,** to receive financial aid from them. This may be referring to Tzidkiya's covenant with Egypt.[112] And we went to **Assyria, to be sated with bread;** but help came from neither kingdom.[113]

7 **Our fathers have sinned and are no more, and we have suffered** not only for our own sins, but for **their iniquities** as well.

8 **Servants rule over us.** The true kingdom has fallen, and as naturally happens when the government is weak, people from the bottom of society have risen to greatness. **There is none to deliver us from their hand.**

9 **We bring our bread at the peril of our lives due to the sword of the wilderness.** In order to obtain food, we must put our lives at risk by traveling through the desert, which is frequented by robbers.[114] Alternatively: In order to survive during the war we must bring food from faraway places, even from the wilderness.

10 **Our skin burns like an oven,**[115] or has shriveled as though it were baked in an oven,[116] **due to fear of famine.**

11 When the enemy soldiers invaded the city, **they raped women in Zion, virgins in the cities of Judah.**

12 **Princes were hanged by their hand.** The enemies would hang the dignitaries of Jerusalem by their hands as a punishment, for show, or in order to extract information from them. **The faces of elders were not shown deference.** No one honored the elders.

13 **The young,** strong **men carried the mill;** they were ordered to carry the mill on their shoulders so that this would wear them out.[117] **And the lads,** who were chained, **stumbled on the wood** to which they were chained.[118]

"Princes were hanged by their hand." Men of Judah hanged, Lakhish reliefs, Nineveh, 701 BCE

14 **The elders have ceased from** sitting at **the** city **gate,** as there is no longer anyone to listen to them. **The young men** have ceased **from their music** and parties.

15 **The gladness of our heart has ceased; our** joyous **dance has been transformed into mourning.**

16 **The crown has fallen from our head;** our honor is lost. Alternatively, this may refer to the crown and honor of the monarchy. **Woe to us, for we have sinned.**

17 **For this our heart suffers; for these our eyes are dim:**

18 **for Mount Zion,**[D] the Temple Mount, **which is desolate;** its past vitality is gone, and **foxes,** who commonly dwell in desolate areas, **walk on it.**

19 Despite the anguish, the book ends on a note of acceptance and hope: **You, Lord, are enthroned forever; Your throne is** secure **from generation to generation.** Although God's residency in this world is the mountain of Zion, which is now desolate, His heavenly throne is independent of worldly events, and it will stand forever.[119]

20 But as for us, **why do You forget us forever, forsake us for the length of** our **days?**

21 **Return us to You, Lord, and** if You do so, **we will return;** we will return to You, willingly and actively. **Renew our days as of old,** like the days when You loved us and honored us.

22 **For You have despised us,** or: You have indeed despised us. **You have been exceedingly angry with us.** We have suffered more than enough humiliation; our debt has been paid.

The penultimate verse is repeated in a communal recitation:

Return us to You, Lord, and we will return; renew our days as of old.[D]

א ב זְכֹר יְהוָה מֶה־הָיָה לָנוּ הַבִּיטָ וּרְאֵה אֶת־חֶרְפָּתֵנוּ׃ נַחֲלָתֵנוּ נֶהֶפְכָה לְזָרִים בָּתֵּינוּ
ג ד לְנָכְרִים׃ יְתוֹמִים הָיִינוּ אין אָב אִמֹּתֵינוּ כְּאַלְמָנוֹת׃ מֵימֵינוּ בְּכֶסֶף שָׁתִינוּ עֵצֵינוּ וְאֵין
ה ו בִּמְחִיר יָבֹאוּ׃ עַל צַוָּארֵנוּ נִרְדָּפְנוּ יָגַעְנוּ לא הוּנַח־לָנוּ׃ מִצְרַיִם נָתַנּוּ יָד אַשּׁוּר וְלֹא
ז ח לִשְׂבֹּעַ לָחֶם׃ אֲבֹתֵינוּ חָטְאוּ אינם אנחנו עֲוֹנֹתֵיהֶם סָבָלְנוּ׃ עֲבָדִים מָשְׁלוּ בָנוּ וְאֵינָם וַאֲנַחְנוּ
ט י פֹּרֵק אֵין מִיָּדָם׃ בְּנַפְשֵׁנוּ נָבִיא לַחְמֵנוּ מִפְּנֵי חֶרֶב הַמִּדְבָּר׃ עוֹרֵנוּ כְּתַנּוּר נִכְמָרוּ
יא יב מִפְּנֵי זַלְעֲפוֹת רָעָב׃ נָשִׁים בְּצִיּוֹן עִנּוּ בְּתֻלֹת בְּעָרֵי יְהוּדָה׃ שָׂרִים בְּיָדָם נִתְלוּ
יג יד פְּנֵי זְקֵנִים לֹא נֶהְדָּרוּ׃ בַּחוּרִים טְחוֹן נָשָׂאוּ וּנְעָרִים בָּעֵץ כָּשָׁלוּ׃ זְקֵנִים מִשַּׁעַר
טו טז שָׁבָתוּ בַּחוּרִים מִנְּגִינָתָם׃ שָׁבַת מְשׂוֹשׂ לִבֵּנוּ נֶהְפַּךְ לְאֵבֶל מְחוֹלֵנוּ׃ נָפְלָה עֲטֶרֶת
יז רֹאשֵׁנוּ אוֹי־נָא לָנוּ כִּי חָטָאנוּ׃ עַל־זֶה הָיָה דָוֶה לִבֵּנוּ עַל־אֵלֶּה חָשְׁכוּ עֵינֵינוּ׃
יח יט עַל הַר־צִיּוֹן שֶׁשָּׁמֵם שׁוּעָלִים הִלְּכוּ־בוֹ׃ אַתָּה יְהוָה לְעוֹלָם תֵּשֵׁב כִּסְאֲךָ לְדוֹר
כ כא וָדוֹר׃ לָמָּה לָנֶצַח תִּשְׁכָּחֵנוּ תַּעַזְבֵנוּ לְאֹרֶךְ יָמִים׃ הֲשִׁיבֵנוּ יְהוָה ׀ אֵלֶיךָ וְנָשׁוּב
כב חַדֵּשׁ יָמֵינוּ כְּקֶדֶם׃ כִּי אִם־מָאֹס מְאַסְתָּנוּ קָצַפְתָּ עָלֵינוּ עַד־מְאֹד׃

השיבנו יהוה אליך ונשובה חדש ימינו כקדם

DISCUSSION

5:18 | **Mount Zion:** In the book of Isaiah, the Temple Mount is commonly referred to as the mountain of Zion.

5:21 | **Renew our days as of old:** There are several books in the Bible that conclude on a negative note, and the custom is to repeat the second to last verse, which has a more optimistic tone, in order to finish the book with a positive message (see the final verses of Isaiah, Malachi, and Ecclesiastes). In the context of Lamentations, ending the book with this verse is an expression of the hope to renew Israel's relationship with God and restore it to its state at the beginning of the people's history. A similar aspiration appears in Malachi (3:4): "Then shall the offering of Judah and Jerusalem be pleasant to the Lord, as in the days of old, and as in ancient years." This verse is recited at the end of the *Amida* prayer.

Ecclesiastes

Ecclesiastes

INTRODUCTION TO ECCLESIASTES

Ecclesiastes is not a book of enthusiasm born of faith. Rather, the book of Ecclesiastes is based on human musings and insights. The speaker, Kohelet, critiques the state of affairs in the world in general and the way people conduct their lives in particular. Therefore, much negativity is expressed in it, and the decision to incorporate it into the biblical canon aroused opposition.[1]

Three books of the Bible are attributed to King Solomon: Proverbs, the Song of Songs, in which his authorship is explicitly mentioned, and Ecclesiastes, in which he appears by an alternative name. Although all three books share certain philosophical and linguistic features, overall they differ greatly from each other. It has therefore been suggested that they were composed at various stages of King Solomon's life. According to one opinion in the Midrash, Solomon wrote Song of Songs, which is a love song, in his youth; the book of Proverbs, which contains practical advice and guidance for appropriate behavior, in middle age; and after he had experienced all the adversities of life and grown old, he wrote Ecclesiastes, which deems all the toil and adventures of life, its ups and downs, as mere futility.[2]

This book articulates the thoughts of a wise, mature man who does not presume to offer a unified, coherent picture of reality beyond what he himself understands based on his rich experiences and the vicissitudes of his life. The central theme of the book is stripping the value and meaning from all matters of the world. The book provides some conventional words of wisdom and morality, but concurrently poses an unfathomable question with regard to the patterns of human existence, its significance and stability, and the congruence of visible reality with values of morality and justice. Positive faith in and of itself is not depicted in Ecclesiastes in a systematic, detailed manner, and those positive statements that occasionally surface are not easily reconcilable with its other statements.

Kohelet's recommendations are far more complex than the advice that appears in the book of Proverbs. There, King Solomon instructs the reader unambiguously to choose good and refrain from evil, while the book of Ecclesiastes describes the path of a man considering the world in which he lives and functions with considerable practical success; however, his attempt does not yield the results that he anticipated, and therefore he struggles to find purpose in life.

It is interesting to note that specifically in this book, in which human existence and the reality of this world are described as futile, there are several instances where the existence of the spirit independent of the body surfaces, a ray of optimism in the midst of the futility. Alone among the books of the Bible, Ecclesiastes speaks explicitly of a person's soul that returns to God after the body returns to dust (3:20). Ecclesiastes also mentions the existence of souls not yet born (see, e.g., 4:3).

The circular attempts to address all these topics, the recurring accounts of the author's search for new insights into the nature of human existence, and the frustrating return to the original point that all is futility are consistent with the content of the book. Both by means of the book's internal contradictions, as well as its tortuous structure, which resists any attempt to discover a consistent order or framework, Kohelet is saying that the world, in all its detail, is filled with trouble, confrontation, and pain. Kohelet also reveals that the world and human life are insipid. He repudiates accepted frameworks without suggesting alternatives. The reader, whom Kohelet has convinced that meaning cannot be found in this world, is left with two options: Holding on to that which is beyond this futile existence, that is, fear of God and the observance of His commandments, or living a life of delusion.

Ecclesiastes

Introduction and Summary

ECCLESIASTES 1:1–11

The opening verses of Ecclesiastes are also verses of summation. Its central themes are condensed into these verses: Everything is futile, everything passes, everything recurs, and there is no purpose.

1 1 **The words of Kohelet,** another name for Solomon,[3] whose words of wisdom many people gathered [*nikhalu*] to hear, **son of David,** who was **king in Jerusalem.**

2 **Futility of futilities,** the world is absolute futility, **says Kohelet; futility of futilities, all is futility.**[D] Kohelet characterizes all reality as lacking substance and significance.[4]

3 **What advantage is there for man in all his toil that he toils under the sun**[D] in this world? Many events transpire here, but none of them is significant. Moreover, even when a matter of significance transpires, or a valuable item is discovered, it soon vanishes without a trace. At times, the one responsible for the event or the discovery ultimately realizes its futility himself, while at other times only future generations will arrive at that realization.[5]

4 **A generation goes and a generation comes, and the earth stands forever.** Despite all the activity and the many apparent changes, the earth remains in place. The entire world is bound to a cyclicality that does not lead to any change.

5 **The sun rises and the sun sets and seeks** to continue uninterrupted to **its place; it rises there,** where it rose the previous day.[6] Faced with this fixed circular mechanism, one comes to question how one day differs from another.

"The sun rises"

"And the sun sets"

6 But the movements of the sun change slightly with the seasons: **It goes to the south** of the sky during winter **and turns** more **to the north** in summer; **it turns and turns, goes in a** different **direction [*ruaḥ*], and in its circuit it returns to its** original **direction.**[7] Some commentaries hold that this verse refers not to the movements of the sun but to those of the wind [*ruaḥ*].[8] The wind was one of the four basic elements into which the world was thought to be divided in ancient times, earth, fire, wind, and water, and which are alluded to in these verses.

7 **All the streams go to the sea,** flowing continuously, **yet the sea is** still **not full; to the place that the streams go, there they go again,** in the fixed water cycle.[9]

"The streams go to the sea"

8 **All matters are wearying.** People take action and take action again, and exhaust themselves. **A man is unable to speak** everything that he would want to say, **the eye will not be satisfied to see** everything that it would want to see, **and the ear will not be filled from hearing** what it wants to hear.

9 In summary, **that which was is that which will be, and that which was done is that which will be done; there is nothing new under the sun.** Events transpire over and over again in a recurring cycle.

10 **There is a matter of which one would say: See, this is new. It has already been, in the ages that were before us.** Even when something appears to be novel, upon closer examination one realizes that it is the same old familiar object; perhaps there is a superficial change, but nothing more.

11 Kohelet returns to the subject with which he began:[10] Natural existence is fixed and cyclical, and one's exertion under the sun is of no avail and leaves no trace, as one generation goes and another generation comes, and **there is no memory of the earlier ones,** who have already disappeared. One might then think that later generations will be remembered because their actions will be documented. In response, Kohelet declares:

קהלת

א ב דִּבְרֵי קֹהֶלֶת בֶּן־דָּוִד מֶלֶךְ בִּירוּשָׁלָם׃ הֲבֵל הֲבָלִים אָמַר קֹהֶלֶת הֲבֵל הֲבָלִים הַכֹּל א
ג ד הָבֶל׃ מַה־יִּתְרוֹן לָאָדָם בְּכָל־עֲמָלוֹ שֶׁיַּעֲמֹל תַּחַת הַשָּׁמֶשׁ׃ דּוֹר הֹלֵךְ וְדוֹר בָּא
ה וְהָאָרֶץ לְעוֹלָם עֹמָדֶת׃ וְזָרַח הַשֶּׁמֶשׁ וּבָא הַשָּׁמֶשׁ וְאֶל־מְקוֹמוֹ שׁוֹאֵף זוֹרֵחַ הוּא
ו שָׁם׃ הוֹלֵךְ אֶל־דָּרוֹם וְסוֹבֵב אֶל־צָפוֹן סוֹבֵב ׀ סֹבֵב הוֹלֵךְ הָרוּחַ וְעַל־סְבִיבֹתָיו
ז שָׁב הָרוּחַ׃ כָּל־הַנְּחָלִים הֹלְכִים אֶל־הַיָּם וְהַיָּם אֵינֶנּוּ מָלֵא אֶל־מְקוֹם שֶׁהַנְּחָלִים
ח הֹלְכִים שָׁם הֵם שָׁבִים לָלָכֶת׃ כָּל־הַדְּבָרִים יְגֵעִים לֹא־יוּכַל אִישׁ לְדַבֵּר לֹא־תִשְׂבַּע
ט עַיִן לִרְאוֹת וְלֹא־תִמָּלֵא אֹזֶן מִשְּׁמֹעַ׃ מַה־שֶּׁהָיָה הוּא שֶׁיִּהְיֶה וּמַה־שֶּׁנַּעֲשָׂה
י הוּא שֶׁיֵּעָשֶׂה וְאֵין כָּל־חָדָשׁ תַּחַת הַשָּׁמֶשׁ׃ יֵשׁ דָּבָר שֶׁיֹּאמַר רְאֵה־זֶה חָדָשׁ
יא הוּא כְּבָר הָיָה לְעֹלָמִים אֲשֶׁר הָיָה מִלְּפָנֵנוּ׃ אֵין זִכְרוֹן לָרִאשֹׁנִים וְגַם לָאַחֲרֹנִים
שֶׁיִּהְיוּ לֹא־יִהְיֶה לָהֶם זִכָּרוֹן עִם שֶׁיִּהְיוּ לָאַחֲרֹנָה׃

DISCUSSION

1:2 | **Futility [*havel*]:** Many abstract nouns in biblical Hebrew are based on metaphors. The simple meaning of this term is vapor or fumes. In Ecclesiastes and elsewhere, it is employed as a reference to futility and meaninglessness.

1:3 | **Under the sun:** This expression appears numerous times in Ecclesiastes. Sometimes the parallel expression, "beneath the heavens," which appears elsewhere in the Bible as well (Genesis 6:17; Exodus 17:14; II Kings 14:27), is employed. These phrases, which appear in this context eleven times, refer to the actual world, which is essentially physical. In Ecclesiastes, this conveys the nihility of the world in and of itself, along with criticism of the actions and exertions of people inhabiting it. However, within these pointed statements about that which is performed under the sun, there is an allusion to a potential resolution. This resolution does not exist in this world under the sun or beneath the heavens; rather, it exists above the sun or above the heavens. Kohelet's critiques are directed exclusively at the physical world delineated by time and place, questioning its substance and undermining its pleasures, but does not address that which transcends it (Alsheikh; *Shabbat* 30b).

And also of the latter ones, who will be, there will be no memory among those who will be last, who will come after them, as they will be unaware of the other generations' earlier existence. All actions will ultimately disappear and be forgotten, as nothing lasts forever, not in reality and not in memory.

Personal Trials and Conclusions

ECCLESIASTES 1:12–2:26

The general abstract ideas that Kohelet outlined at the beginning of the book, he now goes on to illustrate by means of his life experiences and the insights that arose from them.

12 **I, Kohelet, was king over Israel in Jerusalem.** All opportunities were open to me.

13 **I directed my heart to seek and to search for wisdom about all that is performed beneath the heavens,** and I reached the following conclusion about the deeds performed beneath the heavens: **It is an evil matter that God has given to the sons of man in which to be engaged,** since all of mankind's endeavors provide no benefit, joy, or fruits.[11]

14 **I have seen** and examined **all the actions that are performed under the sun, and behold, all is futility and herding [*re'ut*] wind.** One who engages in futile actions of this kind is comparable to one who attempts to herd [*ro'eh*] the wind. Whereas one who herds sheep can produce milk, wool, or meat, one who attempts to herd wind will produce nothing from it. Indeed, the challenge of containing or directing the elusive wind is utterly ridiculous.[12]

15 Any action that is performed under the sun is considered **that which is warped** that **cannot be mended and deficiency** that **cannot be restored.**

16 **I spoke with my heart,** I contemplated, **saying: Behold, I have increased and added wisdom, beyond all who were before me over Jerusalem.**[D] **My heart has seen much wisdom and knowledge.**

17 **I directed my heart to know wisdom, and to know debauchery and folly. I knew that this too,** analysis of these subjects and drawing novel conclusions, **is an empty notion,** a futile undertaking. There is no substance or benefit in either wisdom or foolishness.[13]

18 Wisdom does not console a person, nor is it beneficial, **for with great wisdom is great anger.** As a person grows wiser and his powers of discernment become more sensitive, he discovers more truths that anger him. **And one who increases knowledge increases pain** for himself: The pain of life in the world, the pain of his disappointment with the world, and the pain associated with greater knowledge.

2 1 **I said in my heart:** Instead of contemplating abstract problems, **let us go now; I will pour** wine for you, or, alternatively, I will test you, my body, **with joy,**[14] **and** I will **see goodness.** I will live the good life. **But behold, it too,** enjoyment and sensual pleasure, **is futility.** It does nothing to resolve the questions of life, and it fails to calm the soul.

2 **Of laughter, I said: It is debauchery** and wildness; **and of joy,** I said:[15] **What does it achieve,** and what is its purpose? The attempt to live a life of pleasure gradually loses its appeal. People can host a party or two, drink wine, and attempt to rejoice, but over time they begin to question the ultimate objective of their laughter and merriment. Jokes cease to be funny, and joy departs from the heart.

3 Once unbridled debauchery lost its excitement and ceased to be attractive, **I searched in my heart** for another path, **to tempt my flesh with wine**[B] **and have my heart conduct itself with wisdom, and** yet still **grasp folly,** human pleasures, **until I could see what is best for the sons of man that they do beneath the heavens in the numbered,** limited, **days of their lives.** I would try to live a successful and beneficial life without sinking into the depths of wisdom or the shallowness of merriment.

Vineyards

4 Consequently, **I expanded my projects;** I undertook a series of large-scale projects: **I built for myself houses, planted for myself vineyards.**

Gardens and orchards

5 **I made for myself gardens and orchards and planted in them every fruit tree.**

6 **I made for myself pools of water, to irrigate from them a forest of growing trees.** I built a magnificent estate for myself.

7 **I purchased slaves and maidservants, and I had home-born servants; I also had much livestock of cattle and sheep, beyond,** more than, **all who were before me in Jerusalem.**

"Pools of water, to irrigate from them a forest of growing trees." Fresco, Tomb of Nebamun, Egypt, 1380 BCE

יב יג אֲנִי קֹהֶלֶת הָיִיתִי מֶלֶךְ עַל־יִשְׂרָאֵל בִּירוּשָׁלָםִ׃ וְנָתַתִּי אֶת־לִבִּי לִדְרוֹשׁ וְלָתוּר
בַּחׇכְמָה עַל כׇּל־אֲשֶׁר נַעֲשָׂה תַּחַת הַשָּׁמָיִם הוּא ׀ עִנְיַן רָע נָתַן אֱלֹהִים לִבְנֵי
יד הָאָדָם לַעֲנוֹת בּוֹ׃ רָאִיתִי אֶת־כׇּל־הַמַּעֲשִׂים שֶׁנַּעֲשׂוּ תַּחַת הַשָּׁמֶשׁ וְהִנֵּה הַכֹּל
טו טז הֶבֶל וּרְעוּת רוּחַ׃ מְעֻוָּת לֹא־יוּכַל לִתְקֹן וְחֶסְרוֹן לֹא־יוּכַל לְהִמָּנוֹת׃ דִּבַּרְתִּי אֲנִי
עִם־לִבִּי לֵאמֹר אֲנִי הִנֵּה הִגְדַּלְתִּי וְהוֹסַפְתִּי חׇכְמָה עַל כׇּל־אֲשֶׁר־הָיָה לְפָנַי עַל־
יז יְרוּשָׁלָםִ וְלִבִּי רָאָה הַרְבֵּה חׇכְמָה וָדָעַת׃ וָאֶתְּנָה לִבִּי לָדַעַת חׇכְמָה וְדַעַת הֹלֵלוֹת
יח וְשִׂכְלוּת יָדַעְתִּי שֶׁגַּם־זֶה הוּא רַעְיוֹן רוּחַ׃ כִּי בְּרֹב חׇכְמָה רׇב־כָּעַס וְיוֹסִיף דַּעַת
א יוֹסִיף מַכְאוֹב׃ אָמַרְתִּי אֲנִי בְּלִבִּי לְכָה־נָּא אֲנַסְּכָה בְשִׂמְחָה וּרְאֵה בְטוֹב וְהִנֵּה
ב ג גַם־הוּא הָבֶל׃ לִשְׂחוֹק אָמַרְתִּי מְהוֹלָל וּלְשִׂמְחָה מַה־זֹּה עֹשָׂה׃ תַּרְתִּי בְלִבִּי
לִמְשׁוֹךְ בַּיַּיִן אֶת־בְּשָׂרִי וְלִבִּי נֹהֵג בַּחׇכְמָה וְלֶאֱחֹז בְּסִכְלוּת עַד אֲשֶׁר־אֶרְאֶה
ד אֵי־זֶה טוֹב לִבְנֵי הָאָדָם אֲשֶׁר יַעֲשׂוּ תַּחַת הַשָּׁמַיִם מִסְפַּר יְמֵי חַיֵּיהֶם׃ הִגְדַּלְתִּי
ה מַעֲשָׂי בָּנִיתִי לִי בָּתִּים נָטַעְתִּי לִי כְּרָמִים׃ עָשִׂיתִי לִי גַּנּוֹת וּפַרְדֵּסִים וְנָטַעְתִּי
ו בָהֶם עֵץ כׇּל־פֶּרִי׃ עָשִׂיתִי לִי בְּרֵכוֹת מָיִם לְהַשְׁקוֹת מֵהֶם יַעַר צוֹמֵחַ עֵצִים׃
ז קָנִיתִי עֲבָדִים וּשְׁפָחוֹת וּבְנֵי־בַיִת הָיָה לִי גַּם מִקְנֶה בָקָר וָצֹאן הַרְבֵּה הָיָה לִי

BACKGROUND

2:3 | **To tempt [*limshokh*] my flesh with wine:** In the folk medicine of the ancient world, wine was utilized in various ways, among them for medicinal bathing and disinfection, presumably due to the alcohol it contains. In Sparta, they would immerse children in wine as a vaccination or to assess their strength. However, there are no extant records of wine used on the body for pleasure. Perhaps *limshokh* is a lyrical expression representing the flaunting of wealth, physical health, and abundance of wine. If so, it is reminiscent of Jacob's blessing of Judah: "He launders his garments in wine, and in the blood of grapes his clothes" (Genesis 49:11). Perhaps, though, unlike the root *mem-shin-ḥet*, the root *mem-shin-khaf* is not a reference to anointing; rather, it means tempting and enticing the body (see Rabbi Ovadya Bartenura, *Avot* 3:10).

DISCUSSION

1:16 | **Behold, I have increased and added wisdom, beyond all who were before me over Jerusalem:** In the book of I Kings (3:9), God responds favorably to Solomon's request that he be given "an attentive heart to judge Your people, to discern between good and evil." He even promises Solomon: "Behold, I have granted you a wise and discerning heart, that there has not been anyone like you before you, and after you no one will arise like you" (I Kings 3:12). This promise indeed comes to fruition: "Solomon's wisdom exceeded the wisdom of all the people of the East and all the wisdom of Egypt" (I Kings 5:10). The identification of Kohelet with Solomon is partly based on this self-description.

8 **I also gathered for myself silver and gold and the** beautiful,
unique, and rare **treasure of kings and countries,** the rare objects with which kings and the wealthy amuse themselves.[16] **I appointed for myself singers and songstresses** to sing before me, **and the pleasures of the sons of man, chests and wagons**[B] used for storing my collection of treasures.[17] I was constantly in action, living a life of restless luxury.
9 **I grew great, and I increased beyond all** those **who were**
before me in Jerusalem,[D] not only because I am the son of a king, but because **my wisdom too stood by me,** so that I could invest my resources wisely.
10 **Everything that my eyes sought, I did not withhold from**
them;[18] **I did not withhold my heart from any joy, for** rather **my heart rejoiced from all my toil, and that was my portion from all my toil.**
11 After I had invested so heavily in constructing and creating
new entities, **I turned to** comprehend **all the actions that my hands had performed and the toil that I had toiled, and behold,** after a long reflection upon these matters, I discovered that **everything was futility and herding wind.** None of the houses, fields, songs, ornaments, or pleasures provided any real benefit or had any significance. **There was no advantage** to all these **under the sun.**
12 **I** therefore **turned** in a different direction: **To see** the distinc-
tion between **wisdom,**[D] **debauchery, and folly.** Following my unsuccessful attempts to investigate the entire range of activities performed under the sun and the potential to change events, I decided to analyze human wisdom philosophically and to understand the nature of foolishness without seeking to change the world. **For who is the man who would come after the** many acts of the **king to do** other than **that which he already did?**
13 Initially **I saw** and thought **that there is advantage to wisdom**
over folly, like the advantage of light over darkness.
14 **The wise man's eyes are in his head,** and he sees every-
thing clearly, **but the fool walks in darkness.** Foolishness prevents a person from ascertaining the details of reality and understanding the world. Therefore, the wise man, who accurately assesses the situation and resolves problems that present themselves, is superior to the fool, who habitually stumbles in the darkness. **But** on second thought, **I also knew that one fate will befall them all.** Both the wise man and the foolish one will ultimately perish. What, then, remains of all his wisdom?[19]
15 **I said in my heart: Like the fate of the fool, so will befall me,**
I too will die; **why, then, did I become wiser?**[D] What use was my additional wisdom? **Then I said in my heart that this too,** the search for wisdom,[20] **is futility.**
16 **For there is no memory of the wise man with the fool**
forever. The memory of the wisdom of one person or the foolishness of another will not remain forever. **After the passage of the coming days, everything is forgotten.** Future generations will shrug at the wise man who has already left the world. **How can the wise man die with the fool,** without any difference between them?[21]
17 **I hated life, for distressing to me was the deed that is per-**
formed under the sun, for everything is futility and herding wind. Even if one can enjoy, act, and create in this world, nothing lasts forever, and there is no significance to these actions beyond the here and now.
18 **I hated all my toil that I have toiled under the sun,** seeing
that after my death, **I will leave it to the man who will be after me.**
19 **Who knows: Will he** who inherits me **be a wise man or a**
fool? I have no control over this matter. **He will control all my toil that I have toiled and that I have become wise under the sun.** Consequently, all of **that,** all my work **too, is futility.**
20 **I shifted** to a different path, **to cause my heart to despair of**
all the toil that I have toiled under the sun. I decided not to invest any more effort in that toil.[22]
21 **For there is a man whose toil is in wisdom, in knowledge,**
and in skill, and he achieves greatness, **but he will leave his portion to a man who did not toil in it.** Ultimately, the one who inherits the fruit of his labor might lack all wisdom, knowledge, or skill. **This too is futility and a great evil** [*ra'a*]**,** an evil that is worse than herding [*re'ut*] wind (see 1:14).

BACKGROUND

2:8| **Chests and wagons [*shidda veshiddot*]:** The Radak suggests an additional interpretation of this phrase: It is a reference to musical instruments. This suggestion is presumably based on the parallel terms in the preceding phrase, "singers and songstresses [*sharim vesharot*]," or on the phonetic similarity of these phrases. In Akkadian, the term *siddu* means metal utensil.

ח מִכֹּל שֶׁהָיוּ לְפָנַי בִּירוּשָׁלִָם: כָּנַסְתִּי לִי גַּם־כֶּסֶף וְזָהָב וּסְגֻלַּת מְלָכִים וְהַמְּדִינוֹת
ט עָשִׂיתִי לִי שָׁרִים וְשָׁרוֹת וְתַעֲנוּגֹת בְּנֵי הָאָדָם שִׁדָּה וְשִׁדּוֹת: וְגָדַלְתִּי וְהוֹסַפְתִּי
י מִכֹּל שֶׁהָיָה לְפָנַי בִּירוּשָׁלִָם אַף חָכְמָתִי עָמְדָה לִּי: וְכֹל אֲשֶׁר שָׁאֲלוּ עֵינַי לֹא
אָצַלְתִּי מֵהֶם לֹא־מָנַעְתִּי אֶת־לִבִּי מִכָּל־שִׂמְחָה כִּי־לִבִּי שָׂמֵחַ מִכָּל־עֲמָלִי וְזֶה־
יא הָיָה חֶלְקִי מִכָּל־עֲמָלִי: וּפָנִיתִי אֲנִי בְּכָל־מַעֲשַׂי שֶׁעָשׂוּ יָדַי וּבֶעָמָל שֶׁעָמַלְתִּי
יב לַעֲשׂוֹת וְהִנֵּה הַכֹּל הֶבֶל וּרְעוּת רוּחַ וְאֵין יִתְרוֹן תַּחַת הַשָּׁמֶשׁ: וּפָנִיתִי אֲנִי לִרְאוֹת
חָכְמָה וְהוֹלֵלוֹת וְסִכְלוּת כִּי ׀ מֶה הָאָדָם שֶׁיָּבוֹא אַחֲרֵי הַמֶּלֶךְ אֵת אֲשֶׁר־כְּבָר
יג עָשׂוּהוּ: וְרָאִיתִי אָנִי שֶׁיֵּשׁ יִתְרוֹן לַחָכְמָה מִן־הַסִּכְלוּת כִּיתְרוֹן הָאוֹר מִן־הַחֹשֶׁךְ:
יד הֶחָכָם עֵינָיו בְּרֹאשׁוֹ וְהַכְּסִיל בַּחֹשֶׁךְ הוֹלֵךְ וְיָדַעְתִּי גַם־אָנִי שֶׁמִּקְרֶה אֶחָד יִקְרֶה
טו אֶת־כֻּלָּם: וְאָמַרְתִּי אֲנִי בְּלִבִּי כְּמִקְרֵה הַכְּסִיל גַּם־אֲנִי יִקְרֵנִי וְלָמָּה חָכַמְתִּי אֲנִי
טז אָז יֹתֵר וְדִבַּרְתִּי בְלִבִּי שֶׁגַּם־זֶה הָבֶל: כִּי אֵין זִכְרוֹן לֶחָכָם עִם־הַכְּסִיל לְעוֹלָם
יז בְּשֶׁכְּבָר הַיָּמִים הַבָּאִים הַכֹּל נִשְׁכָּח וְאֵיךְ יָמוּת הֶחָכָם עִם־הַכְּסִיל: וְשָׂנֵאתִי
אֶת־הַחַיִּים כִּי רַע עָלַי הַמַּעֲשֶׂה שֶׁנַּעֲשָׂה תַּחַת הַשָּׁמֶשׁ כִּי־הַכֹּל הֶבֶל וּרְעוּת
יח רוּחַ: וְשָׂנֵאתִי אֲנִי אֶת־כָּל־עֲמָלִי שֶׁאֲנִי עָמֵל תַּחַת הַשָּׁמֶשׁ שֶׁאַנִּיחֶנּוּ לָאָדָם
יט שֶׁיִּהְיֶה אַחֲרָי: וּמִי יוֹדֵעַ הֶחָכָם יִהְיֶה אוֹ סָכָל וְיִשְׁלַט בְּכָל־עֲמָלִי שֶׁעָמַלְתִּי
כ וְשֶׁחָכַמְתִּי תַּחַת הַשָּׁמֶשׁ גַּם־זֶה הָבֶל: וְסַבּוֹתִי אֲנִי לְיַאֵשׁ אֶת־לִבִּי עַל כָּל־הֶעָמָל
כא שֶׁעָמַלְתִּי תַּחַת הַשָּׁמֶשׁ: כִּי־יֵשׁ אָדָם שֶׁעֲמָלוֹ בְּחָכְמָה וּבְדַעַת וּבְכִשְׁרוֹן וּלְאָדָם

DISCUSSION

2:9| **I grew great, and I increased beyond all who were before me in Jerusalem:** This description is consistent with what is stated elsewhere about King Solomon. Since he was wise enough to prefer wisdom above other gifts, God promised him: "Also I have granted you that which you did not request, both riches and honor, that there has not been anyone like you among the kings, all your days" (I Kings 3:13). Indeed, Solomon was privileged to own massive amounts of property, to rule over a large kingdom, and to attain worldwide renown (see I Kings 5).

2:12| **I turned to see wisdom:** Kohelet's change of approach is similar to that of many modern philosophers, such as Descartes and Kant, who turned their attention away from concrete reality to abstract human thought, judgment, and philosophy.

2:15| **Why, then, did I become wiser:** Like many other issues raised in this book, the question of the value of wisdom is relevant only to the world that is under the sun. These existential questions lack a metaphysical basis. Man wonders what is the value of the philosophical expertise that he acquired, the broad knowledge that he amassed, or his delving into wisdom literature. In the final analysis, in the real world there is no difference between people who know more and people who know less, as wisdom is essentially valueless and ephemeral.

22 **For what is there**[23] **for a man in all his toil and in the contemplation of his heart that he labors under the sun?** Ultimately, what will he gain from all these deeds and thoughts?
23 **For all his days are pains, and anger is his concern; even at night his heart does not rest.** Even when the body rests, his heart is not at ease. On the contrary, it is specifically then that all the questions unresolved during the day arise. **This too,** his night worries and his day preoccupations,[24] **is futility.**
24 The obvious conclusion from this analysis is that one should refrain from exertion and amassing investments whose profits might never be realized, and simply enjoy the present. Accordingly, **there is nothing better for a man than that he should eat and drink, and indulge his soul through his toil. This too, I saw that it is** a gift **from the hand of God,** which is not dependent on man.
25 **For** after all, **who will eat** my food, **or who will** be quick to **enjoy,** or derive sensuous pleasure from my toil, **other than me?** My experiences are mine alone, and I gain no advantage or real benefit from them.
26 **For to the man who is good before Him,** whose honor God desires, **He gave wisdom, knowledge, and joy,** so that he will feel some satisfaction from his work and reap the benefit. **But to the sinner He gave the matter of gathering and amassing** possessions, in order **to** ultimately **give** them **to him who is good before God.** The property that the sinner has collected will not remain his but will be given to one who finds favor in the eyes of God. Both the righteous and the wicked could have heirs whose paths diverge from the path of their parents. Consequently, **this** matter of amassing possessions or squandering them[25] **too is futility and herding wind.**

The Order of the World

ECCLESIASTES 3:1–17

In the context of the fundamental uncertainties raised by Kohelet, the poem of the times appears. This is a rhythmic, ordered poem containing a series of sayings arranged in pairs of contrasting activities and life events. In this poem, Kohelet is saying that each of the listed matters has its own designated time. The various areas of human existence are organized in a fixed order, as arranged by Divine Providence.

The poem begins and ends with the phrase "a time for every purpose"; however, the knowledge that everything is conducted in accordance with a plan does not resolve the question of the purpose of man's existence. Even if one recognizes that all the events that transpire in the world are arranged and directed from above, he remains ignorant of God's design for the world, and he does not comprehend the meaning of all the events that unfold before his eyes. Nevertheless, certain conclusions do emerge from this poem: One must be aware of his limitations and his place in relation to God. The world is in God's hands, and the person who focuses on conducting his life joyfully and in the performance of good deeds will be privileged to receive His gifts. In addition, one must keep in mind that although the ways of the world might sometimes appear to be perversions of justice, ultimately divine justice will be revealed.

3 1 The section begins with a general statement: **For everything there is a season,** its appropriate time, **and** there is **a** suitable **time for every purpose,** action, desire, or wish, **beneath the heavens.**
2 The song lists the various events that man experiences in life: There is **a time to be born and a time to die; a time to plant and a time to uproot the planted.**

"A time to plant"

"And a time to uproot the planted"

3 There is **a time to kill** and destroy life **and a time to heal** and restore it; **a time to breach,** to demolish, **and a time to build;**
4 **a time to weep and a time to laugh; a time for lamenting and a time for dancing;**
5 **a time to cast stones and a time to gather stones**[B] together; **a time to embrace and a time to refrain from embracing.** In certain situations it is improper to embrace.
6 There is **a time to seek** or desire something **and a time to lose** it; **a time to keep and a time to discard;**
7 **a time to rend and a time to sew; a time to be silent and a time to speak;**
8 **a time to love and a time to hate; a time of war and a time of peace.**
9 In light of this perspective, that all worldly matters are arranged in an organized fashion, Kohelet reiterates his question on the benefit and purpose of the world: **What is the advantage of the doer in that he toils?**
10 **I have seen the concerns that God has given to the sons of man in which to engage,** to occupy themselves with.
11 **He made everything beautiful in its time; He put the world too in their heart,**[D] to think about and engage in its matters, **notwithstanding that man will not**[D] **discover,** understand, **from beginning to end** the significance of **the accomplishment that God has accomplished.**

כב שלא עמל־בו יתננו חלקו גם־זה הבל ורעה רבה: כי מה־הוה לאדם בכל־
כג עמלו וברעיון לבו שהוא עמל תחת השמש: כי כל־ימיו מכאבים וכעס ענינו
כד גם־בלילה לא־שכב לבו גם־זה הבל הוא: אין־טוב באדם שיאכל ושתה
כה והראה את־נפשו טוב בעמלו גם־זה ראיתי אני כי מיד האלהים היא: כי מי
כו יאכל ומי יחוש חוץ ממני: כי לאדם שטוב לפניו נתן חכמה ודעת ושמחה
ולחוטא נתן ענין לאסוף ולכנוס לתת לטוב לפני האלהים גם־זה הבל ורעות
א ב רוח: לכל זמן ועת לכל־חפץ תחת השמים: עת ללדת ועת למות
ג עת לטעת ועת לעקור נטוע: עת להרוג ועת לרפוא
ד עת לפרוץ ועת לבנות: עת לבכות ועת לשחוק
ה עת ספוד ועת רקוד: עת להשליך אבנים ועת כנוס אבנים
ו עת לחבוק ועת לרחק מחבק: עת לבקש ועת לאבד
ז עת לשמור ועת להשליך: עת לקרוע ועת לתפור
ח עת לחשות ועת לדבר: עת לאהב ועת לשנא
ט עת מלחמה ועת שלום: מה־יתרון העושה באשר הוא עמל:
י יא ראיתי את־הענין אשר נתן אלהים לבני האדם לענות בו: את־הכל עשה
יפה בעתו גם את־העלם נתן בלבם מבלי אשר לא־ימצא האדם את־המעשה

BACKGROUND

3:5 | **To cast stones...to gather stones:** Casting and gathering stones were important agricultural activities in the mountains of the Land of Israel. One prepares its hilly slopes for seeding and planting by removing stones from the fields. The stones are subsequently gathered and used in the construction of terraces, for retention of rainwater, and for building watchmen's huts.

DISCUSSION

3:11 | **He put the world [*ha'olam*] too in their heart:** Obviously, a person is located in this world; however, the statement that the world is found within a person is also true. The Sages interpret this phrase in another manner as well: God also placed the ability to forget in their heart. This explanation is based on the linguistic similarity between the word *olam*, world, and *he'elem*, disappearance, and also on the way that *olam* is written here, without the *vav,* as well as the fact that in the Bible the word *olam* also refers to eternity (see *Midrash Tanḥuma, Kedoshim* 8).

Nothwithstanding that man will not [*mibli...lo*]: This expression should not be understood as a double negative; rather, it is a form of emphasis. This linguistic phenomenon is found elsewhere too, such as the rhetorical question "Is there no [*hamibli ein*] God in Israel that you send to inquire of Baal Zevuv, god of Ekron"? (II Kings 1:6).

12 Since no one is privy to God's actions or plans, **I know that there is nothing good for them,** the people,[26] **other than** for each **to rejoice** in his portion, **and to do good during his life.**

13 **Also, each man who eats and drinks and sees good in all his toil,** living a standard, reasonable life, **it is the gift of God.**

14 Regardless of all our actions, **I know that everything that God does, it will be forever; one cannot add to it and cannot subtract from it.** Since God is in charge of the world, man cannot alter it much. **God caused** the helplessness people experience because of the way He runs the world, so **that they would experience fear before Him.** This fear stems from the feeling of a lack of control over the world and all the vicissitudes that befall a person.[27]

15 **That which was already is** present now, **and that which will be** in the future **already was.** Nothing changes in the world. **And** in this state where nothing is under the control of man, it is **God** who **seeks the pursued** and assists him.

16 **Furthermore, I saw under the sun,** in this world: In **the place of judgment, there is the wickedness;** in **the place of justice, there is the wickedness.**[D] In contrast to expectations, the judicial system becomes institutionalized evil. In that case, there is no secure refuge from evil.

17 **I said in my heart: God will judge the righteous and the wicked, as there is a time for every purpose and** ultimately, the day will come when they will be held accountable **for every action** that was done **there,** even if it is not currently evident.[28]

Confrontations with Death

ECCLESIASTES 3:18–4:3

This section expresses in more extreme terms the transitory nature of human existence and the futility of human actions that were described at the beginning of the book. Death is decreed on man and animal alike, although Kohelet notes that in contrast to animals, the human spirit ascends to the heavens upon his death. However, Kohelet immediately proceeds to ignore this concept, preferring to focus on celebrating his actions and his lot in this world over contemplation that extends far beyond the horizon of human perspective.

At the end of this passage, Kohelet relates to death from a different perspective: He prefers the dead, who have already returned to dust, and those who never emerged from the dust of this world, over the world of the living, in light of the severe corruption of human society and the pain it causes.

18 **I said in my heart: It is by the speech of the sons of man that God has distinguished them** from other living creatures and elevated their status above the animal world,[29] **but** I **saw that** in truth, **they,** men, **are animals to themselves.** The difference between them and other life forms is not that significant.

19 **For the fate of the sons of man is the fate of the animal; there is one fate for them.** The demise of the animal awaits man as well. **Like the death of this, so is the death of that, and there is one spirit for all; the superiority of the man over the animal is nothing, as everything is futility.** The most impressive elements of human culture and achievement, e.g., the construction of the pyramids, the composition of brilliant music, and the development of higher-order mathematics, cannot remove the decree of death hovering over man's head as he is a member of the kingdom of the living.[30]

20 When one considers physical existence alone, it is clear that **everything goes to one place; everything was from the dust, and everything returns to the dust** upon death. All material objects begin as raw material and ultimately return to that state.

21 In contrast, with regard to the spirit, **who knows the spirit of the sons of man? Does it ascend upward, and the spirit of the animal, does it descend downward to the earth?** Most people do not consider the difference between the spirit of man and that of the animal.[31]

22 **I saw that there is nothing better,** at least as a temporary solution, a palliative, **than that a man should rejoice in his actions, as that is his portion, for who will bring him to see that which will be after him?** Since knowledge of what awaits him after death is unattainable, it is preferable to live a simple active life and rejoice in the portion that is presently his.

4 1 **I again** considered time after time the events of the world, and I **saw all the exploited,** the victims of corrupt deeds, **who are afflicted under the sun,** in the world. **Behold the tear of the exploited, but there is no comforter for them, and duress from their exploiters but there is no comforter for them.** The world is full of evil and pain.

"The exploited who are afflicted under the sun." Nubian slaves sold in the market, illustration based on sunken relief, Tomb of Horemheb, Egypt

2 **I praise** and prefer **the dead who are already dead,** or, alternatively, I favor them because they have already died, **more than the living who are still alive,** as the dead no longer suffer from the troubles of this world, whereas the living are surrounded by a life of iniquity.[32]

יב אֲשֶׁר־עָשָׂה הָאֱלֹהִים מֵרֹאשׁ וְעַד־סוֹף׃ יָדַעְתִּי כִּי אֵין טוֹב בָּם כִּי אִם־לִשְׂמוֹחַ
יג וְלַעֲשׂוֹת טוֹב בְּחַיָּיו׃ וְגַם כָּל־הָאָדָם שֶׁיֹּאכַל וְשָׁתָה וְרָאָה טוֹב בְּכָל־עֲמָלוֹ מַתַּת ב
יד אֱלֹהִים הִיא׃ יָדַעְתִּי כִּי כָּל־אֲשֶׁר יַעֲשֶׂה הָאֱלֹהִים הוּא יִהְיֶה לְעוֹלָם עָלָיו אֵין
טו לְהוֹסִיף וּמִמֶּנּוּ אֵין לִגְרֹעַ וְהָאֱלֹהִים עָשָׂה שֶׁיִּרְאוּ מִלְּפָנָיו׃ מַה־שֶּׁהָיָה כְּבָר הוּא
טז וַאֲשֶׁר לִהְיוֹת כְּבָר הָיָה וְהָאֱלֹהִים יְבַקֵּשׁ אֶת־נִרְדָּף׃ וְעוֹד רָאִיתִי תַּחַת הַשָּׁמֶשׁ
יז מְקוֹם הַמִּשְׁפָּט שָׁמָּה הָרֶשַׁע וּמְקוֹם הַצֶּדֶק שָׁמָּה הָרָשַׁע׃ אָמַרְתִּי אֲנִי בְּלִבִּי
אֶת־הַצַּדִּיק וְאֶת־הָרָשָׁע יִשְׁפֹּט הָאֱלֹהִים כִּי־עֵת לְכָל־חֵפֶץ וְעַל כָּל־הַמַּעֲשֶׂה
יח שָׁם׃ אָמַרְתִּי אֲנִי בְּלִבִּי עַל־דִּבְרַת בְּנֵי הָאָדָם לְבָרָם הָאֱלֹהִים וְלִרְאוֹת שְׁהֶם־
יט בְּהֵמָה הֵמָּה לָהֶם׃ כִּי מִקְרֶה בְנֵי־הָאָדָם וּמִקְרֶה הַבְּהֵמָה וּמִקְרֶה אֶחָד לָהֶם
כְּמוֹת זֶה כֵּן מוֹת זֶה וְרוּחַ אֶחָד לַכֹּל וּמוֹתַר הָאָדָם מִן־הַבְּהֵמָה אָיִן כִּי הַכֹּל
כ הָבֶל׃ הַכֹּל הוֹלֵךְ אֶל־מָקוֹם אֶחָד הַכֹּל הָיָה מִן־הֶעָפָר וְהַכֹּל שָׁב אֶל־הֶעָפָר׃
כא מִי יוֹדֵעַ רוּחַ בְּנֵי הָאָדָם הָעֹלָה הִיא לְמָעְלָה וְרוּחַ הַבְּהֵמָה הַיֹּרֶדֶת הִיא לְמַטָּה
כב לָאָרֶץ׃ וְרָאִיתִי כִּי אֵין טוֹב מֵאֲשֶׁר יִשְׂמַח הָאָדָם בְּמַעֲשָׂיו כִּי־הוּא חֶלְקוֹ כִּי מִי
א יְבִיאֶנּוּ לִרְאוֹת בְּמֶה שֶׁיִּהְיֶה אַחֲרָיו׃ וְשַׁבְתִּי אֲנִי וָאֶרְאֶה אֶת־כָּל־הָעֲשׁוּקִים
אֲשֶׁר נַעֲשִׂים תַּחַת הַשָּׁמֶשׁ וְהִנֵּה ׀ דִּמְעַת הָעֲשׁוּקִים וְאֵין לָהֶם מְנַחֵם וּמִיַּד
ב עֹשְׁקֵיהֶם כֹּחַ וְאֵין לָהֶם מְנַחֵם׃ וְשַׁבֵּחַ אֲנִי אֶת־הַמֵּתִים שֶׁכְּבָר מֵתוּ מִן־הַחַיִּים

DISCUSSION

3:16| **The place of judgment, there is the wickedness; the place of justice, there is the wickedness:** According to the greatest legal experts in Israel and the world, the purpose of the courts and the legal system is to uphold the law, not necessarily to uphold justice. Indeed, there are times when upholding the law undermines true justice.

3 **Better than both of them,** the living and the dead, **is he who has not yet been,** one who has not yet been born, **who has not seen the evil action that is performed under the sun.** The impression of evil remains upon the dead, and the living experience it, whereas evil has no effect on those not yet born.

Toil and Human Fervor

ECCLESIASTES 4:4–16

In this section, Kohelet emphasizes the costs of the worldview that prioritizes labor and success. He examines the two possible justifications for hard work, helping others and investing on behalf of future generations, and arrives at the conclusion that one who toils on behalf of his descendants is oblivious to the possibility that he will not be at all satisfied with his successors. Therefore, any laboring and stockpiling for the future at the expense of the present is futile.

4 **I saw all toil and all skilled action, that it is** motivated by **each man's envy of his counterpart.** One's talents and success often arouse jealousy among others, but **this too,** the envy of another's property and abilities,[33] **is futility and herding wind.**

5 On the one hand, **the fool folds his hands** in his lap, as he does not work and therefore lacks support and food, **and** ultimately **eats his** own **flesh.**[B] His flesh is consumed, and he dies of hunger.[34] Alternatively, he is ashamed due to frustration and inactivity.

6 On the other hand, **a handful of tranquility is better than two handfuls of toil and herding wind,** of hard yet futile labor.

7 I returned to contemplate the world, and **I again saw** that devotion to toil and diligence is **futility under the sun.**

8 For example, **there is one and no other** with him, or he chooses not to involve others in his activities, **without even a son or a brother. There is no end to all his toil, and his eye is not satisfied with riches,** as he constantly desires more. This person may well ask himself: **For whom** then **do I toil,** if I need not support anyone other than myself, **and** for what purpose do I **deny good from my soul** with my hard work? **This too is futility and a grave concern.**

9 In contrast, there are good reasons to engage in joint efforts: **Two are better than one,**[D] **because they have a good reward for their toil.** Two people who work together can earn a greater profit than the sum of their solitary efforts.[35]

10 The benefits to such a partnership go beyond the financial: **For if they fall, one will raise the other; and the one who falls, there is no other to raise him.**

11 **Also,** there is another advantage: **If two lie** together, at the very least **it is warm for them,** as they will provide each other with heat; **but for one** alone, **how will he be warm?** Who will warm him?

12 **If the one is attacked, both will stand against it.** If someone attacks one of two, neither will stand alone against the attacker. **And a threefold thread is not quickly severed.**[B] Intertwined threads are stronger than individual strands, and likewise a group of three is superior to a pair.[36]

"And a threefold thread is not quickly severed"

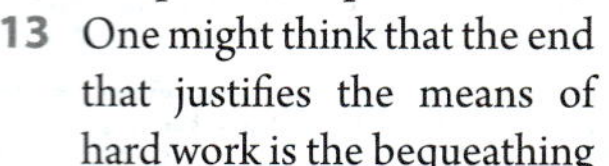

13 One might think that the end that justifies the means of hard work is the bequeathing of the fruit of his toil to future generations. However, the future is not in his control, and the profit garnered from his labor guarantees nothing: **Better an impoverished but wise child** with nothing **than an old and foolish king** with everything but **who no longer knows to be cautious.** Wisdom involves caution and potential success, whereas a fool, even if he is a king, is liable to act impulsively and fail.

14 **For he,** a foolish king, is comparable to someone who was released and **emerged from prison to become king,** as he lacks the requisite tools to rule a kingdom. **For even in his reign he is revealed as poor,** as he is lacking in knowledge as well as leadership skills.

15 **I saw all the living** people, **who walk under the sun, with the child, the successor, who will stand in his stead.** Their hopes were placed in their children, as each generation invests great effort in the succeeding one, hoping that it will be more successful than its predecessor.

16 Indeed, **there is no end to the entire people, to all those,** all generations, **who were before them,** who lived in the past, **and also the later ones,** the generations that will come after; **they will not rejoice in him,** the child from whom the present generation have great expectations. **As this too,** the expectation and hope in the succession of the generations, **is futility and an empty notion.**[37]

ג אֲשֶׁר הֵמָּה חַיִּים עֲדֶנָה׃ וְטוֹב מִשְּׁנֵיהֶם אֵת אֲשֶׁר־עֲדֶן לֹא הָיָה אֲשֶׁר לֹא־רָאָה
ד אֶת־הַמַּעֲשֶׂה הָרָע אֲשֶׁר נַעֲשָׂה תַּחַת הַשָּׁמֶשׁ׃ וְרָאִיתִי אֲנִי אֶת־כָּל־עָמָל וְאֵת
ה כָּל־כִּשְׁרוֹן הַמַּעֲשֶׂה כִּי הִיא קִנְאַת־אִישׁ מֵרֵעֵהוּ גַּם־זֶה הֶבֶל וּרְעוּת רוּחַ׃ הַכְּסִיל
ו חֹבֵק אֶת־יָדָיו וְאֹכֵל אֶת־בְּשָׂרוֹ׃ טוֹב מְלֹא כַף נָחַת מִמְּלֹא חָפְנַיִם עָמָל וּרְעוּת
ז ח רוּחַ׃ וְשַׁבְתִּי אֲנִי וָאֶרְאֶה הֶבֶל תַּחַת הַשָּׁמֶשׁ׃ יֵשׁ אֶחָד וְאֵין שֵׁנִי גַּם בֵּן וָאָח
אֵין־לוֹ וְאֵין קֵץ לְכָל־עֲמָלוֹ גַּם־עֵינָיו לֹא־תִשְׂבַּע עֹשֶׁר וּלְמִי ׀ אֲנִי עָמֵל וּמְחַסֵּר עֵינוֹ
ט אֶת־נַפְשִׁי מִטּוֹבָה גַּם־זֶה הֶבֶל וְעִנְיַן רָע הוּא׃ טוֹבִים הַשְּׁנַיִם מִן־הָאֶחָד אֲשֶׁר
י יֵשׁ־לָהֶם שָׂכָר טוֹב בַּעֲמָלָם׃ כִּי אִם־יִפֹּלוּ הָאֶחָד יָקִים אֶת־חֲבֵרוֹ וְאִילוֹ הָאֶחָד
יא שֶׁיִּפֹּל וְאֵין שֵׁנִי לַהֲקִימוֹ׃ גַּם אִם־יִשְׁכְּבוּ שְׁנַיִם וְחַם לָהֶם וּלְאֶחָד אֵיךְ יֵחָם׃
יב וְאִם־יִתְקְפוֹ הָאֶחָד הַשְּׁנַיִם יַעַמְדוּ נֶגְדּוֹ וְהַחוּט הַמְשֻׁלָּשׁ לֹא בִמְהֵרָה יִנָּתֵק׃
יג יד טוֹב יֶלֶד מִסְכֵּן וְחָכָם מִמֶּלֶךְ זָקֵן וּכְסִיל אֲשֶׁר לֹא־יָדַע לְהִזָּהֵר עוֹד׃ כִּי־מִבֵּית
טו הָסוּרִים יָצָא לִמְלֹךְ כִּי גַּם בְּמַלְכוּתוֹ נוֹלַד רָשׁ׃ רָאִיתִי אֶת־כָּל־הַחַיִּים הַמְהַלְּכִים
טז תַּחַת הַשָּׁמֶשׁ עִם הַיֶּלֶד הַשֵּׁנִי אֲשֶׁר יַעֲמֹד תַּחְתָּיו׃ אֵין־קֵץ לְכָל־הָעָם לְכֹל
אֲשֶׁר־הָיָה לִפְנֵיהֶם גַּם הָאַחֲרוֹנִים לֹא יִשְׂמְחוּ־בוֹ כִּי־גַם־זֶה הֶבֶל וְרַעְיוֹן רוּחַ׃

BACKGROUND

4:5| **Eats his flesh:** In the biological process known as catabolism, a body that fails to receive external sustenance breaks down its own fat and muscle tissue in order to sustain the brain and the nerves. Consequently, a person in that state can be described as eating his own flesh.

4:12| **And a threefold thread is not quickly severed:** Ropes with twisted fibers are made from a minimum of three strands, as the mutual friction of the threads enhances the strength of the rope. Likewise, ropes woven into a braid, like those used by mountain climbers, are entwined from at least three strands.

DISCUSSION

4:9| **Two are better than one:** This comment also constitutes social justification for marriage, as mutual assistance provides the couple with advantages in all realms of life.

Instructions concerning Man's Inferiority before God

ECCLESIASTES 4:17–5:7

In his awareness of man's lowliness before God, Kohelet calls on man to obey God rather than bring offerings without intent and purity of heart. His cautions against impulsive speech lacking requisite accompanying commitment are tied to the fear of God. Ultimately, he reminds man that the scope of his vision is limited; therefore, one must be restrained in judging that which he sees.

17 **Watching your step,** being cautious, **when you go to the House of God,** keeping in mind the purpose of your visit, **and listening attentively** to the Torah and its commandments, **is better than fools giving offerings, for** in their imprudence **they do not** even **know how to perform evil.**[38] Some explain that they know only to perform evil, or that they are unaware that what they have done is evil, or that fools bring offerings erroneously thinking that it can somehow exonerate them of their evil doings.

5 1 **Do not be rash with** the comments of **your mouth, and** also **let your heart,** your thoughts, **not be hasty to express a word before God, as God is in the heavens and you are on earth,** and consequently your knowledge is limited. **Therefore, your words** to God and about Him, and your statements in general,[39] **should be few.**

2 **For a dream comes with a multitude of** diverse **concerns, and** by the same token, **a fool's voice** comes **with a multitude of words.** A fool can invariably be identified by incessant prattle, like the meaningless portions of a dream.[40]

3 **When you take a vow to God, do not delay paying it.** Rather, bring the pledged offering at the proper time, **as He does not desire fools,** who vow indiscriminately and impulsively but do not fulfill their commitments.[41] **That which you vow, pay.**

4 In fact, **it is better that you not vow** at all **than that you vow and not pay.**

5 **Do not allow your mouth to cause your flesh to** let yourself **sin.** Imprecise and inappropriate statements can corrupt and endanger you. **And do not say before the messenger** who is responsible for collecting the money you vowed[42] **that it was a mistake. Why should God become angry at your voice and destroy your handiwork?**[43]

6 **So it is with a multitude of dreams, futilities, and many words.** Alternatively, it is because of the multitude of dreams and vanities and many words that troubles befall a person. **Rather, fear God.** One who fails to honor his word and commitments is likely to harm himself. In addition, it constitutes impertinence toward God.

7 **If you see exploitation of the poor, subversion of judgment and justice in the country, do not wonder at the purpose, for higher than high is watching, and** there are **high ones** who **are over them,** the events that you observe. The world contains many layers built upon other layers. You do not necessarily understand the reasons behind events, and they make you uneasy because you have a low vantage point and your perspective is limited. You are incapable of seeing the bigger picture.[44]

Kohelet Disparages the Accumulation of Money and Possessions for the Future

ECCLESIASTES 5:8–6:10

In this section, Kohelet criticizes the pursuit of money, as thereby the present, and life in general, is mortgaged for the sake of an undefined purpose. It is therefore preferable to celebrate one's accomplishments in the present. Even so, the section concludes with a critique of people who focus exclusively on their own lives, living a static existence with no possibility of effecting change in the world.

8 **The advantage of land is in every way.** Land is superior to all other property, as even **a king is subservient to a field.** The field is the source of life, and everyone is dependent on its cultivation.[45]

9 **A lover of silver will never be satisfied with silver.** One who desires money will never be satiated. **And he who loves abundance** of possessions **has no produce.** Alternatively, one who loves an abundance of possessions will not receive grain or sustenance from them;[46] **this** hoarding of excessive possessions **too is futility.**

10 **With the increase of goodness,** when plenty of food is brought home, **its consumers increase,** more people come to eat it; **and what use is it to its owner,** what does he gain from this abundance, **other than the sight of** his wealth before **his eyes?** He himself does not benefit from it in any other way. Alternatively, all he beholds with his eyes are others consuming his food.[47]

11 **Sweet is the sleep of the worker, whether he eats little or much** beforehand. **But the satiation of the wealthy does not allow him to sleep,** as he does not work hard enough to grow tired. Furthermore, due to

"Wealth kept for its owner." Collection of coins Carmel, first century BCE

יז שְׁמֹור רגליך כַּאֲשֶׁר תֵּלֵךְ אֶל־בֵּית הָאֱלֹהִים וְקָרוֹב לִשְׁמֹעַ מִתֵּת הַכְּסִילִים זָבַח רַגְלְךָ
א כִּי־אֵינָם יוֹדְעִים לַעֲשׂוֹת רָע: אַל־תְּבַהֵל עַל־פִּיךָ וְלִבְּךָ אַל־יְמַהֵר לְהוֹצִיא דָבָר
לִפְנֵי הָאֱלֹהִים כִּי הָאֱלֹהִים בַּשָּׁמַיִם וְאַתָּה עַל־הָאָרֶץ עַל־כֵּן יִהְיוּ דְבָרֶיךָ מְעַטִּים:
ב ג כִּי בָּא הַחֲלוֹם בְּרֹב עִנְיָן וְקוֹל כְּסִיל בְּרֹב דְּבָרִים: כַּאֲשֶׁר תִּדֹּר נֶדֶר לֵאלֹהִים
ד אַל־תְּאַחֵר לְשַׁלְּמוֹ כִּי אֵין חֵפֶץ בַּכְּסִילִים אֵת אֲשֶׁר־תִּדֹּר שַׁלֵּם: טוֹב אֲשֶׁר
ה לֹא־תִדֹּר מִשֶּׁתִּדּוֹר וְלֹא תְשַׁלֵּם: אַל־תִּתֵּן אֶת־פִּיךָ לַחֲטִיא אֶת־בְּשָׂרֶךָ וְאַל־
תֹּאמַר לִפְנֵי הַמַּלְאָךְ כִּי שְׁגָגָה הִיא לָמָּה יִקְצֹף הָאֱלֹהִים עַל־קוֹלֶךָ וְחִבֵּל אֶת־
ו מַעֲשֵׂה יָדֶיךָ: כִּי בְרֹב חֲלֹמוֹת וַהֲבָלִים וּדְבָרִים הַרְבֵּה כִּי אֶת־הָאֱלֹהִים יְרָא:
ז אִם־עֹשֶׁק רָשׁ וְגֵזֶל מִשְׁפָּט וָצֶדֶק תִּרְאֶה בַמְּדִינָה אַל־תִּתְמַהּ עַל־הַחֵפֶץ כִּי גָבֹהַּ
ח מֵעַל גָּבֹהַּ שֹׁמֵר וּגְבֹהִים עֲלֵיהֶם: וְיִתְרוֹן אֶרֶץ בַּכֹּל היא מֶלֶךְ לְשָׂדֶה נֶעֱבָד: הוּא
ט י אֹהֵב כֶּסֶף לֹא־יִשְׂבַּע כֶּסֶף וּמִי־אֹהֵב בֶּהָמוֹן לֹא תְבוּאָה גַּם־זֶה הָבֶל: בִּרְבוֹת
יא הַטּוֹבָה רַבּוּ אוֹכְלֶיהָ וּמַה־כִּשְׁרוֹן לִבְעָלֶיהָ כִּי אִם־ראית עֵינָיו: מְתוּקָה שְׁנַת רְאוּת
יב הָעֹבֵד אִם־מְעַט וְאִם־הַרְבֵּה יֹאכֵל וְהַשָּׂבָע לֶעָשִׁיר אֵינֶנּוּ מַנִּיחַ לוֹ לִישׁוֹן: יֵשׁ
יג רָעָה חוֹלָה רָאִיתִי תַּחַת הַשָּׁמֶשׁ עֹשֶׁר שָׁמוּר לִבְעָלָיו לְרָעָתוֹ: וְאָבַד הָעֹשֶׁר
יד הַהוּא בְּעִנְיַן רָע וְהוֹלִיד בֵּן וְאֵין בְּיָדוֹ מְאוּמָה: כַּאֲשֶׁר יָצָא מִבֶּטֶן אִמּוֹ עָרוֹם
טו יָשׁוּב לָלֶכֶת כְּשֶׁבָּא וּמְאוּמָה לֹא־יִשָּׂא בַעֲמָלוֹ שֶׁיֹּלֵךְ בְּיָדוֹ: וְגַם־זֹה רָעָה חוֹלָה

his preoccupation with his concerns over his possessions, he cannot enjoy his abundance.[48]

12 **There is a grave evil,** or malady, **that I have seen under the sun: Wealth kept for its owner.** He does not enjoy his wealth at all, as he always anticipates greater profit. That wealth is **to his detriment,**

13 because when **that wealth is lost in an ill-fated concern,**[B] an unsuccessful business transaction, then **he,** that individual, **begets a son, and there is nothing** left **in his,** the son's, **hand.**

14 **As he emerged from his mother's womb,** with nothing, **so he will return naked, to go as he came** into the world, **and he will take nothing for his toil that he can carry in his hand.**

15 **This too is a grave evil; just as he came** to the world, **so will he go; and what is the advantage for he who toils for the wind,** for naught?

BACKGROUND

5:13 | **That wealth is lost in an ill-fated concern:** The field of economics involves recurring cycles consisting of peaks of capital growth and valleys of decline. There are recorded cycles of seven to eleven years, of fifteen to twenty-five years, and of forty-five to sixty years.

16 **Indeed,** not only does he derive no benefit from his wealth, but while preoccupied with his business he suffers, as **all his days he eats in darkness,** in the twilight hours, not during the day, as he must work all day, and not at night either, as he needs his sleep. Alternatively, the verse means that he eats in sorrow. **And he has much anger** throughout his life, **illness, and wrath.**[49]

17 Instead of dreaming of wealth, saving for an uncertain future and risking the loss of all one's money, **behold the good that I have seen: That it is fine to eat, and to drink, and to see benefit in all his toil that he toils under the sun,** throughout **the number of days of his life that God has given him,** rather than devising plans that are liable not to materialize,[50] **as that is his portion.**

18 **Also any man to whom God has given wealth and property, and to whom He has given control to eat from it, and to bear,** enjoy, **his portion, and to rejoice in his toil, that,** the possibility that one will actually enjoy his wealth, **is the gift of God.**

19 **Because he will not remember much of the days of his life; rather, it is God who is the solution** and who provides him with his needs, and He will grace a person **with the joy of his heart.** Therefore, it is preferable to enjoy one's state of serenity rather than get caught up in baseless plans for the future.

6 1 **There is an evil that I have seen under the sun,** in this world, **and it is widespread among men,** a pervasive phenomenon:[51]

2 **A man to whom God gives wealth, property, and honor, and he lacks nothing for himself from anything that he desires.** This person has unlimited potential to live a good life, **but God does not grant him the opportunity to consume it,** as he dies before he can fulfill his dreams and ambitions, and **rather, a stranger will consume it,** reaping the benefit of his achievements. **That is futility, and it is a grave illness.**

3 Kohelet presents another example of this same phenomenon: **If a man begets one hundred** children from many wives **and lives many years, and the days of his years are numerous,** more than average, **but** despite all of this goodness, **his soul is not sated from the goodness,** as he is unable to find satisfaction and enjoyment from his accomplishments and he continues to further pursuits, **and moreover, he** ultimately **has no burial,** since that person, despite his toil and achievements, might not receive a dignified burial, a fate common to many who traveled abroad in pursuit of greater wealth and then disappeared, **I say: A stillborn is better than he.** He would have been better off not being born.[52]

4 **For** like a stillborn, **he came in futility and will depart in darkness, and his name will be covered in darkness,** and nothing will remain of it.

5 This person comes into the world empty-handed, works hard, lives a long life, and fathers many offspring. Yet he ultimately dies in a foreign, distant land and leaves this world empty-handed, without benefiting from the fruit of his labor. In contrast, the non-viable newborn, **even the sun he did not see and** he **did not know** any hard toil or evil; therefore, **there is more gratification for that** non-viable newborn **than** for **this** wealthy person;[53]

6 and **even if he,** that rich individual, **had lived one thousand years twice, he would not have seen good,** as he was so obsessed with acquiring more possessions and expanding his options he never settled down to enjoy his possessions. **Doesn't it all go to one place,** the grave, and nothing remains from all that he amassed?[54]

7 **All the toil of man is for his mouth,** in order to eat and sustain himself,[55] **but** in actuality **his soul too is not filled.** In the majority of cases, one leaves this world without having satisfied even half his desires.

8 **For what advantage has the wise over the fool?** Neither of them is immune from the rat race during their lives, or from inevitable death. **Why should the knowing poor man,** who is aware that his spirit will not be sated, **go against life,** rather than take action in the world on behalf of the living?[56]

9 Everything stated until this point indicates that **better is the sight of the eyes,** real life itself, **than the pursuit of desire,** yearning after what has not yet been achieved. **That too,** the clear perception of reality, is preferable, even though reality **is futility and herding wind,**[57]

10 since **that which was, its name was already called.** Past events have already been imprinted upon the world, and they cannot be changed. **It is known that he is a man,** a mere mortal, **and he is unable to contend with that which is mightier than he.** Man cannot change reality, as it is more powerful than he.

What Is Good for Man in Life

ECCLESIASTES 6:11–7:29

The numerous matters and aspects of the world forcefully raise the question of what is good. At the margins of Kohelet's acknowledgment of the limitations of his intellect, he notes two phenomena that he has encountered in his ruminations: The danger posed by and the shortcomings of a seductive woman, and the distortion of the world generated by humanity. Were it not for these two factors, the world could be a simpler, better place.

11 **Since there are many matters,** large and small, in the world, **futility increases.** The richer a person grows, the more he becomes preoccupied with worthless matters, and one who lives confronted with an overabundance of worthless matters will inevitably encounter incalculably more vanity. **What remains for the person?** What will be left to man from all this?

טז כָּל־עֻמַּת שֶׁבָּא כֵּן יֵלֵךְ וּמַה־יִּתְרוֹן לוֹ שֶׁיַּעֲמֹל לָרוּחַ׃ גַּם כָּל־יָמָיו בַּחֹשֶׁךְ יֹאכֵל
יז וְכָעַס הַרְבֵּה וְחָלְיוֹ וָקָצֶף׃ הִנֵּה אֲשֶׁר־רָאִיתִי אָנִי טוֹב אֲשֶׁר־יָפֶה לֶאֱכוֹל וְלִשְׁתּוֹת
וְלִרְאוֹת טוֹבָה בְּכָל־עֲמָלוֹ ׀ שֶׁיַּעֲמֹל תַּחַת־הַשֶּׁמֶשׁ מִסְפַּר יְמֵי־חַיָּו אֲשֶׁר־נָתַן־
יח לוֹ הָאֱלֹהִים כִּי־הוּא חֶלְקוֹ׃ גַּם כָּל־הָאָדָם אֲשֶׁר נָתַן־לוֹ הָאֱלֹהִים עֹשֶׁר וּנְכָסִים
וְהִשְׁלִיטוֹ לֶאֱכֹל מִמֶּנּוּ וְלָשֵׂאת אֶת־חֶלְקוֹ וְלִשְׂמֹחַ בַּעֲמָלוֹ זֹה מַתַּת אֱלֹהִים
יט א הִיא׃ כִּי לֹא הַרְבֵּה יִזְכֹּר אֶת־יְמֵי חַיָּיו כִּי הָאֱלֹהִים מַעֲנֶה בְּשִׂמְחַת לִבּוֹ׃ יֵשׁ רָעָה
ב אֲשֶׁר רָאִיתִי תַּחַת הַשָּׁמֶשׁ וְרַבָּה הִיא עַל־הָאָדָם׃ אִישׁ אֲשֶׁר יִתֶּן־לוֹ הָאֱלֹהִים
עֹשֶׁר וּנְכָסִים וְכָבוֹד וְאֵינֶנּוּ חָסֵר לְנַפְשׁוֹ ׀ מִכֹּל אֲשֶׁר־יִתְאַוֶּה וְלֹא־יַשְׁלִיטֶנּוּ
ג הָאֱלֹהִים לֶאֱכֹל מִמֶּנּוּ כִּי אִישׁ נָכְרִי יֹאכְלֶנּוּ זֶה הֶבֶל וָחֳלִי רָע הוּא׃ אִם־יוֹלִיד
אִישׁ מֵאָה וְשָׁנִים רַבּוֹת יִחְיֶה וְרַב ׀ שֶׁיִּהְיוּ יְמֵי־שָׁנָיו וְנַפְשׁוֹ לֹא־תִשְׂבַּע מִן־הַטּוֹבָה
ד וְגַם־קְבוּרָה לֹא־הָיְתָה לּוֹ אָמַרְתִּי טוֹב מִמֶּנּוּ הַנָּפֶל׃ כִּי־בַהֶבֶל בָּא וּבַחֹשֶׁךְ יֵלֵךְ
ה ו וּבַחֹשֶׁךְ שְׁמוֹ יְכֻסֶּה׃ גַּם־שֶׁמֶשׁ לֹא־רָאָה וְלֹא יָדָע נַחַת לָזֶה מִזֶּה׃ וְאִלּוּ חָיָה
ז אֶלֶף שָׁנִים פַּעֲמַיִם וְטוֹבָה לֹא רָאָה הֲלֹא אֶל־מָקוֹם אֶחָד הַכֹּל הוֹלֵךְ׃ כָּל־עֲמַל
ח הָאָדָם לְפִיהוּ וְגַם־הַנֶּפֶשׁ לֹא תִמָּלֵא׃ כִּי מַה־יּוֹתֵר לֶחָכָם מִן־הַכְּסִיל מַה־
ט לֶּעָנִי יוֹדֵעַ לַהֲלֹךְ נֶגֶד הַחַיִּים׃ טוֹב מַרְאֵה עֵינַיִם מֵהֲלָךְ־נָפֶשׁ גַּם־זֶה הֶבֶל
י וּרְעוּת רוּחַ׃ מַה־שֶּׁהָיָה כְּבָר נִקְרָא שְׁמוֹ וְנוֹדָע אֲשֶׁר־הוּא אָדָם וְלֹא־יוּכַל לָדִין
יא עִם שהתקיף מִמֶּנּוּ׃ כִּי יֵשׁ־דְּבָרִים הַרְבֵּה מַרְבִּים הָבֶל מַה־יֹּתֵר לָאָדָם׃ שֶׁתַּקִּיף

12 **For who knows what is good for man in his life, the number of days of his life of futility that he renders** meaningless **like a shadow? For who can tell a man what will be after him under the sun?**[D] Since no one knows what will endure after his death, one cannot determine what endeavor is worth undertaking.

"The number of days of his life of futility that he renders like a shadow"

7 1 **A good name is better than fragrant oil.**[B] Whereas the fragrance of oil is appreciated only by those proximate to it, a good reputation spreads far and wide and remains in the consciousness of those who hear of it. **And the day of death** is better **than the day of one's birth,** as on the day of death it is clear how the person acquired his good name, whereas on the day of one's birth no one knows what will ultimately become of him.[58]

2 Kohelet elaborates on the advantages of death: **It is better to go to a house of mourning than to go to a house of feasting, as that,** death, **is the end of every man, and** therefore **the living,** one who goes to the house of mourning,[59] **will take it to his heart,** as he will say to himself: Since everything ends in death, I must utilize my life to do something worthwhile. One tends to repress those thoughts in the course one's daily routine, but when faced with the inevitability of death, one can transcend the mundane and choose to change his ways. Kohelet prefers unpleasant situations because they are likely to motivate a person to move forward.

3 Accordingly, Kohelet asserts that another person's **anger is better** and more productive **than laughter, for from a harsh visage the heart** of man **may benefit.** One's character can improve and become more refined in the wake of criticism from another.[60]

4 **The heart of the wise is in a house of mourning.** Wise people often reflect about death, and consequently they frequently contemplate the future and the destiny of man. **But the heart of fools is in a house of rejoicing,** where they can enjoy the present.[61]

"The heart of fools is in a house of rejoicing." Illustration based on Assyrian relief, seventh century BCE

5 **It is better to hear the rebuke of the wise,** unpleasant though it may be, as criticism has the potential to guide a person, **than to be a man who hears the song of fools.** The absurd and nonsensical songs of fools might be pleasant to the ear, but they teach nothing and do not present any challenge to the listener.[62]

6 **For like the sound of brambles**[B] that burn **under a pot, so is the laughter of the fool.** His laughter is insignificant and fleeting, like the momentary crackling of burning thorns. **That too,** the laughter of the fool,[63] **is futility.** Alternatively, Kohelet is referring back to the preference of the rebuke of the wise: Despite all his wisdom and advice, even this individual can lose his status with ease.[64]

Thorny burnet

7 **For exploitation discomfits a wise man,** as it causes even a wise person to lose his judgment,[65] **and destroys the gift of the** understanding **heart** that was given to man.[66]

8 Kohelet returns to addressing the matter of ethics and wisdom that he addressed earlier: His preference for matters that do not provide immediate gratification but whose benefits are longer term. **The end of a matter is better than its beginning.** Although the beginning may be impressive, it is what remains at the end that is genuinely significant. **One of patient spirit**[67] **is better than one of arrogant spirit.**[D]

9 This verse also praises the virtue of patience, and it too refers to the human spirit: **Do not precipitate your spirit to become angry.** Do not allow yourself to be annoyed easily, **as anger abides in the bosom of fools.** Outbursts of rage can provide instant emotional gratification, but hasty, thoughtless expressions of anger are characteristic of fools.

10 In contrast to the focus of the previous verses on the ultimate future, this verse addresses the past. **Do not say: How was it** in the past? And do not say **that the early days were better than these. For it is not from wisdom that you ask about this.** Do

יב כִּי מִי־יוֹדֵעַ מַה־טּוֹב לָאָדָם בַּחַיִּים מִסְפַּר יְמֵי־חַיֵּי הֶבְלוֹ וְיַעֲשֵׂם כַּצֵּל אֲשֶׁר
א מִי־יַגִּיד לָאָדָם מַה־יִּהְיֶה אַחֲרָיו תַּחַת הַשָּׁמֶשׁ: טוֹב שֵׁם מִשֶּׁמֶן טוֹב ג
ב וְיוֹם הַמָּוֶת מִיּוֹם הִוָּלְדוֹ: טוֹב לָלֶכֶת אֶל־בֵּית־אֵבֶל מִלֶּכֶת אֶל־בֵּית מִשְׁתֶּה
ג בַּאֲשֶׁר הוּא סוֹף כָּל־הָאָדָם וְהַחַי יִתֵּן אֶל־לִבּוֹ: טוֹב כַּעַס מִשְּׂחוֹק כִּי־בְרֹעַ פָּנִים
ד ה יִיטַב לֵב: לֵב חֲכָמִים בְּבֵית אֵבֶל וְלֵב כְּסִילִים בְּבֵית שִׂמְחָה: טוֹב לִשְׁמוֹעַ גַּעֲרַת
ו חָכָם מֵאִישׁ שֹׁמֵעַ שִׁיר כְּסִילִים: כִּי כְקוֹל הַסִּירִים תַּחַת הַסִּיר כֵּן שְׂחֹק הַכְּסִיל
ז ח וְגַם־זֶה הָבֶל: כִּי הָעֹשֶׁק יְהוֹלֵל חָכָם וִיאַבֵּד אֶת־לֵב מַתָּנָה: טוֹב אַחֲרִית דָּבָר
ט מֵרֵאשִׁיתוֹ טוֹב אֶרֶךְ־רוּחַ מִגְּבַהּ־רוּחַ: אַל־תְּבַהֵל בְּרוּחֲךָ לִכְעוֹס כִּי כַעַס בְּחֵיק
י כְּסִילִים יָנוּחַ: אַל־תֹּאמַר מֶה הָיָה שֶׁהַיָּמִים הָרִאשֹׁנִים הָיוּ טוֹבִים מֵאֵלֶּה כִּי לֹא

BACKGROUND

7:1 | **A good name is better than fragrant oil:** Fragrances dissolved in oil evaporate in the open air at normal room temperatures and quickly dissipate. These fragrances are typically organic compounds with a low boiling or evaporation point. They evaporate from their liquid state, become concentrated in a small space, and their scent is lost.

7:6 | **Brambles [*sirim*]:** These are generally identified as the thorny burnet, *Sarcopoterium spinosum*, from the rose family. This plant is a small, prickly bush typically found in mountainous regions of Israel. It reaches a height of 30 cm with a diameter of 50 cm. The thorny burnet spreads quickly and covers large tracts of uncultivated land and consequently has become a symbol for abandoned places (see Isaiah 34:13). It is also used as a hedgerow: In the hills of Judea and Samaria one sees vineyards surrounded by fences with thorny burnets on them. Likewise they were placed at the entrances of caves where sheep were tended (see Hosea 2:8). Since this plant is effective as kindling, it was also used for heating and cooking. When it burns, it crackles, as described in the verse.

DISCUSSION

6:12 | **That he renders like a shadow…under the sun:** The life of man passes like a shadow, and when it ends, nothing remains of it under the sun. When the midday sun shines, the shadow dissipates. When the position of the sun is to the east or to the west, a shadow appears in the opposite direction. Similarly, human life is ethereal, like a passing shadow that moves from place to place.

Kohelet wonders whether there is anyone who knows what is worthwhile for man in his life, wonderment intertwined with confusion in light of man's limitations in terms of foreseeing the future and understanding the meaning of existence in general. He seeks to answer this question, though it was initially presented as an unanswerable rhetorical question. In the context of addressing this question, the verses that follow contain statements relating to the relative good in human life from different perspectives.

7:8 | **One of patient spirit [*erekh ruaḥ*] is better than one of arrogant spirit [*gevah ruaḥ*]:** Literally, the verse addresses two dimensions: Length and height. The long-winded, patient person is preferable to the high-winded, arrogant person. One who is long-winded is receptive and will listen to the high-winded one, whereas the high-winded one is unwilling to learn from the long-winded one.

not cling to fond memories of the past, neither with regard to your personal life nor with regard to the broader historical context, as the days of yore were not actually better than present times.[68] Some interpret this statement in accordance with its prevalent meaning that the world deteriorates over the course of the generations: It is unwise to express the pointless wish for a reprisal of the past.[69] Either way, wistful, nostalgic remarks are unproductive; one should accept reality as it is.[70]

11 Kohelet now compiles a series of popular aphorisms, only to refute the accepted understanding of their wisdom: **Wisdom is good with an inheritance,** material possessions. The combination of spiritual assets together with material resources is beneficial for man, **and more so for those revealed to the sun.** A wise and wealthy person derives even greater benefit if the people surrounding him are aware of his riches.[71]

12 **For** one who is **in the shadow of wisdom** and **in the shadow of silver,** wealth, is doubly secure, and his influence on others is great. But **the advantage of knowledge** over wealth[72] **is that wisdom preserves the life of its possessors.** Wisdom and knowledge can bring life to their owner.[73]

13 **See the work of God,** reflect on the world and accept it as God made it, **for who can mend that which He has warped?** Even if you conclude that the world was created distorted, you cannot fix it.[74]

14 Therefore, **on a day of good, enjoy, and on a day of bad, see** what you can do to prevent matters from deteriorating. Alternatively, watch resignedly, accepting the situation.[75] **God made this,** good, **corresponding to that,** evil; **therefore, man cannot discover anything,** he is unable to achieve complete understanding, **about it.** Alternatively, man has no legitimate claim of bias and inequity[76] with regard to good and evil in the world.

15 **I have seen everything in the days of my futility,** my fleeting days. I have seen that **there is a righteous man who perishes in his righteousness,** even though he deserves to continue living, **and** in contrast, **there is a wicked person who endures in his wickedness,** despite the fact that he should perish.

16 Reality is complicated and twisted, and therefore one must be careful. The following recommendations contrast with each other and are juxtaposed in order to balance each other: **Do not be overly righteous,** do not be excessively virtuous, e.g., by being merciful in an exaggerated manner, overly ascetic, or extreme in distancing oneself from sin,[77] **and do not be exceedingly wise; why should you go insane?** One can grow mad or depressed through extreme behavior,[78] and excessive righteousness or wisdom can backfire.

17 Conversely, **do not be overly wicked,**[79] even if you have already performed some evil,[80] **and do not be foolish; why should you die before your time?** Evil and foolish people are more likely to die young.[81]

18 Therefore, **it is good that you grasp this, and from that also do not withdraw your hand.** Adopt the middle road; do not go to any extreme.[82] **For one who fears God,** he is the moderate person, and he **will emerge from them all,** the many problems destined to afflict those who tend toward the extremes.[83]

19 **Wisdom will fortify** and strengthen **the wise more than ten rulers,** a large number of powerful men,[84] **who were in a city.**[D]

20 It is advisable not to be overly righteous,[85] **for there is no righteous man upon the earth who does good and does not sin.** In this imperfect reality, there are no entirely righteous people. No matter how much a person exerts himself, he can never achieve the ideal.

21 **Also do not pay attention to all the matters that they speak** about you, **so that you will not hear your servant cursing you.** If you listen to everything, you will eventually hear comments that are not only insignificant but also unpleasant, e.g., your servant cursing you. It is therefore preferable not to listen to everything people say.[86]

22 Even if you hear speech of that kind, you should not grow angry, **for your heart also knows that many times you too have cursed others.** Just as at times you blurt out inappropriate speech, others do so as well.

23 With regard to the quest for greater wisdom,[87] **all this I attempted with wisdom; I said: I will become wise.** I sought to follow the path of the wise, **but** I discovered that **it,** wisdom, **is distant from me.** Even one who seeks to acquire wisdom cannot obtain it fully.[88]

24 I sought to understand everything, but I eventually realized that **that which was** in the past **is distant** and cannot be properly understood, **and** even that which is not in the past[89] is **exceedingly deep; who can find it?** It is beyond comprehension. I have learned from experience that human wisdom and knowledge are limited.

25 Although one who seeks knowledge and wisdom cannot realize his goal entirely, Kohelet notes that there are positive conclusions at which he arrived through wisdom. First, he warns one who yearns for wisdom and wishes to live a balanced life of the dangers of a seductive woman: **I and my heart went about to know and to search, to seek wisdom and cunning,** sophisticated thoughts, **to know that wickedness is stupidity and foolishness is debauchery.**

26 **I find more bitter than death the** seductive **woman, who, in her heart, is snares and nets, her hands, shackles.**[90] It is therefore fitting that **one who is good before God,** a good and honest man, **will escape from her, but the sinner will be captured by her** trap. Kohelet is not preaching celibacy, but rather is calling upon man to reflect soberly and cautiously upon his passions and the power of women over him, so that he does not get caught in the trap of a woman of that kind.[91]

יא יב מֵחָכְמָה שָׁאַלְתָּ עַל־זֶה: טוֹבָה חָכְמָה עִם־נַחֲלָה וְיֹתֵר לְרֹאֵי הַשָּׁמֶשׁ: כִּי בְּצֵל
יג הַחָכְמָה בְּצֵל הַכָּסֶף וְיִתְרוֹן דַּעַת הַחָכְמָה תְּחַיֶּה בְעָלֶיהָ: רְאֵה אֶת־מַעֲשֵׂה
יד הָאֱלֹהִים כִּי מִי יוּכַל לְתַקֵּן אֵת אֲשֶׁר עִוְּתוֹ: בְּיוֹם טוֹבָה הֱיֵה בְטוֹב וּבְיוֹם רָעָה
רְאֵה גַּם אֶת־זֶה לְעֻמַּת־זֶה עָשָׂה הָאֱלֹהִים עַל־דִּבְרַת שֶׁלֹּא יִמְצָא הָאָדָם אַחֲרָיו
טו מְאוּמָה: אֶת־הַכֹּל רָאִיתִי בִּימֵי הֶבְלִי יֵשׁ צַדִּיק אֹבֵד בְּצִדְקוֹ וְיֵשׁ רָשָׁע מַאֲרִיךְ
טז יז בְּרָעָתוֹ: אַל־תְּהִי צַדִּיק הַרְבֵּה וְאַל־תִּתְחַכַּם יוֹתֵר לָמָּה תִּשּׁוֹמֵם: אַל־תִּרְשַׁע
יח הַרְבֵּה וְאַל־תְּהִי סָכָל לָמָּה תָמוּת בְּלֹא עִתֶּךָ: טוֹב אֲשֶׁר תֶּאֱחֹז בָּזֶה וְגַם־מִזֶּה
יט אַל־תַּנַּח אֶת־יָדֶךָ כִּי־יְרֵא אֱלֹהִים יֵצֵא אֶת־כֻּלָּם: הַחָכְמָה תָּעֹז לֶחָכָם מֵעֲשָׂרָה
כ שַׁלִּיטִים אֲשֶׁר הָיוּ בָּעִיר: כִּי אָדָם אֵין צַדִּיק בָּאָרֶץ אֲשֶׁר יַעֲשֶׂה־טּוֹב וְלֹא יֶחֱטָא:
כא גַּם לְכָל־הַדְּבָרִים אֲשֶׁר יְדַבֵּרוּ אַל־תִּתֵּן לִבֶּךָ אֲשֶׁר לֹא־תִשְׁמַע אֶת־עַבְדְּךָ
כב כג מְקַלְלֶךָ: כִּי גַּם־פְּעָמִים רַבּוֹת יָדַע לִבֶּךָ אֲשֶׁר גַּם־אַתָּ קִלַּלְתָּ אֲחֵרִים: כָּל־זֹה
כד נִסִּיתִי בַחָכְמָה אָמַרְתִּי אֶחְכָּמָה וְהִיא רְחוֹקָה מִמֶּנִּי: רָחוֹק מַה־שֶּׁהָיָה וְעָמֹק ׀
כה עָמֹק מִי יִמְצָאֶנּוּ: סַבּוֹתִי אֲנִי וְלִבִּי לָדַעַת וְלָתוּר וּבַקֵּשׁ חָכְמָה וְחֶשְׁבּוֹן וְלָדַעַת
כו רֶשַׁע כֶּסֶל וְהַסִּכְלוּת הוֹלֵלוֹת: וּמוֹצֶא אֲנִי מַר מִמָּוֶת אֶת־הָאִשָּׁה אֲשֶׁר־הִיא
מְצוֹדִים וַחֲרָמִים לִבָּהּ אֲסוּרִים יָדֶיהָ טוֹב לִפְנֵי הָאֱלֹהִים יִמָּלֵט מִמֶּנָּה וְחוֹטֵא

DISCUSSION

7:19| **Ten rulers who were in a city:** Several allegorical interpretations have been suggested for this phrase, as referring to a person's character traits, inclinations, or limbs. Wisdom is a force that can help one master all these elements (see *Pesikta Zutreta*; *Nedarim* 32b; *Kohelet Rabba* 7:19).

27 **See, this I have found, says** the wisdom of[92] **Kohelet.** I have examined the details of the world, **one by one, to find a scheme,** to reach a kind of statistically valid conclusion:[93]
28 **That,** those matters, **which my soul sought further** in my survey, **I did not find; one** perfect **man out of one thousand I have found, but a** perfect **woman among all these I did not find.** This assertion might be an allusion to Solomon's thousand wives and concubines.[94]

29 I sought many conclusions but emerged empty-handed; what I have discovered is unimportant in my eyes. **However, see, this** is the only insight that **I have found** and which deserves attention: **God made man straight, but they,** men, **have sought out many schemes,** distortions and tricks. I have learned that the world's troubles are caused by humanity. Were it not for the commercial activities, gambling, tricks, and schemes of people, the world could be a far better place.[95]

Obedience, Justice, and the Joy of Life

ECCLESIASTES 8:1–17

This section begins with sayings praising wisdom and the maintenance of the ruling order. Later, Kohelet also directs his attention to the problematic side of human rule and the helplessness of one confronted with what he considers a deviation from justice. However, the absence of just retribution is explained here as a temporary state, stemming from the limited perspective of man and his short life span. Nevertheless, in light of this situation, the wise man recommends that man focus on the simple joy of life, which renders his hard labor pleasant and eases the frustration engendered by the insoluble questions.

8 1 **Who is like the wise man, and who knows the meaning of a matter?** Nobody understands the meaning of matters in the world like a wise man. **The wisdom of a man illuminates his face, and** in his wisdom, **his arrogance**[96] **is ameliorated.** In other words, wisdom influences his character traits.[97]
2 **I keep the king's directive, and** I also observe **the word of an oath to God,** the oath I took to God.[98]
3 **Do not flee; leave his,** the king's, **presence;**[99] go wherever he sends you. **Do not stay in a bad situation, as he will do what he wills.** If you disobey the king, misfortune will befall you,
4 **since governance is by the king's word,** as it is the instrument of his reign, **and who will say to him: What are you doing?** No one can challenge the king's decisions, and all the more so the deeds of God.[100]
5 **One who follows a command** of the king **will not know an evil matter, and a wise man's heart will know the time and judgment.** A wise man remembers that the day of reckoning will ultimately arrive, and he obeys the law in the present with the future judgment in mind.[101] Alternatively, a wise man knows the right time and framework for everything.
6 **For there is a time and a judgment for every purpose, as the evil of man overwhelms him.** Great wisdom is required in order to identify what is right and what is correct in every situation.
7 A person sins because he chooses to overlook the consequences of his deeds, **for he does not know what will be** in the future, **for whatever it,** the consequences of his actions, **will be, who will have told him** now?
8 **There is no man who rules the spirit,** his own living spirit, **to retain the spirit,** to prevent it departing from the body when his time comes;[102] **and there is no ruling** by man **over the day,** the timing, **of** his **death. There is no sending a proxy in war,** one cannot transfer his fate to others,[103] **and maneuvering,** extensive efforts[104] or the amassing of wealth,[105] **will not rescue its owner** from death.
9 **All this I have seen and taken to my heart, for every action that is performed under the sun: Whenever man controlled man, it was to his detriment.** Man's rule over another is detrimental to both the ruler and the ruled.[106] There is a fundamental problem with the very concept of government.

"Whenever man controlled man, it was to his detriment." Pharaoh beating an Asian tribe member, ivory label, Den's tomb, Abydos, Egypt, ca. 3000 BCE

10 **So,** in this light, **I saw the wicked** who are now **buried and gone,** who have vanished; **they went from a holy place** and performed wickedness at will, **but they were forgotten** even **in the city where they acted like that.**[107] **This too,** the fact that the wicked are forgotten, **is futility.**

כז כח יִלְכַּד בָּהּ׃ רְאֵה זֶה מָצָאתִי אָמְרָה קֹהֶלֶת אַחַת לְאַחַת לִמְצֹא חֶשְׁבּוֹן׃ אֲשֶׁר
עוֹד־בִּקְשָׁה נַפְשִׁי וְלֹא מָצָאתִי אָדָם אֶחָד מֵאֶלֶף מָצָאתִי וְאִשָּׁה בְכָל־אֵלֶּה לֹא
כט מָצָאתִי׃ לְבַד רְאֵה־זֶה מָצָאתִי אֲשֶׁר עָשָׂה הָאֱלֹהִים אֶת־הָאָדָם יָשָׁר וְהֵמָּה
א בִקְשׁוּ חִשְּׁבֹנוֹת רַבִּים׃ מִי כְּהֶחָכָם וּמִי יוֹדֵעַ פֵּשֶׁר דָּבָר חָכְמַת אָדָם תָּאִיר פָּנָיו
ב ג וְעֹז פָּנָיו יְשֻׁנֶּא׃ אֲנִי פִּי־מֶלֶךְ שְׁמוֹר וְעַל דִּבְרַת שְׁבוּעַת אֱלֹהִים׃ אַל־תִּבָּהֵל
ד מִפָּנָיו תֵּלֵךְ אַל־תַּעֲמֹד בְּדָבָר רָע כִּי כָּל־אֲשֶׁר יַחְפֹּץ יַעֲשֶׂה׃ בַּאֲשֶׁר דְּבַר־מֶלֶךְ
ה שִׁלְטוֹן וּמִי יֹאמַר־לוֹ מַה־תַּעֲשֶׂה׃ שׁוֹמֵר מִצְוָה לֹא יֵדַע דָּבָר רָע וְעֵת וּמִשְׁפָּט
ו ז יֵדַע לֵב חָכָם׃ כִּי לְכָל־חֵפֶץ יֵשׁ עֵת וּמִשְׁפָּט כִּי־רָעַת הָאָדָם רַבָּה עָלָיו׃ כִּי־אֵינֶנּוּ
ח יֹדֵעַ מַה־שֶּׁיִּהְיֶה כִּי כַּאֲשֶׁר יִהְיֶה מִי יַגִּיד לוֹ׃ אֵין אָדָם שַׁלִּיט בָּרוּחַ לִכְלוֹא אֶת־
הָרוּחַ וְאֵין שִׁלְטוֹן בְּיוֹם הַמָּוֶת וְאֵין מִשְׁלַחַת בַּמִּלְחָמָה וְלֹא־יְמַלֵּט רֶשַׁע אֶת־
ט בְּעָלָיו׃ אֶת־כָּל־זֶה רָאִיתִי וְנָתוֹן אֶת־לִבִּי לְכָל־מַעֲשֶׂה אֲשֶׁר נַעֲשָׂה תַּחַת
י הַשָּׁמֶשׁ עֵת אֲשֶׁר שָׁלַט הָאָדָם בְּאָדָם לְרַע לוֹ׃ וּבְכֵן רָאִיתִי רְשָׁעִים קְבֻרִים וָבָאוּ
יא וּמִמְּקוֹם קָדוֹשׁ יְהַלֵּכוּ וְיִשְׁתַּכְּחוּ בָעִיר אֲשֶׁר כֵּן־עָשׂוּ גַּם־זֶה הָבֶל׃ אֲשֶׁר אֵין־
נַעֲשָׂה פִתְגָם מַעֲשֵׂה הָרָעָה מְהֵרָה עַל־כֵּן מָלֵא לֵב בְּנֵי־הָאָדָם בָּהֶם לַעֲשׂוֹת
יב רָע׃ אֲשֶׁר חֹטֶא עֹשֶׂה רָע מְאַת וּמַאֲרִיךְ לוֹ כִּי גַּם־יוֹדֵעַ אָנִי אֲשֶׁר יִהְיֶה־טּוֹב
יג לְיִרְאֵי הָאֱלֹהִים אֲשֶׁר יִירְאוּ מִלְּפָנָיו׃ וְטוֹב לֹא־יִהְיֶה לָרָשָׁע וְלֹא־יַאֲרִיךְ יָמִים
יד כַּצֵּל אֲשֶׁר אֵינֶנּוּ יָרֵא מִלִּפְנֵי אֱלֹהִים׃ יֶשׁ־הֶבֶל אֲשֶׁר נַעֲשָׂה עַל־הָאָרֶץ אֲשֶׁר ׀
יֵשׁ צַדִּיקִים אֲשֶׁר מַגִּיעַ אֲלֵהֶם כְּמַעֲשֵׂה הָרְשָׁעִים וְיֵשׁ רְשָׁעִים שֶׁמַּגִּיעַ אֲלֵהֶם

11 **Because justice for an evil act is not executed swiftly, therefore,** as retribution is not immediate,[108] **the heart of the sons of man dares to perform evil.** They repress their knowledge of the calamity that will befall them in the distant future.

12 **So a sinner performs one hundred evils,**[109] **and** yet **He,** God, **prolongs for him.** He does not punish him immediately, in accordance with his evil. **For I indeed know that it will be well for the fearers of God, who fear before Him.**

13 **Good will not be for the wicked, and he will not prolong his days,** which are fleeting **like a shadow, since he does not fear before God.**

14 After asserting that retribution will eventually arrive, Kohelet once again reverses course: **There is futility that is done on the earth,** in our world, **in that there are righteous who receive in accordance with the action of the wicked and there are wicked who receive in accordance with the action of the righteous,** and nevertheless people expect to see justice and fairness. **I said that this too is futility,** as it is clear that the world does not operate as people think it should.[110]

15 I therefore **praised** simple **joy, as there is nothing better for a man under the sun than to eat, drink, and rejoice. That** joy **will accompany him**[111] **in his toil during the days of his life that God has given him under the sun.**

16 I reached this conclusion **when I applied my heart to know wisdom and to see,** understand, **the affairs that are carried out upon the earth. As** I discovered, **both during the day and during the night, he,** the one occupied with such matters, **does not see sleep in his eyes.** He finds no rest.

17 **I saw all the work of God, as man is not able to discover,** comprehend, **the work that is performed under the sun. Although man toils to seek,** to understand the meaning of existence, **he will not find; even if a wise man wishes to know, he will not be able to discover** that meaning. I therefore recommend natural, unsophisticated joy. It is good for man when this type of joy accompanies him in his toil, renders his life pleasant, and soothes his soul.

Life in the Face of Death and Danger

ECCLESIASTES 9:1–12

Death is the ultimate fate of both the righteous and the wicked; it consumes everything. Even if it seems better to repress death and instead focus on life in the present with its simple pleasures, this guarantees nothing. The ravages of the future may surprise even talented people. Although wisdom has greater power to protect an individual or his environment than other talents, attributes, and possessions, society does not always value wisdom as it should.

9 1 **For all this,** the present reality, **I have taken to my heart,** as I wish **to clarify all this,** to examine what is true, good, and important and what is false, evil, and inconsequential. I discovered **that the righteous, the wise, and their acolytes,**[112] or their deeds,[113] **are in the hand of God. Both love and hatred, man does not know.** People are not even fully aware of their own feelings, and this prevents them from finding their way in the world. **Everything is** potentially **before them.** All kinds of events over which they have no control can happen to them.

2 **Everything is as it is for everyone.** Anything can happen to any individual.[114] **There is one fate for the righteous and for the wicked, for the good, for the pure and for the impure, for one who sacrifices** offerings **and for one who does not sacrifice; like the good, so is the sinner; one who takes oaths,** and who therefore might occasionally take a false oath, **is like one who is leery of** taking **an oath.**

3 **This is evil among everything that is performed under the sun: That there is one fate for all,** the wicked and the righteous alike. The human eye cannot discern the link between people's deeds and the events of their lives, all their successes and failures, which is one reason man feels that life is meaningless. **Also,** due to the fact that people do not see any necessary connection between actions and consequences, **the heart of the son of man is full of evil, and debauchery** and drunkenness **is in their heart during their lives. And afterward, it,** the heart,[115] **is** destined only **to** join **the dead.**[116]

4 **For** only **whoever is joined to any of the** forms of the **living has hope; for** example, **a living dog is better than a dead lion.** Life, no matter how lowly, is better than death.[117]

5 **For** only **the living know** for a certainty **that they will die; but the dead do not know anything, and** what is more, **they no longer have a reward, as their memory is forgotten.**

6 **Even their love, even their hatred, and even their envy have already perished,** vanished and dissipated after their death; **they will never again have a portion in anything that is performed under the sun.** There is no trace of their history, exploits, and adventures in this world. The confidence gained in that very knowledge, slight or troubling though it may be, renders conscious, living people superior to the dead, who have no knowledge at all.

7 In conclusion, **go, eat your bread with joy, and drink your wine with a good heart.** Find satisfaction in your simple life, and avoid the upheavals of emotions like envy, animosity, and lust, **as** this lifestyle of simple joy will enable you to know that **God has already accepted your actions.**[118]

8 **At all times, may your garments be white.** Wear pleasant, simple, and clean clothes. **And may the oil on your head not be lacking.**[B] Anoint your hair with oil and thereby groom it.

9 **Appreciate life with a woman whom you love all the days of your futile life, which He has given you under the sun, all the days of your futility.** Even if you are not wise, and your life is meaningless, you should still find a way to enjoy your futile existence, **as that is your portion in life and in your toil that you toil under the sun.** This is your fate; be happy with it. Even if your life has no meaning to you, at least take comfort in a reasonable and unpretentious life.

10 **Everything that you are capable of doing with your strength,** whatever you are capable of doing, you should **do,** here and now, **as there is no action, scheme, knowledge, or wisdom in the grave where you are going.** After death, you cannot perform any more deeds,, and considerations of all kinds disappear. Therefore, it is advisable to live a life of comfort, and enjoy a happy marriage, while working in accordance with the possibilities open before you.

טו כְּמַעֲשֵׂ֣ה הַצַּדִּיקִ֑ים אָמַ֕רְתִּי שֶׁגַּם־זֶ֖ה הָֽבֶל׃ וְשִׁבַּ֤חְתִּֽי אֲנִי֙ אֶת־הַשִּׂמְחָ֔ה אֲשֶׁ֨ר
אֵֽין־ט֤וֹב לָֽאָדָם֙ תַּ֣חַת הַשֶּׁ֔מֶשׁ כִּ֛י אִם־לֶאֱכֹ֥ל וְלִשְׁתּ֖וֹת וְלִשְׂמ֑וֹחַ וְה֞וּא יִלְוֶ֣נּוּ
טז בַעֲמָל֗וֹ יְמֵ֥י חַיָּ֛יו אֲשֶׁר־נָֽתַן־ל֥וֹ הָאֱלֹהִ֖ים תַּ֥חַת הַשָּֽׁמֶשׁ׃ כַּאֲשֶׁ֨ר נָתַ֤תִּי אֶת־לִבִּי֙
לָדַ֣עַת חָכְמָ֔ה וְלִרְאוֹת֙ אֶת־הָ֣עִנְיָ֔ן אֲשֶׁ֥ר נַעֲשָׂ֖ה עַל־הָאָ֑רֶץ כִּ֣י גַ֤ם בַּיּוֹם֙ וּבַלַּ֔יְלָה
יז שֵׁ֕נָה בְּעֵינָ֖יו אֵינֶ֥נּוּ רֹאֶֽה׃ וְרָאִיתִי֮ אֶת־כָּל־מַעֲשֵׂ֣ה הָאֱלֹהִים֒ כִּי֩ לֹ֨א יוּכַ֜ל הָאָדָ֗ם
לִמְצוֹא֙ אֶת־הַֽמַּעֲשֶׂה֙ אֲשֶׁ֣ר נַעֲשָׂ֣ה תַֽחַת־הַשֶּׁ֔מֶשׁ בְּשֶׁ֨ל אֲשֶׁ֧ר יַעֲמֹ֛ל הָאָדָ֖ם לְבַקֵּ֣שׁ
א וְלֹ֣א יִמְצָ֑א וְגַ֨ם אִם־יֹאמַ֤ר הֶֽחָכָם֙ לָדַ֔עַת לֹ֥א יוּכַ֖ל לִמְצֹֽא׃ כִּ֣י אֶת־כָּל־זֶ֞ה נָתַ֤תִּי
אֶל־לִבִּי֙ וְלָב֣וּר אֶת־כָּל־זֶ֔ה אֲשֶׁ֨ר הַצַּדִּיקִ֧ים וְהַחֲכָמִ֛ים וַעֲבָדֵיהֶ֖ם בְּיַ֣ד הָאֱלֹהִ֑ים
ב גַּם־אַהֲבָ֣ה גַם־שִׂנְאָ֗ה אֵ֤ין יוֹדֵ֙עַ֙ הָֽאָדָ֔ם הַכֹּ֖ל לִפְנֵיהֶֽם׃ הַכֹּ֞ל כַּאֲשֶׁ֣ר לַכֹּ֗ל מִקְרֶ֨ה
אֶחָ֜ד לַצַּדִּ֣יק וְלָרָשָׁ֗ע לַטּוֹב֙ וְלַטָּה֣וֹר וְלַטָּמֵ֔א וְלַזֹּבֵ֔חַ וְלַאֲשֶׁ֖ר אֵינֶ֣נּוּ זֹבֵ֑חַ כַּטּוֹב֙
ג כַּֽחֹטֶ֔א הַנִּשְׁבָּ֕ע כַּאֲשֶׁ֖ר שְׁבוּעָ֥ה יָרֵֽא׃ זֶ֣ה ׀ רָ֗ע בְּכֹ֤ל אֲשֶׁר־נַעֲשָׂה֙ תַּ֣חַת הַשֶּׁ֔מֶשׁ
כִּֽי־מִקְרֶ֥ה אֶחָ֖ד לַכֹּ֑ל וְגַ֣ם לֵ֣ב בְּֽנֵי־הָ֠אָדָ֠ם מָלֵא־רָ֨ע וְהוֹלֵל֤וֹת בִּלְבָבָם֙ בְּחַיֵּיהֶ֔ם
ד וְאַחֲרָ֖יו אֶל־הַמֵּתִֽים׃ כִּי־מִי֙ אֲשֶׁ֣ר יבחר אֶ֣ל כָּל־הַחַיִּ֔ים יֵ֖שׁ בִּטָּח֑וֹן כִּֽי־לְכֶ֤לֶב חַי֙ יְחֻבַּ֔ר
ה ה֣וּא ט֔וֹב מִן־הָאַרְיֵ֖ה הַמֵּֽת׃ כִּ֛י הַחַיִּ֥ים יוֹדְעִ֖ים שֶׁיָּמֻ֑תוּ וְהַמֵּתִ֞ים אֵינָ֧ם יוֹדְעִ֣ים
ו מְא֗וּמָה וְאֵֽין־ע֤וֹד לָהֶם֙ שָׂכָ֔ר כִּ֥י נִשְׁכַּ֖ח זִכְרָֽם׃ גַּ֧ם אַהֲבָתָ֛ם גַּם־שִׂנְאָתָ֥ם גַּם־
קִנְאָתָ֖ם כְּבָ֣ר אָבָ֑דָה וְחֵ֙לֶק֙ אֵין־לָהֶ֥ם עוֹד֙ לְעוֹלָ֔ם בְּכֹ֥ל אֲשֶׁר־נַעֲשָׂ֖ה תַּ֥חַת הַשָּֽׁמֶשׁ׃
ז לֵ֣ךְ אֱכֹ֤ל בְּשִׂמְחָה֙ לַחְמֶ֔ךָ וּֽשֲׁתֵ֥ה בְלֶב־ט֖וֹב יֵינֶ֑ךָ כִּ֣י כְבָ֔ר רָצָ֥ה הָאֱלֹהִ֖ים אֶת־ ד
ח ט מַעֲשֶֽׂיךָ׃ בְּכָל־עֵ֕ת יִהְי֥וּ בְגָדֶ֖יךָ לְבָנִ֑ים וְשֶׁ֖מֶן עַל־רֹאשְׁךָ֥ אַל־יֶחְסָֽר׃ רְאֵ֨ה חַיִּ֜ים
עִם־אִשָּׁ֣ה אֲשֶׁר־אָהַ֗בְתָּ כָּל־יְמֵי֙ חַיֵּ֣י הֶבְלֶ֔ךָ אֲשֶׁ֤ר נָֽתַן־לְךָ֙ תַּ֣חַת הַשֶּׁ֔מֶשׁ כֹּ֖ל יְמֵ֣י
י הֶבְלֶ֑ךָ כִּ֣י ה֤וּא חֶלְקְךָ֙ בַּֽחַיִּ֔ים וּבַעֲמָ֣לְךָ֔ אֲשֶׁר־אַתָּ֥ה עָמֵ֖ל תַּ֥חַת הַשָּֽׁמֶשׁ׃ כֹּל֩ אֲשֶׁ֨ר
תִּמְצָ֧א יָדְךָ֛ לַעֲשׂ֥וֹת בְּכֹחֲךָ֖ עֲשֵׂ֑ה כִּי֩ אֵ֨ין מַעֲשֶׂ֜ה וְחֶשְׁבּ֗וֹן וְדַ֙עַת֙ וְחָכְמָ֔ה בִּשְׁא֕וֹל

BACKGROUND

9:8| **And may the oil on your head not be lacking:** In ancient times people would rub their heads with oil for hygienic purposes, in order to clean the head from parasites, such as lice. Certain oils repel nits and enable their quick removal with a comb. Applying oil to one's head and face was also an expression of goodwill, decency, and respect. Accordingly, kings and priests were typically anointed with oil.

11 Yet **I again saw under the sun** that even for one who lives a simple life there is no guarantee of security and calm. I saw **that** winning **the race is not** guaranteed **to the swift,** as one who runs fast is not always able to escape or apprehend what he pursues, **and** triumph in **the war is not** assured **to the valiant; also not to the wise is bread,** a livelihood, guaranteed, **and also not to the clever is wealth, and also not to the knowledgeable is favor.** Although wisdom and knowledge are generally beneficial, they are not always appreciated by others. **Rather, time and chance befalls all of them.** The life of any one of these talented people is liable to be destroyed.[119]

12 **For man also does not know his time,** the future that awaits him. He does not know when he will experience failure and from where it will come. Just **like the fish that are trapped,** suffering, **in an evil net, and like the birds that are trapped in the snare, so are the sons of man snared at an evil time, when it falls upon them suddenly.** People can likewise find themselves suddenly in a trap from which they cannot escape. Even one who focuses on the present and represses all troubling thoughts of death, while depending on his inherent or acquired virtues, is not protected from life's trials and tribulations.

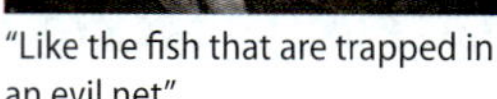

"Like the fish that are trapped in an evil net"

"Like the birds that are trapped in the snare"

Wisdom, Folly, and Their Consequences

ECCLESIASTES 9:13–10:20

In this section, Kohelet levels sharp criticism at a society that lacks proper esteem for wisdom. Alongside his discussion of the relationship between wisdom and folly, Kohelet addresses several related issues: speech in general, the respective statements of the wise man and the fool, the relationship between efforts and their consequences, and the power of money. Kohelet also dispenses various bits of practical advice.

13 **This** phenomenon **too I have I seen under the sun as wisdom, and it is great to me:**

14 **There was a small city, but few men in it, and a great king came against it, and surrounded it, and built great siege works against it,**[B] ready to attack.

"And surrounded it, and built great siege works against it." City besieged with a battering ram on a siege ramp, relief, Nimrud, Iraq, 728 BCE

15 In this situation, it might seem that the city has no chance. But **a poor,**[120] or wretched, **and wise man was found in it, and he saved the city in his wisdom, but** after a while **nobody remembered that poor man.**[D] The leaders of the city took all the credit and praise for themselves, and everyone forgot the poor but wise man.

16 **I said** in conclusion that **wisdom is** still **better than courage,** even **though the wisdom of the poor man is scorned, and his words are not heard,** accepted and remembered, and his deserved fame is taken by others.

17 Nevertheless, in other circumstances a wise man is accorded recognition and people listen to him, thanks to his manner of speech:[121] **The words of the wise, softly spoken, are better heard than the crying out of a ruler of fools.** One who imposes authority over fools often has to raise his voice, but they take no notice of him anyway.

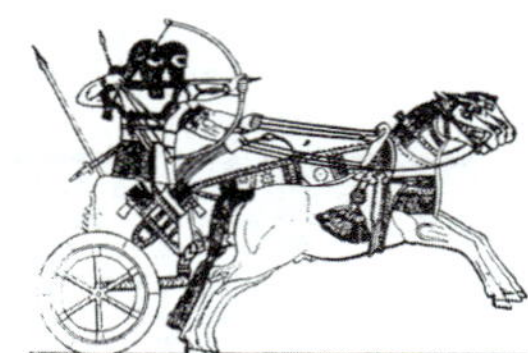
"Weapons of battle." Assyrian army

18 Therefore, **wisdom is** ultimately **better than weapons of battle, and** still, it does not guarantee the wise man's fate, as **one sinner** who fails to recognize the benefit that the wise man provides **destroys much good,** since he causes it to be forgotten. Alternatively, wisdom is better than weapons of war, and yet it does not ensure military success, as even if the army follows the wise man's advice, a single traitor can ruin the entire strategy.

10 1 Similarly,[122] **flies of death,** dead flies, or flies that accompany rot, **putrefy and froth**[123] **the perfumed oil,**[B] an expensive fragrance oil. Although flies are tiny insects, a single one can impair the odor of a lot of perfume. Likewise, **a little folly is weightier than wisdom, than honor.** A small measure of foolishness is sufficient to spoil a delicate and refined environment. This is similar to the statement of the previous verse: One sinner is enough to spoil the works of the wise man.[124]

"Flies of death putrefy and froth the perfumed oil"

יא אֲשֶׁר אַתָּה הֹלֵךְ שָׁמָּה: שַׁבְתִּי וְרָאֹה תַחַת־הַשֶּׁמֶשׁ כִּי לֹא לַקַּלִּים הַמֵּרוֹץ וְלֹא
לַגִּבּוֹרִים הַמִּלְחָמָה וְגַם לֹא לַחֲכָמִים לֶחֶם וְגַם לֹא לַנְּבֹנִים עֹשֶׁר וְגַם לֹא לַיֹּדְעִים
יב חֵן כִּי־עֵת וָפֶגַע יִקְרֶה אֶת־כֻּלָּם: כִּי גַּם לֹא־יֵדַע הָאָדָם אֶת־עִתּוֹ כַּדָּגִים שֶׁנֶּאֱחָזִים
בִּמְצוֹדָה רָעָה וְכַצִּפֳּרִים הָאֲחֻזוֹת בַּפָּח כָּהֵם יוּקָשִׁים בְּנֵי הָאָדָם לְעֵת רָעָה
יג כְּשֶׁתִּפּוֹל עֲלֵיהֶם פִּתְאֹם: גַּם־זֹה רָאִיתִי חָכְמָה תַּחַת הַשָּׁמֶשׁ וּגְדוֹלָה הִיא אֵלָי:
יד עִיר קְטַנָּה וַאֲנָשִׁים בָּהּ מְעָט וּבָא־אֵלֶיהָ מֶלֶךְ גָּדוֹל וְסָבַב אֹתָהּ וּבָנָה עָלֶיהָ
טו מְצוֹדִים גְּדֹלִים: וּמָצָא בָהּ אִישׁ מִסְכֵּן חָכָם וּמִלַּט־הוּא אֶת־הָעִיר בְּחָכְמָתוֹ
טז וְאָדָם לֹא זָכַר אֶת־הָאִישׁ הַמִּסְכֵּן הַהוּא: וְאָמַרְתִּי אָנִי טוֹבָה חָכְמָה מִגְּבוּרָה
יז וְחָכְמַת הַמִּסְכֵּן בְּזוּיָה וּדְבָרָיו אֵינָם נִשְׁמָעִים: דִּבְרֵי חֲכָמִים בְּנַחַת נִשְׁמָעִים
יח מִזַּעֲקַת מוֹשֵׁל בַּכְּסִילִים: טוֹבָה חָכְמָה מִכְּלֵי קְרָב וְחוֹטֶא אֶחָד יְאַבֵּד טוֹבָה
א הַרְבֵּה: זְבוּבֵי מָוֶת יַבְאִישׁ יַבִּיעַ שֶׁמֶן רוֹקֵחַ יָקָר מֵחָכְמָה מִכָּבוֹד סִכְלוּת מְעָט:
ב ג לֵב חָכָם לִימִינוֹ וְלֵב כְּסִיל לִשְׂמֹאלוֹ: וְגַם־בַּדֶּרֶךְ כשהסכל הֹלֵךְ לִבּוֹ חָסֵר וְאָמַר כְּשֶׁסָּכָל

2 **The heart of the wise inclines to his right,** to his benefit, **and the heart of a fool inclines to his left,** the wrong side.[125]

3 **Even while the fool walks on the way, his heart is lacking and says to everyone that he is a fool.** His manner of walking and talking, and his behavior in general, attest to his foolishness.[126]

BACKGROUND

9:14 | And surrounded it, and built great siege works against it: The laying of a siege has been a common war tactic throughout history. In order to subdue an enemy city or military camp, an army will surround it and prevent all access to and from the place. Historically, the army would often construct a dike, a wall surrounding the city that blocked all entrances. Sometimes fortifications were built around the besieged city to allow control of the access roads.

10:1 | Flies of death putrefy and froth the perfumed oil: Drosophilidae are a family of flies that feed on liquids that emerge from fruits, some of which were used in ancient times to produce perfume. These flies spoil the fruit or their juices, causing them to sour or ferment, and their fine odor dissipates. These flies can be found all over the world. Even in ancient times, vessels containing perfumes would be tightly sealed in order to prevent both their evaporation and contact with flies or their larva. The term *zevuvei mavet*, flies of death, possibly stems from the fact that they hover over corpses in a manner similar to larger flies.

DISCUSSION

9:14–15 | There was a small city.... Nobody remembered that poor man: The Sages interpret this story as a parable about man's situation in general: He is attacked by a great king, which is his evil inclination. The poor and wise man is one's good inclination, which saves him by encouraging repentance and good deeds, but when the evil inclination reigns, the individual fails to remember the good inclination (see Ralbag; *Nedarim* 32b; see also *Tanya, Likkutei Amarim* 9–17).

4 Kohelet offers a word to the wise: **If the spirit of the ruler shall be raised against you,** and he is angry with you, **do not abandon your place.** Stay put and do not depart from his presence because of his rebuke or in a state of shame, **for in its abating he will allow great sins.** Even great offenses can be forgiven over time, when the ruler's anger is assuaged, but if you abandon your position in embarrassment, you might lose everything.[127]

5 **There is an evil that I have seen under the sun, like an error that emerges from before the ruler.** One of the great evils in the world is the mistake of one in a position of power. When a person of authority errs, the harm that he is liable to cause is more severe than that of a commoner. Corruption and injustice inevitably follow:

6 Sometimes **folly is set on lofty heights,** as incompetent people can rise to prominence, **and** meanwhile **the wealthy** in spirit[128] **sit in lowliness.**

7 **I have seen servants** conducting themselves like masters, riding **upon horses, and princes walking on the ground like servants.**

8 Some people fail specifically due to their own actions, and against their best intentions:[129] **One who digs a pit, into it he will fall; and one who breaches a fence, a serpent,** hiding in the cracks between the stones of the fence, **will bite him.**[B]

Water pit, Tel Arad, early Bronze Age

9 It is never clear whether labor will yield a commensurate reward, as **one who transports stones** for a constructive purpose will not always achieve his objective, while he **will** certainly **be distressed by them,** as pain and suffering inevitably result from that grueling activity. **And** similarly, **one who splits wood will be endangered by them.**[130] He might be cut or wounded by the wood chips. Alternatively, his body may overheat from the hard labor.[131]

10 **If the iron** of an ax, or any other cutting tool, **is blunt, and one did not whet the edge** of the blade, even if **he intensifies his exertion** it will be to no avail. In that instance, **the advantage is in preparation with wisdom.** Wisdom is advantageous with respect to physical labor, as it enables one to prepare in advance and thus achieve one's objective with minimal effort.[132]

11 **If the serpent bites without a spell,**[D] since the charmer could not control it, **there is no advantage to the charmer [*ba'al halashon*].**[133] Alternatively, the term *ba'al halashon* refers to a person who speaks evil, likening him to a serpent that bites: Just as there are snakebites that no spell can heal, so too one who speaks evil can cause irrevocable harm.[134]

12 In contrast to one who speaks evil,[135] **the words of the mouth of a wise man are grace, but the lips of a fool,** his ill-advised comments, **will destroy him,** lead to his ruin, or cause him to lose the respect of others.

13 **The beginning of the words from his mouth is foolishness, and the end from his mouth is evil debauchery.** His statements are initially merely silly, but ultimately they will lead to insanity.

14 Unlike a wise person, who remains mostly quiet, mindful that silence is a safeguard for wisdom,[136] **the fool will proliferate words.** In his many comments he presumes to be able to foresee the future, but **man knows not what will be, and that which will be after him, who can tell him?**

15 **The toil of the fools will exhaust him, as he will not know how to go to a city.** Since a fool does not know how to reach his objective, he soon becomes weary and wastes his energy for nothing.[137]

16 One's wisdom or foolishness is manifest in his conduct. **Woe is you, land, that your king is a boy,** young and inexperienced, and ruins the land with his vanities, **and your princes dine in the morning,** instead of working on behalf of the country.

17 **Happy are you, land, that your king is a free man,** or the son of an esteemed family, a distinguished individual,[138] **and your princes dine at the proper time,** not immediately upon waking, but at the appropriate time, in accordance with the tasks ahead. If so, they will eat **in valor,** enough for them to be healthy and strong, **and not in drunkenness.**[139]

18 **With laziness,** due to idleness, **the ceiling sags,**[B] the roof collapses. When a roof is not properly maintained, it sags and may eventually collapse. **And with idleness of the hands, the house leaks.** Neglect of a house will lead to a leaky roof.

19 Kohelet lists the power of money alongside the value of wisdom and diligence: **For laughter,** entertainment, **one prepares bread,** a feast, and **wine cheers the living, and money answers everything,** provides a solution for all problems.

20 **Even in your thought do not curse a king,**[140] **and** even when you are alone **in your bedrooms do not curse the rich, as a bird of the heavens will carry the voice, and a winged creature will tell a matter.** Any spoken words will eventually become public, as even if they are not spread by people, they will be disseminated by birds or other airy, imperceptible airborne mediums.[141] Therefore, one must be careful even with regard to his thoughts, and all the more so with regard to his spoken words, which are liable to cause the speaker great trouble.

ד לַכֹּל סָכָל הוּא: אִם־רוּחַ הַמּוֹשֵׁל תַּעֲלֶה עָלֶיךָ מְקוֹמְךָ אַל־תַּנַּח כִּי מַרְפֵּא יַנִּיחַ
ה חֲטָאִים גְּדוֹלִים: יֵשׁ רָעָה רָאִיתִי תַּחַת הַשָּׁמֶשׁ כִּשְׁגָגָה שֶׁיֹּצָא מִלִּפְנֵי הַשַּׁלִּיט:
ו ז נִתַּן הַסֶּכֶל בַּמְּרוֹמִים רַבִּים וַעֲשִׁירִים בַּשֵּׁפֶל יֵשֵׁבוּ: רָאִיתִי עֲבָדִים עַל־סוּסִים
ח וְשָׂרִים הֹלְכִים כַּעֲבָדִים עַל־הָאָרֶץ: חֹפֵר גּוּמָּץ בּוֹ יִפּוֹל וּפֹרֵץ גָּדֵר יִשְּׁכֶנּוּ נָחָשׁ:
ט י מַסִּיעַ אֲבָנִים יֵעָצֵב בָּהֶם בּוֹקֵעַ עֵצִים יִסָּכֶן בָּם: אִם־קֵהָה הַבַּרְזֶל וְהוּא לֹא־פָנִים
יא קִלְקַל וַחֲיָלִים יְגַבֵּר וְיִתְרוֹן הַכְשֵׁיר חָכְמָה: אִם־יִשֹּׁךְ הַנָּחָשׁ בְּלוֹא־לָחַשׁ וְאֵין
יב יג יִתְרוֹן לְבַעַל הַלָּשׁוֹן: דִּבְרֵי פִי־חָכָם חֵן וְשִׂפְתוֹת כְּסִיל תְּבַלְּעֶנּוּ: תְּחִלַּת דִּבְרֵי־
יד פִיהוּ סִכְלוּת וְאַחֲרִית פִּיהוּ הוֹלֵלוּת רָעָה: וְהַסָּכָל יַרְבֶּה דְבָרִים לֹא־יֵדַע הָאָדָם
טו מַה־שֶּׁיִּהְיֶה וַאֲשֶׁר יִהְיֶה מֵאַחֲרָיו מִי יַגִּיד לוֹ: עֲמַל הַכְּסִילִים תְּיַגְּעֶנּוּ אֲשֶׁר לֹא־
טז יז יָדַע לָלֶכֶת אֶל־עִיר: אִי־לָךְ אֶרֶץ שֶׁמַּלְכֵּךְ נָעַר וְשָׂרַיִךְ בַּבֹּקֶר יֹאכֵלוּ: אַשְׁרֵיךְ
יח אֶרֶץ שֶׁמַּלְכֵּךְ בֶּן־חוֹרִים וְשָׂרַיִךְ בָּעֵת יֹאכֵלוּ בִּגְבוּרָה וְלֹא בַשְּׁתִי: בַּעֲצַלְתַּיִם
יט יִמַּךְ הַמְּקָרֶה וּבְשִׁפְלוּת יָדַיִם יִדְלֹף הַבָּיִת: לִשְׂחוֹק עֹשִׂים לֶחֶם וְיַיִן יְשַׂמַּח חַיִּים
כ וְהַכֶּסֶף יַעֲנֶה אֶת־הַכֹּל: גַּם בְּמַדָּעֲךָ מֶלֶךְ אַל־תְּקַלֵּל וּבְחַדְרֵי מִשְׁכָּבְךָ אַל־תְּקַלֵּל

BACKGROUND

10:8 | **And one who breaches a fence, a serpent will bite him:** It was the practice to place dry construction between the boundaries of fields, e.g., stones without cement, as terraces of sorts. Various insects, lizards, and snakes would hide between the cracks and gaps of such fences. During the winter, snakes seek to slow their metabolism and enter a state of sluggishness similar to hibernation. The demolition of a fence in which a snake is hidden can provoke a defensive response from the creature, which might include biting the purported assailant, the one breaching the fence.

10:18 | **With laziness, the ceiling sags:** The roofs of houses in the ancient Land of Israel rested on wooden beams. For a reasonably sized house, the beams would consist of several sections. Therefore, regular inspection and reinforcement of the beams were essential for maintenance of structural integrity. If the beams were neglected, they could bend and break under the weight of the roof. Eventually, the roof was liable to collapse on the occupants of the house.

DISCUSSION

10:11 | **If the serpent bites without a spell:** Alternatively, this phrase means: If the serpent bites before it hisses. The hissing of a snake can result from the exhalation of air or the friction of its scales as it moves. These sounds alert those in proximity to the snake.

Dealing with the Future

ECCLESIASTES 11:1–12:8

This section begins with a series of statements addressing the manner in which people cope with their inability to know the future. Subsequently, Kohelet recommends that a person enjoy life while still young, but he also mentions that in old age there will be no recourse for a person to be taken to account for those uninhibited pleasures.

The section ends with a gradual and harsh description of old age, when God exacts a price for the desire of a person's childhood and the lust of his youth, in which he freely indulged. Through poetic, powerful images, Kohelet depicts the decline of the human body. His description of old age and inevitable death brings Kohelet back to his opening statement with regard to the futility of the world.

11 1 **Cast your bread upon the water,** perform acts of kindness and virtue, even if you receive no immediate remuneration, **for after many days,** at the appropriate time, **you will find it,** your reward.[142]

2 **Distribute a portion to seven, and even to eight;** divide your resources, **as you do not know what evil will be upon the earth,** and which of your possessions, or your land, will be harmed.

3 **If the clouds are filled with rain, they will** certainly **empty onto the earth,** but one cannot know where exactly the rain will fall. In contrast, **if a tree falls in the south or in the north, the place where the tree falls, there it will be.**[143] There are some occurrences whose consequences are predictable in all their details, whereas others are beyond man's grasp.

"If the clouds are filled with rain"

"The place where the tree falls, there it will be"

4 In these ambiguous conditions, the search for certainty and control can lead to paralysis: **One who awaits the wind,** postponing sowing his field until it calms, as it is difficult to sow in a strong wind, **will not** ever **sow, and** likewise, **one who gazes at the clouds,** calculating his steps to schedule his harvest at a time when he can be certain that it will not rain,[144] **will not** ever **reap.** One should act even when conditions are not ideal rather than endlessly delaying.

5 **Just as you do not know the conduct of the wind,** or one's inspiration or will power, **or**[145] **how the fetuses grow in a womb of the pregnant,** as the limbs of the fetus are hidden from the eye,[146] **so you will not know the work of God who does everything.**

6 Therefore, **in the morning sow your seed, and in the evening do not rest your hand.**[D] Do not be lazy, but rather sow again in the evening, even if you already sowed in the morning, **as you do not know which will succeed, this or that, or whether they both alike will be good.**

"Sow your seed"

"Do not rest your hand." Pioneer tossing seeds in a field, Kibbutz Rudgas, Petah Tikva, 1930–36

7 After recommending that one act even in conditions of uncertainty, Kohelet stresses that one should also enjoy the brightness of the world: **The light is sweet, and it is good for the eyes to see the sun.**[B]

8 **For if a man lives many years, let him rejoice in all of them, and** still, **let him remember the days of darkness,** old age, death, and bad times in general, **as they will be many.** He should remember that **everything that is coming is futility.**

9 Likewise, **rejoice, young man, in your childhood. Let your heart cheer you in the days of your youth. Follow the ways of your heart and the sight of your eyes, but** along with your enjoyment of the vast theater of action presented to you in your youth, **know that for all these, God will bring you to judgment.** The suggestion that you should do as you please is limited, as you cannot escape future judgment for your current choices.[147]

10 Therefore, despite the recommendation that one should do as he wishes, **remove anger from your heart,** thereby **purging evil from your flesh, as childhood and youth are futility.** The pleasures of youth will lose all meaning when you reflect upon them from a mature perspective and assess their consequences.

12 1 **Remember your Creator** even **in the days of your youth, before the evil days come, and the years arrive when you will say: I have no desire in them.** The evil days mentioned here do not necessarily feature devastating external events; rather, the verse is referring to a period when you will no longer be able to do as you wish, the period of old age.[148]

2 The following description of old age is detailed and poetic, with numerous images designed to arouse terror of this period

א עָשִׁיר כִּי עוֹף הַשָּׁמַיִם יוֹלִיךְ אֶת־הַקּוֹל וּבַעַל הכנפים יַגֵּיד דָּבָר׃ שַׁלַּח לַחְמְךָ כְּנָפַיִם
ב עַל־פְּנֵי הַמָּיִם כִּי־בְרֹב הַיָּמִים תִּמְצָאֶנּוּ׃ תֶּן־חֵלֶק לְשִׁבְעָה וְגַם לִשְׁמוֹנָה כִּי לֹא
ג תֵדַע מַה־יִּהְיֶה רָעָה עַל־הָאָרֶץ׃ אִם־יִמָּלְאוּ הֶעָבִים גֶּשֶׁם עַל־הָאָרֶץ יָרִיקוּ
ד וְאִם־יִפּוֹל עֵץ בַּדָּרוֹם וְאִם בַּצָּפוֹן מְקוֹם שֶׁיִּפּוֹל הָעֵץ שָׁם יְהוּא׃ שֹׁמֵר רוּחַ לֹא
ה יִזְרָע וְרֹאֶה בֶעָבִים לֹא יִקְצוֹר׃ כַּאֲשֶׁר אֵינְךָ יוֹדֵעַ מַה־דֶּרֶךְ הָרוּחַ כַּעֲצָמִים בְּבֶטֶן
ו הַמְּלֵאָה כָּכָה לֹא תֵדַע אֶת־מַעֲשֵׂה הָאֱלֹהִים אֲשֶׁר יַעֲשֶׂה אֶת־הַכֹּל׃ בַּבֹּקֶר זְרַע
אֶת־זַרְעֶךָ וְלָעֶרֶב אַל־תַּנַּח יָדֶךָ כִּי אֵינְךָ יוֹדֵעַ אֵי זֶה יִכְשָׁר הֲזֶה אוֹ־זֶה וְאִם־
ז ח שְׁנֵיהֶם כְּאֶחָד טוֹבִים׃ וּמָתוֹק הָאוֹר וְטוֹב לַעֵינַיִם לִרְאוֹת אֶת־הַשָּׁמֶשׁ׃ כִּי
אִם־שָׁנִים הַרְבֵּה יִחְיֶה הָאָדָם בְּכֻלָּם יִשְׂמָח וְיִזְכֹּר אֶת־יְמֵי הַחֹשֶׁךְ כִּי־הַרְבֵּה יִהְיוּ
ט כָּל־שֶׁבָּא הָבֶל׃ שְׂמַח בָּחוּר בְּיַלְדוּתֶךָ וִיטִיבְךָ לִבְּךָ בִּימֵי בְחוּרוֹתֶךָ וְהַלֵּךְ בְּדַרְכֵי
י לִבְּךָ ובמראי עֵינֶיךָ וְדָע כִּי עַל־כָּל־אֵלֶּה יְבִיאֲךָ הָאֱלֹהִים בַּמִּשְׁפָּט׃ וְהָסֵר כַּעַס וּבְמַרְאֵה
א מִלִּבֶּךָ וְהַעֲבֵר רָעָה מִבְּשָׂרֶךָ כִּי־הַיַּלְדוּת וְהַשַּׁחֲרוּת הָבֶל׃ וּזְכֹר אֶת־בּוֹרְאֶיךָ
בִּימֵי בְּחוּרֹתֶיךָ עַד אֲשֶׁר לֹא־יָבֹאוּ יְמֵי הָרָעָה וְהִגִּיעוּ שָׁנִים אֲשֶׁר תֹּאמַר אֵין־לִי
ב בָהֶם חֵפֶץ׃ עַד אֲשֶׁר לֹא־תֶחְשַׁךְ הַשֶּׁמֶשׁ וְהָאוֹר וְהַיָּרֵחַ וְהַכּוֹכָבִים וְשָׁבוּ הֶעָבִים

BACKGROUND

11:7| **The light is sweet, and it is good for the eyes to see the sun:** When the eyes absorb sunlight, they signal to the pineal gland in the brain to delay the secretion of melatonin. This hormone causes fatigue, drowsiness, and sleep. Melatonin is an important component of the biological clock, because its secretion induces sleep, whereas its reduction or absence enables one to stay alert.

DISCUSSION

11:6| **In the morning sow your seed, and in the evening do not rest your hand:** The Sages apply this proverb to having children. They state that if one is capable of fathering children in his old age, he should do so, since there is no way of knowing what will become of his offspring, which of them will be righteous (*Yevamot* 62b).

of human life: **Before the sun, the light, the moon, and the**
stars darken,[B] since an aging person, whose eyesight is dim-
ming, feels as though the sun does not shine as brightly as it did
during his youth, and that the moon and stars are dull, **and** as
though **the clouds return** to cast shade,[149] darkening the sun-
light, even **after the rain** has stopped;
3 **on the day that the guards of the house tremble,** the hands
shake and malfunction, **and the infantry men**[150] **are distort-**
ed, and the grinders, the teeth,[151] **cease because they have**
dwindled, as most of them have fallen out, **and it is dark for**
the gazers, the eyes, **through the windows,** as their vision is
impaired;[152]
4 **and the doors to the street are shut,** as the elderly person feels
as though the gates of the marketplace are locked to him,[153] **with**
the fading of the noise of the mill, since he is no longer active in the world, or because he does not eat much and he sees
no reason to run to the marketplace, or alternatively, the doors
to the street are the person's orifices,[154] or his lips,[155] and in that
case, the grinders (verse 3) refer to the digestive organs; **and**
one, the aging person, **arises,** wakes up, even **at the sound of**
the bird, as his sleep is not deep, and he has trouble going back
to sleep after he has woken up, and **yet,** although he awakens
even at the sound of a bird,[156] **all the sources of music are mut-**
ed, as he cannot hear music clearly, either because he is hard of
hearing, or because he no longer has any interest in listening
to music,[157] or, alternatively, the voice of the old person itself is
muted, because he is no longer capable of singing loudly;[158]
5 **when they,** the elderly, **will also be fearful of heights** and look
for ways to circumvent any hill or mound,[159] **and obstacles**
will be on the way. When they were young, they did not even
notice obstacles in the road but simply passed over them; however, in old age, when every step requires effort, it becomes clear
that the road is not smooth. **The almond tree will blossom,**
certain bones begin to bulge,[160] **but the grasshopper will be**
burdened, other parts of the body grow heavy and feel like a
burden,[161] and **the caper berry will fail,** sexual desire wanes
and disappears.[162] **For the man goes to his eternal home,** his
death, **and the mourners will circle in the street.**[B] These are
the people who announce a death and conduct a public eulogy.
6 **Before the silver cord,** human will and strength to live, **is sev-**
ered,[163] **and the golden skull is shattered, and the pitcher is**
broken at the spring, an allusion to the stomach, which holds
food as a spring holds water,[164] **and the wheel** used for drawing
water **is smashed into the cistern** and the body falls into the
grave,[165]

Wheel for drawing water from a well

7 **and the dust returns to the earth as it was, and the spirit re-**
turns to God who provided it.
8 Since every human life flows toward its end, and very few of
a person's accomplishments survive him, **futility of futilities,**
says Kohelet;[D] **all is futility.**

The Conclusion of the Book

ECCLESIASTES 12:9–14

Kohelet's concluding remarks begin with a description of his works of wisdom in the third person. At the end of his book, Kohelet emphasizes the single source of the many and diverse sayings of the Sages and warns against too many literary projects.

Although the book analyzes the various human life experiences and the fluctuations of the mind that seeks meaning in man's world, it ends with an unequivocal statement about the value of the fear of God and the observance of His commandments.

9 **Beyond that Kohelet was wise** himself, **he moreover taught**
the people knowledge, considered,[166] or preached, **and in-**
vestigated, composed many proverbs, both orally and in
writing, e.g., in the book of Proverbs, which contains many sayings and wise maxims.[167]
10 **Kohelet sought to find matters of value, and** to find **that**
which was written with integrity, matters of truth that have
already been written.
11 **The words of the wise are** strong **like prods,** sticks with nails
at their ends, which are used for striking and piercing animals in
order to urge them along,[168]
and like well-fastened[169]
nails are the collectors of
wisdom, statements of the
Sages, whose words of wisdom appear to have been
collected from many sources,
but in reality **they were given**
from one shepherd, God.[170]

Nail from the Persian period, Nahal Tut, Israel

12 At the end of the book, Kohelet advises his reader: **More than**

ג אַחַר הַגָּשֶׁם׃ בַּיּוֹם שֶׁיָּזֻעוּ שֹׁמְרֵי הַבַּיִת וְהִתְעַוְּתוּ אַנְשֵׁי הֶחָיִל וּבָטְלוּ הַטֹּחֲנוֹת
ד כִּי מִעֵטוּ וְחָשְׁכוּ הָרֹאוֹת בָּאֲרֻבּוֹת׃ וְסֻגְּרוּ דְלָתַיִם בַּשּׁוּק בִּשְׁפַל קוֹל הַטַּחֲנָה
ה וְיָקוּם לְקוֹל הַצִּפּוֹר וְיִשַּׁחוּ כָּל־בְּנוֹת הַשִּׁיר׃ גַּם מִגָּבֹהַּ יִרָאוּ וְחַתְחַתִּים בַּדֶּרֶךְ
וְיָנֵאץ הַשָּׁקֵד וְיִסְתַּבֵּל הֶחָגָב וְתָפֵר הָאֲבִיּוֹנָה כִּי־הֹלֵךְ הָאָדָם אֶל־בֵּית עוֹלָמוֹ
ו וְסָבְבוּ בַשּׁוּק הַסֹּפְדִים׃ עַד אֲשֶׁר לֹא־ירחק חֶבֶל הַכֶּסֶף וְתָרֻץ גֻּלַּת הַזָּהָב יֵרָתֵק
ז וְתִשָּׁבֶר כַּד עַל־הַמַּבּוּעַ וְנָרֹץ הַגַּלְגַּל אֶל־הַבּוֹר׃ וְיָשֹׁב הֶעָפָר עַל־הָאָרֶץ כְּשֶׁהָיָה
ח וְהָרוּחַ תָּשׁוּב אֶל־הָאֱלֹהִים אֲשֶׁר נְתָנָהּ׃ הֲבֵל הֲבָלִים אָמַר הַקּוֹהֶלֶת הַכֹּל הָבֶל׃
ט וְיֹתֵר שֶׁהָיָה קֹהֶלֶת חָכָם עוֹד לִמַּד־דַּעַת אֶת־הָעָם וְאִזֵּן וְחִקֵּר תִּקֵּן מְשָׁלִים
י יא הַרְבֵּה׃ בִּקֵּשׁ קֹהֶלֶת לִמְצֹא דִּבְרֵי־חֵפֶץ וְכָתוּב יֹשֶׁר דִּבְרֵי אֱמֶת׃ דִּבְרֵי חֲכָמִים
יב כַּדָּרְבֹנוֹת וּכְמַשְׂמְרוֹת נְטוּעִים בַּעֲלֵי אֲסֻפּוֹת נִתְּנוּ מֵרֹעֶה אֶחָד׃ וְיֹתֵר מֵהֵמָּה

BACKGROUND

12:2 | **Before the sun, the light, the moon, and the stars darken:** One of the characteristics of an aging body is visual impairment. The aging of the lens leads to a decrease in focus and in the flexibility of vision at various distances, turbidity of the lens, cataracts, and a gradual degradation of vision. Glaucoma, which affects the optic nerve, can reduce the nerve's activity to the point of blindness. In the absence of focus, the stars disappear first, then the moon blurs, and finally vision itself, sunlight, entirely vanishes.

12:5 | **And the mourners [*sofedim*] will circle in the street:** A *hesped*, eulogy, or *sipittu* in Akkadian, is a system of ceremonies held around a person's death. In ancient times, professional eulogizers would come to enhance the honor of the deceased by spreading the news of his death in public. They would issue sounds of mourning, wear mourning garments, e.g., sackcloth, spread ashes on their heads, and participate in the funeral and eulogies (see also Esther 4:3).

DISCUSSION

12:8 | **Kohelet [*hakohelet*]:** The word *hakohelet* literally means *the* Kohelet, which indicates that Kohelet was not the name of an individual but a term for a preacher or sage who delivers lectures to the public. This is how the word has been translated into other languages as well (see Rashi; Ibn Ezra).

that, my son, be careful. Alternatively, do not go further than the books that have already been written, with their words of truth:[171] Refrain from **making many books,** as it **is without end, and** in them there is **much prattle** or drivel, and it **is weariness of the flesh.** Reading those books provides little benefit.
13 **The end of the matter, everything,** all I have to say, **has been heard,** and after having established that childhood and adolescence are vanity, old age is terrifying, and everything else is herding wind, only one value remains: **Fear God and observe His commandments, for that is all of man.**[D]
14 **For every action** of man[172] **God will bring to judgment, for every unknown.** You cannot hide or escape. This judgment will encompass even actions that you have forgotten, **whether good or evil.**[D]

The penultimate verse is repeated in a communal recitation:

The end of the matter, everything has been heard: Fear God and observe His commandments, for that is all of man.

DISCUSSION

12:13 | **Fear God and observe His commandments, for that is all of man:** This verse is not a superficial addition designed to end this pessimistic book positively. Rather, it presents the conclusion that emerges from Kohelet's previous observations. The entire book has addressed human life, people's downfalls, and the futility and hope of life under the sun. In his ongoing journey of the mind, many ideas have been voiced that may negatively affect one's attitude toward human reality as such, but they do not refer to, or intend to harm, man's relationship with God. Therefore, Kohelet concludes with the declaration that the fear of God and the observance of His commandments are the only matters of value that remain.

12:14 | **The last verse:** In the public reading of Ecclesiastes, it is customary to repeat this, the penultimate verse of the book, as the last verse ends on a negative note. This is the custom with regard to the books of Isaiah, Malachi, and Lamentations as well.

יג בְּנִ֣י הִזָּהֵ֑ר עֲשׂ֨וֹת סְפָרִ֤ים הַרְבֵּה֙ אֵ֣ין קֵ֔ץ וְלַ֥הַג הַרְבֵּ֖ה יְגִעַ֥ת בָּשָֽׂר׃ ס֥וֹף דָּבָ֖ר הַכֹּ֣ל
יד נִשְׁמָ֑ע אֶת־הָאֱלֹהִ֤ים יְרָא֙ וְאֶת־מִצְוֺתָ֣יו שְׁמ֔וֹר כִּי־זֶ֖ה כָּל־הָאָדָֽם׃ כִּ֧י אֶת־כָּל־
מַעֲשֶׂ֗ה הָאֱלֹהִ֛ים יָבִ֥א בְמִשְׁפָּ֖ט עַ֣ל כָּל־נֶעְלָ֑ם אִם־ט֖וֹב וְאִם־רָֽע׃

סוף דבר הכל נשמע את האלהים ירא
ואת מצותיו שמור כי זה כל האדם

Esther

Esther

INTRODUCTION TO ESTHER

The book of Esther relates an attempt to destroy the entire Jewish people, and its failure due to the interference of Queen Esther. Haman's motivation for his evil plan seems to be a combination of his contempt for Jewish separateness and the Jews' unique lifestyle and religion (3:8) with his personal rivalry with and hatred of Mordekhai and, by extension, of his people (3:4–5). However the motivation is understood, the Jewish people are treated as a single entity with a single fate, despite their exiled state, in which they are "scattered and dispersed among the peoples in all the provinces" (3:8). It is therefore fitting that their salvation is celebrated with a national holiday, Purim, as described at the end of the book (9:20–28). The Sages instituted that the book of Esther be read on Purim in the evening and in the morning.[1]

The book of Esther states that it was written by Mordekhai and Esther as an epistle to the Jewish people throughout the Persian Empire.[2] It is possible that it was composed with the assistance of various sages and advisors as a semi-official document of the Persian Empire.[3] This status accounts for the book's gentle treatment of King Ahashverosh despite his role as one of the central figures in the attempted annihilation of the Jews. Although it is possible to detect unflattering undercurrents with regard to the king, there is not one word of direct criticism of Ahashverosh explicitly stated in the text.

The absence of any direct reference to God is perhaps also a reflection of the book of Esther's status as a Persian imperial document, to be read by all Persia's subjects.[4] Although the Septuagint and the Aramaic translations insert a passage depicting Esther praying to God, it does not appear in the original. In fact, God's name does not appear in the book at all. Nevertheless, there are not-very-subtle allusions to the hidden hand of Divine Providence that pulls the strings in the story: The sequence of events, described so fully and dramatically, contains no peripheral incidents. Each detail is linked to another aspect of the plot, until the complex chain of events directed from on High reaches its inevitable conclusion and is revealed to all. Faith in God is undoubtedly at the heart of the book.

Chronology of Events in the Book of Esther according to the Sages[5]

Kings	Year BCE	Major events	Prophets of the era
Nebuchadnezzar	422	Destruction of the First Temple	Jeremiah, Ezekiel, Daniel
Cyrus the Great and Darius the Mede	369	Conquest of Babylon by Cyrus the Persian and Darius the Mede Founding of the Persian Empire	
Cyrus the Great (3 years)	369	Edict of Cyrus	
	368	Return of Zerubavel (Sheshbatzar) and Yehoshua the High Priest to the Land of Israel Rebuilding of the altar and laying of the foundations of the Second Temple (Ezra 3:10)	
Ahashverosh son of Darius the Mede (14 years)	367	Death of Cyrus	
	368?–350	Temporary cessation of work on the Second Temple due to political interference by Israel's enemies (Ezra 4)	
	363	Ahashverosh's first feast	
	359	Crowning of Esther as queen of Ahashverosh, in the seventh year of his reign	
	354–353	Haman's plot and downfall	
Darius the Persian (Artahshasta, 36 years)	353	Suppression of a revolt in the city of Babylon	Haggai, Zechariah
	348	Completion of work on the Second Temple (Ezra 6:15)	
	347	Return of Ezra to the Land of Israel (Ezra 7)	Malachi
	334	Appointment of Nehemiah as governor Rebuilding of the walls of Jerusalem and renewal of the covenant (Nehemiah 10:1)	
	318	Conquests of Alexander the Great	

Chronology of Events in the Book of Esther according to the Standard Chronology

Kings	Year BCE	Major events	Prophets of the era
Nebuchadnezzar	586	Destruction of the First Temple	Jeremiah, Ezekiel, Daniel
Cyrus the Great	550	Founding of the Persian Empire	
	539	Conquest of Babylon by Cyrus Edict of Cyrus	
	538	Return of Zerubavel (Sheshbatzar) and Yehoshua the High Priest to the Land of Israel Rebuilding of the altar and laying of the foundations of the Second Temple (Ezra 3:10)	
	538?–520	Temporary cessation of work on the Second Temple due to interference by Judah's enemies (Ezra 4)	
Cambyses	530	Succession as emperor after Cyrus	
Darius the Great	522	Beginning of reign with the suppression of a revolt in the city of Babylon and in Persia	
	520	Resumption of work on the Second Temple (Ezra 4:24–6:14)	Haggai, Zechariah
	516	Completion of work on the Second Temple (Ezra 6:15)	
Xerxes (Ahashverosh)	483	Ahashverosh's first feast	Malachi
	479	Crowning of Esther as queen of Ahashverosh, in the seventh year of his reign	
	474–473	Haman's plot and downfall	
Artaxerxes (Artahshasta)	458	Arrival of Ezra in the Land of Israel (Ezra 7)	
	445	Appointment of Nehemiah as governor Rebuilding of the walls of Jerusalem and renewal of the covenant (Nehemiah 10:1)	
Alexander the Great	331	Conquest of the Persian Empire by Alexander	

Esther

The Feasts and the End of Vashti's Reign

ESTHER 1:1–22

As a backdrop to the main story, this prelude vividly represents the hedonistic culture that was prevalent in the kingdom of Persia and Media by detailing a series of ostentatious banquets held for the masses, featuring an abundance of wine and extravagant displays of wealth. However, affairs take a turn for the worse when the queen refuses to obey the king, thereby undermining the self-image of a ruler who was accustomed to being obeyed without question.

1 1 **It was in the days of Ahashverosh,**[D] **that Ahashverosh who reigned from India to Kush,**[B] southern Egypt. The Persian kingdom, which was at its zenith at the time, was divided into **one hundred and twenty-seven provinces.**[B] The empire was divided into large regions that were under the control of governors, called satraps, while a subordinate governor was appointed over each state or province.

Xerxes I, identified as Ahashverosh, stone relief, 560–331 BCE

Map of the Persian Empire

2 It happened that **in those days, when King Ahashverosh sat on the royal throne that was in the Shushan citadel [*habira*].**[B] Shushan, also known as Susa, was a city in Elam, whose ruins are still extant.[6] Inside the city was a royal fortress, or citadel [*bira*], where both the central government and Ahashverosh's palace were located.[7]

3 **In the third year of his reign,** after he had crushed all those who stood in his way,[8] **he made a** large public **banquet for all his princes and his servants.** He did not hold his coronation celebrations immediately upon ascending the throne, possibly because he was preoccupied with settling internal disputes.[9] Once he had firmly established his reign, he invited **the elite of**

King of Persia on his throne receiving a royal audience, stone relief, Persepolis, 560–331 BCE

Persia and Media,[B] two separate states that were partly unified; **the nobles**[B] **and princes** who were appointed to be in charge **of the provinces before him,**

4 **with his showing the riches of his glorious kingdom, and the honor of his splendid majesty, for many days.** The feast, which was designed to publicly display the king's riches and might, lasted **one hundred and eighty days.**

Persian soldiers in flat hats, and Medes in rounded hats, relief, Persepolis, sixth century BCE

5 **Upon the completion of those days,** during which a banquet was held for people who came from afar, **the king made a**

אסתר

א וַיְהִי בִּימֵי אֲחַשְׁוֵרוֹשׁ הוּא אֲחַשְׁוֵרוֹשׁ הַמֹּלֵךְ מֵהֹדּוּ וְעַד־כּוּשׁ שֶׁבַע וְעֶשְׂרִים א
ב וּמֵאָה מְדִינָה: בַּיָּמִים הָהֵם כְּשֶׁבֶת ׀ הַמֶּלֶךְ אֲחַשְׁוֵרוֹשׁ עַל כִּסֵּא מַלְכוּתוֹ אֲשֶׁר
ג בְּשׁוּשַׁן הַבִּירָה: בִּשְׁנַת שָׁלוֹשׁ לְמָלְכוֹ עָשָׂה מִשְׁתֶּה לְכָל־שָׂרָיו וַעֲבָדָיו חֵיל ׀
ד פָּרַס וּמָדַי הַפַּרְתְּמִים וְשָׂרֵי הַמְּדִינוֹת לְפָנָיו: בְּהַרְאֹתוֹ אֶת־עֹשֶׁר כְּבוֹד מַלְכוּתוֹ
ה וְאֶת־יְקָר תִּפְאֶרֶת גְּדוּלָּתוֹ יָמִים רַבִּים שְׁמוֹנִים וּמְאַת יוֹם: וּבִמְלוֹאת ׀ הַיָּמִים

BACKGROUND

1:1 | **From India to Kush:** The Achaemenid, or First Persian, Empire reached its greatest extent under Darius the Great, who reigned 522–486 BCE. By the end of his reign it stretched from the banks of the Indus in the east to the kingdom of Ethiopia (Kush) in the southwest.

One hundred and twenty-seven provinces: The Persian Empire was divided into provinces, each headed by a satrap [*aḥashdarpan*]. In Old Persian, the word *aḥashdarpan* means shield of the kingdom (see 3:12). External sources indicate that the number of provinces established by the Persian government was far fewer than one hundred and twenty-seven, but such provinces were often divided into smaller units ruled by subordinate governors. Taking this into account, one may arrive at 127 provinces.

1:2 | **The Shushan citadel:** In Old Persian this city was called Susha, Susa in Greek and Latin, and Shush in modern Persian. It was the oldest and most important city of the Proto-Elamite kingdom in southwest Persia, in the vicinity of the Karkheh River, at the foot of the Zagros Mountains. Cambyses II (died 522 BCE), the son of Cyrus II, also known as Cyrus the Great, established Shushan as his capital, and during the reign of Darius I, Shushan was the political and administrative capital of Persia and one of its four capital cities, together with Persepolis, Ecbatana, and Babylon. The city lost its prominence after the Alexandrian conquests at the end of the fourth century BCE.

1:3 | **Persia and Media:** Media was an ancient kingdom in the northeast of Persia, south of the Caspian Sea. From the ninth century BCE it was involved in unremitting conflict with Assyria. After Media entered into a pact with Babylon toward the end of the seventh century, the two nations defeated Assyria. In 550 BCE, Cyrus the Great conquered Media and unified it with Persia. Some attribute the difference in the order of the two names, "Persia and Media" or "Media and Persia" (e.g., 10:2; Daniel 5:28, 6:9), to the change of kings from Persian to Median, and vice versa. Others claim that the interchangeability of the order reflects the equality of the two states in the unified kingdom.

The nobles [*partemim*]: From the Old Persian *partema*, meaning the first, those that are closest to the king.

DISCUSSION

1:1 | **Ahashverosh:** Since the Persian name of the king was not Ahashverosh, it is difficult to identify this figure. It is most likely that he is the king known in Greek literature as Xerxes I, or Khshayarsha in Persian. Much of the information about Xerxes I comes from Greek historians, who documented the wars the Greeks fought against the Persians. Their accounts indicate that Xerxes I ascended the throne after the Persian kingdom had suffered civil wars, conspiracies, and betrayals. This may explain why some of Ahashverosh's behavior as related in the book makes him appear paranoid. Even when the king was sitting "on the royal throne" (verse 2), nothing could be taken for granted.

banquet for all the people who were present in the Shushan citadel, from great to small, seven days. He may have treated them to this feast in an attempt to win the trust of the citadel's residents, many of whom were government officials.[10] This banquet took place **in the court of the garden of the king's audience hall,**[B] a courtyard with a garden or orchard, adjacent to the audience hall.

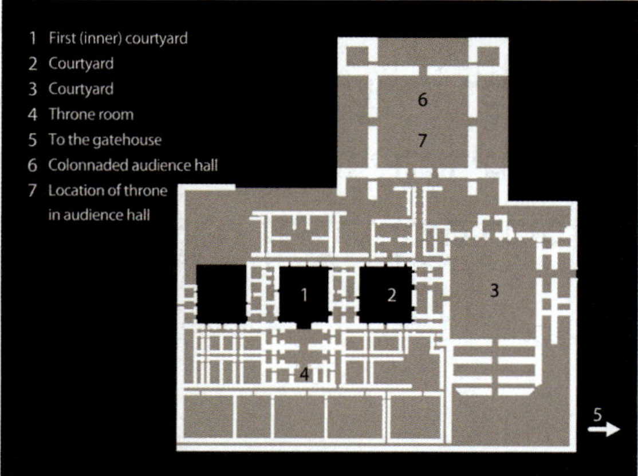

Plan of the ancient palace, Shushan

6 The place was decorated with expensive fabrics: **White linen,**[B] **green cotton [*karpas*],**[B] **and sky-blue wool,** all **bound with**

Remains of pillars from the palace of the kings of Persia, Persepolis, fifth century BCE

cords of fine **linen**[B] **and purple**[B] **wool.** All these fabrics and cords were hung **on silver rods**[B] **and marble pillars,**[B] and there were **couches of gold and silver on a floor of alabaster, marble, mother-of-pearl, and precious stone.**[B]
7 **Serving drink in vessels of gold,** as befitted a royal feast, **and vessels of diverse kinds;** the guests were offered vessels of various shapes and colors, in accordance with their status and needs. **And abundant royal wine** was provided at the king's expense, **in accordance with the king's bounty,** offered freely and without concern for the cost.

Excavated vessels, Shushan

8 **The drinking was as customary,** following the accepted rules of etiquette, and **without constraint.** Since the king wanted the people to feel part of the royal feast, they were free to drink as they pleased. **For so did the king establish,** command,[11] **for all the officials of his palace, to act in accordance with the wishes of each and every man.** The Persian policy was not to try to impose conformity within the multicultural empire, but to grant each nation the freedom to preserve their identity, language, and customs.
9 **Also Vashti**[D] **the queen made a banquet for the women,** in parallel to the great feast for the men, **in** another wing **of the royal palace of King Ahashverosh.** The feast for the women was held separately from that of the men to avoid the undesirable consequences of mixed festivities.[12] Unlike the king's wild feast, the women's banquet was a more dignified affair.
10 **On the seventh day** of the feast, **when the king was merry with wine;** he was in good spirits after much drinking. It is hard to tell whether he was actually drunk, partly due to the rather formal tone of the description here. In any case, **he,** Ahashverosh, **said to Mehuman, Bizeta, Harbona, Bigta, Avagta, Zetar, and Karkas, the seven** special **chamberlains [*sarisim*]**[B] **who attended to King Ahashverosh,** and who were closest to him. The word *sarisim* can also mean eunuchs and it can be assumed that these were actual eunuchs, as their job required them to pass between the men and the women.[13] In the raucous atmosphere of debauchery at the party, the king

DISCUSSION

1:9 | **Vashti:** This sounds like a Persian name (see Ibn Ezra, second commentary), and in a collection of Zoroastrian texts from the tenth century BCE there are two words that are possibly the source of the name: *vashita*, the best, and *ushiti*, the beloved. However, there is no certainty that Vashti was Persian. It is clear from the story that she was more than merely one of the king's many wives and concubines, and that she was well aware of her superior status. According to a tradition of the Sages, Vashti was originally a Babylonian princess (see, e.g., *Megilla* 10b). There are other instances in the Bible where a foreigner who was brought into a royal house was given a new name upon entering the royal household (see Genesis 41:45; Daniel 1:7).

הָאֵלֶּה עָשָׂה הַמֶּלֶךְ לְכָל־הָעָם הַנִּמְצְאִים בְּשׁוּשַׁן הַבִּירָה לְמִגָּדוֹל וְעַד־קָטָן
ו מִשְׁתֶּה שִׁבְעַת יָמִים בַּחֲצַר גִּנַּת בִּיתַן הַמֶּלֶךְ: חוּר ׀ כַּרְפַּס וּתְכֵלֶת אָחוּז בְּחַבְלֵי־
בוּץ וְאַרְגָּמָן עַל־גְּלִילֵי כֶסֶף וְעַמּוּדֵי שֵׁשׁ מִטּוֹת ׀ זָהָב וָכֶסֶף עַל רִצְפַת בַּהַט־וָשֵׁשׁ
ז וְדַר וְסֹחָרֶת: וְהַשְׁקוֹת בִּכְלֵי זָהָב וְכֵלִים מִכֵּלִים שׁוֹנִים וְיֵין מַלְכוּת רָב כְּיַד הַמֶּלֶךְ:
ח וְהַשְּׁתִיָּה כַדָּת אֵין אֹנֵס כִּי־כֵן ׀ יִסַּד הַמֶּלֶךְ עַל כָּל־רַב בֵּיתוֹ לַעֲשׂוֹת כִּרְצוֹן
ט אִישׁ־וָאִישׁ: גַּם וַשְׁתִּי הַמַּלְכָּה עָשְׂתָה מִשְׁתֵּה נָשִׁים בֵּית הַמַּלְכוּת
י אֲשֶׁר לַמֶּלֶךְ אֲחַשְׁוֵרוֹשׁ: בַּיּוֹם הַשְּׁבִיעִי כְּטוֹב לֵב־הַמֶּלֶךְ בַּיָּיִן אָמַר לִמְהוּמָן
בִּזְּתָא חַרְבוֹנָא בִּגְתָא וַאֲבַגְתָא זֵתַר וְכַרְכַּס שִׁבְעַת הַסָּרִיסִים הַמְשָׁרְתִים אֶת־

BACKGROUND

1:5 | **The court of the garden of the king's audience hall [*bitan*]:** The royal palace in Shushan, which has been unearthed in archaeological excavations, was built in the Syrian-western style. It included four inner garden courtyards, while its northern section contained the *bitan*, the audience hall. The word *bitan* is from the Akkadian *bitanu*, meaning an inner part or inner structure of a palace or temple. It has been surmised that this term developed from the Persian word *apadana*, an audience hall with columns. Sometimes tents or canopies were erected for guests in this hall or in an adjoining courtyard. During the excavations of the palace at Shushan, a tablet with cuneiform script was discovered. The text on this tablet describes the glories of the palace, specifically the cost and rarity of the building materials, and the expertise of its builders.

1:6 | **White linen [*hur*]:** A brilliant-white woven linen fabric, from *ḥiver*, meaning pale. Alternatively, this is a perforated [*meḥurar*] woven material, similar to netting (see Genesis 40:16; Isaiah 19:9).

Green cotton [*karpas*]: Apparently a woven cotton fabric, which was brought to the region from India in the time of Sennacherib. It is called *karpasa* in Sanskrit and *kirpas* in Persian.

Sky-blue [*tekhelet*] wool...purple [*argaman*] wool: These are wool fabrics colored with dyes extracted from snails that live in the Mediterranean Sea. *Tekhelet* is a shade of deep blue, extracted from the banded dye-murex, *Murex trunculus*, while *argaman* is the general name for a dark reddish-purple or deep purple dye produced from the spiny dye-murex, *Murex brandaris*. The liquid used for preparing these dyes was extracted from a protective secretion of the snails found in minute quantities in their hypobranchial glands. Many thousands of snails were required in order to dye a fabric or item of clothing and therefore these dyes were very expensive and the fabric dyed with them was used mainly by nobles and kings.

These two dyes were used for coloring the cloth tent-coverings of the Tabernacle (Exodus 26, 36–38) and the cloths with which the vessels of the Tabernacle were covered during journeys (Exodus 39), as well as the vestments of the High Priest (Exodus 28, 39). *Tekhelet* was also the dye used in ritual fringes (Numbers 15:38–39). In the affluent Persian kingdom, the king would have curtains and clothes that were made entirely of *tekhelet*-dyed wool.

Bound with cords of linen [*butz*]: Linen is made from flax, *Linum usitatissimum*, in Akkadian, *busu* (see Onkelos, Leviticus 16). The Sages likewise called the linen of the vestments of the High Priest *butz* (Mishna *Yoma* 3:4). These cords were used to spread the fabrics above the garden of the king's palace, where the feast was held, and to tie them to the silver and marble pillars. Linen cords are particularly strong and therefore well suited for this purpose. It seems that the cords of the Tent of Meeting were also made of linen.

Silver rods: These were poles of silver or a shiny white metal that supported the curtains which were hung to provide shade and decoration in the garden courtyard of the palace.

Marble pillars [*shesh*]: In ancient times, palace courtyards were often surrounded by a colonnade of pillars. These pillars often supported roofs, providing the courtyard with a shaded area. *Shesh* is white marble, which was preferred for monolithic, cylindrical pillars because it can be smoothed or engraved. Possibly, some of the pillars mentioned here did not have a roof over them and instead curtains were hung over them.

A floor of alabaster [*bahat*], marble, mother-of-pearl [*dar*], and precious stone [*soḥaret*]: The palaces and royal gardens of the kings of Persia and Media were paved with ceramic tiles or colorful flagstones, which were both decorative and durable. *Bahat* may not be alabaster, but rather *purfir*, a hard, red stone. *Dar* is mother-of-pearl, a substance produced by mollusks as an inner shell layer. Alternatively, *dar* may mean gold, from the Old Persian *darniya*. *Soḥaret* is probably a light-bluish precious stone, *sikhru* in Akkadian and *saharet* in ancient Egyptian. The Persians were experts in the production of ceramic tiles, in many different colors, including gold with a metallic sheen. It is possible that this list refers to different kinds of tiles in a colorful array.

1:10 | **Chamberlains [*sarisim*]:** While not all chamberlains would have been eunuchs, eunuchs did hold positions of authority in the royal courts of Assyria and Babylon, as well as in the

► Persian

bragged about his power, wealth, wisdom, and success. He also boasted of his beautiful wife.

11 The king, not satisfied with mere boasts, commanded his officials **to bring Queen Vashti before the king with the royal crown,** in order **to display her beauty to** all **the peoples and the princes,**[D] **as she was of fair appearance.**

12 **Queen Vashti refused to come at the king's word,**[B] delivered **by means of the chamberlains.** Her refusal to obey the command of the king, whose authority was absolutely unlimited, is indicative of her high status. She was unwilling to humiliate herself by parading her body before an audience. **The king was very angry, and his fury burned within him.** His rage was provoked by his wife's audacity in rejecting his demand, which was not issued privately but by an official delegation. His sensitivity to any slight to his honor was undoubtedly heightened by his inebriated state. Under the circumstances, he had anticipated that his request would be obeyed immediately and in full. Perhaps Vashti also alluded to his drunkenness, or mocked him, further enflaming his anger.[14] This is possibly the meaning of the phrase in verse 17, "for the matter [*devar*] of the queen," which can also mean the statement of the queen.

13 **The king communicated with the wise men, knowledgeable of the portents,** the astrologers, or his advisors in charge of managing the affairs of the kingdom,[15] **for so was the practice of the king before those learned in custom and law,**[BD] to present his problems before his legal counselors.[16]

14 The verse notes that **those** advisors who were **close to him,** the king, **were Karshena, Shetar, Admata, Tarshish, Meres, Marsena, and Memukhan, the seven princes of Persia and Media, who viewed the king's face,** who would meet with him. The king did not ordinarily appear in public and only his closest courtiers would regularly encounter him face-to-face.[17] It was these advisors **who were seated first in the kingdom,** as the chief ministers of his government.

15 The legal question under discussion was as follows: **As to the policy: What to do to Queen Vashti, in that she did not follow the order of King Ahashverosh by means of the chamberlains?** What is to be done in light of the queen's public refusal to obey the king's command, which was delivered to her by an official delegation?

16 **Memukhan said before the king and the princes** that the queen's sin was even worse than might have been thought: **It is not the king alone that Queen Vashti has wronged,** by failing to obey his instruction; **rather, it is all the princes, and all the peoples, who are in all the provinces of King Ahashverosh.** Since she publicly rebelled against the king, her decision will have ramifications that will spread throughout the entire Persian Empire.

17 **For the matter of the queen will get out to all the women, rendering their husbands contemptible in their eyes.** Although the queen did not issue an explicit declaration to this effect, and did not preach this type of conduct, her personal example here is likely to become the norm, **in their saying,** by women who seek to copy her: **King Ahashverosh said to bring Queen Vashti before him, but she did not come.** The queen has created a dangerous precedent.

18 From **this day** onward, **the princesses of Persia and Media,** the wives of the officials and nobles, **who have heard of the matter of the queen, will recount it to all the king's princes,** they will issue similar statements, and perhaps the wives of commoners will follow suit as well. Vashti's refusal will embolden these women when they quarrel with their husbands, **and** through this incident **there will be no end of contempt and wrath,** or contempt that should arouse our anger. This is not merely a personal slight, which the king could potentially overlook; rather, the broader consequences of the queen's refusal will be severe, as her scandalous behavior, even if not repeated, is likely to serve as a model that will be imitated throughout the kingdom.

19 Therefore, **if it pleases the king, let the royal edict be issued before him.** The decision should be published as a formal decree, **and** furthermore, **let it be written in** the book of **the decrees of Persia and Media,**[B] **not to be repealed,** as despite the king's power and position, he is considered to be

BACKGROUND

Persian court, and were always used in positions which involved the women of the royal court, and the royal harem. In Persia, such officials could achieve the status of senior advisors to the king, or be awarded other governmental posts, including that of generals who commanded military campaigns. The Persian kings relied on eunuchs for the most sensitive roles, such as the king's personal bodyguard, or his cupbearer.

1:12 | **Queen Vashti refused to come at the king's word:** The principal wife of the king of Persia enjoyed a lofty status in the court. She was typically an educated woman in control of her own daily routine who could even be involved in religious matters. Ahashverosh's request that Vashti be summoned in the middle of a feast was in defiance of the accepted practice, whereby only women from the harem were present at drinking parties; the queen would depart at the conclusion of the official meal. In fact, the queen had the right to choose whether or not to be seen by the king. Despite Zoroastrian beliefs according the king significant religious status as the agent of Ahura Mazda, even the king was not permitted to diverge from these ancient rules of the court unless they were changed by consent.

1:13 | **For so was the practice of the king before those learned in custom and law:** Since the rights of the Persian queen were based on ancient law, the discussion about her refusal required the presence of legal scholars.

יא פְּנֵי הַמֶּלֶךְ אֲחַשְׁוֵרוֹשׁ׃ לְהָבִיא אֶת־וַשְׁתִּי הַמַּלְכָּה לִפְנֵי הַמֶּלֶךְ בְּכֶתֶר מַלְכוּת
יב לְהַרְאוֹת הָעַמִּים וְהַשָּׂרִים אֶת־יָפְיָהּ כִּי־טוֹבַת מַרְאֶה הִיא׃ וַתְּמָאֵן הַמַּלְכָּה
וַשְׁתִּי לָבוֹא בִּדְבַר הַמֶּלֶךְ אֲשֶׁר בְּיַד הַסָּרִיסִים וַיִּקְצֹף הַמֶּלֶךְ מְאֹד וַחֲמָתוֹ בָּעֲרָה
יג בוֹ׃ וַיֹּאמֶר הַמֶּלֶךְ לַחֲכָמִים יֹדְעֵי הָעִתִּים כִּי־כֵן דְּבַר הַמֶּלֶךְ לִפְנֵי
יד כָּל־יֹדְעֵי דָּת וָדִין׃ וְהַקָּרֹב אֵלָיו כַּרְשְׁנָא שֵׁתָר אַדְמָתָא תַרְשִׁישׁ מֶרֶס מַרְסְנָא
טו מְמוּכָן שִׁבְעַת שָׂרֵי ׀ פָּרַס וּמָדַי רֹאֵי פְּנֵי הַמֶּלֶךְ הַיֹּשְׁבִים רִאשֹׁנָה בַּמַּלְכוּת׃ כְּדָת
מַה־לַּעֲשׂוֹת בַּמַּלְכָּה וַשְׁתִּי עַל ׀ אֲשֶׁר לֹא־עָשְׂתָה אֶת־מַאֲמַר הַמֶּלֶךְ אֲחַשְׁוֵרוֹשׁ
טז בְּיַד הַסָּרִיסִים׃ וַיֹּאמֶר מומכן לִפְנֵי הַמֶּלֶךְ וְהַשָּׂרִים לֹא עַל־הַמֶּלֶךְ מְמוּכָן
לְבַדּוֹ עָוְתָה וַשְׁתִּי הַמַּלְכָּה כִּי עַל־כָּל־הַשָּׂרִים וְעַל־כָּל־הָעַמִּים אֲשֶׁר בְּכָל־
יז מְדִינוֹת הַמֶּלֶךְ אֲחַשְׁוֵרוֹשׁ׃ כִּי־יֵצֵא דְבַר־הַמַּלְכָּה עַל־כָּל־הַנָּשִׁים לְהַבְזוֹת
בַּעְלֵיהֶן בְּעֵינֵיהֶן בְּאָמְרָם הַמֶּלֶךְ אֲחַשְׁוֵרוֹשׁ אָמַר לְהָבִיא אֶת־וַשְׁתִּי הַמַּלְכָּה
יח לְפָנָיו וְלֹא־בָאָה׃ וְהַיּוֹם הַזֶּה תֹּאמַרְנָה ׀ שָׂרוֹת פָּרַס־וּמָדַי אֲשֶׁר שָׁמְעוּ אֶת־דְּבַר
יט הַמַּלְכָּה לְכֹל שָׂרֵי הַמֶּלֶךְ וּכְדַי בִּזָּיוֹן וָקָצֶף׃ אִם־עַל־הַמֶּלֶךְ טוֹב יֵצֵא דְבַר־
מַלְכוּת מִלְּפָנָיו וְיִכָּתֵב בְּדָתֵי פָרַס־וּמָדַי וְלֹא יַעֲבוֹר אֲשֶׁר לֹא־תָבוֹא וַשְׁתִּי

DISCUSSION

1:11 | **To display her beauty to the peoples and the princes:** Although the book of Esther does not offer any explicit criticism of this command, the Persian king's demand to display the queen was clearly in poor taste. The Sages suggest that the order was in even worse taste than is obvious here, and that when Ahashverosh ordered Vashti to appear with the royal crown, he was actually commanding that she wear nothing *but* the crown, expecting her to display her nakedness before all (see *Megilla* 12b).

1:13 | **The practice of the king before those learned in custom and law:** There is a measure of irony here: Later in the story, the king alone, and apparently without any hesitation, makes decisions that will have dramatic moral and political ramifications. In this situation, by contrast, when he is drunk and angry, he assembles an entire legal team in order to discuss the fate of his wife. His behavior is similar to that of various dictators over the course of history who sought to preserve the image of a law-abiding ruler, and who were careful that everything be documented and performed in a very formal manner.

It should be noted that Ahashverosh's consultation with his ministers is nothing more than a matter of etiquette through which he expresses his respect for the legal establishment; in practice, they are at his mercy: He appointed them, and he can remove them from their posts and have them executed. Therefore, his legal advisors were naturally careful to tailor their comments to fit what they assumed the king would want to hear, as ultimately the law depended upon his whim.

BACKGROUND

1:19 | **And let it be written in the decrees of [*datei*] Persia and Media:** *Data* is the Old Persian word for law. The Persians were committed to preserving their legal records. Persian legal codes were written in cuneiform on clay tablets, as well as on parchment. Their archives were placed in the most fortified sections of the palace walls, as has been discovered by archaeologists at Persepolis.

bound by the laws and proclamations of the kingdom, at least technically (see 8:8), **that Vashti will not come before King Ahashverosh.** Memukhan did not specify her fate; whether she was to be killed, permanently exiled, or simply deposed from her position as queen. **And** it should also be decreed that **the king will give her queenship,** her official status as queen, **to her counterpart who is worthier than she.** The king should dispense with her and choose a more suitable woman to replace her.

20 **The king's edict**[B] **that he will enact will be heard throughout his entire kingdom, although it,** the kingdom, **is vast, and all the wives,** following the dissemination of the royal precedent, **will confer honor on their husbands,** and will not disobey their commands, **from great to small.**

21 **The matter was pleasing in the eyes of the king and the princes.** Memukhan's appraisal of the fundamental problem, with its potentially serious consequences, was greeted with approval. In his speech, Memukhan presented his solution not as a royal whim, but rather as an important precedent in the management of the country. The angry, drunken king was delighted at the opportunity to inflate the incident into an event of imperial importance. **And** therefore **the king acted in accordance with the word of Memukhan.** As noted in the introduction, the book of Esther, with its formal style, does not criticize the king overtly. However, reading between the lines, Ahashverosh emerges as a ridiculous, easily manipulated figure.

22 **He,** Ahashverosh, **sent scrolls** containing the official order **to all the provinces of the king, to each and every province in its script, and to each and every people in its language: Every man shall be ruler in his house.** The king did not mention Vashti by name, but simply declared that each man should be in charge of his house, **and** that he should **speak the language of his people.** People of different nationalities in his kingdom had intermarried, thereby mixing their languages.[18] Consequently, the king took this opportunity to issue a decree that from this point forward the language of the husband should be the one spoken by all members of his household.[19]

"To each and every province in its script." Trilingual inscription of Xerxes I, Van Fortress, Turkey, 485–465 BCE

Esther Is Crowned Queen

ESTHER 2:1–20

This section starts by relating the consequences of the incident described in the previous section, as a search is undertaken to find a queen to replace Vashti. Esther is then introduced, and these two narrative strands intertwine into a single plotline.

2 1 **After these matters, when the fury of king Ahashverosh had abated, he remembered Vashti, and what she had done, and what was decreed against her.** Since it is not explicitly stated that she was executed, and imposition of the death penalty for the nobility was rare, except for the most serious crimes, it can be assumed that she was not put to death. Perhaps Vashti had been exiled, and Ahashverosh missed her.[20]

2 The king's ministers did not merely carry out his commands; they also paid attention to his moods and tried to anticipate his wishes. **The king's lads, his attendants, said:** We can find a replacement for Vashti. **Let there be sought for the king virgin young women who are of fair appearance,** as befits the honor of a king.

3 In keeping with the king's status, this was to be a large and organized project, ensuring that only suitable candidates would be sent: **Have the king appoint officials in all the provinces of his kingdom** to perform an initial selection, **and they will gather every virgin young woman of fair appearance to the Shushan citadel, to the harem, to the custody of Hegai, the king's chamberlain, guardian of the women** in the palace; **and** to complement and enhance their natural beauty, **their** perfumes and **cosmetics will be provided.**

4 **The young woman who will be pleasing in the eyes of the king** at the end of this process **will be crowned queen in place of Vashti. The proposal was pleasing in the eyes of the king and he did so.**

5 **There was a Judean [*Yehudi*] man,**[B] from the land of Judah,[21] the small independent province which the Persians called Yehud, who was **in the Shushan citadel.** It is not clear whether he actually lived there or simply worked there as a court official. **And his name was Mordekhai, son of Ya'ir, son of Shimi, son of Kish, a Benjamite,**[D] from the tribe of Benjamin. Although he came from the land of Judah, he was from the tribe of Benjamin. This was Mordekhai,

כ לִפְנֵי הַמֶּלֶךְ אֲחַשְׁוֵרוֹשׁ וּמַלְכוּתָהּ יִתֵּן הַמֶּלֶךְ לִרְעוּתָהּ הַטּוֹבָה מִמֶּנָּה׃ וְנִשְׁמַע
פִּתְגָם הַמֶּלֶךְ אֲשֶׁר־יַעֲשֶׂה בְּכָל־מַלְכוּתוֹ כִּי רַבָּה הִיא וְכָל־הַנָּשִׁים יִתְּנוּ יְקָר
כא לְבַעְלֵיהֶן לְמִגָּדוֹל וְעַד־קָטָן׃ וַיִּיטַב הַדָּבָר בְּעֵינֵי הַמֶּלֶךְ וְהַשָּׂרִים וַיַּעַשׂ
כב הַמֶּלֶךְ כִּדְבַר מְמוּכָן׃ וַיִּשְׁלַח סְפָרִים אֶל־כָּל־מְדִינוֹת הַמֶּלֶךְ אֶל־מְדִינָה וּמְדִינָה
כִּכְתָבָהּ וְאֶל־עַם וָעָם כִּלְשׁוֹנוֹ לִהְיוֹת כָּל־אִישׁ שֹׂרֵר בְּבֵיתוֹ וּמְדַבֵּר כִּלְשׁוֹן
א עַמּוֹ׃ אַחַר הַדְּבָרִים הָאֵלֶּה כְּשֹׁךְ חֲמַת הַמֶּלֶךְ אֲחַשְׁוֵרוֹשׁ זָכַר אֶת־
ב וַשְׁתִּי וְאֵת אֲשֶׁר־עָשָׂתָה וְאֵת אֲשֶׁר־נִגְזַר עָלֶיהָ׃ וַיֹּאמְרוּ נַעֲרֵי־הַמֶּלֶךְ מְשָׁרְתָיו
ג יְבַקְשׁוּ לַמֶּלֶךְ נְעָרוֹת בְּתוּלוֹת טוֹבוֹת מַרְאֶה׃ וְיַפְקֵד הַמֶּלֶךְ פְּקִידִים בְּכָל־מְדִינוֹת
מַלְכוּתוֹ וְיִקְבְּצוּ אֶת־כָּל־נַעֲרָה־בְתוּלָה טוֹבַת מַרְאֶה אֶל־שׁוּשַׁן הַבִּירָה אֶל־
ד בֵּית הַנָּשִׁים אֶל־יַד הֵגֶא סְרִיס הַמֶּלֶךְ שֹׁמֵר הַנָּשִׁים וְנָתוֹן תַּמְרוּקֵיהֶן׃ וְהַנַּעֲרָה
אֲשֶׁר תִּיטַב בְּעֵינֵי הַמֶּלֶךְ תִּמְלֹךְ תַּחַת וַשְׁתִּי וַיִּיטַב הַדָּבָר בְּעֵינֵי הַמֶּלֶךְ וַיַּעַשׂ
ה כֵּן׃ אִישׁ יְהוּדִי הָיָה בְּשׁוּשַׁן הַבִּירָה וּשְׁמוֹ מָרְדֳּכַי בֶּן יָאִיר בֶּן־שִׁמְעִי ב

BACKGROUND

1:20 | **Edict [*pitgam*]:** In Old Persian, *pratigama* denotes something which goes out to meet something else. In this instance, this is a message from the king to the people. This is the source for the Aramaic term *pitgama*, meaning a publicized command or decree.

2:5 | **A Judean man:** This refers to one who came from the land of Judah, or the Persian province of Yehud. Judah became a Persian province when Cyrus defeated Babylon and took over its empire. He subsequently issued an edict authorizing and encouraging the Judean exiles to return to Judah and rebuild the Temple (see Ezra 1:1–4). The province of Yehud was a sub-province of Avar Nahara, literally "beyond the river," which was the area of the Persian Empire west of the Euphrates River. It was semi-independent, as is clear from the unsuccessful attempts of its governor to suppress rebuilding of the Temple and the successful appeals to the Persian kings made by the leaders of Judah (see Ezra 4–6). The province of Yehud was governed by a satrap appointed from the ranks of the returning exiles. It was divided into administrative areas, centered around five cities: Jerusalem; Beit HaKerem, possibly modern-day Bethlehem; Mitzpa, in the region of Benjamin; Beit Tzur, in modern-day Gush Etzion; and Ke'ila, near modern-day Beit Guvrin (see Nehemiah 3).

DISCUSSION

2:5 | **A Judean man…a Benjamite:** The tribes of Judah and Benjamin inhabited adjacent areas of the Land of Israel. They were both exiled to Babylon, and members of both tribes later returned to the Land of Israel (see Nehemiah 11:7, 25–36). Mordekhai's lineage, specified in this verse, indicates that he was descended from the royal line of King Saul (see *Pirkei deRabbi Eliezer* 48; *Megilla* 16a).

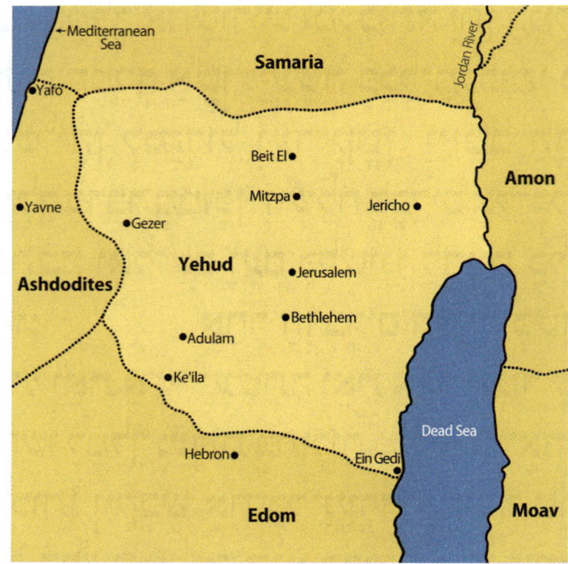

Province of Yehud

6 **who had been exiled from Jerusalem** in his youth, together **with the** first **exile, that was exiled with Yekhonya king of Judah, whom Nebuchadnezzar king of Babylon exiled.**

7 **He was rearing Hadassa** as her guardian, **she was Esther.**[B] Hadassa was her Hebrew name, while Esther was her Persian or Babylonian name. She was **his uncle's daughter** and was much younger than he. Mordekhai had become her guardian **as she had no father or mother. The young woman was of fine form and fair appearance, and with the death of her father and her mother, Mordekhai had adopted her as his own daughter.**

8 **It was when the edict of the king and his** new **decree was heard, and when** there was **the gathering of many young women to the Shushan citadel, to the custody of Hegai, that Esther was taken** against her will[22] **to the king's palace, to the custody of Hegai, guardian of the women.** Presumably, most of the young women were delighted to come from their lands to the capital city and excited at the opportunity the search for the queen provided. The young woman who was chosen would become the queen of the empire. Esther, in contrast, was taken against her will.

9 **The young woman was pleasing in his eyes.** Hegai, who was in charge of the women of the royal household, and was familiar with the king's tastes, considered Esther a serious candidate for the role of queen.[23] **She exhibited grace before him.** In addition to her beauty, he was charmed by her, **and** therefore he took special care of her needs: **He hastened to provide her** with a supply of **cosmetics, and her portions** of food to which she was entitled, **and the seven young women it was requisite to provide her from the king's palace.** It was unbecoming for a candidate for queen of Persia to venture forth by herself, and therefore she was given seven maidservants. **And** he elevated her status, as **he promoted her and her young women to the best** place **of the harem.**

10 Throughout this entire period **Esther did not disclose her people or her birthplace.** She had hidden her ethnic origin and her place of birth, **because Mordekhai had commanded her that she should not disclose it,**[D] her identity. Even after she left his house, and when she later rose to a position of greatness, she remained obedient to Mordekhai.

11 **On each and every day, Mordekhai would walk before the courtyard of the harem, to know Esther's well-being, and what would be done with her.** As her guardian, Mordekhai had both personal affection for Esther and was responsible for her welfare.

12 The young women's preparation for their encounters with the king followed a clearly defined process: **When each and every maiden's turn arrived to come to King Ahashverosh, at the end of her having twelve months, according to the custom of the women,** when she had been readied for the king by completing the standard beauty regimen as instructed, a process lasting twelve months, **for so were prescribed the days for their treatment: Six months** she was anointed **with myrrh oil,** which, among other things, was a depilatory,[24] **and six months** with various **perfumes, and with women's cosmetics,**

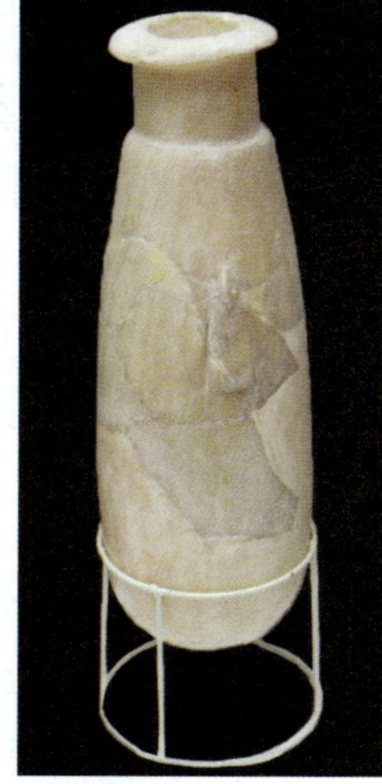

Ivory perfume bottle, Persepolis, 560–331 BCE

13 **and with that the young woman would come to the king,** after she had completed all of the treatments. One of the rules of her arrival was that **whatever she would say,** or request, in order to enhance her beauty **would be given to her, to come with her from the harem to the king's palace.** She was entitled to ask for a special ornament, or escort, or even an entire retinue, and her every wish would be granted.

14 **She would come in the evening** to the king and stay the night, **and return in the morning to the second harem,**[D] **to the custody of Shaashgaz, the king's chamberlain, guardian of the concubines.**[25] She would not go back to the compound where

ו בֶּן־קִ֖ישׁ אִ֥ישׁ יְמִינִֽי׃ אֲשֶׁ֤ר הָגְלָה֙ מִיר֣וּשָׁלַ֔יִם עִם־הַגֹּלָה֙ אֲשֶׁ֣ר הָגְלְתָ֔ה עִ֖ם יְכָנְיָ֣ה
ז מֶֽלֶךְ־יְהוּדָ֑ה אֲשֶׁ֣ר הֶגְלָ֔ה נְבוּכַדְנֶאצַּ֖ר מֶ֥לֶךְ בָּבֶֽל׃ וַיְהִ֨י אֹמֵ֜ן אֶת־הֲדַסָּ֗ה הִ֤יא אֶסְתֵּר֙
בַּת־דֹּד֔וֹ כִּ֛י אֵ֥ין לָ֖הּ אָ֣ב וָאֵ֑ם וְהַנַּעֲרָ֤ה יְפַת־תֹּ֙אַר֙ וְטוֹבַ֣ת מַרְאֶ֔ה וּבְמ֤וֹת אָבִ֙יהָ֙
ח וְאִמָּ֔הּ לְקָחָ֧הּ מָרְדֳּכַ֛י ל֖וֹ לְבַֽת׃ וַיְהִ֗י בְּהִשָּׁמַ֤ע דְּבַר־הַמֶּ֙לֶךְ֙ וְדָת֔וֹ וּֽבְהִקָּבֵ֞ץ נְעָר֥וֹת
רַבּ֛וֹת אֶל־שׁוּשַׁ֥ן הַבִּירָ֖ה אֶל־יַ֣ד הֵגָ֑י וַתִּלָּקַ֤ח אֶסְתֵּר֙ אֶל־בֵּ֣ית הַמֶּ֔לֶךְ אֶל־יַ֥ד הֵגַ֖י
ט שֹׁמֵ֥ר הַנָּשִֽׁים׃ וַתִּיטַ֨ב הַנַּעֲרָ֣ה בְעֵינָיו֮ וַתִּשָּׂ֣א חֶ֣סֶד לְפָנָיו֒ וַ֠יְבַהֵל אֶת־תַּמְרוּקֶ֤יהָ
וְאֶת־מָנוֹתֶ֙הָ֙ לָתֵ֣ת לָ֔הּ וְאֵת֙ שֶׁ֣בַע הַנְּעָר֔וֹת הָרְאֻי֥וֹת לָֽתֶת־לָ֖הּ מִבֵּ֣ית הַמֶּ֑לֶךְ
י וַיְשַׁנֶּ֧הָ וְאֶת־נַעֲרוֹתֶ֛יהָ לְט֖וֹב בֵּ֥ית הַנָּשִֽׁים׃ לֹא־הִגִּ֣ידָה אֶסְתֵּ֔ר אֶת־עַמָּ֖הּ וְאֶת־
יא מֽוֹלַדְתָּ֑הּ כִּ֧י מָרְדֳּכַ֛י צִוָּ֥ה עָלֶ֖יהָ אֲשֶׁ֥ר לֹֽא־תַגִּֽיד׃ וּבְכָל־י֣וֹם וָי֔וֹם מָרְדֳּכַי֙ מִתְהַלֵּ֔ךְ
יב לִפְנֵ֖י חֲצַ֣ר בֵּית־הַנָּשִׁ֑ים לָדַ֙עַת֙ אֶת־שְׁל֣וֹם אֶסְתֵּ֔ר וּמַה־יֵּעָשֶׂ֖ה בָּֽהּ׃ וּבְהַגִּ֡יעַ תֹּר֩
נַעֲרָ֨ה וְנַעֲרָ֜ה לָב֣וֹא ׀ אֶל־הַמֶּ֣לֶךְ אֲחַשְׁוֵר֗וֹשׁ מִקֵּץ֩ הֱי֨וֹת לָ֜הּ כְּדָ֤ת הַנָּשִׁים֙ שְׁנֵ֣ים
עָשָׂ֣ר חֹ֔דֶשׁ כִּ֛י כֵּ֥ן יִמְלְא֖וּ יְמֵ֣י מְרוּקֵיהֶ֑ן שִׁשָּׁ֤ה חֳדָשִׁים֙ בְּשֶׁ֣מֶן הַמֹּ֔ר וְשִׁשָּׁ֤ה חֳדָשִׁים֙
יג בַּבְּשָׂמִ֔ים וּבְתַמְרוּקֵ֖י הַנָּשִֽׁים׃ וּבָזֶ֕ה הַנַּעֲרָ֖ה בָּאָ֣ה אֶל־הַמֶּ֑לֶךְ אֵת֩ כָּל־אֲשֶׁ֨ר תֹּאמַ֜ר
יד יִנָּ֤תֵֽן לָהּ֙ לָב֣וֹא עִמָּ֔הּ מִבֵּ֥ית הַנָּשִׁ֖ים עַד־בֵּ֥ית הַמֶּֽלֶךְ׃ בָּעֶ֣רֶב ׀ הִ֣יא בָאָ֗ה וּ֠בַבֹּקֶר
הִ֣יא שָׁבָ֞ה אֶל־בֵּ֤ית הַנָּשִׁים֙ שֵׁנִ֔י אֶל־יַ֧ד שַֽׁעַשְׁגַ֛ז סְרִ֥יס הַמֶּ֖לֶךְ שֹׁמֵ֣ר הַפִּֽילַגְשִׁ֑ים

BACKGROUND

2:7 | **Esther:** Esther is a Persian name, from *astra*, which means a star in Indo-European languages (see *Megilla* 13a), perhaps referring to the planet Venus (see *Targum*, 10:13), whereas her Hebrew name was Hadassa, from *hadas*, meaning myrtle. It should be noted that the flowers of the myrtle, with their many stamens, resemble ancient drawings of stars. Some suggest that the name Esther is derived from that of the Babylonian goddess Ishtar, while the name Mordekhai is based on the Babylonian god Marduk. In this context, it is interesting to note that documents from ancient Shushan dating back to the reign of Xerxes I, who died in 465 BCE and whom some identify with Ahashverosh, mention a royal treasurer called Marduka.

DISCUSSION

2:10 | **Because Mordekhai had commanded her that she should not disclose it:** The text does not explain Mordekhai's motives, but presumably he thought that Esther could potentially be a secret agent. It can be safely assumed that Mordekhai would have preferred her to marry a Judean man, but that when she was forcibly taken to the house of the king, he quickly adapted to the new situation (see Rashi; Rav Yosef Kara). As one who held a position in the royal court (see 2:19), Mordekhai wanted to keep Esther's identity secret in case he should need to reveal it at an opportune moment, although of course he did not know how necessary that would ultimately be. He realized that it was in his interests to have a sleeper agent in the palace, who would be ready to act in a time of need.

2:14 | **To the second harem:** After a woman had spent the night with the king, she was considered his property, and she was therefore transferred to a special residence for his concubines. It would be disrespectful to the monarch if she were given to another man (Ibn Ezra). An example of this from elsewhere in the Bible is the case of Avishag the Shunamite, King David's companion. After David's death, his son Adoniyahu requested Avishag from King Solomon as a wife for himself, and it can be inferred from Solomon's incensed reaction that a woman who had shared the king's bed was forbidden to any other man, including a member of the royal family (I Kings 1:1–4, 2:13–25; see commentary on II Samuel 20:3).

the candidates were being groomed, but rather to the harem of the concubines, where all the young women went after they had been with the king.[26] **She would not come to the king anymore, unless the king desired her, and she was called by name.** If the king remembered her, he would instruct his minister to call her again, and if not, she would remain with the other concubines in the harem.

15 **With the arrival of the turn of Esther, daughter of Avihayil,** who had been the **uncle of Mordekhai, who had taken her as a daughter for him, to come to the king, she did not request anything except that which Hegai, the king's chamberlain, guardian of the women, said.** The other young women made an effort to impress the king, whereas Esther refrained from taking such measures on her own initiative and merely accepted the recommendations of the expert, Hegai. **And Esther found favor in the eyes of everyone who saw her.**

16 **Esther was taken to King Ahashverosh to his royal palace, in the tenth month, which is the month of Tevet, in the seventh year of his reign.** This was four years after Ahashverosh had dismissed Vashti. During this period the young women had been gathered and had undergone meticulous preparation before presentation to the king.

17 **The king loved Esther more than all the** other **women, and she found favor and grace in his eyes more than all the** other **virgins. He placed the royal crown on her head, and he crowned her queen in place of Vashti.** It is surprising that in Persia and Media a woman who was not of royal blood would be selected as queen. As stated above,[27] it seems likely that although Esther concealed her origins, she was believed to come from a noble family.

18 **The king made a great banquet for all his princes and his servants, the banquet of Esther.** A private celebration to mark the appointment of the new queen did not suffice; rather, he issued an announcement to all the nations. Since everyone had heard about the removal of Vashti, the king decided to declare publicly that her replacement had been found. **He awarded an abatement for the provinces;** he lowered the taxes so his subjects would participate in his joy. **And** furthermore, **he gave gifts in accordance with the king's bounty,** in order to improve the general welfare of his subjects and encourage their devotion.

19 **With the gathering of the virgins a second time;** it seems that some of the candidates who had been gathered had not yet had been presented to the king, and therefore the process continued in some form even after Esther had been chosen,[28] **Mordekhai was sitting at the king's gate,**[BD] that is, he held a position in the royal court, from which he was able to follow the events at the palace.[29]

Gates of the palace of the kings of Persia, Persepolis, fifth century BCE

20 It had been some time since she had entered the house of the king, and still **Esther did not disclose her birthplace or her people, as Mordekhai had commanded her; Esther would perform the directive of Mordekhai, as it was when she was reared by him,** in her childhood.

BACKGROUND

2:19| **The king's gate:** There was a special structure for the king's gate in the palace in Shushan (see image below 1:5). Those who sought the king or his counselors were permitted to approach no further than the gatehouse, where they would wait to be received, or to hear an answer to their request.

2:23| **And the two of them were hanged on a gibbet:** Researchers maintain that the practice of public hanging as a method of execution originated in ancient Persia. This manner of killing is a simple procedure that does not require an expert hangman and does not involve the actual shedding of blood. However, some claim that the hanging referred to in the book of Esther is actually impalement, in which a sharp wood pole is inserted into the chest or between the legs of the condemned until it emerges on the other side of the body. The Persians inherited this method of execution from the Assyrians and Babylonians.

DISCUSSION

2:19| **Mordekhai was sitting at the king's gate:** The name Mordekhai appears in the list of those who initially immigrated to the Land of Israel from Babylonia (see Ezra 2:2; *Megilla* 16b). It is possible that after he arrived in the Land of Israel, Mordekhai was sent back to Shushan to serve in a kind of diplomatic role, representing the interests of the province of Judah in the king's court.

טו לֹא־תָבוֹא עוֹד אֶל־הַמֶּלֶךְ כִּי אִם־חָפֵץ בָּהּ הַמֶּלֶךְ וְנִקְרְאָה בְשֵׁם: וּבְהַגִּיעַ תֹּר־
אֶסְתֵּר בַּת־אֲבִיחַיִל ׀ דֹּד מָרְדֳּכַי אֲשֶׁר לָקַח־לוֹ לְבַת לָבוֹא אֶל־הַמֶּלֶךְ לֹא בִקְשָׁה
דָּבָר כִּי אִם אֶת־אֲשֶׁר יֹאמַר הֵגַי סְרִיס־הַמֶּלֶךְ שֹׁמֵר הַנָּשִׁים וַתְּהִי אֶסְתֵּר נֹשֵׂאת
טז חֵן בְּעֵינֵי כָּל־רֹאֶיהָ: וַתִּלָּקַח אֶסְתֵּר אֶל־הַמֶּלֶךְ אֲחַשְׁוֵרוֹשׁ אֶל־בֵּית מַלְכוּתוֹ
יז בַּחֹדֶשׁ הָעֲשִׂירִי הוּא־חֹדֶשׁ טֵבֵת בִּשְׁנַת־שֶׁבַע לְמַלְכוּתוֹ: וַיֶּאֱהַב הַמֶּלֶךְ אֶת־
אֶסְתֵּר מִכָּל־הַנָּשִׁים וַתִּשָּׂא־חֵן וָחֶסֶד לְפָנָיו מִכָּל־הַבְּתוּלוֹת וַיָּשֶׂם כֶּתֶר־מַלְכוּת
יח בְּרֹאשָׁהּ וַיַּמְלִיכֶהָ תַּחַת וַשְׁתִּי: וַיַּעַשׂ הַמֶּלֶךְ מִשְׁתֶּה גָדוֹל לְכָל־שָׂרָיו וַעֲבָדָיו
יט אֵת מִשְׁתֵּה אֶסְתֵּר וַהֲנָחָה לַמְּדִינוֹת עָשָׂה וַיִּתֵּן מַשְׂאֵת כְּיַד הַמֶּלֶךְ: וּבְהִקָּבֵץ
כ בְּתוּלוֹת שֵׁנִית וּמָרְדֳּכַי יֹשֵׁב בְּשַׁעַר־הַמֶּלֶךְ: אֵין אֶסְתֵּר מַגֶּדֶת מוֹלַדְתָּהּ וְאֶת־
עַמָּהּ כַּאֲשֶׁר צִוָּה עָלֶיהָ מָרְדֳּכָי וְאֶת־מַאֲמַר מָרְדֳּכַי אֶסְתֵּר עֹשָׂה כַּאֲשֶׁר הָיְתָה
כא בְאָמְנָה אִתּוֹ: בַּיָּמִים הָהֵם וּמָרְדֳּכַי יֹשֵׁב בְּשַׁעַר־הַמֶּלֶךְ קָצַף
בִּגְתָן וָתֶרֶשׁ שְׁנֵי־סָרִיסֵי הַמֶּלֶךְ מִשֹּׁמְרֵי הַסַּף וַיְבַקְשׁוּ לִשְׁלֹחַ יָד בַּמֶּלֶךְ אֲחַשְׁוֵרֹשׁ:
כב וַיִּוָּדַע הַדָּבָר לְמָרְדֳּכַי וַיַּגֵּד לְאֶסְתֵּר הַמַּלְכָּה וַתֹּאמֶר אֶסְתֵּר לַמֶּלֶךְ בְּשֵׁם מָרְדֳּכָי:
כג וַיְבֻקַּשׁ הַדָּבָר וַיִּמָּצֵא וַיִּתָּלוּ שְׁנֵיהֶם עַל־עֵץ וַיִּכָּתֵב בְּסֵפֶר דִּבְרֵי הַיָּמִים לִפְנֵי

Discovery of an Assassination Plot against the King

ESTHER 2:21–23

At this stage, an apparently random incident of marginal importance is presented. However, it later becomes clear that this incident is a pivotal link in the chain of events.

21 **In those days, as Mordekhai was sitting at the king's gate, two of the king's chamberlains, Bigtan and Teresh, among the guardians of the threshold, became angry and sought to do violence to King Ahashverosh,** to assassinate him. The royal court in Persia was rife with intrigue, plots, and conspiracies at that time. In some cases it is hard to know whether a particular Persian king took the throne by virtue of his lineage, or essentially successfully performed a coup d'etat.

22 **The matter,** the plot that was being hatched, **became known to Mordekhai.** One suggestion is that Mordekhai discovered the plot because the men conversed in a language they thought no one knew, but which Mordekhai could understand.[30] **And he,** Mordekhai, **told Queen Esther** about it, in order that she pass the message on to Ahashverosh, since Mordekhai himself did not have direct contact with the king, as he was a mere official or representative of the Judeans in the royal court. **And Esther reported** the plot **to the king in the name of Mordekhai,** with whom the king was unfamiliar.

23 **The matter was investigated, and it was revealed** that Bigtan and Teresh were indeed involved in the plot, **and the two of them were hanged on a gibbet.**[B] It seems that hanging was the preferred method of execution by the Persian monarchy, as it served to display publicly the offenders' dishonorable end. **It,** the two men's attempt to assassinate King Ahashverosh on that date, as well as how he was saved, **was recorded in the book of the chronicles before the king.**

Haman and the Plot to Destroy the Jews

ESTHER 3:1–15

In this section Mordekhai refuses to accept the authority of Haman, who has become the most distinguished minister in Persia. Haman, affronted at this personal slight, convinces the king to permit the systematic annihilation of all of Mordekhai's nation, the Jews, in his empire. The word for the members of Mordekhai's nation, *Yehudim*, can be translated as either Judeans or Jews. Elsewhere in the Bible this translation has used Judeans, but in this context it makes use of the term Jews. It is in the book of Esther that the Jewish people's identity is first conceived as not necessarily a function of their origins in Judah. Most of Haman's potential victims did not live in Judah, and their families had not lived there for several generations. They nevertheless maintained a unique religious, ethnic, and cultural identity wherever they were found in the vast Persian Empire.

3 1 **After these matters,** the appointment of Esther and the foiled plot of Bigtan and Teresh, **King Ahashverosh promoted** from among his ministers **Haman son of Hamedata the Agagite,**[BD] **and he elevated him,** raised his status, **and he placed his seat above all the princes who were with him.** Advancing one particular minister to the status of a close confidant of the king was not unheard of, as attested in other documents of the period.[31]
2 **All the king's servants,** his ministers and attendants, **who were at the king's gate, were bowing and prostrating themselves to Haman, for so had the king commanded concerning him; but Mordekhai would not bow and would not prostrate himself,**[D] for an undetermined reason.[32]
3 **The king's servants, who were at the king's gate, said to Mordekhai: Why are you violating the king's commandment** that all must bow before Haman?
4 **It was, when they spoke to him day after day, and he did not listen to them, that they told** this to **Haman.** Perhaps Haman had not noticed Mordekhai's refusal up to that point, as a large crowd would pass before him, all bowing,[33] but those present, seeking to stir up trouble, informed Haman of the situation in order **to see whether Mordekhai's words would prevail,** whether he would remain firm in his decision not to bow to Haman, **for he had told them that he was a Jew** and perhaps for that reason he would not prostrate himself to Haman.[34]
5 **Haman saw that Mordekhai was not bowing and not prostrating himself to him, and Haman was filled with fury** over what he considered a public insult.
6 Haman could have punished Mordekhai for his behavior, or tried to do away with him, but **he disdained to do violence to Mordekhai alone;** merely harming Mordekhai himself was not enough for him, **for he had been told of Mordekhai's people.** This indicates that in those times there was no external sign that made it easy to differentiate between Jews and gentiles. **Haman sought to destroy all the Jews**[D] **in the entire kingdom of Ahashverosh, the people of Mordekhai.** Despite Haman's many duties as senior minister of a massive empire, he developed an obsession with the Jews, because they were Mordekhai's nation, and he sought a way to eliminate them all.
7 Haman was determined to destroy all the Jews, and he plotted how to bring this idea to fruition. **In the first month, which is the month of Nisan, during the twelfth year of King Ahashverosh, he had cast a pur,** a Persian word,[35] **which is the lot** [*goral*] in Hebrew. This was a means of divination through which one would determine the best course of action to take, and the ideal time to take it.[36] The lot was cast **before Haman.** Haman wanted to find the right date, and to that end cast lots **for each day and for each month, to the twelfth month, which is the month of Adar.** He came to the conclusion that the best time to bring about the downfall of the Jews was the month of Adar, presumably in the upcoming year.

Lot of Yahalu, illustration based on stone die, Assyria, ninth century BCE

8 Since Haman had no independent authority, he needed to incite Ahashverosh to approve his initiative. **Haman said to King Ahashverosh: There is one people**[D] **that is scattered and**

BACKGROUND

3:1 | **Haman son of Hamedata the Agagite:** It is possible that the name Haman is derived from the name of the Elamite sky god, Humban or Humman. Alternatively, it relates to a sacred bird in Persian mythology, *homa* or *huma*, whose supposed characteristics were similar to those of the phoenix, specifically long life and resistance to fire. There is also mention in Persian manuscripts of a Persian officer called Humadat, which is similar to Hamedata. The Sages understood Agagite to refer to the fact that Haman was a descendant of Agag king of Amalek (see I Samuel 15:8–9), but the name Agaga also exists in the Elamite language.

א הַמֶּלֶךְ׃ אַחַר ׀ הַדְּבָרִים הָאֵלֶּה גִּדַּל הַמֶּלֶךְ אֲחַשְׁוֵרוֹשׁ אֶת־הָמָן
בֶּן־הַמְּדָתָא הָאֲגָגִי וַיְנַשְּׂאֵהוּ וַיָּשֶׂם אֶת־כִּסְאוֹ מֵעַל כָּל־הַשָּׂרִים אֲשֶׁר אִתּוֹ׃
ב וְכָל־עַבְדֵי הַמֶּלֶךְ אֲשֶׁר־בְּשַׁעַר הַמֶּלֶךְ כֹּרְעִים וּמִשְׁתַּחֲוִים לְהָמָן כִּי־כֵן צִוָּה־
ג לוֹ הַמֶּלֶךְ וּמָרְדֳּכַי לֹא יִכְרַע וְלֹא יִשְׁתַּחֲוֶה׃ וַיֹּאמְרוּ עַבְדֵי הַמֶּלֶךְ אֲשֶׁר־בְּשַׁעַר
ד הַמֶּלֶךְ לְמָרְדֳּכָי מַדּוּעַ אַתָּה עוֹבֵר אֵת מִצְוַת הַמֶּלֶךְ׃ וַיְהִי באמרם אֵלָיו יוֹם וָיוֹם כְּאָמְרָם
וְלֹא שָׁמַע אֲלֵיהֶם וַיַּגִּידוּ לְהָמָן לִרְאוֹת הֲיַעַמְדוּ דִּבְרֵי מָרְדֳּכַי כִּי־הִגִּיד לָהֶם
ה אֲשֶׁר־הוּא יְהוּדִי׃ וַיַּרְא הָמָן כִּי־אֵין מָרְדֳּכַי כֹּרֵעַ וּמִשְׁתַּחֲוֶה לוֹ וַיִּמָּלֵא הָמָן חֵמָה׃
ו וַיִּבֶז בְּעֵינָיו לִשְׁלֹחַ יָד בְּמָרְדֳּכַי לְבַדּוֹ כִּי־הִגִּידוּ לוֹ אֶת־עַם מָרְדֳּכָי וַיְבַקֵּשׁ הָמָן
ז לְהַשְׁמִיד אֶת־כָּל־הַיְּהוּדִים אֲשֶׁר בְּכָל־מַלְכוּת אֲחַשְׁוֵרוֹשׁ עַם מָרְדֳּכָי׃ בַּחֹדֶשׁ
הָרִאשׁוֹן הוּא־חֹדֶשׁ נִיסָן בִּשְׁנַת שְׁתֵּים עֶשְׂרֵה לַמֶּלֶךְ אֲחַשְׁוֵרוֹשׁ הִפִּיל פּוּר
הוּא הַגּוֹרָל לִפְנֵי הָמָן מִיּוֹם ׀ לְיוֹם וּמֵחֹדֶשׁ לְחֹדֶשׁ שְׁנֵים־עָשָׂר הוּא־חֹדֶשׁ
ח אֲדָר׃ וַיֹּאמֶר הָמָן לַמֶּלֶךְ אֲחַשְׁוֵרוֹשׁ יֶשְׁנוֹ עַם־אֶחָד מְפֻזָּר וּמְפֹרָד ג
בֵּין הָעַמִּים בְּכֹל מְדִינוֹת מַלְכוּתֶךָ וְדָתֵיהֶם שֹׁנוֹת מִכָּל־עָם וְאֶת־דָּתֵי הַמֶּלֶךְ

DISCUSSION

3:1 | **The Agagite:** This probably means that he was a descendant of Agag the Amalekite king (see the Aramaic translations of the Bible; *Masekhet Soferim* 13; *Aggadat Esther* 3). The Agag mentioned in the Bible lived during the period of Saul (see I Samuel 15:8–9). It is possible, however, that Agag was the standard royal name for all kings of the Amalekites (see Rashbam, and Ramban, Numbers 24:7; see also Jerusalem Talmud, *Yevamot* 2:6). Haman might have changed his original Amalekite name to one that sounded more Persian.

3:2 | **But Mordekhai would not bow and would not prostrate himself:** It would seem that Mordekhai's refusal to bow before Haman was not motivated by religious concerns. After all, it is related about other righteous figures that they bowed down and prostrated themselves before ministers and kings, and this was not considered a sin (see Genesis 42:6; Exodus 18:7; I Samuel 24:8; I Kings 1:23). Perhaps Mordekhai, who was from Judean nobility, considered the idea of bowing down to Haman an act of humiliation for all Jews (see also *Yalkut Shimoni* 954). It is also possible that his refusal to lower himself before Haman was due to the personal enmity between the men. According to tradition, they had a prior acquaintance, and Mordekhai despised Haman personally (see *Megillat Setarim*; *Megilla* 15a–16a). Some say that he refused to bow down because Haman presented himself as a god, or because he hung an idol from his clothing (see Ibn Ezra; Ralbag; *Megilla* 10b, 19a; *Sanhedrin* 61b).

3:6 | **Haman sought to destroy all the Jews:** This phenomenon of a personal hatred that expands into hatred of an entire people is unusual and puzzling. The background of this enmity is related to Haman's Amalekite roots. Although not a large nation, Amalek hated the nation of Israel from the beginning of its history as a people (see Exodus 17:8–16). Haman's confrontation with Mordekhai was not the only reason for his extreme reaction; it awakened a primeval enmity that he and his people had nurtured against Israel from time immemorial.

3:8 | **There is one people:** The fact that Haman had to tell Ahashverosh about the Jews indicates that the king knew very little about them. Although the Jews were his subjects, and they even had a small state of their own in the area surrounding Jerusalem, it is doubtful whether Ahashverosh had ever thought about this tiny nation. The 127 provinces over which he reigned, some of which were very large and important, contained many peoples and tribes. Even if Ahashverosh had been a conscientious and organized ruler, he would not have been intimately familiar with the Jewish people. However, it is known that he received a letter from Samaritans libeling the exiles who had returned to the Land of Israel (see Ezra 4:6), and therefore it is likely that Haman's comments evoked his existing negative associations, making him receptive to the idea of their destruction.

dispersed[B] **among the peoples in all the provinces of your kingdom;** they are not concentrated in one country;[37] and **their laws,** their practices, their ways of life, **are different from every people's.** A significant proportion of the commandments of the Torah serve to keep Jews apart from gentiles and prevent them from engaging in idolatry. **And** while the Jews observe their own laws, **they do not follow the king's laws,** and therefore **it is not worthwhile for the king to tolerate them.** They are a small nation of no importance, and an annoyance that disrupts the harmony of your kingdom.

9 **If it pleases the king** to accept my proposal, **let it be written** as an official order **to eliminate them,**[D] **and I will weigh ten thousand talents of silver**[D] **into the hands of the king's craftsmen.** I volunteer to give ten thousand silver talents of my own to those who can turn it into silver bullion, **to bring to the king's treasuries.**[B] The donation to the king's treasuries would compensate Ahashverosh for any possible financial costs incurred by the course of action suggested by Haman, as the king might fear the loss of so many taxpayers.

10 Apathetic as he was to the fate of the Jews, Ahashverosh was apparently enthused by the generous gift of his chief minister. Therefore, **the king removed his ring** with the royal seal **from his hand,**[D] **and he gave it to Haman son of Hamedata the Agagite, the adversary of the Jews.** This was not merely a verbal agreement; by giving him his seal, Ahashverosh granted Haman practical permission and authority to sign in the king's name.[38]

Ring seal, Shushan, third century BCE

11 **The king said to Haman: The silver** that you offered to donate **is given to you;** it shall remain in your possession, as the kingdom will bear the cost, **and the people** are also given to you, **to do with them as it is pleasing in your eyes,** in accordance with your wishes.

12 Haman acted with great haste. He cast the lots at the beginning of Nisan, and by the thirteenth of the month everything was ready for the next stage of his plan: **The king's scribes were summoned in the first month, on the thirteenth day of it, and it was written in accordance with everything that Haman commanded to the king's satraps,**[B] who presided over the larger regions, **and to the governors**[B] **who were over each and every province,** the smaller areas, **and to the princes of each and every people, to each and every province in its script, and to each and every people in its language.**[B] **In the name of King Ahashverosh, it,** the missive with the decree, **was written, and it was sealed with the king's ring.**

Illustration of Assyrian scribes, illustration based on stone relief, Nimrud, Iraq, eighth century BCE

13 **The scrolls were sent in the hand of the couriers to all the king's provinces,** in which it was written that the king permitted his subjects **to destroy, to kill, and to eliminate all the Jews, from lad to elder, children and women, in one day, on the thirteenth of the twelfth month, which is the month of Adar, and to plunder their spoils,** their property. The instructions were sent almost a year in advance, perhaps in order to establish the facts on the ground as soon as possible, and so that the missives would reach the farthest corners of the empire in time. Due to Haman's trust in his divination, he was resolute in keeping the determined date, at which point the Jews would be deemed legitimate targets. There does not seem to have been any need to enforce this decree. It simply stated that on such and such a date the Jews would no longer enjoy the protection of the law. Haman assumed that that was sufficient, and that the members of the various nations of the empire would take the opportunity to annihilate the Jews.

DISCUSSION

3:9 | Let it be written to eliminate them: Haman's proposal and his conduct toward Mordekhai is the first case of anti-Semitism in the sense of Jew-hatred. In previous generations various nations had fought against the kingdoms of Israel, but those were not anti-Semitic wars that sought to exterminate the nation, but struggles for power due to conflicts of interest. Similarly, the Israelites suffered in Egypt because they were strangers, and perhaps because the ruling authorities felt threatened by their presence. Most of these wars were not etched in the collective national memory. The attack recorded here is of a different kind entirely. Haman's speech is an ancient model for anti-Semitic propaganda, which has been used, with minor variations, by many anti-Semites in subsequent generations. It is possible to see signs of anti-Semitism in the struggle against the exiles returning to Judah on the part of Sanbalat the Horonite, the leader of the Samaritans, which occurred at roughly the same time as the events described in this book. He and his men sought to sabotage the rebuilding of Jerusalem and the Temple through mockery, the weakening of the Jews' resolve, and scaremongering and informing on them to the authorities, as well general abuse and threats of destruction (see Nehemiah 2–6).

▸ *Ten*

ט אֵינָם עֹשִׂים וְלַמֶּלֶךְ אֵין־שֹׁוֶה לְהַנִּיחָם׃ אִם־עַל־הַמֶּלֶךְ טוֹב יִכָּתֵב לְאַבְּדָם
וַעֲשֶׂרֶת אֲלָפִים כִּכַּר־כֶּסֶף אֶשְׁקוֹל עַל־יְדֵי עֹשֵׂי הַמְּלָאכָה לְהָבִיא אֶל־גִּנְזֵי
י הַמֶּלֶךְ׃ וַיָּסַר הַמֶּלֶךְ אֶת־טַבַּעְתּוֹ מֵעַל יָדוֹ וַיִּתְּנָהּ לְהָמָן בֶּן־הַמְּדָתָא הָאֲגָגִי צֹרֵר
יא הַיְּהוּדִים׃ וַיֹּאמֶר הַמֶּלֶךְ לְהָמָן הַכֶּסֶף נָתוּן לָךְ וְהָעָם לַעֲשׂוֹת בּוֹ כַּטּוֹב בְּעֵינֶיךָ׃
יב וַיִּקָּרְאוּ סֹפְרֵי הַמֶּלֶךְ בַּחֹדֶשׁ הָרִאשׁוֹן בִּשְׁלוֹשָׁה עָשָׂר יוֹם בּוֹ וַיִּכָּתֵב כְּכָל־אֲשֶׁר־
צִוָּה הָמָן אֶל אֲחַשְׁדַּרְפְּנֵי־הַמֶּלֶךְ וְאֶל־הַפַּחוֹת אֲשֶׁר ׀ עַל־מְדִינָה וּמְדִינָה וְאֶל־
שָׂרֵי עַם וָעָם מְדִינָה וּמְדִינָה כִּכְתָבָהּ וְעַם וָעָם כִּלְשׁוֹנוֹ בְּשֵׁם הַמֶּלֶךְ אֲחַשְׁוֵרֹשׁ
יג נִכְתָּב וְנֶחְתָּם בְּטַבַּעַת הַמֶּלֶךְ׃ וְנִשְׁלוֹחַ סְפָרִים בְּיַד הָרָצִים אֶל־כָּל־מְדִינוֹת
הַמֶּלֶךְ לְהַשְׁמִיד לַהֲרֹג וּלְאַבֵּד אֶת־כָּל־הַיְּהוּדִים מִנַּעַר וְעַד־זָקֵן טַף וְנָשִׁים
בְּיוֹם אֶחָד בִּשְׁלוֹשָׁה עָשָׂר לְחֹדֶשׁ שְׁנֵים־עָשָׂר הוּא־חֹדֶשׁ אֲדָר וּשְׁלָלָם לָבוֹז׃

BACKGROUND

3:8 | **Scattered and dispersed:** The Assyrian kings first exiled the ten tribes of Israel to northwest Mesopotamia, after which Nebuchadnezzar exiled the leading Judeans to central and southern Mesopotamia. In some cases, these exiles achieved high social and political status, and they also dealt in international trade. In this manner they spread across the Persian Empire, from Afghanistan and India to Libya, southern Egypt, and western Anatolia. Judeans apparently served on Phoenician ships and conducted business with Sidonian merchants, and they may have even reached distant trading stations in northern Africa and Spain.

3:9 | **The king's treasuries [*ginzei*]:** In Old Persian, *ganzaka* is a small treasure chamber. This word is also the source of the Hebrew terms *ganzakh*, archive, and *gizbar*, treasurer.

3:10 | **The king removed his ring from his hand:** Royal commands were generally etched in cuneiform script on clay tablets which were authorized with the impression of a seal. Some seals were attached to a ring, while others were hung on a chain around the neck. It is possible that the king did not need to be literate, as all his orders were written by scribes, who would read out the texts to him when necessary (see 6:1).

3:12 | **The king's satraps [*aḥashdarpenei*]:** The Persian word originally denoted a shield of the kingdom, but this meaning was broadened to include the rulers of administrative units of the Persian Empire.

The governors [*hapaḥot*]: *Peḥa*, or *pihatu* in Akkadian, was an official of a lower status than a satrap. A *paḥavva*, which was ruled by a *peḥa*, was part of a larger unit.

To each and every province in its script, and to each and every people in its language: According to the standard procedure of the Persian monarchy, the king would dictate his order in Persian, while the Aramean scribes would write it in Aramaic. The missives were sent to the local scribes of each province, who would read the Aramaic and translate it into the local language while reading them aloud. In this instance the missives were sent in different languages due to the importance of their content.

DISCUSSION

Ten thousand talents of silver: If this is referring to sacred talents mentioned in the book of Exodus, then a silver talent weighed roughly 30 kg. According to this calculation, Haman proposed to give the king some 300 metric tons of silver. It is unusual for such a large sum to be in the possession of a private individual. Haman was clearly an immensely wealthy man with the powerful position of the chief minister of the empire (see 5:11; *Bemidbar Rabba* 22:6).

14 **A copy**[39] **of the document**[B] **went out to issue the decree in each and every province, publicizing it to all the peoples: To be ready for that day.** Although it is unlikely that Jews were to be found in every remote corner of the Persian Empire, for bureaucratic reasons the announcement was sent to each province; a general decree of the king had to reach the entire kingdom.

15 **The couriers went out urgently by the word of the king, and the decree was issued in the Shushan citadel. The king and Haman sat to drink** and toast the success of their plan. Ahashverosh and Haman were so delighted that the plan had been put into motion that they held a small feast; **and** meanwhile **the city of Shushan,** mainly its Jewish community, of which Mordekhai[40] was a prominent member, **was confounded** by the sudden harsh decree.

Mordekhai and Esther React to the Decree

ESTHER 4:1–17

Mordekhai's refusal to bow before Haman is the pretext for the decree to destroy the Jews. When the decree is publicized, he reacts without delay, calling upon Esther, his secret representative in the king's palace, to thwart it. The conversation between Mordekhai and Esther reveals both their profound concerns about the king's decree, and their faith and trust in God. At the start of this section, Mordekhai cries out in distress, and at its conclusion, Esther asks for all the Jews to gather together and fast. Even if they are uncertain as to whether their prayers will be accepted, they both believe that their fervent supplications and their fasting will influence the unfolding events.

4 1 **Mordekhai,** who was a court official, **knew everything that was done,** as he was presumably one of the first to read a copy of the decree that had been distributed throughout the kingdom. He understood the severity of the situation and its implications for the future of the Jews, even before the rest of the Jews living in Shushan knew what had transpired. He was deeply concerned by the likely effectiveness of Haman's propaganda, as well as Haman's growing influence in the royal court. **And** consequently, **Mordekhai rent his garments and donned sackcloth, and** placed **ashes** upon his head, all signs of mourning. **He went out in the midst of the city and cried a loud and bitter cry,** a cry of prayer and entreaty to God,[41] and a cry of protest against the authorities.

2 **He came up to before the king's gate;** although he was generally authorized to enter, he did not approach further, **as** in accordance with the royal dress code,[42] **one may not come to the king's gate in a sackcloth garment.**

3 **And in each and every province, any place where the word of the king and his decree reached, there was great mourning among the Jews, fasting, weeping, and keening; sackcloth and ashes were draped by the multitudes;** alternatively, sackcloth and ashes were laid out in the streets for public use.

4 **Esther's young women and her chamberlains came and told her** of Mordekhai's actions. Those who were close to Esther knew about her relationship with him, as Mordekhai would inquire about her welfare every day, and it was she who had passed on Mordekhai's warning about the plot on the king's life (2:11, 22). **And the queen was greatly shocked,** as she had not heard anything about what was going on. The king's decree had not been disclosed to the women, as they were presumed to not be interested in political matters. **And** as Esther wanted to hear from Mordekhai what was happening, and since she knew that he could not enter while wearing sackcloth, **she sent garments to clothe Mordekhai and to remove from upon him his sackcloth, but he would not accept them,** refusing to take off his sackcloth.

5 **Esther called Hatakh, one of the king's chamberlains, whom he had set before her.** Hatakh was no ordinary servant; he had been granted explicit authority to help the queen with whatever she might need. **And** she **commanded him concerning Mordekhai,** in order **to know what this is, and why this is.** She wanted to know the reason for his behavior, and what he wanted.[43]

6 **Hatakh went out to Mordekhai, to the city square that was before the king's gate.** Since Mordekhai did not approach the king's gate, Hatakh came out to the square outside it, where he asked Mordekhai to explain his conduct.

7 **Mordekhai told him everything that had happened to him.** This did not necessarily include his refusal to bow down to Haman, as Mordekhai might have considered Haman's decree no more than his manifestation of a tradition of hatred for Jews he had inherited from his ancestors, the tribe of Amalek. **And** he informed Hatakh of **the matter of the silver that Haman had said to weigh out for the king's treasuries concerning the Jews,** in order **to destroy them.** In addition to the decree

BACKGROUND

3:14 | **A copy [*patshegen*] of the document:** In Old Persian, this means a faithful copy of the source of the law, signed with the seal of the king's ring.

יד פַּתְשֶׁגֶן הַכְּתָב לְהִנָּתֵן דָּת בְּכָל־מְדִינָה וּמְדִינָה גָּלוּי לְכָל־הָעַמִּים לִהְיוֹת עֲתִדִים
טו לַיּוֹם הַזֶּה: הָרָצִים יָצְאוּ דְחוּפִים בִּדְבַר הַמֶּלֶךְ וְהַדָּת נִתְּנָה בְּשׁוּשַׁן הַבִּירָה
א וְהַמֶּלֶךְ וְהָמָן יָשְׁבוּ לִשְׁתּוֹת וְהָעִיר שׁוּשָׁן נָבוֹכָה: וּמָרְדֳּכַי יָדַע אֶת־
כָּל־אֲשֶׁר נַעֲשָׂה וַיִּקְרַע מָרְדֳּכַי אֶת־בְּגָדָיו וַיִּלְבַּשׁ שַׂק וָאֵפֶר וַיֵּצֵא בְּתוֹךְ הָעִיר
ב וַיִּזְעַק זְעָקָה גְדוֹלָה וּמָרָה: וַיָּבוֹא עַד לִפְנֵי שַׁעַר־הַמֶּלֶךְ כִּי אֵין לָבוֹא אֶל־שַׁעַר
ג הַמֶּלֶךְ בִּלְבוּשׁ שָׂק: וּבְכָל־מְדִינָה וּמְדִינָה מְקוֹם אֲשֶׁר דְּבַר־הַמֶּלֶךְ וְדָתוֹ מַגִּיעַ
ד אֵבֶל גָּדוֹל לַיְּהוּדִים וְצוֹם וּבְכִי וּמִסְפֵּד שַׂק וָאֵפֶר יֻצַּע לָרַבִּים: ותבואינה נַעֲרוֹת וַתָּבוֹאנָה
אֶסְתֵּר וְסָרִיסֶיהָ וַיַּגִּידוּ לָהּ וַתִּתְחַלְחַל הַמַּלְכָּה מְאֹד וַתִּשְׁלַח בְּגָדִים לְהַלְבִּישׁ
ה אֶת־מָרְדֳּכַי וּלְהָסִיר שַׂקּוֹ מֵעָלָיו וְלֹא קִבֵּל: וַתִּקְרָא אֶסְתֵּר לַהֲתָךְ מִסָּרִיסֵי הַמֶּלֶךְ
ו אֲשֶׁר הֶעֱמִיד לְפָנֶיהָ וַתְּצַוֵּהוּ עַל־מָרְדֳּכָי לָדַעַת מַה־זֶּה וְעַל־מַה־זֶּה: וַיֵּצֵא
ז הֲתָךְ אֶל־מָרְדֳּכָי אֶל־רְחוֹב הָעִיר אֲשֶׁר לִפְנֵי שַׁעַר־הַמֶּלֶךְ: וַיַּגֶּד־לוֹ מָרְדֳּכַי אֵת
כָּל־אֲשֶׁר קָרָהוּ וְאֵת ׀ פָּרָשַׁת הַכֶּסֶף אֲשֶׁר אָמַר הָמָן לִשְׁקוֹל עַל־גִּנְזֵי הַמֶּלֶךְ
ח ביהודיים לְאַבְּדָם: וְאֶת־פַּתְשֶׁגֶן כְּתָב־הַדָּת אֲשֶׁר־נִתַּן בְּשׁוּשָׁן לְהַשְׁמִידָם נָתַן בַּיְּהוּדִים
לוֹ לְהַרְאוֹת אֶת־אֶסְתֵּר וּלְהַגִּיד לָהּ וּלְצַוּוֹת עָלֶיהָ לָבוֹא אֶל־הַמֶּלֶךְ לְהִתְחַנֶּן־לוֹ
ט י וּלְבַקֵּשׁ מִלְּפָנָיו עַל־עַמָּהּ: וַיָּבוֹא הֲתָךְ וַיַּגֵּד לְאֶסְתֵּר אֵת דִּבְרֵי מָרְדֳּכָי: וַתֹּאמֶר
יא אֶסְתֵּר לַהֲתָךְ וַתְּצַוֵּהוּ אֶל־מָרְדֳּכָי: כָּל־עַבְדֵי הַמֶּלֶךְ וְעַם מְדִינוֹת הַמֶּלֶךְ יֹדְעִים

itself, word had spread of the enormous sum that Haman had proposed to give to the king in his determination to annihilate the Jews.

8 **He** also **gave him,** Hatakh, **a copy of the written decree to destroy them,** the Jews, **that was issued in Shushan** in order **to show it,** the decree, **to Esther, to inform her** of the situation, **and** furthermore **to command her** in his name **to go to the king, to plead with him, and to request before him on behalf of her people.** Only she could stop Haman, who enjoyed such privileged status in the kingdom. Mordekhai himself was not close to the king, whereas Esther lived in the palace and was beloved by Ahashverosh. Since the decree was essentially motivated by emotion, Mordekhai hoped that she had the power to annul it through her entreaties.

9 **Hatakh came and told Esther the words of Mordekhai.**

10 **Esther said to Hatakh, and commanded him** to take back the following message **for Mordekhai:**

11 The rules of entering to see the king are well known: **All the king's servants** in the court, **and the people of the king's provinces, know that for any man or woman who comes to the king to the inner courtyard who has not been summoned** and has not been granted permission, **there is but one rule for him: To be put to death.** It was forbidden to enter without special invitation, as the king had quasi-divine status.

Esther continued: This fate is the rule, **except for one to whom the king will extend the golden scepter,**[B] **who lives.** If the king does not want a person who has entered without permission to be executed, he stretches forth his golden scepter to the person. Esther concludes: And **I have not been summoned to come to the king these thirty days.** Although I am the king's beloved queen, he has thousands of wives and concubines. I do not know his current mood, but the fact that he has not invited me for a month does not bode well. If I simply march in to see him, I will be endangering my life.

12 **They told Mordekhai Esther's words.**

13 **Mordekhai said to respond to Esther:** You feel protected in the palace, and you suppose that you will be spared any harm from Haman's order. However, you are wrong; **do not imagine escaping** because you are **in the king's palace,** that **out of all the Jews** you will be safe.

14 **For if you are silent** and do nothing **at this time,** I trust that **relief and deliverance will arise for the Jews from another place.** The decree does not go into effect for another eleven months, and I have faith in God that He will deliver us before then, **but** I am sure that **you and your father's house will perish,** as you did not act at the opportune time to save the Jews. Destruction will be visited upon you and your family, including myself.[44] **Who knows whether you have attained royalty for a time like this?** You came to a position of power without planning to do so, and now you find yourself in a situation where you can act to change the course of events and thereby save your people. Don't you think that this apparent coincidence is significant? Can't you see that it is a sign from Heaven?

15 Esther, as usual, accepted Mordekhai's instructions. **Esther said to respond to Mordekhai:**

16 **Go, assemble all the Jews who are present in Shushan, and** pray[45] and **fast on my behalf; do not eat and do not drink for three days, night and day,** an unusually severe fast. **Also I and my young women will fast in this manner,** as we must all pray for my success; **and then I will go to the king, against the rule, and if I perish, I perish.** Perhaps the day when I approach the king will be the last of my life.

17 **Mordekhai went on** his way, **and acted in accordance with everything that Esther had commanded him.** He gathered together all the Jews, informed them of the evil decree and of Esther's situation, and instructed them to pray and fast. The Jews' high regard for Mordekhai inspired them to rally behind him and follow his instructions.

Esther Risks Her Life

ESTHER 5:1–14

In dramatic contrast to Vashti, who defied the king by refusing to appear before Ahashverosh when he called her, Esther dares to transgress the law by approaching the king without having been called, thereby putting her life at risk. The feast for the public described at the beginning of the book likewise stands in contrast to the intimate feasts orchestrated by Esther for the king and Haman. As the story continues, the pace of events increases, and all the main characters are placed under stress: Ahashverosh does not understand why Esther risked her life in approaching him, nor why she keeps inviting him and Haman to parties; Haman enjoys the great honor granted to him by the queen and concurrently suffers humiliation in his dealings with Mordekhai; Esther does not know whether her plans and efforts will help her save her brethren, or whether they will bring disaster upon her; meanwhile, a death sentence hovers over Mordekhai's head.

5 1 **It was on the third day;**[D] **Esther donned royalty,**[46] royal apparel, **and stood in the inner courtyard of the king's palace, facing the king's palace; the king was sitting on his royal throne in the royal palace, facing the entrance of the palace,**[B] where he could see who was present in the court.[47]

2 **It was as the king saw Queen Esther standing in the courtyard that she found favor in his eyes;** the affection that he had initially felt toward her when he chose her was rekindled, **and** consequently **the king extended the golden scepter that was in his hand to Esther,** thereby granting her official permission to enter. **Esther approached and touched the top of the scepter,** which was apparently the accepted ceremonial response to receiving royal permission to approach.

Darius seated on throne, holding his scepter, Persepolis, fifth century BCE

3 **The king said to her: What is it with you, Queen Esther, and what is your request?** You clearly want something. In my love for you I will grant it, **up to half of the kingdom, and it will be granted to you.**[B] The king expresses in exaggerated terms his willingness to act for her sake.

4 **Esther said,** in the same formal manner: **If it pleases the king, let the king and Haman,** the most important man in the kingdom and the one closest to the king, **come**[D] **today to the banquet that I have prepared for him,** the king.

אֲשֶׁר כָּל־אִישׁ וְאִשָּׁה אֲשֶׁר־יָבוֹא אֶל־הַמֶּלֶךְ אֶל־הֶחָצֵר הַפְּנִימִית אֲשֶׁר לֹא־
יִקָּרֵא אַחַת דָּתוֹ לְהָמִית לְבַד מֵאֲשֶׁר יוֹשִׁיט־לוֹ הַמֶּלֶךְ אֶת־שַׁרְבִיט הַזָּהָב
יב וְחָיָה וַאֲנִי לֹא נִקְרֵאתִי לָבוֹא אֶל־הַמֶּלֶךְ זֶה שְׁלוֹשִׁים יוֹם׃ וַיַּגִּידוּ לְמָרְדֳּכָי אֵת
יג דִּבְרֵי אֶסְתֵּר׃ וַיֹּאמֶר מָרְדֳּכַי לְהָשִׁיב אֶל־אֶסְתֵּר אַל־תְּדַמִּי בְנַפְשֵׁךְ לְהִמָּלֵט
יד בֵּית־הַמֶּלֶךְ מִכָּל־הַיְּהוּדִים׃ כִּי אִם־הַחֲרֵשׁ תַּחֲרִישִׁי בָּעֵת הַזֹּאת רֶוַח וְהַצָּלָה
יַעֲמוֹד לַיְּהוּדִים מִמָּקוֹם אַחֵר וְאַתְּ וּבֵית־אָבִיךְ תֹּאבֵדוּ וּמִי יוֹדֵעַ אִם־לְעֵת
טו טז כָּזֹאת הִגַּעַתְּ לַמַּלְכוּת׃ וַתֹּאמֶר אֶסְתֵּר לְהָשִׁיב אֶל־מָרְדֳּכָי׃ לֵךְ כְּנוֹס אֶת־כָּל־
הַיְּהוּדִים הַנִּמְצְאִים בְּשׁוּשָׁן וְצוּמוּ עָלַי וְאַל־תֹּאכְלוּ וְאַל־תִּשְׁתּוּ שְׁלֹשֶׁת יָמִים
לַיְלָה וָיוֹם גַּם־אֲנִי וְנַעֲרֹתַי אָצוּם כֵּן וּבְכֵן אָבוֹא אֶל־הַמֶּלֶךְ אֲשֶׁר לֹא־כַדָּת
יז וְכַאֲשֶׁר אָבַדְתִּי אָבָדְתִּי׃ וַיַּעֲבֹר מָרְדֳּכָי וַיַּעַשׂ כְּכֹל אֲשֶׁר־צִוְּתָה עָלָיו אֶסְתֵּר׃
א וַיְהִי ׀ בַּיּוֹם הַשְּׁלִישִׁי וַתִּלְבַּשׁ אֶסְתֵּר מַלְכוּת וַתַּעֲמֹד בַּחֲצַר בֵּית־הַמֶּלֶךְ הַפְּנִימִית
נֹכַח בֵּית הַמֶּלֶךְ וְהַמֶּלֶךְ יוֹשֵׁב עַל־כִּסֵּא מַלְכוּתוֹ בְּבֵית הַמַּלְכוּת נֹכַח פֶּתַח
ב הַבָּיִת׃ וַיְהִי כִרְאוֹת הַמֶּלֶךְ אֶת־אֶסְתֵּר הַמַּלְכָּה עֹמֶדֶת בֶּחָצֵר נָשְׂאָה חֵן בְּעֵינָיו
וַיּוֹשֶׁט הַמֶּלֶךְ לְאֶסְתֵּר אֶת־שַׁרְבִיט הַזָּהָב אֲשֶׁר בְּיָדוֹ וַתִּקְרַב אֶסְתֵּר וַתִּגַּע בְּרֹאשׁ
ג הַשַּׁרְבִיט׃ וַיֹּאמֶר לָהּ הַמֶּלֶךְ מַה־לָּךְ אֶסְתֵּר הַמַּלְכָּה וּמַה־בַּקָּשָׁתֵךְ עַד־חֲצִי
ד הַמַּלְכוּת וְיִנָּתֵן לָךְ׃ וַתֹּאמֶר אֶסְתֵּר אִם־עַל־הַמֶּלֶךְ טוֹב יָבוֹא הַמֶּלֶךְ וְהָמָן הַיּוֹם

BACKGROUND

4:11 | **Scepter [*sharvit*]:** The Akkadian source of *sharvit* is *sabbitu*, a rod, branch, or staff that symbolizes the authority of the bearer. The parallel Hebrew term, *shevet*, is a metonym, as the physical staff represents the monarchy (see Genesis 49:10; II Samuel 7:7; Rashi, I Chronicles 18:5). Throughout history, various kings developed a custom of holding a gold or gold-plated ceremonial scepter, and this is practiced to this day by the monarchs of Britain and Scandinavia.

5:1 | **His royal throne in the royal palace, facing the entrance of the palace:** According to the map of the palace (see image alongside 1:5), the throne room was open, and from there the king could see who was standing in the inner courtyard.

5:3 | **Up to half of the kingdom, and it will be granted to you:** The queen of Persia, the foremost wife of the king, enjoyed a privileged status and great authority. This is supported by the account of Herodotus, who portrayed Atossa, Darius' wife and the mother of Xerxes I, in such terms. She ensured that her son would become king despite the fact that he was not the heir apparent (*The Histories* VII:2).

DISCUSSION

5:1 | **On the third day:** That is, the third day of the fast the Jews had taken upon themselves. This may also have been the third day since Haman's decree had been issued, which was the first day of the festival of Passover, or one or two days later (see Rav Yeshaya of Trani; *Seder Olam Rabba* 29; *Pirkei deRabbi Eliezer* 49; *Esther Rabba* 8; see also the *piyyut*: "Your Mighty Strength You Displayed on Passover," from the Passover Haggadah; *Targum*; Rashi, Esther 4:17; *Megilla* 15a).

5:4 | **Let the king and Haman come:** It seems that Esther's plan was to display personal affection for, and bestow particular honor upon, Haman, in order to sow discord and engender the king's suspicion

▸ that

5 **The king said: Hasten Haman to do Esther's bidding.** The tone of this order is somewhat dismissive of Haman, as the king is treating him like a servant who must instantly obey any desire of the queen.[48] **The king and Haman,** who was very pleased at this honor, **came to the banquet that Esther had prepared.**

6 Ahashverosh understood that this feast was not a celebration for its own sake, but rather was designed to create a favorable opportunity for the queen to state her request. Therefore **the king said to Esther at the wine banquet: What is your wish? It will be granted to you. What is your request? Up to half of the kingdom, and it will be done.**

7 **Esther answered and she said: My wish and my request** is as follows:

8 **If I have found favor in the eyes of the king, and if it pleases the king to grant my wish and to perform my request, let the king and Haman come to the banquet that I will** again **prepare for them, and tomorrow I will do the king's bidding.** Despite the expressions of affection that she had heard from Ahashverosh, Esther still hesitated; she was not yet ready to present her request. She was unsure of her ability to take a drastic step immediately, and she knew that were she to fail, she would also place herself in danger.

9 Ahashverosh left the feast in a state of intense curiosity. Esther had approached him the previous day, against the rules. In light of her repeated deferrals, he realized that she was preparing herself to request something important. In contrast, **Haman emerged on that day joyful and glad of heart.** He felt that he had reached the pinnacle of his success, as he was now not only a confidant of the king, but the queen had also shown him special favor, and he considered this a clear sign of his exalted status. **But upon Haman's seeing Mordekhai at the king's gate,** where Mordekhai had returned in his usual apparel after the end of the fast, **and he did not stand, and he did not move on his account,** but ignored Haman completely, Haman's mood changed for the worse; **Haman became filled with fury against Mordekhai.** The loftier his position in the kingdom, the more uncontrollable his anger over this act of disrespect.

10 Nevertheless **Haman restrained himself,** as he could do nothing at that time,[49] **and** he **entered his house and brought,** gathered, **his supporters, and Zeresh, his** influential **wife.**

11 **Haman** arranged a celebratory gathering of his supporters in order to tell them that he had been invited to the queen's feast, and he **related to them the honor of his wealth, and the multitude of his children, and all** the ways **that the king had promoted him, and that he had elevated him over the princes and servants of the king.** It is mentioned later (9:7–10) that ten sons of Haman were hanged, and he might have had even more children from other wives.[50]

12 **Haman said: Indeed, Queen Esther did not bring anyone but me with the king to the banquet that she prepared; tomorrow too, I am invited to her with the king.** This is the crowning glory. Not only am I the chief minister of the kingdom, but I have become the favorite in the royal household.

13 **But all this is not worthwhile for me**[D] **whenever I see Mordekhai the Jew sitting at the king's gate.** Yes, I have honor, wealth, and a bright future, but Mordekhai treats me with disrespect.

14 **Zeresh his wife and all his supporters said to him,** all in agreement with each other: **Let a gibbet be prepared, fifty cubits high; in the morning say to the king that they should hang Mordekhai upon it.** Do not wait until the feast. Go to the king in the morning and tell him that there is someone who aggravates you and refuses to accept your authority. Request that that person be hanged even before the rest of the Jews are killed. **And** then, in the evening, you can **come joyfully, with the king to the banquet. The matter,** this idea, **was pleasing to Haman, and he prepared the gibbet.** He gave an order that a gibbet of this kind be built in preparation for Mordekhai's hanging, paving the way for Haman's ultimate triumph.

DISCUSSION

that perhaps his chief minister was becoming too powerful. Furthermore, in light of Haman's prominent position, his deviousness, and his influence over the king, it is reasonable to assume that he had enemies in the royal court. Esther's maids and officials would certainly have informed the queen of the goings-on in the court, and she likely assumed that if Haman were to receive preferential treatment from his queen as well, it would inspire suspicion and mistrust in the court. This course of action was a gamble, as the success of Esther's plan depended on the reaction of Ahashverosh, who was not the most stable of men.

There were constant intrigues, conspiracies, and plots at work in the Persian court, and Ahashverosh, who apparently had seized the throne in a not entirely legal manner (see *Yalkut Shimoni* 954; *Megilla* 14a), was well aware of this state of affairs. Upon seeing Esther showing such favoritism to Haman, he might well have thought that a plot of some sort was being hatched against him, and that the queen was signaling to the protagonist her willingness to assist him. Even if an idea of this kind had not entered Haman's mind, Esther hoped to play on the king's fears, so that he would come to view Haman as someone who had gained too much power and who posed a threat to his reign (see *Megilla* 15b).

5:13 | **But all this is not worthwhile for me:** According to some commentaries, Mordekhai and Haman had known each other even before Haman rose to greatness (see *Megilla* 16a). For Haman, the encounter with someone who remembered him from when he was a lowly commoner, and who refused to honor him, would have been especially galling.

ה אֶל־הַמִּשְׁתֶּה אֲשֶׁר־עָשִׂיתִי לוֹ׃ וַיֹּאמֶר הַמֶּלֶךְ מַהֲרוּ אֶת־הָמָן לַעֲשׂוֹת אֶת־דְּבַר
ו אֶסְתֵּר וַיָּבֹא הַמֶּלֶךְ וְהָמָן אֶל־הַמִּשְׁתֶּה אֲשֶׁר־עָשְׂתָה אֶסְתֵּר׃ וַיֹּאמֶר הַמֶּלֶךְ
לְאֶסְתֵּר בְּמִשְׁתֵּה הַיַּיִן מַה־שְּׁאֵלָתֵךְ וְיִנָּתֵן לָךְ וּמַה־בַּקָּשָׁתֵךְ עַד־חֲצִי הַמַּלְכוּת
ז ח וְתֵעָשׂ׃ וַתַּעַן אֶסְתֵּר וַתֹּאמַר שְׁאֵלָתִי וּבַקָּשָׁתִי׃ אִם־מָצָאתִי חֵן בְּעֵינֵי הַמֶּלֶךְ
וְאִם־עַל־הַמֶּלֶךְ טוֹב לָתֵת אֶת־שְׁאֵלָתִי וְלַעֲשׂוֹת אֶת־בַּקָּשָׁתִי יָבוֹא הַמֶּלֶךְ וְהָמָן
ט אֶל־הַמִּשְׁתֶּה אֲשֶׁר אֶעֱשֶׂה לָהֶם וּמָחָר אֶעֱשֶׂה כִּדְבַר הַמֶּלֶךְ׃ וַיֵּצֵא הָמָן בַּיּוֹם
הַהוּא שָׂמֵחַ וְטוֹב לֵב וְכִרְאוֹת הָמָן אֶת־מָרְדֳּכַי בְּשַׁעַר הַמֶּלֶךְ וְלֹא־קָם וְלֹא־
י זָע מִמֶּנּוּ וַיִּמָּלֵא הָמָן עַל־מָרְדֳּכַי חֵמָה׃ וַיִּתְאַפַּק הָמָן וַיָּבוֹא אֶל־בֵּיתוֹ וַיִּשְׁלַח
יא וַיָּבֵא אֶת־אֹהֲבָיו וְאֶת־זֶרֶשׁ אִשְׁתּוֹ׃ וַיְסַפֵּר לָהֶם הָמָן אֶת־כְּבוֹד עָשְׁרוֹ וְרֹב בָּנָיו
יב וְאֵת כָּל־אֲשֶׁר גִּדְּלוֹ הַמֶּלֶךְ וְאֵת אֲשֶׁר נִשְּׂאוֹ עַל־הַשָּׂרִים וְעַבְדֵי הַמֶּלֶךְ׃ וַיֹּאמֶר
הָמָן אַף לֹא־הֵבִיאָה אֶסְתֵּר הַמַּלְכָּה עִם־הַמֶּלֶךְ אֶל־הַמִּשְׁתֶּה אֲשֶׁר־עָשָׂתָה
יג כִּי אִם־אוֹתִי וְגַם־לְמָחָר אֲנִי קָרוּא־לָהּ עִם־הַמֶּלֶךְ׃ וְכָל־זֶה אֵינֶנּוּ שֹׁוֶה לִי בְּכָל־
יד עֵת אֲשֶׁר אֲנִי רֹאֶה אֶת־מָרְדֳּכַי הַיְּהוּדִי יוֹשֵׁב בְּשַׁעַר הַמֶּלֶךְ׃ וַתֹּאמֶר לוֹ זֶרֶשׁ
אִשְׁתּוֹ וְכָל־אֹהֲבָיו יַעֲשׂוּ־עֵץ גָּבֹהַּ חֲמִשִּׁים אַמָּה וּבַבֹּקֶר ׀ אֱמֹר לַמֶּלֶךְ וְיִתְלוּ
אֶת־מָרְדֳּכַי עָלָיו וּבֹא עִם־הַמֶּלֶךְ אֶל־הַמִּשְׁתֶּה שָׂמֵחַ וַיִּיטַב הַדָּבָר לִפְנֵי הָמָן
א וַיַּעַשׂ הָעֵץ׃ בַּלַּיְלָה הַהוּא נָדְדָה שְׁנַת הַמֶּלֶךְ וַיֹּאמֶר לְהָבִיא
ב אֶת־סֵפֶר הַזִּכְרֹנוֹת דִּבְרֵי הַיָּמִים וַיִּהְיוּ נִקְרָאִים לִפְנֵי הַמֶּלֶךְ׃ וַיִּמָּצֵא כָתוּב אֲשֶׁר

The Night between the Two Feasts

ESTHER 6:1–14

The previous section ended at the lowest ebb of the story. Haman, who has been called for the second time to join the queen and king, is overjoyed; Mordekhai is to be hanged; and the decree of destruction still hovers over the Jews. There appears to be no hope on the horizon. However, in this next section the power relations between Mordekhai and Haman begin to reverse themselves. Haman arrives at the king's courtyard in order to request that Mordekhai be hanged on the gibbet that he has prepared at the precise moment when the king is inquiring as to how he can repay Mordekhai for his good deed. Haman is betrayed by his own lust for honor.

6 1 **On that night,** after Esther's feast, **the king's sleep was disturbed,** for no evident reason; **and he said to bring the book of records, the chronicles,** the book of royal history, **and they,** sections of the book, **would be read before the king,** in order to divert his mind with memories of past events.

2 **It was found written,** among the various events that had transpired in the kingdom, **that Mordekhai had reported of Bigtana,** Bigtan, **and Teresh, two of the king's chamberlains, among the guardians of the threshold,** who were very close to the king, **who had sought to do violence to King**

Ahashverosh. Their assassination attempt, the disclosure of the plot, and the fact that they had been hanged, were all recorded in the book.

3 **The king said: What honor or greatness has been bestowed upon Mordekhai**[D] **for this?** Perhaps he had received some form of reward, but as the details did not involve the king, they were not recorded in the book. **The king's lads, his servants, said to him: Nothing was done with him** to reward him.

4 **The king said: Who is in the courtyard?** These events likely occurred in the wee hours of the morning, and the king sought someone with whom he could converse and receive counsel about the matters that were disturbing his rest.[51] Now just at that moment **Haman had come to the outer courtyard of the king's palace,**[B] **to say to the king** his request **to hang Mordekhai on the gibbet that he had prepared for him,** in accordance with the advice he had received from his wife and friends. Although Mordekhai and the Jewish people were associated in his mind, since it was Mordekhai's presence that bothered Haman on a daily basis, he wished to dispose of him without delay.

5 **The king's lads said to him: Behold, Haman is standing in the courtyard. The king said: Let him enter.**

6 **Haman came, and the king said to him: What is to be done to the man whose honoring the king desires,** whom he wishes to honor in public? **Haman said in his heart: Upon whom would the king desire to bestow honor more than I?** Under the circumstances, Haman interpreted the king's question as though it were directed to him personally: How would you wish to be honored?

7 **Haman said to the king:** My advice is, **for the man whose honoring the king desires,**

8 **let them bring royal garments that the king** himself **has worn, and a horse upon which the king has ridden**[B] **while a royal crown was set on his,** the king's, **head,** while he rode the horse.[52] Alternatively, a royal crown was set upon the horse's head, demonstrating that it was the king's horse.

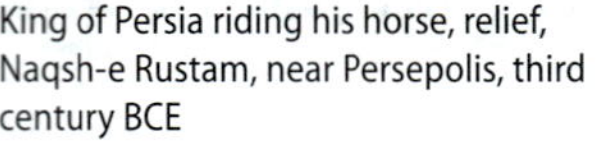

King of Persia riding his horse, relief, Naqsh-e Rustam, near Persepolis, third century BCE

Persian royal crown, relief

9 **And** once all these have been assembled, have them **put the garments and the horse in the hand of one of the king's princes, of the nobles,** a senior minister rather than a lowly servant; **they will dress the man whose honoring the king desires, and they will lead him riding on the horse in the city square, and they,** the nobles who lead him, **will proclaim before him: So shall be done to the man whose honoring the king desires.** Haman had no difficulty imagining himself riding on the horse, wearing royal clothing, after selecting one of the other ministers who would run before him.

10 **The king said to Haman:** This is indeed a good idea. Hurry, **quickly take the garments and the horse, as you have spoken, and do so to Mordekhai the Jew,**[D] **who sits at the king's gate.** Perhaps the king was not greatly familiar with Mordekhai, but he was not an anonymous figure either. His status and position in the royal court were well known. **Do not omit anything**[D] **from all that you have spoken.**

11 The king's order left Haman no choice. **Haman took the garments and the horse, dressed Mordekhai, led him riding through the city square, and proclaimed before him: So shall be done to the man whose honoring the king desires.**

BACKGROUND

6:4| **Haman had come to the outer courtyard of the king's palace:** Even important ministers might soon find themselves on the gibbet if they entered from the outer courtyard without invitation or permission (see commentary on 5:1). However, it is clear from the next verse that when the king sought an advisor at night and was told that Haman was in the outer courtyard, he gave him explicit permission to enter unharmed.

6:8| **And a horse upon which the king has ridden:** According to Herodotus, horses were highly esteemed creatures in Persia and were even considered sacred. Only kings and nobles were permitted what was considered the best breed, called by Herodotus the Nisean, due to its origins in the plains of Nisa in Media. Riding the king's horse was therefore a great honor. The horses' heads were sometimes adorned with a sort of crown. In Old Persian, the word for horse was *aspa*, or *asp*, a word that appears in names of people at the time of the book of Esther, e.g., Aspata, one of Haman's sons (9:7), as well as in contemporary Persian names (see also Song of Songs 1:9, and commentary ad loc.).

הִגִּיד מָרְדֳּכַי עַל־בִּגְתָנָא וָתֶרֶשׁ שְׁנֵי סָרִיסֵי הַמֶּלֶךְ מִשֹּׁמְרֵי הַסַּף אֲשֶׁר בִּקְשׁוּ
ג לִשְׁלֹחַ יָד בַּמֶּלֶךְ אֲחַשְׁוֵרוֹשׁ׃ וַיֹּאמֶר הַמֶּלֶךְ מַה־נַּעֲשָׂה יְקָר וּגְדוּלָּה לְמָרְדֳּכַי
ד עַל־זֶה וַיֹּאמְרוּ נַעֲרֵי הַמֶּלֶךְ מְשָׁרְתָיו לֹא־נַעֲשָׂה עִמּוֹ דָּבָר׃ וַיֹּאמֶר הַמֶּלֶךְ מִי
בֶחָצֵר וְהָמָן בָּא לַחֲצַר בֵּית־הַמֶּלֶךְ הַחִיצוֹנָה לֵאמֹר לַמֶּלֶךְ לִתְלוֹת אֶת־מָרְדֳּכַי
ה עַל־הָעֵץ אֲשֶׁר־הֵכִין לוֹ׃ וַיֹּאמְרוּ נַעֲרֵי הַמֶּלֶךְ אֵלָיו הִנֵּה הָמָן עֹמֵד בֶּחָצֵר וַיֹּאמֶר
ו הַמֶּלֶךְ יָבוֹא׃ וַיָּבוֹא הָמָן וַיֹּאמֶר לוֹ הַמֶּלֶךְ מַה־לַּעֲשׂוֹת בָּאִישׁ אֲשֶׁר הַמֶּלֶךְ
חָפֵץ בִּיקָרוֹ וַיֹּאמֶר הָמָן בְּלִבּוֹ לְמִי יַחְפֹּץ הַמֶּלֶךְ לַעֲשׂוֹת יְקָר יוֹתֵר מִמֶּנִּי׃
ז ח וַיֹּאמֶר הָמָן אֶל־הַמֶּלֶךְ אִישׁ אֲשֶׁר הַמֶּלֶךְ חָפֵץ בִּיקָרוֹ׃ יָבִיאוּ לְבוּשׁ מַלְכוּת
אֲשֶׁר לָבַשׁ־בּוֹ הַמֶּלֶךְ וְסוּס אֲשֶׁר רָכַב עָלָיו הַמֶּלֶךְ וַאֲשֶׁר נִתַּן כֶּתֶר מַלְכוּת
ט בְּרֹאשׁוֹ׃ וְנָתוֹן הַלְּבוּשׁ וְהַסּוּס עַל־יַד־אִישׁ מִשָּׂרֵי הַמֶּלֶךְ הַפַּרְתְּמִים וְהִלְבִּישׁוּ
אֶת־הָאִישׁ אֲשֶׁר הַמֶּלֶךְ חָפֵץ בִּיקָרוֹ וְהִרְכִּיבֻהוּ עַל־הַסּוּס בִּרְחוֹב הָעִיר וְקָרְאוּ
י לְפָנָיו כָּכָה יֵעָשֶׂה לָאִישׁ אֲשֶׁר הַמֶּלֶךְ חָפֵץ בִּיקָרוֹ׃ וַיֹּאמֶר הַמֶּלֶךְ לְהָמָן
מַהֵר קַח אֶת־הַלְּבוּשׁ וְאֶת־הַסּוּס כַּאֲשֶׁר דִּבַּרְתָּ וַעֲשֵׂה־כֵן לְמָרְדֳּכַי הַיְּהוּדִי
יא הַיּוֹשֵׁב בְּשַׁעַר הַמֶּלֶךְ אַל־תַּפֵּל דָּבָר מִכֹּל אֲשֶׁר דִּבַּרְתָּ׃ וַיִּקַּח הָמָן אֶת־הַלְּבוּשׁ ד
וְאֶת־הַסּוּס וַיַּלְבֵּשׁ אֶת־מָרְדֳּכָי וַיַּרְכִּיבֵהוּ בִּרְחוֹב הָעִיר וַיִּקְרָא לְפָנָיו כָּכָה יֵעָשֶׂה

DISCUSSION

6:3 | **What honor or greatness has been bestowed upon Mordekhai:** It can be assumed that when the king was reminded of this earlier effort to assassinate him, he began to wonder: Since there are people in the kingdom who oppose me to such an extent that they will attempt to assassinate me, have I properly rewarded those who protect me? Esther's mysterious invitation to another feast, to which once again the chief minister had been invited, further aroused his suspicions. The king might have reasoned that if he failed to repay those who saved his life, it was no wonder that people concealed their plans from him (Rashi, verse 1; *Megilla* 15b).

6:10 | **And do so to Mordekhai the Jew:** In addition to the great honor that the king sought to bestow upon Mordekhai by having him led by his chief minister, there is no doubt that he also wanted to humiliate Haman. It can be presumed that word of the animosity between Mordekhai and Haman had spread beyond mere servants' gossip to the royal court itself. Although the king had no special connection to Mordekhai, now that he had been reminded of how Mordekhai had helped him, Ahashverosh took advantage of this opportunity to reinforce in his subjects the awareness that all power and status are derived from the crown. From the fact that Haman wished to be displayed in the city square in the manner of the king on the day of his coronation, Ahashverosh came to the conclusion that his chief minister had been granted too much power, and that his megalomaniacal ambitions might undermine the king's own regime. By insisting that Haman be the one to lead Mordekhai, the king thereby publicized his own authority over Haman (see Malbim 10).

Do not omit anything: Some infer from here that Haman tried to persuade the king to exchange this parade for a monetary gift or some other type of honor. Therefore, the king gave him explicit instructions to carry out his suggestion to the letter, without any changes (*Megilla* 16a).

12 **Mordekhai returned to the king's gate.** Even if Mordekhai was pleased at Haman's humiliation, this did not ease the terror in his heart over the fate of the Jews.[53] **And Haman hastened to his house, mourning and with covered head,** as he was humiliated and wanted to hide his shame.

13 **Haman related to Zeresh his wife and to all his supporters everything that had befallen him.** He told them that he had followed their advice, but that he had arrived at the king's courtyard at the wrong moment and had suffered a terrible humiliation. **His wise men** who, perhaps significantly, are no longer described as his supporters, **and Zeresh his wife, said to him** dispassionately: **If Mordekhai, before whom you have begun to fall, is of the progeny of the Jews, you will not prevail against him; rather, you will fall before him.** There is no middle ground in our relations with the Jews. One who fights against them will either crush them or be utterly defeated by them.

14 These comments certainly did not improve Haman's mood. **They were still talking with him, and the king's chamberlains arrived, and they hastened to bring Haman to the banquet that Esther had prepared,** despite the fact that feasts were generally held in the evening hours. As part of the royal formalities, officials were sent to Haman informing him that his presence was requested at the feast immediately.

Haman's Downfall and Mordekhai's Rise to Power

ESTHER 7:1–8:2

Although the humiliation Haman has suffered does not necessarily cause him to change his plans, it can be assumed that he comes to Esther's second party dispirited and discouraged. This second party is also an intimate affair. Esther wants only Ahashverosh, Haman, and herself to be present, so that Haman will suddenly discover that both the king and the queen are against him, and that there is no one to defend him.

Subsequently, Esther lobbies the king to promote Mordekhai in Haman's place, and so the turnabout is complete. Haman is hanged on the gibbet that he had prepared for Mordekhai, and Mordekhai, who had refused to bend his knee to Haman, takes his place.

7 1 **The king and Haman came to** attend the **banquet with Queen Esther.**

2 **The king said to Esther also on the second day at the wine banquet: What is your wish, Queen Esther, and it will be granted to you. What is your request? Up to half the kingdom and it will be done.** The king repeated his earlier question because he knew that Esther wanted something, which she was to reveal at this second feast.

3 **Queen Esther answered** with the customary etiquette **and said: If I have found favor in your eyes, the king, and if it pleases the king, let my life be given me with my wish, and my people with my request.** You have agreed, in principle, to grant me half the kingdom, but all I want is that my life and my people be spared. This dramatic opening statement was designed to have maximum effect upon the king.

4 The queen clarifies her meaning: **For we have been sold, my people and I,** for our enemies **to destroy, to kill, and to eliminate** us. **If we had** only **been sold as slaves and as maidservants, I would have been silent** and would not ask for anything, **as** in that case **the trouble,** such an unfortunate event, **would not have been worth the distress to the king.** It would not be worth upsetting the king if we were only to be enslaved.[54]

5 **King Ahashverosh,** who was caught by surprise, as Esther had not told him that she was a Jew, **said, he said to Queen Esther:**[D] **Who is he, and where is he, who was so presumptuous to do so?** What kind of person would dare seek to destroy you and your people?

6 **Esther said: A man who is an adversary and an enemy, this evil Haman.** Haman advised you to destroy us because he is an enemy of the Jews. Moreover, he is an evil man, and his intentions are far from pure; you should not trust him. Although Haman had been discouraged by his experience with Mordekhai, he was still under the impression that Esther had invited him because she held him in high regard and was entirely unprepared for the queen's accusation. Therefore, **Haman was terrified in the presence of the king and the queen.**

7 **The king rose in his fury**[D] **from the wine banquet and went to the garden of the house.** He had forgotten his own involvement in the decree, and the fact that he had granted permission for Haman's plan. At this point, all he could see was Haman trying to destroy Esther and her people. In order to calm himself, he got up and went to take some air in the garden. **And Haman remained to plead for his life from Queen Esther.** Although by now Haman realized that she did not seek his favor, he hoped that she might have mercy upon him, as he had not yet harmed her in any way. He might also have sought to arouse her innate feminine compassion,[55] **for he saw that harm was resolved against him by the king.**

8 **The king returned from the garden of the house to the chamber of the wine banquet, and** he saw that **Haman was falling upon the couch on which Esther was** lying. According to Persian and Greek custom, wealthy and noble individuals would not sit on chairs during a feast; rather, they would recline on couches.[56] Haman was bending over Esther's couch in supplication but the king interpreted it in the worst way possible. **The king said: Is it also** part of your plan **to conquer**

יב לָאִישׁ אֲשֶׁר הַמֶּלֶךְ חָפֵץ בִּיקָרוֹ׃ וַיָּשָׁב מָרְדֳּכַי אֶל־שַׁעַר הַמֶּלֶךְ וְהָמָן נִדְחַף
יג אֶל־בֵּיתוֹ אָבֵל וַחֲפוּי רֹאשׁ׃ וַיְסַפֵּר הָמָן לְזֶרֶשׁ אִשְׁתּוֹ וּלְכָל־אֹהֲבָיו אֵת כָּל־
אֲשֶׁר קָרָהוּ וַיֹּאמְרוּ לוֹ חֲכָמָיו וְזֶרֶשׁ אִשְׁתּוֹ אִם מִזֶּרַע הַיְּהוּדִים מָרְדֳּכַי אֲשֶׁר
יד הַחִלּוֹתָ לִנְפֹּל לְפָנָיו לֹא־תוּכַל לוֹ כִּי־נָפוֹל תִּפּוֹל לְפָנָיו׃ עוֹדָם מְדַבְּרִים עִמּוֹ
וְסָרִיסֵי הַמֶּלֶךְ הִגִּיעוּ וַיַּבְהִלוּ לְהָבִיא אֶת־הָמָן אֶל־הַמִּשְׁתֶּה אֲשֶׁר־עָשְׂתָה
א ב אֶסְתֵּר׃ וַיָּבֹא הַמֶּלֶךְ וְהָמָן לִשְׁתּוֹת עִם־אֶסְתֵּר הַמַּלְכָּה׃ וַיֹּאמֶר הַמֶּלֶךְ לְאֶסְתֵּר
גַּם בַּיּוֹם הַשֵּׁנִי בְּמִשְׁתֵּה הַיַּיִן מַה־שְּׁאֵלָתֵךְ אֶסְתֵּר הַמַּלְכָּה וְתִנָּתֵן לָךְ וּמַה־
ג בַּקָּשָׁתֵךְ עַד־חֲצִי הַמַּלְכוּת וְתֵעָשׂ׃ וַתַּעַן אֶסְתֵּר הַמַּלְכָּה וַתֹּאמַר אִם־מָצָאתִי
חֵן בְּעֵינֶיךָ הַמֶּלֶךְ וְאִם־עַל־הַמֶּלֶךְ טוֹב תִּנָּתֶן־לִי נַפְשִׁי בִּשְׁאֵלָתִי וְעַמִּי בְּבַקָּשָׁתִי׃
ד כִּי נִמְכַּרְנוּ אֲנִי וְעַמִּי לְהַשְׁמִיד לַהֲרוֹג וּלְאַבֵּד וְאִלּוּ לַעֲבָדִים וְלִשְׁפָחוֹת נִמְכַּרְנוּ
ה הֶחֱרַשְׁתִּי כִּי אֵין הַצָּר שֹׁוֶה בְּנֵזֶק הַמֶּלֶךְ׃ וַיֹּאמֶר הַמֶּלֶךְ אֲחַשְׁוֵרוֹשׁ
וַיֹּאמֶר לְאֶסְתֵּר הַמַּלְכָּה מִי הוּא זֶה וְאֵי־זֶה הוּא אֲשֶׁר־מְלָאוֹ לִבּוֹ לַעֲשׂוֹת כֵּן׃
ו וַתֹּאמֶר אֶסְתֵּר אִישׁ צַר וְאוֹיֵב הָמָן הָרָע הַזֶּה וְהָמָן נִבְעַת מִלִּפְנֵי הַמֶּלֶךְ וְהַמַּלְכָּה׃
ז וְהַמֶּלֶךְ קָם בַּחֲמָתוֹ מִמִּשְׁתֵּה הַיַּיִן אֶל־גִּנַּת הַבִּיתָן וְהָמָן עָמַד לְבַקֵּשׁ עַל־נַפְשׁוֹ
ח מֵאֶסְתֵּר הַמַּלְכָּה כִּי רָאָה כִּי־כָלְתָה אֵלָיו הָרָעָה מֵאֵת הַמֶּלֶךְ׃ וְהַמֶּלֶךְ שָׁב מִגִּנַּת
הַבִּיתָן אֶל־בֵּית ׀ מִשְׁתֵּה הַיַּיִן וְהָמָן נֹפֵל עַל־הַמִּטָּה אֲשֶׁר אֶסְתֵּר עָלֶיהָ וַיֹּאמֶר

DISCUSSION

7:5 | **He said to Queen Esther:** As long as Esther kept her origins secret, her personal status was suspect. It would naturally be assumed that a woman who refused to reveal her ethnicity and background was in fact a maidservant of indeterminate birth, perhaps the daughter of a slave. Even among slaves and maidservants, a slave born to a slave lacked any social standing, and was considered inferior to a freeman who was captured in war. Ahashverosh had no particular familiarity with, or affection for, the Jewish people, but the Sages explain that Esther revealed at this point that she was descended from a royal line. She was no maidservant whom the king had raised up from misery, but a woman of noble descent (*Megilla* 16a).

7:7 | **The king rose in his fury:** The conversation between Ahashverosh and Haman the previous night had changed the image of Haman in the king's eyes. He realized that Haman was power hungry and would attempt to advance his status in the kingdom at any price. This impression that Haman had left upon the king the night before was reinforced by Esther's accusations. The king was therefore filled with great rage.

It should be noted that in royal courts of this kind, the chief minister is accorded great honor, but is also highly exposed. The king will always be wary of the person filling this role becoming too powerful. It is no coincidence that neither Haman nor Mordekhai, the two men whom Ahashverosh appointed to this position, came from the Persian nobility, and in fact were both foreigners. Such individuals could be removed from their posts with relative ease when the need arose. This might well have been one of Pharaoh's motivations for appointing Joseph (Genesis 41:39–44).

the queen with me in the house, to rape the queen in my own presence? **The words emerged from the king's mouth, and Haman's face fell.** He turned pale as he realized that he was facing his demise. Apologizing was futile, as in these circumstances nothing he could say would save him.

9 The feast was served by waiters who were not considered to be attendees. However, when the king revealed his opinion about Haman, one of them dared to interject in support of that sentiment. **Harvona,** who was **one of the chamberlains who was before the king, said: Indeed, behold, the gibbet that Haman prepared for Mordekhai,** who is someone **who spoke beneficially for the king.** This is the true nature of Haman; he is a man who prepares a gibbet for one who helps the king. The gibbet **is standing in the house of Haman,** and is **fifty cubits high.** Perhaps Harvona disliked Haman for reasons of his own, and he now saw the chance to retaliate. **The king said: Hang him on it.** If the gibbet is already prepared, Haman's sentence can be carried out without delay.

10 **They hanged Haman on the gibbet that he had prepared for Mordekhai, and the king's fury abated.**

8 1 Once Haman had been hanged, the king decided to bestow further favors upon Esther. **On that day, King Ahashverosh gave the house of Haman, adversary of the Jews, to Queen Esther.** This gift included the enormous amount of wealth that Haman had accumulated.[57] **And Mordekhai came** for a personal audience **before the king, as Esther had related what he was to her.** She presented him as her cousin, who had adopted, raised, and educated her. Ahashverosh was in good spirits now that Haman was gone, and for her part Esther treated him with affection and gratitude. Furthermore, if Ahashverosh was not yet personally familiar with Mordekhai, he was now given the opportunity to meet this loyal subject who had been instrumental in uncovering the assassination plot against him.

2 **The king removed his ring that he had taken from Haman, and he gave it to Mordekhai,** as a sign of trust. **Esther appointed Mordekhai over the house of Haman.** She appointed him to be in charge of Haman's estate.

The Order against Haman's Decree

ESTHER 8:3–17

Although the problem of Haman himself had been resolved, the decree permitting the annihilation of the Jews still stood. Esther seeks to take advantage of her favor with the king and annul the evil decree that threatens her people.

3 **Esther spoke again before the king, fell before his feet, cried, and besought him to repeal the evil of Haman the Agagite and his plot that he had devised against the Jews.**

4 **The king extended to Esther the golden scepter,** to signal to the queen, who was lying on the floor at his feet, that she was permitted to rise and speak her mind. **And Esther rose and stood before the king.**

5 **She said,** choosing her words carefully in order to arouse all the king's love and affection for her: **If it pleases the king, and if I have found favor before him, and the matter is proper before the king, and I am pleasing in his eyes, let it be written to return the scrolls** that were sent as part of **the plot of Haman son of Hamedata the Agagite that he wrote, to eliminate the Jews who are in all the king's provinces,** and to annul the decree they contain;

6 **for how can I bear and see the harm that will find my people;**[D] **and how can I bear and see the elimination of my birthplace?** By this stage, Esther no longer had any concerns for herself. She knew that she would be left untouched, but she implored the king not to let her people be harmed as a result of the decree.

7 **King Ahashverosh said to Queen Esther and to Mordekhai the Jew,** who was present: **Behold, I gave the house of Haman to Esther,** as a gesture of goodwill, **and they hanged him on the gibbet because he sought to do violence to the Jews.** Once again the king places the blame entirely on Haman while conveniently disregarding his own involvement in the plot against the Jews.

8 **As for you, write concerning the Jews** a different missive **as is pleasing in your eyes, in the king's name, and seal it with the king's ring,** so that the two orders cancel each other out; **for a document that is written in the name of the king, and sealed with the ring of the king, may not be revoked.** According to the laws of the kingdom, not even the king could nullify his own orders, as once written they were considered to be absolute, divine commands. Consequently, another royal communiqué, formulated in such a manner that it bypasses the previous command and limits its significance, must be written.

9 Indeed, **the king's scribes were summoned at that time, in the third month, which is the month of Sivan, on the twenty-third day of it,**[B] roughly three months after Haman was hanged; **it was written according to everything that Mordekhai commanded concerning the Jews.** The missives

המלך הגם לכבוש את־המלכה עמי בבית הדבר יצא מפי המלך ופני המן
ט חפו: ויאמר חרבונה אחד מן־הסריסים לפני המלך גם הנה־העץ אשר־עשה
המן למרדכי אשר דבר־טוב על־המלך עמד בבית המן גבה חמשים אמה
י ויאמר המלך תלהו עליו: ויתלו את־המן על־העץ אשר־הכין למרדכי וחמת
א המלך שככה: ביום ההוא נתן המלך אחשורוש לאסתר המלכה
את־בית המן צרר היהודיים ומרדכי בא לפני המלך כי־הגידה אסתר מה היהודים
ב הוא־לה: ויסר המלך את־טבעתו אשר העביר מהמן ויתנה למרדכי ותשם
ג אסתר את־מרדכי על־בית המן: ותוסף אסתר ותדבר לפני
המלך ותפל לפני רגליו ותבך ותתחנן־לו להעביר את־רעת המן האגגי ואת
ד מחשבתו אשר חשב על־היהודים: ויושט המלך לאסתר את שרבט הזהב
ה ותקם אסתר ותעמד לפני המלך: ותאמר אם־על־המלך טוב ואם־מצאתי
חן לפניו וכשר הדבר לפני המלך וטובה אני בעיניו יכתב להשיב את־הספרים
מחשבת המן בן־המדתא האגגי אשר כתב לאבד את־היהודים אשר בכל־
ו מדינות המלך: כי איככה אוכל וראיתי ברעה אשר־ימצא את־עמי ואיככה
ז אוכל וראיתי באבדן מולדתי: ויאמר המלך אחשורש לאסתר
המלכה ולמרדכי היהודי הנה בית־המן נתתי לאסתר ואתו תלו על־העץ
ח על אשר־שלח ידו ביהודיים: ואתם כתבו על־היהודים כטוב בעיניכם בשם ביהודים
המלך וחתמו בטבעת המלך כי־כתב אשר־נכתב בשם־המלך ונחתום
ט בטבעת המלך אין להשיב: ויקראו ספרי־המלך בעת־ההיא בחדש השלישי

DISCUSSION

8:6 | **For how can I bear and see the harm that will find my people:** A person's concern for his people or family, even when it does not accord with the interests of the kingdom, would not be considered a betrayal, but rather a respectable, appropriate reaction. This is also seen in the response of King Artahshasta to Nehemiah's misery (Nehemiah 2:1–9).

BACKGROUND

8:9 | **In the third month, which is the month of Sivan, on the twenty-third day of it:** One explanation for the long delay between the hanging of Haman and the sending of the missives negating his decree is that they waited for the original messengers to return in order to send them back again, as the return of the very same messengers would reinforce the credibility of the new command (see Vilna Gaon, *Seder Olam Rabba* 29).

were sent **to the satraps, the governors, and princes of the provinces, which are from India to Kush, one hundred and twenty-seven provinces, each and every province according to its script, and each and every people according to its language, and** on this occasion even **to the Jews according to their script, and according to their language.** Since this time Jews were not merely the passive targets of the order but active participants in its implementation, they too received the missives.[58]

10 **He,** Mordekhai, **wrote in the name of King Ahashverosh, and he sealed** the missives **with the ring of the king** that he had received. **He sent scrolls in the hand of the couriers on horses, riders on the finest steeds** owned by the king,[59] **the mules born to mares.**[B]

Horseman, stone relief, Nineveh, 645–635 BCE

11 The missives stated **that the king had authorized the Jews who were in each and every city to assemble and to defend themselves.** Whereas the previous order allowed all those who wished to do so to attack the Jews, under the assumption that the Jews were forbidden to retaliate, here the king permitted them to defend themselves, and even **to destroy, to kill, and to eliminate the forces of people and provinces that are hostile to them, children and women, and to plunder their spoils.** The Jews were granted royal consent to wage total war against any enemy.

12 This order would come into effect **on one day, in all the provinces of King Ahashverosh, on the thirteenth** day **of the twelfth month, which is the month of Adar,** the same date that was previously fixed for their destruction.

13 **A copy of the document went out to issue the decree in each and every province, publicizing it to all the peoples: For the Jews to be ready for that day, to avenge themselves on their enemies.** The same day that had been designated for their destruction would be the day of their salvation.

14 **The couriers, riders on the finest steeds, went out** again **urgently and hastily, by edict of the king,** in order to disseminate the new order as quickly as possible throughout the kingdom, **and the decree was** also **issued in the Shushan citadel** itself.

15 **Mordekhai,** who had recently been appointed the chief minister, **came out from before the king** dressed **in royal garments** made **of sky-blue and white** woven material, **with a great golden crown** upon his head, **and** wrapped in **a cloak**[60] **of fine linen and purple wool,**[B] **and** the Jewish population of **the city of Shushan reveled and rejoiced** upon seeing that their representative had become the most influential man in the kingdom.

16 **For the Jews there was light, and joy, and gladness, and honor,** as instead of the bloody pogrom that had been planned, in which they were not meant to have any right to self-defense whatsoever, they were now legally permitted to protect themselves and fight their enemies.

17 **In each and every province and in each and every city, any place where the king's edict and his decree reached, there was joy and gladness for the Jews, a banquet and a holiday, and many from the peoples of the land pretended to be Jews,**[61] or professed to favor the Jews but without internal conviction, **as the fear of the Jews had fallen upon them.** The missives alone produced such a great impression that even before the decree was put into practice, the Jews began rejoicing and others became fearful.

The Jews' Victory and Its Commemoration

ESTHER 9:1–32

In this section, the order issued by the king together with Esther and Mordekhai is carried out. It is implemented to an even greater extent than Ahashverosh has already authorized. As the book of Esther nears its conclusion, it relates how this miraculous deliverance is to be memorialized in the Jewish national consciousness. This is achieved in two ways: First, the initially spontaneous days of rejoicing over the salvation and the victory are established as permanent dates of feasting and joy for the nation, throughout the generations. Second, Esther and Mordekhai write a record of the events, which is this book.

9 1 **In the twelfth month, which is the month Adar, on the thirteenth day of it,** the date that Haman had set for the destruction of the Jews, **when the time arrived for the king's edict and his decree to be implemented, on the day that the enemies of the Jews had hoped to rule over them, it was** in fact **reversed, so that it was the Jews who ruled over those who hated them.**

הוּא־חֹדֶשׁ סִיוָן בִּשְׁלוֹשָׁה וְעֶשְׂרִים בּוֹ וַיִּכָּתֵב כְּכׇל־אֲשֶׁר־צִוָּה מׇרְדֳּכַי אֶל־
הַיְּהוּדִים וְאֶל הָאֲחַשְׁדַּרְפְּנִים וְהַפַּחוֹת וְשָׂרֵי הַמְּדִינוֹת אֲשֶׁר ׀ מֵהֹדּוּ וְעַד־כּוּשׁ
שֶׁבַע וְעֶשְׂרִים וּמֵאָה מְדִינָה מְדִינָה וּמְדִינָה כִּכְתָבָהּ וְעַם וָעָם כִּלְשֹׁנוֹ וְאֶל־
י הַיְּהוּדִים כִּכְתָבָם וְכִלְשׁוֹנָם׃ וַיִּכְתֹּב בְּשֵׁם הַמֶּלֶךְ אֲחַשְׁוֵרֹשׁ וַיַּחְתֹּם בְּטַבַּעַת
הַמֶּלֶךְ וַיִּשְׁלַח סְפָרִים בְּיַד הָרָצִים בַּסּוּסִים רֹכְבֵי הָרֶכֶשׁ הָאֲחַשְׁתְּרָנִים בְּנֵי
יא הָרַמָּכִים׃ אֲשֶׁר נָתַן הַמֶּלֶךְ לַיְּהוּדִים ׀ אֲשֶׁר ׀ בְּכׇל־עִיר וָעִיר לְהִקָּהֵל וְלַעֲמֹד
עַל־נַפְשָׁם לְהַשְׁמִיד וְלַהֲרֹג וּלְאַבֵּד אֶת־כׇּל־חֵיל עַם וּמְדִינָה הַצָּרִים אֹתָם טַף
יב וְנָשִׁים וּשְׁלָלָם לָבוֹז׃ בְּיוֹם אֶחָד בְּכׇל־מְדִינוֹת הַמֶּלֶךְ אֲחַשְׁוֵרוֹשׁ בִּשְׁלוֹשָׁה עָשָׂר
יג לְחֹדֶשׁ שְׁנֵים־עָשָׂר הוּא־חֹדֶשׁ אֲדָר׃ פַּתְשֶׁגֶן הַכְּתָב לְהִנָּתֵן דָּת בְּכׇל־מְדִינָה
וּמְדִינָה גָּלוּי לְכׇל־הָעַמִּים וְלִהְיוֹת היהודיים עתודים לַיּוֹם הַזֶּה לְהִנָּקֵם מֵאֹיְבֵיהֶם׃ (הַיְּהוּדִים עֲתִידִים)
יד הָרָצִים רֹכְבֵי הָרֶכֶשׁ הָאֲחַשְׁתְּרָנִים יָצְאוּ מְבֹהָלִים וּדְחוּפִים בִּדְבַר הַמֶּלֶךְ וְהַדָּת
טו נִתְּנָה בְּשׁוּשַׁן הַבִּירָה׃ וּמׇרְדֳּכַי יָצָא ׀ מִלִּפְנֵי הַמֶּלֶךְ בִּלְבוּשׁ מַלְכוּת
תְּכֵלֶת וָחוּר וַעֲטֶרֶת זָהָב גְּדוֹלָה וְתַכְרִיךְ בּוּץ וְאַרְגָּמָן וְהָעִיר שׁוּשָׁן צָהֲלָה
טז יז וְשָׂמֵחָה׃ לַיְּהוּדִים הָיְתָה אוֹרָה וְשִׂמְחָה וְשָׂשֹׂן וִיקָר׃ וּבְכׇל־מְדִינָה וּמְדִינָה ה
וּבְכׇל־עִיר וָעִיר מְקוֹם אֲשֶׁר דְּבַר־הַמֶּלֶךְ וְדָתוֹ מַגִּיעַ שִׂמְחָה וְשָׂשׂוֹן לַיְּהוּדִים
מִשְׁתֶּה וְיוֹם טוֹב וְרַבִּים מֵעַמֵּי הָאָרֶץ מִתְיַהֲדִים כִּי־נָפַל פַּחַד־הַיְּהוּדִים עֲלֵיהֶם׃
ט א וּבִשְׁנֵים עָשָׂר חֹדֶשׁ הוּא־חֹדֶשׁ אֲדָר בִּשְׁלוֹשָׁה עָשָׂר יוֹם בּוֹ אֲשֶׁר הִגִּיעַ דְּבַר־
הַמֶּלֶךְ וְדָתוֹ לְהֵעָשׂוֹת בַּיּוֹם אֲשֶׁר שִׂבְּרוּ אֹיְבֵי הַיְּהוּדִים לִשְׁלוֹט בָּהֶם וְנַהֲפוֹךְ

BACKGROUND

8:10| **The couriers on horses, riders on the finest steeds [*rekhesh*], the mules born to mares:** These royal messengers were part of a remarkable system of communication and road networks created by Darius I. In order to increase their speed across the flat terrain of Mesopotamia, the king's messengers would change their horses at waystations. *Rekhesh* is the name for a famously swift breed of horse. The last part of the verse is probably referring to riders of fast mules, the offspring of a select breed of mares, as these could ride through the mountainous regions of central and northern Persia, as well as Anatolia. Perhaps the three different types of messengers specified in this verse, those on "horses," "riders on the finest steeds," and on "mules born to mares," performed different missions, for short, medium, and long distances. Only those messengers sent to the far corners of the kingdom required mules that could cope with mountainous terrain.

8:15| **In royal garments of sky blue and white, with a great golden crown, and a cloak of fine linen and purple wool:** See commentary on 1:6; see also the image of the king with his second-in-command standing behind him, dressed in similar attire, above 1:4.

2 **The Jews assembled in their cities in all the provinces of King Ahashverosh** where there were Jewish communities, **to do violence to those who sought their harm, and no man could withstand them, as fear of them had fallen upon all the peoples.**

3 **All the princes of the provinces, the satraps, the governors, and the king's administrators elevated** or honored **the Jews, because the fear of Mordekhai had fallen upon them.** When the first missives were sent, Haman was chief minister to Ahashverosh. By this point, however, Mordekhai was the foremost of the king's ministers, and therefore everyone granted the Jews the freedom of action they required.

4 **For Mordekhai was great** in status **in the king's palace, and his renown** had **spread in all the provinces, for the man Mordekhai was growing more and more powerful.**

5 **The Jews smote all their enemies a blow of the sword, killing, and destruction, and they did to their enemies as they willed.** Presumably this also took place in the province of Judah, which is not explicitly mentioned here, but whose Jewish residents were experiencing harassment during this time.[62]

Sword, Persepolis, 560–331 BCE

6 **In the Shushan citadel the Jews killed and eliminated five hundred men,** their enemies who had planned to attack the Jews on that day, and who had perhaps taunted the Jews earlier and boasted of their heinous plans.

7 **And Parshandata, Dalfon, Aspata,**

8 **Porata, Adalya, Aridata,**

9 **Parmashta, Arisai, Aridai, and Vayzata,**

10 **the ten sons of Haman the son of Hamedata, the adversary of the Jews, they killed; but they did not extend their hands to the spoils.** The Jews did not consider this conflict a war, but an act of self-defense, and since they wished to avoid provoking hatred against themselves they did not touch their enemies' property, despite the fact that in his missive the king had granted the Jews permission to loot their enemies' possessions.[63]

11 **On that day, the number of those killed in the Shushan citadel came before the king,** through his extensive intelligence network.

12 **The king said to Queen Esther: The Jews have killed and eliminated five hundred men in the Shushan citadel, along with the ten sons of Haman; in the rest of the king's provinces they** presumably **have done likewise.** It can be assumed that the results are comparable in the other provinces, even though the numbers are not yet known. Your people have avenged themselves upon their enemies, as you wished. **What is your wish and it will be granted to you. What else do you request? It will be done.**

13 **Esther said,** realizing that the king wanted to make her happy and to fulfill her every desire: **If it pleases the king, let tomorrow, too, be granted to the Jews who are in Shushan to do in accordance with today's decree.** Although this was not written in the original missives, I would like you to issue a verbal instruction permitting the Jews in Shushan, which was likely the center of Haman's support,[64] to complete the task, **and have them hang Haman's ten sons,** who have already been killed,[65] **upon the gibbet,** as a public display that the king and the authorities support the action that has been taken, and that they consider these men criminals, rather than random victims of indiscriminate rioting.

14 **The king said to do so, and a decree was issued** permitting another day of vengeance **in Shushan, and they hanged Haman's ten sons.**

15 **The Jews who were in Shushan assembled on the fourteenth day of the month of Adar as well, and killed** another **three hundred men in Shushan, but** also in this instance **they did not extend their hand to the spoils.**

16 **The rest of the Jews who were in the king's provinces assembled and defended themselves, and rested from their enemies.** By the end of the day, **they** had **killed seventy-five thousand of those who hated them,** throughout the kingdom, **but** they **did not extend their hand to the spoils.**

17 **It,** all this, **was on the thirteenth day of the month of Adar, and the rest** after the fighting **was on the fourteenth of it, and it was made a day of banqueting and joy,** in honor of the victory.

18 **But the Jews who were in Shushan assembled** together to avenge themselves upon their enemies **on the thirteenth of it and on the fourteenth of it, and rested** after the fighting **on the fifteenth of it, and it was made a day of banqueting and joy.** They celebrated the victory one day later than the rest of the empire.

ב הוּא אֲשֶׁר יִשְׁלְטוּ הַיְּהוּדִים הֵמָּה בְּשֹׂנְאֵיהֶם׃ נִקְהֲלוּ הַיְּהוּדִים בְּעָרֵיהֶם בְּכָל־
מְדִינוֹת הַמֶּלֶךְ אֲחַשְׁוֵרוֹשׁ לִשְׁלֹחַ יָד בִּמְבַקְשֵׁי רָעָתָם וְאִישׁ לֹא־עָמַד לִפְנֵיהֶם
ג כִּי־נָפַל פַּחְדָּם עַל־כָּל־הָעַמִּים׃ וְכָל־שָׂרֵי הַמְּדִינוֹת וְהָאֲחַשְׁדַּרְפְּנִים וְהַפַּחוֹת
וְעֹשֵׂי הַמְּלָאכָה אֲשֶׁר לַמֶּלֶךְ מְנַשְּׂאִים אֶת־הַיְּהוּדִים כִּי־נָפַל פַּחַד־מָרְדֳּכַי עֲלֵיהֶם׃
ד כִּי־גָדוֹל מָרְדֳּכַי בְּבֵית הַמֶּלֶךְ וְשָׁמְעוֹ הוֹלֵךְ בְּכָל־הַמְּדִינוֹת כִּי־הָאִישׁ מָרְדֳּכַי
ה הוֹלֵךְ וְגָדוֹל׃ וַיַּכּוּ הַיְּהוּדִים בְּכָל־אֹיְבֵיהֶם מַכַּת־חֶרֶב וְהֶרֶג וְאַבְדָן וַיַּעֲשׂוּ
ו בְשֹׂנְאֵיהֶם כִּרְצוֹנָם׃ וּבְשׁוּשַׁן הַבִּירָה הָרְגוּ הַיְּהוּדִים וְאַבֵּד חֲמֵשׁ מֵאוֹת
ז אִישׁ׃ וְאֵת ׀ פַּרְשַׁנְדָּתָא וְאֵת ׀
ח דַּלְפוֹן וְאֵת ׀ אַסְפָּתָא׃ וְאֵת ׀
פּוֹרָתָא וְאֵת ׀ אֲדַלְיָא וְאֵת ׀
ט אֲרִידָתָא׃ וְאֵת ׀ פַּרְמַשְׁתָּא וְאֵת ׀
אֲרִיסַי וְאֵת ׀ אֲרִדַי וְאֵת ׀
י וַיְזָתָא׃ עֲשֶׂרֶת בְּנֵי הָמָן בֶּן־הַמְּדָתָא צֹרֵר הַיְּהוּדִים
יא הָרָגוּ וּבַבִּזָּה לֹא שָׁלְחוּ אֶת־יָדָם׃ בַּיּוֹם הַהוּא בָּא מִסְפַּר הַהֲרוּגִים בְּשׁוּשַׁן הַבִּירָה
יב לִפְנֵי הַמֶּלֶךְ׃ וַיֹּאמֶר הַמֶּלֶךְ לְאֶסְתֵּר הַמַּלְכָּה בְּשׁוּשַׁן הַבִּירָה הָרְגוּ הַיְּהוּדִים
וְאַבֵּד חֲמֵשׁ מֵאוֹת אִישׁ וְאֵת עֲשֶׂרֶת בְּנֵי־הָמָן בִּשְׁאָר מְדִינוֹת הַמֶּלֶךְ מֶה עָשׂוּ
יג וּמַה־שְּׁאֵלָתֵךְ וְיִנָּתֵן לָךְ וּמַה־בַּקָּשָׁתֵךְ עוֹד וְתֵעָשׂ׃ וַתֹּאמֶר אֶסְתֵּר אִם־עַל־
הַמֶּלֶךְ טוֹב יִנָּתֵן גַּם־מָחָר לַיְּהוּדִים אֲשֶׁר בְּשׁוּשָׁן לַעֲשׂוֹת כְּדָת הַיּוֹם וְאֵת עֲשֶׂרֶת
יד בְּנֵי־הָמָן יִתְלוּ עַל־הָעֵץ׃ וַיֹּאמֶר הַמֶּלֶךְ לְהֵעָשׂוֹת כֵּן וַתִּנָּתֵן דָּת בְּשׁוּשָׁן וְאֵת
טו עֲשֶׂרֶת בְּנֵי־הָמָן תָּלוּ׃ וַיִּקָּהֲלוּ היהודיים אֲשֶׁר־בְּשׁוּשָׁן גַּם בְּיוֹם אַרְבָּעָה עָשָׂר הַיְּהוּדִים
טז לְחֹדֶשׁ אֲדָר וַיַּהַרְגוּ בְשׁוּשָׁן שְׁלֹשׁ מֵאוֹת אִישׁ וּבַבִּזָּה לֹא שָׁלְחוּ אֶת־יָדָם׃ וּשְׁאָר
הַיְּהוּדִים אֲשֶׁר בִּמְדִינוֹת הַמֶּלֶךְ נִקְהֲלוּ ׀ וְעָמֹד עַל־נַפְשָׁם וְנוֹחַ מֵאֹיְבֵיהֶם וְהָרוֹג
יז בְּשֹׂנְאֵיהֶם חֲמִשָּׁה וְשִׁבְעִים אָלֶף וּבַבִּזָּה לֹא שָׁלְחוּ אֶת־יָדָם׃ בְּיוֹם־שְׁלוֹשָׁה עָשָׂר
יח לְחֹדֶשׁ אֲדָר וְנוֹחַ בְּאַרְבָּעָה עָשָׂר בּוֹ וְעָשֹׂה אֹתוֹ יוֹם מִשְׁתֶּה וְשִׂמְחָה׃ והיהודיים וְהַיְּהוּדִים

19 **Therefore, the unwalled Jews,** that is, those **who live in the unwalled cities,**[B] whose residents were exposed to great danger, **observe the fourteenth day of the month** of **Adar as a day of joy, banqueting, and a holiday, and** furthermore, a day **of sending portions** of food **one to another,** in order to increase joy and publicly express happiness. The date on which they spontaneously celebrated at that time was established as a day of rejoicing in the following years.[66]
20 It was Mordekhai who established the conversion of the spontaneous celebration into a permanent holiday: **Mordekhai wrote these matters,** the events that occurred, **and he sent scrolls to all the Jews who were in all the provinces of King Ahashverosh, near and far,** instructing them
21 **to establish for themselves to observe** the victory celebrations of **the fourteenth day of the month Adar, and the fifteenth day of it, in each and every year,** as permanent days of merriment and feasting:
22 **In accordance with** the dates of **the days that the Jews** of that generation had **rested from their enemies, and the month that was transformed for them from sorrow to joy, and from mourning to holiday, to observe them as days of banquet and joy, and of sending portions one to another, and gifts to the indigent,** so that the poor should also participate in the festivities.
23 **The Jews** as a people **undertook,**[67] or committed to continuing, **that which they had begun to practice** at the time, **and that which Mordekhai wrote to them.**
24 Mordekhai's brief summary of the events, as he wrote to the Jews, went as follows: **Because Haman son of Hamedata the Agagite, adversary of all the Jews,** not only the enemy of Mordekhai alone,[68] **had plotted against the Jews to eliminate them, and he cast the pur, that is the lot,** in order to determine a date on which **to crush them, and eliminate them.**
25 **But when she,** Esther,[69] **came before the king;** alternatively, when it, Haman's intention, came before the king, **he said: By means of the scroll, may his evil plot that he had devised against the Jews return upon his head.** When he summarized what happened, Mordekhai was careful not to mention that Ahashverosh had initially signed Haman's decree. Rather, he described the events in such a manner that it seemed that when the missives appeared, the king was surprised to discover that his minister had used his authority for reprehensible ends, and as a result he commanded that Haman be punished.[70] Subsequently, **they hanged him and his sons on the gibbet.**
26 **Therefore, they called these days Purim, after the lot [*pur*]** cast by Haman. **Therefore, for all the matters of this epistle** of Mordekhai's, **and what they saw about that matter,** that is, what led them to establish these days: Haman's **pur, and what befell them,** how they ultimately achieved victory and rest,
27 **the Jews established and accepted upon themselves, and upon their descendants, and** as these days of Purim were established for the entire people throughout the generations, they were also accepted **upon everyone associated with them,** converts,[71] despite the fact that their biological ancestors were not affected. **And** it was agreed that **it will not be neglected, to observe these two days as they are written, and on their dates, each and every year.**
28 **These days are remembered and observed in each and every generation, each and every family, each and every province, and each and every city.** Celebration of the holiday spread through all Jewish communities. Therefore, **these days of Purim will not pass from among the Jews, and their memory will not perish from their descendants;** they will be commemorated forever. Often, national days of celebration are temporary, and forgotten over the passage of time. By contrast, because this episode involved a plot to destroy the entire nation, it must be commemorated by the entire people through all its generations.
29 **Queen Esther daughter of Avihayil, and Mordekhai the Jew, wrote of all the significant events,**[72] alternatively, they wrote with all their authority, **confirming this second letter of Purim.** The first one, which contained a summary of the events, was sent by Mordekhai. Later they together wrote a revised epistle, signed by the queen.[73]
30 **He,** Mordekhai, **sent scrolls to all the Jews, to one hundred and twenty-seven provinces of the kingdom of Ahashverosh, matters of peace and truth.** These epistles were not binding orders, but inspirational instruction from the spiritual leader of the Jews.

BACKGROUND

9:19 | **The unwalled [*haperazim*] Jews, who live in the unwalled cities:** The authors of the book of Esther may have felt it was necessary to elaborate and precisely define the term *perazim* because of the similar Persian word *perazona*, which means people from diverse origins, similar to the Hebrew term *pezura*, diaspora. It is therefore emphasized that this term denotes specifically Jews who lived outside the fortified capital or other fortified cities, which were protected by soldiers of the Persian kingdom (Tamar Eilam Gindin, *The Book of Esther Unmasked*. Zeresh Publications, 2016 [Hebrew], pp. 144–145).

אֲשֶׁר־בְּשׁוּשָׁן נִקְהֲלוּ בִּשְׁלוֹשָׁה עָשָׂר בּוֹ וּבְאַרְבָּעָה עָשָׂר בּוֹ וְנוֹחַ בַּחֲמִשָּׁה עָשָׂר
יט בּוֹ וְעָשֹׂה אֹתוֹ יוֹם מִשְׁתֶּה וְשִׂמְחָה׃ עַל־כֵּן הַיְּהוּדִים הפרוזים הַיֹּשְׁבִים בְּעָרֵי הַפְּרָזִים
הַפְּרָזוֹת עֹשִׂים אֵת יוֹם אַרְבָּעָה עָשָׂר לְחֹדֶשׁ אֲדָר שִׂמְחָה וּמִשְׁתֶּה וְיוֹם טוֹב
כ וּמִשְׁלֹחַ מָנוֹת אִישׁ לְרֵעֵהוּ׃ וַיִּכְתֹּב מָרְדֳּכַי אֶת־הַדְּבָרִים הָאֵלֶּה וַיִּשְׁלַח סְפָרִים
אֶל־כָּל־הַיְּהוּדִים אֲשֶׁר בְּכָל־מְדִינוֹת הַמֶּלֶךְ אֲחַשְׁוֵרוֹשׁ הַקְּרוֹבִים וְהָרְחוֹקִים׃
כא לְקַיֵּם עֲלֵיהֶם לִהְיוֹת עֹשִׂים אֵת יוֹם אַרְבָּעָה עָשָׂר לְחֹדֶשׁ אֲדָר וְאֵת יוֹם־חֲמִשָּׁה
כב עָשָׂר בּוֹ בְּכָל־שָׁנָה וְשָׁנָה׃ כַּיָּמִים אֲשֶׁר־נָחוּ בָהֶם הַיְּהוּדִים מֵאֹיְבֵיהֶם וְהַחֹדֶשׁ
אֲשֶׁר נֶהְפַּךְ לָהֶם מִיָּגוֹן לְשִׂמְחָה וּמֵאֵבֶל לְיוֹם טוֹב לַעֲשׂוֹת אוֹתָם יְמֵי מִשְׁתֶּה
כג וְשִׂמְחָה וּמִשְׁלֹחַ מָנוֹת אִישׁ לְרֵעֵהוּ וּמַתָּנוֹת לָאֶבְיֹנִים׃ וְקִבֵּל הַיְּהוּדִים אֵת
כד אֲשֶׁר־הֵחֵלּוּ לַעֲשׂוֹת וְאֵת אֲשֶׁר־כָּתַב מָרְדֳּכַי אֲלֵיהֶם׃ כִּי הָמָן בֶּן־הַמְּדָתָא
הָאֲגָגִי צֹרֵר כָּל־הַיְּהוּדִים חָשַׁב עַל־הַיְּהוּדִים לְאַבְּדָם וְהִפִּל פּוּר הוּא הַגּוֹרָל
כה לְהֻמָּם וּלְאַבְּדָם׃ וּבְבֹאָהּ לִפְנֵי הַמֶּלֶךְ אָמַר עִם־הַסֵּפֶר יָשׁוּב מַחֲשַׁבְתּוֹ הָרָעָה
כו אֲשֶׁר־חָשַׁב עַל־הַיְּהוּדִים עַל־רֹאשׁוֹ וְתָלוּ אֹתוֹ וְאֶת־בָּנָיו עַל־הָעֵץ׃ עַל־כֵּן קָרְאוּ
לַיָּמִים הָאֵלֶּה פוּרִים עַל־שֵׁם הַפּוּר עַל־כֵּן עַל־כָּל־דִּבְרֵי הָאִגֶּרֶת הַזֹּאת וּמָה־
כז רָאוּ עַל־כָּכָה וּמָה הִגִּיעַ אֲלֵיהֶם׃ קִיְּמוּ וְקִבְּלֻ הַיְּהוּדִים ׀ עֲלֵיהֶם ׀ וְעַל־זַרְעָם
וְעַל כָּל־הַנִּלְוִים עֲלֵיהֶם וְלֹא יַעֲבוֹר לִהְיוֹת עֹשִׂים אֵת שְׁנֵי הַיָּמִים הָאֵלֶּה כִּכְתָבָם
כח וְכִזְמַנָּם בְּכָל־שָׁנָה וְשָׁנָה׃ וְהַיָּמִים הָאֵלֶּה נִזְכָּרִים וְנַעֲשִׂים בְּכָל־דּוֹר וָדוֹר מִשְׁפָּחָה
וּמִשְׁפָּחָה מְדִינָה וּמְדִינָה וְעִיר וָעִיר וִימֵי הַפּוּרִים הָאֵלֶּה לֹא יַעַבְרוּ מִתּוֹךְ
כט הַיְּהוּדִים וְזִכְרָם לֹא־יָסוּף מִזַּרְעָם׃ וַתִּכְתֹּב אֶסְתֵּר הַמַּלְכָּה בַת־
אֲבִיחַיִל וּמָרְדֳּכַי הַיְּהוּדִי אֶת־כָּל־תֹּקֶף לְקַיֵּם אֵת אִגֶּרֶת הַפֻּרִים הַזֹּאת הַשֵּׁנִית׃
ל וַיִּשְׁלַח סְפָרִים אֶל־כָּל־הַיְּהוּדִים אֶל־שֶׁבַע וְעֶשְׂרִים וּמֵאָה מְדִינָה מַלְכוּת

31 The epistle was sent **to establish these days of Purim on their dates, as Mordekhai the Jew and Queen Esther had established for them, and as they established the matters of the fasts and their lamentations**[D] **for themselves and for their descendants.** Just as all the Jews throughout the kingdom of Ahashverosh had taken part in the communal fast and prayers when the evil decree was issued, it was fitting that the entire people likewise share in the commemoration of the events.
32 **The edict of Esther established these matters of Purim, and it was written in the scroll.** As queen, Esther's affirmation of the holiday by writing and signing the account of these events, i.e., this book, gave great force to the establishment of the holiday.[74]

Scroll of Esther, Fez, Morocco, thirteenth to fourteenth century CE

The Greatness of Ahashverosh and Mordekhai

ESTHER 10:1–3

This short section, which concludes the book of Esther, parallels its opening verses. The book began with a description of the kingdom of Ahashverosh and his lavish feasts; it ends here with a historical record of his reign, conveyed in a formal style.

10 1 **King Ahashverosh imposed a tax on the land, and on the lands of the sea,**[B] as under his rule the kingdom of Persia reached the pinnacle of its greatness and power.
2 **All** the details of **the acts of his,** Ahashverosh's, **authority, and his might, and the episode of the greatness of Mordekhai, that the king promoted him** to the chief minister of the kingdom; **are they not written in the book of the chronicles of the kings of Media and Persia?** These historical matters are not relevant to this book; further descriptions may be found in the chronicles of the kings of Persia and Media. Similar statements directing the reader to the royal chronicles appear elsewhere in the Bible.[75]
3 The book concludes by returning to the matter at hand: **For Mordekhai the Jew** had achieved the high status of a man who **was viceroy to King Ahashverosh, and** as such, he was also **prominent** as a great leader **among the Jews,** and **accepted by most of his brethren.**[D] Mordekhai was **a** constant **seeker of good for his people,** as he tried to help the Jewish population with all the means at his disposal, **and** an unwavering **spokesman of peace for all his descendants.** All his children and grandchildren benefited from his position of greatness.

Alleged tomb of Mordekhai and Esther, Hamadan, western Iran

לא אֲחַשְׁוֵרוֹשׁ דִּבְרֵי שָׁלוֹם וֶאֱמֶת׃ לְקַיֵּם אֶת־יְמֵי הַפֻּרִים הָאֵלֶּה בִּזְמַנֵּיהֶם כַּאֲשֶׁר
קִיַּם עֲלֵיהֶם מָרְדֳּכַי הַיְּהוּדִי וְאֶסְתֵּר הַמַּלְכָּה וְכַאֲשֶׁר קִיְּמוּ עַל־נַפְשָׁם וְעַל־זַרְעָם
לב דִּבְרֵי הַצֹּמוֹת וְזַעֲקָתָם׃ וּמַאֲמַר אֶסְתֵּר קִיַּם דִּבְרֵי הַפֻּרִים הָאֵלֶּה וְנִכְתָּב
א ב בַּסֵּפֶר׃ וַיָּשֶׂם הַמֶּלֶךְ אחשרש ׀ מַס עַל־הָאָרֶץ וְאִיֵּי הַיָּם׃ וְכָל־ אֲחַשְׁוֵרוֹשׁ
מַעֲשֵׂה תָקְפּוֹ וּגְבוּרָתוֹ וּפָרָשַׁת גְּדֻלַּת מָרְדֳּכַי אֲשֶׁר גִּדְּלוֹ הַמֶּלֶךְ הֲלוֹא־הֵם
ג כְּתוּבִים עַל־סֵפֶר דִּבְרֵי הַיָּמִים לְמַלְכֵי מָדַי וּפָרָס׃ כִּי ׀ מָרְדֳּכַי הַיְּהוּדִי מִשְׁנֶה
לַמֶּלֶךְ אֲחַשְׁוֵרוֹשׁ וְגָדוֹל לַיְּהוּדִים וְרָצוּי לְרֹב אֶחָיו דֹּרֵשׁ טוֹב לְעַמּוֹ וְדֹבֵר שָׁלוֹם
לְכָל־זַרְעוֹ׃

DISCUSSION

9:31 | **The matters of the fasts and their lamentations:** Some explain that this is the Fast of Esther, which the Jews accepted upon themselves as a day of prayer and supplication forever (Ra'avad). Many other commentaries disagree, maintaining that the verse is referring to the fast days observed in memory of the destruction of the Temple, which are mentioned in Zechariah 8:19 (see Malbim; Ran, *Ta'anit* 18b).

10:3 | **Accepted by most of his brethren:** The Sages expound that Mordekhai was accepted by most, but not all, of his brethren, as some members of the Sanhedrin parted ways with him, perhaps because he had taken on such a senior position of authority (see Rashi; *Megilla* 16b). Alternatively, there were some who objected to him because the building of Jerusalem and the Temple were not renewed during his tenure. On the other hand, this period of calm may have been a contributing factor that allowed the Jews to later petition the king of Persia and request that the rebuilding of the Temple in Jerusalem, which had been halted, be resumed.

BACKGROUND

10:1 | **The lands of the sea:** At its height, the Persian Empire controlled the Anatolian coast and many of the Greek islands in the Aegean Sea, as well as the island of Cyprus. This was achieved thanks to the powerful Persian navy, which was manned by Phoenician mercenaries.

Daniel

Daniel

INTRODUCTION TO DANIEL

The book of Daniel is unique among the books of the Bible in several respects.

First, parts of it are written in Aramaic, rather than Hebrew. Although there are sections of the book of Ezra that are also in Aramaic, these are only documents or official records cited in their original language, whereas in the case of Daniel it is the actual text of the narrative itself. Furthermore, the portions of the book that are in Hebrew contain many obscure expressions.

Second, the book of Daniel focuses on one central character. While other individuals appear in the book as well, it mainly relates the story of Daniel's life, from his early years, and describes his deeds and visions.

Third, despite Daniel's visions, he is not considered a full-fledged prophet. The fact that the book of Daniel is not listed among the books of Prophets in the Bible, but rather as part of the Writings, is not because of its relatively late date. Daniel was roughly a contemporary of the prophet Ezekiel, who prophesied in Babylonia,[1] and he preceded Haggai, Zechariah, and Malachi, all prophets who were active at the start of the Second Temple period. Rather, Daniel is not one of the books of the Prophets because Daniel has a different status from the prophets whose books were included in that section of the Bible.

A prophet is not simply one who sees heavenly visions, predicts the future, or discloses events occurring in other parts of the world, but a person who receives his words as a prophecy and delivers them as a messenger of God. In the case of Daniel, even when he dealt with general matters and shared the revelations he had experienced through angels or by means of dreams, he was not sent to others as a prophet.[2] Consequently, his book can be described as a biography. The first part relates events of Daniel's life in the third person, while the rest is written in autobiographical style, with Daniel speaking about himself in the first person.

The character of Daniel brings to mind the relatively familiar Jew of the Second Temple period. Daniel's regular prayers and the care he took to refrain from eating non-kosher food call to mind the form of Jewish life that began to take shape during the Second Temple period. Though this way of conducting Jewish life did not originate with him, he is one of its forebears.

The first section of the book of Daniel recounts his deeds and trials, while the second section enumerates his visions. These visions allude to larger patterns of history and are somewhat reminiscent of Nebuchadnezzar's dreams that Daniel interpreted for him at the beginning of the book. Parts of Daniel's visions are difficult to decipher, and they will remain a mystery until the end of days.

Chronology for Book of Daniel

Date BCE	Event	Leader of the Jewish People	Babylonian/ Persian King
605	Daniel, Hananya, Mishael, and Azarya are taken to Babylon as captives in the third year of Yehoyakim's reign	King Yehoyakim	Nebuchadnezzar
603	Nebuchadnezzar's first dream[3]		
597	Exile of Yehoyakhin, the craftsmen, and the smiths to Babylon	King Yehoyakhin	
586	Destruction of First Temple	King Tzidkiyahu Gedalia (governor)	
562	Death of Nebuchadnezzar Evil Merodakh releases Yehoyakhin from prison		Evil Merodakh
539	Daniel interprets the writing on the wall for Belshatzar Conquest of Babylon led by Darius the Mede[4] and Cyrus the Great of Persia		Belshatzar

Daniel

Daniel and His Colleagues Are Trained to Serve the King of Babylon

DANIEL 1:1–21

Daniel and his three colleagues were all talented youths who were taken as captives from Judah and sent to serve in the royal palace in Babylon. Although they were cut off from their homeland, surrounded by a foreign culture, and forced into a restrictive lifestyle, the four youths kept a kosher diet, engaged in an intensive program of intellectual studies, and gained the favor of their overseers.

1 1 **In the third year of the reign of Yehoyakim king of Judah, Nebuchadnezzar king of Babylon came to Jerusalem and besieged it.**[B] This probably refers to the Babylonians' initial subjugation of Judah as part of their suppression of Egyptian influence in the entire area (see II Kings 23–24).

Partial ruins of the ziggurat and temple of the Babylonian deity Nabu, sixth century BCE

2 **The Lord delivered Yehoyakim king of Judah into his hand with some of the vessels of the House of God.**[D] At this stage, Nebuchadnezzar had not yet breached the city to fully conquer it. Nevertheless, the king of Judah submitted to him, bribing him with Temple vessels, and therefore Nebuchadnezzar allowed him to continue his rule in Judah.[5] **And he brought them,** the vessels, **to the land of Shinar,** Babylon,[6] **to the temple of his god, and he brought the vessels to the treasure-house of his god.**

3 **The king said to Ashpenaz chief of his chamberlains,**[D] the supervisor over the king's other officials,[7] **to bring from the children of Israel and from the royal offspring**[B] **and from the nobles,** the best families of Judah,[8]

4 **youths in whom there was no blemish,**[9] **and** who were **handsome, and skillful in all wisdom, knowledgeable and**

Representation of a street in the city of Babylon

perceptive. Nebuchadnezzar sought the most handsome, talented, and intelligent youths, **who would have the ability to stand in the king's palace.** A position in the king's palace imposed great responsibility, and therefore required both physical and psychological strength. **And** as the king did not intend to train them as ordinary officers, but instead wanted them to be part of his senior administration, he decided **to teach them the writing and speech of the Chaldeans.**

5 **The king allotted for them each day's** fixed **portion on its day, from the king's food,** bread, or meat, **and from the wine of his drink.** The youths received portions from the food and wine of the royal household, and the king gave instructions **to raise them,** that they be cared for in his palace, **for three years.**[B] Since they were foreigners their education required time, as merely learning to read and speak in the Chaldean

DISCUSSION

1:2 | **The vessels of the House of God:** On more than one occasion, when kings of Judah were in difficult positions, they brought out their own treasures, the treasures of the House of God, and sometimes even actual Temple vessels, for their enemies to plunder or to give as a bribe (see I Kings 14:25–26, 15:18–19; II Kings 12:19, 15:19, 16:8). In Babylon, these vessels were not used for idolatrous purposes, but were placed in the treasury as part of the property of the pagan temple (see Rashi; *Metzudat David*).

1:3 | **Chief of his chamberlains [*sarisav*]:** In rabbinic Hebrew, the term *saris* refers to a eunuch. It is unclear whether this is true in biblical Hebrew as well. The basic meaning of *saris* is a functionary in the royal household. Certainly in Persia, and perhaps also in Babylon, these servants were sometimes actually castrated. With regard to Daniel and his colleagues, the Sages dispute whether they were simply officials in the king's court, or if they too were physically castrated (see Ibn Ezra; *Sanhedrin* 93b; commentary on Isaiah 56:4; Jeremiah 38:7, and commentary ad loc.; commentary on Esther 1:10).

דניאל

א

א בִּשְׁנַת שָׁלוֹשׁ לְמַלְכוּת יְהוֹיָקִים מֶלֶךְ־יְהוּדָה בָּא נְבוּכַדְנֶאצַּר מֶלֶךְ־בָּבֶל יְרוּשָׁלַםִ
ב וַיָּצַר עָלֶיהָ: וַיִּתֵּן אֲדֹנָי בְּיָדוֹ אֶת־יְהוֹיָקִים מֶלֶךְ־יְהוּדָה וּמִקְצָת כְּלֵי בֵית־הָאֱלֹהִים
ג וַיְבִיאֵם אֶרֶץ־שִׁנְעָר בֵּית אֱלֹהָיו וְאֶת־הַכֵּלִים הֵבִיא בֵּית אוֹצַר אֱלֹהָיו: וַיֹּאמֶר
הַמֶּלֶךְ לְאַשְׁפְּנַז רַב סָרִיסָיו לְהָבִיא מִבְּנֵי יִשְׂרָאֵל וּמִזֶּרַע הַמְּלוּכָה וּמִן־הַפַּרְתְּמִים:
ד יְלָדִים אֲשֶׁר אֵין־בָּהֶם כָּל־מאוּם וְטוֹבֵי מַרְאֶה וּמַשְׂכִּילִים בְּכָל־חָכְמָה וְיֹדְעֵי
דַעַת וּמְבִינֵי מַדָּע וַאֲשֶׁר כֹּחַ בָּהֶם לַעֲמֹד בְּהֵיכַל הַמֶּלֶךְ וּלְלַמְּדָם סֵפֶר וּלְשׁוֹן
ה כַּשְׂדִּים: וַיְמַן לָהֶם הַמֶּלֶךְ דְּבַר־יוֹם בְּיוֹמוֹ מִפַּת־בַּג הַמֶּלֶךְ וּמִיֵּין מִשְׁתָּיו וּלְגַדְּלָם

BACKGROUND

1:1 | **Nebuchadnezzar king of Babylon came to Jerusalem and besieged it:** The Babylonian Chronicles, a series of tablets discovered in archaeological excavations in the city of Babylon, depict the conquest of Jerusalem by Nebuchadnezzar and his crowning of Tzidkiya in the following terms: "In the seventh year, in the month of Kislev, the king of Akkad [Nebuchadnezzar] gathered his troops, marched to the Hatti-land [Syria and the Land of Israel], and encamped against the city of Judah; and on the ninth day of the month of Adar he seized the city and captured the king. He appointed there a king of his own choice and took from it a heavy tribute and brought it to Babylon."

1:3 | **To bring from the children of Israel and from the royal offspring:** Historically, when a kingdom was conquered, the children of its noble families would be taken to the royal palace of the victors, where they would be raised. They were thereby assimilated into the political system, and educated as loyal subjects of their new ruler. Sometimes they were used as political tools by their captors to guarantee against any possibility of rebellion by their fathers, the subjugated kings. Documents dating from the eighteenth century BCE in Mari, Syria, as well as Egyptian records from the beginning of the New Kingdom, attest to this custom.

This is possibly the case with regard to the youths who grew up with Rehavam (I Kings 12:10), and the young princes of Ahav's dominions (I Kings 20:17). Isaiah likewise refers to this practice in his prophecy to Hizkiya: "They will take from your sons, who will descend from you, whom you shall beget, and they will be officials in the palace of the king of Babylon" (II Kings 20:18). The Roman Empire was also known to employ this tactic: Antiochus III was forced to send his sons to Rome as collateral against rebellion as part of the Treaty of Apamea. Moreover, Agrippa, the last king of Judah, was educated in Rome (*Antiquities of the Jews* XVIII:6). Important captives were occasionally granted governmental positions, but they always remained absolutely subordinate to the king.

1:5 | **To raise them for three years:** The Chaldeans were an Aramean tribe or nation that lived in southern Mesopotamia near the Syrian-Arabian desert. Although their name in Hebrew is *Kasdim*, ancient Assyrian documents call them *Kaldim*. According to external sources, from the ninth century BCE the Chaldeans became established in Babylonian cities, where they formed part of the ruling class, and thus Babylon was called "the land of the Chaldeans" (Isaiah 23:13).

The Chaldeans did not have a written alphabet, but they did have cuneiform, with a complex structure. Although their spoken language was similar to Hebrew, their written language and grammar were very different. Accordingly, it could indeed take three years for the captive youths to completely absorb this new language and culture.

language was not easy. In order that they would be ready for their complex roles, these talented youths underwent professional training. They were constantly tested by their overseers, **and** at the end of the three years **the select of them,** the best and most successful, **would stand before the king.**

6 Nebuchadnezzar likely took youths from other nations, and perhaps also Jewish youths from different regions of Israel. **Among them from the children of Judah,** from those Jewish youths whom they considered capable for the task, **were** chosen **Daniel, Hananya, Mishael, and Azarya.**

7 **The chief of the chamberlains gave them** new **names.** The Chaldean king and officers did not care to pronounce foreign names, especially as the youths' Hebrew names had no meaning in Chaldean. Therefore, they were given new Babylonian names. Changing someone's name to one from the local language when he began royal service was practiced in other eras as well.[10] **To Daniel he gave** the name **Beltshatzar,** based on the name of the chief god of Babylon, Baal, pronounced Bel in Babylonian.[11] **And to Hananya,** he gave the name **Shadrakh, and to Mishael, Meshakh, and to Azarya, Aved Nego,** which means worshipper of Nego, possibly the Babylonian god Nabu.[12] Since Daniel was the most gifted of the four, he was given the most distinguished name.

8 Daniel was apparently the leader and spokesman for the group, the one who would take the initiative, and perhaps the oldest as well. **Daniel resolved in his heart that he would not taint himself with the king's food and with the wine of his drink,** because they were not kosher. It can be assumed that they were given meat, which was certainly prohibited to Jews, and possibly rodents, insects, and other forbidden foods. **And** therefore **he requested from the chief of the chamberlains that he** be allowed **not** to **taint himself**[D] by eating that food and wine.

9 The chief officer was not supposed to attend to such a request. After all, there were many youths in his care, and he could not possibly accommodate the dietary preferences of each and every one of them. Furthermore, it was not even his decision to make. And yet, **God granted Daniel kindness and compassion before the chief of the chamberlains.** Daniel had made a favorable impression on the chamberlain, and he took the request seriously.

10 **The chief of the chamberlains said to Daniel:** I am prepared to grant your request, but **I fear my lord the king, who allotted your food and your drink.** I, too, have supervisors, whom I fear, and I am also concerned about the possible intervention of the king himself. **For why should he see your faces distressed more than the youths who are your contemporaries?** If you do not eat the king's food, you will appear gaunt, and less satisfied than the youths who eat all the food. If the king notices that you do not look well, **you would have my head,** i.e., me, **liable to the king.** The king will execute me on your account, as I am responsible not only for your behavior and education but also for your physical well-being.

11 The chamberlain explained his hesitancy, while not completely denying the request. **Daniel** therefore **said to the attendant,** the man in charge of serving the food,[13] **whom the chief of the chamberlains had appointed over Daniel, Hananya, Mishael, and Azarya:**

12 **Please, test your servants,** ourselves, **for ten days; let them give us some vegetables,** seeds, fruits, and vegetables, **and we will eat, and water and we will drink.** The king's meat and wine were almost certainly prohibited for consumption, but seeds and vegetables were kosher.[14]

13 **And our appearance and the appearance of the youths who are eating the king's food will be seen before you.** You can then compare our appearance to that of the other youths, **and as you will see** fit to do, **do with your servants.** Try this as an experiment, which will last several days, and then you can decide how to proceed.

14 **He,** the attendant, **heeded them in this matter, and he tested them for ten days.**

15 **At the end of ten days** it turned out that not only were Daniel and the other youths not sickly, and no thinner in appearance than the others, but **their appearance was better and plumper than all the youths who were eating the king's food.**

16 Upon seeing this result, **the attendant would take their food and the wine for their drink,** to be used for some other purpose. It would make sense that plenty of people would consider it a privilege to eat the king's food, and even to pay for it. **And** instead of giving Daniel and the other youths their standard portions of food, the attendant would **give them vegetables.** It is possible the attendant was not acting in a completely lawful manner. In any case, he would not have wanted this arrangement to become known.

17 Employing youths with fine appearances was only one element of the king's intent. This training period was mainly set aside for them to develop their education and learn how to deport themselves in a way that would reflect their court status. **These youths, the four of them, God granted them knowledge and perception in all writings and wisdom.** They learned to comprehend all kinds of books, and acquired various forms of knowledge. The king wanted them to be the wisest in the kingdom, so that he could use them as a kind of council for advice and leadership. **And** in addition to his knowledge and perception, **Daniel** also **had understanding in all visions and dreams.**

18 **At the end of the days that the king had said to bring them,** once they had finished their set training period,[15] **the chief of the chamberlains brought them before Nebuchadnezzar.**

ו שָׁנִים שָׁלוֹשׁ וּמִקְצָתָם יַעַמְדוּ לִפְנֵי הַמֶּלֶךְ׃ וַיְהִי בָהֶם מִבְּנֵי יְהוּדָה דָּנִיֵּאל חֲנַנְיָה
ז מִישָׁאֵל וַעֲזַרְיָה׃ וַיָּשֶׂם לָהֶם שַׂר הַסָּרִיסִים שֵׁמוֹת וַיָּשֶׂם לְדָנִיֵּאל בֵּלְטְשַׁאצַּר
ח וְלַחֲנַנְיָה שַׁדְרַךְ וּלְמִישָׁאֵל מֵישַׁךְ וְלַעֲזַרְיָה עֲבֵד נְגוֹ׃ וַיָּשֶׂם דָּנִיֵּאל עַל־לִבּוֹ
אֲשֶׁר לֹא־יִתְגָּאַל בְּפַת־בַּג הַמֶּלֶךְ וּבְיֵין מִשְׁתָּיו וַיְבַקֵּשׁ מִשַּׂר הַסָּרִיסִים אֲשֶׁר
ט לֹא יִתְגָּאָל׃ וַיִּתֵּן הָאֱלֹהִים אֶת־דָּנִיֵּאל לְחֶסֶד וּלְרַחֲמִים לִפְנֵי שַׂר הַסָּרִיסִים׃
י וַיֹּאמֶר שַׂר הַסָּרִיסִים לְדָנִיֵּאל יָרֵא אֲנִי אֶת־אֲדֹנִי הַמֶּלֶךְ אֲשֶׁר מִנָּה אֶת־מַאֲכַלְכֶם
וְאֶת־מִשְׁתֵּיכֶם אֲשֶׁר לָמָּה יִרְאֶה אֶת־פְּנֵיכֶם זֹעֲפִים מִן־הַיְלָדִים אֲשֶׁר כְּגִילְכֶם
יא וְחִיַּבְתֶּם אֶת־רֹאשִׁי לַמֶּלֶךְ׃ וַיֹּאמֶר דָּנִיֵּאל אֶל־הַמֶּלְצַר אֲשֶׁר מִנָּה שַׂר הַסָּרִיסִים
יב עַל־דָּנִיֵּאל חֲנַנְיָה מִישָׁאֵל וַעֲזַרְיָה׃ נַס־נָא אֶת־עֲבָדֶיךָ יָמִים עֲשָׂרָה וְיִתְּנוּ־לָנוּ
יג מִן־הַזֵּרֹעִים וְנֹאכְלָה וּמַיִם וְנִשְׁתֶּה׃ וְיֵרָאוּ לְפָנֶיךָ מַרְאֵינוּ וּמַרְאֵה הַיְלָדִים הָאֹכְלִים
יד אֵת פַּת־בַּג הַמֶּלֶךְ וְכַאֲשֶׁר תִּרְאֵה עֲשֵׂה עִם־עֲבָדֶיךָ׃ וַיִּשְׁמַע לָהֶם לַדָּבָר הַזֶּה
טו וַיְנַסֵּם יָמִים עֲשָׂרָה׃ וּמִקְצָת יָמִים עֲשָׂרָה נִרְאָה מַרְאֵיהֶם טוֹב וּבְרִיאֵי בָּשָׂר מִן־
טז כָּל־הַיְלָדִים הָאֹכְלִים אֵת פַּת־בַּג הַמֶּלֶךְ׃ וַיְהִי הַמֶּלְצַר נֹשֵׂא אֶת־פַּת־בָּגָם וְיֵין
יז מִשְׁתֵּיהֶם וְנֹתֵן לָהֶם זֵרְעֹנִים׃ וְהַיְלָדִים הָאֵלֶּה אַרְבַּעְתָּם נָתַן לָהֶם הָאֱלֹהִים מַדָּע
יח וְהַשְׂכֵּל בְּכָל־סֵפֶר וְחָכְמָה וְדָנִיֵּאל הֵבִין בְּכָל־חָזוֹן וַחֲלֹמוֹת׃ וּלְמִקְצָת הַיָּמִים

DISCUSSION

1:8 | **That he not taint himself:** The book of Daniel is important partly because it deals with topics that are not discussed elsewhere in the Bible. The way Jews took great care to avoid forbidden foods, a trait which features in all types of Jewish literature, is barely mentioned in the Bible up to this point. Among other reasons, this is because the problem did not arise often, as a meal shared by Jews and gentiles was a rarity. Here, however, when the Jews had to eat the food that was provided for them by gentiles, the verse notes that they insisted on eating only kosher foods.

19 **The king spoke with them,** all the youths from the different lands who had gone through this training process, **and among all of them none was found** with outstanding qualities **comparable to Daniel, Hananya, Mishael, and Azarya, and they stood before the king** to serve him.
20 **In any matter of wisdom or understanding that the king inquired of them, he found them ten times better than all the magicians[B] and enchanters[B] that were in his entire realm.**

21 **Daniel was there,** and continued to serve as a member of the king's council, not just during Nebuchadnezzar's reign but during those of his son and his grandson as well, **until the first year of King Cyrus,** the Persian ruler during whose reign the Babylonian Empire collapsed and was superseded by the Persian Empire. The Persian attitude toward the Jews differed greatly from that of Babylonia.

Daniel Interprets Nebuchadnezzar's Dream

DANIEL 2:1–49

This section concerns Daniel's first interpretation of a dream, as a result of which he reaches a high status in the Babylonian kingdom.

2 1 **And in the second year of the reign of Nebuchadnezzar,**
from the consolidation of his kingdom, or after the destruction
of the Temple,[16] **Nebuchadnezzar dreamed dreams; and his**
spirit was troubled [*titpa'em*], his spirit pounded against him
like a bell [*pa'amon*], **and his sleep was disrupted** due to his
agitation.
2 **The king said to call the magicians, the enchanters, the**
sorcerers, and the chaldeans,[B] various levels of wise men,[17]
advisors, and priests who divined the future and interpreted
dreams, **to tell the king his dreams. They came and stood**
before the king.
3 **The king said to them: I dreamed a dream, and my spirit is**
troubled to know the dream.
4 **The chaldeans spoke to the king in Aramaic:[D] King,** may you
live forever. Tell your servants the dream, and we will tell
the interpretation. Of course we can tell the king the correct
interpretation, but we must hear the dream first.
5 **The king spoke, saying to the chaldeans: The matter is gone**
from me; I do not remember the details of the dream.[18] **If you**
do not make known to me the dream and its interpretation,
you will be rendered into pieces, and your houses will be
made a dunghill. Not only did the king demand the interpretation of his dream, he also insisted that they tell him the dream itself, and he threatened their lives and their possessions if they were unable to do so. Apparently, when a person committed a severe crime, he would be executed and his house would be destroyed as well.[19]
6 **But if you tell** me **the dream and its interpretation, you will**
receive from me gifts and grants and great honor; therefore, tell me the dream and its interpretation.
7 **They,** the chaldeans, **answered a second time and said: Let**
the king say the dream to his servants, and we will tell the
interpretation. We must hear the dream before we can interpret it.
8 **The king spoke, saying: In truth I know that you are buy-**
ing time, by stalling until I calm down, change my mind, or become distracted by something else;[20] alternatively: In truth I know that now you are going to be executed;[21] or, I know for a fact that this time you are deceiving me, **since you see that the matter has gone from me;** alternatively, you see the thing is certain with me. You are trying to shirk your responsibility, since I have already told you that I do not remember my dream, and yet you still want me to relate it.
9 I therefore declare that **if you do not make known to me the**
dream, there is but one sentence for you; clearly **you intended to say before me false and fraudulent matters until the time would change,** until enough time had passed and I would involve myself in other matters.[22] **Therefore, say to me the dream, and I will know that you can tell me its** correct **interpretation.** First and foremost, tell me the content of my dream, and then I will believe that your interpretation is correct. If you cannot do that, I will conclude that you mean to deceive me, and that your interpretation is false.

DISCUSSION

2:4 | **In Aramaic:** The astrologers, literally chaldeans, were the original Babylonian people, and they spoke to the king in Aramaic because that was their language. However, even after concluding the citation of their speech, the text continues in Aramaic until the end of chapter 7. It seems that the author of this book was very familiar with both Hebrew and Aramaic, and therefore once he had used Aramaic to quote the chaldeans accurately, he continued writing the story in that language. It should be noted that the Aramaic of the book of Daniel is not identical to the Aramaic of the Talmud or the *Targumim* on the Bible. It is a specific dialect that served as an international language in the years of the empires of Babylonia, Persia, and Media. An ornate, flowery language, it is similar to the Aramaic found in ancient manuscripts (see commentary on Ezra 4:7).

יט אשר־אמר המלך להביאם ויביאם שר הסריסים לפני נבכדנצר: וידבר אתם
המלך ולא נמצא מכלם כדניאל חנניה מישאל ועזריה ויעמדו לפני המלך:
כ וכל דבר חכמת בינה אשר־בקש מהם המלך וימצאם עשר ידות על כל־
כא החרטמים האשפים אשר בכל־מלכותו: ויהי דניאל עד־שנת אחת לכורש
א המלך: ובשנת שתים למלכות נבכדנצר חלם נבכדנצר חלמות
ב ותתפעם רוחו ושנתו נהיתה עליו: ויאמר המלך לקרא לחרטמים ולאשפים
ג ולמכשפים ולכשדים להגיד למלך חלמתיו ויבאו ויעמדו לפני המלך: ויאמר
ד להם המלך חלום חלמתי ותפעם רוחי לדעת את־החלום: וידברו הכשדים
ה למלך ארמית מלכא לעלמין חיי אמר חלמא לעבדיך ופשרא נחוא: ענה לעבדך
מלכא ואמר לכשדיא מלתה מני אזדא הן לא תהודעונני חלמא ופשרה הדמין לכשדאי
ו תתעבדון ובתיכון נולי יתשמון: והן חלמא ופשרה תהחון מתנן ונבזבה ויקר
ז שגיא תקבלון מן־קדמי להן חלמא ופשרה החוני: ענו תנינות ואמרין מלכא
ח חלמא יאמר לעבדוהי ופשרה נהחוה: ענה מלכא ואמר מן־יציב ידע אנה די
ט עדנא אנתון זבנין כל־קבל די חזיתון די־אזדא מני מלתא: די הן־חלמא לא
תהודענני חדה־היא דתכון ומלה כדבה ושחיתה הזמנתון למאמר קדמי עד הזדמנתון

BACKGROUND

1:20 | **Magicians [*ḥartumim*]:** The word *ḥartumim* is from the Egyptian, in which it refers to an individual of the priestly caste, whose members were considered particularly knowledgeable in witchcraft.

Enchanters [*ashafim*]: This term refers to experts in sorcery and healing through incantations. The word *ashafim* is related to an Akkadian term for incantations, *shiptu*.

2:2 | **Chaldeans:** The Chaldeans were famous in the ancient world for their mastery of astronomy and their interest in occult practices such as astrology. These were so deeply rooted in Babylonian culture that a type of magician came to be called a chaldean (see *Pesaḥim* 113b; *Wars of the Jews* II:111).

10 **The chaldeans answered before the king, and said: There is**
not a man on earth who can tell the king's matter, just as no king, prince, or ruler has asked a matter of this kind from any magician, or enchanter, or chaldean. You are asking for something that no man can do, which no king has ever even thought to request before.
11 **The matter that the king is asking is difficult; there is no one**
who can tell it before the king other than the gods, whose abode is not with those who are **flesh.** Such a difficult matter can be asked only of the gods, not mere mortals.
12 **For that reason, the king was distressed and very angry,**
and he said, instructed, **to eliminate all the wise men of Babylonia.** Since they were unable to meet his expectations he no longer had any respect for them, and decided that it was best to do away with all of them.
13 **The decree was issued, and the wise men were being put to**
death, and Daniel and his companions were about to be put to death, as they were among those who had studied the wisdom and secrets of the chaldeans.
14 **Then Daniel replied with** some words of **counsel**[23] **and dis-**
cernment to Aryokh the king's executioner, who was in charge of all the executions, and **had come out to put the wise men of Babylonia to death.**
15 **He,** Daniel, **spoke, saying to Aryokh the king's officer: Why**
is the decree so peremptory from before the king? Then Aryokh informed Daniel of the matter of the king's dream, and his demand that his sorcerers tell him its contents, and that when they failed to do so he had decreed they should all be killed.
16 **Daniel entered, and asked from the king that he be given**
time, in order to be able **to tell the interpretation to the king.** He wanted to delay the king's decree of mass execution so that he could have the opportunity to discern the dream and its interpretation.
17 **Then Daniel went to his house, and he informed Hananya,**
Mishael, and Azarya, his companions, of the matter.
18 He told them in order **for them to request mercy from before**
the God of heaven with regard to this secret, of the contents of the king's dream, **so that Daniel and his companions would not be eliminated with the rest of the wise men of Babylonia.**
19 **Then the secret was revealed to Daniel in a nocturnal vi-**
sion. Then Daniel blessed the God of heaven.
20 **Daniel spoke, saying: May the name of God be blessed for-**
ever and ever,[D] **for wisdom and might are His.**
21 **He changes the times and the seasons; He removes kings**
and establishes kings; He grants wisdom to the wise, and knowledge to those who know understanding;
22 **He reveals the profound and the obscure; He knows what is**
in the darkness, and the light rests with Him.
23 **I thank and praise You, God of my fathers; You who have**
granted me wisdom and might, and now You have let me know that which I asked of You; You have let me know the matter of the king.
24 **Thereupon Daniel went in to Aryokh, whom the king had**
appointed to eliminate the wise men of Babylonia. He went to Aryokh **and so he said to him: Do not eliminate the wise men of Babylonia; bring me before the king, and I will tell the king the interpretation.**
25 **Then Aryokh brought Daniel before the king in haste, and**
so he said to him: I found a man, a member of the exile of Judah,[B] **who will inform the king of the interpretation.** Aryokh spoke in this manner to the king because Daniel was young and new to the royal service, and therefore it was possible that the king did not remember him.
26 **The king spoke, saying to Daniel, whose name** among the
gentiles **was Beltshatzar,** and therefore this was the name by which the king addressed him: **Are you able to let me know the dream that I saw, and its interpretation?**
27 **Daniel spoke before the king, saying: Not wise men, en-**
chanters, magicians, or oracles, a type of fortune-teller,[24]

DISCUSSION

2:20 | **May the name of God be blessed forever and ever:** Some of these grand expressions of praise became part of the prayer liturgy over the generations. This clause, for example, appears in a slightly variant form in the *Kaddish* prayer.

BACKGROUND

2:25 | **Judah [*Yehud*]:** This was the Aramaic name for the province of Judah during the period of the Persian Empire. Yehud was a relatively small Persian province, covering about 1600 sq km (see also Ezra 5:8). Its borders incorporated Jerusalem, the southern Jordan Valley to the Dead Sea, Beit El, Mitzpa, Lod, Gezer, Ke'ila, Adulam, and Beit HaKerem, also known as Bethlehem, as well as Beit Tzur and Ein Gedi in the south. Coins and jug handles bearing the word *Yehud* have been found in Judea dating from this period (see commentary on Ezra 5:8).

י די עדנא ישתנא להן חלמא אמרו לי ואנדע די פשרה תהחונני׃ ענו כשדיא כשדאי
קדם־מלכא ואמרין לא־איתי אנש על־יבשתא די מלת מלכא יוכל להחויה
כל־קבל די כל־מלך רב ושליט מלה כדנה לא שאל לכל־חרטם ואשף וכשדי׃
יא ומלתא די־מלכה שאל יקירה ואחרן לא איתי די יחונה קדם מלכא להן
יב אלהין די מדרהון עם־בשרא לא איתוהי׃ כל־קבל דנה מלכא בנס וקצף
יג שגיא ואמר להובדה לכל חכימי בבל׃ ודתא נפקת וחכימיא מתקטלין ובעו
יד דניאל וחברוהי להתקטלה׃ באדין דניאל התיב עטא וטעם
טו לאריוך רב־טבחיא די מלכא די נפק לקטלה לחכימי בבל׃ ענה ואמר לאריוך
שליטא די־מלכא על־מה דתא מהחצפה מן־קדם מלכא אדין מלתא הודע
טז אריוך לדניאל׃ ודניאל על ובעא מן־מלכא די זמן ינתן־לה ופשרא להחויה
יז למלכא׃ אדין דניאל לביתה אזל ולחנניה מישאל ועזריה
יח חברוהי מלתא הודע׃ ורחמין למבעא מן־קדם אלה שמיא על־רזא דנה די
יט לא יהובדון דניאל וחברוהי עם־שאר חכימי בבל׃ אדין לדניאל בחזוא די־
כ ליליא רזא גלי אדין דניאל ברך לאלה שמיא׃ ענה דניאל ואמר להוא שמה
כא די־אלהא מברך מן־עלמא ועד־עלמא די חכמתא וגבורתא די־לה היא׃ והוא
מהשנא עדניא וזמניא מהעדה מלכין ומהקים מלכין יהב חכמתא לחכימין
כב ומנדעא לידעי בינה׃ הוא גלא עמיקתא ומסתרתא ידע מה בחשוכא ונהירא ונהורא
כג עמה שרא׃ לך ׀ אלה אבהתי מהודא ומשבח אנה די חכמתא וגבורתא יהבת
כד לי וכען הודעתני די־בעינא מנך די־מלת מלכא הודעתנא׃ כל־קבל דנה
דניאל על על־אריוך די מני מלכא להובדא לחכימי בבל אזל ׀ וכן אמר־לה
לחכימי בבל אל־תהובד העלני קדם מלכא ופשרא למלכא אחוא׃
כה אדין אריוך בהתבהלה הנעל לדניאל קדם מלכא וכן אמר־לה די־השכחת
כו גבר מן־בני גלותא די יהוד די פשרא למלכא יהודע׃ ענה מלכא ואמר לדניאל
כז די שמה בלטשאצר האיתיך כהל להודעתני חלמא די־חזית ופשרה׃ ענה האיתך

can tell the king the secret that the king asked, that he be informed of both his dream and its interpretation.

28 **But there is a God in the heavens, who reveals secrets, and He has informed King Nebuchadnezzar that which will be at the end of days. This is your dream, and the vision in your head** which you saw **on your bed.** After this brief introduction, Daniel describes the dream:

29 **You, the king, your thoughts arose onto your bed.** Before you went to sleep, you were thinking of **that which will be hereafter.** Since you are a powerful king who rules over a large portion of the known world, you wish to know what will occur in the future. **He who reveals secrets has informed you** of **that which will be.**

30 **But I, it is not due to wisdom that is in me more than all** other **living** beings **that this secret is revealed to me; rather, it is so** that **the interpretation will be made known to the king, and the thoughts of your heart you will know.** I am merely a messenger, sent to tell you matters that you need to know, not in order to display my wisdom, but because God in heaven wants to reveal them to you.

31 **You, king, were seeing, and behold,** there was **a giant image. This image, which was great, and its radiance surpassing** that of all materials, **stood before you; and its appearance was terrifying.**

32 **That image, its head was of fine gold, its breast and its arms of silver, its belly and its thighs** were **of bronze,**

33 **its calves,** from the knees down, were **of iron, its feet part of them of iron and part of them of clay.**

34 **You were watching** that imposing image **until a stone was hewn, not with hands** but rather as if by itself, **and struck the image on its feet of iron and clay, and crushed them.**

35 **Then the iron, the clay, the bronze, the silver, and the gold were pulverized, and became like the chaff of the threshing floors of summer, and the wind carried them, and in no place were they to be found.** They were all completely gone. **The stone that struck the image became a great mountain, and filled the entire earth.**

36 **That is the dream, and we will tell its interpretation before the king.** It seems that when Daniel retold this terrifying and cryptic dream, Nebuchadnezzar remembered it. Daniel proceeded to explain the meaning of the dream:

37 **You, king, are king of kings, to whom the God of the heavens has given the kingdom, the power, the strength, and the glory.**

Chaff carried by the wind

38 **And everywhere the sons of man, the beasts of the field, and the birds of the heavens dwell, He has given into your hand and set your rule over all of them.** You have dominion over man, beasts, and birds, and thus, in the dream, **you are** represented by **the head of gold.**

39 **After you will arise another kingdom, inferior to yours,** represented by the silver, which is under the head of gold; **and afterward** there will be **a third kingdom, of bronze, that will rule over the entire earth.**

40 **The fourth kingdom will be strong as iron; just as iron crushes and flattens everything,**[25] **and like iron that smashes all these** other metals, **it,** this kingdom, **will crush and smash.**

41 **That which you saw the feet and toes, some of them from potter's clay and some of them from iron** – that is because **it will be a divided kingdom. There will be in it of the firmness of the iron, as you saw the iron mixed with earthenware of clay.**

42 **The toes of the feet, some of them iron,** a strong substance, **and some of them earthenware,** a fragile material – this alludes to the fact that **part of the kingdom will be strong, and some of it will be brittle;** the fourth kingdom will be uneven in strength.

43 **That which you saw the iron mixed with the earthenware of clay,** this is the interpretation: **They,** the peoples of the kingdom represented by these substances, **will be mixed together with the offspring of men,** they will marry each other, **but they will not adhere one to another** and form true bonds, **just as iron does not mix together with clay.**

דניאל קדם מלכא ואמר רזא די־מלכא שאל לא חכימין אשפין חרטמין גזרין
כח יכלין להחויה למלכא׃ ברם איתי אלה בשמיא גלא רזין והודע למלכא
נבוכדנצר מה די להוא באחרית יומיא חלמך וחזוי ראשך על־משכבך דנה
כט הוא׃ אנתה מלכא רעיונך על־משכבך סלקו מה די להוא אחרי אַנְתְּ | רַעְיוֹנָךְ
ל דנה וגלא רזיא הודעך מה־די להוא׃ ואנה לא בחכמה די־איתי בי מן־כל־
חייא רזא דנה גלי לי להן על־דברת די פשרא למלכא יהודעון ורעיוני לבבך
לא תנדע׃ אנתה מלכא חזה הוית ואלו צלם חד שגיא צלמא אַנְתְּ
לב דכן רב וזיוה יתיר קאם לקבלך ורוה דחיל׃ הוא צלמא ראשה די־דהב טב
לג חדוהי ודרעוהי די כסף מעוהי וירכתה די נחש׃ שקוהי די פרזל רגלוהי מנהון מִנְּהֵין
לד די פרזל ומנהון די חסף׃ חזה הוית עד די התגזרת אבן די־לא בידין ומחת וּמִנְּהֵין
לה לצלמא על־רגלוהי די פרזלא וחספא והדקת המון׃ באדין דקו כחדה פרזלא ב
חספא נחשא כספא ודהבא והוו כעור מן־אדרי־קיט ונשא המון רוחא וכל־
אתר לא־השתכח להון ואבנא ׀ די־מחת לצלמא הות לטור רב ומלאת
לו לז כל־ארעא׃ דנה חלמא ופשרה נאמר קדם־מלכא׃ אנתה אַנְתְּ
מלכא מלך מלכיא די אלה שמיא מלכותא חסנא ותקפא ויקרא יהב־לך׃
לח ובכל־די דארין בני־אנשא חיות ברא ועוף־שמיא יהב בידך והשלטך בכלהון דָיְרִין
לט אנתה הוא ראשה די דהבא׃ ובתרך תקום מלכו אחרי ארעא מנך ומלכו אַנְתְּ | אֲרַע
מ תליתיא אחרי די נחשא די תשלט בכל־ארעא׃ ומלכו רביעיה תהוא תקיפה תְלִיתָאָה |
כפרזלא כל־קבל די פרזלא מהדק וחשל כלא וכפרזלא די־מרעע כל־אלין רְבִיעָאָה
מא תדק ותרע׃ ודי־חזיתה רגליא ואצבעתא מנהון חסף די־פחר ומנהון פרזל מִנְּהֵין | וּמִנְּהֵין
מלכו פליגה תהוה ומן־נצבתא די־פרזלא להוא־בה כל־קבל די חזיתה פרזלא
מב מערב בחסף טינא׃ ואצבעת רגליא מנהון פרזל ומנהון חסף מן־קצת מלכותא מִנְּהֵין | וּמִנְּהֵין
מג תהוה תקיפה ומנה תהוא תבירה׃ די חזית פרזלא מערב בחסף טינא מתערבין וְדִי
להון בזרע אנשא ולא־להון דבקין דנה עם־דנה הא־כדי פרזלא לא מתערב

44 **In the days of those kings,** from the fourth kingdom, **the God of the heavens will establish a kingdom that will never be destroyed, and kingdom,** dominion, **will not be left to another people. It will crush and eliminate all these kingdoms, but it will stand forever.**
45 Daniel summarized: **That which you saw, that a stone was hewn from the mountain, not with hands, and it crushed the iron, the bronze, the clay, the silver, and the gold – the great God has informed the king that which will be hereafter. The dream is true and its interpretation reliable.** Your dream is not a flight of the imagination, as it actually contains a kind of prophecy of the distant future, and my interpretation of it is the truth.
46 **Then King Nebuchadnezzar fell on his face, and he prostrated himself to Daniel and said for a meal offering** to be brought **and fragrances** to **be poured out to him,** Daniel. Nebuchadnezzar knew that no man could have guessed such a dream; therefore, he saw Daniel as the embodiment of divine holiness, and consequently he bowed down to him.[26]
47 **The king spoke to Daniel, saying: It is the truth that your God is God of gods, and Master of kings, and Revealer of secrets, as you have been able to reveal this secret.**
48 **Then the king elevated Daniel, and gave him many great gifts, and set him ruler over the entire province of Babylonia, and** appointed him **chief prefect,** the senior official, **over all the wise men of Babylonia.**
49 **Daniel requested from the king, and** in response to his request **he,** the king, **appointed Shadrakh, Meshakh, and Aved Nego,** Hananya, Mishael, and Azarya, **over the** political **affairs of the province of Babylonia, and Daniel was** appointed as the chief advisor, and as such he sat **at the gate of the king.** From his lofty position, Daniel was able to delegate the practical task of managing the kingdom to his colleagues Hananya, Mishael, and Azarya.

Hananya, Mishael, and Azarya Sanctify the Name of God

DANIEL 3:1–30

Although Daniel himself is not mentioned in the following story, it deals with the miracles that occurred to his friends, Hananya, Mishael, and Azarya. This is the first written account in Jewish history of individuals who were willing to die out of loyalty to the commandments of their religion. For this reason, the episode has been etched into the collective national memory of the Jewish people, and has become a symbol of religious struggle. Hananya, Mishael, and Azarya express complete confidence that God is capable of saving them. The fact that they are indeed spared death, which did not always happen over the course of history, renders their story all the more significant.

3 1 **King Nebuchadnezzar made an image of gold; its height was sixty cubits,** about thirty meters, **and its width six cubits.** Although it was apparently in human form, the limbs of the image were not entirely proportionate in size.[27] **He erected it in the plain of Dura,** a name that is used in reference to several different locations, **in the province of Babylonia.**
2 **King Nebuchadnezzar sent** a command **to assemble the satraps,**[D] who ruled over large regions, **the** senior **prefects,** second-in-command to the satraps, **and the governors,** rulers over smaller provinces, including, at a later stage, the small state of Judah,[28] **the counselors,**[29] **the treasurers,**[30] **the judges, the officers, and all the rulers of the provinces.** All these functionaries were invited **to come to the dedication of the image that King Nebuchadnezzar had erected.**[D]
3 **Then the satraps, the prefects, and the governors, the counselors, the treasurers, the judges, the officers, and all the rulers of the provinces were assembled for the dedication of the image that King Nebuchadnezzar had erected; and they stood before the image that Nebuchadnezzar had erected.**

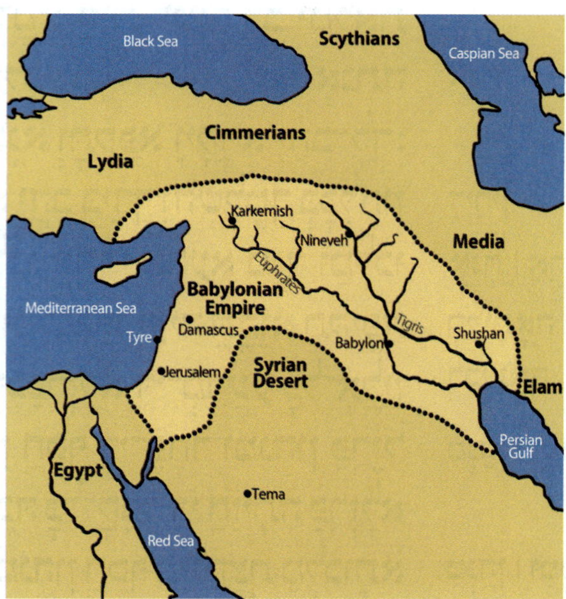

Babylonian Empire

מד עם־חספא: וביומיהון די מלכיא אנון יקים אלה שמיא מלכו די לעלמין לא
תתחבל ומלכותה לעם אחרן לא תשתבק תדק ותסיף כל־אלין מלכותא והיא
מה תקום לעלמיא: כל־קבל די־חזית די מטורא אתגזרת אבן די־לא בידין והדקת
פרזלא נחשא חספא כספא ודהבא אלה רב הודע למלכא מה די להוא אחרי
מו דנה ויציב חלמא ומהימן פשרה: באדין מלכא נבוכדנצר נפל
מז על־אנפוהי ולדניאל סגד ומנחה וניחחין אמר לנסכה לה: ענה מלכא לדניאל
ואמר מן־קשט די אלהכון הוא אלה אלהין ומרא מלכין וגלה רזין די יכלת
מח למגלא רזא דנה: אדין מלכא לדניאל רבי ומתנן רברבן שגיאן יהב־לה
מט והשלטה על כל־מדינת בבל ורב־סגנין על כל־חכימי בבל: ודניאל בעא
מן־מלכא ומני על עבידתא די מדינת בבל לשדרך מישך ועבד נגו ודניאל
ג א בתרע מלכא: נבוכדנצר מלכא עבד צלם די־דהב רומה אמין
ב שתין פתיה אמין שת אקימה בבקעת דורא במדינת בבל: ונבוכדנצר מלכא
שלח למכנש | לאחשדרפניא סגניא ופחותא אדרגזריא גדבריא דתבריא
תפתיא וכל שלטני מדינתא למתא לחנכת צלמא די הקים נבוכדנצר מלכא:
ג באדין מתכנשין אחשדרפניא סגניא ופחותא אדרגזריא גדבריא דתבריא
תפתיא וכל שלטני מדינתא לחנכת צלמא די הקים נבוכדנצר מלכא וקאמין [וקימין]

DISCUSSION

3:2 | **Satraps:** Satrap is a Persian term describing a regional ruler with a high position of power who answered directly to the king (see, e.g., Ezra 8:36; Esther 3:12). It would seem from here that the book of Daniel was written toward the end of Daniel's life, when the Persian Empire had replaced the Babylonian Empire as the dominant force in the region. Therefore, certain positions in the Babylonian Empire were described using terms relevant at the time of the book's writing. The empire Nebuchadnezzar ruled was not as large as the Persian Empire that followed it, but it nevertheless covered a large amount of territory, stretching from Persia and Asia Minor, through the Land of Israel and the eastern side of the Jordan River, all the way to Egypt and even Yemen.

To come to the dedication of the image that King Nebuchadnezzar had erected: Nebuchadnezzar did not desire a small, local celebration but a large ritual with the participation of people from all across the kingdom. He therefore gathered the most important officials from all the lands under his control. The king sought to establish a new form of worship for the entire kingdom (see, e.g., Rashi; Rav Se'adya Gaon; *Vayikra Rabba* 33; *Bemidbar Rabba* 15). It is also possible that he attempted to unify several old gods into a single, new deity. This is why it was important to him that all these dignitaries should attend, so they could inform the constituents under their jurisdiction of the new deity. By contrast, some maintain that this image was merely designed as a monument depicting Nebuchadnezzar, not as full-fledged idolatry (see Abravanel; *Tosafot*, *Pesaḥim* 53b, citing Rabbeinu Tam).

4 **The herald cried out forcefully: It is commanded to you, peoples,** groups defined by the area where they live, **nations,** ethnic groups, **and languages,** groups that speak the same language or dialect:

5 **When you hear the sound**[31] **of the horn,**[B] **the pipe,**[B] **the lyre,**[B] an ornamented string instrument, **the sambuca,**[B] a small, triangular lyre, **the psaltery,**[B] an instrument with many strings or keys, **the bagpipe,**[B] perhaps an instrument that was able to join together many diverse sounds, **and all types of musical instruments,**[B] when this impressive, loud music is played, which serves as a sign for those not in the immediate vicinity as well, **you shall fall** on your faces[32] **and prostrate yourselves before the golden image that King Nebuchadnezzar has erected.**

Playing the lyre, illustration on earthenware vessel, Greece, 440–430 BCE

Double flute, Egypt, 1537–1531 BCE

"Horn"

Trumpet, 550–330 BCE

"Psaltery." Painting of a Persian woman playing the santur at a banquet, early twentieth century

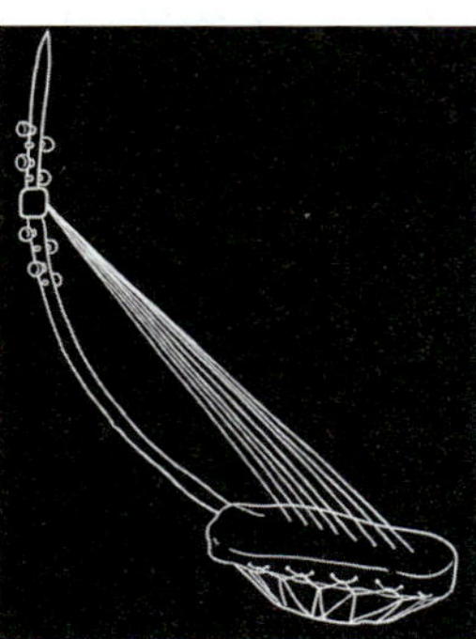

Illustration of sambuca

6 **Whoever does not fall and prostrate himself, at that moment, he will be** sentenced and **cast into a burning fiery furnace.**[B] Nebuchadnezzar's determination was expressed through his invitation to all dignitaries from every state, the instruction concerning the musical signal that would be heard from afar, obligating all residents to bow down to the image, and his warning to anyone who might think of disobeying his decree of the cruel death that awaited them.

7 **Thereupon,** faced with this threat, **at that time, when all the peoples heard the sound of the horn, the pipe, the lyre, the sambuca, the psaltery, and all types of musical instruments, all the peoples, the nations, and the languages,** people who speak the same language or dialect, **fell and prostrated themselves to the golden image that King Nebuchadnezzar had erected.**

8 **Thereupon, at that time, certain Chaldean men approached and informed**[D] **on the Judeans.**

9 **They spoke, saying to King Nebuchadnezzar: O king, live forever.** A call similar to "long live the king," which was and is customary in many languages and countries.

10 **You, O king, issued a directive, that every man who hears the sound of the horn, the pipe, the lyre, the sambuca, the psaltery, the bagpipe, and all types of musical instruments, shall fall and prostrate himself before the golden image,**

11 **and whoever does not fall and prostrate himself will be cast into a burning fiery furnace.**

DISCUSSION

3:8 | **Chaldean men approached and informed [*akhalu kartzeihon*]:** It would seem that although the word *akhalu* literally means to eat [*okhel*], this phrase is idiomatic, and means to slander. It may be related to a practice of gossipers to eat while gossiping, or it may be referring figuratively to one who consumes pieces of human flesh. Alternatively, it may refer to one who emits suggestive sounds hinting at certain ideas (see Rashi; Ibn Ezra; *Metzudat David*; *Metzudat Tzion*; Rashi, Rashbam, and Ramban, Leviticus 19:16).

The Chaldeans were mentioned previously among the magicians and necromancers who surrounded the king (see, e.g., 2:2). They may not only have been members of a particular nation, but may have also held positions in the government. If so, it can be surmised that they did not act solely due to sincere religious fervor.

ד לקבל צלמא די הקים נבכדנצר: וכרוזא קרא בחיל לכון אמרין עממיא אמיא
ה ולשניא: בעדנא די־תשמעון קל קרנא משרוקיתא קיתרס סבכא פסנתרין קתרוס
סומפניה וכל זני זמרא תפלון ותסגדון לצלם דהבא די הקים נבוכדנצר מלכא:
ו ז ומן־די־לא יפל ויסגד בה־שעתא יתרמא לגוא־אתון נורא יקדתא: כל־קבל
דנה בה זמנא כדי שמעין כל־עממיא קל קרנא משרוקיתא קיתרס שבכא קתרוס
פסנטרין וכל זני זמרא נפלין כל־עממיא אמיא ולשניא סגדין לצלם דהבא
ח די הקים נבוכדנצר מלכא: כל־קבל דנה בה זמנא קרבו גברין כשדאין ואכלו
ט קרציהון די יהודיא: ענו ואמרין לנבוכדנצר מלכא מלכא לעלמין חיי: אנתה אנת
מלכא שמת טעם די כל־אנש די־ישמע קל קרנא משרקיתא קיתרס שבכא קתרוס
יא פסנתרין וסיפניה וכל זני זמרא יפל ויסגד לצלם דהבא: ומן־די־לא יפל ויסגד וסופניה

BACKGROUND

3:5 | **Horn [*karna*]:** A wind instrument made from an actual animal's horn [*keren*], like a shofar, or a metal instrument similar to a straight trumpet. This name is used for several wind instruments fashioned from brass, silver, or gold, which range in length from roughly 35 cm to 2 m. According to ancient Persian literature, this instrument was used for religious and royal processions. In the Greek-Roman world they used a round, metal wind instrument in the shape of a horn, called a *cornu*.

Pipe [*mashrokita*]: Apparently an onomatopoeic name which mimics the whistling sound of the instrument, similar to the whistling of one's lips. Since the word *sherika* appears in connection with flocks of sheep (Judges 5:16), some maintain that the *mashrokita* was a flute composed of several pipes used by shepherds, like a pan flute or the double shepherd's flute. Alternatively, the term *mashrokita* does not refer to a specific musical instrument, but is a general name for a type of horn.

Lyre [*katros*]: From the Greek *kitara*, the *katros* is a professional, ornamented string instrument similar to the lyre, which was a folk instrument. The guitar, both the name and the instrument itself, originated from this instrument. *Katros* is mentioned in the Talmud as a name for one of the types of cedar trees (*Rosh HaShana* 23a), and it appears that the instrument was made from the wood of that tree.

Sambuca [*sabekha*]: A string instrument with seven to nine strings whose triangular shape is similar to a small lyre. It bears a similar name in Greek, *sambuki*. Ancient Greek writers used this name also in reference to a siege engine, that could raise and lower a ladder against city walls, as well as with regard to a battleship that had a ladder affixed to its bow, due to the visual similarity between them and this instrument.

Psaltery [*pesanterin*]: In Greek, the word *psaltirion* means lyre, and *pesanterin* is translated accordingly by the Septuagint. Some contend that it is the santur, a Persian instrument built from a trapezoidal wooden box across which many strings are spread out.

Bagpipe [*sumponya*]: From the Greek term *symfonia*, which appears in classical Greek literature; however, there is no consensus as to its meaning. It is not the same as the familiar modern term symphony, although it is possible that in Greek this means a unified sound. Some claim that the *sumponya* is a bagpipe, an enhanced flute with leather bellows which aid the exhalation of air; others contend it is a percussion instrument, while yet others maintain that it means a flute orchestra (Daniel Sperber, *Tarbut Homrit Be'eretz Yisrael Beyemai HaTalmud* ["Material Culture in Eretz Israel during the Talmudic Period"], vol. 2. Jerusalem: Yad Izhak Ben Zvi & Bar Ilan University, 2006, [Hebrew], 89).

And all types of musical instruments: The names of the musical instruments listed above are either in Aramaic or in Greek. The use of Greek names is due to the influence of Greek culture from the fifth century BCE, or because there were Greek musicians in the kingdom of Persia.

3:6 | **Furnace [*attun*]:** This was a pit resembling an enormous earthenware container. It was used for molding vessels, burning lime, and the like.

12 **There are certain Judean men whom you appointed over the affairs of the province of Babylonia: Shadrakh,** Hananya, **Meshakh,** Mishael, **and Aved Nego,** Azarya. Although it was Daniel who initiated the appointment of his friends, since the king approved the appointments (see 2:49), these Chaldeans are correct in ascribing the decision to the king. They continued: **These men, O king, do not pay attention to you,** they take no notice of you: **They do not worship your gods, and they do not prostrate themselves to the golden image that you have erected.** You commanded that all who hear must participate in the ritual you established, and yet your own men, whom you appointed to senior positions in your government, have flouted your order.

13 **Then Nebuchadnezzar, in rage and fury, said to bring Shadrakh, Meshakh, and Aved Nego. Then these men were brought before the king.**

14 **Nebuchadnezzar spoke, saying to them: Impudence!**[33] **Shadrakh, Meshakh, and Aved Nego, you do not worship my gods, and you do not prostrate yourselves to the golden image that I have erected?** Since they refused to obey the king's order, he could have thrown them into the furnace without delay. However, it is possible that since he knew them and was fond of them, he gave them another chance.

15 **Now, if you are prepared that at the time that you hear the sound of the horn, the pipe, the lyre, the sambuca, the psaltery, and the bagpipe, and all types of musical instruments, you fall and prostrate yourselves to the image that I made,** then all is well; **but if you do not prostrate yourselves, at that time you will be cast into the burning fiery furnace; who is the god who will save you from my hands?**

16 **Shadrakh, Meshakh, and Aved Nego spoke, saying to the king: Nebuchadnezzar, we have no need to reply to you,** to ponder or say anything more **in this matter.**

17 **Behold our God, whom we worship, exists; He is able to save us from the burning, fiery furnace, and will save us from your hand, O king.** The false gods of the other nations are unable to save their adherents, but our God will rescue us from both the furnace and from your grasp.

18 **Behold,** even **if** He will **not** deliver us, **let it be known to you, O king, that we will not worship your gods, and we will not prostrate ourselves to the golden image that you have erected.** They could have used an excuse for their inaction, by saying that they didn't hear the instruments, or that they were busy with some administrative task, but instead they admitted that they refused to bow down before the image. Furthermore, they declared sharply and unambiguously that they did not believe in idolatry and would not worship the image.

19 **Then Nebuchadnezzar was filled with fury against Shadrakh, Meshakh, and Aved Nego, and the expression on his face was distorted** with anger; **he spoke, saying** in his rage **to heat the furnace seven times more than it was fit to be heated,** so that the fire would be fierce enough to burn all three men instantly.

20 **He said to mighty warriors who were in his forces to bind Shadrakh, Meshakh, and Aved Nego,** to tie them by their hands and feet, **and to cast them into the burning fiery furnace.**

21 **Then these men were bound in their trousers,** alternatively, their cloaks, **their tunics,**[B] **their hats,**[B] **and their garments, and were cast into the burning fiery furnace.** The three men insisted that they should not enter the fiery furnace in a lowly, demeaned state, but with pride, dressed in their finest garments.[34]

Rightmost figure: Captive Cimmerian wearing a pointed turban, illustration based on Darius' Behistun Inscription, sixth century BCE

22 **Thereupon, because the king's commandment was peremptory, and the furnace was exceedingly hot, a flare of fire killed those men who took up Shadrakh, Meshakh, and Aved Nego** to the mouth of the furnace.[35] Generally, a pillar of fire emerges from a furnace,[36] but in this case the fire was

יב יִתְרְמֵא לְגוֹא־אַתּוּן נוּרָא יָקִדְתָּא׃ אִיתַי גֻּבְרִין יְהוּדָאִין דִּי־מַנִּיתָ יָתְהוֹן עַל־
עֲבִידַת מְדִינַת בָּבֶל שַׁדְרַךְ מֵישַׁךְ וַעֲבֵד נְגוֹ גֻּבְרַיָּא אִלֵּךְ לָא־שָׂמוּ עליך מַלְכָּא עֲלָךְ
טְעֵם לאלהיך לָא פָלְחִין וּלְצֶלֶם דַּהֲבָא דִּי הֲקֵימְתָּ לָא סָגְדִין׃ לֵאלָהָךְ
יג בֵּאדַיִן נְבוּכַדְנֶצַּר בִּרְגַז וַחֲמָא אֲמַר לְהַיְתָיָה לְשַׁדְרַךְ מֵישַׁךְ וַעֲבֵד נְגוֹ בֵּאדַיִן
יד גֻּבְרַיָּא אִלֵּךְ הֵיתָיוּ קֳדָם מַלְכָּא׃ עָנֵה נְבֻכַדְנֶצַּר וְאָמַר לְהוֹן הַצְדָּא שַׁדְרַךְ מֵישַׁךְ
טו וַעֲבֵד נְגוֹ לֵאלָהַי לָא אִיתֵיכוֹן פָּלְחִין וּלְצֶלֶם דַּהֲבָא דִּי הֲקֵימֶת לָא סָגְדִין׃ כְּעַן
הֵן אִיתֵיכוֹן עֲתִידִין דִּי בְעִדָּנָא דִּי־תִשְׁמְעוּן קָל קַרְנָא מַשְׁרוֹקִיתָא קיתרס קַתְרֹס
שַׂבְּכָא פְּסַנְתֵּרִין וְסוּמְפֹּנְיָה וְכֹל ׀ זְנֵי זְמָרָא תִּפְּלוּן וְתִסְגְּדוּן לְצַלְמָא דִּי־עַבְדֵת
וְהֵן לָא תִסְגְּדוּן בַּהּ־שַׁעֲתָה תִתְרְמוֹן לְגוֹא־אַתּוּן נוּרָא יָקִדְתָּא וּמַן־הוּא אֱלָהּ
טז דִּי יְשֵׁיזְבִנְכוֹן מִן־יְדָי׃ עֲנוֹ שַׁדְרַךְ מֵישַׁךְ וַעֲבֵד נְגוֹ וְאָמְרִין לְמַלְכָּא נְבוּכַדְנֶצַּר
יז לָא־חַשְׁחִין אֲנַחְנָה עַל־דְּנָה פִּתְגָם לַהֲתָבוּתָךְ׃ הֵן אִיתַי אֱלָהַנָא דִּי־אֲנַחְנָא
יח פָּלְחִין יָכִל לְשֵׁיזָבוּתַנָא מִן־אַתּוּן נוּרָא יָקִדְתָּא וּמִן־יְדָךְ מַלְכָּא יְשֵׁיזִב׃ וְהֵן לָא
יְדִיעַ לֶהֱוֵא־לָךְ מַלְכָּא דִּי לאלהיך לָא־אִיתַנָא פָלְחִין וּלְצֶלֶם דַּהֲבָא דִּי הֲקֵימְתָּ לֵאלָהָךְ
יט לָא נִסְגֻּד׃ בֵּאדַיִן נְבוּכַדְנֶצַּר הִתְמְלִי חֱמָא וּצְלֵם אַנְפּוֹהִי אשתנו אֶשְׁתַּנִּי
עַל־שַׁדְרַךְ מֵישַׁךְ וַעֲבֵד נְגוֹ עָנֵה וְאָמַר לְמֵזֵא לְאַתּוּנָא חַד־שִׁבְעָה עַל דִּי חֲזֵה
כ לְמֵזְיֵהּ׃ וּלְגֻבְרִין גִּבָּרֵי־חַיִל דִּי בְחַיְלֵהּ אֲמַר לְכַפָּתָה לְשַׁדְרַךְ מֵישַׁךְ וַעֲבֵד נְגוֹ
כא לְמִרְמֵא לְאַתּוּן נוּרָא יָקִדְתָּא׃ בֵּאדַיִן גֻּבְרַיָּא אִלֵּךְ כְּפִתוּ בְּסַרְבָּלֵיהוֹן פטישיהון פַּטְּשֵׁיהוֹן
כב וְכַרְבְּלָתְהוֹן וּלְבֻשֵׁיהוֹן וּרְמִיו לְגוֹא־אַתּוּן נוּרָא יָקִדְתָּא׃ כָּל־קֳבֵל דְּנָה מִן־דִּי

BACKGROUND

3:21 | **In their trousers, their tunics [*besarbaleihon pattsheihon*]:** The identification of these items of clothing is uncertain, as similar names were used in Greek, Aramaic, and Hebrew for different articles of clothing. There is a dispute in the Midrash as to whether the *sarbal* was a garment worn over the upper body, such as a robe, or over the lower body, e.g., trousers (*Bereshit Rabba* 31; *Midrash Yelamedenu, Bereshit* 3; see *Arukh*, s.v. *sarbal*). Linguists note that similar terms (*saru'alin*; *sarbelin*; *salu'ar*) refer to clothes that cover the legs or arms. A *petash* is a shirt or, according to another opinion, legwarmers (*Midrash Yelamedenu, Bereshit* 3).

Their hats [*vekharbelat'hon*]: Based on Akkadian administrative records dating back to the tenth century BCE, this is a linen head covering. According to an inscription in the tomb of Darius, it is a certain type of headgear worn by the Cimmerian people. Indeed, on Darius' Behistun Inscription one can see the figure of a captive Cimmerian wearing a pointed turban, similar to the crest [*karbolet*] of a male bird.

so fierce that the furnace emitted many flames, one of which burned the guards bringing Hananya, Mishael, and Azarya.

23 **And these three men, Shadrakh, Meshakh, and Aved Nego, fell bound into the burning fiery furnace.** It seems that they were brought to the opening of the furnace. When the flames then emerged and burned those standing around them, they were flung inside.

24 **Then King Nebuchadnezzar was astonished and rose** from his seat **in haste, and spoke, saying to his commanders: Didn't we cast three bound men into the midst of the fire? They spoke, saying to the king: True, O king.**

25 **He spoke, saying: I see four unbound men walking in the fire, and no harm comes to them.** They are strolling inside the furnace like people walking on the street, with no signs of suffering any harm. **And the fourth resembles a son of the gods.**

26 **Then Nebuchadnezzar approached the gate of the burning fiery furnace; he spoke, saying: Shadrakh, Meshakh, and Aved Nego, servants of God Most High,**[D] **emerge and come.** I permit you to leave the furnace. **Then Shadrakh, Meshakh, and Aved Nego emerged from within the fire.** The fourth figure did not emerge, as he did not only look like an angel, he actually was an angel.

27 **The satraps, the prefects, the governors, and the king's commanders,** the officials the king had invited, **assembled and saw these men, that the fire did not take hold of their bodies, the hair of their head was not singed, their trousers were unchanged** by the fire, **and the odor of fire did not cover them.** They had emerged from inside a fire that was so powerful that the soldiers who had stood too close were killed by its flames, and yet they were not harmed by it at all, not their bodies, nor their hair, nor their clothing.

28 **Nebuchadnezzar spoke, saying: Blessed is the God of Shadrakh, Meshakh, and Aved Nego, who sent His angel, and saved His servants, who trusted in Him and defied the king's word and sacrificed their bodies so as not to worship and not to prostrate themselves to any god except their God.** Idol worshippers who saw Nebuchadnezzar's new deity were willing to accept the command of the king, who perhaps sought to establish a new religion, as it did not bother them to add one more god to the idols they already worshipped. By contrast, these three men were willing to place themselves in great danger out of loyalty to God.

29 **And from me is issued a decree that any people, nation, or language,** groups that speak the same language or dialect, **that says anything amiss against the God of Shadrakh, Meshakh, and Aved Nego will be rendered into pieces, and their houses will be made a dunghill, since there is no other god that is capable of salvation of this sort.** Nebuchadnezzar was a capricious individual, yet nevertheless he was willing to acknowledge the truth and was not ashamed to admit his error.

30 **Then,** after witnessing the miracle that occurred to them when they fulfilled the will of God, **the king promoted,** or bestowed favors upon, **Shadrakh, Meshakh, and Aved Nego in the province of Babylonia.**

Nebuchadnezzar's Account of His Second Dream

DANIEL 3:31–4:34

The following section is a segment from the memoirs of Nebuchadnezzar, recited in the first person. Nebuchadnezzar recounts an unusual, wondrous event that occurred to him. His recounting is preceded by an announcement to all his subjects, which is in essence a glorious song of praise to God, and was perhaps even longer in the original.[37] This praise and thanksgiving may also be read as a continuation of the story in the previous section. The story concludes with similar words of prayer and tribute.

31 From **King Nebuchadnezzar to all peoples, nations, and languages,** groups that speak the same language or dialect, **that reside in the entire earth: May your peace be abundant.** This is a standard opening of a letter, which bears the name of the sender and the recipients,[38] followed by a greeting of peace.[39]

32 **It is pleasing for me to relate the signs and the wonders that God Most High has performed with me.** I wish to share with you the marvels that God has performed for me.

33 **How great are His signs,** His miracles, **and how mighty are His wonders! His kingdom is an eternal kingdom, and His**

DISCUSSION

3:26| **God Most High:** This expression is used again many years later by Cyrus, and others as well. It would seem that other nations also referred to the God of Israel in this manner (see 4:14, 31, 5:18; Ezra 1:2; Jonah 1:9), as the God who is above all other gods (see Ibn Ezra on 3:32; *Menaḥot* 110a). Apparently, there was a conception even among idolaters, at least the intelligent ones, that there was indeed some sort of supreme Being above everything else. The Torah already records that in the time of Abraham, Malkitzedek king of Shalem was a priest to the God Most High, and he even blessed Abraham in His name (Genesis 14:18–20). However, idolaters assumed that the Most High was so lofty and distant that ordinary individuals were not supposed to worship Him directly, but rather to worship the intermediaries that were subject to His authority. This worldview is still extant in some circles of idol worshippers, even in contemporary times. For this reason, those idol worshippers did not refer to God with the special name used by the Jews, but rather with the more generic term, God Most High (see also Ralbag, I Chronicles 16:26).

מִלַּת מַלְכָּא מַחְצְפָה וְאַתּוּנָא אֵזֵה יַתִּירָה גֻּבְרַיָּא אִלֵּךְ דִּי הַסִּקוּ לְשַׁדְרַךְ מֵישַׁךְ

כג וַעֲבֵד נְגוֹ קַטִּל הִמּוֹן שְׁבִיבָא דִּי נוּרָא׃ וְגֻבְרַיָּא אִלֵּךְ תְּלָתֵּהוֹן שַׁדְרַךְ מֵישַׁךְ

כד וַעֲבֵד נְגוֹ נְפַלוּ לְגוֹא־אַתּוּן־נוּרָא יָקִדְתָּא מְכַפְּתִין׃ אֱדַיִן נְבוּכַדְנֶצַּר

מַלְכָּא תְּוַהּ וְקָם בְּהִתְבְּהָלָה עָנֵה וְאָמַר לְהַדָּבְרוֹהִי הֲלָא גֻבְרִין תְּלָתָה רְמֵינָא

כה לְגוֹא־נוּרָא מְכַפְּתִין עָנַיִן וְאָמְרִין לְמַלְכָּא יַצִּיבָא מַלְכָּא׃ עָנֵה וְאָמַר הָא־אֲנָה

חָזֵה גֻּבְרִין אַרְבְּעָה שְׁרַיִן מַהְלְכִין בְּגוֹא־נוּרָא וַחֲבָל לָא־אִיתַי בְּהוֹן וְרֵוֵהּ דִּי

כו רביעיא דָּמֵה לְבַר־אֱלָהִין׃ בֵּאדַיִן קְרֵב נְבוּכַדְנֶצַּר לִתְרַע אַתּוּן רְבִיעָאָה

נוּרָא יָקִדְתָּא עָנֵה וְאָמַר שַׁדְרַךְ מֵישַׁךְ וַעֲבֵד־נְגוֹ עַבְדוֹהִי דִּי־אֱלָהָא עליא פֻּקוּ עִלָּאָה

כז וֶאֱתוֹ בֵּאדַיִן נָפְקִין שַׁדְרַךְ מֵישַׁךְ וַעֲבֵד נְגוֹ מִן־גּוֹא נוּרָא׃ וּמִתְכַּנְּשִׁין אֲחַשְׁדַּרְפְּנַיָּא

סִגְנַיָּא וּפַחֲוָתָא וְהַדָּבְרֵי מַלְכָּא חָזַיִן לְגֻבְרַיָּא אִלֵּךְ דִּי לָא־שְׁלֵט נוּרָא בגשמיהון בְּגֶשְׁמְהוֹן

כח וּשְׂעַר רֵאשְׁהוֹן לָא הִתְחָרַךְ וְסַרְבָּלֵיהוֹן לָא שְׁנוֹ וְרֵיחַ נוּר לָא עֲדָת בְּהוֹן׃ עָנֵה

נְבוּכַדְנֶצַּר וְאָמַר בְּרִיךְ אֱלָהֲהוֹן דִּי־שַׁדְרַךְ מֵישַׁךְ וַעֲבֵד נְגוֹ דִּי־שְׁלַח מַלְאֲכֵהּ

וְשֵׁיזִב לְעַבְדוֹהִי דִּי הִתְרְחִצוּ עֲלוֹהִי וּמִלַּת מַלְכָּא שַׁנִּיו וִיהַבוּ גשמיהון דִּי לָא־ גֶּשְׁמְהוֹן

כט יִפְלְחוּן וְלָא־יִסְגְּדוּן לְכָל־אֱלָהּ לָהֵן לֵאלָהֲהוֹן׃ וּמִנִּי שִׂים טְעֵם דִּי כָל־עַם אֻמָּה

וְלִשָּׁן דִּי־יֵאמַר שלה עַל־אֱלָהֲהוֹן דִּי־שַׁדְרַךְ מֵישַׁךְ וַעֲבֵד נְגוֹא הַדָּמִין יִתְעֲבֵד שָׁלוּ

וּבַיְתֵהּ נְוָלִי יִשְׁתַּוֵּה כָּל־קֳבֵל דִּי לָא אִיתַי אֱלָה אָחֳרָן דִּי־יִכֻּל לְהַצָּלָה כִּדְנָה׃

ל בֵּאדַיִן מַלְכָּא הַצְלַח לְשַׁדְרַךְ מֵישַׁךְ וַעֲבֵד נְגוֹ בִּמְדִינַת בָּבֶל׃ ג

לא נְבוּכַדְנֶצַּר מַלְכָּא לְכָל־עַמְמַיָּא אֻמַיָּא וְלִשָּׁנַיָּא דִּי־דארין בְּכָל־אַרְעָא שְׁלָמְכוֹן דָּיְרִין

לב לג יִשְׂגֵּא׃ אָתַיָּא וְתִמְהַיָּא דִּי עֲבַד עִמִּי אֱלָהָא עליא שְׁפַר קָדָמַי לְהַחֲוָיָה׃ אָתוֹהִי עִלָּאָה

כְּמָה רַבְרְבִין וְתִמְהוֹהִי כְּמָה תַקִּיפִין מַלְכוּתֵהּ מַלְכוּת עָלַם וְשָׁלְטָנֵהּ עִם־דָּר

dominion is from generation to generation, in each and every generation. King Nebuchadnezzar declares to all the nations, both those who are under his dominion and those who are not, the content of the revelation he received: There is a supreme God who reigns over all places and all times.

4 1 **I, Nebuchadnezzar, was tranquil in my house, and flourishing in my palace.**

2 **I saw a dream and it frightened me, and ponderings** that arose to me **on my bed and visions in my head have terrified me.** This dream, which appeared against a calm backdrop, was strange and frightening.

3 As I was very anxious about it, **I issued a decree to bring all the wise men of Babylonia before me,** dream interpreters, **to make known to me the interpretation of the dream.**

4 **Then,** perhaps that same night, **the magicians, the enchanters, the chaldeans, and the oracles,** various types of fortune-tellers,[40] **entered, and I related the dream before them, but they did not make its interpretation known to me.** In this case, Nebuchadnezzar remembered his dream, but once again its interpretation eluded him.

5 **Ultimately, Daniel,** or: The last man who came before me was Daniel, **whose name was Beltshatzar, after the name of my god,** he was renamed on the king's command, after Bel the chief god of Babylon (see 1:7, 5:12), **and in whom there is the spirit of the holy God, entered before me and I related the dream before him:**

6 I said to him as follows: **Beltshatzar, chief magician,** as stated earlier, Daniel had been appointed head of all wise men of Babylon (2:48), **as I know that the spirit of the holy God is in you, and no secret overcomes you,** you can reveal all mysteries, **relate the visions of my dream that I have seen, and its interpretation.**

7 **In the visions in my head while on my bed;** the king knew this vision came from within, not from external sources: **I saw** in my dream, **behold, a tree** planted **in the midst of the land, and its height was great.**

8 **The tree grew and became strong, and its height reached the heavens, and** the ends of **its boughs** stretched **to the ends of the whole earth.**

9 **Its foliage,** its array of branches and leaves,[41] **was beautiful, and its fruit abundant, and there was food for all in it; the beasts of the field had shade beneath it, and the birds of the heavens,** which generally live in trees, **dwelled in its branches, and all flesh would be sustained from it.** This was an enormous tree that provided shade and sustenance for the entire world.

10 **I saw in the visions in my head while on my bed, and behold, a messenger and a holy one,** an angel, **descending from heaven.**

11 **He,** this angel, **called loudly, and thus he said: Hew down the tree and cut off its branches, strip its foliage and scatter its fruit; the beasts will move from beneath it and the birds from its branches.**

12 **But** even though you must sever the tree, **leave the stump of its roots in the ground, and** the stump should be encircled **in a band of iron and bronze,** and **it shall be with the grass of the field. It will be soaked with the dew of the heavens, and its portion will be with the beasts in the vegetation of the earth.** It shall remain in the ground.

13 **Let its heart,** the tree's heart, **be altered from that of a man, and a beast's heart be given to it, and let seven seasons pass over it** in this state.

14 **The matter is by the decree of the messengers,** angels, **and the verdict by the statement of the holy ones,** also angels, **so that all the living know that the Most High rules in the kingdom of men, and He will give it,** kingship, **to whomever He wishes, and the lowliest of men He may set over it.** God can establish a king from the lowliest of men, as all depends on His will alone.

15 **This dream, I, King Nebuchadnezzar, saw, and** now **you, Beltshatzar, state the interpretation, since all the wise men of my kingdom are unable to make known to me the interpretation, and you are capable because the spirit of the holy God is in you.** Daniel himself likewise had declared that his ability to interpret dreams was not due to his own wisdom alone. Rather, the spirit of God spoke through him (see 2:27–30).

16 Nebuchadnezzar continues narrating the episode: **Then Daniel, whose name was Beltshatzar, was astonished for some time, and his thoughts terrified him.** Upon seeing that Daniel was sitting and contemplating, **the king spoke, saying: Beltshatzar, do not let the dream or the interpretation terrify you.** The attempt of the powerful king to ease Daniel's worries attests to the unusually close relationship between them. **Beltshatzar spoke, saying: My lord, the dream is for your enemy, and its interpretation for your foe.** This is an evil dream; I wish that its message would fall upon the heads of your enemies.

17 **The tree that you saw that grew and became strong, whose height reached to the heavens, and its boughs to the entire earth,**

18 **its foliage was beautiful, its fruit abundant, and there was food for all in it; the beasts of the field had shade beneath it, and the birds of the heavens dwelled in its branches;**

א ב וְדָר: אֲנָה נְבוּכַדְנֶצַּר שְׁלֵה הֲוֵית בְּבֵיתִי וְרַעְנַן בְּהֵיכְלִי: חֵלֶם חֲזֵית וִידַחֲלִנַּנִי
ג וְהַרְהֹרִין עַל־מִשְׁכְּבִי וְחֶזְוֵי רֵאשִׁי יְבַהֲלֻנַּנִי: וּמִנִּי שִׂים טְעֵם לְהַנְעָלָה קֳדָמַי לְכֹל
ד חַכִּימֵי בָבֶל דִּי־פְשַׁר חֶלְמָא יְהוֹדְעֻנַּנִי: בֵּאדַיִן עללין חַרְטֻמַיָּא אָשְׁפַיָּא כשדיא עָלִּין | כַּשְׂדָּאֵי
ה וְגָזְרַיָּא וְחֶלְמָא אָמַר אֲנָה קֳדָמֵיהוֹן וּפִשְׁרֵהּ לָא־מְהוֹדְעִין לִי: וְעַד אָחֳרֵין עַל
קֳדָמַי דָּנִיֵּאל דִּי־שְׁמֵהּ בֵּלְטְשַׁאצַּר כְּשֻׁם אֱלָהִי וְדִי רוּחַ־אֱלָהִין קַדִּישִׁין בֵּהּ
ו וְחֶלְמָא קֳדָמוֹהִי אַמְרֵת: בֵּלְטְשַׁאצַּר רַב חַרְטֻמַיָּא דִּי ׀ אֲנָה יִדְעֵת דִּי רוּחַ אֱלָהִין
ז קַדִּישִׁין בָּךְ וְכָל־רָז לָא־אָנֵס לָךְ חֶזְוֵי חֶלְמִי דִי־חֲזֵית וּפִשְׁרֵהּ אֱמַר: וְחֶזְוֵי רֵאשִׁי
ח עַל־מִשְׁכְּבִי חָזֵה הֲוֵית וַאֲלוּ אִילָן בְּגוֹא אַרְעָא וְרוּמֵהּ שַׂגִּיא: רְבָה אִילָנָא וּתְקִף
ט וְרוּמֵהּ יִמְטֵא לִשְׁמַיָּא וַחֲזוֹתֵהּ לְסוֹף כָּל־אַרְעָא: עָפְיֵהּ שַׁפִּיר וְאִנְבֵּהּ שַׂגִּיא וּמָזוֹן
לְכֹלָּא־בֵהּ תְּחֹתוֹהִי תַּטְלֵל ׀ חֵיוַת בָּרָא וּבְעַנְפוֹהִי ידרון צִפֲּרֵי שְׁמַיָּא וּמִנֵּהּ יִתְּזִין יְדוּרָן
י כָּל־בִּשְׂרָא: חָזֵה הֲוֵית בְּחֶזְוֵי רֵאשִׁי עַל־מִשְׁכְּבִי וַאֲלוּ עִיר וְקַדִּישׁ מִן־שְׁמַיָּא
יא נָחִת: קָרֵא בְחַיִל וְכֵן אָמַר גֹּדּוּ אִילָנָא וְקַצִּצוּ עַנְפוֹהִי אַתַּרוּ עָפְיֵהּ וּבַדַּרוּ אִנְבֵּהּ
יב תְּנֻד חֵיוְתָא מִן־תַּחְתּוֹהִי וְצִפְּרַיָּא מִן־עַנְפוֹהִי: בְּרַם עִקַּר שָׁרְשׁוֹהִי בְּאַרְעָא
שְׁבֻקוּ וּבֶאֱסוּר דִּי־פַרְזֶל וּנְחָשׁ בְּדִתְאָא דִּי בָרָא וּבְטַל שְׁמַיָּא יִצְטַבַּע וְעִם־חֵיוְתָא
יג חֲלָקֵהּ בַּעֲשַׂב אַרְעָא: לִבְבֵהּ מִן־אנושא יְשַׁנּוֹן וּלְבַב חֵיוָא יִתְיְהִב לֵהּ וְשִׁבְעָה אֲנָשָׁא
יד עִדָּנִין יַחְלְפוּן עֲלוֹהִי: בִּגְזֵרַת עִירִין פִּתְגָמָא וּמֵאמַר קַדִּישִׁין שְׁאֵלְתָא עַד־דִּבְרַת
דִּי יִנְדְּעוּן חַיַּיָּא דִּי־שַׁלִּיט עליא בְּמַלְכוּת אנושא וּלְמַן־דִּי יִצְבֵּא יִתְּנִנַּהּ וּשְׁפַל עִלָּאָה | אֲנָשָׁא
טו אֲנָשִׁים יְקִים עליה: דְּנָה חֶלְמָא חֲזֵית אֲנָה מַלְכָּא נְבוּכַדְנֶצַּר ואנתה בֵּלְטְשַׁאצַּר עֲלַהּ | וְאַנְתְּ
פשרא אֱמַר כָּל־קֳבֵל דִּי ׀ כָּל־חַכִּימֵי מַלְכוּתִי לָא־יָכְלִין פִּשְׁרָא לְהוֹדָעוּתַנִי פִּשְׁרֵהּ
טז ואנתה כָּהֵל דִּי רוּחַ־אֱלָהִין קַדִּישִׁין בָּךְ: אֱדַיִן דָּנִיֵּאל דִּי־שְׁמֵהּ בֵּלְטְשַׁאצַּר וְאַנְתְּ
אֶשְׁתּוֹמַם כְּשָׁעָה חֲדָה וְרַעְיֹנֹהִי יְבַהֲלֻנֵּהּ עָנֵה מַלְכָּא וְאָמַר בֵּלְטְשַׁאצַּר חֶלְמָא
ופשרא אַל־יְבַהֲלָךְ עָנֵה בֵלְטְשַׁאצַּר וְאָמַר מָרִאי חֶלְמָא לשנאיך וּפִשְׁרֵהּ וּפִשְׁרֵהּ | לְשָׂנְאָךְ
יז לעריך: אִילָנָא דִּי חֲזַיְתָ דִּי רְבָה וּתְקִף וְרוּמֵהּ יִמְטֵא לִשְׁמַיָּא וַחֲזוֹתֵהּ לְכָל־ לְעָרָךְ
יח אַרְעָא: וְעָפְיֵהּ שַׁפִּיר וְאִנְבֵּהּ שַׂגִּיא וּמָזוֹן לְכֹלָּא־בֵהּ תְּחֹתוֹהִי תְּדוּר חֵיוַת בָּרָא

19 **it,** this massive tree, **is you, O king, who has grown and be-**
come strong; your greatness has grown, and reached the
heavens, and your dominion is so overarching that it stretches **to the ends of the earth.**
20 **That which the king saw, a messenger and a holy one de-**
scending from the heavens, and he said: Hew down the
tree, and destroy it; but leave the stump of its roots in the
ground, and let it be tied **in a band of iron and bronze,** and **it**
shall be with the grass of the field. It will be soaked with the
dew of the heavens, and its portion will be with the beasts
of the field until seven seasons pass over it. The meaning of
this command is simple:
21 **This is the interpretation, O king, and it is the decree of the**
Most High that is coming upon my lord the king.
22 **You will be driven from** the company of **men, and your**
dwelling will be with the beasts of the field,[B] **and you will be**
fed grass like oxen, and you will be soaked with the dew of
the heavens, and seven seasons will pass over you, until you
know that the Most High rules in the kingdom of men, and
He gives it to whomever He wishes.
23 Concerning **that which was stated** in the dream **to leave the**
stump of the roots of the tree, this means that **your kingdom**
will remain yours, and it will wait for you to return **after you**
come to know that the heavens rule. You have been informed
that you will not be entirely destroyed. After a lengthy period,
you will come to recognize that the Most High God rules over
everything, and then your redemption will come. The king
is informed through this harsh prophecy that he will lose his
mind and will be unable to live among people, and he will have
to go out to the fields and act like an animal.
24 **Therefore, O king, let my counsel be acceptable to you, and**
redeem your sins with charity, and atone for **your iniquities**
with favor to the poor; then, or: Perhaps,[42] **there will be an**
extension of your tranquility. The dream will be fulfilled, but
if you give charity and perform kindness with the needy, you
can stave off the decree against you.[43] Some explain: If your
kingdom is lengthened, then you should act with charity and
show mercy toward the poor.
25 Nebuchadnezzar further relates how the dream came to pass, although when describing his loss of sanity he refers to himself in
the third person:[44] **All this came upon King Nebuchadnezzar.**
26 **At the end of twelve months he,** Nebuchadnezzar, **was walk-**
ing upon the roof of **the royal palace of Babylon,** in his
customary manner.[45]
27 **The king spoke, saying: Isn't this great Babylon, which I**
built as a royal residence, with the might of my power and
for the glory of my majesty? Babylon was a major city even before the time of Nebuchadnezzar, but he turned it into the large, grand capital of a great empire. When the king strolled upon the roof of his palace and gazed at the view of his city, he was filled with wonder at his own greatness, as he had successfully conquered many kingdoms and nations as well as constructed such an important city.

"Great Babylon." Model of the entrance to Babylon through the Ishtar Gate

28 Presumably, he had forgotten about the frightening dream he
had experienced roughly a year earlier, but **while the matter,**
his self-aggrandizement in his glory, **was yet in the mouth of**
the king, a voice fell from the heavens: To you it is said,
King Nebuchadnezzar: The kingdom is removed from you.
29 **You will be driven from men, and your dwelling will be with**
the beasts of the field; you will be fed grass like oxen, and
seven seasons will pass over you, until you know that the
Most High rules in the kingdom of men, and He gives it to
whomever He wishes.
30 **At that moment, the matter was determined for Nebu-**
chadnezzar, and he was driven away from men, and would
eat grass like oxen, and his body was soaked with the dew of
the heavens, until his hair grew like that of **eagles, and his**
nails like those of **birds.** Since he no longer considered himself
a man, but behaved like an animal in all regards, no one took
care of him, and his hair and nails grew long.[46]
31 When Nebuchadnezzar describes his return to his normal self,
he once again speaks in the first person: **At the end of the days**
of my punishment, **I, Nebuchadnezzar, lifted my eyes to the**

BACKGROUND

4:22 | **You will be driven from men, and your dwelling will be with the beasts of the field:** Some explain that it was decreed upon Nebuchadnezzar that he would be afflicted with clinical lycanthropy, a rare psychological disease similar to schizophrenia. The affected person believes that an animal is trapped in his body, and he adopts certain behavioral patterns of that animal. He experiences hallucinations, his speech is disorganized, and he has difficulty communicating with those around him. Nevertheless, he does not lose his inner awareness, and he retains the ability to change his behavior while he is sick.

יט וּבְעַנְפ֫וֹהִי יִשְׁכְּנָן צִפֲּרֵי שְׁמַיָּא׃ אנתה־הוּא מַלְכָּא דִּי רבית וּתְקִפְתְּ וּרְבוּתָךְ אַנְתְּ־ | רְבַת
כ רְבָת וּמְטָת לִשְׁמַיָּא וְשָׁלְטָנָךְ לְסוֹף אַרְעָא׃ וְדִי חֲזָה מַלְכָּא עִיר וְקַדִּישׁ נָחִת ׀
מִן־שְׁמַיָּא וְאָמַר גֹּדּוּ אִילָנָא וְחַבְּלוּהִי בְּרַם עִקַּר שָׁרְשׁוֹהִי בְּאַרְעָא שְׁבֻקוּ וּבֶאֱסוּר
דִּי־פַרְזֶל וּנְחָשׁ בְּדִתְאָא דִּי בָרָא וּבְטַל שְׁמַיָּא יִצְטַבַּע וְעִם־חֵיוַת בָּרָא חֲלָקֵהּ
כא עַד דִּי־שִׁבְעָה עִדָּנִין יַחְלְפוּן עֲלוֹהִי׃ דְּנָה פִשְׁרָא מַלְכָּא וּגְזֵרַת עליא הִיא דִּי עִלָּאָה
כב מְטָת עַל־מראי מַלְכָּא׃ וְלָךְ טָרְדִין מִן־אֲנָשָׁא וְעִם־חֵיוַת בָּרָא לֶהֱוֵה מְדֹרָךְ
וְעִשְׂבָּא כְתוֹרִין ׀ לָךְ יְטַעֲמוּן וּמִטַּל שְׁמַיָּא לָךְ מְצַבְּעִין וְשִׁבְעָה עִדָּנִין יַחְלְפוּן
עליך עַד דִּי־תִנְדַּע דִּי־שַׁלִּיט עליא בְּמַלְכוּת אֲנָשָׁא וּלְמַן־דִּי יִצְבֵּא יִתְּנִנַּהּ׃ עֲלָךְ | עִלָּאָה
כג וְדִי אֲמַרוּ לְמִשְׁבַּק עִקַּר שָׁרְשׁוֹהִי דִּי אִילָנָא מַלְכוּתָךְ לָךְ קַיָּמָה מִן־דִּי תִנְדַּע
כד דִּי שַׁלִּטִן שְׁמַיָּא׃ לָהֵן מַלְכָּא מִלְכִּי יִשְׁפַּר עליך וחטיך בְּצִדְקָה פְרֻק וַעֲוָיָתָךְ עֲלָךְ | וַחֲטָאָךְ
כה בְּמִחַן עֲנָיִן הֵן תֶּהֱוֵה אַרְכָה לִשְׁלֵוְתָךְ׃ כֹּלָּא מְטָא עַל־נְבוּכַדְנֶצַּר מַלְכָּא׃
כו כז לִקְצָת יַרְחִין תְּרֵי־עֲשַׂר עַל־הֵיכַל מַלְכוּתָא דִּי בָבֶל מְהַלֵּךְ הֲוָה׃ עָנֵה מַלְכָּא
וְאָמַר הֲלָא דָא־הִיא בָּבֶל רַבְּתָא דִּי־אֲנָה בֱנַיְתַהּ לְבֵית מַלְכוּ בִּתְקַף חִסְנִי וְלִיקָר
כח הַדְרִי׃ עוֹד מִלְּתָא בְּפֻם מַלְכָּא קָל מִן־שְׁמַיָּא נְפַל לָךְ אָמְרִין נְבוּכַדְנֶצַּר מַלְכָּא
כט מַלְכוּתָה עֲדָת מִנָּךְ׃ וּמִן־אֲנָשָׁא לָךְ טָרְדִין וְעִם־חֵיוַת בָּרָא מְדֹרָךְ עִשְׂבָּא כְתוֹרִין
לָךְ יְטַעֲמוּן וְשִׁבְעָה עִדָּנִין יַחְלְפוּן עליך עַד דִּי־תִנְדַּע דִּי־שַׁלִּיט עליא בְּמַלְכוּת עֲלָךְ | עִלָּאָה
ל אֲנָשָׁא וּלְמַן־דִּי יִצְבֵּא יִתְּנִנַּהּ׃ בַּהּ־שַׁעֲתָא מִלְּתָא סָפַת עַל־נְבוּכַדְנֶצַּר וּמִן־
אֲנָשָׁא טְרִיד וְעִשְׂבָּא כְתוֹרִין יֵאכֻל וּמִטַּל שְׁמַיָּא גִּשְׁמֵהּ יִצְטַבַּע עַד דִּי שַׂעְרֵהּ
לא כְּנִשְׁרִין רְבָה וְטִפְרוֹהִי כְצִפְּרִין׃ וְלִקְצָת יוֹמַיָּא אֲנָה נְבוּכַדְנֶצַּר עַיְנַי ׀ לִשְׁמַיָּא

heavens, and my knowledge returned to me, and I blessed the Most High, and I praised and glorified Him who lives forever, whose dominion is an everlasting dominion, and His kingdom from generation to generation. It is possible that before the evil that befell him Nebuchadnezzar did not look up to heaven at all, but now he gives thanks to God and recognizes that He rules the world.

32 And **all the inhabitants of the earth are considered as nothing,** or as something insubstantial, such as dust,[47] or spiders' webs, before the Most High God; **and He does as He wishes with the host of the heavens and the inhabitants of the earth. No one can reprimand Him, or say to Him: What have You done?**[48]

33 **At that time, my knowledge returned to me, and to the glory of my kingdom I returned, and my splendor was given back to me;**[49] some read: I was restored to the glory of my kingdom, and my splendor returned to me; and **my commanders and my lords sought me;** they had not been able to communicate with Nebuchadnezzar when he was temporarily insane, **and I was** again firmly **established over my kingdom, and exceeding greatness was added to me.**

34 **Now I, Nebuchadnezzar, praise, and exalt, and glorify the King of heaven, for all His actions are truth, His ways are justice,** truth and righteousness, **and He is able to humble those who walk in arrogance.**

The Fall of Babylon and Its King

DANIEL 5:1–30

The previous story occurred during the prime of Nebuchadnezzar's reign. Many years have passed since then; Nebuchadnezzar has died, and his son who reigned after him, Evil Merodakh, has also departed from the world. The king in the following story is Belshatzar, also from the dynasty of Nebuchadnezzar, although historical records indicate that Belshatzar was not an official king.

5 1 **King Belshatzar**[B] **made a great banquet for one thousand of his noblemen, and before the thousand he drank wine,** or he drank the amount imbibed by a thousand men.[50]

2 **Belshatzar said, as he tasted the wine,** or while he was under the influence of the wine, **to bring the gold and silver vessels that Nebuchadnezzar his father,** one of his ancestors, **had removed from the Sanctuary that was in Jerusalem, so that the king, his noblemen, his consorts, and his concubines could drink from them.** For some reason the drunk king decided to use the Temple vessels for his feast, despite the fact that most of them were very large. Typically, captured vessels of this kind were melted down, or preserved solely to commemorate the occasion of the capture; acts of desecration of this kind were generally considered unacceptable.

3 **Then they brought the gold vessels that had been removed from the Sanctuary of the House of God that was in Jerusalem, and the king, his noblemen, his consorts, and his concubines drank from them.**

4 **They drank wine, and praised the gods of gold, silver, bronze, iron, wood, and stone** while they were sitting, drunk, during the feast at which they used the sacred vessels.

5 **At that time, fingers of a human hand emerged, and wrote opposite the** large **candelabrum on the plaster of the wall of the king's palace, and the king saw the hand that was writing.** An image of the palm of a hand suddenly appeared before the king, and it wrote a message on the wall of its own accord.

6 **Then the king's demeanor changed** for the worse, **and his thoughts terrified him; the joints of his hips,** or his loins, **went slack,** lost their stability, as his body was weakened, **and his knees knocked one against another.**

7 **The king cried loudly,** or forcefully, **to bring in the enchanters, the chaldeans, and the oracles,** who were the experts in interpreting dreams and revealing secrets, to come and give their opinion. **The king spoke, saying to the wise men of Babylonia: Whoever can read this script, and tell me its interpretation, will wear purple.**[B] In many places the color purple was set aside for the sole use of kings and outstanding individuals. The donning of a garment entirely made of purple was considered a royal honor. **And** he will **have a chain of gold** placed **around his neck, and will rule as one among three,** a senior position, perhaps one of the three highest ministers **in the kingdom.** The drunk Belshatzar issued lavish promises and assurances of great honor for whoever would solve the riddle.

Gold chain necklace, Greece, 360 BCE

נטלת ומנדעי עלי יתוב ולעליא ברכת ולחי עלמא שבחת והדרת די שלטנה ולעלאה
לב שלטן עלם ומלכותה עם־דר ודר: וכל־דארי ארעא כלה חשיבין וכמצביה דירי
עבד בחיל שמיא ודארי ארעא ולא איתי די־ימחא בידה ויאמר לה מה ודירי
לג עבדת: בה־זמנא מנדעי | יתוב עלי וליקר מלכותי הדרי וזיוי יתוב עלי ולי
לד הדברי ורברבני יבעון ועל־מלכותי התקנת ורבו יתירא הוספת לי: כען אנה
נבכדנצר משבח ומרומם ומהדר למלך שמיא די כל־מעבדוהי קשוט וארחתה
דין ודי מהלכין בגוה יכל להשפלה:

ה א בלשאצר מלכא עבד לחם רב לרברבנוהי אלף ולקבל אלפא חמרא שתה:
ב בלשאצר אמר | בטעם חמרא להיתיה למאני דהבא וכספא די הנפק
נבוכדנצר אבוהי מן־היכלא די בירושלם וישתון בהון מלכא ורברבנוהי
ג שגלתה ולחנתה: באדין היתיו מאני דהבא די הנפקו מן־היכלא די־בית
ד אלהא די בירושלם ואשתיו בהון מלכא ורברבנוהי שגלתה ולחנתה: אשתיו
ה חמרא ושבחו לאלהי דהבא וכספא נחשא פרזלא אעא ואבנא: בה־שעתה
נפקו אצבען די יד־אנש וכתבן לקבל נברשתא על־גירא די־כתל היכלא נפקה
ו די מלכא ומלכא חזה פס ידא די כתבה: אדין מלכא זיוהי שנוהי ורעינהי
ז יבהלונה וקטרי חרצה משתרין וארכבתה דא לדא נקשן: קרא מלכא בחיל
להעלה לאשפיא כשדיא וגזריא ענה מלכא ואמר | לחכימי בבל די כל־ כשדאי
אנש די־יקרה כתבה דנה ופשרה יחונני ארגונא ילבש והמונכא די־דהבא והמניכא

BACKGROUND

5:1 | **Belshatzar:** In documents from the reign of Nabonidus, the last ruler of Babylon, his son Belshatzar is often mentioned as second-in-command to his father, and he is called the son of the king. Apparently, Belshatzar substituted for the king when Nabonidus was in the city of Tema, when he went to wage war in that region. Belshatzar is not mentioned at all by the Greek historians, perhaps because their lists of kings included only official monarchs.

5:7 | **Purple:** This is a general name for a reddish-purple dye extracted from the spiny dye-murex, *Murex brandaris*, a sea snail. Early documents indicate that wool dyed with this substance was four times more expensive than other dyed wool. Together with sky-blue, purple was used in the building of the Tabernacle, the covers of its vessels and the vestments of the High Priest (see Exodus 25–28; Numbers 4:13). In addition, the dye appears in external sources dating from the fourteenth century BCE. In the Roman period, purple dye was used by priests, kings, and ministers. Due to its importance and high price, its production was monitored, and free commerce with the dye was prohibited.

8 **Then all the king's wise men entered, but they could not read the script and make the interpretation known to the king.**
9 **Then King Belshatzar was extremely terrified, and his demeanor changed upon him, and his noblemen were confused.** After they became sober following the frightening sight of the disembodied hand writing something apparently incomprehensible on the wall, a great commotion ensued.
10 **The queen, due to the words of the king and his noblemen,** when she heard of their comments and saw their panicky behavior, she **entered the banquet hall;** it seems that the banquet was mainly for men,[51] and **the queen spoke, saying: O king, live forever. May your thoughts not terrify you and may your demeanor not be changed;** calm down, as I have an idea:
11 **There is a man in your kingdom that the spirit of the holy God is in him.** You are surrounded by wise and learned men who are familiar with their own specific rituals, but this is a very different individual, a special man, as the spirit of God rests upon him. **And in the days of your father, enlightenment, sense, and wisdom, like the wisdom of the gods, was found in him,** in this man. **King Nebuchadnezzar your father,** ancestor, **set him as chief of the magicians, enchanters, chaldeans, and oracles for your father the king.**
12 **Since extraordinary spirit, knowledge, sense, interpretation of dreams, solving riddles, and unraveling conundrums were found in Daniel, whom the king,** Nebuchadnezzar, **named Beltshatzar,** therefore **now let Daniel be called, and he will tell the interpretation.** It can be assumed that Daniel was no longer widely known. Perhaps he did not visit the palace as often as he had in his early years, or he might have at this point preferred a private life. The queen, who was a daughter of royalty and who was probably not drunk, like the other people present, remembered this interpreter of dreams and revealer of secrets, and suggested that he be summoned.
13 **Then Daniel was brought in before the king. The king spoke, saying to Daniel: You are Daniel, who is of the members of the exile of Judah, whom the king my father brought from Judah.**
14 **I have heard about you that the spirit of God is in you, and that enlightenment, and sense, and exceeding wisdom is found in you.**
15 **Now, the wise men, the enchanters, have been brought in before me, so that they would read this script** in order **to make known to me its interpretation; but they were unable to tell me the interpretation of the matter.**
16 **I have heard about you that you are able to expound interpretations and unravel conundrums. Now, if you are able to read the script, and make known to me its interpretation, you will wear purple, and have a chain of gold** placed **around your neck, and you will rule as one among three in the kingdom.**
17 **Then Daniel spoke, saying before the king: Let your gifts be for you, and your** generous **grants**[52] **give to another; however, I will read the script to the king, and I will make known to him the interpretation.** Daniel declares that he is not interested in gifts; his reason will become apparent below.
18 **You, O king, God Most High gave Nebuchadnezzar your father the kingdom, greatness, honor, and glory;**
19 **due to the greatness that He gave him, all the peoples, the nations, and the languages,** groups that speak the same language or dialect, **trembled and were afraid before him. Those whom he wished** to kill, **he killed, and those whom he wished, he smote;**[53] alternatively, he kept alive;[54] **and those whom he wished, he elevated, and those whom he wished, he lowered.** He held all the power in his hands.
20 **But when his heart was haughty, and his spirit was hardened to perform evil, he was deposed from the throne of his kingdom, and they removed his honor from him.**
21 **He was driven away from the sons of man; his heart was placed with the beasts, and his dwelling place was with the onagers; he was fed grass like oxen, and his body was soaked with the dew of the heavens.** As related in the previous section, Nebuchadnezzar had to leave the company of humans, as he lost his sanity and became like an animal, living with the beasts; **until he knew that God Most High rules in the kingdom of men, and that whomever He wishes, He sets over it.**

Oxen eating grass

ח עַל־צַוְּארֵהּ וְתַלְתִּי בְמַלְכוּתָא יִשְׁלַט׃ אֱדַיִן עָלְלִין כֹּל חַכִּימֵי מַלְכָּא עָלִּין
ט וְלָא־כָהֲלִין כְּתָבָא לְמִקְרֵא וּפִשְׁרָא לְהוֹדָעָה לְמַלְכָּא׃ אֱדַיִן מַלְכָּא בֵלְשַׁאצַּר וּפִשְׁרֵהּ
י שַׂגִּיא מִתְבָּהַל וְזִיוֹהִי שָׁנַיִן עֲלוֹהִי וְרַבְרְבָנוֹהִי מִשְׁתַּבְּשִׁין׃ מַלְכְּתָא לָקֳבֵל מִלֵּי
מַלְכָּא וְרַבְרְבָנוֹהִי לְבֵית מִשְׁתְּיָא עַלְלַת עֲנָת מַלְכְּתָא וַאֲמֶרֶת מַלְכָּא לְעָלְמִין חֱיִי עַלַּת
יא אַל־יְבַהֲלוּךְ רַעְיוֹנָךְ וְזִיוָיךְ אַל־יִשְׁתַּנּוֹ׃ אִיתַי גְּבַר בְּמַלְכוּתָךְ דִּי רוּחַ אֱלָהִין וְזִיוָךְ
קַדִּישִׁין בֵּהּ וּבְיוֹמֵי אֲבוּךְ נַהִירוּ וְשָׂכְלְתָנוּ וְחָכְמָה כְּחָכְמַת־אֱלָהִין הִשְׁתְּכַחַת
בֵּהּ וּמַלְכָּא נְבֻכַדְנֶצַּר אֲבוּךְ רַב חַרְטֻמִּין אָשְׁפִין כַּשְׂדָּאִין גָּזְרִין הֲקִימֵהּ אֲבוּךְ
יב מַלְכָּא׃ כָּל־קֳבֵל דִּי רוּחַ ׀ יַתִּירָה וּמַנְדַּע וְשָׂכְלְתָנוּ מְפַשַּׁר חֶלְמִין וְאַחֲוָיַת אֲחִידָן ד
וּמְשָׁרֵא קִטְרִין הִשְׁתְּכַחַת בֵּהּ בְּדָנִיֵּאל דִּי־מַלְכָּא שָׂם־שְׁמֵהּ בֵּלְטְשַׁאצַּר כְּעַן
יג דָּנִיֵּאל יִתְקְרֵי וּפִשְׁרָה יְהַחֲוֵה׃ בֵּאדַיִן דָּנִיֵּאל הֻעַל קֳדָם מַלְכָּא עָנֵה
מַלְכָּא וְאָמַר לְדָנִיֵּאל אנתה־הוּא דָנִיֵּאל דִּי־מִן־בְּנֵי גָלוּתָא דִּי יְהוּד דִּי הַיְתִי אַנְתְּ־
יד מַלְכָּא אַבִי מִן־יְהוּד׃ וְשִׁמְעֵת עליך דִּי רוּחַ אֱלָהִין בָּךְ וְנַהִירוּ וְשָׂכְלְתָנוּ וְחָכְמָה עֲלָךְ
טו יַתִּירָה הִשְׁתְּכַחַת בָּךְ׃ וּכְעַן הֻעַלּוּ קֳדָמַי חַכִּימַיָּא אָשְׁפַיָּא דִּי־כְתָבָה דְנָה יִקְרוֹן
טז וּפִשְׁרֵהּ לְהוֹדָעֻתַנִי וְלָא־כָהֲלִין פְּשַׁר־מִלְּתָא לְהַחֲוָיָה׃ וַאֲנָה שִׁמְעֵת עליך דִּי־ עֲלָךְ
תוכל פִּשְׁרִין לְמִפְשַׁר וְקִטְרִין לְמִשְׁרֵא כְּעַן הֵן תוכל כְּתָבָא לְמִקְרֵא וּפִשְׁרֵהּ תִּכֻּל | תִּכֻּל
לְהוֹדָעֻתַנִי אַרְגְּוָנָא תִלְבַּשׁ והמונכא דִי־דַהֲבָא עַל־צַוְּארָךְ וְתַלְתָּא בְמַלְכוּתָא וְהַמְנִיכָא
יז תִּשְׁלַט׃ בֵּאדַיִן עָנֵה דָנִיֵּאל וְאָמַר קֳדָם מַלְכָּא מַתְּנָתָךְ לָךְ לֶהֶוְיָן
יח וּנְבָזְבְּיָתָךְ לְאָחֳרָן הַב בְּרַם כְּתָבָא אֶקְרֵא לְמַלְכָּא וּפִשְׁרָא אֲהוֹדְעִנֵּהּ׃ אנתה אַנְתְּ
מַלְכָּא אֱלָהָא עליא מַלְכוּתָא וּרְבוּתָא וִיקָרָא וְהַדְרָא יְהַב לִנְבֻכַדְנֶצַּר אֲבוּךְ׃ עִלָּאָה
יט וּמִן־רְבוּתָא דִּי יְהַב־לֵהּ כֹּל עַמְמַיָּא אֻמַּיָּא וְלִשָּׁנַיָּא הֲווֹ זאעין וְדָחֲלִין מִן־קֳדָמוֹהִי זָיְעִין
דִּי־הֲוָא צָבֵא הֲוָה קָטֵל וְדִי־הֲוָה צָבֵא הֲוָה מַחֵא וְדִי־הֲוָה צָבֵא הֲוָה מָרִים וְדִי־
כ הֲוָא צָבֵא הֲוָה מַשְׁפִּל׃ וּכְדִי רִם לִבְבֵהּ וְרוּחֵהּ תִּקְפַת לַהֲזָדָה הָנְחַת מִן־כָּרְסֵא
כא מַלְכוּתֵהּ וִיקָרֵה הֶעְדִּיו מִנֵּהּ׃ וּמִן־בְּנֵי אֲנָשָׁא טְרִיד וְלִבְבֵהּ ׀ עִם־חֵיוְתָא שוי שַׁוִּיו
וְעִם־עֲרָדַיָּא מְדוֹרֵהּ עִשְׂבָּא כְתוֹרִין יְטַעֲמוּנֵּהּ וּמִטַּל שְׁמַיָּא גִּשְׁמֵהּ יִצְטַבַּע עַד

22 **And you his son,** descendant, **Belshatzar, have not humbled**
your heart, although you knew all this. Your ancestor learned
his lesson, and yet you have learned nothing from his example.
23 But **you have been haughty toward,** raised yourself up against,
the Lord of heaven: They brought vessels of His House be-
fore you, and you, your noblemen, your consorts, and your
concubines drank wine from them, and you praised the
gods of silver, gold, bronze, iron, wood, and stone, which
do not see, do not hear,
and do not know. You did
not glorify the God that
your breath is by His hand,
and all your ways are His.
He is the God who gives you
life, and yet you have turned
in the opposite direction
from Him.
24 Daniel continues: **Then the**
hand that was seen by the
king **was sent from before**
Him, God, **and this script**
was inscribed.
25 **This is the writing that was**
inscribed: Mene Mene,
Tekel Ufarsin.[B] It is unclear whether these words appeared
in the ancient Hebrew script, which is why Belshatzar and his
ministers could not read them, or if they were written in some
other script, or if they appeared as symbols, or in a particular
order which only Daniel could decipher.[55]
26 **This is the interpretation of the matter: Mene** means that
God has tallied [***mena***] the days of **your kingdom, and com-**
pleted it. The portion of [*menat*] your kingdom has come to an
end.
27 **Tekel** means that **you have been weighed** [***tekilta***] **on the**
scale and found lacking.
28 The last word, *parsin*, has a double meaning: **Peres – your**
kingdom is divided [***perisat***] **and given to Media and Persia**
[***Paras***].
29 Although Belshatzar was drunk and frightened, he was also
very impressed by the Jewish sage. **Then Belshatzar said that**
they should clothe Daniel in purple, and a chain of gold was
placed **around his neck, and they proclaimed about him**
that he should be a ruler, one among three in the kingdom.
30 **During that night, Belshatzar the Chaldean king was**
killed.[B] The king had time to adorn Daniel with the symbols
of glory and declare that he was a senior ruler, but this was of
no practical consequence, as the city fell that very night, and
Belshatzar was killed.

Half-mina weight dedicated by King Shulgi of Ur, 2094–2047 BCE

Daniel in the Lions' Den

DANIEL 6:1–29

This section deals with a later period, the reign of Media and Persia, but it too recounts Daniel's greatness and deeds.

6 1 **Darius the Mede**[B] **received**
the kingdom of Babylon
after the fall of Belshatzar,
when he was sixty-two
years old. This was actually
the result of a collaboration
between Darius and Cyrus,
as together they defeated the
Babylonian Empire and es-
tablished the joint kingdom of Persia and Media.
2 **It was pleasing before Darius to set over the kingdom one**
hundred and twenty satraps,[B] governors or state rulers, **who**
would be spread **throughout the entire kingdom;**

Darius I or Xerxes I, surrounded by his ministers and advisors, relief, Persepolis, 558–465 BCE

Achaemenid Persian Empire and its provinces

BACKGROUND

5:25 | **Mene Mene, Tekel Ufarsin:** It is possible that this cryptic phrase refers to forms of counting, weighing, and distribution; perhaps these are names of measures and weights. If that is the case, then the word "Mene" would refer to the *maneh*, the word "Tekel" would refer to the shekel, and the word "Ufarsin" would refer to the *peras*.

The *maneh* is the oldest known weight. It appears in the Sumerian and Akkadian languages as well, and it is known as *mina* in the Greek pronunciation. The Hitites, Phoenicians, Assyrians, and Egyptians used this name in reference to different weights, and the *maneh* was also used later as the name of a weight and coin in Greece.

▸ *According*

די־ידע די־שליט אלהא עליא במלכות אנשא ולמן־די יצבא יהקים עליה: עלאה | עלה
ואנתה ברה בלשאצר לא השפלת לבבך כל־קבל די כל־דנה ידעת: ועל ואנת כב כג
מרא־שמיא | התרוממת ולמאניא די־ביתה היתיו קדמיך ואנתה ורברבניך קדמך | ואנת |
שגלתך ולחנתך חמרא שתין בהון ולאלהי כספא־ודהבא נחשא פרזלא אעא ורברבנך
ואבנא די לא־חזין ולא־שמעין ולא ידעין שבחת ולאלהא די־נשמתך בידה
וכל־ארחתך לה לא הדרת: באדין מן־קדמוהי שליח פסא די־ידא וכתבא כד
דנה רשים: ודנה כתבא די רשים מנא מנא תקל ופרסין: דנה פשר מלתא כה כו
מנא מנה־אלהא מלכותך והשלמה: תקל תקלתא במאזניא והשתכחת חסיר: כז
פרס פריסת מלכותך ויהיבת למדי ופרס: באדין | אמר בלשאצר והלבשו כח כט
לדניאל ארגונא והמונכא די־דהבא על־צואריה והכרזו עלוהי די־להוא שליט והמניכא
תלתא במלכותא: בה בליליא קטיל בלאשצר מלכא כשדיא: כשדאה ל
ודריוש מדיא קבל מלכותא כבר שנין שתין ותרתין: שפר קדם דריוש והקים מדאה א ב
על־מלכותא לאחשדרפניא מאה ועשרין די להון בכל־מלכותא: ועלא מנהון ג

3 **and over them were three** senior **officials** in the Persian kingdom, **of whom Daniel was one, to whom these satraps would give counsel, so that** thereby **no harm would come to the king.** In this enormous kingdom, each of the satraps

BACKGROUND

According to Ezekiel (45:12), who prophesied in Babylon, the weight of a *maneh* in Babylon was sixty shekels, which suits the Babylonian base-sixty counting system. However, according to Canaanite weights found in Ugarit, the *maneh* weighed fifty shekels, and this fits the system of counting in base ten, which was practiced in Egypt and Canaan. In modern measurements, the weight of a Babylonian *maneh* was roughly 1 kg, and the shekel approximately 16 g, while the Canaanite-Israelite *maneh* was roughly 480–650 g. Tekel is the shekel, which weighs some 10 g, and the *peras* [Ufarsin] is half a *maneh*.

5:30 | **During that night, Belshatzar the Chaldean king was killed:** According to Greek historians from the fifth through fourth centuries BCE, Herodotus (*The Histories* I:191) and Xenophon (in his biography of Cyrus, the *Cyropaedia*, book 7), the Persians and their allies were unable to overcome the fortifications of the city of Babylon. Therefore, Cyrus instructed his soldiers to divert the Euphrates River, which crossed the city upstream. This in turn lowered the water level, allowing the Persian soldiers to enter the city and surprise its inhabitants while they were busy with celebrations and drinking.

6:1 | **Darius the Mede:** Babylon was conquered by a coalition between the kingdoms of Media and Persia, headed by Darius the Mede and his son-in-law Cyrus the Persian (*Josippon* III; *Antiquities of the Jews* X:248). Darius died a year after the conquest. It should be noted that Darius the Mede does not appear by this name in the sources of the Greek historians on which the research is based, although Xenophon (fourth century BCE) speaks of a Darius son of Astyages, who conquered Babylon together with his relative Cyrus.

6:2 | **One hundred and twenty satraps:** The Persian Empire was divided into satrapies, or provinces, each of which was headed by a satrap, which literally means protector of the province. A similar number appears at the beginning of the book of Esther: One hundred and twenty-seven provinces (Esther 1:1). According to Herodotus (*The Histories* III:89), the system was more complex: Darius divided his empire into twenty satrapies, each divided into sub-provinces. Thus, for example, the satrapy of Avar Nahara or Ever-Nari, meaning "Beyond the [Euphrates] River" in Aramaic and Persian, respectively, included the province of Judah, the province of Moav, and others (see, e.g., Ezra 6:7, 8:4; Nehemiah 5:14;

▸ commentary

was in effect the ruler of a state, sometimes a very large one. Consequently, the king needed officials to supervise the satraps, by receiving reports from them and ensuring that the matters of the kingdom were run smoothly. Daniel was appointed above the officials because he was already considered the wisest man in Babylon, even though it was generally known that he was not Babylonian.

4 **Then this Daniel would supervise,** in his official position, **the officials and the satraps, since an extraordinary spirit was in him; and the king considered setting him over the entire realm,** to appoint him as a kind of prime minister for the king of Persia.

5 **Then the officials and the satraps sought to find a pretext against Daniel with regard to matters of the kingdom.** They wanted to prove to the king that Daniel was not fulfilling his functions properly. Apparently, it was for the very reason that Daniel was not one of them that he noticed any discrepancies in the financial accounts of the realm, and was diligent in transferring taxes, raising armies, and the like. Consequently, the other officials were displeased that Daniel was placed in charge of them. **But they could find no pretext or corruption, since he was faithful, and no fault or corruption was found in him.**

6 **Then these men said that we will not find any pretext against this Daniel,** as his administrative service and loyalty to the king are impeccable; **therefore,** they said, **we will find** some claim **against him with regard to the law of his God.** We shall use Daniel's faith in the Torah of Israel to bring about his downfall.

7 **Then these officials and satraps stormed** in excitement, causing a commotion, **into the king,**[56] into his chambers, **and so did they say to him: King Darius, live forever.**

8 They continued: **All the officials of the kingdom, the prefects, the satraps, the commanders, and the governors consulted to establish the law of the king and to institute a ban** stating **that whoever will petition any god or man for** the next **thirty days, except you, O king, will be cast into the lions' den.** They suggested to the king that he reaffirm his status and enhance his power through a law stating that the king is the sole source for any blessing or assistance. It would be forbidden to issue a request or pray to a god of any kind. Only addressing the king with such issues would be permitted, as the ruler of an empire was treated at the time as a kind of demigod.

9 **Now, O king, set the prohibition, and write the script,** enact a law, **not to be changed, according to the law of Media and Persia, which will not be abrogated.** They asked the king not only to impose this decree, but to also establish it as an unalterable law. Clearly, they did not merely wish to prevent others from changing the law; their main aim was to preempt any possibility that the king himself might change his mind. Similarly, it is stated in the book of Esther (8:8) that something written in the king's name and sealed with the king's ring cannot be changed, even by the king.

10 **Thereupon, King Darius wrote the script and the ban.**

11 **When Daniel knew that the script,** the decree, **had been written, he entered his house, and windows were open for him in his upper chamber facing Jerusalem, and three times a day he knelt on his knees, and prayed,**[D] **and gave thanks before his God, as he had always done.**

12 **Then these men stormed in** hurriedly, or: they paid careful attention, **and** they **found Daniel petitioning and supplicating before his God.**

13 **Then they approached and said before the king, concerning the king's ban: Didn't you write a ban that any man who petitions any god or man within thirty days, except you, O king, will be cast into the lions' den? The king spoke, saying: The matter is true, in accordance with the law of Media and Persia, which will not be abrogated.**

14 **Then they,** those men, **spoke, saying before the king that Daniel, who is from the members of the exile of Judah, does not heed you, O king, or the ban that you wrote, and three times a day he petitions.**

15 **Then the king, when he heard this matter, was extremely upset, and set his heart on Daniel to save him, and until sunset he endeavored to save him.** The king, who was very fond of Daniel, sought to find a way to spare him from the harsh decree.

16 **Then these men stormed into the king, and they said to the king: Know, O king, that it is a law of Media and Persia, that no ban or statute that the king establishes may be altered.** They knew that the king was not at all pleased at having to punish Daniel as stated in the law, and that he was seeking a way to save him. They therefore stressed that the order had become an integral part of the laws of Media and Persia, and could not be annulled.

BACKGROUND

commentary on Nehemiah 2:10). It seems that provinces were occasionally divided or combined, and therefore their internal divisions into regions may have reached such high numbers as stated here. It should be noted that there is no definitive distinction in the historical records between the terms state, province, and satrapy, and it is not even clear if these terms refer to ethnic or administrative groupings (see commentary on Ezra 8:36).

DISCUSSION

6:11 | **Windows were open for him in his upper chamber facing Jerusalem, and three times a day he knelt on his knees, and prayed:** Daniel prayed three times a day toward Jerusalem, just as Jews have always done and continue to do today (see I Kings 8:44, and commentary ad loc.; Psalms 55:18). This is one of the few instances in the Bible where the daily order of prayer practiced throughout all the generations is mentioned.

סָרְכִין תְּלָתָה דִּי דָנִיֵּאל חַד מִנְּהוֹן דִּי־לֶהֱוֺן אֲחַשְׁדַּרְפְּנַיָּא אִלֵּין יָהֲבִין לְהוֹן טַעְמָא
ד וּמַלְכָּא לָא־לֶהֱוֵא נָזִק׃ אֱדַיִן דָּנִיֵּאל דְּנָה הֲוָא מִתְנַצַּח עַל־סָרְכַיָּא וַאֲחַשְׁדַּרְפְּנַיָּא
ה כָּל־קֳבֵל דִּי רוּחַ יַתִּירָא בֵּהּ וּמַלְכָּא עֲשִׁית לַהֲקָמוּתֵהּ עַל־כָּל־מַלְכוּתָא׃ אֱדַיִן
סָרְכַיָּא וַאֲחַשְׁדַּרְפְּנַיָּא הֲווֹ בָעַיִן עִלָּה לְהַשְׁכָּחָה לְדָנִיֵּאל מִצַּד מַלְכוּתָא וְכָל־
עִלָּה וּשְׁחִיתָה לָא־יָכְלִין לְהַשְׁכָּחָה כָּל־קֳבֵל דִּי־מְהֵימַן הוּא וְכָל־שָׁלוּ וּשְׁחִיתָה
ו לָא הִשְׁתְּכַחַת עֲלוֹהִי׃ אֱדַיִן גֻּבְרַיָּא אִלֵּךְ אָמְרִין דִּי לָא נְהַשְׁכַּח לְדָנִיֵּאל דְּנָה
ז כָּל־עִלָּא לָהֵן הַשְׁכַּחְנָא עֲלוֹהִי בְּדָת אֱלָהֵהּ׃ אֱדַיִן סָרְכַיָּא
וַאֲחַשְׁדַּרְפְּנַיָּא אִלֵּן הַרְגִּשׁוּ עַל־מַלְכָּא וְכֵן אָמְרִין לֵהּ דָּרְיָוֶשׁ מַלְכָּא לְעָלְמִין חֱיִי׃
ח אִתְיָעַטוּ כֹּל ׀ סָרְכֵי מַלְכוּתָא סִגְנַיָּא וַאֲחַשְׁדַּרְפְּנַיָּא הַדָּבְרַיָּא וּפַחֲוָתָא לְקַיָּמָה
קְיָם מַלְכָּא וּלְתַקָּפָה אֱסָר דִּי כָל־דִּי־יִבְעֵא בָעוּ מִן־כָּל־אֱלָהּ וֶאֱנָשׁ עַד־יוֹמִין
ט תְּלָתִין לָהֵן מִנָּךְ מַלְכָּא יִתְרְמֵא לְגֹב אַרְיָוָתָא׃ כְּעַן מַלְכָּא תְּקִים אֱסָרָא וְתִרְשֻׁם
י כְּתָבָא דִּי לָא לְהַשְׁנָיָה כְּדָת־מָדַי וּפָרַס דִּי־לָא תֶעְדֵּא׃ כָּל־קֳבֵל דְּנָה מַלְכָּא
יא דָּרְיָוֶשׁ רְשַׁם כְּתָבָא וֶאֱסָרָא׃ וְדָנִיֵּאל כְּדִי יְדַע דִּי־רְשִׁים כְּתָבָא עַל לְבַיְתֵהּ וְכַוִּין ה
פְּתִיחָן לֵהּ בְּעִלִּיתֵהּ נֶגֶד יְרוּשְׁלֶם וְזִמְנִין תְּלָתָה בְיוֹמָא הוּא ׀ בָּרֵךְ עַל־בִּרְכוֹהִי
יב וּמְצַלֵּא וּמוֹדֵא קֳדָם אֱלָהֵהּ כָּל־קֳבֵל דִּי־הֲוָא עָבֵד מִן־קַדְמַת דְּנָה׃ אֱדַיִן גֻּבְרַיָּא
יג אִלֵּךְ הַרְגִּשׁוּ וְהַשְׁכַּחוּ לְדָנִיֵּאל בָּעֵא וּמִתְחַנַּן קֳדָם אֱלָהֵהּ׃ בֵּאדַיִן קְרִבוּ וְאָמְרִין
קֳדָם־מַלְכָּא עַל־אֱסָר מַלְכָּא הֲלָא אֱסָר רְשַׁמְתָּ דִּי כָל־אֱנָשׁ דִּי־יִבְעֵא מִן־כָּל־
אֱלָהּ וֶאֱנָשׁ עַד־יוֹמִין תְּלָתִין לָהֵן מִנָּךְ מַלְכָּא יִתְרְמֵא לְגוֹב אַרְיָוָתָא עָנֵה מַלְכָּא
יד וְאָמַר יַצִּיבָא מִלְּתָא כְּדָת־מָדַי וּפָרַס דִּי־לָא תֶעְדֵּא׃ בֵּאדַיִן עֲנוֹ וְאָמְרִין קֳדָם
מַלְכָּא דִּי דָנִיֵּאל דִּי מִן־בְּנֵי גָלוּתָא דִּי יְהוּד לָא־שָׂם עליך מַלְכָּא טְעֵם וְעַל־ עֲלָךְ
טו אֱסָרָא דִּי רְשַׁמְתָּ וְזִמְנִין תְּלָתָה בְּיוֹמָא בָּעֵא בָּעוּתֵהּ׃ אֱדַיִן מַלְכָּא כְּדִי מִלְּתָא
שְׁמַע שַׂגִּיא בְּאֵשׁ עֲלוֹהִי וְעַל דָּנִיֵּאל שָׂם בָּל לְשֵׁיזָבוּתֵהּ וְעַד מֶעָלֵי שִׁמְשָׁא הֲוָא
טז מִשְׁתַּדַּר לְהַצָּלוּתֵהּ׃ בֵּאדַיִן גֻּבְרַיָּא אִלֵּךְ הַרְגִּשׁוּ עַל־מַלְכָּא וְאָמְרִין לְמַלְכָּא דַּע
מַלְכָּא דִּי־דָת לְמָדַי וּפָרַס דִּי־כָל־אֱסָר וּקְיָם דִּי־מַלְכָּא יְהָקֵים לָא לְהַשְׁנָיָה׃

17 **Then the king,** seeing that he had no choice, **said,** gave instructions, **and they brought Daniel, and cast him into the lions' den. The king spoke, saying to Daniel: Your God whom you serve regularly, He will deliver you,** as there is nothing I can do.

Daniel in the lions' den, decoration on lintel stone, synagogue in Ein Nashut, Golan Heights

18 **One stone was brought and was placed over the mouth of the den, and the king sealed it with his signet,**[B] **and with the signet of his noblemen, so that nothing would be altered concerning Daniel,** that they should not try to rescue him from the lions' den. Perhaps the lords added their own signets because they suspected the king might remove his seal.

Cylinder seal and its imprint, Persia, Achaemenid period

19 **Then the king went to his palace, and spent the night fasting; no diversions,** or tables of food, **were brought before him, and his sleep eluded him,** due to his worry about Daniel.
20 **Then the king arose at the first light of dawn, and he went in haste to the lions' den.**
21 **When he approached the den, he cried out to Daniel in a sad voice.** Daniel was inside the den and could not be seen from without. **The king spoke, saying to Daniel: Daniel, servant of the living God, your God, whom you serve regularly, has He been able to save you from the lions?**
22 **Then Daniel said to the king: O king, live forever.**
23 **My God sent His angel and he shut the lions' mouths, and they did not harm me, since merit was found in me before Him. Also before you, O king, I have done no harm;** I have never wronged you.
24 **Then the king was exceedingly glad, and he said to raise Daniel from the den. Daniel was raised from the den, and no harm was found upon him, because he trusted in his God.**
25 **The king said,** gave instructions, **and they brought those men who had informed on Daniel** (see commentary on 3:8) **and cast them into the lions' den, them, their children, and their wives. They did not reach the ground of the den before the lions overpowered them, and crushed all their bones.** It seems that the lions had been starved so that they would eat Daniel. Since the beasts were not able to touch Daniel, they were now so hungry and frustrated that they pounced on the people thrown into their den and devoured them immediately.
26 **Then King Darius wrote to all the peoples, the nations, and the languages,** groups that speak the same language or dialect, **that reside in the entire earth: May your peace be abundant.**
27 **A decree is issued before me, that in the entire dominion of my kingdom men shall tremble and fear before the God of Daniel, as He is the living God, and exists forever, and His is a kingdom that will not be destroyed, and** it is **His dominion** that **will** endure and **be until the end** of days;
28 **He saves and delivers, and performs signs and wonders in the heavens and on earth. He saved Daniel from the grasp of the lions.** Darius publicized throughout his kingdom that the God of Daniel is above all the gods, and he commanded that everyone should act toward God with respect and awe.
29 After relating the story of Daniel's rescue from the lions' den, the chapter summarizes his career: **This Daniel prospered during the reign of Darius and during the reign of Cyrus the Persian,** who reigned after Darius and was apparently his son-in-law.[57]

יז בֵּאדַ֨יִן מַלְכָּ֜א אֲמַ֗ר וְהַיְתִיו֙ לְדָ֣נִיֵּ֔אל וּרְמֹ֖ו לְגֻבָּ֣א דִּ֣י אַרְיָוָתָ֑א עָנֵ֤ה מַלְכָּא֙ וְאָמַ֣ר
יח לְדָֽנִיֵּ֔אל אֱלָהָ֗ךְ דִּ֤י אנתה פָּֽלַח־לֵהּ֙ בִּתְדִ֣ירָ֔א ה֖וּא יְשֵׁיזְבִנָּֽךְ׃ וְהֵיתָ֙יִת֙ אֶ֣בֶן חֲדָ֔ה אַנְתְּ
וְשֻׂמַ֖ת עַל־פֻּ֣ם גֻּבָּ֑א וְחַתְמַ֨הּ מַלְכָּ֜א בְּעִזְקְתֵ֗הּ וּבְעִזְקָת֙ רַבְרְבָנ֔וֹהִי דִּ֛י לָא־תִשְׁנֵ֥א
יט צְב֖וּ בְּדָנִיֵּֽאל׃ אֱדַ֨יִן אֲזַ֤ל מַלְכָּא֙ לְהֵ֔יכְלֵהּ וּבָ֣ת טְוָ֔ת וְדַחֲוָ֖ן לָא־הַנְעֵ֣ל קָדָמ֑וֹהִי
כ וְשִׁנְתֵּ֖הּ נַדַּ֥ת עֲלֽוֹהִי׃ בֵּאדַ֣יִן מַלְכָּ֔א בִּשְׁפַרְפָּרָ֖א יְק֣וּם בְּנָגְהָ֑א וּבְהִתְבְּהָלָ֔ה
כא לְגֻבָּ֥א דִֽי־אַרְיָוָתָ֖א אֲזַֽל׃ וּֽכְמִקְרְבֵ֤הּ לְגֻבָּא֙ לְדָ֣נִיֵּ֔אל בְּקָ֥ל עֲצִ֖יב זְעִ֑ק עָנֵ֨ה מַלְכָּ֜א
וְאָמַ֣ר לְדָנִיֵּ֗אל דָּנִיֵּאל֙ עֲבֵד֙ אֱלָהָ֣א חַיָּ֔א אֱלָהָ֗ךְ דִּ֤י אנתה פָּֽלַח־לֵהּ֙ בִּתְדִ֣ירָ֔א אַנְתְּ
כב הַיְכִ֥ל לְשֵׁיזָבוּתָ֖ךְ מִן־אַרְיָוָתָֽא׃ אֱדַ֨יִן דָּנִיֵּ֔אל עִם־מַלְכָּ֖א מַלִּ֑ל מַלְכָּ֖א לְעָלְמִ֥ין
כג חֱיִֽי׃ אֱלָהִ֞י שְׁלַ֣ח מַלְאֲכֵ֗הּ וּסֲגַ֛ר פֻּ֥ם אַרְיָוָתָ֖א וְלָ֣א חַבְּל֑וּנִי כָּל־קֳבֵ֗ל דִּ֤י קָֽדָמ֙וֹהִי֙
כד זָכוּ֙ הִשְׁתְּכַ֣חַת לִ֔י וְאַ֣ף קדמיך מַלְכָּ֔א חֲבוּלָ֖ה לָ֥א עַבְדֵֽת׃ בֵּאדַ֨יִן מַלְכָּ֜א שַׂגִּ֣יא קֳדָמָךְ
טְאֵ֣ב עֲל֔וֹהִי וּֽלְדָנִיֵּ֔אל אֲמַ֖ר לְהַנְסָקָ֣ה מִן־גֻּבָּ֑א וְהֻסַּ֤ק דָּנִיֵּאל֙ מִן־גֻּבָּ֔א וְכָל־חֲבָל֙
כה לָא־הִשְׁתְּכַ֣ח בֵּ֔הּ דִּ֥י הֵימִ֖ן בֵּאלָהֵֽהּ׃ וַאֲמַ֣ר מַלְכָּ֗א וְהַיְתִ֞יו גֻּבְרַיָּ֣א אִלֵּךְ֮ דִּֽי־אֲכַ֣לוּ
קַרְצ֘וֹהִי֮ דִּ֣י דָנִיֵּאל֒ וּלְגֹ֤ב אַרְיָוָתָא֙ רְמ֔וֹ אִנּ֖וּן בְּנֵיה֣וֹן וּנְשֵׁיה֑וֹן וְלָֽא־מְט֞וֹ לְאַרְעִ֣ית
כו גֻּבָּ֗א עַ֣ד דִּֽי־שְׁלִ֤טוּ בְהוֹן֙ אַרְיָ֣וָתָ֔א וְכָל־גַּרְמֵיה֖וֹן הַדִּֽקוּ׃ בֵּאדַ֗יִן דָּרְיָ֣וֶשׁ מַלְכָּ֡א
כז כְּתַ֗ב לְכָל־עַֽמְמַיָּ֞א אֻמַּיָּ֧א וְלִשָּׁנַיָּ֛א דִּֽי־דארין בְּכָל־אַרְעָ֖א שְׁלָמְכ֥וֹן יִשְׂגֵּֽא׃ מִן־ דָּיְרִין
קֳדָמַי֮ שִׂ֣ים טְעֵם֒ דִּ֣י ׀ בְּכָל־שָׁלְטָ֣ן מַלְכוּתִ֗י לֶהֱוֺ֤ן זאעין וְדָֽחֲלִין֙ מִן־קֳדָ֖ם אֱלָהֵ֣הּ זָיְעִין
דִּֽי־דָנִיֵּ֑אל דִּי־ה֣וּא ׀ אֱלָהָא֩ חַיָּ֨א וְקַיָּ֜ם לְעָלְמִ֗ין וּמַלְכוּתֵהּ֙ דִּֽי־לָ֣א תִתְחַבַּ֔ל וְשָׁלְטָנֵ֖הּ
כח עַד־סוֹפָֽא׃ מְשֵׁיזִ֣ב וּמַצִּ֗ל וְעָבֵד֙ אָתִ֣ין וְתִמְהִ֔ין בִּשְׁמַיָּ֖א וּבְאַרְעָ֑א דִּ֚י שֵׁיזִ֣יב לְדָנִיֵּ֔אל
כט מִן־יַ֖ד אַרְיָוָתָֽא׃ וְדָנִיֵּ֣אל דְּנָ֔ה הַצְלַ֖ח בְּמַלְכ֣וּת דָּרְיָ֑וֶשׁ וּבְמַלְכ֖וּת כּ֥וֹרֶשׁ פרסיא׃ פָּרְסָאָה

BACKGROUND

6:18 | **And the king sealed it with his signet:** In the ancient Middle East there were several different ways of attaching a seal to a document. One method involved attaching a piece of clay or bitumen, known as a bulla, to a document and impressing upon it a mark with a signet. At other times, lumps of clay were placed over the knot that tied documents together, so that the knot could not be undone without breaking the seal. Another method used by Persian kings was to roll a cylinder seal across soft clay. The manufacturers of such seals had to take into account the fact that the desired picture would be the reverse of how it appeared on the seal, in the form of indentations rather than protrusions. A fourth method was to place a large lump of clay on top of a document or a bale of merchandise and then impress it with a mark, in order to indicate ownership, or the control of a government official (*Encyclopædia Iranica*, http://www.iranicaonline.org/articles/bullae-sealings). It is likely that this fourth method was the one used for the seals at the entrance to the lions' den mentioned in this verse.

Visions of the Kingdoms and of the End of Days

DANIEL 7:1–12:13

The remainder of the book of Daniel does not discuss Daniel's activities. Rather, it consists of his visions of future events. Among these visions are some that contain elements with symbolic significance. Prophets sometimes received these types of visions rather than a direct revelation of the word of God (see Ibn Ezra, 10:5; Rambam, *Guide of the Perplexed* 2:45). These visions closely resemble the prophecies of the Second Temple-era prophets such as Zechariah.

Daniel was similar to a prophet in that heavenly forces spoke to him, but was not entirely like a prophet in that his visions do not include instructions or words of reproof, and he was not sent to relate his prophecy to others. Indeed, he was asked to conceal certain parts of his visions.

The Four Kingdoms and the Kingdom That Follows Them

DANIEL 7:1–28

In this vision, which Daniel receives in a dream, he sees large animals and other figures. An angel deciphers the dream's main message, which relates to various kingdoms that will arise and fall from the stage of history in the future. Despite the angel's assistance, the meaning of many of the details noticed by Daniel remain obscure.

7 1 **In the first year of Belshatzar king of Babylon, Daniel saw a**
dream and visions in his head which arose **while** he was
dreaming **on his bed; then he wrote** down **the dream** for posterity, **and stated the principal things,** the beginning of the
dream; alternatively, the headings.[58]
2 **Daniel spoke, saying: I was seeing in my vision at night, and**
behold, the four winds of the heavens were **bursting forth to**
the great sea.
3 **Four great beasts arose from the sea, each different from**
the other.
4 **The first was like a lion, and it had wings of an eagle.**[B] **I was**
looking at it **until its wings were torn off, and it was lifted**
from the ground and set on its feet like a man, and a man's
heart was given to it. The beast was given a somewhat human
form.

Lion with wings of an eagle, neck of a horse, and horns; relief, Persepolis, reign of Darius, 522–486 BCE

5 **Behold, another** figure appeared; **a second beast, resem-**
bling a bear, and it was positioned on one side, and there
were three ribs in its mouth between its teeth; so they said
to it: Arise, devour much flesh.
6 **After this I saw, and behold,** there was **another** animal, **like a**
leopard, which had upon it four wings of a bird; the beast
had four heads, and dominion was given to it.
7 **After this** array of creatures that **I was seeing in the night vi-**
sions, I looked **and behold, a fourth beast** appeared,
fearsome, and **terrifying, and very strong, and it had great**
iron teeth. It devoured and crushed with those teeth, **and**
stomped and sullied **the remains with its feet. It was differ-**
ent from all the beasts that were before it, and it had ten
horns.
8 **I was looking at the horns, and behold, another, small horn**
arose among them, and three of the original horns were up-
rooted from before it. Behold, there were eyes like the eyes
of a man in this small **horn, and a mouth speaking arrogant-**
ly, making prideful statements.
9 **I was seeing** these visions **until thrones were set in place,**
and the Ancient One, ap-
parently a reference to God,
sat. His garment was like
white snow, and the hair of
His head was also white, **like**
pure wool. His throne was
fashioned from **sparks of**
fire, and its wheels, of the
throne, were **blazing fire.**

"Sparks of fire"

Snowy mountain

Wool, before and after whitening

א בִּשְׁנַת חֲדָה לְבֵלְאשַׁאצַּר מֶלֶךְ בָּבֶל דָּנִיֵּאל חֵלֶם חֲזָה וְחֶזְוֵי רֵאשֵׁהּ עַל־מִשְׁכְּבֵהּ
ב בֵּאדַיִן חֶלְמָא כְתַב רֵאשׁ מִלִּין אֲמַר: עָנֵה דָנִיֵּאל וְאָמַר חָזֵה הֲוֵית בְּחֶזְוִי עִם־
ג לֵילְיָא וַאֲרוּ אַרְבַּע רוּחֵי שְׁמַיָּא מְגִיחָן לְיַמָּא רַבָּא: וְאַרְבַּע חֵיוָן רַבְרְבָן סָלְקָן
ד מִן־יַמָּא שָׁנְיָן דָּא מִן־דָּא: קַדְמָיְתָא כְאַרְיֵה וְגַפִּין דִּי־נְשַׁר לַהּ חָזֵה הֲוֵית עַד דִּי־
מְּרִיטוּ גפיה וּנְטִילַת מִן־אַרְעָא וְעַל־רַגְלַיִן כֶּאֱנָשׁ הֳקִימַת וּלְבַב אֱנָשׁ יְהִיב לַהּ: גַּפַּהּ
ה וַאֲרוּ חֵיוָה אָחֳרִי תִנְיָנָה דָּמְיָה לְדֹב וְלִשְׂטַר־חַד הֳקִמַת וּתְלָת עִלְעִין בְּפֻמַּהּ בֵּין
ו שניה וְכֵן אָמְרִין לַהּ קוּמִי אֲכֻלִי בְּשַׂר שַׂגִּיא: בָּאתַר דְּנָה חָזֵה הֲוֵית וַאֲרוּ אָחֳרִי שִׁנַּהּ
כִּנְמַר וְלַהּ גַּפִּין אַרְבַּע דִּי־עוֹף עַל־גביה וְאַרְבְּעָה רֵאשִׁין לְחֵיוְתָא וְשָׁלְטָן יְהִיב גַּבַּהּ
ז לַהּ: בָּאתַר דְּנָה חָזֵה הֲוֵית בְּחֶזְוֵי לֵילְיָא וַאֲרוּ חֵיוָה רביעיא דְּחִילָה וְאֵימְתָנִי רְבִיעָאָה
וְתַקִּיפָא יַתִּירָה וְשִׁנַּיִן דִּי־פַרְזֶל לַהּ רַבְרְבָן אָכְלָה וּמַדְּקָה וּשְׁאָרָא ברגליה רָפְסָה בְּרַגְלַהּ
ח וְהִיא מְשַׁנְּיָה מִן־כָּל־חֵיוָתָא דִּי קדמיה וְקַרְנַיִן עֲשַׂר לַהּ: מִשְׂתַּכַּל הֲוֵית בְּקַרְנַיָּא קָדָמַהּ
וַאֲלוּ קֶרֶן אָחֳרִי זְעֵירָה סִלְקָת ביניהון וּתְלָת מִן־קַרְנַיָּא קַדְמָיָתָא אתעקרו מִן־ בֵּינֵיהֵן | אֶתְעֲקַרָה
ט קדמיה וַאֲלוּ עַיְנִין כְּעַיְנֵי אֲנָשָׁא בְּקַרְנָא־דָא וּפֻם מְמַלִּל רַבְרְבָן: חָזֵה הֲוֵית עַד קָדָמַהּ
דִּי כָרְסָוָן רְמִיו וְעַתִּיק יוֹמִין יְתִב לְבוּשֵׁהּ ׀ כִּתְלַג חִוָּר וּשְׂעַר רֵאשֵׁהּ כַּעֲמַר נְקֵא
י כָּרְסְיֵהּ שְׁבִיבִין דִּי־נוּר גַּלְגִּלּוֹהִי נוּר דָּלִק: נְהַר דִּי־נוּר נָגֵד וְנָפֵק מִן־קֳדָמוֹהִי

10 **A river of fire flowed and emerged from before Him; thousands upon thousands** of angels **served Him, and tens of thousands upon tens of thousands** of angels **stood before Him; the court convened, and the books were opened.**

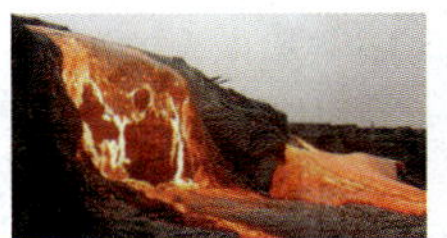
"River of fire." Burning lava

BACKGROUND

7:4 | **A lion, and it had wings of an eagle:** The image of a lion was common in the sculptural arts of the Ancient East; it appeared on statues, murals, vessels, and ritual artifacts. The lion was also frequently used in written descriptions as a symbol of courage, cruelty, and great power. Occasionally, the lion represented the qualities of kings and gods, while at other times it made its appearance as a beast defeated by the gods or kings.

In Mesopotamia, wings added to the image of a lion signified enhanced strength. Sometimes the face of a man and the body of a lion were amalgamated, as in the Sphinx in Egypt, which features the head of the king on a lion's body. In Assyria, Babylonia, and Persia, winged lions were thought to guard the city from evil spirits, and were therefore positioned at the city gates. It should be noted that statues of winged oxen with human heads would also be placed near gates of cities.

11 **I was seeing then, from the sound of the arrogant words that the** small **horn spoke; I was seeing** this vision **until the beast was slain, its body destroyed, and it was relegated to the burning of fire.** As a result of the many boastful statements of the horn, the judgment was issued that the entire animal must be destroyed.

12 As for **the rest of the beasts, their dominion was removed, and an extension of their lives was given them for a time and** for a certain **epoch,** but not forever.[59]

13 **I was seeing in night visions, and behold, among the clouds of the heavens** one cloud **like** the form of **a person was coming, and he reached the Ancient One, and** this "person" **was presented before Him.**

14 **To him was given dominion, honor, and kingship, and all the peoples, nations, and languages,** groups that speak the same language or dialect, **would serve him; his dominion is an everlasting dominion that will not be abrogated, and his kingdom, one that will not be destroyed.** This concludes the vision that Daniel saw, but he did not understand its meaning.

15 **I, Daniel, my spirit was distressed,** or removed from,[60] or was excited, or became impatient, **in my body, and the visions of my head terrified me.**

16 **I approached one of those standing,** one of the angels, **and I asked him for the truth concerning all this,** the vision of the beasts and these figures. **He said to me and made known to me the interpretation of the matters:**

17 **These great beasts, which are four, are** alluding to **four kings;** kingdoms, dynasties, or levels of governments. **They will arise from the earth,** appear in the world.

18 **The holy** ones **of the Most High,** angels, or the righteous, **will receive the kingdom,** dominion over the world, **and take possession of the kingdom forever, forever and ever.** The kingdom of God will last forever.

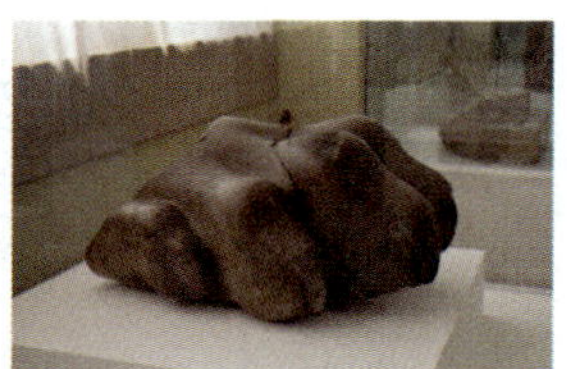

Lion claw, showing the nails, fragment from a stone statue, Persia, 539–531 BCE

19 **Then I wished for the truth concerning the fourth beast, wanting to know** the significance of this creature, **which was different from them all, exceedingly fearsome; its teeth were of iron and its nails were of bronze; it devoured and crushed its prey, and as for the remains, it stomped on them with its feet,**

20 **and concerning the ten horns that were on its head, and the other** horn **that arose, and before which three** horns **fell; that horn that had eyes, and a mouth that spoke arrogantly, and its,** the beast's, **appearance was greater than that of its counterparts.**

21 Daniel further describes what he saw after the appearance of the terrible beast, in an attempt to discover its meaning: **I was seeing, and that horn made war with the holy** ones, the angels or the righteous, **and overcame them.** Everything about this horn was negative;

22 **until the Ancient One came, and passed judgment in favor of the holy** ones **of the Most High;** He brought their judgment to light and fought on their behalf, **and the time arrived, and the holy** ones of the Most High **took possession of the kingdom** represented by that horn, which was at the extremity of the fourth beast.

23 **So he,** the angel, **said: The fourth beast will be a fourth kingdom upon the earth that will be different from all the** other **kingdoms, and will devour,** destroy or plunder, **the entire earth, and will stomp it and crush it.**

24 **And** as for **the ten horns,** the meaning is that **from this kingdom, ten kings will arise, and another will arise after them, and he will be different from the earlier ones, and he will subdue three kings.**

25 **He will speak words against the Most High** God, **and will demolish the holy of the Most High; he will think of changing** the holy and commemorative **times;** he will change or eliminate their observance, **and** will do away with the **law, and they,** the holy ones, **will be delivered into his hand until an epoch, and epochs, and half an epoch** will have passed (see 12:7).

26 Then **the court will convene, and his dominion,** of this king, **will be removed,** for him **to be destroyed and eliminated completely.**

27 **The kingdom, the dominion, and the greatness of the kingdoms under the entire heavens will be given to the people of the holy of the Most High,** the nation of Israel. **Their kingdom is** to be **an everlasting kingdom, and all dominions will serve and obey them.**

28 **Here is the end of the matter. I, Daniel, my thoughts greatly terrified me, and my demeanor was changed in me and I kept the matter in my heart.** In his dream, Daniel saw predators rising from the sea and the image of a man coming from the heights. God also appeared in the vision, with an entourage of His ministers. One of the angels explained to Daniel that the vision symbolizes future events in the world, as different kingdoms will follow one another, until the eventual redemption.

יא אֶלֶף אלפים יְשַׁמְּשׁוּנֵּהּ וְרִבּוֹ רבון קֳדָמוֹהִי יְקוּמוּן דִּינָא יְתִב וְסִפְרִין פְּתִיחוּ׃ חָזֵה אַלְפִּין | רִבְבָן
הֲוֵית בֵּאדַיִן מִן־קָל מִלַּיָּא רַבְרְבָתָא דִּי קַרְנָא מְמַלֱּלָה חָזֵה הֲוֵית עַד דִּי קְטִילַת
יב חֵיוְתָא וְהוּבַד גִּשְׁמַהּ וִיהִיבַת לִיקֵדַת אֶשָּׁא׃ וּשְׁאָר חֵיוָתָא הֶעְדִּיו שָׁלְטָנְהוֹן
יג וְאַרְכָה בְחַיִּין יְהִיבַת לְהוֹן עַד־זְמַן וְעִדָּן׃ חָזֵה הֲוֵית בְּחֶזְוֵי לֵילְיָא וַאֲרוּ עִם־
עֲנָנֵי שְׁמַיָּא כְּבַר אֱנָשׁ אָתֵה הֲוָא וְעַד־עַתִּיק יוֹמַיָּא מְטָה וּקְדָמוֹהִי הַקְרְבוּהִי׃
יד וְלֵהּ יְהִב שָׁלְטָן וִיקָר וּמַלְכוּ וְכֹל עַמְמַיָּא אֻמַיָּא וְלִשָּׁנַיָּא לֵהּ יִפְלְחוּן שָׁלְטָנֵהּ
טו שָׁלְטָן עָלַם דִּי־לָא יֶעְדֵּה וּמַלְכוּתֵהּ דִּי־לָא תִתְחַבַּל׃ אֶתְכְּרִיַּת
טז רוּחִי אֲנָה דָנִיֵּאל בְּגוֹא נִדְנֶה וְחֶזְוֵי רֵאשִׁי יְבַהֲלֻנַּנִי׃ קִרְבֵת עַל־חַד מִן־קָאֲמַיָּא
יז וְיַצִּיבָא אֶבְעֵא־מִנֵּהּ עַל־כָּל־דְּנָה וַאֲמַר־לִי וּפְשַׁר מִלַּיָּא יְהוֹדְעִנַּנִי׃ אִלֵּין חֵיוָתָא
יח רַבְרְבָתָא דִּי אִנִּין אַרְבַּע אַרְבְּעָה מַלְכִין יְקוּמוּן מִן־אַרְעָא׃ וִיקַבְּלוּן מַלְכוּתָא
יט קַדִּישֵׁי עֶלְיוֹנִין וְיַחְסְנוּן מַלְכוּתָא עַד־עָלְמָא וְעַד עָלַם עָלְמַיָּא׃ אֱדַיִן צְבִית
לְיַצָּבָא עַל־חֵיוְתָא רְבִיעָיְתָא דִּי־הֲוָת שָׁנְיָה מִן־כלהון דְּחִילָה יַתִּירָה שניה כָּלְּהֵין | שִׁנַּהּ
כ דִּי־פַרְזֶל וטפריה דִּי־נְחָשׁ אָכְלָה מַדֱּקָה וּשְׁאָרָא ברגליה רָפְסָה׃ וְעַל־קַרְנַיָּא וְטִפְרַהּ | בְּרַגְלַהּ
עֲשַׂר דִּי בְרֵאשַׁהּ וְאׇחֳרִי דִּי סִלְקַת ונפלו מִן־קדמיה תְּלָת וְקַרְנָא דִכֵּן וְעַיְנִין וּנְפַלָה | קֳדָמַהּ
כא לַהּ וּפֻם מְמַלִּל רַבְרְבָן וְחֶזְוַהּ רַב מִן־חַבְרָתַהּ׃ חָזֵה הֲוֵית וְקַרְנָא דִכֵּן עָבְדָא
כב קְרָב עִם־קַדִּישִׁין וְיָכְלָה לְהֹן׃ עַד דִּי־אֲתָה עַתִּיק יוֹמַיָּא וְדִינָא יְהִב לְקַדִּישֵׁי
כג עֶלְיוֹנִין וְזִמְנָא מְטָה וּמַלְכוּתָא הֶחֱסִנוּ קַדִּישִׁין׃ כֵּן אֲמַר חֵיוְתָא רְבִיעָיְתָא
מַלְכוּ רביעיה תֶּהֱוֵא בְאַרְעָא דִּי תִשְׁנֵא מִן־כָּל־מַלְכְוָתָא וְתֵאכֻל כָּל־אַרְעָא רְבִיעָאָה
כד וּתְדוּשִׁנַּהּ וְתַדְּקִנַּהּ׃ וְקַרְנַיָּא עֲשַׂר מִנַּהּ מַלְכוּתָה עַשְׂרָה מַלְכִין יְקֻמוּן וְאׇחֳרָן
כה יְקוּם אַחֲרֵיהוֹן וְהוּא יִשְׁנֵא מִן־קַדְמָיֵא וּתְלָתָה מַלְכִין יְהַשְׁפִּל׃ וּמִלִּין לְצַד עליא עִלָּאָה
יְמַלִּל וּלְקַדִּישֵׁי עֶלְיוֹנִין יְבַלֵּא וְיִסְבַּר לְהַשְׁנָיָה זִמְנִין וְדָת וְיִתְיַהֲבוּן בִּידֵהּ עַד־עִדָּן
כו וְעִדָּנִין וּפְלַג עִדָּן׃ וְדִינָא יִתִּב וְשָׁלְטָנֵהּ יְהַעְדּוֹן לְהַשְׁמָדָה וּלְהוֹבָדָה עַד־סוֹפָא׃
כז וּמַלְכוּתָא וְשָׁלְטָנָא וּרְבוּתָא דִּי מַלְכְוָת תְּחוֹת כׇּל־שְׁמַיָּא יְהִיבַת לְעַם קַדִּישֵׁי
כח עֶלְיוֹנִין מַלְכוּתֵהּ מַלְכוּת עָלַם וְכֹל שָׁלְטָנַיָּא לֵהּ יִפְלְחוּן וְיִשְׁתַּמְּעוּן׃ עַד־כָּה

The Kingdoms of Media-Persia and Greece

DANIEL 8:1–27

The following of Daniel's visions are related in Hebrew. Like the previous vision, which occurred in the first year of King Belshatzar's reign, this next one, which Daniel experiences in the third year of his reign, deals with kingdoms of the future, and here too, they are represented by animals.

8 1 **In the third year of the reign of King Belshatzar a vision ap-**
peared to me, I, Daniel, after that which appeared to me at
first, the vision described in the previous section, which also
depicts future kingdoms.
2 **I saw in the vision, and it was as I was seeing** myself in the
vision. **I was in the Shushan citadel,**[B] the administrative complex at the heart of the city of Shushan, **which is in the**
province of Elam; I saw in the vision, and I was beside a
channel of a river called **the Ulai.**[BD]

Karkheh River

3 **I lifted my eyes and I saw,**
and behold, there was one
ram standing before the
channel; it had horns, and
the horns were high and
one was higher than the
other, and the higher grew,
sprouted, **last.** Alternatively,
it started to sprout behind the lower horn.

Ram with horns

4 **I saw the ram,** with its great horns, **goring to the west, and to**
the north, and to the south, and no beasts could withstand
it, it felled them all, **and there was no savior from its hand; it**
did as it willed, and became great; the animal grew in size and
strength.
5 **I was looking,** reflecting on this scene, **and behold, a goat**
came from the west and
moved **over the surface of**
the entire earth, and it was
not touching the ground;
it did not walk but appeared
to float. **The goat had a con-**
spicuous horn between its
eyes.

Goat

6 **It,** the goat with the single
horn, **came to the horned**
ram that I saw standing before the channel, and it ran to it
with the fury of its power.
7 **I saw it reaching the ram, and it stormed against it,** it charged
in rage, **and struck the ram, and it shattered its two horns,**
and the ram had no strength to withstand it. It, the goat, **cast**
it, the ram, **to the ground and trampled it, and there was no**
savior for the ram from its hand.
8 **The goat became exceedingly great, and when it became**
powerful, the great horn on its forehead **was broken, and**
in its place, there were four conspicuous horns directed **to-**
ward the four winds of the heavens.
9 **From one of them, a horn emerged from smallness and ex-**
panded greatly, grew in strength more than the others; **it was**
turned **to the south, and to the east, and toward the magnifi-**
cent, splendid, and desirable **land,** the Land of Israel.
10 **It,** this horn, **expanded up to the host of the heavens,** to the
constellations, **and it threw some of the host and some of**
the stars to the ground and trampled them. It reached such
heights that it even overshadowed the stars.
11 **It grew great,** as the horn grew **up to the prince of the host;**
and the continual burnt **offering was removed from before**
him, the prince of the host, **and the place of His Sanctuary**
was cast down. The horn struck down the Temple.

DISCUSSION

8:2 | **I saw in the vision, and I was beside a channel of the Ulai:** The Sages note that prophecies that were received by prophets outside the Land of Israel, such as by Daniel here and below (10:4), as well as by Ezekiel (1:3), were generally given next to water, which is considered a place of purity (see *Mekhilta, Bo, Mesekhta dePiseḥa*).

סוֹפָא דִי־מִלְּתָא אֲנָה דָנִיֵּאל שַׂגִּיא ׀ רַעְיוֹנַי יְבַהֲלֻנַּנִי וְזִיוַי יִשְׁתַּנּוֹן עֲלַי וּמִלְּתָא
בְּלִבִּי נִטְרֵת׃
א בִּשְׁנַת שָׁלוֹשׁ לְמַלְכוּת בֵּלְאשַׁצַּר הַמֶּלֶךְ חָזוֹן נִרְאָה אֵלַי אֲנִי דָנִיֵּאל אַחֲרֵי
ב הַנִּרְאָה אֵלַי בַּתְּחִלָּה׃ וָאֶרְאֶה בֶּחָזוֹן וַיְהִי בִּרְאֹתִי וַאֲנִי בְּשׁוּשַׁן הַבִּירָה אֲשֶׁר
ג בְּעֵילָם הַמְּדִינָה וָאֶרְאֶה בֶּחָזוֹן וַאֲנִי הָיִיתִי עַל־אוּבַל אוּלָי׃ וָאֶשָּׂא עֵינַי וָאֶרְאֶה
וְהִנֵּה ׀ אַיִל אֶחָד עֹמֵד לִפְנֵי הָאֻבָל וְלוֹ קְרָנָיִם וְהַקְּרָנַיִם גְּבֹהוֹת וְהָאַחַת גְּבֹהָה
ד מִן־הַשֵּׁנִית וְהַגְּבֹהָה עֹלָה בָּאַחֲרֹנָה׃ רָאִיתִי אֶת־הָאַיִל מְנַגֵּחַ יָמָּה וְצָפוֹנָה וָנֶגְבָּה
ה וְכָל־חַיּוֹת לֹא־יַעַמְדוּ לְפָנָיו וְאֵין מַצִּיל מִיָּדוֹ וְעָשָׂה כִרְצֹנוֹ וְהִגְדִּיל׃ וַאֲנִי ׀ הָיִיתִי
מֵבִין וְהִנֵּה צְפִיר־הָעִזִּים בָּא מִן־הַמַּעֲרָב עַל־פְּנֵי כָל־הָאָרֶץ וְאֵין נוֹגֵעַ בָּאָרֶץ
ו וְהַצָּפִיר קֶרֶן חָזוּת בֵּין עֵינָיו׃ וַיָּבֹא עַד־הָאַיִל בַּעַל הַקְּרָנַיִם אֲשֶׁר רָאִיתִי עֹמֵד
ז לִפְנֵי הָאֻבָל וַיָּרָץ אֵלָיו בַּחֲמַת כֹּחוֹ׃ וּרְאִיתִיו מַגִּיעַ ׀ אֵצֶל הָאַיִל וַיִּתְמַרְמַר אֵלָיו
וַיַּךְ אֶת־הָאַיִל וַיְשַׁבֵּר אֶת־שְׁתֵּי קְרָנָיו וְלֹא־הָיָה כֹחַ בָּאַיִל לַעֲמֹד לְפָנָיו וַיַּשְׁלִיכֵהוּ
ח אַרְצָה וַיִּרְמְסֵהוּ וְלֹא־הָיָה מַצִּיל לָאַיִל מִיָּדוֹ׃ וּצְפִיר הָעִזִּים הִגְדִּיל עַד־מְאֹד
וּכְעָצְמוֹ נִשְׁבְּרָה הַקֶּרֶן הַגְּדוֹלָה וַתַּעֲלֶנָה חָזוּת אַרְבַּע תַּחְתֶּיהָ לְאַרְבַּע רוּחוֹת
ט הַשָּׁמָיִם׃ וּמִן־הָאַחַת מֵהֶם יָצָא קֶרֶן־אַחַת מִצְּעִירָה וַתִּגְדַּל־יֶתֶר אֶל־הַנֶּגֶב
י וְאֶל־הַמִּזְרָח וְאֶל־הַצֶּבִי׃ וַתִּגְדַּל עַד־צְבָא הַשָּׁמָיִם וַתַּפֵּל אַרְצָה מִן־הַצָּבָא
יא וּמִן־הַכּוֹכָבִים וַתִּרְמְסֵם׃ וְעַד שַׂר־הַצָּבָא הִגְדִּיל וּמִמֶּנּוּ הרים הַתָּמִיד וְהֻשְׁלַךְ הוּרַם

BACKGROUND

8:2 | **The Shushan citadel:** Shushan, the capital of the Elamite kingdom, is one of the oldest cities in the world. It was destroyed by the Assyrians between the years 645–640 BCE, and as a result, the Elamite kingdom was divided, and subsequently declined. Some twenty years after the death of Belshatzar, in 539 BCE, Darius the Great built his royal palace in the city and turned it into his capital (*The Histories* III:140).

A channel [*uval*] of the Ulai: Assyrian inscriptions from the palace of Ashurbanipal in Nineveh, with its relief carvings depicting the Battle of Til-Tuba in 653 BCE, in which Ashurbanipal defeated the Elamites, refer to a river by the name of Ulai. This is apparently the river known today as Karkheh, which flows west of Shushan. Pliny the Elder, in the first century BCE, mentions a river with a similar name, Eulaeus, which was near the city of Shushan. However, the precise identification of the river remains uncertain, as the routes of the tributaries of rivers that flowed east and west of the city have changed, and some have been given new names.

Uval refers to a tributary or a large, wide water channel that once linked the tributaries of rivers. This channel passed north-east of Shushan, and its traces can be seen even today.

12 **A host,** or war, or a fixed period of time, **was given for** the nullification of **the continual** burnt **offering, for,** due to, **transgression; it,** the horn, **cast** down and trampled **truth to the ground, and it acted and succeeded.** The horn's successes continued.

13 **Then I heard one of the holy,** an angel, **speaking, and** beforehand **another holy one** had **said to that anonymous one,** the angel **who was speaking: Until when will the vision of the continual** burnt **offering and the desolating transgression be;** how long will the vision last? Alternatively, until when will there be idolatry;[61] And how much time will be granted for **giving the Sanctuary and the host** of heaven **over for trampling?**

14 The answer is as cryptic as the vision itself: **He,** that holy one, **said to me: Until evening-morning two thousand three hundred;** this state of affairs is supposed to continue for 2,300 units of a specific time period, perhaps days, **and** then **the Sanctuary will be vindicated,** it will be recognized that the Temple is victorious and righteous. It will no longer be broken and shattered, but will triumph and be rebuilt. These are the matters that Daniel saw and heard.

15 **It was when I, Daniel, saw the vision, that I requested understanding; behold, there was** a figure who had **the appearance of a man standing before me,** but who was actually an angel.

16 **I heard the voice of a man by** the thickets of **the** River **Ulai, and he called** to the angel that looked like a man, **and said: Gavriel, explain the vision to this one.** The voice Daniel heard instructed the angel to explain his vision to him.

17 **He,** the angel, **came to where I was standing, and when he came, I was terrified and fell upon my face,** due to the force of the angelic revelation. **He said to me: Understand, son of man, for the vision is for the end time** of history,[62] or for a very late period.[63]

18 **As he was speaking with me, I fell asleep, my face to the ground.** Even though Daniel did not hear the voice of God directly, his mere proximity to the angel so terrified him that he fell and fainted. **And he touched me** and thereby gave me strength, **and** once again **stood me up where I was standing.**

19 **He said: Behold, I will make known to you what will be at the end of the fury, for there is an appointed time for the end;** at the designated time, the events will be revealed before everyone.

20 He elaborates: **The ram that you saw with the horns: The kings of Media and Persia,** as the Persian Empire was comprised of two nations. First the king of Media reigned, followed by the king of Persia, the greater king, who was represented by the larger animal.

21 **The goat is the king of Yavan,** Greece, **and the great horn that is between his eyes is the first king**[B] who will reign in Greece.

Alexander the Great fighting Darius III, detail from the Alexander Mosaic, Pompeii, second century BCE

22 And as for the meaning of **the broken one, and the four** horns **that arose in its place: Four kingdoms will arise,** develop, **from the nation,** Greece, **but** this will **not** be **from its power.** They will not be built by the first king, but will arise and be established of their own accord.

23 **At the end of their kingdom, when the transgressors are finished, there will arise a brazen king, who understands subtleties.**[B] This intelligent king is represented by the small horn that will sprout and grow between the eyes.

Coin of Antiochus Epiphanes, Syria, 175–164 BCE

24 **His power will increase mightily, but** this will **not** be **by his own power;**[64] and **he will destroy wondrously,** in astonishing ways, **and will succeed and accomplish, and he will destroy the mighty and** will mainly harass **the people of the holy,** Israel.

25 It will be **by his cunning,** his stratagems, that this king will establish himself, not by any special military prowess, and **deceit will succeed in his hand,** as he will cheat those whom he cannot defeat in battle; **he will grow arrogant, and in tranquility,** when others are complacent and are not paying attention, **he will destroy many; he will rise** to fight **against the prince of princes,** the "prince of the host" in the dream; **but** ultimately **he will be broken, by no one's hand**[B] striking him. When the time comes, he will stumble by himself, without external force.

26 **The vision of the evening and the morning that was said is true,** even though the meaning of these dates is unclear to you; **and you, suppress,** conceal, **the vision, for it** will not come to pass immediately, as it **relates to many days** to come, since the kingdom of Media and Persia lasted for centuries after Daniel's time.

27 **I, Daniel, was weakened** after the dream, **and was sick for days; I rose,** I strengthened myself, **and** again **performed the king's business, and I was astonished at the vision, and no one understood** its details. The prophecy referred to the very distant future, so during Daniel's time, it remained wrapped in mystery.

יב מְכוֹן מִקְדָּשׁוֹ׃ וְצָבָא תִּנָּתֵן עַל־הַתָּמִיד בְּפָשַׁע וְתַשְׁלֵךְ אֱמֶת אַרְצָה וְעָשְׂתָה
יג וְהִצְלִיחָה׃ וָאֶשְׁמְעָה אֶחָד־קָדוֹשׁ מְדַבֵּר וַיֹּאמֶר אֶחָד קָדוֹשׁ לַפַּלְמוֹנִי הַמְדַבֵּר
יד עַד־מָתַי הֶחָזוֹן הַתָּמִיד וְהַפֶּשַׁע שֹׁמֵם תֵּת וְקֹדֶשׁ וְצָבָא מִרְמָס׃ וַיֹּאמֶר אֵלַי
טו עַד עֶרֶב בֹּקֶר אַלְפַּיִם וּשְׁלֹשׁ מֵאוֹת וְנִצְדַּק קֹדֶשׁ׃ וַיְהִי בִּרְאֹתִי אֲנִי דָנִיֵּאל אֶת־
טז הֶחָזוֹן וָאֲבַקְשָׁה בִינָה וְהִנֵּה עֹמֵד לְנֶגְדִּי כְּמַרְאֵה־גָבֶר׃ וָאֶשְׁמַע קוֹל־אָדָם בֵּין
יז אוּלָי וַיִּקְרָא וַיֹּאמַר גַּבְרִיאֵל הָבֵן לְהַלָּז אֶת־הַמַּרְאֶה׃ וַיָּבֹא אֵצֶל עָמְדִי וּבְבֹאוֹ
יח נִבְעַתִּי וָאֶפְּלָה עַל־פָּנָי וַיֹּאמֶר אֵלַי הָבֵן בֶּן־אָדָם כִּי לְעֶת־קֵץ הֶחָזוֹן׃ וּבְדַבְּרוֹ
יט עִמִּי נִרְדַּמְתִּי עַל־פָּנַי אָרְצָה וַיִּגַּע־בִּי וַיַּעֲמִידֵנִי עַל־עָמְדִי׃ וַיֹּאמֶר הִנְנִי מוֹדִיעֲךָ
כ אֵת אֲשֶׁר־יִהְיֶה בְּאַחֲרִית הַזָּעַם כִּי לְמוֹעֵד קֵץ׃ הָאַיִל אֲשֶׁר־רָאִיתָ בַּעַל הַקְּרָנָיִם
כא מַלְכֵי מָדַי וּפָרָס׃ וְהַצָּפִיר הַשָּׂעִיר מֶלֶךְ יָוָן וְהַקֶּרֶן הַגְּדוֹלָה אֲשֶׁר בֵּין־עֵינָיו הוּא
כב הַמֶּלֶךְ הָרִאשׁוֹן׃ וְהַנִּשְׁבֶּרֶת וַתַּעֲמֹדְנָה אַרְבַּע תַּחְתֶּיהָ אַרְבַּע מַלְכֻיוֹת מִגּוֹי
כג יַעֲמֹדְנָה וְלֹא בְכֹחוֹ׃ וּבְאַחֲרִית מַלְכוּתָם כְּהָתֵם הַפֹּשְׁעִים יַעֲמֹד מֶלֶךְ עַז־פָּנִים
כד וּמֵבִין חִידוֹת׃ וְעָצַם כֹּחוֹ וְלֹא בְכֹחוֹ וְנִפְלָאוֹת יַשְׁחִית וְהִצְלִיחַ וְעָשָׂה וְהִשְׁחִית
כה עֲצוּמִים וְעַם־קְדֹשִׁים׃ וְעַל־שִׂכְלוֹ וְהִצְלִיחַ מִרְמָה בְּיָדוֹ וּבִלְבָבוֹ יַגְדִּיל וּבְשַׁלְוָה
כו יַשְׁחִית רַבִּים וְעַל שַׂר־שָׂרִים יַעֲמֹד וּבְאֶפֶס יָד יִשָּׁבֵר׃ וּמַרְאֵה הָעֶרֶב וְהַבֹּקֶר
כז אֲשֶׁר נֶאֱמַר אֱמֶת הוּא וְאַתָּה סְתֹם הֶחָזוֹן כִּי לְיָמִים רַבִּים׃ וַאֲנִי דָנִיֵּאל נִהְיֵיתִי

BACKGROUND

8:21 | **The goat is the king of Yavan, and the great horn that is between his eyes is the first king:** Based on the context, this would seem to be referring to Alexander the Great, who conquered all kingdoms, including the Persian Empire, which he crushed almost effortlessly. However, his dominion did not last long and, indeed, Alexander's realm was divided after his death into four kingdoms (see, e.g., Rashi).

8:23 | **There will arise a brazen king, who understands subtleties:** Some explain that this last king is Antiochus IV, known as Epiphanes, the Seleucid king who reigned between the years 175–164 BCE. The image of the small horn that rises and overcomes the host of heaven has been interpreted to refer to Antiochus IV because he rose to power by gaining the upper hand in the struggle for the throne, and killed many Jews, until he was defeated by the Hasmoneans (see verses 9–11; Rashi and Malbim, verse 9). Antiochus IV Epiphanes was more of a politician than a man of war. With his political acumen he sought to unify the kingdom and build it afresh (see Rashi; Ibn Ezra).

8:25 | **But he will be broken, by no one's hand:** Following the decisive defeat of Antiochus III in the Battle of Magnesia, the kingdom declined and succumbed to Rome, as expressed in the Treaty of Apamea and its aftermath. Antiochus IV was thus limited in his ability to undertake any independent military campaign. Consequently, those events have been seen as the fulfillment of this prophecy of Daniel, that he was "broken, by no one's hand." Antiochus IV occupied himself mainly with the internal establishment of his reign and with diverse diplomatic efforts, apart from a war against the Ptolemaic kingdom of Egypt in 170 BCE, from which he withdrew under Roman pressure, and with his attempts to suppress the revolts of the Hasmoneans and other rebellions in the east of his kingdom.

Daniel's Supplication and Gavriel's Response regarding the End of the Destruction of the Temple

DANIEL 9:1–27

A year after the previous vision, the content of which had already begun to materialize with the fall of the kingdom of Babylon to Media and Persia, Daniel seeks to know the end of the vision. In the earlier vision, the angel Gavriel had explained to Daniel the meaning of what he had seen, and here he informs him of further details. In fact, almost all of the visions until the end of the book include conversations with Gavriel.[65]

9 1 **In the first year of Darius son of Ahashverosh, of Median**
descent, Darius I, **who was crowned king over the king-**
dom of the Chaldeans, Babylon, after his victory over the
Babylonians (see 5:30, 6:1);
2 **in the first year of his reign, I, Daniel, examined the books**[D]
of calculations: **The number of the years according to the**
word of the Lord that was with Jeremiah the prophet to
complete the term of the desolations of Jerusalem was sev-
enty years. Daniel read Jeremiah's prophecy that Jerusalem
would remain destroyed for seventy years, after which Israel
would be redeemed, but this did not seem to have occurred.
The kingdom of Babylon no longer ruled over the Land of
Israel, but the redemption had not arrived.[66]
3 **I directed my attention,** my thoughts, **to the Lord God, to**
request with prayer and supplications, with fasting, sack-
cloth, and ashes.
4 **I prayed to the Lord my God, and I confessed and said,** in
my prayer and confession: **Please O Lord, the great and awe-**
some God, who maintains the covenant and kindness for
those who love Him and who observe His commandments.
5 Daniel follows his opening words of praise with the confession:
We have sinned, have performed iniquity, been wicked, re-
belled, and strayed[67] **from Your commandments and from**
Your ordinances.
6 **We did not heed Your servants the prophets, who spoke in**
Your name to our kings, our princes, and our fathers, and to
all the people of the land. You warned us through Your prophets against sinning, but we did not listen.
7 **With You, O Lord, is the righteousness, and with us the**
shame, as it is this day, as we can currently see;[68] **with the men**
of Judah and with the inhabitants of Jerusalem, and with all
Israel, near and far, who are scattered **in all the lands where**
You have driven them. Apart from the tribe of Judah, all of
Israel had been exiled many years earlier by the Assyrians, and
apparently there were other known communities of exiles in
various places,[69] **because of the trespass they have commit-**
ted against You; due to their treacherous sins toward You.
8 **O Lord, with us is the shame, with our kings, with our**
princes, and with our fathers, who have sinned against You.
All of us, from the highest levels of leadership to the lowliest
commoner, should be ashamed of ourselves.
9 **With the Lord our God is mercy and forgiveness, as we have**
rebelled against Him, and therefore all we can do is request
His mercy and forgiveness;
10 **and we did not heed the voice of the Lord our God, to**
follow His laws that He put before us by means of His ser-
vants, the prophets. We received the Torah, and we also heard
the prophets' words of reproof and instruction.
11 **All Israel have violated Your Torah, straying** from the upright path **in not heeding Your voice; and you poured out**
upon us the curse and the oath that is written in the Torah
of Moses servant of God, for we have sinned against Him.
Since we have abandoned God, all the curses that were written
in sections of the Torah said upon our entrance into the covenant with God have come to pass.[70]
12 **He fulfilled His word that He had spoken against us, and**
against our rulers who ruled us, to bring upon us great
harm that had not been done under the entire heavens as
had been done to Jerusalem.[B]

DISCUSSION

9:2 | **I, Daniel, examined the books:** The Sages explain that Daniel erred in his calculation because he calculated the start of the seventy years from when he was taken captive. At that time, which was during the rule of Yehoyakim, he was a young boy, and at this point he would have been close to eighty years old, and he had yet to see any signs of the redemption. He probably should have calculated seventy years from the destruction of Jerusalem, which occurred many years later, during the time of Tzidkiya (see Rashi; Ibn Ezra; *Megilla* 12a). Another related ambiguity involves the timing of Cyrus' announcement (see Ezra 1:1) permitting the Jews to rebuild the Temple. It would seem that there was some overlap between the rule of Darius and that of Cyrus. Darius reigned first; Cyrus, who may have been the greater warrior during their joint conquest of the Babylonian kingdom, was the younger of the two. Some even say that Cyrus was Darius' son-in-law. If so, perhaps the time of the announcement was only after Cyrus himself ascended to power, which had not yet occurred.

וְנֶחֱלֵיתִי יָמִים וָאָקוּם וָאֶעֱשֶׂה אֶת־מְלֶאכֶת הַמֶּלֶךְ וָאֶשְׁתּוֹמֵם עַל־הַמַּרְאֶה
וְאֵין מֵבִין׃
א בִּשְׁנַת אַחַת לְדָרְיָוֶשׁ בֶּן־אֲחַשְׁוֵרוֹשׁ מִזֶּרַע מָדָי אֲשֶׁר הָמְלַךְ עַל מַלְכוּת
ב כַּשְׂדִּים׃ בִּשְׁנַת אַחַת לְמָלְכוֹ אֲנִי דָּנִיֵּאל בִּינֹתִי בַּסְּפָרִים מִסְפַּר הַשָּׁנִים אֲשֶׁר
הָיָה דְבַר־יְהוָה אֶל־יִרְמְיָה הַנָּבִיא לְמַלֹּאות לְחָרְבוֹת יְרוּשָׁלִַם שִׁבְעִים שָׁנָה׃
ג וָאֶתְּנָה אֶת־פָּנַי אֶל־אֲדֹנָי הָאֱלֹהִים לְבַקֵּשׁ תְּפִלָּה וְתַחֲנוּנִים בְּצוֹם וְשַׂק וָאֵפֶר׃
ד וָאֶתְפַּלְלָה לַיהוָה אֱלֹהַי וָאֶתְוַדֶּה וָאֹמְרָה אָנָּא אֲדֹנָי הָאֵל הַגָּדוֹל וְהַנּוֹרָא שֹׁמֵר ו
ה הַבְּרִית וְהַחֶסֶד לְאֹהֲבָיו וּלְשֹׁמְרֵי מִצְוֹתָיו׃ חָטָאנוּ וְעָוִינוּ והרשענו וּמָרָדְנוּ וְסוֹר הִרְשַׁעְנוּ
ו מִמִּצְוֹתֶךָ וּמִמִּשְׁפָּטֶיךָ׃ וְלֹא שָׁמַעְנוּ אֶל־עֲבָדֶיךָ הַנְּבִיאִים אֲשֶׁר דִּבְּרוּ בְּשִׁמְךָ
ז אֶל־מְלָכֵינוּ שָׂרֵינוּ וַאֲבֹתֵינוּ וְאֶל כָּל־עַם הָאָרֶץ׃ לְךָ אֲדֹנָי הַצְּדָקָה וְלָנוּ בֹּשֶׁת
הַפָּנִים כַּיּוֹם הַזֶּה לְאִישׁ יְהוּדָה וּלְיוֹשְׁבֵי יְרוּשָׁלִַם וּלְכָל־יִשְׂרָאֵל הַקְּרֹבִים וְהָרְחֹקִים
ח בְּכָל־הָאֲרָצוֹת אֲשֶׁר הִדַּחְתָּם שָׁם בְּמַעֲלָם אֲשֶׁר מָעֲלוּ־בָךְ׃ יְהוָה לָנוּ בֹּשֶׁת
ט הַפָּנִים לִמְלָכֵינוּ לְשָׂרֵינוּ וְלַאֲבֹתֵינוּ אֲשֶׁר חָטָאנוּ לָךְ׃ לַאדֹנָי אֱלֹהֵינוּ הָרַחֲמִים
י וְהַסְּלִחוֹת כִּי מָרַדְנוּ בּוֹ׃ וְלֹא שָׁמַעְנוּ בְּקוֹל יְהוָה אֱלֹהֵינוּ לָלֶכֶת בְּתוֹרֹתָיו אֲשֶׁר
יא נָתַן לְפָנֵינוּ בְּיַד עֲבָדָיו הַנְּבִיאִים׃ וְכָל־יִשְׂרָאֵל עָבְרוּ אֶת־תּוֹרָתֶךָ וְסוֹר לְבִלְתִּי
שְׁמוֹעַ בְּקֹלֶךָ וַתִּתַּךְ עָלֵינוּ הָאָלָה וְהַשְּׁבֻעָה אֲשֶׁר כְּתוּבָה בְּתוֹרַת מֹשֶׁה עֶבֶד־
יב הָאֱלֹהִים כִּי חָטָאנוּ לוֹ׃ וַיָּקֶם אֶת־דבריו ׀ אֲשֶׁר־דִּבֶּר עָלֵינוּ וְעַל־שֹׁפְטֵינוּ אֲשֶׁר דְּבָרוֹ
שְׁפָטוּנוּ לְהָבִיא עָלֵינוּ רָעָה גְדֹלָה אֲשֶׁר לֹא־נֶעֶשְׂתָה תַּחַת כָּל־הַשָּׁמַיִם כַּאֲשֶׁר

BACKGROUND

9:12 | **Great harm that had not been done under the entire heavens as had been done to Jerusalem:** The failure of Nebuchadnezzar's war campaign against Egypt at the start of the sixth century BCE and the rise of Egyptian power caused instability in the Land of Israel in general, and Judah in particular. As a result, the Babylonians changed their policy and established their control through direct rule over areas of the land, rather than through the medium of vassal kingdoms. The Babylonians acted mercilessly in their efforts to neutralize the center of the Judean revolt by wiping out the Davidic dynasty, exiling the elites, and destroying Jerusalem in a focused, systematic manner. Nevertheless, they left the rural agricultural system intact, so that it would provide food and taxes for the besieging troops. The extreme measures of the Babylonians are evident in the scale of the devastation, the destruction of the Temple and the king's palace, the great fire, the smashing of the city walls, and the transfer of the central government to Mitzpa (see II Kings 25). It is likewise clear from the books of Ezra and Nehemiah that at the start of the Second Temple period the city of Jerusalem was essentially still in ruins. The walls were breached, the houses derelict, and the city as a whole deserted and in need of fundamental reconstruction (see Ezra 4; Nehemiah 1:2–3, 7:4).

13 **As it is written in the Torah of Moses, all this harm came upon us and we did not implore the Lord our God, to repent of our iniquities, and to become wise in Your truth,** to learn and reflect on Your truth. As predicted in the sections in the Torah that speak of retribution, minor misfortunes occurred, but we paid no attention; greater disasters befell us and still we ignored them. Therefore, we are deserving of punishment.[71]

14 **The Lord was intent on harm,** punishing us at the appropriate time, **and He brought it upon us, as the Lord our God is righteous in all His actions that He has done, and** we can have no complaints, as He warned us ahead of time, and **we did not heed His voice.**

15 **Now, O Lord our God, who took Your people from the land of Egypt with a mighty hand, and you have made for Yourself a name,** the fame of Your greatness and deeds has spread through the world, **as it is** known **this day;**[72] we confess before You: **We have sinned,** and **we have acted wickedly.**

16 **O Lord, with all Your righteousness, please may Your anger and Your fury** be diminished and **turn from Your city Jerusalem, Your sacred mountain;** after You have stricken us, please forgive us, **for with our sins, and the iniquities of our fathers, Jerusalem and Your people are in disgrace to all those around us.** It is a disgrace that Israel has become the archetype of a nation without a land and a safe haven.

17 **Our God, heed now the prayer of Your servant and his supplications, and shine Your face upon Your Sanctuary that is desolate, for the Lord's sake.** Act for Your sake; that is all I can hope to ask.

18 **Incline Your ear, My God, and hear, open Your eyes, and see our desolations, and the city upon which Your name is called;** observe the terrible state of the city that was once Your city and in which Your Temple stood. **For it is not based on our righteousness that we lay,** spread out, **our supplications before You,** as we do not claim to be righteous and worthy, **but** rather, it is based **on Your great mercy.** We appeal to Your boundless mercy.

19 **O Lord, hear, O Lord, forgive, O Lord, listen and act,** fulfill our request, and **do not delay;** all this do **for Your sake, my God, because Your name is called upon Your city and Your people.** Since Your name is upon us, and Jerusalem is Your city, we ask for forgiveness and pardon in order to prevent a desecration of Your name.

20 **I was still speaking, and praying, and confessing my sin and the sin of my people Israel,**[D] **and laying my supplication before the Lord my God on behalf of the holy mountain of my God,**

21 **and I was still speaking in prayer, and the man Gavriel,** the angel **whom I had seen** in the form of a man **in the previous vision, was flying swiftly; he reached**[73] **me at the time of the** daily **evening offering** in the Temple, toward the end of the day, when the second daily offering and the meal offering and libations that accompanied it were offered.[74] It seems that Daniel fasted and prayed all day, until the angel visited him at the end of the day.[75]

22 **He explained, and spoke with me, and said: Daniel, I have now come out to teach you understanding.**

23 Already **at the beginning of your supplications the word came out,** it was decreed that you deserve a response, **and I have come to relate it,** to tell you what you wish to know, **as you are splendid,**[D] a dear and precious man; **comprehend the word,** focus your mind on the matter,[76] **and understand** the meaning of **the vision.**

24 **Seventy periods of seven,** seven units of time in exile, which might be seven years or seventy years, **are decreed upon your people and upon your holy city.** The purpose of the lengthy exile and the extended suffering until that time is **to eliminate the transgression, to expiate sins, to atone for iniquity, to bring everlasting righteousness,** an indication that this vision is not referring to the near future but to the distant future, **to**

DISCUSSION

9:20 | **My sin and the sin of my people Israel:** Daniel did not pray here for his own personal redemption. As an individual, he had already achieved the highest spiritual level possible, and he was certainly not concerned about himself. Rather, he was praying on behalf of the entire Jewish people and perceived himself as a representative of the nation. It is not coincidence that portions of this prayer of Daniel's have been incorporated into the permanent daily prayer service of the Jewish people, as well as into the special prayer services conducted during times of repentance and on fast days. Although this confession was recited by an individual, nevertheless, it laid the foundation for the manner in which the Jewish people as a whole have confessed their sins throughout history.

9:23 | **As you are splendid:** Daniel is referred to a number of times in the book as being splendid, as he is described as being of superior character in every possible way. In some parts of the book, he himself is the speaker, and it is certainly possible that he also authored the portions of the book that refer to him in third person and in an objective manner. Daniel was a wise, successful, God-fearing person. He was willing to give up his life to sanctify God's name, he was scrupulous in his proper performance of the commandments, and he constantly turned to God in prayer. He also possessed other superior traits, both in spirit as well as physically. Therefore, it is logical that the individual Daniel, who is mentioned in the book of Ezekiel as one of the great righteous individuals in the world at that time, refers to the Daniel of this book (see Ezekiel 14:14, and commentary ad loc.).

יג נֶעֶשְׂתָ֖ה בִּירוּשָׁלִָֽם׃ כַּאֲשֶׁ֤ר כָּתוּב֙ בְּתוֹרַ֣ת מֹשֶׁ֔ה אֵ֛ת כָּל־הָרָעָ֥ה הַזֹּ֖את בָּ֣אָה
עָלֵ֑ינוּ וְלֹֽא־חִלִּ֜ינוּ אֶת־פְּנֵ֣י ׀ יְהוָ֣ה אֱלֹהֵ֗ינוּ לָשׁוּב֙ מֵעֲוֺנֵ֔נוּ וּלְהַשְׂכִּ֖יל בַּאֲמִתֶּֽךָ׃
יד וַיִּשְׁקֹ֤ד יְהוָה֙ עַל־הָ֣רָעָ֔ה וַיְבִיאֶ֖הָ עָלֵ֑ינוּ כִּֽי־צַדִּ֞יק יְהוָ֣ה אֱלֹהֵ֗ינוּ עַל־כָּל־מַעֲשָׂיו֙
טו אֲשֶׁ֣ר עָשָׂ֔ה וְלֹ֥א שָׁמַ֖עְנוּ בְּקֹלֽוֹ׃ וְעַתָּ֣ה ׀ אֲדֹנָ֣י אֱלֹהֵ֗ינוּ אֲשֶׁר֩ הוֹצֵ֨אתָ אֶֽת־עַמְּךָ֜
טז מֵאֶ֤רֶץ מִצְרַ֙יִם֙ בְּיָ֣ד חֲזָקָ֔ה וַתַּֽעַשׂ־לְךָ֥ שֵׁ֖ם כַּיּ֣וֹם הַזֶּ֑ה חָטָ֖אנוּ רָשָֽׁעְנוּ׃ אֲדֹנָ֗י כְּכָל־
צִדְקֹתֶ֙ךָ֙ יָשָׁב־נָ֤א אַפְּךָ֙ וַחֲמָ֣תְךָ֔ מֵעִירְךָ֥ יְרוּשָׁלִַ֖ם הַר־קָדְשֶׁ֑ךָ כִּ֤י בַחֲטָאֵ֙ינוּ֙ וּבַעֲוֺנ֣וֹת
יז אֲבֹתֵ֔ינוּ יְרוּשָׁלִַ֧ם וְעַמְּךָ֛ לְחֶרְפָּ֖ה לְכָל־סְבִיבֹתֵֽינוּ׃ וְעַתָּ֣ה ׀ שְׁמַ֣ע אֱלֹהֵ֗ינוּ אֶל־תְּפִלַּ֤ת
יח עַבְדְּךָ֙ וְאֶל־תַּ֣חֲנוּנָ֔יו וְהָאֵ֣ר פָּנֶ֔יךָ עַל־מִקְדָּשְׁךָ֖ הַשָּׁמֵ֑ם לְמַ֖עַן אֲדֹנָֽי׃ הַטֵּ֨ה אֱלֹהַ֥י ׀
אָזְנְךָ֮ וּֽשֲׁמָע֒ פקחה עֵינֶ֗יךָ וּרְאֵה֙ שֹֽׁמְמֹתֵ֔ינוּ וְהָעִ֕יר אֲשֶׁר־נִקְרָ֥א שִׁמְךָ֖ עָלֶ֑יהָ כִּ֣י ׀ פְּקַ֣ח
יט לֹ֣א עַל־צִדְקֹתֵ֗ינוּ אֲנַ֨חְנוּ מַפִּילִ֤ים תַּחֲנוּנֵ֙ינוּ֙ לְפָנֶ֔יךָ כִּ֖י עַל־רַחֲמֶ֥יךָ הָרַבִּֽים׃ אֲדֹנָ֤י ׀
שְׁמָ֙עָה֙ אֲדֹנָ֣י ׀ סְלָ֔חָה אֲדֹנָ֛י הַקְשִׁ֥יבָה וַעֲשֵׂ֖ה אַל־תְּאַחַ֑ר לְמַֽעַנְךָ֣ אֱלֹהַ֔י כִּֽי־שִׁמְךָ֣
כ נִקְרָ֔א עַל־עִירְךָ֖ וְעַל־עַמֶּֽךָ׃ וְע֨וֹד אֲנִ֤י מְדַבֵּר֙ וּמִתְפַּלֵּ֔ל וּמִתְוַדֶּה֙ חַטָּאתִ֔י וְחַטַּ֖את
כא עַמִּ֣י יִשְׂרָאֵ֑ל וּמַפִּ֣יל תְּחִנָּתִ֗י לִפְנֵי֙ יְהוָ֣ה אֱלֹהַ֔י עַ֖ל הַר־קֹ֥דֶשׁ אֱלֹהָֽי׃ וְע֛וֹד אֲנִ֥י
מְדַבֵּ֖ר בַּתְּפִלָּ֑ה וְהָאִ֣ישׁ גַּבְרִיאֵ֡ל אֲשֶׁר֩ רָאִ֨יתִי בֶחָז֤וֹן בַּתְּחִלָּה֙ מֻעָ֣ף בִּיעָ֔ף נֹגֵ֣עַ אֵלַ֔י
כב כְּעֵ֖ת מִנְחַת־עָֽרֶב׃ וַיָּ֖בֶן וַיְדַבֵּ֣ר עִמִּ֑י וַיֹּאמַ֕ר דָּֽנִיֵּ֕אל עַתָּ֣ה יָצָ֔אתִי לְהַשְׂכִּילְךָ֖ בִינָֽה׃
כג בִּתְחִלַּ֨ת תַּחֲנוּנֶ֜יךָ יָצָ֣א דָבָ֗ר וַאֲנִי֙ בָּ֣אתִי לְהַגִּ֔יד כִּ֥י חֲמוּד֖וֹת אָ֑תָּה וּבִין֙ בַּדָּבָ֔ר
כד וְהָבֵ֖ן בַּמַּרְאֶֽה׃ שָׁבֻעִ֨ים שִׁבְעִ֜ים נֶחְתַּ֥ךְ עַֽל־עַמְּךָ֣ ׀ וְעַל־עִ֣יר קָדְשֶׁ֗ךָ לְכַלֵּ֨א הַפֶּ֜שַׁע
ולחתם חטאות וּלְכַפֵּ֣ר עָוֺ֔ן וּלְהָבִ֖יא צֶ֣דֶק עֹֽלָמִ֑ים וְלַחְתֹּם֙ חָז֣וֹן וְנָבִ֔יא וְלִמְשֹׁ֖חַ וּלְהָתֵ֣ם חַטָּ֔את

conclude vision and prophecy, and to anoint, raise up and
crown, **sacred sacrament,** the holy Temple, which will return
in all its glory.[77] When this period of time is concluded, the
kingdom will be rebuilt once again. It is possible that the "seventy weeks" is a reference to the Second Temple period rather
than the period of exile.[78]
25 **You should know and understand, from the issuing of the
word** from God **about restoring and rebuilding Jerusalem
until the anointing of a ruler** of Jerusalem; during these seventy "weeks," there will be periods of ups and downs, and these
will be in seven periods of seven, in a time that lasts for **sixty-
two periods of seven,** and then **it will be rebuilt, a plaza and
a moat;** the streets of the city and its defenses will be rebuilt,
and this will occur **in times of distress.**
26 **After the sixty-two periods, the anointed one will be eliminated, and will be no more,**[79] or will no longer have a place.
**The ruling people who will come will destroy the city and
the Sanctuary; its end,** the end that this people will bring,
will be quick and intense; **and by the end of the** final **war, it
will be devastated to desolation,** Jerusalem will be ruined and
deserted.[80]
27 **He will promote a covenant,** or the covenant will be strengthened[81] **with the multitudes for one period of seven;** there
will be a period of widespread unity; and **half of the period
of seven he will abolish the offering and the meal offering,
and upon it,** upon the place of the offerings, **the wing of a
detestable thing,** the winged idol, **that causes desolation,**[D]
the destructive force, as the idol will stand in the place of the
sacrifice and offering; and that situation will last **until elimination and devastation,** all the destruction and the expurgation,
will be poured out on the desolation, or upon the devastated
place. Daniel does not receive words of comfort here, nor even
a clear answer to his question concerning Jeremiah's prophecy. Perhaps due to his greatness he is allowed a glimpse of
the broader picture, and therefore the angel Gavriel explains
to him that the end will arrive only after a period that will last
hundreds, if not thousands of years. In the future there will be
a great war, leaving desolation and destruction in its wake, as
is recorded in a number of other places in the Bible as well.[82]
There might be some betrayers, while others will remain faithful, but there is hope for the end of the process, as will be stated
below.

The Clashes between the Kings

DANIEL 10:1–11:39

The sections in this portion of the book do not relate a consecutive series of events. Here, for example, the narrative leaps forward to a vision that Daniel saw many years after the previous one. Likely the last vision Daniel experienced, it begins with current affairs before moving on to the distant future. There have been attempts to associate this prophecy with specific periods and particular wars in history. Although these efforts do clarify some of the details of the vision, other aspects remain obscure.

10 1 **In the third year of Cyrus king of Persia a matter was revealed to Daniel, whose name was called Beltshatzar** (see
1:7), **the truth of the matter and all the details;** the vision itself and its fulfillment in all its details were revealed to Daniel.
He understood the matter and had understanding given to
him **of the vision.**[83]
2 From this point, Daniel narrates the events in the first person.
In those days, I, Daniel was mourning again for the destruction of the Temple and its aftermaths, **for three weeks of
days.**[84]
3 I did not mourn or fast completely; however, **I ate no tasty,**
good-quality **bread,** but only plain, cheap bread; this is reminiscent of the dietary limitations imposed upon the prophet
Ezekiel,[85] **and meat and wine did not enter my mouth. I did
not anoint myself,** my body with oil, **until the completion of
three weeks of days.** For three weeks I lived in the simplest
fashion, without delicacies or pleasure.
4 **On the twenty-fourth day
of the first month, I was
alongside the great river,
the Tigris,** not far from the
city of Babylon;
5 **I lifted my eyes and I saw,
and behold a man dressed
in linen, and his loins were girded with** belts of choice **gold
of Ufaz.**[B]

"The great river, the Tigris"

DISCUSSION

9:27 | **And upon it, the wing of a detestable thing that causes desolation:** The expression "a detestable thing that causes desolation" also appears in Maccabees vol. I, but its meaning is unclear. Some scholars claim that this is referring to an image of Zeus, while others contend that it is the *bimus*, or platform, which was a kind of small stone idolatrous altar with a base, which was placed upon the large altar in the Temple (see *Avoda Zara* 47b). Yet others maintain that this detestable thing was an idol, or a pig. Many commentaries explain this verse as a reference to events that occurred during the time of the Hasmoneans or the time of the destruction of the Second Temple. The wing of a detestable thing was the section of the Temple where they built idols at that time (see Rashi; *Metzudat David*; *Ta'anit* 28b; *Yoma* 54a; *Pesikta deRav Kahana* 13:10).

כה קֹדֶשׁ קָדָשִׁים׃ וְתֵדַע וְתַשְׂכֵּל מִן־מֹצָא דָבָר לְהָשִׁיב וְלִבְנוֹת יְרוּשָׁלִַם עַד־מָשִׁיחַ
נָגִיד שָׁבֻעִים שִׁבְעָה וְשָׁבֻעִים שִׁשִּׁים וּשְׁנַיִם תָּשׁוּב וְנִבְנְתָה רְחוֹב וְחָרוּץ וּבְצוֹק
כו הָעִתִּים׃ וְאַחֲרֵי הַשָּׁבֻעִים שִׁשִּׁים וּשְׁנַיִם יִכָּרֵת מָשִׁיחַ וְאֵין לוֹ וְהָעִיר וְהַקֹּדֶשׁ
כז יַשְׁחִית עַם נָגִיד הַבָּא וְקִצּוֹ בַשֶּׁטֶף וְעַד קֵץ מִלְחָמָה נֶחֱרֶצֶת שֹׁמֵמוֹת׃ וְהִגְבִּיר
בְּרִית לָרַבִּים שָׁבוּעַ אֶחָד וַחֲצִי הַשָּׁבוּעַ יַשְׁבִּית ׀ זֶבַח וּמִנְחָה וְעַל כְּנַף שִׁקּוּצִים
מְשֹׁמֵם וְעַד־כָּלָה וְנֶחֱרָצָה תִּתַּךְ עַל־שֹׁמֵם׃

י א בִּשְׁנַת שָׁלוֹשׁ לְכוֹרֶשׁ מֶלֶךְ פָּרַס דָּבָר נִגְלָה לְדָנִיֵּאל אֲשֶׁר־נִקְרָא שְׁמוֹ בֵּלְטְשַׁאצַּר
ב וֶאֱמֶת הַדָּבָר וְצָבָא גָדוֹל וּבִין אֶת־הַדָּבָר וּבִינָה לוֹ בַּמַּרְאֶה׃ בַּיָּמִים הָהֵם אֲנִי
ג דָנִיֵּאל הָיִיתִי מִתְאַבֵּל שְׁלֹשָׁה שָׁבֻעִים יָמִים׃ לֶחֶם חֲמֻדוֹת לֹא אָכַלְתִּי וּבָשָׂר
וָיַיִן לֹא־בָא אֶל־פִּי וְסוֹךְ לֹא־סָכְתִּי עַד־מְלֹאת שְׁלֹשֶׁת שָׁבֻעִים יָמִים׃
ד וּבְיוֹם עֶשְׂרִים וְאַרְבָּעָה לַחֹדֶשׁ הָרִאשׁוֹן וַאֲנִי הָיִיתִי עַל יַד הַנָּהָר הַגָּדוֹל הוּא
ה חִדָּקֶל׃ וָאֶשָּׂא אֶת־עֵינַי וָאֵרֶא וְהִנֵּה אִישׁ־אֶחָד לָבוּשׁ בַּדִּים וּמָתְנָיו חֲגֻרִים

BACKGROUND

10:5 | **Gold of Ufaz [*ketem ufaz*]:** It seems that *ketem* is gold, based on an Egyptian or Akkadian term. Some claim that *ketem* was originally the name of a geographical region where gold was extracted, and over time it became a general term for gold (see Jeremiah 10:9; Naftali Herz Tur-Sinai, cited in *Encyclopaedia Biblica*, vol 5, s.v. *"zahav,"* [Hebrew], 663). Apparently, *ufaz* denotes a high-quality gold. The ancients distinguished between various types of gold in accordance with the metal's place of origin, quality, and method of production. Examples include *paz*, or fine gold (see, e.g., Isaiah 13:12), pure gold (see, e.g., Exodus 25:39), refined gold (see, e.g., I Chronicles 28:18), *sagur* gold (see, e.g., I Kings 6:20), gold of Ofir (see, e.g., Isaiah 13:12), beaten gold (see, e.g., I Kings 10:16), Parvayim gold (II Chronicles 3:6), and *ḥarutz* gold (see, e.g., Proverbs 8:19). The precise differences between these types of gold are no longer known.

6 **His body was like beryl,**[B] **his face** was ablaze, **like the appearance of lightning, his eyes** were bright **like torches of fire, his arms and his legs like burnished bronze, and the sound of his speech, like the noise of a multitude.**[86] He was a mighty, entirely glowing figure.

Peridot

Aquamarine

"The appearance of lightning"

7 **I, Daniel, alone, saw the vision, and the men who were with me,** perhaps Hananya, Mishael, and Azarya,[87] or Haggai, Zechariah, and Malachi,[88] **did not see the vision;** the man Daniel saw was not flesh and blood, but a prophetic vision that was only meant for him; **however, a great trembling overcame them,** for although they could not see the vision sharply and clearly, like Daniel, nevertheless as they were great men, they experienced a vague feeling of terror,[89] **and** therefore **they fled into hiding.**
8 **I remained alone, and I saw this great vision, and no strength remained in me** to stand and bear the vision; **my glory,** the countenance of my face, **was transformed for me into destruction,** as though it were destroyed, **and I retained no strength.**
9 **I heard the sound of his words,** of the man; **and when I heard the sound of his words, I was asleep on my face, with my face toward the ground.**
10 **Behold,** while I was still lying on the ground, the form of **a hand touched me, and it moved** and lifted **me** so that I could get up **onto my knees and the palms of my hands.**
11 **He said to me: Daniel, splendid man,** chosen one, **understand the matters that I am speaking to you, and stand in your place,** or stand in your place to listen to my statement; **for now I have been sent to you. While he was speaking this matter to me, I stood trembling.** Daniel managed to stand, but he still shook in great terror at the angel's presence.
12 **He,** the man clothed in linen, identified as the angel Gavriel,[90] **said to me: Do not fear, Daniel, for from the first day that you set your heart to understand, and to fast before your God, your words have been heard** by God; **and I have come because of your words.**[91]
13 Gavriel continued: **The prince,** the angel who represents the power **of the kingdom of Persia, was standing opposite me,** and we struggled against each other **for twenty-one days,** in my efforts to protect Israel from the angel of the kingdom of Persia, an active force in the world;[92] **and behold, Mikhael, one of the chief princes,** angels, **came to help me, and** throughout the period of your ascetic practices[93] **I remained there, with the kings of Persia.**
14 **I have come to explain to you that which will befall your people at the end of days; for there will yet be** another **vision** designated **for** showing what will happen in **the days** to come.
15 **As he was speaking with me these words, I lowered my gaze toward the ground and was silent.** I could not speak or react at all.
16 **Behold, one in the image of a person was touching my lips, and** as a result, **I opened my mouth, and I spoke and said** as follows **to the one standing opposite me: My lord, at the vision,** at the very sight of you, I felt as though **my** internal **organs were overturned, and I retained no strength.**
17 **How can this servant of my lord,** I, **speak with this my lord,** with you? **As for me, from now, strength will not endure in me, and breath is not left in me.**
18 The same **one with the appearance of a man touched me again, and he strengthened me.** I felt him give me strength.
19 **He said: Splendid man, do not fear. Peace to you, be strong, be strong. As he was speaking with me, I grew stronger, and I said: Speak my lord, as you have strengthened me,** and now I can focus on your words.
20 **He said: Do you know why I have come to you?** It is in order to inform you what is currently happening and what will occur in the future. **Now I will return to fight with the prince of Persia.**[D] **When I go out** from my battle with the prince of Persia, **behold, the prince of Yavan is coming.** After the confrontation with the kingdom of Persia, the kingdom of Yavan, Greece, will rule the world.[94]

BACKGROUND

10:6 | **Beryl [*tarshish*]:** *Tarshish* is the name of a blue or green precious stone, perhaps aquamarine or peridot (*Metzudat David*). It also refers to a city on the Mediterranean Sea, either Tarsus in Asia Minor or perhaps a city of the same name in Iberia. It is likely that Tarshish came to be identified with the sea itself (see Rashi), as seagoing ships are referred to in several places as "ships of Tarshish" (I Kings 22:49; Isaiah 23:1, 14, 60:9; Ezekiel 27:25; Psalms 48:8; II Chronicles 9:21). It is possible that this description refers both to the color of the body and to its size (see Rambam, *Guide of the Perplexed* 2:10; see also commentary on Isaiah 2:16 and Ezekiel 1:16).

ו בְּכֶתֶם אוּפָז׃ וּגְוִיָּתוֹ כְתַרְשִׁישׁ וּפָנָיו כְּמַרְאֵה בָרָק וְעֵינָיו כְּלַפִּידֵי אֵשׁ וּזְרֹעֹתָיו
ז וּמַרְגְּלֹתָיו כְּעֵין נְחֹשֶׁת קָלָל וְקוֹל דְּבָרָיו כְּקוֹל הָמוֹן׃ וְרָאִיתִי אֲנִי דָנִיֵּאל לְבַדִּי
אֶת־הַמַּרְאָה וְהָאֲנָשִׁים אֲשֶׁר הָיוּ עִמִּי לֹא רָאוּ אֶת־הַמַּרְאָה אֲבָל חֲרָדָה גְדֹלָה
ח נָפְלָה עֲלֵיהֶם וַיִּבְרְחוּ בְּהֵחָבֵא׃ וַאֲנִי נִשְׁאַרְתִּי לְבַדִּי וָאֶרְאֶה אֶת־הַמַּרְאָה הַגְּדֹלָה
ט הַזֹּאת וְלֹא נִשְׁאַר־בִּי כֹּחַ וְהוֹדִי נֶהְפַּךְ עָלַי לְמַשְׁחִית וְלֹא עָצַרְתִּי כֹּחַ׃ וָאֶשְׁמַע
אֶת־קוֹל דְּבָרָיו וּכְשָׁמְעִי אֶת־קוֹל דְּבָרָיו וַאֲנִי הָיִיתִי נִרְדָּם עַל־פָּנַי וּפָנַי אָרְצָה׃
י יא וְהִנֵּה־יָד נָגְעָה בִּי וַתְּנִיעֵנִי עַל־בִּרְכַּי וְכַפּוֹת יָדָי׃ וַיֹּאמֶר אֵלַי דָּנִיֵּאל אִישׁ־חֲמֻדוֹת
הָבֵן בַּדְּבָרִים אֲשֶׁר אָנֹכִי דֹּבֵר אֵלֶיךָ וַעֲמֹד עַל־עָמְדֶךָ כִּי עַתָּה שֻׁלַּחְתִּי אֵלֶיךָ
יב וּבְדַבְּרוֹ עִמִּי אֶת־הַדָּבָר הַזֶּה עָמַדְתִּי מַרְעִיד׃ וַיֹּאמֶר אֵלַי אַל־תִּירָא דָנִיֵּאל כִּי ׀
מִן־הַיּוֹם הָרִאשׁוֹן אֲשֶׁר נָתַתָּ אֶת־לִבְּךָ לְהָבִין וּלְהִתְעַנּוֹת לִפְנֵי אֱלֹהֶיךָ נִשְׁמְעוּ
יג דְבָרֶיךָ וַאֲנִי בָאתִי בִּדְבָרֶיךָ׃ וְשַׂר ׀ מַלְכוּת פָּרַס עֹמֵד לְנֶגְדִּי עֶשְׂרִים וְאֶחָד יוֹם
וְהִנֵּה מִיכָאֵל אַחַד הַשָּׂרִים הָרִאשֹׁנִים בָּא לְעָזְרֵנִי וַאֲנִי נוֹתַרְתִּי שָׁם אֵצֶל מַלְכֵי
יד פָרָס׃ וּבָאתִי לַהֲבִינְךָ אֵת אֲשֶׁר־יִקְרָה לְעַמְּךָ בְּאַחֲרִית הַיָּמִים כִּי־עוֹד חָזוֹן
טו טז לַיָּמִים׃ וּבְדַבְּרוֹ עִמִּי כַּדְּבָרִים הָאֵלֶּה נָתַתִּי פָנַי אַרְצָה וְנֶאֱלָמְתִּי׃ וְהִנֵּה כִּדְמוּת
בְּנֵי אָדָם נֹגֵעַ עַל־שְׂפָתָי וָאֶפְתַּח־פִּי וָאֲדַבְּרָה וָאֹמְרָה אֶל־הָעֹמֵד לְנֶגְדִּי אֲדֹנִי
יז בַּמַּרְאָה נֶהֶפְכוּ צִירַי עָלַי וְלֹא עָצַרְתִּי כֹּחַ׃ וְהֵיךְ יוּכַל עֶבֶד אֲדֹנִי זֶה לְדַבֵּר עִם־
יח אֲדֹנִי זֶה וַאֲנִי מֵעַתָּה לֹא־יַעֲמָד־בִּי כֹחַ וּנְשָׁמָה לֹא נִשְׁאֲרָה־בִי׃ וַיֹּסֶף וַיִּגַּע־בִּי
יט כְּמַרְאֵה אָדָם וַיְחַזְּקֵנִי׃ וַיֹּאמֶר אַל־תִּירָא אִישׁ־חֲמֻדוֹת שָׁלוֹם לָךְ חֲזַק וַחֲזָק
כ וּכְדַבְּרוֹ עִמִּי הִתְחַזַּקְתִּי וָאֹמְרָה יְדַבֵּר אֲדֹנִי כִּי חִזַּקְתָּנִי׃ וַיֹּאמֶר הֲיָדַעְתָּ לָמָּה־
בָּאתִי אֵלֶיךָ וְעַתָּה אָשׁוּב לְהִלָּחֵם עִם־שַׂר פָּרָס וַאֲנִי יוֹצֵא וְהִנֵּה שַׂר־יָוָן בָּא׃

DISCUSSION

10:20 | **I will return to fight with the prince of Persia:** The angel is returning to fight with the prince of Persia so that the Persians do not weaken or destroy the nation of Israel. Some explain that the twenty-one days of struggle correspond to the twenty-one kings that ruled the kingdom of Persia over the course of its history (see *Yoma* 77a).

21 **However, I will tell you that which is inscribed in the**
script of truth; there is no one who helps me, aids me in my
struggle **against these** princes **except Mikhael, your prince.**
Mikhael is one of the higher angels; just as there are angels that
represent the kingdoms of Persia and Greece, so Mikhael is
the prince that represents Israel. When Gavriel sought to help,
to fight against the nations of the world that subjugate Israel,
Mikhael arrived to assist him.
11 1 Gavriel continues: At present Mikhael is aiding me in my war,
and **I,** in the past, **in the first year of Darius the Mede, stood**
as a supporter and a bastion for him, Mikhael.[95]
2 **Now I will tell you the truth** about the future. **Behold, three**
more kings remain for Persia;[B] **the fourth** king **will become**
wealthy with greater wealth than all. When he grows strong
through his wealth, he will goad everyone to fight **with the**
kingdom of Yavan; alternatively: He shall stir up all to fight
against him, especially the kingdom of Yavan.
3 **A mighty king will arise** in Yavan, **and he will rule with ex-**
tensive dominion, or over a broad area, **and will act as he**
wills.
4 **When he has arisen,** at the height of his powers,[96] or: when his
life comes to its end,[97] **his kingdom will be broken, and will**
be divided to the four winds of heaven,[B] **and** his realm **will**
not go to his posterity;[98] **it will not be like his dominion**
with which he ruled so forcefully any longer, **as his kingdom**
will be uprooted and transferred **for others,** to other kings,[99]
beside those divisions into the four winds.

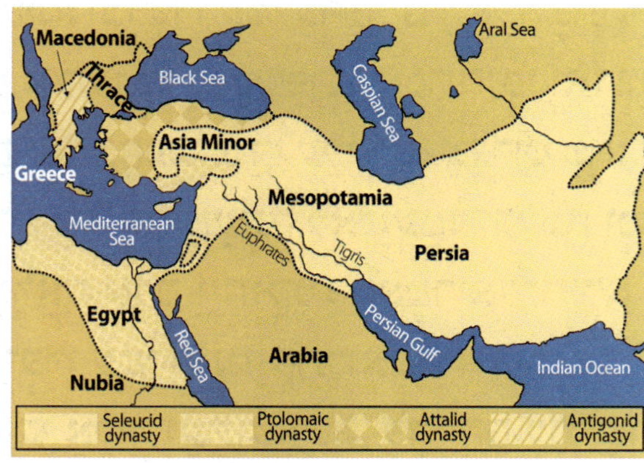

Alexander's empire after his death

5 **The king of the South**[B] **will become stronger** and more powerful than his rival who will control other areas, and he will be
even stronger **than** one of **his** rival's **princes,** or he will overpower an individual who was one of his princes; **and he,** the
king of the South, **will overpower him and rule; his**
dominion will be a great
dominion, powerful and
long-lasting.
6 **At the end of years they will**
join together, try to make
peace with each other, **and**
the daughter of the king
of the South will come to
the rival **king of the North**[B]
to bring about reconcilia-
tion, in an effort to enact a
formal treaty between them;
but she will not restrain the
strength of her arm, or she
will be unable to block their
strength of arms; **and he and**
his arm will not endure,
as the king of the South
will not be strong enough
militarily. **She, those who**
brought her, her companions, **he who begot her,** her
father; alternatively, her son;
and her supporter in those
times, who strengthens her
in the difficult times; alternatively, her husband, **will be given**
up. Some explain that she will not endure but will die, as none
of these will survive; they will all die or be killed.

"The king of the South." Coin portrait of Ptolemy I, Alexandria, 367–283 BCE

"The king of the North." Coin portrait of Antiochus II, 255–235 BCE

7 **A shoot,** a descendant, **from her roots,** from the daughter of
the king of the South, **will stand,** sprout, **in his** own, proper,
place; this descendant will recapture the throne **and will come**
to the forces, or the treasury, **and enter the stronghold of the**
king of the North; he will act against them, destroy them,
or pressure them, **and** will **take possession** of parts of the
kingdom.
8 **Also their gods, with their cast images, with their pre-**
cious vessels, silver and gold, he will bring into captivity to
Egypt. For years he will remain in the land that he conquered
from the king of the North.
9 After a time **he will** once again **come** back **to** the region of **the**
kingdom of the king of the South, and he will return to his
own **land.**
10 **His,** the king of the North's, **sons, will make a provocation**
against him, **and** will **assemble a horde of great forces; it,** the
army of the North **will come, surging and passing through,**
with his army, he will gallop with force to the south; **he will**
again make a provocation, commence a war, **against his,** the
king of the South's, **stronghold.**

כא אֲבָל אַגִּיד לְךָ אֶת־הָרָשׁוּם בִּכְתָב אֱמֶת וְאֵין אֶחָד מִתְחַזֵּק עִמִּי עַל־אֵלֶּה כִּי ז
א אִם־מִיכָאֵל שַׂרְכֶם׃ וַאֲנִי בִּשְׁנַת אַחַת לְדָרְיָוֶשׁ הַמָּדִי עָמְדִי לְמַחֲזִיק
ב וּלְמָעוֹז לוֹ׃ וְעַתָּה אֱמֶת אַגִּיד לָךְ הִנֵּה־עוֹד שְׁלֹשָׁה מְלָכִים עֹמְדִים לְפָרַס
וְהָרְבִיעִי יַעֲשִׁיר עֹשֶׁר־גָּדוֹל מִכֹּל וּכְחֶזְקָתוֹ בְעָשְׁרוֹ יָעִיר הַכֹּל אֵת מַלְכוּת יָוָן׃
ג ד וְעָמַד מֶלֶךְ גִּבּוֹר וּמָשַׁל מִמְשָׁל רַב וְעָשָׂה כִּרְצוֹנוֹ׃ וּכְעָמְדוֹ תִּשָּׁבֵר מַלְכוּתוֹ
וְתֵחָץ לְאַרְבַּע רוּחוֹת הַשָּׁמָיִם וְלֹא לְאַחֲרִיתוֹ וְלֹא כְמָשְׁלוֹ אֲשֶׁר מָשָׁל כִּי תִנָּתֵשׁ
ה מַלְכוּתוֹ וְלַאֲחֵרִים מִלְּבַד־אֵלֶּה׃ וְיֶחֱזַק מֶלֶךְ־הַנֶּגֶב וּמִן־שָׂרָיו וְיֶחֱזַק עָלָיו וּמָשָׁל
ו מִמְשָׁל רַב מֶמְשַׁלְתּוֹ׃ וּלְקֵץ שָׁנִים יִתְחַבָּרוּ וּבַת מֶלֶךְ־הַנֶּגֶב תָּבוֹא אֶל־מֶלֶךְ
הַצָּפוֹן לַעֲשׂוֹת מֵישָׁרִים וְלֹא־תַעְצֹר כֹּחַ הַזְּרוֹעַ וְלֹא יַעֲמֹד וּזְרֹעוֹ וְתִנָּתֵן הִיא
ז וּמְבִיאֶיהָ וְהַיֹּלְדָהּ וּמַחֲזִקָהּ בָּעִתִּים׃ וְעָמַד מִנֵּצֶר שָׁרָשֶׁיהָ כַּנּוֹ וְיָבֹא אֶל־הַחַיִל
ח וְיָבֹא בְּמָעוֹז מֶלֶךְ הַצָּפוֹן וְעָשָׂה בָהֶם וְהֶחֱזִיק׃ וְגַם אֱלֹהֵיהֶם עִם־נְסִכֵיהֶם עִם־
ט כְּלֵי חֶמְדָּתָם כֶּסֶף וְזָהָב בַּשְּׁבִי יָבִא מִצְרָיִם וְהוּא שָׁנִים יַעֲמֹד מִמֶּלֶךְ הַצָּפוֹן׃ וּבָא
י בְּמַלְכוּת מֶלֶךְ הַנֶּגֶב וְשָׁב אֶל־אַדְמָתוֹ׃ וּבָנָו יִתְגָּרוּ וְאָסְפוּ הֲמוֹן חֲיָלִים רַבִּים

BACKGROUND

11:2 | **Behold, three more kings remain for Persia:** According to *Seder Olam Rabba*, these kings are Cyrus, Cambyses II, and Darius the Great, while the fourth king of Persia is Xerxes, who was defeated by the Greeks in the battles of Thermopylae and Salamis (480–479 BCE). These conflicts formed a turning point in the history of the Persian Empire, as they signaled the start of its gradual decline, a process which took some one hundred and fifty years. From that point, the kingdom of Yavan, Greece, began to expand, which culminated in the rise of Alexander the Great (see Rashi; Ibn Ezra; Abravanel, *Ma'ayanei HaYeshu'a*, 11:3).

11:4 | **His kingdom will be broken, and will be divided to the four winds of heaven:** This prophecy is generally interpreted as a reference to Alexander the Great, who conquered all of Persia. After his death in 323 BCE, there were several wars between his successors, known as *Diadochi*, who fought between themselves over who would inherit Alexander's empire. This warfare went on for nearly fifty years, during which time the original *Diadochi* all died and the wars were continued by their successors. Eventually, by around 275 BCE, the situation stabilized, with the empire divided into four main blocks of power: Egypt, under Ptolemy II son of Ptolemy I; Mesopotamia, Syria, and Persia, under Antiochus I son of Seleucus; Macedonia and Greece, under the control of Antigonus Gonatas, grandson of Antigonus; and the city of Pergamon and much of Asia Minor under Philetaerus, Lysimachus's general (Attalid dynasty). The Ptolemaic dynasty, whose king is called "the king of the South" in the verse below, and the Seleucid Empire, whose king is called "the king of the North" in verse 6, constantly fought each other, without either side emerging victorious. Among other places, they waged war in the border regions, such as the Land of Israel, while they also occasionally sought to enact treaties with each other, as described here.

11:5 | **The king of the South:** The king of the South mentioned here and the king of the North mentioned below do not necessarily refer to a particular king but possibly to a dynasty. Thus the king of the South could be one of several Ptolemys and the king of the North one of the rulers of the Seleucid Empire.

11:6 | **The daughter of the king of the South will come to the king of the North:** As part of the efforts to improve relationships between the Seleucid and Ptolemaic kingdoms, Berenice Syra, the daughter of Ptolemy II, "the king of the South," married Antiochus II, "the king of the North." This diplomatic marriage did not last long, as in 246 BCE, Laodice, Antiochus' first wife, whom he had divorced, poisoned the king, Berenice, and their son, and appointed her own son, Seleucus II, to the throne. This murderous act renewed the tensions and wars between the Ptolemaic and the Seleucid kingdoms.

11 **The king of the South will be galled,** be filled with bitterness and anger at the invasion of the king of the North into his territory, **and will come out and wage war with him, with the king of the North; he,** the king of the South, **will mobilize a great horde, and the horde** of the king of the North **will be delivered into his hand.**[100]

12 **The horde will be carried away** in captivity, **and his,** the king of the South's, **heart will grow haughty, and he will fell tens of thousands** of enemy troops; **but** even so **he will not prevail;** despite his successes against the king of the North, the king of the South will not emerge completely victorious or in full control.[101]

13 **The king of the North will again mobilize a horde,** a large army, even **greater than the first, and at the end of the times,** after the passage **of years, he will come with a great army and with much** military **equipment,** or he will return from the battle with much plunder.[102]

14 **In those times, many** enemies,[103] or helpers,[104] **will stand against the king of the South. The lawless among your people,** Daniel, **will presume,** have pretentions, **to establish a vision,** their ideal world, **but they will fail.**[B]

15 **The king of the North will come** to fight, **and erect a ramp,** a mound of dirt alongside the city wall, **and capture** many **fortified cities, and the armies of the South will not endure** the attack, **and his choice people,** the select soldiers of his army, **will have no strength to endure.**[105]

16 **The one,** the king of the North, **who comes against him,** the king of the South, **will act as he wills, and none will stand before him; he will stand** triumphant **in the magnificent land,** the Land of Israel, **and extermination will be by his hand;** he will cause widespread destruction.

17 **He,** the king of the North, **will direct his attention to come** further south **with the strength of his entire kingdom, and conciliators,** or statements of reconciliation, will be **with him, and he will accomplish it,** a peace treaty. **He will give him,** the king of the South,[106] or the king of the North,[107] **a daughter from among the women to destroy it,** the kingdom, through her, **but she will not last** as his wife; alternatively, it, the plan, will not last; **and she will not be for him.**[108] Some explain that this daughter is a metaphor for the people of Israel, which will be subject to decrees of persecution.[109]

18 **He,** the king of the North, **will turn his attention to the coastlands, and he will capture many, but a commander will put an end to his,** the king of the North's, **affront.** A military officer who is not a king will arise against the king of the North and cause his reproaches to cease. **He will pay back his affront to him,** but he will not vanquish the king.[110]

19 **He,** the king of the North, **will redirect his attention to the strongholds of his** own **land, and he will stumble and fall, and not be found,** as he will be destroyed.

20 As the internal upheavals in the two kingdoms continue, **in his place,** taking over the king of the North's throne, **will stand one who will depose the oppressor** [***ma'avir nogeis***], **one with the glory of royalty;** one who will remove the governor from his post, and that king will possess the glory of the kingdom. However, he will not last long, as **within a few days he will be broken, but not in wrath,**[111] in a powerful uprising, **and not in war.**[112] Some interpret the phrase *ma'avir nogeis* to mean that the new king will transfer oppressors from one place to another in an effort to plunder the glory of the kingdom.

21 **In his place will stand a despicable one, upon whom the glory of royalty was not bestowed,**[B] as he will not have the appearance of a king, and will have no royal ties; **he will come in serenity and will seize the kingdom with smooth talk.** He will claim the throne and seize it through deceitful, underhanded means.[113]

22 **The surging** enemy **armies will be swept away from before him and will be broken, and the ruler of the covenant as well,** the ruler in the Land of Israel, will also be swept away by him.[114]

23 **In his making alliances,** with the strength this connection grants him, **he will engage in deceit, and he will ascend and become mighty,** he will grow increasingly powerful, even though he is **with but a small nation,** as few men will be on his side.[115]

24 **With serenity and with the riches of the province,** the treasuries of the land, **he will come, and he will do that which his fathers and the fathers of his fathers did not do. He will distribute spoils, and loot, and property to them,** the residents of the country. **He will think his thoughts about fortresses,** he will plan to establish and populate new fortresses, but only **until the** right **time** comes to set out and conquer.[116]

25 **He will rouse his strength and his heart against the king of the South with a great force, and the king of the South will be provoked** against him and set out **to war with an extremely great and mighty force, but he will not** be able to **stand** up to him, the king of the North, **as they,** the king of the South's own men, **will plot against him,** will use ploys to revolt against him.[117]

26 **Those who eat his food,** or his mercenaries, **will destroy him, and his,** the king of the North's, **forces will sweep away,** will attack, **and many** of them, the soldiers of the king of the South, **will fall slain.**[118]

27 **Both of them, the kings,** the king of the North and the king of the South, **their hearts will be** planning **for evil, and at**

יא וּבָא בוֹא וְשָׁטַף וְעָבָר וְיָשֹׁב ויתגרו עַד־מָעֻזֹּה: וְיִתְמַרְמַר מֶלֶךְ הַנֶּגֶב וְיָצָא וְיִתְגָּרֶה
יב וְנִלְחַם עִמּוֹ עִם־מֶלֶךְ הַצָּפוֹן וְהֶעֱמִיד הָמוֹן רָב וְנִתַּן הֶהָמוֹן בְּיָדוֹ: וְנִשָּׂא הֶהָמוֹן
יג ירום לְבָבוֹ וְהִפִּיל רִבֹּאוֹת וְלֹא יָעוֹז: וְשָׁב מֶלֶךְ הַצָּפוֹן וְהֶעֱמִיד הָמוֹן רַב מִן־ וְרָם
יד הָרִאשׁוֹן וּלְקֵץ הָעִתִּים שָׁנִים יָבוֹא בוֹא בְּחַיִל גָּדוֹל וּבִרְכוּשׁ רָב: וּבָעִתִּים הָהֵם
רַבִּים יַעַמְדוּ עַל־מֶלֶךְ הַנֶּגֶב וּבְנֵי ׀ פָּרִיצֵי עַמְּךָ יִנַּשְּׂאוּ לְהַעֲמִיד חָזוֹן וְנִכְשָׁלוּ:
טו וְיָבֹא מֶלֶךְ הַצָּפוֹן וְיִשְׁפֹּךְ סוֹלְלָה וְלָכַד עִיר מִבְצָרוֹת וּזְרֹעוֹת הַנֶּגֶב לֹא יַעֲמֹדוּ
טז וְעַם מִבְחָרָיו וְאֵין כֹּחַ לַעֲמֹד: וְיַעַשׂ הַבָּא אֵלָיו כִּרְצוֹנוֹ וְאֵין עוֹמֵד לְפָנָיו וְיַעֲמֹד
יז בְּאֶרֶץ־הַצְּבִי וְכָלָה בְיָדוֹ: וְיָשֵׂם ׀ פָּנָיו לָבוֹא בְּתֹקֶף כָּל־מַלְכוּתוֹ וִישָׁרִים עִמּוֹ
יח וְעָשָׂה וּבַת הַנָּשִׁים יִתֶּן־לוֹ לְהַשְׁחִיתָהּ וְלֹא תַעֲמֹד וְלֹא־לוֹ תִהְיֶה: וישב ׀ פָּנָיו וְיָשֵׂם
יט לָאִיִּים וְלָכַד רַבִּים וְהִשְׁבִּית קָצִין חֶרְפָּתוֹ לוֹ בִּלְתִּי חֶרְפָּתוֹ יָשִׁיב לוֹ: וְיָשֵׁב פָּנָיו
כ לְמָעוּזֵּי אַרְצוֹ וְנִכְשַׁל וְנָפַל וְלֹא יִמָּצֵא: וְעָמַד עַל־כַּנּוֹ מַעֲבִיר נוֹגֵשׂ הֶדֶר מַלְכוּת
כא וּבְיָמִים אֲחָדִים יִשָּׁבֵר וְלֹא בְאַפַּיִם וְלֹא בְמִלְחָמָה: וְעָמַד עַל־כַּנּוֹ נִבְזֶה וְלֹא־
כב נָתְנוּ עָלָיו הוֹד מַלְכוּת וּבָא בְשַׁלְוָה וְהֶחֱזִיק מַלְכוּת בַּחֲלַקְלַקּוֹת: וּזְרֹעוֹת הַשֶּׁטֶף
כג יִשָּׁטְפוּ מִלְּפָנָיו וְיִשָּׁבֵרוּ וְגַם נְגִיד בְּרִית: וּמִן־הִתְחַבְּרוּת אֵלָיו יַעֲשֶׂה מִרְמָה
כד וְעָלָה וְעָצַם בִּמְעַט־גּוֹי: בְּשַׁלְוָה וּבְמִשְׁמַנֵּי מְדִינָה יָבוֹא וְעָשָׂה אֲשֶׁר לֹא־עָשׂוּ
אֲבֹתָיו וַאֲבוֹת אֲבֹתָיו בִּזָּה וְשָׁלָל וּרְכוּשׁ לָהֶם יִבְזוֹר וְעַל מִבְצָרִים יְחַשֵּׁב מַחְשְׁבֹתָיו
כה וְעַד־עֵת: וְיָעֵר כֹּחוֹ וּלְבָבוֹ עַל־מֶלֶךְ הַנֶּגֶב בְּחַיִל גָּדוֹל וּמֶלֶךְ הַנֶּגֶב יִתְגָּרֶה
לַמִּלְחָמָה בְּחַיִל־גָּדוֹל וְעָצוּם עַד־מְאֹד וְלֹא יַעֲמֹד כִּי־יַחְשְׁבוּ עָלָיו מַחֲשָׁבוֹת:
כו כז וְאֹכְלֵי פַת־בָּגוֹ יִשְׁבְּרוּהוּ וְחֵילוֹ יִשְׁטוֹף וְנָפְלוּ חֲלָלִים רַבִּים: וּשְׁנֵיהֶם הַמְּלָכִים

BACKGROUND

11:14 | **The lawless among your people will presume to establish a vision, but they will fail:** This is perhaps an allusion to the Hellenists. Already during the days of the Ptolemaic dynasty, many Jews began to assimilate and strayed after Hellenistic culture (see *Metzudat David*; see also *Avot deRabbi Natan*, version A, 5).

11:21 | **In his place will stand a despicable one, upon whom the glory of royalty was not bestowed:** This individual is traditionally identified as Antiochus IV Epiphanes who gained the throne through subterfuge and intrigue, supplanting the legitimate heir, Demetrius (see Maccabees I:1:10).

one table they will speak falsehood. They will sit at the same table as though there is no quarrel between them, and yet they will deceive each other;[119] **but it will not succeed,** they will not achieve anything, and ultimately both will return home, **as there is yet an end for the appointed time.** The time for their downfall will not yet have arrived.[120]

28 **He,** the king of the North, **will return to his land with a great deal of property, and his heart,** his desire and thoughts, **will be against the holy covenant,** the holy people, to act wickedly against them; and **he will take action and return to his land.**[121]

29 **At the appointed time,** at a later stage,[122] **he,** the king of the North, **will return and come into the South, and it will not be like the first time or like the last time.** This attempt will neither be as successful as the first effort nor as the last, which is either the last attack mentioned above or the one described below.[123]

30 **Ships of Kitim will come against him,**[B] **and he will be** cowed and **broken, and** he **will return** from his painful failure in the south, **and rage against the holy covenant,** he will take out his anger upon the people of Israel, **and he will take** evil **action** against them, or gather an army against them, or pressure them; **and he will again attend to the forsakers of the holy covenant.** He will attempt to establish a relationship with those who leave the holy covenant.[124]

31 **Armies of his will rise up and profane the Temple,** which is **the stronghold, and will abolish the continual** burnt **offering,** they will annul the daily offering, **and they will set up** in the Temple **the desolating detestable thing,**[B] an idolatrous image (see commentary on 9:27).

32 **He,** the king, **will flatter with smooth talk those who act wickedly against the covenant,** as he will seek to maintain good relationships with them, **but the people that knows its God will maintain** the covenant **and perform it,** God's commandments.

33 **The wise of the people will explain** matters **to the multitudes, yet they will fall by sword, by flame, by captivity, and by plunder, for days.**[125]

34 **When they fall, they will receive little help;** they will not have many who remain loyal to them; **and many will join them with smooth talk.**

35 **Among the wise, some will fall,** in their attempts **to refine them, to clarify, and to make clear, until the end time;** they will fail, **as it is** not **yet the appointed time.** The time will not yet have arrived.

36 **The king** of the North **shall do as he wills and will exalt and magnify himself**[B] **over every god,** he will present himself as greater than all the gods, a kind of supreme god, **and against the God of gods, he will speak with conceit. He will succeed until the fury is abated, when that which was decreed is accomplished.**

37 **He will pay no regard,** will not reflect upon or pay attention **to the gods of his fathers, or to the splendor of women, and he will not pay regard to any god;** he will be a strange man, detached from women, from his ancestral religion, and from any other religion,[126] **as he will magnify himself over all.** He will be occupied solely with the lust of honor and self-aggrandizement.

38 Even so, **he will honor the god of strongholds**[B] when **that** idol **is on its base,** he will support some sort of idolatry, **and** that god, **a god whom his fathers did not know, he will honor with gold, with silver, with precious stones, and with** valuable **ornaments.**

39 **He will make a fortified stronghold with a foreign god;** he will place his foreign god in the strong fortresses; **he will greatly honor those he knows,** or those who acknowledge his god, **and have them rule over the multitudes, and he will distribute land for a** small **price.**[127]

The Time of the End

DANIEL 11:40–12:3

The following prophecy related to Daniel by the angel Gavriel is vague and obscure. The previous sections are understood to refer to specific historical events that occurred in the Land of Israel during the period of Seleucid control. The first part of this section may also be referring to the Seleucids, specifically the death of Antiochus IV Epiphanes, but it is also possible that it is referring to events that occurred many generations later, or even to events that have not yet happened, that will occur at the end of days, as indicated at the end of the section. The fact is that this book is not meant to be fully understood, and therefore many details of the events it describes appear only as allusions.

40 **At the end time, the king of the South will lock horns with him,** the king of the North, **and the king of the North will storm against him** in a massive attack, **with chariots, with horsemen, and with many ships. He will come into lands, and** his army **will surge** like a powerful stream of water, **and pass through.**

כח לְבָבָם לְמֵרָע וְעַל־שֻׁלְחָן אֶחָד כָּזָב יְדַבֵּרוּ וְלֹא תִצְלָח כִּי־עוֹד קֵץ לַמּוֹעֵד: וְיָשֹׁב
כט אַרְצוֹ בִּרְכוּשׁ גָּדוֹל וּלְבָבוֹ עַל־בְּרִית קֹדֶשׁ וְעָשָׂה וְשָׁב לְאַרְצוֹ: לַמּוֹעֵד יָשׁוּב
ל וּבָא בַנֶּגֶב וְלֹא־תִהְיֶה כָרִאשֹׁנָה וְכָאַחֲרוֹנָה: וּבָאוּ בוֹ צִיִּים כִּתִּים וְנִכְאָה וְשָׁב
לא וְזָעַם עַל־בְּרִית־קוֹדֶשׁ וְעָשָׂה וְשָׁב וְיָבֵן עַל־עֹזְבֵי בְּרִית קֹדֶשׁ: וּזְרֹעִים מִמֶּנּוּ
לב יַעֲמֹדוּ וְחִלְּלוּ הַמִּקְדָּשׁ הַמָּעוֹז וְהֵסִירוּ הַתָּמִיד וְנָתְנוּ הַשִּׁקּוּץ מְשֹׁמֵם: וּמַרְשִׁיעֵי
לג בְרִית יַחֲנִיף בַּחֲלַקּוֹת וְעַם יֹדְעֵי אֱלֹהָיו יַחֲזִקוּ וְעָשׂוּ: וּמַשְׂכִּילֵי עָם יָבִינוּ לָרַבִּים
לד וְנִכְשְׁלוּ בְּחֶרֶב וּבְלֶהָבָה בִּשְׁבִי וּבְבִזָּה יָמִים: וּבְהִכָּשְׁלָם יֵעָזְרוּ עֵזֶר מְעָט וְנִלְווּ
לה עֲלֵיהֶם רַבִּים בַּחֲלַקְלַקּוֹת: וּמִן־הַמַּשְׂכִּילִים יִכָּשְׁלוּ לִצְרוֹף בָּהֶם וּלְבָרֵר וְלַלְבֵּן
לו עַד־עֵת קֵץ כִּי־עוֹד לַמּוֹעֵד: וְעָשָׂה כִרְצֹנוֹ הַמֶּלֶךְ וְיִתְרוֹמֵם וְיִתְגַּדֵּל עַל־כָּל־אֵל
לז וְעַל אֵל אֵלִים יְדַבֵּר נִפְלָאוֹת וְהִצְלִיחַ עַד־כָּלָה זַעַם כִּי נֶחֱרָצָה נֶעֱשָׂתָה: וְעַל־
אֱלֹהֵי אֲבֹתָיו לֹא יָבִין וְעַל־חֶמְדַּת נָשִׁים וְעַל־כָּל־אֱלוֹהַּ לֹא יָבִין כִּי עַל־כֹּל
לח יִתְגַּדָּל: וְלֶאֱלֹהַּ מָעֻזִּים עַל־כַּנּוֹ יְכַבֵּד וְלֶאֱלוֹהַּ אֲשֶׁר לֹא־יְדָעֻהוּ אֲבֹתָיו יְכַבֵּד
לט בְּזָהָב וּבְכֶסֶף וּבְאֶבֶן יְקָרָה וּבַחֲמֻדוֹת: וְעָשָׂה לְמִבְצְרֵי מָעֻזִּים עִם־אֱלוֹהַּ נֵכָר
מ אֲשֶׁר הכיר יַרְבֶּה כָבוֹד וְהִמְשִׁילָם בָּרַבִּים וַאֲדָמָה יְחַלֵּק בִּמְחִיר: וּבְעֵת קֵץ יַכִּיר
יִתְנַגַּח עִמּוֹ מֶלֶךְ הַנֶּגֶב וְיִשְׂתָּעֵר עָלָיו מֶלֶךְ הַצָּפוֹן בְּרֶכֶב וּבְפָרָשִׁים וּבָאֳנִיּוֹת

BACKGROUND

11:30 | **Ships of Kitim will come against him:** This is apparently referring to ships of the Romans, who threatened King Antiochus. After his failure in Egypt, he joined forces with the Hellenists and took out his rage upon Judah.

11:31 | **And will abolish the continual offering, and they will set up the desolating detestable thing:** This description matches the decrees of Antiochus that appear in the writings of the Hasmoneans and other historical sources (e.g., Diodorus Siculus, *Bibliotheca Historica* 34 1–5 (1), first century BCE). However, these sources do not explicitly mention the annulment of the daily offering, but refer to the general impairment of the Temple service and the cessation of its activities.

11:36 | **The king shall do as he wills and will exalt and magnify himself:** Antiochus IV's sense of self-importance is expressed in his name Epiphanes, which means "God Manifest." According to one opinion, the countenance of Zeus on the coins he issued was similar to the features of his own face (Victor Tcherikover, *The Jews and Greeks in the Hellenistic Period*. Tel Aviv: Dvir, 1982 [Hebrew], 145–150, note 13). He considered himself a patron of various religions and heavily invested in the construction of pagan places of worship. Nevertheless, there is no direct testimony of his attitude toward the gods of his fathers, apart from what is stated in this verse and the following ones.

11:37–38 | **He will pay no regard...to the splendor of women...he will honor the god of strongholds:** It is possible that the phrase "the splendor of women" is a reference to the temple of the goddess Diana, also known as the Greek goddess Artemis, which Antiochus sought to conquer and plunder (Maccabees II:1:13, see also 9:2; Maccabees I:1:6). Some researchers claim that "the splendor of women" alludes to Adonis, the god of fertility, passion, and beauty, a central figure in the pagan rites of Greek women. In contrast, "the god of strongholds" is Zeus, whom Antiochus preferred over Apollo, the god favored by his fathers.

41 **He will come into the magnificent land,** the Land of Israel,
and many will fall because of him, either through battle or by
him forcing them to abandon their religion. But **these** lands
will flee from his hand: Edom, and Moav, and the finest, the
choice,[128] or the edge of the land,[129] **of the children of Amon.**
42 **He will extend his hand against the lands, and the land of**
Egypt will not escape, as he will conquer it as well.
43 **He will rule over the hidden treasures of gold and silver,**
and all the ornaments of Egypt; even **Libyans and Kushites,**
of neighboring countries, who were subjugated to Egypt, and
who have gold and silver mines in their countries,[130] **will be under his feet,** defeated by him.
44 But bad and threatening **reports from** the lands of **the East**
and from the North will terrify him, and he will come out
with great fury to destroy and obliterate, kill, **multitudes.**
45 **He will pitch the tents of his** temporary **abode between seas**
and the magnificent holy mountain, the hills of the Land of
Israel,[131] **and he will come to his end,** he will ultimately die,
and there will be no one to help him.

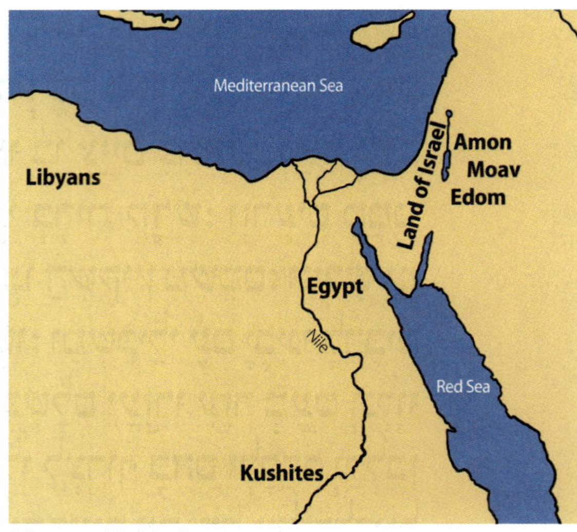

"Libyans and Kushites"

12 1 The following prophecy, which is a continuation of the angel's
speech to Daniel, deals with the end of days. It depicts, in a
highly favorable light, events that will occur in the distant future. **At that time Mikhael the great prince, who stands by**
the members of your people, will stand up to plead Israel's
case and pray for the nation; alternatively, this means that he
will cease to speak on Israel's behalf (see 10:21). At that hour
there will be a time of trouble that has not been from its becoming a nation of Israel **until this time,** the end of days. **At**
that time your people will escape, everyone will be saved of
your people **who is found written in the book,** the Book of
Life.[132]
2 **Many of the sleepers in the dust of the earth,** the dead, **will**
awaken. This is one of the rare prophecies in the Bible that
deals explicitly with the resurrection.[133] **These** will awaken **to**
eternal life, a happy existence, **and those** others, the wicked,
will indeed be resurrected, but **to reviling and eternal disgrace.** They will be subject to curses and unremitting shame.[134]
3 **The wise** of the people **will shine like the radiance of the**
firmament; and those who lead the multitudes to righteousness, who are not only wise but who also care for others
and perform good deeds for the populace, will shine **like the**
stars in heaven **forever and ever.**[135] According to the Sages this
is referring to teachers of children.[136]

The End of the Visions and the Conclusion of the Book

DANIEL 12:4–13

4 **But you, Daniel,** even if you know or understand more than I
have stated, **obscure the words,** leave them vague and unclear,
and seal the book until the end time, when **many will roam,**
seeking God, **and knowledge will increase.** At that stage the
wise might understand what is written in this book.[137]
5 **I, Daniel, saw, and behold, two others,** angels, **were standing, one here on the bank of the river, and one there on the**
bank of the river, on the two banks of the river.
6 **One** of them **said to the man clothed in linen,** apparently the
angel Gavriel, or perhaps Mikhael, **who was** standing **above**
the waters of the river: How long will it be delayed[138] **until**
the wondrous end? When will the end arrive, when all these
wonderful events will occur? In the meantime, times are bad.
7 **I heard the man clothed in linen, who was above the waters**
of the river, speaking, **and he lifted his right and his left to**
the heavens, a gesture of an oath, **and he took an oath by the**
Ever-Living One, God, **that for a time, times, and one-half,**
after the passage of a defined period of time, whose duration is
not stated here, and then again that period, and half of that period, **and with the conclusion of the breaking of the power**
of the holy people, all these troubles **will conclude,** and then
the end will arrive.

מא רַבּוֹת וּבָא בַאֲרָצוֹת וְשָׁטַף וְעָבָר׃ וּבָא בְּאֶרֶץ הַצְּבִי וְרַבּוֹת יִכָּשֵׁלוּ וְאֵלֶּה יִמָּלְטוּ
מב מִיָּדוֹ אֱדוֹם וּמוֹאָב וְרֵאשִׁית בְּנֵי עַמּוֹן׃ וְיִשְׁלַח יָדוֹ בַּאֲרָצוֹת וְאֶרֶץ מִצְרַיִם לֹא
מג תִהְיֶה לִפְלֵיטָה׃ וּמָשַׁל בְּמִכְמַנֵּי הַזָּהָב וְהַכֶּסֶף וּבְכֹל חֲמֻדוֹת מִצְרָיִם וְלֻבִים
מד וְכֻשִׁים בְּמִצְעָדָיו׃ וּשְׁמֻעוֹת יְבַהֲלֻהוּ מִמִּזְרָח וּמִצָּפוֹן וְיָצָא בְּחֵמָא גְדֹלָה לְהַשְׁמִיד
מה וּלְהַחֲרִים רַבִּים׃ וְיִטַּע אָהֳלֵי אַפַּדְנוֹ בֵּין יַמִּים לְהַר־צְבִי־קֹדֶשׁ וּבָא עַד־קִצּוֹ
א וְאֵין עוֹזֵר לוֹ׃ וּבָעֵת הַהִיא יַעֲמֹד מִיכָאֵל הַשַּׂר הַגָּדוֹל הָעֹמֵד עַל־בְּנֵי עַמֶּךָ
וְהָיְתָה עֵת צָרָה אֲשֶׁר לֹא־נִהְיְתָה מִהְיוֹת גּוֹי עַד הָעֵת הַהִיא וּבָעֵת הַהִיא יִמָּלֵט
ב עַמְּךָ כָּל־הַנִּמְצָא כָּתוּב בַּסֵּפֶר׃ וְרַבִּים מִיְּשֵׁנֵי אַדְמַת־עָפָר יָקִיצוּ אֵלֶּה לְחַיֵּי
ג עוֹלָם וְאֵלֶּה לַחֲרָפוֹת לְדִרְאוֹן עוֹלָם׃ וְהַמַּשְׂכִּלִים יַזְהִרוּ כְּזֹהַר הָרָקִיעַ וּמַצְדִּיקֵי
ד הָרַבִּים כַּכּוֹכָבִים לְעוֹלָם וָעֶד׃ וְאַתָּה דָנִיֵּאל סְתֹם הַדְּבָרִים וַחֲתֹם
ה הַסֵּפֶר עַד־עֵת קֵץ יְשֹׁטְטוּ רַבִּים וְתִרְבֶּה הַדָּעַת׃ וְרָאִיתִי אֲנִי דָנִיֵּאל וְהִנֵּה שְׁנַיִם
ו אֲחֵרִים עֹמְדִים אֶחָד הֵנָּה לִשְׂפַת הַיְאֹר וְאֶחָד הֵנָּה לִשְׂפַת הַיְאֹר׃ וַיֹּאמֶר לָאִישׁ
ז לְבוּשׁ הַבַּדִּים אֲשֶׁר מִמַּעַל לְמֵימֵי הַיְאֹר עַד־מָתַי קֵץ הַפְּלָאוֹת׃ וָאֶשְׁמַע אֶת־
הָאִישׁ ׀ לְבוּשׁ הַבַּדִּים אֲשֶׁר מִמַּעַל לְמֵימֵי הַיְאֹר וַיָּרֶם יְמִינוֹ וּשְׂמֹאלוֹ אֶל־הַשָּׁמַיִם
וַיִּשָּׁבַע בְּחֵי הָעוֹלָם כִּי לְמוֹעֵד מוֹעֲדִים וָחֵצִי וּכְכַלּוֹת נַפֵּץ יַד־עַם־קֹדֶשׁ תִּכְלֶינָה

8 **I heard** all of this, **but I did not understand;** I did not know
to what he was referring, **and I said: My lord, what will be the
end of** all **these** calculations you stated?
9 **He said: Go, Daniel, as the matters** that you wish to know
are to remain **obscured and sealed until the end time.** Only
when the redemption arrives will everything become clear.
10 **Many things will be clarified;** many issues will become clearer
over time,[139] and through the sufferings and troubles much will
be **made clear, and refined, and the wicked will act wickedly. All of the wicked will not understand** these prophecies;
but the wise will understand.
11 **From the time of the abolishing of the continual** daily burnt
offering, and the setting of the desolating detestable thing
in the Temple, **there will be one thousand two hundred and
ninety days.** It is unclear whether this is referring to actual
days. Many interpret these "days" of suffering as years.[140]
12 **Happy is one who waits** another forty-five days, or years,[141]
**and reaches one thousand three hundred and thirty-five
days.** It is unknown when this counting starts, when it will end,
or what the indicated dates signify. These matters were left unclear to Daniel himself.
13 **But you,** Daniel, **go to the end,** until the end of your own days,
and rest, die, **and** after you have lain down in death, **you will
arise to your fate at the end of the days.**[142] You will be among
those who will arise at the end of days, and will then understand the meaning of your prophecy.

ח ט כָּל־אֵֽלֶּה׃ וַאֲנִ֥י שָׁמַ֖עְתִּי וְלֹ֣א אָבִ֑ין וָאֹֽמְרָה֙ אֲדֹנִ֔י מָ֖ה אַחֲרִ֥ית אֵֽלֶּה׃ וַיֹּ֖אמֶר לֵ֣ךְ
י דָּנִיֵּ֑אל כִּֽי־סְתֻמִ֧ים וַחֲתֻמִ֛ים הַדְּבָרִ֖ים עַד־עֵ֥ת קֵֽץ׃ יִתְבָּרְר֨וּ וְיִתְלַבְּנ֜וּ וְיִצָּרְפ֨וּ
יא רַבִּ֗ים וְהִרְשִׁ֙יעוּ֙ רְשָׁעִ֔ים וְלֹ֥א יָבִ֖ינוּ כָּל־רְשָׁעִ֑ים וְהַמַּשְׂכִּלִ֖ים יָבִֽינוּ׃ וּמֵעֵת֙ הוּסַ֣ר
יב הַתָּמִ֔יד וְלָתֵ֖ת שִׁקּ֣וּץ שֹׁמֵ֑ם יָמִ֕ים אֶ֖לֶף מָאתַ֥יִם וְתִשְׁעִֽים׃ אַשְׁרֵ֥י הַֽמְחַכֶּ֖ה וְיַגִּ֑יעַ
יג לְיָמִ֕ים אֶ֕לֶף שְׁלֹ֥שׁ מֵא֖וֹת שְׁלֹשִׁ֥ים וַחֲמִשָּֽׁה׃ וְאַתָּ֖ה לֵ֣ךְ לַקֵּ֑ץ וְתָנ֛וּחַ וְתַעֲמֹ֥ד לְגֹרָלְךָ֖
לְקֵ֥ץ הַיָּמִֽין׃

Ezra Nehemiah

Ezra and Nehemiah

INTRODUCTION TO EZRA AND NEHEMIAH

The book of Ezra, which is followed by the book of Nehemiah as a kind of appendix, describes the return to Zion at the start of the Second Temple period. It does not begin with the story of Ezra and his deeds, but rather several years beforehand, when the immigrants from Babylonia first came to the Land of Israel. The main significance of the books of Ezra and Nehemiah lies in the fact that they focus on the last chapters of the children of Israel in the Bible, and the event they describe is one of the most significant in Jewish history.

With regard to Nehemiah, it should be noted that according to rabbinic and later sources, the book of Ezra includes the chapters that are today called the book of Nehemiah.[1] For example, throughout his commentary on the Talmud, Rashi does not mention the book of Nehemiah, but calls its chapters the book of Ezra. Some label these books I Ezra and II Ezra.

Like the book of Chronicles, the books of Ezra and Nehemiah include many technical and detailed lists, which were probably copied from ancient genealogical texts. The major part of the book, however, deals with the formation of a new type of Kingdom of Judah. During the First Temple period, the service of God centered mainly on the Temple and the monarchy. By contrast, the exiles returning to Zion sought not only to resettle the places where they or their ancestors had lived many years earlier, but to establish a different style of Judean state in its structure and essence. The books of Ezra and Nehemiah portray the dilemmas, the struggles, the conflicts, and the overcoming of internal and external troubles that accompanied the building of the Second Temple and the establishment of a lasting Judean kingdom. It was in these years that a new manner of Jewish life was created, one that endured for generations. Beginning from the days of the Second Temple, Judaism became the basis for a whole way of life. If beforehand an Israelite identified mainly as the member of a particular nation or tribe, whose life to a certain extent was circumscribed by the leader of his clan, in this period being an Israelite started to take on a broader meaning. This change has left its mark on the nation of Israel to this day.

The process of this change was led by several talented individuals. The purpose of the book's presentation of certain details of their lives is not merely to tell the protagonists' stories, but to explain how this new form of the people of Israel came into being. Just as the return to Zion was the fulfillment of the prophets' visions, as explicitly stated at the beginning of the book, it was also a significant attempt of the leadership and community of the returnees to actualize the spirit of the prophets and their Torah, which had not been fully achieved up to that point. Hence the great importance of these books and their place in Jewish history.

Chronology for Books of Ezra and Nehemiah

Date BCE	Event	Prophet	Leader of the Jewish People	Babylonian/ Persian King
539	Conquest of Babylon by Darius the Mede and Cyrus the Great of Persia Cyrus' Proclamation[2] Return of first group to Judah under the leadership of Zerubavel and Yehoshua		 Zerubavel (Sheshbatzar) and Yehoshua the High Priest	Belshatzar Cyrus the Great
538	Construction of the altar and laying of the foundation of the Second Temple, followed by initial attempt to rebuild the Temple[3]			
538?–520	The gentile residents of Judah interfere with the rebuilding of the Temple[4]			
520	Resumption of work on the Second Temple[5]			Darius the Great
516	Completion of the building of the Second Temple under the leadership of Zerubavel and Yehoshua[6]	Haggai 520 BCE Zechariah 520-516 BCE		
520?–459?	Libelous letters sent by enemies of Judah and Benjamin[7]	Malachi 500-470 BCE		
479	Esther becomes Queen		Mordekhai and Esther	Ahashverosh
474–473	Haman's decree against the Jews, and their triumph over their enemies			
458	Arrival of Ezra in Judah[8]		Ezra	Artahshasta
445	Nehemiah appointed satrap over Judah Completion of the rebuilding of the walls of Jerusalem[9] Renewal of covenant[10]		Ezra and Nehemiah	

Ezra

The Return to Zion from Babylonia following Cyrus' Decree

EZRA 1:1–2:70

The book of Ezra does not begin with the story of Ezra himself, but with the history of the exiles' return to Zion. It can be assumed that the exiled Judeans living in Babylonia were aware of the condition of the Land of Israel. They knew that for better or for worse, the surrounding nations had not conquered Judah, and that areas of the land were in ruins due to neglect. They also knew that despite some conflict on the borders, the inhabitants of Jerusalem and other settlements had not been exiled.

The events described here occur after the Persians and the Medes join forces to break Babylon's control over the region. They first conquer lands under Babylonian rule as well as other countries, before Cyrus king of Persia eventually becomes ruler over Babylon. In this context it may be noted that although Cyrus is Persian, and is called the king of Persia in this book, once he conquers Babylonia his kingdom is also referred to by the more ancient name of Babylon.

Cyrus grants permission for the exiled Israelites to establish autonomy in the region of Judah, and even encourages them to rebuild the Temple. It is only at this point that Judah is first used as a territorial and political name. The land of Judah becomes a defined political area, with the official name of Yehud.

During this period, certain people living in Jerusalem are not from the tribe of Judah, but had returned to the Land of Israel together with the people of Judah and Benjamin. Nevertheless, all those who returned to the land, even those not from the tribe of Judah, Yehuda, are called Judeans.

1 1 It was **in the first year** of the newly independent rule **of Cyrus**
king of Persia, once the end of the allotted time according to
the word of the Lord from the mouth of Jeremiah had been
fulfilled. Jeremiah had prophesied that the exiles would return
from Babylonia after seventy years. The exact calculation was
unclear, but it was broadly recognized that the return of Judeans
to their land was a fulfillment of that prophecy.[11] In that year,
the Lord roused the spirit of Cyrus[BD] **king of Persia, and**
he, Cyrus, **circulated a proclamation throughout his entire**
kingdom. Although most Judeans lived in one specific area,
there were some scattered throughout the kingdom. **And** Cyrus
not only issued an oral declaration, he put it **also in writing.**
These documents would be very important at a later stage, when
problems arose with regard to the building of the Temple and it
became necessary to examine these letters sent by Cyrus.[12] Cyrus
proclaimed, **saying:**

Winged figure, possibly Cyrus, relief on a post, Pasargadae, Cyrus' capital, sixth century BCE

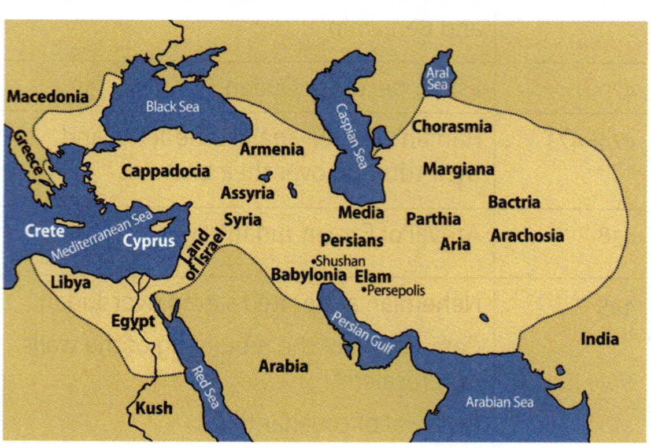

"The Lord, God of the heavens, has given me all the kingdoms of the earth." The empire of Cyrus

2 **So said Cyrus king of Persia: The Lord, God of the heavens,**
has given me all the kingdoms of the earth. My reign is a gift
from the Lord, the God of Israel. A skillful diplomat, Cyrus
would frequently identify himself with the customs and religion
of the people to whom he was speaking. Therefore, in this case,
when addressing the Judeans, he emphasized that the God of

עזרא

א ובשנת אחת לכורש מלך פרס לכלות דבר־יהוה מפי ירמיה העיר יהוה את־ א
ב רוח כרש מלך־פרס ויעבר־קול בכל־מלכותו וגם־במכתב לאמר: כה אמר
כרש מלך פרס כל ממלכות הארץ נתן לי יהוה אלהי השמים והוא־פקד עלי
ג לבנות־לו בית בירושלם אשר ביהודה: מי־בכם מכל־עמו יהי אלהיו עמו ויעל
לירושלם אשר ביהודה ויבן את־בית יהוה אלהי ישראל הוא האלהים אשר
ד בירושלם: וכל־הנשאר מכל־המקמות אשר הוא גר־שם ינשאוהו אנשי מקמו
בכסף ובזהב וברכוש ובבהמה עם־הנדבה לבית האלהים אשר בירושלם:

Israel had given him all the land he controlled. **And He has commanded me to build Him a House in Jerusalem, which is in Judah.** This command came to me from God, and I wish to fulfill it. Cyrus spoke almost like a king of Israel. His statement expressed a sense of obligation to thank God for granting him power as a ruler, and he stated that he was motivated by gratitude to encourage the building of the Temple in Jerusalem.

Cyrus Cylinder, 539 BCE

3 The previous declaration had certain practical ramifications: **Any among you from His entire people,** the people of the God of heaven, the nation of Israel, **may his God be with him, and he may go up to Jerusalem, which is in Judah, and build the House of the Lord, God of Israel; He is the God who is in Jerusalem.** Cyrus did not decree that all Judeans must go back to their land. Rather, he called upon those Judeans who felt as he did, that the Temple should be rebuilt, and invited them to arise and travel to the Land of Israel out of their own desire.

4 It was clear to Cyrus that not all Judeans would respond to his call, as Babylonia was far from the Land of Israel and the journey was grueling. Therefore, he said: **Whoever** of the Judeans **remains, from any place where he,** one who has decided to return to the Land of Israel, **resides, let the people of his place load him,** thereby helping financially, by providing him[13] **with silver, with gold, with goods, and with livestock, along with** a contribution toward **the gift to the House of God that is in Jerusalem.** Cyrus exhorted any Judeans who had decided not to return to at least help those who had chosen to go. He even urged them to send a free-will offering to Jerusalem. Cyrus may

BACKGROUND

1:1 | **Cyrus:** According to the Babylonian Chronicles, as well as Herodotus, Cyrus was already ruling the Persians in 559 BCE. It was only after many conquests and struggles, lasting some twenty years, that he conquered the city of Babylon and became ruler of the Persian Empire, which stretched from northeast India to Asia Minor, incorporating Syria, Lebanon, and the Land of Israel. In that year, a royal decree was issued, similar in spirit to Cyrus' declaration to the Judeans in this chapter, which has been discovered on a cylinder of clay. Called the Cyrus Cylinder, it was found in Babylon in 1897 and is currently located in the British Museum.

DISCUSSION

1:1 | **The Lord roused the spirit of Cyrus:** Cyrus returned the Judeans to their homeland. The Persian king permitted and even encouraged them to reestablish their national identity. Granted, Cyrus was generally tolerant toward other nations and religions as well, but his attitude toward Israel was exceptional, and the verse states that this was due to special divine inspiration (see Isaiah 44:28–45:13, and commentaries ad loc.).

or may not have known that the returning Judeans were about to encounter a virtually desolate land. However, he realized that they would require more money than what was required for mere travel expenses. Another reason for Cyrus' exhortation that the remaining Judeans help their emigrating brothers is that he himself, along with several other kings, donated money and goods to the Temple, and was therefore adamant that the Judeans themselves should participate in this voluntary enterprise as well. Thus Cyrus' statement was more than just the granting of permission to return to the Land of Israel. He was actively encouraging them to return, to build the Temple, and to establish for themselves a national home.

5 **The heads of the patrilineal families of Judah and Benjamin, and the priests and the Levites, everyone whom God had roused his spirit, rose to go up to build the House of the Lord that is in Jerusalem.**
6 **All those surrounding them,** those who had chosen not to return to the Land of Israel, **supported them with vessels of silver, with gold, with goods, with livestock, and with delicacies** or gifts,[14] **besides everything that was donated** to the Temple for when it would be built.

Gold vessel, Mycenae, Greece, 1500 BCE

7 **King Cyrus took out the vessels of the House of the Lord** from his treasury, those **that Nebuchadnezzar had taken out of Jerusalem and put in the house of his god.** The vessels taken from the First Temple had been kept in the treasury of the king of Babylon and were now in the possession of the king of Persia.[15]
8 **Cyrus king of Persia had them taken out by Mitredat, the treasurer,**[B] **and he itemized them,** handed them over while counting them, **for Sheshbatzar,**[D] **the prince,** leader, **of Judah.**
9 **This is their,** the vessels', **number:** Large **gold basins,**[B] **thirty; silver basins, one thousand; and** slaughtering **knives,**[16] which were probably knives of special quality or uniquely decorated, **twenty-nine;**

Golden oil jug

Knives, ancient Egypt, 600-200 BCE

10 **gold bowls,**[B] receptacles used for the sprinkling of blood of atonement upon the altar,[17] or a kind of platter,[18] **thirty; silver secondary bowls,** bowls of secondary importance, **four hundred and ten; and other** unspecified Temple **vessels, one thousand.** It is possible these included appurtenances for the candelabrum or the table for the showbread, both of which were made of pure gold.
11 **All the gold and silver vessels,**[D] including vessels not listed above, **were five thousand four hundred,** of all types and sizes. **All of it was brought by Sheshbatzar with the ascent of the exile from Babylonia to Jerusalem.** Cyrus gave these vessels to Sheshbatzar on condition that he would bring them to Jerusalem, so that they would be the first vessels used in the Temple.

Silver receptacle

2 1 **These are the people of the province** of Babylonia,[19] or of Judah, **who went up from the captivity of the exile, whom Nebuchadnezzar king of Babylon had exiled to Babylonia, and they returned to Jerusalem and Judah; each** returned **to his city.**
2 These are the people **who came with Zerubavel,** the leader of the Judeans: **Yeshua,** the High Priest;[20] **Nehemiah,** probably not

BACKGROUND

1:8| **Treasurer [*gizbar*]:** This is the chief financial officer of the kingdom. The term *gizbar*, which also appears in Akkadian and Old Persian, is a combination of two separate words: *Ganza*, meaning treasury, as in *ginzei hamelekh*, the king's treasuries (Esther 3:9), or *ganzakav*, its treasuries (I Chronicles 28:11); and *bara*, regent, holder, bearer.

1:9| **Basin [*agartal*]:** Either a general term for a vessel (Rashi), or the name of a particular vessel. Some claim that *agartal* is a jug with two handles, designed for washing the hands (Ibn Janaḥ), while according to the Septuagint it is a vessel for cooling wine. The Latin translation (Vulgate) renders it as a flat bowl. Due to the unusual form of the word, various theories have been suggested that it originates from the Sumerian, Hitite, Persian, or Greek language, but these ideas have not been sufficiently substantiated.

1:10| **Bowl [*kefor*]:** This is a receptacle, similar to a jug or a bucket, used in the Temple service for holding blood. The same root is used for atonement [*kapara*] and wiping away (see *Zevaḥim* 25a; *Yalkut Shimoni* 469). Likewise, the Akkadian term *kaparu* also means to wipe away.

ה וַיָּקוּמוּ רָאשֵׁי הָאָבוֹת לִיהוּדָה וּבִנְיָמִן וְהַכֹּהֲנִים וְהַלְוִיִּם לְכֹל הֵעִיר הָאֱלֹהִים
ו אֶת־רוּחוֹ לַעֲלוֹת לִבְנוֹת אֶת־בֵּית יְהֹוָה אֲשֶׁר בִּירוּשָׁלִָם: וְכָל־סְבִיבֹתֵיהֶם חִזְּקוּ
בִידֵיהֶם בִּכְלֵי־כֶסֶף בַּזָּהָב בָּרְכוּשׁ וּבַבְּהֵמָה וּבַמִּגְדָּנוֹת לְבַד עַל־כָּל־הִתְנַדֵּב:
ז וְהַמֶּלֶךְ כּוֹרֶשׁ הוֹצִיא אֶת־כְּלֵי בֵית־יְהֹוָה אֲשֶׁר הוֹצִיא נְבוּכַדְנֶצַּר מִירוּשָׁלִַם
ח וַיִּתְּנֵם בְּבֵית אֱלֹהָיו: וַיּוֹצִיאֵם כּוֹרֶשׁ מֶלֶךְ פָּרַס עַל־יַד מִתְרְדָת הַגִּזְבָּר וַיִּסְפְּרֵם
ט לְשֵׁשְׁבַּצַּר הַנָּשִׂיא לִיהוּדָה: וְאֵלֶּה מִסְפָּרָם אֲגַרְטְלֵי זָהָב שְׁלֹשִׁים
י אֲגַרְטְלֵי־כֶסֶף אָלֶף מַחֲלָפִים תִּשְׁעָה וְעֶשְׂרִים: כְּפוֹרֵי זָהָב שְׁלֹשִׁים כְּפוֹרֵי כֶסֶף
יא מִשְׁנִים אַרְבַּע מֵאוֹת וַעֲשָׂרָה כֵּלִים אֲחֵרִים אָלֶף: כָּל־כֵּלִים לַזָּהָב וְלַכֶּסֶף חֲמֵשֶׁת
אֲלָפִים וְאַרְבַּע מֵאוֹת הַכֹּל הֶעֱלָה שֵׁשְׁבַּצַּר עִם הֵעָלוֹת הַגּוֹלָה מִבָּבֶל לִירוּשָׁלִָם:
א וְאֵלֶּה ׀ בְּנֵי הַמְּדִינָה הָעֹלִים מִשְּׁבִי הַגּוֹלָה אֲשֶׁר הֶגְלָה נבוכדנצור מֶלֶךְ־בָּבֶל נְבוּכַדְנֶצַּר
ב לְבָבֶל וַיָּשׁוּבוּ לִירוּשָׁלִַם וִיהוּדָה אִישׁ לְעִירוֹ: אֲשֶׁר־בָּאוּ עִם־זְרֻבָּבֶל יֵשׁוּעַ נְחֶמְיָה
שְׂרָיָה רְעֵלָיָה מָרְדֳּכַי בִּלְשָׁן מִסְפָּר בִּגְוַי רְחוּם בַּעֲנָה מִסְפַּר אַנְשֵׁי עַם יִשְׂרָאֵל:

DISCUSSION

1:8 | **Sheshbatzar:** There is an accepted tradition that Sheshbatzar was the foreign name of Zerubavel, who is mentioned below (2:2) as the leader of the immigrants (Ibn Ezra; Ralbag; *Metzudat David*). It was no coincidence that Zerubavel was chosen to be prince, as he was a descendant of the Judean royal household, from the sons of King Yehoyakhin (see *Sanhedrin* 37b–38a). Naturally, Cyrus did not deal with the structure of the social or political leadership of the immigrants, but rather he turned to the person who was accepted by all as the prince of Judah. In later generations, there were exilarchs in Babylonia, who were also leaders of the Judeans from the royal house of David.

1:11 | **All the gold and silver vessels:** The list of the plunder that Nebuchadnezzar's general, Nevuzaradan, took at the destruction of the First Temple (II Kings 25:13–17) does not include the major vessels of the Temple: the ark, the candelabrum, the table for the showbread, and the golden altar. Many ornamental objects are mentioned in the descriptions of the building of King Solomon's Temple, and other items were presumably added over the generations. However, many of them, such as the pillars, the sea, which was a very large water basin (see I Kings 7:23), and the castings in the image of oxen upon which it stood, were too heavy to be taken to a distant land, and were probably broken up or melted down. It stands to reason that the spoilers of the Temple who carried their loot were interested mainly in the gold and silver vessels and other precious items, such as the garments of the High Priest (see II Kings 24:13).

It is likely that at the time of the destruction of the First Temple most of the important sacred vessels were no longer in their required places. Some conclude, based on statements of the Sages, that the Ark of the Covenant had already been removed in the days of King Menashe or King Yoshiya (see *Tosefta*, *Sota* 13:1; *Yoma* 52b; *Horayot* 12a). There are several traditions with regard to the places where they were stored away: The Ark of the Covenant was buried in the Chamber of the Woodshed on the Temple Mount (see Mishna *Shekalim* 6:1–2; *Yoma* 54a); the ark and the golden altar were hidden away in a cave by the prophet Jeremiah (see Maccabees II:2:4–5); and according to the Copper Scroll from the third century BCE, found near Khirbet Qumran, certain vessels were buried by King Tzidkiya in an unknown location called Kahelet or Ein Kahal. The same tradition is cited in "The Tractate of the Vessels of the Temple," which is mentioned in the book *Emek HaMelekh* by the seventeenth-century kabbalist Rabbi Naftali Bacharach (see Ibn Ezra, 2:63).

the famous Nehemiah son of Hakhalya, the eponymous figure of the book of Nehemiah, who became leader of Judah at a later stage; **Seraya; Re'elaya; Mordekhai; Bilshan.** Some say that Bilshan is another name for Mordekhai,[21] due to his linguistic expertise, as *lashon* means language, whereas others maintain that Bilshan was a different person.[22] **Mispar, Bigvai, Rehum, Baana.** The following is **the** total **number,** or some **of the** important[23] **men of the people of Israel:**

3 The following section provides a list of family heads and their sums: **The children of Parosh, two thousand one hundred and seventy-two;**

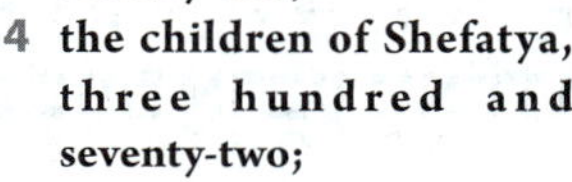

4 **the children of Shefatya, three hundred and seventy-two;**

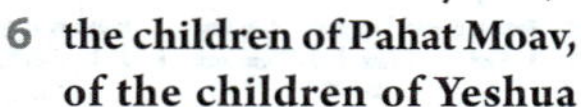

Seal with inscription: "To Neriyahu (son of) Parosh," Tel Lakhish, Iron Age

5 **the children of Arah, seven hundred and seventy-five;**
6 **the children of Pahat Moav, of the children of Yeshua and Yoav,**[24] **two thousand eight hundred and twelve.** The name Pahat Moav probably indicates that he was an officer in the Moavite government when it was under Judean control, or at least from one of the important families that had lived there at some time in the past (see commentary on 8:4);

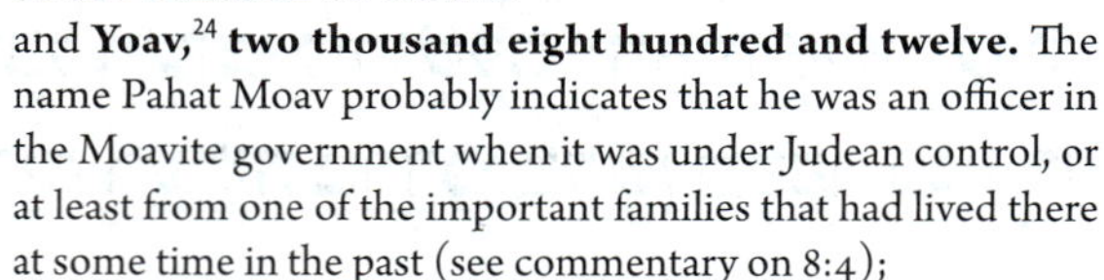

7 **the children of Elam, one thousand two hundred and fifty-four;**

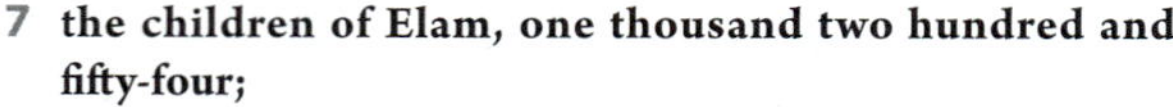

8 **the children of Zatu, nine hundred and forty-five;**
9 **the children of Zakai, seven hundred and sixty;**
10 **the children of Bani, six hundred and forty-two;**
11 **the children of Bevai, six hundred and twenty-three;**
12 **the children of Azgad, one thousand two hundred and twenty-two;**
13 **the children of Adonikam, six hundred and sixty-six;**
14 **the children of Bigvai, two thousand and fifty-six;**
15 **the children of Adin, four hundred and fifty-four;**
16 **the children of Ater,** who were born **to Hizkiya, ninety-eight.**[25] Some explain that the children of Ater denotes a separate family that was appended to Hizkiya;
17 **the children of Betzai, three hundred and twenty-three;**
18 **the children of Yora, one hundred and twelve;**
19 **the children of Hashum, two hundred and twenty-three;**
20 **the children of Gibar, ninety-five.**
21 After the previous list of names of heads of families, the chapter enumerates groups of people who are called after the places where they lived: **The children of Bethlehem, one hundred and twenty-three;**
22 **the men** of the settlement **of Netofa,**[B] **fifty-six;**
23 **the men** of the village **of Anatot,**[B] **one hundred and twenty-eight;**
24 **the children of Azmavet,**[B] **forty-two;**

Village of Hizma

25 **the children of Kiryat Arim,**[B] **Kefira,**[B] **and Be'erot,** cities in Benjamin, were **seven hundred and forty-three;**
26 **the children of Rama**[B] **and Geva,**[B] **six hundred and twenty-one;**
27 **the men of Mikhmas,**[B] **one hundred and twenty-two;**
28 **the men of Beit El and the Ai, two hundred and twenty-three;**
29 **the children of Nevo,**[B] **fifty-two;**
30 **the children of Magbish, one hundred and fifty-six;**
31 **the children of the other Elam,**[B] not the same Elam as the

BACKGROUND

2:21–22 | **Bethlehem and Netofa:** These two settlements are mentioned together elsewhere in the Bible (e.g., II Samuel 23:28; Nehemiah 7:26; I Chronicles 2:54). Some identify them with sites south of Jerusalem: The well-known Bethlehem of modern times, and Umm Tuba or Khirbet Bedd Faluh, roughly 1 km west of Herodion and north of present-day Tekoa, next to a spring called Ein e-Natuf. However, since the Bible often juxtaposes these settlements with other places in the area of Benjamin, they should perhaps be identified with two sites located on the ridge along the Kefira Ravine in Benjamin: Bethlehem with Khirbet Abu Lehem, about 1 km north of Ma'ale Hahamisha; and Netofa with Khirbet Nataf, approximately 4.2 km west of Ma'ale Hahamisha.

2:23 | **Anatot:** A city in Benjamin that was given to the priests (Joshua 21:18), located 5 km northeast of Jerusalem. It has been identified with one of two sites near the contemporary village of Anata: Khirbet Deir es-Sidd and Ras el-Kharrubeh. The fields adjacent to Anatot were owned and worked by priests (see Numbers 35:3–4; Jeremiah 32:7–32).

ג ד בְּנֵי פַרְעֹשׁ אַלְפַּיִם מֵאָה שִׁבְעִים וּשְׁנָיִם׃ בְּנֵי שְׁפַטְיָה שְׁלֹשׁ מֵאוֹת שִׁבְעִים וּשְׁנָיִם׃
ה ו בְּנֵי אָרַח שְׁבַע מֵאוֹת חֲמִשָּׁה וְשִׁבְעִים׃ בְּנֵי־פַחַת מוֹאָב לִבְנֵי יֵשׁוּעַ יוֹאָב אַלְפַּיִם
ז ח שְׁמֹנֶה מֵאוֹת וּשְׁנֵים עָשָׂר׃ בְּנֵי עֵילָם אֶלֶף מָאתַיִם חֲמִשִּׁים וְאַרְבָּעָה׃ בְּנֵי זַתּוּא
ט י תְּשַׁע מֵאוֹת וְאַרְבָּעִים וַחֲמִשָּׁה׃ בְּנֵי זַכָּי שְׁבַע מֵאוֹת וְשִׁשִּׁים׃ בְּנֵי בָנִי שֵׁשׁ מֵאוֹת
יא יב אַרְבָּעִים וּשְׁנָיִם׃ בְּנֵי בֵבָי שֵׁשׁ מֵאוֹת עֶשְׂרִים וּשְׁלֹשָׁה׃ בְּנֵי עַזְגָּד אֶלֶף מָאתַיִם
יג יד עֶשְׂרִים וּשְׁנָיִם׃ בְּנֵי אֲדֹנִיקָם שֵׁשׁ מֵאוֹת שִׁשִּׁים וְשִׁשָּׁה׃ בְּנֵי בִגְוָי אַלְפַּיִם חֲמִשִּׁים
טו טז וְשִׁשָּׁה׃ בְּנֵי עָדִין אַרְבַּע מֵאוֹת חֲמִשִּׁים וְאַרְבָּעָה׃ בְּנֵי־אָטֵר לִיחִזְקִיָּה תִּשְׁעִים
יז יח וּשְׁמֹנָה׃ בְּנֵי בֵצָי שְׁלֹשׁ מֵאוֹת עֶשְׂרִים וּשְׁלֹשָׁה׃ בְּנֵי יוֹרָה מֵאָה וּשְׁנֵים עָשָׂר׃
יט כ כא בְּנֵי חָשֻׁם מָאתַיִם עֶשְׂרִים וּשְׁלֹשָׁה׃ בְּנֵי גִבָּר תִּשְׁעִים וַחֲמִשָּׁה׃ בְּנֵי בֵית־לָחֶם
כב כג מֵאָה עֶשְׂרִים וּשְׁלֹשָׁה׃ אַנְשֵׁי נְטֹפָה חֲמִשִּׁים וְשִׁשָּׁה׃ אַנְשֵׁי עֲנָתוֹת מֵאָה עֶשְׂרִים
כד כה וּשְׁמֹנָה׃ בְּנֵי עַזְמָוֶת אַרְבָּעִים וּשְׁנָיִם׃ בְּנֵי קִרְיַת עָרִים כְּפִירָה וּבְאֵרוֹת שְׁבַע
כו כז מֵאוֹת וְאַרְבָּעִים וּשְׁלֹשָׁה׃ בְּנֵי הָרָמָה וָגָבַע שֵׁשׁ מֵאוֹת עֶשְׂרִים וְאֶחָד׃ אַנְשֵׁי
כח כט מִכְמָס מֵאָה עֶשְׂרִים וּשְׁנָיִם׃ אַנְשֵׁי בֵית־אֵל וְהָעָי מָאתַיִם עֶשְׂרִים וּשְׁלֹשָׁה׃ בְּנֵי
ל לא נְבוֹ חֲמִשִּׁים וּשְׁנָיִם׃ בְּנֵי מַגְבִּישׁ מֵאָה חֲמִשִּׁים וְשִׁשָּׁה׃ בְּנֵי עֵילָם אַחֵר אֶלֶף

BACKGROUND

2:24 | **Azmavet:** This has been identified with the present-day village of Hizma, northeast of Jerusalem, due to the similarity of the names. The settlement is in the portion of Benjamin, and Azmavet was a common name in that tribe (see II Samuel 23:31; I Chronicles 8:36, 9:42, 11:33, 12:3). The place was possibly named after one of those men; alternatively, they were named after their place of residence.

2:25 | **Kiryat Arim:** This has been identified with the hill overlooking Abu Ghosh to the west. Since Kiryat Arim was a border town, its ownership changed over the course of history. It was formerly ruled by Canaanites and Givonites, and was later taken over jointly by the tribes of Judah and Benjamin. Its many names, Giva, Kiryat Ye'arim, Har Ye'arim, Ja'ara, Baala, Kiryat Baal, and Sadeh Ya'ar, not only reflect political and religious changes but refer to different geographical areas within the city itself. Thus, Giva (Joshua 18:28; I Samuel 7:1) is the name of a special site inside Kiryat Arim, one of the places where the Ark of the Covenant was brought in its travels.

Kefira: A city inside the portion of Benjamin, one of the five Givonite cities (Joshua 9:17, 18:26). Kefira is identified with Khirbet Kefireh, about 2 km west of the settlement of Har Adar, where remains from the eras of the First and the Second Temples have been found.

2:26 | **Rama:** Generally identified nowadays with A-ram, north of Jerusalem.

Geva: One of the cities of the tribe of Benjamin that was given to the priests (Joshua 18:24, 21:17; Isaiah 10:29). It is identified with Jaba, an Arab village north of Adam Junction.

2:27 | **Mikhmas:** Identified with the Arab village of the same name, located on the border of the Judean Desert, northeast of Jerusalem. Mikhmas controlled the road that ascended from Jericho to the mountain ridge and which connected to a route that ran from north to south, east of Mikhmas and parallel to the watershed line of the Dead Sea.

2:29 | **Nevo:** This is probably Nov, the city of priests in Benjamin, which is also mentioned in Nehemiah (11:32) alongside Anatot. It is generally identified as a place in the vicinity of the modern-day villages of 'Anata and Beit Hanina, in the area of the village of Shuafat outside of Jerusalem. This location suits the description of Sennacherib's travels in Isaiah (10:32): "Even today he will stand at Nov; he will wave his hand at the mountain of the daughter of Zion, the hill of Jerusalem." A different suggestion places Nov on the slope that overlooks Wadi Joz, near Mount Scopus in present-day Jerusalem.

2:31 | **The other Elam:** This might be referring to Almon, located in the portion of Benjamin (Joshua 21:18).

one mentioned above (2:7), **one thousand two hundred and fifty-four;**
32 **the children of Harim,**[B] **three hundred and twenty;**
33 **the children of Lod,**[B] **Hadid,**[B] **and Ono,**[B] adjacent cities on the same plain, **seven hundred and twenty-five;**
34 **the children of Jericho,**[B] **three hundred and forty-five;**
35 **the children of Senaa,**[B] **three thousand six hundred and thirty.**
36 **The priests: The children** of the watch **of Yedaya, of the house of Yeshua** son of Yotzadak the High Priest[26] were **nine hundred and seventy-three;**
37 **the children of Imer,** another priestly watch, **one thousand and fifty-two;**
38 **the children of Pashhur, one thousand two hundred and forty-seven;**
39 **the children of Harim, one thousand and seventeen.**

Tel el-Haditheh

Tel es-Sultan

40 **The Levites: The children of Yeshua and Kadmiel, of the children of Hodavya, seventy-four.**
41 **The** Levite **singers: The children of Asaf, one hundred and twenty-eight.**
42 **The children of the** Levite **gatekeepers** were from different families: **The children of Shalum, the children of Ater, the children of Talmon, the children of Akuv, the children of Hatita, the children of Shovai; in all, one hundred and thirty-nine.**
43 **The Netinim**[B] were descendants of the Givonites, who lived with the Judeans and were servants responsible for the Temple maintenance.[27] These are the names of their families: **The children of Tziha, the children of Hasufa, the children of Tabaot;**
44 **the children of Keros, the children of Siaha, the children of Padon;**
45 **the children of Levana, the children of Hagava,**[B] **the children of Akuv;**
46 **the children of Hagav, the children of Salmai, the children of Hanan;**

Archer and inscription "For Hagav," illustration based on seal found in Western Wall excavations, seventh century BCE

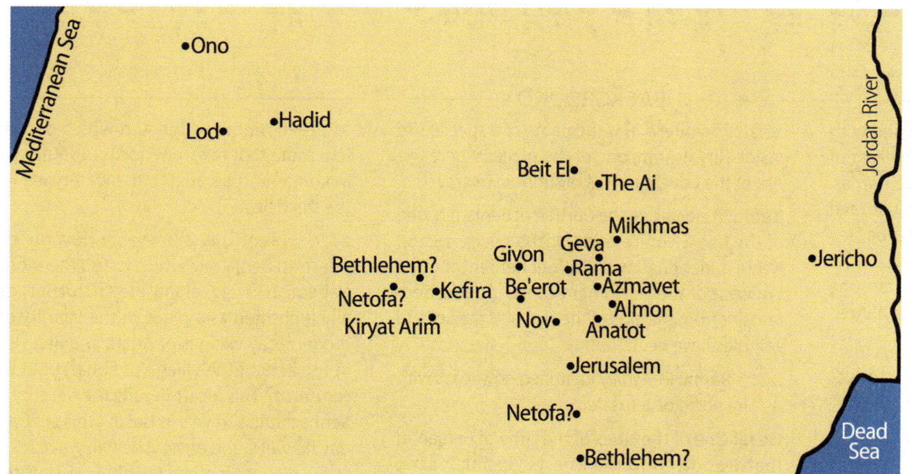

Settlements of the immigrants

Illustration based on seal with inscription "Hagava" above the image of a grasshopper, Jerusalem, eighth century BCE

לב לג מָאתַיִם חֲמִשִּׁים וְאַרְבָּעָה׃ בְּנֵי חָרִם שְׁלֹשׁ מֵאוֹת וְעֶשְׂרִים׃ בְּנֵי־לֹד חָדִיד וְאוֹנוֹ
לד לה שְׁבַע מֵאוֹת עֶשְׂרִים וַחֲמִשָּׁה׃ בְּנֵי יְרֵחוֹ שְׁלֹשׁ מֵאוֹת אַרְבָּעִים וַחֲמִשָּׁה׃ בְּנֵי
לו סְנָאָה שְׁלֹשֶׁת אֲלָפִים וְשֵׁשׁ מֵאוֹת וּשְׁלֹשִׁים׃ הַכֹּהֲנִים בְּנֵי יְדַעְיָה לְבֵית יֵשׁוּעַ
לז לח תְּשַׁע מֵאוֹת שִׁבְעִים וּשְׁלֹשָׁה׃ בְּנֵי אִמֵּר אֶלֶף חֲמִשִּׁים וּשְׁנָיִם׃ בְּנֵי פַשְׁחוּר אֶלֶף
לט מ מָאתַיִם אַרְבָּעִים וְשִׁבְעָה׃ בְּנֵי חָרִם אֶלֶף וְשִׁבְעָה עָשָׂר׃ הַלְוִיִּם בְּנֵי־יֵשׁוּעַ
מא וְקַדְמִיאֵל לִבְנֵי הוֹדַוְיָה שִׁבְעִים וְאַרְבָּעָה׃ הַמְשֹׁרְרִים בְּנֵי אָסָף מֵאָה עֶשְׂרִים
מב וּשְׁמֹנָה׃ בְּנֵי הַשֹּׁעֲרִים בְּנֵי־שַׁלּוּם בְּנֵי־אָטֵר בְּנֵי־טַלְמוֹן בְּנֵי־עַקּוּב בְּנֵי חֲטִיטָא
מג בְּנֵי שֹׁבָי הַכֹּל מֵאָה שְׁלֹשִׁים וְתִשְׁעָה׃ הַנְּתִינִים בְּנֵי־צִיחָא בְנֵי־חֲשׂוּפָא בְּנֵי
מד מה מו טַבָּעוֹת׃ בְּנֵי־קֵרֹס בְּנֵי־סִיעֲהָא בְּנֵי פָדוֹן׃ בְּנֵי־לְבָנָה בְנֵי־חֲגָבָה בְּנֵי עַקּוּב׃ בְּנֵי־

BACKGROUND

2:32 | **Harim:** The name of one of four priestly watches who returned from the Babylonian exile (*Ta'anit* 27a; *Tosefta*, *Ta'anit* 2:1). There is no record of a place of this name.

2:33 | **Lod:** Located on the crossroad between Jaffa and the inland plains, which intersects the Via Maris, Lod is near the valley of Ayalon. It is mentioned in the list of conquered sites of Thutmose III (fifteenth century BCE), and is one of the cities surrounded by a wall from the days of Joshua (*Megilla* 4a). According to I Chronicles 8:12, it was restored by Elpaal of Benjamin (see Judges 21:23; Jerusalem Talmud, *Megilla* 1:5).

Hadid: Identified with Tel el-Haditheh, about 6 km northeast of Lod. Archaeological evidence indicates that this site was already inhabited at the beginning of the Iron Age. According to the Mishna (*Arakhin* 9:6), it was one of the walled cities from the days of Joshua. Bills of sale found there indicate that exiled foreigners settled in the area at the end of the seventh century BCE. Apparently, Israelites resettled the region during the days of King Yoshiya.

Ono: An ancient city in the Ono Valley. Its name is preserved in the Arab village Kafr 'Ana, whose remains are located near modern-day Or Yehuda. Like Lod, Ono is mentioned in the list of the conquests of Thutmose III from the fifteenth century BCE, and it too is considered one of the walled cities from the days of Joshua (*Megilla* 4a). According to I Chronicles 8:12, Ono, like Lod, was rebuilt by Elpaal of Benjamin after its destruction in the war of the concubine of Giva (see Judges 20:48). The city was possibly restored in the days of King Uziya (see II Chronicles 26:6).

2:34 | **Jericho:** Also known as the city of the date palms, Jericho is located in the portion of Benjamin (Deuteronomy 34:3; Judges 1:16, and commentary ad loc., 3:13; II Chronicles 28:15). Jericho controlled the road from the area east of the Jordan River to Jerusalem. It is identified with Tel es-Sultan, approximately 2 km north of the center of present-day Jericho.

2:35 | **Children of Senaa:** A family from the tribe of Benjamin (Mishna *Ta'anit* 4:5; *Tosefta*, *Ta'anit* 2:6). Eusebius mentions a place called Magdalsenna, northeast of Jericho (Eusebius, *Onomasticon*. Erich Klosterman, ed. Leipzig: Hirichs, 1904 [Greek and Latin], 154, 16, 17). This identification is supported by the story of the children of Senaa, who built part of the wall of Jerusalem, next to the construction of the children of Jericho (see Nehemiah 3:2–3).

2:43 | **Netinim:** This term refers to the descendants of the Givonites who were a distinct minority group that lived with the Judeans. The Netinim were assigned by Joshua to be hewers of wood and drawers of water in the service of the Temple (see Joshua 9) and apparently maintained their identity as servants or attendants of the Temple even through the Babylonian captivity and the return of the exiles to the Land of Israel. Despite their relatively undignified line of work and their lowly status, they felt a connection with the Temple and were dedicated to its maintenance, and they were so attached to the people that they preferred to return, and even to resume their previous role.

2:45 | **The children of Hagava:** A seal from the eighth century BCE has been discovered which includes the inscription *hagava* and a picture of a grasshopper, *ḥagav*. The word *gava* is similar to *govai*, locusts (see Amos 7:1; Nahum 3:17). Names which begin with the definite article *ha*, meaning "the," are common in the Bible. They generally refer to craftsmen, or people from noble houses or important functionaries, such as *harakaḥim*, the son of perfumers (Nehemiah 3:8); *benei hakotz*, the son of the calligraphers (Ezra 2:61); and son of Halohesh (Nehemiah 3:12). It is likely that the owner of this seal was from a noble family that performed important roles in the government or the Temple.

A different seal with the name Hagav on it was discovered in 2008, but it is not clear if it is connected to the biblical Hagava family named in this verse. The seal was apparently for an individual named Hagav, who may have served in a senior military role in Judah, as seen in his image as an archer on the seal.

47 **the children of Gidel, the children of Gahar, the children of Re'aya;**
48 **the children of Retzin, the children of Nekoda, the children of Gazam;**
49 **the children of Uza, the children of Pase'ah, the children of Besai;**
50 **the children of Asna, the children of Meunim, the children of Nefusim;**
51 **the children of Bakbuk, the children of Hakufa, the children of Harhur;**
52 **the children of Batzlut, the children of Mehida, the children of Harsha;**
53 **the children of Barkos, the children of Sisera, the children of Temah;**
54 **the children of Netziah, the children of Hatifa.** Many of these names have no meaning in Hebrew, as some of the families maintained their ancient Givonite names.
55 **The children of Solomon's servants,** descendants of Solomon's foreign servants,[28] who also decided to return to Jerusalem: **The children of Sotai, the children of Soferet, the children of Peruda;**
56 **the children of Yaala, the children of Darkon, the children of Gidel;**
57 **the children of Shefatya, the children of Hatil; the children of Pokheret-Hatzeva'im,** a phrase that originally meant a deer trap, and which became a personal name; **the children of Ami.**
58 **All the Netinim and the children of Solomon's servants were three hundred and ninety-two.** All these were Canaanite slaves who lived in the midst of the children of Israel for hundreds of years.
59 **These were those who went up** with the Judeans **from Tel Melah,** from **Tel Harsha,**[B] from **Keruv,** from **Adan,** and from **Imer; and they were not able to tell whether their fathers' houses and their offspring were of Israel,** as their lineage was unknown:
60 **The children of Delaya, the children of Toviya,**[B] **the children of Nekoda, six hundred and fifty-two.**
61 **From the children of the priests: The children of Havaya, the children of Hakotz,** and **the children of Barzilai, who** were called by this name because their father **took a wife from the daughters of Barzilai the Giladite and was called after their name.** Their family is called Barzilai because he was their ancestor on their mother's side.
62 **These** men, who claimed to be priests, **sought their genealogical registry,** which would prove that they were indeed priests, **but it was not found, and they were banned from the priesthood.**
63 The Tirshata was an honorary Persian title, meaning governor.[29] Nehemiah son of Hakhalya, governor of the Judeans, was called by this title.[30] Alternatively, this Tirshata was a different governor of unknown identity.[31] Either way, **the Tirshata said to them,** the priests of questionable lineage, **that they may not eat from the sacred sacraments,** which only the priests are permitted to eat, **until there stands a priest with the Urim and with the Tumim.** Since they could not prove they were priests, they had to remain in a state of questionable priesthood until the arrival of a priest who could use the Urim and Tumim to confirm their lineage.[32]
64 **The entire congregation together was forty-two thousand three hundred and sixty** people,
65 **besides their slaves and their maidservants; these were seven thousand three hundred and thirty-seven; and they had** accompanying them **two hundred male singers and female singers.** Many wealthy families retained singers among their retinue of servants.
66 **Their horses, seven hundred and thirty-six; their mules, two hundred and forty-five;**
67 **their camels, four hundred and thirty-five; their donkeys,** of which they possessed many, more than all the other animals combined, were **six thousand seven hundred and twenty.** This ends the highly detailed account of the first wave of emigrants who returned to the Land of Israel.
68 **Some of the heads of the patrilineal families, upon their arrival at** the ruins of **the House of the Lord that is in Jerusalem, donated** money and other items **to the House of God to establish it in its place,** to restore it afresh;
69 **in accordance with their means, they gave to the treasury of the labor,** for the construction of the Temple: **Gold, sixty-one thousand darics,**[B] a Persian coin; **and silver, five thousand maneh,** either units of weights or coins;[33] **and priests' tunics, one hundred,** whose manufacture requires great skill.

Daric, obverse and reverse, Achaemenid Empire, 522–486 BCE

מז מח חָגָב בְּנֵי־שַׁמְלַי בְּנֵי חָנָן׃ בְּנֵי־גִדֵּל בְּנֵי־גַחַר בְּנֵי רְאָיָה׃ בְּנֵי־רְצִין בְּנֵי־נְקוֹדָא בְּנֵי שַׁלְמַי
מט נ נא גַזָּם׃ בְּנֵי־עֻזָּא בְנֵי־פָסֵחַ בְּנֵי בֵסָי׃ בְּנֵי־אַסְנָה בְנֵי־מְעוּנִים בְּנֵי נְפִיסִים׃ בְּנֵי־בַקְבּוּק נְפוּסִים
נב נג בְּנֵי־חֲקוּפָא בְּנֵי חַרְחוּר׃ בְּנֵי־בַצְלוּת בְּנֵי־מְחִידָא בְּנֵי חַרְשָׁא׃ בְּנֵי־בַרְקוֹס בְּנֵי־
נד נה סִיסְרָא בְּנֵי־תָמַח׃ בְּנֵי נְצִיחַ בְּנֵי חֲטִיפָא׃ בְּנֵי עַבְדֵי שְׁלֹמֹה בְּנֵי־סֹטַי בְּנֵי־הַסֹּפֶרֶת
נו נז בְּנֵי פְרוּדָא׃ בְּנֵי־יַעְלָה בְנֵי־דַרְקוֹן בְּנֵי גִדֵּל׃ בְּנֵי שְׁפַטְיָה בְנֵי־חַטִּיל בְּנֵי פֹּכֶרֶת
נח הַצְּבָיִים בְּנֵי אָמִי׃ כָּל־הַנְּתִינִים וּבְנֵי עַבְדֵי שְׁלֹמֹה שְׁלֹשׁ מֵאוֹת תִּשְׁעִים
נט וּשְׁנָיִם׃ וְאֵלֶּה הָעֹלִים מִתֵּל מֶלַח תֵּל חַרְשָׁא כְּרוּב אַדָּן אִמֵּר
ס וְלֹא יָכְלוּ לְהַגִּיד בֵּית־אֲבוֹתָם וְזַרְעָם אִם מִיִּשְׂרָאֵל הֵם׃ בְּנֵי־דְלָיָה בְנֵי־טוֹבִיָּה
סא בְּנֵי נְקוֹדָא שֵׁשׁ מֵאוֹת חֲמִשִּׁים וּשְׁנָיִם׃ וּמִבְּנֵי הַכֹּהֲנִים בְּנֵי
חֳבַיָּה בְּנֵי הַקּוֹץ בְּנֵי בַרְזִלַּי אֲשֶׁר לָקַח מִבְּנוֹת בַּרְזִלַּי הַגִּלְעָדִי אִשָּׁה וַיִּקָּרֵא עַל־
סב סג שְׁמָם׃ אֵלֶּה בִּקְשׁוּ כְתָבָם הַמִּתְיַחְשִׂים וְלֹא נִמְצָאוּ וַיְגֹאֲלוּ מִן־הַכְּהֻנָּה׃ וַיֹּאמֶר
הַתִּרְשָׁתָא לָהֶם אֲשֶׁר לֹא־יֹאכְלוּ מִקֹּדֶשׁ הַקֳּדָשִׁים עַד עֲמֹד כֹּהֵן לְאוּרִים
סד סה וּלְתֻמִּים׃ כָּל־הַקָּהָל כְּאֶחָד אַרְבַּע רִבּוֹא אַלְפַּיִם שְׁלֹשׁ־מֵאוֹת שִׁשִּׁים׃ מִלְּבַד
עַבְדֵיהֶם וְאַמְהֹתֵיהֶם אֵלֶּה שִׁבְעַת אֲלָפִים שְׁלֹשׁ מֵאוֹת שְׁלֹשִׁים וְשִׁבְעָה וְלָהֶם
סו מְשֹׁרְרִים וּמְשֹׁרְרוֹת מָאתָיִם׃ סוּסֵיהֶם שְׁבַע מֵאוֹת שְׁלֹשִׁים וְשִׁשָּׁה פִּרְדֵיהֶם
סז מָאתַיִם אַרְבָּעִים וַחֲמִשָּׁה׃ גְּמַלֵּיהֶם אַרְבַּע מֵאוֹת שְׁלֹשִׁים וַחֲמִשָּׁה חֲמֹרִים שֵׁשֶׁת
סח אֲלָפִים שְׁבַע מֵאוֹת וְעֶשְׂרִים׃ וּמֵרָאשֵׁי הָאָבוֹת בְּבוֹאָם לְבֵית
סט יְהוָה אֲשֶׁר בִּירוּשָׁלִָם הִתְנַדְּבוּ לְבֵית הָאֱלֹהִים לְהַעֲמִידוֹ עַל־מְכוֹנוֹ׃ כְּכֹחָם נָתְנוּ

BACKGROUND

2:59 | **Tel Melah, Tel Harsha:** These were settlements in Babylonia to which Judeans were exiled. It seems that the area of Nippur in southern Babylonia, where several nations were exiled, was already destroyed during the Assyrian wars with the Babylonians. The book of Ezekiel (3:15) also mentions Tel Aviv as a place where Judeans lived in Babylonia. As *tel* means mound, i.e., the site of a destroyed city, these names possibly attest to a Babylonian policy of settling exiled nations in areas that had been destroyed.

2:60 | **The children of Toviya:** Some researchers connect this family with the Toviya family of Amon (see Nehemiah 13:5–8), who, like the sons of Pahat Moav (Ezra 2:6), were exiled to Babylonia earlier, during the campaigns of Tiglat Pileser III across the Jordan in the second half of the eighth century BCE. For this reason, they did not have a written genealogy (see Ezra 2:62).

2:69 | **Daric:** A Persian gold coin weighing about 8.4 g, and which bears the image of the Persian king holding a bow in his right hand and in his left a spear, which is *daric* in Persian. According to Julius Pollux and Herodotus, *daric* is a corruption of the name of King Darius, who minted the coins. Contemporary researchers claim that the name comes from a Persian word meaning gold. Others suggest it is a combination of the Persian words for king and bow (see also commentary on Nehemiah 7:70).

70 **The priests, and the Levites, and some of the people, and the singers, and the gatekeepers, and the Netinim settled in their cities,** where their families had previously lived, **and all** the rest of **Israel,** members of various tribes who had resided in other areas, dwelt **in their cities.**[34]

Building the Altar and Setting the Foundations of the Temple

EZRA 3:1–13

The returnees to the Land of Israel do not have the capability to rebuild the Temple quickly, as the dimensions of the structure are too large and complex. However, in the meantime they are able at least to build the altar, as they have a tradition that it is permitted to offer sacrifices on the altar even without the Temple, just as the Israelites did in the periods before the First Temple.

3 1 The immigrants likely arrived in the Land of Israel in the summer, when such long journeys are feasible. **The seventh** Hebrew **month,** Tishrei, **arrived with the children of Israel** settled **in the cities; the people assembled, as one man, to Jerusalem.**
2 **Yeshua son of Yotzadak,**[B] the High Priest, **and his brethren the priests, and Zerubavel son of She'altiel,** the leader of royal lineage, a descendant of King Yehoyakhin, **and his brethren stood and built the altar of the God of Israel, to offer up burnt offerings upon it, as it is written in the Torah of Moses, the man of God.**

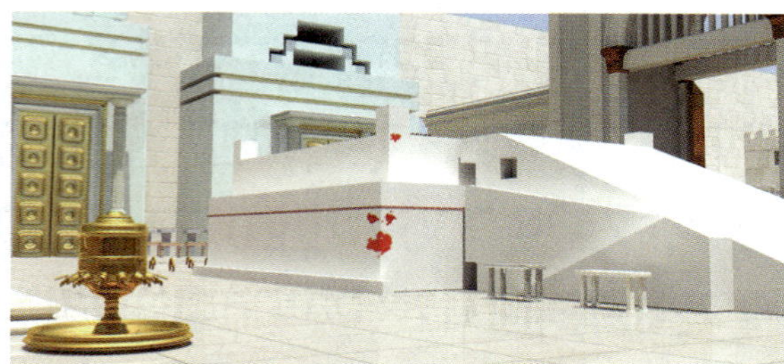

The altar of burnt offerings

3 **They established the altar on its** original **foundations, for they were fearful of the peoples of the land.** They were apprehensive with regard to the nations of the area, and were too afraid to rebuild Jerusalem completely. Therefore, they merely reestablished the altar on its foundations, avoiding any steps that might appear threatening or overly conspicuous.[35] **And they offered up burnt offerings to the Lord upon it,** the two **burnt offerings** that constitute the daily offerings, which are brought **morning and evening.**[36]
4 **They observed the Festival of the Tabernacles, as it is written** in the Torah, **with daily burnt offerings by** the specific **number, in accordance with the ordinance, each day's quantity on its day.** Each day of the festival they would bring a different number of burnt offerings, as required by the Torah,[37]
5 **and thereafter** they continued even in the following days, when the festival had ended, to bring **the** daily **continual burnt offering, and for the new moons, and for all the sacred appointed times of the Lord, and for everyone who proffered a gift offering to the Lord.**
6 **From the first day of the seventh month,** Rosh HaShana, **they began to offer up burnt offerings to the Lord; but the foundation of the Sanctuary of the Lord was not laid.** The altar alone was built, but nevertheless offerings could be burnt upon it.

Handle of a vessel with the inscription "Offering," Second Temple period

7 Meanwhile, **they gave silver to the masons** of stone, **and to the craftsmen** who worked with hard materials; **and** they gave **food, drink, and oil to the Sidonians and to the Tyrians,** in order **to bring cedar trees from Lebanon**[B] **to the sea, to Yafo,**[B] Jaffa, **in accordance with their license** that they had received **from Cyrus king of Persia** to rebuild the Temple.

Craftsmen

Kibbutz members working in the stone quarry of Ein Harod, 1941

Sidonians rowing and transporting cedar trees from Lebanon, stone relief, palace of Sargon II, Dur-Sharrukin, Assyria, 716–713 BCE

View of Yafo from the sea, early twentieth century

לְאוֹצַר הַמְּלָאכָה זָהָב דַּרְכְּמוֹנִים שֵׁשׁ־רִבֹּאות וָאָלֶף וְכֶסֶף מָנִים חֲמֵשֶׁת אֲלָפִים

ע וְכָתְנֹת כֹּהֲנִים מֵאָה׃ וַיֵּשְׁבוּ הַכֹּהֲנִים וְהַלְוִיִּם וּמִן־הָעָם וְהַמְשֹׁרְרִים

א וְהַשּׁוֹעֲרִים וְהַנְּתִינִים בְּעָרֵיהֶם וְכָל־יִשְׂרָאֵל בְּעָרֵיהֶם׃ וַיִּגַּע הַחֹדֶשׁ

ב הַשְּׁבִיעִי וּבְנֵי יִשְׂרָאֵל בֶּעָרִים וַיֵּאָסְפוּ הָעָם כְּאִישׁ אֶחָד אֶל־יְרוּשָׁלִָם׃ וַיָּקָם יֵשׁוּעַ

בֶּן־יוֹצָדָק וְאֶחָיו הַכֹּהֲנִים וּזְרֻבָּבֶל בֶּן־שְׁאַלְתִּיאֵל וְאֶחָיו וַיִּבְנוּ אֶת־מִזְבַּח אֱלֹהֵי

ג יִשְׂרָאֵל לְהַעֲלוֹת עָלָיו עֹלוֹת כַּכָּתוּב בְּתוֹרַת מֹשֶׁה אִישׁ־הָאֱלֹהִים׃ וַיָּכִינוּ הַמִּזְבֵּחַ

עַל־מְכוֹנֹתָיו כִּי בְּאֵימָה עֲלֵיהֶם מֵעַמֵּי הָאֲרָצוֹת וַיַּעַל עָלָיו עֹלוֹת לַיהוה עֹלוֹת

ד לַבֹּקֶר וְלָעָרֶב׃ וַיַּעֲשׂוּ אֶת־חַג הַסֻּכּוֹת כַּכָּתוּב וְעֹלַת יוֹם בְּיוֹם בְּמִסְפָּר כְּמִשְׁפַּט

ה דְּבַר־יוֹם בְּיוֹמוֹ׃ וְאַחֲרֵי־כֵן עֹלַת תָּמִיד וְלֶחֳדָשִׁים וּלְכָל־מוֹעֲדֵי יהוה הַמְקֻדָּשִׁים

ו וּלְכֹל מִתְנַדֵּב נְדָבָה לַיהוה׃ מִיּוֹם אֶחָד לַחֹדֶשׁ הַשְּׁבִיעִי הֵחֵלּוּ לְהַעֲלוֹת עֹלוֹת

ז לַיהוה וְהֵיכַל יהוה לֹא יֻסָּד׃ וַיִּתְּנוּ־כֶסֶף לַחֹצְבִים וְלֶחָרָשִׁים וּמַאֲכָל וּמִשְׁתֶּה

וָשֶׁמֶן לַצִּדֹנִים וְלַצֹּרִים לְהָבִיא עֲצֵי אֲרָזִים מִן־הַלְּבָנוֹן אֶל־יָם יָפוֹא כְּרִשְׁיוֹן כּוֹרֶשׁ

BACKGROUND

3:2 | **Yeshua son of Yotzadak:** Yeshua, or Yehoshua, who was the first High Priest of the Second Temple, returned from Babylonia with Zerubavel. Yeshua came from the priestly family of Tzadok, which was the family of the majority of the High Priests going back to the time of King David. His grandfather, Seraya the High Priest, was executed by Nevuzaradan at the time of the destruction of the Temple (see II Kings 25:18; I Chronicles 5:38–41; *Shir HaShirim Rabba* 5).

3:7 | **Cedar trees from Lebanon:** The cedar, *Cedrus*, is a conifer tree from the pine family. The tree is impressive in size and appearance; it reaches a height of 30 m, and its trunk can be as thick as 2–3 m. It grows in elevated and cold regions, mainly in Lebanon. Due to its strength, as well as the length and straightness of its branches, cedar wood is often used as building material, especially for public structures and castles. Indeed, cedar is a symbol of strength and fortitude.

According to Egyptian and Assyrian records from the first and second millennia BCE, the forests of Lebanon were the main source of construction materials for grand buildings, ships, and boats used for ritual purposes, as well as for furniture and coffins. As early as during the days of Solomon, wood was imported from Lebanon for the construction of the First Temple (see I Kings 5:20–32).

Yafo: A port city whose earliest remains date back to the beginning of the second millennium BCE. Most ancient artifacts that have been found there are Egyptian, and indeed, Yafo is mentioned in Egyptian documents. Among the significant facts about ancient Yafo are: It marks the border of Dan (Joshua 19:46), wood from Lebanon for the First Temple was imported through its port (II Chronicles 2:15), and the prophet Jonah sailed from there to Tarshish (Jonah 1:3). In the Persian period the city was under the control of the Sidonians, like other coastal cities.

8 **In the second year after their arrival at the House of God in Jerusalem, in the second month,** Iyar, **Zerubavel son of She'altiel,** the governor, **and Yeshua son of Yotzadak,** the High Priest, **and the rest of their brethren, the priests and the Levites, and everyone who came from the captivity,** from the exile, **to Jerusalem, commenced** work on this sacred project. To this end **they appointed the Levites, from twenty years old and above, to supervise**[38] **the labor of** rebuilding **the House of the Lord.**
9 **Yeshua, his sons and his brethren, Kadmiel and his sons, of the children of Judah,** all of them **stood together to supervise the craftsmen in the House of God; the children of Henadad** also accompanied them, with **their sons, and their brethren the Levites.**
10 **The builders laid the foundation,**[D] and perhaps had begun to build the walls **of the Sanctuary of the Lord, and they set** up **the attired priests,** who blew **with trumpets, and the Levites, children of Asaf,** the chief singers in the time of King David,[39] played music **with cymbals, to praise the Lord, by means of** the psalms of praise of **David king of Israel.**[40]
11 **They called out with praise and thanksgiving to the Lord: For He is good, for His mercy endures forever over Israel.** This was likely a familiar refrain of praise that featured in various songs. **All the people cheered a great cheer** of joy, **in praise to the Lord on the laying of the foundation of the House of the Lord.**
12 **But many of the priests and Levites and heads of patrilineal families, the elders, who had seen the first House** when

Stone excavated from southern wall of Temple Mount, with inscription "To the Trumpeting Place," first century CE

it was still **standing on its foundation, wept in a loud voice when this** partly rebuilt **House was** presented **before their eyes.** Roughly seventy years had passed since Nebuchadnezzar captured Yehoyakhin, but the great exile in the days of Tzidkiya and destruction of the Temple occurred many years later, and thus there were people some seventy years old who could still remember the appearance of the First Temple. They viewed this new Temple as a shadow of the glory of the magnificent Temple of Solomon. The difference was most conspicuous in the early stages of the rebuilding project. Even if the building would be enlarged, it would still be less impressive than the First Temple. **And** yet in contrast to them, **many** others, younger individuals, **cheered with joy, raising voices.**
13 **The people could not distinguish the sound of the cheer of joy from the sound of the weeping of the people.** The sounds of weeping and joy blended together, **for the people were cheering a great cheer, and the sound was heard from afar.**

Construction of the City Walls and the Sanctuary Is Halted

EZRA 4:1–24

The work of rebuilding the city walls of Jerusalem and the Temple has been delayed for many years, due to harassment and threats by the surrounding communities, who hated the Judeans. Following a letter of libel against the Judeans sent to the king of Persia, all construction work is halted. Not long after these events, Nehemiah describes Jerusalem as a city half in ruins, whose walls were breached. It remained in this state even after the Temple was completed.

4 1 **The adversaries of Judah and Benjamin,**[D] from the nations that had been settled in Samaria by the king of Assyria, **heard that the exiles were building a Sanctuary to the Lord, God of Israel.**

ח מֶֽלֶךְ־פָּרַ֖ס עֲלֵיהֶֽם׃ וּבַשָּׁנָ֨ה הַשֵּׁנִ֜ית לְבוֹאָ֨ם אֶל־בֵּ֣ית הָאֱלֹהִים֮
לִירֽוּשָׁלִַם֒ בַּחֹ֖דֶשׁ הַשֵּׁנִ֑י הֵחֵ֡לּוּ זְרֻבָּבֶ֣ל בֶּן־שְׁ֠אַלְתִּיאֵל וְיֵשׁ֨וּעַ בֶּן־יֽוֹצָדָ֜ק וּשְׁאָ֥ר
אֲחֵיהֶ֣ם ׀ הַכֹּהֲנִ֣ים וְהַלְוִיִּ֗ם וְכָל־הַבָּאִים֙ מֵֽהַשְּׁבִ֣י יְרוּשָׁלִַ֔ם וַיַּעֲמִ֣ידוּ אֶת־הַלְוִיִּ֗ם
ט מִבֶּ֨ן עֶשְׂרִ֤ים שָׁנָה֙ וָמַ֔עְלָה לְנַצֵּ֖חַ עַל־מְלֶ֥אכֶת בֵּית־יהוה׃ וַיַּעֲמֹ֣ד יֵשׁ֡וּעַ בָּנָ֣יו
וְאֶחָ֡יו קַדְמִיאֵ֣ל וּבָנָיו֩ בְּנֵֽי־יְהוּדָ֨ה כְּאֶחָ֜ד לְנַצֵּ֗חַ עַל־עֹשֵׂ֤ה הַמְּלָאכָה֙ בְּבֵ֣ית
י הָאֱלֹהִ֔ים בְּנֵי֙ חֵֽנָדָ֔ד בְּנֵיהֶ֥ם וַאֲחֵיהֶ֖ם הַלְוִיִּֽם׃ וְיִסְּד֥וּ הַבֹּנִ֖ים אֶת־הֵיכַ֣ל יהוה וַיַּעֲמִידוּ֩
הַכֹּהֲנִ֨ים מְלֻבָּשִׁ֜ים בַּחֲצֹֽצְר֗וֹת וְהַלְוִיִּ֤ם בְּנֵֽי־אָסָף֙ בַּֽמְצִלְתַּ֔יִם לְהַלֵּל֙ אֶת־יהוה
יא עַל־יְדֵ֖י דָּוִ֥יד מֶֽלֶךְ־יִשְׂרָאֵֽל׃ וַֽ֠יַּעֲנוּ בְּהַלֵּ֨ל וּבְהוֹדֹ֜ת לַיהוה כִּ֣י ט֔וֹב כִּֽי־לְעוֹלָ֥ם
חַסְדּ֖וֹ עַל־יִשְׂרָאֵ֑ל וְכָל־הָעָ֗ם הֵרִ֜יעוּ תְרוּעָ֤ה גְדוֹלָה֙ בְהַלֵּ֣ל לַֽיהוה עַ֖ל הוּסַ֥ד
יב בֵּית־יהוה׃ וְרַבִּ֡ים מֵהַכֹּהֲנִ֣ים וְהַלְוִיִּם֩ וְרָאשֵׁ֨י הָאָב֜וֹת הַזְּקֵנִ֗ים אֲשֶׁ֨ר רָא֜וּ אֶת־
הַבַּ֤יִת הָֽרִאשׁוֹן֙ בְּיָסְד֔וֹ זֶ֤ה הַבַּ֙יִת֙ בְּעֵ֣ינֵיהֶ֔ם בֹּכִ֖ים בְּק֣וֹל גָּד֑וֹל וְרַבִּ֛ים בִּתְרוּעָ֥ה
יג בְשִׂמְחָ֖ה לְהָרִ֥ים קֽוֹל׃ וְאֵ֣ין הָעָ֗ם מַכִּירִים֙ ק֤וֹל תְּרוּעַ֣ת הַשִּׂמְחָ֔ה לְק֖וֹל בְּכִ֣י הָעָ֑ם ב
כִּ֣י הָעָ֗ם מְרִיעִים֙ תְּרוּעָ֣ה גְדוֹלָ֔ה וְהַקּ֖וֹל נִשְׁמַ֥ע עַד־לְמֵרָחֽוֹק׃
א וַֽיִּשְׁמְע֔וּ צָרֵ֥י יְהוּדָ֖ה וּבִנְיָמִ֑ן כִּֽי־בְנֵ֤י הַגּוֹלָה֙ בּוֹנִ֣ים הֵיכָ֔ל לַיהוה אֱלֹהֵ֖י יִשְׂרָאֵֽל׃

DISCUSSION

3:10 | **The builders laid the foundation:** Of the roughly forty thousand immigrants, there were many who could not actively participate in the massive project of building the Temple. Some of them were children, who certainly did not perform construction work, while others were elderly, and were at the most given the honor of laying down a little mortar. Furthermore, not all those who were fit to work had the time to do so, as they needed to provide for their families as well. They had returned to resettle the abandoned cities and towns of Judah, as well as work for their livelihoods. It should also be kept in mind that not everyone knew how to perform construction work. There were skilled architects, craftsmen, and managers in charge of the labor, but not all the people were qualified in these fields, and acquiring the appropriate skills took time.

Furthermore, the complexity of the building, which was partly constructed from stone and partly from wood, and the need to import raw materials from outside the country, also served to complicate matters. It will later be related that there were other external factors that interrupted the work and caused further delays, but even if the labor had been performed with great industry and effort without those disturbances, it would have taken a long time to complete the building. In his time, King Solomon had 150,000 workers at his disposal, who could perform various tasks, apart from his supervisors and managers (see I Kings 5:29), and even so it took him several years to construct the First Temple (I Kings 6:1, 38). For all these reasons many years passed, encompassing the reigns of several kings, until the immigrants from Babylonia were able to finish the construction of the Second Temple.

4:1 | **Adversaries of Judah and Benjamin:** Among the enemies of the returnees were the Samaritans, descendants of various ethnic groups that had been exiled to Samaria by the king of Assyria. The book of Kings describes the forced population transfer performed by the Assyrians, where people from other conquered lands were brought to Samaria to take the place of its Israelite residents who had themselves been exiled to other distant lands. After a number of incidents in which the new residents were attacked by lions, they sensed that in the Land of Israel they needed to be protected by God, and therefore they made an effort to become connected in some manner to the Israelite religion (see Rashi; II Kings 17:24–41). Eventually the Samaritans organized and built various centers for themselves, but it is not clear if at that time they had already attempted to set up a temple.

2 **They approached Zerubavel,** the governor appointed over the
Judeans by the king of Persia, **and the heads of the patrilineal
families, and said to them: Let
us build** together **with you, for
we seek your God like you, and
to Him we have been sacrific-
ing since the days of Esar
Hadon**[B] **king of Assyria, who
brought us up to here.** Since
the king of Assyria brought us
here to the Land of Israel, we
have offered sacrifices to the
God of Israel. Therefore, we can
join you in your labor.
3 **Zerubavel, and Yeshua,** the
High Priest, **and the rest of the
heads of the patrilineal families of Israel said to them: It
is not for you and us**[D] **to build
a House to our God;** we absolutely object to any partnership
of this kind. **Rather, we our-
selves together,** alone, **will build for the Lord, God of Israel,
as King Cyrus king of Persia has commanded us.**
4 The response of the adversaries of Judah was predictable: **The
people of the land,** the local residents, **weakened the hands of
the people of Judah, and intimidated them from building.**
Excluded from the project, they decided to disrupt it in whatever
manner possible. They could not embark on an open military
conflict, as there was an imperial governor appointed over
Samaria, just as Zerubavel oversaw Judah. Granted, Persia was a
less centralized empire than its predecessors Babylonia and
Assyria, but, perhaps due to its size and nature, it was far more

Victory stele of Esar Hadon, Tel Zincirli, Höyük, Assyria, 671 BCE

organized than its predecessors had been, at least in its
early years.
5 **And** the adversaries **from
among the local populations
hired counselors,** advisors,
**against them to thwart
their plans,** throughout **all
the days of Cyrus king of
Persia, and into the reign of Darius**[B] **king of Persia.** They
continuously sought to frustrate the work, create problems, and
thereby prevent the construction of the Temple. Even without
these disturbances, the construction process by a small group of
immigrants would have advanced at a slow pace. The persistent
harassment, alongside the poor economic situation resulting
from the difficulties of farming uncultivated land that had been
abandoned for more than fifty years, eventually led to the complete cessation of work.
6 **In the reign of** King **Ahashverosh**[B] of Persia, **at the beginning
of his reign, they,** these plotters, **wrote a libel,** a libelous document, to him **against the inhabitants of Judah and Jerusalem.**
7 **And in the days of** King **Artahshasta**[B] of Persia, **Bishlam,** the
name of one of the adversaries of Judah, and also **Mitredat,
Tave'el, and the rest of his companions**[41] **wrote** a letter **to
Artahshasta king of Persia; the document was written in
Aramaic script and translated into Aramaic.**[D] Both the script
and the language of the letter were Aramaic.[42] Since the text
cites the letter from the original Aramaic, the narrative likewise
switches to Aramaic.
8 **Rehum,** which was the name of **the commander,** or advisor,
**and Shimshai the scribe, wrote one letter against Jerusalem
to King Artahshasta, as stated** below.
9 **Then Rehum the commander, and Shimshai the scribe, and**

Silver shekel depicting King Darius, Persia, 500–490 BCE

DISCUSSION

4:3 | **It is not for you and us:** The text does not provide detailed explanations as to why the men of Judah refused to cooperate with the Samaritans. It can be assumed that this was largely because they viewed these people as strangers. Although the Samaritans had drawn close to the Israelite religion, in practice they remained gentiles. Thus, the leaders of the Judean population had no interest in any partnership with them, and were even reluctant to grant equal legal status to their neighbors. External sources indicate that certain foreign nations did not realize that these were two distinct groups, but considered the Judeans and the Samaritans as a single entity, and this was possibly another reason for the Babylonian immigrants' wish to avoid cooperation. In any case, their unequivocal refusal created a rift between Israel and the Samaritans, which has lasted until the present day. At times, there was relatively peaceful coexistence between the two communities, but there were also periods of great hostility. In modern-day Israel the Samaritans are a recognized community and enjoy full civic rights, although their numbers are small. The events recounted here mark the start of this complex relationship (see also Mishna *Shekalim* 1:5; *Arakhin* 5b).

4:7 | **Translated into Aramaic:** Scholars believe that this was the royal Aramaic that Cyrus imposed as the language of his administration. Anyone who negotiated with the government had to know this language. This form of Aramaic was not identical to Late Aramaic; it was not the Aramaic that was spoken by contemporary Judeans in the Land of Israel or Babylon, nor was it the same language spoken by the Arameans themselves in their various locales. Rather, this formal Aramaic, which also appears in official documents, was already a diplomatic language back in the days of the Chaldeans and Assyrians, and its use was continued by the Persians (see also II Kings 18:26). The grammar of this language differs somewhat from regular Aramaic, and certain pedantic linguistic features that had already disappeared from spoken Aramaic are meticulously observed in this written form.

ב וַיִּגְּשׁוּ אֶל־זְרֻבָּבֶל וְאֶל־רָאשֵׁי הָאָבוֹת וַיֹּאמְרוּ לָהֶם נִבְנֶה עִמָּכֶם כִּי כָכֶם נִדְרוֹשׁ
לֵאלֹהֵיכֶם וְלֹא ׀ אֲנַחְנוּ זֹבְחִים מִימֵי אֵסַר חַדֹּן מֶלֶךְ אַשּׁוּר הַמַּעֲלֶה אֹתָנוּ וְלוֹ ׀
ג פֹּה׃ וַיֹּאמֶר לָהֶם זְרֻבָּבֶל וְיֵשׁוּעַ וּשְׁאָר רָאשֵׁי הָאָבוֹת לְיִשְׂרָאֵל לֹא־לָכֶם וָלָנוּ
לִבְנוֹת בַּיִת לֵאלֹהֵינוּ כִּי אֲנַחְנוּ יַחַד נִבְנֶה לַיהוה אֱלֹהֵי יִשְׂרָאֵל כַּאֲשֶׁר צִוָּנוּ
ד הַמֶּלֶךְ כּוֹרֶשׁ מֶלֶךְ־פָּרָס׃ וַיְהִי עַם־הָאָרֶץ מְרַפִּים יְדֵי עַם־יְהוּדָה ומבלהים וּמְבַהֲלִים
ה אוֹתָם לִבְנוֹת׃ וְסֹכְרִים עֲלֵיהֶם יוֹעֲצִים לְהָפֵר עֲצָתָם כָּל־יְמֵי כּוֹרֶשׁ מֶלֶךְ פָּרַס
ו וְעַד־מַלְכוּת דָּרְיָוֶשׁ מֶלֶךְ־פָּרָס׃ וּבְמַלְכוּת אֲחַשְׁוֵרוֹשׁ בִּתְחִלַּת מַלְכוּתוֹ כָּתְבוּ
ז שִׂטְנָה עַל־יֹשְׁבֵי יְהוּדָה וִירוּשָׁלִָם׃ וּבִימֵי אַרְתַּחְשַׁשְׂתָּא כָּתַב בִּשְׁלָם
מִתְרְדָת טָבְאֵל וּשְׁאָר כְּנָוֺתָו עַל־אַרְתַּחְשַׁשְׂתָּא מֶלֶךְ פָּרָס וּכְתָב הַנִּשְׁתְּוָן כָּתוּב
ח אֲרָמִית וּמְתֻרְגָּם אֲרָמִית׃ רְחוּם בְּעֵל־טְעֵם וְשִׁמְשַׁי סָפְרָא כְּתַבוּ
ט אִגְּרָה חֲדָה עַל־יְרוּשְׁלֶם לְאַרְתַּחְשַׁשְׂתְּא מַלְכָּא כְּנֵמָא׃ אֱדַיִן רְחוּם בְּעֵל־טְעֵם
וְשִׁמְשַׁי סָפְרָא וּשְׁאָר כְּנָוָתְהוֹן דִּינָיֵא וַאֲפַרְסַתְכָיֵא טַרְפְּלָיֵא אֲפָרְסָיֵא אַרְכְּוָי

BACKGROUND

4:2 | **Esar Hadon:** The heir of Sennacherib king of Assyria, he reigned during 680–669 BCE, which coincided with the rule of Menashe king of Judah. In response to the military activities of Taharqa, the king of Ethiopia and Egypt, Esar Hadon embarked on several war campaigns in Phoenicia, the Land of Israel, and Egypt. Apart from the testimony of the adversaries of Judah and Benjamin which appears here, there is no record, Assyrian or otherwise, of Esar Hadon exiling a population to Samaria.

4:5 | **Darius:** This apparently refers to Darius the Great, who reigned between the years 522–486 BCE. This king exhibited tolerance toward various religions, reorganized the administration of his entire empire, and developed transportation routes. There were other Persian rulers with the same name: Darius the Mede, who reigned before Cyrus (see commentary on Daniel 6:1), Darius II, who ruled between 423–405 BCE, and Darius III, 380–330 BCE. Some claim that "Darius" is a title which means "holding firm the good" in Persian, and can therefore be used to refer to any of the kings of Persia (*Encyclopedia Iranica*, http://www.iranicaonline.org/articles/darius-iii).

4:6 | **Ahashverosh:** The son of Darius the Great, he ruled between the years 486–465 BCE. Unlike his father, he was known for the weakness of his reign and his intolerance of foreign religions and nations (see *The Histories*, especially VI and VII). His character fits the descriptions of the Ahashverosh in the book of Esther.

4:7 | **Artahshasta:** Several Persian kings had similar names. According to one opinion, "Artahshasta" is not the personal name of a specific individual but a general royal title, like the Egyptian title pharaoh or the Philistine *avimelekh*. It is stated in *Seder Olam Rabba* (30): "Cyrus is the same as Darius who is the same as Artahshasta, as the entire royal line is called Artahshasta." Indeed, according to Josephus, the first letter of accusation was sent to Cyrus (*Antiquities of the Jews* XI:2).

Alternatively, the name Artahshasta in this verse may refer to Artahshasta I, the son of Ahashverosh, who reigned between the years 465–424 BCE. According to ancient historians, Artahshasta was renowned as a peace-loving ruler who performed acts of charity. It was during his reign that Nehemiah immigrated to Israel. The letter of libel cited in this section was apparently sent in the early years of his rule.

The change from Ahashverosh in the previous verse to Artahshasta in this verse is somewhat puzzling, and might be explained in accordance with the aforementioned opinion that Artahshasta was a general title for Persian kings, or that it is another name for Ahashverosh. Alternatively, it is possible that there was a change of leadership just when the letter was sent, and therefore it was addressed to one king but received by another (see Ibn Ezra here and Esther 1:1; *Seder Olam Rabba* 28; *Rosh HaShana* 3a; *Esther Rabba* 1:3; Rashi, Ezra 6:14).

the rest of their companions: the Dinites, and the Afaresatekhites, the Tarpelites, names of ethnic groups living in the Land of Israel that were subsumed under the Persians, **the Afaresites,** or Persians, **the Arkevites,**[B] from the city of Uruk, **the Babylonians, the Shushankhites, the Dehites, the Elamites,**[D] names of various groups which had united but still preserved their own identity, in accordance with their place of origin,

10 **and the rest of the nations whom the great and honored Asenapar,**[B] apparently a name for the king of Assyria, had **exiled**[D] **and settled in the city of Samaria, and in the rest of Avar Nahara,**[B] on the western side of the Euphrates River [*nahar*]: **Now,**[43] a term signaling that the letter is reaching its main point, and perhaps also a way of indicating that some of the original has been omitted from the citation, similar to the term, "etc.";[44]

Stone relief of Ashurbanipal, Babylon, 669–655 BCE

11 **this is a copy of the letter that they sent to him, to King Artahshasta, your servants, the men of Avar Nahara.** Such letters would typically begin by specifying the addressee and the senders. Presumably, at this juncture they would insert titles of honor and praise for the king, which are omitted by the author of the book of Ezra. **Now,**

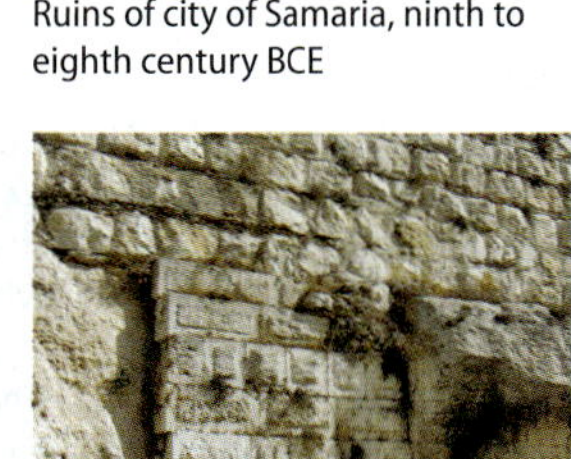
Ruins of city of Samaria, ninth to eighth century BCE

12 **let it be known to the king that the Judeans who went up from** among **you to us have come to Jerusalem. They are building the rebellious and wicked city, and they are completing the walls, and are connecting**[45] or digging out,[46] **the foundations.**

Rows of ancient stones forming the foundation for Ottoman-era walls built in Jerusalem, second century BCE

13 **Now, let it be known to the king, that if this city is built, and its walls finished, they will not pay property tax,** which is imposed in accordance with the size of the specific plot of land,[47] or the **poll tax, or** the road **toll,** which is given for the soldiers who are constantly on the move.[48] These payments included border crossing tolls, customs duties, or payment for postal services,[49] **and** certainly, or eventually, **the royal revenue**[50] **of the kings will be harmed.** When the Judeans will rebuild the city and receive an official status, even if they will not actively rebel against you, they will certainly stop paying taxes.

Tax and tribute brought to the king of Persia, stone relief, Persepolis, fifth century BCE

14 **Now, for the reason that the salt of the** royal **palace is our salt,** meaning we derive benefit from the king's table and are obligated toward it, as salt is a symbol of a covenant,[51] **and we do not desire,**[52] or it is not fitting for us, **to see the king's dishonor, therefore we have sent** this letter **and informed the king.** Although we are not required to do so, we wish to inform the king because of our loyalty to him,

15 **that he should examine in the book of the records of your fathers,** in the official historical accounts, **and you will find in the book of the records and know that this city is a rebellious city, and harmful to kings and provinces, and within it they have engaged in insurrection**[53] **since ancient times; for that, this city was destroyed.**

16 **We inform the king that if this city is built and the walls finished, for that reason a portion** of land under your command **of Avar Nahara will not be subject to you.** If they are allowed to complete the reconstruction of their city, the Judeans will grow ever stronger, and not only will you lose control over this small area, they will eventually push you out of the entire area west of the Euphrates. From the start, the Persian Empire was massive, and the land of Judah was not one of its larger provinces. However, these adversaries warn the king that if its inhabitants are allowed to become more powerful, they will ignite the entire region, as they did to earlier kingdoms.

This letter was designed to bring a halt to the construction of Jerusalem. It does not refer directly to the Temple, as the Temple itself did not pose a political threat. Rather, it draws attention to the building of the city walls, which would provide Jerusalem with protection, independence, and power, and transform it into

י בַבְלָיֵא שֽׁוּשַׁנְכָיֵא דהוא עֵלְמָיֵא׃ וּשְׁאָר אֻמַּיָּא דִּי הַגְלִי אָסְנַפַּר רַבָּא וְיַקִּירָא דֶּהָיֵא
יא וְהוֹתֵב הִמּוֹ בְּקִרְיָה דִּי שָׁמְרָיִן וּשְׁאָר עֲבַר־נַהֲרָה וּכְעֶנֶת׃ דְּנָה פַּרְשֶׁגֶן
אִגַּרְתָּא דִּי שְׁלַחוּ עֲלוֹהִי עַל־אַרְתַּחְשַׁשְׂתְּא מַלְכָּא עבדיך אֱנָשׁ עֲבַר־נַהֲרָה עַבְדָךְ
יב וּכְעֶנֶת׃ יְדִיעַ לֶהֱוֵא לְמַלְכָּא דִּי יְהוּדָיֵא דִּי סְלִקוּ מִן־לְוָתָךְ עֲלֶינָא
אֲתוֹ לִירוּשְׁלֶם קִרְיְתָא מָרָדְתָּא וּבִאישְׁתָּא בָּנַיִן וְשׁוּרַיָּ אשכללו וְאֻשַּׁיָּא יַחִיטוּ׃ שַׁכְלִלוּ
יג כְּעַן יְדִיעַ לֶהֱוֵא לְמַלְכָּא דִּי הֵן קִרְיְתָא דָךְ תִּתְבְּנֵא וְשׁוּרַיָּא יִשְׁתַּכְלְלוּן מִנְדָּה־
יד בְלוֹ וַהֲלָךְ לָא יִנְתְּנוּן וְאַפְּתֹם מַלְכִים תְּהַנְזִק׃ כְּעַן כָּל־קֳבֵל דִּי־מְלַח הֵיכְלָא
מְלַחְנָא וְעַרְוַת מַלְכָּא לָא־אֲרִיךְ לַנָא לְמֶחֱזֵא עַל־דְּנָה שְׁלַחְנָא וְהוֹדַעְנָא
טו לְמַלְכָּא׃ דִּי יְבַקַּר בִּסְפַר דָּכְרָנַיָּא דִּי אֲבָהָתָךְ וּתְהַשְׁכַּח בִּסְפַר דָּכְרָנַיָּא וְתִנְדַּע
דִּי קִרְיְתָא דָךְ קִרְיָא מָרָדָא וּמְהַנְזְקַת מַלְכִין וּמְדִנָן וְאֶשְׁתַּדּוּר עָבְדִין בְּגַוַּהּ
טז מִן־יוֹמָת עָלְמָא עַל־דְּנָה קִרְיְתָא דָךְ הָחָרְבַת׃ מְהוֹדְעִין אֲנַחְנָה לְמַלְכָּא דִּי
הֵן קִרְיְתָא דָךְ תִּתְבְּנֵא וְשׁוּרַיַּהּ יִשְׁתַּכְלְלוּן לָקֳבֵל דְּנָה חֲלָק בַּעֲבַר נַהֲרָא לָא

BACKGROUND

4:9 | **The Arkevites:** This is apparently the equivalent of the Persian and ancient Indian term Aryan, meaning "master," or "freeman." This title served to distinguish the true Persians, the Aryans, from those considered slaves, the non-Aryans, which included the Babylonians, Shushankhites, and the Elamites-Susanites. The Elamites mentioned here were considered inferior to authentic Persians (Naphtali Herz Torczyner (Tur-Sinai), "Aryans and Non-Aryan Persians in the Bible" (Ezra IV, 9), *Bulletin of the Jewish Palestine Exploration Society*, Autumn 1940, 14:1–2 [Hebrew], 6).

4:10 | **Asenapar:** The standard identification of this ruler is Ashurbanipal, although Josephus maintains that it is Shalmaneser (*Antiquities of the Jews* XI:4:3).

Avar Nahara: Avar Nahara is the Aramaic name for the Persian province or satrapy that included much of present-day Syria, Lebanon, Jordan, Iraq, and Israel. The literal meaning of the name is "beyond the river," referring to the lands west of the Euphrates River. This river served as a natural border between these and other countries, and those regions on the eastern side of the Euphrates. The administrative unit of Avar Nahara was also defined by its residents, who were mainly speakers of Semitic languages. Although the Babylonians also spoke a Semitic tongue, their dialect was very different. It is possible that a man who came from this region would define himself as an *ivri*, a Hebrew (see Genesis 14:13; Jonah 1:9), in the broad meaning of those who belong to the other side [*ever*] of the river, that is, the Semitic peoples or the Semitic language-speakers who lived west of the Euphrates (see Ramban, Genesis 11:28, 12:1). The province was divided into sub-units of which Yehud, or Judah, was one.

DISCUSSION

4:9 | **The Dinites, and the Afaresatekhites… the Elamites:** Among other reasons, the writers of the letter mentioned their ancestry in order to emphasize that they had been part of the Persian Empire from its earliest days. They were exiled from countries in the north of the Assyrian Empire, and some even came from the same region from where the Persian Empire would later arise.

4:10 | **Whom the great and honored Asenapar exiled:** The kings of Babylon who conquered Assyria sought to establish the legitimacy of their rule, like the kings of Assyria who had earlier vanquished other nations. To this end, they presented themselves as the followers of the previous regime. Therefore, the mention of the precedents of the kings of Assyria in addressing the king of Persia can be seen as a form of flattery: We turn to you as the successor to and descendant of the great and mighty kings who performed such and such deeds.

a center for future revolts. The adversaries argued that a reflection on the rebellious history of the city will prove to the king
the truth of their claims.
17 After receiving the letter and examining the case, **the king
sent** an official **dispatch to Rehum the commander, and to
Shimshai the scribe,** who were the leaders, **and to the rest of
their companions who live in Samaria, and in the rest of Avar
Nahara,** saying: **Peace** to you. **Now,**
18 **the document that you sent to us has been explicitly read,**
explained, or translated, **before me.** It is possible that the king of
Persia had not learned Aramaic, as he was surrounded by experts
in many languages who could read and translate such dispatches
for him.
19 **From me a decree was issued** to my officials to look into the
matter, **and they investigated** in the book of records **and found
that this city from ancient times has risen against kings, and
rebellion and insurrection have been undertaken in it.**
20 **Mighty kings have been over Jerusalem, who ruled over the
entire Avar Nahara, and property tax, poll tax, and toll were
given to them.** Apparently, the king had consulted old historical
accounts which did not depict a small province of Judah, but
the kingdom of David and Solomon, whose rule extended to
the provinces near the Euphrates, from the northern border of
Syria all the way to Egypt.[54]
21 **Now, issue a decree to stop these men** from their labor. **This
city shall not be built until a** different **decree from me will be
issued.** This is a temporary injunction, until further orders are
issued.
22 **Be wary of performing an error in this regard;**[D] **why should
misconduct increase to the harm of kings?** You sent me the
original letter, and you are hereby receiving my instructions to
pass on the message and ensure that the city is not rebuilt. Take
care of the matter; do not be tempted to be negligent.
23 **Then, once the copy of King Artahshasta's letter was read before Rehum and Shimshai the scribe, and their companions,
they went hastily to Jerusalem to the Judeans, and stopped
them** from working **with violence and force.** An order from
the king of Persia carried exceptional weight.[55] The official letter
in their possession indeed led to the cessation of the work.
24 **Then the work of** constructing **the House of God that is in
Jerusalem stopped; and it was stopped until the second year
of the reign of Darius king of Persia.**

Completion of the Temple's Construction, and Its Inauguration

EZRA 5:1–6:22

The construction of the Temple is renewed in accordance with the instructions of the prophets Haggai and Zechariah.

Tatenai, the governor of the area on the western side of the Euphrates, receives notice of developments in Jerusalem, probably from the same plotters who sent the letter described in the previous chapter. He is informed that the elders of Judah claim that their construction work had been authorized by an explicit order of the first king of Persia. As Tatenai has not heard of such an order, he sends the matter to his superiors for clarification. The king does not take long to respond. Not only does Darius refuse to delay the construction work as his predecessor had done, he chooses to rely on the original order of Cyrus, the founder of the empire, instructing that assistance be provided to the builders in the form of money, as well as items required for sacrifices.

The Temple is completed four years after the renewal of the construction work, some twenty years after permission had first been granted to rebuild it, and is inaugurated in a joyous public ceremony.

5 1 In those years **Haggai the prophet, and Zechariah son of Ido,
prophets of the Judeans who were in Judah and Jerusalem,**[56]
prophesied in the name of the God of Israel about them, the
Judeans. The content of these prophecies does not appear here,
but in their respective prophetic books. It is stated there that
the time had come for the Temple to be rebuilt, that the builders should not be concerned for their own safety, and that God
guarantees the enduring leadership of Zerubavel and the priesthood of Yeshua.[57]
2 **Then Zerubavel son of She'altiel,** a descendant of the royal
house of David, who was still the governor, **and Yeshua son of
Yotzadak,** the High Priest, **rose and began to build the House
of God that is in Jerusalem, and with them were the prophets
of God, helping them.** The two leaders decided to heed the
instructions of the prophets and resume the construction work.
3 **At that time,** when they started to build, **Tatenai,** who was
the governor of Avar Nahara, the official appointed by the
Persian regime over the large province on the western side of
the Euphrates, **and Shetar Bozenai,** apparently Tatenai's second-in-command, **and their companions came to them,**[D] the
builders; **so they said to them: Who issued a decree for you**
allowing you **to build this house, and to finish this wall,**[58] or
to complete its furnishings?
4 The respondent, one of the builders of the Temple, reports in
the first person: **Then, as stated, we said to them** in the letter
that will be cited in this section, **the names of the men who
are building this building.** Tatenai, the powerful leader of the
province, and his assistants came as administrators of the Persian
ruling authorities, and they wished to know the names of those
responsible.

יז איתי לך: פתגמא שלח מלכא על־רחום בעל־טעם ושמשי ספרא
יח ושאר כנותהון די יתבין בשמרין ושאר עבר־נהרה שלם וכעת: נשתונא די
יט שלחתון עלינא מפרש קרי קדמי: ומני שים טעם ובקרו והשכחו די קריתא
כ דך מן־יומת עלמא על־מלכין מתנשאה ומרד ואשתדור מתעבד־בה: ומלכין
תקיפין הוו על־ירושלם ושליטין בכל עבר נהרה ומדה בלו והלך מתיהב
כא להון: כען שימו טעם לבטלא גבריא אלך וקריתא דך לא תתבנא עד־מני
כב טעמא יתשם: וזהירין הוו שלו למעבד על־דנה למה ישגא חבלא להנזקת
כג מלכין: אדין מן־די פרשגן נשתונא די ארתחששתא מלכא קרי
קדם־רחום ושמשי ספרא וכנותהון אזלו בבהילו לירושלם על־יהודיא ובטלו
כד המו באדרע וחיל: באדין בטלת עבידת בית־אלהא די בירושלם
והות בטלא עד שנת תרתין למלכות דריוש מלך־פרס:
א והתנבי חגי נביאה וזכריה בר־עדוא נביאיא על־יהודיא די ביהוד ובירושלם נביא
ב בשם אלה ישראל עליהון: באדין קמו זרבבל בר־שאלתיאל וישוע בר־יוצדק
ושריו למבנא בית אלהא די בירושלם ועמהון נביאיה די־אלהא מסעדין להון:
ג בה־זמנא אתה עליהון תתני פחת עבר־נהרה ושתר בוזני וכנותהון וכן אמרין
ד להם מן־שם לכם טעם ביתא דנה לבנא ואשרנא דנה לשכללה: אדין כנמא

DISCUSSION

4:22 | **Be wary of performing an error in this regard:** The adversaries succeeded not because of the great strength of the Samaritans in the kingdom, but mainly because they knew people of social or political influence and power, and because the king was either sympathetic to their concerns or could be easily manipulated. Since the empire was highly diverse, it is reasonable to assume that there were people, like Haman in his day, who had motives to harm the Jews. Some of those with nefarious aims of this kind were familiar with the king's personality and knew how to address him in such a manner that the complaint would be accepted.

Letters of this type, dealing with large-scale political problems, would be given directly to the king, who was possibly a hater of Israel or perhaps simply a suspicious ruler. Either way, he accepted the offer and ordered an examination of the book of records to see how much trouble Jerusalem had caused over time. His officials found all the relevant documents and were able to inform the king without difficulty about the history of Jerusalem as a focus of rebellions. It was undoubtedly true that there were uprisings in Jerusalem, as indeed was the case for Samaria. When these places grew in strength, opposition to foreign rule arose, and their inhabitants rebelled against Assyria, Babylon, and Egypt. The information gathered from the official records led the king to order a halt to all construction. Consequently, for years Jerusalem remained a city in ruins.

5:3 | **At that time Tatenai...came to them:** It seems that when the previous king had ordered a halt to the construction work, he did not send someone to properly investigate the matter. Since people had come to the king professing to be concerned with his welfare and declaring that the reconstruction of Jerusalem was a threat to the security of the kingdom, he authorized

▸ *them*

5 **And the eye of their God was** looking favorably **upon the el-**
ders of the Judeans, and through His providence **they,** Tatenai
and his colleagues, **could not stop them**[D] from continuing with
the construction work, **until the matter would be brought to**
Darius, the king, **and then they would reply with a letter con-**
cerning this.
6 The text of the letter is preceded by a heading: This is **the copy**
of the letter that Tatenai the governor of Avar Nahara, and
Shetar Bozenai, and his companions the Afarsekhites, the
Persians[59] **who were in Avar Nahara, sent to Darius the king:**
7 **They sent the matter,** an official document, **to him, and so it**
was written in it, an official opening: **To King Darius, com-**
plete peace [*shelama khola*].[60] Others interpret *khola* as an
expression meaning "etc." In any case, it was an official, respectful
greeting, similar to "Your Majesty."
8 **Let it be known to the king that we went to the** autonomous
province of Judah,[B] which was under the control of the gover-
nors of the region Avar Nahara, **to the House of the great God, and it is built with large,** cut **stones [*even gelal*],** which are transported by rolling [*golel*] them from one place to another, **and wood is set in the walls,** as construction with large stones is a complex and slow process and therefore timber was added between the layers of the building, **and** therefore **this work is being**
accomplished diligently, or with precision, **and** the task **is suc-**
ceeding in their, the Judeans', **hands.** They did not know God's
name, but had presumably heard from the Judeans that this was
a Temple for the great God.

Etching of coin from province of Judah

9 **Then we asked those elders, and so we said to them: Who**
issued you a decree that said you were permitted **to build this**
House, and to finish this wall?
10 **We even asked them** for **their names,** in order **to inform you,**
so we could write the names of the men that were at their
head; a list of the leaders heading the project was appended to
the document.
11 **With these words they,** the Judeans, **replied, saying: We are**
the servants of the God of the heavens and the earth, and we
are building the House, the Temple, **that was** first **built many**
years beforehand; a great king of Israel built and finished it.

Model of the Second Temple

12 **However, because our fathers angered the God of the heav-**
ens, He delivered them into the hand of Nebuchadnezzar
king of Babylon, the Chaldean, and he demolished this
House and exiled the people to Babylon.
13 **But in the first year of Cyrus king of Babylon, King Cyrus**
issued a decree to build this House of God. Moreover, he did
not only grant permission, he issued an order that the Temple
should be built.
14 **Even the gold and silver vessels of the House of God that**
Nebuchadnezzar had removed from the Sanctuary that
was in Jerusalem, and transported them to the sanctuary of
Babylon, King Cyrus removed them from the sanctuary of
Babylon and gave them to Sheshbatzar; that is the name of
he, the official, **whom he had appointed governor.** It is possible that Sheshbatzar was the Persian or Chaldean name for
Zerubavel, the governor of Judah appointed by the king. There
is an opinion in the Midrash that Sheshbatzar was Daniel, who
came to Israel from Babylon during this period.[61]

BACKGROUND

5:8 | **The province of Judah [*yehud*]:** This was the official name of the province, as corroborated from archaeological finds. The name appears on coins and seals dated to the time, and contemporary Greek writers also used the same name. Judah was the only province in the region of Syria-Israel which was granted the right to issue its own currency. Researchers suggest two possible reasons for this privilege: First, Cyrus' proclamation, which raised the status of Jerusalem until it became a fortified city that housed the Temple; and second, the possibility that, despite the conquest, the Persian government continued the practices of the previous Babylonian administration, which had allowed the continued existence of Judah, and this also gave it a certain legitimacy (see commentary on Daniel 2:25).

ה אֱמַרְנָא לְּהֹם מַן־אִנּוּן שְׁמָהָת גֻּבְרַיָּא דִּי־דְנָה בִנְיָנָא בָּנַיִן׃ וְעֵין אֱלָהֲהֹם הֲוָת
עַל־שָׂבֵי יְהוּדָיֵא וְלָא־בַטִּלוּ הִמּוֹ עַד־טַעְמָא לְדָרְיָוֶשׁ יְהָךְ וֶאֱדַיִן יְתִיבוּן נִשְׁתְּוָנָא
ו עַל־דְּנָה׃ פַּרְשֶׁגֶן אִגַּרְתָּא דִּי־שְׁלַח תַּתְּנַי ׀ פַּחַת עֲבַר־נַהֲרָה וּשְׁתַר
ז בּוֹזְנַי וּכְנָוָתֵהּ אֲפַרְסְכָיֵא דִּי בַּעֲבַר נַהֲרָה עַל־דָּרְיָוֶשׁ מַלְכָּא׃ פִּתְגָמָא שְׁלַחוּ
ח עֲלוֹהִי וְכִדְנָה כְּתִיב בְּגַוֵּהּ לְדָרְיָוֶשׁ מַלְכָּא שְׁלָמָא כֹלָּא׃ יְדִיעַ ׀ לֶהֱוֵא לְמַלְכָּא
דִּי־אֲזַלְנָא לִיהוּד מְדִינְתָּא לְבֵית אֱלָהָא רַבָּא וְהוּא מִתְבְּנֵא אֶבֶן גְּלָל וְאָע
ט מִתְּשָׂם בְּכֻתְלַיָּא וַעֲבִידְתָּא דָךְ אָסְפַּרְנָא מִתְעַבְדָא וּמַצְלַח בְּיֶדְהֹם׃ אֱדַיִן שְׁאֵלְנָא
לְשָׂבַיָּא אִלֵּךְ כְּנֵמָא אֲמַרְנָא לְּהֹם מַן־שָׂם לְכֹם טְעֵם בַּיְתָא דְנָה לְמִבְנְיָה וְאֻשַּׁרְנָא
י דְנָה לְשַׁכְלָלָה׃ וְאַף שְׁמָהָתְהֹם שְׁאֵלְנָא לְהֹם לְהוֹדָעוּתָךְ דִּי נִכְתֻּב שֻׁם־גֻּבְרַיָּא
יא דִּי בְרָאשֵׁיהֹם׃ וּכְנֵמָא פִתְגָמָא הֲתִיבוּנָא לְמֵמַר אֲנַחְנָא הִמּוֹ עַבְדוֹהִי דִי־
אֱלָהּ שְׁמַיָּא וְאַרְעָא וּבָנַיִן בַּיְתָא דִּי־הֲוָא בְנֵה מִקַּדְמַת דְּנָה שְׁנִין שַׂגִּיאָן וּמֶלֶךְ
יב לְיִשְׂרָאֵל רַב בְּנָהִי וְשַׁכְלְלֵהּ׃ לָהֵן מִן־דִּי הַרְגִּזוּ אֲבָהֳתַנָא לֶאֱלָהּ שְׁמַיָּא
יְהַב הִמּוֹ בְּיַד נְבוּכַדְנֶצַּר מֶלֶךְ־בָּבֶל כסדיא וּבַיְתָה דְנָה סַתְרֵהּ וְעַמָּה הַגְלִי כַּסְדָּאָה
יג לְבָבֶל׃ בְּרַם בִּשְׁנַת חֲדָה לְכוֹרֶשׁ מַלְכָּא דִּי בָבֶל כּוֹרֶשׁ מַלְכָּא
יד שָׂם טְעֵם בֵּית־אֱלָהָא דְנָה לִבְּנֵא׃ וְאַף מָאנַיָּא דִי־בֵית־אֱלָהָא דִּי דַהֲבָה וְכַסְפָּא

DISCUSSION

them to order an immediate halt to the work. He did this without asking those involved in the construction to justify their actions, and nobody told him about Cyrus' proclamation. As has often been the case throughout history regarding documents that those in charge do not want made public, this proclamation seems to have been buried in the royal archives. However, once the regional governor Tatenai, who was based in Damascus or further north, received word of what was happening in Jerusalem (probably from the adversaries who were trying to stop the construction), he decided to conduct a full investigation.

5:5 | **They could not stop them:** Tatenai was an important leader, and ruled over an area which today comprises at least four countries. But in spite of the significant authority which he no doubt wielded, he refrained from ordering a halt to the construction, pending clarification of the matter, as the elders of Judah had succeeded in convincing him that this was a national diplomatic matter that was above the governor's authority and needed to be decided by the king himself. They claimed that their work was in fulfillment of an explicit order of the first Persian king.

Although Tatenai was not personally aware of such an order, he suspected that they might be telling the truth, and therefore refrained from acting unilaterally. It is possible that he may have even known about the previous order to halt construction, but as he realized that any decision he made might cause problems, he elected to refer the matter to his superiors.

There is no doubt that the elders of Judah were certainly aware of the earlier royal decree that had stopped the construction. Nevertheless, they preferred to ignore that detail and request a current ruling on the matter, in order to buy time. Their request was reasonable, since letters traveled fairly quickly in the Persian Empire. The Persians were essentially the first to set up a postal system, with branches in all the districts of the empire. Letters and official documents were delivered to their destinations swiftly by horse-drawn carriages, known as "the finest steeds, the mules born to mares" (Esther 8:10). This royal postal system covered the entire empire, and probably was also used by private citizens to send personal letters.

15 **He,** the king, **said to him,** Sheshbatzar: **Carry these vessels, go, place them in the Sanctuary that is in Jerusalem, and let the House of God be built in its** designated **place.** This was Cyrus' order.

16 **Then, that** same **Sheshbatzar came and set the foundations of the House of God that is in Jerusalem, and from then until now it,** the Temple, **is being built, and it is not completed.** In this brief account of events, the elders omitted the order of the previous Persian king to cease the construction work. They stated simply that Sheshbatzar had fulfilled the order of Cyrus, the great ruler and the first Persian king. It was this celebrated king who had commanded that the House of God be built and had provided assistance in other ways. However, the construction had taken a long time, and was still in progress.

17 Tatenai and his colleagues had no way of authenticating the claim of the Judean elders, as the relevant documents were not in their possession. The historic decree in question involves a matter that was of great concern to the Samaritans, but that was not particularly important to Tatenai, who ruled over a large region and presumably had many other pressing matters at hand. Therefore, Tatenai and his men requested in their letter: **Now, if it pleases the king,**[62] **let it be checked in the king's treasury,** which also served as the royal archives, **which is there, in Babylon,** to determine **whether it is so,** whether there is in fact a document attesting **that a decree was issued by King Cyrus to build this House of God in Jerusalem.** And **may the king's will in this** matter **be sent to us.**

6 1 **Then King Darius issued a decree** to investigate the claim of the elders of Judah, **and they checked in the house of the archives where the treasures were placed, there in Babylon.**

2 **A scroll,** an official document or a copy, **was found in Ahmeta,**[B] **in the capital;** alternatively, this can mean that it was found in a waterskin [*ḥemet*] in the fortress or tower, **that is in the province of Media, and so it was written in it: Memorandum:**

Ruins of Ecbatana, Iran

3 **In the first year of King Cyrus, King Cyrus issued a decree** titled: Concerning **the House of God in Jerusalem,** which said: **Let the House, the place where they slaughter offerings, be built and its foundation laid,** or raised. **Its,** the building's, **height shall be sixty cubits and its width sixty cubits;**

4 they shall build **three rows of great stones,** chiseled for building purposes, **and** an additional **row of new wood, and the expenses will be given from the king's palace,** a detail that was not mentioned in the first version of King Cyrus' proclamation (see 1:1–4).

5 **And** in addition, **also the gold and silver vessels of the House of God, which Nebuchadnezzar removed from the Sanctuary that is in Jerusalem and transported to Babylon, shall be restored, and** let all of them be **returned to the Sanctuary that is in Jerusalem, to its place, and** all **shall be placed in the House of God.**

6 This summary of Cyrus' order is now followed by an instruction from King Darius: **Now, Tatenai the governor of Avar Nahara, Shetar Bozenai, and their companions the Afarsekhites, who are in Avar Nahara, distance yourselves from there.** Do not interfere in the construction work of the Judeans;

7 **allow the work of this House of God; the governor of the Judeans and** with him **the elders of the Judeans shall build this House of God in its** designated **place.**

8 **From me a decree is issued with regard to what you shall do for these elders of the Judeans for the building of this House of God: From the king's property,** raised **from the property tax of Avar Nahara, expenses will be given diligently,** or with exactitude, **to these men, so that they will not be stopped** in their labor.

9 Not only are the requirements for the construction to be provided from the property of the king, but **that which is needed, young bulls, rams, and lambs, for burnt offerings to the God of the heavens, wheat, salt, wine, and oil, in accordance with the word of the priests who are in Jerusalem, shall be given to them each day without fail.** Be conscientious in this matter; do not be negligent;

Ram

Wheat

דִּי נְבוּכַדְנֶצַּר הַנְפֵּק מִן־הֵיכְלָא דִּי בִירוּשְׁלֶם וְהֵיבֵל הִמּוֹ לְהֵיכְלָא דִּי בָבֶל הַנְפֵּק
הִמּוֹ כּוֹרֶשׁ מַלְכָּא מִן־הֵיכְלָא דִּי בָבֶל וִיהִיבוּ לְשֵׁשְׁבַּצַּר שְׁמֵהּ דִּי פֶחָה שָׂמֵהּ׃
טו וַאֲמַר־לֵהּ | אלה מָאנַיָּא שֵׂא אֵזֶל־אֲחֵת הִמּוֹ בְּהֵיכְלָא דִּי בִירוּשְׁלֶם וּבֵית אֱלָהָא אֵל
טז יִתְבְּנֵא עַל־אַתְרֵהּ׃ אֱדַיִן שֵׁשְׁבַּצַּר דֵּךְ אֲתָא יְהַב אֻשַּׁיָּא דִּי־בֵית
יז אֱלָהָא דִּי בִירוּשְׁלֶם וּמִן־אֱדַיִן וְעַד־כְּעַן מִתְבְּנֵא וְלָא שְׁלִם׃ וּכְעַן הֵן עַל־מַלְכָּא
טָב יִתְבַּקַּר בְּבֵית גִּנְזַיָּא דִּי־מַלְכָּא תַמָּה דִּי בְּבָבֶל הֵן אִיתַי דִּי־מִן־כּוֹרֶשׁ מַלְכָּא
שִׂים טְעֵם לְמִבְנֵא בֵּית־אֱלָהָא דֵךְ בִּירוּשְׁלֶם וּרְעוּת מַלְכָּא עַל־דְּנָה יִשְׁלַח
א עֲלֶינָא׃ בֵּאדַיִן דָּרְיָוֶשׁ מַלְכָּא שָׂם טְעֵם וּבַקַּרוּ | בְּבֵית סִפְרַיָּא דִּי
ב גִנְזַיָּא מְהַחֲתִין תַּמָּה בְּבָבֶל׃ וְהִשְׁתְּכַח בְּאַחְמְתָא בְּבִירְתָא דִּי בְּמָדַי מְדִינְתָּא
ג מְגִלָּה חֲדָה וְכֵן־כְּתִיב בְּגַוַּהּ דִּכְרוֹנָה׃ בִּשְׁנַת חֲדָה לְכוֹרֶשׁ מַלְכָּא
כּוֹרֶשׁ מַלְכָּא שָׂם טְעֵם בֵּית־אֱלָהָא בִירוּשְׁלֶם בַּיְתָא יִתְבְּנֵא אֲתַר דִּי־דָבְחִין
ד דִּבְחִין וְאֻשּׁוֹהִי מְסוֹבְלִין רוּמֵהּ אַמִּין שִׁתִּין פְּתָיֵהּ אַמִּין שִׁתִּין׃ נִדְבָּכִין דִּי־אֶבֶן
ה גְּלָל תְּלָתָא וְנִדְבָּךְ דִּי־אָע חֲדַת וְנִפְקְתָא מִן־בֵּית מַלְכָּא תִּתְיְהִב׃ וְאַף מָאנֵי
בֵית־אֱלָהָא דִּי דַהֲבָה וְכַסְפָּא דִּי נְבוּכַדְנֶצַּר הַנְפֵּק מִן־הֵיכְלָא דִּי־בִירוּשְׁלֶם
וְהֵיבֵל לְבָבֶל יַהֲתִיבוּן וִיהָךְ לְהֵיכְלָא דִּי־בִירוּשְׁלֶם לְאַתְרֵהּ וְתַחֵת בְּבֵית
ו אֱלָהָא׃ כְּעַן תַּתְּנַי פַּחַת עֲבַר־נַהֲרָה שְׁתַר בּוֹזְנַי וּכְנָוָתְהוֹן אֲפַרְסְכָיֵא
ז דִּי בַּעֲבַר נַהֲרָה רַחִיקִין הֲווֹ מִן־תַּמָּה׃ שְׁבֻקוּ לַעֲבִידַת בֵּית־אֱלָהָא דֵךְ פַּחַת
ח יְהוּדָיֵא וּלְשָׂבֵי יְהוּדָיֵא בֵּית־אֱלָהָא דֵךְ יִבְנוֹן עַל־אַתְרֵהּ׃ וּמִנִּי שִׂים טְעֵם לְמָא
דִּי־תַעַבְדוּן עִם־שָׂבֵי יְהוּדָיֵא אִלֵּךְ לְמִבְנֵא בֵּית־אֱלָהָא דֵךְ וּמִנִּכְסֵי מַלְכָּא דִּי
מִדַּת עֲבַר נַהֲרָה אָסְפַּרְנָא נִפְקְתָא תֶּהֱוֵא מִתְיַהֲבָא לְגֻבְרַיָּא אִלֵּךְ דִּי־לָא
ט לְבַטָּלָא׃ וּמָה חַשְׁחָן וּבְנֵי תוֹרִין וְדִכְרִין וְאִמְּרִין | לַעֲלָוָן | לֶאֱלָהּ שְׁמַיָּא חִנְטִין

BACKGROUND

6:2 | **Ahmeta:** The city of Hamadan, in northwestern Iran, located at a central crossroads some 280 km west of Teheran, is believed to be the site of Ahmeta, which was one of the four capital cities of Persia together with Shushan, Babylon, and Persepolis. Its more familiar Persian name was Ecbatana. Ahmeta was conquered by Cyrus in 550 BCE (*The Nabonidus Chronicle*). According to Josephus, Daniel built an elegant tower there (*Antiquities of the Jews* X:11:7).

10 **so that they may present pleasing aromas to the God of the heavens, and pray for the life of the king and his sons.**
11 **From me a decree is issued that any man who shall alter this matter, a beam will be removed from his house, and he will be hanged upright on it,** on the beam of his own house, **and his house will be made a dunghill for this** transgression. Apparently, for especially severe crimes, the offender would be executed and his home would be confiscated from his surviving family.[63]
12 **And may the God who rested His name there,** in that House, **eradicate every king or people that extends his hand to modify** this decree, and **to damage this House of God that is in Jerusalem. I, Darius, have issued a decree; let it be performed diligently,** or with precision. In this letter, Darius encourages the building of the Temple, is quick to provide gifts for its needs, and even issues decisive threats against anyone who would dare to disturb the laborers.
13 **Then Tatenai the governor of Avar Nahara, Shetar Bozenai, and their companions, because of what King Darius had sent, as stated, acted diligently,** or precisely.
14 **The elders of the Judeans were building and prospering,** as was stated to them **in accordance with the prophecy of Haggai the prophet and Zechariah son of Ido, and** they **built and finished** the Temple, **by the decree of the God of Israel, and by the decree of Cyrus, and Darius, and Artahshasta king of Persia.** In truth, they never received any communication prohibiting the construction. There had been a letter which ordered a delay, but from this point forward all was performed with the king's permission and indeed his active backing.
15 **This House,** the Temple, **was completed by the third day of the month Adar that was in the sixth year of the reign of King Darius.**
16 **The children of Israel, the priests, and the Levites, and the rest of the exiles,** who were called by this name because they were still recent immigrants, **performed the dedication of this House of God with joy.**
17 **They presented for the dedication of this House of God one hundred bulls, two hundred rams, four hundred lambs, and twelve goats as a sin offering for all Israel, according to the number of the tribes of Israel.**

Goat

18 **They established the priests in their divisions,** into the priestly watches, according to their families, **and the Levites in their sections for the service of God who is in Jerusalem, as it is written in the book of** the Torah of **Moses** with regard to the functions of the priests and Levites.
19 **The exiles performed the paschal offering on the fourteenth day of the first month,** the month of Nisan.
20 **For the priests and the Levites had purified themselves as one; all of them were pure.** As there was no reason to delay the ritual, **they slaughtered the paschal offering for all the exiles, and for their brethren the priests, and for themselves.**
21 **They ate: The children of Israel who had returned from the exile and anyone who had separated himself from the impurity of the nations of the land to seek the Lord, God of Israel, with them,** all those who had converted or detached themselves from idol worship, ate the paschal offering.
22 **They observed the Festival of Unleavened Bread seven days joyfully, as the Lord had caused them to rejoice, and had inclined the heart of the king of Assyria toward them** for good, **to encourage them in the labor of the House of God, God of Israel.** This "king of Assyria" is a reference to the king of Persia, who considered himself as having taken over the authority of the kings of Assyria and Babylon.[64] It is possible that the people could have made a paschal offering a few years earlier, as the altar had already been erected, even though the Temple had not been completely rebuilt. However, as they had managed to complete the construction of the Temple in time for Passover, this provided a perfect opportunity to celebrate both the inauguration of the Temple and the festival of Passover simultaneously in a full, public manner.

מְלַח ׀ חֲמַר וּמְשַׁח כְּמֵאמַר כָּהֲנַיָּא דִי־בִירוּשְׁלֶם לֶהֱוֵא מִתְיְהֵב לְהֹם יוֹם ׀ בְּיוֹם
י דִּי־לָא שָׁלוּ׃ דִּי־לֶהֱוֺן מְהַקְרְבִין נִיחוֹחִין לֶאֱלָהּ שְׁמַיָּא וּמְצַלַּיִן לְחַיֵּי מַלְכָּא
יא וּבְנוֹהִי׃ וּמִנִּי שִׂים טְעֵם דִּי כָל־אֱנָשׁ דִּי יְהַשְׁנֵא פִּתְגָמָא דְנָה יִתְנְסַח אָע מִן־
יב בַּיְתֵהּ וּזְקִיף יִתְמְחֵא עֲלֹהִי וּבַיְתֵהּ נְוָלוּ יִתְעֲבֵד עַל־דְּנָה׃ וֵאלָהָא דִּי שַׁכִּן שְׁמֵהּ
תַּמָּה יְמַגַּר כָּל־מֶלֶךְ וְעַם דִּי ׀ יִשְׁלַח יְדֵהּ לְהַשְׁנָיָה לְחַבָּלָה בֵּית־אֱלָהָא דֵךְ דִּי
יג בִירוּשְׁלֶם אֲנָה דָרְיָוֶשׁ שָׂמֶת טְעֵם אָסְפַּרְנָא יִתְעֲבִד׃ אֱדַיִן תַּתְּנַי
פַּחַת עֲבַר־נַהֲרָה שְׁתַר בּוֹזְנַי וּכְנָוָתְהוֹן לָקֳבֵל דִּי־שְׁלַח דָּרְיָוֶשׁ מַלְכָּא כְּנֵמָא
יד אָסְפַּרְנָא עֲבַדוּ׃ וְשָׂבֵי יְהוּדָיֵא בָּנַיִן וּמַצְלְחִין בִּנְבוּאַת חַגַּי נביאה וּזְכַרְיָה בַּר־ נְבִיָּא
עִדּוֹא וּבְנוֹ וְשַׁכְלִלוּ מִן־טַעַם אֱלָהּ יִשְׂרָאֵל וּמִטְּעֵם כּוֹרֶשׁ וְדָרְיָוֶשׁ וְאַרְתַּחְשַׁשְׂתְּא
טו מֶלֶךְ פָּרָס׃ וְשֵׁיצִיא בַּיְתָה דְנָה עַד יוֹם תְּלָתָה לִירַח אֲדָר דִּי־הִיא שְׁנַת־שֵׁת
טז לְמַלְכוּת דָּרְיָוֶשׁ מַלְכָּא׃ וַעֲבַדוּ בְנֵי־יִשְׂרָאֵל כָּהֲנַיָּא וְלֵוָיֵא וּשְׁאָר
יז בְּנֵי־גָלוּתָא חֲנֻכַּת בֵּית־אֱלָהָא דְנָה בְּחֶדְוָה׃ וְהַקְרִבוּ לַחֲנֻכַּת בֵּית־אֱלָהָא דְנָה
תּוֹרִין מְאָה דִּכְרִין מָאתַיִן אִמְּרִין אַרְבַּע מְאָה וּצְפִירֵי עִזִּין לחטיא עַל־כָּל־ לְחַטָּאָה
יח יִשְׂרָאֵל תְּרֵי־עֲשַׂר לְמִנְיָן שִׁבְטֵי יִשְׂרָאֵל׃ וַהֲקִימוּ כָהֲנַיָּא בִּפְלֻגָּתְהוֹן וְלֵוָיֵא ג
בְּמַחְלְקָתְהוֹן עַל־עֲבִידַת אֱלָהָא דִּי בִירוּשְׁלֶם כִּכְתָב סְפַר מֹשֶׁה׃
יט כ וַיַּעֲשׂוּ בְנֵי־הַגּוֹלָה אֶת־הַפָּסַח בְּאַרְבָּעָה עָשָׂר לַחֹדֶשׁ הָרִאשׁוֹן׃ כִּי הִטַּהֲרוּ
הַכֹּהֲנִים וְהַלְוִיִּם כְּאֶחָד כֻּלָּם טְהוֹרִים וַיִּשְׁחֲטוּ הַפֶּסַח לְכָל־בְּנֵי הַגּוֹלָה וְלַאֲחֵיהֶם
כא הַכֹּהֲנִים וְלָהֶם׃ וַיֹּאכְלוּ בְנֵי־יִשְׂרָאֵל הַשָּׁבִים מֵהַגּוֹלָה וְכֹל הַנִּבְדָּל מִטֻּמְאַת
כב גּוֹיֵ־הָאָרֶץ אֲלֵהֶם לִדְרֹשׁ לַיהוָה אֱלֹהֵי יִשְׂרָאֵל׃ וַיַּעֲשׂוּ חַג־מַצּוֹת שִׁבְעַת יָמִים
בְּשִׂמְחָה כִּי ׀ שִׂמְּחָם יְהוָה וְהֵסֵב לֵב מֶלֶךְ־אַשּׁוּר עֲלֵיהֶם לְחַזֵּק יְדֵיהֶם בִּמְלֶאכֶת

The Return of Ezra to the Land of Israel

EZRA 7:1–8:36

Up to this point, the book has recounted the events following the return of the exiles to the Land of Israel, led by Zerubavel and Yeshua, and how they eventually succeeded in completing the construction of the House of God. Here another episode in history begins, the story of Ezra the priest, after whom the book is named.

7 1 **After these matters, during the reign of Artahshasta king of Persia,** there was a man called **Ezra, son of Seraya, son of Azarya, son of Hilkiya,**

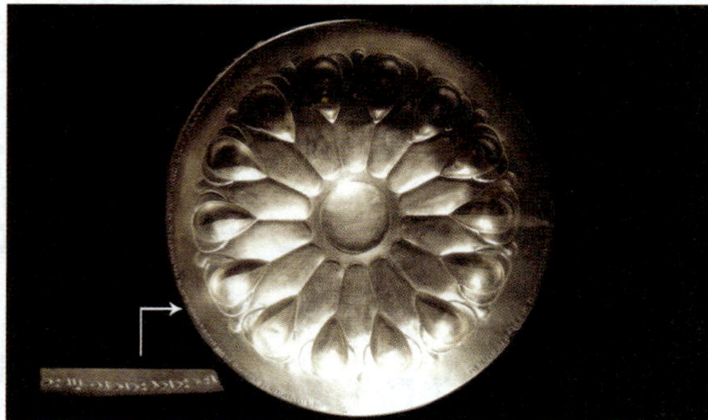

Artahshasta's name on the side of a silver bowl, fifth century BCE

2 **son of Shalum, son of Tzadok, son of Ahituv,**
3 **son of Amarya, son of Azarya, son of Merayot,**
4 **son of Zerahya, son of Uzi, son of Buki,**
5 **son of Avishua, son of Pinhas, son of Elazar, son of Aaron**
the High Priest.[65] Ezra's lineage, at least in part, is a list of High Priests;[66]
6 **he** is the renowned **Ezra** who **went up from Babylonia,**[67] at the head of another wave of immigration; **and he was an expert scribe in the Torah of Moses, which the Lord, God of Israel, had given.** The title of scribe is not given to one who merely knows how to write the Torah, but to a scholar who is also expert in its contents.[68] **The king granted him his entire request, in accordance with** the blessing Ezra received from **the hand of the Lord his God upon him.**[69] The nature of the relationship between the king of Persia and Ezra is unknown, but as Ezra was an important personage among the Judeans, it is likely that King Artahshasta had encountered him and accorded him the respect befitting an esteemed holy man. Consequently, when Ezra expressed his desire to travel to the Land of Israel with a group of people, the king supported him and offered his assistance in anything he might request.
7 **Some of the children of Israel, and some of the priests, and the Levites,** among them **the singers and the gatekeepers, and the Netinim,** descendants of the Givonites (see 2:43), **went up** with Ezra **to Jerusalem in the seventh year of Artahshasta the king.**
8 **He,** Ezra, **arrived** with his congregation **in Jerusalem in the fifth month** of that year, the month of Av; **it was in the seventh year of the** reign of the **king.** Such long voyages were generally undertaken in the summer, as it is easier to travel far when there is no rain.
9 **For on the first** day **of the first month,** Nisan, **was the forming of the emigration from Babylonia,** as on that day the immigrants finalized their decision to leave, **and on the first** day **of the fifth month he,** Ezra, **came to Jerusalem, in accordance with the benevolent hand of his God upon him,** with the assistance of God in His mercy.
10 **For Ezra had prepared his heart,** readied himself, **to study the Torah of the Lord, and to enforce** it, put it into practice, and amend the people's ways, **and teach law and justice in Israel.** Ezra was the spiritual leader of the generation, and he made great efforts to teach Torah to all Israel, while also enacting decrees for the entire nation.
11 The above brief summary of Ezra's immigration to Israel is followed by a detailed description: **This is a copy of the document that King Artahshasta gave to Ezra the priest, the scribe,** a title meaning **a scribe,** an examiner and analyzer **in the matters of the commandments of the Lord, and of His laws** that He commanded and ordained **for Israel:**
12 The king formulated his order in friendly terms: **Artahshasta, king of kings,** delivers this letter **to Ezra the priest, the perfect,**[70] or learned,[71] **scribe of the law of the God of the heavens;** alternatively, the phrase can be read as: The scribe of the law of the God of the heavens and so forth.[72] **Now,**[73]
13 **from me a decree is issued that everyone in my realm from the people of Israel, and its priests, and Levites, who volunteers to go with you to Jerusalem, may go.** Nobody has the right to prevent anyone who wishes to leave from doing so. Furthermore, you, Ezra, will lead the immigrants.[74]
14 **Since it is from before the king and his seven counselors**[75] **that you are sent, to supervise Judah and Jerusalem, in accordance with the law of your God that is in your hand;** and thus you are the messenger of the king and his ministers to deal with religious matters there;
15 **and to transport the silver and gold that the king and his counselors have donated to the God of Israel, whose dwelling is in Jerusalem.** The king and his advisors declare that they will donate a gift to the House of God;
16 **and** Ezra is also entrusted to transport **all silver and gold that you find in the entire province of Babylonia, with the donations of the people, and of the priests, who donate to the House of their God that is in Jerusalem.**

ז א בֵּית־הָאֱלֹהִים אֱלֹהֵי יִשְׂרָאֵל׃ וְאַחַר הַדְּבָרִים הָאֵלֶּה בְּמַלְכוּת
ב אַרְתַּחְשַׁסְתְּא מֶלֶךְ־פָּרָס עֶזְרָא בֶּן־שְׂרָיָה בֶּן־עֲזַרְיָה בֶּן־חִלְקִיָּה׃ בֶּן־שַׁלּוּם
ג ד בֶּן־צָדוֹק בֶּן־אֲחִיטוּב׃ בֶּן־אֲמַרְיָה בֶן־עֲזַרְיָה בֶּן־מְרָיוֹת׃ בֶּן־זְרַחְיָה בֶן־עֻזִּי
ה ו בֶּן־בֻּקִּי׃ בֶּן־אֲבִישׁוּעַ בֶּן־פִּינְחָס בֶּן־אֶלְעָזָר בֶּן־אַהֲרֹן הַכֹּהֵן הָרֹאשׁ׃ הוּא עֶזְרָא
עָלָה מִבָּבֶל וְהוּא־סֹפֵר מָהִיר בְּתוֹרַת מֹשֶׁה אֲשֶׁר־נָתַן יְהוָה אֱלֹהֵי יִשְׂרָאֵל
ז וַיִּתֶּן־לוֹ הַמֶּלֶךְ כְּיַד־יְהוָה אֱלֹהָיו עָלָיו כֹּל בַּקָּשָׁתוֹ׃ וַיַּעֲלוּ מִבְּנֵי־יִשְׂרָאֵל
וּמִן־הַכֹּהֲנִים וְהַלְוִיִּם וְהַמְשֹׁרְרִים וְהַשֹּׁעֲרִים וְהַנְּתִינִים אֶל־יְרוּשָׁלִָם בִּשְׁנַת־שֶׁבַע
ח לְאַרְתַּחְשַׁסְתְּא הַמֶּלֶךְ׃ וַיָּבֹא יְרוּשָׁלִַם בַּחֹדֶשׁ הַחֲמִישִׁי הִיא שְׁנַת הַשְּׁבִיעִית
ט לַמֶּלֶךְ׃ כִּי בְּאֶחָד לַחֹדֶשׁ הָרִאשׁוֹן הוּא יְסֻד הַמַּעֲלָה מִבָּבֶל וּבְאֶחָד לַחֹדֶשׁ
י הַחֲמִישִׁי בָּא אֶל־יְרוּשָׁלִַם כְּיַד־אֱלֹהָיו הַטּוֹבָה עָלָיו׃ כִּי עֶזְרָא הֵכִין לְבָבוֹ לִדְרוֹשׁ
יא אֶת־תּוֹרַת יְהוָה וְלַעֲשֹׂת וּלְלַמֵּד בְּיִשְׂרָאֵל חֹק וּמִשְׁפָּט׃ וְזֶה ׀ פַּרְשֶׁגֶן
הַנִּשְׁתְּוָן אֲשֶׁר נָתַן הַמֶּלֶךְ אַרְתַּחְשַׁסְתְּא לְעֶזְרָא הַכֹּהֵן הַסֹּפֵר סֹפֵר דִּבְרֵי מִצְוֺת־
יב יְהוָה וְחֻקָּיו עַל־יִשְׂרָאֵל׃ אַרְתַּחְשַׁסְתְּא מֶלֶךְ מַלְכַיָּא לְעֶזְרָא כָהֲנָא
יג סָפַר דָּתָא דִּי־אֱלָהּ שְׁמַיָּא גְּמִיר וּכְעֶנֶת׃ מִנִּי שִׂים טְעֵם דִּי כָל־מִתְנַדַּב בְּמַלְכוּתִי
יד מִן־עַמָּא יִשְׂרָאֵל וְכָהֲנוֹהִי וְלֵוָיֵא לִמְהָךְ לִירוּשְׁלֶם עִמָּךְ יְהָךְ׃ כָּל־קֳבֵל דִּי מִן־
קֳדָם מַלְכָּא וְשִׁבְעַת יָעֲטֹהִי שְׁלִיחַ לְבַקָּרָא עַל־יְהוּד וְלִירוּשְׁלֶם בְּדָת אֱלָהָךְ דִּי
טו בִידָךְ׃ וּלְהֵיבָלָה כְּסַף וּדְהַב דִּי־מַלְכָּא וְיָעֲטוֹהִי הִתְנַדַּבוּ לֶאֱלָהּ יִשְׂרָאֵל דִּי
טז בִירוּשְׁלֶם מִשְׁכְּנֵהּ׃ וְכֹל כְּסַף וּדְהַב דִּי תְהַשְׁכַּח בְּכֹל מְדִינַת בָּבֶל עִם הִתְנַדָּבוּת
יז עַמָּא וְכָהֲנַיָּא מִתְנַדְּבִין לְבֵית אֱלָהֲהֹם דִּי בִירוּשְׁלֶם׃ כָּל־קֳבֵל דְּנָה אָסְפַּרְנָא
תִקְנֵא בְּכַסְפָּא דְנָה תּוֹרִין ׀ דִּכְרִין אִמְּרִין וּמִנְחָתְהוֹן וְנִסְכֵּיהוֹן וּתְקָרֵב הִמּוֹ עַל־

17 **You shall therefore diligently** and scrupulously, or speedily, **purchase with this silver** that I am donating, **bulls, rams, lambs, with their meal offerings and their libations, and present them on the altar of the House of your God that is in Jerusalem.** The king is instructing Ezra to bring offerings for the Temple.

18 **Whatever will be good for you and for your brethren to do with the remaining silver and gold, do, in accordance with the will of your God.** Apparently, the king and his advisors gave a handsome gift, not all of which was required for the sacrifices. Therefore, he granted permission for the rest of the money to be used for other purposes.
19 **The vessels that are given to you for service in the House of your God, deliver** faithfully[76] and in their entirety **before the God of Jerusalem.**
20 **The rest of the needs of the House of your God that it will be appropriate for you to give, give from the king's treasury.** If you require more funds for the Temple in addition to this gift of mine, part of which is for sacrifices while the remainder is for you to use as you see fit, you will receive whatever you need from the royal treasury.
21 **From me, King Artahshasta, issue a decree to all the treasurers who are in Avar Nahara** (see 4:10) **that whatever Ezra the priest, scribe of the law of the God of the heavens, will request of you, it will be done diligently,** or speedily,
22 **up to** this amount: **One hundred talents of silver;**[B] a silver talent is a unit of weight equal to at least 30 kg; **up to one hundred kor of wheat;** a *kor* is a unit of volume that is more than 210 L; **up to one hundred bat of wine;** the *bat* is also a unit of volume, equal to one-tenth of a *kor*;[77] **and up to one hundred bat of oil, and salt unquantified,** an unlimited amount; however much salt you need.
23 **Everything that is decreed by the God of the heavens shall be performed with alacrity,** or faithfully, **for the House of the God of the heavens; for why should there be anger** from Heaven **against the realm of the king and his sons?**[D] I must therefore offer sacrifices to God and obey His will.
24 **We inform you,** the treasurers, **that with regard to all the priests, the Levites, the singers, the gatekeepers, Netinim, or workers of this House of God, there is no authority to impose upon them property tax, poll tax, or toll.**[D]
25 **And you, Ezra, in accordance with the wisdom of your God that is in your possession, appoint magistrates and judges, who will judge all the people who are in Avar Nahara, everyone who knows the laws of your God, and educate those who do not know,** who are unacquainted with those laws. In addition to the royal support for his journey and the exemption from taxes, Ezra is granted the authority to appoint judges and lawmakers. It is clear from the wording of this command that the king greatly esteemed Ezra as a wise and holy man.
26 **Anyone who does not observe** and uphold **the law of your God**[D] **and the law of the king, let judgment be executed upon him diligently,** or speedily, **whether by death, by ostracism,** excommunication,[78] pressure, or excision from the world,[79] or perhaps the cutting off of limbs; **by fine of property, or by incarceration.** This concludes the king's letter. Not only did Artahshasta permit Ezra to ascend to the Temple in Jerusalem and to take with him many people and a large amount of assets, he even granted him supreme judicial control over the state, and perhaps also sent soldiers with him to help him put his authority into practice. Ezra had the right to appoint judges and to impose corporal and monetary punishments, not only those enumerated in the Torah, as he saw fit. Nehemiah's discretionary power, by way of comparison, was not nearly as extensive.
27 There was no question that Ezra had found special favor in the eyes of the king and his advisors. Ezra therefore concludes by reciting a blessing: **Blessed is the Lord, God of our fathers, who placed this in the heart of the king, to glorify the House of the Lord that is in Jerusalem,**
28 **and** who **has extended kindness** and mercy **for me before the king and his counselors, and to all the king's mighty princes. I took courage according to** the assistance of **the hand of the Lord my God upon me, and I assembled leaders from Israel,** or heads of families together with their families, **to go up with me.**
8 1 **These are the heads of their patrilineal families and those affiliated with them who came up with me from Babylonia during the reign of King Artahshasta:**

DISCUSSION

7:23 | **Why should there be anger against the realm of the king and his sons?:** The king of Persia's desire that Ezra sacrifice offerings on behalf of the king and his children in the Temple is also mentioned above in the letter of Darius (6:9–10). This request may have been part of a religious syncretism that pervaded the Persian kingdom. Alternatively, the Persians may have bestowed a special status upon the Temple of God, despite their tendency not to worship one specific god or religion (see commentary on Isaiah 45:13).

7:24 | **There is no authority to impose upon them property tax, poll tax, or toll:** This order later served as a precedent for the *halakha* that Torah scholars are not required to pay certain types of taxes (see *Bava Batra* 8a; Rambam, *Sefer HaMadda, Hilkhot Talmud Torah* 6:10).

7:26 | **Anyone who does not observe the law of your God:** The journey to the Land of Israel that Ezra and those who accompanied him undertook was a far more idealistic one than that of the preceding group. While the first group of returning immigrants was led by two upright and righteous leaders, the High Priest and the governor from the house of David, Ezra's group was led by one person, who was a priest and a scribe. Most of the people who returned with Yeshua and Zerubavel simply wished to return home to the land of their forefathers, while those who accompanied Ezra were not only interested in coming to live in the Holy Land, they also wished to imbue it with an element of holiness. This aspiration would also be expressed in the character of the state that was being created in the land of Judah.

יח מדבחה די בית אלהכם די בירושלם: ומה די עליך ועל־אחיך ייטב בשאר עלך | אחך
יט כספא ודהבה למעבד כרעות אלהכם תעבדון: ומאניא די־מתיהבין לך לפלחן
כ בית אלהך השלם קדם אלה ירושלם: ושאר חשחות בית אלהך די יפל־לך
כא למנתן תנתן מן־בית גנזי מלכא: ומני אנה ארתחשסתא מלכא שים טעם
לכל גזבריא די בעבר נהרה די כל־די ישאלנכון עזרא כהנא ספר דתא די־
כב אלה שמיא אספרנא יתעבד: עד־כסף ככרין מאה ועד־חנטין כורין מאה
כג ועד־חמר בתין מאה ועד־בתין משח מאה ומלח די־לא כתב: כל־די מן־טעם
אלה שמיא יתעבד אדרזדא לבית אלה שמיא די־למה להוא קצף על־מלכות
כד מלכא ובנוהי: ולכם מהודעין די כל־כהניא ולויא זמריא תרעיא נתיניא ופלחי
כה בית אלהא דנה מנדה בלו והלך לא שליט למרמא עליהם: ואנת עזרא
כחכמת אלהך די־בידך מני שפטין ודינין די־להון דאנין לכל־עמא די בעבר דינין
כו נהרה לכל־ידעי דתי אלהך ודי לא ידע תהודעון: וכל־די־לא להוא עבד
דתא די־אלהך ודתא די מלכא אספרנא דינה להוא מתעבד מנה הן למות
כז הן לשרשו הן־לענש נכסין ולאסורין: ברוך יהוה אלהי אבתינו לשרשי
כח אשר נתן כזאת בלב המלך לפאר את־בית יהוה אשר בירושלם: ועלי הטה־
חסד לפני המלך ויועציו ולכל־שרי המלך הגברים ואני התחזקתי כיד־יהוה
אלהי עלי ואקבצה מישראל ראשים לעלות עמי:
א ואלה ראשי אבתיהם והתיחשם העלים עמי במלכות ארתחשסתא המלך:

BACKGROUND

7:22 | **One hundred talents [*kakerin*] of silver:** A silver *kikkar* was worth sixty *maneh*, and weighed roughly 30 kg. It was the Babylonian equivalent of the Greek talent. According to Greek historians from the fifth century BCE, a silver *kikkar* was the cost of hiring a boat with a crew of two hundred rowers for a full month.

2 **From the children,** the descendants, **of Pinhas,** son of Elazar, son of Aaron the High Priest, the head of the family who ascended was called **Gershom; from the sons of Itamar** son of Aaron, the name of the man who immigrated was **Daniel; from the sons of David,** it was **Hatush.**
3 **From the children of Shekhanya,** a well-known figure, perhaps one of the descendants of Zerubavel, mentioned in I Chronicles (3:21–22): **From the sons of Parosh,** the head of a branch in the family of Shekhanya, the man who came was called **Zekharya; and with him were affiliated,** the males who were counted with him, **one hundred and fifty males.**
4 **From the children of Pahat Moav**[B] (see 2:6): **Elyehoanai son of Zerahya, and with him, the males were two hundred.**
5 **From the children of Shekhanya: Son of Yahaziyel, and with him, the males were three hundred.**
6 **From the children of Adin,** a man came named **Eved son of Yonatan, and with him, the males were fifty.**
7 **From the children of Elam: Yeshaya son of Atalya, and with him, the males were seventy.**
8 **From the children of Shefatya: Zevadya son of Mikhael, and with him, the males were eighty.**
9 **From the children of Yoav: Ovadya son of Yehiel, and with him, the males were two hundred and eighteen.**
10 **From the children of Shelomit: Son of Yosifya, and with him, the males were one hundred and sixty.** In I Chronicles 3:19, a woman called Shelomit is listed among the children of Zerubavel.
11 **From the children of Bevai: Zekharya son of Bevai, and with him, the males were twenty-eight.**
12 **From the children of Azgad: Yohanan son of Hakatan, and with him, the males were one hundred and ten.**
13 **From the children of Adonikam, who were the last** of this family who remained in exile, as many hundreds of Adonikam's descendants had already immigrated beforehand;[80] **and these are their names: Elifelet, Ye'iel, and Shemaya, and with them, the males were sixty.**
14 **From the children of Bigvai: Utai and Zakur, and with him, the males were seventy.** In total, this list includes some fifteen hundred males, and it can be assumed that most of them came with their families.
15 Since the immigrants were coming from different places within the Babylonian Empire, it was necessary to bring them into one camp so that they could travel together. **I assembled them at the river that runs to Ahava,**[B] the name of a place, or a larger river than the one mentioned in the verse.[81] In those times, there were already man-made water canals that were so large that they were considered rivers in their own right. Such huge water channels were used to link the Euphrates to the Tigris, or for irrigation. **And we camped there three days. I assessed the people and the priests** who had gathered there, **and I did not find there** anyone **from the children of Levi.**
16 **I sent for Eliezer, for Ariel, for Shemaya, for Elnatan, for Yariv, for Elnatan, for Natan, for Zekharya, and for Meshulam,** who were **the leaders, and** also **for Yoyariv and for** another **Elnatan,** who were **the wise men** and scholars.
17 **I appointed them with regard to,** to approach, **Ido, the leader at the place Kasifya;**[B] **and I set words in their mouths to speak to Ido and his brothers, the attendants in the place Kasifya,** who performed the holy service in Kasifya, **to bring to us those who will serve,** Levites and others, **for the House of our God.** Ezra requested that they bring him the men who were needed for the various services and tasks in the Temple.
18 **By the benevolent hand of our God upon us,** with God's assistance, **they brought us a sagacious man,** intelligent and successful men, **from the sons of Mahli,** the son of Merari,[82] **son of Levi, son of Israel,** Jacob; **and Sherevya, and his brothers and his sons, eighteen** men;
19 **and Hashavya, and with him Yeshaya, from the children of Merari, his brothers and their sons, twenty** men; these are the Levites who joined him;
20 **and from the Netinim, whom David and the princes** [*sarim*], the officials,[83] or those who heed [*sarim*] your command,[84] **had**

BACKGROUND

8:4| **Pahat Moav:** It is possible that this name, with its mention of Moav, was a term that stuck to the family over the generations, similar to "the children of Solomon's servants" (2:55; Nehemiah 7:57). The title Pahat, governor, which was not used in earlier periods, is an anachronism, and it alludes to their ancient origin from the family of a minister or prince. According to the Talmud, this name hints at the family of the house of David, or Yoav son of Tzeruya, and it was called after Moav in light of the family's earlier lineage (*Ta'anit* 28a, and Rashi ad loc.).

8:15| **The river that runs to Ahava:** It is difficult to identify this place, which is not mentioned in Babylonian sources. The fact that it is called a river indicates it was a particularly large body of water, and therefore it has been suggested that Ahava is the city of Hit, above the Euphrates, approximately 200 km north of the city of Babylon. Alternatively, the verse is referring to the Naru Itu, the River Itu, which was near the city of Sippar, a region inhabited by exiles from many nations (Oded Bustenay, *The Early History of the Babylonian Exile* (*8th-6th Centuries BCE*). Haifa: Pardes Publications, 2010 [Hebrew]).

8:17| **Kasifya:** Although the location of this city has not been identified, it was an important center for the exiles, where Levites, priests, and Netinim congregated. Due to the fact that it is called "the place Kasifya," some suggest there was a temple there, similar to the temple of the Jewish community at Yeb, Egypt.

ב ג מִבָּבֶל: מִבְּנֵי פִינְחָס גֵּרְשֹׁם מִבְּנֵי אִיתָמָר דָּנִיֵּאל מִבְּנֵי דָוִיד חַטּוּשׁ: מִבְּנֵי שְׁכַנְיָה
ד מִבְּנֵי פַרְעֹשׁ זְכַרְיָה וְעִמּוֹ הִתְיַחֵשׂ לִזְכָרִים מֵאָה וַחֲמִשִּׁים: מִבְּנֵי פַּחַת מוֹאָב
ה אֶלְיְהוֹעֵינַי בֶּן־זְרַחְיָה וְעִמּוֹ מָאתַיִם הַזְּכָרִים: מִבְּנֵי שְׁכַנְיָה בֶּן־יַחֲזִיאֵל וְעִמּוֹ
ו ז שְׁלֹשׁ מֵאוֹת הַזְּכָרִים: וּמִבְּנֵי עָדִין עֶבֶד בֶּן־יוֹנָתָן וְעִמּוֹ חֲמִשִּׁים הַזְּכָרִים: וּמִבְּנֵי
ח עֵילָם יְשַׁעְיָה בֶּן־עֲתַלְיָה וְעִמּוֹ שִׁבְעִים הַזְּכָרִים: וּמִבְּנֵי שְׁפַטְיָה זְבַדְיָה בֶּן־מִיכָאֵל
ט וְעִמּוֹ שְׁמֹנִים הַזְּכָרִים: מִבְּנֵי יוֹאָב עֹבַדְיָה בֶּן־יְחִיאֵל וְעִמּוֹ מָאתַיִם וּשְׁמֹנָה עָשָׂר
י יא הַזְּכָרִים: וּמִבְּנֵי שְׁלוֹמִית בֶּן־יוֹסִפְיָה וְעִמּוֹ מֵאָה וְשִׁשִּׁים הַזְּכָרִים: וּמִבְּנֵי בֵבַי
יב זְכַרְיָה בֶּן־בֵּבָי וְעִמּוֹ עֶשְׂרִים וּשְׁמֹנָה הַזְּכָרִים: וּמִבְּנֵי עַזְגָּד יוֹחָנָן בֶּן־הַקָּטָן וְעִמּוֹ
יג מֵאָה וַעֲשָׂרָה הַזְּכָרִים: וּמִבְּנֵי אֲדֹנִיקָם אַחֲרֹנִים וְאֵלֶּה שְׁמוֹתָם אֱלִיפֶלֶט יְעִיאֵל
יד וּשְׁמַעְיָה וְעִמָּהֶם שִׁשִּׁים הַזְּכָרִים: וּמִבְּנֵי בִּגְוַי עוּתַי וזבוד וְעִמָּהֶם שִׁבְעִים הַזְּכָרִים: וְזַכּוּר
טו וָאֶקְבְּצֵם אֶל־הַנָּהָר הַבָּא אֶל־אַהֲוָא וַנַּחֲנֶה שָׁם יָמִים שְׁלֹשָׁה וָאָבִינָה בָעָם
טז וּבַכֹּהֲנִים וּמִבְּנֵי לֵוִי לֹא־מָצָאתִי שָׁם: וָאֶשְׁלְחָה לֶאֱלִיעֶזֶר לַאֲרִיאֵל לִשְׁמַעְיָה
וּלְאֶלְנָתָן וּלְיָרִיב וּלְאֶלְנָתָן וּלְנָתָן וְלִזְכַרְיָה וְלִמְשֻׁלָּם רָאשִׁים וּלְיוֹיָרִיב וּלְאֶלְנָתָן
יז מְבִינִים: ואוצאה אוֹתָם עַל־אִדּוֹ הָרֹאשׁ בְּכָסִפְיָא הַמָּקוֹם וָאָשִׂימָה בְּפִיהֶם וָאֲצַוֶּה
דְּבָרִים לְדַבֵּר אֶל־אִדּוֹ אָחִיו הנתונים בְּכָסִפְיָא הַמָּקוֹם לְהָבִיא־לָנוּ מְשָׁרְתִים הַנְּתִינִים
יח לְבֵית אֱלֹהֵינוּ: וַיָּבִיאוּ לָנוּ כְּיַד־אֱלֹהֵינוּ הַטּוֹבָה עָלֵינוּ אִישׁ שֶׂכֶל מִבְּנֵי מַחְלִי
יט בֶּן־לֵוִי בֶּן־יִשְׂרָאֵל וְשֵׁרֵבְיָה וּבָנָיו וְאֶחָיו שְׁמֹנָה עָשָׂר: וְאֶת־חֲשַׁבְיָה וְאִתּוֹ יְשַׁעְיָה
כ מִבְּנֵי מְרָרִי אֶחָיו וּבְנֵיהֶם עֶשְׂרִים: וּמִן־הַנְּתִינִים שֶׁנָּתַן דָּוִיד וְהַשָּׂרִים

given to the service of the Levites, two hundred and twenty attendants; all of them designated by name. There were detailed lists of all the Netinim who went with them.
21 **I proclaimed a fast there, by the Ahava River,** before we set on our way, **to afflict ourselves before our God, to seek from Him a straight way,** that our journey will be easy, successful, and without mishaps, **for us, and for our children, and for all our property,** as this was a not particularly large group of civilians for a trip covering the great distance to Israel, and they were loaded with silver, gold, and precious items.
22 Generally, when the central government is strong and stable, there is less danger from bandits and other problems on the roads. But despite the support of a powerful king, there was still room for concern, as the group did not have sufficient protection. However, Ezra was reluctant to ask for such assistance: **For I was ashamed to request from the king**[D] **soldiers and horsemen to help us against an enemy on the way; for we had said to the king, stating: The hand of our God is on those who seek Him for good;** God helps those who pray to him, **and His power and wrath is against all those who forsake Him,** and they will suffer harm. After I had informed the king that God would assist us, I was reluctant to ask him for a protective guard. The king was willing to give anything required, and he certainly would have sent a cavalry unit to protect the immigrants had he been asked.

"Soldiers and horsemen." Lakhish reliefs, 700–692 BCE

23 **We fasted and we requested from our God about this, and He acceded,** and therefore we had a peaceful journey.
24 While we were still at Ahava, **I set aside from the leaders of the priests twelve** men, and appointed them temporary treasurers: **Sherevya, Hashavya, and with them** another **ten of their brethren,**
25 **and I weighed out for them** and gave to them **the silver, and the gold, and the vessels, the gift for the House of our God that the king, his counselors, and his princes, and all Israel that were present,** in Babylon, **had donated.** These men were responsible for all the silver, gold, and vessels received as gifts for the Temple from the king and others.
26 **I weighed,** or counted, **for them: Silver, six hundred and fifty talents,** a substantial sum (see 7:22); and **silver vessels, one hundred,** in addition to the **talents; gold, one hundred talents;**
27 and **gold bowls,** used for sprinkling the blood of sacrifices upon the altar for atonement, **twenty; of darics,** gold Persian coins (see 2:69), **one thousand; and two vessels of fine golden bronze, as nice** and pleasing **as gold.** It was not entirely pure brass, but an admixture of brass and a different material, possibly copper. Nevertheless, it was good quality and glittered, and thus both vessels appeared to be made of gold.

Bronze dining and serving vessels from Dan, Akhziv, and Arad, Israel, ninth to sixth century BCE

Byzantine-era bronze oil flask, found in excavations of the Jewish quarter of the Old City of Jerusalem

28 **I said to them:** As priests, **you are consecrated to the Lord, and the vessels are consecrated, and the silver and the gold are a donation to the Lord, God of your fathers.** Therefore, it is fitting that they be kept with you.
29 **Be vigilant and guard them,** these valuable articles, **until you weigh them out before the princes of the priests and the Levites, and the princes,** the representatives, **of the patrilineal families of Israel in Jerusalem,** until you deliver them to the Temple in precise number, **in the chambers,** for use in the chambers, **of the House of the Lord.**

"And the vessels are consecrated." Serving vessel for meal offerings, reconstruction

Gates to chambers on the northern side of the Temple, model of Temple, Israel Museum

כא לעבדת הלוים נתינים מאתים ועשרים כלם נקבו בשמות: ואקרא שם צום
על־הנהר אהוא להתענות לפני אלהינו לבקש ממנו דרך ישרה לנו ולטפנו
כב ולכל־רכושנו: כי בשתי לשאול מן־המלך חיל ופרשים לעזרנו מאויב בדרך
כי־אמרנו למלך לאמר יד־אלהינו על־כל־מבקשיו לטובה ועזו ואפו על
כג כד כל־עזביו: ונצומה ונבקשה מאלהינו על־זאת ויעתר לנו: ואבדילה משרי
כה הכהנים שנים עשר לשרביה חשביה ועמהם מאחיהם עשרה: ואשקולה ‏(ואשקלה)
להם את־הכסף ואת־הזהב ואת־הכלים תרומת בית־אלהינו ההרימו המלך
כו ויעציו ושריו וכל־ישראל הנמצאים: ואשקלה על־ידם כסף ככרים שש־
כז מאות וחמשים וכלי־כסף מאה לככרים זהב מאה ככר: וכפרי זהב עשרים
כח לאדרכנים אלף וכלי נחשת מצהב טובה שנים חמודת כזהב: ואמרה אלהם
אתם קדש ליהוה והכלים קדש והכסף והזהב נדבה ליהוה אלהי אבתיכם:
כט שקדו ושמרו עד־תשקלו לפני שרי הכהנים והלוים ושרי־האבות לישראל
ל בירושלם הלשכות בית יהוה: וקבלו הכהנים והלוים משקל הכסף והזהב
לא והכלים להביא לירושלם לבית אלהינו: ונסעה מנהר אהוא
בשנים עשר לחדש הראשון ללכת ירושלם ויד אלהינו היתה עלינו ויצילנו
לב לג מכף אויב ואורב על־הדרך: ונבוא ירושלם ונשב שם ימים שלשה: וביום

30 **The priests and the Levites accepted the weight of the silver, the gold, and the vessels,** in order **to bring them to Jerusalem to the House of our God.** They accepted the task and took the items into their possession.

31 **We traveled from the Ahava River on the twelfth of the first month,** Nisan, **to go to Jerusalem, and the hand of our God was upon us, and He saved us from the hand of enemy and ambush on the way.**

32 **We came to Jerusalem and we stayed there three days.**

33 **And on the fourth day the silver, the gold, and the vessels were weighed in the House of our God by Meremot son of Uriya the priest,** who was the officiating priest in the Temple;

DISCUSSION

8:22 | **For I was ashamed to request from the king:** One can infer much from Ezra's autobiographic letter with regard to his personality and character. It is clear that Ezra was a modest person, and sensitive to how words and actions would be understood and received by others. This quality is also evident in the continuation of the narrative, when he arrived in Jerusalem. Although he was given a large amount of power and influence by the Persian king, his governing style was not particularly forceful and his reputation was not one of a typical governor.

and with him Elazar son of Pinhas, and with them Yozavad son of Yeshua and Noadya son of Binui, the Levites.

34 **Everything by number and by weight;** we specified the number of all the vessels and coins, as well as the sum weight of the metals, **and the entire weight was recorded at that time.**

35 **Those coming from captivity, the exiles, presented burnt offerings to the God of Israel: Twelve bulls,** corresponding to the twelve tribes, as atonement **for all Israel;** and **ninety-six rams,** which is twelve times eight; **seventy-seven lambs;** and **twelve goats as a sin offering; everything was a burnt offering to the Lord.** As a provisional edict, all these unique offerings were burned in their entirety upon the altar, in the manner of burnt offerings.[85]

36 **They conveyed the king's orders,** the official letters containing the orders, **to the king's satraps,**[B] the rulers of districts, **and to the governors,** rulers of the states **of Ever HaNahar,**[B] **and** when they saw the direct orders from the king to embrace the immigrants and support them, **they exalted,** honored, **the people and the House of God.** All the ministers and officials provided them with assistance and took care of all the Temple's requirements.

The Separation from the Nations of the Land and the Removal of Foreign Women

EZRA 9:1–10:44

Immediately upon entering the land, Ezra hears about the increasing number of intermarriages. He begins his career as a leader with a campaign to purify the people and transform them into an independent, autonomous group with no ties to any other community in the land.

Assimilation is a mortal danger in all times and places, both because it presents a spiritual threat to the soul and because the nation as a whole thereby loses members and will eventually disappear. In order to deal with the spiritual assimilation posed by intermarriage, a broad cooperative effort is required.

9 1 **With the conclusion of all this,** the rituals of bringing the gifts of the immigrants to the Temple treasury and the offering of sacrifices for atonement, purification, and general inspiration, **the princes approached me, saying: The people of** the tribes of **Israel,** who arrived in the first wave of immigration and who have been living in the land for several years already, **the priests, and the Levites have not separated themselves from the peoples of the lands,** the local nations. Rather, **their abominations are like those of the Canaanites, the Hitites, the Perizites, the Yevusites, the Amonites, the Moavites, the Egyptians, and the Emorites.**

2 The Judeans feel close to these nations, **for they have taken from their,** the nations', **daughters as wives for themselves and for their sons, and they have mingled the holy seed with the peoples of the lands.** What is more, **the hand of the princes and the prefects,** the senior officials, close to the governor, **has been first in this** act of **trespass.** It can happen that the simple folk at the margins of society might fall prey to assimilation, as the lower members of different societies are less particular about such matters and sometimes intermingle with each other. However, in this case the leaders of the people had married gentiles, perhaps women of noble status. This was a very serious situation, as they served as a bad example for others. Apparently, Ezra was unaware of all this.

Egyptian women, Tomb of Nebamun, Thebes, Egypt, 1350 BCE

3 **When I heard this matter, I rent my garment and my robe, and I ripped out some of the hair of my head and my beard,** as a sign of mourning, **and I sat desolate,** silent, angry, and shocked at what I had heard.[86] Ezra had ascended to the Holy Land with a sizeable number of people, and he had been granted the authority and the opportunity to become a great spiritual leader. He intended to raise the status of the local Judean population to a high spiritual level, and yet he discovered that the society was in need of a far more basic, fundamental transformation.

4 **Everyone fervent for the words of the God of Israel gathered around me because of the trespass of the** earlier returnees from **exile.** Upon seeing my reaction, more people who were upset over the sins of the earlier immigrants gathered around me, **and I sat desolate until** the time of **the evening offering,** the late afternoon.[87]

5 **At** the time of **the evening offering I arose from my fast,** for I had not eaten in my sorrow, **and with my garment and my robe rent,** and in my torn clothing, **I bowed on my knees and extended my hands to the Lord my God.** Ezra began to pray, probably as part of a communal prayer rather than a strictly private supplication,

6 **and said: My God, I am ashamed and humiliated to raise my face to You, my God, as our iniquities are higher than our head,** they are too many to number, **and our guilt has grown to the heavens.**

7 **Since the days of our fathers we,** the people in exile, **have been exceedingly guilty, to this day, and due to our iniquities we, our kings,** and **our priests have been delivered into the hand**

הָֽרְבִיעִי נִשְׁקַל הַכֶּסֶף וְהַזָּהָב וְהַכֵּלִים בְּבֵית אֱלֹהֵינוּ עַל יַד־מְרֵמוֹת בֶּן־אוּרִיָּה
הַכֹּהֵן וְעִמּוֹ אֶלְעָזָר בֶּן־פִּינְחָס וְעִמָּהֶם יוֹזָבָד בֶּן־יֵשׁוּעַ וְנוֹעַדְיָה בֶן־בִּנּוּי הַלְוִיִּם׃
לד לה בְּמִסְפָּר בְּמִשְׁקָל לַכֹּל וַיִּכָּתֵב כָּל־הַמִּשְׁקָל בָּעֵת הַהִיא׃ הַבָּאִים ד
מֵהַשְּׁבִי בְנֵי־הַגּוֹלָה הִקְרִיבוּ עֹלוֹת ׀ לֵאלֹהֵי יִשְׂרָאֵל פָּרִים שְׁנֵים־עָשָׂר עַל־כָּל־
יִשְׂרָאֵל אֵילִים ׀ תִּשְׁעִים וְשִׁשָּׁה כְּבָשִׂים שִׁבְעִים וְשִׁבְעָה צְפִירֵי חַטָּאת שְׁנֵים עָשָׂר
לו הַכֹּל עוֹלָה לַיהוָה׃ וַיִּתְּנוּ ׀ אֶת־דָּתֵי הַמֶּלֶךְ לַאֲחַשְׁדַּרְפְּנֵי הַמֶּלֶךְ וּפַחֲווֹת עֵבֶר
א הַנָּהָר וְנִשְּׂאוּ אֶת־הָעָם וְאֶת־בֵּית הָאֱלֹהִים׃ וּכְכַלּוֹת אֵלֶּה נִגְּשׁוּ
אֵלַי הַשָּׂרִים לֵאמֹר לֹא־נִבְדְּלוּ הָעָם יִשְׂרָאֵל וְהַכֹּהֲנִים וְהַלְוִיִּם מֵעַמֵּי הָאֲרָצוֹת
כְּתֹעֲבֹתֵיהֶם לַכְּנַעֲנִי הַחִתִּי הַפְּרִזִּי הַיְבוּסִי הָעַמֹּנִי הַמֹּאָבִי הַמִּצְרִי וְהָאֱמֹרִי׃
ב כִּי־נָשְׂאוּ מִבְּנֹתֵיהֶם לָהֶם וְלִבְנֵיהֶם וְהִתְעָרְבוּ זֶרַע הַקֹּדֶשׁ בְּעַמֵּי הָאֲרָצוֹת וְיַד
ג הַשָּׂרִים וְהַסְּגָנִים הָיְתָה בַּמַּעַל הַזֶּה רִאשׁוֹנָה׃ וּכְשָׁמְעִי אֶת־הַדָּבָר הַזֶּה קָרַעְתִּי
ד אֶת־בִּגְדִי וּמְעִילִי וָאֶמְרְטָה מִשְּׂעַר רֹאשִׁי וּזְקָנִי וָאֵשְׁבָה מְשׁוֹמֵם׃ וְאֵלַי יֵאָסְפוּ
כֹּל חָרֵד בְּדִבְרֵי אֱלֹהֵי־יִשְׂרָאֵל עַל מַעַל הַגּוֹלָה וַאֲנִי יֹשֵׁב מְשׁוֹמֵם עַד לְמִנְחַת
ה הָעָרֶב׃ וּבְמִנְחַת הָעֶרֶב קַמְתִּי מִתַּעֲנִיתִי וּבְקָרְעִי בִגְדִי וּמְעִילִי וָאֶכְרְעָה עַל־בִּרְכַּי
ו וָאֶפְרְשָׂה כַפַּי אֶל־יְהוָה אֱלֹהָי׃ וָאֹמְרָה אֱלֹהַי בֹּשְׁתִּי וְנִכְלַמְתִּי לְהָרִים אֱלֹהַי פָּנַי
ז אֵלֶיךָ כִּי עֲוֺנֹתֵינוּ רָבוּ לְמַעְלָה רֹּאשׁ וְאַשְׁמָתֵנוּ גָדְלָה עַד לַשָּׁמָיִם׃ מִימֵי אֲבֹתֵינוּ
אֲנַחְנוּ בְּאַשְׁמָה גְדֹלָה עַד הַיּוֹם הַזֶּה וּבַעֲוֺנֹתֵינוּ נִתַּנּוּ אֲנַחְנוּ מְלָכֵינוּ כֹהֲנֵינוּ

BACKGROUND

8:36 | **Satrap [*aḥashdarpan*]:** This is the Hebrew form of the name for the ruler of a province, which comprises the two ancient Persian words *khsatra-pava*, meaning a shield of the kingdom. The Persian Empire was divided into twenty provinces, or states, each headed by an *aḥashdarpan*, which was corrupted into the word satrap in Greek (see also commentary on Daniel 6:2).

Ever HaNahar: Ever HaNahar is the Hebrew translation of the Aramaic name of the province of Avar Nahara mentioned in chapters 4–7.

of the kings of the lands, to the sword, to captivity and to spoils, and to shame, as it is clear to us **this day.**

8 **Now, for a brief moment,** temporarily, **there has been pardon from the Lord our God, to leave us a remnant, and to give us a stake,** a small, but permanent foundation, **in the place of His holiness, for God to brighten our eyes, and to provide us with sustenance,** some sort of existence, **in our** period of **enslavement.**

9 **For** ultimately we must keep in mind that **we are slaves,** not independent; **but our God has not forsaken us in our enslavement; He has extended favor toward us before the kings of Persia, to provide us sustenance, to raise the House of our God, to restore its ruins, and to give us a holding in Judah and in Jerusalem.** Although we are still subjugated to foreign rule, a gracious kingdom supports our spiritual development and provides us with protection.

10 **Now, what can we say, our God, after** all **this** good that You have bestowed upon us, **as we have forsaken Your commandments**

11 **that You commanded through Your servants the prophets, saying: The land to which you are coming to take possession of it is a defiled land with the defilements of the peoples of the lands, through their abominations with which they filled it from one end to another,** in its entirety, **with their impurity.** They have befouled the land, so that it is now utterly filthy and impure.

12 **Now, do not give your daughters to their sons, and do not marry their daughters to your sons, and do not seek their peace or their prosperity forever,** as is written several times in the Torah;[88] **so that you will be strong, and eat the goodness of the land, and bequeath it to your children forever.**

"And eat the goodness of the land"

Grapes Figs

13 **After all that has come upon us** over the generations **due to our evil actions, and due to our immense guilt, though You, our God, have mitigated our iniquities, and** You **have given us a remnant like this,**

14 **will we go back to violating Your commandments** now, **and to marry into these peoples of abominations? Wouldn't You** then **be incensed with us to** the point of our entire **destruction, with no remainder or remnant?** We have survived only due to Your mercy, and now with these intermarriages we are spoiling all that we merited to receive from Your hand.

15 **Lord, God of Israel, You are righteous, for we** still **remain as a remnant, as it is this day; behold, we are** here **before You in our guilt, as no one can stand,** or we have no merit to stand, **before You for this** transgression.

10 1 Ezra did not simply recite a prayer to God; he also sought to rouse Israel to repent from the sin of assimilation: **While Ezra was praying and while he was confessing, weeping, and prostrating himself before the House of God, a very great assembly, men, women, and children from Israel, gathered to him, for the people were weeping a great weeping.** He arranged a great display of mourning, and he was joined by many of the people.

2 **Shekhanya**[D] **son of Yehiel, one of the children of Elam,** which was one of the families of immigrants, **responded** on behalf of the people **and said to Ezra: We have trespassed against our God and have settled down with foreign women from the peoples of the land, but now, there is** still **hope for this** matter **for Israel.**[89] Some read this as a question: Is there still hope left for us?[90]

3 **Now, let us establish a covenant with our God to send away all the** foreign **wives, and those born from them,** all their children, **according to the counsel of the Lord and** through the religious awakening **of those fervent for the commandment of our God, and let it be done in accordance with** the command of **the Torah.**

4 **Rise, for,** as the leader, **the task is yours and we are with you,** we will cooperate; **be strong and take action.**

5 **Ezra rose and administered an oath to the princes of the priests, the Levites, and all Israel that they would act in accordance with this matter,** to obey him and do all it would take to remedy the situation; **and they took the oath.**

6 **Ezra rose from before** the site of **the House of God, and went to the chamber of Yehohanan son of Elyashiv. He went there; he did not eat bread, and he did not drink water, for he was**

DISCUSSION

10:2 | **Shekhanya:** The Talmud notes that although Shekhanya confessed that "we have trespassed against our God and have settled down with foreign women from the peoples of the land," he himself was not actually one of the sinners. Rather, he spoke on behalf of the entire people (see *Sanhedrin* 11a).

ח בְּיַד ׀ מַלְכֵי הָאֲרָצוֹת בַּחֶרֶב בַּשְּׁבִי וּבַבִּזָּה וּבְבֹשֶׁת פָּנִים כְּהַיּוֹם הַזֶּה: וְעַתָּה
כִּמְעַט־רֶגַע הָיְתָה תְחִנָּה מֵאֵת ׀ יְהוָה אֱלֹהֵינוּ לְהַשְׁאִיר לָנוּ פְּלֵיטָה וְלָתֶת־
לָנוּ יָתֵד בִּמְקוֹם קָדְשׁוֹ לְהָאִיר עֵינֵינוּ אֱלֹהֵינוּ וּלְתִתֵּנוּ מִחְיָה מְעַט בְּעַבְדֻתֵנוּ:
ט כִּי־עֲבָדִים אֲנַחְנוּ וּבְעַבְדֻתֵנוּ לֹא עֲזָבָנוּ אֱלֹהֵינוּ וַיַּט־עָלֵינוּ חֶסֶד לִפְנֵי מַלְכֵי
פָרַס לָתֶת־לָנוּ מִחְיָה לְרוֹמֵם אֶת־בֵּית אֱלֹהֵינוּ וּלְהַעֲמִיד אֶת־חָרְבֹתָיו וְלָתֶת־
י לָנוּ גָדֵר בִּיהוּדָה וּבִירוּשָׁלִָם: וְעַתָּה מַה־נֹּאמַר אֱלֹהֵינוּ אַחֲרֵי־זֹאת כִּי עָזַבְנוּ
יא מִצְוֺתֶיךָ: אֲשֶׁר צִוִּיתָ בְּיַד עֲבָדֶיךָ הַנְּבִיאִים לֵאמֹר הָאָרֶץ אֲשֶׁר אַתֶּם בָּאִים
לְרִשְׁתָּהּ אֶרֶץ נִדָּה הִיא בְּנִדַּת עַמֵּי הָאֲרָצוֹת בְּתוֹעֲבֹתֵיהֶם אֲשֶׁר מִלְאוּהָ מִפֶּה
יב אֶל־פֶּה בְּטֻמְאָתָם: וְעַתָּה בְּנוֹתֵיכֶם אַל־תִּתְּנוּ לִבְנֵיהֶם וּבְנֹתֵיהֶם אַל־תִּשְׂאוּ
לִבְנֵיכֶם וְלֹא־תִדְרְשׁוּ שְׁלֹמָם וְטוֹבָתָם עַד־עוֹלָם לְמַעַן תֶּחֶזְקוּ וַאֲכַלְתֶּם אֶת־
יג טוּב הָאָרֶץ וְהוֹרַשְׁתֶּם לִבְנֵיכֶם עַד־עוֹלָם: וְאַחֲרֵי כָּל־הַבָּא עָלֵינוּ בְּמַעֲשֵׂינוּ
הָרָעִים וּבְאַשְׁמָתֵנוּ הַגְּדֹלָה כִּי ׀ אַתָּה אֱלֹהֵינוּ חָשַׂכְתָּ לְמַטָּה מֵעֲוֺנֵנוּ וְנָתַתָּה
יד לָּנוּ פְּלֵיטָה כָּזֹאת: הֲנָשׁוּב לְהָפֵר מִצְוֺתֶיךָ וּלְהִתְחַתֵּן בְּעַמֵּי הַתֹּעֵבוֹת הָאֵלֶּה
טו הֲלוֹא תֶאֱנַף־בָּנוּ עַד־כַּלֵּה לְאֵין שְׁאֵרִית וּפְלֵיטָה: יְהוָה אֱלֹהֵי
יִשְׂרָאֵל צַדִּיק אַתָּה כִּי־נִשְׁאַרְנוּ פְלֵיטָה כְּהַיּוֹם הַזֶּה הִנְנוּ לְפָנֶיךָ בְּאַשְׁמָתֵינוּ
א כִּי אֵין לַעֲמוֹד לְפָנֶיךָ עַל־זֹאת: וּכְהִתְפַּלֵּל עֶזְרָא וּכְהִתְוַדֹּתוֹ
בֹּכֶה וּמִתְנַפֵּל לִפְנֵי בֵּית הָאֱלֹהִים נִקְבְּצוּ אֵלָיו מִיִּשְׂרָאֵל קָהָל רַב־מְאֹד אֲנָשִׁים
וְנָשִׁים וִילָדִים כִּי־בָכוּ הָעָם הַרְבֵּה בֶכֶה:
ב וַיַּעַן שְׁכַנְיָה בֶן־יְחִיאֵל מִבְּנֵי עולם וַיֹּאמֶר לְעֶזְרָא אֲנַחְנוּ מָעַלְנוּ בֵאלֹהֵינוּ עֵילָם
וַנֹּשֶׁב נָשִׁים נָכְרִיּוֹת מֵעַמֵּי הָאָרֶץ וְעַתָּה יֵשׁ־מִקְוֶה לְיִשְׂרָאֵל עַל־זֹאת:
ג וְעַתָּה נִכְרָת־בְּרִית לֵאלֹהֵינוּ לְהוֹצִיא כָל־נָשִׁים וְהַנּוֹלָד מֵהֶם בַּעֲצַת אֲדֹנָי
ד וְהַחֲרֵדִים בְּמִצְוַת אֱלֹהֵינוּ וְכַתּוֹרָה יֵעָשֶׂה: קוּם כִּי־עָלֶיךָ הַדָּבָר וַאֲנַחְנוּ עִמָּךְ
ה חֲזַק וַעֲשֵׂה: וַיָּקָם עֶזְרָא וַיַּשְׁבַּע אֶת־שָׂרֵי הַכֹּהֲנִים הַלְוִיִּם
ו וְכָל־יִשְׂרָאֵל לַעֲשׂוֹת כַּדָּבָר הַזֶּה וַיִּשָּׁבֵעוּ: וַיָּקָם עֶזְרָא מִלִּפְנֵי בֵּית הָאֱלֹהִים

mourning over the trespass of the earlier immigrants from **exile.**

7 **They circulated a proclamation in Judah and Jerusalem to all the exiles to assemble in Jerusalem:**

8 **Whoever does not come in three days, according to the counsel of the princes and the elders, all his property shall be confiscated.** Here Ezra utilized the authority the king had granted him in his letter, which gave him the right to confiscate the property of anyone who failed to obey him.[91] **And** furthermore, the proclamation added, **he shall be banished,** excommunicated, **from the congregation of the exile.**

9 **All the men of Judah and Benjamin assembled in Jerusalem within the three days; it,** the date, **was the ninth month,** Kislev, **on the twentieth of the month. All the people sat in the plaza of the House of God, trembling** both **over this matter** itself, **and due to the rains,** as they were sitting in the open streets during the cold, rainy season.

10 **Ezra the priest arose and said to them: You,** who sinned through intermarriage, **have trespassed and have settled down with foreign women, to exacerbate the guilt of Israel.**

11 **Now, make confession to the Lord,**[92] **God of your fathers, and perform His will; and separate yourselves from the peoples of the land, and from the foreign women.**

12 **The entire congregation responded and said in a great voice: In accordance with your words, it is incumbent upon us to act.**

13 **But the people are many and it is the rainy season; there is no strength to stay outside, and the labor,** the matter of clarifying the marital status of each person, **is not for one day and not for two, as we have transgressed exceedingly in this matter.** We require substantial time in order to perform a thorough inspection.

14 **Let our princes,** the representatives, **stay on behalf of the entire congregation, and let everyone who is in our cities who settled down** in their houses **with foreign women come at scheduled times, and with them the elders of each and every city and its judges, until** they change their behavior so that **the enflamed wrath of our God will be averted from us due to this matter.**[93] There is no need for the entire people to participate in this campaign.

15 **Only Yonatan son of Asael, and Yahzeya son of Tikva, insisted on this,** put forth great effort to ensure that the matter would be taken care of; **and Meshulam and Shabetai the Levite assisted them.**

16 **The exiles did so. Ezra the priest,** with[94] certain **heads of patrilineal families, according to their patrilineal houses, all** specified **by their names, sequestered themselves** for this task, as a list was compiled of those appointed to deal with the problem; **they convened on the first day of the tenth month,** Tevet, **to examine** and find a remedy for **the matter.**

17 **They finished** evaluating and dealing **with all the men who had settled down with foreign women by the first day of the first month,** Nisan.

18 Men **from the sons of the priests were found to have settled down with foreign women: From the sons of Yeshua son of Yotzadak,** the High Priest, **and** from **his,** Yeshua's, **brothers, Maaseya, and Eliezer, and Yariv, and Gedalya.**

19 **They committed,** in the form of an obligation, **to sending away their wives and** also **to** bring **guilt offerings, a ram of the flock for their guilt,** for their atonement.

20 **From the children of Imer,** who were also priests: **Hanani and Zevadya;**

21 **from the children of Harim: Maaseya, and Eliya, and Shemaya, and Yehiel, and Uziya.**

22 **From the children of Pashhur: Elyo'einai, Maaseya, Yishmael, Netanel, Yozavad, and Elasa.**

23 **From the Levites: Yozavad, and Shimi, and Kelaya, he is Kelita,** probably his name in Aramaic, **Petahya, Yehuda, and Eliezer.**

24 **From the** Levites who were **singers: Elyashiv, and from the** Levites who were **gatekeepers: Shalum, and Telem, and Uri.**

25 **From Israel: From the children of Parosh: Ramya, and Yiziya, and Malkiya, and Miyamin, and Elazar, and Malkiya, and Benaya.**

וַיֵּלֶךְ אֶל־לִשְׁכַּת יְהוֹחָנָן בֶּן־אֶלְיָשִׁיב וַיֵּלֶךְ שָׁם לֶחֶם לֹא־אָכַל וּמַיִם לֹא־שָׁתָה
ז כִּי מִתְאַבֵּל עַל־מַעַל הַגּוֹלָה׃ וַיַּעֲבִירוּ קוֹל בִּיהוּדָה וִירוּשָׁלִַם לְכֹל בְּנֵי הַגּוֹלָה
ח לְהִקָּבֵץ יְרוּשָׁלִָם׃ וְכֹל אֲשֶׁר לֹא־יָבוֹא לִשְׁלֹשֶׁת הַיָּמִים כַּעֲצַת הַשָּׂרִים וְהַזְּקֵנִים
יָחֳרַם כָּל־רְכוּשׁוֹ וְהוּא יִבָּדֵל מִקְּהַל הַגּוֹלָה׃
ט וַיִּקָּבְצוּ כָל־אַנְשֵׁי־יְהוּדָה וּבִנְיָמִן ׀ יְרוּשָׁלִַם לִשְׁלֹשֶׁת הַיָּמִים הוּא חֹדֶשׁ הַתְּשִׁיעִי
בְּעֶשְׂרִים בַּחֹדֶשׁ וַיֵּשְׁבוּ כָל־הָעָם בִּרְחוֹב בֵּית הָאֱלֹהִים מַרְעִידִים עַל־הַדָּבָר
י וּמֵהַגְּשָׁמִים׃ וַיָּקָם עֶזְרָא הַכֹּהֵן וַיֹּאמֶר אֲלֵהֶם אַתֶּם מְעַלְתֶּם וַתֹּשִׁיבוּ נָשִׁים
יא נָכְרִיּוֹת לְהוֹסִיף עַל־אַשְׁמַת יִשְׂרָאֵל׃ וְעַתָּה תְּנוּ תוֹדָה לַיהוָה אֱלֹהֵי־אֲבֹתֵיכֶם
יב וַעֲשׂוּ רְצוֹנוֹ וְהִבָּדְלוּ מֵעַמֵּי הָאָרֶץ וּמִן־הַנָּשִׁים הַנָּכְרִיּוֹת׃ וַיַּעֲנוּ
יג כָל־הַקָּהָל וַיֹּאמְרוּ קוֹל גָּדוֹל כֵּן כדבריך עָלֵינוּ לַעֲשׂוֹת׃ אֲבָל הָעָם רָב וְהָעֵת כִּדְבָרְךָ
גְּשָׁמִים וְאֵין כֹּחַ לַעֲמוֹד בַּחוּץ וְהַמְּלָאכָה לֹא־לְיוֹם אֶחָד וְלֹא לִשְׁנַיִם כִּי־הִרְבִּינוּ
יד לִפְשֹׁעַ בַּדָּבָר הַזֶּה׃ יַעֲמְדוּ־נָא שָׂרֵינוּ לְכָל־הַקָּהָל וְכֹל ׀ אֲשֶׁר בֶּעָרֵינוּ הַהֹשִׁיב
נָשִׁים נָכְרִיּוֹת יָבֹא לְעִתִּים מְזֻמָּנִים וְעִמָּהֶם זִקְנֵי־עִיר וָעִיר וְשֹׁפְטֶיהָ עַד לְהָשִׁיב
טו חֲרוֹן אַף־אֱלֹהֵינוּ מִמֶּנּוּ עַד לַדָּבָר הַזֶּה׃ אַךְ יוֹנָתָן בֶּן־עֲשָׂהאֵל וְיַחְזְיָה בֶן־תִּקְוָה
טז עָמְדוּ עַל־זֹאת וּמְשֻׁלָּם וְשַׁבְּתַי הַלֵּוִי עֲזָרֻם׃ וַיַּעֲשׂוּ־כֵן בְּנֵי הַגּוֹלָה וַיִּבָּדְלוּ עֶזְרָא
הַכֹּהֵן אֲנָשִׁים רָאשֵׁי הָאָבוֹת לְבֵית אֲבֹתָם וְכֻלָּם בְּשֵׁמוֹת וַיֵּשְׁבוּ בְּיוֹם אֶחָד
יז לַחֹדֶשׁ הָעֲשִׂירִי לְדַרְיוֹשׁ הַדָּבָר׃ וַיְכַלּוּ בַכֹּל אֲנָשִׁים הַהֹשִׁיבוּ נָשִׁים נָכְרִיּוֹת עַד
יח יוֹם אֶחָד לַחֹדֶשׁ הָרִאשׁוֹן׃ וַיִּמָּצֵא מִבְּנֵי הַכֹּהֲנִים אֲשֶׁר הֹשִׁיבוּ
יט נָשִׁים נָכְרִיּוֹת מִבְּנֵי יֵשׁוּעַ בֶּן־יוֹצָדָק וְאֶחָיו מַעֲשֵׂיָה וֶאֱלִיעֶזֶר וְיָרִיב וּגְדַלְיָה׃ וַיִּתְּנוּ
כ יָדָם לְהוֹצִיא נְשֵׁיהֶם וַאֲשֵׁמִים אֵיל־צֹאן עַל־אַשְׁמָתָם׃ וּמִבְּנֵי אִמֵּר חֲנָנִי וּזְבַדְיָה׃
כא כב וּמִבְּנֵי חָרִם מַעֲשֵׂיָה וְאֵלִיָּה וּשְׁמַעְיָה וִיחִיאֵל וְעֻזִּיָּה׃ וּמִבְּנֵי פַּשְׁחוּר אֶלְיוֹעֵינַי
כג מַעֲשֵׂיָה יִשְׁמָעֵאל נְתַנְאֵל יוֹזָבָד וְאֶלְעָשָׂה׃ וּמִן־הַלְוִיִּם יוֹזָבָד וְשִׁמְעִי וְקֵלָיָה
כד הוּא קְלִיטָא פְּתַחְיָה יְהוּדָה וֶאֱלִיעֶזֶר׃ וּמִן־הַמְשֹׁרְרִים אֶלְיָשִׁיב וּמִן־הַשֹּׁעֲרִים
כה שַׁלֻּם וָטֶלֶם וְאוּרִי׃ וּמִיִּשְׂרָאֵל מִבְּנֵי פַרְעֹשׁ רַמְיָה וְיִזִּיָּה וּמַלְכִּיָּה וּמִיָּמִן וְאֶלְעָזָר

26 **From the children of Elam: Matanya, Zekharya, and Yehiel,**
and Avdi, and Yeremot, and Eliya.
27 **From the children of Zatu: Elyo'einai, Elyashiv, Matanya,**
and Yeremot, and Zavad, and Aziza.
28 **From the children of Bevai: Yehohanan, Hananya, Zabai,**
Atlai.
29 **From the children of Bani: Meshulam, Malukh, and Adaya,**
Yashuv, and She'al, and Ramot.
30 **From the children of Pahat Moav: Adna, and Kelal, Benaya,**
Maaseya, Matanya, Betzalel, and Binui, and Menashe.
31 **From the children of Harim: Eliezer, Yishiya, Malkiya,**
Shemaya, Shimon;
32 **Binyamin, Malukh, Shemarya.**
33 **From the children of Hashum: Matenai, Matata, Zavad,**
Elifelet, Yeremai, Menashe, Shimi.
34 **From the children of Bani: Maadai, Amram, and U'el,**
35 **Benaya, Bedeya, Keluhu,**
36 **Vanya, Meremot, Elyashiv,**
37 **Matanya, Matenai, and Yaasai,**
38 **and Bani, and Binui, Shimi,**
39 **and Shelemya, and Natan, and Adaya,**
40 **Makhnadevai, Shashai, Sharai,**
41 **Azarel, and Shelemyahu, Shemarya,**
42 **Shalum, Amarya, Yosef.**
43 **From the children of Nevo: Ye'iel, Matitya, Zavad,**[D] **Zevina,**
Yadai, and Yoel, Benaya.
44 **All these had married foreign wives, and among them had**
wives by whom in the meantime **they had** fathered **children.**
All these wives and children were separated from the people,
and sent to their nations and families of origin. The Judeans in
the Land of Israel were thereby purified from intermarriage.

DISCUSSION

10:43 | **Ye'iel, Matitya, Zavad, etc.:** Nearly all the individuals who appear on this list are unknown. It appears from the usage of some of the names here that in that generation, they had already begun to use names of famous personalities from earlier generations, such as Benjamin [*Binyamin*], Simeon [*Shimon*], or Benaya.

כו וּמַלְכִּיָּ֖ה וּבְנָיָֽה׃ וּמִבְּנֵ֖י עֵילָ֑ם מַתַּנְיָ֤ה זְכַרְיָה֙ וִֽיחִיאֵ֣ל וְעַבְדִּ֔י וִירֵמ֖וֹת וְאֵלִיָּֽה׃
כז כח וּמִבְּנֵ֖י זַתּ֑וּא אֶלְיוֹעֵנַ֤י אֶלְיָשִׁיב֙ מַתַּנְיָ֣ה וִירֵמ֔וֹת וְזָבָ֖ד וַעֲזִיזָֽא׃ וּמִבְּנֵ֖י בֵּבָ֑י יְהוֹחָנָ֥ן
כט ל חֲנַנְיָ֖ה זַבַּ֥י עַתְלָֽי׃ וּמִבְּנֵ֖י בָּנִ֑י מְשֻׁלָּ֤ם מַלּוּךְ֙ וַעֲדָיָ֔ה יָשׁ֥וּב וּשְׁאָ֖ל ירמות׃ וּמִבְּנֵ֖י   וְרָמֽוֹת
לא פַּ֣חַת מוֹאָ֑ב עַדְנָ֣א וּכְלָ֗ל בְּנָיָ֤ה מַעֲשֵׂיָה֙ מַתַּנְיָ֣ה בְצַלְאֵ֔ל וּבִנּ֖וּי וּמְנַשֶּֽׁה׃ וּבְנֵ֖י חָרִ֑ם
לב לג אֱלִיעֶ֣זֶר יִשִּׁיָּ֗ה מַלְכִּיָּ֛ה שְׁמַֽעְיָ֖ה שִׁמְעֽוֹן׃ בִּנְיָמִ֥ן מַלּ֖וּךְ שְׁמַרְיָֽה׃ מִבְּנֵ֖י חָשֻׁ֑ם מַתְּנַ֤י
לד לה מַתַּתָּה֙ זָבָ֣ד אֱלִיפֶ֔לֶט יְרֵמַ֥י מְנַשֶּׁ֖ה שִׁמְעִֽי׃ מִבְּנֵ֖י בָנִ֑י מַעֲדַ֥י עַמְרָ֖ם וְאוּאֵֽל׃ בְּנָיָ֥ה
לו לז לח בֵדְיָ֖ה כלוהי׃ וַנְיָ֥ה מְרֵמ֖וֹת אֶלְיָשִֽׁיב׃ מַתַּנְיָ֥ה מַתְּנַ֖י ויעשו׃ וּבָנִ֥י וּבִנּ֖וּי שִׁמְעִֽי׃   כְּלוּהוּ | וְיַעֲשָֽׂי
לט מ וְשֶֽׁלֶמְיָ֥ה וְנָתָ֖ן וַעֲדָיָֽה׃ מַכְנַדְבַ֥י שָׁשַׁ֖י שָׁרָֽי׃ עֲזַרְאֵ֥ל וְשֶֽׁלֶמְיָ֖הוּ שְׁמַרְיָֽה׃
מא מב מג מד שַׁלּ֥וּם אֲמַרְיָ֖ה יוֹסֵֽף׃ מִבְּנֵ֖י נְב֑וֹ יְעִיאֵ֤ל מַתִּתְיָה֙ זָבָ֣ד זְבִינָ֔א ידו וְיוֹאֵ֖ל בְּנָיָֽה׃ כָּל־   יַדַּ֥י
אֵ֖לֶּה נשאי נָשִׁ֣ים נָכְרִיּ֑וֹת וְיֵ֣שׁ־מֵהֶ֔ם נָשִׁ֖ים וַיָּשִׂ֥ימוּ בָּנִֽים׃   נָשְׂא֖וּ

Nehemiah

Nehemiah's Efforts to Build Jerusalem

NEHEMIAH 1:1–2:9

Little is known about Nehemiah's lineage, but his role as royal cupbearer in the Persian court indicates that he was one of those noble sons who were taken from Judah in order to serve in the Babylonian kings' court.[1] Although Nehemiah served in the court of the king of Persia, not Babylon, presumably this practice of noble Judeans serving in the royal court was continued when the Persians took over the Babylonian Empire. It is there, in the king's court, that Nehemiah begins to act for the sake of his brethren in Judah and for the sake of the city of Jerusalem.

1 1 **The words of Nehemiah son of Hakhalya: It was in the month of Kislev, the twentieth year** of King Artahshasta, **and I was in the Shushan citadel.**[B] Shushan was a fortified city that contained the administrative center of the Persian Empire.[2]

2 **Hanani, one of my brothers,** colleagues,[3] or his actual brother (see 7:2), **he and some** additional **men from Judah came** to Shushan. Hanani had traveled to the Land of Israel while Nehemiah had remained in exile, serving the king. **And I asked them about the Judeans** in Judah, **the survivors that remained from the captivity,** meaning the exiles from Babylonia that had reached Judah previously;[4] alternatively, it refers to an unknown event that occurred closer to that time, in which Judean captives were taken from Jerusalem,[5] **and about** the situation in **Jerusalem.** Nehemiah probably also asked about his family that had immigrated there.

3 **They said to me: The remaining** Judeans **who remain from the captivity there in the province are** living **in great trouble and in disgrace.** Their situation is dire, both economically and otherwise. **The wall of Jerusalem is breached** and in ruins, **and its gates were set on fire.** Perhaps the walls were somewhat breached when Ezra had arrived thirteen years before, and by Nehemiah's time they were in an even worse state.

4 **It was when I heard these words that I sat down and cried and mourned for days; I was fasting and praying before God of the heavens,** as I shared in the misery of Israel.

5 **I said: Please, Lord God of the heavens, the great and awesome God, who maintains the covenant and kindness for those who love Him and those who observe His commandments.** This description of God "who maintains the covenant…" appears in the book of Deuteronomy (7:9), and Daniel also uses it when addressing God in prayer.[6] A similar phrase can be found in Solomon's prayer as well.[7]

6 **Please let Your ear be attentive, and Your eyes open, to hear the prayer of Your servant that I am praying before You today, day and night, about the children of Israel Your servants. I confess the sins of the children of Israel that we have sinned against You; and that I and my father's house have sinned.** Nehemiah includes himself in his confession for his people, just as Daniel did.[8]

7 In our sins, **we have done injury,** caused various harms, **to You, and have not observed the commandments, the statutes, and the ordinances that You commanded Your servant Moses.**

8 **Remember, please, the matter that You commanded Your servant Moses, saying: You will trespass** and betray Me, **and I will scatter you among the peoples;**

9 and if you regret your former ways **and you will return to Me, and observe My commandments and perform them,** then **if your banished** brethren **will be at the ends of the heavens,** the far-flung corners of the world, **from there I will gather them, and I will bring them to the place where I have chosen to rest My name.**[9]

10 **They are Your servants and Your people, whom You redeemed with Your great power, and with Your strong hand.**

11 **Please Lord, let now Your ear be attentive to the prayer of Your servant, and to the prayer of Your servants, who desire to fear Your name,** as Nehemiah is praying on behalf of the community; and **please cause Your servant to succeed today, and dispose him for mercy before this man,** the king. Nehemiah is about to seek permission from the king to take steps to amend the situation in Jerusalem. He therefore prays to God for success in the mission, that he will find favor in the eyes of the king. Before continuing the narrative, Nehemiah provides information about his official function, which is indicative of his closeness to the king: **I was cupbearer to the king.**[B]

Serving wine in the Achaemenid Empire, stone relief, Persepolis, 456–452 BCE

נחמיה

א דִּבְרֵי נְחֶמְיָה בֶּן־חֲכַלְיָה וַיְהִי בְחֹדֶשׁ־כִּסְלֵו שְׁנַת עֶשְׂרִים וַאֲנִי הָיִיתִי בְּשׁוּשַׁן
ב הַבִּירָה: וַיָּבֹא חֲנָנִי אַחַד מֵאַחַי הוּא וַאֲנָשִׁים מִיהוּדָה וָאֶשְׁאָלֵם עַל־הַיְּהוּדִים
ג הַפְּלֵיטָה אֲשֶׁר־נִשְׁאֲרוּ מִן־הַשֶּׁבִי וְעַל־יְרוּשָׁלִָם: וַיֹּאמְרוּ לִי הַנִּשְׁאָרִים אֲשֶׁר
נִשְׁאֲרוּ מִן־הַשְּׁבִי שָׁם בַּמְּדִינָה בְּרָעָה גְדֹלָה וּבְחֶרְפָּה וְחוֹמַת יְרוּשָׁלִַם מְפֹרָצֶת
ד וּשְׁעָרֶיהָ נִצְּתוּ בָאֵשׁ: וַיְהִי כְּשָׁמְעִי ׀ אֶת־הַדְּבָרִים הָאֵלֶּה יָשַׁבְתִּי וָאֶבְכֶּה
ה וָאֶתְאַבְּלָה יָמִים וָאֱהִי צָם וּמִתְפַּלֵּל לִפְנֵי אֱלֹהֵי הַשָּׁמָיִם: וָאֹמַר אָנָּא יהוה אֱלֹהֵי
הַשָּׁמַיִם הָאֵל הַגָּדוֹל וְהַנּוֹרָא שֹׁמֵר הַבְּרִית וָחֶסֶד לְאֹהֲבָיו וּלְשֹׁמְרֵי מִצְוֺתָיו:
ו תְּהִי נָא אָזְנְךָ־קַשֶּׁבֶת וְעֵינֶיךָ פְתוּחוֹת לִשְׁמֹעַ אֶל־תְּפִלַּת עַבְדְּךָ אֲשֶׁר אָנֹכִי
מִתְפַּלֵּל לְפָנֶיךָ הַיּוֹם יוֹמָם וָלַיְלָה עַל־בְּנֵי יִשְׂרָאֵל עֲבָדֶיךָ וּמִתְוַדֶּה עַל־חַטֹּאות
ז בְּנֵי־יִשְׂרָאֵל אֲשֶׁר חָטָאנוּ לָךְ וַאֲנִי וּבֵית־אָבִי חָטָאנוּ: חֲבֹל חָבַלְנוּ לָךְ וְלֹא־
שָׁמַרְנוּ אֶת־הַמִּצְוֺת וְאֶת־הַחֻקִּים וְאֶת־הַמִּשְׁפָּטִים אֲשֶׁר צִוִּיתָ אֶת־מֹשֶׁה עַבְדֶּךָ:
ח זְכָר־נָא אֶת־הַדָּבָר אֲשֶׁר צִוִּיתָ אֶת־מֹשֶׁה עַבְדְּךָ לֵאמֹר אַתֶּם תִּמְעָלוּ אֲנִי אָפִיץ
ט אֶתְכֶם בָּעַמִּים: וְשַׁבְתֶּם אֵלַי וּשְׁמַרְתֶּם מִצְוֺתַי וַעֲשִׂיתֶם אֹתָם אִם־יִהְיֶה נִדַּחֲכֶם
בִּקְצֵה הַשָּׁמַיִם מִשָּׁם אֲקַבְּצֵם והבואותים אֶל־הַמָּקוֹם אֲשֶׁר בָּחַרְתִּי לְשַׁכֵּן אֶת־ וַהֲבִיאוֹתִים
י יא שְׁמִי שָׁם: וְהֵם עֲבָדֶיךָ וְעַמֶּךָ אֲשֶׁר פָּדִיתָ בְּכֹחֲךָ הַגָּדוֹל וּבְיָדְךָ הַחֲזָקָה: אָנָּא ה

BACKGROUND

1:1 | **The Shushan citadel:** Shushan, also known as Susa, was one of the capital cities of the Persian Empire. At its center was a fortified complex [*bira*], translated here as citadel, containing the royal palace and the administrative center of the empire.

1:11 | **Cupbearer to the king:** The royal cupbearer was a senior position in royal courts from ancient times to the Middle Ages (see Genesis 40:1–41:9). He was invariably a trusted servant who was necessarily close to the king, as the king had to rely on his assurance that his wine was not poisoned. The courtyards of Media and Persia witnessed many rebellions and attempts to conspire against the king (see, e.g., Esther 2:21). The person responsible for bringing the king's drink had to supervise all his servants and personally guarantee their loyalty. The title of cupbearer is also mentioned in chronicles recorded on clay tablets that have been found in the palace of Darius in Persepolis, as well as in the writings of Herodotus and Josephus Flavius. In addition to his responsibility for the royal drinks, the cupbearer would also advise the king and direct diplomatic missions. The expanded role of the cupbearer or butler is preserved in European languages, such as *buticularius* in Latin and *botellier* in Old French, which are related to the word bottle. In the Middle Ages, this was the title of the servant in charge of matters involving the royal household.

2 1 **It was in the month of Nisan, the twentieth year of
Artahshasta the king; wine was before him, and I,** as the royal
cupbearer, **carried the wine,
and I gave it to the king. I
had never** until that point
been wretched in his presence. I was always at my best
when before the king, and for
his part he always showed
fondness toward me.
2 **The king said to me: Why is
your face wretched, and you
are not ill?** You do not look
good today; **this is nothing
other than heartache.** If you
are not ill, you must be preoccupied by negative thoughts.
I was exceedingly afraid.
The king of Persia was not accountable to anyone. It was enough
for this supreme leader, who had the virtual status of a demigod,
to suspect someone of wrongdoing, for that person to be
executed.

Artahshasta III, stone relief on his tomb, Persepolis, 425 BCE

3 **I said to the king: May the king live forever. Why wouldn't
my face be wretched;** why would I not appear worried and miserable, **when the city,** which
is **the place of the graves of
my fathers,**[D] **is in ruins, and
its gates have been consumed by fire?** I feel terrible
and restless due to the state of
Jerusalem.
4 **The king said to me:** If you
are that upset, **what is it that
you request?** What is your
desire? The close relationship between Nehemiah
and the king mentioned above is clearly evident here. **And I,**
Nehemiah, **prayed** in my heart **to the God of the heavens** that
I should find the right words and that they would be accepted
by the king. Nehemiah knew that this short conversation could
have important ramifications.
5 **I said to the king: If it pleases the king, and if your servant
has found favor before you, would that you send me,** grant
me permission to go, **to Judah, to the city of the graves of my
fathers, and I will build it** anew.

Royal graves from the First Temple period, City of David, Jerusalem

6 **The king said to me, and the consort,**[D] his queen or concubine,
was sitting with him. Nehemiah depicts the king as dining in a
highly intimate setting, with no strangers around. The king was
in a fine mood, and responded positively to his request: **Until
when will your journey be?** For how long do you wish to go?
**And when will you return? It found favor before the king to
send me.** He allowed me to go, **and I set him a time** for my return. It is known that Nehemiah returned to the king after twelve
years, although sometime later he went back to Jerusalem again.

Western part of the Persian Empire

7 **I said to the king: If it pleases the king, have them give me**[D]
letters to the governors, the rulers of the province, **of Ever
HaNahar**[B] **so that they grant me passage until I arrive in
Judah.** I need some sort of letter of recommendation that will
allow me to pass safely through their territory. Nehemiah required the assistance of the local rulers beyond the Euphrates
for his journey, and missives written and signed by the king were
considered direct orders with unquestionable authority.

BACKGROUND

2:7 | **Ever HaNahar:** Ever HaNahar is the Hebrew translation of the Aramaic name of the province of Avar Nahara mentioned in Ezra (chaps. 4–7).

אֲדֹנָי תְּהִי נָא אׇזְנְךָ־קַשֶּׁבֶת אֶל־תְּפִלַּת עַבְדְּךָ וְאֶל־תְּפִלַּת עֲבָדֶיךָ הַחֲפֵצִים
לְיִרְאָה אֶת־שְׁמֶךָ וְהַצְלִיחָה־נָּא לְעַבְדְּךָ הַיּוֹם וּתְנֵהוּ לְרַחֲמִים לִפְנֵי הָאִישׁ
א הַזֶּה וַאֲנִי הָיִיתִי מַשְׁקֶה לַמֶּלֶךְ׃ וַיְהִי ׀ בְּחֹדֶשׁ נִיסָן שְׁנַת עֶשְׂרִים
לְאַרְתַּחְשַׁסְתְּא הַמֶּלֶךְ יַיִן לְפָנָיו וָאֶשָּׂא אֶת־הַיַּיִן וָאֶתְּנָה לַמֶּלֶךְ וְלֹא־הָיִיתִי רַע
ב לְפָנָיו׃ וַיֹּאמֶר לִי הַמֶּלֶךְ מַדּוּעַ ׀ פָּנֶיךָ רָעִים וְאַתָּה אֵינְךָ חוֹלֶה אֵין זֶה כִּי־אִם רֹעַ לֵב
ג וָאִירָא הַרְבֵּה מְאֹד׃ וָאֹמַר לַמֶּלֶךְ הַמֶּלֶךְ לְעוֹלָם יִחְיֶה מַדּוּעַ לֹא־יֵרְעוּ פָנַי אֲשֶׁר
ד הָעִיר בֵּית־קִבְרוֹת אֲבֹתַי חֲרֵבָה וּשְׁעָרֶיהָ אֻכְּלוּ בָאֵשׁ׃ וַיֹּאמֶר
ה לִי הַמֶּלֶךְ עַל־מַה־זֶּה אַתָּה מְבַקֵּשׁ וָאֶתְפַּלֵּל אֶל־אֱלֹהֵי הַשָּׁמָיִם׃ וָאֹמַר לַמֶּלֶךְ
אִם־עַל־הַמֶּלֶךְ טוֹב וְאִם־יִיטַב עַבְדְּךָ לְפָנֶיךָ אֲשֶׁר תִּשְׁלָחֵנִי אֶל־יְהוּדָה אֶל־עִיר
ו קִבְרוֹת אֲבֹתַי וְאֶבְנֶנָּה׃ וַיֹּאמֶר לִי הַמֶּלֶךְ וְהַשֵּׁגַל ׀ יוֹשֶׁבֶת אֶצְלוֹ עַד־מָתַי יִהְיֶה
ז מַהֲלָכְךָ וּמָתַי תָּשׁוּב וַיִּיטַב לִפְנֵי־הַמֶּלֶךְ וַיִּשְׁלָחֵנִי וָאֶתְּנָה לוֹ זְמָן׃ וָאוֹמַר לַמֶּלֶךְ
אִם־עַל־הַמֶּלֶךְ טוֹב אִגְּרוֹת יִתְּנוּ־לִי עַל־פַּחֲווֹת עֵבֶר הַנָּהָר אֲשֶׁר יַעֲבִירוּנִי עַד

DISCUSSION

2:3 | **The place of the graves of my fathers:** Nehemiah's choice of words here, of referring to Jerusalem as "the place of the graves of my fathers," and his style of speech, attest to his diplomatic prowess. Though Nehemiah himself was not one of those exiled from Judah, his family, which must have been a prominent one, had been exiled. Nevertheless, he did not refer to Jerusalem as the capital of his birthplace, or as his home, but merely described it as the place of the graves of his fathers. He wished to appear as a loyal, patriotic Persian, whose birthplace was Persia, and whose capital city and home was Shushan. He therefore employed an expression illustrating no more than a familial connection to Jerusalem. In this way, his request would be perceived as merely a wish to renovate and refurbish a place to which he felt a personal and emotional bond.

The leaders who had previously gone to the Land of Israel, such as the leaders of the first wave of immigration, Zerubavel and Yehoshua, did not have any direct relationship with the ruling authorities. Even Ezra, who enjoyed the support of the king, spoke in a different fashion. The first wave of immigrants presumably took the wishes of the king and the interests of the authorities into account, but they were not experienced in diplomacy.

2:6 | **The consort [*shegal*]:** The root *shin-gimmel-lamed* is quite rare in the Bible and it is used as a direct expression for intercourse between a man and a woman. Therefore, it is usually not pronounced, and when read, the root *shin-khaf-beit*, meaning to lie down, is substituted (see Deuteronomy 28:30; Isaiah 13:16; Jeremiah 3:2). It is possible that the word *shegal* here refers to the queen, but it would seem inappropriate to use such a word with regard to her. Therefore, it is more likely that it refers to a concubine who was beloved to the king (see Ibn Ezra; Ralbag; *Metzudat David*; *Metzudat Tzion*; see also Psalms 45:10).

2:7 | **If it pleases the king, have them give me:** Both Ezra and Nehemiah requested assistance from the king, but the differences with regard to the manner of the request highlight the differences between their personalities. Ezra was a religious leader, a scribe who was a master of the laws of God and His Torah, and he declared to the king that God supports and protects those who believe in Him. He therefore refrained from requesting technical assistance or military protection from the king (see Ezra 8:22). In contrast, Nehemiah did not present himself as a holy man, but as a man of action, for whom the word of God and His Torah were close to his heart. In this role as practical, political leader, he made use of his connections with the authorities to receive what he desired.

8 **And** also send with me an additional **letter, to Asaf, the keeper of the king's forests,** who was in charge of the royal gardens and woods, **so that he will provide me with timber** from which **to roof the gates of the complex that abuts the House,** the gates of the Temple Mount, **and for the wall of the city, and for the house into which I will come,** to live there.[10] **The king granted me** all that I requested, **according to the benevolent hand of my God upon me,** generously.

9 **I came to the governors of Ever HaNahar, and gave them the king's letters. The king had** also **sent with me army and cavalry officers.** Since Nehemiah was a senior state official, the king had a group of soldiers and horsemen accompany him, to provide him with protection.

The Construction of the Walls of Jerusalem and a List of Its Builders

NEHEMIAH 2:10–4:17

In this section, Nehemiah prepares a plan of action that is well suited to his personality. He conscripts the people of Judah, and together they rebuild the walls of Jerusalem. His role is not merely technical; Nehemiah acts out of deep emotion and profound commitment to all aspects of Judaism. When he speaks to his brethren, his intention is not to preach, but to encourage them and motivate them to fulfill their sacred tasks.

10 **Sanbalat the Horonite,**[B] perhaps the governor of Samaria, **and Toviya the Amonite servant,**[B] possibly a relatively minor governor in Amon, whom Nehemiah derisively called a servant, **heard, and they were exceedingly displeased that a person had come to seek the welfare of the children of Israel.**

Etching by Claude Conder of cave found in 1881 with the inscription "Toviya," Iraq el-Amir, near Rabat Amon, second century BCE

Ancient well, commonly identified with Ein Rogel, photo from 1930–1935

11 **I came to Jerusalem and was there three days,** as a visitor. It is likely that Nehemiah's appearance, accompanied by horsemen and soldiers, made a great impression on the local populace.

12 **I arose** stealthily **at night, I and a few men with me; I did not tell any person what my God had put in my heart to do for Jerusalem; no animal was with me, other than the animal on which I was riding,** probably a horse or a mule.

13 **I emerged through the Valley Gate,**[B] one of the gates of Jerusalem, **at night, to opposite the Jackals' Spring,**[B] which might be Ein Rogel, based on the direction he was walking, **and to the Dung Gate,**[B] **and I surveyed the walls of Jerusalem, which were breached, and its gates were consumed by fire.**

14 **I passed to the Gate of the Spring and to the King's Pool; but** when I tried to enter I discovered that **there was no room for the animal under me to pass.** Due to the collapse of the gate, the entrance was too low for a man riding on an animal to pass through.[11] Alternatively, the animal he was riding could not walk along the blocked path.[12]

15 **I went up the ravine at night and surveyed the** state of the **wall; I came around and entered** once again **through the Valley Gate, and** I **returned** to my starting point after traversing all the way around the city walls. Perhaps Nehemiah made notes and diagrams for himself, or he simply tried to form a mental picture of the appearance of the walls and gates, in order to plan how they could be rebuilt.

16 **The prefects,** senior officials, who were with me,[13] **did not know where I had gone, or what I was doing, and I had not yet told** the rest of **the Judeans, the priests, the nobles, the prefects, and the rest of the laborers** until that point.[14] I did not tell anyone what I had done. The dignified status of the visitor who had

ח אֲשֶׁר־אָבוֹא אֶל־יְהוּדָה׃ וְאִגֶּרֶת אֶל־אָסָף שֹׁמֵר הַפַּרְדֵּס אֲשֶׁר לַמֶּלֶךְ אֲשֶׁר יִתֶּן־לִי
עֵצִים לְקָרוֹת אֶת־שַׁעֲרֵי הַבִּירָה אֲשֶׁר־לַבַּיִת וּלְחוֹמַת הָעִיר וְלַבַּיִת אֲשֶׁר־אָבוֹא
ט אֵלָיו וַיִּתֶּן־לִי הַמֶּלֶךְ כְּיַד־אֱלֹהַי הַטּוֹבָה עָלָי׃ וָאָבוֹא אֶל־פַּחֲווֹת עֵבֶר הַנָּהָר
וָאֶתְּנָה לָהֶם אֵת אִגְּרוֹת הַמֶּלֶךְ וַיִּשְׁלַח עִמִּי הַמֶּלֶךְ שָׂרֵי חַיִל וּפָרָשִׁים׃
י וַיִּשְׁמַע סַנְבַלַּט הַחֹרֹנִי וְטוֹבִיָּה הָעֶבֶד הָעַמֹּנִי וַיֵּרַע לָהֶם רָעָה גְדֹלָה אֲשֶׁר־בָּא
יא אָדָם לְבַקֵּשׁ טוֹבָה לִבְנֵי יִשְׂרָאֵל׃ וָאָבוֹא אֶל־יְרוּשָׁלָ͏ִם וָאֱהִי־שָׁם יָמִים שְׁלֹשָׁה׃
יב וָאָקוּם ׀ לַיְלָה אֲנִי וַאֲנָשִׁים ׀ מְעַט עִמִּי וְלֹא־הִגַּדְתִּי לְאָדָם מָה אֱלֹהַי נֹתֵן אֶל־
לִבִּי לַעֲשׂוֹת לִירוּשָׁלָ͏ִם וּבְהֵמָה אֵין עִמִּי כִּי אִם־הַבְּהֵמָה אֲשֶׁר אֲנִי רֹכֵב בָּהּ׃
יג וָאֵצְאָה בְשַׁעַר־הַגַּיְא לַיְלָה וְאֶל־פְּנֵי עֵין הַתַּנִּין וְאֶל־שַׁעַר הָאַשְׁפֹּת וָאֱהִי שֹׂבֵר
יד בְּחוֹמֹת יְרוּשָׁלַ͏ִם אֲשֶׁר־המפרוצים וּשְׁעָרֶיהָ אֻכְּלוּ בָאֵשׁ׃ וָאֶעֱבֹר אֶל־שַׁעַר הֵם ׀ פְּרוּצִים
טו הָעַיִן וְאֶל־בְּרֵכַת הַמֶּלֶךְ וְאֵין־מָקוֹם לַבְּהֵמָה לַעֲבֹר תַּחְתָּי׃ וָאֱהִי עֹלֶה בַנַּחַל
טז לַיְלָה וָאֱהִי שֹׂבֵר בַּחוֹמָה וָאָשׁוּב וָאָבוֹא בְּשַׁעַר הַגַּיְא וָאָשׁוּב׃ וְהַסְּגָנִים לֹא יָדְעוּ
אָנָה הָלַכְתִּי וּמָה אֲנִי עֹשֶׂה וְלַיְּהוּדִים וְלַכֹּהֲנִים וְלַחֹרִים וְלַסְּגָנִים וּלְיֶתֶר עֹשֵׂה

BACKGROUND

2:10 | **Sanbalat the Horonite:** His name indicates that he was likely not from Judah or Israel. Several explanations have been offered for the name Horonite: He came from the region of the land of Havran, or Bashan; from Beit Horon, on the southern slopes of the highlands of Ephraim, or Huwara, south of Shekhem, both of which were settlements in Samaritan areas; or from Horonayim in Moav, which is mentioned both in Isaiah 15:5 and on the Mesha Stele. Some claim that this is a derogatory name that serves to accentuate his being a foreigner, and perhaps to suggest that he was a devotee of the god Horon.

Toviya the Amonite servant: The name Toviya would seem to indicate that he came from Israel or Judah. The title of servant is likely a mocking critique of his devotion to Sanbalat, while the appellation Amonite is perhaps an indication that he was born from a mixed marriage (see Nehemiah 6:18–19). Alternatively, "servant" is an honorable title, meaning that he was a servant to the king of Persia, serving as one of his governors. Others suggest that "Amonite" means that he came from Amonah, a city in the northern portion of the tribe of Benjamin (Joshua 18:24).

2:13 | **The Valley Gate [*Sha'ar haGai*]:** This gate faced the valley [*gai*] west of the City of David, which descends to join the Valley of the Son of Hinom. This valley is identified with the Tyropoeon Valley mentioned in the writings of Josephus Flavius. In archaeological excavations of the northern part of the valley, conducted in 1927, a gate was discovered that could be the one described in the verse.

To opposite the Jackals' Spring: This place is unidentified, but the fact that Nehemiah turned southward indicates that it is possibly Ein Rogel, which is south of the city.

The Dung Gate: This gate was located on the southern edge of the city walls. It is likely the same gate as the one called the Gate of the Potsherd (Jeremiah 19:2, and see commentary ad loc.), and "the gate between the two walls" through which Tzidkiya fled (Jeremiah 39:4). Some claim that it was named for the various types of rubbish and dung that were flung there, such as the waste parts of sacrifices or other forms of garbage (Menashe Har-El, *Ancient Landscapes of the Land of Israel*. Or Yehuda: Zemorah-Bitan, 2005 [Hebrew], 109). Others connect the name to the cheese industry (Yossef Freund, "Multitudes, Multitudes in the Valley of Decision: A study in the Book of Joel," *Beit Mikra* 21:2 (65) Spring 1976, [Hebrew], 271–277, based on II Samuel 17:29), as the gate is located on the edge of the valley that was called the Tyropoeon in the Second Temple period, which possibly means the valley of the cheese makers.

arrived from the royal capital, under direct appointment of the king, enabled him to act as he wished without having to report to anyone. Nehemiah knew not only how to speak well, but also when to remain silent.

17 After my nocturnal reconnaissance, I turned to the ministers and rulers, and **I said to them: You see the wretched state which we are in, that Jerusalem is in ruins, and its gates were set on fire.** Since our city is entirely unprotected, **let us come and build the wall of Jerusalem, and we will not continue to be a disgrace.**

18 **I told them of the hand of my God that was benevolent upon me,** how God had helped me, **and also of the king's words that he had said to me;** the explicit permission he had granted me to rebuild the city. **They said: Let us rise and build. They were encouraged for the good.** When they heard that Nehemiah had received governmental assistance, they were encouraged to start the work. Nehemiah did not bring with him enough money or the means to resolve all the problems of Jerusalem, but thanks to the royal support and license he had been granted, he was able to motivate the residents of the city to take action with him.

19 **Sanbalat the Horonite and Toviya the Amonite servant and Geshem the Arabian,**[B] probably a leader of a group of Arabians, **heard, and they mocked us and scorned us, and said: What is this thing that you are doing? Are you rebelling against the king?** Given the situation, the enemies of Jerusalem had no option left but to resort to propaganda and slander.

20 **I answered them and said to them: The God of the heavens, He will cause us to succeed, and we, His servants, will rise and build; but** we will take no notice of you, as **you have no share, or right, or vestige in Jerusalem.**[D]

3 1 **Elyashiv the High Priest rose with his brethren the priests, and they built the Sheep Gate,**[B] which was probably called by this name because sheep were brought to the Temple through this gate.[15] **They consecrated it,** prepared the gate, and appended it to the holy city,[16] **and set up its doors, and consecrated it,** the wall, **up to the Tower of the Hundred,**[B] and they continued to build and sanctify it[17] **up to the Tower of Hananel.**[B] The priests accepted upon themselves the construction of that section of the wall.

Pools near the Sheep Gate, from model of Jerusalem from the Second Temple period, Israel Museum

Wall of Jerusalem

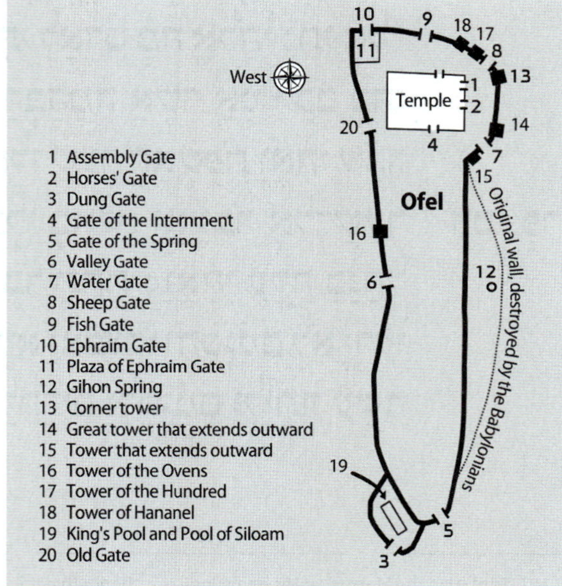

Walls of Jerusalem in the days of Nehemiah

2 **Next to him,** near the section of the wall that was constructed by Elyashiv and his brethren the priests, **the men of Jericho built** part of the wall. **Next to him,** Elyashiv and his colleagues,

DISCUSSION

2:20 | **But you have no share, or right, or vestige in Jerusalem:** Nehemiah emphasized the inhabitants of Judah's rejection of cooperation with surrounding nations in this sacred labor. Since they were acting with the authorization of the king, the enemies of the Judeans could say nothing against the residents of Jerusalem. This knowledge that they had firm diplomatic support strengthened the Judeans in their resolve to build the wall.

Nehemiah had the necessary building materials at his disposal. Although the walls were ruined, they were made of stone, and as fallen stones generally do not shatter, they could be reused. Some of the stones that were part of the walls of Jerusalem fifteen hundred years ago have survived to this day. Wood cannot be preserved in the same manner, but Nehemiah expected to receive whatever wood was needed from the king. The challenge that lay before him was in organizing the labor needed to accomplish the construction. To this end, groups of volunteers from Jerusalem and all of Judah divided the labor among themselves. The list of people below can be seen as a historical description of how the project was carried out, as well as a means of honoring those men who participated. Nehemiah recorded their names in the book so that their efforts in the construction of the walls of Jerusalem would be remembered forever.

יז הַמְּלָאכָה עַד־כֵּן לֹא הִגַּדְתִּי׃ וָאוֹמַר אֲלֵהֶם אַתֶּם רֹאִים הָרָעָה אֲשֶׁר אֲנַחְנוּ
בָהּ אֲשֶׁר יְרוּשָׁלַם חֲרֵבָה וּשְׁעָרֶיהָ נִצְּתוּ בָאֵשׁ לְכוּ וְנִבְנֶה אֶת־חוֹמַת יְרוּשָׁלַם
יח וְלֹא־נִהְיֶה עוֹד חֶרְפָּה׃ וָאַגִּיד לָהֶם אֶת־יַד אֱלֹהַי אֲשֶׁר־הִיא טוֹבָה עָלַי וְאַף־
דִּבְרֵי הַמֶּלֶךְ אֲשֶׁר אָמַר־לִי וַיֹּאמְרוּ נָקוּם וּבָנִינוּ וַיְחַזְּקוּ יְדֵיהֶם לַטּוֹבָה׃
יט וַיִּשְׁמַע סַנְבַלַּט הַחֹרֹנִי וְטֹבִיָּה ׀ הָעֶבֶד הָעַמּוֹנִי וְגֶשֶׁם הָעַרְבִי וַיַּלְעִגוּ לָנוּ וַיִּבְזוּ
עָלֵינוּ וַיֹּאמְרוּ מָה־הַדָּבָר הַזֶּה אֲשֶׁר אַתֶּם עֹשִׂים הַעַל הַמֶּלֶךְ אַתֶּם מֹרְדִים׃
כ וָאָשִׁיב אוֹתָם דָּבָר וָאוֹמַר לָהֶם אֱלֹהֵי הַשָּׁמַיִם הוּא יַצְלִיחַ לָנוּ וַאֲנַחְנוּ עֲבָדָיו
נָקוּם וּבָנִינוּ וְלָכֶם אֵין־חֵלֶק וּצְדָקָה וְזִכָּרוֹן בִּירוּשָׁלָם׃
ג א וַיָּקָם אֶלְיָשִׁיב הַכֹּהֵן הַגָּדוֹל וְאֶחָיו הַכֹּהֲנִים וַיִּבְנוּ אֶת־שַׁעַר הַצֹּאן הֵמָּה קִדְּשׁוּהוּ
ב וַיַּעֲמִידוּ דַּלְתֹתָיו וְעַד־מִגְדַּל הַמֵּאָה קִדְּשׁוּהוּ עַד מִגְדַּל חֲנַנְאֵל׃ וְעַל־יָדוֹ בָנוּ

BACKGROUND

2:19 | **Geshem the Arabian:** Some maintain that he was the leader of the province of Arabia, which included the southeastern side of the Jordan River, Sinai, and northern Arabia, and which is mentioned in Persian and Greek sources. This is supported by the fact that two contemporary inscriptions mention a Geshem king of Kedar, one of which was found in Dedan, in northern Arabia, while the other was discovered in the eastern section of the Nile delta (Tel el-Maskhuta). Others claim that he was the governor of southern Judah, which was infiltrated by Edomites and Arabians after the destruction of the First Temple, and that the title "Arabian" is a derogatory allusion to his ties with Arabians.

3:1 | **The Sheep Gate:** Due to its placement as the first gate when traversing east to west along the northern wall of Jerusalem, some identify this with the Benjamin Gate that is mentioned in the books of Jeremiah (e.g., 37:13; see commentary on Jeremiah 20:2) and Zechariah (14:10). It seems that there was a goat and sheep market near this gate. According to external documents from the end of the Second Temple period, adjacent to the gate there were pools for sheep, which were later called the pools of Beit Hesda. These pools were likely used for water reserves and as ritual baths. Their remains can be seen today north of the Temple Mount.

Set up its doors and consecrated it up to the Tower of the Hundred: Some of the walls of Jerusalem and the towers mentioned here, including the Tower of Hananel, the Fish Gate, and the Ephraim Gate, date back to the First Temple period. Others, such as the Sheep Gate and the Tower of the Hundred, were new. There are also certain gates of Jerusalem that are not mentioned in the book of Nehemiah, e.g., Benjamin Gate and the Corner Gate. Due to the devastation left by the Babylonians and various changes in the routes of the walls, there is no certainty that the gates and towers that were built or reconstructed at this time were identical in location and name to the original towers and gates. Archaeological findings that date from the Persian period are relatively meager, and therefore there is much speculation with regard to this issue.

The Tower of the Hundred…the Tower of Hananel: The Tower of Hananel is described in the book of Jeremiah (31:37, and see commentary ad loc.) as located in the north of the city, and in Zechariah (14:10) as being near the Corner Gate. Some claim that these two towers were located alongside one another, while others maintain that they were both part of the Fish Gate, standing on either side of it.

Zakur son of Imri, probably a member of an important family, also **built.**

3 **The sons of Hasenaa,** a family from the tribe of Benjamin,[18] **built the Fish Gate;**[B] **they roofed it, and set up its doors, its locks, and its bars.** The construction of the gate was more complex than building a simple wall, and it therefore required more effort and craftsmanship.

House of Ahiel, City of David, ninth to eighth century BCE

4 **Next to them, Meremot, son of Uriya, son of Hakotz made repairs** on the adjacent section of the wall. **Next to them, Meshulam, son of Berekhya, son of Meshezavel made repairs. Next to them, Tzadok son of Baana made repairs.**

5 **Next to them, the Tekoites**[B] **made repairs;** the ordinary inhabitants of Tekoa, which was an active, patriotic city,[19] joined in the building work, **but their nobles** and wealthy individuals [***addireihem***] **did not put their necks into the work of their lord.** They did not participate in the labor.[20] Some explain that the verse is praising these people: The owners of great flocks [*addarim*] did not place the necks of their young shepherds in the yoke of their usual labor with the sheep, but rather they allowed them to help in the construction of the walls.

Tel Tekoa

6 **The Old**[21] **Gate,**[B] **Yoyada son of Pase'ah and Meshulam son of Besodeya repaired; they roofed it, and set up its doors, its locks, and its bars.**

7 **Next to them, Melatya the Givonite and Yadon the Meronotite,** who were the **men of Givon and of the Mitzpa, made repairs.** They declared that their share of the construction was **for** the honor of **the seat of the governor of Ever HaNahar,** possibly because he provided them with support. Perhaps they set aside a place for the governor's throne in that location for when he came to Jerusalem.[22] Although the Givonites were presumably members of the group known as Netinim,[23] they apparently did not consider themselves inferior and downtrodden, but as full partners with Israel.

Remains of ancient well in Tel Givon, second millennium BCE

8 **Next to him,** them, **Uziel son of Harhaya,** both of whom were **the smiths, made repairs. Next to him, Hananya,** one **of the perfumers, made repairs. They restored,** or built a sealed layer,[24] in **Jerusalem up to the Broad Wall.**[B]

Remains of the Broad Wall, Jewish Quarter, Jerusalem

9 **Next to them, Refaya son of Hur,** who was **ruler of half the district,** province, **of Jerusalem, made repairs.** He had limited responsibilities, as the population of the city was not large.[25]

10 **Next to them, Yedaya son of Harumaf,** a personal name, or a nickname meaning one whose nose [*af*] is sunken.[26] He **made repairs** in the area **opposite his house. Next to him, Hatush son of Hashavneya made repairs.**

11 **Malkiya son of Harim and Hashuv son of Pahat Moav repaired a second section** of the wall, or a portion identical in size to the previous one,[27] **and** they also built **the Tower of the Ovens.**[B] This is the name of a tower in the city, which was probably at the edge of the section of the wall that they built.

12 **Next to it, Shalum son of Halohesh,** who was **ruler of** the other **half** of **the district of Jerusalem, made repairs, he and his daughters,** perhaps because he had no sons. Presumably these daughters did not build the walls with their own hands. It is more likely that they were noble and wealthy women who helped by donating funds to the cause, as well as sending members of their families to assist in the labor.

13 **The Valley Gate, Hanun and the inhabitants of Zano'ah repaired; they built it, and set up its doors, its locks, and its bars, and** in addition to the construction of the gate, they agreed to build **one thousand cubits of the wall until the Dung Gate** (see commentary on 2:13).

ג אַנְשֵׁי יְרֵחוֹ וְעַל־יָדוֹ בָּנָה זַכּוּר בֶּן־אִמְרִי׃ וְאֵת שַׁעַר הַדָּגִים בָּנוּ בְּנֵי הַסְּנָאָה
ד הֵמָּה קֵרוּהוּ וַיַּעֲמִידוּ דַּלְתֹתָיו מַנְעוּלָיו וּבְרִיחָיו׃ וְעַל־יָדָם הֶחֱזִיק מְרֵמוֹת בֶּן־
אוּרִיָּה בֶּן־הַקּוֹץ וְעַל־יָדָם הֶחֱזִיק מְשֻׁלָּם בֶּן־בֶּרֶכְיָה בֶּן־מְשֵׁיזַבְאֵל וְעַל־יָדָם
ה הֶחֱזִיק צָדוֹק בֶּן־בַּעֲנָא׃ וְעַל־יָדָם הֶחֱזִיקוּ הַתְּקוֹעִים וְאַדִּירֵיהֶם לֹא־הֵבִיאוּ
ו צַוָּרָם בַּעֲבֹדַת אֲדֹנֵיהֶם׃ וְאֵת שַׁעַר הַיְשָׁנָה הֶחֱזִיקוּ יוֹיָדָע בֶּן־פָּסֵחַ וּמְשֻׁלָּם
ז בֶּן־בְּסוֹדְיָה הֵמָּה קֵרוּהוּ וַיַּעֲמִידוּ דַּלְתֹתָיו וּמַנְעֻלָיו וּבְרִיחָיו׃ וְעַל־יָדָם הֶחֱזִיק
מְלַטְיָה הַגִּבְעֹנִי וְיָדוֹן הַמֵּרֹנֹתִי אַנְשֵׁי גִבְעוֹן וְהַמִּצְפָּה לְכִסֵּא פַּחַת עֵבֶר הַנָּהָר׃
ח עַל־יָדוֹ הֶחֱזִיק עֻזִּיאֵל בֶּן־חַרְהֲיָה צוֹרְפִים וְעַל־יָדוֹ הֶחֱזִיק חֲנַנְיָה בֶּן־הָרַקָּחִים
ט וַיַּעַזְבוּ יְרוּשָׁלִַם עַד הַחוֹמָה הָרְחָבָה׃ וְעַל־יָדָם הֶחֱזִיק רְפָיָה בֶן־חוּר שַׂר חֲצִי
י פֶּלֶךְ יְרוּשָׁלִָם׃ וְעַל־יָדָם הֶחֱזִיק יְדָיָה בֶן־חֲרוּמַף וְנֶגֶד בֵּיתוֹ וְעַל־יָדוֹ הֶחֱזִיק
יא חַטּוּשׁ בֶּן־חֲשַׁבְנְיָה׃ מִדָּה שֵׁנִית הֶחֱזִיק מַלְכִּיָּה בֶן־חָרִם וְחַשּׁוּב בֶּן־פַּחַת
יב מוֹאָב וְאֵת מִגְדַּל הַתַּנּוּרִים׃ וְעַל־יָדוֹ הֶחֱזִיק שַׁלּוּם בֶּן־הַלּוֹחֵשׁ שַׂר חֲצִי פֶּלֶךְ
יג יְרוּשָׁלִָם הוּא וּבְנוֹתָיו׃ אֵת שַׁעַר הַגַּיְא הֶחֱזִיק חָנוּן וְיֹשְׁבֵי זָנוֹחַ הֵמָּה בָנוּהוּ

BACKGROUND

3:3 | **The Fish Gate:** This gate is also mentioned in the book of Zephaniah (1:10), though its location is subject to dispute. Some identify it with the Corner Gate, while according to another opinion, it is the Gate of Ephraim (Michael Avi-Yonah, "Topography," in *Sefer Yerushalayim*: Michael Avi-Yonah ed. 2 vols, Jerusalem: Bialik Institute and Dvir, 1956–87, [Hebrew], 161). The name of the gate indicates that there was a fish market nearby, which is mentioned elsewhere in the book of Nehemiah (13:16). The existence of a fish trade in the capital is also attested by archaeological findings in the vicinity of the House of Ahiel in the City of David, including the discovery of bones of edible fish, such as Nile perch, mullet, bream, and clarias, a type of catfish, dating back to the eighth and ninth centuries BCE.

3:5 | **Tekoites:** Tekoa was a small but important town on the edge of the Judean Desert, located about 15 km south of Jerusalem, on the road from Ein Gedi to Bethlehem at the site of what is called Khirbet Taqua nowadays. Tekoa is mentioned several times in the Bible (II Samuel 14:2; Amos 1:1; I Chronicles 27:9; II Chronicles 11:5–12). According to Josephus, the Seleucids fortified Tekoa during the Hasmonean revolt (*Antiquities of the Jews* XIII:1:3). There is a tradition dating back to the fourth century CE that the grave of the prophet Amos is located there.

3:6 | **The Old [*Yeshana*] Gate:** The verse indicates that this gate was located between the Fish Gate and the Tower of the Ovens (see verse 11), on the western wall of the city. It is assumed to have been near the Broad Wall (see verse 8). However, according to the description given later in the book (12:39), it was situated on the northern wall (see Malbim). Perhaps this gate was on the road leading to the city of Yeshana, now known as Burj el-Isaneh, on the border between Jerusalem and Samaria (see II Chronicles 13:19). Some identify this gate with the Corner Gate (II Kings 14:13; Zechariah 14:10), whose precise location is also subject to dispute.

3:8 | **The Broad Wall:** This is generally identified with the remains of a wall, some 7 m thick, which was built in the days of King Hizkiya, toward the end of the eighth century BCE. This wall closed off Jerusalem to the north, to protect it from the Assyrian army. Its remains have been found in the Jewish Quarter of the Old City.

3:11 | **The Tower of the Ovens:** Some claim that the residents of Jerusalem baked their bread in this tower, in accordance with the statement in the Talmud that no furnaces may be kindled in Jerusalem (*Bava Kamma* 82b). It is possibly the "bakers' street" mentioned in the book of Jeremiah (37:21).

14 **The Dung Gate** itself, **Malkiya son of Rekhav, ruler of the district of Beit HaKerem**[B] **repaired; he built it, and set up its doors, its locks, and its bars.**
15 **The Gate of the Spring,**[B] **Shalun son of Kol Hozeh,** a personal name, or a nickname meaning one who sees [*ḥozeh*] all [*kol*], or perhaps one who has great insight,[28] **ruler of the district of the Mitzpa, repaired; he built it, and covered it** with a roof, **and set up its doors, its locks, and its bars, and** he also built **the wall of the pool of the Shela, to the king's garden,**[B] **until the stairs that descend from the City of David.**
16 **After him, Nehemiah son of Azbuk, ruler of half the district of Beit Tzur, made repairs, up to opposite the graves of David**[B] **and** further on from there, or on a different side,[29] **up to the artificial**[30] **pool,**[B] **and up to the House of the Mighty.**
17 **After him,** of **the Levites, Rehum son of Bani, made repairs. Next to him, Hashavya, ruler of half the district of Ke'ila, made repairs for,** on behalf of, **his district.**
18 **After him, their brethren, Bavai son of Henadad, ruler of** the other **half** of **the district of Ke'ila, made repairs.**
19 **Next to him, Ezer son of Yeshua, ruler of the Mitzpa, repaired another section.** Ezer initially participated in the construction of one length of the wall, and when he finished his section he volunteered to build another part that was **opposite the ascent to the armory,** perhaps a structure where weapons were placed,[31] which was located **at the angle,** near the corner of the wall.
20 **After him, Barukh son of Zakai repaired another portion with alacrity, from the angle,** the corner, **to the door of the house of Elyashiv the High Priest.**
21 **After him, Meremot, son of Uriya, son of Hakotz repaired another section, from the door of the house of Elyashiv until the end of the house of Elyashiv.** This house of the High Priest was a large structure that was probably situated adjacent to the wall. Meremot built the section of the wall that ran parallel to this house.
22 **After him, the priests, men of the plain** surrounding Jerusalem (see 12:28), **made repairs.**
23 **After him, Benjamin and Hashuv made repairs opposite their house. After him, Azarya, son of Maaseya, son of Ananya made repairs near his house.** These men owned houses in Jerusalem, and they undertook to build the sections of the wall near their homes.
24 **After him, Binui son of Henadad repaired another section, from the house of Azarya until the angle,** the edge of the wall, **until the corner** tower.[32]
25 **Palal son of Uzai was** working **from opposite the angle, and the tower that emerges from the upper house of the king, which is near,** or part of, **the courtyard of internment,** which served as a detention center within the king's house.[33] It seems that they built the wall opposite this tower, which had not been destroyed. **After him was Pedaya son of Parosh.**
26 **The Netinim were living in the Ofel,**[B] a raised area or building,[34] and they too helped in constructing the wall in their area; **they were building up to opposite the Water Gate to the east, and the tower that extends outward.**[B]

The Ofel, north of the City of David, Israel Museum model

BACKGROUND

3:14 | **Beit HaKerem:** This was the name of a town that was situated on an elevated spot near Jerusalem, to the south (see Jeremiah 6:1). The Mishna states that this was the location from which stones were brought for the altar in the Temple (*Middot* 3:4). Some identify Beit HaKerem with Herodion and the surrounding area, which Josephus describes as a center of commerce during the Roman period (*Antiquities of the Jews* XIV:3, 9). Others suggest that it is the site of present-day Ramat Rachel, where an administrative center from the Persian period has been discovered, or the area known today as Ein Kerem, southwest of Jerusalem.

3:15 | **The Gate of the Spring [*ha'ayin*]:** This is named for the pool which was constructed at the outlet point of Hizkiya's tunnel to contain the water brought into the city from the Gihon spring. It is generally identified with a gate that was discovered near the Pool of Siloam by Raymond Weill in the early twentieth century. Some say that its name is derived from the fact that it faces the direction of Ein Rogel, to the south.

The pool of the Shela, to the king's garden: According to most researchers, this is Birket el-Hamra, near the opening of the Siloam Tunnel, in the southwestern part of the City of David. If so, the name is derived from the Shilo'ah mentioned in Isaiah 8:6. Some claim that this is referring to a pool that was located outside the city walls, in the Kidron Valley, from which the king's garden was watered.

3:16 | **The graves of David:** The graves of David were inside Jerusalem, near a staircase (see II Chronicles 32:33). A tunnel led from the tombs to the Kidron Valley (*Tosefta*, *Bava Batra* 1:11). Excavations conducted by Raymond Weill (1913–1914) uncovered caves hewn in an outcropping bedrock in the south of the city, some of which were ruined by a quarry that was later established on the site. A staircase hewn into the rock descended from the top of the outcropping. Some researchers maintain that the bones in these graves were removed at the end of the Second Temple period, when the people of Israel began to be stringent about the laws of ritual purity and "ritual purity broke out in Israel" (Yoel Elitzur, "*Akhen! Kivrei Beit David*," *Al Atar* 11 2003, [Hebrew], 15–27; see *Shabbat* 13a).

► *The*

יד וַיַּעֲמִידוּ דַּלְתֹתָיו מַנְעֻלָיו וּבְרִיחָיו וְאֶלֶף אַמָּה בַּחוֹמָה עַד שַׁעַר הַשְּׁפוֹת׃ וְאֵת
שַׁעַר הָאַשְׁפּוֹת הֶחֱזִיק מַלְכִּיָּה בֶן־רֵכָב שַׂר פֶּלֶךְ בֵּית־הַכָּרֶם הוּא יִבְנֶנּוּ וְיַעֲמִיד
טו דַּלְתֹתָיו מַנְעֻלָיו וּבְרִיחָיו׃ וְאֵת שַׁעַר הָעַיִן הֶחֱזִיק שַׁלּוּן בֶּן־כׇּל־חֹזֶה שַׂר פֶּלֶךְ
הַמִּצְפָּה הוּא יִבְנֶנּוּ וִיטַלְלֶנּוּ ויעמידו דַּלְתֹתָיו מַנְעֻלָיו וּבְרִיחָיו וְאֵת חוֹמַת בְּרֵכַת וְיַעֲמִידוּ
טז הַשֶּׁלַח לְגַן־הַמֶּלֶךְ וְעַד־הַמַּעֲלוֹת הַיּוֹרְדוֹת מֵעִיר דָּוִיד׃ אַחֲרָיו הֶחֱזִיק נְחֶמְיָה
בֶן־עַזְבּוּק שַׂר חֲצִי פֶּלֶךְ בֵּית־צוּר עַד־נֶגֶד קִבְרֵי דָוִיד וְעַד־הַבְּרֵכָה הָעֲשׂוּיָה
יז וְעַד בֵּית הַגִּבֹּרִים׃ אַחֲרָיו הֶחֱזִיקוּ הַלְוִיִּם רְחוּם בֶּן־בָּנִי עַל־יָדוֹ הֶחֱזִיק חֲשַׁבְיָה
יח שַׂר־חֲצִי־פֶלֶךְ קְעִילָה לְפִלְכּוֹ׃ אַחֲרָיו הֶחֱזִיקוּ אֲחֵיהֶם בַּוַּי בֶּן־חֵנָדָד שַׂר חֲצִי פֶּלֶךְ
יט קְעִילָה׃ וַיְחַזֵּק עַל־יָדוֹ עֵזֶר בֶּן־יֵשׁוּעַ שַׂר הַמִּצְפָּה מִדָּה שֵׁנִית מִנֶּגֶד עֲלֹת הַנֶּשֶׁק
כ הַמִּקְצֹעַ׃ אַחֲרָיו הֶחֱרָה הֶחֱזִיק בָּרוּךְ בֶּן־זבי מִדָּה שֵׁנִית מִן־הַמִּקְצוֹעַ עַד־פֶּתַח זַכַּי
כא בֵּית אֶלְיָשִׁיב הַכֹּהֵן הַגָּדוֹל׃ אַחֲרָיו הֶחֱזִיק מְרֵמוֹת בֶּן־אוּרִיָּה בֶּן־הַקּוֹץ מִדָּה
כב שֵׁנִית מִפֶּתַח בֵּית אֶלְיָשִׁיב וְעַד־תַּכְלִית בֵּית אֶלְיָשִׁיב׃ וְאַחֲרָיו הֶחֱזִיקוּ הַכֹּהֲנִים
כג אַנְשֵׁי הַכִּכָּר׃ אַחֲרָיו הֶחֱזִיק בִּנְיָמִן וְחַשּׁוּב נֶגֶד בֵּיתָם אַחֲרָיו הֶחֱזִיק עֲזַרְיָה בֶן־
כד מַעֲשֵׂיָה בֶּן־עֲנָנְיָה אֵצֶל בֵּיתוֹ׃ אַחֲרָיו הֶחֱזִיק בִּנּוּי בֶּן־חֵנָדָד מִדָּה שֵׁנִית מִבֵּית
כה עֲזַרְיָה עַד־הַמִּקְצוֹעַ וְעַד־הַפִּנָּה׃ פָּלָל בֶּן־אוּזַי מִנֶּגֶד הַמִּקְצוֹעַ וְהַמִּגְדָּל הַיּוֹצֵא
כו מִבֵּית הַמֶּלֶךְ הָעֶלְיוֹן אֲשֶׁר לַחֲצַר הַמַּטָּרָה אַחֲרָיו פְּדָיָה בֶן־פַּרְעֹשׁ׃ וְהַנְּתִינִים

BACKGROUND

The artificial pool: Scholars offer a variety of possible identifications of this pool. Some say it was in the Kidron Valley, whereas others suggest that it is the King's Pool mentioned earlier (2:14). A third possibility is that it is the Upper Pool mentioned in I Kings (18:17) and Isaiah (7:3, 36:2).

3:26 | **Ofel:** A topographically descriptive name for the high, fortified part of the city, an Acropolis. It was called Ofel because it was the place of the people who ascended [*ma'apilim*] (see Rav Se'adya Gaon). The name appears in II Kings (5:24) in connection to the city of Samaria, and in the Mesha Stele of the king of Moav in relation to the city of Qarho. In the case of Jerusalem, the Ofel refers to the saddle between the City of David and the Temple Mount. Already in the earliest periods this area was fortified and raised, and later it probably became the spot of the Seleucid fortified compound known as the Acra, which is depicted in the books of Maccabees. The site was destroyed and leveled by Simeon the Hasmonean in the second half of the second century BCE (see *Wars of the Jews* V:4:1; *Antiquities of the Jews* XIII:6:7).

The Water Gate to the east, and the tower that extends outward: These are generally identified with a large tower built on the wall of the Ofel, south of the southeastern corner of the Temple Mount, which was first unearthed in the 1860s. Some claim that parts of this complex belonged to the upper house of the king, mentioned in the previous verse (Eilat Mazar and Benjamin Mazar, "Excavations in the South of the Temple Mount: The Ofel of Biblical Jerusalem," *Qedem* 29. Jerusalem: The Hebrew University, 1989, 32–35).

27 **After him, the Tekoites,** who had already volunteered for and completed one undertaking, as stated above (3:5), accepted upon themselves a further task and **repaired another section, from opposite the great tower that extends outward, up to the wall of the Ofel.**
28 **Above the Horses' Gate**[B] **the priests made repairs, each opposite his house.** The priests agreed to build the section of the wall that was opposite their houses.
29 **After him, Tzadok son of Imer made repairs opposite his house. After him, Shemaya son of Shekhanya, keeper of the East Gate, made repairs.**
30 **After him, Hananya son of Shelemya, and Hanun,** who was the **sixth [*hashishi*] son of Tzalaf,**[35] **repaired another section.** Some explain that Hanun was an expert craftsman in linen [*shesh*].[36] **After him, Meshulam son of Berekhya made repairs opposite his chamber,** which was on the inside of the wall.
31 **After him, Malkiya, son of the smith, made repairs until the house of the Netinim and the merchants, opposite the Assembly Gate,**[B] **and to the corner tower.**
32 **Between the corner tower and the Sheep Gate** (see commentary on 3:1) **the smiths and the merchants made repairs.** These were professional guilds of sorts, that undertook to perform the labor together.
33 **It was when Sanbalat heard that we were building the wall that he became incensed and was greatly angered, and he mocked the Judeans.**
34 **He stated before his brethren and the forces of Samaria, saying: What are these miserable** and broken **Judeans doing? Will they restore** the wall at will? Could they possibly strengthen it? **Will they slaughter offerings?** When they finish, will they manage to sacrifice anything, as they plan? **Will they finish in a day,** be able to complete the work on time,[37] when the day arrives? **Will they revive the stones from the dust heaps, and,** i.e., although, **they are burned?** Although stones cannot actually be burned, if they are greatly heated they will crack, and thereby be rendered unsuitable for building.[38]
35 **Toviya the Amonite was** standing **near him,** Sanbalat, perhaps serving as one of his deputies, **and said: Even that which they are building,** what kind of a wall would it be? **If a fox were to go up, he would breach the wall of their stones.** Even a mere fox could breach it and knock it down.

Fox

36 Upon hearing their statements, Nehemiah turned to God in prayer: **Hear, our God, for we have become an object of scorn, and return their disgrace on their head,**[D] **and give them up as loot in a land of captivity,** as those men deserve to be exiled from their homes, as captives.
37 **Do not cover over their iniquity, and let their sin not be expunged from before You.** Remember their sins and punish them accordingly when the time comes, **for they have angered You against,** in the presence of, **the builders.**
38 Nehemiah resumes the narrative: **We built the wall** further, **and all the wall,** with its various sections constructed by the different groups of builders, **was connected up to half its height, for the people had heart,** they were happy and enthusiastic, and they had a mind **to work.**

4 1 **It was when Sanbalat and Toviya and the Arabians and the Amonites and the Ashdodites,** who dwelled in the surrounding regions, **heard that healing had come to the walls of Jerusalem, and that the breaches had begun to be sealed, that they were very incensed;**

Tel Ashdod

2 **they all conspired to come and make war against Jerusalem, and to wreak harm upon them,** the people of Jerusalem.[39]
3 **We prayed to our God, and set upon them,** the residents of Jerusalem, **a watch** to guard **day and night, because of them.**
4 The people of **Judah said,** after all the construction efforts and the conscription of the guards: **The strength of the bearer is**

BACKGROUND

3:28 | **The Horses' Gate:** The Horses' Gate and the Assembly Gate (verse 31) were located in the northern section of the eastern wall. Archaeological excavations indicate that the new eastern wall, in its northeastern section, did not follow the same route as the old wall from before the destruction of the First Temple; rather, it was to its west. It is thus possible that the wall of the Temple became the city wall, in which case these gates were located along that wall. It is difficult to pinpoint the precise location of the Horses' Gate. A verse in II Chronicles (23:15) indicates that it was possibly situated in the house of the king himself, or on the Temple wall, while a verse in Jeremiah (31:39) indicates that it was in the city walls.

3:31 | **Opposite the Assembly Gate:** It can be inferred from the fact that the house of the Netinim and of the merchants was opposite the Assembly Gate that this gate was on the inside of the city walls. The gate was located on the eastern side of the Temple walls, and it is also called the East Gate (verse 29). Some claim that it was situated on the northern wall of the Temple.

כז היו ישבים בעפל עד נגד שער המים למזרח והמגדל היוצא: אחריו החזיקו
כח התקעים מדה שנית מנגד המגדל הגדול היוצא ועד חומת העפל: מעל ׀
כט שער הסוסים החזיקו הכהנים איש לנגד ביתו: אחריו החזיק צדוק בן־אמר
ל נגד ביתו ואחריו החזיק שמעיה בן־שכניה שמר שער המזרח: אחרי החזיק אַחֲרָיו
חנניה בן־שלמיה וחנון בן־צלף הששי מדה שני אחריו החזיק משלם בן־
לא ברכיה נגד נשכתו: אחרי החזיק מלכיה בן־הצרפי עד־בית הנתינים והרכלים אַחֲרָיו
לב נגד שער המפקד ועד עלית הפנה: ובין עלית הפנה לשער הצאן החזיקו
לג הצרפים והרכלים: ויהי כאשר שמע סנבלט כי־אנחנו בונים
לד את־החומה ויחר לו ויכעס הרבה וילעג על־היהודים: ויאמר ׀ לפני אחיו
וחיל שמרון ויאמר מה היהודים האמללים עשים היעזבו להם היזבחו היכלו
לה ביום היחיו את־האבנים מערמות העפר והמה שרופות: וטוביה העמני אצלו
לו ויאמר גם אשר־הם בונים אם־יעלה שועל ופרץ חומת אבניהם: שמע אלהינו
לז כי־היינו בוזה והשב חרפתם אל־ראשם ותנם לבזה בארץ שביה: ואל־תכס
לח על־עונם וחטאתם מלפניך אל־תמחה כי הכעיסו לנגד הבונים: ונבנה את־ ו
החומה ותקשר כל־החומה עד־חציה ויהי לב לעם לעשות:

א ויהי ׀ כאשר שמע סנבלט וטוביה והערבים והעמנים והאשדודים כי־עלתה
ב ארוכה לחמות ירושלם כי־החלו הפרצים להסתם ויחר להם מאד: ויקשרו
ג כלם יחדו לבוא להלחם בירושלם ולעשות לו תועה: ונתפלל אל־אלהינו
ד ונעמיד משמר עליהם יומם ולילה מפניהם: ויאמר יהודה כשל כח הסבל

DISCUSSION

3:36 | **Return their disgrace on their head:** Nehemiah's style of speech is not humble like that of those described by the Talmud as "those who are insulted but do not insult others, who hear their shame but do not respond" (see *Gittin* 36b). Instead, he is assertive, even when referring to a prominent, successful local leader, such as Sanbalat.

failing; it is hard for us to bear the loads, **and the dirt is abundant; we cannot build the wall.**

Bearers and builders, Thebes, Egypt, sixteenth to thirteenth century BCE

5 In addition to our physical weakness, the threat hanging over us
also impairs our resolve, as **our enemies said: They,** the Judeans,
**will not know and will not see until we come into their midst
and kill them, and put a stop to the labor.** Our enemies are
planning a surprise attack against us.
6 **It was when the Judeans who lived with them,** among the nations, **came** to us, **and ten times,** on numerous occasions, **they
said to us,** informed us, **of all
the places from which they
would assail us.** Judeans
who lived among the enemy
nations revealed the places
where the enemies would
attack.[40]
7 Therefore, when I heard all
these warnings, **I deployed**
men **in the lower levels
of the space,** in low spots,
hidden in the ground, **behind the wall,** and **in the
crevices,** between the rocks,
**and I deployed the people
according to their families
with their swords, their
spears, and their bows.**

"With their swords, their spears, and their bows." Warriors from the Persian period, palace of Darius I, Susa, 510 BCE

8 **I looked** and examined our defenses, or I saw fit to act, **and I
rose and said to the nobles, to the** senior **prefects, and to the
rest of the people: Do not fear them; remember the great
and awesome Lord, and fight for your brethren, your sons
and your daughters, your wives, and your homes.**
9 **It was when our enemies heard that it,** their plot, **had become
known to us,** and that we were ready to do battle, **that God
thwarted their counsel** and their plans were nullified, **and all
of us returned to the wall, each** man **to his labor.**
10 **It was from that day that half of my lads** who came with
me from Babylonia **would
engage in labor, and half
of them would hold the
spears, the shields, and the
bows, and the armor. The
princes** who accompanied
me **were** constantly marching **behind the entire house
of Judah,** to protect them.

Persian soldiers and their shields, Persepolis, Persia, fifth century BCE

11 **The builders in the wall and
the bearers of burdens were burdened,** those who would lift
and transport the loads, each one of them **with one hand** was
performing labor, and at the same time **with one,** the other
hand, **holding a weapon [*shalaḥ*];** alternatively, *shalaḥ* refers
specifically to a sword;
12 **and** as for **the builders,** who required the use of both hands
to perform their labor, **each** man **had his sword girded at his
side while building. The
sounder of the shofar was**
standing **with me,** to call a
general alarm in case of an
attack.[41]
13 **I said to the nobles and to
the prefects and to the rest
of the people: The labor is
abundant and spread out**
over a broad area, **and we are separated on the wall, each far
from the other,** and therefore we cannot know what is happening in every place.

Shofar

14 **In the place where you hear the sound of the shofar, there
you shall gather to us.** The sound of the shofar will signal the
spot from where the ambush or attack is coming, and **our God
will wage war for us.**
15 **We were performing the labor, and half of them were holding
the spears from dawn until the emergence of the stars.** We
utilized all the available daylight hours for our labor.
16 **It was also at that time that I said to the people: Let each man
and his lad stay the night inside Jerusalem,** rather than return
home, **and the night will be for guarding;** they will perform
guard duty at night, **and the day** is **for labor.**
17 **As for me, and my brethren, and my lads, and the men of the
guard who followed me, we did not remove our garments** at
night, **each man** was **with his weapon,** his sword, drawn, when
he went **to the water.** Even when one of us bathed or performed
his bodily functions, he kept his weapon accessible.[42]

ה וְהֶעָפָר הַרְבֵּה וַאֲנַחְנוּ לֹא נוּכַל לִבְנוֹת בַּחוֹמָה׃ וַיֹּאמְרוּ צָרֵינוּ לֹא יֵדְעוּ וְלֹא יִרְאוּ
ו עַד אֲשֶׁר־נָבוֹא אֶל־תּוֹכָם וַהֲרַגְנוּם וְהִשְׁבַּתְנוּ אֶת־הַמְּלָאכָה׃ וַיְהִי כַּאֲשֶׁר־בָּאוּ
הַיְּהוּדִים הַיֹּשְׁבִים אֶצְלָם וַיֹּאמְרוּ לָנוּ עֶשֶׂר פְּעָמִים מִכָּל־הַמְּקֹמוֹת אֲשֶׁר־תָּשׁוּבוּ
ז עָלֵינוּ׃ וָאַעֲמִיד מִתַּחְתִּיּוֹת לַמָּקוֹם מֵאַחֲרֵי לַחוֹמָה בצחחיים וָאַעֲמִיד אֶת־הָעָם בַּצְּחִיחִים
ח לְמִשְׁפָּחוֹת עִם־חַרְבֹתֵיהֶם רָמְחֵיהֶם וְקַשְּׁתֹתֵיהֶם׃ וָאֵרֶא וָאָקוּם וָאֹמַר אֶל־
הַחֹרִים וְאֶל־הַסְּגָנִים וְאֶל־יֶתֶר הָעָם אַל־תִּירְאוּ מִפְּנֵיהֶם אֶת־אֲדֹנָי הַגָּדוֹל וְהַנּוֹרָא
ט זְכֹרוּ וְהִלָּחֲמוּ עַל־אֲחֵיכֶם בְּנֵיכֶם וּבְנֹתֵיכֶם נְשֵׁיכֶם וּבָתֵּיכֶם׃ וַיְהִי
כַּאֲשֶׁר־שָׁמְעוּ אוֹיְבֵינוּ כִּי־נוֹדַע לָנוּ וַיָּפֶר הָאֱלֹהִים אֶת־עֲצָתָם ונשוב כֻּלָּנוּ אֶל־ וַנָּשָׁב
י הַחוֹמָה אִישׁ אֶל־מְלַאכְתּוֹ׃ וַיְהִי ׀ מִן־הַיּוֹם הַהוּא חֲצִי נְעָרַי עֹשִׂים בַּמְּלָאכָה
וְחֶצְיָם מַחֲזִיקִים וְהָרְמָחִים הַמָּגִנִּים וְהַקְּשָׁתוֹת וְהַשִּׁרְיֹנִים וְהַשָּׂרִים אַחֲרֵי כָּל־בֵּית
יא יְהוּדָה׃ הַבּוֹנִים בַּחוֹמָה וְהַנֹּשְׂאִים בַּסֶּבֶל עֹמְשִׂים בְּאַחַת יָדוֹ עֹשֶׂה בַמְּלָאכָה
יב וְאַחַת מַחֲזֶקֶת הַשָּׁלַח׃ וְהַבּוֹנִים אִישׁ חַרְבּוֹ אֲסוּרִים עַל־מָתְנָיו וּבוֹנִים וְהַתּוֹקֵעַ
יג בַּשּׁוֹפָר אֶצְלִי׃ וָאֹמַר אֶל־הַחֹרִים וְאֶל־הַסְּגָנִים וְאֶל־יֶתֶר הָעָם הַמְּלָאכָה הַרְבֵּה
וּרְחָבָה וַאֲנַחְנוּ נִפְרָדִים עַל־הַחוֹמָה רְחוֹקִים אִישׁ מֵאָחִיו׃
יד בִּמְקוֹם אֲשֶׁר תִּשְׁמְעוּ אֶת־קוֹל הַשּׁוֹפָר שָׁמָּה תִּקָּבְצוּ אֵלֵינוּ אֱלֹהֵינוּ יִלָּחֶם לָנוּ׃
טו וַאֲנַחְנוּ עֹשִׂים בַּמְּלָאכָה וְחֶצְיָם מַחֲזִיקִים בָּרְמָחִים מֵעֲלוֹת הַשַּׁחַר עַד צֵאת
טז הַכּוֹכָבִים׃ גַּם בָּעֵת הַהִיא אָמַרְתִּי לָעָם אִישׁ וְנַעֲרוֹ יָלִינוּ בְּתוֹךְ יְרוּשָׁלִָם וְהָיוּ־
יז לָנוּ הַלַּיְלָה מִשְׁמָר וְהַיּוֹם מְלָאכָה׃ וְאֵין אֲנִי וְאַחַי וּנְעָרַי וְאַנְשֵׁי הַמִּשְׁמָר אֲשֶׁר
אַחֲרַי אֵין־אֲנַחְנוּ פֹשְׁטִים בְּגָדֵינוּ אִישׁ שִׁלְחוֹ הַמָּיִם׃

Nehemiah's Efforts to Help the Poor

NEHEMIAH 5:1–19

All those qualified for labor and guard duty are recruited, but this leads to other difficulties. Although Nehemiah is initially not supposed to deal with the economic situation of the people, many are unable to work for their livelihood because of the building project. They therefore complain to him about their struggles.

5 1 **The cry of the people and their wives was great about** the actions of **their brethren, the** wealthier **Judeans.**

2 **There were some** among those who cried out **who were saying: Our sons, our daughters,**[43] **are numerous;**[44] alternatively: We are trying to raise our children;[45] **we must acquire grain that we may eat and live,** as we must feed our families. Some commentaries explain: We are forced to hand over our children to creditors to pay the interest they imposed on us when we borrowed money to buy food.

"We must acquire grain that we may eat." Ancient tools for grinding grain into flour

3 **There were some who were saying: We have mortgaged our fields, our vineyards, and our houses that we may buy grain for our hunger.**

4 **There were some who were saying: We borrowed silver for the king's tax,** to pay the royal property tax,[46] and to do so we mortgaged **our fields and our vineyards.**

Vineyard

5 **Now our flesh is like the flesh of our** wealthier **brethren, our children like their children, and** nevertheless, **behold, we are forcing our sons and our daughters into servitude, and some of our daughters are being forced** to serve as maidservants; **and we are powerless,** we cannot do anything, **and our fields and our vineyards are for others.** The wealthy lent money to the poor and then took advantage of their debts in order to take over the borrowers' property and to enslave their children.[47]

6 **I was greatly incensed when I heard their outcry and these words.**

7 **I pondered in my heart,** I thought about the problem, **and argued with the nobles and the prefects,** the wealthy individuals in positions of power, **and said to them: Is each of you claiming a debt from his brethren?** How dare you act as creditors toward your brethren and oppress them. This violates the command of the Torah: "If you shall lend silver to My people, to the poor who is with you, you shall not be as a creditor to him."[48] **I set against them a great assembly** to protest their actions.

8 Nehemiah delivered a severely critical speech to the assembly: **I said to them:** When we were in exile, **we purchased our brethren the Judeans, who were sold to the nations, according to our means;** we always made every effort to redeem our captive brothers from gentiles. **As for you, will you sell your brethren, that they will be sold to us?** Will you now enslave your brothers who are among us here, and force us to have to redeem them in the same manner? **They were silent and could not find a word.** They had no answer.

9 **I said: The thing that you are doing is no good; truly, you should walk in,** act with, **the fear of our God.** Don't you seek **to avoid the disgrace of the nations, our enemies,** when they see us oppressing our own people?

10 You are not the only ones to whom money is owed, as **I, my brethren, and my lads also have a claim of silver and grain from them.** I too lent them money. **Let us now abandon this debt.** We should all nullify these debts.[49]

11 **Restore to them now, as of today, their fields, their vineyards, their olive trees, and their houses, also the hundred pieces of silver,** or the great sums of money,[50] **and the grain, the wine, and the oil that you are claiming from them.**

Ancient olive trees, Israel

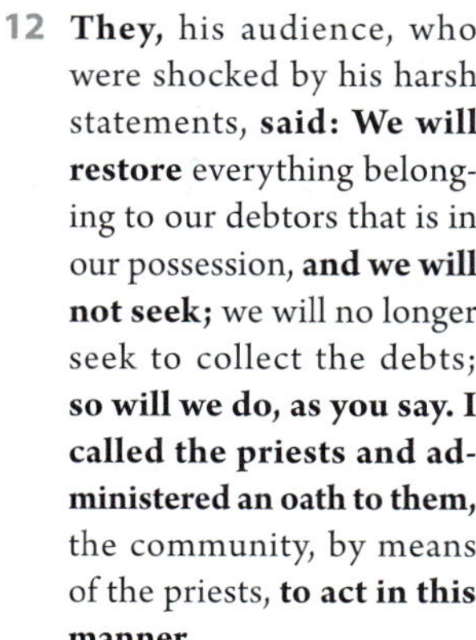

12 **They,** his audience, who were shocked by his harsh statements, **said: We will restore** everything belonging to our debtors that is in our possession, **and we will not seek;** we will no longer seek to collect the debts; **so will we do, as you say. I called the priests and administered an oath to them,** the community, by means of the priests, **to act in this manner.**

Remains of priestly living quarters from the Second Temple period, Herodian Quarter, Jerusalem

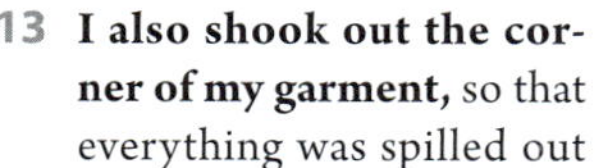

13 **I also shook out the corner of my garment,** so that everything was spilled out as a symbolic act, **and said: So may God shake every man who does not fulfill this matter from his house and from his**

ה א ב וַתְּהִי צַעֲקַת הָעָם וּנְשֵׁיהֶם גְּדוֹלָה אֶל־אֲחֵיהֶם הַיְּהוּדִים׃ וְיֵשׁ אֲשֶׁר אֹמְרִים בָּנֵינוּ
ג וּבְנֹתֵינוּ אֲנַחְנוּ רַבִּים וְנִקְחָה דָגָן וְנֹאכְלָה וְנִחְיֶה׃ וְיֵשׁ אֲשֶׁר אֹמְרִים שְׂדֹתֵינוּ
ד וּכְרָמֵינוּ וּבָתֵּינוּ אֲנַחְנוּ עֹרְבִים וְנִקְחָה דָגָן בָּרָעָב׃ וְיֵשׁ אֲשֶׁר אֹמְרִים לָוִינוּ כֶסֶף
ה לְמִדַּת הַמֶּלֶךְ שְׂדֹתֵינוּ וּכְרָמֵינוּ׃ וְעַתָּה כִּבְשַׂר אַחֵינוּ בְּשָׂרֵנוּ כִּבְנֵיהֶם בָּנֵינוּ וְהִנֵּה
אֲנַחְנוּ כֹבְשִׁים אֶת־בָּנֵינוּ וְאֶת־בְּנֹתֵינוּ לַעֲבָדִים וְיֵשׁ מִבְּנֹתֵינוּ נִכְבָּשׁוֹת וְאֵין לְאֵל
ו יָדֵנוּ וּשְׂדֹתֵינוּ וּכְרָמֵינוּ לַאֲחֵרִים׃ וַיִּחַר לִי מְאֹד כַּאֲשֶׁר שָׁמַעְתִּי אֶת־זַעֲקָתָם וְאֵת
ז הַדְּבָרִים הָאֵלֶּה׃ וַיִּמָּלֵךְ לִבִּי עָלַי וָאָרִיבָה אֶת־הַחֹרִים וְאֶת־הַסְּגָנִים וָאֹמְרָה
ח לָהֶם מַשָּׁא אִישׁ־בְּאָחִיו אַתֶּם נשאים וָאֶתֵּן עֲלֵיהֶם קְהִלָּה גְדוֹלָה׃ וָאֹמְרָה לָהֶם נְשִׁים
אֲנַחְנוּ קָנִינוּ אֶת־אַחֵינוּ הַיְּהוּדִים הַנִּמְכָּרִים לַגּוֹיִם כְּדֵי בָנוּ וְגַם־אַתֶּם תִּמְכְּרוּ
ט אֶת־אֲחֵיכֶם וְנִמְכְּרוּ־לָנוּ וַיַּחֲרִישׁוּ וְלֹא מָצְאוּ דָּבָר׃ ויאמר לֹא־טוֹב הַדָּבָר וָאֹמַר
י אֲשֶׁר־אַתֶּם עֹשִׂים הֲלוֹא בְּיִרְאַת אֱלֹהֵינוּ תֵּלֵכוּ מֵחֶרְפַּת הַגּוֹיִם אוֹיְבֵינוּ׃ וְגַם־
יא אֲנִי אַחַי וּנְעָרַי נֹשִׁים בָּהֶם כֶּסֶף וְדָגָן נַעַזְבָה־נָּא אֶת־הַמַּשָּׁא הַזֶּה׃ הָשִׁיבוּ נָא
לָהֶם כְּהַיּוֹם שְׂדֹתֵיהֶם כַּרְמֵיהֶם זֵיתֵיהֶם וּבָתֵּיהֶם וּמְאַת הַכֶּסֶף וְהַדָּגָן הַתִּירוֹשׁ
יב וְהַיִּצְהָר אֲשֶׁר אַתֶּם נֹשִׁים בָּהֶם׃ וַיֹּאמְרוּ נָשִׁיב וּמֵהֶם לֹא נְבַקֵּשׁ כֵּן נַעֲשֶׂה כַּאֲשֶׁר
יג אַתָּה אוֹמֵר וָאֶקְרָא אֶת־הַכֹּהֲנִים וָאַשְׁבִּיעֵם לַעֲשׂוֹת כַּדָּבָר הַזֶּה׃ גַּם־חָצְנִי
נָעַרְתִּי וָאֹמְרָה כָּכָה יְנַעֵר הָאֱלֹהִים אֶת־כָּל־הָאִישׁ אֲשֶׁר לֹא־יָקִים אֶת־הַדָּבָר
הַזֶּה מִבֵּיתוֹ וּמִיגִיעוֹ וְכָכָה יִהְיֶה נָעוּר וָרֵק וַיֹּאמְרוּ כָל־הַקָּהָל אָמֵן וַיְהַלְלוּ אֶת־

earnings, his wealth; **so shall he be shaken and emptied.** He will forfeit all his property and be left with nothing. **The entire congregation said** to the oath: **Amen, and they praised the Lord and the people acted in this manner.** Despite the difficulties such a move entailed, they agreed to relinquish their debts, and they praised God for the opportunity to help the downtrodden live in dignity.

14 When writing the book, Nehemiah added a comment here: **Moreover, from the day that he had commanded,** appointed,[51] **me to be governor in the land of Judah,**[52] **from the twentieth year until the thirty-second year of Artahshasta the king, for twelve years, I and my brethren,** my colleagues who accompanied me to the Land of Israel, **did not eat the food of the governor.** Although I was entitled to various payments and provisions from the people while serving as ruler, the king's representative, I did not take anything.

15 **But the first governors, who were prior to me, oppressed the people, and took** taxes **from them for bread and wine in addition to** the collection of **forty silver shekels;**[53] **also their lads lorded over the people.** They took advantage of their power to render life difficult for the local residents, **but** in contrast to them, **I did not do so, due to the fear of God.** Perhaps it was somewhat unseemly for Nehemiah to issue such a self-serving declaration,[54] but he was a very forthright man.

16 **Also,** not only did I refuse to take anything from the people for my own needs, **I supported the labor** of the construction **of this wall, and we did not purchase any field, and all my lads were gathered** together **there for the labor.** Even though I brought money with me and I had the prerogatives of a ruler, I did not acquire anything, nor did my servants, as all our actions were for the public good.

17 **The Judeans and the** royal **prefects, one hundred and fifty men, and those** people **coming to** assist **us from the nations that were around us,** they **were** all **at my table.**

18 **That which was prepared** at my table on their behalf **for one day: One bull, six select sheep, and birds were prepared for me, and every ten days** I would give them to drink from **all sorts of wine in abundance;**[55] alternatively: We would renew the store of wine every ten days. **Nevertheless, I did not seek the food of the governor,** the tax for maintenance to which I was entitled as governor, **because the work was heavy upon this people.**

19 **Remember me, my God, for good, all that I have done for this people.**

Taking Precautionary Measures, Nehemiah Completes the Wall

NEHEMIAH 6:1–7:4

Nehemiah continues to relate how the leaders of the surrounding nations made every effort to interfere with his construction project, both through direct means and by stirring up disputes and intrigue within Jerusalem.

6 1 **It was when it was heard by Sanbalat and Toviya, and by Geshem the Arabian, and by the rest of our enemies, that I had built the wall, and that no breach remained in it.** The wall had not been in complete ruin, but it had been full of breaches that required repair, **though** they also heard that **until that time,** after the walls were finished, **I had not** yet **set doors in the gates.** This was a dangerous situation, as even though the city was almost completely fortified, it could still be easily penetrated.

2 **Sanbalat and Geshem sent to me, saying: Come, let us meet together in one of the** small **villages**[B] **in the Valley of Ono.** We should hold a joint conference, you, the leader of the province of Judah, with us, the rulers of other provinces. **And** in fact, **they thought to do me harm.** Nehemiah was generally suspicious of such ideas, perhaps because he was familiar with the frequent political intrigues of the Persian royal court. He was certainly wary of these men, who were hardly his friends.

3 **I sent messengers to them, saying: I am doing a great labor, and I cannot come down.** I am currently too busy for such meetings. **Why should the labor cease when I desist** from working **and come down to you?**

"I had not set doors in the gates." Gate in a wall, Mycenae, Greece, thirteenth century BCE

4 **They sent to me in this manner four times, and I answered them in this manner.** They sent me more invitations, and on each occasion, I replied that I did not have the time.

יד יְהוָה וַיַּעַשׂ הָעָם כַּדָּבָר הַזֶּה׃ גַּם מִיּוֹם ׀ אֲשֶׁר־צִוָּה אֹתִי לִהְיוֹת פֶּחָם בְּאֶרֶץ
יְהוּדָה מִשְּׁנַת עֶשְׂרִים וְעַד שְׁנַת שְׁלֹשִׁים וּשְׁתַּיִם לְאַרְתַּחְשַׁסְתְּא הַמֶּלֶךְ שָׁנִים
טו שְׁתֵּים עֶשְׂרֵה אֲנִי וְאַחַי לֶחֶם הַפֶּחָה לֹא אָכַלְתִּי׃ וְהַפַּחוֹת הָרִאשֹׁנִים אֲשֶׁר־
לְפָנַי הִכְבִּידוּ עַל־הָעָם וַיִּקְחוּ מֵהֶם בְּלֶחֶם וָיַיִן אַחַר כֶּסֶף־שְׁקָלִים אַרְבָּעִים גַּם
טז נַעֲרֵיהֶם שָׁלְטוּ עַל־הָעָם וַאֲנִי לֹא־עָשִׂיתִי כֵן מִפְּנֵי יִרְאַת אֱלֹהִים׃ וְגַם בִּמְלֶאכֶת
הַחוֹמָה הַזֹּאת הֶחֱזַקְתִּי וְשָׂדֶה לֹא קָנִינוּ וְכָל־נְעָרַי קְבוּצִים שָׁם עַל־הַמְּלָאכָה׃
יז וְהַיְּהוּדִים וְהַסְּגָנִים מֵאָה וַחֲמִשִּׁים אִישׁ וְהַבָּאִים אֵלֵינוּ מִן־הַגּוֹיִם אֲשֶׁר־סְבִיבֹתֵינוּ
יח עַל־שֻׁלְחָנִי׃ וַאֲשֶׁר הָיָה נַעֲשֶׂה לְיוֹם אֶחָד שׁוֹר אֶחָד צֹאן שֵׁשׁ־בְּרֻרוֹת וְצִפֳּרִים
נַעֲשׂוּ־לִי וּבֵין עֲשֶׂרֶת יָמִים בְּכָל־יַיִן לְהַרְבֵּה וְעִם־זֶה לֶחֶם הַפֶּחָה לֹא בִקַּשְׁתִּי
יט כִּי־כָבְדָה הָעֲבֹדָה עַל־הָעָם הַזֶּה׃ זָכְרָה־לִּי אֱלֹהַי לְטוֹבָה כֹּל אֲשֶׁר־עָשִׂיתִי
א עַל־הָעָם הַזֶּה׃ וַיְהִי כַאֲשֶׁר נִשְׁמַע לְסַנְבַלַּט וְטוֹבִיָּה וּלְגֶשֶׁם
הָעַרְבִי וּלְיֶתֶר אֹיְבֵינוּ כִּי בָנִיתִי אֶת־הַחוֹמָה וְלֹא־נוֹתַר בָּהּ פָּרֶץ גַּם עַד־הָעֵת
ב הַהִיא דְּלָתוֹת לֹא־הֶעֱמַדְתִּי בַשְּׁעָרִים׃ וַיִּשְׁלַח סַנְבַלַּט וְגֶשֶׁם אֵלַי לֵאמֹר לְכָה
ג וְנִוָּעֲדָה יַחְדָּו בַּכְּפִירִים בְּבִקְעַת אוֹנוֹ וְהֵמָּה חֹשְׁבִים לַעֲשׂוֹת לִי רָעָה׃ וָאֶשְׁלְחָה
עֲלֵיהֶם מַלְאָכִים לֵאמֹר מְלָאכָה גְדוֹלָה אֲנִי עֹשֶׂה וְלֹא אוּכַל לָרֶדֶת לָמָּה תִשְׁבַּת
ד הַמְּלָאכָה כַּאֲשֶׁר אַרְפֶּהָ וְיָרַדְתִּי אֲלֵיכֶם׃ וַיִּשְׁלְחוּ אֵלַי כַּדָּבָר הַזֶּה אַרְבַּע פְּעָמִים

BACKGROUND

6:2 | **Villages [*kefirim*]:** There are many terms in the Bible for settlements, such as: city [*ir*], settled city [*ir moshav*], walled city [*ir ḥoma*], city of ancestral holdings [*aḥuzat ir*], settlement [*moshav*], small cities [*benot ir*], ranch [*ḥava*], courtyard [*ḥatzer*], village [*kefar*], and small village [*kefir*]. The term *kefir* as meaning a small village is also found in Aramaic documents from the eighth century BCE, in Zincirli, northwest Syria. There is also an opinion that Kefirim is the name of an unknown place.

5 **Sanbalat sent his servant to me in this manner a fifth time with an open letter in his hand,** rather than the usual sealed communication, which meant that it could be read by anyone, perhaps in a deliberate attempt to publicize its contents.
6 **In it was written: It has been heard among the nations, and Gashmu,** Geshem the Arabian, **says,** or the body of the letter says: **You and the Judeans are thinking to rebel** against the Persian Empire; **therefore, you are building the wall and you would be king for them and so on;** the letter contained other such statements of this kind.
7 **You have also appointed prophets to proclaim about you in Jerusalem, saying: There is a king in Judah, and now it will be heard by the king,** Artahshasta, **and so on.** We ourselves do not yet believe these insinuations, but rumors abound, and they may well reach the king. **Now, come, and let us confer together.** Let us discuss the matter and announce together that there is no truth to these reports.
8 **I sent to him,** Sanbalat, **saying: Nothing like these things that you are saying has been,** there are no plans or even rumors, **for you have fabricated them from your heart.** These are lies that you have made up.
9 **For they,** those accusing us, **all threaten us,**[56] **saying: Let them desist from the labor, and let it not be done. But now,** if indeed you have my best interests in mind,[57] **support me.**
10 **As for me, I went to the house of Shemaya, son of Delaya, son of Meheitavel,** apparently an important individual, perhaps someone considered a prophet, **and he was housebound,** due to illness or for some other reason. **He said** to me: **Let us meet,** us two, **in the House of God, in the Sanctuary, and let us shut the doors of the Sanctuary, as they are coming to kill you. At night, they are coming to kill you.** Danger awaits you tonight. Since the Temple is closed and empty of people at night, you will be safe there.

Representation of Sanctuary in the Second Temple

11 **I said: Would a man like me flee?** I absolutely will not flee. **Who like me could come to the Sanctuary and live?** Since I am not a priest, it is prohibited for me to enter the Sanctuary. **I will not come.**
12 **I realized, and behold, it was not God who sent him that he spoke the** supposed **prophecy about me** that people were planning to kill me that night, **and** yet that was not the word of God, as in actual fact, **Toviya and Sanbalat had hired him** to speak such matters to me.
13 **For he was hired** to issue that pronouncement **so that I would be intimidated, and do so,** act as he suggested, **and** thereby **sin, and it would serve for them as a bad report, so that they could discredit me.** Had I listened to Shemaya's advice, my adversaries would have publicized the matter, which would lead to people shaming and cursing me. The advice I received from the false prophet would not have harmed me directly, but it would have led to widespread slander against me.
14 **Remember, my God, against Toviya and Sanbalat in accordance with these actions of theirs, and also against the prophetess Noadya,**[D] **and the rest of the prophets who were threatening me.** There were other prophets who sought to intimidate Nehemiah in a similar manner.
15 **The wall was completed on the twenty-fifth day of Elul, after fifty-two days** had passed from the start of the rebuilding project.
16 **When all our enemies heard, all the nations that were around us were frightened, and they were humbled in their own eyes, and they knew that this labor was accomplished from our God.** They realized that our ability to complete the work in a relatively short time was thanks to divine assistance.
17 **Moreover, in those days many letters of the nobles of Judah were going,** were being sent by them, **to Toviya,**[B] **and** many letters **of Toviya were coming to them.** Some people, who did not dare to speak against Nehemiah openly, corresponded with Toviya and his men. At that time, the difference between the Judeans and the Samaritans was not that pronounced, as the Samaritans claimed that they too were members of the people of Israel and wished to participate in the sacred construction project. Thus, various ties were established between the two groups, and many thought that this was an internal dispute between different factions of the same nation.[58]
18 **For many** men **in Judah** were close to Toviya and **were sworn to him,** had established a covenant with him, **because he was a son-in-law of Shekhanya son of Arah, and Yehohanan his,** Toviya's, **son had taken the daughter of Meshulam son of Berekhya** as a wife. They had married into the most distinguished families of Jerusalem.[59]

DISCUSSION

6:14 | **The prophetess Noadya:** Noadya is not a known prophetess. Presumably, just as there were true prophetesses, there were also false prophetesses, and she was such an individual (see Ezekiel 13:17–23). Although it was impossible to hire a true prophet to deliver a specific prophecy, it was possible to purchase the services of a false prophet. During this time period, these false prophets would warn people about the troubles and wars that would break out if Nehemiah continued to build the wall (see Rashi).

ה וְאָשִׁיב אוֹתָם כַּדָּבָר הַזֶּה׃ וַיִּשְׁלַח אֵלַי סַנְבַלַּט כַּדָּבָר הַזֶּה פַּעַם חֲמִישִׁית אֶת־
ו נַעֲרוֹ וְאִגֶּרֶת פְּתוּחָה בְּיָדוֹ׃ כָּתוּב בָּהּ בַּגּוֹיִם נִשְׁמָע וְגַשְׁמוּ אֹמֵר אַתָּה וְהַיְּהוּדִים
חֹשְׁבִים לִמְרוֹד עַל־כֵּן אַתָּה בוֹנֶה הַחוֹמָה וְאַתָּה הֹוֶה לָהֶם לְמֶלֶךְ כַּדְּבָרִים
ז הָאֵלֶּה׃ וְגַם־נְבִיאִים הֶעֱמַדְתָּ לִקְרֹא עָלֶיךָ בִירוּשָׁלִַם לֵאמֹר מֶלֶךְ בִּיהוּדָה
ח וְעַתָּה יִשָּׁמַע לַמֶּלֶךְ כַּדְּבָרִים הָאֵלֶּה וְעַתָּה לְכָה וְנִוָּעֲצָה יַחְדָּו׃ וָאֶשְׁלְחָה אֵלָיו
ט לֵאמֹר לֹא נִהְיָה כַּדְּבָרִים הָאֵלֶּה אֲשֶׁר אַתָּה אוֹמֵר כִּי מִלִּבְּךָ אַתָּה בוֹדָאם׃ כִּי
כֻלָּם מְיָרְאִים אוֹתָנוּ לֵאמֹר יִרְפּוּ יְדֵיהֶם מִן־הַמְּלָאכָה וְלֹא תֵעָשֶׂה וְעַתָּה חַזֵּק
י אֶת־יָדָי׃ וַאֲנִי בָאתִי בֵּית שְׁמַעְיָה בֶּן־דְּלָיָה בֶּן־מְהֵיטַבְאֵל וְהוּא עָצוּר וַיֹּאמֶר
נִוָּעֵד אֶל־בֵּית הָאֱלֹהִים אֶל־תּוֹךְ הַהֵיכָל וְנִסְגְּרָה דַּלְתוֹת הַהֵיכָל כִּי בָּאִים
יא לְהָרְגֶךָ וְלַיְלָה בָּאִים לְהָרְגֶךָ׃ וָאֹמְרָה הַאִישׁ כָּמוֹנִי יִבְרָח וּמִי כָמוֹנִי אֲשֶׁר־יָבוֹא
יב אֶל־הַהֵיכָל וָחָי לֹא אָבוֹא׃ וָאַכִּירָה וְהִנֵּה לֹא־אֱלֹהִים שְׁלָחוֹ כִּי הַנְּבוּאָה דִּבֶּר
יג עָלַי וְטוֹבִיָּה וְסַנְבַלַּט שְׂכָרוֹ׃ לְמַעַן שָׂכוּר הוּא לְמַעַן־אִירָא וְאֶעֱשֶׂה־כֵּן וְחָטָאתִי
יד וְהָיָה לָהֶם לְשֵׁם רָע לְמַעַן יְחָרְפוּנִי׃ זָכְרָה אֱלֹהַי לְטוֹבִיָּה וּלְסַנְבַלַּט
כְּמַעֲשָׂיו אֵלֶּה וְגַם לְנוֹעַדְיָה הַנְּבִיאָה וּלְיֶתֶר הַנְּבִיאִים אֲשֶׁר הָיוּ מְיָרְאִים אוֹתִי׃
טו טז וַתִּשְׁלַם הַחוֹמָה בְּעֶשְׂרִים וַחֲמִשָּׁה לֶאֱלוּל לַחֲמִשִּׁים וּשְׁנַיִם יוֹם׃ וַיְהִי ז
כַּאֲשֶׁר שָׁמְעוּ כָּל־אוֹיְבֵינוּ וַיִּרְאוּ כָּל־הַגּוֹיִם אֲשֶׁר סְבִיבֹתֵינוּ וַיִּפְּלוּ מְאֹד בְּעֵינֵיהֶם
יז וַיֵּדְעוּ כִּי מֵאֵת אֱלֹהֵינוּ נֶעֶשְׂתָה הַמְּלָאכָה הַזֹּאת׃ גַּם ׀ בַּיָּמִים הָהֵם מַרְבִּים חֹרֵי
יח יְהוּדָה אִגְּרֹתֵיהֶם הוֹלְכוֹת עַל־טוֹבִיָּה וַאֲשֶׁר לְטוֹבִיָּה בָּאוֹת אֲלֵיהֶם׃ כִּי־רַבִּים
בִּיהוּדָה בַּעֲלֵי שְׁבוּעָה לוֹ כִּי־חָתָן הוּא לִשְׁכַנְיָה בֶן־אָרַח וִיהוֹחָנָן בְּנוֹ לָקַח

BACKGROUND

6:17 | **Many letters...to Toviya:** It has been suggested that the family of Toviya were Judeans who had possessed an inheritance in the land of Toviya in Gilad throughout the monarchical period. In the Second Temple era as well, members of this family enjoyed a high status along with economic and political prestige. The remains of a palace and grave site can be seen to this day in Iraq al-Amir, 17 km west of Amman. Some claim that one of the heads of this family is the "son of Tave'al" whom Retzin king of Aram wished to crown instead of Ahaz (Isaiah 7:6), and who was exiled to Assyria by Tiglat Pileser. Another suggestion is that the children of Toviya, who are listed among the immigrants from Babylonia who returned to Zion (Ezra 2:60; Nehemiah 7:62), were members of a family whose forebears returned to their inheritance east of the Jordan River (see Jeremiah 50:19; Zechariah 10:10).

19 **They would also say his,** Toviya's, **praises before me,** they
would praise him to me, **and** in contrast, **they would report**
my words to him.[D] They would tell him any gossip they could
find against me. Consequently, **Toviya sent letters to threaten**
me. Although Nehemiah had arrived with royal authorization,
he was new to the region and did not belong to any of the local
factions. The people did not doubt his integrity, but as he was
not one of their own it was only natural that they would have
various grievances and quarrels with him. Even after the wall was
completed, the land was not at peace. Time and again, people
attempted to cause unrest in the city and help the enemies of the
Judeans outside Jerusalem's walls.
7 1 **It was when the wall was built, and I had set up the doors,** so
that the city was properly fortified, **and the gatekeepers and**
the Levite **singers and the** other **Levites were appointed** and
had begun to perform their respective roles,
2 **that I commanded my brother Hanani,** possibly Nehemiah's
actual brother, **and Hananya officer of the capital, over**
guarding **Jerusalem; for he,** Hananya, **was a reliable man, and**
feared God as acknowledged by many; alternatively: He feared
God and was esteemed by many people.
3 **I said to them: The gates of Jerusalem shall not be opened**
until the sun grows hot. The gates are to remain closed all night,
and should be opened only when the heat of the day begins,
which would be at about ten o'clock in the morning.[60] They shall
remain open **while**[61] **they,** the gatekeepers, **are still standing** at
the entrance, and **they shall close and bar the doors** firmly in
the evening;[62] alternatively, hold firm to this matter and do not
neglect it;[63] **and set watches of the inhabitants of Jerusalem,**
each on his watch, and each opposite his house.
4 The reason for this is that **the city was spacious and large,** as
the rebuilt wall roughly followed the route of the old wall, which
served Jerusalem when it was prosperous and populated; **and**
now **the people in it were few, and there were no houses**
built. The immigrants had rebuilt only a few of the city's houses.

A List of the First Immigrants from Babylonia, and Their Property and Donations

NEHEMIAH 7:5–71

This list is almost identical to one that appears in the book of Ezra,[64] with a few variations in the names and numbers. It seems that slightly different versions of this list were recorded at the time, and perhaps they were not entirely accurate. It is also possible that the division of families changed over the years, and when the list was later reconstructed, the names were written in accordance with the new state of affairs.[65]

5 **My God put it,** the thought, **in my heart, and I gathered the**
nobles, and the prefects, and the people, in order **to establish**
their lineage. I found the book of the lineage of the initial
immigrants, and I found written in it:
6 **These are the children of the province, who came up from**
the captivity of the exile, whom Nebuchadnezzar king
of Babylon exiled, and they returned to Jerusalem and to
Judah, each to his city;
7 **those who came with Zerubavel,** the leader of the immigrants,
were Yeshua, Nehemiah, presumably not the Nehemiah of this
book, **Azarya, Raamya, Nahamani, Mordekhai, Bilshan,**
Misperet, Bigvai, Nehum, Baana. Now follows a heading for
the ensuing list: **The number of the men of the people of Israel**
was: Some explain: These are the numbers of the important
men of Israel.[66]
8 **The children of Parosh, two thousand one hundred and**
seventy-two.
9 **The children of Shefatya, three hundred and seventy-two.**
10 **The children of Arah, six hundred and fifty-two.**
11 **The children of Pahat Moav, of the children of Yeshua and**
Yoav, two thousand eight hundred and eighteen.
12 **The children of Eilam, one thousand two hundred and**
fifty-four.
13 **The children of Zatu, eight hundred and forty-five.**
14 **The children of Zakai, seven hundred and sixty.**

יט אֶת־בַּת־מְשֻׁלָּם בֶּן בֶּרֶכְיָה׃ גַּם טוֹבֹתָיו הָיוּ אֹמְרִים לְפָנַי וּדְבָרַי הָיוּ מוֹצִיאִים
לוֹ אִגְּרוֹת שָׁלַח טוֹבִיָּה לְיָרְאֵנִי׃
א וַיְהִי כַּאֲשֶׁר נִבְנְתָה הַחוֹמָה וָאַעֲמִיד הַדְּלָתוֹת וַיִּפָּקְדוּ הַשּׁוֹעֲרִים וְהַמְשֹׁרְרִים
ב וְהַלְוִיִּם׃ וָאֲצַוֶּה אֶת־חֲנָנִי אָחִי וְאֶת־חֲנַנְיָה שַׂר הַבִּירָה עַל־יְרוּשָׁלִָם כִּי־הוּא
ג כְּאִישׁ אֱמֶת וְיָרֵא אֶת־הָאֱלֹהִים מֵרַבִּים׃ ויאמר לָהֶם לֹא יִפָּתְחוּ שַׁעֲרֵי יְרוּשָׁלִַם וָאֹמַר
עַד־חֹם הַשֶּׁמֶשׁ וְעַד הֵם עֹמְדִים יָגִיפוּ הַדְּלָתוֹת וֶאֱחֹזוּ וְהַעֲמֵיד מִשְׁמְרוֹת יֹשְׁבֵי
ד יְרוּשָׁלִַם אִישׁ בְּמִשְׁמָרוֹ וְאִישׁ נֶגֶד בֵּיתוֹ׃ וְהָעִיר רַחֲבַת יָדַיִם וּגְדֹלָה וְהָעָם מְעַט
ה בְּתוֹכָהּ וְאֵין בָּתִּים בְּנוּיִם׃ וַיִּתֵּן אֱלֹהַי אֶל־לִבִּי וָאֶקְבְּצָה אֶת־הַחֹרִים וְאֶת־
הַסְּגָנִים וְאֶת־הָעָם לְהִתְיַחֵשׂ וָאֶמְצָא סֵפֶר הַיַּחַשׂ הָעוֹלִים בָּרִאשׁוֹנָה וָאֶמְצָא
ו כָּתוּב בּוֹ׃ אֵלֶּה ׀ בְּנֵי הַמְּדִינָה הָעֹלִים מִשְּׁבִי הַגּוֹלָה אֲשֶׁר הֶגְלָה
ז נְבוּכַדְנֶצַּר מֶלֶךְ בָּבֶל וַיָּשׁוּבוּ לִירוּשָׁלִַם וְלִיהוּדָה אִישׁ לְעִירוֹ׃ הַבָּאִים עִם־
זְרֻבָּבֶל יֵשׁוּעַ נְחֶמְיָה עֲזַרְיָה רַעַמְיָה נַחֲמָנִי מָרְדֳּכַי בִּלְשָׁן מִסְפֶּרֶת בִּגְוַי נְחוּם
ח ט בַּעֲנָה מִסְפַּר אַנְשֵׁי עַם יִשְׂרָאֵל׃ בְּנֵי פַרְעֹשׁ אַלְפַּיִם מֵאָה וְשִׁבְעִים וּשְׁנָיִם׃ בְּנֵי
י יא שְׁפַטְיָה שְׁלֹשׁ מֵאוֹת שִׁבְעִים וּשְׁנָיִם׃ בְּנֵי אָרַח שֵׁשׁ מֵאוֹת חֲמִשִּׁים וּשְׁנָיִם׃ בְּנֵי־
יב פַחַת מוֹאָב לִבְנֵי יֵשׁוּעַ וְיוֹאָב אַלְפַּיִם וּשְׁמֹנֶה מֵאוֹת שְׁמֹנָה עָשָׂר׃ בְּנֵי עֵילָם אֶלֶף
יג יד מָאתַיִם חֲמִשִּׁים וְאַרְבָּעָה׃ בְּנֵי זַתּוּא שְׁמֹנֶה מֵאוֹת אַרְבָּעִים וַחֲמִשָּׁה׃ בְּנֵי זַכָּי

DISCUSSION

6:19 | **Report my words to him:** It is evident from the narrative that Nehemiah did not have a gentle personality. Although both Ezra and Nehemiah were completely devoted to God and the Torah and had been authorized by the king to act for the benefit of the people of Judah, they were very different personalities. Ezra was primarily a spiritual leader while Nehemiah was a man of action, who did not hesitate to use force to accomplish his goals. Such people are often not well liked by the populace.

The people also had difficulty dealing with Nehemiah for other reasons, such as the fact that they considered him a foreigner. Some of the inhabitants of Judah had arrived with the first wave of immigrants to Israel, while others came with the second. Nehemiah arrived after them and had no association with either of those groups. The inhabitants of Judah likely found his accent and speaking style strange.

This was not the first time that a leader of Israel was resented, either justly or unjustly. Even Moses was constantly maligned by the people, and it is likely that only some of these complaints are recorded in the Torah. King David also had many enemies, some for justifiable reasons and others out of envy or malice. These enemies cast suspicion on his lineage and his fitness to become king. Moreover, when his son Solomon became king, not everyone unquestioningly accepted his authority immediately. In order to establish his kingdom, he needed to first execute a number of individuals, mostly based on the deathbed advice of his father, David. This type of resentment against a strong leader has manifested itself throughout history, especially with regard to individuals who came to power from outside the local population.

15 **The children of Binui, six hundred and forty-eight.**
16 **The children of Bevai, six hundred and twenty-eight.**
17 **The children of Azgad, two thousand three hundred and twenty-two.**
18 **The children of Adonikam, six hundred and sixty-seven.**
19 **The children of Bigvai, two thousand and sixty-seven.**
20 **The children of Adin, six hundred and fifty-five.**
21 **The children of Ater,** of the children **of Hizkiya, ninety-eight.**
22 **The children of Hashum, three hundred and twenty-eight.**
23 **The children of Betzai, three hundred and twenty-four.**
24 **The children of Harif, one hundred and twelve.**
25 **The children,** residents, **of** the city of **Givon, ninety-five.**
26 **The men of Bethlehem and Netofa, one hundred and eighty-eight.**
27 **The men of Anatot, one hundred and twenty-eight.**

Anatot

28 **The men of Beit Azmavet, forty-two.**
29 **The men of Kiryat Ye'arim, Kefira, and Be'erot,**[B] **seven hundred and forty-three.**

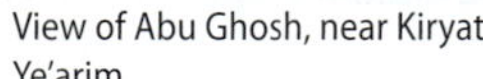
View of Abu Ghosh, near Kiryat Ye'arim

"Be'erot." Khirbet el-Burj, structure from the Crusader period

30 **The men of Rama and Geva, six hundred and twenty-one.**
31 **The men of Mikhmas, one hundred and twenty-two.**
32 **The men of Beit El and the Ai, one hundred and twenty-three.**
33 **The men of Nevo Aher, fifty-two.**
34 **The children of the other Eilam,** not the Eilam mentioned above (verse 12), even though their numbers are identical;[67] **one thousand two hundred and fifty-four.**
35 **The children of Harim, three hundred and twenty.**
36 **The children of Jericho, three hundred and forty-five.**
37 **The children of Lod, Hadid, and Ono,** three cities that were adjacent to one another,[68] **seven hundred and twenty-one.**
38 **The children of Senaa,** who were from the tribe of Benjamin, according to the tradition of the Sages,[69] **three thousand nine hundred and thirty.**
39 **The priests: the children of Yedaya, of the house of Yeshua, nine hundred and seventy-three.**
40 **The children of Imer,** another priestly watch, **one thousand and fifty-two.**
41 **The children of Pashhur, one thousand two hundred and forty-seven.**
42 **The children of Harim, one thousand and seventeen.**
43 **The Levites: the children of Yeshua of Kadmiel,**[70] **of the children of Hodeva,** who is called Hodavya in the book of Ezra (2:40), **seventy-four.**
44 **The singers: the children of Asaf,** who had their own special role and were therefore arranged in a separate watch from the other singers, **one hundred and forty-eight.**
45 **The gatekeepers,** who were **the children of Shalum, the children of Ater, the children of Talmon, the children of Akuv, the children of Hatita, the children of Shovai, one hundred and thirty-eight.**
46 **The Netinim,** the descendants of the Givonites, whom Joshua assigned to service of the people and the altar,[71] and who were therefore connected to the Temple: **the children of Tziha, the children of Hasufa, the children of Tabaot,**
47 **the children of Keiros, the children of Sia, the children of Padon,**
48 **the children of Levana, the children of Hagava, the children of Shalmai,**
49 **the children of Hanan, the children of Gidel, the children of Gahar,**
50 **the children of Re'aya, the children of Retzin, the children of Nekoda,**
51 **the children of Gazam, the children of Uza, the children of Pase'ah,**
52 **the children of Besai, the children of Meunim, the children of Nefishesim,**

טו טז שְׁבַע מֵאוֹת וְשִׁשִּׁים׃ בְּנֵי בִנּוּי שֵׁשׁ מֵאוֹת אַרְבָּעִים וּשְׁמֹנָה׃ בְּנֵי בֵבָי שֵׁשׁ מֵאוֹת
יז יח עֶשְׂרִים וּשְׁמֹנָה׃ בְּנֵי עַזְגָּד אַלְפַּיִם שְׁלֹשׁ מֵאוֹת עֶשְׂרִים וּשְׁנָיִם׃ בְּנֵי אֲדֹנִיקָם שֵׁשׁ
יט כ מֵאוֹת שִׁשִּׁים וְשִׁבְעָה׃ בְּנֵי בִגְוָי אַלְפַּיִם שִׁשִּׁים וְשִׁבְעָה׃ בְּנֵי עָדִין שֵׁשׁ מֵאוֹת
כא כב חֲמִשִּׁים וַחֲמִשָּׁה׃ בְּנֵי־אָטֵר לְחִזְקִיָּה תִּשְׁעִים וּשְׁמֹנָה׃ בְּנֵי חָשֻׁם שְׁלֹשׁ מֵאוֹת
כג כד עֶשְׂרִים וּשְׁמֹנָה׃ בְּנֵי בֵצָי שְׁלֹשׁ מֵאוֹת עֶשְׂרִים וְאַרְבָּעָה׃ בְּנֵי חָרִיף מֵאָה שְׁנֵים
כה כו עָשָׂר׃ בְּנֵי גִבְעוֹן תִּשְׁעִים וַחֲמִשָּׁה׃ אַנְשֵׁי בֵית־לֶחֶם וּנְטֹפָה מֵאָה שְׁמֹנִים וּשְׁמֹנָה׃
כז כח כט אַנְשֵׁי עֲנָתוֹת מֵאָה עֶשְׂרִים וּשְׁמוֹנָה׃ אַנְשֵׁי בֵית־עַזְמָוֶת אַרְבָּעִים וּשְׁנָיִם׃ אַנְשֵׁי
ל קִרְיַת יְעָרִים כְּפִירָה וּבְאֵרוֹת שְׁבַע מֵאוֹת אַרְבָּעִים וּשְׁלֹשָׁה׃ אַנְשֵׁי הָרָמָה וָגָבַע
לא לב שֵׁשׁ מֵאוֹת עֶשְׂרִים וְאֶחָד׃ אַנְשֵׁי מִכְמָס מֵאָה וְעֶשְׂרִים וּשְׁנָיִם׃ אַנְשֵׁי בֵית־אֵל
לג לד וְהָעָי מֵאָה עֶשְׂרִים וּשְׁלֹשָׁה׃ אַנְשֵׁי נְבוֹ אַחֵר חֲמִשִּׁים וּשְׁנָיִם׃ בְּנֵי עֵילָם אַחֵר
לה לו אֶלֶף מָאתַיִם חֲמִשִּׁים וְאַרְבָּעָה׃ בְּנֵי חָרִם שְׁלֹשׁ מֵאוֹת וְעֶשְׂרִים׃ בְּנֵי יְרֵחוֹ שְׁלֹשׁ
לז לח מֵאוֹת אַרְבָּעִים וַחֲמִשָּׁה׃ בְּנֵי־לֹד חָדִיד וְאֹנוֹ שְׁבַע מֵאוֹת וְעֶשְׂרִים וְאֶחָד׃ בְּנֵי
לט סְנָאָה שְׁלֹשֶׁת אֲלָפִים תְּשַׁע מֵאוֹת וּשְׁלֹשִׁים׃ הַכֹּהֲנִים בְּנֵי יְדַעְיָה לְבֵית יֵשׁוּעַ
מ מא תְּשַׁע מֵאוֹת שִׁבְעִים וּשְׁלֹשָׁה׃ בְּנֵי אִמֵּר אֶלֶף חֲמִשִּׁים וּשְׁנָיִם׃ בְּנֵי פַשְׁחוּר
מב מג אֶלֶף מָאתַיִם אַרְבָּעִים וְשִׁבְעָה׃ בְּנֵי חָרִם אֶלֶף שִׁבְעָה עָשָׂר׃ הַלְוִיִּם בְּנֵי־יֵשׁוּעַ
מד לְקַדְמִיאֵל לִבְנֵי לְהוֹדְוָה שִׁבְעִים וְאַרְבָּעָה׃ הַמְשֹׁרְרִים בְּנֵי אָסָף מֵאָה אַרְבָּעִים
מה וּשְׁמֹנָה׃ הַשֹּׁעֲרִים בְּנֵי־שַׁלֻּם בְּנֵי־אָטֵר בְּנֵי־טַלְמֹן בְּנֵי־עַקּוּב בְּנֵי חֲטִיטָא בְּנֵי
מו מז שֹׁבָי מֵאָה שְׁלֹשִׁים וּשְׁמֹנָה׃ הַנְּתִינִים בְּנֵי־צִחָא בְנֵי־חֲשֻׂפָא בְּנֵי טַבָּעוֹת׃ בְּנֵי־
מח מט קֵירֹס בְּנֵי־סִיעָא בְּנֵי פָדוֹן׃ בְּנֵי־לְבָנָה בְנֵי־חֲגָבָא בְּנֵי שַׁלְמָי׃ בְּנֵי־חָנָן בְּנֵי־גִדֵּל
נ נא נב בְּנֵי־גָחַר׃ בְּנֵי־רְאָיָה בְנֵי־רְצִין בְּנֵי נְקוֹדָא׃ בְּנֵי־גַזָּם בְּנֵי־עֻזָּא בְּנֵי פָסֵחַ׃ בְּנֵי־בֵסַי

BACKGROUND

7:29 | **Be'erot:** Be'erot is mentioned in the book of Joshua (9:17) as one of the four Givonite cities located in the portion of the tribe of Benjamin. It was probably situated south or southeast of Givon. Several suggestions have been made with regard to its precise location, including Nebi Samuel and Khirbet el-Burj on the outskirts of the present-day Ramot neighborhood of Jerusalem (see commentary on Joshua 9:17).

53 **the children of Bakbuk, the children of Hakufa, the children of Harhur,**
54 **the children of Batzlit, the children of Mehida, the children of Harsha,**
55 **the children of Barkos, the children of Sisera, the children of Temah,**
56 **the children of Netziah, the children of Hatifa.**
57 **The children of Solomon's servants,** who apparently kept their status as slaves, even though they observed the commandments of the Torah and had close ties to the people of Israel: **the children of Sotai, the children of Soferet, the children of Perida,**
58 **the children of Yala, the children of Darkon, the children of Gidel,**
59 **the children of Shefatya, the children of Hatil, the children of Pokheret HaTzevayim,** a personal name that means deer trap, **the children of Amon.**
60 **All the Netinim, and the children of Solomon's servants,** who were not full-fledged Judeans but had established ties with the children of Israel and in practice were integrated into the nation, **were three hundred and ninety-two.**
61 **These were those who came up from Tel Melah, Tel Harsha, Keruv, Adon, and Imer, and they could not tell their patrilineal houses and their ancestry whether they were from Israel.** Since their lineage was uncertain, it was hard to determine whether or not they were from Israel.
62 They were: **the children of Delaya, the children of Toviya, the children of Nekoda, six hundred and forty-two.**
63 Those **from the priests** whose lineage was uncertain: **the children of Havaya, the children of Hakotz, the children of Barzilai, who** were called accordingly, not because Barzilai was their father but because their father **took a wife from the daughters of Barzilai the Giladite and was called by their name.**
64 **These sought their writ of lineage,** the records of their genealogy, which would prove that they were indeed priests, as they claimed, **but it was not found; and they were disqualified from the priesthood.**
65 **The Tirshata,** an honorary Persian or Aramean title for the ruler of the Judeans, which was also given to Nehemiah (see 8:9, 10:2), **said to them that they may not eat of the sacred sacrament,** the consecrated food of the most sacred order, which only the priests are permitted to eat, **until a priest stands with Urim and Tumim.** Since they could not prove that they were priests, they were prohibited from partaking of this sacrificial meat until the arrival of a priest who could use the Urim and the Tumim to confirm their lineage.[72]
66 **The entire congregation in total was forty-two thousand three hundred and sixty,**
67 **besides their slaves and maidservants; these were seven thousand three hundred and thirty-seven; they had two hundred and forty-five men and women singers.** Some versions of the text[B] add the following line: Their horses, seven hundred and thirty-six; their mules, two hundred and forty-five.
68 **Camels, four hundred and thirty-five; donkeys, six thousand seven hundred and twenty.**
69 **A few of the heads of the patrilineal houses gave** a donation **for the labor. The Tirshata,** the ruler of the Judeans, **gave to the treasury one thousand darics,**[B] which were units **of gold, fifty basins,** large receptacles for the blood that is sprinkled on the altar, **five hundred and thirty priests' tunics.**
70 **Some of the heads of the patrilineal houses gave to the treasury for the labor twenty thousand darics of gold, and two thousand two hundred maneh of silver.** The Tirshata donated a large amount as a private individual, but since the heads of the fathers' houses were a larger group, together they gave a far larger sum overall.
71 **That which the rest of the people,** who were not heads of patrilineal houses, **gave: twenty thousand darics of gold, and two thousand maneh of silver, and sixty-seven priests' tunics.**

BACKGROUND

7:67 | **Some versions of the text:** Though the different manuscript traditions of the Tanakh text are remarkably consistent overall, discrepancies do exist. Most of these discrepancies are very small, having to do with the correct spelling or pronunciation of a word or two. On a few occasions, like here, whole verses, or parts of verses, are included in one version and do not appear in another. This edition of Tanakh follows the text of the Koren Tanakh, which is based on the text of the *Mikraot Gedolot* published in Venice in 1523–1525, and according to the textual glosses of *Minḥat Shai* (see *Minḥat Shai*; see also Joshua 21:35–36, and *Minḥat Shai* ad loc.).

7:69 | **Darics:** Since no Persian *daric* coins have yet been discovered in archaeological excavations in Israel, it is likely that they gave gold bars, each of which weighed about 8.4 g, like the Persian *daric*. If so, the twenty thousand darics weighed roughly 170 kg (Ya'akov Meshorer, "Means of Payment Prior to Coinage and the First Coinage," *Qadmoniot: A Journal for the Antiquities of Eretz-Israel and Bible Lands* 2–3 [34–35], 1976, [Hebrew], 55); see commentary on Ezra 2:69).

נג נד בְּנֵי־מְעוּנִים בְּנֵי נפושסים׃ בְּנֵי־בַקְבּוּק בְּנֵי־חֲקוּפָא בְּנֵי חַרְחוּר׃ בְּנֵי־בַצְלִית נְפִישְׁסִים
נה נו בְּנֵי־מְחִידָא בְּנֵי חַרְשָׁא׃ בְּנֵי־בַרְקוֹס בְּנֵי־סִיסְרָא בְּנֵי־תָמַח׃ בְּנֵי נְצִיחַ בְּנֵי
נז נח חֲטִיפָא׃ בְּנֵי עַבְדֵי שְׁלֹמֹה בְּנֵי־סוֹטַי בְּנֵי־סֹפֶרֶת בְּנֵי פְרִידָא׃ בְּנֵי־יַעְלָא בְנֵי־
נט ס דַרְקוֹן בְּנֵי גִדֵּל׃ בְּנֵי שְׁפַטְיָה בְנֵי־חַטִּיל בְּנֵי פֹּכֶרֶת הַצְּבָיִים בְּנֵי אָמוֹן׃ כָּל־
סא הַנְּתִינִים וּבְנֵי עַבְדֵי שְׁלֹמֹה שְׁלֹשׁ מֵאוֹת תִּשְׁעִים וּשְׁנָיִם׃ וְאֵלֶּה
הָעוֹלִים מִתֵּל מֶלַח תֵּל חַרְשָׁא כְּרוּב אַדּוֹן וְאִמֵּר וְלֹא יָכְלוּ לְהַגִּיד בֵּית־אֲבֹתָם
סב וְזַרְעָם אִם מִיִּשְׂרָאֵל הֵם׃ בְּנֵי־דְלָיָה בְנֵי־טוֹבִיָּה בְּנֵי נְקוֹדָא שֵׁשׁ מֵאוֹת וְאַרְבָּעִים
סג וּשְׁנָיִם׃ וּמִן־הַכֹּהֲנִים בְּנֵי חֳבַיָּה בְּנֵי הַקּוֹץ בְּנֵי בַרְזִלַּי אֲשֶׁר לָקַח
סד מִבְּנוֹת בַּרְזִלַּי הַגִּלְעָדִי אִשָּׁה וַיִּקָּרֵא עַל־שְׁמָם׃ אֵלֶּה בִּקְשׁוּ כְתָבָם הַמִּתְיַחְשִׂים
סה וְלֹא נִמְצָא וַיְגֹאֲלוּ מִן־הַכְּהֻנָּה׃ וַיֹּאמֶר הַתִּרְשָׁתָא לָהֶם אֲשֶׁר לֹא־יֹאכְלוּ מִקֹּדֶשׁ
סו הַקֳּדָשִׁים עַד עֲמֹד הַכֹּהֵן לְאוּרִים וְתֻמִּים׃ כָּל־הַקָּהָל כְּאֶחָד אַרְבַּע רִבּוֹא אַלְפַּיִם
סז שְׁלֹשׁ־מֵאוֹת וְשִׁשִּׁים׃ מִלְּבַד עַבְדֵיהֶם וְאַמְהֹתֵיהֶם אֵלֶּה שִׁבְעַת אֲלָפִים שְׁלֹשׁ
מֵאוֹת שְׁלֹשִׁים וְשִׁבְעָה וְלָהֶם מְשֹׁרְרִים וּמְשֹׁרְרוֹת מָאתַיִם וְאַרְבָּעִים וַחֲמִשָּׁה׃

בקצת ספרים כתוב כאן:

סוּסֵיהֶם שְׁבַע מֵאוֹת שְׁלֹשִׁים וְשִׁשָּׁה פִּרְדֵיהֶם מָאתַיִם אַרְבָּעִים וַחֲמִשָּׁה׃

סח גְּמַלִּים אַרְבַּע מֵאוֹת שְׁלֹשִׁים וַחֲמִשָּׁה חֲמֹרִים שֵׁשֶׁת אֲלָפִים שְׁבַע מֵאוֹת
סט וְעֶשְׂרִים׃ וּמִקְצָת רָאשֵׁי הָאָבוֹת נָתְנוּ לַמְּלָאכָה הַתִּרְשָׁתָא
נָתַן לָאוֹצָר זָהָב דַּרְכְּמֹנִים אֶלֶף מִזְרָקוֹת חֲמִשִּׁים כָּתְנוֹת כֹּהֲנִים שְׁלֹשִׁים וַחֲמֵשׁ
ע מֵאוֹת׃ וּמֵרָאשֵׁי הָאָבוֹת נָתְנוּ לְאוֹצַר הַמְּלָאכָה זָהָב דַּרְכְּמוֹנִים שְׁתֵּי
עא רִבּוֹת וְכֶסֶף מָנִים אַלְפַּיִם וּמָאתָיִם׃ וַאֲשֶׁר נָתְנוּ שְׁאֵרִית הָעָם זָהָב דַּרְכְּמֹנִים שְׁתֵּי

The Gathering of the People on the Festivals

NEHEMIAH 7:72–8:18

Although the immigrants are not a large group, they successfully build a state, which gradually develops and expands. The following sections describe how a new form of national existence is established. The majority of those who returned to the Land of Israel are uneducated migrants who until this point have not lived within a framework that can connect them as a people with a well-defined identity.

Ezra and Nehemiah sought to build a state that would serve as a means of expressing Israel's nature and its mission as God's holy people. Nehemiah was the man of action who organized the people politically and economically, while Ezra addressed the content of their spiritual and moral lives. From this point forward, it is possible to see how the political and spiritual infrastructure has been developed for the nation's collective acceptance of the Torah.

72 **The priests, the Levites, the gatekeepers, the singers, some of the people** of the tribe of Judah, **the Netinim, and all Israel** from the other tribes **settled in their cities.**[73] They did not settle all the way to the edge of the territory of Judah. Their settlement reached only to the area of Lod. **The seventh month,** Tishrei, **arrived, and the children of Israel were** dwelling **in their cities.**

8 1 **All the people gathered as one man to the plaza that was before the Water Gate, and they said to Ezra the scribe to bring the scroll of the Torah of Moses, which the Lord had commanded to Israel.** It seems that Ezra was not serving in an active leadership role at that time but was mainly a scholar and spiritual figure. As a scribe who would write copies of the Torah, he had a Torah scroll in his possession.

2 **Ezra the priest brought the Torah before the congregation, including men and women and everyone who could hear to understand,** who could comprehend the text, **on the first day of the seventh month,** Rosh HaShana.

3 **He,** Ezra, **read from it before the plaza that was before the Water Gate, from dawn until midday, facing the men and the women, and** all **those who understand. And all the people's ears were to the Torah scroll.** They all listened to the words he read aloud.

4 The event was organized as follows: **Ezra the scribe stood on a wooden tower, which they had made** especially **for the matter,** this event, so that all those assembled could hear him; **and Matitya, Shema, Anaya, Uriya, Hilkiya, and Maaseya stood by him on his right, and on his left were Pedaya, Mishael, Malkiya, Hashum, Hashbadana, Zekharya,** and **Meshulam.** He was flanked on both sides by his disciples and colleagues. These were the most prominent scribes, who probably served as members of the court that later became known as the Great Assembly.

5 **Ezra opened the scroll before the eyes of all the people, for** all could see him as **he was above all the people,** on the wooden tower, **and when he opened it,** the Torah scroll, **all the people stood** as a demonstration of reverence.[74]

6 **Ezra blessed the Lord, the great God,** before he began to read. **All the people answered: Amen, amen, with a hand upraised** heavenward, a form of salute at the time; **and** they **bowed and prostrated themselves to the Lord with their faces to the ground.**

7 Some of those present had spoken only Aramaic while in exile. Consequently, it is likely that those individuals did not understand the Hebrew text, and required assistance: **Yeshua, Bani, Sherevya, Yamin, Akuv, Shabetai, Hodiya, Maaseya, Kelita, Azarya, Yozabad, Hanan, Pelaya, and the Levites explained the Torah** that was read **to the people, and the people stood in their place.**

8 **They read in the scroll, in the Torah of God,** by **translating** the text, and perhaps also by commenting on its meaning while elucidating certain words and terms; **and with the appropriate elocution;** they read with the correct vowels, and with precise punctuation and intonation, **and they,** those present, **understood the reading,** all that was read.[75]

9 **Nehemiah, he was the Tirshata,** a Persian title of honor, **and Ezra the priest, the scribe, and the Levites who explained** the Torah **to the people, said to all the people: Today,** Rosh HaShana, **is sacred to the Lord your God; do not mourn, and do not weep, for all the people were weeping when they heard the words of the Torah.** Apparently, Ezra read aloud sections from the book of Deuteronomy, which includes many passages of rebuke and retribution that those present had not heard before, as even before they were exiled from Jerusalem not all of them had been familiar with the Written Law. Upon hearing the commandments of the Torah that they had not fulfilled up to that point, they were distraught about their wrongdoings.

10 **He,** Nehemiah and Ezra, **said to them,** the people, at midday: **Go** to your homes, **eat rich foods,** delicacies, **and drink sweet beverages.** Enjoy your festive meals. **And send gifts** of food **to whomever does not have anything prepared, as this day is holy to our Lord.** Sending food to the poor, which is performed in a somewhat ritual manner on Purim,[76] was an accepted custom on festivals in general, as no one should be left without food on a festival.[77] Not only are the people to rejoice on a festival themselves, they must also gladden the hearts of the needy. **Do not be saddened** over your concerns about possible improper behavior in the past, **as joy in the Lord,** your delight in God, **is your strength** and source of protection.[78]

עב רִבּ֥וֹא וְכֶ֖סֶף מָנִ֣ים אַלְפָּ֑יִם וְכָתְנֹ֣ת כֹּהֲנִ֔ים שִׁשִּׁ֖ים וְשִׁבְעָֽה׃ וַיֵּשְׁב֣וּ הַכֹּהֲנִ֣ים וְהַלְוִיִּ֡ם

וְהַשּׁוֹעֲרִ֣ים וְהַמְשֹׁרְרִ֡ים וּמִן־הָעָ֠ם וְהַנְּתִינִ֛ים וְכָל־יִשְׂרָאֵ֖ל בְּעָרֵיהֶ֑ם וַיִּגַּע֙

א הַחֹ֣דֶשׁ הַשְּׁבִיעִ֔י וּבְנֵ֥י יִשְׂרָאֵ֖ל בְּעָרֵיהֶֽם׃ וַיֵּאָסְפ֤וּ כָל־הָעָם֙ כְּאִ֣ישׁ אֶחָ֔ד אֶל־הָ֣רְח֔וֹב

אֲשֶׁ֖ר לִפְנֵ֣י שַֽׁעַר־הַמָּ֑יִם וַיֹּֽאמְרוּ֙ לְעֶזְרָ֣א הַסֹּפֵ֔ר לְהָבִ֗יא אֶת־סֵ֙פֶר֙ תּוֹרַ֣ת מֹשֶׁ֔ה

ב אֲשֶׁר־צִוָּ֥ה יְהֹוָ֖ה אֶת־יִשְׂרָאֵֽל׃ וַיָּבִ֣יא עֶזְרָ֣א הַ֠כֹּהֵן אֶֽת־הַתּוֹרָ֞ה לִפְנֵ֣י הַקָּהָ֗ל

ג מֵאִ֣ישׁ וְעַד־אִשָּׁ֔ה וְכֹ֖ל מֵבִ֣ין לִשְׁמֹ֑עַ בְּי֥וֹם אֶחָ֖ד לַחֹ֥דֶשׁ הַשְּׁבִיעִֽי׃ וַיִּקְרָא־ב֡וֹ לִפְנֵ֣י

הָרְח֡וֹב אֲשֶׁ֣ר ׀ לִפְנֵ֣י שַֽׁעַר־הַמַּ֗יִם מִן־הָאוֹר֙ עַד־מַחֲצִ֣ית הַיּ֔וֹם נֶ֥גֶד הָאֲנָשִׁ֛ים

ד וְהַנָּשִׁ֖ים וְהַמְּבִינִ֑ים וְאָזְנֵ֥י כָל־הָעָ֖ם אֶל־סֵ֥פֶר הַתּוֹרָֽה׃ וַֽיַּעֲמֹ֞ד עֶזְרָ֣א הַסֹּפֵ֗ר עַֽל־

מִגְדַּל־עֵץ֮ אֲשֶׁ֣ר עָשׂ֣וּ לַדָּבָר֒ וַיַּעֲמֹ֣ד אֶצְל֡וֹ מַתִּתְיָ֡ה וְשֶׁמַע֩ וַעֲנָיָ֨ה וְאֽוּרִיָּ֧ה וְחִלְקִיָּ֛ה

וּמַעֲשֵׂיָ֖ה עַל־יְמִינ֑וֹ וּמִשְּׂמֹאל֗וֹ פְּ֠דָיָה וּמִֽישָׁאֵ֧ל וּמַלְכִּיָּ֛ה וְחָשֻׁ֥ם וְחַשְׁבַּדָּ֖נָה זְכַרְיָ֥ה

ה מְשֻׁלָּֽם׃ וַיִּפְתַּ֨ח עֶזְרָ֤א הַסֵּ֙פֶר֙ לְעֵינֵ֣י כָל־הָעָ֔ם כִּֽי־מֵעַ֥ל כָּל־הָעָ֖ם

ו הָיָ֑ה וּכְפִתְח֖וֹ עָֽמְד֥וּ כָל־הָעָֽם׃ וַיְבָ֣רֶךְ עֶזְרָ֔א אֶת־יְהֹוָ֥ה הָאֱלֹהִ֖ים הַגָּד֑וֹל וַיַּעֲנ֨וּ כָל־

ז הָעָ֜ם אָמֵ֤ן ׀ אָמֵן֙ בְּמֹ֣עַל יְדֵיהֶ֔ם וַיִּקְּד֧וּ וַיִּשְׁתַּחֲוֻּ֛ לַיהֹוָ֖ה אַפַּ֥יִם אָֽרְצָה׃ וְיֵשׁ֡וּעַ וּבָנִ֡י

וְשֵׁרֵבְיָ֡ה ׀ יָמִ֡ין עַקּ֡וּב שַׁבְּתַ֡י ׀ הֽוֹדִיָּה֩ מַעֲשֵׂיָ֨ה קְלִיטָ֜א עֲזַרְיָ֣ה יוֹזָבָ֗ד חָנָן֙ פְּלָאיָ֔ה

ח וְהַלְוִיִּ֔ם מְבִינִ֥ים אֶת־הָעָ֖ם לַתּוֹרָ֑ה וְהָעָ֖ם עַל־עָמְדָֽם׃ וַֽיִּקְרְא֥וּ בַסֵּ֛פֶר בְּתוֹרַ֥ת

ט הָאֱלֹהִ֖ים מְפֹרָ֑שׁ וְשׂ֣וֹם שֶׂ֔כֶל וַיָּבִ֖ינוּ בַּמִּקְרָֽא׃ וַיֹּ֣אמֶר נְחֶמְיָ֣ה ה֣וּא

הַתִּרְשָׁ֡תָא וְעֶזְרָ֣א הַכֹּהֵ֣ן ׀ הַסֹּפֵ֡ר וְהַלְוִיִּם֩ הַמְּבִינִ֨ים אֶת־הָעָ֜ם לְכָל־הָעָ֗ם הַיּ֤וֹם

קָדֹֽשׁ־הוּא֙ לַיהֹוָ֣ה אֱלֹֽהֵיכֶ֔ם אַל־תִּֽתְאַבְּל֖וּ וְאַל־תִּבְכּ֑וּ כִּ֤י בוֹכִים֙ כָּל־הָעָ֔ם כְּשָׁמְעָ֖ם

י אֶת־דִּבְרֵ֥י הַתּוֹרָֽה׃ וַיֹּ֣אמֶר לָהֶ֡ם לְכוּ֩ אִכְל֨וּ מַשְׁמַנִּ֜ים וּשְׁת֣וּ מַֽמְתַקִּ֗ים וְשִׁלְח֤וּ מָנוֹת֙ ח

לְאֵ֣ין נָכ֣וֹן ל֔וֹ כִּֽי־קָד֥וֹשׁ הַיּ֖וֹם לַאֲדֹנֵ֑ינוּ וְאַל־תֵּ֣עָצֵ֔בוּ כִּֽי־חֶדְוַ֥ת יְהֹוָ֖ה הִ֥יא מָֽעֻזְּכֶֽם׃

11 **The Levites were quieting all the people, saying: Hush,** cease your crying and mourning, **for the day is holy; do not be sad.** Although this gathering was similar to the solemn assemblies held on fast days, it was designed for a very different purpose, so that the people would hear the words of the Torah before departing to celebrate the festival.

12 **All the people went to eat and drink, to send gifts, and to make great rejoicing, because they understood the matters that they had related to them.**

13 **On the second day,** the following day, only **the heads of the patrilineal houses of all the people,** as well as **the priests and the Levites, gathered,** but not all the people, **to Ezra the scribe, and** they gathered **to become wise in the matters of the Torah.**

14 **They found written in the Torah that the Lord had commanded by means of Moses that the children of Israel should dwell in booths during the festival of** Sukkot in **the seventh month.** Many of them were unfamiliar with the festival of Sukkot or had forgotten it. When they now listened to the reading of the Torah, they learned about this festival, which is celebrated in the seventh month, Tishrei.

15 **And** the leaders of the people further commanded[79] **that they,** messengers, **should announce and circulate a proclamation in all their cities, and in Jerusalem, saying: Go out to the highlands, and bring olive branches, pine branches,**[B] **myrtle branches, date palm branches, and branches of a leafy tree,** in order **to make booths, as it is written** in the Torah. At least two of the four species that are taken on the festival of Sukkot come from these trees: the *lulav*, which is a palm branch, and the myrtle.[80] It seems that these branches served a double purpose: Some of them were used for the four species, while those that were less beautiful or less suitable were placed on the booths, the *sukkot*, as *sekhakh*, the roofing of the booths.[81]

"Booths"

Pine branches

Myrtle branches

Palm branches

Olive branches

16 **The people went out and brought them, and made themselves booths, each on his roof and in their courtyards, and in the courtyards of the House of God, and in the plaza of the Water Gate, and in the plaza of the Ephraim Gate.**[B] It seems that these plazas in front of city gates were used for markets and gatherings.[82]

17 **The entire congregation of those who returned from the captivity made booths, and they lived in the booths, for the children of Israel had not done so from the days of Joshua son of Nun until that day.** It is possible that over the years only certain lone individuals celebrated the festival, but the nation of Israel as a whole had forgotten it, and now all the people participated together in the festivities.[83] **And the rejoicing was very great.**

18 **He,** Ezra or his representative, **read from the Torah of God day by day, from the first day** of the festival **until the last day.** This indicates that our practice of reading from the Torah on festivals is a very ancient custom.[84] **They observed the festival for seven days, and on the eighth day was an assembly,**[D] **in accordance with the ordinance,** as written in the Torah.[85]

DISCUSSION

8:18 | **They observed the festival for seven days, and on the eighth day was an assembly:** The description given here of the people's celebration of the festivals appears to highlight only activities in which all the people participated. There is no mention of blowing the shofar on Rosh HaShana, perhaps because it was not actually blown by every individual. Rosh HaShana is instead depicted as a festival on which the people do not grieve and do not mourn, as this was how they were taught to celebrate the festival. There is also mention of some form of a second day of Rosh HaShana, on which the heads of the people gathered together again, though it is unclear whether they declared it as an actual festival or whether it was a continuation of the assembly that took place on the first day (verse 13, and Rashi and *Metzudat David* ad loc.; *Rosh HaShana* 19b, and *Tosafot* ad loc.). There is no mention of Yom Kippur, which may indicate that they did not hold any communal ceremony to commemorate it. By contrast, the narrative relates how they reinstituted the celebration of Sukkot for the entire nation by having everyone dwell in *sukkot*, just as it had been when the people of Israel first entered the Land of Israel.

יא יב וְהַלְוִיִּ֞ם מַחְשִׁ֤ים לְכָל־הָעָם֙ לֵאמֹ֣ר הַ֔סּוּ כִּ֥י הַיּ֖וֹם קָדֹ֑שׁ וְאַל־תֵּעָצֵֽבוּ׃ וַיֵּלְכ֣וּ כָל־
הָ֠עָם לֶאֱכֹ֨ל וְלִשְׁתּ֜וֹת וּלְשַׁלַּ֣ח מָנ֗וֹת וְלַעֲשׂ֖וֹת שִׂמְחָ֣ה גְדוֹלָ֑ה כִּ֤י הֵבִ֙ינוּ֙ בַּדְּבָרִ֔ים
יג אֲשֶׁ֥ר הוֹדִ֖יעוּ לָהֶֽם׃ וּבַיּ֣וֹם הַשֵּׁנִ֡י נֶאֶסְפוּ֩ רָאשֵׁ֨י הָאָב֜וֹת לְכָל־הָעָ֗ם
יד הַכֹּהֲנִים֙ וְהַלְוִיִּ֔ם אֶל־עֶזְרָ֖א הַסֹּפֵ֑ר וּלְהַשְׂכִּ֖יל אֶל־דִּבְרֵ֥י הַתּוֹרָֽה׃ וַיִּמְצְא֖וּ כָּת֣וּב
בַּתּוֹרָ֑ה אֲשֶׁ֨ר צִוָּ֤ה יהוה֙ בְּיַד־מֹשֶׁ֔ה אֲשֶׁר֩ יֵשְׁב֨וּ בְנֵֽי־יִשְׂרָאֵ֧ל בַּסֻּכּ֛וֹת בֶּחָ֖ג בַּחֹ֥דֶשׁ
טו הַשְּׁבִיעִֽי׃ וַאֲשֶׁ֣ר יַשְׁמִ֗יעוּ וְיַעֲבִ֨ירוּ ק֜וֹל בְּכָל־עָרֵיהֶם֮ וּבִירוּשָׁלִַ֣ם לֵאמֹר֒ צְא֣וּ הָהָ֗ר
וְהָבִ֙יאוּ֙ עֲלֵי־זַ֙יִת֙ וַעֲלֵי־עֵ֣ץ שֶׁ֔מֶן וַעֲלֵ֤י הֲדַס֙ וַעֲלֵ֣י תְמָרִ֔ים וַעֲלֵ֖י עֵ֣ץ עָבֹ֑ת לַעֲשֹׂ֥ת
טז סֻכֹּ֖ת כַּכָּתֽוּב׃ וַיֵּצְא֣וּ הָעָם֮ וַיָּבִיאוּ֒ וַיַּעֲשׂוּ֩ לָהֶ֨ם סֻכּ֜וֹת אִ֣ישׁ עַל־גַּגּ֗וֹ וּבְחַצְרֹֽתֵיהֶ֔ם
יז וּבְחַצְר֖וֹת בֵּ֣ית הָאֱלֹהִ֑ים וּבִרְחוֹב֙ שַׁ֣עַר הַמַּ֔יִם וּבִרְח֖וֹב שַׁ֥עַר אֶפְרָֽיִם׃ וַיַּעֲשׂ֣וּ כָֽל־
הַ֠קָּהָל הַשָּׁבִ֨ים מִן־הַשְּׁבִ֥י ׀ סֻכּוֹת֮ וַיֵּשְׁב֣וּ בַסֻּכּוֹת֒ כִּ֣י לֹֽא־עָשׂ֡וּ מִימֵי֩ יֵשׁ֨וּעַ בִּן־נ֥וּן
יח כֵּ֚ן בְּנֵ֣י יִשְׂרָאֵ֔ל עַ֖ד הַיּ֣וֹם הַה֑וּא וַתְּהִ֥י שִׂמְחָ֖ה גְּדוֹלָ֥ה מְאֹֽד׃ וַיִּקְרָ֡א בְּסֵפֶר֩ תּוֹרַ֨ת
הָאֱלֹהִ֜ים י֣וֹם ׀ בְּי֗וֹם מִן־הַיּוֹם֙ הָֽרִאשׁ֔וֹן עַ֖ד הַיּ֣וֹם הָאַחֲר֑וֹן וַיַּעֲשׂוּ־חָג֙ שִׁבְעַ֣ת יָמִ֔ים
וּבַיּ֧וֹם הַשְּׁמִינִ֛י עֲצֶ֖רֶת כַּמִּשְׁפָּֽט׃

BACKGROUND

8:15 | **Pine branches:** The verse indicates that this was a tree that grew in the hills of Jerusalem, and its wood was used for building timber. The cherubs in the Temple and the doors of the Sanctuary were built from this wood (I Kings 6:23, 31, and commentary ad loc.). It was also used for the arrangement of the wood on the altar and for lighting the torches to signal the New Moon (Mishna *Tamid* 2:3; Mishna *Rosh HaShana* 2:3). It is apparently the Aleppo pine, *Pinus halepensis*, from which a large amount of resin can be extracted, which burns well (Radak; *Arukh*; Abravanel). It is interesting to note that there are mosaics in Samaritan synagogues, such as in Khirbet Samara, which feature a pine tree with its cones alongside the seven species of the Land of Israel.

8:16 | **Ephraim Gate:** This was one of the gates of the northern wall of Jerusalem, which was situated on its western side (II Kings 14:13; II Chronicles 25:23). It was called by this name because it faced in the direction of the portion of the tribe of Ephraim. Some identify it with the Fish Gate.

An Assembly for Fasting, Confessions, and Supplications

NEHEMIAH 9:1–37

After the festivals and the joyous celebrations, the people and its leaders take advantage of the great gathering to sharpen the separation between Israel and the other nations.

9 1 **On the twenty-fourth day of that month** of Tishrei, **the children of Israel assembled, with fasting, and with sackcloth and earth upon them.** The twenty-second of Tishrei is the festival of Shemini Atzeret, while the twenty-third, the day after the festival, is also a somewhat festive day, known in later generations as *Isru Ḥag*.[86] On the following day, all the people gathered together, fasting and wearing sackcloth, to express their mourning and sorrow.[87]

2 **The descendants of Israel separated themselves from all foreigners, and they stood and confessed their sins and the iniquities of their fathers.** The leaders took this opportunity to deal with the thorny issue of the intermarriages which had spread among the people over the course of time.[88]

3 **They stood in their place and read in the scroll of the Torah of the Lord their God a quarter of the day,**[89] **and** another **quarter of the day they were confessing** their sins **and prostrating themselves** and praying **to the Lord their God.**

4 **Yeshua, and Bani, Kadmiel, Shevanya, Buni, Sherevya,** another **Bani, and Kenani stood on the platform**[90] **of the Levites and cried out in a loud voice to the Lord their God.** They prayed aloud on behalf of all Israel. This prayer was essentially a preface to the ensuing events.

5 **The Levites Yeshua, Kadmiel, Bani, Hashavneya, Sherevya, Hodiya, Shevanya, and Petahya,** some of whom were standing on the platform, **said** to the people: **Stand and bless the Lord your God forever and ever, and,** addressing God, **may they bless the name of Your glory; exalted above all blessing and praise.**

6 **You alone are the Lord; You made the heavens, the heaven of heavens, and all their host, the earth and everything that is on it, the seas and everything that is in them,** all the creatures of the sea, **and You sustain them all, and the host of the heavens prostrates itself to You.**

"The heaven of heavens, and all their host"

"The seas and everything that is in them"

7 **You are the Lord the God, who chose Abram,** which was his name when God chose him, **and took him out of Ur of the Chaldeans, and** later, when he was already in the Land of Israel, You changed his name and **set his name as Abraham.**

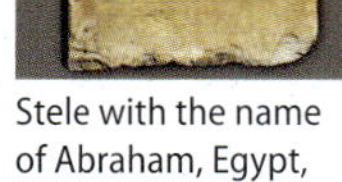
Stele with the name of Abraham, Egypt, second century BCE

Remains of the city of Ur, Iraq

8 **You found his heart faithful before You and established a covenant with him,** which included, among other promises, the promise **to give him the land of the Canaanites, the Hitites, the Emorites, the Perizites, the Yevusites, and the Girgashites, to give to his descendants, and** several generations later **You fulfilled Your words, for You are righteous,** You act justly.

9 **You saw the affliction,** the distress, **of our fathers in Egypt, and You heard their cry at** the shores of **the Red Sea.**

10 **You produced signs and wonders against Pharaoh, and against all his servants, and against all the people of his land, for You knew that they had been deliberately malicious to them.** The Egyptians did not employ the children of Israel as hired workers; rather they forced them to toil in hard labor. Furthermore, not only did they intend to utilize the children of Israel as a source of manpower, they actively sought to destroy them. **And You made a name for Yourself,** You publicized Your greatness, **as this day,** as clear as the day;[91] alternatively, the name and renown that You established for Yourself has lasted from that time to this day.[92]

11 **You divided the sea before them, and they crossed in the midst of the sea on the dry land; You cast their pursuers into the depths, like a stone in mighty waters.**

12 **You led them by day with a pillar of cloud, and with a pillar of fire by night,** in order **to illuminate for them the way that they should go.**

13 The Levites continued to relate the kindnesses of God, in chronological order: **You came down upon Mount Sinai, and spoke**

א וּבְיוֹם עֶשְׂרִים וְאַרְבָּעָה לַחֹדֶשׁ הַזֶּה נֶאֶסְפוּ בְנֵי־יִשְׂרָאֵל בְּצוֹם וּבְשַׂקִּים וַאֲדָמָה
ב עֲלֵיהֶם׃ וַיִּבָּדְלוּ זֶרַע יִשְׂרָאֵל מִכֹּל בְּנֵי נֵכָר וַיַּעַמְדוּ וַיִּתְוַדּוּ עַל־חַטֹּאתֵיהֶם וַעֲוֺנוֹת
ג אֲבֹתֵיהֶם׃ וַיָּקוּמוּ עַל־עָמְדָם וַיִּקְרְאוּ בְּסֵפֶר תּוֹרַת יְהוָה אֱלֹהֵיהֶם רְבִעִית הַיּוֹם
ד וּרְבִעִית מִתְוַדִּים וּמִשְׁתַּחֲוִים לַיהוָה אֱלֹהֵיהֶם׃ וַיָּקָם עַל־מַעֲלֵה
הַלְוִיִּם יֵשׁוּעַ וּבָנִי קַדְמִיאֵל שְׁבַנְיָה בֻּנִּי שֵׁרֵבְיָה בָּנִי כְנָנִי וַיִּזְעֲקוּ בְּקוֹל גָּדוֹל אֶל־
ה יְהוָה אֱלֹהֵיהֶם׃ וַיֹּאמְרוּ הַלְוִיִּם יֵשׁוּעַ וְקַדְמִיאֵל בָּנִי חֲשַׁבְנְיָה שֵׁרֵבְיָה הוֹדִיָּה
שְׁבַנְיָה פְתַחְיָה קוּמוּ בָּרְכוּ אֶת־יְהוָה אֱלֹהֵיכֶם מִן־הָעוֹלָם עַד־הָעוֹלָם וִיבָרְכוּ
ו שֵׁם כְּבֹדֶךָ וּמְרוֹמַם עַל־כָּל־בְּרָכָה וּתְהִלָּה׃ אַתָּה־הוּא יְהוָה לְבַדֶּךָ אַתָּה עָשִׂיתָ
אֶת־הַשָּׁמַיִם שְׁמֵי הַשָּׁמַיִם וְכָל־צְבָאָם הָאָרֶץ וְכָל־אֲשֶׁר עָלֶיהָ הַיַּמִּים וְכָל־אֲשֶׁר
ז בָּהֶם וְאַתָּה מְחַיֶּה אֶת־כֻּלָּם וּצְבָא הַשָּׁמַיִם לְךָ מִשְׁתַּחֲוִים׃ אַתָּה הוּא יְהוָה
הָאֱלֹהִים אֲשֶׁר בָּחַרְתָּ בְּאַבְרָם וְהוֹצֵאתוֹ מֵאוּר כַּשְׂדִּים וְשַׂמְתָּ שְּׁמוֹ אַבְרָהָם׃
ח וּמָצָאתָ אֶת־לְבָבוֹ נֶאֱמָן לְפָנֶיךָ וְכָרוֹת עִמּוֹ הַבְּרִית לָתֵת אֶת־אֶרֶץ הַכְּנַעֲנִי
הַחִתִּי הָאֱמֹרִי וְהַפְּרִזִּי וְהַיְבוּסִי וְהַגִּרְגָּשִׁי לָתֵת לְזַרְעוֹ וַתָּקֶם אֶת־דְּבָרֶיךָ כִּי צַדִּיק
ט י אָתָּה׃ וַתֵּרֶא אֶת־עֳנִי אֲבֹתֵינוּ בְּמִצְרָיִם וְאֶת־זַעֲקָתָם שָׁמַעְתָּ עַל־יַם־סוּף׃ וַתִּתֵּן
אֹתֹת וּמֹפְתִים בְּפַרְעֹה וּבְכָל־עֲבָדָיו וּבְכָל־עַם אַרְצוֹ כִּי יָדַעְתָּ כִּי הֵזִידוּ עֲלֵיהֶם
יא וַתַּעַשׂ־לְךָ שֵׁם כְּהַיּוֹם הַזֶּה׃ וְהַיָּם בָּקַעְתָּ לִפְנֵיהֶם וַיַּעַבְרוּ בְתוֹךְ־הַיָּם בַּיַּבָּשָׁה
יב וְאֶת־רֹדְפֵיהֶם הִשְׁלַכְתָּ בִמְצוֹלֹת כְּמוֹ־אֶבֶן בְּמַיִם עַזִּים׃ וּבְעַמּוּד עָנָן הִנְחִיתָם
יג יוֹמָם וּבְעַמּוּד אֵשׁ לַיְלָה לְהָאִיר לָהֶם אֶת־הַדֶּרֶךְ אֲשֶׁר יֵלְכוּ־בָהּ׃ וְעַל הַר־סִינַי
יָרַדְתָּ וְדַבֵּר עִמָּהֶם מִשָּׁמַיִם וַתִּתֵּן לָהֶם מִשְׁפָּטִים יְשָׁרִים וְתוֹרוֹת אֱמֶת חֻקִּים

with them from heaven, and gave them right principles and
laws of truth, good statutes and commandments.
14 **You informed them of Your holy Sabbath, and commanded**
them commandments, and statutes, and Torah, by means of
Moses Your servant. The Torah contains numerous laws and
commandments, which are meant to structure both public and
personal life, but some are put into practice only occasionally.
By contrast, the Sabbath occurs every week; it was also given to
Israel even before the revelation at Sinai.[93] The Sabbath is not
merely a statute and a commandment, but a permanent, unique
gift that God bestowed upon His people, which is why it is given
special mention here.[94]
15 **You gave them bread from the heavens,** manna, **for their**
hunger, and extracted for them water from the rock for their
thirst, and You said to them to come to take possession of
the land that You lifted up Your hand, You swore, **to give to**
them. The raising of a hand is an act that expresses the taking of
an oath. In relation to God, this expression is, of course, meant
metaphorically.[95]
16 **But they, and** they were **our fathers,**[96] **deliberately sinned,**
and they stiffened their neck, were stubborn, **and they did**
not heed Your commandments.
17 **They refused to heed** Your voice **and did not remember Your**
wonders that You had performed with them; they stiffened
their neck, and in their defiance appointed a leader to return
to their enslavement. They did not wish to enter the Land of
Israel; even worse, they preferred to return to slavery in Egypt
rather than conquering the Promised Land. **But You are a God**
of forgiveness, gracious and merciful, slow to anger, and
abounding in kindness, and You did not forsake them, despite all their sins,
18 **even when they made themselves a cast figure of a calf and**
said: This is your God who took you up from Egypt, and they
performed great offenses.
19 **And** despite all that, **You in Your great mercy did not forsake**
them in the wilderness, even when You disciplined them; **the**
pillar of cloud did not withdraw from over them by day,
leading them on the way, and the pillar of fire was by night,
illuminating for them, and the way on which they should go.
Although You punished them, You did not abandon them.
20 **You gave Your benevolent spirit to educate them, and** despite
all their sins, **You did not withhold Your manna from their**
mouth, and You gave them water for their thirst.
21 **Forty years You sustained them in the wilderness; they did**
not lack anything; **their garments did not grow worn and**
their feet did not swell.
22 **You gave to them kingdoms and peoples, whom You scat-**
tered to the edge of the earth;[97] **and they,** the children of Israel,
took possession of the land of Sihon, and the land of the king
of Heshbon, and the land of Og king of Bashan.
23 **You multiplied their children like the stars of the heavens,**
and You brought them to the land that You said to their fa-
thers to come and to take possession.
24 **The children came and took possession of the land, and**
You subdued before them the inhabitants of the land, the
Canaanites, and delivered them into their hand, and their
kings, and the peoples of the land, to do with them as they
would.
25 **They captured fortified cities, and fat land, and took pos-**
session of houses full of
everything good, hewn
cisterns, vineyards, olive
trees and food trees in
abundance. Since they conquered a previously inhabited
land, everything was ready for
them as soon as they entered.
They ate, and were sated,
and grew fat, and luxuriated
in Your great goodness.

Hewn-out water cistern, Tel Hatzor, late second millennium BCE

"Food trees in abundance." Almond tree and pomegranates on tree

26 Then **they were defiant, and rebelled against You, and they**
cast Your Torah behind their back, and killed Your proph-
ets who warned them to return to You, and they performed
great offenses.
27 **You delivered them into the hand of their enemies, and they**
made trouble for them; and in the time of their trouble, they
would cry to You, and You would hear their cries **from the**
heavens; and in accordance with Your abounding mercy You
would provide saviors for them, and they would save them
from the hand of their enemies. This occurred repeatedly, both
in the era of the judges and in later periods.
28 **And when they experienced relief** from their troubles, **they**
would return to doing evil before You, and You again **for-**
sook them in the hand of their enemies, and they oppressed
them; they repented and cried out to You and called for You to
take action, **and You would hear** them **from the heavens, and**
would rescue them in accordance with Your mercy, many
times over and again.
29 **You warned them, to cause them to return to Your Torah,**
and they deliberately sinned, and did not heed Your

יד וּמִצְוֺת טוֹבִים: וְאֶת־שַׁבַּת קָדְשְׁךָ הוֹדַעְתָּ לָהֶם וּמִצְווֹת וְחֻקִּים וְתוֹרָה צִוִּיתָ
טו לָהֶם בְּיַד מֹשֶׁה עַבְדֶּךָ: וְלֶחֶם מִשָּׁמַיִם נָתַתָּה לָהֶם לִרְעָבָם וּמַיִם מִסֶּלַע הוֹצֵאתָ
לָהֶם לִצְמָאָם וַתֹּאמֶר לָהֶם לָבוֹא לָרֶשֶׁת אֶת־הָאָרֶץ אֲשֶׁר־נָשָׂאתָ אֶת־יָדְךָ
טז לָתֵת לָהֶם: וְהֵם וַאֲבֹתֵינוּ הֵזִידוּ וַיַּקְשׁוּ אֶת־עָרְפָּם וְלֹא שָׁמְעוּ אֶל־מִצְוֺתֶיךָ:
יז וַיְמָאֲנוּ לִשְׁמֹעַ וְלֹא־זָכְרוּ נִפְלְאֹתֶיךָ אֲשֶׁר עָשִׂיתָ עִמָּהֶם וַיַּקְשׁוּ אֶת־עָרְפָּם
וַיִּתְּנוּ־רֹאשׁ לָשׁוּב לְעַבְדֻתָם בְּמִרְיָם וְאַתָּה אֱלוֹהַּ סְלִיחוֹת חַנּוּן וְרַחוּם אֶרֶךְ־
יח אַפַּיִם וְרַב־וחסד וְלֹא עֲזַבְתָּם: אַף כִּי־עָשׂוּ לָהֶם עֵגֶל מַסֵּכָה וַיֹּאמְרוּ זֶה אֱלֹהֶיךָ חֶסֶד
יט אֲשֶׁר הֶעֶלְךָ מִמִּצְרָיִם וַיַּעֲשׂוּ נֶאָצוֹת גְּדֹלוֹת: וְאַתָּה בְּרַחֲמֶיךָ הָרַבִּים לֹא עֲזַבְתָּם
בַּמִּדְבָּר אֶת־עַמּוּד הֶעָנָן לֹא־סָר מֵעֲלֵיהֶם בְּיוֹמָם לְהַנְחֹתָם בְּהַדֶּרֶךְ וְאֶת־עַמּוּד
כ הָאֵשׁ בְּלַיְלָה לְהָאִיר לָהֶם וְאֶת־הַדֶּרֶךְ אֲשֶׁר יֵלְכוּ־בָהּ: וְרוּחֲךָ הַטּוֹבָה נָתַתָּ
כא לְהַשְׂכִּילָם וּמַנְךָ לֹא־מָנַעְתָּ מִפִּיהֶם וּמַיִם נָתַתָּה לָהֶם לִצְמָאָם: וְאַרְבָּעִים שָׁנָה
כב כִּלְכַּלְתָּם בַּמִּדְבָּר לֹא חָסֵרוּ שַׂלְמֹתֵיהֶם לֹא בָלוּ וְרַגְלֵיהֶם לֹא בָצֵקוּ: וַתִּתֵּן לָהֶם
מַמְלָכוֹת וַעֲמָמִים וַתַּחְלְקֵם לְפֵאָה וַיִּירְשׁוּ אֶת־אֶרֶץ סִיחוֹן וְאֶת־אֶרֶץ מֶלֶךְ
כג חֶשְׁבּוֹן וְאֶת־אֶרֶץ עוֹג מֶלֶךְ־הַבָּשָׁן: וּבְנֵיהֶם הִרְבִּיתָ כְּכֹכְבֵי הַשָּׁמָיִם וַתְּבִיאֵם
כד אֶל־הָאָרֶץ אֲשֶׁר־אָמַרְתָּ לַאֲבֹתֵיהֶם לָבוֹא לָרָשֶׁת: וַיָּבֹאוּ הַבָּנִים וַיִּירְשׁוּ אֶת־
הָאָרֶץ וַתַּכְנַע לִפְנֵיהֶם אֶת־יֹשְׁבֵי הָאָרֶץ הַכְּנַעֲנִים וַתִּתְּנֵם בְּיָדָם וְאֶת־מַלְכֵיהֶם
כה וְאֶת־עַמְמֵי הָאָרֶץ לַעֲשׂוֹת בָּהֶם כִּרְצוֹנָם: וַיִּלְכְּדוּ עָרִים בְּצֻרוֹת וַאֲדָמָה שְׁמֵנָה
וַיִּירְשׁוּ בָּתִּים מְלֵאִים־כָּל־טוּב בֹּרוֹת חֲצוּבִים כְּרָמִים וְזֵיתִים וְעֵץ מַאֲכָל לָרֹב
כו וַיֹּאכְלוּ וַיִּשְׂבְּעוּ וַיַּשְׁמִינוּ וַיִּתְעַדְּנוּ בְּטוּבְךָ הַגָּדוֹל: וַיַּמְרוּ וַיִּמְרְדוּ בָּךְ וַיַּשְׁלִכוּ אֶת־
תּוֹרָתְךָ אַחֲרֵי גַוָּם וְאֶת־נְבִיאֶיךָ הָרָגוּ אֲשֶׁר־הֵעִידוּ בָם לַהֲשִׁיבָם אֵלֶיךָ וַיַּעֲשׂוּ
כז נֶאָצוֹת גְּדוֹלֹת: וַתִּתְּנֵם בְּיַד צָרֵיהֶם וַיָּצֵרוּ לָהֶם וּבְעֵת צָרָתָם יִצְעֲקוּ אֵלֶיךָ וְאַתָּה
מִשָּׁמַיִם תִּשְׁמָע וּכְרַחֲמֶיךָ הָרַבִּים תִּתֵּן לָהֶם מוֹשִׁיעִים וְיוֹשִׁיעוּם מִיַּד צָרֵיהֶם:
כח וּכְנוֹחַ לָהֶם יָשׁוּבוּ לַעֲשׂוֹת רַע לְפָנֶיךָ וַתַּעַזְבֵם בְּיַד אֹיְבֵיהֶם וַיִּרְדּוּ בָהֶם וַיָּשׁוּבוּ
כט וַיִּזְעָקוּךָ וְאַתָּה מִשָּׁמַיִם תִּשְׁמַע וְתַצִּילֵם כְּרַחֲמֶיךָ רַבּוֹת עִתִּים: וַתָּעַד בָּהֶם

commandments, but sinned against Your ordinances, despite the fact that these are commandments **which a person shall perform and live by them; they presented a wayward** [*soreret*] **shoulder;** alternatively, a shoulder which one pulls back [*mesir*] from its burden so that the load placed upon it falls away, or a shoulder that one moves in order to turn away from his friend;[98] **and stiffened their neck, and did not heed.**
30 **You continued with them for many years,** waiting for them to repent,[99] **and warned them through Your spirit by means of Your prophets, but they did not listen, and You delivered them into the hand of the peoples of the lands.** You eventually delivered them into the hands of the gentile nations.
31 **But in Your abounding mercy You did not make an end of them.** Despite all their transgressions, You did not destroy Israel, **and did not forsake them, as You are a gracious and merciful God.**
32 **Now, our God, the great, the mighty, and the awesome God, who maintains the covenant and kindness, let it not be trivial before You all the adversity that has found us, our kings, our princes, and our priests, our prophets, our fathers, and all Your people, from the days of the kings of Assyria to this day.** Israel suffered from wars and troubles even before those years, but it was the Assyrians who first actively exiled them from their land, and this exile continued into the subsequent generations.
33 **And You are righteous in everything that comes upon us.** Everything that You have brought upon us is just. We have no complaints, **as You have acted with truth, and we,** all of us, **have acted wickedly.**
34 **Our kings, our princes, our priests, and our fathers,** all of them **did not observe Your Torah, did not heed Your commandments or Your testimonies about which you warned them.**
35 **They, in their kingdom, and with Your great goodness that You gave them, and in the broad and fat land that You put before them, did not serve You and did not repent from their evil exploits.**
36 **Behold, we are servants today.** Although we are not actually enslaved, we are not a free people either, but rather we are subjects of the king of Persia. **And the land that You gave to our fathers to eat its fruit and its goodness, behold, we are servants in it** to foreign rulers. We dwell in the land, but it is not entirely ours.
37 **Its produce is abundant for the kings whom You placed over us in our sins, and they rule over our bodies and over our cattle as they please,** they do as they wish with our livestock, **and we are in great trouble.**

The People Enact a Pact

NEHEMIAH 10:1–40

After the lengthy introductory speech, which enumerated the troubles of Israel over the course of history until that time, the leaders make a pact with God outlining the public and private obligations of the people for the forthcoming years. This is in essence the first known constitution in history. It is almost certain that the much later constitutions of the United States, France, and other countries drew inspiration from here. Modern constitutions follow more or less the same pattern: A historical overview is first presented describing major events in the story of the nation, and then a list of the principles that are the practical content of the constitution.

10 1 **Nevertheless,** even though we are subjugated to foreign rulers, **we are** now **making a pact** with God, **and writing it, signed by our princes, our Levites, and our priests.**
2 **Signed by,** in detail: **Nehemiah,** whose Persian title of honor was **the Tirshata son of Hakhalya.** As the political leader of the people, he was the first to sign; **and Tzidkiya** signed after him.
3 Then **Seraya, Azarya,** and **Yirmeya,** who were probably priests. Some claim that this Azarya was Ezra the scribe, as the name Ezra does not appear among the signatories of the covenant, despite the fact that he was present and was one of the initiators of this assembly. It is therefore possible that Ezra is a shortened, Aramaic version of the Hebrew name Azarya, similar to the way the name Ovadya becomes Avda.[100] When officially signing the new covenant of the Judean state, Ezra used his formal Hebrew name.
4 **Pashhur, Amarya, Malkiya,**
5 **Hatush, Shevanya, Malukh,**
6 **Harim, Meremot, Ovadya,**
7 **Daniyel, Gineton, Barukh,**
8 **Meshulam, Aviya, Miyamin,**
9 **Maazya, Bilgai,** a well-known priestly watch from later generations as well,[101] and **Shemaya. These were the priests.**
10 **The Levites: Yeshua son of Azanya, Binui from the sons of Henadad, Kadmiel.** Some understand this verse as follows: Yeshua son of Azanya, and Binui; and of the sons of Henadad, Kadmiel signed;
11 **and their brethren, Shevanya, Hodiya, Kelita, Pelaya, Hanan,**
12 **Mikha, Rehov, Hashavya,**
13 **Zakur, Sherevya, Shevanya,** a Levite who had the same name as one of the priests who signed the covenant (verse 5) and one of the other Levites (verse 11),
14 a second **Hodiya** (see verse 11), **Bani, Beninu.** Some of these names are familiar from the list of Levites who spoke at the gathering, while many others appear in various lists recorded in the books of Ezra and Nehemiah.
15 **The heads of the people** who signed: **Parosh, Pahat Moav, Eilam, Zatu, Bani,**

לְהֲשִׁיבָם אֶל־תּוֹרָתֶךָ וְהֵמָּה הֵזִידוּ וְלֹא־שָׁמְעוּ לְמִצְוֹתֶיךָ וּבְמִשְׁפָּטֶיךָ חָטְאוּ־
בָם אֲשֶׁר־יַעֲשֶׂה אָדָם וְחָיָה בָהֶם וַיִּתְּנוּ כָתֵף סוֹרֶרֶת וְעָרְפָּם הִקְשׁוּ וְלֹא שָׁמֵעוּ׃
ל וַתִּמְשֹׁךְ עֲלֵיהֶם שָׁנִים רַבּוֹת וַתָּעַד בָּם בְּרוּחֲךָ בְּיַד־נְבִיאֶיךָ וְלֹא הֶאֱזִינוּ וַתִּתְּנֵם
לא בְּיַד עַמֵּי הָאֲרָצֹת׃ וּבְרַחֲמֶיךָ הָרַבִּים לֹא־עֲשִׂיתָם כָּלָה וְלֹא עֲזַבְתָּם כִּי אֵל־חַנּוּן
לב וְרַחוּם אָתָּה׃ וְעַתָּה אֱלֹהֵינוּ הָאֵל הַגָּדוֹל הַגִּבּוֹר וְהַנּוֹרָא שׁוֹמֵר הַבְּרִית וְהַחֶסֶד
אַל־יִמְעַט לְפָנֶיךָ אֵת כָּל־הַתְּלָאָה אֲשֶׁר־מְצָאַתְנוּ לִמְלָכֵינוּ לְשָׂרֵינוּ וּלְכֹהֲנֵינוּ
לג וְלִנְבִיאֵינוּ וְלַאֲבֹתֵינוּ וּלְכָל־עַמֶּךָ מִימֵי מַלְכֵי אַשּׁוּר עַד הַיּוֹם הַזֶּה׃ וְאַתָּה צַדִּיק
לד עַל כָּל־הַבָּא עָלֵינוּ כִּי־אֱמֶת עָשִׂיתָ וַאֲנַחְנוּ הִרְשָׁעְנוּ׃ וְאֶת־מְלָכֵינוּ שָׂרֵינוּ כֹּהֲנֵינוּ
וַאֲבֹתֵינוּ לֹא עָשׂוּ תּוֹרָתֶךָ וְלֹא הִקְשִׁיבוּ אֶל־מִצְוֹתֶיךָ וּלְעֵדְוֹתֶיךָ אֲשֶׁר הַעִידֹתָ
לה בָּהֶם׃ וְהֵם בְּמַלְכוּתָם וּבְטוּבְךָ הָרָב אֲשֶׁר־נָתַתָּ לָהֶם וּבְאֶרֶץ הָרְחָבָה וְהַשְּׁמֵנָה
לו אֲשֶׁר־נָתַתָּ לִפְנֵיהֶם לֹא עֲבָדוּךָ וְלֹא־שָׁבוּ מִמַּעַלְלֵיהֶם הָרָעִים׃ הִנֵּה אֲנַחְנוּ הַיּוֹם
עֲבָדִים וְהָאָרֶץ אֲשֶׁר־נָתַתָּה לַאֲבֹתֵינוּ לֶאֱכֹל אֶת־פִּרְיָהּ וְאֶת־טוּבָהּ הִנֵּה אֲנַחְנוּ
לז עֲבָדִים עָלֶיהָ׃ וּתְבוּאָתָהּ מַרְבָּה לַמְּלָכִים אֲשֶׁר־נָתַתָּה עָלֵינוּ בְּחַטֹּאותֵינוּ וְעַל
גְּוִיֹּתֵינוּ מֹשְׁלִים וּבִבְהֶמְתֵּנוּ כִּרְצוֹנָם וּבְצָרָה גְדוֹלָה אֲנָחְנוּ׃
א ב וּבְכָל־זֹאת אֲנַחְנוּ כֹּרְתִים אֲמָנָה וְכֹתְבִים וְעַל הֶחָתוּם שָׂרֵינוּ לְוִיֵּנוּ כֹּהֲנֵינוּ׃ וְעַל ט
ג ד הַחֲתוּמִים נְחֶמְיָה הַתִּרְשָׁתָא בֶּן־חֲכַלְיָה וְצִדְקִיָּה׃ שְׂרָיָה עֲזַרְיָה יִרְמְיָה׃ פַּשְׁחוּר
ה ו ז אֲמַרְיָה מַלְכִּיָּה׃ חַטּוּשׁ שְׁבַנְיָה מַלּוּךְ׃ חָרִם מְרֵמוֹת עֹבַדְיָה׃ דָּנִיֵּאל גִּנְּתוֹן בָּרוּךְ׃
ח ט י מְשֻׁלָּם אֲבִיָּה מִיָּמִן׃ מַעַזְיָה בִלְגַּי שְׁמַעְיָה אֵלֶּה הַכֹּהֲנִים׃ וְהַלְוִיִּם וְיֵשׁוּעַ בֶּן־אֲזַנְיָה
יא יב בִּנּוּי מִבְּנֵי חֵנָדָד קַדְמִיאֵל׃ וַאֲחֵיהֶם שְׁבַנְיָה הוֹדִיָּה קְלִיטָא פְּלָאיָה חָנָן׃ מִיכָא
יג יד טו רְחוֹב חֲשַׁבְיָה׃ זַכּוּר שֵׁרֵבְיָה שְׁבַנְיָה׃ הוֹדִיָּה בָנִי בְּנִינוּ׃ רָאשֵׁי הָעָם פַּרְעֹשׁ פַּחַת

16 **Buni, Azgad, Bevai,**
17 **Adoniya, Bigvai, Adin,**
18 **Ater, Hizkiya, Azur,**
19 **Hodiya, Hashum, Betzai,**
20 **Harif, Anatot, Nebai,**
21 **Magpiash, Meshulam, Hezir,**
22 **Meshezavel, Tzadok, Yadua,**
23 **Pelatya, Hanan, Anaya,**
24 **Hoshe'a, Hananya, Hashuv,**
25 **Halohesh, Pilha, Shovek,**
26 **Rehum, Hashavna, Maaseya,**
27 **and Ahiya, Hanan, Anan,**
28 **Malukh, Harim, Baana.** Presumably, the signatories were all family heads or firstborn sons. In effect, these were the leaders of the people in that generation. The Tirshata signed first because he was the governor and most important political leader. He was followed by the most important priests, the distinguished Levites, and finally the heads of the people.[102] It seems that they signed together as a single body. Some claim this list was the kernel of a High Court that later became known as the Great Assembly.[103]
29 With regard to **the rest of the people, the priests, the Levites, the gatekeepers, the singers, the Netinim, and everyone who had separated from the peoples of the lands** and had come **to the Torah of God, their wives, their sons, and their daughters, everyone knowledgeable and understanding** of the Torah,
30 they all **join with** and support **their brethren, their nobles,** the highest leaders, **and enter into a curse, and into an oath.** Not everyone signed the covenant, but they all agreed with, and accepted, the content of the scroll that was signed by the leaders, committing **to follow in the Torah of God that was given by means of Moses the servant of God, and to observe and perform all the commandments of the Lord our Lord, and His ordinances and His statutes.** They accepted this upon themselves as the law of the land.
31 The chapter now lays out the various clauses of the covenant, some of which are general obligations while others are more specific: **And that we shall not give our daughters to the peoples of the land, and their daughters we will not take for our sons.**
32 **The peoples of the land,** the gentiles, **who bring merchandise** for purchase, **or any provision on the Sabbath day to sell, we shall not purchase from them on the Sabbath,**[D] **or on a holy day,** a festival. **And we shall forgo** working the land **in the seventh year,** the Sabbatical Year, **and** refrain from the **exaction of every debt.** The remittal of debts is one of the obligations of the seventh year.
33 **We set upon ourselves commandments;** we accepted additional obligations upon ourselves. Each of us agreed **to impose**

Remnant of earthenware Sabbath lamp, with the word "Sabbath" etched onto it, Horvat Uza, 410–340 BCE

Field left fallow in the Sabbatical Year

upon us one-third shekel for the requirements of **the service of the House of our God.** The exact sum of the fixed yearly donation to the Temple changed slightly over the generations.[104]
34 These shekels were required **for the showbread,**[105] **and for the continual meal offering, and for the continual burnt offering,** the burnt offering that is brought each day, in the morning and afternoon, with its accompanying meal offering; and the offerings on **the Sabbaths, the New Moons, for the appointed times, and for the sacraments, and for the sin offerings,** which are brought **to atone for Israel, and for all** the other items needed for **the labor of the House of our God.**

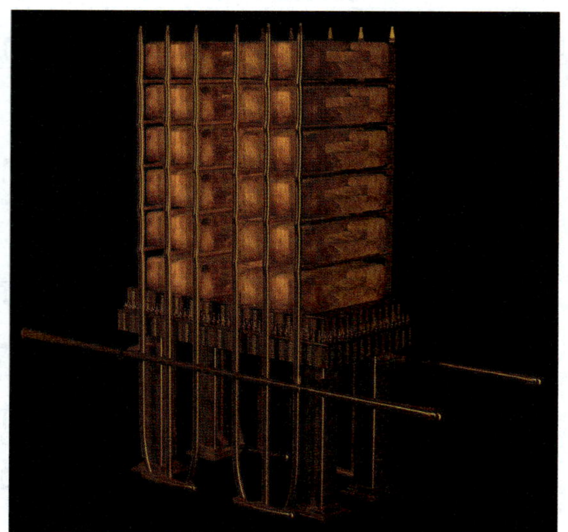
Table for the showbread

35 **We cast lots concerning the wood offering,**[D] which included **the priests, the Levites, and the people, to bring** the wood **to the House of our God, according to our patrilineal houses, at times appointed,** on fixed dates, **year by year,** in order **to burn** the fire **on the altar of the Lord our God, as it is written**

טז יז יח מואב עילם זתוא בני: בני עזגד בבי: אדניה בגוי עדין: אטר חזקיה עזור:
יט כ כא כב הודיה חשם בצי: חריף ענתות נובי: מגפיעש משלם חזיר: משיזבאל צדוק ניבי
כג כד כה ידוע: פלטיה חנן עניה: הושע חנניה חשוב: הלוחש פלחא שובק:
כו כז כח כט רחום חשבנה מעשיה: ואחיה חנן ענן: מלוך חרם בענה: ושאר העם הכהנים
הלוים השוערים המשררים הנתינים וכל־הנבדל מעמי הארצות אל־תורת
ל האלהים נשיהם בניהם ובנתיהם כל יודע מבין: מחזיקים על־אחיהם אדיריהם
ובאים באלה ובשבועה ללכת בתורת האלהים אשר נתנה ביד משה עבד־
לא האלהים ולשמור ולעשות את־כל־מצות יהוה אדנינו ומשפטיו וחקיו: ואשר
לב לא־נתן בנתינו לעמי הארץ ואת־בנתיהם לא נקח לבנינו: ועמי הארץ
המביאים את־המקחות וכל־שבר ביום השבת למכור לא־נקח מהם בשבת
לג וביום קדש ונטש את־השנה השביעית ומשא כל־יד: והעמדנו עלינו מצות
לד לתת עלינו שלשית השקל בשנה לעבדת בית אלהינו: ללחם המערכת ומנחת
התמיד ולעולת התמיד השבתות החדשים למועדים ולקדשים ולחטאות לכפר
לה על־ישראל וכל מלאכת בית־אלהינו: והגורלות הפלנו על־קרבן
העצים הכהנים הלוים והעם להביא לבית אלהינו לבית־אבתינו לעתים

DISCUSSION

10:32 | **We shall not purchase from them on the Sabbath:** This is the first explicit mention of the prohibition against trade on the Sabbath in the Bible, although it is clear that commerce on the holy day was prohibited in the First Temple period as well (see Jeremiah 17:19–22, and commentary ad loc.; Amos 8:5). Commerce in and of itself is not included in the category of "labor" prohibited by the Torah on the Sabbath, but it goes against the character of the day, which is defined by the Torah as "a sabbatical rest, a holy convocation" (Leviticus 23:3; see Ramban, Leviticus 23:24). This covenant states not only that the Sabbath must be observed in general terms, and that all trade between Jews within the city will cease, but also that Jews should refrain from buying merchandise from gentiles on the holy day.

10:35 | **The wood offering:** It is likely that at that time, there was not a large amount of funds in the Temple treasury. However, over time, the treasury filled up as the number of people who donated money increased, and additional donations were no longer required. Nevertheless, the custom of the wood offering continued, and the Mishna and the Talmud relate that certain families took it upon themselves to continue bringing wood on a regular basis. Some families were privileged to bring the wood offering on a specific date every year, a day which became a holiday for the entire family. These families continued to bring this wood until the destruction of the Second Temple, and it is possible that they continued to celebrate these days even after that time (see Mishna *Ta'anit* 4:5; *Ta'anit* 28a; *Megillat Ta'anit* with regard to the fifteenth of Av).

in the Torah. Since the fire had to burn continuously, a large amount of wood was required. Therefore, lots were cast among the people to determine their turns for supplying the wood.

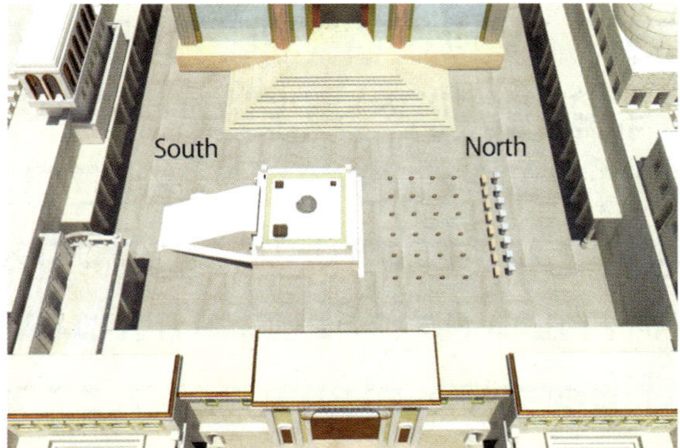

Altar in Temple courtyard

36 We also committed **to bring the first fruits of our land,**[D] **and the first fruits of every fruit from every tree, year by year, to the House of the Lord,** as stated several times in the Torah,[106]

"First fruits of our land"

37 **and** the money for the redemption of **the firstborn of our sons, and** the firstborn **of our animals, as it is written in the Torah,**[107] **and the firstborn of our cattle and our flocks, to bring to the House of our God, to the priests who serve in the House of our God,**

38 **and the first** portion of dough **of our kneading baskets,** the portion separated from the dough when it is kneaded, known as *ḥalla,* **and our gifts** from produce, **and the fruit of every tree, wine and oil, to the priests, to the chambers of the House of our God, and the tithes of our land,**[D] called the first tithe, which is given **to the Levites, and they, the Levites who tithe,** who receive tithes, **in all the cities of our cultivation.**

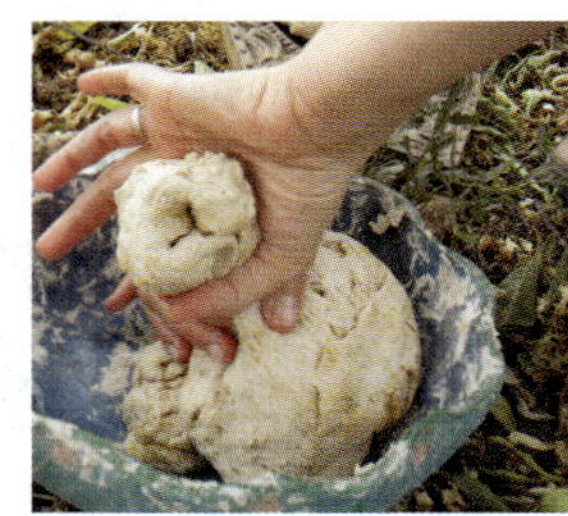
"First of our kneading baskets." Separating a portion of the dough

39 **The priest, son of Aaron, shall be** present **with the Levites when the Levites tithe,**[108] **and the Levites shall raise,** separate, **the tithe of the tithe,** *teruma* of the tithe as explained above, **to the House of our God, to the chambers, to the treasure house.** It shall be given to the priests, as stated in the Torah.[109]

40 **For it is to the chambers that the children of Israel and the children of Levi shall bring the gifts of the grain, of the wine, and of the oil;** both the donations given directly by the children of Israel to the priests, as well as the *teruma* of the tithe, which is the donation the Levites separate from their tithe for the priests. **There,** in the chambers, **are the vessels of the Sanctuary, and the priests who serve, and the gatekeepers, and the singers;** in this manner **we will not forsake,** neglect, **the House of our God** (see 13:10–12).

Populating Jerusalem

NEHEMIAH 11:1–2

Jerusalem is a relatively large capital city for a tiny state that has only just begun to develop. Because it is sparsely inhabited, people are hesitant to move there. Work is found for the residents of other cities near their residences, but life is harder in Jerusalem, and therefore it is decided to take active steps to populate the city.

11 1 Although **the princes of the people settled in Jerusalem,** nevertheless, once the walls were built it became clear that they enclosed a relatively large area, and that the city was sparsely inhabited. **And** therefore, **the rest of the people cast lots, to bring one in ten to settle in Jerusalem the holy city, and** the other **nine parts** would live **in the** various other **cities.** It was decided that one-tenth of the population should move to Jerusalem, as determined by lot.

2 **The people blessed all the people who volunteered to settle in Jerusalem.** Since one had to be dedicated to live in Jerusalem, the people encouraged and blessed those who agreed to move there.

DISCUSSION

10:36 | **The first fruits of our land:** The inhabitants of the land would bring the first fruits of the seven special species of the Land of Israel (see Deuteronomy 8:8) to the Temple. At times, other fruits were also brought as gifts for the priests, as the verse refers to the first fruits of every tree. However, only fruits of the seven species constitute the primary obligation (see Rashi; *Metzudat David*; Malbim; Mishna *Bikkurim* 1:3, 3:9; Ran, *Ḥullin* 120b).

The minimum amount of produce one must bring for this commandment is not mentioned in the Bible, and the Sages ruled that each individual may bring whatever amount he desires (Mishna *Pe'a* 1:1). According to the *halakha*,

▸ *one*

לו מְזֻמָּנִים שָׁנָה בְשָׁנָה לְבַעֵר עַל־מִזְבַּח יהוה אֱלֹהֵינוּ כַּכָּתוּב בַּתּוֹרָה: וּלְהָבִיא
לז אֶת־בִּכּוּרֵי אַדְמָתֵנוּ וּבִכּוּרֵי כָּל־פְּרִי כָל־עֵץ שָׁנָה בְשָׁנָה לְבֵית יהוה: וְאֶת־
בְּכֹרוֹת בָּנֵינוּ וּבְהֶמְתֵּנוּ כַּכָּתוּב בַּתּוֹרָה וְאֶת־בְּכוֹרֵי בְקָרֵינוּ וְצֹאנֵינוּ לְהָבִיא
לח לְבֵית אֱלֹהֵינוּ לַכֹּהֲנִים הַמְשָׁרְתִים בְּבֵית אֱלֹהֵינוּ: וְאֶת־רֵאשִׁית עֲרִיסֹתֵינוּ
וּתְרוּמֹתֵינוּ וּפְרִי כָל־עֵץ תִּירוֹשׁ וְיִצְהָר נָבִיא לַכֹּהֲנִים אֶל־לִשְׁכוֹת בֵּית־אֱלֹהֵינוּ
לט וּמַעְשַׂר אַדְמָתֵנוּ לַלְוִיִּם וְהֵם הַלְוִיִּם הַמְעַשְּׂרִים בְּכֹל עָרֵי עֲבֹדָתֵנוּ: וְהָיָה הַכֹּהֵן
בֶּן־אַהֲרֹן עִם־הַלְוִיִּם בַּעְשֵׂר הַלְוִיִּם וְהַלְוִיִּם יַעֲלוּ אֶת־מַעֲשַׂר הַמַּעֲשֵׂר לְבֵית
מ אֱלֹהֵינוּ אֶל־הַלְּשָׁכוֹת לְבֵית הָאוֹצָר: כִּי אֶל־הַלְּשָׁכוֹת יָבִיאוּ בְנֵי־יִשְׂרָאֵל וּבְנֵי
הַלֵּוִי אֶת־תְּרוּמַת הַדָּגָן הַתִּירוֹשׁ וְהַיִּצְהָר וְשָׁם כְּלֵי הַמִּקְדָּשׁ וְהַכֹּהֲנִים הַמְשָׁרְתִים
א וְהַשּׁוֹעֲרִים וְהַמְשֹׁרְרִים וְלֹא נַעֲזֹב אֶת־בֵּית אֱלֹהֵינוּ: וַיֵּשְׁבוּ שָׂרֵי־הָעָם בִּירוּשָׁלִָם
וּשְׁאָר הָעָם הִפִּילוּ גוֹרָלוֹת לְהָבִיא ׀ אֶחָד מִן־הָעֲשָׂרָה לָשֶׁבֶת בִּירוּשָׁלִַם עִיר
ב הַקֹּדֶשׁ וְתֵשַׁע הַיָּדוֹת בֶּעָרִים: וַיְבָרְכוּ הָעָם לְכֹל הָאֲנָשִׁים הַמִּתְנַדְּבִים לָשֶׁבֶת

DISCUSSION

one may bring the first fruits starting from the holiday of Shavuot, on which the first wheat was used to bring the two loaves offering, until the conclusion of the holiday of Sukkot. First fruits are accepted until Hanukkah (Mishna *Bikkurim* 1:3, 6). Although the first fruits may be brought individually, in the period of the Second Temple, they were generally brought communally, as described in the Mishna (*Bikkurim* 3:2): The residents of a particular city or region would ascend together to Jerusalem in a dramatic and ceremonious manner, which included decorated baskets and oxen as well as much singing and celebration.

10:38 | **The first of our kneading baskets, and our gifts...and the tithes of our land:** The portions separated from the kneading baskets or from the produce at the threshing floor, and given to the priests, are called *ḥalla* and *teruma*, respectively. The Torah does not set a minimum amount that must be given; rather, each person may give as much as he wishes. Nowadays, only a minimal amount is separated, and it is not given to the priests, but rather is burned or buried. This is because a priest must be ritually pure in order to consume *ḥalla* or *teruma*, and today everyone is assumed to be ritually impure.

First tithe, which is one-tenth of the produce, is given to a Levite. Unlike *teruma*, it does not have any sanctity, and there are no special conditions for its consumption. Since Levites today generally cannot prove their lineage conclusively, an Israelite is not obligated according to the *halakha* to give them first tithe, though some individuals even today customarily give their tithe to those with the presumed status of being a Levite. Either way, one must still declare one-tenth of the produce as being tithe, as there are two distinct obligations: designating the tithes and giving the tithes. Even if one does not give the tithe to a Levite, the tithe must still be designated.

Teruma of the tithe, which is separated from the first tithe and is given to the priests, still has halakhic relevance today even if one does not give first tithe to the Levite. Since it is termed "the gift of the Lord" and has sanctity just like *teruma* (Numbers 18:28), it is forbidden to consume it in a state of impurity. Therefore, one is obligated to separate *teruma* of the tithe, which is one percent of the produce, and treat it in the same manner as *teruma*.

Aside from the tithes given to the priest and the Levite that are mentioned here, there is one more tithe that must be separated from one's produce. When the Temple was standing, one would bring a second tithe of one's produce to Jerusalem to be eaten there. Every third year, instead of bringing it to Jerusalem, this tithe is given to the poor, and is known as the poorman's tithe (see Deuteronomy 14:22–29, 26:12, and commentary ad loc.).

The List of the Residents of Jerusalem and Their Lineage

NEHEMIAH 11:3–24

3 **These** people detailed below **are the heads of the province** of
Judah **who settled in Jerusalem. In the** other **cities of Judah**
each man settled in his ancestral portion in their cities:
Israelites, the priests, and the Levites, and the Netinim, and
the children of Solomon's servants.
4 **In Jerusalem,** it was mainly[110] **some of the children of Judah**
and some of the children of Benjamin who **settled. From the**
children of Judah: Ataya, son of Uziya, son of Zekharya, son
of Amarya, son of Shefatya, son of Mahalalel, from the chil-
dren of Peretz son of Judah,
5 **and Maaseya, son of Barukh, son of Kol Hozeh,** a personal
name or a nickname, **son of Hazaya, son of Adaya, son of**
Yoyariv, son of Zekharya, son of the Shilonite, Shela son of
Judah.
6 **All the sons,** descendants, **of Peretz who resided in Jerusalem**
were four hundred and sixty-eight valiant men.
7 **These are the sons of Benjamin** who lived in Jerusalem: Their
leader was **Salu, son of Meshulam, son of Yoed, son of Pedaya,**
son of Kolaya, son of Maaseya, son of Itiel, son of Yeshaya.
8 **After him** in rank[111] **were Gabai** and **Salai.** The sum total of all
members of the tribe of Benjamin in Jerusalem was **nine hun-**
dred and twenty-eight.
9 **Yoel son of Zikhri was the official in charge of them,** those
leaders; **and Judah son of Hasenua was** appointed **deputy over**
the city, second-in-command to Yoel son of Zikhri.[112]
10 **From the priests** in Jerusalem **were Yedaya son of Yoyariv,**
Yakhin,
11 **Seraya, son of Hilkiya, son of Meshulam, son of Tzadok, son**
of Merayot, son of Ahituv; who was the **chief official** in charge
of the House of God, the High Priest,[113]
12 **and their brethren,** all **craftsmen of the House,** inside the
Temple, were **eight hundred and twenty-two; and Adaya, son**
of Yeroham, son of Pelalya, son of Amtzi, son of Zekharya,
son of Pashhur, son of Malkiya,
13 **and his brethren, heads of the patrilineal houses,** heads of
families, **two hundred and forty-two; and Amashsai, son of**
Azarel, son of Ahzai, son of Meshilemot, son of Imer,
14 **and their brethren, mighty warriors,** numbered **one hundred**
and twenty-eight; the official in charge of them was Zavdiel
son of Hagedolim, either a personal name or a nickname, as
gedolim means great ones, the mighty.
15 **From the Levites, Shemaya, son of Hashuv, son of Azrikam,**
son of Hashavya, son of Buni.
16 **Shabetai and Yozavad were in charge of the labor of outside**
the House of God, they were **from the heads of the Levites,**
for example, officers and those in charge of the treasuries;[114]
17 **Matanya, son of Mikha, son of Zavdi, son of Asaf, was the**
head, who would commence giving thanks in the prayer; he
was the man appointed to start the prayer, as Matanya headed the Levites who sang the psalms of praise to God;[115] **and**
Bakbukya was deputy to Matanya **among his brethren, and**
Avda, son of Shamua, son of Galal, son of Yedutun.
18 **All the Levites** who resided **in the holy city were two hundred**
and eighty-four.
19 **The gatekeepers,** who were also Levites but who fulfilled a special role, **were Akuv, Talmon, and their brethren who would**
guard at the gates; they were one hundred and seventy-two.
20 As stated, **the rest of Israel, the priests, the Levites,** dwelled
in all the cities of Judah, each was in his inheritance.
21 **The Netinim lived in the Ofel,** a raised compound or fortress
in the city (see commentary on 3:26), **and Tziha and Gishpa**
were Givonites, or Netinim, who were the leaders **in charge of**
the Netinim.
22 **The officer of the Levites in Jerusalem was Uzi, son of Bani,**
son of Hashavya, son of Matanya, son of Mikha, from the
sons of Asaf the singers; he was appointed **in charge of the**
labor of the House of God. Uzi was the supervisor responsible
for the work and for the various assignments.
23 **For the commandment of the king was upon them.** Part of
the service in the Temple was performed at the directive of the
king of Persia, and in this regard their service was the fulfillment
of a royal command. **And an obligation** was imposed **upon the**
singers, to sing **the matter,** the song, **of each day on its day.**
24 **Petahya son of Meshezavel, from the children of Zerah son of**
Judah, was at the hand of the king, he was the king's appointee,
in all matters for the people, for all the people's needs.

ג בירושלם: ואלה ראשי המדינה אשר ישבו בירושלם ובערי
יהודה ישבו איש באחזתו בעריהם ישראל הכהנים והלוים והנתינים ובני
ד עבדי שלמה: ובירושלם ישבו מבני יהודה ומבני בנימן מבני יהודה עתיה
ה בן־עזיה בן־זכריה בן־אמריה בן־שפטיה בן־מהללאל מבני פרץ: ומעשיה
ו בן־ברוך בן־כל־חזה בן־חזיה בן־עדיה בן־יויריב בן־זכריה בן־השלני: כל־בני־
פרץ הישבים בירושלם ארבע מאות ששים ושמנה אנשי־חיל:
ז ואלה בני בנימן סלא בן־משלם בן־יועד בן־פדיה בן־קוליה בן־מעשיה בן־
ח ט איתיאל בן־ישעיה: ואחריו גבי סלי תשע מאות עשרים ושמנה: ויואל בן־
זכרי פקיד עליהם ויהודה בן־הסנואה על־העיר משנה:
י יא מן־הכהנים ידעיה בן־יויריב יכין: שריה בן־חלקיה בן־משלם בן־צדוק בן־
יב מריות בן־אחיטוב נגד בית האלהים: ואחיהם עשה המלאכה לבית שמנה
מאות עשרים ושנים ועדיה בן־ירחם בן־פלליה בן־אמצי בן־זכריה בן־פשחור
יג בן־מלכיה: ואחיו ראשים לאבות מאתים ארבעים ושנים ועמשסי בן־עזראל
יד בן־אחזי בן־משלמות בן־אמר: ואחיהם גברי חיל מאה עשרים ושמנה ופקיד
טו עליהם זבדיאל בן־הגדולים: ומן־הלוים שמעיה בן־חשוב בן־
טז עזריקם בן־חשביה בן־בוני: ושבתי ויוזבד על־המלאכה החיצנה לבית
יז האלהים מראשי הלוים: ומתניה בן־מיכא בן־זבדי בן־אסף ראש התחלה
יהודה לתפלה ובקבקיה משנה מאחיו ועבדא בן־שמוע בן־גלל בן־ידיתון: ידותון
יח יט כל־הלוים בעיר הקדש מאתים שמנים וארבעה: והשוערים עקוב
כ טלמון ואחיהם השמרים בשערים מאה שבעים ושנים: ושאר ישראל הכהנים
כא הלוים בכל־ערי יהודה איש בנחלתו: והנתינים ישבים בעפל וציחא וגשפא
כב על־הנתינים: ופקיד הלוים בירושלם עזי בן־בני בן־חשביה בן־
כג מתניה בן־מיכא מבני אסף המשררים לנגד מלאכת בית־האלהים: כי־מצות
כד המלך עליהם ואמנה על־המשררים דבר־יום ביומו: ופתחיה בן־

The Inhabited Cities of Judah and Benjamin

NEHEMIAH 11:25–36

Following the previous list of those who came to live in Jerusalem, the book provides a list of all the places in which the returnees settle. Gradually, the immigrants rebuild the ancient cities, including some in remote areas. In this manner, the state of Judah expands and develops.

25 **In the villages,** the settlements that were not surrounded by a
wall, **with their fields, some of the children of Judah settled
in Kiryat Arba,** Hebron, **and its environs,** the nearby settlements, **and in Divon and its environs, and in Yekavtze'el and
its villages,** semi-permanent residential areas;

Cities of the returning exiles to Judah; Hatzar Shual and Mekhona have not been identified

26 **and in Yeshua, and in Molada, and in Beit Pelet,**
27 **and in Hatzar Shual, and in Beersheba and its environs.**
These cities were initially located in the portion of the tribe of
Simeon,[116] but it seems that at this stage Simeon was no longer a
clearly-defined tribe in its own right.[117]
28 **And in Tziklag,** which had belonged to the house of David,[118]
and in Mekhona and in its environs,
29 **and in Ein Rimon, and in
Tzora, and in Yarmut,**
30 **Zanoah, Adulam, and their
villages, Lakhish and its
fields, Azeka and its environs. They encamped from
Beersheba up to the Valley
of Hinom,** which is adjacent
to Jerusalem.

Tel Shera, identified as Tziklag

31 **The children of Benjamin
were from Geva, Mikhmas,
Aya, Beit El and its environs,**

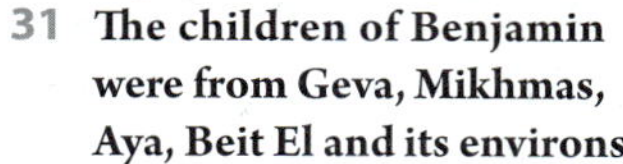

Ruin at Tel Adulam above the Valley of Ela

Tel Azeka

32 **Anatot, Nov, Ananya,**
33 **Hatzor, Rama, Gitayim,**
34 **Hadid, Tzvo'im, Nevalat,**
35 **Lod, Ono, and Gei
Harashim.** Some of these are
known to have been cities of
the tribe of Benjamin from
ancient times.[119]

Tel Hatzor

36 **From the Levites,** there **were divisions,** groups, that came **to**
the land of **Judah and** also **to Benjamin.**

The Priests and Levites, and Their Lineages

NEHEMIAH 12:1–26

12 1 **These are the priests and the Levites that went up with
Zerubavel son of She'altiel, and Yeshua,** the High Priest:
Seraya, Yirmeya, Ezra,
2 **Amarya, Malukh, Hatush,**
3 **Shekhanya, Rehum, Meremot,**
4 **Ido, Ginetoi, Aviya,**
5 **Miyamin, Maadya, Bilga,**
6 **Shemaya, Yoyariv, Yedaya,**
7 **Salu, Amok, Hilkiya, Yedaya. These were the heads of the
priests and their brethren in the days of Yeshua.**

כה מְשֵׁיזַבְאֵל מִבְּנֵי־זֶרַח בֶּן־יְהוּדָה לְיַד הַמֶּלֶךְ לְכָל־דָּבָר לָעָם׃ וְאֶל־הַחֲצֵרִים
בִּשְׂדֹתָם מִבְּנֵי יְהוּדָה יָשְׁבוּ בְּקִרְיַת הָאַרְבַּע וּבְנֹתֶיהָ וּבְדִיבֹן וּבְנֹתֶיהָ וּבִיקַּבְצְאֵל
כו כז וַחֲצֵרֶיהָ׃ וּבְיֵשׁוּעַ וּבְמֹלָדָה וּבְבֵית־פָּלֶט׃ וּבַחֲצַר שׁוּעָל וּבִבְאֵר שֶׁבַע וּבְנֹתֶיהָ׃
כח כט ל וּבְצִקְלַג וּבִמְכֹנָה וּבִבְנֹתֶיהָ׃ וּבְעֵין רִמּוֹן וּבְצָרְעָה וּבְיַרְמוּת׃ זָנֹחַ עֲדֻלָּם וְחַצְרֵיהֶם
לא לָכִישׁ וּשְׂדֹתֶיהָ עֲזֵקָה וּבְנֹתֶיהָ וַיַּחֲנוּ מִבְּאֵר־שֶׁבַע עַד־גֵּיא הִנֹּם׃ וּבְנֵי בִנְיָמִן
לב לג מִגָּבַע מִכְמָשׂ וְעַיָּה וּבֵית־אֵל וּבְנֹתֶיהָ׃ עֲנָתוֹת נֹב עֲנָנְיָה׃ חָצוֹר ׀ רָמָה גִּתָּיִם׃
לד לה לו חָדִיד צְבֹעִים נְבַלָּט׃ לֹד וְאוֹנוֹ גֵּי הַחֲרָשִׁים׃ וּמִן־הַלְוִיִּם מַחְלְקוֹת יְהוּדָה
יב א לְבִנְיָמִין׃ וְאֵלֶּה הַכֹּהֲנִים וְהַלְוִיִּם אֲשֶׁר עָלוּ עִם־זְרֻבָּבֶל בֶּן־שְׁאַלְתִּיאֵל
ב ג ד ה וְיֵשׁוּעַ שְׂרָיָה יִרְמְיָה עֶזְרָא׃ אֲמַרְיָה מַלּוּךְ חַטּוּשׁ׃ שְׁכַנְיָה רְחֻם מְרֵמֹת׃ עִדּוֹא
ו ז גִּנְּתוֹי אֲבִיָּה׃ מִיָּמִין מַעַדְיָה בִּלְגָּה׃ שְׁמַעְיָה וְיוֹיָרִיב יְדַעְיָה׃ סַלּוּ עָמוֹק חִלְקִיָּה
ח יְדַעְיָה אֵלֶּה רָאשֵׁי הַכֹּהֲנִים וַאֲחֵיהֶם בִּימֵי יֵשׁוּעַ׃ וְהַלְוִיִּם יֵשׁוּעַ בִּנּוּי קַדְמִיאֵל
ט שֵׁרֵבְיָה יְהוּדָה מַתַּנְיָה עַל־הֻיְּדוֹת הוּא וְאֶחָיו׃ וּבַקְבֻּקְיָה וענו אֲחֵיהֶם לְנֶגְדָּם וְעֻנִּי
י לְמִשְׁמָרוֹת׃ וְיֵשׁוּעַ הוֹלִיד אֶת־יוֹיָקִים וְיוֹיָקִים הוֹלִיד אֶת־אֶלְיָשִׁיב וְאֶלְיָשִׁיב
יא יב אֶת־יוֹיָדָע׃ וְיוֹיָדָע הוֹלִיד אֶת־יוֹנָתָן וְיוֹנָתָן הוֹלִיד אֶת־יַדּוּעַ׃ וּבִימֵי יוֹיָקִים הָיוּ
יג כֹהֲנִים רָאשֵׁי הָאָבוֹת לִשְׂרָיָה מְרָיָה לְיִרְמְיָה חֲנַנְיָה׃ לְעֶזְרָא מְשֻׁלָּם לַאֲמַרְיָה לִמְלִיכוּ |
יד טו טז יְהוֹחָנָן׃ למלוכי יוֹנָתָן לִשְׁבַנְיָה יוֹסֵף׃ לְחָרִם עַדְנָא לִמְרָיוֹת חֶלְקָי׃ לעדיא זְכַרְיָה לְעִדּוֹא
יז יח לְגִנְּתוֹן מְשֻׁלָּם׃ לַאֲבִיָּה זִכְרִי לְמִנְיָמִין לְמוֹעַדְיָה פִּלְטָי׃ לְבִלְגָּה שַׁמּוּעַ לִשְׁמַעְיָה

8 **The Levites were Yeshua, Binui, Kadmiel, Sherevya, Yehuda, and Matanya, who was in charge of the** psalms of **thanksgiving,**[120] **he and his brethren.**

9 **Bakbukya and Uni, their brethren, were** divided into groups **opposite them,** corresponding to them, **in the watches.**

10 The following is a genealogical list of priests, possibly High Priests: **Yeshua begot Yoyakim, and Yoyakim begot Elyashiv, and Elyashiv begot Yoyada,**

11 **and Yoyada begot Yonatan, and Yonatan begot Yadua.**

12 **In the days of Yoyakim,** the son of Yehoshua the High Priest, these **were priests, heads of the patrilineal houses: For** the family of **Seraya,** who lived in the generation of the first immigrants, the head of the fathers' house was **Meraya; for Yirmeya,** the head of the fathers' house was **Hananya;**

13 **for Ezra, Meshulam; for Amarya, Yehohanan;**

14 **for Melikhu, Yonatan; for Shevanya, Yosef;**

15 **for Harim, Adna; for Merayot, Helkai;**

16 **for Ido, Zekharya,** perhaps the well-known prophet Zekharya son of Ido, who was active in the days of Darius;[121] **for Gineton, Meshulam;**

17 **for Aviya, Zikhri; for Minyamin** and **for Moadya, Piltai;**

18 **for Bilga, Shamua; for Shemaya, Yehonatan;**

19 **and for Yoyariv, Matenai; for Yedaya, Uzi;**
20 **for Salai, Kalai; for Amok, Ever;**
21 **for Hilkiya, Hashavya; for Yedaya, Netanel.**
22 **The Levites in the days of Elyashiv** the priest, son of Yoyakim: **Yoyada and Yohanan and Yadua were recorded as the heads of the patrilineal houses and so too the priests** were likewise inscribed[122] in a book **during the reign of Darius the Persian.** This is no longer referring to the days of the first immigration to Israel, but to a later period.
23 **The sons of Levi, heads of the patrilineal houses, are written in a book of chronicles, up to the days of Yohanan son of Elyashiv.**
24 **The heads of the Levites were Hashavya, Sherevya, and Yeshua son of Kadmiel, with their brethren opposite them, to praise and give thanks, according to the command of David the man of God, watch opposite watch.** Long before, King David had divided the Levites into watches of singers.[123]
25 In addition to the Levites who served as singers, there were Levites who served as gatekeepers: **Matanya and Bakbukya, Ovadya, Meshulam, Talmon,** and **Akuv were guards, gatekeepers of the watch at the thresholds**[124] **of the gates.**
26 **These** were **in the days of Yoyakim, son of Yeshua, son of Yotzadak, and in the days of Nehemiah the governor, and of Ezra the priest, the scribe.**

The Inauguration of the Wall of Jerusalem

NEHEMIAH 12:27–47

Since the wall of Jerusalem marked the city boundaries and determined its special sanctity, it was dedicated in an official ceremony. The ritual inauguration of the wall that is described here, with the participation of priests, Levites, members of the high court, and the king, represented by the governor, became the standard method of dedicating the walls over the generations.[125]

27 **At the dedication of the wall of Jerusalem they sought,** invited, **the Levites from all their places, to bring them to Jerusalem,** in order **to perform the dedication and rejoicing, with thanks,**[126] **with song, cymbals, lyres, and with harps.**

"Plain surrounding Jerusalem." Jerusalem on the Madaba Map, Jordan, sixth century CE

28 **The sons of the singers gathered** from all the places; **from the plain surrounding Jerusalem,**[B] **from the villages of the Netofatites,**[B] which were camps of sorts for the patrilineal houses, located near Netofa;

Archaeological remains, Umm Tuba, Second Temple period

29 **from Beit Gilgal,**[B] **and from the fields of Geva**[B] **and Azmavet,**[127] **as the** Levite **singers** did not live within Jerusalem itself, but **had built for themselves villages around Jerusalem** (see 13:10).
30 **The priests and the Levites purified themselves and purified the people, the gates, and the wall.** They ensured that there was nothing ritually impure in the city.[128]
31 Nehemiah describes in detail the inauguration ceremony of the city walls: **I took the princes of Judah up upon the wall, and set two great thanks offerings,**[129] **with processions to the right upon the wall to the Dung Gate.**
32 **Hoshaya and half of the princes of Judah followed them,**
33 **with Azarya, Ezra, Meshulam,**
34 **Yehuda, Binyamin, Shemaya, Yirmeya,**

יט כ כא יהונתן: ולויריב מתני לידעיה עזי: לסלי קלי לעמוק עבר: לחלקיה חשביה
כב לידעיה נתנאל: הלוים בימי אלישיב יוידע ויוחנן וידוע כתובים ראשי אבות
כג והכהנים על־מלכות דריוש הפרסי: בני לוי ראשי האבות כתובים
כד על־ספר דברי הימים ועד־ימי יוחנן בן־אלישיב: וראשי הלוים חשביה שרביה
וישוע בן־קדמיאל ואחיהם לנגדם להלל להודות במצות דויד איש־האלהים
כה משמר לעמת משמר: מתניה ובקבקיה עבדיה משלם טלמון עקוב שמרים
כו שוערים משמר באספי השערים: אלה בימי יויקים בן־ישוע בן־יוצדק ובימי
כז נחמיה הפחה ועזרא הכהן הסופר: ובחנכת חומת ירושלם בקשו י
את־הלוים מכל־מקומתם להביאם לירושלם לעשת חנכה ושמחה ובתודות
כח ובשיר מצלתים נבלים ובכנרות: ויאספו בני המשררים ומן־הככר סביבות
כט ירושלם ומן־חצרי נטפתי: ומבית הגלגל ומשדות גבע ועזמות כי חצרים בנו
ל להם המשררים סביבות ירושלם: ויטהרו הכהנים והלוים ויטהרו את־העם
לא ואת־השערים ואת־החומה: ואעלה את־שרי יהודה מעל לחומה ואעמידה
לב שתי תודת גדולת ותהלכת לימין מעל לחומה לשער האשפת: וילך אחריהם
לג לד הושעיה וחצי שרי יהודה: ועזריה עזרא ומשלם: יהודה ובנימן ושמעיה
וירמיה:

BACKGROUND

12:28 | **The plain [*kikkar*] surrounding Jerusalem:** *Kikkar* is a geographical term that denotes a low area surrounded by hills. It seems that this particular *kikkar* is the basin in which Jerusalem is located, as it is stated: "Jerusalem, mountains surround it" (Psalms 125:2). This region surrounding Jerusalem apparently served as the agricultural area from which the city received its food (Hugh Godfrey Maturin Williamson, "Ezra, Nehemiah," *World Biblical Commentary* 16. Waco, Texas: Word Books, 1985, 198, 208; Yitzhak Meitlis, "On the Term: 'Surrounding Jerusalem,' at the end of the First Temple Period," *Morashtenu* 9, 1995, [Hebrew], 151–155; see II Kings 23:5; Jeremiah 17:26, 32:44).

The villages of [*ḥatzrei*] the Netofatites: A *ḥatzer* is a type of settlement. It has two basic meanings: a settlement characteristic of nomads, comprised of a cluster of scattered houses; or a single farmhouse in the agricultural area surrounding an urban center.

Netofa has been identified either with Umm Tuba, south of Jerusalem, or with Khirbet Bedd Faluh, roughly 1 km west of Herodion and north of present-day Tekoa. A nearby spring is called Ein e-Natuf.

12:29 | **Beit Gilgal:** From its place in the list it can be inferred that Beit Gilgal was a town in the region of Benjamin, east or north of Jerusalem. Some claim that it is the well-known Gilgal near Jericho, which is featured in the book of Joshua (e.g., Joshua 4:19), and whose precise location is unknown, while others identify it with Khirbet Jiljal, near the village of Rammun, northeast of Jerusalem.

The fields of Geva: This is probably Geva of Benjamin (see, e.g., I Kings 15:22), identified with Jaba, an Arab town north of Adam Junction. The phrase "fields of" preceding the name of a city is a geographical term that refers to the agricultural terrain surrounding a city, and which provides it with its sustenance.

35 **and some of the sons of the priests** who were blowing **with**
trumpets: Zekharya, son of Yonatan, son of Shemaya, son of
Matanya, son of Mikhaya, son of Zakur, son of Asaf,
36 **and his brethren, Shemaya, Azarel, Milalai, Gilalai, Maai,**
Netanel, Yehuda, and **Hanani, with the musical instruments,**
or songs,[130] **of David, the man of God; Ezra the scribe was**
marching **before them.**
37 **They were** continuing to march **at the Gate of the Spring, and**
opposite them, there were those, other people, **who ascended**
the stairs of the City of David, at the stairs to the wall, above
the house of David, up to the Water Gate on the east.
38 **The second thanks offering proceeded opposite it,** the first
company, **with me,** Nehemiah, walking **after it, and half the**
people next to the wall,[131] **from above the Tower of the Ovens**
to the Broad Wall,
39 **and above the Ephraim**
Gate, and near the Old
Gate, the gate of the old wall,
and near the Fish Gate, and
the Tower of Hananel, and
the Tower of the Hundred,
until the Sheep Gate; they
stopped, the procession with
the thanks offering loaves
halted, **at the Gate of the**
Internment.[B]

"Gate of the Internment"

40 **The two thanks offerings stopped at the House of God, with**
me and half of the senior **prefects who were with me.**
41 **The priests, Elyakim, Maas-**
eya, Minyamin, Mikhaya,
Elio'enai, Zekharya, and
Hananya, were blowing **on**
the trumpets
42 **with Maaseya, Shemaya,**
Elazar, Uzi, Yehohanan,
Malkiya, Eilam, and Ezer.
The singers sang the song
aloud, and Yizrahya was
acting as **the officer** over
them.

Trumpets of the Temple, illustration based on coin, period of bar Kokheva rebellion

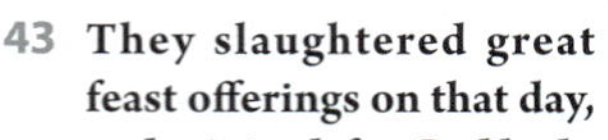

43 **They slaughtered great**
feast offerings on that day,
and rejoiced, for God had caused them to rejoice with great
joy, as Jerusalem was rebuilt and finally surrounded by a wall;
also the women and the children rejoiced, and the joy of
Jerusalem was heard from afar.
44 **On that day, men were appointed** to their various tasks **over**
the chambers for the treasures, for the gifts, for the first
fruits, and for the tithes, to collect in them, from the fields
of the cities, portions according to the Torah for the priests
and Levites; for the joy of Judah was upon the priests and
for the Levites who were present.
45 **They observed the charge** of the service **of their God, and the**

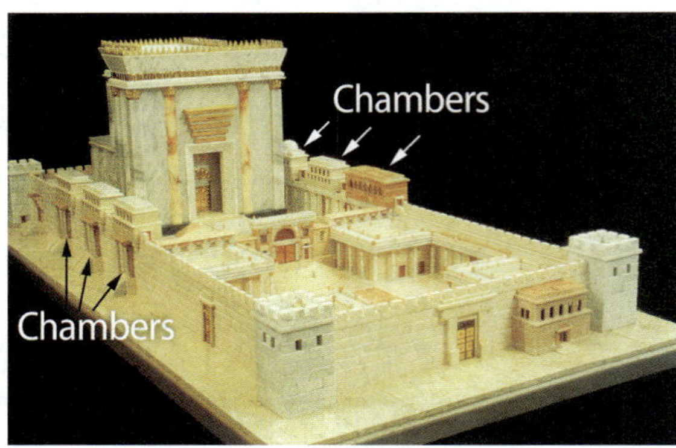

Temple chambers

charge of the purity, to ensure that consecrated items did not
become ritually impure, **the singers and the gatekeepers** began
fulfilling their duties, **in accordance with the command of**
David and Solomon his son.
46 **For it was from the days of David and Asaf of old, the heads**
of the singers, and songs of
praise and the thanksgiv-
ing to God. The practices of
the singing had already been
established in King David's
time, and now the ancient
customs were fully restored.
47 **All Israel in the days of**
Zerubavel and in the days
of Nehemiah would give
the portions of the singers
and the gatekeepers, each day's matter on its day; they con-
secrated them **for the Levites, and the Levites consecrated**
the tithe from their tithe **for the sons of Aaron.**

King David playing a harp, ancient synagogue of Gaza, 508 CE

לה וּמִבְּנֵי הַכֹּהֲנִים בַּחֲצֹצְרוֹת זְכַרְיָה בֶן־יוֹנָתָן בֶּן־שְׁמַעְיָה בֶּן־מַתַּנְיָה בֶּן־מִיכָיָה
לו בֶּן־זַכּוּר בֶּן־אָסָף׃ וְאֶחָיו שְׁמַעְיָה וַעֲזַרְאֵל מִלְלַי גִּלְלַי מָעַי נְתַנְאֵל וִיהוּדָה
לז חֲנָנִי בִּכְלֵי־שִׁיר דָּוִיד אִישׁ הָאֱלֹהִים וְעֶזְרָא הַסּוֹפֵר לִפְנֵיהֶם׃ וְעַל שַׁעַר הָעַיִן
וְנֶגְדָּם עָלוּ עַל־מַעֲלוֹת עִיר דָּוִיד בַּמַּעֲלֶה לַחוֹמָה מֵעַל לְבֵית דָּוִיד וְעַד שַׁעַר
לח הַמַּיִם מִזְרָח׃ וְהַתּוֹדָה הַשֵּׁנִית הַהוֹלֶכֶת לְמוֹאל וַאֲנִי אַחֲרֶיהָ וַחֲצִי הָעָם מֵעַל
לט לְהַחוֹמָה מֵעַל לְמִגְדַּל הַתַּנּוּרִים וְעַד הַחוֹמָה הָרְחָבָה׃ וּמֵעַל לְשַׁעַר־אֶפְרַיִם
וְעַל־שַׁעַר הַיְשָׁנָה וְעַל־שַׁעַר הַדָּגִים וּמִגְדַּל חֲנַנְאֵל וּמִגְדַּל הַמֵּאָה וְעַד שַׁעַר
מ הַצֹּאן וְעָמְדוּ בְּשַׁעַר הַמַּטָּרָה׃ וַתַּעֲמֹדְנָה שְׁתֵּי הַתּוֹדֹת בְּבֵית הָאֱלֹהִים וַאֲנִי
מא וַחֲצִי הַסְּגָנִים עִמִּי׃ וְהַכֹּהֲנִים אֶלְיָקִים מַעֲשֵׂיָה מִנְיָמִין מִיכָיָה אֶלְיוֹעֵינַי זְכַרְיָה
מב חֲנַנְיָה בַּחֲצֹצְרוֹת׃ וּמַעֲשֵׂיָה וּשְׁמַעְיָה וְאֶלְעָזָר וְעֻזִּי וִיהוֹחָנָן וּמַלְכִּיָּה וְעֵילָם וָעָזֶר
מג וַיַּשְׁמִיעוּ הַמְשֹׁרְרִים וְיִזְרַחְיָה הַפָּקִיד׃ וַיִּזְבְּחוּ בַיּוֹם הַהוּא זְבָחִים גְּדוֹלִים וַיִּשְׂמָחוּ
כִּי הָאֱלֹהִים שִׂמְּחָם שִׂמְחָה גְדוֹלָה וְגַם הַנָּשִׁים וְהַיְלָדִים שָׂמֵחוּ וַתִּשָּׁמַע שִׂמְחַת
מד יְרוּשָׁלִַם מֵרָחוֹק׃ וַיִּפָּקְדוּ בַיּוֹם הַהוּא אֲנָשִׁים עַל־הַנְּשָׁכוֹת לָאוֹצָרוֹת לַתְּרוּמוֹת
לָרֵאשִׁית וְלַמַּעַשְׂרוֹת לִכְנוֹס בָּהֶם לִשְׂדֵי הֶעָרִים מְנָאוֹת הַתּוֹרָה לַכֹּהֲנִים
מה וְלַלְוִיִּם כִּי שִׂמְחַת יְהוּדָה עַל־הַכֹּהֲנִים וְעַל־הַלְוִיִּם הָעֹמְדִים׃ וַיִּשְׁמְרוּ מִשְׁמֶרֶת
אֱלֹהֵיהֶם וּמִשְׁמֶרֶת הַטָּהֳרָה וְהַמְשֹׁרְרִים וְהַשֹּׁעֲרִים כְּמִצְוַת דָּוִיד שְׁלֹמֹה בְנוֹ׃
מו כִּי־בִימֵי דָוִיד וְאָסָף מִקֶּדֶם רָאשׁ הַמְשֹׁרְרִים וְשִׁיר־תְּהִלָּה וְהֹדוֹת לֵאלֹהִים׃
מז וְכָל־יִשְׂרָאֵל בִּימֵי זְרֻבָּבֶל וּבִימֵי נְחֶמְיָה נֹתְנִים מְנָיוֹת הַמְשֹׁרְרִים וְהַשֹּׁעֲרִים
דְּבַר־יוֹם בְּיוֹמוֹ וּמַקְדִּשִׁים לַלְוִיִּם וְהַלְוִיִּם מַקְדִּשִׁים לִבְנֵי אַהֲרֹן׃

BACKGROUND

12:39 | **The Gate of the Internment [*ham-matara*]:** Some explain that this name is derived from the Aramaic root *nun-tet-reish*, meaning guarding (see Jeremiah 3:5; Nahum 1:2). It seems that this was the gate for the site known as the Court of Internment which was near the king's house. This is the equivalent expression to the "place of custody" (see Genesis 42:19), which means a detention center (see Jeremiah 32:2, and commentary ad loc.; Jeremiah 33:1, 38:6, 28). Others claim that this was the eastern gate, located in the city walls, or the southern gate of the Temple.

Nehemiah's Enactments for the Observance of the Commandments

NEHEMIAH 13:1–31

Nehemiah was a man of action but also one who was very scrupulous about the observance of the Torah's commandments. Not only did he preach about their importance, and arrange public gatherings to speak about these issues, as did Ezra the scribe, the spiritual leader of the generation, he also used all the means at his disposal to ensure their fulfillment. Although his power was limited, nevertheless, since the people essentially supported him, his efforts met with success.

Nehemiah concludes his book with a description of the deeds he performed to strengthen the House of God and the observance of the commandments.

13 1 **On that day,** on one of those days,[132] **they read in,** from, **the scroll of Moses**[D] **in the ears of the people, and it was found written in it that an Amonite and a Moavite may not enter into the assembly of God forever,**[133]

2 **because they,** the Amonites and Moavites, **did not greet the children of Israel** on their path through the wilderness **with bread and with water, and** instead Moav **hired Bilam**[B] **against them,** Israel, **to curse them, and our God transformed the curse into a blessing.**

Bilam son of Be'or Inscription, Deir Alla, Gilad, near Sukkot, eighth century BCE

3 **It was when they heard** this section read from **the Torah** that **they separated from Israel all the intermingled,** all the foreigners from the nations of Amon and Moav.

4 **Before this, Elyashiv the priest had been appointed over the chambers of the House of our God; he was close with Toviya** the Amonite, an enemy of Judah,[134]

5 **and** Elyashiv had **made for him,** Toviya, **a great chamber** on the Temple Mount, **where earlier they would place the meal offerings, the frankincense,**[B] white pellets extracted from the resin of the frankincense tree, which is used for meal offerings, the showbread, and the incense,[135] **and the vessels, and the tithe of the grain, the wine, and the oil, that which was the commandment for the Levites,** they were the Levites' rightful dues, **and the singers, and the gatekeepers, and the gifts for the priests.**

Pellets of frankincense resin

Vessel for cleaning the lamps of the candelabrum

6 **During all this** time, while all this was happening, **I had not been in Jerusalem, as in the thirty-second year of Artahshasta king of Babylon,** who was actually the king of Persia, but was also called the king of Babylon,[136] **I came to the king** to fulfill my duties after spending twelve years in Jerusalem (see 2:1, 6, 5:14), **and at the conclusion of a** certain period of **time,** perhaps a year,[137] **I requested from the king** to return to Jerusalem;

Tomb of Artahshasta II, among the graves of the kings of Persia, Persepolis, 465 BCE

7 **and I came to Jerusalem, and I understood,** observed, **the evil that Elyashiv had performed for Toviya,** our enemy, **to prepare a chamber for him in the courtyards of the House of God.**

8 **I was greatly displeased, and I cast all the vessels of Toviya's household out of the chamber.** Nehemiah did not sit back and wait for events to unfold. When he saw that this man had illicitly appropriated for himself a chamber in the House of God, he threw out all of his belongings.

9 **I said,** issued a command, **and they purified the chambers, and I returned to there the vessels of the House of God, the meal offerings, and the frankincense.**

10 Another act of Nehemiah: **I knew that the portions of the Levites had not been given.** The tithes that used to be brought to that chamber for the Levites had ceased to arrive, **and each of the Levites and the singers, the craftsmen, had fled to his field.** Those who were supposed to serve in the Temple had left because no one was providing them with sustenance. Instead, they had returned to work their fields for their livelihoods.[138]

11 **I quarreled with the prefects, and said: Why is the House of God forsaken? I gathered them,** the Levites, together once again, **and set them in their** former **place.**

12 **All Judah** again **brought the tithe of the grain and the wine and the oil to the treasuries.**

א בַּיּ֣וֹם הַה֗וּא נִקְרָ֛א בְּסֵ֥פֶר מֹשֶׁ֖ה בְּאׇזְנֵ֣י הָעָ֑ם וְנִמְצָ֤א כָּתוּב֙ בּ֔וֹ אֲשֶׁ֨ר לֹא־יָב֜וֹא
ב עַמֹּנִ֧י וּמֹאָבִ֛י בִּקְהַ֥ל הָאֱלֹהִ֖ים עַד־עוֹלָֽם׃ כִּ֣י לֹ֤א קִדְּמוּ֙ אֶת־בְּנֵ֣י יִשְׂרָאֵ֔ל בַּלֶּ֖חֶם
ג וּבַמָּ֑יִם וַיִּשְׂכֹּ֨ר עָלָ֤יו אֶת־בִּלְעָם֙ לְקַֽלְל֔וֹ וַיַּהֲפֹ֧ךְ אֱלֹהֵ֛ינוּ הַקְּלָלָ֖ה לִבְרָכָֽה׃ וַיְהִ֖י
ד כְּשׇׁמְעָ֣ם אֶת־הַתּוֹרָ֑ה וַיַּבְדִּ֥ילוּ כׇל־עֵ֖רֶב מִיִּשְׂרָאֵֽל׃ וְלִפְנֵ֣י מִזֶּ֔ה אֶלְיָשִׁיב֙ הַכֹּהֵ֔ן
ה נָת֖וּן בְּלִשְׁכַּ֣ת בֵּית־אֱלֹהֵ֑ינוּ קָר֖וֹב לְטוֹבִיָּֽה׃ וַיַּ֣עַשׂ ל֡וֹ לִשְׁכָּ֣ה גְדוֹלָ֡ה וְשָׁ֣ם הָיוּ֩
לְפָנִ֨ים נֹתְנִ֜ים אֶת־הַמִּנְחָ֗ה הַלְּבוֹנָה֮ וְהַכֵּלִים֒ וּמַעְשַׂ֨ר הַדָּגָ֜ן הַתִּיר֣וֹשׁ וְהַיִּצְהָ֗ר מִצְוַת֙
ו הַלְוִיִּ֔ם וְהַמְשֹׁרְרִ֖ים וְהַשֹּׁעֲרִ֑ים וּתְרוּמַ֖ת הַכֹּהֲנִֽים׃ וּבְכׇל־זֶ֕ה לֹ֥א הָיִ֖יתִי בִּירוּשָׁלָ֑͏ִם
כִּי֩ בִּשְׁנַ֨ת שְׁלֹשִׁ֤ים וּשְׁתַּ֙יִם֙ לְאַרְתַּחְשַׁ֣סְתְּא מֶֽלֶךְ־בָּבֶל֙ בָּ֣אתִי אֶל־הַמֶּ֔לֶךְ וּלְקֵ֥ץ
ז יָמִ֖ים נִשְׁאַ֥לְתִּי מִן־הַמֶּֽלֶךְ׃ וָאָב֖וֹא לִירוּשָׁלָ֑͏ִם וָאָבִ֣ינָה בָֽרָעָ֗ה אֲשֶׁ֨ר עָשָׂ֤ה אֶלְיָשִׁיב֙
ח לְטֽוֹבִיָּ֔ה לַעֲשׂ֥וֹת לוֹ֙ נִשְׁכָּ֔ה בְּחַצְרֵ֖י בֵּ֥ית הָאֱלֹהִֽים׃ וַיֵּ֥רַע לִ֖י מְאֹ֑ד וָֽאַשְׁלִ֜יכָה אֶת־
ט כׇּל־כְּלֵ֧י בֵית־טוֹבִיָּ֛ה הַח֖וּץ מִן־הַלִּשְׁכָּֽה׃ וָאֹ֣מְרָ֔ה וַֽיְטַהֲר֖וּ הַלְּשָׁכ֑וֹת וָאָשִׁ֣יבָה שָּׁ֗ם
י כְּלֵי֙ בֵּ֣ית הָאֱלֹהִ֔ים אֶת־הַמִּנְחָ֖ה וְהַלְּבוֹנָֽה׃ וָאֵ֣דְעָ֔ה כִּֽי־מְנָי֥וֹת הַלְוִיִּ֖ם לֹ֣א נִתָּ֑נָה
יא וַיִּבְרְח֧וּ אִישׁ־לְשָׂדֵ֛הוּ הַלְוִיִּ֥ם וְהַמְשֹׁרְרִ֖ים עֹשֵׂ֥י הַמְּלָאכָֽה׃ וָאָרִ֙יבָה֙ אֶת־הַסְּגָנִ֔ים
יב וָֽאֹמְרָ֔ה מַדּ֖וּעַ נֶעֱזַ֣ב בֵּית־הָאֱלֹהִ֑ים וָֽאֶקְבְּצֵ֔ם וָאַעֲמִדֵ֖ם עַל־עׇמְדָֽם׃ וְכׇל־יְהוּדָ֗ה

— DISCUSSION —

13:1 | **They read in the scroll of Moses:** This is referring to the Torah as a whole (see II Kings 14:6), or specifically to the book of Deuteronomy, which begins with the sentence: "These are the words that Moses spoke to all Israel" (Deuteronomy 1:1).

BACKGROUND

13:2 | **Bilam:** Bilam's name has been found in in the Deir Alla Inscription which was discovered in an archaeological excavation in 1967 in Deir Alla, Jordan. The inscription has been dated to 880–770 BCE, and it makes reference to "[Bi]lam [son of Be]or, the man who was a seer of the gods," indicating that Bilam was famous throughout the entire region. The inscription, whose meaning remains obscure to this day, apparently contains one of his prophecies or curses and was painted in ink on a plastered wall. Translated into English, it states: "The sayings of [Bi]lam [son of Be]or, the man who was a seer of the gods. Lo! [Gods came to him in the night] and spoke to him according to these words. Then they said to [Bila]m son of Beor, thus: Let someone make a [ ] hereafter, so that [what] you have hea[rd may be se]en!...And he said to them, Si[t do]wn!...Now come, see the deeds of the g[o]ds!" (See image).

13:5 | **Frankincense [*levona*]:** Frankincense is a fragrant whitish-yellow resin produced from the frankincense or olibanum tree, *Boswellia sacra*, from the Burseraceae family. The Hebrew term *levona* is attributed to its whitish [*levana*] color. These trees grow in the regions of Somalia, Ethiopia, and the southern Arabian Peninsula. The resin is extracted by means of an incision in the tree's bark, from which the sap drips and is collected into a vessel. The liquid sap then slowly coagulates into pellets.

13 **I appointed treasurers over the treasuries; Shelemya the priest, and Tzadok the scribe, and Pedaya from the Levites, next to them,** to assist them, **was Hanan, son of Zakur, son of Matanya, as they were considered faithful, and it was incumbent upon them to distribute** the tithe **to their brethren.**

14 **Remember me, my God, for this, and do not expunge my kindnesses that I performed in the House of my God, and in its watches,** by restoring the orders and watches to their proper places.

15 **In those days I saw in Judah some** people **treading winepresses on the Sabbath, and transporting heaps** of produce, **and loading on donkeys, as well as wine, grapes, and figs, and all burdens, and bringing them to Jerusalem on the Sabbath day; I warned them on the day that they sold provisions.**

Treading grapes

Loaded donkey

16 **Tyrians,** merchants from the maritime city of Tyre, **were residing in it,** the city and the surrounding area, **bringing fish and all merchandise, and selling** them **on the Sabbath to the children of Judah, and in Jerusalem.**

17 **I quarreled with the nobles of Judah, and said to them: What is this evil matter that you are doing, and desecrating the Sabbath day?**

18 **Didn't your fathers do so, and our God brought all this evil upon us and upon this city** because of such actions? **Yet you exacerbate wrath upon Israel by desecrating the Sabbath.**

19 **It was when the gates of Jerusalem began to be shadowed before the Sabbath,** when the sun was setting on Friday, **I said,** issued an order, **and the doors were shut, and I said that they should not open them until after the Sabbath,** so that no one should enter the city on the holy day; **I positioned some of my lads,** the military personnel at my disposal, **at the gates,** to ensure **that no burden should come on the Sabbath day.**

20 **The peddlers and merchants of all merchandise stayed the night outside Jerusalem** on Friday night, in order to sell to the residents of the city who would come out of the city early in the morning of the Sabbath. They did this **once or twice.**

21 **I warned them and said to them: Why are you staying the night opposite the wall? If you do so again, I will send against you** and harm you. Thus, **from that time, they did not come on the Sabbath.**

22 Also with regard to the Sabbath, **I said to,** commanded, **the Levites that they should purify themselves** beforehand, **and come guard the gates,** in order **to sanctify the Sabbath day.** Nehemiah instructed them to ritually purify themselves in honor of the Sabbath when they came to guard at the Temple gates.[139] **Remember this also for me,** to my merit, **my God,** that I enhanced the sanctity of the Sabbath, **and have mercy on me, in accordance with Your abounding mercy.**

23 **Also in those days I saw that the Judeans had married Ashdodite, Amonite, and Moavite women;** they had taken for themselves foreign wives who were forbidden to them;

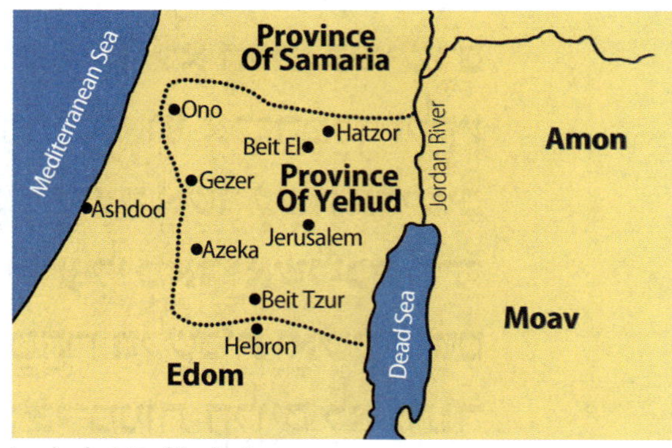

Lands of origin of the foreign women

24 **and half their children** of mixed heritage **spoke Ashdodite,** like the residents of Ashdod, **and did not know to speak** the **Judean** language, even though they were children of Judeans, **but** rather, being the offspring of mothers from the various nations, they would speak **each and every people according to its language.**

25 **I quarreled with them, and cursed them, and I struck some men from among them, and pulled out their hair.** Nehemiah responded very differently from Ezra, who wept when faced with a similar situation.[140] By contrast, Nehemiah acted in a most decisive, forceful manner. **And I administered an oath to them by God: You shall not give your** Judean **daughters to their sons** of the foreign nations, **and you shall not marry their daughters to your sons, or to yourselves.**

26 **Wasn't it over these,** the foreign women whom he married, **that Solomon king of Israel sinned? Among the many nations there was no king** wise and influential[141] **like him, and he was beloved to his God, and God set him king over all Israel; even him, the foreign women caused to sin.**

27 **Shall it be heard of you, performing all this great evil?** Do you wish to repeat that same mistake, **to trespass against our God to marry foreign women?**

יג הֵבִיאוּ מַעְשַׂר הַדָּגָן וְהַתִּירוֹשׁ וְהַיִּצְהָר לָאוֹצָרוֹת׃ וָאוֹצְרָה עַל־אוֹצָרוֹת שֶׁלֶמְיָה
הַכֹּהֵן וְצָדוֹק הַסּוֹפֵר וּפְדָיָה מִן־הַלְוִיִּם וְעַל־יָדָם חָנָן בֶּן־זַכּוּר בֶּן־מַתַּנְיָה כִּי
יד נֶאֱמָנִים נֶחְשָׁבוּ וַעֲלֵיהֶם לַחֲלֹק לַאֲחֵיהֶם׃ זָכְרָה־לִּי אֱלֹהַי עַל־זֹאת
טו וְאַל־תֶּמַח חֲסָדַי אֲשֶׁר עָשִׂיתִי בְּבֵית אֱלֹהַי וּבְמִשְׁמָרָיו׃ בַּיָּמִים הָהֵמָּה רָאִיתִי
בִיהוּדָה ׀ דֹרְכִים־גִּתּוֹת ׀ בַּשַּׁבָּת וּמְבִיאִים הָעֲרֵמוֹת וְעֹמְסִים עַל־הַחֲמֹרִים וְאַף־
יַיִן עֲנָבִים וּתְאֵנִים וְכָל־מַשָּׂא וּמְבִיאִים יְרוּשָׁלִַם בְּיוֹם הַשַּׁבָּת וָאָעִיד בְּיוֹם מִכְרָם
טז צָיִד׃ וְהַצֹּרִים יָשְׁבוּ בָהּ מְבִיאִים דָּאג וְכָל־מֶכֶר וּמוֹכְרִים בַּשַּׁבָּת לִבְנֵי יְהוּדָה
יז וּבִירוּשָׁלִָם׃ וָאָרִיבָה אֵת חֹרֵי יְהוּדָה וָאֹמְרָה לָהֶם מָה־הַדָּבָר הָרָע הַזֶּה אֲשֶׁר
יח אַתֶּם עֹשִׂים וּמְחַלְּלִים אֶת־יוֹם הַשַּׁבָּת׃ הֲלוֹא כֹה עָשׂוּ אֲבֹתֵיכֶם וַיָּבֵא אֱלֹהֵינוּ
עָלֵינוּ אֵת כָּל־הָרָעָה הַזֹּאת וְעַל הָעִיר הַזֹּאת וְאַתֶּם מוֹסִיפִים חָרוֹן עַל־יִשְׂרָאֵל
יט לְחַלֵּל אֶת־הַשַּׁבָּת׃ וַיְהִי כַּאֲשֶׁר צָלֲלוּ שַׁעֲרֵי יְרוּשָׁלִַם לִפְנֵי הַשַּׁבָּת
וָאֹמְרָה וַיִּסָּגְרוּ הַדְּלָתוֹת וָאֹמְרָה אֲשֶׁר לֹא יִפְתָּחוּם עַד אַחַר הַשַּׁבָּת וּמִנְּעָרַי
כ הֶעֱמַדְתִּי עַל־הַשְּׁעָרִים לֹא־יָבוֹא מַשָּׂא בְּיוֹם הַשַּׁבָּת׃ וַיָּלִינוּ הָרֹכְלִים וּמֹכְרֵי כָל־
כא מִמְכָּר מִחוּץ לִירוּשָׁלִָם פַּעַם וּשְׁתָּיִם׃ וָאָעִידָה בָהֶם וָאֹמְרָה אֲלֵיהֶם מַדּוּעַ אַתֶּם
לֵנִים נֶגֶד הַחוֹמָה אִם־תִּשְׁנוּ יָד אֶשְׁלַח בָּכֶם מִן־הָעֵת הַהִיא לֹא בָאוּ בַּשַּׁבָּת׃
כב וָאֹמְרָה לַלְוִיִּם אֲשֶׁר יִהְיוּ מִטַּהֲרִים וּבָאִים שֹׁמְרִים הַשְּׁעָרִים לְקַדֵּשׁ אֶת־יוֹם
כג הַשַּׁבָּת גַּם־זֹאת זָכְרָה־לִּי אֱלֹהַי וְחוּסָה עָלַי כְּרֹב חַסְדֶּךָ׃ גַּם ׀ בַּיָּמִים
כד הָהֵם רָאִיתִי אֶת־הַיְּהוּדִים הֹשִׁיבוּ נָשִׁים אשדודיות עמוניות מוֹאֲבִיּוֹת׃ וּבְנֵיהֶם
כה חֲצִי מְדַבֵּר אַשְׁדּוֹדִית וְאֵינָם מַכִּירִים לְדַבֵּר יְהוּדִית וְכִלְשׁוֹן עַם וָעָם׃ וָאָרִיב עִמָּם
וָאֲקַלְלֵם וָאַכֶּה מֵהֶם אֲנָשִׁים וָאֶמְרְטֵם וָאַשְׁבִּיעֵם בֵּאלֹהִים אִם־תִּתְּנוּ בְנֹתֵיכֶם
כו לִבְנֵיהֶם וְאִם־תִּשְׂאוּ מִבְּנֹתֵיהֶם לִבְנֵיכֶם וְלָכֶם׃ הֲלוֹא עַל־אֵלֶּה חָטָא־שְׁלֹמֹה
מֶלֶךְ־יִשְׂרָאֵל וּבַגּוֹיִם הָרַבִּים לֹא־הָיָה מֶלֶךְ כָּמֹהוּ וְאָהוּב לֵאלֹהָיו הָיָה וַיִּתְּנֵהוּ
כז אֱלֹהִים מֶלֶךְ עַל־כָּל־יִשְׂרָאֵל גַּם־אוֹתוֹ הֶחֱטִיאוּ הַנָּשִׁים הַנָּכְרִיּוֹת׃ וְלָכֶם הֲנִשְׁמַע
לַעֲשֹׂת אֵת כָּל־הָרָעָה הַגְּדוֹלָה הַזֹּאת לִמְעֹל בֵּאלֹהֵינוּ לְהֹשִׁיב נָשִׁים נָכְרִיּוֹת׃

אַשְׁדֳּדִיּוֹת | עַמֳּנִיּוֹת

28 **From the sons of Yoyada, son of Elyashiv the High Priest, there was a son-in-law of Sanbalat the Horonite.** The leaders of the Samaritans married into the best families of Judah (see 6:18). **And I drove him away from me;** I banished him from my presence. Apparently, the descendants of this High Priest ultimately became priests for the Samaritans.

29 **Remember it for them, my God, their defiling of the priesthood, and** how they profaned **the covenant of the priesthood and of the Levites.**

30 **I purified them,** the Judeans, **from everything foreign, and appointed watches for the priests and for the Levites, each at his task.**

31 **And for the wood offering,** I took pains that it should come **at appointed times,** on fixed dates, **and** did likewise **for the first fruits. Remember me, my God, favorably.** Nehemiah concludes his book with a description of all the deeds he performed to restore the proper functioning of the House of God and to reinforce the people's observance of the commandments of the Torah. Unusually for a great leader, he explicitly asks God to remember his merits. As Nehemiah was one of those who molded the way of life in the Kingdom of Judah for future generations, he is worthy of being remembered for the good.

כח וּמִבְּנֵ֨י יֽוֹיָדָ֜ע בֶּן־אֶלְיָשִׁיב֙ הַכֹּהֵ֣ן הַגָּד֔וֹל חָתָ֖ן לְסַנְבַלַּ֣ט הַחֹרֹנִ֑י וָאַבְרִיחֵ֖הוּ מֵעָלָֽי׃
כט ל זָכְרָ֥ה לָהֶ֖ם אֱלֹהָ֑י עַ֚ל־גָּאֳלֵ֣י הַכְּהֻנָּ֔ה וּבְרִ֥ית הַכְּהֻנָּ֖ה וְהַלְוִיִּֽם׃ וְטִהַרְתִּ֖ים מִכׇּל־נֵכָ֑ר
לא וָאַעֲמִ֤ידָה מִשְׁמָרוֹת֙ לַכֹּהֲנִ֣ים וְלַלְוִיִּ֔ם אִ֖ישׁ בִּמְלַאכְתּֽוֹ׃ וּלְקֻרְבַּ֨ן הָעֵצִ֜ים בְּעִתִּ֧ים
מְזֻמָּנ֛וֹת וְלַבִּכּוּרִ֖ים זָכְרָה־לִּ֥י אֱלֹהַ֖י לְטוֹבָֽה׃

Chronicles

I Chronicles

II Chronicles

Chronicles

INTRODUCTION TO CHRONICLES

The book of Chronicles focuses mainly on the history of the Kingdom of Judah, beginning its recounting from Adam, until the destruction of the First Temple and the Babylonian exile. Much of Chronicles parallels the narrative in the book of Samuel and the book of Kings, but its focus is often different. Chronicles is less devoted to political matters and wars, and instead relates a great deal about the king and his court's relationship with the Sanctuary.[1]

Unlike other historical books in the Bible, Chronicles is not part of the biblical section called Prophets but rather is part of the section known as Writings, and accordingly it has a lower level of sanctity.[2] From the language, the mention of Cyrus at the end of the book, and the mention of Zerubavel's descendants in one of the genealogies,[3] it appears to have been composed sometime after the Persian conquest of Babylon, after the Judeans had been given permission to return to the Land of Israel and rebuild the Temple.

The book of Chronicles contains more genealogical lists than all the other books of the Bible combined. Some of these lists are nearly complete, but frequently only a partial genealogy is reported, with the less prominent members of a line of descent being skipped over.[4] At other times, the genealogies appear to be fragmentary remnants of earlier lists, or histories that were only partially preserved.[5] Much of the detail of these parts of Chronicles is not fully comprehensible, as we lack a great deal of background information, and the Sages in fact point out that a lot of supplemental material and interpretive traditions relevant to Chronicles have been irretrievably lost.[6] Because of the nature of these genealogical lists, and the difficulty in understanding their significance, the Sages often read these parts of the book homiletically, admitting that parts of the book remain enigmatic.[7] Most of the time, the details related in Chronicles match those in the books of the Bible that offer parallel accounts of the same events. When they occasionally differ, there is no general principle that explains the differences, and each case requires a careful investigation to resolve them.[8]

The division of Chronicles into two books, like the division of the books of Samuel and Kings, is based on a Christian tradition, whose source is perhaps the Septuagint. It is preserved here only for the purpose of the chapter divisions.

I Chronicles

A List of the Generations of Humanity until the Birth of the Nation of Israel

I CHRONICLES 1:1–54

The book begins with an abbreviated genealogical list of humanity in general, a list with a specific direction. It begins with Adam, the first man, and the generations of his offspring until Noah, and continues with the generations of Noah's offspring, until the birth of the fathers of the Israelite nation. Lists of the other nations that descended from Abraham are then presented, albeit in the form of brief, tangential lists. These lists, which are also scattered throughout the book of Genesis, are not the central focus of the book of Chronicles, which deals primarily with the tribe of Judah and the Davidic dynasty.

1 1 The book opens with a simple list of fathers and sons, starting
with Adam. It presents them without noting that each man fathered the person listed next: **Adam, Seth, Enosh,**
2 **Kenan, Mahalalel, Yered,**
3 **Hanokh, Methuselah, Lemekh.** This is one specific line of the
descendants of Adam, the first man, which, for example, does
not include Cain and his sons, as that branch of the family did
not survive.[9]
4 **Noah,** and his sons: **Shem, Ham, and Yefet.** The text does not
explicitly state that all three were Noah's sons, as it is presumably common knowledge.
5 The chapter specifies some of the nations and kingdoms that
descended from Noah's sons and spread throughout the world:
The sons of Yefet: Gomer,[B] Magog,[B] Madai, Yavan, Tuval,
Meshekh,[B] and Tiras.[B]
6 **The sons of Gomer: Ashkenaz,[B] Difat,[B]** called Rifat in the
book of Genesis,[10] **and Togarma.[B]**
7 **The sons of Yavan: Elisha,[B]**
possibly related to the former name for Greece, Hellas;
and **Tarshish,[B] Kitim,[B] and**
Rodanim,[B] called Dodanim
in Genesis (10:4). This completes the genealogical list of
the children of Yefet, perhaps
Noah's eldest son.[11]
8 **The sons of Ham: Kush,**
Mitzrayim, Put,[B] and
Canaan.
9 **The sons of Kush: Seva,[B]**
Havila,[B] Savta, Raama,
and Savtekha.[B] The sons of
Raama:[B] Sheva and Dedan.[B]

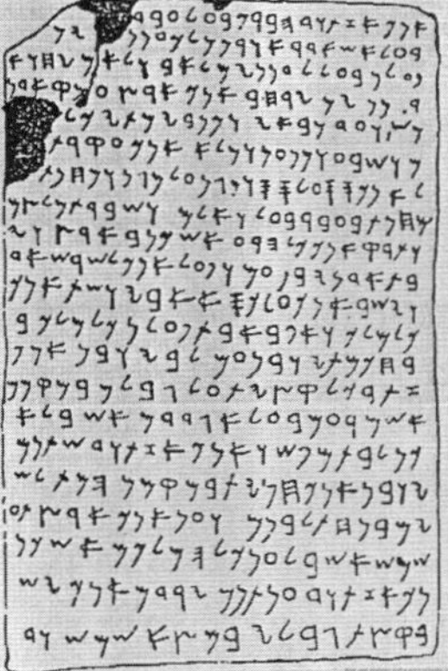

Text with Phoenician alphabet

BACKGROUND

1:5 | **Gomer:** Gomer is mentioned elsewhere as a nation that lives in the uttermost parts of the North (Ezekiel 38:6). The Sages identify Gomer with Germamiya of Rome, the Germanic tribes (*Yoma* 10a). Assyrian documents from the eighth century BCE mention the land of Gamir, near the kingdom of Urartu in the vicinity of Lake Van in the Ararat Mountains, which is in modern-day Armenia. According to the historian Herodotus, from the fifth century BCE, this nation was the Cimmerian people who settled in the Crimean Peninsula; Josephus, on the other hand, identifies them as the Galatians who lived in central Asia Minor.

Magog: In the book of Ezekiel (39:6), Magog is mentioned alongside the inhabitants of the Greek islands: "I will send fire against Magog and against the inhabitants of the islands in security." In *Yoma* (10a), Magog is identified as Kandiya, which is Crete, while in the Jerusalem Talmud (*Megilla* 1:9), it is identified as Gutia, one of the Germanic tribes. Josephus claimed that Magog is a reference to the Scythians, a nomadic nation that dwelled north of the Black Sea.

Tuval, Meshekh: These two people are mentioned together in several places. In the list of nations in Genesis (10:2), they appear as two of the descendants of Yefet, while in Isaiah (66:19), a place called Tuval is listed together with Yavan, commonly identified as Greece. The Sages identify Tuval as Beit Unaiki, which is the land of Bithynia, in northwest Asia Minor, along the coast of the Black Sea (*Yoma* 10a).

The name Tuval is also mentioned in Assyrian documents dating from the ninth to eighth centuries BCE as a people living in central and southern Asia Minor, and is identified by ancient historians, among them Herodotus, as the Tibareni tribe, who lived along the shores of the Black Sea.

Assyrian documents refer to a people with a name similar to Meshekh living in Asia Minor and in the Caucasus Mountains east of the Black Sea, in modern-day Abkhazia.

Tiras: Some Sages identify Tiras as Persia; others as Beit Teraiki, which is Thrace, the eastern portion of the Balkan Peninsula, northeast of Greece (*Yoma* 10a). Ancient Egyptian documents dating back to the end of the thirteenth century BCE list Teresh among the sea peoples, otherwise referred to as the Philistines.

1:6 | **Ashkenaz:** Ashkenaz is mentioned in Jeremiah (51:27) as one of the kingdoms of Ararat. The Sages (Jerusalem Talmud, *Megilla* 1:9) identify it as Asya in central Asia Minor. Some modern scholars say that the term Ashkenaz refers to the Scythians, a group of nomadic tribes

▸ *who*

דברי הימים א

א ב ג ד אָדָם שֵׁת אֱנוֹשׁ: קֵינָן מַהֲלַלְאֵל יָרֶד: חֲנוֹךְ מְתוּשֶׁלַח לָמֶךְ: נֹחַ שֵׁם חָם וָיָפֶת: א
ה ו בְּנֵי יֶפֶת גֹּמֶר וּמָגוֹג וּמָדַי וְיָוָן וְתֻבָל וּמֶשֶׁךְ וְתִירָס: וּבְנֵי גֹּמֶר אַשְׁכֲּנַז וְדִיפַת
ז ח וְתוֹגַרְמָה: וּבְנֵי יָוָן אֱלִישָׁה וְתַרְשִׁישָׁה כִּתִּים וְרוֹדָנִים: בְּנֵי חָם כּוּשׁ
ט וּמִצְרַיִם פּוּט וּכְנָעַן: וּבְנֵי כוּשׁ סְבָא וַחֲוִילָה וְסַבְתָּא וְרַעְמָא וְסַבְתְּכָא וּבְנֵי רַעְמָא

BACKGROUND

who lived on the plains north of the Black and Caspian Seas. The use of the name Ashkenaz in reference to the region of Germany dates back only to the tenth century CE.

Difat: This name appears in Genesis (10:3) as Rifat. The Sages identify it as the kingdom of Adiabene on the east bank of the Tigris River, or as the Ural Mountains (*Bereshit Rabba* 37:1; Jerusalem Talmud, *Megilla* 1:9), which were formerly called the Riphean Mountains and are mentioned in classical Greek literature (Pliny the Elder, *The Natural History* 4:27). According to the *Targum Yerushalmi*, Rifat is Parkhon, or Parkhoi, southeast of the Caspian Sea. Josephus maintains that it is Paphlagonia, in north-central Asia Minor, along the coast of the Black Sea, east of Bithynia.

Togarma: Togarma is mentioned in Ezekiel (27:14) as a country in the far north that traded in horses. It is also mentioned in Assyrian documents as a major commercial city in central Asia Minor. Some identify it as the city of Gürün, in Turkey, while in the Jerusalem Talmud it is identified as Germanica, a city and region in Commagene, which was a Roman province in Asia Minor; others say that it is Barbaria in northern Africa (*Targum*). In later periods, the Ottoman Empire was called Togarma by the Jews.

1:7| **Elisha:** Elisha is mentioned in Ezekiel (27:7) as the name of a group of islands that traded with Tyre. The Midrash (*Bereshit Rabba* 37:4) identifies Elisha as Ellas. Many scholars suggest that it is Cyprus, while Josephus claims that it refers to the Aeolian Islands, also known as the Lipari Islands, between Italy and Sicily. *Targum* translates it as Italia.

Tarshish: Tarshish has been identified as Tarsus in southeastern Asia Minor, and possibly as Tartessos, in the southwestern part of the Iberian Peninsula.

Kitim: The Kitim are mentioned among the descendants of Yefet in Genesis (10:4) and in a number of other places in the Bible (Numbers 24:24; Isaiah 23:12; Jeremiah 2:10; Ezekiel 27:6; Daniel 11:6). They appear to have been a maritime people with ties to the Sidonians and Tyrians, i.e., the Phoenicians. Several of the traditional commentaries identify the Kitim with the Macedonian Empire, and others with Rome. A similar identification is found in the Dead Sea Scrolls. Josephus suggests that they lived in the ancient port city of Kition in the district of Larnaca on the eastern coast of Cyprus (*Antiquities of the Jews* I:6:1) which, according to the archaeological evidence, was a city populated by Phoenicians.

Rodanim: The name appears in Genesis (10:4) as Dodanim. Phoenician inscriptions from the eighth century BCE refer to Orakh king of Dananim and his city Adana in southern Cilicia in Asia Minor. The Septuagint identifies Dodanim as Rhodes.

1:8| **Put:** Put has been identified as a tribe located in Libya, west of Egypt. Alternatively, it is the land of Punt, south of Egypt, which is mentioned in ancient Egyptian documents. Its military was expert in defense and they were allies of Egypt (see Jeremiah 46:9; Ezekiel 30:5; Nahum 3:9).

1:9| **Seva:** The inhabitants of Seva are mentioned in Isaiah (45:14) as men of stature who engaged in commerce, and in Psalms (72:10), as merchants. Accordingly, they have been identified as the Nubians of Kush, a nation of tall individuals, who lived in Meroe, north of Khartoum.

Havila: Havila appears as the name of a region rich in gold, surrounded by the Pishon River (Genesis 2:11); as one of the descendants of Shem (I Chronicles 1:23); and as the home of the children of Ishmael (Genesis 25:18). The Havila located in today's Sudan, home of the descendants of Ham, is apparently not the same as the Havila located in the deserts east of Egypt, where the children of Ishmael lived. Some researchers argue that Havila is not a place name at all; rather, it comes from the root *ḥet-vav-lamed*, which means "sand," and is a general term for sandy deserts.

Savta...and Savtekha: According to the *Targum*, these are peoples and tribes who lived south of Sudan. Savta refers to the Semburai, while Savtekha refers to the Lezingai, who might be members of the Zande tribe. Josephus identifies them as the Estabri, who lived along the Black Nile in Sudan. Alternatively, these are Scythian tribes, nomadic Asiatic peoples located north of the Caspian and Black Seas (*Yoma* 10a).

Raama: Raama is also mentioned in Ezekiel (27:22), together with Sheva, as a city of merchants. It has been identified as Regmah, a major city located on the trade route between Sheva and Dodan, which also appears in ancient south Arabian inscriptions. Alternative suggestions include Libya and Moritinos, whose identity is unknown (*Targum*).

Sheva and Dedan: Sheva and Dedan are listed in Genesis as sons of Kush son of Yefet (Genesis 10:7). Two of Abraham's sons by Ketura bear the

▸ same

10 **Kush begot Nimrod,** among others; **he began to be a mighty one on the earth.** Nimrod appears to have been the first powerful king whose reign extended beyond the confines of his own people. This fact merits mention, but no further details of the events of his life are recorded.
11 **Mitzrayim,** the man who eventually became the Egyptian nation, **begot Ludim,**[B] **Anamim,**[B] **Lehavim,**[B] and **Naftuhim,**[B]
12 **Patrusim,**[B] who sometimes appear in the Bible parallel to the residents of Egypt,[12] **and Kasluhim,**[B] **from which the Philistines**[B] **and Kaftorim emerged,** the residents of the island of Kaftor, modern-day Crete. Consequently, the Philistines are a mixed race, descended from the Patrusim and the Kasluhim, or a people that came from the same place as those nations.[13] Although the Philistines settled in the Land of Israel, they were undoubtedly a foreign nation that invaded from overseas.

Philistine warriors, illustration based on relief, Temple of Rameses III, Habu, Egypt, twelfth to eleventh century BCE

13 **Canaan begot Sidon his firstborn, Het,**
14 **the Yevusites, the Emorites, the Girgashites,**
15 **the Hivites, the Arkites, the Sinites,**
16 **the Arvadites, the Tzemarites, and the Hamatites.** Some of these peoples are mentioned as having lived in the land of Canaan, while others dwelled in the nearby regions.
17 **The sons of Shem: Elam, Ashur, Arpakhshad,** whom some consider the father of the Chaldeans, the Babylonians, and **Lud, Aram, Utz, Hul, Geter, and Meshekh.** It seems that there were two people named Meshekh, one among the descendants of Yefet, and the other among the descendants of Shem. In Genesis (10:23), the latter is called Mash.

Northern Canaanite nations

18 **Arpakhshad begot Shela, and Shela begot Ever.**
19 **To Ever were born two sons: The name of the one was Peleg,**
as in his days the earth was divided [*niflega*], as people began

BACKGROUND

same names (Genesis 25:3; I Chronicles 1:32). The identity of the nations descended from Sheva and Dedan the sons of Kush are unknown, but is has been suggested that they dwelled in eastern Africa near the Red Sea, since two places in that region bear similar names.

1:11 | **Ludim:** Ludim is mentioned elsewhere together with the nations of Kush and Put, who lived close to Egypt (Isaiah 66:19; Ezekiel 27:10, 30:5). The Ludim are also depicted as a mercenary people in the service of the Tyrians, the Sidonians, and the Egyptians. Historical documents mention Lod, or Lydia, as a nation on the western coast of Asia Minor. It has therefore been suggested that they were a nomadic people that originated in Egypt.

Anamim: The Anamim were a nation in the region of Alexandria, Lower Egypt (see *Targum* and Rav Se'adya Gaon).

Lehavim: This name has no parallels in the Bible or in external documents. Some have identified Lehavim as the Libyans, who lived west of Egypt (Septuagint; Josephus).

Naftuhim: This name also has no parallels in the Bible or in external documents. The Septuagint and *Targum* identify the Naftuhim as the residents of the northeastern part of the Nile delta.

1:12 | **Patrusim:** Patros in Egyptian means the southern country, Upper Egypt. The verse: "I will restore the returnees of Egypt, and I will return them to the land of Patros, to the land of their origins" (Ezekiel 29:14), indicates that Patros is the original land of the Egyptians. According to the *Targum Yerushalmi*, the Patrusim are the Pelosai, who lived in the northeastern part of the Nile delta.

Kasluhim: No parallel to this name is found in the Bible or in external documents. *Targum* calls these people Penatsakhnaei, residents of the region of Cyrenaica in Libya.

Philistines: Modern research has not reached an unequivocal conclusion with regard to the origins of the Philistines. There are different indications in the Bible itself: In the list of nations here, as well as in the *parashot* of Bereshit and Noah, they appear as descendants of Ham, from the region of Egypt; however, certain features of later stories in Genesis (chaps. 20, 21, 26) suggest that they were Semites (the name Avimelekh, their occupation with livestock, and their tilling of the land). According to the books of the Prophets, the Philistines came from Kaftor, or Crete (Amos 9:7; Jeremiah 47:4). External Egyptian sources (thirteenth to eleventh century BCE) mention "sea peoples" who invaded [*palshu*] the shores of the Mediterranean Basin, arriving from the area of the Aegean Sea. In contrast, they refer to Philistine mercenaries called "Shardana" who served in the ranks of the Egyptian army. Some archaeological findings in Philistine sites are characteristic of shepherds, but others reveal Egyptian forms of burial (anthropoid-shaped coffins) as well as Egyptian elements in their ceramics, which support the theory that they were descendants of Ham. The name "Philistines" includes various ethnic groups.

י שְׁבָא וּדְדָן׃ וְכוּשׁ יָלַד אֶת־נִמְרוֹד הוּא הֵחֵל לִהְיוֹת גִּבּוֹר בָּאָרֶץ׃
יא יב וּמִצְרַיִם יָלַד אֶת־לודיים וְאֶת־עֲנָמִים וְאֶת־לְהָבִים וְאֶת־נַפְתֻּחִים׃ וְאֶת־פַּתְרֻסִים לוּדִים
יג וְאֶת־כַּסְלֻחִים אֲשֶׁר יָצְאוּ מִשָּׁם פְּלִשְׁתִּים וְאֶת־כַּפְתֹּרִים׃ וּכְנַעַן יָלַד
יד טו אֶת־צִידוֹן בְּכֹרוֹ וְאֶת־חֵת׃ וְאֶת־הַיְבוּסִי וְאֶת־הָאֱמֹרִי וְאֵת הַגִּרְגָּשִׁי׃ וְאֶת־הַחִוִּי
טז יז וְאֶת־הַעַרְקִי וְאֶת־הַסִּינִי׃ וְאֶת־הָאַרְוָדִי וְאֶת־הַצְּמָרִי וְאֶת־הַחֲמָתִי׃ בְּנֵי
שֵׁם עֵילָם וְאַשּׁוּר וְאַרְפַּכְשַׁד וְלוּד וַאֲרָם וְעוּץ וְחוּל וְגֶתֶר וָמֶשֶׁךְ׃
יח יט וְאַרְפַּכְשַׁד יָלַד אֶת־שָׁלַח וְשֶׁלַח יָלַד אֶת־עֵבֶר׃ וּלְעֵבֶר יֻלַּד שְׁנֵי בָנִים שֵׁם הָאֶחָד

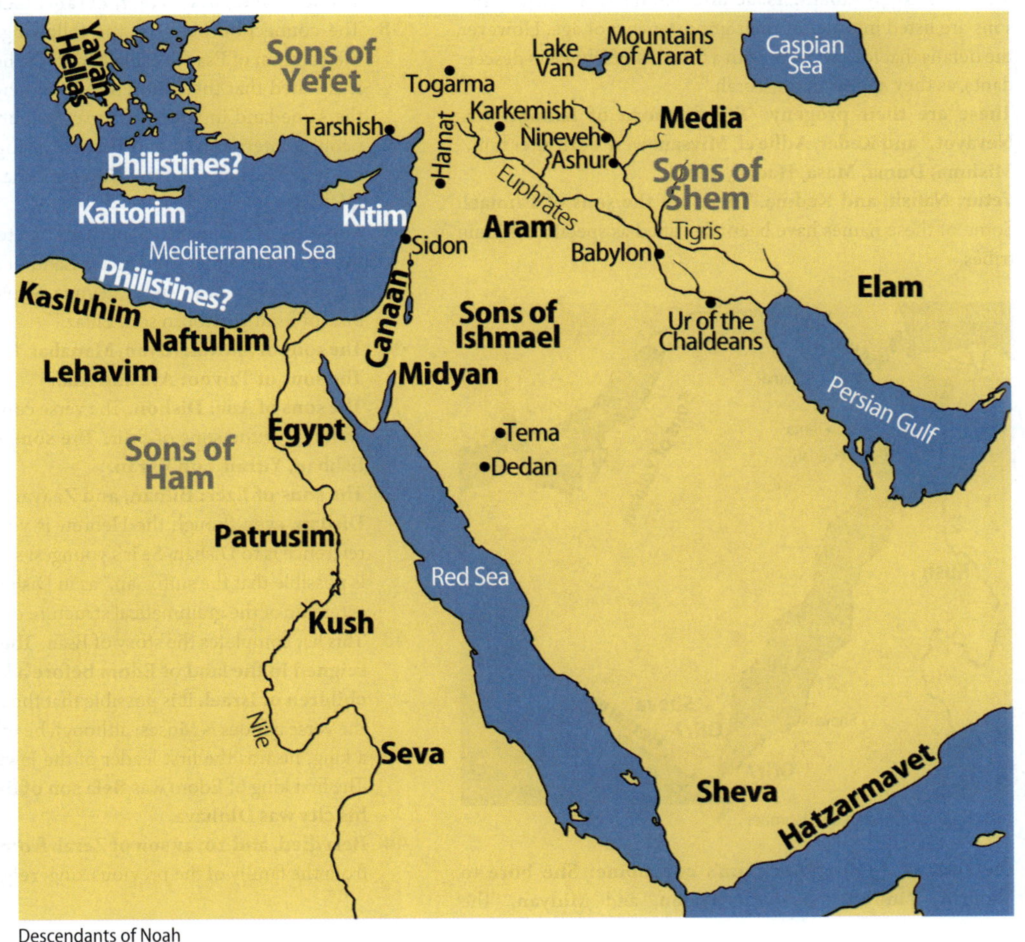

Descendants of Noah

to separate into different nations and languages, **and the name of his brother was Yoktan.**

20 **Yoktan,** apparently the younger [*katan*] of the two brothers, was the father of several nations, as he **begot Almodad, Shelef, Hatzarmavet,**[B] who lived in Yemen, and **Yerah,**

21 **Hadoram, Uzal, Dikla,**

22 **Eival, Avimael, Sheva,**

23 **Ofir,**[B] **Havila, and Yovav.** These nations may have dwelled in Africa or in the Indian Ocean region. **All these were the sons of Yoktan.**

24 The direct genealogical tree of Abraham is now presented: **Shem, Arpakhshad, Shalah,**

25 **Ever, Peleg, Re'u,**

26 **Serug, Nahor, Terah,**

27 **Abram,** the son of Terah, **he is Abraham.** The text emphasizes that Abram will no longer appear by that name, as God changed his name to Abraham.[14]

28 **The sons of Abraham: Isaac and Ishmael.** Abraham's two sons are listed in order of their importance, not age. However, the details that follow begin with a brief list of Ishmael's descendants, as they appear in the Torah.[15]

29 **These are their progeny: The firstborn of Ishmael was Nevayot,**[B] **and Kedar, Adbe'el, Mivsam** were born after him,

30 **Mishma, Duma, Masa, Hadad, Tema,**

31 **Yetur, Nafish, and Kedma. These are the sons of Ishmael.** Some of these names have been identified as specific Bedouin tribes.

Descendants of Yoktan and Ishmael

32 **The sons of Ketura, Abraham's concubine: She bore** to Abraham **Zimran, Yokshan, Medan,** and **Midyan.** The descendants of Midyan, with whom the people of Israel had extensive contact over the course of history, both as individuals and as a nation, could be considered cousins of Israel. Ketura's other two sons were **Yishbak and Shuah; the sons of Yokshan were Sheva and Dedan,** names which already appeared in these lists (verse 9). Perhaps these different groups of people lived together in the same place or they are different nations with identical names.

33 **The sons of Midyan: Efa, Efer, Hanokh, Avida, and Eldaa. All these were the sons of Ketura.**

34 **Abraham begot Isaac. The sons of Isaac: Esau and Israel.** This is Jacob, who was not named Israel at birth, but received that name later in life.[16]

35 **The sons of Esau: Elifaz, Re'uel, Yeush, Yalam, and Korah.**

36 **The sons of Elifaz: Teman, Omar, Tzefi, Gatam, Kenaz, Timna, and Amalek,** whose descendants are mentioned on several occasions as enemies of Israel.[17]

37 **The sons of Re'uel: Nahat, Zerah, Shama, and Miza.**

38 The connection between the following genealogical list and the children of Esau is explained in the book of Genesis, where it is stated that the children of Se'ir were a tribe who lived in the same land in which Esau settled, until over time the two peoples intermingled and became a single nation.[18] **The sons of Se'ir: Lotan, Shoval, Tzivon, Ana, Dishon, Ezer, and Dishan.**

39 **The sons of Lotan: Hori,** perhaps tied to the tribe or nation of the same name that lived in the Land of Israel,[19] **and Homam; Timna was Lotan's sister.** Timna would become the concubine of Esau's firstborn son, Elifaz.[20]

40 **The sons of Shoval: Alyan, Manahat, Eval, Shefi, and Onam. The sons of Tzivon: Aya and Ana.**

41 **The sons of Ana: Dishon.** The verse continues its listing of the children of the sons of Se'ir: **The sons of Dishon: Hamran, Eshban, Yitran, and Keran.**

42 **The sons of Ezer: Bilhan, and Zaavan, Yaakan. The sons of Dishan,** even though the Hebrew is vocalized as Dishon, the reference is to Dishan, Se'ir's youngest son:[21] **Utz and Aran.**[22] It is possible that the suffix "an," as in Dishan and Aran, was characteristic of the grammatical structure of their language.

43 This list completes the story of Esau: **These are the kings who reigned in the land of Edom before a king reigned over the children of Israel.** It is possible that the Israelite king to whom the verse alludes is Moses; although he was not explicitly called a king, he was the first leader of the Jewish nation as a whole. The first king of Edom was **Bela son of Beor; and the name of his city was Dinhava.**

44 **Bela died, and Yovav son of Zerah from Botzra,** who was not from the family of the previous king, **reigned in his stead.**

כ פֶּלֶג כִּי בְיָמָיו נִפְלְגָה הָאָרֶץ וְשֵׁם אָחִיו יָקְטָן׃ וְיָקְטָן יָלַד אֶת־אַלְמוֹדָד וְאֶת־שָׁלֶף
כא כב וְאֶת־חֲצַרְמָוֶת וְאֶת־יָרַח׃ וְאֶת־הֲדוֹרָם וְאֶת־אוּזָל וְאֶת־דִּקְלָה׃ וְאֶת־עֵיבָל וְאֶת־
כג אֲבִימָאֵל וְאֶת־שְׁבָא׃ וְאֶת־אוֹפִיר וְאֶת־חֲוִילָה וְאֶת־יוֹבָב כָּל־אֵלֶּה בְּנֵי
כד כה כו כז יָקְטָן׃ שֵׁם ׀ אַרְפַּכְשַׁד שָׁלַח׃ עֵבֶר פֶּלֶג רְעוּ׃ שְׂרוּג נָחוֹר תָּרַח׃ אַבְרָם
כח כט הוּא אַבְרָהָם׃ בְּנֵי אַבְרָהָם יִצְחָק וְיִשְׁמָעֵאל׃ אֵלֶּה תֹּלְדוֹתָם
ל בְּכוֹר יִשְׁמָעֵאל נְבָיוֹת וְקֵדָר וְאַדְבְּאֵל וּמִבְשָׂם׃ מִשְׁמָע וְדוּמָה מַשָּׂא חֲדַד וְתֵימָא׃
לא לב יְטוּר נָפִישׁ וָקֵדְמָה אֵלֶּה הֵם בְּנֵי יִשְׁמָעֵאל׃ וּבְנֵי קְטוּרָה פִּילֶגֶשׁ אַבְרָהָם
יָלְדָה אֶת־זִמְרָן וְיָקְשָׁן וּמְדָן וּמִדְיָן וְיִשְׁבָּק וְשׁוּחַ וּבְנֵי יָקְשָׁן שְׁבָא וּדְדָן׃
לג וּבְנֵי מִדְיָן עֵיפָה וָעֵפֶר וַחֲנוֹךְ וַאֲבִידָע וְאֶלְדָּעָה כָּל־אֵלֶּה בְּנֵי קְטוּרָה׃
לד לה וַיּוֹלֶד אַבְרָהָם אֶת־יִצְחָק בְּנֵי יִצְחָק עֵשָׂו וְיִשְׂרָאֵל׃ בְּנֵי עֵשָׂו אֱלִיפָז
לו רְעוּאֵל וִיעוּשׁ וְיַעְלָם וְקֹרַח׃ בְּנֵי אֱלִיפָז תֵּימָן וְאוֹמָר צְפִי וְגַעְתָּם
לז קְנַז וְתִמְנָע וַעֲמָלֵק׃ בְּנֵי רְעוּאֵל נַחַת זֶרַח שַׁמָּה וּמִזָּה׃
לח לט וּבְנֵי שֵׂעִיר לוֹטָן וְשׁוֹבָל וְצִבְעוֹן וַעֲנָה וְדִישֹׁן וְאֵצֶר וְדִישָׁן׃ וּבְנֵי לוֹטָן
מ חֹרִי וְהוֹמָם וַאֲחוֹת לוֹטָן תִּמְנָע׃ בְּנֵי שׁוֹבָל עַלְיָן וּמָנַחַת וְעֵיבָל שְׁפִי
מא וְאוֹנָם וּבְנֵי צִבְעוֹן אַיָּה וַעֲנָה׃ בְּנֵי עֲנָה דִּישׁוֹן וּבְנֵי דִישׁוֹן
מב חַמְרָן וְאֶשְׁבָּן וְיִתְרָן וּכְרָן׃ בְּנֵי־אֵצֶר בִּלְהָן וְזַעֲוָן יַעֲקָן בְּנֵי דִישׁוֹן עוּץ
מג וַאֲרָן׃ וְאֵלֶּה הַמְּלָכִים אֲשֶׁר מָלְכוּ בְּאֶרֶץ אֱדוֹם לִפְנֵי מְלָךְ־מֶלֶךְ לִבְנֵי
מד יִשְׂרָאֵל בֶּלַע בֶּן־בְּעוֹר וְשֵׁם עִירוֹ דִּנְהָבָה׃ וַיָּמָת בָּלַע וַיִּמְלֹךְ תַּחְתָּיו יוֹבָב בֶּן־

BACKGROUND

1:20| **Hatzarmavet:** The name of a kingdom and geographical region in the south of the Arabian Peninsula, on the coast of the Indian Ocean. Hatzarmavet is mentioned in external documents from various periods, and the name has been preserved to this day. It is known as Hadhramaut in English. Based on inscriptions that have been uncovered, it is surmised that the kingdom existed until the third century BCE.

1:23| **Ofir:** There are three main opinions with regard to the location of this land, which was known as a source of fine-quality gold: eastern Africa, southern Arabia, or India. According to one theory, the name Africa derives from the word Ofir.

1:29| **Nevayot:** The descendants of Nevayot have been identified as the Bedouin tribe known as the Nabaiates, who lived along the desert that bordered the Land of Israel and are mentioned many times in Assyrian documents dating back to the seventh century BCE. According to those sources, this tribe lived east or southeast of the children of Kedar. They are not to be confused with the tribes known as the Nabateans, who arrived in the region of the Land of Israel from northern Arabia and whose name was given to them by the Greeks in the fourth century BCE.

45 **Yovav died, and Husham from the land of the Temanites,** the province of one of the chieftains of Esau,[23] **reigned in his stead.**
46 **Husham died, and Hadad son of Bedad, who smote Midyan in the field of Moav, reigned in his stead; and the name of his city was Avit.** The Midyanites were a nomadic tribe. Even if there was a place called the land of Midyan, it is unclear whether that place was a fixed, demarcated area. The king who ruled Edom fought Midyan in the territory of Moav, where he routed the Midyanites.
47 **Hadad died, and Samla from Masreka reigned in his stead.**
48 **Samla died, and Shaul from Rehovot on the River reigned in his stead.**
49 **Shaul died, and Baal Hanan son of Akhbor reigned in his stead.**
50 **Baal Hanan died, and Hadad reigned in his stead;**[D] **the name of his city was Pa'i.** In the Torah he is called Hadar, and his city is Pa'u.[24] **And his wife's name was Mehetavel, daughter of Matred, daughter of Mei Zahav.** It is unclear whether these were their actual names, the titles of their professions, or epithets that allude to other aspects of their lives.
51 **Hadad died. The chieftains,** civil governors, small-scale princes who headed the tribes, **of Edom**[B] **were: The chieftain of Timna, the chieftain of Alva, the chieftain of Yetet,**
52 **the chieftain of Oholivama, the chieftain of Ela, the chieftain of Pinon,**
53 **the chieftain of Kenaz, the chieftain of Teman, the chieftain of Mivtzar,**
54 **the chieftain of Magdiel, the chieftain of Iram. These are the chieftains of Edom.**

Genealogical Lists of the Tribes of Israel

I CHRONICLES 2:1–9:44

These are genealogical lists of Israelite families. They are not arranged according to direct lineage; rather, they move from one family to another. As stated previously, the information in the book of Chronicles is fragmentary, and extensive background information is required in order to properly understand the details recorded in it.

Jacob's Sons

I CHRONICLES 2:1–2

2 1 **These are the sons of Israel,** i.e., Jacob: **Reuben, Simeon, Levi, Judah, Issachar,** and **Zebulun,** the sons of Leah in order of their birth;
2 **Dan, Joseph, Benjamin, Naphtali, Gad, and Asher.** Although Naphtali, Gad, and Asher were all born before Joseph and Benjamin, they are mentioned after them because Joseph and Benjamin were the sons of Rachel, Jacob's most beloved wife.[25] The tribes are listed in the Bible fifteen times, on each occasion in a different order.[26]

The Descendants of Judah until the Family of David

I CHRONICLES 2:3–17

3 **The sons of Judah: Er, Onan, and Shela; three were born to him from Bat Shua, the Canaanite woman. Er, Judah's firstborn, was evil in the eyes of the Lord, and He put him to death.** The same fate befell Onan, Judah's second son.
4 **Tamar, his,** Judah's, **daughter-in-law, bore him Peretz and Zerah,** as related in detail in the book of Genesis.[27] **All the sons of Judah were five.** These five sons were not all alive at the same time; in the words of the Sages, they did not live in one world.[28] The first two, who died young, apparently left no heirs, and yet their names and the circumstances of their deaths are repeated in Judah's genealogical lists.[29] The same is true with regard to Aaron's sons, Nadav and Avihu.[30]
5 **The sons of Peretz: Hetzron and Hamul.**
6 **The sons of Zerah: Zimri, Eitan, Heiman, Kalkol, and Dara; all of them were five.** Eitan and Heiman are the names of singers mentioned both in this book and in Psalms.[31] A verse below mentions another Heiman, who was one of the leading singers in the Temple (6:18). Although there is no certainty that the verses are referring to the same individuals, it is possible that Eitan the Ezrahite and Heiman the Ezrahite who appear in the book of Psalms were these sons of Zerah. The pair, together with Kalkol and Dara, also called Darda, are mentioned as men renowned for their wisdom.[32]
7 **The sons of Karmi,** who is not identified here but is known from the book of Joshua as one of the sons of Zerah,[33] included **Akhar,** called Akhan in the book of Joshua. Here he is called Akhar because **he** was the one **who tainted** [*okher*] **Israel,**

מה מו זֶרַח מִבָּצְרָֽה׃ וַיָּמָת יוֹבָב וַיִּמְלֹךְ תַּחְתָּיו חוּשָׁם מֵאֶרֶץ הַתֵּימָנִֽי׃ וַיָּמָת חוּשָׁם
וַיִּמְלֹךְ תַּחְתָּיו הֲדַד בֶּן־בְּדַד הַמַּכֶּה אֶת־מִדְיָן בִּשְׂדֵה מוֹאָב וְשֵׁם עִירוֹ עיות׃ עֲוִית
מז מח וַיָּמָת הֲדָד וַיִּמְלֹךְ תַּחְתָּיו שַׂמְלָה מִמַּשְׂרֵקָֽה׃ וַיָּמָת שַׂמְלָה וַיִּמְלֹךְ תַּחְתָּיו שָׁאוּל
מט נ מֵרְחֹבוֹת הַנָּהָֽר׃ וַיָּמָת שָׁאוּל וַיִּמְלֹךְ תַּחְתָּיו בַּעַל חָנָן בֶּן־עַכְבּֽוֹר׃ וַיָּמָת בַּעַל
חָנָן וַיִּמְלֹךְ תַּחְתָּיו הֲדַד וְשֵׁם עִירוֹ פָּעִי וְשֵׁם אִשְׁתּוֹ מְהֵיטַבְאֵל בַּת־מַטְרֵד בַּת
נא מֵי זָהָֽב׃ וַיָּמָת הֲדָד וַיִּהְיוּ אַלּוּפֵי אֱדוֹם אַלּוּף תִּמְנָע אַלּוּף עליה אַלּוּף יְתֵֽת׃ עַלְוָה
נב נג אַלּוּף אָהֳלִיבָמָה אַלּוּף אֵלָה אַלּוּף פִּינֹֽן׃ אַלּוּף קְנַז אַלּוּף תֵּימָן אַלּוּף מִבְצָֽר׃
נד א אַלּוּף מַגְדִּיאֵל אַלּוּף עִירָם אֵלֶּה אַלּוּפֵי אֱדֽוֹם׃ אֵלֶּה בְּנֵי יִשְׂרָאֵל
ב רְאוּבֵן שִׁמְעוֹן לֵוִי וִיהוּדָה יִשָּׂשכָר וּזְבֻלֽוּן׃ דָּן יוֹסֵף וּבִנְיָמִן נַפְתָּלִי גָּד
ג וְאָשֵֽׁר׃ בְּנֵי יְהוּדָה עֵר וְאוֹנָן וְשֵׁלָה שְׁלוֹשָׁה נוֹלַד לוֹ מִבַּת־שׁוּעַ
ד הַכְּנַעֲנִית וַיְהִי עֵר ׀ בְּכוֹר יְהוּדָה רַע בְּעֵינֵי יְהוָה וַיְמִיתֵֽהוּ׃ וְתָמָר כַּלָּתוֹ יָלְדָה לּוֹ
ה אֶת־פֶּרֶץ וְאֶת־זָרַח כָּל־בְּנֵי יְהוּדָה חֲמִשָּֽׁה׃ בְּנֵי פֶרֶץ חֶצְרוֹן וְחָמֽוּל׃
ו ז וּבְנֵי זֶרַח זִמְרִי וְאֵיתָן וְהֵימָן וְכַלְכֹּל וָדָרַע כֻּלָּם חֲמִשָּֽׁה׃ וּבְנֵי כַּרְמִי

DISCUSSION

1:50 | **Hadad reigned in his stead:** It seems that Hadad, or Hadar, was the last important king of Edom in that period, as no kings are listed after him. There was a monarchy in Edom for many years, although not continuously. In certain periods, officials appointed by the king of Judah ruled Edom (see II Samuel 8:14; I Kings 11:15–16, 22:48; I Chronicles 18:12–13), while in other eras, the Edomites rebelled against Judah and established an independent realm (see II Kings 8:20–22; Psalms 137:7). Edom was divided into tribes and provinces, whose leaders were called *alufim*, meaning chieftains (see Rashi; Radak; Malbim; *Derashot HaRan*, 2, s.v. *zeh*). During periods when the monarchy was weak or non-existent, these *alufim* were de facto independent rulers.

BACKGROUND

1:51 | **The chieftains of [*alufei*] Edom:** Here, and in the Ugarit tablets (*allupu*), the title "chieftain" does not refer to a military office. It is possible that these rulers, who were dynastic heads of tribes, called themselves by this name due to the original meaning of the noun *aluf*, a bull (see Psalms 144:14; *Targum* and Rashi, Deuteronomy 28:4). In the Song at the Sea, the term *aluf* parallels "the powers of [*elei*] Moav" (Exodus 15:15). Some claim that the term *aluf* is derived from the name given to a sheep that is trained [*ulaf*] to lead a flock (see Jeremiah 13:21).

who committed a trespass with the proscribed spoils of Jericho, resulting in a military defeat for Israel.[34]

8 **The sons,** the son[35] or one of the sons,[36] **of Eitan,** son of Zerah: **Azarya.**

9 After mentioning some of the descendants of Zerah, whose line was not historically dominant in the tribe of Judah, the chapter returns to focus on the dominant line of the sons of Peretz. **The sons of Hetzron, who were born to him: Yerahme'el, Ram, and Keluvai.**

10 **Ram begot Aminadav, and Aminadav begot Nahshon,** who was the famous **prince of the children of Judah** at the time of the exodus from Egypt;[37]

11 **and Nahshon begot Salma,** and **Salma begot Boaz,** who was the first of this genealogical line to enter and settle in the Land of Israel;

12 **Boaz begot Oved,** as related in the book of Ruth,[38] and **Oved begot Yishai,**

13 **and Yishai,** spelled "Ishai" here,[39] **begot his firstborn Eliav, and Avinadav, the second** son, **and Shima the third.** The sons of Shima are mentioned in several places in the book of Samuel.[40]

14 **Netanel the fourth, Radai the fifth,**

15 **Otzem the sixth,** and **David** was **the seventh** son, albeit not the last.[41]

16 **Their sisters,** the sisters of the sons of Yishai, **were Tzeruya and Avigayil; the sons of Tzeruya,** their lineage linked here to their mother rather than their father in deference to David,[42] were **Avshai, Yoav, and Asael, three.** The sons of Tzeruya, the nephews of David, are among the principal characters in the book of Samuel.

17 **Avigayil bore Amasa,**[D] **and the father of Amasa was** a man called **Yeter the Ishmaelite.**

Hetzron and His Descendants

I CHRONICLES 2:18–55

18 **Caleb son of Hetzron,**[D] son of Peretz, son of Judah, **begot children with Azuva his wife,**[43] **and** he also fathered children **with** his second wife, **Yeriot, and these are her sons: Yesher, Shovav, and Ardon.**

19 **Azuva died, and Caleb took for himself** another wife, **Efrat,** and **she bore him Hur.** Nothing further is stated about Efrat, but a rabbinic tradition identifies her as Miriam, Moses' sister.[44] Hur appears in the Torah as a confidant of Moses until the revelation at Sinai.[45] Moses trusted Hur, and when Moses ascended Mount Sinai, he left him, along with Aaron, in charge of the people, perhaps because he was his sister's son.

20 **Hur begot Uri, and Uri begot Betzalel,** the chief architect of the Tabernacle,[46] who therefore earns special mention here.

21 **Thereafter,** after he had already fathered several sons, **Hetzron,** Caleb's father, **consorted with the daughter of Makhir.** Makhir was the son of Manasseh and the **father of Gilad.** The family of Gilad son of Makhir became so important that an entire region on the east side of the Jordan River was named after him.[47] **He took her when he was sixty years old.** Hetzron married her when he was a widower, or in addition to his previous wives. **And she bore him Seguv.**

22 **Seguv begot Ya'ir, and he had twenty-three cities in the land of the Gilad.**[B] The book of Numbers (32:41) mentions that Ya'ir conquered parts of Gilad, but his precise lineage is not given there. This list teaches that he was patrilineally descended from the tribe of Judah, but was a descendant of Makhir from his mother's side.[48] When Makhir conquered Gilad, Ya'ir joined him and took possession of a certain portion of the land, which was called Havot Ya'ir after him.[49] This region seems to have bordered a foreign kingdom, as indicated in the next verse.

23 Havot Ya'ir did not remain under Israel's control for long, as it was conquered by neighboring nations: **Geshur and Aram,** kingdoms northeast of Israel, **took Havot Ya'ir from them,**[B] Israel, **with Kenat**[B] **and its environs, sixty cities; all these were the sons of Makhir father of Gilad.** This is not a full

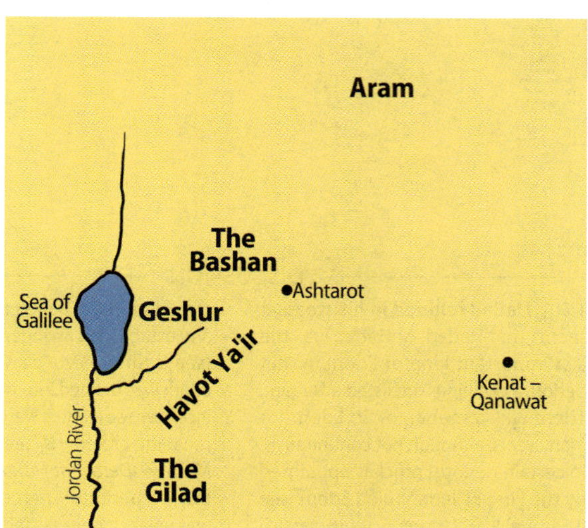

Havot Ya'ir and Kenat

ח עָכָר עוֹכֵר יִשְׂרָאֵל אֲשֶׁר מָעַל בַּחֵרֶם׃ וּבְנֵי אֵיתָן עֲזַרְיָה׃
ט י וּבְנֵי חֶצְרוֹן אֲשֶׁר נוֹלַד־לוֹ אֶת־יְרַחְמְאֵל וְאֶת־רָם וְאֶת־כְּלוּבָי׃ וְרָם הוֹלִיד אֶת־
יא עַמִּינָדָב וְעַמִּינָדָב הוֹלִיד אֶת־נַחְשׁוֹן נְשִׂיא בְּנֵי יְהוּדָה׃ וְנַחְשׁוֹן הוֹלִיד אֶת־שַׂלְמָא
יב יג וְשַׂלְמָא הוֹלִיד אֶת־בֹּעַז׃ וּבֹעַז הוֹלִיד אֶת־עוֹבֵד וְעוֹבֵד הוֹלִיד אֶת־יִשָׁי׃ וְאִישַׁי
יד הוֹלִיד אֶת־בְּכֹרוֹ אֶת־אֱלִיאָב וַאֲבִינָדָב הַשֵּׁנִי וְשִׁמְעָא הַשְּׁלִישִׁי׃ נְתַנְאֵל הָרְבִיעִי
טו טז רַדַּי הַחֲמִישִׁי׃ אֹצֶם הַשִּׁשִּׁי דָּוִיד הַשְּׁבִעִי׃ וְאַחְיֹתֵיהֶם צְרוּיָה וַאֲבִיגָיִל וּבְנֵי צְרוּיָה
יז אַבְשַׁי וְיוֹאָב וַעֲשָׂה־אֵל שְׁלֹשָׁה׃ וַאֲבִיגַיִל יָלְדָה אֶת־עֲמָשָׂא וַאֲבִי עֲמָשָׂא יֶתֶר
יח הַיִּשְׁמְעֵאלִי׃ וְכָלֵב בֶּן־חֶצְרוֹן הוֹלִיד אֶת־עֲזוּבָה אִשָּׁה וְאֶת־יְרִיעוֹת וְאֵלֶּה
יט בָנֶיהָ יֵשֶׁר וְשׁוֹבָב וְאַרְדּוֹן׃ וַתָּמָת עֲזוּבָה וַיִּקַּח־לוֹ כָלֵב אֶת־אֶפְרָת וַתֵּלֶד לוֹ
כ כא אֶת־חוּר׃ וְחוּר הוֹלִיד אֶת־אוּרִי וְאוּרִי הוֹלִיד אֶת־בְּצַלְאֵל׃ וְאַחַר
בָּא חֶצְרוֹן אֶל־בַּת־מָכִיר אֲבִי גִלְעָד וְהוּא לְקָחָהּ וְהוּא בֶּן־שִׁשִּׁים שָׁנָה וַתֵּלֶד
כב לוֹ אֶת־שְׂגוּב׃ וּשְׂגוּב הוֹלִיד אֶת־יָאִיר וַיְהִי־לוֹ עֶשְׂרִים וְשָׁלוֹשׁ עָרִים בְּאֶרֶץ
כג הַגִּלְעָד׃ וַיִּקַּח גְּשׁוּר־וַאֲרָם אֶת־חַוֹּת יָאִיר מֵאִתָּם אֶת־קְנָת וְאֶת־

DISCUSSION

2:17| **Amasa:** This individual is also mentioned in II Samuel (17:25) as the man whom Avshalom appointed over the army, but his lineage is not clearly described there. The fact that Amasa was the son of David's sister explains both his appointment and Yoav's motivation for killing him later; all these events occurred within the family circle. Amasa's father is here called an Ishmaelite, whereas in II Samuel he is referred to as Yitra the Israelite. Perhaps this title is indicative not of his lineage, but of his place of residence (see Rashi; Radak; Malbim; Jerusalem Talmud, *Yevamot* 8:3).

2:18| **Caleb son of Hetzron:** This Caleb is not mentioned elsewhere. He might be Caleb son of Yefuneh, an important personage in the Torah (see Numbers 13–14). This would not be the only instance of someone whose father is mentioned with different names, either because the father had two names, or because the son had a surrogate father after whom he is sometimes called (see Radak here and verse 49; *Sota* 11b; Jerusalem Talmud, *Kiddushin* 1:2). The reason for the discrepancy in names in this case is unclear. It may be due to previous marriages in the generation of Caleb's parents; we are informed, for example, that Caleb had a brother whose father was called Kenaz (see Radak; Ralbag; Malbim; Joshua 15:17; commentary on Joshua 14:6; *Sota* 11b; *Adderet Eliyahu*, verse 9).

BACKGROUND

2:22| **In the land of the Gilad:** This is the hilly region in the center and north of the territory east of the Jordan, bordering on the Bashan. Gad, Reuben, and half the tribe of Manasseh settled in this territory. It is depicted in the Bible as land that was good for grazing, with many forests (Numbers 32:4; II Samuel 17:26–18).

2:23| **Geshur and Aram took Havot Ya'ir from them:** Havot Ya'ir was a region in the northern territory east of the Jordan, between northern Gilad and the Bashan (the Golan Heights). The word *ḥavva* is either borrowed from Hurrian, meaning a stone fence surrounding a field, or may be derived from an Arabic term meaning a circle of tents. The archaeological findings in the region include collar-rimmed jugs, which are characteristic of the period of the Israelite conquest. These *ḥavvot* were located near the kingdom of Geshur, which was not conquered during Joshua's lifetime (Joshua 13:13). Relations between Israel and Geshur were unstable. In David's time, a close relationship was manifest in David's marriage to Maakha the daughter of the king of Geshur (II Samuel 3:3). Later, the *ḥavvot* were conquered by Geshur and Aram, as stated here. The kingdom of Geshur is mentioned in Egyptian documents (Tel el-Amarna) dating back to the fourteenth century BCE.

Kenat: Kenat is generally identified as Qanawat in Syria, a provincial city on the slopes of Jabal al-Druze, in the area of Hauran. Kenat is mentioned in early Egyptian documents dating back to the first half of the second millennium BCE. Under the Roman Empire, it was one of the Decapolis, a group of ten cities that enjoyed a certain measure of autonomy. In the period of the Mishna, Kenat marked the border of the Land of Israel for the separation of tithes (*Tosefta*, *Shevi'it* 4:11).

genealogical list of the descendants of Makhir, but a few fragments of information recorded here because of Makhir's family relationship to Hetzron.[50]

24 **After the death of Hetzron, Caleb consorted with Efrat [*bekhalev efrata*], his wife.** Some explain this phrase as meaning that Caleb came to the town of Efrat near Bethlehem, in the territory he ruled. He may have named the town itself after his wife.[51] **The wife of Hetzron was Aviya and she bore him Ashhur, father** of the settlement **of Tekoa.**

25 The following genealogical lists are cited here apropos the previous one: **The sons of Yerahme'el,** who was the **firstborn of Hetzron, were Ram the firstborn,** which was also the name of Hetzron's son. Several names in I Chronicles recur within the same families. In addition, there were **Buna, Oren, Otzem,** and **Ahiya.** All these were sons of Yerahme'el, presumably from the same wife.

26 **Yerahme'el had another wife, and her name was Atara; she was the mother of Onam.**

27 **The sons of Ram, firstborn of Yerahme'el, were Maatz, Yamin, and Eker.**

28 **The sons of Onam,** another of Yerahme'el's sons, **were Shamai and Yada, and the sons of Shamai: Nadav and Avishur.**

29 **The name of Avishur's wife was Avihayil; she bore him Ahban and Molid.**

30 **The sons of Nadav** son of Shamai were **Seled and Apayim, and Seled died without children,** perhaps without any descendants at all. He certainly did not leave behind sons to continue his name in the genealogical list.

31 **The sons of Apayim,** Nadav's other son, included only **Yishi. The sons of Yishi: Sheshan. The sons of Sheshan: Ahlai.**

32 **The sons of Yada, brother of** the aforementioned **Shamai,** were **Yeter and Yonatan; Yeter died without children.**

33 **The sons of Yonatan: Pelet and Zaza.** All **these were the sons of Yerahme'el.**

34 **Sheshan had no sons, but only daughters.** Ahlai, listed above as his son (verse 31) either died during his father's lifetime or was born after his father's death.[52] **Sheshan had an Egyptian slave, and his name was Yarha.**

35 **Sheshan gave his daughter to Yarha his slave as a wife, and she bore him Atai.** It is not known how this anomalous match came about. It is possible that Yarha was accepted in his master's household and found favor in his eyes; that Yarha later converted, and his employer gave him his daughter in marriage.

36 **Atai begot Natan, and Natan begot Zavad,**

37 **Zavad begot Eflal, and Eflal begot Oved,**

38 **Oved begot Yehu, and Yehu begot Azarya,**

39 **Azarya begot Heletz, and Heletz begot Elasa,**

40 **Elasa begot Sisemai, and Sisemai begot Shalum;**

41 **Shalum begot Yekamya, and Yekamya begot Elishama.** It is unclear why this list appears here, nor is it known who Elishama was. He is the last to be listed in the family dynasty, and was therefore perhaps its most important personage. Some identify him as the grandfather of Yishmael son of Netanya, who killed Gedalya son of Ahikam,[53] although the verses themselves do not indicate that he is that person.[54]

42 **The sons of Caleb, brother of Yerahme'el,** Hetzron's eldest son: **Meisha his firstborn, who was the father of Zif.**[B] This is also the name of a place in the land of Judah, perhaps because it was settled by Zif or Meisha.[55] **And the sons of** Zif were **Maresha, father of Hevron.**[56]

43 **The sons of Hevron: Korah, Tapuah, Rekem, and Shema.**

44 **Shema begot Raham, father** of the settlement **of Yorke'am, and Rekem begot Shamai.**

45 **The son of Shamai was Maon, and Maon was the father of** the settlement of **Beit Tzur.**

46 **Eifa, Caleb's concubine, bore Haran, Motza, and Gazez, and Haran begot Gazez,** another son in that family with the same name.

47 **The sons of Yahdai,** who was not previously mentioned, but was certainly another of Eifa's children,[57] were **Regem, Yotam, Geshan, Pelet, Eifa, and Shaaf.**

48 **Maakha** was the name of **Caleb's concubine,** and she **bore Shever and Tirhana.**

49 **She** also **bore**[58] **Shaaf, father** of the settlement **of Madmana, and Sheva, father** of the settlement **of Makhbena and father** of the settlement **of Giva. The daughter of Caleb was** called **Akhsa.**[D]

BACKGROUND

2:42 | **The father of Zif:** A city in the tribal territory of Judah (Joshua 15:55), identified as Tel Zif. The tel is located approximately 7 km south of Hebron, near the village of Yatta. Remnants of a wall have been discovered at this site, as have other artifacts from the era of the Israelite monarchy. The wilderness of Zif is an area of grazing land near the city of Zif, a place to which David fled from Saul. The Zifites are portrayed in the book of Samuel in a negative light, as they sought to hand David over to Saul (see I Samuel 23:19, 26:1).

כד בְּנֹתֶיהָ שִׁשִּׁים עִיר כָּל־אֵלֶּה בְּנֵי מָכִיר אֲבִי־גִלְעָד׃ וְאַחַר מוֹת־חֶצְרוֹן בְּכָלֵב
כה אֶפְרָתָה וְאֵשֶׁת חֶצְרוֹן אֲבִיָּה וַתֵּלֶד לוֹ אֶת־אַשְׁחוּר אֲבִי תְקוֹעַ׃ וַיִּהְיוּ בְנֵי־
כו יְרַחְמְאֵל בְּכוֹר חֶצְרוֹן הַבְּכוֹר ׀ רָם וּבוּנָה וָאֹרֶן וָאֹצֶם אֲחִיָּה׃ וַתְּהִי אִשָּׁה אַחֶרֶת
כז לִירַחְמְאֵל וּשְׁמָהּ עֲטָרָה הִיא אֵם אוֹנָם׃ וַיִּהְיוּ בְנֵי־רָם בְּכוֹר יְרַחְמְאֵל
כח כט מַעַץ וְיָמִין וָעֵקֶר׃ וַיִּהְיוּ בְנֵי־אוֹנָם שַׁמַּי וְיָדָע וּבְנֵי שַׁמַּי נָדָב וַאֲבִישׁוּר׃ וְשֵׁם אֵשֶׁת
ל אֲבִישׁוּר אֲבִיהָיִל וַתֵּלֶד לוֹ אֶת־אַחְבָּן וְאֶת־מוֹלִיד׃ וּבְנֵי נָדָב סֶלֶד וְאַפָּיִם וַיָּמָת
לא סֶלֶד לֹא בָנִים׃ וּבְנֵי אַפַּיִם יִשְׁעִי וּבְנֵי יִשְׁעִי שֵׁשָׁן וּבְנֵי שֵׁשָׁן
לב אַחְלָי׃ וּבְנֵי יָדָע אֲחִי שַׁמַּי יֶתֶר וְיוֹנָתָן וַיָּמָת יֶתֶר לֹא בָנִים׃
לג לד וּבְנֵי יוֹנָתָן פֶּלֶת וְזָזָא אֵלֶּה הָיוּ בְּנֵי יְרַחְמְאֵל׃ וְלֹא־הָיָה לְשֵׁשָׁן בָּנִים כִּי אִם־בָּנוֹת
לה וּלְשֵׁשָׁן עֶבֶד מִצְרִי וּשְׁמוֹ יַרְחָע׃ וַיִּתֵּן שֵׁשָׁן אֶת־בִּתּוֹ לְיַרְחָע עַבְדּוֹ לְאִשָּׁה וַתֵּלֶד
לו לז לוֹ אֶת־עַתָּי׃ וְעַתַּי הוֹלִיד אֶת־נָתָן וְנָתָן הוֹלִיד אֶת־זָבָד׃ וְזָבָד הוֹלִיד אֶת־אֶפְלָל
לח וְאֶפְלָל הוֹלִיד אֶת־עוֹבֵד׃ וְעוֹבֵד הֹלִיד אֶת־יֵהוּא וְיֵהוּא הֹלִיד אֶת־עֲזַרְיָה׃
לט מ וַעֲזַרְיָה הֹלִיד אֶת־חָלֶץ וְחֶלֶץ הֹלִיד אֶת־אֶלְעָשָׂה׃ וְאֶלְעָשָׂה הֹלִיד אֶת־סִסְמָי
מא וְסִסְמַי הֹלִיד אֶת־שַׁלּוּם׃ וְשַׁלּוּם הוֹלִיד אֶת־יְקַמְיָה וִיקַמְיָה הֹלִיד אֶת־
מב אֱלִישָׁמָע׃ וּבְנֵי כָלֵב אֲחִי יְרַחְמְאֵל מֵישָׁע בְּכֹרוֹ הוּא אֲבִי־זִיף וּבְנֵי
מג מד מָרֵשָׁה אֲבִי חֶבְרוֹן׃ וּבְנֵי חֶבְרוֹן קֹרַח וְתַפֻּחַ וְרֶקֶם וָשָׁמַע׃ וְשֶׁמַע הוֹלִיד אֶת־רַחַם
מה מו אֲבִי יָרְקְעָם וְרֶקֶם הוֹלִיד אֶת־שַׁמָּי׃ וּבֶן־שַׁמַּי מָעוֹן וּמָעוֹן אֲבִי בֵית־צוּר׃ וְעֵיפָה
פִּילֶגֶשׁ כָּלֵב יָלְדָה אֶת־חָרָן וְאֶת־מוֹצָא וְאֶת־גָּזֵז וְחָרָן הֹלִיד אֶת־גָּזֵז׃
מז מח וּבְנֵי יָהְדָּי רֶגֶם וְיוֹתָם וְגֵישָׁן וָפֶלֶט וְעֵיפָה וָשָׁעַף׃ פִּלֶגֶשׁ כָּלֵב מַעֲכָה יָלַד שֶׁבֶר
מט וְאֶת־תִּרְחֲנָה׃ וַתֵּלֶד שַׁעַף אֲבִי מַדְמַנָּה אֶת־שְׁוָא אֲבִי מַכְבֵּנָה וַאֲבִי גִבְעָא וּבַת־

DISCUSSION

2:49 | **The daughter of Caleb was Akhsa:** This too is evidence as to the identification of the Caleb mentioned here (see commentary on 2:18), with Caleb son of Yefuneh; he also had a daughter called Akhsa (see Joshua 15:13–16).

50 **These were the sons of Caleb son of Hur** who was **the first-born of** his mother **Efrat: Shoval,**[59] **father of** the settlement of **Kiryat Ye'arim.**[B] This Hur was, as stated, the son of the elder Caleb son of Hetzron, or Yefuneh.[60]
51 He was followed by **Salma,** perhaps the father of Boaz, mentioned above,[61] who was the **father** of the settlement **of Bethlehem;** and **Haref, father** of the settlement **of Beit Gader.**
52 **Shoval, father** of the settlement **of Kiryat Ye'arim, had sons: Haro'eh,** and **Hatzi HaMenuhot.** Some explain that this these last two are actually one name, referring to a son of Shoval who ruled over half of a place called Menuhot.[62] Some of these names have clear interpretations, while others allude to obscure actions, memories, and perhaps even dreams. It is therefore difficult to ascertain the meaning of all these names.[63]
53 **The families of Kiryat Ye'arim** were **the Yitrites, the Putites, the Shumatites, and the Mishraites; from them,** these families, **the Tzoratites and the Eshtaolites emerged,** the residents of Tzora and Eshtaol. These two cities appear in the list of cities in the portion of Dan, but since the two tribes were close to one another and intermingled, it is possible that their residents traced their lineage to the tribe of Judah.[64]

54 **The sons of Salma:** the inhabitants of **Bethlehem, the Netofatites,**[B] residents of Netofa,[65] and the residents of **Atrot Beit Yoav, and half of the Manahatites**[B] were **the Tzorites,** who had ties to Tzora.[66]

Umm Tuba, archaeological remains from the Second Temple period

55 Alongside the list of the families of Judah and their cities, the chapter notes other families who lived in the same region. **The families of scribes,** who copied Torah scrolls and who were probably also wise men and experts in the Torah,[67] **who dwelled at** a place called **Yabetz,**[68] possibly founded by a man named Yabetz, of unknown lineage.[69] Those families were called **the Tiratites, the Shime'atites,** and **the Sukatites. These are the Kenites,** perhaps the descendants of the Kenites, the family of Yitro, Moses' father-in-law,[70] **that came from Hamat,** the name of a person who was **the father of the house of Rekhav.** The people of Rekhav were a tribe who lived on their own and maintained an unusual lifestyle.[71] It is possible that their father was Yehonadav son of Rekhav, who appears in II Kings 10:15–17.[72]

The House of David and Its Kings

I CHRONICLES 3:1–24

This section details the genealogical lineage of the house of David, focusing mainly on its first and final generations.

3 1 **Now these were the sons of David, who were born to him in Hebron: The firstborn was Amnon, from Ahino'am the Yizre'elitess; second was Daniel, from Avigayil the Carmelitess,** the widow of Naval the Carmelite. Elsewhere, this son is called Kilav;[73]
2 **the third was Avshalom,**[74] who was the **son of Maakha, daughter of Talmai king of Geshur.** Avshalom's ties to Geshur explain why he went there when he fled from his father.[75] **The fourth** son **was Adoniya son of Hagit;**
3 **the fifth was Shefatya,** born **to Avital; the sixth was Yitre'am, to Egla his wife.**
4 **Six** sons **were born to him,** David, **in Hebron; he reigned there seven years and six months, and he reigned thirty-three years in Jerusalem.**
5 **These** sons **were born to him in Jerusalem: Shima, Shovav, Natan, and Solomon, four** born **to Bat Shua daughter of Amiel,** who elsewhere is known as Batsheva, the daughter of Eliam;[76]
6 **Yivhar, Elishama, Elifelet,**
7 **Noga, Nefeg, Yafia,**
8 **Elishama, Elyada, and Elifelet, nine** additional sons. It is somewhat surprising that both the name Elishama and the name Elifelet were assigned twice to different sons. Perhaps two of David's sons died, and he called two of his later-born sons after them.[77]
9 **All these** listed here **are the sons of David, beside the sons of the concubines,** who are not included, **and Tamar was their sister,** of the sons of David. It seems that she was not their actual sister, as nowhere is she described as David's daughter. Rather, she was Avshalom's maternal sister.[78]
10 **Solomon's son was Rehavam; Aviya** was **his son,** the son of Rehavam, and he reigned after Rehavam, and thus the dynasty continued: **Asa his son, Yehoshafat his son,**
11 **Yoram his son, Ahazyahu his son, Yoash his son,**
12 **Amatzyahu his son, Azarya his son,** frequently called Uziyahu, **Yotam his son,**
13 **Ahaz his son, Hizkiyahu his son, Menashe his son,**
14 **Amon his son, Yoshiyahu his son.**
15 **The sons of Yoshiyahu: The firstborn was** named **Yohanan, the second Yehoyakim, the third Tzidkiyahu,** and **the fourth Shalum.**

נ כָּלֵ֖ב עַכְסָֽה׃ אֵ֥לֶּה הָיוּ֙ בְּנֵ֣י כָלֵ֔ב בֶּן־ח֖וּר בְּכ֣וֹר אֶפְרָ֑תָה שׁוֹבָ֕ל אֲבִ֖י קִרְיַ֥ת יְעָרִֽים׃
נא נב שַׂלְמָא֙ אֲבִ֣י בֵֽית־לָ֔חֶם חָרֵ֖ף אֲבִ֥י בֵית־גָּֽדֵר׃ וַיִּהְי֣וּ בָנִ֗ים לְשׁוֹבָ֛ל אֲבִ֖י קִרְיַ֣ת יְעָרִ֑ים
נג הָרֹאֶ֖ה חֲצִ֥י הַמְּנֻחֽוֹת׃ וּמִשְׁפְּחוֹת֙ קִרְיַ֣ת יְעָרִ֔ים הַיִּתְרִי֙ וְהַפּוּתִ֔י וְהַשֻּׁמָתִ֖י וְהַמִּשְׁרָעִ֑י
נד מֵאֵ֗לֶּה יָֽצְאוּ֙ הַצָּ֣רְעָתִ֔י וְהָאֶשְׁתָּאֻלִֽי׃ בְּנֵ֣י שַׂלְמָ֗א בֵּ֣ית לֶ֙חֶם֙ וּנְטוֹפָ֔תִי
נה עַטְר֖וֹת בֵּ֣ית יוֹאָ֑ב וַחֲצִ֥י הַמָּנַחְתִּ֖י הַצָּרְעִֽי׃ וּמִשְׁפְּח֨וֹת סֹפְרִ֜ים ישבו יַעְבֵּ֗ץ יֹשְׁבֵ֣י
תִּרְעָתִ֥ים שִׁמְעָתִ֖ים שׂוּכָתִ֑ים הֵ֚מָּה הַקִּינִ֣ים הַבָּאִ֔ים מֵחַמַּ֖ת אֲבִ֥י בֵית־
א רֵכָֽב׃ וְאֵ֗לֶּה הָיוּ֙ בְּנֵ֣י דָוִ֔יד אֲשֶׁ֥ר נֽוֹלַד־ל֖וֹ בְּחֶבְר֑וֹן הַבְּכ֣וֹר ׀ אַמְנֹ֗ן
ב לַאֲחִינֹ֙עַם֙ הַיִּזְרְעֵאלִ֔ית שֵׁנִי֙ דָּֽנִיֵּ֔אל לַאֲבִיגַ֖יִל הַכַּרְמְלִֽית׃ הַשְּׁלִשִׁי֙ לְאַבְשָׁל֔וֹם
ג בֶּֽן־מַעֲכָ֔ה בַּת־תַּלְמַ֖י מֶ֣לֶךְ גְּשׁ֑וּר הָרְבִיעִ֖י אֲדֹנִיָּ֥ה בֶן־חַגִּֽית׃ הַחֲמִישִׁ֥י שְׁפַטְיָ֖ה
ד לַאֲבִיטָ֑ל הַשִּׁשִּׁ֥י יִתְרְעָ֖ם לְעֶגְלָ֥ה אִשְׁתּֽוֹ׃ שִׁשָּׁה֙ נֽוֹלַד־ל֣וֹ בְחֶבְר֔וֹן וַיִּמְלָךְ־שָׁ֕ם
שֶׁ֥בַע שָׁנִ֖ים וְשִׁשָּׁ֣ה חֳדָשִׁ֑ים וּשְׁלֹשִׁ֤ים וְשָׁלוֹשׁ֙ שָׁנָ֔ה מָלַ֖ךְ בִּירוּשָׁלִָֽם׃
ה וְאֵ֥לֶּה נוּלְּדוּ־ל֖וֹ בִּירֽוּשָׁלָ֑יִם שִׁ֠מְעָא וְשׁוֹבָ֞ב וְנָתָ֤ן וּשְׁלֹמֹה֙ אַרְבָּעָ֔ה לְבַת־שׁ֖וּעַ
ו ז ח בַּת־עַמִּיאֵֽל׃ וְיִבְחָ֥ר וֶאֱלִישָׁ֖מָע וֶאֱלִיפָֽלֶט׃ וְנֹ֥גַהּ וְנֶ֖פֶג וְיָפִֽיעַ׃ וֶאֱלִישָׁמָ֧ע וְאֶלְיָדָ֛ע
ט וֶאֱלִיפֶ֖לֶט תִּשְׁעָֽה׃ כֹּ֚ל בְּנֵ֣י דָוִ֔יד מִלְּבַ֖ד בְּנֵֽי־פִֽילַגְשִׁ֑ים וְתָמָ֖ר אֲחוֹתָֽם׃
י יא וּבֶן־שְׁלֹמֹ֖ה רְחַבְעָ֑ם אֲבִיָּ֥ה בְנ֛וֹ אָסָ֥א בְנ֖וֹ יְהוֹשָׁפָ֥ט בְּנֽוֹ׃ יוֹרָ֥ם בְּנ֛וֹ אֲחַזְיָ֥הוּ בְנ֖וֹ
יב יג יוֹאָ֥שׁ בְּנֽוֹ׃ אֲמַֽצְיָ֥הוּ בְנ֛וֹ עֲזַרְיָ֥ה בְנ֖וֹ יוֹתָ֥ם בְּנֽוֹ׃ אָחָ֥ז בְּנ֛וֹ חִזְקִיָּ֥הוּ בְנ֖וֹ מְנַשֶּׁ֥ה בְנֽוֹ׃
יד טו אָמ֥וֹן בְּנ֖וֹ יֹאשִׁיָּ֥הוּ בְנֽוֹ׃ וּבְנֵי֙ יֹאשִׁיָּ֔הוּ הַבְּכ֖וֹר יֽוֹחָנָ֑ן הַשֵּׁנִי֙ יְהוֹיָקִ֔ים הַשְּׁלִשִׁ֖י צִדְקִיָּ֑הוּ

BACKGROUND

2:50 | **Kiryat Ye'arim:** This city in the tribal territory of Judah has multiple names in the Bible: Giva, Kiryat Ye'arim, Givat Ye'arim, Yaara, Baala, Kiryat Baal, and Sde Yaar. The various names refer to the geographical and religious dimensions of the location, and they also reflect the political and religious changes that the city underwent, both through its conquest from the Canaanites, and due to its situation as a border city between two tribes. Kiryat Ye'arim has been identified as Deir el-Azar, a hilltop located above and to the west of Abu Ghosh.

2:54 | **Netofatites:** Netofa has been identified either with Umm Tuba, south of Jerusalem, or with Khirbet Bedd Faluh, roughly 1 km west of Herodion and north of present-day Tekoa. A nearby spring is called Ein en-Natuf.

Half of the Manahatites [*ḥatzi hamenaḥati*]: It has been suggested that this is the name of a person who was so called because he traced his lineage through two fathers. Alternatively, the city of Manahat was administratively divided into the jurisdictions of Bethlehem and Kiryat Ye'arim. Some contend that the Benjamites were banished to Manahat after the civil war that followed the tragic incident of the concubine at Giva, and thus half of Manahat was inhabited by members of the tribe of Judah, while the tribe of Benjamin lived in the other half.

16 **The sons of Yehoyakim: Yekhonya his son,** also known as Yehoyakhin, who was taken captive to Babylonia, where he remained for many years until his death, and **Tzidkiya his son.**

17 **The sons of Yekhonya: Asir, She'altiel his son.** It is possible to understand that Asir was Yekhonya's son and that She'altiel was Asir's son, but it can also be explained that Yekhonya Asir is the name of a single person, and She'altiel was his son.[79]

18 **Malkiram, Pedaya, Shenatzar, Yekamya, Hoshama, and Nedaviya.**

19 **The sons of Pedaya: Zerubavel and Shimi. The sons of Zerubavel were Meshulam, and** his brother **Hananya, and Shelomit** was **their sister;**

20 **Hashuva, Ohel, Berekhya, Hasadya, Yushav Hesed,** a total of **five** sons listed after Shelomit. The number is needed here to clarify that although Yushav Hesed is two words in the Hebrew, it is the name of a single person.[80]

21 **The son of Hananya: Pelatya and** after him **Yeshaya,**[81] and here the verse provides a brief mention of the families that came after Yeshaya: **the sons of Refaya; the sons of Arnan; the sons of Ovadya; the sons of Shekhanya.**

22 **The sons of Shekhanya: Shemaya; and the sons of Shemaya: Hatush, Yigal, Bariah, Ne'arya, and Shafat,** a total of **six** sons and grandsons.[82]

23 **The sons of Ne'arya: Elyo'einai, Hizkiya, and Azrikam, three** sons.

24 **The sons of Elyo'einai: Hodavyahu, Elyashiv, Pelaya, Akuv, Yohanan, Delaya, and Anani,** a total of **seven** sons. This genealogical list continues for several generations after the construction of the Second Temple, for Zerubavel (verse 19, above) is likely the well-known Zerubavel son of She'altiel,[83] who was one of the leaders of Israel at the beginning of the Second Temple period. The list continues for several generations after him.

Additional Genealogical Lists of the Tribe of Judah

I CHRONICLES 4:1–23

4 1 This chapter provides another partial genealogical list of the tribe of Judah. **The sons,** descendants, **of Judah: Peretz,** and his son **Hetzron,**[84] and **Karmi,** a descendant of Zerah son of Judah,[85] and **Hur, and Shoval,** both of whom were mentioned above.[86]

2 **Re'aya son of Shoval begot Yahat, and Yahat begot Ahumai and Lahad. These are the families of the Tzoratites,** families who lived in Tzora.

3 **These are the fathers of** the place called **Eitam: Yizre'el, Yishma, Yidbash; the name of their sister was Hatzlelponi,** who, according to the Midrash, was the unnamed mother of Samson in the book of Judges;[87]

4 **Penuel was father** of the settlement **of Gedor, and Ezer was** the **father** of the settlement **of Husha.** All **these are the sons of Hur the firstborn of Efrat.** Hur was **the father** of the settlement **of Bethlehem.** Perhaps this is the reason that the city is called both Bethlehem and Efrat.[88]

5 **Ashhur, father** of the settlement **of Tekoa, had two wives: Hela,** probably from the same root as the word *ḥali*, which means an ornament,[89] just as the name Adi is derived from a word meaning ornament; **and Naara.**

6 **Naara bore him Ahuzam, Hefer, Teimeni, and Ahashtari. These are the sons of Naara.**

7 **The sons of Hela: Tzeret, Tzohar, and Etnan.**

8 **Kotz begot Anuv, Hatzoveva, and the families of Aharhel son of Harum.** Kotz was one of the sons of Hela, even though his name is not mentioned in the previous verse; this is a frequent occurrence in the book of Chronicles. Some read these two verses as though the word Kotz appears twice: And Etnan and Kotz; and Kotz begat, etc. The same can be applied to all similar instances.[90]

9 There was a man in this family called **Yabetz** who **was honored more than his brethren; his mother called his name Yabetz, saying,** in a kind of play on words: **Because I bore him in pain [*be'otzev*].**

10 **Yabetz called,** prayed, **to the God of Israel, saying: If only You would,**[91] alternatively, this is an introductory term that signifies a vow,[92] **bless me and expand my border,** or my success, **and Your hand would be with me** to assist me, **and You would keep me from harm, not causing me pain,** so that I will not suffer. **God granted him that which he requested.** Although his requests were perhaps excessive, God fulfilled his wishes, and he indeed became a successful and important man.

11 **Keluv brother of Shuha begot Mehir, who was the father** of the settlement **of Eshton.**

12 **Eshton begot Beit Rafa, Pase'ah, and Tehina,** who was the **father of** the settlement of **Ir Nahash. These are the men of** the family of **Rekha,** although it is not revealed why they were called by this name.[93]

13 **The sons of Kenaz: Otniel,** who is referred to elsewhere as a great man, a mighty warrior, the first of the judges, and a relation of Caleb,[94] **and Seraya; the sons of Otniel: Hatat.**

14 **Meonotai begot Ofra, and Seraya begot Yoav, father** of the city **of Gei Harashim, for they were craftsmen [*ḥarashim*].**

טז יז הָרְבִיעִי שַׁלּוּם׃ וּבְנֵי יְהוֹיָקִים יְכָנְיָה בְנוֹ צִדְקִיָּה בְנוֹ׃ וּבְנֵי יְכָנְיָה אַסִּר שְׁאַלְתִּיאֵל
יח יט בְּנוֹ׃ וּמַלְכִּירָם וּפְדָיָה וְשֶׁנְאַצַּר יְקַמְיָה הוֹשָׁמָע וּנְדַבְיָה׃ וּבְנֵי פְדָיָה זְרֻבָּבֶל וְשִׁמְעִי
כ וּבֶן־זְרֻבָּבֶל מְשֻׁלָּם וַחֲנַנְיָה וּשְׁלֹמִית אֲחוֹתָם׃ וַחֲשֻׁבָה וָאֹהֶל וּבֶרֶכְיָה וַחֲסַדְיָה
כא יוּשַׁב חֶסֶד חָמֵשׁ׃ וּבֶן־חֲנַנְיָה פְּלַטְיָה וִישַׁעְיָה בְּנֵי רְפָיָה בְּנֵי אַרְנָן בְּנֵי עֹבַדְיָה
כב בְּנֵי שְׁכַנְיָה׃ וּבְנֵי שְׁכַנְיָה שְׁמַעְיָה וּבְנֵי שְׁמַעְיָה חַטּוּשׁ וְיִגְאָל וּבָרִיחַ
כג כד וּנְעַרְיָה וְשָׁפָט שִׁשָּׁה׃ וּבֶן־נְעַרְיָה אֶלְיוֹעֵינַי וְחִזְקִיָּה וְעַזְרִיקָם שְׁלֹשָׁה׃ וּבְנֵי
אֶלְיוֹעֵינַי הודיוהו וְאֶלְיָשִׁיב וּפְלָיָה וְעַקּוּב וְיוֹחָנָן וּדְלָיָה וַעֲנָנִי שִׁבְעָה׃ הוֹדַוְיָהוּ
א ב בְּנֵי יְהוּדָה פֶּרֶץ חֶצְרוֹן וְכַרְמִי וְחוּר וְשׁוֹבָל׃ וּרְאָיָה בֶן־שׁוֹבָל הוֹלִיד אֶת־יַחַת
ג וְיַחַת הוֹלִיד אֶת־אֲחוּמַי וְאֶת־לָהַד אֵלֶּה מִשְׁפְּחוֹת הַצָּרְעָתִי׃ וְאֵלֶּה
ד אֲבִי עֵיטָם יִזְרְעֶאל וְיִשְׁמָא וְיִדְבָּשׁ וְשֵׁם אֲחוֹתָם הַצְלֶלְפּוֹנִי׃ וּפְנוּאֵל אֲבִי גְדֹר
ה וְעֵזֶר אֲבִי חוּשָׁה אֵלֶּה בְנֵי־חוּר בְּכוֹר אֶפְרָתָה אֲבִי בֵּית לָחֶם׃ וּלְאַשְׁחוּר אֲבִי
ו תְקוֹעַ הָיוּ שְׁתֵּי נָשִׁים חֶלְאָה וְנַעֲרָה׃ וַתֵּלֶד לוֹ נַעֲרָה אֶת־אֲחֻזָּם וְאֶת־חֵפֶר וְאֶת־
ז ח תֵּימְנִי וְאֶת־הָאֲחַשְׁתָּרִי אֵלֶּה בְּנֵי נַעֲרָה׃ וּבְנֵי חֶלְאָה צֶרֶת יצחר וְאֶתְנָן׃ וְקוֹץ וְצֹחַר
ט הוֹלִיד אֶת־עָנוּב וְאֶת־הַצֹּבֵבָה וּמִשְׁפְּחֹת אֲחַרְחֵל בֶּן־הָרֻם׃ וַיְהִי יַעְבֵּץ נִכְבָּד
י מֵאֶחָיו וְאִמּוֹ קָרְאָה שְׁמוֹ יַעְבֵּץ לֵאמֹר כִּי יָלַדְתִּי בְּעֹצֶב׃ וַיִּקְרָא יַעְבֵּץ לֵאלֹהֵי ב
יִשְׂרָאֵל לֵאמֹר אִם־בָּרֵךְ תְּבָרְכֵנִי וְהִרְבִּיתָ אֶת־גְּבוּלִי וְהָיְתָה יָדְךָ עִמִּי וְעָשִׂיתָ
יא מֵּרָעָה לְבִלְתִּי עָצְבִּי וַיָּבֵא אֱלֹהִים אֵת אֲשֶׁר־שָׁאָל׃ וּכְלוּב אֲחִי־שׁוּחָה
יב הוֹלִיד אֶת־מְחִיר הוּא אֲבִי אֶשְׁתּוֹן׃ וְאֶשְׁתּוֹן הוֹלִיד אֶת־בֵּית רָפָא וְאֶת־פָּסֵחַ
יג וְאֶת־תְּחִנָּה אֲבִי עִיר־נָחָשׁ אֵלֶּה אַנְשֵׁי רֵכָה׃ וּבְנֵי קְנַז עָתְנִיאֵל וּשְׂרָיָה
יד וּבְנֵי עָתְנִיאֵל חֲתַת׃ וּמְעוֹנֹתַי הוֹלִיד אֶת־עָפְרָה וּשְׂרָיָה הוֹלִיד אֶת־יוֹאָב אֲבִי

This city was famous for the craftsmen who lived there.[95] Since Yoav is not a common name, some contend that this is the famous Yoav son of Tzeruya, who is usually referred to by his mother's name; according to this verse, his father was called Seraya.[96]

15 **The sons of Caleb son of Yefuneh,** who belonged to the same
family: **Iru, Ela, and Naam; and the sons of Ela**: **Kenaz.**[97] Some read the verse as follows: The sons of Naam were Ela and Kenaz.[98]

16 **The sons of Yehalelel: Zif, Zifa, Tirya, and Asarel.**

17 **The sons of Ezra: Yeter, Mered, Efer, and Yalon. She,** Caleb's
wife,[99] **bore Miriam, Shamai, and Yishbah, father** of the settlement **of Eshtemoa,**

18 **and his Judean wife,** the wife of Caleb or perhaps Mered, **bore**
Yered, father of the settlement **of Gedor; Hever, father** of the settlement **of Sokho; and Yekutiel, father** of the settlement **of Zano'ah; these are the sons of Bitya daughter of Pharaoh**[D] **whom Mered took as a wife.** Bitya daughter of Pharaoh is perhaps the same woman who earlier in the verse is called his Judean, or Jewish wife.

19 **The sons of the wife of Hodiya, the sister of Naham: the father** of the settlement **of Ke'ila of the Garmites and Eshtemoa of the Maakhatites.**

20 **The sons of Shimon,** who was perhaps sufficiently well known
that there was no need to mention his lineage:[100] **Amnon, Rina, Ben Hanan, and Tilon. The sons of Yishi: Zohet and Ben Zohet,** probably a name rather than "son of [*ben*] Zohet."[101]

21 Some of the people mentioned up to this point were descen-
dants of Zerah son of Judah, although the majority were sons of Peretz. The chapter now cites a very short list of another branch of the tribe. **The sons of Shela son of Judah: Er,** named by Shela after his brother who had died young,[102] the **father** of the settlement **of Lekha, and Lada, father** of the settlement **of Maresha, and the families of the house of the craft of fine linen,**[103] **of the house of Ashbe'a;**

22 **and Yokim, the men of Kozeva** were from these families,
Yo'ash, Saraf, who married into Moav, or who married women from Moav, **and Yashuvi Lehem; the matters are ancient**[D] [*atikim*]; alternatively, the records are copied [*mu'atakim*] from other lists and books.

23 **They are the potters and the inhabitants of Neta'im and**
Gedera; alternatively, this means that they were those who dwelt among plantations [*neta'im*] and hedges [*gedera*];[104] **they dwelt there in the king's employ.** The residents of these places performed the king's labor and were perhaps famous on this account. This concludes an extremely abbreviated list of the descendants of Judah.

The Families of the Tribe of Simeon and Their Cities

I CHRONICLES 4:24–43

This is also a very general list, but it does relate certain key events in the history of the tribe of Simeon. This tribe began as subordinate to the tribe of Judah, but later made a name for itself as a tribe of warriors.

24 **The sons of Simeon**: **Nemuel, Yamin, Yariv, Zerah, Shaul,**

25 **Shalum his,** Shaul's, **son; Mivsam his son,** the son of Shalum;
and thus the generations continue: **Mishma his,** Shalum's, **son.**

26 **The sons of Mishma: Hammuel his son, Zakur his son,**
Shimi his son.

27 **Shimi had sixteen sons and six daughters, but his broth-**
ers did not have many children, and their entire family, the descendants of Simeon, **did not multiply like the children of Judah.** They were always far fewer in number than the tribe of Judah.

28 **They,** the children of Simeon, **dwelled in Beersheba, Molada,**
and Hatzar Shual,

29 **and in Bilha, in Etzem, in Tolad,**

30 **in Betuel, in Horma, in Tziklag,**

31 **in Beit Markavot, in Hatzar Susim, in Beit Biri, and in**
Shaarayim. These were their cities, the cities of the children of Simeon, **until the reign of David.** These are more or less the same places that are listed in the book of Joshua as the cities of Simeon. The tribe of Simeon was virtually subsumed into the tribe of Judah; the members of Judah provided them with

Cities of Simeon

protection, but their territory was swallowed up within the territory of Judah.[105]

טו גִּ֣יא חֲרָשִׁ֔ים כִּ֥י חֲרָשִׁ֖ים הָיֽוּ׃ וּבְנֵי֙ כָּלֵ֣ב בֶּן־יְפֻנֶּ֔ה עִ֥ירוּ אֵ֖לָה וָנָ֑עַם וּבְנֵ֥י

טז יז אֵלָ֖ה וּקְנַֽז׃ וּבְנֵ֖י יְהַלֶּלְאֵ֑ל זִ֣יף וְזִיפָ֔ה תִּירְיָ֖א וַאֲשַׂרְאֵֽל׃ וּבֶן־עֶזְרָ֔ה יֶ֥תֶר וּמֶ֖רֶד וְעֵ֣פֶר

יח וְיָל֑וֹן וַתַּ֙הַר֙ אֶת־מִרְיָ֣ם וְאֶת־שַׁמַּ֔י וְאֶת־יִשְׁבָּ֖ח אֲבִ֥י אֶשְׁתְּמֹֽעַ׃ וְאִשְׁתּ֣וֹ הַיְהֻדִיָּ֗ה

יָֽלְדָ֞ה אֶת־יֶ֙רֶד֙ אֲבִ֣י גְד֔וֹר וְאֶת־חֶ֙בֶר֙ אֲבִ֣י שׂוֹכ֔וֹ וְאֶת־יְקֽוּתִיאֵ֖ל אֲבִ֣י זָנ֑וֹחַ וְאֵ֗לֶּה

יט בְּנֵי֙ בִּתְיָ֣ה בַת־פַּרְעֹ֔ה אֲשֶׁ֥ר לָקַ֖ח מָֽרֶד׃ וּבְנֵי֙ אֵ֣שֶׁת הֽוֹדִיָּ֔ה אֲח֖וֹת נַ֑חַם

כ אֲבִ֖י קְעִילָ֣ה הַגַּרְמִ֑י וְאֶשְׁתְּמֹ֖עַ הַמַּעֲכָתִֽי׃ וּבְנֵ֣י שִׁימ֔וֹן אַמְנ֣וֹן וְרִנָּ֔ה בֶּן־חָנָ֖ן ותולון וְתִילֽוֹן

כא וּבְנֵ֣י יִשְׁעִ֔י זוֹחֵ֖ת וּבֶן־זוֹחֵֽת׃ בְּנֵ֗י שֵׁלָ֤ה בֶן־יְהוּדָה֙ עֵ֚ר אֲבִ֣י לֵכָ֔ה וְלַעְדָּ֖ה אֲבִ֣י מָֽרֵשָׁ֑ה

כב וּמִשְׁפְּח֛וֹת בֵּית־עֲבֹדַ֥ת הַבֻּ֖ץ לְבֵ֥ית אַשְׁבֵּֽעַ׃ וְיוֹקִ֞ים וְאַנְשֵׁ֣י כֹזֵבָ֗א וְיוֹאָ֧שׁ וְשָׂרָ֛ף

כג אֲשֶׁר־בָּעֲל֥וּ לְמוֹאָ֖ב וְיָ֣שֻׁבִי לָ֑חֶם וְהַדְּבָרִ֖ים עַתִּיקִֽים׃ הֵ֚מָּה הַיּ֣וֹצְרִ֔ים וְיֹשְׁבֵ֥י נְטָעִ֖ים

כד וּגְדֵרָ֑ה עִם־הַמֶּ֛לֶךְ בִּמְלַאכְתּ֖וֹ יָ֥שְׁבוּ שָֽׁם׃ בְּנֵ֖י שִׁמְע֑וֹן נְמוּאֵ֣ל וְיָמִ֔ין

כה כו יָרִ֖יב זֶ֥רַח שָׁאֽוּל׃ שַׁלֻּ֥ם בְּנ֛וֹ מִבְשָׂ֥ם בְּנ֖וֹ מִשְׁמָ֥ע בְּנֽוֹ׃ וּבְנֵ֖י מִשְׁמָ֑ע חַמּוּאֵ֥ל בְּנ֛וֹ

כז זַכּ֥וּר בְּנ֖וֹ שִׁמְעִ֥י בְנֽוֹ׃ וּלְשִׁמְעִ֞י בָּנִ֨ים שִׁשָּׁ֤ה עָשָׂר֙ וּבָנ֣וֹת שֵׁ֔שׁ וּלְאֶחָ֕יו אֵ֥ין בָּנִ֖ים

כח רַבִּ֑ים וְכֹל֙ מִשְׁפַּחְתָּ֔ם לֹ֥א הִרְבּ֖וּ עַד־בְּנֵ֥י יְהוּדָֽה׃ וַיֵּשְׁב֛וּ בִּבְאֵֽר־שֶׁ֖בַע וּמוֹלָדָ֥ה

כט ל לא וַחֲצַ֥ר שׁוּעָֽל׃ וּבְבִלְהָ֥ה וּבְעֶ֖צֶם וּבְתוֹלָֽד׃ וּבִבְתוּאֵ֥ל וּבְחָרְמָ֖ה וּבְצִֽקְלָֽג׃ וּבְבֵ֤ית

מַרְכָּבוֹת֙ וּבַחֲצַ֣ר סוּסִ֔ים וּבְבֵ֥ית בִּרְאִ֖י וּבְשַׁעֲרָ֑יִם אֵ֥לֶּה עָרֵיהֶ֖ם עַד־מְלֹ֥ךְ דָּוִֽיד׃

DISCUSSION

4:18 | **Bitya daughter of Pharaoh:** It is not clear from the verse whether the "Judean wife" is the same as Bitya daughter of Pharaoh, and whether she was the wife of Caleb or Mered. According to *midrashim*, this Bitya was the same daughter of Pharaoh who raised Moses, after which she joined the children of Israel and married a man called Mered, who some claim was none other than Caleb son of Yefuneh himself, based on the context here. Since all the men and women listed here are from the tribe of Judah, it can be surmised that the title "Judean wife" signifies that she was not originally from the tribe of Judah but later became part of that tribe (see Radak; *Megilla* 13a; *Sanhedrin* 19b). Alternatively, this is referring to a different woman known as Bitya daughter of Pharaoh, a woman who was a member of the tribe of Judah from birth (see *Adderet Eliyahu*; *Vayikra Rabba* 1).

4:22 | **The matters are ancient:** The Sages identify Yoash and Saraf as Mahlon and Kilyon, who married Moavite women (Ruth 1:4). If so, Mahlon and Kilyon were not their real names; rather, they were monikers indicative of their tragic, early demise. The name or phrase Yashuvi Lehem is also expounded by the Sages in reference to the same episode. They explain that it signifies the family's eventual return [*shava*] to Bethlehem. On these lines, the word *atikim* means that these matters are copied [*mu'atakim*] from the book of Ruth, where the story appears in full (see Rashi; Radak; *Adderet Eliyahu*; *Bava Batra* 91b; *Sifrei*, *Bemidbar* 78).

32 **Their** open, unwalled **villages were Eitam and Ayin, Rimon**
and Tokhen, and Ashan, a total of **five cities;**
33 **and all their villages that were surrounding these cities, up**
to Baal. These were their dwellings, and their relationship
to them.[B] This was the area in which they lived and the cities
to which they were related.[106] There were several central cities,
surrounded by villages and small towns.
34 Over time, the tribe of Simeon increased and spread out:
Meshovav, Yamlekh, Yosha son of Amatzya,
35 **Yoel, Yehu son of Yoshivya, son of Seraya, son of Asiel,**
36 **Elioeinai, Yaakova, Yeshohaya, Asaya, Adiel, Yesimiel,**
Benaya,
37 **and Ziza son of Shifi, son of Alon, son of Yedaya, son of**
Shimri, son of Shemaya.
38 All **these mentioned by name were** not ordinary individuals;
rather, they were **princes in their families,** as each was the
leader of a large group of people, **and their patrilineal houses**
increased greatly. Their families multiplied, and as their territory was in the Negev, which is not very suitable for agriculture,
they earned their living mainly by shepherding.
39 **They went to the approach to Gedor, up to the east of the**
valley, to seek pasture for their flocks.
40 **They found** an area of **lush and good pasture, and the land**
was spacious, serene, and tranquil, for the inhabitants
beforehand were from the children of **Ham.** The descendants
of Ham who lived in that region were not belligerent.
41 **Those** princes **recorded by name came in the days of**
Yehizkiyahu king of Judah, and smote their tents, and the
Maonites, people of the tribe of Maon, who harassed Israel,[107]
who were found there, and destroyed them to this day, until the day this verse was written.[108] **They settled** there **in their**
stead, for there was pasture for their flocks there. It seems
that they wandered in search of land fit for grazing until they
came to an inhabited area, which they then conquered and
settled. It is not clear whether this refers to a portion of the inheritance of Judah that the tribe had never captured, or if the
children of Simeon traveled south of the border of the land of
Judah.
42 **Some of them from the sons of Simeon,** a different section of
the tribe, **went to the highlands of Se'ir, five hundred men,**
and Pelatya, Ne'arya, Refaya, and Uziel, sons of Yishi, were
at their head. Mount Se'ir was the region of the Edomites,
among whom lived the remnant of Amalek that Saul had failed
to destroy.
43 **They,** the sons of Simeon, **smote the surviving remnant of**
the Amalekites and dwelled there to this day.

The Genealogy and Cities of the Tribes of the Eastern Side of the Jordan

I CHRONICLES 5:1–26

These too are fragmentary genealogical lists, which deal with the tribes that lived on the eastern side of the Jordan: Reuben, Gad, and half the tribe of Manasseh.

5 1 **The sons of Reuben, the firstborn of Israel; for he was the**
firstborn in order of age, strictly speaking, **but when he des-**
ecrated his father's couch, as related in Genesis (35:22), **his**
birthright was given to the sons of Joseph son of Israel. This
transfer of the birthright was expressed by the double inheritance given to Joseph's sons. Furthermore, it seems that some
of Joseph's descendants enjoyed a special status in Israel.[109]
But Joseph is **not to be reckoned as firstborn.** Joseph is still
considered among the youngest of Jacob's sons; regarding the
matter of lineage, he is not the firstborn of Israel.[110]
2 **For Judah prevailed over his brothers;** he became greater
and more important than his brothers, as his was the dominant
personality among them, **as the prince would come from**
him, the royal line descended from Judah, **but the right of pri-**
mogeniture with regard to the inheritances and social status
was to Joseph.
3 The previous introduction concerning Reuben's status among
the tribes is followed by a genealogical list. **The sons of**
Reuben, the firstborn of Israel: Hanokh, Palu, Hetzron,
and Karmi.
4 This verse begins a list of important personages among the descendants of Reuben over the subsequent generations.[111] **The**
sons of Yoel, who was not included in the above list: **Shemaya**
his, Yoel's, **son, Gog his,** Shemaya's, **son,** and thus the generations continued: **Shimi his son,**
5 **Mikha his son, Re'aya his son, Baal his son,**
6 **Be'era his son, whom Tilgat Pilneser,** also called Tiglat
Pileser,[112] **king of Assyria, exiled; he,** Be'era, **was prince of the**
Reubenites. The Assyrians exiled the tribes who lived on the
eastern side of the Jordan first, and at that time, Be'era was the
leader of the tribe of Reuben. There is an opinion that identifies this Be'era with Be'eri, the father of the prophet Hosea, but
there is no clear proof of this from the verses themselves.[113]
7 **His brethren,** others of that same tribe, **according to their**
families in establishing their lineage[114] **for their progeny**
were as follows: **The leader was Ye'iel, and Zekharyahu** succeeded him,
8 **and Bela, son of Azaz, son of Shema, son of Yoel; he set-**
tled in Aroer,[B] **up to Nevo**[B] **and Baal Meon,**[B] or he went from

לב לג וְחַצְרֵיהֶם עֵיטָם וָעַיִן רִמּוֹן וְתֹכֶן וְעָשָׁן עָרִים חָמֵשׁ: וְכָל־חַצְרֵיהֶם אֲשֶׁר סְבִיבוֹת
לד הֶעָרִים הָאֵלֶּה עַד־בָּעַל זֹאת מוֹשְׁבֹתָם וְהִתְיַחְשָׂם לָהֶם: וּמְשׁוֹבָב וְיַמְלֵךְ וְיוֹשָׁה
לה לו בֶּן־אֲמַצְיָה: וְיוֹאֵל וְיֵהוּא בֶּן־יוֹשִׁבְיָה בֶּן־שְׂרָיָה בֶּן־עֲשִׂיאֵל: וְאֶלְיוֹעֵינַי וְיַעֲקֹבָה
לז וִישׁוֹחָיָה וַעֲשָׂיָה וַעֲדִיאֵל וִישִׂימִאֵל וּבְנָיָה: וְזִיזָא בֶן־שִׁפְעִי בֶן־אַלּוֹן בֶּן־יְדָיָה
לח בֶּן־שִׁמְרִי בֶּן־שְׁמַעְיָה: אֵלֶּה הַבָּאִים בְּשֵׁמוֹת נְשִׂיאִים בְּמִשְׁפְּחוֹתָם וּבֵית
לט אֲבוֹתֵיהֶם פָּרְצוּ לָרוֹב: וַיֵּלְכוּ לִמְבוֹא גְדֹר עַד לְמִזְרַח הַגָּיְא לְבַקֵּשׁ מִרְעֶה לְצֹאנָם:
מ וַיִּמְצְאוּ מִרְעֶה שָׁמֵן וָטוֹב וְהָאָרֶץ רַחֲבַת יָדַיִם וְשֹׁקֶטֶת וּשְׁלֵוָה כִּי מִן־חָם הַיֹּשְׁבִים
מא שָׁם לְפָנִים: וַיָּבֹאוּ אֵלֶּה הַכְּתוּבִים בְּשֵׁמוֹת בִּימֵי | יְחִזְקִיָּהוּ מֶלֶךְ־יְהוּדָה וַיַּכּוּ
אֶת־אָהֳלֵיהֶם וְאֶת־הַמְּעִינִים אֲשֶׁר נִמְצְאוּ־שָׁמָּה וַיַּחֲרִימֻם עַד־הַיּוֹם הַזֶּה וַיֵּשְׁבוּ הַמְּעוּנִים
מב תַּחְתֵּיהֶם כִּי־מִרְעֶה לְצֹאנָם שָׁם: וּמֵהֶם | מִן־בְּנֵי שִׁמְעוֹן הָלְכוּ לְהַר שֵׂעִיר
מג אֲנָשִׁים חֲמֵשׁ מֵאוֹת וּפְלַטְיָה וּנְעַרְיָה וּרְפָיָה וְעֻזִּיאֵל בְּנֵי יִשְׁעִי בְּרֹאשָׁם: וַיַּכּוּ
ה א אֶת־שְׁאֵרִית הַפְּלֵטָה לַעֲמָלֵק וַיֵּשְׁבוּ שָׁם עַד הַיּוֹם הַזֶּה: וּבְנֵי רְאוּבֵן
בְּכוֹר־יִשְׂרָאֵל כִּי־הוּא הַבְּכוֹר וּבְחַלְּלוֹ יְצוּעֵי אָבִיו נִתְּנָה בְּכֹרָתוֹ לִבְנֵי יוֹסֵף בֶּן־
ב יִשְׂרָאֵל וְלֹא לְהִתְיַחֵשׂ לַבְּכֹרָה: כִּי יְהוּדָה גָּבַר בְּאֶחָיו וּלְנָגִיד מִמֶּנּוּ וְהַבְּכֹרָה
ג ד לְיוֹסֵף: בְּנֵי רְאוּבֵן בְּכוֹר יִשְׂרָאֵל חֲנוֹךְ וּפַלּוּא חֶצְרוֹן וְכַרְמִי: בְּנֵי
ה ו יוֹאֵל שְׁמַעְיָה בְנוֹ גּוֹג בְּנוֹ שִׁמְעִי בְנוֹ: מִיכָה בְנוֹ רְאָיָה בְנוֹ בַּעַל בְּנוֹ: בְּאֵרָה בְנוֹ
ז אֲשֶׁר הֶגְלָה תִּלְּגַת פִּלְנְאֶסֶר מֶלֶךְ אַשֻּׁר הוּא נָשִׂיא לָראוּבֵנִי: וְאֶחָיו לְמִשְׁפְּחֹתָיו
ח בְּהִתְיַחֵשׂ לְתֹלְדוֹתָם הָרֹאשׁ יְעִיאֵל וּזְכַרְיָהוּ: וּבֶלַע בֶּן־עָזָז בֶּן־שֶׁמַע בֶּן־יוֹאֵל

BACKGROUND

4:33 | **These were their dwellings, and their relationship to them:** This list is similar to the one that appears in the book of Joshua (19:1–9), apart from some slight differences in spelling. In addition, the places Beit Biri and Shaarayim appear here instead of Beit Leva'ot and Sharuhen, unidentified locations.

5:8 | **Aroer:** A city on the northern bank of the Arnon Stream, whose name is preserved in Khirbet Arair, around 5 km southeast of Divon.

Nevo: A city in the territory of the tribe of Reuben, in the plains of northern Moav (see Numbers 32:38), at the foot of the mountains of Moav, near Mount Nevo, from where Moses viewed the Land of Israel. Nevo is recorded in the Mesha Stele (ninth century BCE) as having been captured from Israel in a cruel fashion by the Moavites. There is no certain identification of the city. Modern scholars have sought to identify it as one of the settlements on the slopes descending from the mountains of Moav to the plains of Moav.

Baal Meon: Baal Meon has been identified as the Christian town of Ma'in, 7 km southwest of Madaba.

Aroer to Nevo and Baal Meon, as Aroer belonged to the portion of Gad;[115]
9 **and he,** either the tribe or the aforementioned head of the tribe,
settled eastward until the approach to the wilderness, and
because their path was not blocked they continued to spread
from there to a place **adjacent to the Euphrates River,** the
place where the Euphrates River is closest to Israel, **for their**
cattle multiplied in the land of Gilad, and since no political
force halted their advance, they penetrated further and further
into the Syrian Desert.[116]
10 **In the days of Saul, they,** the children of Reuben, **waged war**
with the Hagrites,[B] a Bedouin tribe from the descendants of
Hagar,[117] **who fell into their hand, and they dwelled in their**
tents across all the east of the Gilad.[118]
11 **The sons of Gad dwelled opposite them,** across from the
tribe of Reuben, or near them, **in the land of Bashan,**[B] on the
eastern side of the Jordan, **up to Salkha,** north of the border of
Reuben's territory:
12 **Yoel** was **the chief** in one generation, **Shafam** was **the deputy**
to him, **Yanai, Shafat;** these people lived **in the Bashan,**
13 **and their brethren,** the chiefs,[119] **by their patrilineal houses**
were: **Mikhael, Meshulam, Sheva, Yorai, Yakan, Zia, and**
Ever, a total of **seven.**
14 **These** seven men[120] **are the sons,** descendants, **of Avihayil, son**
of Huri, son of Yaro'ah, son of Gilad, son of Mikhael, son of
Yeshishai, son of Yahdo, son of Buz;
15 **Ahi, son of Avdiel, son of Guni,** was the **chief of their patri-**
lineal houses.
16 **They dwelled in** the broad expanse of **Gilad in the Bashan,**
in its environs, and in all the fields of Sharon,[B] **up to** and including **their borders.**
17 **All of them were established in their lineage in the days of**
Yotam king of Judah and in the days of Yorovam II, **king of**
Israel. This was a period of relative quiet, as Yorovam II expanded Israel's borders almost until the northern edge of
Syria.[121] The tranquil period of his reign provided the peace of
mind that allowed for the organization of these genealogical
lists.
18 **The sons of Reuben, and the Gadites, and half the tribe**
of Manasseh, of the military men, men able to bear shield

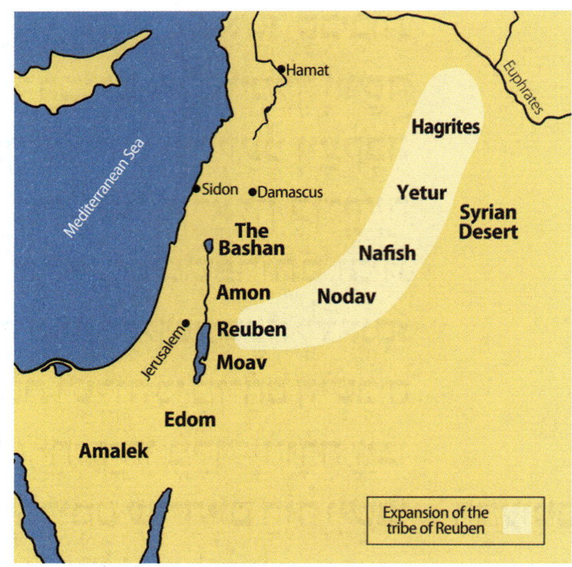

Expansion of the tribe of Reuben

and sword, archers, and those who were **skillful in war,** were
counted: **Forty-four thousand seven hundred and sixty** men
who would go forth to war. This census was presumably performed in the days of Yotam and Yorovam.[122]
19 **They waged war with the Hagrites, Yetur,**[B] **Nafish, and**
Nodav.
20 **They were aided** by God **against them,** their enemies, **and the**
Hagrites and all the smaller tribes or nations **who were with**
them were delivered into their hand, for they cried out to
God in the battle, and He acceded to their entreaty because
they trusted in Him.
21 **They captured their livestock,** from these nations: **Camels**
– fifty thousand; sheep – two hundred and fifty thousand;
donkeys – two thousand. And human beings – one hundred
thousand.
22 **For many fell slain;** they achieved great victory despite being relatively few in number, **because the war was from God.**
They dwelled in their stead, in place of those tribes, **until the**
exile to Assyria.[123]

BACKGROUND

5:10| **The Hagrites:** The Hagrites are also mentioned in the book of Psalms (83:7) as part of a group of tribes or nations that were hostile to Israel and lived in the wildernesses on the eastern side of the Jordan. The descriptions indicate that they were shepherds, and it is possible that Yaziz the Hagrite (I Chronicles 27:31), who was responsible for King David's flocks, was from this nation.

ט הוּא יוֹשֵׁב בַּעֲרֹעֵר וְעַד־נְבוֹ וּבַעַל מְעוֹן׃ וְלַמִּזְרָח יָשַׁב עַד־לְבוֹא מִדְבָּרָה לְמִן־
י הַנָּהָר פְּרָת כִּי מִקְנֵיהֶם רָבוּ בְּאֶרֶץ גִּלְעָד׃ וּבִימֵי שָׁאוּל עָשׂוּ מִלְחָמָה עִם־
הַהַגְרִאִים וַיִּפְּלוּ בְּיָדָם וַיֵּשְׁבוּ בְּאָהֳלֵיהֶם עַל־כָּל־פְּנֵי מִזְרָח לַגִּלְעָד׃
יא יב וּבְנֵי־גָד לְנֶגְדָּם יָשְׁבוּ בְּאֶרֶץ הַבָּשָׁן עַד־סַלְכָה׃ יוֹאֵל הָרֹאשׁ וְשָׁפָם הַמִּשְׁנֶה וְיַעְנַי
יג וְשָׁפָט בַּבָּשָׁן׃ וַאֲחֵיהֶם לְבֵית אֲבוֹתֵיהֶם מִיכָאֵל וּמְשֻׁלָּם וְשֶׁבַע וְיוֹרַי וְיַעְכָּן וְזִיעַ
יד וָעֵבֶר שִׁבְעָה׃ אֵלֶּה ׀ בְּנֵי אֲבִיחַיִל בֶּן־חוּרִי בֶּן־יָרוֹחַ בֶּן־גִּלְעָד בֶּן־
טו מִיכָאֵל בֶּן־יְשִׁישַׁי בֶּן־יַחְדּוֹ בֶּן־בּוּז׃ אֲחִי בֶּן־עַבְדִּיאֵל בֶּן־גּוּנִי רֹאשׁ לְבֵית
טז אֲבוֹתָם׃ וַיֵּשְׁבוּ בַּגִּלְעָד בַּבָּשָׁן וּבִבְנֹתֶיהָ וּבְכָל־מִגְרְשֵׁי שָׁרוֹן עַל־תּוֹצְאוֹתָם׃
יז כֻּלָּם הִתְיַחְשׂוּ בִּימֵי יוֹתָם מֶלֶךְ־יְהוּדָה וּבִימֵי יָרָבְעָם מֶלֶךְ־יִשְׂרָאֵל׃
יח בְּנֵי־רְאוּבֵן וְגָדִי וַחֲצִי שֵׁבֶט־מְנַשֶּׁה מִן־בְּנֵי־חַיִל אֲנָשִׁים נֹשְׂאֵי מָגֵן וְחֶרֶב וְדֹרְכֵי
קֶשֶׁת וּלְמוּדֵי מִלְחָמָה אַרְבָּעִים וְאַרְבָּעָה אֶלֶף וּשְׁבַע־מֵאוֹת וְשִׁשִּׁים יֹצְאֵי צָבָא׃
יט כ וַיַּעֲשׂוּ מִלְחָמָה עִם־הַהַגְרִיאִים וִיטוּר וְנָפִישׁ וְנוֹדָב׃ וַיֵּעָזְרוּ עֲלֵיהֶם וַיִּנָּתְנוּ בְיָדָם
הַהַגְרִיאִים וְכֹל שֶׁעִמָּהֶם כִּי לֵאלֹהִים זָעֲקוּ בַּמִּלְחָמָה וְנַעְתּוֹר לָהֶם כִּי־בָטְחוּ
כא בוֹ׃ וַיִּשְׁבּוּ מִקְנֵיהֶם גְּמַלֵּיהֶם חֲמִשִּׁים אֶלֶף וְצֹאן מָאתַיִם וַחֲמִשִּׁים אֶלֶף וַחֲמוֹרִים
כב אַלְפָּיִם וְנֶפֶשׁ אָדָם מֵאָה אָלֶף׃ כִּי־חֲלָלִים רַבִּים נָפָלוּ כִּי מֵהָאֱלֹהִים הַמִּלְחָמָה

BACKGROUND

5:11| **Bashan:** This is the fertile region at the northern end of the eastern side of the Jordan. The Bashan sprawls from the Yarmuk River to Mount Hermon and from the Jordan Valley in the west to Jabal al-Druze in the east, and includes the Golan Heights. The region is mainly a plateau, and because little water is lost in its clayish, basalt soil, the Bashan grows lush grass most of the year and was therefore considered an ideal location for grazing animals. Consequently, the cattle and sheep raised there were of especially high quality (see, e.g., Deuteronomy 32:14; Ezekiel 39:18; Amos 4:1; Psalms 22:13, see also commentary ad loc.).

5:16| **The fields of Sharon:** There are divergent opinions with regard to this place. Some claim that the word *sharon* is not a place name, but a geographical description of an area that is suitable only for pasture; *sharnu* means "forest" in Akkadian. However, the majority of scholars maintain that *Sharon* is the name of a specific region. Some associate it with Siryon, one of the names for Mount Hermon (see Deuteronomy 3:9), in the north of Bashan. They explain that, until recently, shepherds would bring their sheep to graze on the slopes of the Hermon when the pastures in Gilad and the south of Bashan gradually decreased at the end of spring (Pessah Bar-Adon, "Light on a Biblical Passage from Modern Observation," *Bulletin of the Jewish Palestine Exploration Society,* Spring 1934 [Hebrew], 24). Others claim that this is the familiar Sharon area in western Israel, on the coastal region of Samaria, as the shepherds of the tribe of Gad would wander there with their flocks (see also 27:29). The expression "they dwelled" could also refer to the area of shepherds' wanderings.

5:19| **Yetur:** A nation named after one of the sons of Ishmael, who lived as nomads in the Arabian wilderness. A similarly named people who lived in the Beqaa Valley and on the slopes of the Hermon is mentioned in the writings of Josephus and other writers from the Second Temple period. Modern scholars speculate that they were nomads who wandered north to these regions in the eighth century BCE. According to Josephus, the Yeturites converted to Judaism at the end of the second century BCE, during the reign of Judah Aristobulus I.

23 **The children of half the tribe of Manasseh dwelled in the
land, from Bashan** in the north, westward **to Baal Hermon,
and Senir, and Mount
Hermon;**[B] **they,** the tribe of
Manasseh, **increased in
number.** Although it is stated in the Torah that Senir is
another name for Hermon, it
is possible that various sections of this great mountain
were called by different
names.[124]

Mount Hermon

24 **These are the heads of their patrilineal houses: Efer, and
Yishi.** Literally the verse reads "and Efer and Yishi," but the
first "and" is probably a mere stylistic flourish.[125] **And Eliel, and
Azriel, and Yirmeya, and Hodavya, and Yahdiel, mighty
warriors, men of renown** whose names were well known,[126]
and who were **heads of their patrilineal houses.**
25 **They,** these tribes, **trespassed against the God of their fathers and strayed after the gods of the peoples of the land
whom God had destroyed before them.**
26 **The God of Israel roused the spirit of Pul king of Assyria**[B]
and the spirit of Tilgat Pilneser, also called Tiglat Pileser,
**king of Assyria, and they exiled the Reubenite, the Gadite,
and half the tribe of Manasseh and brought them to Halah,**[B]
Havor, Hara, and to the river of Gozan,[B] **until this day.** These
places were in the northwestern portion of the kingdom of
Assyria, in the northern part of the land of the Medes; present-
day northern Syria and Iraq.

The Levites and the Cities Allocated to Them

I CHRONICLES 5:27–6:66

Following the discussion concerning Reuben and the mention of Simeon as an adjunct to the children of Judah, the chapter turns to the tribe of Levi, whose families are spelled out in the first list in an exceedingly incomplete manner:

27 **The sons of Levi: Gershon, Kehat, and Merari.**
28 **The sons of Kehat: Amram, Yitzhar, Hevron, and Uziel.**
29 **The children of Amram** were: **Aaron, Moses, and Miriam.
The sons of Aaron: Nadav and Avihu, Elazar and Itamar.**
As is well known, Nadav and Avihu died in their father's lifetime without sons, perhaps without any children whatsoever,
and Elazar and Itamar were left as the two families of the High
Priesthood.
30 **Elazar begot Pinhas, Pinhas begot Avishua,**
31 **Avishua begot Buki, Buki begot Uzi,**
32 **Uzi begot Zerahya, Zerahya begot Merayot,**
33 **Merayot begot Amarya, Amarya begot Ahituv,**
34 **Ahituv begot Tzadok,**[D] **Tzadok begot Ahimaatz,**
35 **Ahimaatz begot Azarya, Azarya begot Yohanan,**
36 **and Yohanan begot Azarya** the second; **it is he who served
as priest in the House that Solomon built in Jerusalem.** This
Azarya and his sons after him were High Priests or well-known
priests in the First Temple.[127]
37 **Azarya begot Amarya, Amarya begot Ahituv,**
38 **Ahituv begot Tzadok, Tzadok begot Shalum,**

BACKGROUND

5:23| **Baal Hermon, and Senir, and Mount Hermon:** These are different names for the mountain range that faces Lebanon. The range has two additional names that are mentioned in the book of Deuteronomy: Siryon and Sion (Deuteronomy 3:9, 4:48). These names also appear in Ugaritic, Hurrian, Akkadian, and Egyptian documents. The Sages explain that the many names attest to the importance of this mountain to the various nations that lived in the surrounding area (*Sifrei Zuta* 27:12). It is unclear whether these names were applied to the entire range or only to parts of it; some contend that Siryon and Senir refer to the range's northern section, while Hermon is the name of the southern, higher part, where sites of religious worship have been discovered.

5:26| **Pul king of Assyria:** According to Babylonian documents which list the kings of Babylon, and the Phoenician Inscription of the Incirli Trilingual (south-central Turkey), Pul was the original Assyrian name of Tiglat Pileser III. He adopted the Akkadian name Tiglat Pileser, Tukulti-Apil-Esara in Akkadian, after having seized the throne in 745 BCE and after having wiped out the royal family. In an apparent attempt to legitimize his reign, he adopted an Akkadian name in accordance with the custom of the Assyrian kings, and traced his lineage to Tiglat Pileser I. Some, however, claim that Pul was actually Ashur-nirari V, who came before Tiglat Pileser III, and of whom little is known.

Halah: It is surmised that this place was located northeast of Nineveh, as the northeast-facing gate of Nineveh was called Halahhu. Like Damascus Gate and Jaffa Gate in Jerusalem, the gates of Nineveh were named after the places that would be reached if one left the city from that direction.

Gozan: Gozan was a city located on the upper portion of the Havor River, one of the tributaries of the Euphrates River. It is identified as Tel Halaf, in northern Syria on the Turkish border. According to Assyrian documents, Gozan was the capital city of an Aramaean kingdom called Bit Bahiani, which was sacked by the Assyrians in 858 BCE and became an Assyrian tributary.

כג וַיֵּשְׁבוּ תַחְתֵּיהֶם עַד־הַגֹּלָה׃ וּבְנֵי חֲצִי שֵׁבֶט מְנַשֶּׁה יָשְׁבוּ בָּאָרֶץ מִבָּשָׁן
כד עַד־בַּעַל חֶרְמוֹן וּשְׂנִיר וְהַר־חֶרְמוֹן הֵמָּה רָבוּ׃ וְאֵלֶּה רָאשֵׁי בֵית־אֲבוֹתָם וְעֵפֶר
וְיִשְׁעִי וֶאֱלִיאֵל וְעַזְרִיאֵל וְיִרְמְיָה וְהוֹדַוְיָה וְיַחְדִּיאֵל אֲנָשִׁים גִּבּוֹרֵי חַיִל אַנְשֵׁי
כה שֵׁמוֹת רָאשִׁים לְבֵית אֲבוֹתָם׃ וַיִּמְעֲלוּ בֵּאלֹהֵי אֲבֹתֵיהֶם וַיִּזְנוּ
כו אַחֲרֵי אֱלֹהֵי עַמֵּי־הָאָרֶץ אֲשֶׁר־הִשְׁמִיד אֱלֹהִים מִפְּנֵיהֶם׃ וַיָּעַר אֱלֹהֵי יִשְׂרָאֵל
אֶת־רוּחַ ׀ פּוּל מֶלֶךְ־אַשּׁוּר וְאֶת־רוּחַ תִּלְגַת פִּלְנֶסֶר מֶלֶךְ אַשּׁוּר וַיַּגְלֵם לָראוּבֵנִי
וְלַגָּדִי וְלַחֲצִי שֵׁבֶט מְנַשֶּׁה וַיְבִיאֵם לַחְלַח וְחָבוֹר וְהָרָא וּנְהַר גּוֹזָן עַד הַיּוֹם
כז כח הַזֶּה׃ בְּנֵי לֵוִי גֵּרְשׁוֹן קְהָת וּמְרָרִי׃ וּבְנֵי קְהָת עַמְרָם יִצְהָר וְחֶבְרוֹן
כט וְעֻזִּיאֵל׃ וּבְנֵי עַמְרָם אַהֲרֹן וּמֹשֶׁה וּמִרְיָם וּבְנֵי אַהֲרֹן נָדָב וַאֲבִיהוּא
ל אֶלְעָזָר וְאִיתָמָר׃ אֶלְעָזָר הוֹלִיד אֶת־פִּינְחָס פִּינְחָס הֹלִיד אֶת־אֲבִישׁוּעַ׃
לא לב וַאֲבִישׁוּעַ הוֹלִיד אֶת־בֻּקִּי וּבֻקִּי הוֹלִיד אֶת־עֻזִּי׃ וְעֻזִּי הוֹלִיד אֶת־זְרַחְיָה וּזְרַחְיָה
לג הוֹלִיד אֶת־מְרָיוֹת׃ מְרָיוֹת הוֹלִיד אֶת־אֲמַרְיָה וַאֲמַרְיָה הוֹלִיד אֶת־אֲחִיטוּב׃
לד לה וַאֲחִיטוּב הוֹלִיד אֶת־צָדוֹק וְצָדוֹק הוֹלִיד אֶת־אֲחִימָעַץ׃ וַאֲחִימַעַץ הוֹלִיד
לו אֶת־עֲזַרְיָה וַעֲזַרְיָה הוֹלִיד אֶת־יוֹחָנָן׃ וְיוֹחָנָן הוֹלִיד אֶת־עֲזַרְיָה הוּא אֲשֶׁר
לז כִּהֵן בַּבַּיִת אֲשֶׁר־בָּנָה שְׁלֹמֹה בִּירוּשָׁלִָם׃ וַיּוֹלֶד עֲזַרְיָה אֶת־אֲמַרְיָה וַאֲמַרְיָה
לח הוֹלִיד אֶת־אֲחִיטוּב׃ וַאֲחִיטוּב הוֹלִיד אֶת־צָדוֹק וְצָדוֹק הוֹלִיד אֶת־שַׁלּוּם׃

DISCUSSION

5:34 | **Tzadok:** According to the account in I Kings (2:27), David promoted Tzadok over Evyatar, a descendant of the house of Eli. The house of Eli was eventually rejected entirely from the lofty position of the High Priesthood by King Solomon (see Rashi; *Yoma* 73b).

39 **Shalum begot Hilkiya, Hilkiya begot Azarya,**

40 **Azarya begot Seraya, and Seraya begot Yehotzadak;**

41 **Yehotzadak** was the priest who **went with the Lord's exiling of Judah and Jerusalem by the hand of Nebuchadnezzar.** These verses indicate that the High Priests who served in the First Temple were all members of a single dynasty. It is, however, possible that certain High Priests in the First Temple came from families that are not mentioned in this list. For example, mention is made elsewhere of the High Priest Yehoyada, and he is not listed here.[128]

6 1 This chapter opens once again with the beginning of the family chain, in order to list the families of Levites who were not priests. **The sons of Levi: Gershom, Kehat, and Merari.**

2 **These are the names of the sons of Gershom: Livni and Shimi.**

3 **The sons of Kehat: Amram, Yitzhar, Hevron, and Uziel.**

4 **The sons of Merari: Mahli and Mushi. These are the families of the Levites according to their patrilineal houses.** The same lineage of the family of Levi appears in the Torah.[129]

5 **For Gershom: Livni** was **his son,** as stated, and **Yahat** was **his son,** the son of Livni, and thus the chain of generations continued: **Zima his son,**

6 **Yoah his son, Ido his son, Zerah his son, Ye'aterai his son.** These are the descendants of Gershom.

7 **The sons,** descendants, **of Kehat: Aminadav,** apparently the same individual as the aforementioned Yitzhar,[130] who was **his,** Kehat's **son, Korah his son,** the son of Aminadav, **Asir his son,**

8 **Elkana his son, Evyasaf his son, Asir his son,**

9 **Tahat** was **his,** Asir's, **son, Uriel his son, Uziya his son, and Shaul his son.**

10 **The** additional **sons of** the **Elkana** mentioned above (verse 8) were **Amasai and Ahimot.** Some explain that this Elkana was the same son of Shaul mentioned in the previous verse and that the verse is truncated, a stylistic feature of the book of Chronicles.[131]

11 As for **Elkana,** a different person in this line who had the same name as the previously mentioned Elkana: **The sons,** descendants, **of Elkana: Tzofai his son, Nahat his son,**

12 **Eliav his son, Yeroham his son, Elkana his son.** This Elkana is the father of the prophet Samuel.[132] For some reason Samuel himself is not mentioned as Elkana's son, but the genealogical list continues:

13 **The sons of Samuel: The firstborn was Vashni and the second** son **was Aviya.** Some explain: The firstborn and the second [*vehasheni*] son was Aviya. However, it is more likely that the name of the firstborn was Vashni. Like many of the other names listed in the book of Chronicles, the meaning of Vashni is unclear.[133] These were the descendants of Kehat.

14 **The sons of Merari,** Levi's third son: The firstborn was **Mahli; Livni** was **his son, Shimi his son, Uza his son,**

15 **Shima his son, Hagiya his son, Asaya his son.**

16 **These are those whom David installed in charge of**[134] **the song in the House of the Lord.** They were made responsible for the singing in the House of God **once the ark came to rest,** after which the Levites were no longer required to perform what had been their regular task of carrying the Ark of the Covenant and the other vessels of the Tabernacle.

17 **They served with song before the Tabernacle of the Tent of Meeting;** their service had partly consisted of singing in the Tabernacle **until Solomon built the House of the Lord in Jerusalem; and** then **they remained in their service in accordance with their practice,** their custom; they continued to serve as singers in the Temple.[135]

18 **These are those who stood** over, were involved in, the song, **and** they were joined in this task by **their sons.** The singers were not from one specific Levite family; rather, they came from all branches of the tribe. **From the sons of the Kehatites: Heman the singer, son of Yoel, son of Samuel,** probably Samuel the prophet. If so, Heman was Samuel's grandson.[136]

19 Samuel was the **son of Elkana, son of Yeroham, son of Eliel, son of To'ah,**

20 **son of Tzuf, son of Elkana, son of Mahat, son of Amasai,**

21 **son of Elkana, son of Yoel, son of Azarya, son of Tzefanya,**

22 **son of Tahat, son of Asir, son of Evyasaf, son of Korah,**

23 **son of Yitzhar, son of Kehat, son of Levi, son of Israel.** This is Heman's genealogical lineage.

24 **His brother** from the same tribe, although not from the line of Kehat, **was Asaf,** mentioned by name several times in the book of Psalms (50:1; 73–83), **who stood on his right.** It seems that Heman was the lead singer, while Asaf was secondary to him; **Asaf, son of Berekhyahu, son of Shima,**

25 **son of Mikhael, son of Baaseya, son of Malkiya,**

26 **son of Etni, son of Zerah, son of Adaya,**

27 **son of Eitan, son of Zima, son of Shimi,**

28 **son of Yahat, son of Gershom, son of Levi.**

29 **Their brethren, the sons of Merari, were on the left.** Whereas Asaf stood on Heman's right side, the sons of Merari were positioned to Heman's left:[137] **Eitan, son of Kishi, son of Avdi, son of Malukh,**

30 **son of Hashavya, son of Amatzya, son of Hilkiya,**

31 **son of Amtzi, son of Bani, son of Shemer,**

32 **son of Mahli, son of Mushi, son of Merari, son of Levi.** The book of Psalms mentions a singer named Eitan, but since that singer is called Eitan the Ezrahite, he may not be the same person referred to here in Chronicles.[138]

33 **Their brethren the Levites,** those who were not singers, **were**

לט מ וְשַׁלּוּם הוֹלִיד אֶת־חִלְקִיָּה וְחִלְקִיָּה הוֹלִיד אֶת־עֲזַרְיָה׃ וַעֲזַרְיָה הוֹלִיד אֶת־שְׂרָיָה
מא וּשְׂרָיָה הוֹלִיד אֶת־יְהוֹצָדָק׃ וִיהוֹצָדָק הָלַךְ בְּהַגְלוֹת יְהוָה אֶת־יְהוּדָה וִירוּשָׁלִָם
ו א ב בְּיַד נְבֻכַדְנֶאצַּר׃ בְּנֵי לֵוִי גֵּרְשֹׁם קְהָת וּמְרָרִי׃ וְאֵלֶּה שְׁמוֹת בְּנֵי־
ג ד גֵרְשׁוֹם לִבְנִי וְשִׁמְעִי׃ וּבְנֵי קְהָת עַמְרָם וְיִצְהָר וְחֶבְרוֹן וְעֻזִּיאֵל׃ בְּנֵי מְרָרִי מַחְלִי
ה וּמֻשִׁי וְאֵלֶּה מִשְׁפְּחוֹת הַלֵּוִי לַאֲבוֹתֵיהֶם׃ לְגֵרְשׁוֹם לִבְנִי בְנוֹ יַחַת בְּנוֹ זִמָּה בְנוֹ׃
ו ז יוֹאָח בְּנוֹ עִדּוֹ בְנוֹ זֶרַח בְּנוֹ יְאָתְרַי בְּנוֹ׃ בְּנֵי קְהָת עַמִּינָדָב בְּנוֹ קֹרַח בְּנוֹ אַסִּיר
ח ט בְּנוֹ׃ אֶלְקָנָה בְנוֹ וְאֶבְיָסָף בְּנוֹ וְאַסִּיר בְּנוֹ׃ תַּחַת בְּנוֹ אוּרִיאֵל בְּנוֹ עֻזִּיָּה בְנוֹ
י יא וְשָׁאוּל בְּנוֹ׃ וּבְנֵי אֶלְקָנָה עֲמָשַׂי וַאֲחִימוֹת׃ אֶלְקָנָה בנו אֶלְקָנָה צוֹפַי בְּנוֹ וְנַחַת בְּנֵי
יב יג יד בְּנוֹ׃ אֱלִיאָב בְּנוֹ יְרֹחָם בְּנוֹ אֶלְקָנָה בְנוֹ׃ וּבְנֵי שְׁמוּאֵל הַבְּכֹר וַשְׁנִי וַאֲבִיָּה׃ בְּנֵי
טו מְרָרִי מַחְלִי לִבְנִי בְנוֹ שִׁמְעִי בְנוֹ עֻזָּה בְנוֹ׃ שִׁמְעָא בְנוֹ חַגִּיָּה בְנוֹ עֲשָׂיָה בְנוֹ׃
טז יז וְאֵלֶּה אֲשֶׁר הֶעֱמִיד דָּוִיד עַל־יְדֵי־שִׁיר בֵּית יְהוָה מִמְּנוֹחַ הָאָרוֹן׃ וַיִּהְיוּ מְשָׁרְתִים
לִפְנֵי מִשְׁכַּן אֹהֶל־מוֹעֵד בַּשִּׁיר עַד־בְּנוֹת שְׁלֹמֹה אֶת־בֵּית יְהוָה בִּירוּשָׁלִָם וַיַּעַמְדוּ
יח כְמִשְׁפָּטָם עַל־עֲבוֹדָתָם׃ וְאֵלֶּה הָעֹמְדִים וּבְנֵיהֶם מִבְּנֵי הַקְּהָתִי הֵימָן הַמְשׁוֹרֵר
יט כ בֶּן־יוֹאֵל בֶּן־שְׁמוּאֵל׃ בֶּן־אֶלְקָנָה בֶּן־יְרֹחָם בֶּן־אֱלִיאֵל בֶּן־תּוֹחַ׃ בֶּן־ציף בֶּן־ צוּף
כא כב אֶלְקָנָה בֶּן־מַחַת בֶּן־עֲמָשָׂי׃ בֶּן־אֶלְקָנָה בֶּן־יוֹאֵל בֶּן־עֲזַרְיָה בֶּן־צְפַנְיָה׃ בֶּן־תַּחַת
כג כד בֶּן־אַסִּיר בֶּן־אֶבְיָסָף בֶּן־קֹרַח׃ בֶּן־יִצְהָר בֶּן־קְהָת בֶּן־לֵוִי בֶּן־יִשְׂרָאֵל׃ וְאָחִיו
כה אָסָף הָעֹמֵד עַל־יְמִינוֹ אָסָף בֶּן־בֶּרֶכְיָהוּ בֶּן־שִׁמְעָא׃ בֶּן־מִיכָאֵל בֶּן־בַּעֲשֵׂיָה בֶּן־
כו כז כח מַלְכִּיָּה׃ בֶּן־אֶתְנִי בֶן־זֶרַח בֶּן־עֲדָיָה׃ בֶּן־אֵיתָן בֶּן־זִמָּה בֶּן־שִׁמְעִי׃ בֶּן־יַחַת
כט בֶּן־גֵּרְשֹׁם בֶּן־לֵוִי׃ וּבְנֵי מְרָרִי אֲחֵיהֶם עַל־הַשְּׂמֹאול אֵיתָן בֶּן־קִישִׁי
ל לא בֶּן־עַבְדִּי בֶּן־מַלּוּךְ׃ בֶּן־חֲשַׁבְיָה בֶּן־אֲמַצְיָה בֶּן־חִלְקִיָּה׃ בֶּן־אַמְצִי בֶן־בָּנִי בֶּן־
לב לג שָׁמֶר׃ בֶּן־מַחְלִי בֶּן־מוּשִׁי בֶּן־מְרָרִי בֶּן־לֵוִי׃ וַאֲחֵיהֶם הַלְוִיִּם נְתוּנִים

given for all the service of the Tabernacle, the House of God.

34 **But Aaron and his sons** had a special function, as they **offered on the altar of the burnt offerings and on the altar of incense, for all the labor of the sacred sanctities,** or of the most holy things; the sacred offerings of especially high sanctity which were burned upon the altar,[139] **and to atone for Israel, in accordance with everything that Moses the servant of God had commanded.** Some of the Levites were singers, and the lineage of some of them is traced here. The rest of the Levites performed ancillary services in the Temple, while the actual service of the Temple was reserved for the priests alone.

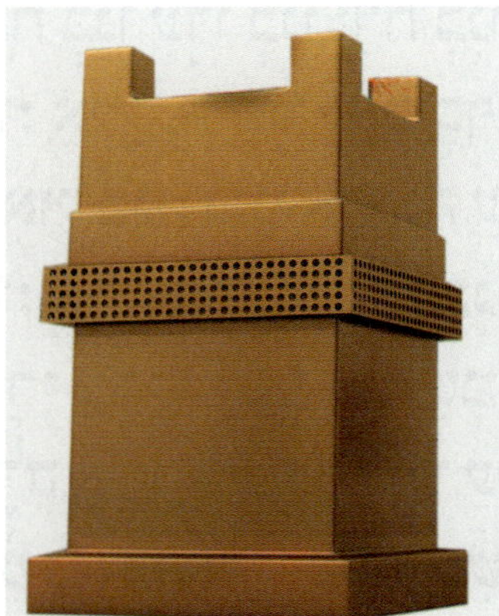

Altar of the burnt offerings

Altar of incense

35 A second list of priests until the generation of Solomon is presented here, which is identical to the list above (5:29). **These are the sons of Aaron: Elazar his son,** the son of Aaron, **Pinhas his son,** the son of Elazar, and so the generations continue: **Avishua his son,**

36 **Buki his son, Uzi his son, Zerahya his son,**

37 **Merayot his son, Amarya his son, Ahituv his son,**

38 **Tzadok his son, Ahimaatz his son.**

39 A list of the cities that were given to the priests and the Levites from the inheritances of the various tribes is provided here, similar to the details given in the book of Joshua (chap. 21). **These are their dwellings,** the dwellings of the priests and Levites, **according to their residences,**[B] fenced-in tent encampments or places of residence, **in their borders:** They were given first **to the sons of Aaron, for the families of the Kehatite, for theirs was the** first **lot.** They received the first lot that determined their cities;[140]

40 **they allotted to them Hebron in the land of Judah, and its perimeter fields,** the open areas **around it,**

Cities of priests and cities of Levites

41 **but the fields of the city and its villages,** the small, surrounding settlements, **they allotted to Caleb son of Yefuneh.** Elsewhere, it is stated that Hebron belonged to Caleb. It is therefore explained here that the city of Hebron itself, together with the open land surrounding it, was given to the priests, the sons of Kehat, while Caleb received the fields and villages.[141]

42 **To the sons of Aaron, they allotted the** following **cities of refuge: Hebron,** which was one of the major cities of refuge,[142] **Livna**[B] **and its perimeter fields, Yatir,**[BD] **and Eshtemoa**[B] **and its perimeter fields.** They were given only the city and its open land, but not the fields and villages, as the Levites and priests did not receive a proper inheritance in Israel, but merely residences and sufficient space for their basic needs.[143]

43 **And Hilen**[B] **and its perimeter fields, Devir**[B] **and its perimeter fields,**

44 **and Ashan and its perimeter fields, and Beit Shemesh**[B] **and its perimeter fields.**

לד לְכֹל־עֲבוֹדַת מִשְׁכַּן בֵּית הָאֱלֹהִים: וְאַהֲרֹן וּבָנָיו מַקְטִירִים עַל־מִזְבַּח הָעוֹלָה ג
וְעַל־מִזְבַּח הַקְּטֹרֶת לְכֹל מְלֶאכֶת קֹדֶשׁ הַקֳּדָשִׁים וּלְכַפֵּר עַל־יִשְׂרָאֵל כְּכֹל
לה אֲשֶׁר־צִוָּה מֹשֶׁה עֶבֶד הָאֱלֹהִים: וְאֵלֶּה בְּנֵי אַהֲרֹן אֶלְעָזָר בְּנוֹ פִּינְחָס
לו לז בְּנוֹ אֲבִישׁוּעַ בְּנוֹ: בֻּקִּי בְנוֹ עֻזִּי בְנוֹ זְרַחְיָה בְנוֹ: מְרָיוֹת בְּנוֹ אֲמַרְיָה בְנוֹ אֲחִיטוּב
לח לט בְּנוֹ: צָדוֹק בְּנוֹ אֲחִימַעַץ בְּנוֹ: וְאֵלֶּה מוֹשְׁבוֹתָם לְטִירוֹתָם בִּגְבוּלָם
מ לִבְנֵי אַהֲרֹן לְמִשְׁפַּחַת הַקְּהָתִי כִּי לָהֶם הָיָה הַגּוֹרָל: וַיִּתְּנוּ לָהֶם אֶת־חֶבְרוֹן
מא בְּאֶרֶץ יְהוּדָה וְאֶת־מִגְרָשֶׁיהָ סְבִיבֹתֶיהָ: וְאֶת־שְׂדֵה הָעִיר וְאֶת־חֲצֵרֶיהָ נָתְנוּ
מב לְכָלֵב בֶּן־יְפֻנֶּה: וְלִבְנֵי אַהֲרֹן נָתְנוּ אֶת־עָרֵי הַמִּקְלָט אֶת־חֶבְרוֹן
מג וְאֶת־לִבְנָה וְאֶת־מִגְרָשֶׁיהָ וְאֶת־יַתִּר וְאֶת־אֶשְׁתְּמֹעַ וְאֶת־מִגְרָשֶׁיהָ: וְאֶת־חִילֵן
מד וְאֶת־מִגְרָשֶׁיהָ אֶת־דְּבִיר וְאֶת־מִגְרָשֶׁיהָ: וְאֶת־עָשָׁן וְאֶת־מִגְרָשֶׁיהָ וְאֶת־בֵּית

BACKGROUND

6:39 | **To their residences [*letirotam*]:** A *tira* is an encampment surrounded by a stone fence, which is a nomadic form of settlement (see Genesis 25:16). Many derive the word from the root *tav-vav-reish*, meaning perimeter, that is, an encampment surrounded by rows of stones. It is only in later periods that the word *tira* was used in the sense of a fortress or castle.

6:42 | **Livna:** Livna is mentioned in the book of Joshua (10:29–32, 12:15) alongside the cities of Makeda, Lakhish, and Adulam in the Judean lowlands, and in the book of II Kings (23:31, 24:18) as the place of origin of Hamutal the daughter of Jeremiah, who was also the mother of Yeho'ahaz and Tzidkiyahu, two of the last kings of Judah. Due to its central location, it was one of the cities besieged by Sennacherib (II Kings 19:8). Some identify it as Tel es-Safi, near Kfar Menahem, which is located alongside an ancient road leading from the coast to the Judean mountains, via the Valley of Ela. This identification is partly due to the white [*lavan*] color of the rocks of that tel. Others suggest that it is Tel Burna, near Kibbutz Gal On.

Yatir: Based on the preservation of the name and a description by Eusebius, Yatir is generally identified as Khirbet Yattir, south of Mount Hebron, around 4 km west of the present-day settlement of Yatir.

Eshtemoa: This is the village of as-Samu, approximately 4 km west of Susya and around 15 km south of Hebron. A large hoard of silver from the eleventh century BCE was unearthed at Eshtemoa.

6:43 | **Hilen:** Hilen, or Hilaz, according to the Aleppo Codex, Leningrad Codex, and the Sassoon Codex, appears in the book of Joshua (15:51) as Holon, alongside the cities of Goshen and Gilo, which are situated southwest of Hebron. The exact location of Hilen is unclear.

Devir: Devir is identified as Khirbet Rabud, 13 km southwest of Hebron, near the present-day settlement of Otniel. Near this tel, there are two springs, which are possibly the upper springs and the lower springs mentioned in the book of Joshua (15:14–19). The remains of a city from that period have also been unearthed.

6:44 | **Beit Shemesh:** A city located at the western foot of the Judean highlands, along the Sorek Stream and at the intersection of the important east-west route from Philistia to Jerusalem and the north-south road that ran along the base of the Judean highlands. The ruins of the site cover an area of around 30 dunams, and many findings from the biblical period have been discovered there. It should be noted that other cities of the same name have been found in the territories of Asher and Naphtali, as well as in Egypt.

DISCUSSION

6:42 | **Cities of refuge, Hebron, Livna and its perimeter fields, Yatir:** This proves that the Levite cities also served as cities of refuge, as stated by the Sages (see *Makkot* 10a; *Metzudat David*). The six cities of refuge specified in the Torah and in the book of Joshua were the main ones, while the other cities given to the Levites were secondary cities of refuge. There are halakhic differences in the manner in which these cities absorbed unwitting murderers. For example, according to some opinions, the unwitting murderers in the major cities were provided with financial support by the residents of the city, whereas in the secondary cities they were not permitted to become a burden upon the inhabitants; rather, they were required to provide for themselves (see *Makkot* 13a; commentary on Numbers 25:6).

45 **From the tribe of Benjamin,** they gave **Geva**[B] **and its perime-**
ter fields, Alemet[B] **and its perimeter fields, and Anatot**[B] **and**
its perimeter fields.[144] **All their cities,** the cities of the priests
from the portion of Benjamin, **were thirteen cities,**[B] where
they dwelled **with their families.**[145]
46 **For the remaining sons of Kehat from the family of the**
tribe, all those who were not priests, **from half,** part of, **the**
tribe of the **half of Manasseh** that dwelled on the western side
of the Jordan River, **ten cities** were divided among them **by**
lots. They also received cities from the inheritances of Ephraim
and Dan, as explained below (verses 51–55) and in the book of
Joshua (21:20–24).
47 **For the sons of Gershom by,** according to, **their families,** cities were given to them **from the tribe of Issachar, from the**
tribe of Asher, from the tribe of Naphtali, and from the
tribe of Manasseh, the other half of Manasseh, which dwelled
in Bashan, thirteen cities.
48 **For the sons of Merari by,** according to, **their families,** cities
were given **from the tribe of Reuben, from the tribe of Gad,**
and from the tribe of Zebulun, twelve cities were divided
among them **by lot.**
49 **The children of Israel allotted to the Levites the cities and**
their perimeter fields.
50 **They allotted them by lot from the tribe of the children of**
Judah, from the tribe of the children of Simeon, and from
the tribe of the children of Benjamin, these aforementioned
cities that they will call them by name. The chapter does not
specify which of the cities were given from the children of
Simeon, whose tribal territory was incorporated within that of
Judah.
51 **For** the rest of **the families of the sons of Kehat, the cities of**
their borders were from the tribe of Ephraim.
52 **They allotted to them the cities of refuge: Shekhem,** another
major city of refuge, **and its**
perimeter fields, in the
highlands of Ephraim, and
Gezer[B] **and its perimeter**
fields;
53 **and Yokme'am**[B] **and its**
perimeter fields, and Beit
Horon and its perimeter
fields,

Tel Balata, remains of ancient Shekhem

54 **and Ayalon**[B] **and its perim-**
eter fields, and Gat Rimon[B] **and its perimeter fields.**
55 **From half the tribe of Manasseh: Aner and its perimeter**
fields, and Bilam[B] **and its perimeter fields, for the remain-**
ing family of the sons of Kehat.
56 **For the sons of Gershom: From the family of half the tribe**
of Manasseh: Golan[B] **in the Bashan,** which was also one of
the main cities of refuge, listed among the cities that Moses
dedicated for this purpose,[146] **and its perimeter fields, and**
Ashtarot[B] **and its perimeter fields.**
57 **From the tribe of Issachar** they gave **Kedesh,**[B] called Kishyon
in the book of Joshua in order to differentiate it from Kedesh
Naphtali, the major city of refuge listed below, **and its perim-**
eter fields, Dovrat and its perimeter fields,

BACKGROUND

6:45 | **Geva:** Identified as Jeb'a, an Arab village slightly north of Adam Junction.

Alemet: Based on the preservation of the same name, Alemet is generally identified as Khirbet Almit, approximately 4 km northeast of Mount Scopus and around 1.5 km south of Hizma (Azmavet). Both Alemet and Azmavet were named for descendants of Benjamin (see 8:36).

Anatot: A city in the territory of Benjamin, 5 km northeast of Jerusalem. It has been identified as two sites near the present-day village of Anata: Deir es-Sid and Ras el-Kharrubeh. The books of Numbers (35:3–4) and Jeremiah (32:7–32) indicate that the fields adjacent to the city were owned and worked by priests.

Thirteen cities: There are only eleven cities in this list, while Givon and Yutta appear in the corresponding list in Joshua. It is possible that those cities were desolate when the book of Chronicles was written (Malbim).

6:52 | **Gezer:** A central, fortified city, located in the western entranceway to the Valley of Ayalon, along an important intersection of the Via Maris and the route leading from the coastal region to the Judean mountains. Archaeological digs have unearthed ruins there from the period of the Israelite conquest of Canaan in the thirteenth century BCE.

6:53 | **Yokme'am:** Yokme'am is listed as a city in the fifth district of Solomon's governorships (I Kings 4:12). The name Yokme'am appears on a Hebrew inscription from the third century BCE found on Mount Gerizim. The parallel list in Joshua (21:22) mentions the city of Kivtzayim instead of Yokme'am; perhaps the city's name was changed after the Levites settled there. Some identify it as Tel Sheikh edh-Dhiab, at the source of the Fatzael Stream, adjacent to the town of Fatzael; others suggest that it is Tel el-Mazar, approximately 10 km to the north, about 2 km north of the town Masua (Benjamin Mazar ed., *Encyclopaedia Biblica*, vol 6, 166). Yet another opinion is that it is Tel Kaon, roughly 9 km southwest of Beit She'an.

6:54 | **Ayalon:** The Valley of Ayalon, or the city of that name. The city is identified as the ruins of the Arab village Yalo, located in Park Canada, on a hill that overlooks the Valley of Ayalon from the east, approximately 2 km south of Mevo Horon.

Gat Rimon: A city in the portion of the tribe of Dan (Joshua 19:45), which is mentioned in the tribute lists of the Egyptian pharaoh Thutmose III (fifteenth century BCE). Two sites have been proposed for Gat Rimon, both in the area of the Yarkon Stream, where findings from the Iron Age have been unearthed: Tel Abu Ziton,

▸ *north*

מה שֶׁמֶשׁ וְאֶת־מִגְרָשֶׁיהָ׃ וּמִמַּטֵּה בִנְיָמִן אֶת־גֶּבַע וְאֶת־מִגְרָשֶׁיהָ וְאֶת־עָלֶמֶת וְאֶת־
מִגְרָשֶׁיהָ וְאֶת־עֲנָתוֹת וְאֶת־מִגְרָשֶׁיהָ כָּל־עָרֵיהֶם שְׁלֹשׁ־עֶשְׂרֵה עִיר
מו בְּמִשְׁפְּחוֹתֵיהֶם׃ וְלִבְנֵי קְהָת הַנּוֹתָרִים מִמִּשְׁפַּחַת הַמַּטֶּה מִמַּחֲצִית
מז מַטֵּה חֲצִי מְנַשֶּׁה בַּגּוֹרָל עָרִים עָשֶׂר׃ וְלִבְנֵי גֵרְשׁוֹם לְמִשְׁפְּחוֹתָם
מִמַּטֵּה יִשָּׂשכָר וּמִמַּטֵּה אָשֵׁר וּמִמַּטֵּה נַפְתָּלִי וּמִמַּטֵּה מְנַשֶּׁה בַּבָּשָׁן עָרִים שְׁלֹשׁ
מח עֶשְׂרֵה׃ לִבְנֵי מְרָרִי לְמִשְׁפְּחוֹתָם מִמַּטֵּה רְאוּבֵן וּמִמַּטֵּה־גָד וּמִמַּטֵּה
מט זְבוּלֻן בַּגּוֹרָל עָרִים שְׁתֵּים עֶשְׂרֵה׃ וַיִּתְּנוּ בְנֵי־יִשְׂרָאֵל לַלְוִיִּם אֶת־הֶעָרִים וְאֶת־
נ מִגְרְשֵׁיהֶם׃ וַיִּתְּנוּ בַגּוֹרָל מִמַּטֵּה בְנֵי־יְהוּדָה וּמִמַּטֵּה בְנֵי־שִׁמְעוֹן וּמִמַּטֵּה
בְּנֵי בִנְיָמִן אֵת הֶעָרִים הָאֵלֶּה אֲשֶׁר־יִקְרְאוּ אֶתְהֶם בְּשֵׁמוֹת׃
נא נב וּמִמִּשְׁפְּחוֹת בְּנֵי קְהָת וַיְהִי עָרֵי גְבוּלָם מִמַּטֵּה אֶפְרָיִם׃ וַיִּתְּנוּ לָהֶם אֶת־עָרֵי
נג הַמִּקְלָט אֶת־שְׁכֶם וְאֶת־מִגְרָשֶׁיהָ בְּהַר אֶפְרָיִם וְאֶת־גֶּזֶר וְאֶת־מִגְרָשֶׁיהָ׃ וְאֶת־
נד יָקְמְעָם וְאֶת־מִגְרָשֶׁיהָ וְאֶת־בֵּית חוֹרוֹן וְאֶת־מִגְרָשֶׁיהָ׃ וְאֶת־אַיָּלוֹן וְאֶת־מִגְרָשֶׁיהָ
נה וְאֶת־גַּת־רִמּוֹן וְאֶת־מִגְרָשֶׁיהָ׃ וּמִמַּחֲצִית מַטֵּה מְנַשֶּׁה אֶת־עָנֵר וְאֶת־מִגְרָשֶׁיהָ
נו וְאֶת־בִּלְעָם וְאֶת־מִגְרָשֶׁיהָ לְמִשְׁפַּחַת לִבְנֵי־קְהָת הַנּוֹתָרִים׃ לִבְנֵי
גֵּרְשׁוֹם מִמִּשְׁפַּחַת חֲצִי מַטֵּה מְנַשֶּׁה אֶת־גּוֹלָן בַּבָּשָׁן וְאֶת־מִגְרָשֶׁיהָ וְאֶת־עַשְׁתָּרוֹת
נז וְאֶת־מִגְרָשֶׁיהָ׃ וּמִמַּטֵּה יִשָּׂשכָר אֶת־קֶדֶשׁ וְאֶת־מִגְרָשֶׁיהָ אֶת־דָּבְרַת

BACKGROUND

north of Pardes Katz, and Tel Gerisa, just east of Hahalakha Junction, within the boundaries of the city of Ramat Gan.

6:55 | **Aner…and Bilam:** The corresponding account in Joshua (21:25) mentions Taanakh and (a second) Gat Rimon, rather than Aner and Bilam. Some suggest that the names of these places were changed in the days of Ezra (Malbim). Others contend that Aner is a corruption of Taanakh and that Bilam is a corruption of Yible'am, which is in the same area. Taanakh and Yible'am are mentioned together in other places (see Joshua 17:11; Judges 1:27).

6:56 | **Golan:** Golan is mentioned in the *Tosefta* and in external sources from the period of the Mishna and Talmud. It is identified as the village Saham al-Jawlan, southeast of Ashtarot.

Ashtarot: Ashtarot is a city in the portion of Manasseh in Bashan. In the Bible, it is also called Be'eshtera, which is perhaps a shortened form of Beit Ashtarot (see Joshua 13:31, 21:27). The city controlled the main road in Bashan. It was the capital city of the province of Karnayim, in which Og king of Bashan lived. It has been identified as Tel Ashtereh in Syria.

6:57 | **From the tribe of Issachar, Kedesh:** The location of this city is uncertain; some identify it as Tel Abu Qudeis, near Givat Oz, in the west of the Valley of Megiddo, while others contend, in light of the account in the book of Judges (4:11, and commentary ad loc.), that it was located near Mount Tavor, but its precise location is unknown.

The name Kedesh was common in the Land of Israel and its neighboring countries. There was a Kedesh Naphtali, a Kedesh in the Negev, and a Kedesh on the Orontes River in northern Lebanon. To this day, there are sites that preserve the name, such as Ein Qedeis near Kadesh Barnea and Khirbet Qadis near Poriya, west of the Sea of Galilee.

58 **Ramot and its perimeter fields, and Anem and its perimeter fields.**
59 **From the tribe of Asher: Mashal and its perimeter fields, and Avdon and its perimeter fields,**
60 **Hukok and its perimeter fields, and Rehov and its perimeter fields.**
61 **From the tribe of Naphtali: Kedesh in Galilee,** one of the three main cities of refuge on the western side of the Jordan, **and its perimeter fields, Hamon and its perimeter fields, and Kiryatayim and its perimeter fields.**
62 **For the remaining** Levites, the **sons of Merari,** cities were given **from the tribe of Zebulun: Rimono and its perimeter fields, Tavor and its perimeter fields.**

Mount Tavor

63 **Beyond the Jordan, at Jericho, east of the Jordan,** the Levites received **from the tribe of Reuben: Betzer in the wilderness,** also a major city of refuge that was dedicated by Moses, **and its perimeter fields, and Yatza and its perimeter fields,**
64 **Kedemot and its perimeter fields, and Meifaat and its perimeter fields.**
65 **From the tribe of Gad: Ramot in the Gilad,** the third major city of refuge on the eastern side of the Jordan, **and its perimeter fields, and Mahanayim and its perimeter fields,**
66 **and Heshbon and its perimeter fields, and Yazer and its perimeter fields.** This list of cities is incomplete. The book of Joshua provides a more orderly account of the manner in which the children of Levi settled by family in the cities they received from each of the tribes of Israel.[147]

Short Lists of the Five Additional Tribes

I CHRONICLES 7:1–40

This chapter provides short genealogical lists of the five additional tribes who were not previously mentioned. These lists are also truncated. Some of them are continued or completed elsewhere, but overall it seems that these genealogical lists were copied from other sources.

7 1 **The sons of Issachar:** **Tola, Pua, Yashuv, and Shimron, four.**
2 **The sons of Tola:** **Uzi, Refaya, Yeriel, Yahmai, Yivsam, and Shmuel,** who were **heads of their patrilineal houses,** all their descendants, were counted **for Tola,** and they were **mighty warriors in their legacy; their number in the days of David,** when a census was conducted to ascertain the number of military men,[148] **was twenty-two thousand six hundred.**
3 **The sons,** descendants, **of Uzi,** the son of Tola, were: his son **Yizrahya; and the sons of Yizrahya** were: **Mikhael, Ovadya, Yoel, Yishiya,** a total of **five; all of them** were **leaders.**
4 **With them,**[149] **by their progeny, by their patrilineal houses, were** counted **units of the army for war,** a sum of **thirty-six thousand** men. This family had more offspring than was common in other corresponding families, **for they had many wives and** thus more **sons.**
5 Together with **their brethren among all the families of Issachar,** these **mighty warriors, all established in their lineage,** were **eighty-seven thousand.** These were all the soldiers who traced their genealogy to all of the heads of the fathers of the tribe.[150]
6 The chapter provides one of various genealogical lists for the tribe of Benjamin (see chap. 8). Some understand that the reference here is not to the tribe of Benjamin, but rather to another descendant of Issachar who was also named Benjamin.[151]
The sons of **Benjamin: Bela, Bekher, and Yediael, three.**
7 **The sons of Bela: Etzbon, Uzi, Uziel, Yerimot, and Iri, five;** they were the **heads of** their **patrilineal houses, mighty warriors;** there were **twenty-two thousand and thirty-four** soldiers **in their lineage.**
8 **The sons of Bekher: Zemira, Yoash, Eliezer, Elyoeinai, Omri, Yeremot, Aviya, Anatot, and Alemet. All these are the sons of Bekher.**
9 **Their lineage through their progeny,** who were the **heads of their patrilineal houses, mighty warriors, was** a total of **twenty thousand two hundred** men.
10 **The sons of Yediael: Bilhan; and the sons of Bilhan: Yeush, Binyamin, Ehud, Kenaana, Zeitan, Tarshish, and Ahishahar.**
11 **All these are sons of Yediael,** who were the **heads of their patrilineal houses, mighty warriors, seventeen thousand two hundred, fit for military service.**
12 **Shupim and Hupim were sons of Ir,** perhaps the Iri mentioned above,[152] **Hushim was the son of Aher.** Some understand this verse as meaning: Son of another [*aḥer*], as the author of the book of Chronicles may have been uncertain whether the members of these families belonged to the tribe of Benjamin; therefore, he counted them separately.[153]
13 **The sons of Naphtali** are presented in an extremely truncated form. They were: **Yahtziel, Guni, Yetzer, and Shalum,** who were **sons,** descendants, **of Bilha,** wife of Jacob. It is possible that "sons of Bilha" also includes Hushim, mentioned in the previous verse, who might have been the son of Dan, the son of Bilha.[154]

נח וְאֶת־מִגְרָשֶׁיהָ׃ וְאֶת־רָאמוֹת וְאֶת־מִגְרָשֶׁיהָ וְאֶת־עָנֵם וְאֶת־מִגְרָשֶׁיהָ׃
נט ס וּמִמַּטֵּה אָשֵׁר אֶת־מָשָׁל וְאֶת־מִגְרָשֶׁהָ וְאֶת־עַבְדּוֹן וְאֶת־מִגְרָשֶׁהָ׃ וְאֶת־חוּקֹק
סא וְאֶת־מִגְרָשֶׁיהָ וְאֶת־רְחֹב וְאֶת־מִגְרָשֶׁיהָ׃ וּמִמַּטֵּה נַפְתָּלִי אֶת־קֶדֶשׁ בַּגָּלִיל
וְאֶת־מִגְרָשֶׁיהָ וְאֶת־חַמּוֹן וְאֶת־מִגְרָשֶׁהָ וְאֶת־קִרְיָתַיִם וְאֶת־
סב מִגְרָשֶׁהָ׃ לִבְנֵי מְרָרִי הַנּוֹתָרִים מִמַּטֵּה זְבוּלֻן אֶת־רִמּוֹנוֹ וְאֶת־
סג מִגְרָשֶׁהָ אֶת־תָּבוֹר וְאֶת־מִגְרָשֶׁהָ׃ וּמֵעֵבֶר לְיַרְדֵּן יְרֵחוֹ לְמִזְרַח הַיַּרְדֵּן מִמַּטֵּה
סד רְאוּבֵן אֶת־בֶּצֶר בַּמִּדְבָּר וְאֶת־מִגְרָשֶׁהָ וְאֶת־יַהְצָה וְאֶת־מִגְרָשֶׁהָ׃ וְאֶת־קְדֵמוֹת
סה וְאֶת־מִגְרָשֶׁיהָ וְאֶת־מֵיפַעַת וְאֶת־מִגְרָשֶׁהָ׃ וּמִמַּטֵּה־גָד
סו אֶת־רָאמוֹת בַּגִּלְעָד וְאֶת־מִגְרָשֶׁהָ וְאֶת־מַחֲנַיִם וְאֶת־מִגְרָשֶׁהָ׃ וְאֶת־חֶשְׁבּוֹן
ז א וְאֶת־מִגְרָשֶׁיהָ וְאֶת־יַעְזֵיר וְאֶת־מִגְרָשֶׁהָ׃ וְלִבְנֵי יִשָּׂשכָר תּוֹלָע
ב וּפוּאָה יָשִׁיב וְשִׁמְרוֹן אַרְבָּעָה׃ וּבְנֵי תוֹלָע עֻזִּי וּרְפָיָה וִירִיאֵל וְיַחְמַי וְיִבְשָׂם יָשׁוּב
וּשְׁמוּאֵל רָאשִׁים לְבֵית־אֲבוֹתָם לְתוֹלָע גִּבּוֹרֵי חַיִל לְתֹלְדוֹתָם מִסְפָּרָם בִּימֵי
ג דָוִיד עֶשְׂרִים־וּשְׁנַיִם אֶלֶף וְשֵׁשׁ מֵאוֹת׃ וּבְנֵי עֻזִּי יִזְרַחְיָה וּבְנֵי יִזְרַחְיָה
ד מִיכָאֵל וְעֹבַדְיָה וְיוֹאֵל יִשִּׁיָּה חֲמִשָּׁה רָאשִׁים כֻּלָּם׃ וַעֲלֵיהֶם לְתֹלְדוֹתָם לְבֵית
ה אֲבוֹתָם גְּדוּדֵי צְבָא מִלְחָמָה שְׁלֹשִׁים וְשִׁשָּׁה אָלֶף כִּי־הִרְבּוּ נָשִׁים וּבָנִים׃ וַאֲחֵיהֶם
לְכֹל מִשְׁפְּחוֹת יִשָּׂשכָר גִּבּוֹרֵי חֲיָלִים שְׁמוֹנִים וְשִׁבְעָה אֶלֶף הִתְיַחְשָׂם
ו ז לַכֹּל׃ בִּנְיָמִן בֶּלַע וָבֶכֶר וִידִיעֲאֵל שְׁלֹשָׁה׃ וּבְנֵי בֶלַע אֶצְבּוֹן וְעֻזִּי וְעֻזִּיאֵל
וִירִימוֹת וְעִירִי חֲמִשָּׁה רָאשֵׁי בֵּית אָבוֹת גִּבּוֹרֵי חֲיָלִים וְהִתְיַחְשָׂם עֶשְׂרִים וּשְׁנַיִם
ח אֶלֶף וּשְׁלֹשִׁים וְאַרְבָּעָה׃ וּבְנֵי בֶכֶר זְמִירָה וְיוֹעָשׁ וֶאֱלִיעֶזֶר וְאֶלְיוֹעֵינַי
ט וְעָמְרִי וִירֵמוֹת וַאֲבִיָּה וַעֲנָתוֹת וְעָלָמֶת כָּל־אֵלֶּה בְּנֵי־בָכֶר׃ וְהִתְיַחְשָׂם לְתֹלְדוֹתָם
י רָאשֵׁי בֵּית אֲבוֹתָם גִּבּוֹרֵי חָיִל עֶשְׂרִים אֶלֶף וּמָאתָיִם׃ וּבְנֵי יְדִיעֲאֵל
יא בִּלְהָן וּבְנֵי בִלְהָן יְעִישׁ וּבִנְיָמִן וְאֵהוּד וּכְנַעֲנָה וְזֵיתָן וְתַרְשִׁישׁ וַאֲחִישָׁחַר׃ כָּל־ יְעוּשׁ
אֵלֶּה בְּנֵי יְדִיעֲאֵל לְרָאשֵׁי הָאָבוֹת גִּבּוֹרֵי חֲיָלִים שִׁבְעָה־עָשָׂר אֶלֶף וּמָאתַיִם
יב יג יֹצְאֵי צָבָא לַמִּלְחָמָה׃ וְשֻׁפִּם וְחֻפִּם בְּנֵי עִיר חֻשִׁם בְּנֵי אַחֵר׃ בְּנֵי נַפְתָּלִי

14 **The sons of Manasseh: Asriel, who was borne by his Aramean concubine, who bore Makhir, father** of the settlement **of Gilad.** Some explain the verse as follows: Asriel was borne by his concubine, the Aramean woman, who also bore Makhir the father of Gilad.[155]

15 **Makhir took a wife for Hupim and Shupim; his sister's name,** either Shupim's sister or the sister of both of them,[156] **was Maakha. The name of the second** child of Manasseh or Asriel[157] **was Tzelofhad, and Tzelofhad had** only **daughters.** The Torah relates how the daughters of Tzelofhad demanded from Moses their right to their father's inheritance.[158]

16 **Maakha the wife of Makhir bore a son, and she called his name Peresh; the name of his brother was Sheresh, and his sons were Ulam and Rekem.**

17 **The sons of Ulam: Bedan. These are the sons of Gilad, son of Makhir, son of Manasseh.**

18 **His sister,** who had the unusual name of **Hamolekhet,**[159] **bore Ishhod, Aviezer, and Mahla.**

19 **The sons of Shemida were Ahyan, Shekhem, Lik'hi, and Aniyam,** who also belonged to the expanded family of Makhir. These were the children of Manasseh.

20 **The sons,** descendants, **of Ephraim** were: **Shutelah, Bered his,** Shutelah's **son, Tahat his son,** the son of Bered, and thus the generations continued: **Elada his son, Tahat his son,**

21 **Zavad his son, Shutelah his son, and Ezer and Elad; the men of Gat, who were born in the land, killed them when they came down to take their livestock.**[D]

22 **Ephraim their father mourned many days** over his slain sons, **and his brethren came to comfort him.**

23 **He consorted with his wife** after the period of mourning, **and she conceived and bore a son, and he called his name Beria, because "in evil" [*bera'a*] was in his house.** The child was born in the evil time of the tragic deaths of his brothers.

24 **His daughter was** called **She'era, and she built Lower and Upper Beit Horon**[B] **and Uzen She'era.**[B]

25 **Refah was his son, and Reshef and Telah his son, and Tahan his son,**

26 **Ladan his son, Amihud his son, Elishama his son;** Elishama son of Amihud was the prince of the tribe of Ephraim, as stated in the Torah.[160]

27 **Non his son,** the son of Elishama, **Joshua his son,**[D] the son of Non, or Nun. This teaches that Joshua son of Nun was the grandson of the prince of the tribe of Ephraim, which might shed light on his character.

28 **Their portion and dwellings,** those of the children of Ephraim, **were Beit El and its environs, and to the east Naaran,**[B] **and**

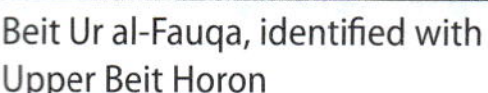

Beit Ur al-Fauqa, identified with Upper Beit Horon

Beit Ur al-Tahta, identified with Lower Beit Horon

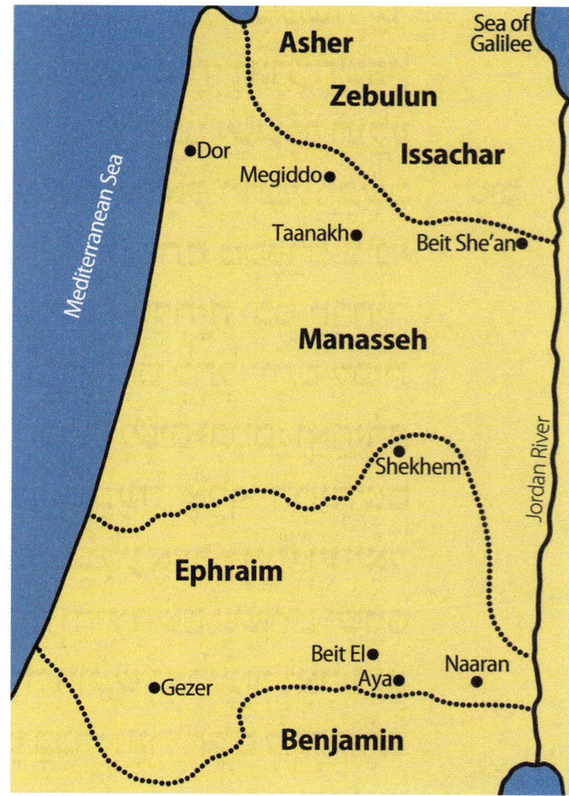

Cities of Ephraim and Manasseh

DISCUSSION

7:21 | **When they came down to take their livestock:** This story of the children of Ephraim who were killed in the Land of Israel by the men of Gat is highly obscure. There is a tradition that the tribe of Ephraim in Egypt thought that they could return to the Land of Israel on their own. They set out by the shorter path, through the land of the Philistines, where they were killed in battle by the Philistine residents of Gat (see Radak; Vilna Gaon; Malbim; *Sanhedrin* 92b; *Shemot Rabba* 20:11). Alternatively, this verse refers to a much earlier episode that occurred in the first generations of the Israelites' stay in Egypt. Perhaps at that stage they still felt a connection to the Land of Israel, as they had an

▸ *inheritance*

יד יַחְצִיאֵל וְגוּנִי וְיֵצֶר וְשַׁלּוּם בְּנֵי בִלְהָה׃ בְּנֵי מְנַשֶּׁה אַשְׂרִיאֵל אֲשֶׁר
טו יָלָדָה פִּילַגְשׁוֹ הָאֲרַמִּיָּה יָלְדָה אֶת־מָכִיר אֲבִי גִלְעָד׃ וּמָכִיר לָקַח אִשָּׁה לְחֻפִּים
טז וּלְשֻׁפִּים וְשֵׁם אֲחֹתוֹ מַעֲכָה וְשֵׁם הַשֵּׁנִי צְלָפְחָד וַתִּהְיֶנָה לִצְלָפְחָד בָּנוֹת׃ וַתֵּלֶד
מַעֲכָה אֵשֶׁת־מָכִיר בֵּן וַתִּקְרָא שְׁמוֹ פֶּרֶשׁ וְשֵׁם אָחִיו שָׁרֶשׁ וּבָנָיו אוּלָם וָרָקֶם׃
יז יח וּבְנֵי אוּלָם בְּדָן אֵלֶּה בְּנֵי גִלְעָד בֶּן־מָכִיר בֶּן־מְנַשֶּׁה׃ וַאֲחֹתוֹ הַמֹּלֶכֶת יָלְדָה
יט אֶת־אִישׁ הוֹד וְאֶת־אֲבִיעֶזֶר וְאֶת־מַחְלָה׃ וַיִּהְיוּ בְּנֵי שְׁמִידָע אַחְיָן וָשֶׁכֶם וְלִקְחִי
כ וַאֲנִיעָם׃ וּבְנֵי אֶפְרַיִם שׁוּתָלַח וּבֶרֶד בְּנוֹ וְתַחַת בְּנוֹ וְאֶלְעָדָה בְנוֹ
כא וְתַחַת בְּנוֹ׃ וְזָבָד בְּנוֹ וְשׁוּתֶלַח בְּנוֹ וְעֵזֶר וְאֶלְעָד וַהֲרָגוּם אַנְשֵׁי־גַת הַנּוֹלָדִים
כב בָּאָרֶץ כִּי יָרְדוּ לָקַחַת אֶת־מִקְנֵיהֶם׃ וַיִּתְאַבֵּל אֶפְרַיִם אֲבִיהֶם יָמִים רַבִּים וַיָּבֹאוּ
כג אֶחָיו לְנַחֲמוֹ׃ וַיָּבֹא אֶל־אִשְׁתּוֹ וַתַּהַר וַתֵּלֶד בֵּן וַיִּקְרָא אֶת־שְׁמוֹ בְּרִיעָה כִּי בְרָעָה
כד הָיְתָה בְּבֵיתוֹ׃ וּבִתּוֹ שֶׁאֱרָה וַתִּבֶן אֶת־בֵּית־חוֹרוֹן הַתַּחְתּוֹן וְאֶת־הָעֶלְיוֹן וְאֵת
כה כו אֻזֵּן שֶׁאֱרָה׃ וְרֶפַח בְּנוֹ וְרֶשֶׁף וְתֶלַח בְּנוֹ וְתַחַן בְּנוֹ׃ לַעְדָּן בְּנוֹ עַמִּיהוּד בְּנוֹ
כז כח אֱלִישָׁמָע בְּנוֹ׃ נוֹן בְּנוֹ יְהוֹשֻׁעַ בְּנוֹ׃ וַאֲחֻזָּתָם וּמֹשְׁבוֹתָם בֵּית־אֵל

DISCUSSION

inheritance there, and the famine of the days of Joseph had ended. It is likewise possible that before the servitude in Egypt began they would return to Canaan from time to time. If so, they might have had business dealings with the men of Gat, and on one of the occasions when they went there to collect their cattle, they were killed by the local residents (see commentary of *Talmid HaRasag* on Chronicles, Kirchheim ed., 12; Rav Yehuda HaḤasid, Exodus 1:7).

7:27 | **Joshua his son:** Nothing is stated here about Joshua's sons. Admittedly, the accounts in Chronicles are often tructated and do not mention everything, but other sources likewise indicate that Joshua fathered no sons. According to a tradition of the Sages, he had daughters who became mothers of important families in Israel (see *Megilla* 14b; *Pesaḥim* 119b).

BACKGROUND

7:24 | **Lower and Upper Beit Horon:** Two adjacent settlements (4 km apart) along a major east-west route from the lowlands to the mountains. They were named after a Canaanite goddess, Horon, whose Temple was possibly located there. Nowadays, they are called Beit Ur al-Tahta and Beit Ur al-Fauqa. The two places are also mentioned in Egyptian documents from the ninth century BCE.

Uzen She'era: Other words derived from the root *alef-zayin-nun* are also used in place names; Aznot Tavor (Joshua 19:34), as well as Aznat Par'an in the Samaria Ostraca (14). Some contend that the word *ozen*, which means ear, became a geographical term, just as many human limbs are used in Hebrew to describe features of the landscape, e.g., "the head of Pisga" (see Deuteronomy 3:27), the "shoulder of the Sea of Galilee" (see Number 34:11), or a "mountain rib" (see II Samuel 16:13), which is the literal meaning of the Hebrew term for a mountainside. If so, the terms Uzen and Aznot refer to an elevated place that is lower than the top of a nearby mountain or hill, just as the ear is slightly lower than the top of the head.

In light of the similarity between the names, some identify Uzen She'era as the Arab village of Beit Sira.

7:28 | **Naaran:** In the book of Joshua (16:7), this place is called Naara. Its identification is subject to debate. Some say that it is Khirbet el-Auja el-Fauqa, around 2 km west of Kibbutz Yitav, where the remnants of a large fortified settlement from the Iron Age have been discovered. Others identify it as the area of the ancient synagogue of Naaran from the Byzantine period, which is near the springs of Ein Nu'eimeh and Ein Duq.

to the west Gezer (see 6:52) **and its environs, and Shekhem and its environs, up to Aya and its environs.**

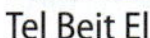
Tel Beit El

Tel Gezer, remains from the tenth century BCE

29 **Alongside them,** the children of Ephraim, **were** situated **the children of Manasseh;** those who crossed the Jordan River together with the rest of Israel rather than remaining on its eastern side like the sons of Makhir. They settled in **Beit She'an and its environs, Taanakh and its environs, Megiddo and its environs, Dor and its environs. In these** places **settled** Ephraim and Manasseh, **the children of Joseph son of Israel.**

Tel Megiddo

Tel Dor

The descendants of Joseph initially inherited Samaria, in central Israel, before spreading to Megiddo in the north and Dor in the west, on the coast.

30 **The sons of Asher: Yimna, Yishva, Yishvi, Beria, and Serah their sister.** It is not clear why Serah is mentioned here and whether she was married and if so, to whom. Serah is also mentioned in the Torah,[161] and many stories are related about her.[162] However, the Bible itself reveals nothing of her life.

31 **The sons of Beria: Hever and Malkiel; he was the father of** a place called **Birzayit.**[163]

32 **Hever begot Yaflet, Shomer, Hotam, and Shua their sister** who, like Serah, is probably also mentioned because she was an important woman.

33 **The sons of Yaflet: Pasakh, Bimhal, and Asvat. These are the sons of Yaflet.** Some of these names do not appear to be of Hebrew origin.

34 **The sons of Shemer: Ahi, Roga, Huba, and Aram.**

35 **The sons of Helem,** who was **his brother: Tzofah, Yimna, Shelesh, and Amal.**

36 **The sons of Tzofah: Suah, Harnefer,**[B] which both sound like Egyptian names, **Shual, Beri,**[B] **Yimra,**

37 **Betzer, Hod, Shama, Shilsha, Yitran, and Be'era.**

38 **The sons of Yeter: Yefuneh, Pispa, and Ara.**

39 **The sons of Ula,** a name that would become famous in the Talmudic period: **Arah, Haniel, and Ritzya.**

40 **All these** people **are the children of Asher, heads of the patrilineal houses, select**[164] **mighty warriors, heads of the princes. Their lineage,** people who were counted **for military service, was twenty-six thousand men.**

Another Genealogical List of the Tribe of Benjamin

I CHRONICLES 8:1–40

This list is not complete either, but it presents a more comprehensive picture of the members of this tribe than the previous list. This list, which traces the lineage of King Saul and his descendants, touches slightly on the lineage of Mordekhai, who is introduced in the book of Esther as "son of Ya'ir, son of Shimi, son of Kish, a Benjamite" (Esther 2:5). It seems that the individuals in these lists lived chronologically very close to each other, although it is not clear whether the names that appear together are invariably those of a father and son or if certain generations are skipped. Consequently, many questions with regard to the precise order of the generations remain unanswered.

8 1 **Benjamin begot Bela his firstborn, Ashbel the second, Ahrah the third,**

2 **Noha the fourth, and Rafa the fifth.** Some of these names correspond to the names that appear in the Torah, occasionally with slight differences,[165] while others are hard to identify. As is the case throughout this book, it seems that many individuals had two names, or nicknames.[166]

3 **Bela had sons,** descendants, **Adar, Gera, Avihud,**

4 **Avishua, Naaman, Aho'ah,**

5 **Gera, Shefufan, and Huram,**

6 **these** people mentioned above **are the sons of Ehud. These are the heads of patrilineal houses,** the heads of families, **of the inhabitants of Geva, and they were exiled to** a place

וּבְנֹתֶיהָ וְלַמִּזְרָח נַעֲרָן וְלַמַּעֲרָב גֶּזֶר וּבְנֹתֶיהָ וּשְׁכֶם וּבְנֹתֶיהָ עַד־עַיָּה וּבְנֹתֶיהָ׃
כט וְעַל־יְדֵי בְנֵי־מְנַשֶּׁה בֵּית־שְׁאָן וּבְנֹתֶיהָ תַּעְנַךְ וּבְנֹתֶיהָ מְגִדּוֹ וּבְנוֹתֶיהָ דּוֹר וּבְנוֹתֶיהָ
ל בְּאֵלֶּה יָשְׁבוּ בְּנֵי יוֹסֵף בֶּן־יִשְׂרָאֵל׃ בְּנֵי אָשֵׁר יִמְנָה וְיִשְׁוָה וְיִשְׁוִי וּבְרִיעָה
לא לב וְשֶׂרַח אֲחוֹתָם׃ וּבְנֵי בְרִיעָה חֶבֶר וּמַלְכִּיאֵל הוּא אֲבִי ברזות׃ וְחֶבֶר הוֹלִיד אֶת־ בִּרְזָיִת
לג יַפְלֵט וְאֶת־שׁוֹמֵר וְאֶת־חוֹתָם וְאֵת שׁוּעָא אֲחוֹתָם׃ וּבְנֵי יַפְלֵט פָּסַךְ וּבִמְהָל
לד לה וְעַשְׁוָת אֵלֶּה בְּנֵי יַפְלֵט׃ וּבְנֵי שָׁמֶר אֲחִי ורוהגה יחבה וַאֲרָם׃ וּבֶן־הֵלֶם אָחִיו וְרָהְגָּה וְחֻבָּה
לו לז צוֹפַח וְיִמְנָע וְשֵׁלֶשׁ וְעָמָל׃ בְּנֵי צוֹפַח סוּחַ וְחַרְנֶפֶר וְשׁוּעָל וּבֵרִי וְיִמְרָה׃ בֶּצֶר
לח לט וָהוֹד וְשַׁמָּא וְשִׁלְשָׁה וְיִתְרָן וּבְאֵרָא׃ וּבְנֵי יֶתֶר יְפֻנֶּה וּפִסְפָּה וָאֲרָא׃ וּבְנֵי עֻלָּא
מ אָרַח וְחַנִּיאֵל וְרִצְיָא׃ כָּל־אֵלֶּה בְנֵי־אָשֵׁר רָאשֵׁי בֵית־הָאָבוֹת בְּרוּרִים גִּבּוֹרֵי
חֲיָלִים רָאשֵׁי הַנְּשִׂיאִים וְהִתְיַחְשָׂם בַּצָּבָא בַּמִּלְחָמָה מִסְפָּרָם אֲנָשִׁים עֶשְׂרִים
וְשִׁשָּׁה אָלֶף׃
ח א ב וּבִנְיָמִן הוֹלִיד אֶת־בֶּלַע בְּכֹרוֹ אַשְׁבֵּל הַשֵּׁנִי וְאַחְרַח הַשְּׁלִישִׁי׃ נוֹחָה הָרְבִיעִי
ג ד וְרָפָא הַחֲמִישִׁי׃ וַיִּהְיוּ בָנִים לְבָלַע אַדָּר וְגֵרָא וַאֲבִיהוּד׃ וַאֲבִישׁוּעַ וְנַעֲמָן וַאֲחוֹחַ׃
ה ו וְגֵרָא וּשְׁפוּפָן וְחוּרָם׃ וְאֵלֶּה בְּנֵי אֵחוּד אֵלֶּה הֵם רָאשֵׁי אָבוֹת לְיוֹשְׁבֵי גֶבַע וַיַּגְלוּם

BACKGROUND

7:36 | **Harnefer:** Some argue that this name was originally Egyptian, comprised of two words: *Hor*, which refers to the Egyptian deity Horus, and *nefer*, meaning good, beautiful. It should be noted that there are other names of Israelites in the Bible which are derived from the Egyptian language, such as Ahira (Numbers 1:15), Pashhur (Jeremiah 20:1), and Amon (II Kings 21:18). Others, however, suggest that the name Harnefer refers to a species of horse, the name of which is derived from the root *nun-ḥet-reish*, referring to a snort [*neḥira*] and from the root *nun-peh-reish*, which in Syriac means the neighing of a horse. It is not surprising that a person would be given this name, just as people are called after other animals, e.g., Dov, meaning bear, and Ze'ev, wolf. This opinion is supported by the fact that other animal names appear in this verse: Shual, fox, and Suah, foal [*siyaḥ*].

Tzofah…Shual, Beri: It has been suggested that some of the names of the children of Asher mentioned in these verses refer to places in the portion of Benjamin and Mount Ephraim, where members of the tribe of Asher lived. Thus, Yaflet is a place name (see Joshua 16:3); Tzofah alludes to the land of Tzuf; Shelesh to the land of Shalisha; Shual to the land of Shaalim (see I Samuel 9:4–5); and Beri to Be'era, or Be'erot (see II Samuel 4:2).

called **Manahat,**[B] although it is unclear when and why this happened.

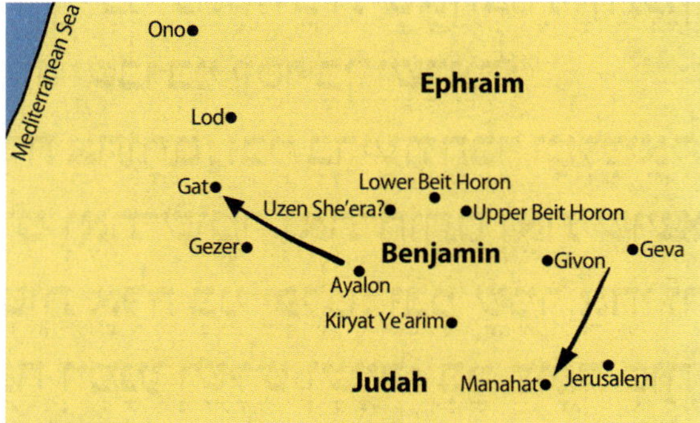

Cities of Benjamin, and movement between cities

7 **As for Naaman and Ahiya, it was Gera who exiled them, and he,** Gera, who banished them or caused them to depart, stayed in his place, and **begot Uza and Ahihud.**
8 **After he sent them away, Shaharayim had children in the field of Moav;**[D] after Gera had banished the heads of the families from Giva, Shaharayim went to the field of Moav,[167] where he fathered children **with Hushim and Baara,**[168] who were **his wives.**
9 And **he begot from Hodesh,** the name of **his** other **wife:**[169] **Yovav, Tzivya, Meisha, Malkam,**
10 **Yeutz, Sakhya, and Mirma.** All **these** men **are his sons, heads of the patrilineal houses.**
11 **From** his wife **Hushim, he begot Avituv and Elpaal.**
12 **The sons of Elpaal: Ever, Misham, and Shemed; he built Ono**[B] **and Lod**[B] **and its environs,** nearby towns and villages. These places were located within the borders of the territory of Benjamin, in its western portion.
13 **Beria and Shema,** from the sons of Elpaal, perhaps other names for Ever and Misham,[170] **they were heads of patrilineal houses of the inhabitants of Ayalon; they caused the inhabitants of Gat**[B] **to flee.**
14 **Ahyo, Shashak, Yeremot,**
15 **Zevadya, Arad, Eder,**
16 **Mikhael, Yishpa, and Yoha,** all these men **were the sons of Beria.**
17 **Zevadya, Meshulam, Hizki, Hever,**
18 **Yishmerai, Yizliah, and Yovav were the sons of Elpaal,** who was mentioned above, together with some of his sons (verses 11–12).
19 **Yakim, Zikhri, Zavdi,**
20 **Eli'enai, Tziletai, Eliel,**
21 **Adaya, Beraya, and Shimrat were the sons of Shimi.**
22 **Yishpan, Eved, Eliel,**
23 **Avdon, Zikhri, Hanan;**
24 **Hananya, Elam, Antotiya,**
25 **Yifdeya and Penuel were the sons of Shashak.**
26 **Shamsherai, Sheharya, Atalya,** which is apparently the name of a man here, as opposed to the well-known Atalya, the royal mother and queen;[171]
27 **Yaareshya, Eliya,**[D] **and Zikhri were the sons of Yeroham.**
28 **These are heads of patrilineal houses by their progeny,** in order of birth; **these heads settled in Jerusalem,** part of which was in the territory of Benjamin.[172]
29 **In Givon, the father** of the settlement **of Givon settled, and his wife's name was Maakha;**
30 **his firstborn son was** called **Avdon, and** the rest of his sons were called **Tzur, Kish, Baal, Nadav,**
31 **Gedor, Ahyo, and Zekher.**
32 **Miklot,** who was also a son of the man known as the father of the settlement of Givon,[173] **begot Shima. They too,** the members of this family, **settled like their brethren in Jerusalem,** like their brothers, they lived in Jerusalem[174] **with their brethren.**

DISCUSSION

8:8 | **Shaharayim had children in the field of Moav:** It seems that in certain periods, relations between the children of Israel and the Moavites were good, and the two nations were even very close. The men of the tribe of Benjamin listed here emigrated to Moav, like Elimelekh of the book of Ruth (chap. 1; see Radak; Jerusalem Talmud, *Yevamot* 8:3). In fact, the Moavite and Israelite nations share a common root, as Moav, the father of the nation, was the son of Lot, a nephew of the patriarch Abraham (Genesis 19:37). Likewise, surviving ancient documents indicate that the Moavite language was highly similar to the Hebrew tongue. Thus, these emigrating families remained in a broadly shared cultural environment, despite the internal differences between the two nations (see also Ezra 2:6, 8:4, 10:30–44; Nehemiah 13:2, 23).

8:27 | **Eliya:** Eliya is not a common name. It is perhaps for this reason that the Sages identify this individual as Elijah the prophet (see *Bereshit Rabba* 71:9), who is also called Eliya (II Kings 1:3–8; Malachi 3:23). However, virtually nothing is known about his origins. It is stated that he was from the inhabitants of Gilad (I Kings 17:1), but this does not necessarily mean that he was from the sons of Gilad or from the tribe of Gad. His mention here among the children of Benjamin is in keeping with a statement that the midrash attributes to Elijah the prophet: I am from none other than the descendants of Rachel (see Radak; *Tanna deVei Eliyahu Rabba* 18).

אֶל־מָנַחַת׃ וְנַעֲמָן וַאֲחִיָּה וְגֵרָא הוּא הֶגְלָם וְהוֹלִיד אֶת־עֻזָּא וְאֶת־אֲחִיחֻד׃ ז
וְשַׁחֲרַיִם הוֹלִיד בִּשְׂדֵה מוֹאָב מִן־שִׁלְחוֹ אֹתָם חוּשִׁים וְאֶת־בַּעֲרָא נָשָׁיו׃ וַיּוֹלֶד ח ט
מִן־חֹדֶשׁ אִשְׁתּוֹ אֶת־יוֹבָב וְאֶת־צִבְיָא וְאֶת־מֵישָׁא וְאֶת־מַלְכָּם׃ וְאֶת־יְעוּץ י
וְאֶת־שָׂכְיָה וְאֶת־מִרְמָה אֵלֶּה בָנָיו רָאשֵׁי אָבוֹת׃ וּמֵחֻשִׁים הוֹלִיד אֶת־אֲבִיטוּב יא
וְאֶת־אֶלְפָּעַל׃ וּבְנֵי אֶלְפַּעַל עֵבֶר וּמִשְׁעָם וָשָׁמֶד הוּא בָּנָה אֶת־אוֹנוֹ וְאֶת־לֹד יב
וּבְנֹתֶיהָ׃ וּבְרִעָה וָשֶׁמַע הֵמָּה רָאשֵׁי הָאָבוֹת לְיוֹשְׁבֵי אַיָּלוֹן הֵמָּה הִבְרִיחוּ אֶת־ יג
יוֹשְׁבֵי גַת׃ וְאַחְיוֹ שָׁשָׁק וִירֵמוֹת׃ וּזְבַדְיָה וַעֲרָד וָעָדֶר׃ וּמִיכָאֵל וְיִשְׁפָּה וְיוֹחָא בְּנֵי יד טו טז
בְרִיעָה׃ וּזְבַדְיָה וּמְשֻׁלָּם וְחִזְקִי וָחָבֶר׃ וְיִשְׁמְרַי וְיִזְלִיאָה וְיוֹבָב בְּנֵי אֶלְפָּעַל׃ וְיָקִים יז יח יט
וְזִכְרִי וְזַבְדִּי׃ וֶאֱלִיעֵינַי וְצִלְּתַי וֶאֱלִיאֵל׃ וַעֲדָיָה וּבְרָאיָה וְשִׁמְרָת בְּנֵי שִׁמְעִי׃ וְיִשְׁפָּן כ כא כב
וָעֵבֶר וֶאֱלִיאֵל׃ וְעַבְדּוֹן וְזִכְרִי וְחָנָן׃ וַחֲנַנְיָה וְעֵילָם וְעַנְתֹתִיָּה׃ וְיִפְדְיָה וּפְנִיאֵל כג כד כה — וּפְנוּאֵל
בְּנֵי שָׁשָׁק׃ וְשַׁמְשְׁרַי וּשְׁחַרְיָה וַעֲתַלְיָה׃ וְיַעֲרֶשְׁיָה וְאֵלִיָּה וְזִכְרִי בְּנֵי יְרֹחָם׃ אֵלֶּה כו כז כח
רָאשֵׁי אָבוֹת לְתֹלְדוֹתָם רָאשִׁים אֵלֶּה יָשְׁבוּ בִירוּשָׁלִָם׃ וּבְגִבְעוֹן יָשְׁבוּ כט
אֲבִי גִבְעוֹן וְשֵׁם אִשְׁתּוֹ מַעֲכָה׃ וּבְנוֹ הַבְּכוֹר עַבְדּוֹן וְצוּר וְקִישׁ וּבַעַל וְנָדָב׃ וּגְדוֹר ל לא
וְאַחְיוֹ וָזָכֶר׃ וּמִקְלוֹת הוֹלִיד אֶת־שִׁמְאָה וְאַף־הֵמָּה נֶגֶד אֲחֵיהֶם יָשְׁבוּ בִּירוּשָׁלִַם לב

BACKGROUND

8:6| **Manahat:** Manahat is identified as the present-day Jerusalem neighborhood of Malha or Manahat, situated around 4.5 km west of the location of biblical Jerusalem; an ancient village stood there, dating back to the Iron Age. The verses above (2:52–54) state that two families from the tribe of Judah, the sons of Shoval from the family of Caleb, and the family of the Tzorites, who came from Kiryat Ye'arim, dwelled in "the half of the Manahatites." This unusual name may refer to the fact that the place was split into two by the tribe of Judah. Alternatively, half of Manahat was inhabited by members of the tribe of Judah, while the other half was settled by the tribe of Benjamin, who were exiled there from Giva due to an incident that is not described in the Bible. There might also be echoes here of the civil war which broke out following the incident of the concubine at Giva (see commentary on 2:54). Indeed, there is an allusion to this in the account in the book of Judges itself: "They surrounded the Benjamite and pursued him, and at Menuhah, trampled him" (20:43).

8:12| **Ono:** An ancient city on the plain of Ono, whose name is preserved in the Arab village of Kafr 'Ana as well as in nearby Kiryat Ono. Its remnants have been found near Or Yehuda. Ono is mentioned in the list of the conquests of Thutmose III (fifteenth century BCE) and was one of the cities surrounded by a wall from the days of Joshua (*Megilla* 4a). The construction of Ono referred to here probably occurred after it was destroyed following the incident of the concubine at Giva.

Lod: Lod is located at the intersection of the road connecting Yafo to the inland plains and the Via Maris, near the Valley of Ayalon. Like Ono, it is also mentioned in the list of the conquests of Thutmose III (fifteenth century BCE) and was one of the cities surrounded by a wall from the days of Joshua (*Megilla* 4a).

8:13| **Gat:** According to the geographical description, this place was located in the Valley of Ayalon, in the northern lowlands, on the border between Ephraim and Benjamin. Some maintain that it is the city of Gitayim, identified as Ras Abu Hamid, near the moshav Yad Rambam, east of Ramla (Benjamin Mazar ed., *Encyclopaedia Biblica*, vol 2, 574). This is the city mentioned in II Samuel 4:3, Nehemiah 11:33, and I Chronicles 7:21–23. It is not the Philistine Gat, located in the portion of the tribe of Judah, which is identified as Tel Tzafit.

33 **Ner begot Kish, and Kish begot Saul.** This teaches that Avner son of Ner was a close relative of Saul.[175] This accounts for his unique relationship with the house of Saul.[176] **And Saul begot Yehonatan,** about whom much is related in the book of Samuel, **Malki Shua, Avinadav, and Eshbaal,** also called Ish Boshet in the book of Samuel. This is the same name, but as the Baal is an idol, this part of the name was replaced by the derogatory term *boshet*, or shame.[177]
34 **The son of Yehonatan was Meriv Baal,** more frequently called Mefivoshet,[178] **and Meriv Baal begot Mikha.**
35 **The sons of Mikha: Piton, Melekh, Taare'a, and Ahaz.**
36 **Ahaz begot Yehoada; Yehoada begot Alemet, Azmavet, and Zimri; Zimri begot Motza;**
37 **Motza begot Bine'a; Rafa was his,** Bine'a's **son,** and thus the generations continued: **Elasa his son, Atzel his son.**
38 **Atzel had six sons and these are their names: Azrikam, Bokhru, Yishmael, Shearya, Ovadya, and Hanan. All these are the sons of Atzel.**
39 **The sons of Eshek his brother,** the brother of Atzel:[179] **Ulam his firstborn, Yeush the second, and Elifelet the third.**
40 **The sons of Ulam were mighty warriors, archers, and had many children and grandchildren,** and the family numbered **one hundred and fifty** men in total. **All these are of the children of Benjamin.**[D]

Archers, relief, Nineveh, 645–635 BCE

The Inhabitants of Jerusalem and the Tasks of the Levites among Them

I CHRONICLES 9:1–34

This section provides lists that apparently belong to the early years of the Second Temple period, when Jerusalem was being rebuilt after the return from the exile. These lists consist mainly of priests and Levites. Parallel lists appear in the books of Ezra and Nehemiah, with minor differences. There it is mentioned with regard to families that lacked documented genealogies, "their register, that is, the genealogy" (Ezra 2:62), meaning that if they claimed any kind of special status, the claim was accepted only partially.

9 1 After having provided genealogical lists for several tribes, the text notes that the books of lineage were more comprehensive than those lists. **All Israel were established in their lineage.** In general, the people had orderly, reliable genealogical lists. **Behold they,** those records of family lineage, which do not deal with the historical events of the nation and its kings, **are recorded with the book of the kings of Israel,** as a kind of appendix to that work. Perhaps this is the origin of the book of Chronicles itself.[180] The people of **Judah,** together with the residents of the nearby areas, **were exiled to Babylon because of their trespass,** due to their sins.
2 **The first settlers** that returned from the exile and **who were in their portions,** their inheritances **in their cities:** Some of the **Israelites,** regular Jews, who were neither priests nor Levites, and some of **the priests, the Levites, and the Netinim,** descendants of the Givonites, who lived with Israel while serving as menial laborers for the Temple.[181] They too returned from Babylon.
3 **In Jerusalem settled some of the children of Judah, some of the children of Benjamin,** as the city was located on the border between these two tribes, **and some of the children of Ephraim and Manasseh:**[D]
4 **Utai son of Amihud, son of Omri, son of Imri, son of Bani, from the children of Peretz son of Judah.**
5 **From the Shilonite,** the descendants of Shela son of Judah: **Asaya the firstborn and his sons.**
6 **From the sons of Zerah** son of Judah: **Yeuel, and their brethren,** the rest of the members of the tribe of Judah, numbered **six hundred and ninety.**
7 **From the sons of Benjamin,** those who returned from the exile and came to Jerusalem at the start of the Second Temple period: **Salu, son of Meshulam,** who was the **son of Hodavya,** who was the **the son of Hasenua;**
8 **Yivneya son of Yeroham; Ela son of Uzi, son of Mikhri; Meshulam son of Shefatya, son of Re'uel, son of Yivneya;**
9 **and their brethren, by their progeny,** the branches of their families, were **nine hundred and fifty-six. All these** counted **men,** important individuals, **were heads of patrilineal houses by their patrilineal houses.**

לג עם־אחיהם: ונר הוליד את־קיש וקיש הוליד את־שאול ושאול
לד הוליד את־יהונתן ואת־מלכי־שוע ואת־אבינדב ואת־אשבעל: ובן־יהונתן
לה מריב בעל ומריב בעל הוליד את־מיכה: ובני מיכה פיתון ומלך ותארע ואחז:
לו ואחז הוליד את־יהועדה ויהועדה הוליד את־עלמת ואת־עזמות ואת־זמרי
לז וזמרי הוליד את־מוצא: ומוצא הוליד את־בנעא רפה בנו אלעשה בנו אצל
לח בנו: ולאצל ששה בנים ואלה שמותם עזריקם | בכרו וישמעאל ושעריה
לט ועבדיה וחנן כל־אלה בני אצל: ובני עשק אחיו אולם בכרו יעוש השני
מ ואליפלט השלשי: ויהיו בני־אולם אנשים גברי־חיל דרכי קשת ומרבים ד
א בנים ובני בנים מאה וחמשים כל־אלה מבני בנימן: וכל־ישראל
התיחשו והנם כתובים על־ספר מלכי ישראל ויהודה הגלו לבבל במעלם:
ב והיושבים הראשנים אשר באחזתם בעריהם ישראל הכהנים הלוים והנתינים:
ג ד ובירושלם ישבו מן־בני יהודה ומן־בני בנימן ומן־בני אפרים ומנשה: עותי
ה בן־עמיהוד בן־עמרי בן־אמרי בן־בנימן־בני פרץ בן־יהודה: ומן־השילוני בני מן־
ו ז עשיה הבכור ובניו: ומן־בני זרח יעואל ואחיהם שש־מאות ותשעים: ומן־בני
ח בנימן סלוא בן־משלם בן־הודויה בן־הסנאה: ויבניה בן־ירחם ואלה בן־עזי
ט בן־מכרי ומשלם בן־שפטיה בן־רעואל בן־יבניה: ואחיהם לתולדתם תשע
מאות וחמשים וששה כל־אלה אנשים ראשי אבות לבית אבתיהם:

DISCUSSION

8:40 | **All these are of the children of Benjamin:** The last descendant of King Saul mentioned in the book of Samuel is Mikha, Mefivoshet's young son (II Samuel 9:12). Here it is revealed that he had sons and grandsons and that the dynasty lasted for generations. The family of Saul came from a fine lineage, at least one branch of which continued for many generations and perhaps even enjoyed the patronage of the kings of Judah.

9:3 | **Some of the children of Ephraim and Manasseh:** It seems that people from tribes other than Judah and Benjamin also lived in Jerusalem, which means that descendants of those tribes might well have survived to this day, although there is no clear evidence for this theory. Most of today's Jews are from the tribes of Judah, Benjamin, and Levi, but it is likely that in the Second Temple period, and thus in later generations as well, there were individuals who came from other tribes, even if they themselves might have been unaware of this fact (see introduction to Jeremiah 30, and commentary ad loc.; Jeremiah 50:4; II Chronicles 34:6, 9).

10 **From the priests,** only some of the priestly families returned from the exile: **Yedaya, Yehoyariv, and Yakhin;**
11 **Azarya son of Hilkiya, son of Meshulam, son of Tzadok, son of Merayot, son of Ahituv,** who was in his day **the chief official,** the man who had been appointed in charge **of the House of God.** This title may refer back to Azarya rather than to Ahituv.[182]
12 **Adaya son of Yeroham, son of Pashhur, son of Malkiya; and Masai, son of Adiel, son of Yahzera, son of Meshulam, son of Meshilemit, son of Imer;**
13 **and their brethren, heads of their patrilineal houses, one thousand seven hundred and sixty; mighty warriors for the labor of the service of the House of God.**
14 **From the Levites: Shemaya son of Hashuv, son of Azrikam, son of Hashavya, from the sons of Merari;**
15 **and Bakbakar, Heresh, and Galal; and Matanya, son of Mikha, son of Zikhri, son of Asaf;**
16 **and Ovadya son of Shemaya, son of Galal, son of Yedutun; and Berekhya son of Asa, son of Elkana, who dwells in the villages of the Netofatites.** It is possible that all these men belonged to families of singers, some of them tracing their lineage to the singers Asaf and Yedutun.
17 **The gatekeepers: Shalum, Akuv, Talmon, and Ahiman; their** aforementioned **brother Shalum was the leader,** the chief official.
18 **Until now,** currently, at the time of writing,[183] **he is in the king's gate to the east; they were the gatekeepers for the camps of the children of Levi.**
19 **Shalum, son of Koreh, son of Evyasaf, son of Korah, and his brethren of his patrilineal house the Korahites,** the family of Korah, **were** appointed **in charge of the labor of the service, guardians of the threshold of the Tent,** they stood guard at the gate of the Tent of Meeting already in the time of David;[184] **their fathers** in the wilderness **had been** appointed **in charge of the camp of the Lord, guardians of the entrance.**
20 The following comment refers to the early generations: **Pinhas son of Elazar had been the chief official** appointed **over them in the** distant **past; the Lord was with him,** and therefore he was the leader of the priests.[185] Alternatively, the verse can be read as follows: In time past, the Lord was with him. This might be teaching that Pinhas was at some point a prophet, but did not remain a prophet for his entire life.[186]
21 The chapter returns to the later generations: **Zekharya son of Meshelemya was** also **the gatekeeper for the entrance of the Tent of Meeting.**
22 **All of those selected as gatekeepers were two hundred and twelve; their lineage was established in** accordance with **their villages.**[187] **It was they who were established by David and Samuel the seer,** the prophet, for the order of the Levite porters, **in their entrusted task,** to fulfill their tasks faithfully and steadily. Alternatively, this last clause is referring to David and Samuel: They ordained the Levites by virtue of their faithful, trustworthy office. Although the Temple had not yet been built in David's lifetime, he prepared for it as much as he possibly could. Not only did he amass the many materials required for its construction, but he also built the administrative systems for the future Temple. Furthermore, Samuel apparently sat with David and shared with him his vision of the pattern of the Temple, which included the watches of the priests and Levites.[188]
23 **They,** the porters, **and their children, were in charge of the gates of the House of the Lord, for the house of the Tent, by watches,** by the groups appointed to guard the Temple.
24 **On the four sides were the gatekeepers: east, westward, northward, and southward.**
25 **Their brethren,** who were living **in their villages,** the Levite cities, **were** charged **to come for seven days at fixed times,** intervals, in order **to be with** and assist **them.** Both the priests and the Levites were divided into watches, each of which served a week at a time.[189]
26 **For the** aforementioned (verse 17) **four head gatekeepers had an entrusted task;** they fulfilled their tasks faithfully and steadily. **They are the Levites,** the permanent staff who managed the Temple, **who were** also appointed **over the chambers and over the treasuries in the House of God.** Apart from the priests and Levites who would come at fixed times to perform the Temple service itself, there was a need for a permanent, dependable team to handle the administrative and logistical requirements of the Sanctuary.
27 **They lodged around the House of God** so that they should always be close to the Temple, **because upon them was** cast **the watch, and they were in charge of the opening** of the doors of the Temple **each and every morning,** some of which were locked at night.
28 **Some of them were in charge of the vessels of service,** the vessels for the regular service, such as those used for carrying the blood of the offerings and sprinkling it upon the altar, as well as the forks and shovels for transporting the sacrificial parts and the ashes; **as they would count when bringing them out and count when removing them.** Due to the importance of the sacred vessels in the Temple, they were all numbered and counted, and brought out only when needed.
29 **From them were those appointed over the vessels,** those vessels that were not directly connected to the sacred service, such as cooking implements,[190] **over all the sacred vessels,** e.g., the table for the showbread and its appurtenances,[191] **and over the high-quality flour, the wine, the oil, the frankincense, and the spices.**

י יא ומן־הכהנים ידעיה ויהויריב ויכין: ועזריה בן־חלקיה בן־משלם בן־צדוק בן־
יב מריות בן־אחיטוב נגיד בית האלהים: ועדיה בן־ירחם בן־פשחור
בן־מלכיה ומעשי בן־עדיאל בן־יחזרה בן־משלם בן־משלמית בן־אמר:
יג ואחיהם ראשים לבית אבותם אלף ושבע מאות וששים גבורי חיל מלאכת
יד עבודת בית־האלהים: ומן־הלוים שמעיה בן־חשוב בן־עזריקם בן־חשביה
טו טז מן־בני מררי: ובקבקר חרש וגלל ומתניה בן־מיכא בן־זכרי בן־אסף: ועבדיה
בן־שמעיה בן־גלל בן־ידותון וברכיה בן־אסא בן־אלקנה היושב בחצרי
יז יח נטופתי: והשערים שלום ועקוב וטלמן ואחימן ואחיהם שלום הראש: ועד־
יט הנה בשער המלך מזרחה המה השערים למחנות בני לוי: ושלום בן־קורא בן־
אביסף בן־קרח ואחיו לבית־אביו הקרחים על מלאכת העבדה שמרי הספים
כ לאהל ואבתיהם על־מחנה יהוה שמרי המבוא: ופינחס בן־אלעזר נגיד היה
כא כב עליהם לפנים יהוה | עמו: זכריה בן משלמיה שער פתח לאהל מועד: כלם
הברורים לשערים בספים מאתים ושנים עשר המה בחצריהם התיחשם המה
כג יסד דויד ושמואל הראה באמונתם: והם ובניהם על־השערים לבית־יהוה
כד לבית האהל למשמרות: לארבע רוחות יהיו השערים מזרח ימה צפונה ונגבה:
כה כו ואחיהם בחצריהם לבוא לשבעת הימים מעת אל־עת עם־אלה: כי באמונה
המה ארבעת גבורי השערים הם הלוים והיו על־הלשכות ועל־האצרות בית
כז האלהים: וסביבות בית־האלהים ילינו כי־עליהם משמרת והם על־המפתח
כח ולבקר לבקר: ומהם על־כלי העבודה כי במספר יביאום ובמספר יוציאום:
כט ומהם ממנים על־הכלים ועל כל־כלי הקדש ועל־הסלת והיין והשמן והלבונה

30 **Some of the sons of the priests were the blenders of the blend of the spices.** A specific family was assigned this role.[192]

31 **Matitya of the Levites, he was the firstborn of Shalum the Korahite, was entrusted with the preparation of pancakes.** This is referring to the meal offering prepared on a griddle, especially the unique meal offering baked on a griddle that was brought by the High Priest every day. An especially appointed, trustworthy person would perform the complex preparation of this meal offering every day, before sunrise. Half of the meal offering was brought in the morning, and the other half in the afternoon.[193]

32 **Some of the children of the Kehatites of their brethren,** of those mentioned above, **were** put **in charge of the bread of the arrangement, to prepare it each and every Sabbath.** Before each Sabbath, they would prepare a fresh set of loaves to place on the table for the showbread in the Sanctuary.

33 **These are the singers,** who were **heads of the patrilineal houses of the Levites, in the chambers, who were exempt** from other service in the Temple **because the labor is incumbent upon them, day and night.** The singers, who were occupied with their special job, did not deal with the administrative tasks of running the Temple and preparing the requisite materials; that was left to the other Levites. Many Temple rites were accompanied by music, but few of the vocal and instrumental arrangements are known to us. There were certain regular songs that were chanted in public, while others were performed only on certain days.[194]

34 **These** men **are heads of patrilineal houses of the Levites, by their progeny; these heads dwelled in Jerusalem.**

The Lineage of the Family of Saul

I CHRONICLES 9:35–44

After having dealt with the priests and Levites, the chapter returns to the genealogical list of the tribe of Benjamin, especially the house of King Saul. In effect, it reiterates the last statement at the end of the previous list (8:29–38).

35 **In Givon settled the father** of the settlement **of Givon,** who was called **Ye'iel, and the name of his wife was Maakha.**

36 **His firstborn son was Avdon, and** his subsequent sons were called **Tzur, Kish, Baal, Ner, Nadav,**

37 **Gedor, Ahyo, Zekharya, and Miklot.**

38 **Miklot begot Shime'am,** called Shima above (8:32), **and they,** the members of this family, **also dwelled like their brethren in Jerusalem,** like their brothers, they lived in Jerusalem **with their brethren.**

39 The following short list provides the lineage of the family of King Saul and his descendants: **Ner begot Kish, and Kish begot Saul,** who later became king, **and Saul begot Yehonatan, Malki Shua, Avinadav, and Eshbaal.**

40 **The son of Yehonatan was Meriv Baal,** more generally known as Mefivoshet, **Meriv Baal begot Mikha.**

41 **The sons of Mikha: Piton, Melekh, and Tahre'a.**

42 **Ahaz begot Yara,** who was earlier called Yehoada (8:36); **and Yara begot Alemet, Azmavet, and Zimri; Zimri begot Motza.**

43 **Motza begot Bina, and Refaya,** who was earlier called Rafa (8:37), was **his son, Elasa his son, Atzel his son.**

44 **Atzel had six sons, and these are their names: Azrikam, Bokhru, Yishmael, She'arya, Ovadya, and Hanan; these are the sons of Atzel.** This too is an abbreviated list of the descendants of Benjamin, some of whom were already mentioned earlier. However, these last few lists serve to complete the account of the Temple and Jerusalem, as well as the dynasty of King Saul.

The Death of Saul and the Start of David's Reign

I CHRONICLES 10:1–11:9

Following the genealogical lists, in which short explanatory remarks were interspersed, the book begins to relate the history of the Kingdom of Judah. Whereas the Kingdom of Israel is mentioned in this book only incidentally, the Kingdom of Judah, commencing with the reign of David over all of Israel, is portrayed in great detail. While David first appears in the book of Samuel as a lad, one of the sons of Yishai, in the book of Chronicles the narrative of David's reign over Israel begins with the death of Saul.

10 1 **The Philistines waged war,** one of the most devastating wars there were **against Israel; and the men of Israel fled from before the Philistines and fell, slain, on Mount Gilboa**[B] and its environs, where the battle took place.

Gilboa Mountains

2 In addition to the general conflict between the Israelites and the Philistines, there was a more focused battle: **The Philistines pursued after Saul and after his sons.** The Philistines sought not merely to defeat the Israelites, but to kill their leaders as well. **And the Philistines smote Yonatan, Avinadav, and Malkishua, sons of Saul.** One son, Ish Boshet, also known as Eshbaal, remained alive, and later assumed his father's throne for a brief period.[195] Following this defeat, the Israelites ceased

ל לא והבשמים: ומן־בני הכהנים רקחי המרקחת לבשמים: ומתתיה מן־הלוים

לב הוא הבכור לשלם הקרחי באמונה על מעשה החבתים: ומן־בני הקהתי מן־

לג אחיהם על־לחם המערכת להכין שבת שבת: ואלה המשררים

לד ראשי אבות ללוים בלשכת פטירים כי־יומם ולילה עליהם במלאכה: אלה (פְּטוּרִים)

ראשי האבות ללוים לתלדותם ראשים אלה ישבו בירושלם:

לה לו ובגבעון ישבו אבי־גבעון יעואל ושם אשתו מעכה: ובנו הבכור עבדון וצור (יְעִיאֵל)

לז לח וקיש ובעל ונר ונדב: וגדור ואחיו וזכריה ומקלות: ומקלות הוליד את־שמאם

לט ואף־הם נגד אחיהם ישבו בירושלם עם־אחיהם: ונר הוליד את־

קיש וקיש הוליד את־שאול ושאול הוליד את־יהונתן ואת־מלכי־שוע ואת־

מ אבינדב ואת־אשבעל: ובן־יהונתן מריב בעל ומרי־בעל הוליד את־מיכה:

מא מב ובני מיכה פיתן ומלך ותחרע: ואחז הוליד את־יעדה ויעדה הוליד את־עלמת

מג ואת־עזמות ואת־זמרי וזמרי הוליד את־מוצא: ומוצא הוליד את־בנעא ורפיה

מד בנו אלעשה בנו אצל בנו: ולאצל ששה בנים ואלה שמותם עזריקם | בכרו

וישמעאל ושעריה ועבדיה וחנן אלה בני אצל:

א ופלשתים נלחמו בישראל וינס איש־ישראל מפני פלשתים ויפלו חללים

ב בהר גלבע: וידבקו פלשתים אחרי שאול ואחרי בניו ויכו פלשתים את־

BACKGROUND

10:1 | **Mount Gilboa:** Gilboa is a mountain range connected to the Samarian Hills. The description of the war indicates that the battle spread from the Yizre'el Valley to its hilly perimeter, the Gilboa Mountains.

fighting as an organized combat force, and split into scattered groups of warriors who fled the advancing Philistines.

3 **The fighting was intense against Saul,** and only a small group of warriors remained to protect him. Although they were unaware of his exact location, the Philistines closed in on him, **and the** Philistine **archers located him.** There were apparently not many skilled archers in the Israelite army; rather, they fought primarily with swords and spears. **And he feared greatly because of the archers** who were closing in on him. Alternatively, the latter phrase of this verse may be translated to mean that he was mortally wounded by the archers.

4 **Saul said to his armor-bearer,** who was always at his side: **Draw your sword, and stab me** to death **with it, lest these uncircumcised** Philistines **come** and find me alive, **and abuse me.** Even if they abuse my body, at least I will not suffer their torture alive. **His armor-bearer was unwilling. As** the closest and most loyal person to his commander, he was so attached to Saul that he was even willing to die for him, and **he was** therefore **very afraid** to perform such a deed. **Saul took his sword and fell on it,** in an attempt to commit suicide. It is not easy to kill oneself by falling on a sword. From one of the descriptions of this incident in the book of Samuel,[196] it seems that Saul's attempt was not entirely successful. Although he was mortally wounded, he remained somewhat conscious until he was killed by an Amalekite lad.

Armor-bearer of the king, palace of Xerxes, Persepolis, fifth century BCE

5 **His armor-bearer saw that Saul was dead, and he too fell on his sword and died.** Due to his profound connection to Saul, when he saw that Saul was dead, the armor-bearer felt that he too had no reason to live.

6 **Saul died, and his three sons and his entire household together died.**

7 **All the men of Israel who were in the valley,** Yizre'el, **saw that they,** the warriors, **had fled** after their defeat, **and that Saul and his sons died, and they** too **abandoned their cities and fled.** Any Israelites who remained in the area after the defeat had no means of defense against the Philistines. Therefore, they abandoned their homes and moved to more secure areas, **and the Philistines came and settled in them,** the abandoned Israelite areas.

8 Apparently, the battle ended at nightfall, as it is pointless to conduct a battle in the dark. **It was on the next day that the Philistines came to strip the corpses** of any clothes or articles of value and take them as spoils of war, standard practice throughout the generations, **and** unexpectedly, **they found Saul and his sons fallen on Mount Gilboa.** Saul could have escaped the battlefield under the cover of night; they were unaware that he had remained until the end.

9 **They stripped him, carried his head,** which they had severed, **and his** personal **armor, and sent** them **all around the** regions of the **land of the Philistines, to bring the news to their idols and to the people.** In their celebration of their victory, they brought the symbolic objects of their triumph to their houses of worship before presenting them to the entire people.

10 Afterward, **they placed his,** Saul's, **armor in the house of their gods, and they fastened his skull in the house of** their deity **Dagon.**[B]

11 **All** the inhabitants of **Yavesh Gilad,**[B] who had had very close ties to the tribe of Benjamin, and to Saul in particular, over the course of many years,[197] **heard everything that the Philistines had done to Saul.**

12 **All the valiant men rose and carried the body of Saul and the bodies of his sons, and brought them to Yavesh.** They stole Saul's remains and the remains of his sons that had been displayed in the Philistine cities. Although the bodies were not heavily guarded, it took bold men to infiltrate the Philistine cities and extract them. **They buried their bones under the terebinth** in a designated area **in Yavesh, and they fasted seven days.**

Ancient terebinth, Ramot Naftali

13 After concluding its description of the tragic events, the chapter provides an explanation for them, as is often the case in the Bible: **Saul died for his trespass that he trespassed against the Lord,** in the war against Amalek and other instances, **in that he did not keep the word of the Lord** precisely,[198] **and also** for another sin, toward the end of his life; **for consulting the medium to seek counsel** of the dead,[199]

ג יוֹנָתָן וְאֶת־אֲבִינָדָב וְאֶת־מַלְכִּי־שׁוּעַ בְּנֵי שָׁאוּל׃ וַתִּכְבַּד הַמִּלְחָמָה עַל־שָׁאוּל
ד וַיִּמְצָאֻהוּ הַמּוֹרִים בַּקָּשֶׁת וַיָּחֶל מִן־הַיּוֹרִים׃ וַיֹּאמֶר שָׁאוּל אֶל־נֹשֵׂא כֵלָיו שְׁלֹף
חַרְבְּךָ ׀ וְדָקְרֵנִי בָהּ פֶּן־יָבֹאוּ הָעֲרֵלִים הָאֵלֶּה וְהִתְעַלְּלוּ־בִי וְלֹא אָבָה נֹשֵׂא
ה כֵלָיו כִּי יָרֵא מְאֹד וַיִּקַּח שָׁאוּל אֶת־הַחֶרֶב וַיִּפֹּל עָלֶיהָ׃ וַיַּרְא נֹשֵׂא־כֵלָיו כִּי מֵת
ו שָׁאוּל וַיִּפֹּל גַּם־הוּא עַל־הַחֶרֶב וַיָּמֹת׃ וַיָּמָת שָׁאוּל וּשְׁלֹשֶׁת בָּנָיו וְכָל־בֵּיתוֹ
ז יַחְדָּו מֵתוּ׃ וַיִּרְאוּ כָּל־אִישׁ יִשְׂרָאֵל אֲשֶׁר־בָּעֵמֶק כִּי נָסוּ וְכִי־מֵתוּ שָׁאוּל וּבָנָיו
ח וַיַּעַזְבוּ עָרֵיהֶם וַיָּנֻסוּ וַיָּבֹאוּ פְלִשְׁתִּים וַיֵּשְׁבוּ בָהֶם׃ וַיְהִי מִמָּחֳרָת וַיָּבֹאוּ
פְלִשְׁתִּים לְפַשֵּׁט אֶת־הַחֲלָלִים וַיִּמְצְאוּ אֶת־שָׁאוּל וְאֶת־בָּנָיו נֹפְלִים בְּהַר גִּלְבֹּעַ׃
ט וַיַּפְשִׁיטֻהוּ וַיִּשְׂאוּ אֶת־רֹאשׁוֹ וְאֶת־כֵּלָיו וַיְשַׁלְּחוּ בְאֶרֶץ־פְּלִשְׁתִּים סָבִיב לְבַשֵּׂר
י אֶת־עֲצַבֵּיהֶם וְאֶת־הָעָם׃ וַיָּשִׂימוּ אֶת־כֵּלָיו בֵּית אֱלֹהֵיהֶם וְאֶת־גֻּלְגָּלְתּוֹ תָקְעוּ
יא בֵּית דָּגוֹן׃ וַיִּשְׁמְעוּ כֹּל יָבֵישׁ גִּלְעָד אֵת כָּל־אֲשֶׁר־עָשׂוּ פְלִשְׁתִּים
יב לְשָׁאוּל׃ וַיָּקוּמוּ כָּל־אִישׁ חַיִל וַיִּשְׂאוּ אֶת־גּוּפַת שָׁאוּל וְאֵת גּוּפֹת בָּנָיו וַיְבִיאוּם
יג יָבֵישָׁה וַיִּקְבְּרוּ אֶת־עַצְמוֹתֵיהֶם תַּחַת הָאֵלָה בְּיָבֵשׁ וַיָּצוּמוּ שִׁבְעַת יָמִים׃ וַיָּמָת
שָׁאוּל בְּמַעֲלוֹ אֲשֶׁר־מָעַל בַּיהוָה עַל־דְּבַר יְהוָה אֲשֶׁר לֹא־שָׁמָר וְגַם־לִשְׁאוֹל

BACKGROUND

10:10 | **Dagon:** This deity is mentioned three times in the Bible (see Judges 16:23; I Samuel 5:2–7), and a settlement in Philistine territory with that name appears twice. According to both the biblical account and historical records, Dagon was not part of the Canaanite pantheon, but was worshipped in areas further north, e.g., Syria, northern Mesopotamia, and Phoenicia, as the god of land and grain [*dagan*]. Interestingly, in Indo-European languages, there is a root similar to *dagan* meaning land or earth. Some suggest that the Philistines brought the cult of Dagon with them from Syria, as they passed through that region on their way to the Land of Israel. Alternatively, they adopted it from the Phoenicians after settling in the area. Ultimately, Dagon became the primary god of the Philistines.

Based on the god's name, some commentaries on the Bible suggest that the idol was an amalgamation of a fish [*dag*] and a person, but there is no evidence supporting that theory.

10:11 | **Yavesh Gilad:** The location of this city is unknown. Researchers have proposed several possible locations along the length of Wadi Yabis. These include Tel el-Maqlub, el-Deir, Tel Abu el-Kharaz, and Deir el-Halawa.

14 **and he did not seek counsel of the Lord.** Although Saul had sought unsuccessfully to seek God at that time, he should have persisted in his efforts.[200] **And He put him to death; He transferred the kingdom to David son of Yishai.** This story is related to the demise of the house of Saul and his royal line. The book does not relate anything about the lives of Saul or of the rest of his family; rather, it relates his death in war, in the wake of which the monarchy was transferred to David. At this juncture, the book begins its treatment of the history of King David and his deeds.

11 1 Once Saul had been killed, and his surviving son, who had ruled for a brief period, had also been assassinated,[201] there was no designated heir to the throne. **All Israel gathered to David, to Hebron, saying: Behold, we are your bone and your flesh.** We are all one people; you are not a stranger to us. Although at that point David ruled only over the tribe of Judah, representatives from other tribes approached him in order to reestablish the monarchy over the entire people, just as Saul had ruled over the entire people.

2 **In times past, even when Saul was king, you were the one who led Israel out and led them in.** Even during Saul's reign, you were a leader in military and other matters.[202] Although, over time, you were partially removed from those roles, you have always been a central figure for us; **and the Lord your God said to you: You shall shepherd My people Israel, and you shall be ruler over My people Israel.** This, of course, is a reference to David's anointment as king by Samuel.

3 **All the elders of Israel** ultimately **came to the king, to Hebron, and David established a covenant with them in Hebron before the Lord.** They agreed that David would be their king, and he accepted the position. **They anointed David king over Israel, in accordance with the word of the Lord** conveyed **by means of Samuel.** Although David had already been anointed by Samuel, that anointment was private, and of limited significance. His anointment in Hebron signified a national decision to crown him as king.

4 David could not rule over all Israel from Hebron, as the city is situated in the middle of the tribal territory of Judah, far removed from the other tribes, and associated exclusively with the tribe of Judah. Therefore, one of David's first actions was to search for an alternative center for his monarchy. While doing so, he also proved his might.[203] **David and all Israel went to Jerusalem, which is** the city that was then called **Yevus, and the Yevusites,** one of the Canaanite tribes, **inhabitants of the land, were** living **there.**

5 **The inhabitants of Yevus said to David: You shall not come here.** Yevus was an enclave that had never been completely conquered by the Israelites when they entered the Land of Israel. However, relations between the Yevusites of Jerusalem and the Israelites[204] were apparently civil. Although the Yevusites were not a populous people and were not full-fledged soldiers, they resisted David's army when it came to conquer the city. In the first stage, **David captured** a fortress adjacent to the city, in the environs of the Temple Mount, which was later called **the stronghold of Zion, which is the City of David.** It seems this was a specific point through which one could enter the city. The parallel account in II Samuel (5:6–8) indicates that control over this spot would enable an army to breach the city.

6 **David said: Whoever smites the Yevusite,** breaks their resistance **first, will be a leader and an officer;** he will be appointed to a senior position. **Yoav son of Tzeruya ascended** to the city **first, and he became a leader.**

7 **David dwelled in the stronghold,** the fortified area of the city; **therefore they called it,** and the area later built around it,[205] **the City of David.**

Stone wall dated to period of David and Solomon, tenth century BCE

8 **He built the city around, from the Milo until the surrounding wall.** There were empty areas between the stronghold and the wall of the city, which David and his son Solomon filled [*millu*].[206] Originally, Jerusalem was not entirely fortified and protected, but after the construction of the Milo, the entire city was surrounded by a wall. **Yoav restored,** or provided for, **the rest of the city.** David's palace was initially located in the City of David, but later an actual palace was built for him.[207] The other side of the city, where David did not reside, was Yoav's responsibility.

9 **David grew steadily greater, as the Lord of hosts was with him.** David became a great king who waged wars, conquered countries, and expanded the borders of Israel.

David's Mighty Men and His Supporters

I CHRONICLES 11:10–12:41

Again, a number of lists are cited in the book with a few truncated descriptions interspersed. However, these are not the genealogical lists cited earlier. Rather, these are lists of David's mighty men, and a partial listing of those who came to celebrate with David when he was crowned king. These names, recorded at the time by nondescript individuals, were then included in the book of Chronicles.

10 The following is a list of David's mighty men, men in special positions and ranks; a parallel list appears in the book of Samuel.[208] **These are the heads of the mighty**[B] **who were with David, who exerted themselves with him** to assist him **in his**

יד בָּאוֹב לִדְרוֹשׁ: וְלֹא־דָרַשׁ בַּיהוָה וַיְמִיתֵהוּ וַיַּסֵּב אֶת־הַמְּלוּכָה לְדָוִיד בֶּן־יִשָׁי:

א א ב וַיִּקָּבְצוּ כָל־יִשְׂרָאֵל אֶל־דָּוִיד חֶבְרוֹנָה לֵאמֹר הִנֵּה עַצְמְךָ וּבְשָׂרְךָ אֲנָחְנוּ: גַּם־
תְּמוֹל גַּם־שִׁלְשׁוֹם גַּם בִּהְיוֹת שָׁאוּל מֶלֶךְ אַתָּה הַמּוֹצִיא וְהַמֵּבִיא אֶת־יִשְׂרָאֵל
וַיֹּאמֶר יְהוָה אֱלֹהֶיךָ לְךָ אַתָּה תִרְעֶה אֶת־עַמִּי אֶת־יִשְׂרָאֵל וְאַתָּה תִּהְיֶה נָגִיד
ג עַל עַמִּי יִשְׂרָאֵל: וַיָּבֹאוּ כָּל־זִקְנֵי יִשְׂרָאֵל אֶל־הַמֶּלֶךְ חֶבְרוֹנָה וַיִּכְרֹת לָהֶם דָּוִיד
בְּרִית בְּחֶבְרוֹן לִפְנֵי יְהוָה וַיִּמְשְׁחוּ אֶת־דָּוִיד לְמֶלֶךְ עַל־יִשְׂרָאֵל כִּדְבַר יְהוָה בְּיַד־
ד שְׁמוּאֵל: וַיֵּלֶךְ דָּוִיד וְכָל־יִשְׂרָאֵל יְרוּשָׁלִַם הִיא יְבוּס וְשָׁם הַיְבוּסִי
ה יֹשְׁבֵי הָאָרֶץ: וַיֹּאמְרוּ יֹשְׁבֵי יְבוּס לְדָוִיד לֹא תָבוֹא הֵנָּה וַיִּלְכֹּד דָּוִיד אֶת־מְצֻדַת
ו צִיּוֹן הִיא עִיר דָּוִיד: וַיֹּאמֶר דָּוִיד כָּל־מַכֵּה יְבוּסִי בָּרִאשׁוֹנָה יִהְיֶה לְרֹאשׁ וּלְשָׂר
ז וַיַּעַל בָּרִאשׁוֹנָה יוֹאָב בֶּן־צְרוּיָה וַיְהִי לְרֹאשׁ: וַיֵּשֶׁב דָּוִיד בַּמְצָד עַל־כֵּן קָרְאוּ־
ח לוֹ עִיר דָּוִיד: וַיִּבֶן הָעִיר מִסָּבִיב מִן־הַמִּלּוֹא וְעַד־הַסָּבִיב וְיוֹאָב יְחַיֶּה אֶת־שְׁאָר
ט הָעִיר: וַיֵּלֶךְ דָּוִיד הָלוֹךְ וְגָדוֹל וַיהוָה צְבָאוֹת עִמּוֹ: ה
י וְאֵלֶּה רָאשֵׁי הַגִּבּוֹרִים אֲשֶׁר לְדָוִיד הַמִּתְחַזְּקִים עִמּוֹ בְמַלְכוּתוֹ עִם־כָּל־יִשְׂרָאֵל

BACKGROUND

11:10 | **The mighty:** Some commentaries maintain that these mighty men constituted an elite military unit, and over time some of them became leaders in David's army, e.g., Avishai, who was appointed the commander of an extremely large military unit, and Benaya son of Yehoyada, who ascended the ranks of command until he became the commander of the entire army during King Solomon's reign. Others hold that "mighty men" and "officers" were also descriptive terms for an organization or institution of the senior military officers in David's army, like the general staff of modern-day armies, and therefore this title is not merely a description of their character and their courageous acts. Indeed, some of these mighty men are also mentioned later in I Chronicles (chap. 27) as senior officers in the army (Samuel Klein, "David's Mighty Men," *Bulletin of the Jewish Palestine Exploration Society*, Summer 1940 [Hebrew], 95–106; Yigael Yadin, *The Art of Warfare in Biblical Lands in the Light of Archaeological Discovery*. Ramat Gan: The International Publishing Co., 1963 [Hebrew], 249). They explain that the place in Jerusalem called the "house of the mighty" (Nehemiah 3:16) was the headquarters of this institution. During Solomon's reign, the organization expanded, and "sixty valiant men" are mentioned as members of that organization (Song of Songs 3:7).

kingdom, with all Israel, to crown him king, in accordance with the word of the Lord concerning Israel. Some of them performed acts of individual heroism, as related here; others grew close to David as courageous individuals and over time were appointed commanders in his army; some filled senior, prominent positions.

11 **This is the number of the mighty who were with David:**[B] The first on the list is **Yoshovam son of Hakhmoni,** who was **head of the officers; he wielded his spear against three hundred** men who were **slain** by him **on one occasion,** in a single encounter, with his own unique strength.

12 **After him, Elazar son of Dodo the Ahohite,** the name of the patriarch of his family; alternatively, Ahohite refers to a place; **who was among the three mighty ones,** an outstanding team of warriors notable for their exploits, as related in the following verses.

13 **He was with David at** a place called **Pas Damim,** or Efes Damim.[209] The reason for either of these names is unknown. **And the Philistines gathered there for war.** This is referring to the early clashes between the Philistines and David, when the Philistines sent a force to weaken David and to contain and damage his kingdom. The Philistines sought to prevent the kingdom of Israel from posing a threat to them. They knew David both as an ally, from the time he spent in their camp, and as a formidable adversary. In their wars, they sought to preserve their hegemony in the region, and their superior status. **There was a tract of a field full of barley, and the people fled from before the Philistines,** and some hid in that field.

Barley field

14 **They stood,** Elazar and another hero, or Elazar and his men,[210] **in the midst of the tract, and saved it, and they smote the Philistines.** They successfully halted the Philistine advance, and even protected the produce of the field from damage. **The Lord rescued them with a great salvation.**

15 **Three of the thirty leaders went down to the rock** that served as a fortress and shelter, **to David, to the cave of Adulam.**[B] It is unclear whether this occurred before or after he conquered Jerusalem. **And the Philistine camp was encamped in the Valley of Refaim,**[B] an open area near Jerusalem.

16 **David was then in the stronghold,** the rock adjacent to the cave of Adulam, **and a Philistine garrison was then in Bethlehem.** After the defeat of Israel at Gilboa, and Saul's death, the Philistines extended their rule into the land of Judah. Therefore, a Philistine governor ruled the city of Bethlehem and its environs, and a garrison defended it.

Tel Adulam

17 **David had a craving and said: Who will give me water to drink from the cistern of Bethlehem, which is at the gate?** Bethlehem was not far from the Valley of Refaim. David was raised in Bethlehem, and he remembered it from its peaceful days. It does not appear that David made a special request; rather he was merely waxing nostalgic about that water, as he could have easily obtained water collected in waterholes in the desert, or elsewhere.[211]

18 When three of David's men heard his wish, **the three** mighty men, who were great admirers of David, fought and **breached the** fortified **Philistine camp, and drew water from the cistern of Bethlehem, which was at the gate. They carried it and brought it to David, but David was unwilling to drink it, and** instead **he poured it** out **to the Lord,** as a water libation to God.

19 **He,** David, **said: Far be it from me by my God to do this,** to drink this water; **shall I drink the blood of these men who risked their lives? For at the risk of their lives they brought it.** Since these men put their lives at risk for this water, it is as though their own blood is mixed with it. It is therefore inappropriate for me to drink this water that was acquired with blood. **He was unwilling to drink it. These were done by the mighty three.** These three mighty men achieved renown through this extraordinary deed.

20 **Avshai,** here called Avshai but consistently referred to as Avishai in the book of Samuel, **brother of Yoav, he was head of the three. He wielded his spear against three hundred**[B] **slain, and he had renown among the three.**

21 **Of the three,** Tahkemoni, Elazar, and Shama,[212] **he was more esteemed,** in his personal courage, **than two, and he became their commander.** Avishai rose in the ranks of command and over time became one of David's great commanders, **but he did not come with the three.** Although Avishai was their leader, he was not included as one of the three.

יא לְהַמְלִיכוֹ כִּדְבַר יְהוָה עַל־יִשְׂרָאֵל׃ וְאֵלֶּה מִסְפַּר הַגִּבֹּרִים אֲשֶׁר לְדָוִיד
יָשָׁבְעָם בֶּן־חַכְמוֹנִי רֹאשׁ השלושים הוּא־עוֹרֵר אֶת־חֲנִיתוֹ עַל־שְׁלֹשׁ־מֵאוֹת הַשָּׁלִישִׁים
יב חָלָל בְּפַעַם אֶחָת׃ וְאַחֲרָיו אֶלְעָזָר בֶּן־דּוֹדוֹ הָאֲחוֹחִי הוּא בִּשְׁלוֹשָׁה הַגִּבֹּרִים׃
יג הוּא־הָיָה עִם־דָּוִיד בַּפַּס דַּמִּים וְהַפְּלִשְׁתִּים נֶאֶסְפוּ־שָׁם לַמִּלְחָמָה וַתְּהִי חֶלְקַת
יד הַשָּׂדֶה מְלֵאָה שְׂעוֹרִים וְהָעָם נָסוּ מִפְּנֵי פְלִשְׁתִּים׃ וַיִּתְיַצְּבוּ בְתוֹךְ־הַחֶלְקָה
טו וַיַּצִּילוּהָ וַיַּכּוּ אֶת־פְּלִשְׁתִּים וַיּוֹשַׁע יְהוָה תְּשׁוּעָה גְדוֹלָה׃ וַיֵּרְדוּ שְׁלוֹשָׁה מִן־
הַשְּׁלוֹשִׁים רֹאשׁ עַל־הַצֻּר אֶל־דָּוִיד אֶל־מְעָרַת עֲדֻלָּם וּמַחֲנֵה פְלִשְׁתִּים חֹנָה
טז יז בְּעֵמֶק רְפָאִים׃ וְדָוִיד אָז בַּמְּצוּדָה וּנְצִיב פְּלִשְׁתִּים אָז בְּבֵית לָחֶם׃ וַיִּתְאָו דָּוִיד
יח וַיֹּאמַר מִי יַשְׁקֵנִי מַיִם מִבּוֹר בֵּית־לֶחֶם אֲשֶׁר בַּשָּׁעַר׃ וַיִּבְקְעוּ הַשְּׁלֹשָׁה בְּמַחֲנֵה
פְלִשְׁתִּים וַיִּשְׁאֲבוּ־מַיִם מִבּוֹר בֵּית־לֶחֶם אֲשֶׁר בַּשַּׁעַר וַיִּשְׂאוּ וַיָּבִאוּ אֶל־דָּוִיד
יט וְלֹא־אָבָה דָוִיד לִשְׁתּוֹתָם וַיְנַסֵּךְ אֹתָם לַיהוָה׃ וַיֹּאמֶר חָלִילָה לִּי מֵאֱלֹהַי מֵעֲשׂוֹת
זֹאת הֲדַם הָאֲנָשִׁים הָאֵלֶּה אֶשְׁתֶּה בְנַפְשׁוֹתָם כִּי בְנַפְשׁוֹתָם הֱבִיאוּם וְלֹא אָבָה
כ לִשְׁתּוֹתָם אֵלֶּה עָשׂוּ שְׁלֹשֶׁת הַגִּבּוֹרִים׃ וְאַבְשַׁי אֲחִי־יוֹאָב הוּא
הָיָה רֹאשׁ הַשְּׁלוֹשָׁה וְהוּא עוֹרֵר אֶת־חֲנִיתוֹ עַל־שְׁלֹשׁ מֵאוֹת חָלָל ולא־שֵׁם וְלוֹ־
כא בַּשְּׁלוֹשָׁה׃ מִן־הַשְּׁלוֹשָׁה בַשְּׁנַיִם נִכְבָּד וַיְהִי לָהֶם לְשָׂר וְעַד־הַשְּׁלוֹשָׁה לֹא־

BACKGROUND

11:11 | **The number of the mighty who were with David:** There are several discrepancies between this list and the one that appears in the book of Samuel. First, the names in Samuel are generally written with deficient spelling, that is without a *yod-vav*, and other vowels, while in Chronicles their spelling is plene, or full. Second, some of the names in Chronicles are corrupted, although one can find similarities between them and those of the parallel list in Samuel. Third, the thirty mighty men in Samuel are primarily from Benjamin and Judah, while in Chronicles there are sixteen additional men, whose names, e.g., Ashteratite, Reubenite, and Aroerite, indicate that they originated east of the Jordan.

11:15 | **The cave of Adulam:** The city of Adulam is identified with Khirbet Madkour, above Wadi el-Tzur, which extends from Mount Hebron into the Judean plain, and served as an important regional path. Near Adulam, the path of the wadi intersects with the Valley of Ela. Several large caves are situated adjacent to Adulam.

The Valley of Refaim: According to the delineation of the borders of the territory of Judah in the book of Joshua: "The border went up to the top of the highlands that were on the western side of the Valley of Hinom, which is at the northern edge of the Valley of Refaim" (Joshua 15:8). The Valley of Refaim is a plateau that extends south and west of Jerusalem, with its southern section reaching the ridge upon which Bethlehem is situated, some 9 km south of Jerusalem. Bethlehem itself is identified with the hill that extends eastward from the plaza of the modern-day city of that name.

11:20 | **Three hundred:** The repeated incidence of the figure three hundred, both in the Bible (e.g., verse 11) and in rabbinic literature (e.g., Mishna *Shekalim* 8:5, *Middot* 3:8; *Ḥullin* 90b), indicates that it is a typological number, indicating an unusually large amount, and should not necessarily be taken literally (see *Ḥullin* 90b).

22 Another mighty man, **Benaya son of Yehoyada, was the son
of an accomplished, valiant man from** a place called
Kavtze'el,[B] and **he smote the two champions** [*ariel*],[B] a term
that also appears on the Mesha Stele of King Mesha of Moav,
and which apparently means "special forces,"[213] who were in the
camp **of Moav. And** in another episode that displays Benaya's
personal valor, he **went down and smote the lion inside the
pit on the snowy day.** Benaya descended alone into a pit on a
snowy day, and managed to overcome a distressed lion that he
found there.[214]

Assyrian king wrestling a lion, Ashurbanipal's Palace, Nineveh, seventh century BCE

23 **He smote the Egyptian man,** who was **a man of** large **dimensions,** roughly **five cubits high; in the Egyptian's hand was a**
great **spear like a** large **weaver's beam** that is found at the top
of the loom; **and he,** Benaya, **went against him with a staff,**
not a spear, **and snatched the spear from the hand of the
Egyptian and killed him with his own spear.** Perhaps Benaya
managed to snatch the spear from the Egyptian's hand because
the latter's armor encumbered him, similar to the story of David
and Goliath.

Weaver's beam

24 **These, Benaya son of Yehoyada did, and he had renown
among the three mighty ones.** Even the three mighty men
considered him a remarkable hero.
25 **He was** considered **more esteemed than the thirty** mighty
men listed below (see 27:6), **but he did not reach the three.**
He was not as mighty as the three, who had become arche-
types of courage and valor. **And David appointed him over
his guard.** David gave Benaya command responsibilities; he
was appointed commander of the Keretites and the Peletites,
David's personal guard detail.[215]
26 **The** names of the **mighty warriors,**[D] including the aforementioned thirty mighty men, were:[216] **Asael,** the younger **brother
of Yoav,** who was killed by Avner,[217] and **Elhanan son of Dodo,**
both **from Bethlehem;**
27 **Shamot the Harorite,**[B] **Heletz the Pelonite.**[B] It is possible that
he was from a place called Peloni; alternatively, he was called
Peloni, a placeholder name in Hebrew, because his place of origin was unknown.
28 **Ira son of Ikesh the Tekoite,** from the city of Tekoa in Judah,
Aviezer the Anatotite, from Anatot in Benjamin;
29 **Sibekhai the Hushatite,**[B] **Ilai the Ahohite,**[B] the name of a family from the tribe of Benjamin (see 8:4);

DISCUSSION

11:26| **The mighty warriors:** The list of David's mighty men includes individuals from various places and backgrounds who gathered and fought alongside him. Some of them hailed from the nobility, while others were foreigners, who were amalgamated into a band of warriors that accompanied David when he fled Saul. Due to his situation at that time, David could not afford to be too particular about the men who joined him, and they were appraised mainly for their military prowess and their devotion to the cause. It is possible that the mighty men who were with him in those early days later formed a foreign legion of sorts in the army that he established as king. Some of the mighty men on this list were renowned for their daring military exploits and successes, even though they did not have designated positions, while others became commanders in David's army.

כב בָּא׃ בְּנָיָה בֶן־יְהוֹיָדָע בֶּן־אִישׁ־חַיִל רַב־פְּעָלִים מִן־קַבְצְאֵל
הוּא הִכָּה אֵת שְׁנֵי אֲרִיאֵל מוֹאָב וְהוּא יָרַד וְהִכָּה אֶת־הָאֲרִי בְּתוֹךְ הַבּוֹר
כג בְּיוֹם הַשָּׁלֶג׃ וְהוּא הִכָּה אֶת־הָאִישׁ הַמִּצְרִי אִישׁ מִדָּה ׀ חָמֵשׁ בָּאַמָּה וּבְיַד
הַמִּצְרִי חֲנִית כִּמְנוֹר אֹרְגִים וַיֵּרֶד אֵלָיו בַּשָּׁבֶט וַיִּגְזֹל אֶת־הַחֲנִית מִיַּד הַמִּצְרִי
כד וַיַּהַרְגֵהוּ בַּחֲנִיתוֹ׃ אֵלֶּה עָשָׂה בְּנָיָהוּ בֶּן־יְהוֹיָדָע וְלוֹ־שֵׁם בִּשְׁלוֹשָׁה הַגִּבֹּרִים׃
כה מִן־הַשְּׁלוֹשִׁים הִנּוֹ נִכְבָּד הוּא וְאֶל־הַשְּׁלֹשָׁה לֹא־בָא וַיְשִׂימֵהוּ דָוִיד עַל־
כו מִשְׁמַעְתּוֹ׃ וְגִבּוֹרֵי הַחֲיָלִים עֲשָׂהאֵל אֲחִי יוֹאָב אֶלְחָנָן בֶּן־דּוֹדוֹ
כז כח מִבֵּית לָחֶם׃ שַׁמּוֹת הַהֲרוֹרִי חֶלֶץ הַפְּלוֹנִי׃ עִירָא
כט בֶן־עִקֵּשׁ הַתְּקוֹעִי אֲבִיעֶזֶר הָעַנְּתוֹתִי׃ סִבְּכַי הַחֻשָׁתִי עִילַי הָאֲחוֹחִי׃

BACKGROUND

11:22 | **Kavtze'el:** According to the verse in Joshua (15:21), Kavtze'el is a city located on the slopes of the Hebron Mountains in the southeastern portion of the tribal territory of Judah. Some identify this with Tel Arad, while others claim that it is Tel Aira.

Two [*shenei*] champions [*ariel*]: Some interpret the term *ariel* as referring to a lion, *arye*. Similar stories of valor in battle, involving a lion [*arye*] and even a bear, are attributed to David himself (I Samuel 17:34). There are comparable accounts in external sources, e.g., the inscriptions and reliefs of the royal Lion Hunt of King Ashurbanipal, who boasts that he grabbed a lion by its tail and killed it with a sword or spear. Researchers have proffered several suggestions for the meaning of the term *shenei ariel*. Some associate *shenei* with *shinayim*, teeth, so the phrase indicates the breaking of a lion's jaw. As stated in the commentary, the term *ariel* appears on the Mesha Stele, of King Mesha of Moav, dated to the ninth century BCE. Some claim that in that instance the reference is to a ritual object used in a temple. If so, it is possible that these were carvings of lions, which served as symbols of divine power, or images of guards, the likes of which can be found on the gates and temples of many nations and cultures. In the Bible, the name Ariel denotes divine strength, as it was accorded to objects in the Temple that had special importance or powers, such as the ark and altar (see Isaiah 29:1–2; Ezekiel 43:15).

11:27 | **The Harorite:** In the parallel passage in II Samuel (23:25), the name is Ḥarodite. This is common, as the letters *heh* and *ḥet* are interchangeable in Hebrew, as are *dalet* and *reish*. This might be identical to Beit Ḥiddudo, or Ḥadduro, mentioned in the Mishna (*Yoma* 6:8), and which has been identified with Khirbet Haradhan, some 20 km southeast of Jerusalem (Samuel Klein, "David's Mighty Men," *Bulletin of the Jewish Palestine Exploration Society*, Summer 1940 [Hebrew], 95–106). Some suggest that this was close to Ein Harod, the Spring of Harod, in the territory of Issachar.

Heletz the Pelonite: The parallel passage in II Samuel (23:26) refers to Heletz the Paltite. Since it is stated later in this book that Heletz the Pelonite was an officer from the children of Ephraim (27:10), some suggest that he was from the Yafeletite family mentioned in the book of Joshua (16:3), which lived at the border of the territory of the tribes of Joseph (Samuel Klein, "David's Mighty Men," *Bulletin of the Jewish Palestine Exploration Society*, Summer 1940 [Hebrew], 95–106). It is also possible that he was from the Pelet family of the descendants of Caleb, mentioned earlier (2:47), or from a place called Beit Pelet, in the Negev region of Judah, mentioned in the book of Joshua (15:27).

11:29 | **Hushatite:** Husha in Judah (4:4), identified with the Arab village of Husan about 6 km west of Bethlehem, south of Jerusalem.

Ahohite: Aho'ah is mentioned earlier (8:4) as one of the family heads of the tribe of Benjamin.

30 **Mahrai the Netofatite,**[B] **Heled son of Baana the Netofatite,**
both from the town of Netofa;
31 **Itai son of Ribai from Giva of the Benjaminites,**[B] **Benaya the**
Piratonite,[B] from Piraton in Ephraim;
32 **Hurai of Nahalei Gaash,**[B] **Aviel the Arvatite,**[B]
33 **Azmavet the Baharumite,**[B] from a place called Bahurim, east
of Jerusalem, **Elyahba the Shaalvonite,**[B] from Shaalvin,
34 **the sons of Hashem the Gizonite,**[B] **Yonatan son of Shageh**
the Hararite,
35 **Ahiam son of Sakhar the Hararite, Elifal son of Ur,**
36 **Hefer the Mekheratite,**[B] **Ahiya the Pelonite,**
37 **Hetzro the Carmelite, Naarai son of Ezbai,**[B]
38 **Yoel brother of Natan;** perhaps the prophet Natan, which may
explain why he is linked to his brother; **Mivhar son of Hagri,**[B]
39 **Tzelek the Amonite, Nahrai the Berotite,**[B] from Be'erot,[218]
who was the **armor-bearer,** close assistant, **of Yoav son of**
Tzeruya,[219]
40 **Ira the Yitrite, Garev the Yitrite,**[B]
41 **Uriya the Hitite, Zavad son of Ahlai,**[B]
42 **Adina son of Shiza the Reubenite,** who eventually became
head of the Reubenites, and with him were **thirty** men,
43 **Hanan son of Maakha, and Yoshafat the Mitnite,**[B]
44 **Uziya the Ashteratite,**[B] **Shama and Ye'iel the sons of Hotam**
the Aroerite,[B]
45 **Yediael son of Shimri, and Yoha his brother, the Tizite,**[B]
46 **Eliel the Mahavite, and Yerivai and Yoshavya sons of**
Elnaam, and Yitma the Moavite,
47 **Eliel, and Oved, and Yaasiel the Metzova'ite.**[B]

12 1 The following list of names, consisting of some names clear
and obvious and some obscure, details David's followers before he rose to power, as well
as those who rallied around
him after he was crowned.
These are those who came
to David, to Tziklag.[B]
Tziklag was a city in the Land
of Israel conquered by the
Philistines. They gave it to
David, and it remained part
of the inheritance of the royal house of David for generations.[220]
These men joined David **while he was still constrained** and
detained there **due to Saul son of Kish.** While David resided

Tel Sera

BACKGROUND

11:30| **Netofatite:** Netofa, near Jerusalem, is mentioned several times in the Bible as being adjacent to Bethlehem in Judah (II Samuel 23:28; Ezra 2:22; Nehemiah 7:26). Some identify it with Khirbet Bedd Faluh, roughly 1 km north of modern-day Tekoa. It should be noted that there was also a city in Benjamin called Netof, some 2.5 km west of modern-day Maaleh HaHamisha.

11:31| **Giva of the Benjaminites:** Elsewhere in the Bible this place is called Givea or Givat Shaul (see, e.g., I Samuel 11:4). It is identified with Tel el-Ful, some 6 km north of Jerusalem.

Piratonite: It is stated in the book of Judges (12:15) that the judge Avdon lived and was buried in Piraton, in the territory of Ephraim. Some identify Piraton with the village of Farata, some 10 km west of Shekhem, roughly 4.5 km northwest of the modern-day city of Imanuel. Others claim that it is the village of Farha, about 4.5 km south of the modern-day city of Ariel.

11:32| **Hurai of Nahalei Gaash:** Most identify Nahalei Gaash with the area of Khirbet Tibneh, about 2 km west of Halamish, south of which flows the Natuf Stream, where there are many water sources. The term Nahalei Gaash can refer either to a strong current of water (see Jeremiah 5:22, 46:7), or to volcanic activity (II Samuel 22:8). Gaash is also near the burial site of Joshua son of Nun (Joshua 24:30).

Arvatite: This is possibly Beit Arava which is close to Jericho, and mentioned in Joshua (18:22).

11:33| **Baharumite:** A place just east of Jerusalem, on the road that descends to Jericho, beyond the ridge of the Mount of Olives. According to the itinerarium of the anonymous pilgrim of Piacenza, Italy, from the sixth century CE, there was a town northeast of the Mount of Olives called Boarim, but its exact location is unknown.

Shaalvonite: Shaalabin, or Shaalvim, is close to Ayalon (Judges 1:35; I Kings 4:9), one of the cities of Dan (Joshua 19:42). Its name is preserved in the Arab town of Salbit, abandoned in 1948, and is located south of modern-day Kibbutz Shaalvim, which overlooks the Valley of Ayalon from the northeast.

11:34| **Gizonite:** A similar name, Gazez, is mentioned above (2:46), among the descendants of Judah. Due to the similarity of names, some identify it with the village of Bayt Jiz, whose remains are located near Kibbutz Harel, some 3 km southeast of Nahshon Junction in the Judean plain.

11:36| **Mekheratite:** Due to the similarities in name, some have suggested that this is the village of Makr, near Acre. However, no archaeological remains from that era have been unearthed in this location.

11:37| **Son of Ezbai:** In the parallel passage in II Samuel (23:35), the name is Paarai the Arvite, meaning "of Arav," which is one of the cities of Judah in the Hebron region, mentioned in the book of Joshua (15:52). It is identified with Khirbet a-Rabiya, just south of modern-day Otniel.

11:38| **Son of Hagri:** Some claim that this is referring to the Hagrite people, mentioned earlier as cattle herders east of the Jordan (chap. 5). It is possible that Yaziz the Hagrite (27:31), appointed by David as his shepherd, was from this nation. According to many commentaries, these were descendants of Abraham's wife Hagar (Ibn Ezra; Radak). There were many converts [*gerim*] and men from other nations among the ranks of David's mighty men.

11:39| **Berotite:** This is likely Be'erot in the territory of Benjamin, which was one of the four Givonite cities, mentioned in Joshua 9:17. It was probably situated south or southeast of Givon. There are several suggestions with regard to

▸ *its*

ל לא מַהְרַי הַנְּטֹפָתִי חֵלֶד בֶּן־בַּעֲנָה הַנְּטוֹפָתִי׃ אִיתַי בֶּן־רִיבַי מִגִּבְעַת בְּנֵי
לב בִנְיָמִן בְּנָיָה הַפִּרְעָתֹנִי׃ חוּרַי מִנַּחֲלֵי גָעַשׁ אֲבִיאֵל הָעַרְבָתִי׃
לג לד עַזְמָוֶת הַבַּחֲרוּמִי אֶלְיַחְבָּא הַשַּׁעַלְבֹנִי׃ בְּנֵי הָשֵׁם הַגִּזוֹנִי יוֹנָתָן בֶּן־
לה שָׁגֵה הַהֲרָרִי׃ אֲחִיאָם בֶּן־שָׂכָר הַהֲרָרִי אֱלִיפַל בֶּן־אוּר׃
לו לז חֵפֶר הַמְּכֵרָתִי אֲחִיָּה הַפְּלֹנִי׃ חֶצְרוֹ הַכַּרְמְלִי נַעֲרַי בֶּן־אֶזְבָּי׃
לח לט יוֹאֵל אֲחִי נָתָן מִבְחָר בֶּן־הַגְרִי׃ צֶלֶק הָעַמּוֹנִי נַחְרַי הַבֵּרֹתִי נֹשֵׂא
מ מא כְּלֵי יוֹאָב בֶּן־צְרוּיָה׃ עִירָא הַיִּתְרִי גָּרֵב הַיִּתְרִי׃ אוּרִיָּה
מב הַחִתִּי זָבָד בֶּן־אַחְלָי׃ עֲדִינָא בֶן־שִׁיזָא הָרְאוּבֵנִי רֹאשׁ לָרְאוּבֵנִי
מג מד וְעָלָיו שְׁלֹשִׁים׃ חָנָן בֶּן־מַעֲכָה וְיוֹשָׁפָט הַמִּתְנִי׃ עֻזִיָּא
מה הָעַשְׁתְּרָתִי שָׁמָע ויעואל בְּנֵי חוֹתָם הָעֲרֹעֵרִי׃ יְדִיעֲאֵל בֶּן־שִׁמְרִי וִיעִיאֵל
מו וְיֹחָא אָחִיו הַתִּיצִי׃ אֱלִיאֵל הַמַּחֲוִים וִירִיבַי וְיוֹשַׁוְיָה בְּנֵי אֶלְנָעַם וְיִתְמָה
מז הַמּוֹאָבִי׃ אֱלִיאֵל וְעוֹבֵד וְיַעֲשִׂיאֵל הַמְּצֹבָיָה׃
יב א וְאֵלֶּה הַבָּאִים אֶל־דָּוִיד לְצִיקְלַג עוֹד עָצוּר מִפְּנֵי שָׁאוּל בֶּן־קִישׁ וְהֵמָּה בַּגִּבּוֹרִים

BACKGROUND

its precise location, including Nebi Samuel and Khirbet el-Burj on the outskirts of the modern-day Ramot neighborhood in Jerusalem.

11:40 | **Yitrite…Yitrite:** This is the name of one of the families in the tribe of Judah, which resided in Kiryat Ye'arim (2:53). This might also refer to its place of origin, Yatir, one of the cities of the priests in the southern Hebron Mountains in the territory of Judah. The name of this city is preserved in Khirbet Attir, some 20 km south of Hebron.

11:41 | **Son of Ahlai:** Ahlai was mentioned earlier in this book (2:31) as one of the descendants of Yerahme'el, from the Hetzron family of the tribe of Judah.

11:43 | **Yoshafat the Mitnite:** Earlier (5:12), "Shafat in the Bashan" of the sons of Gad is mentioned, and in the Aramaic translations of the Bible (Onkelos and *Targum*), Bashan is called Mitnan. Some say that it is el-Mettan, mentioned in the Samaria Ostraca. Due to the similarity of names, it has been identified with Kafr Amatin, approximately 10 km southwest of Shekhem.

11:44 | **Ashteratite:** This Uziya might have been from Ashterot Karnayim (see, e.g., Genesis 14:5, Deuteronomy 1:4), also known as Ashtara, or Beit Ashterot. This was a city in the territory of Manasseh, in Bashan, which was given to the Levites (Joshua 13:31, 21:27; I Chronicles 6:56). The city controlled the main road of Bashan and is identified with Tel Ashterah, in modern-day Syria.

Aroerite: Aroer was a city on the northern bank of the Arnon River, or Wadi Mujib, whose name is preserved in Khirbet Ar'arah, about 5 km southeast of Divon.

11:45 | **Tizite:** Location unknown. Some have suggested that this is the place called Yasot that is mentioned in the Samaria Ostraca, with the letters transposed. If so, it is in the territory of Manasseh, in Samaria. It has been identified with Yasid, 8 km east of Samaria (Samuel Klein, "David's Mighty Men," *Bulletin of the Jewish Palestine Exploration Society*, Summer 1940 [Hebrew], 95–106).

11:47 | **Yaasiel the Metzova'ite:** Yaasiel son of Avner is listed below (27:21) as one of the heads of the tribe of Benjamin. It is possible that the name Metzova'ite is a reference to Tzova, which, according to the Septuagint translation of Joshua 15:59, was one of the towns adjacent to Bethlehem. Some identify it with the site of the former Arab village of Suba, approximately 10 km west of Jerusalem.

12:1 | **Tziklag:** The city of Tziklag, located in the territory of Judah, is mentioned in Joshua (15:31). It is generally identified with Tel Sera, or Tel esh-Sharia in Arabic, on the banks of the Gerar Ravine, in the northern Negev, approximately 5 km west of Rahat. Findings from the Late Bronze Age, as well as Philistine artifacts, have been unearthed at the site.

in Tziklag he was not a free man. Saul, who considered him a traitor, pursued him, and might well have killed him. During his time of need, various men came to David's side; **and they were** considered **among the mighty** men,[221] **supporters in war.**

2 **They** included some who **were armed with bows, both right and left-handed,** who could attack **with stones, and with arrows with the bow.** These men were ambidextrous fighters,[222] which provided a great advantage on the battlefield. They also included some who were **from Saul's brethren from Benjamin.** It has been suggested that left-handedness was a hereditary trait of the tribe of Benjamin, as left-handed individuals are mentioned more than once in connection with this tribe.[223] It has been common throughout time for many left-handed people to learn to use their right hand as well to perform various tasks, whether for convenience or social conformity. Whatever the reasons, they were effectively ambidextrous.[224]

3 **The leader** of them **was Ahiezer, and** with him was **Yo'ash;** both were **sons of Shemaa the Givatite,** of Givat Binyamin; **and Yeziel and Pelet, sons of Azmavet, and Berakha, and Yehu the Anatotite,** from Anatot,

4 **and Yishmaya the Givonite,** from Givon, **who was mighty among the thirty,** one of the thirty mighty men who formed a separate fighting unit, **and** was even appointed **in charge of the thirty;**[225]

5 **and Yirmeya, Yahaziyel, Yohanan, Yozabad the Gederatite,**

6 **Eluzai, Yerimot, Be'alya, Shemaryahu, Shefatyahu the Harifite,**

7 **Elkana, Yishiyahu, Azarel, Yoezer, and Yoshovam, the Korahites,** possibly descendants of Korah the Levite;[226]

8 **and Yoela and Zevadya, sons of Yeroham from Gedor.**

9 **Some of the Gadites,** men from the tribe of Gad, **went over to David, to the stronghold in the wilderness; mighty warriors, soldiers of war,** who engaged in hand-to-hand combat and were skilled **wielders of shield and spear;**[B] **their faces were** fearsome in appearance, like **the faces of the lion, and they were fast like gazelles on the mountains.** These men of Gad came all the way from east of the Jordan, despite the fact that they had no personal stake in the wars. It seems that the legion of soldiers who initially gathered to David's side were men who came from different places, some of them fleeing local persecution for various reasons, e.g., debt.[227] Presumably, they were also joined by men who simply sought adventure and excitement.

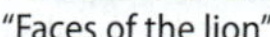

"Faces of the lion"

"Fast like gazelles"

Spear in the hands of an Assyrian warrior, illustration from the Lakhish reliefs, Nineveh, 700–692 BCE

10 **Ezer** was **the head, Ovadya the second, Eliav the third,**

11 **Mishmana the fourth, Yirmeya the fifth,**

12 **Atai the sixth, Eliel the seventh,**

13 **Yohanan the eighth, Elzavad the ninth,**

14 **Yirmeyau the tenth, Makhbenai the eleventh.**

15 **These of the sons of Gad were heads of the army** in their places;[228] **the smallest** among them **was one** commander **over one hundred, and the greatest was one** commander **over one thousand.**[229]

16 A short episode to demonstrate the great power and determination of these captains is now related: **These are those who crossed the Jordan in the first month,**[B] Nisan, after the rainy season, **when it had filled all its banks.** Crossing the river then was both difficult and dangerous. One could easily drown in the Jordan at high tide, especially in the areas in the middle of the river where the current was strongest at that time of year. **And they caused all** who dwelled **in the valleys,** who had harassed them and perhaps sought to prevent them from joining David, **to flee eastward and westward** of the Jordan.

17 **They** also **came from the children of Benjamin and Judah to the stronghold to David.**

18 **David emerged to meet them and he proclaimed and said to them: If you have come to me in peace to support me, my heart will be with you in togetherness,** we will be fully united as though we share the same heart;[230] **but if you come to betray me** by delivering me **to my enemies for no villainy in my hand, let the God of our fathers look and let Him chastise.** God will judge and determine which of us has justice on his side. David repeatedly claimed, and rightly so, that he had neither rebelled against the previous king nor committed any evil, and that he had been undeservedly persecuted.

ב עֹזְרֵי הַמִּלְחָמָה: נֹשְׁקֵי קֶשֶׁת מַיְמִינִים וּמַשְׂמְאִלִים בָּאֲבָנִים וּבַחִצִּים בַּקָּשֶׁת
ג מֵאֲחֵי שָׁאוּל מִבִּנְיָמִן: הָרֹאשׁ אֲחִיעֶזֶר וְיוֹאָשׁ בְּנֵי הַשְּׁמָעָה הַגִּבְעָתִי ויזואל וִיזִיאֵל
ד וָפֶלֶט בְּנֵי עַזְמָוֶת וּבְרָכָה וְיֵהוּא הָעַנְּתֹתִי: וְיִשְׁמַעְיָה הַגִּבְעוֹנִי גִּבּוֹר בַּשְּׁלֹשִׁים
ה ו וְעַל־הַשְּׁלֹשִׁים: וְיִרְמְיָה וְיַחֲזִיאֵל וְיוֹחָנָן וְיוֹזָבָד הַגְּדֵרָתִי: אֶלְעוּזַי וִירִימוֹת וּבְעַלְיָה
ז וּשְׁמַרְיָהוּ וּשְׁפַטְיָהוּ החריפי: אֶלְקָנָה וְיִשִּׁיָּהוּ וַעֲזַרְאֵל וְיוֹעֶזֶר וְיָשָׁבְעָם הַקָּרְחִים: הַחֲרוּפִי
ח ט וְיוֹעֵאלָה וּזְבַדְיָה בְּנֵי יְרֹחָם מִן־הַגְּדוֹר: וּמִן־הַגָּדִי נִבְדְּלוּ אֶל־דָּוִיד לַמְצַד מִדְבָּרָה
גִּבֹּרֵי הַחַיִל אַנְשֵׁי צָבָא לַמִּלְחָמָה עֹרְכֵי צִנָּה וָרֹמַח וּפְנֵי אַרְיֵה פְּנֵיהֶם וְכִצְבָאיִם
י עַל־הֶהָרִים לְמַהֵר: עֵזֶר הָרֹאשׁ עֹבַדְיָה הַשֵּׁנִי אֱלִיאָב הַשְּׁלִשִׁי:
יא יב יג מִשְׁמַנָּה הָרְבִיעִי יִרְמְיָה הַחֲמִשִׁי: עַתַּי הַשִּׁשִּׁי אֱלִיאֵל הַשְּׁבִעִי: יוֹחָנָן הַשְּׁמִינִי
יד טו אֶלְזָבָד הַתְּשִׁיעִי: יִרְמְיָהוּ הָעֲשִׂירִי מַכְבַּנַּי עַשְׁתֵּי עָשָׂר: אֵלֶּה מִבְּנֵי־גָד
טז רָאשֵׁי הַצָּבָא אֶחָד לְמֵאָה הַקָּטָן וְהַגָּדוֹל לְאָלֶף: אֵלֶּה הֵם אֲשֶׁר עָבְרוּ אֶת־הַיַּרְדֵּן
בַּחֹדֶשׁ הָרִאשׁוֹן וְהוּא מְמַלֵּא עַל־כָּל־גדיתיו וַיַּבְרִיחוּ אֶת־כָּל־הָעֲמָקִים לַמִּזְרָח גְּדוֹתָיו
יז יח וְלַמַּעֲרָב: וַיָּבֹאוּ מִן־בְּנֵי בִנְיָמִן וִיהוּדָה עַד־לַמְצַד לְדָוִיד: וַיֵּצֵא דָוִיד
לִפְנֵיהֶם וַיַּעַן וַיֹּאמֶר לָהֶם אִם־לְשָׁלוֹם בָּאתֶם אֵלַי לְעָזְרֵנִי יִהְיֶה־לִּי עֲלֵיכֶם לֵבָב
לְיָחַד וְאִם־לְרַמּוֹתַנִי לְצָרַי בְּלֹא חָמָס בְּכַפַּי יֵרֶא אֱלֹהֵי אֲבוֹתֵינוּ וְיוֹכַח:

BACKGROUND

12:9| **Spear [*romah*]:** The fact that the Bible praises these men for their ability to handle a spear indicates that a *romah* is a type of spear that is long and heavy. This is also evident elsewhere in the Bible, e.g., in the case of Pinhas, when he thrust a spear through Zimri and Kozbi: "He took a spear [*romah*] in his hand. He went after the man of Israel into the tent, and stabbed both of them" (Numbers 25:7–8). This is not the same weapon as a *hanit*, a short spear, which was thrown, as in the phrase: "And Saul cast the spear [*hanit*]" (I Samuel 18:11, 20:32).

12:16| **The first month:** After the rain of the winter season and the melting of the snow on Mount Hermon, the water of the Jordan River swells and fills the river channel. During the summer, the width of the channel ranges from 10 to 40 m, while during the spring months the channel can widen to hundreds of meters, with its current doubling in speed. The book of Joshua (3:15) describes this season: "And when the bearers of the ark came to the Jordan, and the feet of the priests, bearers of the ark, were immersed in the edge of the water, and the Jordan was overflowing on all its banks all the days of harvest."

19 An animated **spirit,** divine inspiration,[231] **clothed Amasai,** probably Amasa, the son of David's sister,[232] **head of the officers** of the group of mighty men.[233] Through this spirit he spoke almost poetically, unlike the style of a typical professional soldier: **To you, David, and with you, son of Yishai; peace, peace be to you, and peace be to your supporters, for your God supports you.** Since David had turned to them in his time of trouble, and had essentially requested their support, Amasai declared on their behalf that their loyalty was fully with David. **David accepted them and set them as the heads of the troop.**

20 **From** the tribe of **Manasseh some fell in with David,** that is, they joined David's side,[234] **when he came with the Philistines against Saul to war.** David was still serving the Philistines when they came to wage war against Saul, as related in the book of Samuel.[235] This put David in a difficult situation. He could not fight in the Israelite army, as Saul continued pursuing him, but he also did not wish to wage war against his own people. **But** ultimately, **they,** David and his men, **did not help them,** the Philistines in waging war, **for the lords,** the leaders **of the Philistines** in the battlefield, **took counsel, sending him away,** as they did not trust him and were worried that he might betray them, **saying: He will fall upon our heads for** reconciliation with **his master Saul.**

21 Then, **upon his** return from the battlefield and **going to Tziklag, some** men **from Manasseh fell in with him: Adnah, Yozabad, Yediael, Mikhael, Yozabad, Elihu, and Tziletai,** who were **heads of thousands that were of Manasseh.**

22 **They assisted David** in his attack **against the troop** of Amalekites who had razed Tziklag, and captured David's family and the families of his men who had emerged from the city, **for they were all mighty warriors, and they were commanders in the army.**

23 **For from day to day,** every day more **men came to David to support him, until there was** with him **a great camp, like the camp of God,** a massive camp.[236] This marks the end of the list of the mighty men who supported David before he became king.

24 The following list of names refers to a later period. **These are the numbers of the heads of the vanguard of the army, who came to David, to Hebron,** in order **to transfer the kingdom of Saul to him, in accordance with the word of the Lord.**

25 **The children of Judah, bearers of shield and spear, were six thousand eight hundred mobilized soldiers.** This was the unit of warriors sent by the tribe of Judah.

26 **From the children of Simeon,** the **mighty warriors** who came **for the army were seven thousand one hundred;**

27 **from the children of Levi, four thousand six hundred.**

28 **Yehoyada was the chief official for Aaron,** the priests,[237] **and with him were three thousand seven hundred** men;

29 **and Tzadok** the priest was **a lad, a mighty warrior, and his patrilineal house of princes** were **twenty-two.**

30 **From the children of Benjamin, the brethren of Saul,** there came **three thousand; until then most of them had kept their allegiance to the house of Saul** as they were his supporters, but now they moved to David's camp to crown him.

31 **From the children of Ephraim, twenty thousand eight hundred; mighty warriors, men of renown**[238] **in their patrilineal houses.**

32 **From half the tribe of Manasseh** there were **eighteen thousand, who were designated** specifically **by name to come and crown David king.**

33 **From the children of Issachar** there came men who were **possessors of understanding of the times,** who possessed great insight and would give good advice, suitable for the time and place, who were able **to know what Israel should do** both in civilian life and in the military; **their leaders were two hundred, and all their brethren** were acting **at their command.** This group of chief advisors later evolved into the leaders of the Sanhedrin, who were experts in determining the months and the intercalation of years.[239]

34 **From Zebulun,** there came men who were **fit for military service, wagers of war with all instruments of war,** were **fifty thousand, and to wage war,** or perform work in other areas,[240] **wholeheartedly.** They were fully devoted to their tasks.[241]

35 **From Naphtali** there came **one thousand captains, and with them** warriors **with shield and spear were thirty-seven thousand.**

36 **From the Danites** came men who were **wagers of war,** they **were twenty-eight thousand six hundred.**

37 **From Asher,** there came men who were **fit for military service, to wage war, forty thousand.**

38 **From the other side of the Jordan,** there came **from the Reubenites, and the Gadites, and half the tribe of Manasseh,** soldiers armed **with all military instruments of war,** they **were one hundred and twenty thousand.**

39 **All these, men of war, wagers of campaigns, came wholeheartedly to Hebron, to crown David king over all Israel; and all the rest of Israel too were wholehearted to crown David king.** These representatives expressed the collective national desire that David should be king over all Israel.

יט וְרוּחַ לָֽבְשָׁה אֶת־עֲמָשַׂי רֹאשׁ השלושים לְךָ דָוִיד וְעִמְּךָ בֶן־יִשַׁי שָׁלוֹם ׀ שָׁלוֹם לְךָ הַשָּׁלִישִׁים
וְשָׁלוֹם לְעֹֽזְרֶךָ כִּי עֲזָרְךָ אֱלֹהֶיךָ וַיְקַבְּלֵם דָּוִיד וַֽיִּתְּנֵם בְּרָאשֵׁי הַגְּדוּד׃
כ וּמִֽמְנַשֶּׁה נָפְלוּ עַל־דָּוִיד בְּבֹאוֹ עִם־פְּלִשְׁתִּים עַל־שָׁאוּל לַמִּלְחָמָה וְלֹא עֲזָרֻם
כִּי בְעֵצָה שִׁלְּחֻהוּ סַרְנֵי פְלִשְׁתִּים לֵאמֹר בְּרָאשֵׁינוּ יִפּוֹל אֶל־אֲדֹנָיו שָׁאוּל׃
כא בְּלֶכְתּוֹ אֶל־צִיקְלַג נָפְלוּ עָלָיו ׀ מִֽמְּנַשֶּׁה עַדְנַח וְיוֹזָבָד וִידִיעֲאֵל וּמִיכָאֵל וְיוֹזָבָד
כב וֶאֱלִיהוּא וְצִלְּתָי רָאשֵׁי הָאֲלָפִים אֲשֶׁר לִמְנַשֶּׁה׃ וְהֵמָּה עָזְרוּ עִם־דָּוִיד עַל־הַגְּדוּד
כג כִּי־גִבּוֹרֵי חַיִל כֻּלָּם וַיִּהְיוּ שָׂרִים בַּצָּבָא׃ כִּי לְעֶת־יוֹם בְּיוֹם יָבֹאוּ עַל־דָּוִיד לְעָזְרוֹ
כד עַד־לְמַחֲנֶה גָדוֹל כְּמַחֲנֵה אֱלֹהִים׃ וְאֵלֶּה מִסְפְּרֵי רָאשֵׁי הֶחָלוּץ
לַצָּבָא בָּאוּ עַל־דָּוִיד חֶבְרוֹנָה לְהָסֵב מַלְכוּת שָׁאוּל אֵלָיו כְּפִי יְהוָה׃
כה בְּנֵי יְהוּדָה נֹשְׂאֵי צִנָּה וָרֹמַח שֵׁשֶׁת אֲלָפִים וּשְׁמוֹנֶה מֵאוֹת חֲלוּצֵי צָבָא׃
כו כז מִן־בְּנֵי שִׁמְעוֹן גִּבּוֹרֵי חַיִל לַצָּבָא שִׁבְעַת אֲלָפִים וּמֵאָה׃ מִן־בְּנֵי הַלֵּוִי
כח אַרְבַּעַת אֲלָפִים וְשֵׁשׁ מֵאוֹת׃ וִיהוֹיָדָע הַנָּגִיד לְאַהֲרֹן וְעִמּוֹ שְׁלֹשֶׁת
כט אֲלָפִים וּשְׁבַע מֵאוֹת׃ וְצָדוֹק נַעַר גִּבּוֹר חָיִל וּבֵית־אָבִיו שָׂרִים עֶשְׂרִים
ל וּשְׁנָיִם׃ וּמִן־בְּנֵי בִנְיָמִן אֲחֵי שָׁאוּל שְׁלֹשֶׁת אֲלָפִים וְעַד־הֵנָּה מַרְבִּיתָם
לא שֹׁמְרִים מִשְׁמֶרֶת בֵּית שָׁאוּל׃ וּמִן־בְּנֵי אֶפְרַיִם עֶשְׂרִים אֶלֶף וּשְׁמוֹנֶה
לב מֵאוֹת גִּבּוֹרֵי חַיִל אַנְשֵׁי שֵׁמוֹת לְבֵית אֲבוֹתָם׃ וּמֵחֲצִי מַטֵּה מְנַשֶּׁה
שְׁמוֹנָה עָשָׂר אָלֶף אֲשֶׁר נִקְּבוּ בְּשֵׁמוֹת לָבוֹא לְהַמְלִיךְ אֶת־דָּוִיד׃
לג וּמִבְּנֵי יִשָּׂשכָר יוֹדְעֵי בִינָה לָעִתִּים לָדַעַת מַה־יַּעֲשֶׂה יִשְׂרָאֵל רָאשֵׁיהֶם מָאתַיִם
לד וְכָל־אֲחֵיהֶם עַל־פִּיהֶם׃ מִזְּבֻלוּן יוֹצְאֵי צָבָא עֹרְכֵי מִלְחָמָה בְּכָל־כְּלֵי
לה מִלְחָמָה חֲמִשִּׁים אָלֶף וְלַעֲדֹר בְּלֹא־לֵב וָלֵב׃ וּמִנַּפְתָּלִי שָׂרִים אָלֶף
לו וְעִמָּהֶם בְּצִנָּה וַחֲנִית שְׁלֹשִׁים וְשִׁבְעָה אָלֶף׃ וּמִן־הַדָּנִי עֹרְכֵי מִלְחָמָה
לז עֶשְׂרִים־וּשְׁמוֹנָה אֶלֶף וְשֵׁשׁ מֵאוֹת׃ וּמֵאָשֵׁר יוֹצְאֵי צָבָא לַעֲרֹךְ מִלְחָמָה
לח אַרְבָּעִים אָלֶף׃ וּמֵעֵבֶר לַיַּרְדֵּן מִן־הָרְאוּבֵנִי וְהַגָּדִי וַחֲצִי ׀ שֵׁבֶט מְנַשֶּׁה
לט בְּכֹל כְּלֵי צְבָא מִלְחָמָה מֵאָה וְעֶשְׂרִים אָלֶף׃ כָּל־אֵלֶּה אַנְשֵׁי מִלְחָמָה עֹדְרֵי

40 **They,** all those guests, both military and civilian, who were sent by all the tribes, **were there with David three days, eating and drinking** to celebrate the coronation of the king; **for their brethren,** probably the local population, **had prepared** foods **for them.**

41 **Also those** tribes **who were close to them,** David's men, plus those who were **as far** away **as Issachar and Zebulun and Naphtali, brought food on donkeys, on camels, on mules, and on cattle; provisions of flour, dried figs, raisins, wine and oil, and cattle and sheep, in abundance, for there was rejoicing in Israel.**

David Establishes the Royal Palace and the Sanctuary in Jerusalem

I CHRONICLES 13:1–17:27

During the war with the Philistines, in which the Tabernacle at Shilo was destroyed, the Philistines captured the Ark of the Covenant. Although the ark was later returned to Israel,[242] it had not yet been brought to Jerusalem. Following the mass celebration of his coronation, the new king, David, sought to bring the Ark of the Covenant, with great fanfare, to Jerusalem. However, an unexpected catastrophe brings the process to a halt.

Transporting the Ark of the Covenant from Kiryat Ye'arim

I CHRONICLES 13:1–14

13 1 **David consulted with the captains of thousands and of hundreds, with every high official.**
2 **David said to the entire assembly of Israel: If it pleases you, and if it,** this matter,[243] **is from the Lord our God,** if it is in accordance with God's will, **let us go out and send to our brethren who remain in all the** tribal **territories of Israel,** who have not come here, **and with them the priests and Levites who are in the cities with their perimeter fields, and gather them to us,** so that there will be a great assembly here;
3 **and let us transfer the ark of our God to us,** to Jerusalem; **for we had not sought it,** we did not address the matter, **in the days of Saul** until now.
4 **The entire assembly said** they desired **to do so, for the matter was right in the eyes of the entire people.** The people agreed that the ark should be moved to a central site where they could renew the service of God.
5 **David assembled all Israel, from Shihor,**[B] the river marking the eastern border **of Egypt until Levo Hamat**[B] in the north, in order **to bring the Ark of God from Kiryat Ye'arim.**
6 **David and all Israel went up to** a place called **Baala,**[B] **to Kiryat Ye'arim which is of Judah,** in order **to bring up from there the Ark of God, the Lord who is seated amidst the cherubs,**[D] **upon which the Name is called.**[244] The ark, over which the cherubs spread their arched wings, symbolizes the Divine Presence in Israel, and for this reason God is called the One who sits upon the cherubs. This is the focal point of the Sanctuary.

View of Abu Ghosh, near Kiryat Ye'arim

7 The Torah explicitly states that the ark may not be transported in a cart; rather, it must be borne by the Levites on their shoulders.[245] The Philistines had returned the ark in a cart, because they were afraid to touch it.[246] **They,** the Israelites tasked with moving the ark, **mounted the Ark of God on a new cart,** as they too did not want to touch it, and they took it **from the house of Avinadav; and Uza and Ahyo were directing the cart.**

Ark of the Covenant

מַעֲרָכָה בְּלֵבָב שָׁלֵם בָּאוּ חֶבְרוֹנָה לְהַמְלִיךְ אֶת־דָּוִיד עַל־כָּל־יִשְׂרָאֵל וְגַם כָּל־
מ שֵׁרִית יִשְׂרָאֵל לֵב אֶחָד לְהַמְלִיךְ אֶת־דָּוִיד׃ וַיִּהְיוּ־שָׁם עִם־דָּוִיד יָמִים שְׁלוֹשָׁה
מא אֹכְלִים וְשׁוֹתִים כִּי־הֵכִינוּ לָהֶם אֲחֵיהֶם׃ וְגַם הַקְּרוֹבִים־אֲלֵיהֶם עַד־יִשָּׂשכָר ו
וּזְבֻלוּן וְנַפְתָּלִי מְבִיאִים לֶחֶם בַּחֲמוֹרִים וּבַגְּמַלִּים וּבַפְּרָדִים ׀ וּבַבָּקָר מַאֲכָל קֶמַח
א דְּבֵלִים וְצִמּוּקִים וְיַיִן וְשֶׁמֶן וּבָקָר וְצֹאן לָרֹב כִּי שִׂמְחָה בְּיִשְׂרָאֵל׃ וַיִּוָּעַץ
ב דָּוִיד עִם־שָׂרֵי הָאֲלָפִים וְהַמֵּאוֹת לְכָל־נָגִיד׃ וַיֹּאמֶר דָּוִיד לְכֹל ׀ קְהַל יִשְׂרָאֵל
אִם־עֲלֵיכֶם טוֹב וּמִן־יְהוָה אֱלֹהֵינוּ נִפְרְצָה נִשְׁלְחָה עַל־אַחֵינוּ הַנִּשְׁאָרִים בְּכֹל
ג אַרְצוֹת יִשְׂרָאֵל וְעִמָּהֶם הַכֹּהֲנִים וְהַלְוִיִּם בְּעָרֵי מִגְרְשֵׁיהֶם וְיִקָּבְצוּ אֵלֵינוּ׃ וְנָסֵבָּה
ד אֶת־אֲרוֹן אֱלֹהֵינוּ אֵלֵינוּ כִּי־לֹא דְרַשְׁנֻהוּ בִּימֵי שָׁאוּל׃ וַיֹּאמְרוּ כָל־הַקָּהָל לַעֲשׂוֹת
ה כֵּן כִּי־יָשַׁר הַדָּבָר בְּעֵינֵי כָל־הָעָם׃ וַיַּקְהֵל דָּוִיד אֶת־כָּל־יִשְׂרָאֵל מִן־שִׁיחוֹר
ו מִצְרַיִם וְעַד־לְבוֹא חֲמָת לְהָבִיא אֶת־אֲרוֹן הָאֱלֹהִים מִקִּרְיַת יְעָרִים׃ וַיַּעַל דָּוִיד
וְכָל־יִשְׂרָאֵל בַּעֲלָתָה אֶל־קִרְיַת יְעָרִים אֲשֶׁר לִיהוּדָה לְהַעֲלוֹת מִשָּׁם אֵת אֲרוֹן
ז הָאֱלֹהִים ׀ יְהוָה יוֹשֵׁב הַכְּרוּבִים אֲשֶׁר־נִקְרָא שֵׁם׃ וַיַּרְכִּיבוּ אֶת־אֲרוֹן הָאֱלֹהִים

BACKGROUND

13:5 | **Shihor:** The Shihor River both symbolizes Egypt (Jeremiah 2:18) and served as its eastern border (Joshua 13:3). It is identified with what was in ancient times the eastern, or Pelusiac, branch of the Nile delta. The various routes from Egypt to the northeast were referred to by the Egyptians as the ways of Hor, and in Egyptian the term "Shihor" means "the water of Hor." Hor, usually referred to as Horus, was one of the primary gods of Egypt, and is often depicted as a man with the head of a falcon.

Until Levo Hamat: Some explain that this is the name of a city in the land of Hamat, which they identify with the village of Labweh, north of Baalbek in the Beqaa Valley. Others claim that this refers to the route from the coast approaching [*levo*] Hamat.

13:6 | **Baala:** As early as the book of Joshua (15:9), Baala is identified with Kiryat Ye'arim: "The border curved to Baala, which is Kiryat Ye'arim." It is generally thought to be Deir el-Azar, a hilltop located above and to the west of Abu Ghosh, which even today is known as Kiryat Ye'arim. Since it was a border city, which changed hands between the Canaanites and Givonites, and was later shared by two tribes of Israel, Judah and Benjamin, it has multiple names in the Bible: Giva, Givat Ye'arim, Kiryat Ye'arim, Kiryat Arim, Mount Ye'arim, Yaara, Baala, Kiryat Baal, and Sde Yaar. The various names reflect the geographical and religious dimensions of the location, and they reflect the political and religious changes as well.

DISCUSSION

13:6 | **Who is seated amidst the cherubs:** The spread wings of the cherubs over the ark cover the seat upon which the glory of God dwells, as it were. For this reason God is called: "The Lord who is seated amidst the cherubs." He would speak to His prophet from there, as it is stated: "And I will tell you, from upon the ark cover, from between the two cherubs that are upon the Ark of the Testimony" (Exodus 25:22; see also commentary on Exodus 24:9).

8 **David and all Israel were reveling before God with all their might,** dancing with enthusiasm and great fervor, **and with songs, and with harps, and with lyres, and with drums, and with cymbals,**[B] **and with trumpets.**

Bronze trumpet, Persepolis, Achaemenid period, 550–330 BCE

Lyre illustration on jug, Greece, 440–430 BCE

"Harps." Ngombi, African musical instrument that resembles a psaltery

"Drums." Tambourine

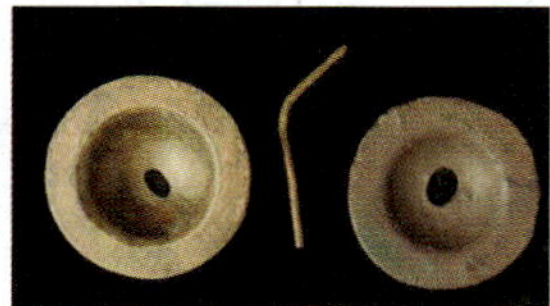
"Cymbals." Timbrels, Khirbet Karkur Illit, Byzantine period

9 **They came to** a place known as **the threshing floor of Kidon, and Uza extended his hand to grasp the ark** to prevent it from falling, **as the oxen had stumbled.** Apparently, it was a cart open on all sides and they feared that the ark would fall. Instinctively, Uza quickly extended his hand to grasp the ark and prevent it from falling.[247]

10 **The wrath of the Lord was enflamed against Uza, and He smote him, because he extended his hand to the ark; and he died there before God.**

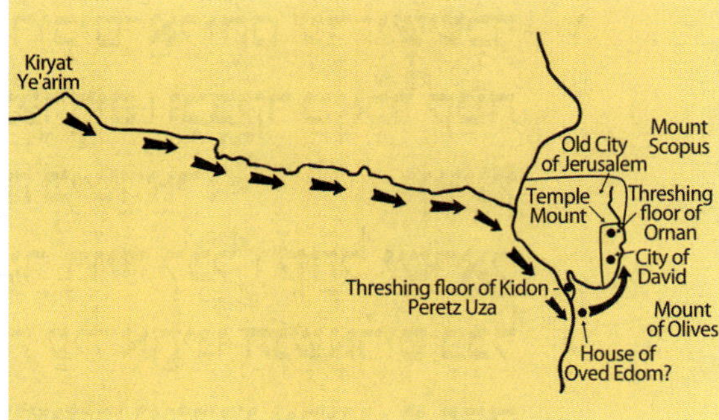

Journey of the Ark of the Covenant from Kiryat Ye'arim to the City of David

11 **David was distressed because the Lord had lashed out in a breach [*peretz*] against Uza,** killing him;[248] **and he called that place,** which was previously known as Kidon, **Peretz Uza to this day.** David was distraught as Uza's intentions were certainly worthy, even if his actions were not.

12 **David feared God on that day, saying: How can I bring the Ark of God to me?** If one whose intentions were good was instantly killed when he touched the ark, what is liable to befall us?

13 **David did not move the ark to him to the City of David, and** instead **he diverted it to the house of Oved Edom the Gitite,** a Levite[249] who lived outside the city.

14 **The Ark of God remained with the household of Oved Edom, in his house three months, and the Lord blessed the house of Oved Edom, and everything that he had.** David was worried that proximity to the ark might lead to calamity, but in fact the opposite occurred in the house of Oved Edom, as his home and family were privileged to receive special blessings. The Sages say that all the women in his house were blessed with children at that time.[250] This teaches that one who treats the Ark of God with the proper deference suffers no harm; rather, he receives God's blessing and salvation.

BACKGROUND

13:8 | **Cymbals [*metziltayim*]:** These are brass percussion instruments, called *tzeltzelim* in II Samuel 6:5. Many instruments of this kind, with a diameter of up to 10 cm, have been excavated in the Land of Israel. They produce their sound when they are clanged together, or when one is struck against a stone or piece of metal, or struck with a stick. It is related that the *tziltzal* used in the Temple, although it was merely one instrument among many, had a powerful sound that could be heard from afar (see *Arakhin* 13b; *Tamid* 30b).

14:1 | **Cedar trees:** The cedar, *Cedrus*, is a conifer tree from the pine family. The tree is impressive in size and appearance; it reaches a height of some 40 m, and its trunk can be as thick as 2–3 m. It grows in cold, elevated regions, primarily in Lebanon. Due to its strength, as well as its long and straight branches, cedar wood was often used in the ancient world as building material, especially in public structures and palaces.

ח על־עגלה חדשה מבית אבינדב ועזא ואחיו נהגים בעגלה: ודויד וכל־ישראל
משחקים לפני האלהים בכל־עז ובשירים ובכנרות ובנבלים ובתפים ובמצלתים
ט ובחצצרות: ויבאו עד־גרן כידן וישלח עזא את־ידו לאחז את־הארון כי שמטו
י הבקר: ויחר־אף יהוה בעזא ויכהו על אשר־שלח ידו על־הארון וימת שם
יא לפני אלהים: ויחר לדויד כי־פרץ יהוה פרץ בעזא ויקרא למקום ההוא פרץ
יב עזא עד היום הזה: ויירא דויד את־האלהים ביום ההוא לאמר היך אביא אלי
יג את ארון האלהים: ולא־הסיר דויד את־הארון אליו אל־עיר דויד ויטהו אל־
יד בית עבד־אדם הגתי: וישב ארון האלהים עם־בית עבד אדם בביתו שלשה
חדשים ויברך יהוה את־בית עבד־אדם ואת־כל־אשר־לו:
א וישלח חירם מלך־צר מלאכים אל־דויד ועצי ארזים וחרשי קיר וחרשי עצים חורם
ב לבנות לו בית: וידע דויד כי־הכינו יהוה למלך על־ישראל כי־נשאת למעלה

Strengthening the Kingdom and Smiting the Philistines

I CHRONICLES 14:1–17

David is accepted as king over all Israel and establishes the borders of his dominion. At the same time, the impression is created among the neighboring powers that the kingdom of Israel is growing stronger.

14 1 **Huram king of Tyre sent messengers to David,** as an expression of goodwill and in order to establish positive diplomatic ties; and in addition he sent **cedar trees,**[B] **and masons, and carpenters,** in order **to build him a house.** The king of Tyre volunteered to help David construct a house from expensive cedar wood, in the style of the magnificent structures to which the king of Tyre was accustomed. This substantial gesture shows that Huram considered David a great king who was worthy of respect. It was not payment of tribute in any sense; rather it was a valuable gift sent in deference to David to cultivate a close relationship between the rulers.

Transporting cedar trees by boat from Lebanon, relief from palace of Sargon II, Dur-Sharrukin, Assyria, 716–713 BCE

Cedar trees

2 David, however, did not interpret this generous gesture as a personal gift. **David knew that the Lord had established him king over Israel, for his kingdom was highly exalted for the sake of His people Israel.** He viewed the action of the king of Tyre as a sign that the status of the kingdom of Israel was elevated among the nations.[251] David's kingdom was no longer a local phenomenon; the nations of the region were aware of its power and its influence. Since the kingdom of Israel was far larger than Tyre, its increased strength brought Huram to seek closer relations with Israel's king.

3 The text inserts another short genealogical list, similar to one cited earlier: (3:5–9) **David took more wives in Jerusalem,** in addition to those he had in Hebron, **and David begot more sons and daughters.**
4 **These are the names of the children whom he had in Jerusalem: Shamua, Shovav, Natan, and Solomon,**
5 **Yivhar, Elishua, Elpelet,**
6 **Noga, Nefeg, Yafia,**
7 **Elishama, Be'elyada, and Elifelet.** Elpelet and Elifelet are versions of the same name, meaning that God [*El*] has saved [*pelet*]. Similarly, the names Elishua and Elishama serve as a reminder that God [*El*], has heard [*shama*] and rescued [*hoshia*] David from his troubles (see commentary on 3:8).
8 **The Philistines heard that David was anointed king over all Israel, and all the Philistines went forth to seek** the life of **David.** They wished to make war against him and end the threat he posed to them. **David heard, and he came out to meet them.**
9 **The Philistines came** and penetrated deep into the Land of Israel, **and raided in the Refaim Valley,**[B] near Jerusalem.
10 **David inquired of God, saying: Shall I go up** to war **against the Philistines, and will You deliver them into my hand? The Lord said to him: Go up, and I will deliver them into your hand.**
11 **They went up to** a place called **Baal Peratzim,**[B] **and David smote them there. David said: God has breached [*paratz*]** and scattered **my enemies by my hand, like a burst [*peretz*] of water** from a narrow spot in all directions, destroying all that lies in its path. The Philistines did not even attempt to fight, but fled for their lives and dispersed.[252] **Therefore they called the name of that place Baal Peratzim.**
12 As the Philistines fled the battlefield in haste, **they abandoned their gods there,** the idols they had taken out with them to war; **David said** to burn them, **and they were burned in fire,** as stated in the Torah.[253]
13 **The Philistines continued** to attack **and raided in the valley.**
14 **David again inquired of God; and God said to him: You shall not go up** directly **after them,** as you did the first time; rather, **turn away from them,** go around, **and come to them opposite the mastic trees,**[B] or bushes; so that they do not sense your approach.

Mastic trees

15 **It shall be when you hear** the unnatural **sound of** men **marching above the tops of the mastic trees,** this will be a sign for you that **then you shall come out to** wage **war, as God has come out before you to smite the Philistine camp.**
16 **David did as God commanded him, and they smote the Philistine camp from Givon to Gezer.** Apparently, they pushed the Philistine army back to the Judean plain, where they smote them.
17 After the impressive victory over the Philistines, **David's renown circulated in all lands, and the Lord imposed fear of him upon all nations.** David's double routing of the Philistines enhanced his reputation and his power over all the surrounding nations.

The Ark Is Brought to Jerusalem

I CHRONICLES 15:1–16:43

After his successes on the battlefield, David turns his attention to building his city, Jerusalem, and preparing a place for the Ark of the Covenant. He gathers the Levites to carry the ark and accompany the procession with music, as the ark is transported to its permanent place in Jerusalem. David participates joyfully with dance, with offerings, and with blessings, and he composes a song of praise and gives gifts to the celebrants. Furthermore, he designates the Levites to permanently serve alongside the ark as singers and as a garrison, and instructs the priests to sacrifice the offerings.

15 1 **He made houses for himself in the City of David, and,** as part of this project, **he prepared a place for the Ark of God and pitched a tent for it.**
2 **Then David said not to bear the Ark of God,** by any other means, e.g., a cart, **excepting the Levites,** who should carry it on their shoulders; **as the Lord has chosen them to bear the Ark of the Lord and to serve Him forever.** Bearing the ark is a task exclusive to the Levites.

ג מַלְכוּתוֹ בַּעֲבוּר עַמּוֹ יִשְׂרָאֵל׃ וַיִּקַּח דָּוִיד עוֹד נָשִׁים בִּירוּשָׁלָ͏ִם וַיּוֹלֶד
ד דָּוִיד עוֹד בָּנִים וּבָנוֹת׃ וְאֵלֶּה שְׁמוֹת הַיְלוּדִים אֲשֶׁר הָיוּ־לוֹ בִּירוּשָׁלָ͏ִם שַׁמּוּעַ
ה ו ז וְשׁוֹבָב נָתָן וּשְׁלֹמֹה׃ וְיִבְחָר וֶאֱלִישׁוּעַ וְאֶלְפָּלֶט׃ וְנֹגַהּ וְנֶפֶג וְיָפִיעַ׃ וֶאֱלִישָׁמָע
ח וּבְעֶלְיָדָע וֶאֱלִיפָלֶט׃ וַיִּשְׁמְעוּ פְלִשְׁתִּים כִּי־נִמְשַׁח דָּוִיד לְמֶלֶךְ עַל־כָּל־יִשְׂרָאֵל
ט וַיַּעֲלוּ כָל־פְּלִשְׁתִּים לְבַקֵּשׁ אֶת־דָּוִיד וַיִּשְׁמַע דָּוִיד וַיֵּצֵא לִפְנֵיהֶם׃ וּפְלִשְׁתִּים בָּאוּ
י וַיִּפְשְׁטוּ בְּעֵמֶק רְפָאִים׃ וַיִּשְׁאַל דָּוִיד בֵּאלֹהִים לֵאמֹר הַאֶעֱלֶה עַל־פלשתיים פְּלִשְׁתִּים
יא וּנְתַתָּם בְּיָדִי וַיֹּאמֶר לוֹ יְהוָה עֲלֵה וּנְתַתִּים בְּיָדֶךָ׃ וַיַּעֲלוּ בְּבַעַל־פְּרָצִים וַיַּכֵּם
שָׁם דָּוִיד וַיֹּאמֶר דָּוִיד פָּרַץ הָאֱלֹהִים אֶת־אוֹיְבַי בְּיָדִי כְּפֶרֶץ מָיִם עַל־כֵּן קָרְאוּ
יב שֵׁם־הַמָּקוֹם הַהוּא בַּעַל פְּרָצִים׃ וַיַּעַזְבוּ־שָׁם אֶת־אֱלֹהֵיהֶם וַיֹּאמֶר דָּוִיד וַיִּשָּׂרְפוּ
יג יד בָּאֵשׁ׃ וַיֹּסִיפוּ עוֹד פְּלִשְׁתִּים וַיִּפְשְׁטוּ בָּעֵמֶק׃ וַיִּשְׁאַל עוֹד דָּוִיד בֵּאלֹהִים
וַיֹּאמֶר לוֹ הָאֱלֹהִים לֹא תַעֲלֶה אַחֲרֵיהֶם הָסֵב מֵעֲלֵיהֶם וּבָאתָ לָהֶם מִמּוּל
טו הַבְּכָאִים׃ וִיהִי כְּשָׁמְעֲךָ אֶת־קוֹל הַצְּעָדָה בְּרָאשֵׁי הַבְּכָאִים אָז תֵּצֵא בַמִּלְחָמָה
טז כִּי־יָצָא הָאֱלֹהִים לְפָנֶיךָ לְהַכּוֹת אֶת־מַחֲנֵה פְלִשְׁתִּים׃ וַיַּעַשׂ דָּוִיד כַּאֲשֶׁר צִוָּהוּ
יז הָאֱלֹהִים וַיַּכּוּ אֶת־מַחֲנֵה פְלִשְׁתִּים מִגִּבְעוֹן וְעַד־גָּזְרָה׃ וַיֵּצֵא שֵׁם־דָּוִיד בְּכָל־
א הָאֲרָצוֹת וַיהוָה נָתַן אֶת־פַּחְדּוֹ עַל־כָּל־הַגּוֹיִם׃ וַיַּעַשׂ־לוֹ בָתִּים בְּעִיר דָּוִיד
ב וַיָּכֶן מָקוֹם לַאֲרוֹן הָאֱלֹהִים וַיֶּט־לוֹ אֹהֶל׃ אָז אָמַר דָּוִיד לֹא לָשֵׂאת אֶת־אֲרוֹן

BACKGROUND

14:9 | **Refaim Valley:** The book of Joshua (15:8) describes the tribal territory of Judah: "The border went up to the top of the highlands that were on the western side of the Valley of Hinom, which is at the northern edge of the Refaim Valley." If so, the Refaim Valley is the plain that sprawls south and west of the Old City of Jerusalem, until Bethlehem.

14:11 | **Baal Peratzim:** Identified with one of the ranges overlooking the Refaim Valley from the south or east. Some claim that this is the same as the Mount Peratzim mentioned in Isaiah (28:21). It could also be the area where the modern-day neighborhood of Gilo is situated or the area where Ramat Rahel is situated. It should be noted that places that contain "Baal" in their names were located on mountaintops, e.g., Baal Tzefon, Baal Maon, and Baal Gad.

14:14 | **Mastic trees [*bekha'im*]:** The name of this tree may be derived from the word *bokheh*, crying. According to a midrash (*Shoḥer Tov* 27:2, s.v. *davar aḥer*), this is a prickly tree, full of thorns, and whoever touches them immediately starts crying. Some explain that the tree is described as crying because it drips with resin. Accordingly, it has been suggested that this is the mastic tree, a shrub with dense, broad branches and hard rustling leaves that emit a resin when they are broken. The diameter of its foliage ranges up to 4 m, and it typically grows to a height of 0.5–1.5 m, although in unusual cases it can grow like a tree, up to a height of 5 m. The mastic tree is common in the valleys and the slopes of the Judean highlands (Yehuda Felix, *Trees: Aromatic, Ornamental, and of the Forest in the Bible and Rabbinic Literature*. Jerusalem: Rubin Mass Press, 1997 [Hebrew], 169–71; Yehuda Felix, *Nature and Land in the Bible: Chapters on Biblical Ecology*. Jerusalem: Reuven Mass Press, 1992 [Hebrew], 136–37).

3 **David** again **assembled all of Israel to** gather in **Jerusalem, to take up the Ark of the Lord to its place,** the tent in Jerusalem **that he had prepared for it.**

4 **David gathered the sons of Aaron and the Levites,** to prepare them to take up the ark;

5 those who gathered **from the sons of Kehat: Uriel the captain,** who was in charge of them, **and his brethren,** the members of his patrilineal house, **one hundred and twenty** men;

6 **from the sons of Merari: Asaya the captain and his brethren, two hundred and twenty** men;

7 **from the sons of Gershom: Yoel the captain and his brethren, one hundred and thirty** men;

8 **from the sons of Elitzafan: Shemaya the captain and his brethren, two hundred** men;

9 **from the sons of Hevron: Eliel the captain and his brethren, eighty** men;

10 **from the sons of Uziel: Aminadav the captain and his brethren, one hundred and twelve** men.

11 **David called for Tzadok and Evyatar the** chief **priests,**[254] **and for the** heads of the aforementioned families of **Levites: For Uriel, Asaya, Yoel, Shemaya, Eliel, and Aminadav.**

12 **He said to them: You are the heads of the patrilineal houses of the Levites; sanctify yourselves,** prepare and purify yourselves, **you and your brethren, and you shall take up the Ark of the Lord, God of Israel, to that** place **which I have prepared for it.**

13 **Because you initially,** on the first occasion, **did not** take it up; therefore, **the Lord our God breached against us,** killing Uza, **because we did not seek Him appropriately.** We failed to conduct ourselves properly, in accordance with protocol. Had we carried the ark in the correct manner from the outset, the tragedy would have been avoided.

14 **The priests and the Levites sanctified themselves** in order **to take up the Ark of the Lord, God of Israel.**

15 **The children of the Levites carried the Ark of God as Moses had commanded** in the Torah,[255] **in accordance with the word of the Lord, on their shoulders with the poles on them.**

16 **David said to the captains of the Levites to stand their brethren the singers with the musical instruments, lyres, harps, and cymbals, playing loudly with joy.**

17 **The Levites set** as singer, **Heiman son of Yoel, and from his brethren, Asaf son of Berekhyahu; and from the sons of Merari their brethren, Eitan son of Kushayahu;** these individuals might be the psalmists Heiman, Asaf, and Eitan.[256]

18 Those were the chief singers, **and with them their brethren of the second rank: Zekharyahu, Ben, and Yaaziel, and Shemiramot, and Yehiel, and Uni, Eliav, and Benayahu, and Maaseyahu, and Matityahu, and Elifelehu, and Mikneyahu, and Oved Edom, and Ye'iel,** who were **the gatekeepers.**

19 **The singers, Heiman, Asaf, and Eitan, were** designated for **playing bronze cymbals;**

20 **Zekharya, Aziel, Shemiramot, Yehiel, Uni, Eliav, Maaseyahu, and Benayahu,** who generally served as gatekeepers, played music in this procession,[257] and **were with lyres on alamot,**[B] either another type of musical instrument,[258] or perhaps lyres,[259] which were generally played by young women [*alamot*];

21 **Matityahu, Elifelehu, Mikneyahu, Oved Edom, Ye'iel, and Azazyahu, were with harps on the sheminit,**[B] **playing.**[260]

22 **Kenanyahu was captain of the Levites in song.** He himself did not sing, perhaps because he was too old or his voice was not pleasant; rather, **he was conductor** and arranger **of the song, because he was an expert.** He conducted the choir and arranged the singing.[261]

23 **Berekhya and Elkana were gatekeepers for the ark.** These Levites stood alongside the ark.

24 **Shevanyahu, Yoshafat, Netanel, Amasai, Zekharyahu, Benayahu, and Eliezer, the priests, sounded the trumpets,** as they proceeded **before the Ark of God; and Oved Edom and Yehiya were gatekeepers for the ark.** They too walked alongside the ark, on the side of the priests.

BACKGROUND

15:20 | **Alamot:** This term might refer to the soft and subtle quality of the sound produced by this instrument, from *ne'elam*, concealed, and in contrast to *maalot*, as in *Shir HaMaalot*, Song of Ascents (see, e.g., Psalms 120:1), which indicates a raised sound (Rav Se'adya Gaon). Alternatively, it means a high-pitched sound, like the singing of a young woman [*alma*].

15:21 | **Sheminit:** Ancient drawings and reliefs feature stringed instruments with anywhere between three and fourteen strings. The term *sheminit* indicates that this particular one had eight [*shemona*] strings. It may have been the stringed instrument called *sammu* in Akkadian.

הָאֱלֹהִים כִּי אִם־הַלְוִיִּם כִּי־בָם ׀ בָּחַר יְהוָה לָשֵׂאת אֶת־אֲרוֹן יְהוָה וּלְשָׁרְתוֹ
ג עַד־עוֹלָם׃ וַיַּקְהֵל דָּוִיד אֶת־כָּל־יִשְׂרָאֵל אֶל־יְרוּשָׁלָםִ לְהַעֲלוֹת
ד אֶת־אֲרוֹן יְהוָה אֶל־מְקוֹמוֹ אֲשֶׁר־הֵכִין לוֹ׃ וַיֶּאֱסֹף דָּוִיד אֶת־בְּנֵי אַהֲרֹן וְאֶת־
ה הַלְוִיִּם׃ לִבְנֵי קְהָת אוּרִיאֵל הַשָּׂר וְאֶחָיו מֵאָה וְעֶשְׂרִים׃
ו ז לִבְנֵי מְרָרִי עֲשָׂיָה הַשָּׂר וְאֶחָיו מָאתַיִם וְעֶשְׂרִים׃ לִבְנֵי גֵרְשׁוֹם יוֹאֵל
ח הַשָּׂר וְאֶחָיו מֵאָה וּשְׁלֹשִׁים׃ לִבְנֵי אֱלִיצָפָן שְׁמַעְיָה הַשָּׂר וְאֶחָיו
ט י מָאתָיִם׃ לִבְנֵי חֶבְרוֹן אֱלִיאֵל הַשָּׂר וְאֶחָיו שְׁמוֹנִים׃ לִבְנֵי
יא עֻזִּיאֵל עַמִּינָדָב הַשָּׂר וְאֶחָיו מֵאָה וּשְׁנֵים עָשָׂר׃ וַיִּקְרָא דָוִיד לְצָדוֹק
וּלְאֶבְיָתָר הַכֹּהֲנִים וְלַלְוִיִּם לְאוּרִיאֵל עֲשָׂיָה וְיוֹאֵל שְׁמַעְיָה וֶאֱלִיאֵל וְעַמִּינָדָב׃
יב וַיֹּאמֶר לָהֶם אַתֶּם רָאשֵׁי הָאָבוֹת לַלְוִיִּם הִתְקַדְּשׁוּ אַתֶּם וַאֲחֵיכֶם וְהַעֲלִיתֶם
יג אֵת אֲרוֹן יְהוָה אֱלֹהֵי יִשְׂרָאֵל אֶל־הֲכִינוֹתִי לוֹ׃ כִּי לְמַבָּרִאשׁוֹנָה לֹא אַתֶּם פָּרַץ
יד יְהוָה אֱלֹהֵינוּ בָּנוּ כִּי־לֹא דְרַשְׁנֻהוּ כַּמִּשְׁפָּט׃ וַיִּתְקַדְּשׁוּ הַכֹּהֲנִים וְהַלְוִיִּם לְהַעֲלוֹת
טו אֶת־אֲרוֹן יְהוָה אֱלֹהֵי יִשְׂרָאֵל׃ וַיִּשְׂאוּ בְנֵי־הַלְוִיִּם אֵת אֲרוֹן הָאֱלֹהִים כַּאֲשֶׁר
טז צִוָּה מֹשֶׁה כִּדְבַר יְהוָה בִּכְתֵפָם בַּמֹּטוֹת עֲלֵיהֶם׃ וַיֹּאמֶר דָּוִיד לְשָׂרֵי
הַלְוִיִּם לְהַעֲמִיד אֶת־אֲחֵיהֶם הַמְשֹׁרְרִים בִּכְלֵי־שִׁיר נְבָלִים וְכִנֹּרוֹת וּמְצִלְתָּיִם
מַשְׁמִיעִים לְהָרִים־בְּקוֹל לְשִׂמְחָה׃
יז וַיַּעֲמִידוּ הַלְוִיִּם אֵת הֵימָן בֶּן־יוֹאֵל וּמִן־אֶחָיו אָסָף בֶּן־בֶּרֶכְיָהוּ וּמִן־בְּנֵי מְרָרִי
יח אֲחֵיהֶם אֵיתָן בֶּן־קוּשָׁיָהוּ׃ וְעִמָּהֶם אֲחֵיהֶם הַמִּשְׁנִים זְכַרְיָהוּ בֵּן וְיַעֲזִיאֵל
וּשְׁמִירָמוֹת וִיחִיאֵל ׀ וְעֻנִּי אֱלִיאָב וּבְנָיָהוּ וּמַעֲשֵׂיָהוּ וּמַתִּתְיָהוּ וֶאֱלִיפְלֵהוּ וּמִקְנֵיָהוּ
יט וְעֹבֵד אֱדֹם וִיעִיאֵל הַשֹּׁעֲרִים׃ וְהַמְשֹׁרְרִים הֵימָן אָסָף וְאֵיתָן בִּמְצִלְתַּיִם נְחֹשֶׁת
כ לְהַשְׁמִיעַ׃ וּזְכַרְיָה וַעֲזִיאֵל וּשְׁמִירָמוֹת וִיחִיאֵל וְעֻנִּי וֶאֱלִיאָב וּמַעֲשֵׂיָהוּ וּבְנָיָהוּ
כא בִּנְבָלִים עַל־עֲלָמוֹת׃ וּמַתִּתְיָהוּ וֶאֱלִיפְלֵהוּ וּמִקְנֵיָהוּ וְעֹבֵד אֱדֹם וִיעִיאֵל וַעֲזַזְיָהוּ
כב בְּכִנֹּרוֹת עַל־הַשְּׁמִינִית לְנַצֵּחַ׃ וּכְנַנְיָהוּ שַׂר־הַלְוִיִּם בְּמַשָּׂא יָסֹר בַּמַּשָּׂא כִּי מֵבִין
כג כד הוּא׃ וּבֶרֶכְיָה וְאֶלְקָנָה שֹׁעֲרִים לָאָרוֹן׃ וּשְׁבַנְיָהוּ וְיוֹשָׁפָט וּנְתַנְאֵל וַעֲמָשַׂי וּזְכַרְיָהוּ

25 **David, and the elders of Israel, and the captains of thousands, who were walking to take up the Ark of the Covenant of the Lord from the house of Oved Edom, were joyful.** The ark was transported from the house of Oved Edom, who was himself a Levite, and taken up to Jerusalem in a great procession that included dignitaries and which was led by the king.

26 **It was as God helped the Levites, carriers of the Ark of the Covenant of the Lord, and they sacrificed seven bulls and seven rams,** in joy and thanksgiving to God that everything was progressing smoothly.[262]

27 **David was wrapped in a fine linen robe,** an unadorned white garment,[263] **along with all the Levites who were carrying the ark, and the singers, and Kenanya the captain of the song of the singers; upon David there was** also **an ephod of linen,** a short cloak like an apron, fastened with a belt and perhaps supported with shoulder straps.[264]

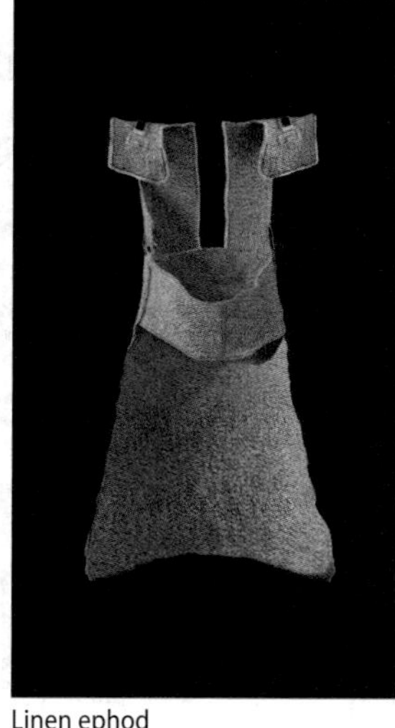
Linen ephod

28 **All Israel were taking up the Ark of the Covenant of the Lord with shouts, and with** the **sound of a shofar, and with trumpets, and with** the **sounding of cymbals,** and **with lyres and harps.**

29 **It was as the Ark of the Covenant of the Lord came to the City of David, Mikhal daughter of Saul looked through the window, and saw King David dancing and reveling** together with the entire assembly, and with the free movements of a dancer, **and she despised him in her heart.** He looked like a common man, and Mikhal, the daughter of a king, could not bear that conduct, which in her mind was undignified.[265]

16 1 **They brought the Ark of God and positioned it in the tent that David had pitched for it, and they presented burnt offerings and peace offerings before God.**

2 **David concluded presenting the burnt offering and the peace offering, and he blessed the people in the name of the Lord.**

3 **He distributed to each person of Israel, both men and women,** a gift in honor of the great occasion of the arrival of the ark. **To each person,** all those present, he gave **a loaf of bread; and a piece of meat [*eshpar*],** which some say was one-sixth [*shishit*] of a bull [*par*]; **and a raisin cake,** a food or drink made of grapes, or a jug of wine.[266]

4 **He set** men, appointed to a permanent position, **from among the Levites before the Ark of the Lord, to be servants and to invoke [*ulhazkir*],** or recite a song that causes the memory [*mazkir*] of Israel to come before God, as it were, or proclaims the deeds of God,[267] **and to thank and to praise the Lord, God of Israel.** Although the Temple had not yet been built, a sanctified tent already stood; therefore, it was appropriate for men to stand alongside the ark and serve there on a permanent basis.

5 These were **Asaf the leader, and his deputy Zekharya,** and with them **Ye'iel, Shemiramot, Yehiel, Matitya, Eliav, and Benayahu; Oved Edom and Ye'iel were** playing **on lyres and on harps, and Asaf was sounding the cymbals;**

6 **Benayahu and Yahaziel the priests were** sounding **with trumpets continually, before the Ark of the Covenant of God.**

7 **On that day David initiated thanking the Lord,** meaning that he was the first to recite the song of thanks to God, **by means of Asaf and his brethren.** It is unclear whether David composed this hymn,[268] or if he merely determined the content of the song or its framework, and one of the singers composed it.

8 The following verses with minor variations appear as part of a longer psalm in the book of Psalms (105): **Give thanks to the Lord, call in His name; proclaim His exploits among the peoples.**

9 **Sing to Him; sing praises to Him; speak of all His wonders.**

10 **Glory in His sacred name;** since Israel is God's nation, their faith in Him and the blessings they receive from Him are the glorification of God's name;[269] **let the heart of the seekers of the Lord rejoice** when they hear all these matters.[270]

11 **Search for the Lord and His strength; seek His face continually.**

12 **Remember His wonders that He performed, His marvels, and the judgments of His mouth,** those deeds which He commanded us to perform.

13 **Descendants of Israel His servant, children of Jacob, His chosen ones,**

14 **He is the Lord our God; His judgments,** decrees, **are** carried out **throughout the earth.**

15 **Remember His** eternal **covenant forever, a matter commanded for one thousand generations,** for generation after generation;

16 this is the covenant **that He** first **made with Abraham, and** it is **His oath to Isaac;**

17 **He established it,** the oath, **for Jacob as a** fixed **statute, for Israel** as **an eternal covenant,**

18 **saying: To you will I give the land of Canaan, the tract,** portion, **of your inheritance.** The promise regarding the inheritance of the land was part of the covenant that God made with the patriarchs.

וּבְנָיָהוּ וֶאֱלִיעֶזֶר הַכֹּהֲנִים מחצצרים בַּחֲצֹצְרוֹת לִפְנֵי אֲרוֹן הָאֱלֹהִים וְעֹבֵד מַחְצְרִים
כה אֱדֹם וִיחִיָּה שֹׁעֲרִים לָאָרוֹן: וַיְהִי דָוִיד וְזִקְנֵי יִשְׂרָאֵל וְשָׂרֵי הָאֲלָפִים הַהֹלְכִים
לְהַעֲלוֹת אֶת־אֲרוֹן בְּרִית־יְהוָה מִן־בֵּית עֹבֵד־אֱדֹם בְּשִׂמְחָה:
כו וַיְהִי בֶּעְזֹר הָאֱלֹהִים אֶת־הַלְוִיִּם נֹשְׂאֵי אֲרוֹן בְּרִית־יְהוָה וַיִּזְבְּחוּ שִׁבְעָה־פָרִים
כז וְשִׁבְעָה אֵילִים: וְדָוִיד מְכֻרְבָּל ׀ בִּמְעִיל בּוּץ וְכָל־הַלְוִיִּם הַנֹּשְׂאִים אֶת־הָאָרוֹן
כח וְהַמְשֹׁרְרִים וּכְנַנְיָה הַשַּׂר הַמַּשָּׂא הַמְשֹׁרְרִים וְעַל־דָּוִיד אֵפוֹד בָּד: וְכָל־יִשְׂרָאֵל
מַעֲלִים אֶת־אֲרוֹן בְּרִית־יְהוָה בִּתְרוּעָה וּבְקוֹל שׁוֹפָר וּבַחֲצֹצְרוֹת וּבִמְצִלְתָּיִם
כט מַשְׁמִעִים בִּנְבָלִים וְכִנֹּרוֹת: וַיְהִי אֲרוֹן בְּרִית יְהוָה בָּא עַד־עִיר דָּוִיד וּמִיכַל
בַּת־שָׁאוּל נִשְׁקְפָה ׀ בְּעַד הַחַלּוֹן וַתֵּרֶא אֶת־הַמֶּלֶךְ דָּוִיד מְרַקֵּד וּמְשַׂחֵק וַתִּבֶז
טז א לוֹ בְּלִבָּהּ: וַיָּבִיאוּ אֶת־אֲרוֹן הָאֱלֹהִים וַיַּצִּיגוּ אֹתוֹ בְּתוֹךְ הָאֹהֶל אֲשֶׁר
ב נָטָה־לוֹ דָּוִיד וַיַּקְרִיבוּ עֹלוֹת וּשְׁלָמִים לִפְנֵי הָאֱלֹהִים: וַיְכַל דָּוִיד מֵהַעֲלוֹת
ג הָעֹלָה וְהַשְּׁלָמִים וַיְבָרֶךְ אֶת־הָעָם בְּשֵׁם יְהוָה: וַיְחַלֵּק לְכָל־אִישׁ יִשְׂרָאֵל מֵאִישׁ
ד וְעַד־אִשָּׁה לְאִישׁ כִּכַּר־לֶחֶם וְאֶשְׁפָּר וַאֲשִׁישָׁה: וַיִּתֵּן לִפְנֵי אֲרוֹן יְהוָה מִן־הַלְוִיִּם
ה מְשָׁרְתִים וּלְהַזְכִּיר וּלְהוֹדוֹת וּלְהַלֵּל לַיהוָה אֱלֹהֵי יִשְׂרָאֵל: אָסָף
הָרֹאשׁ וּמִשְׁנֵהוּ זְכַרְיָה יְעִיאֵל וּשְׁמִירָמוֹת וִיחִיאֵל וּמַתִּתְיָה וֶאֱלִיאָב וּבְנָיָהוּ וְעֹבֵד
ו אֱדֹם וִיעִיאֵל בִּכְלֵי נְבָלִים וּבְכִנֹּרוֹת וְאָסָף בַּמְצִלְתַּיִם מַשְׁמִיעַ: וּבְנָיָהוּ וְיַחֲזִיאֵל
ז הַכֹּהֲנִים בַּחֲצֹצְרוֹת תָּמִיד לִפְנֵי אֲרוֹן בְּרִית־הָאֱלֹהִים: בַּיּוֹם הַהוּא אָז נָתַן דָּוִיד
בָּרֹאשׁ לְהֹדוֹת לַיהוָה בְּיַד־אָסָף וְאֶחָיו:
ח ט הוֹדוּ לַיהוָה קִרְאוּ בִשְׁמוֹ הוֹדִיעוּ בָעַמִּים עֲלִילֹתָיו: שִׁירוּ לוֹ זַמְּרוּ־לוֹ שִׂיחוּ
י יא בְּכָל־נִפְלְאֹתָיו: הִתְהַלְלוּ בְּשֵׁם קָדְשׁוֹ יִשְׂמַח לֵב מְבַקְשֵׁי יְהוָה: דִּרְשׁוּ יְהוָה
יב יג וְעֻזּוֹ בַּקְּשׁוּ פָנָיו תָּמִיד: זִכְרוּ נִפְלְאֹתָיו אֲשֶׁר עָשָׂה מֹפְתָיו וּמִשְׁפְּטֵי־פִיהוּ: זֶרַע
יד טו יִשְׂרָאֵל עַבְדּוֹ בְּנֵי יַעֲקֹב בְּחִירָיו: הוּא יְהוָה אֱלֹהֵינוּ בְּכָל־הָאָרֶץ מִשְׁפָּטָיו: זִכְרוּ
טז לְעוֹלָם בְּרִיתוֹ דָּבָר צִוָּה לְאֶלֶף דּוֹר: אֲשֶׁר כָּרַת אֶת־אַבְרָהָם וּשְׁבוּעָתוֹ לְיִצְחָק:
יז יח וַיַּעֲמִידֶהָ לְיַעֲקֹב לְחֹק לְיִשְׂרָאֵל בְּרִית עוֹלָם: לֵאמֹר לְךָ אֶתֵּן אֶרֶץ־כְּנָעַן חֶבֶל

19 Even **while you were a few men, very few, and** temporarily **re-**
siding in it. You were not yet permanent residents of the land,
and were few and weak.
20 **They,** your forefathers, **went about** wandering, **from nation**
to nation, and from one kingdom to another people, within
the borders of the Land of Israel, and at times beyond those
borders, e.g., when Abraham went to Egypt and to the land of
the Philistines.
21 Although they were uprooted strangers, **He did not allow any**
man to exploit them, to cheat or steal from them, **and He**
warned and **rebuked kings for their sake,** as related with regard to Abraham and Isaac in the incidents involving Pharaoh
and Avimelekh.[271] God said to those kings:
22 **Do not touch My anointed ones,** whom I anointed to be My
princes. Even if they do not appear to be great kings, they are
My kings. **And do not harm My prophets,** the patriarchs, who
were also prophets.[272]
23 These verses also appear, with slight variations, as a separate
psalm in the book of Psalms.[273] **Sing to the Lord, all the earth;**
herald His salvation anew **daily,** each and every day.
24 **Relate His glory among the nations;** relate **His wonders**
among all the peoples.
25 **For the Lord is great and exceedingly praised; He is awe-**
some, lofty and awe evoking, **above all gods.**
26 **For all the gods of the peoples are** no more than **idols,** an
expression of derision and disparagement, indicating they are
like toys;[274] **but** it is **the Lord** who **made the heavens.**
27 **Glory and grandeur are before Him; might and joy are in**
His place.
28 **Accord to the Lord, families of peoples, accord to the Lord**
honor and might, or splendor.
29 **Accord to the Lord the** appropriate **honor of His name;**[275]
bring an offering and come before Him; prostrate yourself
to the Lord in the grandeur of holiness.
30 **Tremble before Him, all** dwellers on **the earth; indeed, the**
world will stand firm, not to be moved. The world, which
sometimes seems shaky, will stand firm when all its inhabitants
honor God and submit to His will. Joy and song will then encompass the entire creation.
31 **Let the heavens rejoice, and let the earth be happy; let them**
say among the nations: The Lord reigns.
32 **Let the sea and that which fills it rage.** The sounds of the sea's
waves are perceived as its song. **Let the field and everything**
that is in it exult;
33 **then the trees of the forest will sing before the Lord, for,** or
when, **He has come to judge the earth.** Even those parts of nature that are not under human control will be filled with joy and
excitement when God reveals Himself in the world through His
judgment.
34 The end of this song echoes its beginning (verse 8): **Give**
thanks to the Lord for He is good, for His kindness is
eternal.
35 **Say: Save us, God of our salvation, and gather us and rescue**
us from the nations, to give thanks to the name of Your holi-
ness, to be glorified in Your praise.
36 **Blessed is the Lord, God of Israel, from everlasting to ever-**
lasting, forever. This was David's song in honor of the arrival of
the Ark of God to its permanent abode. **All the people said:**
Amen, and: Praise the Lord.
37 **He,** David, **left Asaf and his brethren there, before the Ark**
of the Covenant of the Lord, in order **to serve before the ark**
continually, each day's work on its day, in accordance with
the needs of each day.
38 **Oved Edom and their brethren,** the singers,[276] **were** a total of
sixty-eight; Oved Edom son of Yeditun, and Hosa were appointed **to be gatekeepers,**
39 **and Tzadok the priest, and his brethren the priests, were**
those David appointed to serve **before the Tabernacle of the**
Lord in the shrine, a raised spot upon which an altar was erected, **that was at Givon,**[B] where there was a quasi-temple,

Al-Jib, thought to be the biblical Givon, illustration from 1888

40 **to offer up burnt offerings** there **to the Lord on the altar of**
burnt offering continually, morning and evening, in accor-
dance with everything that is written in the Torah of the
Lord, which He commanded to Israel. The ark was brought
to a more central and dignified place, near the king and his
army, and remained there until the building of the Temple. In
the meantime, the daily offerings were offered at the central
shrine in Givon, where later King Solomon would also present
offerings.[277]
41 **With them,** the priests who presented the burnt offerings,
were **Heiman and Yedutun, and the rest of the selected,**[278]
who were designated by name, to give thanks to the Lord,
for His kindness is eternal. It was their task to sing during the
sacrifice of the communal offerings.

יט כ נַחֲלַתְכֶם: בִּהְיוֹתְכֶם מְתֵי מִסְפָּר כִּמְעַט וְגָרִים בָּהּ: וַיִּתְהַלְּכוּ מִגּוֹי אֶל־גּוֹי
כא כב וּמִמַּמְלָכָה אֶל־עַם אַחֵר: לֹא־הִנִּיחַ לְאִישׁ לְעָשְׁקָם וַיּוֹכַח עֲלֵיהֶם מְלָכִים: אַל־
כג תִּגְּעוּ בִּמְשִׁיחָי וּבִנְבִיאַי אַל־תָּרֵעוּ: שִׁירוּ לַיהוָה כָּל־הָאָרֶץ בַּשְּׂרוּ מִיּוֹם־אֶל־יוֹם
כד כה יְשׁוּעָתוֹ: סַפְּרוּ בַגּוֹיִם אֶת־כְּבוֹדוֹ בְּכָל־הָעַמִּים נִפְלְאֹתָיו: כִּי גָדוֹל יְהוָה וּמְהֻלָּל
כו מְאֹד וְנוֹרָא הוּא עַל־כָּל־אֱלֹהִים: כִּי כָּל־אֱלֹהֵי הָעַמִּים אֱלִילִים וַיהוָה שָׁמַיִם
כז כח עָשָׂה: הוֹד וְהָדָר לְפָנָיו עֹז וְחֶדְוָה בִּמְקֹמוֹ: הָבוּ לַיהוָה מִשְׁפְּחוֹת עַמִּים הָבוּ
כט לַיהוָה כָּבוֹד וָעֹז: הָבוּ לַיהוָה כְּבוֹד שְׁמוֹ שְׂאוּ מִנְחָה וּבֹאוּ לְפָנָיו הִשְׁתַּחֲווּ לַיהוָה
ל לא בְּהַדְרַת־קֹדֶשׁ: חִילוּ מִלְּפָנָיו כָּל־הָאָרֶץ אַף־תִּכּוֹן תֵּבֵל בַּל־תִּמּוֹט: יִשְׂמְחוּ
לב הַשָּׁמַיִם וְתָגֵל הָאָרֶץ וְיֹאמְרוּ בַגּוֹיִם יְהוָה מָלָךְ: יִרְעַם הַיָּם וּמְלוֹאוֹ יַעֲלֹץ הַשָּׂדֶה
לג וְכָל־אֲשֶׁר־בּוֹ: אָז יְרַנְּנוּ עֲצֵי הַיָּעַר מִלִּפְנֵי יְהוָה כִּי־בָא לִשְׁפּוֹט אֶת־הָאָרֶץ:
לד לה הוֹדוּ לַיהוָה כִּי טוֹב כִּי לְעוֹלָם חַסְדּוֹ: וְאִמְרוּ הוֹשִׁיעֵנוּ אֱלֹהֵי יִשְׁעֵנוּ וְקַבְּצֵנוּ
לו וְהַצִּילֵנוּ מִן־הַגּוֹיִם לְהֹדוֹת לְשֵׁם קָדְשֶׁךָ לְהִשְׁתַּבֵּחַ בִּתְהִלָּתֶךָ: בָּרוּךְ יְהוָה אֱלֹהֵי ז
יִשְׂרָאֵל מִן־הָעוֹלָם וְעַד־הָעֹלָם וַיֹּאמְרוּ כָל־הָעָם אָמֵן וְהַלֵּל לַיהוָה:
לז וַיַּעֲזָב־שָׁם לִפְנֵי אֲרוֹן בְּרִית־יְהוָה לְאָסָף וּלְאֶחָיו לְשָׁרֵת לִפְנֵי הָאָרוֹן תָּמִיד
לח לִדְבַר־יוֹם בְּיוֹמוֹ: וְעֹבֵד אֱדֹם וַאֲחֵיהֶם שִׁשִּׁים וּשְׁמוֹנָה וְעֹבֵד אֱדֹם בֶּן־יְדִיתוּן
לט וְחֹסָה לְשֹׁעֲרִים: וְאֵת ׀ צָדוֹק הַכֹּהֵן וְאֶחָיו הַכֹּהֲנִים לִפְנֵי מִשְׁכַּן יְהוָה בַּבָּמָה
מ אֲשֶׁר בְּגִבְעוֹן: לְהַעֲלוֹת עֹלוֹת לַיהוָה עַל־מִזְבַּח הָעֹלָה תָּמִיד לַבֹּקֶר וְלָעָרֶב
מא וּלְכָל־הַכָּתוּב בְּתוֹרַת יְהוָה אֲשֶׁר צִוָּה עַל־יִשְׂרָאֵל: וְעִמָּהֶם הֵימָן וִידוּתוּן וּשְׁאָר

BACKGROUND

16:39 | **In the shrine that was at Givon:** The city of Givon, located in the territory of the tribe of Benjamin, is where the family of King Saul originated (8:29–33). The city is also mentioned in the book of Samuel (II Samuel 2:13, 24) as having a pool and an irrigation system. Givon has been identified with the village of al-Jib, near modern-day Givat Ze'ev, where a large water project has been discovered, together with the remains of ancient manufacturing plants. Following the destruction of Shilo and Nov, the Tabernacle was moved to Givon, along with all the ritual vessels other than the Ark of the Covenant. The Tabernacle at Givon differed from that of Shilo and Nov in that the altar there was called "the Great Shrine" (I Kings 3:4). It is possible that due to the absence of the Ark of the Covenant, the focus of the Tabernacle was the ritual offerings, and consequently, it was called the Great Shrine. The book of Samuel (II Samuel 20:8) mentions a great stone at Givon, evoking the great stone that Joshua established in the Sanctuary of the Lord at Shekhem (Joshua 24:26). A great stone also served as a shrine or an altar in the days of Saul (I Samuel 14:33). Some researchers identify the great stone with the large stone surface that is still found in nearby Nebi Samuel, rather than al-Jib.

42 The verse reiterates, in greater detail: **With them were Heiman**
and Yedutun, playing and **sounding trumpets and cymbals**
and the rest of the **musical instruments for God; the sons of**
Yedutun did not sing but **were** appointed **to be at the gate.**

43 When the celebrations concluded, **all the people went, each**
man to his house, and after taking his leave of the people,
David turned to bless the members of **his household** and rejoice with them.[279]

David's Desire to Build a House for God, and the Tidings of the Establishment of His Royal House

I CHRONICLES 17:1–27

David places the Ark of the Covenant in his city in a temporary abode, and now his desire is to build a permanent home for it.

17 1 **It was when David dwelled in his house, David said to Natan**
the prophet: Behold, I dwell in a magnificent **house of cedar,**
which Huram king of Tyre built for me (14:1), **and** yet **the Ark**
of the Covenant of the Lord is in a tent **under curtains.** This
is unseemly. I wish to begin construction of a house for God.
2 **Natan said to David:**[D] **Everything that is in your heart, do,**
as God is with you. Rise and fulfill the grand idea that you are
contemplating.
3 Yet **it was that night,** when **the word of God was with Natan,**
saying:
4 **Go and tell David My servant: So says the Lord: It will not**
be you who will build for Me a house in which to dwell,
5 **for I have not dwelled in a** permanent **house since the day**
that I took up Israel from Egypt **to this day; I have been in**
one tent or another, and in a Tabernacle. The Tabernacle in
Shilo was still a tent, as only its walls were made of stone; its
roof was composed of the curtains of the original Tabernacle.
After the destruction of Shilo, there was no permanent structure that served as a place of worship and a place for the ark.
6 **Wherever,** or whenever, **I have made my way among all**
Israel, have I spoken a word to any of the judges of Israel,
whom I commanded to shepherd My people, saying: Why
didn't you build Me a house of cedar? Over the course of
centuries, none of the judges, some of whom were great and
prominent leaders, were commanded to build a Temple.
7 **Now, so shall you say to My servant David: So says the Lord**
of hosts: You were a young rural shepherd, and **I took you**
from the pasture, from after the flock, to be a ruler over My
people Israel;
8 **I have been with you wherever you went and have eliminat-**
ed all your enemies from before you, and I **have given you a**
name, like the name of the great ones who are on the earth,
as you are the first leader since Joshua whose name is renowned
outside your own land.
9 **I will make a place for My people Israel, and I will plant**
it, and they will dwell in their place, and will no longer be
disturbed. Some read this in the past tense: I have established
My people Israel in its place, and they will no longer be fearful. During David's reign, Israel had achieved a status of relative
peace. **And evil people will not wear them down,** destroy
them, **anymore, as in the past,**
10 **during the days when I appointed judges over My people**
Israel, when the nation was subject to the domination of various enemies and most of its wars were fought to defend it from
invaders and harassers. **I will subdue all your enemies.** This
too can be read in the past tense: The situation has changed
since then, as I have subdued your enemies. **And I will pro-**
claim you, and the Lord will establish a royal **house,** a
dynasty, **for you.** Some read the first part of this sentence as a
continuation of the previous one, and explain it slightly differently: Moreover, I have displayed you to all.
11 Your dynasty will last, as **it will be, that when your days are**
completed to go with your fathers, when the time comes for
you to pass away, **I will set up your offspring after you who**
will be from your sons. A son will be born to you who will succeed you. **And I will establish his kingdom,** so that his reign
will be firmly established. The sons of judges did not assume
their fathers' positions, with the exception of Avimelekh, who
forcibly seized power. King Saul did have a son who assumed
his position, but his reign was tenuous and brief.
12 **He,** your son and heir, **will build a house for Me, and I will**
establish his throne forever.
13 **I will be a father to him, and he will be a son to Me; I will**
not remove My kindness from him, as I removed it from the
one, the king, **who was before you.** Your dynasty, in contrast,
will be eternal:
14 **I will install him in My House and in My kingdom forever,**
and his throne will be established forever.

מב הַבְּרוּרִים אֲשֶׁר נִקְּבוּ בְּשֵׁמוֹת לְהֹדוֹת לַיהוָה כִּי לְעוֹלָם חַסְדּוֹ: וְעִמָּהֶם הֵימָן
וִידוּתוּן חֲצֹצְרוֹת וּמְצִלְתַּיִם לְמַשְׁמִיעִים וּכְלֵי שִׁיר הָאֱלֹהִים וּבְנֵי יְדוּתוּן לַשָּׁעַר:
ז מג א וַיֵּלְכוּ כָל־הָעָם אִישׁ לְבֵיתוֹ וַיִּסֹּב דָּוִיד לְבָרֵךְ אֶת־בֵּיתוֹ:   וַיְהִי כַּאֲשֶׁר
יָשַׁב דָּוִיד בְּבֵיתוֹ וַיֹּאמֶר דָּוִיד אֶל־נָתָן הַנָּבִיא הִנֵּה אָנֹכִי יוֹשֵׁב בְּבֵית הָאֲרָזִים
ב וַאֲרוֹן בְּרִית־יְהוָה תַּחַת יְרִיעוֹת: וַיֹּאמֶר נָתָן אֶל־דָּוִיד כֹּל אֲשֶׁר בִּלְבָבְךָ עֲשֵׂה
ג כִּי הָאֱלֹהִים עִמָּךְ:   וַיְהִי בַּלַּיְלָה הַהוּא וַיְהִי דְּבַר־אֱלֹהִים אֶל־נָתָן
ד לֵאמֹר: לֵךְ וְאָמַרְתָּ אֶל־דָּוִיד עַבְדִּי כֹּה אָמַר יְהוָה לֹא אַתָּה תִּבְנֶה־לִּי הַבַּיִת
ה לָשָׁבֶת: כִּי לֹא יָשַׁבְתִּי בְּבַיִת מִן־הַיּוֹם אֲשֶׁר הֶעֱלֵיתִי אֶת־יִשְׂרָאֵל עַד הַיּוֹם הַזֶּה
ו וָאֶהְיֶה מֵאֹהֶל אֶל־אֹהֶל וּמִמִּשְׁכָּן: בְּכֹל אֲשֶׁר־הִתְהַלַּכְתִּי בְּכָל־יִשְׂרָאֵל הֲדָבָר
דִּבַּרְתִּי אֶת־אַחַד שֹׁפְטֵי יִשְׂרָאֵל אֲשֶׁר צִוִּיתִי לִרְעוֹת אֶת־עַמִּי לֵאמֹר לָמָּה לֹא־
ז בְנִיתֶם לִי בֵּית אֲרָזִים: וְעַתָּה כֹּה־תֹאמַר לְעַבְדִּי לְדָוִיד כֹּה אָמַר יְהוָה צְבָאוֹת
ח אֲנִי לְקַחְתִּיךָ מִן־הַנָּוֶה מִן־אַחֲרֵי הַצֹּאן לִהְיוֹת נָגִיד עַל עַמִּי יִשְׂרָאֵל: וָאֶהְיֶה
עִמְּךָ בְּכֹל אֲשֶׁר הָלַכְתָּ וָאַכְרִית אֶת־כָּל־אוֹיְבֶיךָ מִפָּנֶיךָ וְעָשִׂיתִי לְךָ שֵׁם כְּשֵׁם
ט הַגְּדוֹלִים אֲשֶׁר בָּאָרֶץ: וְשַׂמְתִּי מָקוֹם לְעַמִּי יִשְׂרָאֵל וּנְטַעְתִּיהוּ וְשָׁכַן תַּחְתָּיו
י וְלֹא יִרְגַּז עוֹד וְלֹא־יוֹסִיפוּ בְנֵי־עַוְלָה לְבַלֹּתוֹ כַּאֲשֶׁר בָּרִאשׁוֹנָה: וּלְמִיָּמִים אֲשֶׁר
צִוִּיתִי שֹׁפְטִים עַל־עַמִּי יִשְׂרָאֵל וְהִכְנַעְתִּי אֶת־כָּל־אוֹיְבֶיךָ וָאַגִּד לָךְ וּבַיִת יִבְנֶה־
יא לְּךָ יְהוָה: וְהָיָה כִּי־מָלְאוּ יָמֶיךָ לָלֶכֶת עִם־אֲבֹתֶיךָ וַהֲקִימוֹתִי אֶת־זַרְעֲךָ אַחֲרֶיךָ
יב אֲשֶׁר יִהְיֶה מִבָּנֶיךָ וַהֲכִינוֹתִי אֶת־מַלְכוּתוֹ: הוּא יִבְנֶה־לִּי בָּיִת וְכֹנַנְתִּי אֶת־כִּסְאוֹ
יג עַד־עוֹלָם: אֲנִי אֶהְיֶה־לּוֹ לְאָב וְהוּא יִהְיֶה־לִּי לְבֵן וְחַסְדִּי לֹא־אָסִיר מֵעִמּוֹ כַּאֲשֶׁר
יד הֲסִירוֹתִי מֵאֲשֶׁר הָיָה לְפָנֶיךָ: וְהַעֲמַדְתִּיהוּ בְּבֵיתִי וּבְמַלְכוּתִי עַד־הָעוֹלָם וְכִסְאוֹ

DISCUSSION

17:2 | **Natan said to David:** Natan the prophet supported David's initiative. Although his encouragement of the king was not on the basis of a direct prophecy, his comments were also not received like those of a regular person; rather, they were received as the advice of one imbued with the spirit of God (see *Shoḥer Tov* 62:4). There are other instances in the Bible where a prophet issues a statement inspired by his holy spirit, and God subsequently communicates to him an explicit statement contrary to what he initially thought and felt (see I Samuel 16:6–7).

15 **In accordance with all these matters, and in accordance with this entire vision, so Natan spoke to David.** Along with the negative message that Natan relayed to David that he would not be privileged to build the Temple, he informed him that his kingdom would continue, and that his son who would succeed him would build the House of God.

16 **King David came and sat before the Lord.** There are no seats in the House of God, and it is apparently prohibited to sit before God. The Sages discuss this case from a halakhic perspective, and some conclude that special permission was granted to the kings of the house of David to sit in the Temple.[280] Alternatively, the verse means that David remained before God.[281] **And** he **said,** in response to the prophecy: **Who am I, Lord God, and who is my house, that You have brought me to this point** and crowned me king over Israel?

17 **This did not suffice in Your eyes, God;** that kindness was not enough for You, **and You have** even **spoken of** the establishment of **Your servant's house in the distant future, and have regarded me as**[282] **a man of** great **distinction,** worthy of initiating a royal dynasty, **Lord God.**

18 **What more can David add for You for the honor of Your servant?** What additional honor could I ask of You, as **You know Your servant.** You are aware of my sins, flaws, and errors, and yet You chose me, as You know that my intentions were for Your sake.

19 **Lord, for Your servant's sake, and according to Your heart,** Your will, **You have done all this greatness, to make known all these great things.**

20 **Lord, there is no one like You;** You are the King of the world, **and there is no God other than You, in accordance with everything**[283] **that we heard with our ears.**

21 **Who is like Your people Israel, one nation,** special, **on the earth, whom God went to redeem for Himself as a people, to make for Yourself renown by** means of **great,** marvelous, **and awesome acts, to drive out nations from before Your people, whom You redeemed from Egypt.** We are the first and only chosen people; not only did You redeem us from slavery in Egypt, but You banished other nations from before us.

22 **You made Your people Israel as a people for You forever; and You, Lord, became their God.**

23 **Now, Lord,** all that I can ask is: **Let the matter that You have spoken about Your servant and about his house be fulfilled forever, and do as You have spoken.**

24 **Let it be fulfilled, and let Your name be glorified forever, saying: The Lord of hosts, God of Israel is God to Israel, and the house of David Your servant will be established,** firm and strong, **before You.** You have promised that we will continue to be the chosen nation, and on the personal level You have likewise chosen the royal house of David.

25 **For You, my God, have revealed to the ear of Your servant** that You wish **to build him a** royal **house; therefore Your servant has found it in his heart to pray before You** this prayer, to thank You for what You have given me, and to inquire about Your promise for the future.

26 **Now, Lord, You are God,** who controls everything and has the power to fulfill His promises, **and** You **have spoken this good about Your servant;**

27 **now You have decided,** and it is Your desire **to bless the house of Your servant, to be before You forever; for You, Lord, have blessed, and** we **are blessed forever** from Your blessings. David understood Natan's prophecy as a divine endorsement from above: God has approved his good intentions and informed him that in reward for his initiative he will merit goodness and blessings. However, in practice he himself will not build the Temple, as he had hoped. The gift that he sought to bestow upon God will be accepted only later. The precise reason for the deferral is not explained to David. He is merely told that the Temple will be constructed not as an act of war; rather, it will be only after the kingdom is fully established and peace reigns in the land. The verses that follow describe how David was determined to prepare all that he could for the building of the Temple.

David's Conquests of the Neighboring Nations

I CHRONICLES 18:1–20:8

After David settles in Jerusalem, he is free to address foreign affairs. All is quiet on the home front, and Israel is no longer under attack by its enemies. David feels ready to expand his territory and become a regional power.

18 1 **It was thereafter that David smote the Philistines** and **subdued them.** In the past, the Philistines had invaded the land of Judah in order to capture David, or at least restrict his movement (14:8–17). On this occasion it is David who initiates the conflict, from which he emerges victorious and even conquers Philistine territory: **And** he **took Gat,**[B] an important Philistine city, **and** the villages in **its environs, from the hand of the Philistines.** From this point, the Philistines no longer pose a serious threat to Israel.

2 **He smote Moav; and the Moavites became servants to David, bearers of tribute.** They were forced to pay tribute to David. The land of Moav now came under the protection of the king of Israel, and the payment of levies was an accepted way of expressing subjugation, acceptance of authority, and quasi-servitude.

טו יִהְיֶה נָכוֹן עַד־עוֹלָם׃ כְּכֹל הַדְּבָרִים הָאֵלֶּה וּכְכֹל הֶחָזוֹן הַזֶּה כֵּן דִּבֶּר נָתָן אֶל־
טז דָּוִיד׃ וַיָּבֹא הַמֶּלֶךְ דָּוִיד וַיֵּשֶׁב לִפְנֵי יהוה וַיֹּאמֶר מִי־אֲנִי יהוה אֱלֹהִים
יז וּמִי בֵיתִי כִּי הֲבִיאֹתַנִי עַד־הֲלֹם׃ וַתִּקְטַן זֹאת בְּעֵינֶיךָ אֱלֹהִים וַתְּדַבֵּר עַל־בֵּית־
יח עַבְדְּךָ לְמֵרָחוֹק וּרְאִיתַנִי כְּתוֹר הָאָדָם הַמַּעֲלָה יהוה אֱלֹהִים׃ מַה־יּוֹסִיף עוֹד
יט דָּוִיד אֵלֶיךָ לְכָבוֹד אֶת־עַבְדֶּךָ וְאַתָּה אֶת־עַבְדְּךָ יָדָעְתָּ׃ יהוה בַּעֲבוּר עַבְדְּךָ
כ וּכְלִבְּךָ עָשִׂיתָ אֵת כָּל־הַגְּדוּלָּה הַזֹּאת לְהֹדִיעַ אֶת־כָּל־הַגְּדֻלּוֹת׃ יהוה אֵין כָּמוֹךָ
כא וְאֵין אֱלֹהִים זוּלָתֶךָ בְּכֹל אֲשֶׁר־שָׁמַעְנוּ בְּאָזְנֵינוּ׃ וּמִי כְּעַמְּךָ יִשְׂרָאֵל גּוֹי אֶחָד
בָּאָרֶץ אֲשֶׁר הָלַךְ הָאֱלֹהִים לִפְדּוֹת לוֹ עָם לָשׂוּם לְךָ שֵׁם גְּדֻלּוֹת וְנוֹרָאוֹת לְגָרֵשׁ
כב מִפְּנֵי עַמְּךָ אֲשֶׁר־פָּדִיתָ מִמִּצְרַיִם גּוֹיִם׃ וַתִּתֵּן אֶת־עַמְּךָ יִשְׂרָאֵל ׀ לְךָ לְעָם עַד־
כג עוֹלָם וְאַתָּה יהוה הָיִיתָ לָהֶם לֵאלֹהִים׃ וְעַתָּה יהוה הַדָּבָר אֲשֶׁר דִּבַּרְתָּ עַל־
כד עַבְדְּךָ וְעַל־בֵּיתוֹ יֵאָמֵן עַד־עוֹלָם וַעֲשֵׂה כַּאֲשֶׁר דִּבַּרְתָּ׃ וְיֵאָמֵן וְיִגְדַּל שִׁמְךָ
עַד־עוֹלָם לֵאמֹר יהוה צְבָאוֹת אֱלֹהֵי יִשְׂרָאֵל אֱלֹהִים לְיִשְׂרָאֵל וּבֵית־דָּוִיד עַבְדְּךָ
כה נָכוֹן לְפָנֶיךָ׃ כִּי ׀ אַתָּה אֱלֹהַי גָּלִיתָ אֶת־אֹזֶן עַבְדְּךָ לִבְנוֹת לוֹ בָּיִת עַל־כֵּן מָצָא
כו עַבְדְּךָ לְהִתְפַּלֵּל לְפָנֶיךָ׃ וְעַתָּה יהוה אַתָּה־הוּא הָאֱלֹהִים וַתְּדַבֵּר עַל־עַבְדְּךָ
כז הַטּוֹבָה הַזֹּאת׃ וְעַתָּה הוֹאַלְתָּ לְבָרֵךְ אֶת־בֵּית עַבְדְּךָ לִהְיוֹת לְעוֹלָם לְפָנֶיךָ כִּי־
יח א אַתָּה יהוה בֵּרַכְתָּ וּמְבֹרָךְ לְעוֹלָם׃ וַיְהִי אַחֲרֵי־כֵן וַיַּךְ דָּוִיד אֶת־
ב פְּלִשְׁתִּים וַיַּכְנִיעֵם וַיִּקַּח אֶת־גַּת וּבְנֹתֶיהָ מִיַּד פְּלִשְׁתִּים׃ וַיַּךְ אֶת־מוֹאָב וַיִּהְיוּ

BACKGROUND

18:1 | **Gat:** One of the five Philistine cities, it is typically identified with Tel Tzafit. This is due both to its location, and archaeological finds unearthed there.

3 **David smote Hadadezer king of Tzova at Hamat,**[B] in the northwestern part of modern-day Syria, **when he,** Hadadezer, **had gone to establish his border at the Euphrates River.** Hadadezer, who was king over a large Aramean state, sought to expand in the direction of eastern Syria and reach the Euphrates. David took to the battlefield in order to prevent him from doing so, seeking to halt the formation of a powerful political force in close proximity. When David concluded his military campaigns, all the territory from the Euphrates to the river of Egypt was subject to the supreme command of the king of Israel, even if not under his direct rule.

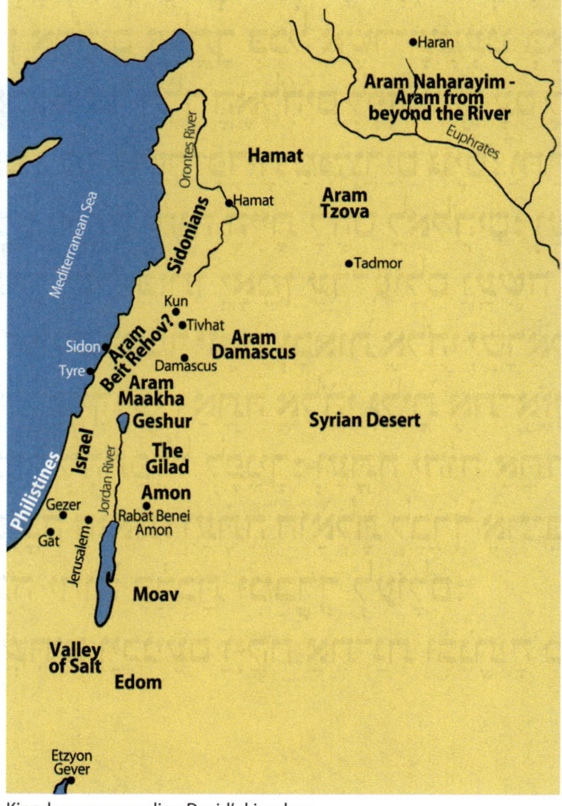

Kingdoms surrounding David's kingdom

4 **David captured from him** as plunder **one thousand chariots and seven thousand horseman and twenty thousand infantry** as captives; **David incapacitated all the chariots,** either by damaging the horses' hooves so that they could no longer run fast, or by incapacitating the chariots themselves, which were made of sturdy wood or iron. **But** he **preserved from them,** the one thousand, **one hundred chariots.** David did not conquer Hadadezer's land, but he sought to control it, and for that reason he destroyed Hadadezer's primary offensive weapon, his chariots of war.

5 The army of **Aram of Damascus**[B] **came to assist Hadadezer king of Tzova,** as the two Aramean kingdoms maintained close ties, **and David smote of the Arameans** of Damascus **twenty-two thousand men.**

6 **David placed** his representative, a supreme commissioner of sorts,[284] **in Aram of Damascus;** alternatively, he altered the market forces and established for himself special commercial rights, as many rulers had done before him throughout history. **And the Arameans became servants and bearers of tribute to David. The Lord saved David wherever he went,** both in his wars with the Philistines to the west, and in his campaigns against the Aramean kings in the far north.

7 **David took** as spoils **the shields of gold that were on the servants of Hadadezer,** as their king was powerful and wealthy, **and brought them to Jerusalem.**

Shield, Crete, eighth century BCE

8 **From Tivhat**[B] **and from Kun,**[B] **the cities of Hadadezer,** wealthy cities with diverse commercial activities, **David took a great deal of bronze,**[B] **with which Solomon** later **made the bronze sea,** an enormous water container, **and the** two huge **pillars,** each of which was more than 10 m tall,[285] **and the bronze vessels,** all for the Temple. Such large castings necessitated a massive quantity of bronze, and the requisite raw materials came partly from the plunder that David brought back from Aram.

Bronze ingot, Crete, 1200–1150 BCE

Representation of bronze pillars in Temple

Representation of bronze sea in Temple

ג מוֹאָב עֲבָדִים לְדָוִיד נֹשְׂאֵי מִנְחָה׃ וַיַּךְ דָּוִיד אֶת־הֲדַדְעֶזֶר מֶלֶךְ־צוֹבָה חֲמָתָה
ד בְּלֶכְתּוֹ לְהַצִּיב יָדוֹ בִּנְהַר פְּרָת׃ וַיִּלְכֹּד דָּוִיד מִמֶּנּוּ אֶלֶף רֶכֶב וְשִׁבְעַת אֲלָפִים
פָּרָשִׁים וְעֶשְׂרִים אֶלֶף אִישׁ רַגְלִי וַיְעַקֵּר דָּוִיד אֶת־כָּל־הָרֶכֶב וַיּוֹתֵר מִמֶּנּוּ מֵאָה
ה רָכֶב׃ וַיָּבֹא אֲרַם דַּרְמֶשֶׂק לַעְזוֹר לַהֲדַדְעֶזֶר מֶלֶךְ צוֹבָה וַיַּךְ דָּוִיד בַּאֲרָם עֶשְׂרִים־
ו וּשְׁנַיִם אֶלֶף אִישׁ׃ וַיָּשֶׂם דָּוִיד בַּאֲרַם דַּרְמֶשֶׂק וַיְהִי אֲרָם לְדָוִיד עֲבָדִים נֹשְׂאֵי
ז מִנְחָה וַיּוֹשַׁע יהוה לְדָוִיד בְּכֹל אֲשֶׁר הָלָךְ׃ וַיִּקַּח דָּוִיד אֵת שִׁלְטֵי הַזָּהָב אֲשֶׁר
ח הָיוּ עַל עַבְדֵי הֲדַדְעָזֶר וַיְבִיאֵם יְרוּשָׁלִָם׃ וּמִטִּבְחַת וּמִכּוּן עָרֵי הֲדַדְעֶזֶר לָקַח

BACKGROUND

18:3 | **David smote Hadadezer king of Tzova at Hamat:** In the accounts of David's wars (here and II Samuel 8:9–10), several northern kingdoms located in the territory of modern-day Syria, Lebanon, and southern Turkey are mentioned. They were a group of small Aramean principalities, including the kingdoms of To'u (called To'i in the book of Samuel) king of Hamat, Aram Naharayim, Aram Tzova, Aram Beit Rehov, Aram of Damascus, and Aram Maakha. Information from non-biblical sources with regard to the relationships between these kingdoms and their precise boundaries is meager and unclear. From the eleventh century BCE, with the decline of the Assyrian kingdom, these principalities came under the control of Aram Tzova, until their defeat during the reign of David. With the decline of the Kingdom of Israel in the ninth century BCE, Aram of Damascus rebelled against Israel and became the greatest and most significant of the kingdoms of Aram. During this period, especially after the division of the united monarchy into the kingdoms of Judah and Israel, and the unification of the Arameans under Aram of Damascus, the united Aramean kingdom became a dominant force in the region, and Aramaic became the diplomatic language of the region for more than one thousand years.

Archaeological finds in northern Syria, dated to the tenth century BCE, support the hypothesis that the Aramean kingdoms flourished during that period, following the collapse of the Hitite Empire. They struggled for control of these areas with "Walistin" or "Patin," which was the kingdom of the Sea Peoples, also known as the northern Philistines. David made a military alliance with them, just as he did with the southern Philistines from Gat, and this helped him expand the border of Israel from the Sinai Peninsula to the Euphrates.

Inscriptions and archaeological findings with Philistine characteristics from the tenth century BCE have been discovered in northern Syria. An inscription at Tel Tayinat mentions a "King Taita, ruler of Walistin," whom some suggest is To'u king of Hamat.

18:5 | **Damascus [*Darmesek*]:** Some maintain that Darmesek is the ancient version of the name of the city Damascus, but in fact it is a later form, as it appears in the Bible only in the book of Chronicles, and in non-biblical sources it appears only from the fourth century BCE. The "r" phoneme was added under the influence of the Aramaic, in place of a *dagesh*, as in *karsei* (Daniel 5:20) instead of *kisei*, chair; *saraf* instead of *se'af*, boughs (Ezekiel 31:5, 6); and *sharvit* (Esther 4:11) instead of *shevet*, scepter (Yechezkel Kutscher, *The Language and Linguistic Background of the Isaiah Scroll*. Jerusalem: Magnes Press, Hebrew University, 1959 [Hebrew], 77, 4–5).

18:8 | **Tivhat:** There is no certain identification of the location of Tivhat. Egyptian documents from the second half of the second millennium BCE, that refer to the area that is modern-day northern Syria and Lebanon, mention a settlement called Tubihi. However, in the parallel account in II Samuel 8:8, the name Betah is mentioned: "From Betah and from Berotai, cities of Hadadezer, King David took a great deal of bronze." Two additional factors render identification difficult: First, the borders and territory of the kingdom of Hadadezer (Aram Tzova) are not clearly defined. Second, although there are iron deposits in these regions there is, as yet, no archaeological evidence for the production of bronze. Nevertheless, several suggestions have been raised with regard to the location of Tivhat. Some say it was on the eastern descent of the Anti-Lebanon Mountains. Others claim that it was proximate to the city of Kadesh on the Orontes River, while yet others maintain that it is Baalbek in the Beqaa Valley. It is noteworthy that Tevah is the name of a family, and a tribe of one of the descendants of Nahor, Abraham's brother (Genesis 22:24).

Kun: While there is reference to this place in ancient Egyptian documents, its location is uncertain. Some say it is the village of Ras Baalbek, in the northern Beqaa Valley, approximately 35 km north of Baalbek. According to local testimonies, this village used to be called Conna, and is mentioned in Roman sources (Antonine Itinerary, second century CE).

A great deal of bronze: Based on what is known of the metal trade in the ancient world, there was no mining or metal industry in the region of Syria and Lebanon. Rather, these were typically imported from Asia Minor, the islands of the Aegean Sea, Tarshish, and even from the distant mountains of Persia. It is therefore likely that, at that time, the kingdom of Aram Tzova and the cities of Tivhat and Kun were centers of commerce or storage for these metals.

9 **To'u king of Hamat heard that David had smitten all the forces of Hadadezer king of Tzova,** who was his neighbor to the north,

10 **and he sent his son Hadoram** as a diplomatic envoy **to King David, to greet him, and to congratulate him on** the fact **that he had made war against Hadadezer and smitten him, for Hadadezer had been a man of wars of To'u.** The king of Tzova and the nearby king of Hamat had been involved in disputes for years; therefore, when Hadadezer was defeated in war, perhaps on his way to wage war with Hamat,[286] To'u was very pleased and even thanked David for not attacking him. Not only did he send his son to David, but he also sent **with** him valuable gifts, **all vessels of gold, and silver, and bronze.** David did not seek to capture the entire area of Syria, and therefore he did not attack the king of Hamat. He gained a certain degree of control over the kingdom of Aram without actually conquering it. Accordingly, this region has a unique halakhic status.[287]

11 **King David consecrated those too to the Lord, with the silver and the gold that he carried from all the nations, from Edom, from Moav, from the children of Amon, from the Philistines, and from Amalek.** David did not deposit these gifts in his personal coffers, but rather earmarked them for the Temple treasury. He stockpiled these large amounts of valuable raw materials that would be required for construction of the Temple.

12 Simultaneous with David's campaign against Aram, **Avshai son of Tzeruya smote Edom in the Valley of Salt,**[B] **eighteen**

"Valley of Salt." Landscape characteristic of the northern Arava

thousand. Avishai, here called Avshai, was sent to battle Edom, which was deemed a lesser threat, while David went with the commander of his army to wage the more difficult war against Aram. Avishai was also victorious, decisively routing the Edomites.[288]

13 **He placed** Israelite **officials in Edom, and all of Edom became servants to David.** David maintained a more constrictive reign over Edom than he did over other lands. He may not have even permitted them to retain their own king. Edom was economically significant because of its copper deposits, and because of the commercial routes that traversed its territory and led to the Red Sea. **The Lord saved David wherever he went.**

14 While David occasionally acted as a military commander, at least officially, and directed military campaigns, he also filled the everyday role of the king, which was not necessarily the case with regard to all kings. **David reigned over all Israel, and he executed justice and righteousness for his entire people.** He preserved the legal system in his kingdom and tended to the needs of the public.

15 **Yoav son of Tzeruya was** the supreme commander **over the army,** probably the official ranked just below the king on the army's frequent military forays, **and Yehoshafat son of Ahilud was chancellor,** a man under the king's direct command and in charge of the government.

16 **Tzadok son of Ahituv,** a descendant of Pinhas son of Elazar the priest, **and Avimelekh son of Evyatar,** from the house of Eli, a descendant of Itamar, **were priests.** At that stage, David had not yet chosen between them, and both served as priests. **And Shavsha was a** royal **scribe.** Shavsha is not an Israelite name; this official was probably a convert. His origins suited his role as scribe; a foreign minister of sorts who would have been engaged in diplomatic relations.

17 **Benayahu son of Yehoyada was** appointed **over the Keretites and the Peletites,**[D] regiments of foreign mercenaries; **and the sons of David were prominent alongside the king.** David appointed his sons to senior positions in government. However, the most important positions were filled by other, apparently more qualified, men.

19 1 **It was after this that Nahash the king of the children of Amon died, and his son reigned in his stead.**

2 **David said: I will act with kindness to Hanun son of Nahash, because his father acted with kindness to me.** Apparently the

DISCUSSION

18:17| **The Keretites and the Peletites:** These were special units of a foreign legion, who were perhaps of Philistine origin (see Rashi; commentary on II Samuel 8:18). Unlike the majority of the army of Israel, which was based on reserve units that were mobilized when the need arose, the Keretites and the Peletites constituted a standing army tasked with maintaining the stability of the military and protecting the king. Consequently, they displayed extreme loyalty to King David (see II Samuel 15:18, 20:7; I Kings 1:44).

דָּוִיד נְחֹשֶׁת רַבָּה מְאֹד בָּהּ ׀ עָשָׂה שְׁלֹמֹה אֶת־יָם הַנְּחֹשֶׁת וְאֶת־הָעַמּוּדִים וְאֵת
ט כְּלֵי הַנְּחֹשֶׁת׃ וַיִּשְׁמַע תֹּעוּ מֶלֶךְ חֲמָת כִּי הִכָּה דָוִיד אֶת־כָּל־חֵיל
י הֲדַדְעֶזֶר מֶלֶךְ־צוֹבָה׃ וַיִּשְׁלַח אֶת־הֲדוֹרָם־בְּנוֹ אֶל־הַמֶּלֶךְ דָּוִיד לשאול־לוֹ לִשְׁאָל־
לִשְׁלוֹם וּלְבָרְכוֹ עַל אֲשֶׁר נִלְחַם בַּהֲדַדְעֶזֶר וַיַּכֵּהוּ כִּי־אִישׁ מִלְחֲמוֹת תֹּעוּ הָיָה
יא הֲדַדְעָזֶר וְכֹל כְּלֵי זָהָב וָכֶסֶף וּנְחֹשֶׁת׃ גַּם־אֹתָם הִקְדִּישׁ הַמֶּלֶךְ דָּוִיד לַיהוה עִם־
הַכֶּסֶף וְהַזָּהָב אֲשֶׁר נָשָׂא מִכָּל־הַגּוֹיִם מֵאֱדוֹם וּמִמּוֹאָב וּמִבְּנֵי עַמּוֹן וּמִפְּלִשְׁתִּים
יב וּמֵעֲמָלֵק׃ וְאַבְשַׁי בֶּן־צְרוּיָה הִכָּה אֶת־אֱדוֹם בְּגֵיא הַמֶּלַח שְׁמוֹנָה עָשָׂר אָלֶף׃
יג וַיָּשֶׂם בֶּאֱדוֹם נְצִיבִים וַיִּהְיוּ כָל־אֱדוֹם עֲבָדִים לְדָוִיד וַיּוֹשַׁע יהוה אֶת־דָּוִיד בְּכֹל
יד אֲשֶׁר הָלָךְ׃ וַיִּמְלֹךְ דָּוִיד עַל־כָּל־יִשְׂרָאֵל וַיְהִי עֹשֶׂה מִשְׁפָּט וּצְדָקָה לְכָל־עַמּוֹ׃
טו טז וְיוֹאָב בֶּן־צְרוּיָה עַל־הַצָּבָא וִיהוֹשָׁפָט בֶּן־אֲחִילוּד מַזְכִּיר׃ וְצָדוֹק בֶּן־אֲחִיטוּב
יז וַאֲבִימֶלֶךְ בֶּן־אֶבְיָתָר כֹּהֲנִים וְשַׁוְשָׁא סוֹפֵר׃ וּבְנָיָהוּ בֶּן־יְהוֹיָדָע עַל־הַכְּרֵתִי
וְהַפְּלֵתִי וּבְנֵי־דָוִיד הָרִאשֹׁנִים לְיַד הַמֶּלֶךְ׃
יט א ב וַיְהִי אַחֲרֵי־כֵן וַיָּמָת נָחָשׁ מֶלֶךְ בְּנֵי־עַמּוֹן וַיִּמְלֹךְ בְּנוֹ תַּחְתָּיו׃ וַיֹּאמֶר דָּוִיד אֶעֱשֶׂה־
חֶסֶד ׀ עִם־חָנוּן בֶּן־נָחָשׁ כִּי־עָשָׂה אָבִיו עִמִּי חֶסֶד וַיִּשְׁלַח דָּוִיד מַלְאָכִים לְנַחֲמוֹ
ג עַל־אָבִיו וַיָּבֹאוּ עַבְדֵי דָוִיד אֶל־אֶרֶץ בְּנֵי־עַמּוֹן אֶל־חָנוּן לְנַחֲמוֹ׃ וַיֹּאמְרוּ שָׂרֵי
בְנֵי־עַמּוֹן לְחָנוּן הַמְכַבֵּד דָּוִיד אֶת־אָבִיךָ בְּעֵינֶיךָ כִּי־שָׁלַח לְךָ מְנַחֲמִים הֲלֹא

king of Amon had supported David when he fled from Saul, and had even provided for his brothers.[289] It is also possible that Nahash had sided with David because King Saul had previously waged war against Nahash.[290] **David sent messengers** to the new king **to console him over** the death of **his father, and David's servants came to the land of the children of Amon, to Hanun,** to pay a courtesy visit and **to console him.**

3 **The princes of the children of Amon said to Hanun: Is David honoring your father in your eyes, as he sent consolers to you?** Do you really suppose that David has sent

BACKGROUND

18:12 | **The Valley of Salt:** Identified with an area in the northern Arava, south of the Dead Sea, a region that was under Edomite rule. It was a focal point of wars between Judah and Edom throughout the generations, as control of the Arava was strategically significant both because of the copper deposits in the region, and because there were major commercial routes that traversed the area.

these men in deference to your father? **Surely it is in order to examine, to reconnoiter** your territory from all perspectives, **and to spy out the land, that his servants came to you.** They are nothing other than spies, seeking to scrutinize the land and gather information. This delegation of comforters is diplomatic cover for David's true objectives. Hanun was persuaded by these claims and did not properly investigate the matter.

4 **Hanun took David's servants, and shaved them.** As detailed elsewhere,[291] he shaved their beards on only one side of the face, which was a clear mark of disgrace. **And** furthermore he **cut their** long **garments in the middle, until their groin,** so that they remained half-naked up to the groin, **and sent them away** in a most ridiculous and miserable state. This crude treatment of David's messengers was undoubtedly a message from Amon, with the aim of demeaning David himself.

5 **They went and** it was **reported to David about** the state in which **the men** had returned. **He sent** people **to meet them, for the men were greatly humiliated** about having to travel in that condition from Amon back to their land. **The king said:** You do not have to return to me immediately. Instead, **stay in Jericho until your beards grow, and** then **return.**

"Jericho." Tel es-Sultan

6 **The children of Amon saw that they had made themselves odious** and contemptible **to David,** as such an act is a direct challenge and even a declaration of war, and the Amonites knew that David was likely to retaliate. **And Hanun and the children of Amon sent one thousand talents of silver to hire for themselves** an auxiliary army of **chariots and horsemen from Aram Naharayim,**[B] **from Aram Maakha,**[B] **and from Tzova,**[B] which is also an Aramean state.

7 **They hired for themselves thirty-two thousand chariots,**[B] a very large force, **with the king of Maakha and his people, and they came and encamped before Medeva,**[B] in the land of Amon. **The children of Amon gathered from their cities and came to war.** They declared a general mobilization and determined a site for the battle, as was customary in those days.

8 **David heard** that the Amonites were gathered for battle, **and he sent Yoav and the entire army of the mighty** men to war.

9 **The children of Amon came forth and arrayed for war at the entrance of the city.** Apparently, they sought to avoid open conflict on a remote terrain, preferring instead to rely on the fortifications of the city of Rabat Amon. **And the kings who came** as mercenaries **were by themselves in the field,** and attacked Yoav's camp from behind.

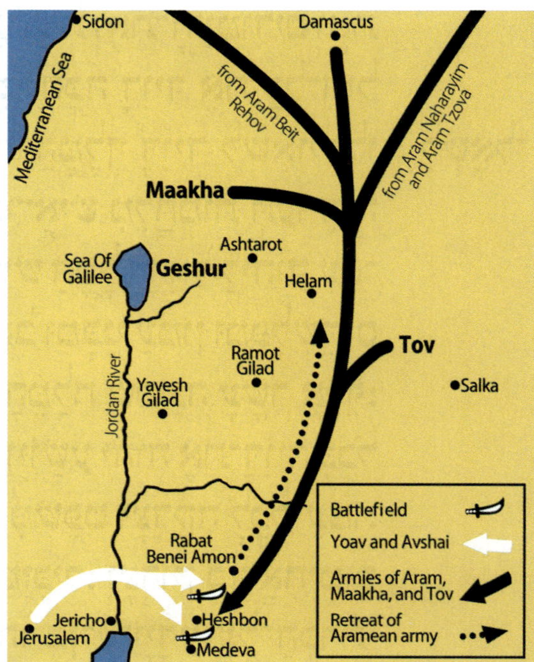

First battle: Yoav and Avshai against Amon and Moav

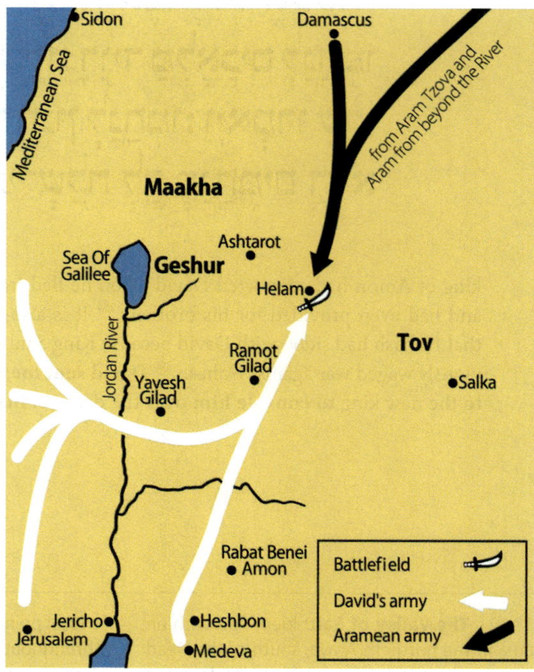

Second battle: David against Aramean states

ד בַּעֲבוּר לַחְקֹר וְלַהֲפֹךְ וּלְרַגֵּל הָאָרֶץ בָּאוּ עֲבָדָיו אֵלֶיךָ: וַיִּקַּח חָנוּן אֶת־עַבְדֵי
ה דָוִיד וַיְגַלְּחֵם וַיִּכְרֹת אֶת־מַדְוֵיהֶם בַּחֵצִי עַד־הַמִּפְשָׂעָה וַיְשַׁלְּחֵם: וַיֵּלְכוּ וַיַּגִּידוּ
לְדָוִיד עַל־הָאֲנָשִׁים וַיִּשְׁלַח לִקְרָאתָם כִּי־הָיוּ הָאֲנָשִׁים נִכְלָמִים מְאֹד וַיֹּאמֶר
ו הַמֶּלֶךְ שְׁבוּ בִירֵחוֹ עַד אֲשֶׁר־יְצַמַּח זְקַנְכֶם וְשַׁבְתֶּם: וַיִּרְאוּ בְּנֵי עַמּוֹן
כִּי הִתְבָּאֲשׁוּ עִם־דָּוִיד וַיִּשְׁלַח חָנוּן וּבְנֵי עַמּוֹן אֶלֶף כִּכַּר־כֶּסֶף לִשְׂכֹּר לָהֶם מִן־
ז אֲרַם נַהֲרַיִם וּמִן־אֲרַם מַעֲכָה וּמִצּוֹבָה רֶכֶב וּפָרָשִׁים: וַיִּשְׂכְּרוּ לָהֶם שְׁנַיִם וּשְׁלֹשִׁים
אֶלֶף רֶכֶב וְאֶת־מֶלֶךְ מַעֲכָה וְאֶת־עַמּוֹ וַיָּבֹאוּ וַיַּחֲנוּ לִפְנֵי מֵידְבָא וּבְנֵי עַמּוֹן נֶאֶסְפוּ
ח מֵעָרֵיהֶם וַיָּבֹאוּ לַמִּלְחָמָה: וַיִּשְׁמַע דָּוִיד וַיִּשְׁלַח אֶת־יוֹאָב וְאֵת כָּל־
ט צָבָא הַגִּבּוֹרִים: וַיֵּצְאוּ בְּנֵי עַמּוֹן וַיַּעַרְכוּ מִלְחָמָה פֶּתַח הָעִיר וְהַמְּלָכִים אֲשֶׁר־בָּאוּ

BACKGROUND

19:6| **Aram Naharayim:** This was the name of the northern Aramean kingdom located in the area of the tributaries of the Euphrates, the Balikh River and the Khabur River. It was the territory of the Mitanni kingdom until the twelfth century BCE, which is called Naharin in ancient Egyptian texts. Some contend that the suffix *rayim* did not necessarily indicate a pair or a multitude, as it does in Hebrew. Rather, it signifies a connection to a place; in this case it means the Aram beside the river, *nahar* (see Numbers 22:5, and Onkelos ad loc.). It should be noted that the parallel account in the book of Samuel refers to the Arameans of Beit Rehov, not Aram Naharayim. It is possible that Hadadezer, who was from the Rehov dynasty (see II Samuel 8:3), expanded the territory under his control all the way to Aram on the Euphrates, and therefore the place is named for the dynasty.

Aram Maakha: Maakha is mentioned in Genesis (22:21–24) among the descendants of Nahor, Abraham's brother. It is also the name of one of the regions of the Land of Israel that was not conquered by Joshua (Joshua 13:13). In addition, it is mentioned in Egyptian execration texts from the second millennium BCE. It seems that during the reign of King Solomon it was incorporated and absorbed as part of Aram of Damascus. According to the description in the book of Joshua, the Maakhatite domain was located in the modern-day northern Golan Heights.

Tzova: According to Egyptian documents dating to the second millennium BCE, there were various Aramean tribes in the region south of Haran. There is also testimony from the end of the eleventh century BCE of the establishment of an Aramean kingdom called Aram Tzova, centered in the northern Beqaa Valley. This kingdom, which was a union of those Aramean tribes, spread to southern Syria and the northern region east of the Jordan. It controlled the roads leading from Mesopotamia until it was defeated by David. The kingdom was later replaced by Aram of Damascus.

19:7| **Thirty-two thousand chariots:** This is an extremely large number of chariots; there is no known case of a comparable force in the armies of that period. For example, in the Battle of Qarqar, a massive coalition of twelve states gathered against the Assyrians. This army, which included the Arameans, Egypt, and Israel, contained only 3940 chariots, according to Assyrian sources. It seems that both the number thirty-two and the mention of thousand are typological figures, signifying a large number and a variety of chariots (see, e.g., Judges 7:3; I Kings 20:1, 22:31). The term "thousand" often indicates only a portion, and an irregular one at that, of a larger unit, e.g., a patrilineal house (Ephraim Hareuveni, "*Aleph* in the Bible," *Beit Mikra* 7:3 (15) Spring 1963, [Hebrew], 12–17). For further examples of exaggerations in the language of the Sages, see *Tamid* 29a; *Ḥullin* 90b.

Medeva: The city of Medeva, or Madaba, is in the territory of the tribe of Reuben, and located on a plateau in the middle of a ridge, a plateau that reached the outskirts of Rabat Amon. It is a terrain suitable for warfare involving chariots and cavalry. The modern-day city, which has retained the name, is located approximately 30 km southwest of Amman. Modern-day Medeva is renowned primarily for a mosaic that was discovered there, the Madaba Map, which contains a cartographic depiction of Israel during the Byzantine period.

10 **Yoav saw that the face of the battle was in front and in back,** and that it was necessary to wage war on two fronts, with the Amonites before him and the Arameans behind, **and he chose of all the select of Israel, and he arrayed against Aram.** Yoav assumed that the Aramean mercenaries were better trained and perhaps more numerous than the Amonites, and he therefore selected his finest warriors under his direct command, and attacked Aram.

11 **The rest of the people he placed into the hand of Avshai his brother, and they arrayed,** went to war, **against the children of Amon.**

12 **He said: If the Arameans overpower me** in battle, **you will be my salvation, and if the children of Amon overpower you, I will save you.** Although we are fighting on two fronts, our forces can assist one another. If one is in dire straits, the other can support him with a reserve force. Yoav concluded his speech in a manner befitting a commander on a battlefield:

13 **Be strong, and let us grow stronger for the sake of our people, and for the sake of the cities of our God;** we must be strong and seek to wage war to the best of our abilities,[292] **and the Lord will do what is good in His eyes.**

14 **Yoav and the people who were with him approached Aram to war, and they fled from before him.** As a skilled military leader, he was able to rout the large Aramean force, which was apparently less organized than his own.

15 **The children of Amon saw that Aram,** upon whom they had been relying for assistance, **had fled, and they too fled from before Avshai, his,** Yoav's, **brother, and they came into the city.** They returned to their fortified city. Then **Yoav came** back **to Jerusalem** in order to inform David of the results of the battle and to prepare for future developments.

16 **Aram saw that it was routed before Israel, and sent messengers.** The Arameans knew that David would not forgive them for their alliance with Amon in the battle against Israel, and therefore they readied themselves for another attack, in which they hoped to overpower David, or at least prevent him from attacking them. **And** they **brought out Aram from beyond the River.** There was an additional, perhaps even greater Aramean kingdom beyond the Euphrates, and its men, too, were mobilized to wage war with Israel, **with Shofakh,** or Shobakh in the parallel account,[293] **commander of the army of Hadadezer, before them.** Apparently, Hadadezer reigned over this Aramean kingdom as well.

17 **It was reported to David, and he gathered all of Israel, and he crossed the Jordan and came to them, and arrayed** his forces to fight **against them.** In order to confront the entire Aramean army, both the troops of the smaller kingdoms on the western side of the Euphrates as well as those from the eastern side, David recruited additional warriors. **David arrayed in war against the Arameans and they waged war against him.**

18 **Aram** again **fled from before Israel,**[D] **and David killed from Aram seven thousand chariot drivers and forty thousand infantry, and Shofakh, commander of the army, he put to death.** It seems that this commander was a very dominant figure, and therefore his death signaled a reversal from which Hadadezer's men could not easily recover.

19 **The servants of Hadadezer saw that they were routed before Israel, and they made peace with David and served him.** David certainly did not conquer the kingdom of Aram of the eastern side of the Euphrates; then again, the Arameans closer to Israel were not fully subjugated to his rule either. Rather, they were under his overall control. **Aram was unwilling to save the children of Amon anymore.** They decided that this experience sufficed for them, and they reached an agreement of non-belligerence or even capitulation to David.

20 1 **It was at the turn of the year, at the time when the kings go on** military **campaign,**[D] in the spring or summer, **that Yoav led the army forces and ravaged the land of the children of Amon,**[D] a small land that could no longer rely on the assistance of the Arameans. The army of Israel was larger and undoubtedly better trained than that of the Amonites. **He approached and besieged Raba,**[B] the capital of Amon. **And David stayed in Jerusalem,** as his participation was unnecessary. **Yoav smote Raba and destroyed it.** Elsewhere it is stated that Yoav gave David the honor of entering the city as its official conqueror.[294]

BACKGROUND

20:1 | **Raba:** The capital of the kingdom of Amon (see Joshua 13:25). The city controlled the eastern King's Highway trade route, from Damascus to the Dead Sea, and the westward road toward Judah.

י לְבַדָּם בַּשָּׂדֶה׃ וַיַּרְא יוֹאָב כִּי־הָיְתָה פְנֵי־הַמִּלְחָמָה אֵלָיו פָּנִים וְאָחוֹר וַיִּבְחַר
יא מִכָּל־בָּחוּר בְּיִשְׂרָאֵל וַיַּעֲרֹךְ לִקְרַאת אֲרָם׃ וְאֵת יֶתֶר הָעָם נָתַן בְּיַד אַבְשַׁי אָחִיו
יב וַיַּעַרְכוּ לִקְרַאת בְּנֵי עַמּוֹן׃ וַיֹּאמֶר אִם־תֶּחֱזַק מִמֶּנִּי אֲרָם וְהָיִיתָ לִּי לִתְשׁוּעָה
יג וְאִם־בְּנֵי עַמּוֹן יֶחֶזְקוּ מִמְּךָ וְהוֹשַׁעְתִּיךָ׃ חֲזַק וְנִתְחַזְּקָה בְּעַד־עַמֵּנוּ וּבְעַד עָרֵי ח
יד אֱלֹהֵינוּ וַיהוָה הַטּוֹב בְּעֵינָיו יַעֲשֶׂה׃ וַיִּגַּשׁ יוֹאָב וְהָעָם אֲשֶׁר־עִמּוֹ לִפְנֵי אֲרָם
טו לַמִּלְחָמָה וַיָּנוּסוּ מִפָּנָיו׃ וּבְנֵי עַמּוֹן רָאוּ כִּי־נָס אֲרָם וַיָּנוּסוּ גַם־הֵם מִפְּנֵי אַבְשַׁי
טז אָחִיו וַיָּבֹאוּ הָעִירָה וַיָּבֹא יוֹאָב יְרוּשָׁלִָם׃ וַיַּרְא אֲרָם כִּי נִגְּפוּ לִפְנֵי
יִשְׂרָאֵל וַיִּשְׁלְחוּ מַלְאָכִים וַיּוֹצִיאוּ אֶת־אֲרָם אֲשֶׁר מֵעֵבֶר הַנָּהָר וְשׁוֹפַךְ שַׂר־צְבָא
יז הֲדַדְעֶזֶר לִפְנֵיהֶם׃ וַיֻּגַּד לְדָוִיד וַיֶּאֱסֹף אֶת־כָּל־יִשְׂרָאֵל וַיַּעֲבֹר הַיַּרְדֵּן וַיָּבֹא אֲלֵהֶם
יח וַיַּעֲרֹךְ אֲלֵהֶם וַיַּעֲרֹךְ דָּוִיד לִקְרַאת אֲרָם מִלְחָמָה וַיִּלָּחֲמוּ עִמּוֹ׃ וַיָּנָס אֲרָם מִלִּפְנֵי
יִשְׂרָאֵל וַיַּהֲרֹג דָּוִיד מֵאֲרָם שִׁבְעַת אֲלָפִים רֶכֶב וְאַרְבָּעִים אֶלֶף אִישׁ רַגְלִי וְאֵת
יט שׁוֹפַךְ שַׂר־הַצָּבָא הֵמִית׃ וַיִּרְאוּ עַבְדֵי הֲדַדְעֶזֶר כִּי נִגְּפוּ לִפְנֵי יִשְׂרָאֵל וַיַּשְׁלִימוּ
א עִם־דָּוִיד וַיַּעַבְדֻהוּ וְלֹא־אָבָה אֲרָם לְהוֹשִׁיעַ אֶת־בְּנֵי־עַמּוֹן עוֹד׃ וַיְהִי כ
לְעֵת תְּשׁוּבַת הַשָּׁנָה לְעֵת ׀ צֵאת הַמְּלָכִים וַיִּנְהַג יוֹאָב אֶת־חֵיל הַצָּבָא וַיַּשְׁחֵת ׀
אֶת־אֶרֶץ בְּנֵי־עַמּוֹן וַיָּבֹא וַיָּצַר אֶת־רַבָּה וְדָוִיד יֹשֵׁב בִּירוּשָׁלִָם וַיַּךְ יוֹאָב אֶת־רַבָּה

DISCUSSION

19:18 | **Aram fled from before Israel:** In the wake of this significant victory in the two campaigns against Aram, David sang a special paean of praise, which was incorporated into the book of Psalms (Psalms 60; see also Psalms 108).

20:1 | **At the time when the kings go on campaign:** The spring and summer seasons were convenient times for military maneuvers and for war in general, especially for attacking forces. When people in a predominantly agrarian society fled an approaching enemy in order to seek refuge in the fortified cities, the advancing army could find produce in the fields, orchards, and vineyards for their own use. This meant that the attacked party would suffer compound damages: In addition to the ravages of the war itself, the destruction of its fields would engender a famine both that year and the following year (see Rashi, and Malbim, II Samuel 11:1).

Yoav led the army forces and ravaged the land of the children of Amon: The book of Chronicles focuses mainly on the kings of the Davidic dynasty. On occasion, it discusses other personalities, but only marginally. Although there is a conspicuous bias in favor of the Davidic dynasty, that bias does not manifest itself in actual falsehoods; but there are certainly some omissions (see, e.g., Rashi, 10:1, 15:29, 17:13). The war against the Amonites is described in detail in II Samuel (chaps. 10–12), but the book of Samuel also relates the contemporaneous incident involving Bathsheba, which, despite its obvious severity, is omitted from the narrative related in the book of Chronicles. An account of a different sin committed by David, his census of the people, is related, because the ramifications of that sin affected the entire nation, while the ramifications of the sin with Bathsheba were more limited in scope.

2 **David took the crown of their king**[D] [***malkam***], possibly a reference to the chief god of Amon, called Molekh or Milkom,
**from upon his head, and found its weight a talent of gold,
and in it a precious stone, and it was on David's head; he
took out a great deal of spoils from the city.**
3 **He,** David, **took out the people who were in it,** who resisted
him, **and cut**[295] **them with saws, with iron picks, and with
axes.**[B] He punished some of
the people severely; it is possible that many of them were
killed by torture. **So David
would do,** not only to the residents of Rabat Amon but **to**
the residents of **all the cities
of the children of Amon.**[D]
He passed through Amon, and
killed many of its inhabitants.
In II Samuel 17:27 it is related
that an important personage
from Rabat Amon supported
David when he fled from Avshalom. Apparently, David left a
measure of autonomous government in Amon. **David and all
the people returned to Jerusalem.**

Fresco depicting sawing, Tomb of Nebamun and Ipuki, Egypt, 1350–1300 BCE

4 **It was after this that a war arose in Gezer,** on the western border of Israel, **with the Philistines.** Apparently, the land of the
Philistines was never conquered by David, and the Philistines
would periodically attack Israel. For better or worse, the
Philistine governors were like minor, semi-autonomous kings in
their own cities, and every so often one of them would decide to
stage an attack to achieve some objective, or to amuse himself.
Then Sibekhai the Hushatite, one of David's mighty warriors,
**smote Sipai, from the offspring of the giants [*refaim*], and
they surrendered.** This was an enormous man, who helped the
Philistines in battle or merely stood among the Philistine warriors in order to frighten the enemy. Therefore, killing this giant
was a bold act. The Refaim were men of great size who belonged
to an ancient race that had dwindled over time; a few isolated individuals remained alive even in later generations. The Philistines
might have employed these men in combat.
5 **There was another war with the Philistines, and Elhanan
son of Ya'ir smote Lahmi, the brother of Goliath the Gitite,**
who had earlier been killed by David. Elhanan killed Goliath's
brother, Lahmi, despite his enormous size: **The shaft of his
spear was like a weaver's beam,** the long, heavy wooden beam
to which the threads of the warp are attached. Only a very tall
and powerful man could wield a spear that large.
6 **There was another war in Gat. There was a man of stature,**
of great dimension, or literally, a man of measure. Ordinary
men are not typically measured, but since giants are so extraordinarily tall, people tend to estimate their great height.[296]
And his fingers and toes were six on each, a total of **twenty-
four.** Genetic mutations of this kind occur even in the modern
world. Although there is no reason to assume that the additional fingers and toes gave him any advantage in combat over
others, they intensified the effect of his frightening image. **And
he too was born to the giant [*rafa*],** a surviving member of
the ancient Refaim. Apparently, several sons born to the same
Rafa waged war alongside the Philistines.[297] Every so often, descendants of ancient races, who were larger than typical people
today, are discovered in various lands. Apparently, individuals
of this type remained in Israel and assisted the Philistines.
7 **He taunted Israel,** with both his might and actual taunting,
and Yehonatan, son of Shima brother of David, smote him.
8 **These** enormous brothers **were born to the giant in Gat, and
they fell by the hand of David and by the hand of his servants.** David killed Goliath, who was the first of these giants to
fall at the hands of Israel.[298] The others were killed by David's
men. The last battles of David and his warriors were waged on
the borders of the kingdom, as time and again he was forced to
confront enemies on the periphery of his kingdom. Israel never
fully conquered the land of the Philistines, who retained control of the coastal strip until the Greek conquest. Nevertheless,
at the time of his death, David was the most significant king in
the entire region west of the Euphrates. Not all the countries in
this area were under his complete control, but they all accepted
his authority. This was the political situation that David left for
the kings who succeeded him.

The Census of Israel

I CHRONICLES 21:1–6

21 1 **An adversary,** an evil inclination, **rose against Israel and incited David**[D] **to take a census of Israel.** David's own thoughts
and musings led him to the decision to count the children of
Israel.[299]
2 **David said to Yoav and to the princes of the people: Go,
count Israel from Beersheba to Dan, and bring it,** the results,
to me, and I will know their number. There does not seem
to have been any real military or civil benefit to the census, although David was no doubt induced to think that the move was

ב וַיֶּהֶרְסֶהָ: וַיִּקַּח דָּוִיד אֶת־עֲטֶרֶת־מַלְכָּם מֵעַל רֹאשׁוֹ וַיִּמְצָאָהּ ׀ מִשְׁקַל כִּכַּר־זָהָב
ג וּבָהּ אֶבֶן יְקָרָה וַתְּהִי עַל־רֹאשׁ דָּוִיד וּשְׁלַל הָעִיר הוֹצִיא הַרְבֵּה מְאֹד: וְאֶת־הָעָם
אֲשֶׁר־בָּהּ הוֹצִיא וַיָּשַׂר בַּמְּגֵרָה וּבַחֲרִיצֵי הַבַּרְזֶל וּבַמְּגֵרוֹת וְכֵן יַעֲשֶׂה דָּוִיד לְכֹל
ד עָרֵי בְנֵי־עַמּוֹן וַיָּשָׁב דָּוִיד וְכָל־הָעָם יְרוּשָׁלִָם: וַיְהִי אַחֲרֵי־כֵן וַתַּעֲמֹד
מִלְחָמָה בְּגֶזֶר עִם־פְּלִשְׁתִּים אָז הִכָּה סִבְּכַי הַחֻשָׁתִי אֶת־סִפַּי מִילִדֵי הָרְפָאִים
ה וַיִּכָּנֵעוּ: וַתְּהִי־עוֹד מִלְחָמָה אֶת־פְּלִשְׁתִּים וַיַּךְ אֶלְחָנָן בֶּן־יָעוּר אֶת־ יָעִיר
ו לַחְמִי אֲחִי גָּלְיָת הַגִּתִּי וְעֵץ חֲנִיתוֹ כִּמְנוֹר אֹרְגִים: וַתְּהִי־עוֹד מִלְחָמָה
בְּגַת וַיְהִי ׀ אִישׁ מִדָּה וְאֶצְבְּעֹתָיו שֵׁשׁ־וָשֵׁשׁ עֶשְׂרִים וְאַרְבַּע וְגַם־הוּא נוֹלַד
ז ח לְהָרָפָא: וַיְחָרֵף אֶת־יִשְׂרָאֵל וַיַּכֵּהוּ יְהוֹנָתָן בֶּן־שִׁמְעָא אֲחִי דָוִיד: אֵל נוּלְּדוּ
א א לְהָרָפָא בְּגַת וַיִּפְּלוּ בְיַד־דָּוִיד וּבְיַד־עֲבָדָיו: וַיַּעֲמֹד שָׂטָן עַל־יִשְׂרָאֵל
ב וַיָּסֶת אֶת־דָּוִיד לִמְנוֹת אֶת־יִשְׂרָאֵל: וַיֹּאמֶר דָּוִיד אֶל־יוֹאָב וְאֶל־שָׂרֵי הָעָם לְכוּ
סִפְרוּ אֶת־יִשְׂרָאֵל מִבְּאֵר שֶׁבַע וְעַד־דָּן וְהָבִיאוּ אֵלַי וְאֵדְעָה אֶת־מִסְפָּרָם:

DISCUSSION

20:2 | **David took the crown of their king:** The considerable weight of this crown could attest to the fact that the crown was not worn by a king; rather, it was placed on the head of an idol (see *Targum* and Rashi, II Samuel 12:30; *Avoda Zara* 44a). Since a talent of gold weighs at least 30 kg, it would be very uncomfortable to wear it on one's head. Perhaps this magnificent crown was placed on David's head only briefly, to underscore his victory over Amon (see Radak).

20:3 | **So David would do to all the cities of the children of Amon:** The war between Israel and Amon was part of an ancient struggle also mentioned in the era of Yiftah (Judges 10–11). Although the Amonites were not a large nation, their kingdom remained stable for a great many years. Following the national insult involving the disgracing of the emissaries of the king of Israel, David sought to break the power of this kingdom for an extended period, to intimidate the surrounding nations and restore Israel's national pride (see Abravanel, II Samuel 12:31).

21:1 | **And incited David:** The verse creates the impression that counting Israel was a prohibited act with dangerous consequences. This conclusion can also be indirectly inferred from the Torah. It has been suggested that reducing Israel into defined classifications and mere numbers minimizes the kindness of God, which is unquantifiable. Therefore, the attempt to count and delineate the people leads to the antithesis of the outpouring of divine grace. A census threatens the very essence of Israel, and consequently the people should be counted only indirectly (see Genesis 15:5, 32:12; Exodus 30:11–16, and commentary ad loc.; I Samuel 15:4; Hosea 2:1; I Chronicles 27:23; *Yoma* 22b).

BACKGROUND

20:3 | **With saws, with iron picks, and with axes:** These are different tools used in quarrying, cutting, and smoothing stone. Some explain that David punished the Amonites by imposing upon them forced labor in quarries. However, others assert that these were instruments of torture. There is an opinion that iron picks are heavy wooden boards with iron teeth on the bottom used for threshing. An animal drags the board over the grain, which separates the kernels from chaff (see also Isaiah 41:15).

both important and necessary. It is possible that the king was motivated by a desire to act in the manner of the rest of the civilized countries.

3 **Yoav said: May the Lord add to His people as they are, one hundred times; surely, my lord the king, they are all servants to my lord.** There is no agitation, or revolt, for which you must prepare. **Why would my lord request this** matter? Since it is unnecessary, **why should it,** the census, **be a cause of guilt for Israel?** Yoav, who typically followed David's orders even when there was room for hesitation, feels that in this situation it is preferable to refrain from following the king's orders, as this census is liable to bring guilt upon Israel.

4 **The king's directive prevailed over Yoav.** David was decisive in his order. In other instances the king accepted Yoav's counsel even when it did not please him, but here the idea that had entered David's mind allowed him no rest, even though it was unclear what he stood to gain from the census. **And Yoav,** despite his reservations, **went out and traveled throughout Israel,** to conduct a census of the population, **and came** back **to Jerusalem.**

5 **Yoav gave the number of the census of the people to David. All of Israel was one million one hundred thousand men, wielders of the sword.** The census did not include women and children. Even David's greatest campaigns did not require that large a number of warriors,[300] but it seems that the official justification for the census was military, and therefore only men who could serve in the military were counted. **And Judah,** which was considered a distinct military unit and was therefore counted separately,[301] **was four hundred seventy thousand men, wielders of the sword.** It is likely that these round figures were based on estimates rather than a precise number of counted individuals, but Yoav nonetheless objected to the idea.

6 **He did not count Levi,** which was scattered among the other tribes, and did not have its own territory or participate in the military, **and Benjamin,** a small tribe, which had suffered many casualties in a civil war, from which it had not yet entirely recovered, **among them,** the rest of Israel, **for the king's directive was abhorrent** and unacceptable **to Yoav.** He therefore sought to avoid fully implementing the king's command.[302]

The Punishment in the Wake of the Census

I CHRONICLES 21:7–17

7 **It was displeasing in the eyes of God about this matter, and He smote Israel.** Presumably, a disease or plague spread among the people.[303]

8 **David said to God: I have sinned greatly in that I have performed this action; now, please excuse,** forgive, **the iniquity of Your servant, as I have been very foolish.**

9 **The Lord spoke to Gad, David's seer.** In addition to Natan the prophet, Gad, who was also a prophet, occasionally advised David. God instructed Gad, **saying:**[304]

10 **Go and speak to David, saying: So said the Lord: Three** options **I am extending against you,** or presenting to you; **choose for yourself one of them, and I will do it to you.** One of these will be your punishment.

11 **Gad came to David, and said to him: So said the Lord:** You must decide. **Accept upon yourself**

12 **either three years of famine,** which is one option; **or three months to be killed before your foes,** with your men killed, **and the sword of your enemies will be able to reach you.** You will not suffer a complete defeat, but many of your soldiers will die in battle. **Or** the third option: For **three days the sword of the Lord** will come, **and** there will be **pestilence,** a severe, contagious disease, **in the land, and the angel of the Lord ravaging throughout the borders of Israel. Now consider what word I shall return to my sender.** As God's messenger, I must deliver your response to Him.

13 **David said to Gad: I am greatly distressed,** as I have caused this tragedy through my own sins. Nevertheless, as I must choose between these possibilities, **please let me fall into the hand of the Lord;** I prefer the plague of pestilence, which is dependent upon the hand of God alone, **as His mercies are great,** and one can pray for the cessation of the plague; **and let me not fall into the hand of man.** I do not wish to lose in battle, or to fall prey to famine, which is an ongoing cause of suffering, and which can also be considered in the hands of man, as the hungry become dependent upon the compassion of other people.[305]

14 **The Lord set a pestilence against Israel, and seventy thousand men fell from Israel.**

15 At a certain stage **God sent an angel to Jerusalem in order to ravage it, and when he was** about **to ravage** the city, **God saw and reconsidered the evil,** for just as David had said, God's mercies are great. **He said to the ravaging angel: Enough, now release your hand** from striking Israel further. **The angel of the Lord was standing at the threshing floor of Ornan the Yevusite.**

16 Details of how these events unfolded are now related: **David lifted his eyes and saw the angel of the Lord standing between the earth and the heavens, and his sword was drawn in his hand, outstretched over Jerusalem,** as a sign that he was about to destroy the city. **David and the elders, covered**

ג וַיֹּאמֶר יוֹאָב יוֹסֵף יְהוָה עַל־עַמּוֹ ׀ כָּהֵם מֵאָה פְעָמִים הֲלֹא אֲדֹנִי הַמֶּלֶךְ כֻּלָּם
ד לַאדֹנִי לַעֲבָדִים לָמָּה יְבַקֵּשׁ זֹאת אֲדֹנִי לָמָּה יִהְיֶה לְאַשְׁמָה לְיִשְׂרָאֵל׃ וּדְבַר־
ה הַמֶּלֶךְ חָזַק עַל־יוֹאָב וַיֵּצֵא יוֹאָב וַיִּתְהַלֵּךְ בְּכָל־יִשְׂרָאֵל וַיָּבֹא יְרוּשָׁלִָם׃ וַיִּתֵּן יוֹאָב
אֶת־מִסְפַּר מִפְקַד־הָעָם אֶל־דָּוִיד וַיְהִי כָל־יִשְׂרָאֵל אֶלֶף אֲלָפִים וּמֵאָה אֶלֶף אִישׁ
ו שֹׁלֵף חֶרֶב וִיהוּדָה אַרְבַּע מֵאוֹת וְשִׁבְעִים אֶלֶף אִישׁ שֹׁלֵף חָרֶב׃ וְלֵוִי וּבִנְיָמִן לֹא
ז פָקַד בְּתוֹכָם כִּי־נִתְעַב דְּבַר־הַמֶּלֶךְ אֶת־יוֹאָב׃ וַיֵּרַע בְּעֵינֵי הָאֱלֹהִים עַל־הַדָּבָר
ח הַזֶּה וַיַּךְ אֶת־יִשְׂרָאֵל׃ וַיֹּאמֶר דָּוִיד אֶל־הָאֱלֹהִים חָטָאתִי מְאֹד אֲשֶׁר
עָשִׂיתִי אֶת־הַדָּבָר הַזֶּה וְעַתָּה הַעֲבֶר־נָא אֶת־עֲווֹן עַבְדְּךָ כִּי נִסְכַּלְתִּי
ט מְאֹד׃ וַיְדַבֵּר יְהוָה אֶל־גָּד חֹזֵה דָוִיד לֵאמֹר׃ לֵךְ וְדִבַּרְתָּ אֶל־דָּוִיד
לֵאמֹר כֹּה אָמַר יְהוָה שָׁלוֹשׁ אֲנִי נֹטֶה עָלֶיךָ בְּחַר־לְךָ אַחַת מֵהֵנָּה וְאֶעֱשֶׂה־לָּךְ׃
יא יב וַיָּבֹא גָד אֶל־דָּוִיד וַיֹּאמֶר לוֹ כֹּה־אָמַר יְהוָה קַבֶּל־לָךְ׃ אִם־שָׁלוֹשׁ שָׁנִים רָעָב
וְאִם־שְׁלֹשָׁה חֳדָשִׁים נִסְפֶּה מִפְּנֵי־צָרֶיךָ וְחֶרֶב אוֹיְבֶיךָ ׀ לְמַשֶּׂגֶת וְאִם־שְׁלֹשֶׁת
יָמִים חֶרֶב יְהוָה ׀ וְדֶבֶר בָּאָרֶץ וּמַלְאַךְ יְהוָה מַשְׁחִית בְּכָל־גְּבוּל יִשְׂרָאֵל וְעַתָּה
יג רְאֵה מָה־אָשִׁיב אֶת־שֹׁלְחִי דָּבָר׃ וַיֹּאמֶר דָּוִיד אֶל־גָּד צַר־לִי מְאֹד
יד אֶפְּלָה־נָּא בְיַד־יְהוָה כִּי־רַבִּים רַחֲמָיו מְאֹד וּבְיַד־אָדָם אַל־אֶפֹּל׃ וַיִּתֵּן יְהוָה
טו דֶּבֶר בְּיִשְׂרָאֵל וַיִּפֹּל מִיִּשְׂרָאֵל שִׁבְעִים אֶלֶף אִישׁ׃ וַיִּשְׁלַח הָאֱלֹהִים ׀ מַלְאָךְ ׀
לִירוּשָׁלִַם לְהַשְׁחִיתָהּ וּכְהַשְׁחִית רָאָה יְהוָה וַיִּנָּחֶם עַל־הָרָעָה וַיֹּאמֶר לַמַּלְאָךְ
הַמַּשְׁחִית רַב עַתָּה הֶרֶף יָדֶךָ וּמַלְאַךְ יְהוָה עֹמֵד עִם־גֹּרֶן אָרְנָן הַיְבוּסִי׃
טז וַיִּשָּׂא דָוִיד אֶת־עֵינָיו וַיַּרְא אֶת־מַלְאַךְ יְהוָה עֹמֵד בֵּין הָאָרֶץ וּבֵין הַשָּׁמַיִם וְחַרְבּוֹ
שְׁלוּפָה בְּיָדוֹ נְטוּיָה עַל־יְרוּשָׁלִָם וַיִּפֹּל דָּוִיד וְהַזְּקֵנִים מְכֻסִּים בַּשַּׂקִּים עַל־פְּנֵיהֶם׃

in sackcloth, fell on their faces. Some interpret the verse in this manner: David fell on his face in terror or respect, whereas the elders did not see the angel, as they were clothed in sackcloth that covered their faces.

17 **David said to God: Wasn't it I who said to count the peo-**
ple? It is I who sinned and I who have done harm, and these sheep, Israel, **what have they done?** It is not right for them to be harmed. **Lord my God, please, let Your hand be against me, and against my father's house;** it is better for the punishment to fall upon myself and my family, **but as for Your people, there should be no plague.**

The Altar and the End of the Plague

I CHRONICLES 21:18–22:1

18 **The angel of the Lord said to Gad** in a prophetic vision,[306] **to**
say to David, that David should go up and establish an altar to the Lord on the threshing floor of Ornan the Yevusite.[D] David did not require an intermediary in order to pray, but as he lacked the power to receive the word of God directly, Gad once again served as the intermediary.

19 **David went up at the word of Gad that he spoke in the name of the Lord.**

20 **Ornan turned and saw the angel; his four sons were with**
him, hiding on the threshing floor, as they thought it best to hide during the plague. **And Ornan** emerged from his hiding place and **was threshing wheat.**

21 **David came to Ornan; Ornan looked and saw David, and he**
emerged from the threshing floor, and he prostrated himself to David with his face to the ground.

22 **David said to Ornan: Give me the site of this threshing**
floor, and I will build upon it an altar to the Lord; give it to me for a full price and then **the plague will cease from the people.**

23 **Ornan said to David: Take it for yourself** as a gift, **and let**
my lord the king do what is good in his eyes. Furthermore, **see, I have given you the cattle** that are here **for burnt offerings, and the threshing sledges,**[B] the boards that are typically dragged by the animals, **for wood** with which to burn the offerings, **and the wheat** on the threshing floor **for the meal offering; I have given it all.** I am prepared to give all of it, free of charge.

Threshing with a threshing sledge

Wheat kernels

24 **King David said to Ornan: No, but I will buy it for full price;**
I insist on purchasing the site, **as I will not take that which is yours for the Lord and offer up a burnt offering for free.** I cannot bring an offering to God on a site that does not belong to me. Since I wish to build an altar here, I will pay for the site.

Threshing sledge

25 **David gave to Ornan for**
the place six hundred shekels of gold by weight. Apparently, David did not purchase the threshing floor alone; rather, he purchased a larger plot of land.[307] According to the continuation of the story, a large part of the mountain, or perhaps even all of it, belonged to Ornan. David acquired the entire area of Moriah, which at that time was located outside the city, in order to establish the Temple there.

26 **David built there an altar to the Lord, and he offered up**
burnt offerings and peace offerings. He called to the Lord, and He answered him from the heavens with fire that descended **on the altar of burnt offering.** The descent of the fire was a sign for David, of his reconciliation with God.

27 **The Lord said to the angel,** God instructed him to abandon
the attack, **and he returned his sword to its sheath.** Up to this point, the angel had remained in a state of waiting, ready to continue or desist.

28 **At that time, when David saw that the Lord had answered**
him on the threshing floor of Ornan the Yevusite, he slaughtered offerings there.

29 At this point, some background information is provided: **The**
Tabernacle of the Lord, which Moses had made in the wilderness, and the altar of burnt offering were, at that time, at the shrine in Givon, not in Jerusalem.

30 **David had not been able to go before it,** the altar at Givon,
to seek God, as he had been afraid due to the sword of the

יז ויאמר דויד אל-האלהים הלא אני אמרתי למנות בעם ואני-הוא אשר-חטאתי
והרע הרעותי ואלה הצאן מה עשו יהוה אלהי תהי נא ידך בי ובבית אבי
יח ובעמך לא למגפה: ומלאך יהוה אמר אל-גד לאמר לדויד כי ׀
יט יעלה דויד להקים מזבח ליהוה בגרן ארנן היבסי: ויעל דויד בדבר-גד אשר
כ דבר בשם יהוה: וישב ארנן וירא את-המלאך וארבעת בניו עמו מתחבאים
כא וארנן דש חטים: ויבא דויד עד-ארנן ויבט ארנן וירא את-דויד ויצא מן-הגרן
כב וישתחו לדויד אפים ארצה: ויאמר דויד אל-ארנן תנה-לי מקום הגרן ואבנה-
כג בו מזבח ליהוה בכסף מלא תנהו לי ותעצר המגפה מעל העם: ויאמר ארנן
אל-דויד קח-לך ויעש אדני המלך הטוב בעיניו ראה נתתי הבקר לעלות
כד והמורגים לעצים והחטים למנחה הכל נתתי: ויאמר המלך דויד לארנן לא
כי-קנה אקנה בכסף מלא כי לא-אשא אשר-לך ליהוה והעלות עולה חנם:
כה כו ויתן דויד לארנן במקום שקלי זהב משקל שש מאות: ויבן שם דויד מזבח
ליהוה ויעל עלות ושלמים ויקרא אל-יהוה ויענהו באש מן-השמים על מזבח
כז כח העלה: ויאמר יהוה למלאך וישב חרבו אל-נדנה: בעת ההיא
כט בראות דויד כי-ענהו יהוה בגרן ארנן היבוסי ויזבח שם: ומשכן יהוה אשר-
ל עשה משה במדבר ומזבח העולה בעת ההיא בבמה בגבעון: ולא-יכל דויד

DISCUSSION

21:18 | **Ornan the Yevusite:** No background information is provided here for Ornan. Some claim that he was the former king of Jerusalem, as elsewhere he is called Aravna the king (II Samuel 24:23). He continued to live among the Yevusites, and David treated him with respect. The Sages relate that his descendants remained in Jerusalem for generations, as due to a certain tradition of theirs they did not wish to leave the city. It is possible that Ornan and his descendants achieved the status of *ger toshav* as gentiles who observed the seven Noahide commandments, and Israel allowed them to continue to live in the city while providing them with a livelihood and a stipend (see *Avoda Zara* 24b; Jerusalem Talmud, *Pe'a* 8:7).

BACKGROUND

21:23 | **Threshing sledges [*morigim*]:** A *morag* is an agricultural implement that is dragged on the ground, consisting of a wooden board to which sharp stones or pieces of iron are appended. In the book of Isaiah (41:15) it is called a threshing board with teeth. According to linguistic scholars, the name *morag* refers to the most critical part of the implement, the stone chips or metal blades that are appended to the board, and which crumble and separate the wheat kernels from the chaff.

angel of the Lord. As long as the angel was standing above him with sword in hand, David feared to leave the city. Therefore, he could not sacrifice offerings in the appropriate place. Instead of traveling to Givon, David built a new altar at Gad's command, upon which he sacrificed offerings of atonement.[308] The Ark of the Covenant had been brought to Jerusalem because David wanted it near him, but he was not certain that this was the suitable site for it. In the meantime, therefore, he situated the ark in a tent rather than in a permanent structure, and also refrained from transferring the rest of the vessels of the Tabernacle to Jerusalem.

22 1 **David said,** after seeing the angel in a vision, and seeing the fire descend from heaven: **This is** the site where **the House of the Lord God** will eventually be built,[309] **and this is the altar of burnt offerings for Israel.**

David's Preparations and Plans for Construction of the Temple

I CHRONICLES 22:2–19

2 **David said to assemble the strangers,**[D] foreigners, **who were in the Land of Israel,** in order to task them with the preparatory stages of the construction of the Temple; **and he appointed masons to hew hewn stones,** in order to use them **to build the House of God.**

Preparing hewn stones, illustration based on fresco in the tomb of Rekhmire, Egypt, Eighteenth Dynasty, sixteenth to thirteenth century BCE

3 **David prepared iron in abundance for the nails for the doors of the gates, and for the couplings,** devices or beams that connected the parts of the building. Although none of the Temple vessels contained iron,[310] it was used in the preparation of certain parts of the structure that required strength and height. **And bronze in abundance without weight;** there was so much bronze, they didn't even weigh it.

4 **And cedar trees without number, for the Sidonians and Tyrians brought cedar trees in abundance to David.**

5 **David said: Solomon my son is young and tender** in years,[311] **and the House to be built for the Lord is to be raised upward, for renown and for splendor throughout all the**

Delivery of cedar trees from Lebanon, illustration based on relief from palace of Sargon II, Dur-Sharrukin, Iraq, 716–713 BCE

lands. It will take time for Solomon to assume full control over the kingdom, and to be able to build such a marvelous structure. **I will prepare now for him. David prepared** materials for the Temple **in abundance before his death.**

6 **He called for Solomon his son and commanded him to build a House for the Lord God of Israel.** This is the first command that David gave his son after he was crowned king of Israel and became the official heir to the throne.

7 **David said to Solomon: My son, I had it in my heart,** I wanted, **to build a House to the name of the Lord my God.**

8 **The word of the Lord was upon me, saying: You have shed blood in abundance, and have waged great wars; you shall not build a House to My name, because you have shed much blood on the earth before Me.** No one is accusing you of murder, but you have killed many people. This explanation for why David was barred from building the Temple does not appear anywhere else.[312]

9 **Behold, a son is born to you, he will be a man of rest,** not a warrior like you,[313] **and I will give him rest from all his**

כב א לָלֶכֶת לְפָנָיו לִדְרֹשׁ אֱלֹהִים כִּי נִבְעַת מִפְּנֵי חֶרֶב מַלְאַךְ יְהוָה: וַיֹּאמֶר דָּוִיד זֶה
ב הוּא בֵּית יְהוָה הָאֱלֹהִים וְזֶה־מִּזְבֵּחַ לְעֹלָה לְיִשְׂרָאֵל: וַיֹּאמֶר דָּוִיד
לִכְנוֹס אֶת־הַגֵּרִים אֲשֶׁר בְּאֶרֶץ יִשְׂרָאֵל וַיַּעֲמֵד חֹצְבִים לַחְצוֹב אַבְנֵי גָזִית לִבְנוֹת
ג בֵּית הָאֱלֹהִים: וּבַרְזֶל ׀ לָרֹב לַמִּסְמְרִים לְדַלְתוֹת הַשְּׁעָרִים וְלַמְחַבְּרוֹת הֵכִין
ד דָּוִיד וּנְחֹשֶׁת לָרֹב אֵין מִשְׁקָל: וַעֲצֵי אֲרָזִים לְאֵין מִסְפָּר כִּי־הֵבִיאוּ הַצִּידֹנִים
ה וְהַצֹּרִים עֲצֵי אֲרָזִים לָרֹב לְדָוִיד: וַיֹּאמֶר דָּוִיד שְׁלֹמֹה בְנִי נַעַר וָרָךְ
וְהַבַּיִת לִבְנוֹת לַיהוָה לְהַגְדִּיל ׀ לְמַעְלָה לְשֵׁם וּלְתִפְאֶרֶת לְכָל־הָאֲרָצוֹת אָכִינָה
ו נָּא לוֹ וַיָּכֶן דָּוִיד לָרֹב לִפְנֵי מוֹתוֹ: וַיִּקְרָא לִשְׁלֹמֹה בְנוֹ וַיְצַוֵּהוּ לִבְנוֹת בַּיִת לַיהוָה
ז אֱלֹהֵי יִשְׂרָאֵל: וַיֹּאמֶר דָּוִיד לִשְׁלֹמֹה בנו אֲנִי הָיָה עִם־לְבָבִי לִבְנוֹת בְּנִי
ח בַּיִת לְשֵׁם יְהוָה אֱלֹהָי: וַיְהִי עָלַי דְּבַר־יְהוָה לֵאמֹר דָּם לָרֹב שָׁפַכְתָּ וּמִלְחָמוֹת
ט גְּדֹלוֹת עָשִׂיתָ לֹא־תִבְנֶה בַיִת לִשְׁמִי כִּי דָּמִים רַבִּים שָׁפַכְתָּ אַרְצָה לְפָנָי: הִנֵּה־
בֵן נוֹלָד לָךְ הוּא יִהְיֶה אִישׁ מְנוּחָה וַהֲנִיחוֹתִי לוֹ מִכָּל־אוֹיְבָיו מִסָּבִיב כִּי שְׁלֹמֹה
י יִהְיֶה שְׁמוֹ וְשָׁלוֹם וָשֶׁקֶט אֶתֵּן עַל־יִשְׂרָאֵל בְּיָמָיו: הוּא־יִבְנֶה בַיִת לִשְׁמִי וְהוּא
יִהְיֶה־לִּי לְבֵן וַאֲנִי־לוֹ לְאָב וַהֲכִינוֹתִי כִּסֵּא מַלְכוּתוֹ עַל־יִשְׂרָאֵל עַד־עוֹלָם:
יא עַתָּה בְנִי יְהִי יְהוָה עִמָּךְ וְהִצְלַחְתָּ וּבָנִיתָ בֵּית יְהוָה אֱלֹהֶיךָ כַּאֲשֶׁר דִּבֶּר עָלֶיךָ:

surrounding enemies; for Solomon [*Shelomo*] shall be his name, and I will grant for Israel peace [*shalom*] and tranquility in his days.

10 **He will build a House to My name; he,** with his unique status, **will be a son to Me, and I to him a father, and I will establish the throne of his kingdom over Israel forever.**

11 After informing Solomon of what God had told him in a prophecy, David continues with his own blessing: **Now, my son, may the Lord be with you and may you succeed in building the House of the Lord your God, as He has spoken in your regard.** I have attended to matters of security so you will receive a kingdom where all potential enemies are subjugated to you, and the reins of power are under your control.

DISCUSSION

22:2 | **David said to assemble the strangers:** The Land of Israel was divided into tribal portions, which were subdivided into family estates. It was prohibited to permanently sell these estates, as they automatically reverted to their original owners in the Jubilee Year (see Leviticus 25:8–24). Therefore, any land that was suitable for agriculture was already in the possession of the Israelites, and in their hands alone. Due to the unique economic and political structure of the country at that time, all foreigners who arrived in Israel were dispersed throughout the land. It is unlikely that these foreigners were merchants, as successful merchants are not typically migrants. Rather, they were hired to work in the fields of Israelite landowners, or they were untrained artisans who made a living from odd jobs. David assembled these foreigners to prepare the infrastructure for the House of God. He did not impose servitude upon them, but provided them with state-sponsored labor.

12 **Yet may the Lord give you prudence and understanding** to lead the country, **and command you over Israel,** to rule over them appropriately, **to observe the Torah of the Lord your God.**
13 **Then you will succeed, if you take care to perform the statutes and the ordinances that the Lord commanded Moses concerning Israel; be strong and courageous; do not fear, do not be frightened.** In order for your reign to succeed, you must lead the people with wisdom and integrity, while observing the commandments of the Torah.
14 **Behold, in my affliction,** an expression of modesty, **I have prepared for the House of the Lord** a weight of **one hundred thousand talents of gold,** a very large amount, **and one million talents of silver.** Although there were not many silver vessels in the Temple, this silver was also used for payments for purchases for the Temple service. **And of bronze and of iron without weight,** he did not have it weighed, **for it is in abundance, and timber and stones I prepared, and you** too **should add to them,** as presumably even that massive amount will not suffice for the needs of the Temple.
15 **With you there are workmen in abundance, hewers and workers in stone and wood, and everyone who is wise,** skillful, **in all craftsmanship.**
16 **To the gold, the silver, the bronze, and the iron** that have already been amassed, **there is no number. Rise and take action, and may the Lord be with you.**
17 **David commanded all the princes of Israel to help Solomon his son** in this great project, saying to them as follows:
18 **Isn't the Lord your God with you? He has given you respite from** your enemies **all around, as He has delivered the inhabitants of the land into my hand, and the land is conquered before the Lord and before His people.**
19 **Now set your heart and your soul to seek the Lord your God** and act for His sake. **Rise and build the Temple of the Lord God, to bring the Ark of the Covenant of the Lord and the sacred vessels of God into the House that is being built for the name of the Lord.** This is one of David's exhortations to Solomon, although it does not deal with personal matters. David did all he could to prepare for the construction of the Temple and tended to all the organizational aspects that could be coordinated in advance. It is stated elsewhere that David, together with Samuel the prophet, prepared a plan for the service schedule in the future Temple. After amassing the raw materials, he commanded Solomon to accept the sacred task upon himself, and also encouraged the other leaders of Israel to participate in the building of the House of God.

Lists Connected to Those Serving in the Temple

I CHRONICLES 23:1–26:32

This part of the book is comprised of additional genealogical lists, as well as rosters organized by King David related to roles and functions to be performed in the future Temple. These are divided into various divisions or watches, the final formulation of which was devised in David's final year.[314]

The Census and Division of the Levites

I CHRONICLES 23:1–32

This section describes how David assembled the Levites and assigned them different tasks in the Temple, some as gatekeepers and singers, and some in administrative positions.

23 1 **David was old and full of days, and he crowned Solomon his son king over Israel,** as is related in detail in the book of Kings.[315]
2 **He gathered all the princes of Israel, and the priests and the Levites,** for another census; one that did not seek to count all the tribes of Israel. Since this was a necessary census, he is not condemned at all.[316]
3 **The Levites were counted from thirty years old and above,** the age from which they start performing their service,[317] **and their number by their head count of males was thirty-eight thousand.**
4 **Of these, to supervise** and manage **the labor of** the organizational aspects of the service in **the House of the Lord, twenty-four thousand; and** additional **officers and judges, six thousand,**
5 **and four thousand gatekeepers, and four thousand praising the Lord with the instruments that I made for praise.** This is apparently a quote from David, in which he claims that he was involved in the preparation of some of the Temple's musical instruments.
6 **David divided them into divisions** based on their patrilineal houses. **For the sons of Levi** son of Jacob, he divided them into three groups: The families of **Gershon, Kehat, and Merari.**
7 **For the Gershonites: Ladan and Shimi.**
8 **The sons of Ladan: Yehiel** was **the leader, and Zetam and Yoel,** a total of **three** heads of patrilineal houses.
9 **The sons of Shimi: Shelomit,** which here, atypically, is a man's name, **Haziel, and Haran, three. These were the heads of the patrilineal houses of Ladan.** It appears that some of the sons of Shimi were considered heads of the patrilineal houses of the sons of Ladan, their uncle. Alternatively, the reference might be

יב אַךְ יִתֶּן־לְּךָ יְהוָה שֵׂכֶל וּבִינָה וִיצַוְּךָ עַל־יִשְׂרָאֵל וְלִשְׁמוֹר אֶת־תּוֹרַת יְהוָה אֱלֹהֶיךָ׃
יג אָז תַּצְלִיחַ אִם־תִּשְׁמוֹר לַעֲשׂוֹת אֶת־הַחֻקִּים וְאֶת־הַמִּשְׁפָּטִים אֲשֶׁר צִוָּה יְהוָה
יד אֶת־מֹשֶׁה עַל־יִשְׂרָאֵל חֲזַק וֶאֱמָץ אַל־תִּירָא וְאַל־תֵּחָת׃ וְהִנֵּה בְעָנְיִי הֲכִינוֹתִי
לְבֵית־יְהוָה זָהָב כִּכָּרִים מֵאָה־אֶלֶף וְכֶסֶף אֶלֶף אֲלָפִים כִּכָּרִים וְלַנְּחֹשֶׁת וְלַבַּרְזֶל
טו אֵין מִשְׁקָל כִּי לָרֹב הָיָה וְעֵצִים וַאֲבָנִים הֲכִינוֹתִי וַעֲלֵיהֶם תּוֹסִיף׃ וְעִמְּךָ לָרֹב
טז עֹשֵׂי מְלָאכָה חֹצְבִים וְחָרָשֵׁי אֶבֶן וָעֵץ וְכָל־חָכָם בְּכָל־מְלָאכָה׃ לַזָּהָב לַכֶּסֶף
יז וְלַנְּחֹשֶׁת וְלַבַּרְזֶל אֵין מִסְפָּר קוּם וַעֲשֵׂה וִיהִי יְהוָה עִמָּךְ׃ וַיְצַו דָּוִיד לְכָל־שָׂרֵי
יח יִשְׂרָאֵל לַעְזֹר לִשְׁלֹמֹה בְנוֹ׃ הֲלֹא יְהוָה אֱלֹהֵיכֶם עִמָּכֶם וְהֵנִיחַ לָכֶם מִסָּבִיב כִּי ׀
יט נָתַן בְּיָדִי אֵת יֹשְׁבֵי הָאָרֶץ וְנִכְבְּשָׁה הָאָרֶץ לִפְנֵי יְהוָה וְלִפְנֵי עַמּוֹ׃ עַתָּה תְּנוּ ט
לְבַבְכֶם וְנַפְשְׁכֶם לִדְרוֹשׁ לַיהוָה אֱלֹהֵיכֶם וְקוּמוּ וּבְנוּ אֶת־מִקְדַּשׁ יְהוָה הָאֱלֹהִים
לְהָבִיא אֶת־אֲרוֹן בְּרִית־יְהוָה וּכְלֵי קֹדֶשׁ הָאֱלֹהִים לַבַּיִת הַנִּבְנֶה לְשֵׁם־יְהוָה׃
כג א ב וְדָוִיד זָקֵן וְשָׂבַע יָמִים וַיַּמְלֵךְ אֶת־שְׁלֹמֹה בְנוֹ עַל־יִשְׂרָאֵל׃ וַיֶּאֱסֹף
ג אֶת־כָּל־שָׂרֵי יִשְׂרָאֵל וְהַכֹּהֲנִים וְהַלְוִיִּם׃ וַיִּסָּפְרוּ הַלְוִיִּם מִבֶּן שְׁלֹשִׁים שָׁנָה וָמָעְלָה
ד וַיְהִי מִסְפָּרָם לְגֻלְגְּלֹתָם לִגְבָרִים שְׁלֹשִׁים וּשְׁמוֹנָה אָלֶף׃ מֵאֵלֶּה לְנַצֵּחַ עַל־מְלֶאכֶת
ה בֵּית־יְהוָה עֶשְׂרִים וְאַרְבָּעָה אָלֶף וְשֹׁטְרִים וְשֹׁפְטִים שֵׁשֶׁת אֲלָפִים׃ וְאַרְבַּעַת
אֲלָפִים שֹׁעֲרִים וְאַרְבַּעַת אֲלָפִים מְהַלְלִים לַיהוָה בַּכֵּלִים אֲשֶׁר עָשִׂיתִי לְהַלֵּל׃
ו ז וַיֶּחָלְקֵם דָּוִיד מַחְלְקוֹת לִבְנֵי לֵוִי לְגֵרְשׁוֹן קְהָת וּמְרָרִי׃ לַגֵּרְשֻׁנִּי
ח לַעְדָּן וְשִׁמְעִי׃ בְּנֵי לַעְדָּן הָרֹאשׁ יְחִיאֵל וְזֵתָם וְיוֹאֵל שְׁלֹשָׁה׃
ט בְּנֵי שִׁמְעִי שלמות וַחֲזִיאֵל וְהָרָן שְׁלֹשָׁה אֵלֶּה רָאשֵׁי הָאָבוֹת לְלַעְדָּן׃ שְׁלֹמִית

to a different Shimi, who was one of the descendants of Ladan, and not Shimi son of Gershon.[318]

10 **The sons of Shimi** son of Gershon:[319] **Yahat, Zina, Ye'ush, and Beria. These were the sons of Shimi, four.**

11 **Yahat was the leader and Ziza the second. Ye'ush and Beria did not have many sons and they** therefore **became a patrilineal house in one reckoning.** They were classified as a single patrilineal house in terms of their service.

12 **The sons of Kehat: Amram, Yitzhar, Hevron, and Uziel, four.**

13 **The sons of Amram: Aaron and Moses; Aaron was set apart to sanctify him as most holy, he and his sons forever,** as priests, **to burn offerings before the Lord, to serve Him** by bringing offerings upon the altar and within the Sanctuary, **and to bless in His name forever.** These duties of the sons of Aaron distinguished them from the rest of the descendants of Kehat.

14 But as for **Moses,** even though he was **the man of God, his sons will be accounted among the** rest of the **tribe of Levi.**

15 **The sons of Moses: Gershom and Eliezer.**

16 **The sons of Gershom: Shevuel the leader.**

17 **The sons of Eliezer were: Rehavya the leader. Eliezer had no other sons, but the sons of Rehavya were very numerous.** This branch of Moses's family was much larger than most Levite families.

18 **The sons of Yitzhar: Shelomit the leader.**

19 **The sons of Hevron: Yeriyahu the leader, Amarya the second, Yahaziyel the third, and Yekame'am the fourth.**

20 **The sons of Uziel: Mikha the leader and Yishiya the second.**

21 **The sons of Merari: Mahli and Mushi. The sons of Mahli: Elazar and Kish.**

22 **Elazar died, and he had no sons, only daughters; the sons of Kish their brothers married them.** The sons and daughters of the two brothers married each other, thereby keeping the family unified. There are other examples in the Bible where a cousin is referred to as a brother.[320]

23 **The sons of Mushi: Mahli, Eder, and Yeremot, three.**

24 **These were the sons of Levi by their patrilineal houses, the heads of the patrilineal houses by their head count, according to the number of names by their count,** all who were **performers of the labor for the service of the House of the Lord, from twenty years old**[D] **and above.**

25 **For David said: The Lord, God of Israel, has given respite to His people,** as the nation is no longer wandering from place to place, **and He dwells in Jerusalem forever,**

26 **and** therefore **the Levites also need not carry the Tabernacle and all its vessels for its service,** as was the case in the wilderness, as God's Temple will be permanently established in Jerusalem.

27 **For among the last matters of David was** his establishment of **the numbering of the sons of Levi from twenty years old and above,** and not from the age of thirty, as in the wilderness, when the main function of the Levites was to carry the sacred vessels.[321]

28 **For their station was alongside the sons of Aaron for the service of the House of the Lord, in the courtyards, and in the chambers, and in the purification of everything sacred, and the performance of the service of the House of God.** The Levites were tasked with the order and cleanliness of the courtyards and chambers, and the ritual purity of the holy places. It was incumbent upon them to remove all impurity found in the Temple and to ensure that no impure items entered the Temple. Furthermore, they were in charge of the service protocols in the Temple;

29 **and for** the preparation of **the bread of the arrangement,** the showbread, **and for the high-quality flour for meal offerings, and for the unleavened wafers, and for that which is on the pan, and for that which is boiled,** all of which are types of meal offerings, **and for all volume,**[B] vessels for measuring liquids, **and measure,** other kinds of measuring implements. It was the Levites, not the priests, who prepared the foods and vessels, and took pains to watch over them;

"And for all volume and measure." Reconstructions of measuring cups for the Temple service

Limestone measuring cup, Jerusalem, early Roman period

י יא וּבְנֵי שִׁמְעִי יַחַת זִינָא וִיעוּשׁ וּבְרִיעָה אֵלֶּה בְנֵי־שִׁמְעִי אַרְבָּעָה׃ וַיְהִי־יַחַת הָרֹאשׁ
וְזִיזָה הַשֵּׁנִי וִיעוּשׁ וּבְרִיעָה לֹא־הִרְבּוּ בָנִים וַיִּהְיוּ לְבֵית אָב לִפְקֻדָּה אֶחָת׃
יב יג בְּנֵי קְהָת עַמְרָם יִצְהָר חֶבְרוֹן וְעֻזִּיאֵל אַרְבָּעָה׃ בְּנֵי עַמְרָם אַהֲרֹן
וּמֹשֶׁה וַיִּבָּדֵל אַהֲרֹן לְהַקְדִּישׁוֹ קֹדֶשׁ קָדָשִׁים הוּא־וּבָנָיו עַד־עוֹלָם לְהַקְטִיר לִפְנֵי
יד יהוה לְשָׁרְתוֹ וּלְבָרֵךְ בִּשְׁמוֹ עַד־עוֹלָם׃ וּמֹשֶׁה אִישׁ הָאֱלֹהִים בָּנָיו יִקָּרְאוּ עַל־
טו טז שֵׁבֶט הַלֵּוִי׃ בְּנֵי מֹשֶׁה גֵּרְשׁוֹם וֶאֱלִיעֶזֶר׃ בְּנֵי גֵרְשׁוֹם שְׁבוּאֵל הָרֹאשׁ׃
יז וַיִּהְיוּ בְנֵי־אֱלִיעֶזֶר רְחַבְיָה הָרֹאשׁ וְלֹא־הָיָה לֶאֱלִיעֶזֶר בָּנִים אֲחֵרִים וּבְנֵי רְחַבְיָה
יח יט רָבוּ לְמָעְלָה׃ בְּנֵי יִצְהָר שְׁלֹמִית הָרֹאשׁ׃ בְּנֵי חֶבְרוֹן יְרִיָּהוּ
כ הָרֹאשׁ אֲמַרְיָה הַשֵּׁנִי יַחֲזִיאֵל הַשְּׁלִישִׁי וִיקַמְעָם הָרְבִיעִי׃ בְּנֵי עֻזִּיאֵל מִיכָה
כא הָרֹאשׁ וְיִשִּׁיָּה הַשֵּׁנִי׃ בְּנֵי מְרָרִי מַחְלִי וּמוּשִׁי בְּנֵי מַחְלִי אֶלְעָזָר וְקִישׁ׃
כב כג וַיָּמָת אֶלְעָזָר וְלֹא־הָיוּ לוֹ בָּנִים כִּי אִם־בָּנוֹת וַיִּשָּׂאוּם בְּנֵי־קִישׁ אֲחֵיהֶם׃ בְּנֵי מוּשִׁי
כד מַחְלִי וְעֵדֶר וִירֵמוֹת שְׁלוֹשָׁה׃ אֵלֶּה בְנֵי־לֵוִי לְבֵית אֲבֹתֵיהֶם רָאשֵׁי הָאָבוֹת
לִפְקוּדֵיהֶם בְּמִסְפַּר שֵׁמוֹת לְגֻלְגְּלֹתָם עֹשֵׂה הַמְּלָאכָה לַעֲבֹדַת בֵּית יהוה מִבֶּן
כה עֶשְׂרִים שָׁנָה וָמָעְלָה׃ כִּי אָמַר דָּוִיד הֵנִיחַ יהוה אֱלֹהֵי־יִשְׂרָאֵל לְעַמּוֹ וַיִּשְׁכֹּן
כו בִּירוּשָׁלַםִ עַד־לְעוֹלָם׃ וְגַם לַלְוִיִּם אֵין־לָשֵׂאת אֶת־הַמִּשְׁכָּן וְאֶת־כָּל־כֵּלָיו
כז לַעֲבֹדָתוֹ׃ כִּי בְדִבְרֵי דָוִיד הָאַחֲרוֹנִים הֵמָּה מִסְפַּר בְּנֵי־לֵוִי מִבֶּן עֶשְׂרִים שָׁנָה
כח וּלְמָעְלָה׃ כִּי מַעֲמָדָם לְיַד־בְּנֵי אַהֲרֹן לַעֲבֹדַת בֵּית יהוה עַל־הַחֲצֵרוֹת וְעַל־
כט הַלְּשָׁכוֹת וְעַל־טָהֳרַת לְכָל־קֹדֶשׁ וּמַעֲשֵׂה עֲבֹדַת בֵּית הָאֱלֹהִים׃ וּלְלֶחֶם הַמַּעֲרֶכֶת
וּלְסֹלֶת לְמִנְחָה וְלִרְקִיקֵי הַמַּצּוֹת וְלַמַּחֲבַת וְלַמֻּרְבֶּכֶת וּלְכָל־מְשׂוּרָה וּמִדָּה׃

DISCUSSION

23:24 | **From twenty years old:** Here, these younger Levites are included in the count of their respective groups, despite the fact that they were not completely initiated into service. The Levites would apparently begin their training as assistants to the other Levites at the age of twenty, and only when they reached the age of thirty would they perform their services independently (Numbers 4:3, 30, 39; see Malbim). Elsewhere in the Torah, it states that the Levites served from the age of twenty-five (Numbers 8:24). The Sages explain that this five-year difference accounts for their training period (See *Ḥullin* 24a).

BACKGROUND

23:29 | **Volume [*mesura*]:** A *mesura* is a small vessel for liquid measurement. It is mentioned in Leviticus (19:35): "You shall do no injustice in judgment, in measure, in weight, or in volume [*uvamesura*]," and twice in the book of Ezekiel: "You shall drink water by measure [*bimsura*]" (Ezekiel 4:11); "and they will drink water by measure [*bimsura*] and in desolation" (Ezekiel 4:16). The Sages state (*Bava Batra* 89b) that the *mesura* is a thirty-sixth, or a thirty-third according to another version, of a *log*, a *log* being roughly 300 cc.

30 **and** another service performed by the Levites was **to stand each and every morning to thank and praise the Lord, and likewise in the evening,**

31 **and** in addition to the fixed songs for every day, **to** sing on every occasion[322] when the priests would **offer up all burnt offerings to the Lord, for the Sabbaths, for the New Moons, and for the appointed times, in number according to their ordinance,** their laws, **continually, before the Lord.**

32 **They shall keep the commission of the Tent of Meeting, the commission of the sacred,** or the charge of the holy items, the vessels and sacrifices, **and the commission of the sons of Aaron their brethren,** as the Levites were also responsible for providing the priests with whatever they needed,[323] **for the service of the House of the Lord.** The Levites dealt with all services that did not have to be performed specifically by the priests, and were in charge of maintaining the Temple and everything in it.

Division of the Priests for Service in the Temple

I CHRONICLES 24:1–19

This section describes how David divided the priests into groups or watches responsible for service in the Temple for specific times of the year.

24 1 **For the sons of Aaron, their division** was also based on the first generation of sons of the priesthood: **The sons of Aaron: Nadav, and Avihu, Elazar, and Itamar.**

2 **Nadav and Avihu died before their father** did, **and they had no children.**[D] **Elazar and Itamar** alone were left to their father, and they **served as priests.**

3 **David,** together with **Tzadok,** who was the highest ranking priest **from** among **the sons of Elazar, and Ahimelekh,** who was **from the sons of Itamar** and the family of Eli, that had held the high priesthood until that time, **divided them,** the priests, **according to their numbers in their service.** It seems that the appointment of Tzadok as a head priest was a relatively recent decision.[324]

4 However, **the sons of Elazar were found** to be **more numerous than** those of **the sons of Itamar by the head count of the males, and they divided them; for the sons of Elazar, sixteen heads of patrilineal houses, and for the sons of Itamar, by their patrilineal houses, eight.** Each of these twenty-four priestly houses served for two non-consecutive weeks every year, while all of the houses served during the weeks of the festivals. This annual cycle was followed throughout the Temple era.[325]

5 **They divided them,** the priestly watches, **by lots, these with those, for there were princes of the Sanctuary and princes of God from the sons of Elazar and from the sons of Itamar.** Since there were important people in both families, the division was performed by lot, neither side being shown any preference.[326] Nevertheless, it seems that over time the sons of Elazar took over almost all the important roles in the Temple.[327]

6 **Shemaya son of Netanel the scribe, from** the tribe of **the Levites, recorded them,** the list of watches, **before the king, the princes, Tzadok the priest, Ahimelekh son of Evyatar, and the heads of the patrilineal houses of the priests and of the Levites: one patrilineal house apportioned to Elazar, and one-half apportioned to Itamar.** For every two patrilineal houses apportioned to Elazar, one patrilineal house was apportioned to Itamar (see verse 4).

7 The twenty-four priestly watches are now recorded: **The first lot emerged for Yehoyariv,** which was the opening watch in the order of the priestly service for many years,[328] **for Yedaya the second,**

8 **for Harim the third, for Seorim the fourth,**

9 **for Malkiya the fifth, for Miyamin the sixth,**

10 **for Hakotz the seventh, for Aviya the eighth,**

11 **for Yeshua the ninth, for Shekhanyahu the tenth,**

12 **for Elyashiv the eleventh, for Yakim the twelfth,**

13 **for Hupa the thirteenth, for Yeshevav the fourteenth,**

14 **for Bilga the fifteenth, for Imer the sixteenth,**

15 **for Hezir the seventeenth, for Hapitzetz the eighteenth,**

16 **for Petahya the nineteenth, for Yehezkel the twentieth,**

17 **for Yakhin the twenty-first, for Gamul the twenty-second,**

18 **for Delayahu the twenty-third, for Maazyahu the twenty-fourth.**[B]

List of the priestly watches, inscription on synagogue, Caesarea, fourth century CE

ל לא וְלַעֲמֹד בַּבֹּקֶר בַּבֹּקֶר לְהֹדוֹת וּלְהַלֵּל לַיהוָה וְכֵן לָעָרֶב׃ וּלְכֹל הַעֲלוֹת עֹלוֹת
לַיהוָה לַשַּׁבָּתוֹת לֶחֳדָשִׁים וְלַמֹּעֲדִים בְּמִסְפָּר כְּמִשְׁפָּט עֲלֵיהֶם תָּמִיד לִפְנֵי יְהוָה׃
לב וְשָׁמְרוּ אֶת־מִשְׁמֶרֶת אֹהֶל־מוֹעֵד וְאֵת מִשְׁמֶרֶת הַקֹּדֶשׁ וּמִשְׁמֶרֶת בְּנֵי אַהֲרֹן
ד א אֲחֵיהֶם לַעֲבֹדַת בֵּית יְהוָה׃ וְלִבְנֵי אַהֲרֹן מַחְלְקוֹתָם בְּנֵי אַהֲרֹן נָדָב
ב וַאֲבִיהוּא אֶלְעָזָר וְאִיתָמָר׃ וַיָּמָת נָדָב וַאֲבִיהוּא לִפְנֵי אֲבִיהֶם וּבָנִים לֹא־הָיוּ לָהֶם
ג וַיְכַהֲנוּ אֶלְעָזָר וְאִיתָמָר׃ וַיֶּחָלְקֵם דָּוִיד וְצָדוֹק מִן־בְּנֵי אֶלְעָזָר וַאֲחִימֶלֶךְ מִן־בְּנֵי
ד אִיתָמָר לִפְקֻדָּתָם בַּעֲבֹדָתָם׃ וַיִּמָּצְאוּ בְנֵי־אֶלְעָזָר רַבִּים לְרָאשֵׁי הַגְּבָרִים מִן־בְּנֵי
אִיתָמָר וַיַּחְלְקוּם לִבְנֵי אֶלְעָזָר רָאשִׁים לְבֵית־אָבוֹת שִׁשָּׁה עָשָׂר וְלִבְנֵי אִיתָמָר
ה לְבֵית אֲבוֹתָם שְׁמוֹנָה׃ וַיַּחְלְקוּם בְּגוֹרָלוֹת אֵלֶּה עִם־אֵלֶּה כִּי־הָיוּ שָׂרֵי־קֹדֶשׁ
ו וְשָׂרֵי הָאֱלֹהִים מִבְּנֵי אֶלְעָזָר וּבִבְנֵי אִיתָמָר׃ וַיִּכְתְּבֵם שְׁמַעְיָה בֶן־
נְתַנְאֵל הַסּוֹפֵר מִן־הַלֵּוִי לִפְנֵי הַמֶּלֶךְ וְהַשָּׂרִים וְצָדוֹק הַכֹּהֵן וַאֲחִימֶלֶךְ בֶּן־אֶבְיָתָר
וְרָאשֵׁי הָאָבוֹת לַכֹּהֲנִים וְלַלְוִיִּם בֵּית־אָב אֶחָד אָחֻז לְאֶלְעָזָר וְאָחֻז ׀ אָחֻז
ז ח לְאִיתָמָר׃ וַיֵּצֵא הַגּוֹרָל הָרִאשׁוֹן לִיהוֹיָרִיב לִידַעְיָה הַשֵּׁנִי׃ לְחָרִם הַשְּׁלִשִׁי
ט י לִשְׂעֹרִים הָרְבִעִי׃ לְמַלְכִּיָּה הַחֲמִישִׁי לְמִיָּמִן הַשִּׁשִּׁי׃ לְהַקּוֹץ הַשְּׁבִעִי לַאֲבִיָּה
יא יב הַשְּׁמִנִי׃ לְיֵשׁוּעַ הַתְּשִׁעִי לִשְׁכַנְיָהוּ הָעֲשִׂרִי׃ לְאֶלְיָשִׁיב עַשְׁתֵּי עָשָׂר לְיָקִים שְׁנֵים
יג יד עָשָׂר׃ לְחֻפָּה שְׁלֹשָׁה עָשָׂר לְיֶשֶׁבְאָב אַרְבָּעָה עָשָׂר׃ לְבִלְגָּה חֲמִשָּׁה עָשָׂר לְאִמֵּר
טו טז שִׁשָּׁה עָשָׂר׃ לְחֵזִיר שִׁבְעָה עָשָׂר לְהַפִּצֵּץ שְׁמוֹנָה עָשָׂר׃ לִפְתַחְיָה תִּשְׁעָה עָשָׂר
יז יח לִיחֶזְקֵאל הָעֶשְׂרִים׃ לְיָכִין אֶחָד וְעֶשְׂרִים לְגָמוּל שְׁנַיִם וְעֶשְׂרִים׃ לִדְלָיָהוּ שְׁלֹשָׁה

DISCUSSION

24:2 | **They had no children [*banim*]:** This is not the only case of a genealogical list in the Bible which mentions people who died without leaving any children (see Genesis 46:12; Numbers 3:4, and commentary ad loc.; Exodus 6:23; Numbers 26:19, 61; I Chronicles 2:4, and Vilna Gaon ad loc.). However, in Hebrew, *banim* can also strictly mean sons, just like any masculine plural can either be strictly masculine or include females. Therefore, this verse may be saying that Nadav and Avihu had no sons, but they may have had daughters, who in turn may have married their cousins. If so, Nadav and Avihu still had descendants among the priests.

BACKGROUND

24:18 | **For Delayahu the twenty-third, for Maazyahu the twenty-fourth:** Apparently, not all the priestly watches returned from Babylonia to the Land of Israel during the Second Temple period. Nevertheless, the leaders of Israel at that time redivided the present priests into twenty-four watches (see *Ta'anit* 24a). Most of the names of those watches remain unknown to us, but some are known by chance. For example, we know that there was still a watch of Bilga from an incident that occurred involving one of its daughters (*Sukka* 56b). The watch of Hezir is not mentioned in any literary source, but a magnificent burial cave in the Kidron Valley has an inscription that bears its name.

19 **These were their assignments,** the roles of the priests, **for**
their service, to come to the House of the Lord in accordance with their practice; they were in the hand of Aaron their father. The priests, the descendants of Aaron, continue their forefather's role and serve as his replacement, **as the Lord, God of Israel, commanded him.**[329]

The Other Levite Heads of the Watches

I CHRONICLES 24:20–31

The following section completes the list of Levite families that began above (23:6–23), and focuses on the Levites from the sons of Kehat and some of the sons of Gershon.

20 **The remaining sons of Levi,** apart from those counted previously:[330] **From the sons of Amram: Shuvael; from the sons of Shuvael: Yehdeyahu;**
21 **from Rehavyahu, from the sons of Rehavyahu: Yishiya** was
the leader;
22 **from** the family of **the Yitzharites: Shelomot; from the sons**
of Shelomot: Yahat.
23 **The sons of Yeriyahu: Amaryahu was the second, Yahaziyel**
the third, Yekame'am the fourth.
24 From **the sons of Uziel: Mikha; from the sons of Mikha:**
Shamir.
25 **The brother of Mikha: Yishiya; from the sons of Yishiya:**
Zekharyahu.
26 **The sons of Merari: Mahli and Mushi; the sons of Yaaziyahu,**
who was also a descendant of Merari, **his son,**
27 **the sons of Merari by Yaaziyahu his son: Shoham, Zakur,**
and Ivri.
28 **For Mahli was Elazar, and he had no sons.** As above (com-
mentary on 23:22), it is still possible that Elazar had daughters who were married to Mushi's sons or grandsons.
29 **From Kish, the sons of Kish,** headed by **Yerahme'el.**
30 **The sons of Mushi: Mahli, and Eder, and Yerimot. These**
were the sons of the Levites according to their patrilineal houses.
31 **They too cast lots** for twenty-four watches,[331] **in parallel to**
their brethren, the sons of Aaron, and the lots were cast **before King David, Tzadok, and Ahimelekh, and the heads of the patrilineal houses of the priests and of the Levites.** It seems that each Levite watch was assigned to a particular priestly watch, and those two watches would come together from their places of residence to perform the Temple service.[332] **The head of a patrilineal house was parallel to his younger brother.** No preference was shown to a supposedly important watch over a minor watch.

Temple Singers and Musicians

I CHRONICLES 25:1–31

This section is comprised of a list of the singers and musicians in the Temple. They too were divided into watches, specific time periods when they were responsible for carrying out their duties in the Temple.

25 1 **David and the captains of the company of service,** the com-
pany that served in the Sanctuary, **set apart the sons of Asaf, Heiman, and Yedutun, who played harps, lyres, and cymbals.** The three fathers, who are also mentioned in the book of Psalms, were not only singers and musicians, but talented composers of some of the psalms that were recited in the Temple throughout the generations. **Their number of craftsmen, according to their service,** who were qualified to perform the service, **was** as follows:
2 The watches **for the sons of Asaf: Zakur, Yosef, Netanya, and**
Asarela, the sons of Asaf who sang **under the hand,** under the auspices, or under the instruction **of** their father **Asaf, who composed**[D] his songs **alongside,** or according to the direction of, **the king.**
3 **For Yedutun, the sons of Yedutun: Gedalyahu, and Tzeri,**
and Yeshayahu, Hashavyahu, and Matityahu, six including Shimi, mentioned below (verse 17), who may have become an official singer at a later stage;[333] they performed **under the hand of their father Yedutun,** who played **with the harp,** and **who composed in thanks,** psalms of thanksgiving, **and praise to the Lord.**
4 **For Heiman, the** many **sons of Heiman: Bukiyahu,**
Matanyahu, Uziel, Shevuel, Yerimot, Hananya, Hanani, Eliata, Gidalti and Romamti Ezer,[D] a single name (verse 31), **Yoshbekasha, Maloti, Hotir, Mahaziot;**
5 **all of these were sons of Heiman, the king's seer in matters**
of God, and whose songs were sung **for** the Temple's and the king's **greater glory.**[334] **God gave to Heiman** a large family of **fourteen sons and three daughters.**
6 **All these** heads of watches **were under the hand of their**
father in playing **the song of the House of the Lord, with cymbals, lyres, and harps, for the service of the House of God, under the hand of the king;** and their fathers were, as stated earlier, **Asaf, Yedutun, and Heiman.**

יט וְעֶשְׂרִים לְמַעַזְיָהוּ אַרְבָּעָה וְעֶשְׂרִים: אֵלֶּה פְקֻדָּתָם לַעֲבֹדָתָם לָבוֹא
לְבֵית־יהוה כְּמִשְׁפָּטָם בְּיַד אַהֲרֹן אֲבִיהֶם כַּאֲשֶׁר צִוָּהוּ יהוה אֱלֹהֵי יִשְׂרָאֵל:
כ כא וְלִבְנֵי לֵוִי הַנּוֹתָרִים לִבְנֵי עַמְרָם שׁוּבָאֵל לִבְנֵי שׁוּבָאֵל יֶחְדְּיָהוּ: לִרְחַבְיָהוּ לִבְנֵי
כב כג רְחַבְיָהוּ הָרֹאשׁ יִשִּׁיָּה: לַיִּצְהָרִי שְׁלֹמוֹת לִבְנֵי שְׁלֹמוֹת יָחַת: וּבְנֵי יְרִיָּהוּ אֲמַרְיָהוּ
כד הַשֵּׁנִי יַחֲזִיאֵל הַשְּׁלִישִׁי יְקַמְעָם הָרְבִיעִי: בְּנֵי עֻזִּיאֵל מִיכָה לִבְנֵי מִיכָה שמור: שָׁמִיר
כה כו אֲחִי מִיכָה יִשִּׁיָּה לִבְנֵי יִשִּׁיָּה זְכַרְיָהוּ: בְּנֵי מְרָרִי מַחְלִי וּמוּשִׁי בְּנֵי יַעֲזִיָּהוּ בְנוֹ:
כז כח בְּנֵי מְרָרִי לְיַעֲזִיָּהוּ בְנוֹ וְשֹׁהַם וְזַכּוּר וְעִבְרִי: לְמַחְלִי אֶלְעָזָר וְלֹא־הָיָה לוֹ בָּנִים:
כט ל לְקִישׁ בְּנֵי־קִישׁ יְרַחְמְאֵל: וּבְנֵי מוּשִׁי מַחְלִי וְעֵדֶר וִירִימוֹת אֵלֶּה בְּנֵי הַלְוִיִּם לְבֵית
לא אֲבֹתֵיהֶם: וַיַּפִּילוּ גַם־הֵם גּוֹרָלוֹת לְעֻמַּת ׀ אֲחֵיהֶם בְּנֵי־אַהֲרֹן לִפְנֵי דָּוִיד הַמֶּלֶךְ
וְצָדוֹק וַאֲחִימֶלֶךְ וְרָאשֵׁי הָאָבוֹת לַכֹּהֲנִים וְלַלְוִיִּם אָבוֹת הָרֹאשׁ לְעֻמַּת אָחִיו
כה א הַקָּטָן: וַיַּבְדֵּל דָּוִיד וְשָׂרֵי הַצָּבָא לַעֲבֹדָה לִבְנֵי אָסָף וְהֵימָן וִידוּתוּן
הנביאים בְּכִנֹּרוֹת בִּנְבָלִים וּבִמְצִלְתָּיִם וַיְהִי מִסְפָּרָם אַנְשֵׁי מְלָאכָה לַעֲבֹדָתָם: הַנִּבְּאִים
ב לִבְנֵי אָסָף זַכּוּר וְיוֹסֵף וּנְתַנְיָה וַאֲשַׂרְאֵלָה בְּנֵי אָסָף עַל יַד־אָסָף הַנִּבָּא עַל־יְדֵי
ג הַמֶּלֶךְ: לִידוּתוּן בְּנֵי יְדוּתוּן גְּדַלְיָהוּ וּצְרִי וִישַׁעְיָהוּ חֲשַׁבְיָהוּ וּמַתִּתְיָהוּ שִׁשָּׁה עַל
ד יְדֵי אֲבִיהֶם יְדוּתוּן בַּכִּנּוֹר הַנִּבָּא עַל־הֹדוֹת וְהַלֵּל לַיהוָה: לְהֵימָן
בְּנֵי הֵימָן בֻּקִּיָּהוּ מַתַּנְיָהוּ עֻזִּיאֵל שְׁבוּאֵל וִירִימוֹת חֲנַנְיָה חֲנָנִי אֱלִיאָתָה גִּדַּלְתִּי
ה וְרֹמַמְתִּי עֶזֶר יָשְׁבְּקָשָׁה מַלּוֹתִי הוֹתִיר מַחֲזִיאוֹת: כָּל־אֵלֶּה בָנִים לְהֵימָן חֹזֵה
הַמֶּלֶךְ בְּדִבְרֵי הָאֱלֹהִים לְהָרִים קָרֶן וַיִּתֵּן הָאֱלֹהִים לְהֵימָן בָּנִים אַרְבָּעָה עָשָׂר
ו וּבָנוֹת שָׁלוֹשׁ: כָּל־אֵלֶּה עַל־יְדֵי אֲבִיהֶם בַּשִּׁיר בֵּית יהוה בִּמְצִלְתַּיִם נְבָלִים

DISCUSSION

25:2 | **Who composed [*haniba*]:** This expression is connected to the word *niv*, which means speech, and often is translated as "prophesied." Asaf and his colleagues were not prophets in the usual sense of the term; nevertheless, both Asaf and Heiman are called "seers" (see 25:5; II Chronicles 29:30; see also II Chronicles 35:15). Their songs were written with divine inspiration (see Radak; *Metzudat David*; *Metzudat Tzion*; Malbim), and therefore, they are mentioned in the introduction to several psalms: Asaf in 50, 73–83; Heiman in 88; and Yedutun in 39, 62, and 77.

25:4 | **Gidalti and Romamti Ezer:** The fact that these two unique names are connected by the conjunctive *vav* brings to mind the expression: "I have reared children and raised them up [*banim giddalti veromamti*]" (Isaiah 1:2). It is possible that when the prophet Isaiah chose that phrase he was influenced by his memory of these two brothers who served as singers in the Temple.

7 **Their number,** the heads of watches, **with their brethren** who
were **trained in singing to the Lord, everyone expert** in song,
was two hundred and eighty-eight.
8 **They cast lots, watches parallel to each other, small and**
great alike, an **expert with** a **student,** one who had yet to
come of age. All were equal in the lot.
9 Once again a detailed list of the order of the lots is provided:
The first lot emerged for Asaf, for his son **Yosef; Gedalyahu**
was the second; he and his brethren and sons were twelve.
It seems that all of these subsequent groups were intentionally comprised of twelve close relatives who knew how to play music.
10 **The third was Zakur; his sons and his brethren were twelve;**
11 **the fourth** lot **was for Yitzri,** Yedutun's second son, called
Tzeri above;[335] **his sons and his brethren were twelve;**
12 **the fifth was Netanyahu his sons and his brethren were twelve;**
13 **the sixth was Bukiyahu his sons and his brethren were twelve;**
14 **the seventh was Yesarela; his sons and his brethren were twelve;**
15 **the eighth was Yeshayahu; his sons and his brethren were twelve;**
16 **the ninth was Matanyahu; his sons and his brethren were twelve;**
17 **the tenth was Shimi; his sons and his brethren were twelve;**
18 **the eleventh was Azarel; his sons and his brethren were twelve;**
19 **the twelfth** lot **was for Hashavya; his sons and his brethren were twelve;**
20 **for the thirteenth** lot, **it was Shuvael; his sons and his brethren were twelve;**
21 **for the fourteenth** lot, **it was Matityahu; his sons and his brethren were twelve;**
22 **for the fifteenth, it was for Yeremot; his sons and his brethren were twelve;**
23 **for the sixteenth, it was for Hananyahu; his sons and his brethren were twelve;**
24 **for the seventeenth, it was for Yoshbekasha; his sons and his brethren were twelve;**
25 **for the eighteenth, it was for Hanani; his sons and his brethren were twelve;**
26 **for the nineteenth, it was for Maloti; his sons and his brethren were twelve;**
27 **for the twentieth, it was for Eliyata,** Heiman's eighth son,
called Eliata above; **his sons and his brethren were twelve;**
28 **for the twenty-first, it was for Hotir; his sons and his brethren were twelve;**
29 **for the twenty-second, it was for Gidalti; his sons and his brethren were twelve;**

וְכִנֹּר֔וֹת לַעֲבֹדַ֖ת בֵּ֣ית הָאֱלֹהִ֑ים עַ֚ל יְדֵ֣י הַמֶּ֔לֶךְ
ז אָסָ֥ף וִֽידוּת֖וּן וְהֵימָֽן׃ וַיְהִ֤י מִסְפָּרָם֙ עִם־אֲחֵיהֶ֔ם מְלֻמְּדֵי־שִׁ֖יר לַֽיהוָ֑ה כָּל־הַמֵּבִ֕ין
ח מָאתַ֖יִם שְׁמוֹנִ֥ים וּשְׁמוֹנָֽה׃ וַיַּפִּ֨ילוּ גּוֹרָל֜וֹת מִשְׁמֶ֗רֶת לְעֻמַּת֙ כַּקָּטֹ֣ן כַּגָּד֔וֹל מֵבִ֖ין
ט עִם־תַּלְמִֽיד׃ וַיֵּצֵ֞א הַגּוֹרָ֧ל הָרִאשׁ֛וֹן לְאָסָ֖ף לְיוֹסֵ֑ף גְּדַלְיָ֙הוּ֙ הַשֵּׁנִ֔י
י הֽוּא־וְאֶחָ֥יו וּבָנָ֖יו שְׁנֵ֥ים עָשָֽׂר׃ הַשְּׁלִשִׁ֣י זַכּ֔וּר
יא בָּנָ֥יו וְאֶחָ֖יו שְׁנֵ֥ים עָשָֽׂר׃ הָֽרְבִיעִי֙ לַיִּצְרִ֔י
יב בָּנָ֥יו וְאֶחָ֖יו שְׁנֵ֥ים עָשָֽׂר׃ הַחֲמִישִׁ֣י נְתַנְיָ֔הוּ
יג בָּנָ֥יו וְאֶחָ֖יו שְׁנֵ֥ים עָשָֽׂר׃ הַשִּׁשִּׁי֙ בֻּקִּיָּ֔הוּ
יד בָּנָ֥יו וְאֶחָ֖יו שְׁנֵ֥ים עָשָֽׂר׃ הַשְּׁבִיעִ֣י יְשַׂרְאֵ֔לָה
טו בָּנָ֥יו וְאֶחָ֖יו שְׁנֵ֥ים עָשָֽׂר׃ הַשְּׁמִינִ֣י יְשַֽׁעְיָ֔הוּ
טז בָּנָ֥יו וְאֶחָ֖יו שְׁנֵ֥ים עָשָֽׂר׃ הַתְּשִׁיעִי֙ מַתַּנְיָ֔הוּ
יז בָּנָ֥יו וְאֶחָ֖יו שְׁנֵ֥ים עָשָֽׂר׃ הָעֲשִׂרִ֣י שִׁמְעִ֔י
יח בָּנָ֥יו וְאֶחָ֖יו שְׁנֵ֥ים עָשָֽׂר׃ עַשְׁתֵּֽי־עָשָׂ֣ר עֲזַרְאֵ֔ל
יט בָּנָ֥יו וְאֶחָ֖יו שְׁנֵ֥ים עָשָֽׂר׃ הַשְּׁנֵ֣ים עָשָׂר֙ לַחֲשַׁבְיָ֔ה
כ בָּנָ֥יו וְאֶחָ֖יו שְׁנֵ֥ים עָשָֽׂר׃ לִשְׁלֹשָׁ֣ה עָשָׂר֙ שׁוּבָאֵ֔ל
כא בָּנָ֥יו וְאֶחָ֖יו שְׁנֵ֥ים עָשָֽׂר׃ לְאַרְבָּעָ֣ה עָשָׂר֙ מַתִּתְיָ֔הוּ
כב בָּנָ֥יו וְאֶחָ֖יו שְׁנֵ֥ים עָשָֽׂר׃ לַחֲמִשָּׁ֣ה עָשָׂר֙ לִֽירֵמ֔וֹת
כג בָּנָ֥יו וְאֶחָ֖יו שְׁנֵ֥ים עָשָֽׂר׃ לְשִׁשָּׁ֣ה עָשָׂר֙ לַחֲנַנְיָ֔הוּ
כד בָּנָ֥יו וְאֶחָ֖יו שְׁנֵ֥ים עָשָֽׂר׃ לְשִׁבְעָ֣ה עָשָׂר֙ לְיָשְׁבְּקָ֔שָׁה
כה בָּנָ֥יו וְאֶחָ֖יו שְׁנֵ֥ים עָשָֽׂר׃ לִשְׁמוֹנָ֣ה עָשָׂר֙ לַחֲנָ֔נִי
כו בָּנָ֥יו וְאֶחָ֖יו שְׁנֵ֥ים עָשָֽׂר׃ לְתִשְׁעָ֣ה עָשָׂר֙ לְמַלּ֔וֹתִי
כז בָּנָ֥יו וְאֶחָ֖יו שְׁנֵ֥ים עָשָֽׂר׃ לְעֶשְׂרִים֙ לֶאֱלִיָּ֔תָה
כח בָּנָ֥יו וְאֶחָ֖יו שְׁנֵ֥ים עָשָֽׂר׃ לְאֶחָ֤ד וְעֶשְׂרִים֙ לְהוֹתִ֔יר
כט בָּנָ֥יו וְאֶחָ֖יו שְׁנֵ֥ים עָשָֽׂר׃ לִשְׁנַ֤יִם וְעֶשְׂרִים֙ לְגִדַּלְתִּ֔י

30 **for the twenty-third, it was for Mahaziot; his sons and his brethren were twelve;**

31 **for the twenty-fourth, it was for Romamti Ezer; his sons and his brethren were twelve.**

Gatekeepers and Guards, Judges and Officers

I CHRONICLES 26:1–32

26 1 **For the divisions of the gatekeepers: Meshelemyahu son of Korei, from the sons of Asaf, was for the Korahites.**
2 **Meshelemyahu had sons: Zekharyahu the firstborn, Yedi'ael the second, Zevadyahu the third, Yatniel the fourth,**
3 **Eilam the fifth, Yehohanan the sixth, Elyeho'einai the seventh.**
4 **Oved Edom** also **had sons: Shemaya the firstborn, Yehozavad the second, Yo'ah the third, and Sakhar the fourth, and Netanel the fifth,**
5 **Amiel the sixth, Yisakhar the seventh, Peuletai the eighth, for God had blessed him,** Oved Edom, because he had kept the Ark of the Covenant in his house (see 13:14).
6 **To Shemaya his,** Oved Edom's, firstborn **son, were born sons who ruled**[336] **over the house of their father,** holding various positions of leadership, **as they were mighty warriors.**
7 **The sons of Shemaya: Otni, Refael, Oved, Elzavad, Ehav, Benei Hayil,**[337] **Elihu, and Semakhyahu.**
8 **All these were of the sons of Oved Edom, they and their sons and their brethren, capable men with strength for the service:** a total of **sixty-two** men **for Oved Edom.**
9 **For** the aforementioned **Meshelemyahu, sons and brethren, capable men: eighteen.**
10 **Hosa,** one of the gatekeepers, **of the children of Merari, had sons: Shimri** was **the leader, although he was not the firstborn; his father appointed him leader,** perhaps in place of an older, deceased brother.
11 **Hilkiyahu was the second, Tevalyahu the third, Zekharyahu the fourth; all the sons and brethren for Hosa were** a total of **thirteen.**
12 **These were the divisions of the gatekeepers, for the heads of the men, parallel to** the watches of **their brethren,** the Levites who sang in the Temple, and the priests, **to serve in the House of the Lord.**
13 **They,** the watches of the gatekeepers, **cast** equal **lots, the small and the great alike, in accordance with their patrilineal houses, for each and every gate,** to determine which of them would be in charge of each of the gates.
14 The lots were initially divided according to the four directions of the compass. Each head of a branch received one of the sides around the Temple, with several watch posts allocated on each side. **The lot for the east fell to Shelemyahu. They** also **cast lots for Zekharyahu his son,** his firstborn, who was **a wise counselor, and his lot,** of Zekharyahu, **came out for the north.**
15 **For Oved Edom, the** lot for the **south** fell, **and the** Temple **storehouse** [***beit ha'asupim***] area **was** the responsibility **for his sons.** Alternatively, this *beit ha'asupim* was a place where people gathered [*hitasfut*].[338]
16 **For Shupim and for Hosa** fell the lot **for the west, with the Shalekhet Gate, on the path that ascends,** a **watch** positioned **opposite** another **watch,** perhaps on the two sides of the gate or the causeway.
17 The division of the watches in each of the four directions is detailed: **On the east, the Levites were** divided into **six** watches, **on the north** there were **four** watches, **on the south four a day,** every day and all day,[339] **and for the storehouses two each;** two watches in each of the two storehouses.
18 **For the extension on the west,** a pavilion or some other area that jutted out from the Sanctuary,[340] there **were four** Levites guarding **at the path, and two at the extension** itself.[341]
19 **These were the divisions of the gatekeepers for the sons of the Korahites and for the sons of Merari.**
20 **The Levites** who had other roles: **Ahiya** was appointed **over the treasuries of the House of God, and over the treasuries of the sacraments,** the dedicated items and the offerings.[342]
21 **The sons of Ladan** were among **the sons of the Gershonites,** descendants of Gershon son of Levi; **for Ladan, the heads of the patrilineal houses of Ladan the Gershonite were from** the sons of **Yehieli,** who was the head of the sons of Ladan (see 23:8). The reiteration of "for Ladan" and "of Ladan" perhaps serves to differentiate him from a different Ladan.
22 **The sons of Yehieli: Zetam and Yoel his brother,** who **were** appointed **over the treasuries of the House of the Lord.** A number of people were placed in charge of the treasuries, due to the various responsibilities that the position entailed.[343]
23 The chapter lists other officials from the Kehatite families: **For the Amramites, for the Yitzharites, for the Hebronites,** and **for the Uzielites:**

ל בָּנָ֥יו וְאֶחָ֖יו שְׁנֵ֥ים עָשָֽׂר׃ לִשְׁלֹשָׁ֣ה וְעֶשְׂרִ֗ים לְמַֽחֲזִיאוֹת֙

לא בָּנָ֥יו וְאֶחָ֖יו שְׁנֵ֥ים עָשָֽׂר׃ לְאַרְבָּעָ֣ה וְעֶשְׂרִ֗ים לְרֽוֹמַמְתִּי֙ עֶ֔זֶר

א בָּנָ֥יו וְאֶחָ֖יו שְׁנֵ֥ים עָשָֽׂר׃ לְמַחְלְק֖וֹת לְשֹׁעֲרִ֑ים לַקָּ֣רְחִ֔ים

ב מְשֶׁלֶמְיָ֥הוּ בֶן־קֹרֵ֖א מִן־בְּנֵ֥י אָסָֽף׃ וְלִמְשֶׁלֶמְיָ֖הוּ בָּנִ֑ים זְכַרְיָ֤הוּ הַבְּכוֹר֙ יְדִיעֲאֵ֣ל

ג הַשֵּׁנִ֔י זְבַדְיָ֙הוּ֙ הַשְּׁלִישִׁ֔י יַתְנִיאֵ֖ל הָרְבִיעִֽי׃ עֵילָם֙ הַחֲמִישִׁ֔י יְהוֹחָנָ֖ן הַשִּׁשִּׁ֑י אֶלְיְהוֹעֵינַ֖י

ד הַשְּׁבִיעִֽי׃ וּלְעֹבֵ֥ד אֱדֹ֖ם בָּנִ֑ים שְׁמַעְיָ֤ה הַבְּכוֹר֙ יְהוֹזָבָ֣ד הַשֵּׁנִ֔י יוֹאָ֙ח הַשְּׁלִשִׁ֔י וְשָׂכָ֥ר

ה הָרְבִיעִ֖י וּנְתַנְאֵ֥ל הַחֲמִישִֽׁי׃ עַמִּיאֵ֤ל הַשִּׁשִּׁי֙ יִשָׂשכָר֙ הַשְּׁבִיעִ֔י פְּעֻלְּתַ֖י הַשְּׁמִינִ֑י כִּ֥י

ו בֵרְכ֖וֹ אֱלֹהִֽים׃ וְלִשְׁמַעְיָ֤ה בְנוֹ֙ נוֹלַ֣ד בָּנִ֔ים הַֽמִּמְשָׁלִ֖ים לְבֵ֣ית אֲבִיהֶ֑ם

ז כִּֽי־גִבּ֥וֹרֵי חַ֖יִל הֵֽמָּה׃ בְּנֵ֣י שְׁמַעְיָ֗ה עָתְנִ֧י וּרְפָאֵ֛ל וְעוֹבֵ֥ד אֶלְזָבָ֖ד אֶחָ֑יו

ח בְּנֵי־חַ֔יִל אֱלִיה֖וּ וּסְמַכְיָֽהוּ׃ כָּל־אֵ֜לֶּה מִבְּנֵ֣י ׀ עֹבֵ֣ד אֱדֹ֗ם הֵמָּה֙ וּבְנֵיהֶ֣ם וַאֲחֵיהֶ֔ם

ט אִישׁ־חַ֥יִל בַּכֹּ֖חַ לָעֲבֹדָ֑ה שִׁשִּׁ֥ים וּשְׁנַ֖יִם לְעֹבֵ֥ד אֱדֹֽם׃ וְלִמְשֶׁלֶמְיָ֖הוּ בָּנִ֣ים וְאַחִ֑ים

י בְּנֵי־חַ֖יִל שְׁמוֹנָ֥ה עָשָֽׂר׃ וּלְחֹסָ֛ה מִן־בְּנֵֽי־מְרָרִ֖י בָּנִ֑ים שִׁמְרִ֣י הָרֹ֗אשׁ כִּ֠י

יא לֹא־הָיָ֤ה בְכוֹר֙ וַיְשִׂימֵ֣הוּ אָבִ֔יהוּ לְרֹֽאשׁ׃ חִלְקִיָּ֤הוּ הַשֵּׁנִי֙ טְבַלְיָ֣הוּ הַשְּׁלִשִׁ֔י זְכַרְיָ֖הוּ

יב הָרְבִיעִ֑י כָּל־בָּנִ֥ים וְאַחִ֖ים לְחֹסָ֥ה שְׁלֹשָׁ֖ה עָשָֽׂר׃ לְאֵ֜לֶּה מַחְלְק֤וֹת הַשֹּֽׁעֲרִים֙ לְרָאשֵׁ֣י

יג הַגְּבָרִ֔ים מִשְׁמָר֖וֹת לְעֻמַּ֣ת אֲחֵיהֶ֑ם לְשָׁרֵ֖ת בְּבֵ֥ית יהוה׃ וַיַּפִּ֙ילוּ גוֹרָל֜וֹת כַּקָּטֹ֣ן

יד כַּגָּד֛וֹל לְבֵ֥ית אֲבוֹתָ֖ם לְשַׁ֥עַר וָשָֽׁעַר׃ וַיִּפֹּ֧ל הַגּוֹרָ֛ל מִזְרָ֖חָה לְשֶֽׁלֶמְיָ֑הוּ

טו וּזְכַרְיָ֨הוּ בְנ֜וֹ יוֹעֵ֣ץ ׀ בְּשֶׂ֗כֶל הִפִּ֙ילוּ֙ גֹּֽרָל֔וֹת וַיֵּצֵ֥א גוֹרָל֖וֹ צָפֽוֹנָה׃ לְעֹבֵ֥ד אֱדֹ֖ם נֶ֑גְבָּה

טז וּלְבָנָ֖יו בֵּ֥ית הָאֲסֻפִּֽים׃ לְשֻׁפִּ֣ים וּלְחֹסָ֗ה לְֽמַעֲרָב֙ עִ֚ם שַׁ֣עַר שַׁלֶּ֔כֶת בַּֽמְסִלָּ֖ה הָעוֹלָ֑ה

יז מִשְׁמָ֖ר לְעֻמַּ֥ת מִשְׁמָֽר׃ לַמִּזְרָ֜ח הַלְוִיִּ֣ם שִׁשָּׁ֗ה לַצָּפ֤וֹנָה לַיּוֹם֙ אַרְבָּעָ֔ה לַנֶּ֥גְבָּה לַיּ֖וֹם

יח אַרְבָּעָ֑ה וְלָאֲסֻפִּ֖ים שְׁנַ֥יִם שְׁנָֽיִם׃ לַפַּרְבָּ֕ר לַֽמַּעֲרָ֑ב אַרְבָּעָה֙ לַֽמְסִלָּ֔ה שְׁנַ֖יִם לַפַּרְבָּֽר׃

יט כ אֵ֙לֶּה֙ מַחְלְק֣וֹת הַשֹּׁעֲרִ֔ים לִבְנֵ֥י הַקָּרְחִ֖י וְלִבְנֵ֥י מְרָרִֽי׃ וְהַלְוִיִּ֕ם אֲחִיָּ֕ה עַל־אוֹצְרוֹת֙

בֵּ֣ית הָאֱלֹהִ֔ים וּלְאֹצְר֖וֹת הַקֳּדָשִֽׁים׃

כא כב בְּנֵ֣י לַעְדָּ֗ן בְּנֵ֤י הַגֵּרְשֻׁנִּי֙ לְלַעְדָּ֔ן רָאשֵׁ֧י הָאָב֛וֹת לְלַעְדָּ֥ן הַגֵּרְשֻׁנִּ֖י יְחִיאֵלִֽי׃ בְּנֵ֖י יְחִיאֵלִ֑י

כג זֵתָ֞ם וְיוֹאֵ֣ל אָחִ֔יו עַל־אֹצְר֖וֹת בֵּ֥ית יהוה׃ לַעַמְרָמִ֥י לַיִּצְהָרִ֖י לַֽחֶבְרוֹנִ֥י לָעָזִּיאֵלִֽי׃

24 **Shevuel, son of Gershom, son of Moses** (see 23:14–16) **was the chief official in charge of the treasuries.**
25 **His brethren by Eliezer,** the other son of Moses: **Rehavyahu his,** Eliezer's, **son, Yeshayahu his son, Yoram his son, Zikhri his son, and Shelomit his son.**
26 **This Shelomot,** Shelomit, **and his brethren were** appointed to be **in charge of all treasuries of the sacraments, which King David, and the heads of the patrilineal houses, the leaders of the thousands and the hundreds, and the commanders of the army, had consecrated.** This refers to the goods that were consecrated to the Temple by various officials, but which had not yet been deposited in the House of God.
27 **They had consecrated from the wars and from the spoils to support the House of the Lord.**
28 **All that was consecrated by Samuel the seer,**[344] who himself had been involved in wars and had consecrated some of the spoils to God,[345] **and Saul son of Kish,** who also dedicated items to the Temple, **and Avner son of Ner, and Yoav son of Tzeruya,** the great former commanders of the army, and **all that anyone** else **had consecrated** to the Temple, **was under the hand of Shelomit and his brethren,** who were in charge of these consecrated items.
29 **For the Yitzharites,** the sons of Yitzhar son of Kehat: **Kenanyahu and his sons were** responsible **for the external affairs of Israel,** Temple matters that were taken care of outside the Temple, and they were appointed **as officers and judges.**[346]
30 **For the Hebronites: Hashavyahu and his brethren, one thousand seven hundred capable men, in charge of the labor of Israel;** they were appointed over the services that were the responsibility of Israel **beyond the Jordan to the west, for all the labor of the Lord, and for the service of the king.** The Temple treasury, the royal treasury, and the national treasury were not entirely separate from one another, and therefore there were men who dealt with all of them together.
31 And furthermore **for the Hebronites: Yeriya** was **the leader of the Hebronites by their progeny, by patrilineal houses. In the fortieth year of the reign of David they were sought, and there were found among them mighty warriors at Yazer Gilad.**
32 **His brethren, capable men, were two thousand seven hundred, heads of the patrilineal houses, and King David appointed them over the Reubenites, the Gadites, and half the tribe of the Manassites, for every matter of God and every matter of the king.** These Levites served as royal officials, and were placed in charge of the territory east of the Jordan.

Lists Pertaining to the Public Sector and to the Senior Officials of the Kingdom

I CHRONICLES 27:1–34

Until this point, the book focused on the priests and the Levites. The lists that follow pertain to the entire kingdom and its governmental structure. They divide the people into divisions composed of twenty-four thousand men, with each division tasked with government service one month a year. The names of the leaders, who were officers from the warriors of David, indicate that this is an army reserve unit of sorts.

The Public Sector

I CHRONICLES 27:1–15

27 1 **The children of Israel by their number** were also divided into divisions, like the watches of the priests and Levites, directed by **the heads of the patrilineal houses and the captains of the thousands and of the hundreds, and their officers who served the king, for all matter** of the management **of the divisions that came and went each and every month for all the months of the year; each division was twenty-four thousand** men.
2 **Over the first division for the first month was** appointed **Yoshovam son of Zavdiel; in his division were twenty-four thousand.**
3 **He was from the children of Peretz** son of Judah, **and** he **was the head of all the commanders of the armies for the first month.**
4 **Over the division of the second month was** appointed **Dodai the Ahohite and his division, with Miklot the prince** as his assistant; **in his division were twenty-four thousand.**
5 **The third commander of the army, for the third month, was Benayahu son of Yehoyada the priest, leader; in his division were twenty-four thousand.** Benayahu's primary role was as a military figure. Although he was a high-ranking official and a priest, it is not stated that he actually served as a priest.[347]
6 **He is Benayahu, the mighty man of the thirty** and one of David's powerful warriors, **and** he was appointed **over the thirty;** and leadership of **his division was** together **with Amizavad his son.**
7 **The** commander of the **fourth** division, **for the fourth month, was** under the leadership of **Asael brother of Yoav, and Zevadya his son was after him,** his successor; **in his division were twenty-four thousand.**
8 **The fifth** division, **for the fifth month, was** under the authority of **the commander** called **Shamhut the Yizrahite; in his division were twenty-four thousand.**

כד כה וּשְׁבֻאֵל בֶּן־גֵּרְשׁוֹם בֶּן־מֹשֶׁה נָגִיד עַל־הָאֹצָרוֹת׃ וְאֶחָיו לֶאֱלִיעֶזֶר רְחַבְיָהוּ בְנוֹ
כו וִישַׁעְיָהוּ בְנוֹ וְיֹרָם בְּנוֹ וְזִכְרִי בְנוֹ ושלמות בְּנוֹ׃ הוּא שְׁלֹמוֹת וְאֶחָיו עַל כָּל־ וּשְׁלֹמִית
אֹצְרוֹת הַקֳּדָשִׁים אֲשֶׁר הִקְדִּישׁ דָּוִיד הַמֶּלֶךְ וְרָאשֵׁי הָאָבוֹת לְשָׂרֵי־הָאֲלָפִים
כז וְהַמֵּאוֹת וְשָׂרֵי הַצָּבָא׃ מִן־הַמִּלְחָמוֹת וּמִן־הַשָּׁלָל הִקְדִּישׁוּ לְחַזֵּק לְבֵית יהוה׃
כח וְכֹל הַהִקְדִּישׁ שְׁמוּאֵל הָרֹאֶה וְשָׁאוּל בֶּן־קִישׁ וְאַבְנֵר בֶּן־נֵר וְיוֹאָב בֶּן־צְרוּיָה
כט כֹּל הַמַּקְדִּישׁ עַל יַד־שְׁלֹמִית וְאֶחָיו׃ לַיִּצְהָרִי כְּנַנְיָהוּ וּבָנָיו לַמְּלָאכָה
ל הַחִיצוֹנָה עַל־יִשְׂרָאֵל לְשֹׁטְרִים וּלְשֹׁפְטִים׃ לַחֶבְרוֹנִי חֲשַׁבְיָהוּ וְאֶחָיו
בְּנֵי־חַיִל אֶלֶף וּשְׁבַע־מֵאוֹת עַל פְּקֻדַּת יִשְׂרָאֵל מֵעֵבֶר לַיַּרְדֵּן מַעְרָבָה לְכֹל
לא מְלֶאכֶת יהוה וְלַעֲבֹדַת הַמֶּלֶךְ׃ לַחֶבְרוֹנִי יְרִיָּה הָרֹאשׁ לַחֶבְרוֹנִי לְתֹלְדֹתָיו לְאָבוֹת
בִּשְׁנַת הָאַרְבָּעִים לְמַלְכוּת דָּוִיד נִדְרָשׁוּ וַיִּמָּצֵא בָהֶם גִּבּוֹרֵי חַיִל בְּיַעְזֵיר גִּלְעָד׃
לב וְאֶחָיו בְּנֵי־חַיִל אַלְפַּיִם וּשְׁבַע מֵאוֹת רָאשֵׁי הָאָבוֹת וַיַּפְקִידֵם דָּוִיד הַמֶּלֶךְ עַל־
הָראוּבֵנִי וְהַגָּדִי וַחֲצִי שֵׁבֶט הַמְנַשִּׁי לְכָל־דְּבַר הָאֱלֹהִים וּדְבַר הַמֶּלֶךְ׃
ז א וּבְנֵי יִשְׂרָאֵל ׀ לְמִסְפָּרָם רָאשֵׁי הָאָבוֹת ׀ וְשָׂרֵי הָאֲלָפִים ׀ וְהַמֵּאוֹת וְשֹׁטְרֵיהֶם
הַמְשָׁרְתִים אֶת־הַמֶּלֶךְ לְכֹל ׀ דְּבַר הַמַּחְלְקוֹת הַבָּאָה וְהַיֹּצֵאת חֹדֶשׁ בְּחֹדֶשׁ
ב לְכֹל חָדְשֵׁי הַשָּׁנָה הַמַּחֲלֹקֶת הָאַחַת עֶשְׂרִים וְאַרְבָּעָה אָלֶף׃ עַל
הַמַּחֲלֹקֶת הָרִאשׁוֹנָה לַחֹדֶשׁ הָרִאשׁוֹן יָשָׁבְעָם בֶּן־זַבְדִּיאֵל וְעַל מַחֲלֻקְתּוֹ עֶשְׂרִים
ג וְאַרְבָּעָה אָלֶף׃ מִן־בְּנֵי־פֶרֶץ הָרֹאשׁ לְכָל־שָׂרֵי הַצְּבָאוֹת לַחֹדֶשׁ
ד הָרִאשׁוֹן׃ וְעַל מַחֲלֹקֶת ׀ הַחֹדֶשׁ הַשֵּׁנִי דּוֹדַי הָאֲחוֹחִי וּמַחֲלֻקְתּוֹ
ה וּמִקְלוֹת הַנָּגִיד וְעַל מַחֲלֻקְתּוֹ עֶשְׂרִים וְאַרְבָּעָה אָלֶף׃ שַׂר הַצָּבָא
הַשְּׁלִישִׁי לַחֹדֶשׁ הַשְּׁלִישִׁי בְּנָיָהוּ בֶן־יְהוֹיָדָע הַכֹּהֵן רֹאשׁ וְעַל מַחֲלֻקְתּוֹ עֶשְׂרִים
ו וְאַרְבָּעָה אָלֶף׃ הוּא בְנָיָהוּ גִּבּוֹר הַשְּׁלֹשִׁים וְעַל־הַשְּׁלֹשִׁים וּמַחֲלֻקְתּוֹ עַמִּיזָבָד
ז בְּנוֹ׃ הָרְבִיעִי לַחֹדֶשׁ הָרְבִיעִי עֲשָׂהאֵל אֲחִי יוֹאָב וּזְבַדְיָה בְנוֹ אַחֲרָיו
ח וְעַל מַחֲלֻקְתּוֹ עֶשְׂרִים וְאַרְבָּעָה אָלֶף׃ הַחֲמִישִׁי לַחֹדֶשׁ הַחֲמִישִׁי

9 **The sixth** division, **for the sixth month, was** under the command of **Ira son of Ikesh the Tekoite; in his division were
twenty-four thousand.**
10 **The seventh** division, **for the seventh month, was** under
the command of **Heletz the Pelonite, from the children of
Ephraim; in his division were twenty-four thousand.**
11 **The eighth** division, **for the eighth month, was** under the
command of **Sibekhai the Hushatite,** from the family **of the
Zerahite; in his division were twenty-four thousand.**
12 **The ninth** division, **for the ninth month, was** under the
command of **Aviezer the Anatotite, of the Benjamite,** from
the tribe of Benjamin; **in his division were twenty-four
thousand.**
13 **The tenth** division, **for the tenth month, was** under the
command of **Mahrai the Netofatite, of the Zerahite; in his
division were twenty-four thousand.**
14 **The eleventh** division, **for the eleventh month, was** under
the command of **Benaya the Piratonite, of the children of
Ephraim; in his division were twenty-four thousand.**
15 **The twelfth** division, **for the twelfth month, was** under the
command of **Heldai the Netofatite, of Otniel; in his division
were twenty-four thousand.**

Heads of the Tribes

I CHRONICLES 27:16–24

During the monarchy, the division into tribes becomes increasingly obscured even though the tribes are still in existence. Each tribe is headed by a prince.

16 **Over the tribes of Israel** there was another appointment, in
addition to the commanders of the quasi-military units: **For
the Reubenite, the chief official** was **Eliezer son of Zikhri;
for the Simeonite, Shefatyahu son of Maakha;**
17 **for Levi, Hashavya son of Kemuel; for** the priests, sons of
Aaron, Tzadok;
18 **for Judah, Elihu, from the brothers of David,** perhaps referring to his eldest brother, Eliav; **for Issachar, Omri son of
Mikhael;**
19 **for Zebulun, Yishmayahu son of Ovadyahu; for Naphtali,
Yerimot son of Azriel;**
20 **for the children of Ephraim, Hoshe'a son of Azazyahu; for**
the **half** of **the tribe of Manasseh** west of the Jordan, **Yoel son
of Pedayahu;**
21 **for half the tribe of Manasseh** that dwelled **in Gilad,** east of
the Jordan, **Ido son of Zekharyahu; for Benjamin, Yaasiel
son of Avner,** apparently referring to Avner son of Ner;
22 **for Dan, Azarel son of Yeroham. These were the princes of
the tribes of Israel.**
23 **David did not take the number of them,** he did not count the
youths of Israel, **from twenty years of age and under, because
the Lord had said** He was going **to increase Israel like the
stars of heaven,** and David did not want to conduct a full and
detailed census of the entire, numerous, nation.
24 **Yoav son of Tzeruya began to count, and he did not finish.**
Yoav did not want to fulfill David's command[348] completely.
He therefore based his count on estimates and omitted certain
groups from the census, **but** even so, **there was wrath on Israel
for this. The number did not enter into** writing in **the tally,** or
the narrative,[349] **in the chronicles of King David.**

The Ministers in David's Government and His Advisors

I CHRONICLES 27:25–34

This is an expanded list of David's government and the names of those responsible for the different areas of his administration.

25 The official **in charge of the king's treasuries was Azmavet
son of Adiel, and in charge of the treasuries in the field, in
the cities, in the villages, and in the towers,**[B] **was Yehonatan
son of Uziyahu;**

BACKGROUND

27:25 | **And in charge of the treasuries in the field, in the cities, in the villages, and in the towers:** Establishing his monarchy required David to organize and institutionalize a more centralized economic system, both for administrative purposes, including those of the royal court, as well as for the sake of international trade. The verses that follow indicate that the organization was accomplished by means of separation into branches of activity that were also geographically distinct. There was also a division in the management of the various labors in the framework of each branch, e.g., growing, cultivating, and storing grapes and olives are all separate divisions. Most of the agricultural branches mentioned were annexed to the kingdom in the wake of David's conquests, while only a few of the branches were on tribal land. This underscores the initial difficulties encountered by David in his efforts to unite the kingdom.

ט הַשַּׂר שַׁמְהוּת הַיִּזְרָח וְעַל מַחֲלֻקְתּוֹ עֶשְׂרִים וְאַרְבָּעָה אָלֶף׃ הַשִּׁשִּׁי
לַחֹדֶשׁ הַשִּׁשִּׁי עִירָא בֶן־עִקֵּשׁ הַתְּקוֹעִי וְעַל מַחֲלֻקְתּוֹ עֶשְׂרִים וְאַרְבָּעָה
י אָלֶף׃ הַשְּׁבִיעִי לַחֹדֶשׁ הַשְּׁבִיעִי חֶלֶץ הַפְּלוֹנִי מִן־בְּנֵי אֶפְרָיִם וְעַל
יא מַחֲלֻקְתּוֹ עֶשְׂרִים וְאַרְבָּעָה אָלֶף׃ הַשְּׁמִינִי לַחֹדֶשׁ הַשְּׁמִינִי סִבְּכַי
יב הַחֻשָׁתִי לַזַּרְחִי וְעַל מַחֲלֻקְתּוֹ עֶשְׂרִים וְאַרְבָּעָה אָלֶף׃ הַתְּשִׁיעִי
לַחֹדֶשׁ הַתְּשִׁיעִי אֲבִיעֶזֶר הָעַנְּתוֹתִי לבנימיני וְעַל מַחֲלֻקְתּוֹ עֶשְׂרִים וְאַרְבָּעָה לַבֶּן ׀ יְמִינִי
יג אָלֶף׃ הָעֲשִׂירִי לַחֹדֶשׁ הָעֲשִׂירִי מַהְרַי הַנְּטוֹפָתִי לַזַּרְחִי וְעַל מַחֲלֻקְתּוֹ
יד עֶשְׂרִים וְאַרְבָּעָה אָלֶף׃ עַשְׁתֵּי־עָשָׂר לְעַשְׁתֵּי עָשָׂר הַחֹדֶשׁ בְּנָיָה
טו הַפִּרְעָתוֹנִי מִן־בְּנֵי אֶפְרָיִם וְעַל מַחֲלֻקְתּוֹ עֶשְׂרִים וְאַרְבָּעָה אָלֶף׃ הַשְּׁנֵים
עָשָׂר לִשְׁנֵים עָשָׂר הַחֹדֶשׁ חֶלְדַּי הַנְּטוֹפָתִי לְעָתְנִיאֵל וְעַל מַחֲלֻקְתּוֹ עֶשְׂרִים
טז וְאַרְבָּעָה אָלֶף׃ וְעַל שִׁבְטֵי יִשְׂרָאֵל לָרְאוּבֵנִי נָגִיד אֱלִיעֶזֶר בֶּן־זִכְרִי
יז לַשִּׁמְעוֹנִי שְׁפַטְיָהוּ בֶּן־מַעֲכָה׃ לְלֵוִי חֲשַׁבְיָה בֶן־קְמוּאֵל לְאַהֲרֹן
יח צָדוֹק׃ לִיהוּדָה אֱלִיהוּ מֵאֲחֵי דָוִיד לְיִשָּׂשכָר עָמְרִי בֶּן־
יט מִיכָאֵל׃ לִזְבוּלֻן יִשְׁמַעְיָהוּ בֶּן־עֹבַדְיָהוּ לְנַפְתָּלִי יְרִימוֹת בֶּן־
כ עַזְרִיאֵל׃ לִבְנֵי אֶפְרַיִם הוֹשֵׁעַ בֶּן־עֲזַזְיָהוּ לַחֲצִי שֵׁבֶט מְנַשֶּׁה יוֹאֵל
כא בֶּן־פְּדָיָהוּ׃ לַחֲצִי הַמְנַשֶּׁה גִּלְעָדָה יִדּוֹ בֶּן־זְכַרְיָהוּ לְבִנְיָמִן יַעֲשִׂיאֵל
כב כג בֶּן־אַבְנֵר׃ לְדָן עֲזַרְאֵל בֶּן־יְרֹחָם אֵלֶּה שָׂרֵי שִׁבְטֵי יִשְׂרָאֵל׃ וְלֹא־נָשָׂא
דָּוִיד מִסְפָּרָם לְמִבֶּן עֶשְׂרִים שָׁנָה וּלְמָטָּה כִּי אָמַר יְהוָה לְהַרְבּוֹת אֶת־יִשְׂרָאֵל
כד כְּכוֹכְבֵי הַשָּׁמָיִם׃ יוֹאָב בֶּן־צְרוּיָה הֵחֵל לִמְנוֹת וְלֹא כִלָּה וַיְהִי בָזֹאת קֶצֶף עַל־
כה יִשְׂרָאֵל וְלֹא עָלָה הַמִּסְפָּר בְּמִסְפַּר דִּבְרֵי הַיָּמִים לַמֶּלֶךְ דָּוִיד׃ וְעַל
אֹצְרוֹת הַמֶּלֶךְ עַזְמָוֶת בֶּן־עֲדִיאֵל וְעַל הָאֹצָרוֹת בַּשָּׂדֶה בֶּעָרִים וּבַכְּפָרִים

26 **in charge of the performers of labor of the field for working the land was Ezri son of Keluv;**

27 **in charge of the vineyards was Shimi the Ramatite; in charge of that which was in the vineyards,** the grapes earmarked **for the wine cellars, was Zavdi the Shifmite;**

Vineyard in the Golan

28 **in charge of the olive trees and the sycamores**[B] **that were in the plain was Baal Hanan the Gederite; and in charge of the oil stores was Yo'ash;**

Olive trees

Sycamore tree

29 **and in charge of the cattle that grazed in the Sharon, Shirtai the Sharonite; in charge of the cattle in the valleys was Shafat son of Adlai;**

"The cattle that grazed"

30 **in charge of the camels was Ovil the Ishmaelite,** whose expertise with camels can be attributed to the fact that he dwelled among the Ishmaelites or was himself an Ishmaelite; **and in charge of the female donkeys**[B] **was Yehdeyahu the Meronotite;**

31 **and in charge of the flocks was Yaziz the Hagrite,**[B] whose expertise in tending to flocks can be attributed to his Arabian origins. **All these were the officers of the property that was King David's.**

Camels

Donkeys

"Flocks"

32 **Yehonatan, David's uncle, was counselor; he was a man of understanding,** an intelligent, learned individual, **and a scribe,** who also knew how to write in foreign languages; **Yehiel son of Hakhmoni was with the king's sons;** he was responsible for teaching them wisdom and royal protocol.[350] Some read the verse as saying that both Yehonatan and Yehiel were with the king's sons.

33 **Ahitofel was counselor to the king,** concerning all matters on the public agenda; **Hushai the Arkite was the king's confidant.** This was not an official position, like that of a counselor; rather, it was a personal appointee of the king who advised the king outside the official framework of his government. He was typically an individual with a very close relationship with the king.

34 **After Ahitofel,** below him in rank in the government, or after him in the order of decision makers,[351] **was Yehoyada son of Benayahu, and Evyatar** the priest. Some of the early commentaries explain the verse as follows: After Ahitofel died, he was followed by Yehoyada. **And the commander of the army for the king** was **Yoav.** In many respects, this was the central and most important office in David's kingdom.

David's Proclamation about the Temple

I CHRONICLES 28:1–29:9

David is the first king of Israel to crown his son during his lifetime. In the presence of all the ministers of the government and with great fanfare, David commands that the House of God be built under the management of Solomon, the new king, who is still very young at the time. He hands over to Solomon detailed plans of the Temple and its vessels, exhorts him to start the construction work, and encourages him to serve God. In addition to the extensive preparations for the Temple, which David performs himself in amassing the requisite building materials, bringing together craftsmen, establishing who would serve in the Temple, and arranging the order of their service, he also sets aside a large donation of precious metals from his treasuries for plating and decorating the Temple. Likewise, he takes advantage of the opportunity to call upon all those present to donate to the Temple. The people respond fullheartedly and with joy.

28 1 **David assembled all the princes of Israel,** as listed above, including the ministers of his government, **the princes of the tribes, and the officials in charge of the divisions who served the king, the captains of the thousands, and the captains of the hundreds, and the officials in charge of all the property and livestock of the king, and his sons,** who gathered **with the officers,**[B] **and the mighty, and all the mighty warriors, to Jerusalem.**

כו וּבַמִּגְדָּלוֹת יְהוֹנָתָן בֶּן־עֻזִּיָּהוּ׃ וְעַל עֹשֵׂי מְלֶאכֶת הַשָּׂדֶה לַעֲבֹדַת
כז הָאֲדָמָה עֶזְרִי בֶּן־כְּלוּב׃ וְעַל־הַכְּרָמִים שִׁמְעִי הָרָמָתִי וְעַל שֶׁבַּכְּרָמִים
כח לְאֹצְרוֹת הַיַּיִן זַבְדִּי הַשִּׁפְמִי׃ וְעַל־הַזֵּיתִים וְהַשִּׁקְמִים אֲשֶׁר בַּשְּׁפֵלָה
כט בַּעַל חָנָן הַגְּדֵרִי וְעַל־אֹצְרוֹת הַשֶּׁמֶן יוֹעָשׁ׃ וְעַל־הַבָּקָר הָרֹעִים בַּשָּׁרוֹן
ל שטרי הַשָּׁרוֹנִי וְעַל־הַבָּקָר בָּעֲמָקִים שָׁפָט בֶּן־עַדְלָי׃ וְעַל־הַגְּמַלִּים שִׁרְטַי
לא אוֹבִיל הַיִּשְׁמְעֵאלִי וְעַל־הָאֲתֹנוֹת יֶחְדְּיָהוּ הַמֵּרֹנֹתִי׃ וְעַל־הַצֹּאן יָזִיז
לב הַהַגְרִי כָּל־אֵלֶּה שָׂרֵי הָרְכוּשׁ אֲשֶׁר לַמֶּלֶךְ דָּוִיד׃ וִיהוֹנָתָן דּוֹד־דָּוִיד
לג יוֹעֵץ אִישׁ־מֵבִין וְסוֹפֵר הוּא וִיחִיאֵל בֶּן־חַכְמוֹנִי עִם־בְּנֵי הַמֶּלֶךְ׃ וַאֲחִיתֹפֶל יוֹעֵץ
לד לַמֶּלֶךְ וְחוּשַׁי הָאַרְכִּי רֵעַ הַמֶּלֶךְ׃ וְאַחֲרֵי אֲחִיתֹפֶל יְהוֹיָדָע בֶּן־בְּנָיָהוּ וְאֶבְיָתָר
ח א וְשַׂר־צָבָא לַמֶּלֶךְ יוֹאָב׃ וַיַּקְהֵל דָּוִיד אֶת־כָּל־שָׂרֵי יִשְׂרָאֵל
שָׂרֵי הַשְּׁבָטִים וְשָׂרֵי הַמַּחְלְקוֹת הַמְשָׁרְתִים אֶת־הַמֶּלֶךְ וְשָׂרֵי הָאֲלָפִים וְשָׂרֵי
הַמֵּאוֹת וְשָׂרֵי כָל־רְכוּשׁ־וּמִקְנֶה ׀ לַמֶּלֶךְ וּלְבָנָיו עִם־הַסָּרִיסִים וְהַגִּבּוֹרִים וּלְכָל־

BACKGROUND

27:28 | **Sycamores:** The sycamore, *Ficus sycomorus*, from the Moraceae family, is one of the most conspicuous and impressive trees in the southern coastal plain, primarily in areas of high groundwater. In light of this verse, the Sages stated: A good sign for the plain is a sycamore tree (*Pesaḥim* 53a). Its trunk can reach 3 m in thickness, and the tree can reach 20 m in height. The sycamore is an important material in the furniture and construction industries, due to the length and the strength of the beams produced from it, and moreover, it is lightweight and durable. In Egypt, well-preserved coffins for embalmed corpses, made of sycamore wood, have been unearthed. In addition, the fruit of the sycamore is edible. The importance of these trees is indicated not only by the appointment of Baal Hanan the Gederite over them, but also by the fact that several places are named for the sycamore, such as Shikmona (see Mishna *Demai* 1:1) and Gimzo, which is derived from *gimziyot*, branches of sycamore trees, as they are called in the Mishna (*Pesaḥim* 4:8). The prophet Amos is also characterized as a tender of sycamores (Amos 7:14).

27:30 | **Female donkeys:** In the ancient world, donkeys played a significant role in transportation, hauling loads, and agricultural work. Official Ugaritic documents mention donkey herdsmen. Female donkeys were in greater demand than males due to the female's calm disposition relative to the male, who can be difficult to control when he smells the odor of, or comes in contact with, the female. Therefore, several times in the biblical narrative one finds dignitaries and the wealthy riding female donkeys, e.g., Bilam (Numbers 22), the Shunamite woman in the story of Elisha (II Kings 4:22), and Job (Job 1:3, 42:12).

27:31 | **Hagrite:** The Hagrites are also mentioned earlier in this book (5:10, 19) and in the book of Psalms (83:7) as one of a group of tribes or nations that dwelled east of the Jordan that were hostile to Israel during the reign of Saul, and during the reigns of Yotam king of Judah, and Yorovam son of Yo'ash, king of Israel. According to the depiction here, the Hagrites were shepherds. Some commentaries suggest that they were descendants of Hagar (Ibn Ezra; Radak).

28:1 | **The officers [*sarisim*]:** It can be inferred from here and elsewhere that the original meaning of *saris* is unrelated to castration, its meaning in modern Hebrew. The term is probably derived from Akkadian, and its original meaning was a servant in the king's palace or harem (see Genesis 39:1). In ancient times it was standard practice to castrate these men, in order to protect the women of the palace from them and to limit their threat potential. Over time, the term came to refer to administrative officials as well, such as Potiphar, who is called a *saris* of Pharaoh (Genesis 37:36), yet had a wife. The Bible uses the term in both of its meanings.

2 **King David rose on his feet, and said: Hear me, my breth-**
ren and my people. As for me, it was in my heart, it was my desire, my passion, **to build a resting place for the Ark of the Covenant of the Lord, and for the footstool of our God, and I prepared** all that is required **to build.**
3 **But God said to me: You shall not build a house to My name, because you are a man of war, and you have shed blood.**
4 **The Lord, God of Israel, chose me from all the house of my father to be king over Israel forever. For He has** long since **chosen Judah to be ruler.** It is possible that already during Jacob's lifetime Judah was the leader of his brothers, even though he was not the firstborn and had not received any official appointment.[352] **And in the house of Judah, the house of my father** was chosen, **and among the sons of my father He preferred me to crown king over all Israel;**
5 **and from all my sons, as the Lord has given me numerous sons, He has chosen Solomon my son to sit upon the throne of the kingdom of the Lord over Israel.** The selection of Solomon was based both on David's promise to Bathsheba[353] and the message delivered to David by Natan the prophet at the time of Solomon's birth.[354]
6 **He said to me: Solomon your son, he will build My house and My courtyards, as I have chosen him to be a son to Me, and I will be a father to him.**
7 **I will establish his kingdom forever, if he will be vigilant to perform My commandments and My ordinances, like this day.** This stipulation, which will later be stated to Solomon as well,[355] can be read as a broad statement directed to the people of Israel, but it might also have important practical implications for them, in that the people are obligated to monitor the king's conduct and assess whether that conduct accords with the will of God.
8 **Now,** I command **before the eyes of all Israel,** before you, **the assembly of the Lord, and in the ears of our God, observe and seek all the commandments of the Lord your God, so that you may possess this good land** in the years to come as well, **and bequeath it to your children after you forever.**
9 The following two verses contain lofty ideas formulated in a poetic style. Some sections were stated by David publicly before the assembly, while others were stated in private. **As for you, Solomon my son, know the God of your father**[D] **and serve Him with a whole heart and with a willing mind; for** God's knowledge does not extend merely to man's deeds, as **the Lord** also **seeks out all hearts, and all inclinations of the thoughts He understands. If you seek** and follow **Him, He will be found for you, but if you forsake Him, He will abandon you forever.**
10 **See now, for the Lord has chosen you to build a house for the Temple; be strong, and act.**
11 After informing Israel of his grand plans and explaining that it would be Solomon, and not he, who would realize them, David entrusts Solomon with this task in private as well. **David gave Solomon his son the configuration of the Hall** of the Temple, **its houses, and its repositories**[356] [***ganzakav***], a word of Persian origin; **its upper chambers and its inner chambers, and the place of the ark cover,** the Holy of Holies;
12 **and the configuration of everything that was with him through** prophetic **inspiration for the courtyards of the House of the Lord, and for all the surrounding chambers, for the treasuries of the House of God, and for the treasuries of the consecrated items;** David had consolidated these plans with the assistance of the prophet Samuel.[357]
13 **And for the divisions of the priests and the Levites, and for all the labor of the service of the House of the Lord, and for all the vessels of service of the House of the Lord.** David also gave Solomon the designs of the vessels:
14 **Of gold by** the required **weight for** fashioning **the gold for all vessels of each and every service;** and similarly, **for all the silver vessels by weight, for all vessels of each and every service.** Solomon received detailed lists of the available materials and their use in each and every vessel.
15 **And the weight for the gold candelabra and their gold**
lamps, receptacles for oil, **by** a specific **weight for each and every candelabrum and its lamps.** Although there was only one candelabrum in the Tabernacle, and the commandment to kindle the lamps was fulfilled with that vessel alone, there were several gold candelabra in

"For each and every candelabrum and its lamps"

DISCUSSION

28:9| **Know the God of your father:** Many consider these words an early expression of the commandment of faith in God. Faith is not merely a passive inner experience within one's soul and consciousness; rather, it is an objective toward which one must strive, and therefore, there is a commandment to have faith in God (see introduction of Rabbeinu Baḥya; *Emunot VeDeot* 3). The Rambam, in formulating this commandment, states that one is obligated "to believe" in and "to know" the existence of God (see Rambam, *Sefer HaMadda, Hilkhot Yesodei HaTorah* 1:1; *Sefer HaMitzvot*, positive commandment 1; Rambam, *Guide of the Perplexed* 3:51).

ב גִּבּוֹר חַיִל אֶל־יְרוּשָׁלִָם׃ וַיָּקָם דָּוִיד הַמֶּלֶךְ עַל־רַגְלָיו וַיֹּאמֶר שְׁמָעוּנִי אַחַי וְעַמִּי
אֲנִי עִם־לְבָבִי לִבְנוֹת בֵּית מְנוּחָה לַאֲרוֹן בְּרִית־יְהוָה וְלַהֲדֹם רַגְלֵי אֱלֹהֵינוּ
ג וַהֲכִינוֹתִי לִבְנוֹת׃ וְהָאֱלֹהִים אָמַר לִי לֹא־תִבְנֶה בַיִת לִשְׁמִי כִּי אִישׁ מִלְחָמוֹת
ד אַתָּה וְדָמִים שָׁפָכְתָּ׃ וַיִּבְחַר יְהוָה אֱלֹהֵי יִשְׂרָאֵל בִּי מִכֹּל בֵּית־אָבִי לִהְיוֹת לְמֶלֶךְ
עַל־יִשְׂרָאֵל לְעוֹלָם כִּי בִיהוּדָה בָּחַר לְנָגִיד וּבְבֵית יְהוּדָה בֵּית אָבִי וּבִבְנֵי אָבִי
ה בִּי רָצָה לְהַמְלִיךְ עַל־כָּל־יִשְׂרָאֵל׃ וּמִכָּל־בָּנַי כִּי רַבִּים בָּנִים נָתַן לִי יְהוָה וַיִּבְחַר
ו בִּשְׁלֹמֹה בְנִי לָשֶׁבֶת עַל־כִּסֵּא מַלְכוּת יְהוָה עַל־יִשְׂרָאֵל׃ וַיֹּאמֶר לִי שְׁלֹמֹה בִנְךָ
ז הוּא־יִבְנֶה בֵיתִי וַחֲצֵרוֹתָי כִּי־בָחַרְתִּי בוֹ לִי לְבֵן וַאֲנִי אֶהְיֶה־לּוֹ לְאָב׃ וַהֲכִינוֹתִי
ח אֶת־מַלְכוּתוֹ עַד־לְעוֹלָם אִם־יֶחֱזַק לַעֲשׂוֹת מִצְוֹתַי וּמִשְׁפָּטַי כַּיּוֹם הַזֶּה׃ וְעַתָּה
לְעֵינֵי כָל־יִשְׂרָאֵל קְהַל־יְהוָה וּבְאָזְנֵי אֱלֹהֵינוּ שִׁמְרוּ וְדִרְשׁוּ כָּל־מִצְוֹת יְהוָה
אֱלֹהֵיכֶם לְמַעַן תִּירְשׁוּ אֶת־הָאָרֶץ הַטּוֹבָה וְהִנְחַלְתֶּם לִבְנֵיכֶם אַחֲרֵיכֶם עַד־
ט עוֹלָם׃ וְאַתָּה שְׁלֹמֹה־בְנִי דַּע אֶת־אֱלֹהֵי אָבִיךָ וְעָבְדֵהוּ בְּלֵב שָׁלֵם וּבְנֶפֶשׁ חֲפֵצָה
כִּי כָל־לְבָבוֹת דּוֹרֵשׁ יְהוָה וְכָל־יֵצֶר מַחֲשָׁבוֹת מֵבִין אִם־תִּדְרְשֶׁנּוּ יִמָּצֵא לָךְ
י וְאִם־תַּעַזְבֶנּוּ יַזְנִיחֲךָ לָעַד׃ רְאֵה ׀ עַתָּה כִּי־יְהוָה בָּחַר בְּךָ לִבְנוֹת־בַּיִת לַמִּקְדָּשׁ יא
יא חֲזַק וַעֲשֵׂה׃ וַיִּתֵּן דָּוִיד לִשְׁלֹמֹה בְנוֹ אֶת־תַּבְנִית הָאוּלָם וְאֶת־בָּתָּיו
יב וְגַנְזַכָּיו וַעֲלִיֹּתָיו וַחֲדָרָיו הַפְּנִימִים וּבֵית הַכַּפֹּרֶת׃ וְתַבְנִית כֹּל אֲשֶׁר הָיָה בָרוּחַ
עִמּוֹ לְחַצְרוֹת בֵּית־יְהוָה וּלְכָל־הַלְּשָׁכוֹת סָבִיב לְאֹצְרוֹת בֵּית הָאֱלֹהִים וּלְאֹצְרוֹת
יג הַקֳּדָשִׁים׃ וּלְמַחְלְקוֹת הַכֹּהֲנִים וְהַלְוִיִּם וּלְכָל־מְלֶאכֶת עֲבוֹדַת בֵּית־יְהוָה וּלְכָל־
יד כְּלֵי עֲבוֹדַת בֵּית־יְהוָה׃ לַזָּהָב בַּמִּשְׁקָל לַזָּהָב לְכָל־כְּלֵי עֲבוֹדָה וַעֲבוֹדָה לְכֹל
טו כְּלֵי הַכֶּסֶף בְּמִשְׁקָל לְכָל־כְּלֵי עֲבוֹדָה וַעֲבוֹדָה׃ וּמִשְׁקָל לִמְנֹרוֹת הַזָּהָב וְנֵרֹתֵיהֶם
זָהָב בְּמִשְׁקַל־מְנוֹרָה וּמְנוֹרָה וְנֵרֹתֶיהָ וְלִמְנֹרוֹת הַכֶּסֶף בְּמִשְׁקָל לִמְנוֹרָה וְנֵרֹתֶיהָ

the Temple.[358] **And for the silver candelabra, by weight for the candelabrum and its lamps, according to the service of each and every candelabrum.** In actual practice, nowhere is it stated that there were silver candelabra in the Temple, nor were there any decorative silver vessels in the Tabernacle.[359]

16 **And the gold by weight,** which was **for the tables of the arrangement,** for the showbread, **for each and every table; and silver for the tables of silver,** which were used in various services;[360]

17 **and the forks,** similar to pitchforks, for holding the meat of the offerings, **and the basins,** receptacles for the blood sprinkled on the altar, **and the tubes,** which formed a layered frame above the table on which the showbread was placed,[361] or which were vessels for holding libations and the like,[362] which were **of pure gold, and for the golden bowls,** or plates used as lids,[363] **by weight for each and every bowl, and for the silver bowls by weight for each and every bowl;**

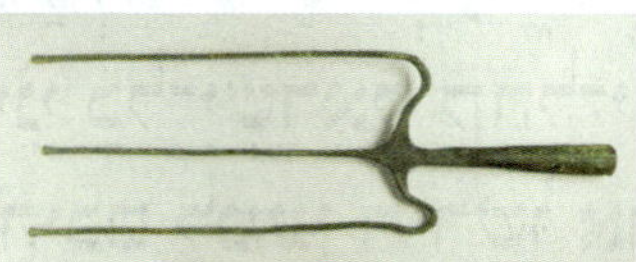

Fork found at Tel Megiddo, Middle Bronze Age, 1400–1300 BCE

Basin

18 **and for the altar of incense** there was **refined gold by weight, and gold for the configuration of the chariot,** which is **the cherubs, for spreading above and shielding the Ark of the Covenant of the Lord.**[364]

19 David summarizes: **Everything in writing from the hand of the Lord upon me that made me wise, all the labors of the configuration.** Solomon received not only instructions, but a complete and detailed plan, including both the architecture and the particulars of the contents of the structure. Although the Temple was not constructed in the same manner as the Tabernacle, in which every detail was given by direct order from God, David nevertheless emphasized that the plans he was presenting to his son were also divinely inspired. When Solomon later executed the project, he followed the plans he received from his father, even if those responsible in practice for its implementation were architects and craftsmen from Tyre.

20 There was concern that a young man facing a daunting project of that magnitude and complexity in the early years of his reign might grow anxious or postpone the project. Therefore, **David said to Solomon his son: Be strong and courageous, and act; do not fear, and do not be frightened. For the Lord God, my God, is with you; He will not fail you and will not forsake you, until the conclusion of all the labor of the service of the House of the Lord.** Be assured that you will receive assistance from Heaven.

21 **Behold the divisions of the priests and the Levites,** who are prepared **for all the service of the House of God; they will be with you in any labor, all who are generous with** their **wisdom** and volunteer their talents **for all service, and the princes and all the people are there for all your directives.** Everything is ready for you: the plans, the materials, and the human organization.

29 1 **King David**[D] **said to the entire assembly: Solomon my son** is only one man, and **God chose him alone;** moreover, he **is a lad** and a **tender youth.** Solomon ascended the throne when he was in his teens,[365] and might also have been youthful in appearance, with soft features. **And the labor is great, as the citadel is not** built **for man, but for the Lord God.** Palaces were typically constructed for show, to flaunt the king's glory, or as fortifications. This palace is not being built for me or for any other flesh-and-blood king; rather, it is for God. How is it possible for a man to fashion a dwelling place for God Almighty? It is incumbent upon him to dedicate himself to this tremendous project and not recoil in fear of failure, as one is not expected to perform any task beyond his human capabilities.[366]

2 **With all my might, I have prepared for the house of my God the gold** required **for the** items of **gold,**[367] **and the silver for the silver, and the bronze for the bronze, the iron for the iron, and the wood for the wood; onyx stones,**[B] **and stones** fashioned **for setting, carbuncle stones,**[B] **and** colorful and

DISCUSSION

29:1 | **King David:** The words attributed to King David include lofty expressions of spiritual inspiration alongside statements of encouragement and exhortation; they are a mixture of practical and material matters blended with themes of the spirit. David is characterized as the prototypical king, because he was not satisfied to merely sit on his throne and tend to administration of the kingdom, as many kings before and after him did. Rather, he considered matters with both a broad perspective from above and with an eye for their practical and systematic implementation. His spiritual and poetic qualities merged with the more practical and prosaic aspects to form his personality.

טז כַּעֲבוֹדַת מְנוֹרָה וּמְנוֹרָה: וְאֶת־הַזָּהָב מִשְׁקָל לְשֻׁלְחֲנוֹת הַמַּעֲרֶכֶת לְשֻׁלְחָן

יז וְשֻׁלְחָן וְכֶסֶף לְשֻׁלְחֲנוֹת הַכָּסֶף: וְהַמִּזְלָגוֹת וְהַמִּזְרָקוֹת וְהַקְּשָׂוֹת זָהָב טָהוֹר

וְלִכְפוֹרֵי הַזָּהָב בְּמִשְׁקָל לִכְפוֹר וּכְפוֹר וְלִכְפוֹרֵי הַכֶּסֶף בְּמִשְׁקָל לִכְפוֹר וּכְפוֹר:

יח וּלְמִזְבַּח הַקְּטֹרֶת זָהָב מְזֻקָּק בַּמִּשְׁקָל וּלְתַבְנִית הַמֶּרְכָּבָה הַכְּרֻבִים זָהָב לְפֹרְשִׂים

יט וְסֹכְכִים עַל־אֲרוֹן בְּרִית־יְהוָה: הַכֹּל בִּכְתָב מִיַּד יְהוָה עָלַי הִשְׂכִּיל כֹּל מַלְאֲכוֹת

כ הַתַּבְנִית: וַיֹּאמֶר דָּוִיד לִשְׁלֹמֹה בְנוֹ חֲזַק וֶאֱמַץ וַעֲשֵׂה אַל־תִּירָא

וְאַל־תֵּחָת כִּי יְהוָה אֱלֹהִים אֱלֹהַי עִמָּךְ לֹא יַרְפְּךָ וְלֹא יַעַזְבֶךָּ עַד־לִכְלוֹת כָּל־

כא מְלֶאכֶת עֲבוֹדַת בֵּית־יְהוָה: וְהִנֵּה מַחְלְקוֹת הַכֹּהֲנִים וְהַלְוִיִּם לְכָל־עֲבוֹדַת בֵּית

הָאֱלֹהִים וְעִמְּךָ בְכָל־מְלָאכָה לְכָל־נָדִיב בַּחָכְמָה לְכָל־עֲבוֹדָה וְהַשָּׂרִים וְכָל־

כט א הָעָם לְכָל־דְּבָרֶיךָ: וַיֹּאמֶר דָּוִיד הַמֶּלֶךְ לְכָל־הַקָּהָל שְׁלֹמֹה בְנִי אֶחָד

בָּחַר־בּוֹ אֱלֹהִים נַעַר וָרָךְ וְהַמְּלָאכָה גְדוֹלָה כִּי לֹא לְאָדָם הַבִּירָה כִּי לַיהוָה

ב אֱלֹהִים: וּכְכָל־כֹּחִי הֲכִינוֹתִי לְבֵית־אֱלֹהַי הַזָּהָב ׀ לַזָּהָב וְהַכֶּסֶף לַכֶּסֶף וְהַנְּחֹשֶׁת

לַנְּחֹשֶׁת הַבַּרְזֶל לַבַּרְזֶל וְהָעֵצִים לָעֵצִים אַבְנֵי־שֹׁהַם וּמִלּוּאִים אַבְנֵי־פוּךְ וְרִקְמָה

ג וְכֹל אֶבֶן יְקָרָה וְאַבְנֵי־שַׁיִשׁ לָרֹב: וְעוֹד בִּרְצוֹתִי בְּבֵית אֱלֹהַי יֶשׁ־לִי סְגֻלָּה זָהָב

specially cut stones for a **mosaic, and all precious stones, and marble stones in abundance.**

3 **Moreover, out of my desire for the House of my God, I have** a special **treasure of gold and silver that I have given to the House of my God, beyond everything,** all the materials **that I prepared for** specific uses in **the sacred House,** as part of the Temple plans:

Onyx stone

"Carbuncle stones"

BACKGROUND

29:2 | **Onyx [*shoham*] stones:** These precious stones are described in the Bible as originating in the land of Havila (Genesis 2:11–12), which is identified with modern-day Sudan. It is clear from the verse: "You shall take two onyx stones and engrave on them the names of the children of Israel" (Exodus 28:9), that these stones are suitable for engraving. Some identify *avnei shoham* with sardonyx. Both onyx and sardonyx are soft quartz stones, and were used in fashioning seals, rings, necklaces, and other ornaments. In Amharic they are known as *samu*, which evokes the word *shoham*.

Carbuncle [*pukh*] stones: This is presumably the same as the *nofekh*, one of the stones in the breast piece of the High Priest (Exodus 28:18). Some theorize, based on the term used in the Septuagint, that this is a red stone, and hence the translation of this term as carbuncle, which is a generic term for a red gemstone. However, others claim that this stone was actually blue or black. Some maintain that *pukh* is a cementing substance, used to fill the gaps between the precious stones in order to hold and highlight them.

4 This special donation is **three thousand talents of gold,** an exceedingly large amount, **from the gold of Ofir,**[B] **and seven thousand talents of refined silver, to overlay the walls of the houses,** referring to the Sanctuary and the Holy of Holies.[368] Instead of regular plaster, the Temple will be coated with gold and silver.

5 The quantity **of gold** is **for the** items of **gold, and of silver for the silver, and for all labor in the hands of** the **craftsmen.** I have given as much of the requisite materials as I can, and I have even left some money for incidental expenses and for the purchase of ornaments. David proceeds to call upon Israel to donate to the Temple treasuries: **Who** of you then **offers to devote himself today to the Lord?**

6 **The princes of the patrilineal houses, the princes of the tribes of Israel, the captains of the thousands and the hundreds, and the leaders of the king's labor donated;**

7 **they gave for the work of the House of God,** in addition to the three thousand talents of gold that David had donated, **five thousand talents and** the equivalent of another **ten thousand darics**[B] **of gold.** As these were Persian gold coins, this may be a later term that is employed here somewhat anachronistically. They also donated **ten thousand talents of silver, eighteen thousand talents of bronze, and one hundred thousand talents of iron.** Some of this massive donation was used for the requirements of the Temple service and vessels, while the rest was placed in the treasury.

Daric, fifth to fourth century BCE

8 **Those with whom precious stones were found** in their possession **gave to the treasury of the House of the Lord, into the hand of Yehiel the Gershonite,** the official in charge of these donations to the Temple.

9 Even when people respond to a king's call, they do not always act joyfully. But here, **the people rejoiced in their donation, because they donated to the Lord wholeheartedly, and King David too rejoiced with great joy** upon seeing the people adding their own donations.

David's Valediction and the Coronation of Solomon

I CHRONICLES 29:10–25

This is apparently King David's final speech before a large audience. Although there is no precise date, it is likely that the speech is presented toward the end of his life. Despite his frailty, the king is of sound mind, and he is able to withstand the exertion required to deliver a public discourse. Consequently, it stands to reason that this is not during David's final days.

The internal religious tension that courses through David's address to God here is reminiscent of many of his compositions in the book of Psalms.

10 **David blessed the Lord before the eyes of the entire assembly, and David said: Blessed are You, Lord, God of Israel, our father, forever and ever.**

11 **Yours, Lord, is the greatness, and the might, and the splendor, and the triumph, and the glory, for everything that is** found **in the heavens and on the earth. Yours, Lord, is the kingdom, and the preeminence over every head,** over all rulers.

12 **The riches and the honor are from before You, and You rule over all; in Your hand is power and might, and it is in Your hand to render everyone great and strong.**

13 **Now, our God, we thank You, and praise Your name of splendor.**

14 **For who am I, and who are my people, that we have the capacity to donate in this manner?** What is the source of our ability to give such substantial donations? In light of Israel's subjugation to its enemies prior to David's ascendancy, together with the many armed conflicts that continued throughout his reign, it is especially impressive that the leaders of the people donated those considerable sums. **For everything comes from You, and from Your own hand we have given to You.** You are the source of everything we possess, and therefore when we consecrate anything to You, it is as though it is given from Your own hand, which bestowed it upon us.

15 **For we** people **are strangers before You, and** temporary **residents, like all our fathers.** Human existence in this world is ephemeral, and we live here according to Your will. **Our days on earth are like a shadow,** which constantly changes and has no fixed, steady form, and which also lacks substance. Similarly, our lives are transient and our existence lacks substance.[369] **And there is no hope** of escaping death.[370]

16 **Lord our God, all this abundance**[371] **that we have prepared to build You a house to Your sacred name, it is from Your hand, and everything is Yours.** We cannot say that anything belongs to us. We give to You from that which You have granted us.

ד וְכֶסֶף נָתַתִּי לְבֵית־אֱלֹהַי לְמַעְלָה מִכָּל־הֲכִינוֹתִי לְבֵית הַקֹּדֶשׁ: שְׁלֹשֶׁת אֲלָפִים
כִּכְּרֵי זָהָב מִזְּהַב אוֹפִיר וְשִׁבְעַת אֲלָפִים כִּכַּר־כֶּסֶף מְזֻקָּק לָטוּחַ קִירוֹת הַבָּתִּים:
ה לַזָּהָב לַזָּהָב וְלַכֶּסֶף לַכֶּסֶף וּלְכָל־מְלָאכָה בְּיַד חָרָשִׁים וּמִי מִתְנַדֵּב לְמַלֹּאות יָדוֹ
ו הַיּוֹם לַיהוָה: וַיִּתְנַדְּבוּ שָׂרֵי הָאָבוֹת וְשָׂרֵי ׀ שִׁבְטֵי יִשְׂרָאֵל וְשָׂרֵי הָאֲלָפִים וְהַמֵּאוֹת
ז וּלְשָׂרֵי מְלֶאכֶת הַמֶּלֶךְ: וַיִּתְּנוּ לַעֲבוֹדַת בֵּית־הָאֱלֹהִים זָהָב כִּכָּרִים חֲמֵשֶׁת־
אֲלָפִים וַאֲדַרְכֹנִים רִבּוֹ וְכֶסֶף כִּכָּרִים עֲשֶׂרֶת אֲלָפִים וּנְחֹשֶׁת רִבּוֹ וּשְׁמוֹנַת אֲלָפִים
ח כִּכָּרִים וּבַרְזֶל מֵאָה־אֶלֶף כִּכָּרִים: וְהַנִּמְצָא אִתּוֹ אֲבָנִים נָתְנוּ לְאוֹצַר בֵּית־יְהוָה
ט עַל יַד־יְחִיאֵל הַגֵּרְשֻׁנִּי: וַיִּשְׂמְחוּ הָעָם עַל־הִתְנַדְּבָם כִּי בְּלֵב שָׁלֵם הִתְנַדְּבוּ
י לַיהוָה וְגַם דָּוִיד הַמֶּלֶךְ שָׂמַח שִׂמְחָה גְדוֹלָה: וַיְבָרֶךְ דָּוִיד אֶת־יְהוָה
לְעֵינֵי כָּל־הַקָּהָל וַיֹּאמֶר דָּוִיד בָּרוּךְ אַתָּה יְהוָה אֱלֹהֵי יִשְׂרָאֵל אָבִינוּ מֵעוֹלָם
יא וְעַד־עוֹלָם: לְךָ יְהוָה הַגְּדֻלָּה וְהַגְּבוּרָה וְהַתִּפְאֶרֶת וְהַנֵּצַח וְהַהוֹד כִּי־כֹל בַּשָּׁמַיִם
יב וּבָאָרֶץ לְךָ יְהוָה הַמַּמְלָכָה וְהַמִּתְנַשֵּׂא לְכֹל ׀ לְרֹאשׁ: וְהָעֹשֶׁר וְהַכָּבוֹד מִלְּפָנֶיךָ
יג וְאַתָּה מוֹשֵׁל בַּכֹּל וּבְיָדְךָ כֹּחַ וּגְבוּרָה וּבְיָדְךָ לְגַדֵּל וּלְחַזֵּק לַכֹּל: וְעַתָּה אֱלֹהֵינוּ
יד מוֹדִים אֲנַחְנוּ לָךְ וּמְהַלְלִים לְשֵׁם תִּפְאַרְתֶּךָ: וְכִי מִי אֲנִי וּמִי עַמִּי כִּי־נַעְצֹר כֹּחַ
טו לְהִתְנַדֵּב כָּזֹאת כִּי־מִמְּךָ הַכֹּל וּמִיָּדְךָ נָתַנּוּ לָךְ: כִּי־גֵרִים אֲנַחְנוּ לְפָנֶיךָ וְתוֹשָׁבִים
טז כְּכָל־אֲבֹתֵינוּ כַּצֵּל ׀ יָמֵינוּ עַל־הָאָרֶץ וְאֵין מִקְוֶה: יְהוָה אֱלֹהֵינוּ כֹּל הֶהָמוֹן הַזֶּה

BACKGROUND

29:4| **The gold of Ofir:** This is high-quality gold from East Africa, southern Arabia, or India, and is also called "the pure gold of Ofir" (Isaiah 13:12; Psalms 45:10; Job 28:16). Some suggest that the name Africa is derived from Ofir. The ancients distinguished between various types of gold, in accordance with the metal's place of origin, quality, and method of production, employing distinct terms: *paz*, fine gold (see, e.g., Isaiah 13:12); pure gold (see, e.g., Exodus 25:39); refined gold (see, e.g., 28:18); *sagur* gold, also translated as "pure gold" (see, e.g., I Kings 6:20); beaten gold (see, e.g., I Kings 10:16); gold of Parvayim (II Chronicles 3:6), and a type of gold known as *ḥarutz* (see, e.g., Proverbs 8:19). The precise difference between these types of gold is unknown.

29:7| **Darics:** This is the first actual coin mentioned in the Bible. This gold Persian coin weighed roughly 8.4 g and was imprinted with the image of the Persian king holding a bow in his right hand and a spear in his left. Despite the similarity of the name, the daric was not identical to the Greek drachma. There are several suggestions for the derivation of the name. According to the Greek writers Julius Pollux and Herodotus, "daric" is a corruption of the name of King Darius who minted the coins, whom they called Dareikós. Modern-day scholars claim that the name is derived from the Persian word *dari*, meaning gold. Others contend that it is a combination of two Persian words, *dara*, king, and *kaman*, bow.

17 **I know, my God, that You examine the heart, and desire uprightness. I, in the uprightness of my heart, have donated all these, and now I have seen** that **Your people, who are present here,** are also **donating to You with joy.** I knew what was in my own heart, and now I see that the leaders of the people who likewise donated have done so joyfully. We cannot claim ownership over the property in our possession, but we can at least dedicate our hearts and desires to God.

18 David requests: **Lord, God of Abraham, Isaac, and Israel our fathers, preserve this forever, the inclination,** the motivating force **of the thoughts of the heart of Your people;** remember forever that the people donated wholeheartedly, **and fortify their heart** to turn **toward You.**

19 **And give to Solomon my son a whole heart, to observe Your commandments, Your testimonies, and Your statutes, and to perform them all, and to build the citadel for which I have prepared.**

20 **David said to the entire assembly: Bless now the Lord your God. All the assembly blessed the Lord, God of their fathers, and bowed and prostrated themselves to the Lord and before the king.**

21 **They sacrificed peace offerings to the Lord and offered up burnt offerings to the Lord, on the morrow of that day, one thousand bulls, one thousand rams, and one thousand lambs, and their libations,** the wine poured onto the altar alongside the offering, and the high-quality flour offering burned on the altar together with the animal offering. All these were given by the king or the community, **and** private **peace offerings** were brought **in abundance for all Israel.**

22 **They ate and drank before the Lord on that day with great joy. They crowned Solomon son of David king a second time, and anointed him to the Lord as ruler.** Although Solomon had already been crowned, in accordance with the wishes and explicit order of David, his coronation had been discreet. Several of the prominent people of the realm had supported the move, but in a private ceremony. Here, by contrast, the crowning and anointing of Solomon is performed before all of Israel. **And Tzadok** they appointed **as** High **Priest.** This was also apparently David's choice, as he preferred that Tzadok lead the priests, rather than Ahimelekh, who was descended from the house of Eli.

23 **Solomon sat on the throne of the Lord as king in place of David his father, and he prospered, and all Israel heeded him,** accepting his authority.

24 **All the princes, and the mighty** men, who served as army officers and in other important positions, **and all the sons of King David, gave a hand in support of King Solomon** and vowed to obey him. Virtually everyone united in support of Solomon. Even those who could have raised claims against him remained silent and accepted his rule.

25 **The Lord exalted Solomon before the eyes of all Israel and bestowed upon him the glory of royalty that had not been on any king over Israel before him.** Not only was he an extraordinarily successful ruler of state, but no other king of Judah or Israel, past or future, could rival the splendor of Solomon's kingdom.[372]

Summary of David's Life

I CHRONICLES 29:26–30

26 **David son of Yishai reigned over all Israel.**

27 **The days that he reigned over Israel were forty years,** divided into two periods: A little more than **seven years he reigned in Hebron,**[373] **and in Jerusalem he reigned thirty-three years.** The numbers indicate that David became king when he was a relatively young man, about thirty years old. During the forty years of his reign, with all its vicissitudes, he consolidated and strengthened the kingdom.

28 **He died at a good old age, full of days, wealth, and honor; Solomon his son reigned in his stead.**

29 **The acts of King David, first and last,** all the events of his life, **behold, they are written in the words of Samuel the seer.** This may refer to a lost work, or to the biblical book of Samuel, which describes the reign of King David.[374] **And** his deeds likewise appear **in the words of Natan the prophet, and in the words of Gad the seer.** Here too, it is possible that the verse is referring to books written by Natan and Gad which are no longer extant.[375] Alternatively, these are the latter parts of the book of Samuel, which was certainly not written in its entirety by Samuel himself, as his death is depicted roughly halfway through the book. It is reasonable to assume that Natan the prophet and Gad the seer, who assumed Samuel's prophetic role, also completed his book.

30 The prophets of Israel wrote the history of King David, **along with all his dominion and his might, and the times that befell him and Israel, and all the kingdoms of the lands.** The book of Chronicles relates these events based on those earlier sources.

יז אֲשֶׁר הֲכִינוֹנוּ לִבְנוֹת־לְךָ בַיִת לְשֵׁם קָדְשֶׁךָ מִיָּדְךָ הִיא וּלְךָ הַכֹּל׃ וְיָדַעְתִּי אֱלֹהַי הוא
כִּי אַתָּה בֹּחֵן לֵבָב וּמֵישָׁרִים תִּרְצֶה אֲנִי בְּיֹשֶׁר לְבָבִי הִתְנַדַּבְתִּי כָל־אֵלֶּה וְעַתָּה
יח עַמְּךָ הַנִּמְצְאוּ־פֹה רָאִיתִי בְשִׂמְחָה לְהִתְנַדֶּב־לָךְ׃ יְהוָה אֱלֹהֵי אַבְרָהָם יִצְחָק
וְיִשְׂרָאֵל אֲבֹתֵינוּ שָׁמְרָה־זֹּאת לְעוֹלָם לְיֵצֶר מַחְשְׁבוֹת לְבַב עַמֶּךָ וְהָכֵן לְבָבָם
יט אֵלֶיךָ׃ וְלִשְׁלֹמֹה בְנִי תֵּן לֵבָב שָׁלֵם לִשְׁמוֹר מִצְוֺתֶיךָ עֵדְוֺתֶיךָ וְחֻקֶּיךָ וְלַעֲשׂוֹת
כ הַכֹּל וְלִבְנוֹת הַבִּירָה אֲשֶׁר־הֲכִינוֹתִי׃ וַיֹּאמֶר דָּוִיד לְכָל־הַקָּהָל בָּרְכוּ־
נָא אֶת־יְהוָה אֱלֹהֵיכֶם וַיְבָרְכוּ כָל־הַקָּהָל לַיהוָה אֱלֹהֵי אֲבֹתֵיהֶם וַיִּקְּדוּ וַיִּשְׁתַּחֲווּ
כא לַיהוָה וְלַמֶּלֶךְ׃ וַיִּזְבְּחוּ לַיהוָה ׀ זְבָחִים וַיַּעֲלוּ עֹלוֹת לַיהוָה לְמָחֳרַת הַיּוֹם הַהוּא
כב פָּרִים אֶלֶף אֵילִים אֶלֶף כְּבָשִׂים אֶלֶף וְנִסְכֵּיהֶם וּזְבָחִים לָרֹב לְכָל־יִשְׂרָאֵל׃ וַיֹּאכְלוּ
וַיִּשְׁתּוּ לִפְנֵי יְהוָה בַּיּוֹם הַהוּא בְּשִׂמְחָה גְדוֹלָה וַיַּמְלִיכוּ שֵׁנִית לִשְׁלֹמֹה בֶן־דָּוִיד
כג וַיִּמְשְׁחוּ לַיהוָה לְנָגִיד וּלְצָדוֹק לְכֹהֵן׃ וַיֵּשֶׁב שְׁלֹמֹה עַל־כִּסֵּא יְהוָה ׀ לְמֶלֶךְ תַּחַת־
כד דָּוִיד אָבִיו וַיַּצְלַח וַיִּשְׁמְעוּ אֵלָיו כָּל־יִשְׂרָאֵל׃ וְכָל־הַשָּׂרִים וְהַגִּבֹּרִים וְגַם כָּל־בְּנֵי
כה הַמֶּלֶךְ דָּוִיד נָתְנוּ יָד תַּחַת שְׁלֹמֹה הַמֶּלֶךְ׃ וַיְגַדֵּל יְהוָה אֶת־שְׁלֹמֹה לְמַעְלָה לְעֵינֵי
כָּל־יִשְׂרָאֵל וַיִּתֵּן עָלָיו הוֹד מַלְכוּת אֲשֶׁר לֹא־הָיָה עַל־כָּל־מֶלֶךְ לְפָנָיו עַל־
כו כז יִשְׂרָאֵל׃ וְדָוִיד בֶּן־יִשָׁי מָלַךְ עַל־כָּל־יִשְׂרָאֵל׃ וְהַיָּמִים אֲשֶׁר מָלַךְ עַל־
יִשְׂרָאֵל אַרְבָּעִים שָׁנָה בְּחֶבְרוֹן מָלַךְ שֶׁבַע שָׁנִים וּבִירוּשָׁלִַם מָלַךְ שְׁלֹשִׁים וְשָׁלוֹשׁ׃
כח כט וַיָּמָת בְּשֵׂיבָה טוֹבָה שְׂבַע יָמִים עֹשֶׁר וְכָבוֹד וַיִּמְלֹךְ שְׁלֹמֹה בְנוֹ תַּחְתָּיו׃ וְדִבְרֵי
דָּוִיד הַמֶּלֶךְ הָרִאשֹׁנִים וְהָאַחֲרֹנִים הִנָּם כְּתוּבִים עַל־דִּבְרֵי שְׁמוּאֵל הָרֹאֶה וְעַל־
ל דִּבְרֵי נָתָן הַנָּבִיא וְעַל־דִּבְרֵי גָּד הַחֹזֶה׃ עִם כָּל־מַלְכוּתוֹ וּגְבוּרָתוֹ וְהָעִתִּים אֲשֶׁר
עָבְרוּ עָלָיו וְעַל־יִשְׂרָאֵל וְעַל כָּל־מַמְלְכוֹת הָאֲרָצוֹת׃

II Chronicles

The Grandeur of Solomon's Kingdom

II CHRONICLES 1:1–18

In the original Jewish division of the books of the Bible, there is only one book of Chronicles. The following section is a direct continuation of the events with which I Chronicles concluded, the death of King David and the coronation of his son Solomon.

1 1 **Solomon son of David grew stronger in his kingdom,** his
rule was well established, **and the Lord his God was with him,**
and God **exalted him upward.** Solomon had a firm grip on the
reins of power, and his kingdom grew gradually greater.
2 **Solomon spoke with all Israel: To the leaders of the thou-**
sands and of the hundreds, to the judges, and to every
prince in all Israel, the heads of the patrilineal houses. He
gathered together all his military and governmental officials,
and also all the local leaders.
3 **Solomon and all the assembly with him went to the shrine**
that was at Givon,[1] **as there was the Tent of Meeting of**
God, which Moses servant of the Lord had crafted in the
wilderness. The remains of the Tabernacle that was initially
constructed in the wilderness, and which had stood in Shilo,
had later been transferred to Givon.

Nebi Samuel, identified by some as the location of the shrine at Givon

4 **But** the ark was not in the Tabernacle in Givon, as **David had**
taken up the Ark of God from Kiryat Ye'arim to the place
that David had prepared for it, for he had pitched a tent for
it in Jerusalem.
5 **The** great **bronze altar** which had been in the Tabernacle,
that Betzalel, son of Uri, son of Hur, had crafted, had also
been brought to the Land of Israel, and **he,** Solomon,[2] **placed**
it **before the Tabernacle of the Lord, and Solomon and the**
assembly sought it; they turned to it. All the leaders gathered
before the altar to sacrifice offerings upon it.
6 **Solomon presented,** that is, at his command they sacrificed
there, on the bronze altar before the Lord, which was at the
Tent of Meeting; he, the priests at his command, **presented**
on it one thousand burnt offerings.
7 **On that night,** after the offerings had been sacrificed, **God ap-**
peared to Solomon in a prophetic vision, **and** He **said to him:**
Ask; what shall I give you?
8 **Solomon said to God: You acted with great kindness to**
David my father, as You made him a victorious and powerful
king, **and You crowned me king in his stead.**
9 **Now, Lord God, let Your word to David my father be sub-**
stantiated, as You have crowned me king over a people
numerous like the dust of the earth, the entire people of
Israel.
10 **Now, grant me wisdom and knowledge, and I will go out**
and come before this people. This expression, "go out and
come before," which appears in several instances in the Bible,
means "to lead."[3] **As who can judge this great people of**
Yours? Who can properly judge an entire nation, and lead the
people while providing for all their needs, both material and
spiritual?
11 **God said to Solomon: Because this was in your heart, and**
you did not request wealth, property, or honor, or the life
of your enemies, and you also did not request long life, but
instead **you requested wisdom and knowledge for yourself**
so that you can judge My people, over whom I crowned you
king;
12 therefore, **the wisdom and the knowledge is granted to you**
as you requested, **and** in addition, despite the fact that you did
not request them, **I will grant you wealth, and property, and**
honor, the like of which none of the kings before you had,
and the like of which there will not be after you.
13 **Solomon came to the shrine that was in Givon** on the day
following his vision, in order to give thanks for the good tidings
he had received that night. He continued **to Jerusalem,**[4] **from**
before the Tent of Meeting in Givon, **and he reigned over**
Israel.

דברי הימים ב

א א וַיִּתְחַזֵּק שְׁלֹמֹה בֶן־דָּוִיד עַל־מַלְכוּתוֹ וַיהוָה אֱלֹהָיו עִמּוֹ וַיְגַדְּלֵהוּ לְמָעְלָה׃
ב וַיֹּאמֶר שְׁלֹמֹה לְכָל־יִשְׂרָאֵל לְשָׂרֵי הָאֲלָפִים וְהַמֵּאוֹת וְלַשֹּׁפְטִים וּלְכֹל נָשִׂיא
ג לְכָל־יִשְׂרָאֵל רָאשֵׁי הָאָבוֹת׃ וַיֵּלְכוּ שְׁלֹמֹה וְכָל־הַקָּהָל עִמּוֹ לַבָּמָה אֲשֶׁר בְּגִבְעוֹן
ד כִּי־שָׁם הָיָה אֹהֶל מוֹעֵד הָאֱלֹהִים אֲשֶׁר עָשָׂה מֹשֶׁה עֶבֶד־יְהוָה בַּמִּדְבָּר׃ אֲבָל
אֲרוֹן הָאֱלֹהִים הֶעֱלָה דָוִיד מִקִּרְיַת יְעָרִים בַּהֵכִין לוֹ דָּוִיד כִּי נָטָה־לוֹ אֹהֶל
ה בִּירוּשָׁלִָם׃ וּמִזְבַּח הַנְּחֹשֶׁת אֲשֶׁר עָשָׂה בְּצַלְאֵל בֶּן־אוּרִי בֶן־חוּר שָׂם לִפְנֵי מִשְׁכַּן
ו יְהוָה וַיִּדְרְשֵׁהוּ שְׁלֹמֹה וְהַקָּהָל׃ וַיַּעַל שְׁלֹמֹה שָׁם עַל־מִזְבַּח הַנְּחֹשֶׁת לִפְנֵי יְהוָה
ז אֲשֶׁר לְאֹהֶל מוֹעֵד וַיַּעַל עָלָיו עֹלוֹת אָלֶף׃   בַּלַּיְלָה הַהוּא נִרְאָה אֱלֹהִים
ח לִשְׁלֹמֹה וַיֹּאמֶר לוֹ שְׁאַל מָה אֶתֶּן־לָךְ׃ וַיֹּאמֶר שְׁלֹמֹה לֵאלֹהִים אַתָּה עָשִׂיתָ
ט עִם־דָּוִיד אָבִי חֶסֶד גָּדוֹל וְהִמְלַכְתַּנִי תַּחְתָּיו׃ עַתָּה יְהוָה אֱלֹהִים יֵאָמֵן דְּבָרְךָ
י עִם דָּוִיד אָבִי כִּי אַתָּה הִמְלַכְתַּנִי עַל־עַם רַב כַּעֲפַר הָאָרֶץ׃ עַתָּה חָכְמָה וּמַדָּע
תֶּן־לִי וְאֵצְאָה לִפְנֵי הָעָם־הַזֶּה וְאָבוֹאָה כִּי־מִי יִשְׁפֹּט אֶת־עַמְּךָ הַזֶּה הַגָּדוֹל׃
יא וַיֹּאמֶר אֱלֹהִים ׀ לִשְׁלֹמֹה יַעַן אֲשֶׁר הָיְתָה זֹאת עִם־לְבָבֶךָ וְלֹא־שָׁאַלְתָּ עֹשֶׁר
נְכָסִים וְכָבוֹד וְאֵת נֶפֶשׁ שֹׂנְאֶיךָ וְגַם־יָמִים רַבִּים לֹא שָׁאָלְתָּ וַתִּשְׁאַל־לְךָ חָכְמָה
יב וּמַדָּע אֲשֶׁר תִּשְׁפּוֹט אֶת־עַמִּי אֲשֶׁר הִמְלַכְתִּיךָ עָלָיו׃ הַחָכְמָה וְהַמַּדָּע נָתוּן לָךְ
וְעֹשֶׁר וּנְכָסִים וְכָבוֹד אֶתֶּן־לָךְ אֲשֶׁר ׀ לֹא־הָיָה כֵן לַמְּלָכִים אֲשֶׁר לְפָנֶיךָ וְאַחֲרֶיךָ
יג לֹא יִהְיֶה־כֵּן׃ וַיָּבֹא שְׁלֹמֹה לַבָּמָה אֲשֶׁר־בְּגִבְעוֹן יְרוּשָׁלִַם מִלִּפְנֵי אֹהֶל מוֹעֵד וַיִּמְלֹךְ

14 These are some depictions of the grandeur of Solomon's kingdom: **Solomon accumulated chariots and horsemen; he had one thousand four hundred chariots and twelve thousand horsemen, and he deployed them,** the horsemen, **in the chariot cities,**[B] e.g., Megiddo, where there were very large stables where the chariots were stored, **and** some of the chariots and horsemen remained **with the king in Jerusalem,** probably as his garrison.

"Chariot cities." Ruins of stable, Tel Megiddo, 790–784 BCE

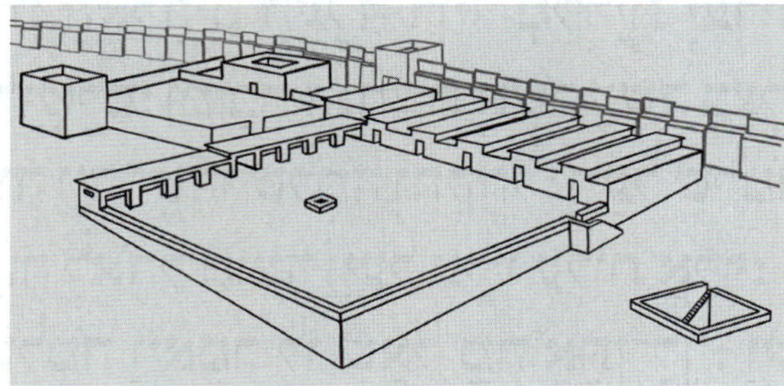
Megiddo stables, sketch based on archaeological findings

15 **The king rendered,** through his wise actions, **the silver and the gold in Jerusalem like stones.** Due to its abundance, people considered silver as no more precious than stones.[5] Israel was a primarily agricultural society in which silver had not been a particularly valuable commodity. However, in Solomon's days, the structure of the country's economy began to change, and gold and silver became valuable. Even then, due to the great amounts of silver and gold that flowed into the land, the people considered it unremarkable. **And the cedars, he,** Solomon, **rendered like the sycamores,**[6] **that are** grown **on the plain in abundance.** The king brought so many cedar trees to Jerusalem that the sight of this tree, imported from Lebanon, became similarly unremarkable for the city's residents.

16 **The origin of the horses of Solomon was Egypt,**[B] which was a great center of horse breeding; **and collection [*mikve*]**[B] **was by the king's,** Solomon's, **merchants, who would purchase a collection for a price.** As King Solomon had been granted the concession to trade in horses,[7] he had a collection center in Egypt, from where the king's merchants would sell them. Alternatively, *mikve* means from Keveh, another province that sold horses to Solomon.[8]

17 **They took up and took out of Egypt a chariot for six hundred silver shekels, and a horse for one hundred and fifty** silver shekels; **and so it was for all the kings of the Hitites, and the kings of Aram; by their hand they would take them out,** at the behest of King Solomon's merchants. These Hitite and Aramean kings were forced to purchase the horses from Solomon's merchants, and Solomon therefore earned a substantial profit as the intermediary. It was lucrative to trade in these horses and chariots, as the horses were utilized as warhorses, and the chariots in armored battles.[9]

Egyptian chariot, Tomb of Tutankhamun, Egypt, Late Bronze Age

18 After his kingdom was established, **Solomon resolved** to fulfill his father's will and **to build a house for the name of the Lord,** the Temple, **and** to also build **a house,** a royal palace, **for his kingdom.**

Solomon Builds the Temple

II CHRONICLES 2:1–5:1

After a brief description of the economic and military structure of Solomon's kingdom, the text provides an elaborate account of the building of the Temple, including its planning and execution. There is a more detailed description of the vessels and the Temple itself in the book of Kings.

2 1 **Solomon mustered** and organized **seventy thousand porters,** whose job was to carry the stones for the Temple, **and** an additional **eighty thousand quarrymen**[D] **in the mountains, and supervising them were three thousand six hundred.** Those appointed to supervisory roles were apparently men who enjoyed prominent social status in Israel, e.g., Yorovam son of Nevat, who would ultimately establish the independent Kingdom of Israel after King Solomon's death.[10]

2 **Solomon sent to Huram king of Tyre, saying: As you did with David my father, and you sent him cedars to build himself a house in which to dwell,**

3 **behold, I am building a house for the name of the Lord my God, to dedicate it to Him,** to exalt His name, **and to burn before Him incense of spices, and a continual arrangement** of the showbread,[11] **and burnt offerings for the morning and for the evening, for Sabbaths and for the New Moons, and for the appointed times of the Lord our God. This is** a worship ritual incumbent **upon Israel forever.**

"To burn before Him incense of spices, and a continual arrangement"

יד עַל־יִשְׂרָאֵל׃ וַיֶּאֱסֹף שְׁלֹמֹה רֶכֶב וּפָרָשִׁים וַיְהִי־לוֹ אֶלֶף וְאַרְבַּע־מֵאוֹת
טו רֶכֶב וּשְׁנֵים־עָשָׂר אֶלֶף פָּרָשִׁים וַיַּנִּיחֵם בְּעָרֵי הָרֶכֶב וְעִם־הַמֶּלֶךְ בִּירוּשָׁלִָם׃ וַיִּתֵּן
הַמֶּלֶךְ אֶת־הַכֶּסֶף וְאֶת־הַזָּהָב בִּירוּשָׁלִַם כָּאֲבָנִים וְאֵת הָאֲרָזִים נָתַן כַּשִּׁקְמִים
טז אֲשֶׁר־בַּשְּׁפֵלָה לָרֹב׃ וּמוֹצָא הַסּוּסִים אֲשֶׁר לִשְׁלֹמֹה מִמִּצְרָיִם וּמִקְוֵא סֹחֲרֵי הַמֶּלֶךְ
יז מִקְוֵא יִקְחוּ בִּמְחִיר׃ וַיַּעֲלוּ וַיּוֹצִיאוּ מִמִּצְרַיִם מֶרְכָּבָה בְּשֵׁשׁ מֵאוֹת כֶּסֶף וְסוּס
יח בַּחֲמִשִּׁים וּמֵאָה וְכֵן לְכָל־מַלְכֵי הַחִתִּים וּמַלְכֵי אֲרָם בְּיָדָם יוֹצִיאוּ׃ וַיֹּאמֶר שְׁלֹמֹה
ב א לִבְנוֹת בַּיִת לְשֵׁם יהוה וּבַיִת לְמַלְכוּתוֹ׃ וַיִּסְפֹּר שְׁלֹמֹה שִׁבְעִים אֶלֶף אִישׁ סַבָּל
וּשְׁמוֹנִים אֶלֶף אִישׁ חֹצֵב בָּהָר וּמְנַצְּחִים עֲלֵיהֶם שְׁלֹשֶׁת אֲלָפִים וְשֵׁשׁ מֵאוֹת׃
ב וַיִּשְׁלַח שְׁלֹמֹה אֶל־חוּרָם מֶלֶךְ־צֹר לֵאמֹר כַּאֲשֶׁר עָשִׂיתָ עִם־דָּוִיד אָבִי וַתִּשְׁלַח־
ג לוֹ אֲרָזִים לִבְנוֹת־לוֹ בַיִת לָשֶׁבֶת בּוֹ׃ הִנֵּה אֲנִי בוֹנֶה־בַּיִת לְשֵׁם ׀ יהוה אֱלֹהָי יב
לְהַקְדִּישׁ לוֹ לְהַקְטִיר לְפָנָיו קְטֹרֶת־סַמִּים וּמַעֲרֶכֶת תָּמִיד וְעֹלוֹת לַבֹּקֶר וְלָעֶרֶב

BACKGROUND

1:14 | **Chariot cities:** Whereas David removed the chariots and hamstrung the horses of his enemies (see II Samuel 8:4; I Chronicles 18:4), his son Solomon established a chariot corps. Its establishment necessitated the formation of a permanent, professional army, and the preparation of an infrastructure of stables based on the following requirements: proximity to important roads and central intersections, availability of horse feed, and open areas for training chariot warriors. Consequently, Solomon constructed his chariot cities in areas adjacent to valleys: Gezer and Beit Horon, near the Ayalon Valley; Hatzor, near the Hula Valley, and Megiddo, alongside the plains of the Yizre'el Valley.

1:16 | **The origin of the horses of Solomon was Egypt:** There are several verses in the Bible that indicate a close connection between Egypt, and horses and chariots (Deuteronomy 17:16; II Kings 18:24, Isaiah 31:1; Ezekiel 17:15; Song of Songs 1:9). This characteristic link is also found in Assyrian documents dating to the eighth century BCE, in which Egypt is mentioned as the source for the imported Nubian horses used in the Assyrian cavalry.

Collection [*mikve*]: Some maintain that the verse is referring to the kingdom of Que, a Hitite kingdom that was located on the Cilician Plains in southeast Turkey (see Abravanel). This kingdom was located on the trade route from Mesopotamia to Anatolia and the islands of the Aegean Sea, and its inhabitants engaged in trading horses.

DISCUSSION

2:1 | **Porters and...quarrymen:** Vast numbers of workers were required due to the unique specifications of the building of the Temple. Unlike other buildings, the Temple was not constructed from stones that could be carried on shoulders; rather, it was built with very large stones. In order to build a structure of stone that large, it was necessary to find a special quarrying site, as well as a way to transport the stones to Jerusalem. Even today, transporting extremely heavy loads is very difficult, all the more so in those days, when the stones were moved without modern means of transportation.

4 **The house that I am building is great, as our God is greater than all the gods.**

5 **Who** indeed **has the capacity to build Him a house, as the heavens and the heaven of heavens cannot contain Him?** I am certainly not trying to build a place in which God will dwell. **Who am I that I should build Him a house, except** only that I desire **to burn offerings** there **before Him.** The Temple does not constrict the place of God, which is impossible; rather, it is to serve as a place to worship Him.[12]

6 **Now send me a wise man** who is able **to craft with the gold, and with the silver, and with the bronze, and with the iron, and with the purple [*argevan*],**[B] wool dyed reddish-purple, the same as the more common term *argaman*, **and the crimson**[B] **and sky-blue wool, and knows how to engrave engravings, to be** working **with the wise men who are with me in Judah and in Jerusalem, whom David my father prepared.** David trained experts who could perform the work for the Temple, and now Solomon requires an executive director for the project.

Spiny dye-murex, from which purple dye is extracted

Scale insects, from which crimson dye is produced

Banded dye-murex, from which blue dye is extracted

7 **Send me cedar, juniper,**[B] **and sandalwood [*algumim*]**[B] **trees from Lebanon.** The precise identity of this wood, which grows in Lebanon, is unclear, but it is certainly not coral, which is *almogim* in modern Hebrew. **As I know that your servants know how to cut the trees of Lebanon** properly; **behold, my servants are** sent **with your** expert **servants**

8 **to prepare me timber in abundance, for the house that I am building will be** exceedingly **great and wondrous.** That is why I need so much material.

Juniper

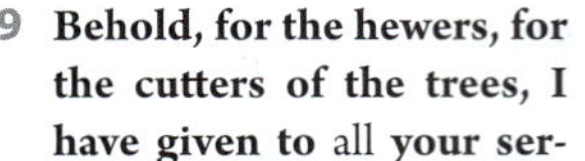

9 **Behold, for the hewers, for the cutters of the trees, I have given to** all **your servants twenty thousand kor of crushed wheat, and** I will give **twenty thousand kor of barley;** a kor is a measure of volume of more than 210 L, **and twenty thousand bat of wine;** a *bat* is a liquid measurement which is one-tenth of a kor,[13] **and twenty thousand bat of oil.**[B] Solomon speaks respectfully, employing diplomatic formulations. He clarifies to Huram that he is not asking for a gift or collecting a tax. Rather, he intends to pay for the work with agricultural produce. In later periods as well, Judah, like the Land of Israel in general, was an exporter of grain and oils.

10 Huram was pleased with Solomon's friendly tone, and with the fact that so significant a client had approached him. **Huram king of Tyre stated in writing, and sent to Solomon: In the love of the Lord of His people, He placed you king over them.**

11 **Huram said: Blessed is the Lord, God of Israel, who made the heavens and the earth, who gave King David a wise son, endowed with sagacity and understanding, who will build a house for the Lord, and a house,** palace, **for his kingdom.**

12 **Now I have sent a wise man, endowed with understanding, the distinguished Huram.**[D] He shared the same name as the king himself, as Huram was apparently not an unusual name.[14]

13 This Huram is the **son of a woman from the daughters of Dan,** and thus he is basically one of your own, **and his father is a man of Tyre.** He is one **knowledgeable to work with the gold, with the silver, with the bronze, with the iron, with the stones, with the wood, with the purple wool, with the sky-blue wool, with fine linen, with crimson wool, to**

DISCUSSION

2:12 | **The distinguished [*avi*] Huram:** *Avi* is an honorific, like "Sir" or "Excellency." This title is found in the Bible (see, e.g., II Kings 2:12, 13:14), and in rabbinic literature, where distinguished Sages are occasionally called Abba, e.g., Abba Binyamin (*Berakhot* 6a).

BACKGROUND

2:6 | **Purple [*argevan*]:** This is a general term for the reddish-purple dye extracted from the spiny dye-murex, *Murex brandaris*. Early documents indicate that wool dyed with this substance was four times more expensive than other dyed wool. It is frequently mentioned in the Bible; it was used in the construction of the Tabernacle, in the weaving of the covers of the Tabernacle and the vestments of the High Priest (see Exodus 25–28; Numbers 4:13). There is also mention of the dye in external sources dating from the fourteenth century BCE. In the Roman period, purple dye was used primarily in the clothing of priests, kings, and ministers. Due to the prestige it accorded those who wore it, as well as its high price, its production was monitored, and free commerce in the dye was prohibited.

Crimson [*karmil*]: This is the same as *tola'at shani*; a bright shade of red, almost orange, which is produced from the blood of a certain insect; *kermes* in Arabic. This is also the name for *tola'at shani* in European

▸ languages

ד לַשַּׁבָּתוֹת וְלֶחֳדָשִׁים וּלְמוֹעֲדֵי יהוה אֱלֹהֵינוּ לְעוֹלָם זֹאת עַל־יִשְׂרָאֵל: וְהַבַּיִת
ה אֲשֶׁר־אֲנִי בוֹנֶה גָּדוֹל כִּי־גָדוֹל אֱלֹהֵינוּ מִכׇּל־הָאֱלֹהִים: וּמִי יַעֲצׇר־כֹּחַ לִבְנוֹת־
לוֹ בַיִת כִּי הַשָּׁמַיִם וּשְׁמֵי הַשָּׁמַיִם לֹא יְכַלְכְּלֻהוּ וּמִי אֲנִי אֲשֶׁר אֶבְנֶה־לּוֹ בַיִת כִּי
ו אִם־לְהַקְטִיר לְפָנָיו: וְעַתָּה שְׁלַח־לִי אִישׁ־חָכָם לַעֲשׂוֹת בַּזָּהָב וּבַכֶּסֶף וּבַנְּחֹשֶׁת
וּבַבַּרְזֶל וּבָאַרְגְּוָן וְכַרְמִיל וּתְכֵלֶת וְיֹדֵעַ לְפַתֵּחַ פִּתּוּחִים עִם־הַחֲכָמִים אֲשֶׁר
ז עִמִּי בִּיהוּדָה וּבִירוּשָׁלַ͏ִם אֲשֶׁר הֵכִין דָּוִיד אָבִי: וּשְׁלַח־לִי עֲצֵי אֲרָזִים בְּרוֹשִׁים
וְאַלְגּוּמִּים מֵהַלְּבָנוֹן כִּי אֲנִי יָדַעְתִּי אֲשֶׁר עֲבָדֶיךָ יוֹדְעִים לִכְרוֹת עֲצֵי לְבָנוֹן וְהִנֵּה
ח עֲבָדַי עִם־עֲבָדֶיךָ: וּלְהָכִין לִי עֵצִים לָרֹב כִּי הַבַּיִת אֲשֶׁר־אֲנִי בוֹנֶה גָּדוֹל וְהַפְלֵא:
ט וְהִנֵּה לַחֹטְבִים לְכֹרְתֵי הָעֵצִים נָתַתִּי חִטִּים ׀ מַכּוֹת לַעֲבָדֶיךָ כֹּרִים עֶשְׂרִים אֶלֶף
וּשְׂעֹרִים כֹּרִים עֶשְׂרִים אָלֶף וְיַיִן בַּתִּים עֶשְׂרִים אֶלֶף וְשֶׁמֶן בַּתִּים עֶשְׂרִים אָלֶף:
י וַיֹּאמֶר חוּרָם מֶלֶךְ־צֹר בִּכְתָב וַיִּשְׁלַח אֶל־שְׁלֹמֹה בְּאַהֲבַת יהוה אֶת־עַמּוֹ נְתָנְךָ
יא עֲלֵיהֶם מֶלֶךְ: וַיֹּאמֶר חוּרָם בָּרוּךְ יהוה אֱלֹהֵי יִשְׂרָאֵל אֲשֶׁר עָשָׂה אֶת־הַשָּׁמַיִם
וְאֶת־הָאָרֶץ אֲשֶׁר נָתַן לְדָוִיד הַמֶּלֶךְ בֵּן חָכָם יוֹדֵעַ שֵׂכֶל וּבִינָה אֲשֶׁר יִבְנֶה־בַּיִת
יב יג לַיהוה וּבַיִת לְמַלְכוּתוֹ: וְעַתָּה שָׁלַחְתִּי אִישׁ־חָכָם יוֹדֵעַ בִּינָה לְחוּרָם אָבִי: בֶּן־

BACKGROUND

languages. Current research suggests that *tola'at shani* is the scale insect *Kermes echinatus*. This identification also fits the descriptions of the Sages (*Pesikta Rabbati* 20). The dye is extracted by drying the insects and then grinding and heating them.

2:7| **Juniper [*beroshim*]:** The term *beroshim* is not referring to the tree known in modern Hebrew as the cypress, *Cupressus*, but rather to the Greek juniper, *Juniperus excelsa*. This tree, which is common in the high mountains of Lebanon, can reach a height of 30 m. These trees were used in the manufacture of the doors, furniture, and paneling in Solomon's Temple. This tree appears as *berotim* in Song of Songs 1:17: "The beams of our houses are cedars, and our rafters are junipers [*berotim*]."

Sandalwood [*algumim*]: In the Jerusalem Talmud (*Ketubot* 7:9) and the Midrash (*Bereshit Rabba* 15:1), these are called *alvum* or *alvus*, or *alvua* based on the Greek. These trees, whose scientific name is *Aquilaria agallocha*, also grow in India, and are used in the production of wooden ornamentation, jewelry, and spices. Some identify *algumim* as an expensive red tree, *Pterocarpus santalinus*, used in luxury wood products whose origins are also in India (Noga Hareuveni, *Tree and Shrub in Our Biblical Heritage*. Neot Kedumim, 1984).

2:9| **The export of produce, wine, and oil from the Land of Israel:** These verses that laud the Land of Israel for its agricultural produce are corroborated by external documents from the ancient world. For example, in an excerpt from the story of Sinuhe, that appears in an Egyptian document dating back to the twentieth century BCE, it is written regarding the goodly land of Yaa, a region in the land of Canaan: "Figs were in it, and grapes, and its wine was more abundant than its water. Plentiful was its honey, many were its olives; all manner of fruits were upon its trees. Wheat was in it and spelt…and there were made for me many dainties, and milk prepared in every way." Evidence for the export of oil, wine, and grain is found over the course of many periods: in the prophecy of Hosea to the Kingdom of Israel (Hosea 12:2); during the days of the return to Zion (Ezra 3:7); in the records of the Ptolemaic minister of finance in Egypt during the Hellenistic period; and in accounts of the export of grain, wine, and oil left behind by historians, e.g., Pliny, and Christian sources, e.g., Jerome from the Roman-Byzantine period (see *Sifrei*, *Devarim* 33), which speak of the export of oil from the Land of Israel to Tyre and Latakia.

engrave all engravings, and to devise all designs; to prepare all types of craftsmanship **that will be given him.** He has the skills to oversee and work **with your wise men, and with the wise men of my lord David your father.** He is certainly qualified to be appointed as your supervisor.

14 **Now, the wheat and the barley, the oil and the wine, of which my lord has spoken, let him send to his servants,** to the workers in your service. We accept your terms, and you can begin remitting the payments;

15 **and we will cut timber from Lebanon, in accordance with all your needs;** and rather than transporting them on dry land, a complicated and expensive procedure, **we will bring them to you on rafts,**[B] **by sea**[15] **to Yafo,** the port city nearest to Jerusalem; **and you will** merely need to **take it up** from Yafo **to Jerusalem.**

The sea at Yafo, 1899

16 **Solomon counted all the foreign men who were in the Land of Israel, after the count that David his father** had **counted them,** since their number might have changed; **and they were found to be one hundred and fifty-three thousand six hundred.**

17 **He tasked from them seventy thousand porters, and eighty thousand quarrymen in the mountains, and three thousand six hundred would supervise,** as managers appointed **to work the people.**

3 1 **Solomon began to build the House of the Lord in Jerusalem on Mount Moriah,** in the place **where He,** the Lord, **had appeared to David his father;** the house **that he,** Solomon,[16] **had prepared in the place of** the altar that **David** had built **on the threshing floor of Ornan the Yevusite.**[17]

2 **He began to build on the second** day **of the second month,**[18] **in the fourth year of his reign.** Apparently, it took four years to complete preparations for the construction of the building.

3 **These are** the measurements of **what Solomon laid**[19] **as foundation for building the House of God. The length in cubits for the first** [*harishona*] **measure was sixty cubits, and the breadth twenty cubits.** Alternatively, *harishona* is not referring to the first chronologically, but to the first building block of the construction, its foundation.[20]

"Mount Moriah." Temple Mount

4 **The Hall, whose length was along the width of the House, was twenty cubits.** The length of the Hall, which served as an entryway to the Temple, was twenty cubits, corresponding to the width of the Temple. **And the height** of the Hall **was one hundred and twenty** cubits, **and he plated it,** the Temple, **within, with pure gold.**

5 **The great House,** the entire Sanctuary, **he overlaid with juniper wood, which he overlaid with fine gold, and fashioned upon it** adornments in the shape of **palm trees**[21] **and chains.**

6 **He adorned the House with** beautiful and **precious stones for splendor; and the gold was gold of Parvayim.** Gold of Parvayim might be reddish gold, like the blood of cows, *parim.*[22]

7 **He overlaid the House, the beams, the thresholds, its walls, and its doors with gold, and engraved** adornments in the shape of **cherubs on the walls.**

8 **He made the chamber of the Holy of Holies,** the innermost chamber of the Temple; **its length was along the width of the House, twenty cubits, and its width was twenty cubits;** it was square, **he overlaid it with** a huge amount of **fine gold, totaling six hundred talents.**

9 **The weight of the nails in shekels was fifty of gold, and he overlaid the upper chambers with gold.**

10 **He made in the chamber of the Holy of Holies two sculpted cherubs,** carved adornments.[23] These were not the same cherubs as the ones on the cover of the Ark of the Covenant, but other cherubs modeled after them. **And they plated them with gold.**

אִשָּׁה מִן־בְּנוֹת דָּן וְאָבִיו אִישׁ־צֹרִי יוֹדֵעַ לַעֲשׂוֹת בַּזָּהָב־וּבַכֶּסֶף בַּנְּחֹשֶׁת בַּבַּרְזֶל
בָּאֲבָנִים וּבָעֵצִים בָּאַרְגָּמָן בַּתְּכֵלֶת וּבַבּוּץ וּבַכַּרְמִיל וּלְפַתֵּחַ כָּל־פִּתּוּחַ וְלַחְשֹׁב
יד כָּל־מַחֲשָׁבֶת אֲשֶׁר יִנָּתֶן־לוֹ עִם־חֲכָמֶיךָ וְחַכְמֵי אֲדֹנִי דָּוִיד אָבִיךָ׃ וְעַתָּה הַחִטִּים
טו וְהַשְּׂעֹרִים הַשֶּׁמֶן וְהַיַּיִן אֲשֶׁר אָמַר אֲדֹנִי יִשְׁלַח לַעֲבָדָיו׃ וַאֲנַחְנוּ נִכְרֹת עֵצִים
מִן־הַלְּבָנוֹן כְּכָל־צָרְכֶּךָ וּנְבִיאֵם לְךָ רַפְסֹדוֹת עַל־יָם יָפוֹ וְאַתָּה תַּעֲלֶה אֹתָם
טז יְרוּשָׁלָםִ׃ וַיִּסְפֹּר שְׁלֹמֹה כָּל־הָאֲנָשִׁים הַגֵּירִים אֲשֶׁר בְּאֶרֶץ יִשְׂרָאֵל
אַחֲרֵי הַסְּפָר אֲשֶׁר סְפָרָם דָּוִיד אָבִיו וַיִּמָּצְאוּ מֵאָה וַחֲמִשִּׁים אֶלֶף וּשְׁלֹשֶׁת
יז אֲלָפִים וְשֵׁשׁ מֵאוֹת׃ וַיַּעַשׂ מֵהֶם שִׁבְעִים אֶלֶף סַבָּל וּשְׁמֹנִים אֶלֶף חֹצֵב בָּהָר
א וּשְׁלֹשֶׁת אֲלָפִים וְשֵׁשׁ מֵאוֹת מְנַצְּחִים לְהַעֲבִיד אֶת־הָעָם׃ וַיָּחֶל שְׁלֹמֹה לִבְנוֹת
אֶת־בֵּית־יהוה בִּירוּשָׁלַםִ בְּהַר הַמּוֹרִיָּה אֲשֶׁר נִרְאָה לְדָוִיד אָבִיהוּ אֲשֶׁר הֵכִין
ב בִּמְקוֹם דָּוִיד בְּגֹרֶן אָרְנָן הַיְבוּסִי׃ וַיָּחֶל לִבְנוֹת בַּחֹדֶשׁ הַשֵּׁנִי בַּשֵּׁנִי בִּשְׁנַת אַרְבַּע
ג לְמַלְכוּתוֹ׃ וְאֵלֶּה הוּסַד שְׁלֹמֹה לִבְנוֹת אֶת־בֵּית הָאֱלֹהִים הָאֹרֶךְ אַמּוֹת בַּמִּדָּה
ד הָרִאשׁוֹנָה אַמּוֹת שִׁשִּׁים וְרֹחַב אַמּוֹת עֶשְׂרִים׃ וְהָאוּלָם אֲשֶׁר עַל־פְּנֵי הָאֹרֶךְ
עַל־פְּנֵי רֹחַב־הַבַּיִת אַמּוֹת עֶשְׂרִים וְהַגֹּבַהּ מֵאָה וְעֶשְׂרִים וַיְצַפֵּהוּ מִפְּנִימָה
ה זָהָב טָהוֹר׃ וְאֵת ׀ הַבַּיִת הַגָּדוֹל חִפָּה עֵץ בְּרוֹשִׁים וַיְחַפֵּהוּ זָהָב טוֹב וַיַּעַל עָלָיו
ו תִּמֹרִים וְשַׁרְשְׁרוֹת׃ וַיְצַף אֶת־הַבַּיִת אֶבֶן יְקָרָה לְתִפְאָרֶת וְהַזָּהָב זְהַב פַּרְוָיִם׃
ז וַיְחַף אֶת־הַבַּיִת הַקֹּרוֹת הַסִּפִּים וְקִירוֹתָיו וְדַלְתוֹתָיו זָהָב וּפִתַּח כְּרוּבִים עַל־
ח הַקִּירוֹת׃ וַיַּעַשׂ אֶת־בֵּית־קֹדֶשׁ הַקֳּדָשִׁים אָרְכּוֹ עַל־פְּנֵי רֹחַב־הַבַּיִת
אַמּוֹת עֶשְׂרִים וְרָחְבּוֹ אַמּוֹת עֶשְׂרִים וַיְחַפֵּהוּ זָהָב טוֹב לְכִכָּרִים שֵׁשׁ מֵאוֹת׃
ט וּמִשְׁקָל לְמִסְמְרוֹת לִשְׁקָלִים חֲמִשִּׁים זָהָב וְהָעֲלִיּוֹת חִפָּה זָהָב׃
י וַיַּעַשׂ בְּבֵית־קֹדֶשׁ הַקֳּדָשִׁים כְּרוּבִים שְׁנַיִם מַעֲשֵׂה צַעֲצֻעִים וַיְצַפּוּ אֹתָם זָהָב׃

BACKGROUND

2:15 | **Rafts [*rafsodot*]:** This term probably has the same meaning as its modern Hebrew equivalent, and refers to wooden planks tied together to form a vessel. It might be of Akkadian origin. The origin of the parallel word employed by the Sages, *asda*, is the Aramaic *sadda*, or the Greek *skhedia*.

11 **The wings of the cherubs: Their length was twenty cubits,** in the following manner: **The wing of the one** cherub **was five cubits** long, **reaching the wall of the House, and the other wing was** likewise **five cubits** long, **reaching the wing of the other cherub.**

12 **The wing of the one cherub was five cubits, reaching the wall of the House, and the other wing was five cubits, adjacent to the wing of the other cherub.** In sum, the two wings of each cherub were together ten cubits long, and therefore, the wings of both cherubs equaled twenty cubits, which meant they stretched from one wall to the other.

13 **The wings of these cherubs spread twenty cubits, and they were standing on their feet, and their faces were** facing **towards the House.** Unlike the cherubs atop the Ark of the Covenant, these cherubs were not placed one opposite the other, but rather they faced toward the open space of the Sanctuary.[24] These cherubs evidently had wings and legs, but there is no description of their bodies. Apparently, the width of their bodies was incorporated within the space occupied by their wings.

14 **He made the curtain** at the entrance of the Holy of Holies **of sky-blue, purple, and crimson wool, and fine linen, and fashioned** the shape of **cherubs on it,** the curtain.

15 **He made at the front of the House two pillars, thirty-five cubits long, and the** ornamented **capital that was atop each one was five cubits.**[25]

16 **He made chains in** the entrance to **the Sanctum,** the Holy of Holies,[26] **and put them,** the chains,[27] **atop the pillars, and he made one hundred** shapes of **pomegranates, and put them in the chains.**

17 **He established the pillars before the Sanctuary,** at the entrance, **one to the right and one to the left, and he called the name of the one on the right Yakhin, and the name of the one on the left Boaz.**

4 1 **He made an altar of bronze** for the Temple; **its length was twenty cubits,** roughly 10 m, **its width was twenty cubits, and its height was ten cubits.** This altar was very large, as it had to hold all the offerings that would be brought to the Temple. It was four times larger in area than the altar of the Tabernacle, which was also relatively big.[28]

2 **He made the sea,**[D] a large basin of sorts, **cast, ten cubits from brim to brim,** and it was **circular around, and its height was five cubits; a thirty-cubit** measuring **line would circle around it.**

3 **The image of cattle [*bekarim*] was under it,** as its foundation, **encircling around beneath it, for ten cubits surrounding the sea all around.** The Sages explain that the sea had a square foundation, each side measuring ten cubits.[29] Alternatively, the verse is referring to bulb ornaments, *peka'im*, which is the term that appears in the parallel account in I Kings (7:24). These bulbs are also described as being arranged ten per cubit, and in two rows, encompassing the sea. **The oxen were** divided **in two rows,** perhaps with one row at the front of the sea and the other at the rear, and they were **cast with its,** the sea's, **casting.** They were cast together with the sea itself, rather than fashioned separately and then joined to the sea.

Front of the Temple, with Yakhin and Boaz pillars, sea with oxen

4 Thus **it,** the sea, **stood upon twelve oxen, three** of them **facing to the north, and three facing to the west, and three facing to the south, and three facing to the east; the sea was upon them from above, and all their hind parts,** the parts at the back, **were** facing **inward** and were not visible.

5 **Its,** the sea's, **thickness was a handbreadth, but its brim was** thin, **like the craftsmanship of the brim of a lily blossom cup.** It was like the delicate ornaments on the rim of a cup hammered into the form of a wreath of lilies. The walls had to be very thick to contain the water, but the upper edges could be very thin. The sea was so

"Lily blossom"

DISCUSSION

4:2 | **Sea:** On the problem of the discrepancy between the circumference and diameter of the sea, see commentary on I Kings 7:23.

יא וְכַנְפֵי֙ הַכְּרוּבִ֔ים אָרְכָּ֖ם אַמּ֣וֹת עֶשְׂרִ֑ים כְּנַ֨ף הָאֶחָ֜ד לְאַמּ֣וֹת חָמֵ֗שׁ מַגַּ֙עַת֙ לְקִ֣יר
יב הַבַּ֔יִת וְהַכָּנָ֤ף הָאַחֶ֙רֶת֙ אַמּ֣וֹת חָמֵ֔שׁ מַגִּ֕יעַ לִכְנַ֖ף הַכְּר֥וּב הָאַחֵֽר׃ וּכְנַ֨ף הַכְּר֜וּב
הָאֶחָ֗ד אַמּ֣וֹת חָמֵ֔שׁ מַגִּ֖יעַ לְקִ֣יר הַבָּ֑יִת וְהַכָּנָ֤ף הָאַחֶ֙רֶת֙ אַמּ֣וֹת חָמֵ֔שׁ דְּבֵקָ֖ה לִכְנַ֥ף
יג הַכְּר֥וּב הָאַחֵֽר׃ כַּנְפֵי֙ הַכְּרוּבִ֣ים הָאֵ֔לֶּה פֹּרְשִׂ֖ים אַמּ֣וֹת עֶשְׂרִ֑ים וְהֵ֤ם עֹמְדִים֙ עַל־
יד רַגְלֵיהֶ֔ם וּפְנֵיהֶ֖ם לַבָּֽיִת׃ וַיַּ֙עַשׂ֙ אֶת־הַפָּרֹ֔כֶת תְּכֵ֥לֶת וְאַרְגָּמָ֖ן וְכַרְמִ֣יל
טו וּב֑וּץ וַיַּ֥עַל עָלָ֖יו כְּרוּבִֽים׃ וַיַּ֜עַשׂ לִפְנֵ֣י הַבַּ֗יִת עַמּוּדִ֣ים שְׁנַ֔יִם אַמּ֕וֹת
טז שְׁלֹשִׁ֥ים וְחָמֵ֖שׁ אֹ֑רֶךְ וְהַצֶּ֛פֶת אֲשֶׁר־עַל־רֹאשׁ֖וֹ אַמּ֥וֹת חָמֵֽשׁ׃ וַיַּ֤עַשׂ
שַׁרְשְׁרוֹת֙ בַּדְּבִ֔יר וַיִּתֵּ֖ן עַל־רֹ֣אשׁ הָעַמֻּדִ֑ים וַיַּ֤עַשׂ רִמּוֹנִים֙ מֵאָ֔ה וַיִּתֵּ֖ן בַּשַּׁרְשְׁרֽוֹת׃
יז וַיָּ֤קֶם אֶת־הָֽעַמּוּדִים֙ עַל־פְּנֵ֣י הַהֵיכָ֔ל אֶחָ֥ד מִיָּמִ֖ין וְאֶחָ֣ד מֵהַשְּׂמֹ֑אול וַיִּקְרָ֤א שֵֽׁם־
א הימיני֙ יָכִ֔ין וְשֵׁ֥ם הַשְּׂמָאלִ֖י בֹּֽעַז׃ וַיַּ֛עַשׂ מִזְבַּ֥ח נְחֹ֖שֶׁת עֶשְׂרִ֨ים אַמָּ֜ה הַיְמָנִ֙י
ב אָרְכּ֗וֹ וְעֶשְׂרִ֥ים אַמָּ֖ה רָחְבּ֑וֹ וְעֶ֥שֶׂר אַמּ֖וֹת קוֹמָתֽוֹ׃ וַיַּ֥עַשׂ אֶת־הַיָּ֖ם
מוּצָ֑ק עֶ֣שֶׂר בָּֽאַמָּ֡ה מִשְּׂפָת֣וֹ אֶל־שְׂפָת֣וֹ עָגֹ֣ול ׀ סָבִ֡יב וְחָמֵ֤שׁ בָּֽאַמָּה֙ קֽוֹמָת֔וֹ וְקָו֙
ג שְׁלֹשִׁ֣ים בָּֽאַמָּ֔ה יָסֹ֥ב אֹת֖וֹ סָבִֽיב׃ וּדְמ֣וּת בְּקָרִ֗ים תַּ֤חַת לוֹ֙ סָבִ֣יב ׀ סָבִיב֙ סֽוֹבְבִ֣ים
אֹת֔וֹ עֶ֚שֶׂר בָּֽאַמָּ֔ה מַקִּיפִ֥ים אֶת־הַיָּ֖ם סָבִ֑יב שְׁנַ֤יִם טוּרִים֙ הַבָּקָ֔ר יְצוּקִ֖ים בְּמֻצַקְתּֽוֹ׃
ד עוֹמֵ֞ד עַל־שְׁנֵ֧ים עָשָׂ֣ר בָּקָ֗ר שְׁלֹשָׁ֣ה פֹנִ֣ים ׀ צָפ֡וֹנָה וּשְׁלוֹשָׁה֩ פֹנִ֨ים ׀ יָ֜מָּה וּשְׁלֹשָׁ֣ה ׀
פֹּנִ֣ים נֶ֗גְבָּה וּשְׁלוֹשָׁה֙ פֹּנִ֣ים מִזְרָ֔חָה וְהַיָּ֥ם עֲלֵיהֶ֖ם מִלְמָ֑עְלָה וְכָל־אֲחֹרֵיהֶ֖ם בָּֽיְתָה׃
ה וְעָבְי֣וֹ טֶ֔פַח וּשְׂפָתוֹ֙ כְּמַעֲשֵׂ֣ה שְׂפַת־כּ֔וֹס פֶּ֖רַח שׁוֹשַׁנָּ֑ה מַחֲזִ֣יק בַּתִּ֔ים שְׁלֹ֥שֶׁת

strong that **it would hold** great amounts of water, as much as **three thousand bat,** which is approximately 70 cubic m, **which it contained.**
6 **He made ten** bronze **lavers,**[30] **and placed five to the right** side of the Temple,[31] **and five to the left, to wash with them; they would rinse the parts of the burnt offering,** the meat of the burnt offering that was placed upon the altar, **with them, and the sea was for the priests to wash with it,** a ritual bath of sorts; alternatively, the priests would use ducts that emerged from the sea for washing.[32]

Bronze laver

7 **He crafted the ten gold candelabra in accordance with ordinance about them,** the description in the Torah, **and put them in the Sanctuary, five to the right and five to the left.** It is likely that there was one primary candelabrum, the one crafted by Moses that was brought from the Tabernacle, and this was perhaps the only one they would light, while ten identical candelabra were placed around it.[33]
8 Similarly, **he crafted ten tables, and placed them in the Sanctuary, five to the right, and five to the left. He crafted one hundred gold bowls,** receptacles for holding the blood of the offerings and for sprinkling the blood upon the altar.
9 **He made the Courtyard of the Priests, and the Great Courtyard,** a large, unroofed courtyard for the people who came to the Temple. This was the main area of the Temple. **And** they built **doors to the courtyard, and he plated their doors,** of the Courtyard of the Priests and the Great Courtyard, **with bronze.**

"Gold bowls"

10 **He placed the sea on the right** corner **side** of the House, **on the east, to the south.** The sea was placed on the eastern side of the Temple, slightly to the south, so that it should not be positioned directly across from the entrance to the porch, but to the side.[34]
11 **Huram,** the master artisan, **crafted the pots, the shovels, and the bowls. Huram concluded performing the labor** of his expertise, casting metals and fashioning the vessels **that he performed for King Solomon in the House of God.**
12 The following is a list of Huram's work: the massive bronze **pillars,** which were wrought by a special casting, **two; and the orbs and the capitals that were atop the pillars, two; and the screens, two,** which served **to cover the two orbs of the capitals that were atop the pillars;**
13 **and the** shapes of **pomegranates, four hundred for the two screens: two rows of pomegranates for each screen, to cover the two orbs of the capitals that were atop the pillars.**
14 **He crafted the bases,** the foundations upon which the lavers were placed,[35] **and made the lavers atop the bases;**
15 **one sea, and the twelve oxen beneath it.**
16 **The distinguished Huram,** or Huram the master craftsman, **crafted the pots,** or vats, **the shovels, the forks** for holding meat, **and all their vessels** that were accessories in the Temple were fashioned **of burnished bronze, for King Solomon, for** use in **the House of the Lord.**
17 **The king cast**[B] **them in the Jordan plain, in an excavation in the ground between Sukot**[B] **and Tzeredata.**[B]
18 **Solomon crafted all these vessels in great abundance, as the weight of the bronze** was so great that it **could not be measured.** There was not even an attempt to calculate the weight of the bronze.
19 **Solomon crafted all the vessels that were** used **in the House of God, and the golden altar, and the tables that the showbread was** arranged **upon them,**
20 **and the candelabra and their lamps,** in order **to burn in accordance with the ordinance,** and they set them **before the Sanctum,** all of them made **of pure gold,** a highly valuable type of gold;[36]

Golden altar and altar for sacrifices

Showbread table

ו אֲלָפִים יָכִיל׃ וַיַּעַשׂ כִּיּוֹרִים עֲשָׂרָה וַיִּתֵּן חֲמִשָּׁה מִיָּמִין וַחֲמִשָּׁה
מִשְּׂמֹאול לְרָחְצָה בָהֶם אֶת־מַעֲשֵׂה הָעוֹלָה יָדִיחוּ בָם וְהַיָּם לְרָחְצָה לַכֹּהֲנִים
ז בּוֹ׃ וַיַּעַשׂ אֶת־מְנֹרוֹת הַזָּהָב עֶשֶׂר כְּמִשְׁפָּטָם וַיִּתֵּן בַּהֵיכָל חָמֵשׁ
ח מִיָּמִין וְחָמֵשׁ מִשְּׂמֹאול׃ וַיַּעַשׂ שֻׁלְחָנוֹת עֲשָׂרָה וַיַּנַּח בַּהֵיכָל חֲמִשָּׁה
ט מִיָּמִין וַחֲמִשָּׁה מִשְּׂמֹאול וַיַּעַשׂ מִזְרְקֵי זָהָב מֵאָה׃ וַיַּעַשׂ חֲצַר הַכֹּהֲנִים
י וְהָעֲזָרָה הַגְּדוֹלָה וּדְלָתוֹת לָעֲזָרָה וְדַלְתוֹתֵיהֶם צִפָּה נְחֹשֶׁת׃ וְאֶת־הַיָּם נָתַן מִכֶּתֶף
יא הַיְמָנִית קֵדְמָה מִמּוּל נֶגְבָּה׃ וַיַּעַשׂ חוּרָם אֶת־הַסִּירוֹת וְאֶת־הַיָּעִים
וְאֶת־הַמִּזְרָקוֹת וַיְכַל חִירָם לַעֲשׂוֹת אֶת־הַמְּלָאכָה אֲשֶׁר עָשָׂה לַמֶּלֶךְ שְׁלֹמֹה חוּרָם
יב בְּבֵית הָאֱלֹהִים׃ עַמּוּדִים שְׁנַיִם וְהַגֻּלּוֹת וְהַכֹּתָרוֹת עַל־רֹאשׁ הָעַמּוּדִים שְׁתָּיִם
וְהַשְּׂבָכוֹת שְׁתַּיִם לְכַסּוֹת אֶת־שְׁתֵּי גֻּלּוֹת הַכֹּתָרוֹת אֲשֶׁר עַל־רֹאשׁ הָעַמּוּדִים׃
יג וְאֶת־הָרִמּוֹנִים אַרְבַּע מֵאוֹת לִשְׁתֵּי הַשְּׂבָכוֹת שְׁנַיִם טוּרִים רִמּוֹנִים לַשְּׂבָכָה
יד הָאֶחָת לְכַסּוֹת אֶת־שְׁתֵּי גֻּלּוֹת הַכֹּתָרוֹת אֲשֶׁר עַל־פְּנֵי הָעַמּוּדִים׃ וְאֶת־הַמְּכֹנוֹת
טו עָשָׂה וְאֶת־הַכִּיֹּרוֹת עָשָׂה עַל־הַמְּכֹנוֹת׃ אֶת־הַיָּם אֶחָד וְאֶת־הַבָּקָר שְׁנֵים־עָשָׂר
טז תַּחְתָּיו׃ וְאֶת־הַסִּירוֹת וְאֶת־הַיָּעִים וְאֶת־הַמִּזְלָגוֹת וְאֶת־כָּל־כְּלֵיהֶם עָשָׂה חוּרָם
יז אָבִיו לַמֶּלֶךְ שְׁלֹמֹה לְבֵית יְהוָה נְחֹשֶׁת מָרוּק׃ בְּכִכַּר הַיַּרְדֵּן יְצָקָם הַמֶּלֶךְ בַּעֲבִי
יח הָאֲדָמָה בֵּין סֻכּוֹת וּבֵין צְרֵדָתָה׃ וַיַּעַשׂ שְׁלֹמֹה כָּל־הַכֵּלִים הָאֵלֶּה לָרֹב מְאֹד כִּי
יט לֹא נֶחְקַר מִשְׁקַל הַנְּחֹשֶׁת׃ וַיַּעַשׂ שְׁלֹמֹה אֵת כָּל־הַכֵּלִים אֲשֶׁר בֵּית
כ הָאֱלֹהִים וְאֵת מִזְבַּח הַזָּהָב וְאֶת־הַשֻּׁלְחָנוֹת וַעֲלֵיהֶם לֶחֶם הַפָּנִים׃ וְאֶת־הַמְּנֹרוֹת

BACKGROUND

4:17 | **Casting:** Evidence suggests that casting was performed with a mold, much like today. A vessel such as the sea, for example, is essentially a very large molded block, with a 5 m opening. It was more than likely that there were no containers to create a cast of this size. Instead, soft material in which such a mold could be fashioned in the ground would be created. The ceramic material required for this process is abundant in the Jordan plain (see Rashi; Radak; *Metzudat David*).

Sukot: Sukot is identified with Deir Alla, which is located in the Sukot Valley (see Psalms 60:8), near an estuary of the Zarqa River, whose soil contains the calcium sulfate deposits that are required for the molds used for casting bronze. Indeed, archaeological excavations at the site have unearthed remnants of a copper industry, including furnaces, the spouts of bellows, and kilns.

Tzeredata: Some suggest that Tzeredata is Tel es-Sa'idiyeh, in the northern part of the Sukot Valley east of the Jordan. Others identify it with the Tzaretan mentioned in Joshua (3:16), which was near the city of Adam, west of the Jordan River. Yet others claim that it is the Tzereda in the territory of the tribe of Ephraim, the birthplace of Yorovam (I Kings 11:26).

21 even **the flower, the lamps, and the tongs,** all
these **were of gold, completely of gold,** with
no admixtures;[37]
22 **the musical instruments, the bowls, the**
ladles, and the pans were of pure gold; the
entrance of the House, its inner doors, which
opened **into the Holy of Holies, and the doors**
of the House, which opened **into the Sanctuary,** those too
were of gold.[38]

Pan

5 1 **All the labor that Solomon performed for the House of the**
Lord was completed. Solomon brought the consecrated
items of David his father, and the silver, the gold, and all the
vessels, and he placed them in the treasuries of the House
of God.

Inauguration of the Temple: Revelation, Blessing, Prayer, and Celebration

II CHRONICLES 5:2–7:22

The Ark of the Covenant is brought in a celebratory procession to Mount Moriah, at which point divine approval is bestowed, in the form of a cloud. At this climactic moment, as the glory of God descends to rest in its permanent abode, Solomon speaks to both God and the assembled people. As part of his prayer, Solomon expresses a detailed request tied to the power of the place that links earth to Heaven, and that connects the people who pray to He who hears their prayers. Solomon receives an explicit verbal response from Heaven.

2 **Then,** when the labor was completed, **Solomon assembled**
the elders of Israel, and all the heads of the tribes and the
princes of the patrilineal houses, of the children of Israel,
to Jerusalem, in order **to take up the Ark of the Covenant of**
the Lord to the Temple on Mount Moriah, **from the City of**
David, which is Zion.[B]

Scale model of City of David (foreground) and Mount Moriah (background) in the period of Solomon

3 **All the men of Israel assembled to the king on the Festival**
of Tabernacles, **which is** in **the seventh month,**[39] now known
by its Babylonian name of Tishrei.
4 **All the elders of Israel came, and the Levites carried the**
ark.
5 **They took up the ark,** and also the parts of the structure of
the Tent of Meeting, to the treasuries in the Temple, **and all**
the sacred vessels that were in the Tent; the priests and the
Levites took them up.
6 In honor of the ascent of the ark to the House of God, **King**
Solomon and all the congregation of Israel who were con-
gregated with him, and walking **before the ark, were offering**
sheep and cattle that were so abundant they **could not be**
numbered and could not be counted. Portions from these
offerings were distributed as gifts to those participating in the
celebrations.
7 **The priests brought the Ark of the Covenant**[D] **of the Lord**
to its place, to the inner **Sanctum of the House, to the Holy**
of Holies, to beneath the wings of the cherubs which had
been constructed by Solomon (3:10) and which filled the inner
Sanctum.
8 **The cherubs had their wings spread over the area of the**
ark, and the cherubs and their wings **covered the ark and its**
staves[40] **from above.** The staves served for carrying the ark.
9 **They pulled out the staves** toward the entrance of the
Sanctum,[41] as they apparently brought the ark in only as far as
the middle of the chamber, **and** the outline of **the ends of the**
staves were visible extending from the ark through the curtain that hung **at the front of the Sanctum, but they were not**
visible from outside because the curtain covered them.[42] **And**
it, the ark with its staves, **is there to this day.**
10 **There is nothing in the ark but the two Tablets** of the
Covenant **that Moses placed there at Horev, with which the**
Lord established a covenant with the children of Israel,
upon their exodus from Egypt.
11 **It was with the emergence of the priests from the Sanctuary**
after having situated the ark in its designated location; and here
it is noted, parenthetically,[43] that no details are given about the
identity of these priests, or the priestly watch with which they
were affiliated, **for all the priests who were present were** prepared and had **sanctified** themselves and arrived as one, and at

כא וְנֵרֹתֵיהֶם לְבַעֲרָם כַּמִּשְׁפָּט לִפְנֵי הַדְּבִיר זָהָב סָגוּר: וְהַפֶּרַח וְהַנֵּרוֹת וְהַמֶּלְקַחַיִם
כב זָהָב הוּא מִכְלוֹת זָהָב: וְהַמְזַמְּרוֹת וְהַמִּזְרָקוֹת וְהַכַּפּוֹת וְהַמַּחְתּוֹת זָהָב סָגוּר
וּפֶתַח הַבַּיִת דַּלְתוֹתָיו הַפְּנִימִיּוֹת לְקֹדֶשׁ הַקֳּדָשִׁים וְדַלְתֵי הַבַּיִת לַהֵיכָל זָהָב:
ה א וַתִּשְׁלַם כָּל־הַמְּלָאכָה אֲשֶׁר־עָשָׂה שְׁלֹמֹה לְבֵית יְהוָה וַיָּבֵא שְׁלֹמֹה אֶת־קָדְשֵׁי
דָּוִיד אָבִיו וְאֶת־הַכֶּסֶף וְאֶת־הַזָּהָב וְאֶת־כָּל־הַכֵּלִים נָתַן בְּאֹצְרוֹת בֵּית
ב הָאֱלֹהִים: אָז יַקְהֵיל שְׁלֹמֹה אֶת־זִקְנֵי יִשְׂרָאֵל וְאֶת־כָּל־רָאשֵׁי הַמַּטּוֹת
נְשִׂיאֵי הָאָבוֹת לִבְנֵי יִשְׂרָאֵל אֶל־יְרוּשָׁלִָם לְהַעֲלוֹת אֶת־אֲרוֹן בְּרִית־יְהוָה מֵעִיר
ג דָּוִיד הִיא צִיּוֹן: וַיִּקָּהֲלוּ אֶל־הַמֶּלֶךְ כָּל־אִישׁ יִשְׂרָאֵל בֶּחָג הוּא הַחֹדֶשׁ הַשְּׁבִעִי:
ד ה וַיָּבֹאוּ כֹּל זִקְנֵי יִשְׂרָאֵל וַיִּשְׂאוּ הַלְוִיִּם אֶת־הָאָרוֹן: וַיַּעֲלוּ אֶת־הָאָרוֹן וְאֶת־אֹהֶל
ו מוֹעֵד וְאֶת־כָּל־כְּלֵי הַקֹּדֶשׁ אֲשֶׁר בָּאֹהֶל הֶעֱלוּ אֹתָם הַכֹּהֲנִים הַלְוִיִּם: וְהַמֶּלֶךְ
שְׁלֹמֹה וְכָל־עֲדַת יִשְׂרָאֵל הַנּוֹעָדִים עָלָיו לִפְנֵי הָאָרוֹן מְזַבְּחִים צֹאן וּבָקָר אֲשֶׁר
ז לֹא־יִסָּפְרוּ וְלֹא יִמָּנוּ מֵרֹב: וַיָּבִיאוּ הַכֹּהֲנִים אֶת־אֲרוֹן בְּרִית־יְהוָה אֶל־מְקוֹמוֹ
ח אֶל־דְּבִיר הַבַּיִת אֶל־קֹדֶשׁ הַקֳּדָשִׁים אֶל־תַּחַת כַּנְפֵי הַכְּרוּבִים: וַיִּהְיוּ הַכְּרוּבִים
פֹּרְשִׂים כְּנָפַיִם עַל־מְקוֹם הָאָרוֹן וַיְכַסּוּ הַכְּרוּבִים עַל־הָאָרוֹן וְעַל־בַּדָּיו מִלְמָעְלָה:
ט וַיַּאֲרִיכוּ הַבַּדִּים וַיֵּרָאוּ רָאשֵׁי הַבַּדִּים מִן־הָאָרוֹן עַל־פְּנֵי הַדְּבִיר וְלֹא יֵרָאוּ הַחוּצָה
י וַיְהִי־שָׁם עַד הַיּוֹם הַזֶּה: אֵין בָּאָרוֹן רַק שְׁנֵי הַלֻּחוֹת אֲשֶׁר־נָתַן מֹשֶׁה בְּחֹרֵב
יא אֲשֶׁר כָּרַת יְהוָה עִם־בְּנֵי יִשְׂרָאֵל בְּצֵאתָם מִמִּצְרָיִם: וַיְהִי בְּצֵאת
הַכֹּהֲנִים מִן־הַקֹּדֶשׁ כִּי כָּל־הַכֹּהֲנִים הַנִּמְצְאִים הִתְקַדָּשׁוּ אֵין לִשְׁמוֹר לְמַחְלְקוֹת:

BACKGROUND

5:2 | **Zion:** This is generally a name for Jerusalem (see commentary on I Kings 8:1), and sometimes for the Temple Mount and the Temple itself (Isaiah 4:5, 8:18, 29:8; Lamentations 5:18). The accepted modern-day use of the term Mount Zion for the hill west of the City of David is a Christian corruption from the Byzantine era.

DISCUSSION

5:7 | **Ark of the Covenant:** The Ark of the Covenant was placed inside the Holy of Holies, from where only a select few could ever view it. Its precise contents and the items placed beside it are shrouded in mystery and subject to dispute among the Sages. Most agree that the second Tablets of the Covenant were the "Testimony" that Moses placed in the ark (5:10; Exodus 40:20), while other sources indicate that the first, broken, Tablets of the Covenant were also stored in the ark. There are differences of opinion as to whether the Torah scroll that Moses wrote was stored inside the ark, and precisely where the jar of manna and Aaron's staff were placed, as they too were supposed to have been there (see Exodus 16:33; Numbers 17:25; Deuteronomy 31:26; *Bava Batra* 14a).

that time **the divisions** into priestly watches **were not maintained,** but they all participated at the same time,

12 **and the Levites, the singers, all of them, Asaf, Heiman, Yedutun, and their sons and their brethren,** who were **garbed in fine linen, were standing east of the altar, with cymbals and lyres and harps, and with them were one hundred and twenty priests sounding the trumpets.** These trumpets were not musical instruments in the standard sense; rather, they produced staccato blasts, which might have been incorporated into the music.

13 **It was when the trumpeters and singers were as one,** a fully coordinated orchestra, **to sound one voice to praise and thank the Lord, and as they raised their voice with,** and started to play, **the trumpets and cymbals, and with the** other **musical instruments, and** together with the instruments they sang **with praise to the Lord, for He is good, for His kindness is forever, that** behold, **the House was filled with a cloud, the House of the Lord.**

14 **The priests were unable to stay to serve due to the cloud, for the glory of the Lord filled the House of God.** The cloud symbolized the glory of God, resting upon and revealing itself in the Temple.

6 1 **Then Solomon said: The Lord said that He would rest in the fog.** It is evident that the glory of God resides in our midst.

2 **I built You an abode and a** permanent, established **seat for Your dwelling forever.**

3 After that opening statement that was directed toward God, and delivered while facing the Sanctuary, **the king turned his face** to the people, **and blessed the entire assembly of Israel, and the entire assembly of Israel was standing** and listening to his oration.

4 **He said: Blessed is the Lord, God of Israel, who spoke with His mouth of David my father, and with His hands,** His rule, **fulfilled it,** His promise, **saying:**

5 **Since the day that I took My people out of the land of Egypt, I have not chosen a city from all the tribes of Israel to build a House,** a complete, permanent stone structure, **for My name to be there,** but rather I dwelled in provisional Tabernacles, roofed with the same curtains that covered the original Tabernacle in the wilderness; **and I have not chosen a man to be ruler,** king, **over My people Israel.** Although Saul had reigned over Israel, Solomon does not mention him, as he had not been promised a royal dynasty, and his monarchy was indeed transitory;

6 **but I have chosen** the city of **Jerusalem for My name to be there, and I have chosen David to be** king **over My people Israel.**

7 **It was in the heart of David my father to build a House for the name of the Lord, God of Israel.**

8 **The Lord said to David my father,** through a prophet: **Because it was in your heart to build a House for My name, you did well, that it was in your heart;** your thoughts and intentions are in themselves praiseworthy.

9 **However, you will not build the House; rather, your son who will emerge from your loins, he will build the House for My name.** Solomon does not state the reason for this decision, i.e., that David was a man of war. In any case, the fact is that Solomon, a man of tranquility and peace, completed the task that his father had sought to perform.

10 **The Lord fulfilled His word that He had spoken, and I have risen in place of David my father, and I have taken my seat on the** royal **throne of Israel, as the Lord spoke, and I have built the House for the name of the Lord, God of Israel.**

11 **I placed there the ark, in which there is the Covenant of the Lord, which He established with the children of Israel,** written on the tablets. Inscribed on the tablets are the Ten Precepts, which can be considered the essence of the Torah, a marriage contract of sorts that God gave His people at Sinai, which details the covenant that God enacted with the children of Israel.

12 **He,** Solomon, **stood before the altar of the Lord, facing the entire assembly of Israel, and spread his hands** upward.[44]

13 **For Solomon had made a bronze laver five cubits long, and five cubits broad, and three cubits high, and had set it in the midst of the court,** some understand this as a reference to the laver used for washing the hands and feet of the priests; and since this laver was raised, **he stood upon it, and kneeled down upon his knees, facing all the assembly of Israel, and spread his hands to the heavens.** This prayer was presumably heard by the people who were present. This is one of the longest, most complex, and comprehensive prayers in the Bible. In addition to its many requests, Solomon's speech also includes a broad vision of the essence and meaning of the Temple.

14 **He said: Lord, God of Israel, there is none like you, God, in the heavens, or on the earth, keeping the covenant and kindness to Your servants, who walk before You with all their heart;**

15 **who has kept for Your servant David, my father, that of which You spoke to him; You spoke with Your mouth, and You have fulfilled it with Your hand;** You fulfilled the promise as it is **this day,** as we see before us at this time.

יב וְהַלְוִיִּם הַמְשֹׁרְרִים לְכֻלָּם לְאָסָף לְהֵימָן לִידֻתוּן וְלִבְנֵיהֶם וְלַאֲחֵיהֶם מְלֻבָּשִׁים
בּוּץ בִּמְצִלְתַּיִם וּבִנְבָלִים וְכִנֹּרוֹת עֹמְדִים מִזְרָח לַמִּזְבֵּחַ וְעִמָּהֶם כֹּהֲנִים לְמֵאָה מַחְצְּרִים
יג וְעֶשְׂרִים מחצררים בַּחֲצֹצְרוֹת׃ וַיְהִי כְאֶחָד למחצצרים וְלַמְשֹׁרְרִים לְהַשְׁמִיעַ לְמַחְצְּרִים
קוֹל־אֶחָד לְהַלֵּל וּלְהֹדוֹת לַיהוָה וּכְהָרִים קוֹל בַּחֲצֹצְרוֹת וּבִמְצִלְתַּיִם וּבִכְלֵי
יד הַשִּׁיר וּבְהַלֵּל לַיהוָה כִּי טוֹב כִּי לְעוֹלָם חַסְדּוֹ וְהַבַּיִת מָלֵא עָנָן בֵּית יְהוָה׃ וְלֹא־ יג
יָכְלוּ הַכֹּהֲנִים לַעֲמוֹד לְשָׁרֵת מִפְּנֵי הֶעָנָן כִּי־מָלֵא כְבוֹד־יְהוָה אֶת־בֵּית
ו א ב הָאֱלֹהִים׃ אָז אָמַר שְׁלֹמֹה יְהוָה אָמַר לִשְׁכּוֹן בָּעֲרָפֶל׃ וַאֲנִי בָּנִיתִי
ג בֵית־זְבֻל לָךְ וּמָכוֹן לְשִׁבְתְּךָ עוֹלָמִים׃ וַיַּסֵּב הַמֶּלֶךְ אֶת־פָּנָיו וַיְבָרֶךְ אֵת כָּל־קְהַל
ד יִשְׂרָאֵל וְכָל־קְהַל יִשְׂרָאֵל עוֹמֵד׃ וַיֹּאמֶר בָּרוּךְ יְהוָה אֱלֹהֵי יִשְׂרָאֵל אֲשֶׁר דִּבֶּר
ה בְּפִיו אֵת דָּוִיד אָבִי וּבְיָדָיו מִלֵּא לֵאמֹר׃ מִן־הַיּוֹם אֲשֶׁר הוֹצֵאתִי אֶת־עַמִּי מֵאֶרֶץ
מִצְרַיִם לֹא־בָחַרְתִּי בְעִיר מִכֹּל שִׁבְטֵי יִשְׂרָאֵל לִבְנוֹת בַּיִת לִהְיוֹת שְׁמִי שָׁם
ו וְלֹא־בָחַרְתִּי בְאִישׁ לִהְיוֹת נָגִיד עַל־עַמִּי יִשְׂרָאֵל׃ וָאֶבְחַר בִּירוּשָׁלַםִ לִהְיוֹת
ז שְׁמִי שָׁם וָאֶבְחַר בְּדָוִיד לִהְיוֹת עַל־עַמִּי יִשְׂרָאֵל׃ וַיְהִי עִם־לְבַב דָּוִיד אָבִי לִבְנוֹת
ח בַּיִת לְשֵׁם יְהוָה אֱלֹהֵי יִשְׂרָאֵל׃ וַיֹּאמֶר יְהוָה אֶל־דָּוִיד אָבִי יַעַן אֲשֶׁר הָיָה עִם־
ט לְבָבְךָ לִבְנוֹת בַּיִת לִשְׁמִי הֱטִיבוֹתָ כִּי הָיָה עִם־לְבָבֶךָ׃ רַק אַתָּה לֹא תִבְנֶה הַבָּיִת
י כִּי בִנְךָ הַיּוֹצֵא מֵחֲלָצֶיךָ הוּא־יִבְנֶה הַבַּיִת לִשְׁמִי׃ וַיָּקֶם יְהוָה אֶת־דְּבָרוֹ אֲשֶׁר
דִּבֵּר וָאָקוּם תַּחַת דָּוִיד אָבִי וָאֵשֵׁב ׀ עַל־כִּסֵּא יִשְׂרָאֵל כַּאֲשֶׁר דִּבֶּר יְהוָה וָאֶבְנֶה
יא הַבַּיִת לְשֵׁם יְהוָה אֱלֹהֵי יִשְׂרָאֵל׃ וָאָשִׂים שָׁם אֶת־הָאָרוֹן אֲשֶׁר שָׁם בְּרִית יְהוָה
יב אֲשֶׁר כָּרַת עִם־בְּנֵי יִשְׂרָאֵל׃ וַיַּעֲמֹד לִפְנֵי מִזְבַּח יְהוָה נֶגֶד כָּל־קְהַל יִשְׂרָאֵל
יג וַיִּפְרֹשׂ כַּפָּיו׃ כִּי־עָשָׂה שְׁלֹמֹה כִּיּוֹר נְחֹשֶׁת וַיִּתְּנֵהוּ בְּתוֹךְ הָעֲזָרָה חָמֵשׁ אַמּוֹת
אָרְכּוֹ וְחָמֵשׁ אַמּוֹת רָחְבּוֹ וְאַמּוֹת שָׁלוֹשׁ קוֹמָתוֹ וַיַּעֲמֹד עָלָיו וַיִּבְרַךְ עַל־בִּרְכָּיו
יד נֶגֶד כָּל־קְהַל יִשְׂרָאֵל וַיִּפְרֹשׂ כַּפָּיו הַשָּׁמָיְמָה׃ וַיֹּאמַר יְהוָה אֱלֹהֵי יִשְׂרָאֵל אֵין־
כָּמוֹךָ אֱלֹהִים בַּשָּׁמַיִם וּבָאָרֶץ שֹׁמֵר הַבְּרִית וְהַחֶסֶד לַעֲבָדֶיךָ הַהֹלְכִים לְפָנֶיךָ
טו בְּכָל־לִבָּם׃ אֲשֶׁר שָׁמַרְתָּ לְעַבְדְּךָ דָּוִיד אָבִי אֵת אֲשֶׁר־דִּבַּרְתָּ לוֹ וַתְּדַבֵּר בְּפִיךָ

16 **Now Lord, God of Israel, keep with Your servant David my father that which You spoke to him, saying: A man of yours will not cease to be before Me, sitting on the throne of Israel, provided that your children keep their way, to walk in** the path of **My Torah as you walked before Me.** That promise to David was conditional on his sons' adherence to the path of God.

17 **Now Lord, God of Israel, may Your word that You spoke to Your servant David be confirmed.**

18 Solomon explains the inner meaning of the Temple to all those present: **For will God indeed dwell with men on the earth?** Can one really build an earthly home for God? **Behold,** even **the heavens and the heavens of the heavens cannot contain You, certainly not this House that I have built.** I know that no place can actually contain You. Nevertheless, at this place of contact, this gate to the heavens, You will reveal Yourself to man and answer him.[45]

19 **May You turn to the prayer of Your servant, and to his entreaty,** that is, to my prayer and entreaty, **Lord my God, to hear the song** and praise **and the prayer that Your servant prays before You.** The essence of this prayer is that the Temple should indeed serve as a house of prayer and a gate to heaven;

20 **for Your eyes to be open toward this House day and night, toward the place of which You said that You would place Your name there, to hear the prayer that Your servant will pray toward this place.**

21 **May You hear the entreaties of Your servant and of Your people Israel that they will pray toward this place** (see verse 34), or pray in this place;[46] **may You hear from Your dwelling place, from the heavens; may You hear** our petition, **and forgive** our sins.

22 **If a man sins against his neighbor, and** that neighbor **utters a curse to curse him, and the curse comes,** meaning that he comes to curse the person who wronged him or to pray about this matter **before Your altar in this House;**

23 **may You hear** him **from the heavens, and act, and judge Your servants, to exact retribution upon the wicked** as he deserves, **to bring his way upon his head, and to vindicate the righteous, to grant him according to his righteousness.** You will issue a true judgment. The Temple will be the place where all those who have suffered harm can come and ask God to perform justice in His world.

24 Similarly, **if Your people Israel are routed before an enemy when they sin against You, and they repent and confess with Your name,** they admit that they sinned and deserved their punishment, **and pray and entreat You in this House;**

25 **may You hear** their supplication **from the heavens, and forgive the sin of Your people Israel, and** if they are taken as captives, **restore them to the land that You gave to them and to their fathers.**

26 **When the heavens are restrained, and there is no rain,** and this too occurs **because they sinned against You, they will pray toward this place, and confess with Your name and repent from their sin, so that You will answer them.**[47]

"When the heavens are restrained, and there is no rain." Cracked earth during a famine

27 **May You hear in** or from **the heavens, and forgive the sin of Your servants, and of Your people Israel, for You will teach them the good way that they should follow, and You will give rain upon Your land, which You have given to Your people as an inheritance.**

28 **If there is famine in the land, if there is pestilence, if there is blight,** an agricultural disease resulting in loss of crops or cattle, or **rust,**[B] which results from the blight, **locusts,**[B] **Moroccan locusts,**[B] or **if their enemies besiege** and oppress **them in the land at their gates;** and in general, if **any plague or any illness** befalls them,

Swarm of locusts attacking crops

BACKGROUND

6:28 | **Rust [*yerakon*]:** A wide range of diseases can decimate crops. Blight is caused by an eastern wind that blackens stalks and prevents the growth of the grain. Rust, which follows blight, is a disease that causes the stalks to turn greenish-yellow, causing their premature germination, before the kernels are ripe. The term *yerakon* is derived from *yarok*, which means green in modern Hebrew. However, in biblical Hebrew, in talmudic terminology, and also in Akkadian, the term can also refer to yellow. According to researchers, *yerakon* is wheat rust, a devastating disease affecting grain that is caused by a fungus. This disease can ruin the crops of an entire country in a single season, leading to famine.

Locusts: These are *Schistocerca gregaria*, one of several species of desert locusts found in East Africa. These creatures undergo two phases of existence: In its first phase, the desert locust appears green and is a mostly solitary creature. However, under certain harsh climate conditions, it will enter a second phase, in which it undergoes both physiological and behavioral changes. It becomes shorter, turns a blackish-red color, and is no longer solitary, but unites with other desert locusts to form enormous groups. A swarm of up to ten billion locusts will begin to move north, along the length of the Red Sea, aided by winds. Each desert locust consumes its weight in vegetation every day; it will attack any form of vegetation, even the bark of a tree. Consequently, the ecological devastation

▸ wrought

טז וּבְיָדְךָ מִלֵּאתָ כַּיּוֹם הַזֶּה׃ וְעַתָּה יְהוָה ׀ אֱלֹהֵי יִשְׂרָאֵל שְׁמֹר לְעַבְדְּךָ דָוִיד אָבִי
אֵת אֲשֶׁר דִּבַּרְתָּ לּוֹ לֵאמֹר לֹא־יִכָּרֵת לְךָ אִישׁ מִלְּפָנַי יוֹשֵׁב עַל־כִּסֵּא יִשְׂרָאֵל
יז רַק אִם־יִשְׁמְרוּ בָנֶיךָ אֶת־דַּרְכָּם לָלֶכֶת בְּתוֹרָתִי כַּאֲשֶׁר הָלַכְתָּ לְפָנָי׃ וְעַתָּה יְהוָה
יח אֱלֹהֵי יִשְׂרָאֵל יֵאָמֵן דְּבָרְךָ אֲשֶׁר דִּבַּרְתָּ לְעַבְדְּךָ לְדָוִיד׃ כִּי הַאֻמְנָם יֵשֵׁב אֱלֹהִים
אֶת־הָאָדָם עַל־הָאָרֶץ הִנֵּה שָׁמַיִם וּשְׁמֵי הַשָּׁמַיִם לֹא יְכַלְכְּלוּךָ אַף כִּי־הַבַּיִת
יט הַזֶּה אֲשֶׁר בָּנִיתִי׃ וּפָנִיתָ אֶל־תְּפִלַּת עַבְדְּךָ וְאֶל־תְּחִנָּתוֹ יְהוָה אֱלֹהָי לִשְׁמֹעַ
כ אֶל־הָרִנָּה וְאֶל־הַתְּפִלָּה אֲשֶׁר עַבְדְּךָ מִתְפַּלֵּל לְפָנֶיךָ׃ לִהְיוֹת עֵינֶיךָ פְתֻחוֹת
אֶל־הַבַּיִת הַזֶּה יוֹמָם וָלַיְלָה אֶל־הַמָּקוֹם אֲשֶׁר אָמַרְתָּ לָשׂוּם שִׁמְךָ שָׁם לִשְׁמוֹעַ
כא אֶל־הַתְּפִלָּה אֲשֶׁר יִתְפַּלֵּל עַבְדְּךָ אֶל־הַמָּקוֹם הַזֶּה׃ וְשָׁמַעְתָּ אֶל־תַּחֲנוּנֵי עַבְדְּךָ
וְעַמְּךָ יִשְׂרָאֵל אֲשֶׁר יִתְפַּלְלוּ אֶל־הַמָּקוֹם הַזֶּה וְאַתָּה תִּשְׁמַע מִמְּקוֹם שִׁבְתְּךָ
כב מִן־הַשָּׁמַיִם וְשָׁמַעְתָּ וְסָלָחְתָּ׃ אִם־יֶחֱטָא אִישׁ לְרֵעֵהוּ וְנָשָׁא־בוֹ אָלָה לְהַאֲלֹתוֹ
כג וּבָא אָלָה לִפְנֵי מִזְבַּחֲךָ בַּבַּיִת הַזֶּה׃ וְאַתָּה ׀ תִּשְׁמַע מִן־הַשָּׁמַיִם וְעָשִׂיתָ וְשָׁפַטְתָּ
אֶת־עֲבָדֶיךָ לְהָשִׁיב לְרָשָׁע לָתֵת דַּרְכּוֹ בְּרֹאשׁוֹ וּלְהַצְדִּיק צַדִּיק לָתֶת לוֹ
כד כְּצִדְקָתוֹ׃ וְאִם־יִנָּגֵף עַמְּךָ יִשְׂרָאֵל לִפְנֵי אוֹיֵב כִּי יֶחֶטְאוּ־לָךְ וְשָׁבוּ
כה וְהוֹדוּ אֶת־שְׁמֶךָ וְהִתְפַּלְלוּ וְהִתְחַנְּנוּ לְפָנֶיךָ בַּבַּיִת הַזֶּה׃ וְאַתָּה תִּשְׁמַע מִן־
הַשָּׁמַיִם וְסָלַחְתָּ לְחַטַּאת עַמְּךָ יִשְׂרָאֵל וַהֲשֵׁיבוֹתָם אֶל־הָאֲדָמָה אֲשֶׁר־נָתַתָּה
כו לָהֶם וְלַאֲבֹתֵיהֶם׃ בְּהֵעָצֵר הַשָּׁמַיִם וְלֹא־יִהְיֶה מָטָר כִּי יֶחֶטְאוּ־לָךְ
כז וְהִתְפַּלְלוּ אֶל־הַמָּקוֹם הַזֶּה וְהוֹדוּ אֶת־שְׁמֶךָ מֵחַטָּאתָם יְשׁוּבוּן כִּי תַעֲנֵם׃ וְאַתָּה ׀
תִּשְׁמַע הַשָּׁמַיִם וְסָלַחְתָּ לְחַטַּאת עֲבָדֶיךָ וְעַמְּךָ יִשְׂרָאֵל כִּי תוֹרֵם אֶל־הַדֶּרֶךְ
הַטּוֹבָה אֲשֶׁר יֵלְכוּ־בָהּ וְנָתַתָּה מָטָר עַל־אַרְצְךָ אֲשֶׁר־נָתַתָּה לְעַמְּךָ
כח לְנַחֲלָה׃ רָעָב כִּי־יִהְיֶה בָאָרֶץ דֶּבֶר כִּי־יִהְיֶה שִׁדָּפוֹן וְיֵרָקוֹן אַרְבֶּה

BACKGROUND

wrought by a swarm of these locusts is both massive and enduring.

Moroccan locusts [*ḥasil*]: Some contend that this is a type of locust, specifically the Moroccan locust, *Dociostaurus maroccanus*. Others claim that it refers to a locust at one of the stages of its development. Its name is derived from the fact that the creature devours and destroys [*meḥasel*] all the crops of a field (see Deuteronomy 28:38).

29 **any prayer, any entreaty, from any man, or by Your entire people Israel, each knowing his affliction and his own pain;** I do not know everything, but each supplicant is aware of what ails him; **he shall spread his hands** in supplication **toward this House,** as he will pray for his troubles here.

30 **May You hear from the heavens, Your dwelling place, and forgive, and grant to each man according to all his ways, as You know his heart, as You alone know the hearts of people,** and therefore You alone can punish or reward each person in an appropriate manner,

31 **so that they will fear You, to walk in Your ways all the days that they live on the land that You gave to our fathers.** When they understand that all prayers are heard in the Temple, they will realize that falsehoods cannot be spoken there, and they will come to fear You and follow Your ways. The Temple is Israel's house of prayer, and Solomon asks God to respond to the prayers issuing from it.

32 **Also for the foreigner, who is not of Your people Israel, and came from a distant land for the sake of Your great name, Your mighty hand, and Your outstretched arm,** which is renowned even among the gentile nations, **and** this foreigner **comes and prays toward this House,**

33 **may You hear from the heavens, from Your dwelling place, and act according to all that the foreigner calls to You, so that all the peoples of the earth will know Your name, and fear You, like Your people Israel do, and know that Your name is called upon this House that I have built.** The Temple is not designated for Israel alone; it is a house of prayer for all nations.

34 **When Your people goes out to war against its enemies on the way that You will send them,** and therefore they are far-removed from the Temple physically, **and they pray to You via this city that You have chosen, and the House**[D] **that I built for Your name,**

35 **may You hear their prayer and their entreaty from the heavens, and enact justice for them.**

36 Also, **when they sin against You,** which is natural, **as there is no person who does not sin** and it is the manner of people to sin; if they err, or even transgress deliberately, **and** due to their sin **You become angry with them, and deliver them before an enemy, and their captors take them captive to a land distant or near,**

37 **they will restore their hearts,** consider what they have done, **in the land where they have been taken captive, and they will repent and entreat You in the land of their captors, saying: We have sinned, we have been iniquitous, and we have been wicked.**

38 **They will return to You with all their heart and with all their soul in the land of their captors who took them captive, and pray via their land that You gave to their fathers, and the city that You have chosen, and toward the House that I built for Your name.** Even when they are in exile in a foreign land, far from the Temple, they will pray to You via this land, this city, and the House of God.

39 **May You hear from the heavens, from Your dwelling place, their prayer and their entreaties, and enact justice for them, and forgive Your people who have sinned against You.**

40 **Now, my God, please may Your eyes be open, and Your ears be attentive, to the prayer of this place.** This is the essence of the prayer. Solomon asks that the Temple should be a gate to the heavens through which all prayers will ascend, from near and far, the supplications of both Israelites and non-Israelites alike.

41 **Now, rise, Lord God, to Your resting place,** dwell in Your permanent abode, **You, and the ark of Your might,** which symbolizes revelation of the Divine Presence, and **may Your priests, Lord God, be garbed,** surrounded by and wrapped in Your **salvation,**[48] **and may Your virtuous ones rejoice in good.**

42 **Lord God, do not reject the face of Your anointed,** he whom You anointed as king; **remember the kindness of David Your servant.**

7 1 **When Solomon had concluded praying, the fire descended from the heavens, and consumed the burnt offering and the feast offerings, and the glory of the Lord filled the House.**

DISCUSSION

6:34 | **Via this city...and the House:** Over the generations, Jerusalem became the center toward which all Jews turn in their prayers. It is customary to turn physically toward Jerusalem when praying. Those who are in Jerusalem face the Temple Mount, and those on the Temple Mount look toward the Temple, where there is a special connection between man and God (see Daniel 6:11; Mishna *Berakhot* 4:5; *Tosefta, Berakhot* 4:15; see II Chronicles 6:38; Isaiah 56:7).

כט וְחָסִיל כִּי יִהְיֶה כִּי יָצַר־לוֹ אֹיְבָיו בְּאֶרֶץ שְׁעָרָיו כָּל־נֶגַע וְכָל־מַחֲלָה׃ כָּל־תְּפִלָּה
כָּל־תְּחִנָּה אֲשֶׁר יִהְיֶה לְכָל־הָאָדָם וּלְכֹל עַמְּךָ יִשְׂרָאֵל אֲשֶׁר יֵדְעוּ אִישׁ נִגְעוֹ
ל וּמַכְאֹבוֹ וּפָרַשׂ כַּפָּיו אֶל־הַבַּיִת הַזֶּה׃ וְאַתָּה תִּשְׁמַע מִן־הַשָּׁמַיִם מְכוֹן שִׁבְתֶּךָ
וְסָלַחְתָּ וְנָתַתָּה לָאִישׁ כְּכָל־דְּרָכָיו אֲשֶׁר תֵּדַע אֶת־לְבָבוֹ כִּי־אַתָּה לְבַדְּךָ יָדַעְתָּ
לא אֶת־לְבַב בְּנֵי הָאָדָם׃ לְמַעַן יִירָאוּךָ לָלֶכֶת בִּדְרָכֶיךָ כָּל־הַיָּמִים אֲשֶׁר־הֵם חַיִּים
לב עַל־פְּנֵי הָאֲדָמָה אֲשֶׁר נָתַתָּה לַאֲבֹתֵינוּ׃ וְגַם אֶל־הַנָּכְרִי אֲשֶׁר לֹא־
מֵעַמְּךָ יִשְׂרָאֵל הוּא וּבָא ׀ מֵאֶרֶץ רְחוֹקָה לְמַעַן שִׁמְךָ הַגָּדוֹל וְיָדְךָ הַחֲזָקָה וּזְרוֹעֲךָ
לג הַנְּטוּיָה וּבָאוּ וְהִתְפַּלְלוּ אֶל־הַבַּיִת הַזֶּה׃ וְאַתָּה תִּשְׁמַע מִן־הַשָּׁמַיִם מִמְּכוֹן
שִׁבְתֶּךָ וְעָשִׂיתָ כְּכֹל אֲשֶׁר־יִקְרָא אֵלֶיךָ הַנָּכְרִי לְמַעַן יֵדְעוּ כָל־עַמֵּי הָאָרֶץ אֶת־
שְׁמֶךָ וּלְיִרְאָה אֹתְךָ כְּעַמְּךָ יִשְׂרָאֵל וְלָדַעַת כִּי־שִׁמְךָ נִקְרָא עַל־הַבַּיִת הַזֶּה אֲשֶׁר
לד בָּנִיתִי׃ כִּי־יֵצֵא עַמְּךָ לַמִּלְחָמָה עַל־אֹיְבָיו בַּדֶּרֶךְ אֲשֶׁר תִּשְׁלָחֵם
וְהִתְפַּלְלוּ אֵלֶיךָ דֶּרֶךְ הָעִיר הַזֹּאת אֲשֶׁר בָּחַרְתָּ בָּהּ וְהַבַּיִת אֲשֶׁר־בָּנִיתִי לִשְׁמֶךָ׃
לה לו וְשָׁמַעְתָּ מִן־הַשָּׁמַיִם אֶת־תְּפִלָּתָם וְאֶת־תְּחִנָּתָם וְעָשִׂיתָ מִשְׁפָּטָם׃ כִּי יֶחֶטְאוּ־לָךְ
כִּי אֵין אָדָם אֲשֶׁר לֹא־יֶחֱטָא וְאָנַפְתָּ בָם וּנְתַתָּם לִפְנֵי אוֹיֵב וְשָׁבוּם שׁוֹבֵיהֶם
לז אֶל־אֶרֶץ רְחוֹקָה אוֹ קְרוֹבָה׃ וְהֵשִׁיבוּ אֶל־לְבָבָם בָּאָרֶץ אֲשֶׁר נִשְׁבּוּ־שָׁם וְשָׁבוּ ׀
לח וְהִתְחַנְּנוּ אֵלֶיךָ בְּאֶרֶץ שִׁבְיָם לֵאמֹר חָטָאנוּ הֶעֱוִינוּ וְרָשָׁעְנוּ׃ וְשָׁבוּ אֵלֶיךָ בְּכָל־
לִבָּם וּבְכָל־נַפְשָׁם בְּאֶרֶץ שִׁבְיָם אֲשֶׁר־שָׁבוּ אֹתָם וְהִתְפַּלְלוּ דֶּרֶךְ אַרְצָם אֲשֶׁר
לט נָתַתָּה לַאֲבוֹתָם וְהָעִיר אֲשֶׁר בָּחַרְתָּ וְלַבַּיִת אֲשֶׁר־בָּנִיתִי לִשְׁמֶךָ׃ וְשָׁמַעְתָּ מִן־
הַשָּׁמַיִם מִמְּכוֹן שִׁבְתְּךָ אֶת־תְּפִלָּתָם וְאֶת־תְּחִנֹּתֵיהֶם וְעָשִׂיתָ מִשְׁפָּטָם וְסָלַחְתָּ
מ לְעַמְּךָ אֲשֶׁר חָטְאוּ־לָךְ׃ עַתָּה אֱלֹהַי יִהְיוּ־נָא עֵינֶיךָ פְּתֻחוֹת וְאָזְנֶיךָ קַשֻּׁבוֹת
מא לִתְפִלַּת הַמָּקוֹם הַזֶּה׃ וְעַתָּה קוּמָה יְהוָה אֱלֹהִים לְנוּחֶךָ אַתָּה וַאֲרוֹן
מב עֻזֶּךָ כֹּהֲנֶיךָ יְהוָה אֱלֹהִים יִלְבְּשׁוּ תְשׁוּעָה וַחֲסִידֶיךָ יִשְׂמְחוּ בַטּוֹב׃ יְהוָה אֱלֹהִים
א אַל־תָּשֵׁב פְּנֵי מְשִׁיחֶךָ זָכְרָה לְחַסְדֵי דָּוִיד עַבְדֶּךָ׃ וּכְכַלּוֹת שְׁלֹמֹה
לְהִתְפַּלֵּל וְהָאֵשׁ יָרְדָה מֵהַשָּׁמַיִם וַתֹּאכַל הָעֹלָה וְהַזְּבָחִים וּכְבוֹד יְהוָה מָלֵא

2 **The priests were unable to enter the House of the Lord, because the glory of the Lord filled the House of the Lord.**

3 **All the children of Israel saw as the fire descended, and the glory of the Lord** was revealing itself **upon the House,** whether by way of a cloud or some other manner of revelation, **and they knelt with their faces to the ground on the floor and prostrated themselves, and gave thanks to the Lord: For He is good, for His kindness is forever.**

4 **And the king and all the people were slaughtering feast offerings before the Lord.**

5 **King Solomon slaughtered a feast offering of twenty-two thousand bulls, and one hundred and twenty thousand sheep, and the king and the entire people dedicated the House of God.** Most of these sacrifices were peace offerings, the meat of which could be eaten by any Israelite who was not ritually impure.[49]

6 **The priests stood at their watches and the Levites were with the musical instruments of the Lord, which David the king had made to give thanks to the Lord, for His kindness is forever, with David's songs of praise in their hand.** These songs were probably in written form, and the Levites held them in their hands and sang them from a written text; alternatively, this means that they sang David's songs of praise accompanied by the musical instruments in their hands.[50] **And the priests sounded trumpets opposite them, and all Israel were standing.**

"Priests sounded trumpets opposite them"

7 **Solomon** also **consecrated the inside of the courtyard that was before the House of the Lord, for there he presented the burnt offerings, and the fat of the peace offerings.** He sanctified the floor of the courtyard so that it should be holy like the altar, **because the bronze altar that Solomon had crafted was unable to accommodate the burnt offerings,** which are burnt in their entirety upon the altar, **the meal offerings, and the fats,** the parts of the peace offering burnt upon the altar. Although the altar was very large, it could not contain so large a number of offerings, and therefore these were burnt on the floor of the Temple courtyard.[51]

8 **Solomon made the Festival** of the Tabernacles, Sukkot, **at that time, for seven days, and all Israel were with him, a very great assembly,** as Israelites dwelled at the time throughout the expansive borders of the land, **from Levo Hamat,** or the entrance of Hamat, in northern Syria, **up to the Ravine of Egypt,** the southern tip of the territory under Solomon's control.[52]

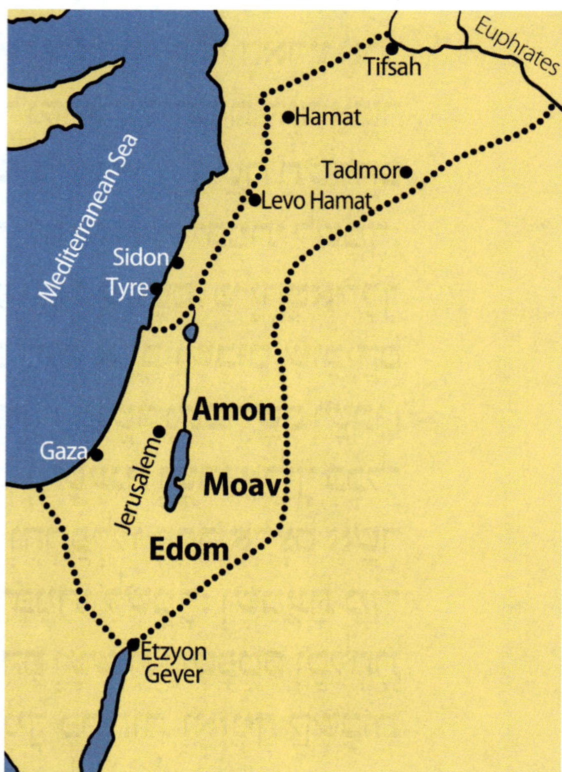

Borders of Solomon's kingdom

9 **On the eighth day** of Sukkot **they held an assembly, for they performed the dedication of the altar for seven days** before Sukkot, **and** afterward **the festival** of Sukkot, **for seven days.** In that year, the children of Israel did not fast on Yom Kippur, as it was one of the days on which they offered and partook of

ב אֶת־הַבָּֽיִת׃ וְלֹא יָֽכְלוּ הַכֹּהֲנִים לָבוֹא אֶל־בֵּית יְהוָה כִּֽי־מָלֵא כְבוֹד־יְהוָה אֶת־
ג בֵּית יְהוָֽה׃ וְכֹל ׀ בְּנֵי יִשְׂרָאֵל רֹאִים בְּרֶדֶת הָאֵשׁ וּכְבוֹד יְהוָה עַל־הַבָּיִת וַיִּכְרְעוּ
אַפַּיִם אַרְצָה עַל־הָֽרִצְפָה וַיִּֽשְׁתַּחֲווּ וְהוֹדוֹת לַֽיהוָה כִּי טוֹב כִּי לְעוֹלָם חַסְדּֽוֹ׃
ד ה וְהַמֶּלֶךְ וְכָל־הָעָם זֹבְחִים זֶבַח לִפְנֵי יְהוָֽה׃ וַיִּזְבַּח הַמֶּלֶךְ שְׁלֹמֹה אֶת־
זֶבַח הַבָּקָר עֶשְׂרִים וּשְׁנַיִם אֶלֶף וְצֹאן מֵאָה וְעֶשְׂרִים אָלֶף וַֽיַּחְנְכוּ אֶת־בֵּית
ו הָאֱלֹהִים הַמֶּלֶךְ וְכָל־הָעָֽם׃ וְהַכֹּהֲנִים עַל־מִשְׁמְרוֹתָם עֹמְדִים וְהַלְוִיִּם בִּכְלֵי־שִׁיר
יְהוָה אֲשֶׁר עָשָׂה דָּוִיד הַמֶּלֶךְ לְהֹדוֹת לַיהוָה כִּֽי־לְעוֹלָם חַסְדּוֹ בְּהַלֵּל דָּוִיד בְּיָדָם
ז וְהַכֹּהֲנִים מחצצרים נֶגְדָּם וְכָל־יִשְׂרָאֵל עֹמְדִֽים׃ וַיְקַדֵּשׁ שְׁלֹמֹה אֶת־ מַחְצְרִים
תּוֹךְ הֶחָצֵר אֲשֶׁר לִפְנֵי בֵית־יְהוָה כִּֽי־עָשָׂה שָׁם הָעֹלוֹת וְאֵת חֶלְבֵי הַשְּׁלָמִים
כִּֽי־מִזְבַּח הַנְּחֹשֶׁת אֲשֶׁר־עָשָׂה שְׁלֹמֹה לֹא יָכוֹל לְהָכִיל אֶת־הָעֹלָה וְאֶת־הַמִּנְחָה
ח וְאֶת־הַחֲלָבִֽים׃ וַיַּעַשׂ שְׁלֹמֹה אֶת־הֶחָג בָּעֵת הַהִיא שִׁבְעַת יָמִים וְכָל־יִשְׂרָאֵל
ט עִמּוֹ קָהָל גָּדוֹל מְאֹד מִלְּבוֹא חֲמָת עַד־נַחַל מִצְרָֽיִם׃ וַיַּעֲשׂוּ בַּיּוֹם הַשְּׁמִינִי עֲצָרֶת
י כִּי ׀ חֲנֻכַּת הַמִּזְבֵּחַ עָשׂוּ שִׁבְעַת יָמִים וְהֶחָג שִׁבְעַת יָמִֽים׃ וּבְיוֹם עֶשְׂרִים וּשְׁלֹשָׁה
לַחֹדֶשׁ הַשְּׁבִיעִי שִׁלַּח אֶת־הָעָם לְאָהֳלֵיהֶם שְׂמֵחִים וְטוֹבֵי לֵב עַל־הַטּוֹבָה אֲשֶׁר
יא עָשָׂה יְהוָה לְדָוִיד וְלִשְׁלֹמֹה וּלְיִשְׂרָאֵל עַמּֽוֹ׃ וַיְכַל שְׁלֹמֹה אֶת־בֵּית יְהוָה וְאֶת־ יד
בֵּית הַמֶּלֶךְ וְאֵת כָּל־הַבָּא עַל־לֵב שְׁלֹמֹה לַעֲשׂוֹת בְּבֵית־יְהוָה וּבְבֵיתוֹ
יב הִצְלִֽיחַ׃ וַיֵּרָא יְהוָה אֶל־שְׁלֹמֹה בַּלָּיְלָה וַיֹּאמֶר לוֹ שָׁמַעְתִּי אֶת־תְּפִלָּתֶךָ
יג וּבָחַרְתִּי בַּמָּקוֹם הַזֶּה לִי לְבֵית זָֽבַח׃ הֵן אֶעֱצֹר הַשָּׁמַיִם וְלֹא־יִהְיֶה מָטָר וְהֵן־

sacrifices. Exceptional practices of this type required the authorization of a prophet.[53]

10 **On the twenty-third day of the seventh month,** after the seven days of Sukkot and the eighth day of the festival, Shemini Atzeret, **he sent the people to their tents, joyful and glad of heart for the benevolence that the Lord had performed for David, and for Solomon, and for Israel His people.**

11 **Solomon completed the House of the Lord, and the house of the king, and in everything that entered Solomon's heart,** all that he thought **to accomplish in the House of the Lord and in his house, he was successful.**

12 **The Lord** again **appeared to Solomon at night, and said to him: I have heard your prayer, and have chosen this place,** this Temple that you have built **for Me, as a house of offerings,** where offerings will be sacrificed in My name.

13 I have also heard the rest of your prayer:[54] **If I restrain the heavens and there is no rain, or if I command the locust to devour the land, or if I send pestilence among My people;**

14 if any of these afflictions occur, **and My people upon whom
My name is called humble themselves, and pray, and seek
My presence, and repent from their evil ways, then I will
hear** their prayers **from the heavens, and will forgive their
sin, and will heal their land.**
15 **Now My eyes will be open, and My ears attentive, to the
prayer of this place.**
16 **Now I have chosen and sanctified this House, for My name
to be there forever; and My eyes and My heart will be there
always.** This place will indeed be very important to Me, as you
requested in your prayer.
17 **And you, if you will walk before Me as David your father
walked, and** take care to **act in accordance with all that I**
have **commanded you, and observe My statutes and My
ordinances,**
18 **I will establish the throne of your kingdom, as I established
a covenant with David your father, saying: A man of yours
will not cease to be ruler in Israel.** Your dynasty will endure
for generations.
19 **But if you turn away,** stray, **and forsake My statutes and My
commandments which I have placed before you, and go
and serve other gods, and prostrate yourselves to them,**
20 **I will displace them from My land which I have given them,
and this House, which I have sanctified for My name, I will
cast from before Me,** it will be destroyed, **and I will render it
a proverb,** an archetype of disaster, **and an adage** of mockery
among all peoples.
21 **This House, which had been exalted, everyone who passes
by it will be astonished, and say: For what did the Lord do
so to this land, and to this House?**
22 **They,** those who will speak of this matter, **will say: It is because they forsook the Lord, God of their fathers, who took
them out of the land of Egypt, and they embraced other
gods, and prostrated themselves to them, and worshipped
them; therefore, He brought all this evil upon them.** God
agrees that this will be His chosen house for prayer and supplications, but He also warns that this determination depends
on the deeds of Israel and their king. The continued reign of
Solomon's dynasty throughout the generations, the status of
the Temple, and even the very presence of Israel upon its land,
are all liable to be compromised if Israel sins.

The Grandeur and Success of Solomon's Projects

II CHRONICLES 8:1–9:31

The primary focus of the book of Chronicles is on the monarchy, the Temple, and the service of God. Following the accounts of the construction of the Temple, the book summarizes Solomon's other grand construction projects, the successful international relations he establishes, and the financial wealth he accumulates. Other aspects of Solomon's personal life, detailed in the book of Kings, are omitted here. The section ends with the death of King Solomon.

8 1 **It was at the end of twenty years, during which Solomon
had built the House of the Lord, and his** own **house,**
2 **and the cities that Huram had given to Solomon; Solomon
built them, and settled the children of Israel there.** These
are apparently the cities that Solomon gave to Huram king of
Tyre, rather than the opposite. However, according to the book
of Kings,[55] Huram was dissatisfied with these places, as they
produced little of value. The transfer of these areas to Huram's
control was in payment for some of Solomon's debts. Solomon
took them back from the king of Tyre, built and settled them,
and was able to pay Huram what he owed him from their agricultural produce.[56]
3 **Solomon went to Hamat Tzova,**[B] **and overcame it.** There was
no actual war waged there. Solomon merely stabilized his control there.
4 **He built Tadmor in the wilderness.**[B] If this is the same place
as modern-day Tadmor, it is a desert oasis in the Syrian Desert,
in eastern Syria. Solomon built a large city there, and indeed it

BACKGROUND

8:3 | **Hamat Tzova:** The center of the kingdom of Aram Tzova was located in the northern section of the Lebanon Valley. Although David had defeated Aram Tzova early in his reign (see II Samuel 10), it seems that the city of Hamat, which was an ally of Israel, came under Aramean control in the last days of his rule, as the influence of the kingdom of David in the region waned. This is probably why Solomon had to strengthen it. During the period of the division of the Israelite kingdom, Aram Damascus would inherit Aram Tzova, with its final destruction coming later at the hands of Tiglat Pileser III, the king of Assyria.

8:4 | **Tadmor in the wilderness:** This city served as an ancient trade station and oasis in the Syrian Desert. Tadmor controlled an important international trade route that stretched from the Land of Israel and Syria to Babylonia and Assyria. It is mentioned in Babylonian and Assyrian documents as early as the nineteenth century BCE.

▸ *Following*

יד אֲצַוֶּה עַל־חָגָב לֶאֱכוֹל הָאָרֶץ וְאִם־אֲשַׁלַּח דֶּבֶר בְּעַמִּי׃ וְיִכָּנְעוּ עַמִּי אֲשֶׁר נִקְרָא־
שְׁמִי עֲלֵיהֶם וְיִתְפַּלְלוּ וִיבַקְשׁוּ פָנַי וְיָשֻׁבוּ מִדַּרְכֵיהֶם הָרָעִים וַאֲנִי אֶשְׁמַע מִן־
טו הַשָּׁמַיִם וְאֶסְלַח לְחַטָּאתָם וְאֶרְפָּא אֶת־אַרְצָם׃ עַתָּה עֵינַי יִהְיוּ פְתֻחוֹת וְאָזְנַי
טז קַשֻּׁבוֹת לִתְפִלַּת הַמָּקוֹם הַזֶּה׃ וְעַתָּה בָּחַרְתִּי וְהִקְדַּשְׁתִּי אֶת־הַבַּיִת הַזֶּה לִהְיוֹת־
יז שְׁמִי שָׁם עַד־עוֹלָם וְהָיוּ עֵינַי וְלִבִּי שָׁם כָּל־הַיָּמִים׃ וְאַתָּה אִם־תֵּלֵךְ לְפָנַי כַּאֲשֶׁר
יח הָלַךְ דָּוִיד אָבִיךָ וְלַעֲשׂוֹת כְּכֹל אֲשֶׁר צִוִּיתִיךָ וְחֻקַּי וּמִשְׁפָּטַי תִּשְׁמוֹר׃ וַהֲקִימוֹתִי
אֵת כִּסֵּא מַלְכוּתֶךָ כַּאֲשֶׁר כָּרַתִּי לְדָוִיד אָבִיךָ לֵאמֹר לֹא־יִכָּרֵת לְךָ אִישׁ מוֹשֵׁל
יט בְּיִשְׂרָאֵל׃ וְאִם־תְּשׁוּבוּן אַתֶּם וַעֲזַבְתֶּם חֻקּוֹתַי וּמִצְוֺתַי אֲשֶׁר נָתַתִּי לִפְנֵיכֶם
כ וַהֲלַכְתֶּם וַעֲבַדְתֶּם אֱלֹהִים אֲחֵרִים וְהִשְׁתַּחֲוִיתֶם לָהֶם׃ וּנְתַשְׁתִּים מֵעַל אַדְמָתִי
אֲשֶׁר־נָתַתִּי לָהֶם וְאֶת־הַבַּיִת הַזֶּה אֲשֶׁר הִקְדַּשְׁתִּי לִשְׁמִי אַשְׁלִיךְ מֵעַל פָּנָי
כא וְאֶתְּנֶנּוּ לְמָשָׁל וְלִשְׁנִינָה בְּכָל־הָעַמִּים׃ וְהַבַּיִת הַזֶּה אֲשֶׁר הָיָה עֶלְיוֹן לְכָל־עֹבֵר
כב עָלָיו יִשֹּׁם וְאָמַר בַּמֶּה עָשָׂה יהוה כָּכָה לָאָרֶץ הַזֹּאת וְלַבַּיִת הַזֶּה׃ וְאָמְרוּ עַל
אֲשֶׁר עָזְבוּ אֶת־יהוה ׀ אֱלֹהֵי אֲבֹתֵיהֶם אֲשֶׁר הוֹצִיאָם מֵאֶרֶץ מִצְרַיִם וַיַּחֲזִיקוּ
בֵּאלֹהִים אֲחֵרִים וַיִּשְׁתַּחֲווּ לָהֶם וַיַּעַבְדוּם עַל־כֵּן הֵבִיא עֲלֵיהֶם אֵת כָּל־הָרָעָה
הַזֹּאת׃

ח א ב וַיְהִי מִקֵּץ ׀ עֶשְׂרִים שָׁנָה אֲשֶׁר בָּנָה שְׁלֹמֹה אֶת־בֵּית יהוה וְאֶת־בֵּיתוֹ׃ וְהֶעָרִים
ג אֲשֶׁר נָתַן חוּרָם לִשְׁלֹמֹה בָּנָה שְׁלֹמֹה אֹתָם וַיּוֹשֶׁב שָׁם אֶת־בְּנֵי יִשְׂרָאֵל׃ וַיֵּלֶךְ
ד שְׁלֹמֹה חֲמָת צוֹבָה וַיֶּחֱזַק עָלֶיהָ׃ וַיִּבֶן אֶת־תַּדְמֹר בַּמִּדְבָּר וְאֵת כָּל־עָרֵי הַמִּסְכְּנוֹת

BACKGROUND

Following the Arab conquest in the seventh century CE, it lost much of its importance. Its English and Greek name is Palmyra, which means date, probably after the palm trees that grew in that oasis. In a parallel account in I Kings (9:18), the name is written as Tamar, although it is also read as Tadmor.

had always been an important commercial center. **And** he built **all the storehouse cities,** which were also trade centers, **which he built in Hamat,** in the north of the land.

Ancient Tadmor

5 **He built Upper Beit Horon and Lower Beit Horon,**[57] rural settlements that Solomon transformed into **fortified cities, with walls, gates, and bars,**

6 **and Baalat,**[B] a city in the south, **and all the storehouse cities that Solomon had, and all the cities for chariots,** the cities where the chariots were stationed, **and the cities for** his **horsemen,** cities of horse stables, **and all of Solomon's ventures that he ventured to build in Jerusalem, and in the Lebanon, and in all the land of his dominion.** Solomon constructed buildings, walls, and cities throughout his kingdom. These massive construction projects led to an increase in the tax burden (see 10:4).

7 After describing the fortifications and the extensive construction projects, the chronicler turns to the levy: From **all the remaining people** of the Canaanite nations; **from the Hitites, the Emorites, the Perizites, the Hivites, and the Yevusites, who were not of Israel,**

8 **Solomon raised a levy of bondservants to this day from their children who remained after them in the land, whom the children of Israel** had been commanded to expel from the Land of Israel, but **had not eradicated.** They were conscripted by Solomon as laborers for the king's construction projects.

9 **But it was from the children of Israel,** in contrast, **that Solomon did not make slaves for his labor, as they were** his **men of war, and the captains of his** military **officials, and the captains of his chariots and of his horsemen.** The king did not want to entrust those positions to foreigners; therefore, the strangers who lived in the land worked mainly as construction workers and simple porters.

10 **These** people of the children of Israel were not merely captains of the army; they **were** also **the chief officials of King**

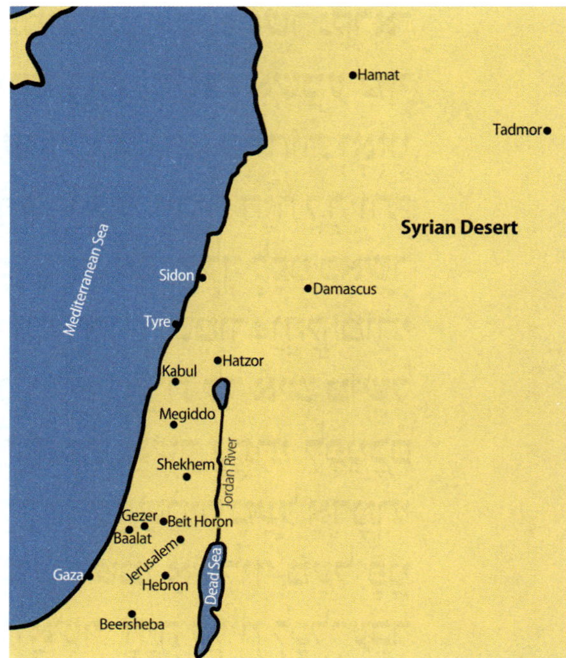

Cities built by Solomon, including cities mentioned in the book of Kings

Solomon, in charge of supervising the work of the many laborers, and of general civil responsibilities, **two hundred and fifty** men **who ruled over the people.**

11 **Solomon took the daughter of Pharaoh up from the City of David to the house that he had built for her.** As she was the daughter of a great ruler, Solomon's marriage to Pharaoh's daughter was undoubtedly a significant diplomatic achievement, and she enjoyed elevated status among his many wives and concubines.[58] However, once the ark was in the City of David, he transferred her to a house in a different location, **as he said: A wife of mine will not dwell in houses of David king of Israel, because they are sacred, as the Ark of the Lord has come there.**

12 **Then Solomon presented burnt offerings to the Lord on the altar of the Lord, which he had built before the Hall,**

13 **and the matter of each day on its day, to present** the daily offerings, **in accordance with the commandment of Moses,** and the offerings brought **on the Sabbaths, and on the New Moons, and at the appointed times, three times a year: On the Festival of Unleavened Bread, and on the Festival of Weeks, and on the Festival of Tabernacles.**

14 **He appointed, in accordance with the practice of David his father, the divisions of the priests for their service, and the Levites for their watches, to praise and to serve opposite the priests, the matter of each day on its day; the gatekeepers**

ה אֲשֶׁר בָּנָה בַּחֲמָת׃ וַיִּבֶן אֶת־בֵּית חוֹרוֹן הָעֶלְיוֹן וְאֶת־בֵּית חוֹרוֹן הַתַּחְתּוֹן עָרֵי
ו מָצוֹר חוֹמוֹת דְּלָתַיִם וּבְרִיחַ׃ וְאֶת־בַּעֲלָת וְאֵת כָּל־עָרֵי הַמִּסְכְּנוֹת אֲשֶׁר־הָיוּ
לִשְׁלֹמֹה וְאֵת כָּל־עָרֵי הָרֶכֶב וְאֵת עָרֵי הַפָּרָשִׁים וְאֵת ׀ כָּל־חֵשֶׁק שְׁלֹמֹה אֲשֶׁר
ז חָשַׁק לִבְנוֹת בִּירוּשָׁלִַם וּבַלְּבָנוֹן וּבְכֹל אֶרֶץ מֶמְשַׁלְתּוֹ׃ כָּל־הָעָם הַנּוֹתָר מִן־
ח הַחִתִּי וְהָאֱמֹרִי וְהַפְּרִזִּי וְהַחִוִּי וְהַיְבוּסִי אֲשֶׁר לֹא מִיִּשְׂרָאֵל הֵמָּה׃ מִן־בְּנֵיהֶם אֲשֶׁר
נוֹתְרוּ אַחֲרֵיהֶם בָּאָרֶץ אֲשֶׁר לֹא־כִלּוּם בְּנֵי יִשְׂרָאֵל וַיַּעֲלֵם שְׁלֹמֹה לְמַס עַד הַיּוֹם
ט הַזֶּה׃ וּמִן־בְּנֵי יִשְׂרָאֵל אֲשֶׁר לֹא־נָתַן שְׁלֹמֹה לַעֲבָדִים לִמְלַאכְתּוֹ כִּי־הֵמָּה אַנְשֵׁי
י מִלְחָמָה וְשָׂרֵי שָׁלִישָׁיו וְשָׂרֵי רִכְבּוֹ וּפָרָשָׁיו׃ וְאֵלֶּה שָׂרֵי הנציבים אֲשֶׁר־לַמֶּלֶךְ הַנִּצָּבִים
יא שְׁלֹמֹה חֲמִשִּׁים וּמָאתָיִם הָרֹדִים בָּעָם׃ וְאֶת־בַּת־פַּרְעֹה הֶעֱלָה שְׁלֹמֹה מֵעִיר
דָּוִיד לַבַּיִת אֲשֶׁר בָּנָה־לָהּ כִּי אָמַר לֹא־תֵשֵׁב אִשָּׁה לִי בְּבֵית דָּוִיד מֶלֶךְ־יִשְׂרָאֵל
כִּי־קֹדֶשׁ הֵמָּה אֲשֶׁר־בָּאָה אֲלֵיהֶם אֲרוֹן יהוה׃
יב יג אָז הֶעֱלָה שְׁלֹמֹה עֹלוֹת לַיהוה עַל מִזְבַּח יהוה אֲשֶׁר בָּנָה לִפְנֵי הָאוּלָם׃ וּבִדְבַר־
יוֹם בְּיוֹם לְהַעֲלוֹת כְּמִצְוַת מֹשֶׁה לַשַּׁבָּתוֹת וְלֶחֳדָשִׁים וְלַמּוֹעֲדוֹת שָׁלוֹשׁ פְּעָמִים
יד בַּשָּׁנָה בְּחַג הַמַּצּוֹת וּבְחַג הַשָּׁבֻעוֹת וּבְחַג הַסֻּכּוֹת׃ וַיַּעֲמֵד כְּמִשְׁפַּט דָּוִיד־אָבִיו
אֶת־מַחְלְקוֹת הַכֹּהֲנִים עַל־עֲבֹדָתָם וְהַלְוִיִּם עַל־מִשְׁמְרוֹתָם לְהַלֵּל וּלְשָׁרֵת נֶגֶד
הַכֹּהֲנִים לִדְבַר־יוֹם בְּיוֹמוֹ וְהַשּׁוֹעֲרִים בְּמַחְלְקוֹתָם לְשַׁעַר וָשָׁעַר כִּי כֵן מִצְוַת

BACKGROUND

8:6 | **Baalat:** This location is mentioned in the book of Joshua (19:44) as a city in the southern tribal portion of Dan. Since the chapter lists it alongside Gezer, some identify it with Mount Baala, roughly 2 km north of modern-day Gedera, which is within the boundaries of Dan. Others claim, in light of the fact that it appears in the text adjacent to Tadmor (verse 4), that it is the northern city of Be'alot (I Kings 4:16), located in the territory of the tribe of Asher, but whose precise location is unknown. There are some who contend that it is Kiryat Ye'arim, one of whose names is Baala (see Joshua 15:9, 18:14; I Chronicles 13:6).

were **in their divisions at each and every gate, as so was the commandment of David, man of God.**[D]

15 **They did not deviate from the commandment of the king to the priests and Levites for any matter, or for** the matters of **the treasures.**

16 **All the labor of Solomon was arranged,** performed in the proper manner and established, **from the day of the laying of the foundation of the House of the Lord and until its completion. The House of the Lord was complete.**

17 The text mentions another royal project that testifies to the expanse and power of Solomon's kingdom: **Then Solomon went**[B] **to Etzyon Gever,**[B] **and to Eilot,**[B] **on the seashore** of the Red Sea, **in the land of Edom.**

18 **Huram sent to him, by means of his servants, ships and servants who were knowledgeable of the sea,** experienced seamen. It is possible that Solomon himself did not yet have his own experienced sailors, and therefore he hired sailors from the major maritime cities of Tyre and Sidon. **And they came with the servants of Solomon,** military men who led the expedition, **to Ofir,** apparently located in East Africa,[59] **and took from there four hundred and fifty talents of gold, and brought them to King Solomon.** This was another source of the great wealth amassed by King Solomon.

"Ships and servants who were knowledgeable of the sea." Phoenician boat, carving on a sarcophagus, second century BCE

Ostracon mentioning thirty shekels of Ofir gold, Tel Qasile, eighth century BCE

9 1 **The queen of Sheba,** a state located in southern Arabia, in the region of Yemen, or in eastern Africa, perhaps modern-day Ethiopia, **heard of the renown of Solomon,** that he was a great king, wiser than the rest. Perhaps she even encountered his ships making their way southward. It is possible that Sheba was always ruled by women or the queen was the heir and successor of a king with no sons. **And she came** from afar, not for political reasons, but **to test Solomon with riddles in Jerusalem,** to ask him clever questions, **with a very great retinue, and camels bearing spices and gold in abundance,**[B] **and precious stones. She came to Solomon and she spoke with him everything that was in her heart.**

Camel train bearing burdens

2 **Solomon responded to all her concerns,** answering all her queries; **there was no matter obscured from Solomon that he could not tell her.**

3 **The queen of Sheba saw the wisdom of Solomon, and the House that he had built,**

4 **and the food of his table, and the seating of his servants,** his officials, **and the standing of his ministers,** their work hierarchy, **and their garments, his cupbearers,** who poured his drinks, **and their garments, and his ascent,** his grand staircase, **that he,** the king, **would ascend to the House of the Lord.** She saw the structure and management of Jerusalem under his reign, all of which was new to her. **And it took her breath away.** She was astonished by what she saw.

5 **She said to the king: The account that I had heard in my land about your words and your wisdom is true.**

6 **I did not believe their accounts until I came** here, **and my eyes saw** the reality; **behold,** it is clear that **half the greatness of your wisdom was not told to me.** The stories which I thought were exaggerations do not cover even half of what I have found; **you exceed the report that I heard.**

7 Your wisdom is so glorious: **Happy are your men, and happy are these servants of yours, who stand before you continually and hear your wisdom.** She praises King Solomon for his greatness, in his presence.

8 **May the Lord your God be blessed, who favored you to place you on His throne, to be king for the Lord your God;**

DISCUSSION

8:14 | **David, man of God:** King David is called by this name because he prepared the general plans of the Temple as well as the inner workings of its service. Although the House of God was not built during his reign, when Solomon became king and constructed the Temple, he followed all of his father's plans. Therefore, the measures originally established by David were implemented.

BACKGROUND

8:17 | **Then Solomon went:** Although this region was located beyond the southern boundary of the Land of Israel (see Numbers 34:3–5; Ezekiel 47:19), for many generations it was annexed to the kingdom of Israel, and under Israelite rule. This area was of great strategic and economic importance, as it provided access to all the kingdoms on the other side of the Red Sea. There was major commercial competition on the Mediterranean Sea between the Tyrians and the Sidonians, the Philistines, the Egyptians, and the other nations that engaged in maritime trade. Solomon enjoyed an advantage due to his control of the entrance to the Red Sea and the navy that he established there.

▸ Etzyon

טו דויד איש־האלהים: ולא סרו מצות המלך על־הכהנים והלוים לכל־דבר
טז ולאצרות: ותכן כל־מלאכת שלמה עד־היום מוסד בית־יהוה ועד־כלתו
יז שלם בית יהוה: אז הלך שלמה לעציון־גבר ואל־אילות על־שפת
יח הים בארץ אדום: וישלח־לו חורם ביד־עבדיו אוניות ועבדים יודעי ים ויבאו אניות
עם־עבדי שלמה אופירה ויקחו משם ארבע־מאות וחמשים ככר זהב ויביאו
ט א אל־המלך שלמה: ומלכת־שבא שמעה את־שמע שלמה ותבוא
לנסות את־שלמה בחידות בירושלם בחיל כבד מאד וגמלים נשאים בשמים
וזהב לרב ואבן יקרה ותבוא אל־שלמה ותדבר עמו את כל־אשר היה עם־
ב לבבה: ויגד־לה שלמה את־כל־דבריה ולא־נעלם דבר משלמה אשר לא הגיד
ג ד לה: ותרא מלכת־שבא את חכמת שלמה והבית אשר בנה: ומאכל שלחנו
ומושב עבדיו ומעמד משרתיו ומלבושיהם ומשקיו ומלבושיהם ועליתו אשר
ה יעלה בית יהוה ולא־היה עוד בה רוח: ותאמר אל־המלך אמת הדבר אשר
ו שמעתי בארצי על־דבריך ועל־חכמתך: ולא־האמנתי לדבריהם עד אשר־
באתי ותראינה עיני והנה לא הגד־לי חצי מרבית חכמתך יספת על־השמועה
ז אשר שמעתי: אשרי אנשיך ואשרי עבדיך אלה העמדים לפניך תמיד ושמעים
ח את־חכמתך: יהי יהוה אלהיך ברוך אשר ׀ חפץ בך לתתך על־כסאו למלך
ליהוה אלהיך באהבת אלהיך את־ישראל להעמידו לעולם ויתנך עליהם

BACKGROUND

Etzyon Gever: Some suggest that this is Tel el-Kheleifeh, which is located between Aqaba and modern-day Eilat, some 500 m north of the shore. Fortifications have been unearthed at the site, as well as a gate from the period of Solomon, and a royal seal inscribed "Belonging to Yotam," perhaps from the days of King Yotam son of Uziya. Others claim that Etzyon Gever is Pharaoh's Island, but there are no findings to support this hypothesis. An additional opinion posits that Etzyon Gever was located within the boundaries of the city of Aqaba.

Eilot: This name is preserved in the Roman name for the city of Aqaba (Aila), which has freshwater sources within its borders, but its exact location and the relationship between it and Etzyon Gever is unknown. Based on I Kings (9:26), it is possible that Eilot is the region where Etzyon Gever was located, while some maintain that Etzyon Gever was the name of the port of the city of Eilot.

9:1 | **Spices and gold in abundance:** The geographical location of the kingdom of Sheba was blessed with a unique ecological confluence that enabled the natural growth of myrrh and frankincense, and the kingdom of Sheba was renowned in ancient times for the cultivation and trade of perfumes. It is related in Assyrian documents dating back to the days of Sargon II, in the eighth century BCE, that the king of Sheba brought spices, horses, and camels to the king of Assyria. Similar inscriptions also exist from the reign of Sennacherib. Sheba was also a source in the gold trade (see Jeremiah 6:20; Ezekiel 27:22; Psalms 72:15).

in your God's love of Israel, He wished **to establish them,** the people of Israel, **forever. He appointed you king over them to execute justice and righteousness.**

9 **She gave the king one hundred and twenty talents of gold,** which was a very large gift, **and spices in great abundance, and precious stones; there was nothing like the spice that the queen of Sheba gave to King Solomon.** Some of the expensive spices that were used in the Temple did not grow in Israel or its immediate environs. Rather, they were imported from India, and perhaps even from farther away. For thousands of years, the spice trade was one of the great international commercial enterprises. On this occasion, the most select spice was brought via the most direct route, and it was considered exceptional in its quantity and quality.

10 Apropos the treasures that the queen of Sheba brought to Solomon, the chronicler lists other riches that arrived from the south, via the sea: **Also the servants of Huram and the servants of Solomon, who had brought gold from Ofir, brought sandalwood and precious stones.**

11 **The king made the sandalwood into paths,** stairs, or bannisters for the ascents,[60] **to the House of the Lord, and to the house of the king, and harps and lyres for the musicians; there were none like them seen previously in the land of Judah,** as they were brought from the distant south.

12 **King Solomon gave to the queen of Sheba all her wishes that she requested, beyond that** which he gave her to correspond to those gifts[61] **which she had brought to the king.** Officially they exchanged gifts, but perhaps there was also a commercial aspect to their meeting. **She** then **turned around and went to her land, she and her servants.** The story of the queen of Sheba is mentioned here because she came from afar to hear Solomon's wisdom, an unusual purpose for a journey that long. She honored Solomon in a manner unlike that of other nations. She did so of her own initiative, motivated by her admiration for him.

13 **The weight of the gold that came to Solomon in one year,** or in one of those years, perhaps the same year during which the queen of Sheba arrived with such a large amount of additional gold, **was six hundred and sixty-six talents of gold,**

14 and all this was **besides that which** was brought by **the itinerant traders,** who traveled to various places to examine merchandise and engage in trade, **and the merchants would bring** goods to the Land of Israel; **all the Arabian kings and the** regional **governors of the land would bring gold and silver to Solomon.**

15 **King Solomon crafted two hundred shields,** large shields that surrounded the warrior from three sides,[62] which had a coating **of beaten gold,**[B] perhaps highly malleable gold that was so soft that it could be stretched out like thread;[63] **six hundred** coins or units **of beaten gold would go into each shield,**

16 **and three hundred bucklers,** small round shields carried by a handle or worn on the forearm, fashioned **of beaten gold; three hundred gold would go into each buckler.** The various types of shields must have been coated with a large amount of gold, so that they too would be effective in battle. **The king put them in the House of the Forest of Lebanon,** the king's palace.[64]

Decorative objects made from ivory, Megiddo, second millennium BCE

17 **The king crafted a great throne of ivory, and he plated it with pure gold.**

18 **There were six stairs to the throne, and a ramp of gold,** upon which one would ascend to the throne, **fastened** tight **to the throne,**[65] **armrests on this side and on that side on the place of the seat, and two lions standing near the armrests** for ornamentation,

19 **and twelve lions standing there on the six stairs on this side and on that side,** on both sides; **nothing like it,** so glorious, **was crafted for any** other **kingdom** in the world.

Throne with carved lions, Tutankhamun's tomb, Egypt, fourteenth century BCE

20 **All the drinking vessels of King Solomon were** made of **gold, and all the vessels of the House of the Forest of Lebanon were pure gold;** relative to the massive amounts of gold, **silver was not considered anything** particularly valuable **in the days of Solomon.**

21 **For the king had ships that went to Tarshish,** which is probably not the city of this name in the area of Spain, as these ships sailed southward, perhaps in the direction of India. These ships sailed **with the servants of Huram.** Due to the great distance, **once every three years the ships of Tarshish would come.** When the ships returned, they would be **bearing gold, silver, ivory,**[B] **monkeys,**[66] **and peacocks.**[B]

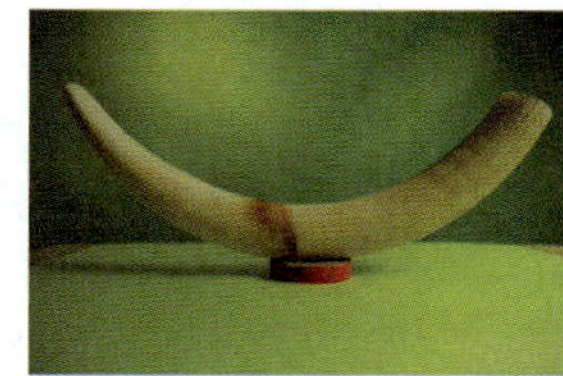
Ivory

ט לְמֶלֶךְ לַעֲשׂוֹת מִשְׁפָּט וּצְדָקָה: וַתִּתֵּן לַמֶּלֶךְ מֵאָה וְעֶשְׂרִים ׀ כִּכַּר זָהָב וּבְשָׂמִים
לָרֹב מְאֹד וְאֶבֶן יְקָרָה וְלֹא הָיָה כַּבֹּשֶׂם הַהוּא אֲשֶׁר נָתְנָה מַלְכַּת־שְׁבָא לַמֶּלֶךְ
י שְׁלֹמֹה: וְגַם עַבְדֵי חירם וְעַבְדֵי שְׁלֹמֹה אֲשֶׁר־הֵבִיאוּ זָהָב מֵאוֹפִיר הֵבִיאוּ עֲצֵי חוּרָם
יא אַלְגּוּמִּים וְאֶבֶן יְקָרָה: וַיַּעַשׂ הַמֶּלֶךְ אֶת־עֲצֵי הָאַלְגּוּמִּים מְסִלּוֹת לְבֵית־יהוה
וּלְבֵית הַמֶּלֶךְ וְכִנֹּרוֹת וּנְבָלִים לַשָּׁרִים וְלֹא־נִרְאוּ כָהֵם לְפָנִים בְּאֶרֶץ יְהוּדָה:
יב וְהַמֶּלֶךְ שְׁלֹמֹה נָתַן לְמַלְכַּת־שְׁבָא אֶת־כָּל־חֶפְצָהּ אֲשֶׁר שָׁאָלָה מִלְּבַד אֲשֶׁר־
יג הֵבִיאָה אֶל־הַמֶּלֶךְ וַתַּהֲפֹךְ וַתֵּלֶךְ לְאַרְצָהּ הִיא וַעֲבָדֶיהָ: וַיְהִי מִשְׁקַל
יד הַזָּהָב אֲשֶׁר־בָּא לִשְׁלֹמֹה בְּשָׁנָה אֶחָת שֵׁשׁ מֵאוֹת וְשִׁשִּׁים וָשֵׁשׁ כִּכְּרֵי זָהָב: לְבַד
מֵאַנְשֵׁי הַתָּרִים וְהַסֹּחֲרִים מְבִיאִים וְכָל־מַלְכֵי עֲרַב וּפַחוֹת הָאָרֶץ מְבִיאִים זָהָב
טו וָכֶסֶף לִשְׁלֹמֹה: וַיַּעַשׂ הַמֶּלֶךְ שְׁלֹמֹה מָאתַיִם צִנָּה זָהָב שָׁחוּט שֵׁשׁ מֵאוֹת זָהָב
טז שָׁחוּט יַעֲלֶה עַל־הַצִּנָּה הָאֶחָת: וּשְׁלֹשׁ־מֵאוֹת מָגִנִּים זָהָב שָׁחוּט שְׁלֹשׁ מֵאוֹת
יז זָהָב יַעֲלֶה עַל־הַמָּגֵן הָאֶחָת וַיִּתְּנֵם הַמֶּלֶךְ בְּבֵית יַעַר הַלְּבָנוֹן: וַיַּעַשׂ
יח הַמֶּלֶךְ כִּסֵּא־שֵׁן גָּדוֹל וַיְצַפֵּהוּ זָהָב טָהוֹר: וְשֵׁשׁ מַעֲלוֹת לַכִּסֵּא וְכֶבֶשׁ בַּזָּהָב
לַכִּסֵּא מָאֳחָזִים וְיָדוֹת מִזֶּה וּמִזֶּה עַל־מְקוֹם הַשָּׁבֶת וּשְׁנַיִם אֲרָיוֹת עֹמְדִים אֵצֶל
יט הַיָּדוֹת: וּשְׁנֵים עָשָׂר אֲרָיוֹת עֹמְדִים שָׁם עַל־שֵׁשׁ הַמַּעֲלוֹת מִזֶּה וּמִזֶּה לֹא־נַעֲשָׂה
כ כֵן לְכָל־מַמְלָכָה: וְכֹל כְּלֵי מַשְׁקֵה הַמֶּלֶךְ שְׁלֹמֹה זָהָב וְכֹל כְּלֵי בֵית־יַעַר הַלְּבָנוֹן
כא זָהָב סָגוּר אֵין כֶּסֶף נֶחְשָׁב בִּימֵי שְׁלֹמֹה לִמְאוּמָה: כִּי־אֳנִיּוֹת לַמֶּלֶךְ הֹלְכוֹת

BACKGROUND

9:15 | **Beaten gold [*zahav shaḥut*]:** According to most commentaries, the expression *zahav shaḥut* refers to gold that has been stretched in some manner, either through heating or beating. The Septuagint renders the expression "beaten gold," while the Sages interpret it either as "highly malleable gold that was spun like thread" (*Yoma* 55a), or "gold stretched out as wax" (Jerusalem Talmud, *Yoma* 4:4; see also Rashi; Radak).

9:21 | **Ivory [*shenhabim*]:** The name *shenhav* is comprised of *shen*, meaning tooth, and *hav*, which means elephant in Egyptian (*eb*). The parallel term in Sanskrit is *ubba*. This is also the source for the island named Abu in the center of the Nile, near modern-day Aswan, called Elephantine in Greek.

Monkeys [*kofim*] and peacocks [*tukiyyim*]: It is accepted that the term *kof* refers to the monkey, just as it does in modern Hebrew, while the *tuki* is a bird, perhaps a peacock (Rashi; Radak). Since the source languages of these terms are unknown, and they appear in the same context as ivory, it has been suggested that these creatures' origins were in India. There are linguists who see a similarity between the name *kof* and the word *kapi* in Sanskrit, one of whose meanings is monkey. They likewise note a similarity between the name *tuki* and *tôgai* or *tôghai*, which means peacock in the language spoken in the Malabar province of southern India. The description in the verse of the rarity of this voyage also corresponds with the long journey to India. Nevertheless, to date, no clear evidence of direct commercial and cultural relations with India during this period has been discovered.

22 **King Solomon became greater than all the kings of the earth in wealth and wisdom.**

23 **All the kings of the earth would seek the presence of Solomon, to hear his wisdom that God had placed in his heart.**

24 **Each would** come to visit him, and **bring his tribute: silver vessels, gold vessels, garments, weapons, spices, horses, and mules, each year's due in its year.** In this way, Solomon was able to collect a vast assortment of great treasures.

25 **Solomon had four thousand stalls for horses and chariots, and twelve thousand horsemen, and he placed them in the chariot cities and with the king in Jerusalem.** It appears that in order to prevent looting, or for organizational reasons, he placed some of the horses and chariots in chariot cities, while others were kept with him, in Jerusalem.

26 **He,** Solomon, **was ruler over all the kings from the** Euphrates **River to the land of the Philistines, and to the border of Egypt.** The kingdom of Solomon incorporated almost all of Syria and the entire southern region of the Land of Israel, all the way to Egypt.

27 **The king caused the silver in Jerusalem to be like stones;** due to the preponderance of available silver it was not considered a precious commodity, **and cedars** that were brought in large amounts from the mountains of Lebanon, **he caused to be as abundant as the sycamores that are in the foothills.** The cedar trees were no longer considered rare but were treated like sycamores, which grew plentifully in the coastal plain.

Sycamore trees

28 **They would bring out horses for Solomon from Egypt, and from all the lands.** Solomon traded in horses that were bred in Egypt. His servants sold them to nations that sought trained horses for their chariots (see 1:16–17).

29 **The rest of the early and late matters of Solomon,** at the beginning and end of his reign, **aren't they written in the words of Natan the prophet, and in the prophecy of Ahiya the Shilonite, and in the visions of Yedo the seer regarding Yorovam the son of Nevat?**[D]

30 **Solomon reigned in Jerusalem, over all Israel, for forty years,**[D] during which time the small kingdom, based on agriculture and a people's army, became a state with diverse foreign relations, a trained military force, and broad maritime trade. This transformation created the foundations for projects in various areas of endeavor in subsequent generations.

31 **Solomon lay with his fathers and,** appropriately, **they buried him in the city of David his father; and Rehavam his son reigned in his stead.**

The Division of the Kingdom

II CHRONICLES 10:1–11:17

After a detailed portrayal of the lives of David and Solomon and a description of the Temple, this section begins the main chronicles of the kings of Judah.

10 1 **Rehavam,** Solomon's son and the heir to his throne, **went to Shekhem;**[BD] **for all Israel had come to Shekhem to crown him** in a coronation ceremony.

2 **It was when Yorovam son of Nevat heard** of Solomon's death, **and he was** then **in Egypt, where he had fled from before King Solomon, that Yorovam returned** to Israel **from Egypt.** It is related in the book of Kings that Yorovam was an officer who rebelled against King Solomon and apparently criticized him harshly. The king pursued him and possibly attempted to imprison him, but Yorovam fled to Egypt.[67] The Egyptians granted him asylum, perhaps in order to preserve a balance of power among Israelite leaders.

Shekhem, photochrom print, late nineteenth century

3 **They,** the leaders of the people, **sent to summon him,** Yorovam, to serve as their

BACKGROUND

10:1 | **Shekhem:** The biblical Shekhem is identified with Tel Balata, and was located on a major intersection in the center of Samaria, on "the path of the setting of the sun" (Deuteronomy 11:30). This path extends from the Jordan Valley to the Mediterranean coast through the Samarian hills. Remains of massive walls have been found at the tel. According to archaeological findings, the city was founded at the beginning of the second millennium BCE, and it is mentioned in Egyptian documents dating from that period.

תַרְשִׁישׁ עִם עַבְדֵי חוּרָם אַחַת לְשָׁלוֹשׁ שָׁנִים תָּבוֹאנָה ׀ אֳנִיּוֹת תַּרְשִׁישׁ נֹשְׂאוֹת
כב זָהָב וָכֶסֶף שֶׁנְהַבִּים וְקוֹפִים וְתוּכִּיִּים: וַיִּגְדַּל הַמֶּלֶךְ שְׁלֹמֹה מִכֹּל מַלְכֵי הָאָרֶץ
כג לְעֹשֶׁר וְחָכְמָה: וְכֹל מַלְכֵי הָאָרֶץ מְבַקְשִׁים אֶת־פְּנֵי שְׁלֹמֹה לִשְׁמֹעַ אֶת־חָכְמָתוֹ
כד אֲשֶׁר־נָתַן הָאֱלֹהִים בְּלִבּוֹ: וְהֵם מְבִיאִים אִישׁ מִנְחָתוֹ כְּלֵי כֶסֶף וּכְלֵי זָהָב וּשְׂלָמוֹת טו
כה נֵשֶׁק וּבְשָׂמִים סוּסִים וּפְרָדִים דְּבַר־שָׁנָה בְּשָׁנָה: וַיְהִי לִשְׁלֹמֹה אַרְבַּעַת
אֲלָפִים אֻרְיוֹת סוּסִים וּמַרְכָּבוֹת וּשְׁנֵים־עָשָׂר אֶלֶף פָּרָשִׁים וַיַּנִּיחֵם בְּעָרֵי הָרֶכֶב
כו וְעִם־הַמֶּלֶךְ בִּירוּשָׁלָםִ: וַיְהִי מוֹשֵׁל בְּכָל־הַמְּלָכִים מִן־הַנָּהָר וְעַד־אֶרֶץ פְּלִשְׁתִּים
כז וְעַד גְּבוּל מִצְרָיִם: וַיִּתֵּן הַמֶּלֶךְ אֶת־הַכֶּסֶף בִּירוּשָׁלַםִ כָּאֲבָנִים וְאֵת הָאֲרָזִים נָתַן
כח כַּשִּׁקְמִים אֲשֶׁר־בַּשְּׁפֵלָה לָרֹב: וּמוֹצִיאִים סוּסִים מִמִּצְרַיִם לִשְׁלֹמֹה וּמִכָּל־
כט הָאֲרָצוֹת: וּשְׁאָר דִּבְרֵי שְׁלֹמֹה הָרִאשֹׁנִים וְהָאַחֲרוֹנִים הֲלֹא־הֵם כְּתוּבִים עַל־
דִּבְרֵי נָתָן הַנָּבִיא וְעַל־נְבוּאַת אֲחִיָּה הַשִּׁילוֹנִי וּבַחֲזוֹת יעדי הַחֹזֶה עַל־יָרָבְעָם יֶעְדּוֹ
ל לא בֶּן־נְבָט: וַיִּמְלֹךְ שְׁלֹמֹה בִירוּשָׁלַםִ עַל־כָּל־יִשְׂרָאֵל אַרְבָּעִים שָׁנָה: וַיִּשְׁכַּב שְׁלֹמֹה
עִם־אֲבֹתָיו וַיִּקְבְּרֻהוּ בְּעִיר דָּוִיד אָבִיו וַיִּמְלֹךְ רְחַבְעָם בְּנוֹ תַּחְתָּיו:
י א ב וַיֵּלֶךְ רְחַבְעָם שְׁכֶמָה כִּי שְׁכֶם בָּאוּ כָל־יִשְׂרָאֵל לְהַמְלִיךְ אֹתוֹ: וַיְהִי כִּשְׁמֹעַ יָרָבְעָם
בֶּן־נְבָט וְהוּא בְמִצְרַיִם אֲשֶׁר בָּרַח מִפְּנֵי שְׁלֹמֹה הַמֶּלֶךְ וַיָּשָׁב יָרָבְעָם מִמִּצְרָיִם:
ג וַיִּשְׁלְחוּ וַיִּקְרְאוּ־לוֹ וַיָּבֹא יָרָבְעָם וְכָל־יִשְׂרָאֵל וַיְדַבְּרוּ אֶל־רְחַבְעָם לֵאמֹר:

DISCUSSION

9:29 | **In the words of Natan the prophet, and in the prophecy of Ahiya the Shilonite, and in the visions of Yedo the seer regarding Yorovam the son of Nevat:** There were books of prophecy that addressed the reign of King Solomon that did not survive. Since their content was not relevant to the book of Chronicles they were not included here. One of these books was written by the prophet Natan, who was active at the beginning of Solomon's reign. Some maintain that the end of the book of Samuel was also written by Natan, but there is no clear proof for this claim from the verses (see *Bava Batra* 15a; Malbim, I Chronicles 29:29). With regard to Ahiya the Shilonite, it is known that he lived toward the end of Solomon's reign, and after his death. The vision of Yedo about Yorovam son of Nevat relates to a later period (see Rashi; *Metzudat David*; *Metzudat Tzion*).

9:30 | **Solomon reigned in Jerusalem, over all Israel, for forty years:** Apparently, Solomon died in his fifties, as he ascended the throne in his youth. Nothing is known of his health, but it is clear that he lived a very intense life. In sharp contrast to the account in I Kings (chap. 11), there is no criticism of Solomon cited here, certainly not explicit criticism.

10:1 | **Shekhem:** Shekhem was an especially important city for the children of Israel, as it was the first place held by the patriarchs in the Land of Israel (Genesis 12:6). Moses (Deuteronomy 11:29, 27:4–13) was referring to Shekhem when he spoke about the construction of an altar where a covenant would be enacted at the start of the conquest of the land (see Joshua 24:25, and commentary ad loc.).

unofficial representative. **And Yorovam and all Israel came**
and spoke with Rehavam, detailing their specific complaints,
saying:
4 **Your father made our yoke difficult,** as he taxed the people
heavily to offset the expenses of his extensive construction
projects throughout the kingdom. Although the king received
a great deal of gold from external sources, that amount was insufficient, and he was obliged to raise taxes.[68] The people and
Yorovam continued: **Ease now from the difficult labor of**
your father, and his heavy yoke that he put upon us, and we
will serve you. We are prepared to accept your authority, but it
is difficult for us to do so under the present conditions.
5 **He said to them:** I must consider the issue; **return to me in**
three more days, and the people departed.
6 **King Rehavam consulted with the elders,** the mature and
experienced ministers, **who had stood before Solomon his**
father while he was alive, saying: How do you counsel to
respond to this people?
7 **They spoke to him, saying: If you will be good to this peo-**
ple, and appease them, and speak kind, conciliatory **words**
to them, then they will be your servants, loyal to you **for-**
ever. Rehavam required fewer expenditures than Solomon,
and therefore the older ministers advised him to accede to the
request. They were perhaps aware of the prevailing feeling of resentment among the people, and they knew that the new king's
authority was not yet firmly established.
8 **He abandoned the counsel of the elders who had counseled**
him, as he considered their suggestion beneath him, **and he**
consulted the youths who had grown up with him, and who
lacked political or general experience, **who were standing be-**
fore him at that time.
9 **He said to them: What do you counsel, and we will respond**
to this people, who spoke to me, saying: Ease the yoke that
your father placed upon us?
10 **The youths who had grown up with him spoke with him,**
saying: So you shall say to the people who spoke to you,
saying: Your father made our yoke heavy; you, ease it for
us. So you shall say to them: My little finger is thicker than
my father's waist. My father was mighty, but I will be far more
powerful.[69]
11 **Now my father burdened you with a heavy yoke, and I will**
add to your yoke; my father chastised you with whips, but
I will chastise you with barbed lashes, whips with knots,
hooks, or spikes. The king's young advisors were familiar only
with Solomon's firmly established rule, and they assumed that
Rehavam's authority was unshakable under any circumstances.
Therefore they advised him not to appease the people, in order
to demonstrate to Yorovam and the entire nation the full extent
of his power.
12 **Yorovam and all the people came to Rehavam on the third**
day, as the king had spoken, saying: Return to me on the
third day.
13 **The king answered them harshly; King Rehavam aban-**
doned the counsel of the elders, who had recommended that
he seek compromise and conciliation.
14 Instead **he spoke to them in accordance with the counsel**
of the youths, saying: I will make your yoke heavy, and I
will add to it; my father chastised you with whips, but I will
chastise you with barbed lashes.
15 **The king did not heed the people** despite the fact that he
should have discerned their resentment toward his policy.
Moreover, there was no need for him to take any immediate
steps to increase their burden; since Solomon's grand projects
would not be continuing at the same pace, he could have cut
taxes without incurring any loss. Nevertheless, Rehavam was
insensitive to these factors, **as it was a plan from God, so that**
the Lord would fulfill His word, which He had spoken by
means of Ahiya the Shilonite to Yorovam son of Nevat. The
prophecy itself is not cited here, but it is recounted at length
in I Kings (chap. 11). There, the prophet Ahiya the Shilonite
informed Yorovam that he would reign over Israel due to the
foreign cults that had infiltrated the kingdom during Solomon's
reign.
16 **All Israel, when the king did not heed them, the people**
responded to the king, saying: What share, inherent connection, **is there in** the house of **David for us? There is no**
inheritance for us in the son of Yishai. Each man to your
tents, Israel. Sheva son of Bikhri, who had rebelled against
King David years before, had employed this same rallying
cry.[70] The people concluded: **Now see to,** reign over, **your** own
house, David; confine your rule to your own tribe. **And all**
Israel went to their tents. The tribes of Israel declared their
secession from the unified kingdom and their rejection of the
central authority in Judah.
17 **But** as for **the children of Israel who resided in the cities of**
Judah and the surrounding areas, **Rehavam** still **reigned over**
them.
18 **King Rehavam sent Hadoram** to the people, he **who was**
appointed **over the levy,** and had apparently been the tax col-
lector during David's reign as well. It seems that Hadoram was
an elderly, prominent individual,[71] although he was unpopular
and by this point the people rejected his authority. Rehavam
sent him to collect taxes, pretending that nothing had changed.
And the children of Israel stoned him, Hadoram, **with**
stones, and he died. King Rehavam, who witnessed the mass
riot, **hastened to mount his chariot to flee to Jerusalem.**
19 **Israel rebelled against the house of David to this day.**

ד אָבִיךָ הִקְשָׁה אֶת־עֻלֵּנוּ וְעַתָּה הָקֵל מֵעֲבֹדַת אָבִיךָ הַקָּשָׁה וּמֵעֻלּוֹ הַכָּבֵד

ה אֲשֶׁר־נָתַן עָלֵינוּ וְנַעַבְדֶךָּ׃ וַיֹּאמֶר אֲלֵהֶם עוֹד שְׁלֹשֶׁת יָמִים וְשׁוּבוּ אֵלָי וַיֵּלֶךְ

ו הָעָם׃ וַיִּוָּעַץ הַמֶּלֶךְ רְחַבְעָם אֶת־הַזְּקֵנִים אֲשֶׁר־הָיוּ עֹמְדִים לִפְנֵי

ז שְׁלֹמֹה אָבִיו בִּהְיֹתוֹ חַי לֵאמֹר אֵיךְ אַתֶּם נוֹעָצִים לְהָשִׁיב לָעָם־הַזֶּה דָּבָר׃ וַיְדַבְּרוּ

אֵלָיו לֵאמֹר אִם־תִּהְיֶה לְטוֹב לְהָעָם הַזֶּה וּרְצִיתָם וְדִבַּרְתָּ אֲלֵהֶם דְּבָרִים טוֹבִים

ח וְהָיוּ לְךָ עֲבָדִים כָּל־הַיָּמִים׃ וַיַּעֲזֹב אֶת־עֲצַת הַזְּקֵנִים אֲשֶׁר יְעָצֻהוּ וַיִּוָּעַץ אֶת־

ט הַיְלָדִים אֲשֶׁר גָּדְלוּ אִתּוֹ הָעֹמְדִים לְפָנָיו׃ וַיֹּאמֶר אֲלֵהֶם מָה אַתֶּם נוֹעָצִים וְנָשִׁיב

דָּבָר אֶת־הָעָם הַזֶּה אֲשֶׁר דִּבְּרוּ אֵלַי לֵאמֹר הָקֵל מִן־הָעֹל אֲשֶׁר־נָתַן אָבִיךָ

י עָלֵינוּ׃ וַיְדַבְּרוּ אִתּוֹ הַיְלָדִים אֲשֶׁר גָּדְלוּ אִתּוֹ לֵאמֹר כֹּה תֹאמַר לָעָם אֲשֶׁר־דִּבְּרוּ

אֵלֶיךָ לֵאמֹר אָבִיךָ הִכְבִּיד אֶת־עֻלֵּנוּ וְאַתָּה הָקֵל מֵעָלֵינוּ כֹּה תֹּאמַר אֲלֵהֶם

יא קָטָנִּי עָבָה מִמָּתְנֵי אָבִי׃ וְעַתָּה אָבִי הֶעְמִיס עֲלֵיכֶם עֹל כָּבֵד וַאֲנִי אֹסִיף עַל־

יב עֻלְּכֶם אָבִי יִסַּר אֶתְכֶם בַּשּׁוֹטִים וַאֲנִי בָּעַקְרַבִּים׃ וַיָּבֹא יָרָבְעָם וְכָל־

הָעָם אֶל־רְחַבְעָם בַּיּוֹם הַשְּׁלִשִׁי כַּאֲשֶׁר דִּבֶּר הַמֶּלֶךְ לֵאמֹר שׁוּבוּ אֵלַי בַּיּוֹם

יג יד הַשְּׁלִשִׁי׃ וַיַּעֲנֵם הַמֶּלֶךְ קָשָׁה וַיַּעֲזֹב הַמֶּלֶךְ רְחַבְעָם אֵת עֲצַת הַזְּקֵנִים׃ וַיְדַבֵּר

אֲלֵהֶם כַּעֲצַת הַיְלָדִים לֵאמֹר אַכְבִּיד אֶת־עֻלְּכֶם וַאֲנִי אֹסִיף עָלָיו אָבִי יִסַּר אֶתְכֶם

טו בַּשּׁוֹטִים וַאֲנִי בָּעַקְרַבִּים׃ וְלֹא־שָׁמַע הַמֶּלֶךְ אֶל־הָעָם כִּי־הָיְתָה נְסִבָּה מֵעִם

הָאֱלֹהִים לְמַעַן הָקִים יְהוָה אֶת־דְּבָרוֹ אֲשֶׁר דִּבֶּר בְּיַד אֲחִיָּהוּ הַשִּׁלוֹנִי אֶל־יָרָבְעָם

טז בֶּן־נְבָט׃ וְכָל־יִשְׂרָאֵל כִּי לֹא־שָׁמַע הַמֶּלֶךְ לָהֶם וַיָּשִׁיבוּ הָעָם ׀ אֶת־הַמֶּלֶךְ ׀

לֵאמֹר מַה־לָּנוּ חֵלֶק בְּדָוִיד וְלֹא־נַחֲלָה בְּבֶן־יִשַׁי אִישׁ לְאֹהָלֶיךָ יִשְׂרָאֵל עַתָּה

יז רְאֵה בֵיתְךָ דָּוִיד וַיֵּלֶךְ כָּל־יִשְׂרָאֵל לְאֹהָלָיו׃ וּבְנֵי יִשְׂרָאֵל הַיֹּשְׁבִים

יח בְּעָרֵי יְהוּדָה וַיִּמְלֹךְ עֲלֵיהֶם רְחַבְעָם׃ וַיִּשְׁלַח הַמֶּלֶךְ רְחַבְעָם אֶת־הֲדֹרָם אֲשֶׁר

עַל־הַמַּס וַיִּרְגְּמוּ־בוֹ בְנֵי־יִשְׂרָאֵל אֶבֶן וַיָּמֹת וְהַמֶּלֶךְ רְחַבְעָם הִתְאַמֵּץ לַעֲלוֹת

יט בַּמֶּרְכָּבָה לָנוּס יְרוּשָׁלִָם׃ וַיִּפְשְׁעוּ יִשְׂרָאֵל בְּבֵית דָּוִיד עַד הַיּוֹם

11 1 For several decades the children of Israel had lived under a monarchy, and they realized that they could not return to the anarchy that had characterized the period of the Judges. Therefore, they sought to establish an alternative kingdom, headed by Yorovam son of Nevat.[72] **Rehavam came to Jerusalem, and he assembled the house of Judah and Benjamin,**[D] **one hundred and eighty thousand select warriors,**[D] **to wage war against Israel,** in order **to restore the kingdom to Rehavam.** He planned to subdue the uprising by military force. Although the population of the other tribes together was greater than that of Judah, and they may have wielded greater economic power as the land inherited by the tribe of Judah was not as fertile as some of the other portions, nevertheless, Rehavam had an organized and well-prepared army at his disposal.

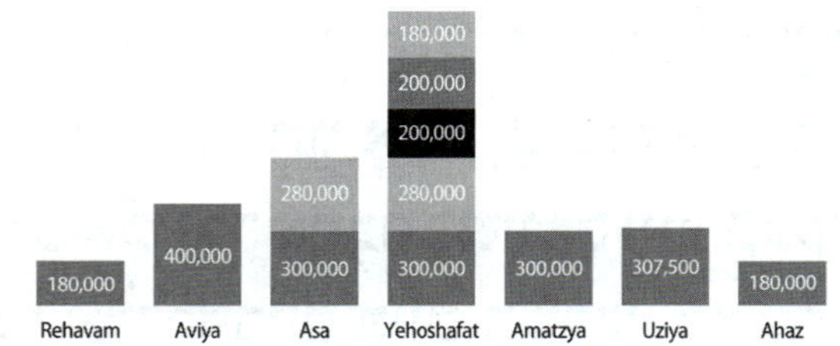

Changes in the number of soldiers of the kings of Judah

2 **The word of the Lord was with Shemayahu, the man of God,** a prophet who was apparently from the land of Judah and who is not mentioned in any other context, **saying:**
3 **Say to Rehavam son of Solomon, king of Judah, and to all Israel in Judah and Benjamin, saying:**
4 **So said the Lord: You shall not go up, and you shall not wage war against your brethren; return, each** military man **to his house, as this matter is from Me.** Do not treat this like any other rebellion, as it is ordained by God. **They heeded the word of the Lord**[D] **and refrained from going** to war **against Yorovam.**
5 **Rehavam dwelled in Jerusalem and built fortified cities**[73] **in Judah** in recognition of the new reality of tense relations with the emerging Kingdom of Israel. Relations between the two kingdoms were often antagonistic and occasionally deteriorated into outright war.
6 **He built Bethlehem, Eitam, Tekoa,**
7 **Beit Tzur, Sokho, Adulam,**
8 **Gat, Maresha, Zif,**
9 **Adorayim, Lakhish,** and **Azeka,**
10 as well as **Tzora,** which had previously been part of the territory of Dan before that tribe had migrated northward,[74] **Ayalon, and Hebron, which are** all **in Judah and in Benjamin;** that is, all these cities were in one or the other of those tribal portions. They were built as **fortified cities.**

Ruins from Adulam

Tel Azeka

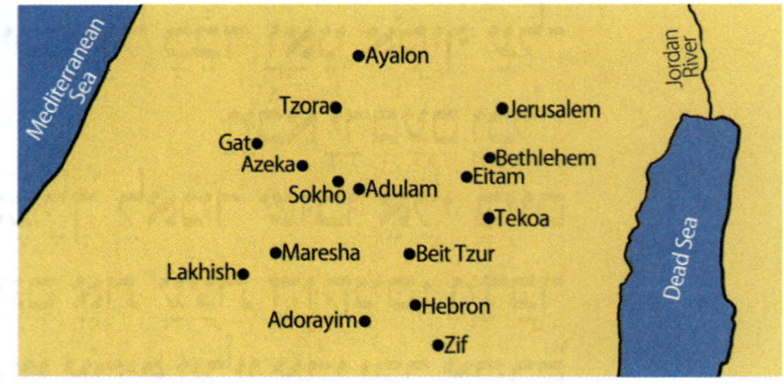

Cities fortified by Rehavam

11 **He strengthened the fortifications, and he installed rulers over them, and** built **storehouses of food, oil, and wine,** for times of siege.
12 **In each and every city were shields and spears, and he strengthened them greatly.** The tribes of **Judah and Benjamin were his,** and he fortified their borders.
13 **The priests and the Levites who were throughout Israel presented themselves to him;** they came to him **from their every border.**
14 **For the Levites left their tracts and their ancestral portions**

DISCUSSION

11:1 | **And he assembled the house of Judah and Benjamin:** The tribe of Benjamin did not have a close familial relationship with the tribe of Judah, but due to the proximity of their territories and especially their sharing of the city of Jerusalem, which was partly in the territory of Judah and partly in Benjamin, a bond had been formed between them. Consequently, the tribe of Benjamin became affiliated with the tribe of Judah and intermingled with them over the generations (see I Chronicles 11:28, 12:1–2, 17).

▸ *One*

א א הַזֶּה׃ וַיָּבֹא רְחַבְעָם יְרוּשָׁלִַם וַיַּקְהֵל אֶת־בֵּית יְהוּדָה וּבִנְיָמִן מֵאָה
וּשְׁמוֹנִים אֶלֶף בָּחוּר עֹשֵׂה מִלְחָמָה לְהִלָּחֵם עִם־יִשְׂרָאֵל לְהָשִׁיב אֶת־הַמַּמְלָכָה
ב ג לִרְחַבְעָם׃ וַיְהִי דְּבַר־יְהוָה אֶל־שְׁמַעְיָהוּ אִישׁ־הָאֱלֹהִים לֵאמֹר׃ אֱמֹר
אֶל־רְחַבְעָם בֶּן־שְׁלֹמֹה מֶלֶךְ יְהוּדָה וְאֶל כָּל־יִשְׂרָאֵל בִּיהוּדָה וּבִנְיָמִן לֵאמֹר׃
ד כֹּה אָמַר יְהוָה לֹא־תַעֲלוּ וְלֹא־תִלָּחֲמוּ עִם־אֲחֵיכֶם שׁוּבוּ אִישׁ לְבֵיתוֹ כִּי מֵאִתִּי
נִהְיָה הַדָּבָר הַזֶּה וַיִּשְׁמְעוּ אֶת־דִּבְרֵי יְהוָה וַיָּשֻׁבוּ מִלֶּכֶת אֶל־יָרָבְעָם׃
ה ו וַיֵּשֶׁב רְחַבְעָם בִּירוּשָׁלִָם וַיִּבֶן עָרִים לְמָצוֹר בִּיהוּדָה׃ וַיִּבֶן אֶת־בֵּית־לֶחֶם וְאֶת־
ז ח עֵיטָם וְאֶת־תְּקוֹעַ׃ וְאֶת־בֵּית־צוּר וְאֶת־שׂוֹכוֹ וְאֶת־עֲדֻלָּם׃ וְאֶת־גַּת וְאֶת־מָרֵשָׁה
ט י וְאֶת־זִיף׃ וְאֶת־אֲדוֹרַיִם וְאֶת־לָכִישׁ וְאֶת־עֲזֵקָה׃ וְאֶת־צָרְעָה וְאֶת־אַיָּלוֹן וְאֶת־
יא חֶבְרוֹן אֲשֶׁר בִּיהוּדָה וּבְבִנְיָמִן עָרֵי מְצֻרוֹת׃ וַיְחַזֵּק אֶת־הַמְּצוּרוֹת וַיִּתֵּן בָּהֶם
יב נְגִידִים וְאֹצְרוֹת מַאֲכָל וְשֶׁמֶן וָיָיִן׃ וּבְכָל־עִיר וָעִיר צִנּוֹת וּרְמָחִים וַיְחַזְּקֵם לְהַרְבֵּה
יג מְאֹד וַיְהִי־לוֹ יְהוּדָה וּבִנְיָמִן׃ וְהַכֹּהֲנִים וְהַלְוִיִּם אֲשֶׁר בְּכָל־יִשְׂרָאֵל
יד הִתְיַצְּבוּ עָלָיו מִכָּל־גְּבוּלָם׃ כִּי־עָזְבוּ הַלְוִיִּם אֶת־מִגְרְשֵׁיהֶם וַאֲחֻזָּתָם וַיֵּלְכוּ

DISCUSSION

One hundred and eighty thousand select warriors: A literary analysis indicates that the listed numbers of the soldiers of the kings of Judah in the book of Chronicles is purposeful and systematic, although it does not necessarily represent the historical facts precisely. In Rehavam's army there were 180,000 men, in Aviya's army there were 400,000, in Asa's 580,000, and in Yehoshafat's 1,160,000. These listings indicate the development of the Kingdom of Judah after the division of the kingdom: Up to Yehoshafat, the number of soldiers increased, which suggests the strengthening of the kingdom. Indeed, the number of soldiers during the reign of each king was identical to the combined number of those of his predecessors, or in the case of Yehoshafat, double the troops of his predecessor, signifying that each king built his reign upon that of the monarch who ruled before him. Matters started to deteriorate from the time of Amatzya, until in the reign of Ahaz the count returned to the initial number from the time of Rehavam, 180,000. The fact that the book does not mention the number of military personnel in the days of Yehoram, Ahazya, Atalya, and Yoash is indicative of the continued process of political and religious decline (Neriah Klein, "The Chronicler's Code: The Rise and Fall of Judah's Army in the Book of Chronicles," *Journal of Hebrew Scriptures*, vol 17, article 3, 2017).

11:4 | **They heeded the word of the Lord:** This episode highlights the great esteem in which the people held the prophets. The unity of the kingdom had been threatened, and politically this may have been the only opportunity Rehavam had to prevent the people of Israel from establishing an independent and stable kingdom of their own. Although Ahiya the Shilonite had already prophesied to Yorovam that the majority of the tribes of Israel would separate from the house of David, and that he would reign over them, it had been a private prophecy (I Kings 11:29–39). Here a prophet ordered the people to halt their preparations for battle and return to their homes, and his instruction carried enough weight that Rehavam refrained from reacting to the rebellion, despite his desire to restore to himself control over the entire nation.

and came to Judah and Jerusalem, because Yorovam and his sons had displaced them from serving the Lord, which meant, in practice, that they had no source of livelihood.
15 **He appointed for himself priests for the shrines, and for the satyrs,** demonic rituals,[75] **and for the calves that he had made.**[D] It is clear from descriptions elsewhere that Yorovam did not engage in full-fledged idolatry; rather, the calves that he made were meant to represent God.[76] In any event, he stripped the priests and Levites of their status, replacing them with any person who was willing and able to fill the role, regardless of their lineage.[77]
16 **After them,** the Levites, came **those from all the tribes of Israel who had set their hearts to seek the Lord, God of Israel.** They **came to Jerusalem to slaughter to the Lord, God of their fathers.** These individuals from the various tribes maintained their devotion and connection to the Temple in Jerusalem and to the service of God, which was practiced there.
17 **They strengthened the Kingdom of Judah and bolstered Rehavam son of Solomon for three years, for they followed the way of David and Solomon for three years.**

The Chronicles of King Rehavam

II CHRONICLES 11:18–12:16

For the first three years of his reign, Rehavam continued in the path of David and Solomon. During those years, he fortified cities and assembled various defenses in preparation for a possible attack by the Kingdom of Israel. However, after three years, Rehavam leads the people on a different path, and the kingdom begins to deteriorate.

18 **Rehavam took for himself a wife, Mahalat, daughter of Yerimot son of David.** There is no record that David had a son of this name; perhaps he was born at the end of David's life or is mentioned elsewhere by another name. And he also married **Avihayil, daughter of Eliav son of Yishai.**[78] Thus, Rehavam married women of royal lineage. Alternatively, the verse is referring to one woman, Mahalat, whose father was Yerimot son of David, and whose mother was Avihayil daughter of Eliav, son of Yishai. She was descended from the house of Yishai from both her mother's and father's sides.[79]
19 **And she,** one of his wives,[80] **bore him sons: Yeush, Shemarya, and Zaham.**
20 **After her he took** another wife, **Maakha daughter of Avshalom,**[D] also from his own extended family, **and she bore him Aviya, Atai, Ziza, and Shelomit.**
21 **Rehavam loved Maakha the daughter of Avshalom more than all his** other **wives and his concubines, as he took eighteen wives and** also had **sixty concubines, and he begot twenty-eight sons and sixty daughters.**
22 As Maakha was his favorite wife, **Rehavam appointed Aviya son of Maakha as head, as ruler among his brethren, in order to make him king.** Although Aviya was not the eldest son, Rehavam decided that he would take his place and inherit the throne.[81]
23 Aviya was granted great power by his father from a young age. **He was prudent** and understood his position.[82] **And he dispersed all his sons, throughout all the lands of Judah and Benjamin, to all the fortified cities,** meaning that he grew stronger and expanded his reach through his many sons, **and he gave them food in abundance.** He too built or strengthened fortified cities industriously. **And** as his ambition was unrestrained and he craved power and status, **he sought** for himself **a multitude of wives.**
12 1 **It was when the kingdom of Rehavam was established, and as he grew strong,** after three years of proper leadership, **that he forsook the law of the Lord, and all Israel with him.** The conduct of Aviya and his other sons may have contributed to his spiritual decline. Rehavam's interest in God's Torah waned, and the people, following his lead, neglected the observance and study of Torah.
2 **It was in the fifth year of King Rehavam** that **Shishak**[B] **king of Egypt went up against Jerusalem, because they had trespassed against the Lord.** Clearly, Shishak was not consciously motivated to attack Judah due to the people's abandonment of

BACKGROUND

12:2| **Shishak:** Due to the similarity of the names, many identify Shishak with Pharaoh Shoshenq I, who reigned around 943–922 BCE. Of Libyan ancestry, Shoshenq was the founder of the twenty-second dynasty, which ruled over Egypt for over two hundred years. This identification is also based on the inscription on the Bubastite Portal gate in the Precinct of Amun-Re temple enclosure in Karnak, which describes Shoshenq's campaign of conquests in Israel and Syria, during which he conquered some fifty cities and towns in the Land of Israel.

טו לִיהוּדָה וְלִירוּשָׁלִָם כִּי־הִזְנִיחָם יָרָבְעָם וּבָנָיו מִכַּהֵן לַיהוָה: וַיַּעֲמֶד־לוֹ כֹּהֲנִים
טז לַבָּמוֹת וְלַשְּׂעִירִים וְלָעֲגָלִים אֲשֶׁר עָשָׂה: וְאַחֲרֵיהֶם מִכֹּל שִׁבְטֵי יִשְׂרָאֵל הַנֹּתְנִים
אֶת־לְבָבָם לְבַקֵּשׁ אֶת־יְהוָה אֱלֹהֵי יִשְׂרָאֵל בָּאוּ יְרוּשָׁלִַם לִזְבּוֹחַ לַיהוָה אֱלֹהֵי
יז אֲבוֹתֵיהֶם: וַיְחַזְּקוּ אֶת־מַלְכוּת יְהוּדָה וַיְאַמְּצוּ אֶת־רְחַבְעָם בֶּן־שְׁלֹמֹה לְשָׁנִים
יח שָׁלוֹשׁ כִּי הָלְכוּ בְּדֶרֶךְ דָּוִיד וּשְׁלֹמֹה לְשָׁנִים שָׁלוֹשׁ: וַיִּקַּח־לוֹ רְחַבְעָם
יט אִשָּׁה אֶת־מָחֲלַת בֶּן־יְרִימוֹת בֶּן־דָּוִיד אֲבִיהַיִל בַּת־אֱלִיאָב בֶּן־יִשָׁי: וַתֵּלֶד לוֹ בַּת־
כ בָּנִים אֶת־יְעוּשׁ וְאֶת־שְׁמַרְיָה וְאֶת־זָהַם: וְאַחֲרֶיהָ לָקַח אֶת־מַעֲכָה בַּת־אַבְשָׁלוֹם
כא וַתֵּלֶד לוֹ אֶת־אֲבִיָּה וְאֶת־עַתַּי וְאֶת־זִיזָא וְאֶת־שְׁלֹמִית: וַיֶּאֱהַב רְחַבְעָם אֶת־
מַעֲכָה בַת־אַבְשָׁלוֹם מִכָּל־נָשָׁיו וּפִילַגְשָׁיו כִּי נָשִׁים שְׁמוֹנֶה־עֶשְׂרֵה נָשָׂא וּפִילַגְשִׁים
כב שִׁשִּׁים וַיּוֹלֶד עֶשְׂרִים וּשְׁמוֹנָה בָּנִים וְשִׁשִּׁים בָּנוֹת: וַיַּעֲמֵד לָרֹאשׁ רְחַבְעָם אֶת־
כג אֲבִיָּה בֶן־מַעֲכָה לְנָגִיד בְּאֶחָיו כִּי לְהַמְלִיכוֹ: וַיָּבֶן וַיִּפְרֹץ מִכָּל־בָּנָיו לְכָל־אַרְצוֹת
ב א יְהוּדָה וּבִנְיָמִן לְכֹל עָרֵי הַמְּצֻרוֹת וַיִּתֵּן לָהֶם הַמָּזוֹן לָרֹב וַיִּשְׁאַל הֲמוֹן נָשִׁים: וַיְהִי
כְּהָכִין מַלְכוּת רְחַבְעָם וּכְחֶזְקָתוֹ עָזַב אֶת־תּוֹרַת יְהוָה וְכָל־יִשְׂרָאֵל עִמּוֹ:
ב וַיְהִי בַּשָּׁנָה הַחֲמִישִׁית לַמֶּלֶךְ רְחַבְעָם עָלָה שִׁישַׁק מֶלֶךְ־מִצְרַיִם עַל־יְרוּשָׁלִַם

DISCUSSION

11:15 | **The calves that he had made:** Notwithstanding the harsh criticism of Yorovam and the Kingdom of Israel (see I Kings 14:7–16), he did not found a new religion. Yorovam did not seek to uproot or deny the Torah of Israel, but to reform it. He did not consider the golden calves he constructed to be gods; rather, he sought to use them to arouse ancient memories. There were images and symbols in the Temple as well, such as the twelve copper oxen under Solomon's sea (I Kings 7:25), the decorative and woven images of lions (I Kings 7:29–36), and the cherubs placed in the Holy of Holies (I Kings 6:23). Similar images are mentioned in prophetic visions that depict the lofty divine chariot (see Ezekiel 1:10, 10:14), and the Sages even point to a connection between the face of the ox on the chariot and the Golden Calf (see *Shemot Rabba* 42:5; Ramban, Exodus 32:1). Accordingly, Yorovam's golden calves were supposed to symbolize the Divine Presence (see Radak, I Kings 12:28). The people who followed Yorovam did not consider themselves idolaters who had abandoned the nation of Israel; rather, they thought that they were simply implementing changes and adjusting the Israelite religion to suit the times.

11:20 | **Maakha daughter of Avshalom:** Despite the connection between Avshalom and the name Maakha, which was his mother's name (see II Samuel 3:3), in light of the chronology it is unlikely that this Maakha was Avshalom's own daughter; she may have been his granddaughter. The book of Samuel mentions almost as an aside that Avshalom had a daughter called Tamar who was beautiful like her father (see II Samuel 14:25, 27). Maakha could have been her daughter. The suggestion that Maakha was actually a granddaughter of Avshalom is supported by the fact that her son Aviya is later (13:2) identified as the son of Mikhayahu daughter of Uriel. Mikhayahu is apparently a variation of the name Maakha (see Rashi and Radak, 13:2), and it seems that Uriel was her father and Avshalom was her grandfather.

the Torah. However, the chronicler is explaining that this is why God brought about these events.

Shoshenq I, possible identification of Shishak; illustration based on relief, Amun-Re temple, Karnak, Egypt, tenth century BCE

3 Shishak attacked Jerusalem **with twelve hundred chariots and sixty thousand horsemen; there was no number for the people who came with him from Egypt: Libyans, Sukiyites,**[B] apparently the inhabitants of a province near Egypt, **and Kushites,** from modern-day northern Sudan.

4 **He,** Shishak, **captured the fortified cities of Judah, and came to Jerusalem.** Apparently, he did not intend to conquer the Land of Israel, and may not even have had the power to do so. Jerusalem was merely an attractive target for his campaign of looting and robbery, as King Solomon had amassed many treasures there.

Inscription of Shoshenq I stating that the fortification fell into his hands, found on a fragment of a stele, Tel Megiddo, 936–925 BCE

5 **Shemaya the prophet,** who had earlier stopped Rehavam from waging war (11:2–5), **came to Rehavam and the princes of Judah, who had gathered to Jerusalem due to Shishak.** When all of the other cities had fallen, the people fled to Jerusalem, which was the largest fortified city. **And he said to them: So said the Lord: You have forsaken Me; therefore I have forsaken you into the hand of Shishak.**

6 **The princes of Israel and the king humbled themselves and said: The Lord is righteous;** we have indeed sinned, and we are deserving of this punishment.

7 **When the Lord saw that they had humbled themselves, the word of the Lord was with Shemaya, saying: They have humbled themselves;** therefore **I will not destroy them, and I will grant them a small measure of deliverance** to preserve them. The kingdom will survive, **and My wrath will not be poured upon Jerusalem by means of Shishak.** The city will be plundered, but it will not be laid waste.

8 **Rather,** Judah will no longer be an independent kingdom. **They will be servants to him,** Shishak, **and they will know** the difference between **My service and the service of the kingdoms of the lands.**[83] Since they have turned away from God's service, they will be exposed to the volatile nature of global politics, and they will experience the taste of subjugation to a foreign power.

9 **Shishak king of Egypt went up against Jerusalem and took the treasures of the House of the Lord and the treasures of the house of the king; he took everything; he took the shields of gold that Solomon had made.** These shields, described earlier (9:16), were designed mainly for ornamental purposes and were valuable artistic works.

10 **King Rehavam made bronze shields,** meant to look similar to shields of gold from a distance, **in their stead. And** he **entrusted them to the hand of the captains of the Runners, who guarded the entrance of the house of the king,** a certain group of the king's bodyguards.

Bronze shield, Delphi, Greece, eighth century BCE

11 **It was, that each time the king entered the House of the Lord, the Runners** who accompanied the king **would come and bear them,** the glittering and impressive shields. **And** afterward they would **bring them back to the chamber of the Runners,** where they were stored. Although these ornamental shields were not made of gold, they still required safekeeping.

12 **When he,** King Rehavam, **humbled himself** before God, **the anger of the Lord was withdrawn from him, not destroying him** and his kingdom **to** the point of **eradication.** Although the king and the people had acted inappropriately, they ultimately humbled themselves before God. **In Judah too, there were good things,** which contributed to God's decision not to destroy the kingdom. David and Solomon's work had not been in vain, as the kingdom did not collapse all at once.

13 **King Rehavam grew strong in Jerusalem and reigned, for Rehavam was forty-one years old when he became king, and he reigned seventeen years in Jerusalem, the city that the Lord chose from all the tribes of Israel to place His name there.** It is likely that Rehavam was Solomon's eldest son, as he assumed the throne at the age of forty-one and his father

ג כִּ֥י מָעֲל֖וּ בַּיהֹוָֽה׃ בְּאֶ֤לֶף וּמָאתַ֙יִם֙ רֶ֔כֶב וּבְשִׁשִּׁ֥ים אֶ֖לֶף פָּרָשִׁ֑ים וְאֵ֣ין מִסְפָּ֗ר לָעָ֞ם
ד אֲשֶׁר־בָּ֤אוּ עִמּוֹ֙ מִמִּצְרַ֔יִם לוּבִ֥ים סֻכִּיִּ֖ים וְכוּשִֽׁים׃ וַיִּלְכֹּ֛ד אֶת־עָרֵ֥י הַמְּצֻר֖וֹת אֲשֶׁ֣ר
ה לִיהוּדָ֑ה וַיָּבֹ֖א עַד־יְרוּשָׁלִָֽם׃ וּשְׁמַֽעְיָ֤ה הַנָּבִיא֙ בָּ֣א אֶל־רְחַבְעָ֔ם וְשָׂרֵ֣י
יְהוּדָ֔ה אֲשֶׁר־נֶאֶסְפ֥וּ אֶל־יְרוּשָׁלִַ֖ם מִפְּנֵ֣י שִׁישָׁ֑ק וַיֹּ֨אמֶר לָהֶ֜ם כֹּֽה־אָמַ֣ר יְהֹוָ֗ה אַתֶּם֙
ו עֲזַבְתֶּ֣ם אֹתִ֔י וְאַף־אֲנִ֛י עָזַ֥בְתִּי אֶתְכֶ֖ם בְּיַד־שִׁישָֽׁק׃ וַיִּכָּנְע֥וּ שָׂרֵֽי־יִשְׂרָאֵ֖ל וְהַמֶּ֑לֶךְ
ז וַיֹּאמְר֖וּ צַדִּ֥יק ׀ יְהֹוָֽה׃ וּבִרְא֤וֹת יְהֹוָה֙ כִּ֣י נִכְנָ֔עוּ הָיָ֨ה דְבַר־יְהֹוָ֜ה אֶל־שְׁמַעְיָ֣ה ׀
לֵאמֹר֙ נִכְנְע֔וּ לֹ֖א אַשְׁחִיתֵ֑ם וְנָתַתִּ֨י לָהֶ֤ם כִּמְעַט֙ לִפְלֵיטָ֔ה וְלֹא־תִתַּ֧ךְ חֲמָתִ֛י
ח בִּירוּשָׁלִַ֖ם בְּיַד־שִׁישָֽׁק׃ כִּ֥י יִֽהְיוּ־ל֖וֹ לַעֲבָדִ֑ים וְיֵדְעוּ֙ עֲב֣וֹדָתִ֔י וַעֲבוֹדַ֖ת מַמְלְכ֥וֹת
ט הָאֲרָצֽוֹת׃ וַיַּ֨עַל שִׁישַׁ֣ק מֶלֶךְ־מִצְרַיִם֮ עַל־יְרוּשָׁלִַם֒ וַיִּקַּ֞ח אֶת־אֹצְר֣וֹת
בֵּית־יְהֹוָ֗ה וְאֶת־אֹֽצְרוֹת֙ בֵּ֣ית הַמֶּ֔לֶךְ אֶת־הַכֹּ֖ל לָקָ֑ח וַיִּקַּח֙ אֶת־מָגִנֵּ֣י הַזָּהָ֔ב אֲשֶׁ֥ר
י עָשָׂ֖ה שְׁלֹמֹֽה׃ וַיַּ֨עַשׂ הַמֶּ֤לֶךְ רְחַבְעָם֙ תַּחְתֵּיהֶ֔ם מָגִנֵּ֖י נְחֹ֑שֶׁת וְהִפְקִ֗יד עַל־יַד֙ שָׂרֵ֣י
יא הָרָצִ֔ים הַשֹּׁ֣מְרִ֔ים פֶּ֖תַח בֵּ֥ית הַמֶּֽלֶךְ׃ וַיְהִ֛י מִדֵּי־ב֥וֹא הַמֶּ֖לֶךְ בֵּ֣ית יְהֹוָ֑ה בָּ֤אוּ הָֽרָצִים֙
יב וּנְשָׂא֔וּם וֶהֱשִׁב֖וּם אֶל־תָּ֥א הָרָצִֽים׃ וּבְהִכָּֽנְעוֹ֙ שָׁ֣ב מִמֶּ֔נּוּ אַף־יְהֹוָ֔ה וְלֹ֥א לְהַשְׁחִ֖ית טז
יג לְכָלָ֑ה וְגַ֗ם בִּיהוּדָ֛ה הָיָ֥ה דְּבָרִ֖ים טוֹבִֽים׃ וַיִּתְחַזֵּ֞ק הַמֶּ֧לֶךְ רְחַבְעָ֛ם
בִּירוּשָׁלִַ֖ם וַיִּמְלֹ֑ךְ כִּ֠י בֶּן־אַרְבָּעִ֨ים וְאַחַ֤ת שָׁנָה֙ רְחַבְעָ֣ם בְּמָלְכ֔וֹ וּשְׁבַ֨ע עֶשְׂרֵ֜ה
שָׁנָ֣ה ׀ מָלַ֣ךְ בִּירוּשָׁלִַ֗ם הָעִ֡יר אֲשֶׁר־בָּחַר֩ יְהֹוָ֨ה לָשׂ֜וּם אֶת־שְׁמ֣וֹ שָׁ֗ם מִכֹּל֙ שִׁבְטֵ֣י

BACKGROUND

12:3 | **Sukiyites:** The mention of the Sukiyites alongside the Libyans and the Kushites indicates that they too lived near Egypt. Apparently, they were the people called Tjuku in Egyptian documents dating from the nineteenth century BCE. Many of the Sukiyites served as policemen and guards in Egypt, and in this sense they resembled the Kushites and Libyans, who were mercenaries in the Egyptian army.

was approximately sixty when he died, meaning that Rehavam was born when his father was eighteen or even younger. **His mother's name was Naama the Amonitess.**

14 **He did evil because he did not set his heart to seek the Lord.** No specific transgressions are attributed to Rehavam, but he did not act in a righteous, God-fearing manner. He lived at a pivotal juncture in history, but he was a weak man who yielded easily to pressure. Indeed, the son of a great king is often inferior to his father.

15 **The early and the late matters concerning Rehavam,** referring to the change in his general conduct over the years, **are they not written in the chronicles of Shemaya the prophet and of Ido the seer,** which were recorded **to establish lineage?** These writings, which included lists of genealogies, were not included in the biblical canon, and were ultimately lost.[84] **There were wars between Rehavam and Yorovam always,** as also described in those accounts. The conflict between Rehavam and Yorovam persisted, although they did not engage in any major wars, because neither side had enough power to defeat the other decisively. Nevertheless, conflicts periodically arose between them, probably with regard to the border between their respective kingdoms.

16 **Rehavam lay with his fathers and was buried in the City of David; Aviya his son reigned in his stead.**

The Chronicles of King Aviya

II CHRONICLES 13:1–23

King Aviya continues in the footsteps of his father, Rehavam. During his reign, the Kingdom of Judah grows stronger than its neighbor, the Kingdom of Israel.

13 1 **In the eighteenth year of** the reign of **King Yorovam** over Israel, **Aviya became king over Judah.**

2 **He reigned three years in Jerusalem, and his mother's name was Mikhayahu daughter of Uriel from** the town of **Giva.**[85] **There was war between Aviya and Yorovam.**

3 **Aviya joined the battle with a force of mighty warriors, four hundred thousand select men, and Yorovam deployed for battle against him with eight hundred thousand select men, mighty warriors.**

4 **Aviya stood** to advance in the initial wave of attack **atop Mount Tzemarayim,**[B] **which is in the highlands of Ephraim, and said: Hear me, Yorovam and all Israel;**

5 **surely you know that the Lord, God of Israel, gave kingship over Israel to David forever, to him and to his sons,** in a dynasty that was established for him **by a covenant of salt,** an eternal covenant.

6 **But Yorovam son of Nevat, servant of Solomon son of David, rose and rebelled against his lord.**

7 **Idle and wicked men gathered around him, and they strove** and rebelled **against Rehavam,** my father, **son of Solomon; and Rehavam was young and fainthearted, and could not withstand them.**

8 **Now you presume to withstand the kingdom of the Lord in the hand of the sons of David, and** although **you are a great multitude, and** your army is large, in whose name are you fighting? After all, **with you are the golden calves that Yorovam made for you for gods.**

Figurine of a calf, found near Samaria, twelfth century BCE

9 **Haven't you dismissed the priests of the Lord, sons of Aaron, and the Levites, and appointed for you priests like the peoples of the** surrounding **land? Anyone who comes to invest himself** and seek appointment as a priest, **with a young bull and seven rams, he may become a priest to the non-gods,** those idols. Your priests are merely individuals who have expressed interest in the position; they are not true priests.

10 **But we,** in contrast, **the Lord is our God, and we have not forsaken Him;** the **priests** who **are serving the Lord** in the Temple are **sons of Aaron, and the Levites are** busy **at their labor** in the Temple.

11 **They burn burnt offerings to the Lord each morning and each evening, and incense of spices; the arrangement of the showbread is on the pure table, and there is the candelabrum of gold and its lamps** that they kindle **to burn every evening, for we keep the commission of the Lord our God, and you have forsaken Him.** You have abandoned God and you practice the customs of gentiles, whereas we observe His service.

יד יִשְׂרָאֵל וְשֵׁם אִמּוֹ נַעֲמָה הָעַמֹּנִית׃ וַיַּעַשׂ הָרָע כִּי לֹא הֵכִין לִבּוֹ לִדְרוֹשׁ אֶת־
טו יְהוָה׃ וְדִבְרֵי רְחַבְעָם הָרִאשֹׁנִים וְהָאַחֲרוֹנִים הֲלֹא־הֵם כְּתוּבִים בְּדִבְרֵי
שְׁמַעְיָה הַנָּבִיא וְעִדּוֹ הַחֹזֶה לְהִתְיַחֵשׂ וּמִלְחֲמוֹת רְחַבְעָם וְיָרָבְעָם כָּל־הַיָּמִים׃
טז וַיִּשְׁכַּב רְחַבְעָם עִם־אֲבֹתָיו וַיִּקָּבֵר בְּעִיר דָּוִיד וַיִּמְלֹךְ אֲבִיָּה בְנוֹ תַּחְתָּיו׃
א ב בִּשְׁנַת שְׁמוֹנֶה עֶשְׂרֵה לַמֶּלֶךְ יָרָבְעָם וַיִּמְלֹךְ אֲבִיָּה עַל־יְהוּדָה׃ שָׁלוֹשׁ שָׁנִים מָלַךְ
בִּירוּשָׁלִָם וְשֵׁם אִמּוֹ מִיכָיָהוּ בַת־אוּרִיאֵל מִן־גִּבְעָה וּמִלְחָמָה הָיְתָה בֵּין אֲבִיָּה
ג וּבֵין יָרָבְעָם׃ וַיֶּאְסֹר אֲבִיָּה אֶת־הַמִּלְחָמָה בְּחַיִל גִּבּוֹרֵי מִלְחָמָה אַרְבַּע־מֵאוֹת
אֶלֶף אִישׁ בָּחוּר וְיָרָבְעָם עָרַךְ עִמּוֹ מִלְחָמָה בִּשְׁמוֹנֶה מֵאוֹת אֶלֶף
ד אִישׁ בָּחוּר גִּבּוֹר חָיִל׃ וַיָּקָם אֲבִיָּה מֵעַל לְהַר צְמָרַיִם אֲשֶׁר
ה בְּהַר אֶפְרָיִם וַיֹּאמֶר שְׁמָעוּנִי יָרָבְעָם וְכָל־יִשְׂרָאֵל׃ הֲלֹא לָכֶם לָדַעַת כִּי יְהוָה ׀
אֱלֹהֵי יִשְׂרָאֵל נָתַן מַמְלָכָה לְדָוִיד עַל־יִשְׂרָאֵל לְעוֹלָם לוֹ וּלְבָנָיו בְּרִית מֶלַח׃
ו ז וַיָּקָם יָרָבְעָם בֶּן־נְבָט עֶבֶד שְׁלֹמֹה בֶן־דָּוִיד וַיִּמְרֹד עַל־אֲדֹנָיו׃ וַיִּקָּבְצוּ עָלָיו
אֲנָשִׁים רֵקִים בְּנֵי בְלִיַּעַל וַיִּתְאַמְּצוּ עַל־רְחַבְעָם בֶּן־שְׁלֹמֹה וּרְחַבְעָם הָיָה נַעַר
ח וְרַךְ־לֵבָב וְלֹא הִתְחַזַּק לִפְנֵיהֶם׃ וְעַתָּה ׀ אַתֶּם אֹמְרִים לְהִתְחַזֵּק לִפְנֵי מַמְלֶכֶת
יְהוָה בְּיַד בְּנֵי דָוִיד וְאַתֶּם הָמוֹן רָב וְעִמָּכֶם עֶגְלֵי זָהָב אֲשֶׁר עָשָׂה לָכֶם יָרָבְעָם
ט לֵאלֹהִים׃ הֲלֹא הִדַּחְתֶּם אֶת־כֹּהֲנֵי יְהוָה אֶת־בְּנֵי אַהֲרֹן וְהַלְוִיִּם וַתַּעֲשׂוּ לָכֶם
כֹּהֲנִים כְּעַמֵּי הָאֲרָצוֹת כָּל־הַבָּא לְמַלֵּא יָדוֹ בְּפַר בֶּן־בָּקָר וְאֵילִם שִׁבְעָה וְהָיָה
י כֹהֵן לְלֹא אֱלֹהִים׃ וַאֲנַחְנוּ יְהוָה אֱלֹהֵינוּ וְלֹא עֲזַבְנֻהוּ וְכֹהֲנִים מְשָׁרְתִים לַיהוָה
יא בְּנֵי אַהֲרֹן וְהַלְוִיִּם בַּמְלָאכֶת׃ וּמַקְטִרִים לַיהוָה עֹלוֹת בַּבֹּקֶר־בַּבֹּקֶר וּבָעֶרֶב־
בָּעֶרֶב וּקְטֹרֶת־סַמִּים וּמַעֲרֶכֶת לֶחֶם עַל־הַשֻּׁלְחָן הַטָּהוֹר וּמְנוֹרַת הַזָּהָב וְנֵרֹתֶיהָ

BACKGROUND

13:4 | **Mount Tzemarayim:** The book of Joshua (18:22) mentions a town called Tzemarayim near Beit El, on the border of the territory of the tribe of Benjamin. It is likely that the mountain was named after the town, and it was located on the boundary between the territory of the tribe of Ephraim, which was part of the Kingdom of Israel, and that of Benjamin, which was part of the Kingdom of Judah. It is generally identified with the summit of the mountain range of al-Bireh, which used to be called Ras et-Tahuneh. This range serves as a natural border between Rama and Beit El.

12 **Behold, God is with us at our head** of our camp, **and His priests** are ready **with the trumpets of alarm to sound an alarm against you. Children of Israel, do not fight against the Lord, God of your fathers, for you will not succeed.**

13 **Yorovam,** who had not stayed to listen to this lecture, had meanwhile **sent the ambush around to come from behind them.** He sent part of his army in a flanking maneuver so that **they,** he and his men, **were before Judah, and the ambush was behind them.**

14 **Judah turned, and behold,** they saw that **the fighting was before and behind** them; **they cried to the Lord, and the priests sounded the trumpets.**

15 **The men of Judah shouted; it was as the men of Judah shouted that God routed Yorovam and all Israel before Aviya and Judah.**

16 **The children of Israel fled from Judah, and God delivered them into their hand.**

17 **Aviya and his people smote them a great blow, and the slain from Israel who fell were five hundred thousand select men.** Most of the army of the Kingdom of Israel fell in battle.

18 **The children of Israel were humbled at that time, and the children of Judah prevailed** over them, **because they relied upon the Lord, God of their fathers.**

19 **Aviya pursued Yorovam,** continuing the advance, **and captured cities from him: Beit El and** the small towns in **its environs;** the city of **Yeshana and its environs; and Efrayin**[B] **and its environs.**

20 **Yorovam did not gain** his **strength again in the days of Aviya; and the Lord afflicted him, and he died.** Yorovam

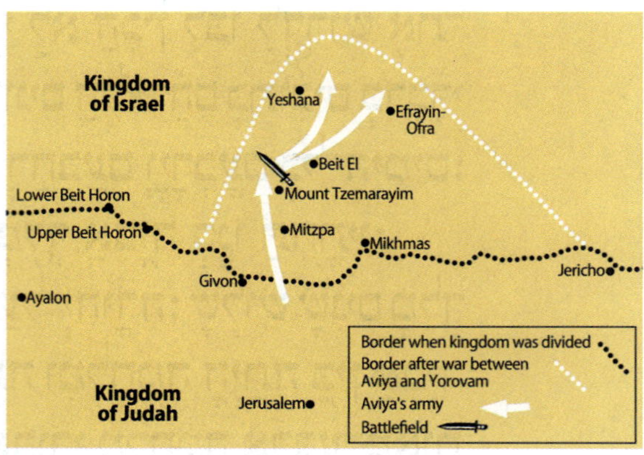

Cities Aviya conquered from Yorovam

could not withstand Aviya, and ultimately he died before the king of Judah.

21 **Aviya grew strong, and he took for himself fourteen wives and begot twenty-two sons and sixteen daughters.**

22 **The rest of the deeds of Aviya, his ways, and his statements, are written in the account of the prophet Ido.**

23 **Aviya lay with his fathers, and they buried him in the City of David.** Elsewhere it is stated that he followed in his father's path, as "his heart was not whole with the Lord his God."[86] Nevertheless, it seems that he did preserve the service of God in the Temple and even fought wars in the name of God. **And Asa his son reigned in his stead; in his days the land was tranquil** and rested from war **for ten years.** Although after the defeat of the army of Israel, the northern kingdom did not mount any further attacks, Asa was not powerful enough to attack them either.

The Chronicles of King Asa

II CHRONICLES 14:1–16:14

Although Aviya took pains to ensure that the Temple was managed properly, he failed to eradicate the foreign cults from the land. His son Asa takes direct action to rid the land of idols. After a period of political calm, Asa is forced to repel an Egyptian attack. He is successful in this war and causes the defeated Egyptian army to flee. However, toward the end of his days, Asa's reign suffers a decline in all aspects: religious, political, and social; even his personal health deteriorates.

14 1 **Asa did what is good and right in the eyes of the Lord his God.**

2 **He removed the foreign altars and the shrines, smashed the monuments, and cut down the sacred trees.**

Remains of shrines and monuments, Tel Gezer

3 **He,** Asa, **said to Judah to seek** closeness with **the Lord, God of their fathers,** to study and reflect upon God's word,[87] **and to fulfill the Torah and the commandments.**

4 **He removed from all the cities of Judah the shrines and the sun pillars,** the idols used in the ritual worship of the sun;[88] **and the kingdom was tranquil before him.**

5 **He built fortified cities in Judah, as the land was tranquil; and there was no war against him in those years, because the Lord had given him respite,** and therefore he could devote time and resources to such projects.

לְבָעֵר בָּעֶרֶב כִּי־שֹׁמְרִים אֲנַחְנוּ אֶת־מִשְׁמֶרֶת יְהוָה אֱלֹהֵינוּ וְאַתֶּם עֲזַבְתֶּם
אֹתוֹ: וְהִנֵּה עִמָּנוּ בָרֹאשׁ הָאֱלֹהִים ׀ וְכֹהֲנָיו וַחֲצֹצְרוֹת הַתְּרוּעָה לְהָרִיעַ עֲלֵיכֶם יב
בְּנֵי יִשְׂרָאֵל אַל־תִּלָּחֲמוּ עִם־יְהוָה אֱלֹהֵי־אֲבֹתֵיכֶם כִּי־לֹא תַצְלִיחוּ: וְיָרָבְעָם הֵסֵב יג
אֶת־הַמַּאֲרָב לָבוֹא מֵאַחֲרֵיהֶם וַיִּהְיוּ לִפְנֵי יְהוּדָה וְהַמַּאֲרָב מֵאַחֲרֵיהֶם: וַיִּפְנוּ יד
מַחְצְרִים יְהוּדָה וְהִנֵּה לָהֶם הַמִּלְחָמָה פָּנִים וְאָחוֹר וַיִּצְעֲקוּ לַיהוָה וְהַכֹּהֲנִים מחצצרים
בַּחֲצֹצְרוֹת: וַיָּרִיעוּ אִישׁ יְהוּדָה וַיְהִי בְּהָרִיעַ אִישׁ יְהוּדָה וְהָאֱלֹהִים נָגַף אֶת־יָרָבְעָם טו
וְכָל־יִשְׂרָאֵל לִפְנֵי אֲבִיָּה וִיהוּדָה: וַיָּנוּסוּ בְנֵי־יִשְׂרָאֵל מִפְּנֵי יְהוּדָה וַיִּתְּנֵם אֱלֹהִים טז
בְּיָדָם: וַיַּכּוּ בָהֶם אֲבִיָּה וְעַמּוֹ מַכָּה רַבָּה וַיִּפְּלוּ חֲלָלִים מִיִּשְׂרָאֵל חֲמֵשׁ־מֵאוֹת יז
אֶלֶף אִישׁ בָּחוּר: וַיִּכָּנְעוּ בְנֵי־יִשְׂרָאֵל בָּעֵת הַהִיא וַיֶּאֶמְצוּ בְּנֵי יְהוּדָה כִּי נִשְׁעֲנוּ יח
עַל־יְהוָה אֱלֹהֵי אֲבוֹתֵיהֶם: וַיִּרְדֹּף אֲבִיָּה אַחֲרֵי יָרָבְעָם וַיִּלְכֹּד מִמֶּנּוּ עָרִים אֶת־ יט
עֶפְרָיִן בֵּית־אֵל וְאֶת־בְּנוֹתֶיהָ וְאֶת־יְשָׁנָה וְאֶת־בְּנוֹתֶיהָ וְאֶת־עפרון וּבְנֹתֶיהָ: וְלֹא־עָצַר כ
כֹּחַ יָרָבְעָם עוֹד בִּימֵי אֲבִיָּהוּ וַיִּגְּפֵהוּ יְהוָה וַיָּמֹת: וַיִּתְחַזֵּק אֲבִיָּהוּ כא
וַיִּשָּׂא־לוֹ נָשִׁים אַרְבַּע עֶשְׂרֵה וַיּוֹלֶד עֶשְׂרִים וּשְׁנַיִם בָּנִים וְשֵׁשׁ עֶשְׂרֵה בָּנוֹת:
וְיֶתֶר דִּבְרֵי אֲבִיָּה וּדְרָכָיו וּדְבָרָיו כְּתוּבִים בְּמִדְרַשׁ הַנָּבִיא עִדּוֹ: וַיִּשְׁכַּב אֲבִיָּה כב כג
עִם־אֲבֹתָיו וַיִּקְבְּרוּ אֹתוֹ בְּעִיר דָּוִיד וַיִּמְלֹךְ אָסָא בְנוֹ תַּחְתָּיו בְּיָמָיו שָׁקְטָה הָאָרֶץ
עֶשֶׂר שָׁנִים: וַיַּעַשׂ אָסָא הַטּוֹב וְהַיָּשָׁר בְּעֵינֵי יְהוָה אֱלֹהָיו: וַיָּסַר אֶת־ א ב
מִזְבְּחוֹת הַנֵּכָר וְהַבָּמוֹת וַיְשַׁבֵּר אֶת־הַמַּצֵּבוֹת וַיְגַדַּע אֶת־הָאֲשֵׁרִים: וַיֹּאמֶר ג
לִיהוּדָה לִדְרוֹשׁ אֶת־יְהוָה אֱלֹהֵי אֲבוֹתֵיהֶם וְלַעֲשׂוֹת הַתּוֹרָה וְהַמִּצְוָה: וַיָּסַר ד
מִכָּל־עָרֵי יְהוּדָה אֶת־הַבָּמוֹת וְאֶת־הַחַמָּנִים וַתִּשְׁקֹט הַמַּמְלָכָה לְפָנָיו: וַיִּבֶן עָרֵי ה
מְצוּרָה בִּיהוּדָה כִּי־שָׁקְטָה הָאָרֶץ וְאֵין־עִמּוֹ מִלְחָמָה בַּשָּׁנִים הָאֵלֶּה כִּי־הֵנִיחַ

BACKGROUND

13:19| **Efrayin:** Generally identified with the biblical Ofra, approximately 7 km northeast of Beit El, in the location of the modern-day Arab town of Tayibe. The reason this place is alternately called Ofra and Efrayin can be attributed to the fact that the ends of place names were pronounced in different ways. Other examples of this phenomenon include Shaalvim, which is also called Shaalabin (see Judges 1:35; Joshua 19:42); Alemet, which is also called Almon (see Joshua 21:18; I Chronicles 6:45); and Samaria, which is called both Shomron and Shomrayin (see I Kings 16:24; Ezra 4:10).

6 **He said to Judah: Let us build these cities, and surround them with a wall, and** with **towers, gates, and bars while the land is still** quiet **before us, because we have sought the Lord our God; we sought, and He has given us respite from** our enemies **all around; and they built** other cities on the border and elsewhere, with the aim of further strengthening and developing the land, **and were successful.**

7 **Asa had a force bearing shield,** which encircles the wearer, **and spear: From Judah there were three hundred thousand** soldiers; **and from Benjamin** he had **bearers of bucklers and archers, two hundred and eighty thousand; all these were mighty warriors.** Clearly, the tribe of Benjamin grew and developed over the years, and it always had especially skilled archers.[89]

8 **Zerah the Kushite,**[B] a king of the Kushite dynasty that ruled over Egypt, **came out** to wage war **against them with a force of one thousand thousands,** one million warriors, **and three hundred chariots, and he came to Maresha,**[B] in the land of Judah.

9 **Asa went out to meet him, and they deployed for war in the Valley of Tzefata at Maresha.**[B]

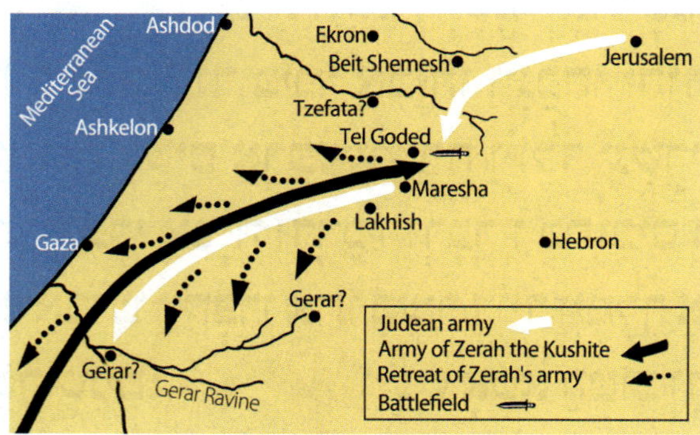

War between Asa and Zerah the Kushite

10 **Asa cried out to the Lord his God, and said: Lord, for helping, there is no difference for you between the great and the powerless.** We are few in number while the Kushites are many, but although we are weak, You can assist us as easily as You could if we were strong.[90] **Help us, Lord our God, for we rely upon You, and in Your name we are coming against this multitude. You are the Lord our God; let no man overcome You** (see 20:6).

11 Indeed, **the Lord routed the Kushites**[B] **before Asa and before Judah; and the Kushites fled.**

12 **Asa and the people who were with him pursued them to Gerar,**[B] **and Kushites were falling to beyond recovery,** they were left with no vitality or hope of rescue, **as they were broken before the Lord and before His camp,** the camp of Israel; **they,** Asa and Judah, **carried a great many spoils.**

Tel Gamma

13 **They smote all the** Philistine **cities around Gerar, because the fear of the Lord was upon them,** the Philistines; **and they plundered all the cities, for there was much plunder in them.**

14 **They also smote the tents of herders, and captured flocks in abundance and camels, and they returned to Jerusalem.**

15 1 **The spirit of God was upon Azarya son of Oded;** he received a prophecy.

2 **He came out before Asa and said to him: Hear me, Asa and all Judah and Benjamin. The Lord is with you when you are with Him, and if you seek Him, He will be found for you; but if you forsake Him, He will forsake you.**

3 The prophet continued: **For many days Israel was without the true God,** as they worshipped idols, **and without a teaching priest, and without Torah.**

4 **They,** the Israelites, **returned to the Lord, God of Israel, in their distress, and sought Him, and He was found for them;** He responded to them.

BACKGROUND

14:8| **Zerah the Kushite:** According to the tradition of the Sages, Zerah was a king of the Kushites who took the treasures of the House of God and of the king's house from Shishak, or Shoshenq I, king of Egypt, who had plundered them from Rehavam (*Pesaḥim* 119a; *Seder Olam Rabba* 16). No king with this name is mentioned in external sources, and researchers have offered several suggestions regarding his identity. Zerah might be the Hebrew name of Orsokon I, son of Shoshenq I, the king of Egypt during the period of Asa. Alternatively, he may have been the ruler over those regions in the south of the Land of Israel that were under Egyptian control, or the leader of nomadic or Kushite tribes that lived there, who sought to expand his control northward into the borders of the Kingdom of Judah, and was supported in this endeavor by the Egyptians and the Kushites (see verse 12).

Maresha: This was an important, fortified city located near an important crossroads in the southwest Judean foothills. This crossroads is where the road that ascends from the west through Wadi Lakhish meets the north–south road at the foot of the Judean highlands. Maresha was situated about 1.5 km south of Beit Guvrin.

14:9| **In the Valley of Tzefata at Maresha:** Some commentaries claim that Tzefata is not the name of a place, but means "the valley that

▸*can*

ו יְהוָה לוֹ׃ וַיֹּאמֶר לִיהוּדָה נִבְנֶה ׀ אֶת־הֶעָרִים הָאֵלֶּה וְנָסֵב חוֹמָה וּמִגְדָּלִים דְּלָתַיִם
וּבְרִיחִים עוֹדֶנּוּ הָאָרֶץ לְפָנֵינוּ כִּי דָרַשְׁנוּ אֶת־יְהוָה אֱלֹהֵינוּ דָּרַשְׁנוּ וַיָּנַח לָנוּ
ז מִסָּבִיב וַיִּבְנוּ וַיַּצְלִיחוּ׃ וַיְהִי לְאָסָא חַיִל נֹשֵׂא צִנָּה וָרֹמַח מִיהוּדָה
שְׁלֹשׁ מֵאוֹת אֶלֶף וּמִבִּנְיָמִן נֹשְׂאֵי מָגֵן וְדֹרְכֵי קֶשֶׁת מָאתַיִם וּשְׁמוֹנִים אֶלֶף כָּל־
ח אֵלֶּה גִּבּוֹרֵי חָיִל׃ וַיֵּצֵא אֲלֵיהֶם זֶרַח הַכּוּשִׁי בְּחַיִל אֶלֶף אֲלָפִים וּמַרְכָּבוֹת שְׁלֹשׁ
ט מֵאוֹת וַיָּבֹא עַד־מָרֵשָׁה׃ וַיֵּצֵא אָסָא לְפָנָיו וַיַּעַרְכוּ מִלְחָמָה בְּגֵיא צְפַתָה לְמָרֵשָׁה׃
י וַיִּקְרָא אָסָא אֶל־יְהוָה אֱלֹהָיו וַיֹּאמַר יְהוָה אֵין־עִמְּךָ לַעְזוֹר בֵּין רַב לְאֵין כֹּחַ
עָזְרֵנוּ יְהוָה אֱלֹהֵינוּ כִּי־עָלֶיךָ נִשְׁעַנּוּ וּבְשִׁמְךָ בָאנוּ עַל־הֶהָמוֹן הַזֶּה יְהוָה אֱלֹהֵינוּ
יא אַתָּה אַל־יַעְצֹר עִמְּךָ אֱנוֹשׁ׃ וַיִּגֹּף יְהוָה אֶת־הַכּוּשִׁים לִפְנֵי אָסָא
יב וְלִפְנֵי יְהוּדָה וַיָּנֻסוּ הַכּוּשִׁים׃ וַיִּרְדְּפֵם אָסָא וְהָעָם אֲשֶׁר־עִמּוֹ עַד־לִגְרָר וַיִּפֹּל
מִכּוּשִׁים לְאֵין־לָהֶם מִחְיָה כִּי־נִשְׁבְּרוּ לִפְנֵי־יְהוָה וְלִפְנֵי מַחֲנֵהוּ וַיִּשְׂאוּ שָׁלָל הַרְבֵּה
יג מְאֹד׃ וַיַּכּוּ אֵת כָּל־הֶעָרִים סְבִיבוֹת גְּרָר כִּי־הָיָה פַחַד־יְהוָה עֲלֵיהֶם וַיָּבֹזּוּ אֶת־
יד כָּל־הֶעָרִים כִּי־בִזָּה רַבָּה הָיְתָה בָהֶם׃ וְגַם־אָהֳלֵי מִקְנֶה הִכּוּ וַיִּשְׁבּוּ צֹאן לָרֹב
טו א וּגְמַלִּים וַיָּשֻׁבוּ יְרוּשָׁלִָם׃ וַעֲזַרְיָהוּ בֶּן־עוֹדֵד הָיְתָה עָלָיו רוּחַ אֱלֹהִים׃
ב וַיֵּצֵא לִפְנֵי אָסָא וַיֹּאמֶר לוֹ שְׁמָעוּנִי אָסָא וְכָל־יְהוּדָה וּבִנְיָמִן יְהוָה עִמָּכֶם בִּהְיוֹתְכֶם
ג עִמּוֹ וְאִם־תִּדְרְשֻׁהוּ יִמָּצֵא לָכֶם וְאִם־תַּעַזְבֻהוּ יַעֲזֹב אֶתְכֶם׃ וְיָמִים
ד רַבִּים לְיִשְׂרָאֵל לְלֹא ׀ אֱלֹהֵי אֱמֶת וּלְלֹא כֹּהֵן מוֹרֶה וּלְלֹא תוֹרָה׃ וַיָּשָׁב בַּצַּר־לוֹ

BACKGROUND

can be seen [*nitzpe*] from Maresha" (*Metzudat David*). The Septuagint, apparently based on a different spelling, translates it as north [*tzafona*] of Maresha. In the spirit of this translation, this place can tentatively be identified with the valley at the foot of Tel Goded, or Tel ej-Judeideh, which is on one of the routes to travel east–west in this area. Alternatively, according to Josephus (*Antiquities of the Jews* VIII:12:1) and the Madaba Map, the reference might be to a town called Tzefata near Beit Guvrin, which some identify with Tel Tzafit, the biblical Gat. This hypothesis is supported by an Egyptian inscription from the Late Bronze Age found at the site. The inscription mentions a prince called Sa-Pa, which sounds like Tzefata.

14:11 | **Kushites:** Some identify these Kushites with the Nubians, who lived in what is now Sudan, south of Egypt, while others claim that they were tribes that dwelled in the southern border regions of Judah and Philistia (see I Chronicles 4:39–40; II Chronicles 21:16).

14:12 | **Gerar:** The name of a city and a region in the eastern Negev (see, e.g., Genesis 10:19, 26:6). The city of Gerar is located near the Gerar Ravine, and has been identified with Tel Gamma near Kibbutz Re'im, or with Tel Hror, south of Melilot in the northern Negev. Over the course of history, Gerar was located in a frontier region that was disputed by Philistia, Judah, and Egypt.

5 **At those times,** when Israel acted improperly, **there was no peace for those going** from their place, **and coming** back, **for great tumults were upon all the inhabitants of the lands,** in all the settled areas of Israel.
6 **Nation,** tribe or family, **was beaten by nation, and city by city,** as there were internal quarrels between different sectors of the people; **for God confounded them [*hamamam*] with every kind of distress.** He afflicted them with various forms of tumult [*mehuma*] and panic.
7 **And you, be strong, and let your hands not slacken;** do not despair or weaken, **as there is reward for your actions.** Since you are following the good and upright path, you will ultimately be rewarded.
8 **When Asa heard these words, and the prophecy of** the son of[91] **Oded the prophet, he was encouraged, and removed the detestable things,** the idols, **from the entire land of Judah and Benjamin, and from the cities that he had captured in the highlands of Ephraim; he restored the altar of the Lord, which was before the Hall of the Lord.**
9 **He gathered all Judah and Benjamin, and those who resided with them from Ephraim and Manasseh, and from Simeon, as many from Israel had joined him,**[92] **when they saw that the Lord his God was with him.** Up to this point, only members of the tribes of Judah, Benjamin, and Levi resided in the Kingdom of Judah. Now they were joined by men from other tribes, as people are generally drawn to affiliate with the strong and successful.
10 **They gathered to Jerusalem in the third month of the fifteenth year of the reign of Asa.**
11 **They slaughtered to the Lord on that day from the spoils they had brought, seven hundred cattle and seven thousand sheep.**
12 **They entered into the covenant to seek the Lord, God of their fathers, with all their heart and with all their soul,**
13 **and** part of the renewed covenant which they accepted upon themselves was that **anyone who would not seek the Lord, God of Israel, would be put to death, both small and great, both man and woman.**
14 **They took an oath to the Lord in loud voice, and with shouting, and with trumpets, and with shofars.**

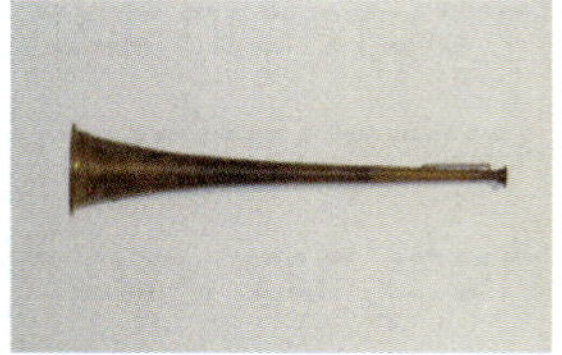
Trumpet

Shofar

15 **All Judah rejoiced over the oath, as with all their heart they had taken the oath and with all their will they sought Him, and He was found to them;** God answered them, **and the Lord gave them respite from all around.**
16 **He,** Asa, **also deposed Maakha mother of Asa the king, who had crafted a monstrosity,**[D] an image that people found horrifying and shocking, **to Ashera,** removing her **from** her official position of **being queen mother. Asa chopped down her monstrosity, pulverized it** into powder, **and burned it in the Kidron Valley.**[B]

Kidron Valley

17 **But** despite these actions, **the shrines were not removed from Israel,** and people continued to offer sacrifices upon them; **nevertheless, Asa's heart was whole all his days.**
18 **He brought the consecrated items of his father and his own consecrated items to the House of God: silver, gold, and vessels.**

DISCUSSION

15:16 | **A monstrosity [*mifletzet*]:** The root *peh-lamed-tzadi* refers to fear and shock. Accordingly, *mifletzet* is an object that provokes an extreme reaction of that kind. There is a similar description of an idol in Ezekiel 8:3: "The seat of the infuriating image of infuriation." The reference here is to a most despicable and repulsive image (see Ibn Janaḥ; Radak). The Sages explain that this *mifletzet* was in the shape of the male reproductive organ, perhaps a tree trunk or a wooden pole, which was positioned alongside the Ashera and used in its rites (see *Avoda Zara* 44a), possibly as a symbol of fertility. Idolatrous objects of this kind were found in Greece, Rome, and other ancient cultures, and similar rites are observed in India to this day.

ה עַל־יְהֹוָה אֱלֹהֵי יִשְׂרָאֵל וַיְבַקְשֻׁהוּ וַיִּמָּצֵא לָהֶם: וּבָעִתִּים הָהֵם אֵין שָׁלוֹם לַיּוֹצֵא
ו וְלַבָּא כִּי מְהוּמֹת רַבּוֹת עַל כָּל־יוֹשְׁבֵי הָאֲרָצוֹת: וְכֻתְּתוּ גוֹי־בְּגוֹי וְעִיר בְּעִיר
ז כִּי־אֱלֹהִים הֲמָמָם בְּכָל־צָרָה: וְאַתֶּם חִזְקוּ וְאַל־יִרְפּוּ יְדֵיכֶם כִּי יֵשׁ שָׂכָר
ח לִפְעֻלַּתְכֶם: וְכִשְׁמֹעַ אָסָא הַדְּבָרִים הָאֵלֶּה וְהַנְּבוּאָה עֹדֵד הַנָּבִיא
הִתְחַזַּק וַיַּעֲבֵר הַשִּׁקּוּצִים מִכָּל־אֶרֶץ יְהוּדָה וּבִנְיָמִן וּמִן־הֶעָרִים אֲשֶׁר לָכַד מֵהַר
ט אֶפְרָיִם וַיְחַדֵּשׁ אֶת־מִזְבַּח יְהֹוָה אֲשֶׁר לִפְנֵי אוּלָם יְהֹוָה: וַיִּקְבֹּץ אֶת־כָּל־יְהוּדָה
וּבִנְיָמִן וְהַגָּרִים עִמָּהֶם מֵאֶפְרַיִם וּמְנַשֶּׁה וּמִשִּׁמְעוֹן כִּי־נָפְלוּ עָלָיו מִיִּשְׂרָאֵל לָרֹב
י בִּרְאֹתָם כִּי־יְהֹוָה אֱלֹהָיו עִמּוֹ: וַיִּקָּבְצוּ יְרוּשָׁלַםִ בַּחֹדֶשׁ הַשְּׁלִישִׁי לִשְׁנַת
יא חֲמֵשׁ־עֶשְׂרֵה לְמַלְכוּת אָסָא: וַיִּזְבְּחוּ לַיהֹוָה בַּיּוֹם הַהוּא מִן־הַשָּׁלָל הֵבִיאוּ בָּקָר
יב שְׁבַע מֵאוֹת וְצֹאן שִׁבְעַת אֲלָפִים: וַיָּבֹאוּ בַבְּרִית לִדְרוֹשׁ אֶת־יְהֹוָה אֱלֹהֵי
יג אֲבוֹתֵיהֶם בְּכָל־לְבָבָם וּבְכָל־נַפְשָׁם: וְכֹל אֲשֶׁר לֹא־יִדְרֹשׁ לַיהֹוָה אֱלֹהֵי־יִשְׂרָאֵל
יד יוּמָת לְמִן־קָטֹן וְעַד־גָּדוֹל לְמֵאִישׁ וְעַד־אִשָּׁה: וַיִּשָּׁבְעוּ לַיהֹוָה בְּקוֹל גָּדוֹל
טו וּבִתְרוּעָה וּבַחֲצֹצְרוֹת וּבְשׁוֹפָרוֹת: וַיִּשְׂמְחוּ כָל־יְהוּדָה עַל־הַשְּׁבוּעָה כִּי בְכָל־ יז
טז לְבָבָם נִשְׁבָּעוּ וּבְכָל־רְצוֹנָם בִּקְשֻׁהוּ וַיִּמָּצֵא לָהֶם וַיָּנַח יְהֹוָה לָהֶם מִסָּבִיב: וְגַם־
מַעֲכָה אֵם ׀ אָסָא הַמֶּלֶךְ הֱסִירָהּ מִגְּבִירָה אֲשֶׁר־עָשְׂתָה לַאֲשֵׁרָה מִפְלָצֶת וַיִּכְרֹת
יז אָסָא אֶת־מִפְלַצְתָּהּ וַיָּדֶק וַיִּשְׂרֹף בְּנַחַל קִדְרוֹן: וְהַבָּמוֹת לֹא־סָרוּ מִיִּשְׂרָאֵל רַק
יח לְבַב־אָסָא הָיָה שָׁלֵם כָּל־יָמָיו: וַיָּבֵא אֶת־קָדְשֵׁי אָבִיו וְקָדָשָׁיו בֵּית הָאֱלֹהִים

BACKGROUND

15:16| **The Kidron Valley:** The Kidron Valley borders the Old City of Jerusalem to the east and water flows in it there from north to south. Approximately 5 km from Jerusalem, the valley winds its way eastward and descends to the Dead Sea. The deeper section of the valley that passes near Jerusalem is called the Valley of Yehoshafat (Joel 4:2), and was named Beit Mikle in the period of the Mishna (*Tosefta, Menaḥot* 10:5). The Gihon and Ein Rogel springs, into which water flows from underground aquifers in this valley, served as a water source for the city, for irrigating the king's garden (II Kings 25:4; Jeremiah 39:4), and for agricultural purposes (Mishna *Yoma* 5:6).

19 **There was no** additional **war,** neither internally nor externally, **until the thirty-fifth year of the reign of Asa,** for roughly twenty years. Before Asa's reign, there were tranquil years, in the wake of Aviya's victory over Yorovam. Later, during Asa's reign, the Kushites, who ruled over Egypt, attacked, and after they too were routed, Asa's control was bolstered, and peace prevailed in his kingdom for many years.

16 1 **In the thirty-sixth year of the reign of Asa, Baasha king of Israel went up against Judah.** Baasha was a man of war who rebelled against Nadav son of Yorovam, established his own royal dynasty in Israel, and destroyed the entire house of Yorovam.[93] When his grip on the throne became firmly established, Baasha rose up against Judah, **and** without yet attacking he **built** fortifications in **Rama,**[B] a city near the southern border of the Kingdom of Israel, **so as not to allow going and coming for Asa king of Judah.** He planned to control the main routes leading from Judah to Israel, and to blockade them before the king of Judah to the best of his ability.

2 While not yet under direct attack, Asa felt threatened. **Asa took out silver and gold from the treasuries of the House of the Lord and the house of the king,** the kingdom's emergency funds, **and he sent to Ben Hadad king of Aram, who lived in Damascus, saying:**

3 **There is a covenant,** peaceful relations, **between me and you, and between my father and your father.** For years relations between us have been good. We do not share a common border, while our mutual enemy, the king of Israel, resides between us. Therefore, **behold, I have sent you silver and gold; go** now, **breach your covenant with Baasha king of Israel,** and attack him, **and he will withdraw from upon me,** as was the accepted practice in alliances in the ancient world. These agreements between nations would quickly dissipate due to bribery or some other means of achieving the interests of a party to the agreement.

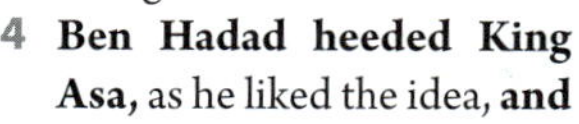

Marjayoun, southeast Lebanon

4 **Ben Hadad heeded King Asa,** as he liked the idea, **and he sent the commanders of his soldiers,** several regiments of his army, **against the cities of Israel; they smote Iyon,**[B] **Dan,**[B] **Avel Mayim,**[B] **and all the storehouse cities of Naphtali,**[B] on the northern border of the Kingdom of Israel.

Worship site at Tel Dan, tenth century BCE

Tel Abel, picture from 1945

5 **It was when Baasha heard** of the attack, **that he ceased building Rama and suspended its labor,** in order to focus on the efforts to stabilize his northern borders. Although there was a historic dimension to his dispute with Judah, the Aramean attack posed a far greater threat.

6 **King Asa took,** gathered, **all Judah, and they carried away the stones of Rama and its wood;** they dismantled the fortified structures **that Baasha had built, and he built with them Geva**[94] **and the Mitzpa**[B] in the Kingdom of Judah.

7 **At that time Hanani the seer,** a prophet not mentioned elsewhere, **came to Asa king of Judah and said to him: For your reliance on the king of Aram** in your quarrel with the king of Israel, and since you gave him the treasures of the House of God and of the king's house **and you did not rely on the Lord your God, the forces of the king of Aram have therefore fled from your hand.** From this

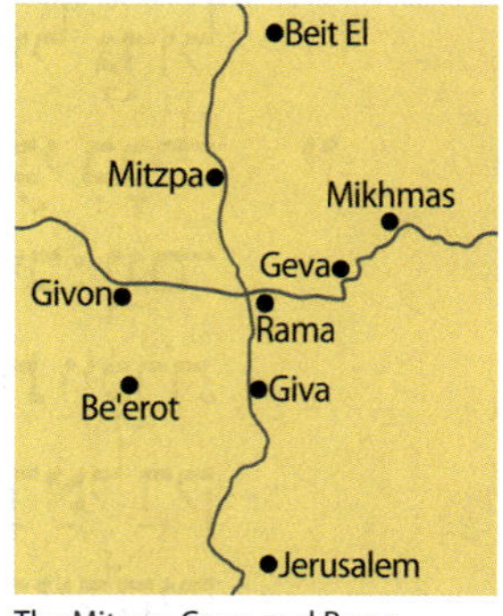

The Mitzpa, Geva, and Rama

BACKGROUND

16:1 | **And built Rama:** Rama is generally identified with the town of a-Ram, some 9 km north of Jerusalem. Rama was situated within the boundaries of the tribe of Benjamin, and overlooked an important crossroads between the central mountain route, which runs north–south between Shekhem and Jerusalem, and the east–west road that ascends from the coastal plains via Beit Horon. This latter road served as the border between the tribes of the Kingdom of Israel and those of the Kingdom of Judah even before the division of the kingdom (see commentary on 8:5). With the division of the kingdom, the Kingdom of Israel sought to gain control of adjacent territories. After the conquests of Aviya king of Judah in northern Benjamin (13:19), Baasha acted to restore the border to its place and even assume control of Rama and Gibeton, near Gezer (see I Kings 15).

16:4 | **Iyon:** Generally identified with Tel Dibbine, in the north of the Marjayoun Valley, near the town of Marjayoun, approximately 7 km north of Metula.

Dan: Identified with Tel Dan, which encompasses an area of some 200,000 sq m. This city, which sat at the foot of Mount Hermon, was a center for idolatry (Judges 18:26–31). It is mentioned in contemporary Egyptian records, and archaeological findings suggest it maintained commercial

▸ ties

יט כֶּסֶף וְזָהָב וְכֵלִים׃ וּמִלְחָמָה לֹא הָיָתָה עַד שְׁנַת־שְׁלֹשִׁים וְחָמֵשׁ לְמַלְכוּת
טז א אָסָא׃ בִּשְׁנַת שְׁלֹשִׁים וָשֵׁשׁ לְמַלְכוּת אָסָא עָלָה בַּעְשָׁא מֶלֶךְ־יִשְׂרָאֵל
ב עַל־יְהוּדָה וַיִּבֶן אֶת־הָרָמָה לְבִלְתִּי תֵּת יוֹצֵא וָבָא לְאָסָא מֶלֶךְ יְהוּדָה׃ וַיֹּצֵא
אָסָא כֶּסֶף וְזָהָב מֵאֹצְרוֹת בֵּית יְהוָה וּבֵית הַמֶּלֶךְ וַיִּשְׁלַח אֶל־בֶּן־הֲדַד מֶלֶךְ אֲרָם
ג הַיּוֹשֵׁב בְּדַרְמֶשֶׂק לֵאמֹר׃ בְּרִית בֵּינִי וּבֵינֶךָ וּבֵין אָבִי וּבֵין אָבִיךָ הִנֵּה שָׁלַחְתִּי
ד לְךָ כֶּסֶף וְזָהָב לֵךְ הָפֵר בְּרִיתְךָ אֶת־בַּעְשָׁא מֶלֶךְ יִשְׂרָאֵל וְיַעֲלֶה מֵעָלָי׃ וַיִּשְׁמַע
בֶּן־הֲדַד אֶל־הַמֶּלֶךְ אָסָא וַיִּשְׁלַח אֶת־שָׂרֵי הַחֲיָלִים אֲשֶׁר־לוֹ אֶל־עָרֵי יִשְׂרָאֵל
ה וַיַּכּוּ אֶת־עִיּוֹן וְאֶת־דָּן וְאֵת אָבֵל מָיִם וְאֵת כָּל־מִסְכְּנוֹת עָרֵי נַפְתָּלִי׃ וַיְהִי כִּשְׁמֹעַ
ו בַּעְשָׁא וַיֶּחְדַּל מִבְּנוֹת אֶת־הָרָמָה וַיַּשְׁבֵּת אֶת־מְלַאכְתּוֹ׃ וְאָסָא הַמֶּלֶךְ
לָקַח אֶת־כָּל־יְהוּדָה וַיִּשְׂאוּ אֶת־אַבְנֵי הָרָמָה וְאֶת־עֵצֶיהָ אֲשֶׁר בָּנָה בַּעְשָׁא וַיִּבֶן
ז בָּהֶם אֶת־גֶּבַע וְאֶת־הַמִּצְפָּה׃ וּבָעֵת הַהִיא בָּא חֲנָנִי הָרֹאֶה אֶל־
אָסָא מֶלֶךְ יְהוּדָה וַיֹּאמֶר אֵלָיו בְּהִשָּׁעֶנְךָ עַל־מֶלֶךְ אֲרָם וְלֹא נִשְׁעַנְתָּ עַל־יְהוָה
ח אֱלֹהֶיךָ עַל־כֵּן נִמְלַט חֵיל מֶלֶךְ־אֲרָם מִיָּדֶךָ׃ הֲלֹא הַכּוּשִׁים וְהַלּוּבִים הָיוּ לְחַיִל ׀

point forward, you will have to deal with the Arameans from a position of inferiority.

8 **Weren't the Kushites** (see 14:12) **and the Libyans,** who attacked you in the past, **a vast force, with very many chariots and horsemen? And** yet, **in your reliance on the Lord, He delivered them into your hand.** The attack of those armies was an immeasurably greater threat than this one, but you were able to defeat them and drive them away because you trusted in God.

BACKGROUND

ties with Mesopotamia, with the cities on the coast of the Mediterranean Sea, and with the Aegean world. Findings identified as Israelite from the twelfth century BCE and afterward have been discovered at the site.

Avel Mayim: Also known as Avel Beit Maakha (see Kings 15:20), this was a city in the territory of the tribe of Naphtali (see II Kings 15:29). Its inhabitants handed over the head of Sheva son of Bikhri to Yoav, after the former rebelled against David and barricaded himself there (II Samuel 20:14–15). The city is also mentioned in contemporary Egyptian records. It is identified with Tel Abel, between modern-day Metula and Kfar Giladi.

And all the storehouse cities of Naphtali: The reference is to fortified cities, which served as storehouses for weapons and food, like the "storehouse cities" mentioned in Exodus (1:11). The term "fortified cities" in the book of Joshua (19:35) refers specifically to the cities of Naphtali. The parallel account in I Kings (15:20) adds: "And all Kinerot, with all the land of Naphtali." It has been suggested that this was a region named for the city of Kineret. Archaeological findings indicate that Kineret was a significant, central city that was destroyed in the days of Tiglat Pileser.

16:6 | **The Mitzpa:** An important city in the tribal portion of Benjamin, which has been identified with Tel Nasbeh, approximately 13 km north of Jerusalem. The Mitzpa overlooked the main road from Shekhem and Samaria to Jerusalem and served as the site for communal and national gatherings (see commentary on I Samuel 7:6, 10:17). It was an administrative center after the destruction of the First Temple (see II Kings 25:23). Some suggest identifying the Mitzpa with the site known today as Nebi Samuel.

9 **For the Lord, His eyes range throughout the entire land;** He watches over everything, **to strengthen those whose heart is whole toward Him** and who trust in Him, and it is clear that you are not completely devoted to God. **You have been foolish in this, as** indeed[95] **from now, there will be wars upon you.**
10 Up to this point, the prophets had invariably encouraged Asa, and he had accepted their words. This was the first time that a prophet rebuked him. **Asa was angry with the seer and placed him in the prison,**[B] perhaps a dungeon or a cage,[96] **as he was in a rage with him over this** matter. Furthermore, after thirty-five years of successful reign, Asa changed his behavior toward his subjects: **Asa afflicted,** oppressed, **some of the people at that time.**
11 **Behold, the early and late matters concerning Asa,** and the changes that occurred between the beginning and the end of his reign; **behold, they are written in the book of the kings of Judah and Israel.**
12 **In the thirty-ninth year of his reign Asa contracted an ailment in his legs,**[B] and **his ailment grew acute. But** even **in his ailment he also did not seek the Lord** and did not pray to Him,[97] **but rather,** he trusted exclusively in **the physicians.**
13 **Asa lay with his fathers, and died in the forty-first year of his reign.** Asa ruled for many years.
14 **They buried him in his graves which he had excavated for himself in the City of David, and laid him in the bed that he had filled with spices and different blends** of spices **in a blend of craft,** the work of an expert in mixing perfumes;[98] **and they kindled a very great conflagration for him.**[B] One of the rites connected to the burial of kings included a burning ritual for a ruler who died peacefully in his bed. This ritual, which also involved burning some of the king's property so that it could not be used by anyone else, was performed in honor of the deceased and to lament his passing.[99]

The Chronicles of King Yehoshafat

II CHRONICLES 17:1–20:37

Yehoshafat continues in the path of his father's good deeds, and succeeds in strengthening his kingdom politically, militarily, and religiously. He is victorious in his wars, sometimes without having to expend any effort, and he seeks to bolster the legal system throughout the cities of his kingdom. Yehoshafat trusts in God and His prophets, and attempts to spread the study of Torah and the observance of its commandments among the people, albeit without complete success. He reconciles with the kings of Israel and establishes family ties with them. Nevertheless, these relationships also lead to errors that later extract a price from him.

17 1 **Yehoshafat his,** Asa's, **son reigned in his stead, and he fortified himself** in his reign **against Israel.**
2 **He positioned forces in all the fortified cities of Judah, and appointed officials** of guard units **in the land of Judah, and in the cities of Ephraim,** border areas **that Asa his father had captured.**
3 **The Lord was with Yehoshafat, because he followed the early ways of his father David and did not seek the Be'alim.**
4 **Rather, he sought the God of his father, and followed His commandments, not like the actions of** the Kingdom of **Israel.**
5 **The Lord established the kingdom in his hand, and all Judah brought tribute to Yehoshafat,** as a sign of their subservience and loyalty;[100] **and he had wealth and honor in abundance.**

"Fortified cities of Judah." Horvat Uza, remains of fortress from reign of Yehoshafat, Judean Desert

Bringing tribute to a king, illustration based on carving on ivory, Megiddo, second millennium BCE

6 **His heart was elevated,** he glorified himself and he courageously walked **in the ways of the Lord;**[101] **moreover,** he surpassed his father's deeds, as **he removed the shrines and the sacred trees from Judah.** The service of God at private altars as well as the worship of idols had reemerged, and it became periodically necessary to remove the remnants of those practices.

ט לרב לרכב ולפרשים להרבה מאד ובהשענך על־יהוה נתנם בידך: כי יהוה
עיניו משטטות בכל־הארץ להתחזק עם־לבבם שלם אליו נסכלת על־זאת
י כי מעתה יש עמך מלחמות: ויכעס אסא אל־הראה ויתנהו בית המהפכת
יא כי־בזעף עמו על־זאת וירצץ אסא מן־העם בעת ההיא: והנה דברי אסא
הראשונים והאחרונים הנם כתובים על־ספר המלכים ליהודה וישראל:
יב ויחלא אסא בשנת שלושים ותשע למלכותו ברגליו עד־למעלה חליו וגם־
יג בחליו לא־דרש את־יהוה כי ברפאים: וישכב אסא עם־אבתיו וימת בשנת
יד ארבעים ואחת למלכו: ויקברהו בקברתיו אשר כרה־לו בעיר דויד וישכיבהו
במשכב אשר מלא בשמים וזנים מרקחים במרקחת מעשה וישרפו־לו שרפה
ז א גדולה עד־למאד: וימלך יהושפט בנו תחתיו ויתחזק על־ישראל:
ב ויתן־חיל בכל־ערי יהודה הבצרות ויתן נציבים בארץ יהודה ובערי אפרים
ג אשר לכד אסא אביו: ויהי יהוה עם־יהושפט כי הלך בדרכי דויד אביו
ד הראשנים ולא דרש לבעלים: כי לאלהי אביו דרש ובמצותיו הלך ולא כמעשה
ה ישראל: ויכן יהוה את־הממלכה בידו ויתנו כל־יהודה מנחה ליהושפט ויהי־
ו לו עשר וכבוד לרב: ויגבה לבו בדרכי יהוה ועוד הסיר את־הבמות ואת־

BACKGROUND

16:10 | **Prison:** A detention facility, either fixed or mobile, which was located in the upper gate of Benjamin (Jeremiah 20:2, 29:26). Rav Yosef Kimḥi explains that it is a pillory, "made from two pieces of wood in which a place is fashioned for the neck, as the [neck of] prisoners was inserted there, and likewise cuffs for the hands" (*Sefer HaGalui*, p. 145).

16:12 | **Asa contracted an ailment in his legs:** The Sages say that he became afflicted with a disease called *padagra*, which affects the feet and causes great pain (see *Sota* 10a). *Padagra*, which comes from Greek and Latin, means a trap for the foot. This is gout, an incurable disease known as *shigadon* or *tzinit* in Hebrew. It is caused by a rise in acidity in the blood, resulting in acid crystals accumulating in various joints in the body, particularly in the toes and sometimes even the kidneys. The acid stones cause inflammation, swelling, and severe pain. In the past, gout was called the disease of kings or the rich man's disease, as it is probably caused by overeating, an unhealthy diet, and subsequent obesity, characteristic of people from pampered groups of the population.

16:14 | **And they kindled a very great conflagration for him:** As opposed to Phoenician burial rites and those of several cultures to this day, in Israel cremation has always been considered disgusting and unacceptable. The prophet Amos included those who burn human bones in his list of sinners (Amos 2:1). Likewise, when King Yoshiya sought to demean idolatry and its priests he burned their bones on the altar (II Kings 23:16). It appears that the burning mentioned here consisted of setting fire to the possessions of the deceased king. This was performed for his honor, so that his personal items would not be used (see Rambam, *Sefer Shofetim*, *Hilkhot Melakhim* 5:1). The same emerges from the story of Yehoram (21:19), and the comments of Jeremiah to Tzidkiyahu (Jeremiah 34:4–5, and commentary ad loc.).

In archaeological excavations of tumuli, ancient burial mounds, southwest of Jerusalem, conducted by Ruth Amiran and Gavriel Barkai, remnants of conflagrations were discovered, which some suggest are from these royal ceremonies.

7 **In the third year of his reign, he sent his princes,** his
ministers: **Ben Hayil, Ovadya, Zekharya, Netanel, and
Mikhayahu, to teach** Torah in public as representatives of the
government, **in the cities of Judah;**
8 **with them were the Levites,** who were apparently professional teachers: **Shemayahu, Netanyahu, Zevadyahu, Asael,
Shemiramot, Yehonatan, Adoniyahu, Toviyahu, and Tov
Adoniya the Levites, and with them were Elishama and
Yehoram the priests.**
9 **They taught in Judah, and with them was a scroll of the
Torah of the Lord; they circulated throughout all the cities
of Judah, and taught among the people.**
10 **Fear of the Lord was upon all the kingdoms of the lands
that surrounded Judah, and they did not wage war against
Yehoshafat.**
11 **The Philistines would bring to Yehoshafat tribute and silver
by load. Also the Arabians would bring him flocks: Seven
thousand seven hundred rams and seven thousand seven
hundred goats.** Although the surrounding nations were not
entirely subjugated to Yehoshafat, they treated him as the greatest of the kings, and each of them brought him gifts, in his own
manner.

Mouflon ram

Goat

12 Enjoying political security, Yehoshafat was free to execute re-
forms in the country and develop the state both spiritually and
materially: **Yehoshafat was growing steadily greater, ever
upward; and he built strongholds,** small, fortified cities, **and
storehouse cities,** which functioned as warehouses, treasuries,
and armories, **in Judah.**
13 **He had great works** and production **in the cities of Judah,
and** he could also call upon **men of war, mighty warriors, in
Jerusalem.**
14 **This was their reckoning,** their total sum, **according to their
patrilineal houses: For Judah,** there were **commanders of**

Remains of a palace and storehouses, Ramat Rachel

**thousands: Adna the commander, and with him were three
hundred thousand mighty warriors;**
15 **next to him was Yehohanan the commander, and with him
were two hundred and eighty thousand;**
16 **next to him was Amasya son of Zikhri, who volunteered** his
services or his property **to the Lord, and with him were two
hundred thousand mighty warriors.** Apparently, these massive divisions were primarily reserve units. It was the custom
in Israel to include in the army rolls anyone who could handle
a weapon, although in practice only a few regiments were in active service.
17 And **from Benjamin: Elyada,** who was **a mighty warrior, and
with him were two hundred thousand armed with bow and
shield;**
18 **alongside him was Yehozavad, and with him were one hundred and eighty thousand mobilized soldiers.**
19 **These were those who served the king besides those** men
**whom the king positioned in the fortified cities throughout
all Judah.** The Kingdom of Judah enjoyed peace, as Yehoshafat
continued in his father's ways, seeking to strengthen and elevate
his subjects both spiritually and materially.

18

1 **Yehoshafat had wealth and honor in abundance; and he
arranged a marriage with Ahav.**[D] He became a member of
Ahav's family through marriage, as his son Yehoram married
Atalya, Ahav's daughter.
2 **After some years, he,** Yehoshafat, **went down to Ahav to
Samaria. Ahav slaughtered sheep and cattle for him in**

ז הָאֲשֵׁרִ֖ים מִֽיהוּדָֽה׃ וּבִשְׁנַ֤ת שָׁלוֹשׁ֙ לְמָלְכ֔וֹ שָׁלַ֣ח לְשָׂרָ֗יו לְבֶן־חַ֨יִל֙
ח וּלְעֹבַדְיָ֧ה וְלִזְכַרְיָ֛ה וְלִנְתַנְאֵ֖ל וּלְמִיכָ֑יְהוּ לְלַמֵּ֖ד בְּעָרֵ֥י יְהוּדָֽה׃ וְעִמָּהֶ֣ם הַלְוִיִּ֗ם
שְֽׁמַֽעְיָ֡הוּ וּנְתַנְיָ֡הוּ וּ֠זְבַדְיָהוּ וַעֲשָׂהאֵ֡ל ושמרימות וִיהוֹנָתָ֡ן וַאֲדֹנִיָּ֧הוּ וְטוֹבִיָּ֛הוּ וְט֥וֹב וּשְׁמִֽירָמ֡וֹת
ט אֲדוֹנִיָּ֖ה הַלְוִיִּ֑ם וְעִמָּהֶ֛ם אֱלִישָׁמָ֥ע וִיהוֹרָ֖ם הַכֹּהֲנִֽים׃ וַֽיְלַמְּדוּ֙ בִּֽיהוּדָ֔ה וְעִמָּהֶ֕ם סֵ֖פֶר
י תּוֹרַ֣ת יְהוָ֑ה וַיָּסֹ֙בּוּ֙ בְּכָל־עָרֵ֣י יְהוּדָ֔ה וַֽיְלַמְּד֖וּ בָּעָֽם׃ וַיְהִ֣י ׀ פַּ֣חַד יְהוָ֗ה עַ֚ל כָּל־
יא מַמְלְכ֣וֹת הָֽאֲרָצ֔וֹת אֲשֶׁ֖ר סְבִיב֣וֹת יְהוּדָ֑ה וְלֹ֥א נִלְחֲמ֖וּ עִם־יְהוֹשָׁפָֽט׃ וּמִן־פְּלִשְׁתִּ֗ים
מְבִיאִ֧ים לִיהוֹשָׁפָ֛ט מִנְחָ֖ה וְכֶ֣סֶף מַשָּׂ֑א גַּ֣ם הָֽעַרְבִיאִ֗ים מְבִיאִ֥ים לוֹ֙ צֹ֔אן אֵילִ֗ים
שִׁבְעַ֤ת אֲלָפִים֙ וּשְׁבַ֣ע מֵא֔וֹת וּתְיָשִׁ֕ים שִׁבְעַ֥ת אֲלָפִ֖ים וּשְׁבַ֥ע מֵאֽוֹת׃
יב וַיְהִ֧י יְהוֹשָׁפָ֛ט הֹלֵ֥ךְ וְגָדֵ֖ל עַד־לְמָ֑עְלָה וַיִּ֧בֶן בִּֽיהוּדָ֛ה בִּירָנִיּ֖וֹת וְעָרֵ֥י מִסְכְּנֽוֹת׃
יג וּמְלָאכָ֤ה רַבָּה֙ הָ֣יָה ל֔וֹ בְּעָרֵ֖י יְהוּדָ֑ה וְאַנְשֵׁ֧י מִלְחָמָ֛ה גִּבּ֥וֹרֵי חַ֖יִל בִּירוּשָׁלִָֽם׃
יד וְאֵ֥לֶּה פְקֻדָּתָ֖ם לְבֵ֣ית אֲבוֹתֵיהֶ֑ם לִֽיהוּדָ֞ה שָׂרֵ֣י אֲלָפִ֗ים עַדְנָ֣ה הַשָּׂ֔ר וְעִמּ֛וֹ גִּבּ֥וֹרֵי
טו חַ֖יִל שְׁלֹ֥שׁ מֵא֥וֹת אָֽלֶף׃ וְעַל־יָד֖וֹ יְהוֹחָנָ֣ן הַשָּׂ֑ר וְעִמּ֕וֹ מָאתַ֥יִם וּשְׁמוֹנִ֖ים
טז אָֽלֶף׃ וְעַל־יָד֗וֹ עֲמַסְיָ֤ה בֶן־זִכְרִי֙ הַמִּתְנַדֵּ֣ב לַֽיהוָ֔ה וְעִמּ֛וֹ מָאתַ֥יִם אֶ֖לֶף
יז גִּבּ֥וֹר חָֽיִל׃ וּמִן־בִּנְיָמִ֔ן גִּבּ֥וֹר חַ֖יִל אֶלְיָדָ֑ע וְעִמּ֛וֹ נֹֽשְׁקֵי־קֶ֥שֶׁת וּמָגֵ֖ן
יח מָאתַ֥יִם אָֽלֶף׃ וְעַל־יָד֖וֹ יְהוֹזָבָ֑ד וְעִמּ֛וֹ מֵאָה־וּשְׁמוֹנִ֥ים אֶ֖לֶף חֲלוּצֵ֥י
יט צָבָֽא׃ אֵ֖לֶּה הַמְשָׁרְתִ֣ים אֶת־הַמֶּ֑לֶךְ מִלְּבַ֞ד אֲשֶׁר־נָתַ֥ן הַמֶּ֛לֶךְ בְּעָרֵ֥י
ח א הַמִּבְצָ֖ר בְּכָל־יְהוּדָֽה׃ וַיְהִ֧י לִיהוֹשָׁפָ֛ט עֹ֥שֶׁר וְכָב֖וֹד לָרֹ֑ב וַיִּתְחַתֵּ֖ן
ב לְאַחְאָֽב׃ וַיֵּ֨רֶד לְקֵ֤ץ שָׁנִים֙ אֶל־אַחְאָב֙ לְשֹׁ֣מְר֔וֹן וַיִּזְבַּח־ל֨וֹ אַחְאָ֜ב צֹ֤אן וּבָקָר֙ לָרֹ֔ב

DISCUSSION

18:1 | **And he arranged a marriage with Ahav:** The prosperity of the kingdom of Yehoshafat and the enhancement of his status enabled him to establish a political relationship through marriage with the family of Ahav king of Israel, who was considered a great king. Although there were ideological and other differences between them, some of which were significant; nevertheless, in light of their extensive shared foundations, those disagreements did not prevent their alliance. As a result, during the reign of Yehoshafat there was no war between the two kingdoms.

Presumably, the king's visit to his son's in-laws, described below, was not on the spur of the moment, and the subject they discussed was not a complete surprise. They had probably already corresponded through emissaries or letters, and at their meeting Ahav persuaded Yehoshafat to join him in war against Aram. Although at times the Arameans established alliances with them and changed allegiances, this was essentially a defensive war against an enemy common to Judah and Israel. Admittedly, Ramot Gilad was under the direct control of the Kingdom of Israel, but in the national perception it was part of the Land of Israel as a whole.

abundance, and for the people who were with him. Ahav gave him a royal welcome, which included the slaughter of sheep and calves, **and** at that meeting[102] Ahav **incited him into going up with him against** Aram in **Ramot Gilad.**[B]

Remains of Ahav's palace, Samaria, ninth to eighth century BCE

3 **Ahav king of Israel said to Yehoshafat king of Judah: Will you go** out **with me to** war in **Ramot Gilad? He,** Yehoshafat, **said to him: I am as you are, my people are as your people, and** we will be **with you in the war.** My army and I will cooperate with you wholeheartedly.

4 **Yehoshafat said to the king of Israel:** However, since there are dangers in initiating a war whose outcome is uncertain, **inquire, please, the word of the Lord today.** I wish to hear the word of God from a prophet.

5 **The king of Israel gathered the prophets** of the God of Israel together, not prophets of the Baal,[103] **four hundred men.** Ahav did not object in principle to hearing the word of God, and at that time the prophets of God were no longer being persecuted. **And** he **said to them: Shall we go to Ramot Gilad to war, or shall I refrain? They said** as one: **Go up** to war; **and may God deliver** your enemy **into the hand of the king.**

6 **But Yehoshafat said,** since his concerns were not allayed by the words of these prophets, as he suspected that they might not be true prophets but merely hired men: **Isn't there still a prophet of the Lord here,**[D] **that we may inquire of him?**

7 **The king of Israel said to Yehoshafat: There is still one man through whom to inquire of the Lord, but I hate him, as he does not prophesy favorably in my regard, but** rather, he **always** prophesies **unfavorably** to me. **He is** named **Mikhayhu son of Yimla.** I did not invite him, because of our mutual enmity. **Yehoshafat said,** politely and respectfully: **Let the king not say so.** Yehoshafat, a God-fearing man, related to the prophets differently than Ahav did. As the less ideologically committed king, Ahav entertained prophets of all sorts, including the prophets of the Baal and Ashera. He saw nothing unique in the prophets of God; therefore, he shunned any prophet he disliked. In contrast, Yehoshafat maintained that one should always heed a true prophet even if he does not bring good tidings.

8 **The king of Israel summoned an officer and said: Quickly,** bring **Mikhayhu son of Yimla.**

9 **The king of Israel and Yehoshafat king of Judah were sitting, each on his throne, dressed in their** ceremonial **raiment, and they were sitting at a threshing floor at the entrance of the gate of Samaria, and all the prophets were prophesying before them,** in the broad open space of the threshing floor. Since Ahav sought to appeal to Yehoshafat, he hosted him in a most accommodating manner; therefore, they sat in the open threshing floor as equals, alongside or opposite one another.[104]

Threshing floor, Hebron region

10 **Tzidkiyahu son of Kenaana,** one of the prophets, **fashioned for himself horns of iron,** which he may have placed on his head in a symbolic gesture, **and said: So said the Lord: With these you will gore Aram, until their destruction.** The prophets of God frequently performed symbolic acts, through which they sought to clarify and illustrate their words. Sometimes an act of this kind was considered to generate effects in the real world.[105]

Helmet with horns of iron, Corinthia, Greece, seventh century BCE

11 **All the prophets were prophesying so,** in the same manner as Tzidkiyahu, who may have been their leader, **saying: Go up to Ramot Gilad, and succeed, and the Lord will deliver** the enemy **into the hand of the king.**

12 **The messenger who went to summon Mikhayhu spoke to him, saying: Behold, the words of the prophets are unanimously good toward the king. Please let your word** also **be like one of them, and speak favorably.** Perhaps you should desist just this once from directing barbed comments at the king and issuing harsh prophecies against him. This was not necessarily a suggestion that the prophet should lie, but an attempt to prompt Mikhayhu to moderate his tone.

13 **Mikhayhu said** in an oath: **As the Lord lives, that which my God will say to me, that I will speak.** I do not conduct myself in that manner. Neither the desires of the king nor his expectations will guide my conduct. I am a prophet of God, a messenger who merely delivers His word.

ג וְלָעָם אֲשֶׁר עִמּוֹ וַיְסִיתֵהוּ לַעֲלוֹת אֶל־רָמֹת גִּלְעָד׃ וַיֹּאמֶר אַחְאָב מֶלֶךְ־יִשְׂרָאֵל
אֶל־יְהוֹשָׁפָט מֶלֶךְ יְהוּדָה הֲתֵלֵךְ עִמִּי רָמֹת גִּלְעָד וַיֹּאמֶר לוֹ כָּמוֹנִי כָמוֹךָ וּכְעַמְּךָ
ד עַמִּי וְעִמְּךָ בַּמִּלְחָמָה׃ וַיֹּאמֶר יְהוֹשָׁפָט אֶל־מֶלֶךְ יִשְׂרָאֵל דְּרָשׁ־נָא כַיּוֹם אֶת־
ה דְּבַר יְהוָה׃ וַיִּקְבֹּץ מֶלֶךְ־יִשְׂרָאֵל אֶת־הַנְּבִאִים אַרְבַּע מֵאוֹת אִישׁ וַיֹּאמֶר אֲלֵהֶם
הֲנֵלֵךְ אֶל־רָמֹת גִּלְעָד לַמִּלְחָמָה אִם־אֶחְדָּל וַיֹּאמְרוּ עֲלֵה וְיִתֵּן הָאֱלֹהִים בְּיַד
ו ז הַמֶּלֶךְ׃ וַיֹּאמֶר יְהוֹשָׁפָט הַאֵין פֹּה נָבִיא לַיהוָה עוֹד וְנִדְרְשָׁה מֵאֹתוֹ׃ וַיֹּאמֶר
מֶלֶךְ־יִשְׂרָאֵל ׀ אֶל־יְהוֹשָׁפָט עוֹד אִישׁ־אֶחָד לִדְרוֹשׁ אֶת־יְהוָה מֵאֹתוֹ וַאֲנִי
שְׂנֵאתִיהוּ כִּי אֵינֶנּוּ מִתְנַבֵּא עָלַי לְטוֹבָה כִּי כָל־יָמָיו לְרָעָה הוּא מִיכָיְהוּ בֶּן־יִמְלָא
ח וַיֹּאמֶר יְהוֹשָׁפָט אַל־יֹאמַר הַמֶּלֶךְ כֵּן׃ וַיִּקְרָא מֶלֶךְ יִשְׂרָאֵל אֶל־סָרִיס אֶחָד וַיֹּאמֶר
ט מַהֵר מיכהו בֶן־יִמְלָא׃ וּמֶלֶךְ יִשְׂרָאֵל וִיהוֹשָׁפָט מֶלֶךְ־יְהוּדָה יוֹשְׁבִים אִישׁ עַל־ מִיכָיְהוּ
כִּסְאוֹ מְלֻבָּשִׁים בְּגָדִים וְיֹשְׁבִים בְּגֹרֶן פֶּתַח שַׁעַר שֹׁמְרוֹן וְכָל־הַנְּבִיאִים מִתְנַבְּאִים
י לִפְנֵיהֶם׃ וַיַּעַשׂ לוֹ צִדְקִיָּהוּ בֶן־כְּנַעֲנָה קַרְנֵי בַרְזֶל וַיֹּאמֶר כֹּה־אָמַר יְהוָה בְּאֵלֶּה
יא תְּנַגַּח אֶת־אֲרָם עַד־כַּלּוֹתָם׃ וְכָל־הַנְּבִאִים נִבְּאִים כֵּן לֵאמֹר עֲלֵה רָמֹת גִּלְעָד
יב וְהַצְלַח וְנָתַן יְהוָה בְּיַד הַמֶּלֶךְ׃ וְהַמַּלְאָךְ אֲשֶׁר־הָלַךְ ׀ לִקְרֹא לְמִיכָיְהוּ דִּבֶּר אֵלָיו
לֵאמֹר הִנֵּה דִּבְרֵי הַנְּבִאִים פֶּה־אֶחָד טוֹב אֶל־הַמֶּלֶךְ וִיהִי־נָא דְבָרְךָ כְּאַחַד
יג מֵהֶם וְדִבַּרְתָּ טּוֹב׃ וַיֹּאמֶר מִיכָיְהוּ חַי־יְהוָה כִּי אֶת־אֲשֶׁר־יֹאמַר אֱלֹהַי אֹתוֹ

BACKGROUND

18:2 | **Ramot Gilad:** A city of refuge in the northern tribal portion of Gad that was given to the Levites (Deuteronomy 4:43; Joshua 20:8). It served as the capital city of Solomon's Gilad district (I Kings 4:13). Due to the similarity between the names, it is generally identified as Tel Ramith, some 6 km south of Ramtha in northern Jordan. The tel overlooks the main road from Damascus to Amman.

DISCUSSION

18:6 | **Still a prophet of the Lord here:** The Sages explain that Yehoshafat's skepticism regarding the credibility of the prophets assembled by Ahav was due to a tradition from his ancestors that no two true prophets prophesy in precisely the same style. When all the speakers employ identical expressions, this might be the result of group hysteria rather than an indication of an authentic prophecy. Although many prophets achieve a state of prophecy through ecstatic inspiration, the true prophet always retains his individuality, even when he is compelled to prophesy. This is comparable to different musical instruments that play the same tune, each with its own unique sound. It was the uniform delivery of the prophets' statement that aroused Yehoshafat's suspicion (see *Sanhedrin* 89a).

14 **He,** Mikhayhu, **came to the king,** Ahav, **and the king said to him: Mikha, shall we go to Ramot Gilad to war, or shall I refrain? He said,** in a mocking tone, mimicking the other prophets: **Go up and succeed, and they will be delivered into your hand.** You wanted to hear from me that which you already heard from the others, so here it is.

15 **The king said to him:** Do not conduct yourself like that. **How many times have I administered an oath to you that you speak to me nothing but the truth in the name of the Lord?** This is a serious matter.

16 **He,** Mikhayhu, **said: I saw** in a vision **all Israel scattered** in every direction **on the mountains, like sheep that do not have a shepherd; and the Lord said: There is no master,** ruler, **for these,** and **let each man return to his house in peace.** In other words, you, their master, will fall in battle, but your soldiers will return from the battlefield unharmed.

17 **The king of Israel said to Yehoshafat: Didn't I tell you** beforehand **that he,** this prophet, **would not prophesy favorably in my regard, but rather unfavorably?**

18 **He,** the prophet, spoke once again and **said: Therefore, hear the word of the Lord.** You think that I am speaking due to some personal interest or due to a quarrel. Not so; this was my vision in full:[106] **I saw the Lord sitting** in His Sanctuary as a king **on His throne, and all the host of the heavens,** the angels, were **attending on His right and His left.**

19 **The Lord said: Who will entice Ahav king of Israel, and he will go up** to war **and fall at Ramot Gilad? He,** each of those present, **said** his response, and **this one says like this and that one says like that.**

20 **The spirit emerged, and it stood before the Lord, and said: I will entice him. The Lord said to him: With what?** How will you do so?

21 **He said: I will go out and be a spirit of falsehood**[D] **in the mouth of all his prophets.** I will give a false message to all the prophets that prophesy for Ahav. **He said: Entice him, and also prevail. Go out and do so.**

22 Mikhayhu said to Ahav: **Now, behold, the Lord placed a spirit of falsehood in the mouth of these prophets of yours, but** in truth, **the Lord has spoken ill of you.**

23 **Tzidkiyahu son of Kenaana,** who, as stated above, was apparently the leader of the prophets, **approached and struck Mikhayhu on the cheek, and said: How is there a way that the spirit of the Lord has passed from me to speak through you?** How dare you claim that the spirit of God has left me and speaks with you? I am the senior prophet.

24 **Mikhayhu said** in absolute confidence: **Behold, you will see on that day,** there will come a time **when you go into a room within a room to hide.** Now you are full of self-righteousness, but when the troubles arrive, you will hide in an inner room in shame.

25 **The king of Israel said: Take Mikhayhu, and return him** to the city, but not to his home; rather, take him **to Amon governor of the city,** one of the king's appointees, **and to Yo'ash the king's son,** who apparently stood in for the king in his absence.

26 **And say** to them: **So said the king: Put this one,** Mikhayhu, whom the king refuses even to mention by name, **in the prison, and feed him scant food and scant water, until I come in peace.** When I return from the war I will settle my account with him for everything he said. In the meantime, detain him in harsh conditions.

27 **Mikhayhu said:** King of Israel, I am not afraid, for **if you return in peace,** that would mean that **the Lord did not speak through me** and I am not a true prophet. **He said** to all those present: **Hear, all the peoples** of Israel and Judah, that which I say. I take full responsibility for my previous statements, as I am entirely convinced of their truth.

28 **The king of Israel and Yehoshafat king of Judah went up to Ramot Gilad.** The entire band of prophets had predicted that they would succeed in the war, with the sole dissenting opinion that of a man whom Ahav said always provided dire prophecies. Moreover, even Mikhayhu had not explicitly prohibited going to war, but had merely declared that the people would scatter and Ahav would fall. Yehoshafat was persuaded to follow the majority.

29 However, Ahav was still troubled by Mikhayhu's prophecy. Therefore, **the king of Israel said to Yehoshafat: I will disguise myself and come to the battle** with different clothes, **but you don your raiment,** as the Arameans will undoubtedly be looking for me rather than you.[107] **The king of Israel disguised himself, and they entered the battle.**

30 **The king of Aram commanded his chariot captains, saying: Do not fight against small or great, only with the king of Israel.** Your sole mission is to smite the king of Israel. Do not wage a comprehensive war; rather focus on a single target, Ahav.

DISCUSSION

18:21 | **A spirit of falsehood:** Some say that the spirit of Navot the Yizre'elite, whose execution was prompted by Ahav, came to avenge his death from the king of Israel (see *Shabbat* 149b; *Sanhedrin* 102b).

יד אֲדַבֵּר: וַיָּבֹא אֶל־הַמֶּלֶךְ וַיֹּאמֶר הַמֶּלֶךְ אֵלָיו מִיכָה הֲנֵלֵךְ אֶל־רָמֹת גִּלְעָד
טו לַמִּלְחָמָה אִם־אֶחְדָּל וַיֹּאמֶר עֲלוּ וְהַצְלִיחוּ וְיִנָּתְנוּ בְּיֶדְכֶם: וַיֹּאמֶר אֵלָיו הַמֶּלֶךְ
עַד־כַּמֶּה פְעָמִים אֲנִי מַשְׁבִּיעֶךָ אֲשֶׁר לֹא־תְדַבֵּר אֵלַי רַק אֱמֶת בְּשֵׁם יְהוָה:
טז וַיֹּאמֶר רָאִיתִי אֶת־כָּל־יִשְׂרָאֵל נְפוֹצִים עַל־הֶהָרִים כַּצֹּאן אֲשֶׁר אֵין־לָהֶן רֹעֶה
יז וַיֹּאמֶר יְהוָה לֹא־אֲדֹנִים לָאֵלֶּה יָשׁוּבוּ אִישׁ־לְבֵיתוֹ בְּשָׁלוֹם: וַיֹּאמֶר מֶלֶךְ־יִשְׂרָאֵל
אֶל־יְהוֹשָׁפָט הֲלֹא אָמַרְתִּי אֵלֶיךָ לֹא־יִתְנַבֵּא עָלַי טוֹב כִּי אִם־לְרָע:
יח וַיֹּאמֶר לָכֵן שִׁמְעוּ דְבַר־יְהוָה רָאִיתִי אֶת־יְהוָה יוֹשֵׁב עַל־כִּסְאוֹ וְכָל־צְבָא הַשָּׁמַיִם יח
יט עֹמְדִים עַל־יְמִינוֹ וּשְׂמֹאלוֹ: וַיֹּאמֶר יְהוָה מִי יְפַתֶּה אֶת־אַחְאָב מֶלֶךְ־יִשְׂרָאֵל
כ וְיַעַל וְיִפֹּל בְּרָמוֹת גִּלְעָד וַיֹּאמֶר זֶה אֹמֵר כָּכָה וְזֶה אֹמֵר כָּכָה: וַיֵּצֵא הָרוּחַ וַיַּעֲמֹד
כא לִפְנֵי יְהוָה וַיֹּאמֶר אֲנִי אֲפַתֶּנּוּ וַיֹּאמֶר יְהוָה אֵלָיו בַּמָּה: וַיֹּאמֶר אֵצֵא וְהָיִיתִי לְרוּחַ
כב שֶׁקֶר בְּפִי כָּל־נְבִיאָיו וַיֹּאמֶר תְּפַתֶּה וְגַם־תּוּכַל צֵא וַעֲשֵׂה־כֵן: וְעַתָּה הִנֵּה נָתַן
כג יְהוָה רוּחַ שֶׁקֶר בְּפִי נְבִיאֶיךָ אֵלֶּה וַיהוָה דִּבֶּר עָלֶיךָ רָעָה: וַיִּגַּשׁ צִדְקִיָּהוּ
בֶן־כְּנַעֲנָה וַיַּךְ אֶת־מִיכָיְהוּ עַל־הַלֶּחִי וַיֹּאמֶר אֵי זֶה הַדֶּרֶךְ עָבַר רוּחַ־יְהוָה מֵאִתִּי
כד לְדַבֵּר אֹתָךְ: וַיֹּאמֶר מִיכָיְהוּ הִנְּךָ רֹאֶה בַּיּוֹם הַהוּא אֲשֶׁר תָּבוֹא חֶדֶר בְּחֶדֶר
כה לְהֵחָבֵא: וַיֹּאמֶר מֶלֶךְ יִשְׂרָאֵל קְחוּ אֶת־מִיכָיְהוּ וַהֲשִׁיבֻהוּ אֶל־אָמוֹן שַׂר־הָעִיר
כו וְאֶל־יוֹאָשׁ בֶּן־הַמֶּלֶךְ: וַאֲמַרְתֶּם כֹּה אָמַר הַמֶּלֶךְ שִׂימוּ זֶה בֵּית הַכֶּלֶא וְהַאֲכִלֻהוּ
כז לֶחֶם לַחַץ וּמַיִם לַחַץ עַד שׁוּבִי בְשָׁלוֹם: וַיֹּאמֶר מִיכָיְהוּ אִם־שׁוֹב תָּשׁוּב בְּשָׁלוֹם
כח לֹא־דִבֶּר יְהוָה בִּי וַיֹּאמֶר שִׁמְעוּ עַמִּים כֻּלָּם: וַיַּעַל מֶלֶךְ־יִשְׂרָאֵל
כט וִיהוֹשָׁפָט מֶלֶךְ־יְהוּדָה אֶל־רָמֹת גִּלְעָד: וַיֹּאמֶר מֶלֶךְ יִשְׂרָאֵל אֶל־יְהוֹשָׁפָט
הִתְחַפֵּשׂ וָבוֹא בַמִּלְחָמָה וְאַתָּה לְבַשׁ בְּגָדֶיךָ וַיִּתְחַפֵּשׂ מֶלֶךְ יִשְׂרָאֵל וַיָּבֹאוּ
ל בַּמִּלְחָמָה: וּמֶלֶךְ אֲרָם צִוָּה אֶת־שָׂרֵי הָרֶכֶב אֲשֶׁר־לוֹ לֵאמֹר לֹא תִּלָּחֲמוּ אֶת־

31 **It was when the** Aramean **commanders of the chariots saw Yehoshafat,**[D] the only person wearing royal garments, **and they said: It is the king of Israel. They,** the commanders of the chariots, **surrounded him to fight against him, and Yehoshafat cried out and the Lord helped him. God caused them to move from him,** and he was spared. It is possible that when Yehoshafat cried out, the enemies recognized that he spoke in a dialect that was slightly different from that of Ahav, or that his voice differed from that of the king of Israel. The Arameans may have been able to distinguish between them because they were familiar with Ahav, as he and the king of Aram had fought wars against each other and had even met on occasion. In any case, they hesitated and did not immediately fire at Yehoshafat.

32 **It was when the commanders of the chariots saw that** indeed **it was not the king of Israel, they withdrew from following him** and left him alone, as they had been commanded to attack only the king of Israel. Although the king of Judah had come to fight against them, with regard to the instructions they had received he was no different from any other officer or captain.

33 Meanwhile, **a** certain **man** from the Aramean camp **drew his bow** toward the enemy **desultorily,** without directing his aim at any specific individual, **and smote the king of Israel between the joints of the armor.** The undirected arrow struck the king of Israel at exactly the right spot, where the parts of his armor joined together. A suit of armor is composed of various segments, to enable movement and flexibility, and the seams are the vulnerable spots of the protective clothing. **He,** Ahav, **said to the driver of the chariot: Reverse your hand** and go backward, **and extract me from the encampment, as I am** mortally **wounded.** The king sensed that the wound was serious; apparently, he was injured in an area that constituted a mortal wound that was liable to lead to massive blood loss.

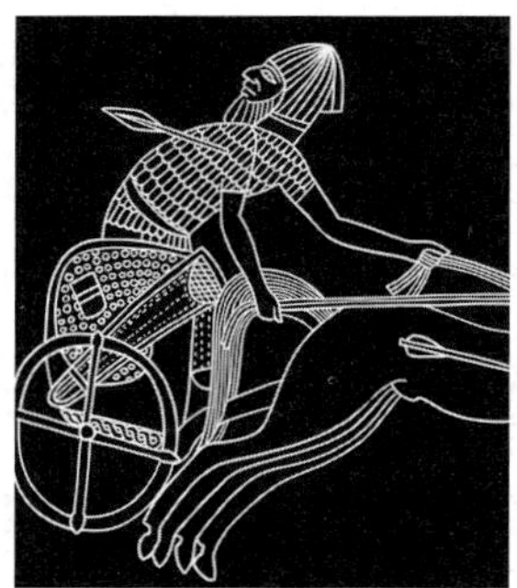

Arrow striking between joints of armor, illustration based on relief, Luxor, Egypt, fifteenth century BCE

34 **The battle continued that day, and the king of Israel,** who did not want to leave the battlefield and thus cause his army to be overthrown, **was propped up in his chariot facing Aram until the evening.** These battle chariots were small and had room for only two or three people in a standing position. Therefore, the king's presence would have been evident to all. He stood bravely, in order to prevent any type of panic, knowing that if his soldiers saw him fleeing, his entire army might disperse. However, he was bleeding throughout. **He died at the time of sunset,** due to blood loss.

19 1 The book of Kings, which deals with the kings of Israel as well as the kings of Judah, describes the events in the Kingdom of Israel following Ahav's death, after his remains were returned to Samaria.[108] This chapter relates only that which pertains to Yehoshafat king of Judah, the part of the story not discussed in Kings. **Yehoshafat king of Judah returned in peace to his house,** unharmed, **to Jerusalem.** The war did not end in absolute defeat, perhaps because the fighting ceased when Ahav died. The king of Aram achieved his objective. It can be assumed that after the Arameans caused the Israelite camp to disperse, they had no further interest in pursuing the war.

2 **Yehu son of Hanani the seer came out to meet him,** Yehoshafat, **and said to King Yehoshafat: Do you** go to **help the wicked, and love haters of the Lord?** How could you go to war together with Ahav? **For that,** because you joined forces with him, **wrath is upon you from before the Lord.** Granted, he is a relative of yours, but even so, it was a mistake to provide assistance to the wicked Ahav.

3 **However,** despite this unworthy campaign of yours, **good things have been found about you, because you eliminated the sacred trees from the land** during the years of your reign, **and directed your heart to seek God.**

4 The king took the prophet's words to heart: **Yehoshafat resided in Jerusalem; and he repeatedly went out among the people from Beersheba to the highlands of Ephraim, and brought them back to the Lord, God of their fathers.** Perhaps as a result of the prophetic message he had received, Yehoshafat realized that he must focus on restoring the service of God to its proper place.

5 **He appointed judges**[D] **in the land in all the fortified cities of Judah, city by city,** in each and every city. The fortified cities are naturally the major cities in every province. Yehoshafat took pains to ensure that there would be enough judges in those cities to maintain civil order.

6 Yehoshafat delivered a short but meaningful speech: **He said to the judges: Consider what you are doing, for you are not judging on behalf of man, but on behalf of the Lord, and He is with you in the matter of judgment.** You issue judgments in the presence of God. It is likewise stated in the book of Psalms: "God stands in the assembly of the Almighty; in the midst of the judges He renders judgment."[109]

7 **Now let the fear of the Lord be upon you; take care and execute** judgment properly, **for there is no injustice, favoritism, and taking bribes with the Lord our God.**

8 **Also, in Jerusalem,** the largest city, **Yehoshafat appointed** judges **from the Levites and the priests, and from the heads**

לא הַקָּטֹן אֶת־הַגָּדוֹל כִּי אִם־אֶת־מֶלֶךְ יִשְׂרָאֵל לְבַדּוֹ: וַיְהִי כִּרְאוֹת שָׂרֵי הָרֶכֶב
אֶת־יְהוֹשָׁפָט וְהֵמָּה אָמְרוּ מֶלֶךְ־יִשְׂרָאֵל הוּא וַיָּסֹבּוּ עָלָיו לְהִלָּחֵם וַיִּזְעַק יְהוֹשָׁפָט
לב וַיהוָה עֲזָרוֹ וַיְסִיתֵם אֱלֹהִים מִמֶּנּוּ: וַיְהִי כִּרְאוֹת שָׂרֵי הָרֶכֶב כִּי לֹא־הָיָה מֶלֶךְ
לג יִשְׂרָאֵל וַיָּשׁוּבוּ מֵאַחֲרָיו: וְאִישׁ מָשַׁךְ בַּקֶּשֶׁת לְתֻמּוֹ וַיַּךְ אֶת־מֶלֶךְ יִשְׂרָאֵל בֵּין
הַדְּבָקִים וּבֵין הַשִּׁרְיָן וַיֹּאמֶר לָרַכָּב הֲפֹךְ ידיך וְהוֹצֵאתַנִי מִן־הַמַּחֲנֶה כִּי הָחֳלֵיתִי: יָדְךָ
לד וַתַּעַל הַמִּלְחָמָה בַּיּוֹם הַהוּא וּמֶלֶךְ יִשְׂרָאֵל הָיָה מַעֲמִיד בַּמֶּרְכָּבָה נֹכַח אֲרָם
יט א עַד־הָעָרֶב וַיָּמָת לְעֵת בּוֹא הַשָּׁמֶשׁ: וַיָּשָׁב יְהוֹשָׁפָט מֶלֶךְ־יְהוּדָה
ב אֶל־בֵּיתוֹ בְשָׁלוֹם לִירוּשָׁלִָם: וַיֵּצֵא אֶל־פָּנָיו יֵהוּא בֶן־חֲנָנִי הַחֹזֶה וַיֹּאמֶר אֶל־
הַמֶּלֶךְ יְהוֹשָׁפָט הֲלָרָשָׁע לַעְזֹר וּלְשֹׂנְאֵי יְהוָה תֶּאֱהָב וּבָזֹאת עָלֶיךָ קֶּצֶף מִלִּפְנֵי
ג יְהוָה: אֲבָל דְּבָרִים טוֹבִים נִמְצְאוּ עִמָּךְ כִּי־בִעַרְתָּ הָאֲשֵׁרוֹת מִן־הָאָרֶץ וַהֲכִינוֹתָ
ד לְבָבְךָ לִדְרֹשׁ הָאֱלֹהִים: וַיֵּשֶׁב יְהוֹשָׁפָט בִּירוּשָׁלִָם וַיָּשָׁב וַיֵּצֵא בָעָם מִבְּאֵר שֶׁבַע
ה עַד־הַר אֶפְרַיִם וַיְשִׁיבֵם אֶל־יְהוָה אֱלֹהֵי אֲבוֹתֵיהֶם: וַיַּעֲמֵד שֹׁפְטִים בָּאָרֶץ בְּכָל־
ו עָרֵי יְהוּדָה הַבְּצֻרוֹת לְעִיר וָעִיר: וַיֹּאמֶר אֶל־הַשֹּׁפְטִים רְאוּ מָה־אַתֶּם עֹשִׂים
ז כִּי לֹא לְאָדָם תִּשְׁפְּטוּ כִּי לַיהוָה וְעִמָּכֶם בִּדְבַר מִשְׁפָּט: וְעַתָּה יְהִי פַחַד־יְהוָה
עֲלֵיכֶם שִׁמְרוּ וַעֲשׂוּ כִּי־אֵין עִם־יְהוָה אֱלֹהֵינוּ עַוְלָה וּמַשֹּׂא פָנִים וּמִקַּח־שֹׁחַד:
ח וְגַם בִּירוּשָׁלִַם הֶעֱמִיד יְהוֹשָׁפָט מִן־הַלְוִיִּם וְהַכֹּהֲנִים וּמֵרָאשֵׁי הָאָבוֹת לְיִשְׂרָאֵל

DISCUSSION

18:31 | **The war against Aram:** While the size of the respective armies is unknown, this clearly was not a mere border skirmish involving a few units, and in fact Ahav brought Yehoshafat with him in an effort to achieve decisive victory. For his part, as the king of Aram faced two armies, it is possible that he feared that his army was too small or would not be able to cope with both kings.

At that time, the fact that the commander did not simply send instructions, but was physically present during military campaigns, was of great importance. Unlike other nations, Israel had a tradition that kings and high military officers would deploy on the front lines; therefore, they were vulnerable to enemy attacks (see Numbers 27:17, and Rashi ad loc.; I Samuel 8:20, 18:16; II Samuel 21:17).

19:5 | **Yehoshafat and the judges:** Since an entire chapter in the history of Yehoshafat deals with judges [*shofetim*], it suggests a connection between the name of the king and his deeds. The meaning of the name Yehoshafat is "God will judge." Indeed, Yehoshafat was especially sensitive to God's judgment, and he took practical steps to ensure that justice was performed throughout his kingdom. Perhaps he chose a royal name for himself that would reflect this special area of interest. This phenomenon of a king selecting his own name was common during various periods, not only in other nations, such as Egypt and Assyria, but also for the kings of Judah and Israel (see commentary on Genesis 11:29; Numbers 1:5; I Kings 15:8). For other names of a king corresponding to the events of his life, see I Chronicles 22:9, II Chronicles 32:5–8, and commentary on II Chronicles 26:1.

of the patrilineal houses of Israel, for executing **the judgment of the Lord, and for** arbitrating **disputes.** After he chose them from the various cities, **they returned to Jerusalem,** to serve in the High Court there. This judicial body included learned representatives from all classes of the people, and it was the equivalent of what would later be called the Great Sanhedrin. It is similarly stated elsewhere that this court comprised priests, Levites, and leaders of Israel, all of whom contributed their own insights and lent authority to the body.[110]

9 **He commanded them, saying: So you shall act in fear of the Lord, faithfully and wholeheartedly.**

10 **Any dispute that comes before you,** as you are the supreme court, **from your brethren who reside in their cities,** of cases left unresolved by the local courts, distinguishing **between blood and blood,** murder cases, when it must be determined who is guilty of shedding blood,[111] or **between Torah and commandment for statutes and ordinances,** questions involving practical halakhic rulings in various fields, **you shall caution them,** or guide them, **that they not bear guilt to the Lord nor wrath be upon you and upon your brethren. So you shall do, and you will not bear guilt.** This verse is reminiscent of the instructions in the book of Deuteronomy with regard to the role of the central court.[112] It seems that when Yehoshafat appointed judges and granted them authority he restored the activity of this highest court in the land.

11 **Behold,** here are your leaders: **Amaryahu the head priest,** the High Priest, **is** appointed **in charge of you for all matters of the Lord.** He represents the word of God. **And Zevadyahu son of Yishmael, the chief official over the house of Judah,** is **for all matters of the king,** the governor appointed by the king and in charge of his affairs. **And the officers of the Levites,** officers from the tribe of Levi, **are before you.** Once the Temple was established in Jerusalem and its vessels no longer had to be transported, the Levites had less work to do, and therefore they were appointed officers. **Be courageous, and the Lord will be with the** performers of **good** deeds.

20 1 **It was** some years **thereafter,** not directly connected to the previous events, **that the children of Moav, and the children of Amon, and with them some Amonites,**[B] a different nation of this name that may have dwelled in areas near the kingdom of Amon,[113] all **came** together from the east **against Yehoshafat to war.**

2 **They came and told Yehoshafat, saying: A great horde has come against you from across the** Dead **Sea, from Aram.**[B] Apparently, the kingdom of Aram also supported this attack, since Yehoshafat had fought Aram alongside Ahav and had failed to defeat them. It is possible that these kingdoms, which came from east of the Jordan, went past the Dead Sea as they moved southward on the eastern side of the Jordan.[114] **And, behold, they are in Hatzetzon Tamar,**[B] **which is Ein Gedi,**[B] as they have chosen to encamp in a place where there is water.

Wadi Ram

Ein Gedi

3 **Yehoshafat was afraid** of the united front of these kingdoms and their large army, **and directed his attention to seek the Lord; and he proclaimed a fast,** a day on which people would come together for communal prayers and supplication,[115] **throughout all Judah.**

4 The men of **Judah gathered to beseech the Lord;** first and foremost, the leaders in Jerusalem, and **they came to seek the Lord also from all the** other **cities of Judah.**

5 **Yehoshafat stood in the assembly of Judah and Jerusalem, in the House of the Lord, before the new courtyard,** one of the new courtyards that was inaugurated after the reign of Solomon,[116]

6 **and said: Lord, God of our fathers, truly You are God in heaven, and You rule over all the kingdoms of the nations; in Your hand is power and might, and no one can withstand You.**[117]

7 **Truly You are our God; You dispossessed the inhabitants of this land before Your people Israel, and gave it to the descendants of Abraham Your beloved** as their inheritance **forever.**

8 **They settled in it, and built You a Sanctuary in it for Your name, saying** that this is one of the purposes of the Temple, as described in Solomon's prayer:[118]

ט לְמִשְׁפַּט יְהוָה וְלָרִיב וַיָּשֻׁבוּ יְרוּשָׁלִָם׃ וַיְצַו עֲלֵיהֶם לֵאמֹר כֹּה תַעֲשׂוּן בְּיִרְאַת
י יְהוָה בֶּאֱמוּנָה וּבְלֵבָב שָׁלֵם׃ וְכָל־רִיב אֲשֶׁר־יָבוֹא עֲלֵיכֶם מֵאֲחֵיכֶם ׀ הַיֹּשְׁבִים
בְּעָרֵיהֶם בֵּין־דָּם ׀ לְדָם בֵּין־תּוֹרָה לְמִצְוָה לְחֻקִּים וּלְמִשְׁפָּטִים וְהִזְהַרְתֶּם אֹתָם
וְלֹא יֶאְשְׁמוּ לַיהוָה וְהָיָה־קֶצֶף עֲלֵיכֶם וְעַל־אֲחֵיכֶם כֹּה תַעֲשׂוּן וְלֹא תֶאְשָׁמוּ׃
יא וְהִנֵּה אֲמַרְיָהוּ כֹהֵן הָרֹאשׁ עֲלֵיכֶם לְכֹל ׀ דְּבַר יְהוָה וּזְבַדְיָהוּ בֶן־יִשְׁמָעֵאל הַנָּגִיד
לְבֵית־יְהוּדָה לְכֹל דְּבַר־הַמֶּלֶךְ וְשֹׁטְרִים הַלְוִיִּם לִפְנֵיכֶם חִזְקוּ וַעֲשׂוּ וִיהִי יְהוָה
עִם־הַטּוֹב׃

כ א וַיְהִי אַחֲרֵי־כֵן בָּאוּ בְנֵי־מוֹאָב וּבְנֵי עַמּוֹן וְעִמָּהֶם ׀ מֵהָעַמּוֹנִים עַל־יְהוֹשָׁפָט
ב לַמִּלְחָמָה׃ וַיָּבֹאוּ וַיַּגִּידוּ לִיהוֹשָׁפָט לֵאמֹר בָּא עָלֶיךָ הָמוֹן רָב מֵעֵבֶר לַיָּם מֵאֲרָם
ג וְהִנָּם בְּחַצְצוֹן תָּמָר הִיא עֵין גֶּדִי׃ וַיִּרָא וַיִּתֵּן יְהוֹשָׁפָט אֶת־פָּנָיו לִדְרוֹשׁ לַיהוָה
ד וַיִּקְרָא־צוֹם עַל־כָּל־יְהוּדָה׃ וַיִּקָּבְצוּ יְהוּדָה לְבַקֵּשׁ מֵיְהוָה גַּם מִכָּל־עָרֵי יְהוּדָה
ה בָּאוּ לְבַקֵּשׁ אֶת־יְהוָה׃ וַיַּעֲמֹד יְהוֹשָׁפָט בִּקְהַל יְהוּדָה וִירוּשָׁלִַם בְּבֵית יְהוָה לִפְנֵי
ו הֶחָצֵר הַחֲדָשָׁה׃ וַיֹּאמַר יְהוָה אֱלֹהֵי אֲבֹתֵינוּ הֲלֹא אַתָּה־הוּא אֱלֹהִים בַּשָּׁמַיִם
ז וְאַתָּה מוֹשֵׁל בְּכֹל מַמְלְכוֹת הַגּוֹיִם וּבְיָדְךָ כֹּחַ וּגְבוּרָה וְאֵין עִמְּךָ לְהִתְיַצֵּב׃ הֲלֹא ׀
אַתָּה אֱלֹהֵינוּ הוֹרַשְׁתָּ אֶת־יֹשְׁבֵי הָאָרֶץ הַזֹּאת מִלִּפְנֵי עַמְּךָ יִשְׂרָאֵל וַתִּתְּנָהּ
ח לְזֶרַע אַבְרָהָם אֹהַבְךָ לְעוֹלָם׃ וַיֵּשְׁבוּ־בָהּ וַיִּבְנוּ לְךָ ׀ בָּהּ מִקְדָּשׁ לְשִׁמְךָ לֵאמֹר׃

BACKGROUND

20:1 | **The Amonites:** According to the Septuagint, this is referring to the Meunite tribes, which dwelled in the frontier wilderness region southwest of the Land of Israel, near Philistia. They are listed among the nations that oppressed Israel (Judges 10:12). It is also stated that they were struck in the days of Uziya (26:7) and in the days of Hizkiya by the tribe of Simeon (I Chronicles 4:41). Assyrian inscriptions from the eighth century BCE describe them as a people: Whose (territory is) below Egypt.

20:2 | **From Aram:** Some maintain that this is referring to the inhabitants of a region in the south of Edom called Jabal Ram, and the nearby wadi, some 40 km east of Aqaba in Jordan.

Hatzetzon Tamar: One of the battles of the four kings in the days of Abraham was waged here (Genesis 14:7). Some claim that Tamar refers to a district, and Hatzetzon is a particular location within it. According to this opinion, the verse should read: "Behold, they are in Hatzetzon of Tamar, toward Ein Gedi," meaning that the Moavites and Amonites advanced from Hatzetzon to Ein Gedi. A different opinion identifies Tamar with Ein Hatzeva, in the northern Arava, where there was a town called Tamar in the Roman-Byzantine period. This town was located at a crossroads and contained important springs and groves of date palms [*temarim*] (see I Kings 9:18; Ezekiel 47:19). Hatzetzon may have been situated within the administrative jurisdiction of Tamar.

Ein Gedi: Ein Gedi is the largest desert oasis on the western coast of the Dead Sea. It is one of the places listed on the eastern border of the portion of the tribe of Judah (Joshua 15:62). Ein Gedi has been identified with Tel Goren, north of the Arugot Ravine. Archaeological remains have been discovered at this tel, attesting to the existence of a permanent settlement from the late eighth century BCE, as well as its destruction at the end of the First Temple period.

9 **If evil should come upon us, a punishing sword,** the sword that punishes through war, or alternatively, the sword of judgment, e.g., drought;[119] or **pestilence,** a general term for a disease that deteriorates into a plague;[120] **or famine, we will stand before this House, and before You, as Your name is in this House, and cry out to You in our distress, and You will hear and grant salvation.**

10 **Now, behold the children of Amon and Moav and Mount Se'ir,** the place of the children of Edom. Although the Edomites were not listed above, it appears that the unified forces of the countries east of the Jordan included them as well. Some commentaries suggest that the "Aram" mentioned earlier is a nation from the land of Edom.[121] These are nations **among whom You did not allow Israel to come** through their territory, **when they came from the land of Egypt; instead, they,** the children of Israel, indeed **turned away from them, and did not destroy them.** God did not permit Israel to pass through their lands against their will, and He certainly did not permit them to destroy those nations, which is why they still remained in their lands.[122]

11 **Behold,** instead of acknowledging that we spared them at a time when we could have done them harm, **they repay us** with evil, **by coming to expel us from Your possession that You bequeathed us.**

12 **Our God, won't You** find them guilty and **punish them? For we do not have strength before this great horde coming against us, and we do not know what to do; rather, our eyes are upon You** for assistance.

13 **All** the men of **Judah were standing before the Lord** in the Temple, **even their young, their wives, and their** older **children.**[123] This was a great gathering of repentance, supplication, and prayer.

14 **The** prophetic **spirit of the Lord was upon Yahaziel, son of Zekharyahu, son of Benaya, son of Ye'iel, son of Matanya, the Levite, from the sons of Asaf,** the well-known Temple singer,[124] while he was standing **in the midst of the assembly.**

15 **He said: Listen, all Judah, inhabitants of Jerusalem, and King Yehoshafat; so said the Lord to you: Do not fear, and do not be frightened** and demoralized **due to this great horde, for the war is not yours, but** it is **God's.**

16 **Tomorrow, descend upon them** to battle; **behold, they are ascending** from Ein Gedi to the land of Judah **at the ascent of Tzitz.**[B] **You shall find them at the end of the ravine, before the wilderness of Yeruel.**[B]

17 **It is not for you to fight in this** battle; **position yourselves,** and **stand and see the salvation of the Lord with you, Judah and Jerusalem; do not fear** and **do not be frightened; tomorrow, go out against them, as the Lord is with you.**

18 This prophecy, which was a direct response to the prayers and supplications, encouraged and strengthened Yehoshafat and all those who had gathered with him. **Yehoshafat bowed with his face to the ground,** as a mark of gratitude, **and all Judah and the inhabitants of Jerusalem fell before the Lord, to prostrate themselves to the Lord.**

19 **The Levites, of the children of the Kehatites and of the children of the Korahites,** from the sons of Korah, who earn special mention in several psalms,[125] **rose to praise the Lord, God of Israel, in an exceedingly**[126] **loud voice.**

20 **They arose early in the morning, and went out to the wilderness of Tekoa.** In the region of the place called by that name today, the area facing eastward is indeed a wilderness. **And as they went out Yehoshafat stood and said: Hear me, Judah and inhabitants of Jerusalem: Have faith in the Lord your God, and your faith will be**

Wilderness area near Tekoa

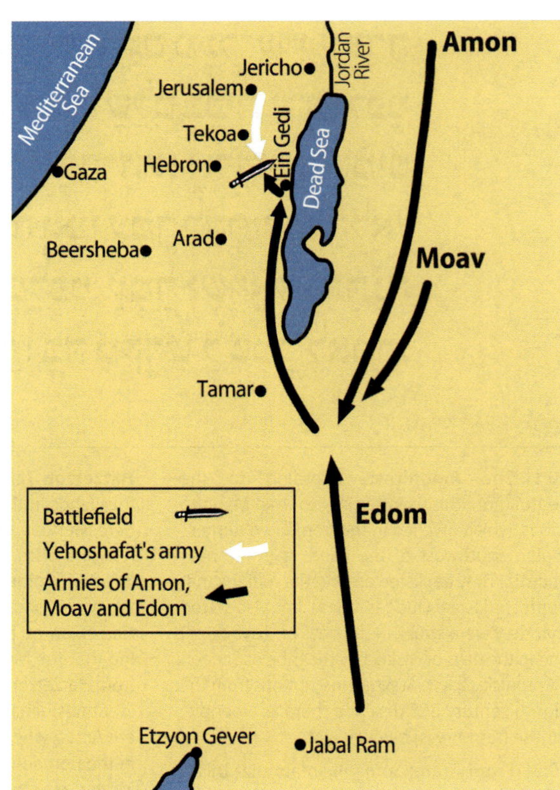

Battle near Tekoa

ט אִם־תָּבוֹא עָלֵינוּ רָעָה חֶרֶב שְׁפוֹט וְדֶבֶר וְרָעָב נַעַמְדָה לִפְנֵי הַבַּיִת הַזֶּה וּלְפָנֶיךָ
י כִּי שִׁמְךָ בַּבַּיִת הַזֶּה וְנִזְעַק אֵלֶיךָ מִצָּרָתֵנוּ וְתִשְׁמַע וְתוֹשִׁיעַ׃ וְעַתָּה הִנֵּה בְנֵי־
עַמּוֹן וּמוֹאָב וְהַר־שֵׂעִיר אֲשֶׁר לֹא־נָתַתָּה לְיִשְׂרָאֵל לָבוֹא בָהֶם בְּבֹאָם מֵאֶרֶץ
יא מִצְרָיִם כִּי סָרוּ מֵעֲלֵיהֶם וְלֹא הִשְׁמִידוּם׃ וְהִנֵּה־הֵם גֹּמְלִים עָלֵינוּ לָבוֹא לְגָרְשֵׁנוּ
יב מִיְּרֻשָּׁתְךָ אֲשֶׁר הוֹרַשְׁתָּנוּ׃ אֱלֹהֵינוּ הֲלֹא תִשְׁפָּט־בָּם כִּי אֵין בָּנוּ כֹּחַ לִפְנֵי הֶהָמוֹן
יג הָרָב הַזֶּה הַבָּא עָלֵינוּ וַאֲנַחְנוּ לֹא נֵדַע מַה־נַּעֲשֶׂה כִּי עָלֶיךָ עֵינֵינוּ׃ וְכָל־יְהוּדָה
יד עֹמְדִים לִפְנֵי יְהוָה גַּם־טַפָּם נְשֵׁיהֶם וּבְנֵיהֶם׃ וְיַחֲזִיאֵל בֶּן־זְכַרְיָהוּ בֶּן־
בְּנָיָה בֶּן־יְעִיאֵל בֶּן־מַתַּנְיָה הַלֵּוִי מִן־בְּנֵי אָסָף הָיְתָה עָלָיו רוּחַ יְהוָה בְּתוֹךְ הַקָּהָל׃
טו וַיֹּאמֶר הַקְשִׁיבוּ כָל־יְהוּדָה וְיֹשְׁבֵי יְרוּשָׁלִַם וְהַמֶּלֶךְ יְהוֹשָׁפָט כֹּה־אָמַר יְהוָה לָכֶם
אַתֶּם אַל־תִּירְאוּ וְאַל־תֵּחַתּוּ מִפְּנֵי הֶהָמוֹן הָרָב הַזֶּה כִּי לֹא לָכֶם הַמִּלְחָמָה כִּי
טז לֵאלֹהִים׃ מָחָר רְדוּ עֲלֵיהֶם הִנָּם עֹלִים בְּמַעֲלֵה הַצִּיץ וּמְצָאתֶם אֹתָם בְּסוֹף
יז הַנַּחַל פְּנֵי מִדְבַּר יְרוּאֵל׃ לֹא לָכֶם לְהִלָּחֵם בָּזֹאת הִתְיַצְּבוּ עִמְדוּ וּרְאוּ אֶת־
יְשׁוּעַת יְהוָה עִמָּכֶם יְהוּדָה וִירוּשָׁלִַם אַל־תִּירְאוּ וְאַל־תֵּחַתּוּ מָחָר צְאוּ לִפְנֵיהֶם
יח וַיהוָה עִמָּכֶם׃ וַיִּקֹּד יְהוֹשָׁפָט אַפַּיִם אָרְצָה וְכָל־יְהוּדָה וְיֹשְׁבֵי יְרוּשָׁלִַם נָפְלוּ לִפְנֵי
יט יְהוָה לְהִשְׁתַּחֲוֺת לַיהוָה׃ וַיָּקֻמוּ הַלְוִיִּם מִן־בְּנֵי הַקְּהָתִים וּמִן־בְּנֵי הַקָּרְחִים לְהַלֵּל
כ לַיהוָה אֱלֹהֵי יִשְׂרָאֵל בְּקוֹל גָּדוֹל לְמָעְלָה׃ וַיַּשְׁכִּימוּ בַבֹּקֶר וַיֵּצְאוּ לְמִדְבַּר תְּקוֹעַ
וּבְצֵאתָם עָמַד יְהוֹשָׁפָט וַיֹּאמֶר שְׁמָעוּנִי יְהוּדָה וְיֹשְׁבֵי יְרוּשָׁלִַם הַאֲמִינוּ בַּיהוָה

BACKGROUND

20:16 | **The ascent of Tzitz:** Generally identified with the ascent from Ein Gedi to the northwest, for approximately 2.5 km, after which the road continues to Tekoa. This was a major route along the width of the Land of Israel, near which remains of Israelite fortresses from the period of the kings have been discovered.

The wilderness of Yeruel: Various areas of the wilderness of Judah were typically named for nearby towns, such as the wilderness of Tekoa and the wilderness of Ein Gedi. Since we have no knowledge of a place called Yeruel, this particular wilderness cannot be identified with certainty, but it seems that it was the western boundary of the wilderness of Tekoa.

reinforced; it will become clear that your faith is firm; **have faith in His prophets, and you will succeed.** Yehoshafat relied both upon God and upon the words of His prophets.
21 **He,** Yehoshafat, **consulted with the people, and he set singers to the Lord, praising with the grandeur of holiness,** in sanctity that contains an awesome beauty, **as they,** the choir and orchestra **went out before the army,**[127] **saying: Give thanks to the Lord, for His kindness is forever.** This was not a victory march, but rather an unusual way to go to war.
22 **At the time that they began with song and praise, the Lord set ambushes against the children of Amon, Moav, and the highlands of Se'ir, who were coming to Judah** for war, **and they were routed.** The identity of the members of this ambush is unclear, but in any case, as the enemy forces were composed of men from three different countries, they were insufficiently organized to deal with surprise attacks from various directions.
23 Even before the army of Judah arrived on the scene, **the children of Amon and Moav stood against the inhabitants of the highlands of Se'ir,** the Edomites, **to annihilate and destroy them.** They began fighting among themselves. The children of Amon and Moav may have suspected the Edomites of betrayal, as the Edomites had been subjugated to the Kingdom of Judah for many years.[128] **And when they had concluded with** the attack against **the inhabitants of Se'ir,** and the battle had dispersed, **each helped** their partners **to destroy his counterpart;** alternatively, as a result of errors or out of a desire to settle old scores, they began fighting among themselves until they destroyed each other.
24 **Judah came to the lookout,** a high observation point **of the wilderness, and they turned to the horde, and behold, they,** their enemies, **were corpses falling to the ground, and there were none remaining.**
25 **Yehoshafat and his people came to plunder their spoils, and they found among them an abundance; there was property, and corpses with precious gear** upon them, such as valuable items and clothing; **they stripped for themselves more than they could carry;**[129] **they were plundering the spoils for three days, as it was abundant.**
26 **On the fourth day they assembled in the Valley of Berakha,**[B] which was called by that name **as there they blessed the Lord** and thanked Him for the victory He granted them without them having to wage war at all, as the prophet had foreseen. All that was left for them to do was to strip the dead. **Therefore, they called the name of that place the Valley of Berakha,** meaning blessing, **to this day.**
27 **All the men of Judah and Jerusalem, with Yehoshafat at their head, turned to return to Jerusalem joyfully, for the Lord had caused them to rejoice over their enemies.** Alternatively, the verse means that all the men of Judah and Jerusalem went to their respective places, while Yehoshaphat turned to return to Jerusalem.
28 **They came to Jerusalem with lyres, harps, and trumpets to the House of the Lord.**
29 **Fear of God was over all the kingdoms of the lands when they heard** the reports from the battlefield, **that the Lord had waged war against the enemies of Israel,** without the children of Israel needing to do anything themselves.
30 **The realm of Yehoshafat became tranquil, and his God provided him respite from all around.** That was the last time that Yehoshafat was compelled to venture out to battle.

Trumpets of the Temple, illustration based on coin, period of bar Kokheva rebellion, early second century CE

31 The chapter summarizes the reign of Yehoshafat: **Yehoshafat reigned over Judah; he was thirty-five years old when he became king, and he reigned twenty-five years in Jerusalem. His mother's name was Azuva daughter of Shilhi.**
32 **He followed in the way of Asa his father,** who was essentially a righteous king, **and** he **did not deviate from it, performing what is right in the eyes of the Lord.**
33 **However, the** private **shrines** for the unlawful service of God, which were scattered around the country, **were not removed, and the people had not yet directed their hearts to the God of their fathers.** On a personal level, the men of Judah still did not fully value the word of God, nor did they strictly observe His commandments. For that to occur, not only was a powerful king required, but also a change in the general atmosphere and a change in the people themselves.
34 **The rest of the early and late deeds of Yehoshafat, behold, they are written in the chronicles of Yehu son of Hanani** the prophet, **which were included**[130] **in the book of the kings of Israel,** a work that is not extant.
35 **Thereafter, Yehoshafat king of Judah allied himself with Ahazya** son of Ahav, **king of Israel;** Ahazya[131] was his family relation, and a king **who acted wickedly.**
36 **He joined with him** in order **to make ships to go to Tarshish.** While the Kingdom of Israel exercised control over a large part of the shore of the Mediterranean Sea, Judah had access to the Red Sea. Thus, the two kings together planned a naval journey, since a commercial trip southward, in the direction of southern Arabia, East Africa, or India, was likely to be lucrative. **They made the ships in Etzyon Gever** (see commentary on 8:17).

כא אלהיכם ותאמנו האמינו בנביאיו והצליחו: ויועץ אל־העם ויעמד משררים
ליהוה ומהללים להדרת־קדש בצאת לפני החלוץ ואמרים הודו ליהוה כי
כב לעולם חסדו: ובעת החלו ברנה ותהלה נתן יהוה | מארבים על־בני עמון
כג מואב והר־שעיר הבאים ליהודה וינגפו: ויעמדו בני עמון ומואב על־ישבי
הר־שעיר להחרים ולהשמיד וככלותם ביושבי שעיר עזרו איש ברעהו
כד למשחית: ויהודה בא על־המצפה למדבר ויפנו אל־ההמון והנם פגרים נפלים
כה ארצה ואין פליטה: ויבא יהושפט ועמו לבז את־שללם וימצאו בהם לרב
ורכוש ופגרים וכלי חמדות וינצלו להם לאין משא ויהיו ימים שלושה בזזים
כו את־השלל כי רב־הוא: וביום הרבעי נקהלו לעמק ברכה כי שם ברכו את־
כז יהוה על־כן קראו את־שם המקום ההוא עמק ברכה עד־היום: וישבו כל־איש
יהודה וירושלם ויהושפט בראשם לשוב אל־ירושלם בשמחה כי־שמחם
כח יהוה מאויביהם: ויבאו ירושלם בנבלים ובכנרות ובחצצרות אל־בית יהוה:
כט ויהי פחד אלהים על כל־ממלכות הארצות בשמעם כי נלחם יהוה עם אויבי
ל לא ישראל: ותשקט מלכות יהושפט וינח לו אלהיו מסביב: וימלך יט
יהושפט על־יהודה בן־שלשים וחמש שנה במלכו ועשרים וחמש שנה מלך
לב בירושלם ושם אמו עזובה בת־שלחי: וילך בדרך אביו אסא ולא־סר ממנה
לג לעשות הישר בעיני יהוה: אך הבמות לא־סרו ועוד העם לא־הכינו לבבם
לד לאלהי אבתיהם: ויתר דברי יהושפט הראשנים והאחרונים הנם כתובים
לה בדברי יהוא בן־חנני אשר העלה על־ספר מלכי ישראל: ואחרי־כן אתחבר
לו יהושפט מלך־יהודה עם אחזיה מלך־ישראל הוא הרשיע לעשות: ויחברהו

BACKGROUND

20:26 | **The Valley of Berakha:** There are several suggestions with regard to the identity of this place: the valley known as Bereikut, at the foot of biblical Tekoa, to the west; the Hyrcania Valley in the wilderness of Judah; or the valley known today as the Valley of Beraka, near Wadi el-Aroub in Gush Etzion.

37 **Eliezer son of Dodavahu of Maresha,** a city in Judah, **prophesied against Yehoshafat, saying: Because you allied yourself with Ahazyahu, the Lord has breached your works.** Indeed, **the ships were wrecked, and they were unable to go to Tarshish.** They were unable to sail that far, and they sank en route.

The Chronicles of King Yehoram

II CHRONICLES 21:1–20

Yehoram does not follow in his father's footsteps, and during his reign the Kingdom of Judah falls to a low point. In every aspect, he fails as a king. He suffers defeat in war, and is left isolated after an attack by the Philistines and Arabians. He even loses the support of his own people, to the extent that a city in Judah rebels against him.

21 1 **Yehoshafat lay with his fathers and was buried with his fathers in the City of David. Yehoram his son reigned in his stead.**

2 **He,** Yehoram, **had brothers, the sons of Yehoshafat: Azarya, Yehiel, Zekharyahu, Azaryahu, Mikhael, and Shefatyahu; all these were the sons of Yehoshafat king of Israel.**

3 **Their father gave them many gifts, of silver, of gold, and of precious items, with fortified cities in Judah;** in addition to the gifts, each of them received a fortified city to rule over as an inheritance; **but the kingdom he gave to Yehoram, because he was the firstborn.** Consequently, the throne passed from Yehoshafat to his son Yehoram.

4 **Yehoram set himself** to rule **over the kingdom of his father, and** he **grew strong, and he killed all his brothers by the sword,**[B] **as well as some of the princes of Israel,** so that they would not challenge him and pose a threat to his rule.

5 **Yehoram was thirty-two years old when he became king, and he reigned eight years in Jerusalem.**

6 **He followed in the way of the kings of Israel, as the house of Ahav had done, for Ahav's daughter became his wife.** Yehoshafat and Ahav had established ties of marriage between their families (see chap. 18). It seems that this daughter of Ahav, who is a dominant figure in the next section (22:10–12), was also Izevel's daughter. Thus, she was a descendant of gentile kings, and she adopted their modes of conduct. It was she who guided Yehoram and wielded influence over him. **And he did evil in the eyes of the Lord.** Due to his close relationship with the house of Ahav, Yehoram departed from the ways of his father and grandfather.

7 Yehoram deserved to be punished for his sins, but **the Lord was unwilling to destroy the house of David, for the sake of the covenant that He had made with David, and as He had said to give him continuity,** a royal dynasty, **through his children always.**

8 For years Edom did not have its own king, but was an autonomous region under the control of the Kingdom of Judah. Then, **in his days,** the days of Yehoram, the people of **Edom rebelled from under the hand of Judah, and they crowned a king over them,** establishing their full independence.[132]

9 **Yehoram crossed over with his commanders and all his chariots with him** to fight the Edomites; **he arose at night, and smote Edom that surrounded him,** whose soldiers had surrounded him and were waiting to ambush him, **and the commanders of the chariots.**

10 Although Yehoram had killed some of the Edomites and escaped from the battle unharmed, he was not victorious and did not manage to conquer their land and subdue them. **Edom rebelled from under the hand of Judah to this day.** Judah lost control over the Edomites, who became its enemies. The tax payments stopped, and Judah's security was undermined. The Edomites in the south were also able to interfere with Judah's trade, as its commercial activities reached all the way to Eilat. **Then,** when Yehoram was weakened, the city of **Livna,**[B] in the land of Judah, also **rebelled at that time from under his hand.** Its inhabitants rebelled against the king **because he forsook the Lord, God of his fathers.** Despite Yehoram's attempt to establish a centralized government, and notwithstanding the killing of his brothers in an effort to concentrate all the power in his own hands, he became unable to control even the cities in his own territory.

Tel es-Safi, possibly the biblical Livna

11 **Also, he made shrines in the highlands of Judah, and perverted the inhabitants of Jerusalem, and led Judah astray** from the service of God.

12 **A letter came to him from Elijah the prophet.** Apparently this letter reached Yehoram after Elijah had already ascended to heaven.[133] Several explanations are offered for this communication, some of which refer to miraculous events.[134] It seems likeliest that Elijah left behind a prophetic letter for Yehoram king of Judah, which came into his possession at a later date. Whatever the precise circumstances, a message from Elijah arrived, **saying: So said the Lord, God of David your father: Because you have not followed in the ways of Yehoshafat your father, and in the ways of Asa king of Judah,** your father's father,

לז עִמּוֹ לַעֲשׂוֹת אֳנִיּוֹת לָלֶכֶת תַּרְשִׁישׁ וַיַּעֲשׂוּ אֳנִיּוֹת בְּעֶצְיוֹן גָּבֶר׃ וַיִּתְנַבֵּא
אֱלִיעֶזֶר בֶּן־דֹּדָוָהוּ מִמָּרֵשָׁה עַל־יְהוֹשָׁפָט לֵאמֹר כְּהִתְחַבֶּרְךָ עִם־אֲחַזְיָהוּ פָּרַץ
א א יְהוָה אֶת־מַעֲשֶׂיךָ וַיִּשָּׁבְרוּ אֳנִיּוֹת וְלֹא עָצְרוּ לָלֶכֶת אֶל־תַּרְשִׁישׁ׃ וַיִּשְׁכַּב יְהוֹשָׁפָט
ב עִם־אֲבֹתָיו וַיִּקָּבֵר עִם־אֲבֹתָיו בְּעִיר דָּוִיד וַיִּמְלֹךְ יְהוֹרָם בְּנוֹ תַּחְתָּיו׃ וְלוֹ־אַחִים
בְּנֵי יְהוֹשָׁפָט עֲזַרְיָה וִיחִיאֵל וּזְכַרְיָהוּ וַעֲזַרְיָהוּ וּמִיכָאֵל וּשְׁפַטְיָהוּ כָּל־אֵלֶּה בְּנֵי
ג יְהוֹשָׁפָט מֶלֶךְ יִשְׂרָאֵל׃ וַיִּתֵּן לָהֶם ׀ אֲבִיהֶם מַתָּנוֹת רַבּוֹת לְכֶסֶף וּלְזָהָב וּלְמִגְדָּנוֹת
עִם־עָרֵי מְצֻרוֹת בִּיהוּדָה וְאֶת־הַמַּמְלָכָה נָתַן לִיהוֹרָם כִּי־הוּא הַבְּכוֹר׃
ד וַיָּקָם יְהוֹרָם עַל־מַמְלֶכֶת אָבִיו וַיִּתְחַזַּק וַיַּהֲרֹג אֶת־כָּל־אֶחָיו בֶּחָרֶב וְגַם מִשָּׂרֵי
ה יִשְׂרָאֵל׃ בֶּן־שְׁלֹשִׁים וּשְׁתַּיִם שָׁנָה יְהוֹרָם בְּמָלְכוֹ וּשְׁמוֹנֶה שָׁנִים מָלַךְ בִּירוּשָׁלִָם׃
ו וַיֵּלֶךְ בְּדֶרֶךְ ׀ מַלְכֵי יִשְׂרָאֵל כַּאֲשֶׁר עָשׂוּ בֵּית אַחְאָב כִּי בַּת־אַחְאָב הָיְתָה לּוֹ
ז אִשָּׁה וַיַּעַשׂ הָרַע בְּעֵינֵי יְהוָה׃ וְלֹא־אָבָה יְהוָה לְהַשְׁחִית אֶת־בֵּית דָּוִיד לְמַעַן
ח הַבְּרִית אֲשֶׁר כָּרַת לְדָוִיד וְכַאֲשֶׁר אָמַר לָתֵת לוֹ נִיר וּלְבָנָיו כָּל־הַיָּמִים׃ בְּיָמָיו
ט פָּשַׁע אֱדוֹם מִתַּחַת יַד־יְהוּדָה וַיַּמְלִיכוּ עֲלֵיהֶם מֶלֶךְ׃ וַיַּעֲבֹר יְהוֹרָם עִם־שָׂרָיו
וְכָל־הָרֶכֶב עִמּוֹ וַיְהִי קָם לַיְלָה וַיַּךְ אֶת־אֱדוֹם הַסּוֹבֵב אֵלָיו וְאֵת שָׂרֵי הָרָכֶב׃
י וַיִּפְשַׁע אֱדוֹם מִתַּחַת יַד־יְהוּדָה עַד הַיּוֹם הַזֶּה אָז תִּפְשַׁע לִבְנָה בָּעֵת הַהִיא
יא מִתַּחַת יָדוֹ כִּי עָזַב אֶת־יְהוָה אֱלֹהֵי אֲבֹתָיו׃ גַּם־הוּא עָשָׂה בָמוֹת בְּהָרֵי יְהוּדָה
יב וַיֶּזֶן אֶת־יֹשְׁבֵי יְרוּשָׁלִַם וַיַּדַּח אֶת־יְהוּדָה׃ וַיָּבֹא אֵלָיו מִכְתָּב מֵאֵלִיָּהוּ
הַנָּבִיא לֵאמֹר כֹּה ׀ אָמַר יְהוָה אֱלֹהֵי דָּוִיד אָבִיךָ תַּחַת אֲשֶׁר לֹא־הָלַכְתָּ בְּדַרְכֵי

BACKGROUND

21:4| **He killed all his brothers by the sword:** The killing of heirs or potential claimants to the throne occurs several times in the Bible, such as the murder of Gideon's sons by their brother Avimelekh, and the slaughter of the sons of Ahav by Yehu. Such actions have been a common feature throughout history. In the Ottoman Empire of the seventeenth century, it was customary for a new sultan to execute all his brothers in order to prevent power struggles over the succession. This practice was halted only because of pressure from the clerics. In Russia, the family of Tsar Nicholas II was liquidated in 1918 in order to prevent any claim to power or future return of the Tsarist regime.

21:10| **Livna:** One of the Levite cities in the Judean foothills (Joshua 10:29, 21:13; I Chronicles 6:42). Due to its central location, it was one of the cities later besieged by Sennacherib (II Kings 19:8). It is mentioned as the place of origin of Hamutal the daughter of Jeremiah, the mother of Yeho'ahaz and Tzidkiya, two of the last kings of Judah (II Kings 23:31, 24:18). Some identify it with Tel es-Safi, near Kfar Menahem, which is located alongside an ancient road leading from the coast to the Judean highlands, via the Valley of Ela. Others suggest it is Tel Burna, near Kibbutz Gal On.

13 **but** you **have followed in the way of the kings of Israel, and perverted Judah and the inhabitants of Jerusalem like the perversion of the house of Ahav, and also you have killed your brothers from your father's house, who were better than you.** You are wicked toward God and wicked toward man;
14 therefore, **behold, the Lord will afflict your people, and your children, and your wives, and all your property with a great plague.**
15 **As for you, there will be great illnesses, an illness of your bowels, until your bowels fall out from the illness, for many days.** Alternatively, the verse means that the illness will last two years (see verse 19).
16 And indeed, **the Lord stirred against Yehoram the spirit of the Philistines.** The Philistines provoked Yehoram. This was after many years in which they did not try to fight Israel, during which their independence was probably limited, as they were under the control of the king of Judah.[135] Once the Edomites cast off the yoke of the Kingdom of Judah, the Philistines also felt confident enough to open a front against them. **And** the Lord also stirred up the spirit **of the Arabians, who were near the Kushites.**[B]
17 **They went up against Judah, and breached it,** the borders and the walls, **and captured all the property that was found in the house of the king, as well as his sons and his wives,** who were killed; (see 22:1) **no son remained for him, except Yeho'ahaz,** who is also called Ahazyahu, a name consisting of the same Hebrew letters, only in a different order. Yeho'ahaz was **the youngest of his sons.**
18 **After all this, the Lord afflicted him,** Yehoram, **in his bowels with an incurable disease.**
19 **It was after a year and the next, at the conclusion of two years** of his disease, **that his bowels fell out with his illness, and he died in dire illness.** He may have suffered from a form of cancer. **His people did not make a** ceremonial **conflagration for him, like the conflagration of his fathers.** They did not bestow great honor upon him in his death.
20 **He was thirty-two years old when he became king, and eight years he reigned in Jerusalem; he departed without contentment,** without any satisfaction from his life. Yehoram's state continuously deteriorated until he died. They did not treat his remains with contempt, as **they buried him in the City of David, but** they did **not** bury him **in the graves of the kings** either. They did not see fit to inter him together with the rest of the kings of the house of David.

The Chronicles of King Ahazyahu

II CHRONICLES 22:1–9

Ahazyahu continues in the ways of his father Yehoram and his mother's parents, Ahav and Izevel. Fittingly, his demise is intertwined with the fate of the house of Ahav.

22 1 **The inhabitants of Jerusalem crowned Ahazyahu his youngest son king in his stead, as the troop that had come with the Arabians to the camp had slain all the older ones.** Consequently, **Ahazyahu son of Yehoram king of Judah became king.**
2 **Ahazyahu was forty-two years old when he became king, and he reigned one year in Jerusalem.** It is difficult to understand that he was literally forty-two years old, as according to the information provided above, his father, Yehoram, was forty when he died. It is likely that this number is based on a different chronology of Ahazyahu's years.[136] **His mother's name was Atalyahu daughter of Omri.**[B] As stated in the previous chapter (21:6), she was the daughter of Ahav, who was the son of Omri. It is not uncommon for the Bible to refer to members of the royal dynasties of Israel as children of the founder of that dynasty.

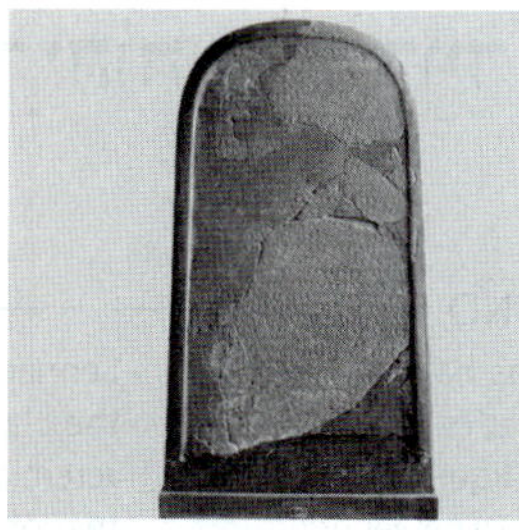

Mesha Stele, which mentions Omri king of Israel; Divon, Jordan

3 **He,** Ahazyahu, **also followed in the ways of the house of Ahav, as his mother was his counselor to act wickedly.** Atalyahu, who was earlier held responsible for the sins of her husband Yehoram, was no less influential over her son Ahazyahu.
4 **He did evil in the eyes of the Lord, like the house of Ahav, as they were his counselors after the death of his father,** and they contributed **to his ruin.** Since his mother the queen was the dominant figure in the royal court, she made sure to fill it with officials who were loyal to her. These advisors had a detrimental effect on the king. Although the Kingdom of Israel did not physically conquer Judah, it greatly influenced the southern kingdom through the figure of Queen Atalyahu.
5 **He also followed their counsel and went with Yehoram son of Ahav, king of Israel, to war against Hazael king of Aram at Ramot Gilad** (see commentary on 18:2). Yehoram continued his father's incessant wars against Aram, **and the Arameans**

Figurine, possibly of Hazael, ivory inlay, Arslan Tash, ninth century BCE

יג יְהוֹשָׁפָט אָבִיךָ וּבְדַרְכֵי אָסָא מֶלֶךְ־יְהוּדָה׃ וַתֵּלֶךְ בְּדֶרֶךְ מַלְכֵי יִשְׂרָאֵל וַתַּזְנֶה
אֶת־יְהוּדָה וְאֶת־יֹשְׁבֵי יְרוּשָׁלִַם כְּהַזְנוֹת בֵּית אַחְאָב וְגַם אֶת־אַחֶיךָ בֵית־אָבִיךָ
יד הַטּוֹבִים מִמְּךָ הָרָגְתָּ׃ הִנֵּה יְהוָה נֹגֵף מַגֵּפָה גְדוֹלָה בְּעַמֶּךָ וּבְבָנֶיךָ וּבְנָשֶׁיךָ וּבְכָל־
טו רְכוּשֶׁךָ׃ וְאַתָּה בָּחֳלָיִים רַבִּים בְּמַחֲלֵה מֵעֶיךָ עַד־יֵצְאוּ מֵעֶיךָ מִן־הַחֹלִי יָמִים
טז עַל־יָמִים׃ וַיָּעַר יְהוָה עַל־יְהוֹרָם אֶת־רוּחַ הַפְּלִשְׁתִּים וְהָעַרְבִים אֲשֶׁר עַל־יַד
יז כּוּשִׁים׃ וַיַּעֲלוּ בִיהוּדָה וַיִּבְקָעוּהָ וַיִּשְׁבּוּ אֵת כָּל־הָרְכוּשׁ הַנִּמְצָא לְבֵית־הַמֶּלֶךְ
יח וְגַם־בָּנָיו וְנָשָׁיו וְלֹא נִשְׁאַר־לוֹ בֵּן כִּי אִם־יְהוֹאָחָז קְטֹן בָּנָיו׃ וְאַחֲרֵי כָּל־זֹאת נְגָפוֹ
יט יְהוָה ׀ בְּמֵעָיו לָחֳלִי לְאֵין מַרְפֵּא׃ וַיְהִי לְיָמִים ׀ מִיָּמִים וּכְעֵת צֵאת הַקֵּץ לְיָמִים
שְׁנַיִם יָצְאוּ מֵעָיו עִם־חָלְיוֹ וַיָּמָת בְּתַחֲלֻאִים רָעִים וְלֹא־עָשׂוּ לוֹ עַמּוֹ שְׂרֵפָה
כ כִּשְׂרֵפַת אֲבֹתָיו׃ בֶּן־שְׁלֹשִׁים וּשְׁתַּיִם הָיָה בְמָלְכוֹ וּשְׁמוֹנֶה שָׁנִים מָלַךְ בִּירוּשָׁלִָם
כב א וַיֵּלֶךְ בְּלֹא חֶמְדָּה וַיִּקְבְּרֻהוּ בְּעִיר דָּוִיד וְלֹא בְּקִבְרוֹת הַמְּלָכִים׃ וַיַּמְלִיכוּ יוֹשְׁבֵי
יְרוּשָׁלִַם אֶת־אֲחַזְיָהוּ בְנוֹ הַקָּטֹן תַּחְתָּיו כִּי כָל־הָרִאשֹׁנִים הָרַג הַגְּדוּד הַבָּא
ב בָעַרְבִים לַמַּחֲנֶה וַיִּמְלֹךְ אֲחַזְיָהוּ בֶּן־יְהוֹרָם מֶלֶךְ יְהוּדָה׃ בֶּן־אַרְבָּעִים
וּשְׁתַּיִם שָׁנָה אֲחַזְיָהוּ בְמָלְכוֹ וְשָׁנָה אַחַת מָלַךְ בִּירוּשָׁלִָם וְשֵׁם אִמּוֹ עֲתַלְיָהוּ
ג בַּת־עָמְרִי׃ גַּם־הוּא הָלַךְ בְּדַרְכֵי בֵּית אַחְאָב כִּי אִמּוֹ הָיְתָה יוֹעַצְתּוֹ לְהַרְשִׁיעַ׃
ד וַיַּעַשׂ הָרַע בְּעֵינֵי יְהוָה כְּבֵית אַחְאָב כִּי הֵמָּה הָיוּ־לוֹ יוֹעֲצִים אַחֲרֵי מוֹת אָבִיו
ה לְמַשְׁחִית לוֹ׃ גַּם בַּעֲצָתָם הָלַךְ וַיֵּלֶךְ אֶת־יְהוֹרָם בֶּן־אַחְאָב מֶלֶךְ יִשְׂרָאֵל לַמִּלְחָמָה

BACKGROUND

21:16 | **The Arabians, who were near the Kushites:** It seems that this is referring to Kushites and Arabians who dwelled in the frontier region, southwest of Philistia (based on I Chronicles 4:39–40; II Chronicles 26:7). Some researchers identify them with the Nubians, who resided in Kush, south of Egypt. If so, the verse is perhaps speaking of tribes from Arabia who passed into the region of Habesh, from where they ascended to attack Yehoram.

22:2 | **Daughter of Omri:** The Kingdom of Israel is referred to in extra-biblical documents as the house of Omri by other nations in the region. Indeed, this name was associated with the kingdom for a hundred years after Yehu destroyed the house of Omri, up to the second half of the eighth century BCE. The name appears in the Mesha Stele from Moav, and in several Assyrian inscriptions from the days of Shalmaneser III, Adad-nirari III, and Tiglat Pileser III to the time of Sargon II, which was the period of the destruction of the Kingdom of Israel.

smote Yoram, Yehoram king of Israel. They did not kill him, but he was wounded in battle.

6 **He,** Yehoram king of Israel, **returned to convalesce in Yizre'el because of the wounds that were struck against him at Rama, when he fought against Hazael king of Aram. Azaryahu,** probably another name for Ahazyahu,[137] **son of Yehoram king of Judah went down to see Yehoram son of Ahav,** his wounded uncle, **in Yizre'el,**[B] **because he was ill.**

Tel Yizre'el

7 **The downfall of Ahazyahu was from God, his coming to Yoram.** His visit to Yehoram was a punishment from God; **and when he came, he went out with Yehoram to Yehu son of Nimshi, whom the Lord had anointed to eliminate the house of Ahav.** Ahazyahu arrived there exactly when a revolt was underway, as Yehu had been given a prophecy instructing him to destroy the house of Ahav, and not to leave any survivors.[138]

8 **It was when Yehu was punishing the house of Ahav that he found** there at the time **the princes of Judah and the sons of the brothers of Ahazyahu,** who were **serving Ahazyahu, and he killed them.** Yehu destroyed not only the family of Ahav; he also killed all the friends and supporters of the king of Israel. Ahazyahu king of Judah was a descendant of Ahav and close to his son Yehoram, and therefore Yehu did not hesitate to kill his men as well.

9 **He,** Yehu, **sought Ahazyahu,** who had fled from him, **and they captured him** from where **he was hiding in** the city of **Samaria. They brought him to Yehu, and he put him to death. They buried him, as they said: He is the son of Yehoshafat, who sought the Lord with all his heart.** He deserves some respect, as he was the grandson of the righteous king, Yehoshafat. Although they did not spare his life, they showed him some honor by burying him rather than tossing his body in the open field, as they had done to Yehoram son of Ahav. **There was no one from the house of Ahazyahu with the capacity to reign.** Yehu had evidently killed all the men of power and status in the Kingdom of Judah.

Ruins of Samaria

The Rise and Fall of Atalyahu as Ruler of Judah

II CHRONICLES 22:10–23:21

Yehu had killed the son of Atalyahu, who was both a wife and mother to kings, as well as all her family, when he seized the throne in the Kingdom of Israel. Now Atalyahu applies the same method toward the royal house of Judah. She eradicates virtually all those who have a claim to the throne and assumes control of the kingdom. However, she fails to fully complete her mission, as Ahazyahu's sister manages to save a one-year-old son of Ahazyahu, whom she hides for six years. Under the guidance of her husband, Yehoyada the High Priest, the throne is eventually restored to the house of David.

10 **Atalyahu,**[D] **mother of Ahazyahu, saw that her son was dead, and she rose and destroyed all the royal offspring of the house of Judah.** Her husband Yehoram had already killed some of his family, and she did her best to destroy anyone who might contest the throne. Consequently, she became the ruler of Judah.

11 **But Yehoshavat,** also called Yehosheva,[139] **daughter of** Yehoram **the king,** though presumably from another woman, not Atalyahu, **took Yo'ash son of Ahazyahu, and spirited him from among the king's sons who were put to death.** Atalyahu had ordered that all the sons of the king be killed, but one small boy remained unnoticed among the corpses. **And she,** Yehoshavat, **put him and his nurse in the bedroom.** The child was so small that he still required a nurse, and his aunt Yehoshavat managed to hide them both away. Some commentaries maintain that this "bedroom" was actually the most concealed place in the Temple, the only spot where they could be sure that the child would remain untouched.[140] **Yehoshavat daughter of King Yehoram, wife of Yehoyada the** High **Priest, concealed him,** Yo'ash, **from Atalyahu, for she was the sister of Ahazyahu, and she,** Atalyahu, **did not put him to death.** The fact that Yehoyada was the High Priest explains why he was given the king's daughter for a wife; it also accounts for their choice of a hiding place. Together, Yehoshavat and Yehoyada sought to preserve a remnant of the house of David from the murderous intentions of Atalyahu.

12 **He was with them in the House of God, hiding, for six years.** The king's son grew up in the Temple without anyone knowing about his existence, as he was under the tutelage and protection of the High Priest, who was in charge of the Temple. **And** throughout these years, **Atalya was reigning over the land.** She had her ministers and advisors, and she proved to be a strong queen who ruled over the land in her own way.

23 1 **In the seventh year, Yehoyada took courage,** as while he knew that he lacked the power to execute his plans by himself, he had gradually established connections with other people.

ו עַל־חֲזָאֵל מֶלֶךְ־אֲרָם בְּרָמוֹת גִּלְעָד וַיַּכּוּ הָרַמִּים אֶת־יוֹרָם: וַיָּשָׁב לְהִתְרַפֵּא
בְיִזְרְעֶאל כִּי הַמַּכִּים אֲשֶׁר הִכֻּהוּ בָרָמָה בְּהִלָּחֲמוֹ אֶת־חֲזָהאֵל מֶלֶךְ אֲרָם וַעֲזַרְיָהוּ
בֶן־יְהוֹרָם מֶלֶךְ יְהוּדָה יָרַד לִרְאוֹת אֶת־יְהוֹרָם בֶּן־אַחְאָב בְּיִזְרְעֶאל כִּי־חֹלֶה
ז הוּא: וּמֵאֱלֹהִים הָיְתָה תְּבוּסַת אֲחַזְיָהוּ לָבוֹא אֶל־יוֹרָם וּבְבֹאוֹ יָצָא עִם־יְהוֹרָם
ח אֶל־יֵהוּא בֶן־נִמְשִׁי אֲשֶׁר מְשָׁחוֹ יְהוָה לְהַכְרִית אֶת־בֵּית אַחְאָב: וַיְהִי כְּהִשָּׁפֵט
יֵהוּא עִם־בֵּית אַחְאָב וַיִּמְצָא אֶת־שָׂרֵי יְהוּדָה וּבְנֵי אֲחֵי אֲחַזְיָהוּ מְשָׁרְתִים
ט לַאֲחַזְיָהוּ וַיַּהַרְגֵם: וַיְבַקֵּשׁ אֶת־אֲחַזְיָהוּ וַיִּלְכְּדֻהוּ וְהוּא מִתְחַבֵּא בְשֹׁמְרוֹן וַיְבִאֻהוּ
אֶל־יֵהוּא וַיְמִתֻהוּ וַיִּקְבְּרֻהוּ כִּי אָמְרוּ בֶּן־יְהוֹשָׁפָט הוּא אֲשֶׁר־דָּרַשׁ אֶת־יְהוָה
י בְּכָל־לְבָבוֹ וְאֵין לְבֵית אֲחַזְיָהוּ לַעְצֹר כֹּחַ לְמַמְלָכָה: וַעֲתַלְיָהוּ אֵם
אֲחַזְיָהוּ רָאֲתָה כִּי־מֵת בְּנָהּ וַתָּקָם וַתְּדַבֵּר אֶת־כָּל־זֶרַע הַמַּמְלָכָה לְבֵית יְהוּדָה:
יא וַתִּקַּח יְהוֹשַׁבְעַת בַּת־הַמֶּלֶךְ אֶת־יוֹאָשׁ בֶּן־אֲחַזְיָהוּ וַתִּגְנֹב אֹתוֹ מִתּוֹךְ בְּנֵי־
הַמֶּלֶךְ הַמּוּמָתִים וַתִּתֵּן אֹתוֹ וְאֶת־מֵינִקְתּוֹ בַּחֲדַר הַמִּטּוֹת וַתַּסְתִּירֵהוּ יְהוֹשַׁבְעַת
בַּת־הַמֶּלֶךְ יְהוֹרָם אֵשֶׁת יְהוֹיָדָע הַכֹּהֵן כִּי הִיא הָיְתָה אֲחוֹת אֲחַזְיָהוּ מִפְּנֵי עֲתַלְיָהוּ
יב וְלֹא הֱמִיתָתְהוּ: וַיְהִי אִתָּם בְּבֵית הָאֱלֹהִים מִתְחַבֵּא שֵׁשׁ שָׁנִים וַעֲתַלְיָה מֹלֶכֶת
כג א עַל־הָאָרֶץ: וּבַשָּׁנָה הַשְּׁבִעִית הִתְחַזַּק יְהוֹיָדָע וַיִּקַּח אֶת־שָׂרֵי
הַמֵּאוֹת לַעֲזַרְיָהוּ בֶן־יְרֹחָם וּלְיִשְׁמָעֵאל בֶּן־יְהוֹחָנָן וְלַעֲזַרְיָהוּ בֶן־עוֹבֵד וְאֶת־

BACKGROUND

22:6 | **Yizre'el:** This city in the territory of the tribe of Issachar (Joshua 19:18) was the location of the second palace of Ahav and the palace of his son Yehoram (I Kings 21:1; II Kings 8:29). It has been identified with Tel Yizre'el, in the center of the Yizre'el Valley, roughly 7 km southeast of the modern-day city of Afula. Royal grounds covering an area of about 60,000 sq m, which also served as a fortified military base, have been unearthed there. It is similar to the site built by Omri in Samaria. Yizre'el was destroyed in the second half of the ninth century BCE, most likely during the rebellion of Yehu.

DISCUSSION

22:10 | **Atalyahu:** It is hard to find a satisfactory explanation for Atalyahu's puzzling deeds. It was certainly rare in that time for a female monarch to rule over a country. In Israel, it took over seven hundred years until another woman would sit on the throne. Furthermore, the decision of a woman to take power into her hands by slaughtering the entire royal household is a unique occurrence. Atalyahu was already a dominant figure during the reign of King Yehoram of Judah, and even more so during the reign of her son Ahazyahu. Her powerful personality enabled her not only to seize the crown but also to hold onto it for several years. It seems that Atalyahu set up a court and surrounded herself with supporters, but her deeds cannot be explained merely as an attempt to prevent competition. She was not a young woman when she took control of the kingdom, and she was not looking to transfer the rule of Judah to her father's house, as the house of Ahav was also completely destroyed. Atalyahu is a tragic figure whose entire world had been lost. It is possible that she became deranged, and this expressed itself in an uncontrollable lust for power that did not take into account the future, just the ability to control the present.

And he **took the commanders of the hundreds: Azaryahu son of Yeroham, Yishmael son of Yehohanan, Azaryahu son of Oved, Maaseyahu son of Adayahu, and Elishafat son of Zikhri,** and brought all of these men **into a** secret **covenant with him,** to restore the monarchy to the dynasty of the house of David.

2 **They,** Yehoyada and the captains, **went around in** the land of **Judah and gathered the Levites from all the cities of Judah and the heads of patrilineal houses of Israel, and they came to Jerusalem.**

3 **The entire congregation** that had assembled specially for this gathering **established a covenant in the House of God with the king. He,** Yehoyada, **said to them: Behold,** this is **the king's son** who **will reign, as the Lord spoke concerning the sons of David,** that the royal line will not cease from his descendants, and His word must be fulfilled.

4 **This is the thing that you shall do** in order to observe the will of God: **One-third of you from among the priests and the Levites will be those arriving on the Sabbath,** in their capacity of the watches that enter the Temple on the Sabbath day,[141] **as gatekeepers at the thresholds.** They will stand in one spot.

5 Another **one-third shall be at the king's house, and** the final **one-third** shall be **at the Gate of the Foundation.** If you position yourselves in different places, there will be no clear sign of the revolt. **All the people will be** located **in the courtyards of the House of the Lord,** the Temple's courtyards.

6 **No one** of the people **shall come into the House of the Lord except the priests, and those among the Levites who serve; they shall enter, as they are holy, and all the people shall keep the watch of the Lord** from the outside.[142]

7 **The Levites shall surround the king all around, each with his weapons in his hand.** Those Levites who are assigned the task of slaughtering the offerings will have knives in their hands. The others will hold various weapons; none shall be empty-handed. **And he who comes into the House,** who is not involved in the conspiracy, **shall be put to death.** The Levites will **be with the king,** serving as his guards, **when he enters and departs,** to ensure that he is protected from danger.

8 **The Levites and all Judah acted in accordance with everything that Yehoyada the priest had commanded; each took his men, those arriving on the Sabbath with those departing on the Sabbath.** Generally, one watch would enter the Temple on the Sabbath to begin its service, while another watch would leave, but in this case both watches remained in the Temple, **for Yehoyada the priest had not dismissed** to their homes **the divisions** who had finished their service, in order to augment the numbers of his supporters on site.

Spear, stele, Jordan, 1200–800 BCE

9 **Yehoyada the priest gave the commanders of the hundreds the spears, bucklers, and shields**[143] **that had been King David's, which were** now located **in the House of God.** There was a large treasury in the Temple, which contained items of historical value, such as David's weapons. Yet, these weapons could also be used in practice. It is also possible that the captains were given these ancient weapons to demonstrate that the legacy of the house of David was in their hands.

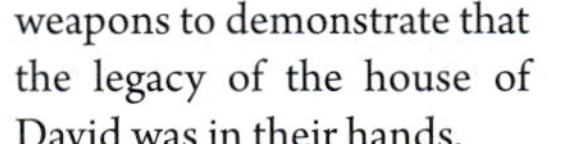

Shield, Tutankhamun's tomb, Egypt, fourteenth century BCE

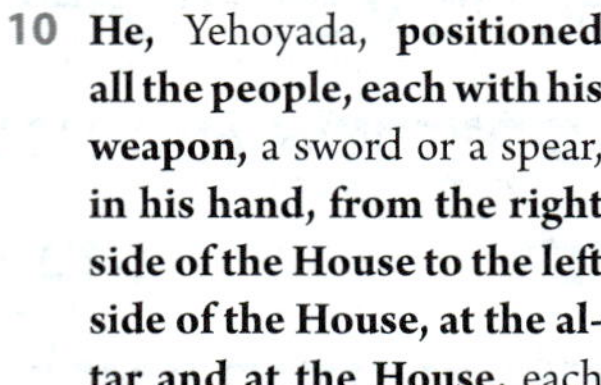

10 **He,** Yehoyada, **positioned all the people, each with his weapon,** a sword or a spear, **in his hand, from the right side of the House to the left side of the House, at the altar and at the House,** each standing with his weapon, to guard **near the king all around.**

11 **They took out the king's son,** Yo'ash, from his hiding place, **and placed the crown and the Testimony,** a Torah scroll,[144] or some sort of royal symbol, **upon him, and crowned him king. Yehoyada and his sons anointed him and said: Long live the king.**

12 **Atalyahu,** whose house was not far from the Temple, **heard the sound of the** many **people who were running about and praising** and crowning **the king, and she came to the people at the House of the Lord.**

13 **She saw, and behold, the king was standing on his platform at the entrance.** They had stood Yo'ash up on a stage, among other reasons because he was still a young child and they wanted everyone to see him. **The leaders and the trumpets were near the king, and all the people of the land rejoiced, sounding the trumpets; the singers** playing **with musical instruments were leading** the assembly in **the praise. Atalyahu rent her garments, and said: Conspiracy, conspiracy!**

14 **Yehoyada the priest brought out** at his orders **the commanders of the hundreds,** the **captains of the army, and said to them: Take her out from** the Temple **among the ranks,** within the lines of guards, so that she cannot escape; **and anyone who follows her,** if anyone tries to accompany her, **shall be put to death by the sword, as the priest said: Do not put her to death in** the compound of **the House of the Lord.**

15 **They cleared a path for her**[145] and pushed her out, **and she went to the entrance of the Horses' Gate to the king's house; and they put her to death there.**

ב מַעֲשֵׂיָהוּ בֶן־עֲדָיָהוּ וְאֶת־אֱלִישָׁפָט בֶּן־זִכְרִי עִמּוֹ בַבְּרִית׃ וַיָּסֹבּוּ בִּיהוּדָה וַיִּקְבְּצוּ
אֶת־הַלְוִיִּם מִכָּל־עָרֵי יְהוּדָה וְרָאשֵׁי הָאָבוֹת לְיִשְׂרָאֵל וַיָּבֹאוּ אֶל־יְרוּשָׁלָ͏ִם׃
ג וַיִּכְרֹת כָּל־הַקָּהָל בְּרִית בְּבֵית הָאֱלֹהִים עִם־הַמֶּלֶךְ וַיֹּאמֶר לָהֶם הִנֵּה בֶן־הַמֶּלֶךְ
ד יִמְלֹךְ כַּאֲשֶׁר דִּבֶּר יְהוָה עַל־בְּנֵי דָוִיד׃ זֶה הַדָּבָר אֲשֶׁר תַּעֲשׂוּ הַשְּׁלִשִׁית מִכֶּם
ה בָּאֵי הַשַּׁבָּת לַכֹּהֲנִים וְלַלְוִיִּם לְשֹׁעֲרֵי הַסִּפִּים׃ וְהַשְּׁלִשִׁית בְּבֵית הַמֶּלֶךְ וְהַשְּׁלִשִׁית
ו בְּשַׁעַר הַיְסוֹד וְכָל־הָעָם בְּחַצְרוֹת בֵּית יְהוָה׃ וְאַל־יָבוֹא בֵית־יְהוָה כִּי אִם־
הַכֹּהֲנִים וְהַמְשָׁרְתִים לַלְוִיִּם הֵמָּה יָבֹאוּ כִּי־קֹדֶשׁ הֵמָּה וְכָל־הָעָם יִשְׁמְרוּ מִשְׁמֶרֶת
ז יְהוָה׃ וְהִקִּיפוּ הַלְוִיִּם אֶת־הַמֶּלֶךְ סָבִיב אִישׁ וְכֵלָיו בְּיָדוֹ וְהַבָּא אֶל־הַבַּיִת יוּמָת
ח וִהְיוּ אֶת־הַמֶּלֶךְ בְּבֹאוֹ וּבְצֵאתוֹ׃ וַיַּעֲשׂוּ הַלְוִיִּם וְכָל־יְהוּדָה כְּכֹל אֲשֶׁר־צִוָּה
יְהוֹיָדָע הַכֹּהֵן וַיִּקְחוּ אִישׁ אֶת־אֲנָשָׁיו בָּאֵי הַשַּׁבָּת עִם יוֹצְאֵי הַשַּׁבָּת כִּי לֹא פָטַר
ט יְהוֹיָדָע הַכֹּהֵן אֶת־הַמַּחְלְקוֹת׃ וַיִּתֵּן יְהוֹיָדָע הַכֹּהֵן לְשָׂרֵי הַמֵּאוֹת אֶת־
הַחֲנִיתִים וְאֶת־הַמָּגִנּוֹת וְאֶת־הַשְּׁלָטִים אֲשֶׁר לַמֶּלֶךְ דָּוִיד אֲשֶׁר בֵּית הָאֱלֹהִים׃
י וַיַּעֲמֵד אֶת־כָּל־הָעָם וְאִישׁ ׀ שִׁלְחוֹ בְיָדוֹ מִכֶּתֶף הַבַּיִת הַיְמָנִית עַד־כֶּתֶף הַבַּיִת
יא הַשְּׂמָאלִית לַמִּזְבֵּחַ וְלַבָּיִת עַל־הַמֶּלֶךְ סָבִיב׃ וַיּוֹצִיאוּ אֶת־בֶּן־הַמֶּלֶךְ וַיִּתְּנוּ עָלָיו כ
אֶת־הַנֵּזֶר וְאֶת־הָעֵדוּת וַיַּמְלִיכוּ אֹתוֹ וַיִּמְשָׁחֻהוּ יְהוֹיָדָע וּבָנָיו וַיֹּאמְרוּ יְחִי
יב הַמֶּלֶךְ׃ וַתִּשְׁמַע עֲתַלְיָהוּ אֶת־קוֹל הָעָם הָרָצִים וְהַמְהַלְלִים אֶת־
יג הַמֶּלֶךְ וַתָּבוֹא אֶל־הָעָם בֵּית יְהוָה׃ וַתֵּרֶא וְהִנֵּה הַמֶּלֶךְ עוֹמֵד עַל־עַמּוּדוֹ בַּמָּבוֹא
וְהַשָּׂרִים וְהַחֲצֹצְרוֹת עַל־הַמֶּלֶךְ וְכָל־עַם הָאָרֶץ שָׂמֵחַ וְתוֹקֵעַ בַּחֲצֹצְרוֹת
וְהַמְשׁוֹרְרִים בִּכְלֵי הַשִּׁיר וּמוֹדִיעִים לְהַלֵּל וַתִּקְרַע עֲתַלְיָהוּ אֶת־בְּגָדֶיהָ וַתֹּאמֶר
יד קֶשֶׁר קָשֶׁר׃ וַיּוֹצֵא יְהוֹיָדָע הַכֹּהֵן אֶת־שָׂרֵי הַמֵּאוֹת ׀ פְּקוּדֵי הַחַיִל
וַיֹּאמֶר אֲלֵהֶם הוֹצִיאוּהָ אֶל־מִבֵּית הַשְּׂדֵרוֹת וְהַבָּא אַחֲרֶיהָ יוּמַת בֶּחָרֶב כִּי אָמַר
טו הַכֹּהֵן לֹא תְמִיתוּהָ בֵּית יְהוָה׃ וַיָּשִׂימוּ לָהּ יָדַיִם וַתָּבוֹא אֶל־מְבוֹא שַׁעַר־הַסּוּסִים
בֵּית הַמֶּלֶךְ וַיְמִיתוּהָ שָׁם׃

16 No one came to Atalyahu's aid, as Yehoyada had already recruited the entire royal guard in support of the new king. Yehoyada did not merely reinstate the king to the throne; he took this opportunity to make a more fundamental change in the kingdom: **Yehoyada established a covenant between himself and the entire people and the king that they should be the people of the Lord.** He did not wish simply to exchange one ruler for another; rather, he sought to eradicate all traces of Atalyahu's reign. As a member of the house of Ahav, she had brought with her idolatrous practices and other foreign customs from her father's house. Now Yehoyada wished to restore the service of God to its rightful place.

17 **The people went to the temple of the Baal,** which had been erected in Jerusalem, perhaps due to the religious tolerance that was prevalent there, or because Atalyahu, who came from a home of Baal worshippers, had established it in the city. **And** they **smashed it** into pieces, **and shattered its altars and its images, and put Matan,** who was the **priest of the Baal, to death before the altars** of Baal.

18 Apparently, during Atalyahu's reign no one took care of the proper management of the Temple. Now[146] **Yehoyada placed the administration of the House of the Lord into the hand of the priests the Levites, whom David had assigned over the House of the Lord.** He restored the watches of priests and Levites to a fully functioning state, in order **to offer up the burnt offerings of the Lord, as it is written in the Torah of Moses, with joy and with song, by means of David.**

19 **He positioned the gatekeepers at the gates of the House of the Lord,** to ensure **that anyone impure in any way,** whoever had contracted any sort of ritual impurity, **shall not enter.**

20 **He took the commanders of the hundreds, and the nobles,** the important and powerful individuals, **and the governors of the people, and all the people of the land, and brought the king down from the House of the Lord; they came through the upper gate** of the Temple **to the king's house and placed the king upon the throne of the kingdom.**

21 **All the people of the land rejoiced** upon the return of the king to his throne, **and the city was tranquil; and they put Atalyahu to death by sword.** As the king was still a young boy, Yehoyada the High Priest, who had saved his life, remained his guardian. With the appointment of the new king, the monarchy was restored to the house of David.

The Chronicles of King Yo'ash

II CHRONICLES 24:1–27

Yo'ash, who was kept hidden in his childhood in the House of God, sees to the maintenance and repair of the Temple building in his adult years. But after the death of Yehoyada the High Priest, Yo'ash's rescuer and patron, the king is led astray by his advisors. Once again the Temple is neglected, and idol worship spreads throughout Judah. The punishment for this sin follows swiftly: The king's enemies, the Arameans, raid Judah, kill its ministers, and abuse its king. Consequently, the king's internal opposition assassinates him.

24 1 **Yo'ash was seven years old when he became king,** as he was kept in hiding for six years (22:12, 23:1). He was only one year old and the sole survivor when his grandmother, Atalya, massacred the entire royal family. **And** he **reigned forty years in Jerusalem. His mother's name was Tzivya from Beersheba.**

2 **Yo'ash did what is right in the eyes of the Lord all the days of Yehoyada the priest.** Yehoyada, a prominent, prestigious man, enjoyed a long life (verse 15) and established a large family:

3 **Yehoyada took for himself two wives** over the course of his life,[147] **and he begot sons and daughters,** a detail that will be important later in the narrative.[148]

4 **It was thereafter,** when the new king had matured into adulthood, **that it entered Yo'ash's heart to restore the House of the Lord.** Not only during the reign of Atalyahu, but also in the days of Ahazyahu, and perhaps even during Yehoram's rule, scant attention had been paid to the Temple, which suffered from neglect.

5 **He gathered the priests and the Levites and said to them: Go out to the cities of Judah, and gather silver from all of Israel from year to year to repair the House of your God;** arrange an annual collection for the upkeep and running of the Temple. He further emphasized: **You shall hasten in this matter. However, the Levites did not hasten.** Evidently, they were not enthusiastic about this mission, possibly because they did not consider it to be their job.

6 **The king called Yehoyada the head** of the priests, **and said to him: Why have you not sought from the Levites,** or inquired about their assignment, **for them to bring from Judah and from Jerusalem the tax of Moses servant of the Lord, and the assembly of Israel,** which they brought **for the Tent of the Testimony,** the requirements of the Tabernacle?[149] I gave clear instructions that a donation of this kind must be given now as well.

7 **For the sons of the wicked Atalyahu had breached the House of God** and looted all its treasures, **and** they **had utilized all the consecrated items of the House of the Lord for the Be'alim.**

8 Therefore, the king devised an alternative method of collecting money from the people: **The king said** his command, **and** in accordance with his order, **they made a chest and placed it at the gate of the House of the Lord, on the outside** of the gate.

טז יז וַיִּכְרֹת יְהוֹיָדָע בְּרִית בֵּינוֹ וּבֵין כָּל־הָעָם וּבֵין הַמֶּלֶךְ לִהְיוֹת לְעָם לַיהוָה׃ וַיָּבֹאוּ
כָל־הָעָם בֵּית־הַבַּעַל וַיִּתְּצֻהוּ וְאֶת־מִזְבְּחֹתָיו וְאֶת־צְלָמָיו שִׁבֵּרוּ וְאֵת מַתָּן כֹּהֵן
יח הַבַּעַל הָרְגוּ לִפְנֵי הַמִּזְבְּחוֹת׃ וַיָּשֶׂם יְהוֹיָדָע פְּקֻדֹּת בֵּית יהוה בְּיַד הַכֹּהֲנִים הַלְוִיִּם
אֲשֶׁר חָלַק דָּוִיד עַל־בֵּית יהוה לְהַעֲלוֹת עֹלוֹת יהוה כַּכָּתוּב בְּתוֹרַת מֹשֶׁה
יט בְּשִׂמְחָה וּבְשִׁיר עַל יְדֵי דָוִיד׃ וַיַּעֲמֵד הַשּׁוֹעֲרִים עַל־שַׁעֲרֵי בֵּית יְהוָה וְלֹא־יָבוֹא
כ טָמֵא לְכָל־דָּבָר׃ וַיִּקַּח אֶת־שָׂרֵי הַמֵּאוֹת וְאֶת־הָאַדִּירִים וְאֶת־הַמּוֹשְׁלִים בָּעָם
וְאֵת ׀ כָּל־עַם הָאָרֶץ וַיּוֹרֶד אֶת־הַמֶּלֶךְ מִבֵּית יהוה וַיָּבֹאוּ בְּתוֹךְ־שַׁעַר הָעֶלְיוֹן
כא בֵּית הַמֶּלֶךְ וַיּוֹשִׁיבוּ אֶת־הַמֶּלֶךְ עַל כִּסֵּא הַמַּמְלָכָה׃ וַיִּשְׂמְחוּ כָל־עַם־הָאָרֶץ
כד א וְהָעִיר שָׁקָטָה וְאֶת־עֲתַלְיָהוּ הֵמִיתוּ בֶחָרֶב׃ בֶּן־שֶׁבַע שָׁנִים יֹאָשׁ
ב בְּמָלְכוֹ וְאַרְבָּעִים שָׁנָה מָלַךְ בִּירוּשָׁלִָם וְשֵׁם אִמּוֹ צִבְיָה מִבְּאֵר שָׁבַע׃ וַיַּעַשׂ יוֹאָשׁ
הַיָּשָׁר בְּעֵינֵי יְהוָה כָּל־יְמֵי יְהוֹיָדָע הַכֹּהֵן׃
ג ד וַיִּשָּׂא־לוֹ יְהוֹיָדָע נָשִׁים שְׁתָּיִם וַיּוֹלֶד בָּנִים וּבָנוֹת׃ וַיְהִי אַחֲרֵי־כֵן הָיָה עִם־לֵב
ה יוֹאָשׁ לְחַדֵּשׁ אֶת־בֵּית יְהוָה׃ וַיִּקְבֹּץ אֶת־הַכֹּהֲנִים וְהַלְוִיִּם וַיֹּאמֶר לָהֶם צְאוּ לְעָרֵי
יְהוּדָה וְקִבְצוּ מִכָּל־יִשְׂרָאֵל כֶּסֶף לְחַזֵּק ׀ אֶת־בֵּית אֱלֹהֵיכֶם מִדֵּי שָׁנָה
ו בְּשָׁנָה וְאַתֶּם תְּמַהֲרוּ לַדָּבָר וְלֹא מִהֲרוּ הַלְוִיִּם׃ וַיִּקְרָא הַמֶּלֶךְ
לִיהוֹיָדָע הָרֹאשׁ וַיֹּאמֶר לוֹ מַדּוּעַ לֹא־דָרַשְׁתָּ עַל־הַלְוִיִּם לְהָבִיא מִיהוּדָה
ז וּמִירוּשָׁלִַם אֶת־מַשְׂאַת מֹשֶׁה עֶבֶד־יְהוָה וְהַקָּהָל לְיִשְׂרָאֵל לְאֹהֶל הָעֵדוּת׃ כִּי
עֲתַלְיָהוּ הַמִּרְשַׁעַת בָּנֶיהָ פָרְצוּ אֶת־בֵּית הָאֱלֹהִים וְגַם כָּל־קָדְשֵׁי בֵית־יְהוָה עָשׂוּ
ח לַבְּעָלִים׃ וַיֹּאמֶר הַמֶּלֶךְ וַיַּעֲשׂוּ אֲרוֹן אֶחָד וַיִּתְּנֻהוּ בְּשַׁעַר בֵּית־יְהוָה חוּצָה׃

9 **They issued a proclamation in Judah and Jerusalem to bring for the Lord the tax of Moses servant of God on Israel in the wilderness.** They commanded that people bring personal donations, just as Moses in the wilderness called upon the children of Israel to bring gifts for the construction of the Tabernacle or to donate shekels for that purpose.
10 **All the princes and all the people rejoiced** over this initiative; **they brought** money **and cast** it **into the chest until it was** entirely **full.**
11 **It was at the time that the chest was brought out at the king's** official **command,**[150] or brought alongside the rest of the money that the king had amassed,[151] **into the hand of the Levites, and when they saw that the silver** in the chest **was plentiful, that the king's scribe and the head priest's official would come and empty** out the contents of **the chest.**[D] **They would pick it up and return it to its place,** in order to collect more money. **They would do so each day, and** thereby **gathered much silver.**
12 **The king and Yehoyada gave it,** the accumulated money, **to** all **the craftsmen of the work of the House of the Lord; and they hired masons and carpenters** in order **to restore the House of the Lord.** Masons were needed to bring new stones, as the Temple and some of its stones had worn with age. Likewise, carpenters, or builders, were required for the maintenance work in the Temple, **as well as smiths of iron and bronze to repair the House of the Lord.**

Carpenters, Tomb of Nebamun, Egypt, 1350–1300 BCE

13 **The craftsmen crafted** in accordance with their skills, **and the** preservation **labor in their hand was successful;** they performed their task well, and they were able to fix that which needed repair. **And they set the House of God in its original form,** or according to its appropriate measurements,[152] **and bolstered it.**
14 **When they concluded** the labor, **they brought the remaining silver** from this donation drive **before the king and Yehoyada, and he made it into vessels for the House of the Lord: service and sacrificial [*veha'alot*] vessels** used for performing [*ha'ala'at*] offerings,[153] or pestles [*eli*] for grinding, or vessels for drawing [*leha'alot*] water, as well as **ladles and gold and silver vessels. They were offering up burnt offerings in the House of the Lord continually all the days of Yehoyada.**
15 **Yehoyada aged and was full of days,** he reached a ripe old age, **and he died. He was one hundred and thirty years old at his death.** He served as High Priest for many years, which enabled him to complete all the above tasks.
16 **They buried him in the City of David with the kings, because he had done good in Israel, and with God and His House.** Yehoyada was buried in the tombs of the kings as a great leader, since he had restored the royal house of David to its rightful place and rehabilitated the House of God.
17 **After the death of Yehoyada the princes of Judah came and prostrated themselves to the king. Then,** after his ministers had paid their respects to him, and perhaps even treated him as a kind of demigod, in the manner that neighboring nations treated their rulers, **the king heeded them** and their seductive suggestions. Yehoyada had gradually transferred effective control of the kingdom to Yo'ash, and as long as the priest was alive the king would seek his advice and accept his guidance. However, once Yo'ash was in sole charge, he was seduced by the great honor bestowed upon him by the princes of Judah, even though that honor was conditional on his willingness to do their bidding. There was no one to admonish him and restrain him from following this path.[154]
18 **They forsook the House of the Lord, God of their fathers, and worshipped the sacred trees and the idols, and there was wrath upon Judah and Jerusalem for this guilt of theirs.**
19 **He,** God, **sent prophets among them, to return them to the Lord, and they admonished them;** the prophets warned the people, **but they would not listen.** The people of Judah returned to the idol worship and cultic rites that were common throughout the nations of the region at that time. Whenever their faith in God wavered, they naturally reverted to the accepted idolatrous trends, as these were the norms of the area.
20 **The spirit of God clothed Zekharya son of Yehoyada the** High **Priest; and he** prophesied and **stood above the people,** probably on an elevated spot in the Temple, **and said to them: So said God: Why are you transgressing the commandments of the Lord, and you will not succeed? Since you have forsaken the Lord, He has forsaken you.**
21 As he was a priest, Zekharya prophesied in the courtyard of the House of God contrary to the inclination of the people and the government. **They conspired against him;** a gang of unruly individuals banded together when they heard his words, **and** in their extreme reaction to his condemnation of them, they **stoned him with stones at the command of the king in the courtyard of the House of the Lord.**
22 It is obligatory to listen to a prophet even when his words are unpleasant and difficult to accept. Yo'ash failed to fulfill this duty, and Zekharya was both a prophet and a priest. What is more, his father had saved the king's life. **King Yo'ash did not remember the kindness that Yehoyada, his,** Zekharya's, **father had performed with him, and he killed his son. As**

ט וַיִּתְּנוּ־קוֹל בִּיהוּדָה וּבִירוּשָׁלַ͏ִם לְהָבִיא לַיהוה מַשְׂאַת מֹשֶׁה עֶבֶד־הָאֱלֹהִים
י עַל־יִשְׂרָאֵל בַּמִּדְבָּר: וַיִּשְׂמְחוּ כָל־הַשָּׂרִים וְכָל־הָעָם וַיָּבִיאוּ וַיַּשְׁלִיכוּ לָאָרוֹן
יא עַד־לְכַלֵּה: וַיְהִי בְּעֵת יָבִיא אֶת־הָאָרוֹן אֶל־פְּקֻדַּת הַמֶּלֶךְ בְּיַד הַלְוִיִּם וְכִרְאוֹתָם
כִּי־רַב הַכֶּסֶף וּבָא סוֹפֵר הַמֶּלֶךְ וּפְקִיד כֹּהֵן הָרֹאשׁ וִיעָרוּ אֶת־הָאָרוֹן וְיִשָּׂאֻהוּ
יב וִישִׁבֻהוּ אֶל־מְקֹמוֹ כֹּה עָשׂוּ לְיוֹם בְּיוֹם וַיַּאַסְפוּ־כֶסֶף לָרֹב: וַיִּתְּנֵהוּ הַמֶּלֶךְ וִיהוֹיָדָע
אֶל־עוֹשֵׂה מְלֶאכֶת עֲבוֹדַת בֵּית־יהוה וַיִּהְיוּ שֹׂכְרִים חֹצְבִים וְחָרָשִׁים לְחַדֵּשׁ
יג בֵּית יהוה וְגַם לְחָרָשֵׁי בַרְזֶל וּנְחֹשֶׁת לְחַזֵּק אֶת־בֵּית יהוה: וַיַּעֲשׂוּ עֹשֵׂי הַמְּלָאכָה
וַתַּעַל אֲרוּכָה לַמְּלָאכָה בְּיָדָם וַיַּעֲמִידוּ אֶת־בֵּית הָאֱלֹהִים עַל־מַתְכֻּנְתּוֹ וַיְאַמְּצֻהוּ:
יד וּכְכַלּוֹתָם הֵבִיאוּ לִפְנֵי הַמֶּלֶךְ וִיהוֹיָדָע אֶת־שְׁאָר הַכֶּסֶף וַיַּעֲשֵׂהוּ כֵלִים לְבֵית־
יהוה כְּלֵי שָׁרֵת וְהַעֲלוֹת וְכַפּוֹת וּכְלֵי זָהָב וָכָסֶף וַיִּהְיוּ מַעֲלִים עֹלוֹת בְּבֵית־יהוה
טו תָּמִיד כֹּל יְמֵי יְהוֹיָדָע: וַיִּזְקַן יְהוֹיָדָע וַיִּשְׂבַּע יָמִים וַיָּמֹת בֶּן־מֵאָה
טז וּשְׁלֹשִׁים שָׁנָה בְּמוֹתוֹ: וַיִּקְבְּרֻהוּ בְעִיר־דָּוִיד עִם־הַמְּלָכִים כִּי־עָשָׂה טוֹבָה
יז בְּיִשְׂרָאֵל וְעִם־הָאֱלֹהִים וּבֵיתוֹ: וְאַחֲרֵי מוֹת יְהוֹיָדָע בָּאוּ שָׂרֵי יְהוּדָה
יח וַיִּשְׁתַּחֲווּ לַמֶּלֶךְ אָז שָׁמַע הַמֶּלֶךְ אֲלֵיהֶם: וַיַּעַזְבוּ אֶת־בֵּית יהוה אֱלֹהֵי אֲבוֹתֵיהֶם
וַיַּעַבְדוּ אֶת־הָאֲשֵׁרִים וְאֶת־הָעֲצַבִּים וַיְהִי־קֶצֶף עַל־יְהוּדָה וִירוּשָׁלַ͏ִם בְּאַשְׁמָתָם
יט זֹאת: וַיִּשְׁלַח בָּהֶם נְבִאִים לַהֲשִׁיבָם אֶל־יהוה וַיָּעִידוּ בָם וְלֹא הֶאֱזִינוּ:
כ וְרוּחַ אֱלֹהִים לָבְשָׁה אֶת־זְכַרְיָה בֶּן־יְהוֹיָדָע הַכֹּהֵן וַיַּעֲמֹד מֵעַל לָעָם וַיֹּאמֶר לָהֶם
כֹּה ׀ אָמַר הָאֱלֹהִים לָמָה אַתֶּם עֹבְרִים אֶת־מִצְוֺת יהוה וְלֹא תַצְלִיחוּ כִּי־עֲזַבְתֶּם
כא אֶת־יהוה וַיַּעֲזֹב אֶתְכֶם: וַיִּקְשְׁרוּ עָלָיו וַיִּרְגְּמֻהוּ אֶבֶן בְּמִצְוַת הַמֶּלֶךְ בַּחֲצַר בֵּית
כב יהוה: וְלֹא־זָכַר יוֹאָשׁ הַמֶּלֶךְ הַחֶסֶד אֲשֶׁר עָשָׂה יְהוֹיָדָע אָבִיו עִמּוֹ וַיַּהֲרֹג אֶת־

DISCUSSION

24:11 | **The donations:** When the chest was filled with the money contributed by those who came to the Temple, or by anyone who wished to donate to the House of God, the money was removed from the chest and accurately counted by two officials, one the representative of the king and the other representing the High Priest. This manner of collection was significant, as it symbolized the notion that the Temple is not the exclusive domain of the king; rather, it is an enterprise in which all Israel are partners.

he died, he, Zekharya, **said: May the Lord see** this wicked act, **and seek retribution** for my blood. May God punish my murderers.
23 **It was at the turn of the year,** when the year had completed a full cycle, a year later, that **the forces of Aram rose against him,** Yo'ash, and they **came to Judah and Jerusalem.** The Aramean forces apparently bypassed the Kingdom of Israel and, in an unusual maneuver, they infiltrated Judah in a looting campaign. **And** they **destroyed all the princes of the people from among the people,**[155] or alternatively, they destroyed them from being a people, from functioning as an army,[156] or they also destroyed some of the people.[157] **And all their spoils they sent to the king, to Damascus,** their capital city.[158]
24 **For** although **the army of Aram came with** only **few men,** they enjoyed the element of surprise, and Yo'ash was incapable of defending himself; **and the Lord delivered a very great force,** or success, **into their hand, because they,** the people of Judah, **had forsaken the Lord, God of their fathers. And to Yo'ash they,** the Arameans, **administered punishment.** They mistreated the king, but did not kill him.
25 **When they,** the Arameans, **departed from him, when they left him in great suffering** after their mistreatment, **his** own **servants** arose and **conspired against him** in vengeance **for the blood of the sons of Yehoyada the priest; and they killed him on his bed,** when he was helpless, injured, and in pain, **and he died.** The mention of the sons of Yehoyada in the plural is possibly an indication that the king killed not only the prophet Zekharya himself but also Yehoyada's other sons, who presumably supported their brother.[159] **They buried him in the City of David, but they did not bury him in the graves of the** other **kings,** because of his conduct, and perhaps also because he died in a demeaning manner after being routed on the battlefield.
26 **These are the** two **conspirators against him: Zavad son of Shimat the Amonitess, and Yehozavad son of Shimrit the Moavitess.** Both of the chief conspirators were ministers or men of other high office in the royal court (see 25:3).
27 **His,** Yo'ash's, **sons, and the abundance of talk about him,** the many prophecies stated in his regard; alternatively, much will be stated about him; **and the reestablishment of the House of God, behold, they,** all these matters, **are written in the account of the book of the kings.** The reference is not to a book of chronicles of the kings of Judah and Israel, but an addendum to, or commentary on, the book of Kings, in which everything was detailed.[160] **Amatzyahu his son reigned in his,** Yo'ash's, **stead.** The killing of Yo'ash was not a revolt against the government, but a local action directed against that specific king due to his ingratitude vis-à-vis Yehoyada the High Priest. Since the people wanted the royal dynasty of David to continue, Yo'ash's son Amatzyahu was crowned in his place.

The Chronicles of King Amatzyahu

II CHRONICLES 25:1–28

Like that of his father, Amatzyahu's conduct worsens over the course of his reign. After defeating Edom, Amatzyahu adopts their idols and worships them. From this point, the kingdom and the status of the king steadily decline, and his rule ends in revolt. The rebellion is probably a reaction to the events of Amatzyahu's reign described here, although there may also have been unspecified personal scores to settle.

25 1 **Amatzyahu was twenty-five years old when he became king, and he reigned twenty-nine years in Jerusalem. His mother's name was Yeho'adan from Jerusalem.**
2 **He did what is right in the eyes of the Lord, but not wholeheartedly.** Although he basically acted properly, he did not seek to go beyond the standard parameters of the kings of Judah, and the spiritual problems of the kingdom remained unresolved.
3 Amatzyahu became king after his father's death at the hands of rebels, which did not establish the new monarch in a clear, stable situation. The deeds of those responsible for the assassination were known to all, but the perpetrators were not immediately punished, due to their prominent positions. **It was when the kingdom was firmly in his control,** when Amatzyahu was confident in the viability of his reign, that **he killed** those of **his servants who had smitten his father the king,** Yo'ash.
4 **But he did not put their children to death,** despite the fact that it was accepted practice to take vengeance upon the entire family of the perpetrators in those situations, **as it is written in the Torah, in the scroll of Moses, that the Lord commanded, saying: Fathers shall not die for** the deeds of **sons, and sons shall not die for fathers, as each shall die for his** own **sin.**[161]
5 **Amatzyahu gathered Judah, and he positioned them in accordance with their patrilineal houses,** their families, **by the commanders of thousands and commanders of hundreds, for all Judah and Benjamin; and he counted them from twenty years old and above, and found them to be three hundred thousand chosen men, fit for military service, handlers of spear and** large **shield.** This is a far smaller army than those at the disposal of his predecessors (see 13:3, 14:7, 17:14–18).
6 Since he thought that he did not have enough warriors, **he hired from Israel,** which was a much larger kingdom, **one hundred thousand mighty warriors for one hundred talents of silver.**

כג בְּנ֖וֹ וּכְמוֹת֣וֹ אָמַ֑ר יֵ֥רֶא יְהוָ֖ה וְיִדְרֹֽשׁ׃ וַיְהִ֣י ׀ לִתְקוּפַ֣ת הַשָּׁנָ֗ה עָלָ֣ה
עָלָיו֮ חֵ֣יל אֲרָם֒ וַיָּבֹ֙אוּ֙ אֶל־יְהוּדָ֣ה וִירֽוּשָׁלִַ֔ם וַיַּשְׁחִ֛יתוּ אֶת־כָּל־שָׂרֵ֥י הָעָ֖ם מֵעָ֑ם
כד וְכָל־שְׁלָלָ֥ם שִׁלְּח֖וּ לְמֶ֥לֶךְ דַּרְמָֽשֶׂק׃ כִּ֡י בְמִצְעַר֩ אֲנָשִׁ֨ים בָּ֜אוּ ׀ חֵ֣יל אֲרָ֗ם וַֽיהוָ֞ה
נָתַ֨ן בְּיָדָ֤ם חַ֙יִל֙ לָרֹ֣ב מְאֹ֔ד כִּ֣י עָֽזְב֔וּ אֶת־יְהוָ֖ה אֱלֹהֵ֣י אֲבוֹתֵיהֶ֑ם וְאֶת־יוֹאָ֖שׁ עָשׂ֥וּ
כה שְׁפָטִֽים׃ וּבְלֶכְתָּ֣ם מִמֶּ֗נּוּ כִּֽי־עָזְב֣וּ אֹתוֹ֮ בְּמַחֲלֻיִ֣ים רַבִּים֒ הִתְקַשְּׁר֙וּ עָלָ֣יו עֲבָדָ֔יו
בִּדְמֵי֙ בְּנֵ֣י יְהוֹיָדָ֣ע הַכֹּהֵ֔ן וַיַּֽהַרְגֻ֥הוּ עַל־מִטָּת֖וֹ וַיָּמֹ֑ת וַֽיִּקְבְּרֻ֙הוּ֙ בְּעִ֣יר דָּוִ֔יד וְלֹ֥א
כו קְבָרֻ֖הוּ בְּקִבְר֥וֹת הַמְּלָכִֽים׃ וְאֵ֖לֶּה הַמִּתְקַשְּׁרִ֣ים עָלָ֑יו זָבָ֗ד בֶּן־שִׁמְעָת֙ הָֽעַמּוֹנִ֔ית
כז וִיה֣וֹזָבָ֔ד בֶּן־שִׁמְרִ֖ית הַמּוֹאָבִֽית׃ וּבָנָ֞יו וְרֹ֤ב הַמַּשָּׂא֙ עָלָ֔יו וִיסוֹד֙ בֵּ֣ית הָאֱלֹהִ֔ים יִרֶב
הִנָּ֣ם כְּתוּבִ֔ים עַל־מִדְרַ֖שׁ סֵ֣פֶר הַמְּלָכִ֑ים וַיִּמְלֹ֛ךְ אֲמַצְיָ֥הוּ בְנ֖וֹ תַּחְתָּֽיו׃
א בֶּן־עֶשְׂרִ֨ים וְחָמֵ֤שׁ שָׁנָה֙ מָלַ֣ךְ אֲמַצְיָ֔הוּ וְעֶשְׂרִ֣ים וָתֵ֗שַׁע שָׁנָ֔ה מָלַ֖ךְ בִּירוּשָׁלִָ֑ם וְשֵׁ֣ם ה
ב ג אִמּ֔וֹ יְהוֹעַדָּ֖ן מִירוּשָׁלָֽיִם׃ וַיַּ֥עַשׂ הַיָּשָׁ֖ר בְּעֵינֵ֣י יְהוָ֑ה רַ֕ק לֹ֖א בְּלֵבָ֥ב שָׁלֵֽם׃ וַיְהִ֕י
ד כַּאֲשֶׁ֛ר חָזְקָ֥ה הַמַּמְלָכָ֖ה עָלָ֑יו וַֽיַּהֲרֹג֙ אֶת־עֲבָדָ֔יו הַמַּכִּ֖ים אֶת־הַמֶּ֥לֶךְ אָבִֽיו׃ וְאֶת־
בְּנֵיהֶ֖ם לֹ֣א הֵמִ֑ית כִּ֣י כַכָּת֣וּב בַּתּוֹרָ֡ה בְּסֵ֣פֶר מֹשֶׁה֩ אֲשֶׁר־צִוָּ֨ה יְהוָ֜ה לֵאמֹ֗ר לֹא־
יָמ֨וּתוּ אָב֜וֹת עַל־בָּנִ֗ים וּבָנִים֙ לֹא־יָמ֣וּתוּ עַל־אָב֔וֹת כִּ֛י אִ֥ישׁ בְּחֶטְא֖וֹ
ה יָמֽוּתוּ׃ וַיִּקְבֹּ֤ץ אֲמַצְיָ֙הוּ֙ אֶת־יְהוּדָ֔ה וַיַּעֲמִידֵ֣ם לְבֵית־אָב֗וֹת לְשָׂרֵ֤י
הָאֲלָפִים֙ וּלְשָׂרֵ֣י הַמֵּא֔וֹת לְכָל־יְהוּדָ֖ה וּבִנְיָמִ֑ן וַֽיִּפְקְדֵ֗ם לְמִבֶּ֨ן עֶשְׂרִ֤ים שָׁנָה֙ וָמַ֔עְלָה
ו וַֽיִּמְצָאֵ֗ם שְׁלֹשׁ־מֵא֨וֹת אֶ֜לֶף בָּח֗וּר יוֹצֵ֣א צָבָ֔א אֹחֵ֖ז רֹ֥מַח וְצִנָּֽה׃ וַיִּשְׂכֹּ֕ר מִיִּשְׂרָאֵ֔ל

7 But an unnamed **man of God came to him, saying: King, let**
the army of Israel not go with you to war, **as the Lord is not**
going **with Israel; all the children of Ephraim** should not join
forces with you. God will not be with them, as they have strayed
from His path. According to a tradition of the Sages, this prophet was Amotz, the brother of King Amatzyahu and the father of
the prophet Isaiah.[162]
8 **For even if you do go** with them and **engage mightily in war,**
God will thwart you before the enemy, as God has power to
help and to thwart.[163]
9 **Amatzyahu said to the man of God: But what is to be done**
with the hundred talents that I gave to the troops of Israel?
I have already paid for these troops. **The man of God said: The**
Lord is capable of giving you more than this. God can restore this money to you, and much more besides.
10 The king listened to the prophet: **Amatzyahu separated them,**
the troops that had come to him from Ephraim, and sent
them **to go** back **to their place.** They were insulted; **their**
wrath was greatly enflamed against Judah, who had dismissed them without allowing them to participate in battle,
and they returned to their place with enflamed wrath.
11 **Amatzyahu took courage, and led his people** on an invasion
into Edom, **and went to the Valley of Salt,**[164] **and smote ten**
thousand of the children of Se'ir, the Edomites. Edom, which
had never been a large nation, was always somewhat subject to
the rule of Judah. Nevertheless, it periodically achieved autonomy, and sometimes even called its leaders kings. Apart from
the need to restrain this neighboring country, the Kingdom of
Judah also had a political and economic interest at stake, since
the Edomites controlled the route to the port of Eilat.
12 **The children of Judah**
captured ten thousand warriors **alive,** as captives, **and**
brought them to the top of
the rock,[B] perhaps Petra, although it was very far away;
and they **cast them from**
the top of the rock, and all
of them were broken. They executed them by throwing them
off the top of the rock.

"Top of the rock"

13 But at the same time,[165] **the members of the troops** of Ephraim,
who were of sufficient numbers to be called an army in their
own right, those **that Amatzyahu had sent back from going**
with him to war, raided in the cities of Judah, from the border with **Samaria to Beit Horon.** They went on a wild spree
of vengeance against the cities of Judah for the insult they had
suffered. **And** they **smote three thousand of them,** the inhabitants of Judah, **and plundered much spoils.**
14 **It was after Amatzyahu came from smiting the Edomites**
that he brought the gods of the children of Se'ir with him to
Judah, as he was attracted to their rituals, **and** he **established**
them as his gods; he would prostrate himself before them
and burn offerings of incense **to them,** as a gesture of brother-
hood or due to a certain closeness he felt toward them.
15 **The wrath of the Lord was enflamed against Amatzyahu,**
and He sent an unidentified **prophet to him, who said to**
him: Why did you seek after the gods of the people that did
not deliver their own people from your hand? Not only did
you turn to idolatry, but you adopted those very same idols that
you had just defeated in war.
16 **It was while** the prophet was **speaking to him that he,** the
king, **said to him: Did we appoint you the king's counselor?**
How dare you tell me what to do and what not to do? **Stop**
this impudence; **why should they,** my counselors, have cause
to **smite you? The prophet stopped** speaking, **and said** only
this: **I know that God has counseled to destroy you because**
you did this and did not heed my counsel. This path you have
chosen will not lead you to glory. Amatzyahu appears to have
been emotionally unstable. He was prone to outbreaks of anger,
and may have suffered from extreme mood swings. Sometimes
he listened to everything a prophet told him, despite the potentially dangerous ramifications of that course of action, whereas
on other occasions he acted as a grand, triumphant king and
refused to accept any criticism.
17 **Amatzyahu king of Judah consulted, and sent to Yo'ash, son**
of Yeho'ahaz, son of Yehu, king of Israel, saying: Come, let
us meet one another[D] in battle.

DISCUSSION

25:17 | **Come, let us meet one another:** In those days, it was customary to engage in warfare in a ceremonial form, at a time and place that had been determined in advance. Perhaps on this occasion the king's declaration was motivated by the actions of the forces of the Kingdom of Israel. Even if the attack of the soldiers of Israel on Judah was not on the order of their king, Amatzyahu had legitimate claims against the king of Israel, as he did nothing to stop the soldiers he sent. King Amatzyahu had hired soldiers from the king of Israel, and paid their wages. While it may have been undignified of him to have canceled their participation, there is no justification for their behavior (see *Metzudat David*; Malbim). Furthermore, the Kingdom of Judah considered the Kingdom of Israel an illegal state that had been founded by rebellion. As a consequence of his victory over the Edomites, Amatzyahu had grown overconfident and challenged the king of Israel.

ז מֵאָה אֶלֶף גִּבּוֹר חָיִל בְּמֵאָה כִכַּר־כָּסֶף׃ וְאִישׁ הָאֱלֹהִים בָּא אֵלָיו לֵאמֹר הַמֶּלֶךְ
ח אַל־יָבוֹא עִמְּךָ צְבָא יִשְׂרָאֵל כִּי אֵין יהוה עִם־יִשְׂרָאֵל כֹּל בְּנֵי אֶפְרָיִם׃ כִּי אִם־
בֹּא אַתָּה עֲשֵׂה חֲזַק לַמִּלְחָמָה יַכְשִׁילְךָ הָאֱלֹהִים לִפְנֵי אוֹיֵב כִּי יֶשׁ־כֹּחַ בֵּאלֹהִים
ט לַעְזוֹר וּלְהַכְשִׁיל׃ וַיֹּאמֶר אֲמַצְיָהוּ לְאִישׁ הָאֱלֹהִים וּמַה־לַּעֲשׂוֹת לִמְאַת הַכִּכָּר
אֲשֶׁר נָתַתִּי לִגְדוּד יִשְׂרָאֵל וַיֹּאמֶר אִישׁ הָאֱלֹהִים יֵשׁ לַיהוה לָתֶת לְךָ הַרְבֵּה
י מִזֶּה׃ וַיַּבְדִּילֵם אֲמַצְיָהוּ לְהַגְּדוּד אֲשֶׁר־בָּא אֵלָיו מֵאֶפְרַיִם לָלֶכֶת לִמְקוֹמָם וַיִּחַר
יא אַפָּם מְאֹד בִּיהוּדָה וַיָּשׁוּבוּ לִמְקוֹמָם בָּחֳרִי־אָף׃ וַאֲמַצְיָהוּ הִתְחַזַּק
יב וַיִּנְהַג אֶת־עַמּוֹ וַיֵּלֶךְ גֵּיא הַמֶּלַח וַיַּךְ אֶת־בְּנֵי־שֵׂעִיר עֲשֶׂרֶת אֲלָפִים׃ וַעֲשֶׂרֶת
אֲלָפִים חַיִּים שָׁבוּ בְּנֵי יְהוּדָה וַיְבִיאוּם לְרֹאשׁ הַסָּלַע וַיַּשְׁלִיכוּם מֵרֹאשׁ הַסֶּלַע
יג וְכֻלָּם נִבְקָעוּ׃ וּבְנֵי הַגְּדוּד אֲשֶׁר הֵשִׁיב אֲמַצְיָהוּ מִלֶּכֶת עִמּוֹ לַמִּלְחָמָה
וַיִּפְשְׁטוּ בְּעָרֵי יְהוּדָה מִשֹּׁמְרוֹן וְעַד־בֵּית חוֹרוֹן וַיַּכּוּ מֵהֶם שְׁלֹשֶׁת אֲלָפִים וַיָּבֹזּוּ
יד בִּזָּה רַבָּה׃ וַיְהִי אַחֲרֵי בוֹא אֲמַצְיָהוּ מֵהַכּוֹת אֶת־אֲדוֹמִים וַיָּבֵא אֶת־
טו אֱלֹהֵי בְּנֵי שֵׂעִיר וַיַּעֲמִידֵם לוֹ לֵאלֹהִים וְלִפְנֵיהֶם יִשְׁתַּחֲוֶה וְלָהֶם יְקַטֵּר׃ וַיִּחַר־אַף
יהוה בַּאֲמַצְיָהוּ וַיִּשְׁלַח אֵלָיו נָבִיא וַיֹּאמֶר לוֹ לָמָּה דָרַשְׁתָּ אֶת־אֱלֹהֵי הָעָם אֲשֶׁר
טז לֹא־הִצִּילוּ אֶת־עַמָּם מִיָּדֶךָ׃ וַיְהִי ׀ בְּדַבְּרוֹ אֵלָיו וַיֹּאמֶר לוֹ הַלְיוֹעֵץ לַמֶּלֶךְ נְתַנּוּךָ
חֲדַל־לְךָ לָמָּה יַכּוּךָ וַיֶּחְדַּל הַנָּבִיא וַיֹּאמֶר יָדַעְתִּי כִּי־יָעַץ אֱלֹהִים לְהַשְׁחִיתֶךָ
יז כִּי־עָשִׂיתָ זֹּאת וְלֹא שָׁמַעְתָּ לַעֲצָתִי׃ וַיִּוָּעַץ אֲמַצְיָהוּ מֶלֶךְ יְהוּדָה
וַיִּשְׁלַח אֶל־יוֹאָשׁ בֶּן־יְהוֹאָחָז בֶּן־יֵהוּא מֶלֶךְ יִשְׂרָאֵל לֵאמֹר לְךָ נִתְרָאֶה פָנִים׃

BACKGROUND

25:12 | **Top of the rock:** It is unclear from the verses whether this is the name of a place or a geographical description of a cliff near the Valley of Salt. The Septuagint translation identifies it with Petra, but that is 50 km south of this valley. Consequently, some researchers claim that it is es-Sela, a rocky fortress with natural defenses, approximately 10 km southwest of present-day Tafileh and about 4 km northwest of present-day Buseirah. However, there are other sites in the Edomite Mountains, also situated on lone peaks, which also fit this description. In all of these spots, archaeological findings have been unearthed which correspond with the representation of Edom in the prophecies of Jeremiah (49:16), and Obadiah (verses 3–4), as a nation that dwells high in the clefts of the rocks.

18 **Yo'ash king of Israel sent** a reply **to Amatzyahu king of Judah, saying,** by means of a parable: **The** small **thistle**[B] **that is in the Lebanon sent to the cedar**[166] **that is in the Lebanon, saying:** Since we are both forms of vegetation in Lebanon, **give your daughter as** a **wife to my son.** In the meantime, **the wild beast that was in the Lebanon passed by and trampled the thistle.** The flimsy thistle should not have been so presumptuous.

Thistle

Cedar of Lebanon

19 To prevent Amatzyahu misunderstanding the meaning of his
parable, Yo'ash explains exactly what he meant: **You said** to
yourself, **behold, you have smitten Edom,** although it is not a
large country; **and** already **your heart has raised you to seek
glory?** After that one minor victory, you wish to declare war
upon me, imagining us as equals. **Sit now at home; why provoke harm? You will fall, you and Judah with you.** It would
be a shame for you and your men to suffer defeat.
20 **But Amatzyahu did not heed** this good advice, **as it,** his obstinacy, **was** decreed **from God, in order to deliver them,** the
men of Judah, **into** the **hand** of their enemies, **because they
had sought the gods of Edom.**
21 **Yo'ash king of Israel went up** to war against Judah, **and he and
Amatzyahu king of Judah met one another,** they engaged in
battle, **in Beit Shemesh, which is in Judah.**[B]
22 **Judah was routed before Israel, and each man fled to his
tent.** The Kingdom of Israel was larger and more experienced in
battle than its southern neighbor, as the borders of the relatively
small Kingdom of Judah were generally quiet. Consequently,
Amatzyahu had been unlikely to win.
23 **Yo'ash king of Israel seized Amatzyahu king of Judah, son of
Yo'ash, son of Yeho'ahaz in Beit Shemesh, and** he did not kill
him, but **brought him to Jerusalem, and breached the wall
of Jerusalem from the Gate of Ephraim**[B] **to the Corner Gate,
four hundred cubits.** This large breach was a display of the
power of the king of Israel, in order to deter Judah from similar
campaigns in the future.
24 He left **with all the gold and silver** as spoils, **and all the vessels that were found in the House of God with Oved Edom,**
who was in charge of guarding them,[167] **and the treasuries of
the king's house, and the hostages.** It was the practice of powerful kings to kidnap children from other nations and tribes, in

Wall, Tel Beit Shemesh, late second millennium BCE

order to ensure their parents' compliance, as the parents knew
that if they took any action against the king, their child would
be harmed.[168] Therefore, these hostages were not merely economic assets, but political resources as well. **He,** the king of
Israel, **returned to Samaria,** after his victory in the war.
25 **Amatzyahu son of Yo'ash, king of Judah, lived for** an additional **fifteen years after the death of Yo'ash son of Yeho'ahaz,
king of Israel.**
26 **The rest of the early** deeds, from when he followed in the path
of God, **and late deeds of Amatzyahu,** his deterioration when
he abandoned God, became haughty, and brought disasters
upon his people, **behold, aren't they written in the book of
the kings of Judah and Israel?**
27 **From the time that Amatzyahu strayed from after the Lord,**
not only did he lose his connection to God, but he lost the support of the people as well, and **they conspired against him,** organizing a revolt **in Jerusalem. He fled to Lakhish,** a fortified city of the kings of Judah, **and they,** the rebels, who were sufficiently powerful, **sent after him to Lakhish, and put him to death there.** In the Kingdom of Israel there were almost no dynasties that lasted more than a few generations. In contrast, the royal dynasty in Judah was relatively stable. These two kings of Judah, Yo'ash and Amatzyahu, who were killed by rebels, are the exception, and even in their cases, the kingdom was not usurped by the rebels but was passed to their sons.

Tel Lakhish, remains of fortifications, period of Judean monarchy

28 **They bore him on horses** from Lakhish **and buried him with
his fathers in the city of Judah,** Jerusalem.[169]

יח וַיִּשְׁלַח יוֹאָשׁ מֶלֶךְ־יִשְׂרָאֵל אֶל־אֲמַצְיָהוּ מֶלֶךְ־יְהוּדָה לֵאמֹר הַחוֹחַ אֲשֶׁר בַּלְּבָנוֹן
שָׁלַח אֶל־הָאֶרֶז אֲשֶׁר בַּלְּבָנוֹן לֵאמֹר תְּנָה־אֶת־בִּתְּךָ לִבְנִי לְאִשָּׁה וַתַּעֲבֹר חַיַּת
יט הַשָּׂדֶה אֲשֶׁר בַּלְּבָנוֹן וַתִּרְמֹס אֶת־הַחוֹחַ׃ אָמַרְתָּ הִנֵּה הִכִּיתָ אֶת־אֱדוֹם וּנְשָׂאֲךָ
לִבְּךָ לְהַכְבִּיד עַתָּה שְׁבָה בְּבֵיתֶךָ לָמָּה תִתְגָּרֶה בְּרָעָה וְנָפַלְתָּ אַתָּה וִיהוּדָה
כ עִמָּךְ׃ וְלֹא־שָׁמַע אֲמַצְיָהוּ כִּי מֵהָאֱלֹהִים הִיא לְמַעַן תִּתָּם בְּיָד כִּי דָרְשׁוּ אֵת
כא אֱלֹהֵי אֱדוֹם׃ וַיַּעַל יוֹאָשׁ מֶלֶךְ־יִשְׂרָאֵל וַיִּתְרָאוּ פָנִים הוּא וַאֲמַצְיָהוּ מֶלֶךְ־יְהוּדָה
כב כג בְּבֵית שֶׁמֶשׁ אֲשֶׁר לִיהוּדָה׃ וַיִּנָּגֶף יְהוּדָה לִפְנֵי יִשְׂרָאֵל וַיָּנֻסוּ אִישׁ לְאֹהָלָיו׃ וְאֵת
אֲמַצְיָהוּ מֶלֶךְ־יְהוּדָה בֶּן־יוֹאָשׁ בֶּן־יְהוֹאָחָז תָּפַשׂ יוֹאָשׁ מֶלֶךְ־יִשְׂרָאֵל בְּבֵית
שֶׁמֶשׁ וַיְבִיאֵהוּ יְרוּשָׁלִַם וַיִּפְרֹץ בְּחוֹמַת יְרוּשָׁלִַם מִשַּׁעַר אֶפְרַיִם עַד־שַׁעַר הַפּוֹנֶה
כד אַרְבַּע מֵאוֹת אַמָּה׃ וְכָל־הַזָּהָב וְהַכֶּסֶף וְאֵת כָּל־הַכֵּלִים הַנִּמְצְאִים בְּבֵית־
הָאֱלֹהִים עִם־עֹבֵד אֱדוֹם וְאֶת־אוֹצְרוֹת בֵּית הַמֶּלֶךְ וְאֵת בְּנֵי הַתַּעֲרֻבוֹת וַיָּשָׁב
כה שֹׁמְרוֹן׃ וַיְחִי אֲמַצְיָהוּ בֶן־יוֹאָשׁ מֶלֶךְ יְהוּדָה אַחֲרֵי מוֹת יוֹאָשׁ בֶּן־
כו יְהוֹאָחָז מֶלֶךְ יִשְׂרָאֵל חֲמֵשׁ עֶשְׂרֵה שָׁנָה׃ וְיֶתֶר דִּבְרֵי אֲמַצְיָהוּ הָרִאשֹׁנִים
כז וְהָאַחֲרוֹנִים הֲלֹא הִנָּם כְּתוּבִים עַל־סֵפֶר מַלְכֵי יְהוּדָה וְיִשְׂרָאֵל׃ וּמֵעֵת אֲשֶׁר־סָר
אֲמַצְיָהוּ מֵאַחֲרֵי יְהוָה וַיִּקְשְׁרוּ עָלָיו קֶשֶׁר בִּירוּשָׁלִַם וַיָּנָס לָכִישָׁה וַיִּשְׁלְחוּ אַחֲרָיו
כח לָכִישָׁה וַיְמִיתֻהוּ שָׁם׃ וַיִּשָּׂאֻהוּ עַל־הַסּוּסִים וַיִּקְבְּרוּ אֹתוֹ עִם־אֲבֹתָיו בְּעִיר יְהוּדָה׃

BACKGROUND

25:18 | **Thistle [*ḥo'aḥ*]:** Described in the Bible as a small, thorny, wild plant, generally despised and easily trampled (see Song of Songs 2:2; Job 31:40). The *ḥo'aḥ* is identified as the spotted golden thistle, *Scolymus maculatus*, a spiny plant with yellow flowers that grows mainly alongside fallow fields. It can reach up to 1.3 m in height.

25:21 | **Beit Shemesh, which is in Judah:** It can be inferred from the fact that the battle was undertaken in the Judean foothills, that those parts of this region that had been conquered by the Arameans in the days of Yo'ash king of Judah (see II Kings 12; II Chronicles 24:23) came under the control of the Kingdom of Israel with the victory of Yo'ash king of Israel over Aram (II Kings 13:23). For more information on Beit Shemesh, see I Chronicles 6:44.

25:23 | **And breached the wall of Jerusalem from the Gate of Ephraim:** The Gate of Ephraim was located in the northern section of the city wall, which was the weak point of Jerusalem throughout the course of history. The breaching of the city without its conquest was an unusual move, indicative of its submission and that it would no longer serve as a stronghold and fortress. Amatzyahu's son, King Uziyahu, would use this military tactic in his war against the Philistine cities of Gat, Yavne, and Ashdod (26:6).

The Chronicles of King Uziyahu

II CHRONICLES 26:1–23

Uziyahu is an accomplished and successful king who brings the kingdom to renewed political and economic heights, and becomes renowned throughout the entire region. Ultimately, his great successes make him arrogant, and he is punished for this in that he contracts leprosy, which prevents him from ruling and forces him to be an outcast until the end of his life.

26 1 **All the people of Judah took Uziyahu,**[D] **who was sixteen years old, and crowned him king instead of his father Amatzyahu.**

2 **He built Eilot,** Eilat, the southern port city (see commentary on 8:17), **and restored it to Judah, after the king,** Amatzyahu, **lay with his fathers.**

3 **Uziyahu was sixteen years old when he became king, and he reigned fifty-two years in Jerusalem.** His reign was one of the longest in the history of the Kingdom of Judah; only Menashe reigned for a longer period, fifty-five years (see 33:1). Uziyahu was able to accomplish much during his lengthy reign. **His mother's name was Yekholya of Jerusalem.**

4 **He did what is right in the eyes of the Lord, in accordance with everything that his father Amatzyahu had done** in the first years of his reign.[170]

5 **He would** frequently[171] **seek God in the days of Zekharyahu,** a prophet or a holy man **who understood the visions of God;** alternatively, Zekharyahu understood what God wanted from people. **During the days that he,** Uziyahu, **sought the Lord** and acted appropriately, **God caused him to succeed.**

6 **He,** Uziyahu, **went out and waged war against the Philistines and breached the wall of Gat,**[172] **the wall of Yavne,**[B] **and the wall of Ashdod,**[B] all Philistine cities. **He built cities in** the area of **Ashdod, and among the Philistines.**[B]

Fortifications and walls, Tel Tzafit, believed to be the biblical Gat, early first millennium BCE

7 **God helped him** to victory **against the Philistines,** who were no longer a large and powerful people, **against the Arabians who lived in Gur Baal,**[B] **and** also **the Meunites** (see commentary on 20:1), a small nation. In Uziyahu's attempts to strengthen the Judean kingdom, he waged war against surrounding enemies, such as the Philistines to the east, and the Arabians and Meunites, in other directions.

8 **The Amonites gave tribute to Uziyahu,** signifying their submission and loyalty.[173] The Amonites' submission to Uziyahu without war is indicative of the strength of the Kingdom of Judah at that time. **And his renown spread to the approach to Egypt, as he grew exceedingly strong.** Even the Egyptians acknowledged the political strength of the Kingdom of Judah under Uziyahu. Although there remained nomadic tribes roaming the region between Egypt and the Land of Israel, as well as the Edomites living in that area, they were not a significant threat to Uziyahu's power.

9 **Uziyahu built towers** for the walls **in Jerusalem, at the Corner Gate, and at the Valley Gate, and at the angle** of the wall, **and he fortified them.**

10 **He built towers in the wilderness and hewed many cisterns, for he had much livestock in the foothills and in the plain.**[B] **He** also **had farmers and viticulturists in the mountains and on the fertile lands,** terrain of fields and vineyards, as he sought to promote agriculture in his kingdom **as he was a lover of the soil.**

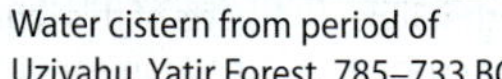

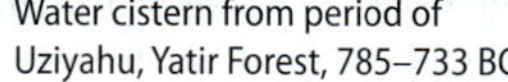

Water cistern from period of Uziyahu, Yatir Forest, 785–733 BCE

Viticulturists

11 **Uziyahu had a force of warriors, fit for military service,**

DISCUSSION

26:1 | **Uziyahu:** Elsewhere this king is called Uziya (e.g., II Kings 15:13, 30; Hosea 1:1; Amos 1:1), and Azarya (e.g., II Kings 14:21, 15:1, 8). He may have been called Azarya because God helped him [*azar*] in his many accomplishments (see verses 5, 7, 15). There are other instances of kings who were given additional names that signified various events in their lives (see commentary on 19:5).

א וַיִּקְחוּ כָּל־עַם יְהוּדָה אֶת־עֻזִּיָּהוּ וְהוּא בֶּן־שֵׁשׁ עֶשְׂרֵה שָׁנָה וַיַּמְלִיכוּ אֹתוֹ תַּחַת
ב אָבִיו אֲמַצְיָהוּ׃ הוּא בָּנָה אֶת־אֵילוֹת וַיְשִׁיבֶהָ לִיהוּדָה אַחֲרֵי שְׁכַב־הַמֶּלֶךְ עִם־ כא
אֲבֹתָיו׃
ג בֶּן־שֵׁשׁ עֶשְׂרֵה שָׁנָה עֻזִּיָּהוּ בְמָלְכוֹ וַחֲמִשִּׁים וּשְׁתַּיִם שָׁנָה מָלַךְ בִּירוּשָׁלִָם וְשֵׁם
ד אִמּוֹ יכיליה מִן־יְרוּשָׁלִָם׃ וַיַּעַשׂ הַיָּשָׁר בְּעֵינֵי יְהוָה כְּכֹל אֲשֶׁר־עָשָׂה אֲמַצְיָהוּ יְכָלְיָה
ה אָבִיו׃ וַיְהִי לִדְרֹשׁ אֱלֹהִים בִּימֵי זְכַרְיָהוּ הַמֵּבִין בִּרְאֹת הָאֱלֹהִים וּבִימֵי דָּרְשׁוֹ
ו אֶת־יְהוָה הִצְלִיחוֹ הָאֱלֹהִים׃ וַיֵּצֵא וַיִּלָּחֶם בַּפְּלִשְׁתִּים וַיִּפְרֹץ אֶת־חוֹמַת גַּת וְאֵת
ז חוֹמַת יַבְנֶה וְאֵת חוֹמַת אַשְׁדּוֹד וַיִּבְנֶה עָרִים בְּאַשְׁדּוֹד וּבַפְּלִשְׁתִּים׃ וַיַּעְזְרֵהוּ
ח הָאֱלֹהִים עַל־פְּלִשְׁתִּים וְעַל־הערביים הַיֹּשְׁבִים בְּגוּר־בָּעַל וְהַמְּעוּנִים׃ וַיִּתְּנוּ הָעַרְבִים
הָעַמּוֹנִים מִנְחָה לְעֻזִּיָּהוּ וַיֵּלֶךְ שְׁמוֹ עַד־לְבוֹא מִצְרַיִם כִּי הֶחֱזִיק עַד־לְמָעְלָה׃
ט וַיִּבֶן עֻזִּיָּהוּ מִגְדָּלִים בִּירוּשָׁלִַם עַל־שַׁעַר הַפִּנָּה וְעַל־שַׁעַר הַגַּיְא וְעַל־הַמִּקְצוֹעַ
י וַיְחַזְּקֵם׃ וַיִּבֶן מִגְדָּלִים בַּמִּדְבָּר וַיַּחְצֹב בֹּרוֹת רַבִּים כִּי מִקְנֶה־רַּב הָיָה לוֹ וּבַשְּׁפֵלָה
יא וּבַמִּישׁוֹר אִכָּרִים וְכֹרְמִים בֶּהָרִים וּבַכַּרְמֶל כִּי־אֹהֵב אֲדָמָה הָיָה׃ וַיְהִי
לְעֻזִּיָּהוּ חַיִל עֹשֵׂה מִלְחָמָה יוֹצְאֵי צָבָא לִגְדוּד בְּמִסְפַּר פְּקֻדָּתָם בְּיַד יעואל יְעִיאֵל

BACKGROUND

26:6 | **Yavne:** A border city in the northwest region of the territory of the tribe of Judah (Joshua 15:11). The city was situated on the ancient Via Maris and has been identified as Tel Yavne, southeast of the modern-day town of Yavne.

Ashdod: One of the main Philistine cities, located on the ancient Via Maris. As a port it was an economically and militarily significant city, and targeted by the Assyrians in their campaigns against Egypt. The biblical Ashdod was situated at Tel Ashdod, southeast of the modern-day city of Ashdod.

He built cities in Ashdod, and among the Philistines: Archaeological surveys attest to the extensive spread of settlement in the region of Philistia in that period, as is described in these verses.

26:7 | **Gur Baal:** The location of Gur Baal is unknown. One speculation is that it is Yagur, in the territory of the tribe of Judah (Joshua 15:21), whose location is also unknown, but was probably situated in the southeast of the territory of Judah.

26:10 | **The plain [*mishor*]:** A geographical term that generally refers to an area of flat terrain, but which also appears to be the name of a specific region east of the Jordan River, north of the Arnon Stream (known today as Wadi Mujib), between the cities of Divon and Heshbon. It is also called the land of the plain, the plain of Divon, and the plain of Medeva (see, e.g., Deuteronomy 3:10, 4:43; Joshua 13:9; Jeremiah 48:8).

mobilized **in troops, in accordance with the number of their tally,** numbered in accordance with their orders and divisions, **at the hand of Ye'iel the scribe and Maaseyahu the official, under the hand of Hananyahu, one of the king's commanders.**

12 **The total number of the heads of the patrilineal houses, the mighty warriors,** the command staff, **was two thousand six hundred.**

13 **Under their hand,** their command, **was an armed force** which numbered **three hundred and seven thousand five hundred, wagers of war with the force of an army,** as their mission was **to help the king against the enemy.**

14 **Uziyahu prepared for them, for the entire army, shields, spears, helmets, mail, bows, and slingstones.** Uziyahu was an effective administrator. In contrast to Amatzyahu's somewhat haphazard approach, Uziyahu steadily and thoroughly improved the country in all areas: agriculture, infrastructure, security, and the provision of equipment and weapons to the army.

Pile of slingstones, Apollonia, Crusader period

Combat with spears and shields, from Stele of the Vultures, Mesopotamia, 2450 BCE

15 **He made in Jerusalem inventions, clever devices, to be on the towers and on the corners,**[B] **with which to shoot arrows and great stones.** These were war engines, similar to catapults. Alternatively, these were structures positioned on top of towers and on the corners of walls, from where arrows could be safely shot.[174] **His,** Uziyahu's, **renown spread far, for he was greatly helped** by all of his innovations, **until he became strong.** Although he ruled over a small country, he greatly upgraded his army and strongholds, with each step leading to further advancements.

16 It had been many years since there was a king in Judah who was as powerful and successful as Uziyahu. **But with his strengthening, his heart grew arrogant, until it became corrupt, and he trespassed against the Lord his God and came into the Sanctuary of the Lord to burn incense on the altar of incense.** Other nations in the region considered their kings holy, and therefore they would be allowed to bring offerings themselves from time to time. This was not the Judean practice; only priests were permitted to burn incense in the Temple, but as Uziyahu became arrogant from all his successes as a major player on the international scene, he decided that he would burn incense himself.

17 **Azaryahu the** High **Priest came after him, and with him** were **eighty priests of the Lord, capable men,** quick and brave.

18 **They stood against Uziyahu the king and said to him: It is not for you, Uziyahu, to burn incense to the Lord; rather, it is for the priests, sons of Aaron, who are sanctified to burn incense. Depart from the Temple, as you have trespassed, and it is not honorable for you from the Lord God.**

19 It can be assumed that Uziyahu had come with a small entourage of his own, but he was followed by a large group of priests who sought to expel him. **Uziyahu was furious, and he** already **had a censer in his hand to burn incense. While he was furious with the priests, leprosy** suddenly **erupted on his forehead before the priests in the House of the Lord,** as he stood **adjacent to the altar of incense.**

20 **Azaryahu the head priest and all the priests turned to him, and behold, he was leprous on his forehead.** Leprosy was considered a disease that necessitated the isolation of the afflicted individual from society, **and** therefore **they rushed him from there; and he too hastened to leave, because** he sensed that **the Lord had afflicted him.**

21 **King Uziyahu was a leper to the day of his death. He lived in the isolation house,**[B] a quarantined area outside the city where lepers were confined. He was still called King Uziyahu, because he had not been formally removed from power,[175] but in practice he no longer ruled the country. He lived **as a leper because he was excised from the House of the Lord. Yotam his son was** appointed **in charge of the king's house, governing the people of the land.** In effect, Yotam took over his father's reign.

22 **The rest of the early** deeds, which were judged favorably, **and the late deeds,** which were not, **of Uziyahu were written by Isaiah son of Amotz, the prophet.** Since the book of Isaiah mentions only that the prophet preached during the days of Uziyahu, and nothing of the king's own actions, this is evidently referring to a different book that did not survive.

יב הַסּוֹפֵר וּמַעֲשֵׂיָהוּ הַשּׁוֹטֵר עַל יַד־חֲנַנְיָהוּ מִשָּׂרֵי הַמֶּלֶךְ׃ כֹּל מִסְפַּר רָאשֵׁי הָאָבוֹת
יג לְגִבּוֹרֵי חָיִל אַלְפַּיִם וְשֵׁשׁ מֵאוֹת׃ וְעַל־יָדָם חֵיל צָבָא שְׁלֹשׁ מֵאוֹת אֶלֶף וְשִׁבְעַת
יד אֲלָפִים וַחֲמֵשׁ מֵאוֹת עוֹשֵׂי מִלְחָמָה בְּכֹחַ חָיִל לַעְזֹר לַמֶּלֶךְ עַל־הָאוֹיֵב׃ וַיָּכֶן
לָהֶם עֻזִּיָּהוּ לְכָל־הַצָּבָא מָגִנִּים וּרְמָחִים וְכוֹבָעִים וְשִׁרְיֹנוֹת וּקְשָׁתוֹת וּלְאַבְנֵי
טו קְלָעִים׃ וַיַּעַשׂ ׀ בִּירוּשָׁלַםִ חִשְּׁבֹנוֹת מַחֲשֶׁבֶת חוֹשֵׁב לִהְיוֹת עַל־הַמִּגְדָּלִים וְעַל־
הַפִּנּוֹת לִירוֹא בַּחִצִּים וּבָאֲבָנִים גְּדֹלוֹת וַיֵּצֵא שְׁמוֹ עַד־לְמֵרָחוֹק כִּי־הִפְלִיא
טז לְהֵעָזֵר עַד כִּי־חָזָק׃ וּכְחֶזְקָתוֹ גָּבַהּ לִבּוֹ עַד־לְהַשְׁחִית וַיִּמְעַל בַּיהוָה אֱלֹהָיו
יז וַיָּבֹא אֶל־הֵיכַל יְהוָה לְהַקְטִיר עַל־מִזְבַּח הַקְּטֹרֶת׃ וַיָּבֹא אַחֲרָיו עֲזַרְיָהוּ הַכֹּהֵן
יח וְעִמּוֹ כֹּהֲנִים ׀ לַיהוָה שְׁמוֹנִים בְּנֵי־חָיִל׃ וַיַּעַמְדוּ עַל־עֻזִּיָּהוּ הַמֶּלֶךְ וַיֹּאמְרוּ לוֹ
לֹא־לְךָ עֻזִּיָּהוּ לְהַקְטִיר לַיהוָה כִּי לַכֹּהֲנִים בְּנֵי־אַהֲרֹן הַמְקֻדָּשִׁים לְהַקְטִיר צֵא
יט מִן־הַמִּקְדָּשׁ כִּי מָעַלְתָּ וְלֹא־לְךָ לְכָבוֹד מֵיְהוָה אֱלֹהִים׃ וַיִּזְעַף עֻזִּיָּהוּ וּבְיָדוֹ
מִקְטֶרֶת לְהַקְטִיר וּבְזַעְפּוֹ עִם־הַכֹּהֲנִים וְהַצָּרַעַת זָרְחָה בְמִצְחוֹ לִפְנֵי הַכֹּהֲנִים
כ בְּבֵית יְהוָה מֵעַל לְמִזְבַּח הַקְּטֹרֶת׃ וַיִּפֶן אֵלָיו עֲזַרְיָהוּ כֹהֵן הָרֹאשׁ וְכָל־הַכֹּהֲנִים
וְהִנֵּה־הוּא מְצֹרָע בְּמִצְחוֹ וַיַּבְהִלוּהוּ מִשָּׁם וְגַם־הוּא נִדְחַף לָצֵאת כִּי נִגְּעוֹ יְהוָה׃
כא וַיְהִי עֻזִּיָּהוּ הַמֶּלֶךְ מְצֹרָע ׀ עַד־יוֹם מוֹתוֹ וַיֵּשֶׁב בֵּית החפשות מְצֹרָע כִּי נִגְזַר הַחָפְשִׁית
כב מִבֵּית יְהוָה וְיוֹתָם בְּנוֹ עַל־בֵּית הַמֶּלֶךְ שׁוֹפֵט אֶת־עַם הָאָרֶץ׃ וְיֶתֶר דִּבְרֵי עֻזִּיָּהוּ

BACKGROUND

26:15 | **Inventions, clever devices, to be on the towers and on the corners:** In the writings and on the monuments of the ancient Near East discovered so far, there is no mention of firing machines such as catapults and ballistae. It is therefore unlikely that such instruments were used in the period of Uziyahu, who lived in the eighth century BCE. A more likely supposition is that the verse is referring to mechanical constructions that were assembled on the towers of the walls. Thanks to these constructions, archers and slingers could fire their weapons. Examples of such towers appear on the Lakhish reliefs (Yigal Sukenik [Yadin], "Engines Invented by Cunning Men," *Bulletin of the Jewish Palestine Exploration Society*, 13 Oct. 1946–Mar. 1947, [Hebrew], 19–24).

26:21 | **The isolation [*haḥofshit*] house:** Ugaritic texts mention the *ḥaftat* house as a reference to the netherworld, whose inhabitants are free [*ḥofshi*] from the sufferings of this world. A similar expression appears in the Bible in descriptions of the state of the dead (see Psalms 88:6; Job 3:17–19), and also in rabbinical literature (see *Shabbat* 30b; Jerusalem Talmud, *Ketubot* 12:3). It seems that from here the concept of a *ḥofshit* house came to refer to places isolated from society, such as lepers' colonies, as lepers were considered like the dead and removed from inhabited areas (see Leviticus 13:46; Numbers 12:12; *Shemot Rabba* 1:34).

23 **Uziyahu lay with his fathers, and they buried him with his**
fathers in the burial field that was for the kings,[B] not in the
actual burial plot of the house of David, but adjacent to it,[176]
as they said: He is a leper.
Yotam his son reigned in
his stead.

Plaque on Uziyahu's tomb, Second Temple period

The Chronicles of King Yotam

II CHRONICLES 27:1–9

Yotam is unique among the kings in that the Bible has nothing bad to say about him. In rabbinic tradition, he is considered an especially righteous person. Despite his piety, he did not have a great influence over the kingdom as a whole.

27 1 **Yotam was twenty-five years old when he became king, and**
he reigned sixteen years in Jerusalem.[D] **His mother's name**
was Yerusha daughter of Tzadok.
2 **He did what is right in the eyes of the Lord,** acting **in ac-**
cordance with everything that his father Uziyahu had
done, who was a good king overall, **except that** in contrast to
his father, **he did not come into the Sanctuary of the Lord**
to serve as a priest. Yotam had no pretensions, as he learned
from his father's mistake.[177] King Yotam was able to protect the
Temple and the area nearby, **but the people were still acting**
corruptly during his reign. He found it hard to have a positive
influence over the people, and they never abandoned their private shrines.[178]
3 Like his father, Yotam was a dynamic king. He continued
Uziyahu's work on infrastructure, security, and the fortification
of the borders. **He built the upper gate of the House of the**
Lord,[B] **and he built extensively on the wall of the Ofel,**[B] a
fortified and raised structure or area.
4 **He built** new **cities in** various places across **the highlands of**
Judah, and in the woodlands he built fortresses and towers,
for protection and to serve as lookout points.
5 **He waged war with the king of the children of Amon and**
prevailed over them. The children of Amon gave him that
year one hundred talents of silver, ten thousand kor of
wheat, a kor being a measure of volume of more than 210 liters,
and ten thousand measures **of barley.** These were respectable
but not huge amounts, as the Amonites did not possess a large
kingdom. **This the children of Amon made restitution to**
him in that year **and in the second year, and in the third.**
6 **Yotam grew strong, because he set,** established and directed,
his ways before the Lord his God.
7 **The rest of the deeds of Yotam, and all his wars and his**

The Ofel, north of the City of David, Israel Museum model

Wheat

Barley

DISCUSSION

27:1 | **He reigned sixteen years in Jerusalem:** As stated above, Yotam "was in charge of the king's house, governing the people of the land" (26:21) during his father's lifetime. He appears to have served as regent in place of Uziyahu, who as a leper was isolated from society and could not reign. It is unclear when this regency began, as the Bible does not specify anywhere how long Uziyahu was a leper. This is perhaps the source of the confusion with regard to the length of Yotam's reign. In several places it says that he reigned for sixteen years, yet it appears from other places that he reigned for longer (see II Kings 15:30, 32, 16:1; *Tosefta, Sota* 12:4; *Seder Olam Rabba* 22).

כג הָרִאשֹׁנִים וְהָאַחֲרֹנִים כָּתַב יְשַׁעְיָהוּ בֶן־אָמוֹץ הַנָּבִיא: וַיִּשְׁכַּב עֻזִּיָּהוּ עִם־אֲבֹתָיו
וַיִּקְבְּרוּ אֹתוֹ עִם־אֲבֹתָיו בִּשְׂדֵה הַקְּבוּרָה אֲשֶׁר לַמְּלָכִים כִּי אָמְרוּ מְצוֹרָע הוּא
כז א וַיִּמְלֹךְ יוֹתָם בְּנוֹ תַּחְתָּיו: בֶּן־עֶשְׂרִים וְחָמֵשׁ שָׁנָה יוֹתָם בְּמָלְכוֹ וְשֵׁשׁ־
ב עֶשְׂרֵה שָׁנָה מָלַךְ בִּירוּשָׁלִָם וְשֵׁם אִמּוֹ יְרוּשָׁה בַּת־צָדוֹק: וַיַּעַשׂ הַיָּשָׁר בְּעֵינֵי
יְהוָה כְּכֹל אֲשֶׁר־עָשָׂה עֻזִּיָּהוּ אָבִיו רַק לֹא־בָא אֶל־הֵיכַל יְהוָה וְעוֹד הָעָם
ג מַשְׁחִיתִים: הוּא בָּנָה אֶת־שַׁעַר בֵּית־יְהוָה הָעֶלְיוֹן וּבְחוֹמַת הָעֹפֶל בָּנָה לָרֹב:
ד ה וְעָרִים בָּנָה בְּהַר יְהוּדָה וּבֶחֳרָשִׁים בָּנָה בִּירָנִיּוֹת וּמִגְדָּלִים: וְהוּא נִלְחַם עִם־מֶלֶךְ
בְּנֵי־עַמּוֹן וַיֶּחֱזַק עֲלֵיהֶם וַיִּתְּנוּ־לוֹ בְנֵי־עַמּוֹן בַּשָּׁנָה הַהִיא מֵאָה כִּכַּר־כֶּסֶף וַעֲשֶׂרֶת
אֲלָפִים כֹּרִים חִטִּים וּשְׂעוֹרִים עֲשֶׂרֶת אֲלָפִים זֹאת הֵשִׁיבוּ לוֹ בְּנֵי עַמּוֹן וּבַשָּׁנָה
ו הַשֵּׁנִית וְהַשְּׁלִשִׁית: וַיִּתְחַזֵּק יוֹתָם כִּי הֵכִין דְּרָכָיו לִפְנֵי יְהוָה אֱלֹהָיו:
ז וְיֶתֶר דִּבְרֵי יוֹתָם וְכָל־מִלְחֲמֹתָיו וּדְרָכָיו הִנָּם כְּתוּבִים עַל־סֵפֶר מַלְכֵי יִשְׂרָאֵל

BACKGROUND

26:23 | **They buried him with his fathers in the burial field that was for the kings:** The exact location of this burial place is unknown. A "Guide to Jerusalem" from the tenth century CE found in the Cairo Geniza describes stairs that led to the top of the Mount of Olives: "And at the end of these steps is the palace of Uziya ... which is called the isolation house." This testimony was bolstered by the discovery of a stone plaque in the collection of the Russian Orthodox Church on the Mount of Olives. It includes an Aramaic inscription (see image on facing page), dated to the Second Temple period, which states: "To this place were brought the bones of Uziyahu the king of Judah; do not open." Alternatively, the writings of Benjamin of Tudela and Judah ben Elijah Hadassi the Karaite, both from the twelfth century CE, record a tradition that Uziyahu's grave is what is nowadays called the Tomb of Zechariah, which is near what is called Absalom's Pillar in the Kidron Valley.

27:3 | **The upper gate of the House of the Lord:** The mention of the building of this gate among Yotam's construction projects attests to its importance and the impression it made on future generations. There is an echo of this in Jeremiah's statement that Barukh son of Neriya read his book: "... in the upper courtyard, at the entrance of the New Gate of the House of the Lord" (Jeremiah 36:10; see also Jeremiah 26:10). The position of the gate in the upper courtyard recalls "the Gate of the Runners" that is mentioned in II Kings (11:19), which is called the upper gate in the parallel account above (23:20). Based on the description, this gate was to the south of the Temple, near the king's palace. It should be noted that the term "upper gate" is also used in reference to the Gate of Benjamin, which was to the north of the Temple (Jeremiah 20:2; Ezekiel 9:2).

The Ofel: A topographically descriptive name for the high, fortified part of the city, equivalent to the Greek acropolis. It is likely called the Ofel due to its being the place to which people ascend, [*ma'apilim*] (see Rav Se'adya Gaon). The name appears in II Kings (5:24) in connection to the city of Samaria, and in the Mesha Stele in relation to the city of Karha. In the case of Jerusalem, it refers to a ridge that connects the City of David to the Temple Mount. In early periods the area was fortified and raised, and later it probably became the spot of the Seleucid Acra fortified compound, which is depicted in the books of Maccabees. The site was destroyed, lowered, and leveled by Simon the Hasmonean in the second half of the second century BCE (see *Wars of the Jews* V:4:1; *Antiquities of the Jews* XIII:6:7).

ways, behold, they are written in the book of the kings of Israel and Judah.

8 **He was twenty-five years old when he became king,** as stated earlier (verse 1), **and he reigned sixteen years in Jerusalem.**

9 **Yotam lay with his fathers, and they buried him in the City of David,** alongside the other worthy kings. **Ahaz his son reigned in his stead.**

The Chronicles of King Ahaz

II CHRONICLES 28:1–27

In contrast to his righteous father Yotam, Ahaz is one of the most wicked kings of Judah. During his reign, the Kingdom of Israel continues its decline, and the Kingdom of Judah begins to feel the pressure exerted by the expanding Assyrian Empire.

28 1 **Ahaz was twenty years old when he became king, and he reigned sixteen years in Jerusalem. He did not do what is right in the eyes of the Lord, as had his father,** his ancestor, King **David.**

2 **Rather, he followed in the ways of the kings of Israel, and also made cast images for** the worship of **the Be'alim.**

3 **He burned offerings,** incense or animals for his idolatrous rites, **in the Valley of the Son of Hinom,**[B] **and ignited his children in the fire.** He probably did not literally burn his children, but merely passed them through fire as a symbolic offering (see II Kings 16:3, and commentary ad loc.; commentary on Leviticus 18:21). Ahaz acted **in accordance with the abominations of the nations whom the Lord had dispossessed from before the children of Israel.**

Altar, Tel Arad, late twelfth century BCE

4 **He slaughtered** animals **and burned offerings in the shrines, and on the hills, and beneath every flourishing tree.**

5 **The Lord his God delivered him into the hand of the king of Aram, and they struck him,** his people, **and took from him a great many captives, and brought** some of **them to Damascus. He was also delivered into the hand of the king of Israel, who struck him a great blow.** The king of Israel also waged war against Judah, perhaps alongside the Arameans, something that had not happened for many years, and he too struck the cities of Judah, although he did not conquer Jerusalem.[179]

6 **Pekah son of Remalyahu,** king of Israel, **killed one hundred and twenty thousand in Judah in one day, all of them capable men, when they forsook the Lord, God of their fathers.**

7 **Zikhri, a mighty one of Ephraim, killed Maaseyahu the king's son, and Azrikam chief official of the** royal **house, and Elkana the viceroy.** Zikhri managed to kill military commanders and leading officials of Judah.

8 **The children of Israel took captive from their brethren two hundred thousand women, boys, and girls, and they also plundered much spoils from them, and brought the spoils to Samaria.** They did not conquer the kingdom, but they were victorious in battle, taking booty and captives.

9 **A prophet of the Lord was there** in Samaria, **Oded was his name. He came out toward the army that was coming** back **to Samaria and said to them: Behold, by the fury of the Lord, God of your fathers, against Judah, He delivered them into your hand, and you killed among them with fury that reached to the heavens,** that is, in a very great rage.

10 **Now you are saying** you wish **to subjugate the children of Judah and Jerusalem as slaves and maidservants for yourselves,** as prisoners of war. **Don't you yourselves have** your own **guilt against the Lord your God,** as you have sinned more than they have?[180]

Slaves, Tomb of Nakht, Thebes, Egypt, second millennium BCE

11 **Now hear me, and return the captives that you have taken captive from your brethren, for the enflamed wrath of the Lord is upon you** even more than upon them. Even if they deserve their punishment, you are even guiltier than they are. Therefore, your retribution will be even more severe if you keep them in captivity.

12 **Men from among the heads of the children of Ephraim, Azaryahu son of Yehohanan, Berekhyahu son of Meshilemot, and Yehizkiyahu son of Shalum, and Amasa son of Hadlai, rose against those who came from the campaign,**

13 **and said to them: You shall not bring the captives here, as you propose to bring guilt against the Lord upon us,** for which we will receive divine punishment, **to add to our sins and to our guilt.** We have committed too many sins already. It would be foolish to increase our culpability through this deed, **for our guilt is great, and there is enflamed wrath against Israel.** It seems that some of the subjects of the Kingdom of Israel understood that the path to which they had become accustomed was not the correct path.

ח ויהודה: בן־עשרים וחמש שנה היה במלכו ושש־עשרה שנה מלך בירושלם:
ט כח א וישכב יותם עם־אבתיו ויקברו אתו בעיר דויד וימלך אחז בנו תחתיו: בן־
עשרים שנה אחז במלכו ושש־עשרה שנה מלך בירושלם ולא־עשה הישר
ב בעיני יהוה כדויד אביו: וילך בדרכי מלכי ישראל וגם מסכות עשה לבעלים:
ג והוא הקטיר בגיא בן־הנם ויבער את־בניו באש כתעבות הגוים אשר הריש
ד יהוה מפני בני ישראל: ויזבח ויקטר בבמות ועל־הגבעות ותחת כל־עץ רענן:
ה ויתנהו יהוה אלהיו ביד מלך ארם ויכו־בו וישבו ממנו שביה גדולה ויביאו
ו דרמשק וגם ביד־מלך ישראל נתן ויך־בו מכה גדולה: ויהרג פקח
בן־רמליהו ביהודה מאה ועשרים אלף ביום אחד הכל בני־חיל בעזבם את־
ז יהוה אלהי אבותם: ויהרג זכרי | גבור אפרים את־מעשיהו בן־המלך
ח ואת־עזריקם נגיד הבית ואת־אלקנה משנה המלך: וישבו בני־
ישראל מאחיהם מאתים אלף נשים בנים ובנות וגם־שלל רב בזזו מהם ויביאו
ט את־השלל לשמרון: ושם היה נביא ליהוה עדד שמו ויצא לפני
הצבא הבא לשמרון ויאמר להם הנה בחמת יהוה אלהי־אבותיכם על־יהודה
י נתנם בידכם ותהרגו־בם בזעף עד לשמים הגיע: ועתה בני־יהודה וירושלם
אתם אמרים לכבש לעבדים ולשפחות לכם הלא רק־אתם עמכם אשמות
יא ליהוה אלהיכם: ועתה שמעוני והשיבו השביה אשר שביתם מאחיכם כי
יב חרון אף־יהוה עליכם: ויקמו אנשים מראשי בני־אפרים עזריהו
בן־יהוחנן ברכיהו בן־משלמות ויחזקיהו בן־שלם ועמשא בן־חדלי על־
יג הבאים מן־הצבא: ויאמרו להם לא־תביאו את־השביה הנה כי לאשמת יהוה

BACKGROUND

28:3 | **The Valley of the Son of Hinom:** This valley descends from the northwest toward Jerusalem, encircles Mount Zion from the west, passes south of the City of David and connects with the Kidron Valley. The Valley of the Son of Hinom served as the border between the tribal territories of Benjamin and Judah (Joshua 15:8, 18:16). In the days of King Menashe the site was also used for the ritual worship of Molekh (II Kings 23).

14 **The vanguard left the captives and the spoils before the princes and the entire congregation,** for the princes to take care of the situation.[181]
15 **The men who were** previously **designated by name,** those who inspired the people to listen to the prophet, **rose and sustained the captives,** provided them with support, **and all the naked among them they clothed from the spoils; they clothed them, gave them shoes, fed them, gave them to drink, and anointed them** with oil, **and transported all the feeble among them,** those who were unable to walk, **on donkeys, and brought them to Jericho, the city of the date palms,**[B] **to their brethren, and they returned to Samaria.** They returned them not due to any external pressure, but because they realized the injustice of keeping them as prisoners of war. It was clear to them that even when Israel and Judah were at war, they were one nation and a single family, and therefore they were forbidden to treat their captives badly.
16 **At that time, King Ahaz sent** messengers **to the kings of Assyria** to ask them **to help him** in his struggle against the Arameans and Israel. He sought help from Assyria, which was already an empire that was expanding rapidly, and whose western border was the eastern border of the Aramean states.
17 However, Israel and the Arameans were not Judah's only problem. **The Edomites came again,** they invaded, **and were smiting at Judah, taking captives.**
18 **The Philistines raided against the cities of the foothills,**[B] **and the south of Judah, and captured Beit Shemesh** (see commentary on 25:21), **Ayalon,**[182] **Gederot,**[B] **Sokho and its environs, Timna**[B] **and its environs, and Gimzo**[B] **and its environs and they settled there.**

Remains at Tel Batash, Late Bronze Age

Tel Sokho, Valley of Ela

19 **For the Lord brought Judah low** before its enemies **because of Ahaz king of Israel, for he corrupted Judah,** alternatively, he had misruled the kingdom, **and committed a trespass against the Lord.**

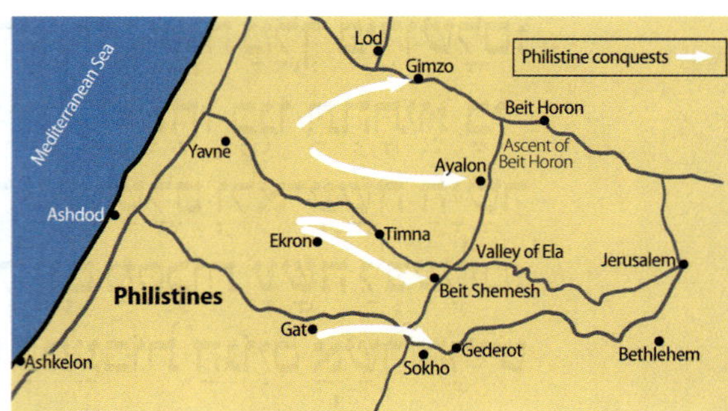

Philistine invasions in the days of Ahaz

20 **Tilgat Pilneser,** also called Tiglat Pileser, **king of Assyria, came against him, and troubled him,** Ahaz, **and did not strengthen him.** Although the king of Assyria arrived, not only did he fail to support Ahaz, he actively caused him more problems.[183]

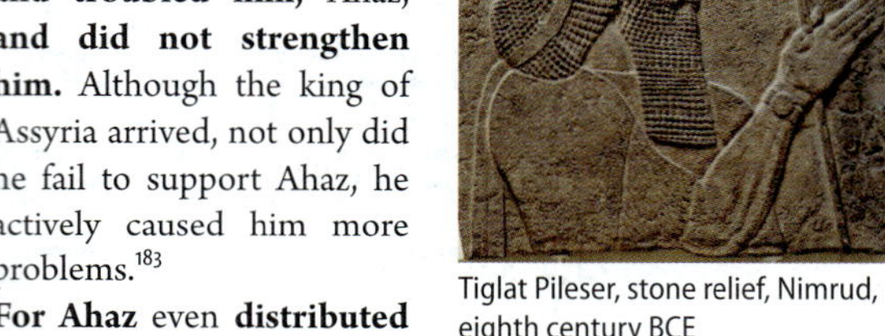
Tiglat Pileser, stone relief, Nimrud, eighth century BCE

21 **For Ahaz** even **distributed** the treasuries of **the House of the Lord, and the** treasuries of the **house of the king and the princes, and he gave them to the king of Assyria, but it did not help him.** Although the king of Assyria would eventually cause the downfall of the Kingdom of Israel, this occurred only much later, and was not a response to the gifts he received from Ahaz.
22 Even **during the time he was being troubled, he continued to trespass against the Lord; he is King Ahaz.** There were occasions when Ahaz refrained from sinning out of respect for God's word, but in general he continued in his wicked ways throughout his life.[184]
23 **He slaughtered to the gods of Damascus, who were striking at him, and he said: Since the gods of the kings of Aram help them, I will slaughter to them, and they will help me. But** in fact **they were what brought about his downfall and that of all Israel.** This idolatry was the cause of his and Israel's suffering.
24 **Ahaz gathered the vessels of the House of God, cut the vessels of the House of God into pieces,** as he needed the valuable materials from which they were fashioned, **and closed the doors of the House of the Lord,** he cancelled the Temple service; **he made altars for himself in every corner of Jerusalem.**

עָלֵינוּ אַתֶּם אֹמְרִים לְהֹסִיף עַל־חַטֹּאתֵנוּ וְעַל־אַשְׁמָתֵנוּ כִּי־רַבָּה אַשְׁמָה לָנוּ
יד וַחֲרוֹן אָף עַל־יִשְׂרָאֵל׃ וַיַּעֲזֹב הֶחָלוּץ אֶת־הַשִּׁבְיָה וְאֶת־הַבִּזָּה לִפְנֵי
טו הַשָּׂרִים וְכָל־הַקָּהָל׃ וַיָּקֻמוּ הָאֲנָשִׁים אֲשֶׁר־נִקְּבוּ בְשֵׁמוֹת וַיַּחֲזִיקוּ בַשִּׁבְיָה וְכָל־
מַעֲרֻמֵּיהֶם הִלְבִּישׁוּ מִן־הַשָּׁלָל וַיַּלְבִּשֻׁם וַיַּנְעִלוּם וַיַּאֲכִלוּם וַיַּשְׁקוּם וַיְסֻכוּם
וַיְנַהֲלוּם בַּחֲמֹרִים לְכָל־כּוֹשֵׁל וַיְבִיאוּם יְרֵחוֹ עִיר־הַתְּמָרִים אֵצֶל אֲחֵיהֶם וַיָּשׁוּבוּ
טז שֹׁמְרוֹן׃ בָּעֵת הַהִיא שָׁלַח הַמֶּלֶךְ אָחָז עַל־מַלְכֵי אַשּׁוּר לַעְזֹר לוֹ׃
יז יח וְעוֹד אֲדוֹמִים בָּאוּ וַיַּכּוּ בִיהוּדָה וַיִּשְׁבּוּ־שֶׁבִי׃ וּפְלִשְׁתִּים פָּשְׁטוּ בְּעָרֵי הַשְּׁפֵלָה
וְהַנֶּגֶב לִיהוּדָה וַיִּלְכְּדוּ אֶת־בֵּית־שֶׁמֶשׁ וְאֶת־אַיָּלוֹן וְאֶת־הַגְּדֵרוֹת וְאֶת־שׂוֹכוֹ
יט וּבְנוֹתֶיהָ וְאֶת־תִּמְנָה וּבְנוֹתֶיהָ וְאֶת־גִּמְזוֹ וְאֶת־בְּנֹתֶיהָ וַיֵּשְׁבוּ שָׁם׃ כִּי־הִכְנִיעַ
יהוה אֶת־יְהוּדָה בַּעֲבוּר אָחָז מֶלֶךְ־יִשְׂרָאֵל כִּי הִפְרִיעַ בִּיהוּדָה וּמָעוֹל מַעַל
כ כא בַּיהוה׃ וַיָּבֹא עָלָיו תִּלְּגַת פִּלְנְאֶסֶר מֶלֶךְ אַשּׁוּר וַיָּצַר לוֹ וְלֹא חֲזָקוֹ׃ כִּי־חָלַק אָחָז
אֶת־בֵּית יהוה וְאֶת־בֵּית הַמֶּלֶךְ וְהַשָּׂרִים וַיִּתֵּן לְמֶלֶךְ אַשּׁוּר וְלֹא לְעֶזְרָה לוֹ׃
כב כג וּבְעֵת הָצֵר לוֹ וַיּוֹסֶף לִמְעוֹל בַּיהוה הוּא הַמֶּלֶךְ אָחָז׃ וַיִּזְבַּח לֵאלֹהֵי דַרְמֶשֶׂק
הַמַּכִּים בּוֹ וַיֹּאמֶר כִּי אֱלֹהֵי מַלְכֵי־אֲרָם הֵם מַעְזְרִים אוֹתָם לָהֶם אֲזַבֵּחַ וְיַעְזְרוּנִי
כד וְהֵם הָיוּ־לוֹ לְהַכְשִׁילוֹ וּלְכָל־יִשְׂרָאֵל׃ וַיֶּאֱסֹף אָחָז אֶת־כְּלֵי בֵית־הָאֱלֹהִים וַיְקַצֵּץ
אֶת־כְּלֵי בֵית־הָאֱלֹהִים וַיִּסְגֹּר אֶת־דַּלְתוֹת בֵּית־יהוה וַיַּעַשׂ לוֹ מִזְבְּחוֹת בְּכָל־

BACKGROUND

28:15 | **Jericho, the city of the date palms:** Already in ancient times Jericho was known as the "city of the date palms" (Deuteronomy 34:3). It is possible that the same epithet or a similar one was also given to other cities, such as Tzoar and Tamar, on the southern reaches of the Dead Sea (see Judges 1:16). Although Jericho was located within the territory of the tribe of Benjamin, it appears that after Ahav rebuilt it (I Kings 16:34), it was ruled by the Kingdom of Israel. During the reigns of Uziyahu and Yotam the control of the Kingdom of Israel over the city weakened, and it had returned to the Kingdom of Judah, as is indicated here (see also commentary on I Kings 16:34).

28:18 | **The cities of the foothills:** These cities were located at important junctures on the roads leading from Philistia to the Jerusalem region: the ascent of Beit Horon, the road adjacent to the Sorek Stream, and the road through the Valley of Ela. It seems that the Philistines gained control over the northern and central areas of the Judean foothills.

Gederot: In the descriptions of the portion of the tribe of Judah, in the book of Joshua (15:35–36), the names Gedera and Gederotayim appear alongside the towns that were near the Valley of Ela. Due to the similarity of the names, this place is generally identified with one of the hills east of Kibbutz Netiv HaLamed-Heh.

Timna: A northern border city in the territory of the tribe of Judah, between Beit Shemesh and Ekron (Joshua 15:10–11). It is identified with Tel Batash, near the Sorek Stream, about 7 km west of Beit Shemesh. Excavations at the site have unearthed Canaanite remains from the eighteenth century BCE, and Philistine remains dating back to the twelfth century BCE.

Gimzo: Generally identified with the ruins of the Arab village of Jimzu, approximately 5 km east of Lod, in the north of the Judean lowlands. It is known as the birthplace of Naḥum man of Gimzo, one of the Sages mentioned in the Mishna.

25 **In every city of Judah he made shrines to burn offerings to other gods, and he angered the Lord, God of his fathers.**
26 **The rest of his deeds, and all his ways, early and late, behold, they are written in the book of the kings of Judah and Israel.** Ahaz was unsuccessful in every aspect of his reign. He was unsuccessful in wars and in defending the land from invaders, and he destroyed Israel's moral and religious integrity.
27 **Ahaz lay with his fathers, and they buried him in the city, in Jerusalem, but they did not bring him to the graves of the kings of Israel,** as he did not deserve such honor; **and Yehizkiyahu his son reigned in his stead.**

The Chronicles of King Hizkiyahu

II CHRONICLES 29:1–32:33

The events of the reign of Hizkiyahu, who is also referred to as Hizkiya[185] and Yehizkiyahu, are related here and elsewhere in the Bible at great length. Hizkiyahu is a righteous king who seeks with all his power to renew the nation's covenant with God in his kingdom. He rises to the throne just as the Kingdom of Israel is being conquered and exiled by Assyria, leaving only a remnant behind.

29 1 **Yehizkiyahu became king when he was twenty-five years old, and he reigned twenty-nine years in Jerusalem. His mother's name was Aviya daughter of Zekharyahu.**
2 **He did what is right in the eyes of the Lord, in accordance with everything that David his father,** his ancestor, **had done.** As was the case with David, some of Hizkiyahu's actions are subject to criticism, but in general he followed in the path of God fully and wholeheartedly.[186]

The Purification of the Temple and the Renewal of Its Service

II CHRONICLES 29:3–36

Already in the early stages of his reign, King Hizkiyahu purifies the Temple and attempts to restore the proper order of its service. He inspires a religious renaissance, awakening the soul of the people of Israel to a renewal and a return to God.

3 **He,** Hizkiyahu, **in the first year of his reign, in the first month, opened the doors of the House of the Lord,** which his father Ahaz had closed or locked (see 28:24), **and** he **refurbished them.**
4 **He brought the priests and the Levites and assembled them in the eastern plaza.**
5 **He said to them: Hear me, Levites: Now, sanctify** and prepare **yourselves, and sanctify the House of the Lord, God of your fathers; remove the abhorrent,** the impurity, **from the Sanctuary.**
6 **For our fathers trespassed, did evil in the eyes of the Lord our God, and forsook Him; they turned their faces away from the dwelling place of the Lord and turned their backs.**
7 **They also closed the doors of the Hall, extinguished the lamps, did not burn incense, and did not offer burnt offerings in the Sanctuary to the God of Israel.**
8 **The wrath of the Lord was upon Judah and Jerusalem, and He made them into an object of horror, desolation,** or astonishment, as people were astounded at how this could happen, **and a cause of whistling** in degradation or in amazement at the depth of their fall,[187] **as you see with your eyes.**
9 **Behold, our fathers fell by the sword, and our sons, our daughters, and our wives are in captivity for this.**
10 **Now it is in my heart,** it is my intention, **to establish a covenant with the Lord, God of Israel, so that His enflamed wrath will be withdrawn from us.**
11 **My sons, do not be misled** or err **now,** do not sin through negligence or complacency,[188] **as it is you,** the priests and Levites, **that the Lord has chosen to stand before Him, to serve Him, and to be his servants and those who burn offerings to Him.**
12 Then leaders of **the Levites rose: Mahat son of Amasai and Yoel son of Azaryahu, from the sons of the Kehatites; and from the sons of Merari: Kish son of Avdi and Azaryahu son of Yehalelel; and from the Gershonites: Yoah son of Zima and Eden son of Yoah;**
13 **and from the sons of Elitzafan: Shimri and Ye'iel; and from the sons of Asaf: Zekharyahu and Matanyahu;**
14 **and from the sons of Heiman: Yehiel and Shimi; and from the sons of Yedutun: Shemaya and Uziel.**
15 **They assembled their brethren and sanctified themselves, and they came in accordance with the command of the king by the words,** instruction,[189] **of the Lord,** or for a purpose concerning the service of God,[190] **to purify the House of the Lord.**
16 **The priests came to the interior of the House of the Lord,** in order **to purify it, and they removed all the impurity,** the various idols and the like, **that they found in the Sanctuary of the Lord, to the Courtyard of the House of the Lord.** They smashed the idols and cleared them out from the Sanctuary to the Courtyard. **The Levites received it,** the pile of smashed idols, **to remove it to the Kidron Valley, outside.**

כה פִּנָּה בִּירוּשָׁלִָם׃ וּבְכָל־עִיר וָעִיר לִיהוּדָה עָשָׂה בָמוֹת לְקַטֵּר לֵאלֹהִים אֲחֵרִים
כו וַיַּכְעֵס אֶת־יְהוָה אֱלֹהֵי אֲבֹתָיו׃ וְיֶתֶר דְּבָרָיו וְכָל־דְּרָכָיו הָרִאשֹׁנִים וְהָאַחֲרוֹנִים
כז הִנָּם כְּתוּבִים עַל־סֵפֶר מַלְכֵי יְהוּדָה וְיִשְׂרָאֵל׃ וַיִּשְׁכַּב אָחָז עִם־אֲבֹתָיו וַיִּקְבְּרֻהוּ
בָעִיר בִּירוּשָׁלִַם כִּי לֹא הֱבִיאֻהוּ לְקִבְרֵי מַלְכֵי יִשְׂרָאֵל וַיִּמְלֹךְ יְחִזְקִיָּהוּ בְנוֹ
כט א תַּחְתָּיו׃ יְחִזְקִיָּהוּ מָלַךְ בֶּן־עֶשְׂרִים וְחָמֵשׁ שָׁנָה וְעֶשְׂרִים וָתֵשַׁע שָׁנָה
ב מָלַךְ בִּירוּשָׁלִָם וְשֵׁם אִמּוֹ אֲבִיָּה בַּת־זְכַרְיָהוּ׃ וַיַּעַשׂ הַיָּשָׁר בְּעֵינֵי יְהוָה כְּכֹל
ג אֲשֶׁר־עָשָׂה דָּוִיד אָבִיו׃ הוּא בַשָּׁנָה הָרִאשׁוֹנָה לְמָלְכוֹ בַּחֹדֶשׁ הָרִאשׁוֹן פָּתַח
ד אֶת־דַּלְתוֹת בֵּית־יְהוָה וַיְחַזְּקֵם׃ וַיָּבֵא אֶת־הַכֹּהֲנִים וְאֶת־הַלְוִיִּם וַיַּאַסְפֵם לִרְחוֹב
ה הַמִּזְרָח׃ וַיֹּאמֶר לָהֶם שְׁמָעוּנִי הַלְוִיִּם עַתָּה הִתְקַדְּשׁוּ וְקַדְּשׁוּ אֶת־בֵּית יְהוָה
ו אֱלֹהֵי אֲבֹתֵיכֶם וְהוֹצִיאוּ אֶת־הַנִּדָּה מִן־הַקֹּדֶשׁ׃ כִּי־מָעֲלוּ אֲבֹתֵינוּ וְעָשׂוּ הָרַע
ז בְּעֵינֵי יְהוָה־אֱלֹהֵינוּ וַיַּעַזְבֻהוּ וַיַּסֵּבּוּ פְנֵיהֶם מִמִּשְׁכַּן יְהוָה וַיִּתְּנוּ־עֹרֶף׃ גַּם סָגְרוּ
דַּלְתוֹת הָאוּלָם וַיְכַבּוּ אֶת־הַנֵּרוֹת וּקְטֹרֶת לֹא הִקְטִירוּ וְעֹלָה לֹא־הֶעֱלוּ בַקֹּדֶשׁ
ח לֵאלֹהֵי יִשְׂרָאֵל׃ וַיְהִי קֶצֶף יְהוָה עַל־יְהוּדָה וִירוּשָׁלִָם וַיִּתְּנֵם לזועה לְשַׁמָּה לְזַעֲוָה
ט וְלִשְׁרֵקָה כַּאֲשֶׁר אַתֶּם רֹאִים בְּעֵינֵיכֶם׃ וְהִנֵּה נָפְלוּ אֲבוֹתֵינוּ בֶּחָרֶב וּבָנֵינוּ וּבְנוֹתֵינוּ
י וּנְשֵׁינוּ בַּשְּׁבִי עַל־זֹאת׃ עַתָּה עִם־לְבָבִי לִכְרוֹת בְּרִית לַיהוָה אֱלֹהֵי יִשְׂרָאֵל וְיָשֹׁב
יא מִמֶּנּוּ חֲרוֹן אַפּוֹ׃ בָּנַי עַתָּה אַל־תִּשָּׁלוּ כִּי־בָכֶם בָּחַר יְהוָה לַעֲמֹד לְפָנָיו לְשָׁרְתוֹ כב
יב וְלִהְיוֹת לוֹ מְשָׁרְתִים וּמַקְטִרִים׃ וַיָּקֻמוּ הַלְוִיִּם מַחַת בֶּן־עֲמָשַׂי וְיוֹאֵל
בֶּן־עֲזַרְיָהוּ מִן־בְּנֵי הַקְּהָתִי וּמִן־בְּנֵי מְרָרִי קִישׁ בֶּן־עַבְדִּי וַעֲזַרְיָהוּ בֶּן־יְהַלֶּלְאֵל
יג וּמִן־הַגֵּרְשֻׁנִּי יוֹאָח בֶּן־זִמָּה וְעֵדֶן בֶּן־יוֹאָח׃ וּמִן־בְּנֵי אֱלִיצָפָן שִׁמְרִי ויעואל וִיעִיאֵל
יד וּמִן־בְּנֵי אָסָף זְכַרְיָהוּ וּמַתַּנְיָהוּ׃ וּמִן־בְּנֵי הֵימָן יחואל וְשִׁמְעִי וּמִן־בְּנֵי יְחִיאֵל
טו יְדוּתוּן שְׁמַעְיָה וְעֻזִּיאֵל׃ וַיַּאַסְפוּ אֶת־אֲחֵיהֶם וַיִּתְקַדְּשׁוּ וַיָּבֹאוּ כְמִצְוַת־הַמֶּלֶךְ
טז בְּדִבְרֵי יְהוָה לְטַהֵר בֵּית יְהוָה׃ וַיָּבֹאוּ הַכֹּהֲנִים לִפְנִימָה בֵּית־יְהוָה לְטַהֵר וַיּוֹצִיאוּ
אֵת כָּל־הַטֻּמְאָה אֲשֶׁר מָצְאוּ בְּהֵיכַל יְהוָה לַחֲצַר בֵּית יְהוָה וַיְקַבְּלוּ הַלְוִיִּם

17 **They began on the first** day **of the first month,** Nisan, **to sanctify** the Levites, **and on the eighth day of the month they came to the Hall of the Lord, and they sanctified the House of the Lord for eight days. On the sixteenth day of the first month they concluded.**

18 **They came inside** the palace **to Hizkiyahu the king, and said: We have purified the entire House of the Lord, the altar of the burnt offering and all its vessels, and the table of the arrangement and all its vessels.**

19 **All the vessels that King Ahaz neglected during his reign, in his trespass** and sinning, **we have prepared and sanctified; behold, they are** purified and ready for service **before the altar of the Lord.**

20 **Yehizkiyahu the king arose early and assembled the princes of the city, and he went up to the House of the Lord.**

21 **They brought seven bulls, seven rams, and seven lambs** as voluntary burnt offerings that were to be burned in their entirety upon the altar,[191] as explained in the verses below;[192] **and seven goats as a sin offering,** an obligatory offering brought to atone for the sins of an individual or a community,[193] **for the kingdom, for the Sanctuary** that was neglected and profaned, **and for Judah. He said to the sons of Aaron, the priests, to offer them up on the altar of the Lord.**

22 **They slaughtered the cattle, and the priests received the blood and sprinkled it on the altar, and they slaughtered the rams and sprinkled the blood on the altar, and they slaughtered the lambs and sprinkled the blood on the altar.**

23 **They presented the goats of the sin offering before the king and the congregation, and they laid their hands upon them,** since one who brings a sin offering must place his hands upon the animal and confess his sin.

24 **The priests slaughtered them and presented their blood as a sin offering on the altar.** They performed the rite of a sin offering by using a finger to spread some of the blood on the altar, as is done with all sin offerings,[194] unlike burnt offerings, whose blood is sprinkled on the altar.[195] They did this in order **to atone for all Israel, for the king had said that the burnt offering and the sin offering were on behalf of all Israel.**

25 **He positioned the Levites in the House of the Lord with cymbals, with lyres, and with harps, in accordance with the command of David, and of Gad, the king's seer,** who was to a certain extent King David's personal prophet,[196] **and Natan the prophet, for the command was by the Lord through His prophets.** The commandments involving the Temple service, including the singing of the Levites, were transmitted by the prophets.[197]

26 **The Levites stood with the** musical **instruments of David, and the priests with the trumpets.**

27 **Hizkiyahu said to offer up the burnt offering upon the altar. At the time that** the sacrifice of **the burnt offering began, the song of the Lord began, and the trumpets,** and the music was played **by means of the instruments of David king of Israel.**

28 **All the congregation prostrated themselves, and the song was sung, and the trumpets were sounded; all this** continued in an orderly fashion **until the conclusion of** the sacrifice of **the burnt offering.**

29 **At the conclusion of the offering, the king and all those present with him knelt and prostrated themselves,** as part of the ritual of the renewed sanctification of the Temple.

30 **Yehizkiyahu the king and the princes said to the Levites to praise the Lord with the words of David, and of Asaf the seer,** called a seer because his compositions were inspired by a divine spirit.[198] Accordingly, **they praised until there was rejoicing,** until the joy spread throughout the congregation, **and they bowed their heads and prostrated themselves** to the ground.[199]

31 **Yehizkiyahu proclaimed and said: Now you have dedicated yourselves to the Lord, approach and bring feast offerings and thanks offerings to the House of the Lord. The congregation brought feast offerings and thanks offerings.** These were peace offerings brought voluntarily, as a mark of gratitude and joy. The major part of such sacrifices is eaten by their owners. **And anyone generous of heart** brought **burnt offerings,** which are not eaten but are entirely burned.

32 **The number of burnt offerings that the congregation brought was seventy bulls, one hundred rams, two hundred lambs; all these were a burnt offering to the Lord.**

יז לְהוֹצִיא לְנַחַל־קִדְרוֹן חוּצָה׃ וַיָּחֵלּוּ בְּאֶחָד לַחֹדֶשׁ הָרִאשׁוֹן לְקַדֵּשׁ וּבְיוֹם שְׁמוֹנָה
לַחֹדֶשׁ בָּאוּ לְאוּלָם יְהוָה וַיְקַדְּשׁוּ אֶת־בֵּית־יְהוָה לְיָמִים שְׁמוֹנָה וּבְיוֹם שִׁשָּׁה
יח עָשָׂר לַחֹדֶשׁ הָרִאשׁוֹן כִּלּוּ׃ וַיָּבוֹאוּ פְנִימָה אֶל־חִזְקִיָּהוּ הַמֶּלֶךְ וַיֹּאמְרוּ
טִהַרְנוּ אֶת־כָּל־בֵּית יְהוָה אֶת־מִזְבַּח הָעוֹלָה וְאֶת־כָּל־כֵּלָיו וְאֶת־שֻׁלְחַן הַמַּעֲרֶכֶת
יט וְאֶת־כָּל־כֵּלָיו׃ וְאֵת כָּל־הַכֵּלִים אֲשֶׁר הִזְנִיחַ הַמֶּלֶךְ אָחָז בְּמַלְכוּתוֹ בְּמַעֲלוֹ הֵכַנּוּ
כ וְהִקְדָּשְׁנוּ וְהִנָּם לִפְנֵי מִזְבַּח יְהוָה׃ וַיַּשְׁכֵּם יְחִזְקִיָּהוּ הַמֶּלֶךְ וַיֶּאֱסֹף אֵת
כא שָׂרֵי הָעִיר וַיַּעַל בֵּית יְהוָה׃ וַיָּבִיאוּ פָרִים־שִׁבְעָה וְאֵילִים שִׁבְעָה וּכְבָשִׂים שִׁבְעָה
וּצְפִירֵי עִזִּים שִׁבְעָה לְחַטָּאת עַל־הַמַּמְלָכָה וְעַל־הַמִּקְדָּשׁ וְעַל־יְהוּדָה וַיֹּאמֶר
כב לִבְנֵי אַהֲרֹן הַכֹּהֲנִים לְהַעֲלוֹת עַל־מִזְבַּח יְהוָה׃ וַיִּשְׁחֲטוּ הַבָּקָר וַיְקַבְּלוּ הַכֹּהֲנִים
אֶת־הַדָּם וַיִּזְרְקוּ הַמִּזְבֵּחָה וַיִּשְׁחֲטוּ הָאֵלִים וַיִּזְרְקוּ הַדָּם הַמִּזְבֵּחָה וַיִּשְׁחֲטוּ
כג הַכְּבָשִׂים וַיִּזְרְקוּ הַדָּם הַמִּזְבֵּחָה׃ וַיַּגִּישׁוּ אֶת־שְׂעִירֵי הַחַטָּאת לִפְנֵי הַמֶּלֶךְ וְהַקָּהָל
כד וַיִּסְמְכוּ יְדֵיהֶם עֲלֵיהֶם׃ וַיִּשְׁחָטוּם הַכֹּהֲנִים וַיְחַטְּאוּ אֶת־דָּמָם הַמִּזְבֵּחָה לְכַפֵּר
כה עַל־כָּל־יִשְׂרָאֵל כִּי לְכָל־יִשְׂרָאֵל אָמַר הַמֶּלֶךְ הָעוֹלָה וְהַחַטָּאת׃ וַיַּעֲמֵד אֶת־
הַלְוִיִּם בֵּית יְהוָה בִּמְצִלְתַּיִם בִּנְבָלִים וּבְכִנֹּרוֹת בְּמִצְוַת דָּוִיד וְגָד חֹזֵה־הַמֶּלֶךְ
וְנָתָן הַנָּבִיא כִּי בְיַד־יְהוָה הַמִּצְוָה בְּיַד־נְבִיאָיו׃
כו כז וַיַּעַמְדוּ הַלְוִיִּם בִּכְלֵי דָוִיד וְהַכֹּהֲנִים בַּחֲצֹצְרוֹת׃ וַיֹּאמֶר חִזְקִיָּהוּ לְהַעֲלוֹת
הָעֹלָה לְהַמִּזְבֵּחַ וּבְעֵת הֵחֵל הָעוֹלָה הֵחֵל שִׁיר־יְהוָה וְהַחֲצֹצְרוֹת וְעַל־יְדֵי כְּלֵי
כח דָּוִיד מֶלֶךְ יִשְׂרָאֵל׃ וְכָל־הַקָּהָל מִשְׁתַּחֲוִים וְהַשִּׁיר מְשׁוֹרֵר וְהַחֲצֹצְרוֹת מחצצרים מַחְצְרִים
כט הַכֹּל עַד לִכְלוֹת הָעֹלָה׃ וּכְכַלּוֹת לְהַעֲלוֹת כָּרְעוּ הַמֶּלֶךְ וְכָל־הַנִּמְצְאִים אִתּוֹ
ל וַיִּשְׁתַּחֲווּ׃ וַיֹּאמֶר יְחִזְקִיָּהוּ הַמֶּלֶךְ וְהַשָּׂרִים לַלְוִיִּם לְהַלֵּל לַיהוָה בְּדִבְרֵי דָוִיד
לא וְאָסָף הַחֹזֶה וַיְהַלְלוּ עַד־לְשִׂמְחָה וַיִּקְּדוּ וַיִּשְׁתַּחֲווּ׃ וַיַּעַן יְחִזְקִיָּהוּ
וַיֹּאמֶר עַתָּה מִלֵּאתֶם יֶדְכֶם לַיהוָה גֹּשׁוּ וְהָבִיאוּ זְבָחִים וְתוֹדוֹת לְבֵית יְהוָה
לב וַיָּבִיאוּ הַקָּהָל זְבָחִים וְתוֹדוֹת וְכָל־נְדִיב לֵב עֹלוֹת׃ וַיְהִי מִסְפַּר הָעֹלָה אֲשֶׁר
הֵבִיאוּ הַקָּהָל בָּקָר שִׁבְעִים אֵילִים מֵאָה כְּבָשִׂים מָאתָיִם לְעֹלָה לַיהוָה כָּל־אֵלֶּה׃

33 **The** animals that the people **consecrated** and brought as peace offerings and thanks offerings **were six hundred cattle and three thousand sheep.**
34 **Only the priests were too few, and were unable to flay all the burnt offerings. Their brethren the Levites supported them until the labor was concluded, until the** rest of the **priests could be sanctified, as the Levites were more conscientious about sanctifying themselves than the priests.** In this instance, the Levites were more diligent and enthusiastic than the priests, who accompanied them. Beforehand as well (29:12, 15), it seems that the heads of the Levite divisions were the first to respond to Hizkiyahu's call.[200]
35 **There were also burnt offerings in abundance, with the fat of the peace offerings, and the libations for each burnt offering,** the flour and wine which must be brought with each burnt offering. **And** thus **the service of the House of the Lord was established** from that point onward.
36 **Yehizkiyahu and all the people rejoiced over God having directed the people,** because He had directed and awakened their hearts to participate in the sacred tasks,[201] **as the matter had happened suddenly.** The Temple had been speedily restored, after generations during which it had ceased its proper functioning. After the neglect of the Temple and its service in the days of Ahaz, and during his father's reign as well, the people who were present saw this ceremony as signaling the start of a new era of renewed interest in the service of God.

The Passover of Hizkiyahu

II CHRONICLES 30:1–31:1

The purification of the Temple continued through the first half of the first month, Nisan. Consequently, the people do not manage to ritually purify themselves in time to offer the paschal offering. Hizkiyahu therefore institutes that in that year they should observe a kind of collective Second Passover in the second month, not only for the inhabitants of Judah but also for the remnant of the Kingdom of Israel. In their great joy, the people extend the celebration of this festival by an additional seven days.

30 1 **Yehizkiyahu sent** messengers not only to his subjects in the Kingdom of Judah, but **to all Israel**[D] **and Judah, and** he **also wrote letters to** the tribes of **Ephraim and Manasseh,**[B] **to come to the House of the Lord in Jerusalem, to perform the paschal offering to the Lord, God of Israel.**
2 **The king and his princes and all the congregation in Jerusalem took counsel,** discussed the matter and came to a decision, **to perform the paschal offering in the second month,** Iyar, instead of the first month, Nisan.[202] There is already a precedent in the Torah that in certain circumstances the paschal offering can be sacrificed on the fourteenth of Iyar, as a substitute for the fourteenth of Nisan.[203] However, it should be noted that the Torah does not state that the entire congregation of Israel may do so, as the king and his men supposed.
3 **For they could not perform it at that time,** on the fourteenth of Nisan, **because** even had they sped up the process of purifying the Temple, there was another problem: **The priests had not sanctified themselves in sufficient number and,** furthermore, **the people had not** yet **gathered in Jerusalem.** Even for those who had set out to Jerusalem, the journey took longer than expected, as they had renewed a pilgrimage that had not been performed in this manner for many years, even from the Kingdom of Judah, and certainly not from the Kingdom of Israel.
4 **The matter,** the postponement of the paschal offering, **was right in the eyes of the king and in the eyes of the entire congregation.**
5 **They reached a decision to issue a proclamation throughout Israel, from Beersheba to Dan,** in all the cities of Israel, **to come to perform the paschal offering to the Lord, God of Israel, in Jerusalem, as they had not often done as it was written.** Even those who knew what the Torah said with regard to the paschal offering had, for many years, treated this commandment as a theoretical idea recorded in the holy book which need not be fulfilled in practice.[204]
6 **The couriers** equipped **with the letters from the hand of the king and his princes went throughout all Israel and Judah,** although the letters were addressed mainly to the people of Israel who were not in Judah, **and in accordance with the command of the king,** the messengers issued a declaration **saying: Children of Israel,** repent and **return to the Lord, God of Abraham, Isaac, and Israel, and He will** have mercy and **return to the remnant** of the Kingdom of Israel **left of you from the hand of the kings of Assyria.**
7 **Do not be like your fathers, and like your brethren, who trespassed against the Lord, God of their fathers, and He rendered them an astonishment [*shamma*],** or desolation [*shemama*], **as you** yourselves can **see.**

לג לד וְהַקֳּדָשִׁים בָּקָר שֵׁשׁ מֵאוֹת וְצֹאן שְׁלֹשֶׁת אֲלָפִים׃ רַק הַכֹּהֲנִים הָיוּ לִמְעָט וְלֹא
יָכְלוּ לְהַפְשִׁיט אֶת־כָּל־הָעֹלוֹת וַיְחַזְּקוּם אֲחֵיהֶם הַלְוִיִּם עַד־כְּלוֹת הַמְּלָאכָה
לה וְעַד־יִתְקַדְּשׁוּ הַכֹּהֲנִים כִּי הַלְוִיִּם יִשְׁרֵי לֵבָב לְהִתְקַדֵּשׁ מֵהַכֹּהֲנִים׃ וְגַם־עֹלָה
לו לָרֹב בְּחֶלְבֵי הַשְּׁלָמִים וּבַנְּסָכִים לָעֹלָה וַתִּכּוֹן עֲבוֹדַת בֵּית־יהוה׃ וַיִּשְׂמַח יְחִזְקִיָּהוּ
ל א וְכָל־הָעָם עַל הַהֵכִין הָאֱלֹהִים לָעָם כִּי בְּפִתְאֹם הָיָה הַדָּבָר׃ וַיִּשְׁלַח
יְחִזְקִיָּהוּ עַל־כָּל־יִשְׂרָאֵל וִיהוּדָה וְגַם־אִגְּרוֹת כָּתַב עַל־אֶפְרַיִם וּמְנַשֶּׁה לָבוֹא
ב לְבֵית־יהוה בִּירוּשָׁלִָם לַעֲשׂוֹת פֶּסַח לַיהוה אֱלֹהֵי יִשְׂרָאֵל׃ וַיִּוָּעַץ הַמֶּלֶךְ וְשָׂרָיו
ג וְכָל־הַקָּהָל בִּירוּשָׁלִָם לַעֲשׂוֹת הַפֶּסַח בַּחֹדֶשׁ הַשֵּׁנִי׃ כִּי לֹא יָכְלוּ לַעֲשֹׂתוֹ בָּעֵת
ד הַהִיא כִּי הַכֹּהֲנִים לֹא־הִתְקַדְּשׁוּ לְמַדַּי וְהָעָם לֹא־נֶאֶסְפוּ לִירוּשָׁלִָם׃ וַיִּישַׁר הַדָּבָר
ה בְּעֵינֵי הַמֶּלֶךְ וּבְעֵינֵי כָּל־הַקָּהָל׃ וַיַּעֲמִידוּ דָבָר לְהַעֲבִיר קוֹל בְּכָל־יִשְׂרָאֵל מִבְּאֵר־
שֶׁבַע וְעַד־דָּן לָבוֹא לַעֲשׂוֹת פֶּסַח לַיהוה אֱלֹהֵי־יִשְׂרָאֵל בִּירוּשָׁלִָם כִּי לֹא לָרֹב
ו עָשׂוּ כַּכָּתוּב׃ וַיֵּלְכוּ הָרָצִים בָּאִגְּרוֹת מִיַּד הַמֶּלֶךְ וְשָׂרָיו בְּכָל־יִשְׂרָאֵל וִיהוּדָה
וּכְמִצְוַת הַמֶּלֶךְ לֵאמֹר בְּנֵי יִשְׂרָאֵל שׁוּבוּ אֶל־יהוה אֱלֹהֵי אַבְרָהָם יִצְחָק וְיִשְׂרָאֵל
ז וְיָשֹׁב אֶל־הַפְּלֵיטָה הַנִּשְׁאֶרֶת לָכֶם מִכַּף מַלְכֵי אַשּׁוּר׃ וְאַל־תִּהְיוּ כַּאֲבוֹתֵיכֶם
וְכַאֲחֵיכֶם אֲשֶׁר מָעֲלוּ בַּיהוה אֱלֹהֵי אֲבוֹתֵיהֶם וַיִּתְּנֵם לְשַׁמָּה כַּאֲשֶׁר אַתֶּם רֹאִים׃

DISCUSSION

30:1 | **Yehizkiyahu sent to all Israel:** Since the book of Chronicles deals almost exclusively with the Kingdom of Judah, and refers to the Kingdom of Israel only incidentally, it does not even mention a highly significant event in the history of the Kingdom of Israel; its conquest in the early years of the reign of Hizkiyahu by the Assyrian Empire, and the exile of its inhabitants from their land (see Rashi on verses 1 and 9). It appears that this exile was not total, as that would require not only great cruelty, but also methods that were not available at the time. Therefore, even if only for technical reasons, the mass exile was left incomplete, and quite a few people remained in the territory of the Kingdom of Israel. True, they were under the control of foreign authorities, but it was at least possible to inspire them to come and celebrate Passover with their brethren in Jerusalem.

BACKGROUND

30:1 | **And also wrote letters to Ephraim and Manasseh:** According to the book of Chronicles, the kingdoms of Judah and Israel maintained mutual contact despite the division of the kingdom in the days of Yorovam and Rehavam, and the Kingdom of Judah had a notable influence over Israel. This can be seen in the activities of Asa king of Judah, in the territory of Ephraim and Manasseh: "When Asa heard…he was encouraged, and removed the detestable things from the entire land of Judah and Benjamin, and from the cities that he had captured in the highlands of Ephraim…He gathered all Judah and Benjamin, and those who resided with them from Ephraim and Manasseh, and from Simeon, as many from Israel had joined him" (15:8–9). The fact that Yehoshafat and Ahaz, who were kings of Judah, are both termed on occasion "king of Israel" is indicative of an identification of sorts between the two kingdoms (see 17:1, 21:2, 28:19). This idea is further supported by the archaeological discovery of seals from the period of Hizkiyahu which were unearthed in the City of David. These seals, which have been dated to the early seventh century BCE, include clearly Israelite names, such as Pinhas, and Ahiav son of Menahem. This shows that certain Israelites served in senior positions in the government of Judah.

8 **Now do not stiffen your necks like your fathers,** but **extend**
a hand to the Lord, and come to His Sanctuary, which He
has sanctified forever, and serve the Lord your God there
and, consequently, **His enflamed wrath will be withdrawn**
from you.
9 **For if you return to the Lord, your brethren and your** exiled and captive **children will be granted compassion before**
their captors. Their captors will have pity upon them, **and** thus
they will have hope that they **will** survive and **return to this**
land, as the Lord your God is gracious and merciful, and
will not turn His face from you, if you return to Him.
10 **The couriers were passing from city to city in the land of**
Ephraim and Manasseh, up to Zebulun, throughout the territory that had once belonged to the Kingdom of Israel; **and**
they, the residents of those areas, **were laughing at them,** the
messengers of the king of Judah, **and mocking them,** as the
messengers had no status or authority in those areas. The idea
of returning to the Temple after hundreds of years during which
their ancestors had not even visited Jerusalem seemed prepos-
terous to many of them.
11 **But** some **people from Asher and from Manasseh and from**
Zebulun humbled themselves and came to Jerusalem.
Apparently no one came from Ephraim, which was a haughty tribe that traditionally refused to accept the authority of
others.[205]
12 **In Judah too, the hand of God,** divine assistance, **was to grant**
them one heart; there was a general spiritual uplifting, and the
people were stirred **to perform the command of the king and**
of the princes regarding the word of the Lord.
13 **Many people assembled in Jerusalem to observe the**
Festival of Unleavened Bread in the second month, a very
great congregation.
14 **They rose,** before they offered the paschal offering, **and re-**
moved the altars that were in Jerusalem, both the shrines that
were designed for the service of God, and the altars dedicated
to idolatry, **and they removed all the censers** for incense, or
the places where incense was burned,[206] **and cast them** all **into**
the Kidron Valley.
15 **They slaughtered the paschal offering on the fourteenth**
of the second month, and the priests and the Levites were
ashamed of their negligence **and they sanctified themselves.**
Since the Temple had been closed and deserted for many
years, the priests were slow to answer Hizkiyahu's call, perhaps because they did not believe that he was ready to carry
out his plans, or they doubted the purity of his intentions.[207]
Nevertheless, at this point they too came **and brought burnt**
offerings to the House of the Lord.
16 **They stood in their** respective **places,** each performing his
tasks, **in accordance with their order, in accordance with**
the Torah of Moses the man of God. The priests sprinkled
the blood which they received from the hand of the Levites,
who slaughtered the offerings. The verses in the Torah indicate
that the slaughtering of an offering need not be performed by a
priest; rather, anyone may perform the act of slaughter. By contrast, receiving the blood in a vessel and sprinkling it upon the
altar are parts of the priestly service and may not be performed
by others.[208]
17 In fact, it was not necessary for the Levites to slaughter, as
in those days every homeowner knew how to slaughter his
animals in the ritually correct manner. Nevertheless, on this occasion the Levites slaughtered, **for there were many**[209] **in the**
congregation who had not sanctified themselves, and the
Levites were in charge of the slaughter of the paschal offer-
ings for everyone impure, and therefore unable themselves **to**
sanctify them, to slaughter the animals **to the Lord.**[210]
18 **For most of the people, many from Ephraim and Manasseh,**
Issachar and Zebulun, had not purified themselves, as they
partook of the paschal offering not as it is written, not according to the guidelines of the Torah, **yet Yehizkiyahu prayed**
on their behalf, saying: The good Lord will atone for
19 **anyone who prepares his heart** and strives **to seek God, the**
Lord, God of his fathers, although he is not able to ritually
purify himself **in accordance with the purity of the conse-**
crated. Most impure people can purify themselves simply by
immersing in a ritual bath, but that is not enough for one who
is impure due to contact with a corpse. Such an individual must
also be sprinkled with the water of purification, as part of a
seven-day process. Thus, many people were unable to purify
themselves properly in time for the fixed date of the paschal
offering.
20 **The Lord heard Yehizkiyahu**[D] **and healed,** forgave, **the peo-**
ple. God apparently consented to the proceedings.
21 **The children of Israel who were present in Jerusalem ob-**
served the Festival of Unleavened Bread for seven days
with great joy, and the Levites and the priests were praising
the Lord day after day with loud instruments to the Lord.
22 **Yehizkiyahu spoke encouragingly to all the Levites who**
were well versed in the song of their service to **the Lord,** or
who were well versed in Torah and could have a positive influence upon the people.[211] **They ate on the festival;** alternatively,
so they ate the offerings of the feast **for the seven days,** while
slaughtering peace offerings and confessing to the Lord,
God of their fathers. Together with their joy upon bringing
the offerings, they also expressed regret for their former deeds,
and returned to God.

ח עַתָּה אַל־תַּקְשׁוּ עָרְפְּכֶם כַּאֲבוֹתֵיכֶם תְּנוּ־יָד לַיהוָה וּבֹאוּ לְמִקְדָּשׁוֹ אֲשֶׁר הִקְדִּישׁ
ט לְעוֹלָם וְעִבְדוּ אֶת־יְהוָה אֱלֹהֵיכֶם וְיָשֹׁב מִכֶּם חֲרוֹן אַפּוֹ: כִּי בְשׁוּבְכֶם עַל־יְהוָה
אֲחֵיכֶם וּבְנֵיכֶם לְרַחֲמִים לִפְנֵי שׁוֹבֵיהֶם וְלָשׁוּב לָאָרֶץ הַזֹּאת כִּי־חַנּוּן וְרַחוּם
י יְהוָה אֱלֹהֵיכֶם וְלֹא־יָסִיר פָּנִים מִכֶּם אִם־תָּשׁוּבוּ אֵלָיו: וַיִּהְיוּ הָרָצִים
עֹבְרִים מֵעִיר ׀ לָעִיר בְּאֶרֶץ־אֶפְרַיִם וּמְנַשֶּׁה וְעַד־זְבֻלוּן וַיִּהְיוּ מַשְׂחִיקִים עֲלֵיהֶם
יא יב וּמַלְעִגִים בָּם: אַךְ אֲנָשִׁים מֵאָשֵׁר וּמְנַשֶּׁה וּמִזְּבֻלוּן נִכְנְעוּ וַיָּבֹאוּ לִירוּשָׁלָם: גַּם
בִּיהוּדָה הָיְתָה יַד הָאֱלֹהִים לָתֵת לָהֶם לֵב אֶחָד לַעֲשׂוֹת מִצְוַת הַמֶּלֶךְ וְהַשָּׂרִים
יג בִּדְבַר יְהוָה: וַיֵּאָסְפוּ יְרוּשָׁלַםִ עַם־רָב לַעֲשׂוֹת אֶת־חַג הַמַּצּוֹת בַּחֹדֶשׁ הַשֵּׁנִי
יד קָהָל לָרֹב מְאֹד: וַיָּקֻמוּ וַיָּסִירוּ אֶת־הַמִּזְבְּחוֹת אֲשֶׁר בִּירוּשָׁלָםִ וְאֵת כָּל־הַמְקַטְּרוֹת
טו הֵסִירוּ וַיַּשְׁלִיכוּ לְנַחַל קִדְרוֹן: וַיִּשְׁחֲטוּ הַפֶּסַח בְּאַרְבָּעָה עָשָׂר לַחֹדֶשׁ הַשֵּׁנִי
טז וְהַכֹּהֲנִים וְהַלְוִיִּם נִכְלְמוּ וַיִּתְקַדְּשׁוּ וַיָּבִיאוּ עֹלוֹת בֵּית יְהוָה: וַיַּעַמְדוּ עַל־עָמְדָם
כְּמִשְׁפָּטָם כְּתוֹרַת מֹשֶׁה אִישׁ־הָאֱלֹהִים הַכֹּהֲנִים זֹרְקִים אֶת־הַדָּם מִיַּד הַלְוִיִּם:
יז כִּי־רַבַּת בַּקָּהָל אֲשֶׁר לֹא־הִתְקַדָּשׁוּ וְהַלְוִיִּם עַל־שְׁחִיטַת הַפְּסָחִים לְכֹל לֹא
יח טָהוֹר לְהַקְדִּישׁ לַיהוָה: כִּי מַרְבִּית הָעָם רַבַּת מֵאֶפְרַיִם וּמְנַשֶּׁה יִשָּׂשכָר וּזְבֻלוּן
לֹא הִטֶּהָרוּ כִּי־אָכְלוּ אֶת־הַפֶּסַח בְּלֹא כַכָּתוּב כִּי הִתְפַּלֵּל יְחִזְקִיָּהוּ עֲלֵיהֶם לֵאמֹר
יט יְהוָה הַטּוֹב יְכַפֵּר בְּעַד: כָּל־לְבָבוֹ הֵכִין לִדְרוֹשׁ הָאֱלֹהִים ׀ יְהוָה אֱלֹהֵי אֲבוֹתָיו
כ וְלֹא כְּטָהֳרַת הַקֹּדֶשׁ: וַיִּשְׁמַע יְהוָה אֶל־יְחִזְקִיָּהוּ וַיִּרְפָּא אֶת־
כא הָעָם: וַיַּעֲשׂוּ בְנֵי־יִשְׂרָאֵל הַנִּמְצְאִים בִּירוּשָׁלַםִ אֶת־חַג הַמַּצּוֹת שִׁבְעַת
יָמִים בְּשִׂמְחָה גְדוֹלָה וּמְהַלְלִים לַיהוָה יוֹם ׀ בְּיוֹם הַלְוִיִּם וְהַכֹּהֲנִים בִּכְלֵי עֹז
כב לַיהוָה: וַיְדַבֵּר יְחִזְקִיָּהוּ עַל־לֵב כָּל־הַלְוִיִּם הַמַּשְׂכִּילִים שֵׂכֶל־טוֹב

DISCUSSION

30:20| **The Lord heard Yehizkiyahu:** The Sages maintain that Hizkiyahu acted improperly here. He should have intercalated the extra month in the year at the correct time, and thereby enabled the people to sacrifice the paschal offering on the appropriate date, in the first month. Intercalation was practiced from the earliest generations, as the Hebrew calendar cannot exclusively follow the lunar cycle, because the festival of Passover must be observed in the springtime. Consequently, the calendar must be adjusted to conform with the solar year (see commentary on Exodus 13:2). However, it appears that Hizkiyahu failed to do this early enough (see *Berakhot* 10b; see also Radak and Malbim, verse 2).

23 **The entire congregation took counsel to celebrate another seven days,** in addition to the first seven days they celebrated, just as was done at the time of the initial inauguration of the Temple in the days of Solomon;[212] **and** indeed **they celebrated for** an additional **seven days joyfully.** They accepted upon themselves this additional period in order to express their gratitude to God.

24 **For** even if the people did not come prepared for this extra period, **Hizkiyahu king of Judah contributed to the congregation one thousand bulls and seven thousand sheep, and the princes contributed to the congregation one thousand bulls and ten thousand sheep.** Thanks to the donations of the king and his princes, there was meat in abundance, **and priests sanctified themselves in large numbers.**

25 **The entire congregation of Judah, the priests and the Levites, the entire congregation that came from Israel, and the strangers who came from the Land of Israel and who lived in Judah, rejoiced.**

26 **There was great joy in Jerusalem, for since the days of Solomon son of David king of Israel there had not been** a celebration **like this in Jerusalem.**

27 **The priests the Levites rose and blessed the people, and their voice was heard; their prayer came to His Holy Abode, to the heavens.**

31 1 **With the conclusion of all this, all Israel who were present** in Jerusalem **went out to the cities of Judah and shattered their** idolatrous **monuments, cut down the sacred trees,** which were worshipped in idolatrous rituals, **and smashed the shrines and the altars from all Judah and Benjamin, and in Ephraim and Manasseh, until they were eradicated.** They made every effort to purify the land from foreign forms of worship, and then, when they had finished, **all the children of Israel returned, each to his portion, to their cities.**

Amulet with the priestly benediction, Ketef Hinom, Jerusalem, seventh century BCE

Reconstructed smashed altar, with a snake etched on its stones, possibly from the days of Hizkiyahu, Beersheba, late eighth century BCE

The Restoration of the Priests and the Levites to Their Former Status in the Temple and throughout the Land

II CHRONICLES 31:2–21

Hizkiyahu, who was one of Israel's greatest kings, acted decisively to eradicate idolatry. He also removed the shrines upon which offerings were presented to God by anyone in any place, a practice that violated the Torah's commandment of centralized sacrifice. Instead, the king reinstituted the service of God in one central location, the Temple in Jerusalem, while at the same time reinforcing the status of the priests and Levites. He also urged the people to give the priestly and Levitical gifts required for sustenance to those who performed the Temple service, and their families. The people responded positively to his request.

2 At this point, the division of the priests and Levites into watches was merely an abstract memory, as the Temple service had not actually been performed in many years, and the Temple had been left mostly deserted. Now it was necessary to renew the service and restore the previous order. **Yehizkiyahu set up the divisions,** or watches, **of the priests and the Levites by their divisions,** their proper order, **each man in accordance with his service, for the priests and for the Levites, for** the sacrifice of **burnt offerings and for peace offerings, to serve, to give thanks, and to praise in the gates of the camps of the Lord,** in the Temple.

3 **The king's portion from his property for the burnt offerings was for the burnt offerings of the morning and the evening,** the daily offerings, **and the** additional **burnt offerings for the Sabbaths, and for the New Moons, and for festivals, as it is written in the Torah of the Lord.**

4 **He,** the king, **said to the people, to the inhabitants of Jerusalem,** that they were obligated **to give the portion,** the gifts, **of the priests and the Levites, so that they would devote themselves to the Torah of the Lord.** It was necessary for the people to give the priests and Levites the *terumot* and tithes that were owed them from the people's agricultural produce[213] to enable them to fulfill their tasks properly, and observe and teach the commandments of the Torah.

5 The people obeyed the king: **When the message** of the king **was disseminated,** or as soon as his command was

לַיהוָה וַיֹּאכְלוּ אֶת־הַמּוֹעֵד שִׁבְעַת הַיָּמִים מְזַבְּחִים זִבְחֵי שְׁלָמִים וּמִתְוַדִּים
כג לַיהוָה אֱלֹהֵי אֲבוֹתֵיהֶם׃ וַיִּוָּעֲצוּ כָּל־הַקָּהָל לַעֲשׂוֹת שִׁבְעַת יָמִים
כד אֲחֵרִים וַיַּעֲשׂוּ שִׁבְעַת יָמִים שִׂמְחָה׃ כִּי חִזְקִיָּהוּ מֶלֶךְ־יְהוּדָה הֵרִים לַקָּהָל אֶלֶף
פָּרִים וְשִׁבְעַת אֲלָפִים צֹאן וְהַשָּׂרִים הֵרִימוּ לַקָּהָל פָּרִים אֶלֶף וְצֹאן עֲשֶׂרֶת אֲלָפִים
כה וַיִּתְקַדְּשׁוּ כֹהֲנִים לָרֹב׃ וַיִּשְׂמְחוּ ׀ כָּל־קְהַל יְהוּדָה וְהַכֹּהֲנִים וְהַלְוִיִּם וְכָל־הַקָּהָל
כו הַבָּאִים מִיִּשְׂרָאֵל וְהַגֵּרִים הַבָּאִים מֵאֶרֶץ יִשְׂרָאֵל וְהַיּוֹשְׁבִים בִּיהוּדָה׃ וַתְּהִי
שִׂמְחָה גְדוֹלָה בִּירוּשָׁלִָם כִּי מִימֵי שְׁלֹמֹה בֶן־דָּוִיד מֶלֶךְ יִשְׂרָאֵל לֹא כָזֹאת
כז בִּירוּשָׁלִָם׃ וַיָּקֻמוּ הַכֹּהֲנִים הַלְוִיִּם וַיְבָרְכוּ אֶת־הָעָם וַיִּשָּׁמַע בְּקוֹלָם
לא א וַתָּבוֹא תְפִלָּתָם לִמְעוֹן קָדְשׁוֹ לַשָּׁמָיִם׃ וּכְכַלּוֹת כָּל־זֹאת יָצְאוּ כָל־
יִשְׂרָאֵל הַנִּמְצְאִים לְעָרֵי יְהוּדָה וַיְשַׁבְּרוּ הַמַּצֵּבוֹת וַיְגַדְּעוּ הָאֲשֵׁרִים וַיְנַתְּצוּ אֶת־
הַבָּמוֹת וְאֶת־הַמִּזְבְּחוֹת מִכָּל־יְהוּדָה וּבִנְיָמִן וּבְאֶפְרַיִם וּמְנַשֶּׁה עַד־לְכַלֵּה וַיָּשׁוּבוּ
ב כָּל־בְּנֵי יִשְׂרָאֵל אִישׁ לַאֲחֻזָּתוֹ לְעָרֵיהֶם׃ וַיַּעֲמֵד יְחִזְקִיָּהוּ אֶת־מַחְלְקוֹת
הַכֹּהֲנִים וְהַלְוִיִּם עַל־מַחְלְקוֹתָם אִישׁ ׀ כְּפִי עֲבֹדָתוֹ לַכֹּהֲנִים וְלַלְוִיִּם לְעֹלָה
ג וְלִשְׁלָמִים לְשָׁרֵת וּלְהֹדוֹת וּלְהַלֵּל בְּשַׁעֲרֵי מַחֲנוֹת יְהוָה׃ וּמְנָת
הַמֶּלֶךְ מִן־רְכוּשׁוֹ לָעֹלוֹת לְעֹלוֹת הַבֹּקֶר וְהָעֶרֶב וְהָעֹלוֹת לַשַּׁבָּתוֹת וְלֶחֳדָשִׁים
ד וְלַמֹּעֲדִים כַּכָּתוּב בְּתוֹרַת יְהוָה׃ וַיֹּאמֶר לָעָם לְיוֹשְׁבֵי יְרוּשָׁלִַם לָתֵת מְנָת הַכֹּהֲנִים
ה וְהַלְוִיִּם לְמַעַן יֶחֶזְקוּ בְּתוֹרַת יְהוָה׃ וְכִפְרֹץ הַדָּבָר הִרְבּוּ בְנֵי־יִשְׂרָאֵל רֵאשִׁית
דָּגָן תִּירוֹשׁ וְיִצְהָר וּדְבַשׁ וְכֹל תְּבוּאַת שָׂדֶה וּמַעְשַׂר הַכֹּל לָרֹב הֵבִיאוּ׃

strengthened, **the children of Israel,** including those living in the Kingdom of Israel, **gave in abundance the first fruits of grain, wine, oil, and** date **honey, and all the produce of the field, and the tithe of everything; they brought in abundance.**

Sheaves of grain piled in heaps

Wine

Olive oil

Date honey

6 **The children of Israel and Judah who lived in the cities of Judah, they too brought the tithes of cattle and sheep, and the tithe of consecrated items that were consecrated to the Lord their God, and piled them in heaps.** They piled them into heaps of grain and fruit, some of which were for the priests, while others were slated for the Levites.[214]

7 **In the third month,** Sivan, **the heaps began to be established.** Throughout the summer, as they gathered in their crops, they separated from them the gifts for the priests and Levites, **and in the seventh month,** Tishrei, **they were completed.**

8 **Yehizkiyahu and the princes came and saw the heaps, and they blessed the Lord,** who had provided them with such great bounty, **and His people Israel,** who had brought the gifts.

9 **Yehizkiyahu inquired of the priests and the Levites concerning the heaps,** asking them whether they had already taken for themselves some of the bounteous crops that had been gathered together.[215]

10 **Azaryahu the chief priest,** the High Priest, **of the house of Tzadok, said to him. He said: Since the gifts began to come to the House of the Lord there has been eating to satisfaction, and a great deal is left over, for the Lord has blessed His people, and this plethora is left over.** The great amount of produce that you see is merely the leftovers of the original amount.[216]

11 **Yehizkiyahu said to prepare the chambers in the House of the Lord** to serve as warehouses, **and they prepared them.**

12 **They faithfully brought in the gifts, the tithes, and the consecrated items, and the chief official** appointed **in charge of them was Konanyahu the Levite, and Shimi his brother was** his **deputy.**

13 **Yehiel, Azazyahu, Nahat, Asael, Yerimot, Yozabad, Eliel, Yismakhyahu, Mahat, and Benayahu were officials under the hand of Konanyahu and Shimi his brother, by appointment of Yehizkiyahu the king, and Azaryahu was the chief official of the House of God,** the High Priest, who was the highest official in charge of the management of the Temple.[217]

14 **Koreh son of Yimna the Levite,** who was **the gatekeeper to the east, was** appointed to be **in charge of the gift offerings of God, allocating** to the priests **the gift of the Lord, and the sacred sacraments.**

15 **Alongside him were Eden, Minyamin, Yeshua, Shemayahu, Amaryahu, and Shekhanyahu,** who were in charge of the distribution **in the cities of the priests, in good faith, to give to their** priestly **brethren by divisions, to great and small alike,** an equal portion to all.

16 Those portions that were distributed in the cities were **besides that which went to males established in their lineage, from three years old and above, any who came to the House of the Lord, each a portion on his day, for their service in their watches according to their divisions.** The priests who served in the watches and their young children would receive portions of the sacrifices and other dues on the days when they performed the Temple service.

17 Here the chapter inserts a parenthetical note. Since the priests were now not only people of status, but had begun to perform public roles, it became necessary to update the lists of their lineage: Therefore, **he,** Hizkiyahu, further commanded that they prepare those lists, and **established the priests in their lineage by their patrilineal houses, and the Levites, from twenty years old and above, in their watches according to their divisions,**

18 **and established the lineage of all their small children, their wives, and their sons, and their daughters, for each** and every **congregation.** Since they reestablished the Temple service, a census was performed, incorporating each priest and Levite in their respective watches; **for in their good faith,** by faithfully observing their unique posts and functions, **they sanctified themselves in sanctity.**

19 And again with regard to the distribution of the gifts in the cities throughout the land: **From the sons of Aaron, the priests, who were** living **in the tracts of the fields of their cities, in each and every city, there were men designated by name** who were charged **to give portions to all the males among**

ו וּבְנֵ֨י יִשְׂרָאֵ֜ל וִיהוּדָ֗ה הַיּֽוֹשְׁבִים֙ בְּעָרֵ֣י יְהוּדָ֔ה גַּם־הֵ֗ם מַעְשַׂ֤ר בָּקָר֙ וָצֹ֔אן וּמַעְשַׂ֣ר
קֳדָשִׁ֔ים הַמְקֻדָּשִׁ֖ים לַיהוָ֣ה אֱלֹהֵיהֶ֑ם הֵבִ֕יאוּ וַֽיִּתְּנ֖וּ עֲרֵמ֥וֹת עֲרֵמֽוֹת׃
ז בַּחֹ֙דֶשׁ֙ הַשְּׁלִשִׁ֔י הֵחֵ֥לּוּ הָעֲרֵמ֖וֹת לִיס֑וֹד וּבַחֹ֥דֶשׁ הַשְּׁבִיעִ֖י כִּלּֽוּ׃
ח וַיָּבֹ֙אוּ֙ יְחִזְקִיָּ֣הוּ וְהַשָּׂרִ֔ים וַיִּרְא֖וּ אֶת־הָעֲרֵמ֑וֹת וַֽיְבָרְכוּ֙ אֶת־יְהוָ֔ה וְאֵ֖ת עַמּ֥וֹ
ט י יִשְׂרָאֵֽל׃ וַיִּדְרֹ֣שׁ יְחִזְקִיָּ֔הוּ עַל־הַכֹּהֲנִ֥ים וְהַלְוִיִּ֖ם עַל־הָעֲרֵמֽוֹת׃ וַיֹּ֣אמֶר כג
אֵלָ֜יו עֲזַרְיָ֧הוּ הַכֹּהֵ֛ן הָרֹ֖אשׁ לְבֵ֣ית צָד֑וֹק וַיֹּ֗אמֶר מֵהָחֵ֨ל הַתְּרוּמָ֜ה לָבִ֣יא בֵית־יְהוָ֗ה
אָכ֨וֹל וְשָׂב֤וֹעַ וְהוֹתֵר֙ עַד־לָר֔וֹב כִּ֤י יְהוָה֙ בֵּרַ֣ךְ אֶת־עַמּ֔וֹ וְהַנּוֹתָ֖ר אֶת־הֶהָמ֥וֹן
יא יב הַזֶּֽה׃ וַיֹּ֣אמֶר יְחִזְקִיָּ֔הוּ לְהָכִ֧ין לְשָׁכ֛וֹת בְּבֵ֥ית יְהוָ֖ה וַיָּכִֽינוּ׃ וַיָּבִ֜יאוּ אֶת־
הַתְּרוּמָ֧ה וְהַֽמַּעֲשֵׂ֛ר וְהַקֳּדָשִׁ֖ים בֶּאֱמוּנָ֑ה וַעֲלֵיהֶ֤ם נָגִיד֙ כונניהו הַלֵּוִ֔י וְשִׁמְעִ֥י אָחִ֖יהוּ כָּֽנַנְיָ֖הוּ
יג מִשְׁנֶֽה׃ וִֽיחִיאֵ֡ל וַ֠עֲזַזְיָהוּ וְנַ֨חַת וַעֲשָׂהאֵ֜ל וִירִימ֤וֹת וְיוֹזָבָד֙ וֶאֱלִיאֵ֔ל וְיִסְמַכְיָ֖הוּ
וּמַ֣חַת וּבְנָיָ֑הוּ פְּקִידִ֗ים מִיַּ֤ד כונניהו וְשִׁמְעִ֣י אָחִ֔יו בְּמִפְקַד֙ יְחִזְקִיָּ֣הוּ הַמֶּ֔לֶךְ וַעֲזַרְיָ֖הוּ כָּֽנַנְיָ֙הוּ֙
יד נְגִ֥יד בֵּית־הָאֱלֹהִֽים׃ וְקוֹרֵ֨א בֶן־יִמְנָ֤ה הַלֵּוִי֙ הַשּׁוֹעֵ֣ר לַמִּזְרָ֔חָה עַ֖ל נִדְב֣וֹת הָאֱלֹהִ֑ים
טו לָתֵת֙ תְּרוּמַ֣ת יְהוָ֔ה וְקָדְשֵׁ֖י הַקֳּדָשִֽׁים׃ וְעַל־יָד֡וֹ עֵ֣דֶן וּ֠מִנְיָמִן וְיֵשׁ֨וּעַ וּֽשְׁמַעְיָ֜הוּ
אֲמַרְיָ֧הוּ וּשְׁכַנְיָ֛הוּ בְּעָרֵ֥י הַכֹּהֲנִ֖ים בֶּאֱמוּנָ֑ה לָתֵ֤ת לַאֲחֵיהֶם֙ בְּמַחְלְק֔וֹת כַּגָּד֖וֹל
טז כַּקָּטָֽן׃ מִלְּבַד֩ הִתְיַחְשָׂ֨ם לִזְכָרִ֜ים מִבֶּ֨ן שָׁל֤וֹשׁ שָׁנִים֙ וּלְמַ֔עְלָה לְכָל־הַבָּ֣א לְבֵית־
יז יְהוָ֔ה לִדְבַר־י֖וֹם בְּיוֹמ֑וֹ לַעֲב֣וֹדָתָ֔ם בְּמִשְׁמְרוֹתָ֖ם כְּמַחְלְקוֹתֵיהֶֽם׃ וְאֵ֨ת הִתְיַחֵ֤שׂ
הַכֹּהֲנִים֙ לְבֵ֣ית אֲבֽוֹתֵיהֶ֔ם וְהַ֨לְוִיִּ֔ם מִבֶּ֛ן עֶשְׂרִ֥ים שָׁנָ֖ה וּלְמָ֑עְלָה בְּמִשְׁמְרֽוֹתֵיהֶ֖ם
יח בְּמַחְלְקוֹתֵיהֶֽם׃ וּלְהִתְיַחֵ֨שׂ בְּכָל־טַפָּ֜ם נְשֵׁיהֶ֧ם וּבְנֵיהֶ֛ם וּבְנוֹתֵיהֶ֖ם לְכָל־קָהָ֑ל כִּ֥י
יט בֶאֱמוּנָתָ֖ם יִֽתְקַדְּשׁוּ־קֹֽדֶשׁ׃ וְלִבְנֵ֨י אַהֲרֹ֜ן הַכֹּהֲנִ֗ים בִּשְׂדֵ֞י מִגְרַ֤שׁ עָרֵיהֶם֙ בְּכָל־עִ֣יר
וָעִ֔יר אֲנָשִׁ֕ים אֲשֶׁ֥ר נִקְּב֖וּ בְּשֵׁמ֑וֹת לָתֵ֣ת מָנ֗וֹת לְכָל־זָכָר֙ בַּכֹּ֣הֲנִ֔ים וּלְכָל־הִתְיַחֵ֖שׂ

the priests, and to all established in their lineage among the Levites. It seems that the Levites had taken less care of their genealogical lists, because their status accorded them less honor than that of the priests and their service was less well-defined than the priestly role, and also because the special marital restrictions of the priesthood did not apply to them. However, now that their status had received new significance, they too came and clarified their lineage.[218]

20 **Yehizkiyahu did so,**[D] or alternatively, Hizkiyahu performed further acts of this kind, **throughout all Judah, and he did what was good and right and true before the Lord his God.**
21 **In every action that he undertook in the service of the House of God, and for the Torah, and for the commandment, to seek his God, he acted with all his heart, and** he **was successful.**

The Downfall of Sennacherib King of Assyria

II CHRONICLES 32:1–23

The story of Sennacherib's campaign against Judah and his ultimate failure is related in detail in the books of Kings and Isaiah, which also cite at length Hizkiyahu's prayer on that occasion. Here the episode appears in brief form, in the general context of the chronicles of Hizkiyahu.

32 1 **After these true matters,** Hizkiyahu's righteous deeds,
Sennacherib king of Assyria came and entered Judah, and
encamped against the fortified cities, intending to breach and capture **them for himself.** He did not head immediately to Jerusalem, the center of the Kingdom of Judah's power, in the manner of other conquerors of the land. This was because Sennacherib was not interested in the conquest of Judah for its own sake, but only as part of his broader attack against Egypt. Since he considered Judah a nuisance in his path to Egypt that had to be removed, he initially besieged and fought against the smaller fortified cities of Judah before approaching Jerusalem.[219]

Sennacherib's Annals, which describe his campaign in Judah, Nineveh, late eighth century BCE

2 **Yehizkiyahu saw that Sennacherib had come, and that his intent was for war against Jerusalem.**
3 **He,** Hizkiyahu, **took counsel with his princes and his mighty ones to plug the waters in the springs that were outside the city** so that the enemies could not access the water, **and they assisted him.**
4 **A great many people were gathered, and they plugged all the springs, and the stream, that flowed through the midst of the land,** the Gihon (see 32:30), **saying: Why should the kings of Assyria come and find abundant water?** Most sieges are conducted in the summer, when water sources are vital.
5 **He took courage and rebuilt the entire breached wall and raised it,** the height of the wall, **above** and beyond **the towers, and** he raised **another wall outside,** a secondary, external wall, which was built to protect the primary wall. **He fortified the Milo,** the area that Solomon had filled in [*mileh*] and built up, in order that there should be no gap between the different sections **in the City of David, and** Hizkiyahu **made weapons** of war **and shields in abundance.**

Remains of the Broad Wall built by Hizkiyahu, Jewish Quarter, Jerusalem

6 **He installed military commanders over the people** of the army, and **he gathered them to himself in the plaza at the gate of the city and spoke encouragingly to them, saying:**
7 **Be strong and courageous, do not fear and do not be frightened of the king of Assyria, and of the entire horde that is with him, as with us there is more,** a Greater Power, **than with him.**
8 **With him is an arm of flesh, but with us is the Lord our God to help us and to fight our wars. The people were bolstered by the words** of encouragement and reassurance **of Yehizkiyahu king of Judah.**
9 **After this, Sennacherib king of Assyria sent his servants to Jerusalem;** in the meantime, **he** himself **was near Lakhish,** besieging that city, a siege that is depicted in highly graphic form in Assyrian reliefs, **and all his command staff was with him.** During his siege of Lakhish he sent messengers to speak to Hizkiyahu, and also to lower the morale of the people, undermine their confidence, and call for their

Relief of Sennacherib sitting on throne, with inscription: "At the entrance of Lakhish…I give permission for its slaughter." Sennacherib's palace, Nineveh, 701 BCE

כ בַּלְוִיִּם: וַיַּעַשׂ כָּזֹאת יְחִזְקִיָּהוּ בְּכָל־יְהוּדָה וַיַּעַשׂ הַטּוֹב וְהַיָּשָׁר וְהָאֱמֶת לִפְנֵי
כא יְהוָה אֱלֹהָיו: וּבְכָל־מַעֲשֶׂה אֲשֶׁר־הֵחֵל ׀ בַּעֲבוֹדַת בֵּית־הָאֱלֹהִים וּבַתּוֹרָה וּבַמִּצְוָה
לִדְרֹשׁ לֵאלֹהָיו בְּכָל־לְבָבוֹ עָשָׂה וְהִצְלִיחַ:
לב א אַחֲרֵי הַדְּבָרִים וְהָאֱמֶת הָאֵלֶּה בָּא סַנְחֵרִיב מֶלֶךְ־אַשּׁוּר וַיָּבֹא בִיהוּדָה וַיִּחַן
ב עַל־הֶעָרִים הַבְּצֻרוֹת וַיֹּאמֶר לְבִקְעָם אֵלָיו: וַיַּרְא יְחִזְקִיָּהוּ כִּי־בָא סַנְחֵרִיב וּפָנָיו
ג לַמִּלְחָמָה עַל־יְרוּשָׁלִָם: וַיִּוָּעַץ עִם־שָׂרָיו וְגִבֹּרָיו לִסְתּוֹם אֶת־מֵימֵי הָעֲיָנוֹת אֲשֶׁר
ד מִחוּץ לָעִיר וַיַּעְזְרוּהוּ: וַיִּקָּבְצוּ עַם־רָב וַיִּסְתְּמוּ אֶת־כָּל־הַמַּעְיָנוֹת וְאֶת־הַנַּחַל
ה הַשּׁוֹטֵף בְּתוֹךְ־הָאָרֶץ לֵאמֹר לָמָּה יָבוֹאוּ מַלְכֵי אַשּׁוּר וּמָצְאוּ מַיִם רַבִּים: וַיִּתְחַזַּק
וַיִּבֶן אֶת־כָּל־הַחוֹמָה הַפְּרוּצָה וַיַּעַל עַל־הַמִּגְדָּלוֹת וְלַחוּצָה הַחוֹמָה אַחֶרֶת וַיְחַזֵּק
ו אֶת־הַמִּלּוֹא עִיר דָּוִיד וַיַּעַשׂ שֶׁלַח לָרֹב וּמָגִנִּים: וַיִּתֵּן שָׂרֵי מִלְחָמוֹת עַל־הָעָם
ז וַיִּקְבְּצֵם אֵלָיו אֶל־רְחוֹב שַׁעַר הָעִיר וַיְדַבֵּר עַל־לְבָבָם לֵאמֹר: חִזְקוּ וְאִמְצוּ אַל־
תִּירְאוּ וְאַל־תֵּחַתּוּ מִפְּנֵי מֶלֶךְ אַשּׁוּר וּמִלִּפְנֵי כָּל־הֶהָמוֹן אֲשֶׁר־עִמּוֹ כִּי־עִמָּנוּ רַב
ח מֵעִמּוֹ: עִמּוֹ זְרוֹעַ בָּשָׂר וְעִמָּנוּ יְהוָה אֱלֹהֵינוּ לְעָזְרֵנוּ וּלְהִלָּחֵם מִלְחֲמֹתֵנוּ וַיִּסָּמְכוּ
ט הָעָם עַל־דִּבְרֵי יְחִזְקִיָּהוּ מֶלֶךְ־יְהוּדָה: אַחַר זֶה שָׁלַח סַנְחֵרִיב מֶלֶךְ־
אַשּׁוּר עֲבָדָיו יְרוּשָׁלַיְמָה וְהוּא עַל־לָכִישׁ וְכָל־מֶמְשַׁלְתּוֹ עִמּוֹ עַל־יְחִזְקִיָּהוּ מֶלֶךְ

DISCUSSION

31:20 | **Yehizkiyahu did so:** Hizkiyahu began great projects and succeeded in bringing about a great revival among the people of Israel. He awakened the people to serve God and, moreover, he and his men were responsible for a literary revival. They transcribed old manuscripts and caused the study of Torah to become widespread throughout the nation (see Proverbs 25:1; *Sanhedrin* 94b; *Sifrei*, *Vaethanan* 32). Although Hizkiyahu's changes did not last for many generations, in his day there was a real transformation of the entire nation, and it was he who initiated these events and issued the relevant commands.

surrender. He sent this message **to Yehizkiyahu king of Judah and to all Judah who were in Jerusalem, saying:**
10 **So said Sennacherib king of Assyria: On what are you trusting and staying under siege in Jerusalem?**
11 **Truly Yehizkiyahu is misleading you, consigning you to die of hunger and of thirst, saying: The Lord our God will deliver us from the hand of the king of Assyria.** Your king's reasoning is that he trusts in God.
12 **Isn't he Yehizkiyahu who removed His shrines and His altars, and stated to Judah and Jerusalem, saying: Before** only **one altar you shall prostrate yourselves, and upon it you shall burn offerings?** Clearly the messengers of the king of Assyria had good intelligence on what had transpired in the land of Judah. Thus, they were aware of Hizkiyahu's efforts to eradicate the shrines, most of which were dedicated to the service of God, not idolatry. Although the removal of those altars was in keeping with the Torah's prohibition against offering sacrifices outside the Temple,[220] the Assyrians attempted to incite the people away from Hizkiyahu by addressing those individuals who had been hurt by the king's initiative and possibly harbored resentment toward him. Such people had perhaps been offering upon their own altars for the past century, and had recently been informed that their families had acted incorrectly all those years; their altars were destroyed, and they were instructed to ascend to Jerusalem. Sennacherib's messengers also assumed that the inhabitants of Judah would agree that the smashing of altars that had been built in order to serve God was likely to reduce His influence and limit His strength.[221]
13 **Don't you know what I and my fathers have done to all the peoples of the lands** throughout this region? **Have** any of **the gods of the nations of the lands** we have already conquered **been able to deliver their land from my hand?**
14 **Who is there among all the gods of those nations that my fathers destroyed, who could deliver his people from my hand, that your God will be able to deliver you from my hand?** They all bowed down to their gods and relied upon them, and yet not one of those nations was saved, neither by its god nor by its army.
15 **Now, do not let Hizkiyahu entice you and do not let him mislead you in this manner, and do not have faith in him, for no god of any nation or kingdom is able to deliver his people from my hand and from the hand of my fathers; also your God will not deliver you from my hand.** Just as no power was able to stop me until now, so too, your God will be unable to stand up against me.
16 **His servants spoke more** of such matters, **against the Lord God, and against Yehizkiyahu His servant.**
17 **He wrote scrolls to blaspheme the Lord, God of Israel, and to speak against Him, saying: Like the gods of the nations of the lands who did not deliver their people from my hand, so the God of Yehizkiyahu will not deliver His people from my hand.**
18 Furthermore, **they called in a loud voice, in the language of Judah [*Yehudit*],** the "Hebrew" that was spoken by the common Jews in Judah [*Yehuda*], **to the people of Jerusalem who were on the wall.** They used the local language rather than their own language, Assyrian, or Aramaic, which served at that time as the international language of diplomacy, in order **to frighten them and to unnerve them, so that they could capture the city.** They were not trying to scare Hizkiyahu, who more or less understood the historical, geographical, and political state of affairs. Their propaganda was directed at the soldiers standing on the walls to protect the city.
19 **They spoke of the God of Jerusalem, as of the gods of the peoples of the land, the handiwork of man.** They blasphemed against God by equating Him with the pagan gods of the other nations, who could not help their people and stop the Assyrians.
20 **Yehizkiyahu the king prayed about this with Isaiah son of Amotz the prophet, and they cried out to the heavens.** The conversation between the king and the prophet, and the content of Hizkiyahu's prayer, appear at length in the books of Isaiah (36) and II Kings (19). Here they are mentioned only in passing.
21 **The Lord sent an angel, and he annihilated every mighty warrior, high official, and commander in the camp of the king of Assyria.** In one night, a heavenly force struck the Assyrians, killing the leaders of the camp, its captains, all its officers, and perhaps other soldiers as well. **He,** the king of Assyria, **returned shamefacedly to his own land,** as he had failed to achieve his goals. The sudden departure of the camp of Sennacherib from Jerusalem was a very great miracle. Furthermore, the king's end proves that he sinned greatly with his derisive comments and his arrogance: **He came to the house of his god** to pray, **and from among those who emerged from his loins, they,** his own offspring, conspired against him and **struck him down by the sword.** As related elsewhere, he was assassinated by two of his own sons.[222]
22 **The Lord saved Yehizkiyahu and the inhabitants of Jerusalem from the hand of Sennacherib king of Assyria, and from the hand of everyone,** all their enemies, **and guided them** toward a peaceful existence,[223] protecting them from their enemies **on every side.**
23 **Many were bringing tribute to the Lord to Jerusalem, and gifts to Yehizkiyahu king of Judah,** as reports of the miracle had naturally reached far and wide; **he became exalted,** the name of Hizkiyahu became renowned, **in the eyes of all the nations**[D] **thereafter.**

י יהודה ועל־כל־יהודה אשר בירושלם לאמר: כה אמר סנחריב מלך אשור
יא על־מה אתם בטחים וישבים במצור בירושלם: הלא יחזקיהו מסית אתכם
לתת אתכם למות ברעב ובצמא לאמר יהוה אלהינו יצילנו מכף מלך אשור:
יב הלא־הוא יחזקיהו הסיר את־במתיו ואת־מזבחתיו ויאמר ליהודה ולירושלם
יג לאמר לפני מזבח אחד תשתחוו ועליו תקטירו: הלא תדעו מה עשיתי אני
ואבותי לכל עמי הארצות היכול יכלו אלהי גויי הארצות להציל את־ארצם
יד מידי: מי בכל־אלהי הגוים האלה אשר החרימו אבותי אשר יכול להציל
טו את־עמו מידי כי יוכל אלהיכם להציל אתכם מידי: ועתה אל־ישיא אתכם
חזקיהו ואל־יסית אתכם כזאת ואל־תאמינו לו כי־לא יוכל כל־אלוה כל־
גוי וממלכה להציל עמו מידי ומיד אבותי אף כי אלהיכם לא־יצילו אתכם
טז יז מידי: ועוד דברו עבדיו על־יהוה האלהים ועל יחזקיהו עבדו: וספרים כתב
לחרף ליהוה אלהי ישראל ולאמר עליו לאמר כאלהי גויי הארצות אשר
יח לא־הצילו עמם מידי כן לא־יציל אלהי יחזקיהו עמו מידי: ויקראו בקול־
גדול יהודית על־עם ירושלם אשר על־החומה ליראם ולבהלם למען ילכדו
יט את־העיר: וידברו אל־אלהי ירושלם כעל אלהי עמי הארץ מעשה ידי
כ האדם: ויתפלל יחזקיהו המלך וישעיהו בן־אמוץ הנביא על־זאת
כא ויזעקו השמים: וישלח יהוה מלאך ויכחד כל־גבור חיל ונגיד ושר
במחנה מלך אשור וישב בבשת פנים לארצו ויבא בית אלהיו ומיציאו מעיו ומיציאי
כב שם הפילהו בחרב: ויושע יהוה את־יחזקיהו ואת ׀ ישבי ירושלם מיד סנחריב
כג מלך־אשור ומיד־כל וינהלם מסביב: ורבים מביאים מנחה ליהוה לירושלם
ומגדנות ליחזקיהו מלך יהודה וינשא לעיני כל־הגוים מאחרי־כן:

DISCUSSION

32:23 | **In the eyes of all the nations:** It is related in II Kings (20:12) that among the men who came to express their admiration and wonder, and to visit Hizkiyahu after they had heard about all the signs and miracles, were emissaries from the city of Babylon, which is farther away than Assyria. This was because the Babylonians also viewed Assyria as an enemy (see Radak and Malbim, II Kings 20:12).

Hizkiyahu's Illness and a Summary of His Works

II CHRONICLES 32:24–33

Generally, this book focuses far more on matters of the Temple and the service of God than on any given king's political, economic, or military record. Nevertheless, on this occasion, the text's summary of Hizkiyahu's reign does include one personal event in his life, his illness, and it also mentions his various achievements.

24 **In those days Yehizkiyahu became deathly ill; he prayed to the Lord, and He,** God, **communicated with him** through the prophet Isaiah, informing him that his prayer had been accepted, **and gave him a sign** that he would recover.[224]

25 **But Yehizkiyahu did not reciprocate according to the reward bestowed upon him.** He did not repay God in accordance with the goodness He had bestowed upon him, **as his heart grew haughty.** Although it was clear that the rout of the Assyrian army was not due to his own army's strength, Hizkiyahu nevertheless took credit for the victory as due to his righteousness.[225] **There was wrath upon him, and upon Judah and Jerusalem.**

26 As a result of his illness and for other reasons, **Yehizkiyahu humbled himself from the haughtiness of his heart,** and changed his arrogant ways,[226] **he and the inhabitants of Jerusalem, and the wrath of the Lord did not come upon them during the days of Yehizkiyahu.** Thus, the land was quiet after the invasion of Sennacherib.

27 **Yehizkiyahu had wealth and honor in great abundance, and he made treasuries,** storehouses, **for himself, for silver, for gold, for precious stones, for spices, for shields, and for all precious vessels.** He was an energetic and successful king, and due to his powerful position and the peace that reigned in his days, he was the recipient of many gifts and levies, and great wealth was once again amassed in Jerusalem;

28 **and** he made **storehouses for produce of grain, wine, and oil, and** he built, or renovated, **stables for each and every animal, and herds for the stables,** with which he filled the royal stables.[227]

29 **He constructed for himself cities, and had livestock of flocks and herds in abundance, for God gave him very many possessions.**

30 **He, Yehizkiyahu, plugged the source of the water of the Upper Gihon,**[B] **and diverted it down to the west side of the City of David,** by digging the Siloam Tunnel. **Yehizkiyahu succeeded in all his actions.**

31 **So it was with the emissaries of the princes of Babylon, who were sent to him to inquire about the wonder that was in the land; God had left him, to test him, to know everything in his heart.** This is an allusion to an episode that is related at length in the books of Isaiah (39) and II Kings (20:11–20): After Sennacherib's downfall, Hizkiyahu received a miraculous sign, alluded to above,[228] which involved a change in the natural order of the world, as time itself went backward. As a result, ministers of the king of Babylon came to visit Hizkiyahu, and

Descent to the upper spring of Gihon

he received them with great, perhaps even excessive, honor. On this occasion, God allowed him to act as he pleased without seeking to restrain him in any way, even though his behavior was not to his credit.[229]

32 **The rest of the deeds of Yehizkiyahu, and his kindnesses,** his acts which bestowed good upon others, **behold, they are written in the vision of Isaiah son of Amotz the prophet, and in the book of the kings of Judah and Israel.** Isaiah was already a prophet many years before Hizkiyahu's reign, and during Hizkiyahu's days was, in fact, the greatest prophet, as his prophecies were being fulfilled. Although some of Hizkiyahu's deeds are indeed recorded in the book of Isaiah, it seems that the prophet wrote another book which included the rest of the chronicles of King Hizkiyahu (see 26:22).

33 **Yehizkiyahu lay with his fathers, and they buried him in the ascent,** the most dignified area,[230] **of the graves of the sons of David.**[B] Apparently, those graves were somewhat scattered, and were not all located in a single cave. **All Judah and the inhabitants of Jerusalem accorded him honor upon his death,** as Hizkiyahu had many achievements to his name, including the fortification of the kingdom, and he was also granted miracles and Heavenly assistance. **Menashe his son reigned in his stead.**

Tombs of the royal house of David, south of the City of David

כד בימים ההם חלה יחזקיהו עד-למות ויתפלל אל-יהוה ויאמר לו ומופת נתן
כה לו: ולא-כגמל עליו השיב יחזקיהו כי גבה לבו ויהי עליו קצף ועל-יהודה
כו וירושלם: ויכנע יחזקיהו בגבה לבו הוא ויושבי ירושלם ולא-בא עליהם קצף
כז יהוה בימי יחזקיהו: ויהי ליחזקיהו עשר וכבוד הרבה מאד ואוצרות עשה-
כח לו לכסף ולזהב ולאבן יקרה ולבשמים ולמגנים ולכל כלי חמדה: ומסכנות
לתבואת דגן ותירוש ויצהר וארות לכל-בהמה ובהמה ועדרים לאורות:
כט ל ועירים עשה לו ומקנה-צאן ובקר לרב כי נתן-לו אלהים רכוש רב מאד: והוא
יחזקיהו סתם את-מוצא מימי גיחון העליון ויישרם למטה-מערבה לעיר דויד ויישרם
לא ויצלח יחזקיהו בכל-מעשהו: וכן במליצי | שרי בבל המשלחים עליו לדרש
המופת אשר היה בארץ עזבו האלהים לנסותו לדעת כל-בלבבו:
לב ויתר דברי יחזקיהו וחסדיו הנם כתובים בחזון ישעיהו בן-אמוץ הנביא
לג על-ספר מלכי יהודה וישראל: וישכב יחזקיהו עם-אבתיו ויקברהו במעלה
קברי בני-דויד וכבוד עשו-לו במותו כל-יהודה וישבי ירושלם וימלך מנשה

BACKGROUND

32:30 | **The source of the water of the Upper Gihon:** Gihon comes from the root *gimmel-yod-ḥet*, which in the Bible means to break out, to gush. The Gihon Spring was the main water source for ancient Jerusalem. It flowed from the foot of the City of David to the east, at the bottom of the slope outside the walls. The need to divert the water to a more accessible and protected location inside the city and to prevent water from reaching the besieging enemy led Hizkiyahu to block the source of the Upper Gihon, so that the waters of the spring would flow through the Siloam Tunnel to the Siloam Pool, which was within the city boundaries, on its western side (see at length Asher Grossberg, "Hizkiya's Water Projects," *Studies of the Ancient City of David and Jerusalem*, 2011, [Hebrew]). This meant that the Siloam provided water for the residents of Jerusalem during times of siege, while the enemies were prevented from access to the waters of the Gihon (see Radak; *Pesaḥim* 56a; Rabbi Ḥanoch Ehrentreu, *Studies in the Words of the Sages and their Language*, Jerusalem, 1978, 42).

32:33 | **In the ascent of the graves of the sons of David:** Some claim that the kings of the house of David were buried in the south-east of the city, near a staircase, which is why it is called "the ascent of the graves of the sons of David." This accords with the statement of the Sages that a tunnel led from David's tomb to the Kidron Valley (*Tosefta*, *Bava Batra* 1:11). The terrain is suitable for such graves, but in the Second Temple period the area was used as a quarry, and therefore it is unknown whether it contained a single royal tomb or several burial caves.

The Chronicles of the Kings Menashe and Amon

II CHRONICLES 33:1–25

Menashe son of Hizkiya rises to the throne at a very young age, and his reign lasts for many years. The period of his rule is of great importance during this time, and has a significant impact on subsequent years. Menashe is wicked in the eyes of God, and his reign is considered a protracted low point in the history of Israel, especially since he can be described as the opposite of his father. Although it is related here that Menashe repents, his previous bad deeds have a lasting effect upon the kingdom.

His son, Amon, follows the wicked ways of his father, and after his assassination he is buried in the same plot.

33 1 **Menashe was twelve years old when he became king;**[D] he ascended to the throne as a child, **and he reigned fifty-five years in Jerusalem.** Menashe's reign was the longest of all the kings of Israel.

2 **He did evil in the eyes of the Lord,**[D] **in accordance with the abominations of the nations that the Lord had dispossessed before the children of Israel.** He reverted to the practice of the sins of the Canaanites.

3 **He rebuilt the** private **shrines** erected for the service of God **that Yehizkiyahu his father had smashed, and he established** new **altars for the Be'alim,** a far more egregious act, **and made** images of **sacred trees.**[B] **And he prostrated himself to the entire host of the heavens, and worshipped them.**

4 Furthermore, **he built altars** for foreign cults **in the House of the Lord,** in the place **of which the Lord said: In Jerusalem My name will be forever.**

5 **He built altars for the entire host of the heavens in the two courtyards,** the outer courtyard and the inner courtyard,[231] **of the House of the Lord.**

6 **He passed his sons through the fire in the Valley of the Son of Hinom, and he engaged in soothsaying,** he sought to predict the future based on the appearance of the clouds or the changing of the seasons, as well as engaging in **divination and witchcraft, and dealt with mediums and oracles,** raising the spirits of the dead in order to discern the future;[232] **he performed much evil in the eyes of the Lord, to anger Him.** This is referring mainly to sins of idolatry and related practices, with regard to which he breached all the boundaries of the service of God.

7 **He placed the idol of the image that he had made in the House of God,** which is the dwelling place **of which God had said to David, and to Solomon his son: In this house, and in** the city of **Jerusalem, which I have chosen from all the tribes of Israel, I will place My name forever [*le'eilom*].**[233] Although *le'eilom* has the same meaning as *le'olam*, forever, this is perhaps also a play on words alluding to the idea that sometimes God is hidden [*ne'elam*] in the world [*olam*].

8 **I will not again remove the foot of Israel from upon the land which I have provided to your fathers** to use.[234] Israel will no longer be a nation of nomads, as they were before they came to Canaan, but they will remain on their land. However, this guarantee is conditional: **Provided that they take care to perform everything that I commanded them, the entire Torah and the statutes and the ordinances by means of Moses.**

9 **Menashe led Judah and the inhabitants of Jerusalem astray, to perform more evil than the nations that the Lord had destroyed from before the children of Israel.** Under his baneful influence, their deeds were even worse than those of the Canaanites, since this idolatrous worship was fresh and novel to them, and therefore they were more enthusiastic in their worship than those who had performed these rites for many years; they were more devoted to the pagan idols than the gentiles.

10 **The Lord spoke to Menashe** by means of His prophets, **and** He delivered words of rebuke **to His people, but they did not listen.**

11 **The Lord brought upon them the commanders of the army of the king of Assyria.** This does not appear to have been a large-scale war, nor does it seem that the king of Assyria sought to destroy Menashe. Rather, the ministers whom the Assyrian king had appointed over Samaria and its environs decided on their own to set out on a limited offensive campaign, which turned out to be very successful. God brought against the king those captains, and **they captured Menashe with fetters,** or rings, with which animals are

Fetters, Roman period

Ancient city of Babylon

לג א בְּנוֹ תַּחְתָּיו׃ בֶּן־שְׁתֵּים עֶשְׂרֵה שָׁנָה מְנַשֶּׁה בְמָלְכוֹ וַחֲמִשִּׁים וְחָמֵשׁ
ב שָׁנָה מָלַךְ בִּירוּשָׁלָם׃ וַיַּעַשׂ הָרַע בְּעֵינֵי יְהוָה כְּתוֹעֲבוֹת הַגּוֹיִם אֲשֶׁר הוֹרִישׁ
ג יְהוָה מִפְּנֵי בְּנֵי יִשְׂרָאֵל׃ וַיָּשָׁב וַיִּבֶן אֶת־הַבָּמוֹת אֲשֶׁר נִתַּץ יְחִזְקִיָּהוּ אָבִיו וַיָּקֶם
מִזְבְּחוֹת לַבְּעָלִים וַיַּעַשׂ אֲשֵׁרוֹת וַיִּשְׁתַּחוּ לְכָל־צְבָא הַשָּׁמַיִם וַיַּעֲבֹד אֹתָם׃
ד ה וּבָנָה מִזְבְּחוֹת בְּבֵית יְהוָה אֲשֶׁר אָמַר יְהוָה בִּירוּשָׁלַם יִהְיֶה־שְּׁמִי לְעוֹלָם׃ וַיִּבֶן
ו מִזְבְּחוֹת לְכָל־צְבָא הַשָּׁמָיִם בִּשְׁתֵּי חַצְרוֹת בֵּית־יְהוָה׃ וְהוּא הֶעֱבִיר אֶת־בָּנָיו
בָּאֵשׁ בְּגֵי בֶן־הִנֹּם וְעוֹנֵן וְנִחֵשׁ וְכִשֵּׁף וְעָשָׂה אוֹב וְיִדְּעוֹנִי הִרְבָּה לַעֲשׂוֹת הָרַע
ז בְּעֵינֵי יְהוָה לְהַכְעִיסוֹ׃ וַיָּשֶׂם אֶת־פֶּסֶל הַסֶּמֶל אֲשֶׁר עָשָׂה בְּבֵית הָאֱלֹהִים אֲשֶׁר
אָמַר אֱלֹהִים אֶל־דָּוִיד וְאֶל־שְׁלֹמֹה בְנוֹ בַּבַּיִת הַזֶּה וּבִירוּשָׁלַם אֲשֶׁר בָּחַרְתִּי
ח מִכֹּל שִׁבְטֵי יִשְׂרָאֵל אָשִׂים אֶת־שְׁמִי לְעֵילוֹם׃ וְלֹא אֹסִיף לְהָסִיר אֶת־רֶגֶל
יִשְׂרָאֵל מֵעַל הָאֲדָמָה אֲשֶׁר הֶעֱמַדְתִּי לַאֲבֹתֵיכֶם רַק ׀ אִם־יִשְׁמְרוּ לַעֲשׂוֹת אֵת
ט כָּל־אֲשֶׁר צִוִּיתִים לְכָל־הַתּוֹרָה וְהַחֻקִּים וְהַמִּשְׁפָּטִים בְּיַד־מֹשֶׁה׃ וַיֶּתַע מְנַשֶּׁה
אֶת־יְהוּדָה וְיֹשְׁבֵי יְרוּשָׁלָם לַעֲשׂוֹת רָע מִן־הַגּוֹיִם אֲשֶׁר הִשְׁמִיד יְהוָה מִפְּנֵי בְּנֵי
י יא יִשְׂרָאֵל׃ וַיְדַבֵּר יְהוָה אֶל־מְנַשֶּׁה וְאֶל־עַמּוֹ וְלֹא הִקְשִׁיבוּ׃ וַיָּבֵא יְהוָה
עֲלֵיהֶם אֶת־שָׂרֵי הַצָּבָא אֲשֶׁר לְמֶלֶךְ אַשּׁוּר וַיִּלְכְּדוּ אֶת־מְנַשֶּׁה בַּחֹחִים וַיַּאַסְרֻהוּ

DISCUSSION

33:1 | **Menashe was twelve years old when he became king:** Based on Hizkiya's age, he could have had children who were twenty years older. The Sages say that Hizkiya did not marry until an advanced age, which is why his son was so young when he died (see *Berakhot* 10a).

33:2 | **He did evil in the eyes of the Lord:** Menashe's behavior is highly surprising. His father was a righteous, God-fearing king, and although Menashe was very young when Hizkiya died, and therefore was not privileged to be brought up by his father for many years, it is still hard to understand the sharp departure from his father's behavior. Moreover, there was not merely a change in the acts of the king, but also in the deeds of the population in general. It appears that despite Hizkiya's efforts to expand the circle of those who worshipped God, his main achievement was the establishment of a strong governmental structure. As a result, King Menashe was able to maintain a firm hold on his kingdom, and it did not occur to his subjects to rebel against him. It is possible that it was precisely by virtue of the governmental mechanism that Hizkiya established that Menashe's evil deeds became possible.

BACKGROUND

33:3 | **Sacred trees [*asherot*]:** This term has several meanings in the Bible: First, a tree that served as a ritual item of worship (Deuteronomy 16:21). Second, Asherot was the name of one of the central Canaanite goddesses, who was considered the partner of the main god, the Baal (see II Kings 23:4). This usage of the word is also found in Ugaritic texts. Third, a manmade ritual object in the form of a wooden post (see I Kings 16:33; II Kings 21:7). Such objects were perhaps used in the service of God, as was the bronze serpent that King Hizkiya eventually crushed (see II Kings 18:4; see also Judges 8:27).

led. They placed these rings around the king's neck, both in order to hold him firmly captive and also to humiliate him. **And** they **bound him in shackles, and led him to Babylon,** for him to give a reckoning before the king of Assyria.

12 **In his distress,** he came to realize that he could rely only upon his Father in Heaven. Therefore, **he implored the Lord his God, and utterly humbled himself before the God of his fathers.**

13 **He prayed to Him, and He acceded to his entreaty;** God accepted his prayer **and heard his supplication, and returned him to Jerusalem to his kingdom. Menashe knew that the Lord, He is God.** Ultimately, the king repented and returned to God.

14 Another detail is provided about King Menashe that is not mentioned elsewhere in the Bible: **Thereafter he,** Menashe, **built an outer wall to the City of David, west of Gihon, in the ravine.** This was an additional wall around Jerusalem, of which nothing remains today; it was probably designed to enclose another part of the city and reached the area which is nowadays known as Mount Zion. This wall was **approaching**[235] **the Fish Gate and going around** the wall **to the Ofel,** a fortress or an elevated, fortified area, **and** Menashe **greatly elevated it,** the wall. **He placed military commanders in all the fortified cities of Judah.**

15 **He,** Menashe, after having repented, **removed the strange gods and the image from the House of the Lord, and all the altars that he had built on the mountain of the House of the Lord, and in Jerusalem, and cast them outside the city.**

16 **He built the altar of the Lord, and slaughtered upon it peace offerings and thanks offerings, and commanded Judah to worship the Lord, God of Israel.** He repented from his former behavior and instructed others to do the same.

17 **But** even after the king returned to God, **the people continued to slaughter at the** private **shrines, albeit to the Lord their God.** Menashe lacked the power to restore the service of God to the only legitimate center of worship in Jerusalem, as his father Hizkiya had successfully done.

18 **The rest of the deeds of Menashe, and his prayer to his God, and the words of the seers,** the prophets, **who spoke to him in the name of the Lord, God of Israel, behold, they are written** and described in detail **among the deeds of the kings of Israel.**

19 **His,** Menashe's, **prayer that He acceded to him,** accepted, and also, in contrast, **all his sins and his trespasses, the places where he built shrines and positioned the sacred trees and the idols before he humbled himself,** all these, **behold, they are written in the words of My seers,** prophets.[236] These matters are recorded in several books written by the prophets of God.

20 **Menashe lay with his fathers,**[D] **and they buried him in his** own **house.** Since he was held in lesser regard toward the end of his days, he was not buried in the tombs of the kings. **Amon his son reigned in his stead.**

21 **Amon was twenty-two years old when he became king, and he reigned two years in Jerusalem.**

22 **He did evil in the eyes of the Lord, like his father Menashe had done; Amon slaughtered offerings to all the idols that Menashe his father had made, and he served them.** Amon continued in his father's path, but not from where his penitent father had left off, as described above. Rather, Amon followed Menashe's previous sinful ways.

23 **He did not humble himself before the Lord, as Menashe his father had humbled himself, rather, Amon incurred much guilt.** Although he did not live a long life, Amon's sins were even more severe than those of his father. The Sages offer various traditions or speculations with regard to the most repulsive sins committed by Amon.[237]

24 **His servants conspired against him, and put him to death in his house.**

25 But afterward, **the people of the land smote all the conspirators against King Amon.** Perhaps King Amon's deeds had been so outrageous that they led certain men to rebel and assassinate him. However, the people still supported the kingdom of David, **and** therefore **the people of the land crowned Yoshiyahu his son king in his stead.** Yoshiyahu would be the last great king of the Kingdom of Judah, and, it follows, of the remnant of Israel.

יב בְּנַחְשְׁתַּיִם וַיּוֹלִיכֻהוּ בָּבֶלָה: וּכְהָצֵר לוֹ חִלָּה אֶת־פְּנֵי יְהוָה אֱלֹהָיו וַיִּכָּנַע מְאֹד
יג מִלִּפְנֵי אֱלֹהֵי אֲבֹתָיו: וַיִּתְפַּלֵּל אֵלָיו וַיֵּעָתֶר לוֹ וַיִּשְׁמַע תְּחִנָּתוֹ וַיְשִׁיבֵהוּ יְרוּשָׁלַ͏ִם
יד לְמַלְכוּתוֹ וַיֵּדַע מְנַשֶּׁה כִּי יְהוָה הוּא הָאֱלֹהִים: וְאַחֲרֵי־כֵן בָּנָה חוֹמָה חִיצוֹנָה ׀
לְעִיר־דָּוִיד מַעְרָבָה לְגִיחוֹן בַּנַּחַל וְלָבוֹא בְשַׁעַר הַדָּגִים וְסָבַב לָעֹפֶל וַיַּגְבִּיהֶהָ
טו מְאֹד וַיָּשֶׂם שָׂרֵי־חַיִל בְּכָל־הֶעָרִים הַבְּצֻרוֹת בִּיהוּדָה: וַיָּסַר אֶת־אֱלֹהֵי הַנֵּכָר
וְאֶת־הַסֶּמֶל מִבֵּית יְהוָה וְכָל־הַמִּזְבְּחוֹת אֲשֶׁר בָּנָה בְּהַר בֵּית־יְהוָה וּבִירוּשָׁלָ͏ִם
טז וַיַּשְׁלֵךְ חוּצָה לָעִיר: ויכן אֶת־מִזְבַּח יְהוָה וַיִּזְבַּח עָלָיו זִבְחֵי שְׁלָמִים וְתוֹדָה וַיֹּאמֶר וַיִּבֶן
יז לִיהוּדָה לַעֲבוֹד אֶת־יְהוָה אֱלֹהֵי יִשְׂרָאֵל: אֲבָל עוֹד הָעָם זֹבְחִים בַּבָּמוֹת רַק
יח לַיהוָה אֱלֹהֵיהֶם: וְיֶתֶר דִּבְרֵי מְנַשֶּׁה וּתְפִלָּתוֹ אֶל־אֱלֹהָיו וְדִבְרֵי הַחֹזִים הַמְדַבְּרִים
יט אֵלָיו בְּשֵׁם יְהוָה אֱלֹהֵי יִשְׂרָאֵל הִנָּם עַל־דִּבְרֵי מַלְכֵי יִשְׂרָאֵל: וּתְפִלָּתוֹ וְהֵעָתֶר־
לוֹ וְכָל־חַטָּאתוֹ וּמַעְלוֹ וְהַמְּקֹמוֹת אֲשֶׁר בָּנָה בָהֶם בָּמוֹת וְהֶעֱמִיד הָאֲשֵׁרִים
כ וְהַפְּסִלִים לִפְנֵי הִכָּנְעוֹ הִנָּם כְּתוּבִים עַל דִּבְרֵי חוֹזָי: וַיִּשְׁכַּב מְנַשֶּׁה עִם־אֲבֹתָיו
וַיִּקְבְּרֻהוּ בֵּיתוֹ וַיִּמְלֹךְ אָמוֹן בְּנוֹ תַּחְתָּיו:
כא כב בֶּן־עֶשְׂרִים וּשְׁתַּיִם שָׁנָה אָמוֹן בְּמָלְכוֹ וּשְׁתַּיִם שָׁנִים מָלַךְ בִּירוּשָׁלָ͏ִם: וַיַּעַשׂ הָרַע
בְּעֵינֵי יְהוָה כַּאֲשֶׁר עָשָׂה מְנַשֶּׁה אָבִיו וּלְכָל־הַפְּסִילִים אֲשֶׁר עָשָׂה מְנַשֶּׁה אָבִיו
כג זִבַּח אָמוֹן וַיַּעַבְדֵם: וְלֹא נִכְנַע מִלִּפְנֵי יְהוָה כְּהִכָּנַע מְנַשֶּׁה אָבִיו כִּי הוּא אָמוֹן
כד כה הִרְבָּה אַשְׁמָה: וַיִּקְשְׁרוּ עָלָיו עֲבָדָיו וַיְמִיתֻהוּ בְּבֵיתוֹ: וַיַּכּוּ עַם־הָאָרֶץ אֵת כָּל־
הַקֹּשְׁרִים עַל־הַמֶּלֶךְ אָמוֹן וַיַּמְלִיכוּ עַם־הָאָרֶץ אֶת־יֹאשִׁיָּהוּ בְנוֹ תַּחְתָּיו:

DISCUSSION

33:20 | **Menashe's historical influence:** The story of Menashe's punishment also appears in the book of Kings (II Kings 21), but his repentance is not described there. Instead, the story of Menashe in the book of Kings ends on a negative note, and it is even stated elsewhere that the bitter fate of Judah and Jerusalem was an eventual consequence of the sins of Menashe (see II Kings 23:26–27, 24:3–4; Jeremiah 15:4). Since he reigned for fifty-five years, a period spanning two generations, Menashe was able to tilt the powerful kingdom left to him by his father in an entirely different direction. Although other evil kings reigned after him, Menashe is considered a colossal historical failure, for if Hizkiya's son had continued along his path, the history of the land of Judah and the First Temple would have been very different. Menashe was such a wicked king that the Sages consign him to everlasting disgrace, as they list him among the few kings who have no share in the World to Come (see *Sanhedrin* 90a). Although this chapter depicts his repentance, it seems that he did not repent with the same strength and vigor as he had sinned, and that he failed to correct all the terrible ramifications of his evil ways. His own son followed in his father's wicked ways, and even outdid him in depravity.

The Chronicles of King Yoshiyahu

II CHRONICLES 34:1–35:27

Once again there is a fundamental change in the leadership of the kingdom. Yoshiyahu son of Amon abandons the path of his father and grandfather, but this time for the better. In many ways, Yoshiyahu is the last great king who reigns over the Kingdom of Judah, as the rulers who follow him are less successful and reign for shorter periods. However, despite his righteousness and his notable efforts to improve the kingdom and purify it from idolatry, Yoshiyahu is unable to nullify the decree of destruction that already hangs over the Kingdom of Judah.

34 1 **Yoshiyahu was eight years old when he became king, and he reigned thirty-one years in Jerusalem.**

2 **He did what is right in the eyes of the Lord, and he followed in the ways of David his father,** his ancestor, **and he did not deviate** from them **right or left.** His behavior was impeccable.

The Removal of the Shrines and the Foreign Cults

II CHRONICLES 34:3–7

Yoshiyahu eradicates all types of foreign worship, not only from Judah but also from the abandoned provinces of the former Kingdom of Israel, where only a few people remain.

3 **In the eighth year of his reign, when he was still a lad,** about sixteen,[238] **he began to seek the God of David his father.** Even as a young man he developed in a particular direction, becoming more and more attached to the service of God and all that that entailed. **And in the twelfth year** of his reign, when he was roughly twenty years old, and his rule was firmly established, **he began to purify Judah and Jerusalem from the shrines, the sacred trees, the idols, and the cast images.**

4 **They smashed at his behest the altars of the Be'alim; he cut down the sun pillars**[239] or other types of symbolic images used in the ritual worship of the sun,[240] **that were set high above them,** the altars; **and the sacred trees [*ha'asherim*], the idols, and the cast images he shattered, ground** into dust, **and threw** the remnants **on the graves of those who slaughtered offerings to them** in their lifetimes.

5 **He burned the bones of the** former **priests** of those cults[241] **on their altars,** in order to demean them and as a sign of their impurity,[242] **and** he **purified Judah and Jerusalem,**

6 **and** so he did also **in the cities of Menashe, Ephraim, and Simeon, up to Naphtali** in the north of the country, **among their surrounding ruins,** after they had been destroyed.[243] The territory of the former Kingdom of Israel was formally under Assyrian control, but Assyria had almost come to the end of its time on the stage of history, and its grip over the land had weakened. After the inhabitants of the Kingdom of Israel had been exiled to distant lands, only remnants of the people were left in its territory, with much of the land remaining vacant. For both political and religious reasons, Yoshiyahu decided to annex those regions de facto, and therefore he continued his campaign of purification there as well.

7 **He smashed the altars, crushed the sacred trees and the idols into dust,** he ground them finely, **and cut down all the sun pillars throughout the Land of Israel, and he returned to Jerusalem.**

The Restoration of the Temple and the Discovery of the Torah Scroll

II CHRONICLES 34:8–21

Yoshiyahu initiates a series of repairs in the Temple, and to his surprise discovers an ancient Torah scroll hidden away there.

8 **In the eighteenth year of his reign, in order to purify the land;** alternatively, when he had finished[244] his campaign and purified the land, **and the House, he,** Yoshiyahu, **sent Shafan son of Atzalyahu.** Shafan and other members of his family held the position of scribes, senior politicians who were involved in foreign relations, among other functions.[245] **And** he sent with him **Maaseyahu governor of the city** of Jerusalem; this was an important job, which required a distinguished and trusted man, **and Yoah son of Yoahaz the chancellor,** a kind of prime minister in King Yoshiyahu's court, **to repair the House of the Lord his God,** to perform the necessary repairs to the Temple.

9 **They came to Hilkiyahu the High Priest and gave over the silver that was brought to the House of God, which the Levites, the gatekeepers** who were in charge of guarding the money or the vessels in the Temple,[246] **had gathered from the hand of Manasseh, Ephraim, from all the remnant of Israel and from all Judah and Benjamin** when they passed through the cities of Israel in order to purify the land, as described above,[247] **and they returned to Jerusalem.**

10 They did not give the money they collected to the priests or Levites. Rather, **they gave it into the hand of the craftsman assigned to the House of the Lord, and the craftsmen who**

לד א ב בֶּן־שְׁמוֹנֶה שָׁנִים יֹאשִׁיָּהוּ בְמָלְכוֹ וּשְׁלֹשִׁים וְאַחַת שָׁנָה מָלַךְ בִּירוּשָׁלִָם: וַיַּעַשׂ כד
הַיָּשָׁר בְּעֵינֵי יְהוָה וַיֵּלֶךְ בְּדַרְכֵי דָּוִיד אָבִיו וְלֹא־סָר יָמִין וּשְׂמֹאול:
ג וּבִשְׁמוֹנֶה שָׁנִים לְמָלְכוֹ וְהוּא עוֹדֶנּוּ נַעַר הֵחֵל לִדְרוֹשׁ לֵאלֹהֵי דָּוִיד אָבִיו וּבִשְׁתֵּים
עֶשְׂרֵה שָׁנָה הֵחֵל לְטַהֵר אֶת־יְהוּדָה וִירוּשָׁלִַם מִן־הַבָּמוֹת וְהָאֲשֵׁרִים וְהַפְּסִלִים
ד וְהַמַּסֵּכוֹת: וַיְנַתְּצוּ לְפָנָיו אֵת מִזְבְּחוֹת הַבְּעָלִים וְהַחַמָּנִים אֲשֶׁר־לְמַעְלָה מֵעֲלֵיהֶם
גִּדֵּעַ וְהָאֲשֵׁרִים וְהַפְּסִלִים וְהַמַּסֵּכוֹת שִׁבַּר וְהֵדַק וַיִּזְרֹק עַל־פְּנֵי הַקְּבָרִים הַזֹּבְחִים
ה לָהֶם: וְעַצְמוֹת כֹּהֲנִים שָׂרַף עַל־מזבחותים וַיְטַהֵר אֶת־יְהוּדָה וְאֶת־יְרוּשָׁלִָם: מִזְבְּחוֹתָם
ו ז וּבְעָרֵי מְנַשֶּׁה וְאֶפְרַיִם וְשִׁמְעוֹן וְעַד־נַפְתָּלִי בחר בתיהם סָבִיב: וַיְנַתֵּץ אֶת־ בְּחַרְבֹתֵיהֶם
הַמִּזְבְּחוֹת וְאֶת־הָאֲשֵׁרִים וְהַפְּסִלִים כִּתַּת לְהֵדַק וְכָל־הַחַמָּנִים גִּדַּע בְּכָל־אֶרֶץ
ח יִשְׂרָאֵל וַיָּשָׁב לִירוּשָׁלִָם: וּבִשְׁנַת שְׁמוֹנֶה עֶשְׂרֵה לְמָלְכוֹ לְטַהֵר הָאָרֶץ
וְהַבָּיִת שָׁלַח אֶת־שָׁפָן בֶּן־אֲצַלְיָהוּ וְאֶת־מַעֲשֵׂיָהוּ שַׂר־הָעִיר וְאֵת יוֹאָח בֶּן־יוֹאָחָז
ט הַמַּזְכִּיר לְחַזֵּק אֶת־בֵּית יְהוָה אֱלֹהָיו: וַיָּבֹאוּ אֶל־חִלְקִיָּהוּ ׀ הַכֹּהֵן הַגָּדוֹל וַיִּתְּנוּ
אֶת־הַכֶּסֶף הַמּוּבָא בֵית־אֱלֹהִים אֲשֶׁר אָסְפוּ־הַלְוִיִּם שֹׁמְרֵי הַסַּף מִיַּד מְנַשֶּׁה
י וְאֶפְרַיִם וּמִכֹּל שְׁאֵרִית יִשְׂרָאֵל וּמִכָּל־יְהוּדָה וּבִנְיָמִן וישבי יְרוּשָׁלִָם: וַיִּתְּנוּ עַל־יַד וַיָּשֻׁבוּ
עֹשֵׂה הַמְּלָאכָה הַמֻּפְקָדִים בְּבֵית יְהוָה וַיִּתְּנוּ אֹתוֹ עוֹשֵׂי הַמְּלָאכָה אֲשֶׁר עֹשִׂים
יא בְּבֵית יְהוָה לִבְדּוֹק וּלְחַזֵּק הַבָּיִת: וַיִּתְּנוּ לֶחָרָשִׁים וְלַבֹּנִים לִקְנוֹת אַבְנֵי מַחְצֵב
וְעֵצִים לַמְחַבְּרוֹת וּלְקָרוֹת אֶת־הַבָּתִּים אֲשֶׁר הִשְׁחִיתוּ מַלְכֵי יְהוּדָה:
יב וְהָאֲנָשִׁים עֹשִׂים בֶּאֱמוּנָה בַּמְּלָאכָה וַעֲלֵיהֶם ׀ מֻפְקָדִים יַחַת וְעֹבַדְיָהוּ הַלְוִיִּם

work in the House of the Lord allotted it to inspecting[248] **and repairing the House.**

11 **They gave it to the artisans,** craftsmen who work with hard materials, **and to the builders,** for them **to buy quarried stones and wood for couplings,** to join together the various parts of the building, **and to make** with them **beams for the structures that the kings of Judah had destroyed.** It was necessary to cover parts of the Temple building with wood and to insert new stones to stabilize the structure. All these matters had been neglected, and perhaps the building had suffered willful damage, for almost sixty years, during the reigns of the two previous kings, Menashe and Amon.

Kibbutz members working in the stone quarry of Ein Harod, 1941

12 **The men worked faithfully, and Yahat and Ovadyahu the Levites from the sons of Merari were in charge of them, and Zekharya and Meshulam, from the sons of the Kehatites,**

were supervising, to instruct and oversee that the work was being performed properly; of **the Levites, anyone expert was with musical instruments,**[249] playing while the repairs were ongoing.
13 **Over the porters were** appointed **those supervising all the craftsmen in every type of work. From the Levites there were** also **scribes, officers, and gatekeepers.** The Levites filled all the routine administrative posts in the Temple.
14 **When they brought out the silver that had been brought to the House of the Lord, Hilkiyahu the priest found the scroll of the Lord's Torah by means of Moses.**[D] For many years no one had inspected the Temple, certainly not its treasuries. Now they apparently found there the original Torah scroll of Moses.
15 **Hilkiyahu proclaimed and said to Shafan the scribe: I found the Torah scroll in the House of the Lord. Hilkiyahu gave the scroll to Shafan.**
16 **Shafan brought the scroll to the king, and furthermore, he brought back a report to the king, saying: Everything that was assigned to your servants, they are doing.** The work is proceeding as it should.
17 **They melted the silver that was found in the House of the Lord.** At that time they did not yet use actual silver coins, but rather pieces of silver which were weighed and stamped. **And they gave it into the hand of those in charge, and into the hand of the craftsmen.** Shafan first reported on the progress of the work for which he was responsible.[250]
18 **Shafan the scribe told the king, saying: Hilkiyahu the priest gave me a scroll. Shafan read in it before the king.**
19 **It was when the king heard the words of the Torah that he rent his garments.** The king's reaction suggests that Shafan read from the sections of rebuke found primarily in the book of Deuteronomy. Perhaps the book happened to be opened before him at those passages which depict the punishments and destruction that will be visited upon Israel if they sin.[251]
20 **The king commanded Hilkiyahu, Ahikam son of Shafan, Avdon son of Mikha, Shafan the scribe, and Asaya the king's servant,** perhaps the chief official appointed over the work, **saying:**
21 **Go inquire of the Lord on my behalf, and on behalf of those remaining in Israel and in Judah, concerning the words of the scroll that has been found, for the wrath of the Lord that is poured upon us is great, in that our fathers did not observe the word of the Lord, to act in accordance with everything that is written in this scroll.**

Hulda's Prophecy and the Assembly of the Covenant

II CHRONICLES 34:22–33

The sections of rebuke written in the Torah give Yoshiyahu no rest, as he knows they are relevant to him and his generation. He therefore sends messengers to Hulda the prophetess, who informs them of the harsh punishments that await them. Consequently, Yoshiyahu gathers together the inhabitants of Judah for a renewal of the covenant with God. Despite Yoshiyahu's emotional and practical religious revival, Hulda's prophecy will still come to pass, although not in the king's own lifetime.

22 **Hilkiyahu,** the High Priest, **and those,** the other men, **with** whom **the king** had spoken,[252] **went to Hulda the prophetess, wife of Shalum son of Tok'hat son of Hasra, keeper of the wardrobe.** Shalum was in charge of the king's clothes, while his wife was a prophetess who sat among her people. **She lived in Jerusalem in the Mishneh,**[B] or the second quarter, an area that was added to the City of David, **and they spoke to her of this,** about the king's concerns over the passages that had been read to him from the Torah scroll.
23 **She said to them** the following prophecy: **So said the Lord, God of Israel: Say to the man who sent you to me,** a somewhat arrogant reference to the king:[253]
24 **So said the Lord: Behold, I am bringing harm upon this place and upon its inhabitants, all the curses that are written in the scroll that they read before the king of Judah,**

DISCUSSION

34:14 | **The scroll of the Lord's Torah by means of Moses:** Torah scrolls in those days were rather large manuscripts, whose copying was both time-consuming and expensive. For this reason, Torah scrolls were much less common than they are nowadays. Moreover, it can be assumed that in the days of Yoshiyahu, after decades of abandoning God's Torah at the directive of the authorities, it was very difficult to find Torah scrolls. Even today, when everyone owns printed books, more than once, a government that sought to prevent the distribution of a particular book has successfully brought about its total disappearance from their country. It is possible that following the reigns of Menashe and Amon, very few whole and worthy Torah scrolls remained, and even these were scattered or hidden in various places. In such a situation, although people knew about the Torah and the commandments, the discovery of a Torah scroll in its entirety took them by surprise, and the appearance of an ancient scroll written by Moses caused quite a commotion.

מִן־בְּנֵי מְרָרִי וּזְכַרְיָה וּמְשֻׁלָּם מִן־בְּנֵי הַקְּהָתִים לְנַצֵּחַ וְהַלְוִיִּם כָּל־מֵבִין בִּכְלֵי־
יג שִׁיר׃ וְעַל הַסַּבָּלִים וּמְנַצְּחִים לְכֹל עֹשֵׂה מְלָאכָה לַעֲבוֹדָה וַעֲבוֹדָה וּמֵהַלְוִיִּם
יד סוֹפְרִים וְשֹׁטְרִים וְשׁוֹעֲרִים׃ וּבְהוֹצִיאָם אֶת־הַכֶּסֶף הַמּוּבָא בֵּית יְהוָה מָצָא
טו חִלְקִיָּהוּ הַכֹּהֵן אֶת־סֵפֶר תּוֹרַת־יְהוָה בְּיַד־מֹשֶׁה׃ וַיַּעַן חִלְקִיָּהוּ וַיֹּאמֶר אֶל־שָׁפָן
הַסּוֹפֵר סֵפֶר הַתּוֹרָה מָצָאתִי בְּבֵית יְהוָה וַיִּתֵּן חִלְקִיָּהוּ אֶת־הַסֵּפֶר אֶל־שָׁפָן׃
טז וַיָּבֵא שָׁפָן אֶת־הַסֵּפֶר אֶל־הַמֶּלֶךְ וַיָּשֶׁב עוֹד אֶת־הַמֶּלֶךְ דָּבָר לֵאמֹר כֹּל אֲשֶׁר־
יז נִתַּן בְּיַד־עֲבָדֶיךָ הֵם עֹשִׂים׃ וַיַּתִּיכוּ אֶת־הַכֶּסֶף הַנִּמְצָא בְּבֵית־יְהוָה וַיִּתְּנוּהוּ
יח עַל־יַד הַמֻּפְקָדִים וְעַל־יַד עוֹשֵׂי הַמְּלָאכָה׃ וַיַּגֵּד שָׁפָן הַסּוֹפֵר לַמֶּלֶךְ לֵאמֹר סֵפֶר
יט נָתַן לִי חִלְקִיָּהוּ הַכֹּהֵן וַיִּקְרָא־בוֹ שָׁפָן לִפְנֵי הַמֶּלֶךְ׃ וַיְהִי כִּשְׁמֹעַ הַמֶּלֶךְ אֵת דִּבְרֵי
כ הַתּוֹרָה וַיִּקְרַע אֶת־בְּגָדָיו׃ וַיְצַו הַמֶּלֶךְ אֶת־חִלְקִיָּהוּ וְאֶת־אֲחִיקָם בֶּן־שָׁפָן וְאֶת־
כא עַבְדּוֹן בֶּן־מִיכָה וְאֵת ׀ שָׁפָן הַסּוֹפֵר וְאֵת עֲשָׂיָה עֶבֶד־הַמֶּלֶךְ לֵאמֹר׃ לְכוּ דִרְשׁוּ
אֶת־יְהוָה בַּעֲדִי וּבְעַד הַנִּשְׁאָר בְּיִשְׂרָאֵל וּבִיהוּדָה עַל־דִּבְרֵי הַסֵּפֶר אֲשֶׁר נִמְצָא
כִּי־גְדוֹלָה חֲמַת־יְהוָה אֲשֶׁר נִתְּכָה בָנוּ עַל אֲשֶׁר לֹא־שָׁמְרוּ אֲבוֹתֵינוּ אֶת־דְּבַר
כב יְהוָה לַעֲשׂוֹת כְּכָל־הַכָּתוּב עַל־הַסֵּפֶר הַזֶּה׃ וַיֵּלֶךְ חִלְקִיָּהוּ וַאֲשֶׁר
הַמֶּלֶךְ אֶל־חֻלְדָּה הַנְּבִיאָה אֵשֶׁת ׀ שַׁלֻּם בֶּן־תוקהת בֶּן־חַסְרָה שׁוֹמֵר הַבְּגָדִים תָּקְהַת
כג וְהִיא יוֹשֶׁבֶת בִּירוּשָׁלַםִ בַּמִּשְׁנֶה וַיְדַבְּרוּ אֵלֶיהָ כָּזֹאת׃ וַתֹּאמֶר לָהֶם כֹּה־אָמַר
יְהוָה אֱלֹהֵי יִשְׂרָאֵל אִמְרוּ לָאִישׁ אֲשֶׁר־שָׁלַח אֶתְכֶם אֵלָי׃
כד כֹּה אָמַר יְהוָה הִנְנִי מֵבִיא רָעָה עַל־הַמָּקוֹם הַזֶּה וְעַל־יוֹשְׁבָיו אֵת כָּל־הָאָלוֹת

BACKGROUND

34:22 | **The Mishneh:** This was probably a residential quarter or compound that was added to the City of David in Jerusalem during the days of King Uziya. It is suggested that this was either the Upper City, located on the western hill of Jerusalem, which is the site of the present-day Jewish Quarter, or the zone of the second wall that was built around the city for added protection (see Rashi, *Metzudat David*, and *Metzudat Tzion*, II Kings 22:14; *Metzudat Tzion*, Zephaniah 1:10).

25 **because they have forsaken Me, and burned offerings to other gods, in order to anger Me with all their handiwork. My wrath will be poured** abundantly **upon this place, and it will not be extinguished.**
26 **To the king of Judah, who sent you to inquire of the Lord, so you shall say to him,** in a rather different tone: **So said the Lord, God of Israel:** With regard to all **the words that you have heard,**
27 **because your heart is tender, and you humbled yourself before God when you heard His words** which He spoke **concerning this place and concerning its inhabitants, and humbled yourself before Me, rent your garments, and wept before Me, I too,** for My part, **have heard you – the utterance of the Lord.**
28 **Behold, I will gather you to your fathers, and you will be gathered to your grave in peace,** you will receive an honorable burial, **and your eyes will not see all the harm that I am bringing upon this place and upon its inhabitants. They,** Yoshiyahu's men, **brought back a report to the king.**
29 Every prophecy of evil is in effect a warning, as the assumption is that if people repent, the dark prophecy will not come to pass.[254] Consequently, Yoshiyahu sought with all his might to reverse the decree: **The king sent and gathered all the elders of Judah and Jerusalem.**
30 **The king went up to the House of the Lord with all the men of Judah, the inhabitants of Jerusalem, the priests, the Levites, and all the people, great and small, and he read in their ears all the words of the book of the covenant that was found in the House of the Lord,** from the Torah scroll itself.
31 **The king stood in his place,** in his specially designated spot in the Temple,[255] **and established a covenant before the Lord, to follow the Lord, and to observe His commandments, His testimonies, and His statutes, with all his heart, and with all his soul, to perform the words of the covenant that are written in this scroll.**
32 **He had everyone who was found in Jerusalem and Benjamin stand,** so that they should participate in the rite of the covenant in an official manner. **And the inhabitants of Jerusalem acted in accordance with** all that is written in **the covenant of God, God of their fathers.**[256] Yoshiyahu brought the people together and had them perform an action that would signify the enactment of the covenant, so that their agreement to the covenant should not be merely a verbal one.
33 **Yoshiyahu removed all the abominations from the lands,** the settled areas, **of the children of Israel, and he obligated,** forced, **everyone who was found in Israel to serve the Lord their God.** And indeed, **they did not deviate from following the Lord, God of their fathers.** Hulda's prophecy came true. Yoshiyahu remained king all his days, and no retribution was visited upon the land of Judah during his reign. However, although the king was buried with his ancestors, he did not die a peaceful death, but was killed in battle. His death signified a turning point; the end of the brief period of tranquility. From that moment onward, the situation in the Kingdom of Judah continuously deteriorated.

The Passover of Yoshiyahu

II CHRONICLES 35:1–19

After hearing Hulda the prophetess' prediction of future retribution, Yoshiyahu reinforced the covenant between the inhabitants of Judah and God, while purifying the land from all types of idolatrous worship. Now he encourages the people to participate in a national ritual of the paschal offering.

35 1 **Yoshiyahu performed the paschal offering to the Lord in Jerusalem, and they slaughtered the paschal offering on the fourteenth day of the first month,** in accordance with the commandment of the Torah.[257]

"Paschal offering." Lamb

2 **He,** the king, **set the priests at their watches, and encouraged them**[258] **in the service of the House of the Lord.**
3 **He said to the Levites who teach all Israel, who were sanctified to the Lord,** and devoted to His service: **Place the Holy Ark**[D] back **in the House,** the Temple, **which Solomon son of David, king of Israel, built;** the previous kings had apparently removed the Holy Ark from its rightful place.[259] Yoshiyahu further stated to the Levites: **You have no** service of **carrying** items **on your shoulders** as you had when you carried the Sanctuary's vessels from place to place in the wilderness; **now serve the Lord your God and His people Israel** through the other tasks assigned to you.[260]

כה הַכְּתוּבוֹת עַל־הַסֵּפֶר אֲשֶׁר קָרְאוּ לִפְנֵי מֶלֶךְ יְהוּדָה׃ תַּחַת ׀ אֲשֶׁר עֲזָבוּנִי ויקטירו וַיְקַטְּרוּ
לֵאלֹהִים אֲחֵרִים לְמַעַן הַכְעִיסֵנִי בְּכֹל מַעֲשֵׂי יְדֵיהֶם וְתִתַּךְ חֲמָתִי בַּמָּקוֹם הַזֶּה
כו וְלֹא תִכְבֶּה׃ וְאֶל־מֶלֶךְ יְהוּדָה הַשֹּׁלֵחַ אֶתְכֶם לִדְרוֹשׁ בַּיהוָה כֹּה תֹאמְרוּ
כז אֵלָיו כֹּה־אָמַר יְהוָה אֱלֹהֵי יִשְׂרָאֵל הַדְּבָרִים אֲשֶׁר שָׁמָעְתָּ׃ יַעַן
רַךְ־לְבָבְךָ וַתִּכָּנַע ׀ מִלִּפְנֵי אֱלֹהִים בְּשָׁמְעֲךָ אֶת־דְּבָרָיו עַל־הַמָּקוֹם הַזֶּה וְעַל־
יֹשְׁבָיו וַתִּכָּנַע לְפָנַי וַתִּקְרַע אֶת־בְּגָדֶיךָ וַתֵּבְךְּ לְפָנָי וְגַם־אֲנִי שָׁמַעְתִּי נְאֻם־יְהוָה׃
כח הִנְנִי אֹסִפְךָ אֶל־אֲבֹתֶיךָ וְנֶאֱסַפְתָּ אֶל־קִבְרוֹתֶיךָ בְּשָׁלוֹם וְלֹא־תִרְאֶינָה עֵינֶיךָ
בְּכֹל הָרָעָה אֲשֶׁר אֲנִי מֵבִיא עַל־הַמָּקוֹם הַזֶּה וְעַל־יֹשְׁבָיו וַיָּשִׁיבוּ אֶת־הַמֶּלֶךְ
כט ל דָּבָר׃ וַיִּשְׁלַח הַמֶּלֶךְ וַיֶּאֱסֹף אֶת־כָּל־זִקְנֵי יְהוּדָה וִירוּשָׁלָ͏ִם׃ וַיַּעַל הַמֶּלֶךְ
בֵּית־יְהוָה וְכָל־אִישׁ יְהוּדָה וְיֹשְׁבֵי יְרוּשָׁלַ͏ִם וְהַכֹּהֲנִים וְהַלְוִיִּם וְכָל־הָעָם מִגָּדוֹל
וְעַד־קָטָן וַיִּקְרָא בְאָזְנֵיהֶם אֶת־כָּל־דִּבְרֵי סֵפֶר הַבְּרִית הַנִּמְצָא בֵּית יְהוָה׃
לא וַיַּעֲמֹד הַמֶּלֶךְ עַל־עָמְדוֹ וַיִּכְרֹת אֶת־הַבְּרִית לִפְנֵי יְהוָה לָלֶכֶת אַחֲרֵי יְהוָה
וְלִשְׁמוֹר אֶת־מִצְוֺתָיו וְעֵדְוֺתָיו וְחֻקָּיו בְּכָל־לְבָבוֹ וּבְכָל־נַפְשׁוֹ לַעֲשׂוֹת אֶת־דִּבְרֵי
לב הַבְּרִית הַכְּתוּבִים עַל־הַסֵּפֶר הַזֶּה׃ וַיַּעֲמֵד אֵת כָּל־הַנִּמְצָא בִירוּשָׁלַ͏ִם וּבִנְיָמִן
לג וַיַּעֲשׂוּ יֹשְׁבֵי יְרוּשָׁלַ͏ִם כִּבְרִית אֱלֹהִים אֱלֹהֵי אֲבוֹתֵיהֶם׃ וַיָּסַר יֹאשִׁיָּהוּ אֶת־כָּל־
הַתּוֹעֵבוֹת מִכָּל־הָאֲרָצוֹת אֲשֶׁר לִבְנֵי יִשְׂרָאֵל וַיַּעֲבֵד אֵת כָּל־הַנִּמְצָא בְּיִשְׂרָאֵל
לַעֲבוֹד אֶת־יְהוָה אֱלֹהֵיהֶם כָּל־יָמָיו לֹא סָרוּ מֵאַחֲרֵי יְהוָה אֱלֹהֵי
ה א אֲבוֹתֵיהֶם׃ וַיַּעַשׂ יֹאשִׁיָּהוּ בִירוּשָׁלַ͏ִם פֶּסַח לַיהוָה וַיִּשְׁחֲטוּ הַפֶּסַח
ב בְּאַרְבָּעָה עָשָׂר לַחֹדֶשׁ הָרִאשׁוֹן׃ וַיַּעֲמֵד הַכֹּהֲנִים עַל־מִשְׁמְרוֹתָם וַיְחַזְּקֵם לַעֲבוֹדַת
ג בֵּית יְהוָה׃ וַיֹּאמֶר לַלְוִיִּם המבונים לְכָל־יִשְׂרָאֵל הַקְּדוֹשִׁים לַיהוָה תְּנוּ אֶת־ הַמְּבִינִים

DISCUSSION

35:3 | **Place the Holy Ark:** The Sages learn from here that the ark had been buried in a hidden place beneath the Temple due to the concern that it might fall into enemy hands (see Rashi; Radak; *Yoma* 52b).

4 **Prepare yourselves according to your patrilineal houses by your divisions,** your watches, as determined **according to the records of David king of Israel, and according to the records of Solomon his son.**
5 **Stand in the Sanctuary according to the** group **divisions of the patrilineal houses of your brethren, the members of the people.** All Israel were called upon to prepare to offer the paschal offering as families, in accordance with the verse: "They shall take for themselves, each one, a lamb for each house of the fathers."[261] **And** let there be **a division according to the patrilineal houses of the Levites** as well.
6 **Slaughter the paschal offering, and sanctify yourselves, and prepare** also **for your brethren,** in order **to act in accordance with the word of the Lord given by Moses.**
7 **Yoshiyahu donated to the members of the people from the flocks, lambs and goats, everything for the paschal offerings for everyone who was present** in Jerusalem, **to the number of thirty thousand, and cattle, three thousand,**[262] for the festival peace offering that is brought together with the paschal offering;[263] **they,** all these animals, **were** brought **from the property of the king.**
8 **His,** the king's, **princes, donated gifts to the people, to the priests, and to the Levites,** they gave the following: **Hilkiyahu, Zekharyahu, and Yehiel, high officials of the House of God, gave to the priests for the paschal offerings two thousand six hundred** sheep, **and three hundred cattle.**
9 **Konanyahu, and Shemayahu and Netanel his brothers, and Hashavyahu, Ye'iel, and Yozabad, the heads of the Levites, gave five thousand** sheep as a donation **to the Levites for the paschal offerings, and five hundred cattle** for the accompanying sacrifices.
10 **The service was established,** performed in the proper, orderly manner, **and the priests stood in their place, and the Levites by their divisions, in accordance with the king's command.**
11 **They slaughtered the paschal offering, and the priests sprinkled** the blood which they received **from their hand,** of those who slaughtered the animals, **and the Levites flayed** the animals.
12 **They removed the portions** of the sacrifices **to be offered up** on the altar, in order **to give them,** the paschal offerings, **to the divisions by the patrilineal houses of the members of the people, to present to the Lord** those portions designated for the altar, **as it is written in the book of Moses; and likewise they did with the cattle.**
13 **They roasted the paschal offering with fire in accordance with the ordinance** of the Torah;[264] **the** other **sacraments they cooked in pots, in cauldrons, and in bowls, and they quickly distributed them to all the members of the people.**
14 **Afterward,** after the Levites had prepared the sacrifices for their brethren, **they prepared for themselves, and for the priests, because** all day **the priests, sons of Aaron, were offering up** on the altar **the portions to be offered up, and the fat,** the choice parts of the meat, **until night; the Levites prepared for themselves, and for the priests, sons of Aaron.**
15 **The singers, sons of Asaf, were** standing **in their place, according to the command of David, Asaf, Heiman, and Yedutun,** each **the king's seer,** called such because the king's singers were inspired with the Holy Spirit.[265] **And the gatekeepers were** standing at their posts **at each and every gate; they did not need to leave their service, as their brethren the Levites prepared for them** as well.
16 **All the service of the Lord was established on that day, to perform the paschal offering, and to offer up burnt offerings on the altar of the Lord, in accordance with the command of King Yoshiyahu.**
17 **The children of Israel who were present** in Jerusalem **performed the paschal offering at that time, and** they celebrated **the Festival of Unleavened Bread for seven days.**
18 **There had been no paschal offering performed like it,** according to the Torah's command and with the participation of so many people,[266] **in Israel, since the days of Samuel the prophet; all the kings of Israel had not performed the paschal offering like that which Yoshiyahu performed, with the priests, and the Levites, and all Judah and Israel who were present, and the inhabitants of Jerusalem.**
19 **In the eighteenth year of the reign of Yoshiyahu, this paschal offering was performed.**

אֲרוֹן־הַקֹּדֶשׁ בַּבַּיִת אֲשֶׁר בָּנָה שְׁלֹמֹה בֶן־דָּוִיד מֶלֶךְ יִשְׂרָאֵל אֵין־לָכֶם מַשָּׂא
ד בַּכָּתֵף עַתָּה עִבְדוּ אֶת־יְהוָה אֱלֹהֵיכֶם וְאֵת עַמּוֹ יִשְׂרָאֵל: והכונו לְבֵית־אֲבוֹתֵיכֶם וְהָכִינוּ
ה כְּמַחְלְקוֹתֵיכֶם בִּכְתָב דָּוִיד מֶלֶךְ יִשְׂרָאֵל וּבְמִכְתַּב שְׁלֹמֹה בְנוֹ: וְעִמְדוּ בַקֹּדֶשׁ
ו לִפְלֻגּוֹת בֵּית הָאָבוֹת לַאֲחֵיכֶם בְּנֵי הָעָם וַחֲלֻקַּת בֵּית־אָב לַלְוִיִּם: וְשַׁחֲטוּ הַפָּסַח כה
וְהִתְקַדְּשׁוּ וְהָכִינוּ לַאֲחֵיכֶם לַעֲשׂוֹת כִּדְבַר־יְהוָה בְּיַד־מֹשֶׁה:
ז וַיָּרֶם יֹאשִׁיָּהוּ לִבְנֵי הָעָם צֹאן כְּבָשִׂים וּבְנֵי־עִזִּים הַכֹּל לַפְּסָחִים לְכָל־הַנִּמְצָא
לְמִסְפַּר שְׁלֹשִׁים אֶלֶף וּבָקָר שְׁלֹשֶׁת אֲלָפִים אֵלֶּה מֵרְכוּשׁ הַמֶּלֶךְ:
ח וְשָׂרָיו לִנְדָבָה לָעָם לַכֹּהֲנִים וְלַלְוִיִּם הֵרִימוּ חִלְקִיָּה וּזְכַרְיָהוּ וִיחִיאֵל נְגִידֵי בֵּית
הָאֱלֹהִים לַכֹּהֲנִים נָתְנוּ לַפְּסָחִים אַלְפַּיִם וְשֵׁשׁ מֵאוֹת וּבָקָר שְׁלֹשׁ מֵאוֹת:
ט וכונניהו וּשְׁמַעְיָהוּ וּנְתַנְאֵל אֶחָיו וַחֲשַׁבְיָהוּ וִיעִיאֵל וְיוֹזָבָד שָׂרֵי הַלְוִיִּם הֵרִימוּ וְכָנַנְיָהוּ
י לַלְוִיִּם לַפְּסָחִים חֲמֵשֶׁת אֲלָפִים וּבָקָר חֲמֵשׁ מֵאוֹת: וַתִּכּוֹן הָעֲבוֹדָה וַיַּעַמְדוּ
יא הַכֹּהֲנִים עַל־עָמְדָם וְהַלְוִיִּם עַל־מַחְלְקוֹתָם כְּמִצְוַת הַמֶּלֶךְ: וַיִּשְׁחֲטוּ הַפָּסַח
יב וַיִּזְרְקוּ הַכֹּהֲנִים מִיָּדָם וְהַלְוִיִּם מַפְשִׁיטִים: וַיָּסִירוּ הָעֹלָה לְתִתָּם לְמִפְלַגּוֹת לְבֵית־
יג אָבוֹת לִבְנֵי הָעָם לְהַקְרִיב לַיהוָה כַּכָּתוּב בְּסֵפֶר מֹשֶׁה וְכֵן לַבָּקָר: וַיְבַשְּׁלוּ הַפֶּסַח
בָּאֵשׁ כַּמִּשְׁפָּט וְהַקֳּדָשִׁים בִּשְּׁלוּ בַּסִּירוֹת וּבַדְּוָדִים וּבַצֵּלָחוֹת וַיָּרִיצוּ לְכָל־בְּנֵי
יד הָעָם: וְאַחַר הֵכִינוּ לָהֶם וְלַכֹּהֲנִים כִּי הַכֹּהֲנִים בְּנֵי אַהֲרֹן בְּהַעֲלוֹת הָעוֹלָה וְהַחֲלָבִים
טו עַד־לָיְלָה וְהַלְוִיִּם הֵכִינוּ לָהֶם וְלַכֹּהֲנִים בְּנֵי אַהֲרֹן: וְהַמְשֹׁרְרִים בְּנֵי־אָסָף עַל־
מַעֲמָדָם כְּמִצְוַת דָּוִיד וְאָסָף וְהֵימָן וִידֻתוּן חוֹזֵה הַמֶּלֶךְ וְהַשֹּׁעֲרִים לְשַׁעַר וָשָׁעַר
טז אֵין לָהֶם לָסוּר מֵעַל עֲבֹדָתָם כִּי־אֲחֵיהֶם הַלְוִיִּם הֵכִינוּ לָהֶם: וַתִּכּוֹן כָּל־עֲבוֹדַת
יְהוָה בַּיּוֹם הַהוּא לַעֲשׂוֹת הַפֶּסַח וְהַעֲלוֹת עֹלוֹת עַל מִזְבַּח יְהוָה כְּמִצְוַת הַמֶּלֶךְ
יז יֹאשִׁיָּהוּ: וַיַּעֲשׂוּ בְנֵי־יִשְׂרָאֵל הַנִּמְצְאִים אֶת־הַפֶּסַח בָּעֵת הַהִיא וְאֶת־חַג הַמַּצּוֹת
יח שִׁבְעַת יָמִים: וְלֹא־נַעֲשָׂה פֶסַח כָּמֹהוּ בְּיִשְׂרָאֵל מִימֵי שְׁמוּאֵל הַנָּבִיא וְכָל־מַלְכֵי
יִשְׂרָאֵל ׀ לֹא־עָשׂוּ כַּפֶּסַח אֲשֶׁר־עָשָׂה יֹאשִׁיָּהוּ וְהַכֹּהֲנִים וְהַלְוִיִּם וְכָל־יְהוּדָה
יט וְיִשְׂרָאֵל הַנִּמְצָא וְיוֹשְׁבֵי יְרוּשָׁלִָם: בִּשְׁמוֹנֶה עֶשְׂרֵה שָׁנָה לְמַלְכוּת

Yoshiyahu's End

II CHRONICLES 35:20–27

King Yoshiyahu does not die a natural death, but is shot with an arrow and killed, in a war he initiates with Pharaoh Nekho.

20 **After all this, when Yoshiyahu had established,** strengthened
and renovated, **the House, Nekho king of Egypt came up to
wage war at Karkemish**[B] **on the Euphrates. Yoshiyahu went
out toward him,** for war. Pharaoh Nekho did not intend to fight against Judah. Rather, he and his army were headed northward to the Euphrates, in order to do battle with the northern empires, for which purpose they had to pass through the territory of the Kingdom of Judah. Yoshiyahu decided to stand in their way and block their progress.

Bronze statuette of Pharaoh Nekho kneeling, 610–595 BCE

Archaeological findings at Karkemish

Campaign of Pharaoh Nekho

21 **He,** the king of Egypt, **sent emissaries to him, saying: What is
there between me and you, king of Judah?** There is no quarrel between us. **It is not against you** that I come to fight **today,
but to the theater of my war,** in the battlefield in Karkemish.
God said that I should make haste; he has encouraged me.
Restrain yourself from the **god who is with me, and he will
not destroy,** kill, **you.** Do not provoke the god who is accompanying me to war.[267]
22 **Yoshiyahu** refused to heed Pharaoh Nekho's warning, and **did
not turn his face from him, but donned armor**[268] **to wage
war with him, and did not heed the words of Nekho from
the mouth of God.** He did not listen to the prophets of Israel who confirmed that the campaign of the king of Egypt was in accordance with God's will.[269] **And he,** King Yoshiyahu, **came
to wage war in the valley of Megiddo.**[B]
23 **The archers shot King Yoshiyahu, and the king said to his
servants: Take me away;** remove me from the battlefield, **as I
am severely wounded.**
24 **His servants took him from the chariot** from which he had
been fighting, **and placed him in the second chariot that he
had,** which was faster and more comfortable, **and brought
him to Jerusalem, and he,** Yoshiyahu, **died. He was buried in
the graves of his fathers. All Judah and Jerusalem mourned
Yoshiyahu.** Not only was Yoshiyahu a righteous and talented king, but he was also esteemed and beloved by his people.
25 **Jeremiah lamented for Yoshiyahu, and all the singers, male
and female, recite their lamentations for Yoshiyahu to
this day; they instituted them as a custom in Israel.** They turned the practice of mentioning Yoshiyahu in their eulogies into a fixed custom in Israel, **and, behold, they,** the words of mourning, **are written in the lamentations,**[D] the book of Lamentations in the Bible.
26 **The rest of the deeds of Yoshiyahu, and his kindnesses**
which he performed, **as it is written** and commanded **in the
Torah of the Lord,**
27 **and his early and late deeds, behold, they are written in the
book of the kings of Israel and Judah.**

כ יֹאשִׁיָּהוּ נַעֲשָׂה הַפֶּסַח הַזֶּה: אַחֲרֵי כָל־זֹאת אֲשֶׁר הֵכִין יֹאשִׁיָּהוּ אֶת־הַבַּיִת עָלָה
כא נְכוֹ מֶלֶךְ־מִצְרַיִם לְהִלָּחֵם בְּכַרְכְּמִישׁ עַל־פְּרָת וַיֵּצֵא לִקְרָאתוֹ יֹאשִׁיָּהוּ: וַיִּשְׁלַח
אֵלָיו מַלְאָכִים ׀ לֵאמֹר ׀ מַה־לִּי וָלָךְ מֶלֶךְ יְהוּדָה לֹא־עָלֶיךָ אַתָּה הַיּוֹם כִּי אֶל־
בֵּית מִלְחַמְתִּי וֵאלֹהִים אָמַר לְבַהֲלֵנִי חֲדַל־לְךָ מֵאֱלֹהִים אֲשֶׁר־עִמִּי וְאַל־
כב יַשְׁחִיתֶךָ: וְלֹא־הֵסֵב יֹאשִׁיָּהוּ פָנָיו מִמֶּנּוּ כִּי לְהִלָּחֶם־בּוֹ הִתְחַפֵּשׂ וְלֹא שָׁמַע
כג אֶל־דִּבְרֵי נְכוֹ מִפִּי אֱלֹהִים וַיָּבֹא לְהִלָּחֵם בְּבִקְעַת מְגִדּוֹ: וַיֹּרוּ הַיֹּרִים לַמֶּלֶךְ
כד יֹאשִׁיָּהוּ וַיֹּאמֶר הַמֶּלֶךְ לַעֲבָדָיו הַעֲבִירוּנִי כִּי הָחֳלֵיתִי מְאֹד: וַיַּעֲבִירֻהוּ עֲבָדָיו
מִן־הַמֶּרְכָּבָה וַיַּרְכִּיבֻהוּ עַל רֶכֶב הַמִּשְׁנֶה אֲשֶׁר־לוֹ וַיּוֹלִיכֻהוּ יְרוּשָׁלִַם וַיָּמָת וַיִּקָּבֵר
בְּקִבְרוֹת אֲבֹתָיו וְכָל־יְהוּדָה וִירוּשָׁלִַם מִתְאַבְּלִים עַל־יֹאשִׁיָּהוּ:
כה וַיְקוֹנֵן יִרְמְיָהוּ עַל־יֹאשִׁיָּהוּ וַיֹּאמְרוּ כָל־הַשָּׁרִים ׀ וְהַשָּׁרוֹת בְּקִינוֹתֵיהֶם עַל־
כו יֹאשִׁיָּהוּ עַד־הַיּוֹם וַיִּתְּנוּם לְחֹק עַל־יִשְׂרָאֵל וְהִנָּם כְּתוּבִים עַל־הַקִּינוֹת: וְיֶתֶר
כז דִּבְרֵי יֹאשִׁיָּהוּ וַחֲסָדָיו כַּכָּתוּב בְּתוֹרַת יְהוָה: וּדְבָרָיו הָרִאשֹׁנִים וְהָאַחֲרֹנִים הִנָּם

BACKGROUND

35:20 | **War at Karkemish:** The city of Karkemish, which is present-day Jarabulus, just south of the Syrian-Turkish border, controlled a crossing of the Euphrates River as well as the road leading to Haran and to Nineveh, the capital of Assyria. When the Babylonian Empire first rose to prominence, the Babylonians conquered Nineveh and Haran, and Karkemish became the new capital of Assyria. The Egyptians came to the assistance of the Assyrians, but they met with failure. In the year 605 BCE, while retreating southwest, they waged battle together with the Assyrian army in the region of Karkemish, with the aim of preventing the Babylonians from crossing the Euphrates. The Egyptian army was destroyed in that fight, and the Babylonians became the dominant empire in the Middle East. Excavations conducted in the city of Karkemish unearthed a layer of ruins that contained seals of Pharaoh Nekho.

35:22 | **The valley of Megiddo:** The valley of Megiddo is located on what was an important international crossroads, where the road from Egypt, the Via Maris, turned east and crossed the Yizre'el Valley before continuing north to Syria. The road coming south from Phoenicia also intersected with the Via Maris at this point. Megiddo's location on the main routes between Egypt and the north and east made it a strategic site in any conflict between the regional powers. The fact that this battle took place in an area that was within an Assyrian province, part of the conquered Kingdom of Israel, is indicative of the disintegration of the Assyrian Empire and the vacuum it left behind. It is likely that the weakness of Assyria contributed to Yoshiyahu's desire to bring the former Kingdom of Israel under Judean sovereignty, and led to his confrontation with Pharaoh Nekho.

DISCUSSION

35:25 | **In the lamentations:** The book of Lamentations deals with a great downfall suffered by Israel. It does not explicitly mention the destruction of the Temple itself. Accordingly, parts of the book can be interpreted as Jeremiah's lamentation over the death of Yoshiyahu (see *Ta'anit* 22b; *Eikha Rabba* 1:53; see introduction to Lamentations; Lamentations 4:20, and commentary ad loc.).

The Chronicles of the Sons of Yoshiyahu

II CHRONICLES 36:1–14

After Yoshiyahu's death, the Kingdom of Judah begins a downward spiral. Although the kingdom retains its independence for a few more years, its strength fades during this period, until its final downfall. Yoshiyahu was the last true hope of the land of Judah, and when he dies, the monarchy effectively comes to an unofficial end. The kings who rule after him are mere shadows of the possibilities that brightened the horizon during Yoshiyahu's reign; Yeho'ahaz is subordinate to the king of Egypt, who then replaces him anyway with Elyakim or Yehoyakim, his brother. For his part, Yehoyakim is under the thumb of the king of Babylon, and his son who reigns after him, Yehoyakhin, is exiled to Babylon. Nebuchadnezzar king of Babylon crowns his brother, Tzidkiyahu, in his place. After a while, Tzidkiyahu rebels against the king of Babylon, in violation of the instruction of the prophet, and the oath he himself swore to Nebuchadnezzar. This decision brings the Babylonian army upon Judah.

36 1 After the death of Yoshiyahu, **the people of the land took Yeho'ahaz son of Yoshiyahu,** who was not his firstborn son, **and crowned him king in his father's stead in Jerusalem.**

2 **Yo'ahaz was twenty-three years old when he became king, and he reigned for three months in Jerusalem.** Three months passed until Pharaoh Nekho returned from his unsuccessful war in Karkemish and passed once again through the land of Judah, probably angry and bitter at his failure. Having killed Yoshiyahu, Pharaoh considered himself the supreme leader over Judah, and therefore refused to accept the appointment of Yeho'ahaz.

3 **The king of Egypt removed him** from the throne **in Jerusalem, and imposed a fine on the land of one hundred talents of silver and a talent of gold.** The king of Egypt was powerful enough to force the inhabitants of Judah to pay this sum.[270]

4 **The king of Egypt crowned Elyakim his brother,** of the deposed Yeho'ahaz, **king over Judah and Jerusalem. He changed his name to Yehoyakim.** The new name bears the same meaning as the old name; Pharaoh probably changed it in order to emphasize the transformation of the Kingdom of Judah's status in relation to Egypt. **Nekho took Yo'ahaz his brother** captive, **and brought him to Egypt.** King Yeho'ahaz did not return from Egypt, and his end is unknown. Some explain that the verse: "Do not weep for the dead, and do not bewail him; weep for him who goes forth, as he will not return again and see the land of his birth,"[271] is a reference to Yeho'ahaz.[272]

5 **Yehoyakim was twenty-five years old when he became king and he reigned eleven years in Jerusalem.** It is clear from the ages given here that Yehoyakim was Yoshiyahu's firstborn, while Yeho'ahaz was the second or third son. Even so, the people chose Yeho'ahaz, probably because they were less fond of his older brother.[273] Indeed, Yehoyakim was not a particularly distinguished or beloved figure: **He did evil in the eyes of the Lord his God.**

6 After a while, **Nebuchadnezzar king of Babylon came up against him.** Although it was Pharaoh who had deposed Yeho'ahaz and crowned Yehoyakim, over the years Nebuchadnezzar developed into a far more powerful ruler than Pharaoh. He captured the entire region, and continued his campaigns of conquest until he reached Egypt. On the way he passed through Judah, where he found King Yehoyakim. **And** since Yehoyakim had been given the throne by a foreign ruler, whom he probably favored, Nebuchadnezzar **bound him in shackles,** in order **to bring him to Babylon.** Elsewhere it is related that Yehoyakim rebelled against the king of Babylon.[274] Nebuchadnezzar captured Yehoyakim with the intention of bringing him down to Babylon, just as Pharaoh Nekho had taken his brother Yeho'ahaz to Egypt. However, it seems that Yehoyakim did not actually reach Babylon, and died along the way.[275]

"And bound him in shackles." Relief of shackled captives at Medinet Habu, Egypt, twelfth century BCE

7 **Nebuchadnezzar brought some of the vessels of the House of the Lord to Babylon and placed them in his temple in Babylon.**

8 **The rest of the deeds of Yehoyakim, and his abominations that he performed,** which are not detailed here, **and that which was found about him,** or that which was written about him,[276] such as the incidents and exchanges related by the prophet Jeremiah, who confronted Yehoyakim on several occasions,[277] **behold, they are written in the book of the kings of Israel and Judah. Yehoyakhin his son reigned in his stead.**

9 **Yehoyakhin was eight years old when he became king.** According to the book of Kings, he was eighteen years old when he rose to the throne;[278] **and he reigned three months and ten days in Jerusalem. He did evil in the eyes of the Lord.** In the short period of his reign, he did not act appropriately in the eyes of God.

10 **At the turn of the year,** the next year, **King Nebuchadnezzar sent and brought him to Babylon, with the precious vessels of the House of the Lord.** Nebuchadnezzar returned to Israel for a second time, after having already looted some vessels from the House of God on the first occasion. This time he sought to assume firmer control over events in Judah. First he

לו א כתובים על־ספר מלכי־ישראל ויהודה: ויקחו עם־הארץ את־
ב יהואחז בן־יאשיהו וימליכהו תחת־אביו בירושלם: בן־שלוש ועשרים שנה
ג יואחז במלכו ושלשה חדשים מלך בירושלם: ויסירהו מלך־מצרים בירושלם
ד ויענש את־הארץ מאה ככר־כסף וככר זהב: וימלך מלך־מצרים את־אליקים
אחיו על־יהודה וירושלם ויסב את־שמו יהויקים ואת־יואחז אחיו לקח נכו
ה ויביאהו מצרימה: בן־עשרים וחמש שנה יהויקים במלכו ואחת
ו עשרה שנה מלך בירושלם ויעש הרע בעיני יהוה אלהיו: עליו עלה נבוכדנאצר
ז מלך בבל ויאסרהו בנחשתים להליכו בבלה: ומכלי בית יהוה הביא
ח נבוכדנאצר לבבל ויתנם בהיכלו בבבל: ויתר דברי יהויקים ותעבתיו אשר־
עשה והנמצא עליו הנם כתובים על־ספר מלכי ישראל ויהודה וימלך יהויכין
ט בנו תחתיו: בן־שמונה שנים יהויכין במלכו ושלשה חדשים
י ועשרת ימים מלך בירושלם ויעש הרע בעיני יהוה: ולתשובת השנה שלח
המלך נבוכדנאצר ויבאהו בבלה עם־כלי חמדת בית־יהוה וימלך את־צדקיהו
יא אחיו על־יהודה וירושלם: בן־עשרים ואחת שנה צדקיהו במלכו
יב ואחת עשרה שנה מלך בירושלם: ויעש הרע בעיני יהוה אלהיו לא נכנע
יג מלפני ירמיהו הנביא מפי יהוה: וגם במלך נבוכדנאצר מרד אשר השביעו
באלהים ויקש את־ערפו ויאמץ את־לבבו משוב אל־יהוה אלהי ישראל:

seized additional Temple vessels, as despite the lowly state Judah was in, the sacred vessels had been replaced. Next he took Yehoyakhin king of Judah to Babylon, as a hostage.[279] **And** Nebuchadnezzar **crowned Tzidkiyahu his brother,** that is, his father's brother,[280] **king over Judah and Jerusalem.** As stated elsewhere, Tzidkiyahu's original name was Matanya, and it was Nebuchadnezzar who gave him his royal name.[281]

11 **Tzidkiyahu was twenty-one years old when he became king, and he reigned eleven years in Jerusalem.**

12 **He did evil in the eyes of the Lord his God. He did not humble himself before Jeremiah the prophet,** who prophesied to him **from the mouth of the Lord;** the king did not accept the prophet's advice.[282]

13 **He also rebelled against King Nebuchadnezzar, who had administered an oath to him by God.** Not only did he rebel against the king of Babylon, but he violated a personal oath he had taken in the name of God. **He stiffened his neck,** he was stubborn, **and hardened his heart from returning to the Lord, God of Israel.** It seems that King Tzidkiyahu was a rather spineless individual. He repeatedly vacillated between his fear of the people and his fear of God.[283]

14 **Also** in his days, **all the leaders of the priests and the**
people trespassed greatly; they betrayed God **like all the**
abominations of the nations, and they defiled the House of
the Lord that He had sanctified in Jerusalem.

The Destruction of Judah and a Sliver of Hope for Redemption

II CHRONICLES 36:15–23

The ensuing events, until the destruction of the Temple and beyond, are described in greater detail in the book of Kings. The book of Chronicles concludes by skipping from the destruction to seventy years later, and the declaration of Cyrus, which signifies the beginning of a new era in Jewish history, as the people of Israel are about to return once again to their homeland.

15 **The Lord, God of their fathers, sent to them by means of**
His messengers, His prophets, **sending time and again;** He
sent the prophets on numerous occasions to exhort Israel to repent **because He had compassion on His people, and on His**
abode, His Temple.
16 **They,** the inhabitants of Judah and Jerusalem, **would insult the**
messengers of God, scorn His words, and abuse and deceive
His prophets, until the wrath of the Lord rose against His
people, until there was no remedy.
17 **He brought against them the king of the Chaldeans,**
Nebuchadnezzar, **and he killed their young men by the**
sword in their Sanctuary, and he did not have pity on young
men or maidens, elderly or aged. All, He gave into his hand.
18 **All the vessels of the House of God,** found in the Temple,
great and small, the treasures of the House of the Lord,
and the treasures of the king and of his princes, all of it,
he brought to Babylon. According to tradition, some of the
Temple vessels had been hidden away earlier by King Yoshiyahu
or others.[284]
19 **They burned the House of God and smashed the wall of**
Jerusalem; all its palaces they burned with fire, and de-
stroyed all its precious vessels.
20 After the king of Babylon devastated Jerusalem, destroyed the
Temple, and looted all that he found there, **all the remnants**
from the sword, those who survived the attack, **he exiled to**
Babylonia, and they became servants to him and his sons
until the reign of the kingdom of Persia. The full story of
Tzidkiyahu appears both in the book of Jeremiah and in Kings,
where it is stated that Nebuchadnezzar blinded the king after
killing his children.[285]
21 The inhabitants of Judah were exiled, **fulfilling the word of**
the Lord as stated **by the mouth of Jeremiah, until the land**
would be repaid for its Sabbaths, the Sabbatical years that
had not been properly observed; **all the days of its desolation**
it rested, to complete seventy years. Jeremiah prophesied
that seventy years after the Babylonian exile Israel would be redeemed,[286] and indeed, the exiles from Zion returned to their
land seventy years after the capture of Tzidkiyahu.[287]
22 In order to conclude this account of the chronicles of the
Kingdom of Judah on an uplifting note, its final verses cite the
proclamation of Cyrus. **And in the first year of Cyrus king**
of Persia, with the completion of the word of the Lord by
the mouth of Jeremiah concerning the seventy years of exile,
the Lord roused the spirit of Cyrus king of Persia, and he
circulated a proclamation throughout his kingdom, and in
addition to this oral announcement, he put his words **also in**
writing, saying:
23 **So said Cyrus**[B] **king of Persia: The Lord, God of the heav-**
ens, has given me all the kingdoms of the earth, and He has
commanded me to build Him a House in Jerusalem, which
is in Judah. This command comes from Above, and I wish to
fulfill it. Therefore, **those among you from all His people,**
may the Lord his God be with him, He will assist him, **and**
let him ascend to Jerusalem.
Any Israelite who wishes to ascend and build the Temple is permitted to return to the Land of Israel. Thus, after the destruction of the Temple, the book, and indeed the entire Bible, concludes with a brief mention of the start of the redemption.

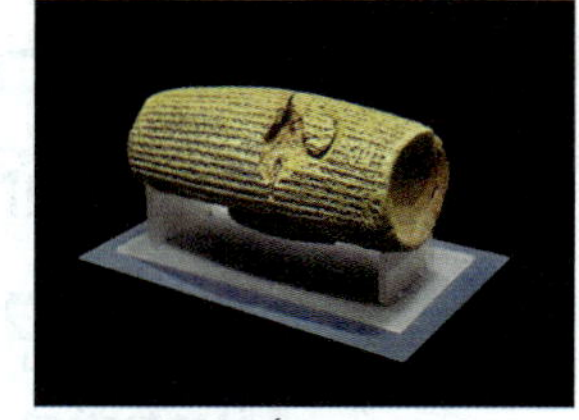

Cyrus Cylinder, Ésagila temple, Babylon, 539 BCE

"The Lord, God of the heavens, has given me all the kingdoms of the earth." The empire of Cyrus

יד גַּם כָּל־שָׂרֵי הַכֹּהֲנִים וְהָעָם הִרְבּוּ למעול־מַעַל כְּכֹל תֹּעֲבוֹת הַגּוֹיִם וַיְטַמְּאוּ לִמְעָל־
טו אֶת־בֵּית יְהוָה אֲשֶׁר הִקְדִּישׁ בִּירוּשָׁלִָם׃ וַיִּשְׁלַח יְהוָה אֱלֹהֵי אֲבוֹתֵיהֶם עֲלֵיהֶם
טז בְּיַד מַלְאָכָיו הַשְׁכֵּם וְשָׁלוֹחַ כִּי־חָמַל עַל־עַמּוֹ וְעַל־מְעוֹנוֹ׃ וַיִּהְיוּ מַלְעִבִים בְּמַלְאֲכֵי
הָאֱלֹהִים וּבוֹזִים דְּבָרָיו וּמִתַּעְתְּעִים בִּנְבִאָיו עַד עֲלוֹת חֲמַת־יְהוָה בְּעַמּוֹ עַד־
יז לְאֵין מַרְפֵּא׃ וַיַּעַל עֲלֵיהֶם אֶת־מֶלֶךְ כשדיים וַיַּהֲרֹג בַּחוּרֵיהֶם בַּחֶרֶב בְּבֵית כַּשְׂדִּים
יח מִקְדָּשָׁם וְלֹא חָמַל עַל־בָּחוּר וּבְתוּלָה זָקֵן וְיָשֵׁשׁ הַכֹּל נָתַן בְּיָדוֹ׃ וְכֹל כְּלֵי בֵּית
הָאֱלֹהִים הַגְּדֹלִים וְהַקְּטַנִּים וְאֹצְרוֹת בֵּית יְהוָה וְאֹצְרוֹת הַמֶּלֶךְ וְשָׂרָיו הַכֹּל
יט הֵבִיא בָבֶל׃ וַיִּשְׂרְפוּ אֶת־בֵּית הָאֱלֹהִים וַיְנַתְּצוּ אֵת חוֹמַת יְרוּשָׁלִָם וְכָל־אַרְמְנוֹתֶיהָ
כ שָׂרְפוּ בָאֵשׁ וְכָל־כְּלֵי מַחֲמַדֶּיהָ לְהַשְׁחִית׃ וַיֶּגֶל הַשְּׁאֵרִית מִן־הַחֶרֶב אֶל־בָּבֶל
כא וַיִּהְיוּ־לוֹ וּלְבָנָיו לַעֲבָדִים עַד־מְלֹךְ מַלְכוּת פָּרָס׃ לְמַלֹּאות דְּבַר־יְהוָה בְּפִי
יִרְמְיָהוּ עַד־רָצְתָה הָאָרֶץ אֶת־שַׁבְּתוֹתֶיהָ כָּל־יְמֵי הָשַּׁמָּה שָׁבָתָה לְמַלֹּאות
כב שִׁבְעִים שָׁנָה׃ וּבִשְׁנַת אַחַת לְכוֹרֶשׁ מֶלֶךְ פָּרַס לִכְלוֹת דְּבַר־יְהוָה בְּפִי
יִרְמְיָהוּ הֵעִיר יְהוָה אֶת־רוּחַ כּוֹרֶשׁ מֶלֶךְ־פָּרַס וַיַּעֲבֶר־קוֹל בְּכָל־מַלְכוּתוֹ וְגַם־
כג בְּמִכְתָּב לֵאמֹר׃ כֹּה־אָמַר כּוֹרֶשׁ ׀ מֶלֶךְ פָּרַס כָּל־מַמְלְכוֹת הָאָרֶץ נָתַן לִי יְהוָה
אֱלֹהֵי הַשָּׁמַיִם וְהוּא־פָקַד עָלַי לִבְנוֹת־לוֹ בַיִת בִּירוּשָׁלִַם אֲשֶׁר בִּיהוּדָה מִי־בָכֶם
מִכָּל־עַמּוֹ יְהוָה אֱלֹהָיו עִמּוֹ וְיָעַל׃

BACKGROUND

36:23 | **Cyrus:** According to the Babylonian Chronicles tablets, as well as Herodotus, Cyrus was already ruling the Persians by 559 BCE. However, it was only after many conquests and struggles, lasting some twenty years, that he conquered the city of Babylon, and became ruler of the Persian Empire, which stretched from northeast India to Asia Minor, incorporating Syria, Lebanon, and Israel. In that year, a royal decree was issued that is similar in spirit to Cyrus' declaration to the Jews cited in this chapter. This so-called Cyrus Cylinder, which was discovered on a cylinder of clay, was found in Babylon in 1897, and is currently located in the British Museum.

Notes

Psalms

1. Genesis 1:27.
2. *Makkot* 24a.
3. See also Exodus 20:18.
4. See Exodus 25:18.
5. See also Deuteronomy 29:28: "The concealed are for the Lord our God, but the revealed are for us and for our children."
6. See, e.g., chap. 68; see Exodus 19:18.
7. See I Samuel 21:11–22:1.
8. See Isaiah 62:6.
9. See I Chronicles 16:41.
10. See introduction to Psalms 32.
11. See Exodus 23:17, 34:23.
12. I Chronicles 29:23.
13. See I Kings 9:28.
14. See Genesis 17:5.
15. See I Kings 19:11–12.
16. Exodus 20:2.
17. See *Vayikra Rabba* 22:10.
18. II Samuel 12:13.
19. See Leviticus 14:4.
20. See Numbers 19:18.
21. See I Samuel 22:9.
22. See I Samuel 23:19–28.
23. See Numbers 16.
24. See I Samuel 27:1–4.
25. See I Samuel 19.
26. See also Judges 5:4–5, which contains similar wording.
27. See Jeremiah 49:19, where the enemy is compared to a lion prowling the banks of the Jordan River.
28. See commentary on 45:1.
29. See, e.g., Genesis 1.
30. Psalms 62.
31. See I Chronicles 7:20–22.
32. See Exodus 16:2–3.
33. See Exodus 16–17; Numbers 11.
34. See Numbers 11:31.
35. See Numbers 11:33–34.
36. See Numbers 14:22–23.
37. See Genesis 10:6.
38. See I Samuel 4.
39. See introduction to Psalms 45.
40. Deuteronomy 14:1.
41. See Exodus 17:7.
42. See Numbers 35:24–25; Mishna *Sanhedrin* 1:4.
43. See Judges 6–7.
44. See Judges 4.
45. See Judges 7:25.
46. See Judges 8.
47. See II Samuel 5:22–24.
48. Almost identical wording appears in Exodus 34:6.
49. See Isaiah 30:7.
50. See I Chronicles 6:18.
51. See I Chronicles 2:6.
52. See I Chronicles 2:6.
53. See I Chronicles 6:29.
54. Genesis 1:21.
55. See I Samuel 16:13.
56. See also *Bereshit Rabba* 68:9: "He is the place of the world, but His world is not His place."
57. See Exodus 32:12.
58. See *Tamid* 33b.
59. Exodus 17:7; Numbers 20:13.
60. Exodus 34:5–7.
61. See Genesis 1:7: "The water that was above the firmament."
62. See Genesis 1:9.
63. Genesis 1:9.
64. See also "pitch darkness" [*mapelya*] in Jeremiah 2:31 and "great conflagration" [*shalhevetya*] in Song of Songs 8:6.
65. See Genesis 17:17–19.
66. See Genesis 20:3.
67. Exodus 5:22–23.
68. See Exodus 7:29.
69. See Exodus 9:24.
70. See, e.g., Genesis 49:3.
71. See Exodus 12:33.
72. Exodus 17:1–7.
73. Exodus 14:10–12.
74. Exodus 15:1–19.
75. Numbers 11:33.
76. Numbers 16.
77. Numbers 16:1.
78. Numbers 16:35.
79. Numbers 25:6–15.
80. Numbers 20:2–12.
81. See Numbers 20:10.
82. See II Samuel 8:18.
83. See also Isaiah 17:12.
84. See II Samuel 24:18–25.
85. See Numbers 10:35–36.
86. I Samuel 24:3.
87. See *Berakhot* 4b for a discussion of the reasons for this omission.

Proverbs

1. See, e.g., Rashi, *Bava Batra* 14b.
2. I Kings 5:11.
3. See Numbers 23:7; I Samuel 10:12; Ezekiel 12:22–23; Job 27:1.
4. See 22:20; *Bava Batra* 15a.
5. See 30:1; Vilna Gaon, 24:23.
6. See *Shir HaShirim Rabba* 1.
7. See Rabbeinu Yona; Rabbeinu Baḥya, introductions to *Shemot* and *Mishpatim*.
8. See, e.g., Ralbag; *Metzudat David*; *Metzudat Tzion*.
9. See *Responsa of the Rashba* 5:55.
10. See Ibn Ezra; Rabbeinu Yona; *Metzudat David*.
11. Rabbeinu Yona.
12. Rabbeinu Yona; Rav Yosef Naḥmias; see also *Tzidkat HaTzaddik* 48.
13. Rav Yosef Naḥmias; see also *Metzudat David*.
14. Rabbeinu Yona.
15. See *Midrash Mishlei*; *Bava Kamma* 119a.
16. See 14:15; Rabbeinu Yona; *Tzidkat HaTzaddik* 259.
17. See Rashi.
18. Ralbag; Malbim.
19. See Rabbeinu Yona; Ralbag; Malbim.
20. See *Midrash Mishlei*; Rabbeinu Yona; *Shir HaShirim Rabba* 1:9; *Sefer HaIkkarim* 3:34.
21. See *Shemot Rabba* 41:3.
22. See Ibn Ezra.
23. See Ibn Ezra; *Metzudat David*.
24. See Rashi; Ralbag.
25. See *Targum*; Radak, *Sefer HaShorashim*, s.v. *nun-samekh-ḥet*; Ramban, Exodus 28:28.
26. See *Berakhot* 63a; *Avodat Yisrael*, *Bereshit*, s.v. *vayasem*; *Tzidkat HaTzaddik* 179.
27. See Rashi; Malbim; *Likkutei Mei HaShiloaḥ*, vol. 1.
28. See Rambam, *Sefer Hafla'a*, *Hilkhot Arakhin* 8:12; Rabbeinu Baḥya, introduction to *Ki Tavo*.
29. See also Ralbag; Malbim.
30. See Rambam, end of *Sefer Zemanim*; Rabbeinu Baḥya, introduction to *Shofetim*.
31. See *Mei HaShiloaḥ*, vol. 2, beginning of *Ki Tetze*.
32. See Rashi, Ibn Ezra, and *Metzudat David*, verse 19.
33. Rashi.
34. *Metzudat David*.
35. See Rambam, *Sefer Mishpatim*, *Hilkhot Sekhirut* 11:5.
36. See *Targum*; Rashi.
37. See *Yevamot* 37b; *Gittin* 90a; Rambam, *Sefer Kedusha*, *Hilkhot Issurei Bia* 21:28.
38. Rambam, *Guide of the Perplexed* 1:34.
39. See Ibn Ezra; *Shabbat* 104a.
40. See Ibn Ezra.
41. *Targum*; *Metzudat David*.
42. *Mei HaShiloaḥ*, vol. 2; *Berakhot* 40a.
43. See *Rosh HaShana* 26b; *Berakhot* 48a.
44. See Genesis 14:20.
45. See Rav Yosef Naḥmias.
46. Rashi; *Metzudat Tzion*.
47. See Malbim.
48. Ibn Janaḥ; Rashi, Exodus 5:4.
49. See Rashi; Ibn Ezra; Rashbam, Exodus 32:25.
50. See Ibn Ezra; Malbim.
51. See *Targum*; Rashi.
52. See *Ohev Yisrael*, beginning of *Tzav*.
53. See Rashi; Ibn Ezra.
54. See Rambam, *Sefer HaMadda*, *Hilkhot Deot* 2:7; Rabbeinu Baḥya, introduction to *Vayikra*.
55. See, e.g., *Avoda Zara* 17a.
56. See Rambam, introduction to *Guide of the Perplexed*. See also Rambam, *Guide of the Perplexed* 3:8; *Sefer HaMadda*, *Hilkhot Yesodei HaTorah* 2:12, *Hilkhot Avoda Zara* 5:2, *Hilkhot Talmud Torah* 5:4.
57. See Rabbeinu Yona; *Metzudat David*.
58. Rav Yosef Naḥmias.
59. See Malbim.
60. See Malbim.
61. See Ramban, Exodus 21:9.
62. See Ibn Ezra.

63. See Rashi.
64. See Ralbag; *Metzudat David.*
65. Rashi; *Metzudat David.*
66. Ibn Ezra.
67. See *Metzudat David.*
68. See Ralbag; Malbim.
69. See also Job 5:19.
70. See *Vayikra Rabba* 16; *Sha'arei Teshuva* 3:41.
71. See Rashi; *Sifrei, Va'ethanan* 34; *Sota* 21a.
72. See *Sota* 21a; *Sefer HaIkkarim* 3:28; *Tzidkat HaTzaddik* 261.
73. See *Midrash Mishlei; Yalkut Shimoni.*
74. See Ibn Ezra; *Midrash Mishlei*; see also 7:7.
75. See *Metzudat David.*
76. See Malbim; *Berakhot* 3b.
77. See Rav Yosef Naḥmias; *Metzudat David.*
78. See Malbim.
79. See *Metzudat David*; Malbim.
80. See Rashi; *Metzudat David.*
81. See commentary on Isaiah 22:3.
82. See Rashi.
83. See also Job 28.
84. See *Avoda Zara* 19a.
85. See commentary on Isaiah 29:21.
86. See *Shabbat* 88b; *Midrash Mishlei*; Rashi; Ralbag; *Da'at Mikra.*
87. See Rabbeinu Yona; Malbim.
88. See *Emunot VeDeot* 3:1.
89. See Rashi; *Metzudat David.*
90. See Rambam, *Guide of the Perplexed* 3:54.
91. See *Avot* 6:1.
92. See *Tzidkat HaTzaddik* 198.
93. See Ibn Ezra; Malbim.
94. See *Targum Yerushalmi, Bereshit* 1:1; *Pirkei deRabbi Eliezer* 3.
95. *Bereshit Rabba* 8:2.
96. See *Metzudat David*; Malbim.
97. See *Sifrei, Ekev* 37.
98. See Rashi; *Metzudat David.*
99. See *Bereshit Rabba* 1:1.
100. See Rashi; Ibn Ezra; *Midrash Mishlei*; *Vayikra Rabba* 11:1–4; Rabbeinu Baḥya, introduction to *Shemini.*
101. Ibn Ezra; Ramban, Exodus 15:10.
102. See Ibn Ezra.
103. See *Mei HaShiloaḥ*, vol. 2, beginning of *Korah.*
104. See *Metzudat David*; Malbim.
105. Yehoshua Meir Greintz, "On the Book of Proverbs," *Iyunim*, vol. 27. Jerusalem: The Department for the Absorption of Children and Youth, 1958 [Hebrew].
106. See Rashi; Ibn Ezra; see also Meiri, 29:15.
107. See Rabbeinu Yona.
108. See Ralbag.
109. See *Midrash Mishlei.*
110. See *Metzudat David*; Vilna Gaon.
111. See Vilna Gaon; Malbim.
112. See Rabbeinu Yona; *Metzudat David.*
113. See Rashi; *Metzudat David*; Ramban, Numbers 5:20; *Likkutei Mei HaShiloaḥ.*
114. See Vilna Gaon; *Tzidkat HaTzaddik* 138.
115. Vilna Gaon.
116. Rashi.
117. See Ibn Ezra; Malbim.
118. See Vilna Gaon.
119. See Rashi.
120. See Ibn Ezra, 18:11.
121. See Rabbeinu Yona.
122. See *Metzudat David.*
123. See *Mesillat Yesharim* 14.
124. See Vilna Gaon, verses 18–19.
125. *Metzudat David*; see introduction to *Emunot VeDeot* 2.
126. See Rambam, *Guide of the Perplexed* 1:39.
127. See Vilna Gaon; Malbim.
128. See Rashi; *Metzudat David.*
129. See Rashi, Genesis 11:18.
130. See Ibn Ezra; Malbim.
131. See *Ta'anit* 4b; *Kiddushin* 45b.
132. See *Sefer HaIkkarim* 3:34.
133. See Vilna Gaon; *Yoma* 72b.
134. See Rashi here and Exodus 7:1; Radak, *Sefer HaShorashim*, on the root *nun-vav-beit.*
135. See Rashi; Rabbeinu Yona; Rashi, Genesis 33:10; see also *Tzidkat HaTzaddik* 98, 235.
136. See Rabbeinu Yona; Ralbag; Vilna Gaon.
137. See Rashi, Deuteronomy 25:17.
138. See Zephaniah 1:15.
139. See Ralbag; *Metzudat David*; *Metzudat Tzion.*
140. See Ibn Ezra.
141. See Rashi; Ralbag; *Metzudat David.*
142. *Emunot VeDeot* 6:4.
143. See Rabbeinu Baḥya, introduction to *Behaalotekha*; *Sefer HaIkkarim* 1:21, 4:40.
144. See Rashi; Ibn Ezra; Ralbag; *Oreḥot Tzaddikim* 24.
145. See Ibn Ezra; Ralbag.
146. See Ibn Ezra.
147. See Ibn Ezra; Rabbeinu Baḥya, introduction to *Vayetze.*
148. Ibn Ezra.
149. See Rashi.
150. See commentary on Isaiah 29:20.
151. See *Vayikra Rabba* 34:3.
152. See Ramban's sermon on Ecclesiastes.
153. See Vilna Gaon; I Kings 7:29.
154. See *Yalkut Shimoni*, Proverbs 847; *Netzaḥ Yisrael* 20.
155. *Tanḥuma, Miketz* 7.
156. See *Midrash Mishlei.*
157. See Rabbeinu Baḥya, introduction to *Korah.*
158. See Rashi; Ibn Ezra; *Metzudat David*; *Metzudat Tzion.*
159. See *Tzidkat HaTzaddik* 113–114.
160. Vilna Gaon; see 24:16.
161. See Vilna Gaon.
162. See Rabbeinu Yona.
163. See Vilna Gaon.
164. See commentary on Job 34:10.
165. See Rav Yosef Naḥmias.
166. See Rabbeinu Yona; Vilna Gaon.
167. See Vilna Gaon.
168. Vilna Gaon.
169. See Meiri; *Da'at Mikra.*
170. *Eiruvin* 65b.
171. See *Metzudat David.*
172. See *Meshekh Ḥokhma*, Leviticus 16:30.
173. See *Sefer HaIkkarim* 4:44.
174. See Rashi; Ralbag.
175. See Rashi, Exodus 12:7.
176. See Ralbag; Malbim.
177. See *Metzudat David*; *Metzudat Tzion.*
178. *Iyyei HaYam, Sota* 42b.
179. See Vilna Gaon; Rashbam, Genesis 26:26.
180. See *Metzudat David*; Vilna Gaon; *Eiruvin* 54b.
181. See Rashi; Rabbeinu Yona.
182. See Rabbeinu Baḥya, introduction to *Vayhi.*
183. See Rashi; Rabbeinu Yona.
184. See Rashi.
185. See Rashi; Ibn Ezra.
186. Ecclesiastes 11:7.
187. See Rabbi Avraham Yitzḥak Kook, *Shemona Kevatzim* 2:107.
188. Rabbeinu Baḥya, introduction to *Behaalotekha.*
189. *Berakhot* 32b; see *Tzidkat HaTzaddik* 211.
190. See Rashi; Vilna Gaon; *Avot* 4:3; *Sha'arei Teshuva* 3:176.
191. Rabbeinu Yona.
192. See Rashi; Ibn Ezra.
193. See Rashi.
194. Rabbeinu Yona.
195. See Rabbeinu Baḥya, introduction to *Lekh Lekha*; Rambam, *Sefer HaMadda, Hilkhot Deot* 6:1, *Hilkhot Teshuva* 4:5.
196. See Rashi; *Metzudat David*; *Tzidkat HaTzaddik* 91; Psalms 34:22, 94:23; *Mikhtav MeEliyahu*, vol. 4, p. 73.
197. See Ibn Ezra; Rabbeinu Yona.
198. See Rabbeinu Yona; Ralbag; *Metzudat David*; Malbim; see also *Midrash Mishlei*; *Bereshit Rabba* 49:5; *Ḥagiga* 4b; *Sefer HaIkkarim* 4:21; *Tzidkat HaTzaddik* 84.
199. See Rambam, *Sefer HaMadda, Hilkhot Deot* 1:4, 5:1; Rambam, *Guide of the Perplexed* 3:12; Ramban, Genesis 25:5.
200. See Rashi.
201. Rashi.
202. See Rashi; Ralbag.
203. See Ibn Ezra; Rabbeinu Yona; *Metzudat David.*
204. See Ibn Ezra; Rabbeinu Yona.
205. See Ibn Ezra.
206. See Ralbag.
207. See *Sefer HaIkkarim* 4:48.
208. See Rashi; Ralbag.
209. Rashi.
210. Rashi; Ramban, Numbers 16:13.
211. See Malbim; *Tanya* 26.
212. See Ralbag.
213. See Ibn Ezra.
214. See Malbim; *Sefer HaIkkarim* 1:21.
215. See, e.g., Rashi; Ramban, Leviticus 20:17.
216. See Ibn Ezra; Ralbag.
217. See *Targum*; Rashbam, Leviticus 20:17.
218. See Rashi; Ibn Ezra; *Bava Batra* 10b.
219. See, e.g., Ralbag; *Metzudat David.*
220. See Rabbeinu Baḥya, introduction to *Yitro.*
221. See Ibn Ezra.
222. See Ralbag; Rabbeinu Baḥya, introductions to *Shemot* and *Nitzavim.*
223. See Ralbag; Malbim; Rabbeinu Baḥya, introduction to *Beshalah.*
224. See Ralbag.
225. See Ralbag.
226. Rabbeinu Baḥya, introduction to *Teruma.*
227. See Ralbag.
228. Rabbeinu Baḥya, introduction to *Behukotai.*
229. See Ibn Ezra; Malbim.
230. See Rashbam, Exodus 15:1.
231. See Ralbag.
232. See Vilna Gaon.
233. See *Metzudat David*; Malbim; Rambam, *Sefer Kinyan, Hilkhot Zekhiya UMattana* 12:17.
234. See Rashi.
235. See Rav Yosef Naḥmias; *Da'at Mikra.*

236. Rabbeinu Baḥya, introduction to *Behar*.
237. Psalms 145:18; see *Sefer HaIkkarim* 2:8.
238. See Ralbag.
239. See Ralbag; *Metzudat David*.
240. See Rashi; Malbim; Rabbeinu Baḥya, introduction to *Tazria*; *Tzidkat HaTzaddik* 116.
241. See Malbim.
242. See Rashi; Psalms 55:23, and Rashi ad loc.; Rabbeinu Yona.
243. See Rambam, *Guide of the Perplexed* 3:13; *Shabbat* 50b; *Yoma* 38a; *Tzidkat HaTzaddik* 173.
244. See Rashi; Rabbeinu Yona; Samuel David Luzzatto.
245. See *Berakhot* 61a.
246. See Rabbeinu Yona; Ralbag.
247. See Ralbag; *Metzudat David*; Rabbeinu Baḥya, introduction to *Bemidbar*.
248. See Ralbag; *Metzudat David*.
249. See Rashi; Ibn Ezra.
250. Ramban, Genesis 32:21.
251. See *Sefer HaIkkarim* 2:29.
252. See Rabbeinu Baḥya, introduction to *Vayera*.
253. See Ralbag; *Tzidkat HaTzaddik* 206.
254. See Malbim.
255. See Rashi; Rabbeinu Yona; *Metzudat David*; Malbim.
256. Ibn Ezra.
257. See Ibn Ezra.
258. See Ibn Ezra.
259. See Rashi; *Metzudat David*.
260. See Rabbeinu Yona.
261. See Ibn Ezra.
262. See Ralbag.
263. See Ralbag.
264. See *Tzidkat HaTzaddik* 88.
265. See Daniel 11:27.
266. See 22:2; *Tanḥuma*, *Behar* 5.
267. See Rashi; Malbim; Rabbeinu Baḥya, introduction to *Toledot*.
268. See Isaiah 32:5.
269. See Malbim.
270. See Rashi; Ralbag; Malbim.
271. See Ralbag.
272. See Rashi.
273. See *Yoma* 72b.
274. See Rashi.
275. See Ralbag.
276. See Rabbeinu Yona.
277. See Ralbag; *Metzudat David*.
278. See *Targum*; Rabbeinu Yona; *Metzudat Tzion*; Ralbag; Rav Yosef Naḥmias.
279. See Malbim.
280. See *Berakhot* 7a.
281. See Ralbag; *Metzudat David*; Rashi, Leviticus 26:21.
282. See Ibn Ezra; Ralbag; *Metzudat David*.
283. See Rabbeinu Yona; Ralbag.
284. See Rashi; Rabbeinu Yona; *Metzudat David*.
285. See Ralbag; *Metzudat David*.
286. See Rashi; Ralbag; Rabbeinu Baḥya, introduction to *Pinhas*; *Mei HaShiloaḥ*, vol. 2, *Va'era*, s.v. *vayikaḥ*.
287. See Ralbag; *Metzudat David*; Rabbeinu Baḥya, introduction to *Pekudei*.
288. See *Eiruvin* 13a.
289. See Rashi; Ramban, Exodus 25:29; Rabbeinu Baḥya, introduction to *Yitro*.
290. See *Targum*; Ralbag; Isaiah 43:26.
291. *Da'at Mikra*, citing *Mishpat HaUrim*.
292. See Rashi; Rabbeinu Yona.
293. See Rashi.
294. See Rabbeinu Yona; *Metzudat David*.
295. See Ralbag.
296. See Malbim.
297. See Rav Yosef Naḥmias.
298. See Ralbag; *Metzudat David*; Vilna Gaon.
299. See Rashi here and *Ta'anit* 9a; Vilna Gaon; Rambam, *Guide of the Perplexed* 3:12.
300. See Ibn Ezra; Vilna Gaon.
301. See Ralbag; *Metzudat David*.
302. See Ralbag; Ibn Ezra, verse 13.
303. See Ralbag.
304. See 22:15, 23:5; Rabbeinu Baḥya, introduction to *Shemot*.
305. See *Midrash Tehillim* 6:7.
306. Rashi.
307. See Rambam, *Guide of the Perplexed* 1:34.
308. *Alei Shur*, vol. 2, p. 252.
309. See Ibn Ezra; Rashi.
310. Ibn Ezra; Ralbag.
311. See Rashi.
312. See Malbim.
313. See Rashi.
314. See Samuel David Luzzatto.
315. See Rabbeinu Baḥya, introduction to *Noah*.
316. See Ibn Ezra; Ralbag; *Ruaḥ Ḥayyim*, *Avot* 5:3.
317. See Malbim.
318. See Ralbag.
319. See Rashi; Ibn Ezra.
320. See Ibn Ezra.
321. See Ibn Ezra; *Metzudat David*.
322. See *Targum*; Ralbag.
323. See Ralbag; Malbim.
324. See Ibn Ezra; Samuel David Luzzatto; Malbim.
325. See *Metzudat David*.
326. See *Metzudat David*; Malbim.
327. See Rabbeinu Yona; Ralbag; *Metzudat David*; 29:26, and Ralbag ad loc.; *Meshekh Ḥokhma*, Deuteronomy 17:15.
328. See Ralbag; Malbim; see, e.g., I Samuel 15:22; Isaiah 1:10–17; Hosea 6:6; commentary on Jeremiah 7:22.
329. See Rashi; Rabbeinu Yona; *Metzudat David*.
330. Rashi; *Metzudat David*; Ralbag; Malbim.
331. See Rashi; *Metzudat David*.
332. See *Metzudat David*; *Metzudat Tzion*; Malbim.
333. See Ralbag.
334. See Rashi; *Metzudat David*.
335. See Ibn Ezra.
336. See Ralbag; *Metzudat David*.
337. See Ralbag; *Metzudat David*.
338. See Rabbeinu Baḥya, introduction to *Naso*.
339. *Sefer HaIkkarim* 3:33.
340. See Rabbeinu Yona; Ralbag.
341. See Malbim.
342. See Rabbeinu Yona; Ralbag.
343. See Rabbeinu Yona; Malbim.
344. See Ibn Ezra.
345. See Ecclesiastes 7:19, 9:14–18.
346. See Ralbag.
347. See Rambam, *Sefer HaMadda*, *Hilkhot Deot* 4:15.
348. See Ralbag.
349. See Ibn Ezra; *Metzudat David*.
350. See Ralbag; *Metzudat David*.
351. See Rabbeinu Yona.
352. See Ralbag; *Metzudat David*.
353. See Rabbeinu Baḥya, introduction to *Shelah*.
354. See Rashi; Ralbag.
355. See Ralbag.
356. See Rabbeinu Yona; Ralbag; *Metzudat David*; Vilna Gaon.
357. See Rashi; Rabbeinu Yona; Ibn Ezra; *Metzudat David*; Rabbeinu Baḥya, introduction to *Vayikra*.
358. See Rashi; Ibn Ezra; *Metzudat David*; *Metzudat Tzion*; Vilna Gaon; Ramban, Numbers 33:55.
359. See *Ketubot* 30a, and Rashi ad loc.
360. See Ibn Ezra; Meiri; Vilna Gaon; Malbim.
361. See Rashi; Ralbag.
362. See *Tzidkat HaTzaddik* 190.
363. See Rabbeinu Yona.
364. See Rabbeinu Yona; *Metzudat David*.
365. See Ibn Ezra; *Metzudat David*.
366. See Ralbag.
367. See Vilna Gaon.
368. See *Metzudat David*.
369. See Rashi, Deuteronomy 12:28.
370. See Rashi; Vilna Gaon; Malbim.
371. See Rashi; *Metzudat David*; see also Vilna Gaon, 30:5; Rabbeinu Baḥya, introduction to *Bo*.
372. See *Targum*; *Mikhlal Yofi*.
373. See *Targum*; Malbim.
374. See Malbim.
375. See Rashi; Malbim.
376. See Rabbeinu Yona; Ralbag; II Samuel 13:4.
377. See *Sanhedrin* 7a.
378. See, e.g., Deuteronomy 14:29, 15:7–8.
379. See Ibn Ezra; Ralbag; commentary on Malachi 3:8.
380. Rambam, *Sefer HaMadda*, *Hilkhot Deot* 6:9.
381. See *Metzudat David*; *Metzudat Tzion*.
382. See Ralbag; *Metzudat David*.
383. See Malbim.
384. See Mishna *Avot* 2:3; Rabbeinu Baḥya, introduction to *Aharei Mot*.
385. See Ibn Ezra; Rabbeinu Yona; Ralbag.
386. See *Metzudat David*.
387. See *Netivot Olam*, *Netiv Ayin Tov*.
388. See Rabbeinu Yona.
389. See Rabbeinu Baḥya, introductions to *Lekh Lekha* and *Shemot*.
390. See Deuteronomy 19:14, 27:17; Isaiah 5:8; Hosea 5:10; Micah 2:2.
391. See Rabbeinu Yona; Ralbag; Vilna Gaon.
392. See Rabbeinu Yona.
393. *Sanhedrin* 105b.
394. See Ralbag; *Metzudat David*.
395. See Ibn Ezra; Rabbeinu Yona; Vilna Gaon; Malbim.
396. See Rashi; Rabbeinu Yona.
397. See *Metzudat David*; Malbim.
398. See Rashi; *Metzudat David*.
399. See *Metzudat David*.
400. See Rashi; Ibn Ezra.
401. *Bekhorot* 29a; Rambam, *Sefer HaMadda*, *Hilkhot Talmud Torah* 1:7.
402. See Rabbeinu Yona.
403. See Rabbeinu Baḥya, introduction to *Ki Tetze*.
404. See Ibn Ezra; *Metzudat David*.
405. Rashi; Ibn Ezra.
406. See also Rambam, *Guide of the Perplexed* 3:8.

407. See Rashi; *Yoma* 74b.
408. See Ralbag.
409. See Vilna Gaon.
410. See Rabbeinu Yona.
411. See Rashi; see also Ecclesiastes 7:19.
412. See Malbim.
413. Ibn Ezra; Alsheikh.
414. See Rashi, Malbim.
415. See *Targum*; Ralbag.
416. See Rashi; Rabbeinu Yona; Vilna Gaon.
417. See *Targum*.
418. See Rashi; Ralbag.
419. See Rabbeinu Yona.
420. See *Tzidkat HaTzaddik* 236.
421. See also Job 31:29.
422. See Ibn Ezra; Rabbeinu Yona.
423. See Ibn Ezra; Ralbag; Vilna Gaon; *Metzudat David*.
424. See Ibn Ezra; Ralbag; *Metzudat David*; Malbim; *Da'at Mikra*.
425. Vilna Gaon.
426. See Rabbeinu Yona; *Metzudat David*.
427. See Rashi; Ralbag; Rabbeinu Baḥya, introduction to *Mishpatim*.
428. See Vilna Gaon; Rabbeinu Baḥya, introduction to *Mishpatim*.
429. See *Metzudat David*.
430. See Rabbeinu Baḥya, introduction to *Emor*.
431. See Rabbeinu Yona.
432. See Malbim.
433. See Rashi; *Bereshit Rabba* 9:1.
434. See Jerusalem Talmud, *Ḥagiga* 2:1; *Bereshit Rabba* 9:1.
435. See Malbim.
436. See Rashbam and Bekhor Shor, Exodus 32:24.
437. See Malbim; *Shemot Rabba* 45:5.
438. See Ralbag.
439. See Vilna Gaon; *Bereshit Rabba* 93:3; introduction to Rambam, *Guide of the Perplexed*; *Emunot VeDeot* 14:10.
440. See Rashi and Rashbam, Leviticus 26:21.
441. See *Metzudat Tzion*; *Metzudat David*.
442. See Ibn Ezra; Ralbag; Malbim.
443. See Ibn Ezra; Vilna Gaon.
444. See Ralbag; *Metzudat David*; Malbim.
445. See Ralbag; *Sefer HaIkkarim* 4:15.
446. See Rabbeinu Baḥya, introduction to *Vayishlah*.
447. See Vilna Gaon; Malbim; Rambam, *Guide of the Perplexed* 1:30, 32.
448. See Ralbag.
449. Rashi.
450. See Rashi; *Metzudat David*.
451. See Rashi; Ralbag; *Metzudat David*; Vilna Gaon.
452. See Vilna Gaon.
453. See Ralbag; *Metzudat David*.
454. See Rashi; Ibn Ezra.
455. See Isaiah 56:11, and commentary ad loc.
456. See Ibn Ezra; *Metzudat David*.
457. See *Metzudat David*; commentary on 19:24.
458. See Meiri.
459. See Ibn Ezra; Malbim.
460. See Rambam, *Sefer HaMadda*, *Hilkhot Deot* 7:4.
461. See Ralbag; *Metzudat David*.
462. See Ralbag.
463. See Rashi, Genesis 25:21.
464. See Ralbag; *Metzudat David*.
465. See Ralbag; Malbim.
466. See Ibn Ezra; Ralbag; *Metzudat David*; Malbim.
467. 20:16; and see, e.g., 6:1, 17:18.
468. See Ralbag; *Metzudat David*; Malbim; *Arakhin* 16a; Rambam, *Sefer HaMadda*, *Hilkhot Deot* 7:4.
469. See Rashi; Ibn Ezra; *Metzudat David*.
470. See Ralbag; *Metzudat David*.
471. See *Targum*; Ralbag; *Metzudat David*; *Midrash Mishlei*.
472. See Ralbag; Malbim; Rashi, Numbers 28:16.
473. See Rashi; *Metzudat David*.
474. Malbim.
475. See Rashi; *Metzudat David*; Vilna Gaon.
476. See Rashi; *Metzudat David*; Vilna Gaon.
477. See Malbim.
478. See *Metzudat David*; Malbim.
479. See *Metzudat David*; Malbim.
480. See Ralbag.
481. See Ramban, Leviticus 25:36.
482. See Ralbag.
483. See Ralbag; Malbim; Rambam, *Sefer HaMadda*, *Hilkhot Teshuva* 2:5.
484. *Metzudat David*; see Rabbeinu Baḥya, introduction to *Bo*.
485. See Rashi; Ralbag.
486. See commentary on Exodus 18:21.
487. See Ibn Ezra; Rambam, *Sefer Nezikin*, *Hilkhot Rotze'aḥ UShmirat HaNefesh* 4:9.
488. *Metzudat David*.
489. Rashi.
490. Vilna Gaon.
491. See Ibn Ezra; Ralbag; *Metzudat David*.
492. See Ibn Ezra; Malbim.
493. See Vilna Gaon.
494. See Malbim.
495. See Rashi; *Metzudat David*.
496. See Rashi; *Metzudat David*; Vilna Gaon.
497. Rambam, *Guide of the Perplexed* 1:40.
498. See Ibn Ezra.
499. See Rashi; Ralbag.
500. See Malbim.
501. See Rashi; Ralbag.
502. See Rambam, *Sefer Nezikin*, *Hilkhot Geneiva* 5:1; Vilna Gaon.
503. See Ralbag; Malbim.
504. See Ibn Ezra, Vilna Gaon, and Malbim, 30:1.
505. See Rav Se'adya Gaon; Ibn Ezra; Vilna Gaon.
506. See II Samuel 12:25.
507. Ecclesiastes 1:1.
508. See *Avot deRabbi Natan* 39:4; *Tanḥuma*, *Va'era* 5.
509. See, e.g., Ibn Ezra; Vilna Gaon.
510. See Rashi; *Tanḥuma*, *Va'era* 5.
511. Vilna Gaon.
512. See Ibn Ezra; *Metzudat David*; Vilna Gaon.
513. See *Metzudat David*.
514. See Rambam, *Guide of the Perplexed* 3:33.
515. See commentary on Amos 1:3.
516. See Rashi; *Metzudat David*; *Avoda Zara* 17a; Rambam, *Sefer HaMadda*, *Hilkhot Teshuva* 8:5.
517. See Ralbag.
518. See Ralbag, verse 15.
519. See Rashi; *Targum*; Bekhor Shor, Genesis 49:10.
520. See Ralbag, verse 15.
521. See Ralbag; *Metzudat David*.
522. See Ralbag; *Metzudat David*.
523. See *Metzudat David*.
524. See *Metzudat David*.
525. See *Metzudat David*.
526. See Ibn Ezra.
527. See Ibn Ezra.
528. See commentary on Jeremiah 23:36.
529. See Exodus 16:7.
530. See Rashi; *Metzudat David*.
531. See Rashi; *Bemidbar Rabba* 10:4.
532. See Ralbag; *Metzudat David*.
533. See, e.g., Ecclesiastes 10:16–17.
534. See Rambam, *Sefer Shofetim*, *Hilkhot Melakhim* 3:5–6.
535. See *Metzudat David*.
536. See *Metzudat David*.
537. See Ibn Ezra; *Metzudat David*.
538. See *Metzudat David*.
539. See, e.g., Exodus 35:25–26; Mishna *Nega'im* 2:4; *Ketubot* 5:5; *Bava Kamma* 10:9.
540. See Ibn Ezra; *Metzudat David*.
541. See Ralbag; *Metzudat David*.
542. See Ibn Ezra; *Metzudat David*.
543. See *Metzudat David*; *Metzudat Tzion*.
544. Rashi; *Metzudat David*.
545. Rashi; Ralbag.
546. Rashi and *Metzudat David*, verse 29.
547. Ibn Ezra.
548. See 12:19; Jeremiah 51:17–18.

Job

1. Rashi; Genesis 10:23.
2. Ibn Ezra; Lamentations 4:21; see also Genesis 36:28; I Chronicles 1:42.
3. Malbim.
4. See *Metzudat David*.
5. See Ramban.
6. See Ramban.
7. See verse 11, 2:9; I Kings 21:10, 13; commentary on Leviticus 24:22.
8. See Rashi.
9. Ibn Ezra.
10. See Rashi; *Ho'il Moshe*.
11. See *Metzudat David*.
12. See *Metzudat David*.
13. See Ibn Ezra.
14. See, e.g., Rashi.
15. See Rashi; Malbim.
16. See *Midrash Iyov* 13.
17. *Metzudat David*.
18. See Jeremiah 49:7; Ezekiel 25:13; Amos 1:12.
19. See Rashi; *Targum*; Malbim.
20. Rashi; Ralbag; Ibn Ezra.
21. Rashi; Ibn Ezra.
22. Ralbag.
23. Rashi.
24. See Rashi.
25. See Malbim.
26. Ralbag.
27. See Rashi.
28. Malbim.
29. See Ibn Ezra.
30. See Rashi; Ralbag.
31. See Rashi; Ralbag.
32. Rashi.
33. See *Metzudat David*.
34. Ibn Ezra.
35. See Rashi; Ibn Ezra.
36. See Rashi; *Metzudat David*.
37. Rashi.
38. Rashi; Ibn Ezra.
39. See Malbim.
40. See Rashi.
41. See Malbim.
42. See commentary on Hosea 5:14.
43. See *Metzudat David*.
44. See *Bereshit Rabba* 52:7.
45. See Rashi.
46. See Rashi; Ibn Ezra; *Metzudat David*.
47. *Targum*.
48. See Rashi; Ibn Ezra.
49. Ibn Ezra.
50. See Rashi; Ibn Ezra.
51. Rashi.
52. See Rashi; *Metzudat David*.
53. See *Metzudat David*.
54. Malbim.
55. Ibn Ezra; *Metzudat Tzion*.
56. Ralbag; Malbim.
57. See Rashi; *Metzudat David*.
58. Ibn Ezra.
59. See Rashi; *Metzudat David*.
60. Malbim.
61. Rashi; Ralbag.
62. See Rashi; Ralbag.
63. See Rashi.
64. See Proverbs 6:16.
65. See Ibn Ezra.
66. Ibn Ezra; *Metzudat David*.
67. See Rashi; Mishna *Kilayim* 8:5.
68. See Rashi; Ibn Ezra.
69. *Targum*; Rashi.
70. See Rashi; *Metzudat David*.
71. Rashi.
72. See Rashi; Ralbag.
73. Ibn Ezra.
74. Rashi.
75. See Ibn Ezra; Malbim.
76. Ibn Ezra.
77. Malbim.
78. Rashi; Ibn Ezra.
79. Rashi.
80. Ralbag.
81. Rashi.
82. *Da'at Mikra*.
83. See Rashi; Ibn Ezra; Ralbag.
84. Rashi.
85. See Rashi; Ralbag.
86. *Da'at Mikra*.
87. See Ibn Ezra.
88. Malbim.
89. *Metzudat David*.
90. Rashi; *Metzudat David*.
91. See Ibn Ezra; *Ho'il Moshe*.
92. Ibn Ezra.
93. *Da'at Mikra*.
94. *Targum*.
95. *Da'at Mikra*.
96. *Metzudat David*.
97. Ralbag.
98. Ibn Ezra.
99. Ibn Ezra; Ralbag.
100. *Targum*.
101. See Ibn Ezra; Ralbag; Isaiah 51:15.
102. Rashi.
103. Rashi.
104. Rashi.
105. See, e.g., Jeremiah 5:22; Psalms 74:13–14.
106. Rashi; Ibn Ezra; *Metzudat David*.
107. Ibn Ezra.
108. See Rambam, *Guide of the Perplexed* 3:16–18.
109. See Ibn Ezra.
110. *Metzudat David*.
111. Ralbag.
112. See *Metzudat David*.
113. Ralbag.
114. See Ibn Ezra.
115. Rashi.
116. Ibn Ezra.
117. See Malbim; Rashi, verse 11.
118. Ibn Ezra; Ralbag.
119. Ralbag.
120. See Malbim.
121. Rav Se'adya Gaon.
122. See Rashi; Ramban; Ralbag.
123. Rashi; Ralbag.
124. See Rashi.
125. See Rashi; Ralbag.
126. *Metzudat David*.
127. See *Ho'il Moshe*.
128. Ibn Ezra.
129. Rashi.
130. Rashi; Ralbag.
131. See Ralbag; *Metzudat David*.
132. *Metzudat David*.
133. Ibn Ezra.
134. See Rashi; *Metzudat David*.
135. Rashi; see Joshua 10:12–13.
136. See Rashi; Ibn Ezra; Ralbag.
137. Ibn Ezra; Ralbag.
138. Rashi.
139. Rashi.
140. Rashi.
141. Rashi.
142. Rashi.
143. Ibn Ezra.
144. *Targum*.
145. Rashi.
146. *Metzudat David*.
147. See Malbim.
148. See *Metzudat David*.
149. Rashi; see I Samuel 1:16.
150. *Targum*.
151. See Rashi; Leviticus 26:17, and commentary ad loc.
152. See *Metzudat David*.
153. See Ibn Ezra.
154. Rashi.
155. Rashi.
156. See *Metzudat David*.
157. See *Metzudat David*.
158. Rashi.
159. Ibn Ezra.
160. Genesis 2:7, 3:19.
161. See Ralbag; *Metzudat David*.
162. Ralbag.
163. See Rashi.
164. Rashi; Ralbag.
165. *Metzudat David*.
166. See Ibn Ezra; *Ho'il Moshe*.
167. See Rashi.
168. See Ibn Ezra; Ralbag.
169. Rashi.
170. *Metzudat David*.
171. See Ibn Ezra; Ralbag.
172. *Targum*.
173. *Da'at Mikra*.
174. See Malbim.
175. See Ibn Ezra.
176. Ralbag; see Ibn Ezra; *Metzudat David*.

177. Rashi.
178. Rashi; Ibn Ezra.
179. Ralbag.
180. Rashi; Ralbag.
181. *Targum*; Malbim.
182. *Metzudat David*.
183. Rashi.
184. *Metzudat David*; Malbim.
185. See, e.g., Isaiah 10:7; Psalms 139:23; Proverbs 6:18.
186. Ibn Ezra; *Metzudat David*.
187. See *Da'at Mikra*.
188. Ibn Ezra; see 31:29; Proverbs 24:22.
189. See Rashi.
190. Ralbag.
191. Rashi.
192. Rashi.
193. See Rashi; Ralbag.
194. See Rashi; *Metzudat David*.
195. See Ralbag; *Metzudat David*.
196. See Malbim.
197. *Targum*.
198. Ibn Ezra.
199. See *Targum*; *Metzudat David*.
200. *Metzudat Tzion*; see *Targum*; Rashi.
201. Rashi; Ralbag.
202. Ralbag.
203. See Rashi; Malbim.
204. *Da'at Mikra*.
205. See Malbim; Judges 12:3; I Samuel 28:21.
206. See Rashi.
207. *Metzudat David*; Malbim.
208. *Targum*; see Ibn Ezra.
209. *Targum*; Ralbag.
210. See Ralbag.
211. See *Metzudat David*.
212. Rashi; Ralbag.
213. Ibn Ezra.
214. *Targum*.
215. Ibn Ezra; Ralbag.
216. See Rashi.
217. Ibn Ezra; Ralbag.
218. *Metzudat David*.
219. *Metzudat David*.
220. See Ibn Ezra; *Metzudat David*.
221. Rashi.
222. See Ramban; Ralbag; *Metzudat David*.
223. Ralbag.
224. Ralbag.
225. Rashi.
226. Ibn Ezra.
227. Malbim.
228. *Metzudat David*.
229. See *Metzudat David*.
230. See Rashi.
231. See Rashi.
232. Rashi.
233. *Da'at Mikra*; see Ralbag; *Metzudat David*.
234. Ibn Ezra.
235. *Targum*.
236. Ralbag.
237. *Targum*.
238. *Da'at Mikra*.
239. Ibn Ezra.
240. Rashi.
241. See Malbim.
242. Rashi.
243. *Targum*.
244. Rashi; Ralbag.
245. Rashi; Ralbag.
246. Ibn Ezra.
247. See Rashi.
248. Rashi.
249. See Malbim.
250. *Metzudat David*.
251. Ralbag.
252. Ralbag.
253. Ralbag; *Metzudat David*.
254. See Rashi.
255. See Ibn Ezra.
256. Ibn Ezra; Malbim.
257. *Ho'il Moshe*.
258. *Metzudat David*; Malbim.
259. Ralbag.
260. Ralbag.
261. Rashi.
262. *Targum*; *Metzudat Tzion*; Malbim.
263. Ibn Ezra; Ramban; Ralbag.
264. Rashi; Ralbag.
265. Ralbag.
266. Ralbag; see *Metzudat David*.
267. Rashi.
268. Malbim.
269. See Ibn Ezra.
270. Ralbag.
271. Ibn Ezra; Ralbag.
272. *Metzudat Tzion*.
273. Ibn Ezra; *Metzudat David*.
274. See *Targum*.
275. *Targum*.
276. Ibn Ezra.
277. See Ibn Ezra.
278. See Proverbs 6:1, 22:26.
279. *Metzudat David*.
280. Ibn Ezra.
281. Ibn Ezra.
282. See Ibn Ezra.
283. See Ramban.
284. *Targum*; Ibn Ezra; Ralbag.
285. Ralbag.
286. Rashi; Ibn Ezra.
287. Malbim.
288. See Rashi; *Metzudat David*.
289. Ralbag; see Ibn Ezra.
290. See Ralbag.
291. Rashi; Ibn Ezra.
292. *Targum*; Rashi.
293. Ibn Ezra; Ralbag.
294. See Rashi; Ibn Ezra; *Ho'il Moshe*.
295. Rashi; Ralbag.
296. Ralbag.
297. See Rashi; *Metzudat David*.
298. Rashi.
299. Ralbag.
300. *Metzudat Tzion*.
301. See *Metzudat David*.
302. *Da'at Mikra*; see Malbim.
303. Ibn Ezra.
304. Malbim.
305. Rashi.
306. See Nahum 2:2.
307. Rashi; *Ho'il Moshe*.
308. See Ibn Ezra.
309. Rashi.
310. See *Targum*.
311. See Malbim.
312. Rashi.
313. See *Metzudat David*.
314. See Ralbag; *Metzudat David*.
315. *Targum*.
316. *Targum*; Malbim.
317. Rashi.
318. Ibn Ezra.
319. Rashi.
320. Malbim.
321. Ibn Ezra.
322. Rashi; see *Metzudat David*; Malbim.
323. Ralbag.
324. Rashi.
325. Rashi; see Malbim.
326. See Ibn Ezra.
327. *Metzudat David*.
328. *Targum*; Ibn Ezra.
329. See Rashi; *Metzudat David*.
330. See Ralbag; *Metzudat David*.
331. See *Metzudat David*.
332. Rashi.
333. *Metzudat David*.
334. *Metzudat David*.
335. Rashi.
336. Rashi.
337. Rashi; see Malbim.
338. *Targum*; Rashi; Ibn Ezra; Ralbag; *Metzudat David*; Malbim.
339. See *Ho'il Moshe*.
340. See Rashi; *Metzudat David*.
341. See *Metzudat David*; Malbim.
342. Ralbag.
343. Ralbag.
344. Ibn Ezra.
345. Ralbag.
346. See Rashi.
347. See Rashi.
348. See *Metzudat David*.
349. Ralbag.
350. Rashi; *Metzudat David*.
351. See Ralbag.
352. Rashi; Ralbag.
353. See Malbim.
354. See Ibn Ezra; *Metzudat David*; Malbim.
355. See Ralbag.
356. See Rashi; Malbim.
357. Rashi; see Ralbag.
358. Rashi.
359. See Ralbag.
360. Ibn Ezra.
361. Ralbag.
362. Ibn Ezra; *Metzudat David*.
363. See *Metzudat Tzion*; Malbim.
364. See Malbim.
365. *Metzudat David*.

366. Rashi; *Metzudat David*; Malbim.
367. See *Metzudat David*.
368. *Targum*; Rashi.
369. Ralbag.
370. Rashi; Ralbag; *Metzudat David*; Malbim.
371. See Ralbag; *Metzudat David*.
372. *Targum*; Rashi; Ibn Ezra; Ralbag.
373. Ibn Ezra; Malbim.
374. Malbim.
375. *Metzudat David*; Malbim.
376. *Metzudat David*.
377. Ibn Ezra.
378. *Metzudat David*.
379. Ibn Ezra; Ralbag.
380. *Metzudat David*.
381. Ralbag; *Metzudat David*.
382. *Metzudat David*.
383. Rashi; *Metzudat David*; Malbim.
384. Rashi; Ibn Ezra.
385. Ralbag; *Metzudat David*.
386. Ibn Ezra.
387. Ibn Ezra.
388. See Malbim.
389. See *Metzudat David*.
390. See *Metzudat David*.
391. Ibn Ezra.
392. Rashi; Ibn Ezra; Ralbag; *Metzudat David*.
393. *Metzudat David*.
394. Ralbag.
395. *Metzudat David*.
396. See *Metzudat David*.
397. *Da'at Mikra*.
398. See *Metzudat David*.
399. *Metzudat David*; see Malbim.
400. See Rashi; *Metzudat David*.
401. Rashi.
402. *Targum*.
403. Rashi; Ibn Ezra; Ralbag.
404. See Rashi; *Ho'il Moshe*.
405. See *Metzudat David*.
406. See *Ho'il Moshe*; *Da'at Mikra*.
407. See Ibn Ezra.
408. Ralbag; see Ibn Ezra.
409. Rashi; Ibn Ezra.
410. Malbim.
411. See Ibn Ezra; Ralbag.
412. Rashi; Ibn Ezra; Ralbag.
413. See Rashi.
414. *Targum*; Rashi; Ibn Ezra; Ralbag.
415. *Metzudat David*.
416. Rashi.
417. Rashi.
418. Rashi; Ibn Ezra.
419. Rashi; Ibn Ezra; Ralbag.
420. *Targum*; Ralbag.
421. See Rashi; Malbim.
422. Malbim.
423. Rashi; Ibn Ezra; Ralbag.
424. See *Targum*; Rashi; *Metzudat David*.
425. Ralbag.
426. *Metzudat David*.
427. *Targum*; Rashi; Ibn Ezra; Ralbag.
428. *Targum*; Rashi; Ibn Ezra; Ralbag.
429. *Metzudat David*.
430. *Targum*; Rashi; Ibn Ezra; Ralbag.
431. *Targum*; Ralbag.
432. Rashi; Ralbag.
433. *Targum*; Rashi; Ibn Ezra; Ralbag.
434. Rashi.
435. Ralbag.
436. *Targum*.
437. See Ibn Ezra.
438. *Targum*; Rashi.
439. Ralbag.
440. Rashi.
441. Ramban.
442. See Rashi.
443. Deuteronomy 24:17.
444. Rashi; Ibn Ezra; Ralbag.
445. *Targum*; Ibn Ezra; Ralbag.
446. Rashi.
447. Malbim.
448. *Targum*; Ibn Ezra.
449. Rashi.
450. See Ibn Ezra; Ralbag.
451. Rashi.
452. See Rashi; *Metzudat David*.
453. Malbim.
454. *Targum*.
455. *Da'at Mikra*.
456. Ibn Ezra.
457. See Rashi.
458. Rashi.
459. Rashi.
460. Ralbag.
461. See Ibn Ezra.
462. See Ibn Ezra.
463. Ralbag.
464. Rashi; Ibn Ezra.
465. See Ralbag.
466. See Rashi; *Metzudat David*; *Metzudat Tzion*.
467. *Da'at Mikra*; see Ralbag.
468. Ibn Ezra.
469. *Da'at Mikra*.
470. See Rashi; *Metzudat David*.
471. *Targum*; Ralbag.
472. *Ho'il Moshe*; *Da'at Mikra*.
473. Rashi; Ralbag.
474. *Targum*; see *Metzudat David*.
475. *Metzudat David*.
476. *Metzudat David*; see Rashi; Ibn Ezra.
477. Ibn Ezra; *Metzudat David*.
478. Rashi; *Metzudat David*; Malbim.
479. *Metzudat Tzion*.
480. Rashi.
481. Ibn Ezra; Ralbag; *Metzudat David*; see Isaiah 66:1.
482. *Targum*; Ibn Ezra; Ralbag.
483. Rashi; Ralbag; Malbim.
484. Rashi; *Metzudat David*; Jeremiah 5:22; Psalms 104:9
485. See Ibn Ezra; *Metzudat David*.
486. See 9:13; *Bava Batra* 74b.
487. See Ibn Ezra; Ralbag.
488. See Malbim; Isaiah 51:9.
489. Ralbag; *Metzudat David*.
490. See Rashi, I Chronicles 16:34.
491. Malbim.
492. See Ramban; *Da'at Mikra* on verse 11.
493. Rashi; Ibn Ezra; see Malbim.
494. *Targum*.
495. Ibn Ezra.
496. See *Ho'il Moshe*; *Da'at Mikra*.
497. See *Targum*; Rashi.
498. *Metzudat David*.
499. *Metzudat David*.
500. Rashi.
501. See *Targum*; *Metzudat David*; *Metzudat Tzion*.
502. See *Metzudat David*.
503. Ibn Ezra.
504. Rashi.
505. See Ralbag; *Metzudat David*.
506. *Da'at Mikra*.
507. Rashi; *Metzudat David*.
508. *Da'at Mikra*.
509. Ralbag.
510. See Malbim.
511. Ralbag; *Metzudat David*.
512. Ralbag.
513. See Malbim.
514. Ibn Ezra; *Metzudat David*.
515. *Metzudat David*.
516. *Da'at Mikra*.
517. See Rashi; *Metzudat David*.
518. Ibn Ezra.
519. See I Kings 6:20–21; II Chronicles 9:20.
520. Rashi.
521. Ibn Ezra; Ralbag.
522. Ibn Ezra; *Metzudat David*.
523. See Ibn Ezra.
524. Rashi.
525. *Targum*; Malbim; *Metzudat David*; *Metzudat Tzion*; see commentary on Proverbs 3:15.
526. Ibn Ezra; Ralbag.
527. *Metzudat David*.
528. Rashi.
529. Ralbag.
530. Rashi; *Ho'il Moshe*.
531. Ralbag.
532. Rashi.
533. See Rashi.
534. Rashi.
535. Rashi; Ibn Ezra; Ralbag.
536. Malbim.
537. Ralbag.
538. See Ibn Ezra; Malbim.
539. *Metzudat David*.
540. See, e.g., Genesis 22:17, 41:49; Joshua 11:4; Hosea 2:1.
541. See Jeremiah 17:8; Psalms 1:3
542. Rashi; Ibn Ezra; Ralbag.
543. See Malbim.
544. Rashi; Ralbag.
545. *Targum*; Ralbag.
546. *Metzudat Tzion*.
547. See Ibn Ezra.
548. *Metzudat David*.
549. Rashi.
550. *Metzudat David*; Malbim.

551. Malbim.
552. Ralbag.
553. Ibn Ezra; Ralbag.
554. See Ralbag.
555. Rashi.
556. *Metzudat David*.
557. See 6:5.
558. Ibn Ezra.
559. See *Metzudat David*.
560. See Malbim.
561. *Da'at Mikra*.
562. See *Targum*; Rashi; Malbim.
563. Malbim.
564. Rashi.
565. *Metzudat David*; Malbim.
566. *Metzudat David*; Malbim.
567. *Metzudat David*.
568. Ibn Ezra.
569. Rashi; see Ralbag.
570. See *Targum*; Rashi.
571. Rashi; Ibn Ezra; Ralbag.
572. *Da'at Mikra*.
573. Ibn Ezra.
574. Ibn Ezra.
575. Ralbag.
576. Ralbag.
577. See Rashi.
578. *Targum*; Ibn Ezra.
579. Rashi; Ralbag.
580. See Rashi.
581. Rashi.
582. Rashi.
583. *Metzudat David*.
584. See Ibn Ezra; Ralbag; Daniel 1:4.
585. *Targum*; Malbim.
586. See *Metzudat David*.
587. Rashi; see *Sota* 10a.
588. Rashi.
589. See Rashi; *Metzudat David*.
590. *Metzudat Tzion*.
591. See *Metzudat David*.
592. Rashi; *Metzudat David*.
593. Rashi.
594. Ralbag.
595. Rashi; Ibn Ezra.
596. Rashi; *Metzudat David*.
597. Rashi; Ibn Ezra.
598. *Da'at Mikra*; see *Metzudat David*.
599. Ibn Ezra.
600. Rashi; Ralbag.
601. Ibn Ezra.
602. Rashi; *Metzudat David*.
603. Rashi.
604. *Metzudat David*.
605. Ibn Ezra.
606. Ibn Ezra.
607. See *Metzudat David*.
608. Rashi; Ibn Ezra; Ralbag; *Metzudat Tzion*.
609. See Rashi; Ralbag; *Metzudat Tzion*.
610. See Rashi.
611. See *Metzudat David*.
612. See Rashi.
613. Ibn Ezra.
614. Rashi.
615. Ralbag; *Metzudat David*.
616. See *Metzudat David*.
617. See *Metzudat David*.
618. *Metzudat David*.
619. Malbim.
620. See Malbim.
621. *Targum*.
622. See Ralbag; Malbim.
623. Rashi; Ibn Ezra; see Ralbag.
624. See Malbim.
625. Ibn Ezra.
626. Rashi; Ibn Ezra; *Metzudat David*.
627. Ralbag.
628. Rashi.
629. Rashi; Ibn Ezra; Ralbag.
630. Ibn Ezra; *Metzudat Tzion*.
631. See Ibn Ezra; *Metzudat David*.
632. *Targum*; Rashi.
633. See Ibn Ezra.
634. *Targum*; Rashi; Ibn Ezra; Ralbag.
635. Ralbag; *Metzudat David*; see Psalms 119:70.
636. *Metzudat David*.
637. Ibn Ezra.
638. Ralbag.
639. *Metzudat Tzion*.
640. *Targum*.
641. Rashi.
642. Rashi.
643. Rashi; Malbim.
644. Ralbag.
645. Rashi; Ibn Ezra; Ralbag; *Metzudat David*.
646. See Rashi; Ibn Ezra.
647. See, e.g., Exodus 31:6; I Kings 3:12; Psalms 49:4; Proverbs 6:18; Ecclesiastes 1:17.
648. See *Targum*.
649. *Targum*; Rashi.
650. Rashi.
651. Ibn Ezra.
652. Rashi.
653. *Targum*; Rashi.
654. Ibn Ezra; Ralbag; see *Metzudat David*.
655. Ibn Ezra.
656. See Rashi; Ralbag.
657. See *Targum*; Ibn Ezra.
658. Rashi; Ramban.
659. *Metzudat David*; Malbim.
660. Ralbag.
661. Ibn Ezra.
662. *Metzudat Tzion*.
663. See Ralbag; *Ho'il Moshe*.
664. Rashi.
665. Rashi.
666. Ibn Ezra.
667. See Genesis 25:23; Psalms 43:1, and Ibn Ezra ad loc.
668. Ibn Ezra; *Metzudat David*.
669. *Metzudat David*.
670. *Metzudat David*.
671. See Ramban.
672. Rashi.
673. See Ralbag; Ibn Ezra.
674. Ralbag.
675. See Ramban.
676. See Rashi.
677. Ibn Ezra.
678. Ibn Ezra; Ralbag.
679. Rashi; Malbim.
680. See *Metzudat David*.
681. See Ralbag.
682. See Rashi.
683. Rashi; Ibn Ezra; Ralbag.
684. *Targum*; Malbim; see *Eiruvin* 100b.
685. See Malbim.
686. Rashi; Ibn Ezra; Ralbag.
687. Ibn Ezra.
688. Rashi; Ibn Ezra; Ralbag; Malbim.
689. See Rashi; *Metzudat David*.
690. Ibn Ezra.
691. See Ibn Ezra.
692. *Targum*; *Metzudat Tzion*.
693. *Targum*; *Metzudat Tzion*.
694. Rashi.
695. *Metzudat David*; Malbim.
696. Rashi.
697. *Metzudat David*.
698. *Targum*.
699. Rashi; *Metzudat David*.
700. Ralbag; *Metzudat David*; *Metzudat Tzion*.
701. See *Metzudat David*; Malbim.
702. *Metzudat David*; Malbim.
703. See Rashi; *Metzudat David*.
704. Rashi.
705. See *Menaḥot* 100a.
706. *Metzudat David*.
707. *Metzudat David*.
708. Rashi.
709. See Rashi.
710. Ralbag.
711. See *Targum*; Malbim.
712. *Da'at Mikra*.
713. *Metzudat Tzion*.
714. Ralbag.
715. *Metzudat David*.
716. Ibn Ezra.
717. See Rashi; Ibn Ezra.
718. *Targum*; Malbim.
719. Malbim.
720. See Ibn Ezra.
721. See Rashi.
722. See Rashi.
723. Ralbag.
724. See *Metzudat David*; *Da'at Mikra*.
725. Ibn Ezra.
726. Ibn Ezra; Ralbag.
727. See Malbim.
728. Malbim.
729. See Ibn Ezra; Malbim.
730. Malbim.
731. Rashi; Ralbag.
732. Rashi; Malbim.
733. Rashi.

734. Ralbag; *Metzudat David*; Malbim.
735. See Ibn Ezra; *Metzudat David*.
736. Ibn Ezra; Ralbag; see Malbim.
737. See Ibn Ezra; *Metzudat David*; Malbim.
738. Ralbag.
739. See Rashi.
740. Rashi; *Metzudat David*; Malbim.
741. See *Metzudat David*.
742. Ralbag; Malbim.
743. Ibn Ezra; Ralbag; *Metzudat David*; Malbim.
744. *Metzudat David*.
745. *Da'at Mikra*.
746. Ibn Ezra.
747. See Rashi; *Metzudat David*.
748. Ibn Ezra.
749. See Ibn Ezra; *Metzudat David*; *Metzudat Tzion*; Malbim.
750. Rashi.
751. *Metzudat David*; Malbim.
752. Ibn Ezra; Ralbag.
753. Rashi.
754. *Metzudat David*.
755. See Rashi; *Metzudat David*.
756. *Metzudat David*.
757. *Metzudat David*.
758. See *Da'at Mikra*.
759. Ibn Ezra; Ralbag.
760. Rashi; Ibn Ezra.
761. Malbim, verse 2.
762. Rashi.
763. See Rashi; *Metzudat David*.
764. Rashi.
765. See *Metzudat Tzion*; Malbim; Rabbeinu Ḥananel, Exodus 19:16.
766. Ibn Ezra; Ralbag.
767. See Rashi; Ramban.
768. See Ibn Ezra.
769. See Jeremiah 5:22.
770. See Ralbag; *Metzudat David*.
771. Ibn Ezra.
772. See Malbim.
773. Ibn Ezra; Ralbag.
774. See Ibn Ezra.
775. Ralbag; Malbim.
776. Ibn Ezra.
777. Ibn Ezra; Ralbag.
778. Ibn Ezra; Ramban.
779. Ralbag.
780. *Metzudat David*.
781. See Ezekiel 13:13; Psalms 11.
782. See Rashi; Ibn Ezra; Ralbag.
783. See Rashi.
784. Rashi; Ralbag.
785. Rashi.
786. See Psalms 42:8.
787. See Malbim.
788. See Rashi.
789. Ibn Ezra; Ralbag.
790. See Ralbag; *Metzudat Tzion*; Malbim.
791. See Rashi; Ibn Ezra.
792. Rashi, based on *Rosh HaShana* 26a; see Ramban.
793. Ibn Ezra.
794. *Metzudat David*.
795. See Ibn Ezra; Ralbag.
796. See Ramban.
797. *Metzudat David*.
798. See Malbim.
799. *Metzudat David*.
800. Rashi.
801. Ibn Ezra.
802. See Ibn Ezra.
803. See Malbim.
804. Ibn Ezra.
805. See Ralbag; *Metzudat David*.
806. Ibn Ezra; Ralbag.
807. *Metzudat David*.
808. *Metzudat David*.
809. Rashi; Ralbag; see Joel 2:4.
810. *Metzudat David*.
811. Ibn Ezra.
812. *Metzudat David*.
813. Rashi; Ibn Ezra; Ralbag.
814. Rashi.
815. See Ibn Ezra.
816. See *Metzudat David*.
817. See Ibn Ezra; *Metzudat David*.
818. *Metzudat David*.
819. Ibn Ezra; Ralbag.
820. *Targum*; Rashi; Ibn Ezra; Ralbag.
821. Ibn Ezra.
822. Ibn Ezra.
823. Ramban.
824. Rashi.
825. See, e.g., Psalms 104:1.
826. See Rashi; Ralbag.
827. See Ibn Ezra; Ralbag; *Metzudat David*.
828. See Psalms 98:1.
829. Ramban.
830. Ibn Ezra; Ralbag; Malbim.
831. See Ibn Ezra.
832. Ralbag; *Metzudat David*.
833. See Ibn Ezra; *Metzudat David*.
834. Ralbag.
835. Ralbag.
836. Ibn Ezra.
837. Rashi; *Metzudat David*.
838. Ibn Ezra.
839. Ibn Ezra; Ralbag.
840. *Targum*; Rashi; Ibn Ezra; see Ralbag.
841. Ibn Ezra; Ralbag.
842. Rashi.
843. See Ibn Ezra; Ralbag; *Metzudat David*; Malbim.
844. Rashi; see *Metzudat David*.
845. See *Targum*; Rashi.
846. Rashi.
847. Rashi; see *Metzudat David*.
848. Rashi; *Metzudat David*.
849. Ralbag.
850. Ibn Ezra; Ralbag.
851. *Targum*; Rashi; Ibn Ezra; Ralbag.
852. See Ibn Ezra; Ralbag.
853. See Ibn Ezra.
854. *Metzudat David*.
855. Rashi; Ralbag.
856. Rashi.
857. Rashi.
858. Rashi; Ibn Ezra.
859. Rashi.
860. Ibn Ezra; Ralbag.
861. Rashi; Ralbag.
862. Rashi; Ralbag.
863. Rashi; Ralbag.
864. Rashi.
865. Rashi.
866. Rashi.
867. Rashi.
868. Rashi.
869. Rashi.
870. Rashi; Ibn Ezra; Ralbag.
871. Ibn Ezra; Ralbag.
872. Rashi.
873. Ibn Ezra.
874. See Ralbag.
875. Ralbag; *Metzudat David*.
876. Ralbag; Malbim.
877. See also Psalms 73.
878. *Targum*.
879. See Rashi.
880. See Rashi.
881. See Rashi.
882. *Metzudat David*.
883. See Rashi.
884. See Rashi.
885. See Rashi.
886. Ibn Ezra.
887. *Targum*; Rashi.
888. Rashi.
889. Rashi.
890. See Psalms 90:10.

The Song of Songs

1. See *Shevuot* 35b; *Shir HaShirim Rabba* 1:11.
2. See, e.g., Isaiah 50:1, 54:4–12; Jeremiah 2:2; Ezekiel 16.
3. See *Soferim* 14.
4. See I Kings 5:12, and commentary ad loc.
5. See Rashi; Ibn Ezra.
6. See Rashbam here and 3:7.
7. See I Samuel 6:19.
8. See Ibn Ezra.
9. See Genesis 29:2–11.
10. See, e.g., Judges 8:21; Ibn Ezra, Esther 6:8, and commentary ad loc.
11. See Ralbag; Radak, I Chronicles 17:20.
12. See Ibn Ezra.
13. See *Shir HaShirim Rabba*.
14. See *Lekaḥ Tov*.
15. See Malbim.
16. See commentary on II Samuel 6:19.
17. See Rashi.
18. See Alsheikh.
19. See Rashi; Onkelos, Genesis 8:22; *Targum*, Jeremiah 36:22.
20. See commentary on Genesis 8:22.
21. See Rav Yeshaya of Trani.
22. See *Metzudat David*; *Metzudat Tzion*.
23. See Joshua 15:19.
24. See Ibn Ezra; Rav Yosef Kara.
25. See Rashbam, Exodus 30:23.
26. See Alsheikh.
27. Jeremiah 2:2.
28. See Ibn Ezra.
29. See Rashi; Rav Yosef Kara; Rav Yeshaya of Trani.
30. See Psalms 22:15; Ruth 1:11.
31. See Rashi.
32. See Daniel 5:10, and the commentaries ad loc.
33. See Leviticus 13:31.
34. See Mishna *Para* 9:3.
35. See Rashi.
36. See Alsheikh.
37. See Ibn Ezra.
38. See Ibn Ezra; Ralbag; I Kings 15:33.
39. See, e.g., Psalms 48:3; Lamentations 2:15; *Kiddushin* 49b.
40. See Rashbam; Ibn Ezra.
41. See Rashi; Rashbam; Rav Yeshaya of Trani.
42. See Rashbam.
43. See Rashi; Alsheikh; *Shir HaShirim Rabba*.
44. See Rav Yeshaya of Trani.
45. See Ramban, Job 8:12.
46. See Ibn Ezra; Rashbam, Exodus 12:13.
47. Rashbam; Ramban, Exodus 25:12.
48. Rav Yeshaya of Trani.
49. See Rashi; Ibn Ezra.
50. See Rashbam.
51. See Rashi.
52. See Rashi; Ibn Ezra.
53. See Rashi; Malbim; *Da'at Mikra*.
54. See Rav Yosef Kara, 1:2.
55. See Rashi; Ibn Ezra.
56. See Ramban, Leviticus 19:20.
57. See Ibn Ezra.
58. See Rashi.
59. See Rashi.

Ruth

1. Psalms 118:22.
2. Rashi; see also Rashi, Ezra 2:2; *Midrash Tanḥuma, Shemini 9*.
3. See Joshua 19:15.
4. See Rashi's second interpretation; commentary on I Samuel 17:12.
5. I Chronicles 4:4.
6. See commentary on Song of Songs 5:4.
7. See *Ruth Rabba 2:15*.
8. Rashi; Ibn Ezra.
9. See Rashi; *Ruth Rabba 3:6*.
10. Ibn Ezra.
11. Rashi.
12. Rashi.
13. Rashi; Ibn Ezra.
14. See Rashi.
15. Rav Yosef Kara.
16. See Ibn Ezra; Gra; Malbim.
17. See Malbim.
18. See II Samuel 16:4.
19. See Rashi; Ibn Ezra.
20. See Rav Yosef Kara; Ralbag; Malbim.
21. See Rashi; Rashbam, Exodus 3:5.
22. See Gra; Malbim.
23. See Ibn Ezra.
24. See Leviticus 25:25; *Kiddushin 21a*.
25. See Rambam, *Hilkhot Shemitta 11:18; Rashi and* Rav Yeshaya of Trani on 3:9.
26. Exodus 34:22.
27. *Ruth Rabba 5:11*.
28. See *Ketubot 7a*.
29. See Ibn Ezra; Malbim.
30. See Alshekh; Malbim.
31. See Ibn Ezra; Ralbag.
32. Rashi.
33. See Rashi.
34. See Malbim; *Ruth Rabba 6:2*.
35. See Alshekh.
36. See Proverbs 12:4; 31:10.
37. See *Kiddushin 21a*.
38. Ibn Ezra; *Bekhor Shor*.
39. *Ruth Rabba 6:4*.
40. See Rashi; Ralbag; Malbim; *Ruth Rabba 6:4*.
41. See Rashi.
42. See *Pesikta Zutreta;* Rav Yeshaya of Trani; Malbim.
43. See *Pesikta Zutreta; Malbim*.
44. See Malbim.
45. Rashi; Rabbi Yosef Caspi; see commentary on Ruth 3:13.
46. See Malbim; Ramban, Leviticus 25:33.
47. See *Targum; Rav Yeshaya of Trani, 3:9; Ramban, Genesis 38:9*.
48. Rashi.
49. See Ibn Ezra; Rav Yeshaya of Trani.
50. See Rashi; Ibn Ezra; *Bava Metzia 47a*.
51. See Deuteronomy 25:5–6.
52. See Rashi; *Bekhor Shor; Ralbag on I Chronicles 10:13; Deuteronomy 25:6, and Ramban ad loc.*
53. Rav Yosef Kara; see Alshekh.
54. See Rashi.
55. See Alshekh.
56. See *Sanhedrin 19b*.
57. See Numbers 1:7.

Lamentations

1. *Bava Batra* 15a.
2. See *Moed Katan* 26a; *Menaḥot* 30a and Rashi ad loc.; Abravanel, Jeremiah 36:4; *Da'at Mikra* on Daniel, summary to chapter 1.
3. II Chronicles 35:25.
4. See Rashi, Lamentations 1:1; *Moed Katan* 26a; *Eikha Rabba* 1:53; Abravanel, Jeremiah 36:2; commentary on 4:20.
5. Ibn Ezra.
6. See Rashi.
7. See Rashi; Ibn Ezra.
8. See Rashi.
9. Rashi.
10. See *Targum Yonatan*; Rashi.
11. *Targum Yonatan*.
12. Rashi.
13. Deuteronomy 23:4.
14. *Targum Yonatan*; Rashi; *Yevamot* 16b.
15. *Targum Yonatan*.
16. *Pesikta Zutreta*; Rav Yosef Kara.
17. *Targum Yonatan*; Ibn Ezra.
18. Rashi.
19. Rashi; Ibn Ezra.
20. See *Targum Yonatan*; Leviticus 20:18.
21. See Rashi.
22. Rashi; Ibn Ezra.
23. See Ibn Ezra.
24. Rashi.
25. Bekhor Shor.
26. Rashi.
27. See *Targum Yonatan*; Rashi.
28. See Ibn Ezra, Job 16:16.
29. Rashi; Ibn Ezra.
30. *Targum Yonatan*; Rashi; see Psalms 132:7; I Chronicles 28:2; commentary on Exodus 24:9.
31. *Targum Yonatan*; Rashi.
32. *Targum Yonatan*; Rashi.
33. See Rashi.
34. *Targum Yonatan*.
35. Rashi; see Rav Yosef Kara, Ezekiel 22:26.
36. Rashi.
37. See Psalms 42:5.
38. *Targum Yonatan*.
39. See Ibn Ezra, Job 16:16.
40. See Rashi; *Pesikta Zutreta*.
41. Ibn Ezra.
42. See *Pesikta Zutreta*.
43. *Targum Yonatan*.
44. *Pesikta Zutreta*.
45. See Rashi.
46. Rashi.
47. Bekhor Shor.
48. See Rashi.
49. *Targum Yonatan*; Rashi.
50. Rashi.
51. Rav Yosef Caspi.
52. Rashi.
53. *Targum Yonatan*.
54. See *Targum Yonatan*; Rashi.
55. Alsheikh.
56. See *Pesikta Zutreta*; Rashi.
57. See Rashi; Ibn Ezra.
58. See *Pesikta Zutreta*.
59. *Pesikta Zutreta*.
60. *Targum Yonatan*; Rashi.
61. See Ibn Ezra.
62. See *Targum Yonatan*; Ibn Ezra.
63. *Targum Yonatan*.
64. See *Pesikta Zutreta*; Rashi.
65. Rashi.
66. *Pesikta Zutreta*.
67. See Rashi.
68. See *Pesikta Zutreta*.
69. See Rashi.
70. See *Eikha Rabba* 3:13.
71. See Rashi.
72. Rashi.
73. *Targum Yonatan*; Rashi.
74. *Targum Yonatan*.
75. Rashi.
76. Rashi.
77. Ibn Ezra.
78. *Targum Yonatan*.
79. Alsheikh.
80. Ibn Ezra; Rav Yosef Caspi.
81. See Rashi.
82. Rashi.
83. See Ibn Ezra.
84. Ibn Ezra.
85. See *Pesikta Zutreta*.
86. Alsheikh.
87. Rashi.
88. Ibn Ezra.
89. *Targum Yonatan*; Rashi.
90. *Targum Yonatan*; Rashi.
91. Rashi; Rav Yeshaya of Trani.
92. Rashi.
93. Rav Yosef Kara; Bekhor Shor.
94. *Pesikta Zutreta*; Rashi.
95. See Rashi.
96. Rashi.
97. See *Targum Yonatan*; *Pesikta Zutreta*.
98. Rashi.
99. See *Pesikta Zutreta*; Rashi.
100. Ibn Ezra.
101. Rashi.
102. Rashi.
103. See Rashi; *Pesikta Zutreta*; Rav Yosef Caspi.
104. *Targum Yonatan*; Rashi.
105. See Rashi; *Pesikta Zutreta*.
106. See Rashi.
107. Rashi.
108. See *Pesikta Zutreta*.
109. Alsheikh.
110. See commentary on 1:1.
111. See Isaiah 55:1.
112. See Ezekiel 17:18.
113. See *Targum Yonatan*; Rashi.
114. *Targum Yonatan*; Rashi.
115. Rashi.
116. See *Pesikta Zutreta*.
117. Rashi.
118. See *Pesikta Zutreta*.
119. See *Targum Yonatan*; Bekhor Shor.

Ecclesiastes

1. See Mishna *Yadayim* 3:5; *Vayikra Rabba* 28:1; *Kohelet Rabba* 1:4.
2. See *Shir HaShirim Rabba* 1:10; *Ramban's Sermon on Ecclesiastes*.
3. Rashi; *Kohelet Rabba* 1:1.
4. See Rashi; *Kohelet Rabba* 1:2.
5. See Alsheikh.
6. See Rashi.
7. See *Targum*; Rashi; *Bava Batra* 25b.
8. Ibn Ezra.
9. See Ibn Ezra.
10. See Rashbam here and Deuteronomy 20:5.
11. See Ibn Ezra.
12. See Ibn Ezra.
13. See Ibn Ezra.
14. Rashi.
15. See Ibn Ezra.
16. Rashi.
17. See Rashi; Mishna *Kelim* 18:1.
18. See *Pesikta Zutreta*.
19. See Rashi; Ibn Ezra.
20. Ibn Ezra.
21. See Ibn Ezra.
22. Rashi; Ibn Ezra.
23. Ibn Ezra.
24. See Ibn Ezra; *Pesikta Zutreta*.
25. Ibn Ezra.
26. Rashi.
27. See Rashi; Ibn Ezra.
28. See Rashi.
29. See Rashi; Ibn Ezra.
30. See Rashi.
31. See Alsheikh.
32. See Ibn Ezra.
33. See *Pesikta Zutreta*.
34. See Ibn Ezra.
35. See Rashi.
36. Rashi.
37. See Ibn Ezra.
38. See Ibn Ezra.

39. See Rambam, *Guide of the Perplexed* 1:59, 3:52.
40. Ibn Ezra.
41. See *Pesikta Zutreta*.
42. Rashi.
43. Ibn Ezra.
44. See Ibn Ezra.
45. Ibn Ezra.
46. See Ibn Ezra.
47. See Ibn Ezra.
48. See Rashi.
49. See Ibn Ezra.
50. Ibn Ezra.
51. See Rashi.
52. See *Pesikta Zutreta*; Rashi.
53. See Ibn Ezra.
54. See Rashi.
55. See Ibn Ezra.
56. See Ibn Ezra.
57. See Ibn Ezra.
58. *Pesikta Zutreta*; Rashi.
59. See Ibn Ezra.
60. See *Pesikta Zutreta*.
61. Rashi; see Ibn Ezra.
62. Ibn Ezra.
63. Rashi; Ibn Ezra.
64. Rav Yeshaya of Trani.
65. See Ibn Ezra.
66. See Rashi.
67. Rashi.
68. See Ibn Ezra; Ralbag.
69. See Rashi; Rashbam.
70. See Rav Yosef Kara.
71. Ibn Ezra.
72. Ibn Ezra.
73. See Rashbam.
74. See Ibn Ezra; Rashbam; Rav Yeshaya of Trani.
75. Rashbam; Rav Yosef Kara.
76. See Ibn Ezra.
77. See Rashi; Ibn Ezra; Rav Yeshaya of Trani.
78. See *Pesikta Zutreta*; Ibn Ezra; Rambam, *Guide of the Perplexed* 1:32.
79. See Ibn Ezra; Rav Yeshaya of Trani; Ralbag.
80. Rashi; Rav Yosef Kara.
81. See Ibn Ezra.
82. See Rambam, *Sefer HaMadda*, *Hilkhot Deot* 1:1; Rambam's introduction to *Avot* 4.
83. See Rashi; Ibn Ezra.
84. See Ibn Ezra here and Daniel 1:20.
85. Ibn Ezra.
86. See Ibn Ezra.
87. Ibn Ezra.
88. See Alsheikh.
89. See Rashi; Ibn Ezra.
90. Rashi.
91. See Ibn Ezra.
92. Ibn Ezra.
93. See Ibn Ezra.
94. Ibn Ezra; I Kings 11:3.
95. See Alsheikh.
96. Ibn Ezra.
97. See Ibn Ezra.
98. See Ibn Ezra.
99. See Rashi.
100. Ibn Ezra.
101. See Rashi.
102. Rashi.
103. Rashi.
104. See, e.g., Job 34:29.
105. See Ibn Ezra; Rashbam.
106. *Kohelet Rabba* 8:9.
107. See Rashi.
108. Rashi; Ibn Ezra.
109. Ibn Ezra.
110. See Rashi.
111. Ibn Ezra.
112. See Rashi.
113. Ibn Ezra; Ralbag; see Job 34:25.
114. See Ibn Ezra; *Pesikta Zutreta*.
115. Ibn Ezra.
116. See *Pesikta Zutreta*.
117. Ibn Ezra.
118. Rav Yosef Kara.
119. Ibn Ezra.
120. See Ibn Ezra; Deuteronomy 8:9.
121. Ibn Ezra.
122. See Rashi; Rashbam; *Emunot VeDeot* 5:3.
123. Rashi.
124. See Ibn Ezra.
125. Rashbam; see Rashi.
126. Rashi; Ibn Ezra.
127. See *Pesikta Zutreta*.
128. See Rashi.
129. See Rashi.
130. Ibn Ezra.
131. Rashi.
132. See Ibn Ezra.
133. Rashbam.
134. See *Pesikta Zutreta*; Ibn Ezra.
135. See Ibn Ezra.
136. *Avot* 3:13.
137. See *Pesikta Zutreta*; Rashi.
138. See, e.g., I Kings 21:8.
139. See Ibn Ezra.
140. Rashi.
141. See Rambam, *Guide of the Perplexed* 2:47.
142. See Rashi.
143. See Ibn Ezra.
144. See Rashi.
145. Rashi.
146. Ibn Ezra.
147. See Rashi; Ibn Ezra.
148. See Ibn Ezra; *Pesikta Zutreta*; *Kohelet Rabba* 12:1.
149. See Ibn Ezra.
150. See *Shabbat* 152a.
151. Rashi.
152. Rashi.
153. *Pesikta Rabbati*; see Rav Yeshaya of Trani.
154. Rashi; *Shabbat* 152a.
155. Ibn Ezra.
156. *Shabbat* 152a.
157. See *Shabbat* 152a.
158. Ibn Ezra; *Pesikta Rabbati*.
159. *Shabbat* 152a.
160. See *Shabbat* 152a.
161. See *Shabbat* 152a.
162. *Shabbat* 152a.
163. See Rashi.
164. *Shabbat* 151b.
165. *Pesikta Rabbati*.
166. See Ibn Ezra.
167. *Targum Kohelet*.
168. See Isaiah 41:7; Jeremiah 10:4.
169. See *Pesikta Zutreta*.
170. Ibn Ezra.
171. See Rashi.
172. Rashi.

Esther

1. *Megilla* 20a.
2. 9:26,29. There seem to have been two epistles out of which the book was assembled.
3. See *Megilla* 7a.
4. See Ibn Ezra's introduction to the book of Esther and his commentary on 5:13, citing Rav Se'adya Gaon.
5. *Seder Olam Rabba*.
6. See Daniel 8:2.
7. Ibn Ezra; Rav Yeshaya of Trani; Vilna Gaon.
8. See, e.g., Rashi; Rashbam; Ibn Ezra.
9. See Ibn Ezra, second commentary.
10. See *Megilla* 12a.
11. Rashi.
12. Based on Rashbam; Bekhor Shor; Ralbag; see also Daniel 5:10.
13. See Ralbag.
14. See *Megilla* 12b.
15. See Ibn Ezra, second commentary; Rav Yosef Kara; Rav Yeshaya of Trani; Ralbag.
16. *Esther Rabba* 1:15; Rashi.
17. Ibn Ezra.
18. See Nehemiah 13:23–24.
19. See, e.g., Rashi.
20. See Rashbam; Ibn Ezra; Rav Yosef Kara; Rav Yeshaya of Trani.
21. Rav Yosef Naḥmias.
22. See *Megilla* 15a; *Targum*; Ibn Ezra.
23. See Malbim.
24. *Targum*; *Megilla* 13a; see Ramban, Exodus 30:23.
25. See Ibn Ezra; Rashbam; Ibn Ezra, second commentary.
26. See, e.g., Rashbam.
27. See discussion on verse 5.
28. See *Megilla* 13a.
29. Ibn Ezra, second commentary; Malbim; see Ruth 4:1; Daniel 2:49.
30. *Megilla* 13a; see *Menaḥot* 65a.
31. See II Kings 25:28; Daniel 5:29.

32. See Rav Yosef Caspi; *Megillat Setarim*.
33. Rav Yosef Kara, verse 5.
34. See the Aramaic translations of the Bible; *Sanhedrin* 61b; *Megilla* 13a.
35. Ibn Ezra.
36. See Ibn Ezra; Ralbag. See also Ezekiel 21:26–27; commentary on Isaiah 36:10.
37. See *Megilla* 13b.
38. See Rashi.
39. Rashbam and Ralbag, 4:8; Ibn Ezra, second commentary, 8:13.
40. See Rashi; Ibn Ezra; Ibn Ezra, 1:2.
41. *Targum*.
42. See Malbim.
43. See Nehemiah 2:4.
44. Ibn Ezra.
45. *Targum*; Ralbag.
46. See Rashi; Ibn Ezra.
47. Ibn Ezra.
48. See Malbim.
49. See Rashi.
50. See *Megilla* 15b.
51. See Rashbam; Rav Yosef Kara.
52. See Malbim.
53. See *Targum*; *Megilla* 16a.
54. See Ibn Ezra; Rav Yosef Kara.
55. Ibn Ezra.
56. See 1:6; Ezekiel 23:41, and Radak ad loc.
57. See *Targum*.
58. See also 3:12.
59. Ibn Ezra.
60. Ibn Ezra.
61. See Ibn Ezra; Rav Yeshaya of Trani.
62. See Ezra 4:6.
63. See Rav Yosef Kara; Esther 8:11.
64. See Ralbag.
65. Rashi; Rashbam.
66. Rambam, *Megilla* 2a, Ibn Ezra.
67. See *Targum*.
68. Malbim.
69. *Targum*; Rashi; Rashbam; Ibn Ezra; see *Megilla* 16b.
70. See Ibn Ezra, 8:8.
71. Rashi.
72. See Rashi.
73. See Ibn Ezra, second commentary.
74. *Targum*; Rashi; Malbim.
75. I Kings 14:29, 15:23; II Kings 14:15; II Chronicles 25:26.

Daniel

1. See commentary on Ezekiel 14:14.
2. See *Megilla* 3a; Rambam, *Guide of the Perplexed* 2:45.
3. Daniel 2.
4. It is difficult to identify Darius the Mede with any particular individual who appears in parallel Greek and Persian sources. In the book of Daniel, he appears to share power with Cyrus the Great after the Persian conquest of Babylon.
5. See II Kings 24.
6. See Genesis 10:10, and commentary ad loc.
7. Ibn Ezra; *Metzudat David*.
8. See commentary on Isaiah 39:7.
9. See commentary on Job 31:7.
10. See Genesis 41:45, and Rashbam, Radak ad loc.; Rashbam, Genesis 1:5; commentary on Esther 1:9, 3:1.
11. See Rashi; Daniel 4:5.
12. See Ibn Ezra, citing Rav Se'adya Gaon.
13. Based on the Akkadian; see Rashi; Ibn Ezra.
14. See Rashi.
15. See Ibn Ezra; *Metzudat David*; Daniel 1:5.
16. *Metzudat David*; Rashi.
17. See *Metzudat David*; *Metzudat Tzion*.
18. Rashi; *Metzudat David*; *Metzudat Tzion*.
19. See Ezra 6:11.
20. See Ibn Ezra; Ralbag.
21. Rashi; *Metzudat David*; *Metzudat Tzion*.
22. See Rav Se'adya Gaon; Rashi; Ibn Ezra.
23. *Metzudat David*.
24. See Rashi; *Metzudat David*; *Metzudat Tzion*; see commentary on Isaiah 47:13.
25. See Rashi.
26. See Ibn Ezra; *Metzudat David*; Malbim; *Sanhedrin* 93a.
27. See Rashi.
28. See Nehemiah 5:14, 12:26.
29. See Ibn Ezra; *Da'at Mikra*.
30. See Ezra 7:21.
31. See Ibn Ezra.
32. See *Megilla* 22b.
33. See Rabbi Tanḥum.
34. See Rashi; *Sanhedrin* 92b.
35. Ralbag.
36. See Genesis 19:28; Exodus 19:18.
37. See *Sanhedrin* 92b.
38. Rashi; see Ezra 4:11, 7:12.
39. See also Ezra 5:7.
40. See commentary on Isaiah 47:13.
41. Rabbi Shmuel of Sanut; see also Ibn Ezra; Radak.
42. Rashi; Rav Se'adya Gaon.
43. Rashi; *Metzudat David*.
44. See Ibn Ezra; *Metzudat David*.
45. See *Metzudat David*.
46. See Rav Se'adya Gaon; Ibn Ezra; Abravanel.
47. See Rashi.
48. See Rashi; *Metzudat David*.
49. See Rav Se'adya Gaon.
50. See, e.g., Rashi; Ibn Ezra.
51. See Esther 1:9.
52. See *Metzudat Tzion*; see 2:6.
53. See Radak; Ralbag.
54. See Rav Se'adya Gaon.
55. See commentaries; *Sanhedrin* 22a.
56. See Ibn Ezra.
57. See Rashi.
58. See Rav Se'adya Gaon.
59. See Rashi; *Metzudat David*.
60. See Rashi; *Metzudat David*; *Metzudat Tzion*.
61. See Rashi.
62. See *Metzudat David*.
63. See Rashi; Ibn Ezra.
64. See, e.g., Ibn Ezra.
65. See commentary on 10:13; *Da'at Mikra*, 10:5; Rashi, 11:1.
66. See Jeremiah 25:11–12, 29:10.
67. See Ibn Ezra.
68. Rashi.
69. See, e.g., Obadiah 1:20.
70. See Leviticus 26:14–46; Deuteronomy 28:15–69.
71. See Malbim; Leviticus 26:18, 21.
72. See *Metzudat David*.
73. Rav Se'adya Gaon.
74. See commentary on Psalms 141:1.
75. See Ibn Ezra.
76. Rashi; *Metzudat David*; *Metzudat Tzion*.
77. See Rashi; *Metzudat David*.
78. See Ibn Ezra; Rashbam, Genesis 5:31; Ramban, *Sefer HaGe'ula* 3.
79. See Rashi; *Metzudat David*.
80. See Ibn Ezra; *Metzudat David*; Malbim.
81. See Ramban, Genesis 7:16.
82. See Isaiah 24, 66:15–16; Ezekiel 38–39; Joel 3; Haggai 2:6–7; Zechariah 12, 14; Malachi 3.
83. See Ibn Ezra; *Metzudat David*.
84. See *Metzudat David*.
85. See Ezekiel 4:9.
86. Rashi; *Metzudat David*.
87. Rav Se'adya Gaon.
88. See *Megilla* 3a.
89. Rashi; see *Megilla* 3a.
90. *Bereshit Rabba* 21:5; *Yoma* 77a.
91. See Rashi.
92. See *Yoma* 77a.
93. See Rashi; *Metzudat David*.
94. See Rashi; *Metzudat David*.
95. See, e.g., Rashi; Ibn Ezra, 10:21.
96. See Rashi.
97. See Rav Se'adya Gaon.
98. See, e.g., Psalms 37:38.
99. See Rashi; Malbim.
100. See Rashi; Ibn Ezra.
101. See Rashi; *Metzudat David*.
102. See Rav Se'adya Gaon.
103. *Metzudat David*.
104. Ibn Ezra, verse 13.
105. See *Metzudat David*.
106. Malbim.
107. Ibn Ezra.
108. See Ibn Ezra; Malbim.
109. Rashi.
110. See Ibn Ezra; Malbim.
111. Rav Se'adya Gaon.
112. See Ibn Ezra; Malbim.
113. See Ibn Ezra; Malbim.
114. See Rashi; *Metzudat David*.
115. See Rashi; *Metzudat David*.
116. See Rashi; *Metzudat David*.
117. See Rashi; Ibn Ezra.

118. See Ibn Ezra; *Metzudat David*.
119. See Malbim.
120. See *Metzudat David*.
121. See Ibn Ezra; *Metzudat David*.
122. Rashi.
123. See Rashi; *Metzudat David*.
124. See Malbim.
125. See Rashi; *Metzudat David*.
126. See Rashi; Ralbag.
127. See Rashi; *Metzudat David*.
128. *Metzudat David*; *Metzudat Tzion*.
129. Rav Se'adya Gaon.
130. See Ibn Ezra; *Metzudat David*.
131. Rav Se'adya Gaon.
132. See Ibn Ezra; *Metzudat David*.
133. See Rambam, "Essay on Resurrection"; see also Isaiah 26:19; Psalms 49:16.
134. See *Metzudat David*.
135. See Ibn Ezra; *Metzudat David*.
136. See *Bava Batra* 8a.
137. See Ibn Ezra; *Metzudat David*.
138. *Metzudat David*.
139. See Rashi; *Metzudat David*.
140. See Rashi; Ibn Ezra.
141. See Rashi.
142. Rav Se'adya Gaon; Rashi; Ibn Ezra; Rashbam, Genesis 35:18.

Ezra

1. See *Bava Batra* 15a; *Sanhedrin* 93b.
2. Ezra 1:1–4.
3. Ezra 3:1–8.
4. Ezra 4:4–5. The reconstruction of the Temple was renewed only in the second year of the reign of Darius the Great.
5. Ezra 4:24–6:14.
6. Ezra 6:15.
7. Apparently, different letters were sent at different times. One letter was sent to Darius (Ezra 5:6), another to Ahashverosh (Ezra 4:6), and another to Artahshasta (Ezra 4:7), although the latter two letters were perhaps the same letter. See commentary on Ezra 4:7.
8. Ezra 7.
9. Nehemiah 6:15.
10. Nehemiah 10:1.
11. See Rashi; *Metzudat David*; Jeremiah 25:11–13; Daniel 9; *Megilla* 11b-12a; *Emunot VeDeot* 8:4.
12. See chaps. 5 and 6.
13. See Ralbag.
14. See Rav Se'adya Gaon; Ralbag; *Metzudat David*; *Metzudat Tzion*.
15. See Daniel 1:2.
16. See, e.g., Rashi.
17. See commentaries; *Menaḥot* 7b; I Chronicles 28:17, and commentaries ad loc.
18. Rav Se'adya Gaon.
19. See Ibn Ezra.
20. Rav Se'adya Gaon; Ibn Ezra.
21. See Esther 2:5–6.
22. See Rashi; Ibn Ezra; Ralbag; Mishna *Shekalim* 5:1; *Megilla* 13b, 16b; *Menaḥot* 65a; Ibn Ezra, Esther 2:21.
23. Rashi.
24. See Ibn Ezra.
25. See Ibn Ezra; *Metzudat David*.
26. See 10:18; Haggai 2:2.
27. See Rashi and Ibn Ezra.
28. See I Kings 9:20–22.
29. See Ibn Ezra.
30. See Nehemiah 8:9.
31. See Ibn Ezra.
32. See Rashi and Ralbag; Exodus 28:30; *Sota* 48b.
33. See commentary on Daniel 5:25.
34. See *Metzudat David*.
35. See Rashi; Rav Se'adya Gaon.
36. Ibn Ezra; see Exodus 29:38–42; Numbers 28:1–8.
37. See Numbers 29:12–34.
38. See Ralbag.
39. See I Chronicles 16:7, 25:1–9.
40. See Rashi; Rav Se'adya Gaon; *Metzudat David*.
41. See Ralbag.
42. See Rashi.
43. See Rav Se'adya Gaon; Ralbag 7:12.
44. See Malbim, verse 11; Samuel David Luzzatto, Exodus 21:10.
45. Ralbag; *Metzudat David*; *Metzudat Tzion*; see Ibn Ezra.
46. Rav Se'adya Gaon.
47. See 6:8; Nehemiah 5:4.
48. See *Nedarim* 62b.
49. See Ibn Ezra.
50. See *Yad Rama*, *Bava Batra* 4:12.
51. See commentary on Leviticus 2:13.
52. See Job 6:11.
53. See Rav Se'adya Gaon; Ramban, Exodus 22:15; Ralbag, Ezra 4:19.
54. See Rashi.
55. See Esther 1:15, 8:8.
56. See Haggai 1:1; Zechariah 1:1, 7.
57. See Haggai 1–2; Zechariah 1:16, 3–4, 6:11–13.
58. See Rashi; Ibn Ezra; *Metzudat David*; *Metzudat Tzion*.
59. See *Tosafot*, *Kiddushin* 2a.
60. See, e.g., Rashi.
61. See *Pesikta Rabbati* 6.
62. See Esther 1:19, 3:9, 5:4; Nehemiah 2:5, 7.
63. See Esther 7:9, 8:1; Daniel 3:29.
64. See *Metzudat David*.
65. See II Kings 25:18; II Chronicles 19:11, 26:20.
66. See I Chronicles 5:30–41; Malbim, I Chronicles 5:30; Ralbag, I Chronicles 5:36; see also Mishna *Para* 3:5, and commentaries ad loc.
67. See *Esther Rabba* 1:2; *Or Ḥadash* 1.
68. See Ralbag; *Metzudat Tzion*; *Kiddushin* 30a; see also I Chronicles 2:55.
69. See Rashi; *Metzudat David*; see also Nehemiah 2:8.
70. See Rav Se'adya Gaon.
71. See Ibn Ezra; Ralbag.
72. *Da'at Mikra*.
73. See 4:10, and Ralbag ad loc.
74. See Rashi; *Metzudat David*.
75. See Esther 1:14.
76. See Rashi; Ralbag; *Metzudat David*; Samuel David Luzzatto, Exodus 13:22.
77. See Ezekiel 45:10–14.
78. See Rav Se'adya Gaon; *Moed Katan* 16a, and Rashi ad loc.; Harkavy, *Responsa of the Ge'onim*, 444.
79. See Rashi.
80. See Malbim; see 2:13.
81. See Rashi; *Metzudat David*; Malbim; see also verse 31.
82. Exodus 6:19; Numbers 3:20.
83. See Rashi.
84. See I Samuel 22:14; Hosea 9:12.
85. See Ralbag; *Metzudat David*; *Temura* 15b; *Horayot* 6a.
86. See Rashi; Rav Se'adya Gaon; Ralbag; *Metzudat David*.
87. See commentary on Psalms 141:2.
88. See Exodus 23:31–33; Deuteronomy 7:1–5, 23:7.
89. See Rashi.
90. Ibn Ezra.
91. See 7:26; *Yevamot* 89b.
92. See Rashi; Joshua 7:19.
93. Ibn Ezra.
94. See Ibn Ezra.

Nehemiah

1. See Daniel 1:3, and commentary ad loc.
2. See commentary on Daniel 8:2.
3. Rashi; *Metzudat David*.
4. See Rashi; see also Ezra 3:8.
5. *Da'at Mikra*.
6. Daniel 9:4.
7. I Kings 8:23.
8. See Daniel 9:5–20, and commentary ad loc.
9. See Deuteronomy 30:4.
10. *Metzudat David*.
11. See Malbim.
12. See Ibn Ezra; *Metzudat David*.
13. See Malbim.
14. Rashi.
15. Rav Se'adya Gaon; Ralbag.
16. See Rashi; Ralbag; *Metzudat David*.
17. *Metzudat David*.
18. See Mishna *Ta'anit* 4:5.
19. See commentary on II Samuel 14:2; commentary on Jeremiah 6:1.
20. Rashi; Ibn Ezra; Ralbag; *Metzudat David*; *Metzudat Tzion*.
21. See Rashi.
22. See Rav Se'adya Gaon.
23. See verse 26; Joshua 9:27; see Ezra 2:43.
24. See Rashi; Ibn Ezra; Rav Se'adya Gaon; *Metzudat David*; *Metzudat Tzion*.
25. See Ibn Ezra.
26. See Leviticus 21:18.
27. See Rashi; see also verse 19.
28. See Rav Se'adya Gaon.
29. See *Metzudat David*; Ralbag.
30. See *Metzudat David*.
31. See, e.g., Rav Se'adya Gaon.
32. See *Metzudat David*; *Metzudat Tzion*; Malbim.
33. See Jeremiah 32:2, and commentary ad loc.; Jeremiah 37:21, and commentary ad loc.
34. See commentary on Isaiah 32:14.
35. Rashi; *Metzudat David*.
36. Rav Se'adya Gaon.
37. See commentary on Isaiah 43:13.
38. See *Metzudat David*.
39. See Ralbag; Ibn Ezra.
40. See Ralbag.
41. See *Metzudat David*.
42. See Rashi; Ibn Ezra; Ralbag.
43. See Ramban, Genesis 31:43.
44. *Metzudat David*.
45. Ralbag.
46. See Ezra 4:13, 6:8.
47. See II Kings 4:1.
48. Exodus 22:24.
49. See *Metzudat David*.
50. See Rashi.
51. Ramban, Numbers 27:19.
52. Rav Se'adya Gaon; *Metzudat David*; see Ibn Ezra.
53. See Rashi.
54. See *Sanhedrin* 93b.
55. See Ibn Ezra; *Metzudat David*.
56. See *Metzudat David*.
57. See Rashi.
58. See Ralbag, verse 18.
59. See Rashi; 13:4, 28.
60. See *Berakhot* 27a.
61. See Haggai 2:19; Job 1:18.
62. See Rashi.
63. *Metzudat David*; *Metzudat Tzion*.
64. See Ezra 2.
65. See Ibn Ezra, verse 6; Rashi, verse 7; *Metzudat David*, verse 66; Malbim, Ezra 2:1.
66. *Metzudat David*; see commentary on Ezra 2:2.
67. *Metzudat David*.
68. See commentary on Ezra 2:33.
69. See, e.g., Mishna *Ta'anit* 4:5.
70. See *Metzudat David*; Ezra 2:40.
71. Joshua 9:27.
72. See Exodus 28:30.
73. *Metzudat David*.
74. See Ibn Ezra; Ralbag; see also *Sota* 39a; *Megilla* 21a; *Shulḥan Arukh, Oraḥ Ḥayyim* 146:4.
75. See Ralbag; *Metzudat David*; *Megilla* 3a; Jerusalem Talmud, *Megilla* 4:1.
76. See Esther 9:19, 22.
77. Deuteronomy 16:11, 16.
78. See Ibn Ezra; Ralbag; *Metzudat David*.
79. See Rashi; *Metzudat David*; *Metzudat Tzion*.
80. See Leviticus 23:40.
81. See Rashi; *Metzudat David*; *Sukka* 12a.
82. See, e.g., Proverbs 1:21, 8:3; commentary on Isaiah 29:21.
83. See Malbim.
84. See *Bava Kamma* 82a.
85. Leviticus 23:36.
86. See Malbim; Jerusalem Talmud, *Avoda Zara* 1:1; *Rosh HaShana* 19b, and *Tosafot* ad loc.
87. See Joshua 7:6; I Samuel 4:12; II Samuel 1:2, 13:19; Isaiah 61:3; Job 2:12; Mishna *Ta'anit* 2:1.
88. See Rashi; Malbim.
89. See *Megilla* 30b.
90. See, e.g., Rashi.
91. See *Metzudat David*.
92. See commentary on Deuteronomy 8:18; Jeremiah 44:6.
93. See Exodus 16:4–30; Rashi, Exodus 15:25.
94. See commentary on Ezekiel 20:13.
95. See commentary on Exodus 6:8.
96. See *Metzudat David*.
97. Ibn Ezra; *Metzudat David*; *Metzudat Tzion*.
98. See *Metzudat David*.
99. See Ibn Ezra.
100. See 11:17; I Chronicles 9:16.
101. See *Sukka* 56b.
102. See Malbim, verse 1.
103. See *Ruth Rabba* 4:8; Jerusalem Talmud, *Megilla* 1:5; Malbim, verse 2.
104. See Malbim; Jerusalem Talmud, *Shekalim* 2:3.
105. See Leviticus 24:5–8.
106. Exodus 23:19, 34:26; Deuteronomy 26:10.
107. E.g., Exodus 13:2, and see commentary ad loc.; commentary on Numbers 18:14.
108. See Ralbag; *Metzudat David*.
109. See Numbers 18:25–32.
110. See *Metzudat David*; I Chronicles 9:3.
111. *Metzudat David*.
112. See *Metzudat David*.
113. See II Kings 25:18; Ezra 7:5, and commentary ad loc.
114. I Chronicles 26:20, 29.
115. See Rashi, I Chronicles 16:7.
116. See Joshua 19:1–3.
117. See Genesis 49:7, and commentary ad loc.; Joshua 19:1–3, and commentary ad loc.
118. I Samuel 27:6.
119. See Joshua 18:21–28, 21:17–18.
120. See Rashi, I Chronicles 16:7.
121. Zechariah 1:1, and see commentary ad loc.; Nehemiah 12:22.
122. See *Metzudat David*.
123. I Chronicles 25; Nehemiah 12:45–46.
124. Rashi; Ibn Ezra.
125. See Rashi; Mishna *Shevuot* 2:2; *Shevuot* 15a.
126. Rashi.
127. See commentary on Ezra 2:24.
128. See Rashi.
129. Rashi; *Shevuot* 15a.
130. See Ralbag.
131. *Metzudat David*; *Metzudat Tzion*, verse 37.
132. See I Samuel 3:2.
133. Deuteronomy 23:4–5.
134. See Rashi; Nehemiah 2:10, 19; 3:35–37; 6:12, 14.
135. See Exodus 30:34; Leviticus 2:1, 24:7.
136. See Ezra 5:13; commentary on Ezra 4:10.
137. See, e.g., Leviticus 25:29; I Samuel 27:7.
138. See Rashi; *Metzudat David*.
139. Ralbag; *Metzudat David*.
140. Ezra 9:4.
141. See *Metzudat David*.

I Chronicles

1. See, e.g., Rashi, II Chronicles 3:8 and introduction to the passage beginning at 2:1.
2. See Rambam, *Guide of the Perplexed* 2:45.
3. 3:19–24.
4. See *Adderet Eliyahu*, 2:26, 6:5.
5. See Rashi 7:13, 8:1, 29; Radak 7:1, 12; Abravanel, I Kings 10:22.
6. See *Pesaḥim* 62b; Radak, I Chronicles 1:36; Malbim, I Chronicles 1:2–3.
7. See *Vayikra Rabba* 1; *Pesaḥim* 62b, and Rashi ad loc.; *Megilla* 13a; *Metzudat David*, I Chronicles 8:1.
8. In his commentary to Chronicles, Malbim consistently argues that the author of Chronicles only mentions events when he can add some detail or insight that was not related in the earlier books.
9. See, e.g., Rashi.
10. Genesis 10:3; see Radak, verse 7; *Metzudat Tzion*, verse 6.
11. See commentary on Genesis 10:21.
12. See Jeremiah 44:1; Ezekiel 29:14, 30:14.
13. See *Metzudat Tzion*.
14. See Malbim.
15. Genesis 25:13.
16. Genesis 32:28, 35:10.
17. See Exodus 17:8–16; Deuteronomy 25:17–19; Judges 6:33; I Samuel 15.
18. See Genesis 36.
19. See Genesis 14:6, 36:20.
20. See Radak; Malbim; Genesis 36:12.
21. See verse 38; Ramban, Genesis 36:29.
22. See Vilna Gaon; Ramban, Genesis 36:29.
23. See Genesis 36:42.
24. Genesis 36:39.
25. See Radak, verse 1; *Bereshit Rabba* 73:4.
26. See *Mei HaShiloaḥ*, *Vayishlah*.
27. Genesis 38.
28. See *Yevamot* 18a.
29. See Vilna Gaon; Genesis 46:12, and commentary ad loc.; Numbers 26:19.
30. See Numbers 3:4, 26:61; I Chronicles 24:2.
31. See 15:19; Psalms 88:1, 89:1.
32. See Rashi; I Kings 5:11; I Chronicles 25:1, 5.
33. See Radak; Joshua 7:1.
34. See Rashi; *Metzudat David*; Joshua 7.
35. See, e.g., Rashi; Radak.
36. See Malbim.
37. See, e.g., Exodus 6:23; Numbers 1:7.
38. Ruth 4:13–22, and commentary ad loc.
39. See Radak.
40. See II Samuel 13:3, 32, 21:21.
41. See Rashi; Radak; 27:18.
42. See commentary on I Samuel 26:6.
43. See Radak; *Metzudat David*; *Adderet Eliyahu*.
44. See *Sota* 12a.
45. See Exodus 17:10–12, 24:14, and commentary ad loc.
46. See Exodus 31:2.
47. See Numbers 26:29, 32:39–40; Joshua 17:1.
48. See Radak; Malbim; Numbers 32:41.
49. See Numbers 32:41.
50. See Malbim.
51. See Rashi; Radak; Malbim.
52. See Rashi; Radak; *Adderet Eliyahu*.
53. See Jeremiah 40–41.
54. See Rashi and Radak, based on the Jerusalem Talmud.
55. See Radak.
56. See Radak; *Metzudat David*.
57. See Rashi.
58. See Malbim.
59. See Rashi.
60. Radak and *Metzudat David*, based on 2:19; see also Malbim.
61. 2:11; see commentary on Ruth 4:22.
62. Rashi; *Adderet Eliyahu*.
63. See Radak; Ralbag; Malbim; Radak, 2:55.
64. See Rashi; Radak; Malbim; Joshua 15:33, 19:41; Judges 13:25.
65. See Rashi; *Metzudat David*.
66. See Malbim.
67. See Radak; Malbim; *Sota* 11a; *Sanhedrin* 104a; commentary on Ezra 7:6.
68. See Radak.
69. See Rashi; Radak; 4:9.
70. See *Sanhedrin* 104a.
71. See Jeremiah 35.
72. See Malbim; *Sifrei*, *Behaalotekha* 78.
73. See Rashi; Radak; II Samuel 3:3; *Berakhot* 4a.
74. See Radak.
75. See II Samuel 13:37–38.
76. See Radak; II Samuel 11:3.
77. Radak; see 14:5–7, and commentary ad loc.
78. See *Sanhedrin* 21a; commentary on II Samuel 13:1.
79. See Radak; Malbim.
80. See Rashi; *Metzudat David*; *Adderet Eliyahu*.
81. See *Adderet Eliyahu*.
82. See *Metzudat David*; Malbim.
83. See Malbim; Haggai 1:1; Ezra 3:2.
84. Genesis 46:12.
85. Joshua 7:1; I Chronicles 2:7.
86. See *Metzudat David*; Malbim.
87. See Judges 13:2–3; *Bava Batra* 91a; *Bemidbar Rabba* 10:5.
88. See Genesis 35:19; I Samuel 17:12; Micah 5:1; Ruth 4:11; see also commentary on I Chronicles 2:24.
89. See, e.g., Proverbs 25:12.
90. See *Adderet Eliyahu*, 2:7; Malbim, 8:31–32, 15:18.
91. See Proverbs 24:11.
92. See Radak; Ralbag; *Temura* 16a.
93. See Rashi; Radak.
94. See Joshua 15:17; Judges 1:13.
95. See Rashi; Radak.
96. See *Responsa of the Ge'onim: Sha'arei Teshuva*, 19.
97. See Radak; Ralbag; *Minḥat Shai*.
98. Vilna Gaon.
99. Malbim.
100. See *Adderet Eliyahu*.
101. See *Metzudat David*; Malbim.
102. See Ralbag, 10:13, "the fourth lesson."
103. Radak; *Adderet Eliyahu*.
104. See Rashi; Radak; *Da'at Mikra*.
105. See Joshua 19:1, 9, and commentary ad loc.; Judges 1:3, 17.
106. See Radak.
107. See Judges 10:12.
108. See Radak.
109. See commentary on Judges 8:1; commentary on II Chronicles 30:11; commentary on I Samuel 1:1.
110. See Rashi; Radak; *Adderet Eliyahu*.
111. See Rashi; Radak; Malbim.
112. II Kings 15:29, 16:7, 10.
113. *Bereshit Rabba* 84; *Pesikta deRav Kahana* 24:9.
114. See Malbim.
115. See Radak.
116. See Radak.
117. Ibn Ezra; Radak.
118. See Rashi.
119. Rashi.
120. Malbim.
121. See II Kings 14:25.
122. See Malbim.
123. See Radak; *Metzudat David*.
124. See Ramban, Deuteronomy 3:9; commentary on Psalms 42:7.
125. Radak; see commentary on Genesis 36:24.
126. See *Metzudat David*.
127. See Ralbag; Malbim, 5:30; II Chronicles 26:17.
128. See Radak here and verse 27; Malbim, verse 30; Ralbag, 10:12, "the sixth lesson"; II Kings 11–12; see also Ezra 7:1–4.
129. Exodus 6:16–19.
130. Verse 3; see Radak; Ralbag; Numbers 16:1.
131. See Radak; Ralbag.
132. See I Samuel 1:1.
133. See Rashi; Radak; Ibn Ezra, second commentary on Esther 1:9.
134. *Adderet Eliyahu*.
135. See Radak.
136. See *Metzudat David*; I Samuel 8:2.
137. See Rashi; Ralbag.
138. See Psalms 89:1; commentary on I Chronicles 2:6.
139. See Numbers 18:9.
140. See Rashi; *Adderet Eliyahu*; Joshua 21:10.
141. See commentary on Joshua 14:13–14.
142. Joshua 20:7.
143. See, e.g., Numbers 18:20–24, 35:1–5; Deuteronomy 10:9, 12:12, 14:27–29.
144. See I Kings 2:26; Jeremiah 1:1, 32:7.
145. *Metzudat David*.
146. See Deuteronomy 4:43.
147. See Ralbag; Malbim; Joshua 21.
148. See II Samuel 24.
149. *Metzudat David*.
150. See Rashi; Ralbag.
151. See Radak; Malbim.
152. 7:7; see Radak.
153. See Rashi.
154. See Malbim.
155. See Malbim.
156. See Radak; *Adderet Eliyahu*.
157. See Radak; *Metzudat David*.
158. See Numbers 27:1–11.
159. See *Adderet Eliyahu*; *Da'at Mikra*.
160. Numbers 1:10.
161. See Genesis 46:17; Numbers 26:46.
162. See *Sota* 13a; *Pirkei deRabbi Eliezer* 48; *Yalkut Shimoni*, *Shemuel*, 152.
163. See Rashi.
164. See Ralbag; *Metzudat David*.
165. See Genesis 46:21; Numbers 26:38–40.

166. See Radak; Ralbag.
167. See Rashi; Ralbag.
168. Radak.
169. Malbim.
170. *Metzudat David*; *Da'at Mikra*.
171. See, e.g., II Kings 8:26.
172. Joshua 18:28.
173. See Malbim; 9:37.
174. See Radak; *Metzudat David*.
175. See Radak; Malbim.
176. See I Samuel 14:50, 20:25; II Samuel 2:8, 3:6–19.
177. See Radak; Malbim; commentary on II Samuel 2:8.
178. See Radak; Ralbag; Malbim; *Shabbat* 56b.
179. *Metzudat David*.
180. See *Metzudat David*; Ralbag, II Chronicles 24:27.
181. See commentary on Joshua 9:27.
182. See II Chronicles 31:13.
183. See Radak; *Metzudat David*; *Adderet Eliyahu*.
184. See Rashi; Malbim.
185. Radak; *Metzudat David*.
186. See, e.g., Rashi; Malbim; Jerusalem Talmud, *Yoma* 1:8; *Bereshit Rabba* 60:3.
187. *Adderet Eliyahu*; Malbim.
188. See Radak; I Samuel 19:18; I Chronicles 28:11–21; *Pesaḥim* 86a; Jerusalem Talmud, *Megilla* 1:1.
189. See Rashi; *Metzudat David*.
190. *Metzudat David*.
191. See *Metzudat David*; Ralbag.
192. See *Yoma* 38a.
193. See Radak; *Metzudat David*; *Adderet Eliyahu*; *Menaḥot* 50b.
194. See Mishna *Sukka* 5; *Ta'anit* 27a; 29a; *Arakhin* 13b.
195. See II Samuel 2.
196. See II Samuel 1:6–10.
197. See Rashi, verse 12; Judges 21; I Samuel 11, and commentary ad loc.
198. See Rashi; Ralbag; I Samuel 28:16–19.
199. See I Samuel 28.
200. See Radak; *Metzudat David*; Radak, 13:2.
201. See II Samuel 4.
202. See commentary on Numbers 27:17; Deuteronomy 31:2.
203. See Malbim.
204. See Joshua 15:63; Judges 1:8, 21, and commentary ad loc.
205. See Malbim.
206. See II Samuel 5:9; I Kings 9:24.
207. See II Samuel 5:11; I Chronicles 14:1.
208. II Samuel 23.
209. See I Samuel 17:1.
210. See Rashi and Ralbag; Radak, I Samuel 23:11.
211. See Rashi; *Metzudat David*.
212. Radak.
213. See Rashi; *Metzudat David*; *Metzudat Tzion*.
214. See Rashi; *Metzudat David*.
215. See Rashi and Malbim; II Samuel 20:23; Radak, II Samuel 23:23.
216. See Malbim.
217. II Samuel 2:18–23.
218. See commentary on II Samuel 4:2.
219. See commentary on I Samuel 14:1.
220. See Joshua 15:31; I Samuel 27:6.
221. *Metzudat David*.
222. See Rashi; Radak.
223. See Malbim; Judges 3:15; Judges 20:16, and commentary ad loc.
224. See II Chronicles 14:7.
225. Rashi.
226. *Targum*.
227. See I Samuel 22:2.
228. Malbim.
229. Ralbag.
230. See *Metzudat David*.
231. See Rambam, *Guide of the Perplexed* 2:45.
232. See *Metzudat David*; Malbim; II Samuel 17:25.
233. See *Metzudat David*; Malbim.
234. See, e.g., Genesis 25:18; I Samuel 29:3; Jeremiah 37:13.
235. I Samuel 29–30.
236. See Rashi; *Metzudat David*.
237. See Rashi and Radak, 27:5.
238. See Numbers 16:2.
239. See *Targum*; Radak; *Adderet Eliyahu*; *Bereshit Rabba* 72:5; *Eruvin* 100b; *Yoma* 26a.
240. See Rashi; Radak.
241. See Radak; *Metzudat David*.
242. I Samuel 4:11–22, chap. 6.
243. Malbim.
244. See Rashi; Malbim.
245. See Numbers 7:9, and commentary ad loc.; commentary on I Samuel 4:4.
246. Rashi; I Samuel 6:11.
247. See *Metzudat David*.
248. See Exodus 19:22.
249. See Rashi; 15:24.
250. See *Adderet Eliyahu*; Jerusalem Talmud, *Yevamot* 4:12; *Berakhot* 63b–64a; *Shir HaShirim Rabba* 2:18; see also I Chronicles 26:4–8, and commentaries ad loc.
251. See *Metzudat David*.
252. See Rashi.
253. See, e.g., Deuteronomy 7:25, 12:3.
254. See Numbers 4:4–20.
255. Numbers 7:9.
256. See, e.g., Psalms 50:1, 88:1, 89:1.
257. See Rashi.
258. See Rashi; Psalms 46:1.
259. See Ralbag.
260. See *Metzudat David*.
261. See Radak; Ralbag; *Metzudat David*; *Metzudat Tzion*; Malbim; Rashi, 29:25.
262. See Radak; *Metzudat David*.
263. See Rashi; Radak; *Adderet Eliyahu*.
264. See Rashi; commentary on Exodus 28:6.
265. See *Metzudat David*; commentary on II Samuel 6:21.
266. See Rashi; *Metzudat David*; *Pesaḥim* 36b; commentary on II Samuel 6:19.
267. See Rashi; Malbim; commentary on Psalms 38:1.
268. See, e.g., II Samuel 22:1; Psalms 3:1, 18:1.
269. See Rashi; Radak; Ralbag; Ralbag, 29:29.
270. See *Metzudat David*.
271. See Rashi; *Metzudat David*; Genesis 12:20, 26:11.
272. Rashi; *Metzudat David*; see Genesis 20:7.
273. See Radak; Rashi, verse 34; Psalms 96.
274. See commentary on Leviticus 19:4.
275. *Metzudat David*.
276. See Rashi.
277. See I Kings 3:4; II Chronicles 1:3–6.
278. See Rashi.
279. See *Bemidbar Rabba* 4:20.
280. See *Yoma* 69b.
281. See Jerusalem Talmud, *Pesaḥim* 5:10.
282. See Radak.
283. See Judges 1:34.
284. See Rashi.
285. See I Kings 7:15–16.
286. See Rashi; verse 3.
287. See *Gittin* 8a; Jerusalem Talmud, *Pe'a* 7:5; commentary on II Samuel 10:18.
288. See Radak; *Da'at Mikra*.
289. See Rashi; *Bemidbar Rabba* 14; *Tanḥuma*, Buber edition, *Vayera* 25.
290. See I Samuel 11.
291. II Samuel 10:4.
292. See Ralbag.
293. II Samuel 10:16; see *Sota* 42b.
294. See II Samuel 12:26–30.
295. See Radak.
296. See Rashi.
297. See Radak.
298. I Samuel 17.
299. See Radak.
300. See 27:1, 23–24.
301. See commentary on I Samuel 11:8 and on II Samuel 2:10.
302. See Rashi; *Metzudat David*; *Metzudat Tzion*.
303. See Malbim.
304. See I Samuel 22:5; II Chronicles 29:25.
305. See *Metzudat David*.
306. See Rambam, *Guide of the Perplexed* 2:42.
307. See *Metzudat David*; Malbim.
308. See Rashi; *Metzudat David*.
309. See II Chronicles 3:1.
310. See I Kings 6:7; *Sota* 48b.
311. See Rashi.
312. See Radak; *Metzudat David*, 28:3–4.
313. See *Metzudat David*; Malbim.
314. See 26:31, and Rashi and Radak ad loc.
315. I Kings 1:11–40.
316. See Ralbag; II Samuel 24:10.
317. See Numbers 4:3.
318. See Radak; Ralbag; *Metzudat David*; *Adderet Eliyahu*.
319. Radak; *Metzudat David*.
320. See commentary on Genesis 20:12.
321. See Radak.
322. *Metzudat David*.
323. See Numbers 3:7.
324. See I Kings 2:27; commentary on Numbers 25:13; commentary on I Samuel 2:30.
325. See *Berakhot* 12a; *Sukka* 55b–56a; *Ta'anit* 27a.
326. See Radak.
327. See I Samuel 2:30–36; Ezekiel 44:15.
328. See *Sukka* 55b; *Ta'anit* 27b.
329. See, e.g., Exodus 28:1; Leviticus 8:8–9; Numbers 25:13.
330. See *Metzudat David*; Malbim.
331. Rambam, *Sefer Avoda*, *Hilkhot Kelei HaMikdash* 3:9.
332. Malbim; Rashi, 25:8; Radak, 25:1.
333. See Radak; Malbim.
334. See Rashi; Malbim.
335. Rashi; Radak.
336. Rashi; Radak; *Metzudat David*; *Metzudat Tzion*.
337. *Metzudat David*.
338. See Ralbag; Radak.
339. See *Metzudat David*.

340. See Rashi; Malbim; *Zevaḥim* 55b; Ramban, Genesis 30:20.
341. See Malbim.
342. See Rashi; *Metzudat David*; Malbim.
343. See Radak, verse 25.
344. *Metzudat David*.
345. See commentary on I Samuel 11:7.
346. See Ralbag; *Metzudat David*.
347. See Rashi; Radak.
348. See Ralbag; *Metzudat David*; 21:1–7.
349. See Judges 7:15.
350. See Rashi; Radak; *Metzudat David*.
351. See Ralbag; *Berakhot* 3b.
352. See Genesis 49:8–10; I Chronicles 5:2; commentary on Joshua 14:6.
353. See I Kings 1:13.
354. See II Samuel 12:24–25; Nehemiah 13:26.
355. See I Kings 3:14; see also II Chronicles 6:16.
356. Rashi; Radak.
357. See Rashi; Radak; 9:22, 28:19.
358. See I Kings 7:49; *Menaḥot* 99a, and Rashi, Rabbeinu Gershom Meor HaGola, and *Keren Ora* ad loc.; *Meshekh Ḥokhma*, beginning of *Parashat Tetzaveh*.
359. See Radak; Malbim.
360. See Rashi; Radak.
361. See Exodus 25:29, and Rashi ad loc.
362. See *Sukka* 48b; Ibn Ezra, Exodus 25:29.
363. See Rashi; Radak; Malbim; *Menaḥot* 7b; Rav Se'adya Gaon, Ezra 1:7.
364. See commentary on Ezekiel 10:15, 18.
365. See Radak; commentary on I Kings 11:41.
366. See Rashi; Ralbag; Malbim.
367. Radak.
368. Ralbag.
369. See also Psalms 102:12, 144:4.
370. See Rashi.
371. See Radak.
372. See II Chronicles 1:12.
373. See *Metzudat David*; commentary on II Samuel 5:5.
374. See Rashi.
375. See Rashi; *Metzudat David*; Malbim.

II Chronicles

1. See commentary on I Chronicles 16:39.
2. See Malbim.
3. See Numbers 27:17; Deuteronomy 31:2; Joshua 14:11; I Samuel 18:13–16; I Kings 3:7.
4. Ralbag.
5. See Radak.
6. See commentary on I Chronicles 27:28.
7. See Rashi; Radak.
8. See *Metzudat David*; *Da'at Mikra*.
9. See Radak.
10. See I Kings 11:26–28.
11. *Metzudat David*.
12. See Rashi; *Metzudat David*.
13. Ezekiel 45:14.
14. See *Metzudat David*.
15. See I Kings 5:23.
16. *Metzudat David*.
17. See I Chronicles 21:28–22:1.
18. See Radak; Ralbag; *Metzudat David*.
19. See *Metzudat David*.
20. See Ralbag.
21. Rashi; Radak.
22. See Rashi; *Yoma* 45a.
23. See Radak.
24. See Radak; *Metzudat David*.
25. See Rashi.
26. See Radak; *Metzudat David*; I Kings 6:21.
27. See Radak; *Metzudat David*.
28. See Exodus 27:1, 38:1.
29. See Rashi; Radak; *Eiruvin* 14b.
30. I Kings 7:38.
31. See I Kings 7:39.
32. See *Pesaḥim* 109b; Rambam, *Sefer Avoda*, *Hilkhot Biat HaMikdash* 5:15–16.
33. See Rashi; *Metzudat David*; Malbim, verse 19; *Menaḥot* 99a, and Rashi and Rabbeinu Gershom Meor HaGola ad loc.; *Meshekh Ḥokhma*, beginning of *Tetzaveh*.
34. See *Metzudat David*; Radak, I Kings 7:39.
35. See I Kings 7:27–38.
36. See commentaries; commentary on I Kings 7:49; *Yoma* 45a.
37. See Rashi; Radak.
38. See Kings 7:50.
39. See Exodus 12:2.
40. Exodus 25:14.
41. See Radak.
42. See Radak; *Yoma* 54a.
43. *Metzudat David*.
44. See I Kings 8:22.
45. See Rashi.
46. *Metzudat David*.
47. *Metzudat David*; Rashi, I Kings 8:35.
48. *Metzudat David*.
49. See I Kings 8:63.
50. See Rashi; Radak.
51. See Rashi; *Zevaḥim* 59a.
52. See I Kings 5:1.
53. See Radak; I Kings 8:65; *Moed Katan* 9a.
54. See Rashi; Malbim.
55. I Kings 9:10–13.
56. See Malbim.
57. See commentary on I Chronicles 7:24.
58. See I Kings 11:1.
59. See commentary on I Chronicles 1:21, 29:4.
60. See Rashi; Malbim.
61. Radak; Malbim.
62. Rashi.
63. See Rashi; *Yoma* 44b–45a; *Ḥullin* 30b; Jerusalem Talmud, *Yoma* 4:4.
64. See Rashi; I Kings 7:1–2.
65. *Da'at Mikra*.
66. See Rashi; Radak.
67. See I Kings 11:26–40.
68. See Rashi.
69. See Rashi.
70. II Samuel 20:1.
71. See Rashi; II Samuel 20:24.
72. See I Kings 12:20.
73. See *Metzudat David*.
74. See Judges 18.
75. See Leviticus 17:7, and commentary ad loc.
76. See I Kings 12:28.
77. See I Kings 12:31.
78. *Targum*; Rashi; Radak.
79. See Rav Se'adya Gaon; *Da'at Mikra*.
80. See Radak.
81. See Radak; Ralbag.
82. Ralbag; see Malbim.
83. See *Metzudat David*; Malbim.
84. See introduction to Isaiah.
85. See 11:20, and commentary ad loc.
86. I Kings 15:3.
87. See commentary on Isaiah 34:16.
88. See *Metzudat David*; *Metzudat Tzion*; Rashi, Leviticus 26:30.
89. See Judges 20:16; I Chronicles 8:40, 12:2; Rashi, I Chronicles 10:3; II Chronicles 17:17.
90. See Rashi.
91. See Radak; see also commentary on Genesis 20:12.
92. See Jeremiah 37:13; I Chronicles 12:20.
93. I Kings 15:25–29.
94. See I Chronicles 6:45.
95. See II Kings 13:7, 23:22.
96. See Rashi; commentary on Jeremiah 20:2.
97. See *Metzudat David*.
98. See Rashi.
99. See Radak; *Metzudat David*; Jeremiah 34:5, and commentary ad loc.; *Avoda Zara* 11a.
100. See commentary on I Samuel 10:27.
101. See Ralbag; Vilna Gaon.
102. See Malbim; *Ḥullin* 4b.
103. Rashi; see 18:21.
104. See *Ḥullin* 5a.
105. See *Metzudat David*; commentaries on Exodus 9:22 and Isaiah 20:2; introduction to Ezekiel 12 and Jeremiah 13.
106. See *Metzudat David*.
107. See Rashi.
108. I Kings 22:35–40.
109. Psalms 82:1.
110. See Deuteronomy 17:8–13; commentary on Deuteronomy 21:5; Malachi 2:1–9; *Sanhedrin* 88b.
111. See Rashi; *Metzudat David*.
112. See Deuteronomy 17:8.
113. See Rashi; Radak.
114. See *Metzudat David*; Malbim, 20:23.
115. See introduction to Isaiah 58.
116. See Radak; *Meshekh Ḥokhma*, *Naso* 5:2.
117. See Rashi; *Metzudat David*; 14:10.
118. I Kings 8:22–53.
119. See Rashi; *Metzudat David*.
120. See commentary on Exodus 9:3.
121. See *Da'at Mikra*, 20:2.
122. See Numbers 20:14–21; Deuteronomy 2; Judges 11:18.
123. See Numbers 16:27.

124. See I Chronicles 6:24.
125. See, e.g., Psalms 42:1, 44:1–49:1.
126. See *Metzudat David*.
127. See *Metzudat David*.
128. See *Metzudat David*, 20:1; Malbim, 20:22; commentary on Genesis 27:40.
129. See *Metzudat David*.
130. See Radak; *Metzudat David*.
131. *Targum*; *Metzudat David*.
132. See Rashi.
133. See Radak; *Seder Olam Rabba* 17.
134. See Radak; Malbim.
135. See Malbim.
136. See Rashi; Radak; Malbim; *Seder Olam Rabba* 17.
137. Rashi.
138. See II Kings 9–10.
139. II Kings 11:2.
140. See Rashi; 22:12; *Shir HaShirim Rabba* 1:2.
141. *Metzudat David*.
142. See Radak.
143. See *Metzudat David*; Song of Songs 4:4.
144. See Rashi; Radak; *Metzudat David*.
145. See, e.g., Rashi.
146. See Malbim.
147. See Malbim.
148. See Rashi; verses 22, 25.
149. See Rashi; Radak.
150. *Metzudat David*; *Metzudat Tzion*.
151. See Isaiah 15:7.
152. Rashi; *Metzudat David*.
153. See Rashi; Ralbag.
154. See Radak; Malbim; *Tanḥuma, Va'era* 9.
155. *Metzudat David*.
156. See Ralbag; *Da'at Mikra*.
157. Radak.
158. See commentary on I Chronicles 18:5.
159. See Radak.
160. See Ralbag; commentary on I Chronicles 9:1.
161. See Deuteronomy 24:16.
162. Radak; *Seder Olam Rabba* 20.
163. See Rashi; Malbim.
164. See commentary on I Chronicles 18:12.
165. See Rashi; Malbim.
166. See commentary on I Chronicles 14:1.
167. See Rashi; *Metzudat David*.
168. See Rashi; *Metzudat David*.
169. See *Metzudat David*.
170. See Rashi; *Metzudat David*.
171. *Metzudat David*.
172. See commentary on I Chronicles 8:13.
173. See commentary on I Samuel 10:27.
174. See Rashi; Ralbag; *Metzudat David*; *Metzudat Tzion*; Malbim.
175. See *Tanna deVei Eliyahu Rabba* 19.
176. Rashi.
177. See Radak; *Metzudat David*.
178. See *Metzudat David*; II Kings 15:35.
179. See Malbim; Isaiah 7:1.
180. See Malbim.
181. See *Metzudat David*.
182. See commentary on I Chronicles 6:54.
183. See Radak; Ralbag.
184. See *Megilla* 11a; see also Isaiah 7; *Sanhedrin* 104a; Jerusalem Talmud, *Sanhedrin* 10:1.
185. See, e.g., II Kings 18; Isaiah 36.
186. See Isaiah 38:3; commentary on Isaiah 38:2; introduction to Isaiah 38.
187. See *Metzudat Tzion*.
188. See Rashi; Radak; Ralbag.
189. See Ralbag.
190. See *Metzudat David*.
191. See Leviticus 1.
192. See also Rashi; Malbim.
193. See Leviticus 4.
194. See Leviticus 4.
195. See, e.g., Leviticus 1:5.
196. See I Chronicles 21:9.
197. See Rashi; Ralbag; *Metzudat David*.
198. See commentary on I Chronicles 25:2.
199. See *Berakhot* 34b.
200. See Rashi; Ralbag; *Metzudat David*.
201. See Rashi; Malbim.
202. See Radak; Malbim; *Sanhedrin* 12b.
203. See Numbers 9:1–14.
204. See Rashi; *Metzudat David*.
205. See Judges 8:1, and commentary ad loc., 12:1; Isaiah 9:8, 28:1.
206. See Rashi; Ralbag; *Metzudat David*; *Metzudat Tzion*.
207. See Rashi.
208. See Rashi; *Metzudat David*; Leviticus 1:5; *Zevaḥim* 32a.
209. Radak.
210. See *Metzudat David*; see also *Menaḥot* 16b; 78b.
211. See Ralbag.
212. See I Kings 8:65.
213. See Rashi; Ralbag; *Metzudat David*.
214. See Rashi; Radak.
215. See Rashi; *Metzudat David*.
216. See Rashi.
217. See I Chronicles 9:20.
218. See Malbim.
219. See commentary on II Kings 18:13.
220. See Deuteronomy 12:11–18.
221. See *Metzudat David*.
222. See Isaiah 38.
223. See *Metzudat David*; Malbim.
224. See *Metzudat David*.
225. See Ralbag; Malbim.
226. See *Targum*.
227. See Rashi; Radak; Malbim.
228. II Chronicles 32:24.
229. Rashi; *Metzudat David*.
230. See Rashi; Radak; *Metzudat David*; *Bava Kamma* 16b.
231. See I Kings 7:12; Ezekiel 8:16.
232. See Deuteronomy 18:10–11.
233. Rashi; Radak.
234. *Da'at Mikra*.
235. *Metzudat David*.
236. Radak; Malbim.
237. See *Sanhedrin* 103b.
238. Malbim.
239. Rashi.
240. See Rashi, Leviticus 26:30; II Kings 23:5, 11.
241. *Metzudat David*.
242. See *Metzudat David*; commentary on II Kings 23:6, 16; commentary on Jeremiah 7:32.
243. Ralbag.
244. See *Metzudat David*.
245. See commentary on Isaiah 36:2; commentary on II Kings 25:22.
246. See Ralbag; II Kings 22:4, and *Targum* and Radak ad loc.
247. See Rashi; Ralbag.
248. *Metzudat Tzion*.
249. See Malbim.
250. See Rashi.
251. See Rashi; Radak; *Tosefta*, *Sota* 13.
252. See Radak.
253. See *Megilla* 14b.
254. See commentary on Jeremiah 28:8.
255. See *Metzudat David*.
256. See Rashi.
257. Exodus 12:6; Leviticus 23:5; Numbers 9:3, 28:16.
258. See *Metzudat David*.
259. See *Metzudat David*; Malbim.
260. See Rashi; Malbim.
261. Exodus 12:3.
262. See *Metzudat David*.
263. See Deuteronomy 16:2, and commentary ad loc.
264. See Ralbag; Exodus 12:9; Deuteronomy 16:7, and Rashi and commentary ad loc.
265. See I Chronicles 25:2, 4, and commentary ad loc.; II Chronicles 29:30.
266. See Rashi; Radak; Malbim.
267. See Radak; *Metzudat David*; *Ta'anit* 22b.
268. See *Metzudat David*.
269. See Rashi; *Metzudat David*.
270. See II Kings 23:35.
271. Jeremiah 22:10.
272. Radak.
273. See I Chronicles 3:15; commentary on Jeremiah 22:11; see *Horayot* 11a.
274. II Kings 24:1.
275. See Rashi; Radak.
276. Malbim.
277. See Radak; Jeremiah 22:13–19, 36:27–31.
278. See Radak; Malbim; II Kings 24:8.
279. See II Kings 25:27–30.
280. See commentary on Genesis 20:12.
281. II Kings 24:17.
282. See Jeremiah 37–38.
283. See Jeremiah 38:14–27; commentary on Jeremiah 23:6; II Kings 24:19.
284. See Rashi; *Yoma* 52b; commentary on Ezra 1:11.
285. See II Kings 25:7; Jeremiah 39:6–7, 52:10–11.
286. See Jeremiah 25:11–12, 29:10.
287. See *Megilla* 11b.

Credits

All images are copyright © Koren Publishers Jerusalem Ltd., except:

PSALMS

p4 upper image © Jarrod; **p4** lower image © Ryan Kilpatrick; **p5** left image © Jun; **p5** right image © public domain; **p6** © garycycles8; **p9** © Joe Mabel; **p10** right image © public domain; **p10** left image © Tropenmuseum, part of the National Museum of World Cultures; **p12** © public domain; **p14** left image © public domain; **p14** center image © Josh Hallett; **p14** right image © Nick Hobgood; **p16** © Gene DiGiovine; **p18** left image © public domain; **p23** © Fée des rêves; **p25** © Bresson Thomas; **p26** left image © Arne Hückelheim; **p26** upper right image © Gift of British Museum/Eric Gaba; **p26** lower right image © Steve Slater - Wildlife Encounters; **p28** © Les Chatfield; **p30** © public domain; **p31** © TheRichic; **p32** left image © public domain; **p32** right image © Walt Stoneburner; **p34** upper image © Josh Plueger; **p34** center image © Marcus Sümnick from Rostock, Germany; **p34** lower image © Evgeni Dinev from Burgas, Bulgaria; **p36** © **courtesy of the Temple Institute**; **p38** © HaRav Menachem Makover, courtesy of *Harenu Bevinyano*; **p40** © Ursus; **p42** left image © BlingBling10; **p42** upper right image © mykaul; **p42** lower right image © Hanay; **p44** © Lior Golgher • ליאור גולגר; **p46** left image © josefstuefer; **p46** right image © carterse; **p48** © public domain; **p52** © יוחנן בן יעקב; **p60** left image © OXLAEY.com; **p60** right image © Carole Raddato; **p62** © public domain; **p64** upper left image © ד״ר אבישי טייכר; **p64** lower left image © public domain; **p66** © Вых Пыхманн; **p68** coin image © Tallenna tiedosto; **p68** painting image © public domain; **p68** myrrh image © shutterstock-50234665; **p68** aloes image © public domain; **p68** cassia image © Simon A. Eugster; **p70** © public domain; **p72** © Elie plus at English Wikipedia; **p75** © public domain; **p77** © Benjamin Shafir; **p78** upper image © Zev Rothkoff; **p78** lower image © public domain; **p80** © Ian Burt; **p83** © Snapshots Of The Past; **p84** left image © Janmad; **p84** upper right image © Wolfgang Sauber; **p84** lower right image © Ji-Elle; **p86** left image © Tambako the Jaguar; **p86** right image © Tony Alter; **p92** © Jean & Nathalie; **p94** upper image © CIMMYT; **p94** lower image © Ggia; **p96** © public domain; **p97** © public domain; **p98** © Ted Rabbitts; **p100** upper image © Dave_S.; **p100** lower image © altonwoods; **p101** © public domain; **p102** © public domain; **p110** © public domain; **p112** © public domain; **p114** © public domain; **p116** upper image © Vmenkov; **p116** lower image © public domain; **p112** © משה רענן; **p122** left image © public domain; **p122** right image © Dynamosquito; **p125** left image © finaldarkworld; **p125** right image © public domain; **p126** © RSCF/www.rarespecies.org; **p132** left image © אלי זהבי, כפר תבור; **p132** right image © public domain; **p136** © C messier; **p137** © public domain; **p138** center image © Dan Lundberg; **p138** right image © jacinta lluch valero from Madrid * Barcelona, Spain; **p144** left image © public domain; **p144** right image © Neitram; **p146** left image © Frank Vassen from Brussels, Belgium; **p146** right image © Trebol-a, modified by Stemonitis; **p148** © Anthere; **p149** © Stefan Krause; **p150** left image © public domain; **p150** right image © public domain; **p152** donkey image © Catatine; **p152** robin image © public domain; **p152** stork image © public domain; **p152** ibex image © public domain; **p152** hyrax image © Mike Bannert; **p154** left image © iStock_000006755209; **p154** right image © Steven W. Dengler; **p156** © Zürich, Braginsky Collection, B317, f. 29; **p159** © public domain; **p160** © Daniel; **p162** © public domain; **p163** © Joe Goldberg; **p171** left image © Smichael21; **p171** right image © louise.helen; **p192** © public domain; **p193** left image © public domain; **p193** right image © public domain; **p194** upper right image © public domain; **p194** left image © shutterstock photo ID: 171932099; **p194** lower right image © Ian Scott; **p196** © Osama Shukir Muhammed Amin FRCP(Glasg) (modified); **p198** © תמר מרום Pikiwiki Israel; **p202** left image © public domain; **p202** center image © sagesolar; **p202** right image © Photograph by Mike Peel (www.mikepeel.net); **p204** left image © Anthony DeLorenzo; **p204** right image © public domain; **p208** left image © HaRav Menachem Makover, courtesy of *Harenu Bevinyano*; **p212** © Diganta Talukdar; **p216** left image © public domain; **p216** right image © Pille Vahtmäe; **p217** left image © public domain; **p217** right image © Darkone; **p218** upper image © Serge Melki; **p218** right image © public domain; **p220** left image © Jan Klimeš; **p220** upper right image © Carole Raddato; **p220** lower right image © Marsyas

PROVERBS

p226 left image © Sailko; **p228** © public domain; **p230** © Hanay; **p232** lower image © James St. John; **p233** left image © derrico_jewelry; **p233** right image © Mauro Cateb; **p236** © public domain; **p238** wormwood image © Karelj; **p238** sword image © public domain; **p238** cistern image © ליאור גולגר • Lior Golgher; **p238** well image © Liadmalone; **p238** Ein Bokek image © ש.י. at Hebrew Wikipedia; **p238** doe image © Marek Szczepanek; **p238** ibex image © Chmee2; **p240** left image © unbekannt, Maler im Alten Ägypten; **p240** right image © public domain; **p242** upper image © Fée des rêves; **p242** lower image © Rama; **p244** myrrh image © shutterstock-50234665; **p244** aloe image © public domain; **p244** iceplant image © Frank Vincentz; **p244** cinnamon image © Simon A. Eugster; **p244** purse image © Wolfgang Sauber; **p244** snare image © Pavla Štrukelj/public domain, colorized; **p248** © צילום: אילנה שקולניק; **p252** © public domain; **p254** © Chamberi; **p256** upper image © Richard New Forest; **p256** lower image © public domain; **p262** © public domain; **p266** left image © Krishna Bhagavatula; **p266** right image © Bernard Gagnon; **p268** © Chamberi; **p269** © public domain; **p271** © H005; **p272** left image © public domain; **p272** right image © Alpenglowmt; **p274** © nava harel Pikiwiki Israel; **p275** © public domain; **p277** left image © mhx from London, United Kingdom; **p277** right image © public domain; **p282** © public domain; **p284** © public domain; **p288** © public domain; **p290** pit image © Georg Waßmuth; **p290** well image © public domain; **p290** viper image © גיא חיימוביץ; **p290** adder image © By Maria Dryfhout. https://www.shutterstock com/image-photo/sneaky-snake-grass-6,187,160; **p290** relief drowning image © Sailko; **p290** mast image © public domain; **p292** © Edominguez6257; **p294** © public domain; **p296** gold ring image © Johnbod; **p296** clouds image © public domain; **p296** honey image © public domain; **p296** arrow image © Clara Amit, Yoram

Lehmann, Yael Yolovitch, Miki Koren, and Mariana Salzberger, courtesy of the Israel Antiquities Authority; **p298** swallow image © Dr. Raju Kasambe; **p298** sparrow image © Richard Hurd; **p298** horse image © Zde; **p298** bit image © Jean; **p300** © Stephen Dann; **p302** © public domain; **p303** upper image © shutterstock_322554950; **p303** lower image © Wildlife Encounters Ltd; **p304** upper image © José-Manuel Benito Álvarez; **p304** lower image © public domain; **p312** leech image © Brian Gratwicke from DC, USA; **p312** raven image © Henrike Mühlichen; **p312** eagle image © Matthias Kabel; **p312** serpent image © public domain; **p312** ship image © public domain; **p312** ant image © public domain; **p314** hyrax image © Mike Bannert; **p314** locust image © Universidad Autónoma de Madrid, modified; **p314** gecko image © James St. John; **p314** hunting dog image © Karen Green; **p314** goats image © Andrzej Otrębski; **p316** left image © distelfliege; **p316** right image © Florian Gerlach (Nawaro); **p317** left image © Daniel P. Diffendale; **p318** field image © public domain; **p318** vineyard image © public domain; **p318** distaff image © public domain; **p318** scarlet wool image © Thomas Quine

JOB

p328 © public domain; **p330** © public domain; **p332** © Frederick L Faulkner III; **p334** upper image © Clemson University - USDA Cooperative Extension Slide Series, Bugwood.org; **p334** lower image © tronics; **p336** leopard image © יוסי אוד; **p336** Samaria image © Netanel h; **p336** sheaves image © Mark Robinson; **p337** left image © Asim Patel; **p337** right image © public domain; **p338** bull mallow image © Krzysztof Ziarnek, Kenraiz; **p338** alkanet image © James Gaither; **p338** marsh mallow image © André Karwath aka Aka; **p338** saltbush image © Mark Marathon; **p338** seablite image © Dinesh Valke; **p338** flooding image © Lehava Kiryat Shmona Pikiwiki Israel; **p338** convoy image © public domain; **p340** © VladimirZhV; **p342** left image © pjt56; **p342** right image © public domain; **p344** upper image © public domain; **p344** lower image © theilr; **p346** reed boat image © public domain; **p346** vulture image © ליאור כסלו; **p346** soapwort image © Hectonichus; **p346** cheese image © public domain; **p348** © Richard Keatinge; **p354** left image © public domain; **p354** upper right image © public domain; **p354** lower right image © צבי שפלטר; **p356** © public domain; **p358** left image © Slippy Slappy; **p358** right image © H. Zell; **p361** © Rémih; **p362** left image © Didier Descouens; **p362** right image © Dan Eckert; **p364** © צבי ספלטר; **p366** upper image © public domain; **p366** lower image © Bernard DUPONT; **p368** birthing image © Rama; **p368** goats image © louise.helen; **p368** drum image © This image was given courtesy of Israel Antiquities Authority/Wikipedia; **p368** harp image © public domain; **p368** pipe image © public domain; **p368** chaff image © Ryan Kilpatrick; **p368** udders image © public domain; **p369** © Dalius Baranauskas; **p374** upper image © A.Poulos (Iya); **p374** lower image © יוחנן בן יעקב; **p378** upper right image © יוחנן בן יעקב; **p378** lower left image © פזיה מילר; **p378** lower right image © public domain; **p380** silver ore image © James St. John; **p380** gold ore image © John St. John; **p380** iron-rich dust image © public domain; **p380** copper ore image © Daniel Schwen; **p380** lava image © public domain; **p380** bonelli's eagle image © Mike Prince; **p380** imperial eagle image © AngMoKio; **p380** honey buzzard image © Доктор рукиноги; **p380** flinty rock image © David J Coombes; **p382** onyx image © Leica; **p382** sapphire crystal image © Géry Parent; **p382** glass vessel image © public domain; **p382** crystal image © Sopivnik I.; **p382** peridot image © Rob Lavinsky, iRocks.com – CC-BY-SA-3.0; **p384** © public domain; **p385** © Don DeBold/donjd2@yahoo.com; **p386** saltbush image © Krzysztof Ziarnek, Kenraiz; **p386** saltwort image © Isidre blanc; **p386** broom image © Frank Vincentz; **p386** caves image © Joe Goldberg; **p388** left image © Вых Пыхманн; **p388** center image © marja kingma; **p388** right image © Muhamad Alfilastini; **p390** left image © Jorge Íñiguez Yarza; **p390** center image © Sleepy Claus; **p390** right image © Arthur Chapman; **p398** © Wolfgang Sauber; **p400** © public domain; **p402** © Wellcome Images; **p404** © public domain; **p406** rooster image © HaleyDara; **p406** clouds image © public domain; **p406** lion image © Gene DeGiovine; **p406** crow image © kees torn; **p406** young image © Pille Vahtmäe; **p406** ibex image © Paul Asman and Jill Lenoble; **p407** left image © Alexxx1979; **p407** right image © public domain, XenonX3; **p408** oxen image © public domain; **p408** ostrich image © ponizej; **p408** archer image © Osama Shukir Muhammed Amin FRCP(Glasg); **p408** hawk image © Dr. Raju Kasambe; **p410** left image © Karunakar Rayker; **p410** right image © public domain; **p411** © Dr. Avishai Teicher Pikiwiki Israel; **p412** right image © Ilkka Jukarainen; **p414** steam image © Brian Hoffman; **p414** millstones image © Chaojoker; **p414** arrows image © Photograph by Mike Peel (www.mikepeel.net); **p414** slingshots image © Photograph by Mike Peel (www.mikepeel.net); **p415** © Deror avi; **p416** bull image © Photo: Myrabella / Wikimedia Commons / CC BY-SA 3.0 & GFDL; **p416** ram image © Andreas Krappweis; **p416** sheep image © SuperJew; **p416** nose rings image © Johnbod

THE SONG OF SONGS

p422 © Etan J. Tal; **p424** lower left image © Myrabella / Wikimedia Commons / CC BY-SA 3.0; **p424** right image © Ippolito Rosellini, Bodleian Libraries, Oxford University; **p425** both images © public domain; **p426** lavender image © Veronique Pagnier; **p426** pendant image © public domain; **p426** myrrh image © Vladimir Melnik https://www.shutterstock.com; **p426** henna image © Tu7uh; **p426** date flower image © Корниенко Виктор; **p426** daffodil image © Zeynel Cebeci; **p426** lily image © Habib M'henni / Wikimedia Commons; **p426** apple tree image © public domain; **p428** upper left image © Ettore Balocchi; **p428** upper right image © Umberto Nicoletti; **p428** lower image © public domain; **p430** nightingale image © Frebeck; **p430** turtledove image © Paco Gómez; **p430** fig tress image © Steve Slater; **p430** dove image © public domain; **p430** jackal image © Shubhamjaincan; **p430** fox image © I, Malene; **p430** mountain image © Bukvoed; **p432** frankincense image © Peter Presslein, modified by Meco; **p432** altar © HaRav Menachem Makover, courtesy of *Harenu Bevinyano*; **p432** crown image © I, Sailko; **p434** dove image © public domain; **p434** goats image © public domain; **p434** pomegranate image © Noa Fisher Pikiwiki Israel; **p434** pendant image © Fabien Dany - www.fabiendany.com / www.datka.kg; **p434** fawn image © public domain; **p436** hermon image © mykaul; **p436** lebanon image © rabiem22; **p436** sealed spring image © Deror Avi; **p436** pomegranate image © public domain; **p436** saffron image © Serpico; **p436** cinnamon image © Simon A. Eugster; **p436** frankincense tree image © Mauro Raffaelli; **p436** aloe tree image © public domain; **p438** upper left image © Luc Viatour / Lucnix.be; **p438** lower left image © public domain; **p438** right image © Waugsberg; **p440** dove image © public domain; **p440** aquamarine image © Kopytin Georgy https://www.shutterstock.com; **p440** ivory image © Dominik Matus; **p440** peridot image © Erik Lernestål; **p440** sapphire image © thisisbossi; **p440** field-bed image © Laslovarga; **p441** © Tamara from Hebrew Wikipedia, modified; **p442** dawn image © public domain; **p442** fruits image © Victor Korniyenko; **p442** dates image © משה רענן; **p442** pomegranate image © public domain; **p442** necklace image © public domain;

p442 pile image © Dûrzan cîrano; **p444** carmel image © ד"ר אבישי טייכר; **p444** headdress image © I, Sailko; **p444** date palms trees image © public domain; **p444** date palm branches © Kakkara; **p444** clusters image © Roberto Vertzo; **p444** grape bud image © Stojanoski Slave; **p444** mandrakes image © tato grasso; **p446** left image © Christopher, Tania and Isabelle Luna; **p446** upper right image © Museo nazionale di Ravenna; **p446** lower right image © Ovedc; **p448** © Tomascastelazo

RUTH

p454 lower left image © DavidB; **p458** upper image © Yann Forget / Wikimedia Commons / CC-BY-SA-3.0; **p458** lower right image © weegiboy; **p459** © Xtuv Photography https://www.shutterstock.com; **p460** upper right image © Yohanan Ben Yaakov; **p460** lower right image © Yohanan Ben Yaakov; **p462** upper left image © Tarish Khan; **p462** upper center image © Mark Robinson; **p462** upper right image © public domain - congerdesign; **p462** lower left image © Yohanan Ben Yaakov; **p463** © A. Davey from Where I Live Now: Pacific Northwest; **p466** © public domain - Daderot; **p468** © Neil Ward

LAMENTATIONS

p474 left image © Osama Shukir Muhammed Amin FRCP(Glasg); **p474** right image © Matt Neale from UK; **p476** left image © Steerpike; **p476** upper right image © Luke; **p476** lower right image © Mike Peel (www.mikepeel.net); **p478** upper image © public domain; **p478** lower left image © Carole Raddato from Frankfurt, Germany; **p478** lower right image © public domain; **p482** upper left image © Mick Talbot from Lincoln (U.K.), England; **p482** center left image © Portable Antiquities Scheme; **p482** lower left image © public domain; **p482** right image © Matt Lavin from Bozeman, Montana, USA; **p484** right image © public domain; **p486** left jackal image © Alastair Rae; **p486** left whale image © Gabriel Barathieu; **p486** lower left ostrich image © Peter Dowley from Dubai, United Arab Emirates; **p486** right sapphire image © Sapphiredge; **p486** right gem image © Mauro Cateb; **p488** left image © public domain; **p490** © kevincellis36109

ECCLESIASTES

p496 left image © public domain; **p496** center image © public domain; **p496** right image © Steve (Sids1); **p498** upper image © Shuhrataxmedov; **p498** middle image © Leonard Bentley; **p498** lower image © public domain; **p502** left image © Pacific Southwest Region 5; **p502** right image © Armando Frazao https://www.shutterstock.com; **p506** © Quinn Dombrowski; **p508** © Hanay; **p512** left image © Ann W; **p512** lower right image © Zeynel Cebeci; **p516** © CaptMondo; **p520** left seige image © public domain; **p520** upper left fish image © Conor Ashleigh, AusAID; **p520** upper right bird image © public domain; **p520** center right chariot image © public domain; **p520** lower right fly image © Sanjay Acharya; **p522** © Sarashany1234; **p524** left cloud image © public domain; **p524** left tree image © Daniel Gonzalez; **p524** right sowing image © Center for Bayanihan Economics; **p524** right pioneer image © public domain; **p526** upper image © Darren Wickham; **p526** lower image © Clara Amit, Yoram Lehmann, Yael Yolovitch, Miki Koren, and Mariana Salzberger, courtesy of the Israel Antiquities Authority

ESTHER

p536 Xerxes image © Jona Lendering, site: www.livius.org; **p536** King of Persia image © alisamii; **p536** Persian soldier image © peteropaliu; **p538** lower left image © Hansueli Krapf; **p538** right image © Siren-Com; **p542** © Philippe Chavin; **p544** right image © public domain; **p546** © Elnaz Sarbar; **p550** left image © Fabien Dany - www.fabiendany.com / www.datka.kg; **p550** right image © public domain; **p554** © public domain; **p558** left image © George Dickie; **p558** right image © public domain; **p564** © Benjamín Núñez González; **p566** © درفش کاویانی; **p570** upper image © Deror avi; **p570** lower image © Philippe Chavin (Simorg)

DANIEL

p576 left image © Osama Shukir Muhammed Amin FRCP(Glasg); **p576** right image © Hamody al-iraqi; **p584** nu chaff image© Ryan Kilpatrick; **p588** lyre image © public domain; **p588** flute image © public domain; **p588** horn image © public domain; **p588** trumpet image © public domain; **p588** santur image © public domain; **p596** © public domain; **p598** © MatthiasKabel; **p600** © public domain; **p602** upper left image © public domain; **p602** lower left image © alisamii; **p606** upper image © Joan Schuman; **p606** lower image © Hjaltland Collection; **p608** lion relief image © dynamosquito; **p608** sparks image © public domain; **p608** mountain image © public domain; **p608** wool image © CSIRO; **p609** © public domain; **p610** © Darafsh; **p612** upper left image © Newager92; **p612** lower left image © Andreas Krappweis; **p612** right image © public domain; **p614** upper image © Berthold Werner; **p614** lower image © Classical Numismatic Group, Inc. http://www.cngcoins.com; **p620** © Bjørn Christian Tørrissen; **p622** left image © Rob Lavinsky, iRocks.com – CC-BY-SA-3.0; **p622** center image © Gunnar Ries Amphibol; **p622** right image © Bresson Thomas; **p624** upper right image © Sailko; **p624** lower right image © Sailko, modified

EZRA/NEHEMIAH

p638 left image © public domain; **p639** © dynamosquito; **p640** gold vessel image © public domain; **p640** oil jug image © **courtesy of the Temple Institute**; **p640** knives image © Wellcome Images; **p640** silver image © **courtesy of the Temple Institute**; **p642** left image © Clara Amit, Yoram Lehmann, Yael Yolovitch, Miki Koren, and Mariana Salzberger, courtesy of the Israel Antiquities Authority; **p642** right image © Dvirraz; **p644** Tel el-Haditheh image © Ori~; **p644** Tel es-Sultan image © Diego Delso; **p646** nu daric image © Ancient Art & Numismatics; **p648** altar image © HaRav Menachem Makover, courtesy of *Harenu Bevinyano*; **p648** handle image © yoav dothan; **p648** craftsmen image © public domain; **p648** quarry image © public domain; **p648** sidonians image © public domain; **p648** view of Yafo image © public domain/ Jenny Bergensten; **p650** © יעל י; **p652** left image © Miguel Hermoso Cuesta; **p652** right image © Marie-Lan Nguyen / Wikimedia Commons; **p654** Ashurbanipal image © public domain; **p654** ruins of Samaria image © Anatbc1; **p654** ancient stones image © תמר הירדני; **p654** tribute relief image © Ziegler175; **p658** right image © Ariely; **p660** left image © ninara; **p660** center image © Keith Evans; **p660** right image © böhringer friedrich; **p662** © public domain; **p664** © Daderot; **p670** lakhish image © Photograph by Mike Peel (www.mikepeel.net); **p670** bronze dining image © public domain; **p670** bronze oil flask image © Clara Amit, Yoram Lehmann, Yael Yolovitch, Miki Koren, and Mariana Salzberger, courtesy of the Israel Antiquities Authority; **p670** serving vessel image © **courtesy of the Temple Institute**; **p670** gates image © מיכאל יעקובסון; **p672** © public domain; **p674** left image © Roberto Vertzo; **p674** right image © public domain; **p680** © درفش کاویانی; **p682** upper left image © Mardetanha; **p682** lower left image © Daniel Ventura; **p684** left image © public domain; **p684** right image © public domain, colorized; **p686** upper left image © Ariely; **p686** upper right image © Ranbar; **p688** upper left image © Deror_avi; **p688** lower left image © שועל; **p688** upper right image © Ar2332; **p688** lower right image © Paul Arps; **p690** © Ariely; **p692** upper image © Malene Thyssen; **p692** lower image © Ori~; **p694** upper left image © public domain; **p694** lower left image © Jakub Halun; **p694** upper right image © Arad; **p694** lower right image © Zachi Evenor; **p696** upper left image © Yelkrokoyade; **p696** lower left image © רזיה ריצ'מן; **p696** upper right image © public domain; **p696** lower right image © Deror avi; **p698** © Andreas Trepte; **p700** © **courtesy of the Temple Institute**; **p704** upper image © Emmanuel DYAN; **p704** lower left image © Hanay; **p704** lower right image © ואן-זיידן עליזה; **p710** booths image © Ori229; **p710** pine image © public domain; **p710** myrtle image © public domain; **p710** palm image © Dan Lundberg; **p710** olive image © public domain; **p712** heavens image © ESO; **p712** seas image © public domain; **p712** stele image © Osama Shukir Muhammed Amin FRCP; **p712** Ur image © M.Lubinski from Iraq,USA; **p714** upper image © האיל הניאוליתי; **p714** lower left image © Lgz01; **p714** lower right image © Makedocreative; **p718** upper left image © courtesy of Israel Antiquities Authority/Wikipedia; **p718** upper right image © public domain; **p718** lower image © HaRav Menachem Makover, courtesy of *Harenu Bevinyano*; **p720** upper left image © public domain; **p720** lower left image © public domain; **p720** right image © courtesy of the Neot Kedumim National Nature Reserve, www.n-k.org.il; **p724** shera image © Danny Gershoni; **p724** adulam image © Davidbena; **p724** azeka image © תמר הירדני; **p724** hatzor image © LeehuZysberg; **p726** left image © public domain; **p726** right image © Israel Antiquities Authority; **p728** upper left image © public domain; **p728** upper right image © unknown; **p728** lower right image © ד"ר אבישי טייכר; **p730** inscription image © http://fontes.lstc.edu/~rklein/images/baltxt.jpg; **p730** frankincense image © public domain; **p730** vessel image © **courtesy of the Temple Institute**; **p730** tomb image © Diego Delso; **p732** left image © Michael Radwin; **p732** center image © public domain

I CHRONICLES

p740 © public domain; **p752** © Israel Antiquities Authority; **p762** © public domain; **p766** both images © HaRav Menachem Makover, courtesy of *Harenu Bevinyano*; **p768** © TrickyH; **p770** © צולם על ידי אלי זהבי 2006; **p772** upper left image © פרופסור אבישי טייכר; **p772** upper right image © מיכאלי; **p774** upper left image © Pessimist2006; **p774** lower left image © Golf Bravo; **p774** lower right image © Bukvoed; **p774** upper right image © public domain; **p778** © Johnbod; **p782** © public domain; **p784** left image © A.Davey; **p784** right image © Avivavi; **p786** left image © Deror_avi; **p788** left image © public domain; **p788** right image © Daniel Ventura; **p790** left image © Carole Raddato; **p790** right image © Einsamer Schütze; **p792** © Danny Gershoni; **p794** left image © public domain; **p794** center image © public domain; **p798** upper image © Hanay; **p798** lower image © HaRav Menachem Makover, courtesy of *Harenu Bevinyano*; **p800** trumpet image © public domain; **p800** lyre image © public domain; **p800** harp image © Ji-Elle; **p800** tambourine image © Catrin; **p800** cymbals image © Israel Antiquities Authority; **p801** left image © public domain; **p801** right image © Jerzy Strzelecki; **p802** © H. Zell; **p806** © **courtesy of the Temple Institute**; **p808** © public domain; **p814** shield image © C messier; **p814** ingot image © Chris 73 / Wikimedia Commons; **p814** lower images © **courtesy of the Temple Institute**; **p816** © Panegyrics of Granovetter; **p818** left image © Diego Delso; **p822** © public domain; **p826** left image © Mark Nesbitt; **p826** center image © public domain; **p826** right image © Deror avi; **p832** left image © **courtesy of the Temple Institute**; **p832** right image © Clara Amit, Yoram Lehmann, Yael Yolovitch, Miki Koren, and Mariana Salzberger, courtesy of the Israel Antiquities Authority; **p834** © From M. Avi-Yona, "Inscription from Caesarea on the Twenty-Four Priestly Watches," *Eretz Yisrael* 7 (1964): 2-28 (Hebrew); **p846** vineyard image © public domain; **p846** olive image © public domain; **p846** sycamore image © public domain; **p846** cattle image © Narek75; **p846** camels image © public domain; **p846** donkeys image © public domain; **p846** flocks image © משה רענן; **p848** © **courtesy of the Temple Institute**; **p850** left image © Clara Amit, Yoram Lehmann, Yael Yolovitch, Miki Koren, and Mariana Salzberger, courtesy of the Israel Antiquities Authority; **p850** right image © **courtesy of the Temple Institute**; **p851** left image © Leica; **p851** right image © Humanfeather / Michelle Jo; **p852** © public domain

II CHRONICLES

p856 © AVRAHAM GRAICER; **p858** ruins of stables image © צילום:ד"ר אבישי טייכר; **p858** sketch image © unknown; **p858** egyptian chariot image © Traumrune; **p858** incense image © **courtesy of the Temple Institute**; **p860** murex images © H. Zell; **p860** insects image © Spodek M, Ben-Dov Y; **p860** juniper image © Vilensija; **p862** left image © public domain; **p862** right image © Andrew Shiva / Wikipedia / CC BY-SA 4.0; **p864** upper image © **courtesy of the Temple Institute**; **p864** lower image © Tom Hilton; **p866** left images © **courtesy of the Temple Institute**; **p866** right images © HaRav Menachem Makover, courtesy of *Harenu Bevinyano*; **p868** upper image © **courtesy of the Temple Institute**; **p868** lower image © יוני שפירא; **p872** upper image © Axel Kristinsson from Reykjavík, Iceland; **p872** lower image © Iwoelbern; **p876** left image © **courtesy of the Temple Institute**; **p880** left image © Marina Milella / DecArch; **p882** left image © Elie plus at English Wikipedia; **p882** center image © Ori~; **p882** right image © Ji-Elle; **p884** upper image © Daderot; **p884** center image © Daderot; **p844** lower image © Save–Elephants; **p886** upper image © תומר קליין; **p886** lower image © public domain; **p890** upper right image © Davidbena; **p890** center right image © Bukvoed; **p894** lower left image © public domain; **p894** right image © Psy guy; **p896** © public domain; **p898** lower left image © Ori~; **p900** right image © Bukvoed; **p902** upper left image © Neitram; **p902** upper right image © ZachiEvenor; **p902** lower image © jimmywee; **p904** lebanon image © Leb500; **p904** Tel Dan image © תמר מרום; **p904** Tel Abel image © The Israel Antiquities Authority scientific Archive 1919–1948; **p906** left image © ליאור גולגר; **p908** left image © Andreas Krappweis; **p908** center image © public domain; **p908** right image © י.ש.; **p910** left image © Ovedc; **p910** upper right image © יוחנן בן יעקב; **p910** lower right image © sailko; **p916** both images © Ester Inbar; **p918** upper image © Deroravi; **p922** © Ori; **p924** right image © public domain; **p924** left image © Mbzt 2012; **p926** right image © Daniel Ventura; **p926** left image © Ori; **p928** upper image © public domain; **p928** lower image © public domain; **p932** © public domain; **p936** © tsur shezaf; **p938** left image © Chenspec; **p938** center image © Patche99z; **p938** upper right image © Bukvoed; **p938** lower right image © Oren Rozen; **p940** left image © Ori; **p940** center image © public domain; **p940** right image © זלדה 10; **p942** upper image © Gilgamesh; **p942** lower image © Eric Gaba; **p944** wheat image © public domain; **p944** barley image © public domain; **p944** tomb image © yoavdothan; **p944** ofel image © Ariely; **p946** left image © hanay; **p946** right image © public domain; **p948** left image © public domain; **p948** center image © Yandud; **p948** Tiglat image © Jastrow (2007); **p958** upper image © Tamar Hayardeni; **p958** lower image © Tamarah; **p960** sheaves image © C:Ben Schonewille; **p960** wine image © public domain; **p960** oil image © public domain; **p960** honey image © public domain; **p962** left image © Justin Ennis; **p962** upper right image © Paul Arps; **p962** lower right image © Knerdler; **p966** upper image © אפי אליאן; **p966** lower image © Daniel Ventura; **p968** upper image © Wolfgang Sauber; **p968** lower image © Osama Sarm; **p973** © public domain; **p976** © Dirk Vorderstraße; **p980** upper left image © Photo: Brooklyn Museum, 71.11_threequarter_PS1.jpg; **p980** upper right image © public domain; **p982** © I, Rimeh; **p984** © dynamosquito

KOREN

Steinsaltz Center